S0-AAK-033
WITHDRAWN

CQ Researcher

CONTENTS January - December 2004

CQ Researcher

Published by CQ Press, a division of Congressional Quarterly Inc.

thecqresearcher.com

Hazing

Should more be done to stop it?

Athletic teams, fraternities and high school groups often initiate new members by hazing them — making them perform embarrassing or degrading stunts. But sometimes hazing switches from silliness to cruelty, criminality or even deadly violence. Last May, five suburban Chicago high school girls were treated at a local hospital for injuries received during a videotaped hazing incident that turned into a melee. In August, varsity football players at a New York high school sodomized junior varsity players with broomsticks, golf balls and pine cones. And dozens of freshmen pledges have died over the years during dangerous fraternity hazings, which are illegal in most states. Experts say more should be done to stamp out hazing, but supporters say the ancient practice builds character and camaraderie.

Scott Krueger, 18, died after an alcohol-related fraternity hazing incident at the Massachusetts Institute of Technology.

INSIDE THIS ISSUE

The CQ Researcher • Jan. 9, 2004 • www.thecqresearcher.com
Volume 14, Number 1 • Pages 1-24

Recipient of Society of Professional Journalists Award for Excellence ◆ American Bar Association Silver Gavel Award

THE ISSUES

BACKGROUND

CURRENT SITUATION

OUTLOOK

SIDEBARS AND GRAPHICS

FOR FURTHER RESEARCH

Cover: Scott Krueger, a freshman from New York, went into a coma and died after binge drinking 15 shots of whiskey during a hazing ritual at MIT for the now-banned Phi Gamma Delta fraternity. (Getty Images)

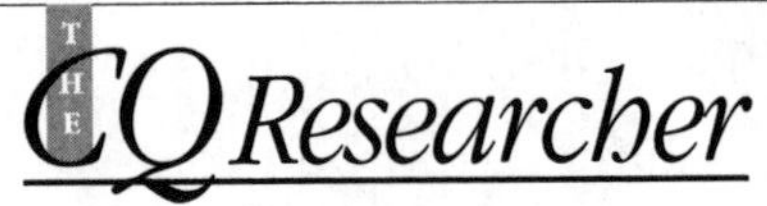

Jan. 9, 2004
Volume 14, No. 1

MANAGING EDITOR: Thomas J. Colin
ASSISTANT MANAGING EDITOR: Kathy Koch
ASSOCIATE EDITOR: Kenneth Jost
STAFF WRITERS: Mary H. Cooper, David Masci, William Triplett
CONTRIBUTING WRITERS: Rachel S. Cox, Sarah Glazer, David Hosansky, Patrick Marshall, Jane Tanner
DESIGN/PRODUCTION EDITOR: Olu B. Davis
ASSISTANT EDITOR: Benton Ives-Halperin

A Division of
Congressional Quarterly Inc.

SENIOR VICE PRESIDENT/GENERAL MANAGER: John A. Jenkins
DIRECTOR, LIBRARY PUBLISHING: Kathryn C. Suárez
DIRECTOR, EDITORIAL OPERATIONS: Ann Davies
CIRCULATION MANAGER: Nina Tristani

CONGRESSIONAL QUARTERLY INC.
CHAIRMAN: Andrew Barnes
VICE CHAIRMAN: Andrew P. Corty
PRESIDENT AND PUBLISHER: Robert W. Merry

The CQ Researcher (ISSN 1056-2036) is printed on acid-free paper. Published weekly, except Jan. 2, April 9, July 2, July 9, Aug. 6, Aug. 13, Nov. 26 and Dec. 31, by CQ Press, a division of Congressional Quarterly Inc. Annual subscription rates for libraries, businesses and government start at $625. Single issues are available for $10. Quantity discounts apply to orders over 10. Additional rates furnished upon request. Periodicals postage paid at Washington, D.C., and additional mailing offices. POSTMASTER: Send address changes to *The CQ Researcher*, 1255 22nd St., N.W., Suite 400, Washington, D.C. 20037.

By Brian Hansen

The Issues

Medically speaking, Walter Dean Jennings, 18, died of hyponatremia, a rare disorder marked by low sodium levels in the blood. But law-enforcement officials in Plattsburgh, N.Y., describe the State University of New York freshman's death in more harrowing terms.

"He was ordered to [drink] very large quantities of water until he vomited," said Police Chief Desmond Racicot. "He died from brain swelling due to water intoxication." [1]

Jennings died last March while undergoing one of several hazing rituals that Psi Epsilon Chi, an "underground" fraternity at the Plattsburgh campus, subjected pledges to before initiating them as new brothers. During the 10-day initiation period, Jennings and other pledges were confined in a tiny room and blasted with strobe lights and deafening music. Members then forced the pledges to drink pitcher after pitcher of water, sometimes pouring it down their throats through a funnel. Fraternity members called the ritual the "water torture," police said.

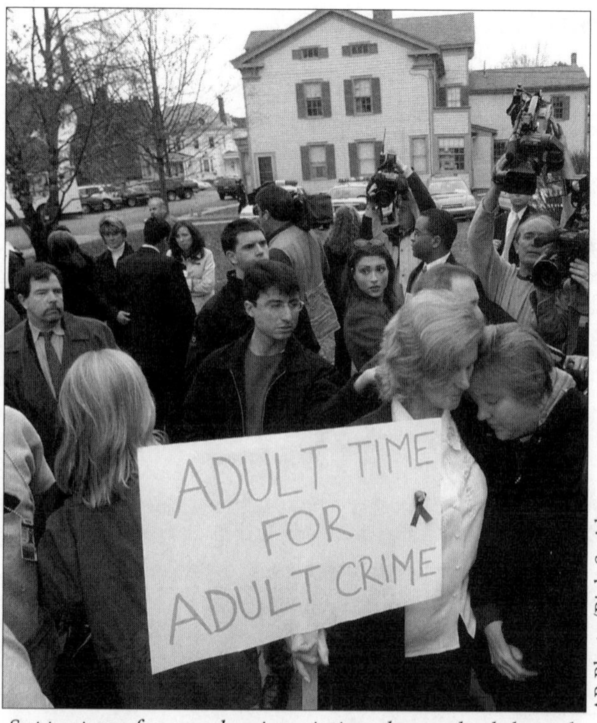

AP Photo/Rick Smith

Supporters of young hazing victims demand adult trials for three varsity football players from Bellmore, N.Y., charged with sodomizing three younger players, ages 13 and 14, with pine cones, broomsticks and golf balls during football camp in Pennsylvania. Hazing is illegal in most states, but experts say high schools, colleges and other institutions must do more to stamp out the increasingly violent practice.

Eleven members of the fraternity recently pleaded guilty to various charges, including criminally negligent homicide, and face additional sanctions by the university. Jennings' death was the latest in a long line of hazing incidents that have caused death or serious injury, but experts don't expect the practice — which has caused concern since ancient times — to disappear anytime soon.

"Hazing is steaming full-speed ahead at many high schools and universities," says Richard Sigal, a sociology professor at the County College of Morris, Randolph, N.J. "Hazing is grounded in tradition, and it's very hard to root out and stop."

No one knows whether hazing is on the rise, because only a handful of researchers have attempted to quantify it. However, it is clearly widespread: Researchers at New York's Alfred University found in 1998-1999 that nearly 80 percent of the nation's college athletes were subjected to "questionable or unacceptable" hazing rituals, and in 2002, 82 percent of the fraternity and sorority members surveyed at Cornell University said they had participated in hazing. Meanwhile, nearly half of the high school students surveyed in 2000 by the researchers said they had participated in hazing-type activities. [2]

"The number of students in our schools that are hazed is incredible," says Norman Pollard, director of Alfred's Counseling and Student Development Center, who co-authored the Alfred hazing studies. "Hazing isn't just harmless fun and games — it can have very serious consequences."

Hazing rituals are used to initiate new members into fraternities, sororities and other "Greek-letter" organizations, athletic teams, marching bands and military units. Hazing can range from seemingly innocuous discomfort, embarrassment or ridicule — such as wearing silly clothing or singing the school fight song in a public place — to what some feel is psychological abuse.

Former North Dakota State University student Sean Burns says he was subjected to psychological abuse when he pledged a fraternity in 1983. Burns — now a University of Minnesota network administrator — remembers "a lot of verbally abusive yelling . . . all mental stuff. They'd make you stand up in front of everyone, and they'd go over your shortcomings as they perceived them."

But hazing can also degenerate into violent, sexually charged abuse or even life-threatening torture — as in the Jennings case — especially when alcohol or mob mentality are involved. Nathan Oates, a Ph.D. candidate at the University of Missouri, Columbia, remembers the violent initiation ceremony of a fraternity-like "drinking society" when he was an undergraduate at the University of Virginia in the mid-1990s.

"As the brothers would get drunker and drunker, they would throw the would-be members down on the ground and kick them extremely

Half of High School Students Are Hazed

More than 1.5 million American high school students experience some form of hazing each year, according to Alfred University researchers, who surveyed 1,541 high school students in 2000.

Percentage of Students Subjected to Hazing

Type of Hazing	Percentage
Any Type	48%
Humiliation	43
Potentially Illegal	29
Substance Abuse	23
Dangerous	22

Source: Nadine C. Hoover and Norman J. Pollard, "Initiation Rites in American High Schools: A National Survey," August 2000

hard," Oates recalls. "I heard these awful thwacking sounds, and I saw one guy get kicked right in the face. It could get pretty out of control."

Some of the most sadistic and cruel recent hazing incidents have involved high school students. Last August, for example, three varsity football players from Mepham High School in Bellmore, N.Y., sodomized three younger players — who were 13 and 14 years old — with broomsticks, golf balls and pine cones during a hazing incident at a school-sanctioned team training camp.

Now even girls are getting into brutalizing one another. In a videotaped, widely publicized high school incident last May, a group of suburban Chicago senior girls (and a few boys) viciously hazed some younger girls by pelting them with feces, fish entrails, blood and other substances. One girl allegedly was strangled with pig intestines and others were kicked, punched and beaten with objects. One of the hazers, a senior boy, placed a bucket over a girl's head, ordered her to kneel on the ground, and kicked her in the head. Five girls were treated at hospitals after the melee: One for a broken ankle, three for bumps and bruises and one who needed 10 stitches in her head, officials said.

The incident revealed society's conflicting attitudes about hazing — which some experts say is one reason the phenomenon has been so hard to stamp out. While parents of the victims were furious and demanded the hazers be punished, parents of the hazers angrily denounced school administrators for punishing their children too harshly. (*See sidebar, p. 8.*)

In fact, experts say hazing has survived for thousands of years precisely because for some people it serves a purpose. Hazing builds character, say some of its advocates, while others see it as a "rite of passage" that forces young adults to put aside their immaturity. Still others say it builds institutional cohesiveness by encouraging bonding among those vying for membership in schools, fraternities and other groups.

But as the number of hazing-related injuries and deaths has mounted, it has become more and more difficult to distinguish between "acceptable" and "unacceptable" hazing rituals. As a result, hazing today is illegal in 43 states, even if no other laws — like assault or battery — are broken in the course of a hazing. Most of the state laws proscribe behavior that threatens to cause severe physical or psychological injury. (*See sidebar, p. 6.*)

Moreover, law enforcement officials in the seven states that do not criminalize hazing per se can still prosecute people — and, in some cases, organizations — that injure, kill or otherwise harm others through hazing.

In addition, most colleges, universities and high schools have anti-hazing policies, as does the U.S. military. All national fraternities and sororities condemn the practice and strongly discourage their chapters from hazing members.

Because most hazing is now illegal, supporters of the practice go to great lengths to hide it from their national leaders, university officials and law enforcement. "Hazing has been driven underground, and there is definitely a code of silence surrounding it," says sociology Professor Sigal. "It's considered to be macho and loyal and an act of brotherhood not to talk about it."

As hazing continues to flourish behind a veil of secrecy, here is a closer look at some of the issues being debated:

Does peer pressure lead to cruel hazing practices?

It was fun and exciting. We felt closer as a group. I got to prove myself. I just went along with it. I was scared to say no.

Those are the top five reasons high school students cite for why they participate in hazing rituals, according to Alfred University's high school hazing survey.

Researcher Pollard, who designed and analyzed the survey, says the responses show that young people have a powerful need to belong to clubs, athletic teams and other groups. They also have a strong need to prove themselves, Pollard says, but contemporary American society affords them few other "rites of passage" to adulthood.

Without acceptable rites of passage in American society, belonging to a club or a sports team "has strong significance for young people," Pollard says. "They partake in hazing rituals to show that they're worthy enough to belong to these groups, which allow them to prove themselves and reinforce their identities."

Ted Feinberg, assistant executive director of the National Association of School Psychologists, agrees. "Hazing serves to affirm the worth and value of social groups," he says. "[Would-be members] think that if others were willing to be hazed, then the group must really be worthwhile."

Peer pressure and the desire to belong motivated Ivery Luckey, a clarinet player who wanted to be fully accepted by his peers in the acclaimed Florida A&M University marching band. Luckey allowed senior band members to beat him on the buttocks with paddles more than 300 times in a 1998 hazing ritual. Luckey succumbed to the beating after being told the ritual was a longstanding "tradition" in the woodwind section of the band, and that he would be ostracized if he refused to participate. He landed in the hospital with severe bruising and acute renal failure.

Police in Tallahassee declined to arrest anyone after determining that Luckey had allowed himself to be hazed. "This was pretty much by [my] choice," Luckey said later. "If you want to be in a fraternity or the cool part of the band, that's kind of what you do." [3]

According to Pollard, many groups don't know how to conduct acceptable initiation ceremonies, so they model their hazing rituals on reckless behaviors glamorized in the popular media. "That's why it can go so horribly wrong," Pollard says. He cites examples like the "Fear Factor" television show, in which contestants perform a series of dangerous and/or disgusting activities — such as jumping from moving vehicles or eating cow brains — to compete for a $50,000 prize, and movies like "Jackass," about people who attempt similarly dangerous or gross stunts.

Moreover, says Pollard, when alcohol plays a prominent role in hazings, "it just escalates the dangers considerably."

People also allow themselves to be hazed because they believe — sometimes wrongly — that everyone in the group has been subjected to the ritual and that nothing can go wrong, points out Professor Sigal. "It's like getting on a ride at Disney World: As scary as it might be, you assume that the people running the show know what they're doing and that the ride isn't going to kill you," he says. "The same is true with hazing — when you're a pledge, you assume that all the stuff they put you through has been tried out, and that it's not going to put you at risk."

In fact, Sigal says, groups sometimes coerce prospective members into doing things they themselves never did. But initiates are in no position to question the group's so-called "tradition." For example, 20-year-old Chuck Stenzel probably didn't object when members of Alfred University's Klan Alpine fraternity locked him in the trunk of a car with a large amount of bourbon, wine and beer and told him he had to drink it all to be released. Stenzel died of alcohol poisoning in the infamous 1978 hazing incident.

"My students always ask me, 'Why didn't he just pour the booze out in the trunk?' " Sigal says. "The answer is: He probably didn't think he was putting his life in danger [but] … assumed that it was a longstanding tra-

Why Students Haze

High school students participate in hazing activities for a variety of reasons, including the thrill, the need to belong and to prove oneself, as well as peer pressure.

Reasons Students Give for Participating in Hazing

Reason Given	Percentage
It was fun and exciting	48%
We felt closer as a group	44
I got to prove myself	34
I just went along with it	34
I was scared to say no	16
I wanted revenge	12
I didn't know what was happening	9
Adults do it, too	9

Source: Nadine C. Hoover and Norman J. Pollard, "Initiation Rites in American High Schools: A National Survey," August 2000

Is Hazing Harmful?

Stripping fraternity pledges naked and beating them with paddles? Clearly that's dangerous hazing. Forcing them to drink alcohol (or even water) until they vomit or pass out? Ditto.

But what about rousting the new team members out of bed at 3 a.m. to make them do push-ups? Or making initiates clean the chapter house? Or having rookie football players carry veteran teammates' equipment or requiring high school freshmen to stand on tables and sing their school song? Those kinds of activities are hazing as well. But are they harmful?

Americans are all over the map when it comes to such questions. Many scoff at the notion that making someone perform minor chores constitutes hazing. Others concede that such activities may be mild forms of hazing but insist that they're not harmful. Still others argue that while such activities may not be hazing per se, they should nevertheless be banned because they are — or have the potential to be — psychologically damaging.

"I don't think that making the rookies carry the equipment is hazing," says Elizabeth Allan, an anti-hazing activist and a professor of education at the University of Maine. "However, it sets up a dynamic in which people who have less power are made to do different things than other people, which can open the door to other, more emotionally and physically harmful activities."

The transformation from "silly, little harmless pranks" to dangerous hazing rituals can occur quickly, she says, especially when alcohol is introduced into the mix. But more typically the transformation is a slower, more incremental process that "creeps up" on people, she says.

"It starts out with just name-calling, and the next week it's personal servitude and by the end, [the hazers] are asking you to do things that you know aren't right," Allan says. "But you keep going because you feel you've come too far and invested too much to quit."

Allan points out that while many hazing victims never suffer psychological problems as a result of their experiences, others do. "You can't predict how people are going to react to different things," says Allan, who once counseled a sorority pledge who was traumatized after she was made to simulate oral sex with a banana. "I've known many students who leave school after being hazed. It can radically alter people's lives, not only in terms of physical injuries, but also psychologically."

Ted Feinberg, assistant executive director of the National Association of School Psychologists, agrees. "Hazing can cause serious psychological-adjustment problems, similar to students who are bullied," he says. Many of the students who opened fire on fellow students in the infamous school shooting incidents of the late 1990s may have been abused and traumatized in a hazing-like manner, he says. [1] "Then there are kids who internalize their feelings and engage in self-destructive behaviors, including committing suicide. So hazing is not a playful, developmental rite of passage for everyone." [2]

But hazing still has its supporters. *Sports Illustrated* writer Richard Hoffer wrote in 1999 that some forms of athletic hazing — forced drinking, ritualistic paddling and activities that cause "bloodshed" — were wrong, but the sports world could benefit from more "wholesome" hazing, he says, because it breaks down players' egos and fosters teamwork.

"Athletics, which increasingly elevates the individual far above the team, needs more hazing," Hoffer wrote. "What's wrong with making a freshman carry a senior's suitcase?" [3]

Frequently, hazing victims themselves do not object to being mildly humiliated. Will Gordon, a sophomore at Glencliff High School in Nashville, Tenn., was tied to a chair and had his head and eyebrows shaved when he was a freshman going out for the football team. "It was all in fun," Gordon said. "We didn't necessarily see it as violence. It was like bonding." [4]

Head shaving, equipment toting and other such activities probably would not constitute hazing under most of the 43 state anti-hazing laws. Maryland's law, for example, prohibits only activities that subject students "to the risk of serious bodily injury." Pennsylvania's statute goes further, banning activities that cause "extreme mental stress" or physical harm.

"Most of the state laws focus on behavior that threatens to cause severe physical or psychological injury," says Douglas E. Fierberg, a Washington, D.C., attorney who specializes in hazing law. "Making someone carry a bucket of water doesn't do that, and making someone sing a fight song at a training table doesn't do that. These things are essentially initiation rituals."

[1] See Kathy Koch, "School Violence," *The CQ Researcher*, Oct. 9, 1998, pp. 881-904.

[2] See Kathy Koch, "Childhood Depression," *The CQ Researcher*, July 16, 1999, pp. 593-616.

[3] Quoted in Richard Hoffer, "Praising Hazing," *Sports Illustrated*, Sept. 13, 1999, p. 31.

[4] Quoted in Tom Weir, "Hazing Rears Ugly Head Across USA," *USA Today*, Dec. 9, 2003, p. C1.

dition. In reality, the 'tradition' could have started with him that year."

Experts say some people impose cruel and potentially dangerous hazing rituals on others to exact revenge for the hazing they themselves were forced to endure as pledges.

Kyle Holtzman, a Justice Department official in Washington, D.C., remembers that phenomenon as a freshman at the Virginia Military Institute (VMI) in the mid-1980s. VMI is famous for its so-called "rat system," in which sophomores, juniors and seniors subject freshmen ("rats") to mental and physical challenges.

"The sophomores were usually the biggest [expletives] because they had

Fraternities and Gangs Haze the Most

More than three-quarters of high school fraternity and sorority members were hazed, compared with less than one-fifth of the members of school newspaper staffs or scholastic clubs.

Percent of Students Hazed to Join Various Groups

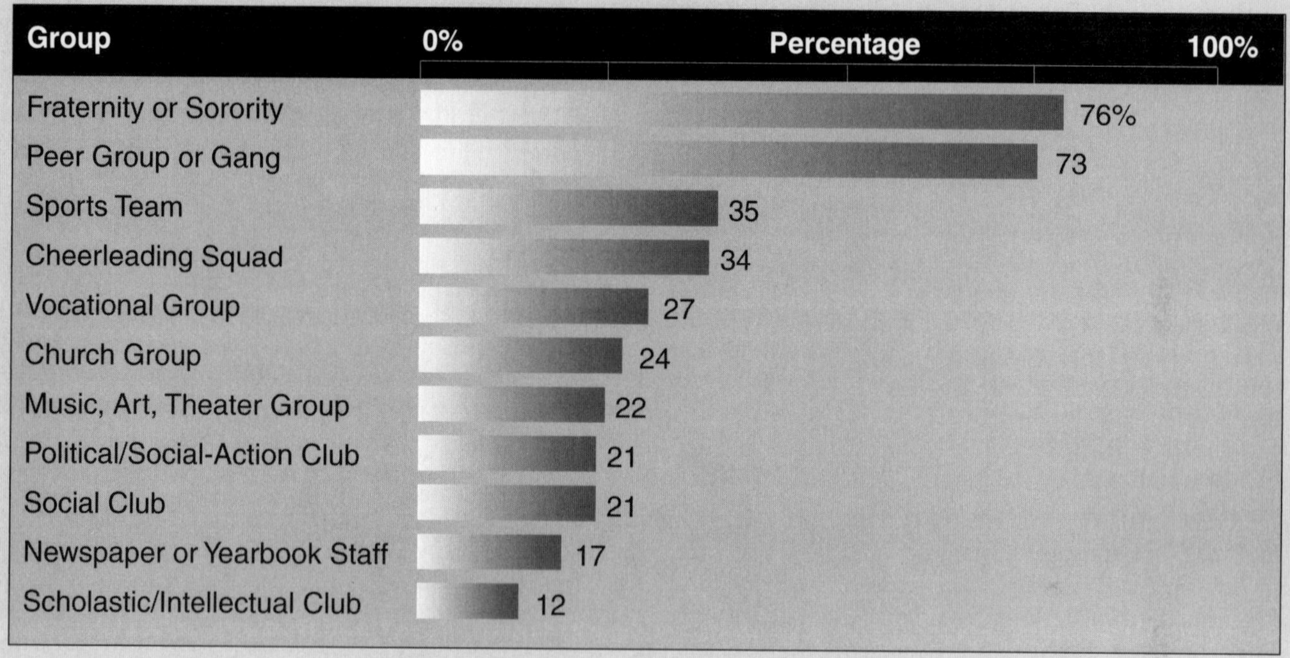

Source: Nadine C. Hoover and Norman J. Pollard, "Initiation Rites in American High Schools: A National Survey," August 2000

just been rats themselves, and their therapy was to inflict the pain — which was still very real for them — on others," he says. "Some of the seniors were pretty rough, but as a whole, it was the [sophomore] class that really messed with the rats."

Hank Nuwer, an assistant professor of journalism at Franklin College in Indiana who has written four books on hazing, doesn't dispute the so-called "revenge" theory. But Nuwer says there's more to it than that. "Some of these hazing incidents clearly look like the acts of sadists," Nuwer says. "The perpetrators appear unable to see the victims as people, because they show absolutely no empathy for the humiliation and pain they cause."

Sean O'Brien can relate to that. In August 2002, two teammates grabbed the 15-year-old football player in the locker room at Central Catholic High School in Pittsburgh, held him down and rubbed their genitals in his face — an act known as tea-bagging. "I was overpowered, O'Brien said. "Nobody tried to help me — they were all just laughing." [4]

When he told police about the incident, O'Brien was harassed further and eventually transferred to another school. His two attackers, who initially faced several criminal charges, recently cut a deal in which they agreed to serve eight months of probation and perform 100 hours of community service.

Feinberg, like many experts, says such violent, sexually charged initiation rituals stem in part from the values articulated by pop culture. "Our society has clearly become more violent and more sexual over the past 20 years," he says. "To some extent, the media have contributed to the notion that this kind of behavior is just good fun, and that it's just what kids these days do."

Does hazing build character or institutional cohesiveness?

In the Middle Ages, hazing was viewed in some circles as a good way to teach young scholars respect for their elders and their academic institutions.

Continued on p. 9

Girls' Hazing Goes Prime Time

Few hazing incidents have spurred more discussion — or more public revulsion — than the melee that was captured on videotape in suburban Chicago last spring. Broadcast repeatedly, the incident provided a rare public look at how brutal and sadistic hazing can be. Atypically, it involved girls.

"What I saw in the film was . . . a complete breakdown of inhibition and all the other painstakingly stitched manners that keep civilization from unraveling," wrote syndicated newspaper columnist Kathleen Parker. [1]

The incident at a public park north of Chicago involved approximately 50 girls from Glenbrook North High School in Northbrook, Ill. Ostensibly, the occasion was a traditional "powder-puff" football game between juniors and seniors. As many as 100 other Glenbrook students and alumni, male and female, also turned out for the event. Two parents brought two kegs of beer.

The juniors expected to be hazed, probably doused with ketchup, mustard, eggs and the like. They also had heard they were supposed to submit willingly. Their turn to "dish it out" would come the following year.

The football game was never even played. Instead, the senior girls (and some boys) pelted the juniors with feces, urine, fish entrails, blood and other vile substances. Some girls were forced to eat raw meat and mud; one girl was choked with pig intestines. Others were kicked and punched.

"It's devastating to our school community," said Glenbrook Principal Mike Riggle. "Hopefully, over time, we will regain the reputation we've always had." [2]

"How could this have possibly happened in our town, in our school?" asked Mary Jo Barrett, director of the Center for Contextual Change, a local therapy center. "What can we learn from this?" [3]

Critics pointed fingers everywhere. Some accused school officials of knowing about and tolerating the hazing tradition. Others blamed the media for glorifying violent behavior. Still others blamed the participants' parents, and many blamed the participants themselves. "Those who choose to be initiated seek acceptance from others due to their inability to accept themselves for who they already are," said Glenbrook alumna Monica Ong, who witnessed hazing at the 1994 powder-puff game. "Those who haze . . . do not believe in developing themselves from the inside, [but instead] try to compensate by proving their superiority to others." [4]

School officials expelled 33 seniors, all but three of them girls. The students were allowed to graduate after undergoing counseling and performing community service. Still, not all of their parents were pleased with the district's punishment. "They made one mistake, and you're punishing them for the rest of their lives," said Glenbrook parent Craig Yudell, whose daughter Valerie was among those expelled. "This may affect college." [5]

But Kim Parks, another Glenbrook parent, accused Yudell of making excuses. "If your daughter had human feces shoved into her mouth, would you feel like that?" Parks demanded. "Your daughter made a bad decision." [6]

In addition to the expulsions, prosecutors brought criminal charges against 16 hazers. All were convicted of, or pleaded guilty to, misdemeanor battery and alcohol charges. Critics were unhappy that most will be eligible to have their records expunged next year. But attorney Alan Davis, who represented one of the hazers, said the punishment fit the crime.

"Most of these kids are really good children who made a mistake," Davis said. "Chances are, you'll never see 99 percent of them in the legal system again." [7]

One of the girls charged with misdemeanor battery, Gina Mengarelli, 18, was found guilty last November and was sentenced to a year of court supervision. She admitted throwing ketchup, mustard and coffee grounds but denied kneeing a girl in the back and pulling another girl's hair and pushing her to the ground, as prosecutors alleged.

Asked if she had intended to harm anyone, Mengarelli responded: "Absolutely not." She told the judge she believed the juniors consented to her actions because they freely participated in the event. [8]

Prosecutors also brought charges against the two mothers who provided the beer. Both women pleaded guilty to misdemeanor charges, but one defiantly maintained that alcohol had nothing to do with the violence, as many experts alleged. "What happened this year is sick, but I don't think the alcohol made them crazy," Marcy Spiwak, 49, told *The Chicago Tribune.* [9]

To prevent future incidents, community and school officials drafted a voluminous report and created a special task force to study hazing. But columnist Parker is one of many observers who remains unimpressed by the response.

"What's disturbing and frankly creepy about the powder-puff implosion is the apparent lack of remorse, empathy or insight — or any of the responses we might expect from well-adjusted, sensitive human beings," she wrote. "There's something very wrong with this picture, and it may well be us." [10]

---

[1] Quoted in Kathleen Parker, "What Are Little Girls Made Of? How About Pig Guts and Beer," *The Chicago Tribune*, May 14, 2003, p. C21.

[2] Quoted in Crystal Yednak, "Hazing Incident Seen Around the Globe," *The Chicago Tribune*, May 9, 2003, p. A3.

[3] Quoted in Mary Jo Barrett, "How a Rite of Passage Crossed Over the Line: Understanding the Powder-Puff Ritual," *The Chicago Tribune*, June 1, 2003, p. C1.

[4] Letter to the editor, *The Chicago Tribune*, May 20, 2003, p. C16.

[5] Quoted in Crystal Yednak and Jimmy Greenfield, "Powder Puff Payback: Crying Girls Escorted Out of School — and No Prom," *The Chicago Tribune*, May 13, 2003, p. A10.

[6] *Ibid.*

[7] Quoted in Lisa Black, "Last Student Sentenced in Hazing," *The Chicago Tribune*, Dec. 2, 2003, p. B1.

[8] Courtney Flynn, "Teen guilty in Glenbrook Hazing," *The Chicago Tribune*, Nov. 4, 2003, p. B1.

[9] Quoted in Lisa Black and Courtney Flynn, "Students' Mothers Charged in Hazing," *The Chicago Tribune*, May 22, 2003, p. C1.

[10] Quoted in Parker, *op. cit.*

AP Photo/Brian Kersey

Three of the hazed Glenbrook North High School students, Lauren Wilner, Marina Fonarev and Cheryl Daley, all 17, were suspended for refusing to sign a school-imposed agreement not to sell their stories.

Continued from p. 7

Then, as now, hazing rituals varied considerably in their mental and physical impacts. Some students were simply required to serve as waiters for their older peers. Others were beaten with books, frying pans or other objects. Occasionally, upperclassmen tried to instill a work ethic in new students by literally holding their noses to a hand-turned grindstone. Early hazing supporters included Protestant reformer Martin Luther, who maintained that it strengthened young adults and enabled them to more easily endure the challenges of adult life. [5]

Hazing was adopted by American students in the mid-17th century for similar reasons. Proponents also viewed it as a way to foster school spirit. By the early 1900s, many college presidents openly advocated some forms of hazing as "an acceptable way for older students to teach newcomers respect for their school or organization," says Franklin College's Nuwer. But when hazing rituals led to serious physical injury or death, Nuwer says, officials quickly condemned it.

Nevertheless, supporters continue to claim that it builds character and institutional cohesiveness, although they rarely articulate those views publicly, now that hazing is so widely proscribed by law and policy. Instead, they tout the benefits of hazing in other forums, such as on Internet bulletin boards, where they can remain anonymous. Several pro-hazing comments are posted on StopHazing.org, a Web site run by University of Maine Professor of Education Elizabeth Allan and other anti-hazing activists. Among them:

- "Hazing made me a better person. I became more responsible. My health improved. My self-esteem and self-confidence skyrocketed. I became more morally conscious. If the rest of the world experienced what I went through, random acts of violence and disrespect would disappear almost at once. There must be order. There must be structure. There must be discipline. Hazing is not evil, nor is it morally wrong. It is something that should be administered well and administered often."
- "I have been hazed, and I now haze our pledges. [Hazing] teaches the pledges togetherness, communication, respect, courage and a huge sense of accomplishment. Granted, a few organizations ruin it for the rest of us, but please, learn the facts. It is NOT HARMFUL! It has a purpose in American society today and it always will."
- "While extreme hazing [such as] anal rape with the hook end of a field hockey stick should be forbidden, regular hazing, which seems to have been blown extremely out of proportion, should be used by institutions to create a sense of unity."

Many high school students voiced similar views when asked about hazing by the Alfred University researchers. More than one-quarter (27 percent) said they had only "positive feelings" about being hazed. Another 32 percent said they had "both negative and positive feelings" about their experiences. [6] Students who found hazing at least partially "positive" said they "gained valuable life experiences," "matured" and "found it challenging."

"Hazing probably has some benefit for some people," says Alfred University's Pollard. "I'm certainly not endorsing it, but we did get a lot of teenagers [in the survey] who said it was a great experience for them. They said it created a sense of unity and bonding."

Dave Westol, executive director of the national Theta Chi fraternity, understands that feeling. He supported hazing in the early 1970s, when he was an undergraduate at Michigan State University. "I believed in hazing for a while because I thought it was the best way to form good [fraternity] brothers," Westol says. Later, he says, "I did learn that it was completely wrong."

Westol's views on hazing changed about the time he graduated. "I started looking around at some of the guys I had verbally hazed and saw that they were not quite as close to me as they might have been because of the things I'd said that had hurt them," he says. "I had actually started to see [that hazing was wrong] before then, but I didn't want to admit it."

Wynn Smiley, CEO of the Alpha Tau Omega (ATO) fraternity, calls the notion that hazing builds character and institutional cohesiveness a "red herring." While hazing may serve to bond together members of a pledge class, he says, it does nothing to promote overall chapter unity. "Hazing ... bonds together people who are being hazed, which may help them to get through whatever it is they're going through," Smiley says. "But that's a very shortsighted approach, because it just polarizes those pledges from the rest of the larger group."

Pete Smithheisler, vice president for community relations at the North American Interfraternity Conference (NIC), a fraternity umbrella group, agrees. "The myth is that hazing will make men better fraternity members, but the reality is that it makes them better pledges," Smithheisler says. "The cohesiveness that's built through hazing is one of 'us against them,' because they rely on each other to stand against whatever's happening to them."

To be sure, not all hazing victims end up inflicting revenge on others. VMI graduate Holtzman says once he became a sophomore he spent less time "messing" with the underclass "rats" than some of his fellow sophomores. "I didn't have time for it," he says. "There were people who would just [expletive] with rats for hours on Saturdays, just for entertainment. I wasn't into that."

Burns, the North Dakota State graduate, felt similarly when he got the chance to haze. "There was no way that I was going to do that to someone else," he says. As for the effectiveness of the hazing in his fraternity, Burns says, "I do think it had some [bonding] effect, but there are other means to achieve the same end that don't involve mentally abusing and dehumanizing fellow human beings."

Are Greek-letter organizations doing enough to stamp out hazing?

High schools, universities, the military and other institutions have made a variety of efforts to stamp out hazing, and all national Greek organizations have banned hazing in their chapters.

National Greek groups generally communicate anti-hazing policies to their members through literature, seminars and other educational programs. Many enlist alumni and volunteers to visit their local chapter houses. Some send paid personnel to visit chapter houses on an annual or more frequent basis to speak about hazing and check up on chapter activities. Many nationals have expelled members who violated their hazing policies, and some have closed houses where hazing has been a problem.

Fraternity leaders say they're doing all they can to stop hazing. "Our communication methods are pretty aggressive in terms of the risk-management documents we provide our chapter officers," says ATO's Smiley. "Every one of our pledges gets a brochure outlining the fact that we don't allow hazing, and if they feel they're being hazed, we have a phone number they can call, anonymously if they want."

ATO staff members check up on chapter houses at least once a year, and volunteers visit more frequently, Smiley says. He acknowledges that the visits, brochures and other educational initiatives have not eradicated hazing altogether, but the fraternity is doing everything it can, Smiley says. "We can't ensure anything. Basically, we're an educational entity, so we can provide the information, and we have staff members who visit our chapters and keep them apprised of our policies. But if we see no reason to believe that our policies are being violated, then that's pretty much the extent of our involvement."

Mark Anderson, president of the Sigma Chi fraternity, offers a similar assessment. "We try to be aggressive in our educational approach so that our pledges, active members and alumni know they have the responsibility to remove themselves from hazing situations," Anderson says. "But just like all fraternities, we're not in a position to control our chapter members. We can't observe every single thing that every member of Sigma Chi does — we just can't."

That argument isn't good enough for some critics, including Washington, D.C., attorney Douglas E. Fierberg, who has represented hazing victims and their families in civil suits against fraternities, sororities and schools. "I don't think many of these organizations are taking the eradication of hazing very seriously," Fierberg says. "They all say they don't allow it, but they're not committing resources in an intelligent way to root out and punish the misconduct they likely know is occurring in their organizations."

Fierberg says many national Greek organizations "rarely or never" visit their local chapters to determine whether hazing is taking place. Such was the case at the Phi Sigma Kappa chapter at the University Maryland, he says. Fierberg is suing the fraternity and two of its members on behalf of the parents of the late Daniel Reardon, who died while pledging the Maryland chapter in February 2002. The civil suit, which seeks $15 million in damages, claims that local members forced the 19-year-old Reardon to drink a large quantity of malt liquor and whiskey as part of his initiation ceremony. Reardon died of alcohol poisoning.

Fierberg says the national fraternity had made no real effort to stop the drinking ritual, which was a longstanding and well-known tradition at the Maryland chapter. "For two years preceding

Continued on p. 12

Chronology

1800s *Hazing comes to America via ancient Greece, North Africa and Western Europe.*

1847
Jonathan Torrance, a freshman at Amherst College dies after upperclassmen wrap him in cold, wet bed sheets.

1873
Cornell University freshman Mortimer Leggett dies in a fall into a gorge after being taken into the countryside, blindfolded and told to walk back to campus as part of a fraternity initiation.

1900-1950s
Hazing incidents range from silly stunts to deadly tragedies.

1901
Congress threatens to close the U.S. military academy at West Point after learning about hazing rituals.

1945
St. Louis University fraternity pledge Robert Perry is burned to death when an electronic device used to shock him ignites a flammable liquid that had been poured over his body.

1950
A University of California pledge is hit by a car and killed after fraternity members abandon him in the country and tell him to walk back to campus.

1956
Six U.S. Marine recruits drown while slogging through swamplands at Parris Island, S.C., under extreme circumstances that some construe as hazing.

1970s-1990s
Alcohol becomes a factor in hazing-related deaths and injuries.

1978
Fraternity pledge Chuck Stenzel dies of alcohol poisoning at Alfred University after being locked in a car trunk and told to drink a large amount of bourbon and beer.

1980
Fraternity pledge Barry Ballou dies of alcohol poisoning at the University of South Carolina.

1993
Chad Saucier, 19, dies of alcohol poisoning while pledging at Alabama's Auburn University.

1997
Marine paratroopers are shown on news videos in January having pronged metal insignias pounded into their chests in the so-called "blood pinning" ritual. . . . Fraternity pledge Scott Krueger, 18, dies after alcohol-related hazing at Massachusetts Institute of Technology. . . . The National Interfraternity Conference urges its 66 member fraternities to maintain alcohol-free chapters. Most enact policies banning drinking by 2001.

August 1999
Researchers at Alfred University find that college athletes are frequently subjected to humiliating and dangerous hazing rituals.

2000-Present
Hazing grows more violent and sexual, especially among high school students.

August 2000
Another Alfred University survey finds hazing widespread among high school students.

2002
Daniel Reardon, 19, dies of alcohol poisoning in February while pledging a fraternity at the University of Maryland, College Park. . . . A high school football player in Pittsburgh is assaulted in August by teammates who rub their genitals in his face. The hazers are sentenced to probation and community service.

2003
Walter Dean Jennings, a freshman at the State University of New York, Plattsburgh, dies of water intoxication in March while pledging an underground fraternity. . . . High school girls in suburban Chicago are videotaped pelting younger girls with feces, fish entrails and other vile substances. . . . Three New York high school football players sodomize three younger teammates in August with broomsticks, golf balls and pine cones. . . . University of Michigan student Evan Loomis is hospitalized with kidney failure in September after fraternity members deprive him of food and water during a three-day initiation rite.

Continued from p. 10

[Reardon's death], the national never visited the local chapter," Fierberg says. "And when it did visit in preceding years, it never uncovered the hazing that had been going on there for years," despite fraternity and university policies banning the use of alcohol in pledge activities.

But Maryland police declined to file any criminal charges against any fraternity members, saying Reardon had a choice not to drink. The fraternity agrees, declaring in a statement that, "College is a time for experimentation and examining adulthood. ... You cannot do so without accepting responsibility for your actions." [7]

Reardon's parents, not surprisingly, reject the fraternity's reasoning. "They are responsible for my son's death," Daniel's father said of the chapter and the national fraternity. "This was a hazing. And no one did anything." [8]

Fierberg says he has seen many such cases. He cites a 2001 incident in which he represented the parents of a Tennessee State University student who died while pledging Omega Psi Phi, a historically black fraternity. Fierberg says the student, 25-year-old Joseph Green, Jr., was rousted out of bed by fraternity members at 3 a.m. and ordered to run multiple laps at a high school track. He collapsed and died of hyperthermia (elevated body temperature) and an acute asthma attack. Fierberg settled the case for a confidential sum.

Fierberg says Omega Psi Phi did nothing to curtail the hazing that he says it knew was occurring at its chapters. Less than a year before Green died, Fierberg notes, the fraternity agreed to pay $1 million to another pledge who was severely beaten in a 1997 hazing incident at the University of Louisville. Also in 1997, hazing lawsuits at Indiana University and the University of Maryland cost the fraternity $1.1 million. Yet, Fierberg says he discovered that Omega Psi Phi budgeted only $250 annually for chapter visitations during those troubled years.

"They pounded their chests [in the Green case] saying, 'We have the strictest rules against hazing,' and ... they spent a total of $250 across 40 to 50 chapters to root out the problem," Fierberg scoffs.

Other hazing experts, such as Franklin College's Nuwer, give more credit to the nationals. "I think most of them are sincere, and I think the civil suits have drawn attention to the problems and put them on a hot seat," he says. "But they haven't done enough to get rid of alumni who tolerate hazing, and that's got to happen." ■

BACKGROUND

Early Hazing

Hazing has a long and controversial history dating back more than 2,000 years to ancient Greece. Then as now, hazing supporters cast the practice as an important rite of passage that taught young people to respect their elders and academic institutions. But, as is the case today, critics condemned it as puerile and pointless at best, and wicked and depraved at worst.

The Greek philosopher Plato likened the hazing of young boys to the acts of ferocious beasts. St. Augustine of Hippo, a fourth-century North African Catholic bishop, compared hazing to the acts of "devils." [9]

In the sixth century, Justinian I outlawed student hazing throughout the Byzantine Empire (the modern-day Balkan states). By the 12th century, hazing was widely proscribed by both policy and law throughout Europe, Asia Minor and North Africa. But the bans only drove the practice underground, where it continued to be carried out with great cruelness and brutality, as upperclassmen sought to assert themselves over younger scholars.

"In the Middle Ages, hazing could be, and frequently was, vicious," says Franklin College's Nuwer. "New students were made to do things such as press their noses to a grindstone, or cut their lips and drink salted water or urine. It was not a benign thing back then."

When hazing came to America in the mid-17th century, institutions like Harvard College moved quickly to ban the practice. But it flourished anyway, primarily directed at first-year students. At Harvard and other schools, upperclassmen handed out fliers describing "class-hazing" rituals to wary freshmen, who were expected to comply.

The rituals consisted largely of forced acts of personal servitude, such as requiring freshmen to run errands for seniors. But some were more dangerous, such as locking freshmen in rooms filled with cigar smoke. At some schools, classwide fighting known as a "battle royal" broke out on a regular basis, in which competing classes fought over such things as ceremonial banners or the right to paint the local water tower. Serious injuries — and later even deaths — occasionally resulted from the melees. Hazers who were caught were typically suspended until they apologized. [10]

Notably, nearly all of the violent hazing rituals of the 17th and 18th centuries were carried out by men. While women did occasionally haze each other at female-only and co-ed institutions, their rituals were far tamer than those favored by their male counterparts.

The first class-hazing death in the United States reportedly occurred at Kentucky's Franklin Seminary in 1838, though details are sketchy because the relevant records were destroyed in a fire. The hazing-related death of Jonathan Torrance at Amherst College in Massachusetts in 1847 is better documented. Torrance, a freshman, became ill and died after upperclassmen wrapped him in cold, wet bed sheets. [11]

The prevalence of class hazing at American colleges and universities began to fade in the 1930s as students began taking a strong stand against the practice. Today, little class hazing occurs at postsecondary institutions.

But as class hazing ebbed in colleges, it began flourishing in high schools. Today, high school seniors, juniors and sophomores frequently subject first-year students — including girls — to cruel, degrading and dangerous hazing rituals.

Fraternity Hazing

Fraternities and sororities began establishing themselves at U.S. colleges and universities in the early 19th century. At first, so-called Greek societies rarely subjected would-be members to formal, organized hazing rituals, though many engaged in horseplay and practical jokes. But by the turn of the 20th century, hazing was commonplace in fraternities, even though many Greek leaders publicly opposed the practice. Fraternities embraced hazing for the same reasons it has persisted through time: Some believed it built character and institutional cohesiveness; some did it for fun or perverted pleasure; and some did it to exact revenge for the hazing they themselves had been forced to endure as pledges.

Initially, most of the more recent Greek hazing rituals were pretty tame. In the mid-19th century, for example, fraternities at Wabash College in Crawfordsville, Ind., made pledges ride broomstick "horses" and hunt bumblebees with bows and arrows. [12] Sororities were even more subdued, as most prohibited pledges from using even moderate amounts of tobacco or alcohol.

Still, early Greek hazing sometimes turned tragic. The first Greek hazing death occurred in 1873, when Cornell University freshman Mortimer Leggett died while pledging the Kappa Alpha Society at the Ithaca, N.Y., school. Fraternity members took Leggett into the countryside, blindfolded him and told him to find his way back to campus. He was killed when he tumbled into a gorge. [13]

In the first decades of the 20th century, Greek hazing became more boorish, reckless and violent. In the 1930s, for example, Phi Delta Gamma pledges at the University of Indiana were forced to walk around naked holding each other's genitals. They were also blindfolded and fed substances said to be human excrement and chicken dung and were subjected to what became the best-known form of fraternity hazing — being beaten on the buttocks with wooden paddles.

"It was easy to accumulate infractions that translated into paddlings," wrote novelist Larry Lockridge in 1994 of his father's experiences as a fraternity pledge in the 1930s. [14]

Although many educators objected to paddling — even when the recipients were allowed to keep their clothes on — the public generally viewed the practice as good, clean fun. Indeed, photographs of real or simulated fraternity paddlings routinely appeared in college and university yearbooks from the 1940s until about 1970. "People considered [paddling] as 'boys just being boys,' " says Theta Chi's Westol.

But other Greek hazing rituals of the era had far more tragic consequences. In 1945, for example, St. Louis University student Robert Perry was burned to death while pledging Phi Beta Pi. Fraternity members ordered Perry to lie naked on a table so they could administer electric shocks to his skin, which they had smeared with a flammable substance. Something sparked during the ritual, turning Perry into a human torch.

Several fraternity and sorority pledges have died over the years during hazing-related "road trips." In 1950, for example, a Sigma Pi pledge at the University of California, Berkeley, was struck and killed by an automobile after fraternity members dropped him off in the country and told him to walk back to campus. Four years later, a Delta Upsilon pledge at Swarthmore College near Philadelphia met the same fate. And in 1973, a Delta Phi pledge at Pennsylvania's Lehigh University died after jumping from a car in an effort to keep fraternity members from driving him into the country far from campus. [15]

Starting in the 1970s, alcohol became a major catalyst in fraternity and sorority deaths and injuries. In 1980, University of South Carolina student Barry Ballou, 20, passed out and choked to death after fraternity members urged him to drink a massive amount of alcohol. And in 1993, 19-year-old Chad Saucier died while pledging Phi Delta Theta at Alabama's Auburn University. Saucier, in keeping with supposed fraternity tradition, drank an entire fifth of Jagermeister liqueur at a pledge party. He passed out and died with a blood-alcohol content of .353 — nearly five times today's .08 legal limit for being considered too drunk to drive in many states.

In the 1990s, colleges and Greek organizations took steps to address alcohol abuse on campus. [16] In 1997, the NIC adopted a resolution encouraging its 66 member fraternities to maintain alcohol-free chapters. The same year, Phi Delta Theta and Sigma Nu banned drinking beginning in 2000. Scores of other fraternities and sororities soon followed suit. Many schools banned alcohol in residence halls and Greek-letter organizations. Some schools, such as Alfred, banned Greek systems on their campuses altogether.

Although the crackdown curbed hazing-related deaths and injuries, it did not eliminate them. Some Greek-letter chapters continue to use alcohol in hazing rituals — despite the policies of their national organizations and their host schools. Some chapters that were dissolved by their national offices or barred from campuses went underground, where they continue to use alcohol. Indeed, Rita Saucier says Phi Delta Theta had ignored its no-alcohol and no-hazing policies when her son Chad died at Auburn.

"They were already on probation for hazing the year before, and they weren't supposed to use alcohol, either," she says. "If they're not going to follow their own policies, what good are the policies?"

Military Hazing

Hazing also has a long and controversial history in the U.S. military and the service academies. Such well-known military figures as Gen. Douglas A. MacArthur and presidential candidate Gen. Wesley Clark experienced hazing when they were cadets at the U.S. Military Academy at West Point. MacArthur, in fact, tried to curtail the practice when he was superintendent at West Point, but his efforts were only partially successful.

In 1901, Congress seriously considered closing West Point after investigating the alleged hazing death of a first-year cadet, or "plebe," named Oscar Booz. Like all plebes, Booz was hazed when he entered West Point in 1898. Booz was beaten and forced to swallow large amounts of hot pepper sauce, among other indignities, by upperclassmen. He left West Point after four months, and — less than a year later — died of tuberculosis of the larynx. His family claimed West Point upperclassmen killed their son by forcing him to ingest the hot sauce, thereby rendering him ripe for infection. [17]

Congress concluded that the forced consumption of hot sauce did not directly cause Booz's fatal throat infection. But many lawmakers were troubled to learn about the hot-sauce ritual, as well as other West Point hazing rites they uncovered in their investigation. Plebes, among other things, were routinely forced to squat for hours over bayonets pointed at their groins, Congress found.

"They wanted to weed out the sissies and the momma's boys," says Col. Philip Leon, an English professor at The Citadel, in Charleston, S.C., who wrote about the West Point hazing scandal. The upperclassmen believed they were strengthening the Army by hazing the plebes, he says. "The Army was a rough place 100 years ago, and you had to be tough. [Upperclassmen] had convinced themselves that they were doing something noble for the Army by purifying and cleaning up the officer ranks."

Nevertheless, Congress outlawed hazing in the armed forces and service academies in the early 1900s, but the practice persisted anyway. In 1956, six U.S. Marine recruits drowned during a forced march through swamplands at Parris Island, S.C., under circumstances that some construed as hazing. And in 1986, a Marine stationed at the U.S. Navy base at Guantánamo Bay, Cuba, was nearly beaten to death by five fellow Marines who believed he had broken an unofficial code of loyalty. The incident inspired the 1992 movie "A Few Good Men," in which actor Jack Nicholson, playing the base commander, orders a "code red" — jargon for hazing — to teach a struggling Marine a lesson.

In 1997, many Americans were shocked when a videotape depicting a graphic, real-life military hazing ritual was broadcast by the news media. It showed graduates of the Marine paratrooper school at Camp Lejeune, N.C., screaming and writhing in pain as fellow Marines pounded metal "jump wing" insignias with half-inch-long mounting posts into their chests. The ritual, known as "blood pinning," has long been illegal in the armed services. William S. Cohen, who was Defense secretary when the videotape surfaced, vowed to enforce a strict, "zero tolerance" hazing policy.

"Abuse such as this has no place in any branch of the United States military," Cohen said.

Still, some soldiers defended the blood-pinning ceremony — anonymously — on military-oriented Web sites. "It's been tolerated throughout all the services for decades," declared a service member on www.enlisted.com. "Compared to having your body ripped to shreds by ground fire as you parachute to Earth, the pinning ceremony is quite civilized." [18] ■

CURRENT SITUATION

High School Brutality

Some of the most sadistic and cruel hazing incidents in recent years have involved high school students, such as the sodomizing incidents involving the New York football players, and the powder-puff football game in suburban Chicago that turned so ugly. Although the videotaped fracas stunned many Americans, sociologists and gender-role experts were not surprised to see girls brutalizing each other, given the violent values emphasized by television, music and other media.

"In our culture we give a lot of status to aggressive masculinity," says the University of Maine's Allan. "Just look at the popularity of the WWF [World Wrestling Federation]. There are certain traits or characteristics that girls learn are ways to gain power, and to me it makes sense that girls are taking on those sorts of behaviors."

Experts say it's not surprising that high school students are engaging in the sort of violent, sexually explicit hazing behaviors exhibited in Chicago and New York. "That's the nature of our society today — everything is violent and sexual," says Sigal, the sociologist at County College of Morris. "Kids today have seen everything by the time they get to high school."

Many adults, meanwhile, maintain that society is going too easy on young people who inflict hazing-related pain and suffering on others. Saucier, for example, remains outraged that Alabama prosecutors didn't charge anyone criminally in the death of her son. "They did an investigation, but it was a joke," she says. "They called it an accident. They basically blamed Chad."

Indeed, law enforcement officials sometimes decline to bring criminal charges if victims consented to being hazed — even when the hazers subject the pledges to extraordinary peer pressure. Such was the case with Evan Loomis, a University of Michigan student. Last September he and other Sigma Chi fraternity pledges were made to crawl over shards of broken beer bottles and perform as many as 1,000 push-ups during the fraternity's three-day initiation period. They were also deprived of adequate amounts of food, water and sleep. Loomis struggled through the initiation period but had to be hospitalized for kidney failure immediately after the ordeal. Upon recovering, he said he kept going because fraternity members told him that none of the pledges would be granted membership if he quit.

University officials quickly booted Sigma Chi off campus. But police declined to arrest anyone after determining that Loomis participated in the initiation ceremony voluntarily. "We have no evidence of a crime here, though obviously, [Loomis] was put through extraordinarily rigorous activity," said Ann Arbor Police Chief Daniel Oates. [19]

College Athletes Often Hazed With Alcohol

Nearly 80 percent of college athletes were hazed; 60 percent of the incidents involved drinking contests or other unacceptable activities.

Percentage of Athletes Subjected to Hazing

(by severity of initiation)

Type of Initiation Activities	%	Estimated Number of Athletes
Acceptable only	19%	61,888
Questionable only	19	61,342
Alcohol-related; no other unacceptable behaviors	39	126,254
Unacceptable, non-alcohol-related	21	68,041
Total Hazed (Questionable/ Unacceptable)	**79%**	**255,637**

Definitions

Acceptable: *positive activities only*

Questionable: *humiliating or degrading — but not dangerous or potentially illegal*

Alcohol-related: *drinking contests, exclusive of other dangerous or potentially illegal behaviors*

Unacceptable and potentially illegal: *activities that carry a high probability of danger or injury, or could result in criminal charges*

Source: Nadine C. Hoover, "National Survey: Initiation Rites and Athletics for NCAA Sports Teams," August 1999

Prosecutors filed dozens of criminal charges in the Chicago and New York high school hazing cases, but critics — especially the victims' families — still weren't satisfied. In the Glenbrook case, 16 students pleaded guilty or were convicted of misdemeanor battery or alcohol charges — but most will be eligible to have their records expunged in a year.

In the New York case, the three attackers were tried as juveniles, not as adults as the victims' families had requested. Juvenile court proceedings are not public, but according to several news reports, two of the three defendants pleaded guilty last November to juvenile counts of involuntary deviate sexual intercourse (the third defendant's case is reportedly still pending).

Relatives of the victims who were in court said the two convicted attackers were taken to a facility where social workers and psychologists will evaluate them and recommend a course of punishment. Their sentences could be as light as probation or community service, outraged relatives said.

One victim's aunt, who identified herself to reporters only as Sue, said the judge in the case should be kicked off the bench. She focused her wrath on one of the attackers, an extremely large 17-year-old who she said pinned her nephew down during the attack. "I want people to see the size of this person who sat on my nephew while he was being raped," she told reporters after a court hearing last November. "He should be walking down a prison hall. But now he's being evaluated." [20]

Blame Game

Critics also say school officials coddle hazers. In St. Amant, La., for example, high school football coach David Swacker came under fire recently for an incident that took place on Oct. 14, 2002, the 16th birthday of one of his players. More than two-dozen players accosted the boy that day in the locker room after practice. They stripped off the boy's pants and underwear, taped him face-down to a bench and beat him on the buttocks with their hands and football cleats. One of the hazers pressed an empty tape dispenser into the victim's buttocks, and another placed his anus over the victim's nose.

Critics — led by the victim's mother — say Swacker knew that older players traditionally hazed younger ones on their birthdays. The mother alleges that several weeks before her son was hazed, Swacker walked in on a similar hazing and told the perpetrators only that they were "wasting good tape."

"The coaches have allowed this to go on for a long time," the mother of the most recent victim says. "I think they should be fired."

Prosecutors charged three of the student hazers with battery. One pleaded guilty and was sentenced to six months of unsupervised probation; the charges against the other two are still pending.

Prosecutors also charged Swacker, 49, with failing to report abuse and neglect of a child. A subpoena issued by the district attorney's office in October 2002 states that Swacker was told about the incident the day it occurred, and that he telephoned the victim at home that night, but that he "failed to immediately report the incident to law enforcement or the minor's parents." [21] The subpoena also alleges that Swacker witnessed, but failed to report, the previous hazing incident.

"Ultimately, the responsibility lies with the coach to make sure that people behave in the locker room," says Robin O'Bannon, the assistant district attorney prosecuting Swacker.

Swacker pleaded not guilty to the failure-to-report charge. His attorney, Tommy Damico, calls the prosecution a "witch hunt" and says the public's "overreaction on this has been unbelievable."

"Coach Swacker lives and dies for those kids," Damico says. "He has never condoned hazing, and he's not aware of any hazing that's going on. He became aware of an incident after the fact, and he immediately notified his superiors. And when we go to trial, everybody is going to realize that."

Divided Communities

There is rarely universal agreement within communities when it comes to hazing, especially in cases involving high school and college teams. Those divisions erupt in particularly nasty ways if the punishment curtails a team's season or jeopardizes athletic scholarships.

After coach Swacker was charged in the St. Amant case, many members of the community's football booster club showed their support for him by wearing bright yellow T-shirts emblazoned with the words "Back Swack" at the team's games.

Assistant District Attorney O'Bannon says Swacker's supporters wore the T-shirts to "harass" the victim and his family. "The booster club has acted deplorably," O'Bannon says. "They've attacked the parents, and they've booed and hissed at [the victim], saying he's a disgrace to St. Amant. They acknowledge what happened to him, but they say he should suck it up like everybody else."

The victim's mother says she was "sickened and appalled" by the "Back Swack" T-shirts. "It's more important to them to have a winning football team than to crack down on these locker-room hazing incidents."

A similar debate galvanized college ice-hockey fans four years ago when a University of Vermont freshman who was vying for a spot on his school's team claimed a group of veteran players forced him to participate in a series of degrading hazing rituals. Corey LaTulippe, then 19, said he and other freshmen were made to parade around naked at a party while holding each other's genitals, among other humiliating stunts.

LaTulippe, who failed to make the team, filed a civil lawsuit against the university, the hockey coach and three players. The university launched its own investigation of the incident and canceled the final 15 games of the season after determining that some players tried to cover it up.

Some hockey fans lauded the university's decision as correct and even "courageous." But others were outraged. In a letter to the editor of a Burlington newspaper, a Waterbury resident called hazing a "harmless rite of passage" and branded LaTulippe a "weakling" and a "whiner" for not being able to "cut the mustard."

"Hazing has been around since the time of the Romans," Greg Ziegler wrote. "Back in the 1960s, when I went to high school, [athletes and other group members] had to go

Continued on p. 18

At Issue

Are fraternities doing enough to stamp out hazing?

EDWARD A. PEASE
PRESIDENT, NORTH-AMERICAN INTERFRATERNITY CONFERENCE

WRITTEN FOR *THE CQ RESEARCHER*, DECEMBER 2003

yes

The North-American Interfraternity Conference (NIC), comprised of 64 national organizations, shares a set of common values and ethics that requires our individual members to respect the dignity of all other people. We do not tolerate hazing in any form.

Fraternities take an aggressive, three-pronged approach to eradicating hazing in all campus organizations. First, we work to make hazing illegal. Second, we enforce the law and our own policies, which are often more comprehensive in defining and prohibiting unacceptable activities. Finally, we make anti-hazing education a priority and recruit members who will not haze or allow hazing to occur.

Fraternities are proud of their efforts to make hazing a crime. Today, 42 states criminalize hazing. We led the push for adoption and enforcement of those laws.

We are uncompromising in policing our organizations. Each national fraternity has its own anti-hazing policies, which often take a more detailed approach than state law in defining and prohibiting hazing. In the rare instances where hazing does occur, we swiftly investigate, penalize those responsible and, where appropriate, sanction or close the chapter for the actions of individual members. We strongly support school and local authorities' efforts to investigate hazing and take appropriate action against the individuals involved, including criminal prosecution, expulsion or loss of a diploma.

Education is our best weapon against hazing. Fraternities have spent millions of dollars in an effort to educate their members about hazing and the harm it can do to a person's physical and mental well being. Hazing is a societal problem that is becoming an alarming rite of passage for a growing number of teenagers engaged in high school sports, bands and clubs, but there is little anti-hazing education before students come to college. In fact, the first time a student receives a clear definition of hazing, why it is illegal and why he won't be hazed, is often after enrolling in a fraternity's new-member program. Our emphasis on proactive education will not stop, and our commitment to eradicate hazing will not waver.

Hazing is not welcome in our organizations. Our student members are too busy serving their communities, pursuing the intellectual development that is the foundation for their future successful careers, and forming relationships that will last a lifetime. Fraternities are the leaders in battling hazing. Attacking us for our efforts only wounds the strongest army in our common struggle.

DOUGLAS E. FIERBERG
PRESIDENT-ELECT, NATIONAL CRIME VICTIM BAR ASSOCIATION;
ANNE R. NOBLE
SENIOR APPELLATE COUNSEL, BODE & GRENIER

WRITTEN FOR *THE CQ RESEARCHER*, DECEMBER 2003

no

The Greek industry knows that hazing is a serious problem but continues to pay little more than lip service to stopping it. That knowledge, moreover, though hard won, is hardly new: By the late 1980s, risk managers ranked these organizations sixth-worst for insurance purposes — just behind hazardous-waste disposal companies and asbestos contractors. Yet, more than a decade later, hazing incidents on American campuses still leave scores of young people seriously injured or dead. Why? A recent incident at a mid-Atlantic university is instructive. There, a pledge died as a result of excessive alcohol at an initiation ritual. After he lost consciousness, fraternity officers delayed summoning emergency medical assistance until he had turned blue from lack of oxygen and all hope for his survival had passed.

In the litigation that ensued, evidence established that the initiation ritual was a "longstanding" tradition at the chapter, which previously had been sanctioned by the university for hazing; that chapter officers had received no risk-management training from the national fraternity; and that the national fraternity, which had not conducted any risk-management inspection of the fraternity for about two years prior to the death, had in fact eliminated the staff position responsible for conducting chapter visitations and inspections, directing the money instead to improving its Web site.

Fraternities cannot plead ignorance. The fraternity chapter president admitted that the chapter's risk-management policy was ineffective. In fact, an Alcohol and Substance Education Committee organized by the national fraternity had studied the problems of hazing and alcohol misuse four years earlier and had concluded that the risk-management policy was "not . . . working." This particular policy is used by approximately 70 percent of fraternities and sororities. Despite the committee's unanimous recommendation that the national fraternity adopt a new policy and convert its chapters into alcohol-free houses, the recommendation was rejected.

The Greek industry routinely resists change. Many fraternities still decline to allow independent risk-management consultants to visit, review or conduct training for their officers and members; fail to disclose the extent of hazing and incidents of serious injury and death; assign key responsibilities to inexperienced, underage chapter officers; and refuse to commit resources and energy to serious risk management. Until the Greek industry addresses these and other issues, hazing will continue and, tragically, young men and women will continue to die or suffer catastrophic injuries as a result.

Verbal Humiliation Is Most Common

The more popular methods of high school hazing include verbal humiliation and being forced to abuse alcohol.

Prevalence of Various Forms of Hazing
(by percentage of victims)

Humiliation Tactics	Male	Female	Average
Being forced to:			
Accept being yelled or cursed at	20%	14%	17%
Restrict associations to certain people	15	16	16
Serve older members	14	11	12
Undress or tell dirty stories or jokes	12	10	11
Embarrass oneself publicly	10	13	11
Be thrown into a pool, ocean, creek, pond or toilet	12	8	10
Skip school or refuse to do schoolwork or chores	10	10	10
Be tattooed, pierced or shaved	11	8	9
Eat or drink disgusting things	8	9	8
Go without food, sleep or cleanliness	8	7	7
Subjected to one or more humiliating activity	**48**	**39**	**43**
Hazing Involving Substance Abuse			
Being forced to:			
Drink alcohol	16%	11%	13%
Participate in drinking contests	13	10	12
Smoke cigarettes or cigars; use tobacco	12	10	11
Use illegal drugs	12	9	11
Drink or exercise until you pass out	11	8	9
Subjected to one or more substance-abuse activity	**24**	**18**	**23**
Dangerous or Illegal Hazing			
Being forced to:			
Make prank phone calls or harass others	11%	9%	10%
Destroy or vandalize property	10	8	9
Steal, cheat, or commit a crime	9	7	8
Beat up others or pick a fight with someone	9	5	7
Inflict pain on or brand self; take part in Satanic rite	5	6	6
Be tied up or exposed to extreme cold	7	5	6
Be physically abused or beaten	8	5	6
Be cruel to animals	4	3	3
Subjected to one or more dangerous activity	**27**	**17**	**22**

Source: Nadine C. Hoover and Norman J. Pollard, "Initiation Rites in American High Schools: A National Survey," August 2000

Continued from p. 16

through the gauntlet of being slapped on the buttocks by wet gym towels or eating live worms. Now, because [LaTulippe] is too much of an emotional weakling to be man enough to go through a harmless rite of passage and whined tearfully to daddy, the hockey careers of dozens of talented youngsters are in jeopardy." [22]

Other Vermont hockey fans called LaTulippe a "rat" and a "wimp," and said his hazing complaint was "sour grapes" for not making the team. "It's the hard-core fans" that are the worst," said Gail Westgate, one of LaTulippe's attorneys. "Sadly, some fans want their sports at any cost." [23]

Things got even uglier last summer after the New York sodomy case. The victims' families and other outspoken anti-hazing members of the Bellmore community received at least six anonymous letters saying they would be sodomized with broomsticks and "executed" if they didn't keep quiet. Police are looking for who mailed the threatening letters, but they have not made any arrests. ■

OUTLOOK

Culture Change

If hazing is to be eradicated, society and its institutions must do more than just ban the practice, experts say.

Many argue that schools, Greek-letter organizations and other groups must offer acceptable alternatives to hazing. "People participate in hazing because it gives them a chance to prove themselves, and we can't ignore that if we're going to change the current hazing culture," says the University of Maine's Allan. "If we just eliminate hazing, we leave people with unfulfilled needs."

Sigma Chi's Anderson agrees. "Saying 'Don't haze' to some fraternity members is like saying 'Don't smoke' to a heavy smoker," he says. "It won't work unless you replace what you're taking away with something good."

To that end, Sigma Chi is putting together a program of "positive, team-building exercises" that can be used to challenge pledges and build brotherhood among members. The activities include "ropes courses"— obstacle courses consisting of rope ladders, log barriers and other impediments — and community-service projects, Anderson says. Other fraternities and sororities are designing similar programs.

High schools are also taking action. At Boulder High School in Colorado, upperclassmen frequently used to haze first-year students by throwing them into a creek near the school. Principal Ronald Cabrera says the number of incidents has dropped considerably since the school initiated a mentoring program that encourages juniors and seniors to engage in academic and after-school activities with first-year students.

"We've really tried to shape the culture and environment of the school so that our upperclassmen will not be so inclined to haze the underclassmen," Cabrera says. "I don't know that we've got [the hazing problem] figured out completely, but I think we're making some substantial inroads."

In nearby Lafayette, Centaurus High School boys' basketball coach Mike Leahy has instituted a similar program. "We match up our freshmen players with our seniors and our lettermen so they feel welcomed and not intimidated," Leahy says. "There's always a worry that somebody is going to pick on the young kids, so we've tried to address it before it becomes a problem."

Experts say that until society — especially those in leadership positions — takes a consistent and strong position against hazing, the practice will not be eradicated. "In my mind, everything starts at the top," says sociologist Sigal, from County College of Morris.

"You have to talk to people and make sure there's no hazing going on, and that's where a lot of school systems are falling down."

— Richard Sigal, Professor of Sociology, County College of Morris, Randolph, N.J.

"If it's a team, it starts with the coach. If it's a school system, it starts with the board and the superintendent and travels downhill to the principals, the coaches, all the way down to the players. The tone has to be set at the top: Officials have to say, 'There will be no hazing, period, or heads will roll.' "

It's easy to see when the top-down model for preventing hazing is not followed, Sigal says. A few years ago, Sigal served as an expert witness in a civil suit involving a Texas high school baseball player who was hazed by teammates on a school bus. Several older boys had held the victim down, stripped off his pants and inserted a Coke bottle filled with tobacco spit into his buttocks. The coaches were riding in the front of the bus at the time, but they did nothing to stop the attack, Sigal says.

"Those bozo coaches in Texas were some of the stupidest men I've ever encountered," Sigal says. "They had no clue what hazing was, they didn't know that it was against the law in Texas, or that it was against their own school policy. I was shocked that they had college degrees."

To prevent such situations, Sigal says, school systems not only should put their anti-hazing policies in print but also conduct in-service workshops and explain them to their staff members. "You really have to put a policy in people's faces and follow it up," she says. "You have to talk to people and make sure there's no hazing going on, and that's where a lot of school systems are falling down."

If school systems don't get a handle on hazing, there may be long-term repercussions for the victims and possibly for society. Hazing victims who "suck it up" and suffer in silence can experience long-lasting psychological problems, experts say, even if they weren't harmed physically.

About the Author

Brian Hansen, a freelance writer in Boulder, Colo., specializes in educational and environmental issues. He previously was a staff writer for *The Researcher* and a reporter for the *Colorado Daily* in Boulder and Environment News Service in Washington. His awards include the Scripps Howard Foundation award for public service reporting and the Education Writers Association award for investigative reporting. He holds a B.A. in political science and an M.A. in education from the University of Colorado.

Researcher Pollard, of Alfred University, agrees. "Hazing can have devastating effects on kids' well being," he says. "They report feeling angry, depressed, anxious and suicidal. Many feel a sense of revenge — and I really worry about that." ■

FOR MORE INFORMATION

Center for the Prevention of School Violence, 1801 Mail Service Center, Raleigh, NC 27699-1801; (800) 299-6054; www.ncdjjdp.org/cpsv. A resource center run by the North Carolina Department of Juvenile Justice and Delinquency Prevention, dedicated to promoting school safety and "positive youth development."

Center for the Study of the College Fraternity, Franklin Hall 206, University of Indiana, Bloomington, IN 47405; (812) 855-1228; www.indiana.edu/~cscf. Encourages and supports research on what roles fraternities and sororities play in higher education.

National Association of Independent Colleges and Universities, 1025 Connecticut Ave., N.W., Suite 700, Washington, DC 20036-5405; (202) 785-8866; www.naicu.edu. Represents private colleges and universities on policy issues.

National Association of Secondary School Principals, 1904 Association Dr., Reston, VA 20191-1537; (703) 860-0200; www.nassp.org. Conducts training for members and serves as an information clearinghouse.

National Association of State Universities and Land Grant Colleges, 1 Dupont Circle N.W., Suite 710, Washington DC 20036; (202) 778-0818. Serves as a clearinghouse for issues involving public higher education.

National Panhellenic Conference, 3905 Vincennes Rd., Suite 105, Indianapolis, IN 46268; (317) 872-3185; www.npcwomen.org. An umbrella group representing 26 national and international women's fraternities and sororities; condemns hazing and prohibits member institutions from using alcohol in recruiting new members.

National School Boards Association, 1680 Duke St., Alexandria, VA 22314; (703) 838-6722; www.nsba.org. Monitors legislation and regulations affecting public-education funding, local governance and education quality.

National School Safety Center, 141 Duesenberg Dr., Suite 11, Westlake Village, CA 91362; (805) 373-9977; www.nssc1.org. A resource center for developing safe-school programs, including anti-hazing strategies.

North-American Interfraternity Conference, 3901 W. 68th St., Suite 390, Indianapolis, IN 46268-1791; (317) 872-1112; www.nicindy.org. An advocacy and educational group representing 64 national fraternities.

www.StopHazing.org. Provides a wealth of information on hazing, anti-hazing laws, alternative initiation rites and other issues.

Notes

[1] Quoted in Kenneth C. Crowe, "11 in Fraternity Face Counts in Man's Death," *The* [Albany, N.Y.] *Times Union*, May 1, 2003, p. A1.

[2] For background on college sports, see Richard L. Worsnop, "College Sports," *The CQ Researcher*, Aug. 26, 1994, pp. 745-768.

[3] Quoted in Jan Pudlow, "Colleges Find Hazing is Nearly Impossible to Squelch," *The Tallahassee Democrat*, Jan. 18, 1999.

[4] Quoted in Thomas Fields-Meyer, *et al.*, "Too Cruel for School," *People*, Nov. 3, 2003, pp. 68-70.

[5] For background, see Hank Nuwer, *Wrongs of Passage: Fraternities, Sororities, Hazing and Binge Drinking* (1999), pp. 98-99.

[6] Another 27 percent said they had only "negative feelings" about hazing, and 13 percent said they wanted to exact "revenge" for their treatment. Percentages do not add up to precisely 100 percent due to rounding.

[7] Phi Sigma Kappa sent the statement to CNN, where it was read on the "Connie Chung Tonight" show on Nov. 21, 2002.

[8] Reardon's parents were interviewed on CNN's "Connie Chung Tonight" show on Nov. 21, 2002.

[9] St. Augustine, *The Confessions of St. Augustine, Books I-X*, translated by Francis Joseph Sheed (1942). For more information, see Nuwer, *op. cit.*, pp. 92-93.

[10] See Samuel Eliot Morison, *Harvard College in the Seventeenth Century* (1936), p. 82.

[11] See Edward Hitchcock, *Reminiscences of Amherst College* (1863), pp. 332-337.

[12] See Nuwer, *op. cit.*, p. 119.

[13] Quoted in *ibid.*, p. 238.

[14] Quoted in Laurence S. Lockridge, *Shade of the Raintree: The Life and Death of Ross Lockridge, Jr.* (1994), pp. 98-99.

[15] For more information on all the incidents described in this paragraph, see Nuwer, *op. cit.*, pp. 242-243.

[16] For more information, see Karen Lee Scrivo, "Drinking on Campus," *The CQ Researcher*, March 20, 1998 pp. 241-264.

[17] See Philip W. Leon, *Bullies and Cowards: The West Point Hazing Scandal, 1898-1901* (2000).

[18] The comment was originally posted at www.enlisted.com/articles/hazing1.html. It was subsequently quoted in Matthew Dolan, "Hazing in the Navy: Commanding Officer Targeted in Inquiry," *The Virginian-Pilot*, Feb. 11, 2002, p. A1.

[19] Quoted in Victoria Edwards, "U. Michigan Sigma Chi Vacates Residence in Light of Hazing Incident," *Michigan Daily*, Oct. 17, 2003, p. 1.

[20] Quoted in Brian Harmon, "'We Brutalized Boys,' HS Athletes Admit," *The* [New York] *Daily News*, Nov. 22, 2003, p. 6.

[21] Motion and order for subpoena duces tecum, 23rd Judicial District Court, Parish of Ascension, State of Louisiana, Oct. 29, 2002.

[22] Letter to the editor, *The Burlington* [Vt.] *Free Press*, Jan. 24, 2000, p. 5A.

[23] Quoted in Leo Roth, "Hockey World Feels High Cost of Hazing," *Rochester* [N.Y.] *Democrat and Chronicle*, Jan. 29, 2000, p. 1D.

Bibliography

Selected Sources

Books

Leon, Philip W., *Bullies and Cowards: The West Point Hazing Scandal, 1898-1901*, Greenwood Publishing Group, 2000.
A Citadel English professor describes how the death of a plebe nearly prompted Congress to close the Army's prestigious service academy.

Nuwer, Hank, *Broken Pledges: The Deadly Rite of Hazing*, Longstreet Press, 1990.
A journalism professor chronicles the death of Chuck Stenzel, who died in an alcohol-related hazing incident at Alfred University in 1978. This was the first of his four books on hazing.

Nuwer, Hank (ed.), *The Hazing Reader*, Indiana University Press, 2004.
Experts in psychology, sociology and education look at hazing in high schools, fraternities, athletics and the military.

Nuwer, Hank, *High School Hazing: When Rites Become Wrongs*, Franklin Watts, 2000.
Nuwer's third book on hazing focuses on peer pressure and initiation rites in high schools, including the role of alcohol.

Nuwer, Hank, *Wrongs of Passage: Fraternities, Sororities, Hazing and Binge Drinking*, Indiana University Press, 1999.
The most comprehensive of Nuwer's four books on hazing examines the phenomenon from its origins in ancient Greece; contains extensive notes and an appendix of U.S. hazing fatalities since 1838.

Articles

Dolan, Matthew, "Navy Officer Gets 5 Days in Brig, Fine for Hazing," *The* [Norfolk] *Virginian-Pilot*, June 5, 2002, p. B1.
A Navy officer was tried, convicted and briefly jailed for hazing sailors under his command.

Fontimayor, Gil Andrei, "Hazed and Confused: A Controversial Tradition of College Initiation Seeps into High Schools," *The* [Norfolk] *Virginian-Pilot*, March 28, 2003, p. E1.
A sportswriter examines why hazing is flourishing in many high school athletic programs, presenting the perspectives of players, coaches and administrators.

Haynes, V. Dion, "Across the U.S., Hazing Lives Despite Laws," *The Chicago Tribune*, May 26, 2003, p. A1.
This overview article on hazing in high schools, colleges, fraternities and other groups focuses on why anti-hazing laws aren't working.

James, Rebecca, "Is it Just a Prank? Or is it Hazing?" *The* [Syracuse, N.Y.] *Post-Standard*, Nov. 2, 2003, p. A1.
A journalist explores attitudes about hazing when it does not result in physical injury or death.

Schuster, Karla, and Keiko Morris, "Mepham Apologies: Two Teenagers Admit Crimes in Hazing Case," *New York Newsday*, Nov. 22, 2003, p. A5.
The authors chronicle legal developments in the case involving three high school varsity football players who sodomized three younger players with broomsticks, golf balls and pine cones.

Ward, Steven, "Coach Charged in Hazing: Official Allegedly Failed to Report Incident," *The* [Baton Rouge, La.] *Advocate*, June 11, 2003, p. A1.
A Louisiana football team hazing incident raises questions about the responsibilities that coaches and school administrators have in preventing hazing.

Weir, Tom, "Hazing Rears Ugly Head Across USA," *USA Today*, Dec. 9, 2003, p. C1.
A broad look at hazing in high schools, athletic teams, school bands and other groups and what educators are doing to stamp out the practice.

Reports and Studies

Hoover, Nadine C., and Norman J. Pollard, "Initiation Rites in American High Schools: A National Survey," Alfred University, August 2000.
The first study of the prevalence of hazing found that it is rampant among high school students across the country. Includes data on why students subject themselves to degrading and dangerous hazing rituals. Available online at: www.alfred.edu/news/html/hazing_study.html.

Hoover, Nadine C., "National Survey: Initiation Rites and Athletics for NCAA Sports Teams," Alfred University, August 1999.
This study by Alfred University researchers is the first national survey designed to quantify hazing among college athletes. It contains numerous data tables and is available online at: http://www.alfred.edu/news/html/hazing_study_99.html.

TV News Reports

"High School Horror: Athletes, Coaches Reportedly Knew of Hazing," ABC News, Dec. 18, 2003; www.abcnews.go.com.
As many as two-thirds of the high school athletes at a summer football camp in Pennsylvania knew some of their young teammates were undergoing vicious, sexually abusive hazing, and even coaches were aware that some form of hazing was going on, but they didn't suspect the severity of the attacks, according to a report today.

The Next Step:

Additional Articles from Current Periodicals

Alcohol and Hazing

Argetsinger, Amy, "Family Sues Fraternity In Death At U-Md.," *The Washington Post*, Nov. 19, 2002, p. B5.
The family of a University of Maryland fraternity pledge who died of an alcohol overdose has sued the national fraternity.

Argetsinger, Amy, "Fraternity Gave Liquor to Pledge Who Later Died," *The Washington Post*, Feb. 28, 2002, p. B1.
A University of Maryland freshman fell into a fatal coma after drinking bourbon with his fellow Phi Sigma Kappa pledges, a member of the fraternity said yesterday.

Clayton, Mark, "Colleges May Be Forced to Curb Alcohol Use," *The Christian Science Monitor*, Sept. 18, 2000, p. 4.
Following the alcohol-related death of an MIT freshman during a fraternity hazing ritual, MIT took steps to curb hazing-related drinking.

Marklein, Mary Beth, "Binge Drinking's Campus Toll," *USA Today*, Feb. 28, 2002, p. D8.
Recent drinking deaths at colleges have prompted college administrators to make alcohol-awareness a priority, while enacting stronger anti-hazing policies.

Wilgoren, Jodi, "Misdemeanor Charges Filed In Teenage Hazing Incident," *The New York Times*, May 17, 2003, p. A12.
Prosecutors filed charges against 15 suburban Chicago teenagers for their involvement this month in a drunken hazing ritual that degenerated into a melee.

Fraternity Hazing

Arenson, Karen W., "University Announces Ban on Fraternities and Sororities," *The New York Times*, May 22, 2002, p. B8.
Critics say the fraternity system leads to drinking, hazing and other dangerous practices that can result in death. Several schools have banned Greek life entirely.

Banks, Sandy, "Rituals Fed by Longing to Belong," *Los Angeles Times*, Sept. 17, 2002, p. E5.
The writer notes that pledging at black fraternities still entails the beatings and other hazing rituals that were common practice 25 years ago.

Childress, Sarah, "Frat Hazing: A Dangerous New Drinking Game," *Newsweek*, Dec. 8, 2003, p. 8.
"Water torture" is a very dangerous form of hazing because fraternity members assume that excessive water drinking can't be as hazardous as alcohol abuse.

Farrell, Elizabeth F., "New Book Profiles History of Black Fraternities and Sororities," *The Chronicle of Higher Education*, Oct. 31, 2003, p. 35.
A recently published book explores dangerous hazing rituals that have evolved at many black fraternities and sororities.

Foderaro, Lisa W., "3 Plead Guilty in Inquiry Into Fatal College Hazing," *The New York Times*, Oct. 11, 2003, p. B5.
Three of the 11 young men charged in a fatal hazing incident at the State University of New York, Plattsburgh, have pleaded guilty.

Foderaro, Lisa W., "Death in Underground Frat's Hazing Ritual Shakes a SUNY Campus," *The New York Times*, Sept. 15, 2003, p. B1.
At the State University of New York, Plattsburgh, a hazing ritual turned deadly when a pledge's brain swelled after he drank too much water.

Gottlieb, Jeff, "UCI Frat Suspended Amid Inquiry," *Los Angeles Times*, Jan. 15, 2002, p. B1.
A University of California, Irvine, fraternity has been suspended while it investigates a pledge's claim that he suffered a grand mal seizure and was hospitalized following a weekend of hazing.

Stockwell, Jamie, "Criminal Charges Studied in Death Of U-Md. Pledge," *The Washington Post*, March 27, 2002, p. A1.
Authorities are considering criminal charges against a University of Maryland fraternity after an autopsy revealed a freshman pledge died of alcohol poisoning.

Wee, Eric L., "Judge Orders Community Service For Two Charged in VMI Hazing," *The Washington Post*, Jan. 16, 1999, p. B4.
Two former Virginia Military Institute cadets accused of criminal hazing must each perform 56 hours of community service.

High School Hazing

Barrett, Mary Jo, "How a Rite of Passage Crossed the Line," *The Chicago Tribune*, June 1, 2003, p. C1.
The origins of violent high school hazing are extremely complex, and it is important to understand the social and personal context within which they occur.

Black, Lisa, "Last Student Sentenced in Hazing," *The Chicago Tribune*, Dec. 2, 2003, p. B1.
The last person facing criminal charges from a brutal hazing last spring involving Glenbrook North High School students pleaded guilty to battery.

Flynn, Courtney, and Lisa Black, "School Will Try to Expel Girls in Hazing Fracas," *The Chicago Tribune*, May 13, 2003, p. C1.
Under national scrutiny after a violent off-campus hazing incident, officials at Illinois' Glenbrook North High School suspended some senior girls for 10 days.

Harrington-Lueker, Donna, "Teenagers' Hazing Becomes Voyeurs' Viewing Pleasure," *USA Today*, May 21, 2003, p. A11.
In the aftermath of the notorious Northbrook, Ill., high school hazing incident, critics say the media and the public are culpable for becoming voyeuristic spectators.

Newman, Maria, "High School Group's Hazing Was Open Secret, Some Say," *The New York Times*, Aug. 8, 2002, p. B5.
After police arrested members of a high school fraternity for assaulting fellow students in a hazing incident, people said the hazing had been an open secret.

Paulson, Amanda, "Hazing Case Highlights Girl Violence," *The Christian Science Monitor*, May 9, 2003, p. 4.
Round-the-clock news coverage of a brutal hazing ritual in a Chicago suburb has renewed the nation's interest in female aggression.

Parents and Hazing

Black, Lisa, "Mother Found Guilty in Hazing," *The Chicago Tribune*, Nov. 14, 2003, p. B1.
A Northbrook, Ill., woman was found guilty of allowing high school students to drink beer in her home before they participated in a violent hazing ritual.

Borgatta, Tina, "Students, Parents Examine Ideas for a Safer School," *Los Angeles Times*, Dec. 16, 2001, p. B4.
At one California school, teachers and administrators are trying to educate parents about the dangers and consequences of hazing rituals.

Hayasaki, Erika, "Victim's Mother Starts Anti-Hazing Group," *Los Angeles Times*, Oct. 13, 2002, p. B3.
A California mother who believes her daughter died while participating in a sorority ritual announced the founding of Mothers Against Hazing.

Kelly, Katy, "Parents in a Haze?" *U.S. News & World Report*, May 26, 2003, p. 44.
Many parents are reluctant to discipline their kids' violations, like hazing, because they're afraid they might be bumped off an athletic team or kept out of an elite college.

Sports and Hazing

"Hazing Shocks Another School," *Los Angeles Times*, Oct. 5, 2003, p. D1.
Three Long Island football players have been accused of sodomizing three teammates during a hazing ritual. The resulting cancellation of the team's season angered some parents.

"High School Coach, Students Charged With Hazing," The Associated Press, June 11, 2003.
In Gonzales, La., a high school head football coach and three former students were charged with hazing a sophomore football player in 2002.

Healy, Patrick, "Coach on L.I. Says He Knew Of No Hazing," *The New York Times*, Oct. 1, 2003, p. B1.
The head coach of Mepham High School's football team, where three team members were sodomized in a hazing incident, said he and his staff did everything they could to ensure the safety of the students.

Weir, Tom, "Move Afoot to Educate Teachers on Hazing," *USA Today*, Dec. 9, 2003, p. C3.
Experts agree that even as many colleges are increasing education for teachers on school violence, hazing in sports has seldom been addressed.

Winzelberg, David, "How Much Supervision Is Enough?" *The New York Times*, Oct. 12, 2003, p. LI14.
At a high school outside New York City, the athletic director has worked hard to remind his coaches and staff that hazing should be stopped.

CITING *THE CQ RESEARCHER*

Sample formats for citing these reports in a bibliography include the ones listed below. Preferred styles and formats vary, so please check with your instructor or professor.

MLA STYLE

Jost, Kenneth. "Rethinking the Death Penalty." The CQ Researcher 16 Nov. 2001: 945-68.

APA STYLE

Jost, K. (2001, November 16). Rethinking the death penalty. *The CQ Researcher, 11*, 945-968.

CHICAGO STYLE

Jost, Kenneth. "Rethinking the Death Penalty." *CQ Researcher*, November 16, 2001, 945-968.

Back Issues

The CQ Researcher *offers in-depth coverage of many key areas.*
Back issues are $10. Quantity discounts available.
Call (866) 427-7737 to order back issues.

Or call for a free CQ Researcher Web trial!
Online access provides:

- *Searchable archives dating back to 1991.*
- *Wider access through IP authentication.*
- *PDF files for downloading and printing.*
- *Availability 48 hours before print version.*

CHILDREN/YOUTH
Preventing Teen Drug Use, March 2002
Sexual Abuse and the Clergy, May 2002
Movie Ratings, March 2003

CRIMINAL JUSTICE
Cyber-Crime, April 2002
Corporate Crime, October 2002
Serial Killers, October 2003

EDUCATION
Charter Schools, December 2002
Combating Plagiarism, September 2003
Home Schooling Debate, January 2003
Black Colleges, December 2003

ENVIRONMENT
Bush and the Environment, October 2002
Crisis in the Plains, May 2003
NASA's Future, May 2003
Water Shortages, August 2003
Air Pollution Conflict, November 2003

HEALTH CARE AND MEDICINE
Fighting SARS, June 2003
Medicare Reform, August 2003
Women's Health, November 2003
Homeopathy Debate Dec. 2003

LEGAL ISSUES
Abortion Debates, March 2003
Race in America, July 2003
Torture, April 2003
Homeland Security, September 2003
Civil Liberties Debates, October 2003

MODERN CULTURE
Gay Marriage, September 2003
Combating Plagiarism, September 2003
Latinos' Future, October 2003
Future of the Music Industry, Nov. 2003

POLITICS/GOVERNMENT
Presidential Power, November 2002
Future of NATO, February 2003
Trouble in South America, March 2003
North Korean Crisis, April 2003
Rebuilding Iraq, July 2003
Aiding Africa, August 2003
State Budget Crises, October 2003

TRANSPORTATION
Auto Safety, October 2001
Future of the Airline Industry, June 2002
Future of Amtrak, October 2002
SUV Debate, May 2003

- ***Stock Market Troubles***
- ***Advertising Overload***
- ***Democracy in the Arab World***

CQ Researcher

Published by CQ Press, a division of Congressional Quarterly Inc.

thecqresearcher.com

Stock Market Troubles

Do recent reforms adequately protect investors?

Accounting scandals at Enron and other large corporations rocked the financial world a few years ago. Now new problems are shaking up the stock market. The $7 trillion mutual fund industry is reeling from revelations that fund managers engaged in unethical trading practices to benefit themselves and a few select clients. Meanwhile, questions about the integrity of governance at the fabled New York Stock Exchange — the world's largest stock market — have led to new leadership and sweeping structural changes. But some analysts contend that the actions taken don't go far enough to protect investors. Others say recent market gains show that the corrective actions are working and that investors retain their faith in the overall integrity of the stock market.

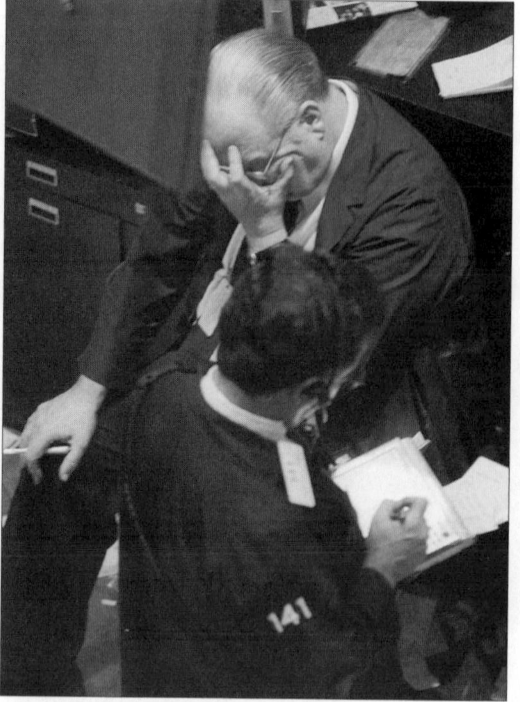

Floor traders at the New York Stock Exchange end a bad trading day.

INSIDE

THIS ISSUE

The CQ Researcher • Jan. 16, 2004 • www.thecqresearcher.com
Volume 14, Number 2 • Pages 25-48

RECIPIENT OF SOCIETY OF PROFESSIONAL JOURNALISTS AWARD FOR EXCELLENCE ◆ AMERICAN BAR ASSOCIATION SILVER GAVEL AWARD

Cover: Traders on the floor of the New York Stock Exchange tally up at the end of a bad day during the 2002 bear market. (AFP Photo/Henny Ray Abrams)

Jan. 16, 2004
Volume 14, No. 2

MANAGING EDITOR: Thomas J. Colin
ASSISTANT MANAGING EDITOR: Kathy Koch
ASSOCIATE EDITOR: Kenneth Jost
STAFF WRITERS: Mary H. Cooper, David Masci, William Triplett
CONTRIBUTING WRITERS: Rachel S. Cox, Sarah Glazer, David Hosansky, Patrick Marshall, Jane Tanner
DESIGN/PRODUCTION EDITOR: Olu B. Davis
ASSISTANT EDITOR: Kenneth Lukas

CQ PRESS

A Division of Congressional Quarterly Inc.

SENIOR VICE PRESIDENT/GENERAL MANAGER: John A. Jenkins
DIRECTOR, LIBRARY PUBLISHING: Kathryn C. Suárez
DIRECTOR, EDITORIAL OPERATIONS: Ann Davies
CIRCULATION MANAGER: Nina Tristani

CONGRESSIONAL QUARTERLY INC.
CHAIRMAN: Andrew Barnes
VICE CHAIRMAN: Andrew P. Corty
PRESIDENT AND PUBLISHER: Robert W. Merry

The CQ Researcher (ISSN 1056-2036) is printed on acid-free paper. Published weekly, except Jan. 2, April 9, July 2, July 9, Aug. 6, Aug. 13, Nov. 26 and Dec. 31, by CQ Press, a division of Congressional Quarterly Inc. Annual subscription rates for libraries, businesses and government start at $625. Single issues are available for $10. Quantity discounts apply to orders over 10. Additional rates furnished upon request. Periodicals postage paid at Washington, D.C., and additional mailing offices. POSTMASTER: Send address changes to *The CQ Researcher*, 1255 22nd St., N.W., Suite 400, Washington, D.C. 20037.

Stock Market Troubles

By David Masci

The Issues

Richard Strong was an American success story, a hardworking Midwesterner who started with nothing in 1974 and built a mutual fund empire and a personal fortune of nearly $1 billion.

But today Strong faces a bleak future. He was forced to resign as chairman of his company — Strong Financial — and faces possible criminal charges by New York state's crusading Attorney General Eliot Spitzer. And Strong Financial, with more than $43 billion in assets under management, is up for sale.

Strong's troubles stem from charges that he personally profited at the expense of his clients by "market-timing," or engaging in quick trades in and out of his own company's funds, even as Strong Financial aggressively discouraged the practice.

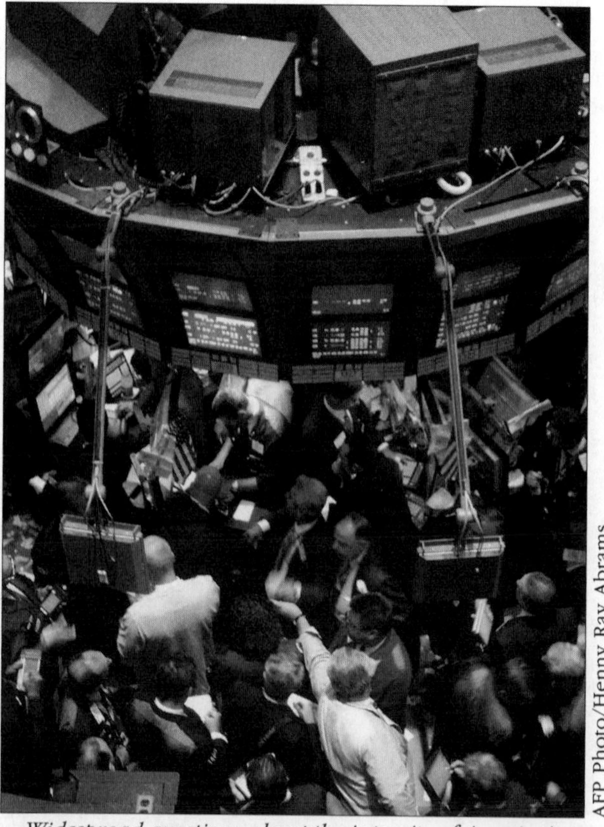

AFP Photo/Henny Ray Abrams

Widespread questions about the integrity of America's financial markets have focused on the busy New York Stock Exchange as well as trading abuses in the mutual fund industry and allegations of unethical practices among investment advisers. Critics say that reforms begun by the exchange don't go far enough to protect investors.

Since September, some two-dozen mutual fund and other financial-services companies have been linked to similarly questionable trading practices, including some of the nation's biggest mutual fund management firms — among them Putnam, Principle, Alliance Capital, Janus and Bank One.

"Our continuing investigations reveal a systemic breakdown in mutual fund governance that allowed directors and managers to ignore the interests of investors," Spitzer said during a Nov. 20 hearing before the Senate Banking Committee. "In fund after fund, what we have seen is the wholesale abandonment of fiduciary responsibilities."

More recently, Spitzer and the Securities and Exchange Commission (SEC) indicated that they would soon begin investigating the banks that financed those trading activities.

And in a stunning development just this week, the SEC announced on Jan. 13 it had uncovered widespread instances of brokers receiving undisclosed payments for steering investors toward specific funds. The revelations followed a nine-month examination of more than a dozen of Wall Street's largest brokerage houses that sell mutual fund shares.

"A customer has the right to know what the incentives are when a broker recommends a particular fund family," said Stephen M. Cutler, chief of the SEC's enforcement division. [1]

During the 1990s, when a booming stock market attracted tens of millions of small investors for the first time, mutual funds grew from a footnote in America's financial markets to its most popular investment tool. Fund assets increased sevenfold during the decade, and by 2003 nearly 100 million people owned shares in mutual funds worth a staggering $7.1 trillion.

Until now, the mutual fund industry had a reputation as a squeaky-clean, relatively safe repository for investors. Indeed, mutual funds — collections of stocks and bonds purchased for investors by professional managers — are the instruments most Americans use to invest in the stock and bond markets.

But several companies and fund managers have been charged with bending or breaking fund-trading rules, encouraging favored clients to time their buying and selling to their advantage. Two of the most common practices are late trading and market-timing, which both take advantage of the fact that mutual fund shares are priced only once a day, at the end of trading at 4 p.m. By contrast, the value of a share of stock is continually in flux.

Late trading involves purchasing or selling mutual fund shares based on information acquired after the price for the next day has been set. The practice has been likened to betting on a race after it's over.

Market-timing involves buying or selling mutual fund shares in anticipation of the setting of the 4 p.m. price, using the changing value of stocks held in the fund to anticipate what that price will be and to profit from it. The practice hurts the fund because the constant buying and selling of shares requires funds to keep more cash on hand to deal with the last-minute trades. That leaves funds with less cash

Confidence in Mutual Funds Remains High

Americans had more than $7 trillion invested in mutual funds in 2003 — a record high — indicating that confidence in mutual funds remains strong despite recent scandals in the industry. Fund assets grew slowly during the bear market from 1999-2001 and declined slightly in 2002.

Total Mutual Fund Assets, 1990-2002
(in $ trillions)

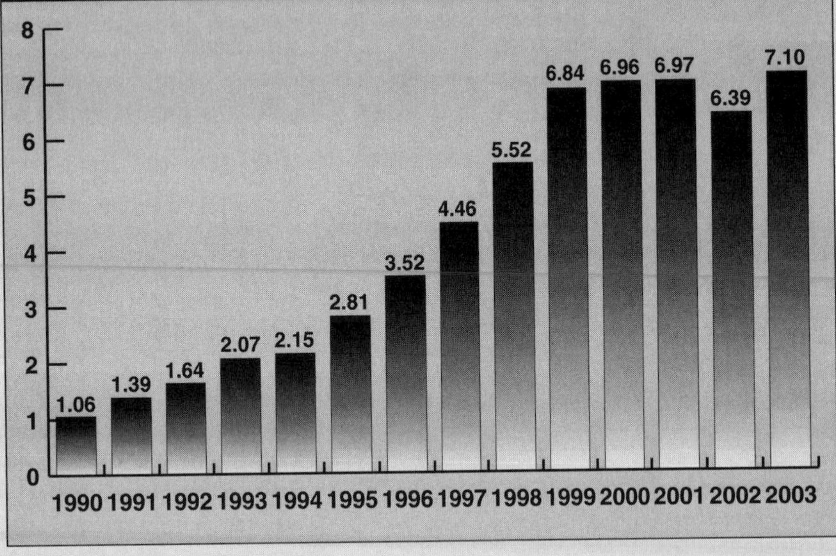

Source: Mutual Fund Fact Book, *Investment Company Institute, 2003*

to invest in financial instruments aimed at benefiting all the fund's investors.

Market-timing violates securities regulations when a fund manager engages in it or encourages a client to do so, because managers have a fiduciary duty to all the fund's investors, not just a few select clients.

Dozens of fund employees, from brokers to top executives, already have been caught up in the scandal and forced to resign. A few have been indicted, and a growing number are under criminal investigation. Some firms, including industry giants like Alliance Capital and Janus, already have agreed to pay investors hundreds of millions of dollars in settlements. And additional firms are likely to be implicated, as internal audits and outside investigations by Spitzer and the SEC seek to uncover more abuses.

"It's like we tapped on the edifice and it crumbled," says New York Assistant Attorney General David Brown, head of the attorney general's Investment Protection Bureau.

The mutual fund scandal comes at the end of a difficult couple of years for the American stock market. On the one hand, the collapse of the "dot com" and telecommunications industries in 2000 helped to trigger a huge drop in overall stock prices, draining billions of dollars from investors' nest eggs.

But plummeting prices were only the beginning. In October 2001, it was revealed that energy giant Enron had altered revenue and earnings numbers to its advantage. Soon, MCIWorldcom and other blue-chip corporations also were being investigated.

The Enron debacle — the firm went bankrupt in December, 2001 — was soon followed by Spitzer's allegations that 10 of the largest Wall Street brokerages, including Citicorp and Merrill Lynch, had been urging customers to buy certain stocks, not because they were good investments but because the companies that issued the securities were clients of the brokerage houses. Under a deal with Spitzer, the 10 firms agreed to pay $1.4 billion in fines. The money would go toward providing better services to investors, including offering new, unbiased research information on stocks. [2]

More recently, the chairman of the nonprofit New York Stock Exchange (NYSE), Richard A. Grasso, resigned on Sept. 19 after the media reported he was slated to receive $188 million in past and deferred pay, approved by his hand-picked board.

The sensational revelations about Grasso's payout came just as the Big Board, as the exchange is known, was grappling with a scandal over alleged abuses by its "specialists" — the 450 experts on the exchange floor who actually execute many of the trades. Like some of the mutual fund managers, the specialists were charged with abusing their positions for their own profit and to the detriment of their clients.

John Reed, the highly regarded former chairman of Citicorp, came out of retirement to rescue the exchange, the world's largest. Less than six weeks after becoming interim chairman, he proposed creating a smaller and more independent board of directors. Later, prodded by the SEC, he agreed to split the job of chairman into two positions — chairman and chief operating officer.

But critics say Reed's new governance plan comes up short, in large part because the new NYSE board of directors is not independent enough and will still be too beholden to members of the exchange, the very people it is charged with regulating.

Many of the same critics say that mutual funds need a similar makeover, blaming their lack of independent boards of directors for at least some of the recent fund scandals.

"Management companies have a board of directors that looks out for their interests; why can't a mutual fund have the same thing instead of this symbiotic relationship between the [mutual fund] board and the management company," says Randall Dodd, president of the Financial Policy Forum, a market watchdog group.

But others argue that the more important issue is disclosure, because even the most independent board cannot stop abuses if it doesn't have enough information.

The SEC moved quickly to issue regulations designed to stop market-timing and late trading and provide fund boards with more information. The agency plans to consider mutual fund board independence later this year. The commission also may review Reed's NYSE restructuring plan, although it has already approved it.

Even Congress has gotten into the act. The House passed a mutual fund reform bill in November, and a similar measure is pending in the Senate.

As lawmakers, regulators and stock market professionals grapple with the investment industry's problems, here are some of the questions being asked:

Mutual Fund Investments Increased

The percentage of U.S. family assets invested in mutual funds has jumped by 11 percentage points in the last dozen years.

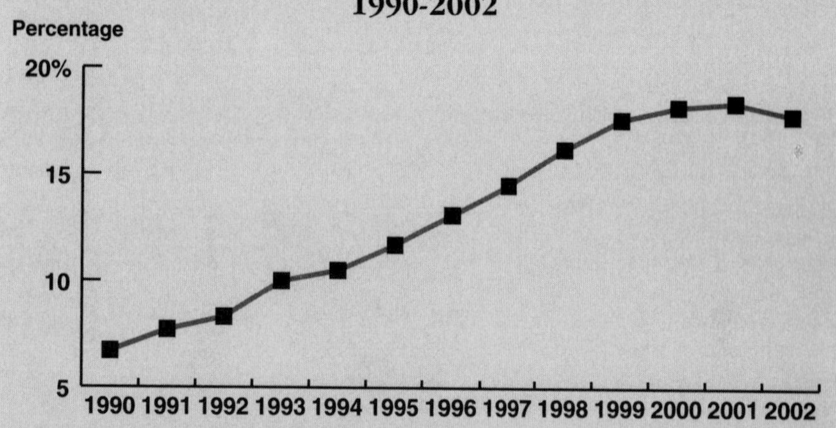

Note: Includes mutual funds held through employer-sponsored pension plans, bank personal trusts and variable annuities.

Sources: Federal Reserve Board, Mutual Fund Factbook, *Investment Company Institute*

Do reforms at the New York Stock Exchange go far enough?

Reed won kudos his first day on the job as NYSE interim chairman when he announced he would accept only $1 in compensation, a far cry from his predecessor's huge pay package. The new chairman also won praise by setting himself a short, ambitious timetable and sticking to it. Already, the exchange has a new governing constitution, an impressive new board of directors and a new chief executive officer.

But Reed's tenure ultimately will be judged on the effectiveness of his reforms, which include replacing the old governance structure — with its powerful chairman and 27-member board — with two separate boards, each with different mandates.

The new center of authority resides in the smaller of the two boards, made up of only eight members who cannot be directly tied to the exchange. Still, although Reed himself chose the first eight members, they had to be approved by NYSE members, as will subsequent directors.

The new board will oversee the exchange's regulations and employee compensation and appoint an advisory board of 20 securities-industry representatives who will run day-to-day exchange operations.

"It is the first time . . . we have had a totally independent board," Reed said on Nov. 5, the day the changes were announced. "And I believe the likelihood of another breakdown in governance is extremely small."

The reorganization plan also divides leadership into two entities: a chairman who will oversee exchange regulations and a CEO who will monitor daily business operations. In addition, a chief regulatory officer will monitor ethical and other issues and report directly to the eight-person board of directors.

Reed and his supporters contend that the new governing structure effectively separates those charged with regulating the exchange from those who administer its operations.

But critics disagree. Sean Harrigan, president of the $145 billion California Public Employees' Retirement System, says Reed has merely reorganized — rather than significantly reformed — the Big Board. "Investors were expecting a home-run proposal. . . . What we got, I believe, is not even a base hit," he said. [3]

Continued on p. 31

New York's Anti-Fraud Crusader

When Noreen Harrington decided to blow the whistle on her employer, Canary Capital Partners, she knew exactly whom she wanted to call. "I went to Eliot [Spitzer] because my perception of him was that if I pointed him in the right direction, he would fix the problem," she said. [1]

In recent years, New York state's energetic attorney general has become the undisputed driving force behind many key investigations into stock market abuses, including the conflict-of-interest charges against 10 powerhouse brokerage firms that led to $1.4 billion in settlement payments last year.

Harrington's confidence in Spitzer was not misplaced. Her descriptions of mutual fund trading abuses at Canary and four other companies prompted Spitzer to launch an industry-wide investigation that so far has implicated more than two-dozen firms and led to scores of resignations and more than $300 million in fines and penalties.

Spitzer did not limit his investigation to mutual fund trading. Less than a month after announcing a settlement in the Canary Capital case, the attorney general was probing mutual fund companies for what he has described as excessive and hidden fees charged to investors. "Fees, fees, fees — that's the big money," he recently said. [2]

He has already negotiated a 20 percent across-the-board reduction in Alliance Capital Management's fee structure and has promised that similar deals will follow.

Rex Features/Erik C. Pendzich

New York state Attorney General Eliot Spitzer

Spitzer's hard-charging style has won him both high praise and criticism. To his supporters he is a hero akin to the legendary Eliot Ness, the Capone-era rackets buster.

"None of these [stock market] abuses would have come out if it weren't for him," says John Freeman, a professor of legal and business ethics at the University of South Carolina. "He's done more to clean up the mutual fund industry in six months than everyone else did in 60 years."

But Spitzer's detractors accuse him of being a self-promoter more interested in seeking headlines than really grappling with problems. "He's a rank opportunist of the first order," says Alan Reynolds, a senior fellow at the Cato Institute, a libertarian think tank.

Moreover, Reynolds says, Spitzer is "dangerous" because he's anti-business. "He's one of these people who thinks that all business is bad and lawyers are angels."

The attorney general also has rankled the Securities and Exchange Commission (SEC) by poaching on its investigative and regulatory turf. But the attorney general is unapologetic. "If the SEC were doing its job, I wouldn't have to," he has said. [3]

Raised in New York City amid affluence, Spitzer attended private schools, spent four years at Princeton University and three at Harvard Law School. But those who know him say that he was greatly influenced by his strong-willed father — a real estate developer and son of immigrants — who preached the need to look out for average people who have little power or influence of their own.

As a young man growing up, Spitzer worked as a field hand and at other menial jobs and later founded (with his wife, public-interest lawyer Silda Wall) the Children for Children Foundation, which encourages young people to volunteer for worthy causes. At the same time, he has a résumé that puts him among the nation's social and professional elite — membership on the *Harvard Law Review*, clerking for a federal district judge and, of course, his election in 1999 as attorney general.

"On paper, he looks like an insider; but in practice, he acts like an outsider," says Delaware Attorney General Jane Brady. "Eliot is a man of contradictions and a loner willing to forge his own path."

That path may next lead to the New York governor's mansion, which Democrat Spitzer is eyeing in 2006. [4] He also has been mentioned as a possible vice presidential candidate this year.

For now, though, Spitzer isn't slowing down as attorney general. He recently launched investigations into the insurance and pharmaceutical industries.

And that's not all. Spitzer intends to examine the Environmental Protection Agency's controversial, recent policy changes on air quality. "What we're doing with the securities markets, we'll do with the environment," Spitzer said. [5]

---

[1] Quoted in Katherine Burton, "Mutual Fund Investigation Started with a Phone Call," *The Washington Post*, Dec. 10, 2003, p. E4.

[2] Quoted in Monica Langley, "As His Ambitions Expand, Spitzer Draws Controversy," *The Wall Street Journal*, Dec. 11, 2003, p. A1.

[3] Quoted in *ibid.*

[4] Jenny Anderson, "Fundraising for a Fund Crusader," *The New York Post*, Dec. 12, 2003, p. 43.

[5] Quoted in Langley, *op. cit.*

Continued from p. 29

And Sarah Teslik, executive director of the Council of Institutional Investors, calls the changes "nearly useless."

Most critics say Reed's plan is flawed at its most basic level because it relies too heavily on self-regulation. "It seems to me that in most cases self-regulation doesn't work," said Sen. Jim Bunning, R-Ky., at a Nov. 20 Senate Banking Committee hearing on the issue. "How can confidence be restored if we still have the fox in the henhouse?"

More specifically, critics contend that since exchange members can still hire and fire members of the board charged with regulating them, that board is not truly independent. "The fact is, the board and managers of the exchange owe their jobs to the NYSE members and therefore will continue to act in their interest rather than in the interest of investors," Teslik says.

Critics also predict that under Reed's plan the 20-person advisory panel will inevitably help regulate the exchange while also running the business operations — two functions that can have conflicting interests.

"When you have one group that's supposed to be generating new business [for the exchange] involved in regulation, there's an inherent conflict of interest," says Dodd, of the Financial Policy Forum. "You need to clearly separate these two responsibilities, which is what they do on the NASDAQ," or the National Association of Securities Dealers Automated Quotation system, a rival stock market that deals heavily in technology stocks.

But Reed and others say there are enough safeguards to ensure independence, pointing out, for example, that no one on the new board can work for a brokerage firm or a company that has shares listed on the exchange.

"Under Reed's plan, the entire board of directors is independent of any interest that owns or operates the NYSE," says Marc E. Lackritz, president of the Securities Industry Association, which represents brokerage houses, investment banks and other financial-services companies. "It's clear that under this structure, the board will represent the interests of the public, of investors."

Moreover, Reed and his supporters say, self-regulation will work because it's very much in the interest of the exchange for it to work. "Regulation of the exchange is like quality control to Toyota," Reed said before the Senate Banking Committee on Nov. 20.

Alan Reynolds, a senior fellow at the Cato Institute, a libertarian think tank, agrees that the NYSE has a strong and natural incentive to preserve its integrity. "If the exchange isn't trusted by those who list on it or those buying stocks on it, people will go someplace else," he says. "So, you can have a self-regulating market, so long as there are alternatives, like the NASDAQ."

Finally, the idea of an outside board is over-hyped and unrealistically seen as a panacea, Reynolds and others say. "There is this standard orthodoxy that board independence is some sort of Holy Grail, but there is absolutely no evidence to suggest that it ultimately means anything," Reynolds says. "Enron had one of the most independent boards of directors in the business, and it didn't do them any good."

Indeed, Reynolds says, too much board independence can be harmful. "If the board is too independent, you end up with a bunch of people who are not really connected to the business at hand and so don't really know enough about it."

Are mutual funds adequately regulated?

American mutual funds hold $7 trillion in wealth, including large portions of the pension funds that pay retirement benefits to tens of millions of Americans. Indeed, 95 million people now own mutual funds, either directly or through retirement funds. [4]

By investing in a mutual fund, investors are essentially giving their money to financial experts and paying them a small fee to pick stocks and other investments on their behalf. As a result, mutual funds are particularly attractive to investors who are unfamiliar with the complexities of the financial markets and who might not buy stocks and bonds on their own. Moreover, although all investments are risky, most experts agree that using mutual funds reduces the risk because most funds are diversified, often owning scores, if not hundreds, of different stocks and bonds.

But now even some of the fundamental benefits of mutual funds are being questioned by critics, who have harshly criticized some fund management companies for loading hidden charges onto investors (*see p. 42*). Such practices show a callous disregard for investors' welfare, many critics of mutual funds say, noting that funds are structured in such a way as to provide investors little or no protection from unscrupulous managers.

The Investment Advisors Act of 1940 requires each fund to have a board of directors responsible for protecting investor interests. But the board does not actually run the fund. Instead, it hires outside advisers to direct the fund's day-to-day operations, from picking stocks to keeping records. And although the board can hire any person or firm to serve as an adviser, in practice, mutual fund boards always assign those duties to the companies that founded the funds. For instance, even though all 343 Fidelity mutual funds have independent boards, they all have contracted out their fund management to Fidelity Investments.

Most boards also have very little authority to oversee the management of their funds. They can fire the company they have hired to run the fund, but that almost never happens, because many of the directors are often tied to the management firm, either as former employees or as shareholders.

The SEC has announced its intention to consider requiring boards to be completely independent of fund managers, an idea also envisioned in some of the legislation pending before Congress.

Critics applaud these moves. "There has to be a sense that board members are not just leashed to the folks who are making the investment decisions," says Sally Greenberg, senior counsel for Consumers Union. "Board members have to be people who in no way benefit from the fund or its investments so they can truly represent the interests of investors."

The boards currently operating most funds, by their very nature, are ill equipped to guard against impropriety, Greenberg says.

"There's an old saying that when you have strong managers, weak directors and passive owners, it's only a matter of time until the looting begins," agrees John Bogle, the celebrated founder and former CEO of the Vanguard Group, one of the few mutual fund management firms with independent boards.

But making boards more independent won't solve the problem, says Matthew Fink, president of the Investment Company Institute, a mutual fund industry group. "It's not a corporate governance problem," Fink says. "There was no system to provide the boards with the information they needed to see that these things were happening. So, even if you'd had the best possible people sitting on the most independent of boards, all of these things still would have happened."

In fact, some of the funds accused of unethical behavior had relatively independent boards, Fink points out. "Look at Putnam: [Their funds] had some of the most independent boards in the industry, and they still have all this trouble," he says.

Board members must understand what is happening in their fund, Fink says, suggesting that a recent SEC proposal to require funds' ethics or compliance officers to report to their boards might solve the problem. "It's a question of disclosure rather than corporate structure."

Still others say the verdict of the marketplace regulates mutual funds better than any boards or government regulations. "When people say they want to strengthen the boards, they assume that it can be a profitable, long-term strategy for the fund to do something that's not in the interests of investors," says Kevin Hassett, a senior fellow at the American Enterprise Institute (AEI). "The punishment the market is inflicting on these funds or anyone who acts improperly dwarfs anything the government can do to them," he adds. Firms involved in the scandal have lost billions of dollars since they came under investigation, he points out. Putnam, for instance, lost $32 billion in November, as nervous investors pulled their money from the company's funds. [5]

But Greenberg says the current system allowed a lot of bad behavior to slip through the cracks, and a lot of investors' hard-earned money to fall into wrongdoers' hands before anything was done. "This stuff has been happening in the mutual fund industry since 1997, so where was the vaunted market for all of those years?" she asks. "It wasn't there, and [that's why] something else is needed to stop these problems before they happen."

"We're told that competition and the integrity of the people involved and their desire to keep their reputations will stop this sort of thing from happening," agrees the Financial Policy Forum's Dodd. "But markets cannot be relied upon to police themselves."

Have recent scandals affected investor confidence?

While many analysts say no one really knows what triggers the ups and downs of the stock market, some contend there's little question the financial scandals contributed to the deep losses in 2001 and 2002 and may have slowed the 2003 rally. "It's hard to see how all of this couldn't have had a big effect," Dodd says.

Yet, optimists note, investors pushed the market to new highs throughout most of 2003. Even though investors pulled some money from the mutual fund firms involved in the market-timing scandal, the mutual fund industry as a whole took in more money last year than in 2002 — an indication that investor confidence is still strong. (*See graph, p. 28.*)

"What we've seen is a loss in confidence in those firms that have gotten into trouble," says Fink. "But confidence has not been shaken in the industry as a whole."

Moreover, Fink says, even the money withdrawn from suspect mutual funds has largely been redirected to other funds. "Those funds that have not had problems are picking up business from those that have, which indicates people still trust the system as a whole."

Indeed, from September through November of 2003 — the height of the scandal — mutual funds took in $63.9 billion in new investments, the highest three-month amount since early 2000. [6] In addition, the overall stock market had a banner year in 2003, with the Dow Jones Industrial Average up 25 percent and the NASDAQ rising 50 percent.

The Cato Institute's Reynolds contends the recent gains show that investors generally ignore scandals and look to more fundamental economic indicators.

"When you look at why markets rise or fall, it comes down to earnings and interest rates, not 'confidence,' " he says. "Stocks moved down [in 2001 and 2002] largely because earnings were lower. They rebounded [in 2003] because profits rose. It's as simple as that."

Even some who think the market should have suffered a loss of confidence concede it has not. The Council of Institutional Investors' Teslik says investor confidence "should be shaken more than it is [since] accountants, the accounting standard setters, analysts, attorneys, stock exchanges, corporate boards, mutual funds, the SEC — all have been shown to be pathetically unable to protect investors."

But Dodd argues the scandals have had a serious impact on investor trust and confidence, even among small investors who might not regularly follow the market. "Just from osmosis, most people have gotten a sense of what is going on," Dodd says. "Main Street now understands that Wall Street isn't on the up-and-up and, of course, that shakes [investors'] confidence."

Mercer Bullard, a University of Mississippi professor of law, agrees. "We're moving toward independent investment decision-making, where more people are getting involved in directing their own assets," he says. "In this environment, people need to feel confident that the market is secure, and I just don't see how they can under the present circumstances."

Moreover, the recent rise in the market doesn't prove that investors are shrugging off the scandals, critics like Dodd say. "It might be that the market isn't going up as high as it would have absent the scandals."

Indeed, says AEI's Hassett, there is evidence that the rise may not have been as high as it could have been. "All you have to do is look at the latest GDP release, and you'll see that corporate profits are way above their past peak, but the Dow [Jones Industrial Average] is way below its peak," he says. "This is at least partly attributable to a fall in investor confidence."

Finally, some critics contend, the scandals' greatest impact may not have been felt yet. "People, especially small investors, are going to scratch their heads, at least in the near term, when they're fed the same old line about how they have to invest in the stock market," Greenberg says. "They had been told that investing was safe, and now they find out the fat cats were skimming off the top and diluting the value of their investments. Of course they're going to be angry and cynical about the market, and it's going to start to show." ■

AFP Photo/Henny Ray Abrams

Former Citigroup Chairman John Reed took over as interim chairman of the New York Stock Exchange on Sept. 21, 2003, and quickly restructured its management practices. The Securities and Exchange Commission unanimously approved his plan on Dec. 17, 2003.

BACKGROUND

Early Scandals

Stock market abuses are as old as the New York Stock Exchange itself. Just months after the exchange opened in 1792, new rules had to be drafted to stop some brokers from improperly selling securities outside the market.

That same year, a leading member of New York's mercantile and banking elite, William Duer, engineered a stock-speculation scheme that ultimately dragged Duer and some of the city's biggest investors into bankruptcy. Duer himself died in debtor's prison.

" 'Tis time there should be a line of separation between honest men and knaves, between respectable stockholders and dealers in funds, and mere unprincipled gamblers," wrote Treasury Secretary Alexander Hamilton of the Duer scandal. [7]

Similar scandals ensued in the years ahead, such as when securities would be sold for companies that existed only on paper — particularly for new ventures like canals and railroads. [8] Yet, the country's entrepreneurial spirit and breakneck growth — both driven by westward expansion — greatly mitigated the impact of the loss of capital and confidence created by such abuses.

Over the years, too, there were efforts, albeit limited ones, to regulate the exchange. One attempt at reform — an early 19th-century New York state law outlawing pyramid schemes — actually helped the NYSE become the nation's largest and most important exchange.

New York also got a boost when the federal government turned to Wall Street's money men to help finance the Civil War, spurring spectacular growth in both the number and size of transactions. By 1865, the NYSE was trading an average of $6 billion in securities and bonds per day, second in size only to London's exchange. [9]

The years following the Civil War in America became known as the "Gilded Age," a time of great economic growth and enormous personal fortunes. In this environment, financial scandals became ever more common — from the manipulation of gold shares, which produced a "gold panic" in 1869, to the great railroad scandals of the 1870s and '80s. [10] But spotty market regulation allowed many of those involved to avoid jail.

Regulatory Stirrings

As the 19th century ended, the ever-increasing size and sophistication of the American economy prompted the federal government to pay more attention to corporate and financial issues. In 1890, Congress passed the Sherman Antitrust Act, which criminalized business monopolies; in 1914, the Federal Reserve was created to help set banking and monetary policy.

The 1929 Wall Street crash shifted the government's attention to the stock market. The crash had been precipitated by a huge, decade-long run-up in prices, fed by rampant stock speculation made possible by the practice of buying on margin, or credit. Although historians still debate whether the crash triggered the Great Depression, at the time Wall Street was seen as the culprit.

President Franklin D. Roosevelt and Congress responded with the Securities Act of 1933 and the Securities Exchange Act of 1934, both aimed at restoring investor confidence. The new laws required publicly traded companies to file regular financial reports and set tough criminal penalties for filing false information.

The Securities and Exchange Commission (SEC) itself was created to enforce the new securities laws and monitor the integrity of the stock market. The exchange, which had resisted serious regulation for almost 150 years, finally had an overseer with real authority.

The SEC's first great test came in 1937. William Whitney, a patrician brokerage owner and former NYSE president, had spent years speculating — mostly unsuccessfully — in stocks. He had been able to hide his losses by stealing millions from his firm, his clients and even his wife.

An SEC audit led to Whitney's arrest — an event that shocked Wall Street. But even more significant, the SEC, led by future Supreme Court Justice William O. Douglas, used the Whitney affair to institute major changes at the NYSE, including tough, new limits on margin buying aimed at preventing the use of debt to finance rampant stock speculation.

The commission also forced the NYSE to draft a new constitution instituting reforms to bolster the exchange's reputation. One reform required the NYSE president to be an independent, salaried employee of the exchange, rather than a member. [11]

The changes helped the market prosper after World War II. The volume of stocks traded and their value more than doubled during the 1950s. The rise continued in the 1960s, bolstered by new technology, such as computers and in 1965 an electronic ticker display. [12]

The expansion spurred the creation in 1971 of the National Association of Securities Dealers Automated Quotation system, or NASDAQ. While there already were alternatives to the NYSE — notably the New York-based American Stock Exchange — all were relatively small. But by the 1980s, the highly automated NASDAQ, with its focus on technology firms, had become a major competitor.

The Roaring '80s

During the mid- and late-1980s, a roaring economy and the pro-business administration of President Ronald Reagan combined to produce a sense of near euphoria on Wall Street. The tone of the decade was perhaps best exemplified by the now-infamous motto "Greed is good" embraced by Gordon Geko, the oily stockbroker in Oliver Stone's 1987 film *Wall Street.*

But greed didn't turn out to be good for everyone, and the decade came to be associated as much with scandal as with financial success.

The trouble began in 1986, when one of Wall Street's most prominent stock speculators, Ivan Boesky, was indicted for insider trading, or acting on information not available to the general public. In exchange for a lighter sentence Boesky pleaded guilty and provided evidence against another leading Wall Street figure: Michael Milken.

Milken had become a Wall Street wonder boy by helping to create a huge market for so-called junk bonds, which often paid high returns because they financed riskier ventures. Milken used junk bonds to back new, innovative businesses, such as the Cable News Network and the long-distance carrier MCI. He also helped perfect the leveraged buyout — purchasing a company almost entirely by borrowing money and then breaking up and selling parts of the firm to pay off the debt.

While many on Wall Street considered Milken an innovative financier and a force for progress, others saw him as a gambler willing to risk healthy, established corporations — and their employees' jobs — in the pursuit of easy money.

Continued on p. 36

Chronology

Before 1900

The stock market is established soon after American independence and expands along with the nation's economy.

1792
New York Stock Exchange (NYSE), a private, nonprofict corporation, opens.

1865
NYSE trades an average of $6 billion in stocks and bonds daily.

1900s-1970s

Stock market crash and the Great Depression lead to strict, new regulations.

1924
First mutual funds are created.

1929
Financial markets crash, leading to calls for new regulation.

1933
Securities Act of 1933 sets new trading standards.

1934
Securities Exchange Act of 1934 authorizes the Securities and Exchange Commission (SEC) to regulate securities markets.

1940
Investment Company Act of 1940 creates a regulatory framework for mutual funds.

1965
NYSE installs an electronic ticker display.

1971
NASDAQ (National Association of Securities Dealers Automatic Quotation) electronic stock exchange is established and quickly becomes home to many of the hottest technology stocks.

1980s-1990s

Financial scandals rock Wall Street but do not lead to significant regulatory changes.

1986
Prominent stock speculator Ivan Boesky is charged with insider-trading and convicted and sentenced the next year to three years in prison.

1990
Junk bond king Michael Milken pleads guilty to securities fraud and is sentenced to 10 years in prison and a $1 billion fine. . . . Investors' assets in U.S. mutual funds reach $1 trillion.

2000 to Present

Corporate and Wall Street scandals lead to regulatory changes.

December 2001
Enron Corp. bankruptcy leads to a broad accounting and corporate scandal.

2002
President Bush signs the Sarbanes-Oxley corporate-reform bill into law on July 30. . . . Ten major brokerage houses accused of unethical practices agree in December to spend $1.4 billion to institute new procedures to educate and protect investors.

2003
ImClone Systems Chairman Sam Waksal pleads guilty on Oct. 15 to insider trading, bank fraud and other charges and draws a seven-year prison sentence. . . . NYSE Chairman Richard A. Grasso's total compensation is reported in August to be $188 million . . . . Four mutual fund companies and Canary Capital Partners, a hedge fund, settle with New York state Attorney General Eliot Spitzer on Sept. 3 over accusations they engaged in mutual fund trading abuses. . . . Grasso resigns on Sept. 17. . . . Former Citicorp Chairman John Reed becomes interim NYSE chairman on Sept. 21 and announces on Oct. 16 that he will fine exchange traders at least $150 million for trading abuses. . . . Reed overhauls NYSE governance on Nov. 5, including a restructured board of directors. . . . SEC approves new rules for mutual fund trading on Dec. 3 and Reed's reform plan on Dec. 17. . . . On Dec. 16, the California Public Employees Retirement System sues the NYSE and seven specialist firms for $150 million alleging improper trading practices. Goldman Sachs President John Thain becomes CEO of the NYSE on Dec. 18. . . . Alliance Capital Management agrees on Dec. 19 to pay $250 million in fines and to lower fees by 20 percent for mutual fund trading abuses.

2004
Spitzer and the SEC begin an investigation into Grasso's pay compensation package. . . . SEC's new mutual fund rules are slated to go into effect.

Mutual Funds Linked to Trading Abuses

More than two-dozen financial-services companies have been implicated in the recent scandal over late trading and market-timing in the mutual fund industry, including:

Alliance Capital Management — The much-vaunted company, which manages some $427 billion in assets, agreed to pay $250 million in fines and reduce the fees it charges investors by 20 percent for the next five years.

Bank of America — The nation's third-largest bank fired several staffers after its assets-management group helped Canary Capital (see below) in late trading of mutual fund shares.

Canary Capital Partners — The once-obscure Secaucus, N.J.-based hedge fund has been at the center of a scandal involving four mutual-fund management firms. After an investigation by New York Attorney General Eliot Spitzer, founder Edward Stern agreed to pay $40 million in fines and restitution to investors.

Fred Alger Management — The asset manager is accused of allowing a hedge-fund client to engage in market timing and late trading; Vice President James Connelly Jr. — one of three suspended employees — pleaded guilty to obstruction of justice and was sentenced to one to three years in jail.

Janus — The nation's ninth-largest mutual fund company has admitted to trading abuses and has agreed to repay investors $31.5 million.

Principal Financial Group — The Des Moines mutual fund company, with more than $92 billion in assets under management, fired two portfolio managers and several other employees for engaging in market timing.

Prudential/Wachovia — Market-timing allegations have led a dozen stockbrokers and managers to resign from the firm, the nation's third-largest brokerage. Several agencies are investigating the firm's trading.

Putnam Investments — The nation's sixth-largest mutual fund group has seen its president and several portfolio managers resign over trading abuses; as part of a settlement with the SEC, the company promised to make full restitution to investors.

Strong Capital Management — The Wisconsin firm, which manages more than $42 billion in assets, allegedly helped Canary Capital engage in unethical market-timing practices; chairman and founder Richard Strong resigned and may be prosecuted.

Continued from p. 34

When Boesky named Milken as the source of some of his illegal inside information, the federal government showed no mercy, indicting the 43-year-old on 98 felony charges. Although he eventually cut a deal, pleading guilty to only a few of the charges, he received the maximum sentence — 10 years in prison — and a $1 billion fine, the largest criminal fine in U.S. history. [13]

Recent Troubles

The recent wave of business-related scandals began with the financial collapse and bankruptcy of Enron in the fall and winter of 2001. As the energy giant imploded, evidence began to emerge that much of Enron's revenue and profit growth had essentially been based on dubious accounting and financing. [14]

Within months, it became clear that Enron was just the tip of the corporate-crime iceberg. By the next summer, other corporate giants, including MCIWorldcom, industrial conglomerate Tyco International and cable television operator Adelphia Communications, had all been implicated in similar accounting scandals. Some, like MCI and Adelphia, were forced into bankruptcy.

Not surprisingly, the accounting industry soon came under fire as well. Accounting giant Arthur Andersen, which had been the auditor for both Enron and MCI, lost many of its biggest clients and partners and went out of business at the end of 2002. Other big accounting firms saw their credibility questioned.

Around the same time, Congress stepped in, enacting a new anti-fraud law that set tough, new financial-disclosure rules and, to prevent potential conflicts of interest, prohibited accounting firms from providing other financial services to companies they audit.

As top corporate officials were being arrested or summoned before congressional committees, the focus started to shift from corporate boardrooms to Wall Street itself. Beginning in late 2001, Attorney General Spitzer began to uncover evidence that stock analysts at the 10 largest and most prestigious brokerage firms were steering clients to buy shares in companies whose stocks the firms were criticizing internally. Moreover, Spitzer discovered that the companies being falsely touted also were banking clients of the analysts.

Particularly egregious were the alleged practices of Citigroup's Jack Grubman, Wall Street's premier stock analyst for the hot telecommunications sector. Grubman continued to issue bullish calls for telecom stocks like MCIWorldcom and Global Crossing, even as evidence mounted that they were in trouble.

Spitzer also uncovered evidence that many of those firms offered executives of their biggest corporate clients an early opportunity to buy initial public offerings, or IPOs, of the best stocks about to be issued. Such favoritism amounted to a conflict of interest since brokers are legally obligated to represent the best interests of all their clients, not just a select few.

Spitzer eventually settled with the 10 firms, requiring them to spend $1.4 billion to purchase independent research from outside analysts that would then be passed on to the firms' clients. Some of the money also was earmarked for investor-education programs. To prevent future conflicts, the Spitzer deal also prohibited direct cooperation between the investment-banking and stock-picking arms of the 10 firms.

In exchange, no criminal charges were filed against the 10 firms or Grubman, and they did not have to publicly admit to any wrongdoing. Nevertheless, they still face hundreds of civil suits filed by investors.

As Spitzer was grappling with the largest financial firms, federal prosecutors began filing charges against several high-profile Wall Street figures, including Credit Suisse's Frank Quattrone, one the leading cheerleaders of the late 1990s technology boom. Quattrone had earned hundreds of millions of dollars engineering IPOs for high-tech leaders like Cisco Systems and Amazon.com. [15]

Prosecutors focused on whether Quattrone and other bankers gave favored investors early opportunities to buy IPOs in exchange for kickbacks. Quattrone was charged with obstructing justice and witness tampering after it was revealed that he had directed hundreds of employees to destroy evidence relevant to the case two days before a grand jury subpoena was issued. [16]

At his trial in fall 2003, Quattrone denied any wrongdoing, arguing that he thought the federal investigation was focused on a different department within his bank and that the order to destroy e-mail messages was part of the company's standard electronic clean-up procedure. After five days of deliberations, the jury was still deadlocked and a mistrial was declared. Quattrone faces a second trial on the same charges later this year. [17]

Another high-profile case emerged in 2002, when it was learned that Sam Waksal, the founder and chairman of ImClone, a cutting-edge drug firm, had tried to sell almost 80,000 ImClone shares right before the Food and Drug Administration (FDA) was slated to reject an anti-cancer drug developed by the firm. Waksal pleaded guilty and was sentenced to seven years in prison. [18]

The ImClone scandal also ensnared Waksal's friend, lifestyle guru Martha Stewart, who was charged with securities fraud and obstruction of justice in connection with her sale of 4,000 ImClone shares right before the FDA's rejection. Stewart has pleaded not-guilty and faces a trial in New York for which jury selection began last week.

AFP Photo/Ronald Sachs

Solomon Smith Barney investment analyst Jack Grubman continued to issue bullish calls for telecom stocks, even as evidence mounted that they were in trouble. Grubman did not face criminal charges, but paid a $15 million fine as part of a 2002 settlement with New York Attorney General Eliot Spitzer.

Grasso's Fall

Many saw Grasso's tenure at the NYSE as a great success. During his eight years as chairman, the exchange added more than 1,500 new listings — nearly double the previous number of companies traded — including 569 firms that transferred from competing exchanges. [19]

Grasso also won high praise for his leadership following the Sept. 11, 2001, terrorist attacks on the nearby World Trade Center and other sites, which forced the exchange to close. The chairman's successful efforts to reopen just six days later were seen as an early sign that the country would rebound from the attacks.

But what many describe as Grasso's lax attitude toward ethical issues marred his record. And as the scandals on Wall Street began to mount during 2002 and into 2003, critics were openly questioning whether there was something fundamentally wrong with NYSE operations.

They were particularly troubled by the growing scandal involving the exchange's specialists. All seven of the exchange's specialist firms have been accused of unfairly using their monopoly role in executing buy and sell orders to profit at the expense of the very investors they are supposed to serve (*see p. 39*). And yet, under Grasso, only a few firms were reprimanded and given (small) fines.

"The specialist scandal is a perfect example of his lack of effective enforcement," says the University of Mississippi's Bullard. "When Grasso was in charge, very little was done to hold these people accountable."

In addition, some who worked with Grasso also chafed under what they call his dictatorial style, accusing the chairman of running the exchange as his personal fiefdom. "He ruled the place as his," said a veteran floor trader. "But different rules at different times seemed to be the order of the day: 'Grasso rules.' " [20]

AFP Photo/New York Stock Exchange

The New York Stock Exchange's iron-fisted chairman, Richard Grasso, was forced to resign on Sept. 19, 2003, after revelations that his hand-picked board had approved a 10-year compensation package worth $188 million, sparking a furor over how the exchange was governed.

Whether or not these criticisms are valid, substantial resentment had been building against Grasso for years. And when he found himself embroiled in his own scandal last summer, much of his support quickly evaporated.

Grasso's troubles began on Aug. 27, when it was disclosed that he was to receive $188 million in existing and deferred compensation through 2006. The figure stunned even many on Wall Street, where huge salaries are not uncommon. Grasso, after all, was charged by federal law with regulating the NYSE's brokers and other members, who had the authority to approve his salary. [21]

"His compensation was outrageous by any measure of what a regulator could be paid and still be credibly called a regulator," Bullard says. "You just can't take that much money from the very people you're charged with overseeing."

At first, Grasso tried to fend off critics by giving back $48 million in deferred retirement benefits and vigorously defending the overall pay package as in line with what other highly paid Wall Street executives make. But the chairman's damage control failed, and on Sept. 17 the NYSE's board voted 13-7 to oust him. [22]

Since Grasso's departure, some have argued that it was unfair to tar him for simply accepting a high salary. "The NYSE is a very profitable monopoly, and there's a lot of money floating around," says AEI's Hassett. "It doesn't strike me as odd that they offered Grasso high compensation, or that he took it."

But many contend that Grasso, as the chairman of a nonprofit organization, should be forced to give at least some of his substantial compensation back to the NYSE. These calls led Spitzer and the SEC to announce, on Jan 8, that they would look into the former chairman's pay package to determine whether it was appropriate and whether regulations or laws were broken. Interim Chairman Reed, who has spoken about suing his predecessor to recover some of the millions already paid, has said that the NYSE would cooperate fully with the joint investigation. [23]

CURRENT SITUATION

Overhauling the NYSE

Since Reed took over as the exchange's interim chairman on Sept. 21, he has pushed through several significant changes in how the country's pre-eminent stock exchange is governed.

Reed quickly made it clear he favored a smaller governing board, prompting the resignations of several prominent board members within a week of his arrival, including former New York state Comptroller Carl McCall and DaimlerChrysler Chairman Jurgen Schrempp. On Nov. 5, Reed announced his new governance plan: Grasso's 27-member board would be replaced with an eight-person body charged with supervising the exchange's regulation, governance, compensation and internal controls.

The new body included two holdovers from the old board: former Secretary of State Madeleine K. Albright and Herbert Allison, chairman of the huge pension fund TIAA-CREF. The six new faces included some with significant industry experience, like former J.P. Morgan Chairman Sir Dennis Weatherstone, and some without, like Shirley Ann Jackson, president of Rensselaer Polytechnic Institute.

Reed's selection criteria permitted no board memberships to be offered to executives of brokerage firms or companies whose stocks are traded on the exchange. Still, future board members would be chosen by the exchange itself, leading many critics to argue the plan did not go far enough.

Despite the reservations about the new plan, Reed quickly lined up the support of the exchange's 1,366 members. On Dec. 17, the SEC approved the plan 5-0, with the caveat that it would re-examine Reed's plan in 2004, possibly requiring future board members to be chosen by outsiders.

In addition, the SEC gave Reed the thumbs up only after he agreed to divide his two posts — chairman and chief executive officer — into two separate jobs. The SEC's Donaldson had pushed for the change, arguing that keeping the positions together — as with Grasso — left too much power in the hands of one man. [24]

Under the new arrangement, the chairman will continue to oversee regulation, compensation and nominations for the board; the CEO will run the exchange's day-to-day operations.

A day after the SEC vote, Reed announced that John A. Thain, president of Goldman Sachs, would become CEO. Reed said he would remain as interim chairman until a replacement was found, probably sometime later this year.

Reed and Thain now face a host of challenges, the most pressing of which is the broadening scandal over the exchange's specialists, who have been accused of using their privileged position on the exchange floor to short-change investors.

Each specialist controls the stocks of a handful of companies listed on the exchange, taking buy and sell orders from both the exchange's computers and its floor brokers. While some floor brokers trade shares among themselves, specialists often match buyers with sellers in exchange for a small fee. They also buy and sell for their own clients and are obliged to buy stock that is being offered for sale when no other buyer can be found.

Every other major exchange in the world uses a purely electronic system to match buy and sell orders, leading many to say that specialists are a costly anachronism. (*See "At Issue," p. 41.*) But defenders of the specialists say they are invaluable because they get investors the best price available. In addition, the defenders say, specialists keep the market running smoothly by buying up unwanted stock.

But critics say the specialists often have used their inside knowledge to "cherry pick" the best deals for themselves, even though other buyers were ready to take the stock. In other words, when specialists saw a stock being sold at a bargain price, they often bought it themselves and then resold it to the buyer instead of letting the buyer reap the benefits. NYSE rules prohibit specialists from stepping in between trades when a seller and buyer have already been matched. More than 2 billion shares were improperly traded in that way over the past three years, at a cost to investors of an estimated $155 million, according to a confidential SEC report leaked to *The Wall Street Journal.* [25]

On Oct. 16, Reed announced that the exchange — at the SEC's request — would fine the five largest specialist firms about $150 million and use the money to reimburse investors.

More recently, on Dec. 16, the huge California Public Employees Retirement System (CALPERS) sued the exchange's seven specialist firms and the NYSE itself for $150 million in damages. The nation's largest public pension fund alleges that the firms engaged in improper trading and that the exchange condoned it. [26] The firms have neither denied nor admitted the accusations, and none has agreed to pay Reed's penalty.

For his part, CEO Thain says he will push for more electronic floor trading, which would shrink the role of the specialists. "All of the orders flow to the floor electronically, and many of them could be matched electronically," he said on the day he was named to his new job. [27]

Mutual Fund Scandal

The illegal-trading scandal that began spreading throughout the mutual fund industry in the fall has tarnished the reputation of mutual funds as solid and trustworthy investment options, though investment experts widely maintain that funds are still a great place for investors, small and large.

But Senate Banking Committee Chairman Richard C. Shelby, R-Ala., has his doubts. Mutual funds were "considered safe" and "above board," he told a Nov. 20 committee hearing. "But that's not really true."

The scandal came to light on Sept. 3, when Spitzer announced a settlement with four fund-management firms that had allowed the manager of the Canary

Greed Among 'Big Problems' Cited by Investors

More than two-thirds of the investors surveyed recently cited greed as a "big problem" for the securities industry, compared with 52 percent in 2001. More than 60 percent of investors also considered the industry's reluctance to punish wrongdoers a serious problem.

Percentage saying the following are "big problems":

	2003	2001
Industry motivated by greed	69%	52%
Industry's reluctance to punish wrongdoers	66	41
Financial advisers or firms putting own interests ahead of investors' interests	61	46
Lack of internal controls to prevent irresponsible or wrongful actions	55	33

Source: Harris Interactive, "Investors' Attitudes Toward the Securities Industry, 2003," November 2003

Capital Partners hedge fund to engage in market-timing and late trading in exchange for promises that Canary would invest large sums in the firms' funds. [28] Spitzer had been tipped off by a whistleblower. (*See sidebar, p. 30.*) Within a month of the settlement, other fund-management companies were being accused of similar behavior.

While late trading is against the law, market-timing is not illegal for the average, individual trader. But it is unethical — and thus a violation of SEC rules — for fund managers to encourage or practice market-timing because the constant buying and selling of shares requires a mutual fund to keep more cash on hand to deal with the quick, last-minute trades. Maintaining large amounts of cash leaves mutual funds with less money to invest in stocks, bonds and other financial instruments aimed at making profits for long-term investors.

At least two-dozen firms have been accused of market-timing and late trading, including some of the nation's biggest fund-management companies. As a group, the firms manage more than $1 trillion in investors' funds. Many other fund-management firms currently are performing self-audits to determine whether they were involved in market-timing or late trading, and additional firms are expected to be implicated.

Moreover, Spitzer and the SEC said on Jan. 8, that they would soon begin investigating the banks that provided the financing for much of the illegal and unethical trading. "Financing activity that you know or have reason to know is illegal is itself an illegal act," said SEC enforcement chief Stephen M. Cutler at a press conference announcing the new investigation. [29]

Critics note that the unethical trading practices occurred with the acquiescence and even encouragement of fund managers. In short, they say, managers ignored their duty to all investors in their funds in favor of the interests of a few special clients and themselves.

"Our continuing investigations reveal a systemic breakdown in mutual fund governance that allowed directors and managers to ignore the interests of investors," Spitzer told the Senate Banking Committee on Nov. 20. "In fund after fund, we have seen the wholesale abandonment of fiduciary responsibilities."

In conjunction with the SEC, Spitzer is negotiating with several management firms to get them to repay investors for losses resulting from the trading improprieties. Alliance Capital Management agreed on Dec. 19 to pay $250 million. [30] Four days later, Janus Fund managers agreed to a $31.5 million payment. The SEC is preparing to file civil fraud charges against several firms, including Putnam and Strong.

In addition, some executives are now facing criminal prosecution, and employees of up to 20 financial-services firms are said to be under investigation. [31]

In response to the abuses, the SEC on Dec. 3 unanimously approved new regulations for mutual fund trades, requiring all orders to be received by 4 p.m. Eastern Standard Time. The new rules also would require each fund to adopt policies aimed at preventing and detecting violations of federal securities laws and have an ethics or compliance officer to administer the policies and report regularly to the mutual fund's board of directors. SEC Chairman Donaldson said the proposed changes would "go a long way toward restoring investor confidence" in mutual funds. [32]

"We need to do this," says the Investment Company Institute's Fink, even though the 4 p.m. rule may be "tough medicine."

Some industry critics also say the SEC should require mutual funds to have boards completely independent of the companies that manage them, a step the commission says it will consider next year.

Despite its recent moves, Spitzer and other critics have complained that the SEC not only was surprised by the mutual fund industry's problems but also was unwilling to act aggressively even when the problem became obvious.

Continued on p. 42

At Issue:

Should the New York Stock Exchange eliminate "specialists"?

yes

KEVIN HASSETT
DIRECTOR, ECONOMIC POLICY STUDIES AMERICAN ENTERPRISE INSTITUTE

WRITTEN FOR THE CQ RESEARCHER, DECEMBER 2003

One of the most significant financial market developments of the last two decades has been the computerization of stock exchanges. In a computerized exchange like the NASDAQ, buyers and sellers communicate instantaneously with each other over a computer network. The advantages of transparency and speedy efficiency are such that just about every stock exchange on Earth is now electronic. The exception is the New York Stock Exchange (NYSE), which still relies on humans with countless slips of paper to execute trades — the specialists.

Why is the NYSE still relying on 19th-century technology? The supporters of the exchange claim that the system of human checks and balances helps the NYSE maintain a smooth-functioning market in the worst of times, an achievement that computerized exchanges have trouble accomplishing. The academic evidence supporting this view is essentially non-existent. Indeed, computerized exchanges generally outperform human ones by most measures.

So why does the NYSE stick to its second-class model? There is only one defensible answer: Computerization would threaten a system that creates almost unfathomable profits for a few insiders — the specialists.

The NYSE is very profitable indeed. If you want to trade a stock on the exchange, you send your order to a specialist on the floor who, in addition to making the market for the stock, also tries to make trading profit for his own account. The specialist is often the only one who has a complete picture of the balance of buying and selling in the market, and this knowledge can be very profitable.

How profitable? A recent study presented at the American Enterprise Institute found that the specialist trading profits were so great that they were, as a group, consistently among the most profitable firms in America.

But the specialists' profits come out of the pockets of ordinary investors. Investors are beginning to strike back. For example, the California Public Employees Retirement System just announced a lawsuit alleging that "the exchange purposefully allowed and specialist firms participated in trade manipulations, enhancing profits to both and cheating investors out of the best prices for stock trades."

One can hope that such lawsuits will lead to a modernization of the NYSE that reluctant regulators should have adopted a decade ago.

no

SEN. CHARLES E. SCHUMER, D-N.Y.
RANKING MINORITY MEMBER, SENATE BANKING SUBCOMMITTEE ON ECONOMIC POLICY

FROM A STATEMENT BEFORE THE SENATE BANKING COMMITTEE, NOV. 20, 2003

I want to comment on what I think is one of the keys to the exchange's success: the unique specialist-based trading system. We clearly need to get to the bottom of charges that a few specialists may have violated the rules and regulations. And it's important we do that quickly.

But some are now arguing that specialists are outdated and that making the quickest trade on an electronic black box is more important than finding and delivering the best price. I couldn't disagree more. The human element at the heart of the specialist system is still critical, and the proof is in the pudding.

The NYSE specialist system beats competing markets, 100 percent electronic markets, and gets the best price 94 percent of the time on listed shares. More importantly, most investors, average investors, want the best price. That's what they think they're getting when they execute a trade.

My father is a small stock trader. I know what he wants. I've asked him. He wants best price. He doesn't care if he has to wait 10 minutes to get the best price. He wants the best price. So it's not how fast. It's . . . getting the best price. And the specialist system beats all others, hands down.

So . . . when we hear some criticism of the specialists, we recognize where it's coming from. It seems to me the cards aren't always on the table. Some of the vocal critics are guilty of their own conflicts of interest through their ownership of rival electronic markets.

I'm not saying the specialist system doesn't need to make adjustments, but if we eliminate the specialist system by design or by accident, we risk fragmenting the market into many little electronic black boxes, where trades are quick but prices suffer. It is in a fragmented, non-transparent market that investors suffer the most. That's where all the behind-the-scenes tricks and things will occur, not in an open system. That's what we've found.

So keeping one efficient, deep and liquid market where orders compete head to head is a goal that serves all investors worldwide. Fragmentation of the markets to me is the greatest nightmare we face, not only for New York, not only for America, but for every investor who wants to be treated fairly worldwide.

Continued from p. 40

"They've been talking about change and reform in mutual funds for 60 years and have done nothing," says John Freeman, a professor of legal and business ethics at the University of South Carolina. "It took Spitzer to push the fund industry toward openness and fair dealing and right business practices with a mere staff of 15 lawyers, compared to the SEC with its hundreds of lawyers."

SEC critics also point to the aggressive actions of Massachusetts Attorney General William F. Galvin, who brought fraud charges against Putnam Investments months after a company whistleblower had tried to warn the SEC, but was ignored. The commission eventually brought its own case against Putnam, but only after the whistleblower had already gone to Massachusetts authorities, and the state charges had become public.

Chairman Donaldson defends the SEC and promises it will be aggressive in its investigations of mutual fund abuses. While the commission hopes that funds will reveal trading abuses on their own, all fund management companies eventually will be examined for problems.

"We're going to get them one way or another," Donaldson told the Senate Banking Committee in November.

Excessive Fees?

Critics have long maintained that mutual funds load too many charges onto investors, some of which are poorly disclosed or hidden. In addition to charges for buying or selling shares in the fund, there are fees for fund managers and their advisers. Even so-called no-load funds — which do not charge for trades and carry low annual charges — have extra costs, such as fees paid to lawyers, accountants and board members, as well as for insurance premiums to protect board members and others from liability.

Getty Images/Stephen Chernin

The first trial of investment banker Frank Quattrone for obstruction of justice and witness tampering ended in a mistrial last year. The charges against Quattrone, who will be retried in March, stem from allegations that his firm, Credit Suisse First Boston, inappropriately doled out shares of initial public offerings of stock.

The fees vary dramatically. Vanguard, for instance, deducts only 0.28 percent of total assets each year, while Alliance Capital Management charges up to 1.69 percent. [33] The industry average is 0.65 percent of assets.

Critics of mutual fund fee policies note that in many funds, many expenses are never clearly disclosed to investors. "The average person is woefully ignorant about things like cost, particularly when you've got an industry that's superb at masking cost," says the University of South Carolina's Freeman.

Others, though, say investors are partly to blame because they pay much more attention to fund performance than fees, leaving companies little reason to compete by driving down costs. Still others say most investors are only concerned with the overall charge. "This whole idea that you need an itemized breakdown of all of the fees is ridiculous," says Cato's Reynolds. "Investors want to know what the final fee is, which is something that is easy enough to find out."

Nevertheless, Spitzer has been pressuring funds to lower fees. On Dec. 18, he said Alliance had agreed to lower its fees by 20 percent for five years, which will save investors an estimated $350 million. [34]

"We are interested in . . . driving fees down to competitive levels," Spitzer said, adding that market forces will prompt other firms to match Alliance's reduction. [35]

But the SEC is among those who say the government has no business negotiating fee reductions. "The government isn't good at setting prices," SEC Commissioner Harvey J. Goldschmid said. "If you have good disclosure, competitive markets and an independent board bargaining hard, that's the way to bring fees down." [36]

Others fear that pressuring mutual funds to lower fees might lead them to lock out small investors. "Funds might raise the minimum needed to invest to say, $20,000 or $25,000, because they have to provide the same customer service to both large and small investors," says Cato's Reynolds. "So if fees are forced down, they might decide it's not worth it to keep these smaller guys on board." ■

OUTLOOK

Action in Congress

Late last year, Congresss took the first step toward imposing new rules on the mutual fund industry. On Nov. 19, the House overwhelmingly passed a measure banning market-timing, sponsored by Rep. Richard H. Baker, R-La.

The bill also would set rigorous new public-disclosure requirements for fund-management companies and require them to adopt an ethics code that would be implemented internally by an ethics-compliance director. In addition, the measure would allow fund companies to discourage short-term trading by eliminating the current 2 percent penalty cap on how much they can charge investors who frequently trade fund shares.

But while these actions could have a significant impact on the industry, most analysts say they will not produce the kind of changes prompted by the so-called Sarbanes-Oxley law, enacted last year to prevent corporate crimes like those uncovered in 2001 and 2002.

"I just don't see a real movement for some sort of major legislative overhaul beyond the mutual fund bills — if even that," says the University of Mississippi's Bullard. "And that's really a shame."

Indeed, the House bill faces an uncertain fate in the Senate, where a similar measure has been introduced by Democrats Jon Corzine of New Jersey and Connecticut Sens. Christopher J. Dodd and Joseph I. Lieberman. Banking Committee Chairman Shelby and other GOP leaders have not indicated whether they believe a legislative overhaul is needed. Shelby has said he would support a new law only if he concludes after committee hearings this spring that the current regulations are inadequate. [37]

The White House and the Federal Reserve also have concerns about the House bill, particularly the disclosure provisions, which they fear could prove too costly for the industry. In a recent letter to Shelby and House Financial Services Committee Chairman Michael G. Oxley of Ohio, Treasury Secretary John W. Snow and Fed Chairman Alan Greenspan said the discloser requirements "should be designed to provide investors with real value rather than serve mainly to increase costs and decrease returns." [38]

Some critics interpret the uncertainties about the bill's future as a sign that Congress probably will not act this year. "This whole thing is already losing its headline appeal," says Cato's Reynolds. "Spitzer and Congress will move onto something else."

Others contend that it is simply unrealistic to think lawmakers will impose real reform on one of the nation's richest and most powerful industries. "The mutual fund industry is worth $7 trillion," the University of South Carolina's Freeman says. "With that much money, you can afford to hire the best lawyers and lobbyists in the business to press your case. With that much power, you're usually going to get your way."

If Congress ends up setting the issue aside or enacting only minor changes, few believe that the mutual fund industry will suffer a long-term drop in business. "If Congress does nothing, it leaves investors in a very difficult position because they don't know where to turn," says the Consumers Union's Greenberg. "People are always told by the experts to put their money into mutual funds. So what are they going to do?"

Indeed, Greenberg says, most consumers are unlikely to pay much attention to what the SEC or Congress does. "I'm not saying that these scandals haven't shaken investors, but this stuff is so dense and complicated that unless you have a lot of time, you usually just trust your financial adviser or the manager of your pension fund and pray for the best."

Freeman agrees that investors will not be put off by lack of significant congressional action. "What are they going to do, put their money under the mattress?"

But that doesn't matter, he says, because real reform will not come from Capitol Hill or the SEC, but from the courts. "Real changes, the kind that benefit investors, are going to come because of lawsuits," Freeman predicts. "And trust me, there are going to be a lot of investor lawsuits against mutual fund companies.

"We've already seen what the threat of a lawsuit can do," he continues, referring to Alliance's settlement with Spitzer, where they agreed to lower fees by 20 percent or $350 million over five years. "Look, Alliance gave up a third of a billion dollars to get rid of Eliot Spitzer. They did it at the point of a knife, not because they're nice guys. That's the kind of change I'm talking about." ■

About the Author

David Masci specializes in science, religion and foreign-policy issues. Before joining *The CQ Researcher* in 1996, he was a reporter at Congressional Quarterly's *Daily Monitor* and *CQ Weekly*. He holds a law degree from The George Washington University and a B.A. in medieval history from Syracuse University. His recent reports include "Rebuilding Iraq" and "Torture."

Notes

[1] Stephen Labaton, "S.E.C Has Found Payoffs in Sales of Mutual Funds," *The New York Times*, Jan. 14, 2004, p. A1.
[2] Patrick McGeehan, "Wall Street Deal Says Little About Investors," *The New York Times*, Dec. 21, 2002, p. C1.
[3] Quoted in Landon Thomas Jr., "Big Pension Fund Objects to Proposal for Big Board," *The New York Times*, Nov. 7, 2003, p. C5.
[4] Figures cited in Amy Borrus and Paula Dwyer, "Funds Need a Radical New Design," *Business Week*, Nov. 17, 2003, p. 47.
[5] John Hechinger, "Putnam is Firing Nine More Workers for Improper Trades," *The Wall Street Journal*, Dec. 17, 2003, p. C1.
[6] Ian McDonald, "Flight to Quality Benefits Three Funds," *The Wall Street Journal*, Dec. 12, 2003, p. C1.
[7] John Steele Gordon, *The Great Game: The Emergence of Wall Street as a World Power, 1653-2000* (2002), p. 43.
[8] *Ibid.*, pp. 101-125.
[9] *Ibid.*, p. 96.
[10] Charles R. Geisst, *Wall Street: A History* (1997), pp. 89-91.
[11] Gordon, *op. cit.*, p. 248.
[12] *Ibid.*, p. 268.
[13] Geisst, *op. cit.*, pp. 356-359.
[14] For background, see Kenneth Jost, "Corporate Crime," *The CQ Researcher*, Oct. 11, 2002, pp. 817-840.
[15] For background on the 1990s boom, see Kenneth Jost, "The Stock Market," *The CQ Researcher*, May 2, 1997, pp. 385-408. For background on mutual funds, see Mary H. Cooper, "Mutual Funds," *The CQ Researcher*, May 20, 1994, pp. 433-456.
[16] Brooke A. Masters and Carrie Johnson, "Banker's Case Ends in Mistrial," *The Washington Post*, Oct. 24, 2003, p. A1.
[17] Brooke A. Masters, "Quattrone to Stand Trial a Second Time, *The Washington Post*, Nov. 5, 2003, p. E2.
[18] Ben White, "ImClone's Waksal Gets Maximum Jail Sentence," *The Washington Post*, June 10, 2003, p. A1.
[19] Gretchen Morgenson, "The Fall of a Wall Street Ward Boss," *The New York Times*, Oct. 19, 2003, p. C1.
[20] Quoted in *ibid.*
[21] Landon Thomas Jr., "Officials in 2 States Urge Big Board Chief to Quit," *The New York Times*, Sept. 17, 2003, p. 1A.
[22] Ben White, "NYSE Ousts Grasso As Chairman," *The Washington Post*, Sept. 18, 2003, p. A1.
[23] Susan Craig and Kate Kelly, "Spitzer Sets Sights on the Pay of Grasso, Once a Great Friend," *The Wall Street Journal*, Jan. 8, 2003, p. C1.
[24] Patrick McGeehan and Landon Thomas Jr., "Stock Exchange Said to Select Chief Executive," *The New York Times*, Dec. 18, 2003, p. A1.
[25] Deborah Solomon and Susanne Craig, "SEC Blasts Big Board Oversight of 'Specialist' Trading Firms," *The Wall Street Journal*, Nov. 11, 2003, p. A1.
[26] Kate Kelly and Susanne Craig, "Calpers Sues Big Board and Specialist Firms," *The Wall Street Journal*, Dec. 16, 2003, p. C1.
[27] Quoted in Kate Kelly, Greg Ip and Ianthe Jeanne Dugan, "For NYSE, New CEO Could Be Just A Start," *The Wall Street Journal*, Dec. 19, 2003, p. C1.
[28] Brook A. Masters, "Spitzer Alleges Mutual Fund Improprieties," *The Washington Post*, Sept. 4, 2003, p. E1.
[29] Brooke A. Masters, "Regulators to Expand Fund Probe," *The Washington Post*, Jan. 9, 2004, p. E1.
[30] Tom Lauricella and John Hechinger, "Alliance Settles Charges," *The Wall Street Journal*, Dec. 19, 2003, p. C1.
[31] Phil Boroff, "First Executive is Sentenced Amid Fund Probe, *The New York Sun*, Dec. 18, 2003, p. 11.
[32] Quoted in Stephen Labaton, "SEC Proposes Rules to End Late Trading in Mutual Funds," *The New York Times*, Dec. 4, 2003, p. C1.
[33] Cited in Christopher Oster and Karen Damato, "Spitzer Gambit May Alter Debate Over Fund-Fees," *The Wall Street Journal*, Dec. 11, 2003, p. C1.
[34] Riva Atlas, "In Settlement, Alliance Agrees to Cut Fees," *The New York Times*, Dec. 17, 2003, p. C1.
[35] Quoted in *ibid.*
[36] Quoted in *ibid.*
[37] Siobhan Hughes, "Senate Banking Chairman Pushes for Government Attention to Mutual Funds," *Congressional Quarterly Daily Monitor*, Nov. 20, 2003.
[38] Quoted in *ibid.*

FOR MORE INFORMATION

Consumers Union of the United States, 1666 Connecticut Ave., N.W., Suite 310, Washington, DC 20009; (202) 462-6262; www.consumersunion.org. Consumer-advocacy group.

Council of Institutional Investors, 1730 Rhode Island Ave., N.W., Suite 512, Washington, DC 20036; (202) 822-0800; www.cii.org. Represents corporate, public and union pension funds.

Investment Company Institute, 1401 H St., N.W., 12th Floor, Washington, DC 20005; (202) 362-5800; www.ici.org. Represents mutual fund management companies.

Investor Responsibility Research Center, 1350 Connecticut Ave., N.W., Suite 700, Washington, DC 20036; (202) 833-0700; www.irrc.com. Analyzes issues affecting investors.

National Association of Securities Dealers, 1735 K St., N.W., Washington, DC 20006; (202) 728-8000; www.nasd.com. Represents investment brokers and dealers.

New York Stock Exchange, 11 Wall St., New York, NY 10005; (212) 656-3000; www.nyse.com. The world's largest stock exchange.

Securities Industry Association, 120 Broadway, 35th Floor, New York, NY 10271; (212) 608-1500; www.sia.com. Represents all segments of the securities industry.

Bibliography

Selected Sources

Books

Geisst, Charles R., *Wall Street: A History*, Oxford University Press, 1997.
A professor of finance at Manhattan College chronicles the rise of America's securities industry and its role in the nation's economic development.

Gordon, John Steele, *The Great Game: The Emergence of Wall Street as a World Power, 1653-2000*, Scribner's, 2002.
A financial journalist colorfully describes past Wall Street conmen.

Articles

"The Scandal Spreads," *The Economist*, Oct. 11, 2003, p. 75.
The piece provides an excellent overview of the expanding mutual fund scandal.

Craig, Susanne, Kate Kelly and Deborah Solomon, "Spitzer, SEC Open Probes Into Grasso's Pay," *The Wall Street Journal*, Jan. 9, 2003, p. C1.
Three experienced financial journalists give a detailed account of how the controversy over former New York Stock Exchange (NYSE) Chairman Richard Grasso's pay package has expanded into a full-blown investigation.

Cohen, Laurie P., and Kate Kelly, "NYSE Turmoil Poses Question: Can Wall Street Regulate Itself?" *The Wall Street Journal*, Dec. 31, 2003, p. A1.
The article assesses the self-regulation system at the New York Stock Exchange.

Damato, Karen, and Tom Lauricella, "Mutual Funds Vow to Fix Their Clocks," *The Wall Street Journal*, Oct. 31, 2003, p. C1.
The article explains the mutual fund industry's proposals to restore investor confidence.

Jost, Kenneth, "Corporate Crime," *The CQ Researcher*, Oct. 11, 2002, p. 817.
A veteran legal journalist provides a comprehensive overview of the corporate-accounting scandals that preceded Wall Street's current troubles.

Labaton, Stephen, "SEC's Oversight of Mutual Funds is Said to be Lax," *The New York Times*, Nov. 16, 2003, p. A1.
Critics complain that the Securities and Exchange Commission (SEC) has not been adequately policing the mutual fund industry.

Langley, Monica, "As His Ambitions Expand, Spitzer Draws Controversy," *The Wall Street Journal*, Dec. 11, 2003, p. A1.
Some critics see political ambition behind New York Attorney General Eliot Spitzer's moves to overhaul Wall Street trading practices.

Morgenson, Gretchen, "The Fall of a Wall Street Ward Boss," *The New York Times*, Oct. 19, 2003, p. C1.
In her inimitable, hard-hitting style, Morgenson examines the rise and fall of NYSE Chairman Richard Grasso.

Norris, Floyd, and Thomas, Landon, "Big Board Head Offers Detailed Overhaul Plan," *The New York Times*, Nov. 6, 2003, p. C1.
Veteran financial reporters examine Interim Chairman John Reed's plan to reform NYSE governance.

Revell, Janice, and David Stires, "Making Sense of the Mutual Fund Scandal," *Fortune*, Nov. 24, 2003, p. 237.
A comprehensive primer on the mutual fund scandals explains why market-timing and late trading are questionable practices.

Reynolds, Alan, "Endless Public Flogging on Wall Street," *The Washington Times*, May 25, 2003, p. A23.
A senior fellow at the libertarian Cato Institute argues that Attorney General Spitzer is more interested in headlines than justice.

Solomon, Deborah, and Susanne Craig, "SEC Blasts Big Board Oversight of 'Specialist' Trading Firms," *The Wall Street Journal*, Nov. 3, 2003, p. A1.
A confidential SEC report blasted the NYSE for ignoring blatant violations by its "specialist" floor traders.

Tully, Shawn, "Bringing Down the Temple," *Fortune*, Nov. 10, 2003, p. 119.
With the fall of NYSE Chairman Grasso, the exchange's 132-year-old "specialist" trading system has lost a powerful protector and is now under increasing pressure from investors who want to eliminate it in favor of a cheaper, all-electronic trading system.

Weiss, Gary, Paula Dwyer and Amy Borrus, "New Broom at the Big Board," *Business Week*, Oct. 6, 2003, p. 44.
A profile describes NYSE Interim Chairman John Reed as "cerebral, worldly" and "somewhat distant and cold."

Reports

"Annual SIA Investor Survey: Investors' Attitudes Toward the Securities Industry," 2003, The Securities Industry Association, November 2003.
The Securities Industry Association poll tracks investors' attitudes toward all aspects of the securities industry.

The Next Step:

Additional Articles from Current Periodicals

Congressional Action

Borrus, Amy, *et al.*, "The Critical Battle for Reform," *Business Week*, Dec. 1, 2003, p. 30.
Big investors, along with Congress and the Securities and Exchange Commission (SEC), are trying to curb abuses in the mutual fund industry.

Peterson, Jonathan, "Fund Overhaul Rises on Congress' To-Do List," *Los Angeles Times*, Nov. 10, 2003, p. C1.
Members of Congress have begun a new push to overhaul controversial mutual fund trading practices.

Petruno, Tom, and Thomas S. Mulligan, "Corporate Reform's Baby Steps," *Los Angeles Times*, July 27, 2003, p. A1.
The law to clean up Wall Street's worst abuses is getting mixed reviews a year after its enactment.

Stone, Peter H., "Mutual Fund Morass," *National Journal*, Nov. 15, 2003.
State regulators, the SEC and members of Congress are moving to crack down on mutual fund trading abuses.

Investor Confidence

Coy, Peter, "Investors are Bullish all Over Again," *Business Week*, Dec. 29, 2003, p. 76.
Many investors are still worried about abuses in the mutual fund industry.

Masters, Brooke A., "Little Guys' Lament," *The Washington Post*, Sept. 14, 2003, p. F1.
Some business analysts think the recent stock research and accounting scandals have hurt investor confidence.

Scherer, Ron, "Grasso Fallout: Is Big Board a Small Clique?" *The Christian Science Monitor*, Sept. 19, 2003, p. 1.
Richard A. Grasso's $140 million retirement package has challenged investor confidence in the New York Stock Exchange.

Waggoner, John, and Thomas A. Fogarty, "Scandals Shred Investors' Faith," *USA Today*, May 2, 2002, p. A1.
A drumbeat of corporate misdeeds has helped crush stock prices, but the biggest victim may be investors' confidence.

White, Ben, "A Crisis Of Trust on Wall Street," *The Washington Post*, May 4, 2003, p. F1.
Investor confidence has been hurt by revelations that stock analysts issued questionable research to boost their companies' business prospects.

Mutual Funds

Atlas, Riva D., *et al.*, "Under Pressure, a Mutual Fund May Lower Fees," *The New York Times*, Dec. 12, 2003, p. C1.
The recent scandals could result in lower fees for investors and less profits for mutual funds.

Day, Kathleen, "SEC Proposes Mutual Fund Curbs," *The Washington Post*, Dec. 4, 2003, p. E1.
The SEC unanimously acted to address widespread trading abuses in the mutual fund industry.

Dwyer, Paula, *et al.*, "Breach of Trust," *Business Week*, Dec. 15, 2003, p. 98.
The mutual fund scandal was a disaster waiting to happen, and many experts think politics had a lot to do with it.

Friedman, Josh, *et al.*, "For the Fund Business, What Went Wrong?" *Los Angeles Times*, Nov. 2, 2003, p. C1.
Growing fraud allegations in the mutual fund business may prompt dramatic changes.

Gray, Steven, "Janus to Pay Investors $31.5 Million to Cover Losses From Scandal," *The Washington Post*, Dec. 20, 2003, p. E1.
Janus Capital Group will reimburse mutual fund investors for the estimated $31.5 million lost because of special trading privileges it gave a hedge fund.

Master, Brooke A., "Regulators to Expand Fund Probe," *The Washington Post*, Jan. 9, 2004, p. E1.
The sprawling investigation into mutual fund abuses will soon target financial institutions that helped bankroll illegal trading by big investors.

Sloan, Allan, and Barney Gimbel, "The Mutual Fund Scandal: Unfair Fight," *Newsweek*, Dec. 8, 2003, p. 42.
Mutual funds were supposed to be the safe choice for small investors, but the latest scandal shows how the little guys take a beating.

Thomas Jr., Landon, "Memo Shows MFS Funds Let Favored Clients Trade When Others Couldn't," *The New York Times*, Dec. 9, 2003, p. C1.
The oldest mutual fund company in the country gave privileged clients unfair trading advantages.

NYSE Reform

"In John Reed's Hands," *The Economist*, Nov. 8, 2003.
In recent years, Wall Street as a whole has been lamentable in making money for anyone but those employed by it.

Dwyer, Paula, *et al.*, "The Big Board's Blueprint: Done Deal?" *Business Week*, Nov. 24, 2003, p. 45.
Some state pension fund trustees question the recent reforms at the New York Stock Exchange.

Farrell, Greg, "Critics Say Human Frailties Taint NYSE," *USA Today*, Oct. 15, 2003, p. B1.
Some of the biggest customers of the New York Stock Exchange are calling for radical changes.

Peterson, Jonathan, "Overhaul of NYSE Approved," *Los Angeles Times*, Dec. 18, 2003, p. C1.
The SEC approved plans to reform the NYSE after the exchange promised to split the roles of chairman and chief executive.

Risen, Clay, "No Respect," *The New Republic*, Nov. 3, 2003, p. 18.
If Richard Grasso was the obvious villain in last month's upheaval at the New York Stock Exchange, SEC Chairman William Donaldson was the unsung hero.

White, Ben, and Kathleen Day, "NYSE to Name New Chief Executive," *The Washington Post*, Dec. 18, 2003, p. E1.
The New York Stock Exchange plans to name John A. Thain, president and chief operating officer of Goldman Sachs, as new chief executive.

Stock Research

Hamilton, Walter, and Thomas S. Mulligan, "Wall Street Will Pay $1.4 Billion," *Los Angeles Times*, April 29, 2003, p. A1.
Securities regulators announced a sweeping legal settlement that will change the brokerage business and require stock analysts to tell the truth.

Masters, Brooke A., "Few Gains for Investors Suing Over Research," *The Washington Post*, Aug. 14, 2003, p. E1.
Investors who blamed misleading research reports for their stock-market losses aren't doing any better in arbitration than they did in the markets.

Morgenson, Gretchen, and Patrick McGeehan, "Wall Street Star May Face Suit By Regulators," *The New York Times*, Jan. 4, 2003, p. A1.
Former stock analyst Henry Blodget has been sued for fraud and other violations of securities regulations.

Thomas Jr., Landon, "Citigroup's Chairman Is Barred From Direct Talks With Analysts," *The New York Times*, April 29, 2003, p. C1.
To prevent bias in future stock research, Citigroup barred senior company officials from talking to Citigroup's research analysts on investment matters.

Vickers, Marcia, "The Myth of Independence," *Business Week*, Sept. 8, 2003, p. 86.
Investors shouldn't be lulled into thinking that independent research is the Holy Grail for stockpicking — some experts think it's ripe for abuse as well.

White, Ben, "Citigroup to Divide Research, Investment Banking," *The Washington Post*, Oct. 31, 2002, p. E1.
Under pressure from regulators, Citigroup separated its stock research from its investment banking.

White, Ben, and Brooke A. Masters, "Investor Suits Against Wall St. Firms Rejected," *The Washington Post*, July 2, 2003, p. E1.
Two federal judges concluded that allegedly biased research reports from stock analysts were not to blame for the market bubble that burst in 2000.

CITING *THE CQ RESEARCHER*

Sample formats for citing these reports in a bibliography include the ones listed below. Preferred styles and formats vary, so please check with your instructor or professor.

MLA STYLE

Jost, Kenneth. "Rethinking the Death Penalty." The CQ Researcher 16 Nov. 2001: 945-68.

APA STYLE

Jost, K. (2001, November 16). Rethinking the death penalty. *The CQ Researcher, 11*, 945-968.

CHICAGO STYLE

Jost, Kenneth. "Rethinking the Death Penalty." *CQ Researcher*, November 16, 2001, 945-968.

Back Issues

The CQ Researcher *offers in-depth coverage of many key areas.*
Back issues are $10. Quantity discounts available.
Call (866) 427-7737 to order back issues.

Or call for a free CQ Researcher Web trial!
Online access provides:

- *Searchable archives dating back to 1991.*
- *Wider access through IP authentication.*
- *PDF files for downloading and printing.*
- *Availability 48 hours before print version.*

CHILDREN/YOUTH
Preventing Teen Drug Use, March 2002
Sexual Abuse and the Clergy, May 2002
Movie Ratings, March 2003

CRIMINAL JUSTICE
Cyber-Crime, April 2002
Corporate Crime, October 2002
Serial Killers, October 2003

EDUCATION
Charter Schools, December 2002
Combating Plagiarism, September 2003
Home Schooling Debate, January 2003
Black Colleges, December 2003

ENVIRONMENT
Bush and the Environment, October 2002
Crisis in the Plains, May 2003
NASA's Future, May 2003
Water Shortages, August 2003
Air Pollution Conflict, November 2003

HEALTH CARE AND MEDICINE
Medicare Reform, August 2003
Women's Health, November 2003
Homeopathy Debate, December 2003

LEGAL ISSUES
Abortion Debates, March 2003
Race in America, July 2003
Torture, April 2003
Homeland Security, September 2003
Civil Liberties Debates, October 2003

MODERN CULTURE
Gay Marriage, September 2003
Combating Plagiarism, September 2003
Latinos' Future, October 2003
Future of the Music Industry, Nov. 2003
Hazing, January 2004

POLITICS/GOVERNMENT
Presidential Power, November 2002
Future of NATO, February 2003
Trouble in South America, March 2003
North Korean Crisis, April 2003
Rebuilding Iraq, July 2003
Aiding Africa, August 2003
State Budget Crises, October 2003

TRANSPORTATION
Auto Safety, October 2001
Future of the Airline Industry, June 2002
Future of Amtrak, October 2002
SUV Debate, May 2003

- ***Advertising Overload***
- ***Democracy in the Arab World***
- ***Medicating Mental Illness***

CQ Researcher

Published by CQ Press, a division of Congressional Quarterly Inc.

thecqresearcher.com

Advertising Overload

Are more restrictions needed?

Consumer advocates say Americans are under siege by advertisers, and that the problem is more serious than just irritating dinnertime phone calls or endless ads during movie previews and commercial names for sports stadiums. The advocates blame increasingly intrusive advertising for such societal ills as childhood obesity, rising health-care costs and lost productivity because workplace e-mail boxes are clogged by unsolicited emails, known as spam. Public outcry has resulted in a national do-not-call list aimed at curbing telemarketing and may soon trigger a do-not-e-mail list to deter spammers. Other advertising critics are seeking greater restrictions on advertising to children. Advertisers and some advocacy groups, however, warn that many of the proposed restrictions violate First Amendment protections for free speech.

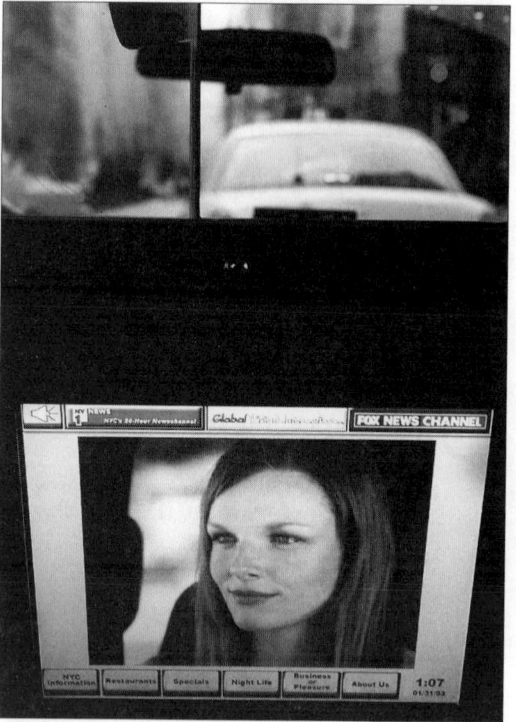

Back-seat televisions in New York City taxi cabs are the latest way to reach consumers.

INSIDE THIS ISSUE

The CQ Researcher • Jan. 23, 2004 • www.thecqresearcher.com
Volume 14, Number 3 • Pages 49-72

RECIPIENT OF SOCIETY OF PROFESSIONAL JOURNALISTS AWARD FOR EXCELLENCE ◆ AMERICAN BAR ASSOCIATION SILVER GAVEL AWARD

THE ISSUES

BACKGROUND

CURRENT SITUATION

OUTLOOK

SIDEBARS AND GRAPHICS

FOR FURTHER RESEARCH

Cover: Interactive television systems showing news, sports and ads are being tested in 178 New York City cabs. (Getty Images/Mario Tama)

THE CQ Researcher

Jan. 23, 2004
Volume 14, No. 3

MANAGING EDITOR: Thomas J. Colin
ASSISTANT MANAGING EDITOR: Kathy Koch
ASSOCIATE EDITOR: Kenneth Jost
STAFF WRITERS: Mary H. Cooper, David Masci, William Triplett
CONTRIBUTING WRITERS: Rachel S. Cox, Sarah Glazer, David Hosansky, Patrick Marshall, Jane Tanner
DESIGN/PRODUCTION EDITOR: Olu B. Davis
ASSISTANT EDITOR: Kenneth Lukas

CQ PRESS

A Division of Congressional Quarterly Inc.

SENIOR VICE PRESIDENT/GENERAL MANAGER: John A. Jenkins
DIRECTOR, LIBRARY PUBLISHING: Kathryn C. Suárez
DIRECTOR, EDITORIAL OPERATIONS: Ann Davies
CIRCULATION MANAGER: Nina Tristani

CONGRESSIONAL QUARTERLY INC.
CHAIRMAN: Andrew Barnes
VICE CHAIRMAN: Andrew P. Corty
PRESIDENT AND PUBLISHER: Robert W. Merry

The CQ Researcher (ISSN 1056-2036) is printed on acid-free paper. Published weekly, except Jan. 2, April 9, July 2, July 9, Aug. 6, Aug. 13, Nov. 26 and Dec. 31, by CQ Press, a division of Congressional Quarterly Inc. Annual subscription rates for libraries, businesses and government start at $625. Single issues are available for $10. Quantity discounts apply to orders over 10. Additional rates furnished upon request. Periodicals postage paid at Washington, D.C., and additional mailing offices. POSTMASTER: Send address changes to *The CQ Researcher*, 1255 22nd St., N.W., Suite 400, Washington, D.C. 20037.

Advertising Overload

By Patrick Marshall

The Issues

It's like the Blob that Steve McQueen faced in the 1961 movie of the same name: a formless horror that threatens to engulf us. At least that's how the critics of advertising see things. Advertising and promotions have gotten so out of hand, they say, the glut of ads is threatening our peace of mind, our privacy and even our health.

Consumers today often cannot escape the onslaught of commercialism, as advertisers — competing for attention in an expanding media environment — inundate classrooms, theaters, cyberspace, sports stadiums, police cars, doctors' offices, garbage cans, airports and even restroom walls. Ads are turning up on parking lot tickets, paper cup insulators, gasoline pump handles and golf scorecards.

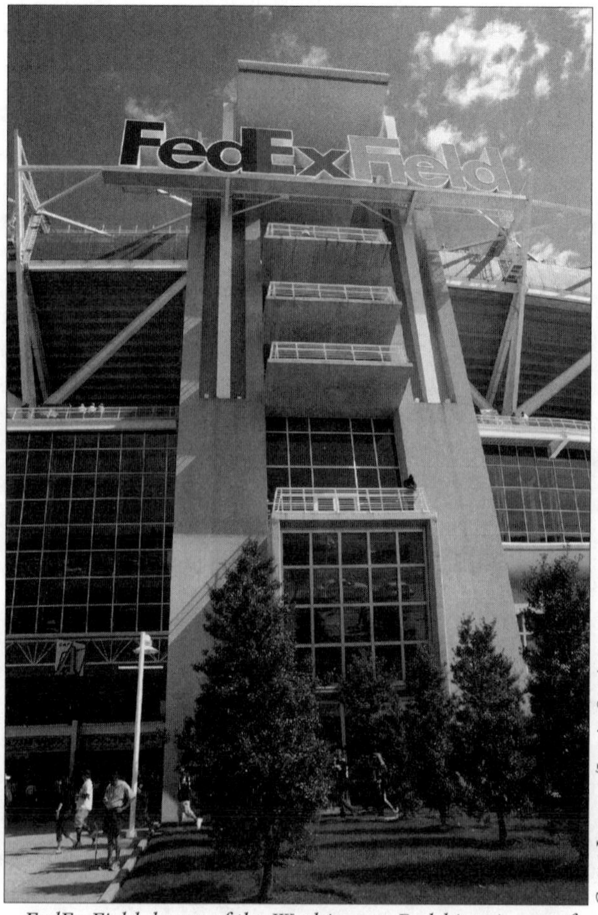

Getty Images/Jamie Squire

FedEx Field, home of the Washington Redskins, is one of dozens of sports stadiums around the country that have sold naming rights to corporate sponsors. Some citizens groups have protested, arguing that putting corporate names on such prominent landmarks is intrusive commercialism. San Francisco recently bought back the naming rights for its Candlestick Park from 3Com.

"There's an effort to hang an ad in front of our eyes at every waking moment of the day and night," says Gary Ruskin, executive director of Commercial Alert, a nonprofit consumer advocacy group in Portland, Ore. "Americans are sick of it."

And consumers cannot even escape the onslaught in their own homes. TV viewers now see nearly a full hour of commercials during a typical night of primetime broadcasts. In addition, telemarketers invade the dinner hour in millions of homes every night, and spammers daily cram bushels of unsolicited ads into millions of private e-mail boxes. [1]

"Advertisements are literally popping up everywhere," says psychologist David Walsh, founder of the National Institute on Media and the Family, in Minneapolis. "It is just overwhelming."

"What advertisers have to come up with each week is the new, new intrusive thing, so we have a steamroller of intrusiveness," said Robert W. McChesney, a professor of communications at the University of Illinois, Urbana-Champaign, and founder of Free Press, a national media-reform organization. "We're locked in a death-spiral of intrusiveness." [2]

Consumers literally can feel like captive audiences of advertisers: Some movie theaters run 20 minutes of ads before showing the movie; airline passengers can find themselves stuck for hours staring at ads plastered across the bottoms of their fold-up trays; and telephone callers must listen to ads repeated over and over while on hold.

But the proliferating ads are more than just annoying or unattractive. Many educators and parents are worried about the impact on students of the increasing number of ads in schools. And the literally billions of spam messages and pop-up ads that daily bombard Internet users raise concerns about privacy, cost and the potential that users will simply be alienated from all ads — even from legitimate retailers.

Seventy percent of e-mail users say spam has made being online unpleasant or annoying, and 80 percent are bothered by what they consider spam's deceptive content, according to the Pew Internet and American Life Project. [3]

The amount of spam being sent out, according to the Pew survey, is "mind-boggling." Researchers estimate that nearly 15 billion spam messages are sent out daily. And the costs imposed on the American economy — primarily in lost productivity and in the cost of filtering and deleting spam — have been estimated at from $10 billion to $87 billion per year. [4]

Despite a significant drop in advertising spending during the economic downturn in 2001, spending on consumer advertising in the United States rose from $128 billion to $162 billion from 1997 to $168 billion in 2003. [5] By 2007, the figure is expected to rise to $220 billion — nearly a quarter-trillion dollars.

Telemarketers Took in $100 Billion

Consumers spent $100 billion in 2002— more than 50 percent more than in 1996— on products sold by telemarketers, mostly on telephone services, magazine subscriptions and cable services. Educational services, Realtors and banks spend the most on telemarketing, and most telemarketers are non-white, working mothers without college degrees.

Most-Popular Products Bought From Telemarketers

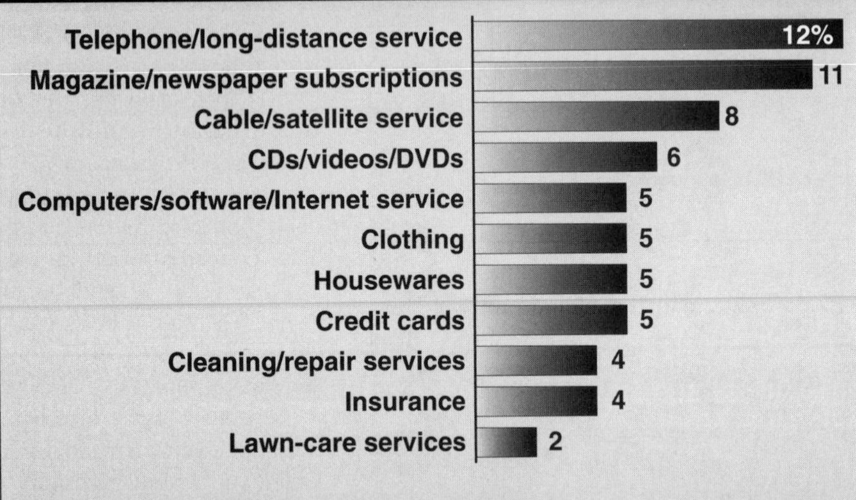

Telemarketing Sales ($ in billions)

Source: DMA Telemarketing Survey, May 2003

A major cause of the advertising boom, analysts say, is the proliferation of new media — from the Internet to hundreds of channels of cable and satellite TV and radio. Increased consumer control over traditional advertising media complicates matters further. DVD rentals and Tivo machines — which allow users to view recorded TV shows without the advertisements — have advertisers searching for additional avenues to reach consumers. Tivo is often cited as one of the reasons more advertisers are turning to "product placements," in which the advertiser pays to have their product used by a character in a TV show or movie.

With so much competition for the consumer's attention, advertisers just keep adding more and more ads. "Advertisers are having to work a lot harder to reach their audiences," says James P. Rutherfurd, executive vice president of Veronis Suhler Stevenson, a media research and investment company in New York City.

"When you're trying to 'break through the clutter,' you have to do more and more things to get the consumers' attention," Walsh explains. "So there is this constant ratcheting up of both the amount and the techniques used to get attention."

Not surprisingly, the ad onslaught has triggered a backlash. In Seattle, recently, moviegoers complained to a theater manager about the interminable advertisements preceding the previews. Last summer, after complaints from the public, San Francisco became the first city to buy back from a corporate sponsor the naming rights of its popular football stadium — tearing down the 3Com Park sign and renaming it Candlestick Park. [6]

While few national-level organizations have yet been formed specifically to fight against the flood of advertising and commercialism, grass-roots groups are springing up, and some national groups are forming to work on specific aspects of the larger issue. The Citizens' Campaign for Commercial-Free Schools, in Washington state, for example, is working toward removing advertising and promotions from schools. And, in Bethesda, Md., parents started the Lion and the Lamb Project to crusade against violence in entertainment. [7]

Much of the most recent legislative action has been aimed at telemarketers and e-mail spam. Over the past several years, dozens of states have passed legislation aimed at curbing telemarketers and spammers, including especially tough laws in California and Virginia. Last month, in fact, Virginia indicted two men under the state's anti-spam law on charges that could result in five years in prison and a $2,500 fine. [8] New York state and Microsoft also announced plans in December to file civil suits against spammers. [9]

Last year the public outcry over telephone and e-mail advertising led to major federal action. In 2003 Congress passed legislation authorizing the

Advertising Expenditures Up 30 Percent

Companies spent nearly a quarter trillion dollars on advertising and marketing to U.S. consumers in 2003, according to industry projections. The amount reflects almost a one-third increase over the 1997 figure.

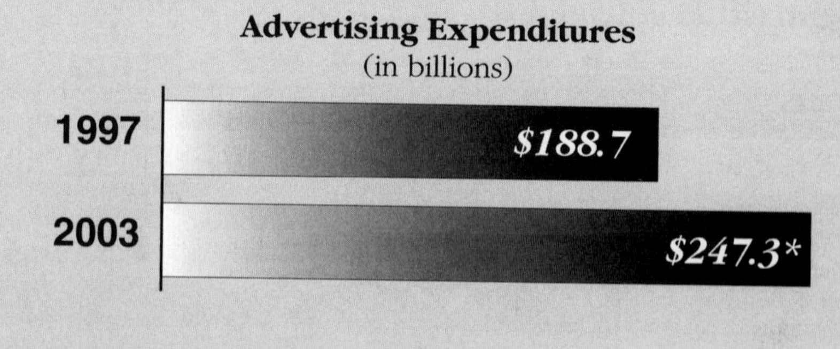

** Projected*

Source: "2003 Commercial Industry Forecast and Report," Veronis Suhler and Stevenson

Federal Trade Commission (FTC) to implement a do-not-call list designed to curb unsolicited calls from telemarketers. Also in 2003, controversial legislation aimed at curbing e-mail spam was enacted.

Nonetheless, some activists say not enough is being done to curb the onslaught of advertising and that certain citizens, especially the very young and the elderly, are not adequately equipped to defend themselves. Commercial Alert, a group founded by consumer activist Ralph Nader in 1998 to fight encroaching commercialism, has called for greater restrictions on advertising to children and recently petitioned the FTC and the Federal Communications Commission (FCC) to require pop-up disclosures when product placements are used in TV shows.

Some physicians and public-health experts also are questioning the increasing use of so-called direct-to-consumer (DTC) advertising by pharmaceutical companies to boost drug sales. While advertisers claim such efforts are purely educational, some experts warn that the advertising may lead to overprescribing and unnecessary increases in health-care costs.

"Drug companies, owing to their clear conflict of interest, are not the ones to educate people about the drugs that they are selling," two former editors of *The New England Journal of Medicine* argue. "DTC ads mainly benefit the bottom line of the drug industry, not the public. They mislead consumers more than they inform them, and they pressure physicians to prescribe new, expensive, and often marginally helpful drugs, although a more conservative option might be better for the patient. That is probably why DTC ads are not permitted in other advanced countries less in the thrall of the pharmaceutical industry." [10]

Others have decried the increasing reliance of government institutions on advertising revenue. Whether it is the Smithsonian Institution soliciting corporate sponsorship for its exhibits or a city government selling advertising space on police cars, "commercial values don't mix with civic values," Nader warns. "The Smithsonian is not a commercial institution. Its job is not to promote General Motors or IBM or whatever company."

The former Green Party presidential candidate says that such advertising deals "blur the line" between marketers and government, creating suspicion that government decisions may not be made on merit. "Our country works best when there's a clear distinction, a bright line between civic and commercial values," Nader says.

But Adonis Hoffman, senior vice president of the American Association of Advertising Agencies, says advertising is an easy target for consumers and regulators. "When products and services come under scrutiny — whether it is prescription drugs or food products or alcoholic beverages — the most likely and expedient target is to go after the marketing. But when you look at what underlies advertising, in fact, it is simply providing information to consumers so that they can make informed choices on a product or service."

Others warn that banning or restricting advertising may run afoul of the First Amendment. "Often, we try to regulate commercial speech because we don't like what the content is," says Marvin Johnson, legislative counsel for the American Civil Liberties Union (ACLU). "That puts us on dangerous territory."

Indeed, says Richard T. Kaplar, vice president of the Media Institute, a nonprofit research foundation, much of the debate over advertising restrictions boils down to the tension between commercial speech and an individual's right to privacy.

"We've got two competing values here," Kaplar says. "It's going be the big question in the future."

As Congress and the public debate what to do about the ever-growing presence of advertising in Americans' lives, here are some of the questions being asked:

Will the new spam-control law work?

Not surprisingly, Congress responded to the public outcry over the deluge of unwanted and often offensive e-mail messages that have clogged cyber mailboxes over the past two years.

Legitimate advertisers and Internet service providers eventually joined consumers in demanding federal anti-spam legislation. They supported federal action partly because they did not want to have to comply with a variety of different state laws and partly because their businesses were being hurt by spammers, most of whom are bent on defrauding the public.

"We need federal legislation in part because a patchwork of 50 state laws would be awful," says Jerry Cerasale, senior vice president of the Direct Marketing Association. Moreover, he adds, "Unlike with telephone marketing, with e-mail the fraud element is sadly the core, and legitimate marketers are the fringe."

"When you are advertising a legitimate product, the last thing you want is to have your target audience turn off and toss your e-mail out," says Hoffman, of the American Association of Advertising Agencies.

By the time Congress took up the issue in earnest, as many as 30 states already had passed anti-spam measures. The toughest is California's, which calls for a $1,000 fine per illegal e-mail. However, the state laws so far have had no noticeable deterrent effect on the flow of spam, partly because enforcing the laws across state borders is virtually impossible.

The cleverly named "Can Spam Act," signed into law by President Bush on Dec. 16, 2003, bans bulk commercial e-mail that falsely identifies senders or uses deceptive subject information. Violators can be fined up to $250 per illegal e-mail — up to $2 million per spam campaign — and sentenced to five years in prison. The law also requires all commercial e-mail to include a valid postal address and to provide recipients an opportunity to opt out of receiving more e-mails.

Some anti-spam advocates wanted the law to require all commercial e-mail to carry a marker that would make it easy to filter out, but the law only requires markers on pornographic e-mails. The law also directs the FTC to study the feasibility of instituting a do-not-spam list comparable to the federal do-not-call list for telemarketers.

Although major advertisers' organizations supported the Can Spam Act, anti-spam activists and some state officials say it is severely flawed. "The Can Spam Act misses most of the major issues with spam," says Scott Hazen Mueller, chairman of the Coalition Against Unsolicited Commercial E-mail. "There might be one or two prosecutions for show, but we don't anticipate any decreased level of spam. In fact, we anticipate that levels will continue to increase."

The act creates neither a do-not-spam registry nor bans unsolicited e-mails, Mueller points out. "The Can Spam Act basically doesn't say that people can't spam," he says. "It actually says that they can spam. We need a stake in the ground that says, 'No, you cannot send unsolicited e-mail advertisements.' "

Critics also complain that the act prohibits individuals from suing spammers, allowing only government agencies to bring actions against senders of e-mails that violate the law. "That pretty much guarantees the law's ineffectiveness," says Jason Catlett, president of Junkbusters, a privacy-advocacy group. The law was "written by online marketers for online marketers. It's going to make for more spam. It's really a tragedy of shortsightedness and corporate lobbying."

Other critics are disappointed that the law pre-empts stronger state laws. "The states take issue with that," said Paula Selis, a spokeswoman for Christine Gregoire, attorney general of Washington state and chairwoman of the National Association of Attorneys Generals' Internet Committee.[11]

Mueller, in fact, believes that concern about the harshness of the impending California law — which would have al-

Getty Images/Tina Hager

President Bush signs the "Can Spam Act" in the Oval Office on Dec. 16, 2003, accompanied by Internet executives and congressional sponsors of the measure, which will help consumers, businesses and families combat unsolicited e-mail.

lowed individuals to sue spammers — caused advertisers to push for federal legislation. "It was such a strong deterrent that certain parties got a little panicky and pushed Congress to establish new national standards," Mueller says, adding that the impact of the California law would have been felt nationwide, since advertisers wouldn't be able to sort out e-mail to Californians from others. "It would effectively have invoked California standards on the nation," he says.

But the federal law's co-sponsor, Sen. Conrad Burns, R-Mont., says that without pre-empting state laws, the measure would have been unworkable. "If the rules change once you cross a state line, it would make legislation almost impossible to enforce and essentially ineffective," he says. "We needed a federal law to make spam legislation cohesive."

Moreover, advertising-industry officials say, spammers would pay no attention to a do-not-spam registry, so it wouldn't be effective either. "It would hurt legitimate marketers more than spammers," Hoffman says.

Cerasale agrees, adding that a do-not-spam list is administratively much more complicated to do than a do-not-call list because there is no control over e-mail addresses as there is over phone numbers. "It won't work," he says.

Despite critics' doubts, Burns says he expects the act, which went into effect on Jan. 1, to produce real results. "Once someone is caught — and the article hits the front page above the fold — the spammers are going to see there are real consequences for their actions and think twice before they proceed," Burns says.

But FTC officials say it may take time to track spammers down and prosecute them. [12] Adding to the difficulty: Many illegitimate spammers are located offshore, beyond the reach of the FTC, and the legislation could simply cause more to move overseas.

Getty Images/Chris Hondros

Blinking electronic billboards were installed on dozens of subway entrances in New York City after the Metropolitan Transportation Authority sold advertising rights to Clear Channel Communications. After citizens protested the "advertising pollution" in their upper West Side neighborhood, the company replaced the illuminated ad at their subway stop with a non-animated sign.

"This is a continuing problem, and one that we have not overlooked," Burns says. "Now that we have passed a law in the United States, it will be important to get other countries on board, and it is clear that many other countries are feeling the same growing pains from the growth of the Internet and the increase in spam.

"But legislation is not a silver bullet that will completely rid the world of spam. It is going to take work from industry and strict enforcement to make a dent in the amount of spam out there," Burns says.

Have existing limits on tobacco advertising worked?

Policymakers considering additional restrictions on advertising for junk food, tobacco or alcohol may be interested in whether earlier restrictions have been effective.

In the past, federal and state governments have limited billboard advertising, alcohol commercials and drug ads, but the most restrictive measures have been imposed on cigarette advertising. Limits on tobacco ads have stemmed from a combination of federal mandates and self-regulation. Tobacco companies insist it is company policy not to market their products to children, but critics say the companies often violate those voluntary restrictions.

Then in the early 1970s, in response to new studies about the dangers of smoking, the federal government mandated that cigarette companies print special health warnings on tobacco products and barred tobacco advertising from radio and television. The 1998 Master Settlement Agreement (MSA) between tobacco companies and 46 states prompted cigarette manufacturers to again adopt voluntary restrictions and agree to pay $1.7 billion over 10 years to promote anti-smoking efforts. Specifically, they agreed not to target youth in the advertising, promotion or marketing of tobacco products. [13]

Continued on p. 57

Do Direct-to-Consumer Drug Ads Raise Health Costs?

When the government relaxed its rules on broadcasting drug commercials in 1997, pharmaceutical companies unleashed a barrage of ads aimed directly at consumers for conditions ranging from arthritis to impotence. In 1998, advertisers spent $1.3 billion on such advertising; the expenditure is expected to jump to $7 billion by 2005. [1]

The problem with so-called direct-to-consumer (DTC) advertising, critics say, is that it encourages consumers to pressure their doctors to prescribe unnecessary or even inappropriate drugs, inflating health-care costs and, in some cases, harming patients. "I'm seeing many more people asking for a particular medication based on their own assessments of their conditions," an internist in Haverhill, Mass., said. "They're basically asking me to rubber-stamp their thought processes." [2]

Advertisers disagree. "We believe that prescription-drug advertising has been one of the great success stories in the advertising world, and that it has been providing tremendous benefit to society at large," says Dan Jaffe, executive vice president for governmental affairs at the Association of National Advertisers. "Millions of people have been going to the doctor to discuss health problems they never discussed before after they had seen an ad that raised that issue. We think that's a tremendously valuable benefit."

In fact, some advocates of DTC ads say that such advertising is still being required to say too much by the Food and Drug Administration (FDA).

"The FDA should reconsider the notion that all DTC advertisements need to balance information about risks and benefits, writes John E. Calfee, resident scholar at the American Enterprise Institute. "Advertising works best as a dynamic medium, filling the most important relevant holes in consumer awareness and emphasizing different product features as dictated by circumstances. This makes information dissemination more efficient, an essential virtue in information-intensive markets such as pharmaceuticals." [3]

But critics say consumers are not getting enough information in the ads because the FDA now allows TV and radio commercials to advertise drugs' benefits without going into detail about potential side-effects. The advertisements only are required to mention major risks and then provide a Web address and toll-free telephone number for more information.

And some researchers contend advertisers are not even adhering to the relaxed requirements. "From late 1997, when the FDA relaxed its broadcast advertising regulations, until early 1999, 33 products were fully advertised on U.S. radio or television — that is, with product name and one or more health claims," write Joel Lexchin and Barbara Mintzes. "Of the 33 products, 17 were found to violate the Federal Food, Drug, and Cosmetic Act." [4]

What is not in dispute, however, is the fact that DTC pharmaceutical ads have paid off big for the pharmaceutical companies. According to the General Accounting Office, "the number of prescriptions dispensed for the most heavily advertised drugs rose 25 percent [from 1999 to 2000], but increased only 4 percent for drugs that were not heavily advertised." [5]

For one drug alone — Claritin, an antihistamine marketed by Schering-Plough — sales jumped $500 million in a single year to a total of $1.9 billion, in large part as a result of DTC ads. [6]

Drugs with Top DTC Advertising Budgets (2000)

Drug	Condition	DTC Spending (in $ millions)	Sales (in $ billions)
Vioxx	Arthritis	$160.8	$1.5
Prilosec	Ulcer/reflux	107.5	4.1
Claritin	Allergy	99.7	2.0
Paxil	Anxiety/depression	91.8	1.8
Zocor	High cholesterol	91.2	2.2
Viagra	Impotence	89.5	0.8
Celebrex	Arthritis	78.3	2.0
Flonase	Allergy	73.5	0.6
Allegra	Allergy	67.0	1.1
Meridia	Obesity	65.0	0.1
Total		$924.3	$16.3*

** Figures do not add up, due to rounding.*

Source: National Institute of Health Care Management, "Prescription Drugs and Mass Media Advertising," 2000; available at www.nihcm.org

---

[1] Phyllis Maquire, "How Direct-to-consumer Advertising is Putting the Squeeze on Physicians," ACP-ASIM Observer, American College of Physicians-American Society of Internal Medicine, http://www.acponline.org/journals/news/ mar99/squeeze.htm.

[2] *Ibid.*

[3] John E. Calfee, "Public Policy Issues in Direct-to-Consumer Advertising of Prescription Drugs," *Journal of Public Policy & Marketing*, Vol. 21, No. 2, fall 2002, p. 174.

[4] Joel Lexchin and Barbara Mintzes, "Direct-to-Consumer Advertising of Prescription Drugs: The Evidence Says No," *Journal of Public Policy & Marketing*, Vol. 21, No. 2, fall 2002, p. 194.

[5] "Prescription Drugs: FDA Oversight of Direct-to-Consumer Advertising Has Limitations," General Accounting Office, October 2002, GAO-03-177, p. 3.

[6] Maquire, *op. cit.*

Continued from p. 55

Advocates of additional advertising limits often cite falling teen smoking rates between the early 1970s and the early '90s as proof that restrictions work.

Some tobacco industry officials agree that advertising restrictions may have helped keep teen smoking rates down. "I suspect . . . that [the restrictions] had a positive impact in reducing youth smoking in this country," says Steven Watson, vice president for external affairs at Lorillard Tobacco Co. "Whatever is going on is working, because youth smoking rates are at the lowest level ever recorded. That's good. We remain committed to the effort and have been in complete compliance with the voluntary [and] mandated restrictions now in place."

Clouding the issue is the fact that teen smoking rates climbed between 1992 and 1996 and then started falling again.

But no researcher has ever been able to show conclusively that the increase was caused by any particular changes in tobacco advertising, although some suspect it was a factor. At least one group of researchers attributes the rise to a drop in cigarette prices, finding that for every 10 percent drop in price, youth smoking rises nearly 7 percent. [14]

In fact, some analysts insist that advertising restrictions have no measurable impact on teen smoking. "I don't find that [advertising bans] have been effective at all, which would suggest the primary impact of advertising generally in [the alcohol and tobacco] industries is to alter brand sales or possibly beverage sales and not to influence the total size of the market," Pennsylvania State University economics Professor Jon P. Nelson says.

Nelson has also studied tobacco advertising bans in Europe, which have been in place longer than American restrictions, and he has found no correlation between the bans and smoking rates. "If [advertising bans] really are effective in altering people's behavior as youths, one might expect them to have some longer-run impact, but I don't find evidence of that," Nelson says.

But other researchers disagree. The Cancer Prevention and Control Program at the University of California, San Diego, found in the early 1990s that "tobacco promotional activities are causally related to the onset of smoking." [15]

Federal researchers found the same results. "Historical analyses show that variations in advertising are associated with concomitant variations in smoking uptake among youths," says a U.S. Department of Health and Human Services report. "A large number of cross-sectional studies have reported associations between exposure to tobacco marketing on the one hand and attitudes toward smoking, susceptibility to smoking, smoking experimentation or regular smoking among youths on the other. These relationships persist even when other factors shown to predict smoking initiation are controlled." [16]

Some analysts say banning tobacco ads has been ineffective because the bans have not been honored. Anti-smoking advocates have charged for years that tobacco companies have continued to target youths in their advertising — in magazines, in-store ads and various other promotions. Indeed, in June 2002, R.J. Reynolds tobacco company was fined $20 million for violating the MSA by running magazine ads aimed at teenagers. [17]

Getty Images/Mark Wilson

Federal Trade Commission Chairman Timothy J. Muris, left, and Federal Communications Commission Chairman Michael K. Powell testify before a Senate committee on the "do-not-call" phone registry created last fall. Some consumer advocates are calling for a similar do-not-spam list.

Cheryl Healton, president of the American Legacy Foundation — an anti-smoking organization funded by the agreement — claims tobacco firms recently have begun using product placements to reach youth audiences, a practice activists call "stealth advertising."

"No matter how much you restrict advertising, if you cannot address the issue of tobacco product placement in TV and movies, it is almost impossible to counteract that," Healton says. "Right now, every single tobacco company is reporting to the FCC that they do not do that. But it defies logic that there would be so high a prevalence of brands appearing both in TV and in first-run movies, and that those product placements are being provided free when virtually no other product placements are ever provided free."

Healton suspects "quid pro quo" arrangements, in which a tobacco company, owned by a company that produces other products, might buy a product placement ad — for mints, for instance — on a TV show like "The West Wing" and the quid pro quo would be having President Bartlett smoke. Getting the proof, however, is "impossible without litigation," Healton says.

Lorillard's Watson takes umbrage at Healton's charges. "That's a very serious allegation to make with absolutely no evidence whatsoever," he says. "It's a part of this continuous effort to try to vilify and demonize tobacco companies, rather than deal with the issue of reducing youth smoking.

"We do not engage in any type of product placement. Furthermore, as stipulated by the master settlement agreement, when our products are placed in movies and TV programs, producers are in violation of the [MSA and] copyright law if they don't request permission, which we would not give them."

If manufacturers use the money saved on advertising to lower prices, that, too, can lessen the anti-smoking impact of advertising bans. "A ban on advertising tends to force liquor and cigarette competitors to compete on the basis of price, because the sellers find it difficult to project their image without ads," writes Dwight Filley, senior fellow at the Independence Institute, a free-market think tank, in Golden, Colo. "A prohibition of advertising reduces the overall cost of production as their ad budgets plummet." [18]

Moreover, some researchers have found that restricting ads in one medium simply shifts the advertising to other media rather than reducing overall advertising.

"If you've got a loose noose, it doesn't do much," says Henry Saffer, an economics professor at Kean University, Union, N.J., and a research associate at the National Bureau of Economic Research. "You have to have fairly draconian restrictions before you get much effect."

Are tougher limits needed on advertising to children?

Advocacy groups have long called for stricter controls on advertising subtly aimed at children, especially if the products being advertised are illegal for minors to purchase — such as tobacco and alcohol. Now, calls are increasingly being heard for restrictions on targeting children with ads for legal — albeit potentially unhealthy — products, like junk food.

AP Photo/Ben Margot

To try to recoup funding lost in budget cuts, a middle school in Scotts Valley, Calif., allows a financial-services company and other firms to advertise at the school. As advertising expands into virtually every aspect of American life, many educators and parents are worried about the impact on students.

"Is the present system adequately protecting children? No way," says Ruskin of Commercial Alert. "There's an epidemic of marketing-related diseases. Our nation's children are suffering from an epidemic of child obesity. Millions of kids are sick and going to die from the marketing of tobacco. Pathological gambling is a terrible problem." [19]

Commercial Alert is asking legislators to impose harsher restrictions on advertising to children, including a ban on all TV advertising to children under 12 and revocation of the business-tax deduction for advertising directed at children.

But advertisers say advertising is not the culprit, especially for so-called junk foods. "People often blame advertising for people making [bad] choices," says Dan Jaffe, executive vice president for governmental affairs of the Association of National Advertisers. "But many low-salt, low-calorie, low-fat products are languishing on the shelves because the public has not really decided to change its eating behavior. Now people are trying to say, 'Well, then they shouldn't even know about these other foods. We should have the government manipulate the information process.' But that isn't what a free society believes in."

Hoffman of the American Association of Advertising Agencies agrees. "The parents are the ultimate decision-makers in the household," Hoffman says. "Kids will be kids, but parents have the responsibility to make sure their kids have a balanced diet, that they're getting foods that have sufficient nutritional content."

The FTC only intervenes if an advertisement is considered misleading or deceptive. An ad hawking junk

Continued on p. 60

Chronology

1900s-1960s

Federal government assembles a regulatory structure to monitor and enforce restrictions on advertising.

1906

Food and Drugs Act calls for a federal agency to oversee full labeling of food and drugs, including those containing alcohol, cocaine and heroin.

1914

Federal Trade Commission is created and charged with ensuring fair competition in business, including regulating advertising, packaging and labeling.

1934

Federal Communications Commission is created and later monitors and regulates advertising on television and radio.

1949

Under the power of the so-called Fairness Doctrine, the Federal Communications Commission begins monitoring programming, including advertisements, for balance and fairness.

1964

A surgeon general's report on the health hazards of smoking prompts the FTC to rule that cigarette advertising is deceptive unless cigarette packages and advertisements bear health warnings.

1970s-1995

Supreme Court rules some commercial speech deserves First Amendment protection, launching a steady stream of commercial-speech litigation.

1970

Cigarette Smoking Act prohibits cigarette ads on radio and television.

1975

Supreme Court rules in *Bigelow v. Virginia* that commercial speech has at least partial protection under the First Amendment.

1980

Supreme Court's *Central Hudson Gas & Electric Corp. v. Public Service Commission* ruling lays out a four-part test — still in use today — for determining whether a federal restriction on commercial speech is permissible under the Constitution.

1982

After Reese's Pieces are featured in the film "E.T," sales of the candy rise 66 percent, sparking the advertising industry's interest in paid product placements in films and television shows.

1986

Supreme Court appears to backtrack on protecting commercial speech in *Posada de Puerto Rico Associates v. Tourism Co.*, allowing a Puerto Rican regulation banning advertisements promoting casino gambling — legal in Puerto Rico — to remain in force.

1989

Channel One educational TV service is launched. In return for loans of television equipment, schools are required to show Channel One programming, including commercials, to students.

1991

Telephone Consumer Protection Act allows Federal Trade Commission to create the do-not-call phone registry, which is implemented in 2003. The law also prohibits sending unsolicited advertising by fax.

1995-Present

Supreme Court gradually increases First Amendment protection for commercial speech.

1995

In *Rubin v. Coors Brewing Co.* the Supreme Court shows a renewed interest in protecting commercial speech when it agrees with a brewery's challenge to a federal regulation that required disclosure of alcohol content on beer labels and in advertisements. Justice Clarence Thomas' majority opinion says First Amendment prevents restrictions on label content.

1998

Master Settlement Agreement between tobacco companies and 46 states requires the tobacco companies not to target youth and to spend $1.45 billion to establish an anti-smoking education organization.

2003

On Sept. 23, a federal judge rules that the FTC is not authorized to implement a do-not-call registry for telemarketers. Congress passes a bill on Sept. 25 authorizing the registry; a U.S. District Court again blocks the registry, after finding its charities exemption violates marketers' free speech. The FTC appeals the ruling on Sept. 26, and the 10th Circuit Court of Appeals decides to allow the list to go into force pending legal challenges. On Sept. 29 President Bush signs the do-not-call law and signs the "Can Spam" Act on Dec. 16. On Dec. 18 the FCC for the first time cites a company for violating the new do-not-call law. . . . By mid-December more than 54 million telephone numbers have been registered with the FTC.

Will Advertisers Resort to 'Mind Reading'?

What is scarier than a spammer obtaining your e-mail address? How about advertisers reading your brain waves?

They aren't doing it yet. But researchers at American universities are studying the brain's responses to advertising, with surprising results.

P. Read Montague, a neuroscientist at Baylor College of Medicine in Houston, monitored the brain activity of test subjects as they participated in a blind taste test of Pepsi and Coca-Cola. As in the taste tests performed on TV, Montague found that most subjects preferred Pepsi, and that Pepsi tended to produce a much stronger response in the region of the brain known as the ventral putamen.

When Montague ran the test again, but with the subjects knowing the identity of both samples, Coke won the test. Moreover, Montague clearly detected brain activity in the medial prefrontal cortex, the brain's center of higher-level logical thought. While the team has not published any conclusions about the finding, some researchers speculate that the subjects' knowledge they were drinking Coke may have summoned up memories and other logical associations that made it the preferred libation, thus affecting their brain activity. [1]

Similar studies are under way at the Harvard Business School's Mind of the Market Laboratory and the BrightHouse Institute for Thought Sciences at Emory University in Atlanta. BrightHouse, in fact, is testing prospective customers' reactions to an unnamed client's products using a magnetic resonance imaging (MRI) machine.

The BrightHouse researchers also detected strong responses in the medial prefrontal cortex when test subjects encountered images of products they liked.

Clint Kilts, the scientific director, recently predicted that neuromarketing will soon become a career niche. "You will actually see this being part of the decision-making process, up and down the company," he told *The New York Times*. "You are going to see more large companies that will have neuroscience divisions." [2]

Kilts' colleague, Chief Operating Officer Adam Koval, is even more boosterish about the technology. "What it really does," Koval told a reporter, "is give unprecedented insight into the consumer mind. And it will actually result in [advertisers] . . . getting customers to behave the way they want them to behave." [3]

The group's Web site denies any attempts to "read" minds. "We are not capable of, nor do we desire, to 'read' people's private thoughts and feelings or use study inferences to induce unwilled behavior," says an explanation of the group's research.

While the various studies have yet to undergo scrutiny by the scientific community, they have stirred up some concern among consumer advocacy groups, among them Commercial Alert. In December the group asked Emory President James Wagner to stop the experiments.

"Universities exist to free the mind and enlighten it," wrote Commercial Alert. "They do not exist to find new ways to subjugate the mind and manipulate it for commercial gain. Emory's quest for a 'buy button' in the human skull is an egregious violation of the very reason that a university exists." [4]

After failing to get a response from Emory, Commercial Alert on Dec. 17, 2003, wrote to the federal Office for Human Research Protections, a unit of the Department of Health and Human Services, seeking an investigation of neuromarketing experiments, calling them "unethical because they will likely be used to promote disease and human suffering." [5]

Pat El-Hinnawy, public affairs specialist at the Office for Human Research Protections, said Jan. 15, "We have received their letter and we're looking into it."

[1] Clive Thompson, "There's a Sucker Born in Every Medial Prefrontal Cortex," *The New York Times*, Oct. 26, 2003, Section 6, p. 54.

[2] *Ibid.*

[3] CBC News, www.cbc.ca/consumers/market/files/money/science_shopping/.

[4] www.commercialalert.org/index.php/category_id/1/subcategory_id/82/article_id/205.

[5] www.commercialalert.org/index.php/category_id/1/subcategory_id/82/article_id/211

Continued from p. 58

food to children would not be considered misleading or deceptive by the FTC unless it made claims that it was nutritious, says Mary Engle, associate director for advertising practices at the FTC. "If, in fact, it was not [nutritious] then that could be deceptive and actionable."

Still, many advertisers concede that — even if they are within the law in advertising to children — they have a special responsibility to the public. "It does not behoove an advertiser to engage in practices that are going to in any way alienate the consuming public," Hoffman says.

But some critics say advertisers are increasingly doing just that — alienating the consuming public — to such an extent that the laws eventually will be changed.

"I'm not one who wants to lay it all at the feet of the advertisers and the fast-food industry," says Walsh of the National Institute on Media and the Family. "But snack-food companies that advertise effectively are influencing people to consume large quantities of foods that contain trans-fatty acids and high-fructose corn syrup, and that's a health problem."

Other critics complain that advertisers have invaded the schools in many communities through exclusive soft-drink marketing agreements, monopolistic TV programming, use of educational support materials that carry advertising and sponsorship of special activities.

"Schools," says Alex Molnar, a professor of education policy at Arizona State University, "have become vectors of marketing."

Marketing on school grounds is increasing dramatically, particularly as more school districts face budget crunches, Molnar says. And he warns that there are hidden dangers beyond the mere clutter of brand names. There is an inherent conflict of interest between the role of schools and the role of marketers, he says, and the result goes far beyond children being encouraged to make unhealthy lifestyle choices.

"Marketers are special interests," Molnar says. "They're not interested in promoting the welfare of children, which is the charge to schools."

Getty Images/Stephen Chernin

New York Attorney General Eliot Spitzer sued major spammers for sending unsolicited e-mails to consumers while hiding behind fake identities and forged e-mail addresses. Microsoft General Counsel Brad Smith, at left, supported the action along with other high-tech firms.

When advertisers sponsor school content through sponsored activities, educational materials or sponsored TV programming, they inevitably control the content of that material, Molnar says. "School programs get distorted in a variety of ways," he says. "Either the curriculum content is made incorrect by omission or commission. A corporate point of view is substituted for a kind of objective, disinterested look."

Molnar urges state or federal legislators to ban marketing to children in schools. "There is no right to market to children in schools," he says. "Schools are protected spaces."

While conceding there is no "right" to advertise in schools, advertisers say it would be inappropriate to exclude advertising by federal or state legislation. "A top-down approach just isn't realistic," says Clark Rector, senior vice president for government affairs of the American Advertising Federation. "The local officials are more than capable. If they decide they don't want to accept advertising within their local schools, they have that absolute right to do it."

At the same time, Rector points out, "a lot of schools are under increasing financial pressure, and if they think that they can accept advertising on a limited basis and it can help them fund future programs, they ought to be able to do that."

School officials say the temptations are great. "Desperate times call for desperate measures," says Bruce Colley, executive director of administrative services for the Bainbridge Island School District in Washington state. "If I'm sitting in a school that doesn't have money available, and some company like Coca-Cola comes up and says they'll put a new scoreboard in there just so long as it says 'Drink Coke,' I can see why people say yes to that."

At the same time, he says, "In a perfect world, if education was funded appropriately, this would be a non-issue."

Even some advocacy groups concerned about the impact of ads on children are skittish about implementing government restrictions. "Once we start banning ads from schools, do we then ban them from children's television programming?" Walsh asks. "Do we draw a line at fast foods or do we ban all advertising from children's programming?"

"I get nervous," he continues. "Some very strong advocacy groups like to keep pushing a line into the next area, and then into the next."

BACKGROUND

Protecting the Public

Policymakers and the courts have struggled over the past 100 years to balance the rights of advertisers to market their products against the responsibility of government to protect the public.

The first major federal effort to regulate advertising was the 1906 Food and Drugs Act. It required federal regulators to make sure that food and drug labels were not misleading and that 11 dangerous but still legal ingredients — including alcohol, co-

What the Law Says

Junk mail — *The Federal Trade Commission's (FTC) prohibition againt false or misleading ads is virtually the only regulation affecting the content of mailed advertisements. The volume of ads mailed is restricted only by the willingness of advertisers to pay postal fees.*

Junk fax — *The 1991 Telephone Consumer Protection Act prohibits sending unsolicited faxes. The law has survived multiple challenges in federal courts, largely because faxes, unlike telephone calls, impose a cost on the recipient. The same law prohibits telemarketing to cellular phones.*

Telephone marketing — *The federal government's new do-not-call registry prohibits telemarketers from calling individuals whose phone numbers are listed in the registry. Solicitations from political organizations, charities and telephone surveyors are excempt.*

caine and heroin — were listed if present.

Then in 1914 Congress created the Federal Trade Commission to ensure fair competition. Besides reviewing corporate mergers and preventing unfair business practices, the FTC regulates advertising, packaging and labeling.

The Federal Communications Commission, created in 1934, is charged with protecting the public interest as it regulates broadcast advertisements. In 1949, under what became known as the Fairness Doctrine, the commission began monitoring programming, including advertisements, to ensure that content was balanced and fair. By 1985, the commission reported that the doctrine was not working as intended and that it might actually be chilling free speech. The Reagan administration abolished the doctrine two years later.

In 1964, the FTC scrutinized cigarette advertising after a U.S. surgeon general's report said smoking was a health hazard. The commission determined that tobacco advertising was deceptive because it failed to inform the consumer of the dangers of smoking and called for warning labels on cigarette packages and advertisements.

The next year, Congress passed the Federal Cigarette Labeling and Advertising Act, which required the warning labels. Congress then passed the Cigarette Smoking Act, which prohibited cigarette ads on radio and television beginning in 1971. Although broadcasters challenged the ban, the courts upheld it.

Notably, the unsuccessful challenge was one of only a handful of cases in which the government's ability to restrict or ban commercial speech was questioned. In fact, the Supreme Court did not rule until 1975 that advertisements and other commercial speech were protected by the First Amendment. In *Bigelow v. Virginia*, the court struck down a state law prohibiting ads for abortion-referral services, holding that "the relationship of speech to the marketplace of products or services does not make [commercial advertising] valueless in the marketplace of ideas." [20] At the same time, however, the court made clear that it was not extending protection to all advertisements, but only to speech that contained "material of clear 'public interest.' " [21]

The next year, the Supreme Court extended First Amendment protections for commercial speech a bit further. In *Virginia State Board of Pharmacy v. Virginia Citizens Consumer Council Inc.*, the court held that a state law barring pharmacies from advertising the price of pharmaceuticals was unconstitutional. Significantly, the court noted that "the particular consumer's interest in the free flow of commercial information . . . may be as keen, if not keener by far, than his interest in the day's most urgent political debate." [22]

In the same decision, however, the court stressed that commercial speech did not warrant the same level of First Amendment protection as other forms of speech and that states could legitimately regulate advertising in the public interest.

Commercial Speech

In 1980, the court handed down its most comprehensive and direct ruling aimed at protecting commercial speech. In *Central Hudson Gas & Electric Corp. v. Public Service Commission*, the court considered whether New York state could bar utilities from advertising to promote the use of electricity. [23] While the court still maintained its previous position that commercial speech was entitled to less protection than other speech, it set out a detailed, four-part test government could use to determine whether an advertising restriction was permitted under the Constitution.

The first test is to determine whether the commercial speech in question is non-misleading and concerns a lawful activity. If it does not meet those requirements, the court said, the speech can be silenced.

In the second part of the test, the court said the government must demonstrate that restricting the advertisement would serve a substantial public interest, and, thirdly, it must show that the restriction directly advances that public interest. Finally, the government must demonstrate that the restriction is only as extensive as necessary to achieve the specified purpose.

Over the next 10 years, the court applied the *Central Hudson* test to a wide variety of cases, with decisions that some analysts have found uneven and potentially confusing.

For example, in the 1986 *Posada de Puerto Rico Associates v. Tourism Co.* decision, the court held that the government of Puerto Rico's ban on ads promoting casino gambling — a legal activity in Puerto Rico — was permissible so long as the advertisements were targeted only at residents of Puerto Rico. [24]

In several subsequent decisions, the court appeared to favor restrictions. [25] In the mid-1990s, however, the tide turned in favor of protections for commercial speech. In *Rubin v. Coors Brewing Co.*, the court agreed with the Colorado brewery's challenge to a federal regulation that required disclosure of alcohol content on beer labels and in advertisements. [26] Justice Clarence Thomas, who has emerged as a champion of protections for commercial speech, wrote the majority opinion, which said bluntly that label-content restrictions were not permitted under the First Amendment.

The *Coors* case "bore the mark of a court bent on ensuring that the *Central Hudson* test be applied with rigor, rather than in a fashion involving unquestioning acceptance of the government's regulatory determinations," an analyst wrote. [27]

Since 1995, the court has shown a decided inclination to strengthen First Amendment protections for commercial speech.

"The Supreme Court got away from its sort of muddled thinking and got back on track in confirming the four-part test for commercial speech," says the Media Institute's Kaplar. "I tend to agree with Justice Thomas that the distinction between commercial and non-commercial speech has become sort of artificial, and we should be giving full protection to all kinds of speech — including commercial speech — provided, of course, that it's not false or misleading or unfair or fraudulent."

Getty Images/William Thomas Cain

Telemarketers at Spectrum Marketing Services, in Philadelphia, work their last shift on Sept. 26, 2003. Establishment of the do-not-call phone registry last fall forced the 30-year-old firm to close.

Gagging Telemarketers

The one significant setback advertisers have experienced in the courts recently — and perhaps only temporarily — came when the advertising industry was unable to stop implementation of a national do-not-call registry, which allows consumers to block most calls from telemarketers.

In 1991, Congress passed the Telephone Consumer Protection Act, which allowed the FTC to create the registry, though it wasn't actually set up to accept consumer telephone numbers until September 2003.

On Sept. 23, Oklahoma City U.S. District Court Judge Lee R. West ruled in a suit filed by the Direct Marketing Association that the FTC was not authorized to implement the registry. Congress responded two days later with legislation specifically authorizing the FTC to implement the do-not-call list. The legislation passed the House 412-8 and the Senate 95-0 and was signed by President Bush on Sept. 29.

But that didn't end the matter. The registry was put on hold yet again by a telemarketing industry lawsuit claiming the registry was an unconstitutional abridgement of marketers' free-speech rights. Judge Edward W. Nottingham of the U.S. District Court in Denver agreed, ruling that exempting charitable organizations from being covered by the registry — as the FTC rule setting up the do-not-call registry permits — would limit what content could be blocked by consumers and would, therefore, violate the free-speech rights of marketers.

"Were the do-not-call registry to apply without regard to the content of the speech . . . it might be a different matter," Nottingham wrote in his decision.

"For them to fix this, you'd have to apply the do-not-call list to charities," said lawyer Deborah Thoren-Peden, who specializes in privacy issues. "I'm guessing this one is going to be fought out more in the courts." [28]

The FTC appealed the ruling to the 10th Circuit Court of Appeals in Denver and was given the go-ahead to put the registry in force while the issue winds its way through the courts, a matter that may take years.

According to the FTC, more than 54 million telephone numbers had been registered by mid-December 2003.

Between mid-October and mid-December, the FTC had received more than 100,000 complaints about potential violations. And on Dec. 18, the FCC, which shares authority with the FTC for enforcing the registry, cited a company for the first time for violating the new restrictions: CPM Funding Inc., a California-based mortgage company. [29] On Nov. 3, the FCC followed up quickly by citing AT&T with violations that could result in a fine of $780,000. [30] Under the law, telemarketers can be fined up to $11,000 per violation. ■

Getty Images/Tom Hauck

The Qualcomm Stadium scoreboard in San Diego gives a plug to Office Depot and Budweiser beer along with the ball scores. Critics say ads are overrunning American society. Supporters cite their First Amendment rights to commercial free speech.

CURRENT SITUATION

Protecting Kids?

Apart from what has been happening in the courts, advertisers today operate in a regulatory environment that is generally friendlier to their interests than it has been in decades — a source of frustration for consumer-advocacy groups and regulators alike.

"Commercial speech shouldn't be protected under the First Amendment, because corporations aren't people," says Ruskin of Commercial Alert. "Corporations deserve no Bill of Rights protection. The state ought to be able to restrict commercial speech in any way it sees fit."

The FTC is feeling handcuffed, too, Engle says, making it hesitant to take regulatory action in areas such as advertising non-nutritious foods to children.

"To regulate, control or prohibit advertising to children we would have to show that the proposed regulation would pass constitutional muster," Engle says. "It's a very high burden on us [since *Central Hudson*]. We can meet the first test, which is to show that there is government interest in preserving children's health. But the next two tests — which are whether the proposed regulation directly advances the government's interest and whether it is narrowly tailored to fit the purpose — would be very hard to meet. You have to show a very strong link between exposure of children to advertising of non-nutritious foods and the health consequences that you're concerned about."

Engle explains that the agency's efforts to regulate advertising to children in the 1970s backfired. "The concern at that time was tooth decay, what with all the sugary foods being advertised," Engle says, pointing out that even 25 years ago there was a "groundswell of public concern" about saturating the airways with ads marketing sugar-filled foods to children.

The agency proposed banning all advertising to kids under age 6, on the theory that advertising to such young children — who lack the cognitive capacity to understand that advertising is trying to sell you something — is unfair. The agency also proposed banning ads for sugary foods directed at children 12 and under.

"Congress passed a law prohibiting us from issuing [that] rule . . . on the grounds it was unfair," Engle says. "They thought we had really overstepped our bounds. There was such an uproar that other industries asked for an exemption because they were so upset with us."

Repercussions from that experience still reverberate at the agency, she says. "[Many] people here now were here back then, so the memory is still very present," Engle says. The FTC's budget also was severely cut in the 1980s, she says. "We have far fewer people than we had back then."

In the final analysis, Engle says, regulating advertising aimed at children is even more difficult now than in the 1970s. "Since that time, Supreme Court decisions [protecting commercial speech] have only gotten stronger," she says. "It would be much more difficult to construct a rule that wouldn't be overturned."

Continued on p. 66

At Issue:

Should pop-up disclosures be required for product placements in TV shows?

GARY RUSKIN
EXECUTIVE DIRECTOR, COMMERCIAL ALERT

WRITTEN FOR THE CQ RESEARCHER, JANUARY 2004

It is a basic principle of law and common morality that advertisers must be honest with viewers. Advertisers can puff and tout and use all the many tricks of their trade. But they must not pretend that their ads are something else.

This principle has been a cornerstone of communications law since the beginning of the broadcast era. Congress first required broadcasters to identify their sponsors in the Radio Act of 1927. The reasoning is obvious: "Listeners are entitled to know by whom they are being persuaded."

Yet current practice in the broadcast industry violates this principle broadly and systematically. Broadcasters not only fail to identify their sponsors; worse, they fail to identify the ads themselves and instead pretend that the ads are merely parts of shows. Such violation has become the new way of doing business.

Put simply, TV networks and stations are shifting advertising from commercial breaks to programming itself. They are inserting branded products directly into programs, in exchange for substantial fees or other consideration. This advertising technique, called "product placement," has become closely integrated into program plots, to the point that the line between programming and "infomercials" has become increasingly blurred. Some commentators see no line at all.

Television networks interweave advertising and programming so routinely that they are, in effect, selling to advertisers a measure of control over aspects of their programming. Some TV programs are so packed with product placements that they approach the appearance of infomercials. The head of a [casino] company that obtained repeated product placements actually called one such program "a great infomercial." Yet these programs typically lack the disclosure required of infomercials to uphold honesty and fair dealing.

Television stations that cram their programs with product placements, yet fail to identify the sponsors in a conspicuous way are brazenly violating the public's right to know who is seeking to persuade them.

This is an affront to basic honesty. We urge the Federal Communications Commission to investigate current TV advertising practices regarding product placement and other embedded ads and to take the steps necessary to restore some honesty and fair dealing to the presentation of these ads by strengthening the sponsorship-identification rules so ads are properly and prominently identified as ads.

yes

DARRYL NIRENBERG
COUNSEL, FREEDOM TO ADVERTISE COALITION

WRITTEN FOR THE CQ RESEARCHER, JANUARY 2004

The proposal offered by Commercial Alert to require that television programs be continually interrupted with "large" and "conspicuous" pop-ups disclosing placements as they appear represents an unconstitutional infringement on commercial speech rights.

The proposal is impractical, would ruin the entertainment experience for viewers and would be unreasonably burdensome on programmers and advertisers. It ignores the facts that existing Federal Communications Commission regulations adequately address the issue of commercial sponsorship and that the Federal Trade Commission, which examines specific issues regarding product placement disclosure on a case-by-case basis, previously denied a petition similar to Commercial Alert's.

Product placement has occupied a well-accepted place in film and television for decades. In the real world, people eat, drink and wear brand-name products. The visual picture painted for the viewer gains vibrancy when products are portrayed as they are used in everyday life. Such products help tell the story and sometimes become the story.

Longstanding disclosure rules permit a program containing product placement to be broadcast as long as the presence of any product placement is noted. The rules protect the artistic integrity of the program and preserve First Amendment rights while properly informing the public of the presence of this form of commercial speech.

Should Commercial Alert's proposal be adopted, television programming would become virtually impossible to watch as scene after scene would be interrupted by pop-ups flashing the word "advertisement." Its likely result will be to censor or ban this means of commercial speech.

The proposed restriction would run afoul of the Supreme Court's holding that the freedom of speech guaranteed by the First Amendment extends to commercial speech as long as it is not misleading and involves a lawful activity. Advertising may be restricted only if: (1) the government has a substantial interest in restricting it; (2) the restriction materially advances the governmental interest; and (3) the restriction is only as extensive as necessary.

Based on its faulty assumption that Americans are unable to discern fact from fiction, Commercial Alert wants the federal government to abandon precedent, ignore the law and force networks to continually interrupt broadcasts with pop-up disclosures. Fortunately, the Constitution stands in the way.

no

Continued from p. 64

New Ad Avenues

Advertisers may face a more welcome reception in the courts, but they nonetheless face serious challenges in reaching overloaded consumers and dealing with rapidly changing technologies. The dual challenges mean advertisers must work ever harder to reach audiences.

While advertisers have been exploring new venues for their ads, including schools and the Internet, the advertising arena that has seen the most dramatic growth — mainly deceptive advertising, some critics say — is in product placements in movies and TV programs.

Advertisers currently spend about $360 million a year on product placements in films and TV programming, according to the Advertising Research Foundation (ARF). [31] The practice of using product placements grows, ARF says, "as marketers cope with increasing commercial clutter, audience fragmentation, media proliferation and — above all — commercial avoidance" with remotes, VCRs and TIVO devices.

The blockbuster Steven Spielberg movie "E.T." has been credited with starting the boom in paid product placements. When the homesick little alien took a liking to Reese's Pieces, sales of the peanut butter candy jumped 66 percent. That inspired the makers of Huggies diapers to pay filmmakers $100,000 to feature their product in the movie "Baby Boom." And Philip Morris reportedly forked over $350,000 to see that James Bond puffed on Lark cigarettes in the movie "License to Kill." [32]

According to the ARF, the No. 1 film in product placement revenues to date is the 2002 James Bond film "Die Another Day." It collected some $160 million by placing 20 products in the feature, including British Airways, Finlandia vodka, Ford, Heineken beer and Sony electronics. [33]

> **"There's an effort to hang an ad in front of our eyes at every waking moment of the day and night. Americans are sick of it."**
>
> ***— Gary Ruskin, Executive director, Commercial Alert, Portland, Ore.***

Critics complain that although the filmmaker must disclose that product-placement fees were paid, viewers usually don't notice the announcements, which occur in the quickly scrolling credits at the end of movies and TV programs. Commercial Alert has petitioned the FTC and FCC to require so-called pop-up disclosures when paid product placements occur in TV programs.

"To prevent stealth advertising and ensure that viewers are fully aware of the efforts of advertisers to embed ads in programming, the commission should require TV networks and stations to prominently disclose to viewers that their product placements are ads. In addition, product placements should be identified when they occur," Commercial Alert said recently. [34] The group has not sought controls of product placements in films, because — unlike broadcasts, which use the public airwaves — movies are not regulated by the federal government.

Advertisers are united in opposition to controls on product placements. "Their proposal is unconstitutional," says Jaffe of the Association of National Advertisers, who argues that current disclosure requirements are sufficient. "People will clearly be on notice, and there's no reason to just bombard people with these types of notices."

Johnson of the American Civil Liberties Union agrees. "When I see Coca-Cola being prominently featured, I know pretty well that Coca-Cola has probably paid for that," he says. "Is it a function of government to control the speech or is it the function of parents? I'm not sure it's the government's function to be saying you have to say X, Y and Z, particularly when the First Amendment specifically prohibits the government from doing certain things in the area of freedom of speech." ■

OUTLOOK

Schools Targeted

Consumer advocates doubt that either the courts or Congress will protect the public from what they characterize as a flood of advertisements.

"Congress is for sale," Commercial Alert's Ruskin says flatly. "Congress is a microcosm of the problem. Congress is basically asleep at the switch."

As for the Supreme Court, analysts say it is not likely to reverse course anytime soon and reduce or eliminate First Amendment protections for commercial speech.

"If there is any good reason for excluding commercial speech from protection, the Supreme Court hasn't stumbled over it yet," says Roger Marzulla, counsel for Defenders of Property Rights.

Even some consumer groups are leery of regulating commercial speech. "We do not come down on the side of regulation of commercial speech," says psychologist Walsh, of the National Institute on Media and the Family. "The First Amendment is such a fragile thing. Erosion of things like the First Amendment don't happen all at once. They happen an inch at a time."

Nevertheless, many consumer groups are beginning to see progress in mobilizing against the onslaught of advertising, especially where it is directed at children. Arizona State University's Molnar says several school districts around the country recently have turned down advertising income after complaints from parents. For example, Molnar notes, districts in Seattle, Rockwell, Texas, and Martin County, Fla., have eliminated their contracts with Channel One, the commercialized in-school television service.

"We found 30 pieces of legislation introduced at either the national or state level that in some way deal with [curbing] school commercialism," Molnar says. "It's a marker of interest. I think we're going to see some kind of legislation shortly, particularly in the area of marketing and nutrition." But ridding schools of advertising may "take a while," he says.

In fact, advertisers say local action rather than federal regulation is more appropriate and effective in controlling advertising. "There are currently sufficient guidelines and regulatory mechanisms in place," says Hoffman of the American Association of Advertising Agencies. "I think the industry is searching for solutions now, given the increased attention by consumers, regulators, the media, activist organizations and others. The industry is very, very sensitive to these things."

"We can do a lot; we have done a lot, basically with persuasion, influence and pressure," Walsh agrees.

Rather than more government regulations, Walsh argues, more attention to public education, especially where children are concerned, can be effective. "We often look for scapegoats," Walsh says. "Right now, the scapegoat in the obesity epidemic is fast food. Unless we can pry kids away from TV screens [and their sedentary lifestyle], we can keep fast food advertising away from kids from now until the cows come home, but we're not going to affect the obesity problem. All this has to do with education." ■

Notes

[1] Steve McClellan, "Ad Clutter Keeps Climbing," *Broadcasting and Cable*, Dec. 22, 2003, p. 13.

[2] Vincent P. Bzdek, "The Ad Subtractors, Making a Difference," *The Washington Post*, July 29, 2003, p. C9.

[3] Deborah Fallows, "Spam: How it is Hurting E-mail and Degrading Life on the Internet," Pew Internet and American Life Project, Oct. 22, 2003, p. i.

[4] *Ibid.*, p. 7.

[5] "2003 Commercial Industry Forecast and Report," Veronis Suhler and Stevenson, p. 133.

[6] Vincent P. Bzdek, "The Ad Subtractors, Making a Difference," *The Washington Post*, July 29, 2003, p. C9.

[7] *Ibid.*

[8] Saul Hansell, "Viginia Indicts Two Under Antispam Law," *The New York Times*, Dec. 12, 2003.

[9] Saul Hansell, "New York and Microsoft Expected to File Civil Suits in Spam Case," *The New York Times*, Dec. 18, 2003.

[10] Arnold S. Relman, and Marcia Angell, "America's Other Drug Problem: How the Drug Industry Distorts Medicine and Politics," *The New Republic*, Dec. 16, 2002, p. 36. For background, see David Hatch, "Drug Company Ethics," *The CQ Researcher*, June 6, 2003, pp. 521-544.

[11] Jennifer S. Lee, "House Accepts Revisions on Antispam Bill," *The New York Times*, Dec. 9, 2003, p. C10.

[12] Saul Hansell, "Spam Keeps Coming, but its Senders are Wary," *The New York Times*, Jan. 7, 2004.

[13] Master Settlement Agreement, p. 14, http://www.naag.org/upload/1032468605_cigmsa.pdf. For background, see Kenneth Jost, "Closing in on Tobacco," *The CQ Researcher*, Nov. 12, 1999, pp. 977-1000, and "High-Impact Litigation," *The CQ Researcher*, Feb. 11, 2000, pp. 89-112.

[14] Jonathan Gruber and Jonathan Zinman, "Youth Smoking in the U.S.: Evidence and Implications," National Bureau of Economic Research, *NBER Working Paper No. 7780*, http://www.nber.org/digest/oct00/w7780.html.

[15] John P. Pierce, *et al.*, "Tobacco Industry Promotion of Cigarettes and Adolescent Smoking," *Journal of the American Medical Association*, Feb. 18, 1998, Vol. 279, No. 7, p. 511. For background, see Richard L. Worsnop, "Teens and Tobacco," *The CQ Researcher*, Dec. 1, 1995, pp. 1065-1088.

[16] "Changing Adolescent Smoking Prevalence: Where It Is and Why," U.S. Depart-

About the Author

CQ Researcher Contributing Writer **Patrick Marshall** is the reviews editor at *Federal Computer Week* and a technology columnist for the *Seattle Times;* he is based in Bainbridge Island, Wash. His recent reports include "Policing the Borders" and "Three-Strikes Laws." He holds a bachelor's degree in anthropology from the University of California at Santa Cruz and a master's in foreign affairs from the Fletcher School of Law and Diplomacy.

ment of Health and Human Services, November 2001, p. 2.

[17] Alyse R. Lancaster and Kent M. Lancaster, "Teenage Exposure to Cigarette Advertising in Popular Consumer Magazines: Vehicle Versus Message Reach and Frequency," *Journal of Advertising*, Sept. 22, 2003," p. 70.

[18] Dwight Filley, "Forbidden Fruit: When Prohibition Increases the Harm it is Supposed to Reduce," *Independent Review*, Dec. 2, 1999, No. 3, Vol. 3, p. 441.

[19] For background, see Patrick Marshall, "Gambling in America," *The CQ Researcher*, March 7, 2003, pp. 201-224, and Alan Greenblatt, "Obesity Epidemic," *The CQ Researcher*, Jan. 31, 2003, pp. 73-104.

[20] *Bigelow v. Virginia* (421 U.S. 809 [1975]), p. 826.

[21] *Ibid.*, p. 822.

[22] *Virginia State Board of Pharmacy v. Virginia Citizens Consumer Council Inc.* (425 U.S. 748 [1976]), p. 763.

[23] *Central Hudson Gas & Electric Corp. v. Public Service Commission*, 447 U.S. 557 (1980).

[24] *Posada de Puerto Rico Associates v. Tourism Co.*, 478 U.S. 328 (1986).

[25] Arlen W. Langvardt, "The Incremental Strengthening of First Amendment Protection for Commercial Speech: Lessons from Greater New Orleans Broadcasting," *American Business Law Journal*, June 22, 2000, No. 4, Vol. 37, p. 587.

[26] *Rubin v. Coors Brewing Co.*, 514 U.S. 476 (1995).

[27] Langvardt, *op. cit.*

[28] Joseph C. Anselmo, "Despite Congress' Best Efforts, Separate Court Rulings Put 'Do Not Call' Registry on Hold," *CQ Weekly*, Sept. 27, 2003, p. 2358.

[29] Griff Witte, "FCC Issues its First 'Do Not Call' Citation," *The Washington Post*, Dec. 19, 2003, p. E3.

[30] Matt Richtel, "Telemarketing Fine Proposed for AT&T," *The New York Times*, Nov. 4, 2003, p. C4.

[31] Denman Maroney, "Top Topic: Product Placement," Informed, Advertising Research Foundation, Vol. 6, No. 4, August 2003.

[32] Michael F. Jacobson and Laurie Ann Mazur, *Marketing Madness: A Survival Guide for a Consumer Society* (1995), p. 67.

[33] Maroney, *op. cit.*

[34] "Commercial Alert Asks FCC, FTC to Require Disclosure of Product Placement on TV," Sept. 30, 2003, www.commercialalert.org/index.php/category_id/1/subcategory_id/79/article_id/191.

FOR MORE INFORMATION

American Advertising Federation, 1101 Vermont Ave., N.W., Suite 500, Washington, DC 20005-6306; (202) 898-0089; www.ana.net. The AAF is a trade association that represents 50,000 professionals in the advertising industry. Their Web site contains much information on regulatory actions and legislative activity.

American Association of Advertising Agencies, 405 Lexington Ave., 18th Floor, New York, NY 10174-1801; (212) 682-2500; www.aaaa.org. The ad industry's lobbying and research organization provides a good deal of accessible information about issues in advertising on its Web site.

American Civil Liberties Union, 125 Broad St., 18th Floor, New York, NY 10004; (212) 549-2666; www.aclu.org. The ACLU aims to "defend and preserve the individual rights and liberties guaranteed to all people in this country by the Constitution and laws of the United States." Its Web site contains information on cases involving commercial-speech issues.

American Legacy Foundation, 2030 M St., N.W., Sixth Floor, Washington, DC 20036; (202) 454-5555; www.americanlegacy.org. The educational foundation created by the Master Settlement Agreement between the tobacco companies and the states develops programs about the health effects of tobacco use.

Center for Science in the Public Interest, 1875 Connecticut Ave. N.W., Suite 300, Washington, DC 20009; (202) 332-9110; www.cspinet.org. The nonprofit advocacy group tracks a broad variety of issues, including advertising and its impacts on nutrition.

Children's Advertising Review Unit, 70 West 36th St., 13th Floor, New York, NY 10018; (866) 334-6272; www.caru.org. CARU was founded in 1974 to promote responsible children's advertising as part of a strategic alliance with major advertising trade associations. The Web site contains "Self-Regulatory Guidelines for Children's Advertising" and relevant laws.

Commercial Alert, 4110 S.E. Hawthorne Blvd, #123, Portland, OR 97214-5426; (503) 235.8012; www.commercialalert.org. The nonprofit activist organization was founded by consumer advocate Ralph Nader in 1998 to fight encroaching commercialism.

Federal Communications Commission, 445 12th St., S.W., Washington, DC 20554; (888) 225-5322; www.fcc.gov. The FCC is the primary federal agency concerned with regulating TV and radio broadcast industries, including advertising on those media.

Federal Trade Commission, 600 Pennsylvania Ave., N.W., Washington, DC 20580; (202) 326-2222; www.ftc.gov. The FTC is the primary federal agency concerned with advertising standards. Its Web site offers a broad variety of historical and current information.

Junkbusters Corp., P.O. Box 7034, Green Brook, NJ 08812; (908) 753-7861; www.junkbusters.com. The for-profit firm offers a wealth of information on how to protect against unwanted advertising.

The Media Institute, 1800 N. Kent St., Suite 1130, Arlington, VA 22209; (703) 243-5060; www.mediainstitute.org. The research foundation specializes in communications policy and the First Amendment. The Web site provides links to a variety of other useful sites.

National Institute on Media and the Family, 606 24th Ave. South, Suite 606, Minneapolis, MN 55454; (612) 672-5437; www.mediafamily.org. The institute is a national resource for information on the impact of media on children and families. Its useful Web site includes movie reviews for parents.

Bibliography

Selected Sources

Books

Jacobson, Michael F., and Laurie Ann Mazur, *Marketing Madness: A Survival Guide for a Consumer Society*, Westview Press, 1995.
The president of the Center for Science in the Public Interest offers an entertaining and image-laden history of advertising and U.S. commercial culture.

Kaplar, Richard T., *Advertising Rights: The Neglected Freedom*, The Media Institute, 1991.
The vice president of The Media Institute argues that commercial speech should have the same First Amendment protections as other speech.

Wright, R. George, *Selling Words: Free Speech in a Commercial Culture*, New York University Press, 1997.
A law professor at Samford University in Birmingham, Ala., examines the legal and social issues surrounding First Amendment protections for commercial speech, arguing there is room within the Constitution for greater restrictions.

Articles

Langvardt, Arlen W., "The Incremental Strengthening of First Amendment Protection for Commercial Speech: Lessons from Greater New Orleans Broadcasting," *American Business Law Journal*, June 22, 2000, p. 587.
A business law professor at the University of Indiana details the Supreme Court's approach to commercial-speech issues over the past 25 years.

McClellan, Steve, "Ad Clutter Keeps Climbing," *Broadcasting and Cable*, Dec. 22, 2003, p. 13.
A new study of commercial "clutter" on the networks reveals that viewers are now exposed to an average 52 minutes of non-program content a night on each of the four major broadcast networks — about 17 minutes per hour.

Nelson, Jon P., "Cigarette Demand, Structural Change and Advertising Bans: International Evidence, 1970-1995," *Contributions to Economic Analysis & Policy*, Vol. 2, Issue 1, 2003.
An economist at Pennsylvania State University concludes from international data that advertising bans have no significant impact on cigarette consumption.

Pierce, John P., Won S. Choi, Elizabeth A. Gilpin, Arthur J. Farkas and Charles C. Berry, "Tobacco Industry Promotion of Cigarettees and Adolescent Smoking," *Journal of the American Medical Association*, Vol. 279, No. 7, Feb. 18, 1998, p. 511.
An influential study at the Cancer Prevention and Control Program at the University of California, San Diego, found no causal effect between cigarette advertising and youths' decisions to begin smoking.

Woellert, Lorraine, "Will the Right to Pester Hold Up?" *Business Week*, Nov. 10, 2003, p. 73.
A U.S. district judge in Denver ruled that the FTC's do not call registry infringes on corporate First Amendment rights, but many question whether commercial free speech doctrine is too permissive.

Reports

"Changing Adolescent Smoking Prevalence: Where It Is and Why," U.S. Department of Health and Human Services, November 2001.
This 272-page report contains 17 articles by top researchers examining such issues as smoking rates among various ethnic groups and the effects of advertising on smoking rates.

"Cigarette Report for 2001," Federal Trade Commission, 2003.
The FTC's annual report on cigarette advertising and sales shows that sales decreased by 15.6 billion cigarettes from 2000 to 2001, while advertising and promotional expenditures rose $1.62 billion to $11.22 billion.

"Exposure to Pro-tobacco Messages Among Teens and Young Adults: Results from Three National Surveys," *The American Legacy*, November 2003.
The anti-smoking group finds that despite restrictions on advertising tobacco products to minors in 1998, youth "continue to be widely exposed to pro-tobacco messages."

"No Student Left Unsold: The Sixth Annual Report on Schoolhouse Commercialism Trends, 2002-2003," Commercialism in Education Research Unit, Arizona State University, October 2003.
The report finds both an increase in marketing activities and "an increasingly vocal resistance to commercializing activities."

"Reducing Tobacco Use: A Report of the Surgeon General," U.S. Department of Health and Human Services, 2000.
This detailed history of efforts to reduce smoking includes a thorough recounting of major court action.

"Spam: How It Is Hurting Email and Degrading Life on the Internet," Pew Internet and American Life Project, Oct. 22, 2003.
Extensive data "suggest that spam is beginning to undermine the integrity of e-mail and to degrade the online experience."

The Next Step:

Additional Articles from Current Periodicals

Ads in Schools

Barboza, David, "If You Pitch It, They Will Eat," *The New York Times*, Aug. 3, 2003, p. C1.
Facing budget shortfalls, many school districts are allowing fast food outlets to market food in their cafeterias to generate revenue, but critics contend that this is encouraging the record levels of obesity among American children.

Clayton, Mark, "Bottomless Pitchers," *Christian Science Monitor*, May 21, 2002, p. 11.
Alcohol advertisements have long been fixtures at colleges, but, with high levels of student alcohol abuse, calls for restrictions are growing.

Day, Sherri, "Coke Moves With Caution To Remain In Schools," *The New York Times*, Sept. 3, 2003, p. C1.
While the Coca-Cola Company vowed to roll back all of its marketing efforts to children, Coke still has not disappeared from the lives of schoolchildren.

Day, Sherri, "Sizing Up Snapple's Drink Deal with New York City," *The New York Times*, Sept. 12, 2003, p. C2.
For $166 million, Snapple signed a deal giving the company exclusive rights to distribute drinks in New York City schools and public buildings for five years.

Garcia, Michelle, "City Seeks to Raise Revenue by Selling Public Spaces to Advertisers," *The Washington Post*, Dec. 7, 2003, p. A3.
New York City school officials named Snapple the official and exclusive "drink of the public schools," sparking complaints over a conflict of interest.

Advertising to Children

"Capturing the Minds of Our Children," *The San Francisco Chronicle*, Dec. 14, 2003, p. D4.
Parents and children are at a huge disadvantage against marketers using sophisticated advertising combined with the latest research into child development.

Kane, Courtney, "TV and Movie Characters Sell Children Snacks," *The New York Times*, Dec. 8, 2003, p. C7.
Ads targeting children are not new, but the increased scope and intensity mean that today's youth become unsuspecting marketing targets at younger and younger ages.

Mayer, Caroline, "Nurturing Brand Loyalty," *The Washington Post*, Oct. 12, 2003, p. F1.
Advertisers and educators say the corporate presence in preschools is a logical extension of companies' commercial presence in elementary and high schools.

Alcohol and Tobacco Advertising Limits

Francis, David, "New Studies to Call for Tighter Reins on Alcohol Industry," *Christian Science Monitor*, Aug. 4, 2003, p. 17.
Two studies on alcohol-industry advertising and on methods to reduce and prevent underage drinking worry the producers of alcohol products.

Howard, Theresa, "Alcohol Advertisers Agree to Raise Standards to Help Keep Their Messages Away from Kids," *USA Today*, Sept. 10, 2003, p. 5B.
Alcohol manufacturers responded to two government reports on alcohol marketing by announcing stricter standards on where and how they advertise.

Rubin, Alissa, "Ads' Impact Debatable, Except to Some Lawmakers," *Los Angeles Times*, March 19, 1998, p. A5.
Lawmakers may be exaggerating the effectiveness that tobacco ads have in hooking young people on cigarettes; experts have decidedly mixed views on the role of advertising in luring new smokers.

Tugend, Alina, "Cigarette Makers Take Anti-Smoking Ads Personally," *The New York Times*, Oct. 27, 2002, p. C4.
Anti-smoking advocates and cigarette makers agree that anti-smoking ads are effective, but cigarette makers say the campaign vilifies their companies and employees.

First Amendment

Greenhouse, Linda, "Nike Free Speech Case Is Unexpectedly Returned to California," *The New York Times*, June 27, 2003, p. A16.
The Supreme Court dismissed Nike's appeal of a California Supreme Court decision requiring the company to stand trial for consumer fraud and unfair trade practices.

Liptak, Adam, "Nike Move Ends Case Over Firms' Free Speech," *The New York Times*, Sept. 13, 2003, p. A8.
A California lawsuit that was expected to produce a landmark ruling on the free-speech rights of corporations ended when Nike paid to settle the case.

Rosenzweig, David, "L.A. Billboard Fees Are Blocked," *Los Angeles Times*, Nov. 1, 2002, p. B3.
A federal judge rules that Los Angeles is violating the First Amendment by collecting annual fees from the owners of outdoor billboards.

Product Placement

Elliott, Stuart, "On ABC, Sears Pays to Be Star of New

Series," *The New York Times*, Dec. 3, 2003, p. C1.
Sears is sponsoring a reality TV program, featuring Craftsman tools and other Sears products, in an effort to reach viewers who avoid commercials.

James, Meg, "Nielsen to Follow Popularity of Product Placement on Prime-Time Television," *Los Angeles Times*, Dec. 5, 2003, p. C1.
Employees at Nielsen have been watching tapes of TV shows and recording products and how long they appear so the data can be sold to networks and advertisers.

Mayer, Caroline, "Buy This! Buy That! Says Cat in the Hat," *The Washington Post*, Nov. 20, 2003, p. E1.
Advertisers and film producers expect the product placement trend in movies to continue to grow, but some advocates for children are concerned.

Spam and Legislation

Hansell, Saul, "An Unrepentant Spammer Vows to Carry On, Within the Law," *The New York Times*, Dec. 30, 2003, p. C1.
Concerned by new penalties, a prolific junk e-mailer pledges to resume his mass marketing after altering his messages to comply with the CAN-SPAM Act.

Kirby, Carrie, "Anti-Spam Law May Benefit Some E-Marketers," *The San Francisco Chronicle*, Jan. 2, 2004, p. B1.
"Legitimate" e-mail marketers are welcoming federal legislation that restricts spam, saying business will improve when "fraudsters" are weeded out.

Lee, Jennifer, "House Accepts Revisions on Anti-Spam Bill," *The New York Times*, Dec. 9, 2003, p. C10.
Congress uses legislation to address proliferating junk e-mail and the associated costs with the CAN-SPAM Act, which requires senders of commercial e-mail to abide by certain rules.

Lee, Jennifer, "We Hate Spam, Congress Says (Except When It's Sent by Us)," *The New York Times*, Dec. 28, 2003, p. A1.
Even though Congress unanimously approved anti-spam legislation, members continue to send out hundreds of thousands of unsolicited messages to constituents.

Mangu-Ward, Katherine, "Canning Spam," *The Daily Standard*, Dec. 11, 2003.
Anti-spam legislation is unlikely to significantly reduce flow of junk e-mails due to lack of a means of ensuring compliance by government.

Telemarketing

Gold, Scott, "It May Not Be a Calling . . .," *Los Angeles Times*, Nov. 7, 2003, p. A1.
The national do-not-call registry may cause the loss of hundreds of thousands of telemarketing jobs, which are held mostly by the economically vulnerable.

Levin, Myron, "Canada Scam Artists Have a Global Reach," *Los Angeles Times*, July 7, 2002, p. B1.
Telemarketing frauds run by Canadians con thousands of American senior citizens out of their savings every year, taking advantage of Canada's lenient white-collar crime statutes and the difficulties involved in extradition.

Richtel, Matt, "No-Call List Dealt Setback in Court Ruling," *The New York Times*, Sept. 25, 2003, p. C1.
According to a federal district court, regulators overstepped their authority in establishing a national do-not-call registry, blocking the national program at least temporarily.

Witte, Griff, "Ringing Around the Rule," *The Washington Post*, Oct. 18, 2003, p. E1.
Companies are acting quickly to take advantage of exemptions in the do-not-call law, such as those that permit calls for surveys.

CITING *THE CQ RESEARCHER*

Sample formats for citing these reports in a bibliography include the ones listed below. Preferred styles and formats vary, so please check with your instructor or professor.

MLA STYLE

Jost, Kenneth. "Rethinking the Death Penalty." The CQ Researcher 16 Nov. 2001: 945-68.

APA STYLE

Jost, K. (2001, November 16). Rethinking the death penalty. *The CQ Researcher, 11*, 945-968.

CHICAGO STYLE

Jost, Kenneth. "Rethinking the Death Penalty." *CQ Researcher*, November 16, 2001, 945-968.

Back Issues

The CQ Researcher *offers in-depth coverage of many key areas.*
Back issues are $10. Quantity discounts available.
Call (866) 427-7737 to order back issues.

Or call for a free CQ Researcher Web trial!
Online access provides:

- *Searchable archives dating back to 1991.*
- *Wider access through IP authentication.*
- *PDF files for downloading and printing.*
- *Availability 48 hours before print version.*

CHILDREN/YOUTH
Preventing Teen Drug Use, March 2002
Sexual Abuse and the Clergy, May 2002
Movie Ratings, March 2003

CRIMINAL JUSTICE
Cyber-Crime, April 2002
Corporate Crime, October 2002
Serial Killers, October 2003

EDUCATION
Charter Schools, December 2002
Combating Plagiarism, September 2003
Home Schooling Debate, January 2003
Black Colleges, December 2003

ENVIRONMENT
Bush and the Environment, October 2002
Crisis in the Plains, May 2003
NASA's Future, May 2003
Water Shortages, August 2003
Air Pollution Conflict, November 2003

HEALTH CARE AND MEDICINE
Medicare Reform, August 2003
Women's Health, November 2003
Homeopathy Debate, December 2003

LEGAL ISSUES
Race in America, July 2003
Torture, April 2003
Homeland Security, September 2003
Civil Liberties Debates, October 2003
Stock Market Troubles, January 2004

MODERN CULTURE
Gay Marriage, September 2003
Combating Plagiarism, September 2003
Latinos' Future, October 2003
Future of the Music Industry, Nov. 2003
Hazing, January 2004

POLITICS/GOVERNMENT
Presidential Power, November 2002
Future of NATO, February 2003
Trouble in South America, March 2003
North Korean Crisis, April 2003
Rebuilding Iraq, July 2003
Aiding Africa, August 2003
State Budget Crises, October 2003

TRANSPORTATION
Auto Safety, October 2001
Future of the Airline Industry, June 2002
Future of Amtrak, October 2002
SUV Debate, May 2003

Future Topics

- ***Democracy in the Arab World***
- ***Medicating Mental Illness***
- ***Youth Suicide***

CQ Researcher

Published by CQ Press, a division of Congressional Quarterly Inc.

thecqresearcher.com

Democracy in the Arab World

Will U.S. efforts to promote democracy succeed?

The monarchs and presidential strongmen who have governed Arab lands since independence in the mid-20th century have been reluctant to share power, allow free elections or permit popular dissent. Following the overthrow of Saddam Hussein, however, President Bush has vowed to establish a working democracy in Iraq — and to promote free elections throughout the region. But democratization faces daunting obstacles, including the Arab world's limited experience with self-rule, imbalanced economic development and the rise of radical Islamist movements. While some experts see encouraging signs in a few countries, prospects for democracy appear dim in many others, including two major U.S. Arab allies: Egypt and Saudi Arabia.

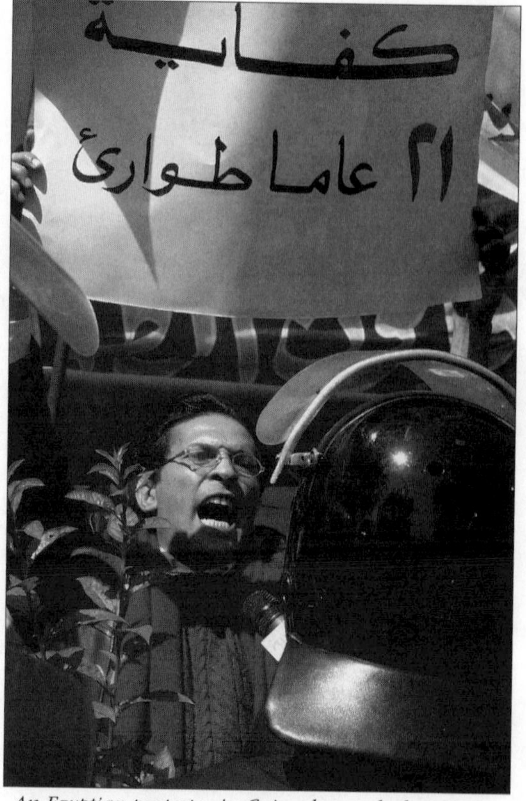

An Egyptian protester in Cairo demands democratic reforms. His banner proclaims: "Enough! 21 years of emergency law."

INSIDE THIS ISSUE

The CQ Researcher • Jan. 30, 2004 • www.thecqresearcher.com
Volume 14, Number 4 • Pages 73-100

RECIPIENT OF SOCIETY OF PROFESSIONAL JOURNALISTS AWARD FOR EXCELLENCE ◆ AMERICAN BAR ASSOCIATION SILVER GAVEL AWARD

Cover: A protester outside Egypt's parliament demands democratic reforms on March 9, 2003. His banner proclaims: "Enough! 21 years of emergency law." (AP Photo/Hasan Jamali)

THE CQ Researcher

Jan. 30, 2004
Volume 14, No. 4

MANAGING EDITOR: Thomas J. Colin

ASSISTANT MANAGING EDITOR: Kathy Koch

ASSOCIATE EDITOR: Kenneth Jost

STAFF WRITERS: Mary H. Cooper, David Masci, William Triplett

CONTRIBUTING WRITERS: Rachel S. Cox, Sarah Glazer, David Hosansky, Patrick Marshall, Jane Tanner

DESIGN/PRODUCTION EDITOR: Olu B. Davis

ASSISTANT EDITOR: Kenneth Lukas

CQ PRESS

A Division of Congressional Quarterly Inc.

SENIOR VICE PRESIDENT/GENERAL MANAGER: John A. Jenkins

DIRECTOR, LIBRARY PUBLISHING: Kathryn C. Suárez

DIRECTOR, EDITORIAL OPERATIONS: Ann Davies

CIRCULATION MANAGER: Nina Tristani

CONGRESSIONAL QUARTERLY INC.

CHAIRMAN: Andrew Barnes

VICE CHAIRMAN: Andrew P. Corty

PRESIDENT AND PUBLISHER: Robert W. Merry

The CQ Researcher (ISSN 1056-2036) is printed on acid-free paper. Published weekly, except Jan. 2, April 9, July 2, July 9, Aug. 6, Aug. 13, Nov. 26 and Dec. 31, by CQ Press, a division of Congressional Quarterly Inc. Annual subscription rates for libraries, businesses and government start at $625. Single issues are available for $10. Quantity discounts apply to orders over 10. Additional rates furnished upon request. Periodicals postage paid at Washington, D.C., and additional mailing offices. POSTMASTER: Send address changes to *The CQ Researcher*, 1255 22nd St., N.W., Suite 400, Washington, D.C. 20037.

Democracy in the Arab World

BY KENNETH JOST AND BENTON IVES-HALPERIN

THE ISSUES

Egyptian sociologist Saad Eddin Ibrahim was lecturing in the United States last November when President Bush called for democratization in the Middle East. "I could not have written a better speech," Ibrahim, a longtime critic of Egyptian strongman Hosni Mubarak, wrote in *The Washington Post.* [1]

Back in Egypt, Ibrahim's op-ed remarks caused an uproar. Pro-government newspapers insinuated that he had actually written Bush's Nov. 6 speech — and that his entire trip was designed to embarrass Egypt and secure U.S. funding for Ibrahim's pro-democracy center in Cairo. Declared a headline in the pro-government weekly *Al-Osbou:* "Saad in Washington to incite the U.S. against Egypt and the Arab world." [2]

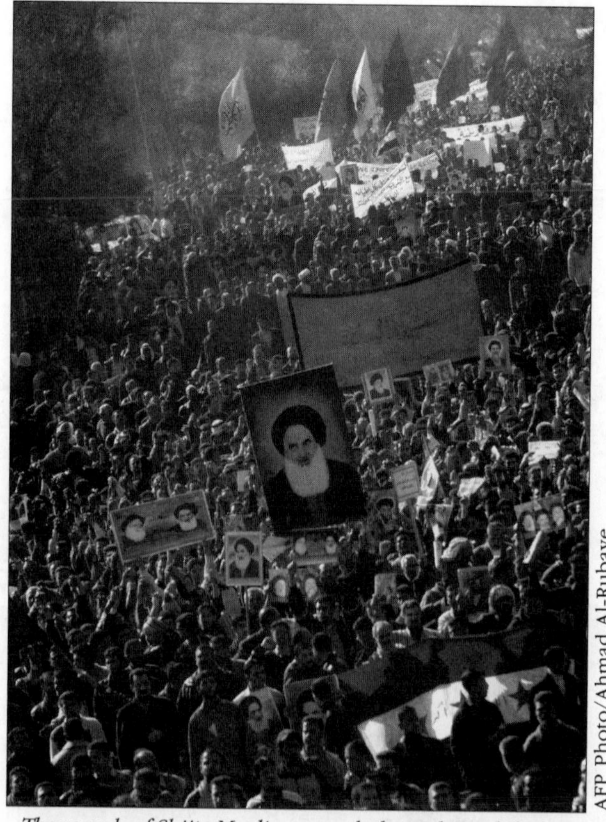

AFP Photo/Ahmad Al-Rubaye

Thousands of Shiite Muslims march through Baghdad on Jan. 19, demanding that Iraq's new government be selected through direct elections rather than caucuses, as the United States has proposed. Some monarchies in the Arab world have taken tentative steps toward electoral governance, but others continue to struggle under the grip of authoritarian regimes. President Bush recently called on all Arab states to join "the global democratic revolution."

Political dissidents in many countries can shrug off newspaper innuendoes. But government critics in Egypt must take care. Ibrahim himself served more than a year in prison and was twice convicted of receiving foreign funds for his Ibn Khaldun Center without permission — a $225,000 grant from the European Union for voter-awareness projects — and spreading defamatory information about Egypt. The convictions sparked international protests that died down only after Ibrahim won a reversal and subsequent acquittal in March 2003. The center, which the government had ordered closed, reopened in November.

Hafez Abu Saada, head of the Egyptian Organization for Human Rights, was arrested five years ago and charged with similar offenses. He was never tried, but he says the government can revive the case any time in the next 15 years. Meanwhile, he has been waiting for more than six months to find out whether the Egyptian Ministry of Social Affairs will allow his group to accept a grant from the U.S.-government-funded National Endowment for Democracy to help pay for its human rights monitoring work.

Egypt's law regulating non-governmental organizations is just one of the many statutes tightly controlling civic life in a country that is a critical American partner in the Middle East and — with about 75 million people — the most populous nation in the Arab world. According to the U.S.-based human rights group Freedom House, a government committee must license all political parties, and the Ministry of the Interior must approve public demonstrations in advance. In addition, the government owns all the broadcast media, along with three major daily newspapers, whose editors are appointed by the president. Direct criticism of the president, his family or the military can result in imprisonment of journalists or closure of publications.

Egypt has an elected president and a bicameral legislature with an elected lower house and a mostly elective upper chamber. But Mubarak — who has ruled by decree since taking office after the assassination of President Anwar el-Sadat in 1981 — is nominated by parliament and then voted on in a single-candidate referendum for a five-year term. Further, the political licensing laws combine with what Freedom House calls "systematic irregularities" in election procedures to assure the ruling National Democratic Party (NDP) a lock on governmental power. "Egyptians cannot change their government democratically," the group concludes. [3]

As in Egypt, so in the rest of the Arab world — which stretches across North Africa, south through the Arabian peninsula and east to Iraq. (*See map, p. 76.*) With around 300 million people, the 22 members of the League of Arab States include only one rated by Freedom House as "free" — tiny Djibouti on the Horn of Africa. None of the other members allows a free election to choose the national leader, and only one — Kuwait — has a parliament with effective power to control the executive branch of government.

Continued on p. 78

Political Freedom Rare in the Arab World

Only one member of the 22-member League of Arab States — tiny Djibouti on the Horn of Africa — is rated "free" by the human-rights group Freedom House. No other Arab country allows free elections of national leaders, and only Kuwait has a parliament that can effectively control the executive branch. Yemen is the only Arab country whose freedom status improved over the past year.

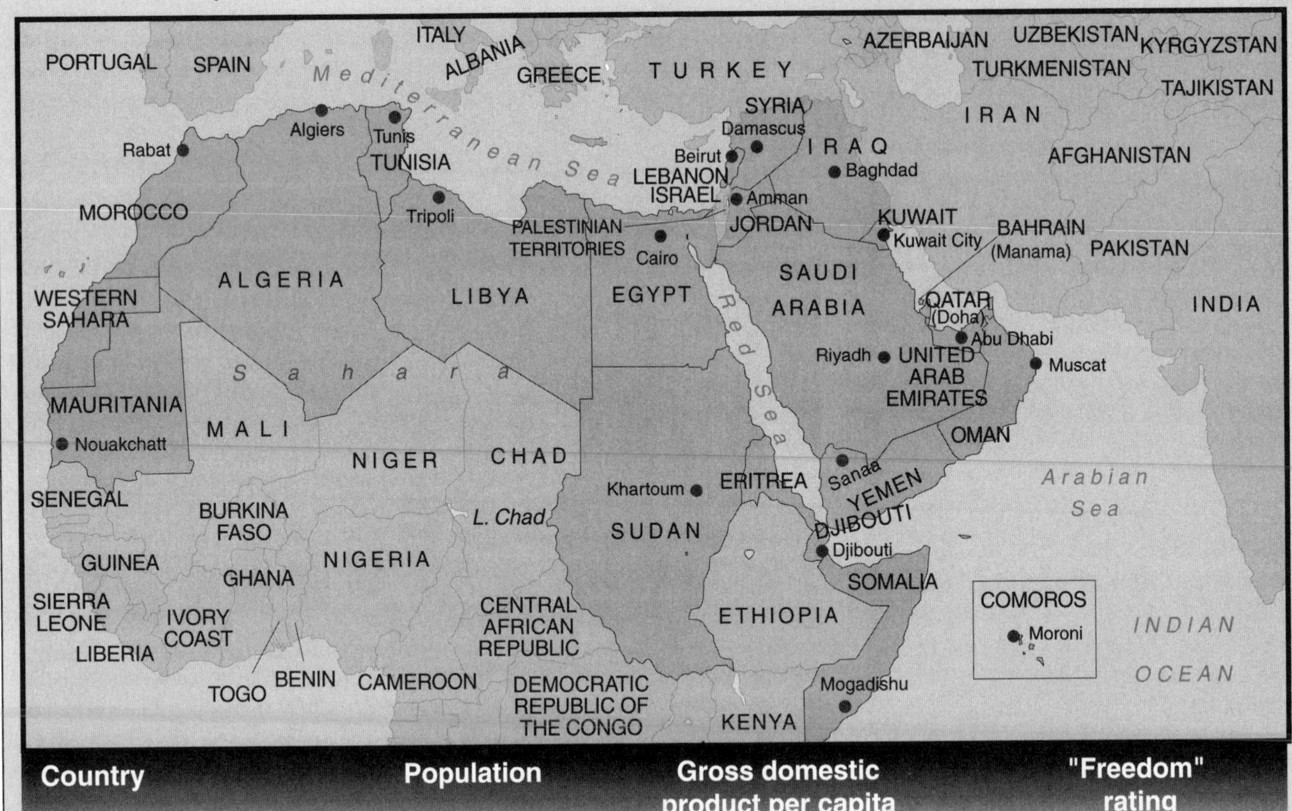

Country	Population	Gross domestic product per capita	"Freedom" rating
Algeria	**32.8 million**	**$5,300**	**Not Free**
Military and intelligence officers dominate government but allow presidential and parliamentary elections. Martial law declared to counter civil war fought by radical Islamists since 1992. Low turnout in 2002 elections because of boycotts by pro-Berber parties and pro-democracy groups.			
Bahrain	**700,000**	**$14,000**	**Partly free**
Parliamentary elections in 2002 — the first in 30 years — were fair and produced victory for opposition groups, especially Islamists. Government is viewed as increasingly committed to democratization.			
Comoros	**600,000**	**$700**	**Partly free**
Legislative elections are scheduled for April against a backdrop of political tension between the country's president and the presidents of the three, semi-autonomous islands that comprise the Indian Ocean archipelago. Political and legal rights are generally respected.			
Djibouti	**500,000**	**$1,300**	**Free**
Parties supporting the president won nearly two-thirds of the popular vote in the country's first multiparty elections recently. Political and legal rights are nominally guaranteed in this strategically located, key base for the U.S. war against terrorism.			

Sources: U.S. Central Intelligence Agency, The World Factbook 2003; *Freedom House,* Freedom in the World 2003; *news reports.*

Country	Population	Gross domestic product per capita	"Freedom" rating
Egypt	**74.7 million**	**$3,900**	**Not free**
President Hosni Mubarak has ruled under a continuous state of emergency since assuming office in 1981 after the assassination of Anwar el-Sadat but said he supports limited reforms drafted by a party committee headed by his son Gamal. Some easing of previous crackdowns on internal dissent has occurred; Islamic militancy is seen as fueled by socioeconomic problems.			
Iraq	**24.7 million**	**$2,400**	**Not free**
The United States is pressing transition to democratic self-rule after a U.S.-led coalition ousted Saddam Hussein last spring. Captured in December 2003, Hussein faces trial by an Iraqi tribunal. L. Paul Bremer III — administrator of the American-led occupation — is working to transfer power to Iraqi entities; elections possible in 2004.			
Jordan	**5.5 million**	**$4,300**	**Not free**
King Abdullah II promises to continue pushing democratic reforms following victory for allies in previously postponed parliamentary elections in June 2003. He dissolved parliament in 2001 to counter Islamist opposition to pro-Western foreign policy he continued after 1999 death of his father, King Hussein.			
Kuwait	**2.2 million**	**$15,000**	**Partly free**
Fundamentalist Muslims and supporters of the royal-backed cabinet improved their standing in parliamentary elections last June; the aging emir appointed his 74-year-old brother as prime minister in July in an apparent effort to boost economic and political reforms, but succession issues still cloud prospects.			
Lebanon	**3.7 million**	**$5,400**	**Not free**
Opposition to Syrian military occupation increasing, although Syria downsized its military presence in 2001. The elected, pro-Syrian government continues to hold power since winning control after the end of Christian-Muslim civil war in 1990.			
Libya	**5.5 million**	**$7,600**	**Not free**
Muammar el-Qaddafi has ruled by decree since seizing power in 1969. Independent political parties and non-authorized Islamic groups are banned. Qaddafi recently has been seeking U.S. goodwill by cooperating in the war against terrorism, while domestic support wanes.			
Mauritania	**2.9 million**	**$1,700**	**Partly free**
Longtime President Maaouiya Ould Taya was re-elected in November after his main opponent was charged with plotting a coup d'etat. Elections in October 2001 were seen as generally fair and open, but Ould Taya's political control was left undisturbed.			
Morocco	**31.7 million**	**$3,900**	**Partly free**
King Mohammed VI instituted political and economic liberalization after assuming the throne in 1999. Free and fair elections for parliament were held in 2002, but turnout was low. Palace still holds decision-making power.			
Oman	**2.8 million**	**$8,300**	**Not free**
An 83-member advisory council was elected by universal-suffrage election in October; parliamentary elections planned in 2004. Political liberalization and economic modernization have been pushed since 1990s by Sultan Qaboos, who overthrew his father in 1970.			
Palestinian Territories	**3.2 million**	**$930**	**Not free**
Progress toward limited self-rule by the Palestinian Authority in the Israeli-occupied West Bank and Gaza Strip has stalled following the outbreak of the Palestinian intifada (uprising) in September 2000, a continuing dispute over Israeli settlements and a stalemate in peace talks. The first popular election in 1996 was seen as legitimate; municipal elections have been postponed since 1998.			

Country	Population	Gross domestic product per capita	"Freedom" rating
Qatar	**800,000**	**$21,500**	**Not free**
Parliamentary elections have been promised for 2004. Liberalization has been directed by the ruling emir, who overthrew his father in 1995. The government's Al-Jazeera all-news satellite TV station and close military ties with the United States have raised the country's profile.			
Saudi Arabia	**24.3 million**	**$10,500**	**Not free**
Crown Prince Abdullah favors political and economic liberalization but faces family opposition. Popular discontent among religious and liberal dissidents fueled by declining living standards has been put down by harsh measures. Under U.S. pressure, the government is moving against al-Qaeda terrorist activities.			
Somalia	**8 million**	**$600**	**Not free**
Delegates to a peace conference agreed in July 2003 to create a new federal government after more than a decade of civil war and virtual anarchy, but the plan has yet to be implemented. The breakaway Republic of Somaliland in the north has not won diplomatic recognition.			
Sudan	**38.1 million**	**$1,420**	**Not free**
The Arab Muslim government reached a cease-fire agreement in September with black African rebels in the south in 20-year-old civil war that has claimed 2 million lives. Accord envisions a six-year transition to autonomy for the southern region and Islamic law in north.			
Syria	**17.6 million**	**$3,500**	**Not free**
President Bashar Assad has mixed record on reform since the death of his autocratic father, Hafez al-Assad, in 2000. Bashar allowed reform movement to form during "Damascus Spring" but began clamping down in February 2001. Calls for reform were renewed last September, but broad political change is seen as unlikely.			
Tunisia	**10 million**	**$6,500**	**Not free**
President Zine el-Abidine Ben Ali gained power in a 1987 coup and won 99 percent approval in a 2002 referendum to seek election for a fourth five-year term. Elections for parliament are heavily orchestrated. The country has a strong, diversified market economy, but political and civil liberties are restricted.			
United Arab Emirates	**2.5 million**	**$22,000**	**Not free**
Council of seven dynastic families have ruled the federation since its formation in 1971. No elections have been held and political parties are banned. The diversified modern economy supports high per capita income. The federation has a moderate foreign policy stance and new anti-money laundering laws to stem terrorism financing.			
Western Sahara	**300,000**	**N/A**	**Not free**
Morocco virtually annexed the country in late 1970s, but the territory is still contested by the so-called Polisario guerrillas; guerrilla activities continued sporadically until a U.N.-monitored cease-fire on Sept. 6, 1991.			
Yemen	**19.3 million**	**$840**	**Partly free**
President Ali Abdullah Saleh, in office since unification of North and South Yemen in 1990, won approval in a 2001 referendum to extend presidential and parliamentary terms. Elections for parliament were deemed free and fair, but it exercises little power. Under U.S. pressure, government is cracking down on al-Qaeda cells and radical Islamist schools.			

Continued from p. 75

"There is no substantial and significant movement toward full democracy in any of the majority-Arab countries," says Adrian Karatnycky, a senior counselor and former president of Freedom House.

Other human rights advocates and experts agree. "Legitimate democracy is non-existent in the Arab world," says James Phillips, a Mideast expert at the conservative Heritage Foundation.

Thomas Carothers, vice president of the more liberal Carnegie Endowment for International Peace, says, "There is very little democratic trend in the region."

Arab leaders, however, profess support for democracy and claim to see progress toward the goal in many countries in the region. "More than a few people are committed to the democratization process, committed to widening and consolidating political participation," says Nassif Hitti, a diplomat in the Paris mission of the League of Arab States. "It's a process. It's moving on, perhaps not as fast as one would like to see it. It's moving on at different speeds depending on different cases."

A leading American spokesman for Arab-Americans also sees advancing democratization in the region. "It's proceeding apace," says James Zogby, president of the Arab American Institute. "While there are problems, to be sure, changes have been occurring that should not be ignored but all too frequently are ignored."

A major 2002 human rights report by a leading Arab development group, however, takes a more critical view. "The wave of democracy . . . has barely reached the Arab States," the Arab Fund for Economic and Social Development said in a 2002 report co-published by the United Nations Development Program. Representative democracy "is not always genuine and sometimes absent," the group said, while freedoms of expression and association are "frequently curtailed." [4]

Bush raised the profile of the issue in his Nov. 6 speech marking the 20th anniversary of the National Endowment for Democracy, calling on the Middle East and North Africa to join what he called "the global democratic revolution." Bush cataloged signs of democratization in many Arab lands — from the first-ever parliamentary elections in the island emirate of Bahrain and planned elections in Saudi Arabia to a new constitution in Qatar and a call by Morocco's king to extend rights to women.

In a widely noted passage, Bush also directly criticized the United States and other Western nations for supporting autocratic governments in the past. "Sixty years of Western nations excusing and accommodating the lack of freedom in the Middle East did nothing to make us safe," Bush said, "because in the long run, stability cannot be purchased at the expense of liberty." [5]

AFP Photo/Luke Frazza

President Bush has urged Egyptian President Hosni Mubarak, left, and other Arab leaders to allow more democracy in the Middle East. "For too long, many people in that region have been victims and subjects — they deserve to be active citizens," Bush said in a Nov. 6 speech.

Bush also vowed to press on with building a democracy in Iraq following last year's U.S.-led invasion and ouster of the country's former dictator, Saddam Hussein. [6] "This work is not easy," he said. But, he added, "We will meet this test."

Egypt merited a mention in the speech, with the president hailing a "great and proud nation" but calling on it to "show the way toward democracy in the Middle East." President Mubarak answered the next month by insisting that Egypt is already a democracy. "We do not need any pressure from anyone to adopt democratic principles," he told a news conference in December. [7]

Indeed, many Arabists say the United States should not try to impose democracy on the Arab world. "It might be considered by many as an interference, for right or wrong reasons, and this might frustrate at some times the progress of this process," Hitti says.

Mubarak's son Gamal, in fact, heads an NDP committee that has called for revising the political licensing laws and invited legal opposition parties and non-governmental organizations to join a "national dialogue." Most Egyptian democracy advocates are unimpressed. "I find all policies unchanged," Abu Saad says. As for Mubarak's assessment, Abu Saad flatly disagrees: "You can't say we have democracy at all."

As the debate on democratic reforms continues in Egypt and elsewhere in the Arab world and in Washington, here are some of the questions being considered:

Is democracy taking root in the Arab world?

The U.S.-led liberation of Kuwait in the first Gulf War in 1991 raised hopes for democratic changes in the oil-rich emirate. Pressure from Washington helped persuade the ruling al-Sabah family to restore the previously suspended national assembly.

Today, Kuwait's parliament is regarded as the only legislative body in an Arab country with the power to check decisions by the executive branch. The parliament's most notable use of that power came in 1999 when it nullified a decree by the ruling emir

Are Islam and Democracy Incompatible?

Politics and religion are a volatile mix in many countries, but nowhere more so than in the Arab world. Islam has a special status in Arab states — not only because it is the nearly universal faith but also because many Muslims view Islam as an essential source of government law.

Even in non-Arab Islamic countries, fundamentalists, or Islamists, often claim a religious basis for repressive policies against political opponents, women and other religions — notably, in Iran after the Islamic revolution of 1979 and in Afghanistan under the now-deposed Taliban. In addition, Islamist groups bring a sometimes deadly religious zeal to their battles against secular Arab regimes, not to mention Israel and the United States.

As a result, many Westerners regard Islam and democracy as inherently incompatible. Muslims in and outside the Arab world resent that view, and human rights advocates take pains to try to refute it.

"Islam, per se, is not an obstacle to democracy," says Thomas Carothers, director of the Project on Democracy and the Rule of Law at the Carnegie Endowment for International Peace. But, Carothers adds, "there are certain patterns of Islam that are inhospitable to democracy."

"There is a long tradition of people who want to combine liberalism with Islam," says Abdelwahab El-Affendi, coordinator of the Project on Democracy in the Muslim World at the University of Westminster in London and a native Sudanese. But he concedes that groups with "illiberal" Islamic views have more adherents in the Arab world today. "They say if liberalism and Islam conflict, then the Islamic way should be supreme," he explains.

In its most recent annual survey, the human rights group Freedom House says there is "no inexorable link between Islam and political repression." [1] Nearly half of the world's 1.5 billion Muslims live in countries with elective democracies, according to the survey. The list includes such majority-Muslim countries as Bangladesh, Nigeria and Turkey as well as more religiously diverse nations like India, Indonesia and the United States.

Nevertheless, the survey reports, "The largest freedom gap exists in countries with a majority-Muslim population, especially in the Arab world." Out of 44 majority-Muslim countries, only eight are electoral democracies — none of them Arab states. And only two are classified as "free": Mali and Senegal in West Africa. The other 42 countries — home to more than 1 billion Muslims — are rated either as "partly free" or "not free."

Human rights advocates blame the limited advance of democracy in the Islamic world more on history and politics than on religion. Radwan Masmoudi, the founding president of the Center for the Study of Islam and Democracy in Washington, says that European colonial rulers of the early 20th century were succeeded by ideologues of various stripes — Arab nationalists, communists and Baathists — who adopted authoritarian policies to hold power.

Properly understood, Islam has been fully consistent with democracy, according to Masmoudi, a Tunisian-born U.S. citizen who founded the center partly with U.S.-government funding in 1999. "From a historical perspective, Islam has been a fairly tolerant religion," Masmoudi says, ever since its birth with the teachings of Muhammad in the seventh century A.D. "The sayings of the Prophet are clearly for freedom, democracy and tolerance," he explains.

Other experts also see support for democratic government in such Islamic principles as consultation (*shurah*), consensus (*ijma*) and independent judgment (*itjihad*). But John Esposito, director of the Center for Christian-Muslim Understanding at Georgetown University in Washington, notes that Islamic thinkers adapt these concepts in ways that reflect criticisms of what they see as the secularism and materialism of Western-style democracy. [2]

Other U.S. scholars, however, say that fundamentalists interpret Islam in ways that are antithetical to democracy. "For [fundamentalists], the truth is knowable, and so there is no need to discuss it in an open forum," says Daniel Pipes, director of the Middle East Forum, a think tank in Philadelphia. "That strikes me as undemocratic." [3]

Islamic fundamentalists "regard liberal democracy as a corrupt and corrupting form of government," writes Bernard Lewis, a leading historian of the Middle East. "They are willing to see it,

to allow women the right to vote. And the prospect for further reforms is clouded by fractiousness within the ruling family and the strong showing by Islamist, or Muslim fundamentalist, forces in the most recent parliamentary elections in 2003.

Kuwait's al-Sabah regime serves as one example of the many obstacles to democratization in the Arab world. While historic, cultural and religious factors are all cited as important, the Carnegie Foundation's Carothers says the most important obstacle is political: the power and survival skills of existing, undemocratic governments.

"These are well-entrenched, nondemocratic regimes that have learned to survive over the years and are able to mobilize resources — either oil or foreign aid — to co-opt opposition movements, to repress and to tell their peoples that they are forces of order that are necessary to keep societies together," Carothers says.

Arab League diplomat Hitti acknowledges that established regimes are part of the problem. "The official elements are in many instances part of the constraining factors," he says. But he declines to comment on specific countries or leaders.

Contemporary political conditions, however, have developed from a history largely without democratic instiat best, as an avenue to power, but an avenue that runs one way only." [4]

Masmoudi and others say that U.S. policymakers must accept that secularism and separation of church and state will not be accepted by most Muslims. "People tend to think that democracy is equal to secularism, that religion will play no role in society whatsoever," he explains. If people view Islam and democracy in conflict, Masmoudi says, "Eighty percent of them will say, 'We want to be good Muslims. We don't care about good democracy — if it is against Islam, we don't want it.' "

AFP Photo/Getty Images/Hani al-Obeidi

Shiite Muslim Iraqis have become increasingly vocal in supporting their spiritual leader Grand Ayatollah Ali al-Sistani's unrelenting call for direct elections. The majority Shiites were repressed by the ruling Sunnis during the regime of deposed President Saddam Hussein.

"The Islamists in the Middle East are there to stay," says Mohamed Ben-Ruwin, an assistant professor of political science at Texas A&M International University in Laredo. "You have to engage them in some kind of dialogue." [5]

"We should have a dialogue of civilizations, not 'a clash of civilizations,' " Ben-Ruwin adds, referring to the widely discussed book by Harvard political scientist Samuel Huntington forecasting an increasing threat of violence from countries and cultures with religiously based policies and traditions. [6]

Democracy advocates point to the success of a moderate Islamic party in Turkey as a promising example for majority-Muslim countries. Since taking office after an overwhelming election victory in November 2002, the Justice and Development Party has moved to expand political rights in a nation founded in 1923 as a secular republic.

"Turkey shows us that Islamists in a democratic environment modify their policies over time," says Adrian Karatnycky, counselor and former president of Freedom House. "Just because this is a religiously informed movement doesn't mean it is going to be anti-democratic."

In Iran, the reform-minded Mohammad Khatami won election as president in 1997 and re-election in 2001 after reformers had also won the overwhelming majority of parliamentary seats in 2000. But hard-line conservatives still dominate the judiciary and security services — producing a stalemate between pro- and anti-liberalization forces. [7]

Many Arab leaders resist free elections by pointing to the danger of a victory for extremist Islamist groups — a fear shared though not always voiced among U.S. policymakers. Masmoudi says the danger is exaggerated.

"I trust the people," he says. "The Islamist parties that will win are not against democracy. I believe it will be the moderate Islamists, not the radical Islamists who are opposed to democracy."

---

1 "Global Freedom Gains Amid Terror, Uncertainty," Freedom House, Dec. 18, 2003 (www.freedomhouse.org).

2 See John L. Esposito and John O. Voll, *Islam and Democracy* (1996), pp. 27-32.

3 Quoted in David Masci, "Islamic Fundamentalism," *The CQ Researcher*, March 24, 2000, pp. 241-264.

4 Bernard Lewis, "A Historical Overview," in Larry Diamond, Marc F. Plattner and Daniel Brumberg (eds.), *Islam and Democracy in the Middle East* (2003), p. 210.

5 See Mohamed Berween, "Leadership Crisis in the Arab Countries and the Challenge of the Islamists," *Middle East Affairs Journal*, Vol. 7, No. 1-2 (winter/spring 2001), pp. 121-132.

6 Samuel P. Huntington, *The Clash of Civilizations and the Remaking of World Order* (2000).

7 For background, see David Masci, "Reform in Iran," *The CQ Researcher*, Dec. 18, 1998, pp. 1097-1120.

---

tutions or procedures. The Heritage Foundation's Phillips says Arab culture itself is ill disposed toward democracy. For example, the Arab word for politics translates most closely as "control," he points out, while the English word derives from a Greek root meaning cooperation.

"Arabs in general don't handle equality very well because in their system you're either giving orders or taking orders," Phillips says.

"The Muslim and Arab countries do not have a culture or heritage or traditions of democratic practices or liberties as such," says Laith Kubba, an Iraqi-born U.S. citizen who is senior program officer for the Middle East and North Africa at the National Endowment for Democracy. "They have more traditional tribal cultures, where consensus is valued and dissent is not appreciated or welcome."

The 2002 Arab human rights report itself acknowledges that "traditional Arab culture and values" are often "at odds with those of the globalizing world." [8] The report calls for Arab countries to adopt an attitude of "openness and constructive engagement" toward other cultures, but Carothers says outside influences are generally unwelcome. "There is a sense in the Arab world that there is a particular Arab way to do things, and they should resist change from the outside," he says.

Arabs and Arab-Americans say cultural factors are less important in inhibiting democracy than historical factors — specifically, the legacy of colonial rule, first by the Ottoman Empire and then by European powers beginning in the 19th century. "During the colonial era, whatever existed before was wiped out," says Radwan Masmoudi, a Tunisian-born U.S. citizen who heads the Center for the Study of Islam and Democracy in Washington.

After independence in the early 20th century, Masmoudi continues, "the new states were created in an ad hoc fashion. They weren't established to represent the will of the people or even to serve the people."

Zogby agrees. "You've got a region that for the last 150 years has not controlled its own destiny," he says. "This region was not free to advance and develop at its own rate, and that's never a positive factor in promoting democracy."

The region's largely Muslim population and character are often cited as another barrier to democratization, but the relationship between Islam and democracy is complex and susceptible to what the Arab League's Hitti calls "contradictory interpretations." Many experts see support for democracy in Islam's central tenets, while others view Islam's fusion of religion and the state as antithetical to democracy.

For his part, President Bush insisted in his Nov. 6 speech that Islam and democracy are not in conflict. And Arab and U.S. experts alike stress the multiplicity of views among Muslims themselves. "There are versions of Islam that are pretty anti-democratic, but they're just versions," Carothers says.

But Abdelwahab El-Affendi, a senior research fellow at the Centre for the Study of Democracy at the University of Westminster, in London, says the strong differences among Muslims themselves are part of the problem. "The many visions are often incompatible," says El-Affendi, a Sudanese. "The holders of each vision are not ready to negotiate."

The Arab human rights report cataloged a host of factors underlying what it called the "freedom deficit" in the region. It listed high rates of illiteracy and low rates of economic development as important factors, along with such political conditions as the unchecked power of executive branches of government, little popular participation and limited freedom of expression or association. "Remedying this state of affairs," the report concluded, "must be a priority of national leaderships." [9]

Will democracy help promote economic development in the Arab world?

Saudi Arabia may be oil-rich, but the kingdom is beset with economic problems, according to Freedom House's most recent annual country profile. The report blames "declining oil prices," "rampant corruption within the royal family" and "gross economic mismanagement" for a steep decline in living standards — represented by a 50 percent drop in per capita income since the 1980s. Meanwhile, unemployment is estimated at 35 percent and expected to rise in coming years. [10]

Saudi Arabia provides just one example — though the most dramatic — of the paradoxical economic conditions in the Arab world. Arab nations control about half of the world's oil reserves, but the region has higher unemployment and poverty than much of the developing world. Unemployment averages 15 percent, according to the Arab human rights report, and more than one out of five people live on less than $2 per day. Combined, the Arab states' gross national product is less than that of Spain — which has less than one-seventh of the Arab world's population. [11]

The region's economic problems are widely seen as an obstacle to democratization, which in turn is viewed as one of the keys to improved economic performance. "Opening up markets is tied directly to opening up the political process," says diplomat Hitti. "There is a direct relationship between the issues."

Many advocates and experts say the region's dependence on oil as its primary source of wealth has had a negative effect on democratization. "Energy-rich societies have been able to use oil and wealth to buy quiescence and consent from portions of their population, and they've used repression to deal with the balance," says Freedom House's Karatnycky.

"Oil is an incredibly corrupting influence," says Stephen Krasner, director of the Center on Democracy, Development and the Rule of Law at Stanford University's Institute of International Studies, in Palo Alto, Calif.

In states with oil wealth, Krasner explains, "People want to get control of the state [because] the state gives you resources that you can use to repress your enemies. You don't have to compromise. You don't have to think about responsive fiscal systems. It's a huge problem."

Michael Ross, a political scientist at the University of California, Los Angeles, says oil dependence also hampers democratization because it fails to produce the kind of social modernization usually associated with democratic change, such as urbanization, education and occupational specialization. Without those changes, Ross writes in a detailed examination of the issue, the public is "demobilized" — ill equipped to organize and communicate and unaccustomed to thinking for itself. [12]

The 2002 Arab human rights report viewed government policies as unhelpful to economic development. "[T]he state's role in promoting, complementing and regulating markets for goods, services and factors of production has been both constrained and constraining," the 2002 report stated. As a result, "the private sector's contribution to development has often been hesitant and certainly below expectations." [13]

Today, however, Hitti claims that Arab governments are adopting free-market policies. "Almost all of our countries are moving along market economic lines," he says.

Some experts say they expect democratic changes will encourage more economic development. "You may liberate a lot of economic free-wheeling activity," says the Heritage Foundation's Phillips. "The Arabs are great traders and merchants, but the problem is that the merchant class has been kept down except in Kuwait, where the merchants run the place."

Other experts, however, caution against expecting democratic change alone to solve the region's economic problems. "No statistical relationship can be shown between democracy and economic growth," Krasner says. He puts greater emphasis on instilling "decent levels of governance," including reducing corruption, adopting a "reasonable level of rule of law" and delivering government services more effectively.

For Saudi Arabia itself, broad democratic changes would have "a huge positive effect" on economic development, says Jean-Francois Seznec, an adjunct professor at Georgetown University's Center for Contemporary Arab Studies, in Washington. "If you have democratization, the private sector will be much more able to invest."

Seznec notes that Saudi Arabia has been developing an industrial base — notably, in petrochemical manufacturing. The Saudi Ministry of Labor is calling for investing $200 billion a year in further industrialization. But investment is hampered by the government's tight control of the economy and the lack of an independent judiciary.

"Right now, the civil service controls the economy, and the royal family is above the law," Seznec explains. An independent judiciary, he says, "would allow people to invest more freely, and there's plenty of money to invest."

Anti-U.S. Views Dominate Arab World

Unfavorable attitudes about the United States were twice as prevalent, on average, as favorable attitudes, according to a poll in five Arab nations.

Country	Favorable	Unfavorable
Lebanon	41%	40%
Kuwait	28	41
Jordan	22	62
Morocco	22	41
Saudi Arabia	16	64
Total	**26%**	**50%**

Note: Percentages are not included for respondents with neither favorable nor unfavorable attitudes.

Source: Gallup Organization, poll of nearly 10,000 residents, February 2002.

Without democratization, Seznec concludes, economic changes "will occur, but very, very slowly."

Should the United States do more to promote democracy in Arab countries?

As Secretary of State Colin L. Powell prepared to visit Morocco, Algeria and Tunisia last December, human rights groups urged him to lobby their leaders for democratic reforms. "Secretary Powell should make bold and specific statements calling for the countries in the region to take serious steps to enhance the rule of law, strengthen independent media and expand democratic freedoms," Freedom House Executive Director Jennifer Windsor urged.

Powell did raise the issue in each country. He praised Morocco's holding of parliamentary elections in 2002, called on Algeria to ensure "free and fair" elections for the national assembly in April 2004 and pressed Tunisia's longtime president, Zine el-Abidine Ben Ali, to move faster on political reforms. But Powell was careful to soften any implied criticism. In Tunis, for example, Powell said that Tunisia "has accomplished so much that people are expecting more to happen."

Human rights groups had mixed reactions. Human rights "was not a major theme of his public statements," Freedom House's Karatnycky commented afterwards. But Tom Malinowski, Washington advocacy director for Human Rights Watch, was more impressed. "Human rights were raised in a manner in which they haven't been raised in the past by the United States in these countries," he remarked.

Powell's careful diplomacy illustrates the recurrent tension between human rights advocacy and present-day strategic considerations. "We still need and value our close cooperation with some of the non-democratic governments in the region — like Egypt and Saudi Arabia — on security matters as well as on economic matters like oil," says the Carnegie Endowment's Carothers. "It's hard for us to take a genuinely tough line toward governments that know we need them."

But human rights advocates and experts also stress that the United States is hampered in pushing for democratic change in the region because of its past record of supporting autocratic Arab governments. "The United States has been, over time, interested in stability and generally indifferent to democracy," Karatnycky says.

"We have very little credibility as a pro-democratic actor," Carothers says. "We will have to earn that credibility by word and deed over a sustained period of time."

Arab-American advocates make the same point, even more critically. "We've never been a supporter of democracy in this region," Zogby says. "We lack both the moral authority and credibility at this point to be an agent for that kind of change."

For their part, Arab governments and Arab-American advocates also say that U.S. support for Israel undermines the United States' position in pushing for democratic changes. "The American position — particularly as it pertains to the Arab-Israeli conflict — has been damaging," Hitti says. He complains today of U.S. "immobilism" in peacemaking efforts in the Mideast. [14]

Bush's Nov. 6 speech drew mixed reactions from U.S. experts and advocates. The Heritage Foundation's Phillips calls it a "great speech," but Joe Stork, acting director for the Middle East and North Africa at Human Rights Watch, is more restrained. "It was a positive signal, but now we have to see if he can walk the walk," Stork says.

"The rhetoric is very dramatic," Karatnycky says, "but as yet the programmatic resources are relatively modest, and the pressure [from the U.S.] is still very, very mild."

The administration's vehicle for pro-democracy programs in the region is the Middle East Partnership Initiative, a State Department program that was headed by Elizabeth Cheney, daughter of the vice president, until her resignation in December 2003 to join President Bush's re-election campaign. Funding for the initiative was $129 million for 2002 and 2003 and up to $120 million for 2004. [15]

For his part, the Arab League's Hitti says Bush's speech failed to resolve concerns about U.S. hypocrisy in pushing for democratization. "There is a great feeling in the region that there is a double standard in America," he says. "You use democracy in certain aspects and not in other aspects."

Apart from any questions about the administration's sincerity, some experts also say that the push for democratization may be too narrowly focused on elections rather than on the full range of political reforms needed to sustain democratic government. Daniel Brumberg, an associate professor of government at Georgetown and a senior associate at the Carnegie Endowment, complains that Bush's speech lacked "any discussion of fundamental constitutional reforms." He points in particular to the need for Arab governments to create what none of them now has: legislative bodies "with the authority and power to speak for elected majorities." [16]

"We are deeply hamstrung by thinking that we must only focus on having free elections," Stanford's Krasner says. "What we should be talking about is good governance and accountability, of which democracy is a part, but only one part."

Despite those criticisms, Kubba at the National Endowment for Democracy believes the United States is on the way to becoming a positive force for democratization — not only for moral reasons but also for national self-interest, particularly after the Sept. 11, 2001, attacks on New York's World Trade Center and the Pentagon by Arab terrorists.

"There has been a genuine shift after Sept. 11 toward supporting democracy in the Middle East," Kubba says, "because [the administration] now believes that democracy-building enhances not only the security and stability in the region but also America's interest and security." ■

BACKGROUND

A Vast Empire

The earliest known Arab governments were established during a period of imperial expansion in the seventh century — shortly after the Islamic religion was established. [17] Led initially by the prophet Muhammad, nomadic peoples of the Arabian Peninsula conquered a vast empire stretching from Spain and North Africa to the Middle East and present-day Pakistan, spreading their religion, language and culture throughout the region. Islam reached Central Asia and the South Caucasus Mountains in the eighth century and spread to India and Indonesia in the 12th and 13th centuries, largely via Muslim traders and explorers.

Arab leaders exercised a tolerant but absolutist rule over their empire. Democratic governance was largely non-existent. Although the empire collapsed in the 15th century, Arabs have remained the principal power in the Middle East well into the modern era.

Pre-imperial Arab society had been organized around tribal allegiances, with little central authority or government and no common legal system. Most Arabs were nomadic shepherds, tending herds of goats, sheep or camels. All males were expected to be warriors, and competition over scarce resources often led to conflict between various tribal groups. Despite their differences, most Mideast tribes shared Arabic as a common language, and overland trade routes required intertribal cooperation and interaction.

The emergence of Islam ("surrender" in Arabic), a new monotheistic religion, on the Arabian Peninsula in 622 A.D. heralded the beginning of the transformation of the Arabs from

Continued on p. 86

Chronology

Before 1900

Arab empire extends from Spain to India; Ottoman Turks conquer the Arabs in 15th century; European powers gain foothold in 1800s.

1900-1945

Britain, France establish "mandates" after defeating Ottomans in World War I; House of Saud establishes kingdom on Arabian peninsula.

1946-1970

Arab nationalism grows with independence after World War II and creation of Israel; U.S. bolsters sitting leaders to protect oil supplies, aid Cold War struggle.

1948-1949
Israel established as Jewish homeland, defeats Arab states in nine-month war; 960,000 Palestinians displaced.

1952
Gamal Abdel Nasser becomes Egypt's president after military coup, promotes pan-Arab unity but loses prestige after Arab defeat in Six-Day War with Israel in 1967.

1967
Israel occupies Gaza Strip, West Bank after victory in Six-Day War.

1968
Sadaam Hussein assumes power in Iraq as leader of Baath Party.

1970s-1980s

Oil, terrorism raise U.S. stakes in Arab lands.

1973
Saudi Arabia leads oil embargo against U.S. by Organization of Petroleum Exporting Countries (OPEC).

1981
Egyptian President Anwar el-Sadat assassinated; new president, Hosni Mubarak, institutes rule by decree that continues to present day.

1990s

U.S. role in Iraq grows after Iraq's defeat in Gulf War; radical Islamist movements advance.

1990-91
Iraq's Hussein invades Kuwait; U.S. leads United Nations coalition in Gulf War to force withdrawal, but President George Bush, the current president's father, decides not to seek Hussein's ouster.

1992
Algerian military cancels legislative elections to forestall victory by radical Islamic Salvation Front, touching off protracted civil war.

1996
With King Fahd ailing, Crown Prince Abdullah gains authority in Saudi Arabia; he later pushes for reforms but faces opposition from other members of royal family.

1999
Jordan's King Hussein, key U.S. ally, dies; his son, Abdullah, succeeds him, continues pro-U.S. policies while promoting limited political reform.

2000-Present

Democracy makes limited gains in region; U.S. promotes democracy after ousting Iraq's Hussein.

2000
Syrian President Hafez al-Assad dies, succeeded by his son, Bashar, who adopts, then backs off from, limited reforms.

2001
Terrorist attacks against U.S. by Osama bin Laden's al-Qaeda leave nearly 3,000 dead; President Bush promises war against global terror.

2002
Bahrain holds first parliamentary elections in 30 years . . . Parliamentary elections in Morocco . . . Arab report criticizes "freedom deficit" in Arab world.

2003
U.S.-led invasion ousts Hussein in Iraq . . . Bush vows transition to democracy, promotes democracy for all Middle East on Nov. 6 . . . Gamal Mubarak, president's son, pushes limited reforms in Egypt.

2004
Democratic elections planned in many Arab states; Saudi Arabia eyes balloting for municipal councils . . . U.S. plans for handoff to Iraqi authorities by June 30 roiled by dispute over timing of elections. . . . Thousands of Shiites march through Baghdad and other major cities on Jan. 19, demanding direct elections to choose a new government. . . . U.N. Secretary-General Kofi Annan announces on Jan. 27 he will send a fact-finding mission to determine whether early elections are feasible.

Women Benefit From Top-Down Reforms

Women's groups are working in many Arab countries to change what an Arab development group describes as a "glaring deficit in women's empowerment" in the region. But recent advances in voting rights and family law in some countries amount to "top-down" reforms pushed by progressive-minded leaders rather than victories for grass-roots women's movements, experts say.

Qatar and Bahrain recently extended the right to vote for women, thanks to changes pushed by the ruling emirs in the tiny Persian Gulf states. Jordan and Morocco have recently given women limited rights to divorce at the behest of their ruling monarchs: King Abdullah II in Jordan and Mohamed VI in Morocco.

Egypt similarly enacted a "personal status" law in 2000 giving women the right to divorce if they relinquish financial rights. Women's associations "indirectly contributed" to passage of the law, according to a 2002 human rights report by the Arab Fund for Economic and Social Development, but the reform ultimately "was decided by the political powers." [1]

"Most of the progress in women's rights has come from progressive-minded rulers or rulers who want to be considered progressive and have tried to impose top-down reforms on society," says Amy Hawthorne, an expert on Mideast politics at the Carnegie Endowment for International Peace in Washington.

Arab countries rank below every other world region except sub-Saharan Africa on a "gender-empowerment measure," according to the Arab human rights report. The statistical measure — created by the United Nations Development Program — combines women's per capita income and the percentages of professional and technical positions and parliamentary seats held by women. [2]

"Women have a lower social and political status" in Arab countries compared to the rest of the world, Hawthorne says. But she also notes that women's status "varies considerably" through the region. She notes that women have had the right to vote in most Arab countries for some time — even if elections in many of those countries are blatantly undemocratic.

Diane Singerman, a professor of political studies at American University in Washington, also says that women are not subjected to second-class status throughout the Arab world. Women's illiteracy is high because education is not encouraged for women, she says, and unemployment is high — especially among educated women.

On the other hand, "there are a lot of very high-powered, very serious professional women," Singerman says. "In many cases, when women do well, they're not discriminated against in ways that are common" in the United States.

Islamic groups inhibit advances for women's rights. Moroccan women's groups mounted a demonstration with some 800,000 marchers in the capital city of Rabat in March 2000 in support of

Continued from p. 84

desert nomads to a world power. Established by an Arab merchant known only as Muhammad, Islam provided a framework for running early Arabian society. The *Koran* — Islam's holy book and a record of God's revelations to Muhammad — provided rules for business contracts, marriages, inheritance and other societal institutions.

Under Muhammad's spiritual and military leadership, early Arab-Islamic society rose to prominence in Arabia, gaining control of religious and trade centers like Mecca and Medina. Muhammad exercised supreme authority over his nascent empire.

Following Muhammad's death in 632 A.D., two factions struggled for control of Arab-Islamic society, producing a schism in Islam. Sunni Arabs believed that a politically selected successor, or caliph, should become ruler. Shiites, on the other hand, claimed that the direct descendents of Muhammad, called imams, were the legitimate rulers of Islam. Sunnis won the power struggle, and the secular caliphs dominated the Arab empire until the 16th century, with Shiite imams wielding only negligible power.

By the middle of the eighth century, the caliphs ruled from Spain to the Indian subcontinent. In theory, a central Arab ruler governed outlying territories with absolute secular and Islamic authority. In practice, the size and breadth of the sprawling empire made direct governance difficult, so Arab rulers often left local administrative and governmental structures intact. Nonetheless, occasional uprisings produced breakaway caliphates in places like North Africa and Egypt.

During the heyday of the Arab-Islamic empire — generally from the eighth to the 10th centuries — poetry, agriculture, trade and intellectual pursuits flourished. Arab scholars made valuable contributions to trigonometry, algebra and philosophy. Religious scholars developed the five pillars of Islam, a framework of prayers and rituals that formed a common and universal religious experience for Arabs.

By the standards of its day, the Islamic empire showed remarkable religious tolerance. Other monotheistic faiths like Christianity or Judaism were protected under the *Koran*. While early caliphs discriminated against non-Arab Muslim converts, later rulers universalized Islam and granted all Muslims equal rights.

Eventually, the increasingly diverse Arab empire proved difficult to govern with only the *Koran* for guidance. Arab leaders and intellectuals developed Sharia, a "legal system that would recognize the proposed divorce law. But on the same day, some 2 million people took to the streets of Casablanca, warning that the proposal was a threat to Islam. Religious conservatives relented only after the king's intervention. [3]

Islamist-minded legislators led the successful opposition to granting women the right to vote in Kuwait in 1999. The strict school of Islam known as Wahhabism serves as the basis for a host of restrictions on women in Saudi Arabia — such as a ban on driving.

Egypt passed its new divorce law, however, after women's groups claimed the *Koran* itself approved dissolving a marriage if a woman gave up financial rights created by the marital contract. "What's happening throughout the area is that women and other people in the region are saying that Islam may say something else," Singerman says. "It's a revisionist history of the record instead of a patriarchal interpretation."

Getty Images/Salah Malkawi

A veiled Jordanian woman casts her ballot. Women have limited voting rights in the Arab world. Bahrain became the first of the Persian Gulf states to allow women to vote in 2002. Kuwait's parliament nullified a decree by the ruling emir in 1999 that would have allowed women to vote.

Improving the status of women is "a critical aspect of human freedom," according to the Arab human rights report. [4] But Hawthorne cautions against assuming that granting women political rights will necessarily lead to political change. Some of the countries with broadest rights for women — for example, Syria — are also among the most autocratic of Arab states, she says.

"In the long run, any country that is going through a genuine process of democratization needs to include the empowerment of women," Hawthorne says. "But the addition of women won't necessarily result [right away] in increased democratization."

[1] United Nations Development Program/Arab Fund for Economic and Social Development Report, "Arab Human Development Report 2002," p. 117.

[2] *Ibid.*, p. 28.

[3] See Kent Davis-Packard, "Morocco Pushes Ahead," *The Christian Science Monitor*, Nov. 12, 2003, p. 15.

[4] "Arab Human Development Report," *loc. cit.*

the requirements of imperial administration and the value of local customs while remaining true to the concept of a community guided by divine [Islamic] revelation," writes William Cleveland, in his book, *A History of the Modern Middle East*. Sharia allowed Islamic officials to interpret Islamic principles to mediate situations not explicitly covered by the *Koran*.

By the 11th century, the central power of the Arab caliphate in Baghdad began to wane. Turkish nomads from Asia — who had converted to Islam — carved out large dynasties of their own within the Arab empire, previewing the coming Ottoman Empire. European crusaders invaded Arab lands and maintained a tenuous occupation of some Arab territory for 200 years. Ultimately, though, the crusades had minimal impact on the Middle East. [18]

Later foreign invasions spelled the end of the Arab empire. In the 13th century, Mongol conquerors from Asia sacked Baghdad and killed the caliph, ending 500 years of Arab imperial rule. And, at the beginning of the 15th century, the armies of Timur Lang (Tamerlane) swept over the empire, splintering it into several, smaller and weakened dynasties.

Ottoman Empire

Beginning in the 15th century, Ottoman Turks established a new empire that encompassed almost all of the Arabic-speaking lands in the Middle East.* But Ottoman imperial rule failed under external pressure from the rising European powers, and after World War I the Middle East fell under European control. Following World War II, the region struggled to shed the yoke of European dominance and adopt independent governments, even as new concepts of Arab identity emerged.

By the late 17th century, the sultans — supreme monarchs of the Ottoman Empire — ruled lands that stretched from Hungary in Europe to Algiers in North Africa to Baghdad in the Middle East. The empire was an agrarian, absolutist monarchy, with a strong bureaucracy of educated ruling elites. The sultans implemented Sharia throughout the empire and conferred with a counsel of advisers on policy issues. [19]

The Ottomans employed a flexible system of imperial governance — similar to earlier Arab empires — that allowed local authorities to retain traditional

* The Ottomans were Turks who organized under Osman I, a tribal chieftain who lived from 1290-1326.

customs, so long as they supplied adequate tax revenue to the Ottoman rulers. The Ottomans also continued Arab traditions of religious tolerance, granting non-Muslims significant civil rights and powers of self-governance.

In the 18th and 19th centuries, faced with the rise of European economic and military might, the Ottoman Empire entered a period of governmental reform and Europeanization. Ottoman officials who knew European languages and supported reforms were promoted, while old-style Ottoman institutions, like the *ulama* (religious scholars), increasingly were bypassed.

The first Ottoman constitution was adopted in 1876, providing for the election of government deputies and an appointed senate. But constitutional reforms proved short-lived, and the sultan reclaimed absolute authority in 1878.

But with central Ottoman authority weakened, several Islamic reformist movements emerged on the rural outskirts of the empire. In Arabia, the puritanical Wahhabi movement rose to power, advocating a return to strict interpretation of the *Koran* and adherence to Sharia.

European 'Mandates'

Elsewhere, intellectuals and scholars called for an Arab cultural renaissance, which reinvigorated the Arabic language and Arab identity, producing a kind of proto-Arab nationalism. And in 1916, an Arab insurrection — supported by the British — founded a short-lived Arab kingdom centered in Damascus.

Although the Ottomans reinstated a constitution in 1908, World War I doomed the empire. The victorious Allies partitioned the empire — which had been allied with Germany — into European-controlled "mandates." Britain maintained control of Egypt — which it had held since 1914 — and gained control over Iraq, Palestine and Transjordan (later called Jordan). France assumed control of Syria.

Under international agreement, Britain and France were expected to guide the Arab mandates toward self-governance. In actuality, the mandates allowed the British and French to protect their interests in the Middle East through the end of World War II. [20]

Not surprisingly, the Arabs chafed under the mandates, and many grew to distrust European-imposed political reforms. In Egypt, the Wafd — a political group opposed to British rule — established a secularist parliamentary constitution in 1924. But continued British influence over Wafd governments spawned popular opposition groups, most notably the fundamentalist Muslim Brotherhood, which advocated a return to an Islamic Egyptian state.

Nominally, Iraq achieved early independence in 1932, with a constitutional monarchy and bicameral legislature, as Britain had little interest in governing Iraq's volatile population of Sunnis, Shiites and ethnic Kurds. But Iraqi nationalists battled British-backed governments until 1958, when they succeeded in evicting the monarch.

Transjordan achieved independence in 1946, although the constitutional monarchy owed much of its authority to British support. In Syria, the French retained almost total control over the government until 1946, despite attempts by the Syrians to form a popular government.

Meanwhile, in Arabia — an area outside of European interest — a strong Islamic government took root in the wake of the Ottoman Empire. The Arabian tribal chief Abd al-Aziz ibn Saud, in an alliance with the Wahhabis, founded the kingdom of Saudi Arabia. Saud gained control of key Islamic religious sites, like Mecca and Medina and instituted strict Sharia law.

Some historians say the period of British and French control in the Middle East marked a high point for Arab democracy. "The Anglo-French domination also gave the Middle East an interlude of liberal economy and political freedom. The freedom was always limited and sometimes suspended but . . . it was on the whole more extensive than anything experienced before or after," writes noted historian Bernard Lewis, in his book, *The Middle East.* [21]

But other historians say Anglo-French domination merely installed a new class of ruling elites. "The same elite that had enjoyed power and prestige before 1914 — the European-educated landed and professional classes in Egypt and the traditional notables in Syria, Lebanon and Palestine — continued to exercise their privileges during the 1920s and 1930s," Cleveland writes. [22]

With the twin failures of Ottoman imperialism and European-backed governments in the Middle East, Arabs increasingly looked to nationalism and Islamism as political organizing principles.

Arab Nationalism

After World War II, the creation of Israel threw much of the Middle East into turmoil. Arab efforts to dislodge the Jewish state failed, and military coups replaced many of the defeated Arab governments. Although Arab military leaders espoused reform and pan-Arabism in the 1960s and '70s, they steadily moved toward authoritarianism. Meanwhile, the Cold War extended U.S. influence throughout the Middle East, and the Arabian oil boom cemented U.S. interests in the region. By the new millennium, Arab governments had stymied democratic reform, and radical Islamic groups increasingly targeted the United States for supporting the autocratic regimes.

After the Nazi Holocaust killed millions of Jews in World War II, international support for a Jewish state rose dramatically, culminating with Israel declaring its independence in 1948. Members of the Arab League — a federation of Arab states including Syria, Egypt and Jordan — promptly declared war on the new state.

Following a nine-month war, Arab forces were defeated, and hundreds of thousands of Arabs fled or were forced out of Palestine. By 1950, more than 960,000 Palestinians were refugees. [23] The Arab League later sponsored the Palestine Liberation Organization (PLO), a resistance group that battled Israel and became a Palestinian government in exile.

Muslims and Freedom

The vast majority of people in Muslim-majority nations are only "partly free" or "not free," according to Freedom House.

Freedom Status in Muslim-Majority Nations

Free Population	Partly Free Population	Not Free Population
20.4 million	577.1 million	532.4 million

Source: CIA Factbook, *www.islamicpopulations.com; Freedom House*

After the 1948 war, many post-imperial Arab governments were swept away by military regimes promising democratic and social reforms. But the new governments reverted to authoritarianism, which some historians attribute to a legacy of authoritarian rule under the European mandates. [24]

In Egypt, a military coup in 1952 led by Col. Gamal Abdel Nasser ousted the old Wafd government and brought some constitutional reforms, including an elected legislature. But Nasser quickly consolidated power and undermined democratic measures by adopting broad presidential powers.

Nasser also championed the cause of pan-Arab unity, hoping to unite all the Arab countries under a single Egyptian-Arab authority. Nasser achieved some success: Egypt and Syria united as a single nation for a short while, and strong Arab alliances formed in opposition to Israel. But the crushing defeat of Egypt (along with Syria and Jordan) by Israel in 1967 — during the so-called Six-Day War — damaged Nasser's reputation and derailed his hopes for pan-Arabism.

Nasser's successor, Sadat, renewed efforts to liberalize Egyptian politics. But Sadat's Western-style reforms failed to satisfy calls for democratic reform. Resistance groups, including the Muslim Brotherhood, called for a return to the successful theocratic governments of the past, and Muslim dissidents assassinated Sadat in 1981. Hosni Mubarak's autocratic government, which assumed power after Sadat's death, continued to control the electoral process and brutally suppress rising Islamic dissent.

In other Arab nations, radical nationalist movements — more focused on ejecting Western-influenced leaders and social reform than in democratization — installed similarly autocratic regimes. A series of military coups in Syria eventually empowered the radical Baath Party, which advocated social reform, pan-Arab unity and nationalism. But Baathist rule brought little reform, prompting militant Islamic groups to battle with the government for power throughout the 1980s and '90s.

Baathist radicals — under Hussein's leadership — assumed power in Iraq in 1968. Hussein's regime produced some social reforms, like increased literacy, but opposition and dissent were violently snuffed out.

Democratic reforms also remained elusive in Arab countries that avoided military insurrection. Jordan's King Hussein assumed power in 1953 and ruled over a monarchy until his death in 1999 — a longevity often attributed to Western support. In Lebanon — a state carved out of Syria by the French — democratic governance was pushed aside by Syrian occupation in 1976. And in Algeria's 1991 free elections, voters overwhelmingly chose an Islamic government that vowed a return to Sharia. Military leaders quickly halted the elections, sparking a civil war between radical fundamentalists and the government.

Many of the Arab autocracies received aid from the superpowers during the Cold War. The U.S. provided billions of dollars in military and economic assistance to Israel, Jordan and Iran, while the Soviets armed Syria, Egypt and Iraq. But continued U.S. support for Israel after the Cold War further inflamed anti-American Arab sentiment, even though since 1979 Egypt has been the second-largest recipient of U.S. foreign aid, after President Jimmy Carter brokered the Egypt-Israeli "Camp David" peace accord the year before. [25]

On the Arabian peninsula, the discovery in the early 20th century of vast oil reserves transformed the desert monarchies into world powers. By 1973, Saudi Arabia was producing 13 percent of the world's crude oil, and surging oil wealth strengthened Arabian monarchs' grip on power, enabling them to sidestep democratic reforms.

The monarchies turned to petroleum-hungry Western powers for military protection, particularly the United States. When Hussein invaded the Kuwaiti monarchy in 1990 and threatened Saudi oil fields, a U.S.-led coalition destroyed Iraq's army. [26]

After the Persian Gulf War, popular resistance to the monarchies grew. Radical Islamic groups objected to Western military and social influence in Saudi

Arabia — home of Islam's holiest cities and shrines — and secular interests pushed for more democracy. In Egypt, radicals battled to overthrow the government, while moderates called for democratic reforms.

In the 1990s, America's ties to autocratic regimes and its continued support for Israel led militant Islamic radicals to launch terrorist attacks against American targets. In 1993, Islamic terrorists bombed New York's World Trade Center, killing six and injuring 1,000. And in 1998, hundreds were killed — including 12 Americans — when U.S. embassies in Kenya and Tanzania were bombed by terrorists linked to the al-Qaeda Islamic terrorist organization run by Saudi dissident Osama bin Laden.

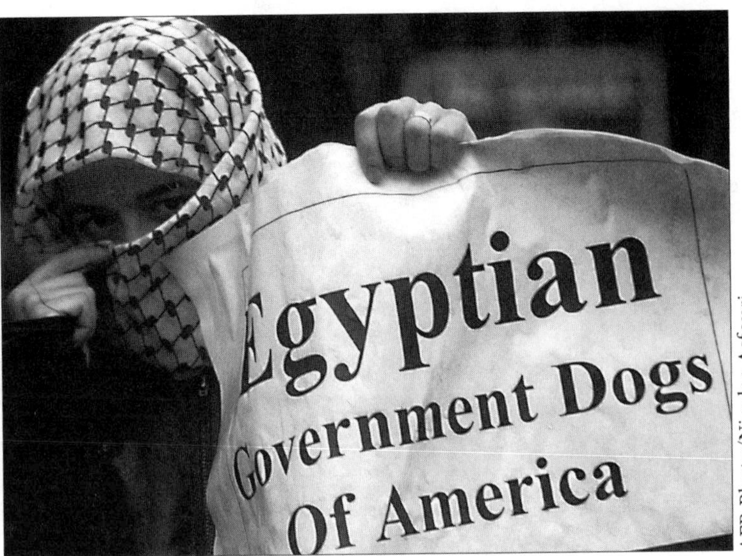

AFP Photo/Nicolas Asfouri

A demonstrator outside No. 10 Downing Street in London, the official residence of British Prime Minister Tony Blair, protests Egypt's arrests, torture and detentions of Islamic activists, scholars and civilians. Egypt's ruling National Democratic Party recently has proposed some democratic reforms, but not competitive presidential elections.

Calls for Reform

In response to the murders of nearly 3,000 people in the Sept. 11 terrorist attacks, many Arab governments helped the United States hunt down the bin Laden followers who had helped put the plan to hijack four airliners into action. [27] Under mounting internal and external pressure, some Arab governments also unveiled new democratization efforts, but widespread reform faltered. Israeli-American ties continued to undermine Arab support for U.S. policies in the Middle East, even though the United States and Britain overthrew the murderously repressive Hussein and tried to establish democracy in Iraq.

The Arab world's initial reaction to the Sept. 11 attacks was mixed. Some news reports showed Arabs celebrating in the Palestinian territories. But heads of Arab governments unanimously condemned the carnage. [28]

American officials pressured Arab governments to crack down on Islamic extremists, and Arab states formerly antagonistic to the U.S. — including Syria, Libya and Sudan — provided intelligence and assistance to the Americans. In Yemen, U.S. forces assassinated a suspected al-Qaeda leader with the government's tacit approval. [29] Security forces in Saudi Arabia — the homeland of 15 of the 19 hijackers — began restricting the activities of Islamic militants. [30]

Some Arab liberals renewed calls for electoral reform, suggesting that political oppression might have been partly responsible for inspiring the hijackers. [31] Even some members of the Arab ruling elite said democratic reforms could curtail extremism. "If people speak more freely and get more involved in the political process, you can really contain them and make them part of the process," said Saudi Prince Walid bin Talal. [32]

A combination of internal dissent and U.S. pressure inspired some Arab democratization efforts after Sept. 11. Reformers gained some ground in Egypt when Mubarak tentatively backed a democratization package put forward by his son, Gamal. Under pressure from the United States, Egypt also freed and later acquitted Egyptian-American democracy advocate Ibrahim, who had been imprisoned by Mubarak's government, some say in an effort to intimidate critics.

On the Arabian Peninsula, some of the monarchies took tentative steps toward electoral governance. Saudi Arabian officials promised municipal elections but did not set a firm date. In Bahrain, parliamentary elections in 2002 established strong support for opposition candidates, particularly Islamists. Qatar approved a constitution in 2003, opening the way for parliamentary elections later this year.

But other Arab states continue to struggle under the grip of authoritarian regimes. Bashar Assad has maintained strict control over Syria since the death of his father in 2000. Pro-democracy groups boycotted the 2002 elections convened by the military in Algeria.

Recent remarks by Jordan's King Abdullah II seem to represent a growing Arab interest in governmental reform. "We are at the beginning of a new stage in terms of democracy and freedom," said Abdullah at a September breakfast with human rights and democracy activists in Washington. "If we are successful, if we can get our act together, we can be an agent other Arabs can use." [33]

Continued on p. 92

At Issue:

Should the United States increase pressure on Arab countries to democratize?

ADRIAN KARATNYCKY
COUNSELOR, SENIOR SCHOLAR, FREEDOM HOUSE

WRITTEN FOR THE CQ RESEARCHER, JANUARY 2004

yes

Over the last 30 years, nearly 50 countries have established democratic governments rooted in the rule of law. Today, countries that provide basic freedoms represent nearly half the world's 192 states. Democracies can be found on all continents, among all races and creeds. They include prosperous and expanding economies as well as poor countries. Yet not one is part of the Arab world.

There are compelling reasons to try to end this Arab exceptionalism and for the United States to press Arab regimes to change by supporting non-violent democratic civic power.

First, it is in the U.S.'s national security interests to do so. It is no coincidence that much global terrorism originates in the least democratic part of the world. The absence of open discourse means ill-informed and misinformed populations fall under the sway of the disinformation of anti-liberal ideas. As a result, extremists prosper. In short, the war on terrorism cannot be won without waging a war of ideas against the extremist ideologies that fuel terror.

Second, Arabs are the main victims of tyrannical regimes and extremist movements, which wreak mayhem on ordinary people and suppress their basic rights. This is why recent polling data show that Arabs strongly favor government elected by and accountable to the people.

Opponents of a U.S. role in promoting democracy in the Arab world suggest that we are hated in that region and our pressure would be counterproductive. Yet, anti-Americanism is rampant because official media in Arab autocracies preach anti-U.S. messages. We are also disliked because over the years, the United States has been indifferent to the massive violations of the basic rights of Arabs.

Others argue that pressing for democracy would only destabilize the Arab world and empower Islamist extremists. Yet the opening of formerly closed societies to genuine freedom of the press, civic activism and electoral competition has served to moderate Islamist political movements — as last year's elections in Turkey showed.

No one says the promotion of democracy in the Arab world will be easy. It will require working with the region's democratic voices to develop a strong latticework of free and diverse media, political parties, civic organizations and think tanks.

But if we fail to exert constructive pressure, we will only help perpetuate the very political environments that produce the fanatics who threaten our well-being today.

JAMES ZOGBY
PRESIDENT, ARAB AMERICAN INSTITUTE

WRITTEN FOR THE CQ RESEARCHER, JANUARY 2004

no

Sadly, given our current foreign policy in the Middle East, I do not believe the United States can, at this time, make a meaningful and positive contribution to democratic transformation in the Arab world.

Positive changes are occurring in many Arab countries, largely in response to the evolving circumstances in those countries and independent of U.S. involvement. In some instances, the United States has served as an impediment to this process: As public opinion has turned against the United States, some Arab governments have become more defensive and resistive to democratic change.

The United States lacks credibility and legitimacy when it claims to support democracy and human rights. While Arabs view U.S. values — democracy, freedom and education — positively, they view U.S. Middle East policy so negatively that overall attitudes toward the United States drop into the single digits.

In other words, Arabs like our values, but do not believe that we have their best interests at heart, especially in Palestine — the central, defining issue of Arab attitudes. We are viewed as biased toward Israel and insensitive to Palestinians' needs and rights. This harms not only our overall standing in the region but also our friends' standings and our ability to function as a partner in the Arab world.

For too long, we have not appreciated Arab history. The current state of affairs for the Arab people is the culmination of more than 100 years of a loss of control. During the past century, some Arab areas were colonized by the West. Others were victims of imperial powers that occupied the region, created states out of whole cloth and implanted regimes.

The neo-conservative "idealism" that sees us establishing democracy in this region is, at best, counterproductive, and, at worst, damaging. Our unilateral occupation of Iraq and our behavior vis-à-vis the Palestinians has us viewed today as a continuation of the Western machinations of the last century. If we fail to understand this, we put ourselves at great risk.

If the United States were to do an about-face on Palestine — for example, by directly and dramatically challenging Israeli expansion on the West Bank — our relationship with the region would improve dramatically. It would significantly contribute to our peacemaking ability, as well as our ability to play a more constructive role as an agent for change in the region.

Continued from p. 90

Some experts say Arab autocrats use Mideast resentment about U.S. support for Israel as a way to divert anger toward the slow rate of reform in their own countries. "The continuing conflict between Israel and Palestine gives [autocratic] regimes an excuse to deflect people's attention away from their own shortcomings," the Carnegie Endowment's Carothers says.

Others say Arab feelings of frustration over the Palestinian issue are more than an excuse. "People see the issue of Palestine as symbolic of their lives," says Zogby, of the Arab American Institute. "It's ever-present, it's very real and it's deeply felt. It's not a game that's being played on them."

The 2003 U.S.-led military campaign to depose Hussein thrust the issue of Arab democracy into the spotlight. While arguing the case for war at the United Nations in September 2002, President Bush said, "Liberty for the Iraqi people is a great moral cause and a great strategic goal." And after a quick and decisive military victory, the U.S. occupying authority established a 25-member Iraqi governing council and organized municipal elections in many Iraqi cities and towns.

But conflict between Iraq's majority-Shiite population and the minority Sunnis has marred efforts to form a popular government. A continued insurgency, thought to be the work of Baathist loyalists, has killed hundreds of American soldiers and further hindered U.S. efforts to democratize Iraq.

Nonetheless, President Bush in his November speech called for more democracy in the Middle East, noting that past U.S. efforts to turn a blind eye to the lack of freedom in the Middle East has made neither America nor the Middle East safer. [34]

But many Arab commentators frostily rejected Bush's calls for reform. "The fundamental problem remains that of Palestine and the scandalous U.S. bias in favor of Israel and against the Arabs, their interests and their aspirations," wrote Lebanese columnist Sahar Baasiri. [35] ■

CURRENT SITUATION

Casting Ballots

Sometime this year, Saudi Arabia will give its people their first opportunity to elect government officials in four decades. But the balloting will be for only half the nation's municipal councils — which have only limited power anyway.

"It's very symbolic," says Georgetown's Seznec. "It doesn't mean anything, especially in terms of democratization per se."

Still, the planned elections — not yet scheduled but likely to be held in the fall — represent a concession by the ruling House of Saud to the need for some form of public participation in a country beset by economic ills and shaken by violent protests, including a deadly terrorist bombing in Riyadh that left 17 people dead in November.

"There is a strong logic to expanding participation for these ruling families," says Michael Herb, an assistant professor of political science at Georgia State University. "It allows them to hear what their people actually have to say, to show a more liberal face to the outside world and to let off steam — all without the risk of actually losing power."

The Saudi elections — the first since similar balloting in the 1950s and '60s — come as more Arab states are allowing their citizens to vote for government officials. As in Saudi Arabia, however, the elections fall far short of full democracy. Women are barred from voting in most countries, political parties often are restricted or prohibited and the media are either government-controlled or tightly regulated.

As President Bush noted in his November speech, some of the strongest stirrings of democracy are in the smallest Arab states: the Persian Gulf emirates of Kuwait, Bahrain, Oman and Qatar. But Bush did not mention the limitations. In Kuwait, for example, voting for the national assembly is limited to less than one-sixth of the population, and political parties are banned. Western-style liberals fared badly in the most recent parliamentary elections in June 2003, winning only three of 50 seats.

Elsewhere, Bahrain became the first of the Gulf states to allow women to vote, but some opposition groups boycotted the 2002 parliamentary elections because of limits on the national assembly's power. As in Kuwait, Islamists led the balloting. Oman is now preparing for universal suffrage parliamentary elections in 2004 following balloting for an advisory council in October 2003. But Herb says that a ban on campaigning makes it impossible to evaluate the results. Qatar is also preparing for legislative elections sometime in 2004, but the constitution approved by voters in 2003 gives the parliament little power, he says.

Outside the Gulf, democracy is less advanced even when voting is allowed. Morocco and Jordan — two countries praised by Bush — held relatively free parliamentary elections in 2002 and 2003, respectively. But King Mohammed VI in Morocco and Jordan's Abdullah both have supreme power, including the right to dissolve parliament and appoint the prime minister and cabinet. Yemen has held free, universal-suffrage elections, but the elected House of Representatives has never exercised its power to initiate legislation.

In Tunisia, balloting for the presidency is highly orchestrated: President Zine el-Abidine Ben Ali claimed 99.4 percent of the vote in 1999 and won approval of a constitutional change in

May 2003 to allow him to seek fourth and fifth five-year terms in 2004 and 2009. Syrian President Assad won 97 percent of the vote in a 2000 referendum after succeeding his father. In Algeria, the electoral process is viewed as highly flawed: All of the rivals to President Abdelaziz Bouteflika withdrew from the 1999 campaign, claiming fraud.

In other countries, elections are simply lacking. Libya's Muammar el-Qaddafi rules by decree, with no signs to date of following his recent moves out of international disgrace with an easing of his domestic powers. The seven ruling families of the United Arab Emirates choose a president and vice president every five years, with no popular elections or political parties. Lebanon holds elections, but Syria effectively controls the government after more than a decade of military occupation.

Democracy also lags in the handful of Arab-minority African countries — all preponderantly Muslim — that belong to the Arab League. Sudan is ravaged by a civil war between the Arab minority in the north and the insurgent black minority in the south, while a secession movement by northern clans racks Somalia. Djibouti — the only Arab League country rated as "free" by Freedom House — held successful multiparty elections in January. A four-party opposition alliance won slightly more than one-third of the vote.

In Egypt, meanwhile, talk of reform is increasing, but the outcome remains uncertain. In a signed editorial, Ibrahim Nafie, editor in chief of the semi-official *Al-Ahram*, praises the ruling National Democratic Party for having taken "big steps" toward reform, but he cautions against moving too fast. Rights advocate Abu Saada notes that the reform package does not call for competitive presidential elections.

In Saudi Arabia as well, experts caution against expecting too much in terms of reform. Former *Washington Post* Mideast correspondent Thomas Lippman, author of a new book on Saudi Arabia, notes that the country's "basic law" — adopted in 1993 — locks in rule by the House of Saud.

"You can talk about the trappings of democracy, various democratic forms, ways in which certain forms of communication with the rulers might be structured to allow more public participation," Lippman says, "but you're not talking about democracy." [36]

AP Photo/Amr Nabil

Egyptian-American human rights activist Saad Eddin Ibrahim, a sociology professor at Cairo's American University, enters Egypt's highest court on Feb. 4, 2003, with his wife. After spending more than a year in jail, he was acquitted of tarnishing Egypt's image with his writings on democracy and human rights.

Building Democracy?

The United States has what seems an unparalleled opportunity to advance democracy in the Arab world in Iraq, where an American administrator heads a U.S.-led military occupation in consultation with an Iraqi advisory council hand-picked by the United States. But forging a stable government — much less a working democracy — is treacherous in a country with longstanding ethnic and religious factionalism and present-day anti-American insurgency.

Bush sees success as important, not only for domestic political reasons but also for the worldwide advance of democracy. "The establishment of a free Iraq at the heart of the Middle East," he said in his November speech, "will be a watershed event in the global democratic revolution."

As 2004 began, however, the administration found itself pressured by the leading cleric of Iraq's majority Shiite Muslims to allow direct elections sooner than envisioned under the U.S. timetable. The United States, citing the difficulties of holding elections, planned instead to hold caucuses around the country to select an interim legislature and executive that would assume responsibility for governing Iraq by June 30. But Grand Ayatollah Ali al-Sistani rejected the plan on Jan. 11, repeating demands he has made since November for direct elections before a U.S. transfer of power.

"The planned transitional assembly cannot represent the Iraqis in an ideal manner," Sistani said after meeting with a delegation of the U.S.-appointed governing council. Sistani described elections as "the ideal mechanism" and insisted balloting could be held in the near future "with an acceptable degree of credibility and transparency." [37]

AFP Photo/Karim Sahib

During voting in Qatar last April 29, Qataris approved the gas-rich monarchy's first written constitution, paving the way for parliamentary elections later this year.

"It's interesting to see Islamic clerics giving the United States lessons in how to conduct democracy," says the Carnegie Endowment's Carothers. "It's funny to see them pushing for early elections and the United States resisting."

Carothers acknowledges that national elections in Iraq would present "huge logistical obstacles," given the lack of security and destruction of Iraqi infrastructure in the invasion. But the dispute is more than procedural. Iraq's 15 million Shiites comprise about 60 percent of the population, but they were politically disadvantaged under Hussein, a Sunni Muslim. The Shiites hope to make political gains with early elections, while the Sunnis and the ethnic Kurds in northern Iraq fear early voting will weaken the influence they currently have with the American-led occupation.

The timing of elections is one of several contentious questions that U.S. Administrator L. Paul Bremer III is grappling with while trying to meet the accelerated timetable for transferring power. One issue — what to do with former members of the ruling Baath Party — appeared in January to be moving toward resolution. The 18-member Governing Council adopted new guidelines that give lower-level party members a better chance to appeal their dismissals or to apply for pensions than under the U.S. "de-Baathification" procedures. American officials were quoted as approving the shift. [38]

The United States appears less content with developments so far on the issue of the Kurds' status in a new Iraq. The Kurds — a non-Arab ethnic group comprising about 17 percent of Iraq's population — were essentially autonomous in Hussein's final 12 years in office following Iraq's defeat in the first Gulf War. They want to maintain their autonomy — or, more ambitiously, gain independence. While the United States supports some form of self-rule, it fears a fragmented Iraq or a weak central government. [39]

Other difficult issues loom in the drafting of the constitution, notably the role of religion. Shiites are widely seen as religiously conservative, the Sunnis and Kurds more liberal. But fears of a religious theocracy appear to have been eased with a formula drawn up by the Governing Council that declares Iraq to be a majority-Muslim community that protects minority rights and in which Islamic law is one — but not the only — source of legislation. [40]

The elections dispute, meanwhile, forced Bremer to return to Washington on Jan. 16 for conferences on how to salvage the administration's timetable. With thousands of Iraqis rallying in the streets demanding prompt elections — the largest protest since the U.S. occupation of Iraq last March — Bremer told reporters that the United States was willing to consider changing the planned method for selecting the interim government.

The administration and the Governing Council also asked the United Nations on Jan. 19 to help broker an agreement with Sistani on transition plans. U.N. Secretary-General Kofi Annan said on Jan. 27 he would send a team to Baghdad to determine whether early elections are feasible. ■

OUTLOOK

Slow Process

Talk of democracy is spreading in the Arab world, but Arab leaders are resisting outside pressure and insisting on definitions and timetables of their own choosing. The result seems all but certain to be slower and less thoroughgoing change than sought by pro-democracy advocates in and outside the Arab world.

Arab ambivalence can be seen in the proceedings of a recent pro-democracy conference, hosted by Yemen and cosponsored by the European Union (EU) and the U.N. Development Program. [41] The January conference in the Yemeni capital of Sanaa drew 600 delegates from 40 countries, including government representatives and democracy activists from most Arab states.

The conference ended with adoption of a declaration embracing the major tenets of so-called Western-style democracy — from elective legislatures and independent judiciaries to fair-trial guarantees and protection of women's rights.

"Democracy is the choice of the modern age for all people of the world and the rescue ship for political regimes," Yemeni President Ali Abdulla Saleh said as he opened the conference.

But Amr Moussa, secretary-general of the Arab League, said democracy should be viewed "as a process, not a decision imposed by others," a point echoed by U.N. Secretary-General Annan. Democracy, Annan told the conference, "cannot be imposed from the outside."

Human rights advocates both in and outside the Arab world discern mounting political pressures for change from the social and economic gaps between Arab countries and the rest of the world. On a variety of socioeconomic measures, Arab states lag behind developing countries in other parts of the world, as well as the United States and other industrialized nations.

Demographics add to the pressure. Population growth rates in all but one of the Arab League states exceed the worldwide average of 1.4 percent per year. Population increases can be "an engine of material development," notes the 2002 Arab human rights report, if other factors are conducive to economic growth — but a "force for immiserization" if not. [42]

Arab leaders say political changes are necessary to respond to the discontent bred by what others more bluntly describe as deteriorating socioeconomic conditions. "There is a great sense in the Arab world about the necessity of having a new social pact," the Arab League's Hitti says. "Democracy is part and parcel of this process."

Still, human rights advocates are generally cautious, at best, in predicting the pace of democratization. "I would be very surprised to see much genuine movement toward democracy in the next five years," says the Carnegie Endowment's Carothers. "The question is whether we can help foster a trend in the next five years. That would be a realistic goal."

Similarly, the Heritage Foundation's Phillips expects little change over the next few years.

Others are somewhat more optimistic. "You've got a little bit of a trend developing," Freedom House's Karatnycky says. He sees prospects for more liberalization in the gulf countries and some larger states, such as Jordan and Morocco. "There's more of a chance for a liberal trend than a retrenchment or some new dark age of anti-liberal ideologies or more repressive regimes," he concludes.

The University of Westminster's El-Affendi also sounds optimistic. "The undemocratic forces are a spent force," he says. "The desire for democracy is very widespread, and the disillusionment with undemocratic governments is at a very high level, and increasing at all times."

El-Affendi says support for democratization from the United States and the European Union is helpful. Others disagree. U.S. pressure, Hitti says, "might fire back." Zogby of the Arab American Institute says American influence has fallen because of increasingly unfavorable public opinion about America due to the invasion of Iraq, the stalemate in the Arab-Israeli peace process and the mistreatment of people of Muslim or Arab backgrounds in the U.S. war on terror. [43]

Apart from government policies, however, El-Affendi says broader global changes — including the Arab peoples' increased exposure to the world beyond — impel democratic advances in the long run.

"The trend is moving in this direction," he says. "It's now very difficult for any ruler in the Muslim world to just hope that he's going to stay in power forever without being responsive to the people. It's just not going to work." ■

Notes

[1] See Saad Eddin Ibrahim, "A Dissident Asks: Can Bush Turn Words Into Action?" *The Washington Post*, Nov. 23, 2003, p. A23. The article and other background can be found on the Web site of the Ibn Khaldun Center: www.democracy-egypt.org.

About the Authors

Associate Editor **Kenneth Jost** graduated from Harvard College and Georgetown University Law Center, where he is an adjunct professor. He is the author of *The Supreme Court Yearbook* and editor of *The Supreme Court from A to Z* (both *CQ Press*). He was a member of *The CQ Researcher* team that won the 2002 American Bar Association Silver Gavel Award.

Benton Ives-Halperin covers House floor votes for Congressional Quarterly's online publication *CQ.com*. He is a former *CQ Researcher* assistant editor and graduated from the University of Virginia with a bachelor's degree in English.

[2] See "Flimsy on Facts," *Al Ahram Weekly*, Nov. 27, 2003 (http://weekly.ahram.org.eg). *Al Ahram Weekly* is an English-language version of the Arabic-language daily *Al Ahram*.
[3] Freedom House, "Freedom in the World 2004" (www.freedomhouse.org).
[4] United Nations Development Programme/Arab Fund for Economic and Social Development, "Arab Human Development Report 2002," p. 2.
[5] For coverage, see David E. Sanger, "Bush Asks Lands in Mideast to Try Democratic Ways," *The New York Times*, Nov. 7, 2003, p. A1; Dana Milbank and Mike Allen, "Bush Urges Commitment to Transform Mideast," *The Washington Post*, Nov. 7, 2003, p. A1.
[6] For background, see David Masci, "Rebuilding Iraq," *The CQ Researcher*, July 25, 2003, pp. 625-648 and David Masci, "Confronting Iraq," *The CQ Researcher*, Oct. 4, 2002, pp. 793-816.
[7] Quoted in Glenn Frankel, "Egypt Muzzles Calls for Democracy," *The Washington Post*, Jan. 6, 2004, p. A1.
[8] United Nations Development Programme, *op. cit.*, p. 8.
[9] *Ibid.*, p. 9.
[10] Country profile in "Freedom in the World 2003," www.freedomhouse.org.
[11] United Nations Development Programme, *op. cit.*, pp. 4-6.
[12] Michael Ross, "Does Oil Hinder Democracy?" *World Politics*, Vol. 53 (April 2001), pp. 336-337.
[13] United Nations Development Programme, *op. cit.*, p. 4.
[14] For background, see David Masci, "Prospects for Middle East Peace," *The CQ Researcher*, Aug. 30, 2002, pp. 673-696, and David Masci, "Israel at 50," *The CQ Researcher*, March 6, 1998, pp. 193-215.
[15] See Glenn Kessler and Robin Wright, "Realities Overtake Arab Democracy Drive," *The Washington Post*, Dec. 3, 2003, p. A22.
[16] See Daniel Brumberg, "Bush Policy or Bush Philosophy," *The Washington Post*, Nov. 16, 2003, p. B3.
[17] Background drawn from William Cleveland, *A History of the Modern Middle East* (2000) and Albert Hourani, *A History of the Arab Peoples* (1992).
[18] Cleveland, *op. cit.*, p. 36.
[19] Bernard Lewis, *The Middle East* (1995), p. 147.
[20] Hourani, *op. cit.*, pp. 315-323.
[21] Lewis, *op. cit.*, p. 355.
[22] Cleveland, *op. cit.*, p. 170.
[23] Cleveland, *op. cit.*, p. 261.
[24] Shibley Telhami, *The Stakes* (2004), p. 161.

FOR MORE INFORMATION

Arab American Institute, 1600 K St. N.W., Suite 601, Washington, DC 20006; (202) 429-9210; www.aaiusa.org.

Arab Information Center/Arab League, 1100 17th St., N.W., Washington, DC 20036; (202) 265-3210; www.arableagueonline.org.

Carnegie Endowment for International Peace, 1779 Massachusetts Ave. N.W., Washington DC 20036-2103; (202) 483-7600; www.ceip.org.

Center for the Study of Islam and Democracy, 1050 Connecticut Ave., N.W., Suite 1000, Washington, DC 20036; (202) 772-2022; www.islam-democracy.org.

Freedom House, 120 Wall St., 26th floor, New York, NY 10005; (212) 514-8040; www.freedomhouse.org.

Heritage Foundation, 214 Massachusetts Ave., N.W., Washington, DC 20002; (202) 546-4400; www.heritage.org.

Human Rights Watch, 350 Fifth Ave. 34th floor, New York, NY 10118-3299; (212) 290-4700; www.hrw.org; Washington office: 1630 Connecticut Ave., N.W., Suite 500, Washington, DC 20009; (202) 612-4321.

National Endowment for Democracy, 1101 15th St., N.W., Suite 700, Washington, DC 20005; (202) 293-9072; www.ned.org.

[25] For background, see Mary H. Cooper, "Foreign Aid After Sept. 11," *The CQ Researcher*, April 26, 2002, pp. 361-392, and Masci, "Prospects for Mideast Peace," *op. cit.*
[26] For background, see Mary H. Cooper, "Oil Diplomacy," *The CQ Researcher*, Jan. 24, 2003, pp. 49-62.
[27] For background, see David Masci and Kenneth Jost, "War on Terrorism," *The CQ Researcher*, Oct. 12, 2001, pp. 817-848.
[28] See Mary H. Cooper, "Hating America," *The CQ Researcher*, Nov. 23 2001, pp. 969-992.
[29] David Johnston and David Sanger, "Fatal Strike in Yemen Was Based on Rules Set Out by Bush," *The New York Times*, Nov. 6, 2002, p. A16.
[30] Douglas Jehl, "Holy War Lured Saudis As Rulers Looked Away," *The New York Times*, Dec. 27, 2001, p. A1.
[31] *Ibid.*
[32] Douglas Jehl, "A Saudi Prince With an Unconventional Idea: Elections," *The New York Times*, Nov. 28, 2001, p. A3.
[33] Jackson Diehl, "Jordan's Democracy Option," *The Washington Post*, Sept. 21, 2003, p. B7.
[34] Sanger, *op. cit.*
[35] Neil MacFarquhar, "Mideast View: Bush Spoke More to U.S. Than to Us," *The New York Times*, Nov. 8, 2003, p. A9.
[36] See Thomas W. Lippman, *Inside the Mirage: America's Fragile Partnership with Saudi Arabia* (2004).
[37] Quoted in Daniel Williams, "Top Shiite Cleric Hardens Call for Early Iraqi Vote," *The Washington Post*, Jan. 12, 2004, p. A12. See also Edward Wong, "Direct Election of Iraq Assembly Pushed by Cleric," *The New York Times*, Jan. 12, 2004, p. A1; Steven R. Weisman, "Bush Team Revising Planning for Iraqi Self-Rule," *The New York Times*, Jan. 13, 2004, p. A1.
[38] See Pamela Constable, "Iraqis Revise Policy on Ex-Baath Members," *The Washington Post*, Jan. 12, 2004, p. A12.
[39] Robin Wright, "Kurds' Wariness Frustrates U.S. Efforts," *The Washington Post*, Jan. 9, 2004, p. A13.
[40] *Ibid.*
[41] Account drawn from John R. Bradley, "Arab Leaders See Democracy Ascendant," *The Washington Times*, Jan. 13, 2004, p. A13. A summary of the conference declaration can be found on the Ibn Khaldun Center's Web site: www.democracy-egypt.org.eg.
[42] United Nations Development Programme, *op. cit.*, pp. 37-38.
[43] For background, see Kenneth Jost, "Civil Liberties Debates," *The CQ Researcher*, Oct. 24, 2003, pp. 893-916.

Bibliography

Selected Sources

Books

Brynen, Rex, Baghat Kornay and Paul Noble, *Political Liberalization and Democratization in the Arab World: Theoretical Perspectives* (Vol. 1), Lynne Rienner, 1996; Brynen, Rex, Baghat Kornay and Paul Noble, *Political Liberalization and Democratization in the Arab World: Comparative Experiences* (Vol. 2), Lynne Rienner, 1998.

Various experts provide an overview of democratization in the region (vol. 1) and the status of democratization in 10 specific countries (vol. 2). Brynen and Noble are McGill University professors; Kornay is now at the American University in Cairo.

Cleveland, William L., *A History of the Modern Middle East* (2d ed.), Westview Press, 2000 (1st edition, 1994).

A professor of Arab political history at Simon Fraser University in Vancouver traces the history of the Middle East, from the rise of Islam through the radical Islamist movements.

Diamond, Larry, Marc F. Plattner and Daniel Brumberg (eds.), *Islam and Democracy in the Middle East*, Johns Hopkins University Press, 2003.

An anthology of *Journal of Democracy* articles by U.S. and Middle Eastern experts examines the status of democratization in the Mideast and the relationship between Islam and democracy.

Esposito, John L., and John O. Voll, *Islam and Democracy*, Oxford University Press, 1996.

The director (Esposito) and assistant director (Voll) of Georgetown University's Center for Muslim-Christian Understanding examine the "heritage and global context" of Islam and democracy, along with the status of democratization in major Islamic countries.

Humphreys, R. Stephen, *Between Memory and Desire: The Middle East in a Troubled Age*, University of California Press, 1999.

A professor of Islamic and Middle Eastern history at the University of California, Santa Barbara, focuses on four basic conditions in the Middle East: economic stagnation, weakness in the international arena, political instability and ideological confusion.

Lewis, Bernard, *What Went Wrong? Western Impact and Middle Eastern Response*, Oxford University Press, 2002 (reissued by Perennial, 2003, with subtitle *The Clash Between Islam and Modernity in the Middle East*).

A distinguished U.S. historian provides a trenchant critique of the Islamic world's failure to modernize. For a comprehensive history of the region, see *The Middle East: A Brief History of the Last 2,000 Years* (Touchstone, 1995).

Magnarella, Paul J. (ed.), *Middle East and North Africa: Governance, Democratization, Human Rights*, Ashgate, 1999.

Experts examine the status of democratization in major Arab countries, Turkey, Israel and the West Bank and Gaza Strip. Magnarella is a professor of anthropology at the University of Florida.

Telhami, Shelby, *The Stakes: America and the Middle East — The Consequences of Power and the Choice for Peace*, Westview Press, 2002.

A professor of government at the University of Maryland and a senior fellow at the Brookings Institution examines public opinion in the Middle East toward the United States and U.S. policy in the Middle East.

Reports and Studies

Ottaway, Marina, *et al.*, "Democratic Mirage in the Middle East," Carnegie Endowment for International Peace, October 2002.

A policy brief forecasts a "long, hard, and slow" path to democratization in the Middle East.

United Nations Development Programme, Arab Fund for Economic and Social Development, "Arab Human Development Report 2002: Creating Opportunities for Future Generations," 2002.

Human development in Arab countries is hampered by "deficits in popular freedoms and in the quality of Arab governance institutions," say the authors. A second report, "Arab Human Development Report 2003: Building a Knowledge Society," focuses on education, communication and technology. Available at www.un.org/publications or www.miftah.org.

Articles

Anderson, Lisa, "Arab Democracy: Dismal Prospects," *World Policy Journal*, Vol. 18, No. 3 (fall 2001), p. 53.

The dean of Columbia University's School of International and Public Affairs critically examines prospects for Arab democracy. For a more favorable assessment by the Arab League's representative to the U.S., see Hussein A. Hassouna, "Arab Democracy: The Hope," *ibid.*, p. 47.

The Next Step:

Additional Articles from Current Periodicals

Country Reports

"Two Countries," *The Economist*, Sept. 13, 2003.
Both Egypt and Morocco have elections and parliaments, but they are beset by social problems, and the governments of both countries face serious challenges from Islamist parties.

Glasser, Susan, "Democracy in Kuwait is Promise Unfulfilled," *The Washington Post*, Feb. 27, 2003, p. A1.
Despite promises by the ruling emir after the Persian Gulf War, political participation and democracy in Kuwait remain limited.

Miller, T. Christian, "Many Disillusioned by Jordan's 'Democracy'," *Los Angeles Times*, July 22, 2003, p. A6.
Often described as a bright spot for democracy in the Middle East, Jordan's political system favors the monarchy over the elected branches of government.

Stack, Megan, "Libya's Slow Trek Out of the Shadows," *Los Angeles Times*, Dec. 12, 2003, p. A1.
After decades of rule by Col. Muammar el-Qaddafi — "The Leader" — Libya may be preparing to reform its economy and shed its status as an international pariah.

Wright, Lawrence, "The Kingdom of Silence," *The New Yorker*, Jan. 5, 2004, p. 48.
An American journalist working at a Saudi Arabian newspaper gets a glimpse of life in the Saudi kingdom, including religious police, censorship and corruption.

Democracy and Islam

Freedberg, Sydney, "The War Within Islam," *National Journal*, May 10, 2003.
Experts say that Islam is not anti-democratic, but that there is a war going on among the world's Muslims on how best to respond to the modern and non-Muslim world.

Lampman, Jane, "Easing into Islamic Democracy," *The Christian Science Monitor*, May 29, 2003, p. 12.
Arabs will choose Islam if asked to choose between Islam and democracy, but Muslim democracy advocates say they do not face that choice.

Remnick, David, "The Experiment," *The New Yorker*, Nov. 18, 2002, p. 50.
Turkey is sometimes viewed as the Muslim nation where secular ideals and democracy have best taken root and could serve as a model for others.

Salopek, Paul, "Imams Exercise Newfound Clout," *Chicago Tribune*, April 23, 2003, p. C1.
In the chaotic aftermath of the fall of Saddam Hussein's secular government, clerics are taking on an increasingly active role in Iraqi politics.

Economic Development

Blustein, Paul, "Unrest a Chief Product of Arab Economies," *The Washington Post*, Jan. 26, 2002, p. A1.
Discontent is rising among Arab citizens who lack prospects for good jobs or upward mobility due to inefficient state-managed economies.

Chen, Edwin, and Maura Reynolds, "Bush Seeks U.S.-Mideast Trade Zone to Bring Peace, Prosperity to Region," *Los Angeles Times*, May 10, 2003, p. A1.
President Bush hopes to foster democracy, stability and peace by stimulating Middle Eastern economies with a free-trade zone.

Murphy, Kim, "Saudis' Quicksand of Poverty," *Los Angeles Times*, May 16, 2003, p. A1.
Once a land of fabled riches, Saudi Arabia increasingly faces economic problems that may fuel political and religious extremism.

Reforms

Brumberg, Daniel, "Liberalization Versus Democracy: Understanding Arab Political Reform," *Carnegie Endowment Working Paper No. 37*, May 2003.
Many Arab governments are "liberal" autocracies; understanding this complexity is a key to engendering democratic transformation within these societies.

Glasser, Susan, "Qatar Reshapes Its Schools, Putting English Over Islam," *The Washington Post*, Feb. 2, 2003, p. A20.
Educational reforms in Qatar and other Arab states are welcomed by political reformers, but Islamists see them as an unwelcome American intrusion.

Haass, Richard, "Toward Greater Democracy in the Muslim World," *The Washington Quarterly* (journal of the Center for Strategic and International Studies), summer 2003, p. 137.
Only the Arabs themselves can choose democracy, but the United States must do what it can to help rather than accepting the status quo, as in the past.

Power, Carla, "Will Tiny Emirates Pave the Way?" *Newsweek*, Nov. 10, 2003, p. 31.
Tiny Qatar and other Persian Gulf states may be the vanguard of democracy in the Arab world as they relax political restrictions.

Repression

Frankel, Glenn, "Egypt Muzzles Calls for Democracy," *The Washington Post*, Jan. 6, 2004, p. A1.
President Bush proclaims support for democracy in the Middle East, but critics say that U.S. aid to Egypt props up an unpopular, dictatorial government.

Shadid, Anthony, "Restrictive Arab Nations Feel Pressure From Within," *The Washington Post*, Feb. 27, 2003, p. A20.
Popular demands for increased economic opportunities and more political openness are challenging governments that have never tolerated dissent.

Taheri, Amir, "The Crackup of Arab Tyrannies?" *The Weekly Standard*, July 7-14, 2003.
The Arab states created after World War I face a crisis, and the events in Iraq could set off a chain reaction that shakes the entire Middle East.

Rights of Women

Dickey, Christopher, and Rod Nordland, "The Fire That Won't Die Out," *Newsweek*, July 22, 2002, p. 34.
A lethal fire at a girls' school in Saudi Arabia may lead to reforms because the religious police interfered with rescue operations.

Parks, Scott, "Women Are Poised to Prosper in Iraq," *Chicago Tribune*, May 7, 2003, p. C7.
Under Saddam Hussein, Iraqi women comprised 20 percent of the work force and held important positions.

Perry, Tony, "In Liberated Kuwait, Some Still Lack Right to Vote," *Los Angeles Times*, March 9, 2003, p. A19.
The heroic deeds of Kuwaiti women during the Iraqi occupation are celebrated, but women's right to vote was defeated in the National Assembly.

U.S. Support for Democracy

Brinkley, Joel, "The Struggle for Iraq: Building Democracy," *The New York Times*, Nov. 30, 2003, p. A24.
American forces are establishing local councils to give Iraqis experience with democracy, but the process is often frustrating for all.

Kessler, Glenn, and Robin Wright, "Realities Overtake Arab Democracy Drive," *The Washington Post*, Dec. 3, 2003, p. A22.
Despite the president's pro-democracy speeches, U.S. pressure on Arab allies is limited because the war on terror remains an overriding priority.

Reynolds, Maura, "Bush Says U.S. Must Spread Democracy," *Los Angeles Times*, Nov. 7, 2003, p. A1.
President Bush's new plan to spread democracy throughout the Middle East reverses a decades-old policy of supporting authoritarian regimes for strategic reasons.

Slavin, Barbara, "Tunisia Needs More Reform, Powell Says," *USA Today*, Dec. 3, 2003, p. 17A.
In an uncommon rebuke to an Arab ally, Secretary of State Colin L. Powell called for political reforms in Tunisia.

Slevin, Peter, and Glenn Kessler, "U.S. to Seek Mideast Reforms," *The Washington Post*, Aug. 21, 2002, p. A1.
As President Bush urges political, educational and economic reforms in the Middle East, the U.S. remains wary of jeopardizing strategic relationships.

CITING *THE CQ RESEARCHER*

Sample formats for citing these reports in a bibliography include the ones listed below. Preferred styles and formats vary, so please check with your instructor or professor.

MLA STYLE

Jost, Kenneth. "Rethinking the Death Penalty." The CQ Researcher 16 Nov. 2001: 945-68.

APA STYLE

Jost, K. (2001, November 16). Rethinking the death penalty. *The CQ Researcher, 11*, 945-968.

CHICAGO STYLE

Jost, Kenneth. "Rethinking the Death Penalty." *CQ Researcher*, November 16, 2001, 945-968.

Back Issues

The CQ Researcher *offers in-depth coverage of many key areas.*
Back issues are $10. Quantity discounts available.
Call (866) 427-7737 to order back issues.

Or call for a free CQ Researcher Web trial!
Online access provides:

- *Searchable archives dating back to 1991.*
- *Wider access through IP authentication.*
- *PDF files for downloading and printing.*
- *Availability 48 hours before print version.*

CHILDREN/YOUTH
Preventing Teen Drug Use, March 2002
Sexual Abuse and the Clergy, May 2002
Movie Ratings, March 2003

CRIMINAL JUSTICE
Cyber-Crime, April 2002
Corporate Crime, October 2002
Serial Killers, October 2003

EDUCATION
Charter Schools, December 2002
Combating Plagiarism, September 2003
Home Schooling Debate, January 2003
Black Colleges, December 2003

ENVIRONMENT
Bush and the Environment, October 2002
Crisis in the Plains, May 2003
NASA's Future, May 2003
Water Shortages, August 2003
Air Pollution Conflict, November 2003

HEALTH CARE AND MEDICINE
Medicare Reform, August 2003
Women's Health, November 2003
Homeopathy Debate, December 2003

LEGAL ISSUES
Abortion Debates, March 2003
Race in America, July 2003
Torture, April 2003
Homeland Security, September 2003
Civil Liberties Debates, October 2003

MODERN CULTURE
Gay Marriage, September 2003
Combating Plagiarism, September 2003
Latinos' Future, October 2003
Future of the Music Industry, Nov. 2003
Hazing, January 2004

POLITICS/GOVERNMENT
Presidential Power, November 2002
Future of NATO, February 2003
Trouble in South America, March 2003
North Korean Crisis, April 2003
Rebuilding Iraq, July 2003
Aiding Africa, August 2003
State Budget Crises, October 2003

TRANSPORTATION
Auto Safety, October 2001
Future of the Airline Industry, June 2002
Future of Amtrak, October 2002
SUV Debate, May 2003

Future Topics

- ***Mental Illness Medication Debate***
- ***Youth Suicide***
- ***Globalization of Jobs***

CQ Researcher

Published by CQ Press, a division of Congressional Quarterly Inc.

thecqresearcher.com

Mental Illness Medication Debate

Should more patients have access to new drugs?

Armed with new findings on the links between brain chemistry and mental illness, drug companies produced a new generation of drugs for schizophrenia, major depression and other severe psychiatric conditions. Most experts say up to 70 percent of the nation's 17.5 million adult sufferers could recover with access to the new drugs and strong social supports. Yet fewer than half receive any treatment, and the situation is eroding as cash-strapped states try to limit public subsidies for the higher-priced new drugs. Some say the new drugs often aren't worth the added costs, but others contend they are cheaper than the alternatives with older drugs — distressing risks and side-effects and more mentally ill people locked up in prison or homeless.

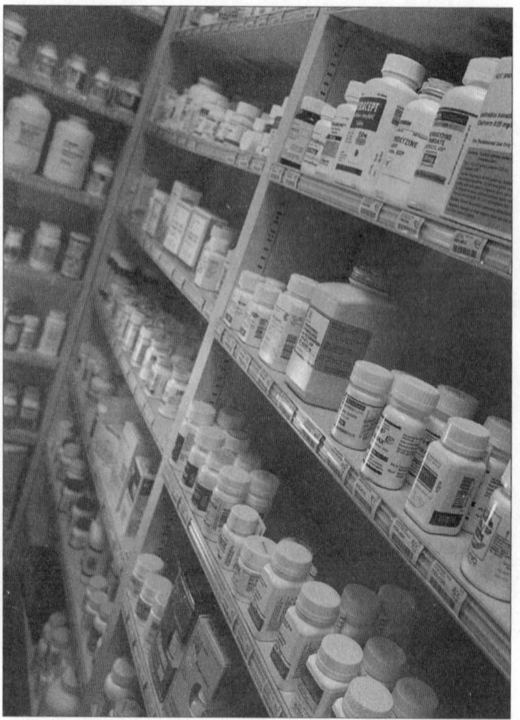

New medications are available for schizophrenia and other disabling mental illnesses, but cash-starved states are limiting public subsidies for the new, higher-priced drugs.

INSIDE THIS ISSUE

The CQ Researcher • Feb. 6, 2004 • www.thecqresearcher.com
Volume 14, Number 5 • Pages 101-124

RECIPIENT OF SOCIETY OF PROFESSIONAL JOURNALISTS AWARD FOR EXCELLENCE ◆ AMERICAN BAR ASSOCIATION SILVER GAVEL AWARD

THE ISSUES

BACKGROUND

CURRENT SITUATION

OUTLOOK

SIDEBARS AND GRAPHICS

FOR FURTHER RESEARCH

Cover: High-priced new psychosis medications have been developed for schizophrenia, major depression and other disabling mental illnesses. (Corbis Images)

Feb. 6, 2004
Volume 14, No. 5

MANAGING EDITOR: Thomas J. Colin

ASSISTANT MANAGING EDITOR: Kathy Koch

ASSOCIATE EDITOR: Kenneth Jost

STAFF WRITERS: Mary H. Cooper, David Masci, William Triplett

CONTRIBUTING WRITERS: Rachel S. Cox, Sarah Glazer, David Hosansky, Patrick Marshall, Jane Tanner

DESIGN/PRODUCTION EDITOR: Olu B. Davis

ASSISTANT EDITOR: Kenneth Lukas

A Division of
Congressional Quarterly Inc.

SENIOR VICE PRESIDENT/GENERAL MANAGER: John A. Jenkins

DIRECTOR, LIBRARY PUBLISHING: Kathryn C. Suárez

DIRECTOR, EDITORIAL OPERATIONS: Ann Davies

CIRCULATION MANAGER: Nina Tristani

CONGRESSIONAL QUARTERLY INC.

CHAIRMAN: Andrew Barnes

VICE CHAIRMAN: Andrew P. Corty

PRESIDENT AND PUBLISHER: Robert W. Merry

The CQ Researcher (ISSN 1056-2036) is printed on acid-free paper. Published weekly, except Jan. 2, April 9, July 2, July 9, Aug. 6, Aug. 13, Nov. 26 and Dec. 31, by CQ Press, a division of Congressional Quarterly Inc. Annual subscription rates for libraries, businesses and government start at $625. Single issues are available for $10. Quantity discounts apply to orders over 10. Additional rates furnished upon request. Periodicals postage paid at Washington, D.C., and additional mailing offices. POSTMASTER: Send address changes to *The CQ Researcher*, 1255 22nd St., N.W., Suite 400, Washington, D.C. 20037.

Mental Illness Medication Debate

By Jane Tanner

The Issues

When Stacey Ferguson was 15, she became convinced her father wanted to kill her. Psychiatrists diagnosed schizophrenia — the most debilitating mental illness, marked by delusions and hallucinations.

Stacey spent the next seven months in a psychiatric hospital about 80 miles from her home in Charlotte, N.C. It was the first of 28 hospitalizations over the next 17 years.

Although doctors tried virtually every available medication for psychosis, none helped much, and most had negative side effects. The first was Thorazine, a powerful drug introduced in 1952 to calm schizophrenic patients. "I felt like I was going to pass out if I moved," she recalls. "I just sat still."

To make matters worse, most of the medications Stacey used carried serious risks, such as possible permanent disfigurement from uncontrollable movements often caused by the drugs, like grimacing or lip smacking.

Courtesy Edward Davis

After more than a decade in halfway houses and group homes, schizophrenia-sufferer Stacey Ferguson moved into her own apartment in Charlotte, N.C., thanks to a new anti-psychosis medication. Advocates for the mentally ill say higher-priced new drugs could help up to 70 percent of the 17.5 million adult Americans with serious mental illness, but they say most lack access to such medications and support. Critics say the new drugs aren't worth the extra cost.

In 1991, when she was 32, Ferguson went on Clozaril, a psychosis drug that had been approved in the U.S. just a year earlier. It changed her life.

"I didn't feel like I was mentally ill," she recalls. After nearly two decades in halfway houses and group homes, Ferguson was able to move into her own apartment, where she still lives. Indeed, Clozaril enables her to work part time consistently. And she has been hospitalized only once, briefly.

Since the late 1980s, growing knowledge about chemical and electrical brain activities has led to a new generation of medications for the most disabling mental illnesses — mainly schizophrenia, bipolar disorder and major depression — which affect 17.5 million adults in the United States. [1]

Clozaril was the first of a handful of new anti-psychotic medications. It carried the risk of causing a dangerous blood disorder, but several alternative, safer medications hit the market within a few years. *

In 1988, pharmaceutical companies began introducing a new class of antidepressants, starting with Prozac, which have all but replaced older depression medications. Today's drugs for psychosis and depression, like their predecessors, do not offer cures. But they are considered as good as or better than the older drugs at managing symptoms and improving functioning. [2] They also produce fewer side effects, though British researchers and the U.S. Food and Drug Administration have raised concerns recently about possible links between antidepressants and youth suicide.

Experts say the new drugs, in combination with talk therapy and other supports, make recovery — living fully despite the disorders — possible for many people. (*See definitions, p. 114.*)

The United Nations' World Health Organization (WHO) reports that eight out of 10 schizophrenics could live without relapses once they have had a full year of optimal, effective drug treatment behind them, and that half could recover fully with additional counseling and support. In addition, WHO estimates that nearly two-thirds of depression sufferers could recover with the proper combination of antidepressants and psychotherapy. [3]

"Medication gets them to the door, and then a good psychosocial program can get them through the door," says Steve Shon, medical director of the Texas Department of Mental Health and Mental Retardation.

Yet, some advocates for the severely mentally ill say most people with the disorders lack access to medications and support. Indeed, according to the federal Substance Abuse and Mental Health Services Administration (SAMHSA), fewer than half the

---

* Clozaril has been available in Europe since 1975, but it was withheld in the United States until 1989, when the government approved its use for cases resistant to other medications.

Mental Illness Is Leading Cause of Disability

Mental illness was by far the largest cause of disability in the United States, Canada and Western Europe in 2000. Mental illness accounts for nearly a quarter of the disabilities — almost twice the amount caused by alcohol and drug disorders.

Causes of Disability for All Ages, 2000*
(U.S., Canada, Western Europe)

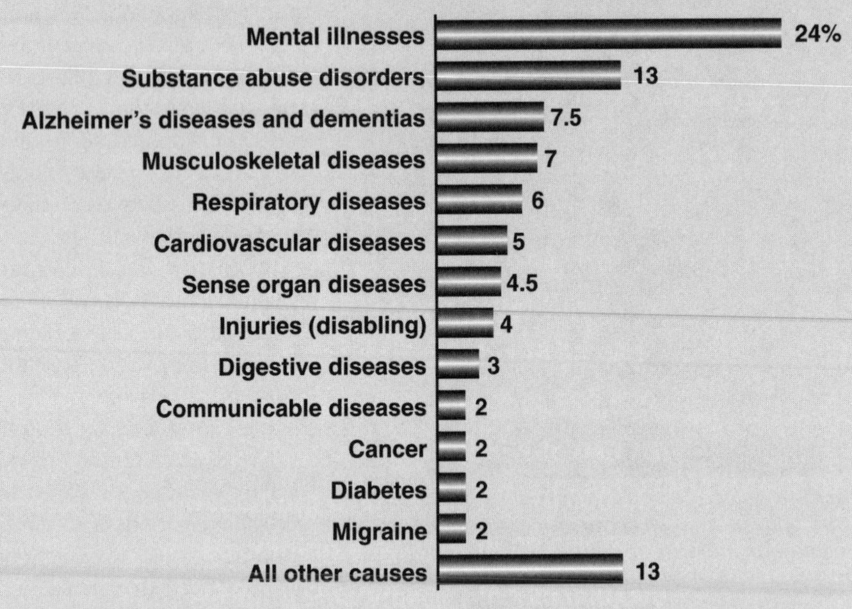

* *Based on the years of healthy life lost with less than full health.*

Source: "The World Health Report, 2001 — Mental Health: New Understanding, New Hope," World Health Organization, 2001

Americans with mental illness get any treatment at all, and fewer still receive proper medication regimes. [4]

President Bush noted the critical gap in a 2002 speech when he announced creation of a federal commission to assess psychiatric care in the United States. "Remarkable treatments exist," he said, "yet too many people remain untreated." [5]

The New Freedom Commission on Mental Health declared U.S. mental health care "in shambles" and "incapable of efficiently delivering and financing effective treatments such as medications, psychotherapies and other services." [6]

The commission, which issued its final report last summer, blamed a fragmented system in which money often flows to outdated, unsuccessful programs. "State-of-the-art treatments, based on decades of research, are not being transferred from research to community settings," a commission report said. [7]

The panel cites several problems, including the difficulty patients and their families have in navigating the patchwork mental-health system and the lack of federal and state resources to treat the most serious illnesses. Moreover, rushed doctors often fail to match patients with optimal medications, and there often isn't outside individual support to help patients stick to drug regimes.

Nevertheless, many debates about medications focus on cost because drug advances carry high price tags. For instance, the new anti-psychosis drug Zyprexa can cost $9,000 a year, compared to $2,100 for the older standby, Haldol, notes a recent U.S. Department of Veterans Affairs (VA) comparison in the *Journal of the American Medical Association* (*JAMA*). [8]

The uproar over high-priced prescriptions, of course, isn't unique to psychiatric conditions. [9] However, experts say the costly, newer psychosis and depression medications contribute most to the double-digit increases in prescription costs. As a result, since 1997 spending on so-called psychotropic drugs has outpaced health and drug spending. [10]

Because it pays the lion's share of the tab for treatment of chronic mental illnesses, Medicaid * is bearing the brunt of the price-escalation pressure. Medicaid spending on anti-psychotic medications alone jumped from a little over $318 million in 1993 to $1.3 billion five years later, while spending on antidepressants rose from $288 million to $980 million during the same period, according to a University of Minnesota analysis of Medicaid prescriptions. [11]

The meteoric rise in spending is linked not only to wider use of the pricier new medications but also to the growing proportion of Medicaid recipients suffering from severe mental illnesses.

Many of them are discouraged from getting work because even meager wages could disqualify them from the program, jeopardizing their public subsidies for the high-cost medications that allow them to function. [12]

---

* Medicaid is the joint federal-state health-insurance program for poor and disabled Americans. Medicare is the public health plan for older Americans.

In fact, many parents are relinquishing custody of their children with severe, often dangerous, behavioral disorders to child welfare or juvenile justice programs — just to get them access to subsidized mental-health treatment — a situation the U.S. General Accounting Office says has reached "crisis proportions." [13]

As the ranks of the mentally ill on Medicaid keep growing, millions of other Americans with severe mental-health disorders are caught in a Catch-22: They are not poor enough to qualify for Medicaid but neither can they afford the expensive medications they need to function. Private health insurers play a minor role in treating severe mental illness, because most people with the chronic disorders have trouble holding down jobs. If they manage to work, it is usually only in part-time or other jobs without medical benefits. Stigma still limits work opportunities for those with mental illness, although the 1990 Americans with Disabilities Act (ADA) provides some legal protection. [14]

The National Mental Health Association (NMHA) says Congress failed to improve access to psychotropic medications when it passed a new prescription-drug benefit for Medicare. [15] Out-of-pocket costs are too high under the plan, and it forces some seniors to give up coverage from former employers, the advocacy group says. Medicare administrators are also expected to restrict mental-health drugs tightly under the new plan. [16]

Even with the limitations, however, the National Alliance for the Mentally Ill (NAMI) says the new benefits "appear to be a major improvement over the status quo." [17]

But due to the skyrocketing medication costs, cash-starved state governments have begun limiting access to psychiatric drugs in public-health programs, claiming they are cutting waste and saving money. [18] But advocates for the mentally ill say patients are suffering as a result.

Costliest Psychosis Drug Dominates Market

The psychosis drug Zyprexa can cost up to $9,000 per year per patient, compared with $2,100 for the older standby Haldol. Some medical experts contend that newer anti-psychotic drugs are not worth their higher cost.

U.S. market share of leading anti-psychotics, 2002

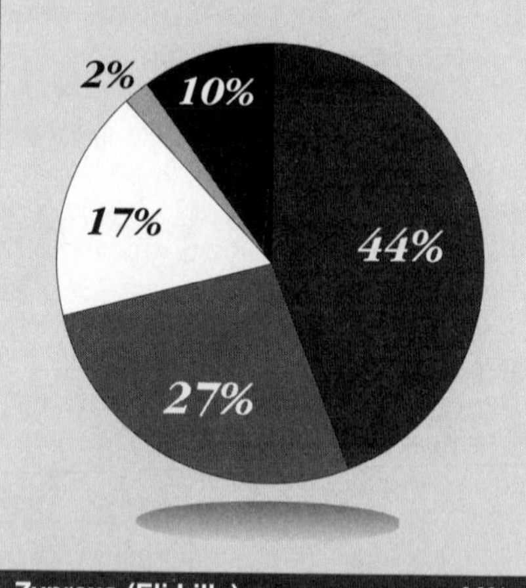

Zyprexa (Eli Lilly)	44%
Risperdal (Johnson & Johnson)	27%
Seroquel (AstraZeneca)	17%
Clozaril (Novartis)	2%
Others, including Haldol	10%

Source: NDC Health

Medicaid is a prime target for cuts since it accounts for 20.8 percent of total state expenditures. [19] Prescriptions are the largest Medicaid expense, with mental-health drugs costing the most. [20]

"Lawmakers are focused on psychotropics, since they are a high-cost category," Cathy Bernasek, a Medicaid specialist at Health Strategies Consultancy, in Washington, D.C., notes. And even though some states have exempted treatments for the most severe psychiatric disorders, as budget woes continue, protections are beginning to erode.

Some advocates for psychiatric patients say they need access to all psychotropic drugs because individual responses to medications vary greatly. Penny pinching on mental-health prescriptions, they say, can end up costing more later, because patients' conditions deteriorate if successful drug regimes are altered or abandoned, often causing them to end up homeless, in jail or repeatedly hospitalized.

But others say careful controls promote patient welfare by eliminating spending on high-priced drugs that don't deliver significant benefits, and then reapplying the savings to expanded treatment. (*See "At Issue," p. 117.*)

"The issue of access isn't just a matter of states coming up with money," says Stephen W. Schondelmeyer, a professor of pharmaceutical economics at the University of Minnesota. "It's also drug companies limiting access by overcharging and by charging more than they charge an HMO for the same drug or more than they charge a hospital for the same drug or more than they charge Canada for the same drug."

In fact, a recent federal study concluded states pay more than federal agencies for the same drugs. [21]

Anne Griffin, spokeswoman for Eli Lilly and Co., which makes Zyprexa and Prozac, says the drugs return significant medical benefits for the costs. "While new medications may cost more than older treatments," Griffin says, "they result in significant savings as patients require less acute treatments and fewer hospitalizations and show signs of recovery."

University of Texas pharmacy Professor Lynn Crismon says drug companies deserve credit for progress, but share responsibility for poor access. "[They] are no more demons than they are angels," Crismon says. "Without their research engines, it is unlikely we would have major advances — and certainly not as rapidly."

As the debate over newer psychiatric drugs continues, these are some of the key questions being asked:

Are Children Being Overmedicated?

Doctors are prescribing psychiatric drugs to children and teenagers at nearly the same rate as adults, even though little is known about how these powerful medications affect young brains and bodies, according to a recent study.

"Are we prescribing the right psychotropic medications to the right children using the right treatment plan?" asked Michael S. Jellinek, head of child psychiatry at Massachusetts General Hospital. [1]

A rise in prescribing mental health drugs to children was reported by University of Maryland researcher Julie Magno Zito. Zito and a group of colleagues looked at nearly 900,000 young people under the age of 20 with both private insurance and public health care from 1986 to 1996, with a spot check again in 2000. [2]

They found two- to threefold increases in mental health drug prescriptions for young people. Drug treatment for anxiety and depression jumped for younger children and early adolescents from the mid-1980s through the mid-1990s, the study showed. Yet, Jellinek said research on clinical treatment of those disorders for those age groups was "largely non-existent." [3]

Zito pointed to a number of factors fueling the trend, including cost-savings by insurers who choose medications instead of other more costly therapies, persuasive marketing by pharmaceutical companies and higher demand by parents and doctors who might be inclined to pick a quick medication solution to childhood problems. [4]

A spokeswoman for the American Association of Health Plans said the study didn't evaluate whether the children received good medical care. "The research doesn't say, 'There is a greater use of drugs and that's having a deleterious effect on children,' " said Susan Pisano. [5] "It just says there is a greater use of drugs."

A backlash started last summer when British health regulators warned doctors there to stop prescribing Paxil, an antidepressant drug, after studies linked it to suicidal thoughts or attempts in children and teenagers. [6]

The U.S. Food and Drug Administration (FDA) has considered imposing restrictions and scheduled hearings on antidepressants and children at the beginning of February. [7]

The FDA, physicians' groups and children's advocates chalked up a victory in December in a long-fought battle for more studies on medications and children. Congress passed a law that requires drug companies to include children in clinical research of proposed new medications. [8] The effects are unknown because the overwhelming majority of studies for new drugs are done on adults.

"No law is perfect, but this goes a long way," says John C. Ring, a member of the American Academy of Pediatrics' drug committee.

The law includes a sunset provision, meaning it expires in four years unless lawmakers extend it or re-enact it. The new federal law mandating studies with children came after a similar FDA rule was struck down in October 2002 by a U.S. district judge after drugmakers sued, arguing the FDA did not have the authority to issue such mandates.

In January 2003, the FDA approved the antidepressant Prozac for children with major depression and obsessive-compulsive disorders. [9] Anne Griffin, a spokeswoman for Prozac's maker, Eli Lilly, says a new drug for attention-deficit disorder has been studied in

Do spending cuts on psychiatric medication raise state costs in other areas?

Most states have instituted cost-savings measures and controls on Medicaid-subsidized prescriptions, using a combination of approaches. Some states press drug manufacturers for discounts or rebates, others cap dosages or strictly limit the number of prescriptions per patient. Other states steer patients to lower-priced generic drugs, forcing those who insist on the more expensive, brand-name drugs to pay higher out-of-pocket costs.

In addition, in the past two years, many states have established formularies, or lists of drugs approved for state reimbursements, and require doctors to apply for special permission before prescribing drugs off the lists. Such controls have been common in private health coverage, and the bureaucratic pre-approval process discourages many doctors from picking drugs outside the formularies.

By using the formularies and other techniques, states say they are saving up to $89 million a year on Medicaid expenses on a broad range of drugs, according to a recent study by the Inspector General of the U.S. Department of Health and Human Services. [22]

Yet, as psychotropic drugs are increasingly restricted, the American Psychiatric Association (APA) has called for across-the-board exemptions for mental-health drugs. They say lawmakers are merely calculating the costs of pills while failing to consider new expenses likely to crop up for hospitalizations, emergency room visits or other health treatments needed when people with chronic psychiatric conditions undergo medication disruptions or changes.

"A patient who does not receive proper medication may become homeless or end up in jail, putting a greater burden on the community's overall social system," the APA said. [23]

William M. Glazer, a psychiatrist and Harvard Medical School professor, says savings in other areas "offset" drug costs. "If you are going to pay $5,000 a year for a drug, and I can prevent children and adults and is approved for both.[10]

Meanwhile, a key goal of the broad research project was to improve basic diagnosis of mental disorders in children.

Today, diagnosis in adults can be difficult and even more problematic in children and adolescents who display a wide range of developmental behaviors that can be misinterpreted, says Steve Shon, medical director of the Texas Department of Mental Health.

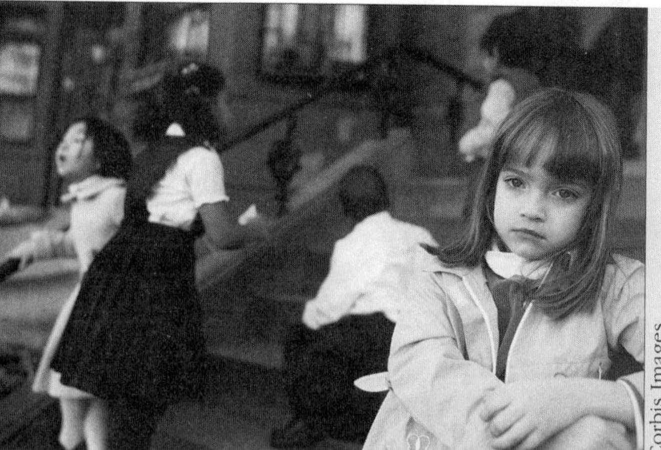

Drug treatment for anxiety and depression jumped for younger children and early adolescents, but little research on clinical treatments was done.

"It's not as easy to nail down a diagnosis," Shon says. "Is it a reaction to something at home or are they developing bipolar? Are they imaginative or are they hallucinating?"

While psychiatrists and other experts in the field are concerned about fine-tuning diagnostic tools, family-practice doctors and pediatricians are more likely to prescribe psychiatric medications to children than mental health specialists, according to a study by the Child and Health Development Institute.[11]

Last spring, the top health official in Massachusetts said doctors were "haphazard" in prescribing psychotropic drugs for children; the state is now developing guidelines.[12]

Bills have been introduced in a handful of states to restrict physicians and teachers from advising parents about mental health drugs for children. In California, a bill would have made it a criminal offense for doctors to prescribe to kids without following strict guidelines.[13]

---

[1] "FDA Statement Regarding the Anti-Depressant Paxil for Pediatric Population," FDA Talk Paper, U.S. Food and Drug Administration, June 19, 2003.

[2] "Achieving the Promise: Transforming Mental Health Care in America," New Freedom Commission on Mental Health, U.S. Department of Health and Human Services, July 2003.

[3] Pediatric Research Equity Act of 2003 Public Law No: 108-155.

[4] Michael Jellinek, "Mirror, Mirror on the Wall," *Archives of Pediatric and Adolescent Medicine*, January 2003, p. 14.

[5] Julie Magno Zito, *et al.*, "Psychotropic Practice Patterns for Youth: A 10-Year Perspective," *Archives of Pediatric and Adolescent Medicine*, January 2003, pp. 17-25.

[6] Jellinek, *op. cit.*

[7] Quoted in Shankar Vedantam, "More Kids Receiving Psychiatric Drugs," *The Washington Post*, Jan. 14, 2003, p. A1.

[8] *Ibid.*

[9] "FDA Approves Prozac for Pediatric Use to Treat Depression and OCD," FDA Talk Paper, U.S. Food and Drug Administration, Jan. 3, 2003.

[10] For more background see Kathy Koch, "Rethinking Ritalin," *The CQ Researcher*, Oct. 22, 1999, pp. 905-928.

[11] "State Echoes U.S. Trend; Psychiatric Drugs Prescribed to Almost 5 % of Children With State-Subsidized Health Insurance, Study Shows," *The Hartford Courant*, June 4, 2001.

[12] Ellen Barry, "Guidelines Pushed on Child Medication," *The Boston Globe*, March 9, 2003.

[13] 2002 California Senate Bill 119.

---

a 10-day hospitalization that costs $600 to $800 a day, I've paid for the drug," he explains. So far, there are no definitive studies making the link between recent cutbacks in psychiatric drugs and higher costs elsewhere.

Lack of compliance with drug regimes is a well-documented problem for psychiatric patients, NAMI warns, and studies show that when higher co-payments are added to brand-name drugs, some people simply quit taking their medications rather than pay more or switch to generics.

This summer Michigan eased earlier Medicaid restrictions on some psychiatric drugs, conceding to these advocates' arguments.[24]

Boston psychiatrist George S. Sigel, who says many of his patients were hospitalized following mandated medication changes, is striking back. Shortly after Massachusetts began restricting psychiatric drugs in its public health plan last summer, Sigel sued Gov. Mitt Romney and state health officials in an effort to repeal the rules.[25] Sigel, clinical director at a South Boston mental health clinic and a Tufts University clinical professor, says the restrictions violate a state constitutional mandate for quality public health care and interfere with his ability to apply his best medical judgments.

"Our patients are fragile," Sigel says. "Yet they are being made to feel they are driving the state to the poorhouse."

State officials in Massachusetts and elsewhere insist the policies and drug lists are based on clinical evidence and protect the quality of health care. Often they are crafted by panels of psychiatrists, pharmacists and even members of patients' advocacy groups, they point out.

Moreover, notes Donna Folkemer, a health analyst with the National Conference of State Legislatures, preferred drug lists often do not single out the cheapest drugs. The formularies comply with Medicaid's dual responsibilities to provide both health care and stewardship of public dollars, she says. "If you have more people using lower-cost drugs that are just as effective,

Suicide Is Leading Cause of Violent Death

Suicide accounts for almost half the violent deaths worldwide. The vast majority of people who commit suicide have a mental illness, often undiagnosed or untreated. In the United States, suicide claims about 30,000 people a year. Overall, suicide was the 11th leading cause of death among Americans in 2000.

Causes of Violent Death Worldwide

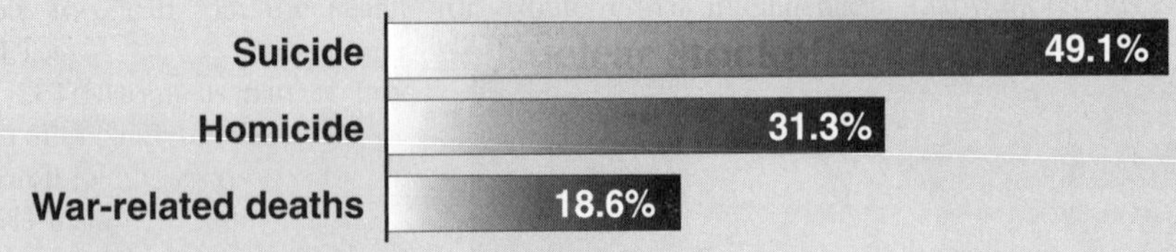

** Totals do not add to 100 due to rounding.*

Source: New Freedom Commission on Mental Health, "Achieving the Promise: Transforming Mental Health Care in America," July 2003

then why would the state want to change from that?" she asks, adding that states are speeding up approval processes for drugs outside preferred-medication lists.

In addition, say some psychiatrists, like Harvard Medical School Professor James Sabin, tighter controls can improve patient welfare, because money saved by limiting payouts for high-cost medications that don't return greater treatment benefits can free up additional money to treat more people. "Paradoxically, in order to promote the widest possible access to needed medications, we must embrace limits," Sabin said. [26]

Massachusetts, along with a few other states, says it is cutting wasteful spending by restricting unnecessary overprescribing or multiple prescriptions in the same drug class — can be the result of heavy marketing by drugmakers. [27]

Glazer says the practice started off in the spirit of good prescribing-pattern reviews, but he fears it could become Draconian if the state is too heavy-handed in controlling doctors' prescription decisions.

Are the newer psychiatric drugs worth the high prices?

As states cut Medicaid funding for prescriptions and restrict medications to a list of preferred drugs, head-to-head comparisons between new psychiatric medications and older, cheaper drugs are taking center stage. Government budget officials and mental health program administrators are asking whether the costs and apparent incremental improvements in patients' conditions are worth the added expense.

The financial stakes are high, running into the billions of dollars. But so are the stakes for individuals, which are measured in personal distress and the debilitating effects of their mental illnesses.

Experts disagree most vociferously over the newer anti-psychotic drugs. The difficult and weighty trade-offs being made between cheaper and more expensive drugs can have dramatic consequences in the treatment of military veterans with psychosis, says Robert Rosenheck, director of the VA's Northeast Program Evaluation Center and the lead investigator in a recent VA study comparing the cost-effectiveness of the new Zyprexa and the older Haldol. [28]

Rosenheck points out that the VA medical program spends $200 million a year on the new antipsychotic drug, but only $25 million on psychological and social rehabilitation for this group of patients — including a well-regarded program that places mentally ill veterans in jobs with strong support to help them succeed.

The jobs program costs about $1,100 per patient per year, while Zyprexa can cost $3,000-$9,000 a year per patient (about $8 a day, compared to six cents a day for Haldol).

"So, for each patient on Zyprexa, you could put between three to nine patients into jobs," Rosenheck points out. "There are a lot of resources at stake, and there's no clear calculus to tell you what to do," adds the Yale Medical School professor of psychiatry and public health.

Rosenheck and his colleagues tracked 309 military veterans for a year concluded that Zyprexa didn't demonstrate sufficient advantages over Haldol to warrant the significantly higher cost.

Their finding, released last November, flies in the face of most other studies that show Zyprexa as a clear favorite. A recent National Institute of Mental Health (NIMH)-funded comparison, for example, found the drugs comparable in many regards but found better patient compliance on Zyprexa. "Retention in treatment is important in this patient population, given their risk of relapse," said the University of North Carolina researchers. [29]

Plus, say many of Rosenheck's peers, the reduced involuntary facial and limb movements and lower risk of permanent disfigurement with the newer drugs warrant the use of Zyprexa, even at the higher cost.

But the VA study results also mirror strong doubts about Lilly's claims that Zyprexa was superior to Haldol, expressed in August 1996 by Paul Leber, director of the FDA's Division of Neuropharmacological Products.

In an internal FDA memo obtained by Rosenheck and his colleagues through a Freedom of Information Act request, Leber wrote: "Who would not want to know that a particular drug, all things considered, gives a 'bigger bang for the buck?' "[30] Nonetheless, Leber went on to explain that Lilly had not made its case. Despite Leber's doubts, the agency approved Zyprexa later that year.[31]

Despite the difficulty of drug comparisons, researchers at the University of North Carolina are currently pitting all the newer antipsychotic medications (except Clozaril) against each other in a clinical study funded by NIMH. In 1999, NIMH awarded the university $42 million to conduct studies comparing the effectiveness of new drugs for schizophrenia and Alzheimer's disease.

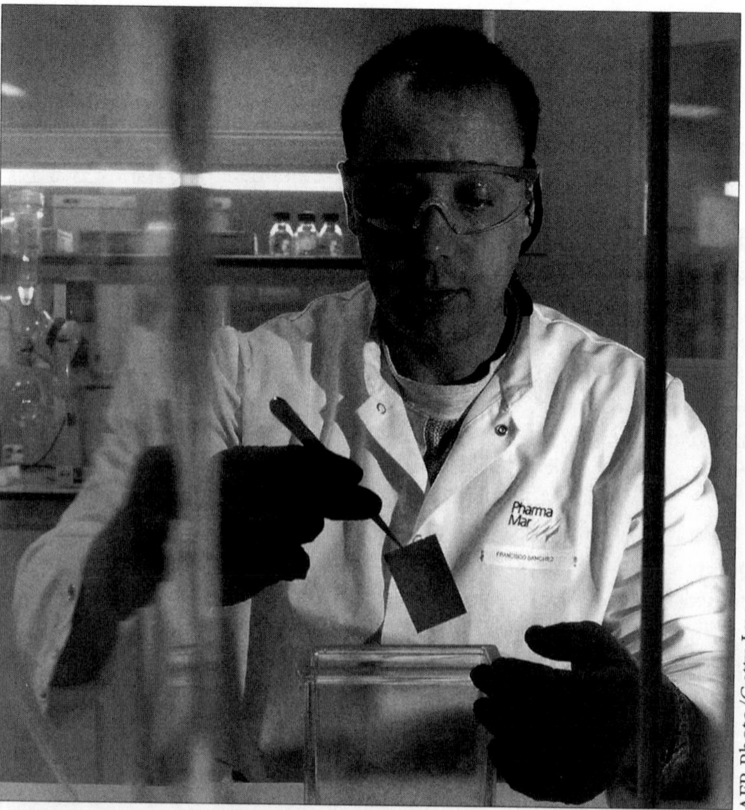

AFP Photo/Getty Images

Drug companies say they must raise prices on new drugs to recoup research and development costs, but critics say marketing and overcharging drive prices up. The New Freedom Commission on Mental Health last year declared U.S. mental health care "in shambles."

For Lilly, government decisions on drug choices are especially paramount. Zyprexa sales reached $4.1 billion during the fiscal year that ended Sept. 30, a large part of the company's overall revenues.[32] In addition, Medicaid and other public health programs account for 70 percent of Zyprexa sales, according to company spokeswoman Griffin.

For APA, NAMI and NMHA, the issue is clear-cut: Psychiatric patients require open access to the entire arsenal of drugs. Those with severe psychiatric disorders respond dramatically differently to medications — more so than non-psychiatric patients — so doctors and patients must try various medications and doses to find the right match-up, they say.

"It's one thing if you've got 50 antibiotics that all work pretty much the same, so you go with the cheapest one," Glazer says. "It's another thing with schizophrenia, where you've got six medications that work differently in different patients."

Glazer says brand-name drugs and generic counterparts are not interchangeable for psychiatric disorders, noting that tests to meet FDA generic-equivalency requirements usually are done on healthy people in short trials. Longer observations of people with severe psychiatric disorders who were switched to generic Clozaril revealed deterioration, he says. "If the generic manufacturer had conducted a one-year study in real patients, it might have noticed the problem," he says.[33]

But Sabin says the generic versions of the pricey brand-name antidepressants, known as SSRIs (selective serotonin reuptake inhibitors), are a clinically sound substitute.

"If I ignore evidence about cost-effectiveness and prescribe the most-expensive SSRIs for all my patients, should I be allowed to indulge my preference if that money could otherwise be used for the care of other patients?" Sabin wrote in a defense of formularies.[34]

Pfizer Inc., maker of Zoloft, a popular brand-name SSRI, pulled out of Michigan's public pharmacy program when the state designated two other drugs as "preferred." A company spokesman said Michigan is "willing to seek cost savings even if that would limit patients' access to the best possible medicines."[35] ■

BACKGROUND

Emerging Science

In the early 20th century, mental illnesses were widely dismissed as caused by personal or character failures, not physical disorders. Advocates for psychiatric patients were a part of a minority that demanded a more scientific approach to treating mental illness. Meanwhile, scientists and physicians around the world had already begun tackling these baffling conditions: Some searched for the origins, while others pursued remedies.

Antonio Egas Moniz, a Portuguese neurologist with ambitions for a Nobel Prize, reported in 1936 his successful surgical treatments for people with anxiety, depression and schizophrenia. Moniz was convinced that unpleasant pathological thoughts were caught in never-ending loops in nerve fibers of the brain. By surgically severing nerves in the front of the brain — a procedure later called a frontal lobotomy — he believed the thought cycles were stopped.

At the time, diagnoses of mental illnesses were on the rise, but no established causes or treatments existed. "Doctors were sometimes willing to try anything to help their most desperately ill patients," according to a historical account. [36]

Indeed, other practitioners started performing frontal lobotomies on patients with schizophrenia, with 5,000 such surgeries in 1949, the same year Moniz won a Nobel Prize in physiology and medicine for his work on the brain. Meanwhile, his procedure was later discredited.

Shortly after Moniz started his treatments, German psychiatrist Franz Kallman became one of the first to theorize a hereditary component to schizophrenia. A recent Émigré to New York, Kallman pioneered the study of twins in his search for genetic links to diseases.

The same year, Italian neuropathologist and psychiatrist Ugo Cerletti started using electric shocks to induce epileptic convulsions in schizophrenics. In part, Cerletti was following up on an earlier theory that schizophrenia and epilepsy produced opposite chemical effects on the brain. Cerletti figured convulsions might alter the brain chemistry of schizophrenics to provide relief. In the end, induced convulsions were most effective with manic-depressive psychosis.

Drug Remedies

Clearly, momentum was building for a grander-scale scientific approach to mental disorders. In 1946, Congress passed the National Mental Health Act, which poured money into research and also training of psychiatrists and mental health workers. Three years later, the creation of the National Institute of Mental Health further advanced research efforts.

Meanwhile, Australian physician John Cade found that manic excitement could be settled with lithium carbonate, a salt. However, because of concern over deaths caused by its overuse by heart patients, lithium was shelved in the United States until the early 1960s.

A turning point in the wider use of medicine for mental illness came in 1952, when French psychiatrist Pierre Deniker began pioneering the use of a surgical anesthesia to calm patients with chronic schizophrenia. The drug, Thorazine (chlorpromazine), became an established pharmacological treatment for psychosis.

In 1958, Haldol joined Thorazine as a widely used drug in the treatment of schizophrenia. Both medications stopped the buildup of dopamine, a chemical messenger in the brain that scientists link to the hallmark symptoms of psychosis — hallucinations, paranoia, delusions and agitation.

Although the drugs relieve hallucinations and other thought problems, they have serious side effects and risks, including lethargy, restlessness, stiffness, difficulty talking and tardive dyskineasia, or involuntary movements of the tongue, facial grimacing and uncontrolled movements of fingers, hands, arms and legs.

Some of the involuntary movements don't dissipate after patients stop taking the drugs, and some of the side effects increase social isolation, because they embarrass patients or cause them to be ridiculed. Because many patients refuse to stay on the drugs, companion drugs are added to help control the side effects. Still, patient non-compliance with the medicines is a common problem.

In 1948, American scientists isolated serotonin, a chemical that shuttles messages between brain cells and the nervous system and is tied to depression. Its role in antidepressant medications began a little more than a decade later.

Deinstitutionalization

While medication breakthroughs improved treatment of major mental illnesses, the infrastructure for administering them and providing support and rehabilitation was being dismantled. The ability to use drugs to control some of the symptoms both prompted and certainly accelerated a push to move people from crowded state hospitals back into communities.

The shift began under President Dwight D. Eisenhower, but it got a big push when President John F. Kennedy signed the Community Mental Health Centers Construction Act in 1963. It set up a funding stream for local programs, with a goal of cutting state mental hospital populations by half.

At the bill-signing ceremony on Oct. 31, Kennedy acknowledged the treatment advances: "It was said, in an earlier age, that the mind of a man is a far country which can neither be approached nor explored. But, today, under present conditions of scientific achievement, it will be possible for a nation as rich in human and material resources as ours to make the remote reaches of the mind accessible." [37]

His next comments addressed the de-institutionalization that would continue for decades: "The mentally ill and the mentally retarded need no

Continued on p. 112

Chronology

1930s-1940s

Scientists recognize physical basis of mental disorders, develop early treatments.

1936
Portuguese neurologist Antonio Egas Moniz reports lobotomies alleviate depression, schizophrenia.

1938
German psychiatrist Franz Kallman theorizes schizophrenia is hereditary. . . . Italian psychiatrist Ugo Cerletti uses electric shocks to treat for schizophrenics.

1946
National Mental Health Act funds psychiatric education and research.

1948
American scientists isolate serotonin, a brain chemical involved in depression, memory and sleep.

1949
Australian physician John Cade reports that lithium treats manic excitement. . . . National Institute of Mental Health (NIMH) is created.

1950s-1960s

Drug treatments become standardized; deinstitutionalization of people with mental illness begins.

1952
French psychiatrist Pierre Deniker uses Thorazine to calm schizophrenics; widespread use eliminates electroshock therapy and lobotomies.

1958
Researchers synthesize Haldol, which, like Thorazine, prevents hallucinations but causes serious side effects.

1963
Congress passes Community Mental Health Centers Construction Act.

1965
Congress creates Medicare and Medicaid insurance programs.

1970s-1990s

New psychiatric drugs are developed; mental health infrastructure deteriorates further.

1970
Food and Drug Administration (FDA) approves lithium to treat mania; four years later, lithium is approved for bipolar illness; suicides and inpatient spending drops dramatically.

1978
Federal commission blames deinstitutionalization for producing neglect and poverty among the mentally ill.

1981
President Reagan repeals community mental health laws, reducing funding for mental health treatment.

1987
Prozac becomes first antidepressant routinely prescribed by family doctors.

1996
Mental Health Parity Act requires equal annual and lifetime coverage limits for mental and medical conditions. Six years later, General Accounting Office finds mental health coverage has not improved. . . . Zyprexa enters market.

1999
First surgeon general's report on mental illness.

2000-Present

States control public spending on prescriptions, question use of high-cost psychiatric drugs.

2001
Florida sets spending controls drugs, demands price discounts and restricts reimbursements but exempts drugs for chronic mental illness; drugmakers sue.

2002
On Jan. 14 Michigan begins prescription controls, including for psychiatric drugs. . . . Drug companies sue Michigan on June 28, arguing its restrictions violate federal health law. . . . U.S. appeals court on Sept. 6 denies pharmaceutical company appeal to gut Florida's prescription program.

2003
Federal district court on March 28 rejects drugmakers' claims in Michigan case; manufacturers appeal on April 15. . . . British health regulators on June 10 warn against prescribing antidepressant Paxil to youths after studies link the drug to suicidal thoughts; FDA warns of prescribing Paxil for children. . . . Michigan eases restrictions on some psychiatric drugs on June 20; Michigan Supreme Court on June 27 denies drugmakers' appeals. . . . On Dec. 3 Congress requires drug companies to research effects on children of proposed medications. A similar FDA requirement was struck down in 2002 after drugmakers argued FDA lacked the authority to impose such a rule.

2004
FDA plans hearings on Feb. 2 on antidepressants and possible links to youth suicide. . . . Psychiatric hospital beds total 40,000 in U.S., down from 550,000 in 1955.

Prison Inmates Often Receive Inadequate Care

As the number of state psychiatric hospital beds fell over the last five decades, jails and prisons began to fill up with people with severe psychiatric disorders.

The two are directly linked, mental health experts say: The lack of promised community supports meant many people moved out of one institution, and when they failed to cope on their own, into another.

"There are hundreds of thousands of people with serious mental illness in other settings not tailored to meet their needs, in nursing homes, jails and homeless shelters," said a federal mental health commission report. [1]

The commission reported that 7 percent of the jail and prison populations suffer from a serious mental illness. The proportion with less serious conditions is higher. [2] The number of mentally ill teens in custody is 106,000, it said.

Human Rights Watch released a 223-page report in October documenting conditions in prisons around the country, where it said some 70,000 inmates are psychotic on any given day. [3]

"All too often, seriously ill prisoners receive little or no meaningful treatment," the report said. "They are neglected, accused of malingering, treated as disciplinary problems."

Many people land in city jails charged with petty offenses, but they might not get out for days or longer, says Bruce Melosh, an adult case-management administrator in the public mental health system in Charlotte, N.C. In many cases, they can't make bail, and then the emotional stress of jail creates disciplinary problems, which can extend their stay.

"It could be a few weeks even for something like loitering," Melosh says.

Charlotte is among cities with psychiatric support in its jail, but it's not foolproof. A nurse stationed in the jail screens prisoners when they are first arrested. If she finds out they are on a drug regimen, she will make sure medication treatments continue. A full-time liaison from community mental health services is stationed in the jail to offer support. But it's a big system, Melosh says, and sometimes people won't report that they are on medications.

"If they don't get flagged for whatever reason, they could [deteriorate] in jail," he says. "There's room for more training and resources and coordination with jails."

In a criminal justice landscape largely grim for people with serious mental illness, advocates have succeeded in making improvements. "Our research reveals significant advances in mental health care services in some prison systems," said the Human Rights Watch report.

Some programs established in communities around the country help improve encounters on the street with police, or divert people to special mental health courts that offer treatment and supervision instead of incarceration, or improve treatment in jails and prisons or provide support for inmates when they are released.

Corbis Images

Jail and prison inmates with serious mental illnesses often receive little or no meaningful treatment, according to Human Rights Watch. Seven percent of American inmates suffer from serious mental illness.

Last October, the Senate Judiciary Committee unanimously passed a bill to offer states and cities $100 million in grants to improve access to mental health treatment for non-violent adults and juveniles in jails and prisons and to bolster other programs. A companion House bill to the Senate's Mentally Ill Offender Treatment and Crime Reduction Act of 2003 was sent on Dec. 10 to the House Subcommittee on Crime, Terrorism and Homeland Security.

Phoenix started a program in 2001 to offer 40-hour voluntary training for officers to help reduce violent scuffles between police and people with mental illnesses.

"These days, all of our officers have to be part-time psychiatrists," said Det. Tony Morales. [4]

1 Interim Report of the President's New Freedom Commission on Mental Health, Oct. 29, 2002.

2 New Freedom Commission on Mental Health, U.S. Department of Health and Human Services, "Achieving the Promise: Transforming Mental Health Care in America," July 2003, p. 32.

3 "Ill Equipped: U.S. Prisoners and Offenders with Mental Illnesses," Human Rights Watch, Oct. 22, 2003.

4 Quoted in Tim Vanderpool, "To deal with mentally ill, cops act as 'social workers,' " *The Christian Science Monitor*, April 8, 2003.

Continued from p. 110

longer be alien to our affections or beyond the help of our communities."

Kennedy's goal of reducing state mental hospital populations by half has been far exceeded: only 40,000 hospital beds exist today for the mentally ill, compared with some 550,000 in 1955. [38]

But communities did not embrace the psychiatric patients who were thrust into their neighborhoods, and most of the money saved by shuttering state hospitals was not put back into community programs. "Jails and prisons have become the new institutions for many with severe mental disorders, with many others left to fend for themselves as homeless street people," Darrel A. Regier, director of research at the American Psychiatric Association, told the federal mental health commission. [39]

Sigel, the Boston psychiatrist, says that when he entered practice in 1971, he and his colleagues were enthusiastic about the new medications and the chance to mainstream people with long-standing mental illnesses into communities. Instead, Sigel now laments the loss of supports — including partially independent housing and work programs — that his patients enjoyed in well-run state hospitals.

States continued to shutter hospitals without enough community support to replace inpatient treatment. In 1980, President Jimmy Carter signed the Mental Health Systems Act, which boosted funding for local treatment programs. However, the following year under the new administration of Ronald Reagan, the one-year-old law was repealed.

Congress passed the Omnibus Budget Reconciliation Act of 1981, which restructured the nation's mental health system by shifting away from direct federal funding to a more flexible program of community block grants that states could apply to mental health treatment if they so chose. Under the new system, funding for community mental health in 1982 was 30 percent lower than the year before. [40]

In the end, medications helped people move out of the hospitals, but drugs alone were not enough, Sigel says. "These medications were, in fact, good enough to allow people to survive in the community," he says. "But no one took the time to go beyond survival and consider quality of life in the community."

AFP Photo

In 1963 President John F. Kennedy signed the Community Mental Health Centers Construction Act., which aimed to cut state mental hospital populations by half. "The mentally ill and the mentally retarded need no longer be alien to our affections or beyond the help of our communities," Kennedy said.

Ad Hoc System

Two years after Kennedy's speech, Medicare and Medicaid were created. Over the years, states shifted psychiatric care under the umbrella of Medicaid instead of creating adequate independent community mental health programs to replace hospitals, as planned. Now, Medicaid has become the nation's largest purchaser of mental health care. [41] Critics say states moved mental health care into Medicaid simply because the federal government picks up half the tab in a matching contribution, and pays up to 75 percent in poorer states. [42]

"Essentially Medicaid has become the dumping ground for mental health patients, and more debilitated HIV patients," the University of Minnesota's Schondelmeyer says. "As a society we've said, 'Let's just dump them all in there and let the states — through the Medicaid program — figure out how to pay for it.'"

With Medicaid serving as the nation's ad hoc mental health system, millions outside the program do not get treatment. "Medicaid doesn't cover people with serious mental illnesses who are homeless or earning a living just above the poverty line but don't have health insurance," said Chris Koyanagi, policy director at the Bazelon Center for Mental Health Law, in Washington. [43] "Without a Medicaid card, these people often can't get access to mental health services."

Nearly two-thirds of the states have created drug-assistance plans to help pay for medications for those too poor to buy drugs but not poor enough for Medicaid. But many of those plans are on hold, now that state budget woes have mounted.

"The current patchwork of state programs is extremely fragile," Bruce Stuart, head of the University of Maryland's Center on Drug Therapy and Aging, said. [44]

People with the most serious mental disorders have higher unemployment rates than most other disabilities groups. Only one in three holds down a job, and many work only part time. [45] Among those who return to full-time jobs, only eight out of 100 have mental-health coverage, according to a recent study. [46]

Although many want to work, they are the largest cohort — 35 percent — of those receiving federal income-assistance checks through the Social Security program for the disabled, called Supplemental Security Income (SSI). [47]

Key Definitions

Severe Mental Illness — *A diagnosable mental, behavioral or emotional disorder of a duration that impairs functioning and substantially interferes with or limits major life activities such as basic self-care — eating, bathing, dressing — household upkeep, managing money and functioning in social, family and work settings.*

Recovery — *The process through which people are able to live, work, learn and participate fully in their communities. For some individuals, recovery means an ability to live fully despite a disability. For others, recovery is reduction or complete remission of symptoms.*

Sources: Diagnostic and Statistical Manual of Mental Disorders, *4th ed.; Public Health Services Act; Federal New Freedom Commission on Mental Health*

"Paradoxically they find that returning to work makes them even poorer, primarily because employment results in losing Medicaid coverage, which is vital in covering the cost of medications and other treatments," the president's commission said. [48]

Monthly expenses for medications vary by individual but can average from $600 to $800, says Patricia Stephens, a mental-health program supervisor in Charlotte, N.C. "Some people are actually afraid to work because they know they won't be able to afford their meds," she says.

Making matters worse, treatment costs have skyrocketed in the last decade because a new line-up of psychiatric medicines largely swept out therapies based on older drugs.

Tricyclic antidepressants, which affect the brain-chemical messengers norepinephrine and serotonin, were the primary treatment for major depression between the 1960s and the 1980s. But in 1987, the new, more expensive SSRI antidepressants, starting with Prozac, quickly edged out the older, cheaper treatments.

In 1989, a new generation of drugs to treat schizophrenia hit the U.S. market, and a handful of new drugs to treat depression were released in the 1990s.

New medications are pricey, in part, because companies who discover and produce them set high prices in the first years the drug is sold to recoup costs for research and development before cheaper copycat drugs are released.

U.S. patent law protects a pharmaceutical company's exclusive rights to sell an original medicine for 20 years. But drugmakers say the window before generics hit the market in reality is only 11 or 12 years, because patent life expires before drugs make it through FDA approvals. [49]

Meanwhile, critics say excessive drug marketing and overcharging drive prices up, and that some companies put out pricey new drugs under patent protection that are merely close copies of existing drugs. ■

CURRENT SITUATION

Escalating Prices

Both individuals and states have trouble keeping up with escalating prescription drug prices.

In 2002, 25 states spent more money for Medicaid services than they had budgeted, and 28 expected to fall short when 2003 figures were tallied, according to the National Association of State Budget Officers. [50] The federal government stepped in with a one-time infusion of extra cash for state Medicaid programs — a total of $10 billion doled out last year and this year. [51]

The Kaiser Commission on Medicaid and the Uninsured confirms that a key culprit in the Medicaid budget woes has been spending on pharmaceuticals. Between 1990 and 2000, Medicaid prescription costs rose fourfold — from $5.1 billion to $20.9 billion, according to the federal Center for Medicare and Medicaid Services. [52]

Moreover, public- and private-sector spending on psychiatric drugs is rising faster than spending on other prescriptions. Starting in 1997, spending on psychotropic medications began to outpace growth in spending on medications as a whole and health care overall, and that trend has continued. [53]

States, of course, feel the pinch because Medicaid is the biggest single purchaser of mental-health drugs. In 2001, Medicaid picked up the tab for 52 percent of all psychiatric drugs and almost 67 percent for anti-psychotic medications. [54]

As state officials consider how to bring down overall Medicaid pharmacy bills, many look to Florida, which in 2001 started requiring a 10 percent rebate from pharmaceutical companies to keep their medications on a state list of preferred drugs. Florida's Medicaid program will automatically pay for drugs on the list but will require doctors to apply for permission to prescribe medications not included. Many times, they won't bother because of the time and paperwork required.

So far, Florida has weathered court challenges by drugmakers, and mental health advocates were relieved that their lobbying efforts succeeded in keeping drugs for severe mental illnesses out of the scheme requiring prior approval.

In early 2002, Michigan began requiring drugmakers to match the lowest available price among peer drugs in each class if they wanted their medications on the state formulary. Mental-health drugs got the same treatment, so NAMI and NMHA pushed lawmakers to exempt psychotropic drugs.

Soon, similar battles cropped up across the country, and many continue to erupt. The mental health groups say medications for behavioral brain disorders need special dispensation, because the drugs affect individuals so differently. Patients may need medications from across the full menu of drugs, they argue.

A key battleground is the new generation of psychosis drugs, which can cost $5,000 or more a year.

State policies on psychiatric medications vary and are still subject to swings in either direction. "There isn't a standard way to treat mental health," Bernasek, of the Health Strategies Consultancy, says. The trend is leaning toward tighter controls, she says, but there are exceptions.

Last June, Michigan eased earlier restrictions over some antidepressants and newer antipsychotic drugs. State officials acceded to advocacy groups' warnings that cutting off drugs for some patients would result in a backlash of higher heath-care costs if patients' conditions deteriorate.

"We recognize the delicate balance of mental health treatment," said Janet Olszewski, director of the Michigan Department of Community Health. [55] "Making more of these critical drugs available without the need for prior-authorization helps to avoid possible setbacks in care due to changes in drug treatment therapy."

Meanwhile, a recent HHS review concluded that states brought the crisis on themselves, in part because they negotiate poorly with drug manufacturers and end up paying as much as 29 percent more for psychotropic drugs than key federal agencies. In fact, the HHS inspector general who issued the report has warned federal officials for years that states are paying too much for drugs in many categories. [56]

For their part, the states say the drug manufacturers do not provide them with enough information on pricing to negotiate better. "[It] is a dysfunctional market in which information on price and relative effectiveness either is not available or is obscured from purchasers, prescribers and consumers," wrote the Reforming States Group, an alliance that includes officials from 40 states. [57]

Parents Surrender

A lack of access to mental health treatment is leading thousands of parents to take desperate measures: surrendering custody of their children with severe psychiatric disorders to child-welfare agencies and juvenile detention solely to get treatment.

Carol Malka, an office manager in Flemington, N.J., reached that point about a year ago after her 14-year-old son Robert trapped her and her two other sons in the family car and then smashed the windows and punched at them. [58]

Malka's health insurance didn't cover the intensive inpatient treatment doctors recommended for her son, who was diagnosed with bipolar disorder. So she relinquished custody to the New Jersey child-welfare system, which paid for hospitalization and treatment.

"I don't think he should be ripped out of his family because I can't pay for treatment," Malka said. [59]

A federal study reported that 12,700 young people with mental illnesses and severe behavior disorders have been turned over to state custody for treatment, about 9,000 into juvenile detention and the rest in foster care. [60]

But the federal mental health commission said the number grossly underestimates the crisis because the study did not include figures from 32 states, including the five largest.

"Loving and responsible parents who have exhausted their savings and health insurance face the wrenching decision of surrendering their parental rights and tearing apart their families," the federal commission said. [61]

In October, senators and representatives from both parties in Congress introduced legislation designed to help stem the breakup of families over mental health care. The Keeping Families Together Act would provide grant money for states to increase mental health care for children — starting with $4.5 million this year, $6.5 million next year and $11 million each year for the following three years.

"The bill is a down payment on building a better mental health care system," said Darcy Gruttadaro, head of NAMI's child and adolescent efforts. [62]

The bill is in subcommittees in both the House and Senate.

Misdiagnosis

Yet even when people are getting new medications, they often are not getting the full benefits of the drugs, says Shon, of the Texas Department of Mental Health and Mental Retardation.

Physicians often fail to prescribe the best drug choices or doses for each patient, he says, and as a consequence, treatments don't work well. "A lot of prescribing is not really following what the science tells us needs to be done; therefore it's not really effective," Shon says.

Sometimes it's the right medication but the wrong dose. A study in the late 1990s comparing the prescriptions of hundreds of patient charts in Ohio and Georgia with the latest guidelines, found only 29 percent of the patients were on the right dose, Shon says.

There are plenty of errors in diagnosis, too, which throw off the medication match-up, he says. "You could be treating somebody for schizophrenia, but if they are really bipolar you could be using the best treatments in the world and not get good results," he says.

Shon and his colleagues tested the accuracy of diagnoses by conducting rigorous re-evaluations of hundreds of patients at a Texas clinic. The diagnoses from the new evaluations were compared to the one in the patients' charts, and half the time they didn't match up. Based on their findings, most of the physicians treating the patients decided to adopt the newer diagnosis and found better results when they adjusted the treatments, Shon says.

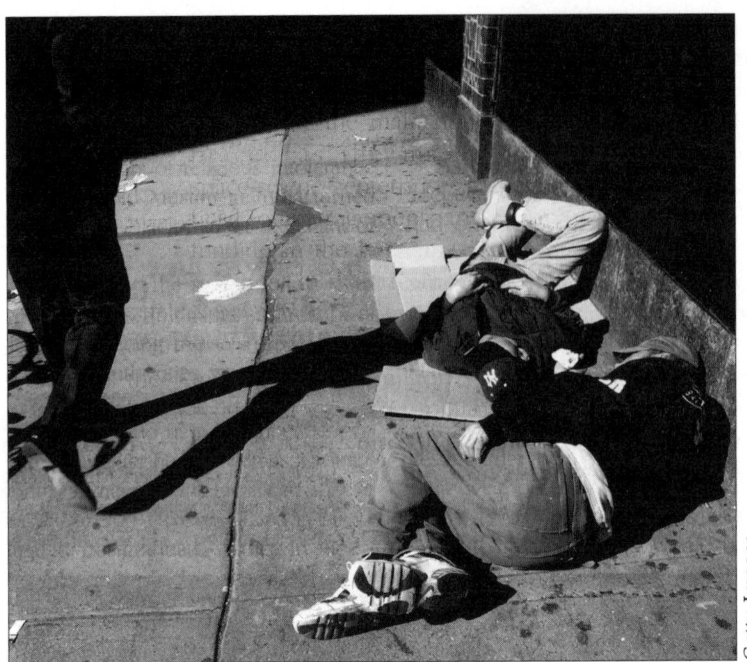
Getty Images

Patients with mental illness who do not receive proper medication may become homeless or end up in jail. When higher co-payments are added to brand-name drugs, some people simply stop taking their medications rather than pay more or switch to generics.

Many doctors said they accepted the previous diagnoses because "that's what the last four doctors had down," Shon says. "That's not as good as we'd like it."

In other cases, doctors keep patients on medications that are helping, but not helping much, he says. "The criteria might be, 'Well, they are not going to the emergency room or getting arrested, so that is enough.' " It's what Shon and his colleagues call the "partial-success syndrome," and it was among the concerns that led them to develop algorithms to help improve prescribing.

The federal mental health commission pointed to the Texas Medications Algorithm Project as one of the success stories in a troubled mental-health care system.

The algorithms offer step-by-step guidelines that help steer doctors to optimal medication choices. They incorporate the latest science into a series of standardized patient evaluations as doctors try different drugs or doses.

A commission report said patients do better — reduced symptoms and higher functioning — when the algorithms are used in the prescribing process. More than a dozen states have adopted the algorithms in pilot programs in their public mental health programs. Shon says they bring psychiatry up to date with other areas of medicine that have used algorithms as a tool for decades, such as diabetes and asthma.

The algorithms help catch diagnosis errors, he says, because failure to get good medication results early on triggers a re-diagnosis.

They also offer a standardized record of drug treatments that can be useful when patients move to new doctors. Shon says doctors often start the prescribing process over with new patients, in part, because they can't make sense of handwritten chart notes from the previous physicians.

When prescribing procedures were introduced years ago at the beginning of managed care, many doctors complained they were merely cost-cutting tools of managed care. Shon agrees, noting that the procedures often recommended "a lot of old, cheap medicines."

But the Texas algorithms, he says, are "totally driven by science" and generally direct doctors to newer treatments early in the algorithm process.

Ironically, Shon's staff in clinics around Texas can't always stick to algorithm recommendations. The budgets for medications are tight, he says, and clinics can only afford to keep a limited number of patients on newer anti-psychotic medications. Once clinics reach their budget cap, new psychiatric patients are prescribed the older, cheaper drugs regardless of algorithm results. "They must wait until somebody leaves the system before they can be put on the new meds," Shon says.

Troubleshooting

Prescribing practices are coming under scrutiny in several states where officials hope to cut wasteful spending on multiple medications for a single patient that they say don't produce meaningful clinical benefits.

Continued on p. 118

At Issue:

Should states public-health programs restrict psychiatric drugs?

WILLIAM M. GLAZER, M.D.
ASSOCIATE CLINICAL PROFESSOR OF PSYCHIATRY, MASSACHUSSETTS GENERAL HOSPITAL

WRITTEN FOR *THE CQ RESEARCHER*, JANUARY 2004

yes

I fear that the arguments for restrictions on psychiatric medications by states are more concerned with costs than with any rational, clinically scientific concern. Budget shortfalls are real, but when restrictions to psychiatric medications occur, politics and economics are speaking louder than science.

This issue is so important that the American Psychiatric Association, the National Alliance of the Mentally Ill and the National Mental Health Association have formed a coalition to advocate against these restrictions.

My position is based on the following arguments:

- There is no expert consensus to support restricted access. While a study here or there might support the interchangeability of some drugs within their classes, no definitive studies lend clear scientific support to this notion. No knowledgeable expert can say with certainty that anti-psychotics or antidepressants are "equally" substitutable. In fact, some studies caution that restricting psychiatric formularies may cost more when you look at the consequences, which include extra use of the emergency room, the hospital bed and the clinic.
- Psychiatric patients are like all people — they are individuals. We all know that the chemical structures of these agents vary tremendously, and with that, we see individuality of response based on gender, race and age. One person's side effect might be another's miracle cure.
- It is absurd to limit one aspect of treatment without knowing what the consequences of that decision would be for all aspects of treatment. Rarely is any system of care able or willing to measure the impact of formulary decisions on long-term (greater than six months) consequences.
- The restricted formulary is not the only strategy available to assure efficient practice. Less-intrusive mechanisms — such as drug-utilization reviews, prescriber education and administrative incentives to prescribe efficiently — also are available.
- Not all medications have the same Food and Drug Administration indications or the same formulations. Not all have been studied in children or in the elderly. There are clinically significant differences in the availability of psychiatric drugs by delivery system — regular pills, rapidly dissolving pills, intramuscular injections, long-acting forms that require administration once every few weeks. No one or two medications hit all of these variations.

JAMES E. SABIN, M.D.
CLINICAL PROFESSOR OF PSYCHIATRY, HARVARD MEDICAL SCHOOL; DIRECTOR, ETHICS PROGRAM, HARVARD PILGRIM HEALTH CARE

WRITTEN FOR *THE CQ RESEARCHER*, JANUARY 2004

no

Exempting psychotropic medications from state formulary restrictions is an attractive advocacy position. After all, patient response to psychiatric medications is highly variable. Formulary restrictions could appear to be one more example of the discrimination that those with mental illnesses have experienced since the colonial era.

But exemption is bad policy. It promotes profit, not patient welfare. By costing states more without producing additional patient benefit, exemption ultimately reduces access to needed medications and other crucial psychiatric services.

For new medications like the selective serotonin reuptake inhibitor (SSRI) antidepressants or the "second generation" anti-psychotics, it is impossible to predict which medication will work best for a first-time user. All of the commonly used SSRIs are equally effective and equally well tolerated. Mr. Jones may respond to Prozac and not Zoloft, whereas for Ms. Smith the opposite may be true. But if they have never taken an SSRI, there is no way to know this in advance.

That is why many states ask prescribers to choose the least costly member of a statistically equal class of medications for first-time users unless there are patient-specific reasons for using a different drug.

Paradoxically, embracing the right kinds of limits actually promotes patient well-being. If I prefer to prescribe the costliest SSRI to a first-time user, should I be allowed to spend money that would otherwise be available for other forms of patient care to indulge my preference when that preference runs counter to the best evidence we have? The commonly asserted mantra that "only the patient's physician should make the decision which drug to prescribe" suggests that I should be given free rein to do so. That's just plain wrong.

Clinicians and advocates should join public officials in ensuring that public expenditures produce the best possible results per dollar spent. The exceptions process must be fast and hassle-free. If the preferred medication does not work, prescribers should have immediate access to alternative drugs. In some circumstances — like the Veterans Affairs and Kaiser Permanente programs — psychiatrists themselves manage the exceptions process.

Since services for persons with mental illness are underfunded, savings from formulary restrictions should be used to enhance patient welfare, through services like improved job training or better housing. Policies of this kind help patients. Stonewalling against state formulary restrictions does not.

Continued from p. 116

Massachusetts became the first state to start systematic scrutiny of prescribing practices, in mid-2002.

"Does our prescribing reflect modern medicine — what patients need — or is there some effective marketing that is resulting in high usage?" said David N. Osser, a Harvard Medical School professor and past president of the Massachusetts Psychiatric Society, who has helped state officials craft the program. [63]

But Boston psychiatrist Sigel and other doctors are concerned that the state will interfere with vital multiple-drug regimes, or cocktails, common with all types of chronic illnesses.

NAMI supports reducing Medicaid pharmaceutical costs through prescription reviews and other alternatives to formularies, prior authorizations or excluding selected drugs outright. "States are struggling mightily; we need new approaches and ideas on how to control costs and at the same time provide appropriate treatment," says Joel Miller, a NAMI policy adviser.

A shortage of psychiatrists in many regions of the country is cited as another reason why psychiatric patients don't receive the right dosage of the optimum medications. While, most big cities with medical schools have plenty of psychiatrists, smaller cities often do not have enough, and rural areas typically have none.

In mountainous western North Carolina, a clinic serving seven counties spent months trying to fill two posts for psychiatrists. "It means we have people waiting to see a psychiatrist to get medications they need," Doug Trantham, service management director of the Smokey Mountain Center, says. As a general rule, public health systems do not use doctors outside of psychiatry to prescribe psychotropic medications.

It is tough to draw doctors with low Medicaid reimbursements and high inpatient work demands, including obligatory, unscheduled trips to hospitals to visit patients within an hour of seclusion or restraints, says Donison Willis, chief of administrative support in the N.C. division of mental health.

Like many states, North Carolina may start to fill the gap with so-called physician extenders, such as nurse practitioners and physician's assistants. New Mexico recently made it legal for certified psychologists to prescribe psychiatric medications, and other states are considering it.

The American Psychiatric Association objects to such practices and is campaigning to boost the number of psychiatrists available. ■

OUTLOOK

States' Solutions

Psychiatric medications likely will remain the focus of contentious battles in state capitals, at least for the next few years. As budgets are cut and spending controls are adopted, the newest and most costly psychotropic medications will no doubt be at the center of tugs of war.

Advocates for psychiatric patients will continue to push for open access to psychotropic drugs, and the other side will push for tighter reins on escalating costs. Few states are likely to offer carte blanche exemptions for psychotropic drugs, says Bernasek, the health consultant specializing in Medicaid. "If they have exemption policies, they will be narrowed into specific types of drugs instead of the category altogether," she says.

Most likely, policies and rules will zigzag, as states institute restrictions and then modify them as outside pressures bear down. Or, if budget pressures get too bad states may retreat on open stances.

Overall, officials in individual states are taking short-term views of spending and savings in the hustle to patch up annual budgets, policy experts say. Yet, decisions made over the next few years in legislative chambers, if viewed collectively and over a longer time frame, could influence the direction for mental health medications, they warn.

"Aggressive price controls and highly restrictive formularies . . . risk . . . overemphasiz[ing] today's cost containment at the expense of tomorrow's therapies," warned a report to the federal mental health commission. [64]

In other words, heavy-handed price cuts by Medicaid could dampen enthusiasm for research and development of new antipsychotic agents, cautions Haiden A. Huskamp, a Harvard Medical School economics professor. [65] "If [drugmakers] are concerned about potential revenue because of the way prices are being set or cost-containment initiatives, that could influence their thinking," Huskamp says.

Drugmaker Lilly counts on its antipsychotic drug Zyprexa to bring in a big share of company revenues, and Medicaid buys half of all Zyprexa sold. "Lilly is committed to the study of neuroscience and has been for decades," spokeswoman Griffin says. Lilly continues to pursue innovations and recognizes a significant unmet need for mental health treatment, she says. "This is our research and development incentive."

But, critics say, Medicaid and other payers have been such compliant customers, drug companies have already moved their focus to marketing and selling rather than research and development. "We are creating incentives for drug companies to heavily market products that may not be worth their value," Yale Professor Rosenheck says.

Crismon, at the University of Texas, says drug companies also are manufacturing "me too" drugs, or copycats sold at new drug prices.

Instead, she says, it makes sense to set prices for new drug products based on the degree of innovation. "That would be a rational approach to pricing and would emphasize unique new drug development," Crismon says. ■

Notes

[1] "Results from the 2002 National Survey on Drug Use and Health: Detailed Tables," Office of Applied Studies, Substance Abuse and Mental Health Services Administration, U.S. Department of Health and Human Services, September 2003, Table 6.1A.

[2] For background, see Mary H. Cooper, "Prozac," *The CQ Researcher*, Aug. 19, 1994, pp. 721-744.

[3] "Mental Disorders Affect One in Four People: Treatment Available but not Being Used," press release: "The World Health Report 2001," World Health Organization, Oct. 4, 2001, p. 2.

[4] Substance Abuse and Mental Health Services Administration, *op. cit.*, Tables 6.16A, 6.23A.

[5] "Mental health reform languishes year after big push; Iraqi war, state budget crises hinder cause's political progress," *The Dallas Morning News*, June 15, 2003.

[6] "Interim Report of the President's New Freedom Commission on Mental Health," Oct. 29, 2002, introductory letter.

[7] *Ibid.*, p. 16.

[8] Robert Rosenheck, *et al.*, "Effectiveness and Cost of Olanzapine and Haloperidol in the Treatment of Schizophrenia," *Journal of the American Medical Association*, Nov. 26, 2003, pp. 2693-2702.

[9] For background, see David Hatch, "Drug Company Ethics," *The CQ Researcher*, June 6, 2003, pp. 521-544.

[10] Richard G. Frank, *et al.*, "Mental Health Policy and Psychotropic Drugs," revised version of report prepared for the New Freedom Commission on Mental Health, Aug. 27, 2003, pp. 3, 5.

[11] PRIME Institute, University of Minnesota, from data collected through the Centers for Medicare and Medicaid.

[12] New Freedom Commission on Mental Health, "Achieving the Promise: Transforming Mental Health Care in America," July 2003, p. 13.

[13] "Child Welfare and Juvenile Justice," U.S. General Accounting Office, April 2003, GAO-03-397.

[14] For background, see Thomas J. Billetteri, "Mental Health Policy," *The CQ Researcher*, Sept. 12, 1997, pp. 793-816.

[15] Medicare Prescription Drug, Improvement, and Modernization Act of 2003, Public Law 108-173.

[16] "NMHA Cannot Support Medicare Prescription Drug Agreement," *NMHA Legislative Alert*, National Mental Health Association, Nov. 19, 2003.

[17] "House-Senate Negotiators Reach Agreement on Medicare Prescription Drug Legislation," *NAMI E-News*, Nov. 18, 2003.

[18] Michael Janofsy, "Governors Unite to Urge Shifting Costs of Medicaid," *The New York Times*, Aug. 18, 2003. For background, see William Triplett, "State Budget Crisis," *The CQ Researcher*, Oct. 3, 2003, pp. 821-844.

[19] National Association of State Budget Officers, "State Expenditure Report 2002," November 2003, p. 46.

[20] Office of Inspector General, U.S. Department of Health and Human Services, "Medicaid's Mental Health Drug Expenditures," Report OEI-05-02-00080, August 2003, p. 1.

[21] *Ibid.*

[22] Office of Inspector General, U.S. Department of Health and Human Services, "State Strategies to Contain Medicaid Drug Costs," October 2003, p. 18.

[23] American Psychiatric Association, "Medicaid Alert: Medicaid in Crisis," Public Policy Advocacy: Action Alerts and Announcements.

[24] "Michigan Department of Community Health Releases Update to Preferred Drug List," press release State of Michigan, June 27, 2003.

[25] Commonwealth of Massachusetts, Norfolk Superior Court, Civil Action No. 03-01464, Aug. 7, 2003.

[26] James Sabin, "Viewpoints: The Realities of Today's Formularies," *Psychiatric News*, April 4, 2003, p. 34.

[27] "Mass. Seeks to limit multiple prescribing in single drug class," *Mental Health Weekly*, July 22, 2002, p. 1.

[28] Rosenheck, *op. cit.*

[29] Jeffrey A. Lieberman, *et. al.*, "Comparative efficacy and safety of atypical and conventional antipsychotic drugs in first-episode psychosis," *American Journal of Psychiatry*, August 2003, Abstract.

[30] Internal memoranda dated Aug. 18, 1996, and Aug. 30, 1996, from Paul Leber, FDA director of the Division of Neuropharmacological Drug Products, to Robert Temple, director of New Drug Evaluation, Department of Health and Human Services Public Health Service Food and Drug Administration Center for Drug Evaluation and Research.

[31] *Ibid.*

[32] Patricia Callahan, "Lilly's Zyprexa Acted Similarly to Cheaper Drug," *The Wall Street Journal*, Nov. 26, 2003.

[33] Larry Ereshefsky, and William M. Glazer, "Comparison of the Bioequivalence of Generic Versus Branded Clozapine," *Journal of Clinical Psychiatry*, Vol. 62, 2001.

[34] *Ibid.*

[35] Quoted in Peter Landers, "States Jointly Seek Drug Discounts Under Medicaid," *The Wall Street Journal*, Feb. 20, 2003.

[36] "Moniz develops lobotomy for mental illness 1935," *A Science Odyssey: People and Discoveries*, www.wgbh.com.

[37] John F. Kennedy, "Remarks Upon Signing Bill for the Construction of Mental Retardation Facilities and Community Mental Health Centers," *Public Papers of the Presidents of the United States: John F. Kennedy, January 1 to November 22, 1963*, U.S. Government Printing Office, p. 826.

[38] Testimony of Darrel A. Regier, American Psychiatric Association, before New Freedom Commission on Mental Health, July 19, 2002.: Interim Report of Federal Commission, p. 5.

[39] *Ibid.*

[40] "Community Mental Health Centers at the 40-year Mark: The Quest for Survival," National Council for Community Behavioral Healthcare, 2003, p. 6.

[41] New Freedom Commission on Mental Health, *op. cit.*, pp. 21, 33.

About the Author

Jane Tanner is a contributing writer in Charlotte, N.C., who writes for *The New York Times* and other publications. She earned her B.A. (social policy) and M.A. (journalism) degrees from Northwestern University. Her recent *CQ Researcher* reports include "Mental Health Insurance" and "Future Job Market."

[42] Robert Bernstein and Chris Koyanagi "Disintegrating Systems: The State of States' Public Mental Health Systems," Bazelon Center for Mental Health Law, Dec. 21, 2001.

[43] Quoted in Christine Lehmann, "Government News: Stressed Budgets Lead States To Cut MH Resources," *Psychiatric News*, Feb. 1, 2002, p. 1.

[44] "Expanding Coverage of Prescription Drugs in Medicare," Hearing before the Committee on Ways and Means, U.S. House of Representatives, 108th Congress, First Session, April 9, 2003, U.S. Government Printing Office, Serial No. 108-7, p.78.

[45] H.S. Kaye, "Employment and Social Participation Among People with Mental Health Disabilities," 2002.

[46] New Freedom Commission, *op. cit.*, p. 34.

[47] *Ibid*, p. 29.

[48] *Ibid.*

[49] Pharmaceutical Research and Manufacturers of America, "Pharmaceutical Industry Profile 2003," p. 61.

[50] National Association of State Budget Officers, *op. cit.*, p. 46.

[51] The funds were included in the Jobs and Growth Reconciliation Act enacted May 2003.

[52] Centers for Medicare and Medicaid Services, Office of the Actuary, "Prescription Drug Expenditures Aggregate and Per Capital Amounts . . . : Selected Calendar Years 1980-2012," Feb. 11, 2003, Table 11.

[53] Richard G. Frank, Howard H. Goldman and Michael Hogan. "Medicaid and Mental Health: Be Careful What You Ask For," *Health Affairs*, January/February, 2003.

[54] *Ibid.*

[55] State of Michigan, *op. cit.*

[56] "Medicaid's Mental Health Drug Expenditures," *op. cit.*, p. 7.

[57] "State Initiatives on Prescription Drugs: Creating a More Functional Market," *Health Affairs*, July/August 2003, p. 128.

[58] Kathy Boccella, "Letting go to get care," *The Philadelphia Inquirer*, June 10, 2003.

[59] *Ibid.*

[60] U.S. General Accounting Office, "Child Welfare and Juvenile Justice: Federal Agencies Could Play a Stronger Role in Helping States Reduce the Number of Children Placed Solely to Obtain Mental Health Services," April 2003.

[61] President's New Freedom Commission, *op. cit.*, pp. 33-34.

[62] "NAMI Supports Bill to End Child Custody Scandal," *PR Newswire*, Oct. 2, 2003.

[63] "Mass. Seeks to Limit Multiple Prescribing in Single Drug Class," *op. cit.*

[64] Frank, *et al.*, *op. cit.*, p. 21.

[65] Haiden A. Huskamp, "Managing Psychotropic Drug Costs: Will Formularies Work?" *Health Affairs*, Vol. 22, Number 5, September/October 2003, p. 91.

FOR MORE INFORMATION

American Psychiatric Association, 1000 Wilson Blvd., Suite 1825, Arlington, VA 22209-3901; (703) 907-7300; www.psych.org. Promotes the availability of high-quality psychiatric care and calls for across-the-board exemptions from state formularies for mental-health drugs.

Bazelon Center for Mental Health Law, 1101 15th St., N.W., Suite 1212, Washington, DC 20005; (202) 467-5730; www.bazelon.org. Public-interest law firm that conducts test-case litigation to defend rights of persons with mental disabilities.

Kaiser Commission on Medicaid and the Uninsured, 1330 G St., N.W., Washington, DC 20005; (202) 347-5270; www.kff.org/about/kcmu.cfm. A unit of the Kaiser Family Foundation that studies health care for low-income people.

National Alliance for the Mentally Ill, 2107 Wilson Blvd., Colonial Pl. III, #300 Arlington, VA 22201-3042; (703) 524-7600; www.nami.org. Advocacy group argues that psychiatric patients require open access to all mental-health drugs.

National Institute of Mental Health, 6001 Executive Blvd., Suite 8235, Rockville, MD 20892; (301) 443-3673; www.nimh.nih.gov. Conducts research on the cause, diagnosis and treatment of mental disorders; commissioned a recent study that found better patient compliance on the new anti-psychosis drug Zyprexa.

National Mental Health Association, 2001 N. Beauregard St., 12th Floor, Alexandria, VA 22311; (703) 684-7722; www.nmha.org. Advocacy group works to increase accessible and appropriate care for adults and children with mental disorders; argues that mental-health drugs should be exempt from state formularies.

National Mental Health Information Center, P.O. Box 42557 Washington, DC 20015; 1 (800) 662-4357; www.mentalhealth.samhsa.gov. A federal agency charged with providing information about mental health.

Pharmaceutical Research and Manufacturers of America (PhRMA), 1100 Fifteenth St., N.W., Washington, DC 20005; (202) 835-3400; www.phrma.org. An industry trade group for pharmaceutical companies.

Policy Research Institute, National Alliance for the Mentally Ill,, 2107 Wilson Blvd., Suite 300, Arlington, VA 22201; (703) 524-7600; www.nami.org. A unit of the advocacy group devoted to government policy concerning severe psychiatric illnesses.

Bibliography

Selected Sources

Books

Whitaker, Robert, *Mad in America: Bad Science, Bad Medicine, and the Enduring Mistreatment of the Mentally Ill*, Perseus Press, 2001.

A medical journalist argues that due to flawed government policy the 2 million-plus Americans with schizophrenia have fared worse over the last quarter-century, despite the introduction of new drugs.

Articles

"States' Initiatives on Prescription Drugs: Creating A More Functional Market," *Health Affairs*, July/August 2003, pp. 128-136.

Lawmakers and officials from a majority of states call for drugmakers to disclose information on pricing and comparative costs and benefits of medications so states can negotiate better prices.

"Three associations unite to protect psychotropic medications," *Mental Health Weekly*, Feb. 24, 2003.

A coalition of the American Psychiatric Association, the National Alliance for the Mentally Ill and the National Mental Health Association advocates preservation of Medicaid beneficiaries' access to psychiatric medications.

Albert, Tanya, "Physician sues Massachusetts over prior authorization rule," *American Medical Association News*, Oct. 27, 2003.

A Boston psychiatrist has asked the courts to repeal Massachusetts' restrictions on Medicaid psychiatric medications, which he says harm patients and force him to discriminate against public-health patients.

Carroll, John, "Drug Companies Crying Foul Over Medicaid's Formulary Push," *Managed Care Magazine*, Nov. 2, 2002.

Carroll explains the drug companies' position that state prescription restrictions harm the country's poorest, sickest and most vulnerable patients and fail to recognize that new drugs produce savings through reduced hospital stays.

Reports and Studies

"Achieving the Promise: Transforming Mental Health Care in America," New Freedom Commission on Mental Health, U.S. Department of Health and Human Services, July 22, 2003.

A federal commission concludes that psychiatric care in America is in "shambles" and recommends better coordination of services and a focus on recovery.

"Medicaid's Mental Health Drug Expenditures," Office of Inspector General, U.S. Department of Health and Human Services, August 2003.

A federal review of Medicaid purchases of psychiatric drugs concludes that states negotiate poorly with drug manufacturers and end up paying as much as 29 percent more for mental-health drugs than large federal agencies.

"State Strategies to Contain Medicaid Drug Costs," Office of Inspector General, U.S. Department of Health and Human Services, October 2003.

A federal survey of Medicaid controls on prescriptions shows that many states are saving millions of dollars by requiring discounts from drugmakers, selecting preferred drugs and increasing patients' out-of-pocket payments.

Hall, Laura Lee, *et al.*, "Shattered Lives: Results of a National Survey of NAMI Members Living with Mental Illnesses and Their Families," *TRIAD Report*, July 2003.

The advocacy group's survey showed most people with severe psychiatric conditions are unemployed and depend on their families for basic functioning. Medications are the best treatment, the survey concluded, but they are often difficult to obtain consistently.

Huskcamp, Haiden A., "Managing Psychotropic Drug Costs: Will Formularies Work?" *Health Affairs*, September/October 2003, pp. 84-96.

An assistant professor of health economics at Harvard Medical School says new state controls on public-health prescriptions are less likely to work for psychiatric drugs because of the very diverse reactions individual patients have to the drugs and Medicaid's dominance as a customer for some drugmakers.

Jellinek, Michael S., "Mirror, Mirror on the Wall: Are We Prescribing the Right Psychotropic Medications to the Right Children Using the Right Treatment Plan?" Editorial, *Archive of Pediatric & Adolescent Medicine*, January 2003.

A pediatric psychiatrist analyzes the results of a recent benchmark study showing a rapid rise in the use of psychotropic drugs by children and warns of scant clinical evidence of the drugs' effects on young people.

Rosenheck, Robert, *et al.*, "Effectiveness and Cost of Olanzapine and Haloperidol in the Treatment of Schizophrenia," *Journal of American Medical Association*, Nov. 26, 2003.

The authors say a clinical comparison of the widely used schizophrenia drug Zyprexa and the older Haldol showed no significant advantages for Zyprexa, raising questions about public spending on the newer drug.

The Next Step:

Additional Articles from Current Periodicals

Causes of Mental Illness

Duenwald, Mary, "Gene Is Linked to Susceptibility to Depression," *The New York Times*, July 18, 2003, p. A14.
Researchers find a gene that determines how well people cope with stress.

Marsa, Linda, "Mental Illness Clues," *Los Angeles Times*, Sept. 29, 2003, p. F3.
A Columbia University researcher thinks infections in the womb may explain why certain people predisposed to mental illness develop disorders while others do not.

Wade, Nicholas, "Gene May Play a Role in Schizophrenia," *The New York Times*, Dec. 13, 2003, p. A37.
Studies of schizophrenics in different countries indicate that inheritors of a certain gene variant may have double the risk of developing schizophrenia.

Drug Side Effects

Goode, Erica, "Anti-Psychotic Approved to Treat Suicidal Behavior," *The New York Times*, Dec. 20, 2002, p. A30.
Despite a potentially lethal side effect, clozapine may save lives; one in 10 patients with schizophrenia commit suicide.

Goode, Erica, "3 Schizophrenia Drugs May Raise Diabetes Risk, Study Says," *The New York Times*, Aug. 25, 2003, p. A8.
Compared to older antipsychotic medications, newer, more expensive drugs may increase patients' chance of developing diabetes.

Kluger, Jeffrey, "Medicating Young Minds," *Time*, Nov. 3, 2003, p. 48.
The long-term effects of psychiatric drugs on children are unknown, but there are fears they may interfere with the brain's natural development.

Escalating Costs

Dewan, Shaila, "Parents of Mentally Ill Children Trade Custody for Care," *The New York Times*, Feb. 16, 2003, p. A35.
Unable to afford care for their mentally ill children, parents are forced to place them in state custody to get them the drugs they need.

Heredia, Christopher, "Health Care System Plays Mind Games With Emotionally Ill, Critics Say," *San Francisco Chronicle*, March 23, 2003, p. F4.
Health-care companies often focus on medication as a less costly alternative to therapy for the mentally ill, but this may not be the most effective approach for all.

Vedantam, Shankar, "Study: Thousands Give Up Children to Get Care," *The Washington Post*, April 22, 2003, p. A2.
Because private insurance often doesn't cover costs for treating mental illness, some parents give up their children to social services or to the police in order to get them the care they need.

Generic vs. Brand-name Drugs

Appleby, Julie, and Jayne O'Donnell, "Consumers Pay as Drug Firms Fight Over Generics," *USA Today*, June 6, 2002, p. 1A.
Paxil and other drugs are at the center of a controversy as drug manufacturers attempt to place multiple patents on a single drug to increase profitability.

Milbank, Dana, "New Drug Rules Aim to Speed Generics," *The Washington Post*, June 13, 2003, p. A27.
The Food and Drug Administration, supported by President Bush, passes new regulations making it easier for generic drugs to enter the market.

Pear, Robert, "Patent Law Change Urged to Speed Generic Drugs," *The New York Times*, July 30, 2002, p. A14.
The FTC calls on Congress to revise patent laws to prevent new generic drugs from being delayed by legal challenges from brand-name drug companies.

Petersen, Melody, "Bristol-Myers Squibb to Pay $670 Million to Settle Numerous Lawsuits," *The New York Times*, Jan. 8, 2003, p. C9.
Bristol-Myers Squibb agreed to pay $670 million to settle numerous lawsuits claiming it used illegal tactics to keep generic versions of its medicines out of the market.

New Psychiatric Drugs

Goode, Erica, "Leading Drugs for Psychosis Come Under New Scrutiny," *The New York Times*, May 20, 2003, p. A1.
After being hailed for miraculous results, some experts are now questioning the superiority of new antipsychosis medications, known as atypicals.

Grady, Denise, "An Older Bipolar Drug Is Linked to Fewer Suicides in a Study," *The New York Times*, Sept. 17, 2003, p. A19.
Lithium may be better at preventing suicides by those with manic-depressive illness than a much newer and more expensive drug, Depakote.

Mestel, Rosie, "New Schizophrenia Treatment at Issue," *Los Angeles Times*, Nov. 26, 2003, p. A13.
A new study finds that an older drug is as effective as a newer one that costs 100 times more; psychiatrists say more studies are needed.

Overprescription of Psychotropic Drugs

Davis, David, "Losing the Mind," *Los Angeles Times Magazine*, Oct. 26, 2003, p. 20.
The "Mad Pride" movement believes drugs are overused in treating mental disorders and the American mental health care system is dysfunctional.

Kelly, Timothy, "Misguided Medicine," *The Washington Post*, July 29, 2002, p. A19.
New studies showing that antidepressant drugs sometimes are no more effective than placebos indicate that treatment options should be more varied.

Reforming Regulations

Colliver, Victoria, "Pharmacies, State Battle Over Medi-Cal Cutbacks," *San Francisco Chronicle*, Dec. 17, 2003, p. B1.
Some pharmacies threaten to end participation in the Medi-Cal program, arguing that cuts to California's drug-subsidy program for the needy may cut into pharmacies' profit margins.

Connolly, Ceci, "States Sued for Pushing Cheaper Drugs Via Medicaid," *The Washington Post*, Aug. 26, 2002, p. A1.
Drug manufacturers are suing state governments that are steering doctors and patients toward cheaper medications to control Medicaid costs.

Grady, Denise, "Major Change in Mental Health Care Is Urged," *The New York Times*, July 23, 2003, p. A13.
A presidential commission on mental health recommended an overhaul of the nation's mental health system, including a call for "mental health parity" legislation requiring equal insurance coverage for physical and mental ailments.

Harris, Gardiner, "States Try to Limit Drugs in Medicaid, but Makers Resist," *The New York Times*, Dec. 18, 2003, p. A1.
Advocates for the mentally ill and drugmakers unite to fight state efforts to create preferred-drug lists that require cheaper medications to be tried first; Zyprexa, an expensive new antipsychotic medication, is often the largest Medicaid drug expense.

Satel, Sally, and Keith Humphreys, "Mind Games," *The Weekly Standard*, Oct. 13, 2003.
The authors argue a Senate bill designed to force insurers to provide more coverage for mental illnesses would reduce care for the worst off.

Sontag, Deborah, "When Politics Is Personal," *The New York Times Magazine*, Sept. 15, 2002, p. 90.
Congressional leaders' personal experiences with mental illness have influenced their attempts to gain equal insurance coverage for physical and mental ailments.

Treating Mental Illness

Genn, Adina, "For the Mentally Ill, a Long Search for a Bed," *The New York Times*, Jan. 26, 2003, p. 14LI-1.
Finding housing for mentally ill people who cannot survive on their own is increasingly difficult.

Kotulak, Ronald, "New Drugs, Social Support Offer Hope for a Normal Life," *Chicago Tribune*, Feb. 23, 2003, p. C15.
Treatment combining new drugs and psychosocial support allows at least 90 percent of schizophrenics to live almost normal lives.

Levy, Clifford, "For Mentally Ill, Death and Misery," *The New York Times*, April 28, 2003, p. A1.
Decades after closing psychiatric wards following scandals, today's adult homes are often filled with the same mismanagement and neglect of their occupants.

CITING *THE CQ RESEARCHER*

Sample formats for citing these reports in a bibliography include the ones listed below. Preferred styles and formats vary, so please check with your instructor or professor.

MLA STYLE

Jost, Kenneth. "Rethinking the Death Penalty." The CQ Researcher 16 Nov. 2001: 945-68.

APA STYLE

Jost, K. (2001, November 16). Rethinking the death penalty. *The CQ Researcher, 11*, 945-968.

CHICAGO STYLE

Jost, Kenneth. "Rethinking the Death Penalty." *CQ Researcher*, November 16, 2001, 945-968.

Back Issues

***The CQ Researcher* offers in-depth coverage of many key areas.**
Back issues are $10. Quantity discounts available.
Call (866) 427-7737 to order back issues.

Or call for a free CQ Researcher Web trial!
Online access provides:

- *Searchable archives dating back to 1991.*
- *Wider access through IP authentication.*
- *PDF files for downloading and printing.*
- *Availability 48 hours before print version.*

CHILDREN/YOUTH
Preventing Teen Drug Use, March 2002
Sexual Abuse and the Clergy, May 2002
Movie Ratings, March 2003

CRIMINAL JUSTICE
Cyber-Crime, April 2002
Corporate Crime, October 2002
Serial Killers, October 2003

EDUCATION
Charter Schools, December 2002
Combating Plagiarism, September 2003
Home Schooling Debate, January 2003
Black Colleges, December 2003

ENVIRONMENT
Bush and the Environment, October 2002
Crisis in the Plains, May 2003
NASA's Future, May 2003
Water Shortages, August 2003
Air Pollution Conflict, November 2003

HEALTH CARE AND MEDICINE
Medicare Reform, August 2003
Women's Health, November 2003
Homeopathy Debate, December 2003

LEGAL ISSUES
Abortion Debates, March 2003
Race in America, July 2003
Torture, April 2003
Homeland Security, September 2003
Civil Liberties Debates, October 2003

MODERN CULTURE
Gay Marriage, September 2003
Combating Plagiarism, September 2003
Latinos' Future, October 2003
Future of the Music Industry, Nov. 2003
Hazing, January 2004

POLITICS/GOVERNMENT
Future of NATO, February 2003
Trouble in South America, March 2003
North Korean Crisis, April 2003
Rebuilding Iraq, July 2003
Aiding Africa, August 2003
State Budget Crises, October 2003
Democracy in the Arab World, January 2004

TRANSPORTATION
Auto Safety, October 2001
Future of the Airline Industry, June 2002
Future of Amtrak, October 2002
SUV Debate, May 2003

Future Topics

- ***Youth Suicide***
- ***Globalization of Jobs***
- ***Future of the United Nations***

CQ Researcher

Published by CQ Press, a division of Congressional Quarterly Inc.

thecqresearcher.com

Youth Suicide

Should government fund more prevention programs?

This year, about 2,800 young people will kill themselves, including about 1,600 in the emotionally volatile 15-to-19-year-old age group. Suicidal tendencies are so common that about one in five high school students seriously considers suicide. To reduce the teen suicide rate, mental health experts say it is vital to identify and treat at-risk youngsters. But suicidal youths are difficult to identify. Some experts worry that talking about suicide may actually exacerbate the problem. Others point to studies indicating antidepressant drugs, increasingly prescribed for children, may trigger suicide in certain cases. Meanwhile, limited government funds have been allocated for the problem, few schools have screening or counseling programs and many states lack comprehensive suicide-prevention plans.

Most suicidal teens have underlying emotional problems — especially depression — but parents, teachers and friends often think they are simply normal, moody teenagers.

INSIDE THIS ISSUE

The CQ Researcher • Feb. 13, 2004 • www.thecqresearcher.com
Volume 14, Number 6 • Pages 125-148

RECIPIENT OF SOCIETY OF PROFESSIONAL JOURNALISTS AWARD FOR EXCELLENCE ◆ AMERICAN BAR ASSOCIATION SILVER GAVEL AWARD

THE ISSUES

BACKGROUND

CURRENT SITUATION

OUTLOOK

SIDEBARS AND GRAPHICS

FOR FURTHER RESEARCH

Cover: Suicide is seriously considered each year by about one in five American high school students, or about 3 million youths. (Corbis Images)

Feb. 13, 2004
Volume 14, No. 6

MANAGING EDITOR: Thomas J. Colin

ASSISTANT MANAGING EDITOR: Kathy Koch

ASSOCIATE EDITOR: Kenneth Jost

STAFF WRITERS: Mary H. Cooper, David Masci, William Triplett

CONTRIBUTING WRITERS: Rachel S. Cox, Sarah Glazer, David Hosansky, Patrick Marshall, Jane Tanner

DESIGN/PRODUCTION EDITOR: Olu B. Davis

ASSISTANT EDITOR: Kenneth Lukas

CQ PRESS

A Division of Congressional Quarterly Inc.

SENIOR VICE PRESIDENT/GENERAL MANAGER: John A. Jenkins

DIRECTOR, LIBRARY PUBLISHING: Kathryn C. Suárez

DIRECTOR, EDITORIAL OPERATIONS: Ann Davies

CIRCULATION MANAGER: Nina Tristani

CONGRESSIONAL QUARTERLY INC.

CHAIRMAN: Andrew Barnes

VICE CHAIRMAN: Andrew P. Corty

PRESIDENT AND PUBLISHER: Robert W. Merry

The CQ Researcher (ISSN 1056-2036) is printed on acid-free paper. Published weekly, except Jan. 2, April 9, July 2, July 9, Aug. 6, Aug. 13, Nov. 26 and Dec. 31, by CQ Press, a division of Congressional Quarterly Inc. Annual subscription rates for libraries, businesses and government start at $625. Single issues are available for $10. Quantity discounts apply to orders over 10. Additional rates furnished upon request. Periodicals postage paid at Washington, D.C., and additional mailing offices. POSTMASTER: Send address changes to *The CQ Researcher*, 1255 22nd St., N.W., Suite 400, Washington, D.C. 20037.

Youth Suicide

By David Hosansky

The Issues

When his girlfriend broke up with him, 16-year-old Joe Muñoz was devastated. "I decided I'd show her; I'd kill myself," recalls Muñoz, now 42 and a Dallas freelance journalist.

But after taking two bottles of sleeping pills, the heartbroken teenager realized he had made a mistake. Instead of peacefully drifting into death as he had expected, his heart started painfully racing. Terrified, he told his younger brother to call the police. After being in a coma for two days, he found himself in the hospital — weak and frightened, but alive.

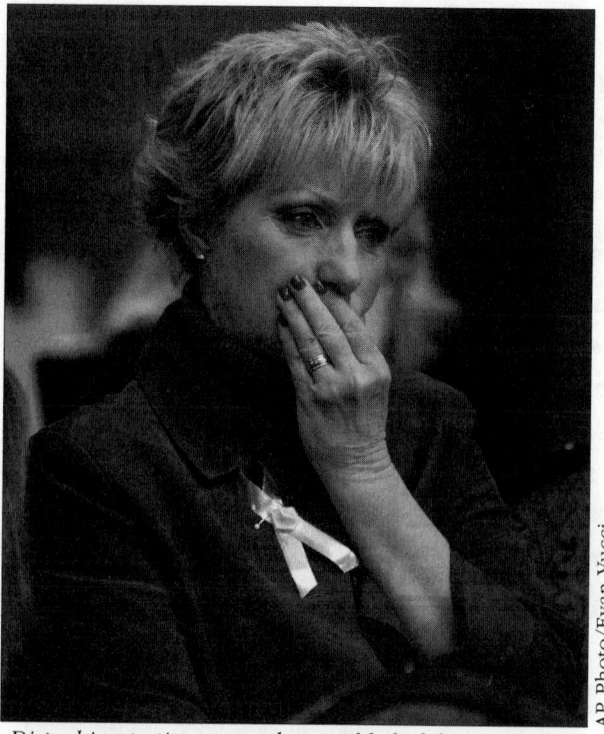

AP Photo/Evan Vucci

Disturbing testimony on the possible link between youth suicide and antidepressants troubles Arizona parent Lorrie Weight during a hearing in Bethesda, Md., on Feb. 2, 2004. The hearing was held by a Food and Drug Administration scientific panel, which urged the FDA to issue stronger warnings to doctors prescribing antidepressants to anyone under age 18.

"You're a teenager, you've got hormones flooding your body, your girlfriend breaks up with you and all of a sudden it's the most horrible thing in the world, and you're never going to get better," he says. "You get so wrapped up in your teenage angst that it blinds you to everything else."

Muñoz' experience is not unusual. In recent years, about 2,800 young people between 10 and 21 have killed themselves annually, including about 1,600 in the emotionally volatile 15-to-19-year-old age group. [1] Millions more suffer from emotional problems and are at risk of suicide. In fact, every year more than 3 million high school students — one in five — consider or imagine committing suicide, according to the Centers for Disease Control and Prevention (CDC). About a third of those actually make an attempt, with some 400,000 requiring medical attention.

"If this were an infectious disease, we would call this an epidemic," said Joseph Woolston, chief of child psychiatry at Yale-New Haven Hospital. [2]

Suicide is a significant public health problem for all age groups, but especially among the elderly. Adults 65 and older have had the highest suicide rate of all age groups since 1933, when states began reporting suicide deaths.

While suicide is viewed as tragic at any age, it is perhaps more understandable among the elderly, who may be suffering from serious, end-of-life physical ailments. But when a young person commits suicide, experts say it is often because youths have trouble coping with both the rapid physiological changes that occur during adolescence and social pressures — such as dating, applying for college and possibly beginning to drink or take drugs.

"A lot of the kids are dealing with depression, loss, frustration, acute disappointment, rejection; sometimes they don't make the team, they break up with their boyfriend or girlfriend," explains David Fassler, a child psychiatrist in Burlington, Vt., and an associate professor at the University of Vermont. "You mix that kind of fairly common incident with impulsivity and substance abuse," and the result may be suicide.

Experts began seeing youth suicide as a major problem in recent decades, after the youth suicide rate nearly tripled between 1952 and 1996. Although the rate has decreased in recent years, suicide remains the third leading cause of death among 15-to-21-year-olds (after accidents and homicides). More American teens die at their own hands than from cancer, heart disease, AIDS, birth defects, stroke, pneumonia, influenza and chronic lung disease — combined. [3]

Similar high tolls overseas have caught the attention of the World Health Organization, which in 1996 urged member nations to address the suicide problem. In 1999 Surgeon General David Satcher called for a concerted effort to reduce suicide rates in the United States.

"The nation must address suicide as a significant public health problem and put into place national strategies to prevent the loss of life and the suffering suicide causes," Satcher said. [4]

But suicidal youngsters are difficult to identify and treat, and only limited government funds have been allocated for the problem. Few schools have programs to screen or counsel emotionally troubled students, rural areas often lack appropriate treatment facilities, and many states have not developed comprehensive suicide prevention plans.

Recognizing Suicide Warning Signs

Suicidal tendencies among adolescents often go undiagnosed, in part because emotional instability is often misinterpreted as normal teenage mood swings. Here are some important warning signs to watch for among adolescents.

Makes suicide threats, direct and indirect
Is obsessed with death
Writes poems, essays or makes drawings about death
Exhibits dramatic change in personality or appearance
Shows irrational or bizarre behavior
Has an overwhelming sense of guilt, shame or reflection
Eating or sleeping patterns change
School performance shows severe drop
Gives away belongings

Source: National Mental Health Association

Most suicidal teens have underlying emotional problems — especially depression — but parents, teachers and friends often miss the warning signs, thinking their moody youngsters are simply acting like normal teenagers.

"Many parents don't recognize when adolescents are depressed," says Lawrence Riso, a psychology professor at Georgia State University. "When their mood fluctuates quite a bit, they're seen as just being an adolescent. They may be depressed and one hour later look fine and go out and play basketball."

In contrast, he adds, "When you're an adult and you're depressed, you tend to not look good for weeks or months."

Contrary to popular belief, suicidal youngsters are often successful and full of energy. Laurie Flynn, director of the Carmel Hill Center for Early Diagnosis and Treatment at Columbia University, was shocked when her 17-year-old daughter, a top student, attempted suicide. "She was one of those kids who was a little star, active in the community," Flynn says. "I thought if she was depressed, I would see it. The truth is, you don't know."

Flynn later learned about a history of depression in the family. Her daughter has since graduated from college and is married.

Suicide rates are higher among whites — particularly white males — than among blacks. But certain minorities, such as Native Americans and Native Alaskans, have even higher rates. In fact, suicidal children come from all racial and socioeconomic backgrounds.

"This is an equal-opportunity event," warns child psychiatrist Harold Koplewicz, director of the Child Study Center at New York University.

Suicide is especially prevalent among youths in rural areas, perhaps because of widely scattered mental health services and the easy availability of firearms. Some experts argue that stricter gun control laws would help reduce the youth suicide rate, but others say youngsters would simply turn to other means to end their lives. (*See sidebar, p. 131.*)

Some research indicates that childhood emotional problems are on the rise. [5] An extensive analysis found that almost one in five children suffers from an emotional or behavioral illness. That's nearly triple the level of 20 years ago. [6] Experts are divided over whether the increase is due to societal changes — such as higher rates of substance abuse and fewer tight-knit families and communities — or to some other cause. Some studies indicate that kids who are bullied, gay or bisexual are particularly prone to depression and suicide.

Controversy also rages over the use of antidepressants to treat emotionally troubled and potentially suicidal teens. Doctors are writing 2 million antidepressant prescriptions a year for young people — sometimes in combination with therapy and sometimes without it. Some studies indicate that Paxil, Zoloft and other new-generation antidepressants may help reduce youth suicide rates, but other data indicate that such drugs may actually spur suicide attempts. [7]

Concerned by data linking the new antidepressants with suicidal thoughts and behavior in children and adolescents, British regulators in December warned doctors not to prescribe some of those drugs for young people. [8] The U.S. Food and Drug Administration (FDA) last year recommended that doctors refrain from giving them to children.

The FDA launched hearings on the highly charged issue on Feb. 2, 2004. Several bereaved parents urged officials to ban antidepressant use by children. "You have an obligation today [to prevent] this tragic story from being repeated over and over again," said Mark Miller of Kansas City, Mo., whose son Matt hanged himself after taking his seventh Zoloft tablet.

Other parents said antidepressants benefited their children immeasurably. "My children have had tremendous improvement with their illnesses," said Dr. Suzanne Vogel-Scibilia of the National Alliance for the Mentally Ill, who has two sons using the drugs.

After the testimony, the scientific advisory panel holding the hearing urged the FDA to issue stronger warnings —

Experts Differ on Why Suicide Rate Is Declining

The number of youth suicides in the United States peaked in 1994 and has been declining ever since. Some experts say the rate has decreased because of a greater usage of antidepressants by youths, but new evidence indicates the new drugs may actually spur suicide attempts in younger patients.

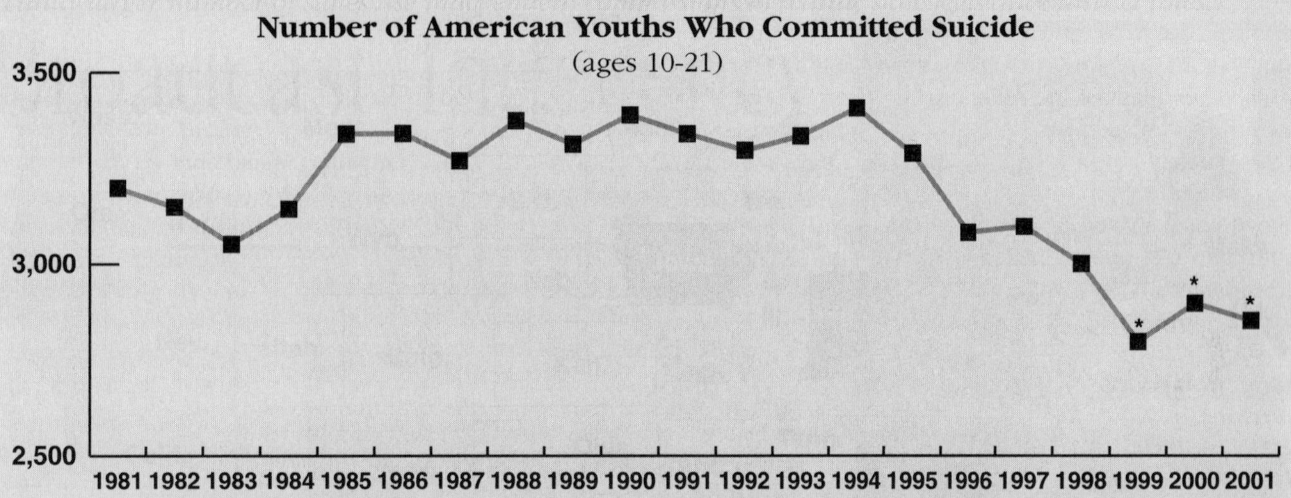

** The way in which suicide is recorded changed significantly in 1999, making it difficult to compare the number of deaths and death rates from 1998 and before with data after 1999.*

Sources: Centers for Disease Control and Prevention, www.cdc.gov/ncipc/wisqars and National Center for Health Statistics, Vital Statistics System

even while waiting for final studies — to doctors prescribing the new antidepressants to anyone under age 18. [9]

The FDA is expected to hold more hearings and issue additional recommendations this spring or summer.

Although less controversial, traditional psychotherapy sometimes doesn't work as well for teens, who tend to assert their independence from adults and thus may resist suggestions from a psychologist. In addition, troubled kids often live in dysfunctional families, which have trouble making sure the patient gets to psychotherapy sessions every week. Still, Riso says, psychotherapy can improve teens' moods and "decrease the frequency of suicidal behavior."

Unfortunately, most children never get the help they need. Mental health experts estimate that less than one-third of children with emotional problems — and as few as one-fifth of children with depression — receive treatment. "Earlier diagnoses and more vigorous treatment can lower the rate," says psychiatrist David C. Clark, director of the Center for Suicide Research and Prevention at Rush University Medical Center in Chicago. "Most people who die from suicide aren't getting psychiatric treatment."

To reduce the teen suicide rate, experts say it is vital to identify at-risk youngsters and get them into treatment. Several public schools have programs to train parents, teachers and students to spot potentially depressed children, and some experts say screening for suicidal tendencies should be as widespread as screening for hearing problems. (*See sidebar, p. 136.*)

However, the programs have earned mixed reviews, and officials in many schools are leery of raising the topic of suicide. Even mental health professionals who say school-based programs may help reduce the suicide rate say the topic needs to be approached carefully so as not to inadvertently spur suicide attempts and "clusters," in which several youths in the same community kill themselves.

"Teens are so impressionable that it's important that the information not be presented in a way that glamorizes suicide and makes a teen at risk consider suicide just because someone talks about it," says Lee Judy, certification coordinator of the American Association of Suicidology.

Meanwhile, few schools have counselors trained to help suicidal youngsters, and many regions lack counselors who specialize in emotionally troubled young people.

"It's a huge problem, and there aren't enough dollars," says Cheryl DiCara, coordinator of the Maine Youth Suicide Prevention Program.

Millions of dollars are spent each year on substance abuse prevention in schools, but youth suicide "is not getting the attention it needs as a public-health problem," says John Kalafut, a Rutgers University psychology professor and president of the American Association of Suicidology.

As society grapples with the problem of youth suicide, here are some questions it must address:

Is society to blame for youth suicide?

More than 20 years ago, when Kalufut began asking high-schoolers whether they knew anyone who had ever attempted suicide, 30 to 40 percent would raise their hands, the Rutgers professor recalls. "Now it's 100 percent," he says.

Rare from the time the government began compiling records in 1933 until the 1950s, youth suicide peaked in the early 1990s with the suicide rate for teens ages 15-19 reaching 11.1 per 100,000 population. Since then, the rate has declined significantly, to 7.9 per 100,000 in 2001. But that's still much higher than in 1950, when it was just 4.5 per 100,000. [10]

Moreover, suicide rates rose alarmingly in the 1990s for certain populations: The rate for youngsters 10-14 doubled between 1980 and 1996 — even though psychologists once thought children so young were immune to depression. The rate among that age group has been declining since it peaked in 1995, except for an increase in 1998. The rate for teenage girls stayed level in the mid-1990s after the rate for older boys began to decline, but the rate of girls' suicides has also begun to decline in recent years.

"For most people, [suicide] is probably a squeamish topic," said Dan Casseday, whose 16-year-old son committed suicide in 2002. "But if people understood the statistics about suicide, there'd be panic about [it]." [11]

No one knows what triggered the enormous jump in youth suicides, but many experts say societal changes could be a factor. The American Academy of Pediatrics, for example, lists four possible causes: easy access to firearms and other means of suicide; increasing pressures of modern life; stiff scholastic competition; and increased media violence. [12]

Other mental health professionals point to the breakdown of the nuclear family, manifested by higher divorce rates and more children living in single-parent households. Our increasingly mobile society also may play a role: Multiple changes of homes and schools can lead to emotional isolation, a key factor in youth suicide. Work demands keep many parents at the office until after dinnertime, or on their computers even after they come home, while neglected kids watch television or play video games.

"The reasons are probably broad societal types of things — people not living near extended families, less involvement in religion and other traditional supports," says David Brent, a professor of psychiatry, pediatrics and epidemiology at the University of Pittsburgh and a nationally recognized expert on youth suicide.

"I see a breakdown in the community's involvement in raising children," Kalafut adds. "The postwar generation of parents is the first in history to raise children without significant input from the community."

Others cite increased rates of alcohol and drug abuse, noting that many youths are impaired when they kill themselves. "From the 1960s forward, the biggest driver was the increasing availability of substances — drugs and alcohol," says the Carmel Hill Center's Flynn. "These substances allow youngsters to act on impulse because they take away inhibition."

A 1986 government survey found that half of the youths at risk of killing themselves cited family conflicts, more than one-third mentioned physical or sexual abuse and 17 percent blamed alcohol or drug abuse. [13] All three prob-

Continued on p. 132

AP Photo/Ralph Wilson

After three local teenage boys killed themselves recently, Judge John B. Leete of Coudersport, Pa., helped bring the Yellow Ribbon suicide-prevention program to town. Across the country, few schools have suicide screening or counseling programs, and many states lack comprehensive suicide-prevention plans. An estimated 1,600 youths ages 15-19 will take their own lives this year.

Would Gun Control Reduce Suicides?

"Probably the single, most effective thing we could do to reduce the incidence of completed suicide is restrict access to firearms," says David Fassler, a child psychiatrist in Burlington, Vt., and an associate professor at the University of Vermont. "If you're impulsive and having thoughts about hurting yourself, you shouldn't be near them."

More than half of teen suicides are committed with guns. [1] Although girls are twice as likely to attempt suicide, boys are four times more likely to succeed in killing themselves, because they tend to use more lethal means, such as guns. According to a 1999 report by Surgeon General David Satcher, the increase in the rate of suicide during the 1980s and early '90s was almost entirely due to more young people using firearms to end their lives.

After his girlfriend broke up with him, 16-year-old Joe Muñoz, wanted to kill himself with one of his father's guns, but it was locked up. "Had his guns been out of the gun case, I would have shot myself," recalls Muñoz, now 42 and a freelance journalist in Dallas. Instead he took two bottles of sleeping pills, realized what he had done when his heart started palpitating and called for help.

"What I tell parents whose kids are at high risk of suicide is just get the guns out of the house for now," says John Kalafut, a professor of psychology at Rutgers University and president of the American Association of Suicidology. "I have sat with kids who said to me, 'If there had been a gun in my house a year ago, I wouldn't be talking with you today.' "

Although gun-control measures enjoy little political support in Washington, a few states have tightened controls. A new Maryland law requires guns to be sold with trigger locks and requires buyers to take a two-hour gun safety class. Last year, New Jersey passed a law that eventually will require guns to be sold with "smart gun" technology, which allows them to be fired only by an authorized user.

Other proposals — such as making it harder for people under 21 to buy or possess guns — are not getting much political traction.

The politically powerful National Rifle Association (NRA) and other advocates of gun ownership say the restrictions are misguided. The New Jersey law is flawed, they say, because the technology to create smart guns does not exist. And Maryland's restrictions will do little to prevent crimes and accidents with guns, in part because the safety locks are ineffective, they add.

David Eccles, an Annapolis gun shop owner who taught his 3-year-old son how a gun works, contends that it's more effective to explain guns to a child than to use safety locks. "It's not going to be any trick [for a child] to figure out where the keys are kept or how to rip the lock off," he said. [2]

The NRA supports educating children, rather than keeping them away from guns, using a mascot known as Eddie Eagle to teach youngsters four basic steps to follow if they see a gun: Stop, don't touch, leave the area, tell an adult.

"The purpose of the Eddie Eagle Program isn't to teach whether guns are good or bad, but rather to promote the protection and safety of children," the NRA's Web site says. "The program makes no value judgments about firearms, and no firearms are ever used in the program. Like swimming pools, electrical outlets, matchbooks and household poison, they're treated simply as a fact of everyday life. With firearms found in about half of all American households, it's a stance that makes sense." [3]

But gun-control advocates cite a new study, published in the January issue of the journal *PEDIATRICS*, which found the gun lobby's educational programs were ineffective. [4] "They fail at keeping kids safe from guns," Mike Barnes, president of the Brady Campaign to Prevent Gun Violence United With the Million Mom March, says. "All they do is teach kids to recite the gun lobby's slogans. From an industry standpoint, it's a great marketing tool for introducing young people to guns."

Research on the issue is mixed. Last year, a Centers for Disease Control and Prevention (CDC) task force reviewed 51 studies of whether gun laws prevent violent crimes, suicides or accidents and concluded that the studies were contradictory, incomplete or poorly designed. It called for more research, concluding that there is "insufficient evidence to determine the effectiveness of any of the firearms laws." [5]

But the government is unlikely to conduct much research into the issue. In 1997 Congress forbade the CDC from promoting gun control, and the center's funds for gun research have been slashed from $2.6 million in 1995 to $400,000 in 2002. [6]

"No one knows if better gun control would reduce the suicide rate," says David C. Clark, director of the Center for Suicide Research and Prevention at Rush-Presbyterian-St. Luke's Medical Center, in Chicago.

He notes that some countries with strict gun-control laws, such as Canada, have youth suicide rates that are comparable to or even higher than those in the United States.

"People would shift to other means such as hanging and pills," he says, but he concedes, "We might make a small decrease in youth suicide."

Even though the evidence is mixed, he adds, it might be worthwhile trying to restrict guns and measure the impact on youth suicide. "I, for one, would love to see such an experiment."

---

[1] A report by the Child Trends DataBank concluded that firearms were used in 60 percent of teen suicides in 1999.

[2] Scott Albright, "Unlock and load: Handgun bill brings out emotions on both sides," *The* [Annapolis, Md.] *Capital*, April 9, 2000, p. A1.

[3] See http://www.nrahq.org/safety/eddie/

[4] Michael B. Himle, *et al.*, "An Evaluation of Two Procedures for Training Skills to Prevent Gun Play in Children," *PEDIATRICS*, January 2004, pp. 70-77.

[5] David Wahlberg, "CDC: Impact of gun laws cloudy," *Los Angeles Times*, Oct. 3, 2003, p. A1.

[6] *Ibid.*

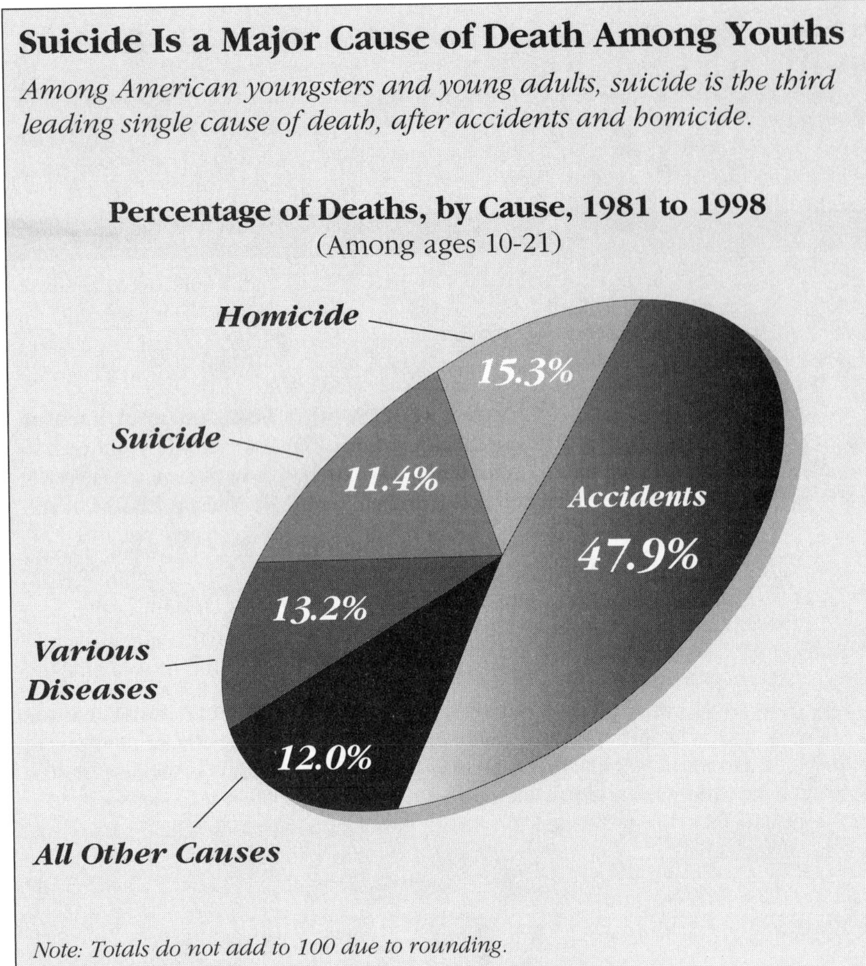

Continued from p. 130

lems became especially prevalent in the second half of the 20th century.

But other experts are not persuaded. Clark at the Center for Suicide Research and Prevention says the youth suicide rate waxed and waned even before the 1930s, when the government began keeping statistics. Although exact statistics are not available, evidence points to a particularly high rate around 1910, he says — a time when society was far different than it is today.

"None of the things we might point to today existed in 1910," he says, adding that more research is needed. "It really takes a major epidemiological study to tease this out. We have to look at thousands and thousands of cases."

Mental health professionals also caution that complex and poorly understood physiological factors should be taken into account, such as how chemical imbalances in the brain can lead to depression and suicide. A 1985 study even suggested that youth suicide victims tend to have mothers who received less prenatal care or smoked and drank during pregnancy. [14]

Others question whether suicide statistics are accurate. Some of the earlier increases could be due to society's greater acceptance today of recording deaths as suicides rather than as accidents. "Coroners were more likely to report suicides in the 1960s [than in earlier decades]," says Koplewicz of the Child Study Center.

Some experts say the jump in suicide rates was driven by a growing prevalence of emotional distress in the young. According to Koplewicz, more than 3 million American youths suffer from depression, even though childhood depression wasn't even recognized as a disorder until the last 25 years. [15] *The Journal of the American Academy of Child and Adolescent Psychiatry* concluded that increasing numbers of children are depressed and that they are showing more severe symptoms earlier in their lives. In Washington state, more children are hospitalized for psychiatric illnesses than for any other single reason. [16]

Children are aware of the pressures that can lead to emotional distress and even suicide. After the suicide of a 14-year-old student at Palo Alto High School in Silicon Valley, a third of the 756 respondents to a school newspaper poll said they felt very stressed, and an additional 44 percent said they were somewhat stressed.

"So many times we hear kids say, 'I can't go home tonight because I got a B+ on that test, and my parents will kill me,' " said Philippe Rey, associate director of Adolescent Counseling Services in Palo Alto, which works with area schools. [17]

But adults typically struggle to acknowledge or accept such distress in their own children. "We don't like to think of our children and our teenagers having mental disorders," Koplewicz says. "We think, 'What does a kid have to be sad about? It just doesn't make any sense.' "

Are schools and governments doing enough to prevent youth suicide?

Sue Eastgard is on a sometimes lonely quest. In Washington state, where an average of two youths a week commit suicide, she is both the director and sole full-time employee of the state Youth Suicide Prevention Program. With an annual budget of less than 25 cents

Depression Differs Among Adults, Youths

Major depression manifests itself differently in adults, adolescents and children. If a person exhibits four or more symptoms of depression for more than two weeks, experts say he or she should consult a physician.

Typical Signs of Depression:

Adults

Persistent sad or "empty" mood.

Feeling hopeless, helpless, worthless, pessimistic and/or guilty.

Substance abuse.

Fatigue or loss of interest in ordinary activities, including sex.

Disturbances in eating and sleeping patterns.

Irritability, increased crying, anxiety or panic attacks.

Difficulty concentrating, remembering or making decisions.

Thoughts of suicide; makes plans to commit suicide or attempts suicide.

Persistent physical symptoms or pains that do not respond to treatment.

Adolescents

Eating disorders.

Drug or alcohol abuse.

Sexual promiscuity.

Risk-taking behavior, such as reckless driving, unprotected sex or carelessness when walking across busy streets or on bridges or cliffs.

Social isolation, running away, difficulty cultivating relationships.

Constant disobedience, getting into trouble with the law, physical or sexual assaults against others, obnoxious behavior.

Failure to care about appearance/hygiene.

No sense of self or of values/morals.

Inability to establish/stick with occupational/educational goals.

Dizziness, headaches, stomach aches, neck aches, arms or legs hurt due to muscle tension, digestive disorders.

Persistent unhappiness, negativity or irritability.

Uncontrollable anger or outbursts of rage.

Overly self-critical, unwarranted guilt, low self-esteem.

Inability to concentrate, remember or make decisions, possibly resulting in refusal to study or an inability to do schoolwork.

Slowed or hesitant speech or body movements, restlessness (anxiety).

Loss of interest in once-pleasurable activities.

Low energy, chronic fatigue or sluggishness.

Change in appetite, noticeable weight loss or gain, or abnormal eating patterns.

Chronic worry, excessive fear.

Preoccupation with death themes in literature, music and/or drawings; speaking of death repeatedly, fascination with guns/knives.

Suicidal thoughts, plans or attempts.

Children

School phobia or avoidance.

Social phobia or avoidance.

Excessive separation anxiety, running away.

Obsessions, compulsions or everyday rituals, such as having to go to bed at the exact time each night for fear something bad may happen.

Chronic illnesses (depression weakens the immune system).

Persistent unhappiness, negativity, complaining, chronic boredom, lack of initiative.

Uncontrollable anger with aggressive or destructive behavior, possibly hitting themselves or others, kicking, self-biting, head banging.

Harming animals.

Continual disobedience.

Easily frustrated, frequent crying, low self-esteem, overly sensitive.

Inability to pay attention, remember, or make decisions, easily distracted, mind goes blank.

Energy fluctuations from lethargic to frenzied activity, with periods of normalcy.

Eating or sleeping problems.

Bedwetting, constipation or diarrhea.

Impulsiveness or being accident-prone.

Chronic worry and fear, clingy, panic attacks.

Extreme self-consciousness.

Slowed speech and body movements.

Disorganized speech.

Dizziness, headaches, stomachaches, arms or legs ache, nail-biting, pulling out hair or eyelashes.

Suicidal talk or attempts.

Source: Suicide Awareness Voices of Education, www.save.org.

per child, she can't reach most of the state's large schools and communities to help them with their programs.

"You can't do a program for $230,000 a year," says Eastgard, who sometimes has to drive three hours each way just to reach a single school. "We need funding to hire more people."

Maine faces a similar situation. The state won a three-year CDC grant to bolster crisis services and help school employees and students recognize at-risk youths in a dozen schools. The grant also pays for several other suicide prevention programs, including a statewide crisis hotline, an information resource center and various training programs. But the funding amounts to less than $300,000 a year, and it runs out next year.

"We want to continue doing this," says DiCara, of the Maine Youth Suicide Prevention Program. "But when this grant goes away, we won't have any money."

Such situations are common. Facing tight budgets and conflicting information about how best to reduce youth suicide rates, states and localities are devoting comparatively few resources to the issue. On the federal level, policymakers have focused more attention on the problem since a 1997 congressional resolution recognizing suicide as a national problem and Surgeon General Satcher's 1999 call for a national suicide prevention strategy.

In the last few years, federal grants for some state-based suicide prevention programs have increased slightly, and the government has helped fund the new national Suicide Prevention Resource Center in Newton, Mass.

States have stepped in as well. For example, nine states fund school-based mental health or suicide prevention programs. Oklahoma has created a Youth Suicide Prevention Council to help community anti-suicide efforts and make policy recommendations, and Washington funds a 24-hour crisis hotline. [18] But advocates warn that most states and communities still lack youth suicide prevention programs, and many people, especially in rural areas, cannot easily obtain counseling services.

"What is lacking is sufficient funding for program development, evaluation, training and initiatives," says Jerry Reed, executive director of the Suicide Prevention Action Network (SPAN). "A solid federal funding commitment to these efforts would undoubtedly reduce the suicide rate among our youth."

Suicide prevention programs are cost-effective, many experts say. Every emergency room visit for a suicide attempt costs taxpayers an average of $33,000. [19] In addition, untreated suicidal youths are more prone to other problems, including dropping out of school, abusing alcohol and drugs and committing violent crimes, including homicide.

"Every juvenile I've represented in a murder case has tried to kill himself," said William Lafond, a defense lawyer in San Diego. "Many of these kids feel helpless and depressed and don't understand why they did what they did. When they try to understand their feelings, they can't handle it." [20]

But even if the government provided more funds for youth suicide prevention programs, the evidence is mixed on how much can be achieved.

Some programs — such as Lifeline — strive to build communities in which at-risk youths are identified and guided into treatment. Designed by Rutgers' Kalafut and used in Maine and some jurisdictions in New Jersey, the program teaches parents, children, teachers and other school employees how to identify youths who appear troubled.

"The emphasis is building a community in which the leaders are committed to creating a safe and supportive environment," Kalafut explains. "Everybody feels responsible for everyone else and is competent to know how to get help for them."

Eastgard says it's important that kids know to look out for each other. She explains, "You say to your friend, 'You look down. Are you feeling so down you're thinking about suicide? Let's go talk to so-and-so' . . . The skills are not to be the junior counselor. The skill is to be comfortable to ask them the question and drag them to help. We're suggesting you don't have to have fancy psychological letters after your name to be an intervener."

There is some evidence such programs can be effective. Youth suicide rates in Bergen County, N.J., dropped by half over a 10-year period in which the local schools used the program, while the rest of the state showed no comparable decline, Kalafut said.

DiCara is heartened when she hears about troubled children who are identified and steered into counseling. "I know it's helping," she says. "We're hearing from a lot of people in these 12 schools that they're already getting kids into services. That's huge."

Other studies, however, raise serious questions about the effectiveness of school programs and even warn that talking about suicide may stir up suicidal thoughts in children. The National Institute of Mental Health (NIMH) concluded: "Many of these programs are designed to reduce the stigma of talking about suicide and encourage distressed youth to seek help. By describing suicide and its risk factors, some curricula may have the unintended effect of suggesting that suicide is an option for many young people who have some of the risk factors and in that sense 'normalize' it — just the opposite of the message intended," the report said. "Of the programs that were evaluated, none has proven to be effective." [21]

Experts particularly criticize the common tactic of having children attend a schoolwide talk after a student commits suicide. Such an approach, they say, can backfire by portraying suicide as a feasible option, sometimes inducing a cluster of suicides in a single school or community.

The University of Pittsburgh's Brant suggests that rather than focusing on suicide, "It's better to educate students more generically about mental health and substance abuse."

But counselors say children are already aware of suicide. Instead of avoiding the subject, they believe, schools should confront it in a sensitive way. "Most of the kids I've talked to were very relieved that suicide was discussed," says Margie

Continued on p. 137

Chronology

1950s *Psychiatric researchers Leon Cytryn and Donald K. McKnew Jr., note that chronically ill and hospitalized children often exhibit symptoms of classical adult depression.*

1950
Youth suicide rate reaches about 4.5 per 100,000 population.

1960s *Youth suicide rate begins a decades-long climb. . . . Teens have more access to alcohol and drugs, and families appear more fractured. . . . First epidemiological study of a child population identifies depression in less than 1 percent of youngsters.*

1970s *Psychiatric researchers begin noting that depressed children present different symptoms than depressed adults. Cytryn and McKnew suggest three types of childhood depression: acute, chronic and masked.*

1980s *Youth suicide rate continues to climb, as childhood depression is recognized for the first time; schools begin establishing prevention programs.*

1980
Authoritative *Diagnostic and Statistical Manual on Mental Disorders* (*DSM-III*) recognizes depression in children and youths as a distinct disorder.

1983
California creates the first state-funded pilot programs to prevent suicide.

1986
Congress considers the Youth Suicide Prevention Act, which would have authorized the secretary of Education to make grants to local agencies and nonprofit organizations for suicide prevention programs. Instead, lawmakers roll the funding into a general program of state block grants. . . . Government survey of suicide experts finds that many at-risk youths cope with troubled families, physical or sexual abuse or alcohol/drug usage.

1987
Drugmaker Eli Lilly introduces Prozac, a powerful antidepressant.

1990s *Youth suicide rate peaks for various populations, reaching 11.1 per 100,000 for older teenagers before beginning to decline.*

1994
Food and Drug Administration (FDA) addresses concerns that untested drugs are being given to children by proposing that pediatric data be required on all drug products that might be prescribed for children "off-label," or for uses not originally intended.

1997
Congress passes a resolution recognizing suicide as a national problem.

1999
Concerns about youth violence are crystallized when two gun-wielding seniors at Columbine High School outside Denver on April 20 murder a dozen students and a teacher before killing themselves. . . . Surgeon General David Satcher declares suicide a public health problem and proposes initiatives to reduce the rate of suicides nationwide.

2000s *Researchers question safety of antidepressant usage among children.*

October 2000
A study in the *Archives of Dermatology* indicates that teenagers who take the acne drug Accutane are no more likely to attempt suicide than those who do not. Accutane has been associated with youth suicide and requires an FDA warning label.

2002
National Suicide Prevention Resource Center begins operation as part of a national suicide prevention strategy.

June 2003
FDA advises that antidepressant Paxil should not be prescribed for teens and younger children until further study.

Dec. 10, 2003
British health regulators warn doctors against prescribing most newer antidepressant drugs to children, arguing benefits are outweighed by risks of triggering suicidal thoughts, self-injury and agitation.

Feb. 2, 2004
FDA scientific advisory board opens hearings on the controversy over antidepressants and their possible role in youth suicide.

Summer 2004
FDA ruling on antidepressants is expected.

Screening Program Identifies Suicide-Prone Kids

American youngsters are checked for everything from flat feet and crooked teeth to tuberculosis and mumps, but few are screened for one of the most dangerous afflictions they could face — the impulse to take their own lives.

"You take your kids in for a physical checkup every year, but the chances of finding anything wrong in adolescents — who are in the best health they'll ever be in — is very remote," says Laurie Flynn, director of the Carmel Hill Health Center for Early Diagnosis and Treatment at Columbia University. "Yet we've got a half-million kids every year trying suicide seriously enough to warrant medical attention, and that's something to pay attention to."

Columbia's TeenScreen Program aims to change that. Developed by Columbia Professor David Shaffer and overseen by the health center, it uses questionnaires and interviews to identify youngsters who may be at risk for depression and suicide, as well as for eating disorders and substance abuse. The program is used in more than 100 communities in some 30 states.

Once parental permission is obtained, students fill out a brief survey that includes questions about depression, substance abuse and suicide. Students who score positive on any of the questions answer a series of questions designed to gain insights into their emotional well-being. The questions probe for possible signs of distress, such as, "Do you have trouble staying awake in school?" Each time the student answers "Yes," the program asks a follow-up question — for example, "Does it happen every day?"

Students are asked specifically if they have thought about committing suicide. If the answer is yes, the computer asks follow-up questions, such as, "This week?" "Have you made a plan?"

A health-care professional must be on site to assess the results and recommend appropriate action. About 10-15 percent of the youngsters tested have been referred for treatment.

Counselors give the program high marks and say the kids enjoy taking the test. "I think it's very effective," says Margie Wright, executive director of the Suicide and Crisis Center in Dallas, which has used the program in several schools. "Kids will tell computers things they don't tell people face to face."

The idea for the program arose from research indicating that the majority of teens who are at risk for suicide are never diagnosed. Shaffer and his colleagues, for example, investigated 120 teenage suicides over a two-year period and found that 90 percent had a mental disorder that had gone undetected. Although parents generally believe they can tell when their kids are depressed, many emotional problems are dismissed as typical adolescent mood swings.

"Teenagers go to great pains to hide emotional distress from their parents," Shaffer said. [1]

Wright says TeenScreen has shown that kids at greatest risk for suicide often appear relatively energetic or happy. This correlates with research showing that many youngsters who kill themselves are successful in their classes and relationships but often impulsive or predisposed toward depression.

"Kids who are depressed don't look like adults who are depressed," she explains. "They're doing well in school, doing well in sports. They may be popular kids. For some kids, enough is never enough. Some kids are beautiful, but they don't see themselves that way. Or they're not living up to their parents' expectations."

But experts warn that TeenScreen has several shortcomings. For one thing, some youngsters become suicidal very suddenly — and the danger signs may not be picked up by a test administered only infrequently.

"When it comes to psychopathology and mental health, a lot of the problems are on and off. You catch me this month and I'm depressed; you catch me next month and I'm not," says David C. Clark, director of the Center for Suicide Research and Prevention at Rush-Presbyterian-St. Luke's Medical Center in Chicago. "Some of the suicidal impulses that kill children can literally sweep in like a storm and take a kid who six weeks before was strong and sturdy."

Moreover, many localities lack appropriate care for those who test positive. When school officials in Florida saw a presentation on TeenScreen, they were impressed, but they worried about what would happen to the children after diagnosis. "We felt that we could not set up a system to provide the necessary services for students identified to need treatment," said Linda Jones, supervisor for Safe and Drug Free Schools in Pinellas County (St. Petersburg). "It's not a good idea to screen unless you can provide care." [2]

Money can also be a factor. Although TeenScreen software is provided for free, schools need to pay to implement the program and provide follow-up evaluations for youngsters who appear to be at risk.

Gwen Luney, assistant school superintendent for supportive services and federal programs in Hillsborough County (Tampa), estimated TeenScreen would have cost the school district about $200,000 a year. "We're hesitant to commit to a new program if there's a strong possibility [of budget] shortfalls. Also, are we going to find a place for this [diagnosed] child to go? If so, what if the child doesn't have insurance? Who picks up the cost?" [3]

TeenScreen has appeared on Washington's radar screen. Rep. Rosa DeLauro, D-Conn., has introduced legislation to create 10 federally funded TeenScreen demonstration projects. Some school officials are warming to the idea, in part because identifying at-risk youth early may help prevent problems down the road, including criminal behavior.

Flynn acknowledges the problems of implementing a successful screening and treatment program, but she asks if society has a feasible alternative. "Would we rather not do this and wait until the kids get worse?" she asks.

---

[1] Quoted in Carol Vinzant, "Suicide Mission; Teens Are Screened for Many Conditions, but Rarely for a Real Killer," *The Washington Post*, Feb. 25, 2003, p. F1.

[2] Eric Snider, "Climbing Out of Hell; We Could Do More To Help Kids Stay Alive," *Weekly Planet Tampa*, June 5-11, 2003.

[3] Quoted in *ibid*.

Continued from p. 134

Wright, executive director of the Suicide and Crisis Center in Dallas. "You can't plant that idea in someone's head. You're either suicidal or not. The more people are educated, the better off we'll be."

But all of the school programs in the world cannot help if there are insufficient counseling services for youngsters, critics say. Some school districts, especially in isolated areas, lack conveniently located counseling services, and there are only 7,000 board-certified child and adolescent psychiatrists in the United States and fewer than 6,000 child psychologists to treat the several million youths with diagnosable psychiatric disorders. [22]

"The schools can do whatever they want, but if there isn't adequate, competent treatment in the community, then the whole program won't achieve its own goals," Kalafut says. "Every piece has to be in place or the whole thing doesn't work."

Are antidepressant drugs helping to reduce the suicide rate?

British health authorities grabbed the attention of medical professionals around the world in December when they warned against prescribing most of the newer antidepressant drugs to children. Britain's equivalent of the FDA said the benefits of popular medications like Zoloft, Celexa and Lexapro were outweighed by the risks that the drugs could cause harmful side effects, including suicidal thoughts, self-injury and agitation. Only with Prozac did the benefits outweigh the risks, they said.

"These medicines may do more harm than good in the treatment of depression in under-18s," the British agency warned. [23]

The FDA had previously cautioned doctors against prescribing the antidepressants to children. Now it is undertaking a more sweeping review of the safety of antidepressants for children, examining about 20 studies, both published and unpublished and mostly conducted by pharmaceutical companies, of children who took antidepressants.

But many psychiatrists say the drugs are essential for treating severely depressed young people, and may even be responsible for the recent drop in the overall youth suicide rate. "I tend to believe they're enormously helpful and save lives," says the Center for Suicide Research and Prevention's Clark. "Clinical depressions can be mild or moderate or severe. If it's severe, I'll always talk about medication."

The antidepressants under scrutiny are called selective serotonin reuptake inhibitors, or SSRIs. They are so popular that total worldwide sales in 2001 hit $15.9 billion, third behind ulcer medications and cholesterol and triglyceride reducers. [24] SSRI use has become increasingly widespread among the young, even though only Prozac has been approved for treating childhood depression (and some researchers even question Prozac's safety, noting that it has been linked to suicide attempts in adults). [25] About 2.1 million prescriptions were written for youths in 2002, compared to only 50,000 in 1992, according to a recent estimate. [26] Even though the drugs are recommended only for severe depression, more than half of American children being treated for depression are given antidepressants, according to a study published in December. [27]

Health experts have raised concerns about whether the drugs are being overprescribed, especially by pediatricians and general practitioners in managed-care plans. The drugs represent a less expensive alternative for treating depression than traditional therapy, which can cost more than $100 for a weekly visit and last for months or even years. A month's supply of Prozac, in contrast, costs about $140 (and as little as $20 for its generic version). Taking a pill is also easier for patients than driving to a therapist for a nearly hourlong session.

But some experts question whether the drugs are effective. One much-quoted study showed 69 percent of children improved while taking Zoloft, only slightly better than the 59 percent who improved while taking a placebo. Other studies, funded by the pharmaceutical industry, reportedly indicate that the drugs are no more effective than placebos — but those studies have not been published. [28] "Some people offer up these [medications] as a panacea," says the University of Pittsburgh's Brent. "They're better than nothing, but they don't work that well."

Still, some studies indicate SSRIs are reducing the youth suicide rate. *The Archives of General Psychiatry* reported in October that between 1990 and 2000 the increase in the use of antidepressants among children was associated with a decrease in teen suicides.

Mark Olfson, one of the study's authors, said that although it is too early to credit the antidepressants for the decrease, "It's a plausible hypothesis, and there's accumulating data."

Studies in Sweden and other European countries also have shown a correlation between antidepressant use and decreased suicide rates, but a study in Italy did not.

"These SSRIs can very possibly be lifesaving medicines," says Koplewicz of New York University's Child Study Center. "If someone really has depression, the first line of attack should be cognitive behavioral therapy. * It works in mild to moderate cases. Within 12 to 16 sessions, you're going to see a difference. If they don't get better, then adding medicine makes a lot of sense."

Although SSRIs appear to be safer than an earlier class of antidepressants known as tricyclic antidepressants, they still can have dangerous side effects. By boosting serotonin levels, they may cause physical and emotional agitation — a condition called akathisia. Some

---

* In cognitive behavioral therapy, also called "talk" therapy, patients discuss their feelings with a psychologist or psychiatrist over a long period of time.

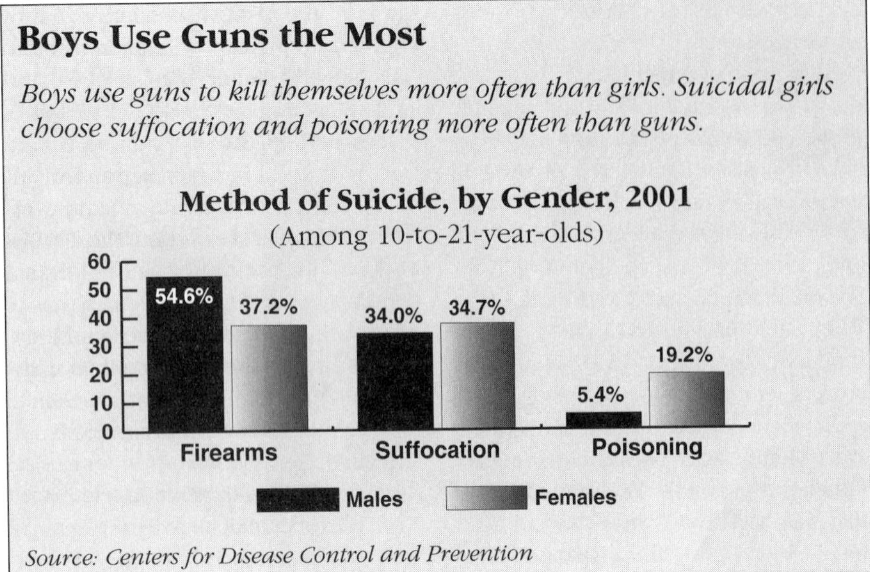

Boys Use Guns the Most

Boys use guns to kill themselves more often than girls. Suicidal girls choose suffocation and poisoning more often than guns.

Source: Centers for Disease Control and Prevention

children can have a paradoxical reaction to the drugs, which causes them to become extremely restless or impulsive, and children with undiagnosed manic-depression can become unstable.

Some SSRIs are metabolized by the body very quickly and can cause a variety of reactions, including mood shifts, when abruptly halted. In three studies of Paxil examined by British regulators, 20 of 34 events "possibly related to suicidality" occurred during the 30 days after the children stopped taking the drug, compared with eight out of 17 in the placebo group in the same period.

Antidepressants are not the only drugs under scrutiny for links to youth suicide. A popular acne drug, Accutane, has been associated with suicide and requires an FDA warning label. The link, however, is not clear, and an extensive study published in the October 2000 issue of *Archives of Dermatology* indicated that teenagers who take Accutane are no more likely to try to kill themselves than those who do not.

Accutane is derived from vitamin A, which is involved with the growth and maintenance of skin. Some studies indicate that people who consume large amounts of vitamin A and related molecules suffer from depression, and concerns have been raised about individual cases of people taking Accutane who killed themselves.

Among the most publicized was the case of B.J. Stupak of Menominee, Mich., who shot himself in 2000. His father, Rep. Bart Stupak, D-Mich., has worked to publicize his son's story and others like it, and to have the drug taken off the market. Stupak said his son acted "out of the blue." The benefits of Accutane are "just not worth the side effects," he said. [29] ■

BACKGROUND

Studying Depression

Before the 20th century, youth suicide almost invariably was associated in literature with a traumatic event, such as the end of a relationship — perhaps most famously in Shakespeare's *Romeo and Juliet*. It briefly took center stage in the 18th century with publication of Goethe's landmark novel, *The Sorrows of Young Werther*. The tragic tale of the doomed young man's unrequited love reportedly impelled dozens of young men throughout Europe to also commit suicide. [30]

Before the 1970s, youth suicide generally garnered little attention. In fact, many psychologists believed young people were incapable of long-term depression, although some psychologists had begun to discover signs of depression in children shortly after World War II. As early as 1946, Viennese psychiatrist Rene A. Spitz described what he called "anaclitic depression" in infants in orphanages, who failed to thrive when deprived of sufficient human contact. And, beginning in the 1950s, psychiatric researchers Leon Cytryn and Donald K. McKnew Jr. noted that chronically ill and hospitalized children often exhibited the same symptoms as classical adult depression, which had been recognized for millennia.

In the 1960s and '70s, several pioneering researchers attempted to differentiate between adult and childhood depression. Meanwhile, the first epidemiological study of a child population, in England in the mid-1960s, identified depression in less than 1 percent of youngsters. A 1967 report by the U.S.-based Group for the Advancement of Psychiatry asserted that depression in children often presented itself differently than in adults.

By the early 1970s, Cytryn and McKnew had suggested there were three types of childhood depression: acute, chronic and masked. But the psychiatric community was not ready to recognize childhood depression as a separate pathology. "The absence of a name for this entity [in diagnostic manuals] forces many professionals to misdiagnose their depressive patients," they wrote in the 1979 *Basic Handbook of Child Psychiatry*. "This in turn perpetuates the misconception that the condition does not exist."

Throughout the 1970s, a handful of psychiatrists began diagnosing depression in children more frequently, and doctors began to realize it had been underestimated in the past. In

1980, childhood depression finally was listed as a diagnosable psychiatric condition in the authoritative *Diagnostic and Statistical Manual on Mental Disorders (DSM-III)*. By then, the youth suicide rate was rising dramatically — and mental health experts had become concerned that emotional problems in the young were a major risk factor.

Rising Toll

Modern thinking about suicide in general was largely shaped by Emile Durkheim, a French sociologist, and Sigmund Freud, the father of psychoanalysis. In *Le Suicide*, published in 1897, Durkheim listed three types of suicide: (1) altruistic suicide, where the customs and mores of a particular society dictate it (as with defeated warriors in certain cultures); (2) egotistical suicide, in which the victim is not sufficiently identified with the institutions of society and is forced to assume more individual responsibility than he can handle; and (3) anomic suicide, in which an individual's adjustment to society is suddenly broken or changed, as by financial reverses. To Freud, who wrote about man's inner destructivity, suicide represented the precocious victory of the inner drive toward death. None of these theories focused on youth suicide.

In 1933, the U.S. government began collecting statistics on morbidity. Although the data showed the nation's overall suicide rate remaining somewhat constant, the youth suicide rate increased dramatically after World War II with the emergence of the so-called Baby Boom generation. The rate of 4.5 suicides per 100,000 population in 1950 tripled over the next four decades. The trends initially coincided with a rebellious younger generation that was associated with drugs, sex and rock music.

But the alarming numbers persisted throughout the 1980s and even into the '90s, long after the turmoil of the '60s had subsided. Experts hypothesized about a variety of causes, including the breakdown of traditional families and communities, growing substance abuse and increasing violence — both in movies and rock songs and in real life. The increased suicide rate forced psychologists and policymakers in the 1990s to begin viewing mental health disorders in the young as a significant public health problem.

Meanwhile, mental health experts had become increasingly aware of the widespread problems of psychiatric disorders in the young. By then, an estimated 10 million children and adolescents had such disorders, according to Koplewicz of New York University. More than half of depressive adults said they had their first bout with the disease before age 20, a fact cited by many as proof of the urgency of catching and treating depression early in life.

Traditionally, mental health programs for the young in the United States have been the province of local care providers — churches, community mental health centers and private practitioners. But in 1983, amid rising concerns about teenage suicide, California created the first state-funded pilot programs to prevent suicide. High school teachers, administrators and students received instruction in sound decision-making, suicide warning signs, community suicide services, the relationship between substance abuse and suicide and how to improve interactions among students, teachers and school counselors.

Two years later, California expanded the pilot programs to encompass the entire state, and New Jersey launched its own program. Since then, about 15 other states have followed suit.

Federal Efforts

The federal government began to tackle the problem of mental illness — particularly the severely mentally ill — more aggressively in the 1960s. In February 1963, President John F. Kennedy asked Congress to adopt a "bold new approach" to those hospitalized with mental illness. Kennedy urged the creation of a nationwide network of community mental health centers to replace existing state mental hospitals. A shift to community-based care was widely seen as humane, since numerous abuses of patients had come to light at state-operated institutions.

Kennedy's goal of reducing mental hospital populations by half has been far exceeded: The number of hospital beds for the mentally ill has dropped from 550,000 in 1955 to only 40,000 today. But most of the money saved by shuttering state hospitals was not put back into the community mental health programs.

States continued to shutter hospitals, and by 1980, 2.4 million persons were receiving some sort of treatment at the nation's 750 mental health centers, 20 percent of which had been weaned off federal support. That same year President Jimmy Carter signed the Mental Health Systems Act, designed to boost funding for local treatment programs. But the following year, under the new administration of Ronald Reagan, the one-year-old law was repealed.

In 1981, as part of Reagan's proposals to curtail federal health programs, the Omnibus Budget Reconciliation Act restructured the nation's mental health system by shifting away from direct federal funding to a program of community block grants that states could apply to mental health treatment. Under the new system, funding for community mental health in 1982 dropped 30 percent below the previous year's level. [31]

In the 1990s, much of the national debate turned to the issue of "parity" — the concept that health insurance policies should cover mental health on a par with physical health. But the insurance industry has resisted the idea, which it warns would be costly and lead to higher premiums. [32]

In the meantime, government-funded research had begun shedding light on the causes of youth suicide. A 1986 survey of suicide experts found that many at-risk youths experienced troubled families, physical or sexual abuse, or alcohol or drug usage. The survey also pointed out that high achievers could also be at risk, because they tend to impose unrealistically high standards on themselves or feel a need to impress others. [33] Sexual orientation also appeared to play a role. A 1989 U.S. Department of Health and Human Services (HHS) study found homosexual teenagers were three times as likely as heterosexuals to attempt suicide. [34]

Even as youth suicide rates began to decline in the 1990s, several sensational school murder-suicides galvanized the nation's attention. Most dramatically, on April 20, 1999, two gun-wielding seniors at Columbine High School outside Denver murdered a dozen students and a teacher and wounded more than 20 others before killing themselves. [35] Many schools responded by establishing anti-bullying programs and trying to identify isolated or troubled students.

The same year, Surgeon General Satcher declared suicide a public health problem and proposed initiatives to reduce the rate of suicides nationwide, including youth suicides. The steps focused on increasing public awareness of suicide risk factors, enhancing services for potentially suicidal people and advancing research into suicide prevention. In 2001, Satcher unveiled the first installment of the national suicide prevention strategy, which focused on increased screening and increasing the number of states that require "parity" in health insurance — providing the same insurance coverage for mental health and substance abuse care as for regular health care.

Washington also has approved several grants for state and local suicide prevention programs, and for a nationwide toll-free suicide hotline (1-800-SUICIDE).

The Brain's Role

Research has shown a strong correlation between depression and suicide, and scientists are finding that some children are genetically predisposed to depression. [36]

Emotional disorder is often accompanied by abnormalities within and between the brain's neurotransmitters, composed of chemical compounds called amines. Neural impulses traveling in and out of the brain are accompanied by the release of these amines — manufactured and stored within nerve cells — which convey information from one nerve cell to another. Chemical messages from the neurotransmitters are passed along from cell to cell across the synapses, or small gaps between nerve cells.

An imbalance of brain amines — or an imbalance between the systems they are connected with — may impair the transmission of messages across the synapses, thus affecting the entire central nervous system and potentially producing symptoms of depression. Three amines in particular — dopamine, norepinephrine and serotonin — have been identified with depression.

In 1987, drug manufacturer Eli Lilly introduced Prozac, an antidepressant that increased levels of serotonin in the brain. Prozac proved highly popular among adults, and other SSRIs — including Paxil, Zoloft and Celexa — soon followed. With concern mounting about depressed children, doctors began prescribing the drugs for youngsters as well, even though the drugs' safety for use by children had never been tested.

From the start, some researchers worried about the new antidepressants' side effects. Some doctors noticed that their Prozac patients felt so uncomfortable they wanted to jump out of their skins. Controversies over the use of antidepressants for both children and adults has grown since then, culminating last year with the FDA warning for doctors not to prescribe Paxil to children and the British government cautioning against most popular antidepressants except Prozac. ■

CURRENT SITUATION

Federal Funds

Federal funding for youth suicide prevention has risen in recent years but still falls short of what's needed, advocates say.

Reed, of the Suicide Prevention Action Network, says funding has been on the upswing since 1997, when Congress passed a resolution recognizing suicide as a national problem. Since then, legislators have held three hearings on suicide prevention and authorized a suicide prevention resource center and a national hotline. The programs are slated to receive $3 million each in the omnibus appropriations bill for fiscal 2004, the same as last year.

Meanwhile, the Children's Mental Health Services Program — part of which goes to youth suicide prevention efforts — is set to increase by nearly $5 million in 2004, to $103 million.

"They've been very receptive," to our requests, Reed says. "They see that this is an important area to proceed on."

Appropriators also have ramped up funding for NIMH suicide research, increasing its appropriation by $2 million in fiscal 2003 and $1 million in the pending omnibus appropriations measure. NIMH is expected to receive $29.3 million for suicide research this year, $17 million of it targeted to youth issues.

Continued on p. 142

At Issue:

Would stricter gun controls reduce the youth suicide rate?

yes

MARY LEIGH BLEK
PRESIDENT EMERITUS, MILLION MOM MARCH

WRITTEN FOR *THE CQ RESEARCHER*, FEB. 3, 2004

After my son was shot and killed, I took a long hard look at how our nation protects our young people. We have a lot of work to do. When it comes to the very difficult issue of teenage suicide, there are fundamental truths that all parents know, but which policymakers typically ignore. A teenager's world is very different from an adult's.

One moment, young adults are soaring into the clouds, and the next they're crashing into the ground. Judgment and communication skills are still developing. As a mom and a former school nurse, I am intimately aware of the ups and downs that teenagers experience.

But I also know that it isn't always easy to learn when a teenager is having trouble.

Our job as parents is to show them our love and to offer them a safe environment. But we can't be everywhere, all the time. That's why we need a caring society and policymakers who are willing to help us build it.

I have often heard young adults say that if there had been a gun available to them, they would be dead. If we acknowledge that a teenager's world is different from our own, then we must make some choices about the world we both inhabit. It's the adult thing to do.

There are many issues concerning teenage depression and their mental well-being that must be examined by policymakers. But we do know that easy access to firearms greatly increases the risks of homicide and suicide.

A fleeting moment of despair combined with a teen's impulsivity and easy access to firearms is a recipe for disaster. The more lethal something is, the more likely death will occur. It's that simple. A recent study from the Harvard School of Public Health concluded that regions in the United States with higher levels of household handgun ownership experience higher suicide rates.

In many cases, technology holds the key. Cars are designed to be safer; guns should be, too. Technology that locks guns, or only permits the user to access it, offers policymakers opportunities to respect gun owners and safety. Many states have made the responsible decision to close loopholes in their laws that otherwise would allow young people to buy or possess guns.

It's time for Congress to act. We must also renew the ban on assault weapons and strengthen it. Sensible gun laws can help us prevent suicides, as well as homicides and injuries.

no

JOHN LOTT
RESIDENT SCHOLAR, AMERICAN ENTERPRISE INSTITUTE

WRITTEN FOR *THE CQ RESEARCHER*, FEB. 5, 2004

Unfortunately, stricter gun-control laws will not reduce youth suicide. There are too many alternative ways for people to kill themselves. A few studies by economists and criminologists indicate that gun regulations may reduce gun suicides, but even they do not find evidence that total suicides decline.

In 2001, 90 American children under age 15 committed suicide with guns, and an additional 361 teens ages 15 to 17. With the National Institute of Mental Health estimating that more than 4.9 percent of 9-to-17-year-olds suffer severe depression during a six-month period, that makes gun suicide rare, even assuming that only the severely depressed commit suicide: The rate is about one in 10,000 of these depressed juveniles.

The problem with gun-control laws is the unintended drawbacks. Recent research in my book, *The Bias Against Guns*, covered juvenile accidental gun deaths and suicides for all the states from 1977 to 1998. I found that safe-storage laws had no impact on either type of death. In fact, in the states that adopted safe-storage laws, juvenile suicides using handguns actually rose very slightly relative to states without those laws.

In addition, law-abiding citizens were less able to defend themselves against crime. The 16 states that adopted these laws during the period faced more than 300 more murders and 4,000 additional rapes per year. Burglaries also increased dramatically.

Guns clearly deter criminals, with Americans using guns defensively over 2 million times each year — more than four times more frequently than the 500,000 times guns were used to commit crimes in 2001. Even though the police are extremely important at reducing crime, they virtually always end up at the crime scene after the crime has been committed. Having a gun is by far the safest course of action when confronting a criminal.

Locked guns (or gun-free households) mean that guns are not as readily accessible for self-defense. Moreover, many mechanical locks (such as barrel or trigger locks) also require that the gun be stored unloaded. Loading a gun obviously requires yet more time to respond to a criminal.

Even if one has young children, it does not make sense to lock up a gun if one lives in a high-crime urban area. Exaggerating the risks involved in gun ownership will make people lock up their guns or cause them not to own a gun in the first place, resulting in more, not fewer deaths.

Continued from p. 140

And the CDC is expected to spend at least $2.8 million on suicide prevention in fiscal 2004, $2 million of it on research and $800,000 on data analysis and school-based suicide prevention pilot programs in Maine and Virginia, spokesperson Dagny Putman says.

Recent research suggests that school-based skills training and direct screening programs can increase coping skills and identify individuals at risk of committing suicide. Other studies suggest that programs aimed at training school personnel to recognize warning signs also may help reduce suicide risk. [37]

Additional funding for other school-based programs is provided in the Commerce, Justice and State department sections of the omnibus appropriations measure, as well as in the Labor, Health and Human Services portions of the bill. Among them are $150,000 for an online suicide prevention demonstration project in New York City and $1.1 million for prevention and awareness programs in Pennsylvania.

Still, mental health advocates did not get all they wanted from Congress. The Suicide Prevention Action Network was denied $8 million in grants to fund state and community suicide prevention plans, while the Mental Health Liaison Group — a nonprofit umbrella group representing families, advocates and mental health providers — lobbied fruitlessly for funds for a suicide prevention program for children and adolescents. The program was authorized in 2000 as part of a broader children's health bill sponsored by Rep. Michael Bilirakis, R-Fla., but has never been funded.

Paul Seifert, director of government affairs for the International Association of Psychosocial Rehabilitation Services — representing agencies, researchers, educators, practitioners and administrators — blames the delay on competing priorities. "If they give money to fund [Bilirakis' bill], they will have to take it from somewhere else," he says.

But Julio Abreu, director of government affairs at the National Mental Health Association, says it's more a matter of misplaced priorities. "There has been a general lack of commitment to issues relating to mental health," he laments.

Funding for the mental health block grant is expected to drop by $22 million in fiscal 2004, to $415 million.

Meanwhile, advocates perennially have failed to pass a mental health parity bill, which would prevent health plans from charging higher deductibles, copayments and out-of-pocket expenses for the treatment of mental illness than for other illnesses. House Republican leaders, warning it would drive up health care costs, have blocked the bill.

But supporters counter that the bill could cut employers' costs by reducing absenteeism and disability claims. Reed's organization plans to renew lobbying for the bill this year.

In states and localities across the country, tight budgets are imperiling anti-suicide programs. Just last month, for example, Massachusetts Gov. Mitt Romney proposed eliminating $125,000 for suicide prevention. [38] Far to the west, cash-strapped city officials in Santa Fe, N.M., have shut down a program to help adolescents in crisis and cut back funding for suicide programs in schools. "It points to a downturn in the economy and a lack of adequate gross receipts that we depend on for our budget," said Santa Fe City Councilor Miguel Chavez. [39]

Suicide on Campus

Colleges and universities across the country are feeling the brunt of the increase in youth depression. From 1989 to 2001, the number of depressed students seeking help doubled, and those at risk for suicide tripled, according to a much-cited Kansas State University study. [40]

"No doubt, over the last 10 years people are coming in with more severe depressions," says Jaquelyn Liss Resnick, president the Association of University and College Counseling Center Directors. "The types of problems have not changed over time, but the severity has."

Suicide is the second-leading cause of death among college students, with an estimated 7.5 deaths per 100,000 students per year, according to a study of Big 10 campuses from 1980 to 1990. A nationwide study found that 9 percent of college students seriously considered suicide between one and 10 times in the 2002-3 school year, and just over 1 percent actually tried to kill themselves. [41]

Resnick and other experts say college students always have been under stress, due to academic and social pressures and being separated from their families. In addition, many are exposed to drugs and alcohol for the first time in college. Moreover, emotional vulnerabilities become more apparent during the intense work and sometimes sleepless nights typical of college life.

In addition, more children with serious mental illnesses today are being diagnosed and treated with antidepressants, which can enable some to attend and cope with college who years ago perhaps would not have even considered applying to college.

"All across the country, we're seeing a significant increase in people coming in who are on psychiatric medication," Resnick says.

The Miami Herald recently profiled one such woman, Caitlin Stork, who attempted suicide when she was 15, then tried again shortly after being discharged from the hospital. Doctors eventually diagnosed her as having a bipolar disorder and put her on the mood stabilizer lithium. Now a senior at Harvard, Stork also takes the anti-psychotic Seroquel.

"You would never believe how much I can hide from you," Stork wrote for a campus display on mental health. "I'm a Harvard student like any other; I take notes during lecture, goof off . . . but I never let on how much I hurt."

Some experts believe the situation is getting worse. "This is just the beginning," said Peter Lake, a professor of law at Stetson University who co-authored *The Rights and Responsibilities of the Modern University: Who Assumes the Risks of College Life?* He believes mental illness — particularly self-inflicted injury — will soon eclipse alcohol as the No. 1 issue on campuses. [42]

In response to growing needs, colleges have hired more psychiatrists, expanded the hours at counseling centers and instituted outreach programs. Teachers are being instructed to keep an eye on potentially overstressed students during exam times.

Congress also may step in. Last year, two House lawmakers introduced the Campus Care and Counseling Act, which would provide $10 million in fiscal 2005 for campus mental and behavioral health service centers.

Resnick believes campuses are a good place for troubled youths to get help, because they are tight-knit communities. "The vast majority of students come here to create a community," she says. "This allows for quite a bit of exposure to faculty and staff, campus ministers and other groups that can be on the alert for people who seem especially distressed. If you do a good job of outreaching, this can be a very good first-alert system."

But some students who need help sometimes don't know about the counseling services or are reluctant to use them because of the stigma attached to emotional problems. "A lot of students aren't that comfortable going up to a psychiatrist, and saying, 'Hey, I need some help,' " said Peter Maki, a University of Miami student and a member of a student outreach group. [43]

Seeking to close that gap, the non-profit Jed Foundation last year launched a free Web site, Ulifeline.org, which links students to mental health centers, information about emotional problems and anonymous screening for depression, eating disorders and other problems. The foundation was founded by Donna and Phil Satow, whose son Jed hanged himself while a sophomore at the University of Arizona in 1998.

"The ability to access a Web site confidentially, in the privacy of your dorm room, has distinct advantages," said Morton Silverman, director of the National Suicide Prevention Center in Newton, Mass. "And university students today are very adept at using the information . . . so having a resource there to check on their mental health is an important thing." [44] ■

OUTLOOK

Positive Trends?

The youth suicide rate has dropped steadily in recent years. The rate for older adolescents (15-19), for example, has declined 29 percent since 1994, according to the National Center for Vital Statistics. But is it just a temporary downswing or a sign that society is finally finding solutions to the problem of youth suicide?

"It doesn't look like it's just a little blip," the Carmel Hill Center's Flynn says. "It looks like a trend, a very positive trend. The optimist in me believes we are beginning to get a handle on it."

In fact, she sees several positive trends, including improved treatment options such as antidepressants and a better understanding of the underlying factors that contribute to suicide.

The University of Vermont's Fassler also believes society may be turning the corner. "I am optimistic," he says. "We're having success in reducing the stigma associated with mental health treatment, and we're getting better at identifying kids earlier and making sure they get appropriate treatment."

Others are less optimistic about the future, warning that experts have yet to figure out precisely what drives the rate up and down. They also point out that rates have declined unevenly for different groups. For example, while the rate for those in the 10-to-14-year-old age group has dropped slightly in recent years, it is still more than double the 1970 rate. [45]

"It's like tides. The rates seem to go in and out," says Clark of Chicago's Center for Suicide Research and Prevention. "It's very hard to predict what's going to happen next."

He and others agree that many suicides are preventable with proper diagnosis and treatment. A major challenge remains in overcoming the stigma associated with mental illness and persuading those who need treatment to get it. But it can be an uphill battle, especially in small towns where traditional values hold more sway and people keep an eye on which cars are parked at the local crisis center.

"We have lots of people who would rather die than come and see a mental health professional," Clark says.

Other challenges include mobilizing societal resources by better equipping schools and local crisis centers to handle youth suicide and providing financial support for patients without insurance coverage. That could be an expensive proposition, especially in lo-

About the Author

David Hosansky is a freelance writer in Denver who specializes in environmental issues. He previously was a senior writer at *CQ Weekly* and the *Florida Times-Union* in Jacksonville, where he was twice nominated for a Pulitzer Prize. His recent *Researcher* reports include "Invasive Species" and "Food Safety."

calities with high budget deficits. But failing to help troubled youths carries its own costs, mental health professionals note. Suicidal tendencies go hand-in-hand with other high-risk behavior, such as substance abuse, teen pregnancy and dropping out of school.

As Fassler puts it, treating youth depression is a "lot less expensive than dealing with the consequences and repercussions in the long run." ■

FOR MORE INFORMATION

American Association of Suicidology, 4201 Conn. Ave., N.W., Suite 408, Washington, DC 20008; (202) 237-2280; suicide hotline 1-800-SUICIDE; WWW.SUICIDOLOGY.ORG.

National Institute of Mental Health, 6001 Executive Blvd., Suite 8235, Rockville, MD, 20852; (301) 443-3673; www.nimh.nih.gov.

National Mental Health Association, 2001 N. Beauregard St., Alexandria, VA 22311; (703) 684-7722; www.nmha.org.

Suicide Prevention Action Network USA, 1025 Vermont Ave., N.E., Washington, DC, 20005; (202) 449-3600; www.spanusa.org. An educational and advocacy organization that seeks to reduce the suicide rate.

Suicide Prevention Resource Center, 55 Chapel St., Newton, MA 02458-1060; (877) 438-7772; www.sprc.org.

Notes

[1] U.S. Division of Vital Statistics data, www.cdc.gov/ncipc/wisqars.

[2] Andrew Julien, "The Kids Are Hurting," *The Hartford Courant*, Dec. 15, 2002, p. A1.

[3] These numbers, based on studies by the Centers for Disease Control and other agencies, were cited by then-Surgeon General David Satcher in a 1999 document, "The Surgeon General's Call to Prevent Suicide."

[4] Satcher, *ibid.*

[5] For background, see Kathy Koch, "Childhood Depression," *The CQ Researcher*, July 16, 1999, pp. 593-617.

[6] Quoted in Julien, *op. cit.*

[7] See Jane Tanner, "Mental Illness Medication Debate," *The CQ Researcher*, Feb. 6, 2004, pp. 101-124.

[8] Shankar Vedantam, "Britain Warns Against Giving Newer Antidepressants to Kids; Only Prozac's Benefits Outweigh Risks, Health Officials Say," *The Washington Post*, Dec. 11, 2003, p. A2.

[9] Lauran Neergard, "FDA hearing whether some drugs can trigger suicides by kids," The Associated Press, Feb. 2, 2004.

[10] Division of Vital Statistics, *op. cit.*

[11] Eric Snider, "Climbing Out of Hell; We Could Do More To Help Kids Stay Alive," *Daily Planet Tampa*, June 5-11, 2003.

[12] The academy Web site is: http://www.aap.org/advocacy/childhealthmonth/prevteensuicide.htm

[13] See Richard L. Worsnop, "Teenage Suicide," *The CQ Researcher*, June 14, 1991, pp. 369-392.

[14] The 1985 study was led by Dr. Lee Salk, a family and child expert. It was cited by Bill Briggs in "Suicide: Isolation, access to guns tied to West's soaring rate," *The Denver Post*, Aug. 27, 2000, p. A1.

[15] Harold S. Koplewicz, *More Than Moody* (2002).

[16] Julien, *op. cit.*

[17] Katherine Seligman and Diana Walsh, "Palo Alto High School shaken by 2 suicides; Students, parents, teachers seek help in learning signs of distress in teenagers," *San Francisco Chronicle*, Nov. 24, 2003, p. A1.

[18] The states are California, Connecticut, Florida, Hawaii, Kentucky, Maryland, New Jersey, New York and Virginia. For background, see Julie Thomerson, "Violent acts of sadness: The tragedy of youth suicide," *State Legislatures*, May 1, 2002, p. 30.

[19] *Ibid.*

[20] *Ibid.*

[21] Carol Vinzant, "Suicide Mission; Teens Are Screened for Many Conditions, but Rarely for a Real Killer," *The Washington Post*, Feb. 5, 2003, p. F1.

[22] Koplewicz, *op. cit.*

[23] Vedantam, *op. cit.*

[24] IMS Health, a pharmaceutical market research and business analysis firm; www.ims-global.com//insight/news_story/0204/news_story_020430.htm

[25] Michael D. Lemonick, "Prescription for Suicide?" *Time*, Feb. 9, 2004.

[26] Virginia Anderson, "Teens and Depression," *The Atlanta Journal and Constitution*, Oct. 19, 2003, p. 1LS.

[27] Mark Olfson, *et al.*, "Outpatient Treatment of Child and Adolescent Depression in the United States," *Archives of General Psychiatry*, December 2003, pp. 1236-1242.

[28] Anderson, *op. cit.*, and Shankar Vedantam, "Antidepressant Makers Withhold Data on Children," *The Washington Post*, Jan. 29, 2004, p. A1.

[29] Quoted in Mary Duenwald, "Debate on Acne Drug's Safety Persists Over Two Decades," *The New York Times*, Jan. 22, 2002, p. F7.

[30] For a good description of early attitudes toward youth suicide, see Worsnop, *op. cit.*

[31] "Community Mental Health Centers at the 40-year Mark: The Quest for Survival," National Council for Community Behavorial Healthcare, 2003, p. 6.

[32] For background, see Jane Tanner, "Mental Health Insurance," *The CQ Researcher*, March 29, 2002, pp. 265-288.

[33] Worsnop, *op. cit.*

[34] *Ibid.*

[35] For background, see Kathy Koch, "School Violence," *The CQ Researcher*, Oct. 9, 1998, pp. 881-904.

[36] See "Childhood Depression," *op. cit.*

[37] Madelyn S. Gould *et al.*, "Youth Suicide Risk and Preventive Interventions: A Review of the Past 10 Years," *Research Update Review*, April 2003, pp. 394-396.

[38] Scott S. Greenberger, "Romney Sets a $22.98B Blueprint," *The Boston Globe*, Jan. 29, 2004, p. A1.

[39] Deborah Davis, "Budget Cuts Would Wound Crisis Response," *Santa Fe New Mexican*, Dec. 31, 2003, p. A1.

[40] Sherry A. Benton, *et al.*, "Changes in Counseling Center Client Problems Across 13 Years," *Professional Psychology: Research and Practice*, Vol. 34, No. 1, 2003, pp. 66-72.

[41] Daniela Lamas, "The Breaking Point: The dark side of college life," *The Miami Herald*, Dec. 9, 2003, p. E11.

[42] Quoted in *ibid.*

[43] *Ibid.*

[44] Shannon Dininny, "Colleges sign on to Web site aimed at reducing youth suicide," The Associated Press, Oct. 6, 2003.

[45] Division of Vital Statistics, *op. cit.*

Bibliography

Selected Sources

Books

Fassler, David G., and Lynne S. Dumas, *"Help Me, I'm Sad,"* Penguin, 1997.

A child psychiatrist (Fassler) and writer (Dumas) examine the causes, symptoms and treatments of depression in youth, noting that young people often exhibit far different symptoms than adults. Includes first-person accounts from children and parents.

Koplewicz, Harold S., *More Than Moody*, G.P. Putnam's Sons, 2002.

A psychiatrist discusses childhood depression and suicide, including the diagnosis and treatment of college students suffering from emotional disorders.

Articles

Briggs, Bill, "Suicide: Isolation, access to guns tied to West's soaring rate," *The Denver Post*, Aug. 27, 2000, p. A1.

The suicide rate in the Mountain States is up to triple the rate in Eastern cities or Southern agricultural areas. The article raises pertinent issues about how high suicide rates may be related to rural isolation and easy access to guns.

Goode, Erica, "British Ignite a Debate on Drugs and Suicide," *The New York Times*, Dec. 16, 2003, p. F1.

Regulators in Britain surprised many U.S. psychiatrists when they told British doctors to stop prescribing several common antidepressants for young people. The article discusses studies that indicate antidepressants may cause suicidal thoughts and behavior in the young, but also quotes experts who tout the drugs' benefits.

Harris, Gardiner, "FDA Intensely Reviews Depression Drugs," *The New York Times*, Oct. 28, 2003, p. F8.

The FDA is reviewing Paxil and similar drugs amid claims that they may increase the likelihood of suicide for teenagers and children.

Julien, Andrew, "The Kids Are Hurting," *Hartford Courant*, Dec. 15, 2002, p. A1.

Experts believe many children today are suffering from emotional and behavioral disorders because of unrelenting pressure to succeed and disintegrating families.

Lamas, Daniela, "The Breaking Point: The dark side of college life," *The Miami Herald*, Dec. 9, 2003, p. E11.

Growing numbers of college students are coping with mental illness and suicidal tendencies, due to increased academic pressure, access to drugs and alcohol, and a greater number of adolescents using psychiatric drugs who now are able to graduate from high school and enroll in college.

Lemonick, Michael D., "Prescription For Suicide? British authorities say some antidepressants can be deadly for kids. Now the FDA is investigating," *Time*, Feb. 9, 2004, p. 59.

For years, a small but vocal group of patients and doctors has insisted that certain antidepressants, including Paxil, Zoloft, Prozac and other medications known as selective serotonin reuptake inhibitors (SSRIs) carry an unacceptable risk of antisocial behavior and suicide. Now the U.S. Food and Drug Administration is about to hold hearings on the controversy.

Seligman, Katherine, and Diana Walsh, "Palo Alto High School shaken by two suicides," *The San Francisco Chronicle*, Nov. 24, 2003, p. A1.

The authors examine the high levels of stress that afflict children in affluent areas of Silicon Valley.

Thomerson, Julie, "Violent Acts of Sadness: The Tragedy of Youth Suicide," *State Legislatures*, May 1, 2002, p. 30.

Suicide is the third-biggest cause of death among 15-to-24-year-olds. State legislators are trying to understand the reasons for this epidemic so they can design programs to help.

Vinzant, Carol, "Suicide Mission; Teens Are Screened for Many Conditions, but Rarely for a Real Killer," *The Washington Post*, Feb. 25, 2003, p. F1.

Columbia University's TeenScreen Program is designed to identify youngsters at highest risk of suicide so they can be steered into treatment.

Reports and Studies

Benton, Sherry A., *et al*, "Changes in Counseling Center Client Problems Across 13 Years," *Professional Psychology: Research and Practice*, Vol. 34, Nov. 1, 2003, pp. 66-72.

A 13-year study of students seeking help at college counseling centers found the number of depressed students doubled, suicidal students tripled, and students seen after sexual assaults quadrupled.

Olfson, Mark, *et al*, "Relationship Between Antidepressant Medication Treatment and Suicide in Adolescents," *Archives of General Psychiatry*, October 2003, pp. 978-82.

Researchers found a correlation between antidepressant prescriptions and lower suicide rates, although the correlation did not hold for girls or younger adolescents.

The Next Step:

Additional Articles from Current Periodicals

Causes of Suicide

Curwen, Thomas, "Psychache," ***Los Angeles Times Magazine*****, June 3, 2001, p. 12.**
The nation's psychiatric community is sharply divided over why suicide rates are rising and how to stop this alarming trend.

Duff-Brown, Beth, "Exam Time Torments Students in India," ***The Washington Post*****, June 29, 2003, p. A19.**
India's extremely competitive educational system can mean that poor performance on exams can be a cause for suicide.

Guthrie, Julian, "When Success Turns to Suicide," ***San Francisco Chronicle*****, June 2, 2002, p. A17.**
High-achieving students can be at risk of suicide because of their own sense that they are not achieving enough.

Heredia, Christopher, "More Suicide Attempts Found Among Gay Teens," ***San Francisco Chronicle*****, Aug. 7, 2001, p. A3.**
Gay teenagers are twice as likely to attempt suicide as heterosexual teenagers, often because of feelings of familial or social rejection.

Peterson, Karen, "Study Suggests Teen Sex Linked to Depression, Suicide Tries," ***USA Today*****, June 4, 2003, p. 8D.**
A study by the conservative Heritage Foundation finds a correlation between sexual activity and depression and suicide attempts by teenagers.

Rose, Devin, "It's Not the Season of Suicide," ***Chicago Tribune*****, Dec. 7, 2003, p. Q9.**
Contrary to popular belief, a new study shows that most suicides do not occur during the holiday season.

Drugs and Suicide

Elias, Marilyn, "Antidepressants and Suicide," ***USA Today*****, Jan. 22, 2004, p. 8D.**
The FDA is holding its first public hearing on whether antidepressants increase the risk of suicide among teenagers and children.

Goode, Erica, "British Ignite a Debate on Drugs and Suicide," ***The New York Times*****, Dec. 16, 2003, p. F1.**
British drug regulators order doctors to stop prescribing several antidepressants to children under 18 because of possible links to suicidal thoughts.

Goode, Erica, "Study Links Prescriptions to Decrease in Suicides," ***The New York Times*****, Oct. 14, 2003, p. F5.**
Columbia University researchers believe a decline in the teenage suicide rate may be linked, at least partially, to the increasing use of antidepressants.

Harris, Gardiner, "Panel Says Zoloft and Cousins Don't Increase Suicide Risk," ***The New York Times*****, Jan. 22, 2004, p. A14.**
A panel of respected researchers issued a report saying that antidepressants are safe and effective; critics questioned their methodology and ties to drugmakers.

Weiss, Mike, "Suicide Watch," ***San Francisco Chronicle Magazine*****, April 27, 2003, p. 7.**
Accutane, a powerful acne drug, reportedly can cause numerous severe side effects, including contributing to suicidal thoughts.

Prevention

"Teen Suicide Scare Shakes Des Moines," ***Los Angeles Times*****, Dec. 28, 2003, p. A35.**
After the death of a friend, many high school students became suicidal; authorities struggle with how to recognize and prevent suicide attempts.

Helderman, Rosalind, "Suicide Program Urges Peer Input," ***The Washington Post*****, Feb. 20, 2003, p. T3.**
A new suicide program in Virginia brings students together with counselors to talk frankly about suicide, fighting the idea that talking about suicide encourages it.

MacDonald, G. Jeffrey, "When Silence Can Be Fatal," ***The Christian Science Monitor*****, Nov. 18, 2003, p. 12.**
Schools are unsure what can be done to prevent teen suicide; some fear that discussing suicide may actually make the problem worse.

Surendran, Aparna, "Suicidal Behavior May Not Be Contagious After All," ***Los Angeles Times*****, July 23, 2001, p. S3.**
Researchers have long believed that hearing about suicide might encourage "copycat" behavior, but new research indicates this may not be true.

Vinzant, Carol, "Suicide Mission," ***The Washington Post*****, Feb. 25, 2003, p. F1.**
Suicide is the third most frequent cause of death for adolescents; with the TeenScreen program, it may be possible to identify those at highest risk.

Suicide on Campus

Giegerich, Steve, "Colleges Embrace Suicide Prevention Programs," ***The Washington Post*****, Dec. 14, 2003, p. A10.**
After a spate of suicides at New York University, universities are seeking help in recognizing and treating students who may be at risk of suicide.

Gose, Ben, "Elite Colleges Struggle to Prevent Student Suicides," *The Chronicle of Higher Education*, Feb. 25, 2000, p. A54.
More students at selective universities seek counseling than ever before, but most of those who commit suicide do not; administrators' responses to suicides are questioned.

Hoover, Eric, "Ferrum College Concedes 'Shared Responsibility' in a Student's Suicide," *The Chronicle of Higher Education*, Aug. 8, 2003, p. 31.
As part of a legal settlement brought by a deceased student's family, a Virginia college admitted "errors in judgment and communication" leading up to the student's death.

Hoover, Eric, "More Help For Troubled Students," *The Chronicle of Higher Education*, Dec. 5, 2003, p. 25.
Colleges are concerned about legal liability when students commit suicide; they are increasing their mental health efforts as mental illness among students increases.

Tavernise, Sabrina, "In College and in Despair, With Parents in the Dark," *The New York Times*, Oct. 26, 2003, p. A31.
Privacy laws often make it impossible for colleges to keep parents informed about the mental health of their children.

Suicide Rates

Fernandez, Maria Elena, "Cultural Conflict," *Los Angeles Times*, Dec. 13, 1999, p. B3.
Latina teens are at a high risk of feeling depressed or suicidal due to stress and cultural conflict, but overall Latino suicide rates are lower than for whites or blacks.

Jordan, Mary, "As Doors Close, a Generation Grows Desperate," *The Washington Post*, Oct. 4, 2003, p. A15.
Suicides are rising in Mexico as young people feel that their chances of a bright future are dim.

Sontag, Deborah, "Who Was Responsible For Elizabeth Shin?" *The New York Times Magazine*, April 28, 2002, p. 57.
The parents of an M.I.T. student who committed suicide are suing the institute for wrongful death, but schools' high-stress environments are becoming increasingly common.

Warning Signs and Diagnosis

Brody, Jane, "Adolescent Angst or a Deeper Disorder? Tips For Spotting Serious Symptoms," *The New York Times*, Dec. 24, 2002, p. F5.
Looking for signs of adult depression in teenagers may be misleading; many symptoms are dismissed as merely a phase or mood swings.

McFadden, Robert, and Robert Worth, "Few Heeded the Distress Signals as a Teenager Lost Control," *The New York Times*, May 14, 2003, p. B1.
A young man in New York tried to kill his girlfriend and then killed himself after numerous threats; the girl's mother is suing the school district for negligence.

Seligman, Katherine, and Diana Walsh, "Palo Alto High School Shaken By 2 Suicides," *San Francisco Chronicle*, Nov. 24, 2003, p. A1.
The suicides of two outwardly happy students raise the question of how parents and teachers can recognize signs of mental distress.

Wingert, Pat, and Barbara Kantrowitz, "Young and Depressed," *Newsweek*, Oct. 7, 2002, p. 52.
As many as 8 percent of adolescents show signs of depression, but they often fail to receive help due to a failure to recognize the signs of mental illness.

Citing *The CQ Researcher*

Sample formats for citing these reports in a bibliography include the ones listed below. Preferred styles and formats vary, so please check with your instructor or professor.

MLA Style

Jost, Kenneth. "Rethinking the Death Penalty." The CQ Researcher 16 Nov. 2001: 945-68.

APA Style

Jost, K. (2001, November 16). Rethinking the death penalty. *The CQ Researcher, 11*, 945-968.

Chicago Style

Jost, Kenneth. "Rethinking the Death Penalty." *CQ Researcher*, November 16, 2001, 945-968.

Back Issues

The CQ Researcher *offers in-depth coverage of many key areas.*
Back issues are $10. Quantity discounts available.
Call (866) 427-7737 to order back issues.

Or call for a free CQ Researcher Web trial!
Online access provides:

- *Searchable archives dating back to 1991.*
- *Wider access through IP authentication.*
- *PDF files for downloading and printing.*
- *Availability 48 hours before print version.*

CIVIL LIBERTIES
Race in America, July 2003
Gay Marriage, September 2003
Civil Liberties Debates, October 2003

CRIME/LAW
Cyber-Crime, April 2002
Corporate Crime, October 2002
Serial Killers, October 2003

ECONOMY (OLD)
Stimulating the Economy, January 2003
State Budget Crises, October 2003
Stock Market Troubles, January 2004

EDUCATION
Home Schooling Debate, January 2003
Combating Plagiarism, September 2003
Black Colleges, December 2003

ENERGY/TRANSPORTATION
Future of the Airline Industry, June 2002
Future of Amtrak, October 2002
SUV Debate, May 2003

ENVIRONMENT
Water Shortages, August 2003
Air Pollution Conflict, November 2003

HEALTH AND SAFETY
Medicare Reform, August 2003
Women's Health, November 2003
Homeopathy Debate, December 2003
Mental Illness Medication Debate, Feb. 2004

POLITICS AND PUBLIC POLICY
Abortion Debates, March 2003
State Budget Crises, October 2003
Democracy in the Arab World, January 2004

SOCIAL TRENDS
Latinos' Future, October 2003
Future of the Music Industry, Nov. 2003

TECHNOLOGY
NASA's Future, May 2003

TERRORISM/DEFENSE
Homeland Security, September 2003
North Korean Crisis, April 2003

WORLD AFFAIRS
Future of NATO, February 2003
Trouble in South America, March 2003
Rebuilding Iraq, July 2003
Aiding Africa, August 2003

YOUTH
Preventing Teen Drug Use, March 2002
Sexual Abuse and the Clergy, May 2002
Movie Ratings, March 2003
Hazing, January 2004

Future Topics

- ***Exporting Jobs***
- ***Future of the United Nations***
- ***Search for Extra-terrestrials***

CQ Researcher

Published by CQ Press, a division of Congressional Quarterly Inc.

thecqresearcher.com

Exporting Jobs

Do low-paid foreign workers hurt or help the economy?

The U.S. economy is recovering, but employment continues to lag. Experts blame some of the joblessness on the job-exporting phenomenon known as offshoring. Well-trained, low-wage workers in India, China and other developing countries make exporting American jobs attractive, along with the widespread availability of high-speed Internet connections. In addition, millions of foreign professionals have entered the U.S. work force using temporary visas, while millions more undocumented foreign workers from Mexico and Latin America have found low-wage jobs in the U.S. thanks to lax immigration and border-control policies. Offshoring proponents say paying lower wages reduces the cost of goods and raises profits, ultimately enabling U.S. companies to create better-paying jobs for Americans. Critics say offshoring simply eliminates good jobs.

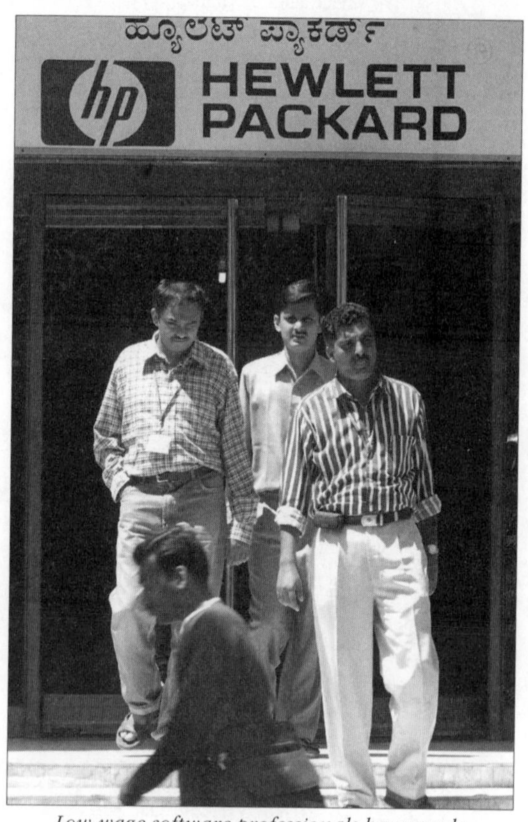

Low-wage software professionals have made Bangalore, India, an outpost for U.S. high-tech firms.

INSIDE THIS ISSUE

The CQ Researcher • Feb. 20, 2004 • www.thecqresearcher.com
Volume 14, Number 7 • Pages 149-172

CQ PRESS

RECIPIENT OF SOCIETY OF PROFESSIONAL JOURNALISTS AWARD FOR EXCELLENCE ◆ AMERICAN BAR ASSOCIATION SILVER GAVEL AWARD

THE ISSUES

BACKGROUND

CURRENT SITUATION

OUTLOOK

SIDEBARS AND GRAPHICS

FOR FURTHER RESEARCH

Cover: Skilled, low-wage workers have turned Bangalore, India, into a major outpost for Hewlett Packard and other firms seeking software programming and other services. (AFP Photo/Indranil Mukherjee)

Feb. 20, 2004
Volume 14, No. 7

MANAGING EDITOR: Thomas J. Colin

ASSISTANT MANAGING EDITOR: Kathy Koch

ASSOCIATE EDITOR: Kenneth Jost

STAFF WRITERS: Mary H. Cooper, David Masci, William Triplett

CONTRIBUTING WRITERS: Sarah Glazer, David Hatch, David Hosansky, Patrick Marshall, Tom Price, Jane Tanner

DESIGN/PRODUCTION EDITOR: Olu B. Davis

ASSISTANT EDITOR: Kenneth Lukas

A Division of Congressional Quarterly Inc.

SENIOR VICE PRESIDENT/GENERAL MANAGER: John A. Jenkins

DIRECTOR, LIBRARY PUBLISHING: Kathryn C. Suárez

DIRECTOR, EDITORIAL OPERATIONS: Ann Davies

CIRCULATION MANAGER: Nina Tristani

CONGRESSIONAL QUARTERLY INC.

CHAIRMAN: Andrew Barnes

VICE CHAIRMAN: Andrew P. Corty

PRESIDENT AND PUBLISHER: Robert W. Merry

The CQ Researcher (ISSN 1056-2036) is printed on acid-free paper. Published weekly, except Jan. 2, April 9, July 2, July 9, Aug. 6, Aug. 13, Nov. 26 and Dec. 31, by CQ Press, a division of Congressional Quarterly Inc. Annual subscription rates for libraries, businesses and government start at $625. Single issues are available for $10. Quantity discounts apply to orders over 10. Additional rates furnished upon request. Periodicals postage paid at Washington, D.C., and additional mailing offices. POSTMASTER: Send address changes to *The CQ Researcher*, 1255 22nd St., N.W., Suite 400, Washington, D.C. 20037.

Exporting Jobs

BY MARY H. COOPER

THE ISSUES

Computer programmer Robin Tauch rode the technology boom to a salary of nearly $100,000 a year at Dallas-based Computer Sciences Corp. But the ride ended last August, when she joined legions of fellow computer professionals on the unemployment rolls.

"I've got tons of friends who are looking for work," she says. "We're all people who have been employed for 20-some years. For the first time in our lives, we've just been dumped on the street."

But losing her job was doubly painful to Tauch because she had to train the two technology workers brought in from India to replace her.

Similar scenarios are playing out across the United States. Eager to reduce labor costs, a U.S. firm imports qualified foreign information technology (IT) workers by obtaining temporary visas for the new employees. Once they learn the host company's specific needs, the foreign workers often return home to establish an IT department for the firm. Or they replace the workers who trained them.

India is one of several countries with relatively low-wage, highly educated, English-speaking populations — Ireland and the Philippines among them — benefiting from U.S. cost-cutting efforts.

Workers in such countries provide a broad range of business services, such as answering customer-service calls, accounting, reviewing insurance claims and processing bills.

The export of American jobs has touched so many sectors of the economy, in fact, that it has generated a new term to describe the trend — "offshoring," short for offshore outsourcing.

"A lot of these offshored positions replace very high-wage jobs," says Lester Thurow, dean of the Sloan School of Business at Massachusetts Institute of Technology (MIT). "Here in Boston, for example, Massachusetts General Hospital is even outsourcing radiologists. Instead of having a $450,000 radiologist read an X-ray or an MRI here, they send it to India and have it read by a $50,000 radiologist."

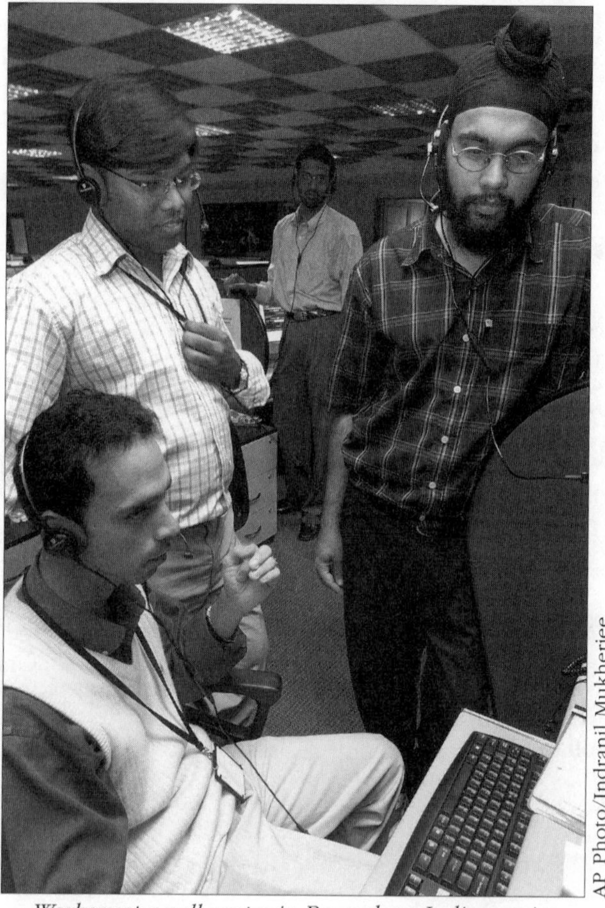

AP Photo/Indranil Mukherjee

Workers at a call center in Bangalore, India, service customers from around the world 24 hours a day. U.S. and other firms are increasingly outsourcing their service operations to India, the Philippines, Russia and other sources of skilled, cheap labor. Proponents of so-called "offshoring" say it ultimately helps the U.S. economy, but critics say sending high-paying jobs overseas forces laid-off Americans into less desirable jobs.

Meanwhile, General Electric, Microsoft and other big firms are expanding their operations in India to include everything from basic customer service to high-end research and development. [1]

Business advocates say offshoring is nothing more than the latest cost-saving technique and that it will benefit Americans in the long run by allowing companies to be more efficient and to invest the savings in more valuable, cutting-edge U.S. jobs of the future.

Labor advocates counter that offshoring threatens U.S. living standards by forcing Americans whose jobs have gone overseas to take lower-wage positions. The debate over whether offshoring helps or hurts the economy also is emerging as a key issue in the coming presidential campaign.

U.S. job outsourcing began in the manufacturing sector in the 1980s, when disappearing worldwide trade barriers forced U.S. companies to compete with foreign manufacturers using cheap labor. To survive, U.S. manufacturers exported factory jobs from the higher-wage, heavily unionized Northeast and Midwest to Asia and Latin America, as well as to the largely non-unionized and lower-wage Southern United States.

In addition, many factory jobs fall victim to computerization and robotization.

As a result, many blue-collar workers and middle managers were "downsized," forcing many former assembly-line workers to seek lower-paid jobs in the rapidly expanding retail and business-service industries. Nearly 5 million U.S. factory jobs have been lost in the United States since 1979, more than half of them — 2.8 million — since 2000 alone. [2]

Nearly 3 Million Factory Jobs Were Lost

More than 2.8 million U.S. factory jobs have been lost since 2000, mainly in the computer/electronics and textile industries. Offshoring accounted for about 10 percent of the losses, according to one estimate. In the next 15 years, other studies predict the loss of up to 14 million service jobs, such as answering customer calls, accounting, insurance claim review and bill processing.

Lost U.S. Manufacturing Jobs
Selected Industries, 2000-2003

Industry	Jobs Lost
Computers and electronics	455,000
Textiles and apparel	395,000
Machinery	301,000
Transportation equipment	297,000
Fabricated materials	288,000
Primary metals	154,000
Electrical equipment/appliances	135,000
Plastics	131,000
Printing	132,000
Furniture	107,000

Source: Labor Department, Bureau of Labor Statistics, Feb. 4, 2004; www.bls.gov.

Lately, however, American businesses have been offshoring more of their highly paid professional staffs, who until now had been insulated from job insecurity by their specialized skills, usually acquired after years of costly college and graduate education.

"The Web makes it much easier for a skilled job to move to India, where you have plenty of people trained not just at MIT but at various high-tech Indian academic institutions," says Susan Aaronson, director of globalization studies at the University of North Carolina's Kenan Institute of Private Enterprise, in Washington, D.C. "The only thing that's new about this is that middle-class jobs are now being affected."

Estimates of the number of American jobs lost to the trend vary widely, largely because U.S. companies are not required to report their offshoring practices. One report blames offshoring for 300,000 of the 2.4 million total jobs lost since 2001. Various studies project that from 3 to 14 million service jobs could go overseas in the next 15 years. [3]

Economists say offshoring helps explain why the nation is undergoing its so-called jobless recovery. Since the last recession ended in 2001, the U.S. economy has rebounded — except for employment.

Last year, America's output of goods and services, or gross domestic product (GDP), rose by 3.1 percent, up from 2.2 percent in 2002 and just 0.5 percent in 2001. [4] Business investment and consumer spending also has picked up. [5] But employment, which typically improves during recoveries, has lagged: Only 112,000 new jobs were added to private payrolls in January, about 38,000 fewer than economists had expected. [6]

President Bush declared on Feb. 9, 2004, that "America's economy is strong and getting stronger" and predicted the creation of 2.6 million jobs this year, increasing non-farm payroll employment to 132.7 million. Last February, the White House predicted that 1.7 million jobs would be created in 2003. In fact, non-farm payrolls showed a small decline. Since Bush took office, the country has lost 2.2 million payroll jobs, as non-farm employment dipped to 130.2 million.

One explanation for the disappointing employment numbers lies in the economy's blistering productivity rate — 9.4 percent in the third quarter of last year.

"Moving all the low-productivity stuff from the American economy to China or India raises the productivity level of what's left," Thurow says. "Outsourcing is the big reason why — even though we've got an economic recovery in terms of rate of growth — we don't have an economic recovery in terms of jobs."

Proponents of offshoring say it simply reflects the way the U.S. economy is evolving and that bumps in the road must be expected. "This trend of moving jobs to other locations, both onshore and offshore, started when we moved from an agrarian-based society to where we are today, and it's been a continuous evolution," says Robert Daigle, co-founder of Evalueserve, an offshoring company in Chappaqua, N.Y. Evalueserve's far-flung staff includes 270 people in India who conduct market research and write patent applications for corporate clients worldwide. "Companies are outsourcing and offshoring to remain competitive."

Business representatives say that attempts to block the hiring of foreign workers would only hurt the economy, and eventually American workers. In addition to cutting labor costs, they say, globalizing work forces lets companies offer round-the-clock customer service, with workers in the Philippines and other overseas call centers answering customers when American employees are sleeping.

But critics say offshoring reflects the corporate quest for profits no matter the human cost. "Every time we hear a story like the one about the young lady [Tauch] in Texas, it just drives us crazy," says Mike Gildea, executive director of the AFL-CIO's Department for Professional Employees.

In addition, he says, offshoring could send a negative signal to the next generation of workers about the value of a college education. "These are American workers who have tried to do the right thing to get the American dream," Gildea says. "They've gone through years of schooling. Collectively, we're talking about billions of dollars invested in education going to waste. It makes no economic sense."

Nevertheless, offshoring is a $35-billion-a-year business and reportedly is growing 30-40 percent annually, gobbling up 1 percent of the world's service sector, according to the *Financial Times*. [7] As Nandan Nilekani, chief executive of Infosys Technologies, said at the World Economic Forum in Davos, Switzerland, recently: "Everything you can send down a wire is up for grabs." [8]

Still, offshoring advocates insist the threat to U.S. jobs has been overblown. According to the British information firm Datamonitor, only 2 percent of the world's 4 million call-center agents work outside the parent company's territory. [9]

Meanwhile, with the presidential campaign intensifying, candidates for the Democratic Party's nomination are beginning to blame offshoring for the loss of good jobs. And labor groups complain that a new immigration amnesty plan recently proposed by President Bush could flood the country with even more low-wage workers from Mexico, depressing U.S. wages for low-end jobs.

Here are some of the issues likely to fuel the coming debate:

Outsourced Jobs Abroad Pay Lower Wages

Computer programmers in countries where U.S. companies are outsourcing their technology jobs earn far less than American programmers (top). Similarly, low wages are paid in other countries, like India, where U.S. firms also are outsourcing non-technology jobs (bottom).

Average Salaries of Programmers
(by country)

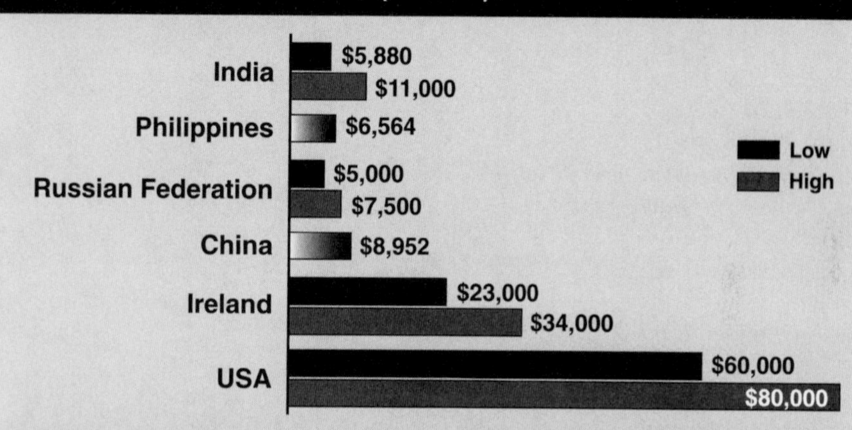

Hourly Wages for Selected Jobs
(2002/2003)

Occupation	U.S.	India
Telephone operator	$12.57	Under $1
Health record technologists & medical transcribers	$13.17	$1.50-$2
Payroll clerk	$15.17	$1.50-$2
Legal assistant/paralegal	$17.86	$6-$8
Accountant	$23.35	$6-$15
Financial researcher/analyst	$33-$35	$6-$15

Source: Ashok Deo Bardhan and Cynthia A. Kroll, "The New Wave of Outsourcing," Fisher Center for Real Estate and Urban Economics, University of California, Berkeley, fall 2003

Does offshoring threaten Americans' standard of living?

Traditionally during recessions, American workers were laid off with the implicit promise they would be rehired when demand for goods and services picked up again. Unemployment benefits generally lasted long enough to tide workers over until they returned to work, and pre-recession living standards were typically restored.

But the downsizing and offshoring trend of the past several decades marks a structural, or permanent, shift in the U.S. labor market, many economists say.[10] Domestic and offshore outsourcing often causes job losses. Unemployment benefits are no longer used to wait out recessions but to help workers retrain and find entirely different jobs — a process that frequently outlasts the benefits themselves.

Terminated workers frequently are forced to take jobs at much lower wages, forcing families to accept reduced living standards or compensate for the loss by sending a second family member to work. In the past, a single worker with a factory job could support a family, but today two-thirds of all working households are supported by two or more workers.[11] Even so, the shifting labor market is shutting many American workers out of the middle class: The Census Bureau reports that 67 percent of full-time workers earn less than $45,000 a year; half of all American workers make less than $33,636, hardly enough for a family to purchase the trappings of the American dream.[12]

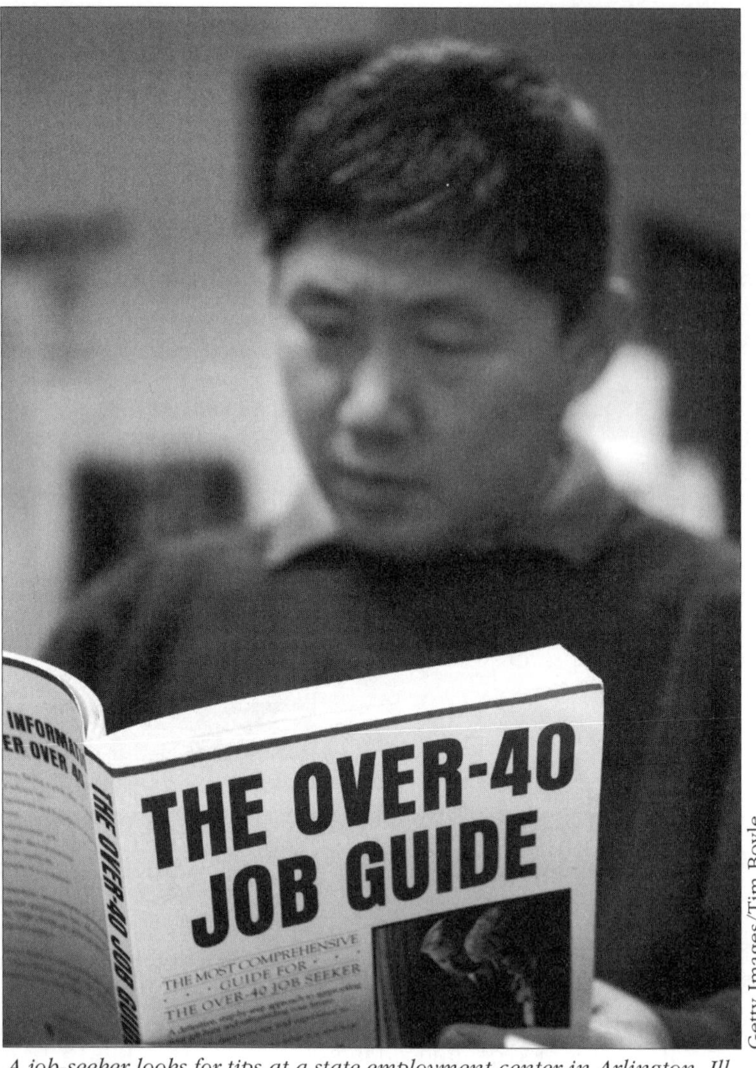

Getty Images/Tim Boyle

A job-seeker looks for tips at a state employment center in Arlington, Ill., last October. Although the economy is improving, economists call it a "jobless" recovery because of sluggish job growth. In December, manufacturers shed 26,000 jobs, bringing to 516,000 the number of U.S. factory jobs that disappeared last year. Moreover, a half-million tech jobs have been lost since 2001.

But most economists cite the result of the 1980s downsizings — the economic boom of the 1990s — as evidence that offshoring will improve living standards for Americans and other workers over the long term.

"Globalization and the movement of jobs offshore are creating new markets for goods and services for U.S. companies," Daigle says. "In India, an emerging middle class lives the same lifestyle we Americans are familiar with; it didn't exist a decade or two ago. Not only are we bringing jobs to a place that sorely needs them, but there's a benefit to U.S. companies as well."

But critics of work force globalization say the benefits to developing countries and American companies are not trickling down to U.S. workers in all sectors of the economy. "We dispute the notion that workers have come out well in the end," Gildea says. "Any number of studies have shown that the lost manufacturing jobs have been replaced by jobs principally in the service sector, which are much, much lower-paying and have few, if any, benefits."

Workers' advocates say the same thing is happening to higher-paid technology specialists whose jobs are going overseas. "We are becoming a Wal-Martized country, where the only place you can afford to shop is at Wal-Mart, and the only thing you can get there is stuff made in China," says John A. Bauman, president of The Organization for the Rights of American Workers (T.O.R.A.W.), an advocacy group formed in 2002 to raise public awareness of IT offshoring. Bauman's job as a computer programmer was terminated in 2002, ending his 25-year career. Unable to find work, he says he delivered FedEx packages over the holidays.

Both sides agree on one thing: Globalization produces winners and losers. "Outsourcing doesn't threaten everybody's standard of living," says Josh Bivens, an economist at the Economic Policy Institute. "What it really does is redistribute a lot of income." Outsourcing boosts corporate profits, he explains, benefiting stockholders but not workers whose only income comes from wages.

Income redistribution already has widened the gap between rich and poor Americans. The share of aggregate income going to the wealthiest 5 percent of U.S. households has risen from 16 percent to 22 percent since 1980, while that received by the poorest 20 percent of all households has fallen by more than 80 percent, to just 3.5 percent of total U.S. income. [13]

Bivens says the trend is only likely to worsen as the offshoring of U.S. jobs escalates. "The winners are going to be people who own stock in large corporations," he says, "while people who get most of their money from a paycheck are going to see their standard of living hurt — the blue-collar workers who have had it rough for the past couple of decades."

Former U.S. Trade Representative Carla Hills likens the current anxiety about offshoring to the 1980s, when Americans feared the exodus of high-tech jobs to Japan. "They were going to make the computer chips, we were going to be left with the potato chips," she recalled. "But that didn't happen. Computer prices came down . . . and all of us, every business could afford a computer. We created jobs not only in computers, but across the spectrum." [14]

The new jobs may take longer than usual to materialize after the recent recession, she said, because the economy has undergone a major "structural change," and recovering from such changes "takes longer to get over the hump than when it's just cyclical." [15]

But Sen. Charles E. Schumer, D-N.Y., says the structural changes represent a fundamental, triple-threat, "paradigm shift" in the world economy, which may prevent classic economic theories from bearing fruit. First, capital flows more freely across borders, allowing American companies to invest in facilities abroad. Second, broadband allows information and jobs to be sent "around the world at no cost in the blink of an eye," he said. [16]

"Thirdly, and most importantly, we have 50 to 100 million well-educated, highly motivated Chinese and Indians coming on the market that can compete" with American workers, Schumer says. "If high-end jobs, middle-end jobs and low-end jobs can all be done better overseas, . . . what's left here?

"Yes, our companies will do better, but if 80 percent, 90 percent of their employees are overseas and if American wages are forced to go down in the new jobs [that are created], what do we do?" he asked. [17]

Craig R. Barrett, CEO of Intel, the world's leading computer chip maker, would seem to agree. "The structure of the world has changed," he said. "The U.S. no longer has a lock on high-tech, white-collar jobs." [18]

The solution, says Hills, is tax incentives to encourage "investment in human capital" so Americans could do the higher-end jobs that will be created in the coming decade. [19]

Manufacturers defend outsourcing as the only way they can stay in business and protect their remaining U.S. jobs. "Manufacturing, more than any other economic activity, is on the world stage," says Hank Cox, spokesman for the National Association of Manufacturers. "The service or retail companies compete with the business in the next block, but our guys compete with China, Korea and the rest of the world, so they face a relentless downward pressure on prices."

Cox says that while prices for manufactured goods have dropped by about 1 percent a year over the past seven years, production costs — including wages and especially health benefits — continue to rise. "A lot of our members have gone under, and we've lost a lot of jobs because of that. A lot of them have been faced with a choice between outsourcing and closing their doors."

Indeed, proponents of offshoring say Americans should embrace the practice, not deplore it. A study by the McKinsey Global Institute shows the U.S. economy gets up to $1.14 in profits for every dollar outsourced. [20]

Furthermore, the proponents say, given America's huge budget deficit, rather than restricting the offshoring of government jobs, the country should be shipping even more government jobs overseas — in order to save taxpayers money. [21]

Would better education and job training protect American jobs?

During the 1980s downsizing, factory workers were encouraged to retrain for the computer-related jobs the fledgling high-tech revolution was creating. While some did get retrained, others took service positions, though generally at lesser wages and benefits than their old jobs.

Now, as offshoring begins taking the jobs of higher-wage workers, many experts are once again urging unemployed Americans to retrain for the new, highly skilled positions expected to become available.

President Bush echoed the call. "Many of the fastest-growing occupations require strong math and science preparation, and training beyond the high school level," Bush said in his State of the Union address in January. "I propose increasing our support for America's fine community colleges, so they can train workers for the industries that are creating the most new jobs." The president announced a Jobs for the 21st Century proposal that would provide $100 million for education and training, including retraining of displaced workers, in fiscal 2005. [22]

But Bush's initiative ignores the plight of specialists with advanced degrees

College Graduates Were Hit Hardest

Highly educated American workers suffered a greater drop in employment rates in the current economic recovery than less well-educated workers. In the previous two recoveries, by contrast, employment rates dropped farther for less-educated workers.

Changes in Employment Rates by Education Level

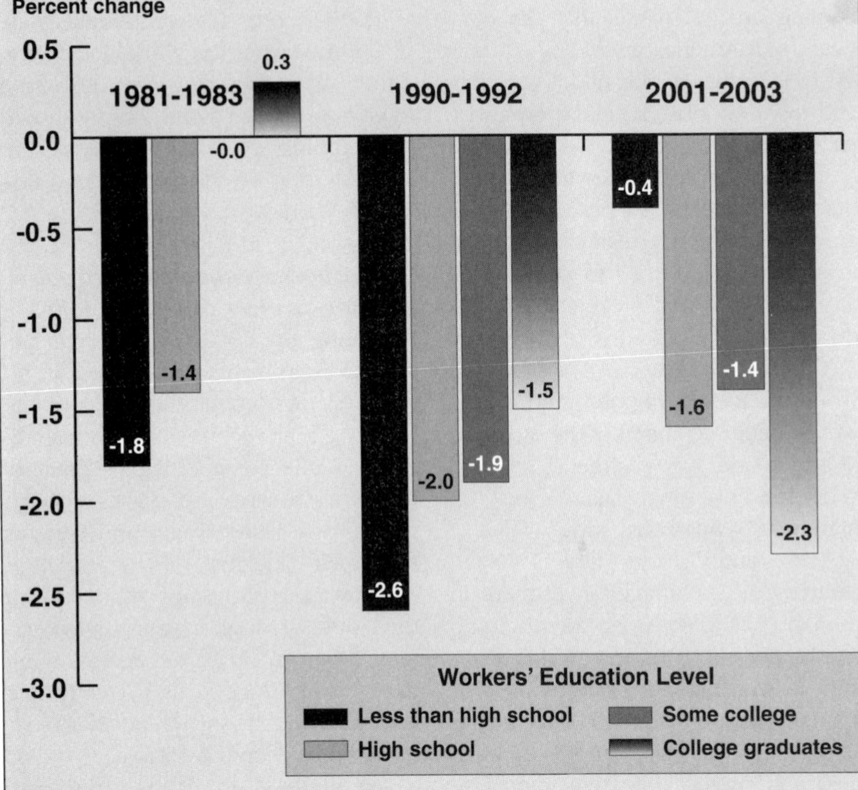

Source: Jared Bernstein and Lawrence Mishel, "Labor Market Left Behind," Economic Policy Institute Briefing Paper, August 2003

who are already unemployed or underemployed. The unemployment rate among science and engineering Ph.D.s stands at around 10 percent. [23] Gene Nelson, a biophysicist in Dallas, Texas, says he cannot find a job in his field that pays a living wage. "As a condition of being a postdoctoral worker, you must have a science or engineering doctorate, which is a very substantial investment of time and money," he says. "Postdocs today, by and large, are paid less than the high school graduate who manages the fast-food restaurant down the road. So there you are. You've earned your Ph.D., and there are no jobs; people are being trained for nonexistent positions at the Ph.D. level."

Nelson attributes the lack of demand for postdoctoral workers in part to an influx of foreign advanced-dgree holders that followed dire warnings in the late 1990s that the United States was not graduating enough engineers and scientists. [24] Unless Congress increased the number of non-immigrant, H-1B, visas for skilled foreign workers, American firms argued, they could not maintain their competitive edge in the high-tech revolution. "Basically, we had a situation designed by employers and lobbied for by government agencies that was totally fraudulent," Nelson says, "because they alleged that we faced a looming shortage of scientists and engineers. Nothing could be further from the truth."

Thurow says the warnings were justified for IT specialists, but only temporarily. "In the late 1990s, there was a huge shortfall of IT professionals in the United States," he says. Even though many out-of-work, older programmers questioned whether there truly was a shortage, Congress expanded the temporary visa program for high-tech workers and those with advanced degrees. Between 1995 and 2000, millions of workers entered the country under the program.

But then the bubble burst. "When the dot-coms collapsed, they disgorged hundreds of thousands of experienced IT professionals," Thurow says. Today, about 800,000 American IT professionals are unemployed. [25]

Workers who lost IT jobs to offshoring doubt education and training will ease their plight. After she lost her job at CSC, Tauch went to a community college to update her bachelor's degree in computer science. "But once you get the training and look for a job, they won't give it to you unless you have experience," she says. "President Bush keeps telling us to go to community college, but it's a joke."

Nevertheless, U.S. manufacturers agree with Bush on the need for a better-educated work force, particularly among high school graduates. "Our members say education is one of their biggest concerns," says the NAM's Cox. "They say the kids coming out of school today can't pass a writing test, can't pass a reading test, can't pass a math test and can't pass a drug test."

Cox supports Bush's community-college initiative and thinks it will help high school graduates transition to an increasingly demanding workplace. "The modern manufacturing workplace is like Star Trek," Cox says. "It's high-tech, and a dummy can't just go in there and handle it. These are advanced jobs that pay well, and we have to start directing some of our brightest young people into manufacturing."

Yet veterans of the labor-market turbulence of recent decades dispute the value of education and training, even for young people entering the job market. For instance, among computer programmers — the sector that has taken one of the biggest hits from outsourcing — unemployment has risen from just 1.6 percent two years ago to 7.1 percent today, significantly higher than the overall U.S. unemployment rate of 5.7 percent. [26]

"They tell you that if you take computer courses you're going to get a job in the computer field," says IT specialist Bauman. "You can go and get an education, but for what jobs? Those of us who are already underemployed are working as FedEx drivers, selling cars and selling insurance. I've got two kids who have all their certifications, and they can't find jobs. It's all because they listened to Dad, and this is one time I wish they hadn't."

Do current work-visa rules hurt American workers?

Bringing foreign workers into the United States on a temporary basis is an indirect form of exporting American jobs, critics of U.S. work-visa programs say. Although the work contributes to the U.S. economy, many of the workers will likely return to their native lands when their visas expire. Although some end up getting green cards and working in the United States permanently, many are hired with the understanding that they will open satellite U.S. offices back home after their training in the United States.

"Importing visa workers facilitates the offshoring of American jobs," Bauman says. "The foreign workers learn about the technology from people here in the United States, figure out how to use that technology in their own countries and then take the jobs offshore." In the meantime, he says, the foreign workers are performing the computer support for which they were hired. "The Americans are already gone."

Temporary work-visa programs were created to satisfy employers' demands for workers during perceived labor shortages. [27] In the early 20th century, Mexican field hands entered the country under the "Bracero" program supported by Western farm interests, followed by Basque sheepherders, Caribbean sugar cane harvesters and academic researchers from Europe and Asia.

In 1990, responding to what industry said was an impending critical shortage of skilled high-tech workers, Congress passed the 1990 Immigration Act. It expanded several existing non-immigrant visas for technical professionals — notably the H-1B visa, granted to foreign professionals for up to six years to take jobs that employers said they could not find qualified U.S. workers to fill. The visa also has been used to import physical therapists and, more recently, elementary and kindergarten teachers. In addition, the L-1 visa program, introduced in 1970, permits foreign executives and managers of U.S.-based multinationals to work in the United States for up to seven years; workers with special knowledge of an employer's products can stay up to five years.

Last year, more than 217,000 work visas were approved for foreign nationals under the H-1B program. [28] Since 1985, more than 17 million H-1B foreign workers have been admitted to the United States, according to ZaZona.com, an online monitoring service run by a critic of the programs. It estimates that almost 900,000 H-1B workers were in the United States at the end of 2001. [29]

Industry supporters say the visas help ensure American competitiveness in the global marketplace. "Access to the best-educated engineering talent around the world is critical to [our] company's future success," said Patrick J. Duffy, human resources attorney for Intel Corp. The U.S. semiconductor giant, with some $27 billion in revenues, employs almost 80,000 workers worldwide, and H-1B workers account for around 5 percent of its U.S. work force. "We expect . . . to sponsor H-1B employees in the future for the simple reason that we cannot find enough U.S. workers with the advanced education, skills and expertise we need." [30]

Moreover, supporters say, the visa programs help protect American jobs by keeping U.S. companies competitive. "When companies are competing in an international market, the inability to effectively manage their work force can mean the difference between gaining the edge and being put out of business," wrote Randel K. Johnson, a vice president of the U.S. Chamber of Commerce. "The result can mean even greater job losses in the long run." [31]

But critics say the visa programs simply have been used to replace American professionals with lower-wage foreigners. Although the visa law specifically says imported workers must receive prevailing wages, critics say enforcement is nearly nonexistent and that H-1B workers make between 15 and 33 percent less than their American counterparts. [32]

Dallas biophysicist Nelson says American universities took an early lead in promoting the visa programs, depressing wages for American scientists across the board. "This was all about bringing in cheap labor," he says.

Furthermore, Nelson says, because H-1B visa holders may only work for the employer who submitted their visa application, they are unlikely to object to adverse working conditions — such as lower pay scales or longer hours.

"This visa was designed to give the employer incredible leverage," Nelson says. "It is conditioned on the foreign national maintaining continuous employment. So if the employer gets unhappy and terminates that worker, the worker is immediately subject to deportation. In practice, it's been rarely done, but this is a very, very powerful tool."

That leverage extends beyond the foreign workers themselves, critics say. "By robbing the foreign workers of bargaining power, the visa program robs everyone else in the industry of that bargaining power as well," says the Economic Policy Institute's Bivens. If employers have access to cheaper labor, he explains, they can ignore American workers' demands for higher wages.

"There's nothing intrinsically wrong with guest workers, or even immigrants who wish to become citizens, having these jobs," Bivens adds. "What's wrong is the way the program is structured, which is quite bad for wages overall in these industries."

Many critics want work-visa programs eliminated altogether. "The H-1B program amounts to a government subsidy, because it provides economic benefits to a narrow class of entities, while the rest of us either have no benefit or — in the case of people like me — a negative benefit," Nelson says. "Our investment in our education, training and experience has been reduced to an economic value approaching zero."

In fact, he adds, because he's considered overqualified for most of the jobs now open — such as retail clerks and administrative assistants — "I've actually had to keep it a secret that I have a Ph.D." ■

BACKGROUND

Postwar Boom

As Western Europe, Japan and the Soviet bloc struggled to rebuild after World War II, U.S. manufacturing enjoyed a golden age. Expanding production and exports brought new jobs by the millions, feeding a rapidly growing American middle class.

Bolstered by union protections, a blue-collar wage earner in the leading manufacturing sectors — steel, appliances and automobiles — took home "family wages" sufficient to support an entire family, plus employer-provided health insurance and pensions. Even low-wage textile jobs offered opportunities for betterment to impoverished Southern farm workers.

For most of the 1950s and '60s, the United States was largely self-sufficient. As Europe and East Asia rebuilt their economies, they provided a vast market for U.S. goods while slowly emerging as significant trade competitors. Japan expanded its manufacturing sector by applying U.S. production techniques and became a leading exporter of plastic toys and other inexpensive products, and eventually high-end electronics and automobiles. Europe focused on exporting cars and other high-value manufactured goods to American consumers.

U.S. manufacturers began building factories in the South and overseas, where wages were much lower. The practice accelerated in the 1970s, when a series of energy crises signaled the beginning of the end of U.S. self-reliance in oil production — the basic fuel driving the U.S. economy. Rising energy prices caused a series of recessions, and steel- and automakers and other manufacturers laid off thousands of workers.

For their part, American consumers sought cheaper imported products, including the increasingly popular Japanese cars. Labor unions responded with "Buy-American" campaigns intended to shore up the beleaguered Midwest, which became known as the Rust Belt for its numerous shuttered factories.

But by the mid-1980s, rising production costs and growing foreign competition had prompted more and more industries to restructure. Many permanently downsized their work forces, often using automation. Others outsourced at least part of the production, either to lower-cost — non-union — domestic producers or overseas, where labor was cheaper still. The textile and apparel industries, usually in Southern mill towns, were among the first to export large numbers of American jobs, especially to emerging economies in Asia.

In the early 1980s, U.S. makers of auto and electronic equipment pioneered the overseas production of basic components for U.S. assembly — providing the technological foundation for other countries to develop their own industries. [33]

With Japan emerging as a major industrial power, Hong Kong, Taiwan, Malaysia, South Korea and Singapore assumed Japan's earlier role of low-cost producer of components shipped to the United States for assembly into finished products.

Meanwhile, to reduce the cost of transporting their own finished products to the U.S. market, foreign companies began opening factories in the United States, partly offsetting the loss of American jobs offshore. European and Japanese automakers, in particular, created thousands of new jobs for Americans in the late 1980s. But they mostly built their facilities outside the industrial heartland, hiring non-union workers for less pay than their unionized peers in the upper Midwest.

Continued on p. 160

Chronology

1970s-1980s

Growing international competition prompts U.S. companies to reduce labor costs by moving factories to lower-wage countries.

1970
Congress establishes the L-1 visa program to permit foreign executives and managers of U.S.-based multinationals to work in the United States.

1976
The Immigration and Nationality Act Amendments increase the number of visas allocated to foreign workers and their families.

1990s

Americans flock to information-technology (IT) jobs after government and industry vow that manufacturing jobs shifted overseas would be replaced by domestic computer jobs and warn of a coming high-tech labor shortage.

1990
The Immigration Act expands the H-1B non-immigrant visa program. It permits up to 65,000 foreign technical professionals a year to work in the U.S. for up to six years at jobs employers claim cannot be filled by U.S. workers.

1993
Congress approves the North American Free Trade Agreement (NAFTA) removing trade barriers among the United States, Canada and Mexico. U.S. manufacturers set up plants just south of the border hiring low-wage Mexican workers.

1998
Congress expands the number of H-1B visas issued each year after U.S. businesses plead for more foreign computer specialists to help prevent widespread computer failures at the turn of the millennium.

2000s

High-tech unemployment increases after the "Y2K" crisis never materializes, the technology boom collapses and U.S. companies begin shifting high-tech and other white-collar jobs offshore.

October 2000
Congress again raises the annual H-1B visa cap, to 195,000.

November 2001
The current "jobless" recovery begins, featuring rising stock prices, economic output and productivity, loss of manufacturing jobs and few new jobs.

2002
Recently fired technology professionals establish the Organization for the Rights of American Workers (T.O.R.A.W.) to raise public awareness of IT offshoring. . . . Forrester Research predicts that 3.3 million service-sectors jobs will move offshore by 2015.

July 10, 2003
Rep. Rosa DeLauro, D-Conn., and Sen. Saxby Chambliss, R-Ga., introduce the L-1 Non-Immigrant Reform Act to address reported abuses of the L-1 visa program.

July 24, 2003
Sen. Christopher J. Dodd, D-Conn., and Rep. Nancy L. Johnson, R-Conn., introduce the USA Jobs Protection Act, which would beef up enforcement of the H-1B and L-1 visa programs to prevent companies from illegally replacing qualified American workers and underpaying foreign workers.

Sept. 30, 2003
Rising unemployment in the high-tech industry prompts Congress to slash the annual cap on H-1B visas from 195,000 to 65,000 in response to concern over the impact of guest workers on U.S. jobs.

December 2003
On the 10th anniversary of NAFTA, studies show that more U.S. jobs have been created than lost since the law was passed.

Jan. 7, 2004
President Bush proposes a plan to offer temporary legal status to illegal immigrants working in the United States.

Jan. 20, 2004
In his State of the Union address, Bush calls for a new education and job-retraining program to be based in the nation's community colleges.

Jan. 23, 2004
Bush signs into law a measure prohibiting American companies from subcontracting some government jobs to companies outside the United States.

Feb. 6, 2004
Labor Department reports that American employers added only 112,000 new jobs in January, about 38,000 fewer than economists had expected.

Poor Nations Thrive on Job Exporting

For all the controversy surrounding the offshore outsourcing of American white-collar jobs, one of its consequences is undisputed — higher living standards in developing countries that have just joined the global economy.

In the late 1980s, when U.S. corporations first began exporting "back-office" work like bill processing, they turned to developed countries with large English-speaking populations but lower prevailing wages, such as Ireland and Israel. Many were allies, reducing the political risks associated with outsourcing.

But by the 1990s, the end of the Cold War had opened up new labor markets in the former Soviet bloc, while the embrace of free markets and the gradual lowering of trade barriers by many formerly closed economies — such as India and China — made still more countries attractive targets for offshoring. [1]

Today, U.S. and European companies are shifting a growing array of white-collar jobs — 500,000 in the past five years — to poorer countries all over the world, from the Philippines to Russia and its former allies in Hungary, Romania and the Czech Republic — virtually any country with broadband Internet access and a technically literate work force. [2]

But no country has benefited more from recent white-collar job outsourcing by American industry than India, where such work now accounts for 2.5 per cent of gross domestic product. [3] After gaining independence in 1947, India missed out on the industrial revolution that had enriched its imperial overlord, Britain, remaining mired in poverty along with the rest of the Third World.

Successive Indian governments adopted protectionist policies to promote self-sufficiency as the engine of India's economy, but they also invested heavily in education, notably a large university system focusing on engineering and science. In addition, the colonial experience left most of India's 1 billion inhabitants with an enduring asset: proficiency in English.

In short, India offers highly educated, English-speaking workers for about a tenth of Americans' salaries. White-collar outsourcing has helped fuel a 33-percent increase in India's share of global economic output since 1991. [4]

Some of the newfound wealth is ending up in the pockets of Indian high-tech workers, whose wages are climbing. [5] Young college graduates are flocking to offshore centers such as Bangalore and Mumbai (formerly Bombay) and gaining the independence that comes with a generous paycheck. In addition, India's strict class and caste divisions are loosening, and a newly emerging middle class of young professionals is adopting the consumption habits of their American peers and casting aside such time-honored traditions as arranged marriages.

India may soon face stiff competition from such budding offshore locations as Bangladesh, Brazil, Singapore, Thailand, Venezuela and Vietnam, the United Nations reports. [6] As wages rise in India, it is likely to see competition from China, whose fast-growing industrial base and even bigger labor pool are making it a tempting alternative for cost-cutting American firms. China is likely to overcome its big shortcoming — a dearth of English speakers — as a new generation of workers graduates from China's schools, where English instruction is now mandatory.

Outsourcing of manufacturing jobs from the United States and other industrial countries has already benefited workers in special economic zones located along China's coastline that were opened to trade in the 1980s. "There are 300 million people in those eastern coastal provinces who have seen an extraordinary pickup in their standard of living," said Edmund Harriss, portfolio manager of the Guinness Atkinson China and Hong Kong Fund. [7]

In 2001, China was granted normal trade status by the United States after joining the World Trade Organization, two moves that forced it to significantly liberalize its trade policies. "You're seeing an economy that is just about to take wing because you now have consumers who were never able to participate in the economy before," Harriss said.

China's opening to foreign investment, including job offshoring, is being felt beyond the U.S. As a result of the 1993 North American Free Trade Agreement, Mexico enjoyed a decade of rapid job growth as U.S. firms seeking low-wage workers set up factories south of the border. But today Mexico is losing many of those jobs to even lower-wage countries, including China.

"Five years ago, Mexico was the logical place for manufacturers to go," said Jonathan Heath, an economist with LatinSource, a consulting firm in Mexico City. "Now China is logical." [8]

---

[1] See Andy Meisler, "Where in the World Is Offshoring Going?" *Workforce Management*, January 2004, p. 45.

[2] Christopher Caldwell, "A chill wind from offshore," *Financial Times*, Feb. 7, 2004.

[3] *Ibid.*

[4] International Monetary Fund, "IMF Survey," Feb. 2, 2004.

[5] See David E. Gumpert, "U.S. Programmers at Overseas Salaries," *Business Week Online*, Dec. 2, 2003.

[6] U.N. Conference on Trade and Development, "E-Commerce and Development Report 2003," Nov. 20, 2003.

[7] Quoted by Erika Kinetz, "Who Wins and Who Loses as Jobs Move Overseas?" *The New York Times*, Dec. 7, 2003, p. A5.

[8] Quoted by Chris Kraal, "NAFTA 10 Years Later," *Los Angeles Times*, Jan. 2, 2004, p. A1.

Continued from p. 158

Wages also suffered as the manufacturing sector declined. Laid-off factory workers often took low-paying, non-union jobs in the burgeoning service sector as retail clerks and cashiers.

NAFTA and More

The export of U.S. manufacturing jobs accelerated in the 1990s, especially after Congress in 1993 approved the North American Free Trade Agreement (NAFTA), which removed trade barriers among the United States, Canada and Mexico. U.S. companies seeking cheap labor close to the American market built hundreds of factories, called *maquiladoras*, just south of the border, employing tens of thousands of Mexicans. By 2000, American textile workers — already hit by outsourcing to Asia — had lost more than 80,000 additional jobs to Mexico as a result of NAFTA. [34]

But according to Mack McLarty, former chief of staff and special envoy for the Americas under President Bill Clinton, NAFTA created more U.S. jobs than it eliminated. While about 500,000 American factory jobs went to Mexico because of NAFTA, U.S. private-sector employment grew by 15 million jobs — with hourly wages up 10 percent — in the decade since the law went into effect, McLarty wrote recently. [35]

Even as traditional manufacturing jobs continued to disappear during the 1990s, increasing productivity transformed several U.S. manufacturing sectors. A newly organized American steel industry emerged, even after such industry leaders as Bethlehem Steel and LTV went under, crushed by lower-cost imports from Japan and other countries. Incorporating the latest technologies, International Steel Group and other new companies over the past two decades increased U.S. steel production from 75 million tons to 102 million tons. But they did so by increasing productivity, not jobs: Today there are just 74,000 U.S. steelworkers, down from 289,000 in the early 1980s. And while wages remain high, at $18 to $21 an hour, the generous pension and health benefits their predecessors enjoyed are gone. [36]

Still, the enormous shift from traditional manufacturing to telecommunications, retail trade, finance and other industries continued apace. Between 1980 — when manufacturers began downsizing — and 2002, General Motors eliminated 53 percent of its work force, Kodak 46 percent and Goodyear 36 percent. Over the same period, United Parcel Service boosted its payroll by 224 percent, McDonald's by 253 percent and Wal-Mart by a whopping 4,715 percent. [37] A quarter of the factory workers who found new jobs took pay cuts of at least 25 percent, according to the Institute for International Economics. [38]

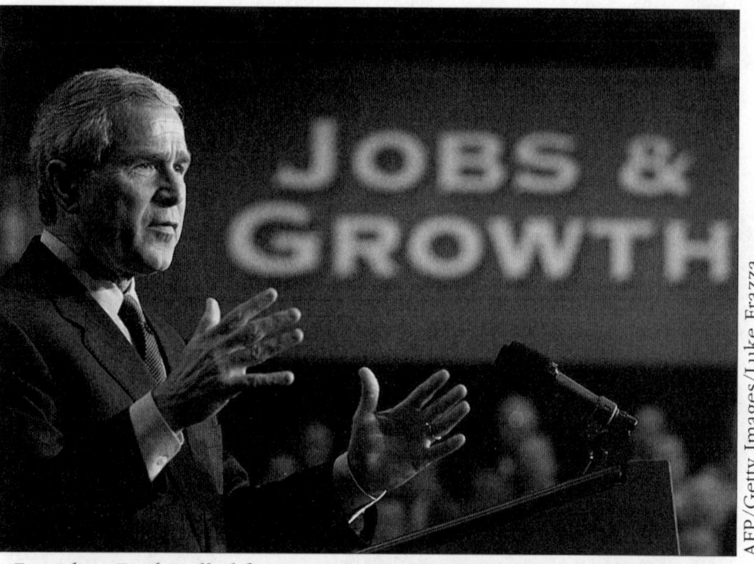

AFP/Getty Images/Luke Frazza

President Bush called for "stronger math and science preparation" in his State of the Union address in January. "I propose increasing our support for America's fine community colleges, so they can train workers for the industries that are creating the most new jobs," he said.

During the 1990s, makers of electronic equipment and computers began emulating older manufacturers by sending production overseas. Despite rapid productivity improvements — accompanied by high profits and rising stock prices — high-tech companies were eager to improve their competitive edge in a rapidly globalizing industry.

The service sector also sought cheaper labor overseas. [39] Software companies led the way, quickly establishing Bangalore, India, as a major U.S. outpost. Other countries benefited from U.S. offshoring as well. Ireland, which largely had missed Europe's postwar boom, blossomed in the 1990s as American corporations outsourced their billing and other "back-office" operations. The Philippines and Malaysia emerged as leading call-center locations, China became an important back-office service center, and Russia and Israel began providing customized software and computer systems.

Several unrelated developments further energized offshoring during the 1990s. Access to the Internet through high-speed broadband connection spread from the industrial countries to the developing world, enabling managers in the U.S. to communicate quickly and cheaply with satellite offices. The use of English as the *lingua franca* of businesses around the world enabled workers in India, the Philippines and other English-speaking countries to take part in the outsourcing boom. And locating offices in different time zones allowed call centers to service customers around the clock.

Y2K Impact

Before U.S. employers began exporting large numbers of IT and other white-collar jobs, they clamored for relaxation of the laws limiting non-immigrant visas. Fueling these efforts were dire predictions by the National Science Foundation and the conservative Hudson Institute that American universities were not turning out enough skilled technical professionals. [40]

Congress cited the studies in 1990, when it substantially increased the number of skilled workers allowed into the country. The Immigration Act of 1990 nearly tripled the number of permanent, work-based admissions allowed each year and created tens of thousands of slots for various types of temporary skilled workers, including 65,000 under the controversial H-1B program. The 1990 law also created new visas for other skilled temporary workers, including nurses, scientists, teachers and entertainers, and expanded the L-1 program enabling multinational corporations to bring key executives to the United States for up to seven years.

As the 20th century came to an end, there was widespread fear that computer systems would crash worldwide on Jan. 1, 2000, because their internal clocks were not set to change from 1999 to 2000. [41] As U.S. companies scrambled to hire extra workers to circumvent the so-called Y2K bug, programmers became scarce. Employers renewed their claims of a dire shortage of skilled American workers and brought in thousands of foreign programmers under the H-1B program.

Either the fears had been overblown — or enough computers had been fixed to avert the problem. In any event, the new century arrived without incident. But companies that had hired costly specialists to rewrite their codes were left with a new incentive to cut costs.

"When 2000 came, employers started laying off more employees," says T.O.R.A.W. President Bauman. "But the foreign visa workers, who were supposedly getting a fair wage, were costing them less." Seasoned professionals like Bauman received higher compensation than H-1B workers, who often were just out of college. "Employers were saving on salaries with foreign workers, and they decided to keep them on."

As the new millennium began, the elimination of U.S. high-tech jobs only accelerated when the nation went into recession after the telecom "bubble" burst. The economy took a further nosedive after the Sept. 11, 2001, terrorist attacks. U.S. employers decided to more fully tap India's vast, cheap, labor pool, setting up operations in Bangalore and other cities. The offshoring boom had begun. ■

AP Photo/Richard Vogel

Vietnamese computer programmers attend a job fair in Hanoi in April 2002. Vietnam has emerged as a major outsourcing base for U.S., European and Japanese high-tech firms.

CURRENT SITUATION

'Jobless' Recovery

The U.S. economy continues on its uneven path to recovery. The Dow Jones Industrial Average rose an encouraging 25 percent last year after two disappointing previous years. GDP growth — 8.2 percent in the third quarter and 4 percent in the fourth — suggests that the recovery, which officially began in November 2001, is finally picking up. Business investments in equipment and software are up, and inflation remains low, prompting the Federal Reserve to keep interest rates at their lowest levels in decades. [42]

"Exports are growing," Bush declared during his State of the Union address. "Productivity is high, and jobs are on the rise."

But Labor Department data show why economists call the recovery "jobless." A net total of just 1,000 jobs were added to industry payrolls in December. Temp agencies and other service companies hired 45,000 workers; construction workers and health-services workers also posted gains. But the new-job gains were offset by the continuing hemorrhaging of manufacturing jobs, which tend to pay middle-class wages and benefits. In December, manufacturers shed 26,000 jobs, bringing to 516,000 the number of U.S. factory jobs that disappeared last year. Moreover, in addition to the 2.8 million manufacturing jobs lost since July 2000, a half-million tech jobs have been lost since 2001. [43]

Although no figures are kept on how much of the job loss can be attributed to outsourcing or offshoring, economists are sure that outsourcing is a factor.

"It certainly plays a role in manufacturing," M.I.T.'s Thurow says. "A lot of the automobile components that used to be made in the United States are now made in various Third World countries. And that basically leads some blue-collar workers and their managers to lose their jobs. This outsourcing started back in the '90s, but the economy was growing so fast in the high-tech sector, we didn't notice it."

Former Labor Secretary Robert B. Reich contends most manufacturing jobs are not disappearing due to offshoring but because of the higher productivity that comes with enhanced efficiency and new technology. "I recently toured a U.S. factory containing two employees and 400 computerized robots," Reich wrote in *The Wall Street Journal*. [44]

Moreover, he noted, although more than 22 million factory jobs worldwide vanished between 1995 and 2002, the United States lost fewer than many other countries, both rich and poor. The United States lost 11 percent of its manufacturing jobs during the period, he noted, while Japan lost 16 percent, China 15 percent and Brazil 20 percent. [45]

Several business-research firms have estimated the extent of offshoring today and its likely growth in the future. The Information Technology Association of America found that 12 percent of its member companies had opened offshore operations, usually for programmers and software engineers. [46] Forrester Research predicts that 3.3 million U.S. service jobs — mostly IT-related positions like software developers and help-desk operators — will move offshore over the next 15 years. [47] Goldman Sachs estimates that 200,000 service jobs have been lost to offshoring so far — with 6 million more to follow over the next decade. [48] A University of California, Berkeley, study put the number at close to 14 million over the next 15 years. [49]

Lower costs for software and other services will allow "huge segments" of the economy to improve productivity, said former U.S. Trade Representative Hills, creating 20 million new American jobs in the coming decade. "That's faster than last decade," she said, noting that even the booming 1990s only created 15 million jobs. "Every metric study shows that . . . job growth [will rise] faster than it did in the last decade. This is an amazing prospect." [50]

Some economists say the estimates ignore the economy's ability to absorb job losses. "The number of high-tech jobs outsourced abroad still accounts for a tiny proportion of America's 10-million strong IT work force," Reich also has noted. "When the U.S. economy fully bounces back from recession (as it almost certainly will within the next 18 months), a large portion of high-tech jobs that were lost after 2000 will come back in some form." [51]

But MIT's Thurow says white-collar outsourcing is still in its infancy — totaling only about $8 billion in a $400 billion, U.S.-dominated global software market. "White-collar outsourcing is rising very rapidly," Thurow says. "The issue is a little bit like rape. Not that many women have been raped, but you don't need a very large fraction of women who've been raped before everybody's worried about it."

Those fears seem likely to intensify as more American technology companies announce they are moving key jobs offshore. America Online reportedly is planning to hire additional Indian software engineers for its facility in Bangalore to help build its Internet software. Yahoo and Google may soon follow AOL's lead. [52] IBM plans to move as many as 4,730 white-collar jobs from the United States. [53] They would be joining the ranks of such American icons as AT&T, Dell, Microsoft, Proctor & Gamble and Verizon.

Legislative Action

Offshoring is turning into a hot political issue in this presidential election year, as the economic recovery fails to generate all the new jobs anticipated by the administration. The shortfall is prompting Congress and the states to consider proposals aimed at stemming the loss of American jobs.

A bipartisan measure pending in Congress would close what critics see as major loopholes in the H-1B and L-1 visa programs. The USA Jobs Protection Act, cosponsored by Democratic Sen. Christopher J. Dodd and GOP Rep. Nancy L. Johnson — both from Connecticut — would beef up federal enforcement of the programs to prevent companies from illegally replacing qualified American workers and underpaying the temporary workers.

Another proposal, sponsored in the House by Rep. Rosa DeLauro, D-Conn., and in the Senate by Sen. Saxby Chambliss, R-Ga., addresses reported abuses of the L-1 program. Since Sept. 30, 2003, when Congress slashed the annual cap on H-1B visas from 195,000 to 65,000, critics charge that companies have abused the L-1 program, which has no annual cap, to import non-managerial tech workers.

"The availability of the L-visa category to those applying under 'specialized knowledge' — a vague term at best open to multiple and elastic interpretations — has done clear harm to the American work force and contributed directly to the job loss since the most recent recession began," House International Relations Committee Chairman Henry J. Hyde, R-Ill., told a Feb. 4, 2004, committee hearing on visa reform. "Lax procedures, for L visas or any other category of non-immigrant visa, are clearly a prescription for chaos in both visa policy and border security. It is time for reform."

Business representatives counter that any attempt to restrict corporate America's ability to hire workers anywhere in the world would only hurt the U.S. economy, and eventually American workers. "The use of certain categories of visas, such as the

H-1B or the L-1, by multinational companies has been an effective means of maintaining our competitive edge," the Chamber of Commerce's Johnson wrote. "In the long run, expansion of international trade and investment in the United States is in the best interests of all." [54]

"Unless U.S. and foreign companies are able to bring key personnel to their American operations, U.S. companies will be put at a competitive disadvantage and foreign companies will be unlikely to establish or expand their presence in our country," Harris N. Miller, president of the Information Technology Association of America, told the committee. Foreign investment "means more U.S. factories, offices and jobs, and the L-1 program facilitates these investments."

Another measure, introduced by Sens. John Kerry, D-Mass., the current front-runner for the Democratic presidential nomination, and Minority Leader Tom Daschle, D-S.D., seeks to help Americans understand how widespread the offshoring phenomenon really is by requiring employees at overseas call centers of U.S.-based companies to disclose the center's physical location.

On Jan. 23, President Bush signed into law a measure preventing American companies from subcontracting some government jobs to companies outside the United States. The ban, originally sponsored by Sens. George V. Voinovich, R-Ohio, and Craig Thomas, R-Wyo., was included in the fiscal 2004 omnibus appropriations bill. It remains uncertain how many of the 1.8 million civilians who work for the federal government will be affected. The Bush administration has accelerated the pace of outsourcing of federal jobs, and 102,000 jobs are currently slated to come up for competitive bidding. [55]

Anti-outsourcing bills are now pending in a dozen legislatures, and up to 20 could consider such measures before the legislative season ends.

—Justin Marks, Analyst, National Conference of State Legislatures

Some states that have been especially hard-hit by IT outsourcing are considering prohibiting government work from being contracted to non-Americans or barring employers from requiring workers slated for layoff to train their foreign replacements. Anti-outsourcing bills are now pending in a dozen legislatures, and up to 20 could consider such measures before the legislative season ends, according to Justin Marks, an analyst at the National Conference of State Legislatures (NCSL). Marks said eight states debated such bills last year, but none passed — largely due to Republican opposition. [56]

Even California — home to Silicon Valley companies that have been heavy users of offshoring and H-1B visas — is considering anti-offshoring legislation. A bill introduced by Assemblywoman Carol Liu, D-Pasadena, would prevent the use of overseas call centers for state services like welfare and food stamps. "There's a great irony here that we're telling people on welfare to find jobs, and the kind of jobs they could do are not here anymore," said Richard Johnson, Liu's legislative aide. [57]

At least one of the bills to be introduced in California is expected to apply to private employers that handle customers' confidential information. Controversies have erupted around the country in recent months when patients learned that insurance companies increasingly are having confidential medical records transcribed by companies overseas, where U.S. medical-privacy laws do not apply. During an employment dispute in October, a Pakistani contract worker handling confidential medical records from California threatened to disclose the information. [58]

Marks says political pressure to pass anti-outsourcing measures this year is growing in some states. "In any event, I think we'll see a ripple effect in policymaking," he said, "with greater efforts at local job creation in places most affected by outsourcing." [59]

Marks says offshoring public-sector jobs may not end up saving taxpayers money in the long run, because hidden long-term costs could outweigh short-term taxpayers' savings. "If you compare the savings to the loss in taxable income [from local workers laid off due to the offshoring] with the state's cost of paying unemployment benefits [to those laid off], it's possible states are not saving that much money," Marks said. [60]

Northeastern University labor economist Paul E. Harrington warns of another hidden, long-term cost: the erosion of a state's middle-class base. States that value "full employment, upward

Continued on p. 166

At Issue:

Should the government slow the outsourcing of high-tech jobs?

yes

RON HIRA
CHAIRMAN, R&D POLICY COMMITTEE, INSTITUTE OF ELECTRICAL AND ELECTRONICS ENGINEERS

FROM TESTIMONY BEFORE THE HOUSE SMALL BUSINESS COMMITTEE, OCT. 20, 2003

According to the most recent data from the Bureau of Labor Statistics, electrical, electronics and computer hardware engineers continue to face a higher unemployment rate than the general population, and over double the rate for other managers and professionals. The news for engineering managers is even worse, with an unemployment rate of 8 percent. . . .

To put this in historical context, in the 30-plus years that the Department of Labor has been collecting statistics, the past two years are the first in which unemployment rates for electrical, electronics and computer engineers are higher than the unemployment rate for all workers. . . . And throughout the 1980s, at a time when unemployment rates for all workers got as high as 9.5 percent, electrical and electronics engineering unemployment rates never rose above 2 percent. . . .

It is entirely misleading to describe offshore outsourcing as a "win-win" proposition for America and other countries, as free-trade advocates so often do. Those advocates [should be required] to demonstrate how workers who have been adversely affected will be compensated and helped to become productive citizens once again.

These advocates assume, as part of their argument, that displaced American workers will be redeployed. Instead of assuming, we should ensure that such workers are redeployed in equally high-skill and highly paid positions. . . .

The federal government must begin regularly tracking the volume and nature of the jobs that are moving offshore. Companies should be required to give adequate notice of their intentions to move work offshore, so displaced employees can make appropriate plans to minimize the financial hardship, and government support agencies can prepare to provide the necessary transition assistance. Congress should rethink how U.S. work force assistance programs can be designed to help displaced high-tech workers become productive again.

We are in a new era of work and lifelong learning, and new and more flexible methods are needed to provide meaningful assistance. Congress should strengthen H-1B and L-1 work force protections and their enforcement to ensure that the programs serve their respective purposes without adversely affecting employment opportunities for U.S. high-tech workers.

The United States needs a coordinated national strategy designed to sustain its technological leadership and promote job creation in response to the concerted strategies being used by other countries to attract U.S. industries and jobs.

no

HARRIS N. MILLER
PRESIDENT, INFORMATION TECHNOLOGY ASSOCIATION OF AMERICA

FROM TESTIMONY BEFORE THE HOUSE SMALL BUSINESS COMMITTEE, OCT. 20, 2003

In statistical terms, the trend towards offshore outsourcing is a cloud on the horizon, not a hurricane sweeping everything in its midst. We should keep our eye on how the weather pattern is changing, but we should not start boarding up our windows and stashing the patio furniture. The U.S. IT industry is facing new challenges, but it is not disappearing.

Over 10 million Americans earn their living in the IT work force . . . nine out of 10 of [them] employed by businesses outside of the IT industry: banks, law firms, factories, stores and the like. Eight out of 10 of these jobs are found in small businesses — the firms arguably least likely to [send their jobs offshore]. Even the most doom-and-gloom analysts predict that fewer than 500,000 computer-specific jobs will move offshore in the next 10 years. . . .

If we have seen any storm at all, it has been the three-year "perfect storm" of trends converging to depress the short-term demand for U.S. IT workers: the dot-com bust, the telecom collapse, the recession and jobless recovery and slow customer spending — domestically and globally — for new IT products and services. . . .

I do not mean to downplay the very real impacts of offshore competition to American IT workers or their families. Thousands of IT professionals have played by the rules: studied hard in school, worked long hours, made a sweat equity investment in the future of their companies, only to find themselves now unemployed or underemployed. A more vibrant economy and greater capital spending by the private sector will greatly help these individuals. Not all of the current concerns, however, can be attributed to the economy, and we need to better understand this new competitive reality, using logic — not emotion — as our filter. . . .

While it may be emotionally satisfying to try to protect jobs by throwing up barriers, free trade and global markets spark investment, trade and job creation. For Americans caught in the riptide of a transitioning job market, economic abstractions like positive trade balances and expanding free markets may be the source of cold comfort. I reject, however, the notion that offshore development is a zero sum game or that every job shipped offshore is a job permanently lost to an American worker. On the contrary, evidence abounds that the working capital that U.S. companies save by moving jobs and operations offshore results in new investment, innovation and job creation in this country.

Continued from p. 164

mobility and a solid middle class as an important and essential feature" of their economies should warn their companies to "think about this outsourcing issue," Harrington advised. [61]

Business spokesmen say anti-outsourcing measures amount to protectionism and will only hurt American workers. "The focus should be making sure that America stays a nimble, highly educated, forward-thinking, innovative economic presence, not one that's trying to hold onto things while the world around them is changing," says Daigle of Evalueserve. "That strategy is a going-out-of-business strategy."

But Bauman says displaced IT workers are counting on the offshoring bills. "If we don't see any action on this problem soon," he says, "we can kiss our careers good-bye forever."

Bush's Amnesty Plan

On Jan. 7, President Bush announced an initiative to permit the estimated 8 million illegal immigrants to remain in the United States for six years as long they are employed. The undocumented workers would receive identification cards enabling them to travel between the United States and their home countries. Employers also could bring in additional "guest workers" under the same conditions if they cannot find qualified American workers.

"We must make our immigration laws more rational and more humane," Bush said. "I believe we can do so without jeopardizing the livelihoods of American citizens." [62]

Critics say the proposal would worsen working conditions for American employees just as existing visa programs do — by tying a worker's legal status to steady employment with a single employer. "One of the ways you get ahead in the U.S. labor market is by making employers bid for you, and it doesn't sound like these guest workers are going to have that ability at all," says Bivens of the Economic Policy Institute. If employers can rely on low-wage immigrants to fill their job openings, he says, they will have no incentive to hire American workers who demand higher wages. "It doesn't really provide a big improvement over the status quo for the undocumented," Bivens says, "and it is one more way to subvert the bargaining power of other workers here."

Business groups welcome the proposal, saying immigrants would take jobs Americans don't want, not manufacturing or white-collar positions. "Manufacturing workers tend to be more sophisticated, higher-level workers," says Cox of the NAM. "Guys don't come here from Guatemala or Mexico and go to work in manufacturing. You have to know too much high-tech stuff."

But critics say similar efforts in other industrial countries offer little grounds for encouragement. "Guest-worker systems haven't worked anywhere in the world because eventually people just don't go home," MIT's Thurow says.

But Switzerland's program works, Thurow says, because every worker must return home for a certain period each year and is barred from bringing family members into the country. "The only way you can deport temporary workers is the way Switzerland does it," he says, "and they are just ferocious."

Few observers expect Congress to take up Bush's immigration plan this year. Many Republicans oppose any immigration initiative that rewards illegal immigrants for breaking the law, while many Democrats say the plan does not do enough to help them gain U.S. citizenship.

A bipartisan alternative presented on Jan. 21 by Sens. Daschle and Chuck Hagel, R-Neb., calls for eventual citizenship for illegal immigrants who meet a series of requirements and would admit no more than 350,000 new temporary workers each year. [63] ■

OUTLOOK

Election Debate

As presidential campaign rhetoric intensifies, many observers expect the globalization of American jobs to become an increasingly important issue, especially if offshoring continues to threaten white-collar jobs.

"If I were President Bush, professional white-collar outsourcing would give me nightmares," Thurow says. "When a factory moves to China or India, that's blue-collar jobs. They're Democratic voters anyway. But white-collar outsourcing? That's Republican voters."

The administration recently got a taste of how politically sensitive the offshoring issue is. N. Gregory Mankiw, chairman of the White House Council of Economic Advisers, stunned Democrats and Republicans alike when he recently described offshoring as "just a new way to do international trade. Outsourcing is a growing phenomenon, but it's something that we should realize is probably a plus for the economy in the long run." [64]

House Speaker J. Dennis Hastert, R-Ill., issued a stern rebuttal to his fellow Republican. "I understand that Mr. Mankiw is a brilliant economic theorist, but his theory fails a basic test of real economics," Hastert said. "An economy suffers when jobs disappear. Outsourcing can be a problem for American workers, and for the American economy. We can't have a healthy economy unless we have more jobs here in America." [65]

Mankiw subsequently hedged his statement. "It is regrettable whenever anyone loses a job," he wrote. "At the same time, we have to acknowledge that any economic change, whether arising from trade or technology, can cause painful dislocations for some workers and their families. The goal of policy should be to help workers prepare for the global economy of the future."

But the basic thrust of Bush's policy on outsourcing stands, as reflected in this year's "Economic Report of the President": "When a good or service is produced more cheaply abroad, it makes more sense to import it than to make or provide it domestically." [66]

President Bush asserts that his income tax cuts, which the administration says will total $1.3 trillion over 10 years, are the key to speeding the recovery and stimulating job growth. "Americans took those dollars and put them to work, driving this economy forward," Bush said during his State of the Union address.

The president went on to ask Congress to fund new programs to improve science and math education at the middle- and high-school levels and help community colleges "train workers for the industries that are creating the most new jobs."

The job-export issue is creeping into the tax debate. Democratic candidates have lambasted a tax loophole that enables corporations to avoid paying U.S. taxes on offshore revenues that already have been taxed by foreign governments.

"George Bush continues to fight for incentives to encourage Benedict Arnold companies to ship jobs overseas at the same time he cuts job training for our workers and cuts help for small businesses that create jobs here at home," Kerry charged. [67]

But the campaign oratory does not impress T.O.R.A.W. President Bauman and other Americans who have lost their jobs to foreign workers.

"Neither side is addressing this problem adequately," Bauman says. "Some of the candidates have outwardly said they would do something, but nobody has come out and said exactly what they would do to stop offshoring. I don't want to wait until November. I want to see action now."

"The issue is going to be exaggerated and manipulated by both sides in the political debate," predicted Dean Davison, an analyst at the Meta Group, a technology research and advisory firm in Stamford, Conn. [68]

Former Trade Representative Hills warns, "We really must be very wary about making the wrong economic move, even when it's politically attractive to be sloganistic." [69] ■

Notes

[1] Saritha Rai, "Indians Fearing Repercussions Of U.S. Technology Outsourcing," *The New York Times*, Feb. 9, 2004, p. C4.

[2] See Nelson D. Schwartz, "Will 'Made in USA' Fade Away?" *Fortune*, Nov. 24, 2003, p. 98, and "Employees on Nonfarm Payrolls by Major Industry Sector, 1954 to Date," Bureau of Labor Statistics.

[3] See Karl Schoenberger, "Kerry, Dean Compete to Stress Hot Issue," *San Jose Mercury News*, Jan. 30, 2004.

[4] The Commerce Department released its most recent GDP data on Jan. 30, 2004.

[5] See Nell Henderson, "Growth Again, but Slower," *The Washington Post*, Jan. 31, 2004.

[6] See "Unemployment Rate Falls; Few Jobs Added," The Associated Press, Jan. 9, 2004.

[7] Christopher Caldwell, "A chill wind from offshore," *Financial Times*, Feb. 7, 2004.

[8] *Ibid.*

[9] "Global Offshore Call Center Outsourcing: Who Will Be the Next India?" *Datamonitor*, Jan. 8, 2004.

[10] See Erica L. Groshen and Simon Potter, "Has Structural Change Contributed to a Jobless Recovery?" *Current Issues in Economics and Finance*, Federal Reserve Bank of New York, August 2003.

[11] Census Bureau, 2002. See Andrew Hacker, "The Underworld of Work," *The New York Review of Books*, Feb. 12, 2004, pp. 38-40.

[12] *Ibid.*

[13] U.S. Census Bureau, "Historical Income Tables — Income Equality," Table IE-3, www.census.gov. For background, see Mary H. Cooper, "Income Inequality," *The CQ Researcher*, April 17, 1998, pp. 337-360.

[14] Quoted on ABC's "This Week," Feb. 15, 2004. Hills was citing a study by Catherine L. Mann, "Globalization of IT Services and White Collar Jobs: The Next Wave of Productivity Growth," International Economics Policy Briefs, Institute for International Economics, December 2003.

[15] *Ibid.*

[16] *Ibid.*

[17] *Ibid.*

[18] Quoted in Steve Lohr, "Many New Causes for Old problem of Jobs Lost Abroad," *The New York Times*, Feb. 15, 2004, p. A17.

[19] ABC, *op. cit.*

[20] www.mckinsey.com/knowledge/mgi/offshore/.

[21] Caldwell, *op. cit.*

[22] From Bush's State of the Union address, Jan. 20, 2004.

[23] See Peter D. Syverson, "Coping with Conflicting Data: The Employment Status of Recent Science and Engineering Ph.D.s," Council of Graduate Schools, 1997.

[24] See, for example, Committee for Economic Development, "Reforming Immigration: Helping Meet America's Need for a Skilled Workforce," 2001.

[25] *Ibid.*

[26] See Eric Chabrow, "The Programmer's Future," *InformationWeek*, Nov. 17, 2003, pp. 40-52.

[27] For background, see Kathy Koch, "High-Tech Labor Shortage," *The CQ Researcher*, April 24, 1998, pp. 361-384.

[28] U.S. Citizenship and Immigration Services Fact Sheet, "H-1B Petitions Received and Approved in FY 2003," Oct. 22, 2003. Citizenship and Immigration Services, part of the Department of Homeland Security, has ad-

About the Author

Mary H. Cooper specializes in defense, energy and environmental issues. Before joining *The CQ Researcher* as a staff writer in 1983, she was Washington correspondent for the Rome daily newspaper *l'Unitá*. She is the author of *The Business of Drugs* (CQ Press, 1990) and holds a B.A. in English from Hollins College in Virginia. Her recent reports include "Weapons of Mass Destruction" and "Bush and the Environment."

ministered work-visa programs since the department absorbed the Immigration and Naturalization Service in 2003.

[29] Ron Sanchez administers ZaZona.com as a source of information on the H-1B program.

[30] Duffy testified Sept. 16, 2003, before the Senate Judiciary Committee.

[31] From a June 18, 2003, letter to House Small Business Committee Chairman Donald A. Manzullo, R-Ill.

[32] Norman Matloff, "Needed Reform for the H-1B and L-1 Work Visas: Major Points," Feb. 5, 2003, http://heather.cs.ucdavis.edu/itaa.html.

[33] See "The Impact of Global Sourcing on the U.S. Economy, 2003-2010," *Evalueserve*, 2003.

[34] See Jane Tanner, "Future Job Market," *The CQ Researcher*, Jan. 11, 2002, p. 14.

[35] See Mack McLarty, "Trade Paves Path to U.S. Prosperity," *Los Angeles Times*, Feb. 1, 2004, p. M2.

[36] Schwartz, *op. cit.*

[37] Hacker, *op. cit.*

[38] See Steve Lohr, "Questioning the Age of Wal-Mart," *The New York Times*, Dec. 28, 2003.

[39] Information in the following paragraphs is based on Ashok Deo Bardhan and Cynthia A. Kroll, "The New Wave of Outsourcing," Research Report, Fisher Center for Real Estate and Urban Economics, University of California, Berkeley, fall 2003.

[40] Koch, *op. cit.*

[41] For background, see Kathy Koch, "Y2K Dilemma," *The CQ Researcher*, Feb. 19, 1999, pp. 137-160.

[42] See Bureau of Economic Analysis, Commerce Department, "Growth Moderates in Fourth Quarter but Is Up for the Year," Jan. 30, 2004.

[43] Bureau of Labor Statistics, Department of Labor, "Employment Situation Summary," Jan. 9, 2004. Also see Jonathan Krim, "Grove Says U.S. Is Losing Edge in Tech Sector," Forbes.com, Oct. 10, 2003.

[44] See Robert B. Reich, "Nice Work If You Can Get It," *The Wall Street Journal*, Dec. 26, 2003, p. A10.

[45] *Ibid.*

[46] Information Technology Association of America, "2003 IT Workforce Survey," May 5, 2003.

[47] John C. McCarthy *et al.*, "3.3 Million U.S. Services Jobs to Go Offshore," *Forrester Tech Strategy Brief*, Nov. 11, 2002.

FOR MORE INFORMATION

Bureau of Labor Statistics, U.S. Labor Department, 2 Massachusetts Ave., N.E., Suite 4040, Washington, DC 20212; (202) 691-7800; www.bls.gov.

Department for Professional Employees, AFL-CIO, 1025 Vermont Ave., N.W., Suite 1030, Washington, DC 2000; (202) 638-0320; www.dpeaflcio.org. This labor group representing more than 4 million white-collar workers calls for policy changes to stem the export of U.S. jobs.

Economic Policy Institute, 1660 L St., N.W., Suite 1200, Washington, DC 20036; (202) 775-8810; www.epinet.org. This nonprofit research group contends Americans lose jobs because of free-trade agreements.

National Association of Manufacturers, 1331 Pennsylvania Ave., N.W., Washington, DC 20004-1790; (202) 637-3000; www.nam.org. The 14,000-member organization defends outsourcing as essential to U.S. competitiveness.

Organization for the Rights of American Workers (T.O.R.A.W.), PO Box 2354, Meriden, CT 06450-1454; www.toraw.org. A worker-advocacy group demanding that U.S. jobs be preserved for American citizens and calling for legislation to limit offshoring and worker-visa programs.

U.S. Chamber of Commerce, 1615 H St., N.W., Washington, DC 20062-2000; (202) 659-6000; www.uschamber.com. The largest U.S. business lobby opposes legislative obstacles to offshore outsourcing.

[48] Andrew Tilton, "Offshoring: Where Have All the Jobs Gone?" Goldman, Sachs & Co., *U.S. Economics Analyst*, Sept. 19, 2003.

[49] Bardhan, *op. cit.*

[50] ABC, *op. cit.*

[51] Robert Reich, "High-Tech Jobs Are Going Abroad! But That's OK," *The Washington Post*, Nov. 2, 2003, p. B3.

[52] See Jim Hu and Evan Hansen, "AOL Takes Passage to India," CNET News.com, Dec. 22, 2003.

[53] See William M. Bulkeley, "IBM to Export Highly Paid Jobs to India, China," *The Wall Street Journal*, Dec. 15, 2003, p. B1.

[54] Johnson, *op. cit.*

[55] Andrew Mollison, "GOP Ban on 'Offshoring' Federal Jobs Angers Business Groups," Cox News Service, Jan. 29, 2004.

[56] Karl Schoenberger, "Legislator wants to keep jobs in state, limits sought on overseas contracts," *San Jose* [California] *Mercury News*, Feb. 5, 2004.

[57] *Ibid.*

[58] *Ibid.*

[59] *Ibid.*

[60] Quoted on "Marketplace," National Public Radio, Feb. 16, 2004.

[61] *Ibid.*

[62] Quoted in Mike Allen, "Bush Proposes Legal Status for Immigrant Labor," *The Washington Post*, Jan. 8, 2004, p. A1. For background, see David Masci, "Debate Over Immigration," *The CQ Researcher*, July 14, 2000, pp. 569-592.

[63] See Helen Dewar, "2 Senators Counter Bush on Immigrants," *The Washington Post*, Jan. 22, 2004, p. A4.

[64] Mankiw spoke as he released the "Economic Report of the President 2004" on Feb. 9, 2004.

[65] Statement, "Hastert Disagrees With President's Economic Advisor On Outsourcing," Feb. 11, 2004, http://speaker.house.gov. See Mike Allen, "Hastert Rebukes Bush Adviser," *The Washington Post*, Feb. 12, 2004, p. A17.

[66] "Economic Report of the President 2004," Chapter 12, International Trade and Cooperation.

[67] From a Feb. 3, 2004, statement posted at Kerry's campaign Web site, johnkerry.com.

[68] Quoted in Karl Schoenberger, "Offshore Job Losses on Voters' Agendas," *San Jose Mercury News*, Jan. 30, 2004.

[69] ABC News, *op. cit.*

Bibliography

Selected Sources

Books

Bardhan, Ashok Deo, *et al.*, *Globalization and a High-Tech Economy*, Kluwer Academic Publishers, 2003.
High-tech U.S. firms are outsourcing white-collar jobs offshore to cut labor costs, according to a University of California, Berkeley, economist and his colleagues.

Thurow, Lester C., *Fortune Favors the Bold: What We Must Do to Build a New and Lasting Global Prosperity*, HarperBusiness, 2003.
The dean of MIT's business school calls on policymakers to take steps to reduce the threat of problems that could result from rapid globalization.

Articles

Cullen, Lisa Takeuchi, "Now Hiring!" *Time*, Nov. 24, 2003, p. 48.
The stagnant U.S. labor market is slowly improving, but the average job search today takes four to six months, while senior-level positions take more than a year.

Fox, Justin, "Where Your Job Is Going," *Fortune*, Nov. 10, 2003, p. 84.
Bangalore, India, has become a major center for call centers and computer services for U.S. businesses.

Hacker, Andrew, "The Underworld of Work," *The New York Review of Books*, Feb. 12, 2004, pp. 38-40.
Three recent books on U.S. employment trends describe the shift from high-wage manufacturing jobs to low-wage service jobs over the past 20 years.

Irwin, Douglas A., "'Outsourcing' Is Good for America," *The Wall Street Journal*, Jan. 28, 2004, p. A16.
Outsourcing gives consumers lower prices and employers higher profits that they can use to create high-skilled U.S. jobs.

Krugman, Paul, "For Richer," *The New York Times Magazine*, Oct. 20, 2003, pp. 62-142.
Tax policies favoring the wealthiest Americans are widening the income gap and worsening living standards for American workers.

Lind, Michael, "Are We Still a Middle-Class Nation?" *The Atlantic Monthly*, January/February 2004, pp. 120-128.
As the number of well-paid jobs shrinks, low-wage service jobs are growing, but the cost of living for middle-class workers is rising.

Overby, Stephanie, "U.S. Stays on Top," *CIO Magazine*, Dec. 15, 2003.
As companies continue to outsource computer jobs overseas, information-technology professionals will find high-level jobs in strategy, implementation and design.

Reich, Robert, "High-Tech Jobs Are Going Abroad! But That's OK," *The Washington Post*, Nov. 2, 2003, p. B3.
The former secretary of Labor explains why he believes the flow of high-tech jobs abroad is not a problem.

Risen, Clay, "Missed Target: Is Outsourcing Really So Bad?" *The New Republic*, Feb. 2, 2004, p. 10.
Instead of banning outsourcing, Congress should create a new program to retrain displaced manufacturing workers and help white-collar workers find alternative jobs.

Reports and Studies

Bernstein, Jared, and Lawrence Mishel, "Labor Market Left Behind," Briefing Paper, Economic Policy Institute, August 2003.
The current recovery has produced fewer jobs than any other during the post-World War II era.

Evalueserve, "The Impact of Global Sourcing on the U.S. Economy, 2003-2010," Oct. 9, 2003.
Some 1.3 million U.S. jobs will be shifted offshore from 2003-2010, compensating for the shrinking of the work force as the Baby Boomers retire.

Information Technology Association of America, "2003 IT Workforce Survey," May 5, 2003.
Twelve percent of U.S. information-technology companies outsourced jobs overseas, primarily programming jobs.

Matloff, Norman, "On the Need for Reform of the H-1B Non-Immigrant Work Visa in Computer-Related Occupations," *University of Michigan Journal of Law Reform*, Dec. 12, 2003.
In a special issue on immigration, a University of California expert on the H-1B visa program contends that employers abuse the program to import low-wage programmers and other professionals.

U.S. Department of Commerce, Economics and Statistics Administration, "Digital Economy 2003," December 2003.
The information-technology sector promises to continue on a modest, steady growth path, thanks in part to offshoring.

The Next Step:

Additional Articles from Current Periodicals

Coping with Outsourcing

Altman, Daniel, "New Economy: Enhancing Education, Not Protecting Beleaguered Industries, Will Help the Economy, Experts Say," *The New York Times*, July 28, 2003, p. C3.

A pilot program offers eligible workers who lose their jobs and take new ones at lower wages half the difference in wages for up to two years, paid by the government.

Ginsburg, Marsha, "From Mouses to Houses," *San Francisco Chronicle*, Nov. 10, 2002, p. H1.

Laid-off tech workers are frequently starting new careers in an area that requires relatively little investment and is open to almost anyone: real estate.

Goldstein, Amy, "Bush Promotes Training in Ohio Area Losing Jobs," *The Washington Post*, Jan. 22, 2004, p. A8.

President Bush tries to create momentum for his "Jobs for the 21st Century" proposal outlined in the State of the Union address.

Henry, Shannon, "From the Dot-Com Crash to What Truly Drives Them," *The Washington Post*, Sept. 26, 2002, p. E1.

Technology workers are often embarking on new careers in fields unrelated to their old jobs and that are more idiosyncratic and enjoyable.

Koeppel, David, "Tech Workers Struggle to Answer Overseas Threat," *The New York Times*, Nov. 23, 2003, Section 10, p. 1.

Experienced tech workers, some with decades of experience, are forced to adapt as their jobs are sent abroad.

Munro, Neil, "High-Tech Job Flight," *National Journal*, Oct. 4, 2003.

Lawmakers are preparing legislation to fight global outsourcing, spurred on by meetings with concerned constituents as this issue looms larger politically.

Postrel, Virginia, "Economic Scene: A Researcher Sees an Upside in the Outsourcing of Programming Jobs," *The New York Times*, Jan. 29, 2004, p. C2.

A researcher cites historical precedents to argue that outsourcing abroad will increase productivity and ultimately lead to higher wages and better jobs for Americans.

Schneider, Greg, "Anxious About Outsourcing," *The Washington Post*, Jan. 31, 2004, p. E1.

A provision in the spending bill signed Jan. 23 prohibits the federal government from awarding certain contracts to companies that would perform the work overseas.

Schumer, Charles, and Paul Craig Roberts, "Second Thoughts on Free Trade," *The New York Times*, Jan. 6, 2004, p. A23.

The economic theory of comparative advantage, crucial to arguments supporting free trade, is questioned in the context of the outsourcing trend.

Exporting Jobs

Dickerson, Marla, " 'Offshoring' Trend Casting a Wider Net," *Los Angeles Times*, Jan. 4, 2004, p. C1.

American workers facing a jobless recovery are finding out that almost any job not requiring face-to-face contact can be digitized and shipped overseas.

Greenhouse, Steven, "The $100,000 Longshoreman," *The New York Times*, Oct. 6, 2002, p. D1.

Many blue-collar workers have suffered from globalization's effects, but longshoremen can earn rich salaries and benefits due to their bottleneck position.

Iritani, Evelyn, and Marla Dickerson, "Tech Jobs Become State's Unwanted Big Export," *Los Angeles Times*, Dec. 12, 2002, p. A1.

California, the home of Silicon Valley, may not see the return of tech jobs lost after the technology crash as companies like Hewlett-Packard look at saving costs in India and China.

Kinetz, Erika, "Who Wins and Who Loses as Jobs Move Overseas?" *The New York Times*, Dec. 7, 2003, p. C5.

White-collar workers long thought they were invulnerable to overseas outsourcing; that is changing and the jobs flowing overseas are becoming a political issue as experts debate these trends' meaning.

Lochhead, Carolyn, "Tech Bosses Defend Overseas Hiring," *San Francisco Chronicle*, Jan. 8, 2004, p. A1.

Technology-industry executives respond to criticism by saying that the government must increase research and educational spending for America to stay competitive.

Pollack, Andrew, "Who's Reading Your X-Ray?" *The New York Times*, Nov. 16, 2003, Section 3, p. 1.

After outsourcing some radiology work to India, the hate mail directed at Massachusetts General Hospital revealed the vulnerability to outsourcing felt even by doctors.

Teicher, Stacy, "White-collar Jobs Moving Abroad," *The Christian Science Monitor*, July 29, 2003, p. 1.

No longer are just manufacturing jobs moving abroad — software engineering, accounting and product development also are being outsourced to other countries.

Thottam, Jyoti, "Where the Good Jobs Are Going," *Time*, Aug. 4, 2003, p. 36.

American businesses are enthusiastic about offshore outsourcing in their efforts to lower costs and stay competitive, but American workers are under increasing pressure.

India and China

Einhorn, Bruce, and Manjeet Kripalani, "Move Over, India," *Business Week*, Aug. 11, 2003, p. 42.
With even lower wages than India, companies are flocking to outsource their back-office functions to Chinese cities like Shenzhen, Dalian and Wuxi.

Hale, David, and Lyric Hughes Hale, "China Takes Off," *Foreign Affairs*, November/December 2003, p. 36.
In a few decades, China has increasingly turned into an exporter of sophisticated technological goods with a rapidly modernizing economy and well-educated population.

Kripalani, Manjeet, and Pete Engardio, "The Rise of India," *Business Week*, Dec. 8, 2003, p. 66.
IT jobs aren't the only ones moving to India; tax preparation, scientific and financial jobs are leaving for India's pool of low-cost, highly skilled workers.

Waldman, Amy, "Sizzling Economy Revitalizes India," *The New York Times*, Oct. 20, 2003, p. A1.
India's economic boom, typified by Bangalore's success in luring IT work, is beginning to change the lifestyles and living standards of this giant nation.

Problems With Outsourcing

Ante, Spencer, "Shifting Work Offshore? Outsourcer Beware," *Business Week*, Jan. 12, 2004, p. 36.
Companies rushing to outsource to India may lose more money than they save due to poor quality, bad customer service and security problems.

Hagenbaugh, Barbara, "Moving Work Abroad Tough For Some Firms," *USA Today*, Dec. 3, 2003, p. 1B.
Facing risks and unexpected complications abroad, some firms are returning previously outsourced work to the United States.

Schwartz, John, "Experts See Vulnerability as Outsiders Code Software," *The New York Times*, Jan. 6, 2003, p. C1.
The risk of sabotage, theft or espionage may increase as companies send their software-development work overseas, where supervision is more difficult.

Shinal, John, "No Smooth Sailing For Offshoring," *San Francisco Chronicle*, Nov. 16, 2003, p. I1.
Companies rushing to send work offshore are finding that non-salary costs and rising pay for Indian workers mean that without careful planning the move may not be justified.

Vittachi, Imran, "Boeing Outsourcing Gives Wing to Concerns," *Chicago Tribune*, Dec. 21, 2003, p. C1.
Some fear that Boeing's decision to use Japanese manufacturers for the wings of a new jet will give away crucial technological information to a possible competitor.

Visas

Grow, Brian, "Skilled Workers — Or Indentured Servants?" *Business Week*, June 16, 2003, p. 54.
Fearing deportation, many foreign workers in the United States are abused by their employers but are afraid to speak out.

Hafner, Katie, and Daniel Preysman, "Special Visa's Use For Tech Workers Is Challenged," *The New York Times*, May 30, 2003, p. C1.
Many American technology workers say their jobs are going not only to foreign workers abroad but also to workers who enter the United States under visa category L-1.

McCarthy, Ellen, "Paring a Foreign Guest List," *The Washington Post*, Sept. 18, 2003, p. E1.
The issue of H-1B visas peaked in 2001, but with companies hiring less, Congress is letting the number of visas issued decline to help American workers.

Citing *The CQ Researcher*

Sample formats for citing these reports in a bibliography include the ones listed below. Preferred styles and formats vary, so please check with your instructor or professor.

MLA Style

Jost, Kenneth. "Rethinking the Death Penalty." The CQ Researcher 16 Nov. 2001: 945-68.

APA Style

Jost, K. (2001, November 16). Rethinking the death penalty. *The CQ Researcher, 11*, 945-968.

Chicago Style

Jost, Kenneth. "Rethinking the Death Penalty." *CQ Researcher*, November 16, 2001, 945-968.

Back Issues

The CQ Researcher *offers in-depth coverage of many key areas.*
Back issues are $10. Quantity discounts available.
Call (866) 427-7737 to order back issues.

Or call for a free CQ Researcher Web trial!
Online access provides:

- *Searchable archives dating back to 1991.*
- *Wider access through IP authentication.*
- *PDF files for downloading and printing.*
- *Availability 48 hours before print version.*

CIVIL LIBERTIES
Race in America, July 2003
Gay Marriage, September 2003
Civil Liberties Debates, October 2003

CRIME/LAW
Cyber-Crime, April 2002
Corporate Crime, October 2002
Serial Killers, October 2003

ECONOMY
Stimulating the Economy, January 2003
State Budget Crises, October 2003
Stock Market Troubles, January 2004

EDUCATION
Home Schooling Debate, January 2003
Combating Plagiarism, September 2003
Black Colleges, December 2003

ENERGY/TRANSPORTATION
Future of the Airline Industry, June 2002
Future of Amtrak, October 2002
SUV Debate, May 2003

ENVIRONMENT
Crisis in the Plains, May 2003
Water Shortages, August 2003
Air Pollution Conflict, November 2003

HEALTH AND SAFETY
Medicare Reform, August 2003
Women's Health, November 2003
Homeopathy Debate, December 2003

POLITICS AND PUBLIC POLICY
Abortion Debates, March 2003
State Budget Crises, October 2003
Democracy in the Arab World, January 2004

SOCIAL TRENDS
Latinos' Future, October 2003
Future of the Music Industry, Nov. 2003

TECHNOLOGY
NASA's Future, May 2003

TERRORISM/DEFENSE
Homeland Security, September 2003
North Korean Crisis, April 2003

WORLD AFFAIRS
Trouble in South America, March 2003
Rebuilding Iraq, July 2003
Aiding Africa, August 2003

YOUTH
Preventing Teen Drug Use, March 2002
Sexual Abuse and the Clergy, May 2002
Movie Ratings, March 2003
Hazing, January 2004
Youth Suicide, February 2004

Future Topics

- ***Future of the U.N.***
- ***Search for Extraterrestrials***
- ***Redistricting Debate***

CQ Researcher

Published by CQ Press, a division of Congressional Quarterly Inc.

thecqresearcher.com

The United Nations and Global Security

Can it deal with today's threats?

The United Nations was founded after World War II to promote global security. But following the bitter divisions created in the Security Council last year by the U.S.-led Iraq war, some observers question whether the U.N. can foster global peace and stability. Critics contend that Article 51 of the U.N. charter, which grants nations the right to self-defense, doesn't allow them to act against rogue states and terrorists. Others say the Security Council lacks credibility because many of today's big powers — like Japan and India — are not permanent members. But U.N. supporters say the charter does allow nations to counter threats, even pre-emptively, and that the Security Council can effectively promote peace and security.

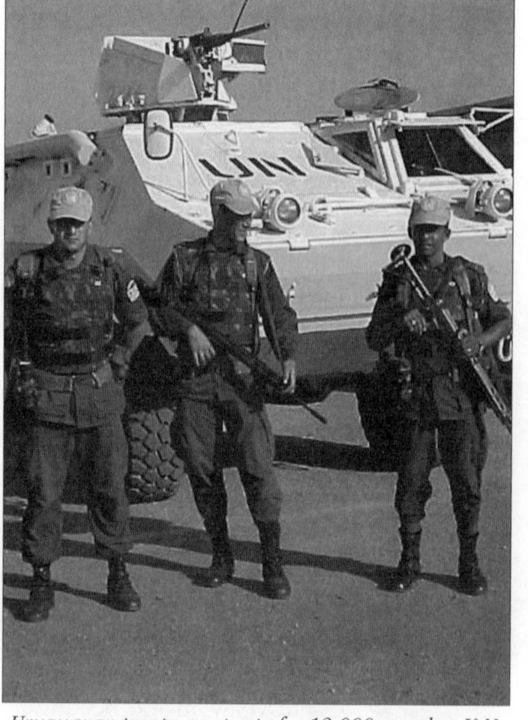

Uruguayan troops are part of a 12,000-member U.N. peacekeeping mission helping to maintain stability in Congo after a brutal civil war.

INSIDE

THIS ISSUE

The CQ Researcher • Feb. 27, 2004 • www.thecqresearcher.com
Volume 14, Number 8 • Pages 173-196

RECIPIENT OF SOCIETY OF PROFESSIONAL JOURNALISTS AWARD FOR EXCELLENCE ◆ AMERICAN BAR ASSOCIATION SILVER GAVEL AWARD

THE UNITED NATIONS AND GLOBAL SECURITY

Cover: U.N. peacekeepers from Uruguay are helping maintain a fragile cease-fire in Congo following a civil war that killed 3 million people. Thirteen U.N. peacekeeping missions currently are deployed around the world. (AFP Photo/Peter Busomokie)

Feb. 27, 2004
Volume 14, No. 8

MANAGING EDITOR: Thomas J. Colin

ASSISTANT MANAGING EDITOR: Kathy Koch

ASSOCIATE EDITOR: Kenneth Jost

STAFF WRITERS: Mary H. Cooper, David Masci, William Triplett

CONTRIBUTING WRITERS: Sarah Glazer, David Hatch, David Hosansky, Patrick Marshall, Tom Price, Jane Tanner

DESIGN/PRODUCTION EDITOR: Olu B. Davis

ASSISTANT EDITOR: Kenneth Lukas

CQ PRESS

A Division of Congressional Quarterly Inc.

SENIOR VICE PRESIDENT/GENERAL MANAGER: John A. Jenkins

DIRECTOR, LIBRARY PUBLISHING: Kathryn C. Suárez

DIRECTOR, EDITORIAL OPERATIONS: Ann Davies

CIRCULATION MANAGER: Nina Tristani

CONGRESSIONAL QUARTERLY INC.

CHAIRMAN: Andrew Barnes

VICE CHAIRMAN: Andrew P. Corty

PRESIDENT AND PUBLISHER: Robert W. Merry

The CQ Researcher (ISSN 1056-2036) is printed on acid-free paper. Published weekly, except Jan. 2, April 9, July 2, July 9, Aug. 6, Aug. 13, Nov. 26 and Dec. 31, by CQ Press, a division of Congressional Quarterly Inc. Annual subscription rates for libraries, businesses and government start at $625. Single issues are available for $10. Quantity discounts apply to orders over 10. Additional rates furnished upon request. Periodicals postage paid at Washington, D.C., and additional mailing offices. POSTMASTER: Send address changes to *The CQ Researcher*, 1255 22nd St., N.W., Suite 400, Washington, D.C. 20037.

The United Nations and Global Security

BY DAVID MASCI

THE ISSUES

On Aug. 19, 2003, a gleaming, new cement truck packed with explosives crashed through a chain-link fence and into a corner of the Canal Hotel, the U.N.'s headquarters in Baghdad, Iraq. The resulting explosion was massive, virtually destroying the three-story building.

The bombing killed 22 people and wounded more than 100, prompting the U.N. to withdraw all its non-Iraqi staff. Among the dead was the apparent target of the attack, Brazilian diplomat Sergio Viera de Mello, the U.N.'s special representative in Iraq and a key player in efforts to rebuild the war-torn nation.

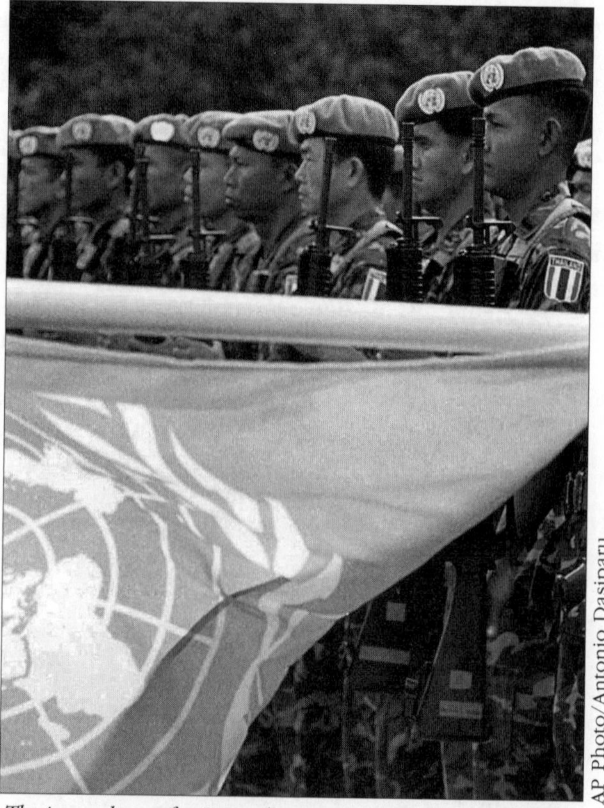

AP Photo/Antonio Dasiparu

Thai members of a United Nations peacekeeping force in East Timor participate in a ceremony marking the handover of authority to the new country's military in July 2002. U.N. intervention in the former Indonesian province ended with the creation of a stable, new state, a rare success for the organization.

But the destruction of U.N. headquarters was more than just the worst attack on the U.N. in its history. To many observers, the strike at the very heart of U.N. efforts in Iraq symbolized the political battering the 59-year-old organization has been taking lately.

"They've been getting it from all sides," says Stephen Zunes, an associate professor of politics at the University of San Francisco. "The right in the United States thinks the U.N. is irrelevant and that the U.S. doesn't need it, while a lot of people on the left don't want it legitimizing what the U.S. has done in Iraq."

The Iraq war severely strained relations between the U.N. and its most important member, the United States. After months of bitter debate between America and other permanent Security Council members — notably France and Russia — the United States and Britain invaded Iraq without U.N. authorization. Moreover, after toppling Saddam Hussein's regime, President Bush made it clear he envisioned only a limited U.N. role in rebuilding Iraq. [1]

The war and its aftermath have prompted many, Bush included, to question whether the United Nations — founded at the end of World War II to promote global security through dialogue and consensus — can still play a significant geopolitical role in the world following the Sept. 11, 2001, terrorist attacks.

"When it comes to the U.N. and issues of security, the world is moving on," says Daniel Goure, vice president of the Lexington Institute, a defense and foreign policy think tank. "The major centers of power either act unilaterally or within the context of regional alliances like NATO — not the U.N."

Even U.N. Secretary-General Kofi Annan has questioned whether his organization can remain relevant in the new world of terrorists and rogue states with weapons of mass destruction — a world in which U.N. members like the U.S. and Britain feel justified in launching pre-emptive attacks without the organization's blessing.

"We have come to a fork in the road," Annan told the U.N. General Assembly on Sept. 23. "We must decide whether . . . to continue on the basis agreed upon or whether radical changes are needed."

Many U.N. critics say radical changes are indeed needed, starting with the organization's all-important Security Council, which has the power to authorize sanctions or even military action. Critics say the council's permanent members — the United States, Russia, Britain, France and China — reflect bygone geopolitical realities. Only if important countries like India and Japan became permanent members would the council truly reflect today's world, they say.

Other critics trace many of the U.N.'s problems to its charter, specifically Article 51 — which allows nations to defend themselves if attacked. They say it is an anachronism in an era when terrorists armed with weapons of mass destruction (WMDs) could leave millions dead in an instant.

"We need to redraft the charter" to give nations more freedom to respond to these new threats, says Nile Gardiner,

Most U.N. Peacekeepers Serve in Africa

The oldest U.N. peacekeeping operation — in the Middle East — was deployed in 1948, soon after the creation of Israel. Today, 70 percent of the U.N.'s 55,000 peacekeepers are deployed in Africa.

Current U.N. Peacekeeping Operations

Location	Date Begun	Total U.N. personnel deployed (military and civilian)
Middle East	1948	367
India/Pakistan	1949	115
Cyprus	1964	1,402
Golan Heights	1974	1,162
Lebanon	1978	2,406
Western Sahara	1991	497
Georgia	1993	408
Kosovo	1999	7,570
Sierra Leone	1999	12,527
Democratic Republic of the Congo	1999	12,068
Ethiopia/Eritrea	2000	4,498
East Timor	2002	3,369
Liberia	2003	8,994

Source: U.N. Department of Peacekeeping Operations

a senior fellow at the Heritage Foundation, a conservative think tank.

But others counter that countries would merely use an expanded charter to justify military action against one another. "What would keep us from just whacking each other whenever we felt like it?" responds William J. Durch, a senior associate at the Henry L. Stimson Center, a national-security think tank.

U.N. peacekeeping efforts also have come under fire. In particular, critics have questioned the organization's ability to enforce its own treaty outlawing genocide. Genocide has killed more than 20 million people worldwide since the U.N.'s founding in 1945, according to Gregory Stanton, president of Genocide Watch and coordinator of the International Campaign to End Genocide.

"The United Nations has been ineffective in preventing genocide," because its members "wave the flag of national sovereignty whenever anyone challenges their 'domestic jurisdiction,' " he writes. [2] Such criticisms were raised in the 1990s, when U.N. troops failed to stop the slaughter of hundreds of thousands of civilians in Bosnia, Rwanda and Kosovo.

More recently, the organization's ability to stop the proliferation of WMDs, especially nuclear weapons, also has come under scrutiny.

But it was the U.N.'s unwillingness to sanction an invasion of Iraq, many critics say, that most seriously undercut its credibility, especially after the overthrow of Hussein revealed that the regime had tortured and murdered hundreds of thousands of civilians. The U.N. can only regain credibility — both as a political player and protector of human rights — if it returns to Iraq in a significant political and humanitarian capacity, critics say.

Tentative steps in this direction have been taken by both the United States and the U.N. On Jan. 19, the U.S. administrator in Iraq, L. Paul Bremer III, traveled to U.N. headquarters in New York to personally ask Annan to send a team to Iraq to assess the prospects for direct elections before the United States turns over power to local authorities on June 30. On Feb. 7, a U.N. team went to Baghdad and spent almost a week trying to resolve disagreements among Iraqi political leaders over upcoming elections.

But some observers think the world body should play more than an advisory role and that the United States should turn over significant amounts of authority to U.N. officials now. "The U.N. should be put in control of the whole political process immediately, replacing Bremer and the Americans," says Robert Boorstin, senior vice president for national security and international policy at the Center for American Progress, a liberal think tank. "They have the most experience at policing, reconstruction and institution-building."

Others say the U.N. has a mixed record on nation-building and would likely fail in Iraq — a large country plagued by ethnic tensions and a low-level insurgency. "It would be a disaster," Goure says. "The U.N. bureaucracy has a slow and consensual style of decision making, which would make everything much harder to accomplish in a country that needs things to move forward quickly and decisively."

Meanwhile, the decades-old battle over differing perceptions of what the U.N. can and cannot accomplish continues — a Catch-22 situation prophetically recognized by the first secretary-general, Trygve Lie.

"Some have too great expectations and others too little faith in what the United Nations can do," he once said. [3]

Not surprisingly, some foreign policy experts today say the United Nations will become increasingly irrelevant while others predict it will play a much greater role in promoting peace and security.

As U.N.-watchers ponder the organization's future role in the world, here are some of the questions they are asking:

Should the Security Council be expanded to include new members?

The Security Council is the most important arm of the United Nations grappling with vital issues of war and peace. It dispatches peacekeepers to war-torn countries and authorizes economic and other sanctions and even military action against aggressors. And unlike General Assembly resolutions, those passed by the Security Council are binding.

When the U.N. was established shortly before the end of World War II, the principal victors in the conflict — the United States, Britain, France, the Soviet Union and China — became the council's five permanent members, each with veto power over all decisions. Six non-permanent members were to be elected by the General Assembly to two-year terms.

Nearly 60 years later, that system remains largely in place — changed only once, in 1965, when the number of non-permanent members was increased from six to 10. The same five permanent members — called the P5 — still preside over the body.

For decades, Security Council critics have said the arrangement is out of date. "The current council in no way reflects the reality of today's world," says Boorstin of the Center for American Progress. "We don't need representation exactly according to [current] population and geography, but we need some new, realistic approximation of the two."

Rich Countries Pay, Poor Ones Send Troops

Developed countries — led by the United States — largely pay for U.N. peacekeeping (top graph), but the troops themselves primarily come from the Third World (bottom). The current peacekeeping budget is $2.17 billion.

Largest Contributors to U.N. Peacekeeping Operations
(in 2002, in $ millions)

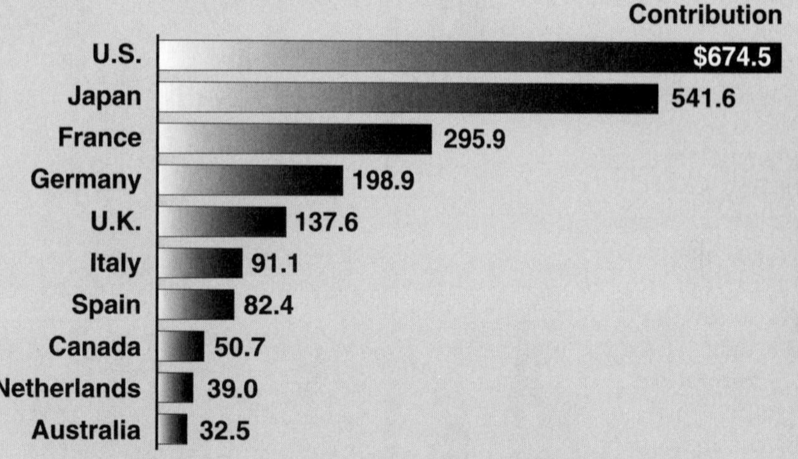

Major Personnel Contributions to U.N. Peacekeeping Forces *
(as of Dec. 31, 2003)

Country	% of U.N. Total	Country	% of U.N. Total
Pakistan	13.6%	Jordan	4.0%
Bangladesh	10.3	South Africa	3.1
Nigeria	7.3	Ethiopia	2.3
India	6.3	U.K.	1.2
Ghana	5.0	U.S.	1.1
Nepal	5.0	Germany	0.8

** Includes troops, civilian police and military observers.*

Sources: U.S. Bureau of the Census, U.N. Department of Peacekeeping Operations

A new Security Council should at least include some economic or regional powers as new permanent members, Boorstin says. India, the world's largest democracy, could easily represent South Asia, and Japan and Germany — the world's second- and third-largest economies — also should be included. In addition, mammoth Brazil could be Latin America's representative while important Muslim and African countries could represent those peoples, he suggests.

Adding new permanent members also would renew the U.N.'s standing in the world, supporters of expansion argue. "For the council to be credible in the world today, it has to include the real powers of the world," the Lexington Institute's Goure says.

Bringing on new members would also facilitate more cooperation in solving international crises, say others.

"Things are so difficult today partly because those who feel excluded are less cooperative than they otherwise might be," says Johanna Mendelson-Forman, senior program officer for peace, security and human rights at the U.N. Foundation. "These countries could use their energies more productively. They wouldn't be spoilers like they often are now."

But Tom Weiss, a professor of political science at Columbia University, thinks new permanent members would "cripple the council with infighting," because existing permanent members won't want to give up power.

AFP Photo/Don Emmert

The United Nations' distinctive headquarters was built in New York City in 1953. The U.N. was founded in 1945 in the wake of both World War II and the failed League of Nations.

Indeed, deciding who would get the new permanent slots would "[tick] off a lot of countries that didn't make it," agrees the Stimson Center's Durch. "You're going to end up with a lot of resentment, and nobody's going to win."

Others say it is in America's interest to maintain the status quo. "Bringing in the countries they always point to — like India, Brazil and Indonesia — means there will simply be more members who are likely to oppose the United States and Britain," says the Heritage Foundation's Gardiner.

Finally, even if agreement could be reached on new members, the larger council would be too big to be effective, expansion opponents say. "This would make it much harder to get anything done," Weiss says. "Adding new members translates into adding new agendas and interests, and this would become even more unwieldy than it is now."

Should the U.N. change its charter to broaden a nation's right to self-defense?

During Security Council debates before the Iraq war, the United States and its allies sought authorization to depose Hussein for his violations of more than a dozen U.N. resolutions passed since the end of the first Persian Gulf War in 1991. Chief among them was Resolution 1441 — which called on Iraq to dismantle its alleged weapons of mass destruction.

But, in making its case for war to the American people and the world community, the Bush administration also argued that Iraq posed a threat to the region and, ultimately, to the United States. Indeed, since the Sept. 11 terrorist attacks, the administration has repeatedly argued that it has the right to take pre-emptive action, alone if necessary, against any potential threat to the country's safety.

"America will never seek a permission slip to defend the security of our country," President Bush said in his State of the Union address on Jan. 20, 2004.

However, the U.N. charter requires member states to "refrain from the threat or use of force" and to settle international disputes by peaceful means. [4] Military force is allowed — under Article 51 — only when a nation is threatened or attacked and is acting in self-defense.

Secretary-General Annan argues that by ignoring the letter and spirit of Article 51, the United States and its allies have made the world more dangerous, because now other nations will justify pre-emptive strikes against other countries by claiming they posed potential threats.

"If nations discount the legitimacy provided by the U.N. and feel they can and must use force unilaterally and pre-emptively, the world will become even more dangerous," Annan told the General Assembly on Sept. 23, 2003. [5]

But critics of Article 51 say the U.N. does not offer countries the right to deal with threats *before* they become imminent — an approach the critics say is more appropriate in the dangerous environment that has emerged since the attacks on the World Trade Center and the Pentagon. "If we wait for threats to materialize," Bush said, "we will have waited too long." [6]

The Heritage Foundation's Gardiner agrees. "We are now living in an age of international terrorism and rogue states, but that's not reflected in Article 51," he says. The article should be updated to allow nations "to attack countries that harbor terrorists," Gardiner says. "This has to be explicit."

"This debate is not about terrorists or even weapons of mass destruction," adds the Lexington Institute's Goure. "It's about failed states that allow terrorists to thrive. Terrorists cannot be effective without access to state assets — like banks, training bases and laboratories to develop weapons."

According to Goure, countries should be allowed to take "anticipatory self-defense" actions against entities that might threaten them. "This needs to be written simply and directly" into the U.N. charter, he says.

But Columbia University's Weiss counters that Article 51 already has evolved to encompass new global realities. "The U.N. charter — like the U.S. Constitution — is a living document that changes with the times," Weiss says. "No one, not even international lawyers, dispute the fact that Article 51 now gives you a right to pre-emptively defend yourself if you're threatened. But that has always meant that a verifiable threat is pointed in your direction."

Christopher Preble, director of foreign policy studies at the libertarian Cato Institute, notes, "The United Nations wouldn't have opposed our intervention in Iraq if the majority of member states believed that Iraq was a threat to the U.S. That was the problem: They didn't believe that we were genuinely threatened."

Indeed, the Stimson Center's Durch points out, the Security Council had no qualms about authorizing American action against Afghanistan. "It came under the purview of Article 51 and was fine, because, in this case, the United States had legitimately been threatened." [7]

Should the U.N. have a greater role in running Iraq?

Even before the fall of Baghdad, debate had begun over the U.N.'s role in postwar Iraq. President Bush said he favored a "vital" role for the international body, but the administration ultimately decided its primary responsibility should be to deliver humanitarian assistance. Britain — America's primary ally in the war — wanted the U.N. to help build political and other institutions while the French, Russians and others — who had opposed the war — argued for direct U.N. administration of the country.

Last May, it was agreed that a U.N. special representative would be sent to Baghdad to assist in reconstruction efforts. Although his job description was not entirely spelled out, de Mello quickly found ways to meaningfully aid reconstruction efforts. [8] Most notably, he helped create the Iraqi governing council, convincing American administrator Bremer to grant the 25-person body greater authority.

Then came the Aug. 19 attack on U.N. headquarters, leading Annan to withdraw all non-Iraqi staff. After the U.N. elections team visited Baghdad in February, there was talk of U.N. staff returning to Iraq, but nothing has been decided.

Some U.N. supporters say the only way for Iraq to evolve into a stable, democratic state is for the United States to hand over day-to-day authority to the United Nations. "It seems more and more necessary all the time," says the University of San Francisco's Zunes. "Things are getting worse, with even the Shiite community — which has been quiescent until now — getting more restless. It's time to bring in someone else to do the job."

The Center for American Progress' Boorstin agrees. "The U.N. should be given control of the whole political process," he says. "If we had done this earlier, many fewer Americans would be dead, and the American taxpayer wouldn't be footing the bill for reconstruction."

Indeed, Boorstin says, the United Nations is better suited to nation-building than the U.S.-led coalition running the country, partly because Iraqis perceive it as more even-handed and trustworthy. "No institution is completely trusted by Iraqis, but the United Nations is trusted more than any other," he says.

"The U.N. still has a lot of legitimacy in Iraq," agrees Durch. "After all, they kept about half the country's population alive for more than a decade with their oil-for-food program." Established after the 1991 Persian Gulf War, the program embargoed oil exports except to finance food and medicine imports.

Moreover, he adds, if the United Nations had a greater role in rebuilding Iraq, it would unleash a flood of

U.S. and Japan Contribute the Most

Five countries contribute 63 percent of the U.N.'s $1.6 billion annual budget, with the United States and Japan paying almost 43 percent of the total.

Largest Contributors to the U.N. Budget*
(in 2003)

Contributor	Percent of Budget	Contribution (in $millions)
U.S.	22.0 %	$341
Japan	19.5	303
Germany	9.8	152
France	6.5	100
UK	5.5	86
Others	37.4	587

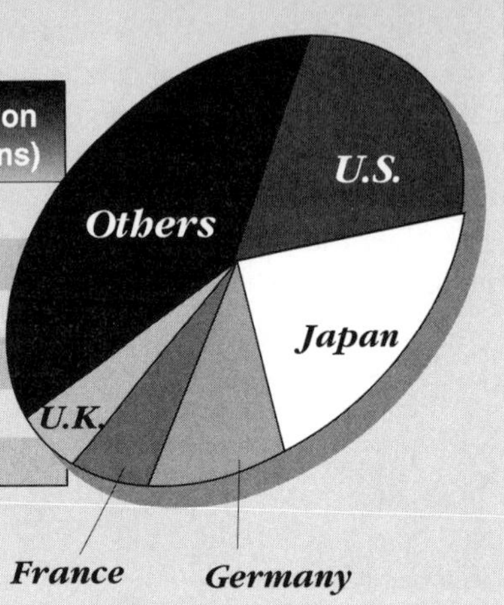

Note: Percentages do not add up to 100 due to rounding.

** Peacekeeping funds not included. The United States and Japan are also the largest contributors to the peacekeeping budget, which currently is $2.17 billion.*

Sources: United Nations; U.S. Census Bureau; Global Policy Forum

additional outside help now being withheld because the U.N. isn't involved.

"The U.N. isn't just the U.N., it's the whole U.N. system," Durch says. "So when they come in, they bring in the NGOs [non-governmental organizations], and they do a lot of the work on the ground. They also bring the World Bank with them, and that means there will be a lot of money to spend."

But getting the United Nations more involved would significantly slow down the hand-over of power to the Iraqis, opponents of the idea say. "The United Nations, by its nature, is a very slow and cumbersome organization because it is a government of governments," says Cato's Preble. "Decisions will be made by committee, and you're going find yourself with too many cooks spoiling the broth, so it will inevitably be less effective than the U.S."

Others contend that — based on its experience with nation-building elsewhere — the United Nations simply can't deal with the kinds of potentially explosive issues that could erupt. "You have a lot of immediate, right and wrong issues that pop up, but the U.N. doesn't have the political inclination to handle them because they are trying to treat all sides equally," Goure says. "In Bosnia, you had the U.N. trying to balance three ethnic groups — Serb, Croat and Muslim — to the point of not moving effectively to stop the Serbs [from committing genocide]." As a result, he adds "you had things like the massacre at Srebrenica," where an estimated 10,000 Muslim men and boys were executed.

The same scenario could unfold in Iraq, Goure says, where three major ethnic and religious groups — the Kurds, Sunni Arabs and Shiite Arabs — are jockeying for power. "If the U.N. replaced Bremer, they would have much less strength and inclination to keep these groups apart, and the chances for ethnic conflict would be much greater."

Finally, some observers disagree that Iraqis would view the United Nations as evenhanded or trustworthy. "The U.N. really isn't liked or seen as part of the solution by most people in Iraq," largely because of its role in imposing and administering the post-Gulf War sanctions, says Edward Luck, director of the Center on International Organizations at Columbia University.

Indeed, the U.N.'s comprehensive economic sanctions (which were partially softened by the oil-for-food program) took a heavy toll on the country's civilian population.

"For the Iraqis, foreigners are foreigners, whether they are wearing the blue helmets of U.N. peacekeepers or the patch of the 82nd Airborne," Preble adds. "They'll be seen as occupiers, just like the U.S. is today." ■

BACKGROUND

Outgrowth of War

The United Nations arose from the ashes of the failed League of Nations and the devastation of World War II.

Continued on p. 182

Kofi Annan's U.N. Balancing Act

When Kofi Annan became the U.N.'s seventh secretary-general in early 1997, he quickly found himself in the midst of a crisis.

The organization was on the brink of bankruptcy, in part because the United States and other key members were refusing to pay their back dues. The United States alone had withheld $1.6 billion in funds, largely in an effort to pressure the institution — which many Americans saw as wasteful and corrupt — to reform itself.

Annan responded by immediately traveling to Washington to lobby Congress, promising to trim staff and spending. Annan's reform plan, combined with his personal charm, won the support of even the U.N.'s toughest critics on Capitol Hill, including Sen. Jesse Helms, R-N.C., and prompted the United States to pay the bulk of its dues.

But those first few months were merely a warm-up for the challenges he was to face in the years ahead, from "ethnic cleansing" in Kosovo to the bitter debate over the invasion of Iraq.

"You're always dealing with crisis, and some country or countries are always upset with you, and then you always have to placate the U.S. and other big powers," says Stephen C. Schlesinger, director of the World Policy Institute at New School University in New York City and author of *Acts of Creation: The Founding of the United Nations*. "No doubt: It's a tough job."

"It's a Catch-22 kind of job," says Johanna Mendelson-Forman, a senior program officer at the U.N. Foundation. "You're the most powerful man in the world with limited resources, which can be very frustrating."

Despite the challenges, the 66-year-old Ghanaian generally gets high marks from U.N.-watchers.

"He's the best secretary-general since Dag Hammarskjold" of Sweden, Schlesinger says. "He's been able to restore the U.N.'s moral authority by bringing people together and stressing the original ideals of the U.N."

"He's an extremely patient and calm man, which is needed in that job," Mendelson-Forman says. "Also, he's a creature of the system, which means that he knows all about the U.N.'s internal problems and understands its great potential."

Annan was a popular and respected senior U.N. officer when he was elected to the post in 1996 as a compromise candidate after a bitter battle between the United States and France over whether the controversial Egyptian diplomat Boutros Boutros-Gali, should serve a second term.

During his tenure, Annan has worked hard to heal the rift that developed in the last few decades between the U.N. and its most important member: the United States. Most recently, he went against the advice of his own staff and, in response to a request from President Bush, sent a high-level representative, Algerian diplomat Lakhdar Brahimi, to Iraq to assess the country's political future.

"He understands that he basically doesn't have any choice but to try to keep the United States happy, since the U.N. is so dependent on the U.S. for money and other things," says Frederick D. Barton, a senior adviser at the Center for International and Strategic Studies' International Security Program.

AFP Photo/Gerard Cerles

U.N. Secretary-General Kofi Annan.

On occasion, however, Annan has opposed the United States and other big powers. "In 1999, for instance, he said the need for humanitarian intervention in places like Bosnia and Rwanda overrode national sovereignty — something the United States was not comfortable with," Schlesinger says.

More recently, in a speech to the General Assembly last November, Annan chided the United States for unilaterally attacking Iraq. At the same time, he criticized opponents of the war — and the U.N. itself — for not adequately taking America's legitimate security concerns into account. "He's good, very good, at balancing interests," Barton says. "That's one of his great strengths."

After Annan joined the U.N. in 1962 as a budget analyst for the World Health Organization, he quickly moved up the U.N. ladder — taking a break in 1972 to obtain a master's degree in management from the Massachusetts Institute of Technology. He became under-secretary for peacekeeping in 1993.

His three-year tenure as head of peacekeeping coincided with one of the most active periods in U.N. peacekeeping history, with blue helmets deployed in Bosnia, Cambodia, Somalia and Rwanda, among others. At one point in 1995, the under-secretary was overseeing 70,000 military and civilian personnel from 77 countries. [1]

Annan's term ends in 2006, and he says he will not seek a third term. Still, Schlesinger says, "it's not impossible to imagine the big powers asking him to stay on one more term, since he's so well respected. Given the divisions at the U.N. right now, they may just be looking for someone they can all agree upon."

---

[1] Figure cited in the secretary-general's official biography at www.un.org/News/ossg/sg/pages/sg_biography.html.

Continued from p. 180

The league, established in 1919 by the Treaty of Versailles following World War I, was the world's first attempt to prevent war by creating an international forum to air grievances. But the U.S. Senate refused to ratify America's membership, and without U.S. support the league soon became ineffective.

In 1931, Japan left the league after invading Manchuria in northern China. Germany withdrew in 1933, the year Adolf Hitler came to power. And in 1937, Italy left after the organization condemned its unprovoked invasion of Ethiopia.

Germany, Japan and Italy, of course, were the primary "Axis powers" responsible for the Second World War. Although the league continued to function after the war began in 1939, it had little impact.

The notion of replacing the league with something more effective emerged two years before the war ended, in 1943, when the major allies — the United States, the Soviet Union, Britain and China — began discussing proposals for a new international body.

Problems that arose during the talks foreshadowed many of the issues that would arise later: The Soviets were wary of a body that might block its own geopolitical ambitions, and Britain worried such an institution might try to control its many colonies.

But President Franklin D. Roosevelt pushed the negotiations forward. Although he died in April 1945 — less than two weeks before the allies were to meet in San Francisco to hammer out a final agreement — the new president, Harry S Truman, strongly supported the project, and a final accord emerged.

All 51 nations attending the San Francisco negotiations ratified the new U.N. charter on Oct. 24. Its primary goal was "saving succeeding generations from the scourge of war," promoting fundamental human rights, establishing "justice and respect" for international law and treaties and working for "social progress." [9]

The General Assembly — comprised of all U.N. members, each with one vote — was given responsibility for overseeing operations and considering non-binding resolutions on international issues. The Security Council was charged with maintaining international peace, authorizing economic and military sanctions and approving the use of force to restore peace.

The five major World War II victors — the United States, the Soviet Union, Britain, France and China — were designated as veto-wielding permanent members of the council, to ensure that every council decision was supported by the globe's strongest nations. The General Assembly elected the council's six non-permanent members — increased to 10 in 1965 — to two-year terms.

The assembly met for the first time on Jan. 10, 1946, in London. "It is in your hands to make or mar the happiness of millions yet unborn," King George VI told the delegates. "It is for you to lay the foundations of a new world where such a conflict as that which lately brought our world to the verge of annihilation must never be repeated." [10]

Early Tests

The new organization's first test, in 1947, involved the fate of British-ruled Palestine, which was claimed by both Arabs and Jews. A fierce debate ensued over whether to create an Arab-Jewish federation, favored by Arab states, or to partition the country into ethnic enclaves, which the United States favored.

The U.N's decision in 1948 to partition prompted the first of several regional wars between Jews and Arabs. [11] After Israel repelled the attacking Arabs and established a new state, U.N. "military observers" went to the Middle East to monitor the cease-fire between Israel and its neighbors. Their mission continues to this day in the Golan Heights, Egypt and along the border of Israel and Lebanon. [12]

The U.N.'s next big test occurred in Korea, where U.S.-Soviet Cold War rivalry had split the country into the communist north and pro-Western south. Although the superpowers eventually agreed to withdraw from the Korean peninsula, the Soviets left behind a well-armed, North Korean army that invaded the south in 1950. [13]

The United States and its allies condemned the invasion, and the U.N. authorized an international force to defend the south. The resulting Korean War dragged on for three years, with U.N. forces trading huge swaths of territory several times with the north and its Chinese communist allies. The war ended in 1953 with Korea still divided. [14]

Secretary-General Lie declared the Korean War a triumph for collective security, but others said it proved the U.N.'s ineffectiveness. Indeed, many Americans argued an international organization could not deal with communism — the major threat of the day — and that the United States should develop regional alliances to meet the challenge.

In 1956, the United Nations enjoyed its first real triumph as a peacemaker. Egypt had nationalized the Suez Canal, taking control from Britain. The British, along with France and Israel, attacked and retook the canal, but the United States condemned the action.

The legendary Secretary-General Dag Hammarskjold — who coined the term "peacekeeping" — stepped into the stalemate and proposed that U.N. troops supervise a truce. The allies withdrew, and 6,000 lightly armed U.N. soldiers from 10 countries took up positions between Israeli and Egyptian troops along their borders. The force remained until May 1967.

Continued on p. 184

Chronology

1940s
United Nations is founded in the closing days of World War II.

June 26, 1945
Delegates from 51 countries sign the U.N. charter; it is formally approved on Oct. 24.

1948
U.N. observers monitor a shaky cease-fire between newly independent Israel and its Arab neighbors.

1950s-1980s
Cold War rivalry hampers but does not entirely quash U.N. efforts to promote peace and security.

June 25, 1950
U.N. authorizes a U.S.-led international force to help defend South Korea after communist North Korea invades.

November 1956
The first U.N. peacekeepers are sent to the Suez Canal to monitor a cease-fire between Israel and Egypt.

1957
International Atomic Energy Agency is founded with U.N. support to promote the peaceful use of nuclear power.

July 14, 1960
The first large-scale U.N. peacekeeping force is sent to Congo, where independence from Belgium has led to civil unrest.

1965
U.N. peacekeepers begin patrolling the India-Pakistan border following warfare over the disputed Kashmir region.

Nov. 29, 1982
U.N. General Assembly condemns Soviet Union's 1979 invasion of Afghanistan.

Oct. 25, 1983
United States invades Grenada without seeking Security Council authorization.

1990s-Present
Cold War ends, leading to increased U.N. peacekeeping operations.

1990
Iraq's Aug. 2 invasion of Kuwait prompts Security Council on Nov. 29 to authorize intervention by an American-led coalition.

1991
Coalition forces liberate Kuwait. . . . U.N. arms inspectors search Iraq for weapons of mass destruction (WMDs) as part of a postwar peace agreement; none are found.

1993
U.N. sends 28,000 peacekeepers to Somalia to alleviate famine and restore order during a civil war. U.S. and other casualties lead to a U.N. withdrawal in 1995.

1994
Almost 1 million civilians die in ethnic fighting in Rwanda between the Hutus and Tutsis. A small U.N. force in the country takes no action.

1995
U.N. efforts to establish "safe havens" in Bosnia to prevent genocide fail as Serbs overrun Srebrenica and kill thousands of civilians.

1996
Kofi Annan, a U.N. official from Ghana, is elected secretary-general.

1998
Iraqi leader Saddam Hussein expels U.N. weapons inspectors.

1999
NATO intervenes in the Yugoslav province of Kosovo without seeking U.N. Security Council authorization.

Sept. 12, 2002
President Bush addresses the General Assembly on WMDs and Iraq and challenges the U.N. to be "relevant."

March 22, 2003
United States and Great Britain lead an invasion of Iraq without seeking Security Council authorization, toppling Hussein's regime in a month.

Aug. 1, 2003
Security Council passes a resolution authorizing the dispatch of U.N. peacekeepers to Liberia.

Aug. 19, 2003
Suicide bomber destroys U.N. headquarters in Baghdad killing U.N. Representative Sergio Viera de Mello and 21 other people.

Nov. 23, 2003
President Bush returns to the U.N. to ask the international community to assist in rebuilding Iraq.

Feb. 7, 2004
Secretary-General Annan sends a U.N. team to Baghdad to assess the prospects for direct elections.

June 30, 2004
United States is scheduled to turn over sovereignty in Iraq to Iraqi authorities.

Dec. 31, 2006
Secretary-General Annan's second term ends.

Continued from p. 182

In the following decades, U.N. peacekeepers were involved in several other conflicts. In 1962, 20,000 so-called blue helmets were dispatched to newly independent Congo to restore order and supervise the withdrawal of Belgian troops. Three years later, peacekeepers took up positions along the India-Pakistan border, after the two countries fought a war over the Indian province of Kashmir. Later missions included Cyprus, Namibia and Sri Lanka.

But Cold War rivalries severely hampered the U.N.'s peacekeeping success. Although the United States largely dominated the organization, the Soviets repeatedly vetoed Security Council resolutions authorizing interventions, resulting in U.N. missions that were too narrowly defined to be effective.

During the 1960s, '70s and '80s, the United Nations did little to halt civil wars in Vietnam, Angola, Mozambique and El Salvador, which were often seen as surrogate struggles in the Cold War, because the two superpowers supported the opposing sides.

New World Order

In the late 1980s, the geopolitical situation started to change as communist governments in the Soviet Union and its client states began collapsing. By the early 1990s, the Cold War rivalry that long had dominated international relations was gone, and the United States emerged as the world's sole superpower.

President George Bush, the current president's father, declared a "new world order" based on respect for the rule of law and human rights. His rhetoric was soon put to the test when Iraq invaded and occupied Kuwait in August 1990. Bush quickly sought an international coalition at the United Nations that drove the Iraqis out of Kuwait in early 1991.

AFP Photo/Mark Garten

The U.N. Security Council, which can impose economic sanctions and authorize military action, has five permanent members — the United States, Russia, Britain, France and China. Reformers say other great powers, like India and Japan, should be added to the exclusive club to reflect contemporary global realities.

Many saw the Persian Gulf War as the beginning of a new, bold era for the United Nations. As historian William Jay Jacobs notes in his book *Search for Peace:* "Although leadership [in the Gulf War] undoubtedly came from Washington, it was the United Nations that had broadened the wartime alliance, even isolating Iraq from most of the Arab world. In a major way, the United Nations had served as a unifying force, bringing together nations of widely different backgrounds — including former communist governments — for the task of armed peacekeeping." [15]

Around this time, the U.N. began taking on greater peacekeeping and nation-building challenges. From 1988 to 1993, it established 14 new peacekeeping efforts — more than in its first four decades. In 1992 alone, the number of blue helmets in the field quadrupled, along with peacekeeping expenses, which grew from $700 million to $2.8 billion. [16]

The role of peacekeepers also began to change. Past U.N. forces had been deployed to keep opposing armies apart following cease-fires. Now, U.N. forces were entering ongoing conflicts in war-torn countries like Cambodia, Somalia and Bosnia.

But the peacekeepers were unable to establish stability in any of the conflicts. In Somalia, for instance, 28,000 U.N. forces (including Americans) could not stop the violence between rival clans that had brought chaos and famine to the East African nation. While the U.N. efforts did alleviate the devastating famine, attempts in 1993 to end the civil war resulted in some 18 U.S. fatalities and prompted the withdrawal of the entire peacekeeping mission by 1995. [17]

Genocide and the U.N.

A genocidal civil war that began in Bosnia in 1992 also proved intractable for the United Nations. A European-led U.N. force proved unwilling to stand up to Serbian troops, who murdered tens of thousands of ethnic Muslims. A tenuous cease-fire took hold in 1995, only after American-led NATO military forces intervened in the wake of an international outcry.

"In places like Bosnia and Somalia, you had active civil wars going on and the U.N. just wasn't equipped to deal with all of that," says the Stimson Center's Durch. "There was a shortage of troops and money, and an overage of optimism that led to the problems on these missions."

Optimism eventually turned to fatigue, both at the United Nations and in the international community. When another ethic conflict erupted in the central African nation of Rwanda in 1994, the U.N. and its members reacted without energy or commitment.

A small group of U.N. peacekeepers had been sent to Rwanda at the end of 1993 to quell rising ethnic tensions, but they could not prevent the wholesale slaughter the following year. Indeed, U.N. troops stood aside as an estimated 800,000 mostly Tutsi Rwandans were massacred by the Hutu majority.

Four years later, on his first visit to Rwanda since the genocide, Secretary-General Annan — after touring gravesites and buildings filled with victims' skulls — apologized for his organization's inaction. "Now we know that what we did was not nearly enough," he said, "not enough to save Rwanda from itself, not enough to honor the ideals for which the United Nations exists." [18]

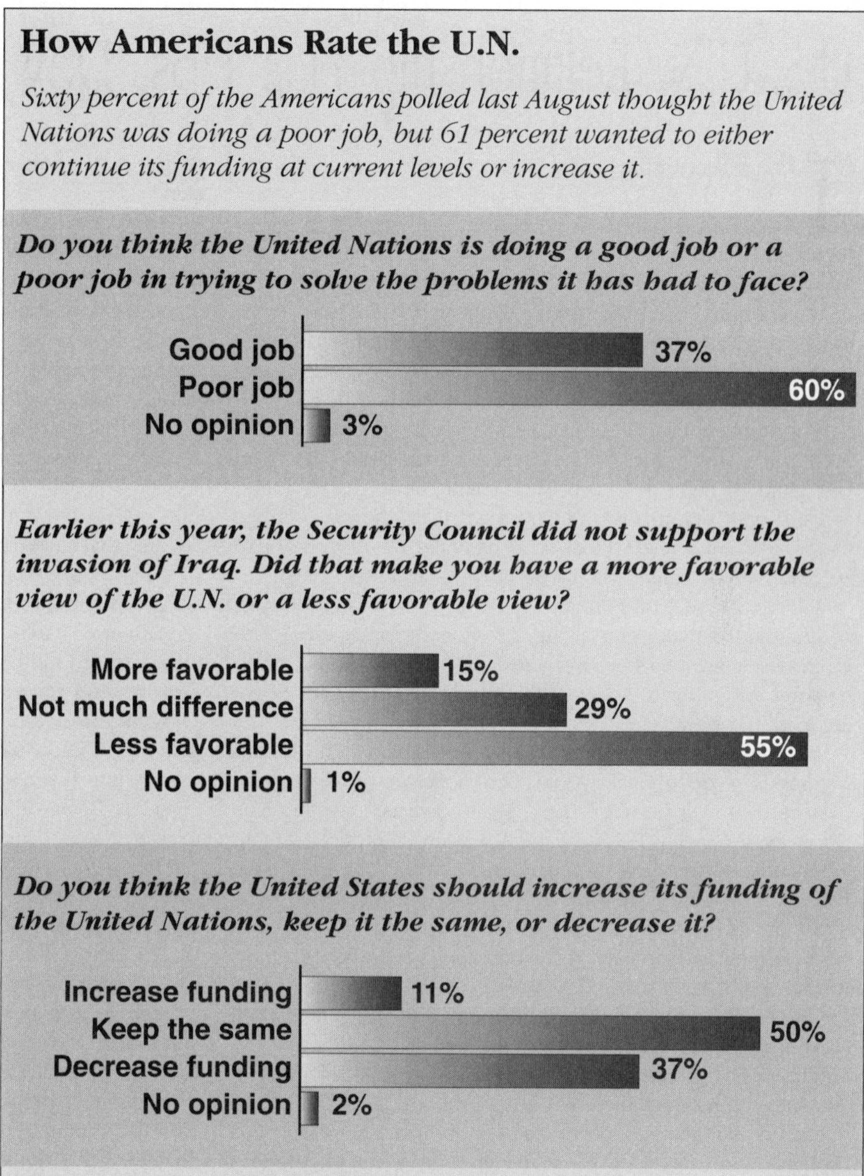

How Americans Rate the U.N.
Sixty percent of the Americans polled last August thought the United Nations was doing a poor job, but 61 percent wanted to either continue its funding at current levels or increase it.
Do you think the United Nations is doing a good job or a poor job in trying to solve the problems it has had to face?
Good job 37%
Poor job 60%
No opinion 3%
Earlier this year, the Security Council did not support the invasion of Iraq. Did that make you have a more favorable view of the U.N. or a less favorable view?
More favorable 15%
Not much difference 29%
Less favorable 55%
No opinion 1%
Do you think the United States should increase its funding of the United Nations, keep it the same, or decrease it?
Increase funding 11%
Keep the same 50%
Decrease funding 37%
No opinion 2%

Source: CNN/USA Today/Gallup poll, conducted Aug. 25-26, 2003.

President Bill Clinton later echoed Annan's apology: "We did not act quickly enough after the killing began. We did not immediately call these crimes by their right name: genocide." [19]

The Security Council later established international tribunals to prosecute war crimes, genocide and crimes against humanity in Bosnia and Rwanda. But the U.N.'s earlier inaction raised serious questions as to whether it is able or willing to act before mass murders happen. The U.N. Convention on the Prevention and Punishment of the Crime of Genocide — established after Nazi Germany's atrocities during World War II — requires its 129 signatory countries to intervene to halt genocide if they determine that it is occurring.

Criticism about the U.N.'s slowness in responding to atrocities erupted again in 1999, when evidence emerged of "ethnic cleansing" by the Serbians against Albanians in Kosovo. "It is right to stop the ethnic cleansing, war crimes, crimes against humanity and other indicators of genocide that we see," Secretary of State Madeleine K. Albright said in April 1999. [20]

Although the Security Council passed several resolutions demanding the hostilities in Kosovo cease, it did not step in to stop the slaughter, which continued. Once again, NATO bypassed the Security Council and launched an American-led bombing

U.S.-U.N. Relationship Has Ups, Downs

The recent dispute over America's decision to go to war with Iraq was not the first time the United States and the United Nations have been at loggerheads. In recent decades, the two have sparred on issues ranging from the Kyoto treaty on global warming to U.N. family-planning programs.

Some observers find the tension surprising, even ironic, since the United Nations is largely an American creation, established despite Soviet and British ambivalence about creating a successor to the failed League of Nations.

But Stephen C. Schlesinger, author of *Act of Creation: The Founding of the United Nations*, sees no contradiction between U.S. attitudes then and now. The United Nations "was bound to clash with our need to get our own way," he says. "We're the biggest guy on the block, and naturally we don't want to be restricted or limited by anyone else — including the U.N."

Johanna Mendelson-Forman, senior program officer for peace, security and human rights at the U.N. Foundation, agrees. "The U.S. doesn't want to be constrained by the U.N., and it doesn't want to live up to some of the international obligations we made in the past," she says.

Yet others blame the nature of the institution. "The United Nations is wedded to the Cold War model of preserving the balance of power between the U.S. and Soviets," says Thomas Donnelly, a resident fellow at the American Enterprise Institute who studies defense and foreign policy issues. "But times have changed. Although we don't live in a multipolar world anymore, the U.N. is still acting like we do."

According to Donnelly, the world body should help America, not block it. "The United States is the most effective agent for peace and order in the world today," he says. "The U.N. should be trying to support U.S. goals, not just in Iraq and the Middle East, but elsewhere too, as we work to open markets and bring democracy."

Others say that as decolonization in the 1950s and '60s brought more and more new members from the developing world into the United Nations family, the institution became less amenable to America's interests. In addition, right-wing and white-supremacist militia groups in America have long seen the United Nations as bent on dismantling the United States in favor of a world government. And anti-abortionists have attacked the institution's family-planning efforts. [1]

In recent years, several issues have produced new U.N.-U.S. friction. In the 1990s, the two sparred over U.N. efforts — or lack of them, critics said — to reform its large bureaucracy. In fact, Congress refused to pay its back dues until the U.N. adopted reforms, a tactic it has used more than once to force policy changes. [2] Eventually, the United States paid the bulk of its back dues, after the U.N. cut its staff and improved efficiency.

In 2002, the United States withheld $34 million in funds earmarked for the U.N. Population Fund, which promotes family planning in the developing world. Anti-abortionists in America argued that the fund supports China's one-child population program, which critics say forces women to have abortions. In defending the move, State Department spokesman Richard Boucher said, "After careful consideration, we came to the conclusion that U.N. Population Fund moneys go to Chinese agencies that support coercive abortions." [3]

But Secretary-General Kofi Annan denied there was coercion. "We have made it clear [the fund] does not go around encouraging abortions," he said. [4]

The U.S. government also rejected the 1997 Kyoto Protocol, a U.N.-sponsored treaty designed to reduce global emissions of "greenhouse" gases believed to cause global warming. The protocol required the United States to reduce its emissions by 7 percent by 2008 compared with 1990 levels. [5]

While American officials helped negotiate the treaty, President Bill Clinton did little to promote it before a hostile U.S. Senate, which feared it would severely slow economic growth. President Bush, similarly concerned about its economic impact, rejected the document soon after taking office in 2001.

"Bush, by dismissing Kyoto and the whole Kyoto process, is really dismissing the United Nations and the international community," says Kert Davies, research director of Greenpeace U.S.A., an environmental advocacy group. "He's done incalculable damage to the [U.N.] and the environment."

Still, some experts say that for all their differences, the U.N. and United States have a more cooperative and productive relationship than appearances would indicate. After all, the United States still provides the largest share — 22 percent — of the U.N.'s annual budget.

"The U.S. supports the U.N. a lot more than people think," Mendelson-Forman says. "In areas like refugee assistance, food aid and health care, the U.S. and U.N. work very closely and very well together."

[1] For background, see Mary H. Cooper, "United Nations at 50," *The CQ Researcher*, April 18, 1995, pp. 729-752.

[2] *Ibid.*

[3] Quoted in "U.S. to Withhold Family Planning Funds, CNN.com, www.cnn.com/2002/US/07/22/un.funds/. For background, see Mary. H. Cooper, "Population and the Environment," *The CQ Researcher*, July 17, 1998, pp. 601-624.

[4] Quoted in CNN, *op. cit.*

[5] For background, see Mary H. Cooper, "Global Warming," *The CQ Researcher*, Jan. 26, 2001, pp. 41-64.

campaign in March, which brought the Serbians to the peace table three months later. The NATO countries did not seek U.N. authorization for the bombings because they knew permanent Security Council members China and Russia — which have been accused of ethnic atrocities in Tibet and Chechnya — would veto the plan.

"If military intervention is used against a country for a human rights issue, that will create a very bad precedent for the world," Chinese Premier Zhu Rongji said. "With that, people will wonder whether foreign powers should take military actions" against China over ethnic issues in Tibet. [21]

Frustrated with the U.N.'s marginalization in the Kosovo affair, Annan criticized both the Security Council's "inaction in the face of genocide" and NATO's unauthorized action. "Unless the Security Council is restored to its pre-eminent position as the sole source of legitimacy on the use of force," Annan said, "we are on a dangerous path to anarchy." [22]

After the peace accord, NATO and Russian peacekeepers helped maintain the ceasefire in Kosovo, and U.N. administrators came in to help restore civil government.

Since Kosovo, U.N. peacekeepers have had some successes, primarily in smaller conflicts. In 1999, for instance, the organization helped shepherd the former Indonesian province of East Timor toward democracy and independence, after decades of bloody conflict between separatists and the Indonesian government.

Confronting Iraq

The terrorist attacks on Sept. 11, 2001, like the end of the Cold War a decade before, imbued the U.N. with a new, if brief, sense of unity and focus. With smoke still rising from the World Trade Center just three miles south of U.N. headquarters, the Security Council authorized several anti-terrorism operations, including military action against Afghanistan, where Osama bin Laden and his al Qaeda terrorist group were operating.

AFP Photo/Atta Kenare

International Atomic Energy Agency (IAEA) chief Mohamed ElBaradei (left), shown with Iranian President Mohammad Khatami in Tehran last year, has been criticized for not demanding more accountability from Iran and other nations suspected of trying to produce nuclear weapons. The U.N.-supported IAEA is charged with ensuring that civilian nuclear programs are not used to create nuclear weapons.

But within a year of the 9/11 attacks, the U.N.'s newfound unity began to crack. With Afghanistan under American control and al Qaeda on the run, the U.S. turned its attention to Iraq's Hussein, who continued to defy U.N. mandates to publicly account for his alleged WMDs.

In his first post 9/11 State of the Union address, on Jan. 29, 2002, President Bush put Iraq and the world on notice that continued defiance of the United Nations would prompt American military action: "The Iraqi regime has plotted to develop anthrax, and nerve gas, and nuclear weapons for over a decade. . . . America will do what is necessary to ensure our nation's safety."

In fall 2002, the United States and Britain began lobbying other Security Council members for a resolution that would give Iraq a time limit to reveal and destroy its WMDs or face invasion. Permanent members France and Russia were strongly opposed, as was Germany, which held one of the rotating council seats. Along with other countries, they argued that any effort to disarm Iraq should work within the U.N. system and that no U.N. resolution demanding Iraqi cooperation should be used to justify a war.

Finally, in November, a compromise emerged. Security Council Resolution 1441, which passed 15-0, authorized the return of U.N. arms inspectors to Iraq, required Baghdad to account for all WMDs within 90 days and promised "serious consequences" for non-cooperation. The U.N. quickly dispatched International Atomic Energy Agency (IAEA) inspectors to look at Iraq's nuclear program and the Monitoring, Verification and Inspection Commission to search for chemical and biological weapons.

The passage of 1441 initially was hailed as a triumph for international cooperation and for the United Nations system. But the resolution, with its vague threat of "consequences," had merely delayed the inevitable big clash over whether war would ever be justified.

By the end of January, head U.N. arms inspector Hans Blix had reported back to the Security Council that Iraq "appears not to have come to a genuine acceptance . . . of the disarmament that was demanded of it," leaving the great powers once again deadlocked over what to do next. [23] France and its allies favored expanded arms inspections while the United States and Britain wanted authorization for the use of force unless Iraq immediately disarmed.

Negotiations dragged on for weeks with each side growing increasingly critical of the other. German Chancellor Gerhard Schröeder dismissed U.S. plans to invade Iraq as "an adventure," an anti-American position that had helped him secure re-election the year before. For his part, Secretary of Defense Donald Rumsfeld ruffled feathers when he labeled France and Germany as part of "old Europe," compared to the ex-communist Central and Eastern European states that supported the U.S. position.

In February, the opposition, led by France, threatened to veto any American or British resolution authorizing military action. French President Jacques Chirac argued that he would never opt for war when there was still a chance that Iraq could be disarmed peacefully. Some observers say France was trying to create a new bloc of powerful countries to serve as a counterweight to the United States, which the French had labeled a "hyperpower."

But the U.S said it would invade Iraq with or without the U.N.'s blessing. The old cooperative spirit evident during the first Persian Gulf War and Afghanistan was gone.

The split in the Security Council endured right up to the war on March 17 and despite last-minute efforts to reach a compromise. Miscalculations apparently played a part. The French held out hope that America and Britain would not really attack on their own, while the Americans continued to believe the French ultimately would not oppose ousting Hussein.

But the biggest loser in the struggle may have been the U.N. itself. "This was a terrible blow to the U.N. system," the U.N. Foundation's Mendelson-Forman says. "By excluding the U.N. from the process, by taking a unilateral as opposed to a multilateral approach to this problem, we ended up saying that the U.N. didn't matter. We made a laughing stock of the U.N." ■

CURRENT SITUATION

Peacekeeping Lessons

Although its charter requires the U.N. to help ensure the "collective security of nations," it does not actually authorize peacekeeping missions. Secretary-General Hammarskjold half-jokingly said peacekeeping — the term he coined — was authorized by "Chapter Six and a Half" of the charter because it fell between resolving disputes peacefully (Chapter 6) and using embargos and other more forceful means (Chapter 7).

In the past, critics have called the U.N.'s peacekeeping efforts ineffective and even negligent. But U.N.-watchers of varying political stripes say the international community sends insufficient numbers of peacekeepers to deal with intractable problems. "People try to throw in U.N. forces as a substitute either for a lack of will by the parties involved to settle their differences or lack of willingness by the great powers to deal with the issue," says Columbia University's Luck. "So, of course, peacekeeping missions turn out badly. What do people expect?"

The so-called safe havens created in Bosnia were just the kind of situation where the U.N. was expected to perform miracles, Luck says.* "The fighting was still raging in Bosnia, and no one really wanted to put outside forces on the ground," he says. "So they put inadequate peacekeepers on the ground and substituted words like 'safe haven' in lieu of real protection."

Nancy Soderberg, vice president of the International Crisis Group, a conflict-resolution think tank in New York, agrees. "The Serbs wanted to keep fighting, so everything quickly got out of control," she says. "The situation didn't improve until the U.S. bombed, and a NATO force was put in place, which should have happened in the first place."

Indeed, Bosnia taught the U.N. some valuable lessons about peacekeeping. Soderberg says. "They've learned they can't fight the war or enforce the peace," she says. "Those things have to be taken care of before they come in."

Soderberg says Kosovo and — more recently Sierra Leone and Ivory Coast — are examples of the U.N.'s more practical approach to peacekeeping. "They're not rushing into these places," she says. Peacekeepers went into Liberia and the Congo only after military forces from the region, the United States or France had established peace. "The U.N. can come in when there's truly a peace to keep."

Peacekeeping is now among the U.N.'s most important and visible activities, along with humanitarian efforts, such as assisting refugees and providing food aid. [24] The mission to

* The havens were areas set aside to protect Muslim refugees, but Serb troops entered the areas with no resistance from U.N. guards and murdered thousands of Muslims.

Continued on p. 190

At Issue:

Should the U.S. transfer administrative power in Iraq to the U.N.?

STEPHEN ZUNES
ASSOCIATE PROFESSOR OF POLITICS, UNIVERSITY OF SAN FRANCISCO; AUTHOR, TINDERBOX: U.S. MIDDLE EAST POLICY AND THE ROOTS OF TERRORISM

WRITTEN FOR *THE CQ RESEARCHER*, FEBRUARY 2004

yes

With the original justifications for the U.S. invasion of Iraq in doubt and discontent growing over U.S. occupation policies, increasing numbers of Iraqis are challenging the U.S. role in their country — even those who opposed Saddam Hussein's brutal regime.

Although extremist elements would not be satisfied if administrative responsibilities were transferred from U.S. occupation forces to the United Nations, such a move would dramatically decrease the extremists' support and facilitate restoring basic services, maintaining stability and establishing peaceful and democratic self-governance.

U.S. forces could remain in Iraq under U.N. command. However, even if the Bush administration chose to withdraw, there would still be sufficient forces available from other U.N. member states for peacekeeping and administrative responsibilities. Several Western European and South Asian governments, which refused to contribute troops under what they see as an illegal U.S. occupation, would do so under the U.N. flag.

It is unlikely that any Iraqi regime that emerges from the U.S. occupation — particularly under the proposed system of caucuses chosen by U.S. appointees — would be accepted as legitimate. Both popular resistance and terrorism would therefore continue, requiring an ongoing presence of U.S. forces.

By contrast, an Iraqi government that would emerge under an international mandate through the United Nations would be far more credible, both inside and outside Iraq, and could thereby take responsibility for its own security needs a lot sooner.

The financial burdens of administrative and security functions in Iraq have thus far fallen upon the American taxpayer. Under U.N. leadership, the United States would be responsible for no more than 20 percent of the costs.

The challenges facing any interim administration in Iraq are daunting, and the United Nations, like other intergovernmental bodies, is an imperfect organization. The U.N. has had a lot more experience in nation-building, however, than the U.S. armed forces, whose primary function should be defending America.

East Timor was a U.N. trusteeship for two years after the withdrawal of Indonesian forces in 1999; the new East Timorese government is a stable democracy and a strong U.S. ally. The U.N. also successfully administered postwar Kosovo, even as NATO remained in charge of security. Turning administration of Iraq over to the U.N. makes sense for Iraq, for America and for the world.

THOMAS DONNELLY
RESIDENT FELLOW, AMERICAN ENTERPRISE INSTITUTE

WRITTEN FOR *THE CQ RESEARCHER*, FEBRUARY 2004

no

The recent visit by U.N. envoy Lakhdar Brahimi to Iraq invites a question as to what role the U.N. can play in American-occupied Iraq, and whether the United States should shape its policies to attract greater international support.

Brahimi's trip was a whopping success, to judge by the headlines. He got in to see the leading Shi'a cleric, Grand Ayatollah Ali Sistani, something Ambassador Paul Bremer III hasn't accomplished. And Brahimi seemed to broker a deal that split the difference between the American plan for a quick transfer of Iraqi sovereignty through regional caucuses and Sistani's demand for direct elections.

Moreover, the U.N. saved Iraq from civil war and conferred a long-sought legitimacy on post-Saddam Iraq, according to the press.

But whether the U.N. can serve as a real powerbroker in Iraq remains very doubtful. First of all, the U.N. has little in the way of real power to bring to the table, and that's what Iraqis and the American-led coalition are jockeying over at the moment. Just because some negotiations may be held in the U.N.'s tent does not mean the U.N. is actually participating in the talks. And, to Iraqi factions trying to summon a minimum of political trust, there is little doubt that the United States is the most trustworthy and most attractive partner.

Two indisputable facts underscore this truth. First is the matter of political legitimacy. As the American Founders wrote repeatedly, the source of a government's legitimacy lies in its ability and commitment to secure the natural political rights of its citizens. This is as true in Iraq today as it was in the English colonies two centuries ago. But the U.N. was founded on state sovereignty and political stability — the principles that helped preserve Saddam Hussein in power for decades, a fact not forgotten by the Iraqi people. Iraqi factions know what the various warring factions in the Balkans knew: America and its real allies are most likely to be their honest broker.

Secondly, in a less-than-utopian world, legitimacy without power is meaningless — indeed, worse than meaningless. The U.N. already has been a target for Iraqi rejectionists, as U.N. forces in the Balkans were. This suggests something less than a respect for the legitimacy of the U.N.

While the Bush administration rightly welcomes the positive contributions of the U.N. to the immense task of reconstruction in Iraq, it cannot delude itself that the world body can be any substitute for the exercise of U.S. power.

Continued from p. 188

Congo is the largest of the 13 active operations, with 10,500 U.N. troops helping maintain a fragile ceasefire following a brutal civil war that left 3 million dead.

Some experts have suggested the U.N. should establish a permanent peacekeeping force. Currently, the U.N. must ask members to contribute troops or money whenever peacekeepers are needed — a time-consuming process that prevents rapid response.

"Better early-warning systems must be developed, and the international community must become willing to react in the early stages of a conflict," Sir Brian Urquhart, former U.N. undersecretary for peacekeeping operation and perhaps the most well-regarded proponent of a permanent peacekeeping force, said. "Some sort of highly trained standing force seems needed." [25]

However, many U.N.-watchers doubt that a permanent force would help. "They could never afford to have the kind of force that could operate without the assistance of the great powers," Luck says. "And if the great powers are on board, you don't need some sort of U.N. group, because they can raise a sufficient force to deal with the problem."

To make peacekeeping more effective, the Security Council should pass "sober and realistic resolutions and stop overreaching in its goals," says Luck at the Center on International Organizations.

The operational quality of U.N. peacekeepers also needs improvement, Soderberg says. "Most of the troops come from developing countries, and they are often not well-equipped or trained," she says. "The U.S. should help train and equip U.N. forces."

Thomas Donnelly, a resident fellow at the American Enterprise Institute, agrees, arguing that troops from many of the peacekeeping nations can't "do much more than man roadblocks."

"The international community must become willing to react in the early stages of a conflict."

— Sir Brian Urquhart, Former U.N. Undersecretary for Peacekeeping

Nuclear Watchdog

When the United Nations was created in 1945, only the United States had nuclear weapons. Today, eight countries are nuclear powers and several others — North Korea and Iran among them — either possess nuclear weapons or are close to developing them. [26]

Moreover, there is widespread fear that terrorist groups like al Qaeda will attack civilian targets using a nuclear device or conventional explosives packed with nuclear material — so-called "dirty bombs."

The U.N-affiliated IAEA promotes the peaceful use of nuclear power. It inspects nuclear-power and research facilities to ensure that they are not being used to produce weapons. Under the 1970 Nuclear Non-Proliferation Treaty — signed by 187 nations — countries with nuclear facilities must follow certain safeguards and allow IAEA inspections. [27]

Recently, the IAEA has played a constructive role in several anti-proliferation efforts. For instance, after the first Persian Gulf War in 1991, Iraq was found to have a much more advanced nuclear weapons program than anyone had suspected. Under the peace agreement following the war, the IAEA supervised the dismantling of the program while inspectors from the ad hoc U.N. Special Commission (UNSCOM) searched for chemical and biological weapons.

In the months leading up to the invasion of Iraq last March, IAEA inspectors returned to determine whether Hussein was continuing to develop nuclear weapons. They found little evidence that the program had been resuscitated.

But critics complain that several countries have "gone nuclear," unbeknown to the IAEA, including India, Israel and Pakistan. In fact, North Korea claims to have built one or more bombs while a small IAEA team was in the country monitoring a plutonium reactor. More recently, Libya admitted to the existence of four nuclear sites that were part of its secret WMD program. [28]

The agency has also drawn fire because Iran allegedly has been developing nuclear weapons, despite the past presence of IAEA inspectors. Iran finally agreed to new IAEA oversight only after Britain, France and Germany brought pressure on Iranian officials.

Critics of the agency say it has been too trusting of some states. "They told countries that if they would forgo nuclear weapons, they could get access to nuclear technology for civilian use," the Lexington Institute's Goure says. "Well guess what? Iran and North Korea ended up using the technology to develop a nuclear weapons program." *

Goure says the agency tries to be evenhanded, even with states that are less responsible about the use of their civilian nuclear programs. "The IAEA sees this as an equality issue, but the fact of the matter is that some of these countries, like Iran, just shouldn't be getting this technology, period."

Others say the agency's current director general, Egyptian scientist Mohamed ElBaradei, sympathizes more with nations seeking nuclear weapons than with those trying to halt their spread. ElBaradei "has routinely acted in a way better calculated to thwart U.S. counterproliferation efforts than to prevent the spread of nuclear weaponry," according to Frank Gaffney, president of the Center for Security Policy, a defense think tank. [29]

"ElBaradei has gone to great lengths to prevent the Bush administration from bringing Iran's illegal nuclear-weapons program before the U.N. Security Council," Gaffney writes, a step mandated by the Nuclear Non-Proliferation Treaty. ElBaradei also has slanted IAEA reports on Iran "to make sure the conclusions do not support a Security Council referral, often by inserting unjustified findings that obscure or downplay the actual evidence," Gaffney charges. [30]

IAEA supporters acknowledge past mistakes by the agency but say it has made the best of what has often been a bad situation. The "bleeding between civilian and military nuclear programs" is inevitable because of the "Siamese-twin relationship" that exists between the two, points out Rose Gottemoeller, a senior associate at the Carnegie Endowment for International Peace and former head of Department of Energy non-proliferation policy. "This leaves the IAEA with a very tough job." But the agency has taken the lead on important issues and "generally done good work," she adds. "I think you can call them a success."

In addition, Goure says, "ElBaradei is getting much tougher," in part because the United States and the Europeans are pressing him not to be too soft.

But Gottemoeller says his tougher attitude is driven more by recent developments than outside pressure. "I talked to him after he returned from Iran, and he's deadly serious about getting a handle on this," she says. "The problem cases, like Iran and North Korea, have really made him want to deal with these issues." ■

* Iran continues to deny accusations from many in the international community that it has a nuclear weapons program.

OUTLOOK

Regaining Relevance?

In a speech before the U.N. on Sept. 12, 2002, President Bush asked: "Will the United Nations serve the purpose of its founding, or will it be irrelevant?" [31]

Although Bush was referring to the U.N.'s lack of action in Iraq, the question resonated beyond the Middle East. Some U.N.-watchers contend the organization has proven incapable of meeting the president's challenge.

The Lexington Institute's Goure says the major powers already acknowledge in their actions, if not always their words, the U.N.'s lack of importance in global security issues. "The U.S. has shown that it's willing to act alone if it needs to," he says, "and you have other players like the Europeans forming an E.U. [European Union] rapid-reaction force. Recently, even the ASEAN [Association of Southeast Asian Nations] nations created a security structure to deal with these kinds of issues. All of this points away from the U.N. and toward alternatives."

Indeed, Goure argues, "Since the early 1950s, [the U.N.] hasn't lived up to its mandate 'To prevent wars and chase down aggressors.' Recent events just showed how much this is the case."

Other skeptics contend that the U.N. could still carve out an important role if it took a tougher line on the world's biggest security threat: the development of WMDs by rogue states. "A lot hinges on how the U.N. handles the biggest security concerns we're facing right now: namely Iran and North Korea," says the Heritage Foundation's Gardiner. "And I'm not optimistic.

"If the U.N. were to disarm these countries, then they would be a serious player," he continues. "But if there is more inaction and appeasement, then the organization will be written off. And, given the bipolar power structure at the Security Council — with the U.S. and Britain on one side and France and Russia on the other — I really don't see any strong response from the U.N. on this issue any time soon."

But the University of San Francisco's Zunes says the United Nations plays too important a role in the world to

About the Author

David Masci specializes in science, religion and foreign-policy issues. Before joining *The CQ Researcher* in 1996, he was a reporter at Congressional Quarterly's *Daily Monitor* and *CQ Weekly.* He holds a law degree from The George Washington University and a B.A. in medieval history from Syracuse University. His recent reports include "Rebuilding Iraq" and "Torture."

sink into irrelevance. "Eventually, we'll realize how much we need the United Nations to help keep the peace and make the world a better place," he says. "Unfortunately, given the attitude of the current administration, we'll probably hobble the U.N. more than help it in the short run, but I'm optimistic over the longer term."

Columbia University's Luck also sees signs of the U.N.'s future relevance. "Even when you look at Iraq, which was supposed to be the U.N.'s darkest hour, you see evidence that it is terribly relevant," he says. "Why has the United States gone back to the United Nations over and over again with regard to Iraq? Because the U.N. is a vital part of the furniture of international relations, and the U.S. knows that."

Indeed, Luck says, most states see the continued existence of the U.N. as very much in their interest. "On one hand, smaller countries want to have a voice — especially on the big issues of war and peace — and where else can they go except the U.N.?" he asks. "On the other hand, big powers, even the U.S., need partners and help, and the U.N. is still the best place for that."

Others share the view that the U.N. will always be seen as necessary for global stability. "No matter how often we criticize the U.N., it's necessary to have a forum like it," says Boorstin of the Center for American Progress. "If the U.N. didn't exist, we'd have to build it." ■

FOR MORE INFORMATION

American Enterprise Institute, 1150 17th St., N.W., Washington, DC 20036; (202) 862-5800; www.aei.org. A major Washington think tank.

Center for American Progress, 805 15th St., N.W., Suite 400, Washington, DC 20005; (202) 682-1611; www.americanprogress.org. A nonpartisan research and educational institute.

International Crisis Group, 1629 K St., N.W., Suite 450, Washington, DC 20006; (202) 785-1601; www.crisisweb.org. A nonprofit, non-governmental organization devoted to resolving conflicts around the globe.

United Nations Association, 801 2nd Ave., 2nd Fl., New York, N.Y. 10017; (212) 907-1300; www.unausa.org. A nonprofit group that supports the U.N.

United Nations Foundation, 1225 Connecticut Ave., N.W., Suite 400, Washington, DC 20036; (202) 887-9040; www.unfoundation.org. Supports U.N. activities through grants and public-private partnerships.

World Policy Institute, New School University, 66 5th Ave., Suite 900, New York, NY 10011; (212) 229-5808; www.worldpolicy.org. An international-relations think tank.

Notes

[1] See David Masci, "Confronting Iraq," *The CQ Researcher*, Oct. 4, 2002, pp. 793-816, and David Masci, "Rebuilding Iraq," *The CQ Researcher*, July 25, 2003, pp. 625-648.

[2] Gregory Stanton, "Create a United Nations Genocide Prevention Focal Point and Genocide Prevention Center," *Genocide Watch*; www.genocidewatch.org/UnitedNationsGenocidePreventionFocalPoint.htm.

[3] Quoted in Bill Spindle, "U.N. Strives to Define Its Role in a Single-Superpower World," *The Wall Street Journal*, Aug. 21, 2003, p. A1.

[4] See www.un.org/aboutun/charter/

[5] Quoted in "Binding the Colossus," *The Economist*, Nov. 20, 2003.

[6] *Ibid.*

[7] See David Masci and Kenneth Jost, "War on Terrorism," *The CQ Researcher*, Oct. 12, 2001, pp. 817-848, and Kenneth Jost, "Rebuilding Afghanistan," *The CQ Researcher*, Dec. 21, 2001, pp. 1041-1064.

[8] Spindle, *op. cit.*

[9] For background, see Mary H. Cooper, "United Nations at 50," *The CQ Researcher*, Aug. 18, 1995, pp. 729-752.

[10] Quoted in Max Harrelson, *Fires All Around the Horizon: The U.N.'s Uphill Battle to Preserve the Peace* (1989), p. 5.

[11] For background, see David Masci, "Prospects for Mideast Peace," *The CQ Researcher*, Aug. 30, 2002, pp. 673-696.

[12] *Ibid.*, pp. 31-39.

[13] For background, see Kenneth Jost, "Future of Korea," *The CQ Researcher*, May 19, 2000, pp. 425-448.

[14] William Jay Jacobs, *Search For Peace: The Story of the United Nations* (1994), p. 44.

[15] Quoted in *ibid.*, pp. 90-91.

[16] Figures cited in *ibid.*, p. 85.

[17] For background, see David Masci, "Aiding Africa," *The CQ Researcher*, Aug. 29, 2003, pp. 697-720.

[18] Quoted in James C. McKinley Jr., "Annan Given Cold Shoulder by Officials in Rwanda," *The New York Times*, May 8, 1998, p. A9.

[19] Quoted in Brad Knickerbocker, "Grappling with the century's most heinous crimes," *The Christian Science Monitor*, April 12, 1999, p. 1.

[20] *Ibid.*

[21] Quoted in Peter Ford, "World weighs in on NATO's war," *The Christian Science Monitor*, April 14, 1999, p. 1.

[22] Judith Miller, "Annan Takes Critical Stance on U.S. Actions in Kosovo," *The New York Times*, May 19, 1999, p. A11.

[23] Quoted in "When Squabbling Turns Too Dangerous," *The Economist*, Feb. 15, 2003.

[24] For background, see Mary H. Cooper, "Global Refugee Crisis," *The CQ Researcher*, July 9, 1999, pp. 569-592, and Brian Hansen, "Children in Crisis," *The CQ Researcher*, Aug. 31, 2001, pp. 657-688.

[25] Urquhart's 1995 speech is at www.colorado.edu/conflict/peace/example/urqu5486.htm.

[26] See Mary H. Cooper, "North Korean Crisis," *The CQ Researcher*, April 11, 2003, pp. 321-344.

[27] Treaty at www.un.org/Depts/dda/WMD/treaty/; for more information on the IAEA see www.iaea.org. For background, see Mary H. Cooper, "Non-Proliferation Treaty at 25," *The CQ Researcher*, Jan. 27, 1995, pp. 73-96.

[28] Patrick Tyler, "Libya's Atom Bid in Early Phases," *The New York Times*, Dec. 30, 2003, p. A1.

[29] Frank Gaffney, "A Fateful Choice," *The Washington Times*, Feb. 10, 2004, p. A17.

[30] *Ibid.*

[31] Full speech at www.whitehouse.gov/news/releases/2002/09/20020912-1.html.

Bibliography

Selected Sources

Books

Harrelson, Max, *Fires All Around the Horizon: The U.N.'s Uphill Battle to Preserve the Peace*, Praeger, 1989.

An Associated Press foreign correspondent and editor details the U.N.'s various efforts to promote peace and security, from its founding to the late 1980s.

Schlesinger, Stephen C., *Acts of Creation: The Founding of the United Nations*, Westview Press, 2003.

The director of the World Policy Institute chronicles the negotiations and intrigues that accompanied creation of the United Nations, including the crucial, persistent efforts of President Harry S Truman and Secretary of State Edward Stettinius.

Articles

"Binding the Colossus," *The Economist*, Nov. 20, 2003.

The article examines the tension between the world's sole superpower, the United States, and its premier international institution, the United Nations.

Barringer, Felicity, "U.N. Senses It Must Change, Fast, or Fade Away," *The New York Times*, Sept. 19, 2003, p. A3.

Barringer looks at the debate over the United Nations' relevance after the Iraq war.

Block, Robert, and Alix Freedman, "U.N. Peacekeeping is a Troubled Art," *The Wall Street Journal*, Oct. 1, 2003, p. A1.

The article examines the difficulties of organizing and executing a peacekeeping operation, especially in a place embroiled in civil war, like Congo.

Cooper, Mary H., "United Nations at 50," *The CQ Researcher*, Aug. 18, 1995, pp. 729-752.

Cooper's overview is still on target almost a decade after it was written.

ElBaradei, Mohamed, "Toward a Safer World," *The Economist*, Oct. 18, 2003.

The head of the International Atomic Energy Agency lays out his vision for improving nuclear non-proliferation.

Freedman, Alix, and Bill Spindle, "Now at the Top of the U.N.'s Agenda: How to Save Itself," *The Wall Street Journal*, Dec. 19, 2003, p. A1.

Part of a six-part series on the U.N. examines how the organization is determining its role in a post-Iraq war environment.

Fuerth, Leon, "America Need Not be a Law Unto Itself," *The Financial Times*, May 12, 2003, p. 17.

Vice President Al Gore's former national security adviser argues the United States can operate effectively as a world power within the parameters set by Article 51 of the U.N. charter, which grants a nation the right of self-defense.

Jordan, Michael J., "Who's In, Who's Out: U.N. Security Council Mulls Reform," *The Christian Science Monitor*, Oct. 16, 2002, p. 7.

The author reviews the various arguments for reforming the Security Council.

Khanna, Parag, "One More Seat at the Table," *The New York Times*, Dec. 6, 2003, p. A15.

A research analyst at the Brookings Institution proposes reforms to make the Security Council more effective, including eliminating the five permanent members' veto.

Lander, Mark, "U.N. Atom Agency Gives Iran Both a Slap and a Pass," *The New York Times*, Nov. 27, 2003, p. A22.

The author details recent efforts to contain Iran's alleged nuclear weapons development program.

Urquhart, Brian, "A Force Behind the U.N." *The New York Times*, Aug. 7, 2003, p. A23.

Urquhart, who served as U.N. under secretary-general for political affairs from 1974 to 1986, proposes development of a permanent U.N. peacekeeping force.

Weiss, Thomas G., "The Illusion of U.N. Security Council Reform," *The Washington Quarterly*, Autumn 2003, p. 147.

A political science professor at Columbia University argues that the Security Council, in its current configuration, is more than capable of effectively working toward the promotion of international peace and security.

Reports

"Enhancing U.S. Leadership at the United Nations," Council on Foreign Relations and Freedom House, 2002.

Analysts urge the United States to work more closely with other democratic nations at the United Nations to promote democracy and increase counterterrorism efforts.

Gardiner, Nile, and Baker Spring, "Reform the United Nations," *The Heritage Foundation*, Oct. 27, 2003.

Conservative analysts call for significant changes at the United Nations, including the broadening of a nation's right to self-defense and the removal from the U.N. Human Rights Commission of regimes that abuse human rights.

The Next Step:

Additional Articles from Current Periodicals

Nuclear Proliferation

"Binding the Colossus — America and the World," ***The Economist*****, Nov. 22, 2003.**

Interpretations of Article 51 of the U.N. charter, granting nations the right to self-defense, have broadened over time; some form of pre-emption has long been thought justifiable.

Beals, Gregory, "U.N. Nuclear Chief Presses for Better Antiproliferation Efforts," ***The Christian Science Monitor*****, Dec. 5, 2003, p. 7.**

Mohamed ElBaradei, director general of the International Atomic Energy Agency (IAEA), believes enhanced nuclear-inspection protocols will limit nuclear proliferation.

Frantz, Douglas, "Iran Discloses Nuclear Activities," ***Los Angeles Times*****, Oct. 24, 2003, p. A3.**

Responding to an IAEA resolution, Iran details its nuclear activities to prove it is not pursuing nuclear weapons.

Gera, Vanessa, "U.S., U.N. Trade Barbs on Iran," ***The Washington Post*****, Nov. 22, 2003, p. A18.**

The U.S. representative to the IAEA questions the agency's report on Iran's efforts to build nuclear weapons.

Landler, Mark, "As 2 Crises Swirl, U.N. Nuclear Agency Gains a Bigger Profile, and Bigger Problems," ***The New York Times*****, Jan. 6, 2003, p. A11.**

With nuclear weapons programs in the news more than ever, the IAEA gets increasing attention — and criticism.

Slevin, Peter, "Bush to Outline Plan For Limiting Nuclear Arms," ***The Washington Post*****, Feb. 11, 2004, p. A22.**

President Bush's plan to fight nuclear proliferation also envisions changes to the IAEA.

Slevin, Peter, and Joby Warrick, "U.S. Will Work with U.N. Agency in Libya," ***The Washington Post*****, Jan. 20, 2004, p. A13.**

The U.S., Britain and the IAEA will cooperate in the dismantling of Libya's atomic weapons program.

Peacekeeping

Barringer, Felicity, "Peacekeeping Is Back, With New Faces and Rules," ***The New York Times*****, July 20, 2003, Section 4, p. 4.**

Today the developed world supplies the money, and poorer nations provide the troops.

Dougherty, Carter, "Broken Record," ***The New Republic*****, July 21, 2003, p. 10.**

U.N. peacekeeping operations in Congo follow the same erroneous pattern of previous missions and won't stop the bloodshed, the author argues.

Durch, William, ***et al.*****, "The Brahimi Report and the Future of U.N. Peace Operations," Henry L. Stimson Center, December 2003. (available at www.stimson.org)**

A report on the U.N. study of its peacekeeping operations includes recommendations for improvements.

Gourevitch, Philip, "The Congo Test," ***The New Yorker*****, June 2, 2003, p. 33.**

The true test of the U.N.'s success is whether or not it can succeed in areas like Congo, where vital interests of Security Council members are not at stake.

Prusher, Ilene, "U.N. Aims to Disarm Afghan Fighters," ***The Christian Science Monitor*****, Dec. 2, 2003, p. 6.**

The U.N. campaign to eliminate warlord armies is moving slowly two years after the defeat of the Taliban; corrupt commanders and poor job prospects hinder disarmament.

Schrader, Esther, "U.S. Looks at Organizing Global Peacekeeping Force," ***Los Angeles Times*****, June 27, 2003, p. A1.**

Bush administration officials are considering a U.S.-led permanent peacekeeping force separate from both the U.N. and NATO.

Sengupta, Somini, "Congo War Toll Soars as U.N. Pleads for Aid," ***The New York Times*****, May 27, 2003, p. A1.**

Outnumbered and outgunned, U.N. peacekeepers in Congo watched helplessly as civilians and U.N. observers were slaughtered.

Wax, Emily, "French Peacekeepers Arrive in Congo," ***The Washington Post*****, June 7, 2003, p. A14.**

The arrival of French peacekeepers in Bunia, Congo, gave citizens reason for hope.

Rebuilding Iraq

Efron, Sonni, "U.N. in Pivotal, Difficult Iraq Role," ***Los Angeles Times*****, Jan. 19, 2004, p. A4.**

The U.N. must weigh security risks against the danger of looking weak and irrelevant in deciding whether or not to re-engage in Iraq.

Efron, Sonni, and Alissa Rubin, "U.S. Asks U.N. to Go to Iraq, Assess Feasibility of Vote," ***Los Angeles Times*****, Jan. 20, 2004, p. A1.**

Despite its reluctance to involve the U.N. in Iraq, the Bush administration needs the U.N. to help achieve a solution to demands by Iraqis for direct elections.

Hoge, Warren, "Iraqi Official Criticizes Security Council for Quibbling and Failing to Help Depose Hussein," ***The New York Times*****, Dec. 17, 2003, p. A24.**

Hoshyar Zebari, Iraq's interim foreign minister, criticized the U.N. for failing to do more to oust Saddam Hussein.

Sanders, Edmund, and Charles Duhigg, "Iraqis Hope to Sway Experts," *Los Angeles Times*, Feb. 8, 2004, p. A9.
The U.N. assessment team sent to Iraq to study the feasibility of elections will face the competing demands of various Iraqi groups with an interest in the results.

Slevin, Peter, "Aug. 19 Blast Reverberating in U.N. Debate on Role in Iraq," *The Washington Post*, Sept. 14, 2003, p. A21.
United Nations staff feels the U.N. should refrain from returning to any meaningful role in Iraq unless the U.S. gives it substantial authority.

Weisman, Steven, "Bush Presses U.N. to Mediate Iraqi Clash on Rule," *The New York Times*, Feb. 4, 2004, p. A1.
Faced with a divided Governing Council and objections from a leading cleric, the Bush administration wants the U.N. to play a bigger role in finding a solution in Iraq.

Williams, Daniel, "Blast Devastates U.N. Baghdad Offices," *The Washington Post*, Aug. 20, 2003, p. A1.
A truck bomb shattered the U.N. headquarters in Baghdad and killed many U.N. staff members, including Special Representative Sergio Vieira de Mello.

Reforming the U.N.

Curiel, Jonathan, "Who Needs the U.N.? (The World Does)," *San Francisco Chronicle*, Jan. 11, 2004, p. D1.
Despite often seeming powerless, the requests by the U.S. for the U.N. to help in Iraq demonstrate its continuing influence.

Farley, Maggie, "Annan to Propose Overhaul of U.N.," *Los Angeles Times*, Sept. 23, 2003, p. A1.
Kofi Annan lays out ambitious plans to reform the U.N. to help it regain influence.

Glennon, Michael, "Why the Security Council Failed," *Foreign Affairs*, May/June 2003, p. 16.
The author argues that the U.N.'s rules regarding the use of force undermine the U.N. because they do not reflect the way states actually behave.

Hukill, Traci, "Time for Radical Reform at the U.N.?" *The National Journal*, Nov. 1, 2003.
Many agree the Security Council is in need of reform, but if it were made more representative, it might be even less effective.

Jordan, Michael, "New Calls for Reform of U.N. Rights Commission," *The Christian Science Monitor*, May 7, 2003, p. 7.
With nations like China, Saudi Arabia and Libya sitting on the U.N.'s Commission on Human Rights, even human rights organizations question its credibility.

Jordan, Michael, "Who's In, Who's Out: U.N. Security Council Mulls Reform," *The Christian Science Monitor*, Oct. 16, 2002, p. 7.
The permanent members of the Security Council don't represent today's international community but the leading powers of 60 years ago.

Khanna, Parag, "One More Seat at the Table," *The New York Times*, Dec. 6, 2003, p. A15.
Security Council members must give up their veto powers and make room at the table for India and Japan, Khanna argues.

Smith, Patrick, "Annan Tackles Remaking the U.N.," *The Christian Science Monitor*, Sept. 25, 2003, p. 6.
Annan tells the General Assembly the U.N. has come to a "fork in the road" and asks whether its current structure is tenable.

Tharoor, Shashi, "Why America Still Needs the United Nations," *Foreign Affairs*, September/October 2003, p. 67.
The U.N. excels at peacekeeping at bargain rates, provides much-needed international legitimacy and has the expertise to assist in the reconstruction of shattered nations.

CITING *THE CQ RESEARCHER*

Sample formats for citing these reports in a bibliography include the ones listed below. Preferred styles and formats vary, so please check with your instructor or professor.

MLA STYLE

Jost, Kenneth. "Rethinking the Death Penalty." The CQ Researcher 16 Nov. 2001: 945-68.

APA STYLE

Jost, K. (2001, November 16). Rethinking the death penalty. *The CQ Researcher, 11*, 945-968.

CHICAGO STYLE

Jost, Kenneth. "Rethinking the Death Penalty." *CQ Researcher*, November 16, 2001, 945-968.

Back Issues

The CQ Researcher *offers in-depth coverage of many key areas. Back issues are $10. Quantity discounts available. Call (866) 427-7737 to order back issues.*

Or call for a free CQ Researcher Web trial! Online access provides:

- *Searchable archives dating back to 1991.*
- *PDF files for downloading and printing.*
- *Wider access through IP authentication.*
- *Availability 48 hours before print version.*

CIVIL LIBERTIES
Race in America, July 2003
Gay Marriage, September 2003
Civil Liberties Debates, October 2003

CRIME/LAW
Cyber-Crime, April 2002
Corporate Crime, October 2002
Serial Killers, October 2003

ECONOMY
State Budget Crises, October 2003
Stock Market Troubles, January 2004
Exporting Jobs, February 2004

EDUCATION
Home Schooling Debate, January 2003
Combating Plagiarism, September 2003
Black Colleges, December 2003

ENERGY/TRANSPORTATION
Future of the Airline Industry, June 2002
Future of Amtrak, October 2002
SUV Debate, May 2003

ENVIRONMENT
Crisis in the Plains, May 2003
Water Shortages, August 2003
Air Pollution Conflict, November 2003

HEALTH AND SAFETY
Medicare Reform, August 2003
Women's Health, November 2003
Homeopathy Debate, December 2003

POLITICS AND PUBLIC POLICY
Abortion Debates, March 2003
State Budget Crises, October 2003
Democracy in the Arab World, January 2004

SOCIAL TRENDS
Latinos' Future, October 2003
Future of the Music Industry, Nov. 2003

TECHNOLOGY
NASA's Future, May 2003

TERRORISM/DEFENSE
Homeland Security, September 2003
North Korean Crisis, April 2003

WORLD AFFAIRS
Trouble in South America, March 2003
Rebuilding Iraq, July 2003
Aiding Africa, August 2003

YOUTH
Preventing Teen Drug Use, March 2002
Sexual Abuse and the Clergy, May 2002
Movie Ratings, March 2003
Hazing, January 2004
Youth Suicide, February 2004

Future Topics

▶ ***Search for Extraterrestrials***

▶ ***Redistricting Debate***

▶ ***Reforming College Sports***

CQ Researcher

Published by CQ Press, a division of Congressional Quarterly Inc.

thecqresearcher.com

The Search for Extraterrestrials

Does new evidence suggest we aren't alone?

Recent discoveries have given renewed prominence to the search for intelligent life beyond Earth, including dramatic new evidence Mars once had water. NASA is already planning more missions similar to the current $1 billion exploration of the Red Planet by unmanned rovers. And President Bush recently proposed establishing a base on the moon to prepare for an eventual manned mission to Mars. While NASA will be looking for microbial life, the chance that evidence of an intelligent civilization might show up has not been dismissed. Critics of the search for extraterrestrial intelligence (SETI) say the money being spent on research should be used for more promising projects. But supporters argue that even if the search fails, it may lead to spin-off benefits for all humankind.

If intelligent extraterrestrials exist, they won't look anything like "Star Trek's" Mr. Spock and other Hollywood aliens, say scientists searching for evidence that humans are not alone in the universe.

INSIDE THIS ISSUE

The CQ Researcher • March 5, 2004 • www.thecqresearcher.com
Volume 14, Number 9 • Pages 197-220

CQ PRESS

RECIPIENT OF SOCIETY OF PROFESSIONAL JOURNALISTS AWARD FOR EXCELLENCE ◆ AMERICAN BAR ASSOCIATION SILVER GAVEL AWARD

The Search for Extraterrestrials

The Issues

Background

Current Situation

Outlook

Sidebars and Graphics

For Further Research

Cover: Hollywood often portrays aliens as human-like bipeds such as "Star Trek's" Mr. Spock, played by Leonard Nimoy. But scientists say if living creatures exist beyond Earth, it's doubtful they will resemble us. (Getty Images/Bertil Unger)

March 5, 2004
Volume 14, No. 9

Managing Editor: Thomas J. Colin

Assistant Managing Editor: Kathy Koch

Associate Editor: Kenneth Jost

Staff Writers: Mary H. Cooper, David Masci, William Triplett

Contributing Writers: Sarah Glazer, David Hatch, David Hosansky, Patrick Marshall, Tom Price, Jane Tanner

Design/Production Editor: Olu B. Davis

Assistant Editor: Kenneth Lukas

CQ Press

A Division of Congressional Quarterly Inc.

Senior Vice President/General Manager: John A. Jenkins

Director, Library Publishing: Kathryn C. Suárez

Director, Editorial Operations: Ann Davies

Circulation Manager: Nina Tristani

Congressional Quarterly Inc.

Chairman: Andrew Barnes

Vice Chairman: Andrew P. Corty

President and Publisher: Robert W. Merry

The CQ Researcher (ISSN 1056-2036) is printed on acid-free paper. Published weekly, except Jan. 2, April 9, July 2, July 9, Aug. 6, Aug. 13, Nov. 26 and Dec. 31, by CQ Press, a division of Congressional Quarterly Inc. Annual subscription rates for libraries, businesses and government start at $625. Single issues are available for $10. Quantity discounts apply to orders over 10. Additional rates furnished upon request. Periodicals postage paid at Washington, D.C., and additional mailing offices. POSTMASTER: Send address changes to *The CQ Researcher*, 1255 22nd St., N.W., Suite 400, Washington, D.C. 20037.

The Search for Extraterrestrials

By William Triplett

The Issues

As the world marvels at the images of Mars' dusty, red landscape being transmitted to Earth by NASA's two golf-cart-sized rovers, more than 150 scientists wait anxiously for fresh data at the Jet Propulsion Laboratory (JPL) in Pasadena, Calif.

The experts include planetary geologists Philip R. Christensen of Arizona State University, JPL's Matt P. Golombek and NASA's Nathalie A. Cabrol. They want to know about the rocks on Mars. Are there carbonates such as limestone? Rounded, smooth rocks? Or really big boulders?

When the two rovers, *Spirit* and *Opportunity*, aren't transmitting their stunning pictures to a fascinated world — NASA's Web site experienced a billion hits in the first 48 hours it posted images from the Red Planet — they are digging into the Martian soil and conducting mineralogical tests on rocks. Then scientists on Earth eagerly review the results. *

NASA/JPL/Caltech/Harvard-Smithsonian Center for Astrophysics

A cluster of 130 newborn stars 3,330 light years from Earth was captured by NASA's new Spitzer Space Telescope using infrared detectors. The space agency's current Rover mission to Mars, and recent discoveries by astronomers, have given new prominence to the search for intelligent extraterrestrials. But critics say the most effective technologies aren't being used in the search and that, in any event, the money being spent could be more profitably used on other projects.

The scientists were trying to find out whether — as they strongly suspect — water once flowed abundantly on Mars' surface. And in a dramatic press conference on March 2, NASA's chief mission scientist, Steve Squyres, announced that their suspicions had been confirmed. "Liquid water once drenched the surface" of Mars, he said. But while the planet had been moist enough to support life, no signs of life were found. Water would indicate an atmosphere that would have been able to support some kind of life. And rocks were a key to the puzzle, because mineral content and shape reveal how a rock was formed and in what kind of environment.

Determining whether life ever existed on Mars is the primary goal of the twin-rover mission. Ultimately, however, it is really just trying to answer a question that humankind has spiritedly debated for millennia, long before it ever dreamed of sending robotic devices 100 million miles into space: Are we alone?

"Now if the atoms are so abundant that all generations of living creatures could not count them, and if the same force and nature remains with the power to throw each kind of atom into its place in the same way as they have been thrown here, you must admit that in other parts of the universe there are other worlds and different races of men and species of wild beasts." [1]

Thus declaimed the Roman poet Lucretius more than 2,000 years ago, and he was hardly the first to weigh in on the subject. Aristotle had contended 300 years earlier that no world but ours could exist, and before him the Epicureans espoused a universe full of inhabited worlds.

While the intensity of the debate over extraterrestrial life has waxed and waned over the centuries, the possibility of it has never been far from the popular imagination. The history of literature and cinema is filled with speculation about alien civilizations. Some of the earliest books written explored the subject.

A raft of intriguing discoveries — such as new planets, the signs of water on Mars and one of Jupiter's moons and exotic organisms found living in places on Earth thought uninhabitable — have reinvigorated the hunt for signs of life in our galaxy. Now, after nearly a decade of shying away from the search for extraterrestrial intelligence (SETI), NASA is already planning several more missions similar to the Mars rovers.

* The Mars pictures can be seen at http://marsrovers.jpl.nasa.gov/gallery/

What Are the Odds?

Believers in extraterrestrial intelligence often point to the sheer size of the universe to support the contention that life must be out there. The Milky Way Galaxy — Earth's galaxy — alone is estimated to have up to 400 billion stars, and astronomers estimate the universe has 100 billion galaxies. Some believers in ET life hypothesize that even if only 1 in a billion stars has intelligent life orbiting around it, then there would be 100 intelligent species in our galaxy alone.

Compared to the odds of intelligent extraterrestrial life, here are the odds of:

Flying on a plane with a drunken pilot: 1 in 117

Having your identity stolen: 1 in 200

A golf pro hitting a hole in one: 1 in 2,491

Being struck by lightning: 1 in 3,000

Dating a supermodel: 1 in 88,000

Dying of a spider bite: 1 in 592,829

Being dealt a royal flush: 1 in 649,739

Becoming president: 1 in 10,000,000

Becoming a saint: 1 in 20,000,000

Winning Powerball: 1 in 120,000,000

A meteorite hitting your house: 1 in 182,138,880,000,000

NASA/JPL/Hubble Heritage Team

Sources: National Weather Service, NASA, Encyclopedia Britannica, newspaper reports

Moreover, President Bush recently proposed establishing a base on the moon to prepare for a future manned mission to Mars. While the NASA missions will largely be looking for microbial life, the chance that evidence of an intelligent civilization might show up has not been dismissed.

How likely is it that intelligent extraterrestrial life exists? And if it does, how likely are we to make contact with it? With the current mission to Mars alone costing almost $1 billion, the questions raise more than highly charged scientific or philosophical arguments.

Proponents of the search for extraterrestrials say a billion dollars isn't much compared to what would be arguably the most important discovery in history. But skeptics maintain that looking for extraterrestrial life (ET) simply wastes resources that could support other research much more likely to deliver results. [2]

The pro-ET side insists that the magnitude of the numbers strongly suggests that we are not alone. The Milky Way contains up to 400 billion stars, while the number of stars in the entire universe is estimated at up to 10 to the 22nd power — or 1 followed by 22 zeroes.

Yet, even if we were able to send rovers to all the planets in our solar system and the 100 recently discovered planets in nearby parts of the galaxy — and each proved lifeless — we would still be far from a definitive answer. Some known stars would require 12 billion years to reach, assuming a spacecraft could travel at the speed of light.

Those who believe we humans are not alone in the universe say that in such a huge universe, it is illogical to think that life exists only in our infinitesimal corner of the galaxy. "The number of stars is so huge that you could cut it down by a factor of 10, and it would still be huge," says Christopher Chyba, director of the Center for the Study of Life in the Universe at the SETI Institute in Mountain View, Calif. Chyba thinks that discoveries made in the last decade offer several "exciting" and "compelling" reasons to believe in the possibility of intelligent life elsewhere.

But skeptics argue that only a fraction of stars would be the right age and size to support life, and only a minute number of planets would be the right size and distance from their star to support life. Moreover, they say, the development of life here on Earth depended on so many flukes of astronomy, biology and geology that the odds are against it happening again.

Frank Tipler, a professor of mathematical physics at Tulane University, thinks searching for extraterrestrial intelligence is just "a desperate hope," while Michael Hart, a retired professor of astronomy and former SETI proponent, thinks the SETI community is stubbornly romanticizing the possibility of intelligent life elsewhere. "The evidence of the last 30 years makes my position seem more likely," he says.

NAIC — Arecibo Observatory, National Science Foundation

The world's largest radio telescope — 1,000 feet in diameter — scans 168 million radio frequencies from its base in Arecibo, Puerto Rico, in hope of picking up stray radio signals from an alien civilization in outer space.

"Yet the SETI community, in the face of increasing amounts of negative evidence, get ever more certain they're right."

The sheer, mind-boggling vastness of the universe might argue for the likelihood of extraterrestrial life elsewhere, but it also argues against our making any meaningful contact. For the last 40 years, SETI has searched many of the nearest stars — the closest being four light years away. Yet no sign of life has been detected. A sign, perhaps an electronic signal, might indeed come at any moment, but the odds are it would come from a distance of hundreds of light years away. Moreover, even SETI believers expect it would not be immediately recognizable or understandable. Deciphering it, then replying and waiting for a response would take hundreds of years, at the least.

And yet, short of manned or robotic missions visiting or inspecting every corner of the universe, it would be impossible to rule out the possibility of extraterrestrial intelligence, ET proponents say.

In the frequently polarized debate, questions inevitably arise over whether both sides' accepted assumptions and premises are valid. One might also wonder whether a world that still hasn't resolved Earth's most enduring problems — famine, poverty, disease and war — should devote much time and resources to looking for other kinds of life. The other side responds: Perhaps another civilization has resolved these problems — and could teach us how.

Both sides agree that answering the question of how life began here on Earth would yield vital clues about life elsewhere. But science and faith eye each other uneasily in the debate about extraterrestrial life, so the claims and counterclaims are often intensely emotional. As the debate heats up, here are some of the questions being asked:

Does the existence of life on Earth necessarily mean life exists elsewhere?

From our relatively short time exploring outer space — the last 50 of Earth's 4 billion years of existence — scientists have determined that the laws of physics are the same throughout the universe. Moreover, while an alien life form might assume any shape, the basic chemistry and biology of Earth-like life appear to be possible in an extraterrestrial environment.

Life on Earth is based heavily on carbon, with a strong supporting mix of hydrogen and oxygen — three of the four most common elements in the universe (the fourth is helium). And organic chemists have been learning that molecules containing carbon are not unique to Earth. [3]

"The necessary ingredients for life seem to be ubiquitous," Michael Meyer, senior NASA astrobiologist, says. "Looking into interstellar clouds, we see lots of organic chemistry going on. We find molecules that are related to the carbon compounds we use in life as we know it, and we see organic chemistry going on in space. So, the suspicion is that other parts of the universe are just as capable of getting life started as this part of the universe."

Water also is present elsewhere in our solar system. In 1995, when the NASA spacecraft *Galileo* photographed Jupiter's four moons, one of them, Europa, was covered in what scientists determined was freshwater ice six miles thick in some places. Icebergs seemed to have formed, broken away, floated to another destination and frozen again in place — suggesting a liquid ocean beneath the surface ice.

Then in 2000, NASA's *Mars Global Surveyor* spacecraft found that some kind of liquid had flowed on Mars' surface within the last million years. Detailed photographs showed ancient gullies and beds formed by, if not water, then something very water-like — spurring the rover missions and NASA's current "follow the water" strategy.

"Liquid water is not, after all, extremely rare," the SETI Institute's Chyba says.

Nor, it seems, are planets. The discoveries within the last decade of roughly 100 planets orbiting other stars in the Milky Way were "a huge shot in the arm" for the pro-ET side, says David Grinspoon, principal scientist in the Department of Space Studies at the Southwest Research Institute, in Boulder, Colo. After centuries without evidence of planets outside our solar system, the proof was welcome validation of the old hypothesis that, based on the odds, other worlds must exist.

But skeptics remain unimpressed. "I enjoyed the bar scene in the original 'Star Wars' as much as anyone else," James Trefil, a physics professor at George Mason University, in Fairfax, Va., says. "That scene is a visualization of this idea of a galactic club of billions of civilizations, because [proponents of ET life] always say, no matter how small you make the odds, look at how many stars are out there! Well, they have to be the right kind of stars with the right kind of planets, and the numbers start coming down pretty fast."

For example, almost all the recently discovered planets are like Jupiter or Saturn — too large and hot to maintain an Earthlike atmosphere. "If life is going to be chemical, it has to take place in a fluid," Trefil continues, "and the fluid can only be water, because it's the only one that has the right properties to allow the reactions to go on. That means there has to be liquid water on the surface of the planet, so the surface can't be too hot or too cold."

To permit that, temperatures typically would have to be between zero and 100 degrees Celsius (C). Curiously, temperatures in the areas on Mars showing geologic evidence of surface liquid routinely drop to -100°C, raising doubts that the gullies and beds were caused by water. [4]

SETI Institute

Christopher Chyba, director of the Center for the Study of Life in the Universe, at the SETI Institute, in Mountain View, Calif., thinks recent discoveries offer "exciting" and "compelling" reasons to believe in the possibility of intelligent life elsewhere. Jill Tarter, director of the institute's Center for SETI Research, adds, "There's a lot we don't know, and anyone who makes categorical statements is just deluding themselves."

In the mid-1970s, Hart proposed his theory of the Continuously Habitable Zone, which holds that a planet must be positioned a perfect distance from its star in order to develop and sustain a life-supporting atmosphere. Trefil supports the theory, noting that if Earth were just 2 percent either closer to or farther from the Sun, our atmosphere would either burn up or freeze.

Recently, Guillermo Gonzalez, an assistant professor of astronomy and physics at Iowa State University, in Ames, advanced his own theory of a Galactic Habitable Zone. A life-supporting solar system, he contends, must be far enough from the galaxy center, where exploding stars known as supernovae frequently occur, but not too far out to preclude heavy elements, which he says are the building blocks of an Earth-type planet. "The heavy-element abundance goes down as you go out from center," Gonzalez says.

Peter Ward, a professor of Earth sciences at the University of Washington, brings a geologist's perspective to the debate. "The global thermostat on our planet — how the Earth has been able to maintain constant temperature — is caused by plate tectonics," he says. "For the longest time, nobody knew this. So, much of the argument [about life elsewhere] comes down to: How common is plate tectonics in the universe?"

Nobody knows the answer — which is precisely why ET proponents say further exploration and experimentation are needed. "There's a lot we don't know, and anyone who makes categorical statements is just deluding themselves," says Jill Tarter, director of the Center for SETI Research at the SETI Institute. "It all could go either way."

Perhaps most intriguing, scientists in the last decade have discovered so-called extremophiles — microorganisms living on Earth in environments and temperatures previously thought uninhabitable. Thus, ET proponents say, space explorers could possibly encounter an alien life form that resembles some as-yet undiscovered life form on Earth.

Are scientists using the best strategy to detect intelligent extraterrestrial life?

In 1959, two physicists at Cornell University proposed that radio-astronomy technology could be used to detect radio signals coming from another technological civilization. Scientists know that radio signals — which include television and radar transmissions traveling at the speed of light — leak out of Earth's atmosphere. Another intelligent civilization would have developed radio just as we had, the two scientists argued, and leaking radio signals from that civilization might be streaking our way. In fact, if they wanted to contact us, they might have aimed radio signals directly at us, they wrote in the journal *Nature*. [5]

Although they weren't the first to suggest communicating with other civilizations, the two scientists were the first to propose the attempt using scientific deliberation and rigor. However, that would require finding the right radio frequency in a vast electromagnetic bandwidth often plagued by significant background noise. The scientists recommended searching for deliberately sent signals, which would most likely be transmitted at 1420 megahertz — a generally quiet frequency at which hydrogen hums naturally and the presumed logical choice of technologically advanced beings.

The *Nature* article helped spawn the SETI movement, led by eminent scientists like astronomer Carl Sagan, physicist Freeman Dyson and Frank Drake, the first radio astronomer to conduct a SETI search. The movement grew over the next two decades, and in 1984 its leading members founded the SETI Institute. Since the first detection efforts in 1960, radio astronomers have tuned in to more than 1,000 nearby stars, all of which have been utterly silent.

But with billions more stars to listen to, the SETI Institute's Tarter isn't the least concerned about the initial failures. "Radio makes an awful lot of sense because radio can travel huge distances without being perturbed," says Tarter, whose optimism extends to keeping a bottle of champagne in the office refrigerator to celebrate the first alien signal.

Thanks largely to generous private donations, the institute eventually will have its own extensive series of radio telescopes. Until then, it will continue to buy whatever time is available on multiple-use radio telescopes. When the Allen Telescope Array, more than 300 radio telescopes to be erected in northern California, is fully operating in 2007, SETI will increase its search speed by a factor of 300 and cover five times more bandwidth.

"That'll begin to take a big bite out of the cosmic haystack," Tarter says. Indeed, according to her colleague Chyba, over the next decade the Allen project will tune in to at least 100,000 stars, possibly as many as 1 million. "That almost starts to mean something statistically," Chyba says.

The National Academy of Sciences (NAS) supports SETI's radio-astronomy project. "No known remote-sensing technique can detect the presence of intelligent versus complex life forms, other than by listening for electromagnetic forms of communication leaking from or deliberately sent from another world," a NAS committee wrote. "The SETI Institute has forged a unique endeavor out of private and public funds, maintained a high standard of scientific research through its peer-reviewed research activities, and articulated clearly and authoritatively the rationale for approaches to a comprehensive search for extraterrestrial intelligence." [6]

But the chairman of the University of Virginia's astronomy department questions the efficacy of radio-telescope searches. "I wouldn't put my career in it," Robert Rood says, mainly because leakage provides too weak a signal. Even if a signal were detected once, confirming it — for scientific validity — would be nearly impossible, he says. Moreover, the period of leakage during the life of a technological society would be small, he maintains, noting that Earthbound broadcasters already are trying to prevent leakage.

With minimum distances of hundreds, if not thousands, of light years involved, Rood says the chances of a deliberately aimed signal's reaching us during our lifetime are minuscule.

And George Mason's Trefil argues the hydrogen frequency or channel is no more likely to carry a signal than any other. "Everyone has their favorite frequency, but it's all [bunk]," he says. "Nobody has any real data."

Continued on p. 205

You, Too, Can Join the Hunt for ET!

Since 1999, some 4.5 million participants from around the world have been using their personal computers to help search for anomalous radio signals from outer space. In fact, SETI@Home may be the world's largest, single-focus computing operation. [1]

All you need is a computer with access to the Internet, and you, too, can join the search for extraterrestrial intelligence (SETI).

SETI@Home is part of Project SERENDIP, a radio-telescope search jointly sponsored by the SETI Institute, the Planetary Society and the Friends of Serendip, a fund-raising group headed by famed science fiction writer Arthur C. Clarke (whose island home in Sri Lanka is known as Serendip). The project scans the skies for alien radio signals using the largest — 1,000 feet in diameter — radio telescope in the world, which is located in Arecibo, Puerto Rico.

But in simultaneously scanning 168 million radio frequencies, the Arecibo telescope harvests more data than the project's computers can analyze quickly for signals of unnatural origin. That's where the volunteers with home computers come in.

AFP Photo/Sena Vidanagama

Arthur C. Clarke, whose 60 science fiction books have sold 50 million copies, wrote the prescient 1968 book 2001: A Space Odyssey. *He helped establish the SETI Institute.*

After downloading the free software, SETI@Home participants then let their computers do the rest. Whenever the computer is idle for a certain period of time (which the participant can specify), the software automatically connects to the Internet and the SERENDIP data site, downloads a 300-kilobyte chunk of data, and then analyzes it for signals. When the analysis is completed, the computer sends the results back to SERENDIP, and then downloads another chunk to analyze.

In the four years since volunteers have been "loaning" their home computers to SETI@Home, the program has collectively analyzed the amount of data that a single computer would need 1.5 million years to analyze.

As an adjunct research tool, SETI@Home has its advantages and disadvantages. All 4.5 million home computers can only analyze a 2.5-megahertz piece of the observed spectrum at one time, and the data processing does not occur "real time," so interesting signals must be followed up at a later date. However, the collective computing power also can detect weaker signals than a targeted search could pick up, and the software allows users to view the downloaded data on their screens.

The program's greatest asset may be public relations, since many thousands of interested folks will become active participants in SETI. Almost from its inception, the project has captivated space enthusiasts from Laos and the Gaza Strip to Vanuatu, Zimbabwe and Iraq.

Of course, public fascination with the possibility of extraterrestrial beings is hardly new. Still, when a University of California, Berkeley, graduate student suggested the idea, no one had an inkling that the response would be so large — and immediate. "At first we thought we could get 50,000 participants," said SETI@Home Director David Anderson. "We got that in the first couple of hours." [2]

Aside from feeling like they're helping a worthy scientific research effort, participants know that, should one of their computers identify an alien signal, they will be part of one of the most profound discoveries in history. Skeptics, of course, doubt such a discovery will ever come and point out that in four years, nothing has been found. [3]

Then again, the galaxy — not to mention the universe — is vast and old. In addition, SETI@Home has recently joined forces with other online research projects. Through software developed at Berkeley, SETI@Home participants now are interconnected with participants who donate their computer time to analyze research data on weather, biological proteins and even an AIDS cure.

"When one project doesn't have any work to do, the other projects can receive the benefit," Anderson said. [4]

---

[1] The SETI Web site is at http://setiathome.ssl.berkeley.edu/.

[2] See Irene Brown, "Alien Hunt Pioneers New Computing Realm," United Press International, July 18, 2003.

[3] See Mike Toner, "NASA to Fund Extraterrestrial Life Study," *The Atlanta Journal and Constitution*, September 8, 2003.

[4] See Joan Oleck, "Getting More from a PC's Spare Time," *The New York Times*, Sept. 11, 2003, p. G5.

Continued from p. 203

Moreover, according to Tipler at Tulane, the chance of another civilization developing technologically at the same rate as ours is almost statistically impossible in a 14-billion-year-old universe. A less-developed civilization would be unable to send or receive radio signals; one that is several billion years older than ours presumably would have gone on to vastly superior technology.

Indeed, Tipler argues, a radically advanced civilization would dispatch self-repairing and self-replicating probes throughout the universe — a capability he says humans should be able to achieve in the next 100 years. We should be looking for robot probes, he says, because they are "the best way to contact another civilization."

Rood favors the relatively new approach of optical searches, or scanning deep space for pulses of laser light. "If I'd have spent my career doing [radio-astronomy searches] and then learned about optical laser, I'd have been depressed," he says. "If I were an ET, this is how I'd send the signals." The advantage of laser light is it's stronger; the disadvantage is that it can be hard to see because filtering out interfering starlight is difficult.

The SETI Institute also mounts optical searches, but radio astronomy continues to be the preferred method, and, as Tarter acknowledges, radio astronomy "may take a while to succeed."

Should the federal government spend money searching for alien intelligence?

In the late 1960s, NASA began providing some funding for SETI radio searches, but controversy erupted when astronomers argued over whether the program constituted reputable science or a quest for tabloid publicity.

Some members of Congress questioned the fiscal wisdom of federal funding for SETI, dismissing it as a hunt for "little green men." Indeed, as more and more SETI projects detected nothing but silence, Sen. William Proxmire, D-Wis., in 1978 gave the institute one of his infamous "Golden Fleece" Awards, reserved for programs he believed were bilking taxpayers. SETI pioneer Drake, who later helped found the SETI Institute, responded by nominating Proxmire for membership in the Flat Earth Society.

In 1993, Congress finally zeroed out the roughly $10 million a year NASA was providing for radio searches; the institute has since generated its funding from private sources.

However, the institute also performs astrobiology research, and last summer NASA's astrobiology program awarded the first federal money — $10 million — to the SETI Institute since 1993, to research small, stable stars. No radio-astronomy activity is involved, says NASA's Meyer, who evaluated the proposal. But he acknowledges that the research will allow SETI to "build up a library of potential stars that would be good to look at [with] radio astronomy."

The University of Washington's Ward, who doubts the value of radio searches, concedes that the institute "does lots of good stuff" in astrobiology. "But the scary thing is, once they got that grant, a lot of their [radio-astronomy] people started saying, 'See! We're justified!' That got a little spooky." He would rather see the money go toward preserving endangered species in the Amazon rain forest.

"What would happen if we did discover intelligent life out there?" he asks. "They're going to be light years away. Even if it's only 50 light years, you're going to take 50 years to get back to them, and another 50 for them to get back to you. Yet you're still going to have 35 or 40

NASA/JPL/U.S. Geology Survey

The rocky surface of Mars is seen in a photo transmitted by Spirit, *one of the two rovers NASA landed on the Blue Planet. The golf cart-size vehicles are digging into the Martian soil and conducting mineralogical tests on rocks. Their size and composition helped scientists determine that water once flowed on Mars, indicating it may have had an atmosphere able to support life.*

million people in this country without health insurance. It would be a great moment, wonderful — wow, really cool! — but it won't change anything. And there are a lot of problems on planet Earth."

"We're not going to get any answers through radio signals," Hart says. "If people are willing to donate privately to it, fine. I just don't want them using my money. Not that $10 million is a serious figure, but government budgets do tend to creep up."

Iowa State's Gonzalez concurs, arguing that any scientist seeking federal money should first demonstrate a reasonable chance of success, which, he says, the SETI record has not been able to do. *(See "At Issue," p. 213.)*

But even skeptics like Trefil feel SETI should continue to receive federal help. "First, this is about the only experiment where either answer is exciting," he says. "If we find somebody, that's fantastic. If we're alone in the galaxy, that's fantastic. You've got to look because you can never be sure if you don't. And since it's so cheap — this isn't even walking-around change in Washington — I don't see any reason why government shouldn't spend more on this."

The Southwest Research Institute's Grinspoon agrees. "We're not talking billions and billions" of dollars, he says. "The hallmark of a wise, intelligent species is to commit some small fraction of its resources to future-looking and maybe high-risk efforts that have high-potential payoff, like SETI."

SETI's Tarter — upon whom the 1997 movie "Contact" starring Jodie Foster loosely was based — "absolutely" believes Congress should restore funding for the searches. "When you have NASA in its strategic plan addressing the question of are we alone, it's a little disingenuous to say that the American public thinks you're looking for microbes," she says, referring to NASA's Origins program, which is devoted primarily to searching for signs of microbial life in our solar system. *

In 2001, Rep. Lamar Smith, R-Texas, asked the House Subcommittee on Space and Aeronautics to review current federal efforts to fund explorations into the possibility of life in the universe. "The discovery of life in the universe would be one of the most astounding discoveries in human history," said Smith, a strong NASA supporter and believer in extraterrestrial life. "Funding should match public interest, and I don't believe it does." [7]

Although memories of Sen. Proxmire's 1978 Golden Fleece Award had faded, there was no real support for restoring funding for SETI, but there was no discernible opposition either. Congress didn't authorize new funds, and NASA didn't push for it. As NASA's Meyer put it back then, "There's [the issue of] once burnt, twice shy."

Nevertheless, Meyer says, SETI's astrobiology program is "fantastically popular" with the public, the Office of Management and Budget, Congress and even NASA. But if SETI radio searches were included in the astrobiology program, he says, "all of a sudden the enthusiasm you had gets turned back into, 'Why are we looking for little green men?' " [8]

NASA has yet to seek any more funds from Congress for SETI radio searches. ■

BACKGROUND

Early Theories

In the 4th and 5th centuries B.C., the Greek philosophers Leucippus, Democritus and Epicurus articulated the first scientific cosmology, called atomism, which held that an ordered system of life existed beyond the observable world. Epicurus spoke extensively about the premise that still underpins belief in extraterrestrial life today — that the numbers favor its chances. As Epicurus reasoned, since the observable world seemed to be composed of an infinite number of atoms, there must be an infinite number of worlds elsewhere.

Astronomer and science historian Steven J. Dick has summed up the thrust of atomism: "As our world was created by the chance collision of atoms in an entirely natural process, so must other worlds be created in like manner." [9] Atomism eventually gave rise to a doctrine the Greeks referred to as the "plurality of worlds."

The Greek philosopher Aristotle, however, argued that the Earth was the center of a cosmology that precluded the existence of any other world, triggering a debate that continues to rage today. The Sun, moon and stars orbit the Earth, Aristotle argued, but they were subject to different physical laws and composed of matter completely different from the four elements that constitute all life on Earth, which he listed as earth, air, fire and water.

As the cosmological center, Aristotle argued, only Earth exerted any gravitational pull. No other worlds like ours could form, because Earth pulled all the four elements toward itself.

The first significant attempt to refute Aristotelian physics occurred in the 1st-century B.C., when the Roman poet Lucretius expanded on atomism. In *On the Nature of Things*, Lucretius insisted that other worlds must exist "since there is illimitable space in every direction, and since seeds innumerable in number and unfathomable in sum are flying about in many ways driven in everlasting motion." [10]

Continued on p. 208

* The *Spirit* and *Opportunity* rover expeditions to Mars are part of the Origins program.

Chronology

5th-4th Centuries B.C.

Greek philosophers develop theory about extraterrestrial life.

4th-century B.C.
Aristotle argues that Earth is the center of the universe and the sole home of life, a view that comports with later Christian beliefs.

1500s-1600s

Astronomers suggest Earth is not the center of the solar system.

1543
Polish astronomer Nicolaus Copernicus argues that the Sun, not the Earth, is the center of our world.

1609
German astronomer Johannes Kepler demonstrates laws of elliptical planetary motion. Italian astronomer Galileo Galilei supports Copernicus' heliocentric theory.

1686
Catholic Church fails to stop spread of Copernican theory as *Conversations on the Plurality of Worlds*, about the possibility of extraterrestrial life, is published in France.

19th Century

Hard science advances, and the modern ET debate begins.

1853
William Whewell, a Cambridge don, publishes *Plurality of Worlds*, the first scientific argument against the possibility of extraterrestrial life.

1859
British naturalist Charles Darwin publishes his landmark study, *On the Origin of Species*. ET believers hail Darwin's thesis that life adapts to its environment as evidence life can exist almost anywhere.

1895
American astronomer Percival Lowell's book, *Mars*, popularizes belief in intelligent life on the Red Planet.

The 20th Century

The debate over ET becomes more technical and precise.

1920s
New telescope technology disproves Lowell's theories, damaging the pro-ET side's credibility.

1959
Two researchers argue in *Nature* that radio transmissions could detect an alien technological civilization.

1960
American astronomer Frank Drake carries out the first radio-telescope search for extraterrestrial intelligence (SETI). By decade's end, NASA is funding SETI searches.

1975
American astronomer Michael Hart develops theory of the Continuously Habitable Zone, reducing the chances that life may exist elsewhere in the Milky Way galaxy.

1984
SETI Institute is founded in California, and NASA continues to fund radio-astronomy searches; criticism of the program as a wasteful hunt for "little green men" increases.

1993
Congress eliminates federal funding of SETI searches; SETI Institute finds private donors to continue its work.

Mid-to-late 1990s
Astronomers discover the first extra-solar-system planets . . . NASA spacecraft send photographs showing signs of water on one of Jupiter's moons and possibly on Mars. . . . On Earth, researchers examining a meteorite from Mars believe they discover fossils embedded in the rock. . . . Microorganisms known as extremophiles are discovered on Earth. . . . NASA's Origins program begins to search for microbial life in the solar system.

2000s

SETI searches continue, but more carefully.

January 2004
NASA rovers *Spirit* and *Opportunity* land on Mars to take mineralogical samples and transmit the data back to the Jet Propulsion Laboratory in California, where scientists examine it for evidence of liquid water.

March 2, 2004
NASA announces it has solid proof Mars once was "drenched" in water.

2007
The Allen Telescope Array in northern California is slated to become operational, using more than 300 telescopes dedicated to radio searches. SETI proponents say the powerful system offers the best chance yet for success in the search for ET.

Continued from p. 206

He also advanced another principle that remains a fundamental precept for those who believe life exists elsewhere: the notion that nothing about Earth is so special that it cannot be repeated elsewhere.

Lucretius popularized the doctrine of the plurality of worlds throughout the rest of Europe, but for several reasons Aristotelian physics and its model of the universe dominated early Western thinking. For instance, Aristotle's one-world thesis comported more easily with Christianity, while a plurality of worlds raised troubling questions not answered in the Bible.

By the dawn of the Renaissance, Christianity had firmly embraced the idea that God had not only created the Earth as the center of the universe but also, as the *Book of Genesis* suggested, the sole home for life. "Like hand in glove, [the Bible's] human-centered narrative fits snugly into Aristotle's cosmos, in which perfect, untouchable heavens envelop an Earth that is unique, central, separate, stationary and inferior," writes Grinspoon in his latest book. [11]

The first to try peeling the glove off was, of course, Nicolas Copernicus, the Polish astronomer who in the mid-16th century made the radical deduction that the Sun, not Earth, was the center around which everything else turned. A few decades after Copernicus died, the German astronomer Johannes Kepler — genius to some, madman to others — refined Copernican theory by revising the shape of the paths by which Earth and the other planets were thought to orbit the Sun. Copernicus had said they were circular; Kepler said they were elliptical.

For the most part, though, Copernicus and Kepler only offered theory. In the early-17th century, the Italian astronomer Galileo, who despised the Catholic Church, gleefully offered proof. Summoned to appear before the Inquisition, he eventually recanted his views — influenced perhaps by the fate of Giordano Bruno, a defrocked monk who preached Copernican theory along with the existence of multiple worlds and civilizations. Bruno also believed in devil worship and refused to recant anything. The Inquisition had burned him at the stake shortly before bringing Galileo in.

But the church could not stop the spread of Copernican thought, which ultimately led to widespread belief that all the stars were individual suns with their own planets, and that all were inhabited by life of some sort. For instance, in 1644 the French philosopher René Descartes published *Principia Philosophiae*, in which he proposed a schematic of the universe that implied the existence of other heliocentric systems similar to our own.

Getty Images/Spencer Arnold

British naturalist Charles Darwin gave hope to believers in extraterrestrial life in 1859 with his revolutionary theory of evolution. If life on Earth had adapted to its environment, as Darwin wrote in On the Origin of Species, *then perhaps life elsewhere also could adapt to its environment, they reasoned.*

Later in the century, another Frenchman, Bernard le Bovier de Fontenelle published *Conversations on the Plurality of Worlds*, which became a huge international bestseller and was, according to Grinspoon, astonishingly prescient. "Fontanelle predicts spaceflight, discusses the habitability of other planets in our solar system and beyond, and offers vivid descriptions, centuries before the Apollo project, of the Earth as seen from space," Grinspoon says. "It is remarkable how many modern scientific arguments about alien life were anticipated by Fontenelle." [12]

Enlightenment philosophers and scholars enlarged prolifically on the once-heretical notion of life existing elsewhere, publishing during the first half of the 18th century nearly a dozen books arguing in its favor. The methodologies don't all hold up today. For example, a 1735 book posited a formula for calculating the size of aliens relative to the size of their planet. But some observations, like those of the German philosopher Immanuel Kant, were monumental.

An astronomer before becoming a philosopher, Kant was the first to observe that the Milky Way, as we see it, is an optical illusion because of our position within it. He also offered a theory on the origin of planetary systems, which was a precursor of today's current thinking.

Less convincingly, Kant speculated that life existed on all planets in our solar system and that a planet's age and the sophistication of its inhabitants were directly proportional to the planet's distance from the sun. In short, creatures on planets close to the Sun were dumb, while geniuses peopled the outer planets, and Earth's population represented "exactly the middle rung . . . on the ladder of beings." He later retracted that formulation, but he remained a believer in a plurality of inhabited worlds. [13]

The English physicist Sir Isaac Newton tried to link the idea of multiple worlds with Christianity, arguing that if other ordered solar systems existed, it was at the consent or will of God and reflected "the glory, power, and wisdom of the Creator." [14]

But his attempt at reconciling Christianity and the nascent field of hard science was short-lived. In 1793, the influential American political thinker Thomas Paine argued that a plurality of worlds essentially made a mockery of the concept of a messiah. Would Jesus have only come to Earth to save this civilization while ignoring others? Paine asked, or was he traveling from world to world, constantly being reincarnated for "an endless succession of death, with scarcely a momentary interval of life"? [15]

Christianity and multiple worlds with intelligent life, Paine concluded, were fundamentally opposing doctrines, which prompted many 19th-century thinkers to try resurrecting and defending Newton's reconciliation.

But as the West began to industrialize, and science developed increasingly into a rigorous discipline, any religious interpretations or implications concerning the possibility of extraterrestrial life rapidly lost credibility. The modern era of the debate, in which scientific arguments alone mattered, had begun.

From Pluralism to SETI

Two 19th-century books heralded new approaches to the question of whether intelligent life exists beyond Earth.

William Whewell's 1853 book, *Plurality of Worlds*, argued that Earth might be the exception to the rule of an otherwise lifeless universe. Whewell pointed out that all the observable planets had surface conditions vastly different from those on Earth, no other planets orbited other stars and intelligent life on Earth was only a recent phenomenon and thus could not be extrapolated elsewhere with any certainty. [16]

Six years later, the British naturalist Charles Darwin's revolutionary *On the Origin of Species* provided dispirited pluralists with the ammunition they desperately needed. If, as Darwin had just demonstrated, life on Earth had adapted to its environment through natural selection, life elsewhere also could adapt to its environment. So what if conditions on other planets were vastly different from Earth's, or no planets were known to orbit other stars? Life could at least be extrapolated to the other known planets of our solar system.

Empiricism now seemed to be on the side of the pluralists, but they were about to suffer a public-relations disaster. The wealthy American astronomer Percival Lowell was convinced that intelligent life existed on Mars, evidenced by what he claimed to be a visible, elaborate system of canals. He wrote books and lectured on the subject, and the public devoured every word. Increasingly, however, he drew conclusions based on slender evidence, specious reasoning and, mostly, his devout belief. But people still believed him, even after his death in 1916.

Lowell did much to popularize astronomy, and he's considered a pioneer of modern planetary science. But in the 1920s, when stronger telescopes disproved all of his claims, he became an embarrassment and his passionate folly nearly eclipsed the credibility pluralists had gained from Darwin.

True, that credibility was already damaged: Alfred Wallace, who had worked with Darwin on the theory of natural selection, had published a book some years earlier arguing that intelligent life probably existed only on Earth. But Lowell had made the pluralist case in general look like reckless sensationalism. [17]

Wallace's book, *Man's Place in the Universe*, appeared just as pluralists were trying to project a more serious, respectable image. They replaced the term "pluralism" with "the more scientific-sounding 'extraterrestrial life debate,' " Grinspoon notes. And as a result of Wallace's argument, the debate's opposing sides now consisted of biologists who agreed with Wallace about life's uniqueness, and astronomers who believed the overwhelming number of stars argued in favor of life's possible existence elsewhere.

Then came the influential article in *Nature* maintaining that radio astronomy could detect signals from another civilization. Within a year, Drake in West Virginia trained his dish in the direction of the two nearest stars resembling the Sun. He tuned into a frequency and almost immediately heard a strange signal. He questioned — wisely, as it turned out — whether it would be so easy to pick up an alien transmission. Subsequent investigation revealed that he had detected a secret military communications test.

Equations and Paradoxes

Nevertheless, several prominent scientists — including Drake, Sagan and American scientist John Lilly,

How Pop Culture Shapes Alien Images

Both sides of the ET debate agree on one thing: If living creatures exist beyond Earth, it's highly unlikely they will resemble us. Yet the image of a human-like biped seems to be the universal idea of what aliens look like.

Why? Maybe it's the movies. As astrophysicist Neil deGrasse Tyson, director of New York's Hayden Planetarium, told a congressional subcommittee, "Given the diversity of life on Earth, one might expect a diversity of life exhibited among Hollywood aliens. But I am consistently amazed by the film industry's lack of creativity. With a few notable exceptions such as life forms in 'The Blob' and in '2001: A Space Odyssey,' Hollywood aliens look remarkably humanoid. No matter how ugly or cute they are, nearly all of them have two eyes, a nose, a mouth, two ears, a head, a neck, shoulders, arms, hands, fingers, a torso, two legs, two feet, and they can walk. If anything is certain, it is that life elsewhere in the universe, intelligent or otherwise, will look at least as exotic as some of Earth's own life forms." [1]

AFP Photo

ET (left) and the director Steven Spielberg.

But Robert Baker, emeritus professor of psychology at the University of Kentucky and an expert on paranormal psychology, suggests that movies and other forms of entertainment are alternately playing to and reflecting a collective, popular imagination that woefully lacks an understanding of basic scientific principles. The fact that so many people seem to accept a human-like image of aliens is proof, Baker says, that the general public really doesn't comprehend evolution.

"The odds are 99 to 1 that, even if we did have aliens visiting us, they would not resemble human beings because we are products of this planet." Another being would reflect the environment and conditions in which it evolved, and which may not have required anything like hands, fingers or even eyes. "So, this stuff on 'Star Trek' and in movies is what we call psychological projection — projecting our own image onto other creatures so that they all look like us and act like us."

Polls consistently show that people are more willing to believe in unidentified flying objects (UFOs) than in certain tenets of science, because most people tend to interpret the world not through critical scientific understanding but through their simple observations — or, more likely, someone else's, as in the case of alien abductions. [2]

"The idea of alien abduction was actually fomented and encouraged by a lack of understanding of hypnosis," says Baker, author of a book on hypnosis. "Hypnosis has nothing to do with mind control, merely suggestion and what we call conforming behavior on the part of the person being hypnotized."

who'd done groundbreaking research on dolphin intelligence — officially launched the SETI movement. The Drake Equation soon emerged — the first attempt to identify and quantify all the critical factors that could answer the question of how likely intelligent ET life might be.

Factors in the equation included the rate at which stars are born each year, the fraction of those that might have planets, the fraction of planets that might have habitable atmospheres, the fraction of those atmospheres that might have produced life, the fraction of life that might have evolved intelligence, etc. After much discussion, the scientists estimated that at least 10,000 intelligent civilizations could exist in our galaxy.

The groups immediately mounted SETI radio-astronomy projects. None detected anything. Soon, a question that Italian nuclear physicist Enrico Fermi had posed in 1950 started to haunt the SETI community: "If extraterrestrial beings exist, why aren't they here already?"

Fermi's Paradox, as it was called, posited that if Earthlings were about to develop the capability to build space colonies, other technological civilizations probably could, too. Depletion of resources and overcrowding would have most likely caused any civilization to move into space colonies, and as colonies became overcrowded, build others farther out. Even at an extremely slow rate of expansion, the entire galaxy could be colonized in 50 million years — a blink of time in a Milky Way 12 billion years old. The conclusion: Any civilization predating ours would have colonized Earth long ago.

Many accounts of alien abduction allege being taken while asleep, just as victims are waking up to a weird sensation akin to floating out of their bodies, Baker says. "But when people relax and are given suggestions, they have those very sensations," he says. "These are very common physical experiences."

Being hypnotized is identical to certain states of light sleep in which imagination and reality are indistinguishable. "And it's so easy to confuse people, to make them believe that what they dreamed or imagined actually happened," Baker says. "That's why courts don't recognize hypnosis."

Baker blames pop culture for spreading the idea — some say the mass hysteria — that people have been abducted by aliens. "The media have blown up this whole idea of aliens and alien abduction into a gigantic modern myth," Baker says. A culture saturated with reports of alien abductions makes some people believe they've been abducted by aliens, Baker explains.

Can the media really implant so powerful a suggestion? Consider the origin of the phrase "flying saucer." In June 1947, a pilot flying near Washington's Cascade Mountains saw "nine brightly glowing lights, moving in a series of jumps," recounts David Grinspoon, principal scientist in the department of space studies at the Southwest Research Institute. Later, talking to a news reporter, the pilot described the movement of the lights — not their appearance — as "like a saucer if you skip it across water." An Associated Press reporter covering the incident later coined the term "flying saucer," and in the half-century since then, that's how UFOs invariably are described. [3]

And that's understandable, because of media hype, Baker says. "If you look up and see something strange going on in the sky, you can conclude one of three possibilities: An alien spacecraft, and that's most unlikely; something in nature you've never seen before or don't understand, and that's most probable; or three, the Air Force has developed a new kind of aircraft. That, too, is plausible. But because of media influence, everyone jumps on the first one."

AFP Photo

Star Wars' Chewbacca (right) and Princess Leia, played by actress Carrie Fisher.

[1] Testimony before House Science Subcommittee on Space and Aeronautics, July 11, 2001.

[2] For background, see Charles S. Clark, "Pursuing the Paranormal," *The CQ Researcher*, March 29, 1996, pp. 265-288. Also see David Grinspoon, *Lonely Planets: The Natural Philosophy of Alien Life* (2003), p. 331.

[3] *Ibid.*, p. 335.

Believers in the possibility of ET life dismissed Fermi's Paradox, arguing that interstellar travel was too arduous and time-consuming for any intelligent civilization to attempt. (Some even argued that aliens had indeed already come to Earth but did not want to reveal their presence.)

But by the late 1970s, astronomers like Hart were asserting that interstellar travel, while extraordinarily long, was indeed possible and even logical under certain circumstances, putting Fermi's question back on the table. Hart also wrote his highly influential paper on the Continuously Habitable Zone, which drastically reduced the number of intelligent civilizations possible under the Drake Equation.

In 1977 an Ohio State University radio astronomer recorded a strong, 72-second-long signal coming from somewhere within the constellation Sagittarius; it bore no trace of earthly origin. But hundreds of subsequent efforts to detect it again failed, and with no confirmation, the event can only be considered an anomaly at best. In the early 1980s, the SETI Institute was established in California, and some 50 separate SETI projects had recorded nothing but silence.

Congress killed all NASA funding for SETI in 1994, denouncing it as a boondoggle.

While the SETI Institute has survived easily on private funding, its reputation has taken longer to recover. Fortunately, discoveries of planets outside our solar system, of possible water on Europa and Mars, of extremophiles living here on Earth — all in the last few years of the 20th century and the first few of the 21st — have brightened SETI's prospects considerably. ■

CURRENT SITUATION

Astrobiology 'Revolution'

The SETI Institute, as well as the SETI community at large, owes a good deal of its renewed respectability to the relatively recent rise of a quasi-new science called astrobiology. In 1997, NASA officially defined it as the study of the origin, evolution, distribution and destiny of life in the cosmos. [18]

Ward and his colleague at the University of Washington, Donald Brownlee, both doubters of intelligent ET life, acknowledge astrobiology as a "revolution" in that it represented a "convergence of widely different scientific disciplines: astronomy, biology, paleontology, oceanography, microbiology, geology and genetics, among others." [19]

Grinspoon says astrobiology is a reconstituted, rehabilitated and rigorously improved version of exobiology, which for decades "had always survived on the fringes of planetary science." Exobiology — or biological studies of life "out there," as the prefix implies — often had to distance itself from people claiming to have been abducted by UFOs and "X Files"-like conspiracy theorists. "It was fed scraps but made to sleep outside," Grinspoon said. "Reborn as astrobiology, it has rather suddenly been invited inside the main house and embraced as the mascot of our space-science enterprise, receiving official encouragement and generous funding in the bargain." [20]

Since it was founded in 1998, NASA's Astrobiology Institute has seen its budget quadrupled — from $5 million to $20 million. But it currently spends $70 million to $100 million researching the possible existence of life in the universe, depending on how much of other NASA programs' budgets are factored in.

SETI Institute

Frank Drake conducted the first radio-astronomy SETI search, from West Virginia in 1960. His Drake Equation attempted to answer the question of how likely intelligent ET life might be. Drake and other leading scientists, including Carl Sagan, founded the SETI Institute in 1984. Since Drake's pioneering efforts, radio astronomers have tuned in to more than 1,000 nearby stars; all have been utterly silent.

While NASA's extensive astrobiology efforts are mainly looking for microbial life, the question of whether microbial life can evolve into more complex and perhaps intelligent forms is implicit. That, combined with continued favorable National Academy of Sciences evaluations of SETI astrobiology efforts, has helped return SETI at least partly to mainstream acceptance.

Astrobiology is driving NASA's Origins program, the primary goal of which is "to discover whether Earth-like planets exist beyond our solar system and whether any of those planets are habitable or even inhabited by primitive life," said Edward Weiler, NASA's associate administrator for space science. [21]

The space agency is planning at least three such missions over the next decade, beginning in 2006 with what it calls the Kepler mission. The mission is based on the phenomenon known as a "transit." When a distant planet passes in front of the star it orbits, the star's light dims; Kepler is expected to detect upward of 30 planets the size of Earth by looking for these telltale transits.

The Space Interferometry Mission (SIM) scheduled for 2009 will survey 200 nearby stars, looking for any horizontal wobbles that planets, via their gravity, exert on starlight. NASA expects SIM to find at least one or two planets like Earth.

Slated for launch in 2014, the Terrestrial Planet Finder mission is expected to focus on the habitable zone — where temperature ranges could allow for liquid water — surrounding 250 stars. The mission will seek planets within 50 light years of Earth, attempting to make detailed observations of the atmospheres of the most promising candidates. Biologists, atmospheric chemists and geologists will analyze those observations to determine whether it is likely that life exists.

Continued on p. 214

At Issue:

Should the federal government spend more money to search for extraterrestrial intelligence?

JILL TARTER
DIRECTOR, CENTER FOR SETI RESEARCH, SETI INSTITUTE

WRITTEN FOR *THE CQ RESEARCHER*, FEBRUARY 2004

yes

That's like asking me if breathing is a good idea! Of course, the government should fund SETI research, but it shouldn't break the bank in doing so. SETI is a scientific lottery, and nobody knows the odds of success — but the payoff would be extraordinary.

Today's funding level from the federal government: $0. Yet, federal funding is a good idea because:

- It reflects the interest and intentions of the majority of the American public.
- It is an integral part of the newly funded and exciting field of astrobiology within NASA. For an agency that asks, "Are we alone?" as part its strategic framework, NASA would be disingenuous to limit its explorations to the detection of extraterrestrial microbes and not also embrace the detection of extraterrestrial mathematicians.
- Detection, if successful, would compel humans to re-evaluate their place in the universe in a more cosmic context. SETI has been described as the "archeology of the future." A signal, traveling at the speed of light, informs us about "their" past and demonstrates that "our" species has a future as a technology-using civilization.
- Meeting with ET electromagnetically would tend to trivialize the differences among humans, when compared to the biology of a truly "alien" creature. Detection would hold up a mirror forcing humans to see themselves as one species, regardless of color, religion or national origin.
- The universe is vast — even our own Milky Way galaxy contains billions of stars like our own Sun. The search may take a while to succeed (if, in fact, it can). Therefore we have a vested interest in training our replacements.
- The lunar far side is protected by international treaty from transmitters. This is an ideal location for SETI systems but is unaffordable and unreachable with only private, philanthropic funding.
- The past 40 years of searching, which have detected nothing, have been relatively easy and inexpensive. The next steps — which require more sophisticated software and hardware — require more investment, perhaps too much for private philanthropy.
- If SETI is successful, humanity will have to decide whether or not to reply and who will speak for Earth. These questions are political and sociological, not strictly scientific. In the absence of any global governance, many nations should be funding the search efforts, as well as parallel efforts in planning for success.

GUILLERMO GONZALEZ
ASSISTANT RESEARCH PROFESSOR OF ASTRONOMY, IOWA STATE UNIVERSITY

WRITTEN FOR *THE CQ RESEARCHER*, FEBRUARY 2004

no

Scientists requesting federal grants from the National Science Foundation and the National Aeronautics and Space Administration (NASA) must compete with their peers for very limited resources. Each year, only a small fraction of proposals receive funding, and then usually for less than requested. Once funded, researchers must often further compete to use public scientific instruments. If SETI researchers want to compete for the same public dollars and instruments, then they should at least demonstrate that they have a reasonable probability of success.

Have SETI researchers made a convincing case for their programs? To answer this question, we need to appreciate the progress made in astrobiology/exobiology over the past few decades. The modern era of the scientific debate on the question of extraterrestrial intelligence (ETI) began in the early 1960s with two important developments. First, scientists began to consider in a systematic way factors relevant to the existence of intelligent life on a planet, such as the concept of the Circumstellar Habitable Zone. Such factors, when multiplied out, form the so-called Drake Equation, first developed by SETI pioneer Frank Drake. The second major development was Drake's initial attempt to search for radio transmissions by ETI.

Astrobiologists have continued to make much progress on both fronts. Radio surveys have become more sensitive and better able to discriminate against false signals. SETI researchers still maintain that tens of thousands of civilizations in the Milky Way could be transmitting radio signals.

The astronomer Carl Sagan considered only a couple of habitability factors in the 1960s when he famously estimated that a million civilizations exist in the Milky Way. Astrobiologists have since discovered many more factors. The accumulation of these factors has led several prominent scientists — among them Donald Brownlee, Simon Conway Morris, Stuart Ross Taylor, Peter Ward and Stephen Webb — to conclude that Earth-like planets are rare. In my book *The Privileged Planet*, I present an updated version of the Drake Equation and conclude that we are very likely alone in the Milky Way.

In summary, the best current estimates of the probability of ETI in the Galaxy indicate that we are indeed alone. Given this, federal funds should not be spent on SETI programs. This would not end them, however, as they still receive large private donations.

Continued from p. 212

The European Space Agency — also keen on astrobiology — plans to launch its own mission in 2015, called Darwin, to detect the chemical composition of the atmosphere surrounding Earth-like planets.

Meanwhile, the SETI Institute is wrapping up Project Phoenix, which the institute calls "the world's most sensitive and comprehensive search for extraterrestrial intelligence." Designed to listen to approximately 1,000 stars within 200 light years of Earth, Phoenix began in 1995, using a radio telescope in Australia to search the Southern Hemisphere. The following year, to scan the Northern Hemisphere, the project moved to a radio telescope in West Virginia, near the very telescope Drake used when he carried out the first radio search almost 40 years earlier. So far Phoenix has detected nothing.

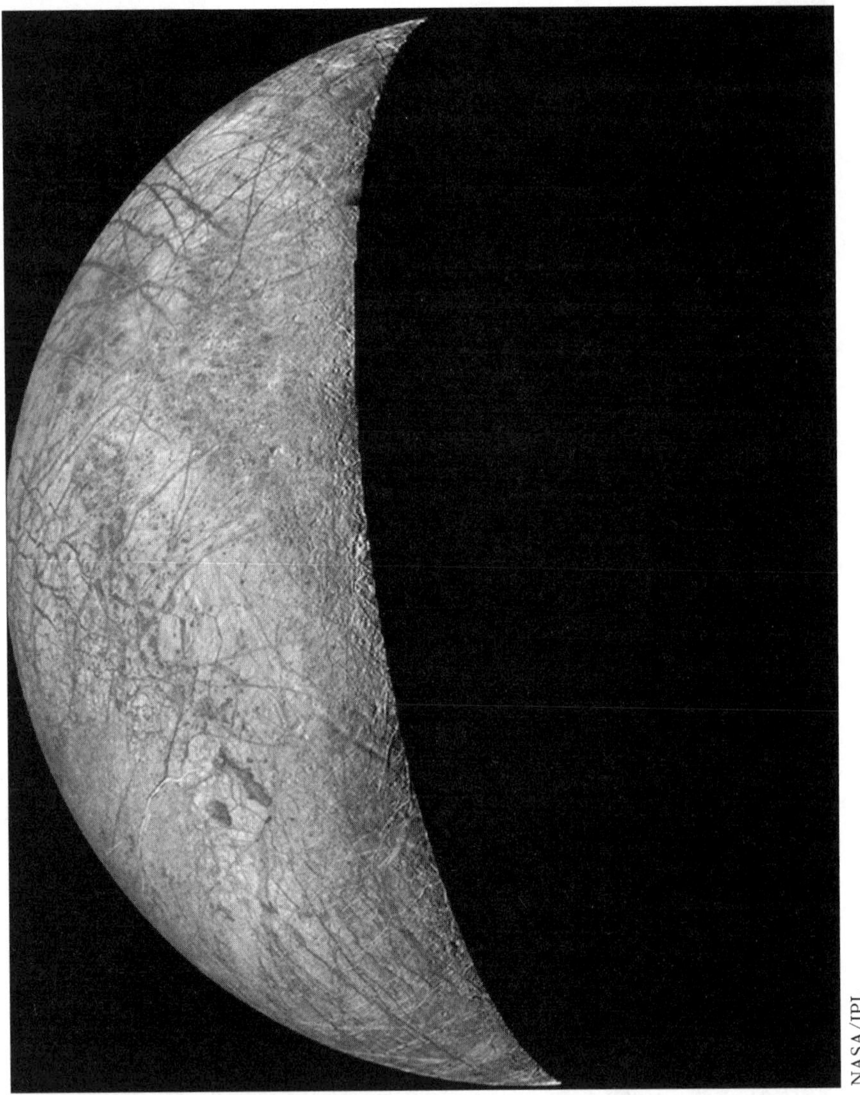
NASA/JPL

Freshwater ice six miles thick in some places is thought to cover Europa, one of Jupiter's four moons. Scientists say icebergs seem to have formed, broken away, floated to another destination and frozen again in place— suggesting a liquid ocean beneath the surface ice. NASA's Galileo *spacecraft made the photograph.*

Shifting Argument

The ET debate is increasingly shifting from arguments about the number of possible ET civilizations to debates over how life began here and whether it can develop elsewhere. Microorganisms are believed to have first appeared on Earth about 4 billion years ago. In the 1950s, scientists came close to determining how life on Earth began, when two researchers placed simple molecules in a pressure vessel containing elements believed common in the early atmosphere. They then charged the vessel with electricity to simulate lightning. Amino acids and sugars — the basic ingredients of life — did form, but life itself did not occur, not then or in repeated attempts. [22]

To the pro-ET community, the experiment demonstrated at the very least that the physical laws and basic elements of the universe favor life, and life has the potential to arise anywhere it possibly can. Skeptics, however, say it requires an enormous leap of faith to assume that something as complicated as DNA — vital to life — could ever assemble itself spontaneously. Hart once calculated those odds as one in 10 to the 30th power, hence his belief that each galaxy likely contains only one habitable planet.

But SETI's Chyba remains undaunted. "We know the galaxy is full of organics," he says. "That's not decisive, I know. But it is encouraging."

Then there's the matter of complex life — the kind with eyes and ears — which has arisen only in the last 540 million years, according to contemporary science. Tulane's Tipler says complex life does not necessarily eventually develop into intelligent life. "There are so many evolutionary pathways life can take, it's more than likely that it will take a path that will not lead to intelligent life," he says.

Contemporary theories on evolution, Tipler says, estimate the chances that single-cell organisms will evolve into intelligent life are "10 to the -1 millionth power," or one chance in 10 to the 1 millionth power. "With 10 to the 22nd stars in the visible universe, assuming every single one has 10 Earth-like planets, that will give you 10 to the 26th chances of possible Earth-like planets where intelligent life can evolve. But 10 to the 26th and 10 to the -1 millionth? That 1 millionth swamps the 26th like a million dollars swamps 26 dollars."

Just because life happened here, does that mean it can happen again? "With a sample of only one," SETI astronomer Tarter says, "it's hard to know what's appropriate to infer." Which is why she insists we must keep looking. ■

OUTLOOK

'Freakish Exception'?

"Tomorrow we could get a signal, or a fleet of flying saucers could land on the White House lawn," George Mason's Trefil says. "Pretty unlikely, though. Things will go on pretty much as they have."

Skeptics believe that the more we search and find nothing, and the more closely we examine the evidence, the numbers continue to shift significantly in their favor. Therefore, they say, don't expect ET to be phoning us any time soon.

For instance, Gonzalez of Iowa State recently reconsidered the Drake Equation by adding in additional factors based on new information, such as his theory that a solar system capable of producing habitable planets must be located within a narrow band of a galaxy. [23] He also included new estimates of the likely effects of deadly gamma-ray bursts, supernovae and giant flares from the host, or Sun-like, star. Figuring in all the new factors, "We arrive at a total number of habitable planets in the Milky Way Galaxy of 0.01. So, the probability that the Milky Way Galaxy contains even one advanced civilization is likely to be much less than one." [24]

How can that be, when we obviously exist? "We are a freakish exception, a rare coincidence," former SETI proponent Hart explains. Yet humans are a coincidence that should come as no surprise, he says, when considering — as the pro-ET side has for more than 2,000 years — the vast numbers of stars and planets that exist. "Given enough tries," he says, "you get very rare coincidences."

Math physicist Tipler agrees. That two such rare coincidences — humans on Earth and intelligent beings on another planet — could occur at or even remotely near the same time is virtually impossible, he says, concluding that the idea of finding or contacting another intelligent civilization is nothing more than "a desperate hope," at least for the next billion years.

Yet neither Drake nor any of his colleagues ever claimed that his equation was anything more than a useful tool for organizing systematic thought about the probability of intelligent life elsewhere. Indeed, his original calculation of 10,000 likely civilizations was never meant to be infallible or immutable. Like his supporters, Drake — now president of the SETI Institute — has been encouraged by the discoveries of the last decade, "all of which add up to life probably being even more prolific than we imagined it 40 years ago," he says.

But he doubts confirmation of that will arrive anytime soon. "We can't predict with any certainty what kind of technology another civilization might have," Drake says. "We've seen our own technology change substantially in the last 40 years. What about in 100 or 1,000 years?"

In other words, future SETI searches might best be carried out with technologies not yet invented. "We'll get an answer about whether there's intelligent life out there. That's easy to say. The hard thing to say is how much searching it's going to take."

The SETI Institute's Chyba thinks scientists will get at least some answers soon. "Because of the Kepler mission, we'll know whether or not this is really a rare Earth by the end of the decade," he says. "We'll understand a lot more about the history of water on Mars, too, from the rover missions."

But he expects more information from the Allen Telescope Array, expected to be fully operational in 2007, and its search of possibly a million stars.

"It may be that Earth is unique," Chyba says. "I'd be surprised by that outcome, but that's possible. Those of us involved in the search for life elsewhere, we'd just like to know whether we're alone. And there's only one way to find out." ■

About the Author

William Triplett recently joined the *CQ Researcher* as a staff writer after covering science and the arts for such publications as *Smithsonian, Air & Space, Nature, Washingtonian* and *The Washington Post.* He also served as associate editor of *Capitol Style* magazine. He holds a B.A. in journalism from Ohio University and an M.A. in English literature from Georgetown University.

Notes

[1] David Koerner and Simon LeVay, *Here Be Dragons: The Scientific Quest for Extraterrestrial Life* (2000), p. 5.

[2] For background, see Mary H. Cooper, "Space Program's Future," *The CQ Researcher*, April 25, 1997, pp. 361-384; and David Masci, "NASA's Future," *The CQ Researcher*, May 23, 2003, pp. 473-496.

[3] Testimony before House Science Subcommittee on Space and Aeronautics, July 11, 2001.

[4] See David Grinspoon, *Lonely Planets: The Natural Philosophy of Alien Life* (2003), p. 186.

[5] See G. Cocconi and P. Morrison, "Searching for an Interstellar Connection," *Nature*, No. 184 (1959), p. 844.

[6] *Life in the Universe: An Assessment of U.S. and International Programs in Astrobiology* (2003), National Academy of Sciences.

[7] See William Triplett, "Search for Alien Life Reasserts its Credibility," *Nature*, July 19, 2001, p. 260.

[8] *Ibid.*

[9] Steven J. Dick, *Life on Other Worlds: The 20th-Century Extraterrestrial Life Debate* (1998), p. 8.

[10] *Ibid.*

[11] Grinspoon, *op. cit.*, p. 15.

[12] *Ibid.*, p. 22.

[13] *Ibid.*, p. 29.

[14] Dick, *op. cit.*, p. 14.

[15] *Ibid.*, p. 16.

[16] Grinspoon, *op. cit.*, p. 35.

[17] *Ibid.*, pp. 39-40.

[18] Testimony before House Science Subcommittee on Space and Aeronautics, July 11, 2001.

[19] Peter D. Ward and Donald Brownlee, *Rare Earth: Why Complex Life is Uncommon in the Universe* (2000), p. xv.

[20] Grinspoon, *op. cit.*, pp. 238-239.

[21] House Science Subcommittee on Space and Aeronautics, *op. cit.*

[22] Gregg Easterbrook, "Are We Alone?" *The Atlantic Monthly*, August 1988, p. 25.

[23] Guillermo Gonzalez and Jay W. Richards, *The Privileged Planet: How Our Place in the Cosmos is Designed for Discovery* (2004), Appendix A, "The Revised Drake Equation;" also see Charles Lineweaver, Yeshe Fenner and Brad K. Gibson, "The Galactic Habitable Zone and the Age Distribution of Complex Life in Our Galaxy," *Science*, Jan. 2, 2004, p. 59.

[24] Gonzalez and Richards, *op. cit.*

FOR MORE INFORMATION

American Astronomical Society, 2000 Florida Ave., N.W., Suite 400, Washington, DC 20009; (202) 328-2010; www.aas.org. The major professional organization for astronomers.

Arecibo Observatory, HC3 Box 53995, Arecibo, PR 00612; (787) 878-2612; www.naic.edu. World's largest radio telescope.

Astronomical Society of the Pacific, 390 Ashton Ave., San Francisco, CA 94112; (415) 337-1100; www.astrosociety.org. An international, nonprofit organization founded in 1889 specializing in astronomy education.

Jet Propulsion Laboratory, 4800 Oak Grove Dr., Pasadena, CA 91109; (818); 354-4321; www.jpl.nasa.gov/index.html. JPL undertakes the robotic exploration of the solar system for NASA. The JPL Web site offers extensive information about current and forthcoming missions.

NASA Astrobiology Institute, Ames Research Center, Moffett Field, CA 94035; (650) 604-0809; www.nai.arc.nasa.gov. Studies possibility of life in the universe.

NASA Center for Mars Exploration, cmex-www.arc.nasa.gov/CMEX/index.html. Information resource for teachers and students.

National Radio Astronomy Observatory, 520 Edgemont Rd., Charlottesville, VA 22903; (434) 296-0211; www.nrao.edu. Designs, builds and operates radio telescopes.

Planetary Society, 65 North Catalina Ave., Pasadena, CA 91106; (626) 793-5100; www.planetary.org. A nonprofit membership group founded in 1980 by the astronomer Carl Sagan and others to encourage the exploration of the solar system and the search for extraterrestrial life.

SETI Institute, 2035 Landings Dr., Mountain View, CA 94043; (650) 961-6633; www.seti.org. A nonprofit founded in 1984 and dedicated to exploring for life in the universe.

SETI@Home, http://setiathome.ssl.berkeley.edu. Available only online, this scientific experiment uses Internet-connected personal computers to help analyze data acquired in SETI radio-astronomy searches.

SETI League, P.O. Box 555, Little Ferry, NJ 07643; (201) 641-1770; www.setileague.org. Grassroots organization scanning electromagnetic spectrum for signs of life.

Bibliography

Selected Sources

Books

Dick, Steven J., *Life on Other Worlds: The 20th-Century Extraterrestrial Life Debate*, Cambridge University Press, 1998.
An astronomer and science historian explores the historical antecedents of all the major themes and issues in the extraterrestrial life debate.

Grinspoon, David, *Lonely Planets: The Natural Philosophy of Alien Life*, Ecco/Harper Collins, 2003.
An astrobiologist and professor of astrophysical and planetary sciences views Western society, evolution and science through the long history of the extraterrestrial life debate.

Koerner, David, and Simon LeVay, *Here Be Dragons: The Scientific Quest for Extraterrestrial Life*, Oxford University Press, 2000.
An astronomer and a biologist review the works of cosmologists, biologists, NASA engineers, computer theorists, UFO believers and debunkers and conclude that the universe is suited to the evolution of other living creatures.

Sagan, Carl, with new material from Freeman Dyson, Ann Druyan and David Morrison, *Carl Sagan's Cosmic Connection: An Extraterrestrial Perspective*, Cambridge University Press, 2000.
This update of Sagan's seminal *The Cosmic Connection* (1973) elaborates on virtually all matters astronomical, from solar system science and astrophysics to colonizing other worlds and the search for extraterrestrials.

Ward, Peter D., and Donald Brownlee, *Rare Earth: Why Complex Life is Uncommon in the Universe*, Copernicus, 2000.
A geologist and an astronomer question many of the assumptions of the pro-ET community, arguing that while life probably does exist elsewhere, it is extremely unlikely to be advanced or intelligent.

Articles

Easterbrook, Gregg, "Are We Alone?" *The Atlantic Monthly*, August 1988, p. 25.
A journalist chronicles modern efforts to answer the question and the implications of each.

Overbye, Dennis, "Where Are Those Aliens?" *The New York Times*, Nov. 11, 2003, p. 15.
Overbye recounts the Fermi Paradox and what contemporary SETI supporters say to counter it.

Triplett, William, "Search for Alien Life Reasserts its Credibility," *Nature*, July 19, 2001, p. 260.
The SETI movement appears to be regaining credibility with Congress, which eight years earlier had cut off all federal funding for SETI radio-astronomy searches.

Triplett, William, "SETI Takes the Hill," *Air & Space/Smithsonian*, October-November, 1992, p. 80.
An account of the SETI Institute's relationship with Congress and NASA.

Vergano, Dan, "Is There Another Earth Out There?" *USA Today*, June 4, 2003, p. 1A.
A detailed look at NASA's forthcoming missions seeking other planets in our galaxy.

Wilford, John Noble, "Mars Rovers in Quest for Holy Grail: Signs of Water," *The New York Times*, Jan. 11, 2004, p. A18.
Scientists from around the world await data transmitted by the rovers on Mars, hoping to determine whether the Martian surface once flowed with water and thus perhaps supported life.

Reports and Studies

Alexander, Amir, "The Search for Extraterrestrial Intelligence: A Short History," 2001, The Planetary Society, www.planetary.org/html/UPDATES/seti/history/History00.htm.
The author provides an overview of the SETI movement's beginnings, evolution and scientific rationale.

Dressler, Alan, "About Origins," National Aeronautics and Space Administration, 2003, http://origins.jpl.nasa.gov/about/index.html.
This detailed brief on NASA's Origins program includes a description of individual missions that will search for signs of life.

National Academy of Sciences, "Life in the Universe: An Assessment of U.S. and International Programs in Astrobiology," Chapter 6: SETI and Astrobiology, (2003).
The academy reviews important astrobiology programs, and describes the SETI Institute's radio-astronomy efforts and its astrobiology research as solid and worthy.

U.S. House of Representatives, 107th Congress, "Life in the Universe," Hearing, Subcommittee on Space and Aeronautics, Committee on Science, July 11, 2001.
Extensive written and oral testimony from a lengthy hearing on the state of research surrounding the question of whether life exists elsewhere is available at http://www.house.gov/science/hearings/index.htm.

The Next Step:

Additional Articles from Current Periodicals

Earth's Extremophiles

Chang, Kenneth, "From Lake's Depths, Frozen Bacteria Are Brought Back to Life," *The New York Times*, Dec. 24, 2002, p. F3.

Deep in the ice of Antarctica's Lake Vida, scientists have thawed and revived microbes frozen 2,800 years ago.

Lemonick, Michael, and Andrea Dorfman, "How Life Began," *Time*, July 29, 2002, p. 42.

Discoveries of life on Earth that can survive in ice or on a diet of nothing but "heat and poison" have implications for the possible nature of extraterrestrial life.

Perlman, David, "From Outer Space to Inner Earth," *San Francisco Chronicle*, Sept. 1, 2003, p. A4.

A biologist at NASA's Astrobiology Institute searches Mono Lake in California for extremophiles like the ones that may be living on the moons of Jupiter or Saturn.

Spotts, Peter, "Life at the Extremes," *The Christian Science Monitor*, May 6, 2003, p. 18.

Biologists are eager to learn more about the vast numbers of terrestrial microbes that live under extreme conditions, the so-called extremophiles.

Life in Our Solar System

McFarling, Usha, "Life on Jupiter Moon Likely on Thin (or Thick) Ice," *Los Angeles Times*, May 23, 2002, p. A12.

Observations of Europa indicate that its icy crust could be 12 miles thick; any probe would be hard-pressed to penetrate to the oceans below.

McFarling, Usha, "Searching for Signs of a Wet Mars," *Los Angeles Times*, June 6, 2003, p. A1.

The 19th-century astronomer Percival Lowell thought he saw canals on Mars; although there are no canals, new probes are beaming back pictures that show evidence of once-flowing water.

Morton, Oliver, "Don't Ignore the Planet Next Door," *Science*, Nov. 29, 2002, p. 1706.

Venus is usually thought a dim prospect for life, but some scientists argue life on Venus may simply be very different from life on Earth.

Perlman, David, "Search for Extraterrestrial Life Moves to Forefront," *San Francisco Chronicle*, Dec. 15, 2003, p. A4.

NASA has redoubled its efforts in recent years to explore the solar system for signs that life exists or has existed outside Earth.

Sawyer, Kathy, "Cutting-Edge Research on the Red Planet," *The Washington Post*, Feb. 8, 2004, p. A15.

Spirit and *Opportunity*, NASA's rovers, are drilling and driving their way across the Martian surface in a search for evidence of water.

Spotts, Peter, "Hello? Anybody Out There?" *The Christian Science Monitor*, May 13, 2003, p. 18.

Scientists plan to send "cryobots" to bore through Europa's crust aboard a large spacecraft called *JIMO*, to be launched in 2011.

Wilford, John, "Looking for a Little Life, 3 Visitors Descend on Mars," *The New York Times*, Dec. 23, 2003, p. F1.

Taking advantage of Mars' closest approach to Earth in millennia, Earthlings sent three craft to the Martian surface to look for signs of life.

Newly Discovered Planets

Harwood, William, "Solar System Akin to Earth's Is Discovered," *The Washington Post*, June 14, 2002, p. A3.

The star known as 55 Cancri may have planets orbiting it in a pattern similar to that of our own solar system.

Heinrichs, Allison, "Distant Solar System Resembles Ours," *Los Angeles Times*, July 3, 2003, p. A24.

Observers using the "Doppler Wobble" technique discovered a solar system with gas giants, but which do not intrude into the space where an Earth-type planet would be.

Kluger, Jeffrey, "A Sister Solar System?" *Time*, June 24, 2002, p. 53.

Our solar system's unique place in the cosmos erodes even further with the discovery of a planet whose location and characteristics make its solar system seem like home.

Monastersky, Richard, "Astronomers Have Found Dozens of Giant Worlds, but They're Really Looking for Something More Like Home," *The Chronicle of Higher Education*, Feb. 15, 2002, p. 20.

Most extra-solar planets observed have been positioned to interfere with an Earth-like planet; but the transit method of observation will make the search easier.

Sawyer, Kathy, "Scientists Discover Planetary Patriarch," *The Washington Post*, July 11, 2003, p. A1.

Almost 13 billion years old, life could have arisen and then died out on a planet orbiting a binary star system, the only planet known in such a system.

Spotts, Peter, "Planet Hunters," *The Christian Science Monitor*, Oct. 24, 2002, p. 11.

Astronomy enthusiasts with backyard equipment are looking for planets around other stars — and finding them.

Vergano, Dan, "Is There Another Earth Out There?" *USA Today*, June 4, 2003, p. 1A.
Improved astronomical techniques and equipment, coupled with scientists' redoubled efforts, cause optimism that an Earth-like planet will soon be found.

Vergano, Dan, "A Planetary Discovery of Astronomical Magnitude," *USA Today*, Jan. 7, 2003, p. 7D.
Researchers detect the first extra-solar planet using the transit method, which measures a star's dimming as a planet passes between the star and Earth.

Wilford, John Noble, "New Method Detects Planet Very Distant," *The New York Times*, Jan. 7, 2003, p. A14.
Some 8,000 light years from Earth, scientists have located a planet closer to its sun than any other, so hot that it likely rains molten iron.

Search for ET Intelligence

Bridges, Andrew, "Are We Alone? SETI Listens for Answer," *The Washington Post*, Sept. 21, 2003, p. A5.
Despite a high level of public interest in extraterrestrial life, the funding and number of people engaged in the search have never been high.

Oleck, Joan, "Getting More From a PC's Spare Time," *The New York Times*, Sept. 11, 2003, p. G5.
Millions of people volunteer their PC's spare processing power to a variety of causes, including the search for life among the stars.

Overbye, Dennis, "NASA Presses Its Search for Extraterrestrial Life," *The New York Times*, June 4, 2002, p. F1.
The Astrobiology Institute, established by NASA, provides an opportunity for physicists, astronomers and biologists to discuss the possible nature of alien life.

Overbye, Dennis, "Search for Life Out There Gains Respect, Bit by Bit," *The New York Times*, July 8, 2003, p. F1.
Once scorned, the SETI Institute won a five-year grant from NASA as a lead team in its Astrobiology Institute.

Overbye, Dennis, "Where Are Those Aliens?" *The New York Times*, Nov. 11, 2003, p. F15.
Enrico Fermi first asked the question: If extraterrestrial life exists, why haven't we heard from them by now?

Perlman, David, "U.C. Researchers Hope to Tap ET's Home Phone," *San Francisco Chronicle*, March 12, 2003, p. A1.
UC-Berkeley scientists identify the first 150 bursts of radio noise to be analyzed for evidence that it might be a signal from extraterrestrial intelligence.

Petit, Charles, "An Ear for ET," *U.S. News & World Report*, June 23, 2003, p. 46.
The Allen Telescope Array, comprising 350 antenna dishes, will be able to scan broad swaths of the sky for possible extraterrestrial transmissions.

Vergano, Dan, "Oceans Suggest Life Beyond," *USA Today*, April 28, 2003, p. 6D.
Scientists speculate that water is extremely abundant in the universe; finding oceans is likely to be a key step in finding life.

Vergano, Dan, "Searching for Signs of ET Life in the Universe," *USA Today*, March 19, 2002, p. 1D.
Engineers are designing space probes to detect potential signs of life, including ozone and nitrous oxide, byproducts of living things.

CITING *THE CQ RESEARCHER*

Sample formats for citing these reports in a bibliography include the ones listed below. Preferred styles and formats vary, so please check with your instructor or professor.

MLA STYLE

Jost, Kenneth. "Rethinking the Death Penalty." The CQ Researcher 16 Nov. 2001: 945-68.

APA STYLE

Jost, K. (2001, November 16). Rethinking the death penalty. *The CQ Researcher, 11*, 945-968.

CHICAGO STYLE

Jost, Kenneth. "Rethinking the Death Penalty." *CQ Researcher*, November 16, 2001, 945-968.

Back Issues

The CQ Researcher *offers in-depth coverage of many key areas.*
Back issues are $10. Quantity discounts available.
Call (866) 427-7737 to order back issues.

Or call for a free CQ Researcher Web trial!
Online access provides:

- *Searchable archives dating back to 1991.*
- *Wider access through IP authentication.*
- *PDF files for downloading and printing.*
- *Availability 48 hours before print version.*

CIVIL LIBERTIES
Race in America, July 2003
Gay Marriage, September 2003
Civil Liberties Debates, October 2003

CRIME/LAW
Cyber-Crime, April 2002
Corporate Crime, October 2002
Serial Killers, October 2003

ECONOMY
State Budget Crises, October 2003
Stock Market Troubles, January 2004
Exporting Jobs, February 2004

EDUCATION
Home Schooling Debate, January 2003
Combating Plagiarism, September 2003
Black Colleges, December 2003

ENERGY/TRANSPORTATION
Future of the Airline Industry, June 2002
Future of Amtrak, October 2002
SUV Debate, May 2003

ENVIRONMENT
Crisis in the Plains, May 2003
Water Shortages, August 2003
Air Pollution Conflict, November 2003

HEALTH AND SAFETY
Medicare Reform, August 2003
Women's Health, November 2003
Homeopathy Debate, December 2003

POLITICS AND PUBLIC POLICY
Abortion Debates, March 2003
State Budget Crises, October 2003
Democracy in the Arab World, January 2004

SOCIAL TRENDS
Latinos' Future, October 2003
Future of the Music Industry, Nov. 2003

TECHNOLOGY
NASA's Future, May 2003

TERRORISM/DEFENSE
Homeland Security, September 2003
North Korean Crisis, April 2003

WORLD AFFAIRS
Rebuilding Iraq, July 2003
Aiding Africa, August 2003
The U.N. and Global Security, Feb. 2004

YOUTH
Preventing Teen Drug Use, March 2002
Sexual Abuse and the Clergy, May 2002
Movie Ratings, March 2003
Hazing, January 2004
Youth Suicide, February 2004

Future Topics

▶ ***Redistricting Debate***

▶ ***Reforming College Sports***

▶ ***Human Trafficking***

CQ Researcher

Published by CQ Press, a division of Congressional Quarterly Inc.

thecqresearcher.com

Redistricting Disputes

Should the courts limit partisan gerrymandering?

Disputes over partisan redistricting, or gerrymandering, date back to the nation's earliest days, and the once-a-decade process was as contentious as ever following the 2000 census. New computer technology now gives map drawers unprecedented precision to make districts nearly impregnable by stuffing them with party loyalists. Republican-drawn maps in some key states helped the GOP gain House seats in the 2002 midterm congressional elections, which saw significantly less turnover than in similar elections during the last 30 years. Then, in an unusual move, Republicans re-opened the redistricting process in Colorado and Texas, prompting the Democrats to try to get mid-decade re-mappings declared unconstitutional. The Supreme Court also is considering a case that could set some limits on partisan gerrymandering. Some citizens' groups say that using independent bodies to redraw the maps would ensure partisan fairness, competitiveness and stability.

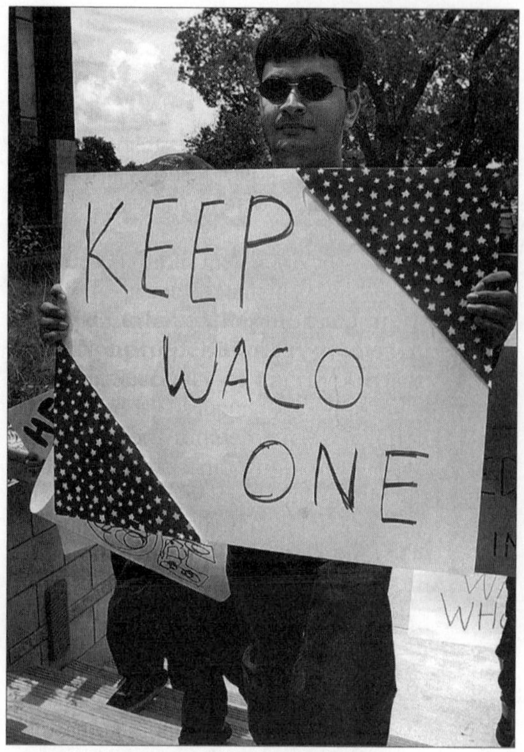

A Waco, Texas, resident opposes a congressional redistricting plan proposed last year by the state's Republicans.

INSIDE

THIS ISSUE

The CQ Researcher • March 12, 2004 • www.thecqresearcher.com
Volume 14, Number 10 • Pages 221-248

CQ Press

Recipient of Society of Professional Journalists Award for Excellence ◆ American Bar Association Silver Gavel Award

Cover: A Waco, Texas, resident opposes a congressional redistricting plan proposed last year by the state's Republicans. Despite opposition from Democrats, Republican lawmakers in Texas last year redrew the state's districts. (AP Photo/ *Waco Tribune-Herald*, Duane A. Laverty)

March 12, 2004
Volume 14, No. 10

MANAGING EDITOR: Thomas J. Colin

ASSISTANT MANAGING EDITOR: Kathy Koch

ASSOCIATE EDITOR: Kenneth Jost

STAFF WRITERS: Mary H. Cooper, David Masci, William Triplett

CONTRIBUTING WRITERS: Sarah Glazer, David Hatch, David Hosansky, Patrick Marshall, Tom Price, Jane Tanner

DESIGN/PRODUCTION EDITOR: Olu B. Davis

ASSISTANT EDITOR: Kenneth Lukas

CQ PRESS

A Division of Congressional Quarterly Inc.

SENIOR VICE PRESIDENT/GENERAL MANAGER: John A. Jenkins

DIRECTOR, LIBRARY PUBLISHING: Kathryn C. Suárez

DIRECTOR, EDITORIAL OPERATIONS: Ann Davies

CIRCULATION MANAGER: Nina Tristani

CONGRESSIONAL QUARTERLY INC.

CHAIRMAN: Andrew Barnes

VICE CHAIRMAN: Andrew P. Corty

PRESIDENT AND PUBLISHER: Robert W. Merry

The CQ Researcher (ISSN 1056-2036) is printed on acid-free paper. Published weekly, except Jan. 2, April 9, July 2, July 9, Aug. 6, Aug. 13, Nov. 26 and Dec. 31, by CQ Press, a division of Congressional Quarterly Inc. Annual subscription rates for libraries, businesses and government start at $625. Single issues are available for $10. Quantity discounts apply to orders over 10. Additional rates furnished upon request. Periodicals postage paid at Washington, D.C., and additional mailing offices. POSTMASTER: Send address changes to *The CQ Researcher*, 1255 22nd St., N.W., Suite 400, Washington, D.C. 20037.

Redistricting Disputes

BY KENNETH JOST

THE ISSUES

Martin Frost knows redistricting. The long-time Democratic congressman from Dallas-Fort Worth helped state lawmakers draw a congressional districting map in the early 1990s that gave Democrats control of Texas' delegation in the U.S. House of Representatives for a decade. Critics called the artfully drawn map a blatant "gerrymander."

During the 2001-2002 redistricting cycle, Frost had a chance to really help Democrats — as leader of the party's efforts to reshape congressional districts across the country.

But last year, Texas Republicans decided it was time to teach Frost a lesson about redistricting he would never forget. Aided by two other redistricting pros from Texas — House Majority Leader Rep. Tom DeLay and President Bush's top political adviser, Karl Rove — they redrew congressional districts so artfully that GOP congressional candidates could win 22 of the state's 32 House seats this November. [1]

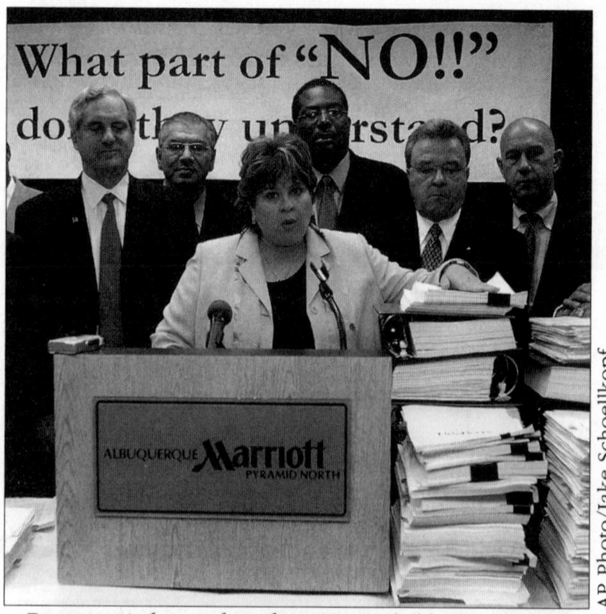

AP Photo/Jake Schoellkopf

Democratic lawmakers from Texas, led by Sen. Leticia Van de Putte, display voter mail last summer opposing redistricting plans that could give Republicans 22 of the state's 32 House seats this November. Democratic lawmakers staged an exodus from the state last summer in an unsuccessful effort to block voting on the new boundaries. Redistricting normally occurs every 10 years, but Texas and Colorado Republicans regained control of their legislatures and decided to redistrict mid-decade.

As for Frost, his once-safe 24th District was decimated, its loyal Democratic voters in Fort Worth's Hispanic and African-American neighborhoods dispersed. Frost decided his best bet to win a 14th term this year would be to move to another district. He set his sights on the new, east-of-Dallas 32nd District and Rep. Pete Sessions — a four-term, conservative incumbent. The campaign is likely to be one of the most expensive, closely watched House contests this fall.

Frost avoids accusing the Republicans of singling him out. "I think they were trying to eliminate as many Democrats as possible," he says. "I happened to be one of the many Democrats that they were targeting."

For his part, Sessions says he is "surprised" that Frost decided to run against him, but adds, "I welcome him, red carpet rolled out. It won't be easy." [2]

Frost is among more than a half-dozen House Democrats who were thrown into new districts against each other or against Republican incumbents or stripped of large segments of their old constituencies. Meanwhile, Republicans in several safe districts shed some of their voters to aid the party's chances in others.

What happened in Texas could determine whether the Democrats regain control of the House next year. The new Texas map (*see p. 238*) could shift the state's House delegation from its current 16-16 partisan balance to a GOP margin as wide as 22-10. A six- or seven-vote pickup for the Republicans would all but dash Democrats' already slim hope of regaining control of the House in November.

Republicans make no secret of their partisan motivations, but insist they were merely trying to bring the state's congressional delegation into line with Republican dominance throughout the state.

"We increased the number of Republican-opportunity districts to reflect the voting trend in the state of Texas," says Andy Taylor, a Houston attorney who represents the state in defending the redistricting plan in federal court. "We undid a Democratic gerrymander instead of creating a Republican gerrymander. We brought balance back to the districts because of the partisan shift in the way Texas voters vote."

But Democrats insist the GOP plan is indeed a partisan gerrymander and should be struck down. "The sole motivation of the Texas plan was to maximize partisan advantage, to discriminate against nearly half of the voters on the basis of their political affiliation," says Sam Hirsch, a Washington attorney representing Democrats challenging the plan. "This map is designed to lock down 22 out of 32 seats for the Republicans for the rest of the decade."

The bitter redistricting fight came after most observers thought the rough-and-tumble game of redrawing congressional district maps — which normally occurs every 10 years after a new census is released — was over until 2011. [3] But after gaining control of their state legislatures in 2002, Republicans in Texas and Colorado decided to revisit the task anew. GOP

Continued on p. 225

GOP-Drawn Map Threatens Texas Democrats

Texas' new congressional redistricting plan, adopted by a Republican-controlled legislature, put 10 incumbent House Democrats in new, politically less favorable districts. One Democrat decided not to seek re-election, and another switched parties; the others are all running for new terms.

Democratic U.S. House member	Term	New political situation
Martin Frost	13th	Old Dallas-Fort Worth district carved up; seeking re-election in new 32nd District against four-term Republican.
Charles W. Stenholm	13th	Senior Agriculture Committee member lost two-thirds of his old Central/West Texas district; running against freshman Republican in 69 percent GOP district.
Ralph M. Hall	12th	Longtime conservative switched to GOP after more Republicans added to East Texas district.
Chet Edwards	7th	Lost major parts of his Central Texas district; new district is 64 percent GOP.
Gene Green	6th	Anglo representing Hispanic-majority Houston district; new district more Hispanic; ran unopposed for renomination in March 9 primary.
Lloyd Doggett	5th	Liberal representative from Austin; new district, heavily Hispanic, stretches to Mexican border; easily won renomination over Hispanic opponent in March 9 primary.
Max Sandlin	4th	East Texas district is 63 percent Republican, with 40 percent of previous constituency.
Jim Turner	4th	Old district virtually eliminated; Turner decided not to run.
Nick Lampson	4th	Lost major parts of his Houston suburban district.
Chris Bell	1st	White freshman elected from mixed Houston district redrawn into majority-black district; Bell lost bid for renomination against black opponent in March 9 primary.

Source: Politics in America 2004 *(CQ Press)*

Legislators Redraw Most Congressional Districts

In 40 states, the legislature or governor redraws new district lines, but the legislators have the final say. In three states, redistricting panels draw the maps and submit them to the legislatures for approval. In seven states, special commissions control both drawing and approving the maps. Seven low-population states have only one congressional district, so they do not regularly go through the process. ** A significantly larger number of states use independent commissions to redraw state legislative district lines.*

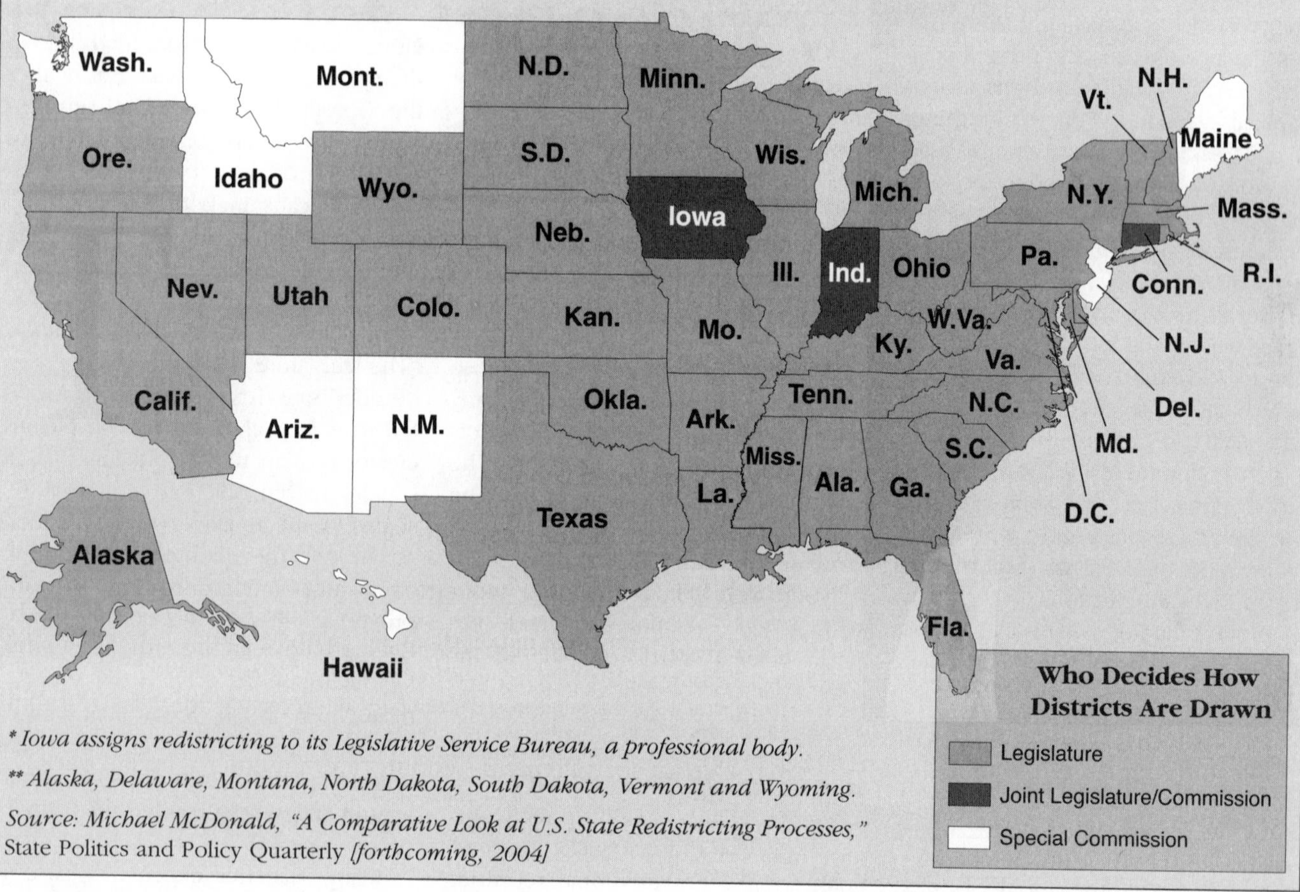

** Iowa assigns redistricting to its Legislative Service Bureau, a professional body.*

*** Alaska, Delaware, Montana, North Dakota, South Dakota, Vermont and Wyoming.*

Source: Michael McDonald, "A Comparative Look at U.S. State Redistricting Processes," State Politics and Policy Quarterly *[forthcoming, 2004]*

Continued from p. 223

leaders in both states insisted they acted because their legislatures had deadlocked on redistricting in 2001, forcing courts to draw the districting plans used in the 2002 elections.

The unusual maneuver prompted Democrats — and many political observers — to say that redistricting is, or should be, allowed only once every 10 years. But Republicans and some academic experts say the Constitution's command to reapportion House seats among the states every 10 years based on census revisions does not limit redistricting to once per decade. Moreover, they say, mid-cycle remappings are more frequent than critics acknowledge.

One thing is certain: Redistricting can mean political life or death.

"It's no secret why everybody fights so hard," says Mark Braden, a Washington attorney for the Republican National Committee. "How you draw the lines has a huge impact on who sits in legislative chambers."

"You can devise districts in such a way that you can not only predict the outcome of the next election but also how they're going to perform in a series of elections over a decade," says Gerald Hebert, a Washington-area lawyer for Democrats. "You can actually rig elections in such a way that you can produce an electoral outcome almost regardless of what happens on Election Day."

Fights over redistricting date back to the nation's earliest days, but they have become more complex since the Supreme Court launched the reapportionment revolution in the 1960s, requiring the states to draw congressional and legislative districts with roughly equal populations.

The high court introduced a new measure of complexity in the 1990s by limiting the use of race to create districts with majority-black or Hispanic populations. (*See box, p. 228.*)

Now the court is considering a constitutional challenge that could fundamentally alter redistricting. Pennsylvania Democrats argue the Republican-written congressional redistricting plan is unconstitutional because it gerrymanders on political — rather than population or racial — grounds. Republicans gained a 12-7 majority in Pennsylvania's congressional delegation under the new map. The court heard arguments in the case on Dec. 10, 2003. The case is *Vieth v. Jubelirer*, 02-1580.

Meanwhile, courts in Colorado and Texas were asked to announce a "once-per-decade" rule to strike down the new GOP redistricting plans. Democrats won in Colorado but failed with a similar argument in Texas. Democrats are appealing to the Supreme Court, but the justices refused to issue a stay — meaning the new map will be used for the Nov. 2 elections.

Political map-drawing is all the more intense today because of computers. "Partisan gerrymandering is becoming easier because of the sophistication of the technology," says Nathaniel Persily, a law professor and redistricting expert at the University of Pennsylvania. Using detailed census maps with racial and ethnic breakdowns and past election results, redistricters can customize a district neighborhood by neighborhood — even block by block.

Moreover, Persily says, "partisan preferences are more stable" today. Predictable voting patterns allow redistricters to use two common techniques for partisan advantage. "Packing" a rival party's voters into overly safe districts gives one's own party a better shot in others, while "cracking" a rival party's voters — dispersing them into several districts — can make the targeted district politically competitive for the party drawing the lines.

Some citizens' groups — such as Common Cause and the League of Women Voters — say that if independent bodies redrew the maps, partisan wrangling would be reduced and political competition enhanced. The Center for Voting and Democracy, in Takoma Park, Md., advocates replacing the single-member, winner-take-all system of congressional and legislative districts with some form of proportional or cumulative voting in multimember districts. Although voters would probably show little interest, politicians would probably adamantly resist either change. (*See sidebar, p. 227.*)

Meanwhile, some academics say redistricting is not really a big problem. "The political system does recover," says Mark Rush, a professor of political science at Washington and Lee University in Lexington, Va. Over time, voting behavior changes, incumbents retire and new candidates emerge, he says. "Elections go back and forth. The system works."

As redistricting cases work their way through the courts, and redistricting issues continue to divide political parties, here are some of the major questions being debated:

Should states redraw congressional district lines in the middle of a decade?

When Colorado's legislature deadlocked on a congressional redistricting plan in 2002, a federal court redrew the maps that were used for the seven House races that November. The result was a GOP-controlled legislature, and in May 2003 it adopted a new plan that favored Republicans in two politically competitive districts.

Democrats sued, complaining that both federal and state constitutions — as well as established political custom — limit redistricting to once a decade following the federal census. In December 2003, the Colorado Supreme Court agreed and threw out the new plan.

But Colorado appears to be one of only about a dozen states with such prohibitions. The Texas constitution limits legislative — but not congressional — redistricting to the session following a census. Constitutional or statutory redistricting provisions in other states are either silent or ambiguous on mid-decade enactments.

The U.S. Constitution requires that House seats be reapportioned among the states after the census. But neither the Constitution nor federal law explicitly says when congressional maps can be — or must be — redrawn.

Republicans in both Colorado and Texas insist they were merely fulfilling their constitutional responsibilities in order to replace court-crafted plans following the earlier legislative deadlock. "The legislature hadn't done its job this decade," says Texas attorney Taylor. "It fell to a federal court, and that court created a plan that we believe was a simple interim solution, not one designed for the remainder of the decade."

Hirsch, the Democrats' lawyer, counters that a redistricting plan approved at the start of a decade should be retained, whether adopted by the legislature or by a court. "If you redistrict more often, you're taking away [voters'] chance to vote for incumbents who've served them well — or against incumbents who've served them poorly," he says.

Many academic experts say successive redistrictings serve no purpose other than the partisan interests of the majority party. "No one in his right mind believes there's a good reason to do mid-decade redistricting except for political gain," says Bernard Grofman, a professor of political science at the University of California, Irvine.

"Redistricting occupies a lot of resources, it engenders litigation — all at taxpayer expense," Rush says. "The taxpayers' coffers are being drained to allow incumbents of one party to put incumbents of the other party out of business."

Reformers Target 'Winner-Take-All' System

About 40 percent of the population in Amarillo, Texas, is African-American or Latino, but during the 1990s no black or Hispanic sat on the school board.

To help minority groups elect a candidate of their choice, the League of United Latin American Citizens (LULAC) and the NAACP jointly filed a federal court suit asking to replace the system of at-large elections with single-member districts.

In a settlement with the Amarillo Independent School District, however, the two groups agreed instead to a different system known as cumulative voting, which allows voters in a multi-office election to cast multiple votes in any combination. For example, in an election for four school board seats, a voter could spread four votes among four candidates or cast all four for the same candidate.

The new system produced the hoped-for results. An African-American and a Hispanic won two of the four seats being filled in the first cumulative-voting election for the seven-member board, held in May 2000. Many voters had cast multiple votes for their respective minority candidates to enable them to win.

"The fact that we got two minorities on the board is awesome," said Nancy Bosquez, a local LULAC leader. "History was made in Amarillo." [1]

Amarillo's experience is often cited by the small number of academic experts and political reformers who want to replace the predominant use of single-member districts and winner-take-all elections for multimember bodies with some form of so-called limit voting designed to enhance representation for political, racial or ethnic minorities.

"Winner-take-all is horse-and-buggy technology," says Steven Hill, Western regional director of the Center for Voting and Democracy. "One side wins all the representation; the other side wins nothing."

Cumulative voting is one of three election systems suggested by reformers as alternatives to winner-take-all, according to Richard Engstrom, a professor of political science at the University of New Orleans. [2] Often imprecisely labeled "proportional representation," the proposed systems differ from those used in Israel and Europe, which allot parliamentary seats to party candidates in mathematical proportion to the party's overall vote. Rather, the U.S. reformers' methods would still focus on individual candidates, but change the methods of casting and counting votes.

Cumulative voting would give cohesive minority groups a chance to aggregate their votes for a select number of candidates. A second, less common method — known as limited voting — would allow voters to vote for fewer candidates than the total number of positions at stake, thus preventing a majority from taking every seat in a multimember election by eliminating the "sweep effect." A voter might get three votes, for example, if four seats are being filled.

A third, more complicated system, known as preference voting, would allow voters to write in a specified number of candidates in order of preference. After an initial tally of the first-preference votes, one or more candidates are eliminated, and the ballots for those candidates are redistributed according to the voters' second preferences. The counting continues until the number of candidates remaining equals the number of seats being filled.

Besides beefing up minority representation, Hill and Engstrom say, the alternatives avoid some of the redistricting problems experienced today. "Alternative election systems take the emphasis off the lines," Engstrom explains.

Some critics say the proposals are too complex, but Engstrom says, "There's nothing all that complicated. That's largely a red herring."

In Amarillo at least, voters appear satisfied. "It's a new system, and it takes some explaining, but we haven't had any resistance to it," Amarillo Assistant School Superintendent Les Hoyt remarked recently. [3]

Cumulative or limited voting has been instituted in 100 communities, according to Engstrom — typically in response to minority groups' suits brought under the federal Voting Rights Act. But Hill says the benefits go beyond minority representation: The alternatives would improve campaign discourse and increase political participation.

Winner-take-all encourages "negative campaigning," Hill says, because candidates are as interested in driving voters away from a rival as attracting voters to themselves. The alternative systems require candidates to "define themselves more precisely," he says.

Alternative systems would also increase turnout, he says, because they would increase competition. "All voters are swing voters, instead of a small select number of voters," he says.

But so far the proposals are only blips on the nation's political radar screen. A bill sponsored by Rep. Melvin Watt, D-N.C., in 1999 would have allowed states to choose House members from multimember districts with alternative voting arrangements. Watt, the African-American candidate elected from the majority-black district that was the focus of the Supreme Court's first ruling on racial redistricting in 1993, got a hearing on the bill, but it advanced no further. [4]

---

[1] Sonny Bohanan, "Voting System Lauded," *The* (Amarillo) *Globe-News*, May 8, 2000. The seven-member board now includes two Hispanics and one African-American.

[2] See Richard L. Engstrom, "The Political Thicket, Electoral Reform, and Minority Voting Rights," pp. 36-44, in Mark E. Rush and Richard L. Engstrom, *Fair and Effective Representation? Debating Electoral Reform and Minority Rights* (2001).

[3] Quoted in Zeke MacCormack, "Like a Candidate? Vote for Him Twice," *San Antonio Express-News*, May 1, 2003, p. 1B.

[4] See Engstrom, *op. cit.*, pp. 51-52.

"Reapportionment and redistricting are done every 10 years," says Paul Herrnson, director of the Center for American Politics and Citizenship at the University of Maryland, College Park. "That is the written law and a norm, practiced for a very long time."

Herrnson acknowledges that legislatures occasionally redraw maps mid-

Court Redistricting Decisions Affecting Race

The Supreme Court issued a series of decisions beginning in 1993 limiting states' ability to consider race in drawing majority-minority congressional and legislative districts.

Case Date of Vote Vote

***Shaw v. Reno*, 509 U.S. 630 (1993); 5-4** — White voters were allowed to challenge a highly irregular-shaped congressional district under the Constitution's Equal Protection Clause as an effort to separate voters by race; the challenge to North Carolina's majority-black 12th District was sent back to the lower court for trial.

***Miller v. Johnson*, 515 U.S. 900 (1995); 5-4** — Use of race as predominant factor in drawing voting-district lines can be upheld only if it serves a compelling government interest and is narrowly tailored to serve that interest; the ruling struck down a Georgia plan with three majority-black districts.

***Bush v. Vera*, 517 U.S. 952 (1996); 5-4** — Three majority-minority congressional districts in Texas were ordered redrawn because they were primarily motivated by race and not justified by legitimate state interests; in a fractured decision, majority of justices nevertheless said states can deliberately create majority-minority districts in some circumstances.

***Shaw v. Hunt*, 517 U.S. 899 (1996); 5-4** — North Carolina's 12th District was ruled unconstitutional because it was racially motivated and not justified by state interests; state responded by redrawing a more compact district with 47 percent black population; in new challenge, a three-judge court ruled the redrawn district was unconstitutional without full trial.

***Hunt v. Cromartie*, 526 U.S. 541 (1999); 9-0** — Federal court must hold a trial in racial gerrymandering case if the state's motivation for creating a challenged districting plan is in dispute; ruling sent challenge to North Carolina's redrawn 12th District back to lower court for full trial.

***Easley v. Cromartie*, 532 U.S. 234 (2001); 5-4** — Redistricting plan challenged on racial grounds must be upheld unless plaintiffs show state had ways to achieve legitimate political objectives with significantly greater racial balance; decision upheld North Carolina's redrawn 12th District.

***Georgia v. Ashcroft*, 539 U.S.___ (2003); 5-4** — States can reduce the number of blacks in majority-minority districts if they offset the reduced voting strength with gains in minority groups' political influence elsewhere; ruling sent challenge to redistricting plan for Georgia Senate back for trial on other issues; three-judge court in February 2004 ruled plan invalid because of excessive population deviations between districts.

Source: Supreme Court Collection, *CQ Press*

decade after a court strikes down lawmakers' first attempt. "What's taken place in Colorado and Texas goes beyond that," he says. "Basically, it's a power grab."

GOP lawmakers in Texas, however, insist they were merely bringing district lines into conformity with the state's predominantly Republican voting pattern. "We tried to make it consistent with general voting patterns," says state Rep. Phil King, R-Weatherford. "We took it from 15 seats to maybe 19, 20, or 21 or 22. That's a long way from a coup."

Grofman scoffs. "The Republican plan will exaggerate the extent to which Texas is a Republican state rather than mirror the politics of the state," he says.

Hebert, the Democrats' lawyer, says the Constitution envisions congressional lines being redrawn only in conjunction with reapportionment of House seats after the decennial census. "The Census Clause makes it pretty clear that the Framers intended for the House to be electorally stable," he says.

"There's no rule against it," counters GOP lawyer Braden. "Maybe there should be, but there isn't."

Academic opinion — even among critics of mid-decade redistricting — appears to side with the Republicans. "It makes sense to have it once a decade, but it's clear that there's no legal rule against it in most states," says Michael McDonald, a professor of government and politics at George Mason University, in Fairfax, Va.

And there's nothing in the Constitution about redistricting at all, Persily notes. "The Constitution does not mandate how the states draw district lines at all."

Democrats plan to press their argument by appealing the Texas decision to the U.S. Supreme Court. Declaring that redistricting should occur only once a decade is "one thing the court could do if it is looking for some clear way to put some brakes on the redistricting process — which has gone completely haywire," Hebert says. Braden notes that Congress also could limit congressional redistricting to once a decade.

But Taylor insists public disapproval is enough to deter legislators from successive redistrictings. "Public sentiment is a sufficient check and balance on the legislative redistricting front," the GOP lawyer says. "If voters don't think state legislatures should be changing districts, they'll let them know, either before or after."

Should courts limit partisan gerrymandering?

After Republicans gained control of both houses of the Pennsylvania legislature in 2000, they began drawing new congressional districts, cutting two districts to reflect declining statewide population. The GOP-crafted plan maximized the party's advantages. It paired Democratic incumbents in three redrawn districts — forcing them to fight against each other. It also put another Democratic incumbent in a district drawn to favor a senior Republican House member, and created two new open seats favorably situated for up-and-coming GOP state senators.

The strategy paid off. The state's congressional delegation shifted from a narrow 11-10 Republican majority in 2000 to a lopsided 12-7 edge for the GOP in 2002.

The Pennsylvania shift, combined with Republican gains from another GOP-drawn redistricting plan in Michigan, helped the Republicans pick up six additional House seats — an unusual midterm gain for a party controlling the White House.

Democrats complained in federal court that by "packing" Democratic voters into Democratic districts, the Republicans locked in a GOP advantage in most districts, regardless of any partisan shift in the statewide population.

"Republican votes count twice as much as a Democrat's vote," says Hirsch, one of the attorneys for Pennsylvania Democrats in the case now before the U.S. Supreme Court. In House races, he contends, "We Democrats could capture a majority of the votes, [but] Republicans would get two-thirds of the seats."

Republicans counter that the new map simply reflects a statewide trend toward the GOP. The state has two Republican senators although it has voted Democratic in the past three presidential elections. [4]

"The state itself was becoming more Republican," says John Krill, a Harrisburg attorney for the Republicans. The predominantly Democratic cities of Philadelphia and Pittsburgh have lost population, and people have moved into Republican areas, such as central Pennsylvania, he says. "The legislature [had to accommodate] very significant demographic shifts."

Library of Congress

The term gerrymander was coined after Massachusetts Gov. Elbridge Gerry approved an irregularly shaped legislative district in 1812 that a critic said resembled "a salamander;" another critic promptly dubbed it "a gerrymander." This cartoon-map first appeared in the Boston Gazette *on March 26, 1812.*

Democrats have asked the high court to breathe life into a 1986 decision, *Davis v. Bandemer*, which allowed federal challenges to political gerrymandering. [5] A redistricting scheme could be unconstitutional if it caused "continued frustration of the will of a majority of the voters or effective denial to a minority of voters of a fair chance to influence the political process," Justice Byron R. White wrote in the main opinion.

"The standard is very hard to meet," says Washington and Lee's Rush. In fact, the Supreme Court upheld, 7-2, the Indiana congressional redistricting plan at issue in the case. Since then, no federal court has used the *Davis v. Bandemer* case to strike down a legislative or congressional redistricting plan. [6]

Critics of gerrymandering hope the Supreme Court will use the Pennsylvania case to establish a new standard that challengers could more readily meet. The Pennsylvania Democrats say a plan drawn by one party should be held unconstitutional if "the rival party's candidates could be consigned to fewer than half the seats even if its candidates consistently won a majority of votes statewide."

Grofman endorses the Democrats' test. "It's a gerrymander when an even split always means one party wins," he says.

Somewhat oddly, Republicans at the national level are not averse to the court limiting partisan gerrymandering. Attorney Braden says he is "sympathetic" to the goal of getting "useful" standards from *Bandemer* and suggests a plan be struck down if the lines are "totally lacking in legitimate state interests."

Some experts, however, caution against judicial intervention in gerrymandering disputes. "There is a real risk that it will seriously affect the integrity of the judiciary," Persily says. Courts "are going to be in this incredible position of having to decide . . . which representatives live and die," he continues. "It would make confirmation fights more difficult, and it would reduce somewhat the impression of an impartial judiciary."

Rush says courts should avoid partisan gerrymandering disputes because — in contrast to racial lines in redistricting cases — voting patterns and voting behavior are inherently changeable. "History indicates that the damage done by a partisan gerrymander simply is not as clear as critics suggest,"

Rush says. For example, within a few years after Indiana Democrats failed to overturn the GOP-crafted redistricting plan challenged in *Bandemer*, the Democrats had regained a majority of the state's congressional delegation, he notes.

Critics of partisan gerrymandering are doubtful about the outcome of the Pennsylvania case. "It's clear from the questions of the justices that they were searching for a standard, and they can't find one," Grofman says.

Krill urged the justices to flatly overrule *Bandemer*. "Any extreme attempts at partisan redistricting are self-correcting," he says, "sometimes in a very short time."

If the court chooses not to limit partisan gerrymandering, Congress could establish new redistricting standards. Congress passed a law in 1901 requiring "contiguous and compact" House districts but it lapsed after 1929.

Should states use nonpartisan or bipartisan bodies to oversee redistricting?

Arizona voters in 2000 approved creation of an independent, five-member, bipartisan commission to draw congressional and state legislative district lines that would encourage competitive political contests.

In January, however, Maricopa County Superior Court Judge Kenneth Fields agreed with Hispanic plaintiffs that the commission had hampered political competition by packing Hispanic voters into Democratic districts, thus giving Republicans too much of an edge elsewhere. [7]

The episode illustrates the difficulty of objective redistricting. Good-government groups — such as Common Cause and the League of Women Voters, which promoted the Arizona initiative — earnestly call for nonpartisan or bipartisan bodies to take the politics out of the process.

Many academic experts agree. Nonpartisan bodies "remove the prima facie basis for challenging a redistricting plan as being predatory," Washington and Lee's Rush says.

"Incumbents are looking to benefit themselves, and their parties are looking for partisan advantage," says the University of Maryland's Herrnson, who calls himself "a big fan" of using commissions.

But others insist that neutrality is simply unattainable in such an inherently partisan undertaking. "You can't just give off to technicians the responsibility for a plan," says the University of California's Grofman. "Any plan involves trade-offs. These are political questions, not purely technical matters."

Currently, 21 states use bipartisan or nonpartisan bodies for either congressional or legislative redistricting. Iowa assigns the task to its professional Legislative Service Bureau. The others use special bipartisan commissions. Typically, commission members include the attorney general, secretary of state or other government officials, or members appointed by the governor or legislative leaders.

The Arizona measure aimed to minimize partisan influence by using a judicial-appointments body to select a pool of potential commission members. Republican and Democratic legislative leaders appoint two members each from the pool. The fifth member is then chosen by the other four.

In some states, commissions propose districting maps for the legislature to consider; in others, the commission itself is the decision-making body. In Florida and Kansas, lawmakers submit a plan to the state supreme court, which can approve it or draw its own.

Iowa is often cited as proof that politics can be removed from the redistricting process. Four out of Iowa's five congressional districts are potentially competitive — a much higher percentage than in other states. "If you believe in representation and accountability, and that political competition leads to that, that's hard not to notice," Herrnson says.

Other experts, however, note that the Iowa legislature has thrice rejected redistricting maps drawn by the professional staff. They also say the Iowa system's relative success stems mostly from the state's somewhat less partisan political culture. "Nothing about the institutional form insulates it from partisan pressures," says Persily, at the University of Pennsylvania. "If you transfer that to New York, it wouldn't be nonpartisan."

Iowa does not have the same kind of racial and ethnic diversity that creates problems in other states, says McDonald, who supports the commission approach. "Iowa is like white bread," he says. "It doesn't matter how you slice it; you get back Iowa."

Elsewhere, commissions either split along party lines and produce a plan that favors the dominant party or reach a "compromise" favorable to both parties. "They tend to behave just like legislatures," Persily says.

GOP attorney Braden is dubious about reform proposals. "Bipartisan commissions are possible," he says, "but they've not been notoriously successful. It's a tricky matter to make it work. Some good intentions have been disasters."

Democratic lawyer Hebert, however, says independent bodies "ultimately are the solution," if they are truly nonpartisan. "It's an idea that needs to be studied." ■

BACKGROUND

Political Conflicts

In structuring the new national legislature, the Framers of the Constitution crafted a compromise to balance the interests of large and small

Continued on p. 232

Chronology

Before 1960

Reapportionment and redistricting engender political conflicts; Congress and Supreme Court leave issues mostly to states.

1787
Constitution requires House of Representatives to reapportion seats following decennial censuses.

1842, 1872, 1901
Congress requires single-member, contiguous districts for House seats; subsequent versions require districts to be nearly equal in population (1872) and "compact" (1901). House declines to void elections for violations; law lapses after 1929.

1946
Supreme Court declines to nullify Illinois' malapportioned congressional districts; main opinion says court should stay out of "political thicket" of redistricting.

1950s
Cities, suburbs gain population, but most states fail to redraw districts to reflect shift.

1960s

Supreme Court launches reapportionment revolution; states forced to redraw legislative, congressional districts, shifting power to cities and suburbs.

1962
Supreme Court rules that redistricting challenges are "justiciable" in federal courts (*Baker v. Carr*).

1963, 1964
Supreme Court establishes equal-population requirement — "one person, one vote" — for congressional districts and state legislatures.

1970s-1980s

Redistricting becomes routine, along with court challenges; partisan maneuvering, incumbent protection are dominant considerations.

1983
Supreme Court limits population deviations for congressional districts unless required for legitimate state interests.

1986
High court opens door slightly to federal court challenges to partisan gerrymandering (*Davis v. Bandemer*); separately, court sets standards for "minority vote dilution" cases under federal Voting Rights Act.

1990s

Supreme Court limits use of race in redistricting.

1993
In *Shaw v. Reno*, Supreme Court rules that white voters can challenge the use of race to create "majority-minority" districts.

1995, 1996
Supreme Court tightens strictures on racial redistricting in cases from Georgia, Texas.

2000-Present

With Republican gains, partisan conflicts over redistricting intensify.

2001-2002
Democrats redraw congressional districts in Georgia to their advantage; Republicans do the same in Michigan, Pennsylvania; lesser partisan shifts approved in other states; Democrats challenge Pennsylvania plan as unconstitutional partisan gerrymander.

November 2002
Redistricting helps Republicans pick up seats in U.S. House; GOP also gains in gubernatorial and state legislative contests.

May 2003
GOP-controlled Colorado state legislature adopts new congressional map to replace court-drawn plan; Democrats file state, federal challenges.

October 2003
Texas legislature, controlled by Republicans, ends months of partisan rancor by approving new congressional map aimed to give Republicans 20-22 out of 32 House seats; Democrats challenge plan in federal court.

December 2003
Colorado Supreme Court bars second-in-decade redistricting on state constitutional grounds (Dec. 1) . . . U.S. Supreme Court hears arguments in Pennsylvania case on constitutional limits to partisan gerrymandering (*Vieth v. Jubelirer*, Dec. 10); decision expected by June 2004.

2004
Three-judge federal court rejects challenge to Texas' second-in-decade congressional redistricting (*Sessions v. Perry*, Jan. 6); Supreme Court refuses to stay ruling, allowing the plan to be used in the Nov. 2 elections.

Racial, Ethnic Politics Complicate Redistricting

Reps. Howard L. Berman and Brad Sherman represent adjoining congressional districts in Los Angeles County's San Fernando Valley, an area with a rapidly growing Hispanic population. The two Anglo Democrats back Latino positions on such issues as immigration and regularly receive Hispanic support in elections.

When it came time to redraw California's congressional map after the 2000 census, however, neither Berman nor Sherman wanted to have too many Latinos in his district — for fear of a successful challenge from a Latino opponent. Fortunately for Berman, the state's Democratic lawmakers had entrusted the task of redrawing congressional districts to his brother Michael, a behind-the-scenes force in the powerful local Democratic machine.

The new map, approved by the state legislature in September 2001 with support from most Latino lawmakers, shifted enough Hispanics out of Berman's district to protect him from a potential Latino rival. But Sherman, who now had double the number of Latino registered voters in his district, opposed the plan, although it still left Latinos far short of the numbers required to threaten him. [1]

The Mexican American Legal Defense and Educational Fund (MALDEF) challenged the configuration in court, arguing that the legislature deliberately fragmented Latino voters, creating "vote dilution" prohibited by the federal Voting Rights Act. MALDEF charged that the legislature had violated the act by removing thousands of Latino voters from Berman's district and placing them in Sherman's.

A three-judge federal court rejected the suit on the ground that Anglo prejudice against Latino candidates has diminished in recent years. "Whites and other non-Latinos are currently far more willing to support Latino candidates for office than in the past," the court ruled. [2]

The episode illustrates some of the complexities of racial and ethnic politics in the redistricting process, especially as it affects the nation's two largest minorities: Hispanics and African-Americans. Race-conscious redistricting in the 1990s contributed to a marked increase in blacks and Hispanics elected to the House. But a series of Supreme Court decisions now limits state legislatures' discretion to create so-called majority-minority districts. [3]

Meanwhile, the partisan implications of racial redistricting have become more evident. For Republicans, creating majority-minority districts can help GOP prospects in other districts with reduced minority voting strength. For Democrats, while the strategy helps elect African-Americans and Hispanics, it can put Anglo incumbents at risk — either from minority challengers in districts with concentrated minority populations or from Republican opponents in districts with fewer minority voters.

In Texas, partisan maneuvering meant that neither of the major parties supported Latino groups' call for an additional Latino majority district in South and West Texas. A Republican-drawn map reduced the Latino voting-age population in one district — the 23rd — below 50 percent to safeguard incumbent Republican Henry Bonilla. The five-term Hispanic Republican depended on Anglo votes to narrowly beat a Hispanic Democrat in 2002.

Democrats opposed the GOP-drawn map as a partisan gerrymander, but did not support the call for a new Latino district. Instead, they focused on line drawing elsewhere that put Anglo Democrats' political fortunes in jeopardy.

"In this round of redistricting, there was less willingness to create Latino-majority districts and little support from either political party to do it," says Nina Perales, a MALDEF regional counsel in San Antonio. "In terms of the redistricting struggle, there are Re-

Continued from p. 230

states. Congress was to consist of a Senate, with two members from each state, and a House of Representatives, with each state allotted a number of representatives tied to its population. Although the plan eased the way for ratification of the Constitution, it also set the stage for recurrent political conflicts over reapportionment and redistricting. [8]

Article I, Section 2, initially allocated 65 representatives among the 13 original states and required population-based reapportionment "within every subsequent term of ten years" — now done after each decennial census. However, the Constitution contained no instructions about how states were to draw congressional districts — or even whether districts were required at all.

Nevertheless, the Framers apparently envisioned the division of states into congressional districts with equal population. In *The Federalist Papers No. 57*, for example, James Madison said each representative "will be elected by five or six thousand citizens." In the absence of a specific requirement, however, the states adopted varying practices. Six states elected representatives by districts, while five used at-large elections. Delaware and Rhode Island each were allotted only a single House member. [9]

More than a century of trial-and-error produced the current system of apportioning representatives among the states. Debates swirled around the size of the House and the method of allocating seats among the states, given the inevitability of "fractional remainders" — the leftover fraction when a state's population is divided by the population of an ideal-size district. [10]

At first, leftover fractions were disregarded (1790-1830). A method used only in 1840 allotted an additional seat to any state with a surplus fraction greater than one-half the size of the ideal district. From 1850-1900, a new plan specified the publicans, there are Democrats and there are Latinos. And our interests don't line up with either of the other two groups."

The push to create majority-minority districts began during the administration of the first President George Bush. The Justice Department interpreted the Voting Rights Act to require states to draw districts with majority-black populations wherever feasible. To comply, some Southern states — with Democratic-controlled legislatures — created bizarre-shaped districts to cover widely separated African-American neighborhoods.

Beginning in 1993, the Supreme Court set limits on the practice, ruling that race could not be the predominant factor in drawing district lines. In 2001, however, the high court gave states somewhat greater leeway by ruling that North Carolina had legitimate political reasons for creating a congressional district challenged on racial grounds. [4]

The court eased the state rules again in 2003 in a ruling on Georgia's Democratic-drawn plan for state Senate districts. Supported by 10 of 11 black senators — all Democrats — the plan reduced the African-American population in some senatorial districts to help spread the predominantly Democratic voters into others. But the Justice Department had said the plan improperly reduced minority voting strength.

In a 5-4 decision, the high court ruled that states could indeed move black voters out of "majority-minority" districts in order to increase the black population in "minority-influence" districts.

"The State may choose," Justice Sandra Day O'Connor wrote for the majority, "that it is better to risk having fewer minority representatives in order to achieve greater overall representation of a minority group by increasing the number of representatives sympathetic to the interests of minority voters." [5]

Minorities Gained in Redistricting

Race-conscious redistricting in the 1990s contributed to a marked increase in the number of blacks and Hispanics elected to the U.S. House of Representatives. But recent Supreme Court decisions now limit legislatures' discretion to create so-called "majority-minority" districts.

African-American and Hispanic Members of U.S. House of Representatives

Year	Blacks	Hispanics
1991	26	11
2001	37	19
2003	37	22

Sources: CQ.com, CQ Weekly, *American Political Leaders: 1789-2000, CQ Press.*

[1] For background, see David Rosenzweig and Michael Finnegan, "Latino Voter Lawsuit Rejected," *Los Angeles Times,* June 13, 2002, p. A1., and Kenneth Reich, "Latino Groups Sue Over Redistricting," *Los Angeles Times,* Oct. 2, 2001, Part 2, p. A1.

[2] The case is *Cano v. Davis,* 211 F.Supp.2d 1208 (C.D. Cal. 2002).

[3] For background, see Nadine Cohodas, "Electing Minorities," *The CQ Researcher,* Aug. 12, 1994, pp. 697-720.

[4] The decision is *Hunt v. Cromartie,* 526 U.S. 541 (2001). The most important of the earlier decisions are *Shaw v. Reno,* 509 U.S. 630 (1993); *Miller v. Johnson,* 515 U.S. 900 (1995) and *Bush v. Vera,* 517 U.S. 952 (1996).

[5] The decision is *Georgia v. Ashcroft,* 539 U.S. ___ (2003). The ruling sent the case back to a three-judge federal court for further consideration. The court struck the plan down because of population deviations. See Rhonda Cook, "Redistricting Shot Down," *The Atlanta Journal-Constitution,* Feb. 13, 2004.

size of the House with each new decade, allocated whole-number seats and assigned any leftover seats to states with the largest leftover fractions.

In 1910, Congress voted that the House would permanently consist of 435 members, and that seats would be apportioned using a system called "major fractions." A decade later, a Congress dominated by members from rural states stalemated when it appeared reapportionment would combine with the fixed-size provision to shift power to more urban states. For the only time in U.S. history, Congress went an entire decade without reapportioning House seats. [11]

Meanwhile, a debate between leading mathematicians produced a new apportionment method, which was eventually adopted in 1950 and remains in use today. The so-called Huntington method — named after its inventor, Edward Huntington of Harvard University — was deemed fairer than the earlier method. It assigns seats to the states based on a division of each state's population by $n(n-1)$, with n being the number of seats given so far to the state. The Supreme Court upheld this method in 1992 in a suit brought by Montana, which lost its second seat under the formula but would have been entitled to two seats under a different method. [12]

Congress followed a similarly meandering path on districting issues. In the early 1800s, the Senate three times approved a constitutional amendment requiring single-member congressional districts, but it failed to reach a vote in the House. Nevertheless, by 1840 most states were using single-member districts. In 1842, Congress required contiguous, single-member districts. The law lapsed after 1850 but was approved again in 1862. A decade later, Congress enacted a seemingly stricter law that required contiguous, single-member districts "as nearly as practicable" equal in population. That requirement was re-enacted in 1881 and 1891 and again in 1901 with an added requirement that districts be "compact."

But none of the laws were enforced. The House in 1844 voted — on partisan lines — to seat representatives from four states that had used at-large elections despite the law requiring single-member districts. In 1901, a House committee rejected a challenge to the election of a Kentucky congressman on the grounds that the state's redistricting law did not conform to federal statutes. Seven years later, a House committee approved a somewhat similar challenge involving a Virginia congressman, but the full House never acted on the recommendation.

Getty Images

James Madison recommended in The Federalist Papers No. 57 *that each representative to Congress "will be elected by five or six thousand citizens."* The Federalist Papers, *written with Alexander Hamilton and John Jay in 1787-88 and published in several New York newspapers, argued for ratification of the proposed Constitution.*

The 1901 single-member districting requirement was not re-enacted when it expired in 1929, but a new version was adopted in 1967, which also barred at-large elections. By then, however, the Supreme Court had transformed the legal landscape by requiring that legislative and congressional districts be roughly equal in population — the "one person, one vote" standard.

Court Battles

Initially, the Supreme Court decided to stay out of what Justice Felix Frankfurter famously called the "political thicket" of legislative and congressional redistricting. In a series of momentous decisions in the 1960s, however, it ruled that federal courts had jurisdiction over equal-protection claims attacking malapportioned districting schemes and required states to devise districts essentially equal in population.

In its first brush with the issue, the Supreme Court in 1932 left standing a Mississippi redistricting law that was challenged as a violation of the 1911 federal statute. The majority ruled that the 1911 law had expired, but four other justices said they would have dismissed the suit "for want of equity" — in effect, a discretionary decision not to exercise jurisdiction.[13]

In 1946, the court shelved a broader attack claiming that an Illinois legislative districting scheme favoring rural areas violated the voting rights of urban and suburban voters under the Equal Protection Clause. Three justices said the court had no jurisdiction. "Courts ought not enter this political thicket," Frankfurter wrote, although three other justices said they would have heard the case. Casting the deciding vote, Justice Wiley Rutledge concluded that courts could hear such claims, but that in this instance the court should refrain because of the potential "collision" with other branches of government.[14]

In the absence of judicial pressure, state lawmakers often did not bother to redistrict, leaving the nation's growing urban and suburban areas underrepresented. The disparity was greatest in state legislative districts: By 1960, all the nation's legislatures featured at least a 2-to-1 disparity between the most and the least heavily populated districts. Congressional districts were less imbalanced, but several states had lopsided plans. The most heavily populated congressional district in Texas, for instance, had four times as many inhabitants as its least populated, while Arizona, Maryland and Ohio had 3-to-1 disparities between districts.

Once again, city-dwellers took the equal-protection issue to the courts, this time in Tennessee, which had not reapportioned its legislature since 1901. The state courts declined to act, as did a lower federal court — citing the Supreme Court's 1946 decision. But the high court reversed itself in 1962, in its landmark *Baker v. Carr* decision. The urban residents' claim that the failure to reapportion violated their equal-protection rights presented "a justiciable constitutional cause of action upon which [they] were entitled to a trial and a decision," Justice William J. Brennan Jr. wrote in the 6-2 ruling. [15]

The decision set no standard and sent the case back to Tennessee. A year later, however, the high court was more explicit. In a legislative-reapportionment suit from Georgia, Justice William O. Douglas wrote for the majority that political equality "can mean only one thing — one person, one vote." The next year, the high court applied the same standard to congressional districting in another case from Georgia. "[A]s nearly as practicable, one man's vote in a congressional election is to be worth as much as another's," Justice Hugo Black wrote. [16] The dual rulings forced state lawmakers subsequently to redraw legislative and congressional district maps — significantly shifting power from rural to urban and suburban areas.

In applying the one-person, one-vote standard, the Supreme Court moved gradually toward strict mathematical equality for congressional districts, while allowing a bit more leeway for legislatures. The series of decisions on congressional maps culminated with a 1983 ruling in a New Jersey case, *Karcher v. Daggett*, which struck down a districting scheme where the disparity between the most and the least populous district was a tiny 0.69 percent — or 4,400 people. The court said that even small deviations were prohibited unless they were necessary to achieve some legitimate state interest. [17]

In separate opinions, Justice John Paul Stevens, who joined the majority, and Justice Lewis F. Powell Jr., who dissented, said they were more concerned about the partisan gerrymandering in New Jersey's plan. The court took up that issue more directly in Indiana's *Bandemer* case three years later, but the split decision fell short of a constitutional command against politically driven districting.

The 6-3 vote established that federal courts could entertain and rule on constitutional claims against political gerrymandering, but the fact that Indiana's politically driven congressional districting plan was upheld — plus the strict legal test set out in the main opinion — gave federal courts scant encouragement to review partisan gerrymandering cases. [18]

Building Blocs

Racial politics, partisan gamesmanship and computerized demographics combined in the 1990s to transform both congressional redistricting and judicial oversight of the process. Under pressure from a Republican Justice Department in the early 1990s, states used newly available, block-by-block census maps to draw intricate schemes concentrating minority voters in select districts to help elect African-American or Hispanic candidates.

White voters challenged the bizarrely shaped districts as "racial gerrymanders" that violated their equal-protection rights. The Supreme Court recognized the claims and told states that race could not be "the predominant factor" in drawing district lines.

Computer-aided redistricting was first proposed in the 1960s as an antidote to overly partisan line-drawing, according to Mark Monmonier, a geography professor at Syracuse University's Maxwell School of Citizenship and Public Affairs and author of a book on the subject. [19] Beginning with the 1970 population count, the Census Bureau started producing computerized street maps that could be used in an interactive computerized process to draw increasingly precise district lines. With the 1990 census, the bureau produced what Monmonier calls "a more powerful and precise database." These electronic files, he explains, enabled redistricters to follow streets, streams, railways or other boundaries to produce districts with specified population counts — and predictable demographic makeups.

Meanwhile, slow, expensive "mainframe" computers were replaced by fast, cheap personal computers, spawning a growing niche industry that gave legislators, political parties, interest groups and others the data needed to fine-tune redistricting schemes to maximize their respective interests.

The new demographic information became available just as the Justice Department — under the first President George Bush — was advancing a new interpretation of the federal Voting Rights Act, which required states to maximize the number of majority-minority congressional and legislative districts. Legally, the department said it was acting to prevent "minority vote dilution," as defined by a pivotal 1986 decision by the Supreme Court. [20] But the legal position also served Republican interests by packing minority voters — overwhelmingly Democratic — into a few districts. Minority groups supported the government's position. Democrats had little choice but to go along, given their dependence on African-American votes.

States subject to the Voting Rights Act's "preclearance" requirement for redistricting plans met the Justice Department directive after the 1990 census by stitching minority neighborhoods together in sprawling, comically intricate districts. North Carolina's 12th wound snakelike through the center of the state to pick up African-American neighborhoods in three cities. Georgia's 11th stretched from Atlanta eastward to pick up black neighborhoods in Augusta and Savannah on the coast. Louisiana's 4th gained the nickname "the mark of Zorro" for its Z-shaped path along the state's northern and eastern borders. Texas produced a congressional map with districts resembling Rorschach inkblots — some designed to elect African-American or Hispanic candidates, others aimed at protecting incumbents.

The Supreme Court had countenanced some use of racial criteria in legislative districting in a 1974 decision. But the racial redistricting of the 1990s — often discarding the traditional principle of compactness — did not sit well with the court's conservative majority. A series of 5-4 decisions challenging the North Carolina, Georgia and Texas maps established constitutional bounds on the practice.

First, the court ruled in the North Carolina case — *Shaw v. Reno* — that white voters could challenge racially drawn districts that were "highly irregular in shape." Two years later, in the Georgia case, the court said a redistricting plan had to meet the high constitutional standard of "strict scrutiny" if race was "the predominant factor" in placing "a significant number of voters" in or outside a district. A year later, the court made clear that the constitutional test was stringent by rejecting Texas' argument that its racially drawn districts were justifiable efforts to preserve minority voting strength or to protect incumbents in other districts. [21]

The court also helped resolve a second reapportionment-related issue over the use of statistical "sampling" in the population counts used to allocate congressional seats. The Census Bureau and most demographers argued that enumerators could not possibly find everybody in a nationwide count and that sampling techniques were reliable methods to adjust for the inevitable "undercount." [22] Democrats agreed, but Republicans said sampling was unreliable, unnecessary and illegal. In 1999, the court sided with the GOP, ruling 5-4 that the Census Act did not allow sampling in congressional apportionment. [23]

By decade's end, the court's decisions in the racial redistricting cases had forced Georgia, North Carolina and Texas to redraw the challenged congressional districts and prompted other states to re-examine the use of race in map drawing. Meanwhile, political winds were blowing in a Republican direction. The GOP gained control of the House in 1994 and held on for the rest of the decade. In 2000, Republicans gained control of the White House and both chambers of Congress and improved their positions in statehouses and state legislatures. The GOP began the new century in a favorable posture and saw an opportunity for further gains in the coming redistricting cycle.

Escalating Warfare

Political pundits expected the post-2000 redistricting season to be the most contentious ever. Three years later, the predictions had proven well-founded. As both parties sought to maximize whatever political control they had over the process, the courts were again called in to referee, but the judiciary appeared reluctant to rein in partisan gerrymandering or limit redistricting to once a decade.

In Texas, a divided state legislature — with a Democratic-controlled House and GOP-controlled Senate — adjourned its regular session in May 2001 without seriously trying to redraw the congressional map to incorporate the two new seats Texas was apportioned following the 2000 census. GOP Gov. Rick Perry decided not to reconvene the legislature for a special session — leaving the matter up to the courts. In approving a new map on Nov. 14, a three-judge federal court relied heavily on the existing, Democratic-drawn map in order to protect incumbents. [24]

Colorado followed a similar course after the Republican-controlled House and Democratic-controlled Senate deadlocked. A state judge adopted a Democratic-backed plan in January 2002 that largely protected the state's six incumbent House members — four Republicans and two Democrats — while favoring a Democratic candidate in a newly created district around Denver. [25]

Democrats already had won a victory in Georgia, where a Democratic-controlled legislature had adopted a redistricting plan. By "packing" GOP districts and pairing incumbent Republicans in two of them, Democrats hoped to shift the state's congressional delegation from an 8-3 GOP majority to a 7-6 Democratic edge. [26]

Some Pennsylvania Republicans cited the Democrats' Georgia remap as grounds for retaliation in their own state later that year. Facing the loss of two of Pennsylvania's 21 House seats, the GOP-controlled legislature threw two pairs of Democratic incumbents together and put another Democrat into a district with an incumbent Republican. The map, approved in early January 2002, appeared likely to enlarge the GOP's narrow 11-10 edge to a more comfortable 12-7 margin. [27]

Michigan, another GOP-controlled state that lost seats after the 2000 census, followed Pennsylvania's example by pairing six Democratic incumbents in three redrawn districts. Likewise, Democratic-controlled legislatures in North Carolina and Tennessee approved maps likely to net their party one seat in each, while a Democratic plan in Maryland added a hefty chunk of Democrats to the district of longtime moderate Republican Rep. Constance A. Morella. In other states, incumbent protection appeared the dominant goal. As the redistricting cycle ended, Republicans and Democrats alike pronounced themselves largely satisfied.

In November, however, redistricting appeared to be a significant factor — along with President Bush's popularity and the population shift toward predominantly Republican Sun Belt states

— in producing a net pickup of six House seats for the GOP. [28] It was only the third time since the Civil War that the president's party gained House seats in a midterm election.

Democrats lost six seats in Michigan and Pennsylvania, while Republicans gained new seats in Florida and Texas (two each) and Arizona and Nevada (one each). In Maryland, Morella fell to a Democratic opponent, but Democrats did not match their expectations in other states. Notably, Republicans held onto an 8-5 majority in the expanded Georgia delegation. In Colorado, a Republican eked out a surprise 122-vote victory for the new seat.

Republicans also made gains in state legislative contests and, significantly, won majority control of both chambers of the Colorado and Texas legislatures. Meanwhile, House Majority Leader DeLay hatched a plan for a second round of redistricting in Texas. Ironically, the idea bore fruit first in Colorado, where a Republican-crafted redistricting plan was introduced, approved and signed into law within five days in early May. Colorado's Democratic attorney general, Ken Salazar, promptly vowed to challenge the mid-cycle redistricting in court.

The path to the second-in-a-decade redistricting in Texas was more protracted. Republicans pushed the measure to the top of the House calendar as the regular legislative session was ending in May. But Democrats thwarted passage by decamping en masse to a motel in Oklahoma for the final four days — putting them beyond the reach of Texas authorities and leaving the chamber without a quorum. When Gov. Perry convened a special legislative session, the Senate's 12 Democrats staged a similar exodus to New Mexico. But the month-long boycott ended on Sept. 2 when one of the Democrats decided to come back home after concluding that Perry could outlast them by calling a succession of special sessions. [29]

The legislature finally adopted the plan on Oct. 13. Democrats immediately sued, claiming the mid-decade redistricting violated the U.S. and state constitutions. Along with the Mexican American Legal Defense and Educational Fund (MALDEF), Democrats also contended that the map improperly diluted minority voter strength in violation of the Voting Rights Act. Republicans countered that the measure actually created a new, third "minority-opportunity" district for African-Americans in Houston and maintained the number of Hispanic opportunity districts at six.

Meanwhile, Pennsylvania Democrats were challenging the redistricting plan the GOP had pushed through in the regular post-census cycle. The measure was an unconstitutional gerrymander, they claimed, even under the Supreme Court's stringent *Davis v. Bandemer* standard. A three-judge federal court rejected the claim in January 2003, but the high court agreed in June to take up the case and scheduled oral arguments for Dec. 10.

As the December arguments approached, the stage was set for some of the most significant legal battles over redistricting since the start of the reapportionment revolution four decades earlier. ■

CURRENT SITUATION

Designing Districts

Pennsylvania Democrats want the Supreme Court to give courts more power to strike down political gerrymandering, but they ran into strong resistance from several justices during arguments on Dec. 10, 2003. Even justices sympathetic to the Democrats' claim of unfairness appeared uncertain about what standard courts could use to police the practice. Meanwhile, lawyers for GOP legislators and the state urged the justices to bar partisan gerrymandering cases from federal courts altogether or give legislatures free rein in drawing district lines for partisan advantage. [30]

For the Democrats, Washington attorney Paul Smith opened the hour-long session by saying that lower courts had "effectively overruled" the high court's 1986 decision allowing challenges to partisan gerrymandering by setting an "impossible" burden of proof for plaintiffs. He urged that redistricting maps be ruled unconstitutional if plaintiffs showed it was "very clear" one party could win a majority of votes but have "no chance" of securing a majority of the seats.

Three justices openly disagreed with Smith — starting with the pivotal moderate conservative Sandra Day O'Connor, a dissenter in the original *Bandemer* decision. "Maybe the way to go is to just say hands off these things," O'Connor declared.

Justice Antonin Scalia reached the same conclusion after noting that the Constitution lets the states or Congress itself prescribe the "time, place, and manner" of House elections. "That suggests to me it is none of our business."

Chief Justice William H. Rehnquist, another of the dissenters in *Bandemer*, also sharply rejected Smith's proposed standard. "You're just pulling this thing out of a hat," he said.

For his part, Justice Anthony M. Kennedy conceded that the GOP-drawn congressional map might be "unfair . . . in common parlance," but still wondered what test courts could use. "It seems to me that we're at sea," he said.

"The government has no business discriminating against people based on their partisan affiliation or their political viewpoint," Smith answered later. "There has to be an outer boundary."

Harrisburg attorney Krill, representing the GOP legislative leaders, urged the justices to bar federal courts from policing politically driven redistricting. Any test "requires inherent political choices" that are "inappropriate for the judiciary to make," Krill said.

Justice John Paul Stevens — who had voted in 1986 not only to allow legal challenges to gerrymandering but also to strike down the Indiana map at issue in the case — asked Krill whether a redistricting plan should be subject to challenge if "maximum partisan advantage" were the only justification for a line-drawing.

Yes, Krill answered, "It's a permissible legislative choice." When Stevens again asked whether the legislature had "any duty" to try to draw districts "impartially," Krill said the Constitution does not require fairness, but that "political forces" might pull lawmakers "in a multitude of directions."

In any event, Krill added, "The system is self-correcting," noting that Indiana Democrats gained control of the state's congressional delegation within a few years of losing their redistricting challenge. In Pennsylvania, he added, Democrats had won the House race in a district seemingly drawn to favor the GOP incumbent. "Voters are not disenfranchised," he concluded.

Representing Pennsylvania, Senior Deputy Attorney General J. Bart DeLone said "the simplest and cleanest way" for the justices to "get out of the political thicket" was to overrule the *Bandemer* decision.

By the close of the argument, court-watchers counted four votes seemingly against the Democrats: Rehnquist, O'Connor, Scalia and the conservative Clarence Thomas, who followed his customary practice of asking no questions. Kennedy, a moderate conservative, seemed a likely fifth vote to reject the Democrats' claim.

Meanwhile, among the four liberal justices, only Stevens strongly favored an aggressive role for the courts on gerrymandering, and he did not embrace the standard proposed by Smith. Justices David H. Souter and Ruth Bader Ginsburg seemed possible votes for the Democrats' position, but Justice Stephen G. Breyer, an active questioner, had asked skeptical questions of both Smith and Krill.

"I expect the Supreme Court will reject the plaintiffs' cause of action," the University of Pennsylvania's Persily commented after attending the arguments. The justices, he said, "are afraid that they will get even more deeply into the political thicket."

A decision is due by July.

Taking Seconds

Democrats are one for two in challenging the mid-cycle congressional redistricting plans approved by GOP legislatures and governors in Colorado and Texas. But the Colorado Supreme Court's decision barring a second-in-a-decade redistricting set no broad precedent, because it depended on a provision in the state's constitution. So Democrats will have only a limited victory unless they can persuade the U.S. Supreme Court to overturn the Texas federal court ruling that the Constitution does not limit congressional redistricting to once every 10 years.

The Colorado court's decision, announced Dec. 1, came on a 5-2 vote, with the court's two Republican-appointed justices dissenting.[31] The ruling relied on a provision in Colorado's constitution requiring the general assembly to redistrict congressional seats whenever "a new apportionment shall be made by Congress." Writing for the majority, Chief Justice Mary Mullarkey said the provision mandated redistricting immediately after the census and barred a second remap — even if the new plan was drawn by a court following a legislative deadlock.

"The state constitution limits redistricting to once per census,

Continued on p. 240

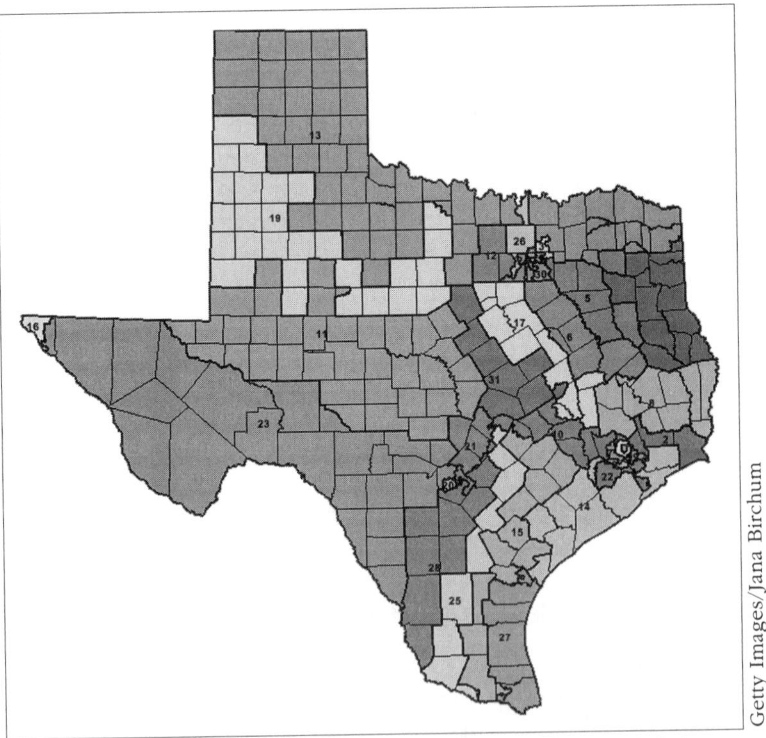

Getty Images/Jana Birchum

Texas' new congressional map threw several House Democrats into new districts against each other or against Republican incumbents or stripped them of large segments of their old districts. Voting in November in Texas could eliminate the Democrats' hopes of regaining control of the House next year.

At Issue:

Should federal courts limit partisan gerrymandering?

yes

SAM HIRSCH
***COUNSEL FOR APPELLANTS IN* VIETH V. JUBELIRER,**
JENNER & BLOCK LLP

WRITTEN FOR *THE CQ RESEARCHER*, FEBRUARY 2004

Inviting federal courts to wade deeper into the "political thicket" always raises difficult issues of federalism and separation of powers. But sometimes the risks are worth taking. That was the case in the 1960s, when malapportionment had effectively doubled the voting strength of rural voters, at the expense of city-dwellers and suburbanites. It is the case again today, when partisan gerrymandering has effectively doubled the power of a class of voters defined solely by their political viewpoint. Like malapportionment 40 years ago, severe gerrymandering today threatens to make a mockery of our democratic system.

In the first general elections after the 2001-2002 redistricting, only four congressional challengers ousted incumbents — a record low. In California, none of the 50 general-election challengers garnered even 40 percent of the vote. Indeed, in 80 of the 435 districts nationwide, one of the two major parties did not even field a candidate. This lack of competition was peculiar to House elections, where redistricting has an impact: On the same day when barely one out of 12 House elections were decided by 10 percentage points or less, roughly half of all gubernatorial and Senate elections were that close. Most of the House is now locked in cement.

While historic levels of uncompetitiveness infected redistricting nationally, severe partisan bias was confined to a handful of states where one political party had unilateral control over the legislature and the governorship. For example, although Florida, Pennsylvania, Ohio and Michigan are all highly competitive "toss-up" states, redistricting handed the Republican Party 51 of their 77 House seats — an artificial 2-to-1 advantage.

Partisan gerrymandering is also transforming Congress. With little reason to fear voters, representatives increasingly cater to party insiders and donors, rather than to the political center where most Americans reside. Bipartisan compromise around moderate policies takes a backseat to party loyalty, resulting in historic levels of polarization. And further polarization only fuels the bitterness that promotes more gerrymandering.

The partisan-gerrymandering wars have spilled out of the legislatures and into the courtrooms. But with little prospect of prevailing on a forthright claim of partisan gerrymandering, aggrieved partisans instead often allege racial gerrymandering or minority-vote dilution under the Voting Rights Act. The incentive to couch partisan disputes in racial terms corrodes our politics. By putting teeth into the constitutional limits on partisan gerrymandering, federal courts can halt the racializing of redistricting, while restoring to the American people a House of Representatives worthy of its name.

no

JOHN P. KRILL, JR.
***COUNSEL FOR APPELLEES IN* VIETH V. JUBELIRER,**
KIRKPATRICK & LOCKHART LLP

WRITTEN FOR *THE CQ RESEARCHER*, FEBRUARY, 2004

Court-imposed limits on partisanship in redistricting would create, not solve, problems. Redistricting is inherently political. Any line drawn anywhere has partisan repercussions, and no criteria are "neutral." For example, trying to follow county and municipal lines would give preference to 19th-century political boundary decisions, while disfavoring emerging communities of interest in our sprawling, non-compact suburbs.

Turning judicial preferences into constitutional principles would create a drag on democratic change. Although legislators are free to envision the future, the judicial role is essentially to apply precedent and past legislative policy choices to restrict future conduct. If the courts had intervened in an earlier age, and had applied principles of so-called partisan fairness based on past electoral strength, they might well have kept the Whig Party from collapsing. But a party whose base is shrinking should not be propped up by judges giving weight to the past preferences of voters who have died, moved or switched.

If judges start second-guessing elected legislatures about fundamental choices for future representation, the judiciary will inevitably be criticized for partisanship. Although the courts often redraw maps in one-person, one-vote cases, they must use past legislative districting decisions as guidance, so as to avoid making political choices. But if the courts start making such policy choices themselves, the unavoidable partisan impact will put judicial legitimacy at risk. We can't afford to have respect for the courts turn into cynicism about political bosses in black robes.

In any event, redistricting, even with the aid of modern computers, cannot control the choices of voters. Good candidates vector toward the politics of their districts, regardless of their party affiliation. That is why Congress has conservative Democrats and liberal Republicans and vice versa. Some districts will elect a conservative regardless of party and vice versa. Recognizing this point leads to the realization that partisan affiliation is not the be-all, end-all of elections, except to the parties themselves. The parties care about partisan control of legislative bodies more than about the politics of the members of their caucuses. Voters care more about the responsiveness and personalities of their representatives.

The states have used districting for partisan effect since the ratification of the Constitution. For example, Pennsylvania enacted different plans for congressional elections in 1788, 1790, 1792 and 1794, as Federalists struggled with Anti-Federalists for control of the delegation. Partisan conflict is no fiercer now. Judicial restraint is just as important now.

Continued from p. 238

and nothing in state or federal law negates this limitation," Mullarkey wrote in her 63-page opinion. "Having failed to redistrict when it should have, the General Assembly has lost its chance to redistrict until after the 2010 federal census."

Mullarkey also cited previous state practice and policy considerations as weighing against a second-in-a-decade redistricting. "The Framers knew that to achieve accountability there must be stability in representation," she wrote. "Limiting redistricting to once per decade maximizes stability."

Justice Rebecca Kourlis, one of the two dissenters, argued that the state constitution's provision specifying redistricting "when" Congress reapportions did not prohibit a subsequent remap, nor did the state court's adoption of new congressional maps prevent the legislature from "reclaiming its authority to redistrict."

In the Texas case, all three federal judges said mid-decade redistricting is not prohibited by the Constitution, federal statute, Texas law or tradition — at least when a new map substitutes for a court-drawn plan. But two of the judges recommended Congress ban the practice, citing "compelling arguments" why states should "abstain from drawing district lines mid-decade." [32]

The judges divided sharply, however, on whether the redistricting violated the Voting Rights Act by improperly weakening Hispanics' political clout. Two Republican-appointed judges upheld the decision to disperse Hispanic voters from a South Texas district held by a Republican incumbent — a Hispanic — because the move was offset by creation of a new Hispanic-majority district. The Democratic-appointed judge on the panel disagreed.

In the main opinion, Judge Patrick Higginbotham — a federal appeals court judge appointed in 1982 by President Ronald Reagan — rejected the Democratic plaintiffs' arguments that the Census Clause limits redistricting to once per decade. The clause, Higginbotham wrote, "does not mention the states or their power to redistrict, and we fail to see how it can limit a power it never references." The Democratic-appointed judge on the panel, John Ward, also said mid-decade redistricting was prohibited, but added, "There may be legitimate state interests advanced by the effort."

In the main opinion, Higginbotham rejected claims by Democrats and minority-advocacy groups that the Voting Rights Act was violated by dispersing blacks and Hispanics — changes affecting 11 of the state's previous districts, including Frost's old 24th. Higginbotham wrote that because the two groups together constituted only 46 percent of the voting-age population in the old district — less than a majority — the argument against the reconfiguration was political, not racial or ethnic.

Higginbotham also upheld the redrawing of GOP Rep. Henry Bonilla's 23rd district to reduce its Hispanic voting-age citizen population to 46 percent from 57 percent — chiefly by splitting the border city of Laredo. The move was aimed at boosting Bonilla, who won only 8 percent of the Hispanic vote when he narrowly defeated a Hispanic Democrat in 2002. But Higginbotham said the offsetting creation of a new Hispanic-majority district — the 25th, stretching 300 miles from the Austin suburbs south to the border — satisfied the Voting Rights Act. Ward — a federal district judge appointed by President Bill Clinton — said the redrawn 23rd district violated Supreme Court rulings against "minority vote retrogression."

Democrats asked the Supreme Court to stay the effect of the ruling and leave the existing districting map in place for the 2004 election, but the justices declined without comment. Democrats now plan a full appeal to the Supreme Court, but Republicans are confident about the outcome.

"We are in very good shape," says GOP lawyer Taylor. If the court does hear the case, oral arguments would not be held until fall 2004. ■

OUTLOOK

Winners Take All?

The House of Representatives undergoes some turnover at the start of each decade when seats are reapportioned among states and districts redrawn within the states. But House elections in 2002 saw considerably less turnover and less political competitiveness than in comparable years in any of the previous three decades — and, in fact, less turnover and less competitiveness than in a typical election year.

Only 16 incumbent House members were defeated in 2002 — compared to an average of 35 following redistricting in 1972, 1982 and 1992. In addition, fewer members retired: 35 in 2002 compared to an average of 48 for the first post-redistricting elections in the previous three decades. And — in a telling statistic compiled by Democratic attorney Hirsch — 338 of the House's 435 members were elected in 2002 with at least 60 percent of the vote in their districts. [33]

Hirsch views the lack of political competitiveness as a consequence of partisan gerrymandering and the courts' refusal to rein in the practice. He wants courts — federal or state — to consider the political effects of redistricting plans and require what he calls "a reasonable degree" of partisan fairness, competitiveness and stability.

Surprisingly, perhaps, Republican attorney Braden agrees on the diagnosis, but not on the cure. "Turnover in 2002 was way too low," Braden says. He blames "partisan" gerrymanders, where both parties used control of the process to protect incumbents, as well as "bipartisan" gerrymanders, where Republicans and Democrats combined to spare incumbents from competitive races.

But Braden says he is "adamantly opposed to the courts getting more politicized." States may want to add competitiveness to the factors to be considered in redrawing districts, he says, but federal courts should keep hands off. "My concern doesn't make it a constitutional issue," he says.

Supporters of redistricting reforms — such as independent commissions or the more far-reaching step of devising some form of proportional representation — also cite lawmakers' self-preservation instinct as a drawback of current practices. Academic experts who worry about the problem see no easy solution.

"No politician likes competitive seats," says the University of California's Grofman. "It's hard to imagine a situation where you will have a lot of seats that will shift back and forth.'

"Incumbents are quite powerful," says Washington and Lee's Rush. "How to repair that, I can't say."

For now, most Supreme Court-watchers do not expect the justices to use the Pennsylvania case to increase the judicial review of partisan gerrymandering. "I'm not very optimistic that *Bandemer* is going to be resuscitated," Grofman adds. "It's more likely that the final nail will be laid."

Without any judicial controls, partisan gerrymandering is likely to continue and perhaps increase, the University of Maryland's Herrnson predicts. "Once the precedent allows for extremely selfish behavior on the part of politicians, it will be followed until things become so out of hand that reform is ultimately enacted," he says.

Predictions about the future of mid-decade redistricting are more tentative. Some experts say if the courts give the practice a green light, both parties will draw new maps for partisan advantage whenever and wherever they can. Others question whether legislators of either party have much stomach for reopening the partisan warfare unless forced to.

For his part, state Sen. Todd Staples, a Republican architect of Texas' mid-decade redistricting, says he has no desire to redraw congressional maps anytime soon. "I want to take up redistricting again in the year 3011," Staples quips.

But Democratic attorney Hirsch notes that GOP lawmakers have not promised to stick with the map approved in 2003, which was designed to elect 22 Republicans. "If they get only 20 or 21 seats, it will be interesting to see if they try again in 2005 or 2007," he says.

Hirsch's Democratic colleague Hebert agrees judicial intervention is necessary to check partisan-driven redistricting. "It won't get better as long as the fox guards the district and just makes more foxes," he says. "It's time for the Supreme Court to step in; it's not going to happen in any other fashion."

But GOP attorney Krill in Pennsylvania says a Supreme Court decision allowing greater review of redistricting cases would damage the political process and the judicial system itself.

"If they adopt a more relaxed standard, then there's litigation all over the country," says Krill — not only over Congress but also over state legislatures, city councils, school districts and so forth. "It will be wasteful litigation that will immerse judges in every level — federal, state and local. It will be bad for the public perception of the judicial system." ■

Notes

[1] For detailed information, including maps, see the Web site of the Texas Legislative Council: www.tlc.state.tx.us.

[2] Quoted in Dave Leventhal, "Sessions, Frost Ready to Rumble," *The Dallas Morning News*, Jan. 18, 2004, p. 1B.

[3] For background, see Jennifer Gavin, "Redistricting," *The CQ Researcher*, Feb. 16, 2001, pp. 113-128.

[4] "Candidate and Office Histories," CQ Voting and Elections Collection, CQ Electronic Library, accessed Feb. 26, 2004; http://library2.cqpress.com/elections/histories.php.

[5] *Davis v. Bandemer*, 478 U.S. 109 (1986).

[6] In the only decision to cite *Davis v. Bandemer* to mandate an electoral change, a federal court in North Carolina required the state to elect state supreme court justices by district rather than statewide; the court said at-large elections disenfranchised Republicans. See *Republican Party v. Martin*, 980 F.2d 943 (4th Cir. 1992).

[7] Chip Scutari and Robbie Sherwood, "Legislative Districts Map Thrown Out; Judge Orders New Boundaries Drawn," *The Arizona Republic*, Jan. 17, 2004, p. 1B. The ruling upheld the commission's congressional district map. For background on the

About the Author

Associate Editor **Kenneth Jost** graduated from Harvard College and Georgetown University Law Center, where he is an adjunct professor. He is the author of *The Supreme Court Yearbook* and editor of *The Supreme Court from A to Z* (both *CQ Press*). He was a member of *The CQ Researcher* team that won the 2002 American Bar Association Silver Gavel Award.

initiative, see Chip Scutari, "Citizens Panel to Redraw Districts," *The Arizona Republic*, Nov. 8, 2000, p. 11E.

8 Background drawn from "Reapportionment and Redistricting," in *Congressional Quarterly's Guide to Congress* (5th ed., 2000), pp. 891-911. See also David Butler and Bruce Cain, *Congressional Redistricting: Comparative and Theoretical Perspectives* (1992), pp. 17-41.

9 "Reapportionment and Redistricting," *op. cit.*, p. 900. States with districts were Maryland, Massachusetts, New York, North Carolina, South Carolina and Virginia; at-large states included Connecticut, Georgia, New Hampshire, New Jersey, and Pennsylvania.

10 A chart summarizing the various formulas can be found in Butler and Cain, *op. cit.*, p. 19.

11 For a history, see Charles W. Eagles, *Democracy Delayed: Congressional Reapportionment and Urban-Rural Conflict in the 1920s* (1990).

12 The case is *Department of Commerce v. Montana*, 503 U.S. 442 (1992).

13 *Wood v. Broom*, 287 U.S. 1 (1932).

14 *Colegrove v. Green*, 328 U.S. 549 (1946).

15 The citation is 369 U.S. 186 (1962). For a history of the case, see Gene Graham, *One Man, One Vote: Baker v. Carr and the American Levelers* (1972).

16 The cases are *Gray v. Sanders*, 372 U.S. 368 (1963), and *Wesberry v. Sanders*, 376 U.S. 1 (1964).

17 The citation is 462 U.S. 725 (1983). The leading case on population deviations in legislative redistricting is *Mahan v. Howell*, 410 U.S. 315 (1973), which approved a Virginia plan with a 16 percent variation between the largest and smallest population districts.

18 The citation is 478 U.S. 109 (1986). Stevens and Powell dissented from the decision to uphold Indiana's districting plan.

19 Mark S. Monmonier, *Bushmanders and Bullwinkles: How Politicians Manipulate Electronic Maps and Census Data to Win Elections* (2001). Background drawn from "What a Friend We Have in GIS [Geographic Information Systems]," pp. 104-120.

20 The case is *Thornburg v. Gingles*, 478 U.S. 30 (1986). The decision held that minority plaintiffs could establish a claim of improper "vote dilution" under the Voting Rights Act by proving racially polarized voting, a legacy of official discrimination in voting or other areas, and campaign appeals to racial prejudice.

21 The citation for *Shaw v. Hunt* is 509 U.S. 630 (1993). The other cases are *Miller v. Johnson*, 515 U.S. 900 (1995) (Georgia) and *Bush v. Vera*, 517 U.S. 952 (1996) (Texas).

22 For background, see Kenneth Jost, "Census 2000," *The CQ Researcher*, May 1, 1998, pp. 385-408.

23 The case is *Department of Commerce v. United States House of Representatives*, 503 U.S. 442 (1999).

24 See Mary Clare Jalonick, "Court-Ordered Remap Aids Texas Incumbents," *CQ Weekly*, Nov. 17, 2001, p. 2758.

25 Gregory L. Giroux, "Judge's Ruling Puts New House District Up for Grabs," *CQ Monitor News*, Jan. 25, 2002.

26 Gregory L. Giroux, "Georgia Remap Merges 2 GOP-Held Districts," *CQ Weekly*, Oct. 6, 2001, p. 2001.

27 Jonathan Allen, "GOP Scores Major Win in Pennsylvania Redistricting," *CQ Monitor News*, Jan. 4. 2002.

28 See Gregory L. Giroux, "Redistricting Helped GOP," *CQ Weekly*, Nov. 9, 2002, p. 2934. See also Gregory L. Giroux, "Redistricting Increases Polarization," in *Politics in America 2004: The 108th Congress* (2003), p. xxiii.

29 See Gregory L. Giroux, "Texas GOP Outlasts Renegades, Prepares for New Congressional Map; Democrats Put Their Hope in Court," *CQ Weekly*, Sept. 6, 2003, p. 2145; Gebe Martinez, "In Texas Redistricting Game, DeLay Holds the High Cards," *CQ Weekly*, July 12, 2003, p. 1728.

30 For coverage, see Stephen Henderson, "Spirited Debate at High Court on Pa. Redistricting," *Philadelphia Inquirer*, Dec. 11, 2003, p. A19; Michael McGough, "Justices Treading Warily in Pa. Case," *Pittsburgh Post-Gazette*, Dec. 11, 2003, p. A12.

31 The decision is *Salazar v. Davidson*, 03SA133. For the most extensive coverage in Colorado newspapers, see John J. Sanko, "Dems Are Big Winners on Congressional Map," *Rocky Mountain News*, Dec. 2, 2004, p. 6A.

32 The decision is *Sessions v. Perry*, 2:03-CV-354. For the most extensive coverage in Texas newspapers, see David Paztor and Chuck Lindell, "Map Survives Court Challenge," *The Austin American-Statesman*, Jan. 7, 2004, p. A1.

33 Sam Hirsch, "The United States House of Unrepresentatives: What Went Wrong in the Latest Round of Congressional Redistricting," *Election Law Journal*, Vol. 2, No. 2 (November 2003), Table 1, p. 3.

FOR MORE INFORMATION

Center for Voting and Democracy, 6930 Carroll Ave., Suite 610, Takoma Park, MD 20912; (301) 270-4616; www.fairvote.org.

Common Cause, 1250 Connecticut Ave., N.W., Suite 600, Washington DC 20036; (202) 833-1200; www.commoncause.org.

Democratic National Committee, 430 South Capitol St., S.E., Washington, DC 20003; (202) 863-8000; www.dnc.org.

National Conference of State Legislatures, 7700 East First Place, Denver, CO 80230; (303) 364-7700; www.ncsl.org.

Republican National Committee, 310 1st St., S.E., Washington, DC 20003; (202) 863-8500; www.rnc.org.

Bibliography

Selected Sources

Books

Butler, David, and Bruce Cain, *Congressional Redistricting: Comparative and Theoretical Perspectives*, Macmillan, 1992.
Surveys the history and contemporary practices of U.S. congressional redistricting; compares practices in other democracies. Butler is a professor at Nuffield College, Oxford, England; Cain is director of the Institute of Governmental Studies, University of California, Berkeley.

Clayton, Dewey M., *African Americans and the Politics of Congressional Redistricting*, Garland, 2001.
An assistant professor of political science at the University of Louisville argues that the case for deliberately drawing majority-black congressional districts "remains compelling."

Grofman, Bernard (ed.), *Political Gerrymandering and the Courts*, Agathon Press, 1990.
Essays by 15 political scientists examine the Supreme Court's decision to allow federal challenges to gerrymandering. Includes 12-page list of references. Grofman is a professor of political science at the University of California, Irvine.

— (ed.), *Race and Redistricting in the 1990s*, Agathon Press, 1998.
Essays by 16 political scientists examine Supreme Court decisions in the 1990s limiting the use of race in redistricting.

Hill, Steven, *Fixing Elections: The Failure of America's Winner Take All Politics*, Routledge, 2002.
The Western regional director of the Center for Voting and Democracy strongly criticizes redistricting and the single-member, winner-take-all system, advocating proportional representation to increase political competition.

Kousser, J. Morgan, *Colorblind Injustice: Minority Voting Rights and the Undoing of the Second Reconstruction*, University of North Carolina Press, 1999.
A professor of social sciences at California Institute of Technology and frequent witness for minority groups in voting-rights cases analyzes the history of minority voting rights during post-Civil War Reconstruction and following passage of the Voting Rights Act in 1965. Includes 36-page bibliography.

Monmonier, Mark S., *Bushmanders and Bullwinkles: How Politicians Manipulate Electronic Maps and Census Data to Win Elections*, University of Chicago Press, 2001.
A professor of geography at Syracuse University's Maxwell School of Citizenship and Public Affairs examines the implications of high-tech, super-precise redistricting.

Rush, Mark E., *Does Redistricting Make a Difference? Partisan Representation and Electoral Behavior*, Johns Hopkins University Press, 1993.
A professor of politics at Washington and Lee University argues that concern about partisan gerrymandering is based on an inaccurate understanding of voting behavior and contributes to political divisiveness.

Rush, Mark E., and Richard L. Engstrom, *Fair and Effective Representation? Debating Electoral Reform and Minority Rights*, Rowman & Littlefield, 2001.
Two political science professors offer conflicting views on using proportional representation instead of winner-take-all, single-member districts. Includes excerpts from nine major Supreme Court decisions. Rush is at Washington and Lee University, Engstrom at the University of New Orleans.

Thernstrom, Abigail M., *Whose Votes Count? Affirmative Action and Minority Voting Rights*, Harvard University Press, 1987.
A senior fellow at the conservative Manhattan Institute argues that maximizing minority office-holding may inhibit political integration.

Articles

Hirsch, Sam, "The United States House of Unrepresentatives: What Went Wrong in the Latest Round of Congressional Redistricting," *Election Law Journal*, Vol. 2, No. 2 (November 2003), pp. 179-216.
A Washington lawyer for Democrats in redistricting cases strongly criticizes courts' reluctance to carefully scrutinize "severely partisan incumbent-protecting gerrymanders."

McDonald, Michael, "A Comparative Look at U.S. State Redistricting Processes," *State Politics and Policy Quarterly* [forthcoming, 2004].
An assistant professor of government and politics at George Mason University analyzes redistricting processes and lawmakers' use of them to influence electoral outcomes.

Persily, Nathaniel, "In Defense of Foxes Guarding Henhouses: The Case for Judicial Acquiescence to Incumbent-Protecting Gerrymanders," *Harvard Law Review*, Vol. 116 (2002), pp. 649-683.
A University of Pennsylvania law professor defends courts' deference to partisan-motivated redistricting.

"Reapportionment and Redistricting," in *Congressional Quarterly's Guide to Congress* (5th ed.), CQ Press, 2000, pp. 891-911.
Overview of relevant issues from the Constitutional Convention to present day. Includes selected bibliography.

The Next Step:

Additional Articles from Current Periodicals

Electoral Reform

Gledhill, Lynda, "Recall Mastermind Focuses on Redistricting Reform," ***San Francisco Chronicle*****, Nov. 1, 2003, p. A5.**
After Republicans and Democrats in the state Legislature struck a bipartisan deal to protect incumbents through redistricting, Ted Costa wants to push through an initiative giving the people authority to approve district maps.

Raspberry, William, "Advantage, Incumbents," ***The Washington Post*****, July 8, 2003, p. A17.**
The syndicated columnist discusses a proposal for multi-member districts to overcome gerrymandering and give a voice to voters in areas dominated by the other party.

Reding, Andrew, "Beyond Gerrymandering and Texas Posses: U.S. Electoral Reform," ***The Christian Science Monitor*****, May 29, 2003, p. 9.**
The sight of Texas Rangers chasing fleeing legislators is a sign that electoral reform in the U.S. is the only way to end gerrymandering; proportional representation, multiple-member districts or some variation may be the answer.

Vogel, Nancy, "Recall Backers Target Districts," ***Los Angeles Times*****, Oct. 31, 2003, p. B1.**
The same advocacy group behind the recall of Gov. Gray Davis launches an initiative drive to reshape legislative districts so that politicians face more competition on election day.

Gerrymandering

"How to Rig an Election," ***The Economist*****, April 27, 2002.**
Unlike most democracies, America puts redistricting in the hands of politicians rather than an independent commission; the results are predictably bizarre.

"Making Votes Count," ***The New York Times*****, Jan. 18, 2004, Section 4, p. 10.**
Noncompetitive elections, flawed voting technology and low voter turnout combine to undermine the "elective government" espoused by Thomas Jefferson.

"Rescuing U.S. Democracy," ***The Washington Post*****, Dec. 15, 2003, p. A30.**
Politicians are unlikely to freely give up the delicious power to construct safe districts for themselves while packing the opposition into fewer seats; the Supreme Court will have to intervene in these partisan disputes.

Axtman, Kris, "Redistricting: the Wars Get More Frequent," ***The Christian Science Monitor*****, May 29, 2003, p. 2.**
Some ask whether democratic legitimacy is being damaged when politicians choose voters rather than voters choosing politicians.

Babington, Charles, "Hey, They're Taking Slash-and-Burn to Extremes!" ***The Washington Post*****, Dec. 21, 2003, p. B1.**
Republicans say they're repaying Democrats for the decades they were in the minority; but this ever-increasing partisanship, exemplified by redistricting, may make cooperation impossible if Democrats retake Congress.

Blumenauer, Earl, and Jim Leach, "Redistricting, a Bipartisan Sport," ***The New York Times*****, July 8, 2003, p. A23.**
Democratic and Republican House members urge redistricting reform for the sake of American democracy.

Halbfinger, David, "Across U.S., Redistricting as a Never-Ending Battle," ***The New York Times*****, July 1, 2003, p. A1.**
House Majority Leader Tom DeLay's desire to win more seats for the GOP in Texas is rendering the bipartisanship of George W. Bush's days in Austin a distant memory.

Hill, Michael, "Political Cut-Outs," ***The Baltimore Sun*****, p. 1F.**
"Gerrymandering" goes back almost to the founding of the nation, but what, if anything, to do about it remains in dispute.

Hulse, Carl, "Democrats Scale Back Ambitions for House," ***The New York Times*****, Feb. 29, 2004, p. A20.**
Through redistricting in Texas, Republicans are gaining seats without elections and building the strength to stop the Democrats' bid to take back the House.

Page, Susan, "More Than Ever, Incumbents in Driver's Seat," ***USA Today*****, Oct. 30, 2002, p. 1A.**
Despite breathless political commentary, almost 90 percent of Americans live in districts where the outcome is so certain that their votes are irrelevant.

Iowa and Redistricting

Barnes, Fred, "Where Incumbents Tremble . . .," ***The Weekly Standard*****, Sept. 30, 2002.**
Iowa bucked the trend of entrenching incumbents in safe seats by turning its redistricting process over to the non-partisan Legislative Research Bureau.

Brownstein, Ronald, "Iowa Puts Politicians Through the Paces," ***Los Angeles Times*****, Oct. 15, 2002, p. A1.**
Rather than staying ensconced in safe districts, incumbents must get out and fight for new voters in competitive districts drawn after the last census.

Clymer, Adam, "Democracy in Middle America," ***The New York Times*****, Oct. 27, 2002, Section 4, p. 5.**
Iowa has nonpartisan redistricting, five House seats and three competitive districts; California has 53 House seats and had only one truly competitive House race in 2002.

Marlantes, Liz, "Iowa: Election Ground Zero," ***The Christian Science Monitor*****, Aug. 21, 2002, p. 1.**
Iowa's numerous competitive House seats and evenly divided electorate attract considerable attention from the national parties as competitive seats become rare.

Local Battles

Anderson, Nick, "GOP Battle Lines Redrawn in Georgia," ***Los Angeles Times*****, June 2, 2002, p. A15.**
Facing off in Georgia, two Republican incumbents battled for a conservative district whose possession would let them cruise to victory for the next decade.

Eilperin, Juliet, "Redistricting Inflames a Few House Races," ***The Washington Post*****, May 26, 2002, p. A5.**
Races between incumbents are particularly fierce because both candidates have incumbents' traditional advantages.

Graham, Judith, "Redistricting Draws Partisan Blood in Colorado," ***Chicago Tribune*****, May 27, 2003, News Section, p. 11.**
Political partisanship in the redistricting process could rise to new heights with decisions to redraw districts between census adjustments.

Green, Andrew, "A District Drawn for Democrat Victories," ***The Baltimore Sun*****, Feb. 29, 2004, p. 1B.**
Maryland's 2nd Congressional District provides an example of how packed districts drive off credible candidates from the other party.

Jacobson, Louis, "Back to the Redrawing Board?" ***National Journal*****, April 12, 2003.**
Colorado, Montana, Georgia, Texas, New Hampshire and New Mexico all have efforts underway to gerrymander legislative districts in the middle of the usual decennial cycle.

Kelly, David, "Colorado Redistricting Plan Illegal, Court Rules," ***Los Angeles Times*****, Dec. 2, 2003, p. A15.**
The Colorado Supreme Court ruled that the redistricting plan drawn up by state Republicans is unconstitutional.

Novak, Viveca, "The Blue Dog Hangs Tough," ***Time*****, Oct. 28, 2002, p. 43.**
A conservative Pennsylvania Democrat fights hard for reelection in a district drawn to ensure that he will lose.

Reid, T.R., "GOP Redistricting: New Boundaries of Politics?" ***The Washington Post*****, July 2, 2003, p. A4.**
The president of the Colorado Senate, a Republican, responded to criticism of the GOP's redistricting by saying that "nonpartisanship is not an option."

West, Paul, "Battle Lines Drawn, Incumbents Face Off," ***The Baltimore Sun*****, July 11, 2002, p. 1A.**
When one party dominates the redistricting contest, it often forces incumbents from the other party to compete for a single new district.

Race and Redistricting

Cohen, Richard, "Fewer Court-Drawn Maps This Time," ***National Journal*****, July 13, 2002.**
Following the 1990 census, federal courts were active in ensuring that redistricting created more black-majority districts to comply with the Voting Rights Act; the courts were relatively silent 10 years later.

Hockstader, Lee, "Supreme Court Hands Texas GOP a Redistricting Victory," ***The Washington Post*****, Jan. 17, 2004, p. A2.**
The Supreme Court gives Texas Republicans a significant political victory by refusing to block a mid-decade redistricting plan targeting white Democratic incumbents.

Melton, R.H., "Va. High Court Uphold GOP-Drawn Redistricting," ***The Washington Post*****, Nov. 2, 2002, p. B6.**
The Virginia Supreme Court unanimously rejected a Democratic challenge to a Republican redistricting plan that allegedly discriminated against black voters.

Rosenbaum, David, "In Georgia, a Shot at Congress for 5 Blacks," ***The New York Times*****, Sept. 24, 2002, p. A25.**
Georgia Democrats redrew the state's House districts after the 2000 census with a strategy called "max black," aimed at getting more blacks elected to Congress.

Tell, David, "Race to the Bottom," ***The Weekly Standard*****, July 21, 2003.**
Republican efforts to segregate the South into black and white districts for political gain, abetted by the courts and civil rights groups, are disgraceful.

Redistricting in the Courts

"Elections With No Meaning," ***The New York Times*****, Feb. 21, 2004, p. A14.**
An editorial urges the Supreme Court to preclude or reduce gerrymandering to give voters meaningful choices.

"Judgment Day," ***The Economist*****, Dec. 13, 2003.**
A suit before the Supreme Court brought by Pennsylvania Democrats argues that the Republican redistricting plan for the state is unconstitutional.

Carman, Diane, "Political Lines Being Drawn in Pa. Case," ***The Denver Post*****, Dec. 3, 2003, p. B1.**
The Colorado Supreme Court's ruling on the GOP redistricting plan failed to address whether partisan advantage may be considered in drawing district boundaries.

Cohen, Richard, "Democratic Turf Slip-Sliding Away," ***National Journal*****, Jan. 24, 2004.**

Democratic hopes that the federal courts will aid the losers in partisan redistricting battles prove to be misplaced as courts repeatedly reject challenges to new, gerrymandered congressional districts.

Hockstader, Lee, "In Texas Senate, a Racial Outburst," *The Washington Post*, Sept. 20, 2003, p. A6.
Texas Democrats accuse the state's Republicans of racism in their redistricting plan; a political scientist says white Democrats are the real targets.

Jordan, Lara, "Did the Pennsylvania Legislature Cross the Line?" *The Washington Post*, Dec. 11, 2003, p. A27.
The Supreme Court considers in *Vieth v. Jubelirer* whether congressional districts awarding two-thirds of Pennsylvania's congressional seats to Republicans when there are more Democratic voters in the state is a constitutional issue.

Plunkett, Chuck, and Howard Pankratz, "Cries of Bias Greet Remapping Ruling," *The Denver Post*, Dec. 3, 2003, p. A1.
The Colorado Supreme Court's ruling in its redistricting decision split along party lines, resulting in at least the appearance of partisanship on the court.

Richey, Warren, "Rigging Election Boundaries: When Does It Go Too Far?" *The Christian Science Monitor*, Dec. 10, 2003, p. 2.
For the first time in 17 years, the U.S. Supreme Court considers a case to determine whether political gerrymandering is so egregious it violates the Constitution.

Rosenbaum, David, "Congressional Redistricting Battle Could Lead to New Rules," *The New York Times*, Feb. 23, 2004, p. A18.
Supreme Court decisions on partisan gerrymandering are due by summer, and the results could help provide some resolution to a complex issue.

Rosenzweig, David, and Michael Finnegan, "Latino Voter Lawsuit Rejected," *Los Angeles Times*, June 13, 2002, p. A1.
Judges rejected a civil rights group's lawsuit challenging California's redistricting, saying that racial discrimination is not the problem it once was.

Taylor, Stuart, "Should the Supreme Court Clean Up Its Own Mess?" *National Journal*, Dec. 20, 2003.
Some argue the Supreme Court itself is responsible for the collapse of reasonable standards in the redistricting process.

Walsh, Edward, "Redistricting by GOP Raises New Questions," *The Washington Post*, Oct. 26, 2003, p. A1.
By redrawing district lines already determined for this decade's census, Republican lawmakers in Texas and Colorado enter uncharted legal and constitutional territory.

Walsh, Edward, "Supreme Court Upholds Mississippi Redistricting Plan," *The Washington Post*, April 1, 2003, p. A5.
After the Supreme Court unanimously ruled that a redistricting plan by three federal judges could stand, Mississippi Democrats claimed the judiciary favors the Republicans.

Wiltenburg, Mary, "High Stakes in Redistricting Fights," *The Christian Science Monitor*, Feb. 5, 2004, p. 16.
Since 2000 the number of successful legal challenges to districts alleged to be illegal or unconstitutional has declined.

Safe Seats

"Politics as Warfare," *The Economist*, Nov. 8, 2003.
Representatives in safe seats need to appeal only to the ideological voters who turn out for primaries; partisanship increases as a result.

Barnes, Fred, "An Election Year With No Races," *The Weekly Standard*, June 24, 2002.
The author decries the lack of true competition in House races due to redistricting efforts that lock incumbents into safe districts.

Cohen, Richard, "When Campaigns Are Cakewalks," *National Journal*, March 16, 2002.
Even Communist Party elections in the Soviet Union were subject to more uncertainty than today's House races.

Dann, Joanne, "Safe But Sorry," *The Washington Post*, Dec. 2, 2001, p. B1.
Partisan redistricting encourages hard-line candidates in safe districts who have no need to be sensitive to constituents' views.

Marlantes, Liz, "Redistricting Shifts Clout, but Plays It Safe," *The Christian Science Monitor*, June 10, 2002, p. 2.
In the aftermath of 9/11, lawmakers decided to make incumbent protection their top priority in redistricting after the 2000 census — the results are Rorschach-like fiefdoms.

Mitchell, Alison, "Redistricting 2002 Produces No Great Shake-Ups," *The New York Times*, March 13, 2002, p. A20.
After a redistricting process that focused on ensuring incumbents' re-elections, the 2002 House elections had about 35 to 55 competitive seats.

Quinn, Tony, "In California, Politicians Choose — and Voters Lose," *Los Angeles Times*, Sept. 29, 2002, Part M, p. 3.
Gerrymandered districts have destroyed any pretense of voter choice in California; the only meaningful elections are primaries limited to the most partisan voters.

Technology and Redistricting

Abramsky, Sasha, "The Redistricting Wars," ***The Nation*****, Dec. 29, 2003, p. 15.**

The author condemns a concerted new gerrymandering effort, aided by inexpensive, easy-to-use mapping software.

Dresser, Michael, "Redistricting Options Grow With Technology," ***The Baltimore Sun*****, May 8, 2001, p. 2B.**

With $3,500 and a standard computer, anyone can use the Caliper Corp.'s Maptitude software to instantly get population recalculations when shifting precincts from one district to another.

Yi, Daniel, "Political Mapping Process Is Redrawn," ***Los Angeles Times*****, Aug. 11, 2001, p. B1.**

A revolution in cheap, accessible mapping software allows political interest groups to draw their own redistricting maps and analyze voter demographics in an effort to influence political leaders during the redistricting process.

Texas

"A West Texas Hamlet Adjusts to Being Split by Redistricting," ***The New York Times*****, Nov. 30, 2003, p. A34.**

The new GOP redistricting plan divides Sonora, Texas, costing it an additional $5,000 to comply with the new districts.

Barnes, Fred, "Texas Chainsaw Gerrymander," ***The Weekly Standard*****, Oct. 13, 2003.**

The GOP's plans in Texas were nearly derailed by internecine squabbling, and popular Democrats like Charlie Stenholm will be hard to beat even in gerrymandered districts.

Blumenthal, Ralph, "After Bitter Fight, Texas Senate Redraws Congressional Districts," ***The New York Times*****, Oct. 13, 2003, p. A1.**

Texas' redistricting plan finally passed in the state Senate, but Democrats warn the genie is out of the box and Democrat-controlled states will now proceed with mid-decade redistricting of their own.

Gold, Scott, "Judges Uphold Texas' Contested Election Maps," ***Los Angeles Times*****, Jan. 7, 2004, p. A10.**

Declaring that they ruled only on the legality of the plan and not its wisdom, federal judges ruled in favor of Texas Republicans' redistricting plan.

Lichtblau, Eric, "Justice Dept. Rejected Idea of Joining Texas Dispute," ***The New York Times*****, Aug. 13, 2003, p. A16.**

Justice Department officials rejected the request by an aide to Tom DeLay, the House majority leader, that they assist in tracking down Democrats who fled to Oklahoma.

Martinez, Michael, "Texas Drama Over Redistricting Heads to Court," ***Chicago Tribune*****, Dec. 9, 2003, News Section, p. 13.**

As the case goes before a federal court, Democrats say that limits in the Texas Constitution on mid-decade redistricting are implied rather than explicit.

Walsh, Edward, "GOP Study Feeds Furor Over Texas Redistricting," ***The Washington Post*****, Oct. 12, 2003, p. A9.**

A candid analysis of the Texas GOP's redistricting plan and its intended effects by a Republican House staff member adds to the plan's controversy.

Walsh, Edward, "Texas Legislature Adjourns Special Session," ***The Washington Post*****, Aug. 27, 2003, p. A4.**

State Senate Democrats in Texas defeat a GOP redistricting plan by fleeing to New Mexico and denying the Senate a quorum with which to vote on the plan.

CITING *THE CQ RESEARCHER*

Sample formats for citing these reports in a bibliography include the ones listed below. Preferred styles and formats vary, so please check with your instructor or professor.

MLA STYLE

Jost, Kenneth. "Rethinking the Death Penalty." The CQ Researcher 16 Nov. 2001: 945-68.

APA STYLE

Jost, K. (2001, November 16). Rethinking the death penalty. *The CQ Researcher, 11,* 945-968.

CHICAGO STYLE

Jost, Kenneth. "Rethinking the Death Penalty." *CQ Researcher,* November 16, 2001, 945-968.

Back Issues

The CQ Researcher offers in-depth coverage of many key areas.
Back issues are $10. Quantity discounts available.
Call (866) 427-7737 to order back issues.

Or call for a free CQ Researcher Web trial!
Online access provides:

- *Searchable archives dating back to 1991.*
- *Wider access through IP authentication.*
- *PDF files for downloading and printing.*
- *Availability 48 hours before print version.*

CIVIL LIBERTIES
Race in America, July 2003
Gay Marriage, September 2003
Civil Liberties Debates, October 2003

CRIME/LAW
Cyber-Crime, April 2002
Corporate Crime, October 2002
Serial Killers, October 2003

ECONOMY
State Budget Crises, October 2003
Stock Market Troubles, January 2004
Exporting Jobs, February 2004

EDUCATION
Home Schooling Debate, January 2003
Combating Plagiarism, September 2003
Black Colleges, December 2003

ENERGY/TRANSPORTATION
Future of the Airline Industry, June 2002
Future of Amtrak, October 2002
SUV Debate, May 2003

ENVIRONMENT
Crisis in the Plains, May 2003
Water Shortages, August 2003
Air Pollution Conflict, November 2003

HEALTH AND SAFETY
Medicare Reform, August 2003
Women's Health, November 2003
Homeopathy Debate, December 2003

POLITICS AND PUBLIC POLICY
Abortion Debates, March 2003
State Budget Crises, October 2003

SOCIAL TRENDS
Latinos' Future, October 2003
Future of the Music Industry, Nov. 2003

TECHNOLOGY
NASA's Future, May 2003

TERRORISM/DEFENSE
Homeland Security, September 2003
North Korean Crisis, April 2003

WORLD AFFAIRS
Trouble in South America, March 2003
Rebuilding Iraq, July 2003
Aiding Africa, August 2003
The U.N. and Global Security, Feb. 2004

YOUTH
Preventing Teen Drug Use, March 2002
Sexual Abuse and the Clergy, May 2002
Movie Ratings, March 2003
Hazing, January 2004
Youth Suicide, February 2004

Future Topics

- ***Reforming Big-Time College Sports***
- ***Slavery and Human Trafficking***
- ***Anniversary of Desegregation***

CQ Researcher

Published by CQ Press, a division of Congressional Quarterly Inc.

thecqresearcher.com

Reforming Big-Time College Sports

Does the emphasis on winning exploit athletes?

The University of Colorado faces charges it used sex, alcohol and drugs to recruit high school players. Colorado is just the latest in a seemingly unending list of educational institutions embroiled in recent sports scandals, spurring widespread demands for reform. A growing number of critics argue college sports actually harms higher education and exploits athletes. Only 54 percent of Division I-A football players and 44 percent of the basketball players ever graduate; rates are lowest for minority players. The critics blame the win-at-all-costs ethic in many big-time athletics programs and the millions of dollars at stake. Meanwhile, the vast majority of schools have to subsidize their intercollegiate athletics programs. And some educators worry that the problems of big-time college programs are drifting into less-prominent sports and smaller schools.

University of Georgia basketball coach Jim Harrick resigned in March after his program was accused of academic fraud and making payments to players.

INSIDE THIS ISSUE

The CQ Researcher • March 19, 2004 • www.thecqresearcher.com
Volume 14, Number 11 • Pages 249-272

CQ PRESS

RECIPIENT OF SOCIETY OF PROFESSIONAL JOURNALISTS AWARD FOR EXCELLENCE ◆ AMERICAN BAR ASSOCIATION SILVER GAVEL AWARD

THE ISSUES

BACKGROUND

CURRENT SITUATION

OUTLOOK

SIDEBARS AND GRAPHICS

FOR FURTHER RESEARCH

Cover: University of Georgia basketball coach Jim Harrick resigned in March after the National Collegiate Athletic Association accused his program of academic fraud and improper payments to players. Harrick previously left the University of Rhode Island and UCLA amid allegations of improper conduct. (Getty Images/Johnathen Daniel)

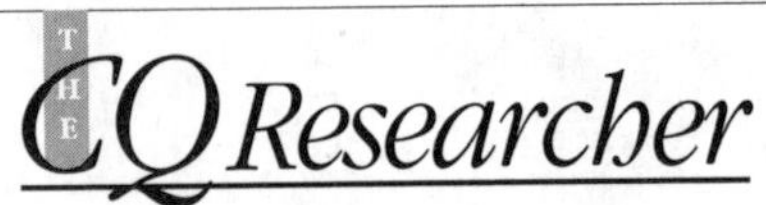

March 19, 2004
Volume 14, No. 11

MANAGING EDITOR: Thomas J. Colin

ASSISTANT MANAGING EDITOR: Kathy Koch

ASSOCIATE EDITOR: Kenneth Jost

STAFF WRITERS: Mary H. Cooper, David Masci, William Triplett

CONTRIBUTING WRITERS: Sarah Glazer, David Hatch, David Hosansky, Patrick Marshall, Tom Price, Jane Tanner

DESIGN/PRODUCTION EDITOR: Olu B. Davis

ASSISTANT EDITOR: Kenneth Lukas

A Division of Congressional Quarterly Inc.

SENIOR VICE PRESIDENT/GENERAL MANAGER: John A. Jenkins

DIRECTOR, LIBRARY PUBLISHING: Kathryn C. Suárez

DIRECTOR, EDITORIAL OPERATIONS: Ann Davies

CIRCULATION MANAGER: Nina Tristani

CONGRESSIONAL QUARTERLY INC.

CHAIRMAN: Andrew Barnes

VICE CHAIRMAN: Andrew P. Corty

PRESIDENT AND PUBLISHER: Robert W. Merry

The CQ Researcher (ISSN 1056-2036) is printed on acid-free paper. Published weekly, except Jan. 2, April 9, July 2, July 9, Aug. 6, Aug. 13, Nov. 26 and Dec. 31, by CQ Press, a division of Congressional Quarterly Inc. Annual subscription rates for libraries, businesses and government start at $625. Single issues are available for $10. Quantity discounts apply to orders over 10. Additional rates furnished upon request. Periodicals postage paid at Washington, D.C., and additional mailing offices. POSTMASTER: Send address changes to *The CQ Researcher*, 1255 22nd St., N.W., Suite 400, Washington, D.C. 20037.

Reforming Big-Time College Sports

BY TOM PRICE

THE ISSUES

Gary Barnett took over the University of Colorado football team in 1999 with a reputation as a disciplinarian who could clean up a troubled program. Five years later, things haven't worked out as planned.

Barnett was placed on paid administrative leave in February 2004 as the university grappled with charges it used sex, alcohol and drugs to recruit promising high school football players.

Seven women — including a former team kicker — claim to have been sexually assaulted by Colorado football players or recruits. Three women have sued the university charging it failed to protect them from rape. The suits reveal stories of alcohol-and-marijuana-fueled parties where strippers danced for recruits, young women willingly entertained them with sex and some women were raped. Other revelations include records of calls from the football recruiting coordinator's cell phone to a Boulder escort service. [1]

Getty Images/Jonathan Daniel

Indiana's Jeff Newton shoots over a University of Michigan defender at the Big Ten Men's Tournament, March 14, 2003. A growing number of critics argue big-time college sports actually harms higher education and exploits college athletes. Only about half of Division I-A football players and 44 percent of the basketball players graduate. The critics blame the coaches' win-at-all-costs ethic and the billions of dollars riding on TV revenues.

Colorado's sports program is just the latest to be caught up in scandal. Baylor University's basketball coach was taped urging players to mislead murder investigators. [2] St. Bonaventure University's president, athletic director and basketball coach left their jobs following a scandal that led the chairman of the school's Board of Trustees to kill himself. [3]

"It's like looking at the Grand Canyon," Jim Haney, executive director of the National Association of Basketball Coaches, said of the many scandals. "You can't take it all in." [4]

The National Collegiate Athletic Association (NCAA) is "treating this as if it were a crime wave," said President Myles Brand. "We are hiring more investigators and taking almost a law-and-order approach to misbehavior. It makes me wonder whether the coaches — because of their marketability, compensation and fan adulation — have come to feel above the morality and societal norms that govern us all." [5]

It's tempting to conclude that this must be the worst time in college sports history. But longtime reformer Richard Lapchick isn't so sure. When he founded the Center for the Study of Sport in Society at Northeastern University in 1984, he recalls, a school administrator told him, "'You have a small window of opportunity with all the scandals that have broken this year. You should be able to seize the moment.'

"The moment has never closed since then," says Lapchick, who now heads the Institute for Diversity and Ethics in Sport at the University of Central Florida. "People have asked me in previous years if that was the worst it's ever been. But it's kind of a continuation of terrible examples."

Even the general public is disenchanted. Two-thirds of those surveyed last year said colleges "place too much emphasis on athletics," and more than three-quarters said college athletes "are not held to the same academic performance standards as other students." Moreover, only a third said athletics is a "somewhat or very important" mission for colleges. [6]

There is general agreement the misconduct tends to be concentrated in big-time football and basketball programs, where television contracts and other lucrative commercial ventures offer enormous financial rewards to winning schools and coaches. Indeed, college sports has become a $4-billion-a-year enterprise, and the elite football and basketball teams — mostly those in the Atlantic Coast, Big East, Big 10, Big 12, Pac-10 and Southeastern conferences — earn multimillion-dollar profits for their universities.

Graduation Rates Improved in the 1990s

The National Collegiate Athletic Association (NCAA) instituted tougher academic standards and new academic support programs in 1996, and graduation rates began to improve. In 2002, 62 percent of Division I athletes who had enrolled six years earlier graduated. However, graduation rates remained lower for black players.

Percentage of Students Graduating Within Six Years

	Percentages	
	Avg. of students who enrolled between 1993-94 and 1996-97	Enrolled in 1996-97
All Division I Students	57%	59%
Blacks	39	41
All Division I Scholarship Athletes	60	62
Blacks	47	52
All Division I Scholarship Men s Basketball Players	42	44
Blacks	36	41
All Division I-A Scholarship Men s Football Players	51	54
Blacks	45	49

Source: NCAA Web site: http://ncaa.org/grad_rates/2003/d1/index.html

"Money seems to be the force that's causing what is happening," says William Friday, president-emeritus of the University of North Carolina and chair of the reformist Knight Foundation Commission on Intercollegiate Athletics. [7]

Because they bring millions of dollars to campus and are treated as celebrities, coaches and players on big-time teams often appear to believe they are above the rules, critics say, pointing out that the worst scandals tend to arise from attempts to recruit top athletes and keep them eligible to play.

For example, in the Southeastern Conference — a perennial basketball and football powerhouse — nine of the 12 schools are on NCAA probation, and two others just got off. Vanderbilt University was the lone exception to censure.

Colorado's travails stemmed from "spoiled, pampered, revered athletes and the coaches and administration that have a blind desire to win at all costs, with no self-examination," said Regina Cowles, president of the National Organization for Women's Boulder chapter. [8]

Critics also blame the drive to win. Coaches, athletic directors and even college presidents at the big-time sports institutions acquire a "winning-at-all-costs" ethic, says Linda Bensel-Meyers, who teaches English at the University of Denver and heads The Drake Group, a sports-reform organization of faculty who emphasize the importance of academic integrity.

Or, as Floyd Keith, executive director of the Black Coaches Association and a former head football coach at two Division I * schools, says: "You don't lose your job as a coach because you don't meet educational objectives. You lose your job because you don't win."

In the case of Nebraska football coach Frank Solich, you lose your job even when you educate *and* win.

Solich's 2003 team placed 84 players on the Big 12 Academic Honor Roll for earning at least a "B" average. The team won 9 of 12 games, ranked in the top 25 teams nationally and was invited to the Alamo Bowl. Throughout his career at Nebraska, Solich won 75 percent of the time, captured one Big 12 championship, was named conference coach of the year twice and played for the national championship in 2001.

Nevertheless, he was fired after the 2003 season. Nebraska Athletic Director Steve Pederson said he fired him because he did not want to let the program "gravitate into mediocrity." Pederson explained, "I understand we aren't going to win the championship every year, but I believe we should be playing for or gaining on the championship on a consistent basis." [9]

A growing number of critics also argue that college sports programs harm higher education and exploit college athletes, at the expense of their education. Although the proportions were up last year, only 54 percent of Division I-A football players and 44 percent of basketball players graduated. The vast majority of

* The NCAA places schools in divisions based on the emphasis they give to intercollegiate sports. Division I schools tend to have the most expensive programs and draw the biggest crowds. Division III schools award no athletic scholarships. Division II schools fall in between. For football, Division I is divided further into I-A, I-AA and I-AAA subdivisions. Division I-A schools spend the most and draw the biggest crowds. Division I-AAA schools don't play football.

schools subsidize their intercollegiate athletics programs at the expense of academic programs. And some educators worry that the problems of big-time athletics are drifting into less-prominent sports and smaller schools.

The recent deluge of scandals — coupled with the knowledge that the problem isn't new — has spurred growing demands for reform, most notably from the Knight Foundation Commission, the leading sports-reform panel, composed primarily of college presidents.

Some reformers suggest wringing the big money out of college sports and treating intercollegiate athletics as just another extracurricular activity. Others want a more equitable distribution of the billions of dollars in television revenue collected by powerhouse football and basketball schools.

Other reformers focus on the athletes themselves, suggesting that sports programs reduce their demands on athletes' time so they can study more and have a life outside of sports. Others say athletes should be paid for generating income for big-time sports programs.

Brand's selection as NCAA president last year appeared to give the reformers a huge boost. The former philosophy professor and president at Indiana University and the University of Oregon had been the first university president to head intercollegiate athletics' top governing body. He had gained national fame in 2000 when he fired legendary Indiana basketball coach Bob Knight for misconduct. He describes himself as an avid reformer, and he has warned college administrators that "without genuine reform, the future of intercollegiate athletics is in peril."

But more aggressive reformers, such as Bensel-Meyers, say Brand's efforts fall short. "Myles Brand's academic reforms are only going to perpetuate the problem," she argues. "We need a package plan that overhauls the whole system and enables regular students to play in a sports atmosphere that is actually part of the college."

As coaches, administrators, students, parents and sports fans debate how to reform college sports, here are some of the questions being asked:

Are intercollegiate athletics too commercial?

After his team crushed West Virginia University, 41-7, in the 2004 Gator Bowl, University of Maryland football coach Ralph Friedgen had a message for his employers: "I'd like more money." [10]

Having led the Terrapins to 31 victories in his first three seasons — compared to 32 wins in the preceding eight years — Friedgen had a powerful argument for improving on his contract. Not that his 10-year, $12-million contract was exactly paltry. Moreover, *The Washington Post* explained how the university could afford to give him a $100,000 raise right away and several hundred thousand more in subsequent years: The university was renegotiating its promotional contract with athletic garment maker Under Armour, and the Terrapins' new winning ways should earn them higher payments. Also, Nike was expected to up the ante when its contract with the school expires. And Maryland's share of ABC and ESPN payments for telecasting Atlantic Coast Conference (ACC) games is scheduled to jump from $2.6 million in 2004 to $3.8 million in 2010. [11]

Friedgen is not alone in the millionaires' club. More than 30 college football and basketball coaches make more than $1 million a year, mostly those whose teams consistently play in the big football bowls and final rounds of the NCAA men's basketball tournament. For instance, after leading LSU to a spot in the Division I national football championships this year, Nick Saban was offered a contract worth at least $2.3 million.

So You Want to Play College Ball?

Basketball players have the lowest chances of making a college or pro team, compared to football and baseball players. The National Collegiate Athletic Association (NCAA) estimates that only about 3 percent of high school basketball players typically play on an NCAA team — and only 1.3 percent of the NCAA players go on to the pros.

Chances of Playing at NCAA or Professional Level

	Men's Basketball	Football	Baseball
Total high school athletes	549,500	983,600	455,300
Total NCAA athletes	15,700	56,500	25,700
Total NCAA senior athletes	3,500	12,600	5,700
NCAA seniors drafted	44	250	600
High school players to NCAA	2.9%	5.8%	5.7%
NCAA seniors to pros	1.3%	2.0%	10.5%

Source: National Collegiate Athletic Association; ncaa.org/research/prob_of_competing/

The coaches command such payments because college sports is a $4-billion-a-year enterprise, and the elite football and basketball teams earn multimillion-dollar profits for their universities. The earnings come not just from selling tickets but also from promo deals from equipment manufacturers, sale of team-related paraphernalia and — most important — enormous television contracts.

CBS paid the NCAA $6.2 billion to televise the Division I basketball tournament for 11 years beginning in 2002, a contract worth about $780,000-per-win for schools that play. ABC paid hundreds of millions more for rights to football's Bowl Championship Series (BCS), dominated by Notre Dame and the six elite conferences. (The NCAA distributes the networks' proceeds to conferences according to how many tournament games their teams play.) Athletic equipment sponsorships also bring in the big bucks. Nike's contract with the University of Michigan alone is estimated to be worth at least $25 million over seven years. [12]

Critics assail these developments, not just because of the vast sums involved but also because of what the universities — and players — must do for the money. To maximize broadcast opportunities, basketball games are played nearly every day and late into the evening, while football teams play on weeknights — taxing the bodies of athletes who have to get up for classes the next morning. Televised games are interrupted for beer commercials, even though universities discourage students from excessive drinking. And the millions of dollars at stake increase the pressure to win.

"The pressure and time demands can be overwhelming," laments Chris Hill, a starting junior on Michigan State's basketball team, who nonetheless insists he loves playing big-time ball on television.

CNN/Getty Images

Former University of Colorado place kicker Katie Hnida is among seven women who claim to have been sexually assaulted by Colorado football players or recruits. Coach Gary Barnett was placed on paid administrative leave in February 2004 as the university grappled with charges it used sex, alcohol and drugs to recruit high school players.

"We played Wednesday night in Minnesota," he says of a recent road game, "and because of TV we played at 9. The game went into overtime, so we didn't get back to [campus] till 3 in the morning. By the time you get home, you're able to grab only a couple hours sleep before class."

To the Knight Commission's Friday, "there's no question commercialization is dominating college sports. There always have been problems, it's just bigger now, more expensive, vastly more involved with money.

"We're running an entertainment business that has no relationship to the academic program in the institution," he continues. "The ultimate problem now is what all of this is doing to the integrity of the institution itself."

University of Texas football coach Mack Brown has described it as being "in the education business Monday through Friday," and "in the entertainment business on Saturday." [13]

NCAA President Brand worries about the balance between the two "businesses" and perceives a drift away from what he calls "the collegiate model" of sports toward "the professional model." If the trend continues, Brand told the annual NCAA convention in Nashville in January, "College sports as we know it will disappear and with it the educational value to student-athletes and the institutional goodwill and support from alumni and fans." [14]

However, he also said, "those who proclaim that commercial interests have no place in intercollegiate athletics have a myopic view of the nature of the modern university. Universities, both private and public, cannot achieve excellence, including paying competitive faculty salaries and constructing necessary academic facilities, without individual and corporate support." [15]

And Georgetown University Athletic Director Joseph Lang warns against painting all schools with the greed of a few.

"Every year there are a certain number of problems. You can take those problems and suggest the sky is falling," Lang says. "But I wouldn't rush to an overgeneralization that everything that's going on is bad. There are an awful lot of good things going on in intercollegiate athletics all over the country."

At a Feb. 2 Knight Commission meeting, commission members expressed concern about extensive advertising during televised games and naming of bowls after corporations.

"Is there a way we can walk back from the ledge" of overcommercialization? University of Georgia President Michael F. Adams asked two ABC-TV executives who were at the meeting.

Said ABC Senior Vice President Loren Matthews: "You charge us less, and we can charge the sponsors less."

Charles E. Young, former CEO of the University of Florida and the University of California, Los Angles, added: "You have to walk back from some money."

The Big 10 already follows Young's suggestion, according to Conference Commissioner James Delany. "We're accused of a lot of things," he said, "but we leave money on the table all the time. People beg us to play football games on Thursday nights, [but] we don't. "We play on Saturday. That's part of our tradition." [16]

Do college sports harm higher education?

The University of Wyoming's Katie Groke and Michigan State's Hill are impressive ambassadors for college sports.

Groke won three letters with Wyoming's Division I women's soccer team and graduated last year with two degrees. She now works for a non-profit organization that supports female entrepreneurs.

Hill hopes to make it to the pros. But he's enrolled in the Honors College, plans to earn his finance degree in four years and has his eyes set on a business career when his basketball days are over.

Hill and Groke say that while college sports places great demands on student athletes, the benefits outweigh the disadvantages. The travel, the bonding and the thrill of competition make the hard work worthwhile, they say. And, because of the demands, they've learned to manage their time, set priorities and overcome challenges.

These are lessons "you'll carry with you for the rest of your life," Hill says.

"When all's said and done at your last senior game," Groke says, "I don't think many athletes would say they would have done it differently."

But their experiences are not universal, and some educators believe big-time sports harm the athletes and damage their schools.

"We violate our most fundamental values by exploiting young people" in big-time sports, says James J. Duderstadt, former president of the University of Michigan. "We bring in people who have no hope of getting a meaningful education, we have them major in eligibility, and we toss them aside when they lose it.

"After 10 years of leading the university, I became convinced that [college sports] actually harms the institution," he continues.

While two-thirds of Wyoming's female athletes graduated, only 18 percent of its men's basketball team did, according to the NCAA. [17] A majority of Michigan State's basketball team graduated, but only 41 percent of the football players. By comparison, only 35 percent of the black football players graduated, reflecting a nationwide trend of lower graduation rates for African-American athletes.

Overall, the Division I-A graduation rate was 42 percent for all basketball players and 36 percent for black players, 51 percent for football players and 45 percent for black football players. And the teams with the most wins often have the least graduates.

Syracuse, the 2003 Division I men's basketball champion, graduated no black players from the entering classes of 1992-95. [18] At the beginning of the 2003 tournament, all four No. 1 seeds had failed to graduate a single black player from the entering class of 1995. [19]

Hill admits that games, practice, travel, injury treatment and studying opponents' film can eat up 40-60 hours a week. Indeed, college athletes often find it necessary to practice and work out year round. Ramogi Huma, a former UCLA linebacker who heads the Collegiate Athletes Coalition, which seeks to improve conditions for players, says he chose a less-demanding major because of football's time demands, although he's glad he played.

Sports proponents argue that athletes benefit from the kinds of experiences described by Hill and Groke and that college sports contribute to a vibrant campus. Winning teams, they assert, bring valuable attention to a college, encourage financial contributions, attract desirable students and — with big-time teams — turn a profit for the universities.

"At great institutions of learning, part of the program is good, broad-based athletics," Georgetown's Lang says. "When teams are doing well, there's a buzz on campus. If you come here on a nice spring day and there's a lacrosse game going on and there's a track meet going and there are people throwing Frisbees, the place is alive."

But critics question the return on sports investments. In what Brand called "myth-breaking" findings, the NCAA reported last year that higher spending on football and basketball teams did not improve won-lost records, attract higher alumni contributions or bring better students to campus. [20]

In fact, only 40 of the 117 NCAA Division I-A schools make money on their athletic programs, according to Daniel Fulks, the Transylvania University accounting program director who

Scandals Likened to 'Crime Wave'

When star high school linebacker Willie Williams agreed to share his experiences as a heavily recruited football player early this year, readers of *The Miami Herald* got a startling look at how far big-time college sports recruiters will go.

Florida State University sent a private jet with a flight attendant to collect the 6-foot-2, 230-pound Miami senior. For dinner, Williams feasted on four lobster tails, two steaks and an order of shrimp scampi — then "we hit the clubs."

Alabama's Auburn University also sent a private plane, but Williams had to share it with six other recruits. Auburn cheerleaders gave the recruits a send-off at the end of the visit, chanting, "We want you, Willie. We want you."

The University of Miami couldn't very well fly Williams across town, so head coach Larry Coker picked Williams up at home in his Cadillac Escalade and deposited him in the Mayfair House Hotel's Paradise Suite, complete with a Jacuzzi on the balcony. Williams ate ribs, shrimp, barbecue chicken, lobster tails and steaks at fancy restaurants. Police escorts ushered the recruits' bus through red lights on their trips across town. The high-schoolers were taken partying on trendy South Beach.

Williams, a "B" student with respectable SAT scores, decided to attend Miami. But then his story took a bad turn.

After his newspaper diaries ran, Williams was charged with hitting a man outside a nightclub, hugging a woman without her permission and setting off fire extinguishers at the hotel during his recruiting trip to the University of Florida at Gainesville. It then was revealed that he had been arrested 10 times for property crimes and was being charged with probation violation. Now he waits for a judge to decide whether to send him to jail and for the Hurricanes to decide whether they still want him. [1]

Getty Images

Baylor University basketball player Carlton Dotson faces murder charges in the death of teammate Patrick Dennehy.

Williams' descriptions of lavish accommodations and partying at nightspots with college athletes raised eyebrows, especially since NCAA rules limit entertaining recruits to "a scale comparable to that of normal student life." [2] But Williams' tales were mild compared with some other recent recruiting scandals — most notably at the University of Colorado — in which strippers, pornography, alcohol and arranged sex were alleged to be part of the entertainment for high school athletes.

Noting the reported recruiting tactics were "morally reprehensible," NCAA President Myles Brand on Feb. 12 announced appointment of a task force to review NCAA recruiting rules and recom-

compiles NCAA financial statistics. The other 1,000 NCAA members lose money — an average of $3.8 million in 2001 at I-A universities and lesser amounts at smaller schools. And "the gap between the haves and the have-nots is getting larger every year," he says. [21]

Division I-A football and Division I men's basketball inspire the most concern, since Division I scholarship athletes who play other sports tend to graduate at higher rates than other students. And graduation rates for big-time football and basketball players rose in the most recent report, an indication that academic reforms are having an impact. [22]

However, critics warn that some of the academic problems are spilling over into non-revenue sports and smaller schools. "I had 22 other [non-revenue] teams chasing that [football/basketball] model," Terry Holland, former basketball coach and athletics director at Division I University of Virginia, told the Knight Commission in February. "When we gave them larger scholarship budgets, the average SATs and GPAs of entering students went down" because teams recruited players with lower academic qualifications. "When we gave them larger travel budgets, the academic performance went down" because players missed more classes.

Even Ivy League universities and elite colleges are shaving standards for athletes, according to William G. Bowen, president of the Andrew W. Mellon Foundation and former president of Princeton University, and Mellon researcher Sarah H. Levin. Although Ivy League schools do not offer athletic scholarships, some give athletes preference in admissions, Bowen and Levin found. As a result, athletes arrive with inferior academic credentials and don't perform as well in class as other students. They also perform worse than would be expected based on their own credentials, perhaps because they devote too much time to sports. [23]

mend needed revisions to the Division I Management Council meeting in April. [3]

The recruiting incidents represent just a fraction of the recent deluge of college sports scandals that Brand has likened to a "crime wave." [4] Other examples include:

- Baylor University basketball coach Dave Bliss caught on tape last summer urging players to mislead murder investigators. Bliss wanted to portray murdered player Patrick Dennehy as a drug dealer to provide an explanation for income Dennehy had received improperly in connection with Baylor's basketball program. Bliss resigned. Carlton Dotson, another Baylor player, was charged with killing Dennehy. [5]
- The departures of St. Bonaventure University's president, athletic director and basketball coach last spring when it was revealed the team's center did not meet NCAA eligibility requirements. President Robert J. Wickenheiser had personally approved the junior-college transfer's eligibility, even though he only had a welding certificate. Distraught by charges the school had compromised its Franciscan values, Trustees Chairman William E. Swan killed himself. [6]
- The suspension or expulsion of six St. John's University basketball team members after they picked up a 38-year-old woman at a suburban strip club after a Feb. 5 game and took her back to the team's hotel, where some of them had sex with her. School President the Rev. Donald J. Harrington lamented "the culture of the team" that had made such conduct acceptable. [7]
- The departures of University of Georgia basketball coach Jim Harrick and his son, assistant coach Jim Harrick Jr., in March after their program was accused of academic fraud and making improper payments to players. The university withdrew from post-season play as self-punishment. NCAA investigators said players received a total of $1,872.66 in improper benefits and that Harrick Jr. had fraudulently awarded "A" grades to three players in a class he taught on "Coaching Principles and Strategies of Basketball." The university said all 39 students in the course received "A"s.

Harrick Sr. had previously left coaching positions at the University of Rhode Island and UCLA amid allegations of improper conduct. [8]

---

[1] Information about Willie Williams comes from the following articles in *The Miami Herald* by Manny Navarro: "Willie Williams' Recruiting Journey," Jan. 13, 2004, p. D1; "Auburn Fails to Get Williams," Jan. 21, 2004, p. D8; "UM Trip Is Paradise for Williams," Jan. 27, 2004, p. D1; "Williams Signs With Miami," Feb. 4, 2004. "Talent, Triumph, Trouble: It's Story of Williams' Life," Feb. 15, 2004, p. C17.

[2] 2003-04 NCAA Division I Manual, Article 13.5, Entertainment, available at http://ncaa.org/library/membership/division_i_manual/2003-04/2003-04_d1_manual.pdf.

[3] "NCAA President Myles Brand Forms Task Force to Review Recruiting Practices," *NCAA News Release*, Feb. 12, 2004, available at http://ncaa.org/releases/miscellaneous/2004/2004021201ms.htm.

[4] Pete Alfano, "NCAA Coaches Slide Down Slippery Slope," *St. Paul Pioneer Press*, Sept. 7, 2003, p. 3C.

[5] Bill Hanna, "Dotson Indicted In Death Of Player," *Fort Worth Star Telegram*, Aug. 28, 2003, Metro Section, p. 1.

[6] Mike Wise, "Picking Up Pieces of a Shattered Program," *The New York Times*, Nov. 4, 2003, p. D1.

[7] Rafael Hermoso, "Ingram Out At St. John's," *The New York Times*, Feb. 11, 2004, p. D1; Hermoso, "At Its Lowest, St. John's Tries to Hold Head High," *The New York Times*, Feb. 9, 2004, p. D1; Ron Dicker, "Expulsion and Suspensions Leave St. John's in Shambles," *The New York Times*, Feb. 6, 2004, p. D1; Roger Rubin, "Harrington-Jarvis Word War Cuts Two Ways," *Daily News* (New York), Feb. 10, 2004. p. 71.

[8] Mark Schlabach, "Scandal Drives UGA's Harrick to Quit," *The Atlanta Journal-Constitution*, March 28, 2003, p. 1A; Schlabach, "NCAA Acts on Harrick Charges," *The Atlanta Journal-Constitution*, Jan. 6, 2004, p. 1C; Christian Red and Michael O'Keeffe, "Trouble U: NCAA May Need Outside Reformers to Step in," *Daily News* (New York), Aug. 31, 2003, p. 90.

However, athletes at elite schools graduate at least as often as other students, sports advocates contend, and their total college experience may be just as worthwhile as non-athletes' — even if their grades are a bit lower, "Given the time and effort that athletes put out, to get a couple of B's isn't so terrible," Princeton Political Science Professor Harold A. Feiveson said. [24]

According to the Institute for Diversity and Ethics in Sport's Lapchick, "The overwhelming majority of universities educate their student athletes," and the problems that exist can be fixed. "The schools that flagrantly violate the rules create the impression that all of college sports is a cesspool. But it's not."

Case in point: The nation's No. 2 Division I basketball team at the end of this year was Stanford, which lost just one game. Its basketball graduation rate for the most recent four classes: 100 percent.

Should college athletics be exempt from antitrust law to better enforce reforms?

From 1952 to 1984, the NCAA negotiated television contracts for all football telecasts. It limited the times the top teams could be televised, provided television opportunities for less prestigious schools and distributed the income widely.

However, the Supreme Court in 1984 ruled that the NCAA was functioning as "a classic cartel," by fixing prices and "seriously restrict[ing] free-market forces." The ruling meant that the Universities of Oklahoma and Georgia — which brought the suits — and other NCAA members were free to cut their own TV deals. [25]

The result, in many reformers' eyes, is today's smorgasbord of televised games — with students playing football in midweek, late at night and in the morning, and enormous TV windfalls for the half-dozen most powerful conferences.

Antitrust laws also knocked down an attempt by the NCAA to restrict some assistant coaches' salaries. After losing in lower courts, the NCAA agreed in 1999 to pay $55 million to former Division I assistant coaches whose annual pay was capped at $16,000 from 1991 to 1995. [26]

Last year, a federal district court in Ohio ruled that NCAA restrictions on basketball schedules violated antitrust laws. The NCAA cannot restrict teams' participation in basketball tournaments organized independently of the NCAA, the court ruled. [27]

Now a growing number of reformers want the NCAA exempted from antitrust laws, believing it's the only way to trim excessive costs and harness rampant commercialism. Without an exemption, proponents say, the NCAA cannot control sports telecasts and sports spending.

NCAA President Brand thinks exemption would create a useful reform tool, but he questions whether it would be worth the effort. [28]

Meanwhile, opponents have attacked the idea on several fronts. Some view antitrust laws as tools for reform; others don't trust the NCAA to use the exemption powers wisely.

Tom McMillen, a former college and professional basketball player, introduced exemption legislation when he was a U.S. representative from Maryland in 1991. Only NCAA regulations could end the "arms race" among colleges that feel a competitive need to constantly spend more on salaries and facilities, he argued. "It's exactly like the arms race in the Cold War," he said, "but instead of two countries it's 100." No one could "unilaterally disarm." [29]

Although McMillen's bill failed, pressure for such a measure is coming now from outside Congress. Transylvania University's Fulks has documented the growing gap between "have and have-not" college athletic programs. He suggests that getting an antitrust exemption from Congress is "the only way you can get it to stop."

Without an exemption, antitrust laws pose "a very important barrier to cost-containment," Pennsylvania State University President Graham Spanier said. [30]

An exemption would allow the NCAA to order colleges to support women's sports without eliminating non-revenue men's teams, an advisory panel told the U.S. Education Department. [31] An exemption, reformers say, also would allow the association to rein in coaches' salaries, which would not only cut spending but also bring athletic departments into mainstream campus life.

"It's crazy to me that coaches get paid $1 million and $2 million," says Smith College economics Professor Andrew Zimbalist, author of several books about the economics of sports.

Tulane University President Scott Cowen wants an exemption so the NCAA can take control of postseason Division I-A football games. Cowen leads the Coalition for Athletic Reform, which is comprised of presidents of schools in conferences that have been shut out of the Bowl Championship Series. [32]

Other reformers argue the BCS violates antitrust laws by excluding the other conferences, a demonstration of why an exemption is not supported universally. [33]

Robert W. Brown, an economist at California State University, San Marcos, who studies the economic value of college athletics, opposes allowing an NCAA monopoly to interfere with natural market forces. Individual colleges are free to limit coaches' salaries and enact reforms, Brown points out. Restrictions imposed by a "classic cartel" like the NCAA, he says, would merely encourage members to cheat. Most scandals now spring from NCAA regulation of players, such as restrictions on payments and requirements that they meet academic standards, he says.

Reformer Bensel-Meyers opposes an exemption because she does not think the NCAA has any real authority over universities. "If the institutions have already sold out to the higher dollars, there's no way the NCAA has any authority to rein in the problems," she says. "A lot of members of The Drake Group think the NCAA should have less of a hand in the pot."

Similarly, attorney Alan C. Milstein says the NCAA "is the problem, not the solution." Milstein employed antitrust laws this year to overturn the National Football League (NFL) rule that players could not be drafted until three years after they graduated from high school. Milstein says his client, former Ohio State University running back Maurice Clarett, challenged the rule because the NCAA and Ohio State mistreated him. He plans to enter the draft.

The NFL and NCAA restrict players, Milstein argues, "so the schools can maintain free farm systems for the pros and make all the money without any of it going to the kids."

For its part, the NFL says younger players are not capable of playing against professional football players. The NCAA says its regulations are designed to preserve amateurism and fair competition in college sports.

The debate notwithstanding, spokespersons for both the House and Senate Judiciary committees say no legislative action is planned this year on exempting the NCAA from antitrust laws. ■

BACKGROUND

Early Scandals

In the first-known college sports contest, the Harvard crew beat Yale's rowers in 1852. Seven years later, Amherst beat Williams in the first-known intercollegiate baseball game by the mind-boggling score of 73-32. [34]

Continued on p. 260

Chronology

Early 1900s
Violence begets first reform demands; cheating, recruitment scandals haunt college sports.

1905
President Theodore Roosevelt demands an end to excessive violence during season in which 18 football players die.

1906
Intercollegiate Athletic Association (IAA) establishes football safety rules.

1910
IAA changes name to National Collegiate Athletic Association (NCAA).

1914
Professor at Ohio's Otterbein College laments recruiting improprieties.

1929
Carnegie Foundation condemns college sports corruption.

1937-1940
Rise of college basketball.

1937
First national basketball tournament organized by small-college National Association of Intercollegiate Basketball (NAIB), later the National Association of Intercollegiate Athletics (NAIA).

1939
Oregon beats Ohio State in first NCAA basketball championship; Fordham defeats Waynesburg in first televised college football game.

1940
NAIB holds first national meeting.

1945-1970
Scandals, television challenge big-time college sports.

1945
Five Brooklyn College basketball players expelled for taking bribes.

1951
Point-shaving indictments returned against 33 basketball players from seven colleges, four in New York.

1952
Three University of Kentucky students are convicted of point shaving during 1949 season. . . . NBC pays $1.1 million to televise football games.

1970s *Colleges open doors to women athletes.*

1971
Association for Intercollegiate Athletics for Women (AIAW) is organized; it disbands in 1983.

1972
Title IX of the Education Amendments of 1972 prohibits sex discrimination in education.

1973
Wayne State University diver Dacia Schileru is first woman to compete in an NCAA championship.

1980s *NAIA establishes women's programs.*

1981-82
Women compete for NCAA championships in basketball, field hockey, swimming, tennis, volleyball.

1984-2004 *Commercial floodgates open, followed by scandals, reforms.*

1984
Supreme Court rules NCAA can't monopolize football telecasts.

1987
NCAA closes Southern Methodist University's football program for two years for serious rules violations.

1989
Knight Foundation creates Commission on Intercollegiate Athletics.

1991
Knight Commission urges college presidents to assert control over intercollegiate sports.

1997
College CEOs take control of NCAA.

1998
Major football conferences create Bowl Championship Series.

2002
CBS pays $6.2 billion to televise Division I basketball tournaments for 11 years.

2003
Myles Brand becomes first college CEO to head NCAA. . . . Rising NCAA admissions and eligibility requirements help raise Division I graduation rates. . . . Avalanche of scandals shake college sports.

2004
Scandal epidemic continues with reports that high school recruits at University of Colorado are plied with alcohol, marijuana and sex.

Continued from p. 258

It was football, however, that produced the first college sports scandals and inspired the first college sports reform — and the problem was violence, not corruption. [35]

Protective equipment was scarce and ineffective. The rules, such as they were, allowed dangerous play. In 1905, 18 players were killed and 149 seriously injured in college football games.

President Theodore Roosevelt — no shrinking violet — was appalled. On Oct. 9, while the deadly 1905 season was still in progress, he summoned representatives from Harvard, Yale, Princeton and Columbia to the White House and gave them a simple message: Clean up football, or abandon it.

Two months later, representatives from 13 schools met to discuss reform. By March 31, 1906, the Intercollegiate Athletic Association of the United States had been born, with 62 schools as members. In 1910, it changed its name to the National Collegiate Athletic Association.

The association was to conduct intercollegiate athletics "on an ethical plane in keeping with the dignity and high purpose of education." But the early NCAA leaders quickly learned that reforming college sports is no easy task.

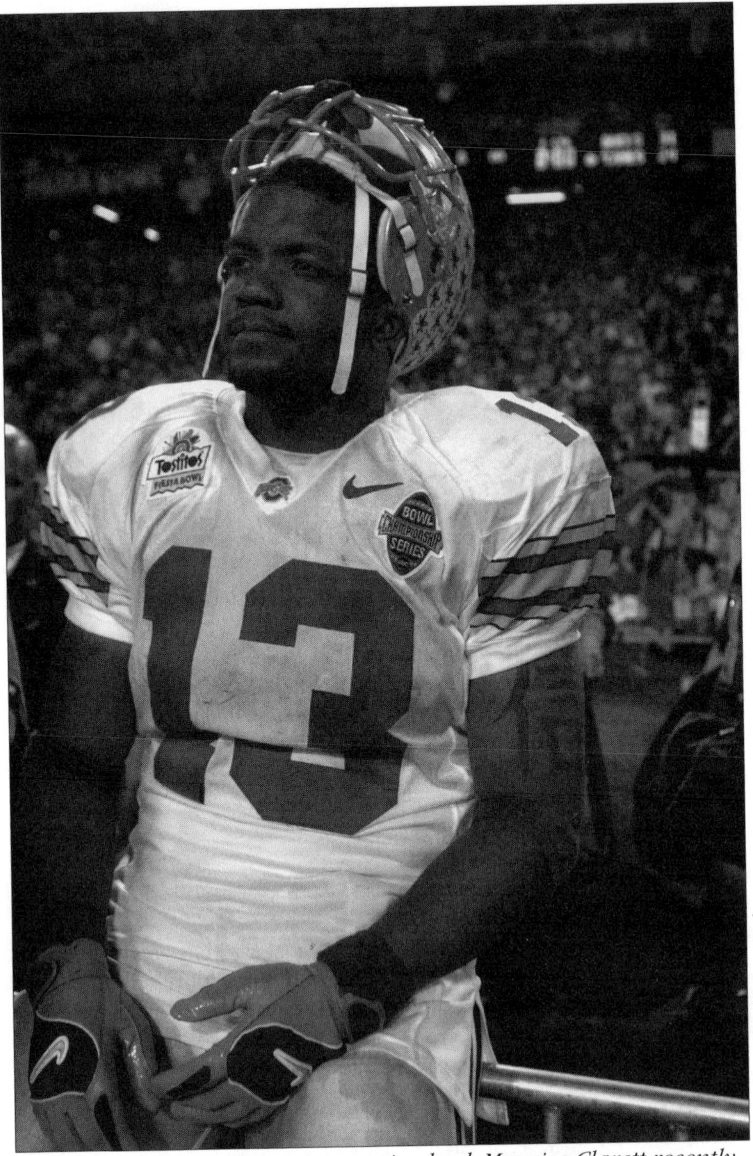

Getty Images/Brian Bahr

Former Ohio State University running back Maurice Clarett recently won his challenge to the National Football League rule preventing college players from entering the NFL draft until three years after their high school graduation. Clarett said he opposed the rule because the NCAA and Ohio State had mistreated him.

In 1906, the association eliminated the most dangerous plays and established the basis for the game we know today — legalizing the forward pass and requiring 10 yards for a first down. Nonetheless, 33 players died on the football field in 1909, and the association adopted more drastic rules changes.

From early on, college sports has been haunted by overly aggressive recruitment of promising players, payment of student athletes and other misconduct familiar today. In a lament with a 21st-century ring, Otterbein College Professor C.W. Savage said in 1914: "Under existing conditions, promising young athletes in high schools and academies are rounded up by alumni scouts or other agencies, they receive inducements of one sort and another, in many cases legitimate and in many other cases such as to prostitute all moral integrity. He thus enters college with the wrong idea of the relative importance of sport and study, [then] lives in an athletic atmosphere that is commercialized and professionalized."

In 1929, a Carnegie Foundation report condemned rampant corruption in college sports.

Yet, despite obvious abuses of NCAA standards, member colleges were allowed to police themselves until 1940, when the executive committee was authorized to investigate alleged violations of the association's amateurism principles.

In 1948, the NCAA adopted a statement of principles that banned athletic scholarships, required athletes to be amateurs and held them to the same academic standards as their fellow students. But the association adopted only one penalty for schools that violated the code — expulsion from the NCAA.

Thus, when the first allegations of violations were brought to the 1950 NCAA convention, members refused to take the extreme step of throwing the alleged violators out of the organization. The association repealed that code in 1951, then adopted a new set of regulations in 1952.

During the same period, college athletes began coming under criminal investigation, as gamblers and fixers paid players to shave points and throw basketball games. In 1945, five Brooklyn College students were expelled for accepting bribes to throw a game. In 1951, 33 players from seven schools — including the 1950 NCAA and NIT basketball champion, City College of New York — were indicted for point shaving, and two were sent to prison. In 1952, three University of Kentucky students were convicted of gambling and point shaving.

Following the Kentucky revelations, the NCAA suspended its basketball program for a year and made it the first team to be officially placed on probation.

TV's Impact

While the NCAA was dealing with the gambling scandals, it was also coming to grips with television. Fordham University had beat Waynesburg College 34-7 in the first televised college football game in 1939, but it did not cause much of a stir. One camera from station W2XBS (now WNBC) sent the action out to the few hundred New York homes with TV sets. Far more fans — 9,000 — saw the game in person, and W2XBS paid no fees for the right to televise the game. [36]

But by 1951, the NCAA realized television could either cripple or promote college sports. Led by Television Committee Chairman Thomas J. Hamilton of the University of Pittsburgh, the NCAA banned live telecasts of football games, except for "controlled telecasts" used to study TV's effect on game attendance.

In 1952, the NCAA decided to sell a TV package covering all member schools. Bought by NBC for $1.1 million in 1952, it allowed a game to be televised nationally on 12 Saturday afternoons. No school could appear more than once, and the games had to involve schools from all parts of the country. Small-college games of regional interest also could be televised, and additional games could be televised if approved by the television committee. Sponsors had to be "organizations of high standards that meet traditional college requirements of dignified presentation."

The NCAA kept control of football telecasts until 1984, when the Supreme Court found the arrangement violated antitrust laws. The universities of Oklahoma and Georgia had sued the NCAA, supported by other football powers that wanted to make their own TV deals. By then, the NCAA television football package was worth more than $30 million a year. [37]

The NCAA retained control of television rights to its basketball tournaments, which grew to the $6.2 billion CBS paid to televise the Division I tournament for 11 years beginning in 2002.

In a 1993 report, however, the National Association of College and University Business Officers warned schools they could harm students by catering to broadcasters' needs. When a student plays an away game at 9 p.m. midweek, he may have a hard time doing well in a morning class the next day, if he doesn't miss it altogether.

Women's Movement

The women's movement also spurred changes in college sports. Until the 1970s, "college sports" at the national level was essentially synonymous with "men's college sports."

Until then, women had nothing like the NCAA to promote and govern their sports. Vassar College fielded two women's baseball teams as early as 1866, Tuskegee Institute offered athletic scholarships to women in the 1920s, when only 22 percent of American colleges sponsored women's teams. The Intercollegiate Women's Fencing Association was organized in 1929. [38]

But not until 1971 did women from 280 schools form the Association for Intercollegiate Athletics for Women (AIAW), and it turned out to be short-lived.

A year later, Congress passed Title IX of the Education Amendments of 1972 — prohibiting sex discrimination in educational institutions. Colleges and college sports associations realized they would have to do more to accommodate women athletes. At the time, only about 31,000 women were playing college sports, less than $100,000 in athletic scholarships was available to women, and the average college sponsored just two women's teams. [39]

The NCAA opened championship competition to women for the first time in 1973, when Dacia Schileru of Wayne State University in Detroit competed in diving. By the 1981-82 school year, women's teams were entering championship competition in basketball, field hockey, swimming, tennis and volleyball, and women's athletic programs were invited to become full NCAA members.

Similarly, the National Association of Intercollegiate Athletics (NAIA) — a rival organization of small colleges that today has about 360 members — established women's programs in 1980; the AIAW went out of business three years later.

Scandals Redux

If the 1980s were good for women's sports, they were a time of continued scandals for big-time men's teams. The most egregious, in the NCAA's view, involved improper

Can Brand Reform the NCAA?

Myles Brand first burst onto the national stage in 2000 after he fired Bob Knight, the legendary and volatile Indiana University basketball coach best known for winning games and losing his temper.

When the National Collegiate Athletic Association (NCAA) made Brand its president in January 2003, it was sending a message that reform was high on the organization's agenda — and not just because he axed Knight. Brand, then Indiana University's president, was the first NCAA chief executive to come from outside college athletics. An ardent college sports reformer, he had delivered a widely publicized 2001 speech at the National Press Club in which he called for "academics first" in college sports reform. [1]

Brand grew up in Brooklyn, an avid Dodgers fan who ran track and played basketball in high school. He also played basketball and lacrosse as a freshman at Rensselaer Polytechnic Institute (RPI) in Troy, N.Y. But "the pull of academics" lured him away from organized sports; today his physical recreation focuses on hiking, canoeing and horseback riding. [2]

The first in his family to graduate from college, Brand earned a B.S. in philosophy at RPI in 1964 and a Ph.D. at the University of Rochester in 1967. He began teaching philosophy at the University of Pittsburgh, moved on to the Universities of Chicago and Arizona and became president of the University of Oregon in 1989 and of Indiana in 1994.

Brand's arrival at the NCAA was greeted with both hope and skepticism. Although he had fired Knight, Brand clearly also enjoyed big-time college sports. And, as president of a voluntary organization of more than 1,000 independent colleges and universities, he would have to reform through persuasion rather than command.

Brand is a "fine leader," Wake Forest University President Thomas K. Hearn Jr. said when he was appointed. "The question is: Can the organization be led?" [3]

As University of Kansas Chancellor Robert Hemenway has noted, "No one ever accused the NCAA of having a streamlined bureaucracy." [4]

"He thinks he can make a difference," said University of Arizona Athletics Director Jim Livengood. "Now, whether he can or not, I don't know." [5]

Brand acknowledges the challenge. When he was asked if he sensed a desire for change in the NCAA, he replied, "Among some, but not all." [6]

Insisting he can achieve reform, Brand likened the NCAA president to a college executive, who can't simply order tenured faculty around. "A university president can move the institution in certain directions, not as a corporate CEO dictator but as a person who sets the agenda, brings people to see a point of view and advocates a certain position," he said. [7] "Running up the hill by yourself doesn't do any good. If the troops aren't with you, and everyone isn't on board, you're not going to get it done." [8]

Brand advocates what he calls the "collegiate model" — as opposed to the "professional model" — of college sports. He also wants athletics integrated into mainstream campus life and insists that college sports put the student first.

"The student has to be at the center of all we do," he told the Knight Foundation Commission on Intercollegiate Athletics in February. "We want them to get a good education. We want to turn them into productive citizens. We want them to achieve

payments to Southern Methodist University (SMU) athletes — done with the knowledge of both the school's Board of Directors and the Texas governor. For the only time in history, the NCAA imposed its "death penalty," shutting down the SMU football program for two years.

Other schools were found to have given improper benefits to athletes, violated recruiting regulations and falsified athletes' academic records. By the end of the decade, polls showed the public believed colleges overemphasized athletics, commonly paid players, inflated athletes' grades and allowed athletes to ignore academic standards required for other students. Among the most shocking revelations were confessions by professional athletes that they had played on collegiate teams without ever learning to read or write.

Concerned that the abuses "had reached proportions threatening the very integrity of higher education," the Knight Foundation created the Knight Commission on Intercollegiate Athletics in October 1989. Co-chaired by Notre Dame University President Theodore M. Hesburgh and UNC's Friday, the panel became the most influential voice for college sports reform.

Its first report, in 1991, called for college presidents to take control of intercollegiate sports and focus on establishing academic integrity, financial integrity and accountability. Those recommendations have remained at the heart of the commission's work ever since.

Many college presidents have asserted more control over their sometimes-independent athletic departments. College CEOs gained full authority to govern the NCAA in 1997. When Myles Brand left Indiana University to become NCAA president in January 2003, he became the first college CEO to run the association.

During the '90s, the association had adopted reforms designed to enhance the "student" part of student-athletes' lives. Athletes-only dormitories were banned and use of specially catered sports training tables in dining halls was curtailed. Athletes were limited to 20 hours of competition and practice per week, but that is regularly their potential, whether it's in academics or athletics."

College athletes also suffer, he says, because college sports "has drifted off from the mainstream of the campus."

After more than a year on the job, Brand gets mixed reviews. Fans laud his attempts to rein in the big-time athletics tail that's been wagging the academic dog, but reformers doubt the NCAA can reform itself.

Floyd Keith, executive director of the Black Coaches Association, says Brand has done "a super job," particularly on behalf of minorities. "It's important that he's trying to separate professionalism from amateurism," Keith says approvingly.

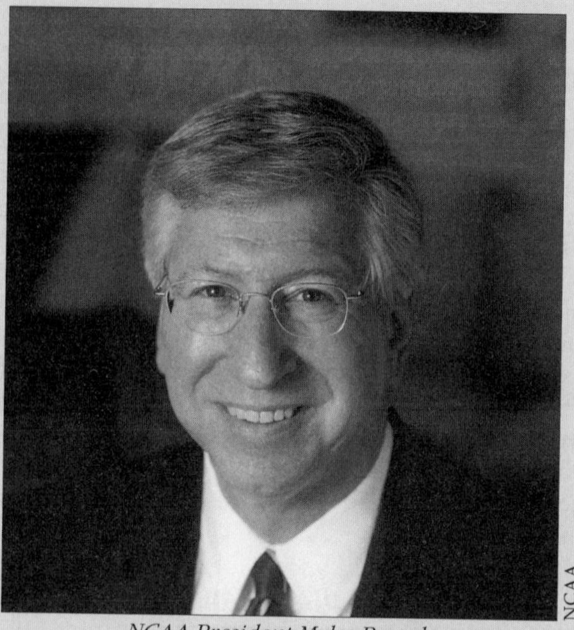

NCAA

NCAA President Myles Brand.

Former University of Wyoming soccer player Katie Groke, who graduated last year with two degrees, says it's "refreshing" that Brand is trying to see the student-athletes' perspective. "I'm excited that he's getting back to academics and being so stern about commercialism," she says.

Former American Council on Education head Robert Atwell calls Brand "a profile in courage" for firing Knight. "If anybody can do that job, he can," Atwell says.

However, he warns, Brand is not in charge of the NCAA. "He is answerable to various groups of presidents, who are in turn answerable back home to constituencies, many of whom are very supportive of the athletic enterprise."

Agreeing that Brand's power is limited, University of Michigan President James J. Duderstadt says, "He's in a position kind of like [U.N. Secretary-General] Kofi Annan."

---

1 Liz Clarke, "It's a Brand New Start for Collegiate Athletics," *The Washington Post*, Dec. 1, 2002, p. D1.

2 Michael Dobie, "Meet the Prez," *Newsday* (New York), Dec. 1, 2002, p. B12.

3 *Ibid.*

4 Lance Purmire, "Brand Urges Academic Reforms," *Los Angeles Times*, Jan. 13, 2003, Sports section, p. 3.

5 Steve Wieberg, "Brand Takes Control, Such As It Is, of NCAA," *USA Today*, Jan. 10, 2003, p. 4C.

6 Joe Lapointe, "The NCAA Selects Brand As Its Chief," *The New York Times*, Oct. 11, 2002, p. D1.

7 Wieberg, *op. cit.*

8 Liz Clarke, "Commission Looks to Fix an Industry in 'Trouble,' " *The Washington Post*, Nov. 25, 2003, p. D2.

exceeded through the use of "voluntary" activities.

In its 1991 report, the NCAA had found that fewer than half of student athletes were earning degrees — and only a quarter of the black athletes. Thus, academic requirements for admission and maintaining eligibility were stiffened, and schools were required to provide tutoring and counseling services to recruited athletes.

As a result, graduation rates rose gradually throughout the decade. In 2002, 62 percent of Division I athletes who had enrolled six years earlier graduated. For men's basketball players, however, the overall graduation rate was 44 percent, and only 41 percent for black players. ■

CURRENT SITUATION

Demands for Reform

An ever-expanding epidemic of college sports scandals has spawned what appears to be an unprecedented level of demands for reform. At least a half-dozen major efforts are examining different aspects of the problem, says the Knight Commission's Friday. "There is movement, and it is gaining strength."

In fact, he says, given the events of the last 14 months, "There is much more agitation about the difficulties in intercollegiate sports than at any time in my experience."

And Friday has more experience than most. Before becoming chairman of the Knight Commission in 1989, he ran the University of North Carolina for 30 years.

The universities have no choice but to reform college sports if they want to maintain "the sense of integrity and honor that they're supposed to manifest," he insists.

Reformer Bensel-Meyers says it's not accurate to talk about a sports-reform movement, because "there's not one unified reform movement going on. Individual reform units are trying to make changes. Things are hitting a crisis; there are enough people who are concerned."

The reform groups espouse several, often conflicting, causes — from stripping commercialism from big-time college sports to sharing the profits of commercialism more widely. And they're forming some unexpected alliances.

In a February meeting between five leaders from the Coalition on Intercollegiate Athletics — a faculty group devoted to athletic reform — and five Division I athletic directors, both groups reported finding a surprising amount of agreement. Last year, the professors met with representatives of the Association of Governing Boards of Universities and Colleges and of the NCAA, and the three groups agreed to form a new organization, the Alliance for Athletic Reform.

The most important reform group is the NCAA itself, which has the power to act. And it is acting.

Division I college athletes' 62 percent graduation rate in 2002 was an all-time high, which NCAA officials attributed in part to tougher eligibility standards implemented in 1996. It was 2 points higher than the year before, 3 points higher than the rate for all students, and the highest percentage recorded since tracking began in 1984. Black athletes continued to graduate at lower rates — 52 percent — but that represented a 5 point increase over the previous year. And the 41 percent graduation rate among black male basketball players was 5 points higher than the previous year.

"This illustrates that changes in NCAA minimum standards can have a positive impact on academic performance," NCAA President Brand said.[40] And the organization has continued to upgrade the standards.

Beginning this academic year, entering students must have completed 14 core courses in high school and maintained a 2.0 grade average. Freshmen must complete 24 hours of college coursework and earn at least a 1.8 average. To maintain eligibility, athletes must complete 40 percent of the requirements for a degree by the end of their sophomore year, and an additional 20 percent in each of the next two years.[41]

In April, the Division I directors will decide whether to reward and punish schools based on athletes' academic performance. Proposed punishments include reducing the number of scholarships available, restricting recruiting activities and exclusion from pre- and postseason competition. Suggested rewards include a larger share from NCAA tournament revenues. Later, directors are expected to discuss reducing payments to schools that fail to meet the standards.[42]

Tougher Proposals

But many teachers, administrators, students, coaches and outsiders think the NCAA reforms don't go far enough. Several prominent retired basketball coaches — John Wooden of UCLA, Dean Smith of North Carolina and Terry Holland of Virginia, for instance — want to ban freshmen from varsity competition, as was the case before 1972. Holland and Smith want to make junior-college transfers sit out for a year as well.

"You have to show you're a student before you can play ball," Smith told the Knight Commission.

Smith and retired Nebraska football coach Tom Osborne (now a Republican representative from Nebraska) have petitioned college presidents to ban alcohol advertising from broadcasts of college sporting events. "This is the leading cause of young deaths, of date rape, and here we are advertising it," Smith said.

Holland wants game schedules changed to minimize missed classes.

Meanwhile, the Black Coaches Association this year is expected to publish a "report card" on how aggressively athletic departments are trying to find minorities to fill important vacancies. It will examine the number of minority candidates interviewed, the diversity of search committees, the university's affirmative-action policy and how well the athletic department followed it, association chief Keith explains.[43]

"We don't say you have to hire an African-American," says Keith, former head football coach at the University of Rhode Island and Howard University. But it's important that minorities have a real opportunity to be considered, he says. Otherwise, schools "will perpetuate the old syndrome that you hire who you know."

Fewer than 5 percent of Division I-A football coaches are black, although most players are black. If coaches from historically black colleges are excluded, only 3.4 percent of NCAA athletics directors are black, Keith points out. Noting that 8.3 percent of U.S. Army generals are black, Keith postulates, "It's easier to become a general in the U.S. Army than an athletics director or Division I-A head football coach."

Athletes' Demands

The Collegiate Athletes Coalition — which claims to represent more than 1,000 college athletes, mostly Division I football and basketball players — has sought reform through the state legislatures. The coalition, which is advised by the United Steelworkers union, wants better health insurance, multiple-year scholarships that cover the full cost of college, less restriction on outside income and more time for academics and social life.

It won an initial victory in California, where the Senate adopted a Student Athletes' Bill of Rights that would override NCAA policies on scholarships, employment, health insurance,

Continued on p. 266

At Issue:

Can the NCAA effectively reform college sports?

MYLES BRAND
PRESIDENT, NATIONAL COLLEGIATE ATHLETIC ASSOCIATION

WRITTEN FOR *THE CQ RESEARCHER*, MARCH 2004

Not only can the NCAA effectively reform college sports, but it has been doing so for nearly a century. The organization was founded in 1906 to reform college football and to bring some order to the rules under which the game was being played. In some form or fashion, reform has been an ongoing priority for the NCAA ever since. In fact, given that the environment is always changing, reform is a constant.

It is important to be precise about what is meant in this instance by "the NCAA." There is often confusion about whether the term means the national office and staff in Indianapolis, or the 1,200 colleges and universities that are members of the NCAA, or the full association — the membership, staff and all the governing bylaws and structure. In this case, college sports can only be reformed by the association. I and the staff in Indianapolis alone certainly cannot successfully change college sports. Nor can the colleges and universities do so by themselves. It will take the discipline and full cooperation of the entire association.

True reform in terms of how behavior within college sports aligns with the values of higher education, also requires discipline from campus to campus. The campus is the first line of defense against cheating, unbridled self-interest and other attacks on the collegiate model of athletics that damage not only the integrity of college sports but also that of the colleges and universities that sponsor intercollegiate athletics. University presidents, therefore, are key to ensuring that athletics reform is played out across higher education in accordance with the association's bylaws and with profound respect for the spirit behind the rules. They must also have the support of faculty, athletics directors, coaches and student athletes.

Indeed, it takes an entire campus to operate an athletics program worthy of the academy.

Through the NCAA, university presidents will continue to examine the state of college sports as both a mirror of society and a window on the campus. By exercising their responsibility for setting national policy, they will guide the administration of intercollegiate athletics by establishing standards that all institutions must follow. The NCAA is the right and proper forum for the debate and adoption of those standards.

As a university president recently said, "If the NCAA ceased to exist this morning, we would have to reinvent it this afternoon."

LINDA BENSEL-MEYERS
DIRECTOR, THE DRAKE GROUP; PROFESSOR OF ENGLISH, UNIVERSITY OF DENVER

WRITTEN FOR *THE CQ RESEARCHER*, MARCH 2004

The NCAA cannot effectively reform college sports. How can it succeed when it places corporate interests before those of higher education? The NCAA essentially is in collusion with the National Football League and National Basketball Association to exploit colleges as a free, professional sports farm system.

The NCAA's role as a regulator of sports trade creates a powerful incentive for higher education to compromise its central mission of preserving and perpetuating those values that capitalism does not encourage — moral integrity, the disinterested search for truth and the civilized and humane treatment of others independent of socioeconomic class, race and gender.

All of these values are compromised by the code of "win at any cost." When maximizing revenues supplants the educational development of the students, when it becomes the end that justifies the means, the NCAA cannot institute reform since it is the source of the problem. The NCAA institutionalized the problem when it chose to create "athletic scholarships" to avoid workman's compensation claims. The NCAA essentially created the myth of the "student athlete" to disguise the fact that athletic scholarships in reality are bogus contracts for participants in high-revenue entertainment sports.

Athletes who want an education are often prevented from getting one due to the demands intercollegiate sports make on their time, particularly when many are recruited without the prerequisite skills of other students; on the other hand, those who don't want an education usually have no choice but to take the college route to enter the pros, seeing it as the only place to develop and showcase their athletic skills. In practice, the athletic scholarship serves the pre-professional players better than the students themselves, particularly when we realize how it takes away enrollment places from non-athletic students who might better profit from access to a college education.

The only way to reform the situation is to separate the universities from the entertainment industry, to remove athletic scholarships and replace them, within the institution, with need-based financial aid, and outside, with professional sports clubs where athletes who are not — and have no wish to be — students can receive pay for their role as the public's gladiators. The NCAA cannot reform collegiate athletics, but it can reform itself by honestly taking on the job of regulating a farm system independent of higher education.

Continued from p. 264

athletes' ability to transfer if their head coach leaves and their right to retain an agent.[44] If the bill, which awaits House action, becomes law, it would force the NCAA to either change its rules, exempt California colleges or kick them out of the association.

Coalition Chairman Huma says his organization is working with state legislatures because "the NCAA is not capable of reforming itself."

The NCAA and its student athlete advisory committees oppose the legislation, although the student panels have expressed concern about many of the issues the coalition is raising.

While most reformers want to take money out of college sports rather than spread it around, one group, the Coalition for Athletic Reform — comprised of college presidents whose schools have little chance of playing in the Bowl Championship Series — want the lucrative competition opened to more schools.

Bensel-Meyers says The Drake Group is pushing for comprehensive reforms that would end college sports' role as a free farm system for professional sports, forcing the pros to establish their own minor leagues for young players who aren't really interested in higher education, and "enable regular students to have their own collegiate sports that actually are part of the college."

Other reformers would accept the commercialization of big-time football and basketball as long as other sports are protected. "[One] solution is to isolate big-time football and basketball," says George H. Hanford, president emeritus of The College Board, who played three sports at Harvard in the late 1930s and early '40s. "You can have courses in football, prepare kids to go into the professional ranks, give them an associate degree in football, and make them take a modicum of other courses so they're about halfway to a legitimate degree and could come back to get it.

"If you build the firewall, you're legitimizing what is going on but keeping it from infecting everybody else."

Similarly, Indiana University English Professor Murray Sperber, a leading advocate of college sports reform, envisions benefits from employing athletes like other staff. "If you want to take a course or two, that's fine," says Sperber, the author of several books critical of college sports, including *Beer and Circus: How Big-Time College Sports Is Crippling Undergraduate Education.* "There would be some athletes who might actually want a degree. You could say, 'If you don't make the pros or your career ends early, we'll guarantee you a scholarship to come back.'

"Not every school would go in that direction," he continues. "I think you'd end up with 60 schools at the top rung, and all the rest would just have to give up the pretense of competing and fall back to something much like the Division III model."

Attorney Milstein agrees big-time athletes should be paid. "If someone were a virtuoso violin player, she could be in the New York Philharmonic," Milstein says. "She could also be attending NYU and be in the school orchestra. It's just ludicrous not to allow athletes the same kind of opportunities.

"It would be one thing if you had a pure system. But you have a system where everybody's making tons of money except for the kids who are earning it," he says. ■

OUTLOOK

Last Chance?

College sports soothsayers offer a wide range of predictions about the future of intercollegiate athletics — from unabashed professionalism to old-fashioned amateurism.

But they all agree on one thing: "I would bet within the next year there will be a scandal in college sports," Indiana's Sperber says. "Coaches who cheat, people who pay money to athletes, people who fix grades. That is as inevitable as the next snowflake that I can see out my window will fall onto the ground."

Many also agree with another Sperber prognostication: If college sports executives don't clean up their own act soon, outsiders — state legislatures, courts, perhaps Congress — will try to do it for them. "The current reform movement is different from all earlier efforts in one important way," he said. "It is probably the final one that will originate within higher education, sponsored by groups with academic interests at heart. If this reform attempt fails, changes to the college-sports system will probably come from outside the academy."[45]

College sports took an indirect hit this year from the court that overturned the NFL rule requiring high school graduates to wait three years before turning pro. If higher courts uphold that decision, big-time college football teams will lose some of their best players early, as basketball teams do now. Moreover, more students could now enter college only for sports, ignoring studies while expecting to leap to the pros in a year or two, NCAA President Brand said.

The court's decision should encourage the NFL and the National Basketball Association to create minor leagues, he said. It also may encourage colleges to declare freshmen ineligible for varsity sports, to discourage high school graduates from viewing college athletics as a brief detour on the way to the pros, he added.[46]

If colleges do not curb excess commercialism, Sperber and others warn, they could lose even more-damaging lawsuits. "Sooner or later, someone's going to figure out to sue us over injuries to players," former Michigan President Duderstadt predicts. "Then you'll begin to see $10-, $20-, $50-million judgments. And maybe finally the federal government will realize these kids really are employees of the institution, and they ought to have the same rights of unemployment, workmen's comp, health care, perhaps even the ability to organize."

Rampant commercialism also could lead taxing agencies or legislatures to remove college sports' nonprofit status, several reformers suggested. "If college sports is left untouched, and it gets bigger and bigger, you're going to see state legislatures and Congress say it is not an academic enterprise, so we're going to treat it like business," Knight Commission Chairman Friday says.

Meanwhile, four legislatures — Colorado, Nebraska, Oklahoma and Texas — have joined California in considering bills that would override NCAA rules in order to aid college athletes.

Without reform, college revenue expert Fulks foresees "a continuation of the growing gap between the financial haves and have-nots, until at some point it splits. I can see a split in Division I-A coming eventually, where the have-nots back off and reach cost-control measures," while the haves continue their big-time spending.

The NCAA is wrapping up its latest round of academic reforms this year, Brand said. Then it will focus on athlete welfare and finances.

Whatever reforms are adopted, University of Texas Athletics Director DeLoss Dodds is confident intercollegiate sports will always be with us. If intercollegiate football were abolished [at Texas], he said, "the intramural program would gather the best athletes to compete against the best at Texas A&M. Pretty soon, they'd draw a crowd. It'd be like stopping the wind from blowing. It would grow back the same way." [47] ■

Notes

[1] Kelli Anderson and George Dohrmann, "Out of Control?" *Sports Illustrated*, Feb. 23, 2004, p. 64; Charlie Brennan and Jody Berger, "Sixth Woman Alleges Assault," *Rocky Mountain News*, Feb. 20, 2004, p. 5A; B.G. Brooks, "Barnett Seen as Determined," *Rocky Mountain News*, Feb. 19, 2004, p.18A.

[2] Bill Hanna, "Dotson Indicted in Death of Player," *Fort Worth Star Telegram*, Aug. 28, 2003, Metro Section, p.1.

[3] Mike Wise, "Picking Up Pieces of a Shattered Program," *The New York Times*, Nov. 4, 2003, p. D-1.

[4] Pete Alfano, "NCAA Coaches Slide Down Slippery Slope," *Saint Paul Pioneer Press*, Sept. 7, 2003, p. 3C.

[5] *Ibid.*

[6] Welch Suggs, "Sports as the University's 'Front Porch'? The Public Is Skeptical," *The Chronicle of Higher Education*, May 2, 2003, p. 17.

[7] For background, see Richard L. Worsnop, "College Sports," *The CQ Researcher*, Aug. 26, 1994, pp. 745-768.

[8] Anderson and Dohrmann, *op. cit.*, p. 64.

[9] Eric Olson, "Pederson Ready to Bear Weight of Decision to Fire Solich," The Associated Press, Dec. 1, 2003.

[10] Barry Svrluga, "Friedgen Has Options, and Would Like More Money," *The Washington Post*, Jan. 2, 2004, p. D7.

[11] Svrluga, "Friedgen Wants Raise; Terps Want Friedgen," *The Washington Post*, Jan. 3, 2004, p. D3.

[12] Figures in these four paragraphs are from: The Knight Foundation Commission on Intercollegiate Athletics, "A Call to Action: Reconnecting College Sports and Higher Education," June 2001; Mike Triplett, "Saban Thanks LSU," *Times-Picayune* (New Orleans), Feb. 21, 2004, Sports Section p. 1.

[13] Kirk Bohls, "Big Games, Big Money, Big Troubles," *Austin American-Statesman*, Aug. 24, 2003, p. C1.

[14] Myles Brand, "State of the Association Speech," January 2004, available at www.ncaa.org/releases/miscellaneous/2004/2004011102m.

[15] Carter Strickland, "Brand's Plan To Be a Hard Sell," *Spokesman Review*, Jan. 21, 2003, p. C1.

[16] Jay Weiner, "Big Ten Is Much More Than Games," *Star Tribune* (Minneapolis), Jan. 11, 2004, p. 1C.

[17] Unless otherwise noted, graduation rates refer to the percentage of athletic scholarship recipients who enrolled between 1993 and 1996 and graduated within six years. The statistics are available at http://ncaa.org/grad_rates.

[18] Institute for Diversity and Ethics in Sport, available at www.bus.ucf.edu/sport/public/downloads/media/ides/men_chart_01.pdf.

[19] Alexander Wolff, "A Matter of Degrees," *Sports Illustrated*, April 7, 2003, p. 23.

[20] Gary T. Brown, "Eight-Year Study of Sports Spending Takes Myths to Task," The NCAA News, Aug. 18, 2003. Available at http://ncaa.org/news/2003/20030818/active/4017n04.html.

[21] Daniel L. Fulks, "Revenues And Expenses of Division I and II Intercollegiate Athletics Programs: Financial Trends and Relationships — 2001," available at www.ncaa.org/library/research/i_ii_rev_exp/2002/d1_d2_revenues_expenses.pdf.

[22] Statistics available at http://ncaa.org/grad_rates.

[23] William G. Bowen and Sarah H. Levin, "Revisiting 'The Game of Life': Athletics at Elite Colleges," *The Chronicle of Higher Education*, Sept. 19, 2003, p. B12.

About the Author

Tom Price is a Washington-based freelance writer who focuses on education, technology and business. Previously he was a correspondent in the Cox Newspapers Washington Bureau and chief politics writer for the *Dayton Daily News* and *The Journal Herald*. He is the author of three major studies of politics and the Internet published by the Foundation for Public Affairs and author of *Washington, D.C. for Dummies*. His work has appeared in *The New York Times*, *Time*, *Rolling Stone* and other publications. He earned a bachelor of science in journalism at Ohio University.

[24] Welch Suggs, "The Big-Time Cost of Small-Time Sports," *The Chronicle of Higher Education*, Sept. 19, 2003, p. 35.
[25] Gordon S. White, "NCAA Telecast Rights on Football Struck Down," *The New York Times*, Sept. 16, 1982, p. B19; "Judge Burciaga Gets Down to Business with College Football," *Sports Illustrated*, Sept. 27, 1982; Fred Barbash, "Supreme Court Breaks NCAA Hold On Televised College Football Games," *The Washington Post*, June 28, 1984, p. A1.
[26] Welch Suggs, "NCAA to Pay $55-Million to Settle Lawsuit by Assistant Coaches," *The Chronicle of Higher Education*, March 19, 1999, p. A47.
[27] "NCAA Is Enjoined from Enforcing 'Two in Four Rule,' " *Entertainment Law Reporter*, January 2004.
[28] Mark Alesia, "Brand Wouldn't Support More Control of College Sports," *The Indianapolis Star*, Jan. 11, 2004, p. 1C.
[29] Mark Alesia, "Brand Wouldn't Support More Control of College Sports," *The Indianapolis Star*, Jan. 11, 2004, p. 1C.
[30] Diana Jean Schemo, "Title IX Panel Favors Lifting Antitrust Laws," *The New York Times*, Jan. 30, 2003, p. D2.
[31] *Ibid.* For background, see See Jane Tanner, "Women in Sports," *The CQ Researcher*, May 11, 2001, pp. 401-424.
[32] Liz Clarke, "Commission Looks to Fix an Industry in 'Trouble,' " *The Washington Post*, Nov. 25, 2003, p. D2.
[33] Welch Suggs, "Presidents See Progress in Opening up Big-Money Bowls to More Colleges," *The Chronicle of Higher Education*, Nov. 28, 2003, p. 38.
[34] Suggs, *op. cit.*, Sept. 19, 2003; "Amherst College & Amherst Athletics Quickfacts," Amherst College Web site, www.amherst.edu/sports/misc/qf.html.
[35] Unless otherwise noted, information in this historical section comes from: "History of the NCAA," available at http://ncaa.org/about/history.html; "The New NAIA: A Proud Past, A Dynamic Future," available at http://naia.org/campaign/history/history.html; and Worsnop, *op. cit.*
[36] Kevin B. Blackistone, "Blame '39 TV Game for Crisis," *The Dallas Morning News*, Nov. 30, 2003, p. 1C.

FOR MORE INFORMATION

Black Coaches Association, 201 S. Capitol Ave., Suite 495, Indianapolis, IN 46225; http://www.bcasports.org. Nonprofit organization that promotes participation and growth of minorities in all facets of sports.

Center for the Study of Sport in Society, Northeastern University, 360 Huntington Ave., Suite 161 CP, Boston, MA 02115-5000; http://www.sportinsociety.org. A leading sports think tank.

Knight Commission on Intercollegiate Athletics, 200 S. Biscayne Blvd., Suite 3300, Miami, FL 33131-2349; http://www.knightfdn.org/athletics/index.html. The leading college sports reform panel, comprised primarily of college presidents.

National Association of Intercollegiate Athletics, 3500 W. 105th St., Olathe, KS 66051-1325; http://naia.org. Smaller counterpart to the NCAA, organizes and governs sports competitions for about 360 small colleges.

National Collegiate Athletic Association, 700 W. Washington St., P.O. Box 6222, Indianapolis, IN 46206-6222; http://ncaa.org. A private, voluntary organization of colleges and universities that serves as college sports' main regulatory body.

Women's Sports Foundation, Eisenhower Park, East Meadow, NY 11554; http://www.womenssportsfoundation.org. Founded by tennis star Billie Jean King to promote equal access for women in sports.

[37] Gordon S. White, "NCAA Telecast Rights on Football Struck Down," *The New York Times*, Sept. 16, 1982, p. B19; "Judge Burciaga Gets Down to Business with College Football," *Sports Illustrated*, Sept. 27, 1982; Fred Barbash, "Supreme Court Breaks NCAA Hold On Televised College Football Games," *The Washington Post*, June 28, 1984, p. A1.
[38] This women's sports history is based on "History of Women in Sports Timeline," from the Web site of the American Association of University Women, St. Lawrence County (New York) Branch, www.northnet.org/stlawrenceaauw/timeline.htm.
[39] For background, see Worsnop, "Gender Equity in Sports," *The CQ Researcher*, April 18, 1997, pp. 337-360.
[40] "NCAA Division I Graduation Rates Rise to 62 Percent," NCAA news release, Sept. 2, 2003, available at http://ncaa.org/releases/research/2003090201re.htm.
[41] "The NCAA and Academic Reform," available at www.ncaa.org/releases/currentTopics/academicReform.html.
[42] "NCAA Division I Framework Related to an Incentives and Disincentives Structure," Version #5 Final, Feb. 9, 2004, available at www1.ncaa.org/eprise/main/administrator/incentives/20040209_whitepaper.pdf.
[43] For background, see Kenneth Jost, "Affirmative Action," *The CQ Researcher*, Sept. 21, 2001, pp. 737-760, and Alan Greenblatt, "Race in America," *The CQ Researcher*, July 11, 2003, pp. 593-523.
[44] California Senate Bill 193, "Student Athletes' Bill of Rights," available at http://info.sen.ca.gov/pub/bill/sen/sb_0151-0200/sb_193_bill_20030617_amended_asm.html.
[45] Murray Sperber, "The NCAA's Last Chance to Reform College Sports," *The Chronicle of Higher Education*, April 19, 2002, p. 121.
[46] Myles Brand, "Fueling False Hopes," *The Sporting News*, Feb. 23, 2004, p. 8.
[47] Kirk Bohls, "Big Games, Big Money, Big Troubles," *Austin American-Statesman*, Aug. 24, 2003, p. C1.

Bibliography

Selected Sources

Books

Bowen, William G., and Sarah A. Levin, *Reclaiming the Game: College Sports and Educational Values*, Princeton University Press, 2003.
The president of the Andrew W. Mellon Foundation (Bowen) and a research assistant conclude that even at elite schools, athletes are admitted with lesser qualifications and don't do as well as their classmates.

Feinstein, John, *The Last Amateurs: Playing for Glory and Honor in Division I Basketball*, Back Bay Books, 2001.
The noted sportswriter spends a season in the Patriot League, where top-notch colleges like Lehigh, Lafayette and Colgate put real students on the court to play Division I basketball. This, he says, is "what college sports are supposed to be about."

Smith, Ronald A., *Play-By-Play: Radio, Television, and Big-Time College Sports*, Johns Hopkins University Press, 2001.
A professor emeritus at Penn State and secretary-treasurer of the North American Society for Sport History for three decades details the history of college sports' relationship with broadcast media — from the first radio broadcasts in the 1920s to today's multibillion-dollar network TV contracts.

Sperber, Murray, *Beer and Circus: How Big-time College Sports Is Crippling Undergraduate Education*, Owl Books, 2001.
A longtime Indiana University English professor and noted sports reformist argues that universities use sports as the Romans used circuses: to distract students from shortcomings in education.

Articles

Anderson, Kelli, and George Dohrmann, "Out of Control?" *Sports Illustrated*, Feb. 23, 2004, p. 64.
The authors review the University of Colorado sex-for-recruits scandal.

Blackistone, Kevin B., "Fixing College Sports," *The Dallas Morning News*, 2003.
A 10-part series examines the problems in intercollegiate athletics and suggests how to fix them; appeared in the sports section on Nov. 30 and Dec. 3, 5, 7, 10, 12, 14, 17, 19 and 21.

Lederman, Douglas, "College Presidents Learn It's Hard to Keep Sports Pure," *USA Today*, Jan. 14, 2004, p. 1A.
Sports reformers have called on college presidents to seize control of college sports from often-independent athletics departments, but the presidents themselves can be a big part of the problem, Lederman writes.

Suggs, Welch, "A Hard Year in College Sports," *The Chronicle of Higher Education*, Dec. 19, 2003, p. 37.
A chronology of college sports in 2003 covers events from the University of Rhode Island's settlement of a sexual-harassment suit against its athletics department in February to the controversial Bowl Championship Series selections in December, with a full course of scandals sandwiched in between.

Weiner, Jay, "Nothing New about Major Scandals in 'U' Men's Athletics," (Minneapolis) *Star Tribune*, Nov. 22, 1999, p. 1A.
A history of sports scandals at the University of Minnesota demonstrates that athletics departments behaving badly have been with us always.

Reports and Studies

"A Call to Action: Reconnecting College Sports and Higher Education," Knight Foundation Commission on Intercollegiate Athletics, June 2001. Available at http://www.knightfdn.org/default.asp?story=athletics/finalreport.html.
The latest report on — and proposals for fixing — intercollegiate athletics, from the most prestigious reform panel examining the subject. Past commission reports are available at: www.knightfdn.org/publications/knightcommission/KnightCommissiononIntercollegiateAthletics.pdf.

"History of Women in Sports Timeline," American Association of University Women, St. Lawrence County (New York) Branch. Available at www.northnet.org/stlawrenceaauw/timeline.htm.
This frequently updated history of women in sports covers everything from the Games of Hera (for women excluded from the Olympics) in 8th-century B.C. Greece to 14-year-old Michelle Wie this year becoming the youngest player in a Professional Golfers' Association Tour event.

"NCAA Graduation-Rates Report," on the NCAA Web site, http://ncaa.org/grad_rates.
Graduation rates for athletic scholarship recipients are shown in the national aggregate and broken down by schools and teams.

Brown, Robert W., "An Estimate of the Rent Generated by a Premium College Football Player," *Economic Inquiry*, October 1993, p. 671.
An economist calculates how much the typical elite football player earns for his college. Answer: More than $500,000 a year.

The Next Step:

Additional Articles from Current Periodicals

Improper Activities

Bernstein, Viv, "Christian Values Meet Athletic Scandal," *The New York Times*, Oct. 23, 2002, p. D1.

Gardner-Webb University, known for its Christian ethos, was rocked when the university president admitted to intervening on behalf of a player whose grades didn't make the cut.

Clarke, Liz, and Steve Fainaru, "The High Cost of Winning," *The Washington Post*, March 18, 2003, p. D1.

Colleges that try to raise their profile through athletic successes face collateral damage in the form of scandals and compromised values.

Freeman, Mike, "Getting a Grip on Recruiting Parties," *The New York Times*, Nov. 21, 2002, p. D1.

The subculture of college recruiting parties for athletes is a disturbing mixture of teenagers, sex, alcohol, drugs and the tacit approval of school authorities.

Lederman, Douglas, "College Presidents Learn It's Hard to Keep Sports Pure," *USA Today*, Jan. 14, 2004, p. 1A.

Presidential participation is touted as a way to reform college sports, but recent scandals involving presidents cast doubts on whether it will change anything.

Milbert, Neil, "Strippers Get Call to Reel in Recruits," *Chicago Tribune*, Feb. 11, 2004, Sports Section, p. 1.

The owner of an adult-entertainment company says strippers are common at recruiting parties for the University of Colorado and other nearby schools.

Weir, Tom, "Scandals Could Produce Reforms," *USA Today*, March 13, 2003, p. 1C.

A rising tide of scandal at collegiate athletic programs could reach a critical mass great enough to start a round of genuine reforms.

Wharton, David, David Kelly, and Chris Dufresne, "University of Colorado Is a Study in Sports Scandal," *Los Angeles Times*, Feb. 20, 2004, p. A1.

A surge of accusations against the Colorado football program is only the latest round of scandals regarding colleges' recruiting of prospective athletes.

Reform Efforts

"Reform and College Sports," *Chicago Tribune*, Dec. 30, 2003, Editorial Section, p. 20.

The NCAA's proposed changes would help restore more dignity to college sports and to pressure presidents, athletic directors and coaches whose programs exploit athletes

Bowen, William, and Sarah Levin, "Reclaim College Athletics-for All," *The Christian Science Monitor*, Sept. 18, 2003, p. 9.

There is a growing "academic-athletic" divide at many colleges, but ending intercollegiate athletics, as some suggest, is not the answer.

Gee, Gordon, "My Plan to Put the College Back in College Sports," *The Washington Post*, Sept. 21, 2003, p. B2.

The chancellor of Vanderbilt University defends replacing the traditional athletics department at Vanderbilt and outlines steps to reform college sports.

Prisbell, Eric, "NCAA Tries to Get Handle on Truth," *The Washington Post*, Feb. 23, 2004, p. D1.

If the NCAA's enforcement committee is the organization's police force and district attorney, then the infractions committee is its judge and jury.

Rozin, Skip, with Susan Zegel, "A Whole New Ball Game?" *Business Week*, Oct. 20, 2003, p. 100.

"Myth-breaking" statistics in a recent study cited by NCAA President Myles Brand show that less than a dozen universities actually make money from sports.

Sperber, Murray, "The NCAA's Last Chance to Reform College Sports," *The Chronicle of Higher Education*, April 19, 2002, p. 12.

The author, a professor at Indiana University, Bloomington, writes an open letter to the next NCAA president detailing the actions needed to purify college sports.

Suggs, Welch, "NCAA Chief Picks His Battles," *The Chronicle of Higher Education*, Jan. 16, 2004, p. 37.

NCAA President Myles Brand picks his battles as he tries to make his organization the "conscience of intercollegiate sports."

Basinger, Julianne, and Welch Suggs, "Trustee Group Plans to Join With Faculty Senates in Bid to Change College Sports," *The Chronicle of Higher Education*, Jan. 31, 2003, p. 39.

College trustees, who have sometimes been involved in questionable aspects of athletics, announce a new initiative to work with the faculty to reform sports programs.

Paying Coaches and Athletes

Bloom, Jeremy, "Show Us the Money," *The New York Times*, Aug. 1, 2003, p. A21.

A University of Colorado football player argues that college athletes should be allowed to benefit from endorsement contracts.

Drape, Joe, "Coaches Receive Both Big Salaries and Big Questions," *The New York Times*, Jan. 1, 2004, p. D1.
Even some prominent coaches wonder about receiving seven-figure salaries while professors and even university presidents earn far less.

Jacobson, Jennifer, "The Perks of Coaching," *The Chronicle of Higher Education*, Oct. 24, 2003, p. 43.
Swank country-club memberships and dealer-provided cars are two of the perks athletic officials often receive; scholars must be content with tenure.

Wharton, David, "What Price Victory? Colleges Learning It Can Be Steep," *Los Angeles Times*, Dec. 29, 2002, p. A1.
The "arms race" in college football coaching is escalating coaches' salaries to levels of $2 million or more per year; coaches say they work hard and demand is high.

Athletes and Academics

Blum, Debra, and Douglas Lederman, "NCAA Plans New Way to Keep Score," *USA Today*, Nov. 19, 2003, p. 1A.
New NCAA rules to help ensure more players earn degrees may cause a host of unintended consequences, including more academic fraud.

Dowling, William, "To Cleanse Colleges of Sports Corruption, End Recruiting Based on Physical Skills," *The Chronicle of Higher Education*, July 9, 1999, p. B9.
The low level of academic preparation among many athletes combined with the rigors of sports participation means that some form of academic fraud is inevitable.

Pugmire, Lance, "Graduation Rates Far From Sweet," *Los Angeles Times*, March 27, 2003, p. B1.
A study detailing low graduation rates for men's basketball players encounters resistance from those who question its methodology and validity.

Suggs, Welch, "Athletes' Graduation Rates Set a Record," *The Chronicle of Higher Education*, Sept. 12, 2003, p. 35.
A report indicates that while academic performance by athletes is improving, the number of black athletes graduating decreased significantly.

Sports as Business

Jenkins, Sally, "How to Curb Big-Time Schools? Hit Them With Big-Time Taxes," *The Washington Post*, May 17, 2003, p. D1.
If athletic programs are going to act like businesses, for example the Bowl Championship Series cartel, then the proceeds should be subject to taxation.

McMillen, Tom, "March Madness Really About Frenzy for Money," *USA Today*, April 1, 2002, p. 13A.
Big-time sports' erosion of integrity at institutions of learning doesn't have to be this way; relaxing antitrust restrictions on the NCAA is a big part of any solution.

Sack, Allen, "College Sports and the Myth of Amateurism," *The Christian Science Monitor*, March 17, 2003, p. 9.
Participation in major college sports has become identical to full-time employment; yearly grants instead of four-year scholarships allow players to be "fired."

Sokolove, Michael, "Football Is a Sucker's Game," *The New York Times Magazine*, Dec. 22, 2002, p. 36.
The University of South Florida's football program is described as "revenue-producing," but there's a big difference between revenue and profit.

Wieberg, Steve, "The Runaway Train," *USA Today*, Nov. 4, 2003, p. 1C.
Since the Supreme Court stripped the NCAA of its control of football television rights in 1984, schools must compete fiercely for a piece of the bowl system money.

CITING *THE CQ RESEARCHER*

Sample formats for citing these reports in a bibliography include the ones listed below. Preferred styles and formats vary, so please check with your instructor or professor.

MLA STYLE

Jost, Kenneth. "Rethinking the Death Penalty." The CQ Researcher 16 Nov. 2001: 945-68.

APA STYLE

Jost, K. (2001, November 16). Rethinking the death penalty. *The CQ Researcher, 11*, 945-968.

CHICAGO STYLE

Jost, Kenneth. "Rethinking the Death Penalty." *CQ Researcher*, November 16, 2001, 945-968.

Back Issues

The CQ Researcher *offers in-depth coverage of many key areas.*
Back issues are $10. Quantity discounts available.
Call (866) 427-7737 to order back issues.

Or call for a free CQ Researcher Web trial!
Online access provides:

- *Searchable archives dating back to 1991.*
- *Wider access through IP authentication.*
- *PDF files for downloading and printing.*
- *Availability 48 hours before print version.*

CIVIL LIBERTIES
Race in America, July 2003
Gay Marriage, September 2003
Civil Liberties Debates, October 2003

CRIME/LAW
Cyber-Crime, April 2002
Corporate Crime, October 2002
Serial Killers, October 2003

ECONOMY
State Budget Crises, October 2003
Stock Market Troubles, January 2004
Exporting Jobs, February 2004

EDUCATION
Home Schooling Debate, January 2003
Combating Plagiarism, September 2003
Black Colleges, December 2003

ENERGY/TRANSPORTATION
Future of the Airline Industry, June 2002
Future of Amtrak, October 2002
SUV Debate, May 2003

ENVIRONMENT
Crisis in the Plains, May 2003
Water Shortages, August 2003
Air Pollution Conflict, November 2003

HEALTH AND SAFETY
Women's Health, November 2003
Homeopathy Debate, December 2003

POLITICS AND PUBLIC POLICY
Abortion Debates, March 2003
State Budget Crises, October 2003
Democracy in the Arab World, January 2004
Redistricting Disputes, March 2004

SOCIAL TRENDS
Latinos' Future, October 2003
Future of the Music Industry, Nov. 2003

TECHNOLOGY
NASA's Future, May 2003

TERRORISM/DEFENSE
Homeland Security, September 2003
North Korean Crisis, April 2003

WORLD AFFAIRS
Trouble in South America, March 2003
Rebuilding Iraq, July 2003
Aiding Africa, August 2003

YOUTH
Preventing Teen Drug Use, March 2002
Sexual Abuse and the Clergy, May 2002
Movie Ratings, March 2003
Hazing, January 2004
Youth Suicide, February 2004

Future Topics

- ***Slavery and Human Trafficking***
- ***Nuclear Proliferation***
- ***Anniversary of Desegregation***

CQ Researcher

Published by CQ Press, a division of Congressional Quarterly Inc.

thecqresearcher.com

Human Trafficking and Slavery

Are the world's nations doing enough to stamp it out?

From the villages of Sudan to the factories, sweatshops and brothels of India and South Asia, slavery and human trafficking still flourish. Some 27 million people worldwide are held in some form of slavery, forced prostitution or bonded labor. Some humanitarian groups buy captives' freedom, but critics say that only encourages slave traders to seize more victims. Meanwhile, nearly a million people are forcibly trafficked across international borders annually and held in captivity. Even in the United States, thousands of women and children from overseas are forced to become sex workers. Congress recently strengthened the Trafficking Victims Protection Act, but critics say it is still not tough enough, and that certain U.S. allies that harbor traffickers are treated with "kid gloves" for political reasons.

Abducted from her village in southern Sudan when she was 6 years old, Akuac Malong was enslaved in northern Sudan until she was freed at age 13.

INSIDE THIS ISSUE

The CQ Researcher • March 26, 2004 • www.thecqresearcher.com
Volume 14, Number 12 • Pages 273-296

CQ PRESS

RECIPIENT OF SOCIETY OF PROFESSIONAL JOURNALISTS AWARD FOR EXCELLENCE ◆ AMERICAN BAR ASSOCIATION SILVER GAVEL AWARD

HUMAN TRAFFICKING AND SLAVERY

Cover: Akuac Malong, a 13-year-old Dinka girl from southern Sudan, was freed after being enslaved for seven years by Arab Muslims in northern Sudan. Tens of thousands of black Christians and followers of tribal religions are thought to be held captive in Sudan. (AP Photo/Jean-Marc Bouju)

THE *CQ Researcher*

March 26, 2004
Volume 14, No. 12

MANAGING EDITOR: Thomas J. Colin

ASSISTANT MANAGING EDITOR: Kathy Koch

ASSOCIATE EDITOR: Kenneth Jost

STAFF WRITERS: Mary H. Cooper, David Masci, William Triplett

CONTRIBUTING WRITERS: Sarah Glazer, David Hatch, David Hosansky, Patrick Marshall, Tom Price, Jane Tanner

DESIGN/PRODUCTION EDITOR: Olu B. Davis

ASSISTANT EDITOR: Kenneth Lukas

A Division of Congressional Quarterly Inc.

SENIOR VICE PRESIDENT/GENERAL MANAGER: John A. Jenkins

DIRECTOR, LIBRARY PUBLISHING: Kathryn C. Suárez

DIRECTOR, EDITORIAL OPERATIONS: Ann Davies

CIRCULATION MANAGER: Nina Tristani

CONGRESSIONAL QUARTERLY INC.

CHAIRMAN: Andrew Barnes

VICE CHAIRMAN: Andrew P. Corty

PRESIDENT AND PUBLISHER: Robert W. Merry

The CQ Researcher (ISSN 1056-2036) is printed on acid-free paper. Published weekly, except Jan. 2, April 9, July 2, July 9, Aug. 6, Aug. 13, Nov. 26 and Dec. 31, by CQ Press, a division of Congressional Quarterly Inc. Annual subscription rates for libraries, businesses and government start at $625. Single issues are available for $10. Quantity discounts apply to orders over 10. Additional rates furnished upon request. Periodicals postage paid at Washington, D.C., and additional mailing offices. POSTMASTER: Send address changes to *The CQ Researcher*, 1255 22nd St., N.W., Suite 400, Washington, D.C. 20037.

Human Trafficking and Slavery

BY DAVID MASCI

THE ISSUES

One morning in May, 7-year-old Francis Bok walked to the market in Nymlal, Sudan, to sell some eggs and peanuts. The farmer's son had made the same trip many times before.

"I was living a very good life with my family," he recalls today. "I was a happy child."

But his happy life ended that day in 1986. Arab raiders from northern Sudan swept into the village, sowing death and destruction. "They came on horses and camels and running on foot, firing machine guns and killing people everywhere," he says. His entire family — mother, father and two sisters — died in the attack.

AFP Photo/Philippe Lopez

Tearful Eastern European women comfort each other after being freed in 2000 from an American-owned hotel in Phnom Penh, Cambodia, where they were forced to have sex with businessmen and government officials. Traffickers in Eastern Europe often lure young women into bondage by advertising phony jobs abroad for nannies, models or actresses.

The raiders grabbed Francis and several other children, lashed them to donkeys and carried them north for two days. Then the children were parceled out to their captors. Francis went to a man named Giema Abdullah.

For the next 10 years, the boy tended his "owner's" goats and cattle. He slept with the animals, never had a day off and was rarely fed properly.

"He treated me like an animal, he even called me an animal, and he beat me," Francis says. "There was no joy. Even when I remembered my happy life before, it only made me sad."

In 1996, Francis escaped to Sudan's capital, Khartoum; then he made his way to Cairo, Egypt, and eventually in 2000 to the United States, which admitted him as a refugee.

As all American students learn, the Civil War ended slavery in the United States in 1865. Internationally, the practice was banned by several agreements and treaties, beginning in 1926 with the Slavery Convention of the League of Nations. But for tens of millions of people around the world, including millions of children like Francis, slavery never ended. An estimated 27 million people currently are held in some form of bondage, according to anti-slavery groups like Free the Slaves. [1] From the villages of Sudan and Mauritania in Africa to the factories, sweatshops and brothels of South Asia, slavery in its rawest, cruelest form is very much alive in the 21st century.

Many of those in bondage were kidnapped, like Francis. Others go voluntarily to different countries, thinking they are heading for a better life, only to be forced into a nightmare of prostitution or hard labor. Many more work as bonded laborers, tied to lifetime servitude because their father or grandfather borrowed money they couldn't repay.

Trafficking people across international borders has become a $12-billion-a-year global industry that touches virtually every country. The U.S. government estimates that between 800,000 and 900,000 people are trafficked internationally every year, many of them women and children, transported as sex workers. [2] The total includes up to 20,000 people forcibly trafficked into the United States annually, according to the Central Intelligence Agency. [3] (*See sidebar, p. 284.*)

Lyudmilla's story is typical. Like many desperately poor young women, the single mother of three from the former Soviet republic of Moldova responded to an advertisement promising work in Italy. Instead she was taken to a brothel in Macedonia, where she spent two horrific years in sexual slavery before escaping in 2002. [4]

Venecija, a Bulgarian, also ended up in a Macedonian brothel. "We were so tired we couldn't get out of bed," she recalled. "But [we had to] put on makeup and meet customers," she said after escaping. Those who refused were beaten until they "changed their minds." [5]

Traffickers control their victims through a variety of coercive means. In addition to rape and beatings, they keep their passports, leaving them with few options if they do manage to escape.

And the violence can follow those who do get away. Mercy, a young West African woman trafficked to Italy, escaped her tormentors only to see her sister killed in retribution after Mercy told human rights groups about her experience. [6]

The vast majority of slaves and victims of human trafficking come from the poorest parts of Africa, Asia, Latin America and Eastern Europe, where, smooth-talking traffickers often easily

Where Human Trafficking Occurs

Human trafficking and slavery take place in virtually every country in the world, but the U.N. and other reliable sources say the most extensive trafficking occurs in the countries below (listed at right).

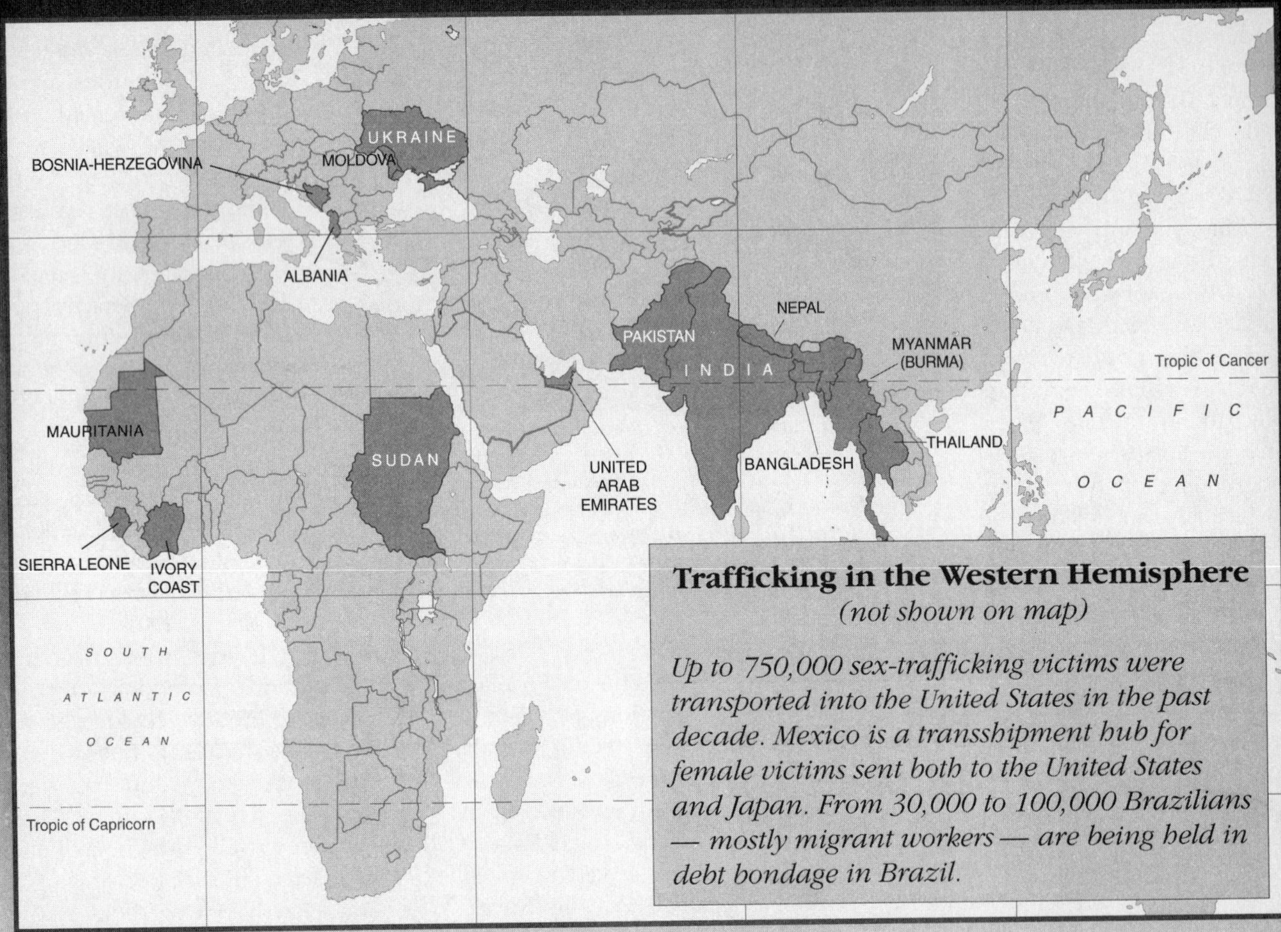

Trafficking in the Western Hemisphere
(not shown on map)

Up to 750,000 sex-trafficking victims were transported into the United States in the past decade. Mexico is a transshipment hub for female victims sent both to the United States and Japan. From 30,000 to 100,000 Brazilians — mostly migrant workers — are being held in debt bondage in Brazil.

Sources: Protection Project at Johns Hopkins University, U.S. State Department, Human Rights Watch, International Labour Organization, American Anti-Slavery Group

deceive desperate victims or their parents into believing that they are being offered a "better life."

"Being poor doesn't make you a slave, but it does make you vulnerable to being a slave," says Peggy Callahan, a spokeswoman for Free the Slaves, based in Washington, D.C.

Some Christian groups and nongovernmental organizations (NGOs) have tried to buy slaves out of bondage, particularly in Sudan, where two decades of civil war have stoked the slave trade. But many humanitarian groups argue that so-called slave redemption merely increases the demand for slaves.

International efforts to fight slavery and trafficking have increased dramatically over the last 10 years, with the United States playing a leading role. President Bush dramatized America's commitment in an address to the U.N. General Assembly on Sept. 23, 2003. The president had been expected to focus on security issues in the Middle East, but he devoted a substantial portion of his remarks to urging the international community to do more to fight trafficking.

"There is a special evil in the abuse and exploitation of the most innocent and vulnerable," Bush said.

Europe	
Albania	Up to 90 percent of the girls in rural areas don't go to school for fear of being abducted and sold into sexual servitude.
Bosnia and Herzegovina	A quarter of the women working in nightclubs claim they were forced into prostitution. The U.N. police task force is suspected of covering up its involvement in the sex trade.
Moldova	Up to 80 percent of the women trafficked as prostitutes in Western Europe may be Moldovans.
Ukraine	Up to 400,000 Ukrainian women have been trafficked for sexual exploitation in the past decade, Ukraine says. Ukrainian sex slaves can fetch up to $25,000 in Israel.
Africa	
Ivory Coast	A girl can allegedly be bought as a slave in Abidjan for about $7; a shipment of 10 children from Mali for work on the cocoa plantations costs about $420.
Mauritania	Light-skinned Arab Berbers today are thought to exploit hundreds of thousands of black African slaves. Slave raids in the 13th century began systemic slavery in Mauritania.
Sudan	Muslim tribesmen from northern Sudan still stage slave raids on non-Muslim Dinka peoples in the south, taking thousands of women and children.
Asia	
Bangladesh	An estimated 25,000 women and children are trafficked annually from Bangladesh.
India	Parents have sold an estimated 15 million children into bonded labor in return for meager loans from moneylenders.
Myanmar	The ruling military junta coerces minorities into forced labor in factories that benefit the regime and foreign corporations.
Nepal	A major source of women trafficked into Indian brothels; in addition, an estimated 75,000 people are trapped as bonded laborers in Nepal.
Pakistan	Millions of Pakistanis, often members of religious minorities, are forced to work as brick makers or in the fields of feudal landowners.
Thailand	Children sold by their parents make up a significant percentage of prostitutes in Thailand, which is a prime destination for pedophile sex tourists.
United Arab Emirates	Many women trafficked from the former Soviet Union end up in the UAE.

"Nearly two centuries after the abolition of the transatlantic slave trade, and more than a century after slavery was officially ended in its last strongholds, the trade in human beings for any purpose must not be allowed to thrive." [7]

The cornerstone of recent American anti-trafficking efforts is the 2000 Trafficking Victims Protection Act, which mandates the cutoff of most non-humanitarian U.S. aid for any nation deemed not trying hard enough to address the problem.

"The act breaks new ground because it actually tries to bring about changes in other countries," says Wendy Young, director of external relations for the Women's Commission for Refugee Women and Children in New York City.

"It's making a difference in countries all over the world," agrees Rep. Christopher H. Smith, R-N.J., one of the law's authors.

But critics contend the act is too weak to force real behavior changes. "It's very easy for countries to avoid sanctions just by taking a few largely meaningless actions," says Katherine Chon, co-director of the Polaris Project, an anti-trafficking advocacy group in Washington. She also accuses the administration of giving a pass to important allies, like Saudi Arabia, regardless of what they do to ameliorate their forced-labor practices.

All sides agree that many countries where trafficking occurs have a long way to go before they attain the level of economic, legal and political maturity needed to entirely eliminate the practice. "I don't think people realize just how desperately poor and chaotic many countries are today," says Linda Beher, a spokeswoman for the New York City-based United Methodist Committee On Relief, which assists trafficking victims.

A tragic consequence of this poverty is child labor, which many experts see as a cousin to slavery. In the developing world today, nearly 200 million children ages 5-14 are put to work to help support their families, according to the International Labour Organization (ILO). Almost half are under age 12, and more than 20 million are engaged in highly hazardous work, such as tanning leather or weaving rugs, exposing them to unhealthy chemicals or airborne pollutants. [8]

Some humanitarian aid workers describe much child labor as inherently coercive, because young children often have no choice.

The ILO argues that eliminating child labor and sending children to school would ultimately benefit nations with child laborers by raising income levels. (*See graph, p. 280.*) But some economists counter that putting even a fraction of the working children in school would be prohibitively expensive.

As experts debate resolving what has been called one of the greatest humanitarian problems of the 21st century, here are some of the questions they are asking:

AP Photo/Jean-Marc Bouju

John Eibner of Christian Solidarity International pays an Arab trader to free 132 slaves in Madhol, northern Sudan, in 1997. Critics of slave-redemption say it only encourages more slave-taking, but supporters say that not trying to free slaves would be unconscionable.

Does buying slaves in order to free them solve the problem?

In recent years, would-be Samaritans — from Christian missionaries to famous rock musicians — have worked to free slaves in Africa. Although slave trading occurs in many countries, the rescue efforts largely have focused on war-torn Sudan, where Muslim raiders from the north have enslaved hundreds of thousands of Christian and animist tribesmen in the south.

The Sudanese government has done virtually nothing to stop the practice and has even encouraged it as a means of prosecuting the war against the rebellious south, according to the U.S. State Department's 2003 "Trafficking in Persons Report."

Since 1995, Christian Solidarity International (CSI) and other slave-redemption groups operating in Sudan say they have purchased the freedom of more than 60,000 people by providing money for local Sudanese to buy slaves and then free them. [9]

"Women and children are freed from the terrible abuse, the rape, the beatings, the forcible conversions [to Islam] — all of the horrors that are an inherent part of slavery in Sudan," said John Eibner, director of CSI's redemption program. [10]

Halfway around the world, *New York Times* columnist Nicholas D. Kristof had his own brush with slave redemption when he traveled to Cambodia and freed two female sex slaves. "I woke up her brothel's owner at dawn," he wrote of his efforts to purchase one of the prostitutes, "handed over $150, brushed off demands for interest on the debt and got a receipt for $150 for buying a girl's freedom. Then Srey Neth and I fled before the brothel's owner was even out of bed." [11]

While experts concede that slave redeemers are well-intentioned, many contend the practice actually does more harm than good. "When you have people running around buying up slaves, you help create market demand for more slaves," says Jim Jacobson, president of Christian Freedom International, a relief group in Front Royal, Va., that stopped its slave-repatriation efforts five years ago. "It's really just simple economics."

Kevin Bales, author of *Disposable People: New Slavery in the Global Economy* and president of Free the Slaves, agrees. "This is like paying a burglar to redeem the television set he just stole," says Bales, a noted expert on contemporary slavery. "It's better to find other ways to free people, like going to the police or taking them out of bondage by force."

Indeed, Jacobson says, redemption only puts more money in the pockets of unscrupulous and often violent slave traders. "These people end up taking the money and buying more guns and hiring more thugs to go out and take more slaves," he says.

In addition, the critics say, many "slaves" pretend to be in bondage to defraud Westerners. "If you talk to aid workers in these places, you'll find that [bogus slave traders] are literally picking up [already free] people from across town and 'selling' them an hour later," Free the Slaves' Callahan says.

"So much of it is a huge scam operation," agrees Jacobson. "A lot of these people aren't really slaves."

But supporters of redemption say it would be unconscionable not to attempt to free slaves, even if slavers will go out searching for new victims. "Slaves are treated so badly, especially the women and children, who have been beaten and raped," says William Saunders, human rights counsel for the Family Research Council, a conservative social-policy group, and co-founder of the Bishop Gassis Sudan Relief Fund, both in Washington. "How can you not try to free these people?"

Saunders and others also contend that slave buyers take steps to avoid creating a bigger market for slaves. "In the Sudan, they use the local currency, because a dollar or a [British] pound is the sort of powerful magnet that might give people incentives to take more slaves or present non-slaves," he says.

In addition, redemption supporters say, they usually cap what they will pay per person — typically $50. "There's a real effort to ensure that we don't inflate the value of slaves," says Tommy Ray Calvert, chief of external operations for the Boston-based American Anti-Slavery Group (AASG).

Calvert contends that the redemptions have helped decrease slave raids in Sudan. The redemptions "brought world attention to the issue and forced our government and others to start pressuring the Sudanese to stop this evil practice," he says.

Moreover, Saunders refutes the charge that redeemers simply set people free without trying to ensure that they are true slaves. "They try to repatriate these people directly to their villages," Saunders says. "They don't just buy their freedom and let them go."

But the critics remain dubious. "It's so hard to get anywhere in Sudan that there is no way that they could

Fighting the Traffickers

The 2000 Trafficking Victims Protection Act requires the State Department to report each year on global efforts to end human trafficking. Last year, 15 countries were placed in Tier 3, for those deemed to be doing little or nothing against trafficking. Countries in Tier 3 for three years in a row can lose all U.S. non-humanitarian aid. Tier 1 countries are considered to be actively fighting trafficking. Seventy-five countries are in Tier 2, indicating they are making some efforts against trafficking.

State Department Anti-Trafficking Ratings

Tier 1 — Actively Fighting Trafficking

Austria	Hong Kong	Poland
Belgium	Italy	Portugal
Benin	South Korea	Spain
Colombia	Lithuania	Sweden
Czech Republic	Macedonia	Switzerland
Denmark	Mauritius	Taiwan
France	Morocco	United Arab Emirates
Germany	The Netherlands	United Kingdom
Ghana		

Tier 3 — Doing Little or Nothing

Belize	Georgia	North Korea
Bosnia and Herzegovina	Greece	Sudan
Myanmar	Haiti	Suriname
Cuba	Kazakhstan	Turkey
Dominican Republic	Liberia	Uzbekistan

Source: "2003 Trafficking in Persons Report," Office to Monitor and Combat Trafficking in Persons, Department of State, June 2003

Economic Benefits Cited for Ending Child Labor

Banning child labor and educating all children would raise the world's total income by 22 percent, or $4.3 trillion, over 20 years, according to the International Labour Organization (ILO). The principal benefit would be the economic boost that most countries would experience if all children were educated through lower secondary school, plus substantial but less dramatic health benefits. The ILO analysis assumes countries that banned child labor would pay poor parents for their children's lost wages, something critics say is unrealistically expensive.

Net Economic Benefits of Eliminating Child Labor

(as a percentage of annual gross national income)

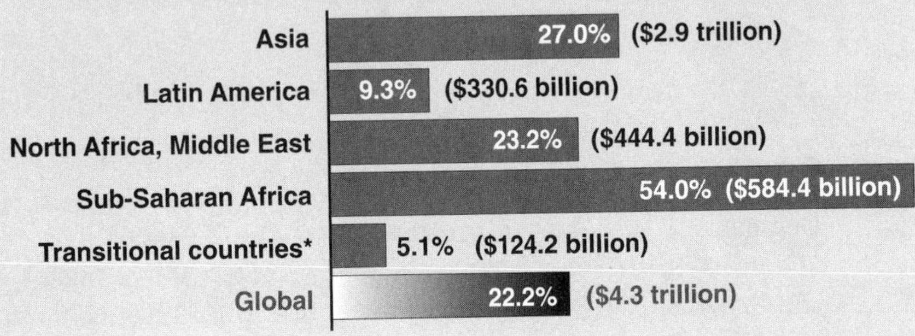

** Transitional countries — such as Taiwan, Singapore and Malaysia — are no longer considered "developing" but not yet classified as fully industrialized.*

Source: "Investing in Every Child," International Programme on the Elimination of Child Labour, International Labour Office, December 2003

actually follow all of these people back to their home villages," Jacobson says. "It would take weeks or months."

Moreover, he says, "they don't have any idea whether the people they've freed have been coached or whether the village they're going to is really their village. It's simply impossible to know."

Is the Trafficking Victims Protection Act tough enough?

The $12 billion human-trafficking industry is now the world's third-largest illegal business, surpassing every other criminal enterprise except the drug and arms trades, according to the United Nations.[12]

In October 2000, the U.S. government zeroed in on the problem, enacting the Trafficking Victims Protection Act (TVPA), which targets the illegal trade both at home and abroad.[13] The law established the State Department's Office to Monitor and Combat Trafficking in Persons, which issues an annual report on what countries are doing to end trafficking.

The report uses a three-tiered system to rank countries — from states that actively fight trafficking (Tier 1) to those doing little (Tier 3). Countries classified as Tier 3 for three years in a row are subject to a cut-off of non-humanitarian U.S. aid. (*See sidebar, p. 284.*)

On the domestic side, the law allows U.S. authorities to charge alleged traffickers in the United States under the tough federal anti-racketeering law (RICO). According to the State Department, 111 persons have been charged with trafficking in the first three years since the law was enacted, a threefold increase over the three-year period before the TVPA went into effect.[14]

The law also makes it easier for trafficked victims to acquire refugee status in the United States and allows them to sue their victimizers for damages in civil court.

President Bill Clinton signed the bill into law on Oct. 28, 2000, saying it would provide "important new tools and resources to combat the worldwide scourge of trafficking."

Today, however, critics argue that while the act is "a step in the right direction," it is ultimately not tough enough to shake up the industry, especially internationally. "Of course, it's good that we have it, but frankly we have an awfully long way to go," says the Polaris Project's Chon.

She especially criticizes provisions requiring countries to fight trafficking or face American penalties. "It's just not strong enough because it allows countries to avoid sanctions with just superficial acts," she says.

For example, she says, Japan responded to U.S. pressure to curtail sex trafficking by "giving Cambodia a few million dollars in anti-trafficking aid and holding a symposium on trafficking." But the Japanese did "not really do anything to substantially crack down on their own widespread problem."

Yet, she adds, the United States has said Japan has been tackling trafficking enough to avoid a Tier 3 classification and the prospect of sanctions. "Japan is an important ally," she says. "Need I say more?"

Other critics allege that certain countries are treated with "kid gloves" for political reasons. "States like Saudi Arabia and countries from the former Soviet Union, which are important American allies, have been pushed up to Tier 2 because stopping slavery isn't the priority [in U.S. foreign relations] it should be," says Calvert of the AASG.

Calvert is especially incensed that the government failed to classify Mauritania, on Africa's northwestern coast, in Tier 3, calling it instead a "special case" because of insufficient information to make an accurate determination. "This is a country with literally hundreds of thousands of people in chattel slavery and everyone knows it, and yet it gets a pass," he says. "That is just unbelievable to me."

AFP Photo

Rescuers return 14 children to their native Bangladesh after they were abducted to India. Children in poor countries sometimes are sold by their parents or kidnapped by traffickers and forced to work without pay, frequently in hazardous conditions.

But supporters contend that the TVPA, while not perfect, helps move problem countries in the right direction. "It's important to have a tool we can use to push foreign governments to act against this terrible abuse of human dignity, and this law does that," says Beher, of the United Methodist Committee On Relief.

In Japan, for instance, the law has helped make the fight against trafficking more effective, raising public awareness of the problem dramatically as a result of the debate over its ranking in the TVPA, supporters add.

"When Japan was dropped from Tier 1 to Tier 2, it was very embarrassing for them, and all of a sudden you saw this real public debate about the trafficking issue — which is a huge problem there," says Diana Pinata, a spokeswoman for Vital Voices, a global woman's advocacy group in Washington. "If nothing else, the [annual State Department trafficking] report and the threat of sanctions keeps the issue in the spotlight in these countries, and that's very positive."

Besides Japan, several other countries, including Russia, Saudi Arabia and Indonesia, have dramatically improved their anti-trafficking efforts as a result of pressure brought to bear by the TVPA, says John Miller, director of the Office to Combat Trafficking. "We've seen real efforts all over the world," he says. "Some have been more substantial than others, but there already has been a lot of progress."

Moreover, Miller rejects the charge of political favoritism. "Look at the Tier 3 list, and you'll see that there are U.S. allies like Greece and Turkey there," he says. "These decisions aren't being made on the basis of politics."

Pinata agrees. "When we speak to NGO workers and others in the field working on this issue, we get the sense that the trafficking report's assessment of these countries is essentially correct," she says.

Should most forms of child labor be eliminated?

Zara Cigay, 12, and her two younger brothers don't go to school. Instead, they help their parents and extended family, migrant farm workers who pick cotton and other crops in southern Turkey.

"Wherever there is a job, we do it," said Huseyin Cigay, Zara's great-uncle. "The children work with us everywhere." [15]

More than 250 million children around the world between the ages of 5 and 17 are working, according to the ILO. Most are in developing countries in Africa and Asia, and nearly half work full time like Zara and her brothers. [16]

Many do strenuous farm labor. In cities, they do everything from retailing and domestic service to manufacturing and construction. In nations beset by civil wars, thousands of children have been forced to fight in rebel armies. [17]

A large portion of child labor is coerced, according to child-welfare experts. Children are often sold by their parents or kidnapped and forced to work virtually as slaves for no pay. In India, children are literally tied to weaving looms so that they cannot run away.

Labor experts uniformly condemn forced and bonded labor. But on the question of child labor in general, the experts are split over whether the practice should be condoned under certain circumstances.

Human rights advocates and others point to the ILO's 1999 Worst Forms of Child Labor Convention, which prohibits all full-time work and any work by children under 12 but sanctions part-time, non-hazardous labor for teenagers that does not interfere with their social development. [18]

"Under international law, children have a right to a basic education," says Karin Landgren, chief of child protection at the United Nations Children's Fund (UNICEF). "Work should never interfere with this."

In addition, Landgren says, "They need to have time to play and participate freely in their country's cultural and social life. This is vitally important if they are to develop into healthy adults."

A recent ILO report says that child labor negatively impacts all levels of society. "Child labor perpetuates poverty, because when children don't have an education and a real chance to develop to their fullest potential, they are mortgaging their future," says Frans Roselaers, director of the organization's international program on the elimination of child labor and author of the report.

Child labor also costs societies economically by producing uneducated adult workers, Roselaers says. "Countries with a lot of child workers are stunting their economic growth," he says, "because they will only end up producing an army of weak and tired workers with no skills."

But some economists counter that child labor, even full-time work, is often a necessity in developing countries. "In an ideal world, children would spend all of their time at school and at play, but poor people in poor countries don't have the kind of options that we in rich countries do," says Ian Vasquez, director of the Project on Global Economic Liberty at the Cato Institute, a libertarian think tank. "When you begin to restrict children's options for work, you can end up hurting children and their families."

Indeed, child labor often is the only thing that stands between survival and starvation, some experts say. "No parents want their child to work, but child labor helps families get by," says Deepak Lal, a professor of international-development studies at the University of California, Los Angeles. "When a country's per capita income rises to about $3,000 or $4,000, child labor usually fades away."

In addition, Lal says, working children often end up with a better education than those who don't work. "The public education system is a failure in many parts of the developing world and really doesn't offer much to the children who attend school," he says. "But if a child works and his family earns enough to send him or his siblings to private school, that can really pay off."

Finally, Vasquez argues that outlawing child labor would only drive the problem underground, where there is no government oversight, and abuses would increase. "In Bangladesh, girls were prevented from continuing to work in textile plants, so many ended up as prostitutes," he says. "People need to make money, and if you deny them one route, they'll take another."

But Roselaers counters that child workers would not be driven to more dangerous and demeaning jobs if the international community eased the transition from work to school. In the case of Bangladesh, he says, the threat of a consumer boycott by Western countries prompted textile factory owners to fire their child employees.

"The factory owners panicked and fired the kids, and so, yes, there were problems," he says. "But when groups like the ILO and UNICEF came in, we started offering the parents stipends to make up for the lost income and easing the children's transition from work to school."

Some 1 million children are now being helped to make the transition from work to school, according to a recent ILO report. [19] In India, for instance, the ILO and the U.S. Department of Labor are spending $40 million this year to target 80,000 children working in hazardous jobs. [20]

Nonetheless, Lal says, such a program could only make a small dent in the problem. "You can't give a stipend to each of the many millions of families that send their children to work," he says. "There isn't enough money to do this, so it's not a realistic solution, just a palliative that make Westerners feel good about themselves." ■

BACKGROUND

Ancient Practice

Slavery is as old as human civilization. All of the world's great founding cultures, including those in Mesopotamia, China, Egypt and India, accepted slavery as a fact of life. [21] The practice also was common in sub-Saharan Africa and the Americas.

Neither the Bible nor the great thinkers of Greece and Rome took firm positions against slavery. Some, like the Greek philosopher Aristotle, vigorously defended it.

It was not until Enlightenment philosophers like John Locke and Voltaire established new definitions of human freedom and dignity in the 17th and 18th centuries, that large numbers of people started questioning the morality of keeping another person in bondage.

Ancient societies typically acquired slaves from outside their borders, usually through war or territorial conquest. Captives and conquered people often served as agricultural workers or domestic servants.

Slavery probably reached its zenith in ancient Greece and then Rome, where human trafficking became a huge and profitable industry. In many Greek cities, including powerful Athens and Sparta, as many as half the residents were slaves. In Rome, slavery was so widespread that even common people could afford to have one or two. [22]

Slaves in the ancient world often did more than just menial tasks. Some, especially in the Roman Empire, became physicians and poets. Others achieved great influence, managing estates or assisting powerful generals or politicians.

Continued on p. 284

Chronology

19th Century

After thousands of years, slavery is abolished in much of the world.

1821
Congress enacts the Missouri Compromise, specifying which new U.S. states will allow slavery.

1833
England outlaws slavery throughout its empire.

1839
The world's first international abolitionist group, Anti-slavery International, is founded in England.

1848
Slavery abolished in French colonies.

1863
President Abraham Lincoln issues Emancipation Proclamation.

December 1865
The 13th Amendment abolishes slavery.

1873
Spain ends slavery in Puerto Rico.

1888
Brazil outlaws slavery.

1900-1990

International treaties to halt slavery are adopted.

1919
International Labour Organization (ILO) is founded.

1926
League of Nations outlaws slavery.

1945
United Nations is founded.

1946
U.N. Children's Fund is established.

1948
U.N.'s Universal Declaration of Human Rights prohibits slavery.

1951
International Organization for Migration is founded to help migrants.

1956
Supplementary Convention on the Abolition of Slavery, the Slave Trade, and Institutions and Practices Similar to Slavery outlaws debt bondage, serfdom and other forced-labor practices.

1978
Human Rights Watch is founded.

1983
Sudan's civil war begins, pitting the Muslim north against the Christian and animist south, leading to slave raids in the south.

1990s

The end of the Cold War and other geopolitical changes allow trafficking and slavery to expand.

1991
Collapse of the Soviet Union leads to a dramatic rise in trafficking in Eastern Europe.

1994
American Anti-Slavery Group is founded.

1995
Christian and non-governmental organizations begin redeeming slaves in Sudan.

June 1, 1999
ILO adopts the Worst Forms of Child Labor Convention.

2000-Present

United States and other countries renew efforts to fight slavery and trafficking.

March 2000
Free the Slaves is founded.

Oct. 28, 2000
President Bill Clinton signs the Trafficking Victims Protection Act.

Nov. 15, 2000
United Nations approves the Protocol to Prevent, Suppress and Punish the Trafficking in Persons.

Feb. 14, 2002
Polaris Project is founded to fight trafficking.

June 10, 2002
State Department's Office to Monitor and Combat Trafficking releases its first "Trafficking in Persons Report."

March 11, 2003
Brazilian President Luiz Inacio Lula da Silva unveils anti-slavery initiative.

Sept. 19, 2003
President Bush signs Trafficking Victims Protection Act Reauthorization.

Sept. 23, 2003
President Bush delivers a major anti-trafficking address at the U.N. General Assembly.

January 2004
U.N. launches year-long commemoration of anti-slavery movement.

Summer 2004
State Department's Fourth Annual "Trafficking in Persons Report" to be released.

Fighting Trafficking in the United States

Seven men were sent to prison on Jan. 29, 2004, for holding several Latin American women against their will in South Texas, forcing them to work without pay and raping them repeatedly.

The case was the latest in a series of sex-trafficking cases prosecuted under the Trafficking Victims Protection Act (TVPA) of 2000, which established stiff penalties for human trafficking and provided mandatory restitution to victims. [1] In the last three years, the Justice Department has prosecuted 132 traffickers — three times the number charged in the three years before the law was enacted. [2]

Last year, Congress updated the law to make trafficking a racketeering offense and allow victims to sue their captors in U.S. courts.

"While we have made much progress in combating human trafficking . . . we have not yet eradicated modern-day slavery," reauthorization sponsor Rep. Christopher H. Smith, R-N.J., said during consideration of the bill by the House International Relations Committee on July 23, 2003.

The Central Intelligence Agency estimates that between 18,000 and 20,000 people are trafficked into the United States each year. [3] Many are women — kidnapped or lured here with promises of marriage or work as nannies, models, waitresses, factory workers and exotic dancers. Once they arrive, they are stripped of their passports and forced to work as sex slaves, laborers or domestic servants until their smuggling or travel "debts" are repaid. The average victim is 20 years old. [4]

"They tell them they'll make a lot of money, they'll be free, they'll have a beautiful life," says Marisa B. Ugarte, executive director of the Bilateral Safety Corridor Coalition, a San Diego organization that assists trafficking victims in Mexico and the United States. "But once they are here, everything changes."

Prior to passage of the TVPA, many of the victims were treated as criminals and subject to deportation. Today, they can apply to the Bureau of Citizen and Immigration Services for one of 5,000 "T" nonimmigrant visas available each year. The visas allow them to remain in the United States if they are assisting in the investigation or prosecution of traffickers. They may then apply for permanent residency if their removal would cause severe hardship. [5]

The Department of Homeland Security had received 721 T-status applications as of June 30, 2003: 301 were granted, 30 were denied and 390 are pending. [6]

Mohamed Mattar, co-director of the Protection Project, a human-rights research institute at Johns Hopkins University, said the visa program has been stymied by victims' reluctance to go to law enforcement authorities for help.

This fear is fed by the fact that many police officers remain unaware of the TVPA and are more likely to arrest the victims than the perpetrators, says Donna M. Hughes, an authority on sex trafficking at the University of Rhode Island.

"We need to start treating [Johns] like the perpetrators they are, and not like lonely guys," Hughes adds. "We need a renewal of ideas at the state and local level."

Under the TVPA, alien trafficking victims who do come forward can receive federal benefits normally available to refugees.

Historically, most trafficked victims have come from Latin America and Southeast Asia, smuggled across the porous Mexican border by "coyotes" or escorted by "jockeys" pretending to be a boyfriend or cousin. [7] Since the early 1990s, however, there has been an influx of women from the former Soviet Union and Central and Eastern Europe, where trafficking rings recruit women with newspaper ads and billboards beckoning them to prosperous futures in the United States.

Undocumented migrant workers are also vulnerable to traffickers. On March 2, 2004, a federal district judge sentenced Flori-

Continued from p. 282

Great Roman thinkers like Pliny the Younger and Cicero urged masters to treat their slaves with kindness and even to let them "share your conversations, your deliberations and your company," Cicero wrote. [23] Perhaps as a result, manumission, or the freeing of slaves by their masters, was commonplace, usually after many years of service.

Ultimately, however, Roman slavery was maintained by cruelty and violence, including the use of severe flogging and even crucifixion. Slave revolts, common in the first and second centuries B.C., were brutally suppressed.

The collapse of the western half of the Roman Empire in the 5th-century A.D. led to a new, more fragmented, power structure in Western Europe often centered around local warlords (knights) and the Catholic Church. The new order did not eliminate slavery, but in many areas slaves became serfs, or peasants tied to the local lord's land and could not leave without his permission. [24]

In the East, meanwhile, a new force — Islam — was on the rise. For the Arabs who swept into the Mediterranean basin and the Near East beginning in the 7th century, traditional slavery was a way of life, just as it had been for the Romans. In the ensuing centuries, the Arabs brought millions of sub-Saharan Africans, Asians and Europeans to the slave markets for sale throughout the Middle East.

Meanwhile, slavery remained commonplace elsewhere. In North America, Indians along the Eastern seaboard and in the Pacific Northwest often enslaved members of other tribes taken in war. The more advanced indigenous civilizations to the south, like the Aztec and Mayans in what is now Mexico, and the Inca of Peru, also relied upon slaves. And on the Indian subcontinent, the strict Hindu caste system held tens of millions in virtual bondage.

da labor contractor Ramiro Ramos to 15 years in prison for holding migrant workers in servitude and forcing them to work in citrus groves until they had paid off their transportation debts. [8]

In some instances, diplomats and international civil servants bring domestic workers — often illiterate women from Africa, Asia and Latin America — into the United States legally, but then force them to work long hours for almost no pay. In one case, an Ethiopian maid for an International Monetary Fund staffer says she worked eight years for seven days a week, 15 hours a day for less than 3 cents an hour. [9]

Although the employer claimed the maid was his guest, he disappeared before a lawsuit filed by the maid, Yeshehareg Teferra, could be prosecuted. "I was not their guest," Teferra told a reporter. "I was their slave " [10]

Foreign diplomats bring 3,800 domestic servants into the United States each year under special temporary work visas, which allow them only to work for the employer who sponsored them. The employer promises to abide by U.S. labor laws, but there is almost no oversight of the program, so the abuse of servants remains under law enforcement's radar screen, human rights advocates say. [11]

But foreign nationals are not the only victims of domestic trafficking. Homeless and runaway American children also are preyed upon by pimps, who troll malls and clubs in search of teenagers they can "turn." Typically, the pimps befriend the girls, ply them with drugs and then use their addiction to turn them into prostitutes. [12]

There are between 100,000 and 300,000 such citizen victims in the United States, though they're more often overlooked by police, says Derek Ellerman, co-founder of the Polaris Project, a grass-roots anti-trafficking organization. "There is a glaring bias in enforcement" of the Mann Act, which bans the transport of children and adults across state lines for prostitution, Ellerman says. "U.S. kids who are being targeted [by traffickers] just are not being protected."

For the traffickers — many of them members of gangs or loosely linked criminal networks — trafficking is much more lucrative than smuggling contraband items, because human slaves can provide a source of long-term income through prostitution and forced labor. "There's a market for cheap labor, and there's a market for cheap sex, and traffickers know they can make money in it," Michele Clark, co-director of the Protection Project, says.

— Kelly Field

[1] Department of Justice press release, Jan. 29, 2004.

[2] Department of Justice press release, March 2, 2004.

[3] Department of Justice, "Assessment of U.S. Activities to Combat Trafficking in Persons," August 2003, p. 3.

[4] Amy O'Neill Richard, "International Trafficking in Women to the United States: A Contemporary Manifestation of Slavery and Organized Crime," DCI Exceptional Intelligence Analyst Program, pp. 3-5.

[5] John R. Miller, "The United States' Effort to Combat Trafficking in Persons," *International Information Program Electronic Journal*, U.S. State Department, June 2003.

[6] Department of Justice, *op. cit.*, August 2003, p. 9.

[7] Peter Landesman, "The Girls Next Door," *The New York Times Magazine*, Jan. 25, 2004.

[8] Justice Department, *op. cit.*, March 2, 2004.

[9] William Branigin, "A Life of Exhaustion, Beatings, and Isolation," *The Washington Post*, Jan. 5, 1999, p. A6.

[10] Quoted in *ibid.*

[11] Richard, *op. cit.*, p. 28,

[12] Janice G. Raymond and Donna M. Hughes, "Sex Trafficking of Women in the United States, International and Domestic Trends," Coalition Against Trafficking in Women, March 2001, p. 52.

Slavery Goes Global

In the 15th century, European explorers and adventurers sailing to new territories in Asia, Africa and the Americas began a new chapter in the history of slavery.

By 1650, the Dutch, Spanish, Portuguese, French and English had established colonies throughout the world. The new territories, especially in the Americas, produced new crops such as sugar and tobacco, as well as gold and other minerals. Initially, enslaved indigenous peoples did the harvesting and mining in South America. But ill treatment and disease quickly decimated native populations, prompting the importation of slaves from Africa.

From the mid-1500s to the mid-1800s, almost 9 million Africans were shipped mostly to Latin America — particularly to today's Brazil, Haiti and Cuba — under the most inhumane conditions. About 5 percent — about 400,000 — of all the African slaves ended up in the United States. [25]

On the sugar plantations of the West Indies and South America, crushing work and brutal punishment were the norm. Although Spain and Portugal had relatively liberal laws concerning the treatment of slaves — they could marry, sue a cruel owner and even buy their freedom — they were rarely enforced.

In the British colonies and later in the United States, slaves enjoyed somewhat better working conditions and medical care. Nonetheless, life was harsh and in some ways more difficult. Since slaves in Latin America and the Caribbean usually outnumbered Europeans, they were able to retain more of their African customs. In British America, where by 1750 whites outnumbered slaves by more than four to one, Africans quickly lost many of their cultural underpinnings.

Most American slavery was tied to the great Southern plantations that grew

Nearly 200 Million Young Kids Must Work

Nearly a fifth of the world's young children have to work, including 110 million in Asia and fully a quarter of all the children in sub-Saharan Africa.

Working Children, Ages 5 to 14, By Region
(in millions)

Region	Total Working	Percentage of children in region
Asia	110.4	18.7%
Latin America	16.5	17.0
North Africa, Middle East	9.0	10.2
Sub-Saharan Africa	37.9	25.3
Transitional countries*	8.3	14.6
Total	**182.1**	**18.5%**

** Transitional countries — such as Taiwan, Singapore and Malaysia — are no longer considered "developing" but not yet classified as fully industrialized.*

Source: "Investing in Every Child," International Programme on the Elimination of Child Labour, International Labour Office, December 2003

tobacco, rice and other cash crops. Although slavery also was practiced in Northern states, it was never as widespread and had been largely abolished by 1800.

By the late 18th century, Southern slavery also appeared headed for extinction, as industrialization and other trends took hold, rendering the plantation system increasingly economically unfeasible. But Eli Whitney's invention of the cotton gin in 1793 gave American slavery a new lease on life. The gin made the labor-intensive process of separating the seeds from the cotton easy, enabling slaves to dramatically increase their output. [26]

Meanwhile, the rise of textile mills in England and elsewhere was creating a new demand for the fluffy, white fiber. By the early 19th century, many Southern plantations that had been unprofitably growing other crops were now making plenty of money using slaves to pick and process cotton.

Around the same time, however, a movement to abolish slavery began to gather steam in the Northern states. For decades, Americans had debated the morality of slavery. During deliberations over independence in 1776, many delegates to the Second Continental Congress — including John Adams, Benjamin Franklin and Virginia slaveholder Thomas Jefferson — had pushed to make the elimination of slavery part of the movement for America's independence. But resistance from the South and the need for colonial unity against the British doomed the proposal.

The debate over slavery, however, did not go away. The issue complicated the new country's efforts to form its governing institutions and to expand westward, forcing increasingly abolitionist Northerners and slaveholding Southerners to craft tortured compromises to keep the nation together.

In 1789, delegates to the Constitutional Convention hammered out the infamous Three-fifths Compromise, permitting each slave to be counted as three-fifths of a person for purposes of apportioning the number of representatives each state had in the new Congress. [27] And in 1821, Congress passed the Missouri Compromise, drawing a line westward along the 36.30 parallel. The new Western states above the line would be admitted to the Union as "free" states, while those below the boundary would be so-called slave states.

Outlawing Slavery

Much of the rest of the world, however, was abolishing slavery. In the early 1800s, many of the newly independent nations of Spanish America won their independence and immediately outlawed human bondage. Simón Bolivár, who liberated much of Latin America, was a staunch abolitionist, calling slavery "the daughter of darkness." [28]

In Europe, the tide also was turning. Largely due to the efforts of abolitionist William Wilberforce, the British Empire outlawed the practice in 1833, although de facto slavery continued in India and some other colonies. In 1848, France also freed the slaves in its colonies.

However, in the United States, peaceful efforts at compromise over slavery failed, and the issue finally helped trigger the Civil War in 1861. In 1863, during the height of the conflict, President Abraham Lincoln issued the "Emancipation Proclamation," freeing all slaves in the Southern, or Confederate, states. Soon after the war ended with Union victory in 1865, the 13th Amendment to the Constitution abolished slavery altogether. [29]

After the Civil War, the worldwide abolition of slavery continued. Spain outlawed the practice in Puerto Rico in 1873 and in Cuba in 1886. More important, Brazil began dismantling its huge slave infrastructure in 1888.

Today, slavery is illegal in every country in the world and is outlawed by several treaties. "In international law, the outlawing of slavery has become what is called *jus cogens*, which means that it's completely accepted and doesn't need to be written into new treaties and conventions," says Bales of Free the Slaves.

The foundation of this complete acceptance rests on several groundbreaking international agreements, beginning with the 1926 Slavery Convention of the League of Nations, which required signatory countries to work to abolish every aspect of the practice. [30]

AFP Photo

Six-year-old Ratan Das breaks rocks at a construction site in Agartala, India, where he earns about 40 cents a day to supplement his widowed mother's 60-cents-per-day income. India has more child laborers than any other country — about 120 million — followed by Pakistan, Bangladesh, Indonesia and Brazil.

Slavery also is banned by the 1948 Universal Declaration of Human Rights, which holds that "no one shall be held in slavery or servitude; slavery and the slave trade shall be prohibited in all their forms." [31]

Other conventions prohibiting the practice include the 1930 ILO Convention on Forced Labor and a 1956 Supplementary Convention on the Abolition of Slavery, the Slave Trade, and Institutions and Practices Similar to Slavery.

More recently, the United Nations in 2001 approved a Protocol to Prevent, Suppress and Punish the Trafficking in Persons as part of a major convention on fighting organized crime. The protocol requires signatories to take action to fight trafficking and protect its victims. It has been signed by 117 countries and ratified by 45. [32] While the United States has not yet ratified the document, it has the support of the White House and is expected to win Senate approval in the near future. ■

CURRENT SITUATION

Human Trafficking

The poorest and most chaotic parts of the developing world supply most trafficking victims — often women and children destined for the sex trade.

In South Asia, young women and children routinely are abducted or lured from Nepal, Pakistan, India, Bangladesh, Cambodia and Myanmar (Burma) to work in brothels in India's large cities, notably Bombay, and the Persian Gulf states. Thousands also end up in Bangkok, Thailand's capital and an infamous sex-tourism mecca.

In Asia, the victims' own families often sell them to traffickers. "In Nepal, entire villages have been emptied of girls," says Pinata of Vital Voices. "Obviously, this could not have happened without the complicity between traffickers and the victims' families."

Parents sell their children for a variety of reasons — virtually all linked to poverty, Pinata says. "Some think the child will have a better life or that their daughter will be able to send money home," she says. "For some, it's just one less mouth to feed."

"Even when they have a sense of what their children will be doing, many parents feel they don't have a choice," adds UNICEF's Landgren. "They feel that literally anything is better than what they have now."

In Eastern Europe, traffickers often lure women into bondage by advertising in local newspapers for nanny positions in the United States or Western Europe. For instance, Tetiana, a Ukrainian woman, was offered 10 times her salary to be an au pair in Italy. Instead she was forced into prostitution in Istanbul, Turkey. [33]

Others are promised work as models or actresses. In some cases, the victims even put up their own money for their travel expenses, only to find themselves prisoners in a European brothel or in Mexico, awaiting transport across the border to the United States. [34]

Even those who understand at the outset that they are going to be prostitutes are not prepared for the brutality they face. "They're unaware of how much abuse, rape, psychological manipulation and coercion is involved," says the Polaris Project's Chon.

Eastern Europe is particularly fertile ground for sex traffickers, she says. The collapse of communism more than a decade ago has left many parts of the region, especially Ukraine, Moldova and Belarus, economically and politically stunted. "These countries are just full of desperate people who will do anything for a chance at a better life," she says.

To make matters worse, brothel owners prize the region's many light-skinned, blonde women. "Lighter women are very popular in places like the United States, Europe and Asia," Chon says. "So these women are in demand."

In Africa, more people are trafficked for forced labor than as sex slaves. "In Africa, you have a lot of people being taken and sent to pick cotton and cocoa and other forms of agricultural labor," says Vital Voices' Pinata.

Regardless of their origin, once victims are lured into a trafficking ring, they quickly lose control over their destiny. "If they have a passport, it's usually taken from them and they're abused, physically and psychologically, in order to make them easier to control," says the United Methodist Committee On Relief's Beher.

When victims of trafficking reach their final destination, they rarely have freedom of any kind. "A 16-year-old girl who had been trafficked into Kosovo to be a prostitute told me that when she wasn't working in the bar, she was literally locked into her room and not allowed out," Beher says. "That's the sort of thing we see all the time."

Organized crime plays a key role in most human trafficking. "Most of what you are dealing with here is criminal networks," says Miller of the Office to Combat Trafficking. "You can't take someone out of the Czech Republic and drive her to the Netherlands and hand her over to another trafficker and then to a brothel without real cooperation."

Indeed, smuggling rings often team up with criminal groups in other countries or maintain "branch offices" there. And most traffickers are involved in other criminal activities, such as drugs and weapons smuggling. "Many drug gangs in Southeast Asia are spinning off into trafficking because it's very low risk and very lucrative," says the Women's Commission's Young, who adds that unlike a shipment of drugs, human cargo can earn traffickers money for years.

AFP Photo/Rob Elliott

A 16-year-old Cambodian girl rescued from a brothel peers from her hiding place in Phnom Penh. An estimated 300,000 women are trapped in slave-like conditions in the Southeast Asian sex trade. Cambodia recently agreed to join the first U.N. program aimed at halting the trafficking of women in the region.

These crime networks, especially in Eastern Europe and Asia, operate freely, in large part because they have corrupted many local officials. "So many people are being moved across borders that it's impossible to believe that government officials aren't cooperating," Young says. "Like drugs and other illegal activities, this is very corrupting, especially in poor countries where the police are poorly paid."

In addition to stepping up law enforcement, countries can do many things to fight trafficking, UNICEF's Landgren says. "For example, the United Kingdom has a new system that keeps tabs on children entering the country," she says. "By keeping track of children that come in from abroad, we can better protect them."

And in Brazil, where landowners often lure peasants to their farms with promises of work only to put them in debt bondage, President Luiz Ignacio Lula da Silva has stepped up efforts to free forced laborers. Lula, as the president is called, also has called for a change in the constitution to allow the confiscation of land for those convicted of enslaving workers.

Even countries that have long allowed trafficking are beginning to address the issue. Moldova, for instance, has begun prosecuting traffickers and has created a database of employment agencies that help people find legitimate work abroad. [35]

NGOs have also taken steps to help. For instance, some groups run safe houses where trafficking victims who escape can find shelter and security. "We provide them with medical and psychological care," says Beher, whose group operates a house in Kosovo's capital, Pristina. "We allow them to stay until they recover and then help them to get home, which is usually somewhere else in Eastern Europe, like Romania or Moldova."

Continued on p. 290

At Issue:

Is the Trafficking Victims Protection Act tough enough?

yes

REP. CHRISTOPHER H. SMITH, R-N.J.
CHAIRMAN, U.S. HELSINKI COMMISSION

WRITTEN FOR *THE CQ RESEARCHER*, MARCH 15, 2004

Each year, nearly a million people worldwide are bought and sold into the commercial sex industry, sweatshops, domestic servitude and other dehumanizing situations.

In October 2000, President Clinton signed into law the Trafficking Victims Protection Act (TVPA), which I authored. It provided a multifaceted approach to halting human trafficking through law enforcement, prevention and aid to victims. It also represented two major policy changes: up to life in prison for those who traffic in humans and treatment of the people trafficked — largely women, children, and teenagers — as victims rather than as criminals. In 2003, the law was expanded and strengthened.

As President Bush noted in his historic speech at the United Nations in September 2003, the global community must do more to eradicate human slavery. But significant progress has been made in just a few years, thanks largely to the law's three-tier system and annual "Trafficking in Persons Report" mandated by the law.

When the first report came out, the State Department listed 23 nations in Tier 3 as the worst offenders. It pulled no punches and did not hesitate to name offending nations, including our allies, if they were not making "serious and sustained" efforts to fight trafficking. Naming names was a measure I fought hard to include in the law, even though it was initially opposed by the previous administration.

Thanks to the report and the threat of sanctions, most nations have improved their record on trafficking. Only 15 countries were in Tier 3 during the most recent 2003 report, and most of them made enough progress in the ensuing months to avoid economic sanctions. The State Department is continually improving the scope of the report so it will present the most accurate and thorough picture of the worldwide trafficking problem.

The message from the United States is loud and clear: If you are committed to the fight against human slavery, we welcome you as an ally. But if you continue to look askance when it comes to this horrible crime and pretend you don't have a trafficking problem, we're going to aggressively push you to make reforms, and we'll use economic sanctions as a means to that end.

no

TOMMY CALVERT, JR.
CHIEF OF EXTERNAL OPERATIONS, AMERICAN ANTI-SLAVERY GROUP

WRITTEN FOR *THE CQ RESEARCHER*, MARCH 15, 2004

Most anti-slavery experts would agree the TVPA is a good law, but that slavery can be defeated in our lifetime only if we give the law priority in attention and funding — and apply it equally to friends and foes alike.

The "Trafficking in Person's Report" (TIPS) required by the law does not reveal the full story on global slavery, but only a snapshot. The criteria used to determine progress in the fight against slavery — by focusing on government action rather than on total slavery within a nation's borders — skew our view of realities on the ground.

South Korea, for example, has a serious problem with trafficking — an estimated 15,000 people trafficked per year — but it is ranked in Tier 1, the best ranking a government can receive. Nations can create many seemingly tough laws and programs to fight slavery. However, organized crime may still run thriving trafficking operations in the face of such policies, which may in reality be weak or ineffectual.

Last year marked the first time that countries designated by the "Trafficking In Persons Report" as the worst offenders — Tier 3 — would automatically be subject to U.S. sanctions, which can only be waived by the president.

The State Department gave wide latitude to the standards for Tier 2, perhaps to keep strategic allies from being hit with sanctions. Both Brazil and Saudi Arabia, for instance, received Tier 2 designations. But Brazil's president has launched one of the world's most ambitious plans to end slavery, while Saudi Arabia has no laws outlawing human trafficking and has prosecuted no offenders. Thus, the report's rankings equate a major national initiative to end slavery with royal lip service.

Some Middle Eastern and North African countries may have advanced in the rankings because they are being courted by the administration to support the war on terror and our plans for change in the region. But there is evidence these countries have not really progressed in the fight against human bondage.

The long-term effect of such discrepancies is to reduce the credibility of the report and lengthen the time it takes to eradicate slavery.

Continued from p. 288

The Polaris Project maintains three 24-hour hotlines (in English, Thai and Korean) in the United States to allow both victims and third parties to report trafficking activity. Polaris also has a trafficking database to help law enforcement and other officials gather information about potential cases.

But international organizations and NGOs can only do so much, says Beher, because impoverished, poorly governed countries will always be breeding grounds for trafficking. "Until the causes disappear, all we in the international aid community can do is fight the symptoms," she says.

"In order to really get rid of this problem," Beher continues, "you need political stability and a strong civil society, which in turn leads to the rule of law and stronger law enforcement. You know, there's a reason why there aren't a lot of Finnish people being trafficked."

But Calvert of the American Anti-Slavery Group says governments and international organizations could virtually shut down the trade in human beings if they wanted to. "The international community is in a state of denial and lacks the commitment to fight this," he says. "Look at Britain: They had whole fleets of ships devoted to stopping the slave trade on the high seas, and it worked."

Calvert says the United Nations and other international groups should be more aggressive and uncompromising in combating slavery. "They had weapons inspectors didn't they?" he asks. "Well that's what we need to fight this. We need that kind of action."

AFP Photo/Saeed Khan

Pakistani Minister for Education Zobaida Jalal and Deputy Labor Under Secretary for International Labor Affairs Thomas Moorhead sign an agreement in Islamabad on Jan. 23, 2002, calling for the U.S. to provide $5 million to help educate working children in Pakistan.

Slavery and Forced Labor

Slavery today bears little resemblance to earlier forms of bondage. For instance, 150 years ago in the American South, a healthy slave was a valuable piece of property, worth up to $40,000 in today's dollars, according to Free the Slaves. [36] By contrast, slaves today are often worth less than $100, giving slaveholders little incentive to care for them.

Although slavery exists nearly everywhere, it is most prevalent in the poorer parts of South Asia, where an estimated 15 million to 20 million people are in bonded labor in India, Pakistan, Bangladesh and Nepal.

Bonded labor usually begins when someone borrows money from someone else and agrees to work for that person until the debt is paid. In most cases, the debt is never paid and the borrower and his immediate family become virtual slaves, working in exchange for basic amenities like food and shelter.

"Often you see a whole family in bondage for three or four generations because once someone borrows a small amount of money you're trapped," says Callahan of Free the Slaves. "You don't pay off the principal of the loan, you just keep paying off the interest."

Bonded laborers work at jobs ranging from making bricks in Pakistan to farming, cigarette rolling and carpet making in India. In the western Indian state of Gujarat, some 30,000 bonded families harvest salt in the marshes. The glare from the salt makes them color-blind. When they die, the laborers cannot even be cremated, according to Hindu custom, because their bodies have absorbed too much salt to burn properly. [37]

Slavery is also widespread in sub-Saharan Africa, where the Anti-Slavery Group estimates that at least 200,000 people are in bondage. Besides Sudan, the largest concentration of African slaves is in Mauritania. For hundreds of years, Mauritania's lighter-skinned ruling elite kept their darker compatriots in a system of chattel slavery, with generations being born into servitude. Although the country formally outlawed slavery in 1980, the practice is thought to still be widespread.

"For the thousands of slaves who were legally freed in 1980, life did not change at all," Bales writes. "No one bothered to tell the slaves about it. Some have never learned of their legal freedom, some did so years later, and for most legal freedom was never translated into actual freedom." Today, slaves are still "everywhere" in Mauritania "doing every job that is hard, onerous and dirty." [38]

Slaves also pick cotton in Egypt and Benin, harvest cocoa and other crops in Ivory Coast and mine diamonds in Sierra Leone.

In addition, hundreds of youngsters are abducted each year and forced to become soldiers for rebel fighters in war zones like Uganda and Congo.

Child soldiers often are made to do horrible things. A girl in Uganda who was kidnapped at 13 was forced to kill and abduct other children during her five years in captivity. [39]

But slavery also flourishes beyond the developing world. Although the problem is not as widespread, forced labor and servitude also occur in Europe and the United States — in brothels, farms and sweatshops. "It's amazing, but there are slaves in the United States doing all kinds of things," says Miller of the Office to Combat Trafficking. "Recently authorities found a group of Mexican [agricultural workers] who had been trafficked to work for no pay in Florida. It's unbelievable."

Moreover, slavery is not confined to just seedy brothels or plantations. In upscale American neighborhoods too, people, usually from other countries, have been enslaved, often as domestics. Last year, for instance, a suburban Maryland couple was convicted of forced labor for coercing an illegal alien from Ghana to work seven days a week as a domestic servant without pay. And from time to time, foreign diplomats are found to be harboring unpaid domestic workers from their home countries who cannot leave to work for someone else because the diplomats hold their visas. [40] ■

OUTLOOK

Impact of Globalization

The increasing ease of travel and communication brought about by globalization has helped many industries, including illegal ones like trafficking and slavery.

"Globalization has certainly made trafficking and slavery easier, but it is a double-edged sword," says Jacobson of Christian Freedom International. "It has also helped us to more quickly and effectively shine a spotlight on the evil thugs who are doing these bad things."

Moreover, Jacobson says, as globalization improves the general standard of living in the developing world, it becomes harder for traffickers to prey on innocents. "When the boats are rising for everyone, poverty and despair are alleviated," he says. "When someone gets a job and education and health care, they are much less susceptible to being abused."

The Polaris Project's Chon is also optimistic, although for different reasons. "I'm very upbeat about all of this, because tackling these problems is a matter of political will, and I think the world is slowly beginning to pay more attention to these issues," she says. "I feel as though we're at the same point as the [American] abolitionist movement at the beginning of the 19th century, in that things are slowly beginning to move in the right direction."

Rep. Smith agrees. "There's a fever all over the world to enact new, tough policies to deal with this," he says. "Because the U.S. is out front on this, a lot of countries are beginning to follow suit."

Moreover, the optimists note, victims themselves are increasingly fighting for their rights. "There is a silent revolution going on right now, in places like India, where people are literally freeing themselves from slavery," says Callahan of Free the Slaves, referring to thousands of quarry slaves in northern India who recently have left their bondage and begun new lives. "If this kind of thing keeps up, in a few decades these problems will be blips on the radar screen compared to what they are today."

But Beher of the United Methodist Committee on Relief sees little change ahead because of continuing poverty and societal dysfunction. "The problems that lead to trafficking and slavery are very complicated, and there are no easy fixes," she says. "We need to build up the economies and the civil society of the places where these things happen in order to get rid of this once and for all. And I'm afraid that that is going to take many decades."

Indeed, "Things could get a lot worse before they get better," warns Young of the Women's Commission for Refugee Women and Children, comparing trafficking to the drug trade.

"It's so profitable, and there is so little risk in getting caught that it seems like there will be plenty of this kind of thing going on for the foreseeable future." ■

Notes

1 See www.freetheslaves.net/slavery_today/index.html.

2 Figure cited in "2003 Trafficking in Persons Report," U.S. Department of State, p. 7.

3 Frank Trejo, "Event Underscores Scope, Toll of Human Trafficking," *Dallas Morning News*, March 4, 2003, p. 3B.

4 Richard Mertens, "Smuggler's Prey: Poor Women of Eastern Europe," *The Christian Science Monitor*, Sept. 22, 2002, p. A7.

5 Quoted in *ibid*.

6 "Trafficking in Persons Report," *op. cit.*, p. 6.

7 The entire text of President Bush's speech can be found at www.whitehouse.gov/news/releases/2003/09/20030923-4.html.

About the Author

David Masci specializes in science, religion and foreign-policy issues. Before joining *The CQ Researcher* in 1996, he was a reporter at Congressional Quarterly's *Daily Monitor* and *CQ Weekly.* He holds a law degree from The George Washington University and a B.A. in medieval history from Syracuse University. His recent reports include "Rebuilding Iraq" and "Torture."

[8] "IPEC Action Against Child Labour: 2002-2003," International Labour Organization, January 2004, p. 15; see also ILO, "Investing in Every Child," December 2003, p. 32.
[9] Figure cited in Davan Maharaj, "Panel Frowns on Efforts to Buy Sudan Slaves' Freedom," *Los Angeles Times*, May 28, 2002, p. A3.
[10] Quoted from "60 Minutes II," May 15, 2002.
[11] Nicholas D. Kristof, "Bargaining For Freedom," *The New York Times*, Jan 21, 2004, p. A27.
[12] Figure cited at "UNICEF Oral Report on the Global Challenge of Child Trafficking," January 2004, at: www.unicef.org/about/TraffickingOralreport.pdf.
[13] Full text of the law is at: www.state.gov/documents/organization/10492.pdf. The law was reauthorized in December 2003.
[14] Figures cited at www.state.gov/g/tip/rls/fs/28548.htm.
[15] Richard Mertens, "In Turkey, Childhoods Vanish in Weary Harvests," *The Christian Science Monitor*, May 8, 2003, p. 7.
[16] ILO, *op. cit.*
[17] See Brian Hansen, "Children in Crisis," *The CQ Researcher*, Aug. 31, 2001, p. 657.
[18] See: www.ilo.org/public/english/standards/ipec/ratify_govern.pdf.
[19] ILO, *op. cit.*, January 2004, p. 37.
[20] "With a Little U.S. Help, ILO Targets Child Labour," *Indian Express*, March 3, 2004.
[21] Hugh Thomas, *World History: The Story of Mankind from Prehistory to the Present* (1996), pp. 54-55.
[22] *Ibid.*, pp. 105-107.
[23] Quoted in Michael Grant, *The World of Rome* (1960), p. 116.
[24] Thomas, *op. cit.*, pp. 107-110.
[25] Figures cited in *ibid.*, p. 279.
[26] John Hope Franklin and Alfred A Moss, Jr., *From Slavery to Freedom: A History of African-Americans* (2000), p. 100.
[27] *Ibid.*, p. 94.
[28] From a speech before the Congress of Angostura in 1819. See http://www.fordham.edu/halsall/mod/1819bolivar.html.
[29] Franklin and Moss, *op. cit.*, p. 244.
[30] The full text of the convention can be found at www.unicri.it/1926%20slavery%20convention.pdf.
[31] Quoted at www.un.org/Overview/rights. html.
[32] A complete list of those countries that have signed and ratified the protocol are at www.unodc.org/unodc/en/crime_cicp_signatures_trafficking.html.
[33] Sylvie Briand, "Sold into Slavery: Ukrainian Girls Tricked into Sex Trade," Agence France Presse, Jan. 28, 2004.
[34] Peter Landesman, "The Girls Next Door, *The New York Times Magazine*, Jan. 25, 2004, p. 30.
[35] "Trafficking in Person's Report," *op. cit.*, p. 107.
[36] See www.freetheslaves.net/slavery_today/index.html.
[37] Christopher Kremmer, "With a Handful of Salt," *The Boston Globe*, Nov. 28, 1999.
[38] Kevin Bales, *Disposable People: The New Slavery in the Global Economy* (1999), p. 81.
[39] Thomas Wagner, "Study Documents Trauma of Child Soldiers," Associated Press Online, March 11, 2004.
[40] Ruben Castaneda, "Couple Enslaved Woman," *The Washington Post*, June 10, 2003, p. B1.

FOR MORE INFORMATION

American Anti-Slavery Group, 198 Tremont St., Suite 421, Boston, MA 02116; (800) 884-0719; www.iabolish.com.

Casa Alianza, 346 West 17th St., New York, N.Y.10011; (212) 727-4000; www.casa-alianza.org. A San Jose, Costa Rica, group that aids street children in Latin America.

Christian Children's Fund, 2821 Emerywood Parkway, Richmond, VA 23294; (800) 776-6767; www.christianchildrensfund.org. CCF works in 28 countries on critical children's issues.

Christian Freedom International, P.O. Box 535, Front Royal, VA 22630; (800) 323-CARE (2273); (540) 636-8907; www.christianfreedom.org. An interdenominational human rights organization that combines advocacy with humanitarian assistance for persecuted Christians.

Christian Solidarity International, Zelglistrasse 64, CH-8122 Binz, Zurich, Switzerland; www.csi-int.ch/index.html. Works to redeem slaves in Sudan.

Defence for Children International, P.O. Box 88, CH 1211, Geneva 20, Switzerland; (+41 22) 734-0558; www.defence-for-children.org. Investigates sexual exploitation of children and other abuses.

Free the Children, 1750 Steeles Ave. West, Suite 218, Concord, Ontario, Canada L4K 2L7; (905) 760-9382; www.freethechildren.org. This group encourages youth to help exploited children.

Free the Slaves, 1326 14th St., N.W., Washington, DC 20005; (202) 588-1865; www.freetheslaves.net.

Human Rights Watch, 350 Fifth Ave., New York, NY 10118; (212) 290-4700; www.hrw.org. Investigates abuses worldwide.

International Labour Organization, 4, route des Morillons, CH-1211, Geneva 22, Switzerland; www.ilo.org. Sets and enforces worldwide labor standards.

Polaris Project, P.O. Box 77892, Washington, DC 20013; (202) 547-7990; www.polarisproject.org. Grass-roots organization fighting trafficking.

United Methodist Committee On Relief, 475 Riverside Dr., New York, NY 10115; (800) 554-8583; gbgm-umc.org. Worldwide humanitarian group.

United Nations Children's Fund (UNICEF), 3 United Nations Plaza, New York, NY 10017; (212) 326-7000; www.unicef.org. Helps poor children in 160 countries.

Women's Commission on Refugee Women and Children, 122 East 42nd St., 12th Floor, New York, NY 10168-1289; (212) 551-3088; www.womenscommission.org. Aids trafficking victims in the developing world.

World Vision International, 800 West Chestnut Ave., Monrovia, Calif. 91016; (626) 303-8811; www.wvi.org. A Christian relief and development organization established in 1950.

Bibliography

Selected Sources

Books

Bales, Kevin, *Disposable People: New Slavery in the Global Economy*, University of California Press, 1999.
The president of Free the Slaves and a leading expert on slavery offers strategies to end the practice.

Bok, Francis, *Escape From Slavery: The True Story of My Ten Years In Captivity and My Journey to Freedom in America*, St. Martin's Press, 2003.
A former slave in Sudan tells the gripping story of his ordeal and eventual journey to the United States.

Franklin, John Hope, and, Alfred Moss Jr., *From Slavery to Freedom: A History of African Americans*, McGraw-Hill, 2000.
Franklin, a renowned professor emeritus of history at Duke University and Moss, an associate professor at the University of Maryland, discuss the slave trade and slavery in the United States up to the Civil War.

Articles

"A Cargo of Exploitable Souls," *The Economist*, June 1, 2002.
The article examines human trafficking of prostitutes and forced laborers into the United States.

Bales, Kevin, "The Social Psychology of Modern Slavery," *Scientific American*, April 2002, p. 68.
A leading expert on slavery examines the psychological underpinnings that may drive both traffickers and slaveholders as well as their victims.

Cockburn, Andrew, "Hidden in Plain Sight: The World's 27 Million Slaves," *National Geographic*, Sept. 2003, p. 2.
A correspondent for London's *Independent* takes a hard look at slavery; includes chilling photographs of victims.

Hansen, Brian, "Children in Crisis," *The CQ Researcher*, Aug. 31, 2001, pp. 657-688.
Hansen examines the exploitation of children around the world, including sexual slaves and forced laborers.

Kristof, Nicolas D., "Bargaining For Freedom," *The New York Times*, Jan. 21, 2004, p. A27.
The veteran columnist describes how he "bought" and freed two sex slaves in Cambodia. The article is part of Kristof's series on his experiences in Southeast Asia.

Landesman, Peter, "The Girls Next Door," *The New York Times Magazine*, Jan. 25, 2004, p. 30.
Landesman's detailed exposé of trafficking focuses on the importation of young girls into the U.S. for prostitution.

Maharaj, Davan, "Panel Frowns on Efforts to Buy Sudan Slaves Freedom," *Los Angeles Times*, May 28, 2002, p. 3.
The article details the controversy surrounding the practice of slave redemption in Sudan.

Mertens, Richard, "Smugglers' Prey: Poor Women of Eastern Europe," *The Christian Science Monitor*, Sept. 25, 2002, p. 7.
The article examines the plight of Eastern European women trafficked into sexual slavery who manage to escape.

Miller, John, R., "Slavery in 2004," *The Washington Post*, Jan. 1, 2004, p. A25.
The director of the State Department's Office to Monitor and Combat Trafficking in Persons argues that the Trafficking Victims Protection Act has prodded other countries to act.

Power, Carla, *et al.*, "Preying on Children," *Newsweek*, Nov. 17, 2003, p. 34.
The number of children being trafficked into Western Europe is rising, helped by more porous borders and the demand for young prostitutes.

Vaknin, Sam, "The Morality of Child Labor," United Press International, Oct. 4, 2002.
UPI's senior business correspondent argues that organizations opposed to most forms of child labor impose unrealistic, rich-world standards on the poorest countries.

Reports

"Investing in Every Child: An Economic Study of the Costs and Benefits of Eliminating Child Labor," International Labour Organization, December 2003.
The ILO contends that ending child labor would improve economic growth in the developing world.

"IPEC Action Against Child Labor: 2002-2003," International Labour Organization, January 2004.
The report charts the progress made by the ILO's International Program on the Elimination of Child Labor (IPEC), which funds anti-child labor initiatives around the world.

"Trafficking in Persons Report," U.S. Department of State, June 2003.
The annual report required by the Trafficking Victims Protection Act assesses global anti-trafficking efforts.

The Next Step:

Additional Articles from Current Periodicals

Children

Byrne, Eileen, "Morocco Wants Children Out of Workshops and Into School," ***Los Angeles Times*****, Dec. 29, 2002, p. A18.**
Children as young as seven earn a dollar a day working a six-day week; intense poverty means laws against child labor go unenforced.

Iritani, Evelyn, "Child Labor Rules Don't Ease Burden in Bangladesh," ***Los Angeles Times*****, May 4, 2003, p. C1.**
Critics of an agreement with Bangladesh to eliminate child labor in garment factories say many children end up in more dangerous jobs.

Kirk, Danica, "Albania Told to Halt Trade of Children," ***The Washington Post*****, Dec. 7, 2003, p. A27.**
In a country so poor government aid sometimes arrives by horse-drawn cart, child trafficking is a low priority for the Albanian government.

McKelvey, Tara, "The Youngest Soldiers," ***Chicago Tribune*****, May 26, 2003, Tempo Section, p. 1.**
A surplus of small arms and a shortage of adults in populations ravaged by war resulted in a surge in the number of child soldiers, up to 300,000 globally.

Power, Carla, "Preying on Children," ***Newsweek*****, Nov. 17, 2003, p. 34.**
Poor economic conditions in Eastern Europe and Africa combine with fractured and sometimes hurtful laws to fuel an increase in European child trafficking.

Sengupta, Somini, "Child Traffickers Prey on Bangladesh," ***The New York Times*****, April 29, 2002, p. A6.**
Thousands of Bangladeshi children are trafficked abroad each year; many boys serve as camel jockeys in the Persian Gulf.

Government Policies

Allen, Mike, "Bush Warns U.N. Assembly About Dangers of Trade in Sex Slaves," ***The Washington Post*****, Sept. 24, 2003, p. A23.**
President Bush for the first time mentioned the fight against human trafficking when he addressed the General Assembly.

Branigin, William, "Va. Aid Group Helps Victims of Human Trade," ***The Washington Post*****, March 6, 2003, p. B8.**
Boat People SOS aids people like Quang Thi Vo, a Vietnamese woman who worked as a virtual slave in a Korean-owned factory in American Samoa.

Continetti, Matthew, "On Human Bondage," ***The Weekly Standard*****, Oct. 6, 2003.**
President Bush's comments to the U.N. urging the fight against human trafficking are mirrored by more aggressive U.S. prosecution of traffickers.

Finley, Bruce, "Human Rights Color Trade Debate," ***The Denver Post*****, April 22, 2002, p. A1.**
A proposal to grant President Bush increased authority to reach trade agreements is influenced by slave-labor concerns in Myanmar and elsewhere.

Haugen, Gary, "State's Blind Eye on Sexual Slavery," ***The Washington Post*****, June 15, 2002, p. A23.**
The author argues that the annual "Trafficking in Persons Report" by the Department of State gives a passing grade to many countries where sex trafficking is unpunished.

McKenzie, Glenn, "Nigeria Targets Traffickers Who Exploit Children," ***Chicago Tribune*****, Oct. 26, 2003, News Section, p. 4.**
Operations in Nigeria aim to free children and teens who labor in granite quarries for 20 cents a day.

Miller, John, "Slavery in 2004," ***The Washington Post*****, Jan. 1, 2004, p. A25.**
The director of the State Department's anti-trafficking section describes how the threat of economic penalties can motivate countries to fight slavery and forced labor.

Sex Trade

Binder, David, "In Europe, Sex Slavery Is Thriving Despite Raids," ***The New York Times*****, Oct. 20, 2002, p. A8.**
A U.S.-funded, multinational anti-trafficking operation in Europe had mixed results.

Faiola, Anthony, "N. Korean Women Find Life of Abuse Waiting in China," ***The Washington Post*****, March 3, 2004, p. A20.**
Female North Korean refugees are regularly forced into sexual servitude in China; their captors threaten them with deportation back to North Korea, where a worse fate awaits.

Macintyre, Donald, "Base Instincts," ***Time Asia*****, Aug. 12, 2002, p. 18.**
Members of Congress demand action to address concerns U.S. troops frequent Korean bars and clubs staffed by women trafficked from the Philippines and Russia.

Mertens, Richard, "Smugglers' Prey: Poor Women of E. Europe," ***The Christian Science Monitor*****, Sept. 25, 2002, p. 7.**
Peacekeepers and international police forces in Bosnia and Kosovo formed the core customers of traffickers who bought and sold women like cattle.

Montlake, Simon, "In Thailand, a Struggle to Halt Human Trafficking," *The Christian Science Monitor*, Aug. 29, 2003, p. 9.
Poverty and exploitation are more common elements in Thai prostitution than outright coercion; some Burmese women return to the brothels voluntarily.

Sulavik, Christopher, "Facing Down Traffickers," *Newsweek*, Aug. 25, 2003, p. 27.
The poverty accompanying the collapse of the Soviet Union made it relatively easy to exploit desperate, young women from impoverished former Soviet satellites.

Situation in America

"A Cargo of Exploitable Souls," *The Economist*, June 1, 2002.
The State Department estimates that every year approximately 50,000 people are forcibly trafficked into the United States.

Lochhead, Carolyn, "Sex Trade Uses Bay Area to Bring in Women, Kids," *San Francisco Chronicle*, Feb. 26, 2003, p. A3.
Trafficking is a bigger problem on the West Coast because of better access from Asia and Mexico.

O'Connor, Anne-Marie, "Gathering Fights Those Who Deal in Human Lives," *Los Angeles Times*, Aug. 25, 2002, p. B10.
Police, human rights activists and social workers from the U.S. and Mexico discussed ways to fight the international sex trade.

Roche, Walter, and Willoughby Mariano, "Trapped in Servitude Far From Their Homes," *The Baltimore Sun*, Sept. 15, 2002, p. 1A.
Micronesians and Marshall Islanders are brought to the United States on false pretenses and forced to labor in virtual servitude for minimal pay.

Wallace, Bill, and Jim Herron Zamora, "Sex Trafficking Ruthless, Lucrative," *San Francisco Chronicle*, Jan. 24, 2004, p. A1.
Raids on San Francisco brothels highlight the nation's $9 billion-a-year trade in human flesh; lured by profit, new operators spring up overnight.

Sudan

"A Modern Tale of Slavery, Survival, and Escape," *The Christian Science Monitor*, Dec. 19, 2003, p. 11.
Excerpts are presented from a book by a young Sudanese boy who was captured by northern militiamen and spent 10 years as a slave.

Kristof, Nicholas, "A Slave's Journey in Sudan," *The New York Times*, April 23, 2002, p. A23.
Applying pressure on the Sudanese government and engaging them rather than applying sanctions is the most effective means to fight slavery.

Lacey, Marc, "Panel Led by U.S. Criticizes Sudan's Government Over Slavery," *The New York Times*, May 23, 2002, p. A17.
A multinational commission formed by the United States condemned Sudan for allowing slavery to flourish.

Maharaj, Davan, "Panel Frowns on Efforts to Buy Sudan Slaves' Freedom," *Los Angeles Times*, May 28, 2002, p. A3.
A U.S.-led commission on slavery in Sudan discourages the buying back of slaves because the money provides an incentive for taking more slaves.

Martin, Randolph, "Sudan's Perfect War," *Foreign Affairs*, March/April 2002, p. 111.
The story of Sudan's endless war is a confluence of tribal enmities, religious fanaticism, political opportunism and access to oil.

CITING *THE CQ RESEARCHER*

Sample formats for citing these reports in a bibliography include the ones listed below. Preferred styles and formats vary, so please check with your instructor or professor.

MLA STYLE

Jost, Kenneth. "Rethinking the Death Penalty." The CQ Researcher 16 Nov. 2001: 945-68.

APA STYLE

Jost, K. (2001, November 16). Rethinking the death penalty. *The CQ Researcher, 11*, 945-968.

CHICAGO STYLE

Jost, Kenneth. "Rethinking the Death Penalty." *CQ Researcher*, November 16, 2001, 945-968.

Back Issues

The CQ Researcher offers in-depth coverage of many key areas.
Back issues are $10. Quantity discounts available.
Call (866) 427-7737 to order back issues.

Or call for a free CQ Researcher Web trial!
Online access provides:

- *Searchable archives dating back to 1991.*
- *Wider access through IP authentication.*
- *PDF files for downloading and printing.*
- *Availability 48 hours before print version.*

CIVIL LIBERTIES
Race in America, July 2003
Gay Marriage, September 2003
Civil Liberties Debates, October 2003

CRIME/LAW
Cyber-Crime, April 2002
Corporate Crime, October 2002
Serial Killers, October 2003

ECONOMY
State Budget Crises, October 2003
Stock Market Troubles, January 2004
Exporting Jobs, February 2004

EDUCATION
Home Schooling Debate, January 2003
Combating Plagiarism, September 2003
Black Colleges, December 2003

ENERGY/TRANSPORTATION
Future of the Airline Industry, June 2002
Future of Amtrak, October 2002
SUV Debate, May 2003

ENVIRONMENT
Crisis in the Plains, May 2003
Water Shortages, August 2003
Air Pollution Conflict, November 2003

HEALTH AND SAFETY
Medicare Reform, August 2003
Women's Health, November 2003
Homeopathy Debate, December 2003

POLITICS AND PUBLIC POLICY
Abortion Debates, March 2003
State Budget Crises, October 2003
Democracy in the Arab World, January 2004

SOCIAL TRENDS
Latinos' Future, October 2003
Future of the Music Industry, Nov. 2003

TECHNOLOGY
NASA's Future, May 2003

TERRORISM/DEFENSE
Homeland Security, September 2003
North Korean Crisis, April 2003

WORLD AFFAIRS
Trouble in South America, March 2003
Rebuilding Iraq, July 2003
Aiding Africa, August 2003

YOUTH
Sexual Abuse and the Clergy, May 2002
Movie Ratings, March 2003
Hazing, January 2004
Youth Suicide, February 2004
Reforming Big-Time College Sports, March 2004

Future Topics

- ***Nuclear Proliferation***
- ***Broadcast Indecency***
- ***Anniversary of Desegregation***

CQ Researcher

Published by CQ Press, a division of Congressional Quarterly Inc.

thecqresearcher.com

Nuclear Proliferation and Terrorism

Can "rogue" states and terrorists acquire nuclear weapons?

The recent discovery of a global black market in nuclear weapons and related technology has intensified concerns that so-called rogue nations and terrorist organizations like Osama bin Laden's al Qaeda network might acquire nuclear bombs. The network run by the "father" of Pakistan's atomic bomb, A.Q. Khan, sold nuclear-weapons materials to Iran and North Korea, which have refused to sign the Nuclear Non-Proliferation Treaty (NPT). Virtually all the other nations of the world are signatories. President Bush responded to the revelations about Khan's network with a plan to strengthen international anti-proliferation efforts, including calling on the U.N. Security Council to require all states to criminalize proliferation of components that could be used to make weapons of mass destruction. While arms experts commended the president for focusing on proliferation, some said his proposals did not go far enough.

The mushroom cloud from Romeo, an 11-megaton hydrogen bomb, rises over Bikini Atoll in the South Pacific on March 26, 1954.

INSIDE

THIS ISSUE

The CQ Researcher • April 2, 2004 • www.thecqresearcher.com
Volume 14, Number 13 • Pages 297-320

CQ PRESS

RECIPIENT OF SOCIETY OF PROFESSIONAL JOURNALISTS AWARD FOR EXCELLENCE ◆ AMERICAN BAR ASSOCIATION SILVER GAVEL AWARD

Nuclear Proliferation and Terrorism

The Issues

Background

Current Situation

Outlook

Sidebars and Graphics

For Further Research

Cover: The mushroom cloud from Romeo, an 11-megaton hydrogen bomb, rises over Bikini Atoll in the South Pacific on March 26, 1954. Most modern nuclear weapons are much weaker; W88 warheads on U.S. submarine-launched ballistic missiles, for example, yield only 475-kilotons, or 32 times the power of the bomb dropped on Hiroshima, Japan, in 1945. A megaton is equivalent to 1 million tons of TNT, a kiloton to 1 thousand tons. (U.S. Department of Energy)

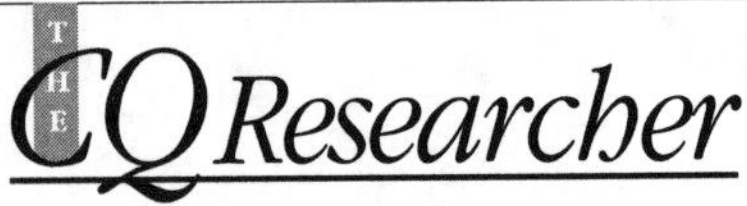

April 2, 2004
Volume 14, No. 13

Managing Editor: Thomas J. Colin

Assistant Managing Editor: Kathy Koch

Associate Editor: Kenneth Jost

Staff Writers: Mary H. Cooper, David Masci, William Triplett

Contributing Writers: Sarah Glazer, David Hatch, David Hosansky, Patrick Marshall, Tom Price, Jane Tanner

Design/Production Editor: Olu B. Davis

Assistant Editor: Kenneth Lukas

A Division of Congressional Quarterly Inc.

Senior Vice President/General Manager: John A. Jenkins

Director, Library Publishing: Kathryn C. Suárez

Director, Editorial Operations: Ann Davies

Circulation Manager: Nina Tristani

Congressional Quarterly Inc.

Chairman: Andrew Barnes

Vice Chairman: Andrew P. Corty

President and Publisher: Robert W. Merry

The CQ Researcher (ISSN 1056-2036) is printed on acid-free paper. Published weekly, except Jan. 2, April 9, July 2, July 9, Aug. 6, Aug. 13, Nov. 26 and Dec. 31, by CQ Press, a division of Congressional Quarterly Inc. Annual subscription rates for libraries, businesses and government start at $625. Single issues are available for $10. Quantity discounts apply to orders over 10. Additional rates furnished upon request. Periodicals postage paid at Washington, D.C., and additional mailing offices. POSTMASTER: Send address changes to *The CQ Researcher*, 1255 22nd St., N.W., Suite 400, Washington, D.C. 20037.

Nuclear Proliferation and Terrorism

BY MARY H. COOPER

THE ISSUES

Concern about nuclear terrorism rose to new levels when A.Q. Khan, the revered father of Pakistan's nuclear bomb, confessed recently to peddling nuclear weapons technology to Libya and other rogue states.

Khan's dramatic confession punctured any remaining illusions that 60 years of nonproliferation efforts had kept the world's most dangerous weapons out of the hands of countries hostile to the United States and its allies. Moreover, he enhanced fears that terrorist groups bent on destroying the United States — like Osama bin Laden's al Qaeda network — may be closer than anyone had realized to acquiring nuclear weapons.

AFP Photo/Philippe Lopez

Terrorist leader Osama bin Laden, left, with his deputy, Ayman al-Zawahiri, has said he wants to use a nuclear bomb against the West. The recent sale of black-market nuclear-weapons technology to North Korea and Iran and the terrorist bombing of passenger trains in Madrid, killing more than 190 people, have intensified concerns about nuclear weapons falling into the hands of "rogue" states or terrorists.

"A nuclear 9/11 in Washington or New York would change American history in ways that [the original] 9/11 didn't," says Graham Allison, director of Harvard University's Belfer Center for Science and International Affairs. "It would be as big a leap beyond 9/11 as 9/11 itself was beyond the pre-attack illusion that we were invulnerable."

Khan's January confession followed the revelation that he had operated a busy black-market trade in centrifuges, blueprints for nuclear-weapons equipment to enrich uranium into weapons-grade fuel and missiles capable of delivering nuclear warheads. Khan's vast network involved manufacturers in Malaysia, middlemen in the United Arab Emirates and the governments of Libya, North Korea and Iran. [1]

Several countries in Khan's network were known to have violated the 1968 Nuclear Non-Proliferation Treaty (NPT) and hidden their weapons programs from inspectors for the U.N.'s International Atomic Energy Agency (IAEA). [2] NPT signatories promise to forgo nuclear weapons in exchange for help from the world's five official nuclear powers — the United States, Russia, China, France and Britain — in building civilian nuclear power plants.

In fact, North Korea has bragged that it is developing nuclear weapons, Iraq tried for years to produce weapons-grade fuel, and Iran recently barred IAEA inspections from its nuclear facilities amid allegations that it was developing a bomb. Libya's admission in December that it, too, had tried to build the bomb blew the cover on Khan's network. (*See sidebar, p. 308.*)

But the extent of Khan's black-market activities stunned even the most seasoned observers. "I was surprised by the level of commerce in the supporting supply network," says Charles B. Curtis, president of the Nuclear Threat Initiative, an advocacy group that calls for stronger measures to stop the spread of nuclear weapons. "While there had been suggestions that the Pakistanis were nefariously engaged in both Iran and North Korea, the extent of the engagement in Libya and indications that there was an attempt to market proliferation technology in Syria exceeded the darkest suspicions of the intelligence community."

Given the grim realities of the post-9/11 world, fear of nuclear terrorism has dominated the international response to Khan's revelations. President Bush has proposed several measures to strengthen international anti-proliferation efforts. "In the hands of terrorists, weapons of mass destruction would be a first resort," Bush said. "[T]hese terrible weapons are becoming easier to acquire, build, hide and transport. . . . Our message to proliferators must be consistent and must be clear: We will find you, and we're not going to rest until you're stopped." [3]

But many experts say the president's proposals will not provide adequate safeguards against these lethal weapons. Wade Boese, research director of the Arms Control Association, a Washington think tank, commends the administration for emphasizing proliferation and pointing out that it is the most serious threat facing the United States today. However, he notes, since 9/11, the Bush administration has only "maintained the status quo" on funding for programs that deal with the threat of nuclear proliferation.

"The Khan network underscores the fact that we're in a race to tighten down security around [nuclear-weapons technology] so the terrorists can't get it," Boese says. "If this is such an urgent priority, which it is, why

Russia Has Most Nuclear Warheads

Russia and the United States have most of the more than 28,000 nuclear warheads stockpiled today. India, Israel and Pakistan — which have not signed the Nuclear Non-Proliferation Treaty (NPT) — have enough nuclear materials to produce more than 300 warheads. North Korea and Iran are both thought to be developing nuclear bombs. It is unknown whether terrorist groups have or are developing nuclear weapons.

Worldwide Nuclear Stockpiles

Country	Nuclear Weapons (estimated)
NPT Signatories	
China	410
France	350
Russia	18,000
United Kingdom	185
United States	9,000
Non-NPT Signatories *	
India	95 (max.)
Israel	200 (max.)
Pakistan	52 (max.)
Maximum total	28,292

** The number of warheads that could be produced with the amount of weapons-grade nuclear material these countries are thought to possess. The total number of assembled weapons is not known.*

Source: Carnegie Endowment for International Peace, 2004

not fund it like it is and recognize that we're in a race with the terrorists?"

During the Cold War, both the United States and the Soviet Union understood that using nuclear weapons would amount to mass suicide. The doctrine of mutual assured destruction — MAD — ensured that a nuclear attack by one superpower would unleash a full-scale response by the other, resulting in annihilation on a national, if not global, scale. Consequently, the theory went, rational leaders would avoid using nuclear weapons at all costs.

But al Qaeda and other radical Islamist organizations don't appear to operate under such constraints. Their suicide bombers embrace death as martyrdom in their quest to destroy the "Great Satan." [4] And because they operate in a number of countries and have no permanent, identifiable headquarters, terrorist groups also have no "return address" to target for a counterattack.

As a result, keeping weapons-grade plutonium and highly enriched uranium out of the hands of terrorists is the only sure way to block terrorists from building nuclear bombs, many experts say.

"The essential ingredients of nuclear weapons are very hard to make and don't occur in nature," notes Matthew Bunn, a nuclear-terrorism expert at the Belfer Center. "But once a well-organized terrorist group gets hold of them, it could make at least a crude nuclear explosive."

Instructions for making a nuclear bomb are not secret; they are even on the Internet. "The secret is in making the nuclear material," Bunn points out, "and that, unfortunately, is the secret that A.Q. Khan was peddling."

While the ability of terrorists to stage a full-scale nuclear attack is of paramount concern, experts say the use of a conventional explosive device containing radioactive waste — a so-called dirty bomb — is far more likely. A dirty bomb in an urban area could contaminate dozens of city blocks, fomenting panic and costing tens of billions of dollars in lost revenues and devalued real estate, even if it claimed no human lives. [5]

"A dirty bomb is pretty likely to happen," says Leonard S. Spector, director of the Center for Nonproliferation Studies' Washington office, a part of the Monterey Institute of International Studies. A dirty bomb can be made easily with radioactive materials, such as cesium, used in X-ray machines and other commonplace diagnostic equipment. Moreover, he points out, civilian nuclear-waste facilities are much easier to penetrate than weapons facilities.

"We have to do our best to control as much of the radioactive material as possible," he says, "but it's already the subject of criminal activities. So we're recommending that people get ready for this one."

As policymakers examine the impact of Khan's nuclear black marketeering on U.S. counterproliferation policy, these are some of the questions being considered:

Is the Non-Proliferation Treaty still an effective shield against the spread of nuclear weapons?

The United States launched the atomic age when it detonated the first atomic bomb in 1945. But After Britain, China, France and the Soviet Union developed their own nuclear weapons, the great powers sought to put the nuclear genie back in the bottle. The landmark 1968 Non-Proliferation Treaty embodied a "grand bargain," by which the five countries with nuclear arsenals agreed to help the rest of the world develop nuclear power for peaceful uses in exchange for the non-nuclear states' promise to forgo nuclear weapons. The IAEA was to oversee compliance with the treaty, which enjoyed near universal support.

However, India, Israel and Pakistan — all of which have since developed nuclear weapons — never signed the treaty. And North Korea, which signed but later renounced the treaty, recently boasted that it is on the threshold of developing nuclear weapons.

Getty Images

Protesters in Seoul, South Korea, burn a North Korean flag and an effigy of Kim Jong Il on Dec. 28, 2003, calling on North Korea's leader to end the country's efforts to build a nuclear bomb.

The absence of universal adherence to the NPT reveals the treaty's basic weakness. "The fact that a very small number of individuals — nobody believes that A.Q. Khan was acting alone — can create a network that provides some of the most worrisome states on the planet with the technology needed to produce nuclear weapons is very troubling," Bunn says. "It shows that the NPT regime is only as strong as its weakest links. We can secure 90 percent of the nuclear material to very high levels, but if the other 10 percent is vulnerable to theft, we still won't have solved the problem because we're dealing with intelligent adversaries who will be able to find and exploit the weak points."

In fact, some experts say that weaknesses doom the NPT to failure. "Arms-control regimes are not capable of dealing with the hard cases," says John Pike, a defense policy expert and founding director of GlobalSecurity.org, a nonprofit organization that studies emerging security threats.

"The logic of the NPT just doesn't get you very far in Tehran [Iran] or Pyongyang [North Korea]," Pike says. "It's not going to matter to India or Pakistan, which have their own fish to fry. And the Israelis are not going to let go of their arsenal until there is a just and lasting peace in the Middle East," Pike says. "I'm afraid we're rapidly approaching a situation in which there are more nuclear-weapons states outside the NPT than inside, and the treaty itself provides no way whatsoever of addressing that problem."

The nonproliferation regime also lacks adequate verification and enforcement provisions, critics say. "The NPT was a confidence-building measure, not a true arms-control treaty," says C. Paul Robinson, director of Sandia National Laboratories, a division of the Energy Department's National Nuclear Security Administration. Robinson also was chief U.S. negotiator of the U.S.-Soviet Threshold Test Ban and Peaceful Nuclear Explosions Treaties, both ratified in 1990. None of the requirements normally found in arms-control treaties to verify compliance were included in the NPT, he says. "So there's nothing in the original NPT designed to catch cheaters."

After the 1991 Persian Gulf War, the nuclear nonproliferation community was surprised to learn that Iraq had been secretly developing nuclear weapons. So an "Additional Protocol" was added to the NPT allowing for more thorough inspections of suspected weapons facilities, but only 38 countries have ratified it. In any case, Robinson dismisses the protocol as little more than a "Band-Aid."

Even IAEA Director Mohamed ElBaradei said the NPT regime does not prevent nuclear proliferation. "You need a complete overhaul of the export-control system," he said. "It is not working right now." [6]

But the Bush administration says if the NPT and the IAEA oversight powers are strengthened, nonproliferation can remain a credible goal. On Feb. 11, Bush outlined seven steps designed to make the regime more effective in

Continued on p. 303

A Chronology of Nuclear Close Calls

The superpowers came close to using nuclear weapons several times during the Cold War, sometimes due to tensions that might have escalated, and sometimes due to simple accidents or mistakes. The end of the Cold War in 1991, however, did not end the threat of nuclear conflict.

First year of Korean War, 1950-51 — President Harry S. Truman sends atomic weapons to Guam for possible use against North Korea; Strategic Air Command makes plans to coordinate an atomic strike. Gen. Douglas MacArthur pushes for attacks on China, possibly using atomic weapons. [1]

The Offshore Islands Crises, 1954-55, 1958 — Testing America's resolve, China bombs Quemoy and Matzu, two Nationalist-held islands near the mainland. U.S. officials warn they will use atomic weapons to defend the islands. [2]

Mistake in Greenland, October 1960 — The American early-warning radar system in Thule, Greenland, mistakenly reports a "massive" Soviet missile launch against the United States. A reflection on the moon 250,000 miles away is thought to be a missile launch 2,500 miles away. [3]

Flashpoint Berlin, 1961 — Soviet threats regarding West Berlin prompt President John F. Kennedy to consider a nuclear first-strike against the U.S.S.R. if it attacks the city. [4]

Cuban Missile Crisis, October 1962 — President Kennedy considers invading Cuba to remove Soviet nuclear missiles, unaware the Soviets plan to respond with nuclear weapons. The Strategic Air Command goes to Defense Condition 2 (DEFCON 2), the second-highest state of readiness, for the only time in U.S. history. After an American naval quarantine of the island, Soviet Premier Nikita Khrushchev withdraws the missiles. [5]

B-52 Crash in Greenland, January 1968 — A B-52 carrying four thermonuclear bombs crashes near the U.S. early-warning base in Greenland. If the bombs' safety features had failed, the detonation could have been viewed as a surprise attack on America's early-warning system, prompting nuclear retaliation. [6]

Sino-Soviet Conflict, 1969 — Soviet Defense Minister Andrei Grechko advocates a nuclear strike against China to deal with what is perceived as an inevitable future war. Fearing the U.S. reaction, the Soviets refrain. [7]

Yom Kippur War, October 1973 — Egypt and Syria attack Israel, and after initial successes face military disaster. The Soviet Union indicates it might intervene to rescue its client states if Israel continues to refuse a cease-fire; Soviet airborne forces are put on alert, and U.S. military forces also go on alert. Israel agrees to a cease-fire and the superpower crisis ends. [8]

War Game Turns 'Real' at NORAD, 1979-80 — In November 1979, a technician at the North American Air Defense (NORAD) facility in Cheyenne Mountain, Colo., accidentally places a training tape simulating a nuclear attack on the United States into the base computer system. The mistake is corrected in six minutes — but after the president's airborne command post is launched. Twice in June 1980, false attack warnings caused by faulty computer chips send bomber crews racing for their planes. [9]

Tension in Europe, Early 1980s — After the Soviet Union deploys new nuclear missiles in Europe, the United States follows suit. Soviet leader Yuri Andropov fears NATO is planning a nuclear first-strike and orders Soviet intelligence to find the non-existent evidence. Tension in Europe decreases when Mikhail Gorbachev replaces Andropov. [10]

Soviet Pacific Fleet, August 1984 — A rogue officer at the Soviet Pacific Fleet in Vladivostok broadcasts an unauthorized war alert to Soviet naval forces, which, like American vessels, are armed with nuclear weapons. Soviet, U.S. and Japanese forces all prepare for battle. After 30 minutes, the alert is determined to be false. [11]

Norwegian Sea, January 1995 — Russian radar detects an inbound missile over the Norwegian Sea, and President Boris N. Yeltsin opens his nuclear command briefcase and confers with his military commanders. The missile turns out to be a Norwegian weather rocket. [12]

Kargil, Kashmir, May-July 1999 — A year after nuclear tests by India and Pakistan, Pakistan invades Kargil, in Indian-controlled Kashmir, and battles Indian forces from May until July. The crisis between the two rival nuclear powers is described as "warlike." Pakistan withdraws in July under heavy international pressure. [13]

Attack on the Indian Parliament, December 2001-January 2002 — Islamic militants probably connected to Pakistan's intelligence service attack India's Parliament. India demands that Pakistan cease supporting Islamic fighters. Hundreds of thousands of troops face off at the Indo-Pakistani border; both sides discuss a possible nuclear exchange. Tensions ease after Pakistan cracks down on Islamist groups. [14]

— Kenneth Lukas

---

1 Burton Kaufman, *The Korean Conflict* (1999).

2 John W. Garver, *Foreign Relations of the People's Republic of China* (1993), pp. 50-60.

3 Center for Defense Information (CDI), www.cdi.org/Issues/NukeAccidents/accidents.htm.

4 Fred Kaplan, "JFK's First Strike Plan," *The Atlantic Monthly*, October 2001, pp. 81-86.

5 Graham Allison and Philip Zelikow, *Essence of Decision* (1999).

6 Scott D. Sagan, *The Limits of Safety* (1993), pp. 180-193.

7 Garver, *op. cit.*, pp. 305-310.

8 P. R. Kumaraswamy (ed.), *Revisiting the Yom Kippur War* (2000).

9 Sagan, *op. cit.*, pp. 228-233.

10 Christopher Andrew and Vasili Mitrokhin, *The Sword and the Shield* (1999).

11 CNN, www.cnn.com/SPECIALS/cold.war/episodes/12/spotlight/.

12 CNN, *op. cit.*

13 Yossef Bodansky, "The Kargil Crisis in Kashmir Threatens to Move into a New Indo-Pak War, With PRC Involvement," *Defense & Foreign Affairs Strategic Policy*, May/June 1999, p. 20.

14 Seymour M. Hersh, "The Getaway," *The New Yorker*, Jan. 28, 2002, p. 36.

Continued from p. 301

dealing with the threat of what the State Department calls "rogue" states and nuclear terrorism, including U.S. Senate approval of the Additional Protocol (*see p. 312*).

Other analysts say world dynamics have changed so dramatically since the NPT took effect that the nonproliferation regime needs a revolutionary overhaul. "The treaty was about controlling states and governments, not rogue individuals or terrorists who get their hands on these weapons," says Boese of the Arms Control Association. "The nonproliferation regime needs to be modified to better address this gap."

"The system has been pretty remarkable and successful, but is now in sufficient need of radical repair that we need a big jump forward," says Allison of the Belfer Center, who as assistant Defense secretary oversaw the Clinton administration's efforts to reduce the former Soviet nuclear arsenal. "We should now build a global alliance against nuclear terrorism, and the core of its strategy should be the doctrine of what I call the three 'Nos:' " [7]

- "No loose nukes" — Allison coined the phrase a decade ago to describe weapons and weapons-grade materials inadequately secured against theft. "These weapons and materials must be protected to a new security standard adequate to prevent nuclear terrorists from attacking us," he says. Under Allison's proposal, all nuclear states would have to be certified by another member of the nuclear club that all their nuclear materials had been adequately secured. The NPT has no such requirement.
- "No new nascent nukes" — New production of highly enriched uranium and plutonium would be barred. "If you don't have either one of them, you don't have a nuclear weapon," Allison says.
- "No new nuclear weapons" — Noting North Korea's nuclear ambitions, Allison acknowledges that this is the most difficult but potentially most important goal. "To accept North Korea as a new member of the nuclear club would be catastrophic," Allison says, "because North Korea historically has been the most promiscuous proliferator on Earth."

North Korea has sold nuclear-capable missiles to Iraq, Pakistan and other would-be nuclear powers. If Pyongyang develops a nuclear arsenal, most experts agree, other countries in the region, including South Korea, Japan and Taiwan, would be tempted to jettison the NPT and develop their own arsenals in defense, setting off a potentially disastrous regional arms race. "A nuclear North Korea," Allison says, "would blow the lid off the previous arms control and nuclear proliferation regime."

Is the United States doing enough to halt nuclear proliferation?

Since the fall of the Soviet Union in 1991, the United States has concentrated its nonproliferation efforts on preventing the theft or sale of nuclear weapons and materials left in Russia, Ukraine and other former Soviet republics. The 1991 Soviet Nuclear Threat Reduction Act — renamed the Cooperative Threat Reduction (CTR) program in 1993 — was designed to help former Soviet satellite countries destroy nuclear, chemical and biological weapons and associated infrastructure. Nicknamed Nunn-Lugar after the law's original sponsors (Sens. Sam Nunn, D-Ga., and Richard G. Lugar, R-Ind.), it also established verifiable safeguards against the proliferation of such weapons.

Recent U.S. efforts to control the worldwide supply of nuclear weapons and materials have focused almost solely on the CTR program: More than 50 former Soviet nuclear-storage sites have been secured and new security systems installed. Besides locking up nuclear materials and establishing security perimeters around the storage sites, says Robinson of Sandia Labs, the CTR program installs detection equipment to warn of any movement of the guarded material. "This material is being locked up and safeguarded," Robinson says. Sandia designs and installs the nuclear-security systems and trains foreign technicians on their use.

But critics say the agreement is woefully inadequate. "Very, very little progress has taken place," says Curtis of the Nuclear Threat Initiative, which Nunn co-founded. "There is an inertia that simply must be overcome with presidential leadership in all the participant countries."

The Bush administration recognizes the importance of securing Russia's nuclear stockpiles. In 2002, the United States, along with Britain, France, Canada, Japan, Germany and Italy, agreed to spend $20 billion over 10 years to support CTR programs — with half of it, or $1 billion a year, to come from the United States.

But that amounts to only about a quarter of 1 percent of the current Defense Department budget of about $401 billion, Bunn points out. "Amazingly," he adds, despite the new terrorist threats throughout the world, U.S. funding for the CTR programs "hasn't increased noticeably since Sept. 11."

Bunn is not alone. A task force led by former Sen. Howard H. Baker Jr., R-Tenn., and former White House Counsel Lloyd Cutler in January 2001 called for a tripling in annual CTR spending — to $3 billion a year. [8]

Inadequate funding has slowed the pace of securing Russia's nuclear sites, critics say. "We're not doing all that we know how to do and all that we must to keep these weapons and materials safe," Curtis says. After more than a decade of Nunn-Lugar efforts, only half of Russia's nuclear weapons have been adequately secured, Curtis points out.

Critics of the war against Iraq suggest that the campaign to topple Saddam Hussein expended precious resources that could have gone toward halting the spread of nuclear materials. The first order of business in combating nuclear terrorism, Allison says, is to list potential sources of nuclear weapons, in order of priority. "Saddam clearly had nuclear ambitions, and the CIA said that over the course of a decade he might realize them," Allison says. "So he deserved to be on the list somewhere down there, but he wasn't in the top dozen for me."

The nuclear weapons and materials that remain vulnerable to theft in Russia are at the top of Allison's list, primarily because of the magnitude of the problem. "We've still got 120 metric tons of highly enriched uranium and plutonium in Russia alone that we haven't even begun security upgrades on," Curtis points out.

Second on Allison's list is North Korea. By repudiating the Clinton administration's "Agreed Framework" with North Korea and refusing to engage in negotiations with the regime until it renounces its nuclear program, Allison says the Bush administration has allowed "North Korea to just about declare itself a nuclear-weapons state. For the past three years, they have been given a pass. And what have they been doing while they got a pass? They've been creating more plutonium every day, as they are today." Recent six-party talks in Beijing aimed at halting North Korea's nuclear-weapons program ended without significant progress. [9]

Third on Allison's priority list is Pakistan. Because it is not a party to the NPT, Pakistan's nuclear-weapons inventory is unknown. But according to a recent CIA analysis, Pakistan's Khan Research Laboratories has been providing North Korea with nuclear fuel, centrifuges and warhead designs since the early 1990s. [10] No one knows how many other customers Khan supplied over the past decade.

"A coherent strategy has got to deal with the most urgent potential sources of supply to terrorists first," Allison says. "When all this other stuff has been happening, why was Iraq the focus of attention for two years?"

Although no evidence that Iraq had recently pursued nuclear weapons has been found since the United States invaded the country over a year ago, Bush continues to defend his decision to overthrow Hussein's regime in the name of counterproliferation.

"The former dictator of Iraq possessed and used weapons of mass destruction against his own people," Bush said on Feb. 11. "For 12 years, he defied the will of the international community. He refused to disarm or account for his illegal weapons and programs. He doubted our resolve to enforce our word — and now he sits in a prison cell, while his country moves toward a democratic future."

Although Russia and Pakistan are widely regarded as the biggest potential sources of nuclear proliferation, the United States has a mixed record on safeguarding its own nuclear materials. The United States exported highly enriched uranium to 43 countries for nearly four decades as part of the Atoms for Peace program, sanctioned by the NPT, to help other countries acquire nuclear technology for peaceful purposes. The uranium was supposed to be returned to the United States in its original form or as spent fuel. But according to a recent report by the Energy Department's inspector general, the United States has made little headway in recovering the uranium, which is enough to make about 1,000 nuclear weapons. [11]

"While we should be locking up materials at risk wherever we can and recovering them when needed, the Department of Energy has been leisurely pursuing its program to recover highly enriched uranium at risk in research facilities around the world," Curtis says. "This is a leisure that we can ill afford."

Should nonproliferation policy aim to eliminate all nuclear weapons?

Article VI of the NPT requires countries with nuclear weapons to take "effective measures" to end the arms race and work toward nuclear disarmament. This was an essential component of the "grand bargain" used to lure the rest of the world to forgo nuclear arms.

As the sole remaining superpower, the United States plays a key role in leading the world toward disarmament. "Nonproliferation strategies have always been linked to U.S. efforts to reduce reliance on its nuclear forces, so there's always been an arms control link to the NPT as part of the essential bargain," says Curtis of NTI. "The world community also considers it a prerequisite for the United States to exercise its moral leadership on nonproliferation, that it be seen to be living up to its side of that bargain."

During the Cold War, the United States and the Soviet Union, which had amassed vast nuclear arsenals, signed a series of treaties that first limited, and then began to reduce, the number of nuclear weapons on each side. [12] On May 24, 2002, President Bush and Russian President Vladimir V. Putin signed the latest of these, the Strategic Offensive Reductions Treaty (SORT). It called on the two countries to reduce their current number of strategic nuclear warheads by nearly two-thirds by Dec. 31, 2012 — to 1,700-2,200 warheads.

"President Putin and I have signed a treaty that will substantially reduce our strategic nuclear warhead arsenals to . . . the lowest level in decades," Bush declared at the Moscow signing ceremony. "This treaty liquidates the Cold War legacy of nuclear hostility between our countries."

But critics say the so-called Moscow Treaty will be far less effective in ridding the world of nuclear weapons than the president's comments suggest. "The agreement doesn't require

Continued on p. 306

Defusing North Korea and Iran

The good news: Only two so-called rogue nations are suspected of trying to build nuclear weapons. (Libya recently promised to end its bomb-making efforts, and Iraq never was close to having a bomb, U.N. inspectors say.) The bad news: The two rogue nations are North Korea and Iran.

North Korea is considered the more immediate threat. The shaky truce that ended the bloody Korean War (1950-53) has not removed the threat of hostilities between the reclusive, authoritarian regime and U.S.-supported South Korea, which relies on a large U.S. military presence for much of its defense.

Under the 1994 Agreed Framework brokered by President Bill Clinton, North Korea agreed to freeze production of plutonium — needed in the production of some nuclear weapons — in exchange for U.S. energy assistance and improved diplomatic relations. That agreement fell apart in October 2002, when the Bush administration accused North Korean leader Kim Jong Il of trying to enrich uranium in violation of the Non-Proliferation Treaty (NPT).

In January 2003, North Korea withdrew from the NPT and kicked out U.N. International Atomic Energy Agency (IAEA) inspectors. North Korea has continued to deny it has a uranium-enrichment program but openly acknowledges its plutonium program, which may already have produced one or two nuclear weapons.

AFP Photo

North Korean leader Kim Jong Il

The most recent talks aimed at ending North Korea's nuclear-weapons ambitions, held in late February 2004 in Beijing, also involved China, Russia, Japan and South Korea. The talks failed to overcome the impasse between the Bush administration, which insists on the "complete, verifiable and irreversible dismantlement " of North Korea's nuclear programs before the United States will agree to improve bilateral relations, provide economic and energy assistance and offer "security guarantees" that it will not invade North Korea.

Prospects for the success of follow-up talks soured further on March 20, when North Korea warned it would expand its nuclear-weapons program if the yearly U.S.-led military exercises in South Korea proceed as scheduled in late March. [1]

Iran's nuclear ambitions raised concern two years ago with the discovery of a large uranium-enrichment plant south of Tehran, the capital. Iran, a signatory to the NPT, claims its nuclear program is used purely to generate electricity. In mid-March, after the IAEA censured Tehran for not fully disclosing its nuclear program, Iran temporarily barred the agency from the country. Inspections were set to resume on March 27.

Meanwhile, IAEA Director Mohamed ElBaradei has appealed to President Bush to launch talks with Iran aimed at improving bilateral relations, which have remained hostile since Islamic clerics wrested control of Iran from the U.S.-supported regime of Shah Mohammed Reza Pahlavi in 1979.

Ending Iran's and North Korea's nuclear ambitions will require convincing both countries that they don't need nuclear weapons to defend themselves, experts say. "To strengthen the international nonproliferation regime, we're going have to provide security assurances as well as economic aid," says Matthew Bunn, a nuclear-weapons expert at Harvard University's Belfer Center for Science and International Affairs. "There's going to have to be some kind of security assurance that the United States isn't going to invade Iran and overthrow its government. That's the center of the discussion with North Korea as well."

Failure to do so may lead to regional arms races that could quickly get out of control. If North Korea produces a nuclear arsenal, predicts John Pike of GlobalSecurity.org, Japan may feel sufficiently threatened to transform some of its civilian power-plant nuclear materials to build nuclear weapons in self-defense. "Then South Korea is going to need them, and Taiwan's going to need them," he says. "That will make China want to have more, which will prompt India to need more, and then Pakistan will, too."

---

[1] United Press International, "N. Korea Warns U.S. over War Exercises," March 20, 2004.

Continued from p. 304

the destruction of a single warhead or a single delivery vehicle," says Boese of the Arms Control Association. Warheads that are removed from deployment could be disassembled or stored rather than destroyed. "Also, the agreement's limit is actually in effect for just one day — Dec. 31, 2012," Boese says. "Because neither side has to destroy anything after that day, presumably they could then rebuild their arsenals."

After the Sept. 11 terrorist attacks, the Bush administration toughened U.S. policy on nuclear weapons and other weapons of mass destruction (WMD). The new national strategy to combat nuclear, biological and chemical weapons, issued in December 2002, called for strengthening "traditional measures — diplomacy, arms control, multilateral agreements, threat-reduction assistance and export controls." But for the first time, the United States openly warned that it would pre-emptively attack adversaries thought to be preparing to use weapons of mass destruction against the United States.

"U.S. military forces . . . must have the capability to defend against WMD-armed adversaries, including, in appropriate cases, through pre-emptive measures," the administration declared. "This requires capabilities to detect and destroy an adversary's WMD assets before these weapons are used." [13]

Meanwhile, the administration's latest Nuclear Posture Review, sent to Congress on Dec. 31, 2001, called for research into new types of nuclear weapons and outlined new uses for them. [14] As part of that policy, the administration has initiated research into the "bunker buster," a missile armed with a low-yield (less than five kilotons) nuclear warhead designed to penetrate and destroy enemy arsenals or other targets buried deep underground. To enable research to proceed, Congress last year overturned a Clinton-era ban on research and development of low-yield nuclear weapons. [15]

"The reason it was important to reduce or get rid of the prohibition on low-yield nuclear weapons was not because we're trying to develop or are developing low-yield nuclear weapons," said National Nuclear Security Administrator Linton Brooks. "That's a misconception. . . . What we said was that the amendment was poorly drawn and it prohibited research that could lead to a low-yield nuclear weapon." [16] In fact, research on high-powered "bunker buster" bombs commenced in 2003, after Congress overturned the ban. [17]

Since taking office, the administration has rejected arms control as an essential tool for reducing the nuclear threat. Shortly after being sworn into office, Bush said he would not resubmit the 1996 Comprehensive Test Ban Treaty to the Senate for ratification. He also abrogated the 1972 U.S.-Soviet Anti-Ballistic Missile Treaty, which barred signatories from building national defense systems to protect against ballistic-missile attack — a move designed to discourage the superpowers from building more nuclear weapons to overcome such defenses.

Bush instead announced he would pursue earlier plans to build a National Missile Defense System while seeking a "new strategic framework" for dealing with Russia that would focus on reductions in nuclear weapons. [18] The first U.S. anti-missile defense facility, scheduled for deployment in Alaska this summer, has faced criticism for its technical flaws and for undermining the United States' credibility as a strong advocate of nuclear disarmament. [19]

"The current U.S. approach to proliferation emphasizes non-treaty methods and military means, including the effort to deploy a national missile defense system," said John Cirincione, director for nonproliferation at the Carnegie Endowment for International Peace. "The system faces formidable technical challenges and is unlikely to be militarily effective anytime in this decade. Every system within the missile-defense program is behind schedule, over budget and underperforming." [20]

While supporters of the administration's nuclear policy say the changes were needed to protect the United States in a new era of uncertainty, critics say they undermine the administration's credibility in its calls to strengthen global anti-proliferation measures.

"If you're trying to build a consensus [on halting proliferation] while at the same time saying we need a few more different nuclear weapons, I would say those are inconsistent arguments," Allison says. "I've negotiated on behalf of the U.S. government many times when I felt I had a weak hand, but I couldn't imagine keeping a straight face in trying to argue these two goals at the same time." ■

BACKGROUND

Manhattan Project

The nuclear age traces its origins to 1938, when scientists in Nazi Germany split the nucleus of a uranium atom, releasing heat and radiation. The potential of nuclear fission, as the process was called, to produce weapons of unparalleled power prompted a recent refugee from Germany — Albert Einstein — to alert President Franklin D. Roosevelt. "[T]he element uranium may be turned into a new and important source of energy in the immediate future," the already-legendary physicist wrote. ["T]his new phenomenon," he added, could lead "to the construction of bombs . . ., extremely powerful bombs of a new type." [21]

In 1939, even before the United States entered World War II or realized the full implications of Einstein's

Continued on p. 308

Chronology

1930s-1980s
Atomic Age begins and evolves into the Cold War.

1938
Scientists in Nazi Germany split the nucleus of a uranium atom. A year later, the U.S. Manhattan Project enters the race to create an atomic bomb.

Aug. 6, 1945
U.S. drops an atomic bomb on Hiroshima, Japan, followed on Aug. 9 by another on Nagasaki, killing a total of more than 250,000 people. Two days later, Japan surrenders, ending World War II.

1949
The Soviet Union tests its first atomic weapon.

Dec. 8, 1953
President Dwight D. Eisenhower's "Atoms for Peace" proposal calls for using fissionable material "to serve the peaceful pursuits of mankind."

1957
International Atomic Energy Agency (IAEA) is created to promote peaceful use of nuclear energy.

May 26, 1958
Eisenhower opens first U.S. nuclear power plant, at Shippingport, Pa.

1964
China joins the United States, Soviet Union, Britain and France in the "nuclear club" of officially recognized nuclear-weapons states.

July 1, 1968
Nuclear Non-Proliferation Treaty (NPT) is signed by 98 countries after a decade of talks.

1969
Treaty of Tlatelolco bars nuclear weapons from Latin America. Brazil and Argentina are the last nations to sign, in the 1990s.

1981
Israel destroys an Iraqi nuclear reactor, claiming it was being used to produce fuel for weapons.

1990s ***Cold War ends, posing new proliferation threats.***

1991
Soviet Union collapses. . . . Persian Gulf War against Iraq, an NPT signatory, reveals that Saddam Hussein had been trying to develop nuclear weapons. . . . Soviet Nuclear Threat Reduction Act sponsored by Sens. Sam Nunn, D-Ga., and Richard G. Lugar, R-Ind., authorizes the United States to help former Soviet-bloc countries destroy nuclear, chemical and biological weapons and establishes verifiable safeguards against their proliferation.

1993
Nunn-Lugar program is broadened and renamed the Cooperative Threat Reduction (CTR) program. . . . South Africa becomes first country with nuclear weapons to renounce its nuclear program and join the NPT.

October 1994
North Korea agrees to freeze its plutonium production in exchange for U.S. assistance in producing energy.

1996
President Bill Clinton signs the Comprehensive Test Ban Treaty.

1998
India and Pakistan join Israel on the list of non-NPT signatories with nuclear weapons.

2000s ***Massive terrorist attacks raise the specter of nuclear terrorism.***

Sept. 11, 2001
Suicide airline hijackers linked to Osama bin Laden's al Qaeda terrorist group kill nearly 3,000 people in the worst terrorist attacks in U.S. history.

2002
President Bush disavows the U.S. pact with North Korea and calls on Kim Jong Il to renounce his nuclear ambitions as a condition of the resumption of U.S. aid.

March 19, 2003
U.S. troops invade Iraq but find no weapons of mass destruction.

Dec. 19, 2003
Libya agrees to terminate its nuclear-weapons program, revealing evidence of a Pakistan-based black market in nuclear technology.

Feb. 6, 2004
Pakistani President Pervez Musharraf pardons Abdul Qadeer Khan, founder of Pakistan's nuclear-weapons program, for selling nuclear technology to Iran, North Korea, Libya and possibly others.

Feb. 11, 2004
President Bush responds to the revelations about Khan's network with a seven-point plan to strengthen the NPT and IAEA's enforcement powers.

Fall of a Nuclear Black Marketeer

As A.Q Khan tells it, the horrors of religious intolerance he witnessed as a 10-year-old Muslim in India turned him into the world's leading black-market merchant of nuclear-bomb materials. [1]

"I can remember trains coming into the station full of dead Muslims," Khan recalled recently, describing the sectarian violence that broke out in Bhopal following Indian independence from Britain. "The [Hindu] Indian authorities were treating the Muslims horribly." [2]

Six years later, Khan fled north to the newly independent Islamic nation of Pakistan. But the slaughter he had seen as a youngster left Khan with an enduring enmity toward India and shaped his life's work, spurring him to develop Pakistan's nuclear bomb.

In the 1960s, Khan pursued postgraduate studies in metallurgy in Western Europe and later worked in the Netherlands at a uranium-enrichment plant run by Urenco, a Dutch-British-German consortium. There he learned about uranium enrichment and the design of sophisticated centrifuges needed to produce weapons-grade nuclear fuel.

Khan reportedly smuggled Urenco's centrifuge designs into Pakistan in the mid-1970s after Prime Minister Zulfikar Ali Bhutto invited him to establish the country's nuclear-weapons program. A Dutch court in 1983 convicted him in absentia of attempted espionage for stealing the designs, but the conviction was overturned.

As the director of Pakistan's nuclear program, Khan became adept at procuring equipment and technology — both legally and on the black market — and did little to conceal his activities. He even published a brochure with a photo of himself and a list of nuclear materials available for sale or barter, including intermediate-range ballistic missiles. Investigators say Khan's network stretched from Europe to Turkey, Russia and Malaysia. Khan himself traveled to North Korea at least 13 times to swap his nuclear technology for Korean missile technology, and U.N. inspectors have discovered documents in Iraq suggesting that he offered to help Saddam Hussein build a nuclear weapon in 1990, just before the first Gulf War. [3]

By 1998, when India first tested nuclear devices, Khan was quick to follow suit. Now the bitter adversaries were both in the "nuclear club."

Khan became an instant hero to Pakistanis, whose hatred of India permeates the national culture. Schools, streets and children were named after him. Indeed, most Pakistanis appeared forgiving when Khan confessed in February following revelations he had illegally supplied nuclear technology to North Korea, Libya and Iran.

But Khan's admissions — and the fact that he was not punished for selling nuclear secrets to rogue states — infuriated many Americans and others in the West. "It sends a horrible signal," said David Albright, president of the Institute for Science and Interna-

Continued from p. 306

warning, Roosevelt established the first federal uranium-research program. Fission research led to further advances, including the 1940 discovery of the element plutonium by physicists at the University of California, Berkeley. After the United States entered the war against Japan, Germany and Italy in December, the race to beat Germany in developing an atomic bomb accelerated under a secret Army Corps of Engineers program known as the Manhattan Project. *

By September 1944, after less than two years of work, Manhattan Project researchers had begun producing plutonium for weapons. On July 16, 1945, they detonated an experimental atomic bomb known as "the Gadget" from a tower in the New Mexico desert. Less than three weeks later, on Aug. 6, U.S. airmen dropped an atom bomb nicknamed "Little Boy" on Hiroshima, followed on Aug. 9 by the detonation of "Fat Man" over Nagasaki. Two days later, Japan surrendered. World War II was over and the "Atomic Age" had begun. Within weeks of the bombings, the death toll had climbed to more than 100,000 people — mainly civilians.

The enormous loss of civilian lives sparked intense debate over the future of atomic weapons. The Manhattan Project cost the U.S. government almost $20 billion (in today's dollars), including the construction of reactors and lab facilities at more than 30 sites, such as Los Alamos, N.M., Oak Ridge, Tenn., and Hanford, Wash. In 1946, the American representative to the newly created United Nations Atomic Energy Commission, Bernard M. Baruch, proposed the elimination of atomic weapons, but the Soviet Union rejected the proposal. In 1947, Congress replaced the Manhattan Project with the civilian Atomic Energy Commission, which assumed control over atomic research and weapons facilities around the country.

The postwar deterioration of relations with the Soviet Union effectively ended the nuclear debate in the United States and prompted the administration of President Harry S Truman to intensify production of nuclear weapons, especially the next generation of more powerful, thermonuclear weapons. The first Soviet atomic bomb test and the rise of communism in China in

* Atomic weapons get their energy from the fission, or breaking apart, of the nucleus of an atom of uranium or plutonium. Hydrogen — or thermonuclear — weapons get their energy largely from fusion, the formation of a heavier nucleus from two lighter ones. Both types of weapons are known collectively as nuclear weapons.

tional Security, a nonpartisan think tank dedicated to educating the public on scientific issues affecting international security. "It basically says, 'Yeah, your wrists will be slapped, but, boy, you're going to make millions of dollars.' " [4]

Khan professes bewilderment at the outrage his proliferation activities have engendered. "They dislike me and accuse me of all kinds of unsubstantiated and fabricated lies because I disturbed all their strategic plans, the balance of power and blackmailing potential in this part of the world," he said. "I am not a madman or a nut. . . . I consider myself a humble, patriotic Pakistani who gave his best for his country."

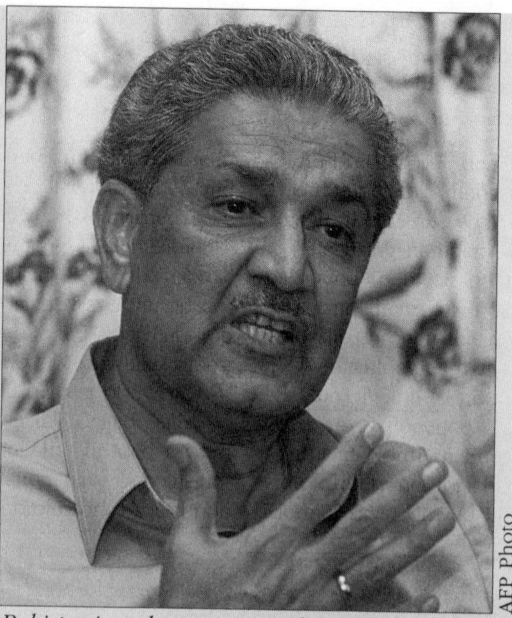

AFP Photo

Pakistani nuclear scientist Abdul Qadeer Khan

Indeed, while Islamic extremism is rising in Pakistan, the moderate Khan is married to a Dutch national, and neither she nor their daughters wear the veil typically worn by conservative Muslims.

Kahn's enduring popularity helps explain why Pakistani President Pervez Musharraf pardoned him — and why the Bush administration accepted Musharraf's claim that he knew nothing of Khan's illicit activities. Others say the United States did not push Musharraf to punish Khan because of a deal in which Pakistan would help U.S. troops find terrorist leader Osama bin Laden, thought to be hiding in Pakistan's northwest territories (*see p. 312*).

"They correctly judged that the United States would blow hot and cold on the question of nuclear proliferation, depending on the temper of the times," says defense-policy analyst John Pike, director of GlobalSecurity.org, a nonprofit organization studying emerging security threats. "Blaming the black market all on A.Q. Khan and letting Musharraf say he had no idea what was going on is just a way for everybody to have their cake and eat it, too."

[1] Unless otherwise noted, information in this section is based on Peter Grier, Faye Bowers and Owais Tohid, "Pakistan's Nuclear Hero, World's No. 1 Nuclear Suspect," *The Christian Science Monitor*, Feb. 2, 2004.

[2] Khan was interviewed by the Human Development Foundation, an expatriate Pakistani group in Shaumburg, Ill., www.yespakistan.com.

[3] "The Black Marketeer," "Nightline," ABC News, March 8, 2004.

[4] *Ibid.*

1949, followed the next year by the outbreak of the Korean War, fueled U.S. policymakers' support of the weapons program. By the early 1950s, both sides in the rapidly escalating Cold War had developed hydrogen bombs.

With momentum building for still more nuclear research, calls to abandon the new technology ran into resistance from those promoting nuclear power as a cheap, virtually inexhaustible source of energy. Fission releases large amounts of heat, which can be harnessed to power a steam turbine to generate electricity.

On Dec. 8, 1953, President Dwight D. Eisenhower presented his "Atoms for Peace" proposal to the United Nations, calling for creation of an international atomic energy agency "to devise methods whereby this fissionable material would be allocated to serve the peaceful pursuits of mankind."

The Soviet Union beat the United States in the race to introduce nuclear power, starting up the world's first plant in 1954. With federal support and AEC oversight, General Electric, Westinghouse Electric and other U.S. companies invested heavily in the new technology. On May 26, 1958, Eisenhower opened the first U.S. nuclear power plant, at Shippingport, Pa.

For the next 20 years — until the partial meltdown at Pennsylvania's Three Mile Island nuclear plant in 1979 and the catastrophic accident at the Soviet plant at Chernobyl in 1986 — nuclear power accounted for a growing percentage of the world's electricity.

Today nuclear power accounts for 16 percent of global electricity generated at some 440 plants in 30 countries. [22] A handful of countries depend on nuclear power for more than half of their electricity, but only about 20 percent of the power generated in the United States comes from nuclear reactors.

Nonproliferation Efforts

Eisenhower's Atoms for Peace proposal bore fruit in 1957, when the IAEA was established as an independent U.N. body charged with promoting the peaceful use of nuclear energy. The agency was responsible for inspecting nuclear research facilities and power plants to ensure that they were not being used to build nuclear weapons. [23]

It already was becoming clear, however, that stronger measures were needed to prevent nuclear proliferation. Britain, which had participated in the U.S. nuclear development program, tested its first nuclear device in

1952 and quickly built several hundred warheads. France developed its nuclear capability independently and began building a nuclear arsenal in 1960. In 1964, China tested its first nuclear weapon, becoming the fifth and last nuclear-weapon state recognized under the NPT.

Faced with the prospect of dozens more countries acquiring the bomb within a few decades, the United States and 17 other countries began talks in 1958 aimed at halting the further spread of nuclear weapons. A proposal by Ireland envisioned a commitment by all nuclear-weapons states not to provide the technology to other countries. In theory, non-nuclear countries would benefit from such an arrangement because it would ensure that their neighbors would also remain nuclear-free. But non-nuclear states called for more incentives to accept this permanent state of military inferiority.

EPA/Wade Payne

Components from Libya's nuclear weapons program are displayed by Secretary of Energy Spencer Abraham at the Y-12 National Security Complex in Oak Ridge, Tenn., on March 15, 2004. Libyan leader Muammar el-Qaddafi ended the country's isolation by renouncing weapons of mass destruction and joining the world nonproliferation regime.

In 1968, after a decade of negotiations, 98 countries signed the Nuclear Non-Proliferation Treaty (NPT). The agreement recognized the original five nuclear-weapons states — the United States, the Soviet Union, France, the United Kingdom and China — defined as countries that had "manufactured and exploded a nuclear weapon or other nuclear explosive device prior to 1 January 1967." The IAEA was charged with monitoring compliance with the treaty. Countries that signed the treaty agreed to refrain from producing, obtaining or stockpiling nuclear weapons.

The treaty expanded on the Irish resolution by offering more incentives to refrain from building nuclear weapons. The nuclear states agreed to help other countries develop civilian nuclear power plants and also, under Article X, to take "effective measures" to end the arms race and work toward nuclear disarmament.

But the treaty set no timetables for disarmament, enabling the nuclear powers to keep their arsenals virtually indefinitely. The NPT's Article X contains another important loophole — it allows signatories to withdraw from the treaty without penalty for unspecified "supreme interests."

With 188 parties, the NPT has the broadest support of any arms control treaty. Only three countries — India, Israel and Pakistan — have not signed the pact and are believed to possess finished nuclear weapons or components that could be rapidly assembled. Israel began developing its nuclear capability in the 1950s with French assistance. The United States has refrained from pressing its chief Middle Eastern ally on its nuclear program, and Israel has never acknowledged its arsenal, thought to number 98-172 warheads. In 1998, India and Pakistan — engaged in a longstanding border dispute — acknowledged their nuclear status. Both India with (50-90 warheads) and Pakistan (30-50 warheads) are believed to store their nuclear weapons in the form of separate components that can be assembled at short notice. [24]

Over the past decade, the international nonproliferation regime has scored some important successes. In the 1990s, Argentina and Brazil agreed to abandon their nuclear-weapons ambitions, signed the NPT and became the last two Latin American countries to sign the 1969 Treaty of Tlatelolco, which barred nuclear weapons from the 33-nation region. After the Soviet Union's collapse, the former Soviet republics of Belarus, Kazakhstan and Ukraine voluntarily relinquished to Russia all the nuclear weapons Moscow had deployed on their territory during the Cold War. And, in 1993, after the fall of apartheid, South Africa became the first nuclear-armed country to voluntarily dismantle its entire nuclear-weapons program.

Mushrooming Nukes

For all the NPT's success in containing nuclear weapons, it has failed to keep non-signatories, and even some "renegade states" that signed the treaty, from pursuing nuclear capabilities. Almost as soon as it signed the NPT in 1968, Iraq began developing nuclear weapons with help from France and Italy, presumably to counter Israel's arsenal. Israel destroyed an Iraqi reactor in 1981, claiming it was being used to produce fuel for weapons. Nevertheless, Iraq continued its clandestine program, as weapons inspectors discovered upon entering Iraq after its defeat in the 1991 Gulf War.

After the war, U.S.-led condemnation of Iraq's nuclear-weapons program resulted in U.N. sanctions that prohibited trade with Iraq. The sanctions were later eased to allow Iraq to sell a limited amount of oil to buy food and medical supplies, but by the end of the 1990s, Iraq was in the throes of an economic crisis.

Although the Bush administration cited evidence that Iraq had continued its nuclear-weapons program to justify last year's invasion and toppling of Hussein, recent inspections have turned up no signs Hussein was pursuing nuclear weapons. "It turns out we were all wrong," said former weapons inspector David Kay of U.S. suspicions that Iraq possessed weapons of mass destruction. "And that is most disturbing." [25]

Another NPT "renegade," North Korea is considered to pose a far greater risk. A party to the NPT since 1985, North Korea launched a clandestine nuclear program centered on production of plutonium, which could be used to make nuclear weapons. Although North Korea insisted that its program was intended only to generate electricity, in 1993 it barred IAEA inspectors from viewing its facilities, precipitating a crisis in the nonproliferation regime. In October 1994, the Clinton administration brokered an "Agreed Framework," whereby North Korea agreed to freeze plutonium production in exchange for U.S. assistance to compensate for any energy lost due to the reactor shutdown. President Bush disavowed the pact in 2002 as bowing to nuclear blackmail and called on North Korea's Kim Jong Il to renounce his nuclear ambitions as a condition of resuming aid to the impoverished country.

Concerned that nuclear weapons or weapons-grade materials might fall into the hands of renegade states or terrorist groups, the United States, the Soviet Union and 38 other countries with nuclear technology established the Nuclear Suppliers Group in 1985, agreeing to control exports of civilian nuclear material and related technology to non-nuclear-weapon states. And to restrict the proliferation of nuclear-capable missiles, the United States and six other countries in 1987 set up the Missile Technology Control Regime, a voluntary agreement that has since been expanded to more than 30 countries.

The collapse of the Soviet Union signaled the end of both the Cold War and the nuclear standoff dominated by the military doctrine of mutual assured destruction But the post-Cold War peace, welcome as it was, ushered in a new era of uncertainty in which concern over nuclear proliferation took the place of superpower nuclear brinkmanship. The resulting economic and political upheavals left Russia — the Soviet successor state — poorly equipped to maintain security over the vast nuclear arsenal it inherited.

Recognizing the proliferation risk posed by Russia's arsenal, Congress passed the so-called Nunn-Lugar measure. Since it became law in 1991, the United States has helped Russia deactivate some 6,000 nuclear warheads, retrain 22,000 nuclear-weapons scientists and remove all the nuclear weapons deployed in the former Soviet republics of Belarus, Kazakhstan and Ukraine. Nunn-Lugar also has helped destroy hundreds of Soviet missiles, seal nuclear test facilities and dismantle submarine-based nuclear warheads. ■

CURRENT SITUATION

Black Market Revealed

A.Q. Khan's black market in nuclear weapons and materials began to unravel on Dec. 19, 2003, when Libya told the United States and Britain it would terminate its nuclear-weapons program. Although the North African country had not developed warheads, it was found to have imported numerous key components, including sophisticated centrifuges needed to enrich uranium into fuel for bombs.

The Bush administration claims much of the credit for this unexpected victory in the fight against nuclear proliferation. "The success of our mission in Libya underscores the success of this administration's broader nonproliferation efforts around the world," said Energy Secretary Spencer Abraham at a special press tour of seized Libyan nuclear materials and equipment on display at the department's Oak Ridge labs on March 15. "What you have witnessed represents a big, big victory in the administration's efforts to combat weapons of mass destruction."

Administration critics dispute this claim, citing reports that Libyan leader Muammar el-Qaddafi had been convinced by his son and presumptive heir, 31-year-old Saif al-Islam Qaddafi, to end the country's isolation by renouncing weapons of mass destruction and joining the world nonproliferation regime. [26] Libya has suffered severe economic privation since coming under U.N.-sponsored economic sanctions for its involvement in the 1988 bombing of a Pan-Am flight over Lockerbie, Scotland, which killed 270 people.

U.N. sanctions, imposed in 1992, were lifted in September 2003, after Libya accepted responsibility for the bombing and agreed to pay $2.7 billion in compensation to families of the Pan Am victims. Although the Bush administration lifted a ban on travel to Libya after it renounced its nuclear program, other U.S. economic sanctions remain in place. [27]

"Muammar's son thought his dad had run the country into a ditch," says Pike of GlobalSecuirity.Org. "But when the dynastic handoff of a country from father to son becomes the primary determinant of our disarmament success, then we're running on a pretty thin reed."

When they entered Libyan facilities in January, IAEA inspectors said they discovered crates of nuclear equipment that only could have come from sources with advanced nuclear programs of their own. Subsequent investigations uncovered a complex web of international transactions that led to a factory in Malaysia, transshipment facilities in Dubai, an intercepted cargo ship in Italy, shipments to Iran and ultimately to Khan himself. In January, after acknowledging his role in establishing the nuclear black market, Khan was pardoned by Pakistani President Pervez Musharraf, who claimed he knew nothing of Khan's undercover business.

Nuclear experts dismiss Musharraf's disavowal as ludicrous. Khan's prominent role as the father of Pakistan's nuclear arsenal made him a highly visible national hero who made no attempt to conceal his lavish lifestyle in his impoverished country and who actually had published brochures describing nuclear materials and equipment that were for sale from his lab for more than a decade.

"The pattern of activity was at such a large scale that it's inconceivable that the Pakistani government didn't know about this all along," Pike says. "It's like asking me to believe that [U.S. nuclear pioneer] Ed Teller was secretly selling hydrogen bombs out of the back of a pickup truck."

But the Bush administration did not question Musharraf's disavowal of knowledge about Khan's activities. Since the Pakistani leader emerged as an outspoken ally of the United States in its war on terrorism after Sept. 11, the administration clearly has been loath to undermine his standing in an Islamic country where anti-American feelings and support for al Qaeda run high. Musharraf has narrowly escaped two assassination attempts, attributed to al Qaeda, in recent months. [28]

AP Photo/Ted S. Warren

Vehicles entering the United States from Canada pass through radiation detectors at the Blaine, Wash., border crossing. Experts say terrorists are far more likely to deploy a small, easily transported conventional explosive device containing radioactive waste — a so-called dirty bomb — than to explode a nuclear bomb.

Moreover, the Bush administration needs Musharraf's cooperation in order to find al Qaeda leader Osama bin Laden — considered by some to be the mastermind of the 9/11 attacks — and his top lieutenants. Some observers suggest that the Bush administration decided to accept Musharraf's denial of knowledge about Khan's network in exchange for permission for U.S. forces to enter the rugged area on the Pakistani side of the border with Afghanistan, believed to be a key stronghold of al Qaeda militants and possibly bin Laden himself. [29] Up to now, U.S. forces have had to limit their searches to the Afghan side of the border.

Although administration spokesmen deny the existence of such a deal, American military officials have announced plans for a "spring initiative" on the Afghan side of the border. [30] Already, signs are emerging that an offensive is under way. On March 16, on the eve of a visit to Pakistan by Secretary of State Colin L. Powell, Pakistani troops suffered numerous casualties in gun battles in the border region. [31]

Bush's Response

President Bush responded to the revelations about Khan's network with a seven-point plan to strengthen the NPT and IAEA's enforcement powers. On Feb. 11, the president called for the expansion of his Proliferation Security Initiative, a year-old

Continued on p. 314

At Issue:

Will U.S. policies keep nuclear weapons away from terrorists?

yes

PRESIDENT GEORGE W. BUSH

FROM A SPEECH AT THE NATIONAL DEFENSE UNIVERSITY, FEB. 11, 2004

On Sept. 11, 2001, America and the world witnessed a new kind of war. We saw the great harm that a stateless network could inflict upon our country, killers armed with box cutters, mace and 19 airline tickets. Those attacks also raised the prospect of even worse dangers — of other weapons in the hands of other men. The greatest threat before humanity today is the possibility of secret and sudden attack with chemical or biological or radiological or nuclear weapons. . . .

America, and the entire civilized world, will face this threat for decades to come. We must confront the danger with open eyes, and unbending purpose. I have made clear to all the policy of this nation: America will not permit terrorists and dangerous regimes to threaten us with the world's most deadly weapons. . . .

We're determined to confront those threats at the source. We will stop these weapons from being acquired or built. We'll block them from being transferred. We'll prevent them from ever being used. One source of these weapons is dangerous and secretive regimes that build weapons of mass destruction to intimidate their neighbors and force their influence upon the world. These nations pose different challenges; they require different strategies. . . .

I propose to expand our efforts to keep weapons from the Cold War and other dangerous materials out of the wrong hands. In 1991, Congress passed the Nunn-Lugar legislation. Sen. [Richard] Lugar had a clear vision, along with Sen. [Sam] Nunn, about what to do with the old Soviet Union. Under this program, we're helping former Soviet states find productive employment for former weapons scientists. We're dismantling, destroying and securing weapons and materials left over from the Soviet . . . arsenal. . . .

Over the last two years, a great coalition has come together to defeat terrorism and to oppose the spread of weapons of mass destruction — the inseparable commitments of the war on terror. We've shown that proliferators can be discovered and can be stopped. We've shown that for regimes that choose defiance, there are serious consequences. The way ahead is not easy, but it is clear. We will proceed as if the lives of our citizens depend on our vigilance, because they do.

Terrorists and terror states are in a race for weapons of mass murder, a race they must lose. Terrorists are resourceful; we're more resourceful. They're determined; we must be more determined. We will never lose focus or resolve. We'll be unrelenting in the defense of free nations, and rise to the hard demands of dangerous times.

no

NATURAL RESOURCES DEFENSE COUNCIL

FROM A STATEMENT, FEB. 12, 2004, WWW.NRDC.ORG.

Nunn-Lugar funds are not being used to "dismantle and destroy" Russian nuclear weapons (as opposed to missile silos and obsolete strategic bombers and submarines). In fact, the recently signed Moscow Treaty between the United States and Russia allows Russia to keep SS-18 "heavy" strategic ballistic missile systems that would otherwise have been destroyed under the START II and START III treaties.

Despite years of cooperation, the United States still has no firm idea of how many and which types of Russian nuclear warheads and bombs have been dismantled. As former Sen. Sam Nunn has indicated, the Nunn-Lugar program suffers from inadequate funding. President Bush cites the 2002 G-8 Summit agreement to provide $20 billion over 10 years, but even here the participating countries used accounting tricks to avoid increasing previous commitments. Moreover, some of this money is earmarked to build a plutonium fuel-fabrication plant in Russia that many observers believe will increase the potential that plutonium will be diverted and used for illicit purposes.

President Bush so far has refused to commit to destroying more than a few hundred of the more than 10,000 nuclear weapons still in the United States' nuclear weapons stockpile. The Strategic Offensive Reduction Treaty (SORT) negotiated with Russia in 2002 — the Moscow Treaty — does not require the elimination of a single nuclear missile silo, submarine, missile warhead, bomber or bomb. . .

President Bush failed to address the longer-term problem, and long-term proliferation pressures, arising from a world permanently and inequitably divided into declared nuclear weapons states under the Non-Proliferation Treaty (NPT), defacto nuclear weapon states outside the treaty (India, Pakistan and Israel), non-weapon states that have abandoned the treaty (North Korea) and states with varying degrees of nuclear expertise (Iran) that are presently bound by their treaty commitment not to acquire nuclear weapons but could elect to withdraw from the NPT at any time.

Nor did President Bush discuss how and when the United States and other nuclear weapon states would take further steps to fulfill their Non-Proliferation Treaty commitments to eliminate their nuclear arsenals. On the contrary, the Bush administration is spending record amounts revitalizing the U.S. nuclear weapons complex. . . .

There are two distinct kinds of threats facing the United States, one having to do with the proliferation of [weapons of mass destruction] by nation states and the second with threats posed by terrorists. The president's proposals focused on threats posed by the spread of nuclear weapons, materials and technologies to nation states rather than those by terrorists.

Continued from p. 312

international effort to seize nuclear materials on the high seas while in transit to or from rogue states. In 1999 and 2000, years before Bush's initiative, Indian and British authorities seized two North Korean shipments of missile components and related equipment en route to Libya. [32]

Bush also called on the U.N. Security Council to adopt a resolution requiring all states to criminalize proliferation of components that could be used to make weapons of mass destruction and to strengthen export controls on them. And he proposed expanding U.S. efforts to secure Russia's nuclear weapons and materials under the Nunn-Lugar program.

In addition, Bush called for closing the loophole in the NPT that allows aspirants to the nuclear club to enrich and reprocess fuel used in civilian nuclear reactors and proposed that only signatories of the Additional Protocol be allowed to import equipment for civilian reactors. To strengthen the IAEA, Bush proposed a new measure to beef up the agency's safeguards and verification powers. Finally, he recommended barring countries being investigated for alleged NPT violations from holding positions of influence in the IAEA.

"We've shown that proliferators can be discovered and can be stopped," Bush said. "Terrorists and terror states are in a race for weapons of mass murder, a race they must lose."

Weapons analysts praised Bush's recommendations. "It was a very important speech," says Curtis of the Nuclear Threat Initiative. "It addressed a number of areas that require U.S. leadership and international cooperation."

But Curtis also says the United States needs to do more to dispel the perception that it holds itself to a different standard than the rest of the world regarding proliferation. "Missing from the speech was some meaningful initiative on addressing the strategic nuclear weapons that the United States and Russia still maintain in very large numbers and, under the Treaty of Moscow, may retain into the indefinite future," Curtis says.

To others, Bush's speech exemplified the administration's unilateral approach to pursuing U.S. interests. "President Bush's speech was a series of measures that would constrain everybody else," says Bunn of Harvard's Belfer Center. "There was no mention of anything that would constrain the United States."

In Pike's view, the Bush administration's nuclear policies have left the United States with few viable options. "Right now, our declaratory policy is one of attacks to disarm our enemies' weapons infrastructure, followed up by military invasion and regime change," he says. That's the policy that led to the war in Iraq, which did not yet possess nuclear weapons. But the same policy cannot be applied to a state like North Korea, which may harbor nuclear weapons, for fear of igniting a global holocaust. "So we have an extraordinarily alarming declaratory policy that's basically frightened the living daylights out of the rest of humanity, [but which] we're not prepared to implement. That puts us in the worst of all possible worlds." ■

OUTLOOK

Crumbling Coalition?

The March 11 bombing of commuter trains in Madrid has lent further urgency to the international war on terrorism. Ten separate explosions at the rush hour ripped through the trains, killing more than 190 commuters and wounding some 1,400. [33] After initially blaming Basque separatists for the attacks, the government announced two days later that it had arrested five people with suspected links to al Qaeda.

The next day, March 14, Spaniards went to the polls and removed Prime Minister José Maria Aznar, a staunch U.S. ally in the war against terrorism, from office. Spain's new leader, Socialist José Luis Rodríguez Zapatero, renewed Spain's commitment to fight terrorism. But he promised to fulfill a campaign pledge to withdraw Spain's 1,300-man contingent of peacekeepers in Iraq by June 30. He is one of Europe's most outspoken critics of the war.

Calling the occupation of Iraq "a fiasco," Zapatero has outlined an approach to fighting terrorism that relies on international cooperation, which he says differs sharply from the administration's tactic. "Fighting terrorism with Tomahawk missiles isn't the way to defeat terrorism," he said. "I will listen to Mr. Bush, but my position is very clear and very firm. . . . Terrorism is combated by the [rule] of law." [34]

Zapatero may be expressing the views of more than a demoralized Spanish electorate. According to a new international survey, opposition to the war in Iraq and U.S. international policies has intensified in Europe. A growing percentage of Europeans polled said they want to distance their fate from the United States by adopting independent foreign and security policies through the European Union. More than half support a European foreign policy independent from that of the United States. Even in Britain, the administration's strongest war on terrorism ally, support for an independent European foreign policy has risen from 47 percent in April 2002 to 56 percent in the current poll. [35]

The Bush administration has downplayed any notion of a rift between the United States and its European allies. "We don't think countries face a choice — being European or being trans-Atlantic," said an administration official following Secretary of State Powell's March 24 trip to Spain to attend a memorial service for victims of the Madrid bombing. "All of us, especially in the NATO alliance, are almost by definition both. . . . European nations don't have to choose between good relations with Europe and good relations with the United States."

Foiling Nuclear Terror

The Madrid bombing — the worst incident of terrorist violence in Europe since the Pan Am bombing — coming as it did on the heels of the exposure of Khan's nuclear-smuggling network, will likely intensify debate over how to deal with the threat of nuclear terrorism. Bin Laden has made no secret of his desire to use a nuclear bomb as the ultimate weapon against the West, and weapons experts say events are fast outpacing policies deigned to avert such a catastrophe.

"The Bush administration and the president himself have rightly said that the ultimate specter is al Qaeda with a nuclear weapon," says Harvard's Allison. "But this administration has no coherent strategy for preventing nuclear terrorism. That's a pretty serious charge, but I think it's correct."

Administration supporters reject that view. "President Bush has transported the fight the terrorists began back to their land," wrote former Sen. Alfonse M. D'Amato, R-N.Y. "He refuses to allow them to contaminate our soil with their hatred. He has stood firm in the face of the terrorist threat, despite constant harping from critics who would second-guess his leadership." [36]

Still, IAEA Director General ElBaradei paints a grim picture of nuclear proliferation's future and calls for a revolutionary overhaul of international systems and policies to prevent nuclear terrorism. "Eventually, inevitably, terrorists will gain access to such materials and technology, if not actual weapons," he wrote. "If the world does not change course, we risk self destruction."

ElBaradei calls for globalization of worldwide security. "We must abandon the traditional approach of defining security in terms of boundaries — city walls, border patrols, racial and religious groupings," he wrote recently in *The New York Times*. "The global community has become irreversibly interdependent, with the constant movement of people, ideas, goods and resources.

"In such a world, we must combat terrorism with an infectious security culture that crosses borders — an inclusive approach to security based on solidarity and the value of human life. In such a world, weapons of mass destruction will have no place." [37] ■

Notes

[1] See Ellen Nakashima and Alan Sipress, "Insider Tells of Nuclear Deals, Cash," *The Washington Post*, Feb. 21, 2004, p. A1.

[2] For background, see Mary H. Cooper, "Non-Proliferation Treaty at 25," *The CQ Researcher*, Jan. 27, 1995, pp. 73-96.

[3] From a speech at the National Defense University in Washington, D.C., Feb. 11, 2004.

[4] For background, see Mary H. Cooper, "Hating America," *The CQ Researcher*, Nov. 23, 2001, pp. 969-992, and David Masci and Kenneth Jost, "War on Terrorism," *The CQ Researcher*, Oct. 12, 2001, pp. 817-840.

[5] See Michael A. Levi and Henry C. Kelly, "Weapons of Mass Disruption," *Scientific American*, November 2002, pp. 76-81.

[6] ElBaradei spoke at IAEA headquarter in Vienna, Feb. 5, 2004. See Peter Slevin, "U.N. Nuclear Chief Warns of Global Black Market," *The Washington Post*, Feb. 6, 2004, p. A18.

[7] For a detailed description, see Graham Allison, "How to Stop Nuclear Terrorism," *Foreign Affairs*, January/February 2004, pp. 64-74.

[8] Howard Baker and Lloyd Cutler, "A Report Card on the Department Of Energy's Nonproliferation Programs with Russia," Jan. 10, 2001.

[9] See Steven R. Weisman, "Lasting Discord Clouds Talks on North Korean Nuclear Arms," *The New York Times*, March 14, 2004. For background, see Mary H. Cooper, "North Korean Crisis," *The CQ Researcher*, April 11, 2003, pp. 321-344.

[10] See David E. Sanger, "U.S. Sees More Arms Ties between Pakistan and Korea," *The New York Times*, March 14, 2004, p. A1.

[11] See Joel Brinkley and William J. Broad, "U.S. Lags in Recovering Fuel Suitable for Nuclear Arms," *The New York Times*, March 7, 2004, p. A8.

[12] For a list of nuclear arms-control treaties and their provisions, see "Treaties and Agreements," U.S. State Department, www.state.gov, and Nuclear Threat Initiative, "WMD411," www.nti.org. For background, see Mary H. Cooper, "Weapons of Mass Destruction," *The CQ Researcher*, March 8, 2002, pp. 193-116.

[13] "National Strategy to Combat Weapons of Mass Destruction," The White House, December 2002, p. 3.

[14] "Findings of the Nuclear Posture Review," U.S. Department of Defense, released Jan. 9, 2002; www.defenselink.mil.

[15] The measure was included in the 1994 Defense Authorization Act.

[16] From an interview with *Arms Control Today*,

About the Author

Mary H. Cooper specializes in defense, energy and environmental issues. Before joining *The CQ Researcher* as a staff writer in 1983, she was Washington correspondent for the Rome daily newspaper *l'Unitá*. She is the author of *The Business of Drugs* (CQ Press, 1990) and holds a B.A. in English from Hollins College in Virginia. Her recent reports include "Exporting Jobs," "Weapons of Mass Destruction" and "Bush and the Environment."

January/February 2004; www.armscontrol.org.
[17] See Joseph C. Anselmo, "Opponents See New Arms Race in Push for Nuclear Research," *CQ Weekly*, Feb. 21, 2004, pp. 498-500.
[18] For background, see Mary H. Cooper, "Bush's Defense Policy," *The CQ Researcher*, Sept. 7, 2001, pp. 689-712.
[19] See Bradley Graham, "Missile Defense Still Uncertain," *The Washington Post*, March 12, 2004.
[20] Cirincione testified before a special meeting of the Danish Parliament, April 24, 2003.
[21] For the text of Einstein's letter, see Robert C. Williams and Philip L. Cantelon, eds., *The American Atom* (1984), cited in Stephen I. Schwartz, ed., *Atomic Audit* (1998). Unless otherwise noted, information in this section is based on Schwartz.
[22] Data from www.iaea.org and the Nuclear Energy Institute, www.nei.org.
[23] For background, see David Masci, "The United Nations and Global Security," *The CQ Researcher*, Feb. 27, 2004, pp. 173-196.
[24] For background, see David Masci, "Emerging India," *The CQ Researcher*, April 19, 2002, pp. 329-360.
[25] Kay testified before the Senate Armed Services Committee, Jan. 28, 2004.
[26] See Michael Evans, "Libya Knew Game Was Up Before Iraq War," *The Times* (London), March 23, 2004, p. 8.
[27] See "Top U.S. Official Visits Libyan Leader," The Associated Press, March 23, 2004.
[28] See Salman Masood, "Link to Qaeda Cited in Effort to Assassinate Pakistan Chief," *The New York Times*, March 17, 2004.
[29] See Seymour M. Hersh, "The Deal," *The New Yorker*, March 8, 2004, pp. 32-37.
[30] See David Rohde, "U.S. Announces New Offensive Against Taliban and al Qaeda," *The New York Times*, March 14, 2004, p. 4.
[31] See Sulfiqar Ali, "Firefight in Pakistan Claims 32 Lives; Troops Hunting for Militants Clash with Tribesmen in a Region Bordering Afghanistan," *Los Angeles Times*, March 17, 2004, p. A13.

FOR MORE INFORMATION

Arms Control Association, 1726 M St., N.W., Washington, DC 20036; (202) 463-8270; www.armscontrol.org. A nonpartisan membership organization dedicated to promoting support for effective arms-control policies.

Belfer Center for Science and International Affairs, John F. Kennedy School of Government, Harvard University, 79 JFK St., Cambridge, MA 02138; (617) 495-1400; http://bcsia.ksg.harvard.edu. Provides information on technical and political aspects of nonproliferation policy.

Bureau of Nonproliferation, U.S. Department of State, 2201 C St., N.W., Washington, DC 20520; (202) 647-4000; www.state.gov. Administers policies to prevent the spread of weapons of mass destruction.

Center for Nonproliferation Studies, Monterey Institute of International Studies, 460 Pierce St., Monterey, CA 93940; (831) 647-4154; http://cns.miis.edu. A nongovernmental organization devoted to research and training on nonproliferation issues.

GlobalSecurity.org, 300 N. Washington St., Suite B-100, Alexandria, VA 22314; (703) 548-2700; www.globalsecurity.org. A Web site maintained by veteran defense-policy analyst John Pike containing exhaustive information on U.S. defense policies, including nonproliferation strategy.

Nonproliferation Policy Education Center, 1718 M St., N.W., Suite 244, Washington, DC 20036; (202) 466-4406; www.npec-web.org. A project of the Institute for International Studies that promotes understanding of proliferation issues.

Nuclear Threat Initiative, 1747 Pennsylvania Ave., N.W., 7th Floor, Washington DC 20006; (202) 296-4810; www.nti.org. Seeks to increase global security by reducing the risk from nuclear, biological and chemical weapons. The Web site contains a wealth of information.

Nuclear Cities Initiative, U.S. Department of Energy, NA-24, 1000 Independence Ave., S.W., Washington, DC 20585; www.nnsa.doe.gov. Helps the Russian Federation downsize its nuclear weapons complex by establishing private business opportunities for nuclear scientists living in three of the former Soviet Union's closed cities.

[32] See J. Peter Scoblic, "Indefensible," *The New Republic*, March 8, 2004, p. 14.
[33] See Aparisim Ghosh and James Graff, "Terror on the Tracks," *Time*, March 22, 2004, p. 32.
[34] From an interview on radio Onda Cero quoted in "New Spain PM Firm on Troop Withdrawal," The Associated Press, March 17, 2004.
[35] Pew Research Center for the People & the Press, "A Year After Iraq War, Mistrust of America in Europe Ever Higher, Muslim Anger Persists," March 16, 2004; people-press.org.
[36] Alfonse D'Amato, "Bush Will Win War on Terrorism," *Newsday*, March 22, 2004.
[37] Mohamed ElBaradei, "Saving Ourselves from Self-Destruction," *The New York Times*, Feb. 12, 2004, p. A37.

Bibliography

Selected Sources

Books

Allison, Graham, *Nuclear Terrorism: The Ultimate Preventable Catastrophe* (Henry Holt), forthcoming.

A former Defense Department official outlines his strategy for strengthening the nuclear nonproliferation regime to prevent the spread of nuclear weapons to terrorists.

Blix, Hans, *Disarming Iraq*, Pantheon, 2004.

The head of the U.N. weapons inspection team in Iraq asserts that the inspectors would have proved conclusively that Iraq no longer possessed weapons of mass destruction had the Bush administration given them more time before invading.

Frum, David, and Richard Perle, *An End to Evil: How to Win the War on Terror*, Random House, 2003.

A former Bush speechwriter (Frum) and a former administration Defense official call current policies in the war on terrorism a choice between "victory or holocaust."

Weissman, Steve, and Herbert Krosney, *The Islamic Bomb*, Times Books, 1981.

Two authors describe how Pakistan and Iraq launched programs to develop nuclear weapons more than two decades ago.

Articles

Cirincione, Joseph, and Jon B. Wolfsthal, "North Korea and Iran: Test Cases for an Improved Nonproliferation Regime?" *Arms Control Today*, December 2003.

Innovative measures to strengthen anti-proliferation measures may be needed to keep North Korea and Iran from developing nuclear weapons.

Hersh, Seymour, "The Deal," *The New Yorker*, March 8, 2004, pp. 32-37.

President Bush may have accepted Pakistani President Pervez Musharraf's pardon of his top nuclear scientist's black marketing activities in exchange for letting U.S. troops pursue al Qaeda inside Pakistan.

Kagan, Robert, and William Kristol, "The Right War for the Right Reasons," *The Weekly Standard*, Feb. 23, 2004.

Although weapons of mass destruction have not been uncovered, two conservative commentators say that ridding the world of Saddam Hussein more than justifies the war against Iraq.

Pollack, Kenneth M., "Spies, Lies, and Weapons: What Went Wrong," *The Atlantic Monthly*, January/February 2004, pp. 78-92.

A former CIA analyst examines how U.S. intelligence wrongfully concluded that Saddam Hussein's regime was actively pursuing nuclear, biological and chemical weapons.

Sokolski, Henry, "Taking Proliferation Seriously," *Policy Review*, October/November 2003.

A conservative analyst argues the United States should call for strong measures to close loopholes in the Nuclear Non-Proliferation Treaty.

Weisman, Steven R., "Lasting Discord Clouds Talks on North Korea Nuclear Arms," *The New York Times*, March 14, 2004, p. 10.

A proposal to overcome an impasse in six-party talks to end North Korea's nuclear-weapons program has failed to gain acceptance, forcing a postponement of future talks.

Reports and Studies

Baker, Howard, and Lloyd Cutler, "A Report Card on the Department of Energy's Nonproliferation Programs with Russia," Russia Task Force, Secretary of Energy Advisory Board, Jan. 10, 2001.

The panel calls for greater efforts to keep nuclear weapons and materials in the former Soviet Union out of the hands of terrorists.

Cochran, Thomas B., and Christopher E. Paine, "The Amount of Plutonium and Highly-Enriched Uranium Needed for Pure Fission Nuclear Weapons," Natural Resources Defense Council, April 15, 1995.

The environmental-protection advocacy organization questions the standards the International Atomic Energy Agency (IAEA) uses to determine the amount of weapons-grade material needed to build a nuclear weapon.

Federation of American Scientists, Natural Resources Defense Council and Union of Concerned Scientists, "Toward True Security: A U.S. Nuclear Posture for the Next Decade," June 2001.

Three organizations that support arms control say drastically reducing the U.S. nuclear arsenal is essential to countering nuclear proliferation.

Ferguson, Charles D., *et al.*, "Commercial Radioactive Sources: Surveying the Security Risks," Center for Nonproliferation Studies, Monterey Institute of International Studies, January 2003.

Numerous sources of commercial radioactive material are vulnerable to terrorist theft. The authors call for an education campaign to prepare the public for a "dirty-bomb" attack.

The White House, "National Strategy to Combat Weapons of Mass Destruction," December 2002.

The Bush administration's post-Sept. 11 strategy contemplates preemptively attacking adversaries armed with nuclear, chemical or biological weapons before they can attack the United States.

The Next Step:

Additional Articles from Current Periodicals

American Actions

Ellis, Jason, "The Best Defense: Counterproliferation and U.S. National Security," *The Washington Quarterly*, spring 2003, p. 115.
A professor at the National Defense University discusses counterproliferation, not just non-proliferation, as a key element of America's foreign policy.

Frantz, Douglas, "Observers Fault U.S. for Pursuing Mini-Nukes," *Los Angeles Times*, Dec. 23, 2003, p. A1.
Critics say U.S. plans for new nuclear weapons damage non-proliferation efforts; the Bush administration says research on new weapons provides necessary flexibility.

McGeary, Johanna, with Scott Macleod and Massimo Calabresi, "What Will Make Them Stop?" *Time*, Nov. 3, 2003, p. 36.
American policy on how to deal with nuclear proliferation is sharply divided between proponents of conciliation and those advocating a tougher approach.

Pasternak, Douglas, and Eleni Dimmler, "A Home-Grown Nuclear Threat," *U.S. News & World Report*, Sept. 23, 2002, p. 40.
The Atoms for Peace program, designed to prevent nuclear proliferation, may help terrorists acquire nuclear materials sent abroad from the U.S.

Sanger, David, "Bush Plans to Focus on Fuel Ban to End Spread of A-Bombs," *The New York Times*, Feb. 11, 2004, p. A1.
President Bush's plan to combat nuclear proliferation focuses on controlling access to the fuel necessary to make nuclear weapons.

Squitieri, Tom, "Bush Pushes for New Nukes," *USA Today*, July 7, 2003, p. 1A.
Small, bunker-busting nuclear bombs designed to destroy buried chemical or biological weapons are the focus of new research.

A.Q. Khan

Broad, William, David Sanger and Raymond Bonner, "A Tale of Nuclear Proliferation: How Pakistani Built His Network," *The New York Times*, Feb. 12, 2004, p. A1.
Working with centrifuge plans stolen from Holland, Pakistani scientist A. Q. Khan was motivated both by ideology and greed to build a black market nuclear network.

Frantz, Douglas, and Josh Meyer, "For Sale: Nuclear Expertise," *Los Angeles Times*, Feb. 22, 2004, p. A1.
The vast scope and relatively open nature of A.Q. Khan's sale of nuclear-weapons technology raises the question of why it was allowed for so long.

Nakashima, Ellen, and Alan Sipress, "Insider Tells of Nuclear Deals, Cash," *The Washington Post*, Feb. 21, 2004, p. A1.
A Sri Lankan businessman provides an insider's view of Khan's global network: cash-filled suitcases and uranium hexafluoride.

Sanger, David, and William Broad, "From Rogue Nuclear Programs, Web of Trails Leads to Pakistan," *The New York Times*, Jan. 4, 2004, p. A1.
A.Q. Khan was a national hero to Pakistanis as well as the proliferator-in-chief of a nuclear arms network embracing rogue governments.

Slevin, Peter, John Lancaster and Kamran Khan, "At Least 7 Nations Tied to Pakistani Nuclear Ring," *The Washington Post*, Feb. 8, 2004, p. A1.
The nuclear smuggling ring run by A.Q. Khan spanned at least seven nations in Africa, Asia and Europe.

Nukes in Russia

Badkhe, Anna, "Nuclear Theft Case Raises Fears About Russia," *San Francisco Chronicle*, Nov. 23, 2003, p. A16.
No one knows exactly why a high Russian official pilfered six pounds of uranium, but the case raises troubling questions about Russian nuclear security.

Efron, Sonni, "Trove of Russian Arms at Risk," *Los Angeles Times*, Dec. 2, 2002, p. A1.
By attaching conditions impossible for the Russians to fulfill, a handful of legislators are blocking U.S. government non-proliferation efforts.

Weir, Fred, "Mothballed Warheads Pose Continuing Threat," *The Christian Science Monitor*, May 23, 2002, p. 12.
Russian nuclear stocks remain vulnerable to theft due to lax oversight and poor funding, despite $400 million per year in U.S. aid.

Perspectives on Proliferation

"A World Wide Web of Nuclear Danger," *The Economist*, Feb. 28, 2004.
Proliferation is a burgeoning danger, and the NPT appears to have failed.

"Don't Ignore Proven Gaps Fueling Nuclear Black Market," *USA Today*, Feb. 19, 2004, p. 12A.
Any new plan to stop nuclear proliferation should meet a new test before it is adopted: Would it have stopped Khan?

Allison, Graham, "How to Stop Nuclear Terror," *Foreign Affairs*, January/February 2004, p. 64.
President Bush is right to call nuclear terrorism America's defining threat.

ElBaradei, Mohamed, "Towards a Safer World," *The Economist*, Oct. 18, 2003.
The head of the International Atomic Energy Agency offers his own suggestions to improve the non-proliferation regime.

Leverett, Flynt, "Why Libya Gave Up on the Bomb," *The New York Times*, Jan. 23, 2004, p. A23.
A foreign-policy expert argues that the Libyan case shows that offering carrots as well as sticks is the only way to get states to give up their weapons of mass destruction ambitions.

McNamara, Robert, "A Plan to Ban Nukes," *Los Angeles Times*, June 22, 2003, Part M, p. 5.
The former secretary of Defense discusses his own proposal, focused on the Security Council, for dealing with proliferation.

Sangillo, Gregg, "Is the Nonproliferation Treaty in Tatters?" *The National Journal*, July 12, 2003.
Both liberal and conservative experts increasingly are coming to the conclusion that the Nuclear Non-proliferation Treaty (NPT) is failing.

Sokolski, Henry, "Nukes on the Loose," *The Weekly Standard*, June 23, 2003.
Loopholes in the NPT mean that a legally enforceable prohibition of trafficking in weapons of mass destruction needs to be created.

Remainder of the Axis: Iran and North Korea

Broad, William, and David Sanger, "U.N. Inspectors Report Evidence That Iran Itself Made Fuel That Could Be Used for A-Bombs," *The New York Times*, Feb. 25, 2004, p. A11.
Traces of highly enriched uranium that appears to have been created in Iran cast doubts on Iran's claims not to have a nuclear weapons program.

Efron, Sonni, and Douglas Frantz, "Secret Iran Nuclear Plan Discovered," *Los Angeles Times*, Feb. 13, 2004, p. A1.
In a breach of its promise to disclose all its nuclear activities, international inspectors found Iranian plans for a device to enrich uranium that had not been reported.

Frantz, Douglas, "Iran Closes In on Ability to Build a Nuclear Bomb," *Los Angeles Times*, Aug. 4, 2003, p. A1.
Iran appears to be in the advanced stages of a nuclear weapons program despite protestations the program is for electrical power only.

Larkin, John, and Donald Macintyre, "Arsenal of the Axis," *Time Asia*, July 14, 2003, p. 30.
Bankrupt North Korea is known to sell ballistic missile technology for hard cash; experts fear nuclear technology may also be for sale.

Sanger, David, "North Korea Says It Seeks to Develop Nuclear Arms," *The New York Times*, June 10, 2003, p. A10.
North Korea openly admits that it seeks nuclear weapons.

Warrick, Joby, "N. Korea Shops Stealthily for Nuclear Arms Gear," *The Washington Post*, Aug. 15, 2003, p. A19.
North Korea's intricately disguised attempts to procure nuclear weapons technology sometimes fail — but analysts assume many others succeed.

Warrick, Joby, "Nuclear Program in Iran Tied to Pakistan," *The Washington Post*, Dec. 21, 2003, p. A1.
Overwhelming evidence points to Pakistan as the source of key technology in Iran's suspected nuclear weapons program.

Wehrfritz, George, and Richard Wolffe, "How North Korea Got the Bomb," *Newsweek*, Oct. 27, 2003, p. 22.
After decades of effort, North Korea almost certainly has enough enriched uranium to produce three to five nuclear bombs.

CITING *THE CQ RESEARCHER*

Sample formats for citing these reports in a bibliography include the ones listed below. Preferred styles and formats vary, so please check with your instructor or professor.

MLA STYLE

Jost, Kenneth. "Rethinking the Death Penalty." The CQ Researcher 16 Nov. 2001: 945-68.

APA STYLE

Jost, K. (2001, November 16). Rethinking the death penalty. *The CQ Researcher, 11*, 945-968.

CHICAGO STYLE

Jost, Kenneth. "Rethinking the Death Penalty." *CQ Researcher*, November 16, 2001, 945-968.

Back Issues

The CQ Researcher *offers in-depth coverage of many key areas. Back issues are $10. Quantity discounts available. Call (866) 427-7737 to order back issues.*

Or call for a free CQ Researcher Web trial! Online access provides:

- *Searchable archives dating back to 1991.*
- *Wider access through IP authentication.*
- *PDF files for downloading and printing.*
- *Availability 48 hours before print version.*

CIVIL LIBERTIES
Race in America, July 2003
Gay Marriage, September 2003
Civil Liberties Debates, October 2003

CRIME/LAW
Cyber-Crime, April 2002
Corporate Crime, October 2002
Serial Killers, October 2003

ECONOMY
State Budget Crises, October 2003
Stock Market Troubles, January 2004
Exporting Jobs, February 2004

EDUCATION
Home Schooling Debate, January 2003
Combating Plagiarism, September 2003
Black Colleges, December 2003

ENERGY/TRANSPORTATION
Future of the Airline Industry, June 2002
Future of Amtrak, October 2002
SUV Debate, May 2003

ENVIRONMENT
Crisis in the Plains, May 2003
Water Shortages, August 2003
Air Pollution Conflict, November 2003

HEALTH AND SAFETY
Medicare Reform, August 2003
Women's Health, November 2003
Homeopathy Debate, December 2003

POLITICS AND PUBLIC POLICY
Abortion Debates, March 2003
State Budget Crises, October 2003
Democracy in the Arab World, January 2004

SOCIAL TRENDS
Latinos' Future, October 2003
Future of the Music Industry, Nov. 2003

TECHNOLOGY
NASA's Future, May 2003

TERRORISM/DEFENSE
Homeland Security, September 2003
North Korean Crisis, April 2003

WORLD AFFAIRS
Trouble in South America, March 2003
Rebuilding Iraq, July 2003
Aiding Africa, August 2003
Human Trafficking and Slavery, March 2004

YOUTH
Movie Ratings, March 2003
Hazing, January 2004
Youth Suicide, February 2004
Reforming Big-Time College Sports, March 2004

Future Topics

- ***Broadcast Indecency***
- ***Anniversary of Desegregation***
- ***Partisan Politics***

CQ Researcher

Published by CQ Press, a division of Congressional Quarterly Inc.

thecqresearcher.com

Broadcast Indecency

Should sexually provocative material be more restricted?

The supposedly accidental "wardrobe malfunction" that exposed Janet Jackson's right breast during the Super Bowl halftime show shouldn't have surprised anyone. Radio shock jocks like Howard Stern and Bubba the Love Sponge have been pushing the decency envelope for years, and TV has been following suit, raising new complaints about its increasingly risqué — some say indecent — content. Defenders of the media say the First Amendment gives them wide latitude to broadcast sexually provocative material, which simply reflects changing contemporary mores. But critics of today's radio and television content say sexually oriented broadcasting can harm society, especially children. With polls showing that Americans want something done about broadcast content, legislation is now pending in Congress to increase indecency fines dramatically. There is even talk of regulating the cable TV industry.

Radio shock jock Howard Stern has pushed the propriety envelope for years.

Inside This Report

The CQ Researcher • April 16, 2004 • www.thecqresearcher.com
Volume 14, Number 14 • Pages 321-344

CQ Press

Recipient of Society of Professional Journalists Award for Excellence ◆ American Bar Association Silver Gavel Award

THE ISSUES

BACKGROUND

CURRENT SITUATION

OUTLOOK

SIDEBARS AND GRAPHICS

FOR FURTHER RESEARCH

Cover: Radio shock jock Howard Stern has been hit with heavy fines for broadcasting indecency. (Getty Images/Robin Platzer)

THE CQ Researcher

April 16, 2004
Volume 14, Number 14

MANAGING EDITOR: Thomas J. Colin

ASSISTANT MANAGING EDITOR: Kathy Koch

ASSOCIATE EDITOR: Kenneth Jost

STAFF WRITERS: Mary H. Cooper, David Masci, William Triplett

CONTRIBUTING WRITERS: Sarah Glazer, David Hatch, David Hosansky, Patrick Marshall, Tom Price, Jane Tanner

DESIGN/PRODUCTION EDITOR: Olu B. Davis

ASSISTANT EDITOR: Kenneth Lukas

CQ PRESS

A Division of Congressional Quarterly Inc.

SENIOR VICE PRESIDENT/GENERAL MANAGER: John A. Jenkins

DIRECTOR, LIBRARY PUBLISHING: Kathryn C. Suárez

DIRECTOR, EDITORIAL OPERATIONS: Ann Davies

CONGRESSIONAL QUARTERLY INC.

CHAIRMAN: Andrew Barnes

VICE CHAIRMAN: Andrew P. Corty

PRESIDENT AND PUBLISHER: Robert W. Merry

The CQ Researcher (ISSN 1056-2036) is printed on acid-free paper. Published weekly, except Jan. 2, April 9, July 2, July 9, Aug. 6, Aug. 13, Nov. 26 and Dec. 31, by CQ Press, a division of Congressional Quarterly Inc. Annual subscription rates for institutions start at $625. For pricing, call 1-800-834-9020, ext. 1906. To purchase a *CQ Researcher* report in print or electronic format (PDF), visit www.cqpress.com or call 866-427-7737. A single report is $10. Bulk purchase discounts and electronic-rights licensing are also available. Periodicals postage paid at Washington, D.C., and additional mailing offices. POSTMASTER: Send address changes to *The CQ Researcher*, 1255 22nd St., N.W., Suite 400, Washington, D.C. 20037.

Broadcast Indecency

By William Triplett

The Issues

Rep. Fred Upton wouldn't have missed this year's exciting Super Bowl game for anything. But the Michigan Republican did miss the fireworks during the halftime show. He was in the kitchen making popcorn when a supposedly accidental "wardrobe malfunction" exposed pop singer Janet Jackson's right breast.

By the time he returned to the TV, the second half had started. For that one day, all he knew was that Super Bowl XXXVIII had been one of those rare, exciting contests between two equally matched teams.

The next day Upton called his 80-year-old father to get his reaction to the game. He expected to hear, "Great!"

"Awful!" his father said. He'd seen singer Justin Timberlake rip Jackson's costume, momentarily exposing her right breast, and it had ruined the entire game for him. Upton felt particularly bad because his father had watched it on the high-definition television set Upton had encouraged him to buy — which gave him a superb view of something he'd rather not have seen at all.

A few weeks later, Rep. Christopher Cox, R-Calif., and his 5-year-old son were horsing around in the living room. Out of breath, Cox called for a break, saying, "Halftime!" That prompted his son to jump on the coffee table, yank off his shirt and shout, "Halftime show!" He had not seen the Timberlake-Jackson incident but had heard other kids and adults talking about it.

Getty Images/Donald Miralle

Justin Timberlake prepares to rip Janet Jackson's costume during their controversial halftime show at Super Bowl XXXVIII on Feb. 1, 2004. Critics say the increasingly indecent content on radio and TV harms society and needs to be regulated more strictly. Defenders of the media say the First Amendment provides wide latitude to broadcast sexually provocative material.

As Upton and Cox discovered, it was impossible to escape the infamous breast-baring — even if one hadn't seen it — and even more difficult not to have a reaction to it.

Ironically, the House Subcommittee on Telecommunications and the Internet, which Upton heads and Cox sits on, had been holding hearings into charges that radio and network television have become regular purveyors of indecent material, in violation of rules set by the Federal Communications Commission (FCC). But neither congressman — nor millions of other Americans — was prepared for such a brazen display of female anatomy in the middle of what had become an annual family-viewing tradition.

Nor, presumably, had viewers been prepared for the NBC comedy special that aired in May 2003 at 8 p.m. — during what the networks once dubbed the "family hour." The show included a sexually suggestive skit featuring comedian Dana Carvey as the Church Lady, a character he'd originated on "Saturday Night Live," interviewing former child star Macaulay Culkin about his "sleep-overs" with pop singer Michael Jackson, who is facing child sex-abuse charges. Crude commentary by TV gangster Michael Imperioli, of "The Sopranos," added to the vulgarity.

In the weeks following the Super Bowl, the FCC ultimately received more than 530,000 complaints about the Jackson incident. The loudest came mostly from those who had been complaining for years that the public airwaves had become increasingly saturated with indecency; to them, the Jackson episode was unavoidable proof of what they'd been saying.

Others argued, however, that while the halftime show was neither tasteful nor smart, it was just another example of television doing what it always does: trying to grab the viewers' attention. Ultimately, no one had gotten hurt, they said, and after all, it was just a TV show in a country where free speech and freedom of expression are constitutionally protected.

Defenders of the media say the First Amendment gives them wide latitude to broadcast sexually provocative material, which simply reflects changing contemporary mores. But critics of today's radio and television content say sexually ori-

Majority of TV Shows Have Sexual Content

Sexual content is in the vast majority of top teen TV shows and nearly two-thirds of all the programs on broadcast TV. During prime time, nearly three-quarters of the shows have sexual content.

Sexual Content in TV Programs
(by percentage, 2001-2002)

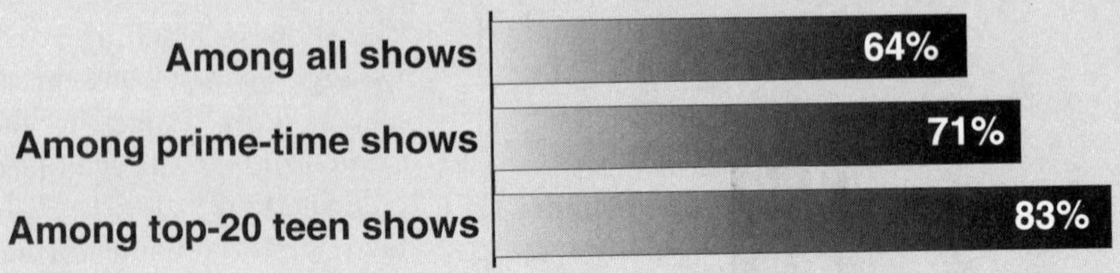

Note: The survey included all types of shows (except sports, news and children's) and all segments of the TV industry, including broadcast network, syndicated programming, basic and premium cable and public TV. Ten channels were included: ABC, NBC, CBS, Fox, Lifetime, TNT, HBO, PBS, USA and the WB affiliate in Los Angeles, KTLA.

Source: "Sex on TV: Content and Context," Kaiser Family Foundation, February 2003

ented broadcasting can harm society, especially children.

They blame the increasing amounts of broadcast indecency on the intense competition between the networks and the cable industry. Networks have been losing market share to cable for the past two decades, mostly, because cable — which is unregulated — offers racier, more violent content. As a result, say some critics, the FCC should be authorized to regulate cable as well as TV broadcasting.

Others say indecency on the airwaves has increased since Congress deregulated the industry in 1996, which has contributed to media concentration into a tiny group of conglomerates. "Deregulation has simply greased the pockets of [broadcast executives], while spawning a fundamental lack of accountability," said James P. Steyer, author of *The Other Parent: The Inside Story of the Media's Effect on Our Children.* [1]

The simmering debate — which perennially erupts during presidential elections — includes questions about whether anyone is really harmed by broadcast indecency. Does a naked body presented as titillating entertainment affect or influence public perceptions — especially children's perceptions — of sex and sexuality? Are the media helping to shape the culture, or just reflecting it?

The current national upset over indecency is just another flareup in a very old debate, says Robert J. Thompson, professor of popular culture and director of the Center for the Study of Popular Television at Syracuse University. "Before television, it was radio, and before radio it was comic books, and before that vaudeville," he says. "Plato talked about whether art should show how the world is or how it should be. We're having the same conversation now."

However, recent studies show there is more sexual content on network prime-time television now than ever before. And some say the problem is even more acute on radio, where some disk jockeys have offered prizes to listeners willing to describe their experiences having sex in public places, invited porn stars into the studio to discuss their work in detail and even castrated a pig during a broadcast.

Left unchecked, some critics say, the networks and cable companies will only compete to outdo each other with increasingly shocking content. A prime-time episode of NBC's "Friends" shows roommates unable to tear themselves away from the television after learning they were mistakenly receiving a pornography channel for free. A rock star says the F-word on live television, followed a few weeks later by a movie star saying the S-word on a similar program. Then a pop singer's breast "accidentally" appears before a U.S. television audience of 143 million people.

The networks are competing in a "race to the bottom," said FCC Commissioner Michael J. Copps. [2]

Some observers and critics say broadcast indecency has seemingly accelerated since the 1980s due to the combined impact of the advent of cable television, videocassette recorders and industry deregulation. And the phenomenon seems even more rapid, according to Thompson, because during the 1950s and '60s, television insisted on presenting an idealized view of the world, while American culture and values were, in fact, changing dramatically.

"Now, you're seeing this catch-up, and it seems to be happening really fast, because nothing happened for 50 years," Thompson recently said. "Cultural standards changed and broadcasting didn't. Now it seems like it's unbelievably out of control." [3]

But some warn that the catching-up can be far from benign. Texas Republican Joe Barton, chairman of the House Energy and Commerce Committee, says an increasing amount of indecency could harm the national culture. "The media can be one of three things: Neutral on values, reinforcing values or dismissive/destructive of values," Barton says. "Some of the music and language you hear on radio and TV have been dismissive, if not destructive of values. Over time, that could be very corrosive."

By itself, Jackson's bared breast might have provoked only momentary outrage. But coming in the wake of growing charges of indecency against radio shock jocks and broadcast television shows — and prompting Rep. Upton to hold hearings — it electrified the indecency debate with contemporary urgency.

In many ways the debate is a Rorschach test revealing our national values. To some, it is nothing less than part of a fight for the very soul of the culture.

"Historically, culture was something for more than just enjoyment," says Robert Peters, president of Morality in Media. "It was what knit a civilization together, to encourage the values that the particular civilization believed were important. When your popular culture begins to undermine everything you think is good in your society, you're headed for trouble. There's a lot of good in America, and, relatively speaking, not much good makes the news or the entertainment media. To me, it's literally a life and death issue for our society."

As the debate over broadcast indecency rages, here are some of the questions being raised over the meaning and implications of recent events:

Sexual Behavior on TV Increased

Although the percentage of shows with sexual content declined slightly in recent years, the percentage exhibiting specific sexual behaviors increased. The percentage of programs that referred to or depicted sexual intercourse in 2001-2002, for instance, was double that of 1997-1998.

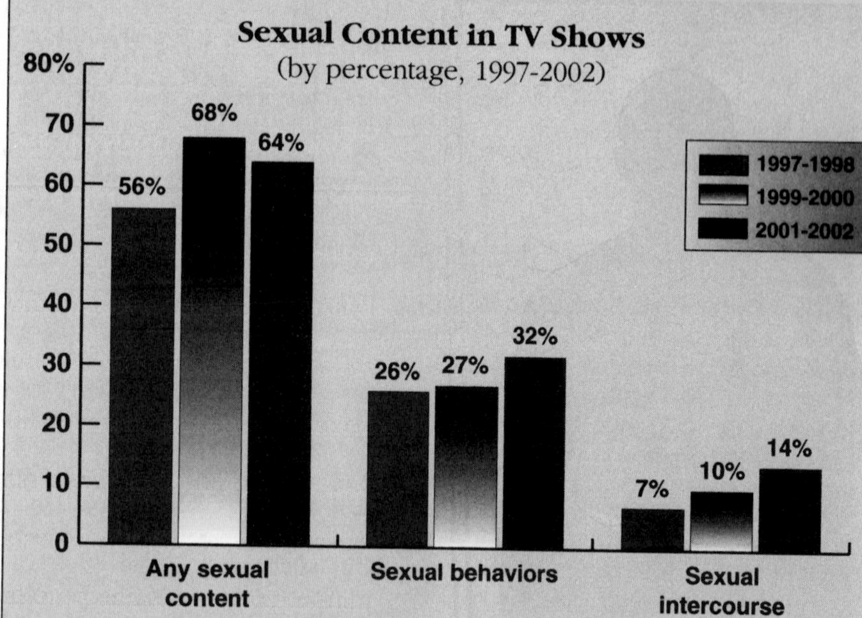

Note: The survey included all types of shows (except sports, news and children's) and all segments of the TV industry, including broadcast network, syndicated programming, basic and premium cable and public TV. Ten channels were included: ABC, NBC, CBS, Fox, Lifetime, TNT, HBO, PBS, USA and the WB affiliate in Los Angeles, KTLA.

Source: "Sex on TV: Content and Context," Kaiser Family Foundation, February 2003.

Does indecency over the airwaves undermine American society?

"It's easy to dismiss how influential television can be or how much power it has to undermine values," says Melissa Caldwell, director of research and publications at the Parents Television Council, a conservative group that supports family-oriented TV programming. "But when you look at the . . . thousands of studies pointing to a causal relationship between media violence and real-life aggression, you see that children who watch lots of violent TV as kids can grow up to be violent adults. There is a huge body of evidence out there for that."

Likewise, a "growing body of evidence shows that kids' sexual behavior is influenced by what they see on television," she says. Although the evidence linking youngsters' behavior to sexual content on TV is still relatively small, it is notable, she says.

For instance, the Medical Institute for Sexual Health, in Austin, Texas, which promotes abstinence as the only foolproof method of birth control and avoidance of sexually transmitted diseases, recently reviewed more than 2,500 biomedical and social science studies conducted over the last 20 years. Only 19 — less than 1 percent — examined the effects of mass media on adolescent sexual behavior or attitudes.

Those 19 studies found that teenagers are exposed to "extensive sexual imagery and content" in mass media. Researchers found that television, for example, showed 6.7 scenes featuring topics related to sexuality every hour, and the average teenager watches three to four hours of television a day. Adolescents exposed to such content were more likely to have more permissive views of premarital sex and more likely to think that "having sex is beneficial," according to the study.[4]

Supreme Court Internet-Indecency Decision Due

Congress has tried twice to limit children's access to sexually explicit material on the Internet, but the effort has been tied up in constitutional knots.

The Supreme Court ruled the first attempt unconstitutional on free-speech grounds. Now, however, a majority of the justices appear receptive to the lawmakers' second try, after hearing a legal challenge to the law in March.

The government is asking the high court to reinstate the 1998 Child Online Protection Act (COPA), which makes it a crime for commercial organizations to make sexual material deemed "harmful to minors" available to children under 17.

"Internet porn is widely accessible, as equally accessible to children as a TV remote," Solicitor General Theodore Olson told the justices during March 2 arguments.

But a lawyer for the American Civil Liberties Union (ACLU) insisted the law violates the First Amendment because it "suppresses" materials that adults have a right to view. "COPA criminalizes speech that adults under any definition have the right to access," Ann Beeson told the justices. The government has "less restrictive alternatives" to controlling minors' access to indecent materials, she said, such as encouraging parents to install software filters that block sexually explicit sites.

The case — *Ashcroft v. American Civil Liberties Union* — marked the third time the Supreme Court has heard arguments on efforts to limit minors' access to Internet pornography. In pre-Internet cases, the Supreme Court ruled the government can prohibit children from having access to sexually explicit materials, but only if the law does not unduly interfere with adults' rights to read or view anything short of the stringent definition of legal obscenity.

In its first ruling on Internet porn, the court in 1997 struck down the 1996 Communications Decency Act. In a mostly unanimous decision, the court in *Reno v. American Civil Liberties Union* agreed with the ACLU's arguments that the law unconstitutionally interfered with adults' access to protected materials.

Congress tried to meet the court's objections when it approved the COPA in 1998. The new law applies only to commercial publishers on the World Wide Web, not to e-mail, chat rooms or news groups. In contrast to the earlier prohibition against "patently offensive" materials, the new law covers material found to be "harmful to minors" — defined as sexually explicit, patently offensive and lacking serious value for minors. The new law — like the earlier one — protects a Web publisher if it requires users to establish their age by a credit card, adult identification number or other device.

Despite the modifications, the ACLU immediately challenged the new law on behalf of an array of Web publishers. Plaintiffs included Internet privacy advocates, gay and lesbian services and the online magazine *Salon* — which publishes a widely read sex-advice columnist, Susie Bright.

The lawsuit had first reached the Supreme Court in 2002 after the statute was ruled unconstitutional, first in a broad ruling by a federal district court in Philadelphia and then on a narrower ground by the federal appeals court in Philadelphia. The high court said the appeals court was wrong to strike the statute on the ground that it allowed local community standards to be used in defining the scope of the law. [1] The decision sent the case back to the appeals court to rule on other issues. The appeals court again ruled the law unconstitutional, and the Bush administration brought the case back to the high court.

Meanwhile, a third law aimed at protecting children from Internet porn — the Children's Internet Protection Act — was upheld by the court in June 2003. It required schools and libraries to install software filters on computers to restrict children's access to sexually explicit materials. [2]

In the March 2 arguments in the COPA suit, Olson stressed Congress' efforts to target commercial pornography. Beeson countered by claiming the law threatened sites that provided safe-sex education. For instance, Bright's *Salon* columns would be covered, Beeson said, because they discuss "sexual pleasure."

Justice Stephen G. Breyer appeared unconvinced. "I don't think that's prurient," he said. "A discussion about sex is a totally different thing from a discussion that is itself supposed to be part of a sexual response." In previous cases, Breyer has sometimes joined with members of the court's conservative majority to uphold government regulation of speech and expression.

Among the nine justices, only two — Anthony M. Kennedy and Ruth Bader Ginsburg — appeared strongly skeptical of the law. Kennedy questioned the breadth of the law, while Ginsburg voiced concerns that adults would be deterred from looking at sexually explicit materials if they had to identify themselves by using a credit card. Justice David H. Souter, who had voted to invalidate other Internet porn laws, was silent during the hourlong argument.

A decision is due by the end of June.

— Kenneth Jost

[1] The 8-1 decision is *Ashcroft v. American Civil Liberties Union*, 535 U.S. ___ (May 13, 2002). Justice John Paul Stevens dissented.

[2] The 6-3 decision is *United States v. American Library Association*, 539 U.S. ___ (June 23, 2003). Justices Stevens, David H. Souter, and Ruth Bader Ginsburg dissented. For background, see Kenneth Jost, "Libraries and the Internet," *The CQ Researcher*, June 1, 2001, pp. 465-488.

"Children exposed to lots of sexual content believe that everyone's having sex," Susan Tortolero, a study author and an epidemiology professor at the University of Texas School of Public Health. "That is bad, especially for young ages," particularly since most sex on television is casual or between unwed couples, and married sex is usually portrayed negatively, she says.

"Psychologists [say] it can confuse children when they're exposed to a lot of sexual material. It can cause harm in that it's too much information," which kids aren't capable of understanding at young ages. "We see lots of kids having oral sex and at early ages. They say they see it on television and hear it in music, mostly rap music."

Similarly, a recent report from the Kaiser Family Foundation — which has been tracking sexual content on television for several years — found that in the top 20 shows watched by teens, eight in 10 episodes included some sexual content and one in five involved sexual intercourse.* And the amount of sexual content was increasing on nearly every channel, the report noted. Approximately 64 percent of all shows now have some kind of sexual content, up from roughly 50 percent just four years ago. And 14 percent of shows specifically include sexual intercourse, either depicted or strongly implied, an increase from 7 percent four years ago. [5] (*See graph, p. 325.*)

However, the report also notes that references on these shows to safe, or at least safer, sex practices are also increasing, thus presenting at least in part an arguably more responsible view toward sex. (*See graph, p. 328.*)

Getty Images

"Dawson's Creek" created waves from its first show, which featured a love affair between a female high school teacher and one of her male students. Most teen-oriented shows today have high amounts of sexual content.

Are kids being corrupted by sexual imagery on television? No, according to a 17-year-old high school girl in North Carolina. "People don't give people our age enough credit," she recently said. "We understand what's going on. We're a lot wiser. [Networks] just have to keep getting more shocking to keep people tuning in."

But asked about Madonna's televised open-mouth kiss with Britney Spears during last year's MTV music video awards show, the girl acknowledged: "It's more common to see girls making out now as a tactic to get guys. Nobody's going to say it's because Britney and Madonna did it, but it is." [6]

And the effect isn't just on children, says Patrick Trueman, senior legal adviser to the conservative Family Research Council. He says formerly inhibited or prohibited behaviors are becoming commonplace as a result of programming standards that he says have hit bottom. "What used to be sort of extreme activity has become normal for a good segment of society," he says.

"The shock-jock routine has taken the shock out of taboo in America," continues Trueman, former chief prosecutor in the Department of Justice's child exploitation and obscenity division. "I was recently with the Philadelphia vice squad on a drive around to 'massage' parlors, and the clientele were normal, regular businessmen — ordinary Joes doing what seems a casual, regular thing." Although Trueman doesn't blame shock jocks for all such adult behavior, indecent programming is partly responsible, he says.

No one argues that the airwaves are pure, or even harmless. The debate surrounds how much harm occurs from broadcast indecency and whether it's appreciably worse now than ever before. "I'm sure indecency undermines some people's values," says Frank Couvares, professor of history and American studies at Amherst College in Massachusetts. "And I'm sure it has no effect on other people."

Others note that as cultural standards in broadcast, print and the newer electronic media have become more permissive, large parts of American life have

* In the past few years, top-rated teen shows have included "Dawson's Creek," "That '70s Show," "One on One," "Just Deal" and "Beverly Hills 90210," all of which contain scenes involving sex or talk of sex.

Teen Shows Often Mention 'Safer Sex'

Among the most-popular teen shows with intercourse-related content, nearly half mentioned safer-sex practices, such as using condoms or practicing abstinence.

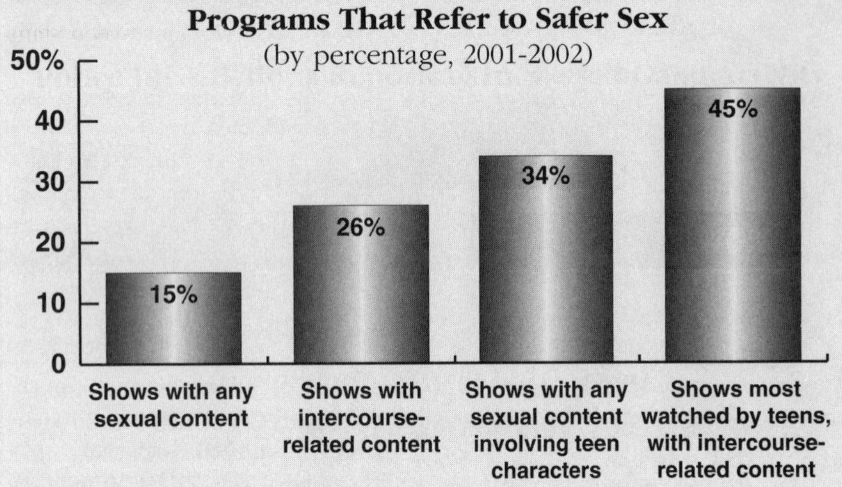

Note: The survey included all types of shows (except sports, news and children's) and all segments of the TV industry, including broadcast network, syndicated programming, basic and premium cable and public TV. Ten channels were included: ABC, NBC, CBS, Fox, Lifetime, TNT, HBO, PBS, USA and the WB affiliate in Los Angeles, KTLA.

Source: "Sex on TV: Content and Context," Kaiser Family Foundation, February 2003

substantially improved. Women and blacks, for example, have achieved a status long previously denied to them. U.S. church attendance remains steady as ever and is significantly higher than in most European societies. Overall, violent crime has been declining since the early 1990s, and more public interest and advocacy groups are fighting poverty, homelessness, hunger and illiteracy today than ever before. [7]

Perhaps most significant: At a time when sexual content increasingly pervades television and radio, pregnancy rates among U.S. teenagers have dropped to the lowest level ever recorded, and fewer teenagers are having sex. [8]

"There's not much [evidence of] children being corrupted by media . . . [or] being led here in radically dysfunctional directions," Couvares says, adding that many children are, however, "being corrupted by abusive parents and terrible events in their lives."

While to some extent television and radio simply reflect the culture, some evidence suggests the media also influences culture. But the influence is minimal, at best, Syracuse's Thompson says. "It always amazes me to hear claims that television sets the agenda," he says, noting that school segregation was ruled unconstitutional in 1954, but not until 1971 did civil rights get regular mention on television, in "All in the Family." "Other institutions push envelopes, television licks the envelope only when it's safe to do so.

"Ultimately," he continues, "if we're looking at the 500 major things threatening American life today — including the welfare of our children — the content of television isn't even in the top 100." If children are suffering any ill effects from exposure to sexual content on either television or radio, he says, then parents are failing to restrict access as they should. (*See "At Issue," p. 337.*)

But parents say that's almost impossible today, given the pervasiveness of sexual content throughout American media and culture.

Does the FCC have sufficient authority to punish broadcasters for indecency?

"Yes, we do have the authority," says FCC Commissioner Copps. "I've been talking about this issue [since] I arrived here two and half years ago." But until recently, he says, the commission had been unwilling to tackle the problem, largely due to institutional fears of running afoul of the First Amendment and the commission's free-market stance that the public was free to turn off the TV or radio if they did not like the content.

"The Super Bowl became a galvanizing incident," Copps says, precisely because "it gave the lie to these arguments. Here's all of America gathered round to watch the Super Bowl, and they're supposed to turn it off?"

The FCC's historical stance of letting market forces influence content has angered some parents. "A major responsibility of the FCC is to ensure that those who use the public airwaves adhere to standards of decency," L. Brent Bozell III, president of the Parents Television Council, recently told a House subcommittee. "Yet, looking at the FCC's track record on indecency enforcement, it becomes painfully apparent that the FCC could care less about community standards of decency or about protecting the innocence of young children."

In the past two years, Bozell continued, the FCC has received "literally hundreds of thousands of complaints of broadcast indecency from fed-up, angry, frustrated parents." Yet it "hasn't seen fit to agree with a single complaint." In fact, in its entire history the

FCC has issued only three fines to television stations for broadcast indecency.

The FCC, he concluded, is "a toothless lion, and its non-actions are not only irresponsible, they're inexcusable. Either the FCC has no idea what it's doing, or it just doesn't care what the public thinks." [9]

Excluding this year's Super Bowl, the FCC has received more than 308,000 complaints of indecent broadcasts over the last 10 years, but issued only 52 notices of liability for violations. [10]

FCC Chairman Michael K. Powell has maintained that regulating content "gets tricky" because it is difficult to define a violation for which a licensee can be fined. [11]

Nevertheless, Copps says, "I don't think commissioners need to sit and debate whether we have the authority. We've been given a law that says when kids are watching television, you shouldn't have obscene, indecent or profane material."

The law stems from a 1978 Supreme Court decision following the 1973 airing by Pacifica Radio of comic George Carlin's now-famous "Seven Words You Can't Say on Television" monologue. After the high court affirmed in *FCC v. Pacifica Foundation* that the FCC has a right to police indecent broadcasts, the commission defined indecency as "language that describes, in terms patently offensive as measured by contemporary community standards . . . sexual or excretory activities or organs," when "there is a reasonable risk that children may be in the audience." [12]

However, Robert Corn-Revere, a former FCC attorney now specializing in communications law, says the *Pacifica* decision — which split the court 5-4 — was a limited affirmation of FCC authority. Moreover, he says, subsequent changes in technology, society and especially the law have weakened the constitutional basis for the FCC's definition of indecency.

For instance, last fall FCC Enforcement Bureau Chief David Solomon decided not to fine rock singer Bono, who exclaimed, "This is really, really f—ing brilliant!" after receiving an award during NBC's 2003 live broadcast of the Golden Globe Awards. Solomon said he was prevented from fining NBC in part because FCC regulations only prohibit such words from being used as verbs or nouns, not as adjectives or adverbs.

Moreover, the Supreme Court's *Pacifica* decision had also said that for a broadcast to be indecent or obscene, the violations must be repeated and willful, so FCC rules also require the context of an alleged violation to be considered.

Solomon didn't have the authority to fine NBC, says Corn-Revere, "because with the Bono case, you were talking about a live, unscripted program and a single, fleeting reference."

The Parents Television Council successfully pressed the FCC to reconsider the Bono decision, and in March the commission declared that the incident did indeed violate decency standards. In the future, the FCC said, use of the F-word in any form would be fined. But the panel again refused to issue a fine, saying no stations had been warned first that broadcasting such profanity would violate FCC decency rules. [13]

However, some observers say the reconsidered decision is consistent with the FCC's longstanding pattern of avoiding fines in indecency cases to prevent being challenged in court on First Amendment grounds. Instead of going to court, the FCC typically collects fines by holding up other business — such as a merger or a license renewal — that the station wants to effect. As such, the agency avoids a legal challenge to whether its indecency standard is constitutional. All the cases filed by the FCC over the last 10 years have been settled out of court.

Thus, for at least the last 20 or 25 years, getting involved in "content stuff" was the "last thing the commission wanted to do," says Christopher Sterling, a former special assistant for media affairs at the FCC and now a professor of media and public affairs at George Washington University. "The FCC has washed its hands [of the matter] and said there's no role it can play here. So [people] write to Congress, which is why we're having hearings."

"The FCC is caught between statutory and constitutional demands in an area that from time to time is highly politicized," says Corn-Revere, who often had to determine whether allegations of indecency merited action when he worked at the commission. "The people who are howling for blood simply don't have a clue about what the [commission's] legal dilemma is."

Chairman Powell acknowledged the statutory-constitutional tension in a statement accompanying the reconsidered Bono decision. "This sends a signal to the industry that the gratuitous use of such vulgar language on broadcast television will not be tolerated," Powell said. "Going forward, as instructed by the Supreme Court, we must use our enforcement tools cautiously. As I have said since becoming a commissioner, government action in this area can have a potential chilling effect on free speech." [14]

However, Rep. Barton doesn't think the FCC needs any additional or revised authority to do its job. "In the past," he says, "they've been lax in enforcement."

Should the FCC regulate cable television?

Radio and network television broadcasts travel over the public airwaves and thus can be tuned in for free by anyone with a TV or radio. The courts have said that because these broadcasts are "pervasive" and an "uninvited guest" in homes, the FCC has authority to regulate them.

But because cable and satellite programs are privately transmitted for a fee and those who watch them must first "invite" them into their homes, cable and satellite programs are not subject to FCC authority.

But that may change.

More than 85 percent of viewers — including those who could receive broadcast directly over the airwaves — now receive their broadcast television through cable or satellite transmissions. [15] And viewers increasingly discern little difference between broadcast and cable, except when changing channels from, say, a Disney show to something like "The Sopranos," the popular HBO Mafia series that includes graphic language, sex and violence.

"That changes the argument a little," says Copps, "especially when the Supreme Court has already said there's a compelling governmental interest in protecting children from indecency on cable." [16]

Nielsen Media Research reported last year that for the first time more viewers watch TV through cable than via broadcast, though the top-rated broadcast shows still draw larger audiences than most top-rated cable programs. But with more families receiving television through cable and satellite transmission — and the prospect that even more people will do so in the future — some argue that the FCC should have domain over cable and satellite as well.

"I'm sympathetic to the many people who ask why our indecency regulations apply only to broadcast," FCC Commissioner Kevin Martin recently testified. "Increasingly, I hear a call for the same rules to apply to everyone, for a level playing field. And if cable and satellite operators continue to refuse to offer parents more tools for blocking unwanted content, then basic indecency and profanity restrictions may be a viable alternative that also should be considered." [17]

Bozell, of the Parents Television Council, agrees. "More and more, the audience is gravitating to cable, so you have to address the sewage that's seeping through there," he said recently. [18]

Even Rep. Barton, who describes himself as a "free-market, pro-competition guy," believes FCC regulation of cable and satellite should be considered. "As satellite and cable become more ubiquitous," he says, "the distinction between over-the-air and cable lowers."

The cable industry says regulation is unnecessary. Cable has become popular precisely because it provides networks offering appropriate programs targeting children and families, says Brian Dietz, a spokesman for the National Cable and Telecommunications Association.

"Cable also has specific technology that allows customers to block out certain channels," Dietz adds. "Analog boxes offer simple technology to block whole channels, while digital boxes offer advanced technology that will allow the channel to come in, but not certain shows if you don't want them."

Parents' groups have complained that children often are more technologically sophisticated than adults and can circumvent such control devices. But Dietz points out that with cable, children cannot access the control system without knowing the parents' password, or PIN number. "If a kid doesn't have the PIN code, he's not going to get in."

The FCC's Martin and others have pressed the cable and satellite industries to at least consider offering family-friendly tiers or à la carte bundles of channels, instead of forcing consumers to subscribe to packages that include every available channel. That way, parents who prefer their kids not to see, for example, "The Sopranos" or anything on MTV, could order packages without those channels.

"Tier or à la carte delivery would undermine the economics of the industry and have a detrimental impact on the diversity and variety of programming," Dietz claims. Cable advertising rates are based on the total number of homes served — about 70 million. "If a network was sold à la carte or by a tier, that base of 70 million might go down to 5 million." With fewer viewers in a tier, the ad rates would have to drop, lowering the company's overall profitability.

"To stay in business," Dietz says, "subscription prices would have to be significantly higher." Consumers currently paying $40 a month for 70-80 channels could end up paying $40 a month for only 10 channels, he says.

Caldwell, of the Parents Television Council, isn't persuaded by such economic arguments. "I don't know what all the economic ramifications are," she says, "but if you're taking a free-market position, let the viewers pay for what they want."

Dietz counters: "Cable is sold as a bundled product similar to a newspaper or a magazine. You can't buy just the business section of *The Washington Post* or *The New York Times.*"

Ultimately, the courts probably will declare it unconstitutional for the FCC to gain authority over the cable and satellite industries, according to attorney Corn-Revere.

"In every other medium and in every other situation, the courts — including the Supreme Court — have struck down attempts to extend an indecency or indecency-type regime outside of the network-broadcasting context," he says. "Broadcasting is the sole and very narrow exception."

Others don't view the situation in such absolute terms. "The First Amendment is to benefit everyone, but that's not to say we can't have laws against indecency," says the Family Research Council's Trueman. "Because it's a freedom that turns into a slavery if we are no longer allowed to protect our children and instead enslave them in this culture we're developing." ■

BACKGROUND

Early TV Taboos

The federal government began regulating America's media industry in the early 1900s, driven by a

Continued on p. 332

Chronology

1950s ***Television experiences its "Golden Age"; networks voluntarily impose decency rules.***

1950-51
Complaints of starlets' plunging necklines prompt the first congressional hearings into TV content. Broadcasters establish a voluntary ethics code.

1952
Network censors forbid the word "pregnant" from being uttered in any "I Love Lucy" episode.

1957
Actress Jayne Mansfield's breasts "accidentally" pop out of her low-cut gown during live TV Oscar show.

1970s ***Television is allowed to show more realism.***

1971
"All in the Family" debuts, addressing taboo subjects like racism, bigotry, homosexuality and rape.

Feb. 4, 1975
National Association of Broadcasters TV code board adopts "Family Viewing Hour" prohibiting programming "inappropriate for general family viewing" during the 7-9 p.m. time period.

Nov. 4, 1976
A federal judge rules the family-viewing hour unconstitutional; the networks voluntarily re-establish it.

1978
Supreme Court's *FCC v. Pacifica Foundation* decision grants the FCC limited authority to regulate broadcast indecency.

1980s-1990s

Advent of unregulated adult fare on cable and video forces commercial broadcasters to compete.

1981
"Hill Street Blues" introduces edgy dialogue and implied or discussed sex to prime-time drama.

1983
Broadcasters abandon voluntary code of ethics after Justice Department alleges it violates antitrust laws.

1987
A character on NBC's "St. Elsewhere" moons his boss.

1988
"Married . . . with Children" debuts, becomes an instant hit.

1992
When unwed TV character "Murphy Brown" decides to have a baby, Vice President Dan Quayle denounces TV's disrespect for "family values."

1993
Premiere episode of "NYPD Blue" shows a woman's dimly lit breast and backside during a lovemaking scene.

1995
FCC fines Infinity Broadcasting a record $1.7 million for indecency by radio shock jock Howard Stern.

1996
Telecommunications Act requires networks to develop content ratings and for all televisions to eventually contain "V-chips" allowing parents to block objectionable programs.

Jan. 1, 1997
Television industry begins ratings system with age-based advisories; made more descriptive later that year.

1999
Critically acclaimed "The Sopranos" debuts on cable's HBO, featuring profanity, graphic violence and sex.

2000s ***Broadcasters continue to push the decency envelope, prompting a regulatory and congressional backlash.***

2000
Contestant Richard Hatch appears naked several times on CBS' reality TV show "Survivor."

2001
Characters on the animated cable satire "South Park" say the S-word 162 times in one episode.

2002
The FCC fines Infinity Broadcasting $357,500 after radio shock jocks Opie and Anthony broadcast a live description of a couple having sex during a church service.

2003
Rock singer Bono says the F-word during a live broadcast; FCC refuses to fine the network.

January 2004
Viewer complaints prompt Congress to hold hearings on broadcast indecency and FCC inaction.

February 2004
Janet Jackson's right breast is exposed during the Super Bowl halftime show.

March 2004
Senate and House pass bills increasing fines against indecency from $27,500 per infraction to as much as $500,000.

Policing the F-word . . . and Its Cousins

Viewers were outraged a year ago, when rock star Bono — in response to receiving a Golden Globe award — said on a live NBC television broadcast, "This is really, really f—ing brilliant."

But they were even more outraged when the Federal Communication Commission's (FCC) Enforcement Bureau announced it would not fine either Bono or NBC for the incident.

The FCC's indecency rules prohibit offensive words describing sexual or excretory acts or organs, but only when used as verbs or nouns. Because Bono had used the word as an adjective, it did not officially violate the FCC rule.

Incensed at what they considered a technicality, many people complained to Congress. In January, Rep. Doug Ose, R-Calif., introduced a bill to amend FCC rules so that any mention in any context of the F-word — as well as several other words and phrases considered obscene or indecent — would violate FCC rules and therefore be subject to fines.

The measure has triggered debate on several topics, including whether such a zero-tolerance policy is artistically harmful. For example, in 2001 ABC aired Steven Spielberg's Academy Award-winning movie "Saving Private Ryan," with its multiple use of the F-word (and gory scenes of battlefield carnage) fully intact. Network censors decided that the context in which the word was used — among soldiers fighting and dying in the bloody D-Day landing of World War II — made the language relevant and necessary.

If Ose's bill passes — it has more than 40 cosponsors and has been referred to the House Subcommittee on the Constitution — uncensored versions of "Saving Private Ryan" or other movies with similar content could not air on network television without incurring fines.

After receiving thousands of outraged letters about the FCC's Bono decision, FCC commissioners recently reconsidered the case and issued a unanimous decision that the rocker's use of the word "is within the scope of our indecency definition because it does depict or describe sexual activities." However, because existing precedents had allowed such utterances, the commission did not fine NBC or Bono. [1]

"Bono may have used the F-word as an adjective, but today's FCC ruling turned it into a verb directed at American families," responded an angry L. Brent Bozell III, president of the Parents Television Council, which advocates family-friendly TV content. [2]

However, the FCC warned that future utterances of the F-word would trigger fines. Ose's bill would simply clarify and strengthen the FCC's statutory authority to do so.

But some in the broadcast industry question the FCC's constitutional authority to police indecency more stringently. For one thing, a 1978 Supreme Court decision on broadcast indecency, *FCC v. Pacifica Foundation*, says that for an utterance to be indecent, it must be "repeated" and "willful" — a standard the single Bono comment, in a moment of excitement, apparently does not meet.

Continued from p. 330

concern that had nothing to do with content. Fearing that the infant broadcast companies might acquire too much market power, possibly violating antitrust laws, Congress passed the 1927 Federal Radio Act, establishing the Federal Radio Commission — a precursor of the FCC.

Seven years later, Congress passed the watershed 1934 Communications Act, which established the FCC as an independent agency and set guidelines for regulating the amount of public airwaves any one company could use.

An infamous science-fiction radio program in 1938 — Orson Welles' eerily realistic adaptation of H.G. Wells' novel, "War of the Worlds"— triggered the government's first interest in controlling broadcast content. On Halloween night, Welles introduced the show as a fictional drama, but most listeners tuned in later and didn't hear the disclaimer. The broadcast, crafted as a breaking news story, convinced thousands of people that Martians had landed and were taking over the Earth. Panic ensued.

In response, the head of the FCC warned radio to police itself and its programming better if it wanted to avoid government intervention. [19]

A dozen years later, however, television presented a bigger problem. "Television in the beginning was almost all live," says Louis Chunovic, author of the 2000 TV history, *One Foot on the Floor: The Curious Evolution of Sex on Television from "I Love Lucy" to "South Park."* "The first people who put shows on reasoned that they were being invited into viewers homes," so they dressed up for the occasion, with men often in tuxedos and women in evening gowns.

"The very first thing that got Congress up in arms was the plunging neckline debate," Chunovic says of the ambitious starlets who wore gowns with revealing necklines, out of which they might "accidentally" tumble. "This was a great way to get publicity in those days, and it happened time after time after time on these live programs."

One buxom starlet — Virginia Ruth Egnor, known to millions as Dagmar — provoked government intervention. "Her job was just to wear spectacular strapless evening gowns and view the proceedings, from a stool set up near the band," Chunovic says. Soon she was receiving 500 fan letters a week.

But other viewers, offended by Dagmar's ample décolletage, complained to Congress, prompting the first congressional hearings into tele-

Moreover, says *Radio Business Report,* an online trade newsletter, the agency's indecency standard is so vague it is hard to enforce.

The standard describes indecency as "language that describes, in terms patently offensive as measured by contemporary community standards . . . sexual or excretory activities or organs, at times of the day when there is a reasonable risk that children may be in the audience." Indeed, the standard is so vague that within the last 10 years the agency has settled all its indecency cases, avoiding taking them to court and risking defeat.

In addition, says the newsletter, the commission's indecency enforcement has been "erratic and inconsistent" and the defense could easily prove that no one at the FCC has a really clear idea of what the FCC's indecency standard really is. [3]

AFP Photo/Jeff Haynes

The rock singer Bono used the F-word on live TV last year, but the FCC declined to fine him or NBC. Here he performs during halftime at the 2002 Super Bowl.

For that reason, says Robert Corn-Revere, a former FCC attorney now specializing in communications law, Ose's bill — if enacted — "would be reversed in 10 minutes" if it were challenged in court. "People will argue the [overall] indecency standard is vague, which it is, so why don't you fix it by making it specific?"

FCC Chairman Michael K. Powell nevertheless believes the agency is moving in the right direction. "We will continue to respect the delicate balance of protecting the interests of the First Amendment with the need to protect our children," he said recently. [4]

[1] See *Radio Business Report,* http://www.rbrepaper.com/epaper/pages/march04/04-55_news6.html]

[2] See Jonathan D. Salant, "FCC cites Howard Stern and Bono for Indecency," The Associated Press, March 18, 2004.

[3] *Radio Business Report, op. cit.*

[4] Statement, March 18, 2004.

vision morality. Knowing that broadcast licenses had to be periodically renewed and that Congress was already hotly pursuing suspected communists in Hollywood, the industry wilted under the political glare. Executives ordered backstage seamstresses to sew gauze onto the tops of low-cut gowns. CBS declared it would henceforth ban any mention, in any context, of the word "sex" over the airwaves.

Most significantly, the industry adopted a voluntary code of conduct dictating what could and could not be broadcast. The National Association of Broadcasters, the industry trade group, specifically banned "profanity, obscenity and smut," including "camera angles that emphasize anatomical details indecently." Moreover, "illicit sexual relations" should not be treated as "commendable." [20]

During the 1950s and the beginning of the '60s, life was depicted on television as remarkably — absurdly, to some — free of almost anything that even hinted at sex or sexuality. For instance, the married characters Lucy and Ricky Ricardo of the "I Love Lucy" show slept in separate twin beds, as did Rob and Laura Petrie of "The Dick Van Dyke Show." When Lucille Ball (Lucy) became pregnant by real-life husband Desi Arnaz (Ricky), and producers incorporated the development into the show's story line, the word "pregnant" could not be used.

On the eve of the social and sexual revolutions of the 1960s, American television remained a safe haven ruled by network censors acutely sensitive to anything that might be the least bit offensive. For example, the still relatively new "Tonight Show" featured host Jack Paar, who could be sharp, edgy and impatient. When a network censor forbade him from telling a joke using the word "W.C." — the abbreviation for water closet, or bathroom toilet — Paar walked off the set.

Television continued to reflect a world in which nothing really sexual or even remotely bad happened, even as the cultural upheavals of the decade burst forth: the rise of the counterculture, the war in Vietnam, the surge of feminism and the appearance of explicit sex in the cinema. In 1968 — the year of North Vietnam's Tet Offensive, the Chicago Democratic convention, the assassinations of The Rev. Martin Luther King Jr. and Sen. Robert F. Kennedy — one of the top-ranked television shows was "Gomer Pyle, USMC." "It was set in the contemporary Marine Corps," notes Thompson of Syracuse University, "but never even once mentioned Vietnam." Meanwhile, NBC ran a comedy series called "I Dream of Jeannie," about an astronaut and the confounding hijinks that always resulted when his 2,000-year-old, live-in genie tried to help him. Costumers dressed Barbara Eden, who played the genie, in stereotypical Middle Eastern female garb, complete with bare midriff, but NBC censors insisted that her navel always be hidden.

Getty Images

The popular HBO Mafia series "The Sopranos" includes graphic language, sex and violence. Some critics say the Federal Communications Commission should regulate cable television because most broadcast TV comes into homes on cable, and viewers increasingly discern little difference between broadcast and cable. From left: Steven Van Zandt as Silvio Dante, James Gandolfini as Tony Soprano and Tony Sirico as Paulie Walnuts.

The first prime-time show to address contemporary issues was "All in the Family," producer Norman Lear's groundbreaking comedy series that debuted on CBS in 1971. One episode dealt with impotence, another with rape and still another with marital problems. Subjects previously taboo — particularly racism — became staples as the show proved a hit with viewers and advertisers.

Chunovic attributes the show's enormous success to the fact that the first generation of Baby Boomers was at the age — the mid-20s — to start demanding a more realistic and representative portrait of the world from network television. Also, as critics pointed out, the show treated its volatile subjects with an unprecedented balance of biting satire and serious respect.

Then in 1973, WBAI, the Pacifica network radio station in New York City, played Carlin's "Seven Words" routine. But in just a few years, technology and market forces enormously complicated the applicability of the Supreme Court's ensuing *Pacifica* ruling.

The Cable Challenge

During the network era, the business model had been one of homogenization, Thompson says. "The networks were airing pretty much the same shows, trying to appeal to the biggest audience possible," he explains. "That made the most marketplace sense at the time. Then cable came along and flipped that business model on its ear."

The cable industry's underlying market theory was "different strokes for different folks." Not everyone liked the same thing, so industry executives figured a bundled subscription package of multiple channels offering diverse programming — effectively fragmenting the audience — would become reasonably profitable. And because cable shows were not broadcast over public airwaves, programmers did not have to abide by the FCC's indecency rules. Cable shows almost immediately pushed the envelope of taste and propriety.

The videocassette recorder (VCR) appeared almost simultaneously with the rise of cable. VCRs allowed viewers not only to tape edgy cable programs but also to watch adult videos in the privacy of their own homes. And Americans quickly displayed a substantial appetite for pornography: By 1984, adult videos accounted for 13 percent of all video rentals nationwide. [21]

Cable and VCRs delivered a powerful one-two punch to the networks. Even with popular shows like "Three's Company" — in which two single young women roomed with a single male who pretended to be homosexual — the networks began to look hopelessly prim and out-of-date compared with the more realistic and gritty programs on cable, not to mention the tantalizing allure of adult videos. Networks felt pressure to compete, and by then they had little reason not to: In 1983, they had abandoned their voluntary code of ethics after the Justice Department ruled that parts of the code violated antitrust laws.

Meanwhile, as the Reagan administration proselytized for deregulation in almost all areas, the White House appointed Mark S. Fowler as FCC chairman. Fowler's FCC essentially left the networks to self-regulate content, per the guidelines established in the *Pacifica* decision. The three major broadcast networks continued to maintain their standards-and-practices departments — the censors' bailiwick.

But then the Fox network appeared in the late 1980s. "When Fox came on the air as the fourth network," Chunovic says, "part of its commercial campaign was to tout, 'Hey, we're the network that doesn't have standards and practices!' "

Fox positioned itself as the only broadcaster offering the kind of edgy, hip material typically reserved for cable. "Married . . . with Children," for example, dished up lowbrow jokes about such topics as menstruation, sexual devices and penis size — raunchy humor never before seen in prime-time television. " 'Married' was immensely influential, both for Fox . . . and for other broadcast networks," Chunovic writes in his history of sex on television. "Not only because it extended the reach of what was permissible for over-the-air TV, but because its no-taste humor was genuinely funny." [22] Fox now has a standards-and-practices department.

Syracuse University's Thompson says until then the barriers establishing what was acceptable on network television had been broken by "classy stuff" — quality shows like "Hill Street Blues" and "St. Elsewhere."

"However, once that's done, one can't make laws that take into account quality, because that's completely subjective," he says.

Getty Images

The gritty ABC-TV police drama "NYPD Blue" debuted in 1993 with violent, sexually oriented content. In recent years, the actors have begun using mild profanity. Dennis Franz, right, still stars as Det. Andy Sipowicz; Jimmy Smits played his partner for several years.

Shock Jocks

With few FCC regulators looking over their shoulders, the networks began ratcheting up sexual content in all sorts of prime-time shows. For instance, the hugely popular '90s series "Seinfeld" devoted an entire episode to a bet over which of the characters could go the longest without masturbating.

Although shock jocks like sex-obsessed Howard Stern in New York were beginning to make names for themselves on radio, television drew most of the criticism at the time. During the 1992 presidential campaign, for example, Vice President Dan Quayle attacked the series "Murphy Brown" as morally irresponsible because the lead character bore a child out of wedlock. (Defenders of the show accused Quayle of playing politics: The previous year the same thing had happened on another show, "The Days and Nights of Molly Dodd," but passed without comment from Washington.)

Sexy talk and double-entendres proliferated on prime time throughout the '90s, and shows that featured such content were among the most critically acclaimed and widely popular, such as "NYPD Blue," "Seinfeld," "Northern Exposure," "Mad About You" and "Law and Order." In the late 1990s, cable's HBO introduced "The Sopranos," a hit almost from the very first episode, featuring not only nudity and sex but also a torrent of four-letter words and violence as a way of life.

However, as both sexual and violent content increased, parents and concerned groups again pressured Washington to do something. President Bill Clinton responded in 1996 with an omnibus telecommunications bill, which, among many other things, mandated that television manufacturers equip new sets with a computerized "V-chip," which could be used in conjunction with a new industry ratings system. Parents could program the chip to block reception of specific shows based on their ratings. [23]

Politicians and cultural critics continued to denounce broadcast indecency. For instance, in 1997 Sen. Joseph I. Lieberman, D-Conn., said in a speech at the University of Notre Dame, "The media [are] speeding the moral breakdown of our society."

Former Secretary of Education William J. Bennett, a Republican, joined forces with Lieberman, calling their movement the "Revolt of the Revolted," which they said represented the "disgust millions of Americans feel toward the growing culture of violence, perversity and promiscuity" in the media. [24]

While groups like the Parents Television Council steadily complained about indecent and violent content on television, radio shock jocks seemed to be pushing the broadcast envelope the farthest, prompting a new round of concern about indecency on the airwaves. Throughout the early '90s, Stern, who seemed to interview a different porn actress almost every time he was on the air, asking detailed questions about their work, racked up indecency fines totaling a record $1.7 million, which station owner Infinity Broadcasting eventually paid.

In 2001, Bubba the Love Sponge, a Florida shock jock whose real name used to be Todd Clem, graphically discussed sex acts during several different broadcasts, resulting in $755,000 in fines against station owner Clear Channel Communications, Inc., a major player in the radio market.

In 2002, the shock duo Opie and Anthony, at WNEW-FM in New York, outraged listeners when they held a contest calling for couples to have sex in risky places. After broadcasting a live encounter between a couple in a Manhattan church during services, Infinity Broadcasting — which owned the station — fired the DJs, and the FCC levied a $375,500 fine against Infinity.

Ironically, the Center for Media and Public Affairs, which studies the news and entertainment media, announced findings around the same time showing that sexual content on television had decreased by almost a third in recent years. But television returned almost instantly to the front of the indecency debate in January 2003, when rock singer Bono uttered the F-word on live television.

The FCC's subsequent decision not to fine NBC for the incident provoked even more outrage, the brunt of which hit Congress. Rep. Upton, who personally signs every letter his office sends in response to constituents' queries or complaints, says, "Last year, I signed about 50,000 letters." Broadcast indecency "was the No. 1 mail item — above Iraq, above abortion — and it only really started coming in the last weeks of 2003, after the FCC's decision on Bono."

Upton began holding hearings on the issue last January, before the Super Bowl incident. ■

CURRENT SITUATION

Raising Fines

In late February, just after the Super Bowl, Clear Channel Radio President John Hogan sat contritely before the House Subcommittee on Telecommunications and the Internet. The subcommittee wanted to know whether increasing the fine for broadcasting indecency from $27,500 per incident to $500,000 would indeed curb indecency on the airwaves.

Hogan answered by announcing that Clear Channel had fired Bubba the Love Sponge. "More than anything else," he said, "I am embarrassed by Bubba's broadcasts." The DJ's shows in general, he added, "are tasteless, they are vulgar and they should not, do not and will not represent what Clear Channel is about." He also said Stern's show would be dropped by the six Clear Channel stations that carried it. Finally, he said that he had begun a "zero tolerance" policy regarding indecency on any Clear Channel airwaves. [25]

Hogan argued that because he had taken these measures without the threat of higher fines, the amount of the fines did not need to be raised. Television executives from ABC, NBC and Fox — all of whom said their networks oppose indecency — supported Hogan's point. They also spoke in conciliatory tones and made clear their desire to cooperate.

But author Steyer questions the media's professed sincerity. "For Clear Channel to say after eight years of Howard Stern, 'Oh, no, he's saying that on the air?' — it's a joke! These guys have laughed all the way to the bank, being completely irresponsible to kids and families as they've pursued the almighty buck," says Steyer, who is executive director of Common Sense Media, which calls itself "the leading nonpartisan organization dedicated to improving media and entertainment choices for kids and families."

Still, broadcast executives have responded positively to some suggestions from Congress, such as airing public-service announcements informing parents how to block programs with certain ratings using the V-chip technology. More than half of parents who own televisions with V-chips don't know how to use them, industry executives say. TV executives also have agreed to flash ratings of shows following every commercial break, so parents tuning in after the start of a program — the only time the ratings now are shown — can be better informed about content.

"The industry will do whatever it has to do, and that includes acceding to censorship of some sort, which they've done repeatedly when they feel a danger of getting caught in the crossfire of public outrage," says Couvares of Amherst College. Moreover, as author Chunovic and others say, the industry believes a willing attitude will result in less governmental intrusion into the marketplace.

Nevertheless, Congress is working on a bill to raise indecency fines to $500,000. The House passed its version on March 11 establishing a $500,000 ceiling, applicable even for first offenses. The Senate version — passed by committee on March 9 but still awaiting a floor vote — would establish a climbing scale, with $500,000 applicable for third and subsequent offenses. Both

Continued on p. 338

At Issue:

Are parents who seek stricter broadcast-indecency rules asking the government to do their job as parents?

yes

ROBERT THOMPSON
PROFESSOR OF POPULAR CULTURE
DIRECTOR, CENTER FOR THE STUDY OF POPULAR TELEVISION, SYRACUSE UNIVERSITY

WRITTEN FOR *THE CQ RESEARCHER*, MARCH 2004

Once upon a time a parent, in reasonably good conscience, could sit a kid in front of just about anything on TV. Not today. The industry has changed, the culture has changed and much of what's on television today is patently inappropriate for the very young.

So what's a parent to do?

Rudimentary childproofing technologies such as the V-chip and the ratings system are available, but most parents never bother to learn how to deploy them. Instead, many depend upon the federal government to tell kids what they can't watch by never letting it go on the air in the first place.

Children are at the center of nearly every discussion about broadcast indecency today. Most adults, after all, aren't going to be damaged by a vulgar word or a peek at an exposed breast. The outrage over the Super Bowl halftime show was nearly always expressed in terms of the fact that there were little kids in the audience.

Citizens have every right to demand more programming in the public interest. But in calling for the enhancement and enforcement of indecency rules, people aren't asking for the introduction of better programming but merely for the elimination of naughty words and sexual content. And millions of parents, many of whom object to the federal government's regulation of prayer in the classroom and resent it when public schools teach sex education, want the FCC to police the airwaves more aggressively than ever before.

The power to enforce the prior restraint of content in any medium, even a regulated one like broadcasting, is not one to be granted lightly, and especially not as a form of child care. If we legislate against anything inappropriate for a child, we may also eliminate good programming for adults. Little children shouldn't listen to Howard Stern; neither should they watch a performance of "King Lear." And, as much as we want to protect them, they shouldn't determine the content of everything seen on TV before 10 p.m.

Like liquor and toxic cleaning products, some TV content is a potential household hazard to children, to be responsibly managed by parents but not necessarily removed by federal fiat.

no

ROBERT PETERS
PRESIDENT, MORALITY IN MEDIA

WRITTEN FOR *THE CQ RESEARCHER*, MARCH 2004

In *FCC v. Pacifica Foundation*, the Supreme Court listed two characteristics of the broadcast media that justify regulation of indecent language. First, broadcasting is "a uniquely pervasive presence in the lives of all Americans" and confronts the citizen in the privacy of the home so that prior warnings alone cannot protect consumers from unexpected program content.

I would add that if adults can use a helping hand in shielding themselves from indecent programming, they can also use some help protecting their children.

Secondly, the court said, "broadcasting is uniquely accessible to children, even those too young to read." The government has an interest in protecting the "well-being of its youth," the court continued, and in "supporting parents' claim to authority in their own household."

Common sense ought to inform us that *Pacifica* was right about the government interests. Many children do not enjoy the blessings of a responsible parent. Consider parents who place no restrictions on what their kids, regardless of age and maturity, watch on TV or how long they watch. Some of these children may need the government's help, regardless of what a parent thinks.

As for the government supporting parents, most parents would welcome government's help in keeping their children away from indecent entertainment on radio and TV. The reasons should be obvious. Parents can't monitor their children every hour of every day from birth to full legal age. And despite their efforts, many parents fail to inculcate their children with a perfect moral sense and the strength to act on it. Moreover, parents can't always control the actions of someone else's kids.

As I see it, parents bear the primary responsibility for raising children, and undoubtedly there are parents who don't fulfill that responsibility and then blame others for their children's problems. But that does not mean that the whole job of raising children should fall on parents!

Human beings are gregarious in nature. We form governments to help order the communities in which we live and to protect us from irresponsible and unscrupulous persons who would harm the community or individuals in it — including children, who often need special protections.

Most parents aren't asking the FCC to do their job; they are asking the FCC to do its job.

Continued from p. 336

versions for the first time would allow the FCC to fine individual artists as well as licensees for indecency violations.

Edward O. Fritts, president and CEO of the National Association of Broadcasters, said voluntary industry initiatives are "far preferable to government regulation" when dealing with programming issues. While the group does not support the legislation as written, he said, "We hear the call of legislators and are committed to taking voluntary action to address this issue." [26]

AFP/Getty Images/Luke Frazza

Federal Communications Commission Chairman Michael K. Powell testifies on Feb. 11, 2004, on Capitol Hill on broadcast indecency following the Janet Jackson incident. "We must use our enforcement tools cautiously," Powell said. "Government action in this area can have a potential chilling effect on free speech."

Media Consolidation

The Senate's version of the bill also includes a temporary moratorium on media mergers or expansions, so Congress can study whether media consolidation is contributing to broadcast indecency. Eighty percent of the 91 major cable TV networks, serving more than 16 million homes, are owned or co-owned by only six media conglomerates. [27]

Both conservative and liberal organizations have claimed that having fewer companies controlling what's on the air leads to less concern for community tastes and standards. In turn, they argue, that allows networks to pursue the large, lucrative market of 18- to 34-year-old (mostly male) viewers with increasingly racy and raunchy content.

Both constituencies were concerned last fall when Congress debated whether to include a provision in the fiscal 2004 omnibus appropriations bill relaxing media-ownership rules. The White House and FCC Chairman Powell had favored allowing individual broadcast companies to own as much as 45 percent of the national television market, up from 35 percent. Congress eventually settled on a compromise of 39 percent, which still angered the two constituencies.

"Congress is basically an un-indicted co-conspirator here," says Jeff Chester, executive director of the Center for Digital Democracy, a media-policy group opposed to relaxing media ownership rules. "Congress has basically given to the broadcasters and cable every special-interest request they have made over the last decade."

FCC Commissioner Copps opposes the continued consolidation of the nation's media. For instance, when the agency last summer approved the merger between Spanish-language broadcaster Univision and the Hispanic Broadcasting Corporation, Copps said the deal would "take consolidation to new and threatening heights for those who receive their news and entertainment in Spanish. It involves not just TV, radio and cable, but Internet portals, recording labels and other promotional enterprises."

Univision was already the fifth-largest network and owns local stations reaching more than 40 percent of the country, Copps noted. [28]

When the agency approved News Corporation's acquisition last December of a multichannel distribution system plus a television station in the same market, Copps called the deal "an unprecedented level of consolidation," and asked rhetorically, "When is 'Big Media' big enough?" [29]

Rep. Barton, however, argues that greater media consolidation may lead to less indecency or vulgarity, rather than more. "If you've got a hundred people trying to get a piece of the market, the probability is that at least one of those hundred will do whatever it takes to get share. But when you have only four or five, there's a higher degree of probability that they're more willing to listen to community standards and are more responsive."

In fact, the Parents Television Council does see progress being made. Caldwell notes that merely the threat of FCC action "has been enough for broadcasters to start doing some things they should've been doing all along," such as firing Bubba the Love Sponge and the networks' recent decision to put live broadcasts — including sporting events — on 10-second delay transmission, which allows them to delete objectionable words. "I hope they continue to be more proactive in restricting content, rather than responding to an FCC fine," he says.

However, Peters of Morality in Media thinks the networks still aren't getting the message. "A lot more people in America would watch any one of the networks," he says, "if they'd stop crapping in our face." ■

OUTLOOK

Political Posturing

"The attention directed toward indecency really tends to be cyclical," FCC Chairman Powell said recently. "The envelope will be pushed until someone barks. Then, we recalibrate again and move forward." [30]

Whether the current debate recedes as part of a cycle depends on some factors that didn't figure into previous clashes over indecent programming. One is the dramatically increased fines. Predictions of their effectiveness vary widely.

"If you're the general manager of a television station [facing] a potential $500,000 fine, and any violation will be considered when you apply for relicensing, that's going to get your attention," says Rep. Heather Wilson, R-N.M. At the network level, though, it might not draw much attention at all. At the Feb. 26 hearing of the House Subcommittee on Telecommunications and the Internet, Rep. John Dingell, D-Mich., asked three network executives if the higher fines would be a credible deterrent. Two replied they didn't think so.

"Some fines may be levied, and some may actually stick," says Sterling of George Washington University. "But I'll be surprised if there's any fundamental change in the industry. You may see it for a season or two, but after that, it'll be business as usual.

"Let's not lose track of the fundamental issue here: money. Lots of it," he continues. "There's huge money to be made, and with the broadcast industry panicking over survival in a multichannel world, one way to do that is to shoot for the lowest common denominator. Clearly that's what's happened, and it's not going to stop. Maybe slow down a little, but not stop."

Others are even less optimistic, saying that the only reason Washington is paying any serious attention to the indecency issue right now is because 2004 is an election year.

"If I were a betting man, I'd bet that after a certain Tuesday in November this will all go away," author Chunovic says.

"It's a front-and-center controversy now," says Chester of the Center for Digital Democracy. "But after the election, this will fade into obscurity."

While hardly optimistic, Peters of Morality in Media is hopeful. "Is all this just a moment of political posturing? Well, the industry isn't going to change on its own," he says. "It's the old carrot-and-stick approach, and if the stick isn't there, they are not going to do what is right. But the potential for change is there." It all depends on whether the FCC maintains its current resolve to crack down on indecent programming, he says. "If they mean business and start taking their responsibility to uphold indecency standards, there's going to be a change."

In theory, the FCC is an independent agency, although the White House designates the commissioners, who must be confirmed by the Senate, and Congress authorizes funding and maintains oversight. Since many argue that the FCC is only as effective and engaged as Congress is, the ultimate question may be whether Congress means business.

"The industry is so powerful and the political leadership so spineless on this that the near-term changes will be small," predicts Steyer of Common Sense Media.

Rep. Wilson acknowledges that Congress hasn't been as diligent on indecency as it could have been, but she and several colleagues vow to follow the issue after the November elections.

Rep. Upton, whose father was appalled by the Super Bowl halftime show, intends to watch the issue, too. "Once our bill is law and it's in effect for a while, we'll come back and see how they're doing, probably around the end of the year," he says. "Are broadcasters and shock jocks meeting limits, or are they still getting fines?"

If they are still exceeding limits, he says, the industry can prepare for more government intervention. ■

Notes

[1] Quoted in Patrick Goldstein, "The Decency Debate: The Zipping Point," *Los Angeles Times*, March 28, 2004.

About the Author

William Triplett recently joined the *CQ Researcher* as a staff writer after covering science and the arts for such publications as *Smithsonian, Air & Space, Nature, Washingtonian* and *The Washington Post*. He also served as associate editor of *Capitol Style* magazine. He holds a B.A. in journalism from Ohio University and an M.A. in English literature from Georgetown University.

FOR MORE INFORMATION

Center for Digital Democracy, 1718 Connecticut Ave., N.W., Suite 200, Washington, DC 20009; (202) 986-2220; www.democraticmedia.org/index.html. A media-policy organization committed to encouraging non-commercial, public-interest programming and free access to the Internet.

Center for the Study of Popular Television, S. I. Newhouse School of Public Communications, Syracuse University, Syracuse, NY 13244; (315) 443-4077; http://newhouse.syr.edu/research/POPTV/mission.htm. Examines the impact of entertainment television on popular culture.

Common Sense Media, 500 Treat Ave., Suite 100, San Francisco, CA 94110; (415) 643-6300; www.commonsensemedia.org. A nonpartisan, nonprofit organization advocating media programming that serves children's interests.

Family Research Council, 801 G St., N.W., Washington, DC 20001; (202) 393-2100; www.frc.org. A public-policy group promoting traditional societal and cultural values.

The Henry J. Kaiser Family Foundation, 2400 Sand Hill Rd., Menlo Park, CA 94025; (650) 854-9400; www.kff.org. A nonpartisan, nonprofit foundation that studies major health-care issues confronting America.

Morality in Media, 475 Riverside Dr., Suite 239, New York, NY 10115; (212) 870-3222; www.moralityinmedia.org. A national, nonprofit organization "established in 1962 to combat obscenity and uphold decency standards in the media."

National Association of Broadcasters, 1771 N St., N.W., Washington, DC 20036; (202) 429-5300; www.nab.org. The main trade association representing television and radio broadcasters, though the Big Four TV networks are no longer members.

National Cable and Telecommunications Association, 1724 Massachusetts Ave., N.W., Washington, DC 20036; (202) 775-3550; www.ncta.com. The major trade association for cable companies.

Parents Television Council, 707 Wilshire Blvd., Suite 2075, Los Angeles, CA 90017; (213) 629-9255; www.parentstv.org. A conservative organization focusing on improving the quality of television programming.

[2] *Ibid.*

[3] See Lynn Smith, "Can You Say That on TV?" *Los Angeles Times*, Jan. 19, 2004, p. E1.

[4] See http://cme.kff.org/Key=1959.CJr.J.D.MW2Tr9.

[5] See Kaiser Family Foundation, *Sex on TV 3: Content and Context*, February 2004.

[6] See Scott Dodd, "America Divided on Decency; Culture War Especially Hot in States Bush Won, Including the Carolinas," *The Charlotte Observer*, Feb. 23, 2004, p. 1A.

[7] See Eric Adler and Steve Paul, "The Debate Over Decency: Media and Morality Face Off," *The Kansas City Star*, Feb. 12, 2004. See also U.S. Department of Justice, "Uniform Crime Reports, January — June 2003," Dec. 15, 2003, p.1.

[8] National Campaign to Prevent Teen Pregnancy, "Recent Trends in Teen Pregnancy, Sexual Activity and Contraceptive Use," Fact Sheet, February 2004. See also Nina Bernstein, "Behind Fall in Pregnancy, A New Teenage Culture of Restraint," *The New York Times*, March 7, 2004, p. A1, and Kathy Koch, "Encouraging Teen Abstinence," *The CQ Researcher*, July 10, 1998, pp. 577-600.

[9] Testimony before U.S. House Subcommittee on Telecommunications and the Internet, Jan. 28, 2004.

[10] Michael K. Powell, FCC chairman, letter to Rep. John Dingell, March 2, 2004.

[11] See "Powell's Agenda for '04; FCC chief discusses initiatives on content, localism, indecency," *Broadcasting and Cable*, Jan. 26, 2004, p. 30.

[12] See Charles S. Clark, "The Obscenity Debate," *The CQ Researcher*, Dec. 20, 1991, pp. 969-992.

[13] See Frank Ahrens, "FCC Says Bono Profanity Violated Standards, but Won't Fine NBC," *The Washington Post*, March 19, 2004, p. E1.

[14] See http://hraunfoss.fcc.gov/edocs_public/attachmatch/FCC-04-43A2.doc.

[15] See Frank Ahrens, "Over the Line? Only if Over the Air," *The Washington Post*, Feb. 3, 2004, p. E1.

[16] In 1996, Playboy Entertainment Group sued the government over the FCC's attempt to force adult cable channels to scramble their signals. Playboy won, but the government appealed, ultimately to the Supreme Court, which upheld the initial decision that the attempt violated First Amendment rights. However, the court asserted that the government did have "compelling interest" in protecting children from indecency on cable. See http://hraunfoss.fcc.gov/edocs_public/attachmatch/FCC-01-340A1.pdf.

[17] Testimony before U.S. House Subcommittee on Telecommunications and the Internet, Feb. 11, 2004.

[18] See Ahrens, *op. cit.*, Feb. 3, 2004.

[19] See Steve Carney, "Around the Dial; FCC Official's Plea Goes Unheeded," *Los Angeles Times*, March 22, 2004, p. 28.

[20] See Louis Chunovic, *One Foot on the Floor: The Curious Evolution of Sex on Television from "I Love Lucy" to "South Park"* (2000), pp. 19, 27.

[21] See Clark, *op. cit.*, p. 973.

[22] See Chunovic, *op. cit.*, p. 114.

[23] See Kenneth Jost, "Children's Television," *The CQ Researcher*, Aug. 15, 1997, p. 736.

[24] Quoted in Koch, *op. cit.*, p. 588.

[25] Testimony before House Subcommittee on Telecommunications and the Internet, Feb. 26, 2004.

[26] Statement, March 3, 2004.

[27] Goldstein, *op. cit.* For background, see David Hatch, "Media Ownership," *The CQ Researcher*, Oct. 10, 2003, pp. 845-868.

[28] Statement, Sept. 22, 2003.

[29] Statement, Dec. 19, 2003.

[30] See "Powell's '04 Agenda," *op. cit.*

Bibliography

Selected Sources

Books

Chunovic, Louis, *One Foot on the Floor: The Curious Evolution of Sex on Television from "I Love Lucy" to "South Park,"* TV Books, 2000.

A former television journalist argues that, despite changing audience tastes and standards, network executives and censors face the same challenges they did when commercial television first appeared, such as: How best to hook large numbers of viewers without offending too many of them?

McChesney, Robert, *Rich Media, Poor Democracy: Communication Politics in Dubious Times*, University of Illinois Press, 1999.

A left-leaning media scholar says television's mercantile demands, including racy material to draw viewers, should be balanced by governmental subsidies for nonprofit television, antitrust suits against media conglomerates and vigorous regulation of commercial broadcasters.

Minow, Newton, and Craig LaMay, *Abandoned in the Wasteland: Children, Television, and the First Amendment*, Hill & Wang, 1995.

As chairman of the Federal Communications Commission (FCC) in 1961, Minow shook the industry with his description of television as "a vast wasteland." Writing with a communications scholar, he charges broadcasters with exploiting children for profit while hiding behind First Amendment guarantees.

Steyer, James P., *The Other Parent: The Inside Story of the Media's Effect on Our Children*, Atria Books, 2002.

A Stanford University professor argues that today's media constantly bombard children with images of commercialism, sex and violence, forcing them to confront an adult world long before they are ready.

Articles

Brown, Patricia Leigh, "Sex Appeals; Hey There, Couch Potatoes: Hot Enough for You?" *The New York Times*, July 27, 2003, Section 4, p. 1.

A cultural reporter asks whether "the current deluge of sex-charged programming indicates a healthy affirmation of American sexuality or the transformation of prime time into a Hooters franchise."

Rutenberg, Jim, "Few Viewers Object as Unbleeped Bleep Words Spread on Network TV," *The New York Times*, Jan. 25, 2003, Section B, p. 7.

Even following rock singer Bono's saying the F-word on live television and other similar incidents, the FCC reported receiving few complaints.

Smith, Lynn, "Can You Say That on TV? Just When It Seems As If Nothing Is Too Profane, Recent Incidents have Gotten the Feds Involved," *Los Angeles Times*, Jan. 19, 2004, Section E, p. 1.

The author reviews the current controversy over FCC indecency standards and television's historical attempts to test their limits.

Teitelman, Bram, "Radio Reacts to Indecency Flak," *Billboard.com*, March 13, 2004.

Major radio corporations have issued guidelines to their stations regarding new limits on indecent content, signaling the industry's willingness to cooperate with Congress and the FCC.

Witte, Griff, "Broadcasters Promise to Curtail Indecency," *The Washington Post*, Feb. 27, 2004, p. E01.

The threat of new legislation to strengthen anti-indecency rules prompts broadcasting executives to tell Congress they will be more vigilant about content

Reports and Studies

"Dereliction of Duty: How the Federal Communications Commission has Failed the Public," Parents Television Council, 2004. See www.parentstv.org/ptc/publications/reports/fccwhitepaper/main.asp.

The group says the FCC has a poor record of holding corporate broadcasters accountable for indecent programming.

"Impact of the Media on Adolescent Sexual Attitudes and Behaviors," Medical Institute for Sexual Health, 2004. See www.medinstitute.org/media/index.htm.

The institute found a significant lack of knowledge about how media sex imagery affects children and youth.

"Middletown Media Studies," Ball State University Center for Media Design, 2004. See www.commonsensemedia.org/information/index.php?article=latestresearch.

A team of researchers discovered that 101 Americans' exposure to media in almost all forms was nearly twice as much as the participants had estimated.

"Sex on Television 3: Content and Context," The Kaiser Family Foundation, 2003. See www.kff.org/entmedia/3325-index.cfm.

The third biennial study sponsored by the prestigious foundation finds that while the amount of sex on television remains high, there are also increased references to safe sex and abstinence.

The Next Step:

Additional Articles from Current Periodicals

Broadcast Industry

Ahrens, Frank, "Critics Blame Big Media for Sleaze Factor," *The Washington Post*, Feb. 11, 2004, p. E1.
Some say massive media conglomerates make broadcasters impervious to the concerns of local viewers.

Carter, Bill, "Broadcasters Wrestle F.C.C. for Remote," *The New York Times*, March 15, 2004, p. C1.
The networks introduce a slew of new measures in response to the indecency outcry, including new time-delay features and additional content oversight.

McKee, Sandra, "NASCAR Drivers Watch Road, Words," *The Baltimore Sun*, March 21, 2004, p. 2E.
NASCAR initiates a policy of serious fines and penalties for drivers who curse on radio or television.

Montgomery, David, and Frank Ahrens, "Howard Stern Booted in Clear Channel Indecency Crackdown," *The Washington Post*, Feb. 26, 2004, p. C1.
Clear Channel Radio dropped Howard Stern's show as part of its indecency crackdown, but the original shock jock stayed on the air in most markets.

Changing Standards

Jonsson, Patrik, "Swearing, Swearers and FCC's New Rulebook," *The Christian Science Monitor*, Dec. 17, 2003, p. 3.
Changing cultural standards that make swearing seem acceptable may have left the Federal Communications Commission's (FCC) regulations behind the times.

Kelly, Katy, *et al.*, "Trash TV," *U.S. News & World Report*, Feb. 16, 2004, p. 48.
American television has come a long way since married couples slept in separate beds.

Peyser, Marc, "Family TV Goes Down the Tube," *Newsweek*, Feb. 23, 2004, p. 52.
Factors influencing TV content are too profound for congressional hearings to make a difference; outrage always increases in election years.

Stanley, Alessandra, "It's a Fact of Life: Prime-Time Shows Are Getting Sexier," *The New York Times*, Feb. 5, 2003, p. E1.
A new study confirms what everyone already knows: Sex sells, and there's more of it on TV than ever before, especially during prime time.

Congress and the FCC

Ahrens, Frank, "FCC Says Bono Profanity Violated Standards, but Won't Fine NBC," *The Washington Post*, March 19, 2004, p. E1.
The FCC reverses an earlier ruling that the "F-word" was not indecent, but declines to issue fine.

Ahrens, Frank, "Over the Line? Only If Over the Air," *The Washington Post*, Feb. 3, 2004, p. E1.
More viewers spent prime time watching cable rather than the broadcast networks in 2003, raising questions about the sensibility of regulating broadcast but not cable TV.

Cook, John, "Will the FCC Go After Cable?" *Chicago Tribune*, Feb. 8, 2004, Arts and Entertainment Section, p. 1.
Media lobbyists say the four main broadcasters are forced to be more risqué by unregulated cable and satellite programs.

Epstein, Edward, "GOP Representative Would Ban Dirty Words From TV," *San Francisco Chronicle*, Jan. 9, 2004, p. A4.
Outraged by the FCC's decision that Bono's use of a curse word in its adjectival form was not indecent, Rep. Doug Ose pushes legislation to ban seven words in all their forms.

Jones, Chris, and John Cook, "Radio Chief Says He's 'Ashamed'," *Chicago Tribune*, Feb. 27, 2004, News Section, p. 9.
The possibility that radio and TV personalities, not just the station owners, would have to pay indecency fines stirs opposition.

Krim, Jonathan, "Congress Acts to Curb Offensive Programs," *The Washington Post*, March 10, 2004, p. E1.
The Senate's new indecency bill would raise fines for indecency and roll back rules passed last year allowing greater media consolidation.

Zurawik, David, "FCC Hearings Seen as Just Theater," *The Baltimore Sun*, Feb. 11, 2004, p. 1E.
Media experts say the current hullabaloo over indecency is unlikely to result in major changes; important issues, like media oligopolies, are not addressed.

Free Speech and the First Amendment

"Collision Course on the Airwaves," *Chicago Tribune*, March 14, 2004, News Section, p. 1.
The renewed vigor of government efforts to regulate TV and radio content raises predictable questions regarding free speech.

Bennett, William, "The First Amendment, Public Pollution and Cultural Air Ducts," *Chicago Tribune*, March 18, 2004, Commentary Section, p. 29.
The virtues "czar" defends government regulations of speech on radio and TV, drawing a distinction between censoring and censuring.

Chapman, Steve, "Indecent Moves Toward Federal Censorship," *Chicago Tribune*, Feb. 12, 2004, Commentary Section, p. 27.
America has a long, mortifying history of censorship; the only TV Michael Powell should be allowed to regulate is the one in his own living room.

Sharma, Amol, "Indecency Bill May Raise First Amendment Issues," *CQ Weekly*, March 13, 2004, p. 635.
Several provisions of the new indecency hill appear dubious to legal experts, who expect it to be challenged in court.

On-Air Indecency

Ahrens, Frank, "Nasty Language on Live TV Renews Old Debate," *The Washington Post*, Dec. 13, 2003, p. A1.
The flaps over swearing by Nicole Richie and Bono illustrate the growing concern over broadcast indecency.

Carney, Steve, "Shock-Jock Antics Stir Up More Tough Talk by FCC," *Los Angeles Times*, Aug. 23, 2002, Part 6, p. 28.
Radio shock jocks Opie and Anthony are canceled after they air a segment featuring a couple having sex in New York's St. Patrick's Cathedral.

Parker, Lonnae O'Neal, "Battle Station in a Rap 'Revolution'," *The Washington Post*, Feb. 2, 2002, p. C1.
The FCC fined a station for indecency when the station aired a song by a feminist poet-performer criticizing the misogyny of contemporary rap music.

Sherman, Ed, "FCC, CBS, NFL Come Undone Over Jackson's Halftime Stunt," *Chicago Tribune*, Feb. 3, 2004, News Section, p. 1.
Indignation and outrage over Janet Jackson's Super Bowl halftime stunt triggered a new round of discussions over entertainment standards.

Parents' Role

Goldstein, Patrick, "The Big Picture: A Parent Who Said 'Enough'," *Los Angeles Times*, March 16, 2004, p. D1.
One parent's 19-month quest to get the FCC to take action against a raunchy popular DJ shows how weak the FCC's enforcement really is.

Kluger, Bruce, "Parents: Talk to Teens About TV's Casual Sex," *USA Today*, Dec. 22, 2003, p. 19A.
Seventy-two percent of 15-to-17-year-olds believe TV influences their peers' attitudes toward sex, but teens can learn positive lessons with the right amount of parental guidance.

Nevius, C.W., "Parents Fear Perils of Media, Poll Shows," *San Francisco Chronicle*, May 22, 2003, p. A1.
A new public-interest group's survey shows that parents are deeply troubled by what is on the air and on screen.

Violence

Bauder, David, "TV Violence Escalating, Study Finds," *Chicago Tribune*, Dec. 10, 2003, Metro Section, p. 2.
A media-watchdog group says that TV violence has increased markedly in the past four years.

Collins, Scott, "CBS Ahead of Curve on 'Helter'," *Los Angeles Times*, Feb. 23, 2004, p. D1.
Concerned about overly graphic violence, CBS decides to alter its adaptation of "Helter Skelter," the 1969 movie about the Charles Manson murders.

Lamb, Gregory, "TV's Higher Threshold of Pain," *The Christian Science Monitor*, Aug. 23, 2002, p. 13.
Contrary to expectations that TV violence would decrease after 9/11, a study found that torture and sadism are being shown at twice the previous rate.

Citing *The CQ Researcher*

Sample formats for citing these reports in a bibliography include the ones listed below. Preferred styles and formats vary, so please check with your instructor or professor.

MLA Style

Jost, Kenneth. "Rethinking the Death Penalty." The CQ Researcher 16 Nov. 2001: 945-68.

APA Style

Jost, K. (2001, November 16). Rethinking the death penalty. *The CQ Researcher, 11,* 945-968.

Chicago Style

Jost, Kenneth. "Rethinking the Death Penalty." *CQ Researcher,* November 16, 2001, 945-968.

CQ Researcher

Published by CQ Press, a division of Congressional Quarterly Inc.

thecqresearcher.com

School Desegregation

How can the promise of equal education be fulfilled?

This May the nation celebrates the 50th anniversary of the Supreme Court's landmark decision declaring racial segregation in public schools unconstitutional. But the promise of equal educational opportunity for all offered by the once-controversial *Brown v. Board of Education* ruling is widely viewed as unfulfilled. Today, an increasing percentage of African-American and Latino students attend schools with mostly other minorities — a situation that critics blame on recent Supreme Court decisions easing judicial supervision of desegregation plans. Black and Latino students also lag far behind whites in academic achievement. School-desegregation advocates call for stronger steps to break down racial and ethnic isolation and to upgrade schools that serve minority students. Critics of mandatory desegregation, however, say stronger accountability, stricter academic standards and parental choice will do more to improve education for all students.

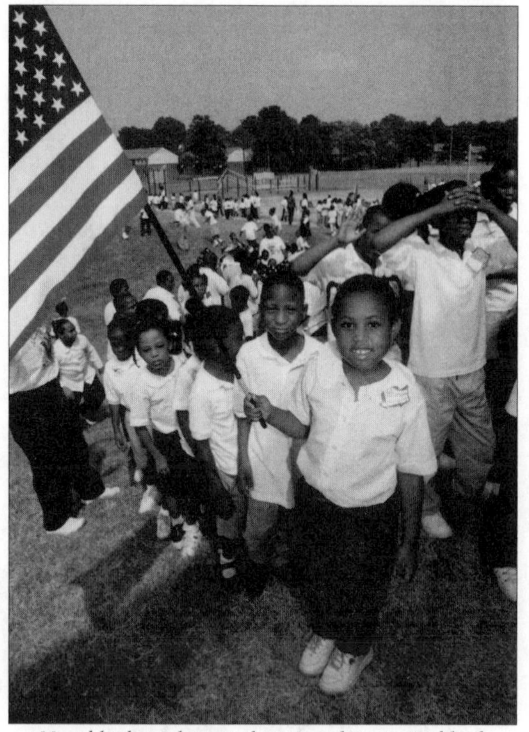

Most black students today attend majority-black schools, evidence of what civil rights advocates call resegregation.

INSIDE THIS REPORT

The CQ Researcher • April 23, 2004 • www.thecqresearcher.com
Volume 14, Number 15 • Pages 345-372

CQ PRESS

RECIPIENT OF SOCIETY OF PROFESSIONAL JOURNALISTS AWARD FOR EXCELLENCE ◆ AMERICAN BAR ASSOCIATION SILVER GAVEL AWARD

THE ISSUES

BACKGROUND

CURRENT SITUATION

OUTLOOK

SIDEBARS AND GRAPHICS

FOR FURTHER RESEARCH

Cover: Most black and Latino students today attend predominantly minority schools. All of the students at the Georgia Avenue Elementary School in Memphis, Tenn., are African-American. (Memphis Public Schools)

April 23, 2004
Volume 14, Number 15

MANAGING EDITOR: Thomas J. Colin

ASSISTANT MANAGING EDITOR: Kathy Koch

ASSOCIATE EDITOR: Kenneth Jost

STAFF WRITERS: Mary H. Cooper, David Masci, William Triplett

CONTRIBUTING WRITERS: Sarah Glazer, David Hatch, David Hosansky, Patrick Marshall, Tom Price, Jane Tanner

DESIGN/PRODUCTION EDITOR: Olu B. Davis

ASSISTANT EDITOR: Kenneth Lukas

A Division of Congressional Quarterly Inc.

SENIOR VICE PRESIDENT/GENERAL MANAGER: John A. Jenkins

DIRECTOR, LIBRARY PUBLISHING: Kathryn C. Suárez

DIRECTOR, EDITORIAL OPERATIONS: Ann Davies

CONGRESSIONAL QUARTERLY INC.

CHAIRMAN: Andrew Barnes

VICE CHAIRMAN: Andrew P. Corty

PRESIDENT AND PUBLISHER: Robert W. Merry

The CQ Researcher (ISSN 1056-2036) is printed on acid-free paper. Published weekly, except Jan. 2, April 9, July 2, July 9, Aug. 6, Aug. 13, Nov. 26 and Dec. 31, by CQ Press, a division of Congressional Quarterly Inc. Annual subscription rates for institutions start at $625. For pricing, call 1-800-834-9020, ext. 1906. To purchase a *CQ Researcher* report in print or electronic format (PDF), visit www.cqpress.com or call 866-427-7737. A single report is $10. Bulk purchase discounts and electronic-rights licensing are also available. Periodicals postage paid at Washington, D.C., and additional mailing offices. POSTMASTER: Send address changes to *The CQ Researcher*, 1255 22nd St., N.W., Suite 400, Washington, D.C. 20037.

School Desegregation

BY KENNETH JOST

THE ISSUES

Civil rights advocates consider Louisville-Jefferson County, Ky., a model of desegregation — but don't tell that to David McFarland.

McFarland says the county's claimed success in racial mixing comes at the expense of his children's education. In his view, Stephen and Daniel were denied admission to the school of their choice simply because they are white. "Diversity should not be used as an excuse for discrimination," he says.

The county's 19 traditional schools — with their reputation for good discipline, structured teaching and parental involvement — are so popular that they cannot accommodate all the students who want to attend. So students are assigned to schools by lottery.

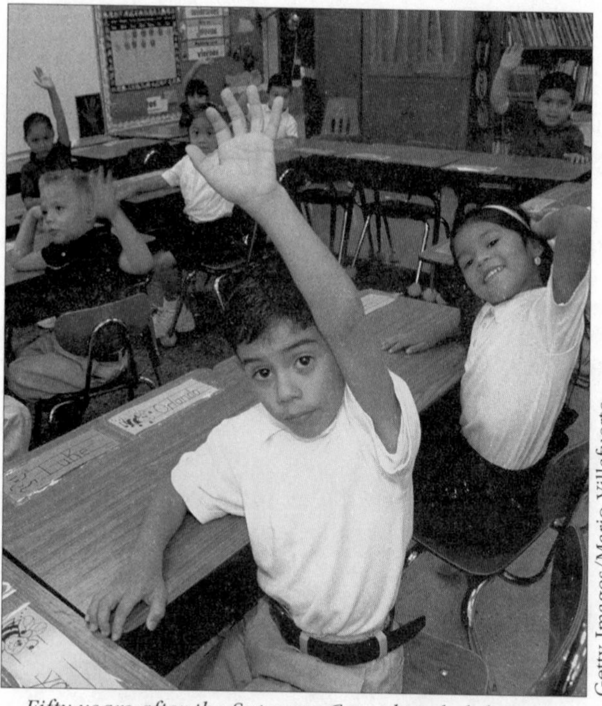

Getty Images/Mario Villafuerte

Fifty years after the Supreme Court handed down its historic Brown v. Board of Education *decision declaring racial segregation in public schools unconstitutional, most black and Latino students attend predominantly minority schools. At Birdwell Elementary in Tyler, Texas, 60 percent of the students are Hispanic.*

To keep enrollments at each school within racial guidelines, a separate list of African-American applicants is maintained. The county's voluntary "managed-choice" program — which replaced a court-ordered desegregation plan in 2000 — is designed to prevent any school from having fewer than 15 percent or more than 50 percent African-American students.

The program works. In a countywide system where African-Americans comprise about one-third of the 96,000 students, only one school has a majority-black enrollment.

Jefferson County was one of the first school systems in the country to begin integrating after the U.S. Supreme Court handed down its historic *Brown v. Board of Education* decision declaring racial segregation in schools unconstitutional. [1]

Today, as the 50th anniversary of the May 17, 1954, ruling approaches, Jefferson County stands in stark contrast to the ethnic and racial patterns in most other school districts. Across the country today, most black students attend majority-black schools, and an even larger percentage of Latino students attend majority-Latino schools — evidence of what civil rights advocates call resegregation.

In Louisville, McFarland and three other families sued in federal court to bar the school system from using race in any student assignments. [2] "It can't be fair to discriminate against a white male because he's a white male," says Ted Gordon, the plaintiffs' attorney. "That can't be fair in anybody's book."

School administrators, however, say a ruling for McFarland would effectively bring back racial segregation in Louisville. "We would be back to majority-white suburban schools and majority-black inner-city schools," says Byron Leet, lead attorney for the school system. "That would not be in the best interest of young people in the community, who have benefited greatly from attending desegregated schools."

The case is being closely watched at a time when school desegregation litigation nationwide is dormant, but parents in some areas are asking courts to block administrators from continuing to use race to promote integration.

"If the court decides that the sensitive way that Louisville has gone about trying to achieve integration is not acceptable, then I worry that there may be little or no way to reap the benefits of integration for our primary and secondary schools," says Chinh Quang Le, assistant counsel for the NAACP Legal Defense and Educational Fund, which filed a friend of the court brief on the side of the Louisville school system. The fund directed the court challenges against racial segregation that produced the *Brown* decision and remains the principal litigation center in school desegregation cases.

Today's pattern of school desegregation litigation underscores the changes in the nation's schools — and in the nation's attitudes toward race — since the *Brown* decision. [3] While the ruling is universally hailed, its promise is widely recognized as unfulfilled and its implications for educational policies today vigorously debated.

"*Brown v. Board of Education* is one of the signal legal events of our time," says Education Secretary Rod Paige, who himself attended racially segregated schools through college in his native Mississippi. But the ruling did not eliminate all the vestiges of segregation, Paige quickly adds. "If the goal

Minority School Districts Receive Less Funding

School districts with high enrollments of minority or low-income students typically receive fewer funds compared to districts with more white or wealthier students. In 11 states, the funding gap between white and minority school districts is more than $1,000 per pupil.

Per-Pupil Funding Gaps Between Districts with High and Low Minority Enrollments

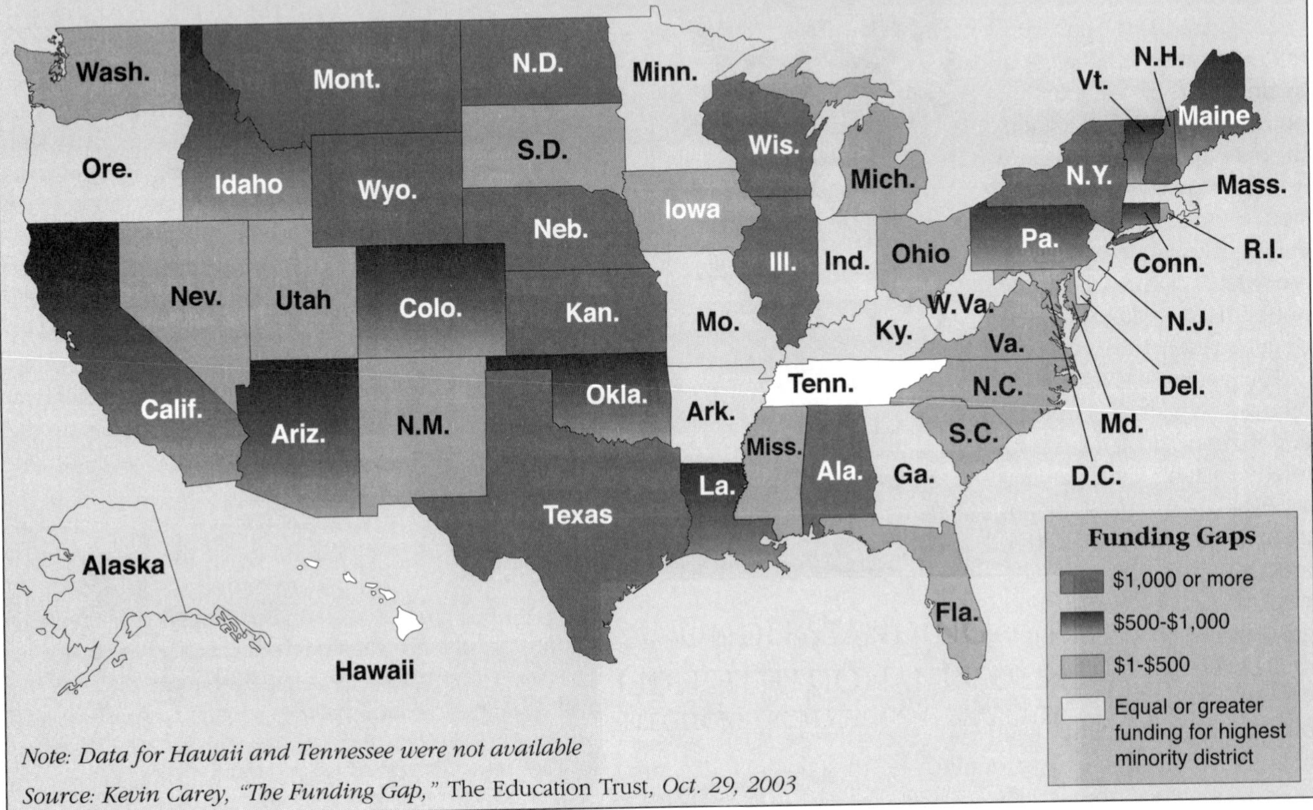

Note: Data for Hawaii and Tennessee were not available

Source: Kevin Carey, "The Funding Gap," The Education Trust, *Oct. 29, 2003*

was equality in education — to level the educational playing field for all children, especially children of color — we've yet to achieve that," he says.

"We have an unfulfilled promise of *Brown*," says Julie Underwood, general counsel for the National School Boards Association, which once resisted and now strongly supports desegregation. "If the civil rights people were actually seeking fully integrated public schools, we have not reached that point."

Civil rights advocates acknowledge that *Brown* fundamentally transformed American schools — and America itself. "Both whites and blacks have been in far more integrated settings than anyone would have imagined before *Brown*," says Gary Orfield, a professor at Harvard's Graduate School of Education and director of the Harvard Civil Rights Project.

But Orfield and other desegregation advocates also maintain that the hard-won progress of the post-*Brown* era has not merely stalled but is now being reversed. "We've been going backward almost every place in the country since the 1990s," Orfield says.

A coterie of educational conservatives from academia and various advocacy groups challenge both this view of present-day conditions and policies for the future. While praising the *Brown* decision, they argue that today's racial separation is not the result of law or policy and that race-conscious assignments violate *Brown*'s central meaning.

Brown "stands for the principles of integration and color-blindness," says Curt Levey, director of legal and public affairs for the Washington-based Center for Individual Rights.

"It's unfortunate that in the past few decades we have abandoned those principles in favor of racial preferences," Levey says. "It's just another form of discrimination." The center has

School-Integration Trend Reversing

The Supreme Court's landmark 1954 Brown v. Board of Education *ruling declared racial segregation in public schools unconstitutional. But after more than three decades, the desegration trend in U.S. schools reversed after 1988 — particularly in the South. Then a series of Supreme Court decisions between 1991 and 1995 eased the pressure on school districts to continue desegregation efforts. Today U.S. classrooms are almost as segregated as they were in the late 1960s, and some experts say the trend is likely to continue.*

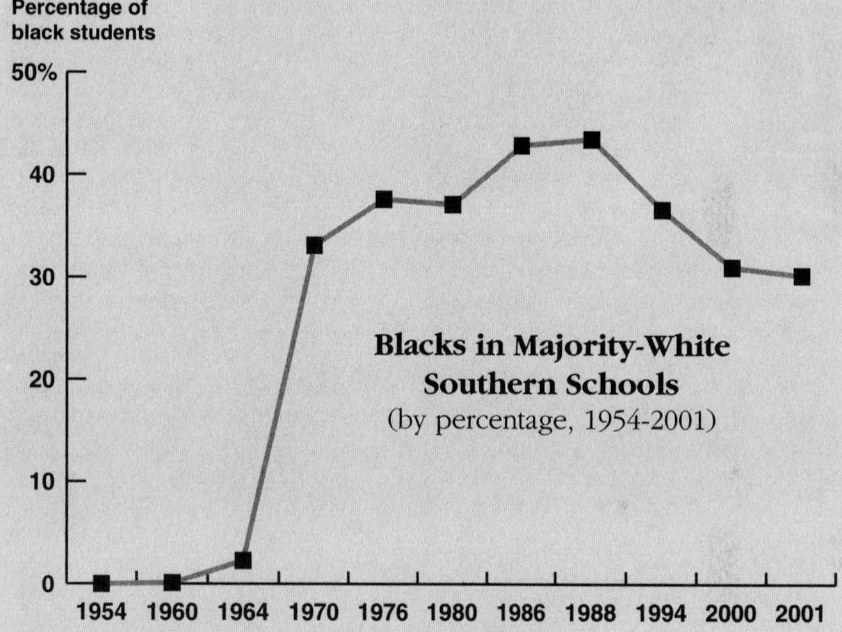

*Source: Gary Orfield and Chungmei Lee, "*Brown *at 50: King's Dream or* Plessy's *Nightmare?" The Harvard Civil Rights Project, January 2004*

represented plaintiffs challenging affirmative action in higher education and, in one case from Minneapolis, racial guidelines in public schools.

"Most of our schools became substantially racially balanced," says David J. Armor, a professor at George Mason University School of Public Policy in Fairfax, Va., and the leading academic critic of mandatory integration. Armor acknowledges that there's been "some resegregation of schools" but attributes the trend to changes in ethnic and racial residential patterns and the higher percentages of blacks and Latinos in public schools.

The debate over desegregation is waged against the disheartening persistence of large gaps in learning and achievement between whites, blacks and Latinos. "The magnitude of the gap is simply appalling," says Abigail Thernstrom, a senior scholar at the Manhattan Institute and co-author with her husband Stephan Thernstrom of a book on the subject. [4]

"A typical black student is graduating from high school with junior high school skills," Thernstrom says, citing figures from the National Assessment of Educational Progress (NAEP) — informally known as "the nation's report card." Hispanics, she says, "are doing only a tad better."

Traditional civil rights advocates acknowledge the gap, but they say that closing the gap requires more thoroughgoing desegregation and better funding for schools with large numbers of minority or low-income students. But educational conservatives discount those solutions, calling instead for changing "school culture" by improving discipline, teaching and student behavior.

One path to those changes, conservatives say, is "school choice" — vouchers that help students pay for private school tuition and charter schools that operate with freedom from traditional regulations. Traditional civil rights groups generally oppose vouchers and voice some doubts about charter schools, saying they drain support from public schools and risk further resegregation of minority students.

The policy debates underscore the shared view that *Brown* — despite its iconic status — has not proved a complete success. "You have to say it was a partial failure," says James Patterson, a professor emeritus of history at Brown University and author of a new account of the ruling and its impact.

Theodore Shaw, director of the Legal Defense Fund, agrees: "*Brown* changed everything and yet did not change everything."

As the nation prepares to unite in celebrating *Brown*, here are some of the issues that divide Americans 50 years later:

Is racial imbalance in schools increasing due to court actions?

North Carolina's Charlotte-Mecklenburg County school system in 1971 became the first in the country to operate under a court-ordered desegregation plan using wide-scale busing to achieve racial balance in school populations. Under the plan, African-Americans comprised between 30 percent and

Latinos' Unheralded Struggles for Equal Education

When school board officials in Lemon Grove, Calif., became concerned in 1930 that Mexican-American students were slowing down the Anglo pupils, they hit upon a simple solution: build a new school solely for the Mexican-Americans.

To the board's surprise, however, Mexican-Americans in the small border community protested, deriding the new facility as a "barn." And — more than two decades before the Supreme Court declared racial segregation in public schools unconstitutional — they won a lower-court order forcing the school board to dismantle the plans for a dual system of education. [1]

The Lemon Grove incident is one of many efforts by Latinos to fight for educational equity well before the Supreme Court's landmark 1954 decision in *Brown v. Board of Education*. The history of those efforts, however, has gone largely untold. "These cases are not taught, even in law school," says Margaret Montoya, a professor at the University of New Mexico School of Law.

Today, Latinos continue to receive far less attention in school desegregation debates than African-Americans even though Latinos now comprise the nation's largest ethnic minority, and Latino students are somewhat more likely than blacks to be in ethnically identifiable schools.

"We don't see an equal commitment on the part of educational equity for Latinos," says James Ferg-Cadima, legislative staff attorney for the Mexican American Legal Defense and Educational Fund (MALDEF) in Washington.

The Lemon Grove ruling was never appealed and had no further impact in California. Chicano families won a similar ruling from a lower court in Texas around the same time. It, too, did nothing to undo the advancing segregation of Mexican-American students in that state. [2]

In 1946, however, a federal appeals court in California ruled in favor of Mexican-American parents contesting school segregation in four districts in Orange County, south of Los Angeles. Ferg-Cadima says the case "could have been a precursor to *Brown v. Board of Education*," but the school districts decided not to appeal. The ruling did lead to a law in 1947, however, that barred school segregation in the state. The act was signed by then-Gov. Earl Warren, who later became chief justice and author of the *Brown* decision. [3]

Perversely, Mexican-American families prevailed in some of their early legal efforts on the grounds that they were white and could not be segregated as black students were. "We have not been treated as a white subgroup, and we don't think of ourselves as a white subgroup," Montoya says. "But when the litigation was being developed, that seemed to be a reasonable way of trying to get kids educational rights." One consequence, Montoya adds, has been "to drive a wedge between Latinos and African-Americans."

The Supreme Court recognized Latinos as a separate group for desegregation purposes only in 1973 in a case from Denver. [4] By that time, however, the justices were about to pull back on school-desegregation remedies. "About the time we could have profited from *Brown* and used it ourselves, the protection starts crumbling," Ferg-Cadima says. Latinos have been the principal beneficiaries, however, of the Supreme Court's unanimous 1974 decision that school districts must make sure that non-English-speaking students are given language skills needed to profit from school attendance. [5]

Language is among the educational barriers distinctive to Latino students. Another, Ferg-Cadima says, is the migratory status of many Latino families, especially in agricultural areas in California, Texas and the Southwest.

Today, most Latino students attend majority-Latino schools in every region of the country, according to The Harvard Civil Rights Project. [6] As with African-American students, ethnic isolation for Latinos increased through the 1990s. The most intense segregation is found in the Northeast, where 45 percent of Hispanic students attend schools that are 90 to 100 percent Hispanic.

As for educational achievement, Latinos lag far behind white students and only slightly ahead of African-Americans. The average Latino student scored around the 25th percentile in both reading and mathematics in the 1999 National Assessment of Educational Performance — the so-called nation's report card. [7]

"The one lesson from *Brown* for all minority communities is that educational equity must be battled for on all fronts — it's something that has to be sought out," Ferg-Cadima says. "The schoolhouse gate isn't always open for our kids, so we have to fight for schools to be open and conducive to learning for all students."

[1] Robert R. Alvarez Jr., "The Lemon Grove Incident: The Nation's First Successful Desegregation Court Case," *The Journal of San Diego History*, Vol. 32, No. 2 (spring 1986). Alvarez is the son of the lead plaintiff in the case, *Alvarez v. Board of Trustees of the Lemon Grove School District*.

[2] See "Project Report: De Jure Segregation of Chicanos in Texas Schools," *Harvard Civil Rights-Civil Liberties Law Review*, Vol. 7, No. 2 (March 1972), pp. 307-391. The authors are Jorge C. Rangel and Carlos M. Alcala.

[3] See Vicki L. Ruiz, "'We Always Tell Our Children They Are Americans': *Méndez v. Westminster* and the California Road to *Brown v. Board of Education*," *The College Board Review*, No. 200 (fall 2003), pp. 20-27. See also Charles Wollenberg, *All Deliberate Speed: Segregation and Exclusion in California Schools, 1855-1975* (1976), pp. 108-135.

[4] The case is *Keyes v. Denver School District No. 1*, 413 U.S. 921 (1973).

[5] The case, brought by non-English-speaking Chinese students in San Francisco, is *Lau v. Nichols*, 414 U.S. 563 (1974).

[6] Gary Orfield and Chungmei Lee, "Brown at 50: King's Dream or Plessy's Nightmare?," Harvard Civil Rights Project, January 2004, p. 21.

[7] Cited in Abigail Thernstrom and Stephan Thernstrom, *No Excuses: Closing the Racial Gap in Learning* (2001), pp. 19-20.

40 percent of the students at most of the schools through the 1970s and '80s. [5]

With public support for desegregation weakening, however, the school system shifted in the 1990s to voluntary measures to maintain racial balance — chiefly by attracting white students to majority-black schools by turning them into magnet schools. Then, at the end of the decade, white families successfully sued the school system, forcing it to dismantle the busing plan altogether. [6]

The result, combined with increasing percentages of African-American and Hispanic students in the system, has been a growing concentration of minorities in many schools. Today, more than one-third of the county's 148 schools have at least 80 percent non-white enrollment.

Civil rights advocates say Charlotte is one of many school systems where political and legal developments have contributed to a trend toward resegregation. "The federal court required Charlotte to resegregate," says Harvard's Orfield, "and they are resegregating — fast."

Critics of mandatory integration, however, say today's concentration of non-white students, particularly in urban school systems, largely reflects residential demographics. Nationwide, whites comprise only about 60 percent of students in public schools, compared to 80 percent in the late 1960s. In Charlotte today, 43 percent of the system's 114,000 students are black, and only 42 percent white.

"It's wrong to say that schools are segregated or becoming resegregated," says Abigail Thernstrom, a former member of the Massachusetts Board of Education. "Cities are becoming more heavily minority. There's nothing we can do about that. You can't helicopter kids in to get more white kids in the schools."

Orfield acknowledges that the increase in non-white enrollment poses "an obstacle" to racial mixing. But he and other desegregation advocates blame resegregation primarily on the courts, including the Supreme Court.

The percentage of black students attending majority-black schools was declining nationwide through the 1980s, Harvard Civil Rights Project reports show, but it increased during the 1990s — just as the Supreme Court was signaling to federal courts that they could ease desegregation orders. "The only basic thing that's changed since [the 1980s] is the Supreme Court of the United States," Orfield maintains. [7]

"This is a demographic process," responds Armor, "and has little to do with what the courts are doing in the desegregation area."

Education Secretary Paige also argues that court rulings are not responsible for the increasing racial isolation of blacks or Latinos. "It's not our impression that these patterns are the result of current legal practices," he says. "Ethnic communities cluster together because of a lot of different factors. Some of these factors include preferences; some are economic."

The Harvard civil rights report found that during the 1990s the trend toward integration was reversed, and the percentage of black students attending majority-black schools increased throughout the country. The percentage of Latino students attending majority-minority schools also increased in every region. Latinos are more likely than African-Americans to be in a racially or ethnically identifiable school, the report shows.

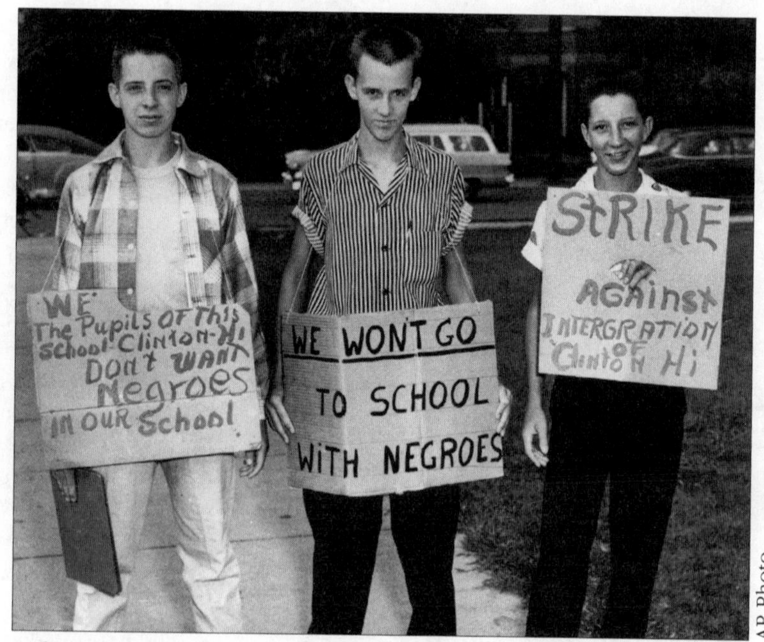

Three high school students in Clinton, Tenn., peacefully register their feelings about their school becoming the first in Tennessee to integrate, on Aug. 27, 1956. Many other protests were violent.

Educational conservatives, however, claim that Orfield presents a misleading picture by focusing exclusively on minority pupils' exposure to white students and not on white students' exposure to blacks and Latinos. "There are fewer white children who have no non-white classmates," says Stephan Thernstrom. "More and more white children have minority classmates."

More broadly, conservatives insist that talk of resegregation ignores the changes wrought by *Brown*. "There is no public school today that is segregated in the way that schools were routinely segregated before *Brown v. Board of Education*," says Roger Clegg, vice president and general counsel of the Center for Equal Opportunity, which opposes racial preferences. "Racial balance in a school that reflects the neighborhood is not segregation in the sense that we had segregation before *Brown*."

Shaw, of the Legal Defense Fund, counters that segregation never was

Minority Students Are Now More Isolated

The 1954 Brown *ruling led to widespread school integration, but today, due to resegregation, an overwhelming percentage of African-American and Latino students attend schools with predominantly non-white student bodies. Segregation has increased nationwide since 1991, when the Supreme Court began to relax pressure on school districts to integrate.*

Percentage of Blacks and Latinos in 50-100% Minority Schools

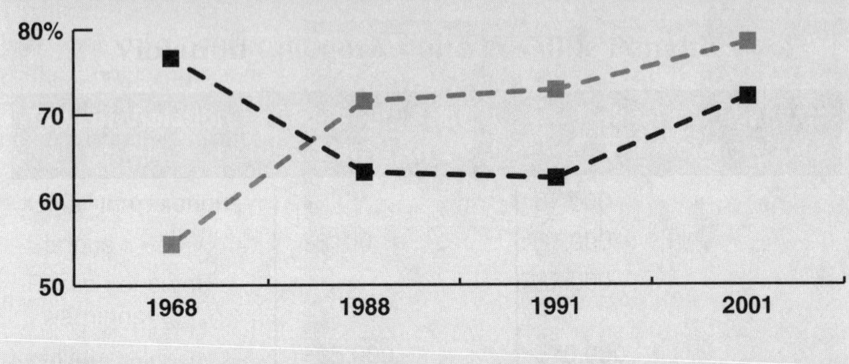

Percentage of Blacks and Latinos in 90-100% Minority Schools

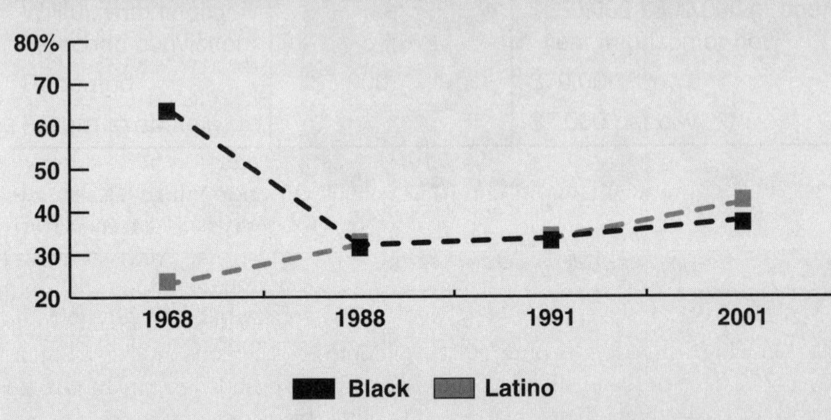

*Source: "*Brown *at 50: King's Dream or* Plessy's *Nightmare?" The Civil Rights Project, Harvard University, January 2004.*

eliminated completely and is increasing today. "The legal fiction is that we've severed the link between present-day segregation and our past segregated and discriminatory actions," Shaw says. "The truth is that the effects of decades and decades of segregation and discrimination were to segregate housing and to segregate other aspects of life.

"The busing remedies didn't eliminate the effects of that discrimination; they neutralized them," Shaw continues. "Once you get rid of the desegregation plans, those effects become operative once again."

Shaw and Orfield both say school boards should be allowed to consider race and ethnicity in pupil-assignment plans in order to promote integration. But educational conservatives oppose policies to deliberately increase racial mixing.

"I like racially mixed schools better than racially homogeneous schools," Abigail Thernstrom says. "But I do not want computer printouts that say you have no choice as to where to send your kids."

Do minorities suffer educationally because of racial isolation?

Black and Latino youngsters lag significantly behind whites (and Asian-Americans) on every significant measure of academic achievement. The "racial gap" in learning deeply troubles advocates and experts on both sides of the desegregation debate.

Traditional civil rights advocates largely blame racial isolation for the lagging performance of blacks and Latinos. There is "a very systematic relation" between segregation and the learning gap, Orfield says. "No one has ever made separate schools equal in American history on any scale."

Some critics of mandatory integration, however, see no solid evidence that racially mixed classrooms significantly benefit learning. "There is absolutely no reason to assume that because schools are heavily Hispanic or black that these children can't learn, that they have to sit next to whites or Asians in order to learn," Abigail Thernstrom says.

The social-science evidence on the issue is voluminous but less than clear-cut. In his review of the literature, George Mason University's Armor concludes that racial composition "by itself" has "no significant effect on black achievement." When combined with other educational improvements, he says, desegregation has improved black achievement "to a limited but significant degree." [8]

Desegregation advocates strongly disagree with this minimalist view. Orfield says the effect of desegregation on achievement is "significant, but not transformative." But he adds that desegregation has a "huge" effect on "life chances," such as graduating from high school, going to college and "being able to live in an interracial world as an adult." [9]

In an examination of data from Charlotte-Mecklenburg schools, Roslyn Mickelson, a professor of sociology at the University of North Carolina in Charlotte, found that black and white students both had higher average scores on standardized tests if they had been in racially integrated schools. "There is a small but significant effect on test scores that cumulates over time," she says. [10]

Orfield and other desegregation advocates say the achievement gap for minority students results in part from underfunding of schools with high percentages of black or Latino students. "The resources aren't equivalent because those are often schools that have a badge of poverty," says Underwood of the school boards association. "So they have fewer resources." U.S. schools traditionally have received most of their funding from property taxes, so schools in wealthier neighborhoods usually had more resources than schools in districts with lower property values. [11]

Armor and the Thernstroms instead blame the racial gap primarily on social and cultural factors. "There are very strong correlations between single-parent households, low birth-weight and performance in school," says Abigail Thernstrom. Armor lists single-parent households as one of 10 "risk factors" for low academic achievement. Some of the others include poverty, limited education of parents, the size of the family and the age of the mother at pregnancy. [12]

The most incendiary aspect of the issue, perhaps, concerns the claim that some black students disdain academic achievement for fear of being accused by their peers of "acting white." The thesis is most often associated with the work of the late John Ogbu, an African-American professor of anthropology at the University of California, Berkeley, who died in 2003. Ogbu first aired the theory in a co-authored article about Washington, D.C., high school students in 1986 and repeated similar views in a book about students in the affluent Cleveland suburb of Shaker Heights. [13]

Education Secretary Paige subscribes to the theory based not only on Ogbu's research but also on his own experience as school superintendent in Houston. "I had a chance to see examples where some kids were not putting their best efforts into this in an effort to keep status among some of their peers," Paige says. "It exists."

Armor, however, discounts the theory, noting that the educational gap for African-Americans can be found at the earliest grades. Abigail Thernstrom also says the evidence is "not very good." She places greater blame on schools' failure to instill educational ambitions in minority youngsters. "Schools are delivering a wrong message — that this is a racist society, and there's a limit to how far you can go," she says.

But the Legal Defense Fund's Shaw says there is evidence of an "acting white" syndrome and says the issue needs more discussion among African-Americans. But he adds that some of the debate over the educational gap for black students has "the lurking sense of racial inferiority.

"If people come to this issue in good faith and they want to focus on the causes, the first thing they have to recognize is that there's still massive inequality," Shaw says. "By the time you get to high school, African-American students have had a completely different experience from white students. Let's not blame the victim. Let's fix the problem."

Would "school choice" policies help reduce the racial gap in educational achievement for African-Americans and Latinos?

President Bush touts school vouchers, not integration, as the best way to help disadvantaged students get a better education. "When we find children trapped in schools that will not change, parents must be given another viable option," Bush told students and teachers at Archbishop Carroll High School in Washington on Feb. 13, 2004. The president used the appearance to plug a new law he had just signed to award vouchers to some 1,700 District of Columbia students per year to help pay tuition at private schools. [14]

Educational conservatives say "school choice" programs such as vouchers or charter schools will help improve schools by promoting innovation and overcoming resistance to change from public school administrators and teachers. Education Secretary Paige claims particular support for school choice among African-American families.

"My reading of the polls shows that African-American parents support choice, vouchers, strongly," Paige says. "The parents are supporters because the parents want the best education for the child."

The public school establishment strongly opposes vouchers, saying they would drain needed money from public schools. Underwood, the school boards association lawyer, says vouchers also "threaten any kind of diversity agenda that a school district may have." Private schools, she says, "can choose to discriminate. They can choose not to serve students with special needs or students who are poor or of a particular culture or ethnicity."

Local voucher programs are already operating in Milwaukee and Cleveland; Florida has a statewide program pushed by Gov. Jeb Bush, the president's brother. The programs are targeted to middle- and low-income families, but are small-scale because of limited funding. "Vouchers are going to be a sideshow for American education," Orfield says.

Charter schools — which operate under public auspices but free from some generally applicable regulations — are more widespread. [15] Some 2,700 charter schools were operating as of the 2002-2003 academic year. Many of them were established by black families and educators to serve the educational needs of African-American students. But Orfield and other desegregation advocates are skeptical that they will be better for black pupils than public schools.

"There is no evidence that charter schools are better than average," Orfield says, "and our studies show that they're more segregated than public schools."

Abigail Thernstrom counters that vouchers and charter schools "have the potential" to improve education for minority youngsters. "They have the potential for one very simple reason," she says. "They are out from under the constraints that make for such mediocre education in so many public schools."

Armor, however, sees no necessary benefit for minority youngsters from school choice programs. "I don't see personally why vouchers or charters would have any automatic impact on school quality," Armor says. "It might or might not. There's nothing intrinsic about charters that says those teachers are going to have a better subject mastery" than teachers at regular schools. As for vouchers, Armor says they "can also be used to go to a school that doesn't have better programs" than regular public schools.

Public-education groups cite underfunding as a major barrier to improving education for minority youngsters. Nationwide, schools with the highest minority or low-income enrollments receive $1,000 less per student than schools with the lowest minority or poverty enrollments, according to a report by the Education Trust, a Washington advocacy group. (*See map, p. 348.*)

"There is definitely a relationship between the amount of funding a district gets and academic performance," says Kevin Carey, a senior policy analyst with the group. "There are important issues besides money: organization, expectations for students, curricula, the way teachers are compensated. But money matters, too."

"We need to pay attention to sending resources where resources are needed," Underwood says, "so students with high educational needs get the resources they need to learn, so you really aren't leaving any child behind."

But Paige and other educational conservatives discount the importance of funding. "I don't accept that the achievement gap is a function of funding issues," Paige says. "It is a factor, but it is not *the* factor. The more important factors are those factors embedded in the No Child Left Behind Act: accountability, flexibility and parental choice — and teaching methods that work."

Orfield, however, says the No Child Left Behind Act has produced "confusion and frustration" for local school districts with scant evidence of help for minority pupils. [16] And the Legal Defense Fund's Shaw insists that school choice proposals could help only some minority students while leaving most of them behind.

"Most African-American students, like most students, are going to remain in public schools," Shaw says. "The promise of *Brown* isn't going to be realized by focusing on those few students who can escape from public schools. If we don't talk about fixing public education, then I think we betray not only *Brown* but also the fundamental notion of what public education is all about." ■

BACKGROUND

Long, Hard Road

The Supreme Court's celebrated decision in *Brown v. Board of Education* marks neither the beginning nor the end of the campaign for equal education for black Americans. It was only a turning point in a struggle with roots in the 19th century that now extends into the 21st. [17]

Black youngsters received no education in the antebellum South and little schooling in the decades immediately after the abolition of slavery. Where blacks did go to school, they were segregated from whites in most (though not all) parts of the country, by law or custom. Some legal challenges to the practice in the 19th century succeeded, but the Supreme Court thwarted any broad attack on segregation with its 1896 decision in *Plessy v. Ferguson* upholding "separate but equal" in public transportation.

The NAACP — founded in 1909 — won its first victory against racial segregation in education in 1935, with a state court ruling to admit a black student to the University of Maryland's law school. Four years later, one of the winning lawyers, Thurgood Marshall, was named to head a separate organization: the NAACP Legal Defense and Educational Fund, Inc. The Inc. Fund — as it was then known — won important victories from the Supreme Court with two unanimous decisions in 1950 striking down segregationist practices in graduate education at state universities in Oklahoma and Texas. [18]

Meanwhile, Marshall had been helping organize local campaigns against segregation in elementary and secondary education in four Southern and Border States. The four cases, which were consolidated in the *Brown* decision, differed in their facts and in their legal histories: Black schools in Clarendon County, S.C., were mostly ramshackle shanties; those in Topeka, Kansas, were more nearly comparable to schools for whites. The federal judge in the Prince Edward County, Va., case found "no hurt or harm to either race" in dual school systems;

Continued on p. 356

Chronology

Before 1950

Racial segregation takes root in public schools — by law in the South, by custom elsewhere; NAACP begins challenging "separate but equal" doctrine in the 1930s.

1950s-1960s

Supreme Court outlaws racial segregation; ruling provokes massive resistance in South.

1950
Supreme Court bars racial segregation in public graduate education.

1954
Supreme Court rules racial segregation in public elementary and secondary schools unconstitutional on May 17, 1954 (*Brown I*).

1955
Court says schools must be desegregated "with all deliberate speed" (*Brown II*).

1957
President Dwight D. Eisenhower calls out Arkansas National Guard to maintain order when Little Rock's Central High School is integrated.

1964
Civil Rights Act authorizes federal government to bring school-desegregation suits and to withhold funds from schools that fail to desegregate.

1968
Impatient with limited desegregation, Supreme Court says school districts must dismantle dual school systems "now."

1970s-1980s

Desegregation advances, but busing triggers battles in many cities.

1971
Supreme Court upholds use of busing as desegregation tool.

1973
Supreme Court orders Denver to desegregate, making it the first non-Southern city ordered to integrate.

1974
Supreme Court bars federal courts from ordering cross-district busing to achieve desegregation . . . Start of busing in Boston provokes fierce opposition.

1975
Coleman report blames white-flight from urban public schools on court-ordered busing; desegregation advocates disagree.

Late 1980s
Integration peaks, with most African-American students still attending predominantly black schools in each of five regions across country.

1990s

Many school systems freed from court supervision; race-conscious assignments challenged as "reverse discrimination."

1991
Supreme Court allows judges to lift court orders if segregation has been eliminated to all "practicable" extent.

1995
Supreme Court says judges in desegregation cases should try to end supervision of school systems.

1998, 1999
Federal courts strike racial preferences used for Boston Latin School, "magnet" schools in two Washington, D.C., suburban districts.

2000-Present

Brown's *promise hailed, impact debated.*

2001
President Bush wins passage of No Child Left Behind Act, providing penalties for school districts that fail to improve students' overall scores on standardized tests. . . . Federal court in September lifts desegregation decree for Charlotte-Mecklenburg schools in North Carolina.

2003
Supreme Court upholds affirmative action for colleges and universities. . . . Federal judge in December hears challenge to racial guidelines for Louisville-Jefferson County Schools; federal appeals court in same month considers suit to bar use of race as "tiebreaker" in pupil assignments in Seattle.

2004
Brown decision widely celebrated as 50th anniversary approaches; civil rights advocates decry "resegregation," while others say emphasis on racial balance is divisive and unproductive. . . . Federal appeals court to hear challenge in June to racial-balance transfer policy for Lynn, Mass., schools.

Success Asian-American Style

"Uncivilized, unclean and filthy beyond all conception . . . they know not the virtues of honesty, integrity or good faith," fulminated Horace Greeley, the 19th-century abolitionist and social reformer, describing Chinese immigrants. [1]

But the numbers today tell a different story. By any measure, Asian-Americans have been phenomenally successful academically. As a result, the concentration of Asian students in top American schools is wildly disproportionate to their ratio in the U.S. population.

For example, Asians make up approximately 70 percent of San Francisco's most prestigious public school, Lowell High, with Chinese-Americans alone constituting over 50 percent, although Chinese make up only 31.3 percent of the school district.

The excellent scholastic record of Asian students dates back at least to the 1930s, when California teachers wrote of "ideal" Japanese students who could serve as an example to other students. Their delinquency rate was one-third that of whites.

Today, although Asians make up only 3.8 percent of the U.S. population, Asian-Americans accounted for 27 percent of the freshman class at the Massachusetts Institute of Technology in the 2000-2001 school year, 25 percent at Stanford, 24 percent at the California Institute of Technology and 17 percent at Harvard; Asians were a phenomenal 40 percent of the freshmen at the University of California, Berkeley, in 1999. One in five American medical students is Asian. [2] Similarly, between 10 and 20 percent of the students at the nation's premier law schools are Asian.

The achievement gap between whites and Asians is greater than the gap between blacks and whites, by some measures. In 2001, 54 percent of Asian-Americans between ages 25 and 29 had at least a bachelor's degree, compared with 34 percent of whites and 18 percent of blacks.

Academics have long disputed the reasons for Asians' stellar performance. The controversial 1994 book, *The Bell Curve*, held that Asians did better because they were inherently more intelligent than others. But numerous academics attacked Richard J. Herrnstein and Charles Murray's methodology and racial conclusions. Some studies show that Asians, particularly Chinese, consistently score higher on IQ tests than other groups. [3] But there is increasing evidence that racial differences are minimal. [4]

Another explanation attributes the relative success of Asians in America to the socioeconomic and educational status of the Asian immigrants who were allowed to enter the United States. In 1965, immigration reforms allotted immigrant visas preferentially to people with needed skills. Many came from India or China with advanced degrees in medicine or technology.

The parents' educational and occupational attainments "far exceed the average for native-born Americans," according to Stephen L. Klineberg, a Rice University sociology professor studying Houston-area demographics. [5] With such parents, the children seem primed for success, but critics of socioeconomic explanations point out that even though many early Asian immigrants were mainly laborers and peasants, they still performed exceptionally well in school.

Most of those early Asian-Americans, mainly Chinese, lived in California, where school segregation developed quickly. By 1863, "Negroes, Mongolians and Indians" were prohibited from attending schools with white children. [6] Statewide restrictions were soon amended so non-white children could attend public schools with whites where no separate schools existed; in areas with fewer Chinese immigrants, they often attended schools with whites. San Francisco responded by building a separate school for Chinese children in 1885.

In 1906, Japanese and Koreans also were ordered to attend the so-called Oriental School in San Francisco, although the Japanese resisted, and by 1929 the vast majority of Japanese children attended integrated schools. [7] The courts and legislature ended legal segregation in California schools in 1947.

However, Chinese immigrants in California have staunchly opposed integration proposals that required their children to be bused out of local neighborhoods. "One time, in the 1960s and '70s, when integration of schools was the big issue, I almost got lynched in Chinatown by Chinese-Americans for supporting integration," said Ling-chi Wang, a professor of ethnic studies at Berkeley and veteran civil rights advocate. [8] More recently, Chinese-American parents successfully challenged a San Francisco school-integration plan, arguing that their children were losing out due to racial quotas at magnet schools. [9]

Today, regardless of their parents' income level or education, Asian students perform better academically than other groups, though

Continued from p. 354

the state judge in the Delaware case declared that state-imposed segregation "adversely affected" education for blacks. The federal judge in Topeka also had agreed that separate schools were harmful for blacks but abided by Supreme Court precedent in rejecting any relief for the plaintiffs.

The four cases were argued before the Supreme Court twice — first in December 1952 and then again in December 1953. The justices were divided after the first argument. Five or six justices appeared inclined to declare segregation unconstitutional, according to later reconstructions of the deliberations. [19] But Chief Justice Fred M. Vinson hesitated to press for a final decision and accepted the suggestion of Justice Felix Frankfurter to ask for a reargument.

Vinson's death in September 1953 paved the way for the appointment of Chief Justice Earl Warren, who as governor of California had signed a law abolishing racial segregation in that their performance does improve as parental education and income increase. The persistent performance gap, even accounting for socioeconomic factors, leads to a third explanation for Asians' success: the great emphasis put on education by Asian parents, higher academic expectations and the attitude that successful achievement is simply a question of hard work.

For instance, a study by Temple University's Laurence Steinberg of 20,000 Wisconsin and California students found that Asian-American students felt any grade below A- would anger their parents; for whites the anger threshold was B-, for blacks and Latinos a C-. And research shows that more than 50 percent of Asian-American high school seniors spend an hour or more per night on homework, compared to 30 percent of Latinos and less than 25 percent of whites. [10]

Education experts often blame the gap between how white children and new immigrants perform educationally on the language barriers faced by the immigrants. But evidence suggests that newly arrived Asians learn English faster than Latinos, thus breaking down those barriers faster. For instance, 1990 Census data showed that 90 to 95 percent of third-generation Asian-American children spoke only English at home, compared to only 64 percent of Mexican-Americans. [11]

But Asian immigrants are not a monolithic "model minority." Asians who arrive already speaking English, such as Filipinos or Indians, fare better educationally and economically. The poverty rate among Filipino immigrants — who come from a country with a 95 percent literacy rate — is only 6.3 percent, compared with 37.8 percent among the Hmong — a mostly uneducated ethnic group from Southeast Asia.

In Sacramento, where Hmong comprise about 8 percent of public school students, they are the lowest-performing group, according to Suanna Gilman-Ponce, director of the school district's multilingual education department. [12] For example, only 3 percent of the Hmong had a bachelor's degree, according to the 1990 census, compared with 24 percent of the nation as a whole.

But there is progress: Among the 25-to-34 age group, the first Hmong generation to grow up in the United States, 13.5 percent had degrees. And of the Vietnamese, many of whom also arrived as refugees, 26.9 percent had a college degree; the national average is 27.5 percent.

— ***Kenneth Lukas***

Library of Congress

Asians were segregated from whites in California schools at the end of the 19th century. In 1885, San Francisco built a separate school for Chinese children.

[1] Quoted in Andrew Gyory, *Closing the Gate* (1998), p. 17.

[2] Abigail Thernstrom and Stephan Thernstrom, *No Excuses: Closing the Racial Gap in Learning* (2003), p. 85.

[3] Jeff Wise, "Are Asians Smarter?" *Time International*, Sept. 11, 1995, p. 60.

[4] Natalie Angier, "Do Races Differ? Not Really, Genes Show," *The New York Times*, Aug. 22, 2000, p. F1 and Steve Olson, "The Genetic Archaeology of Race," *The Atlantic Monthly*, April 2, 2001, p. 69.

[5] Quoted in Mike Snyder, "Survey: Area Asians Have Head Start," *The Houston Chronicle*, Oct. 1, 2002, p. A1.

[6] For background on Asians in California, see Charles Wollenberg, *All Deliberate Speed: Segregation and Exclusion in California Schools, 1855-1975* (1976).

[7] Bill Hosokawa, *Nisei: The Quiet Americans* (2002), pp. 85-89.

[8] Quoted in Sam McManis, "Activist Fights for Asian Americans at U.S. Labs," *San Francisco Chronicle*, March 27, 2002, p. A1.

[9] David J. Hoff, "San Francisco Assignment Rules Anger Parents," *Education Week*, June 4, 2003, p. 9. See also "All Things Considered," National Public Radio, Aug. 10, 2002, and April 5, 2004.

[10] Thernstrom, *op. cit.*, p. 94.

[11] *Ibid.*, pp. 111-113.

[12] Quoted in Erika Chavez, "Hmong Cry for Help Has Been Heard," *Sacramento Bee*, May 28, 2002, p. B1.

state's public schools. [20] Warren used his considerable political skills to forge the unanimous decision on May 17, 1954, which buried the "separate but equal" doctrine, at least in public education. "Separate educational facilities," Warren wrote near the end of the 13-page opinion, "are inherently unequal."

A year later, the justices rejected both Marshall's plea to order immediate desegregation and a federal recommendation that a specific timetable for desegregation be established. Instead, the court in *Brown II* ruled that the four school districts be required to admit pupils on a racially non-discriminatory basis "with all deliberate speed." [21]

Public opinion polls indicated a narrow majority of Americans favored the ruling, but the court's gradualist approach allowed the formation of what became massive resistance. More than 100 members of Congress signed the "Southern Manifesto" in 1956 vowing to use "all lawful means" to reverse the ruling. Most school districts

What Americans Think About School Desegregation

While 60 percent of Americans think classroom racial diversity is "very important," 66 percent think school officials should not try to increase the diversity of local schools.

In elementary school, were your classmates of many different races, or mostly the same race?

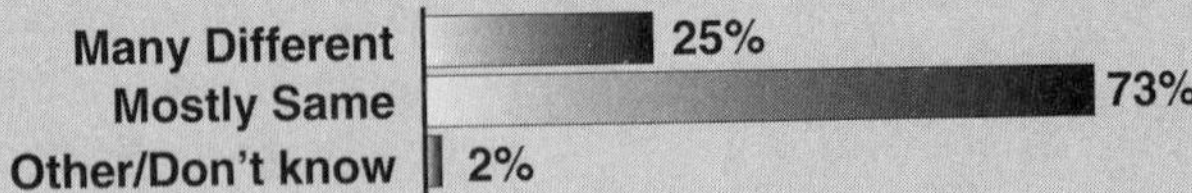

Do the public elementary schools in your community today have kids mostly of the same race, or many different races?

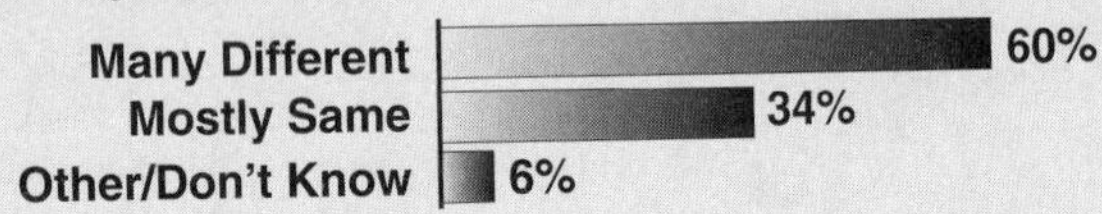

Did the Supreme Court make the right decision to end racial segregation in schools?

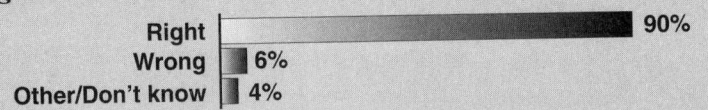

How did ending racial segregation affect the quality of America's schools?

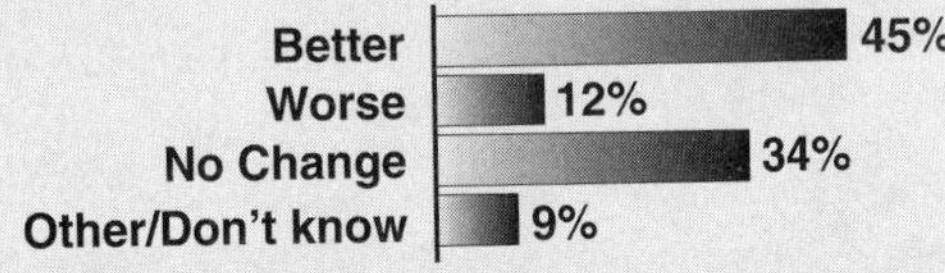

How important is it that students of different races are in class together?

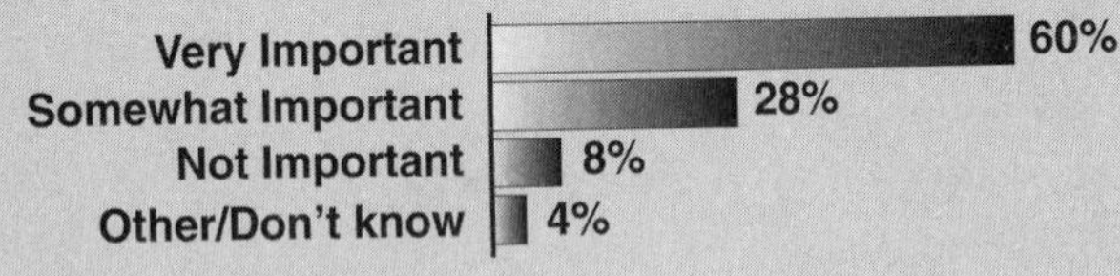

Should school officials try to increase the racial diversity of schools in your community?

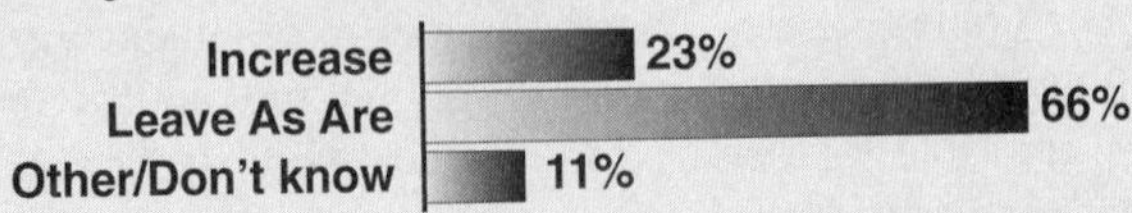

Source: Scripps Survey Research Center, Ohio University, www.newspolls.org. The national telephone survey of 1,013 people was taken Feb. 15-24, 2004.

dragged their feet, while even token integration efforts brought forth scattered bombings and violence and more widespread intimidation and harassment. In the most dramatic instance, President Dwight D. Eisenhower had to call out National Guardsmen in September 1957 to maintain order at Central High School in Little Rock, Ark., after nine black students were enrolled. As of 1964, only 2 percent of black students in the South were attending majority-white schools.

Facing resistance both active and passive, the Supreme Court left local federal courts largely on their own for nearly a decade. In 1964, however, Congress included provisions in the landmark Civil Rights Act that authorized the federal government to file school desegregation suits and to withhold funds from school districts that failed to desegregate. Four years later, the court — with Marshall now serving as the first African-American justice — announced that its patience was at an end. The justices rejected a "freedom of choice" plan offered by a rural Virginia school board and declared that school districts had to develop plans to dismantle dual systems "root and branch" — and to do it "now."

Given patterns of residential segregation, many plans devised by federal judges inevitably involved busing — typically, transporting black students to schools in predominantly white areas. Many white parents objected, but the court — under a new chief justice, Warren Burger — unanimously ruled in the *Charlotte-Mecklenburg* case in 1971 that courts had discretion to order busing as part of a desegregation plan.

Bumps in the Road

In the 1970s and '80s, desegregation advanced generally in the South and in most of the rest of the country. But the use of busing as a principal tool for racial mixing provoked fierce protests in some cities and widespread opposition from officials and the public at large. Meanwhile, Latino enrollment in public schools began to increase dramatically — and so, too, did the percentage of Latino students attending predominantly Latino schools.

The busing issue dominated the headlines and the policy debates in the 1970s, obscuring the less dramatic evidence of changes in public schools, especially in the South. From 1968 to 1988, the percentage of black students attending predominantly minority schools fell sharply in the South — from more than 80 percent to around 55 percent — and declined significantly in every other region except the Northeast.[22] As historian Patterson notes, most of the heavily black schools in the South were more nearly comparable to white schools by the end of the 1980s, salaries for black teachers were more nearly equal to those for whites and teaching staffs were integrated.

Public education in the South, he concludes, "had been revolutionized" — thanks to pressure from the then-Department of Health, Education and Welfare and rulings from federal courts.[23]

For many Americans, however, desegregation came to be understood only as court-ordered transportation of students out of their neighborhoods to distant schools of uncertain character and quality. The polarizing issue erupted most dramatically in ostensibly liberal Boston, where a federal judge ordered racial mixing between heavily white South Boston and predominantly black Roxbury. Patterson notes that on the first day of the plan in September 1974, only 10 of the 525 white students assigned to Roxbury High School showed up, while buses carrying 56 black pupils bound for South Boston High School were stoned.[24]

Busing had few vocal supporters. President Gerald Ford, a Republican, complained that busing "brought fear to black students and white students." President Jimmy Carter, a Democrat, was lukewarm toward the practice. Sociologist James Coleman — who authored an influential report in 1968 documenting the educational achievement gap for African-American students — added respectability to the anti-busing critique with a report in 1975 blaming "white flight" from central-city schools on court-ordered busing and calling instead for voluntary desegregation.[25]

Civil rights supporters countered that opponents were exaggerating the costs and disruption of court-ordered busing when their real objection was to racial mixing altogether. They also sharply disputed Coleman's "white flight" theory, insisting that the movement of whites to the suburbs — and the resulting concentration of African-Americans in inner cities — stemmed from social and economic trends dating from the 1950s unrelated to school desegregation.

The Supreme Court itself acknowledged the logistical problems of busing in some of its decisions, but the justices couched their emerging disagreements on desegregation in legalistic terms. In 1973, the court established a critical distinction between "de jure" segregation — ordered by law — and "de facto" segregation resulting only from residential segregation. The ruling allowed a lower court to enforce a desegregation plan, but only on the grounds that the school district had intentionally drawn zones

Library of Congress

Pioneering civil rights attorney Thurgood Marshall, shown here in 1957, successfully argued the landmark Brown v. Board of Education *case before the U.S. Supreme Court. President Lyndon B. Johnson appointed Marshall to the high court in 1967.*

to separate black and white pupils. (The ruling also recognized Hispanic students as an identifiable class for desegregation purposes.) In a partial dissent, Justice Lewis F. Powell Jr. criticized the distinction between "de facto" and "de jure" segregation, saying any racial separation of students was constitutionally suspect.

A year later, the court dealt integration advocates a more serious setback in a 5-4 ruling that barred transportation of students across school-district lines to achieve desegregation. The ruling struck down a desegregation plan for the heavily black Detroit school district and the predominantly white schools in surrounding Wayne County suburbs. For the majority, Chief Justice Burger said school district lines "could not be casually ignored." In dissent, Marshall called the ruling "a large step backwards."

Three years later, the court dealt another blow to desegregation advocates by ruling — in a case from Pasadena, Calif. — that a school district was not responsible for resegregation of students once it had adopted a racially neutral attendance plan.

The rulings combined with political opposition and socioeconomic trends to stall further increases in racial mixing of students by the end of the 1980s. The percentage of black students attending predominantly minority schools increased after 1988 in the South and West and after 1991 in the Northeast, Midwest and Border States. The Supreme Court, under the leadership of conservative Chief Justice William H. Rehnquist, then eased the pressure on school districts to continue desegregation efforts with three more decisions between 1991 and 1995.

The rulings — in cases from Oklahoma City; suburban DeKalb County, Ga.; and Kansas City — effectively told federal judges to ease judicial supervision once legally enforced segregation had been eliminated to the extent practicable. For the majority, Rehnquist wrote in the Kansas City case that federal judges should remember that their purpose was not only to remedy past violations but also to return schools to the control of local and state authorities.

Police escort school buses carrying African-American students into South Boston in 1974, implementing a court-ordered busing plan to integrate schools.

AP Photo

Reversing Directions?

By the mid-1990s, traditional civil rights advocates were strongly criticizing what they termed the resegregation of African-American and Latino students. Critics of mandatory integration replied that legal segregation and its effects had been largely eliminated and that apparent racial and ethnic separation reflected residential neighborhoods and the growing proportion of African-American and Latino students in public schools.

As federal courts backed away from desegregation suits, white students brought — and in a few cases won — so-called reverse-discrimination suits contesting use of race in school-assignment plans. Meanwhile, some civil rights supporters shifted direction by bringing school-funding cases in state courts.

School-desegregation litigation all but petered out during the 1990s. Nearly 700 cases remain technically alive nationwide, but a law professor's examination of the period 1992-2002 found only 53 suits in active litigation.[26] Professor Wendy Parker of the University of Cincinnati College of Law also showed that school districts had succeeded in every instance but one when they asked for so-called unitary status — in order to get out from under further judicial supervision of desegregation decrees — even if enrollments continued to reflect racial imbalance.

In addition, Parker said judges were somewhat lax in requiring racial balance of teaching staffs and that any racial imbalance in teaching assignments invariably mirrored a school's racial composition: Schools with a disproportionate number of black teachers were predominantly black, those with disproportionate numbers of white teachers were predominantly white.

Meanwhile, a few federal courts were curbing school districts' discretion to consider race in assigning students to elite or so-called magnet schools. In 1998, the 1st U.S. Circuit Court of Appeals had ruled against the use of "flexible race/ethnicity guidelines" for filling about half of the places each year at the elite Boston Latin School. The court said the Boston School Committee had failed to show that the policy either promoted diversity or helped remedy vestiges of past discrimination.[27]

The next year, another federal appeals court ruled in favor of white students' claims that school boards in two suburban Washington, D.C., school districts — Montgomery County, Md., and Arlington, Va. — violated the Constitution's Equal Protection Clause by considering race in magnet-school placements. In both rulings, the 4th U.S. Circuit Court of Appeals said the use of race was not narrowly tailored to achieve the goal of diversity. The Supreme Court refused to hear the school districts' appeals.[28]

With federal courts seemingly uninterested in desegregation initiatives, civil rights groups put more resources into school-funding challenges before state legislatures or courts.[29] The various efforts, pushed in some 40 states, generally aimed at narrowing or eliminating financial disparities between well-to-do and less-well-off school districts. Funding-equity advocates succeeded in part in several states — sometimes through court order, sometimes by legislative changes spurred by actual or threatened litigation.

The initiatives helped cause a shift in education-funding sources away from the historic primary reliance on local property taxes. Today, just over half of local education funding comes from state rather than local revenues, according to Carey, of the Education Trust. Nonetheless, school districts with high minority or low-income enrollments still receive fewer funds compared to districts with more white or wealthier students.

The limited progress on funding issues gave civil rights advocates only slight consolation for the evidence of increasing racial imbalance in public schools. By 2001, at least two-thirds of black students and at least half of Latino students nationwide were enrolled in predominantly minority schools. Significantly, the Northeast is more segregated: More than half of black students (51 percent) and nearly half of Latino students (44 percent) attended intensely segregated schools with 90 to 100 percent minority enrollment. "We've been going backward almost every place in the country since the 1990s," Harvard's Orfield says.

Critics of mandatory integration, however, viewed the figures differently. They emphasized that white students' exposure to African-American and Latino students has continued to increase. In any event, they say, residential patterns, city-suburban boundary lines and the increasing percentages of African-American and Latino students in overall enrollment make it impractical to achieve greater racial mixing in many school districts.

"The proportion of minorities in large districts is growing," says George Mason's Armor. "When it crosses 50 percent, whatever your racial-assignment plan, you're going to have minority schools."

For his part, President Bush has pushed education reform aimed in part at helping low-income students but without adopting traditional civil rights goals or rhetoric. "American children must not be left in persistently dangerous or failing schools," Bush declared as he unveiled — on Jan. 23, 2001, his second full day in office — what eventually became the No Child Left Behind Act. Approved by Congress in May 2001, the law prescribes student testing to measure academic progress among public school students and provides financial penalties for school districts that fail to improve student performance.

Education Secretary Paige says the law seeks to continue the effort to improve educational opportunities for all students started by *Brown v. Board of Education*. The law passed with broad bipartisan support. By 2004, however, many Democrats were accusing the administration of failing to provide funding to support needed changes, while many school administrators were criticizing implementation of the law as excessively rigid and cumbersome. ■

CURRENT SITUATION

Race-Counting

Schools in Lynn, Mass., were facing a multifaceted crisis in the 1980s, with crumbling buildings, tattered textbooks, widespread racial strife and rapid white flight. To regain public confidence, the school board in 1989 adopted a plan combining neighborhood-school assignments with a transfer policy that included only one major restriction: No child could transfer from one school to another if the move would increase racial imbalance at either of the schools involved.

The Lynn school board credits the plan with stabilizing enrollment, easing race relations and helping lift academic performance throughout the 15,000-student system. But lawyers for parents whose children were denied transfers under the plan are asking a federal appeals court to rule that the policy amounts to illegal racial discrimination.

'We've Yet to Achieve' Equality of Education

Secretary of Education Rod Paige was interviewed on March 24, 2004, in his Washington office by Associate Editor Kenneth Jost. Here are verbatim excerpts from that interview.

On his experience attending racially segregated schools:

"The fact that [white students] had a gym was a big deal. They played basketball on the inside. They had a big gym with lights and stuff on the inside. We played basketball on the outside with a clay court. We played up until the time that you couldn't see the hoop any more. . . . I wanted to take band, but there was no music. I wanted to play football, but there was no football team [until senior year]. . . . The concept of separate but equal is not at all academic for me. It is very personal. And even today . . . I don't know what I missed."

Secretary of Education Rod Paige

On the impact of the* Brown v. Board of Education *decision:

"Was the goal to take 'separate but equal' away . . . ? The answer would be [yes], in a very strong and striking way. If the goal was equality education, to level the educational playing field for all children, especially children of color, the answer is we've yet to achieve that."

On the resegregation of black and Latino students:

"Ethnic communities cluster together because of a lot of different factors. Some of these factors include preferences; some are economic. So our goal should be now to provide a quality education for a child no matter where they are in this system."

On efforts to promote racial balance in schools:

"If anybody is in a segregated school based on unfairness, then, yes, they should work against that. But . . . we don't want to get integration confused with educational excellence. We want to provide educational excellence to kids no matter what their location is [or] the ethnic makeup of their community."

On the use of race in pupil assignments:

"A person should not be disadvantaged because of the color of their skin. Nor should that person be advantaged because of the color of their skin. . . . That's the principle I would apply to any set of circumstances."

On "equal" opportunities for African-American and Latino students:

"I've got to come down on the side that there's a large amount of lower expectations for minority kids. . . . If there are lower expectations for a child, then the answer to your question has to be that there is not a fair opportunity."

On causes of the "racial gap" in learning:

"There are three drivers. One is the quality of instructional circumstances. . . . The second is the quantity of it . . . And the third one is student engagement. Learning is an active activity between the teacher and the student. So the student does have some responsibility here in terms of student engagement."

On underfunding of minority and low-income schools:

"I don't accept that the achievement gap is a function of funding issues. I think it is a factor, but it is not *the* factor. . . . The more important factors are those embedded in the No Child Left Behind Act: accountability, flexibility and parental choice — and teaching methods that work."

On school choice proposals — vouchers and charter schools:

"My reading of the polls show[s] that African-American parents support choice, vouchers, strongly. . . . The parents are supporters because [they] want the best education for the child. . . . Enforcing monopolistic tendencies on schools is a detriment to schools. The people who force these monopolistic tendencies on schools deny schools the opportunity to innovate, create and reach their potential."

"They're denying school assignments based on the color of the kid who's asking for the assignment," says Michael Williams, a lawyer with the Boston-based Citizens for the Preservation of Constitutional Rights.

The case — expected to be argued in September 2004 before the 1st U.S. Circuit Court of Appeals in Boston — is one of several nationwide where school boards with voluntary integra-

Continued on p. 364

At Issue:

Should the federal government do more to promote racial and ethnic diversity in public schools?

GARY ORFIELD
DIRECTOR, THE HARVARD CIVIL RIGHTS PROJECT CO-AUTHOR, "BROWN AT 50: KING'S DREAM OR PLESSY'S NIGHTMARE?"

WRITTEN FOR *THE CQ RESEARCHER*, APRIL 2004

yes

The federal government has taken no significant, positive initiatives toward desegregation or even toward serious research on multiracial schools since the Carter administration. In fact, Presidents Richard M. Nixon, Gerald Ford, Ronald Reagan and both George Bushes were generally opposed to urban desegregation and named like-minded appointees to run the major federal civil rights and education agencies. Attorney General John Ashcroft, for example, fought desegregation orders in St. Louis and Kansas City, and Reagan Supreme Court appointee Chief Justice William H. Rehnquist has consistently opposed urban desegregation.

Between 1965 and 1970, federal leadership played a decisive role in ending educational apartheid in the South and transforming it into the nation's most desegregated region. Southern schools were the most integrated for more than three decades, during which time black achievement, graduation and college attendance increased, and educational gaps began to close. But those schools now are seriously resegregating.

President Nixon largely ended enforcement of the 1964 Civil Rights Act in schools and intentionally stirred up national division over busing as part of his "Southern strategy." Then, in two separate 5-4 decisions in 1973 and 1974, four Nixon justices helped block school-finance equalization and desegregation across city-suburban lines. The federal government never enforced the Supreme Court's 1973 decision recognizing Latinos' right to desegregation. And in the 1990s the Rehnquist court thrice ended desegregation orders, effectively producing resegregation. Nearly 90 percent of the heavily segregated minority schools produced by this process have high rates of poverty and educational inequality.

Federal policy could help reverse the resegregation trend. First, leaders must make the compelling case that desegregation, properly implemented, is valuable for all students, preparing them to live and work in a multiracial society. Second, judicial vacancies and civil rights enforcement agencies should be staffed with progressives. Third, the desegregation-aid program could be revived to help suburbs experiencing racial change without preparation or resources.

In addition, serious research needs to be done on resegregation. Educational choice programs should forbid transfers that increase segregation and reward those that diminish it. And magnet school programs should be expanded. Finally, fair-housing enforcement should be greatly increased and policies adopted to help stabilize desegregated neighborhoods.

DAVID J. ARMOR
PROFESSOR OF PUBLIC POLICY, SCHOOL OF PUBLIC POLICY, GEORGE MASON UNIVERSITY

WRITTEN FOR *THE CQ RESEARCHER*, APRIL 2004

no

To answer this question, we must ask three related questions. First, do legal constraints prevent the promotion of diversity in public schools? The answer is yes. The Supreme Court has provided a legal framework for using race in public policy, and the justices recently clarified that framework in two cases involving college admissions in Michigan. Racial diversity can be a compelling government purpose, but policies must be narrowly tailored to reflect the use of race or ethnicity as only one factor, not the predominant factor, in the policy.

Applying this framework to public schools, race could not be used as the primary basis for assigning students to schools (as in old-fashioned busing plans), unless a school district was remedying illegal segregation. The use of race might be justified for controlling enrollment in a voluntary magnet school on the grounds that students should be allowed to choose racially diverse programs, but even this limited use of race is being challenged in the courts. The Supreme Court has yet to rule on diversity for K-12 public schools.

Second, does diversity bring clear social and educational benefits to public school children? Diversity unquestionably has social value, since it allows children from different backgrounds to learn about other cultures and how to work together. However, it is hard to find social outcomes that have consistently benefited from desegregation. For example, race relations have sometimes worsened after desegregation programs, particularly if they involved mandatory busing. Moreover, the formal educational value of diversity has not been proven, since large-scale school-desegregation programs have not reduced the racial gap in academic achievement.

The third question we must ask is what kind of promotion, if any, might be appropriate for the federal government? Federal agencies have an important but limited role in policies for K-12 public schools. They conduct research, sponsor special programs, conduct assessment and recently adopted policies to raise academic standards and accountability under the No Child Left Behind Act. Given the legal constraints on diversity programs and the uncertain educational benefits of diversity in K-12 schools, I do not think promoting diversity should be a high priority at this time.

However, since there is still a debate over the educational benefits of racial diversity programs, it would be appropriate for the federal government to sponsor research to help resolve this important issue.

Continued from p. 362

tion plans are facing legal actions aimed at eliminating any use of race in student assignments. Attorneys for the school boards are vigorously defending race-conscious policies.

"You cannot ignore race and expect that the issue will not be present in your school system," says Richard Cole, senior counsel for civil rights in the Massachusetts attorney general's office, who is defending the Lynn plan. "The only way is to take steps to bring kids of different racial groups together."

Meanwhile, the federal appeals court for Washington state is considering a challenge to the Seattle School District's use of race as one of several factors — a so-called "tiebreaker" — in determining assignments to oversubscribed schools. The 9th Circuit appeals court heard arguments on Dec. 14, 2003, in a three-year-old suit by the predominantly white Parents Involved in Community Schools claiming that the policy violates equal-protection guarantees. [30]

Opposing experts and advocates in the desegregation debate are also closely watching the Louisville case, where U.S. District Judge John Heyburn II is expected to rule by the end of the school year on Jefferson County's racial guidelines for pupil assignments. And in another case, a conservative public-interest law firm is in California state court claiming that a statewide initiative barring racial preferences prevents the Berkeley school system from asking for racial information from students and families or using the information for assignment purposes. [31]

Schools in Lynn, a gritty former mill town 10 miles north of Boston, were in "dire straits" in the 1980s before adoption of the integration plan, according to Cole. Attendance was down; violence and racial conflict were up. White students — who comprised more than 80 percent of the enrollment as of 1977 — were fleeing the schools at the rate of 5 percent a year. There was also evidence that white students were being allowed to transfer out of predominantly black schools in violation of the district's stated rules.

The school board adopted a multipronged strategy to try to stem white flight and improve schools for white and minority youngsters alike, Cole says. A neighborhood-school assignment plan was combined with the construction of new schools, including magnet schools, using funds under a state law to aid racial-balance programs. Cole says attendance rates and achievement levels are up, discipline problems down and enrollment stabilized. The district's students are 58 percent minority, 42 percent white.

The citizens' group, which had earlier filed a suit that forced Boston to drop its use of busing for desegregation, sued Lynn schools in August 1999. Williams acknowledges the school system's past problems and more recent progress. But he says all of the improvements resulted from "race-neutral stuff that could have happened if the plan had not included a racial element."

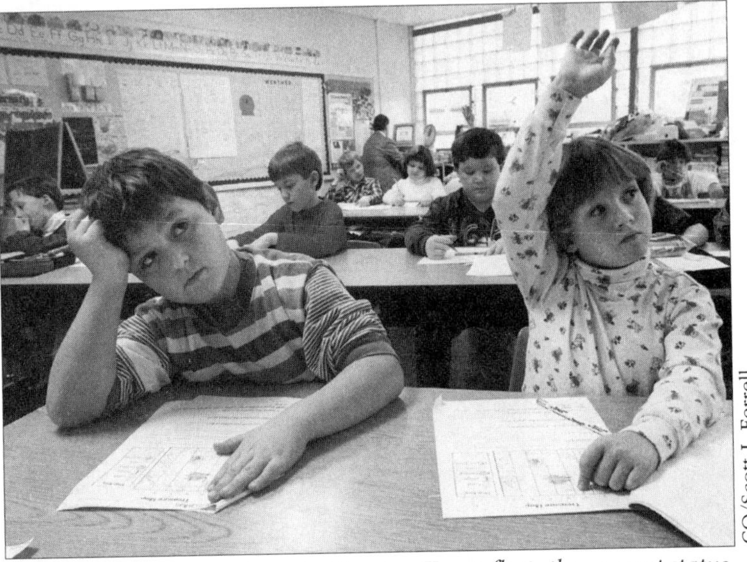

CQ/Scott J. Ferrell

Stanton Elementary School, in Stanton, Ky., reflects the current status of school integration in most of the nation. Most public schools are as segregated today as they were in 1969. During the 2000-2001 school year, for instance, only 30 non-white students were enrolled in the 2,500-student Stanton school district.

U.S. District Judge Nancy Gertner rejected the group's suit in a 156-page ruling in December 2003. "The Lynn plan does not entail coercive assignments or forced busing; nor does it prefer one race over another," said Gertner, who was appointed by President Bill Clinton. "The message it conveys to the students is that our society is heterogeneous, that racial harmony matters — a message that cannot be conveyed meaningfully in segregated schools." [32]

Legal Defense Fund Director Shaw calls the legal challenges to voluntary desegregation plans "Orwellian." "Our adversaries have this perverted sense of the law and the Constitution that holds mere race consciousness — even if it's in support of desegregation — as discriminatory," he says.

But Clegg of the Center for Equal Opportunity says schools should not assign students on the basis of race or ethnicity. "The social benefits to achieving a predetermined racial or ethnic mix are very small compared to the social costs of institutionalized racial and ethnic discrimination," he says.

Race-Mixing?

Some two-dozen Washington, D.C., high school students gathered on a school day in late February for a "dialogue" with the president of the American Bar Association and the city's mayor about *Brown v. Board of Education*. Dennis Archer, a former mayor of Detroit, is black — as is Washington's mayor, Anthony Williams. And so, too, are all but three of Woodson High School's 700 students.

The students — chosen from an advanced-placement U.S. history course — listen respectfully as Archer and Williams relate the story of the *Brown* case and the implementation of the ruling over the ensuing 50 years. The students' questions, however, make clear that they feel little impact from the ruling in their daily lives.

"Why is there such a small percentage of white students in D.C. schools?" Danyelle Johnson asks. Wesley Young echoes the comment: "I feel that to make it better we should be like Wilson [High School] and have different races in schools," he says, referring to a well-regarded integrated school in a predominantly white neighborhood.

"It's really hard for me to make [*Brown*] relevant to them," assistant principal Phyllis Anderson remarks afterward, "because they've been in an all-black environment all their lives, and their parents before them."

With 84 percent of its 65,000 public school students black, another 10 percent Hispanic and only 5 percent white, Washington provides an extreme, but not unrepresentative, example of the situation in central-city school districts throughout the country. Nationwide, central-city black students typically attend schools with 87 percent minority enrollment, according to the Harvard Civil Rights Project. For Latinos, the figure is 86 percent. This "severe segregation" results from residential segregation and the "fragmentation" of large metropolitan regions into separate school districts, the project's most recent survey explains. [33]

The Supreme Court's 1974 ruling barring court-ordered interdistrict desegregation plans virtually eliminated the possibility of racial mixing between inner cities and suburbs except in countywide systems like those in Louisville-Jefferson County and Charlotte-Mecklenburg County. The court's ruling in the Kansas City desegregation case in 1995 also limited federal judges' power to order costly improvements for central-city schools in an effort to attract white students from the suburbs.

Over the past decade or so, middle-class blacks and Latinos have themselves migrated to the suburbs, but because of residential segregation the movement has not fundamentally changed the pattern of racial isolation in the schools, according to the Harvard report. Even in the suburbs of large metropolitan areas, the typical black student attends a school that is 65 percent minority, the typical Latino a school that is 69 percent minority. [34]

Federal courts, meanwhile, have been freeing dozens of school districts from judicial supervision by declaring the segregated systems dismantled and granting the districts "unitary status." In an examination of 35 such districts, the Harvard study found that black students' exposure to whites had fallen in all but four — typically, by at least 10 percent. "Desegregation is declining rapidly in places the federal courts no longer hold accountable," the report concludes. [35]

The Legal Defense Fund's Shaw says the trends result from judicial solicitude for school districts that once practiced segregation. "If a snapshot reveals a desegregated district," he says, "the court can grant judicial absolution, and the district can return to a segregated status."

The Manhattan Institute's Abigail Thernstrom counters that the focus on racial mixing is beside the point. "Teach the kids instead of worrying about the racial composition of the school," she says. "Otherwise, we're chasing demographic rainbows. Cities aren't going to get whiter. And they're not going to get more middle-class." ■

OUTLOOK

Mixed Records

Fifty years after the Supreme Court declared the end of racial segregation, the four communities involved in the historic cases present mixed records on the degree of progress in bringing black and white children together in public schools. [36]

Topeka — home of Oliver Brown and his daughter Linda, then in elementary school — achieved "substantial levels of integration" while under a court-ordered desegregation plan,

About the Author

Associate Editor **Kenneth Jost** graduated from Harvard College and Georgetown University Law Center, where he is an adjunct professor. He is the author of *The Supreme Court Yearbook* and editor of *The Supreme Court from A to Z* (both *CQ Press*). He was a member of *The CQ Researcher* team that won the 2002 American Bar Association Silver Gavel Award.

according to the Harvard Civil Rights Project. But integration has receded slightly since the system was declared unitary and judicial supervision was ended in 1999.

As of 2001, black students in Topeka were in schools with 51 percent white enrollment — down from 59 percent in 1991. Just outside the city limits, however, better-off suburban school districts have predominantly white enrollments. "The city was then, as it is now, physically and emotionally segregated," Ronald Griffin, a black professor at Washburn University Law School in Topeka, remarked at a symposium in 2002. "That has not changed." [37]

The Delaware case "led to the merger and full desegregation of all students" in Wilmington and adjoining suburban districts, the Harvard report says. The federal court lifted judicial supervision in 1996, but Wilmington and the entire state remain as some of the most integrated school systems in the country, according to the report.

The two Southern communities involved in the four cases present a sharp contrast. Prince Edward County, Va., resisted integration to the point of closing all public schools from 1959 until the Supreme Court ordered them reopened in 1964. Today, however, the school system has an integration level "far above the national average" and student achievement in line with other Virginia districts, despite a predominantly black enrollment, according to the Harvard report.

In Clarendon County, S.C., however, School District Number One in tiny Summertown has only 60 white students among a total enrollment of 1,100. Other white students attend a private academy set up at the start of desegregation in 1969. When an *Education Week* reporter recently asked Jonathan Henry — a great-great-grandson of one of the plaintiffs — about his interactions with white students, Henry seemed "bewildered. . . . He really doesn't know any." [38]

The legacy of the *Brown* cases is "mixed," according to historian Patterson. "It seems in the early 2000s to be somewhat more complicated, somewhat more mixed than anybody in the 1970s could have imagined."

"We are miles ahead because of *Brown*," Education Secretary Paige says. "But we have yet to achieve" the goal of equal educational opportunities for all students.

Whatever has or has not been accomplished in the past, the nation's changing demographics appear to be combining with law and educational policy to push ethnic and racial mixing to the side in favor of an increased emphasis on academic performance. Schools "are going to be more racially identifiable," the Legal Defense Fund's Shaw says. "I don't see any public policy right now that's going to turn that around."

Critics of mandatory integration applaud the change. "At the end of the day, what you want to ask is, 'Are the kids getting an education?'," Abigail Thernstrom says. "The right question is what are kids learning, not whom are they sitting next to."

The emphasis on academic performance makes the challenges for schools and education policy-makers all the more difficult, however, not less. "The black kid who arrives at school as a 5- or 6-year old is already way, way behind, and it just gets worse as they go on," historian Patterson says. "There's only so much the schools can do."

Latino youngsters enter school with many of the same socioeconomic deficits, often combined with limited English proficiency. In any event, the debates about educational policy have yet to catch up with the fact that Latinos are now the nation's largest minority group. [39] "We don't see an equal commitment on the part of educational equity for Latinos," says James Ferg-Cadima, an attorney for the Mexican American Legal Defense and Educational Fund.

"It's a major challenge for all of us to work together collegially to make sure that our children get the education they deserve," ABA President Archer says. "We're going to have to do a lot more to make sure all of our children in public schools — or wherever they are — graduate with a good education and can be competitive in a global economy." ■

Notes

[1] The decision is *Brown v. Board of Education of Topeka*, 347 U.S. 483 (1954). The ruling came in four consolidated cases from Topeka; Clarendon County, S.C.; Prince Edward County, Va.; and Wilmington-Kent County, Del. In a companion case, the court also ruled racial segregation in the District of Columbia unconstitutional: *Bolling v. Sharpe*, 347 U.S. 497 (1954).

[2] The case is *McFarland v. Jefferson County Public Schools*, 3:02CV-620-H. For coverage, see Chris Kenning, "School Desegregation Plan on Trial," *The* (Louisville) *Courier-Journal*, Dec. 8, 2003, p. 1A, and subsequent daily stories by Kenning, Dec. 9-13. McFarland's quote is from his in-court testimony.

[3] For background, see Kenneth Jost, "Rethinking School Integration," *The CQ Researcher*, Oct. 18, 1996, pp. 913-936.

[4] Abigail Thernstrom and Stephan Thernstrom, *No More Excuses: Closing the Racial Gap in Learning* (2003). For a statistical overview, see pp. 11-23.

[5] Some background drawn from Roslyn Arlin Mickelson, "The Academic Consequences of Desegregation and Segregation: Evidence From the Charlotte-Mecklenburg Schools," *North Carolina Law Review*, Vol. 81, No. 4 (May 2003), pp. 1513-1562.

[6] The decision is *Belk v. Charlotte-Mecklenburg Board of Education*, 269 F.3d 305 (4th Cir. 2001). For coverage, see Celeste Smith and Jennifer Wing Rothacker, "Court Rules That Schools Unitary," *The Charlotte Observer*, Sept. 22, 2001, p. 1A.

[7] See Gary Orfield and Chungmei Lee, "*Brown* at 50: King's Dream or *Plessy's* Nightmare,"

The Civil Rights Project, Harvard University, January 2004.

[8] David J. Armor, "Desegregation and Academic Achievement," in Christine H. Rossell *et al.*, *School Desegregation in the 21st Century* (2001), pp. 183-184.

[9] See Orfield and Lee, *op. cit.*, pp. 22-26.

[10] Mickelson, *op. cit.*, pp. 1543ff.

[11] For background, see Kathy Koch, "Reforming School Funding," *The CQ Researcher*, Dec. 10, 1999, pp. 1041-1064.

[12] See David J. Armor, *Maximizing Intelligence* (2003).

[13] See John Ogbu, *Black Students in an Affluent Suburb: A Study of Academic Disengagement* (2003).

[14] Quoted in Justin Blum, "Bush Praises D.C. Voucher Plan," *The Washington Post*, Feb. 14, 2004, p. B2. For background, see Kenneth Jost, "School Vouchers Showdown," *The CQ Researcher*, Feb. 15, 2002, pp. 121-144.

[15] For background, see Charles S. Clark, "Charter Schools," *The CQ Researcher*, Dec. 20, 2002, pp. 1033-1056.

[16] See Gary Orfield *et al.*, "No Child Left Behind: A Federal-, State- and District-Level Look at the First Year," The Civil Rights Project, Harvard University, Feb. 6, 2004.

[17] For a recent, compact history, see James T. Patterson, Brown v. Board of Education: *A Civil Rights Milestone and Its Troubled Legacy*, 2001. The definitive history — Richard Kluger, *Simple Justice: The History of* Brown v. Board of Education *and Black America's Struggle for Equality* — was republished in April 2004, with a new preface and final chapter by the author.

[18] The decisions are *Sweatt v. Painter*, 339 U.S. 629, and *McLaurin v. Oklahoma State Regents for Higher Education*, 339 U.S. 637. Sweatt required Texas to admit a black student to its main law school even though a "black" law school was available; McLaurin ruled that the University of Oklahoma could not deny a black student use of all its facilities, including the library, lunchroom and classrooms.

[19] For a recent reconstruction of the deliberations, see National Public Radio, "All Things Considered," Dec. 9, 2003.

[20] See Charles Wollenberg, *All Deliberate Speed: Segregation and Exclusion in California Schools, 1855-1975* (1976), p. 108.

[21] The case is *Brown v. Board of Education of Topeka*, 349 U.S. 294 (1955).

FOR MORE INFORMATION

Center for Equal Opportunity, 14 Pidgeon Hill Dr., Sterling, VA 20165; (703) 421-5443; www.ceousa.org. Opposes the expansion of racial preferences in education, employment and voting.

Center for Individual Rights, 1233 20th St., N.W., Washington, DC 20036; (202) 833-8400; www.cir.org. A nonprofit, public-interest law firm that opposes racial preferences.

Harvard Civil Rights Project, 125 Mt. Auburn St., 3rd floor, Cambridge, MA 02138; (617) 496-6367; www.civilrightsproject.harvard.edu. A leading civil rights advocacy and research organization.

Mexican American Legal Defense and Educational Fund, 1717 K St., N.W. Suite 311, Washington, DC 20036; (202) 293-2828; www.maldef.org. Founded in 1968 in San Antonio, MALDEF is the leading nonprofit Latino litigation, advocacy and educational outreach organization.

NAACP Legal Defense and Educational Fund, Inc., 99 Hudson St., 16th floor, New York, NY 10013; (212) 219-1900; www.naacpldf.org. The fund's nearly two-dozen attorneys litigate on education, economic access, affirmative action and criminal justice issues on behalf of African-Americans and others.

National School Boards Association, 1680 Duke St., Alexandria, VA 22314; (703) 838-6722; www.nsba.org. The association strongly supports school desegregation.

[22] "*Brown* at 50," Harvard Civil Rights Project, *op. cit.*, Appendix: Figure 5.

[23] Patterson, *op. cit.*, p. 186.

[24] *Ibid.*, p. 173.

[25] James S. Coleman, Sara D. Kelly and John A. Moore, *Trends in School Segregation, 1968-1973*, The Urban Institute, 1975. The earlier report is James S. Coleman, *et al.*, *Equality of Educational Opportunity*, U.S. Department of Health, Education and Welfare, 1966.

[26] Wendy Parker, "The Decline of Judicial Decisionmaking: School Desegregation and District Court Judges," *North Carolina Law Review*, Vol. 81, No. 4 (May 2003), pp. 1623-1658.

[27] The case is *Wessmann v. Gittens*, 160 F.3d 790 (1st Cir. 1998).

[28] The decisions are *Tuttle v. Arlington County School Board*, 195 F.3d 698 (4th Cir. 1999) and *Eisenberg v. Montgomery County Public Schools*, 197 F.3d 123 (4th Cir. 1999).

[29] See Koch, *op. cit.*

[30] The case is *Parents Involved in Community Schools v. Seattle School District No. 1*. For coverage, see Sarah Linn, "Appeals Judges Told of Schools' Racial Tiebreaker," The Associated Press, Dec. 16, 2003.

[31] The case is *Avila v. Berkeley Unified School District*, filed in Alameda County Superior Court. For coverage, see Angela Hill, "Suit Accuses District of Racial Bias," *The Oakland Tribune*, Aug. 9, 2003.

[32] The decision is *Comfort v. Lynn Schools Committee*, 283 F Supp, 2d 328 (D.Mass. 2003). For coverage, see Thanassis Cambanis, "Judge OK's Use of Race in School Assigning," *The Boston Globe*, June 7, 2003, p. A1.

[33] Orfield and Lee, *op. cit.*, p. 34.

[34] *Ibid.*

[35] *Ibid.*, pp. 35-39.

[36] *Ibid.*, pp. 11-13, 39 (Table 21).

[37] Quoted in Vincent Brydon, "Panel: Segregation Still Exists in U.S. Schools," *The Topeka Capital-Journal*, Oct. 26, 2002. The Topeka district has a Web site section devoted to the *Brown* case (www.topeka.k12.ks.us).

[38] Alan Richard, "Stuck in Time," *Education Week*, Jan. 21, 2004.

[39] For background, see David Masci, "Latinos' Future," *The CQ Researcher*, Oct. 17, 2003, pp. 869-892.

Bibliography

Selected Sources

Books

Armor, David J., *Forced Justice: School Desegregation and the Law*, Oxford University Press, 1995.

A professor of public policy at George Mason University offers a strong critique of mandatory desegregation. Includes table of cases and seven-page bibliography.

Cushman, Clare, and Melvin I. Urofsky (eds.), *Black, White and* Brown*: The School Desegregation Case in Retrospect*, Supreme Court Historical Society/CQ Press, 2004.

This collection of essays by various contributors — including the lawyer who represented Kansas in defending racial segregation in *Brown* — provides an historical overview of the famous case, from a variety of perspectives.

Klarman, Michael J., *From Jim Crow to Civil Rights: The Supreme Court and the Struggle for Racial Equality*, Oxford University Press, 2004.

A law professor at the University of Virginia offers a broad reinterpretation of racial issues, from the establishment of segregation through the *Brown* decision and passage of the Civil Rights Act of 1964. Includes extensive notes and a 46-page bibliography.

Kluger, Richard, *Simple Justice: The History of* Brown v. Board of Education *and Black America's Struggle for Equality*, Vintage, 2004.

A former journalist and book publisher has written a definitive history of the four school-desegregation suits decided in *Brown v. Board of Education*. Originally published by Knopf in 1976, the book has been reissued with a new chapter by the author.

Ogletree, Charles J., Jr., *All Deliberate Speed: Reflections on the First Half Century of* Brown v. Board of Education, Norton, 2004.

A well-known African-American professor at Harvard Law School offers a critical examination of the unfulfilled promise of the *Brown* decision. Includes notes, case list.

Patterson, James T., Brown v. Board of Education*: A Civil Rights Milestone and Its Troubled Legacy*, Oxford University Press, 2001.

A professor emeritus of history at Brown University provides a new compact history of *Brown* and its impact.

Rossell, Christine H., David J. Armor and Herbert J. Walberg (eds.), *School Desegregation in the 21st Century*, Praeger, 2001.

Various academics examine the history and current issues involving desegregation. Rossell is a professor of political science at Boston University, Armor a professor of public policy at George Mason University and Walberg a professor emeritus of education and psychology at the University of Illinois, Chicago. Includes chapter notes, references.

Thernstrom, Abigail, and Stephan Thernstrom, *No Excuses: Closing the Racial Gap in Learning*, Simon & Schuster, 2003.

An academic-scholar couple provides a strongly argued case for adopting educational reforms, including school choice, instead of racial mixing to reduce the learning gap for African-American and Latino pupils. Abigail Thernstrom is a senior scholar at the Manhattan Institute; Stephan Thernstrom is a professor of history at Harvard. Includes detailed notes.

Articles

Cohen, Adam, "The Supreme Struggle," *Education Life Supplement*, *The New York Times*, Jan. 18, 2004, p. 22.

A *Times* editorial writer offers an overview of the 1954 *Brown* decision and its impact.

Henderson, Cheryl Brown, "*Brown v. Board of Education* at Fifty: A Personal Perspective," *The College Board Review*, No. 200 (fall 2003), pp. 7-11.

The daughter of Oliver Brown, first-named of the 13 plaintiffs in *Brown v. Board of Education of Topeka*, provides a personal reflection on the landmark case. Henderson is executive director of the Brown Foundation for Educational Equity, Excellence and Research in Topeka (www.brownvboard.org).

Hendrie, Caroline, "In U.S. Schools, Race Still Counts," *Education Week*, Jan. 21, 2004.

This broad survey of racial issues in public schools was the first of a five-part series marking the 50th anniversary of *Brown*. Other articles appeared on Feb. 18 (Charlotte-Mecklenburg County, N.C.), March 10 (Chicago; Latinos), April 14 (Arlington, Va., challenges of integration), with a final story scheduled for May 19 (parental choice).

Reports and Studies

Orfield, Gary, and Chungmei Lee, "*Brown* at 50: King's Dream or *Plessy's* Nightmare?" The Civil Rights Project, Harvard University, January 2004.

The project's most recent analysis of school-enrollment figures finds that racial separation is increasing among African-American and Latino students.

The Next Step:

Additional Articles from Current Periodicals

Achievement Gap

Asimov, Nanette, "Testament to Testing," *San Francisco Chronicle*, Dec. 18, 2003, p. A21.

In San Francisco, frequent diagnostic testing to pinpoint students' problem areas in reading and math has made significant headway in closing the achievement gap.

Barnes, Julian, *et al.*, "Unequal Education," *U.S. News & World Report*, March 22, 2004, p. 66.

Legally enforced segregation is no longer an issue in schools, but the disturbing gap in performance between children of different races remains troubling.

Bok, Derek, "Closing the Nagging Gap in Minority Achievement," *The Chronicle of Higher Education*, Oct. 24, 2003, p. 20.

The president emeritus of Harvard University discusses the causes of the achievement gap and recommends ways to reduce it.

Johnson, Darragh, "A Classroom Crusade," *The Washington Post Magazine*, Nov. 10, 2002, p. W22.

Eric Smith is an educational reformer with one mission — to close the racial achievement gap in schools.

Mathews, Jay, "As Data Show Fewer Report Race, Minority Scores on SAT Questioned," *The Washington Post*, April 4, 2004, p. A6.

With 25 percent of SAT takers declining to disclose their race, some question whether it can still be useful in measuring the racial achievement gap.

Olson, Lynn, "Panel Asks for Action on Hispanic Achievement Gap," *Education Week*, April 16, 2003, p. 21.

A presidential commission notes the educational problems faced by Hispanics and proposes measures to help.

Reid, Karla Scoon, " 'Value Added' Study Finds NAEP Gains for Black Students," *Education Week*, March 17, 2004, p. 7.

A study using a new methodology finds that blacks improved their reading assessment scores by a wider margin than whites or Asians.

Taylor, Stuart, "Closing the Racial Gap in Learning: What Does Not Work," *National Journal*, Oct. 25, 2003.

A discussion of Abigail and Stephan Thernstrom's social research, which argues that more integration and more money would not help close the achievement gap between white and minority students.

Winerip, Michael, "In the Affluent Suburbs, an Invisible Race Gap," *The New York Times*, June 4, 2003, p. B8.

Even controlling for economic factors, a performance gap exists between black and white students in prosperous schools.

Elementary and Secondary Schools

Gewertz, Catherine, "Racial Gaps Found to Persist in Public's Opinion of Schools," *Education Week*, May 21, 2003, p. 9.

Whites express the highest levels of satisfaction with their schools and blacks the lowest, reflecting the educational divide facing America.

Hendrie, Caroline, "City Boards Weigh Rules on Diversity," *Education Week*, Nov. 5, 2003, p. 1.

School districts in Boston, Little Rock and San Francisco weigh changes to their racial policies as they ponder possible court challenges.

Olszewski, Lori, and Darnell Little, "Integration a Dream Never Lived," *Chicago Tribune*, March 23, 2003, Metro Section, p. 1.

Chicago's school integration plan achieved very little for $108 million per year; a changing ethnic balance in the city means that old plans are increasingly outdated.

Powell, Michael, "Separate and Unequal in Roosevelt, Long Island," *The Washington Post*, April 21, 2002, p. A3.

The schools in Roosevelt, Long Island, combine segregation and an inequitable property tax system, and the result is some of the nation's poorest performing schools.

Smith, Celeste, "Resegregation; When Busing Ends," *The New York Times*, Jan. 18, 2004, Section 4A, p. 30.

With the end of its decades-old court-ordered desegregation plan, North Carolina's Charlotte-Mecklenburg schools are making extraordinary efforts to maintain high academic success rates.

Winter, Greg, "Schools Resegregate, Study Finds," *The New York Times*, Jan. 21, 2003, p. A14.

As court-ordered desegregation plans end, racial isolation is increasing in America's schools as a result of housing patterns and demographic factors.

Higher Education

Cavanagh, Sean, "Ed. Dept. Report Lists Alternatives to Race Use in College Admissions," *Education Week*, April 9, 2003, p. 28.

The Department of Education releases a report on race-neutral policies to foster diversity; critics call the report misleading.

Dobbs, Michael, "At Colleges, an Affirmative Reaction," *The Washington Post*, Nov. 15, 2003, p. A1.

Most don't realize it, but minority students with strong academic credentials are intensely fought over by selective colleges; selling SAT data is big business.

Fears, Darryl, "At U-Michigan, Minority Students Find Access — and Sense of Isolation," *The Washington Post*, April 1, 2003, p. A3.
The University of Michigan boasts about its commitment to diversity, but black students often feel racially isolated and misunderstood.

Kantrowitz, Barbara, and Pat Wingert, "What's at Stake," *Newsweek*, Jan. 27, 2003, p. 30.
The questions surrounding affirmative action are complex — a 10-step overview to help sort out the issues may make things clearer.

Merritt, Jennifer, "B-Schools: A Failing Grade on Minorities," *Business Week*, May 12, 2003, p. 52.
Only about 12 percent of students at the best business schools are black or Hispanic; outside the best schools, the numbers are slightly lower.

Orfield, Gary, and Susan Eaton, "Back to Segregation," *The Nation*, March 3, 2003, p. 5.
With elementary and secondary schools becoming more segregated, the authors maintain there is a moral duty to allow affirmative action to level the playing field.

Schmidt, Peter, "New Pressure Put on College to End Legacies in Admissions," *The Chronicle of Higher Education*, Jan. 30, 2004, p. 1.
Schools are coming under increased pressure to end legacy admissions, which due to previous segregation are biased against minority students.

Taylor, Stuart, "Racial Preferences in Admissions: The Real Choice We Face," *National Journal*, Jan. 25, 2003.
The affirmative action status quo amounts to pervasive racial discrimination against whites and Asians; x-percent plans could be damaging to academic standards.

Winter, Greg, "Study Challenges Case for Diversity at Colleges," *The New York Times*, March 20, 2003, p. A28.
A new study challenges the idea that more diversity automatically increases racial tolerance and the educational experience.

History

Cohen, Adam, "The Supreme Struggle," *The New York Times*, Jan. 18, 2004, Section 4A, p. 22.
The outcome of *Brown* seems inevitable now, but at the time there were considerable doubts about what verdict the Supreme Court would render.

Ewers, Justin, "Making History," *U.S. News & World Report*, March 22, 2004, p. 76.
The first cracks in segregation had already appeared by 1954, but *Brown v. Board of Education* was the legal thunderbolt that smashed the legal basis of segregation.

Knickerbocker, Brad, "Evolution of Affirmative Action," *The Christian Science Monitor*, June 24, 2003, p. 1.
From President John F. Kennedy to the many major corporations that lined up to support racial preferences at the University of Michigan, affirmative action has a long history in America.

Reid, Karla Scoon, "Va. Expresses 'Regret' for Closures Aimed at Resisting Desegregation," *Education Week*, Feb. 19, 2003, p. 17.
The Virginia state Senate voted to express regret for the closure of the Prince Edward County, Va., public schools for five years to resist integration.

Improving Integration and Performance

Dobbs, Michael, "For Vouchers, a Mixed Report Card," *The Washington Post*, Sept. 23, 2003, p. A1.
Some private schools provide an outstanding education, some not so much; Milwaukee statistics suggest funding for vouchers is not draining public schools.

Hubler, Eric, "Group: Mix Rich, Poor Students," *The Denver Post*, Dec. 8, 2002, p. A1.
After the apparent success of voluntary economic integration in North Carolina, hopes are high in Denver that the same can be achieved there.

MacGillis, Alec, "Basing Affirmative Action on Income Changes Payoff," *The Baltimore Sun*, May 25, 2003, p. 1C.
Studies show that income-based affirmative action, as opposed to race-based, would actually decrease the number of blacks and Latinos at top colleges.

Rimer, Sara, "Schools Try Integration by Income, Not Race," *The New York Times*, May 8, 2003, p. A1.
Cambridge, Mass., is one of a small but growing number of cities that are using economic status as the basis of school integration, not race.

Thernstrom, Abigail, "Education's Division Problem," *Los Angeles Times*, Nov. 13, 2003, p. B17.
A prominent educational researcher decries low educational performance among blacks and Latinos and praises charter schools as a way of closing the achievement gap that exists between white and minority students.

Tienda, Marta, and Sunny Niu, "Texas' 10 Percent Plan: The Truth Behind the Numbers," *The Chronicle of Higher Education*, Jan. 23, 2004, p. 10.
An empirical study of Texas students sets the record straight about the actual effects of the 10 percent admissions plan.

Toppo, Greg, "School Integration Helps in Game of Life," *USA Today*, April 14, 2004, p. 6D.
Interviews with the Class of 1980 show that most valued

an integrated education because it helped them to be more tolerant and to interact with people of other races.

Winerip, Michael, "What Some Much-Noted Data Really Showed About Vouchers," *The New York Times*, May 7, 2003, p. B12.
A much-publicized study detailing the gains of students in voucher programs suffered from flaws in its methodology.

Yardley, Jim, "Desperately Seeking Diversity," *The New York Times*, April 14, 2002, Section 4A, p. 28.
The University of Texas' admissions plan admitting the top 10 percent of high school graduates has had effects on a broad stratum of Texas students, opening doors for some, closing them for others.

Recent Court Decisions

"Judge Accepts Plan to End Chicago Desegregation Case He Calls Outdated," *The New York Times*, March 3, 2004, p. B8.
Saying that it's time "for Big Brother to bow out," a judge indicates he may soon agree to an end for the government's desegregation decree affecting Chicago's schools.

Greenhouse, Linda, "The Supreme Court: Affirmative Action," *The New York Times*, June 24, 2003, p. A1.
Justice O'Connor maintains that race as a factor in a holistic evaluation of an applicant, not in a "mechanical way," is consistent with the earlier *Bakke* ruling.

Greenhouse, Linda, "The Supreme Court: School Tuition," *The New York Times*, June 28, 2002, p. A1.
The court's 5-to-4 ruling upheld the use of public money for tuition at religious schools as part of taxpayer-funded voucher programs.

Lane, Charles, "Affirmative Action for Diversity Is Upheld," *The Washington Post*, June 24, 2003, p. A1.
Although the Michigan decisions upheld the principle of using race in college admissions, swing voter Sandra Day O'Connor noted that in 25 years racial preferences are not expected to be in use.

Lee, Henry K., "Desegregation Plan Ruled OK," *San Francisco Chronicle*, April 8, 2004, p. B5.
A judge rules that a long-standing desegregation plan for Berkeley, Calif., does not violate Proposition 209, the state's law banning racial preferences.

Schmidt, Peter, "Affirmative Action Fight Is Renewed in the States," *The Chronicle of Higher Education*, July 18, 2003, p. 9.
Although the Supreme Court upheld race as a factor in college admissions, affirmative action opponents are still working through referendums and legislation.

Funding Disparities

Olszewski, Lori, and Darnell Little, "School Spending Disparity Revealed," *Chicago Tribune*, March 2, 2004, News Section, p. 1.
With a court prepared to end a decades-old desegregation agreement, a study shows funding gaps; mostly Hispanic schools receive the least money.

Richard, Alan, "Poor Districts Seen to Face 'Funding Gaps' in Many States," *Education Week*, Sept. 4, 2002, p. 28.
The richest quarter of school districts on average receive about $1,000 more per pupil than the poorest quarter, although in some places this tendency is reversed.

Symonds, William, "Closing the School Gap," *Business Week*, Oct. 14, 2002, p. 124.
An outdated system for funding schools results in economic segregation between rich and poor districts; but high-spending districts sometimes have poor results.

Citing *The CQ Researcher*

Sample formats for citing these reports in a bibliography include the ones listed below. Preferred styles and formats vary, so please check with your instructor or professor.

MLA Style

Jost, Kenneth. "Rethinking the Death Penalty." The CQ Researcher 16 Nov. 2001: 945-68.

APA Style

Jost, K. (2001, November 16). Rethinking the death penalty. *The CQ Researcher, 11*, 945-968.

Chicago Style

Jost, Kenneth. "Rethinking the Death Penalty." *CQ Researcher*, November 16, 2001, 945-968.

In-depth Reports on Issues in the News

Are you writing a paper?

Need back-up for a debate?

Want to become an expert on an issue?

For 80 years, researchers have turned to *The CQ Researcher* for in-depth reporting and analysis of issues in the news. Reports on a full range of political and social issues are now available. Following is a selection of recent reports:

Civil Liberties
Civil Liberties Debates, 10/03
Gay Marriage, 9/03

Crime/Law
Serial Killers, 10/03
Corporate Crime, 10/02

Economy
Exporting Jobs, 2/04
Stock Market Troubles, 1/04

Education
Black Colleges, 12/03
Combating Plagiarism, 9/03

Energy/Transportation
SUV Debate, 5/03
Future of Amtrak, 10/02

Environment
Air Pollution Conflict, 11/03
Water Shortages, 8/03

Health/Safety
Homeopathy Debate, 12/04
Women's Health, 11/03

International Affairs
Aiding Africa, 8/03
Rebuilding Iraq, 7/03

Politics/Public Policy
Redistricting Disputes, 3/04
Democracy in Arab World, 1/04

Social Trends
Future of Music Industry, 11/03
Latinos' Future, 10/03

Terrorism/Defense
North Korean Crisis, 4/03
Homeland Security, 9/03

Youth
Youth Suicide, 2/04
Hazing, 1/04

Upcoming Reports

Partisan Politics, 4/30/04
Future of Marriage, 5/7/04
Gang Crisis, 5/14/04
Worker Safety, 5/21/04
Smart Growth, 5/28/04
Re-examining 9/11, 6/4/04

ACCESS

CQ Researcher is available in print and online. For access, visit your library or www.thecqresearcher.com.

PURCHASE

To purchase a *CQ Researcher* report in print or electronic format (PDF), visit www.cqpress.com or call 866-427-7737. A single report is $10. Bulk purchase discounts and electronic rights licensing are also available.

SUBSCRIBE

A full-service *CQ Researcher* print subscription — including 44 reports a year, monthly index updates, and a bound volume — is $625 for academic and public libraries, $605 for high school libraries, and $750 for media libraries. Add $25 for domestic postage.

The CQ Researcher Online offers a backfile from 1991 and a number of tools to simplify research. Available in print and online, *The CQ Researcher en español* offers 36 reports a year on political and social issues of concern to Latinos in the U.S. For pricing and a free trial of either product, call 800-834-9020, ext. 1906, or e-mail librarysales@cqpress.com.

CQ Researcher

Published by CQ Press, a division of Congressional Quarterly Inc.

thecqresearcher.com

The Partisan Divide

Are politics more polarized than ever?

If political ads sound unusually harsh this campaign season, it may be because the major parties are highlighting their differences in hopes of tipping an evenly divided electorate their way. Over the past couple of decades, elected officials and party leaders have become more openly partisan, with greater divisions between the parties across the entire range of political issues, including taxation and government spending, foreign policy and cultural issues. As the politicians present completely opposing views to the public, so-called swing voters are becoming an endangered species. Voters are either becoming more closely aligned with one party or the other, or dropping out of the political process altogether. If this year's presidential race remains as close as polls indicate, it will be the second squeaker in a row — and a further indication that there is no clear majority of political opinion in a divided country.

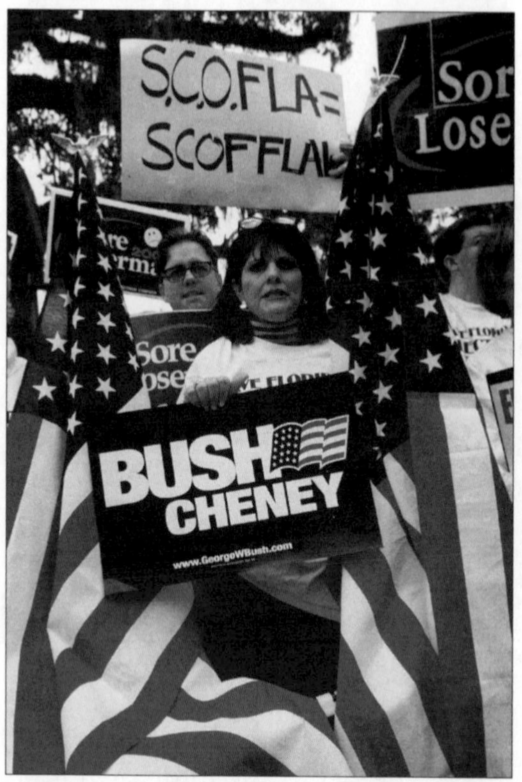

Republicans celebrate the decision to halt the recount of presidential votes in Florida in 2000, reflecting the passion and polarization of today's politics.

INSIDE

THIS REPORT

The CQ Researcher • April 30, 2004 • www.thecqresearcher.com
Volume 14, Number 16 • Pages 373-396

RECIPIENT OF SOCIETY OF PROFESSIONAL JOURNALISTS AWARD FOR EXCELLENCE ◆ AMERICAN BAR ASSOCIATION SILVER GAVEL AWARD

THE PARTISAN DIVIDE

Cover: Republicans celebrate the decision to halt the Florida recount in the 2000 presidential election dispute between Texas Gov. George W. Bush and Vice President Al Gore. (Getty Images)

The CQ Researcher

April 30, 2004
Volume 14, Number 16

MANAGING EDITOR: Thomas J. Colin

ASSISTANT MANAGING EDITOR: Kathy Koch

ASSOCIATE EDITOR: Kenneth Jost

STAFF WRITERS: Mary H. Cooper, David Masci, William Triplett

CONTRIBUTING WRITERS: Sarah Glazer, David Hatch, David Hosansky, Patrick Marshall, Tom Price, Jane Tanner

DESIGN/PRODUCTION EDITOR: Olu B. Davis

ASSISTANT EDITOR: Kenneth Lukas

CQ PRESS

A Division of
Congressional Quarterly Inc.

SENIOR VICE PRESIDENT/GENERAL MANAGER: John A. Jenkins

DIRECTOR, LIBRARY PUBLISHING: Kathryn C. Suárez

DIRECTOR, EDITORIAL OPERATIONS: Ann Davies

CONGRESSIONAL QUARTERLY INC.

CHAIRMAN: Andrew Barnes

VICE CHAIRMAN: Andrew P. Corty

PRESIDENT AND PUBLISHER: Robert W. Merry

The CQ Researcher (ISSN 1056-2036) is printed on acid-free paper. Published weekly, except Jan. 2, April 9, July 2, July 9, Aug. 6, Aug. 13, Nov. 26 and Dec. 31, by CQ Press, a division of Congressional Quarterly Inc. Annual subscription rates for institutions start at $625. For pricing, call 1-800-834-9020, ext. 1906. To purchase a *CQ Researcher* report in print or electronic format (PDF), visit www.cqpress.com or call 866-427-7737. A single report is $10. Bulk purchase discounts and electronic-rights licensing are also available. Periodicals postage paid at Washington, D.C., and additional mailing offices. POSTMASTER: Send address changes to *The CQ Researcher,* 1255 22nd St., N.W., Suite 400, Washington, D.C. 20037.

The Partisan Divide

By Alan Greenblatt

The Issues

Walk into any well-stocked bookstore and it would be hard to miss the strident rhetoric that has become a hallmark of American politics. From the left, recent titles include *Worse Than Watergate; The Bush-Hater's Handbook; The I Hate Republicans Reader* and what might be called the lies trilogy: *The Lies of George W. Bush; Big Lies* and *Lies and the Lying Liars Who Tell Them.*

From the right, titles include: *Slander: Liberal Lies About the American Right; Useful Idiots: How Liberals Got it Wrong in the Cold War and Still Blame America First* and *Bush Country: How Dubya Became a Great President While Driving Liberals Insane.*

Getty Images

Partisan crowds keep a tense vigil at the U.S. Supreme Court on Dec. 1, 2000, during oral arguments in the election dispute between Texas Gov. George W. Bush and Vice President Al Gore. The bitter partisan feelings that resulted from the nearly tied election have only intensified since then, leaving the nation with deep political divisions as it faces another presidential election.

Indeed, some contemporary media outlets specifically target partisan markets, often deliberately cranking up the political rancor.

"You can be plugged into the news all day long and never hear a liberal thought unless it's something responded to very quickly," says Mike Franc, vice president of government relations at the Heritage Foundation. To combat what has been seen as a conservative bias on talk radio, Air America, a new radio network featuring hosts with an avowedly liberal bias, began broadcasting in several major cities on March 31.

However, even with today's media balkanization, Americans are not more divided than they have ever been: The civil rights and Vietnam eras opened larger wounds. But Americans are more perfectly sorted politically than they have been in living memory.

"I like to say that we're evenly divided, not deeply divided," says Karlyn Bowman, a polling expert at the American Enterprise Institute.

President Bush is widely viewed as having failed in his stated mission of "changing the tone in Washington." Instead of being a "healer," he has become a polarizing figure, loved or hated by seemingly equal numbers of people.

The two major parties in general have found more success in highlighting their differences than in working toward consensus, but some of the rancor may have more to do with power. Some conservatives chalk up Democratic anger toward Bush to the fact that Republicans, for the first time in 50 years, control both houses of Congress and the White House.

After searching for decades for someone who could lead them out of the political wilderness, Republicans in the mid-1990s followed the program of Georgia Rep. Newt Gingrich, who instructed a generation of GOP candidates to describe Democrats in terms such as "sick" and "corrupt."

The strategy worked. Republicans gained majorities in both chambers, and Gingrich, for a time, was Speaker of the House, until his attacks on President Bill Clinton backfired in the 1998 elections. Still, Gingrich's tactics have been widely adopted not only in Congress — by today's minority Democrats as well as Republicans — but also in state legislatures.

Political power in the states is also narrowly divided now, having shifted dramatically in 2002, after Democrats lost their half-century-long control over the statehouses. Republicans now enjoy a slight advantage in the number of state legislative seats they hold.

The switch was in part the result of a 20-year grass-roots campaign led by conservative Republicans bent on eliminating moderates and inter-party cooperation, both in Washington and in statehouses. "We are trying to change the tones in the state capitals — and turn them toward bitter nastiness and partisanship," said GOP strategist and one-time Gingrich adviser Grover Norquist, who equates bipartisan behavior by Republicans as betrayal on a par with "date rape." [1]

Norquist and other fiscal conservatives are teaming up with social conservatives across the country to knock off moderates like prominent centrist Republican Sen. Arlen Specter, who on April 27 narrowly survived a challenge from staunchly conservative Rep. Patrick J. Toomey in Pennsylvania's GOP primary. Bush had supported Specter, but anti-tax and Christian Republicans supported Toomey,

Americans Are Now Evenly Divided

For much of the 20th century, more Americans considered themselves Democrats than Republicans. The GOP started making major gains, however, during the administration of Democrat Jimmy Carter in the late 1970s, when there was double-digit inflation and 52 Americans were held hostage in Iran for more than a year. In recent years the country has been split more evenly. In 2003, nearly 31 percent of Americans identified with the Democrats, and 30 percent with the Republicans.

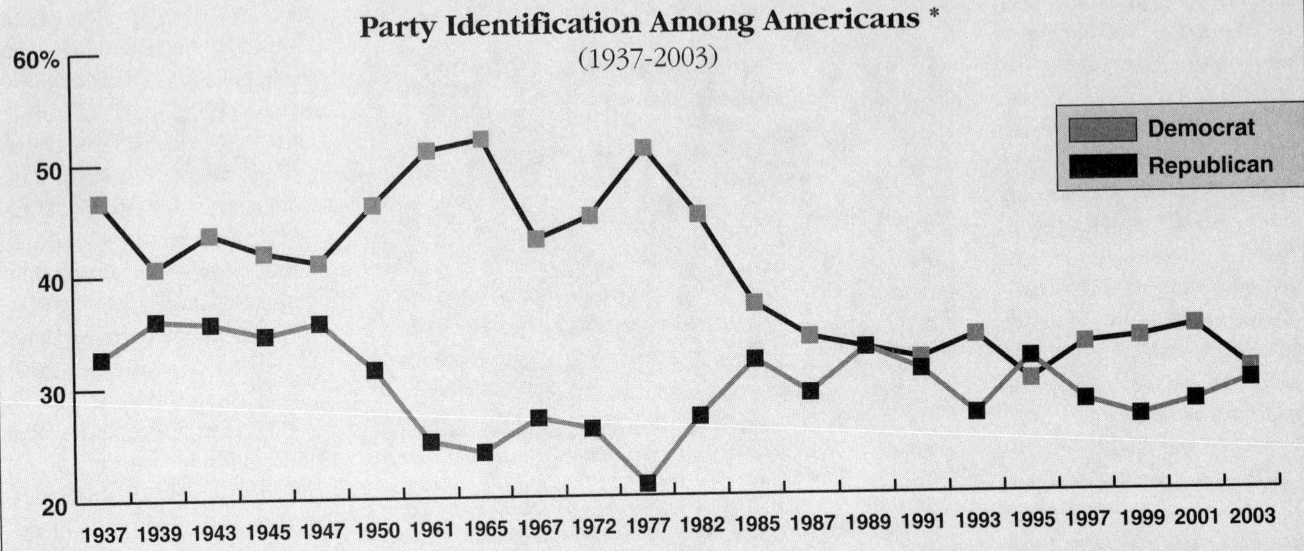

** According to various polls of the general population. Among registered voters in the 29 states and the District of Columbia that require voters to specify a party affiliation, 42 percent are registered as Democrats and 33 percent as Republicans.*

Sources: "2004 Political Landscape: Evenly Divided and Increasingly Polarized," The Pew Research Center for The People & The Press, Nov. 5, 2003; Ballot Access News, *Feb. 1, 2004, available at www.ballot-access.org/2004/0201.html*

claiming Specter was too liberal on abortion and government spending.

Because the voting public is divided right down the middle, politicians both in state capitals and in Washington press for any partisan advantage they can find, playing up the issues that help divide and reinforce their coalitions.

"This country has become polarized in a way that many people have never seen it before," says Sen. Ben Nelson, D-Neb. "For a centrist, you have as many nightmares as you can possibly have because you can't get people together, and they don't want to get together on issues."

That is one reason why, even after a cataclysmic, unifying event such as the terrorist attacks of Sept. 11, 2001, politics today have such a hard, partisan edge. Moreover, parties are sorting themselves out ideologically in ways they never have before.

There has always been disagreement between Republicans and Democrats on some issues, but it was possible to arrive at consensus on others. Once there was considerable mixing and matching within the parties. Plenty of populist Democrats who were liberal on labor issues, for example, opposed abortion, while many anti-tax Republicans supported abortion rights. Both parties had their deficit hawks and their pro-defense members.

Today, elected officials from the major parties can't seem to agree about anything, whether it's gay marriage, tax cuts or the war in Iraq. "The parties are becoming more ideologically polarized on all issues — race, the economy, foreign policy," says Geoffrey Layman, a Vanderbilt University political scientist. "The parties are so divided, there's very little to like from the other side if you're a hardcore Republican or Democrat."

The 2000 election resulted in a near-tie, with Democrat Al Gore winning more popular votes, and Bush barely winning a majority in the Electoral College after the Florida recount dispute went all the way to the U.S. Supreme Court. [2] The bitter partisan feelings that resulted from that fight have only intensified since then, despite a brief moment of bipartisan comity following the Sept. 11 attacks.

Republicans and Democrats have been bitterly divided before, during the Civil War, the '60s, and during Watergate. But no presidential candidate has won a majority of the popular presidential vote since 1988.

In an era of political parity, party leaders fight for every vote they can by magnifying every difference they have with the other side. In the process, centrist voters have come to feel disenchanted and unrepresented, while most others have been transformed into strong supporters of either one party or the other.

"That's why it's so bitter — because the stakes are so high now," says Thomas E. Mann, a senior fellow at the Brookings Institution. "It matters a huge amount which party is in power. It may have mattered less 20 years ago, because of the greater ideological diversity within each party."

Party squabbles have even contaminated foreign policy, where tradition has always dictated that partisanship stopped at the water's edge. For example, the National Commission on Terrorist Attacks Upon the United States, known as the 9/11 Commission, has won praise for its bipartisan investigation into intelligence failures. But its hearings have become highly partisan affairs, with Bush and Clinton administration figures pointing fingers at one another for failures to protect the country against al Qaeda.

Average voters, taking their signals from elected officials and party leaders, also have grown farther apart. "We are used to hearing ordinary Americans described as centrist, pragmatic and non-ideological. Well, it just isn't so [anymore]," Mann says. With today's strong partisanship and ideological polarization, "There is no longer a huge gulf between the activists and the broad public."

Of course, not all voters are hardcore party loyalists, says Morris Fiorina, a Stanford University political scientist who feels the notion of culture wars and "two Americas" — Republican red states and Democratic blue ones — is overblown.

"It's a good theme for the media — the conflict theme plays better than a consensus theme," he says. "The parties are clearly farther apart, but there's no indication that the population as a whole is more divided than it was 30 years ago."

Still, even if voters are not as ideologically polarized as the party leaders, the split between the parties leaves most voters in the position of either loving or hating the current occupant of the White House, regardless of his party. "Clinton mobilized the right, Bush mobilized the left," says William Schneider, a political analyst with the American Enterprise In-

Congress Is Becoming More Polarized

Democrats and Republicans in Congress have become more liberal and more conservative, respectively, over the past 30 years, with GOP members moving farther from the center than Democrats.

Ideological Scores of Congress, 1971-2000

(Higher positive numbers reflect more conservative leanings; higher negative numbers reflect more liberal positions; zero is the ideological center)

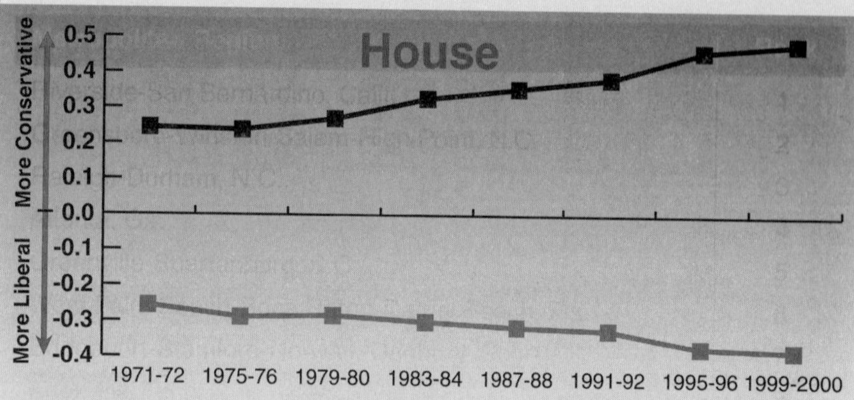

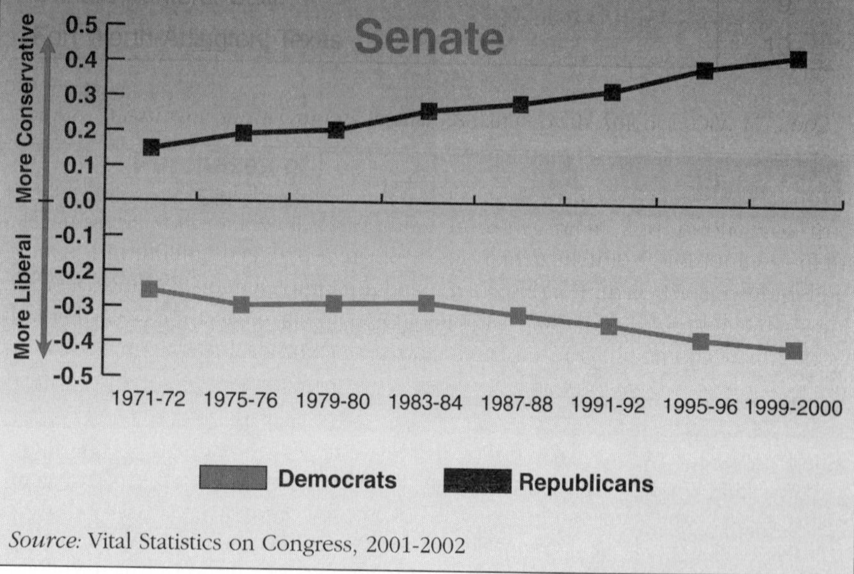

Source: Vital Statistics on Congress, 2001-2002

Bush: a Uniter or a Divider?

All this spring term, Emily Epting, a senior at the University of Georgia, has been wearing buttons that say unkind things about President Bush.

"Every time he opens his mouth, he digs himself deeper into a hole of lies and deceit," she says, criticizing Bush's policies on Iraq, gay marriage and the budget.

Others think Bush has emerged as a great leader, supporting his positions on all the issues that infuriate Epting. "Providence was smiling on the United States of America on that night when George Bush finally became president," Mitch Daniels, the leading Republican candidate for governor in Indiana, told the GOP faithful at a recent Lincoln Day dinner.

Bush, who ran for office as "a uniter, not a divider," has become a polarizing figure as president. Virtually all Democrats plan to vote against him, while Republicans are just as unanimous in supporting him. A March *USA Today*/CNN/Gallup Poll showed that 91 percent of Republicans approved of the job Bush is doing, but only 17 percent of Democrats approved — the largest partisan gap in presidential job performance ratings since Gallup began measuring in 1948. [1]

AFP Photo/Luke Fazza

President Bush campaigned on being "a uniter, not a divider," but critics say he has been a polarizing figure, loved or hated by seemingly equal numbers of people.

In December, *Time* ran a cover story called "The Love Him, Hate Him President." [2] But the question remains whether Bush is to blame for being a divisive figure, or whether half the country is bound to dislike whoever is governing at a time when voters are so evenly divided along partisan lines.

"When Republicans rated Bill Clinton in the late 1990s, they were as negative in terms of strong disapproval about him as Democrats are about President Bush now," says Scott Keeter, associate director of the Pew Research Center for The People & The Press.

The nation was split before Bush took office, after having prevailed in what was about as close to a tied election as you can get. Bush lost the popular vote in 2000 to former Vice President Al Gore but won just one more electoral vote than required. In 18 states, the winning candidate prevailed by 6 percent or less.

Mike Franc, vice president of government relations at the conservative Heritage Foundation, says Bush — the first president to preside over an all-Republican government since Dwight D. Eisenhower — "may have become the poster child for the Democratic Party's frustration at being out of power in ways it hasn't been out of power in many, many decades."

But Rep. David R. Obey, a senior Democrat from Wisconsin, says Bush should have been humbled by his narrow victory. "I'm not saying he had to go around in sackcloth and ashes," Obey says. Instead, Bush "thinks he learned from his father's defeat to never allow one ounce of separation between himself and the most extreme segments of his party."

Other Democrats are dismayed that Bush did not present himself as a unifying figure after the terrorist attacks of Sept. 11, 2001. "After 9/11, there was the inevitable rallying around the president after an unimaginable catastrophe," says Will Marshall, president of the Progressive Policy Institute, a moderate Democratic think tank. "People wanted this president to succeed, and the normal rules of political combat were suspended."

Instead, Bush squandered that goodwill by taking a "my way or the highway approach" to domestic issues like tax cuts and the war in Iraq, Marshall says.

William Schneider, a political analyst for CNN and the conservative American Enterprise Institute, agrees that Bush used up any residual post-9/11 goodwill on Iraq. "He spent his political capital, just like he spent his surplus on a tax cut. It's all gone."

Republicans acknowledge that Bush has become a polarizing figure, but they argue that acting nice and reaching out across party lines matters less than sturdy leadership in wartime.

Franc says politicians and activists are divided between those who think 9/11 was an isolated event and that terrorism is a less pressing concern than health care, the economy and other purely domestic issues, and those who side with Bush in thinking that "terrorism is like an Ebola virus and you have to stamp it out at the expense of everything else.

"To the conservative side of the electorate, the president has been masterful at steering the country through this period of challenge after 9/11," he says.

[1] Richard Benedetto and Judy Keen, "Love Him or Loathe Him: Electorate Polarized Over Bush," *USA Today*, March 10, 2004, p. 4A.

[2] John F. Dickerson and Karen Tumulty, "The Love Him, Hate Him President," *Time*, Dec. 1, 2003, p. 28.

stitute and CNN. "[Ronald] Reagan never had that impact." (*See sidebar, p. 378.*)

A March *USA Today*/CNN/Gallup Poll found that Democrats supported presidential candidate Sen. John Kerry, D-Mass., by 95-3 percent, while Republicans supported Bush by an identical margin. [3] That complete lack of bipartisan support for presidential candidates is also a new development.

In addition, neither party has been able to win a firm majority of support from voters. Although Republicans have enjoyed a great deal of success over the last decade, the GOP hasn't won the popular vote for president since 1988, and Democrats remain competitive at other levels.

Moreover, the polarization process is becoming institutionalized. Political gerrymandering by increasingly sophisticated redistricting experts and software is giving one party or the other a virtual lock on nearly every seat. [4]

"That means the representative pays a lot more attention to the strong partisan backers and appeals to them instead of playing to the center," says former Rep. Lee H. Hamilton, D-Ind., vice chairman of the 9/11 Commission.

In a sense, gerrymandering merely exacerbates a larger tendency among Americans. Demographers nowadays talk about "the big sort," in which people move to live among like-minded individuals with similar lifestyles. Political analyst Charlie Cook notes that Republicans dominate rural districts, Democrats control urban districts and the suburbs are split. In 2002, he quips, "Democrats got killed in every district that didn't have a Starbucks."

Meanwhile, says James G. Gimpel, a professor of government and politics at the University of Maryland, "The more moderate voters are dropping out of the electorate, leaving only the most intensely partisan people."

As politicians and observers seek to understand the increasingly partisan divide, here are some of the questions they're debating:

Are today's congressional Republicans more partisan than the Democrats were when they held power?

In 2003, Congress was more polarized than at any other time during the five decades that Congressional Quarterly has been analyzing "party unity" votes (votes in which a majority of one party voted against a majority of the other). [5] At a news conference on Dec. 9, 2003, Senate Democratic leader Tom Daschle, S.D., called it "the single most partisan session of Congress that I participated in."

Certainly the GOP majorities on the Hill have used their power to ram through legislation over the objections of Democrats, especially in the House. The GOP kept minority members from participating in major conference committees, which draft the final versions of bills. And last November, House Republican leaders held open a floor vote on a Medicare bill for three hours — much longer than the normal 17 minutes — in the middle of the night so they could twist arms for passage.

In another notable instance last year, House Ways and Means Chairman Bill Thomas, R-Calif., called the Capitol police to break up a meeting of committee Democrats. (Thomas later apologized.)

But if Republicans have unabashedly asserted their power, did they do more than the Democrats did when they ran both Congress and the White House?

Of course not, says Rep. Ray LaHood, R-Ill. Being in the minority "is no fun," he says, regardless of which party is in power. "The worst position to be in around here is the minority. You never get to set the agenda, and you're always subject to the will of the majority."

But David R. Obey, a 17-term Democrat from Wisconsin, says the abuse of power today "is far more pernicious than in the past."

Standing in the House Speaker's Lobby under a portrait of Texan Jim Wright, a highly partisan Democratic Speaker in the 1980s, Obey concedes that Democrats sometimes abused their power. But the Republicans are much worse, he says.

"Nine times out of 10 — and that's no exaggeration — they will not allow us to present our preferred alternatives," he says. "That happened occasionally under Jim Wright. It happens almost universally under these guys."

Surprisingly, many members and outside observers agree that Congress is more partisan under GOP control, but they disagree on whether the Republicans are at fault.

Hamilton, now director of the Woodrow Wilson International Center for Scholars, says, without doubt "excessive partisanship has made the congressional environment less welcoming and less civil, and makes it more difficult to get the work done." But, he says, given the general breakdown in civility and the compressed congressional workweek, during which members often spend fewer than 60 hours in Washington, whichever party were currently in power might look bad.

Others point out that the Republican rise to power has coincided with the increased polarization of the two parties. The GOP won its congressional majorities as a result of the partisan realignment in the South following the civil and voting rights movements of the mid-1960s. Seats once held by conservative Democrats have almost all been taken over by Republicans. Meanwhile, the GOP's influence declined in its more moderate "Eastern Establishment" base in the Northeast. As a result, there are fewer conservative Democrats or moderate or liberal Republicans.

"The Republicans are — and probably throughout their history have been — more homogenous and cohesive than the Democrats," says Barbara Sinclair, a political scientist at the University of California, Los Angeles. "Republicans can manage some things that Democrats could never manage to do."

Once Republicans, even when they were in the minority, could find support for their proposals among conservative Southern Democrats and form a working majority called the "conservative coalition." Today, there's seldom reason for the GOP — which has held narrow majorities throughout its decade in power — to try to reach out to Democrats.

"The Republicans have had to be cohesive because they've had a very small margin for error," says former Rep. Robert S. Walker, R-Pa. "There have been so few Democrats willing

GOP Evens Score in 'Swing' States

The GOP has made notable gains among registered voters in 15 key states that pundits say could "swing" the upcoming presidential election. In the late 1990s, Democrats outnumbered Republicans in those states, 36 percent to 30 percent, but since the Sept. 11, 2001, terrorist attacks and the war in Iraq, the two parties have become neck-and-neck.

Party Identification in Swing States
(among registered voters)

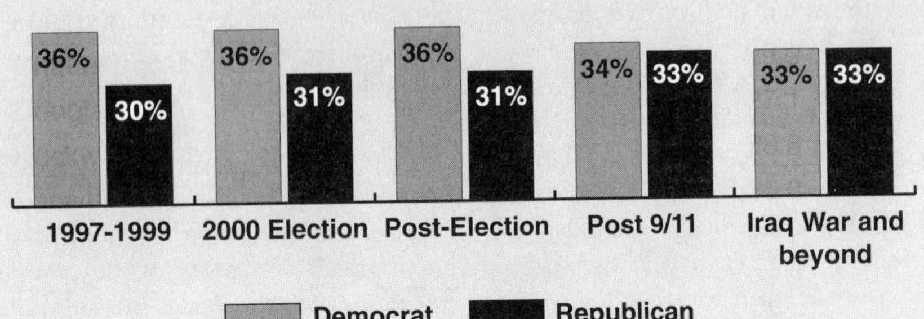

Source: "2004 Political Landscape: Evenly Divided and Increasingly Polarized," The Pew Research Center for The People & The Press, Nov. 5, 2003

to cross over and support their bills."

Moreover, thanks to redistricting, most Republicans and Democrats are in safe, partisan districts in which they only have to worry about answering to their own party's supporters.

"Yes, things are worse," concludes Brookings' Mann, largely because the parties today are so much more "ideologically polarized, unified and balanced in their strength."

Is the center disappearing from American politics?

If the two major parties today are more polarized than at any time in recent memory, has the general populace become polarized as well? "There's still a radical center in American politics that is often forgotten," says Rep. Tom Davis, R-Va., chairman of the Government Reform Committee. "The middle is where you win elections."

The argument that many, if not most, U.S. voters are moderate and centrist has long been a truism. But many people are beginning to doubt its veracity today.

Marc J. Hetherington, a government professor at Bowdoin College, in Brunswick, Maine, believes Americans today are more likely to view "one party positively and one negatively," and "less likely to feel neutral toward either party." They are also better able to list what they like and dislike about the political parties than 20 to 30 years ago, he says. [6]

Hetherington does not believe the public is as partisan as elected officials. Most people like to think of themselves as moderate, and most Americans don't pay all that much attention to politics, he points out. But in recent years, there has been more partisan "sorting," he says. People may still think of themselves as ideological centrists, but they identify more strongly with one major party or the other today than they once did.

"Partisan intensity or even interest in being a partisan is at an unusually high level," says David Hill, a Republican consultant in Texas. "For whatever reason, people today — more than in past decades — are willing to wear a party label, and those who are willing are more intense about it."

Voters may be taking their cues from "hyperpartisan" elected officials and party leaders, Hill suggests. National Democratic Party Chairman Terry McAuliffe "knows just what to say to get the base all up in an uproar," as does House Republican leader Tom DeLay of Texas, he says.

And political gerrymandering has made it less important for either members of Congress or state legislators to appeal to the middle, says Franc, the Heritage Foundation lobbyist. "If you're in a 60 percent Republican district," he says, "it doesn't matter that 15 percent of your constituents are undecided." But when politicians must appeal to a broader constituency — such as in statewide races for governor or senator — candidates will often present themselves as more moderate, Franc says, in order to appeal to centrist voters, who are more crucial in such contests.

"However shrinking, there still are some voters without firm roots in party or ideology, and they can be moved," Mann says. "The middle is important because the parties are so balanced."

The Pew Research Center for The People & The Press released a widely cited survey in March showing that 38 percent of registered voters are committed to Kerry, 33 percent are committed to Bush and 29 percent are swing voters open to persuasion. [7] Those numbers support other polls and registration data suggesting that the country is almost evenly split between Republicans, Democrats and independents.

Most self-described centrist commentators believe there is still a center and that it very much matters politically, because the parties are so close to parity.

"You don't win elections by appealing to Judge Moore supporters in Alabama," says Alan Wolfe, director of the Boisi Center for Religion and American Public Life at Boston College and author of *Marginalized in the Middle.* He was referring to former Alabama Supreme Court Chief Justice Roy Moore, who lost his job after he installed a Ten Commandments monument in the lobby of the Alabama Judicial Building and then refused to remove it. "You win by appealing to [moderate] suburban housewives outside Cincinnati."

Vanderbilt political scientist Layman agrees that the center "does matter," but he says the political parties increasingly are realizing that elections may be won by "mobilizing the base rather than appealing to the center."

Are cultural issues dividing America?

Since Bush and Gore divided up the nation's voters into nearly equal parts in the 2000 election, many have argued that they split the country along cultural and religious lines — with churchgoers and gun owners supporting Bush, and secularists and gun-control and abortion-rights advocates voting for Gore.

"The map of America after the 2000 election delineated cultural fault lines more than economic ones," says Will Marshall, president of the Progressive Policy Institute, a centrist Democratic think tank. [8]

Schneider, of the American Enterprise Institute, agrees that the 2000 map "was a map of cultural America" that was more about church members and gun ownership than about the economy and jobs. Cultural issues "divide voters most closely. That's what leads large numbers of populist voters — who should vote Democratic because of jobs — to vote for Bush, because they're deeply religious and patriotic."

Layman, who has written extensively about the intersection of cultural issues and politics, notes that voters' frequency of church attendance was a greater predictor of voting preferences in 2000 than income, gender, region or any other traditional demographic variable except race. "The party platforms sent out pretty clear signals that there is a big cultural gap between the two parties," Layman says, on issues such as abortion and gun owners' rights.

Bush himself sent strong signals about his cultural conservatism in 2000. As a candidate, he called Jesus Christ his favorite political philosopher and in office has limited stem-cell research involving fetal tissue obtained through abortion and called for a constitutional amendment excluding gays from marrying each other.

"A lot of people support Bush passionately because he's so vocal about his faith," says John J. Pitney Jr., a government professor at Claremont McKenna College in Claremont, Calif., "and for the same reason a lot of people are hostile to him."

Cultural issues are especially polarizing, Pitney argues, because they leave little room for compromise. "With a tax bill or a spending bill," he notes, "you can always find a number in between. You really can't do that with gay marriage." In addition, both parties use cultural issues as a "wedge" to keep voters from supporting their opponents.

Some say Bush's proposed amendment banning same-sex marriages is being used as just such a wedge issue. Because Congress is unlikely to approve such an amendment this year, most pundits say, Bush proposed it this year primarily to motivate conservative voters to go to the polls. Meanwhile, voters in six states will consider constitutional amendments on gay marriage in November.

But many still question whether voters this year will choose candidates based more on their cultural stances than on government budgets and the economy. Marshall predicts that job loss and other economic issues will supplant cultural arguments this time around, and Schneider agrees that cultural issues "wash away" when the economy is a prime concern.

Cultural issues are important, says Republican consultant Hill, but they aren't everything. "There are still some economic issues that are important catalysts," he says. "There are still ardent Republicans who are Republicans because of tax issues, and they share little or none of the social-conservative agenda."

Clyde Wilcox, a political scientist at Georgetown University who specializes in religion and politics, says the idea of a cultural war is overstated. The activists and political elites have trouble compromising on issues like abortion, he says, but only a "really tiny portion" of the population takes extreme positions on such issues. "If we're talking about a culture 'war,' " he says, "we're talking about a lot of non-combatants."

Cultural issues may only be part of the mix, but they're an important part. "The cultural issues and the economic positions have aligned themselves," says Scott Keeter, associate director of the Pew Research Center for The People & The Press. It's not a perfect divide, he says, but for the most part Republicans now embrace the conservative position on cultural issues, tax cuts and the proper role of government, while Democrats take the more liberal or progressive stance. ■

BACKGROUND

Rise of Factionalism

The United States was founded without a political party system. In fact, in his 1796 farewell address to the nation, President George Washington warned "in the most solemn manner against the baneful effects of the spirit of party." Excessive partisanship, he wrote, leads to factionalism and power mongering contrary to the spirit of democracy. [9]

Because Washington was such a popular and unifying figure, his administration passed without the creation of a party system. But historians have noted that even Washington sometimes had to suppress factionalism so that his own positions would prevail.

Other Founders paid lip service to nonpartisanship, but even during Washington's administration "polarization laid the foundation for powerful two-party politics," note his most recent biographers. "A long ideological war had just begun." [10]

The early party factions — the Federalists and Anti-Federalists — were led and largely personified by Alexander Hamilton and Thomas Jefferson. "In every free and deliberating society," Jefferson wrote, "there must, from the nature of man, be opposite parties, and violent discussions and discords; and one of these for the most part, must prevail over the other for a longer or shorter time." [11]

Hamilton and the Federalists, who included powerful bankers and industrialists in the North, favored a strong central government. Jefferson and the Anti-Federalists argued against a "monarchical" rule by the aristocracy, saying that farmers, craftsmen and shopkeepers should control their own interests without interference from the capitol. "If the Federalists had wealth, social standing and political sophistication on their side," writes veteran political journalist Jules Witcover, "Jefferson had the raw numbers." [12]

Jefferson's party — which dominated politics throughout the first half of the 19th century — eventually morphed into today's Democratic Party. The major step came after the controversial presidential election of 1824, which was decided by the House of Representatives and led to the splitting of the party into factions. Four years later, Andrew Jackson won big calling himself the Democratic-Republican candidate, in a campaign loaded with "Old Hickory" clubs and promotional tie-ins, such as badges, plates and pitchers — lending politics some entertainment value. Jackson's anti-corporate, populist appeal made him both loved and hated.

"His blunt words and acts assumed the character of moral gestures which forced men to declare themselves, for or against," according to Jackson biographer Marvin Meyers. [13] His vice president and successor, Martin Van Buren, had long laid the groundwork for a true party organization, reasoning that a party based more on principles than personalities would endure longer. The convention that nominated Van Buren in 1836 released an address to the public that was the forerunner of modern party platforms.

Dozens of parties — including the Whigs, Know-Nothings, Barnburners, Softshells, Hunkers and Free Soilers — emerged during the first half of the 19th century. They all enjoyed some success, but the Jefferson-Jackson Democrats became so dominant that the party eventually split into Northern and Southern factions arguing over the expansion of slavery.

In 1854, a group of Whigs, Free Soilers, abolitionists and anti-slavery Democrats met and formed the Republican Party. The name was a pointed reference to the Democratic Party's previous name, with members of the new party complaining that the Democrats had formed a "slavocracy" in thrall to Southern slaveholders. (*See cartoon, p. 386.*)

Four years later, Democrats lost control of the House, and debate over slavery grew so heated that some members carried pistols onto the House floor. [14] Southern Democrats walked out of the party's 1860 convention and ended up nominating a pro-slavery candidate of their own. The Democratic Party was cut in two, leading to the election of the first Republican president, Abraham Lincoln — who would eventually abolish slavery — in a four-way race. Since then, 17 Republicans and 10 Democrats have been elected president.

Grand New Party

Republicans dominated American politics for most of the 72 years following Lincoln's election, occupying the White House for 56 of those years, controlling the Senate for 60 and the House for 50. But Lincoln's prosecution of the Civil War and the subsequent Reconstruction of the South earned the Republicans intense enmity in the South for the next century, preventing the GOP from becoming a true national party until recent times.

After losing two close presidential elections to Democrat Grover Cleveland in 1884 and 1892, Republicans in 1896 forged a coalition of Northern urbanites, prosperous farmers and industrial workers, solidifying their position as "the majority party of the nation" everywhere but in the solid Democratic South. [15] Republicans held onto the White House until 1932, except in 1912 when former Republican President Theodore Roosevelt ran as a third-party "Bull Moose" candidate and split the GOP vote with President William Howard Taft — leading to the eight-year reign of Democrat Woodrow Wilson. As late as 1928, the GOP candidate, Herbert Hoover, carried 40 states.

Hoover, of course, would bear the blame for the Great Depression and lose to Democrat Franklin D. Roosevelt four years later. FDR's New Deal Coalition combined support from blacks, urban ethnics, Jews, Catholics, organized labor and Southerners to produce a new majority that would last for the next three decades.

The Democrats' presidential run was broken only in 1952 and 1956 by Dwight D. Eisenhower — the latest in a long string of military heroes elected president more on the strength of their personal popularity than their party label. Eisenhower did little to challenge New Deal programs, especially after the

Continued on p. 384

Chronology

1960s-1980s

Republicans eventually dominate the White House, but Democrats maintain control of Congress

1960
John F. Kennedy defeats Richard M. Nixon by 118,550 votes, but Democrats lose seats in both the House and Senate — the first time in a century any winning presidential candidate's party lost seats.

1964
President Lyndon B. Johnson wins by a landslide, carrying 44 states — but five Deep South states oppose him, opening the first cracks in Democratic control of the region.

1966
In a backlash against Johnson's anti-poverty and civil rights programs, Republicans gain 47 House seats, elect three Southern senators and pick up eight new governorships, including Ronald Reagan's in California.

1968
Nixon wins the presidency, narrowly defeating Vice President Hubert H. Humphrey in a three-way race and inaugurating an era of divided federal government that lasts, with few interruptions, until 2002.

1974
In a backlash to the Watergate scandal, 75 new House Democrats are elected, presaging the Democrats' sole White House victory between 1968 and 1988 — Jimmy Carter's in 1976.

1980
Reagan is elected president, heralding the modern GOP message of low taxes, strong defense and conservative stances on cultural issues.

1984
Reagan is re-elected in a 49-state landslide, increasing voter identification with Republicans, particularly among born-again Christians and cutting into Democratic strength in blue-collar union households.

1990s-2000s

Democrats tack to the center but continue to lose power to a decidedly more conservative GOP.

1992
Moderate "New Democrat" Bill Clinton defeats the first President George Bush. Ross Perot takes 19 percent of the presidential vote — the best third-party showing since 1912.

1994
Unpopular Clinton initiatives on health care and gun control help Republicans win majorities in both houses of Congress — for the first time in 40 years, including their first majority of Southern House seats since Reconstruction; Republicans also open up a big lead in governorships.

1998
For the first time since 1934, the president's party gains seats in a midterm election, largely in response to the GOP investigation into Clinton's sex life. Clinton then becomes the second president to be impeached after the House, along party lines, finds him guilty of lying and obstructing investigations into his personal conduct.

1999
The Senate acquits Clinton, voting largely along party lines.

2000
George W. Bush loses the popular vote for the presidency but wins a majority of electoral votes, after the U.S. Supreme Court ends a 36-day recount standoff in Florida. Election reveals Democratic estrangement in the South and much of the nation's midsection.

2001
Sen. James M. Jeffords of Vermont leaves the GOP, putting a tied Senate into Democratic hands. . . . Following the Sept. 11 terrorist attacks, a spirit of bipartisanship is short-lived.

2002
GOP recaptures the Senate and retains control of the House. . . . More Republicans are elected to state legislatures than Democrats for the first time in 50 years.

October 2003
The legislature approves a new congressional-district map increasing the GOP's share of the state's congressional delegation.

November 2003
Republicans hold a House vote open for an unprecedented three hours, starting at 3 a.m., to round up votes to pass Medicare bill.

December 2003
U.S. Supreme Court hears arguments in Pennsylvania case on constitutional limits to partisan gerrymandering.

March 2004
Democrats quickly select Sen. John Kerry of Massachusetts as their presumptive nominee to face Bush in November, showing uncommon solidarity in their desire to find a candidate who is "electable."

April 28, 2004
U.S. Supreme Court, in a 5-4 vote, upholds Pennsylvania redistricting plan.

New Campaign Finance Law Shifts Power

Many people debate whether the 2002 federal campaign finance reform law succeeded in limiting the influence of big money in politics. But they don't disagree over one of the law's unintended consequences: the weakening of America's two major political parties.

The so-called McCain-Feingold law, representing the most profound change in political financing in 30 years, banned national political parties from using "soft money" — unregulated campaign donations from corporations, unions and wealthy individuals. [1]

But in trying to keep soft money out of party officials' hands, the law has prevented the parties from doing the kind of grassroots organizing they traditionally have done. "McCain-Feingold has had a profoundly negative effect on political parties," says Jim Jordan, spokesman for America Coming Together, a new, liberal fundraising group. "They're simply less well funded to do their traditional, core work."

Ironically, the law has actually encouraged *more* campaign donations from special interests. Instead of relying on million-dollar donations from big contributors, parties and candidates are raising record amounts of money by leaning hard on more lobbyists to write $2,000 checks. [2]

Meanwhile, the law has empowered hundreds of new groups like Jordan's — known as 527s after a section of the tax code — to collect multimillion-dollar donations to do the same work once done by political parties: running television ads, registering voters and encouraging supporters to turn out on Election Day. The most prominent 527 so far is the Media Fund, supported by billionaire investor George Soros, which is running millions of dollars' worth of anti-Bush ads in key "swing" states. Another pro-Democratic group, Partnership for America's Families, registered 86,000 Philadelphia voters last fall, helping Mayor John Street eke out an 85,000-vote win.

The rise in the influence of soft money grew out of post-Watergate rule changes that allowed state parties to use unregulated funds for "party-building activities," such as paying for yard signs and voter registration efforts. But the exemption grew into an enormous loophole that transformed state parties into virtual money-laundering machines for each other and the national party committees.

During the 2000 and 2002 election cycles, the two major national parties gave $472 million in soft money to state parties nationwide. [3] But in 2002 — before McCain-Feingold took effect — state parties spent only about $52 million on genuine party-building expenses, devoting most of the rest to broadcast ads that skirted regulations, according to Anthony Corrado, a campaign finance expert at the Brookings Institution.

Under the new law, all nuts-and-bolts party work that occurs within 120 days of a federal election (primary or general) — such as identifying and registering voters or bringing them to the polls — is now considered "federal election activity" and is subject to federal regulation. Even if a county party is merely seeking to support its local sheriff, if a federal candidate is on the same ballot, all party contacts with voters are subject to the new regulations.

"You could interpret this law so broadly that if I tell people to 'vote for the Republican team,' that could trigger federal disclosure and reporting requirements," complains Indiana state Rep. Mike Murphy, chairman of the Marion County (Indianapolis) GOP. "The whole psyche of how people identify with political parties would be damaged if state and local candidates have to put up a Chinese wall between themselves and federal candidates."

Because of the complex nature of the new campaign finance law, that wall is going up. State party officials now avoid contact with federal candidates whenever possible. Moreover, the law inhibits federal candidates from appearing at fundraisers or in ads for state or local candidates. The Federal Election Commission (FEC) ruled in January that President Bush cannot appear in ads this year endorsing other state, local or congressional Republican candidates unless his re-election campaign pays for the ad. Otherwise, the ad would be considered an illegal donation to the Bush campaign. [4] The new restrictions apply to other federal candidates as well.

But American political parties are nothing if not adaptable. The powerful entities that once decided who ran for what office and with how much support had found a new role in recent years as support organs, offering consulting and fundraising support to self-selected aspirants. With those functions now under legal restriction, the parties may be forced into still another role: as clearinghouses of legal advice for avoiding McCain-Feingold's many minefields.

"The bottom line," says Wayne Hamilton, a senior adviser to the Texas GOP, "is we tell our local parties to stay completely away from any type of federal activity unless they have the money to hire attorneys that specialize in FEC regulation and federal campaign laws."

[1] The law was named after its sponsors, Sen. John McCain, R-Ariz., and Russell Feingold, D-Wis. For background, see Kenneth Jost, "Campaign Finance Showdown," *The CQ Researcher*, Nov. 22, 2002, pp. 969-992.

[2] Glen Justice, "New Rules on Fundraising Bring Lobbyists to the Fore," *The New York Times*, April 20, 2004, p. A14.

[3] Denise Barber, "Life Before BCRA: Soft Money at the State Levels in the 2000 & 2002 Election Cycles," *The Institute on Money in State Politics*, Dec. 17, 2003, p. 3 (www.followthemoney.org/press/Reports/200312171.pdf).

[4] Dana Milbank and Thomas B. Edsall, "FEC Curbs 'Endorsement' Ads," *The Washington Post*, Jan. 30, 2004, p. A2.

Continued from p. 382

midterm elections of 1954 provided Democrats with enduring majorities in both houses of Congress.

During the first 20 years after World War II, the parties shared power about equally outside of the South. From 1968 until 2003, control of the White House and at least one chamber of Congress was split between the two parties — except for six and a half years (during Jimmy Carter's administration, Clinton's first two years in office and Bush's first six months in office). With consensus on most domestic issues and agreement on fighting the Cold War, politics were fairly tranquil, with about three-quarters of the public trusting the government in Washington to do "the right thing." [16]

In 1960, Democrat John F. Kennedy barely beat Eisenhower's vice president, Richard M. Nixon, to win the presidency by a mere 118,574 votes. Kennedy pushed an inclusive vision, promoting programs for the poor while offering tax cuts to keep the middle class in the Democratic column. After Kennedy's assassination in 1963, Congress passed the Civil Rights Act in 1964, outlawing discrimination in employment and public accommodations, largely to memorialize the slain president and after strong arm-twisting by Kennedy's successor, Southerner Lyndon B. Johnson. The following year, Congress cleared the Voting Rights Act, which outlawed literacy tests and similar qualification devices used to keep blacks off the rolls. Johnson signed the bill in full knowledge that it would weaken his party in the South. [17]

Johnson won re-election in a landslide in 1964, but that election saw the first GOP inroads into the Deep South, with Barry Goldwater carrying five Southern states, largely in reaction to passage of the Civil Rights Act. In the midterm elections of 1966, Republicans gained 47 House seats and picked up three new Senate seats from the South. They also picked up eight new governorships, including Ronald Reagan's in California. The public generally felt that Johnson had gone too far with his poverty programs and civil rights legislation.

By the late 1960s, courts began ordering the integration of public schools in the South, the delayed result of a 1954 Supreme Court decision — another development that alienated Southerners from the Democratic Party. In 1968, a year punctuated by race riots and the assassinations of civil rights leader the Rev. Dr. Martin Luther King Jr. and Democratic presidential candidate Sen. Robert F. Kennedy, D-N.Y., Nixon tied his Democratic opponent, Hubert H. Humphrey, in the popular vote, but carried the Electoral College. Alabama Gov. George Wallace — running as the American Independent candidate — carried five Southern states.

Nixon's so-called "Southern strategy" had contributed to "a positive polarization of the electorate," in his running mate's phrase, by assuring Southerners that he opposed school busing to achieve integration and favored states' rights on social issues. [18]

New GOP

Nixon's Southern strategy paid immediate dividends. The newfound Republican strength in the South — combined with support in the Mountain West and Plains states — gave the GOP what for a long time looked like a "lock" on the Electoral College. Republicans won five of the six presidential elections from 1968 to 1988, losing only the post-Watergate contest of 1976.

Reagan's 1980 victory also broke the party's 26-year drought in the Senate, creating a majority there that lasted for six years. In addition, it marked the rise of a new, more conservative Republican Party: Reagan stressed lower taxes, smaller government and a robust defense. Social conservatives also favored Reagan, who promoted their agenda rhetorically, if not all that actively once in office. Reagan's ideas had a lasting influence on the GOP, but his personal popularity did not convert itself into a majority for the party in Congress. That would have to wait until 1994.

President Clinton had tried to pull the Democrats back to the center after its disastrous flirtation with the New Left in the 1970s and '80s. But opposition to his ambitious universal health-care plan, his decision to raise taxes to plug a deficit and his support for gun control helped the Democrats lose their 40-year House majority in 1994.

Throughout much of that period out of power, House Republicans often cooperated with the majority in hopes of winning approval for some of their favored projects. At times, particularly early in the Reagan presidency, they were able to join forces with conservative Southern Democrats to create a working majority. Their fortunes began to change after Reagan left office, when Rep. Gingrich joined the leadership.

House Republicans had frequently changed leaders in hopes of selecting one who would more aggressively confront the Democratic majority. [19] With Gingrich, they finally picked a true aggressor. With the help of other Republicans who felt their caucus had been too compliant under Democratic rule, Gingrich in 1983 founded the Conservative Opportunity Society, a rump group dedicated to circumventing the Democratic Party's refusal to address GOP pet issues, such as tax cuts and constitutional amendments to allow school prayer and ban abortion.

Gingrich's signature line at that stage of his career was to decry the "liberal welfare state." After joining the House leadership in 1989 — having contributed to the toppling of heavy-handed House Speaker Wright — Gingrich recruited countless GOP candidates and instructed them to refer to the Democrats in negative terms, such as "pathetic," "sick" and "corrupt."

The strategy paid off but contributed to a heightened level of partisan ill will in Washington. A cornerstone of the GOP's new strategy was the South, which finally was voting Republican for Congress as well as president. In 1994, the GOP won a majority of the region's House seats for the first time since Reconstruction. All of the party's congressional leadership, like Gingrich, hailed from the South.

"As Southerners moved into positions of power and influence within the GOP," writes historian Lewis Gould, "their racial views, cultural conservatism and religious moralism sometimes grated on other sections of the nation. Like the Democrats before them, the Republicans would find that having a 'Solid South' was a mixed advantage." [20]

Perhaps the GOP's biggest political mistake was impeaching Clinton for lying about his sexual conduct in office. The relentless attack led to the GOP losing five House seats in 1998 — the first time the president's party had gained seats in a midterm election since 1934. Gingrich was tossed from power and resigned his seat.

"The Gingrich revolution had a great impact that hasn't left off yet in polarizing things," says Rutgers University political scientist Alan Rosenthal. "For the Republicans to win Congress, they had to play mean, and they continue to do so, and the Democrats saw that that worked."

In 2000, Bush ran for president as "a uniter, not a divider." Gore, who won the popular vote, managed to hold onto many of the states Clinton had brought back into the Democratic column. The Democrats now enjoy an advantage in many former Republican strongholds, such as New Jersey and most of New England — the old "Eastern Establishment" provinces where voters have been put off by the new GOP's socially conservative message.

Consumer advocate Ralph Nader, running as a Green Party candidate, ate into Gore's vote total in toss-up states — most notably Florida. Bush narrowly prevailed in the Electoral College, after the Supreme Court ended a 36-day standoff, during which Florida's voting results were in dispute.

Despite his narrow victory, Bush has governed as an unblinking conservative on domestic and foreign issues. After the Sept. 11 terrorist attacks, Democrats held their fire and largely supported Bush, with many — including presumptive Democratic candidate Kerry — supporting the resolution authorizing the war in Iraq. But rather than rewarding the Democrats' loyalty to Bush, voters in 2002 rallied around the president: Republicans regained control of the Senate.

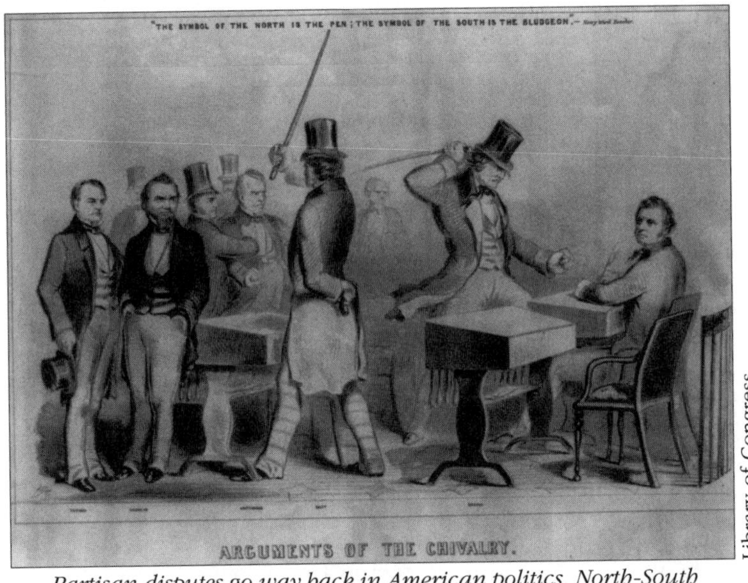

Library of Congress

Partisan disputes go way back in American politics. North-South sectional disputes erupted in Congress on May 22, 1856. South Carolina Rep. Preston S. Brooks attacks seated Massachusetts Sen. Charles Sumner with his cane after Sumner insulted two Senate colleagues. South Carolina Rep. Lawrence M. Keitt, center, raises his own cane to keep other legislators at bay, while hiding a pistol behind his back.

Since then, Democrats have hardened their opposition to Bush's policies. Bush himself has been a polarizing force as president, failing to "change the tone in Washington," as he had promised. He is enormously popular among Republicans but equally reviled among Democrats. So the verdict on the Bush presidency may very well depend on the few voters left in the middle. ■

CURRENT SITUATION

Upcoming Election

The famously divided 2000 presidential election was the third such election in a row in which neither candidate won a majority — the first time that had happened since the period between 1884 and 1892. It also represented the third set of congressional elections in a row in which neither party mustered a majority of the overall vote.

Republicans finally managed a slight majority (51 percent) of the congressional vote in 2002. This November, Bush and the Republicans will try to forge a stable majority coalition. Knowing they will face long years in the wilderness if they again fall short, Democrats will try everything they can to block them.

The presidential race between Bush and Kerry is too close to call at this point. Bush enjoys the advantages of incumbency and a huge fundraising lead, but voters unhappy with Bush's handling of the economy and Iraq have embraced Kerry.

Presidential elections usually amount to referenda on the incumbent. This year, however, most voters' positions appear to be set in stone, months before the nominating conventions — with partisan allegiances and the electoral map strongly resembling the 2000 patterns that resulted in a toss-up.

The Bush and Kerry campaigns already have all but conceded to each other more than 30 states that were not close in 2000, and independent groups have likewise concluded that most states probably will be a lock for one side or the other. Hence, both candidates have targeted their advertising campaigns on 16-18 key states. [21]

"When you have a strong polarizer in the White House in either party, the center tends to shrink," says Larry J. Sabato, director of the University of Virginia's Center for Politics. "People become more emotional about their party ties — you either love him or you hate him, and the center shrinks."

In his recent book *The Two Americas*, Democratic pollster Stanley Greenberg says the Republican base consists of voters in rural areas, fast-growing outer suburbs and the Deep South. "It includes the workingmen who want the government to stop messing with them and the world to stop messing with America," Greenberg writes. "And it is a world for the most privileged." [22]

Meanwhile, Democratic loyalists are found among African-Americans, Hispanics, union households, women with postgraduate degrees and high incomes and voters in "Cosmopolitan States," such as California, New York and New Jersey, Greenberg notes. [23]

"New Deal Democrats were the party of Southern whites, urban ethnics and Midwestern blue-collar workers," writes Democratic demographer Ruy Teixiera. "Now Democrats are the party of teachers, nurses and janitors," along with college-educated white-collar workers, who Teixeira says have voted 52 to 40 percent in favor of Democrats over the last four presidential elections. [24]

Religious Right

Greenberg and other political observers also have noted the divide among voters based on their church attendance, or lack thereof. In 2000, evangelicals who regularly attend church gave Bush, an evangelical Christian, 84 percent of their vote, while nearly 60 percent of those who don't attend church regularly supported Gore. [25] "It's easy to caricature them," said Karl Rove, Bush's top political adviser, "but they're essentially your neighbors who go to church on a regular basis and whose life is a community of faith and who are concerned about values." [26]

Rove has said that 4 million evangelicals failed to vote in 2000, an estimate he and the Bush administration have worked diligently to erase in this year's campaign. (The party's success in the 2002 midterm elections has been widely attributed to improved Republican turnout efforts, particularly in Georgia and other Southern states.)

Several Bush actions have appealed to evangelicals and other culturally conservative voters, including limiting stem-cell research, seeking a constitutional ban on gay marriage and signing a bill making it illegal to harm a fetus while committing another federal crime. Some pundits say such issues and others, like the current case before the Supreme Court challenging use of the phrase "under God" in the Pledge of Allegiance, suggest that the cultural divide remains wide open and may favor Bush. [27] Even debates about the phenomenally popular movie "The Passion of the Christ" — which takes a conservative Christian view of the crucifixion of Jesus Christ — reflect that divide.

Courting the Bases

Meanwhile, Bush has made moves that could eat into the Democrats' traditional base among Latinos and the elderly. His appointment of Miguel Estrada to the federal bench and his proposal to create a temporary guest-worker plan were, at least in part, meant as appeals to the heavily courted Latino vote. Similarly, his education reform initiative and expansion of Medicare to cover prescription drugs were designed to cut into Democratic support among the elderly and voters concerned about the state of public education. [28]

After the Sept. 11 attacks, as the country rallied around its president, congressional Democrats complied with most of Bush's wishes and did not offer a strong alternative platform during the 2002 midterm elections. It cost them dearly in both chambers. Then as the presidential primary season got under way, Vermont Gov. Howard Dean came out swinging, claiming he represented "the Democratic wing of the Democratic Party" (borrowing the line from the late Sen. Paul Wellstone, D-Minn.). Dean's attacks on Bush — particularly on the war in Iraq — resonated with poll respondents, and Dean held a sizeable lead throughout the second half of 2003. But his liabilities — his claim that the United States was not safer after Saddam Hussein's capture, his criticism of Bush's tax cuts for the middle class and his support of civil unions for gays — left Democratic voters worried he would alienate moderates.

Indeed, Democrats during the primary season seemed most concerned with "electability" — finding a candidate who could beat Bush. Kerry seemed to win out on that question, more than on his merit or positions.

"Bush has succeeded in doing something that was almost impossible in the '90s — he's united the Democrats," says Ted Widmer, a historian at Washington College in Chestertown, Md., and former Clinton speechwriter.

With the center diminished — "There is no middle," Rove said — the two parties are tending to their bases, hoping to get the faithful to the polls while picking off just enough independents to cobble a majority. Both sides act as if they'd be satisfied by "winning ugly," grinding out electoral gains with 50.1 percent of the vote. [29]

"All non-voters are irrelevant and unimportant," political analyst Stuart Rothenberg wrote in an online chat, "and I am skeptical about efforts by the right, left or radical center to motivate large numbers of non-voters. It seems that every election we talk about bringing new people into the system, but the 2004 contest is likely to be about which party motivates its base and sways swing voters." [30]

And as for undecided swing voters, most live in states already considered sewn up by one party or the other, such as California and Texas, according to the Pew Research Center. That leaves less than 10 percent of the undecided electorate living in states considered competitive.

"The behavior of the parties is probably not helping this situation," says the center's Keeter. "The parties are not helping people that aren't already on board to think about joining up. There's a lot of maintenance of the base going on."

The notion that less than 10 percent of voters are really in play in the presidential race mirrors the new picture in House races, where most voters' choices, in effect, don't count. Due to modern, technologically sophisticated redistricting, there are very few competitive House seats left — estimates range from 25 to 40 in any given cycle, depending on retirements, out of 435 seats. That means the Democrats would have to win close to about 70 percent of the seats seriously in contention to erase the GOP's current 11-seat majority. Their job is made especially difficult this year because the Texas legislature redrew the state's congressional map, giving Republicans a good chance of picking up a half-dozen additional seats. [31]

A similar mid-decade redistricting in Colorado was ruled to have violated the state's constitution. And the U.S. Supreme Court is set to rule by June in a Pennsylvania case that could determine whether partisan gerrymandering is constitutional. During oral arguments last December, even justices sympathetic to the notion that the court could play a role in limiting districts drawn for maximum partisan advantage did not appear convinced that a workable legal standard could be devised. [32]

Democrats also appear unlikely to regain control of the Senate, even though Republicans currently hold only a two-seat majority. Democrats are defending more seats — including five in the South — being vacated by retirements than the GOP. And, like the Electoral College, rural and underpopulated states have a disproportionate voice in the Senate, further hurting Democrats' chances because they draw more support from urbanites. Of the 21 states with two Republican senators, 18 have 7 million inhabitants or less. In fact, the 36 Republican senators from those 18 states represent only 2 million more inhabitants than California and New York combined, which send four Democrats to the Senate.

Partisanship is increasing in state legislatures as well, for many of the same reasons it's increasing in Congress. For most of the postwar era, Democrats enjoyed healthy leads in both the number of legislators and legislatures they controlled, but Republicans have superseded them in both categories over the last couple of years. The same tight party competition that keeps Congress narrowly divided exists in the states: About 60 percent of the legislative chambers could be won by either party, and every election cycle since 1984 has resulted in at least one tied chamber somewhere.

Republicans increased their number of governorships last year to 28 — including the election of Arnold Schwarzenegger following the recall of Democrat Gray Davis, the first such recall since 1921. Of course, Davis was not above pressing for partisan advantage himself, as displayed most vividly in his $10 million ad campaign against former Los Angeles Mayor Richard Riordan in the 2002 primary, helping to deny the nomination of the candidate Davis least wanted to face in November — part of a growing trend of candidates interfering in the other party's primaries.

The recall occurred four years after the first presidential impeachment in 130 years. Two years later, the presidential election was marred by legal wrangling over voting results in Florida, ended by a narrow majority in the Supreme Court. These trends, along with the mid-decade redistricting efforts, lead University of Kansas political scientist Burdett Loomis to conclude that we're living in an age of "slightly unhinged partisanship."

Formerly extreme and extraordinary political and legal tactics are being used with increasing regularity, he points out. "We will redistrict because we can, we will impeach because we can, we will recall because we can," Loomis says. "We're going to politicize everything. In a sense, partisan advantage becomes everything." ■

OUTLOOK

Continued Parity?

Although Republicans and Democrats have been fighting for 150 years, at the moment, it appears they've fought each other to a draw. "Parity is an anomaly in American politics," says Marshall, of the Progressive Policy Institute. "Usually there is a governing party and an opposition party — a sun and a moon. But we've been so long in this period of parity that I'm beginning to wonder whether we've got a new norm."

"It's sort of like the exhaustion of two boxers fighting it out in the middle of the ring," Rove told *The New Yorker*. "This happened in 1896, where the Civil War party system was in

Continued on p. 390

At Issue:

Are third-party alternatives needed in this year's presidential election?

RICHARD WINGER
EDITOR, BALLOT ACCESS NEWS

WRITTEN FOR *THE CQ RESEARCHER*, APRIL 2004

yes

Voters respond favorably to elections in which they have more than two viable choices. In 1992, when Ross Perot ran as an independent, voter turnout rose for the first time since 1980, another election with three strong presidential candidates.

Ralph Nader's entry in this year's presidential election will attract voters who have a visceral dislike of both major parties. Commentators who presume that all of Nader's voters are those who would otherwise vote Democratic are not paying attention. Nader has been endorsed by many leaders of Perot's Reform Party, including former Chairman Jack Gargan. And Nader has reached out to Perot voters, saying Perot was right about NAFTA and other issues.

People use the term "two-party system" as a synonym for the Democratic and Republican parties, and they talk about candidates operating "outside the two-party system." This is nonsense. Minor parties are not only part of the two-party system but also a key factor in making it work better.

This is true at the state level as well as in presidential contests. In 1998, Minnesota enjoyed a 60-percent voter turnout — by far the best turnout in any state in 1998, or in 2002, for that matter. (The average turnout in both years nationally was below 40 percent). In 1998, Minnesota saw a gubernatorial election with three viable candidates; former professional wrestler Jesse Ventura won, running as a Reform candidate.

Two-party systems are considered healthy when either of the two major parties has a fair chance to win. But sometimes one of the two major parties gets permanently too strong compared to the other one. The United States had this problem from 1860 to 1932, when the Republicans won 14 presidential elections and only lost four. Minor parties kept that imbalance from being even worse than it was. Republicans lost the presidential elections of 1884, 1912 and 1916 because of minor parties.

During the 1980s, many commentators discussed the so-called Republican lock on the Electoral College, arguing that it made a democratic presidential victory impossible. This theory was especially strong after the 1988 election. But then Perot entered the race in 1992, giving the Democrats a chance to win.

Minor parties and independent candidates help keep the two-party system healthy by keeping the two major parties in closer balance.

AMY ISAACS
NATIONAL DIRECTOR, AMERICANS FOR DEMOCRATIC ACTION

WRITTEN FOR *THE CQ RESEARCHER*, APRIL 2004

no

Over the years, numerous third-party candidacies have had a positive impact on the political system. The introduction of new and alternative ideas can — as Teddy Roosevelt's Bull Moose Progressive Party did in 1912 — make our nation healthier and more prosperous.

But, while we stand for the freedoms and benefits attributed to third-party campaigns, they must be judged in their context and on their merit. We must also recognize the potential dangers that can bring more harm than good — both for the causes we champion and the needs of the nation.

The most recent example is the 2000 election. Ralph Nader's Green Party platform was based on many of the same liberal positions that formed the basic platform for many Democrats and the campaign of Vice President Al Gore. Yet, by splitting small majorities in states like Florida and New Hampshire, Nader supporters ultimately contributed to the election of a president with views and eventually policies quite contrary to progressive goals.

Americans for Democratic Action always has and always will support the right of third-party candidacies to vie for national political office. By raising a wider range of issues and forcing major-party candidates to take stances on these issues, minor-party candidates bring a valuable component to any election. For 57 years we have fought to preserve the basic principles of American democracy, including the right to freedom of speech guaranteed by the First Amendment of the U.S. Constitution.

But the 2004 election is one of the most important elections of our time. The Bush administration has threatened the very fabric of that which unites all Americans in the search for life, liberty and the pursuit of happiness. A repeat performance by Mr. Nader in 2004 would represent a disaster at untenable cost.

Perhaps minor parties should petition the major-party candidate that they most identify with to carry their message. However, now is not the time to divide essentially like-minded voters. The world's fortune pivots on a narrow margin of error and that calls for no third-party intervention in this election cycle.

In Kansas, Looks Are Deceiving

To outward appearances, Kansas is one of the most solidly Republican states in the country. Kansans haven't supported a Democrat for president in 40 years and haven't sent one to the U.S. Senate since 1932.

But serious internal rifts have developed within the state's GOP, making it, in effect, the nation's only three-party state. Power is now divided about evenly between moderate Republicans, conservative Republicans and Democrats. The two wings of the GOP run separate candidates for many offices and often cannot coalesce behind the winner in their party primaries.

The state's Board of Education represents, in microcosm, the political schism within Kansas. Although seven of its 10 members are Republicans, the board chose a Democratic chairwoman because the two GOP factions thought she would make a better peacemaker. Republicans on the board split primarily over the teaching of evolution, which has led to heated elections and acrimony.

Besides evolution, most GOP arguments in Kansas surround differing views on social issues — most notably abortion. "We've had, for quite a few years, a strong difference of opinion between two factions of the Republican Party — social conservatives and regular Republicans," says Sen. Pat Roberts, R-Kan., chairman of the Intelligence Committee. "These are building blocks of your personal beliefs, and it's difficult to compromise."

In the 1998 GOP primary, Gov. Bill Graves, a moderate, easily turned back a conservative challenge by a former party chairman. After that, Roberts says, many Republicans hoped the infighting would end. Instead, the conservatives, ousted from control of the party organization, left the incoming moderates — who sometimes call themselves the "mod squad" — with just $500 in the bank. In effect, they had taken their ball and gone home, setting up rump organizations to support their favored candidates. Sen. Sam Brownback became a leader of the more conservative wing after defeating a Republican appointed by Graves to fill a Senate seat in a 1996 primary.

GOP infighting helped Kathleen Sebelius, a Democrat, win election as governor two years ago, even as Roberts was being re-elected without having to face a Democratic opponent. In dealing with the legislature, Sebelius navigates between three competing factions. Whichever wing of the GOP feels most put-upon will often side with Democrats — as conservatives did in 2002 to pass a legislative-redistricting plan designed to hurt moderate members of their own party.

"The governor has to look at the three factions and try to figure out where her majority is coming from," says Burdett Loomis, a political scientist at the University of Kansas. Loomis says state Senate President Dave Kerr recently visited his classroom and told students about his need to elect moderate Republicans in this year's legislative elections. He wasn't interested in electing just any Republicans, Loomis recalls, because more conservatives would threaten his grasp on power.

The fighting in Kansas has a lot to do with one party having been in power for nearly all of the state's history. [1] "When conservatives rail against big government, they can't complain about Democrats because it was the Republicans who built this state government," says Michael Smith, a Kansas State University political scientist. "That's a big cause of the rift."

Fights for control of the state GOP and its nominations are naturally intense and sometimes split along regional lines, such as education-funding disagreements between Republicans in wealthy, suburban Johnson County, outside of Kansas City, and the rest of the largely rural state.

Other states have been long dominated by a single party without developing such intense divisions. Loomis suggests in Kansas the rift is largely a battle between businessmen, such as farmers and bankers — who look to the GOP to support the private sector — and those mostly focused on promoting a socially conservative agenda.

"Indeed, the business community is often looked down on at least as much as Democrats," Loomis says.

Sen. Roberts has a simpler explanation. "It's in the water," he jokes.

[1] For background, see Michael Smith, "Kansas, the Three-Party State," *Campaigns & Elections*, October-November 2003, p. 36.

Continued from p. 388

decline, and the parties were in rough parity and somebody came along and figured it out and helped create a governing coalition that really lasted for the next some-odd years. Similarly, somebody will come along and figure out a new governing scheme through which people could view things and could, conceivably, enjoy a similar period of dominance." [33]

Republicans appear to be in a better position to break through as the new majority party. Their victories at the presidential and congressional levels have been slim — but they have been victories. They appear certain to retain their congressional majorities this year and, if Bush gets re-elected, they'll be able to leverage incumbency into greater power.

"There are five — five! — Democratic seats in the Senate up for grabs in the South," said one Democratic strategist. "We could lose four. I think we will. And the Republicans could have a majority for 30 to 40 years." [34]

Of course, during the 1980s, many political observers spoke of a Republican "lock" on the White House, which Clinton managed to "pick" twice in a row. And since Republicans haven't won the popular presidential vote since 1988, some Democrats believe demographics favor them over the long haul. Some largely Democratic groups, such as Latinos and secular voters, are growing faster than parts of the Republican base.[35] Bush's pollster Matthew Dowd has said that if all the demographic groups vote as they did in 2000, Bush will lose this year — even though the number of electoral votes in states that supported him has increased.[36]

"We are in need of diversity — women, Latin, African-American, Asian," former Republican National Committee Chairman Rich Bond said. "We've taken white guys as far as that group can go."[37]

Republicans, of course, have been actively courting Latinos, Jews and others who traditionally have supported Democrats. Meanwhile, "demography is moving, slowly, toward the Bush nation," says journalist Michael Barone.[38] He notes that the states Bush won in 2000, which were then worth 271 electoral votes, now hold 278 electoral votes after the decennial reapportionment. In 2000, except for California, Bush carried every state that later gained House seats — mostly in the South or West. Complicating the matter for Democrats is the fact that Nader, widely seen as a spoiler during the 2000 campaign, is running again this year.

Both major parties understand which groups are in play and what messages might most appeal to them. "Parties and politicians have gotten very, very sophisticated strategically," says Jim Jordan, a longtime Democratic strategist now with America Coming Together, a new group that supports the party's candidates. "We've hit a type of equilibrium of appeal, and when a party seems to move too far in a certain direction either to the left or the right, there are powerful corrective forces.

"Polling has become so sophisticated," Jordan continues. "We know immediately what the public is thinking, and there are powerful desires to satisfy those urges. In effect, as parties, we won't allow ourselves to take positions that consign us to minority status."

In addition, both parties have "stolen" issues from each other in recent years. Clinton got credit for signing a Republican bill to overhaul welfare, while Bush has paid more attention to education and signed the largest expansion of federal entitlements in 40 years with his Medicare prescription-drug plan.

If both parties speak the same language on certain issues, however, their approaches remain fundamentally different. They use the language of broadest appeal when talking to swing voters but cast competing plans and candidates in the starkest terms when speaking to their supporters.

Creating a majority, says Sabato of the University of Virginia, "takes not just one party being smart, it takes the other party being really stupid and refusing for ideological reasons to get on the right side of some huge emotional issues that really matter to voters."

So what will end this period of parity? "Big events are going to reshape the political landscape," Marshall says.

The most profound event of recent times — the Sept. 11 attacks — has had a major effect on politics, but it's not yet certain what its ultimate political effect will be.

"If Democrats can't compete on national security," Marshall suggests, "then you may see a Republican trend through several election cycles." But Marshall notes that Democrats, partly by nominating Vietnam War veteran Kerry and questioning Bush's handling of Iraq and the war on terror, are trying to neutralize the Republican lead on this issue.

Bush's use of images from Sept. 11 in his first campaign ads this year — and the charges by his former anti-terror chief Richard A. Clarke that Bush was inattentive to international terror before Sept. 11 — suggest that the terrorist attacks have become just one more partisan issue. And the growing number of U.S. casualties in Iraq makes the war increasingly controversial.[39]

In any event, arguments about war haven't precluded arguments about other issues. "Sept. 11 should have ended the culture war," says Wolfe, of Boston College. "The idea that we can still argue about these really trivial wedge issues after this tragedy is just unbelievable."

Self-described centrists like Wolfe are disappointed that leaders of both parties continue to offer partisan approaches to issues, rather than reaching a consensus. But with both parties afraid to abandon their bases amid intense competitiveness, he will no doubt remain disappointed.

Eventually, events and problems will force one party or the other to offer a bold enough position to break the deadlock. The Heritage Foundation's Franc suggests that day will come when the Baby Boomers retire and the costs of major entitlement programs grow by double-digit rates.

"That's going to be the big divide — what's going to be done about keeping all the promises made to Baby Boomers," he says. "If entitlement spending keeps going, will it crowd out defense, or force tax increases?"

Those questions remain a few years down the road. Until then, Franc says, people on either side of the partisan di-

About the Author

Alan Greenblatt is a staff writer at *Governing* magazine. He previously covered elections, agriculture and military spending for *CQ Weekly*, where he won the National Press Club's Sandy Hume Award for political journalism. He graduated from San Francisco State University in 1986 and received a master's degree in English literature from the University of Virginia in 1988.

vide are likely to remain where they are. "Forevermore, presidents will be viewed in very bright, clear colors, and there will be no more grays and pastels," Franc says. "You're either with me or you're not, and you're right or wrong on an issue." ■

FOR MORE INFORMATION

American Enterprise Institute, 1150 17th St., N.W., Washington, DC 20036; (202) 862-5800; www.aei.org. One of the nation's largest think tanks, promoting limited government, private enterprise and a strong national defense.

Brookings Institution, 1775 Massachusetts Ave., N.W., Washington, DC 20036; (202) 797-6000; www.brookings.edu. An independent think tank that focuses on economics, foreign policy and governance.

Center for Politics, University of Virginia, 2400 Old Ivy Rd., Charlottesville, VA 22904; (434) 243-8468; www.centerforpolitics.org. Promotes civic education and participation.

Democratic National Committee, 430 South Capitol St., S.E., Washington, DC 20003; (202) 863-8000; www.dnc.org. The national party organization for Democrats serves as an umbrella for state parties.

Heritage Foundation, 214 Massachusetts Ave., N.E., Washington DC 20002; (202) 546-4400; www.heritage.org. A conservative think tank that promotes free enterprise and limited government.

Pew Research Center for The People & The Press, 1150 18th St., N.W., Suite 975, Washington, DC 20036; (202) 293-3126; www.people-press.org. A foundation-sponsored polling organization.

Progressive Policy Institute, 600 Pennsylvania Ave., S.E., Suite 400, Washington, DC 20003; (202) 546-0007; www.ppionline.org. A moderate Democratic think tank affiliated with the Democratic Leadership Council.

Republican National Committee, 310 1st St., S.E., Washington, DC 20003; (202) 863-8500; www.rnc.org. The GOP's national headquarters.

Notes

[1] Quoted in John Aloysius Farrell, "Rancor becomes top D.C. export; GOP leads charge in ideological war," *Denver Post*, May 26, 2003.

[2] Kenneth Jost and Gregory L. Giroux, "Electoral College," *The CQ Researcher*, Dec. 8, 2000, pp. 977-1008.

[3] Jeffrey M. Jones, "Public Divided on Bush," The Gallup Organization, March 10, 2004, http://www.gallup.com/content/login.aspx?ci=10948.

[4] For background, see Kenneth Jost, "Redistricting Disputes," *The CQ Researcher*, March 12, 2004, pp. 221-248.

[5] John Cochran, "Legislative Season Drawn in Solid Party Lines," *CQ Weekly*, Jan. 3, 2004, p. 10.

[6] Marc J. Hetherington, "Resurgent Mass Partisanship: The Role of Elite Polarization," *American Political Science Review*, September 2001, p. 628.

[7] The Pew Research Center for The People & The Press, "Three-in-Ten Voters Open to Persuasion," March 3, 2004, http://people-press.org/reports/display.php3?ReportID=205.

[8] To see map, go to http://www.sptimes.com/election2000/map.shtml.

[9] The address can be found at http://gwpapers.virginia.edu/farewell/transcript.html.

[10] James MacGregor Burns and Susan Dunn, *George Washington* (2004), p. 116.

[11] Quoted in Jules Witcover, *The Party of the People* (2003), p. 60.

[12] *Ibid.*

[13] Marvin Meyers, *The Jacksonian Persuasion* (1957), p. 15.

[14] Witcover, *op. cit.*, p. 204.

[15] Lewis L. Gould, *Grand Old Party* (2003), p. 127.

[16] Stanley B. Greenberg, *The Two Americas* (2004), p. 36.

[17] For background, see Alan Greenblatt, "Race in America," *The CQ Researcher*, July 11, 2003, pp. 593-624.

[18] *Ibid.*, p. 46, and Gould, *op. cit.*, p. 377.

[19] Jonathan Allen, "John Rhodes, House GOP Leader Noted for Advising Nixon to Quit, Dies of Cancer at Age 86," *CQ Weekly*, Aug. 30, 2003, p. 2099.

[20] *Ibid.*, p. 420.

[21] Dan Balz and Jim VandeHei, "Candidates Narrow Focus to 18 States," *The Washington Post*, March 15, 2004, p. A1.

[22] Greenberg, *op. cit.*, p. 95.

[23] *Ibid.*, p. 118.

[24] Ruy Teixeira, "Emerging Democrats," *Prospect*, Feb. 26, 2004.

[25] Ronald Brownstein, "Attendance, Not Affiliation, Key to Religious Voters," *Los Angeles Times*, July 16, 2001, p. 10.

[26] Quoted in Nicholas Lemann, "The Controller," *The New Yorker*, May 12, 2003, p. 68.

[27] Bill Sammon, " 'Culture Wars' Shaping Election," *The Washington Times*, March 25, 2004, p. A1.

[28] For background, see David Masci, "Latinos' Future," *The CQ Researcher*, Oct. 17, 2003, pp. 869-892; Kenneth Jost, "Testing in Schools," *The CQ Researcher*, April 20, 2001, pp. 321-344; and Adriel Bettelheim, "Medicare Reform, *The CQ Researcher*, Aug. 22, 2003, pp. 673-696.

[29] Quoted in Lemann, *op. cit.*

[30] "Q&A With Bob Levey," washingtonpost.com, Sept. 16, 2003, http://discuss.washingtonpost.com/wp-srv/zforum/03/r_metro_levey091603.htm.

[31] For background, see Richard E. Cohen, "Could Lightning Strike?" *National Journal*, March 27, 2004, p. 970, and Jost, "Redistricting Disputes," *op. cit.*

[32] Jost, *ibid.*, p. 257.

[33] Lemann, *op. cit.*, p. 68.

[34] Philip Gourevitch, "The Shakeout," *The New Yorker*, Feb. 9, 2004, p. 28.

[35] John B. Judis and Ruy Teixeira, *The Emerging Democratic Majority* (2004).

[36] Alan Greenblatt, "The Politics of Parity," *Governing*, January 2002, p. 20.

[37] Thomas B. Edsall, "Census a Clarion Call for Democrats, GOP," *The Washington Post*, July 8, 2001, p. A5.

[38] Barone, Michael, "The 49 Percent Nation," *National Journal*, June 9, 2001.

[39] William Schneider, "Bush's Vanished Capital," *National Journal*, March 27, 2004, p. 996.

Bibliography

Selected Sources

Books

Gould, Lewis L., *Grand Old Party: A History of the Republicans*, Random House, 2003.

The University of Texas historian concludes that contemporary Republicans have rejected the ideas of Lincoln, Theodore Roosevelt and Eisenhower in an embrace of conservatism.

Greenberg, Stanley B., *The Two Americas: Our Current Political Deadlock and How to Break It*, Thomas Dunne Books, 2004.

The Democratic pollster examines today's competing voting blocs and lays out the best cases each major party can make in seeking to win over the public.

Reichley, A. James, *The Life of the Parties: A History of American Political Parties*, Rowman & Littlefield, 2000.

A fellow at the Public Policy Institute explains the cyclical nature of majority-party dominance and concludes with a survey of how national, state and local parties have adapted to their changing roles in contemporary times.

White, John Kenneth, *The Values Divide: American Culture and Politics in Transition*, Chatham House, 2003.

A Catholic University political science professor details how the cultural rift between Americans produced the tied 2000 election and predicts that it will continue to shape electoral politics for years to come.

Witcover, Jules, *Party of the People: A History of the Democrats*, Random House, 2003.

In this companion to Gould (above), the veteran journalist portrays the Democratic Party as always on the side of economic and social justice against moneyed interests represented by a parade of competing parties.

Articles

"Eatanswill Revisited — America's Election," *The Economist*, Jan. 31, 2004, Special Report, p. 1.

The British magazine concludes that with the parties at even strength and competing strictly on turnout, partisanship will become sharper.

Barone, Michael, "The 49 Percent Nation," *National Journal*, June 9, 2001.

An influential article notes the varying partisanship of different regions and argues that religion separates voters more than any other factor.

Cochran, John, "Disorder in the House — and No End in Sight," *CQ Weekly*, April 3, 2004, p. 790.

Although Democrats say the GOP is high-handed, the partisan rancor has been brought about by bad deeds by both sides.

Cochran, John, "Legislative Season Drawn in Solid Party Lines," *CQ Weekly*, Jan. 3, 2004, p. 10.

A journalistic analysis of partisan votes in Congress shows that Congress was more polarized in 2003 than at any other time in the past 50 years.

Cohen, Richard E., Kirk Victor and David Baumann, "The State of Congress," *National Journal*, Jan. 10, 2004, p. 82.

The authors examine a dozen trends in congressional behavior and conclude that the institution of Congress has weakened in the decade since Republicans took control, but they trace many of the trends back to Democratic days.

Goldberg, Jonah, "Division Diversions," *National Review Online*, Feb. 5, 2004, www.nationalreview.com/goldberg/goldberg200402051231.asp.

The conservative columnist says all presidents in this era are divisive because they symbolize different stances in the culture wars, but that Democratic complaints about a divided America are overblown.

Kuttner, Robert, "America as a One-Party State," *The American Prospect*, Feb. 1, 2004, p. 18.

The liberal magazine editor argues that Republicans are gaming the rules in Congress and the courts not only to push their agenda but also to preserve their majority.

Samuelson, Robert J., "Polarization Myths . . .," *The Washington Post*, Dec. 3, 2003, p. A29.

The economics columnist argues that talk of Americans being polarized today is off the mark, especially compared to the civil rights and Vietnam eras.

Reports and Studies

***Evenly Divided and Increasingly Polarized: 2004 Political Landscape*, The Pew Research Center for The People & The Press, Nov. 5, 2003.**

The independent polling organization determines that the national unity prompted by the Sept. 11, 2001, terrorist attacks has evaporated over a partisan divide centered on the war in Iraq and differing views about the role of business and the social safety net.

The Next Step:

Additional Articles from Current Periodicals

Congress

Babington, Charles, "Hey, They're Taking Slash-and-Burn to Extremes!" *The Washington Post*, Dec. 21, 2003, p. B1.
Republicans hope their tough tactics will ensure their majority status; given the ill will it's causing, Sen. John McCain says they'd better be right.

Calmes, Jackie, "Us vs. Them Rules American Politics," *The Wall Street Journal*, Dec. 1, 2003, p. A4.
As polarizing political partisanship increases in Congress, even the old cross-party friendships between members are discouraged by party bosses.

Lewis, Neil A., "Where the Gloves Are Nearly Always Off," *The New York Times*, Oct. 28, 2003, p. A19.
The Senate Judiciary Committee is a prime example of both the politicization of the judicial nomination process and the rancor between Democrats and Republicans.

Stolberg, Sheryl Gay, "The High Costs of Rising Incivility on Capitol Hill," *The New York Times*, Nov. 30, 2003, Section 4, p. 10.
Thomas Jefferson wrote rules of civility for Congress, but today's members are prone to bending them.

Divided Nation

"A Portrait in Red and Blue — American Politics," *The Economist*, Jan. 3, 2004.
The differences between the congressional districts of Dennis Hastert and Nancy Pelosi represent the cultural and political divide between the "red" and "blue" states.

Broder, David, "Tight Race for a Divided Nation," *The Washington Post*, March 3, 2004, p. A1.
Pundits agree that the ferocity of both Republicans and Democrats will guarantee a close, hard-fought race in November.

Brownstein, Ronald, "Survey Finds Americans Are Increasingly Divided," *Los Angeles Times*, Nov. 6, 2003, p. A20.
The national unity generated by 9/11 has disappeared, says a survey showing that the political chasm separating Americans from each other is wider than ever.

Jenkins, Jeffery, "Fed Up With Partisan Politics? Welcome Back to Good Old Days," *Chicago Tribune*, Sept. 28, 2003, Perspective Section, p. 6.
Concerns about increasing levels of partisanship often ignore America's political history; until World War II, extreme partisanship was the norm.

Kotkin, Joel, "Red, Blue and . . . So 17th Century," *The Washington Post*, March 28, 2004, p. B1.
America's cultural divide parallels the split between England's Roundheads and Cavaliers; growth is concentrated in the conservative Roundhead regions.

Kotkin, Joel, and Karen Speicher, "Parting Souls," *Los Angeles Times*, May 11, 2003, Part M, p. 1.
The cultural divide extends even to religion; American clergy are often considerably to the left of their parishioners.

Samuelson, Robert J., "Polarization Myths . . . ," *The Washington Post*, Dec. 3, 2003, p. A29.
The author argues political and cultural polarization isn't as bad as the media make it out to be; overheated rhetoric and exaggerations are a political strategy.

Sterngold, James, "Culture War Being Reshaped," *San Francisco Chronicle*, Feb. 29, 2004, p. A1.
Although society still seems bitterly divided, in many cases the culture wars are shaped by the gradual retreat of conservative positions.

Von Drehle, David, "Political Split Is Pervasive," *The Washington Post*, April 25, 2004, p. A1.
Birds of a feather flock together, and people increasingly choose their neighborhoods and news sources in a way that reinforces their political views.

Effects of Partisanship

"Politics as Warfare," *The Economist*, Nov. 8, 2003.
As American politics becomes more akin to warfare, politicians are more likely to reach for political "weapons of mass destruction," like Bill Clinton's impeachment.

Dann, Joanne, "Safe But Sorry," *The Washington Post*, Dec. 2, 2001, p. B1.
Hard-line candidates in districts rendered totally secure for their party by gerrymandering have no need to consider other viewpoints.

Farrell, John, "Rancor Becomes Top D.C. Export," *The Denver Post*, May 26, 2003, p. A1.
Quoting prominent GOP strategist Grover Norquist, who equates bipartisanship with "date rape" and calls for more "bitter nastiness and partisanship" beyond the Beltway, Farrell describes a 20-year campaign by the GOP to take control of state legislatures and defeat or marginalize moderates in both parties through partisan redistricting.

Rogers, David, "Gloves Come Off in Fight to Control Courts," *The Wall Street Journal*, Oct. 30, 2003, p. A4.
Judges' important role in setting policy means that the partisan rancor over appointing judges to the bench is likely to continue.

Electoral Conflict

Balz, Dan, and Jim VandeHei, "Candidates Narrow Focus to 18 States," *The Washington Post*, March 15, 2004, p. A1.

With most states already a lock for one side or the other, the presidential campaign hinges on the states won or lost by a few percentage points in 2000.

Green, Joshua, "In Search of the Elusive Swing Voter," *The Atlantic Monthly*, Jan./Feb. 2004, p. 102.

The need to target the limited number of swing voters in a small number of states means that in many respects the actual identity of the Democratic candidate is irrelevant.

Judis, John B., and Ruy Teixeira, "Majority Rules," *The New Republic*, Aug. 5, 2002, p. 18.

Cultural and demographic trends in the coming years will transform the American political landscape: A progressive Democratic majority will dominate politics.

Milbank, Dana, "A Move to Satisfy Conservative Base," *The Washington Post*, Feb. 25, 2004, p. A1.

As the culture wars heat up over gay marriage, President Bush is forced to secure his base and announce his support for an amendment banning gay marriage.

Purnick, Joyce, "Data Churners Try to Pinpoint Voters' Politics," *The New York Times*, April 7, 2004, p. A1.

Both political parties maintain massive databases of information on millions of voters in hopes of predicting how people will vote.

Sullivan, Amy, "Do the Democrats Have a Prayer?" *Washington Monthly*, June 2003, p. 30.

The Democrats need to get religion to win elections; they can and have fielded religious candidates, like Jimmy Carter, successfully.

Whitman, Christie, "The Vital Republican Center," *The New York Times*, Jan. 12, 2004, p. A23.

The former GOP governor argues that Republicans must reach out to moderates in order to become a true majority party.

President Bush

Benedetto, Richard, and Judy Keen, "Love Him or Loathe Him: Electorate Polarized Over Bush," *USA Today*, March 10, 2004, p. 4A.

The divided opinion over President Bush is razor sharp; the gap in approval of the president between voters of different parties is bigger than ever before.

Cook, Charlie, "Polarizer-in-Chief," *National Journal*, April 3, 2004.

With solid support from Republicans and just as solid opposition from Democrats, President Bush's support level fluctuates within a narrow band, with little room to grow or shrink.

Hamburger, Tom, and Greg Hitt, "Bush Hardball Leaves Bruises," *The Wall Street Journal*, Dec. 5, 2003, p. A4.

Brass-knuckled tactics used by the Bush administration in dealing with critics of either party are a reflection of the increasingly bitter conflict in Washington.

Jenkins, Jeffery A., "Ideologically, Bush Is Right of Center, But Not Extreme Right," *Chicago Tribune*, March 7, 2004, Perspective Section, p. 3.

A political scientist's assessment of President Bush's place on the political spectrum finds him only slightly more conservative than his moderate father.

Kurtz, Howard, "A Dislike Unlike Any Other?" *The Washington Post*, Oct. 19, 2003, p. D1.

The feelings of many prominent commentators on the left toward President Bush are so negative that even seeing him or hearing his name is painful.

Citing *The CQ Researcher*

Sample formats for citing these reports in a bibliography include the ones listed below. Preferred styles and formats vary, so please check with your instructor or professor.

MLA Style

Jost, Kenneth. "Rethinking the Death Penalty." The CQ Researcher 16 Nov. 2001: 945-68.

APA Style

Jost, K. (2001, November 16). Rethinking the death penalty. *The CQ Researcher, 11*, 945-968.

Chicago Style

Jost, Kenneth. "Rethinking the Death Penalty." *CQ Researcher*, November 16, 2001, 945-968.

In-depth Reports on Issues in the News

Are you writing a paper?
Need back-up for a debate?
Want to become an expert on an issue?

For 80 years, researchers have turned to *The CQ Researcher* for in-depth reporting and analysis of issues in the news. Reports on a full range of political and social issues are now available. Following is a selection of recent reports:

Civil Liberties
Civil Liberties Debates, 10/03
Gay Marriage, 9/03

Crime/Law
Serial Killers, 10/03
Corporate Crime, 10/02

Economy
Exporting Jobs, 2/04
Stock Market Troubles, 1/04

Education
Black Colleges, 12/03
Combating Plagiarism, 9/03

Energy/Transportation
SUV Debate, 5/03
Future of Amtrak, 10/02

Environment
Air Pollution Conflict, 11/03
Water Shortages, 8/03

Health/Safety
Homeopathy Debate, 12/04
Women's Health, 11/03

International Affairs
Aiding Africa, 8/03
Rebuilding Iraq, 7/03

Politics/Public Policy
Redistricting Disputes, 3/04
Democracy in Arab World, 1/04

Social Trends
Future of Music Industry, 11/03
Latinos' Future, 10/03

Terrorism/Defense
North Korean Crisis, 4/03
Homeland Security, 9/03

Youth
Youth Suicide, 2/04
Hazing, 1/04

Upcoming Reports

Future of Marriage, 5/7/04
Gang Crisis, 5/14/04
Worker Safety, 5/21/04
Smart Growth, 5/28/04
Re-examining 9/11, 6/4/04
Nanotechnology, 6/11/04

ACCESS

CQ Researcher is available in print and online. For access, visit your library or www.thecqresearcher.com.

PURCHASE

To purchase a *CQ Researcher* report in print or electronic format (PDF), visit www.cqpress.com or call 866-427-7737. A single report is $10. Bulk purchase discounts and electronic rights licensing are also available.

SUBSCRIBE

A full-service *CQ Researcher* print subscription — including 44 reports a year, monthly index updates, and a bound volume — is $625 for academic and public libraries, $605 for high school libraries, and $750 for media libraries. Add $25 for domestic postage.

The CQ Researcher Online offers a backfile from 1991 and a number of tools to simplify research. Available in print and online, *The CQ Researcher en español* offers 36 reports a year on political and social issues of concern to Latinos in the U.S. For pricing and a free trial of either product, call 800-834-9020, ext. 1906, or e-mail librarysales@cq-press.com.

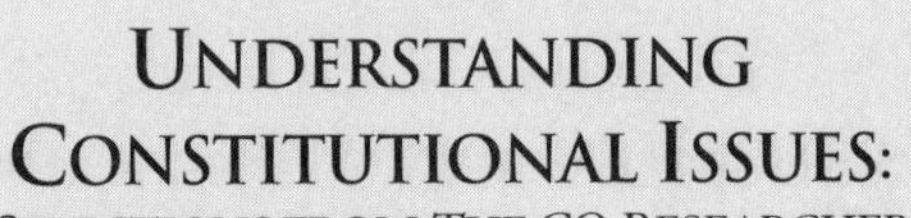

SELECTIONS FROM *THE CQ RESEARCHER*

Understanding Constitutional Issues focuses on four key themes — governmental powers and structure, security, liberty, and equality — to help students develop a deeper understanding of the relation between current events and constitutional issues and principles. Integrating eighteen *CQ Researcher* reports, *Understanding Constitutional Issues* makes important connections clear, such as those between civil liberties and security; and privacy and liberty.

June 2004 • 8 1/2 x 11 • Approx. 432 pages • Paperback • ISBN 1-56802-885-7 • $39.95

To Order: Call Toll-Free: 866.4CQ.PRESS (427.7737)
Fax: 800.380.3810 • Web: www.cqpress.com
E-mail: customerservice@cqpress.com

CQ Press, 1255 22nd Street, NW, Suite 400 • Washington, DC 20037

CQ Researcher

Published by CQ Press, a division of Congressional Quarterly Inc.

thecqresearcher.com

Future of Marriage

Is traditional matrimony going out of style?

In the past 40 years, the nation's marriage rate has dropped from three-quarters of American households to slightly over half. Moreover, nearly 50 percent of all U.S. marriages now end in divorce, and the number of households with unmarried couples has risen dramatically. Some scholars say that although traditional marriage will not disappear entirely, it will never again be the nation's pre-eminent social arrangement. In the future, they say, the United States will look more like Europe, where couples increasingly are opting to cohabit rather than marry. But other experts argue that the recent decrease in the divorce rate and other positive trends point to a brighter future for marriage. Meanwhile, actions by a number of state courts and local officials in favor of same-sex unions have helped ignite a debate over the issue and prompted conservatives to push for a constitutional amendment banning gay marriage.

Fewer and fewer American couples are choosing to walk down the aisle like Washington-area lawyers Melissa Jurgens and Jim Reed.

INSIDE THIS REPORT

The CQ Researcher • May 7, 2004 • www.thecqresearcher.com
Volume 14, Number 17 • Pages 397-420

CQ PRESS

RECIPIENT OF SOCIETY OF PROFESSIONAL JOURNALISTS AWARD FOR EXCELLENCE ◆ AMERICAN BAR ASSOCIATION SILVER GAVEL AWARD

THE ISSUES

BACKGROUND

CURRENT SITUATION

OUTLOOK

SIDEBARS AND GRAPHICS

FOR FURTHER RESEARCH

Cover: Melissa Jurgens and Jim Reed knew that marriage was right for them, but more and more American couples are deciding against matrimony, or ending up divorced. (Courtesy of Melissa Jurgens)

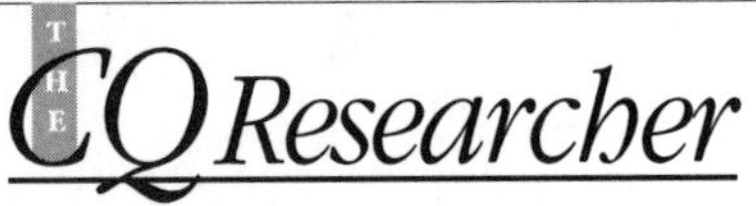

May 7, 2004
Volume 14, Number 17

MANAGING EDITOR: Thomas J. Colin

ASSISTANT MANAGING EDITOR: Kathy Koch

ASSOCIATE EDITOR: Kenneth Jost

STAFF WRITERS: Mary H. Cooper, David Masci, William Triplett

CONTRIBUTING WRITERS: Sarah Glazer, David Hatch, David Hosansky, Patrick Marshall, Tom Price, Jane Tanner

DESIGN/PRODUCTION EDITOR: Olu B. Davis

ASSISTANT EDITOR: Kenneth Lukas

CQ PRESS

A Division of Congressional Quarterly Inc.

SENIOR VICE PRESIDENT/GENERAL MANAGER: John A. Jenkins

DIRECTOR, LIBRARY PUBLISHING: Kathryn C. Suárez

DIRECTOR, EDITORIAL OPERATIONS: Ann Davies

CONGRESSIONAL QUARTERLY INC.

CHAIRMAN: Andrew Barnes

VICE CHAIRMAN: Andrew P. Corty

PRESIDENT AND PUBLISHER: Robert W. Merry

The CQ Researcher (ISSN 1056-2036) is printed on acid-free paper. Published weekly, except Jan. 2, April 9, July 2, July 9, Aug. 6, Aug. 13, Nov. 26 and Dec. 31, by CQ Press, a division of Congressional Quarterly Inc. Annual subscription rates for institutions start at $625. For pricing, call 1-800-834-9020, ext. 1906. To purchase a *CQ Researcher* report in print or electronic format (PDF), visit www.cqpress.com or call 866-427-7737. A single report is $10. Bulk purchase discounts and electronic-rights licensing are also available. Periodicals postage paid at Washington, D.C., and additional mailing offices. POSTMASTER: Send address changes to *The CQ Researcher*, 1255 22nd St., N.W., Suite 400, Washington, D.C. 20037.

Future of Marriage

BY DAVID MASCI

THE ISSUES

For Washington-area lawyers Melissa Jurgens and Jim Reed, their four years of marriage has meant greater happiness and stability than they have ever known.

"After I married Jim, I had someone I could talk to all the time and who could support me in ways that my friends, as wonderful as they are, just can't," Jurgens says. "He's more than a friend: He's committed to me, like I am to him, and that makes all the difference. We're going to be living together for the next 50 years, and so he needs to ensure that I'm OK and happy."

Marriage has been equally transforming for Reed. "I was 35 at the time and had already been a lawyer for 10 years," he says. "But I didn't really feel established until I married my wife. Marrying Melissa committed me to certain things — like my career path and staying here in Washington . . . [in part] because we want to have children."

But Dimitra Hengen, a successful businesswoman in Alexandria, Va., wants no part of the institution. "A lot of people do much better living on their own rather than in a marriage," says Hengen, who divorced her husband in 2001 after 18 years of marriage. "I'm not saying that we don't need companionship, but you need to assess this need against the things you have to give up when you marry, like your independence — and I don't want to give those things up."

Instead, she sees herself having long-term relationships that may be permanent, but will never lead to matrimony. "I have a wonderful boyfriend right now, and he wants to marry me, but I don't even want to live with him," she says. "I want to be able to come and go as I please, to travel, to see friends and family, all without the compromises that come with marriage. I don't need marriage."

Hengen is among a growing number of Americans who see marriage as more of an option than a necessity, according to Laura Kipnis, a professor of media studies at Northwestern University and author of *Against Love: A Polemic*. "As the economic necessity of it has become less pressing, people have discovered that they no longer need marriage," she says. "It restricts our choices and is too confining, which is why fewer people are marrying."

Indeed, in the last 50 years, the percentage of American households headed by married couples has fallen from nearly 80 percent to an all-time low of 50.7 percent, according to the Census Bureau. Meanwhile, the percentage of marriages that end in divorce jumped from roughly 25 percent to 45 percent.

Courtesy Dimitra Hengen

Businesswoman Dimitra Hengen of Alexandria, Va., has no desire to remarry after divorcing her husband of 18 years. She is among a growing number of Americans who no longer see marriage as necessary to their happiness.

As a result of the changing marriage and divorce statistics, married couples with children now comprise only 25 percent of all American households. The number is expected to fall to 20 percent by 2010. By that time, the bureau predicts, single adults will make up 30 percent of all households. [1]

Nonetheless, many marriage scholars argue that despite current trends, marriage will never really go out of style.

"We're a pair-bonding species, and we have a deep need at the species level to love and be loved by another and a need to pass on a part of ourselves to the next generation," says David Blankenhorn, founder and president of the Institute for American Values, a marriage advocacy group. "Marriage is the institution that encompasses these two great needs."

The case for marriage is further bolstered by research showing that married men and women are healthier, wealthier and happier than their single or divorced counterparts, Blankenhorn says. Children, too, are more likely to do better in school and less likely to have disciplinary trouble if they live in homes with married parents, he says. [2]

Marriage advocates note there is already some evidence to support the institution's resiliency, pointing out that divorce rates, for instance, have leveled off and even declined slightly in recent years.

More Americans Remaining Unmarried

The percentage of American men and women who remain unmarried jumped dramatically in the past 30 years. In the 25-29 age group, the percentage of unmarried men rose from just 19 percent in 1970 to 54 percent in 2002; among women it nearly quadrupled, to 40 percent. Marriage experts say increased wealth and new freedoms are largely behind the trend.

Percentage of Americans Who Never Married

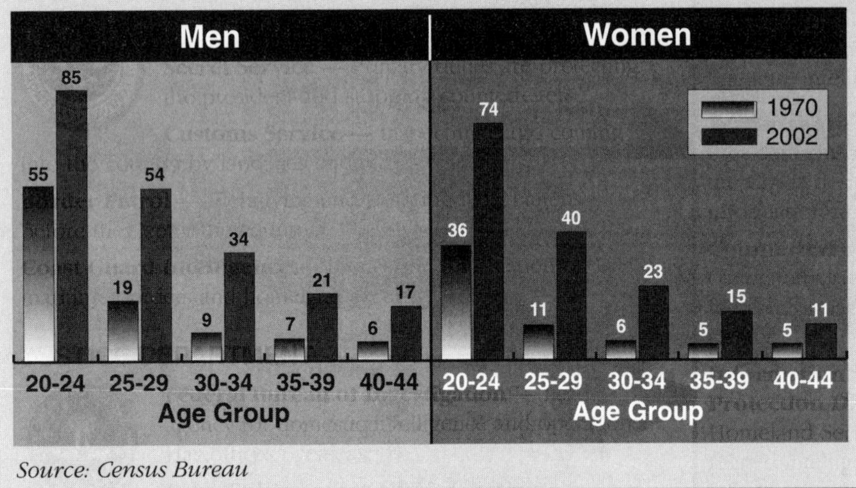

Source: Census Bureau

And compared with Northern Europeans, Americans are still marriage fanatics. In Denmark, for instance, 60 percent of all children are born out of wedlock, compared to 34 percent in the United States. [3] (*See sidebar, p. 405.*)

But many experts worry that the United States eventually will become more like Europe, with cohabitation and single parenthood replacing marriage as the dominant social institution. They point out that between 1996 and 2002, the number of cohabiting couples rose from 2.8 million to nearly 4.3 million, a trend that is expected to continue in the coming years.

Marriage advocates say that increasing rates of cohabitation can and should be stopped with education and other measures. They support a recent $1.5 billion Bush administration proposal to promote marriage among the poor, who are more likely to have children outside wedlock than middle-class Americans.

But critics of the initiative, which is part of a planned reauthorization of the nation's welfare law, argue that marriage-promotion schemes are unlikely to work. And even if they did prove successful, they say, the money could better be spent on education or job training, which help women become more self-sufficient and less in need of a husband.

The Bush administration also has promoted marriage by rewriting the tax code to eliminate the so-called marriage penalty — which required some married couples to pay higher taxes together than if they had remained single. The penalty was eliminated when Congress passed the first Bush tax cuts in 2001, but the provisions expire at the end of the year. On April 28, the House passed legislation making the elimination of the penalty permanent. However, prospects in the Senate are uncertain. [4]

The drive to promote marriage, especially through taxes or benefits, has angered many singles. Unmarried workers, for instance, complain that pension and health benefits favor those with spouses and children. If the percentage of single employees in America were to surpass the percentage of married employees, singles could begin demanding equal treatment with regard to employee benefits and other government policies that currently favor married workers. Already, 40 percent of the nation's largest 500 companies have re-examined their "marriage-centric" benefit policies. For instance, Bank of America has redefined "family" to include non-traditional household members — such as domestic partners or adult children living at home. [5]

At the same time, many widows and widowers feel that they can't afford to remarry because they will lose health, pension and other benefits tied to their deceased spouses.

Ironically, concerns over the state of heterosexual marriage come as more gay couples are forming families by adopting children, and national debate flares over whether same-sex partners should be allowed to wed. While most polls show that roughly two-thirds of Americans oppose same-sex unions, several state courts in recent years have expanded marriage rights for homosexuals — ranging from civil unions now allowed in Vermont to matrimony approved by the Massachusetts Supreme Court in November. In addition, mayors and other public officials in several cities — notably San Francisco and Portland, Ore. — have issued thousands of marriage licenses to gay couples. [6]

Social conservatives have responded by proposing an amendment to the U.S. Constitution defining marriage as the union of a man and a woman — effectively banning same-sex marriages. Supporters of the amendment, including President Bush, argue a constitutional amendment is needed to prevent liberal

Fewer Couples Are Marrying . . .

The percentage of U.S. households headed by married couples has declined steadily from more than three-quarters of all homes in 1950 to barely more than half today.

Percentage of Married-Couple Households

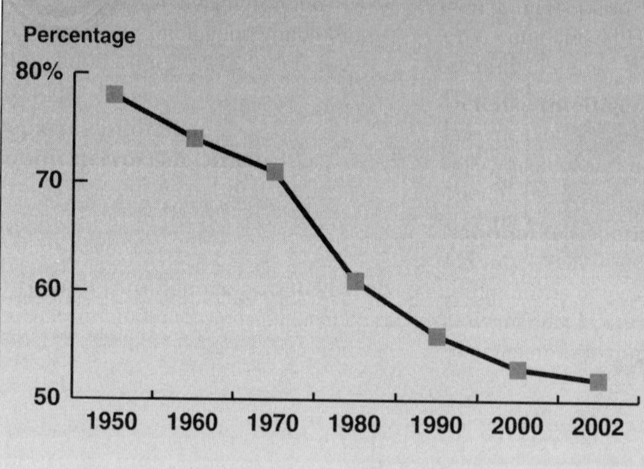

. . . And More Couples Are Cohabiting

More than 4 million unmarried American couples were living together in 2002, a 50 percent increase over the number just six years earlier.

Households Headed by Opposite-Sex Unmarried Couples

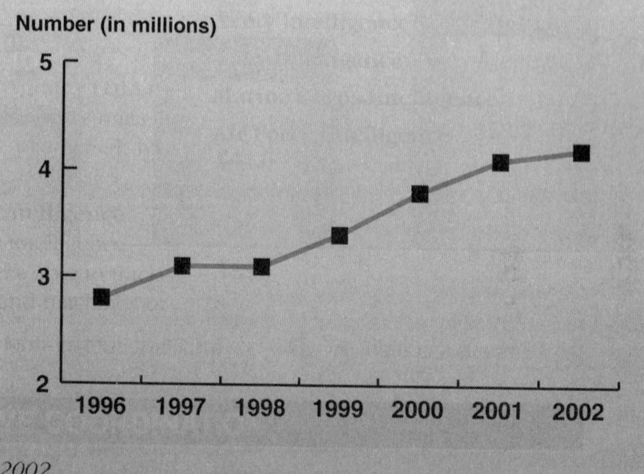

Source: U.S. Census Bureau, Current Population Survey, March 2002

judges and officials from watering down the millennia-old definition of marriage until it loses all meaning and significance.

But the amendment's critics, including gay-rights groups and even some conservatives, note that the Constitution is usually changed to expand rights rather than take them away.

As the experts debate the future of one of the most important social institutions in human history, here are some of the questions they are asking:

Is the future bleak for traditional marriage?

Nearly half of all American marriages end in divorce, according to the U.S. Census Bureau. Meanwhile, the nation's marriage rate has been steadily dropping, from an annual rate of 9.9 marriages per thousand population in 1987 to 8.4 per thousand in 2001. [7] Today, just over 50 percent of all households are headed by married couples, compared with three-quarters of the same group 40 years ago.

At the same time, the number of households with unmarried couples has risen dramatically. In 1977, only 1 million Americans were cohabiting; today, it's 5 million. The percentage of children raised in single-parent households also has jumped, tripling in the last 40 years — from 9.4 percent in 1960 to 28.5 percent in 2002.

Some scholars say that while traditional marriage will not disappear, it will never again be the country's pre-eminent social arrangement. "Ozzie and Harriet are moving out of town, and they're not coming back," says Stephanie Coontz, a professor of history at The Evergreen State College in Olympia, Wash., and author of the upcoming *A History of Marriage*. "Americans now have too many choices — due to new technologies and economic and social opportunities — and it would take a level of repression unacceptable to nearly everyone to force us to begin marrying and stay married at the same levels we once did."

Coontz argues that marriage thrived during more socially and economically restricted times. "For thousands of years, marriage has been humanity's most important economic and social institution," she says. "It gave women economic security and helped men financially, through dowry payments and socially by connecting them to another family."

However, Coontz continues, the recent expansion of individual wealth and freedom — especially among women — makes the economic argument for marriage much less compelling. "We no longer need a spouse for economic security or to [financially] take care of us when we get old," she says. "We can do these things for ourselves now."

Northwestern's Kipnis agrees. "Look, marriage has essentially been an economic institution with some romantic aspects tacked onto it," she says. "Once you take away the economic need, marriage becomes different, and for many people it becomes confining."

Indeed, only 38 percent of Americans in first marriages say that they are happy, Kipnis says, citing a 1999 survey by the National Marriage Project at Rutgers University. [8] "What does that say about everyone else?" she asks.

Some of the unhappiness may be stoked by a consumer culture that emphasizes choice and happiness, raising unrealistic expectations, she says. "Our emotional and physical needs have expanded a lot, and people now expect that the person they are with is going to meet those needs," Kipnis says. "That makes it much harder to find someone else they feel they can marry."

It also increases the likelihood of divorce, says Diane Sollee, founder and director of the Coalition for Marriage, Family and Couples Education, in Washington. "There are a lot of unnecessary divorces because when married people feel unhappy, they assume that they married the wrong person. So they find someone new, and when that person doesn't make them happy, they move on to the next one."

But supporters of marriage believe that the institution is beginning to make a comeback, in part because of the very changes that the pessimists cite. "All of this mobility and freedom also means that we're living in an increasingly impersonal mass society," says William Doherty, director of the Marriage and Family Therapy Program at the University of Minnesota in St. Paul. "Marriage will continue to be important. We will continue to need someone who is permanently and unquestionably in our corner."

Getty Images/Steve Liss

Single mothers would be encouraged to marry under President Bush's Healthy Marriage Initiative, which would provide $1.5 billion to establish marriage-education programs, advertise pro-marriage messages and teach marriage skills.

Others argue that marriage will survive and thrive because it is still the best way to organize society on a personal level. "People are beginning to see how much we need marriage, because it is the only effective way to raise children," says Tom Minnery, vice president of public policy at Focus on the Family, a Christian-oriented advocacy group in Colorado Springs. "And this isn't something that just religious people are saying; it's accepted by the scientific community too." (*For debate over research on the impact of marriage, see "Current Situation," p. 411.*)

There are already signs of a reverse in the trend away from marriage, Minnery says. He points out, for instance, that the annual divorce rate has dropped, from five per 1,000 people in 1982 to four in 2002. [9]

In addition, the upward trend toward working motherhood has halted, Minnery says, noting that the percentage of working mothers (72 percent) has held steady since 1997, after rising dramatically during the previous 20 years. [10]

Optimists also contend that young people today take marriage more seriously than people did 20 or 30 years ago. "I actually think the institution of marriage is going to become more stable in the future," Doherty says. "People are becoming more sober and serious about marriage and doing more to prepare themselves for it, like taking marriage-education classes before they wed."

He attributes the trend, in part, to painful memories. "The children of divorce are keen to not make the same mistakes as their parents," he says. "Even those whose parents stayed together feel this way, because they were able to witness the divorce revolution in other families."

"When you look at young people, they're more conservative and religious than their parents," Minnery agrees. "Just like the Baby Boomers rebelled against what their parents did, the children of Baby Boomers are rebelling against their parents and their lifestyle choices."

Finally, marriage optimists say the institution will endure because it fulfills basic human needs. "There's still a great hunger for stable, loving, intimate relationships," Doherty says, "and marriage is still the best way to have them."

Would President Bush's initiative to promote marriage improve poor people's lives?

In 2001, President Bush proposed a new initiative to promote marriage for lower-income Americans as part of the reauthorization of the federal government's welfare program. Recently, the president expanded his proposal.

Bush's new Healthy Marriage Initiative would provide $1.5 billion over five years in grants to states, local governments and private charities for a variety of activities, including establishing marriage-education programs in schools and community centers and advertising pro-marriage messages. Funds could also be spent to teach marriage skills to people preparing to tie the knot or to mentor troubled married couples. [11]

The proposal was included in the massive Welfare Reform Reauthorization bill passed by the House last year. But the measure stalled in the Senate in March after legislators could not agree on several issues unrelated to the marriage proposal. [12] No new date has been set for the Senate to revisit the bill.

The University of Minnesota's Doherty says Bush's initiative is "well worth the effort" because research shows that marriage can dramatically improve the physical and emotional health of adults and especially children. "We know that the best way to raise children is in a healthy marriage, and yet our welfare policy hasn't reflected that," he says.

Blankenhorn agrees. "We know that in most cases children do better in a home where their biological parents are married," he says. "So we have a real interest in seeing that people with children marry and making those marriages work."

But opponents of the initiative contend it will neither be effective nor do much social good.

"You can't really push people into a decision this big, absent fraud or coercion," Evergreen State's Coontz says. "This will change a few minds, but not many."

Moreover, says Barbara Risman, a sociology professor at North Carolina State University in Raleigh, changing minds in one direction should not be the focus of federal efforts. Instead, she says, the government should better equip people to make their own decisions.

"The focus on marriage, as opposed to self-sufficiency, is a negative issue for women," she says. "The government shouldn't promote marriage. It should promote the ability of anyone to live with the kind of families they want to have."

There are better ways to spend welfare funds, critics like Risman and Coontz add. "No matter what [supporters] say, this is going to divert funds, because at the end of the day you only have so much welfare money to spend," Coontz says. "And we have such pressing needs in child care, health and in so many other areas."

In fact, opponents say, marriage promotion could do more harm than good, in part because the pool of good husbands is likely to be much smaller among the group the administration would target — poor women. "Poor people have a lot of barriers in their lives, like economic instability, substance abuse and a history of being on the giving or receiving end of domestic violence," says Lisalyn Jacobs, vice president for government relations at the National Organization for Women's (NOW) Legal Defense and Education Fund, a women's-rights group. "It may not be such a great idea to get or keep some of these people together, because they're not very stable."

Marriage also might not be such a good idea if the potential marriage partner is abusive, she adds. "Sixty percent of all women on welfare have been victims of domestic violence at some time in their lives," Jacobs says, "so encouraging people to stay together might put many of them at greater risk of injury."

But Sollee disputes that argument. "Women generally get beat up when they're single or in a cohabiting relationship," she says, pointing to the National Crime Victimization Survey, which shows that two-thirds of the violence against women is not committed by husbands but by casual dating partners. [13] "Marriage stabilizes relationships and makes domestic violence much less likely."

Indeed, the idea that those on welfare are different with regard to marriage is "insulting to the poor," she says. "Poor people pair up for the same reason everyone else does: Because they're human, and they want to form love relationships. Given that, we need to give them the skills needed to make the right choices."

Should the Constitution be amended to define marriage as the union of a man and a woman?

After months of pressure from religious and conservative groups alarmed at what they saw as a rising tide of same-sex marriages, President Bush on Feb. 24 publicly endorsed amending the U.S. Constitution to define marriage as the union of a man and a woman. Bush said the decision had been forced upon him by "activist judges and local officials" in Massachusetts, California and elsewhere, who had made "an aggressive attempt" to redefine marriage.

"On a matter of such importance, the voice of the people must be heard," the president said at a White House press conference announcing his support for the amendment. "Activist courts have left the people with

Students' Views of Unmarried Parenthood

The idea of having a child outside of marriage has become more acceptable to high school seniors over the past 20 years — especially among girls.

Percentage of high school seniors who said having a child without being married is experimenting with a "worthwhile lifestyle or not affecting anyone else"

	Boys	Girls
1976-1980	41%	33%
1996-2000	49%	54%

Source: "Monitoring the Future," Survey Research Center, University of Michigan

one recourse. If we are to prevent the meaning of marriage from being changed forever, our nation must enact a constitutional amendment to protect marriage in America." (*See "At Issue," p. 413.*)

The federal government had addressed the issue in 1996, when Congress passed, and President Bill Clinton signed, the Defense of Marriage Act, which defined marriage as being between a man and a woman for purposes of federal law. It explicitly prevents any jurisdiction from being forced to accept another's definition of marriage. In other words, if Massachusetts legalizes same-sex unions and marries two men, New York is not required to acknowledge the marriage if the couple subsequently moves there.

But because the Constitution's Full Faith and Credit Clause requires each state to recognize the lawful actions of other states, Bush and gay marriage opponents say federal courts might overrule the law and require other states to recognize gay marriages performed outside their jurisdiction.

The amendment, proposed by Colorado Republicans Sen. Wayne Allard and Rep. Marilyn M. Musgrave, would still allow states to pass civil-union or domestic-partnership laws that could grant same-sex partners and others the same rights as married couples. But marriage would be strictly limited to heterosexual couples.

Gay-rights activists, civil-liberties organizations and even some conservatives and libertarians oppose the amendment, albeit for different reasons.

"It's a perversion to use our founding document to discriminate against a group of people when it has traditionally been used to expand liberties and rights," says Kevin M. Cathcart, executive director of the Lambda Legal Defense and Education Fund, a gay-rights group in New York. "It's ironic that on the 50th anniversary of the *Brown v. Board of Education* decision, which struck down the doctrine of 'separate but equal,' we're on the verge of writing it back into the Constitution." [14]

Other opponents of gay marriage say a Constitutional amendment is heavy-handed and unnecessary. Former Rep. Bob Barr, who as a conservative Republican from Georgia helped write the 1996 Defense of Marriage Act, calls the amendment an unwarranted intrusion into an area traditionally left to the states.

"Changing the Constitution is just unnecessary — even after the Massachusetts decision, the San Francisco circus and the Oregon licenses," Barr told the House Judiciary Subcommittee on the Constitution on March 30. "We have a perfectly good law on the books that defends marriage on the federal level and protects states from having to dilute their definitions of marriage by recognizing other states' same-sex marriage licenses." [15]

Opponents also call the administration's claim that the amendment process was "forced" on them by activist judges and mayors a cynical election-year ploy. "I don't think this is really about gay marriage at all, but is a distraction meant to focus attention away from the [Iraq] war and the deficit and all of the other problems this administration is dealing with," Cathcart says.

Moreover, by trying to amend the Constitution, they say, conservatives are trying to cut off the emerging national debate on same-sex marriage. "You know, we're really just beginning this debate all over the country, and already they want to amend the Constitution," Cathcart says. "They accuse liberals of trying to use the courts and local officials to circumvent debate, but that's actually what they're doing."

"Amending the Constitution is something that you traditionally do when you've run out of remedies," agrees NOW's Jacobs. "It seems to me that we've only just begun to try to work this one out."

Continued on p. 406

Will U.S. Follow Europe's Cohabitation Trend?

In their 21 years together, Stig Skovlind and Malene Breining Nielsen of Denmark have dated, lived together and raised three children — but they never got married. "We trust each other. We don't need a document," Malene said. [1]

More and more Europeans — particularly from the Nordic countries — are cohabiting. Nineteen percent fewer Europeans got married in 2002 than in 1980, compared to a 5.7 percent drop in the United States during the same period. Meanwhile, almost 20 percent of young Europeans — and 40 percent of Swedes — are cohabiting, compared to 7.7 percent in the United States. [2]

Northern European demographics could be headed toward a point at which "marriage and cohabitation have become indistinguishable," says Kathleen Kiernan, a professor of social policy and demography at the London School of Economics. And many cohabiting Nordic couples are having children. More than half of Swedish mothers ages 25 to 29 give birth to their first child out of wedlock, and more than a quarter of Norwegian mothers.

About 80 percent of those surveyed in Sweden, Finland and Denmark consider cohabiting couples with children a "family." But in mostly Catholic Southern European countries like Italy, Spain and Portugal, attitudes about cohabitation are more conservative; only 44 percent of Italians, for instance, view unwed couples with children as a family.

AFP Photo/Pascal Guyot

Protesters in Paris oppose the Civil Solidarity Pacts (PACS) being considered by the French National Assembly, which would give traditional rights to homosexual and unwed couples.

Still, many European courts now accommodate the emerging class of cohabiting partners and parents. In Sweden, Finland and Denmark, "family law has come to be applied to married and cohabiting couples in the same way," writes Kiernan. And in 1998 the Netherlands began recognizing both homosexual and heterosexual partnerships as if they were "functionally equivalent to marriage," she notes.

In France, so-called PACS (pacte civil de solidarite) offer unwed heterosexual and homosexual couples some of the same rights accorded to marriage; more than 130,000 couples have signed PACS. Even in Italy, the government is considering granting some legal rights to unmarried couples.

Some experts worry the United States may be headed in the same direction as Europe. "Our marriage rate continues to drop, our divorce rate is high and our cohabitation rate continues to climb," says David Popenoe, professor of sociology and co-director of the National Marriage Project at Rutgers University.

And recent U.S. demographic surveys support his concerns: The number of American couples cohabiting rose by 72 percent in the 1990s, with nearly half of them raising children. [3]

The rising numbers worry experts because cohabiting couples tend to break up more than married couples, Popenoe says, and there is no safety net in the United States for kids who slip through the financial cracks when parents separate.

"We can't agree that . . . welfare provisions are proper, and we don't [want] to give up our hard-earned taxes in times of need," says Popenoe.

But in Northern Europe, expansive welfare measures provide a safety net for children when relationships break down, Kiernan says. Unwed European mothers — cohabiting or not — have the same rights as married mothers and, although the law is less clear-cut for men, unwed fathers generally have a financial duty to their children once paternity is established.

Critics of cohabitation note that children of single parents have a higher incidence of psychiatric problems, Popenoe says. "Kids are much better off when raised by two married biological parents than . . . by a single parent or a broken cohabiting couple and are then thrust on the welfare state," he says.

But Stephanie Coontz, national co-chair of the Council on Contemporary Families, notes that while "transitions can be hard on kids," the effects of a parental breakup on kids can be exaggerated.

Americans will have to get used to a broader definition for family, she concludes. "There's been a worldwide transformation of marriage — it will never again have a monopoly on organized child care or on the caring for dependents," she says.

— Benton Ives-Halperin

[1] Jennie James, *et al.*, "All In The Family . . . or Not," *Time*, Sept. 17, 2001, p. 54.

[2] Marriage statistics are from "Demography: EU Population Up by 0.3% in 2002," *European Report*, Sept. 3, 2003, and National Center for Health Statistics; cohabiting statistics — which are for those ages 25 to 34 — come from the U.S. Census Bureau and Kathleen Kiernan, "Unmarried Cohabitation and Parenthood: Here to Stay?" Conference on Public Policy and the Future of the Family, Oct. 25, 2002. Unless otherwise noted, other data are from Kiernan.

[3] Laurent Belsie, "More Couples Living Together, Roiling Debate on Family," *The Christian Science Monitor*, March 13, 2003, p. 1.

Continued from p. 404

But supporters point out that to become law any constitutional amendment must first win the support of two-thirds of Congress and three-quarters of the nation's state legislatures. "This would be a wonderful way to debate the issue, given all of the hurdles that have to be jumped before it became part of the Constitution," says Minnery of Focus on the Family. "There would be a debate in Congress and then in every state legislature in the country. That seems pretty thorough to me."

And while proponents admit the amendment process has traditionally been about expanding rights, they argue that gay marriage presents a unique challenge to American society that calls for a unique solution.

"Our founding documents, like the Declaration of Independence, tell us that our rights have come from our creator or, to put it another way, they are part of natural law," says Ed Vitagliano, pastor of Harvester Church in Pontotoc, Miss., and a spokesman for the conservative American Family Association. "When you talk about redefining marriage, you're really talking about an overthrow of this natural order or natural law, because marriage is something that predates government. So this is a big deal, a once-in-a-lifetime debate about whether to overturn the natural order upon which our rights are based. That requires a big response." ■

BACKGROUND

Origins of Marriage

Marriage has meant very different things in different places at different times. "Marriage has been continually evolving through the centuries, and it's still doing so," the University of Minnesota's Doherty says.

For instance, the idea of choosing a mate or "marrying for love" became commonplace only in the 18th and 19th centuries and only in some cultures. Marriages are still arranged by families throughout much of Asia, Africa and the Middle East today. Moreover polygamy — long rejected by Western cultures — is common in many Muslim countries and among various ethnic groups.

Still, there have been some constants, especially in the West. For instance, until recently, most people saw marriage as a necessary right of passage into adulthood, rather than a choice. Moreover, definitions of marriage were — and to some degree still are — largely dictated by the Judeo-Christian ethic, which sees the institution as a permanent, unbreakable union between a man and a woman.

While polygamy was allowed in early Jewish life, ancient Hebrew laws on marriage eventually came to stress monogamy. Laws strictly forbade adultery (the prohibition is one of the Ten Commandants) and incest. Restrictions against divorce also were enforced, making it almost impossible for Jewish couples to legally separate.

Christian thinkers built on this tradition. St. Mark, in his New Testament gospel, echoed the Old Testament when he said "from the beginning of the creation God made them male and female. For this cause shall a man leave his father and mother, and cleave to his wife; and the twain shall be one flesh: so then they are no more twain, but one flesh. What therefore God hath joined together, let no man put asunder." [16]

But the Christian emphasis on monogamy and fidelity was more than a reaffirmation of ancient Jewish traditions or the teachings of the new church's founders; it also was a reaction to what Christians viewed as the weak marriage laws of Rome, which allowed couples to separate and gave women an unusual amount of personal freedom.

While many of today's matrimonial traditions — such as the wearing of bridal veils and the exchange of wedding rings — date back to ancient Rome, the Christian church rejected Rome's lax marriage laws and instead transformed marriage into a divinely ordained sacrament. Separation or divorce were strictly forbidden, although widows could remarry after a spouse's death. Jesus himself condemned divorce, calling men who leave their wives for others — even if legally sanctioned — adulterers. [17]

The only option for irreconcilable couples was to petition the church for an annulment, which did not dissolve the marriage but declared that it had been invalid from the start and hence had never actually taken place. Annulments were usually employed in cases of bigamy or when a husband and wife were closely related. Otherwise, annulments were difficult to obtain. Petitions, even from kings — like England's Henry VIII — were routinely denied.

Besides fidelity, the church emphasized the dominant role of the husband, continuing the tradition of the Jews and of most other ancient cultures at the time. Ironically, Christian teachings held that men and women were equal in God's eyes but, nonetheless, women were to be "in submission" to their husbands. [18]

Sweeping Changes

Sweeping changes in the state of marriage did not begin to occur until the 16th-century Protestant Reformation, which rejected much of the institutionalization of religion and stressed individual choice. Many Protestants, including the movement's

Continued on p. 408

Chronology

17th-19th Centuries

Less-restrictive ideas and laws concerning marriage develop among colonies and later states in the New World.

1620
Puritans arrive in America and establish more liberal marriage and divorce laws than those in England.

1770s
The struggle for U.S. independence spurs debate on the rights of women and the obligations of marriage.

1800s
Western territories pass liberal divorce laws in the transition to statehood to attract settlers.

1867
All but three states have abolished the most restrictive divorce laws.

1870
Only 3 percent of all U.S. marriages end in divorce.

1900-1960

War and social changes bring women more freedom.

1900
U.S. divorce rate stands at 8 percent.

August 1920
American women get the right to vote after Tennessee becomes the 36th state to ratify the 19th Amendment.

1925
The divorce rate is 25 percent.

1941
U.S. entry into World War II brings millions of American women into the work force.

1947
California Supreme Court rules that the state's miscegenation law violates the state Constitution, making California the first state to abolish limits on interracial marriage.

1960-Present

The civil and women's rights movements and the sexual revolution dramatically change the institution of marriage.

1960
Nation's divorce rate is 26 percent.

1964
Civil Rights Act prohibits discrimination based on gender.

1967
U.S. Supreme Court overturns state miscegenation laws.

1969
Gov. Ronald Reagan, R-Calif., signs the first no-fault divorce law.

1972
The launch of *Ms.* magazine heralds the arrival of the woman's movement. Jessie Barnard's book *The Future of Marriage* argues that marriage is often detrimental to women.

1974
The number of American children whose parents divorce in a year reaches 1 million.

1980
Divorce rate hits 50 percent.

1989
Psychologist Judith Wallerstein argues in her book *Second Chances* that the impact of divorce on kids is worse than previously thought.

1992
Vice President Dan Quayle criticizes decision by TV sitcom character "Murphy Brown" not to wed her child's father.

1996
Hawaiian Supreme Court rules the state cannot ban gay marriages.

1998
Hawaiians amend Constitution to permit ban on gay marriage.

1999
Vermont Supreme Court rules that gay couples are entitled to the same benefits as married people.

2000
The Case for Marriage attempts to counter earlier arguments that many people don't need marriage.

Nov. 18, 2003
Massachusetts Supreme Court rules the state's law prohibiting gay marriage violates the state Constitution.

April 29, 2004
Massachusetts legislature adopts constitutional amendment banning gay marriage but allowing civil unions.

May 17, 2004
Massachusetts must begin issuing marriage licenses to same-sex couples, according to a state Supreme Court order; governor is seeking an emergency stay of the deadline until action is completed on new constitutional amendment.

2006
Massachusetts gay-marriage amendment would take effect, if approved again by the legislature and by a statewide voter referendum.

Can You Click to Find Your Soul Mate?

"Aren't you just a little curious?" purrs an ad on Match.com's Web site. "With 8 million profiles to choose from, imagine the possibilities."

Match.com and other large Internet dating services do offer singles many choices, but most online services are not concerned with whether a potential customer is seeking a friend, a date or a spouse.

But a relatively new online service, eHarmony.com, actively plays cupid, limiting its clientele to those looking to get married. Its Web site is full of pictures of happily married or engaged couples who met through the service. Potential subscribers are urged to join "when you're ready to find the love of your life."

Americans have been seeking love online for more than a decade, but in recent years Internet dating has become much more widespread and socially acceptable.

"The traditional institutionalized means for getting people together are not working as well as they did previously," says Norville Glenn, a sociology professor at the University of Texas. "There's a need for something new, and the Internet is filling it."

Last year an estimated 21 million Americans spent $313 million on Internet dating, a figure likely to more than double by 2008, according to the Internet market research firm Jupiter Communications. [1]

Most of the biggest services, like Match.com and Yahoo Personals, are largely search engines with millions of profiles, each usually containing a photo and personal information ranging from height and weight and likes and dislikes to "latest book read." Users scroll through the results, e-mailing anyone who catches their fancy.

But eHarmony works differently. Founded in August 2000 by clinical psychologist Neil Clark Warren, it does not allow users to choose whom they're going to contact. Instead, it matches people based on an exhaustive personality survey completed by each subscriber.

"I saw more than 7,000 patients over the years, and so many of these troubled people were in bad marriages," he says of his 35 years as a therapist. "It struck me that the most important need we have is to get marriage right."

Warren conducted more than 500 "divorce autopsies," usually interviewing both spouses and sometimes even the children of the divorced parents. He found that most people in failed marriages chose their spouse for the wrong reasons, such as physical appearance, sense of humor or financial status, while neglecting more important concerns. "The true things people need for a happy marriage are on the inside, like character and intellect, rather than the shape of their nose," he says.

Moreover, he found, those who succeed at marriage are usually paired with someone who shares most of their basic values and beliefs. "We're told that opposites attract, but that's not so," he says. "When people have a lot in common, they have much less to negotiate, fewer things to compromise on."

For instance, different work ethics or attitudes about how to raise children might not be a problem on a first or second date, but they can breed resentment when a couple is living together.

eHarmony tries to match clients by requiring all new subscribers to fill out an extensive 436-item questionnaire based on what Warren says are "29 dimensions for compatibility," such as spirituality, education, sexual desire and kindness.

Continued from p. 406

founder, Martin Luther, cast off the notion that marriage was a holy sacrament to be regulated entirely by the church. Instead, Luther wrote, marriage was "a secular and outward thing having to do with wife and children, house and home and with other matters that belong to the realm of the government, all of which have been completely subjected to reason." According to Luther, the laws of marriage and divorce "should be left to the lawyers and made by secular government." [19]

Luther's new attitudes set the stage for ensuing changes. "The Reformation set out a bunch of new ingredients on the table . . . but it took the Enlightenment and the spread of wage labor to bring these ingredients together," says Coontz, who is writing a book on the history of marriage.

The 17th- and 18th-century Enlightenment "brought to dominance the notion that people have the right to organize their lives as they see fit," says Coontz, leading to the belief that "marriage should be a love match." Indeed, during subsequent centuries, more and more people, especially among the educated classes, eschewed family obligation and chose their own mates.

If the Enlightenment gave people the intellectual justification for choosing their spouses, wage labor — brought on by the Industrial Revolution — gave them the means. Having a job with a steady wage disconnected people from rural life and its familial and other controls, giving them both geographic and social mobility.

"If you didn't want to marry the person your parents had chosen for you, you could leave and find someone else," Coontz says.

New World Flexibility

The first European settlers in the New World took with them many

After computers match candidates with similar traits, early communication is limited to e-mail, but eventually, matched singles can move on to calling and then meeting for dates.

Although eHarmony is less than four years old, it has attracted 4 million users and is adding roughly 10,000 new customers per day, Warren says. It has also spawned imitators, such as TrueBeginnings. Even Match.com, the nation's largest online service, is offering a short personality test to its registered users.

Warren claims his company has already connected at least 2,500 couples who have gotten married, and who, for the most part, are "doing very well so far."

Paul Consbruck, 42, of Jacksonville Fla., says he is now happily married to someone he met through eHarmony. "A lot of dating takes place on a very superficial level," he says. "eHarmony tells you to step back and look at what's really important to you before you get attracted to someone physically." [2]

About 15 percent of all eHarmony applicants are turned away for a variety of reasons including emotional difficulties, substance abuse or concerns about truthfulness.

"A lot of people are not ready for marriage, and so we encourage them to get better and then reapply," Warren says. "It's painful, but the alternative is to match them when they're not ready and bring other, healthier people down with them. That's not fair."

Neil Clark Warren, founder of eHarmony.com, says most marriages fail because people choose mates for the wrong reasons.

Because eHarmony takes such an active interest in who and even how its subscribers meet, it has been likened to an old-fashioned matchmaker, a comparison Warren does not reject. In today's increasingly urban and mobile society, he says, a service like eHarmony can provide "the kind of wisdom that people might have found with their family or community in the past," when most people lived in small towns.

Indeed, Warren believes that it is "extremely hard" for a single person to find a suitable partner without a service like eHarmony. "You need to tap into a large pool of people so that you can increase your odds of finding your soul mate," he says. "That's why I think that in 10 or 15 years, virtually every person will find their husband or wife on the Internet."

[1] Figures cited in Adrienne Mand, "Dr. Love is In," ABCNEWS.com, March 26, 2004.

[2] Quoted in Anna Kuchment, "The Internet: Battle of the Sexes," *Newsweek International*, Dec. 2, 2003.

of their old laws and customs, including rules on matrimony. But as the late historian Daniel Boorstin has pointed out, views on marriage in England's American colonies and eventually the United States were always more flexible than those in Europe, in large part to fit the needs of a less socially rigid and more mobile society.

"The rights of married women and their powers to carry on business and to secure divorce were much enlarged," he wrote about matrimony laws in early North America. "The law protected women in ways unprecedented in the English common law." [20]

In colonial Massachusetts and Connecticut, Puritan-influenced law even allowed for divorce if a spouse could prove that the other had neglected a fundamental duty of the marriage, such as providing food and shelter. However, by modern standards, divorce was difficult to obtain in colonial America, so it was rare. In many jurisdictions, divorce could only be granted by legislative action (the passage of a private bill), which meant that usually only the rich had the resources to legally separate.

Between the American Revolution and the Civil War, most states greatly liberalized their divorce laws as part a trend to expand individual freedoms, such as voting and other rights and eventually to abolish slavery. For instance, by 1867, 34 of the 37 states had abolished legislative divorce, giving the courts authority to grant divorces. Still, the divorce rate remained relatively low — about 3 percent in 1870.

During the great westward migration just before and after the Civil War, many of the new states carved out of the Western territories, such as Nevada, passed liberal divorce laws in an effort to attract more settlers.

Around the same time, some Mormon settlers in the Western territory began practicing polygamy. The practice, which only involved men marrying multiple wives, began after the religion's leader, Brigham Young, declared it acceptable in 1852.

While most Mormon marriages involved only two people, a substantial minority of Mormon men had two or three wives. Still, the practice was relatively short-lived due to pressure from the rest of the country. As a condition for Utah joining the Union, the Mormon Church banned new polygamous marriages in 1890. *

Meanwhile, many states, new and old, were also passing so-called miscegenation laws, prohibiting marriage between members of different races. Support for miscegenation goes back to the earliest English settlements and, while largely prompted by a desire to prevent whites and African-Americans from marrying, was not confined to the South or to black-white couplings. Indeed, the first miscegenation law in North America was passed by the Maryland Assembly in 1664. Later, Western states prohibited Asians and whites from marrying.

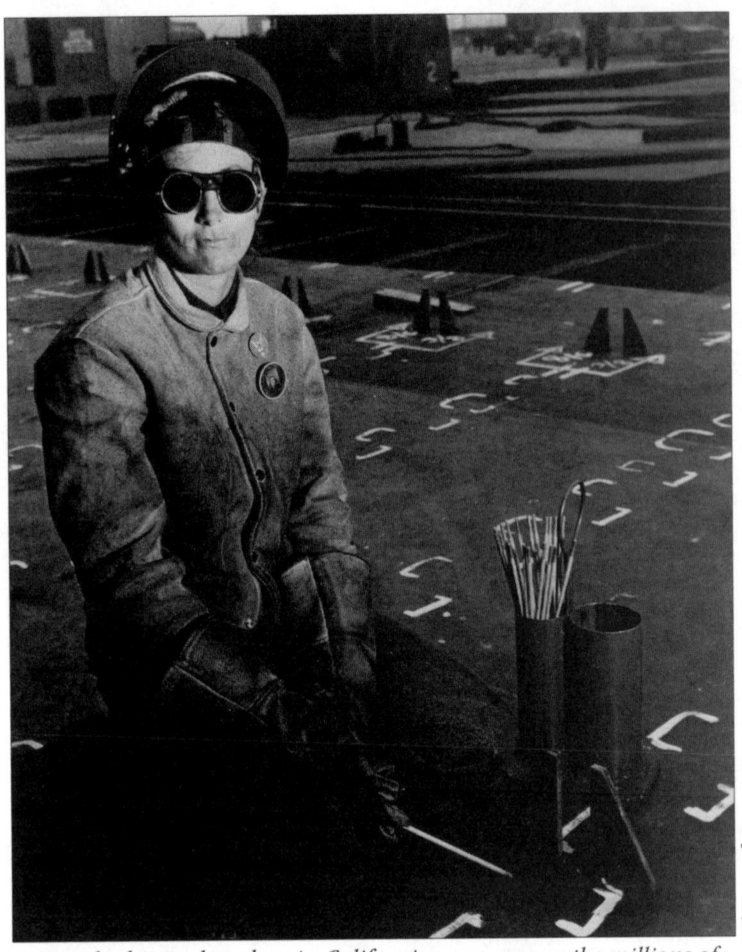

Library of Congress

Female shipyard workers in California were among the millions of women brought into the work force by World War II, helping to plant the seeds for social changes in the 1960s that experts say have contributed to the decline in marriage nationwide.

Miscegenation laws were still common until the second half of the 20th century. In 1948, the California Supreme Court became the first state court to strike down a law banning racial mixing, arguing that it violated the Constitution's 14th Amendment guaranteeing equal protection under the law. [21] Nearly 20 years later, in *Loving v. Virginia*, the Supreme Court followed suit, repealing miscegenation laws nationwide.

* Polygamy is still practiced illegally in parts of Utah.

Shifting Views

The last 50 years have witnessed dramatic, indeed unprecedented, changes in perceptions of marriage in the United States. During the 1960s and '70s, the general purposes and characteristics of marriage changed, reflecting new attitudes about freedom and self-realization, especially for women.

"In the middle of the 20th century, we began to shift away from an institutional view of marriage — that it is based on economic viability, child rearing and a sense that this is something that all adults should do," Doherty says. "And we moved into what is called psychological marriage — the notion that you marry by choice and that you do so primarily for romantic reasons."

This change was prompted by several important social and cultural changes, beginning with the entry of married women into the workplace during World War II. In 1930, only 12 percent of all married women worked outside the home. [22] By 1944, with the labor demands of rising war production and 12 million young men taken out of the work force for military service, that figure had nearly tripled, to 35 percent. [23]

Work brought many women, regardless of their marital status, more than financial independence. "In the absence of men, women found doors suddenly open to them in higher education and in the professions; the Army and Navy admitted women for the first time," writes Nancy F. Cott, a professor of history at Yale University and author of *Public Vows: A History of Marriage and the Nation*. [24]

After the war, as men returned home to resume their lives and jobs, many women — both married and unmarried — left work to focus on starting and raising families. While many women wanted to leave their war jobs, some were pressured or even forced to do so in order to make room for returning soldiers.

But during the 1960s, social changes erupted that significantly altered the marital landscape. The civil rights and anti-war movements, the rise of youth culture and the sexual revolution wrought profound changes in society's mores. Old ideas, such as female premarital chastity or the notion that a woman went to college only to find a suitable husband, began to collapse.

By the early 1970s, the women's-liberation movement was demanding equality in the workplace and elsewhere and advising American women that they had other choices in life besides getting married and having children. Indeed, many feminists declared housework demeaning and encouraged women to "find themselves."

By the 1980s, a majority of married women with children at home were working, driven not only by new freedoms and a desire for a career but also by financial need, as the cost of housing, education and health care rose faster than wages. Today, about 72 percent of married women with children are in the labor force, a figure that has held steady since the mid-1990s.

A dramatic rise in the rate of divorce accompanied these societal changes. From 1955 to 1975, the divorce rate more than doubled, from 23 percent of all marriages to 48 percent, where it has remained, give or take a few points, ever since. [25]

Many say that the advent of no-fault divorce laws across the country in the late 1960s and early '70s helped spur the divorce trend. No-fault laws made it significantly easier to untie the knot. "These new laws did a terrible disservice to couples, but they especially hurt the weakest people in our society — children," says Richard Land, a spokesman for the Southern Baptist Convention. "No-fault divorce sent people the message that it was easy and alright to breakup their families."

But others disagree. "When you look at almost all the reputable research, you find that no-fault divorce was not the cause of the divorce rate rising," says Coontz of Evergreen State. "It was the rising demand for divorce that caused the rising divorce rate. No-fault only speeded up what was going to happen anyway." ■

CURRENT SITUATION

Gay-Marriage Push

Although the debate over same-sex marriage has only recently risen to national attention, the issue is by no means new. Gay-rights advocates have been working for decades to secure matrimonial and related rights for same-sex couples. And they have had some successes, as well as setbacks.

In 1996, Hawaii's Supreme Court ruled that the state government's ban on same-sex marriages violated the state Constitution. Then in 1998, Hawaiian voters amended their state constitution giving the legislature authority to ban same-sex marriage. In 1999, Vermont's highest court ruled that gay couples were entitled to the same benefits as married people, although it stopped short of giving same-sex couples the right to marry.

But developments in the last six months have clearly pushed gay marriage to the top of the national domestic agenda, making it one of the most hotly debated topics of the year and an important issue in the 2004 presidential election.

New interest in same-sex unions was sparked by a Nov. 18 Massachusetts Supreme Court decision holding that denying gay couples the right to marry violated the state constitution's equal protection clause. The court gave the state until May 17 to start allowing same-sex couples to wed.

For gay advocates and some civil-rights proponents, the decision was long overdue. "A court finally had the courage to say that this really is an issue about human equality and human dignity, and it's time that the government treats these people fairly," said Mary Bonauto, the lawyer for Gay & Lesbian Advocates & Defenders who argued the case.

But the decision also prompted a substantial backlash and not just in Massachusetts, where both Republicans and Democrats proposed amending the state Constitution to reverse the court's ruling. President Bush also weighed in, arguing that "activist judges" had no right to rewrite the rules of marriage.

After several months of negotiation, Massachusetts Gov. Mitt Romney, a Republican, and legislative leaders proposed amending the state Constitution defining marriage as a union of a man and a woman, but allowing for gay civil unions. It was approved by the legislature on April 29, but it must be passed again next year and then approved by voters before it would take effect — in 2006 at the earliest.

Meanwhile, Romney has asked the state legislature to pass emergency legislation allowing him to seek a stay of the Massachusetts Supreme Court's May 17 marriage order. The governor contends the state should not be required to issue marriage licenses to same-sex couples while the legislature and citizens are debating the issue.

"This is a decision that is so important it should be made by the people," Romney said on April 15, the day the legislation was filed. [26]

But the Massachusetts court ruling has emboldened gay-marriage supporters elsewhere. On Feb. 12, newly elected San Francisco Mayor Gavin Newsom authorized the city government to begin issuing marriage licenses to gay and lesbian couples. The response surprised even supporters: In the first five days 2,500 couples came from around the country to marry, often waiting for hours in long lines for their chance to get hitched.

In 2000, California voters had approved a ballot measure — Proposition 22 — which defined marriage as a union between a man and a woman, leading many, including the state's popular new governor, Arnold Schwarzenegger, to criticize Newsom for ignoring the law. "If the people change their minds and they want to overrule [Proposition 22], that's fine with me," Schwarzenegger said on March 2. "But right now, that's the law, and I think that every mayor and everyone should abide by the law." [27]

But Newsom justified his decision as an attempt to abide by the U.S. Constitution's requirement to treat all people equally. "I've got an obligation that I took seriously to defend the Constitution," he said. "There is simply no provision that allows me to discriminate." [28]

However, as a result of a court order, San Francisco stopped granting licenses on March 12. The state Supreme Court is currently deciding whether the 4,000 same-sex marriage licenses eventually issued by the city are valid, and a decision is expected in the next month or so. [29]

Even if the marriage licenses are ultimately invalidated, supporters of same-sex unions see developments in San Francisco as the event that most fully energized the gay-marriage movement. "Sometimes when you're in a civil rights struggle, you reach a tipping point," Lambda Legal's Cathcart says. "We reached it in San Francisco when you saw thousands of couples lining up to pay for their license and legally get married. Mayor Newsom lit the spark, and what happened afterwards inspired others around the country to act."

Indeed, mayors in a handful of other cities — including New Paltz, N.Y., and Asbury Park, N.J. — and the commissioners of Multnomah County, Ore., (which includes Portland) followed Newsom's lead.

But conservatives and marriage traditionalists view events in San Francisco differently. "The mayor of San Francisco has done more than anyone else to solidify support behind a federal amendment," the Southern Baptist Convention's Land says. "When a public official defies not only public opinion but [also] the law he's sworn to uphold, average people get outraged."

As evidence, Land points to a March CBS poll showing that 59 percent of Americans favor a constitutional amendment allowing marriage only between a man and woman. In December, only 35 percent favored such an amendment. [30]

But gay-marriage advocates remain optimistic, in part because polls show that resistance to same-sex unions increases with age. "I'm very confident that we're going to win on this issue over the long term, because most young people just don't think this is a big deal," Cathcart says. "The young are already largely with us, and the coming generations will be even more supportive."

Corbis Images

Married life improves the physical and psychological health of both adults and children, according to many social researchers. But skeptics contend that bad marriages aren't counted in the statistics.

Impact of Marriage

In the last decade, a consensus has begun to emerge that marriage can provide tangible benefits, both for adults and their children. Indeed, most sociologists now agree that a good marriage generally improves the lives of all involved.

"Even the skeptics have come around on this," the University of Minnesota's Doherty says. "Marriage, and by that we mean a good marriage, is good for people."

Linda J. Waite, a sociology professor at the University of Chicago and co-author of *The Case for Marriage,* agrees, claiming the amount of evidence available on the benefits of matrimony is "fairly overwhelming."

Waite and Doherty point to a host of studies by sociologists and others, which found that men and women in happy marriages enjoy better mental and physical health and more financial security than similarly situated unmarried counterparts.

Continued on p. 414

At Issue:

Will same-sex marriage hurt traditional marriage?

MAGGIE GALLAGHER
PRESIDENT, INSTITUTE FOR MARRIAGE AND PUBLIC POLICY

WRITTEN FOR *THE CQ RESEARCHER*, APRIL 2004

yes

Same-sex marriage divides people into two camps: Those who say that gay marriage will affect only gays and those who believe that court-ordered same-sex marriage will dramatically alter the legal, shared public understanding of marriage.

If the Massachusetts court had decided the "right to marry" includes the right to polygamy, would that affect only those who want a polygamous marriage? Of course not. The entire marriage culture would shift if polygamy were to become a "normal" marriage variant. Monogamy would no longer be a core part of our definition of marriage.

I'm not saying that same-sex marriage will lead to polygamy. I'm pointing out that legally changing the definition of marriage affects everyone and would radically transform what marriage is. It would hurt the traditional form of marriage by:

- Sending a terrible message to the next generation: The law will say that two men or two women raising children are just the same as a mom and dad; thus, social institutions would be bending to adult sexual desires, regardless of who gets hurt.
- Creating an abyss between "civil" and "religious" marriage. Civil marriage would be divorced from religious traditions that gave rise to marriage and which continue to sustain marriage as a social institution. Government should be more modest about redefining marriage to make it unrecognizable to most religious traditions in this country.
- Neutering our shared language about parenting. You won't be able to say "children need mothers and fathers, and marriage has something important to do with getting this for children" because it will no longer be true, and because the government will be committed to the idea that two mothers or two fathers are just as good as a mom and a dad in raising children.
- Marginalizing or silencing traditional advocates of marriage. Marriage is a public act. Faith-based organizations that fail to endorse and accept same-sex marriage may find themselves driven from the public square: their broadcasting licenses, tax-exempt statuses and school accreditation at risk.

If gay marriage is a civil right, then people who believe that children need moms and dads will be treated like bigots. How will we raise young men to become reliable husbands and fathers in a society that officially promotes the idea that fathers don't matter?

KEVIN CATHCART
EXECUTIVE DIRECTOR, LAMBDA LEGAL DEFENSE AND EDUCATION FUND

WRITTEN FOR *THE CQ RESEARCHER*, APRIL 2004

no

The current, unprecedented dialogue about marriage for same-sex couples isn't an abstract discussion about politics or religion — it's about real people's lives and the human cost of denying basic equality to an entire group of Americans.

Denying marriage to same-sex couples blocks hundreds of thousands of families nationwide from the critical rights and protections that others take for granted. Same-sex couples are left vulnerable and scrambling to cobble together a patchwork of legal documents that still don't provide them with the security and protections they want and need.

To understand why marriage is so important for so many same-sex couples, look no further than Lydia Ramos. Lydia's partner of 14 years died in a car accident, triggering a legal and emotional nightmare. The coroner refused to turn the body over to Lydia, and the daughter they raised together was taken away by her partner's relatives after the funeral. Mother and daughter were kept apart for months — at a time when they most needed each other.

Mother and daughter were finally reunited after Lambda Legal fought a long and gut-wrenching legal battle on their behalf. But if Lydia and her late partner had been able to marry, their daughter would never have been put through such a nightmare.

If they had been able to marry, it would not have changed the marriages of their heterosexual neighbors and co-workers. Heterosexual marriages are not on such shaky ground that they will fall apart simply because loving, committed same-sex couples are given equal access to the rights and protections provided by marriage.

The nation is about to see that in Massachusetts, where lesbian and gay couples will soon begin getting married. That state's highest court — with six of seven justices appointed by Republican governors — ruled that only marriage can fix the inequalities in how the state treats same-sex couples.

Within the next year, our lawsuit on behalf of seven New Jersey couples is expected to reach that state's high court. Our cases in New York, Washington state and California will ask the same fundamental questions addressed by the Massachusetts court.

The courts and political leaders are beginning to recognize that anything less than marriage treats same-sex couples differently, and that separate is never equal. Loving couples are being kept from our nation's promise of fairness, and we'll fight for them for as long as it takes to win equality.

Continued from p. 412

For instance, a 1990 study published in the *Journal of Marriage and Family* found that singles had higher mortality rates than their married counterparts. The mortality rate for single men was a whopping 250 percent higher, while unmarried women had a 50 percent higher rate. The study found the unwed were particularly at greater risk for those diseases that hinged on behavior, like lung cancer and cirrhosis of the liver. [31]

"It helps to have someone around who is a stakeholder in your health," Doherty says. "People do better when there is someone who can push you or nag you to keep to your diet, exercise regularly, take your medicine and just take proper care of yourself."

Likewise, married people are happier — almost twice as happy as singles and roughly three times happier than those who are widowed or divorced, according to studies. [32]

Children growing up in homes where both biological parents are present also do better than those living with a single parent. For instance, they are more likely to graduate from high school and have fewer discipline problems if raised by a married biological mother and father.

But some experts question at least parts of the consensus, arguing that much of the research paints too rosy a picture of the institution. "We need to remember that when we're talking about the benefits of marriage, we're really only talking about good marriages," Evergreen State's Coontz says. "When researchers tell you that marriage in general is good even after they average together good and bad marriages, it's very skewed," she continues. "Good marriages tend to last, while many bad marriages aren't being counted because they end in divorce. So good marriages tend to get overcounted, and the bad ones are undercounted."

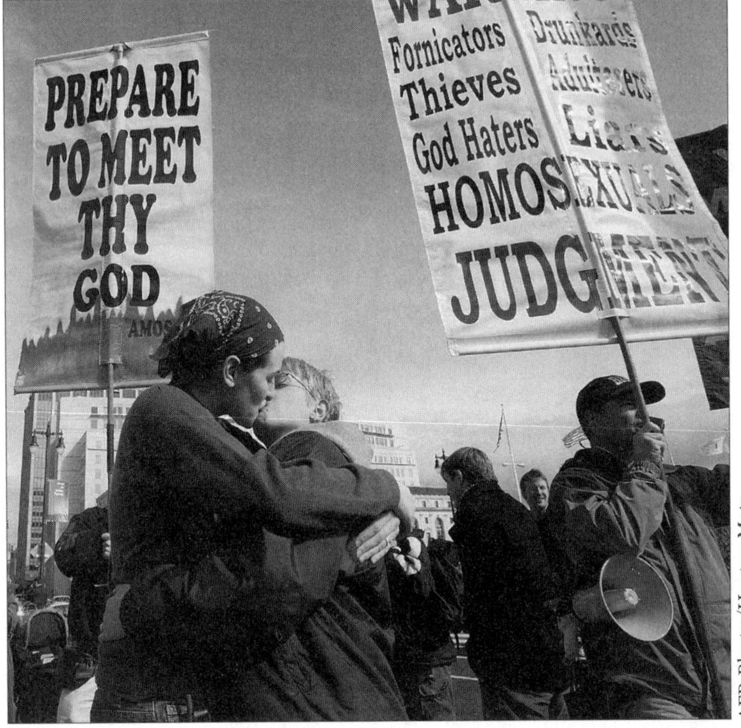

AFP Photo/Hector Mata

Two newly married women ignore demonstrators protesting same-sex marriages at San Francisco City Hall on Feb. 20. San Francisco Mayor Gavin Newsom authorized the city government to begin issuing marriage licenses to gay and lesbian couples on Feb. 12, helping put the controversial issue at the top of the national agenda.

Skeptics also contend that while marriage may provide real benefits for men, it is not necessarily as beneficial for women. "Men are used to being taken care of by women, first their mothers and then their wives," North Carolina State's Risman says. "So, sure, marriage is a good deal for men because without a wife to replace their mother they usually don't take good care of themselves."

But women marry for very different reasons, she says. "In a world where women still earn 75 cents or less for every dollar earned by men, they still have to marry for economic and other practical reasons."

According to Risman, a woman might be mentally or physically healthier in marriage because her husband's income provides health insurance or better food and shelter. "So, yes, maybe she's better off, but only because society's inequalities force her to marry," she says. "We need to construct a society where women don't need to marry in order to have these things."

But researchers who tout the benefits of marriage dispute both arguments. Coontz's contention of research bias is incorrect, they say, because the studies account for both divorce and bad marriages. "The best research looks at transitions into and out of marriage and includes all marriages experienced by respondents, including those prior bad marriages that ended in divorce," Waite says.

Others question the contention that marriage favors men more than women. "There are some areas where men benefit more and some where women are better off," says Maggie Gallagher, president of the Institute for Marriage and Public Policy. "But in all cases, in every area, both benefit." ■

OUTLOOK

Privatizing Marriage

The 20th century witnessed unparalleled changes in married life, at least in rich countries. In the United States, Europe and elsewhere, a trend away from obligations to parents, community and other forms of collective responsibility gave way to more of an emphasis on individual choice. People had more freedom to decide whom to marry and whether to stay in that marriage.

Many scholars predict even more dramatic changes for married life in the coming decades. "People will view their marriages more and more as a private relationship, rather than as a public institution as they did in the past," Blankenhorn of the Institute for American Values says. "You already see this happening, as, for instance, many couples no longer speak the traditional vows but write their own."

Blankenhorn contends that the "privatization of marriage," as he calls it, will make marriages less stable, because the built-in guideposts and expectations that once accompanied married life are disappearing. "Without a set of public expectations — like permanence or total commitment to each other — people are more on their own, and that's more risky."

The University of Minnesota's Doherty agrees that marriage will continue shifting from a public to a private institution. But he sees a positive side to such a change: Future marriages, to some degree, will be on a more equal footing. "Men will look more and more at a woman's earning potential when they decide on a mate and be less interested in women as homemakers," Doherty says. "They're going to want someone who can bring in as much as they do or just a little less. This will bring a new level of gender equality to marriage."

Still, Doherty adds, husbands will continue to want to make at least as much as their wives. "Men are hardwired by evolution to be 'providers,' and this is still backed up by our culture," he says. "So a man who makes less than his wife will still feel 'inadequate.' "

> **"Men will look more and more at a woman's earning potential when they decide on a mate and be less interested in women as homemakers."**
>
> ***— William Doherty,***
> ***Director, Marriage and Family Therapy Program,***
> ***University of Minnesota***

However, some scholars see few, if any, additional changes occurring in married life — at least in the United States. "We've had so much happen in the last 100 years that I think we're entering a period of stability," North Carolina State's Risman says. "We're going to spend the next 50 years absorbing the changes of the last 50."

Risman says several trends bolster her belief. "The divorce rate has stabilized over the last few decades, which to me is a sign that the rate of change has slowed significantly." Moreover, things don't seem to be changing all that much for women at home, she points out.

"Housework remains women's work, and there is no sign that that is changing." The fact that the number of women staying at home with their children and putting off a career is holding steady is a sign that "women still don't think they can have it all, because their husbands still haven't been told that they can't have it all."

Evergreen State's Coontz agrees that marriage won't change too much in the immediate future, but neither will it remain static. "We're going to spend the next few decades sorting through the enormous changes we've seen in marriage."

In particular, she says, couples will have to work through the consequences of gender equality in marriage. "Men

About the Author

David Masci specializes in science, religion and foreign-policy issues. Before joining *The CQ Researcher* in 1996, he was a reporter at Congressional Quarterly's *Daily Monitor* and *CQ Weekly*. He holds a law degree from The George Washington University and a B.A. in medieval history from Syracuse University. His recent reports include "Rebuilding Iraq" and "Human Trafficking and Slavery."

can longer count on being the boss anymore," she says. "So, we're going to see more efforts to develop new habits, new emotional expectations, new time schedules and new negotiating skills as we sort out the details of this new reality." ■

FOR MORE INFORMATION

Coalition for Marriage, Family and Couples Education, 5310 Belt Rd., N.W., Washington, DC 20015-1961; (202) 362-3332; www.smartmarriages.com. Nonpartisan group that promotes marriage education.

Council on Contemporary Families, 208 E. 51st St., Suite 315, New York, NY 10022; www.contemporaryfamilies.org. Left-leaning think tank that researches marriage and other family issues.

Focus on the Family, 8685 Explorer Dr., Colorado Springs, CO, 80995; (719) 531-3400; www.family.org. Christian advocacy group that opposes gay marriage.

Institute for American Values, 1841 Broadway, Suite 211, New York, NY 10023; (212) 246-3942; www.americanvalues.org. Promotes the renewal of marriage and family life.

Lambda Legal Defense and Education Fund, 120 Wall St., Suite 1500, New York, NY 10005-3904; (212) 809-8585; www.lambdalegal.org. National gay-rights organization that represents plaintiffs in a number of gay-marriage cases.

Notes

[1] Figures cited at www.census.gov/population/www/socdemo/ms-la.html.

[2] For background, see David Masci, "Children and Divorce," *The CQ Researcher*, Jan. 19, 2001, pp. 25-40.

[3] Figures cited in *National Vital Statistics Reports*, Centers for Disease Control and Prevention, Vol. 52, No. 10, Dec. 17, 2003, p. 1.

[4] Amy Fagen, "Permanent Tax Cut OK'd," *The Washington Times*, April 29, 2004, p. A1.

[5] Michelle Conlin, "Unmarried America," *Business Week*, Oct. 20, 2003, p. 106.

[6] For background, see Kenneth Jost, "Gay Marriage," *The CQ Researcher*, Sept. 5, 2003, 721-748.

[7] Figures cited in *National Vital Statistics Reports*, Centers for Disease Control and Prevention, Vol. 50, No. 14, Sept. 11, 2002, p. 1.

[8] Barbara Defoe Whitehead and David Popenoe, "The State of Our Unions: The Social Health of Marriage in America," National Marriage Project, Rutgers University, 1999.

[9] Figures cited in *National Vital Statistics Reports*, *op. cit.*, and "U.S. Per Capita Divorce Rates Every Year: 1940-1990," Centers for Disease Control and Prevention, www.cdc.gov/nchs/fastats/pdf/43-9s-t1.pdf.

[10] Figures cited in Claudia Wallis, "The Case for Staying at Home," *Time*, March 22, 2004, p. 51. See also, Sarah Glazer, "Mothers' Movement," *The CQ Researcher*, April 4, 2003, pp. 297-320.

[11] Amy Fagen, "Senate Mulls Pro-Marriage Funds," *The Washington Times*, April 1, 2004, p. A5.

[12] Bill Swindell, "Welfare Reauthorization Becomes Another Casualty in Congress' Partisan Crossfire," *CQ Weekly*, April 3, 2004, p. 805.

[13] Figures cited in Ronet Bachman and Linda E. Saltzman, "Violence Against Women: Estimates from the Redesigned Survey," *National Crime Victimization Survey Special Report*, August 1996, p. 4.

[14] For background, see Kenneth Jost, "School Desegregation," *The CQ Researcher*, April 23, 2004, pp. 345-372.

[15] Barr's testimony available at www.house.gov/judiciary/barr033004.pdf.

[16] *The Gospel According to St. Mark*, 10:6-9.

[17] *The Gospel According to St. Mark*, 10:11-12.

[18] *1 Corinthians* 14:34-35.

[19] Quoted in Daniel J. Boorstin, *The Americans: The Colonial Experience* (1958), p. 67.

[20] *Ibid.*, p. 187.

[21] Nancy Cott, *Public Vows: A History of Marriage and the Nation* (2000), p. 184.

[22] *Ibid.*, p. 167.

[23] *Ibid.*, p. 187.

[24] Quoted in *ibid.*, p. 185.

[25] Figures available from the Bureau of the Census at www.census.gov/prod/2004pubs/03statab/vitstat.pdf.

[26] Cheryl Wetzstein, "Romney Moves to Get Vote on Same-Sex 'Marriage,'" *The Washington Times*, April 16, 2004, p. A3.

[27] Quoted in Dean E. Murphy, "Scwharzenegger Backs Off His Stance Against Gay Marriage," *The New York Times*, March 2, 2004, p. A11.

[28] Quoted in Dean E. Murphy, "San Francisco Mayor Exults in Move on Gay Marriage," Feb. 18, 2004, p. A18.

[29] Maura Dolan, "State High Court Seeks Briefs on Validity of Gay Marriage," *Los Angeles Times*, April 15, 2004, p. B6.

[30] CBS News Poll, March 15, 2004, at www.cbsnews.com/stories/2004/03/15/opinion/polls/main606453.shtml.

[31] Catherine E. Ross, John Mirowsky and Karen Goodsteen, "The Impact of the Family on Health: Decade in Review," *Journal of Marriage and the Family 52* (1990), p. 1061.

[32] Cited in Linda J. Waite and Maggie Gallagher, *The Case for Marriage: Why Married People are Happier, Healthier and Better Off Financially* (2000), p. 67.

Bibliography

Selected Sources

Books

Cott, Nancy F., *Public Vows: A History of Marriage and the Nation*, Harvard University Press, 2000.

A professor of history and American studies at Yale University examines marriage in the United States from European settlement in the New World through social revolutions following World War II.

Waite, Linda J., and Maggie Gallagher, *The Case for Marriage: Why Married People Are Happier, Healthier and Better Off Financially*, Doubleday, 2000.

A sociology professor of at the University of Chicago (Waite) and the director of the Marriage Program at the Institute for American Values (Gallagher) review recent research showing the benefits of marriage.

Articles

"The Case for Gay Marriage," *The Economist*, Feb. 28, 2004, p. 9.

The venerable English news weekly argues that same-sex couples should be allowed to marry, asking: "Why should one set of loving, consenting adults be denied a right that other such adults have and which, if exercised, will do no damage to anyone else?"

Belsie, Laurent, "More Couples Living Together, Roiling Debate on Family," *The Christian Science Monitor*, March 13, 2003, p. A1.

The author explores the social impact of the growth of cohabiting couples in the United States.

Conlin, Michelle, "UnMarried America," *Business Week*, Oct. 20, 2003, pp. 106-116.

Conlin's cover story reports that the dramatic decline in traditional families has significant implications for American business and society.

Crary, David, "Will the Institution of Marriage Continue? It's Debatable," *Los Angeles Times*, Feb. 10, 2002, p. A20.

The article explores the marriage movement, which seeks to promote the social benefits of matrimony.

Gallagher, Maggie, "Massachusetts vs. Marriage," *The Weekly Standard*, Dec. 1, 2003.

A pro-marriage writer argues that expanding the definition of marriage to include same-sex couples will make the institution largely meaningless.

Hubler, Shawn, "Nothing But 'I Do' Will Do Now for Many Gays," *Los Angeles Times*, March 21, 2004, p. A1.

Hubler explores the evolution of attitudes about gay marriage within the homosexual community.

Jost, Kenneth, "Gay Marriage," *The CQ Researcher*, Sept. 5, 2003, pp. 721-748.

The author provides a broad overview of the debate over gay marriage.

Kmiec, Douglas R., "Marriage is Based on Procreation, a Fact No Claim of Gay 'Equality' Can Avoid," *Los Angeles Times*, March 14, 2004, p. M1.

A professor of constitutional law at Pepperdine University argues that marriage is not a matter of rights but a question of public policy.

Lyall, Sarah, "In Europe, Lovers Now Propose: Marry Me a Little," *The New York Times*, Feb. 15, 2004, p. A3.

Lyall looks at legal arrangements short of marriage that are gaining popularity in Europe.

Munro, Neil, "Supporting Marriage, But for What Goal?" *National Journal*, Jan. 3, 2004.

An overview of the debate over the benefits of marriage.

Reich, Robert B., "Marriage Aid That Misses the Point," *The Washington Post*, Jan. 22, 2004, p. A25.

The former secretary of Labor argues that the money President Bush would like to spend on marriage promotion would be better used on job training and education.

Wallis, Claudia, "The Case for Staying At Home," *Time*, March 22, 2004, p. 50.

Wallis examines the trend among professional women who put their careers on hold to care for their children.

Reports and Studies

Coontz, Stephanie, and Nancy Folbre, *Marriage, Poverty and Public Policy*, Council on Contemporary Families, April 2002.

A professor of history and family studies at The Evergreen State College (Coontz) and an economics professor at the University of Massachusetts (Folbre) argue that money devoted to promoting marriage among welfare recipients would be better spent on education and other social services.

***Why Marriage Matters: Twenty-One Conclusions from the Social Sciences*, Center for the American Experiment, Coalition for Marriage, Family and Couples Education and Institute for American Values, 2002.**

Three marriage-advocacy groups catalog many of the arguments traditionally given in favor of marriage.

The Next Step:

Additional Articles from Current Periodicals

Benefits of Marriage

Kimberly, James, "Naperville Is Family Capital of U.S.," *Chicago Tribune*, March 26, 2004, Metro Section, p. 1.
Naperville, Ill., has perhaps the most married, two-parent households in America, but whether that is sufficient to explain its low crime and poverty rates is questionable.

Lerner, Sharon, "Good and Bad Marriage, Boon and Bane to Health," *The New York Times*, Oct. 22, 2002, Section F, p. 5.
Married people are healthier than singles, but bad relationships can also have a negative effect on health.

Rauch, Jonathan, "The Widening Marriage Gap: America's New Class Divide," *National Journal*, May 19, 2001.
Research shows that children raised in single-parent homes are at a greater risk for a variety of ills; married and unmarried could be the class division of the future.

Vedantam, Shankar, "Does a Ring Bring Happiness, or Vice Versa?" *The Washington Post*, April 21, 2003, p. A9.
Some research suggests that, on average, the level of happiness one experiences after marriage is similar to the pre-marriage level.

Zeller, Tom, "Two Fronts: Promoting Marriage, Fighting Poverty," *The New York Times*, Jan. 18, 2004, Section 4, p. 3.
The benefits of two-parent households are generally conceded, but exactly what the government can or should do about the situation is disputed.

Changing Institution

"At Last, Good News on the Family (Probably)," *The Economist*, July 28, 2001.
The proportion of American children living in single-parent homes is decreasing, although why is unclear.

Hampson, Rick, and Karen Peterson, "The State of Our Unions," *USA Today*, Feb. 26, 2004, p. 1A.
While marriage is still often exalted as an ideal, the realities of divorce, adultery, cohabitation and children out of wedlock have eroded the practice.

Kantrowitz, Barbara, "State of Our Unions," *Newsweek*, March 1, 2004, p. 44.
Heterosexuals have altered the meaning of marriage from perpetual commitment to lifestyle choice; gays may be looking for something that doesn't exist.

Lampman, Jane, "Shaping the Future of Marriage," *The Christian Science Monitor*, Oct. 2, 2003, p. 12.
Changing values are leading some to question the very meaning of marriage, and whether it's just another product in our consumer society.

Lewin, Tamar, "For Better or Worse: Marriage's Stormy Future," *The New York Times*, Nov. 23, 2003, Section 4, p. 1.
As in Europe, there is some evidence America is becoming a "post-marital" society; single households outnumber married households with children.

Gay Marriage

Biskupic, Joan, "Same-Sex Couples Are Redefining Family Law in USA," *USA Today*, Feb. 18, 2003, p. 1A.
Same-sex couples seeking child custody and other family-law matters are increasingly spurring judges to reconsider aspects of the law and the nature of parenthood.

Deam, Jenny, "Same-Sex Parents, Foes Clash Over Effect on Kids," *The Denver Post*, April 21, 2002, p. A1.
Critics and proponents of same-sex relationships argue over how such relationships affect children living within them.

Mehren, Elizabeth, "Mass. High Court Backs Gay Marriage," *Los Angeles Times*, Nov. 19, 2003, p. A1.
The decision by Massachusetts' Supreme Judicial Court that gays have a right to marry ultimately pushed the issue into the forefront of politics.

Romney, Lee, "Defiant San Francisco Marries Dozens of Same-Sex Couples," *Los Angeles Times*, Feb. 13, 2004, p. A1.
San Francisco Mayor Gavin Newsom seized the limelight in the gay-marriage debate by unilaterally issuing marriage licenses to gay couples.

Von Drehle, David, and Alan Cooperman, "Same-Sex Marriage Vaulted Into Spotlight," *The Washington Post*, March 8, 2004, p. A1.
A flurry of activity beginning in late January 2004 began to dizzy even veteran gay-marriage advocates.

New Meaning of Family

"Recasting the Definition of Family," *Los Angeles Times*, Sept. 14, 2003, p. A26.
A single gay man and his three adopted sons win the Family of the Year Award from the National Adoption Center in a sign of changing familial attitudes.

Armas, Genaro C., "Census Finds More Teens Are Marrying," *Chicago Tribune*, Nov. 9, 2002, News Section, p. 9.
Although Americans generally are waiting longer to marry, the marriage rate for teenagers has increased, perhaps a reflection of immigration trends.

Gardner, Marilyn, "Life as a Single Dad," *The Christian Science Monitor*, July 9, 2003, p. 15.
Men now comprise one in six single parents, a trend that reflects a societal shift away from the assumption that parenting is intrinsically a maternal duty.

Peterson, Karen S., "Marriage as an Institution Is Abandoning Kids, Report Finds," *USA Today*, June 19, 2003, p. 9D.
Marriage and children are no longer inseparably linked in the United States, according to a new report.

Tyre, Peg, and Daniel McGinn, "She Works, He Doesn't," *Newsweek*, May 12, 2003, p. 44.
The number of families where the woman is the primary breadwinner is small, but economists believe it is poised to continue increasing.

Politics of Marriage

Lochhead, Carolyn, "Big Fights Rage in State Capitols," *San Francisco Chronicle*, March 11, 2004, p. A1.
Lobbying in state capitols is fierce as advocates try to alter marriage laws and constitutions, at least partly in the hope of affecting any later Supreme Court decisions on same-sex marriages.

Pear, Robert, and David Kirkpatrick, "Bush Plans $1.5 Billion Drive for Promotion of Marriage," *The New York Times*, Jan. 14, 2004, p. 1A.
President Bush prepares to roll out a government proposal to encourage marriage, influenced by a desire to strengthen his support among his electoral base.

Perine, Keith, and Jennifer Dlouhy, "Parties Wary of Political Risk in Stands on Gay Marriage," *CQ Weekly*, Jan. 10, 2004, p. 84.
Both parties fear getting burned over gay marriage, a potential "culture war" type of issue that stirs passions among voters.

Peterson, Karen S., "The President's Family Man," *USA Today*, July 30, 2002, p. 1D.
Wade Horn is the president's point man for efforts to promote marriage through changes to welfare-reform proposals.

Promoting Marriage

"Get Me to the Church on Time," *The Economist*, July 12, 2003.
Bush-administration efforts to encourage marriage make some wonder whether this "neo-paternalism" is too intrusive.

Bernstein, Nina, "Strict Limits on Welfare Benefits Discourage Marriage, Studies Say," *The New York Times*, June 3, 2002, p. A1.
The stricter welfare requirements that require more work may also be resulting in fewer single mothers choosing to wed.

Campbell, Kim, "Can Marriage Be Taught?" *The Christian Science Monitor*, July 18, 2002, p. 1.
Oklahoma's programs to teach couples marriage skills are emblematic of a trend to encourage lasting marriages at both the state and federal levels.

Grier, Peter, and Patrik Jonsson, "Should Government Be Trying to Promote Good Marriages?" *The Christian Science Monitor*, Jan. 20, 2004, p. 1.
Proponents and critics of government proposals to encourage marriage dispute the relevance and the appropriateness of government efforts.

Serafini, Marilyn Werber, "Get Hitched, Stay Hitched," *National Journal*, March 9, 2002.
Efforts to encourage marriage through welfare reform unsettle some people; for others, they don't go far enough.

CITING *THE CQ RESEARCHER*

Sample formats for citing these reports in a bibliography include the ones listed below. Preferred styles and formats vary, so please check with your instructor or professor.

MLA STYLE

Jost, Kenneth. "Rethinking the Death Penalty." The CQ Researcher 16 Nov. 2001: 945-68.

APA STYLE

Jost, K. (2001, November 16). Rethinking the death penalty. *The CQ Researcher, 11*, 945-968.

CHICAGO STYLE

Jost, Kenneth. "Rethinking the Death Penalty." *CQ Researcher*, November 16, 2001, 945-968.

CQ Researcher

Published by CQ Press, a division of Congressional Quarterly Inc.

thecqresearcher.com

Gang Crisis

Do police and politicians have a solution?

Once an urban problem, street gangs have now infiltrated U.S. communities large and small. Gang experts say at least 21,500 gangs — with more than 731,000 members — are active nationwide. Long-established domestic gangs like the Bloods and the Crips remain powerful, but the problem has worsened dramatically in recent years. Heavy immigration, particularly from Latin America and Asia, has introduced highly violent gangs like Mara Salvatrucha and the Almighty Latin Kings Nation. Bound by tight ethnic and racial ties, they often stymie police investigations by assaulting or killing potential witnesses. Having already diversified from illegal drugs into auto theft, extortion, property crimes and home invasion, some East Coast gangs have begun trafficking in fraudulent identification papers that could be used by terrorists. While experts agree gangs are more pervasive than ever, few agree on a remedy. Proposed legislation would increase penalties for gang membership and gang crimes, but critics say it won't solve the problem.

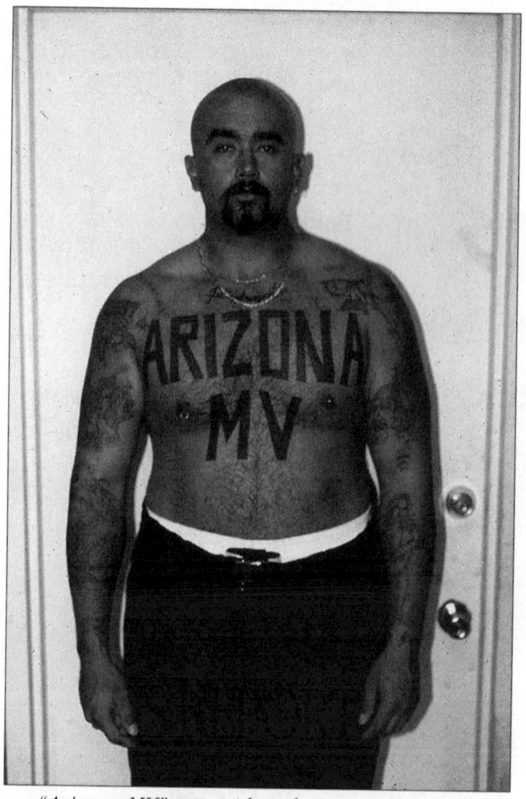

"Arizona MV" tattoo identifies a member of the Arizona Maravilla gang from East Los Angeles.

INSIDE THIS REPORT

The CQ Researcher • May 14, 2004 • www.thecqresearcher.com
Volume 14, Number 18 • Pages 421-444

CQ PRESS

RECIPIENT OF SOCIETY OF PROFESSIONAL JOURNALISTS AWARD FOR EXCELLENCE ◆ AMERICAN BAR ASSOCIATION SILVER GAVEL AWARD

THE ISSUES

BACKGROUND

CURRENT SITUATION

OUTLOOK

SIDEBARS AND GRAPHICS

FOR FURTHER RESEARCH

Cover: Tattoos identify a member of the Arizona Maravilla gang from East Los Angeles' Arizona Street. Nearly half of all U.S. gang members are Latino. (California Gang Investigators Association)

May 14, 2004
Volume 14, Number 18

MANAGING EDITOR: Thomas J. Colin

ASSISTANT MANAGING EDITOR: Kathy Koch

ASSOCIATE EDITOR: Kenneth Jost

STAFF WRITERS: Mary H. Cooper, David Masci, William Triplett

CONTRIBUTING WRITERS: Sarah Glazer, David Hatch, David Hosansky, Patrick Marshall, Tom Price, Jane Tanner

DESIGN/PRODUCTION EDITOR: Olu B. Davis

ASSISTANT EDITOR: Kenneth Lukas

A Division of
Congressional Quarterly Inc.

SENIOR VICE PRESIDENT/GENERAL MANAGER: John A. Jenkins

DIRECTOR, LIBRARY PUBLISHING: Kathryn C. Suárez

DIRECTOR, EDITORIAL OPERATIONS: Ann Davies

CONGRESSIONAL QUARTERLY INC.

CHAIRMAN: Andrew Barnes

VICE CHAIRMAN: Andrew P. Corty

PRESIDENT AND PUBLISHER: Robert W. Merry

The CQ Researcher (ISSN 1056-2036) is printed on acid-free paper. Published weekly, except Jan. 2, April 9, July 2, July 9, Aug. 6, Aug. 13, Nov. 26 and Dec. 31, by CQ Press, a division of Congressional Quarterly Inc. Annual subscription rates for institutions start at $625. For pricing, call 1-800-834-9020, ext. 1906. To purchase a *CQ Researcher* report in print or electronic format (PDF), visit www.cqpress.com or call 866-427-7737. A single report is $10. Bulk purchase discounts and electronic-rights licensing are also available. Periodicals postage paid at Washington, D.C., and additional mailing offices. POSTMASTER: Send address changes to *The CQ Researcher*, 1255 22nd St., N.W., Suite 400, Washington, D.C. 20037.

Gang Crisis

BY WILLIAM TRIPLETT

THE ISSUES

In June 2001, Fredy Reyes-Castillo met four fellow Latino immigrants at a gas station in Reston, an affluent Northern Virginia suburb. With its upscale malls and subdivisions, it's what drug dealers call a "green area" — full of kids with money.

The four were members of Mara Salvatrucha, or MS-13, a nationwide Latino street gang infamous for its drug dealing and violence. Reyes-Castillo, 22, was not a member, but that day he pretended to be. When the real gangsters realized he didn't understand MS-13 slang or sport gang tattoos, they beat him to death so brutally it took weeks to identify his body. [1]

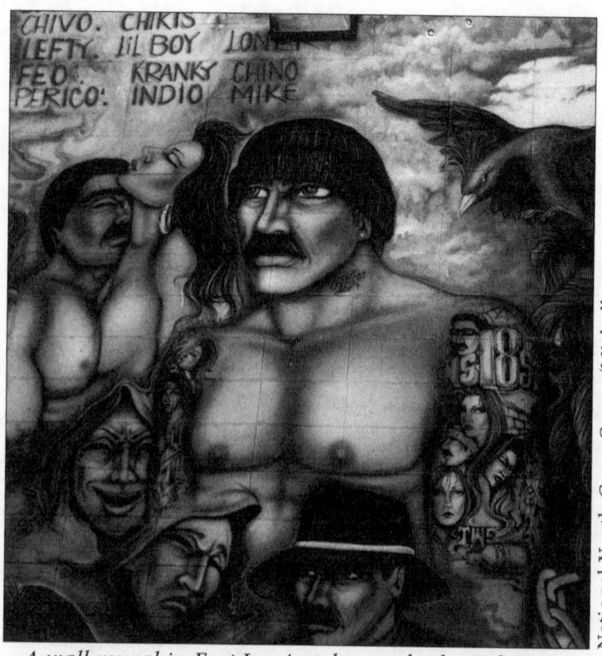

National Youth Gang Center/Michelle Arciaga

A wall mural in East Los Angeles marks the18th Street gang's turf. At least 21,500 gangs are active nationwide, in small communities as well as cities. Recent immigration has energized violent Latino and Asian gangs like Mara Salvatrucha and the Oriental Playboys.

Three months later, in nearby Alexandria, MS-13 members walked into a McDonald's and spotted an acquaintance, Joaquim Diaz, 19. Diaz was not an MS-13 member and didn't pretend to be.

However, one of the gang members, Denis Rivera, suspected Diaz had joined a rival gang. Rivera and another gang member convinced Diaz to accompany them to Washington to buy marijuana. But Diaz soon found himself in a remote area where he was slashed, stabbed, run over and then mutilated.

Rivera's girlfriend, Brenda Paz, later told police Rivera had bragged that he had tried to behead Diaz, comparing it to "preparing a chicken." But his knife had been too dull, so he had cut out Diaz's larynx instead. Paz entered the federal Witness Protection Program but left before Rivera went on trial. Weeks later her pregnant body was found on the banks of the Shenandoah River, stabbed to death. Police believe MS-13 was responsible. [2]

Newspapers across the country report scores of similar crimes in places like Reston that, until now, have not known gang violence. Even Utah, which historically has enjoyed a relatively low crime rate, has at least 250 gangs with 3,000 members operating in the Salt Lake City region alone. [3]

Gang experts say the U.S. gang problem, which had diminished in the 1990s, has worsened dramatically in recent years. In 2001, for instance, 27 percent of police agencies polled by the National Youth Gang Center (NYGC), a research agency funded by the Department of Justice (DOJ), said gang activity was increasing in their jurisdictions. In 2002, however, the figure had jumped to more than 40 percent, with at least 21,500 gangs — and more than 731,000 members — active nationwide. [4] In addition to MS-13, the major groups include the Bloods, Crips, Black Gangster Disciples Nation, Almighty Latin Kings Nation and various so-called Jamaican posses, as well as outlaw motorcycle gangs and prison gangs.

Perhaps most alarmingly, the National Alliance of Gang Investigators Associations (NAGIA) says gangs have morphed from an urban scourge into a nationwide threat. "Gang membership has crossed all socioeconomic, ethnic and racial boundaries and now permeates American society," said an NAGIA report. "The gang problem today is much more pervasive and menacing than at any [other] time in history." [5]

Wesley McBride, president of the California Gang Investigators Association, told a Senate Judiciary Committee hearing on gang violence in September 2003 that while gang activity may wane periodically, it usually roars back at record levels. "While there have been occasional declines in gang activity over the years," McBride said, "the declines never seem to establish a record low [and] the climactic rise at the end of the decline almost always sets a record." [7]

Moreover, authorities say, today's gangs are surprisingly well organized. The organizational chart of Chicago's 7,000-member Gangster Disciples — recovered during execution of a search warrant — was described by a federal prosecutor as "more sophisticated than many corporations." More than half the size of the Chicago Police Department, the gang had formed a political action committee, bought legitimate businesses and even sponsored community events, the prosecutor said. [9]

In the wake of the Sept. 11, 2001, terrorist attacks on the United States,

Gang Activity Jumped 50 Percent in 2002

Forty percent of police agencies reported an increase in local gang activity in 2002, a 50 percent rise over 2001, according to a research agency funded by the Department of Justice. Nationwide, there were some 21,500 gangs and 731,000 gang members in 2002.

Police Jurisdictions Reporting Increased Gang Activity

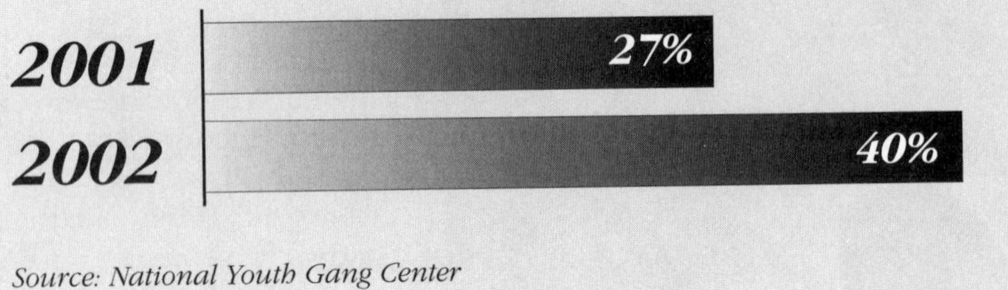

Source: National Youth Gang Center

gangs have even drawn the attention of the State Department and the Department of Homeland Security. Having already diversified from drug dealing into auto theft, extortion, property crimes and home invasion, some East Coast gangs have begun trafficking in fraudulent identification papers that could be used by terrorists trying to enter the country illegally.

While experts agree gangs are a serious problem, few agree on the causes or remedies. Even the definition of a gang is controversial. Some law enforcement officials say a youth gang is three or more 14-to-24-year-olds associating mainly, if not exclusively, to commit crimes. Others, like David Rathbun, a juvenile probation official in Fairfax County, Va., have simpler criteria for identifying gangs: "If it walks like a duck and quacks like a duck, it's probably a duck."

Because different authorities define gangs differently, national figures on gang activity and membership are often only "informed estimates," says NYGC Executive Director John Moore. But according to his organization's "fairly reliable" estimates, he says, 49 percent of U.S. gang members are Latino, 34 percent are black, 10 percent are white and 6 percent are Asian. While Latino and Asian gangs tend to be the most violent, white gangs have expanded into the most new territory over the last decade. [10]

Gangs also commit a disproportionate amount of urban violence. In Rochester, N.Y., for example, gang members who participated in a survey represented only 30 percent of the violent offenders in the region but committed 68 percent of the violent offenses. In Denver, gang members were only 14 percent of those surveyed but admitted to 79 percent of all violent, adolescent offenses committed in the city. [11] In fact, Moore says, 35 percent of Denver's homicides are gang-related.

Many gang victims are potential witnesses, police say. When not killing witnesses, gangs routinely intimidate them, usually through assault or rape. The U.S. attorney in New Orleans recently told Congress that witness intimidation had increased 50 percent in the previous year. [12] "Gangs have even been known to kill police officers who serve as witnesses against them," McBride said. [13]

Yet, the statistics can be tricky. For instance, the data show that overall gang membership and activity in smaller communities have decreased somewhat, but remain as high as ever — if not higher — in large cities and surrounding suburbs, Moore says. "They have decreased in smaller areas, but that's not where their strength ever was," he says.

As law enforcement officials and policymakers try to assess America's gang problem, here are some of the questions under debate:

Is government doing enough to combat the problem?

Traditionally, state and local authorities have dealt with gangs, since they were not considered a federal problem. In addition to law enforcement, policymakers have tried a variety of prevention programs, such as midnight basketball, designed to give adolescents socially acceptable alternative activities. Other programs, such as vocational training, have offered at-risk youth the promise of legitimate jobs, since unemployment is a major reason kids join gangs.

As gangs migrated — or "franchised" themselves, as some officials describe it — from Los Angeles and other major cities, many police departments set up special gang units. Authorities felt they were keeping pace with the problem until gangs began increasing in the late 1980s and early '90s, when insufficient resources prevented police from keeping up. Since then, state and local authorities say they haven't been able to keep up with the increase. If the federal government would provide more resources, local law enforcement authorities say they could do more.

Several federal agencies assist in the fight against gangs. Since gang crime often involves guns, the Bureau of Alcohol, Tobacco, Firearms and Explosives (BATFE) investigates gangs. Similarly, gangs' frequent involvement with illegal drugs draws attention from the Drug Enforcement Administration (DEA).

Perhaps foremost among federal anti-gang agencies are the 75 FBI Safe

Streets Gang Task Forces (SSGTFs) operating around the country. The SSGTFs emphasize "identification of the major violent street gangs [and] drug enterprises [that] pose significant threats," Grant D. Ashley, assistant director of the FBI's Criminal Investigative Division, told the Senate Judiciary Committee. [14]

"SSGTFs operate under the premise of cooperation between local, state and federal agencies," says Jeff Riley, chief of the FBI's Safe Streets and Gang Unit. "Once established, the SSGTFs are charged with bringing the resources of all the participating agencies to bear on the area's gang problem. This includes using sensitive investigative techniques, with an emphasis on long-term, proactive investigations into the violent criminal activities of the gang's leadership and hierarchy."

Moreover, when appropriate, U.S. attorneys "actively and creatively" prosecute gang crimes in federal courts, according to three U.S. attorneys who testified last September before the Judiciary Committee. In addition to using traditional narcotics and firearms statutes, federal prosecutors are using the Racketeer Influenced and Corrupt Organizations (RICO) law — successfully used to weaken the Mafia — against gangs. The U.S. attorney in Southern California recently convicted 75 members of the 18th Street and Mexican Mafia gangs under the RICO law. [15]

The DOJ also administers the Office of Juvenile Justice and Delinquency Prevention (OJJDP) and the Gang Resistance Education and Training (GREAT) program, which tries to develop positive relationships among local law enforcement, families and at-risk youths.

But McBride says federal law enforcement efforts have been ineffective because they have not been properly coordinated with state and local efforts. For instance, he says Los Angeles law enforcement agencies "hardly ever hear from" the FBI task force on gangs based in Los Angeles.

"You can almost compare [the situation] to the 9/11 hearings," says McBride, referring to the recent commission hearings that revealed a crucial lack of communication between various intelligence agencies before the terrorist attacks. "That's much like what's happening in the gang world."

Riley responds that the SSGTF in Los Angeles is located near the heart of the Watts section and focuses on inner-city gang activity, rather than on the more suburban activity McBride has been battling.

Fairfax County's Rathbun says the FBI task force in Northern Virginia, as well as U.S. immigration officials, works well with local officials, but he acknowledges that the level of cooperation varies from region to region.

But McBride, who recently retired from the Los Angeles County Sheriff's Department after 28 years of fighting gangs, contends that federal prosecution has not been effective. "You'd think they're prosecuting gang members right and left," says McBride, referring to the testimony at last September's Senate Judiciary Committee hearing. "I can tell you that U.S. attorneys don't want to see a gang case. They're very

Most Gang Members Are Latino, Black

Nearly half of all U.S. gang members are Latino, and more than a third are black, according to a research agency funded by the Department of Justice. White gangs reportedly have expanded into the most new territory over the last decade, while Asian gangs have moved into the Northeast, and Latino, black and Asian gangs have migrated into the South.

Ethnic Makeup of U.S. Gang Population

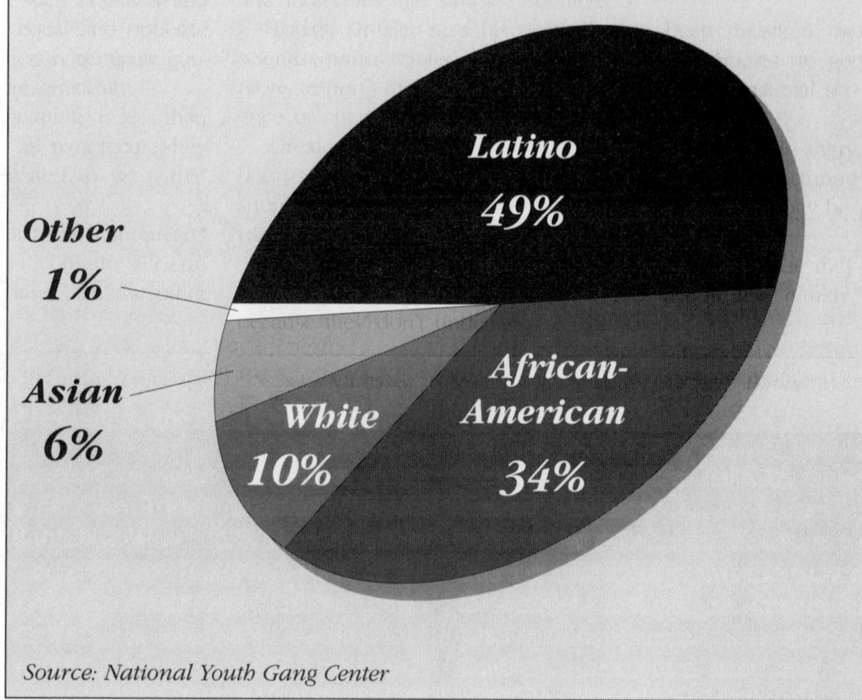

Source: National Youth Gang Center

hard to prosecute, very labor-intensive and in their [U.S. attorneys'] defense, they simply can't handle all the cases — we probably arrest 40,000 gang members a year just in L.A. But don't say the feds are doing a great job of prosecuting gang members."

Many state and local authorities say they are best equipped to prosecute gangs, if the federal government would provide the necessary funding. Robert McCulloch, prosecuting attorney of St. Louis County, Mo., and president of the National District Attorneys Association, says 180 gangs with about 4,000 members are fighting a violent turf war in St. Louis. But he says most cases will never be prosecuted because he can't offer witness protection.

"Prosecutors across the county believe witness intimidation is the single, biggest hurdle facing successful gang prosecution," he said. In Denver, a defendant allegedly ordered a sexual assault on a female witness scheduled to testify in a gang homicide. In Savannah, a gang murder occurred in front of 300 people, but no one would identify the assailant. [16]

Most state and local jurisdictions cannot afford witness-protection programs or the training and overtime needed for gang investigations. The state budget crisis and tax cuts have sapped local funds, and the war on terrorism has forced the redeployment of anti-gang units. [17]

"There are already plenty of laws to prosecute gangs," says Beryl Howell, a former legislative director for Sen. Patrick J. Leahy, D-Vt., who worked on anti-juvenile-crime legislation in the mid-1990s. The obstacles to pursuing gangs effectively, she says, are "resource issues, not legal issues."

Sens. Orrin G. Hatch, R-Utah, and Dianne Feinstein, D-Calif., hope to remedy that with the Gang Prevention and Effective Deterrence Act of 2003. The bill would authorize approximately $100 million in federal funds annually for five years to underwrite area law enforcement efforts in jurisdictions with "high-intensity interstate gang activity." Another $40 million a year would fund prevention programs.

California Gang Investigators Association

Bloods gang members from Los Angeles display their gang signs and colors. Gang members generally don't wear their colors in public nowadays to avoid trouble from police or rival gangs.

The Hatch-Feinstein bill would do more than provide desperately needed funds, says Bill Johnson, executive director of the National Association of Police Organizations and a former Florida prosecutor. It would also make participation in a "criminal street gang" and recruiting people to commit "gang crimes" federal offenses, punishable by 10 to 30 years in prison.

"It won't be the only solution, by any stretch of the imagination," he continues. "But if used properly, it'll help crush some of these gangs that really do overrun neighborhoods and communities."

But others are concerned that the bill would expand the federal role in fighting gangs, and in the process hamper local prosecutions. For instance, by redefining some state offenses as federal crimes, the bill could curtail state prosecutors' discretion in bringing charges and negotiating plea agreements, because defendants would be facing federal as well as state prosecution for gang crimes.

"We should be wary of making a federal crime out of everything," said Sen. Leahy. [18]

But Feinstein argues: "It used to be that gangs were local problems, demanding local, law-enforcement-based solutions. But over the last 12 years, I have seen the problem go from small to large and from neighborhood-based to national in scope. What were once loosely organized groups . . . are now complex criminal organizations whose activities include weapons trafficking, gambling, smuggling, robbery, and, of course, homicide. This is why we need a strong federal response."

Others are concerned about the historic conflicts between federal and state/local investigations and prosecutions. While SSGTFs are designed to work cooperatively with local authorities, differences remain in their investigative priorities. For instance, federal investigators' concentration on building cases over time will usually net more convictions, but local authorities often need to respond more quickly to community complaints, usually with street sweeps that can interfere with federal investigations.

Should gun laws be tightened to combat gang violence?

More than 350,000 incidents of gun violence, including 9,369 homicides, were committed in 2002, according to Michael Rand, chief of victimization statistics at the Justice Department's Bureau of Justice Statistics. But no one knows what percentage of those murders were committed by gang members, partly because of disagreement over what constitutes gang-related crime. To some officials, if two gang members commit an armed robbery, the crime can only be considered gang-related if they share the proceeds with the rest of the gang. To others, any armed robbery committed by gang members qualifies as gang-related.

According to the BATFE, 41 percent of the 88,570 guns used in crimes in 46 large cities in 2000 were traced to people age 24 or younger. [19] Of course, no one knows how many of them were gang members.

But as a recent Justice Department survey concluded: "Although both gang members and at-risk youths admitted significant involvement with guns, gang members were far likelier to own guns, and the guns they owned were larger caliber." More than 80 percent of gang members surveyed said either they or their fellow members had carried concealed guns into school, while only one-third of at-risk youths said they or their friends had done the same. [20] The most popular weapons were 9mm semiautomatic pistols. [21]

"Gangs, like any criminals, can never be as effective without firearms," says Joe Vince, a retired BATFE analyst. "Absolutely, guns are a tool of the trade for gangs — you've never heard of a drive-by with a knife."

Vince regularly investigated gangs' gun-show purchases, where unlicensed firearms dealers are exempt from the Brady Handgun Violence Prevention Act, which requires licensed sellers to perform a criminal background check before selling a weapon. Since it is illegal for anyone to sell a firearm to a buyer with a criminal record, gangs often send buyers who don't have criminal records to gun shows. [22]

Such "straw purchases" are also illegal, but unscrupulous unlicensed dealers pretend not to recognize a suspicious purchase, even when an 18-year-old is trying to buy a dozen guns at once, Vince says. "We found a lot of gangs sending someone who didn't have a record to gun shows, and he'd be on a cell phone talking to the gang leaders and saying, 'Hey, this guy's offering this, and that guy's offering that,' " Vince says.

"Some dealers even advertise that they're not licensed, so you can buy from them no-questions-asked," says Garen Wintemute, director of the Violence Prevention Research Program at the University of California, Davis.

In Chicago — which now may have the nation's largest and most active gang population — gangs are blamed for 45 percent of last year's 598 homicides. [23]

Continued on p. 429

Is There a Gang in Your 'Hood?

The following quiz can help neighborhoods measure potential gang activity. A score of 50 points or more indicates the need for a gang-prevention and intervention program:

In your community:

- Is there graffiti? (5 points)
- Is the graffiti crossed out? (10)
- Do the young people wear colors, jewelry, clothing, flash hand signs or display other behaviors that may be gang related? (10)
- Are drugs available? (10)
- Has there been a significant increase in the number of physical confrontations? (5)
- Is there an increasing presence of weapons? (5)
- Are beepers, pagers or cell phones used by the young people? (10)
- Has there been a "drive-by" shooting? (15)
- Have you had a "show-by" display of weapons? (10)
- Are truancies and/or daytime burglaries increasing? (5)
- Have racial incidents increased? (5)
- Is there a history of local gangs? (10)
- Is there an increasing presence of "informal social groups" with unusual names containing words like: kings, disciples, queens, posse, crew? (15)

Scoring Key

0-20 points = No Problem
25-45 points = Emerging Problems
50-65 points = You Have Problems
70+ points = You Have Serious Problems

Source: Tennessee Gang Investigators Association

The Violence of Mara Salvatrucha

David Rathbun has seen a lot of youngsters come through the juvenile justice system in Fairfax County, Va., near Washington, D.C. But he can't shake the memory of the 11-year-old charged with murder.

The boy and his 16-year-old brother belonged to Mara Salvatrucha, a Latino gang known for its violence. The two boys were out early one morning, "looking for trouble," says Rathbun, a juvenile-probation official. When they thought a youth across the street flashed a rival gang's sign at them — a gesture of disrespect — they crossed the street and stabbed him to death.

Violence is a gang's normal stock-in-trade, but gang experts say Mara Salvatrucha — or MS-13 — has made shootings, stabbings, hackings, beatings and rapes its brazen specialties. The gang originated in Los Angeles among refugees of El Salvador's civil war of the 1980s and rapidly spread around the country. The gang was formed in Los Angeles to protect Salvadoran immigrants from other, hostile Latino immigrants, according to veteran gang investigator Wesley McBride. The theory was: strike back twice as violently as you were attacked, and they'll leave you alone. Many MS-13s had been guerrilla fighters in El Salvador's bloody civil war.

MS-13 began as a merger between immigrants who'd been involved with La Mara — a street gang in El Salvador — and former members of the FMNL, a paramilitary group of Salvadoran guerrilla fighters called "Salvatruchas."

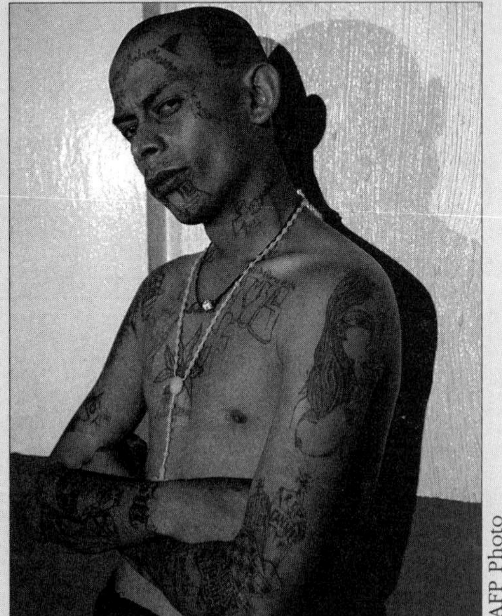
AFP Photo

Police arrested this Mara Salvatrucha leader last year in San Salvador, El Salvador. Thousands of the gang's most violent U.S. members have been deported.

MS-13's victims have included innocent people caught in the middle as well as other gang members. In 2002, MS-13's Los Angeles cell reportedly dispatched several members to Fairfax County with instructions to kill a county police officer "at random." They didn't succeed. [1]

The Justice Department says MS-13 now has about 8,000 members in 27 states and the District of Columbia, and 20,000 more members in Central and South America, particularly El Salvador. The gang is involved in smuggling and selling illegal drugs, but different cells (or cliques, as they're sometimes called) may be involved in other activities, including providing "protection" to houses of prostitution, Rathbun says.

The independent National Gang Crime Research Center (NGCRC) ranks gangs by their violence level, with 1 being least dangerous and 3 the most dangerous. MS-13 is ranked a 3. Center Director George W. Knox describes MS-13's level of violence as "extraordinary." [2]

An investigator with the Orange County, Calif., district attorney's office says the gang participates in a broad range of criminal activities across the country. "MS members have been involved in burglaries, auto thefts, narcotic sales, home-invasion robberies, weapons smuggling, car jacking, extortion, murder, rape, witness intimidation, illegal firearm sales, car theft and aggravated assaults. . . . [C]ommon drugs sold by MS members include cocaine, marijuana, heroin, and methamphetamine. Mara Salvatrucha gang members have even placed a 'tax' on prostitutes and non-gang member drug dealers who are working in MS 'turf.' Failure to pay up will most likely result in violence." [3]

One of the gang's signatures is a military-style booby trap used to protect a stash of illegal drugs. The trap usually consists of a tripwire rigged to an anti-personnel grenade.

Joining the gang requires potential members to be "jumped in." Several gangs observe this ritual, which involves a group-administered beating. Typically, gang members surround the candidate and then attack him; other gang members evaluate how well he defends himself and his ability to endure punches. MS-13's jumping-in lasts for 13 seconds.

Most MS-13 members are between ages 11 and 40, but leaving the gang is often difficult. The father of the two boys who stabbed the suspected rival gang member to death is also an MS-13 member; the mother wholeheartedly supports her husband's and sons' memberships, Rathbun says.

The 16-year-old was tried as an adult and sentenced to a maximum-security prison, but Rathbun has hope for the 11-year-old, who took school classes when he was in the county's juvenile system. "He had a probation officer that worked very closely with him, and his sense of self-worth increased as he did better academically. He stayed in touch with the gang, but he wasn't participating any more. I don't think his father will ever be out of MS-13, but, knock wood, I think we may have changed the son's course."

---

1 "Focus on Gangs: Salvadoran MS-13 Rated Among Most Violent," *EmergencyNet News*, Aug. 24, 2002; http://www.emergency.com/polcpage.htm.

2 *Ibid.*

3 Al Valdez, "A South American Import," National Alliance of Gang Investigators Associations, 2000; http://www.nagia.org/mara_salvatrucha.htm.

Continued from p. 427

Authorities also believe Chicago has more illegal firearms than any other city: In 2003, Chicago police seized more than 10,000 illegal guns; Los Angeles police recovered just under 7,000 and New York City under 4,000. [24]

Gun control advocates maintain that tougher gun laws and more stringent enforcement of them could cut gang violence. "Wherever you can reduce the availability and accessibility of firearms to criminals, you reduce violent crime," Vince says. "People just cannot be as violent without a gun."

However, Erich Pratt, communications director for Gun Owners of America (GOA), says, "We've yet to discover any gun control legislation that successfully keeps guns out of the wrong hands. Washington, D.C., is certainly the epitome of that — you have a draconian gun ban there that doesn't let anybody own any guns, and yet the bad guys continue to get firearms."

Data compiled by the Bureau of Justice Statistics show that handgun homicides started decreasing in 1993 — a year before Congress enacted the Brady law — and continued to fall through 2000.

But a study in the *Journal of the American Medical Association* suggests no link between the decrease and the Brady law. "We find no differences in homicide or firearms homicide rates in the 32 . . . states directly subject to the Brady Act provisions compared with the remaining [18] states," the researchers wrote. [25]

Wintemute says the results could be interpreted in two equally valid ways: "One is that the Brady law never went far enough from the beginning," he says, "or that the Brady law is a failure and we should get rid of it."

Supporters of the law say that at the least it has prevented the crime rate from worsening. But Andrew Arulanandam, public affairs director for the National Rifle Association (NRA), says the law's stringent record-keeping provisions make that unlikely.

"You mean to tell me that some guy who's going to commit a heinous crime is going to leave a paper trail?" Arulanandam asks. Gang members are "not going to be deterred by a firearm law. More often than not, they'll obtain the firearm by illegal means."

But record-keeping is diminishing. Because of a provision in the Omnibus Appropriations bill, passed last January, federal authorities who run criminal background checks on gun buyers are no longer required to keep a record of the check for 90 days. In fact, they must now destroy the record within 24 hours.

Moreover, Eric Howard, spokesman for the Brady Campaign to Prevent Gun Violence, says the Department of Justice recently found that Brady background checks blocked more than a million potential purchasers from buying guns. "This flies in the face of what [the NRA] says all the time: That these guys aren't going to get background checks, they'll get guns elsewhere," Howard says. "Well, these guys aren't the sharpest knives in the drawer." The Brady law could very well have kept the nation's crime rate lower than it might otherwise have been in the past decade, Howard argues. [26]

Nonetheless, some states enforce the Brady law less stringently, so gangs go to those states. For instance, gangs in Chicago have established a gun-running pipeline into Mississippi, where Brady enforcement and local gun laws are generally more relaxed. [27]

Opponents of gun control say this proves their point: Regardless of how many prohibited purchases are blocked, criminals will always find a way to get firearms. The best deterrent, they say, is not to limit the number of guns on the street but to increase them — by allowing law-abiding citizens to carry concealed weapons. "States that have adopted concealed-carry legislation are seeing the greatest and most dramatic decreases in the murder rate," Pratt says.

The gun problem is like the drug problem, says the NRA's Arulanandam. "Drugs are outlawed, but people get their hands on them."

The BATFE's Vince agrees with the comparison, but he and other gun control advocates want to close the gun-show loophole, which the gun lobby says would penalize law-abiding, unlicensed dealers.

"If you focus law enforcement only on gun users but not on dealers," he says, "that's like saying we're going to go after everyone that shoots heroin but not the cartel."

Should more minors be tried as adults for gang crimes?

An undercover Chicago police officer working a drug deal in the depressed Humboldt Park neighborhood in April noticed two young men run into an alley. Seconds later, he heard gunshots and saw the men running out. A third man lay dying in the alley.

As the cop chased the suspects, they turned and fired at him. He continued chasing them and eventually caught them. One was 18, the other 15. Both were members of the Maniac Latin Disciples. "I wanted to shoot a Cobra" — a rival gang — "to prove how tough I was," the 15-year-old reportedly said. He was charged as an adult with first-degree murder. [28]

In colonial days, children sometimes faced adult charges and just as often were incarcerated with adults; sometimes they were executed. [29] In the late 19th century, however, social reformers argued that juveniles were developmentally different from adults and could be rehabilitated. The nation established a juvenile justice system — with separate statutes and penalties — at the beginning of the 20th century.

But in cases involving violent crimes, prosecutors sometimes try minors as adults, triggering debate over the tactic's effectiveness and justification. A surge in juvenile crime beginning in the late 1980s — largely triggered by a crack epidemic — led many minors to be charged as adults. A 1989 Supreme Court ruling allowing states to execute juvenile offenders 16 and older has kept the debate alive.

Currently, state prosecutors decide whether minors charged with violent felonies should be charged as adults. But the proposed Hatch-Feinstein bill would allow federal prosecutors to try any gang member 16 or older as an adult.

The legislation has triggered debates over whether more minors should be tried as adults, and whether the federal government should be trying minors at all. "We're always uncomfortable when furthering policies that take things that should be state matters and throw them into federal courts," the GOA's Pratt says. "We agree that if you do an adult crime, you do the adult time, but we think the states [should] handle it."

"The feds don't have any infrastructure set up to deal with juveniles, so they usually defer to the states, and wisely so," says Rathbun of Fairfax County. "We've had a couple of murder cases where the feds got involved, and it was useful because [the accused] got harsher sentences. But that's just a handful of our cases."

However, former legislative director Howell believes that federal authorities can more effectively prosecute gangs than state or local authorities. "The gang problem warrants federal attention because it quickly overtakes local and state boundaries," she says. "It can overtake national boundaries, too."

For example, as a federal prosecutor Howell once went after members of the Flying Dragons, which ran gambling and Mah Jong parlors in New York's Chinatown. But the gang also smuggled heroin from Hong Kong. The investigation had to contend with the respective requirements and laws affecting New York and Hong Kong authorities, not to mention language and cultural complications between both cities.

But prosecuting juveniles as adults won't solve the gang problem, she says. "Where does that get you?" she asks. "The younger you send kids to prison, the better-educated they become at being criminals. Adult prisons have lost much pretense, if they ever had any, of being rehabilitative. With the juvenile system, there's at least a pretense of rehabilitation."

Federal prosecution of minors as adults would be "a good law to have on the books and threaten with, but it's not going to help much," adds McBride, of the California Gang Investigators Association. States have tougher provisions on minors and gangs than federal agencies, he notes, and states aren't making any demonstrable headway against gangs by prosecuting minors as adults.

Trying minors as adults "is an effective tool the same way a sledge hammer is an effective tool," says the National Association of Police Organizations' Johnson. "It ought to be used sparingly, but in those cases where it's necessary, then it ought to be used."

More than 60 child-advocacy organizations oppose the Senate bill's provision to prosecute juveniles as adults for gang crimes. "I understand the desire to respond to gang violence," said Marc Schindler, a staff attorney for the Youth Law Center. "But this is the wrong way to do it. It's basically going to throw kids away to the adult system." [30]

Even law-and-order hard-liners acknowledge that the threat of severe punishment alone will not deter gangs. "A lot of gang members are in gangs because their parents didn't give a rat's behind about them," says McBride, echoing experts on all sides of the issue. "How do you make a momma care for her kid? You can't legislate that."

The best deterrent to gangs, many experts say, is to have parents involved with their children's lives, but in today's economy, that's often nearly impossible. Some observers attribute the rise in immigrant gangs to the fact that both parents often work multiple jobs and have little time to spend with their kids.

Whatever the causes, the rise in gang crime has made some authorities open to anything that might help. Los Angeles County's sheriff recently estimated that the 96,000 gang members in his jurisdiction commit half the violent offenses each year. "We believe there are teenagers close to 18 who are committing heinous adult acts, and they should be treated as an adult," said Steve Whitmore, a spokesman for the L.A. sheriff's office. [31] ■

BACKGROUND

Early Gangs

The youth gang phenomenon dates back at least to the days of St. Augustine (A.D. 354-430), who wrote in his *Confessions* of the pleasures of stealing pears with adolescent accomplices: "My pleasure was not in those pears, it was in the offense itself, which the company of fellow sinners occasioned." [32]

In 17th-century London, youth gangs with such names as the Mims, the Bugles and the Dead Boys terrorized the citizenry by breaking windows, destroying taverns and fighting, each group wearing different-colored ribbons. And Charles Dickens often wrote about gangs in the 19th century, perhaps most famously the gang of boy orphans run by the money-grubbing Fagin in the classic *Oliver Twist.*

Continued on p. 432

Chronology

1950s *Southern blacks migrate to Northern inner cities; classic era of teen street gangs; wave of Puerto Rican immigrants arrives in New York City.*

Sept. 26, 1957
Leonard Bernstein's hit musical "West Side Story" opens on Broadway. It looks unflinchingly at the growing menace of gang warfare.

1960s *Gangs take on traits from civil rights, Black Muslim and radical youth movements; government channels some gangs into anti-poverty work.*

1961
President John F. Kennedy signs Juvenile Delinquency and Youth Offenses and Control Act, creating a federal committee to address youth crime.

1967
President's Task Force on Juvenile Delinquency calls for community efforts to curb youth crime. . . . Senate probes fraud in federal grant program for Chicago's Blackstone Rangers gang.

1970s *Police officials and academics shift their strategies on gangs from social work to suppression and control.*

Aug. 21, 1974
Congress creates Office of Juvenile Justice and Delinquency Prevention.

1975
Justice Department launches first national gang survey.

1980s *Latino and Asian immigrants make Los Angeles the nation's gang capital; crack cocaine arrives in inner cities; Reagan administration declares war on drugs.*

1982
FBI designates motorcycle gangs as national investigative priority within its organized-crime program.

1985
California creates State Task Force on Youth Gang Violence; L.A. Police Chief Daryl F. Gates vows to eliminate gangs in five years.

Late 1980s
Highly profitable crack cocaine becomes the product of choice for drug-dealing gangs, sparking fights over the most profitable turf and a spike in violent crime.

1988
President Ronald Reagan signs Anti-Drug Abuse Act. . . . California convenes State Task Force on Gangs and Drugs; Los Angeles police crack down on gang neighborhoods.

May 15, 1989
Administration of first President George Bush bans imports of semiautomatic assault weapons used by street gangs.

1990s *Gangs expand out from inner cities; government, police and academics coordinate comprehensive approach to the gang problem.*

1995
Gang homicides in Los Angeles hit a record 809 deaths . . . more than half of all violent crime in Buffalo, N.Y., is gang related.

1997
FBI estimates that 50,000 gang members are active in Chicago. . . . Congress attempts to overhaul the U.S. juvenile justice system, but the bill deadlocks over juvenile sentencing and gun control.

1999
Congress again addresses juvenile justice, but House and Senate negotiators again stall over gun control.

2000s *Police say gang violence begins to rise; Asian and Latino gangs account for most juvenile violence; Congress again attempts to pass anti-gang legislation.*

Sept. 11, 2001
Terrorist strikes against the U.S. cause many police departments to reassign special gang units to counter-terrorist duties.

January 2004
Congress passes Omnibus Appropriations bill, which contains a provision voiding the Brady law's requirement that the National Instant Criminal Background Check system maintain records of criminal checks for 90 days; gun control advocates claim this will make it harder for authorities to trace crime guns to gang members and other criminals.

April 2004
Senate Judiciary Committee begins consideration of the Gang Prevention and Effective Deterrence Act, sponsored by Sens. Dianne Feinstein, D-Calif., and Orrin Hatch, R-Utah. Committee approval is expected in May.

Gangs Commit Most Violent Teen Crimes

Gang members make up a small percentage of violent offenders but commit a disproportionate amount of teenage violent crime, as shown by statistics from Rochester, N.Y., and Denver, Colo.

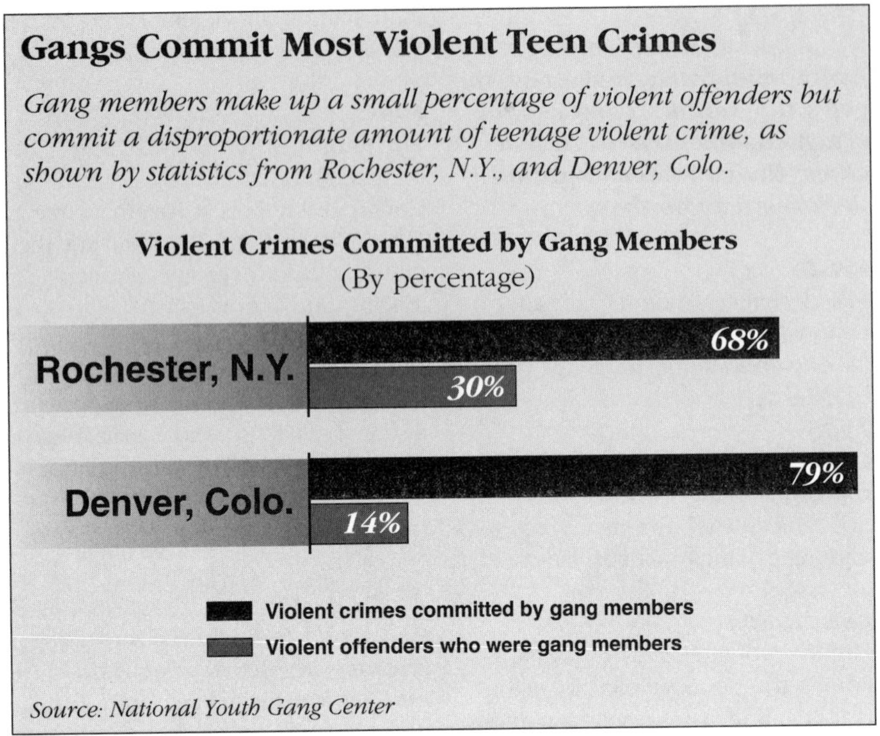

Source: National Youth Gang Center

Continued from p. 430

In the United States, the first recorded youth gang was the Forty Thieves, founded in about 1825 in Lower Manhattan. Others appeared in Philadelphia in the 1840s, such as the Bouncers, the Rats and the Skinners. Mostly they defaced walls with graffiti and carried pistols and knives.

Immigrants usually formed gangs for self-protection. Often not speaking the language of their new country and unfamiliar with its customs, they found assimilation extremely difficult. Discrimination added a sense of victimization to their existing feelings of alienation, and they saw gangs as a refuge from a hostile environment.

Waves of Irish immigrants in New York in the 19th century soon begat such gangs as the Bowery Boys and the Dead Rabbits, who waged three-day rumbles that forced helpless police to call in the Army. Their nonchalance toward violence was remarkable: A member of the Plug Uglies is said to have attacked a stranger and cracked his spine in three places just to win a $2 bet. [33]

Female gang members also were known in the mid-19th century, among them the celebrated street fighters Hellcat Annie and Battle Annie. [34]

Early New York gangs, as brutally portrayed in the 2002 movie "Gangs of New York," often sold their services to labor unions and company operators maneuvering in the rough and tumble world of politics. "By 1855," a city historian wrote, "it was estimated that the Metropolis contained at least 30,000 men who owed allegiance to gang leaders and through them to the leaders of Tammany Hall and the Know Nothing, or Native American Party." [35] During the Civil War, Irish gang members were blamed for the anti-conscription riots in which many blacks were lynched.

The German and Italian immigrants who arrived in the late 19th century produced equally violent gangs. Some would commit crimes for hire: A slash on the cheek with a knife cost $10; throwing a bomb, $50; murder, $100. "It might be inferred that the New York tough is a very fierce individual [but] it is only when he hunts with the pack that he is dangerous," noted social reformer and photographer Jacob Riis. [36]

The most notorious of the early immigrant gangs in New York was, of course, the Mafia, or La Cosa Nostra ("Our Thing"), which originated as a criminal organization in Sicily. The Mafia rose to power by extorting neighborhood shopkeepers for "protection" money against arson. It consolidated its power during Prohibition, when it controlled the illegal distribution of liquor in many U.S. cities.

By the turn of the century, Jewish gangs and Chinese gangs had been added to the ethnic stew in New York's Bowery, Chinatown and in such rough neighborhoods as Hell's Kitchen on the West Side. During Prohibition, many youth gangs became involved with adult bootleggers. In Southern California, waves of Mexican immigrants arrived to form the first so-called barrio gangs.

But the worst gang problems plagued Chicago. In 1927 criminologist Frederick M. Thrasher published the first major book on the problem, *The Gang: A Study of 1,313 Gangs in Chicago*, in which he analyzed gangs of every ethnic and racial stripe: Polish, Irish, Anglo-American, Jewish, Slavic, Bohemian, German, Swedish, Lithuanian, black, Chinese and Mexican. "The gang is a conflict group," Thrasher wrote. "It develops through strife and warfare."

The ethnic character of American gangs continued to manifest itself. In the 1930s, the rising numbers of blacks migrating from the South to New York, as well as new immigrants from the British West Indies, set up the first rivalries among black gangs. In the early 1940s, gangs of Latino youths in Southern California frequently clashed with U.S. servicemen stationed in the area, eventually provoking the so-called Zoot Suit Riots, named for a flashy clothing style then popular among Latinos.

Seeking Respectability

The classic youth-gang era began after World War II, when Americans migrated from the farms to the cities. The first "teenage" subculture emerged in the postwar period, and gangs severed their earlier ties to adult organized crime.

In Los Angeles, two black gangs appeared — the Businessmen and the Home Street Gang. In the 1950s, CBS News correspondent Edward R. Murrow drew nationwide attention to the conditions that produce gangs with the documentary "Who Killed Michael Farmer?" about the death of a handicapped young man at the hands of a Bronx street gang.

Society responded to gangs by trying to build long-term relationships with gang members and by sponsoring dances or athletic contests, such as a New York City Youth Board program that sought to reduce gang tensions. "Participation in a street gang or club," a 1950 Youth Board document read, "like participation in any natural group, is part of the growing-up process. . . . Within the structure of the group the individual can develop such characteristics as loyalty, leadership and community responsibility. . . . Some gangs . . . have developed patterns of anti-social behavior . . . [but] members can be reached and will respond to sympathy, acceptance, affection and understanding when approached by adults who possess those characteristics and reach out to them on their own level." [37]

In the 1960s, the Hell's Angels motorcycle gang gained national exposure and greatly influenced the younger, more ethnic urban gangs. "By 1965," wrote counterculture journalist Hunter S. Thompson, later of *Rolling Stone* fame, "[gangs] were firmly established as All-American bogeymen." Meanwhile, the decade's civil rights movement, urban riots and radical politics spilled over into the world of gangs, particularly among blacks, many of whom would become attracted to revolutionary groups like the Black Panthers.

With President Lyndon B. Johnson's War on Poverty pouring millions of federal grant dollars into inner cities, some criminal youth gangs decided to join the Establishment, heralding either an optimistic or opportunistic approach to addressing social problems, depending on one's viewpoint.

In New York City in 1967, for example, leaders of the Puerto Rican gang Spartican Army decided they wanted a role in bettering the social and economic conditions of their Lower East Side neighborhoods. Borrowing from Johnson's Great Society rhetoric, they took the name the Real Great Society and applied for a grant from the federal Office of Economic Opportunity (OEO). They were turned down, but their well-publicized efforts (profiled in *Life* magazine) attracted private foundation money. They opened a Real Great Society nightclub, a child-care service and a leather-goods store, all of which blossomed briefly but failed within a year. [38] They then organized summer classes for inner-city youths and finally won an OEO grant.

In Chicago, meanwhile, another experiment in gang respectability was under way. In 1967, the Blackstone Rangers, led by a fervent black nationalist, Jeff Fort, began toying with the notion of doing anti-poverty work with a radical white clergyman, John Fry, who was affiliated with a community-organizing group named for Chicago's Woodlawn neighborhood. Because the group opposed Chicago's powerful mayor, Richard J. Daley, its anti-poverty programs had never received federal grant money, over which Daley had de facto control.

But the possible turnaround of the Blackstone Rangers was too tempting to Washington. In June, the OEO awarded the Woodlawn Organization and the Blackstone Rangers $927,000 to operate anti-poverty programs for a year.

Daley was furious at fellow Democrats in the Johnson administration, but he did not have to fume for long. The Woodlawn program quickly became known as a monumental boondoggle: Only 76 of 800 participants in its jobs program got jobs; bookkeeping was lax; gang members encouraged each other to quit school and be paid from the federal grant; by autumn, Fort had been arrested on murder charges. [39]

In Washington, Sen. John L. McClellan, D-Ark., chairman of the Government Operations Committee, held widely publicized hearings into the Woodlawn grant. Many blamed the OEO for poor judgment. While under indictment, Fort appeared as a witness but refused to speak. (The murder charges against him were later dismissed.)

In May 1968, OEO shut down the Woodlawn project, just weeks after the Blackstone Rangers were given credit for keeping Chicago relatively calm during the urban riots that followed the assassination of the Rev. Dr. Martin Luther King, Jr. The idealistic notion of giving government money to reformed gang members had suffered a crippling blow.

The impact of Chicago's gang experiment during the days of the War on Poverty would be felt for decades. Chicago gang members continued to receive foundation money for nearly 20 years. Fort was sentenced to prison in the early 1970s for fraud committed with the OEO grant. In prison, he converted to Islam and changed the Rangers' name to El Rukns (Arabic for "the foundation").

When he and some fellow gang members emerged from prison in the late 1970s, they threw themselves into the violent drug trade. Dozens of El Rukns members were sent to prison in the early 1980s. In 1987, Fort was sentenced to 75 years in prison for soliciting money from Libya to fund terrorist operations in the U.S. [40]

Continued on p. 435

When Girls Join Gangs

In Augusta, Ga., six members of an all-girl gang corner a 22-year-old woman on the street and savagely beat her. [1] In San Antonio, Texas, two girls slash a rival gang girl's face with a broken bottle. [2] In Buffalo, N.Y., female members of a mixed gang transport narcotics and sometimes sell drugs on the streets. [3]

Gang members are usually seen as young men wearing distinctive clothes or colors, using a common slang and hand signals and fighting with gangs from other neighborhoods. If females are in the picture at all, they're usually viewed as supporting players — girlfriends, perhaps, or maybe sisters, but never gang members in their own right. Yet, female gangs have existed in America at least since the 19th century.

Relatively little is known about female gangs, however, and most of the knowledge has been acquired only in the last 20 years. Sexist stereotyping has largely been responsible for the lack of awareness, according to the Justice Department's Office of Juvenile Justice and Delinquency Prevention (OJJDP). Researchers historically perceived gangs in terms of vandalism, theft and assault — generally considered male provinces.

"It was often assumed that females did not take part in such behavior, so early researchers were not interested in the delinquency of female gang members," wrote sociologist Joan Moore and criminologist John Hagedorn in an issue of the *Juvenile Justice Bulletin* devoted to female gangs. [4]

When gang activity escalated in the 1980s and '90s, researchers began noticing that female gangs were either autonomous entities or affiliates of male gangs. With names like Latin Queens, the female counterpart to Latin Kings, and Sisters of the Struggle, they usually had their own identities and structures.

No one knows how many female gangs exist. Law enforcement surveys tend to show that between 4 and 11 percent of gang members are female, but social-service surveys show higher numbers.

Although little is known about female gang activity, some research and anecdotal reports show that most girl gangs are involved in delinquency or non-violent crimes, with drug offenses ranking near the top of the list. Female gang members commit fewer violent crimes than male gang members and in general are more prone to property crime. [5]

"The biggest difference between female gangs and male gangs is violence," says Hagedorn, a professor of criminal justice at the University of Illinois. "Girls are very seldom involved in homicide. The difference between males and females on this issue is massive."

Still, he acknowledges, female gang members can sometimes be just as violent as males. In the mid-1990s, an 11-city survey of eighth-graders revealed that more than 90 percent of male and female gang members admitted to having committed one or more violent acts in the previous 12 months. Moreover, 78 percent of female gang members reported having been in a gang fight, 65 percent acknowledged carrying a weapon and 39 percent said they had attacked someone with a weapon. [6]

Within mixed gangs, males commonly boast that the females are their sex objects, a claim that has perpetuated the "sex slave" stereotype of female gang members. But OJJDP research done in conjunction with the National Youth Gang Center shows that females deny this, insisting that females of any position or authority in the gang are respected precisely because they do not allow the males to exploit them sexually. Sexual exploitation does occur, they say, but almost always involving girls or young women who are not members of the gang.

California Gang Investigators Association

Female gang members commit fewer violent crimes than male gang members, primarily property and drug offenses.

Currently, most female gangs are Latina and African-American, though the numbers of Asian and white female gangs have been increasing.

Regardless of ethnicity or race, many girls join gangs for the same reasons as males — seeking friendship and self-affirmation. Sometimes the lack of job opportunities pushes girls and young women to join gangs, as it does boys and young men. But many female gang members share a common pain of childhood, which they have tried to escape by seeking refuge in a gang. "Research consistently shows that high proportions of female gang members have experienced sexual abuse at home," Hagedorn and Moore write.

There's another important difference between female and male gang members: Females tend to leave a gang sooner because they get pregnant, usually by age 18.

---

[1] See "Woman Reports Gang Assault," *The Augusta Chronicle*, Feb. 22, 2004, p. B3.

[2] See Elda Silva, "'Homegirls' Gets Personal, Introspective," *The San Antonio Express-News*, Jan. 29, 2004, p. 1F.

[3] See Lou Michel, "The Bloods, Settling Debts with Death," *Buffalo News*, Dec. 16, 2003, p. A1.

[4] See Joan Moore and John Hagedorn, "Female Gangs: A Focus on Research," *Juvenile Justice Bulletin*, March 2001, p. 1.

[5] *Ibid*, p. 5.

[6] *Ibid*, p. 6.

Continued from p. 433

In the 1980s, crack cocaine became the product of choice for drug-dealing gangs: Highly addictive and inexpensive, crack provided a profit margin greater than powdered cocaine. Gangs soon were fighting over the most profitable turf — markets — giving rise to drive-by shootings and a spike in violent crime.

War Refugees

In El Salvador, civil war in the early 1980s prompted many refugees — and former guerrillas — to flee to the United States. The Mara Salvatrucha, or MS-13, gang emerged from a rapidly swelling population of Salvadoran immigrants in Los Angeles. Other gangs with roots in the Central American immigrant communities of Southern California also formed, and violence frequently erupted between them and the area's long-established Mexican gangs.

Asian gangs began appearing around the same time, mostly as a result of massive Asian immigration, including the "boat people," refugees from war-ravaged Southeast Asia. The gangs of Vietnamese, Cambodian and Laotian refugees had roots in the region's refugee camps following the Vietnam War and the post-war atrocities committed by the Khmer Rouge in Cambodia. [41] By the late 1980s and early '90s, Asian gangs had footholds from West Valley City, Utah, to Manhattan. "When I was a prosecutor in New York," Howell recalls, "the Vietnamese gangs were as violent as anybody."

Throughout the late 1980s and early '90s, many Latino gang members in L.A. headed north to Chicago, already teeming with black, white and mixed-race gangs. In 1991, the city's homicide rate hit a record 609 deaths. In response, Mayor Richard M. Daley recalled the gang-grant scandal from the era when his famous father had run city hall. The younger Daley lashed out at the liberal "social workers" of the 1960s and '70s who had "coddled" the teenage gang members who were now, as adults, Chicago's drug kingpins.

In an effort to reduce the nation's crime rate, Congress in 1996 enacted a law that allows deportation of noncitizens sentenced to a year or more in prison for anything ranging from petty theft to murder. Since then, in what constitutes the largest dragnet in the country's history, more than 500,000 "criminal aliens" have been deported to more than 130 countries, including many gang members who originally immigrated to the United States with their parents to escape poverty or civil war. [42]

While the tactic has effectively reduced the number of criminals in the United States, it has overwhelmed the receiving countries, particularly in Latin America and the Caribbean, which have seen crime rates skyrocket since 1996.

Many of the deported have joined local gangs — often home-country versions of the gangs they belonged to in the United States. El Salvador and Honduras have suffered particularly sharp rises in violent gang crime, with beheadings, shootings, rapes and hackings now commonplace, police say. Moreover, vigilante groups often hunt down gang members and murder them on sight — a practice both U.S. and Latin American officials say only causes retaliation and escalation. [43]

By 1997, the chief of the FBI's violent-crime section estimated that Chicago had 50,000 active gang members — more than the combined area membership of the Moose, the Elks, the Knights of Columbus and the Shriners. [44] Meanwhile, in the previous 16 years approximately 7,300 people had died in gang violence in Los Angeles.

But Chicago and L.A. were not alone. In 1995, police blamed gangs for 41 percent of Omaha's homicides, and more than half of all violent crime in Buffalo. In Phoenix, gang-related homicides jumped 800 percent between 1990 and '94. [45] While the overall violent-crime rate across the country was dropping, violent juvenile crime remained high.

In response, lawmakers drafted the Violent and Repeat Juvenile Justice Act of 1997. The House passed its version of the bill, but the Senate's version — opposed by countless advocacy groups — never made it to a floor vote. Liberals felt it was too harsh, citing its intention to prosecute juveniles as adults and house them with adults in prison. Conservatives felt it penalized law-abiding gun merchants and owners.

Congress tried again in early 1999 with Democrats and Republicans apparently determined to compromise on the issue. But the bipartisan spirit was shattered in April, when two teenagers in Littleton, Colo., went on a shooting rampage at Columbine High School, killing 13 people before turning the guns on themselves. [46] Both the House and Senate passed juvenile crime bills, but liberals and conservatives deadlocked over gun control, effectively killing the bills in conference.

Starting in 1995, juvenile violent crime began falling, and continued falling through 2001, but in 2002 authorities began seeing an upsurge in gang violence. [47] Latino and Asian gangs were committing the most violent offenses, particularly along the Northeast Corridor. Of the two, the Latinos have drawn the most attention because their numbers are currently the largest. And among the Latinos, MS-13 is widely considered the most dangerous. ■

CURRENT SITUATION

Invisible Crisis

If many Americans are unaware of the country's gang crisis, it may be because some police departments don't want them to know about it. The National Alliance of Gang Investigators Associations says many law enforcement agencies have refused to cooperate with its nationwide survey of gang activities.

"We're getting so many of those forms back from [police] departments refusing to fill them out," McBride says. "The local authorities say, 'We don't want to ruin our economy, because companies won't move here if they know we have gangs!' " McBride says. "I even had one executive tell me that people don't have a right to know, and no sense scaring them. I was flabbergasted. People absolutely have a right to know and need to know how many gangs are out there."

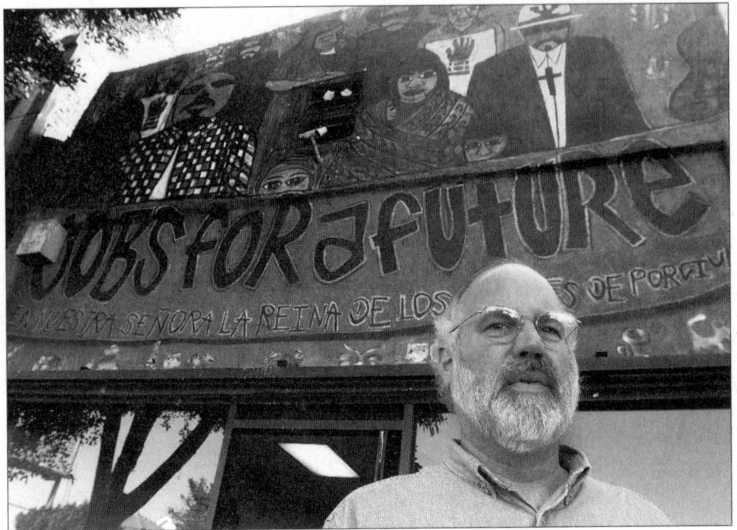

AFP Photo/Mike Nelson

The Rev. Greg Boyle, a Jesuit priest, runs a jobs program in East Los Angeles for gang members who want to stop being criminals.

But sometimes the agencies don't respond because of poor record keeping, he says. In Denver, for example, police records show that the city's 17,000 gang members committed only 89 of the 59,581 crimes in 2002. "I heard that figure, and I just wanted to laugh," said a member of the metropolitan police department's gang crimes unit. [48] Moore, of the National Youth Gang Center, says officers often do not know immediately that a crime is gang related; when they find out, they rarely revise the initial police report.

Another problem is the cyclical nature of gangs and gang prevention. Police departments often set up gang units and then dissolve them once they believe the situation is under control, only to see the problem worsen again. "There's just no continuity of incident reporting," Moore says, so police records on gangs are "notoriously slack."

Four years ago, when acknowledging a gang problem carried less stigma than it does today, the NAGIA assembled a national picture of gangs and gang activities that many say is still essentially accurate. Starting in the late 1990s, gangs began penetrating into suburban areas in the Northeast and Mid-Atlantic regions, particularly in upstate New York, eastern Pennsylvania and Northern Virginia. Increasing numbers of Asian gangs were migrating into the Northeast, while two Latino gangs — the Latin Kings and the Netas — had become involved in political and social causes to establish some legitimacy. [49]

Along with the increase in gangs has come an increase in crime. Last September, for instance, Christopher Christie, U.S. attorney for Newark, N.J., reported that for the third straight year, the city's murder rate had risen, as well as the number of handguns recovered by police. "The rise in violence and unlawful gun possession corresponds directly to a substantial increase in documented gang activity beginning in 1999," he said. [50]

The South also has seen increased activity among established Asian and Latino gangs, and several Latino and black gangs from Chicago have expanded into the region, particularly in drug dealing. [51] In Charlotte, N.C., authorities have been fighting white motorcycle gangs along with the black Kings, but as in Northern Virginia, the most violent and visible gang is MS-13. [52]

In the Chicago area, gangs have been growing more sophisticated and organized. Asian and Latino gangs account for the greatest growth throughout the region, with the latter expanding in direct relation to a widening of the methamphetamine market. Chicago-based gangs have also extended their reach into various regions of the West, where the epicenter of gang activity continues to be Los Angeles.

National Gang Policy?

Investigating gangs that appear to be operating in several regions is complicated, because different gang factions often have different interests. "Gangs are, more often than not, locally based, geographically oriented criminal associations," Sen. Leahy recently said. "Even gangs that purportedly have the same name on the East and West coast are not necessarily affiliated with one another." [53]

What is needed, McBride says, is a national gang policy that spells out an accepted definition of a gang and gang-related activity and a national gang intelligence center, similar to the Department of Justice's National Drug Intelligence Center.

"We need massive federal aid to local government in a multifaceted approach — it can't be just cops," he continues, adding that the approach

Continued on p. 438

At Issue:

Would the Gang Prevention and Effective Deterrence Act proposed by Sens. Orrin Hatch and Dianne Feinstein help in the fight against gangs?

yes

SEN. ORRIN G. HATCH, R-UTAH

FROM A STATEMENT BEFORE THE U.S. SENATE, OCT. 15, 2003

Mr. President, I rise today to introduce a comprehensive, bipartisan bill to increase gang prosecution and prevention efforts.

The Gang Prevention and Effective Deterrence Act of 2003 also increases funding for the federal prosecutors and FBI agents needed to conduct coordinated enforcement efforts against violent gangs.

Additionally, this bill will create new, criminal, gang-prosecution offenses, enhance existing gang and violent-crime penalties to deter and punish illegal street gangs, propose violent-crime reforms needed to prosecute effectively gang members and propose a limited reform of the juvenile-justice system to facilitate federal prosecution of 16- and 17-year-old gang members who commit serious acts of violence.

Once thought to be only a problem in our nation's largest cities, gangs have invaded smaller communities. Gangs now resemble organized-crime syndicates who readily engage in gun violence, illegal gun trafficking, illegal drug trafficking and other serious crimes.

Recent studies confirm that gang violence is an increasing problem in all of our communities. The most current reports indicate that in 2002 alone, after five years of decline, gang membership has spiked nationwide.

While we all are committed to fighting the global war on terrorism, we must redouble our efforts to ensure that we devote sufficient resources to combating this important national problem — the rise in gangs and gang violence in America.

We must take a proactive approach and meet this problem head on if we wish to defeat it. If we really want to reduce gang violence, we must ensure that law enforcement has adequate resources and legal tools, and that our communities have the ability to implement proven intervention and prevention strategies, so that gang members who are removed from the community are not simply replaced by the next generation of new gang members.

Federal involvement is crucial to control gang violence and to prevent new gang members from replacing old gang members. I strongly urge my colleagues to join with me in promptly passing this important legislation.

no

JERALYN MERRITT
CRIMINAL DEFENSE ATTORNEY, DENVER, COLO.

FROM TALKLEFT.COM: THE POLITICS OF CRIME, DEC. 21, 2003

Sens. Diane Feinstein, D-Calif., and Orrin Hatch, R-Utah, have teamed up to sponsor a terrible bill — one that panders to irrational fear but resonates politically.

It is rife with new categories of crimes, added punishments for having a gun or being a gang member and myriad "think twice" measures hoping gang members will reconsider before committing a crime.

Anyone who knows gangs knows that lawmakers cannot conceive of a law that would lead a hard-core gang member to "think twice." We already have enough gang- and gun-related sentencing "enhancements" to send a 17-year-old who has never been in trouble with the law to prison for 35 years to life. And that's without his ever touching a gun or ever being an actual member of a gang. We need to overhaul these enhancements, not add to them.

Gangs are not all that mysterious. Reformers know what works with them and what doesn't. Gang experts, intervention practitioners, social scientists, researchers and enlightened law enforcement officials all agree. What works is prevention, intervention and enforcement.

You prevent kids from joining gangs by offering after-school programs, sports, mentoring and positive engagement with adults. You intervene with gang members by offering alternatives and employment to help redirect their lives. You deal with areas of high gang-crime activity with real community policing.

There are ways that money could make a difference in curbing gangs — but the Feinstein-Hatch bill doesn't acknowledge them.

Law enforcement doesn't need more tools; it needs more officers. Real community policing requires different deployment, which can happen only with increased personnel. Although the Feinstein-Hatch bill would also allocate $200 million for prevention and intervention, more than three-quarters of that money would be administered by law enforcement. That is as misguided as having Homeboy Industries — a gang rehab center — enforce a gang injunction.

What's really going on here is politics. Feinstein and Hatch's ill-advised bill will neither prevent nor deter gang-related crime. It's time to stop funding wasteful law enforcement initiatives and listen to those who know what works — and it's not the politicians. This turkey of a bill needs to die a fast death.

Continued from p. 436

should coordinate probation, corrections and community-based programs, as well as prevention and intervention programs. Coordination and communication among all relevant authorities, which currently is lacking, also must be beefed up, he says. "And it all has to be long term. The problem with going to federal funding agencies is you get little grants for 18 months at most. That's not enough."

Newark's Christie has called for a special, multi-level unit that would target an entire gang operation — much like the Mafia was targeted — not simply the most visible members on the streets. "It is not uncommon for a single gang to be involved in drug dealing, firearms trafficking, murder, robbery, money laundering and, more recently, mortgage fraud," he said. To deal with such broad-based activities, he suggests, the U.S. attorney's office should lead a team consisting of the FBI, DEA, BATFE and the Marshals Service, along with local authorities. [54]

Without such broad-based coordination and information sharing, many investigations and prosecutions languish, authorities say. Investigations are also hindered by the lack of funds to adequately protect witnesses. "For many prosecutors, a witness-protection program simply consists of a bus ticket or a motel room," said McCulloch, of the National District Attorneys Association, who has pleaded for federal funds for such programs. In Denver, he points out, the number of prosecutions has dropped sharply because of the lack of protection while the number of gang crimes "has increased tremendously." [55]

Lately, Congress appears to be listening: In addition to making some gang activities federal offenses, the proposed Gang Prevention and Effective Deterrence Act would provide approximately $100 million of federal assistance for state and local law enforcement and $40 million for prevention programs over five years. In the Senate the bill was scheduled for markup in mid-May and expected to pass largely intact. A House companion bill has yet to be submitted.

Johnson of the National Association of Police Organizations predicts the measure will eventually become law. "Maybe not in this Congress before the [November presidential] election," he says, "but I do think it will pass. It won't be a cure-all but another tool in the box that will marginally and incrementally help bring down gangs and make communities safer."

However, Denver criminal-defense attorney Jeralyn Merritt calls it "a terrible bill" that "panders to irrational fear but resonates politically." In a scathing criticism of the proposal on the Web site *talkleft.com*, she argues: "We already have enough gang- and gun-related sentencing 'enhancements' to send a 17-year-old who has never been in trouble with the law to prison for 35 years to life. And that's without his ever being an actual member of a gang. We need to overhaul these enhancements, not add to them.

"Gangs are not all that mysterious. Reformers know what works with them . . . What works is prevention, intervention and enforcement. You prevent kids from joining gangs by offering after-school programs, sports, mentoring and positive engagement with adults. You intervene with gang members by offering alternatives and employment to help redirect their lives. You deal with areas of high gang-crime activity with real community policing." ■

OUTLOOK

More Violence?

In Northern Virginia, probation official Rathbun thinks authorities at every level of government have begun to realize the size and scope of the gang threat. As he puts it, "It's kind of the problem *du jour* now."

But whether effective policies will soon emerge is an open question, he says. "There's still lots of crazy things," he says. "We've got a directive from our agency now that says we can't question anybody about their immigration status, which seems stupid."

Moore, of the National Youth Gang Center, expects gang violence to continue its cyclical patterns, with upswings followed by downturns. "Some cities experience a big flare-up in gang violence every year," he says. "They've either never recognized the problem and it bubbles up to the surface, or they think they've dealt with the problem, but it comes back up again."

To U.S. Attorney Christie in Newark, nothing short of a full-scale, coordinated assault by law enforcement agencies at all levels is going to make a difference. Gang crime is, he said, "the new organized crime in the United States, an organized crime that destroys families, corrupts our children and lays waste to neighborhoods in our most vulnerable communities. We must mount a fight comparable to the fight against La Cosa Nostra in past decades if we expect to have the same success." [56]

But the FBI's Riley believes the resources are coming "at a slow pace." Given the FBI's priority on combating terrorism, Riley envisions "probably a 10-year progression to get [anti-gang resources] to the point I'd like to see." Meantime, he expects increasing gang activity as a result of continued immigration and "the phenomenon of the media making the 'gangsta' lifestyle appealing."

But he's also somewhat optimistic. "I see more cooperation between federal agencies — the FBI, the [BATFE] and the DEA and even the Marshals Service."

Although federal legislation may help bring the problem under control, changing demographics and the inherent dangerousness of gang activity may help staunch the growth of gangs over the long-term, says Johnson of the National Association of Police Organizations. "The Baby Boomlet will get older, and as they do, they'll mature and calm down," he says. "As this generation ages, there will be a decrease in the general crime rate. Plus, the really bad ones either get caught or killed. Gang [activity] is a very high-risk business."

McBride of the California Gang Investigators Association doubts that either the proposed legislation or more federal funds will eliminate the problem. "After you get some federal grants, the statistics decrease, and then the politicians walk away saying the problem's solved," he says. "Then, surprise, surprise — the problem's right back."

But if done right, he says, the legislation could help. "If the funding goes for local prosecution and for local gang units, that's going to be a tremendous help. But if it stays federally based, it's not going to have the impact they want it to have."

Rathbun, who deals with juvenile gangs daily, is pessimistic. Some gangs that had seemed to disband in Northern Virginia, such as TRG, are revitalizing, and becoming shrewder.

"The kids are less apt to get the tattoos now, and less apt to dress like gang-bangers," he says, so authorities are less apt to immediately recognize them. Their actions, however, won't be any different than before. Rathbun says the rival 18th Street Gang and the Latin Kings, as well as the new South Side Locos, are beginning to move into MS-13 territory.

"We're expecting turf battles," he says. "Machetes, knives and guns. I think it's going to be a bad summer."

It has already begun with machetes. A 16-year-old boy thought to be a South Side Locals member was walking along a suburban street on May 10 when reputed MS-13 members jumped him and nearly hacked his hands off. His screams woke residents, who called police. Doctors saved both hands, but four fingers were permanently lost, and it is too soon to tell if he will recover use of his hands. [57]

"They were trying to send a message," said Robert Walker, a former Drug Enforcement Administration special agent who runs a gang-identification training program for law enforcement officers. "Gangs deal in what we call the three R's. The first is reputation, and they want to do all they can to build that. The second is respect . . . and the third is retaliation or revenge." ■

Notes

[1] See Maria Glod, "Man Gets 30 Years in Gang Slaying; Va. Judge Cites Brutal Beating in Sentencing 1 of 4 Charged," *The Washington Post*, Sept. 28, 2002, p. B6. See also Maria Glod, "Gangs Get Public's Attention: Dozen Actively Contributing to Area Crime," *The Washington Post*, Sept. 18, 2003, p. T1.

[2] See Maria Glod, "Prosecutors Describe Gang-Style Execution as MS-13 Trial Opens," *The Washington Post*, Nov. 6, 2003, p. B6. See also Maria Glod, "Guardian of Slain Woman Replaces Her as Witness; Authorities Believe Teen was Silenced by Gang," *The Washington Post*, Nov. 7, 2003, p. B4.

[3] Sen. Orrin G. Hatch, opening statement before Senate Judiciary Committee hearing on "Combating Gang Violence in America: Examining Effective Federal, State and Local Law Enforcement Strategies," Sept. 17, 2003.

[4] Office of Juvenile Justice and Delinquency Prevention, U.S. Department of Justice, "Highlights of the 2001 National Youth Gang Survey," April 2003. See also Neely Tucker, "Gangs Growing in Numbers, Bravado Across Area," *The Washington Post*, Sept. 18, 2003, p. A1.

[5] National Alliance of Gang Investigators Associations, "Threat Assessment, 2000."

[6] Office of Juvenile Justice and Delinquency Prevention, *op. cit.*

[7] Wesley McBride, testimony before Senate Judiciary Committee hearing, Sept. 17, 2003.

[8] *Ibid.*

[9] Patrick Fitzgerald, testimony before Senate Judiciary Committee hearing, Sept. 17, 2003.

[10] National Youth Gang Center, www.iir.com/nygc/faq.htm#q6.

[11] *Ibid.*

[12] Eddie Jordan, testimony before Senate Judiciary Committee hearing, Sept. 17, 2003.

[13] McBride, *op. cit.*

[14] Grant D. Ashley, testimony before Senate Judiciary Committee hearing, Sept. 17, 2003.

[15] Debra Yang, testimony before Senate Judiciary Committee hearing, Sept. 17, 2003.

[16] Robert McCulloch, testimony before Senate Judiciary Committee hearing, Sept. 17, 2003.

[17] For background, see William Triplett, "State Budget Crisis," *The CQ Researcher*, Oct. 3, 2003, pp. 821-844.

[18] See Keith Perine, "Senators Pushing for Increased Federal Role in Fighting Crime Linked to Gangs," *CQ Today*, April 9, 2004.

[19] Bureau of Alcohol, Tobacco and Firearms and Explosives (BATFE), "Crime Gun Trace Reports: National Report," June 2002, pp. ix, x.

About the Author

William Triplett recently joined the *CQ Researcher* as a staff writer after covering science and the arts for such publications as *Smithsonian, Air & Space, Nature, Washingtonian* and *The Washington Post.* He also served as associate editor of *Capitol Style* magazine. He holds a B.A. in journalism from Ohio University and an M.A. in English literature from Georgetown University.

[20] C. Ronald Huff, "Criminal Behavior of Gang Members and At-Risk Youths," presentation to the National Institute of Justice.
[21] BATFE, *op. cit.*
[22] For background, see Richard L. Worsnop, "Gun Control," *The CQ Researcher*, June 10, 1994, pp. 505-528, and Kenneth Jost, "Gun Control Standoff," *The CQ Researcher*, Dec. 19, 1997, pp. 1105-1128.
[23] Fitzgerald, *op. cit.*
[24] See David Heinzmann, "Gangs Run Gun Pipeline from Delta to Chicago; Lenient Laws Make Buying Weapons Easier in South," *Chicago Tribune*, Feb. 5, 2004, p. C1.
[25] Jens Ludwig and Phil Cook, "Homicide and Suicide Rates Associated with Implementation of the BHVPA," *Journal of the American Medical Association*, Aug. 2, 2000, Vol. 284, p. 585.
[26] Jost, *op. cit.*
[27] Heinzmann, *op. cit.*
[28] See Carlos Sandovi, "Teen Charged in Humboldt Park Gang Rival's Killing; Police say Suspect also Took Shots at Undercover Cop," *Chicago Tribune*, April 21, 2004, p. C2.
[29] For background see Brian Hansen, "Kids in Prison," *The CQ Researcher*, April 27, 2001, pp. 345-376.
[30] See Lisa Friedman, "Anti-Gang Bill Draws Critics; Juvenile Advocacy Groups Oppose Adult Sentencing," *Los Angeles Daily News*, Nov. 24, 2003, p. N4.
[31] *Ibid.*
[32] Quoted in Armando Morales and Bradford W. Sheafor, *Social Work: A Profession of Many Faces* (1989), p. 415.
[33] For background see Charles S. Clark, "Youth Gangs," *The CQ Researcher*, Oct. 11, 1991, pp. 753-776.
[34] Anne Campbell, *The Girls in the Gang* (1984), p. 9.
[35] Quoted in Irving A. Spergel, *Crime and Justice: A Review of Research*, "Youth Gangs: Continuity and Change," Michael Tonry and Norval Morris, eds., Vol. 12 (1990), p. 172.
[36] Quoted in James Haskins, *Street Gangs: Yesterday and Today* (1974), p. 48.
[37] *Ibid*, p. 99.
[38] *Ibid*, p. 112.
[39] See Nicholas Lemann, *The Promised Land* (1991), p. 245.
[40] See Michael Abramowitz, "Street Gang Convictions Challenged in Chicago," *The Washington Post*, Dec. 22, 1992, p. A3.
[41] See Matt Canham and Tim Sullivan, "Asian Gangs a Scourge: Violent Rivals in the Vietnamese, Lao and Cambodia Communities are Settling Scores at Malls, Amusement Parks; Asian Gangs Target Their Own People," *The Salt Lake Tribune*, April 14, 2003, p. D1.
[42] The Associated Press, "U.S. Deportees Cart Crime to Native Lands," *Los Angeles Times*, Jan. 4, 2004, p. A5.
[43] Kevin Sullivan, "Spreading Gang Violence Alarms Central Americans," *The Washington Post*, Dec. 1, 2003, p. A1.
[44] Steven Wiley, testimony before Senate Judiciary Committee hearing on gang violence, April 23, 1997.
[45] Sen. Dianne Feinstein, statement before Senate Judiciary Committee hearing on gang violence, April 23, 1997.
[46] For background, see Sarah Glazer, "Boys' Emotional Needs," *The CQ Researcher*, June 18, 1999, pp. 521-544 and Kathy Koch, "School Violence," *The CQ Researcher*, Oct. 9, 1998, pp. 881-904.
[47] National Center for Juvenile Justice, "Juvenile Arrest Rates by Offense, Sex, and Race," May 31, 2003.
[48] See Chuck Plunkett, "Gangs' Hidden Fingerprint," *The Denver Post*, Nov. 9, 2003, p. A1.
[49] National Alliance of Gang Investigators Associations, *op. cit.*
[50] Christopher Christie, testimony before Senate Judiciary Committee hearing, Sept. 17, 2003.
[51] National Alliance of Gang Investigators Associations, *op. cit.*
[52] See Arian Campo-Flores, "Gangland's New Face," *Newsweek*, Dec. 8, 2003, p. 41.
[53] Sen. Patrick Leahy, opening statement before Senate Judiciary Committee hearing, Sept. 17, 2003.
[54] Christie, *op. cit.*
[55] McCulloch, *op. cit.*
[56] Christie, *op. cit.*
[57] Maria Glod and Tom Jackman, "Teen's Hands Severed In Northern Va. Machete Attack," *The Washington Post*, May 11, 2004, p. B1.

FOR MORE INFORMATION

Bajito Onda, P.O. Box 270246, Dallas, TX 75227; (214) 275-6632; www.bajitoonda.org/bajito.html. Foundation dedicated to giving Latino youths positive alternatives to gangs, drugs and violence through education.

Juvenile Justice Clearinghouse, P.O. Box 6000, Rockville, MD 20849; (800) 851-3420; http://ojjdp.ncjrs.org/programs/ProgSummary.asp?pi=2. A component of the National Criminal Justice Reference Service that maintains information and resources on juvenile-justice topics.

National Alliance of Gang Investigator Associations; www.nagia.org. An online coalition of criminal-justice professionals dedicated to promoting a coordinated anti-gang strategy.

National Criminal Justice Reference Service, P.O. Box 6000, Rockville, MD, 20849; (800) 851-3420; http://virlib.ncjrs.org/juv.asp?category=47&subcategory=66. A federally funded service that provides information on justice and substance abuse to support research, policy and program development worldwide.

National Major Gang Task Force, 338 S. Arlington Ave., Suite 112, Indianapolis, IN 46219; (317) 322-0537; www.nmgtf.org. An independent organization specializing in intervention, management strategies, networking, training and information-sharing regarding gangs.

National Youth Gang Center, P.O. Box 12729, Tallahassee, FL 32317; (800) 446-0912; www.iir.com/nygc. A Department of Justice-funded group that collects and analyzes information on gangs.

Office of Juvenile Justice and Delinquency Prevention, 810 7th St., N.W., Washington, D.C. 20531; (202) 307-5911; http://ojjdp.ncjrs.org. A Justice Department office providing leadership, coordination and resources on preventing juvenile delinquency and victimization.

Bibliography

Selected Sources

Books

***The Truth about Street Gangs*, Gang Prevention Inc., 2001.**
This publication is designed to help communities identify and understand gangs, focusing on how they operate and how they conceal their activities.

Hernandez, Arturo, *Peace in the Streets: Breaking the Cycle of Gang Violence*, Child Welfare League of America, 1998.
Hernandez tells the riveting story of his experience as a young teacher in South Central Los Angeles and the positive effect he had on the gang members who were his students.

Kinnear, Karen L., *Gangs: A Reference Handbook*, ABC-CLIO, 1996.
This compendium on juvenile gangs by a journalist focuses on their activities, membership, motivations and their relation to society and the law.

Lloyd, J.D., ed., *Gangs*, Greenhaven Press, 2002.
A collection of informational essays by a journalist examines why gangs exist, their history, their day-to-day actions and what can be done to lessen the damage they do.

Articles

"U.S. Deportees Cart Crime to Native Lands; More than 500,000 have been banished under 1996 law," The Associated Press, *Los Angeles Times*, Jan. 4, 2004, p A5.
The federal government's tactic of deporting non-U.S. citizens convicted of crimes has sent many gang members back to their homeland, where they resume gang activity.

Campo-Flores, Arian, "Gangland's New Face," *Newsweek*, Dec. 8, 2003, p. 41.
The surge of Latino gangs is reflected in their relatively new and overwhelming presence in Charlotte, N.C.

Canham, Matt, and Tim Sullivan, "Asian Gangs a Scourge; Gunplay: Violent rivals in the Vietnamese, Lao and Cambodian communities are settling scores at malls, amusement parks; Asian Gangs Target Their Own People," *Salt Lake Tribune*, April 14, 2003, p. D1.
Asian gangs wreak havoc in the greater Salt Lake area, mostly within the immigrant community but sometimes outside of it.

Heinzmann, David, "Gangs run pipeline from Delta to Chicago; Lenient laws make buying weapons easier in the South," *Chicago Tribune*, Feb. 5, 2004, p. 1.
To skirt tough gun control laws, Chicago gangs use the proceeds of illegal drug sales to buy weapons in Mississippi.

Jackson, Chriscia, "Asian gangs have reputation for living 'giang ho,' or crazy life," Associated Press, May 25, 2000.
A look at the violence and destructiveness of Asian gangs as seen in the story of two juvenile members of Vietnamese gangs in Port Arthur, Texas.

Plunkett, Chuck, "Gangs' Hidden Fingerprint," *The Denver Post*, Nov. 9, 2003, p. A1.
Plunkett details the extensive gang activity throughout the Denver area and the police department's lack of accurate records on gangs.

Tucker, Neely, "Gangs Growing in Numbers, Bravado Across Area," *The Washington Post*, Sept. 18, 2003, p. A1.
Latino gangs are growing rapidly in Washington, D.C., and other areas of the country not previously known for intense gang activity.

Reports and Studies

"Highlights of the 2001 National Youth Gang Survey," Office of Juvenile Justice and Delinquency Prevention, Department of Justice, April 2003.
This annual survey documents national trends, activities and developments among youth gangs.

"National Youth Gang Center Bibliography of Gang Literature," Office of Juvenile Justice and Delinquency Prevention, U.S. Department of Justice, 1997.
An exhaustive bibliography of gang literature — dating as far back as the 1940s — reviewed and compiled by the National Youth Gang Center for the Office of Juvenile Justice and Delinquency Prevention.

Huff, C. Ronald, "Comparing the Criminal Behavior of Youth Gangs and At-Risk Youths," National Institute of Justice, Department of Justice, October 1998.
A survey shows that criminal activity of youth-gang members is significantly higher than that of at-risk youths.

Moore, Joan, and John Hagedorn, "Female Gangs: A Focus on Research," *Juvenile Justice Bulletin*, Office of Juvenile Justice and Delinquency Prevention, U.S. Department of Justice, March 2001.
This summary of research attempts to address the imbalance between research on male and female gangs.

Reed, Winifred L., and Scott H. Decker, "Responding to Gangs: Evaluation and Research," National Institute of Justice, U.S. Department of Justice, July 2002.
A comprehensive review of recent research about gang behavior as well as anti-gang strategies.

The Next Step:

Additional Articles from Current Periodicals

Expanding Reach

Boorstein, Michelle, "New Police Unit Fights Growing Drug, Gang Activity," *The Washington Post*, March 21, 2004, p. C5.
A growing criminal influence is expanding into less urban parts of America like Spotsylvania County, Va.

Pulitzer, Lisa, "East End Is Seeing Signs of Gang Activity," *The New York Times*, Aug. 10, 2003, Section 14LI, p. 5.
Gang graffiti and gang members are appearing more and more in Long Island's East End, where they had been previously unknown.

Sappenfield, Mark, "Gang Colors Flourish in Farm Country," *The Christian Science Monitor*, Oct. 1, 2001, p. 3.
Although the word gang conjures images of urban ghettoes, the fields and farmlands of rural America are also home to gang activity.

Skoloff, Brian, "Drugs, Guns, Gangs Mark Life in Little Rock," *Los Angeles Times*, Sept. 1, 2002, p. A13.
Little Rock, Ark., began experiencing a major gang problem in the late 1980s that culminated in a homicide rate higher than New York or Chicago's.

Exporting Violence Abroad

Dellios, Hugh, "Central America Targets Gangs," *Chicago Tribune*, Feb. 9, 2004, p. 1.
El Salvador is cracking down on gangs like Mara Salvatrucha and finding strong support from most citizens; critics contend the crackdown ignores larger issues.

Paddock, Richard C., "Cambodia's Black Sheep Return to Fold," *Los Angeles Times*, March 28, 2003, p. A27.
The U.S. policy of deporting criminals, often gang members, may further destabilize already politically fragile Cambodia.

Sullivan, Kevin, "Spreading Gang Violence Alarms Central Americans," *The Washington Post*, Dec. 1, 2003, p. A1.
A rash of beheadings has focused attention on ultra-violent Central American gangs, which often learned the gang lifestyle in America.

Fighting Gangs

Buchanan, Andrew, "Chicago Tries Rapid Response to Curb Gangs," *The Christian Science Monitor*, June 30, 2003, p. 2.
The Cobras, Vice Lords, Latin Kings and Black Souls are a few of the dozen known gangs operating in Chicago's most violent police district.

Butterfield, Fox, "Rise in Killings Spurs New Steps to Fight Gangs," *The New York Times*, Jan. 17, 2004, p. A1.
Chicago and Los Angeles are having some success against gangs with tough, new tactics; in Chicago, the Mafia killed 1,000 people in 80 years, gangs 1,300 in the past five.

Fitzgerald, Patrick J., "We're All Directly in the Line of Fire," *Chicago Tribune*, May 13, 2003, Commentary Section, p. 21.
The U.S. attorney for the Chicago area argues that the culture of acceptance where gangs can cynically be used to get out the vote in elections must change.

Garvey, Megan, and Richard Winton, "City Declares War on Gangs," *Los Angeles Times*, Dec. 4, 2002, p. A1.
Los Angeles Police Chief William Bratton and Mayor James Hahn announce their aggressive new initiative to combat gangs.

Garvey, Megan, and Richard Winton, "Tracking of Gang-Related Crime Falls Short," *Los Angeles Times*, Jan. 24, 2003, p. A1.
Los Angeles police lack reliable statistics on gangs, or even an agreed-upon definition of gang crimes, which hobbles their anti-gang efforts and forces police to rely on "guesstimates."

Perine, Keith, "Senators Pushing for Increased Federal Role in Fighting Crime Linked to Gangs," *CQ Today*, April 9, 2004.
A crime-fighting bill co-sponsored by Sen. Orrin G. Hatch, R-Utah, would toughen penalties for gang activity.

Wood, Daniel, "As Gangs Rise, So Do Calls for U.S.-Wide Dragnet," *The Christian Science Monitor*, Feb. 4, 2004, p. 2.
As gang members migrate across the country and gang-related homicides spike upward, calls for a nationally coordinated law enforcement effort against gangs are increasing.

Gangs and Kids

"In Class and in Prison," *Los Angeles Times*, April 11, 2004, Part M, p. 4.
By allowing gangs to dictate what school a student attends, school officials are sending the wrong message.

Hayasaki, Erika, and Joy Buchanan, "Students Fear Transfer to Rival Turf," *Los Angeles Times*, March 31, 2004, p. B1.
After their school closed, students feared being assigned to another school dominated by a rival gang.

Domash, Shelly Feuer, "Sharks in the Kiddie Pool," *The New York Times*, Aug. 10, 2003, Section 14LI, p. 1.
The age at which gangs recruit members has steadily decreased until 14- and 15-year-olds are now experienced gang members.

Steindorf, Sara, "Police Give Teachers a Primer on Gangs," *The Christian Science Monitor*, June 25, 2002, p. 14.
Teachers in Lynn, Mass., learn about warning signs of gang activity and view a stunning array of weapons.

Gangs in America

Axtman, Kris, "A Street Gang With MBA Order and Mafia Cruelty," *The Christian Science Monitor*, March 3, 2003, p. 1.
The Latin Kings have organizational charts, instruction manuals and a penchant for killing members who disobey gang rules.

Fahrenthold, David, "New Breed of D.C. Gang Emerges," *The Washington Post*, Aug. 11, 2003, p. B1.
Well-organized Hispanic gangs from Los Angeles are beginning to grow in strength in the Washington area, perhaps superseding the mostly black "crews."

Felch, Jason, and Sean Kelly, "Asian Gangs a Growing Issue," *The Denver Post*, June 20, 2003, p. B1.
For some Vietnamese youth, assimilating into American society sometimes means adopting criminal behavior.

Glod, Maria, "A High Price for Belonging," *The Washington Post*, Sept. 18, 2003, p. T1.
Mara Salvatrucha, also known as MS-13, is a violent, well-organized gang with Salvadoran roots that actively recruits young people.

Lee, Denny, "Years of the Dragons," *The New York Times*, May 11, 2003, Section 14, p. 1.
Although peaceful today, New York's Chinatown has a bloody history of gang warfare.

Tucker, Neely, "Girl's Slaying Opens Window on Intimidation," *The Washington Post*, Feb. 2, 2004, p. A1.
The murder of a 14-year-old witness to a homicide focuses attention on witness intimidation and murder by gangs.

Prison Gangs

Grann, David, "The Brand," *The New Yorker*, Feb. 16, 2004, p. 157.
The Aryan Brotherhood makes between a half-million and a million dollars per year selling heroin in a single prison.

Hughes, Jim, "Aryan Brotherhood Makes Home in State," *The Denver Post*, Nov. 24, 2002, p. A1.
Despite ultra-tight security at the federal government's most secure prison, gang leaders continue to run their operations.

Reynolds, Julia, and George Sanchez, "Prison Gang Case Puts Role of FBI Informants Under Scrutiny," *San Francisco Chronicle*, Nov. 29, 2003, p. A1.
The Nuestra Familia gang was running its operations from prison; cracking it was difficult without using informants involved in criminal activities.

Social Attitudes

Huppke, Rex W., "On Streets, Drug Trade the Only Game in Town," *Chicago Tribune*, April 18, 2004, News Section, p. 1.
In places where jobs are hard to come by and drugs are a financial life preserver, the definition of success is a product of the environment.

Huppke, Rex W., and David Heinzmann, "Shoot-First Culture Stalks Streets of Murder Capital," *Chicago Tribune*, Feb. 1, 2004, News Section, p. 1.
A minor argument or just parking in the wrong part of town is enough to justify murder in Chicago.

Gaona, Elena, "Tattoos Draw Picture of Life in L.A. Gangs," *Los Angeles Times*, Jan. 18, 2002, p. B2.
Gang tattoos not only help to identify gang members or provide information about prison time but also represent a total immersion in the gang culture and lifestyle.

Citing *The CQ Researcher*

Sample formats for citing these reports in a bibliography include the ones listed below. Preferred styles and formats vary, so please check with your instructor or professor.

MLA STYLE

Jost, Kenneth. "Rethinking the Death Penalty." The CQ Researcher 16 Nov. 2001: 945-68.

APA STYLE

Jost, K. (2001, November 16). Rethinking the death penalty. *The CQ Researcher, 11*, 945-968.

CHICAGO STYLE

Jost, Kenneth. "Rethinking the Death Penalty." *CQ Researcher*, November 16, 2001, 945-968.

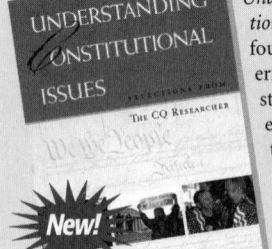

CQ Researcher

Published by CQ Press, a division of Congressional Quarterly Inc.

thecqresearcher.com

Worker Safety

Are government regulations tough enough?

Although workplace fatalities and injuries are on the decline, thousands of workers are still hurt or killed on the job each year, and many mishaps go unreported. But the most flagrant violators of the nation's safety rules remain in business despite racking up hundreds of penalties and losing multiple workers to death or injury, raising tough questions about the effectiveness of the Occupational Safety and Health Administration. And certain groups of workers — including Hispanics — suffer disproportionately higher casualty rates. Labor unions and citizen advocacy groups accuse President Bush of gutting protections and caving to corporate interests, but Republicans deny the accusations and say deregulation actually helps business improve safety. Businesses complain of burdensome, one-size-fits-all rules that drain time and money, hamper international competitiveness and spur companies to move jobs offshore.

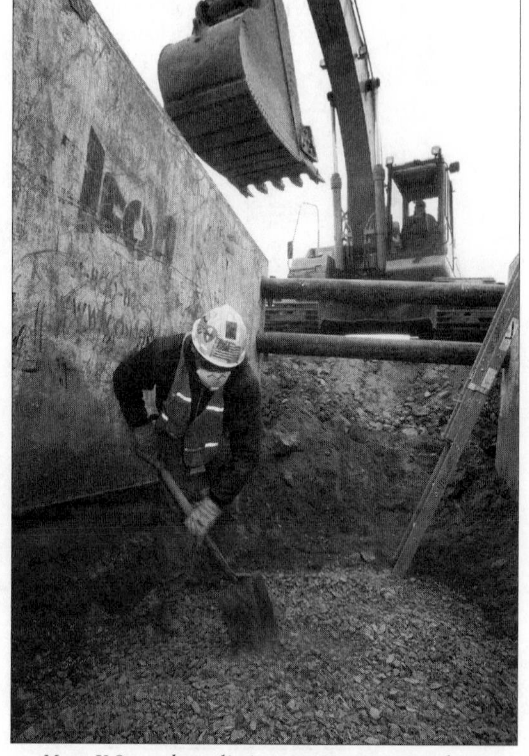

More U.S. workers die in construction accidents than in any other industry.

INSIDE THIS REPORT

The CQ Researcher • May 21, 2004 • www.thecqresearcher.com
Volume 14, Number 19 • Pages 445-468

CQ PRESS

RECIPIENT OF SOCIETY OF PROFESSIONAL JOURNALISTS AWARD FOR EXCELLENCE ◆ AMERICAN BAR ASSOCIATION SILVER GAVEL AWARD

THE ISSUES

BACKGROUND

CURRENT SITUATION

OUTLOOK

SIDEBARS AND GRAPHICS

FOR FURTHER RESEARCH

Cover: Construction work caused 1,121 deaths in the United States in 2002, more than any other industry. (Occupational Safety and Health Administration)

THE CQ Researcher

May 21, 2004
Volume 14, Number 19

CQ PRESS

A Division of Congressional Quarterly Inc.

The CQ Researcher (ISSN 1056-2036) is printed on acid-free paper. Published weekly, except Jan. 2, April 9, July 2, July 9, Aug. 6, Aug. 13, Nov. 26 and Dec. 31, by CQ Press, a division of Congressional Quarterly Inc. Annual subscription rates for institutions start at $625. For pricing, call 1-800-834-9020, ext. 1906. To purchase a *CQ Researcher* report in print or electronic format (PDF), visit www.cqpress.com or call 866-427-7737. A single report is $10. Bulk purchase discounts and electronic-rights licensing are also available. Periodicals postage paid at Washington, D.C., and additional mailing offices. POSTMASTER: Send address changes to *The CQ Researcher*, 1255 22nd St., N.W., Suite 400, Washington, D.C. 20037.

BY DAVID HATCH

THE ISSUES

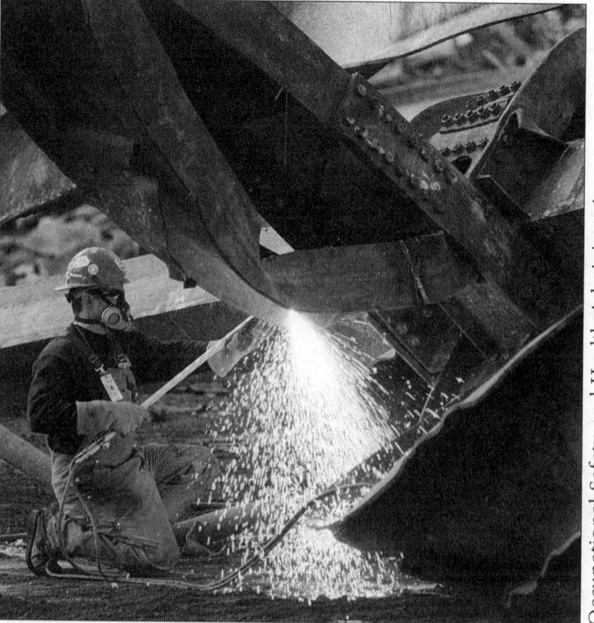

During rescue and demolition work at the World Trade Center after the terrorist attacks, critics faulted the government for not adequately monitoring the health of workers at the smoldering site. Although workplace fatalities and injuries are declining, critics question the effectiveness of the Occupational Safety and Health Administration.

It was dangerous, lousy work, and Rolan Hoskin knew it. Temperatures in the Tyler, Texas, factory reached a blistering 130 degrees; the noise was deafening, the machines treacherous. But the maintenance job paid 10 bucks an hour, and the unemployed electrician needed the cash. [1]

In the wee hours of June 29, 2000, Hoskin tried to clean a large, moving conveyer belt. Co-workers later found his body, trapped between the belt and rollers, one arm crushed and his head split open.

Federal investigators said Hoskin died because government safety regulations were not being followed at the plant, owned by Birmingham, Ala.-based McWane Inc., one of the world's largest manufacturers of cast-iron pipe — and one of the nation's most dangerous employers. [2]

Conditions at the Tyler plant were so hazardous that during a 1999 visit, an inspector with the Occupational Safety and Health Administration (OSHA) — the federal agency charged with protecting U.S. workers — found countless employees with visible scars, burns and other wounds. [3]

"The people, they're nothing," Robert S. Rester, a former McWane plant manager, told a reporter. "If they get hurt or complain about safety, you put a bull's-eye on them." [4]

Ten McWane employees have died on the job since 1995, and 4,600 others have been injured. Although the company has racked up more than 400 federal health and safety violations and paid millions in fines, OSHA has never pursued federal criminal prosecutions against company officials. [5]

Although McWane stands out for its poor safety record, it is not alone. More than 5,500 U.S. workers died on the job in 2002 — about 15 per day — and that doesn't count the 50,000-60,000 workers who die each year from diseases acquired on the job, such as black lung or asbestosis. Another 4.7 million private-sector workers were injured or developed illnesses at work in 2002, according to the Bureau of Labor Statistics (BLS). [6] Occupational injuries and illness cost more than $170 billion a year in health-care expenses, workers' compensation, lost wages and productivity and employee retraining, according to OSHA. [7]

Workplace dangers run the gamut from repetitive-stress injuries, common among office workers and cashiers, to potentially lethal hazards like explosions, exposure to toxic chemicals or asbestos or accidents. Sometimes dangers in the work environment — secondhand smoke in a bar or fire-code violations in a building — pose a greater risk than the job itself.

Construction caused 1,121 deaths in 2002, the most of any industry. [8] But mining had the highest worker-fatality rate: 23.5 miners killed per 100,000 workers in 2002. [9]

Blue-collar workers are not the only ones affected by workplace safety issues. Hundreds of workers have sued IBM in recent years, claiming they were poisoned while making computer chips. [10] And major corporations like Con Edison, U.S. Steel and Corning have paid millions in settlements to employees sickened from exposure to asbestos. [11]

Some groups face disproportionately higher workplace risks. Illegal immigrants routinely accept dangerous, low-wage jobs, where safety protections are few or nonexistent, but poor language skills and fear of deportation keep workers from filing complaints. Hispanics also incur more than their share of workplace injuries, because they often take jobs in high-risk industries. Workplace deaths among Hispanics jumped 11.3 percent from 1999 to 2000, in part reflecting the population growth of this community in the United States. [12]

Despite so many potential workplace safety problems, critics say OSHA is too weak on regulation, enforcement and inspection and waits too long to intervene in hazardous workplaces.

"They normally don't go in until there's some publicity," says Ron Hayes, founder of the nonprofit group Families in Grief Hold Together, in Fairhope, Ala. "They usually wait until there's two or three deaths." Since his 19-year-old son Patrick died in a grain-silo accident in 1993, Hayes has been pressing OSHA to improve. [13]

OSHA Fines Spur Controversy

The typical fine for a willful workplace safety violation dropped from $36,487 in 2000 to $26,888 in 2002 — and fines for failing to fix a violation dropped from $7,687 to $2,448. But in the past two years fines have been rising. OSHA Administrator John Henshaw says the agency imposed $82 million in penalties in the first 11 months of 2003. Critics say big corporations view fines as a cost of doing business, but OSHA says its goal is to bring about workplace changes, not rack up fines. The average penalty for a serious violation was $892 in 2003.

Violation Categories and Possible Penalties

Type of Violation	Minimum Penalty Per Violation	Maximum Penalty Per Violation
Other-than-serious		$7,000
Serious	$100	$7,000
Posting of safety warnings		$7,000
Willful	$5,000	$70,000
Willful, with fatality (first conviction)		$250,000/$500,000 or six months in prison or both
Willful, with fatality (second conviction)		$250,000/$500,000 or one year in prison or both
Repeated	$5,000	$70,000
Failure to abate		$7,000 per day

Source: "All About OSHA," Occupation Safety and Health Administration, 2003; The New York Times, *March 11, 2003, p. A1.*

Critics also claim the Bush administration has been quietly gutting the controversial agency's rules, appointing business-friendly bureaucrats to run the agency and promoting voluntary efforts over regulation.

"Over the years, you've had an ongoing attempt to defang this agency, to weaken the law, to make things voluntary," says Peg Seminario, the AFL-CIO'S director of health and safety. "Everything the agency does is challenged — not only in a legal sense but also in a political sense, because employers in this country have a lot of power and they're not afraid to use it."

Moreover, OSHA is reluctant to impose the stiffest fines allowable and rarely pursues criminal prosecutions against egregious safety violators, Seminario and other critics say. As a result, they claim, many companies would rather pay the fines than implement expensive safer practices.

But OSHA Administrator John Henshaw insists OSHA seeks to safeguard workers without unduly saddling companies with burdensome regulations, noting that in recent months OSHA enforcement procedures have been strengthened for all companies, especially the worst safety violators. "We're focusing our inspection on where we can get the biggest bang for the buck," he says.

Businesses and conservative groups endorse such moves, insisting OSHA is too restrictive and imposes unnecessary, time-consuming and costly one-size-fits-all regulations.

"We don't need to pass more regs. We need to go after the bad guys," says Christopher Tampio, director of employment policy at the National Association of Manufacturers (NAM). He says it's wrong for OSHA to issue sweeping regulations as a means of targeting a few violators.

Henshaw says OSHA is helping improve conditions at McWane, which says it has corrected problems, hired a new safety director and re-energized its safety initiatives. [14] "They're giving us signs that they're making a turnaround," Henshaw says.

Since the Sept. 11, 2001, terrorist attacks, employers' and regulators' usual concerns about workplace safety have been diverted to protecting workers from potential future attacks. And new problems emerge all the time: During California's rolling blackouts in 2001, for instance, businesses pleaded with state officials for advance warning of power failures. "When you've got heavy equipment suddenly shutting down and employees groping around in the dark . . . there is a real concern for worker safety," said Julie Puentes, spokeswoman for the Orange County Business Council. [15]

Meanwhile, as U.S. employers confront an increasingly globalized work force, many labor experts fear that competition from overseas workers — who typically enjoy far fewer workplace protections than Americans — will erode hard-fought protections that labor leaders spent much of the 20th century obtaining.

And the current administration does not appear willing to encumber trade agreements with demands that trading partners protect workers. In April, the Bush administration rejected an AFL-CIO trade petition, endorsed by Democratic presidential contender Sen. John Kerry, requesting that China be punished for suppressing worker rights. U.S. officials dubbed the union petition as "economic isolationism" and said they're working with China on making sure its international labor agreements are upheld.

"Had the administration accepted the petition, there would have been a number of negative consequences," said U.S. Chamber of Commerce President Tom Donahue. "We would have married forever human rights and trade, and that would have been a huge mistake." [16]

As the nation focuses on economic and workplace issues during this presidential election year, here are some safety issues being debated:

Is OSHA effective at safeguarding workers?

In 1989, after a worker for Moeves Plumbing in Ohio died in a trench collapse, OSHA fined the company nearly $14,000 but didn't seek criminal prosecution because the company founder had died recently, and his wife promised major changes. Thirteen years later, a similar mishap occurred at Moeves, with the same lethal consequences. This time, despite the grieving family's efforts to convince OSHA to pursue criminal charges, the agency backed off again, even cutting the fine from $90,000 to $54,000. [17]

Such actions raise tough questions about OSHA's effectiveness, critics say. "There's a culture in the agency that essentially nothing really has import," says the AFL-CIO's Seminario. "This is an agency . . . that has been under attack from the day it was established," she says, arguing that OSHA has effectively been neutralized by controversy surrounding it.

"Are we effective? Yes, we're effective," responds OSHA's Henshaw, who insists agency decisions are governed only by safety concerns. "Can we be more effective? We're going to learn every day," he says. Henshaw said he did not have a role in deciding the Moeves case. [18]

Workplace Fatality Rates Declining

The U.S. worker-fatality rate has dropped steadily since legislation creating OSHA was passed in 1970. However, the Cato Institute and other agency critics note that worker fatalities began dropping well before OSHA's creation.

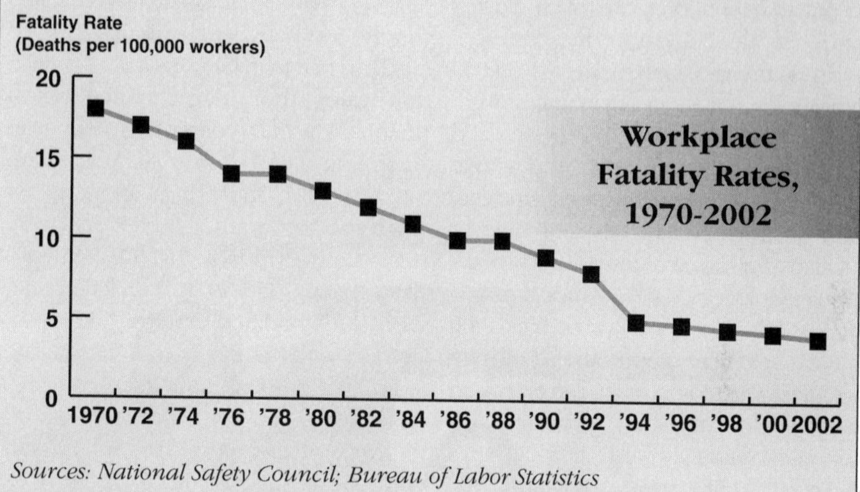

Sources: National Safety Council; Bureau of Labor Statistics

"We're not like law enforcement, where you have a cop on every corner," he adds, noting that the agency's 1,123 inspectors visit only 2 percent of the nation's 7 million worksites each year. "We can't physically protect workers. The employer is the one that can physically protect."

NAM's Tampio praises OSHA for emphasizing compliance and education and not just issuing fines. "Teaching people is the best way," he says. But he wants more follow-up inspections to ensure problems are corrected. "It shouldn't [just] be a fine to try to get money."

But in recent years, the General Accounting Office (GAO), Congress' independent research arm, has criticized the agency for failing to identify the most hazardous worksites for priority inspection and not tracking the impact on employers of its special consultation program for small companies in hazardous industries. [19] In contrast, some state OSHAs, such as California's, have garnered favorable media coverage for their strong enforcement efforts and for tailoring regulations specifically to local industries. [20] And Hayes, of Families in Grief, praises Oregon's agency.

Seminario says OSHA has never aggressively protected workers. And while its mandatory safety standards have substantially reduced worker exposure to lead, benzene and other hazards, she says additional standards for other toxins are needed, and many existing guidelines are based on 1950s data. "The bottom line is: You don't have a body of regulation that protects people," she says. In the 33 years since it was created, OSHA has issued 28 toxic-chemical exposure standards — a number that workers' advocates consider too low.

Henshaw concedes that some standards "are not quite up to date," including '70s-era requirements for operating cranes and derricks and handling explosives. "We're constantly updating, upgrading our standards-setting process — and the old standards as well as the new ones," he says.

In recent years, the agency says it has stepped up its scrutiny of worksites and industries with high injury rates, such as construction, where half its inspections are conducted. And inspections overall rose 6 percent between 2002 and 2003. Moreover, the agency has forged alliances with more than 130 trade associations, urging them to put additional pressure on employers through outreach and education.

In February, OSHA alerted 14,000 companies that their injury rates were higher than most U.S. businesses and recommended generic steps to improve safety, but it did not threaten agency action. Such efforts have resulted in fewer fatalities for ironworkers and chemical plant employees, OSHA officials say. [21]

But last October, after embarrassing media coverage about the deaths at McWane, OSHA announced an enhanced enforcement program to crack down on serious violators. Richard Fairfax, OSHA's director of enforcement programs, said companies are subject to tougher inspections (including mandatory follow-ups), top executives are updated on OSHA findings and employee illness and injury records are carefully reviewed.

"That was put in place to get at . . . the recalcitrant employers who just don't get it — or the ones who've just constantly factored in our fines, our penalties, into the cost of doing business," Henshaw says.

But Seminario contends that the new OSHA enforcement program has "no teeth." Rather than "really bringing anything more to bear on those employers . . . it's just basically more oversight," she says.

BLS data provide a mixed picture for OSHA: The 5,542 work-related fatalities in 2002 represented a 6.6 percent drop from the year before and the lowest number since 1992, when BLS began conducting its national census of fatal occupational injuries. Much of the decline was due to a drop in fatalities involving vehicle accidents, homicides and falls. [22]

But BLS also reported some unflattering findings: Work fatalities in agriculture, forestry and fishing grew about 6 percent during the same period; deaths due to exposure to harmful substances and environments also increased — largely due to a jump in heat stroke — and electrocutions also were up slightly. [23]

And job-safety statistics seem staggering when viewed over time: About 200,000 workers in America were killed on the job between 1972 and 2003. [24]

The libertarian Cato Institute — which advocates abolishing the agency — emphasizes that worker fatalities began dropping well before OSHA was created in 1971. Indeed, in an essay for Cato two economics professors argue there's no evidence that OSHA regulations have led to substantial reductions in job-related injuries. "Most protection on the job comes from state workers'-compensation rules and programs, and tort law," they wrote. [25]

OSHA often touts BLS' annual survey of non-fatal workplace injuries as proof that the agency is helping to sharply reduce employee accidents. But over the years critics have charged that gaps in the data favor OSHA because the survey excludes government employees, farms with fewer than 11 workers and the self-employed. [26]

But OSHA emphasizes that its annual census of workplace fatalities includes those categories of workers.

However, it doesn't mention deaths related to occupational disease — such as black lung, suffered by coal miners and asbestosis suffered by those working around asbestos — critics point out. The National Institute for Occupational Safety and Health (NIOSH) estimates occupational diseases kill 50,000 workers a year, but the AFL-CIO says the figure is closer to 60,000. [27]

OSHA's Henshaw says the annual census of workplace fatalities provides his agency with an important benchmark to help the agency monitor its progress from year to year.

Another concern is underreporting of workplace mishaps. While BLS reported 4.7 million private-sector workplace injuries and illnesses in 2002, the amount could be double that, the AFL-CIO's Seminario says. [28]

The union also points out that BLS statistics miss up to 69 percent of all workplace injuries, according to a recent study in the *Journal of Occupational and Environmental Medicine*. [29]

Henshaw acknowledges there is underreporting but says there's also overreporting by employers who don't understand OSHA procedures. He considers the BLS census on fatalities, which is culled from several sources and reflects all types of workers, to be very complete.

The statistical debate aside, OSHA supporters say the agency could be more effective if it had more money for enforcement and more inspectors. Since 1980, OSHA's real per-worker expenditure on enforcement at both the state and federal levels has been reduced by one-third. [30]

Yet Cato points out that even with the lower enforcement budgets of the last 24 years, workplace injuries have continued to decline. "If a slimmed-down OSHA is not causing workplace safety to deteriorate, then a beefed-up OSHA is unlikely to improve it," Cato argues in its biannual *Handbook for Congress*. [31]

In fact, the group argues, given the lack of evidence of the agency's effectiveness, lawmakers should either further reduce OSHA's enforcement budget or shut the agency down entirely. At the very least, Congress should prevent OSHA from issuing any more mandatory standards, inspecting companies or imposing fines for noncompliance, the group says. State workers' compensation programs have a greater impact on worker safety than OSHA, Cato argues, because employers' premiums go up as the frequency of workers' claims against them rises. Moreover, market forces promote worker safety better than federal regulations, the group argues, because companies must pay higher wages to get workers to take hazardous jobs.

Continued on p. 452

IBM Faces 'Clean Room' Lawsuits

IBM is fighting lawsuits by scores of former workers who allege they weren't adequately protected in the sterile "clean rooms" where computer chips are made. "Big Blue" defends its safety record and says other problems caused the workers' illnesses. But, other chipmakers worry the lawsuits could spawn a flood of additional suits.

Alida Hernandez and James Moore, who worked at IBM in San Jose, Calif., in the 1970s and '80s and were diagnosed with cancer in the '90s, sued IBM in California Superior Court, alleging that workplace chemicals caused their illnesses. [1] In California, workplace injury claims generally are handled through workers' compensation. To win damages outside the workers' comp scheme, plaintiffs' attorneys had to prove that IBM fraudulently withheld information about the dangers posed by the chemicals. [2]

Earlier this year, a Superior Court jury sided with IBM. "The law in California is very restrictive," says Amanda Hawes, whose law firm helped represent the plaintiffs. But IBM's victory could be short-lived. Some 250 workers have sued the company in New York and California, some alleging chemical exposure caused birth defects in offspring.

Two of the suits have been settled out of court. "They wouldn't be settling if they could prove they weren't causing birth defects," says Joseph LaDou, a clinical professor of medicine at the University of California, San Francisco, and an expert on cancer in the semiconductor field. "It's not tough to show that the workers were exposed to carcinogens."

In fact, in March the judge in the California case suspended 44 pending suits against IBM and ordered both sides to settle. [3]

Meanwhile, a class-action lawsuit filed five years ago by employees of Santa Clara, Calif.-based chipmaker National Semiconductor remains pending. [4] Although automation in semiconductor manufacturing has reduced the number of employees who enter clean rooms, observers say problems remain industrywide.

"It's the most secretive industry anyone's ever dealt with," LaDou says. "They present themselves as the clean industry, not traditionally polluting, as the heavy industries of the past."

Actually, he says, computer manufacturing is a "chemically intensive" industry, and although clean-room workers wear protective gear, it is really designed to protect the computer chips from impurities — not to protect the workers from the chemicals. [5]

In fact, concerns about safety in computer manufacturing prompted the formation of a grass-roots organization, the Silicon Valley Toxics Coalition (SVTC), in 1982.

But Martin Sepulveda, vice president of global well-being services and health benefits at IBM, said the company takes the materials it uses very seriously. "We're maniacal about it," he said, adding that IBM restricts chemical exposure to one-fourth of legal limits, carefully trains employees who work with hazardous chemicals and regularly monitors their health. [6]

"OSHA standards are not protective," responds Hawes, who thinks that more should be done to safeguard computer workers. While OSHA has standards for individual chemicals, it lacks standards for the chemical mixtures that clean-room workers encounter, she explains. In addition, environmental laws restrict exposure to these chemicals to a few parts per billion, whereas OSHA and IBM limit contact to parts per million, she says.

LaDou says OSHA and the National Institute for Occupational Safety and Health (NIOSH) have brushed off his requests for stricter standards. "It's just standard operating procedure in Washington that this industry is being treated with favor," he says of technology giants, which wield considerable political and economic clout.

LaDou insists that workplace cancer should be a high priority for the government because dozens of studies show that between 5 percent and 25 percent of U.S. cancer cases are rooted in the workplace. According to NIOSH, roughly 20,000 people die each year from cancer attributable to the workplace, and about 40,000 workers develop cancer each year from workplace environmental factors. [7]

IBM has conducted three cancer studies in the past 15 years. In the mid-1990s, one linked chemicals used at two IBM semiconductor plants to higher miscarriage rates among female workers, prompting the company to stop using them. But a second study concluded that workers in IBM's electronic manufacturing did not have higher rates of brain tumors. A third study, to be released this year, is examining a possible link between cancer and employment at three of the IBM facilities that prompted lawsuits. [8]

In 2002, an independent panel commissioned by the Semiconductor Industry Association found "no affirmative evidence of increased risk of cancer among U.S. semiconductor factory workers." But insufficient data prevented it from drawing any conclusions. [9] At the time, the SVTC said the panel's actions fell short.

"We expect much more from the state-of-art, high-tech electronics industry," Ted Smith, coalition executive director, said. "What we have here is a state-of-the art stall job." [10]

Now LaDou fears the companies are shifting their computer manufacturing to countries that keep few, if any, records on workplace cancer. Computer companies say they've moved manufacturing offshore to cut costs and remain competitive, and that the resultant lower prices for their products will benefit Americans.

---

[1] Laurie J. Flynn, "Trial Against I.B.M. Over Worker Safety Practices Is Nearing a Finish," *The New York Times*, Feb. 23, 2004, p. C4.

[2] *Ibid.*

[3] Therese Poletti, "Judge Tells Sides to Try to Settle Toxics Dispute," *San Jose Mercury News*, March 4, 2004, p. 1.

[4] For background, visit www.svtc.org/svtc/listserv/letter34.htm.

[5] *Ibid.*

[6] Nicholas Varchaver, "What Really Happened in IBM's Clean Room," *Fortune*, Dec. 8, 2003.

[7] For more details, see "NIOSH Safety and Health Topic: Occupational Cancer," at www.cdc.gov/niosh/topics/cancer/.

[8] *Ibid.*

[9] See press release, "Semiconductor Industry Association to Implement Health and Safety Review for fabrication Workers," SIA, available at www.sia-online.org/pre_release.cfm?ID=216.

[10] See press release, "Semiconductor Industry Health Problems Continue to Mount," Silicon Valley Toxics Coalition, March 21, 2002, available at www.svtc.org/hu_health/stalljob.htm.

Construction Work Had Most Deaths

One-fifth of the more than 5,500 Americans who died on the job in 2002 were construction workers.

Worker Fatalities by Industry, 2002*

(Total fatalities: 5,524)**

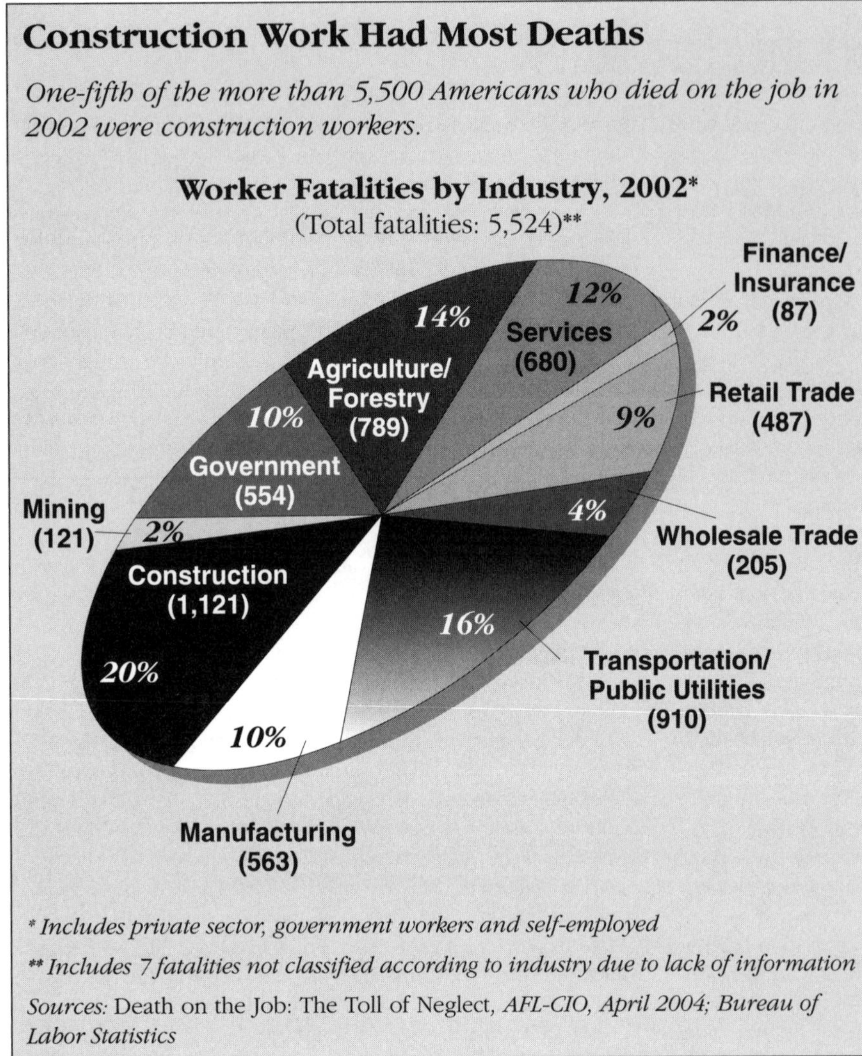

* *Includes private sector, government workers and self-employed*

** *Includes 7 fatalities not classified according to industry due to lack of information*

Sources: Death on the Job: The Toll of Neglect, *AFL-CIO, April 2004; Bureau of Labor Statistics*

Continued from p. 450

But Seminario, of the AFL-CIO, says workers' compensation schemes do not always spur employers to provide safer workplaces because sometimes employers' insurance rates are not tied to their claims experience. And market forces, she says, are skewed by the influx of immigrants, often illegal, willing to work in hazardous jobs for low pay, as evidenced by the large percentage of Hispanic immigrants now working in construction — the nation's most dangerous industry.

Should unsafe companies face stiffer penalties?

At a plant in Portsmouth, Ohio, Dale Livingston died in 2001 after slipping off a hatch into a 2,200-degree oven while shoveling coal. OSHA later found the lid to be faulty. The plant had been regularly cited for a litany of safety violations before it went bankrupt in 2002.

"They didn't give a damn about you," said longtime employee Jim Caldwell, claiming managers routinely denied safety advances costing as little as $500 because it was cheaper to pay the OSHA fines. [32] McWane executives reportedly came to the same conclusion. [33]

Congress — which first established the agency's fines in 1970 and has sole authority to set OSHA penalties — has raised them only once, in the early '90s.

Critics say deep-pocketed corporations see the fines as merely a business cost and not a deterrent. "They're pitiful," says Hayes of Families In Grief Hold Together. "Every company knows that it's cheaper to pay the fine than to protect the worker."

But Henshaw says the fines are adequate. "Our goal is not to cite [for violations]," he says. "Our goal is to assure a safe workplace" using court settlements, inspections and enforcement to effect change.

Business groups agree, but they also note that the fines can be onerous for small players, sometimes forcing them into bankruptcy.

The NAM's Tampio says the penalties are high enough and that some companies receive citations for minor violations even though they may otherwise have strong safety records. He rejects the notion that raising fines only hurts unsafe employers. "It's not black and white when you have someone come into your facility and say, 'Is this up to par?' " he says. "You could have one inspector see something one way, and one another [way]."

But critics note that OSHA often reduces the fines it does impose, usually after negotiating with employers. Hayes says reductions can sometimes be as high as 70 percent of the original fine if the employer is a small business and implements changes.

He should know. OSHA initially fined the grain silo owner responsible for his son's death $530,000, but OSHA reduced it to $30,000 shortly thereafter, arguing that the money was better spent on safety improvements than on fines. After Hayes complained, the agency then bumped the fine up to $42,000.

Penalties for serious violations range from $100 to $7,000 per incident. For a "willful" violation, fines range from $5,000 to $70,000. For the willful death of an employee, which is only a misdemeanor, the maximum fine is $250,000 for an individual or six months in prison, with a maximum fine of $500,000 for a company. (*See chart, p. 448.*) [34] But in practice, Hayes says, the average

OSHA fine for a death on the job is $2,500 to $5,000. In most states, widows or injured workers cannot sue employers but must rely on workers' compensation.

The AFL-CIO's Seminario wants harsher penalties when workers die. Specifically, when worker deaths are caused by serious, willful or repeat safety offenses on the part of the employer, she would like the penalty raised from a misdemeanor to a felony. "Those are significant violations," she says.

The misdemeanor penalty dissuades the government from pursuing criminal charges, she argues. "People aren't going to prosecute because they're just not big cases. So you've had a very dismal history of criminal prosecution," she says. The Justice Department does sometimes prosecute workplace death cases under environmental statutes, if applicable, because the penalties are tougher, she says.

"It is a sad statement that federal law provides for stronger enforcement for harassing a wild burro on federal lands . . . than for willfully killing a worker," writes Seminario. (*See At Issue, p. 461.*)

But OSHA rarely prosecutes a company when a worker dies, even when there were multiple deaths or repeat violations. From 1982 to 2002, OSHA investigated 1,242 workplace deaths, but only made criminal referrals in 7 percent of the cases, *The New York Times* found. In 2003, OSHA made eight criminal referrals to the Justice Department — the second highest number in 10 years and up from five in 2002. [35] In 2002, the DOJ prosecuted all five referrals, according to OSHA.

"The No. 1 problem in OSHA is you have to fight with your own people to prosecute cases," said William M. Murphy, the now-retired director of OSHA in Cincinnati, commenting on the death of the Moeves trench workers. "Very few were taken up. Sometimes I'd know why. Sometimes I wouldn't." [36]

And OSHA rarely slaps companies with maximum fines. In fact, OSHA fines declined sharply at the beginning of the Bush administration, according to an AFL-CIO study. From 2000 to 2002, the typical fine for a willful safety violation dropped 26 percent — from $36,487 to $26,888 — and fines for failing to fix a safety violation dropped 68 percent — from $7,687 to $2,448. [37]

But since a joint, nine-month investigation of OSHA's record by *The New York Times*, PBS's "Frontline" and Canadian Broadcasting's "The Fifth Estate," the agency's fines seem to be on the upswing. Henshaw says OSHA imposed $82 million in penalties in the first 11 months of 2003, and its yearly penalty totals are rising.

OSHA's compliance officers also have a "rigorous process" for determining penalties, Henshaw says. "I think it's a pretty good system. It's fair, it's consistent. We're not here to rack up the dollar amount."

Others complain OSHA doesn't consider the consequences of a violation when it imposes a fine. The end result: The fine is the same for a serious violation whether workers die or not. "It doesn't sound fair to those from the outside," Henshaw says. "But the fact is, all we can do is cite for the violation or the hazard."

Does the Bush administration favor corporate interests over workers?

The AFL-CIO complains the administration has quietly gutted regulations on ergonomics, tuberculosis, beryllium — a metal that is lethal at certain exposure levels — and other hazards, installed pro-business officials in regulatory roles and relies on companies to develop voluntary guidelines instead of issuing mandatory regulations.

"In a direct slap in the face to workers, the president nominated one of the industry's anti-ergonomic leaders, Eugene Scalia, as the Labor Department's top lawyer, clearly demonstrating [Bush's] commitment to big business, rather than workers," the AFL-CIO complains on its Web site. [38]

The Bush administration is "missing in action" when it comes to issuing mandatory safety standards that protect workers, Seminario says. "This will be the first administration in OSHA's history that will go through a four-year term and not set any major safety and health rule — not one — which is pretty astounding given the number of hazards," Seminario says.

"They've come to a practical standstill in the last decade," says Peter Lurie, deputy director of Public Citizen's Health Research Group, charging that Bush's OSHA favors corporate interests; he is equally critical of OSHA under the Clinton administration. "We see . . . a lack of desire to regulate."

Administration officials say they're simply striving for a healthy balance between corporate interests and workers' rights — a stance that business groups are applauding.

OSHA's Henshaw emphasizes that his agency devotes its resources to efforts that are more beneficial than regulations: Establishing partnerships with trade associations that then craft guidelines for member companies. "That's much more effective and lasting than if the federal government did it on its own," he says.

In a 2002 essay in OSHA's *Job Safety and Health Quarterly*, Henshaw said the agency had established 139 partnerships involving 6,200 employers covering almost 216,000 workers. "These partnerships are formal agreements that focus on eliminating specific hazards, establishing comprehensive safety and health-management systems or expanding training opportunities," he wrote. Cooperative alliances with the business community further extend OSHA's reach. [39]

But skeptics are not buying it. "They essentially have gone out of business and totally abdicated responsibility under this administration," counters Seminario. "Every step of the way on these matters, particularly the regulatory matters, they've just taken the position of the employers."

Hayes notes that the administration only began to show an interest in his efforts to provide more protections for Hispanic workers this year — an election year in which the Hispanic vote will be critical. "I'm a great proponent of OSHA. You don't kill it to fix it. Politics is so ingrained in the agency," Hayes says, adding, "It should not be political. Period."

"That's hogwash," Henshaw says. "This is not a political operation. This is a safety and health operation," he says. "Whatever political statements are made for whatever political reasons, it doesn't apply here."

Critics also complain that OSHA has essentially shut workers and labor groups out of its regulation-writing process, relying instead on employers' guidance.

That's a departure from earlier administrations, Seminario says, including those of GOP Presidents Ronald Reagan and the first George Bush, which forged trilateral negotiations among labor unions, companies and OSHA to craft regulations. "There's a whole history of trying to bring people together to deal with serious hazards, and this administration is basically one that is very anti-union and very anti-worker," she says.

The watchdog group Public Citizen and the Paper, Allied-Industrial, Chemical and Energy Workers International Union repeatedly have sued OSHA for allegedly delaying new rules limiting workplace exposure to hexavalent chromium, a lung carcinogen associated with chrome surfaces, certain dyes and welding. Lurie says a million workers a year are exposed to the hazard. Last year, in response to a lawsuit filed by the groups, the Third U.S. Circuit Court of Appeals ordered OSHA to issue a proposed rule on chromium no later than Oct. 4, 2004, and a final rule no later than Jan. 18, 2006. [40]

"It's dreadful that we had to drag them kicking and screaming into federal court to get them to do something that the agency had promised a decade previously," Lurie says. "But you don't get anywhere with OSHA unless you sue them."

OSHA can drag its feet on writing regulations because the labor movement is weaker than it once was and public attention has waned, Lurie says. "Administrations have appointed a series of industry-friendly administrators who have started to look at OSHA as an agency that gets in the way of doing business," he says, noting that corporations have tremendous hostility toward OSHA.

Henshaw says hexavalent chromium had languished on the regulatory agenda of several previous administrations and that his agency decided to start a rulemaking on it "before we got the court order." ■

BACKGROUND

Defining Moments

Of the butchers and floorsmen, the beef-boners and trimmers, and all those who used knives, you could scarcely find a person who had the use of his thumb. . . . There were men who worked in the cooking rooms, in the midst of steam and sickening odors, by artificial light; in these rooms the germs of tuberculosis might live for two years, but the supply was renewed every hour. . . . There were those who worked in the chilling rooms, and whose special disease was rheumatism. . . . and as for the other men, who worked in tank rooms full of steam . . . their particular trouble was that they fell into the vats; and when they were fished out, there was never enough of them left to be worth exhibiting."

— Upton Sinclair, *The Jungle*, 1906

Sinclair's explosive exposé of the grisly, dangerous world of Chicago meatpacking awakened the country to worker safety issues. The book prompted President Theodore Roosevelt to launch a government investigation into the industry, resulting in passage of the Pure Food and Drug Act of 1906, which created the Food and Drug Administration (FDA), and the Meat Inspection Act, which mandated animal inspections and cleanliness in slaughterhouses.

But Eric Schlosser, author of the 2002 best-seller *Fast Food Nation*, says the laws actually did little to improve workplace conditions. Unions would struggle for decades to represent Chicago's slaughterhouses, but meatpacking firms used every obstacle at their disposal — including spies, blacklists and strikebreakers — to undermine them, Schlosser writes. [41]

It would take a calamitous fire in New York City to get the federal government to begin overseeing workplace safety. On March 25, 1911, as workers at the Triangle Shirtwaist Co. in Greenwich Village were about to go home, a fire that had begun in a scrap bin suddenly roared through the 10-story building, fed by the highly flammable sewing fabric, cotton, tissue paper and long wooden tables.

Workers on the upper floors managed to flee, but in the commotion, no one warned the mostly Jewish and Italian immigrants at their sewing machines on the ninth level. By the time most of them saw the smoke and flames, it was too late to escape. [42]

The toll was horrific: 146 workers perished, mostly young women and girls, with many victims leaping from ninth floor windows, their skirts ablaze. The fire moved so swiftly it was over in a half-hour.

Besides the highly flammable materials, the heavy fatalities were blamed on the lack of fire extinguishers or sprinklers, locked exit doors, weak fire escapes (some of which collapsed under the weight of fleeing workers) and ladders too short to rescue workers on the higher floors.

Journalist David Von Drehle, who documents the tragedy in a new book, says the incident was sensational, but not unusual. "Death was an almost routine workplace hazard in those days," he

Continued on p. 456

Chronology

1870-1910s
Workplace tragedies horrify the nation.

1906
Upton Sinclair's *The Jungle* exposes the dangerous world of Chicago's stockyards, prompting a government investigation and passage of meat inspection laws.

1911
Fire ravages a New York City garment factory, adding momentum to a growing labor movement and spurring new worker protections.

1930-1960s
Safety regulation and labor movement gain momentum.

1938
Fair Labor Standards Act creates minimum wage, 44-hour workweek and limits child labor.

1952
A succession of coal-mine accidents spurs Congress to enact the Mine Safety Act, requiring annual inspections, safeguards and penalties for violators.

1955
American Federation of Labor and Congress of Industrial Organizations merge, forming the AFL-CIO.

1960
Edward R. Murrow's "Harvest of Shame" documentary about the plight of migrant farm workers shocks the nation and triggers passage of the Migrant Health Act of 1962.

1969
To combat black lung disease, Congress enacts the Federal Coal Mine Health and Safety Act, establishing limits on coal dust in mines.

1970s ***New federal agencies created to protect workers.***

1970
Occupational Safety and Health Administration (OSHA) Act is signed into law by President Richard M. Nixon, creating the modern framework for protecting employees.

1971
OSHA and NIOSH (National Institute for Occupational Safety and Health) are established.

1977
Federal Mine Safety and Health Act strengthens protections for miners.

1978
OSHA standards on cotton dust, the source of "brown lung disease" at textile factories, and lead poisoning dramatically reduce injuries and deaths.

1979
An explosion and partial meltdown at the Three Mile Island nuclear power plant outside Harrisburg, Pa., raises fears about nuclear safety.

1980-1990s
OSHA issues safety rules.

1980
OSHA updates workplace fire-protection standards and — over the next 16 years — new safety standards for grain elevators, toxic materials, hazardous waste, chemicals, confined workspaces, scaffolds, asbestos and blood-borne pathogens, including AIDS.

1986
Congressional hearings are held on workplace violence after a postal worker in Edmond, Okla., murders 14 colleagues, wounds six and commits suicide.

2000s ***President's workplace policies spark controversy.***

2001
Bush signs repeal of mandatory ergonomics rules issued by Clinton administration. . . . Sept. 11 terrorist attacks make terrorism a major workplace safety concern. . . . Spate of East Coast anthrax attacks targets postal workers, journalists and government officials. . . . Mississippi jury awards $25 million each to six workers sickened by asbestos.

2002
Nine mine workers are dramatically rescued from a flooded section of the Quecreek Mine in Somerset County, Pa. . . . Bush administration announces voluntary ergonomic guidelines.

2003
Sen. Orrin G. Hatch, R-Utah, offers legislation creating trust fund for asbestos victims but barring them from suing employers. . . . OSHA adopts new initiative to crack down on worst safety violators and issues ergonomic recommendations for nursing homes.

February 2004
Lethal ricin powder mailed to Senate Majority Leader Bill Frist, R-Tenn., prompts closure of Senate office buildings, raising fresh concerns about terrorism in the workplace.

Battle Over Ergonomics Rules Continues

The political battle over ergonomic standards has spanned two administrations and is still simmering. In November 2000, during the final months of the Clinton administration, the Occupational Safety and Health Administration (OSHA) issued mandatory regulations designed to prevent ergonomic-related injuries at work.

Labor and watchdog groups hailed the new regulations, designed to cover repetitive stress and over-exertion injuries. "Ergonomic injuries and illnesses are the nation's biggest workplace safety and health problem, causing over 600,000 serious injuries and costing $45-$50 billion every year," the advocacy group Public Citizen said. "OSHA's ergonomics standard is a flexible measure based on science and good employer practices." [1]

But corporate interests fiercely opposed the rules, including the National Association of Manufacturers (NAM) and U.S. Chamber of Commerce. The Labor Department had estimated the new regulations would have cost companies $4.5 billion, but the business community put the potential cost at $100 billion annually, including the cost of lost productivity, new employees and expensive workspace redesigns. [2] In one of his first acts in office, President Bush on March 20, 2001, signed a bill repealing the Clinton ergonomic rules, after Republicans in Congress convinced centrist Democrats to pass a resolution overturning the rules. [3]

NAM, which opposes mandatory ergonomic regulations, nevertheless acknowledges that some ergonomic injuries are work-related. But it emphasizes that the ailments can also be caused by other factors, such as diet or genetic predisposition. "If you can't even know how to treat something that you don't even know how it actually happened, it becomes such an unclear science," says Christopher Tampio, NAM's director of employment policy. "This is another huge burden that you're putting on business, and especially manufacturing."

Labor advocates say mandatory rules are needed to prevent an assortment of repetitive-stress problems, such a carpal-tunnel syndrome and back injuries, resulting from demanding tasks or poorly designed desks and other office equipment.

"This is a huge problem economically, already, and it's a huge source of disability for workers," says Peg Seminario, the AFL-CIO's director of health and safety. "Yes, there may be some costs involved, but the cost of not doing anything is huge."

The AFL-CIO says there were 27,900 serious cases of carpal tunnel in 1999, but many such injuries go unreported. [4] The group also says that since the rules were repealed, more than 1.8 million workers across the country have suffered ergonomic-related injuries. [5]

"Carpal tunnel syndrome is one of the most expensive injuries in terms of time off the job and costs," Seminario says. "So these are very, very expensive injuries, and they are disabling as well. Some employers are taking action, and that's a good thing, but the majority are not."

In April 2002, President Bush announced a new initiative for combating ergonomic ailments through voluntary guidelines. Recommendations were issued for nursing homes in 2003 and are under development for grocery stores, poultry plants and other industries. "[The new plan] is a major improvement over the rejected old rule because it will prevent ergonomics injuries before they occur and reach a much larger number of at-risk workers," Labor Secretary Elaine Chao said in a statement at the time. [6]

Sen. Edward M. Kennedy, D-Mass., and other critics say the new approach falls short. "When it comes to protecting America's workers, this administration's goal is to look the other way and help big business get away with it," Kennedy said. He predicted that women would be impacted the most, because they hold more jobs that cause ergonomic injuries. [7]

Some business representatives, however, think even voluntary guidelines are not needed. Randel Johnson, vice president

Continued from p. 454

writes. "By one estimate, one hundred or more Americans died on the job every day in the booming industrial years around 1911. Mines collapsed on them, ships sank under them, pots of molten steel spilled over their heads, locomotives smashed into them, exposed machinery grabbed them by the arm or leg or hair and pulled them in." [43] Only a few months before the Triangle Shirtwaist fire, he noted, an inferno in a Newark, N.J., garment factory had killed 25 women.

But the scope — and timing — of the Triangle fire would spur New York and the rest of the nation to adopt worker-safety laws. In the years prior to the fire, garment workers had held strikes, including one at the Triangle factory, to protest unsafe working conditions. [44] The fire itself occurred as the American labor movement was beginning to organize an influx of mostly European immigrants toiling in dangerous conditions in factories and sweatshops.

The Triangle owners dodged manslaughter charges because the jury could not ascertain whether they had bolted the doors or if they even knew they were locked. Civil suits filed by relatives of the victims resulted in payouts of $75 per family. [45]

Birth of Regulation

Twenty-seven years later, in 1938, Congress passed the Fair Labor Standards Act, which imposed child-labor restrictions, established a minimum wage of 25 cents an hour and mandated overtime pay and work-weeks no longer than 44 hours. Signed into law by President Franklin D. Roosevelt, the act set the minimum working age for most industries at 16 and barred youths under 18 from dangerous jobs. [46]

for labor and employee benefits at the Chamber of Commerce, worries that recommendations send the wrong message that regulation is needed.

"It bolsters the argument that there is a concern," says Johnson, who serves as co-chairman of the National Coalition on Ergonomics, which represents more than 250 business organizations. He notes that many companies already spend billions of dollars on ergonomic programs tailored to their facilities, but are unwilling to implement sweeping, government-imposed standards that may be of no benefit.

Richard Fairfax, OSHA's director of enforcement programs, explains that while the agency has no explicit requirement that employers reduce ergonomic hazards, companies are liable under the so-called "general duty clause," which requires all employers to provide safe and healthy workplaces. "Employers do have that obligation, and we are enforcing it," he says. As of March 1, the agency had issued 13 citations to employers for ergonomics-related problems.

Much of the debate over ergonomics boils down to opinions about scientific data. Supporters of regulation say the science conclusively links musculoskeletal disorders with work environments, including three major reports since 1997 — one by OSHA and two by the National Academy of Sciences. [8]

Yet Johnson counters, "The science isn't there yet to show what kinds of repetitive motions in the workplace cause what problems."

However, OSHA may never know the extent of work-related ergonomic injuries. In a little-noticed move, OSHA in 2003 revoked a previous requirement that employers report incidents of carpal tunnel and other ergonomic ailments to the agency. [9]

In late January, nearly a dozen researchers boycotted an OSHA-sponsored symposium on ergonomics, insisting the government was distorting the science for political purposes and delaying implementation of safety measures.

"We've had symposia on top of symposia followed by symposia, and all have arrived at the same conclusion: That there is a clear relationship between musculoskeletal disorders and physical loading in the workplace," said Robert Radwin, professor of biomedical engineering at the University of Wisconsin, Madison. [10] But the Chamber's ergonomics coalition complained that speakers at the event favored regulation.

Meanwhile, corporate America has taken its fight to the grass roots. In Washington state last year, after businesses expressed strong opposition to proposed ergonomic rules, voters rejected the initiative. [11]

---

1 Press release, "Hard-won Workplace Safety Standard Fighting for its Life: Protections for Office Workers, Clerks and Assembly Workers on Chopping Block," March 2, 2001, at www.citizen.org/congress/regulations/bush_admin/articles.cfm?ID=1433.

2 Caroline E. Mayer, "Guidelines, Not Rules, on Ergonomics; Labor Dept. Rejects Pay For Repetitive-Stress Injury, *The Washington Post*, April 6, 2002, p. E1.

3 For background, see Rebecca Adams, "GOP-Business Alliance Yields Swift Reversal of Ergonomics Rule," *CQ Weekly*, March 9, 2001.

4 See "Facts About Worker Safety and Health," AFL-CIO, at www.aflcio.org/yourjobeconomy/safety/tools/factsaboutwsh.cfm.

5 See AFL-CIO BushWatch, "Offered toothless, voluntary ergonomic guidelines," April 2002, at www.aflcio.org/issuespolitics/bushwatch/bushwatch_archive.cfm?goButton2.x=14&goButton2.y=2.

6 Mayer, *op. cit.*

7 *Ibid.*

8 David Kohn, "Ergonomic experts boycott conference; Leading scientists accuse government of distorting science for political ends," *The Baltimore Sun*, Jan. 26, 2004, p. A3.

9 AFL-CIO statement, "Injured at Work? New Bush Rules Say Some Injuries Don't Count," July 8, 2003. For more information, go to www.aflcio.org/yourjobeconomy/safety/ns07082003.cfm

10 Kirsten Downey, "OSHA Forum on Ergonomics Draws Fire," *The Washington Post*, Jan. 27, 2004, p. A15.

11 "Workplace Initiatives Give Mixed Results For Business Groups," *The Wall Street Journal*, Nov. 6, 2003, p. A1.

Congress had created the Bureau of Mines in 1910 to curb the death rate for miners, which was surpassing 2,000 a year, but the bureau primarily conducted research and did not begin inspections until 1941. In the 1950s and '60s, lawmakers turned their attention to coal mines, then as now one of the most dangerous workplaces. [47]

Passage of the Federal Coal Mine Safety Act in 1952 stepped up inspections at some mines and gave the bureau more enforcement authority. In 1966, the act was expanded to cover all coal mines. To fight the pervasive "black lung disease," Congress passed the Federal Coal Mine Health and Safety Act in 1969, limiting the amount of coal dust permissible in mines, requiring quarterly mine inspections and providing compensation for miners who contracted the disease.

By 1970, lawmakers had concluded that voluntary safety arrangements by employers and a patchwork of state laws were not protecting workers. As part of Washington's effort to federalize workplace-safety regulation, Congress passed the watershed Occupational Safety and Health Act, which created OSHA a year later.

The legislation also established NIOSH, now part of the U.S. Department of Health and Human Services, to conduct research on worker safety and make recommendations to OSHA. The agency has researchers in labs across the country examining issues ranging from indoor air pollution and mining hazards to cancer in the workplace.

In 1977, the Federal Mine Safety and Health Act provided miners with additional protections and rights and consolidated regulation under the Labor Department's Mine Safety and Health Administration (MSHA). Since the act's passage, mining fatalities have dropped from 272 in 1977 to 56 in 2003. [48]

Hispanic Workers' Deaths Rose

Workplace fatalities among Hispanics rose more than 50 percent in the decade from 1992 to 2002, reflecting Hispanics' population growth in the U.S. and the fact they often take jobs in high-risk industries.

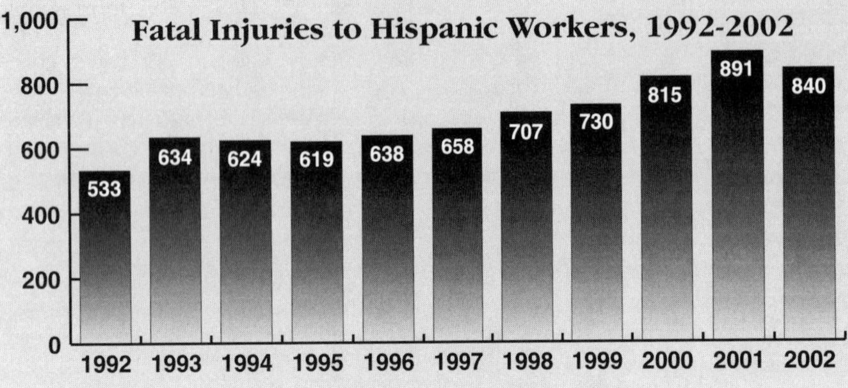

Source: "Death on the Job: The Toll of Neglect," AFL-CIO, April 2004; Bureau of Labor Statistics

Nevertheless, the GAO criticized MSHA last year for failing to complete six-month inspections of ventilation and roof supports on time and failing to follow up to see that problems identified at mines were corrected. The GAO also found omissions and flaws in MSHA's casualty data and said inspectors need better guidance. Moreover, it predicted a shortage of inspectors in the next five years, when nearly half of its investigators will be eligible to retire. [49] MSHA keeps a running tally of annual mine-worker fatalities on its Web site, www.msha.gov.

Golden Era

Many observers, like Public Citizen's Lurie, consider OSHA's earliest years — under Presidents Nixon, Ford and Carter — as the agency's "golden era." Since then, he says, the agency "has been a disaster."

But OSHA Enforcement Director Fairfax thinks the agency has improved over time. In the 1970s and early '80s, OSHA was heavily criticized for issuing inconsistent citations and penalties, he says, but since then it has taken considerable steps to correct the problem.

For most of its existence, OSHA has been in the crosshairs of politicians. "By 1974, OSHA was under attack, fighting for its very life," write journalists Andrew Schneider and David McCumber, in a new book on asbestos poisoning at a Montana mine. "The Nixon administration, sympathetic to business, faced a hostile, Democrat-controlled Congress that was urging tougher regulation." [50]

On March 28, 1979, a malfunctioning cooling system at the Three Mile Island nuclear power plant near Harrisburg, Pa., gave workplace safety a new meaning. [51] Although no one was killed or injured, the explosion and partial meltdown of the nuclear reactor raised concerns about safety conditions at nuclear power plants. Investigators later blamed the near-catastrophe on human error, design flaws and component failure. [52]

During the 1980s and '90s, OSHA issued a succession of safety regulations for dangers related to fires, grain elevators, hazardous waste, electrical machinery, blood-borne pathogens (such as AIDS and Hepatitis B), chemicals, construction, asbestos and scaffolds, among others.

But often those regulations were ignored by states, 21 of which had their own worker-safety regulatory schemes under which they agreed to monitor worker safety themselves in lieu of federal regulation. Although they were supposed to impose standards at least as stringent as the federal safety rules, some states did a better job than others, and OSHA's oversight of the state programs was sometimes lacking.

For instance, on Sept. 3, 1991, 25 mostly poor, black and female workers died in a poultry plant fire in Hamlet, N.C. Investigators said the exits had been padlocked to prevent alleged worker thefts, the plant had no sprinkler system or fire alarm and the state worker-safety agency had never inspected the plant. [53]

Subsequent investigations revealed that North Carolina had one of the most lax worker-protection systems, but the federal OSHA had not properly monitored the state's program. For example, the state had only 27 inspectors, while federal guidelines mandated 116. The state legislature subsequently passed new worker-safety laws, and the chicken plant's owner pleaded guilty to manslaughter and served four years in prison. [54]

Over the years, OSHA's whistle-blower protections — designed to prevent workers from being fired or penalized for complaining about unsafe conditions — have been included in more than a dozen worker-related federal statutes, such as the Solid Waste Disposal Act and the Surface Transportation Assistance Act. [55]

Then in the early-to-mid-'90s, after the Republican House takeover, GOP members unsuccessfully offered legislation to gut OSHA's authority. [56]

Recent Problems

While the federal government is charged with protecting private-sector workers via OSHA and NIOSH, critics say it has failed to protect its own Department of Energy (DOE) workers from hazards in government labs and at DOE cleanup sites.

They point to the defunct Hanford nuclear weapons facility in Washington state, where more than 11,000 DOE workers are involved in a $2 billion cleanup expected to take at least 35 years. Some wonder if the facility poses more risks now than it did while operational.

"Hanford is creating a new generation of sick and injured workers," concludes a report by the Government Accountability Project, a watchdog group representing ill workers who are suing the agency. Some employees complain that onsite doctors are hesitant to link their maladies to Hanford because it would make them eligible for compensation or transfer. [57]

In 2002, the GAO recommended that DOE's science laboratories, which are not regulated or licensed by any outside bodies, come under independent oversight. "The situation is too murky to trust the Department of Energy's self-investigation, and the sooner some independent eyes are trained on Hanford worker safety, the better," said Sen. Ron Wyden, D-Ore. [58]

Ironically, despite the dangers at nuclear plants, meatpacking remains one of the deadliest occupations in America, with slaughterhouse injury rates about three times higher than at other factories. "Every year, about one out of three meatpacking workers in this country — roughly 43,000 men and women — suffer an injury or a work-related illness that requires medical attention beyond first aid," Schlosser writes. [59]

The pressure of maintaining production lines drives some workers to take drugs such as methamphetamines, putting them at greater risks for accidents, he writes. Weak unions make it tougher to complain, and many slaughterhouse workers are non-union. Illegal immigrants often avoid making waves because they fear being fired.

"Again and again, workers told me they are under tremendous pressure not to report injuries," Schlosser writes, because supervisors' annual bonuses are often based in part on whether they have been able to keep workers' injury rates low. Many slaughterhouses try to rid themselves of injured employees because they sap productivity. [60]

Late-night cleaning crews have what Schlosser calls "the worst job in the United States." Many are illegal immigrants working on contract at low wages. They clean the plants with high-pressure hoses that spray a 180-degree mixture of water and chlorine onto everything in the plants, cutting visibility to a few feet. When the machinery is running, the crewmembers can't see or hear each other so they routinely spray each other with burning hot, chemical-laden water, which sickens them, he writes. [61] ■

CURRENT SITUATION

Proposed Legislation

Lawmakers on Capitol Hill are championing several bills aimed at protecting workers and reforming OSHA, but some measures are drawing controversy.

GOP Sen. Mike Enzi of Wyoming, a member of the Senate Health, Education, Labor and Pensions Committee, is drafting legislation that would make willfully causing the death of a worker a felony. Currently, the penalty is a misdemeanor, with a maximum individual fine of $250,000 and up to six months in jail for a first offense. Enzi's bill would increase prison terms to more than a year but would not increase the fines.

A bill introduced by Democratic Sen. John Corzine of New Jersey would increase the six-month jail term for willfully causing the death of a worker to 10 years. [62] The prison term would be 20 years for anyone with similar prior convictions or who has been assessed penalties for violations.

Rep. Charlie Norwood, R-Ga., chairman of the House Workforce Protections Subcommittee, has offered four OSHA reform bills that he says are designed to promote fairness and are strongly supported by the business community. All four passed the House on May 18.

One strengthens the Occupational Safety and Health Review Commission, which reviews OSHA citations challenged by companies, by increasing its size from three to five members. A second would give the panel authority over OSHA to interpret workplace laws in dispute. A third measure would give employers longer than the current 15-day deadline to respond to OSHA citations.

A fourth bill requires the government to pay attorney fees of small businesses that successfully challenge OSHA citations. Randel Johnson, vice president of labor, immigration and employee benefits at the U.S. Chamber of Commerce, says the measure would encourage small businesses, which might not otherwise afford to take on OSHA, the chance to challenge them if they have solid cases.

"If OSHA's correct, the businesses are not going to have to pay a cent," adds a staffer with the House Education and the Workforce Committee, who spoke on condition of anonymity.

But opponents say the bills reduce OSHA's authority. Hayes, of Families In Grief Hold Together, who insists Norwood "has been trying to gut OSHA for years," thinks the congressman is trying to make it easier for businesses to resist regulation.

Overexertion and Falls Cause Many Absences

Bumping into objects or equipment and overexertion caused more than half the days Americans stayed away from work in 2002. Falls and slips caused one-fifth of the absences. Repetitive motion injuries, suffered largely by office workers and cashiers, were blamed for 4 percent of the non-work days.

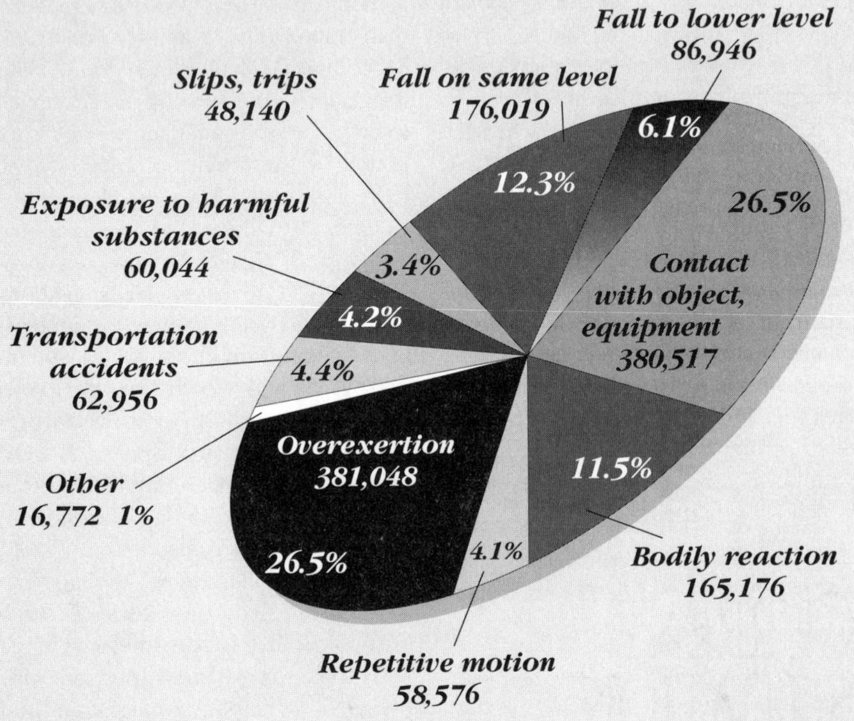

Sources: Death on the Job: The Toll of Neglect, *AFL-CIO, April 2004; Bureau of Labor Statistics*

The following legislation is also in play:

- Sen. Enzi may offer an updated version of his 2003 bill that lets a company use outside consultants to enhance worker safety in exchange for a one-year exemption from OSHA civil penalties for safety violations. To receive the exemption, companies must satisfy the program requirements.
- Senate Majority Leader Bill Frist, R-Tenn., and Senate Judiciary Chairman Orrin G. Hatch, R-Utah, have introduced legislation creating a trust fund — ranging from $108 billion to $115 billion — to compensate workers sickened by asbestos. [63] More than 200,000 pending asbestos lawsuits have overwhelmed the courts and pushed more than 60 companies, some with only tangential connections to asbestos, into bankruptcy. [64] The fund would be financed by asbestos and insurance companies sued by victims. Proponents said it would compensate victims more quickly and unclog the courts.

The watchdog U.S. Action and other opponents said the proposed trust is too small and would bar sickened workers from suing. Both sides have dueling TV ad campaigns. On April 22, Democratic senators who think the trust should be larger blocked a Republican effort to cut off debate on the bill and hold a Senate floor vote. Political negotiations over the legislation are ongoing. [65]

On a related note, the White House has proposed $461.6 million in funding for OSHA in fiscal 2005 — a $4.1 million increase over current funding. While the agency's budget has been rising in recent years, the percentage of OSHA money available for enforcement activities was cut from 38 percent in 1998 to 36 percent in 2003. [66]

Workplace Anti-Terrorism

The Sept. 11, 2001, terrorist attacks, followed by a spate of anthrax-laden letters sent to government offices and news organizations, changed the way Americans view workplace safety.

Spurred by the attacks and the letters — and a steady stream of terror warnings — many companies are proactively planning for the worst. Security has been beefed up in skyscrapers, and employees have been drilled on emergency exit procedures. Some firms have designed "safe" interior rooms in their buildings stocked with emergency supplies. Barriers erected at General Motors' corporate headquarters in Detroit protect against truck bombs. At Coca-Cola headquarters in Atlanta, visitors must use a satellite parking lot a quarter-mile away, where cars undergo rigid security checks. When the government warned in 2001 that terrorists might target the Golden Gate Bridge, the San Francisco-based Bechtel Corp. instructed its 3,000 West Coast workers to remain at home. [67]

After the attacks, the AFL-CIO faulted the government for not adequately

Continued on p. 462

At Issue:

Are OSHA's penalties tough enough?

CHRIS TAMPIO
DIRECTOR, EMPLOYMENT POLICY
NATIONAL ASSOCIATION OF MANUFACTURERS

WRITTEN FOR *THE CQ RESEARCHER*, MAY 2004

yes

The majority of manufacturers understand that preventing injuries makes good business sense. Employers, however, frequently report that they are frustrated by the amount of time they spend on OSHA paperwork and bureaucratic requirements that do not improve safety in their workplaces.

Many employers — based on past experiences — believe that OSHA will find something wrong no matter how great their safety efforts. Some companies believe OSHA inspections take time away from genuine safety efforts because they often involve paperwork violations or trivial citations. If employers have had positive experiences with OSHA in recent years, it has been because of compliance-assistance programs, not the threat of larger fines.

A good example of this can be seen from an experience an NAM member shared with me. This company had injury rates that were higher than the industry average. Concerned about the cost of those injuries to productivity, morale and increased workers'-compensation rates, management redoubled its safety efforts. The "threat" of OSHA enforcement had little impact on spurring this company into action.

OSHA's compliance assistance, however, did play a significant role in reducing injury rates for the company. Using OSHA's voluntary model for safety-program management, the company reduced, within a few years, injury rates in 10 divisions to below the industry average, and its remaining two divisions also showed rapid reductions in injury rates. One division is now in OSHA's Voluntary Protection Program (VPP). Additionally, another division has applied for the VPP, and a third is working on its application. The corporate goal is now to have all divisions in the VPP.

For employers who demonstrate a commitment to safety, OSHA should focus on expanding compliance-assistance programs that increase safety in the workplace. It should focus its inspection and enforcement on recalcitrant employers. OSHA already can issue enormous fines to employers through the current system of willful, repeat and egregious citations, including failure-to-abate citations. OSHA should use all of the current tools in its arsenal to deal with employers who do not act in good faith and who fail to provide safe and healthy workplaces.

By not differentiating between employers who are trying to do the right thing and those who are not, OSHA wastes precious resources. OSHA should assist good employers in creating safe workplaces and punish those few who don't. Larger fines do not make for safer workplaces.

PEG SEMINARIO
DIRECTOR OF HEALTH AND SAFETY, AFL-CIO

WRITTEN FOR *THE CQ RESEARCHER*, MAY 2004

no

Under the Occupational Safety and Health (OSHA) Act of 1970, strong, effective enforcement was to be a cornerstone of government efforts to "assure as far as possible every working man and woman in the nation safe and healthful working conditions."

But more than three decades later, the foundation of the program is shaky and full of holes. OSHA's enforcement is weak and ineffective, failing to provide appropriate sanctions for violations or to send a strong message to employers that failure to protect workers from serious hazards will have serious consequences.

Under the law, the maximum penalty allowable for a violation that poses a substantial risk of death or serious physical harm is $7,000. By comparison, most environmental statutes impose maximum penalties of $25,000 a day for similar violations. And in actuality, OSHA penalties end up being far below statutory levels. For instance, in fiscal 2003, the average serious penalty was only $874, and most penalties are further reduced — often by as much as 35 percent — through settlements with employers.

OSHA's criminal enforcement — limited under current law to cases where a willful violation results in the death of a worker — is even more deficient. The maximum jail term for a first offense is six months in jail, making it a misdemeanor. By comparison, willful violations under virtually every environmental law are felonies and are regularly prosecuted. It is a sad statement that federal law provides for stronger enforcement for harassing a wild burro on federal lands — treating it as a felony punishable by up to a year in jail — than for willfully killing a worker.

As *The New York Times* uncovered in its recent Pulitzer Prize-winning investigation, workplace fatalities are seldom prosecuted. Even worse, at the urging of employer lawyers, OSHA has developed a practice of categorizing violations in fatality cases as "unclassified" — meaning that OSHA cannot criminally prosecute them and undercutting potential civil and criminal actions against employers in other venues.

Despite this sorry situation, employer groups, Republicans in Congress and the Bush administration oppose modest legislation by Sen. John Corzine, D-N.J., to make violations that cause a worker's death a felony, and instead support a bill by Rep. Charlie Norwood, R-Ga., that would weaken OSHA enforcement and penalties.

Is it too much for workers to ask the government to protect their lives, limbs and health the same as we protect wild burros and other natural resources?

Continued from p. 460

monitoring the health of rescue workers at the World Trade Center site in Lower Manhattan, where rescue workers spent months searching the smoldering debris for human remains. The labor group said that shortly after the collapse of the twin towers, the White House pressured the Environmental Protection Agency (EPA) to tone down its reports about health hazards at the site. [68]

Moreover, the AFL-CIO also said that President Bush's August 2002 decision not to release $5.1 billion in congressionally approved funding for homeland security meant the withholding of $90 million to monitor the health of workers at Ground Zero, $150 million for equipment and training requested by the nation's 18,000 fire departments and $100 million to bolster communications equipment for fire, police and other emergency services. [69]

OSHA has said only 57 rescue workers at the World Trade Center site suffered injuries that resulted in lost workdays and that there were no fatalities, despite the nearly 3.7 million work hours spent there. [70]

Since the attacks, NIOSH has set up a Web site offering detailed information on emergency preparedness for businesses in the event of terrorist incidents. [71] In April 2003, it issued guidelines for building managers on how to prevent terrorists from using ventilation systems to spread chemical, biological or radiological agents. The agency also is working with the U.S. Postal Service to determine whether its mail-handling machinery is effective at protecting workers from anthrax.

Voluntary Steps

Some companies that resist generic, mandatory, government safety regulations end up adopting voluntary measures, which they say they can better control and tailor to their specific needs.

And businesses often find that implementing safety measures saves them money. In a 2001 survey conducted by the business insurance company Liberty Mutual, 61 percent of executives polled said they saved $3 or more for every $1 they voluntarily spent on safety programs.

"We absolutely support voluntary actions and programs because they demonstrate that a business is committed," says Karl Jacobson, senior vice president of loss prevention at Liberty Mutual.

"Employers are not out there making their workplaces safer because OSHA tells them to. They're doing it because it's good for business," says the NAM's Tampio. "That's 100 percent of what I hear from my companies."

But watchdog and labor advocates say voluntary efforts are insufficient because not all employers adopt them, and the programs usually fall short of mandatory rules.

Meanwhile, researchers at NIOSH are studying whether emissions from common office equipment and products — such as cleaning supplies, photocopy machines and toner cartridges — endanger workers, especially in contained areas like photocopying rooms. "We don't know at this point what that low level [of exposure] may do," NIOSH spokesman Fred Blosser says. "It's a very exacting and very difficult science." As a precaution, NIOSH has recommended better ventilation for some work spaces and respirators for some workers.

In addition, with more and more teenagers working after school and part time, NIOSH is also studying the risk of injury and illness to those under 19. An average of 67 workers under 18 were killed each year between 1992 and 2000 and in 1998 77,000 were hospitalized. [72]

"Sixteen- and 17-year-old workers die from the leading causes of work-related fatalities — motor vehicle injuries, job-related homicide and injuries associated with machinery — at rates comparable to or slightly higher than those for adult workers," the report said. ■

OUTLOOK

If Kerry Wins

If Sen. Kerry wins the White House in November, he plans to shake up OSHA by adopting a get-tough, regulatory style. In his response to the AFL-CIO's candidate questionnaire, Kerry vowed to make big changes at the agency. President Bush did not respond to the questionnaire

"I'd start by stepping up OSHA inspections, ordering my Justice Department to vigorously prosecute the worst violators and reinstating the standards for ergonomics that the Bush administration cancelled," Kerry said. [73]

Noting that recent statistics show increases in workplace injuries among Hispanics and miners, he wrote, "We need to step up enforcement action and begin to prosecute willful violators of health and safety rules. We also need an administration that recognizes the health and safety threat that workers face, whether in the form of ergonomic injury, exposure to [tuberculosis], or workplace accidents." [74]

The labor group, which represents 13 million workers, has endorsed Kerry despite his support of the 1993 North American Free Trade Agreement (NAFTA). The union strongly opposes the agreement, arguing it has spurred U.S. companies to close up shop here and move factories to Mexico to take advantage of lower wages. While the organization gives Kerry a favorable 91 percent rating for his lifetime voting record, half the votes it objects to were on trade.

Indeed, the net loss of nearly 3 million manufacturing jobs in the last three years has made job growth and globalization key issues in this year's presidential race.

For his part, Kerry has vowed to "fix" NAFTA rather than scuttle it. He would start by eliminating incentives for companies to move jobs overseas, but some observers think Kerry's plan would have only a minor impact, because U.S. employers would still be able to invest in operations overseas.

Unions are betting that despite his stance on NAFTA, Sen. Kerry will do more for them on wages, health care and safety than Bush. "We are obviously an organization with very broad interests," explains Seminario.

In the Senate, Kerry supported efforts to craft a mandatory ergonomic standard and opposed Republican efforts in the mid-1990s to curb workplace safety regulations, Seminario says.

But there's little the Massachusetts lawmaker can do to address the biggest motivation companies have to send jobs elsewhere — the gap between the average U.S. wage of $22.92 per hour ($16.49 base wage, plus $6.43 in benefits) and the significantly lower wages earned by foreign workers. [75]

As companies increasingly slash expenses to stay competitive in a global economy, some observers fear that spending on worker protection will become an increasingly lower priority.

And there are growing concerns that overseas workers for U.S. manufacturers, such as technology companies, are putting themselves at risk in factories that face little regulation and are outside OSHA's purview. "As the high-tech industry has expanded out of Silicon Valley, it has not only exported its technology to countries all over the world but also its toxic chemicals and the resulting health hazards," the watchdog Silicon Valley Toxics Coalition warns on its Web site, www.svtc.org.

"We've had three years of national priorities that placed the special interests of corporations and the wealthy over those of regular workers and their families," AFL-CIO President John Sweeney said upon endorsing Kerry on Feb. 19, 2004. "This is a man who will not sign his name to a single trade agreement that does not include worker protections and environmental protections," he said. [76]

But the Bush administration insists it is safeguarding workers through its international trade agreements. In a March 2004 report, U.S. Trade Representative Robert B. Zoellick noted that free-trade agreements with Chile and Singapore approved by Congress in 2003 "use innovative new mechanisms to meet the labor and environmental objectives set out by Congress in the Trade Act of 2002." Both agreements promote international labor standards and environmental protection through cooperative projects, he said. [77] ■

Notes

[1] David Barstow and Lowell Bergman, "At a Texas Foundry, an Indifference to Life," *The New York Times*, Jan. 8, 2003, p. A1.

[2] *Ibid.*

[3] See "Two Companies, Two Visions," part of PBS' "Frontline" coverage of McWane, at http://www.pbs.org/wgbh/pages/frontline/shows/workplace/mcwane/two.html.

[4] Quoted in David Barstow and Lowell Bergman, "A Family's Fortune, A Legacy of Blood and Tears," *The New York Times*, Jan. 9, 2003, p. A1.

[5] Robin Stein, "Worker Is Crushed to Death At Troubled Foundry Upstate," *The New York Times*, Feb. 21, 2004, p. B5; Barstow and Bergman, Jan. 8, 2003, *op. cit.*; and David Barstow, "Officials at Foundry Face Health and Safety Charges," *The New York Times*, Dec. 16, 2003, p. A 28.

[6] See "National Census of Fatal Occupational Injuries in 2002," Bureau of Labor Statistics, Sept. 17, 2003, at www.bls.gov/news.release/cfoi.nr0.htm, and "Workplace Injuries and Illnesses in 2002," *BLS*, Dec. 18, 2003, at http://stats.bls.gov/news.release/osh.nr0.htm.

[7] See "All About OSHA," Occupational Safety and Health Administration, 2003, p. 3.

[8] BLS "National Census," *op. cit.*

[9] *Ibid.*

[10] Nicholas Varchaver, "What Really Happened in IBM's Clean Room?" *Fortune*, Dec. 8, 2003, p. 90.

[11] For background, see Kenneth Jost, "Asbestos Litigation," *The CQ Researcher*, May 2 2003, pp. 393-416.

[12] See "Safety is Seguridad," National Research Council, The National Academies Press, 2003, pp. 5, 11, 134, 135.

[13] See Jen Wieczorek, "Hellraiser: Ron Hayes," *Mother Jones*, May/June 1998.

[14] See "McWane's memo to N.Y. Attorney General," obtained by PBS's "Frontline," at www.pbs.org/wgbh/pages/frontline/shows/workplace/mcwane/kennedy.html.

[15] Marla Dickerson and Mitchell Landsberg, "Demand Grows for Early Warning of Blackouts; Power: Employee safety and business losses are cited. Utilities' responses vary," *Los Angeles Times*, May 10, 2001, California section, Part 2, p. 1.

[16] Elizabeth Becker, "Bush Rejects Labor's Call to Punish China," *The New York Times*, April 29, 2004, p. C4.

[17] David Barstow, "A Trench Caves In; a Young Worker Is Dead. Is It a Crime?" *The New York Times*, Dec. 21, 2003, Sect. 1, p.1.

[18] *Ibid.*

[19] See "OSHA Can Strengthen Enforcement Through Improved Program Management," General Accounting Office, November 2002, and "OSHA Should Strengthen the Management of its Consultation Program," General Accounting Office, October 2001.

[20] David Barstow and Robin Stein, "California Leads Prosecution of Employers in Job Deaths," *The New York Times*, Dec. 23, 2003, p A1.

[21] View the letter at www.osha.gov/as/opa/foia/letter2004.html.

[22] BLS, "National Census," *op. cit.*

[23] *Ibid.*

[24] "Death in the Workplace," Editorial, *The New York Times*, Jan. 11, 2003, p. A14.

[25] Thomas J. Kniesner and John D. Leeth, "Abolishing OSHA," *The Cato Review of Business and Government*, originally published in 1995. Kniesner and Leeth are economics professors at, respectively, Indiana University and Bentley College.

About the Author

David Hatch is a freelance writer in Arlington, Va., who specializes in media, advertising and consumer issues. A former reporter in the Crain Communications Washington bureau, he holds a B.A. in English from the University of Massachusetts, Amherst.

[26] See AFL-CIO, "Facts About Worker Safety and Health," at www.aflcio.org/yourjobeconomy/safety/tools/factsaboutwsh.cfm.
[27] See U.S. Department of Labor "FY 2003-2008 Strategic Plan," September 2003, p. 35.
[28] See BLS, "Workplace Injuries and Illnesses in 2002," Dec. 18, 2003, at www.bls.gov.
[29] J. Paul Leigh, *et. al.*, "An Estimate of the U.S. Government's Undercount of Nonfatal Occupational Injuries," *Journal of Occupational and Environmental Medicine*, January 2004.
[30] "Occupational Safety and Health Administration," *Cato Handbook for Congress: Policy Recommendations for the 107th Congress*, Cato Institute, pp. 409-417.
[31] *Ibid.*
[32] Geoff Dutton, "Worker's Death Followed Years of Safety Violations," *Columbus Dispatch*, Nov. 23, 2003, p. 2A.
[33] *Ibid.*
[34] Barstow and Stein, *op. cit.*
[35] David Barstow, Remy Gerstein and Robin Stein, "U.S. Rarely Seeks Charges For Deaths in Workplace," *The New York Times*, Dec. 22, 2003, p. A1.
[36] Barstow, Dec. 21, 2003, *op. cit.*
[37] David Barstow and Lowell Bergman, "OSHA to Address Persistent Violators Of Job Safety Rules," *The New York Times*, March 11, 2003, p. A1.
[38] See "BushWatch," www.aflcio.org/issues politics/bushwatch/.
[39] See "Assistant Secretary's Message," *Job Safety & Health Quarterly*, OSHA, summer 2002, p. 2.
[40] The case is *Public Citizen Health Research Group, and Paper, Allied-Industrial, Chemical & Energy Workers International Union v. Elaine Chao, Secretary of Labor, and OSHA.*
[41] *Ibid.*, p. 153.
[42] Quoted on NPR's Morning Edition, "David von Drehle discusses the Triangle Shirtwaist Company fire of 1911," Sept. 1, 2003.
[43] David Von Drehle, *Triangle: The Fire That Changed America* (2003), pp. 2-4, 127-128.
[44] See NPR, *op. cit.*
[45] Douglas Martin, "Rose Freedman, Last Survivor of Triangle Fire, Dies at 107," *The New York Times*, Feb. 17, 2001, p. B8.
[46] For background, see www.dol.gov/asp/programs/history/flsa1938.htm.
[47] Unless otherwise noted, information in this section comes from "History of Mine Safety and Health Legislation," Mine Safety and Health Administration.
[48] See chart listing fatalities of miners at www.msha.gov/stats/daily/d2003bar.pdf.
[49] See "MSHA Devotes Substantial Effort to Ensuring the Safety and Health of Coal Miners, but its Programs Could be Strengthened," General Accounting Office, September 2003, p. 1.
[50] Andrew Schneider and David McCumber, *An Air That Kills: How the Asbestos Poisoning of Libby, Montana Uncovered a National Scandal* (2004), p. 249.
[51] See "Fact Sheet on the Accident at Three Mile Island," Nuclear Regulatory Commission, at www.nrc.gov/reading-rm/doc-collections/fact-sheets/3mile-isle.html.
[52] *Ibid.*
[53] Lacayo, Richard, "Death on the Shop Floor," *Time*, Sept. 16, 1991, p. 28.
[54] Wil Haygood, "After a Deadly Fire, a Town's Losses Were Just Beginning," *The Washington Post*, Nov. 10, 2002, p. F1.
[55] See "All About OSHA," *op. cit.*, pp. 18-19.
[56] Schlosser, *op. cit.*, pp. 185-186.
[57] Sarah Kershaw and Matthew L. Wald, "Lack of Safety Is Charged in Nuclear Site Cleanup," *The New York Times*, Feb. 20, 2004, p. A1.
[58] See testimony by Gary L. Jones, director, Natural Resources and Environment, GAO, before of House Science Committee Energy Subcommittee, July 25, 2002, p. 2; and Matthew L. Wald and Sarah Kershaw, "Wider Investigation Sought at Nuclear Site," *The New York Times*, Feb. 26, 2004, p. A16.
[59] Schlosser, *op. cit.*, pp. 172-178.
[60] *Ibid.*
[61] *Ibid.*
[62] Barstow and Bergman, March 11, 2003, *op. cit.*
[63] Albert B. Crenshaw, "Accord Reached On Asbestos Fund; Manufacturers, Insurers Accept Plan," *The Washington Post*, Oct. 16, 2003, p. E6.
[64] Alex Berenson, "Senate Panel Agrees to Increase Size of Asbestos Trust," *The New York Times*, June 27, 2003, p. C5.
[65] Albert B. Crenshaw, "Asbestos Bill Stalls in Senate; Measure Would Create National Trust Fund for Victims," *The Washington Post*, April 23, 2004, p. E3.
[66] See "Change from FY1998 to FY2004," OSHA.
[67] Michelle Conlin, *et al.*, "When the Office is the War Zone," *Business Week*, Nov. 19, 2001, p. 38.
[68] See Aug. 2003 entry on White House/EPA in "BushWatch" section of www.afl-cio.org.
[69] See "Will block funds to monitor health of World Trade Center rescue and recovery workers and money for firefighters," August 2002, on AFL-CIO "BushWatch" Web site, at www.afl-cio.org.
[70] See "Job Safety & Health Quarterly," OSHA, summer 2002, p.13.
[71] The site is www.cdc.gov/niosh/topics/prepared/
[72] See "NIOSH Alert: Preventing Deaths, Injuries and Illnesses of Young Workers," National Institute for Occupational Safety and Health, at www.cdc.gov/niosh/docs/2003-128/2003-128.htm.
[73] See www.afl-cio.org/issuespolitics/politics/candidates_kerry.cfm.
[74] *Ibid.*
[75] Quoted from "CBS Evening News with Dan Rather," March 15, 2004.
[76] For details, see www.afl-cio.org.
[77] See "The President's Trade Policy Agenda," March 1, 2004 at www.ustr.gov/reports/2004 Annual/overview.pdf.

FOR MORE INFORMATION

American Federation of Labor-Congress of Industrial Organizations, 815 16th St., N.W., Washington, DC 20006; (202) 637-5000; www.aflcio.org.

National Association of Manufacturers, 1331 Pennsylvania Ave., N.W., Washington, DC 20004-1790; (202) 637-3000; www.nam.org.

National Institute for Occupational Health and Safety, Hubert H. Humphrey Bldg., 200 Independence Ave., S.W., Room 715H,Washington, DC 20201; (800) 356-4674; www.cdc.gov/niosh/about.html.

National Safety Council, 1121 Spring Lake Dr., Itasca, IL 60143-3201; (630) 285-1121; www.nsc.org.

Occupational Safety and Health Administration, 200 Constitution Ave., N.W., Washington, DC 20210; (800) 321-OSHA; www.osha.gov.

Public Citizen, 1600 20th St., N.W., Washington, DC 20009; (202) 588-1000; www.citizen.org.

Bibliography

Selected Sources

Books

Drehle, David Von, *Triangle: The Fire that Changed America*, Atlantic Monthly Press, 2003.
A *Washington Post* journalist exhaustively explores the infamous 1911 inferno that killed 146 workers — mostly women and girls — at the Triangle shirtwaist factory in New York City.

Schlosser, Eric, *Fast Food Nation: The Dark Side of the All-American Meal*, Houghton Mifflin, 2001.
This critical examination of American fast-food chains examines the perilous working conditions endured by today's meatpackers and slaughterhouse cleanup crews.

Schneider, Andrew, and David McCumber, *An Air That Kills: How the Asbestos Poisoning of Libby, Montana, Uncovered a National Scandal*, G.P. Putnam's Sons, 2004.
Two journalists conducted a yearlong investigation into asbestos contamination at a W.R. Grace & Co. mine in Libby, Mont. The mine closed in 1990 and the company, sued by thousands of ill employees, recently went bankrupt.

Sinclair, Upton, *The Jungle*, Bantam Books, 1981 (first published 1906).
Upton Sinclair's muckraking classic exposes the dangerous and filthy working conditions of the Chicago stockyards at the turn-of-the-century.

Articles and News Reports

"Dangerous Prescription," "Frontline," Nov. 11, 2003.
A nine-month investigation by PBS's "Frontline" (produced by WGBH-TV in Boston), *The New York Times* and the Canadian Broadcasting Corp.'s "The Fifth Estate" revealed worker fatalities and injuries at plants operated by Alabama-based McWane Inc., a major pipe manufacturer.

Barstow, David, "A Trench Caves In; a Young Worker Is Dead. Is It a Crime?" *The New York Times*, Dec. 21, 2003.
In a three-part series, Barstow contrasts the style of the federal Occupational and Safety and Health Administration (OSHA), which often avoids prosecuting companies and limits fines, with California's state OSHA, which aggressively imposes penalties and seeks criminal charges.

Barstow, David, and Lowell Bergman, "At a Texas Foundry, an Indifference to Life," *The New York Times*, Jan. 8, 2003.
The first article in another three-part series looks at McWane Inc., widely viewed as one of the most hazardous companies to work for in America.

Grimsley, Kirstin Downey, "Danger: People Working; Education, Regulation Aim to Cut Job Deaths," *The Washington Post*, May 28, 2002, p. F1.
Workplace deaths are on the decline in the United States, but new dangers — including terrorism — arise all the time. The article provides an overview of domestic and global worker-safety issues.

Varchaver, Nicholas, "What Really Happened in IBM's Clean Room?" *Fortune*, Dec. 8, 2003.
In a legal battle that could have repercussions for the entire computer industry, hundreds of sickened workers have sued IBM over exposure to dangerous chemicals in the company's "clean rooms," where computer chips are manufactured.

Reports and Studies

"Death on the Job: The Toll of Neglect — A national and state-by-state profile of worker safety and health in the United States," AFL-CIO, April 2004.
This annual review of worker safety by the nation's largest labor group accuses OSHA of failing to regulate aggressively and says the Bureau of Labor Statistics underreports work fatalities, injuries and illness.

"OSHA Can Strengthen Enforcement Through Improved Program Management," General Accounting Office, November 2002.
Congress' investigative arm says OSHA fails to identify the most hazardous worksites for priority inspection because it relies on insufficient data, as well as information furnished by employers that may be incomplete or biased.

Kniesner, Thomas J., and John D. Leeth, "Abolishing OSHA," *The Cato Review of Business and Government*, originally published in 1995.
OSHA's impact on worker safety is marginal, given that fatality rates were declining before the agency was created and OSHA inspects only a fraction of worksites each year, argue two economics professors. Kneisner, of Indiana University, and Leeth, of Bentley College, recommend abolishing OSHA altogether.

Leonard, Jeremy A., "How Structural Costs Imposed on U.S. Manufacturers Harm Workers and Threaten Competitiveness," Manufacturers Alliance (prepared for the National Association of Manufacturers), 2003.
Escalating costs of complying with regulations on worker safety and pollution, coupled with excessive corporate taxation and rising energy costs, are undermining U.S. businesses and making them less competitive with foreign companies.

The Next Step:

Additional Articles from Current Periodicals

Ergonomics

Hamilton, Martha, "U.S. Publishes Guidelines for Nursing Homes," *The Washington Post*, March 14, 2003, p. E3.

The Occupational Safety and Health Administration (OSHA) rolls out new, voluntary guidelines designed to reduce injuries in nursing homes.

Mayer, Caroline E., "Guidelines, Not Rules, on Ergonomics," *The Washington Post*, April 6, 2002, p. E1.

Critics denounce it as a sham, but the voluntary ergonomics guidelines favored by the Bush administration are superior, proponents say.

Schafer, Sarah, and Kenneth Bredemeier, "Firms Get a Grip on 'Repetitive' Injuries," *The Washington Post*, March 18, 2001, p. H1.

Although Congress terminated new ergonomics rules, some companies find that implementing ergonomics-friendly policies voluntarily is good business.

Skrzycki, Cindy, "An Ergonomic Mess in the Grocery Aisles," *The Washington Post*, May 27, 2003, p. E1.

Following its "soft touch" trend in regulation, new OSHA guidelines for grocery workers are purely voluntary and lambasted by unions.

Skrzycki, Cindy, "OSHA Makes No Bones About Ergonomics," *The Washington Post*, Oct. 14, 2003, p. E1.

Amid squabbles over how to define an ergonomics injury, the Department of Labor killed a Clinton-era requirement for recording musculoskeletal ailments.

High-Tech Workplaces

Ante, Spencer E., "Was IBM Hazardous to Workers' Health?" *Business Week*, Oct. 20, 2003, p. 46.

IBM maintained exhaustive documentation of its workers' health, and these records may ultimately play a major role in future trials.

Gaither, Chris, and Terril Yue Jones, "IBM Found Not Liable for Ex-Workers' Cancers," *Los Angeles Times*, Feb. 27, 2004, p. C1.

Two plaintiffs suing IBM for causing their cancer lose at trial, but their attorney pledges to go on with other suits.

Menn, Joseph, "Case Targets High-Tech Manufacturing," *Los Angeles Times*, Oct. 13, 2003, p. C1.

A case filed by two workers against IBM for exposure to carcinogenic chemicals — the first of many — could have major repercussions for the entire semiconductor industry.

Pimentel, Benjamin, "Tech to Study Cancer Data," *San Francisco Chronicle*, March 19, 2004, p. C1.

A major industry study aims to settle the question of whether chemicals used in microchip production cause cancer.

Immigrant Workers

"Mexican-Born Workers More Likely to Die on Job," *Los Angeles Times*, March 14, 2004, p. A1.

Mexican immigrants are the most likely workers to suffer a fatal injury at work.

Aizenman, Nurith C., "Harsh Reward for Hard Labor," *The Washington Post*, Dec. 29, 2002, p. C1.

Despite their increasing share of workplace injuries, undocumented workers are often ineligible for workers' compensation benefits.

Hopkins, Jim, "Fatality Rates Increase for Hispanic Workers," *USA Today*, March 13, 2003, p. 1B.

While deaths among other workers went down, they increased among Hispanics; former OSHA employees say the agency is too emasculated to provide meaningful penalties.

Regulations and Penalties

Barstow, David, "California Leads Prosecution of Employers in Job Deaths," *The New York Times*, Dec. 23, 2003, p. A1.

California pursues employers' safety violations much more aggressively than other states or the federal government.

Barstow, David, "U.S. Rarely Seeks Charges for Deaths in Workplace," *The New York Times*, Dec. 22, 2003, p. A1.

From 1982 to 2002, OSHA only recommended prosecution for 7 percent of the 1,242 worker deaths that resulted from "willful" safety violations by employers.

Barstow, David, and Lowell Bergman, "Deaths on the Job, Slaps on the Wrist," *The New York Times*, Jan. 10, 2003, p. A1.

McWane, Inc., has amassed a record of safety violations and interfering with investigations, but there has been little action by government prosecutors or safety regulators.

Downey, Kirstin, "More OSHA Scrutiny for Riskiest Work Sites," *The Washington Post*, March 12, 2003, p. E2.

Government safety inspectors plan to ramp up their inspections of repeat offenders, companies whose constant safety violations are evidence of bad faith.

Mulkern, Anne C., "Unions Say Workers Under Siege," *The Denver Post*, Aug. 24, 2003, p. K1.

Labor unions and other critics of the Bush administration claim that it has weakened worker protections in order to satisfy donors who represent business.

Safety in the Age of Terrorism

Cohn, Meredith, "Security Tightens Further at the Office," *The Baltimore Sun*, March 28, 2003, p. 1C.
The Iraq war and the associated terror threats cause Baltimore employers and building owners to emphasize security measures at work.

Downey, Kirstin, "New Occupational Hazards," *The Washington Post*, May 28, 2003, p. E1.
With anthrax in the mail and the increased threat of terrorism, jobs once deemed boring and safe, like postal work, have become potentially deadly.

Downey, Kirstin, and Amy Joyce, "At Work, a War of Nerves," *The Washington Post*, March 23, 2003, p. H1.
Biometric identification systems and emergency intranets prepare Washington workers for the threat of terror attacks in the nation's capital.

Merle, Renae, "For U.S. Contractors, a Reminder," *The Washington Post*, May 14, 2003, p. E1.
American companies in Saudi Arabia and elsewhere in the Middle East must remain conscious of security to keep their workers safe.

Wald, Matthew, "Senators Vote to Permit Pilots to Carry Guns," *The New York Times*, Sept. 6, 2002, p. A1.
The Senate joins the House in voting overwhelmingly to allow airline pilots to carry guns.

Unsafe Workplaces

Armour, Stephanie, "Is Butter Flavoring Ruining Popcorn Workers' Lungs?" *USA Today*, June 20, 2002, p. 1A.
Factory workers say their severe lung ailments and skin diseases are a result of prolonged exposure to the butter flavoring used in microwave popcorn.

Armour, Stephanie, "Is Work Giving You Cancer?" *USA Today*, Feb. 2, 2004, p. 1B.
Fears of cancer in the workplace are sometimes true, sometimes false alarms; but many workers remain suspicious of the results of management investigations.

Burns, Greg, "Lack of Safety Rules Reaping Toll on Farms," *Chicago Tribune*, Oct. 19, 2003, News Section, p. 1.
Farming injuries, particularly tractor rollovers, are common and deadly, but farmers oppose increased government safety regulations.

Grady, William, and Ted Gregory, "Fatalities on Power Lines Draw Scrutiny," *Chicago Tribune*, Nov. 23, 2003, News Section, p. 1.
The relatively frequent death of workers for electrical contractor L.E. Myers attracted the attention of prosecutors.

Harden, Blaine, "Waste Cleanup May Have Human Price," *The Washington Post*, Feb. 26, 2004, p. A1.
Financial incentives may have prompted a doctor to falsify medical records to show that employee injuries at the Hanford Nuclear Reservation were not work-related.

Olsson, Karen, "The Shame of Meatpacking," *The Nation*, Sept. 16, 2002, p. 11.
Speed and sharp knives are a dangerous combination for meatpacking workers.

Shipley, Sara, "Snack Food: Is It Hurting Workers Who Make It?" *St. Louis Post-Dispatch*, April 4, 2004, p. A1.
Diacetyl, an ingredient in butter flavoring used in popcorn and other snack foods, is proven to have caused severe respiratory damage to rats.

Treaster, Joseph, "Cost of Insurance for Work Injuries Soars Across U.S.," *The New York Times*, June 23, 2003, p. A1.
Workers' compensation insurance costs have risen 50 percent in recent years, adding another burden to a lethargic economy.

CITING *THE CQ RESEARCHER*

Sample formats for citing these reports in a bibliography include the ones listed below. Preferred styles and formats vary, so please check with your instructor or professor.

MLA STYLE

Jost, Kenneth. "Rethinking the Death Penalty." The CQ Researcher 16 Nov. 2001: 945-68.

APA STYLE

Jost, K. (2001, November 16). Rethinking the death penalty. *The CQ Researcher, 11*, 945-968.

CHICAGO STYLE

Jost, Kenneth. "Rethinking the Death Penalty." *CQ Researcher*, November 16, 2001, 945-968.

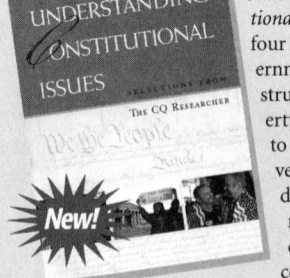

CQ Researcher

Published by CQ Press, a division of Congressional Quarterly Inc.

thecqresearcher.com

Smart Growth

Can managed growth reduce suburban sprawl?

Sprawling suburbs, increasing traffic congestion, strip malls surrounded by acres of parking lots: Are these longstanding features of the modern American landscape only going to get worse? Without a shift in priorities, projected increases in population over the next few decades are expected to accelerate the spread of development away from city and town centers. Critics contend that sprawl eats up valuable open space, worsens air and water pollution and destroys Americans' sense of community. They champion policies that encourage "smart growth" — compact neighborhoods that combine housing, offices, schools and other amenities linked by public transportation and sidewalks. Developers and land-rights advocates call such policies intrusive social engineering and say sprawl is upstoppable — a sign of American prosperity and an efficient market responding to the growing demand for a piece of the American dream.

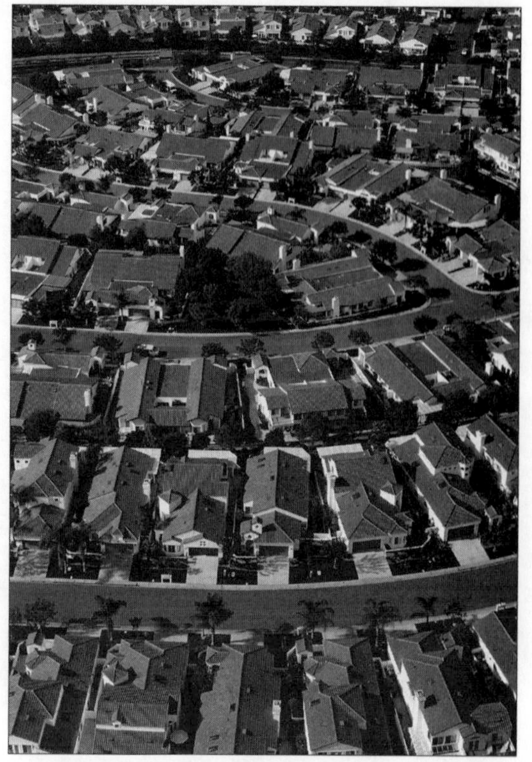

Sprawling suburban developments eat up open space and cause other environmental problems, according to advocates of smart growth.

INSIDE THIS REPORT

The CQ Researcher • May 28, 2004 • www.thecqresearcher.com
Volume 14, Number 20 • Pages 469-492

CQ PRESS

RECIPIENT OF SOCIETY OF PROFESSIONAL JOURNALISTS AWARD FOR EXCELLENCE ◆ AMERICAN BAR ASSOCIATION SILVER GAVEL AWARD

THE ISSUES

BACKGROUND

CURRENT SITUATION

OUTLOOK

SIDEBARS AND GRAPHICS

FOR FURTHER RESEARCH

Cover: Critics say urban sprawl increases traffic and air pollution while devouring open space, but developers say it reflects the popularity of home ownership. (Corbis Images)

THE CQ Researcher

May 28, 2004
Volume 14, Number 20

MANAGING EDITOR: Thomas J. Colin

ASSISTANT MANAGING EDITOR: Kathy Koch

ASSOCIATE EDITOR: Kenneth Jost

STAFF WRITERS: Mary H. Cooper, David Masci, William Triplett

CONTRIBUTING WRITERS: Sarah Glazer, David Hatch, David Hosansky, Patrick Marshall, Tom Price, Jane Tanner

DESIGN/PRODUCTION EDITOR: Olu B. Davis

ASSISTANT EDITOR: Kenneth Lukas

CQ PRESS

A Division of
Congressional Quarterly Inc.

SENIOR VICE PRESIDENT/GENERAL MANAGER: John A. Jenkins

DIRECTOR, LIBRARY PUBLISHING: Kathryn C. Suárez

DIRECTOR, EDITORIAL OPERATIONS: Ann Davies

CONGRESSIONAL QUARTERLY INC.

CHAIRMAN: Paul C. Tash

VICE CHAIRMAN: Andrew P. Corty

PRESIDENT AND PUBLISHER: Robert W. Merry

The CQ Researcher (ISSN 1056-2036) is printed on acid-free paper. Published weekly, except Jan. 2, April 9, July 2, July 9, Aug. 6, Aug. 13, Nov. 26 and Dec. 31, by CQ Press, a division of Congressional Quarterly Inc. Annual subscription rates for institutions start at $625. For pricing, call 1-800-834-9020, ext. 1906. To purchase a *CQ Researcher* report in print or electronic format (PDF), visit www.cqpress.com or call 866-427-7737. A single report is $10. Bulk purchase discounts and electronic-rights licensing are also available. Periodicals postage paid at Washington, D.C., and additional mailing offices. POSTMASTER: Send address changes to *The CQ Researcher*, 1255 22nd St., N.W., Suite 400, Washington, D.C. 20037.

Smart Growth

BY MARY H. COOPER

THE ISSUES

Nestled beside Virginia's Blue Ridge Mountains only 30 miles west of Washington, Loudoun County has long cherished its rolling pastures and dense woodlands.

Today, however, the rooftops of suburban housing developments pepper the bucolic countryside, and the county has emerged as a flashpoint in the acrimonious national debate over policies designed to deal with suburban sprawl.

Indeed, Loudoun was recently "crowned" as America's fastest-growing county. In just over three years, more than 50,000 people moved to Loudoun, boosting the population by more than 30 percent and spurring construction of thousands of new homes. [1]

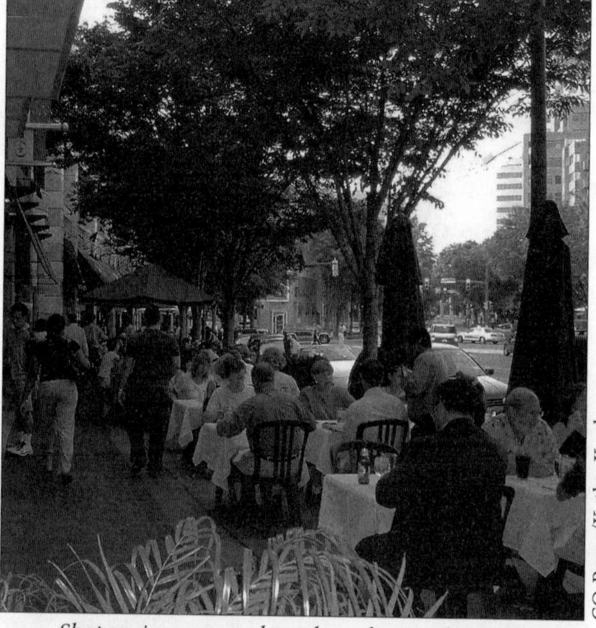

CQ Press/Kathy Koch

Shops, cinemas and outdoor dining share the neighborhood with new high-rise apartment and office buildings in Bethesda, Md. The popular mixed-use "infill" development — an example of the smart-growth trend — is two blocks from a subway stop and a 10-minute train ride from Washington, D.C.

"It is sad to see Loudoun following the lead of [neighboring] Fairfax County in its mass destruction of open space, wetlands and agricultural lands for the sake of development and greed," complained county resident Dennis Desmond. "Each day we see traffic grow, an increase in demand on limited freshwater supplies, and an increase in the pollution of groundwater, streams, ponds and the air." [2]

The county's explosive growth led to controversial, new anti-sprawl, or "smart growth," policies. Alarmed by the pace of development in eastern Loudoun, the county's Board of Supervisors last year set strict new limits on new-home construction in the rural western region, still dominated by dairy farms. The board reduced by 80,000 the number of new homes allowed to be built over the next several years and raised the minimum lot size from three acres per house to 10, 20, and in some areas, 50 acres per house. These restrictions, they hoped, would concentrate growth in the eastern, developed area and protect the remaining open space.

But builders and some property owners complained the policies shut out developers and violated property rights. Farmers said the new rules denied them the right to sell off a few small parcels to pay rising property taxes — thus driving them off their farms.

Last fall, county voters elected a new, pro-development majority to the board, which has since overturned many of the building restrictions, renewing the controversy over Loudoun's future.

"Being No. 1 [in growth] doesn't worry me," says Stephen J. Snow, one of the new county supervisors who led the rollback of building restrictions. "I firmly believe in the American dream. So whatever we can do to help people raise themselves in life through home ownership is a good thing."

Building restrictions, he says, infringe on Americans' right to choose where to live. "People ought to have access to the land," he says. "Take a look at our history, including the Oklahoma land rush, when they gave people land. Why? To create the American dream.

"How can a black or Hispanic family on the rise ever hope to buy 50 acres in Loudoun County?" he asks. "That's only for the wealthy. All we get from these policies is economic segregation. That is just so un-American it's beyond the pale."

With the nation losing 365 acres of open space every hour to developers' bulldozers, it's little wonder that the controversy dividing Loudoun County is echoing in communities across the country. [3] And much of the new growth is occurring in areas that have not had to deal with rapid growth before. While Los Angeles County — the perennial poster child for suburban sprawl — remains the nation's most populated county, rural counties like Loudoun are growing much faster. Indeed, half of the country's 10 fastest-growing counties are in predominantly rural Georgia, as suburban Atlanta development spills onto farmland far from downtown. (*See chart, p. 476.*)

Of course, suburban sprawl has been around for decades. But its environmental and cultural impact is becoming increasingly apparent as development expands farther from urban centers. Besides devouring open space and wildlife habitat, new suburbs degrade the quality of life in other ways, environmentalists say: By spending more time commuting, residents ex-

Many States Are Adopting Smart-Growth Measures

At least 20 states have passed statutes to discourage sprawl and promote smart growth, and many of them are now seeking additional reforms. Fifteen states currently have efforts under way to enact their first anti-sprawl laws.

Status of Smart-Growth Reforms

- Moderate to substantial reforms adopted
- Pursuing additional reforms
- Pursuing first reforms
- Few or no reforms

Source: "Planning for Smart Growth: 2002 State of the States," American Planning Association

acerbate both traffic congestion and air pollution. As runoff-absorbing trees and fields are paved over, stormwater that normally would have been absorbed into the ground ends up in streams, rivers and low-lying areas, often causing flooding or polluting waterways with salt, chemicals and microbes picked up on the way.

Sprawl also has homogenized the American cultural landscape, erasing much of the local character that distinguished a New England village, say, from a Kansas railroad town or a community that grew up around a California mission. Over the course of several decades, local ordinances separating residential from commercial and industrial areas have produced a seemingly endless patchwork of isolated bedroom communities where residents must drive in order to reach shops, schools and other destinations. Miles of strip malls filled with national chain stores flank major roadways, producing little to differentiate one community from another.

Some critics have even demonized sprawl as the source of contemporary ills ranging from homicidal alienation to obesity. (*See sidebar, p. 474.*) The movie "Bowling for Columbine," for instance, largely blamed the 1999 massacre by two teenagers at Columbine High School in suburban Littleton, Colo., on alienation caused in part by their community's sprawling development. In a similar vein, author James Howard Kunstler calls the suburbs "a vast and evil setting," complaining of "the whole destructive, wasteful, toxic, agoraphobia-inducing spectacle that politicians proudly call 'growth.' "[4]

But while environmentalists, historic preservationists and other critics decry sprawl as dehumanizing, developers and property-rights advocates like Snow see sprawl as evidence that the American free-enterprise system works, creating wealth and well-being and allowing people to live where they choose. "For me, growth is neither good nor bad," says Samuel R. Staley, president of the Buckeye Institute for Public Policy Solutions in Columbus, Ohio. "As long as what we're doing is trying to accommodate the housing needs and preferences of people, I'm pretty happy with it." (*See "At Issue," p. 485.*)

Like sprawl itself, smart growth means different things to different people. "To paraphrase the old Supreme Court observation, smart growth is like pornography — there's no uniform definition; you just know it when you see it," says Clayton Traylor, senior vice president for state and local political affairs at the National Association of Home Builders. "The homebuilding industry supports smart growth to the extent that we think better planning at the local level is needed. Good, comprehensive planning is smart, in and of itself, regardless of the pattern of development you're trying to achieve."

Some states, notably Oregon, have taken a stronger stand against sprawl, requiring all towns and cities to establish "urban growth boundaries" barring further development. And a growing number of local and even state governments are looking for ways to improve land-use planning by concentrating new construction in already-developed areas along transit corridors. A pioneer in this approach, known as "infilling," is former Democratic Gov. Parris Glendening of Maryland, who spearheaded Maryland's 1997 Smart Growth and Neighborhood Conservation Act. It required the state to deny or limit subsidies for new roads, sewers and schools outside state-identified "smart-growth" areas.

Infilling in older neighborhoods can help residents avoid driving to work and create people-friendly shopping, dining and entertainment meccas, replete with sidewalk-café ambiance. But infilling has its downsides. Some longtime residents complain that the high-rises dramatically alter a neighborhood's quality of life. And the new commercial areas can become victims of their own popularity if the resultant crowds, traffic congestion and parking problems end up producing more hassle than enjoyment.

Besides government-sponsored managed-growth initiatives, several architects and builders are combating sprawl on their own by creating so-called New Urbanist communities from scratch. They range from free-standing towns like Seaside, Fla., and suburban enclaves like Kentlands, Md., to infill neighborhoods carved out of abandoned urban parcels. They aim to reduce the need for cars and increase social interaction by mixing housing, retail and public construction in walkable communities, many with public transit. Design guidelines bring buildings close to streets and sidewalks, place some housing above stores and move parking lots behind buildings.

"New Urbanism is the design part of the overall smart-growth movement," says Glendening, who now heads the Smart Growth Leadership Institute, a Washington, D.C.-based nonprofit. "The two efforts go hand in hand."

As the controversy in Loudoun County shows, population-driven development is fueling the debate about land-use policies — a debate that seems likely to intensify. As state and local governments examine ways to manage growth, these are some of the questions they are asking:

U.S. Cities With Worst Sprawl

Smart-growth advocates say Riverside, Calif., has the nation's worst sprawl. Two-thirds of Riverside's residents live more than 10 miles from a central business district, and fewer than 1 percent live in areas with enough population to support mass transit. Nearly all of the other most-sprawling cities are in the South or West.

The 10 Most-Sprawling Metropolitan Regions

Metropolitan Region	Rank
Riverside-San Bernardino, Calif.	1
Greensboro-Winston-Salem-High Point, N.C.	2
Raleigh-Durham, N.C.	3
Atlanta, Ga.	4
Greenville-Spartanburg, S.C.	5
West Palm Beach-Boca Raton-Delray Beach, Fla.	6
Bridgeport-Stamford-Norwalk-Danbury, Conn.	7
Knoxville, Tenn.	8
Oxnard-Ventura, Calif.	9
Fort Worth-Arlington, Texas	10

Source: "Measuring Sprawl and its Impact," Smart Growth America, *Oct. 17, 2002*

Sprawl and Obesity Go Hand in Hand

Suburban development has long been criticized for consuming open space and exacerbating air pollution caused by traffic congestion. Now health experts are blaming sprawl for the twin American health ills — obesity and heart disease.

For years, public-health officials have warned of a rising epidemic of obesity in the United States. By 2000, 64 percent of adults in the United States were either overweight or obese, according to the Centers for Disease Control and Prevention (CDC). Both conditions are implicated in the rising incidence of heart disease, adult-onset diabetes and certain cancers. [1]

The trend is especially noticeable among children. Since the 1960s, the incidence of overweight and obesity among American children and adolescents has more than tripled, to about 15 percent. Obesity in children is especially alarming, experts say, because obese children are more likely to become obese adults, when the health consequences of overweight most often arise. [2]

Although overeating and poor diet, including the consumption of fatty junk food and high-calorie sodas, are the primary causes of overweight, the lack of physical exercise is another crucial factor, experts say. More than half of American adults fail to meet the surgeon general's recommendation for 30 minutes of moderate physical activity five days a week. More than a quarter don't get any exercise at all, the CDC reports. [3]

Experts say Americans' love affair with the automobile, encouraged by postwar suburban development, has contributed to the current obesity epidemic. A recent study found that counties with suburban sprawl have higher incidences of obesity and associated chronic illnesses, such as heart disease, than urban or rural counties. [4] By isolating residential areas from other parts of communities, sprawl forces people to drive to stores, schools and work. Even when destinations aren't too far away to reach by walking or bicycle, the lack of sidewalks along noisy, barren roadways usually discourages suburbanites from leaving their cars at home.

Americans' sedentary lifestyle is costing states and businesses billions of dollars in higher health-care premiums, lost productivity and increased workers' compensation payments, according to the National Governors Association. In Michigan, for example, 55 percent of adults are inactive, resulting in diseases that cost the state nearly $9 billion a year. [5]

To address the problem, in 2002 the association helped launch the Active Living Leadership initiative to help state and local governments advance more active lifestyles through zoning-law changes that encourage smart-growth — high-density, mixed-use communities with walkable streets, bike paths and public transit services. Thus far, the initiative has focused primarily on California, Colorado, Kentucky, Michigan and Washington.

Colorado boasts the lowest obesity rate in the country (17 percent of adults), but the state also has experienced the fastest increase in obesity over the past decade, prompting officials to look for ways to counter the trend by fighting sprawl. [6] For example, a 4,700-acre community being developed on the site of the old Stapleton Airport near Denver entices residents out of

Do smart-growth policies contain sprawl?

Oregon's 30-year-old law requiring urban-growth boundaries around cities and towns is the nation's most far-reaching effort to contain sprawl — making it a bellwether for both advocates and opponents of smart-growth policies.

To supporters, the growth boundary around Portland has largely succeeded in fostering the kind of development its authors had intended — smaller houses with smaller yards, mixed-use neighborhoods, a well-utilized transit and bike-lane system, a thriving downtown — while preserving open space outside the city.

Critics acknowledge that the policy has curbed outward growth, but they contend the policy is an excessive intrusion into the free market that denies residents the right to live in traditional suburbs. The American Dream Coalition, a property-rights group in Bandon, Ore., recently hosted a national conference in Portland to demonstrate what coalition leader Randal O'Toole sees as the downsides of smart growth: High-density living and congestion caused by government overreach. "I don't see it as a livable place to live," he said. "Our message is, 'Don't emulate Portland.' " [5]

But supporters of Portland's effort to counter sprawl say the policy is no more intrusive than zoning rules that established minimum lot sizes and separated residential neighborhoods from commercial and retail areas — rules that have spurred suburban sprawl since the late 1940s. "The 'Ozzie and Harriet' version of the American dream was not the result of invisible forces of the market," Rep. Earl Blumenauer, D-Ore., whose district includes Portland, told conferees. "[It] was the result of massive government engineering." [6]

Most other states with growth-management policies have used incentives and other less-stringent tools to focus new construction in and around already-developed areas. Maryland's smart-growth policies, for example, include a mix of tax incentives, siting of schools and other public buildings in developed areas and regulations that discourage construction in rural areas.

"We decided not to manage growth through regulation, but rather with a series of incentives and disincentives," Glendening says. "By doing that, we changed the bottom line. We wanted their cars by incorporating walking and biking trails and public transit, built around a network of linked neighborhoods, each with retail and commercial sites within walking distance of schools and other amenities.

Simply changing land-use ordinances may go a long way toward improving Americans' health. For example, ordinances and school-board guidelines commonly discourage renovation of older, close-in schools and require that new schools be built on large sites, often 10 acres or more. As a result, schools are being shifted from established neighborhoods to the far edges of suburbia, too far for most pupils to walk or ride their bikes. [7]

But some experts say the link between suburban development and obesity is less clear than the studies suggest. "Many nutritionists would argue that diet is much more important than exercise in reaching and maintaining a healthy weight," says Samuel R. Staley, president of the Buckeye Institute, a Columbus, Ohio, organization that opposes strong government control over development. "If you're going to McDonald's every day, you probably aren't going to shave off those extra pounds, no matter where you live."

In any case, Staley says, it's not the government's role to determine where people should live. "People should be allowed to make choices, even if they're poor choices," he says. "In this country you're allowed to be fat."

AFP Photo/Robyn Beck

Americans' love affair with the automobile, encouraged by postwar suburban sprawl, has contributed to the obesity epidemic.

[1] Centers for Disease Control and Prevention (CDC), "National Health and Nutrition Examination Survey, 1999-2000." For background, see Alan Greenblatt, "Obesity Epidemic," *The CQ Researcher*, Jan. 31, 2003, pp. 73-104.

[2] American Heart Association, "Obesity and Overweight in Children," www.americanheart.org.

[3] CDC, "The Importance of Physical Activity," March 31, 2004, www.cdc.gov.

[4] Barbara A. McCann and Reid Ewing, "Measuring the Health Effects of Sprawl: A National Analysis of Physical Activity, Obesity and Chronic Disease," Smart Growth America and Surface Transportation Policy Project, September 2003.

[5] National Governors Association, "Story Idea: Smart Growth = Less Obesity?" March 15, 2004, www.nga.org.

[6] See Kirk Johnson, "Colorado Takes Strides to Polish Thin and Fit Image," *The New York Times*, Feb. 1, 2004, p. A12.

[7] See Constance E. Beaumont and Elizabeth G. Pianca, "Why Johnny Can't Walk to School: Historic Neighborhood Schools in the Age of Sprawl," National Trust for Historic Preservation, October 2002.

investors, builders and homebuyers to realize that they would get a better deal by purchasing in a smart-growth community."

Maryland's approach has had mixed results. A number of urban, infill projects in long-abandoned industrial areas of Baltimore have drawn new residents and retail centers, increasing the tax base and creating jobs in previously impoverished neighborhoods. Glendening cites the American Can factory, once on the Environmental Protection Agency's (EPA) list of polluted industrial "brownfields." * "The site had been run-down, caught fire a number of times and was inhabited by vagrants and drug addicts," he says. With state assistance in cleaning up the site, a private developer built a mixed industrial and retail complex, creating more than 700 high-tech and retail jobs. "The whole neighborhood around the factory has taken off, and it now has the highest increase in assessed value for anyplace in Baltimore City."

But the smart-growth initiatives like Maryland's have been less successful in reducing traffic congestion — one of the main goals of the movement. This is particularly true when local efforts to preserve open space, such as Loudoun County's recently abandoned policies, are not coordinated with neighboring jurisdictions.

"If you prevent the development of land in part of a county in a fast-growing region like the Washington metropolitan area, you force the growth to move out even farther"— beyond the no-growth areas, says Anthony Downs, an expert on urban affairs at the Brookings Institution, a Washington think tank. People who move into new developments beyond the no-growth area must then drive even farther to reach their jobs, adding to air pollution. "So this kind of zoning really doesn't necessarily reduce traffic congestion; it just changes the character of the congestion. [Development just] arises farther out, and commuters are just driving

* A brownfield is a former industrial property whose reuse is limited to non-residential development because it contains a hazardous substance, pollutant or contaminant. The Environmental Protection Agency estimates that there are more than 400,000 brownfields in the United States. See www.epa.gov/brownfields; see also Mary H. Cooper "Environmental Justice," June 19, 1998, pp. 529-552.

Sun Belt Is Burgeoning

Five of America's fastest-growing counties are in Georgia — primarily suburban Atlanta — with the others mostly in suburban communities in Sun Belt states.

Fastest-Growing U.S. Counties
(Percent change, 2000-2003)

County	Nearest Major City	Population Change
Loudoun, Va.	Washington, D.C.	30.7%
Chattahoochee, Ga.	Columbus	29.9
Douglas, Colo.	Denver	27.1
Rockwall, Texas	Dallas	26.8
Forsyth, Ga.	Atlanta	25.8
Henry, Ga.	Atlanta	25.7
Flagler, Fla.	Daytona Beach	24.8
Newton, Ga.	Atlanta	22.8
Paulding, Ga.	Atlanta	22.7
Kendall, Ill.	Chicago	22.0

Source: U.S. Census Bureau, "Population Estimates," April 1, 2000 to July 1, 2003

through the areas being preserved from new development."

Likewise, urban-infill developments that come with smart growth can go too far or have unintended consequences. Many longtime residents of close-in suburban neighborhoods worry that development can reach a tipping point, overwhelming the qualities that drew them to those areas in the first place.

"The towering buildings that are going up now are a bit frightening," says Ellen Showell, a 30-year resident of Arlington County's bustling Rosslyn-Ballston corridor, along the subway line outside Washington, D.C. "Also, I don't like seeing all the streets parked up. Where we used to have one or two cars parked outside our house, we now have a real city parking situation. Even though they've attempted to make this a pedestrian-friendly area, our society is still dependent on cars, and more people have brought more cars."

Showell and her husband supported Arlington's development plans through their local civic association and still embrace many of the changes the county government and developers have introduced. "They've really tried their best to keep a certain urban village feel to the neighborhood," she says. "We always loved the neighborhood's low-key lifestyle and getting to know the independent business owners over the years. We hope this won't be totally lost."

Many experts caution that it's too soon to judge the effectiveness of most smart-growth initiatives. "There is no one model or tool that is going to solve the problem of sprawl," says Glendening. "No one should expect that you can put in place anything that is reasonably acceptable politically that would instantaneously reverse current growth trends.

"We as a nation have worked hard for the last 60 years to get to the position where we are now," he continues, "and it's going to take at least a decade or two to start seeing any significant reversal of sprawl."

Does managed growth reduce the supply of affordable housing?

By calling for a mix of apartments, condominiums, town houses and single-family homes in most new developments, smart-growth and New Urbanist designs attempt to end the longstanding economic segregation of neighborhoods between wealthy suburbs and poor downtowns. But that goal often proves elusive.

Arlington County launched an ambitious managed-growth policy three decades ago, when it decided to site its main segment of Metro, the region's new subway system, along a decaying thoroughfare and focus new development along that corridor. In order to preserve the single-family suburban neighborhoods that lay close to the proposed development area, county planners designated areas within a quarter-mile of each of the five Metro stations for high-rise office, apartment and condominium buildings. Outside those areas, density and building height were reduced, providing a transition to the single-family neighborhoods.

Arlington's gamble paid off; today the Rosslyn-Ballston Corridor, named for the Metro stations at either end of the county, is a bustling community whose eclectic mix of housing, shops, restaurants and county offices won it the EPA's National Award for Overall Excellence in Smart Growth in 2002. [7]

"Arlington's elected officials had the vision 30 years ago to use the Metro system to plan for the revitalization of an aging commercial corridor that was losing out to the new malls" being built in the outer suburbs, says Thomas H. Miller, coordinator of Arlington's planning commission. "The development occurred in a very linear fashion, so the single-family neighborhoods right on the periphery have really stayed intact."

Arlington's smart-growth success story has come at a cost, however. Small Sears bungalows built for a few thousand dollars in the 1920s and '30s now fetch close to $1 million. Even two-bedroom condos are going for $400,000, and affordable housing is scarce.

"Affordability is absolutely the biggest challenge we face," Miller concedes. "The people moving here now have the luxury of owning their automobile and living near Metro. The challenge is to get more affordable units and make sure that the people who need transit the most are actually able to live near transit." The county board is now considering a proposal to require developers to include more affordable units in residential projects along the corridor.

Moreover, so-called "greenfield" communities being built from the ground up in undeveloped areas also frequently fall short of expectations for affordable housing. New towns such as Mountain House, built on an open tract about 60 miles east of pricey, downtown San Francisco, are designed to offer housing for a broad range of income levels. But high demand for housing in the new community has driven prices beyond the reach of most moderate-income buyers. [8]

Some smart-growth critics say land-use regulations that focus development in certain areas and bar it in others inevitably drive up the cost of housing, to the disadvantage of less-affluent Americans. "Downzoning [reducing the number of houses allowed on a given tract of land] only creates more disparity in economic well-being," says Loudoun County's Snow. Most would-be buyers in western Loudoun were disadvantaged under the discontinued smart-growth rules because only the wealthy could afford single-family houses on the huge lots.

But sellers also lost out, in his view. "For many farmers their land is their 401(k) or pension," Snow says. When the county barred those farmers from selling small, single-family parcels — which would fetch more money per acre than the large, single-family parcels mandated under the smart-growth rules — they were deprived of their retirement income. "Under downzoning, a farmer's land that was worth $2 million suddenly fell in value to $700,000. That's a $1.3 million hit in the name of smart growth."

But simply overturning smart-growth rules and relying on market forces to direct development seems unlikely to reverse the lack of adequate affordable housing in wealthy suburban jurisdictions. According to a recent study of the Washington metropolitan area, the wealthiest suburban counties have the fewest affordable housing units. [9] And less-affluent residents are being driven out of housing markets across the country in other fast-growing areas.

"Many young workers cannot stay here," said former Secretary of Housing and Urban Development Henry Cisneros, calling for government intervention to increase the availability of affordable housing in the Los Angeles suburbs. "And those that can't leave are living in overcrowded, declining neighborhoods."

Without such intervention, he said, it will always be more profitable for developers to build higher-priced, single-family houses. "All the factors are against affordability." [10]

Corbis Images

The nation loses 365 acres of open space every hour to developers' bulldozers, much of that growth in areas that have never had to deal with rapid growth before.

Are Americans wedded to suburban life?

The pull of the suburbs has been strong for upwardly mobile Americans since the streetcar and, later, the automobile enabled them to escape the grime, noise and crime of industrial downtowns. A suburban house with a yard is still what comes to mind as the American dream.

"Our polls show that the ideal housing solution is a four-bedroom, two-and-a-half-bath, single-family house with a garage," says Traylor of the National Association of Home Builders. "That's still what 75 percent or more of the people who are purchasing houses say they want."

The past few years of economic turmoil and job loss may have tempered those aspirations somewhat, at least temporarily. "With affordability issues, some buyers are having to make do with something less than that ideal solution, and town houses tend to be the default substitute," Traylor adds.

But the latest census data suggest that the traditional suburban house continues to be the preferred long-term housing goal for many Americans. "The fastest-growing counties are on the periphery of metropolitan areas, such as Atlanta, Washington, D.C., and Dallas," says William Frey, an urban-migration expert at the University of Michigan. "My guess is that there's a continuing desire to live within a major metropolitan area but without having to put up with all the hustle and hassle of living near the center of town, with its congestion and high housing costs."

Indeed, the rising cost of housing and worsening traffic congestion in cities and the close-in suburbs is contributing to the continued allure of the far suburbs, or exurbs. "The price of housing declines by at least 1.5 percent per mile as you move away from the center of a metropolitan area," says Downs at Brookings.

Meanwhile, many jobs are moving to small cities on the fringes of suburbs known as "edge cities," exempting some suburban residents from having to commute all the way into downtown. "The average distance people drive as their housing gets farther and farther from the center does rise," Downs says, "but it doesn't rise as much as their distance from the center."

Apart from such calculations, some property-rights advocates and critics of smart-growth policies say efforts to build more compact communities are doomed to failure because Americans will always prefer the bigger houses and yards that only the suburbs and rural developments can offer.

"Smart growth is the antithesis of the American dream," says Loudoun County's Snow, who sees conspiracy afoot in efforts to contain sprawl. "They're trying to get transit-oriented development and other things that actually deny people real homes," he says. "They want them to move into condos and apartments and ride bicycles. That's fine for [Beijing] and the rest of the communist bloc, but we should be about putting people into houses."

Most developers stop short of such sweeping condemnation of efforts to manage growth. Indeed, many in the building industry see promise in the kind of development that smart-growth planners and New Urbanist designers are promoting. Even the home-builders' association now has a department that deals specifically with smart-growth issues. "We feel it's important to satisfy all housing desires," says Blake Smith, the department's spokesman. "Whether it's the higher-density urban lifestyle or the larger home on a larger lot, people should have a choice of where they live, and the homebuilders believe we need to be satisfying that demand."

In fact, areas where smart-growth policies have been on the books long enough to produce alternative patterns of development, such as Portland and Arlington, tend to be such hot real-estate markets that supporters see a more profound shift in consumer tastes away from the suburbs. What critics see as a failure to provide adequate low-cost housing, smart-growth advocates see as evidence that people are clamoring for more residential density, not less.

"What higher housing prices in smart-growth communities are really telling us is that this is where people want to live," says former Maryland Gov. Glendening. "We say, let people go ahead and choose to live where they want. If someone wants to live in what I consider to be a rather sterile subdivision of two-acre lots where you have to drive to get a quart of milk, let them go ahead and do it. But let's make sure that there are also choices for those people who would prefer to live in an area with a real sense of community, where they can walk down to the corner to get that quart of milk and hop on mass transit to get directly to work."

The retiring Baby Boomers are the wild card in the debate about whether Americans can be pried from their suburbs. City planners hope that retiring "empty nesters" from the huge Boomer generation will decide they no longer need the big yards and wide open spaces of the suburbs, and will begin migrating back into the cities, perhaps into smart-growth enclaves close to commuter lines. (*See "Outlook," p. 487.*) ■

BACKGROUND

Early American Cities

Until the Industrial Revolution, the world's cities and towns typically arose on the banks of rivers, lakes and harbors or along major overland trade routes. [11] Often fortified against enemy attacks, they tended to be compact, densely populated and oriented toward the center, where a cathedral or government building provided an anchoring focal point for civic life.

American cities followed a slightly different model, based on British urban patterns. Protected by the English Channel from attack, London and other British cities began branching outward as early as the 16th century, as wealthy residents built rural estates to escape the crowding, filth and noise of urban life. Colonial cities, such as New York, Boston and Baltimore, also arose beside rivers and harbors that offered dockage for trading ships. Inland communities, such as St. Louis and Richmond, typically arose at the confluence of two rivers or at the "fall lines" of rivers — the point where riverboat traffic gave way to overland transportation. Like their English counterparts, wealthier Americans pushed urban boundaries outward, building fashionable neighborhoods, such as Boston's Beacon Hill, linked to the city center by a "mansion" street flanked by churches, clubs and libraries.

Continued on p. 480

Chronology

1940s-1960s
Suburban development becomes firmly established, spurred by federal policies.

1947
William Levitt sets the pattern for postwar suburban development with his legendary Long Island subdivision, Levittown. With its curved streets, small yards and garages, Levittown becomes a homogeneous residential enclave of middle-class families with children, whose residents depend almost entirely on their cars for transportation.

1956
The federally funded Interstate Highway System begins to take shape, eventually creating a 45,000-mile superhighway network that helps fuel suburban development.

1964
Developer Robert E. Simon builds Reston, on Virginia farmland outside Washington, D.C., as a free-standing new town with shops close to houses so residents won't need to drive to shop and socialize.

1970s-1990s
Some state and local governments try to limit suburban sprawl.

1973
Oregon requires local governments to develop land-use and zoning plans to curb sprawl.

1979
Portland, Ore., adopts an "urban-growth boundary," beyond which most new development is barred.

1981
Miami architects Andres Duany and Elizabeth Plater-Zyberk design Seaside, Fla., as a free-standing, pedestrian-friendly new town that will become a model for New Urbanist designers.

1990
Washington requires fast-growing communities to develop growth-management plans.

1993
The nonprofit Congress for the New Urbanism is founded to promote high-density, mixed-use development along transit lines as an alternative to expanding suburban development.

1995
Minnesota passes the Livable Communities Act, which underwrites development of lightly contaminated "brownfield" sites to encourage retail and commercial use of already-developed areas.

1996
The Environmental Protection Agency (EPA) creates the Smart Growth Network — a partnership of more than 30 government, business and civic organizations — to share information on best practices for development.

1997
Congress approves $500,000 capital-gains tax exemption for a couple on profits from the sale of primary residences, which smart-growth advocates say will induce suburban dwellers to move to less-expensive, close-in housing. Maryland's Smart Growth and Neighborhood Conservation Act requires the state to deny or limit subsidies for new roads, sewers and schools outside state-identified "smart-growth" areas.

1998
President Bill Clinton signs the $217.9 billion Transportation Equity Act that boosts spending for both highways and mass transit systems. Oregon voters overturn an initiative to repeal Portland's urban-growth boundary.

January 1999
Vice President Al Gore identifies sprawl as a major environmental threat.

2000s
Population-growth pressures challenge anti-sprawl efforts.

2000
The Centers for Disease Control and Prevention says 64 percent of Americans are obese and blames the epidemic, in part, on the lack of exercise due to an overreliance on automobiles. The Transportation Department reports that new-road construction has not kept up with the growing demand for roads accompanying suburban development.

2002
The National Governors Association helps launch the Active Living Leadership initiative to promote state and local zoning changes that favor walking, biking and transit over development that relies solely on cars for personal transportation.

2004
The U.S. Census Bureau projects that the number of people living in the United States will exceed 419 million — an additional 126 million people — by 2050.

Teardowns: The Dark Side of Smart Growth?

During the urban-renewal heyday of the 1960s-'70s, city governments routinely demolished abandoned inner-city houses, factories and stores and put up high-rise housing projects and office buildings, hoping to restore social and economic vitality to decaying downtowns.

But urban renewal produced mixed results: Many low-cost and public housing projects, often built in areas that no longer offered job opportunities, soon deteriorated into crime- and drug-ridden slums.

Today, a new wave of demolition and reconstruction is occurring in the nation's wealthier, close-in suburbs — and it is no less controversial. Dubbed by critics as the "teardown tsunami," the trend is rapidly transforming many longstanding neighborhoods, as older houses and mature trees are being replaced with large, multistoried houses that often bump up against property lines, dwarfing neighboring houses, blocking out sunlight, obstructing views and diminishing neighbors' privacy.

Moreover, what some call the "McMansionization" of old neighborhoods can "radically change the fabric of a community," said Richard Moe, president of the National Trust for Historic Preservation. "From 19th-century Victorians to 1920s bungalows, the architecture of America's historic neighborhoods reflects the character of our communities. Without proper safeguards, historic neighborhoods will lose the identities that drew residents to put down roots in the first place." [1]

Ironically, teardowns are largely a reaction to suburban sprawl and a consequence of the very smart-growth policies devised to curb it. Ever-increasing commuting distances, traffic jams and road rage are prompting many residents from the far suburbs, or "exurbs," to move closer to town, and the stock-market boom of the 1990s enabled many middle- and upper-income Americans to do just that.

But instead of trading their spacious suburban dwellings for smaller, older houses in the inner suburbs, these new urban immigrants demand the best of both worlds — large houses close to downtown amenities. Many are willing to pay top dollar for a large house, even if it is one of several squeezed onto a traditional quarter-acre lot. Indeed, the smaller yard, with its limited maintenance requirements, is especially appealing to exurban refugees tired of extensive lawn care.

Consumer demand and economics are driving the teardown trend. Historically, construction enhanced the value of land. Since the late 1990s, however, vacant land in the downtown and inner suburban neighborhoods has become increasingly scarce. As demand for real estate in these areas grew, land became more valuable than the structure on it.

Higher land values, in turn, make it harder for builders to turn a handsome profit by replacing a smaller teardown with just a same-size structure. According to the "Rule of Three," developers typically aim to sell new construction for three times what they paid for the property. [2] In order to maintain traditional profit margins, developers end up building two, three or more large houses — or a single McMansion — on a lot that once accommodated a single, small dwelling.

Similar financial incentives motivate local governments to tolerate and even encourage teardowns. Recent federal income-tax cuts have reduced the flow of revenues to states and localities, which are left to rely more heavily on alternative revenue streams — such as property taxes — to fund libraries, police departments and other vital services. A housing lot that once produced revenues from a single dwelling can generate much more if it ac-

Continued from p. 478

The Industrial Revolution and the growth of the railroad system in the late 19th century accelerated the outward development of American cities. Mills and factories arose along major transportation routes — roads, railroads and rivers, which also provided water power to fuel industrial production. Worker shantytowns that arose around exurban factories evolved into small communities separate from the nearby cities, such as Camden, N.J., across the Delaware River from Philadelphia.

Innovations in transportation continued to influence patterns of urban development. As railroads accelerated the westward migration of people and the creation of new towns and cities in the Midwest and West, local transit systems facilitated the outward migration of city residents. By the early 20th century, while blue-collar workers continued to live within walking distance of their factory jobs, streetcars enabled the growing ranks of middle-class workers to live farther from their downtown offices. Wealthier families moved even farther out to "railroad suburbs," such as Philadelphia's Main Line communities.

This pattern, repeated in cities across the country, established a model for U.S. urban development that would persist for the next half-century — a vibrant downtown commercial district flanked by industrial areas, with residential neighborhoods both in town and extending along train and streetcar lines.

Cars Drive Development

With the advent of the automobile, transportation played an even greater role in shaping American communities. Henry Ford began mass-producing cars in the early 20th century, but it was not until the post-World War II economic boom that car ownership came within the grasp of millions of Americans. The car, more than commodates two or more units, all the more if they are large, opulent houses.

Teardowns are a mixed bag for nearby neighbors. The first teardown in a neighborhood may be welcomed as a signal that local real estate values — the main source of many homeowners' net worth — are rapidly rising. Homeowners already contemplating a move may quickly put their houses on the market to collect the windfall.

Developers who specialize in razing older houses tout the benefits to house sellers in marketing their properties as teardowns. "Until a few years ago, 'teardown' was practically a bad word," said Michael Barofsky, an Illinois Realtor who specializes in selling teardown houses. "Now it's come out of the closet and is almost desirable." [3]

Barofsky said convenience is luring more and more property owners to overcome their reluctance to abandon their homes to the bulldozer. Teardowns eliminate the need for lock boxes, open houses, home inspections, cleanup, costly repairs and the other hassles typical of house sales. Some sellers even leave behind their unwanted furniture, old papers or even groceries. "The builder doesn't care," Barofsky said, "because he wrecks it anyway."

CQ Press/Mary H. Cooper

Huge, multistoried houses that replace smaller, older houses often dwarf neighboring structures, block sunlight, obstruct views and diminish neighbors' privacy.

But not all neighbors welcome the change. Many long-term residents have set down permanent roots in their neighborhoods, leading them to feel entitled to a greater say in the community's appearance and character than a recent buyer — especially a developer interested purely in a money-making operation.

Some residents of older neighborhoods are beginning to take steps to slow or halt the pace of teardowns, aided by guidelines published by the National Trust to help communities and neighborhoods gain some control over local development. Although the Trust acknowledges the benefits of smart growth and channeling new development into already developed areas, it counsels communities to make sure new investment "respects the character and distinctiveness that made these neighborhoods so desirable in the first place." [4]

[1] Quoted in National Trust for Historic Preservation, "Teardowns: Historic Neighborhoods, Nationwide," www.nationaltrust.org.

[2] See Patrick T. Reardon and Blair Kamin, "Paths of Destruction," *Chicago Tribune*, April 24, 2003, p. 1.

[3] Quoted in Rebecca R. Kahlenberg, "Is Your House a 'Teardown' Candidate?" *The Washington Post*, Oct. 25, 2003, p. F1.

[4] National Trust, *op. cit.*

any industrial innovation, was to break the traditional boundaries that had contained urban development, making way for the rise of the suburbs.

Federal policies in the 1950s and '60s facilitated the exodus from the cities. Home ownership became a key goal of federal incentives, particularily the home-mortgage income-tax deduction. Federally subsidized home-mortgage loans enabled returning GIs and other homebuyers of limited means to buy houses. But the loans often were restricted to houses in neighborhoods where housing values were considered safe from devaluation linked to poverty and crime. This restriction fostered the racial segregation of American communities and accentuated a widening divide between poor, minority, downtown neighborhoods and middle-class, white enclaves in the new suburban developments.

"It's a sad but true fact of our history that entire neighborhoods with any significant African-American population were redlined and excluded from eligibility for the home-loan guarantee," says Glendening of the Smart Growth Leadership Institute. "As a result, the federal loan programs were not only about helping people buy homes; they were almost forcing them to buy homes out there as opposed to the urban areas that had black populations."

The Interstate Highway System also fueled suburban development. Launched in 1956, it created a 45,000-mile network of federally financed superhighways. [12] Originally envisioned to speed long-distance passenger and freight traffic, Interstate highways became major commuter arteries as well, enabling downtown workers to move beyond the older, "inner" suburbs to new developments miles from downtown. Because land values generally drop as one moves away from downtown, prospective homebuyers could afford more land and bigger houses in these new suburbs. And the four-lane Interstates made the tradeoff in commuting distances less onerous.

Struever Bros. Eccles and Rouse (Both)

Urban Transformation

Transformation of Baltimore's abandoned American Can Co. factory (top) into a vibrant retail and office center (bottom) exemplifies the urban "infill" development advocated by historic preservationists and other smart-growth proponents.

The design of postwar suburbs generally followed a pattern set by such developers as William Levitt. Levittown, the legendary Long Island subdivision he built beginning in the late 1940s, comprised more than 17,000 small, almost identical, inexpensive houses. With its curved streets and cul-de-sacs, small yards and garages, Levittown became a homogeneous middle-class enclave whose residents depended almost entirely on their cars for transportation.

Today, worsening urban traffic congestion is a major impetus to smart-growth programs across the country. As suburbs continue to spread farther from downtown jobs, commuters spend more and more time stuck in traffic jams. The migration of businesses from downtown to suburban locations has had mixed effects on traffic congestion: While it has eased pressure on roadways leading to and from city centers, it has also made it more difficult for workers to use public transportation.

As commuter traffic disperses in many different directions, mass transit lags behind in meeting commuters' changing needs, so more workers drive to work. As a result, even metropolitan areas with extensive bus and subway service, such as Washington, D.C., continue to suffer from jammed roadways. And because its acclaimed Metro system cannot keep up with the region's rapidly expanding suburban commercial development, the Washington region ranks just behind Los Angeles as the country's most congested metropolitan area. [13]

Moreover, new road construction has not kept up with suburban development. According to the Transportation Department, from 1980 to 2000 the number of vehicle miles traveled in the United States grew by 44 percent, while the total road space grew by less than 2 percent. [14]

Anti-Sprawl Measures

Unlike older cities, which evolve over many years and include a mix of residential, industrial and commercial activities, the American suburbs have been shaped from the beginning by a desire to separate residential areas from commercial and industrial projects. Zoning ordinances created and enforced by local city and county governments have produced bedroom communities separated from industrial parks and commercial strip malls.

As the suburban boom continued in the 1960s-'80s, a few visionaries decided that zoning regulations alone were too blunt a tool to create attractive suburban communities. One of the first was Robert E. Simon, who in 1964 created Reston, a new Virginia town in what at the time was beyond the western suburban perimeter of Washington. Simon envisioned shops so close to houses that residents would not need to drive to shop and socialize. Although the suburbs have long since surrounded Reston, Simon's vision proved to be a success, and residents recently celebrated the town's 40th anniversary as an island of innovative development in one of the country's most congested metropolitan areas. [15]

Frustrated by failed efforts to contain sprawl, some state and local governments adopted stronger measures. In 1973, for instance, Oregon required all local governments to develop land-use and zoning plans to curb sprawl. Although opponents complained the measure violated property-owners' rights and reduced consumers' residential options, Oregon voters rejected efforts to repeal the law. In 1979, the Portland metropolitan area established an "urban-growth boundary" as well as a new regional government, Metro, to enforce the boundary.

In 1995, Minnesota passed the Livable Communities Act, which aimed to underwrite the development of brownfield sites, integrate affordable housing into new developments and develop mixed-use communities. The EPA granted its 2003 smart-growth achievement award to the Minneapolis-St. Paul metropolitan council, which used state funds provided by the Livable Communities Act to transform deteriorating inner suburbs into vibrant, mixed-use communities, such as St. Louis Park, built along Excelsior Boulevard. [16]

In 1997, Maryland's Gov. Glendening launched his smart-growth program. Rather than establishing urban-growth boundaries as Oregon had done, Glendening's program aimed to concentrate new development in partially developed areas with existing roads, utility lines and schools, thereby saving the state from having to build new infrastructure and preserving the state's rapidly dwindling rural green space.

Although most states have stopped short of adopting Oregon's statewide growth policy, many have followed Portland's example and established urban-growth boundaries, including California's fast-growing San Jose and Sonoma County, a largely rural, wine-producing region north of San Francisco.

Other local governments used traditional zoning ordinances to fight sprawl, as Arlington County did in response to construction of the Metro subway system. Arlington planners used zoning ordinances to focus high-density development along the Metro corridor, limiting intensive retail, commercial and high-rise apartment and condominium development to within a quarter-mile of each Metro station. Forty years later, the area is an award-winning, vibrant residential and retail community whose residents can walk to stores and take public transit downtown.

Consumers Prefer Bigger Houses, Lots

American homebuyers prefer larger houses and lots located away from cities, according to the homebuilders association. Meanwhile, they appear less interested in being able to get to work quickly and living closer to public transportation — features promoted by smart-growth advocates.

What Homebuyers Want

(In order of preference)

Feature	Percent saying it was "important" to "very important"
Houses spread out	62%
Less traffic in neighborhood	60
Lower property taxes	55
Bigger home	47
Bigger lot	45
Better schools	44
In a good neighborhood	43
Less developed area	40
Away from city	39
More luxury features	35
Closer to work	28
Shorter commute to work	23
Recreational facilities	22
Closer to public transit	13
Smaller house	10
Smaller lot	9

Source: "Smart Growth, Smart Choices," National Association of Home Builders

New Urbanism

The New Urbanism movement, another effort to create alternatives to the postwar suburban model, attracted support from many planners, architects and developers. Since 1993, the nonprofit Congress for the New Urbanism has called for more investment in central cities and decried sprawl as the leading cause of the separation of neighborhoods by race and income, environmental degradation, loss of open space and the lack of community identity in much of the country. The group's design guidelines for new communities espouse the following principles:

- Grid street layout, with wide sidewalks, bike lanes and, where feasible, public transit;
- Mixed-use development, including shops, offices and residential units of all types, including detached, single-family houses, town houses, condominiums and rental apartments;
- Buildings constructed close to the street, with windows and porches facing sidewalks to foster communication between occupants and pedestrians;
- Parking lots and garages behind buildings, ending the asphalt parking lots that surround strip-mall stores;
- Placement of schools, stores, libraries and other public facilities within safe walking or biking distance from residences;
- Community focal points, such as town squares or neighborhood centers, also within walking distance of residences;
- Clear boundaries around communities, with open space separating communities.

Some of the best-known New Urbanist communities, such as Seaside, in Walton County, Fla., Kentlands, in Gaithersburg, Md., and Laguna West, in Sacramento County, Calif., were built on previously undeveloped sites.

But the goal of saving open space and revitalizing deteriorating downtown areas makes such development especially suited for urban infill projects. City West, a 1,085-unit mix of affordable and market-rate rental units and owner-occupied houses in downtown Cincinnati was recently completed on the site of two failed public-housing projects. The new neighborhood has begun to draw both higher-income buyers eager to live near downtown amenities and lower-income renters, including some former residents who had fled the crime-ridden projects. [17] ■

CURRENT SITUATION

Policy Challenges

A major obstacle to the spread of New Urbanist designs is existing zoning laws, which often discourage mixing residential with commercial and retail uses and mandate large building setbacks from the street.

"Right now, it is easier to pave over a farm or tear down a forest and build a brand new subdivision or office park than to reuse or infill space in existing communities," says Glendening of the Smart Growth Leadership Institute. He cites historic Annapolis — Maryland's capital and one of the state's most popular tourist attractions — as a case in point.

"Everybody loves Annapolis," Glendening says. "It's got narrow streets, a wonderful mixture of single-family and multi-family residences, some over stores, and all the other attributes of the traditional neighborhood development pursued by New Urbanist designers. Yet if you wanted to go out and build a community like Annapolis today, it would be illegal in almost every state, including Maryland. Even after all the changes we've accomplished with our smart-growth program, it would take several years of variances to overcome existing zoning rules to create a town like Annapolis today."

Moreover, zoning rules governing school siting encourage suburban sprawl. [18] When older schools need renovation, most communities build a new, larger school outside of town or even beyond the suburban areas, where land is more plentiful and cheaper. "Common, existing guidelines dictate that schools have at least 30 acres of land, which means in most cases new schools will be built outside of town," Glendening says. "The first thing a family with young children looks for in a community is the condition of its schools. If they discover that the school has not been renovated in 30 years but that they've just built three new schools farther out, then that's where they're going to move."

Not only does this pattern fuel sprawl, but it also contributes to the growing incidence of obesity among American children. (*See sidebar, p. 474.*) [19] Rather than walking to a neighborhood school, Glendening says, "Everyone must either take the car to school, have a parent drive them or take a school bus. And it's all a result of these faulty guidelines that schools need to be on 30 acres."

Zoning regulations that encourage sprawl also drive up local governments' costs, which already are facing the worst budget crises in a half-century. [20] Suburban residential development costs governments more than commercial or retail development, because they require construction of schools, new roads and extensive utility hookups. "Residential development costs more in necessary services for every dollar in tax revenues that it generates," says Scott York, chairman

Continued on p. 486

At Issue:

Are smart-growth policies the best solution for suburban sprawl?

JAMES E. MCGREEVEY
GOVERNOR OF NEW JERSEY (DEM.)

FROM A SPEECH BEFORE THE N.J. ASSOCIATION OF COUNTIES, APRIL 4, 2004

yes

Whether we look at smart growth environmentally, economically or socially, it means the future of New Jersey.

We can't continue as we have in the past. It is not sustainable from any perspective. We must be mindful of where we build and how we build. We must design new policies that encourage the rebirth of our older suburbs, our great inner cities and the planned development of new, rural, town centers. We must preserve what is left of our open space and ensure the sanctity of our drinking-water supplies. . . . We cannot say we are serious about smart growth and continue to have development guidelines that lack enforcement mechanisms.

Our goal is to provide clarity and predictability so developers, municipalities and counties can understand their regulatory obligations prior to proposing any new development projects. . . . Together with the other municipal and county tools to direct and control growth, we will have the ability to reshape New Jersey's development patterns and make them more rational, responsible and predictable. . . .

The impacts of growth and sprawl do not adhere to the boundaries of a single community or town, [so] we cannot realistically address sprawl if we fail to engage in a greater level of regional planning. . . . So I am proposing . . . a mediation forum in which municipalities and counties can try to resolve their issues before heading to the courts. The purpose will be to find regional solutions to regional problems and to encourage municipalities to think about the impacts their development decisions have outside their borders.

Smart growth is about balance. I recognize the importance of economic development, the importance of jobs and the importance of keeping our state profitable. But I also recognize that in addition to our fiscal responsibilities, we have a responsibility to the land and environment that make up our state. Sprawl — and the unrestrained development that has jeopardized our water supplies, made our schools more crowded, our roads congested and our open space disappear — is the single greatest threat to our way of life in New Jersey.

We are trying to reverse decades' worth of thinking and policies in order to preserve our future. It will not be easy, but it is a fight from which we cannot back down or postpone. Every day we lose 50 acres to development — 50 acres of parks, farmland and open space that will never be reclaimed.

SAMUEL R. STALEY
PRESIDENT, BUCKEYE INSTITUTE FOR PUBLIC POLICY SOLUTIONS

WRITTEN FOR *THE CQ RESEARCHER*, APRIL 2004

no

Smart growth is a political response to residential and commercial development outside core urban centers. Shifting land-use decisions to a politically driven planning process can significantly reduce the quality of life for the very people it is supposed to help by limiting housing choice, reducing housing affordability and lengthening commute times.

New Jersey is a case in point. Thirty-seven percent of its land is urbanized and a third is permanently locked up as open space (mainly through state parks), while its population density ranks ninth in the nation. State residents have access to a wide range of housing options, from the revitalized shorefront of Jersey City to the gritty urbanity of Newark to the housing subdivisions sprouting up in central Jersey, while remaining accessible to instate and out-of-state employment centers.

This diversity, however, could be at risk if smart-growth principles are implemented statewide. Leading the charge in New Jersey and perhaps the nation, Gov. McGreevey argues sprawl is the "single greatest threat to our way of life in New Jersey." The state must clearly outline the "regulatory obligations" of developers, cities and other governmental agencies to mitigate this threat — obligations that would presumably include conforming to a state plan to reduce sprawl. While the plan is voluntary for local governments, local officials are expected to ensure their plans conform with the state plan. In other words, housing with large yards and open floor plans should be discouraged as much as possible.

Thus, smart growth is not always about broadening choices. Smart growth can also be about imposing a one-size-fits-all concept of the neighborhood — as compact, high-density and transit-dependent — communitywide.

However, efforts that limit housing choices are likely to create new burdens. The most obvious may be limiting immediate access to open space in the form of yards. Moreover, statewide planning laws and higher densities have been found to increase housing prices, significantly reducing affordability. Research also has shown that transit riders spend a significantly larger share of their time commuting than automobile users.

Local policymakers should be cautious about adopting smart-growth principles too quickly. Housing options become scripted by state and regional planners, not the decisions of thousands of households haggling with developers and real-estate agents in the local housing market. The result could be less affordable, less competitive communities and neighborhoods.

Continued from p. 484

of Loudoun County's Board of Supervisors. "It's important to expand the commercial tax base to help offset the cost of residential services."

In fact, cost containment had been a key justification for Loudoun's earlier smart-growth initiative. As the fastest-growing county in the nation, it accounts for an astounding 70 percent of Virginia's projected growth in public school enrollment over the next five years. [21] The county built 28 schools in the past eight years, and is scheduled to build an additional 23 over the next six years.

"We're piling on debt in order to build school after school after school in order to serve the growing population," York says. "Of course, the traffic situation also is becoming a nightmare around here, but there's very little money coming from the state government to deal with it."

Federal Impact

Although land-use decisions fall primarily within the jurisdiction of state and local governments, federal policies play an important role in shaping local development patterns. Environmental-protection statutes, such as the Clean Air and Clean Water acts, require state and local governments to meet federal mandates in controlling traffic-related smog and protecting waterways from the pollutants that stormwater washes from paved areas into streams and rivers.

The 1970 National Environmental Policy Act (NEPA) requires federal agencies to study and disclose the environmental impact of federally funded projects, like highways, and confer with the public before the projects are built. Supporters of deregulation have sought to undermine the NEPA process, saying it causes costly delays in highway projects, contributing to traffic congestion in fast-growing metropolitan areas. Reflecting that concern, President Bush in 2002 ordered the public-review process streamlined. [22]

Smart-growth supporters say federal policies — from income-tax deductions for interest on home mortgages to federally funded highway construction — have long underwritten suburban development. "The federal government has subsidized sprawl in a major way and continues to do so," says Glendening.

The federal government funds road-building and mass transit projects through a massive highway bill, reauthorized every six years. This year's renewal has bogged down over disagreements in funding levels: While President Bush requested $256 billion, the Senate approved a $318 billion highway bill in February, and the House passed a $284 billion measure in March. Congressional leaders have yet to name members of a conference committee, which will work out a compromise. Meanwhile, Bush has threatened to veto any bill that exceeds the administration proposal. [23]

Developers generally disagree that the federal highway system has driven development away from cities and towns. "Some people think that if you build highways, then growth will follow," says Jim Tobin, legislative director for smart growth and environmental affairs at the National Association of Home Builders. "That's not the way it happens. Population is driving growth, home ownership and housing construction. The growth is already there; the transportation system — be it transit, highways or a mix — needs to accommodate that growth."

Some experts doubt that federal or state funding for new roads will relieve sprawl-related traffic congestion because commuters from the new communities they serve will eventually fill them to capacity. "The idea that traffic congestion can be eliminated through some kind of solution is a myth," says Downs of the Brookings Institution.

Flexible work hours and telecommuting could help alleviate congestion, he says, but only to a limited extent. "Congestion gets worse in part because it's a sign of prosperity and success, not necessarily a sign of defeat," he explains. "Traffic congestion is inevitably going to get worse in major metropolitan areas, and there's nothing we can do about it."

Anti-Sprawl Movement

But as congestion continues to clog metropolitan roadways, smog levels exceed allowable limits, and housing developments consume available open space, support is building in many parts of the country for curtailing sprawl. Reflecting that concern, the EPA has been supporting state and local smart-growth efforts for almost a decade.

EPA says its outreach into the state and local planning process could help protect the environment. "The built environment . . . has both direct and indirect effects on the natural environment," the agency states. "Where and how we develop directly impacts resource areas and animal habitat and replaces natural cover with impervious surfaces, such as concrete or asphalt. Smart growth [has] clear environmental benefits, including improved air and water quality, greater wetlands and open-space preservation and more cleanup and reuse of brownfield sites." [24]

To promote smart growth, EPA in 1996 created the Smart Growth Network, a partnership of more than 30 government, business and civic organizations that shares information on best practices for development. The effort gained momentum in January 1999, when Vice President Al Gore identified sprawl as a major threat to the environment.

But conservative activists criticize the EPA's new role, calling it an unwarranted intrusion into state and local affairs. "The federal government should not subsidize one side of a public-policy debate; doing so undermines the very essence of democracy," said a recent analysis by the CATO Institute, a libertarian think tank. "Congress should shut down the federal government's anti-sprawl lobbying activities and resist the temptation to engage in centralized social engineering." [25] ■

OUTLOOK

More Roads?

America's growing population seems likely to pose a serious challenge to efforts to limit further sprawl. By 2050, the Census Bureau projects, the number of people living in the United States will exceed 419 million — an additional 126 million people.

Although smart-growth proponents worry about the impact of this rapid increase in population, critics of smart growth question their motives. "A lot of concern about growth appears to stem from people's opposition to the idea of growth itself," says Staley of the Buckeye Institute. "But we live in a culture that is supposed to embrace tolerance for diversity and individuals. The whole idea underlying our government system is that just because we don't like more people is not a legitimate reason for preventing people from moving into a new community."

Staley concedes that more suburban development will likely add to the country's traffic congestion problems. "Traffic is a legitimate concern," he says. "But the issue is not so much that we have a lot of people commuting. It's more that we have not invested in the infrastructure upgrades necessary to keep people flowing.

"Our road investments lag development, and the result is all this congestion."

But traffic experts say accelerated road building will never solve the traffic problem. "If you build a lot more roads, you'd have to make the whole metro area a big cement slab," Downs, of the Brookings Institution, says. And expanding public transportation is not feasible, he says, because suburban residential areas are too low-density to support additional transit, and many Americans reject charging freeway tolls during peak hours to cut down on traffic, because it gives an advantage to those with money. "The last thing we could do is wait in line, and that's exactly what we're doing now — it's called congestion."

In Downs' view, traffic congestion is here to stay, regardless of population trends and smart-growth initiatives. "All metropolitan areas throughout the world have the same problem," he says, "and they all solve it the same way, which is with congestion."

Aging Baby Boomers

An important subset of America's growing population may determine the success or failure of future efforts to contain sprawl. The leading edge of the Baby Boom generation — the 78 million Americans born between 1946 and 1964 — is approaching retirement age. Many Boomers, who represent 28 percent of the U.S. population, were born and raised in the suburbs and raised their children there as well.

As the Boomers' children leave the nest, many planners wonder where this huge cohort will decide to spend its retirement years. If a large number decide to abandon the suburbs for alternative living arrangements, they will likely find that developers and local governments are eager to satisfy their housing needs. Retirees are in many ways ideal residents for localities trying to reduce expenses, because many are relatively well-off, with no children requiring schools, libraries and other services.

"Most governments — particularly in the fiscally constrained environment they're operating in right now — want to have their cake and eat it, too," Traylor, of the National Association of Home Builders, says. "They want Yuppie housing, built close to transit so they don't have to build new roads. They don't want children because they're very expensive to educate, and they don't want [less affluent] populations because they tend to require more social services."

Indeed, many local governments already provide attractive incentives for builders to construct specialized housing for aging Boomers and other active retirees.

"In many communities, if you want to build town houses or small single-family houses, the impact fees and other costs imposed by local governments are going to be exponentially higher than what you'd pay if you build a 55-and-older community," Traylor says.

Besides specialized retiree communities, many older Boomers may seek housing that has less space and

About the Author

Mary H. Cooper specializes in defense, energy and environmental issues. Before joining *The CQ Researcher* as a staff writer in 1983, she was Washington correspondent for the Rome daily newspaper *l'Unità*. She is the author of *The Business of Drugs* (CQ Press, 1990) and holds a B.A. in English from Hollins College in Virginia. Her recent reports include "Exporting Jobs," "Weapons of Mass Destruction" and "Bush and the Environment."

no yard to maintain and is close to stores and other services — the kind of housing that New Urbanist communities provide. "In many cases, empty nesters prefer the higher density found with condominiums or apartments that have convenient access to amenities," says Glendening of the Smart Growth Leadership Institute. "If you build a high-density, mixed-use project right around mass transit, you will attract many retirees, who will want to spend the next 20-30 years of their lives there."

If Boomers lead a new reverse migration from the suburbs to the city, they will help relieve some of the pressure to build new suburban housing for America's growing population.

"When empty nesters and other seniors move back into urbanized areas, they leave houses behind in the suburbs that these additional millions of people can move into," Glendening says. ■

FOR MORE INFORMATION

American Planning Association, 1776 Massachusetts Ave., N.W., Washington, DC 20036; (202) 872-0611; www.planning.org. Tracks growth management legislation and provides model bills.

Congress for the New Urbanism, The Hearst Building, 5 Third St., Suite 500A, San Francisco, CA 94103; (415) 495-2255; www.cnu.org. Promotes transit-oriented, mixed-use development as an alternative to traditional residential suburbs.

National Trust for Historic Preservation, 1785 Massachusetts Ave., N.W., Washington, DC 20036; (202) 588-6000;www.nationaltrust.org. Advocates curbing sprawl and revitalizing traditional downtowns and neighborhoods.

Reason Foundation, 3415 S. Sepulveda Blvd., Suite 400, Los Angeles, CA 90034; (310) 391-2245; www.reason.org. A libertarian organization that opposes smart-growth efforts as an unwarranted government intrusion into private life.

Smart Growth Leadership Institute, 1200 18th St., N.W., Suite 801, Washington, DC 20036; (202) 207-3348; www.sgli.org. Founded by former Maryland Gov. Parris N. Glendening to promote policies that curb sprawl.

U.S. Environmental Protection Agency, Development, Community and Environment Division (1808), 1200 Pennsylvania Ave., N.W., Washington, DC 20460; (202) 566-2878; smartgrowth@epa.gov. Manages EPA's Smart Growth program, which provides extensive information on state and local efforts to curb sprawl.

Notes

[1] U.S. Census Bureau figures released April 8, 2004, at *www.census.gov.*

[2] From an April 20, 2004, letter to "Leesburg2Day.com," on online journal covering Loudoun County.

[3] According to the Natural Resources Defense Council, www.nrdc.org.

[4] See John King, "What's Sprawling Is Our Worship of Comfort," *San Francisco Chronicle*, Oct. 2, 2003, p. E1, and James Howard Kunstler, *The Geography of Nowhere* (1993), p. 10.

[5] O'Toole spoke at the "Preserving the American Dream" conference, held April 15-18, 2004, in Portland, Ore. See Aimee Curl, "Conference Promotes Alternatives to Smart Growth," *Daily Journal of Commerce* (Portland, Ore.), April 19, 2004.

[6] Quoted by Laura Oppenheimer, "Visitors Boo Portland Planning," *The Sunday Oregonian*, April 18, 2004, p. B1.

[7] EPA's Smart Growth Program encourages states and localities to adopt managed-growth policies.

[8] See John Ritter, "New Town's Challenge Is to Stick to Blueprint," *USA Today*, April 13, 2004, p. 15A.

[9] Washington Regional Network for Livable Communities, "The Affordable Housing Progress Report," April 2004.

[10] Quoted by Amanda Covarrubias, "'Recycling' Old Neighborhoods Urged," *Los Angeles Times*, April 9, 2004, p. B3.

[11] Unless otherwise noted, information in this section is based on Jonathan Barnett, *The Fractured Metropolis* (1995). See also Mary H. Cooper, "Urban Sprawl in the West," *The CQ Researcher*, Oct. 3, 1997, pp. 865-889.

[12] For background, see Mary H. Cooper, "Transportation Policy," *The CQ Researcher*, July 4, 1997, pp. 577-600.

[13] See David Hosansky, "Traffic Congestion," *The CQ Researcher*, Aug. 27, 1999, pp. 729-752.

[14] See Isaiah J. Poole, "Gas Tax Alternatives for a Nation on the Road," *CQ Weekly*, April 17, 2004, pp. 918-922.

[15] See David Cho, "Reston Tosses a Party for 56,000 Neighbors," *The Washington Post*, April 18, 2004.

[16] See "National Award for Smart Growth Achievement," www.epa.gov.

[17] See Richelle Thompson, "City West Experiment Tests Idea of Mixing Incomes in Neighborhood," *The Cincinnati Enquirer*, Feb. 24, 2002.

[18] For more information, see Rob Gurwitt, "Edge-ucation," *Governing*, March 2004, pp. 22-26.

[19] For background, see Alan Greenblatt, "Obesity Epidemic," *The CQ Researcher*, Jan. 31, 2003, pp. 73-97.

[20] For background, see William Triplett, "State Budget Crises," *The CQ Researcher*, Oct. 3, 2003, pp. 821-845.

[21] See Rosalind S. Helderman, "School Growth Charts Put Loudoun on Top," *The Washington Post*, April 27, 2004, p. B1.

[22] For information on public involvement in federal road-building projects, see Sierra Club and Natural Resources Defense Council, "The Road to Better Transportation Projects: Public Involvement and the NEPA Process" (undated), sierraclub.org.

[23] See Isaiah J. Poole, "Chambers 'Not Close Yet' to Highway Bill Conference as Construction Season Wanes," *CQ Weekly*, April 24, 2004, p. 968.

[24] "Environmental Protection and Smart Growth," www.epa.gov.

[25] Peter Samuel and Randal O'Toole, "Smart Growth at the Federal Trough: EPA's Financing of the Anti-Sprawl Movement," *Policy Analysis*, Cato Institute, Nov. 24, 1999, p. 1.

Bibliography

Selected Sources

Books

Barnett, Jonathan, *The Fractured Metropolis: Improving the New City, Restoring the Old City, Reshaping the Region*, HarperCollins, 1995.

A city planner recounts the history of America's cities and the technologies that have shaped them, from the barge to the automobile. He calls for a national agenda to combat sprawl and improve the quality of city and suburban life.

Duany, Andres, Elizabeth Plater-Zyberk and Jeff Speck, *Suburban Nation: The Rise of Sprawl and the Decline of the American Dream*, North Point Press, 2001.

Leaders of the "New Urbanist" approach to development describe the pitfalls of suburban sprawl and outline design alternatives they say would greatly improve the quality of life in American communities by making it easier to walk or take public transit from home to school, work and other destinations.

Holcombe, Randall G., and Samuel R. Staley, *Smarter Growth: Market-Based Strategies for Land-Use Planning in the 21st Century*, Greenwood Publishing Group, 2001.

With the continuing spread of suburban development, state governments are playing a stronger role in planning decisions, traditionally the purview of local governments. The authors examine this trend and offer market-based alternatives to help shape development patterns.

Kunstler, James Howard, *Home from Nowhere: Remaking Our Everyday World for the 21st Century*, Free Press, 1998.

A noted critic of suburban sprawl calls for revised zoning and tax laws to promote alternative patterns of development that reduce dependence on the automobile and make more vibrant communities by combining residential housing with stores and offices.

Articles

Brooks, David, "Our Sprawling, Supersize Utopia," *The New York Times Magazine*, April 4, 2004, pp. 46-51.

For all the criticism of suburban sprawl, most Americans still choose to inhabit large houses in isolated, residential neighborhoods far from the city center, continuing the pattern that has dominated residential construction since World War II.

Frey, William H., "Gaining Seniors," *American Demographics*, November 201, pp. 18-21.

While Sun Belt communities continue to fill up with retirees, many elderly Americans are choosing to "age in place" in the same suburban communities where they raised their children.

Gurwitt, Rob, "Edge-ucation," *Governing*, March 2004, pp. 22-26.

A movement is taking hold to reverse the trend of building schools so far from most pupils' homes that they can no longer walk or bike to school.

O'Toole, Randal, "The Folly of 'Smart Growth'," *Regulation*, Fall 2001, pp. 20-25, fall 2001.

A critic of government regulation writes that Oregon's experiment with banning development outside urban boundaries has backfired, causing housing prices inside the boundaries to rise and failing to improve residents' quality of life.

Reports and Studies

Downs, Anthony, "Traffic: Why It's Getting Worse, What Government Can Do," *Policy Brief*, Brookings Institution, January 2004.

Because adults need to get to work every day, and children have to go to school, the author sees little hope of eliminating traffic congestion. But cities and states can take steps to reduce congestion, such as encouraging high-density development around transit stops, creating toll lanes on heavily used commuter roads and giving regional transportation authorities more power to coordinate planning in large metropolitan areas.

Heid, Jim, "Greenfield Development Without Sprawl: The Role of Planned Communities," Urban Land Institute, March 2004.

America's growing population cannot be accommodated by urban infill alone. But developing existing open space, or greenfields, need not be as destructive as it often is today. Careful planning can reduce the toxic emissions, stormwater runoff and visual pollution associated with suburban sprawl.

McCann, Barbara A., and Reid Ewing, "Measuring the Health Effects of Sprawl: A National Analysis of Physical Activity, Obesity and Chronic Disease," Smart Growth America and Surface Transportation Policy Project, September 2003.

By forcing residents to use their cars to commute from home to work, school and other destinations, the authors argue that sprawling suburban development is a key underlying cause of an alarming rise in the incidence of obesity, as well as heart disease, diabetes and other diseases related to overweight. McCann is a public-policy expert and Ewing an urban-studies professor at the University of Maryland.

The Next Step:

Additional Articles from Current Periodicals

Affordability

Ritter, John, "New Town's Challenge Is to Stick to Blueprint," *USA Today*, April 13, 2004, p. 15A.
Soaring demand in a new California town designed according to smart-growth plans is pricing out the middle-class inhabitants for whom it was designed.

Sichelman, Lew, "Local Rules: Affordability's Final Frontier?" *Chicago Tribune*, April 4, 2004, p. 5R.
Excessive regulation often drives up housing costs; in heavily regulated California, a median-price home is $200,000 more expensive than the national average.

Zito, Kelly, "Report Decries Housing Rules," *San Francisco Chronicle*, April 15, 2004, p. C1.
Housing policies requiring a certain percentage of new homes to be affordable may boost costs but reduce construction, according to a controversial study.

Effects of Sprawl

Fleishman, Sandra, "Sprawl by the Sea," *The Washington Post*, Aug. 16, 2003, p. F1.
Beachfront property and low taxes in Delaware are fueling a boom in population and construction that critics say is damaging the quality of life.

Johnson, Kirk, "Mostly Sprawling and Warmer," *The New York Times*, Oct. 24, 2002, p. B1.
Climate researchers study how the transition from open fields to a sea of concrete and houses affects weather patterns.

Siegel, Eric, "Urban Sprawl Hurts Minorities, Author Says," *The Baltimore Sun*, Oct. 3, 2002, p. 2B.
An Atlanta professor says that correlates of urban sprawl, such as air pollution, have a disproportionately harmful effect on urban minorities.

Wall, Lucas, "Motorists Pay High Price for Region's Sprawl," *Houston Chronicle*, July 23, 2003, p. A17.
Sprawl necessitates owning a car, which eats a big part of Americans' family budgets, but some note that sprawl generally also leads to lower housing prices.

Growth Disputes

El Nasser, Haya, "Anti-Sprawl Fervor Meets Backlash," *USA Today*, Aug. 26, 2002, p. 3A.
With growth controls increasing housing costs "between a little and a lot," the anti-sprawl movement is taking heat from people facing long commutes.

Emerson, Bo, "Suburb vs. City: Matter of Morality?" *Chicago Tribune*, April 6, 2003, Real Estate Section, p. 7M.
Where someone chooses to live may be a moral choice, but it's definitely inflaming tempers in an already tense situation.

Hevesi, Dennis, "Antidotes to Sprawl Taking Many Forms," *The New York Times*, Oct. 6, 2002, Section 11, p. 1.
Citizens have been concerned about sprawl, meaning unplanned growth, for many decades, but only in recent years has "smart growth" become a political and market issue.

King, John, "When Smart Growth Is Dumb," *San Francisco Chronicle*, June 23, 2002, p. D1.
Smart growth seems like such an obviously appealing concept that one is forced to wonder: Why isn't it making more headway?

Ritter, John, "Calif. Housing Battle Creates an Odd Alliance," *USA Today*, Dec. 10, 2002, p. 13A.
For the first time in its history, the Sierra Club sides with a builder in an effort to support "developers who are doing it right."

Health and Sprawl

McKee, Bradford, "As Suburbs Grow, So Do Waistlines," *The New York Times*, Sept. 4, 2003, p. F1.
Studies finding a tentative causation between suburban living and higher weight and blood pressure may be related to a car-centric culture that can make sidewalks seem superfluous.

Moore, Martha, "Walk/Can't Walk," *USA Today*, April 23, 2003, p. 1A.
A variety of factors including zoning, spread-out neighborhoods and the ubiquity of cars conspire to reduce walking in America, with fattening results.

Seibert, Trent, "'Burbs Prepare for Foot Traffic," *The Denver Post*, July 17, 2003, p. A1.
Both for sentimental and health reasons, many people, particularly retiring Boomers, prefer more pedestrian-friendly neighborhoods.

Lure of Suburbia

Avila, Oscar, and Colleen Mastony, "Immigrants Here in Record Numbers," *Chicago Tribune*, June 16, 2003, Metro Section, p. 1.
New Americans, like old Americans, seem to prefer the suburban life; immigrants are heading for the 'burbs in increasing numbers.

Boxall, Bettina, "Suburbs Still Have Allure, Poll Says," *Los Angeles Times*, Nov. 15, 2002, p. B2.
While residents agree that sprawl-related problems like air

pollution and traffic congestion are problems, they still prefer the suburban lifestyle.

Mann, Leslie, "Circular Argument; Home Buyers Love Cul-de-Sacs, but Critics Fret About Sprawl," *Chicago Tribune*, Nov. 16, 2002, New Homes Section, p. 1.
Cul-de-sac neighborhoods are clearly desirable to many people, but others criticize them for inefficiently using space and contributing to isolated communities.

Medved, Michael, "Real America Relishes Suburbia," *USA Today*, March 13, 2003, p. 13A.
A prominent film critic dissects movies depicting the travails of suburbia and contrasts them with not-so-terrible reality.

Rodriguez, Gregory, "Suburbia Gains an Accent," *Los Angeles Times*, Dec. 28, 2003, p. M6.
Glendale, Calif., which once represented suburban blandness, now boasts the world's second-largest Armenian population after the Armenian capital.

Stopping Sprawl

Clines, Francis X., "Maryland Farmland a Focus in Suburban Sprawl Battle," *The New York Times*, June 25, 2001, p. A10.
Former Maryland Gov. Parris N. Glendening takes on local officials as he battles sprawl in the Old Line state.

El Nasser, Haya, "Counties Try to Preserve Quiet Life," *USA Today*, April 22, 2003, p. 3A.
Rural communities once safely distant from big cities are taking steps to keep from being consumed by the relentless growth of metropolitan areas like Nashville.

Peterson, Iver, "For New Jersey Towns, an Experiment," *The New York Times*, April 21, 2004, p. B5.
It's a dry, technical term — "transfer of development rights" — but it's also a way to manage growth without wiping out farmers who depend on selling their land for development.

Ragland, Jenifer, "Voters to Decide Whether Growth Should Be Stopped in Its Tracts," *Los Angeles Times*, Nov. 4, 2002, p. B1.
California voters often decide on development-related questions because, according to critics, state leaders have abdicated responsibility for dealing with growth issues.

Whoriskey, Peter, "Density Limits Only Add to Sprawl," *The Washington Post*, March 9, 2003, p. A1.
Counties around Washington often require each home to be on four to 25 acres, a measure intended to stop suburban sprawl; but hundreds of large estates are not exactly the same as unspoiled country land.

Urban Planning

Forgey, Benjamin, "Urban Experiment Revisited," *The Washington Post*, June 20, 2003, p. C1.
New Urbanist architects visit Kentlands, Md., to check on the progress of a town begun according to the principles of New Urbanism.

Leigh, Catesby, "It Takes a (Well-Planned) Village: In Praise of the New Urbanism," *National Review*, July 24, 2003.
The emotionless, mechanical view of building can't reflect the sense of community necessary for a thriving nation.

Lewis, Roger, "New Rail Transit Systems Could Be Used to Direct Future U.S. Growth," *The Washington Post*, June 15, 2002, p. H11.
Relatively inexpensive compared to subways, trams could be a way of both successfully adapting to and shaping growth patterns.

Viglucci, Andres, "Living in Past: New Urbanism Catches On," *The Miami Herald*, June 16, 2002, p. B1.
Southern Florida officials and planners cotton to the New Urbanism in a bid to relieve the gridlock and chaotic growth of the Sunshine State.

CITING *THE CQ RESEARCHER*

Sample formats for citing these reports in a bibliography include the ones listed below. Preferred styles and formats vary, so please check with your instructor or professor.

MLA STYLE

Jost, Kenneth. "Rethinking the Death Penalty." The CQ Researcher 16 Nov. 2001: 945-68.

APA STYLE

Jost, K. (2001, November 16). Rethinking the death penalty. *The CQ Researcher, 11*, 945-968.

CHICAGO STYLE

Jost, Kenneth. "Rethinking the Death Penalty." *CQ Researcher*, November 16, 2001, 945-968.

CQ Researcher

Published by CQ Press, a division of Congressional Quarterly Inc.

thecqresearcher.com

Re-examining 9/11

Could the terrorist attacks have been prevented?

After nearly three years, haunting questions remain unanswered about the Sept. 11 terrorist attacks on the United States: How did the 19 hijackers elude detection to carry out their deadly plot? And why did the government fail to take stronger action against al Qaeda earlier? An independent commission is preparing a long-awaited report on what went wrong on 9/11 and what can be done to prevent future catastrophes. Due in late July, the bipartisan panel's report is expected to fault both the Clinton and Bush administrations for failing to recognize the dangers posed by Osama bin Laden and to call for significant changes in U.S. intelligence agencies. But some experts say even major reforms cannot eliminate the danger of future attacks by determined enemies. Indeed, the government is warning that major terrorist attacks are possible in the United States this summer.

Smoke billows from the World Trade Center after terrorists crashed two airliners into the twin towers on Sept. 11, 2001.

INSIDE THIS REPORT

The CQ Researcher • June 4, 2004 • www.thecqresearcher.com
Volume 14, Number 21 • Pages 493-516

CQ PRESS

RECIPIENT OF SOCIETY OF PROFESSIONAL JOURNALISTS AWARD FOR EXCELLENCE ◆ AMERICAN BAR ASSOCIATION SILVER GAVEL AWARD

Cover: People in New Jersey peer across the Hudson River at the burning World Trade Center on Sept. 11, 2001. Minutes later, both towers collapsed. Some 2,700 people died, including passengers in the two planes and office workers in the towers. (AFP Photos/Michael Boesl)

THE CQ Researcher

June 4, 2004
Volume 14, Number 21

MANAGING EDITOR: Thomas J. Colin

ASSISTANT MANAGING EDITOR: Kathy Koch

ASSOCIATE EDITOR: Kenneth Jost

STAFF WRITERS: Mary H. Cooper, David Masci, William Triplett

CONTRIBUTING WRITERS: Sarah Glazer, David Hatch, David Hosansky, Patrick Marshall, Tom Price, Jane Tanner

DESIGN/PRODUCTION EDITOR: Olu B. Davis

ASSISTANT EDITOR: Kenneth Lukas

A Division of Congressional Quarterly Inc.

SENIOR VICE PRESIDENT/GENERAL MANAGER: John A. Jenkins

DIRECTOR, LIBRARY PUBLISHING: Kathryn C. Suárez

DIRECTOR, EDITORIAL OPERATIONS: Ann Davies

CONGRESSIONAL QUARTERLY INC.

CHAIRMAN: Paul C. Tash

VICE CHAIRMAN: Andrew P. Corty

PRESIDENT AND PUBLISHER: Robert W. Merry

The CQ Researcher (ISSN 1056-2036) is printed on acid-free paper. Published weekly, except Jan. 2, April 9, July 2, July 9, Aug. 6, Aug. 13, Nov. 26 and Dec. 31, by CQ Press, a division of Congressional Quarterly Inc. Annual subscription rates for institutions start at $625. For pricing, call 1-800-834-9020, ext. 1906. To purchase a *CQ Researcher* report in print or electronic format (PDF), visit www.cqpress.com or call 866-427-7737. A single report is $10. Bulk purchase discounts and electronic-rights licensing are also available. Periodicals postage paid at Washington, D.C., and additional mailing offices. POSTMASTER: Send address changes to *The CQ Researcher*, 1255 22nd St., N.W., Suite 400, Washington, D.C. 20037.

Re-examining 9/11

BY KENNETH JOST

THE ISSUES

When President Bush's national security adviser, Condoleezza Rice, agreed after weeks of pressure to testify before the independent commission investigating the Sept. 11, 2001, terrorist attacks, relatives of victims filled the first three rows immediately behind her.

AFP/Paul Richards (Rice) and Luke Frazza

National security adviser Condoleezza Rice defended the Bush administration's anti-terrorism policies in April 2004 before the commission investigating the Sept. 11, 2001, attacks. Former U.S. counterterrorism coordinator Richard A. Clarke generally praised the Clinton administration's policies in his testimony but sharply criticized Bush's anti-terrorism record.

Many listened on April 8 with a mixture of frustration and anger as Rice fended off questions about the administration's anti-terrorism policy in the months before the attacks.

"To listen to her not recall things, to hear those kinds of statements was very frustrating," says Carie Lemack, whose mother was on the first plane that crashed into the World Trade Center. "It was all very surreal."

Rice stoutly defended the administration's anti-terrorism policy, saying that the White House was working overtime to develop a comprehensive strategy to eliminate the al Qaeda terrorist organization. She also discounted the importance of an intelligence briefing that Bush had received on Aug. 6 warning of Osama bin Laden's intention to attack within the United States — possibly an airline hijacking. [1]

The so-called Presidential Daily Brief, or PDB, was "historical information based on old reporting," Rice said. "There was no new threat information."

After more than three hours, Rice stepped down from the witness stand, embracing some 9/11 family members on her way out. But Lemack kept her distance. "Accountability, ma'am, accountability," Lemack shouted at her.

"That's the word that resonates with me: accountability," Lemack explains today. "If my mother was the CEO of a company, and somebody messed up, at the end of the day it was her fault. She would be accountable." [2]

Lemack helped found one of the major 9/11 survivors' groups, the Family Steering Committee, which vigorously lobbied a reluctant Bush administration in 2002 to create the independent National Commission on Terrorist Attacks upon the United States, the so-called 9/11 commission. [3] Family groups have kept up the pressure since then. Most recently, they forced an equally reluctant House Speaker J. Dennis Hastert, R-Ill., to give the commission more time to complete its report; it is now due on July 26.

Judging by questions from the 10 commission members and from several "staff statements" already released, the panel's final report is likely to fault the anti-terrorism policies of both Bush and his Democratic predecessor, Bill Clinton. [4] For Bush, the report is likely to intensify the political problems generated by legal attacks on the administration's post-9/11 detention policies and the recent, high-profile disclosures — including shocking photographs — of Iraqi prisoners being abused by U.S. servicemembers. [5]

The commission gained most attention with its reconstruction of events immediately leading up to the four hijackings of Sept. 11, which ultimately took some 3,000 lives. The actions of the 19 hijackers also have been dissected to try to understand how they eluded detection by immigration, law enforcement and aviation-security personnel on Sept. 11 and in the days, months and years beforehand. [6]

In its first interim report, released on Jan. 26, 2004, the commission staff documented numerous holes in immigration procedures that allowed some of the hijackers to enter or remain in the United States despite detectable visa violations. Another staff report released the same day reconstructed how the hijackers exploited "publicly available vulnerabilities of the aviation-security system" to pass through checkpoint screening and board their flights. [7] (*See sidebars, pp. 500, 506.*)

"I would not say that 9/11 was preventable, but I would certainly say we had a chance," says Amy Zegart, an assistant professor of public policy at UCLA who specializes in national security issues. "We could have been better organized than we were. Whether that could have made a difference, we'll never know."

The commission is also examining how the Clinton and Bush administrations dealt with al Qaeda since its first attack: the 1993 truck-bomb explosion at the World Trade Center that killed six persons and injured more than 1,000.

In sharply critical statements in April, the commission staff said the Central Intelligence Agency (CIA) failed through the 1990s to develop a "comprehensive

Can Separate, Secret Agencies . . .

The U.S. intelligence community "was not created and does not operate as a single, tightly knit organization," a congressional commission wrote in 1996. "It has evolved over nearly 50 years and now amounts to a confederation of separate agencies and activities with distinctly different histories, missions and lines of command."

As a result, there is no single place where intelligence-gathering can be coordinated and collected information can be analyzed. In the wake of hearings by the independent Sept. 11 commission, some lawmakers say the intelligence network should be restructured.

DOMESTIC INTELLIGENCE AGENCIES

HOMELAND SECURITY DEPARTMENT

Secret Service — Primary duties are protecting the president and stopping counterfeiters.

Customs Service — Inspecting cargo coming into the country by land, sea and air.

Border Patrol — Identifying and stopping illegal aliens before they enter the country.

Coast Guard Intelligence — Processing information on U.S. maritime borders and homeland security.

JUSTICE DEPARTMENT

Federal Bureau of Investigation — Lead agency for domestic intelligence and operations. Has offices overseas.

Drug Enforcement Administration — Collects intelligence in the course of enforcement of federal drug laws.

DEPARTMENT OF ENERGY

Office of Intelligence — Key player in nuclear weapons and non-proliferation, energy security, science and technology.

TREASURY DEPARTMENT

The Office of Intelligence Support — Collects and processes information that may affect fiscal and monetary policy.

STATE AND LOCAL POLICE AGENCIES

Coordinate with the FBI through joint counterterrorism task forces.

Trying to Pull It All Together

Several agencies were created before and after the Sept. 11 terrorist attacks primarily to analyze and integrate intelligence data. Among them:

Terrorist Threat Integration Center — Created by President Bush in 2003, this analysis center located in the CIA is designed to assess all terrorism-related information from U.S. and foreign intelligence sources.

Counterterrorist Center — CIA unit that coordinates counterterrorist efforts of the intelligence community; feeds information to the Terrorist Threat Integration Center.

Information Analysis and Infrastructure Protection Directorate — Part of the Department of Homeland Security created in 2002 to analyze terrorist-related intelligence and assess threats to critical infrastructure.

Terrorist Screening Center — A multi-agency center administered by the FBI to develop a watch-list database of suspected terrorists.

The Intelligence Community

As director of the CIA, George J. Tenet is the titular head of the U.S. intelligence community, a network of 15 departments and agencies. These agencies conduct both domestic and international intelligence-gathering.*

estimate" of al Qaeda. In a second report, the staff said the FBI had failed to go beyond its law enforcement role to try to detect and prevent possible terrorist incidents. That report also criticized Bush's attorney general, John Ashcroft, for giving terrorism a low priority in the months before 9/11. [8]

Officials from both the Bush and Clinton administrations testified before the panel to defend their actions, including CIA Director George J. Tenet,* who served in both administrations; FBI Director Robert S. Mueller III and his Clinton administration counterpart, Louis Freeh; and Ashcroft and his predecessor, Janet Reno.

* Tenet abruptly resigned "for personal reasons" on June 10, 2004, just after this report went to press. President Bush said Tenet had done a "superb job for the American people" and that CIA Deputy Director John McLaughlin will become acting director after Tenet's resignation takes effect in mid-July.

. . . Learn to Share?

INTELLIGENCE AGENCIES OPERATING OVERSEAS

CIVILIAN AGENCIES

Central Intelligence Agency (CIA) — Lead agency for collecting and analyzing foreign intelligence, including information on terrorism. Briefs the president daily.

Department of State Counterterrorism Office — Coordinates efforts to improve counterterrorism cooperation with foreign governments.

Bureau of Intelligence and Research — Analyzes and interprets intelligence on global developments for secretary of State.

MILITARY AGENCIES

National Security Agency (NSA) — Collects and processes foreign signal intelligence from eavesdropping and signal interception. Also charged with protecting critical U.S. information security systems.

Defense Intelligence Agency (DIA) — Provides intelligence to military units, policymakers and force planners. It has operatives in many U.S. embassies.

National Geospatial-Intelligence Agency (NGA) — The intelligence community's mapmakers, able to track movements of people and machines or changes in topography.

National Reconnaissance Office (NRO) — Builds and maintains the nation's spy satellites. Provides information to the Defense Department and other agencies.

Army Intelligence

Navy Intelligence

Marine Corps Intelligence

Air Force Intelligence

TAKING STEPS TO IMPROVE COORDINATION

The weakest link in the intelligence campaign against terrorism has been the analysis and sharing of millions of bits of raw data swept up by government agencies operating in the United States and abroad.

The original plan for correcting this flaw after the Sept. 11 attacks was to centralize analysis in the Department of Homeland Security, which Congress created in 2002. After the law was passed, however, President Bush changed tack. By executive fiat in early 2003 — no written executive order was issued — Bush created the Terrorism Threat Integration Center (TTIC), housed in the Central Intelligence Agency, to coordinate terrorism-related analysis.

Except for a passage in Bush's 2003 State of the Union speech and an address to FBI employees, the administration did not formally outline the roles and responsibilities of agencies participating in the center. A memorandum signed in 2003 by Attorney General John Ashcroft, Director of Central Intelligence George J. Tenet and Homeland Security Secretary Tom Ridge explained the information-sharing responsibilities of the center's participants.

It was not until an April 13, 2004, letter from Tenet, Ridge, FBI Director Robert S. Mueller III and TTIC Director John O. Brennan to several members of Congress that the administration made clear that terrorism-related intelligence would be analyzed by the threat center Bush had created.

The letter was sent in response to a series of inquiries dating to February 2003 from Susan Collins, R-Maine, chairwoman of the Senate Governmental Affairs Committee, and Carl Levin of Michigan, the panel's second-ranking Democrat.

The letter said Brennan's unit controls "terrorism analysis (except for information relating solely to purely domestic terrorism)," which is the province of the FBI. Homeland Security manages information collected by its own components, such as the Coast Guard and Secret Service, and is responsible for analyzing material "supporting decisions to raise or lower the national warning level."

—Justin Rood

CQ Graphic/Marilyn Gates-Davis

The parade of high-ranking officials came after the commission's most dramatic witness before Rice's appearance: Richard A. Clarke, a career civil servant whom Clinton named in 1998 as the nation's first national counterterrorism coordinator and who continued in that position under Bush for more than two years, though with downgraded status.

Clarke appeared before the panel after publication of his first-person account, *Against All Enemies*, which paints a fairly positive picture of the Clinton administration's counterterrorism policies but sharply criticizes the Bush administration's record. Bush "failed to act prior to Sept. 11 on the threat from al Qaeda despite repeated warnings," Clarke writes. He goes on to blame Bush for having launched "an unnecessary and costly war in Iraq that strengthened the fundamentalist, radical Islamic terrorist organization worldwide." [9]

Zegart, who is writing a book on U.S. intelligence agencies' response to terrorism, faults both the CIA and the FBI for organizational deficiencies and "cultural" blind spots in dealing with the problem. [10] But she also criticizes policymakers in both the Clinton and Bush administrations. "It seems fairly clear that terrorism was not a high enough priority for either administration," she adds. [11]

Under widespread pressure, Bush himself agreed to submit to questioning by the commission, but only after insisting that Vice President Dick Cheney accompany him and that no recording or transcript be made of the closed-door session. (The commission had earlier heard separately from Clinton and former Vice President Al Gore.) The April 29 meeting with Bush and Cheney lasted more than three hours. Afterward, the commission said Bush and Cheney had been "forthcoming and candid." Bush described the meeting as "very cordial."

As the 9/11 commission continues its hearings and deliberations, here are some of the major questions being considered by the panel and by policymakers, experts and the public:

Did the Clinton administration miss good opportunities to take action against al Qaeda?

The CIA's Counterterrorism Center knew enough about bin Laden's role in financing and directing al Qaeda that it created a special "Issue Station" in January 1996 devoted exclusively to tracking his activities. But the unit's "sense of alarm" about bin Laden was not widely shared, according to the 9/11 commission staff. "Employees in the unit told us they felt their zeal attracted ridicule from their peers," the staff's March 24, 2004, statement said. [12]

The skepticism even among intelligence professionals about targeting bin Laden was one of many difficulties the Clinton administration faced in confronting al Qaeda in the late 1990s. Clinton today gets some credit, even from political conservatives, for recognizing the threat. But he is also criticized for failing to mobilize support in or outside the government for strong action or to make effective those initiatives he was willing to authorize — most significantly, an Aug. 20, 1998, cruise missile attack against an al Qaeda base in Afghanistan aimed at killing bin Laden after he was linked to the Aug. 7, 1998, bombings of embassies in Kenya and Tanzania.

Moreover, many of the intelligence agencies' missteps occurred on Clinton's watch — most notably, the CIA's and FBI's mutual failure in 2000 to track two al Qaeda operatives into the United States and their eventual roles as 9/11 hijackers. Many experts fault Clinton for adopting a law enforcement approach toward al Qaeda — focusing on criminal prosecutions inside the United States — instead of a military approach using armed force.

"They continued to have largely a criminal-justice model for al Qaeda rather than a military model, rather than a counterinsurgency model," says John Pike, director of GlobalSecurity.org, an Alexandria, Va., think tank.

Mark Riebling, editorial director at the conservative Manhattan Institute and author of a history of the relationship between the CIA and the FBI, says it was "patently absurd" for Clinton to designate the Justice Department as the lead agency in his 1995 Presidential Decision Directive on terrorism. Both men, however, say Clinton's approach matched what Riebling calls the "conventional wisdom" of the time.

Some other experts are less forgiving of what they regard as the Clinton administration's misdirection. "There was a strategic failure to understand the magnitude of the threat — that the 1993 World Trade Center bombing and the other incidents were part of a larger campaign," says Steven Aftergood, a senior research analyst at the liberal-oriented Federation of American Scientists.

But Aftergood also says the administration's attitude coincided with the public's. "There was a kind of post-Cold War relaxation that did not properly assess the rising hostility in parts of the Islamic world," he says. "It seems to have been a blind spot."

On the other hand, Richard Betts, a professor at Columbia University and member of the Hart-Rudman commission on terrorism in the late 1990s, says Clinton could have done more to mobilize public support for stronger action against al Qaeda. "There would have been political support for much more decisive military action" after the embassy bombings in Africa, Betts says.

Pike gives the administration credit for the strike against the al Qaeda camp in Afghanistan. Stronger action — an invasion of Afghanistan — was unrealistic at the time, he says. "I don't think they could have convinced anybody even if they had convinced themselves," he says.

In any case, Betts notes that Clinton faced personal and political problems in trying to overcome the military's reluctance to go after al Qaeda. "Clinton, being Clinton, had no moral authority to challenge the military on anything," Betts says.

"The other problem is that there was that whole impeachment business," Pike adds. "The last two years of the administration, they were politically paralyzed."

Intelligence experts also emphasize that the administration inherited a decades-old lack of CIA and FBI coordination. "The problem was deeply structural," says Greg Treverton, a RAND Corporation senior research analyst who has held intelligence-related positions in government. "We built these agencies to fight the Cold War. But they set us up to fail in the war on terror." [13]

The "most stunning" of the agencies' missteps, Zegart and others say, was the lack of effective follow-up after two of the eventual hijackers — Nawaf al Hazmi and Khalid al Mihdhar — were observed at an al Qaeda meeting in Kuala Lumpur, Malaysia, in 2000.

9/11 Commission Bucked White House

The special commission created to investigate the 9/11 terrorist attacks has clashed with the Bush administration ever since its creation.

Congress approved creating the 10-member National Commission on Terrorist Attacks upon the United States on Nov. 15, 2002, a month after the White House had blocked a version passed by both the House and the Senate that summer. President Bush signed the bill into law on Nov. 27 and immediately named former Secretary of State Henry Kissinger to chair the commission. [1]

Congressional Democrats chose former Senate Majority Leader George Mitchell of Maine as the vice-chair of the panel. But both men resigned from the posts barely two weeks later: Mitchell cited the time demands of the job; Kissinger refused ethics requirements to disclose the clients of his international consulting firm.

Bush then picked former New Jersey Gov. Thomas F. Kean to chair the panel on Dec. 16. Kean, currently president of Drew University, is well regarded as a political moderate but lacks any foreign policy experience. In the previous week, congressional Democrats had tapped former Rep. Lee Hamilton of Indiana as vice chair. Hamilton had extensive foreign affairs experience during 34 years in the House and was widely respected.

The law creating the commission required it to complete its work within 18 months — by May 27, 2004. The timetable, insisted on by the White House, was aimed at getting the commission's report published before the 2004 presidential campaign. By late 2003, however, the commission was saying that it needed more time to complete its work. House Speaker J. Dennis Hastert, R-Ill., opposed the request, but finally agreed in late February 2004 to a 60-day extension for the commission's report — now due on July 26.

The commission said it needed more time in part because federal agencies — chiefly, the Defense and Justice departments — had responded slowly to requests for information. The commission also tangled with the White House over access to intelligence briefings Bush received on terrorism issues — including the now famous Aug. 6 "Presidential Daily Brief" warning of Osama bin Laden's interest in attacking the United States.

Bush eventually bowed to the commission's demands. He also agreed under pressure in April 2004 to meet and answer questions from all 10 members of the commission. The commission now states on its Web site that it has had access to every document and every witness it has sought, and that Bush has yet to assert executive privilege on any document request.

AFP Photo/Timothy A. Clary

Commission Chairman Thomas Kean, left, and Vice Chairman Lee Hamilton.

Kean and Hamilton have maintained the appearance of bipartisan unity in public statements and hearings. However, Attorney General John Ashcroft complained that Jamie Gorelick, deputy attorney general under President Bill Clinton, should have recused herself from discussions of Justice Department guidelines limiting information sharing between intelligence agencies and the FBI. Both Kean and Hamilton defended Gorelick.

Other Democrats on the panel include Richard Ben-Veniste, a former Watergate prosecutor; former Sen. Bob Kerrey of Nebraska; and former Rep. Timothy Roemer of Minnesota. Besides Kean, the Republican panel members are Fred Fielding, White House counsel under President Ronald Reagan; former Sen. Slade Gorton of Washington; former Navy Secretary John F. Lehman; and former Illinois Gov. James R. Thompson.

[1] The legislation was part of the Intelligence Authorization Act for Fiscal Year 2003, Public Law 107-306. The text of the law is on the commission's Web site: www.9-11commision.gov.

After receiving pictures of the two from Malaysia's security service, the CIA tracked both men into the United States. Subsequent events are bitterly disputed by the agency and FBI. [14]

In one version, the CIA never told the FBI about the two men; in the other, the FBI had access to the information but failed to act on it. In any event, the two men were never put on a terrorism "watchlist" and lived openly in San Diego — under their real names — until the hijackings. The 9/11 commission staff says the episode illustrates the failure "to insure seamless handoffs of information" among intelligence agencies — including the ultrasecret National Security Agency. [15]

Was the CIA or the FBI more to blame for the foul-up? "There's plenty of blame to go around," Zegart says bluntly.

Clinton left office with actions against al Qaeda again under discussion after

Continued on p. 501

Improved Aviation Security Still Has Gaps

The American airline industry was virtually brought to its knees on Sept. 11, 2001, by 19 men with box cutters like those available at any hardware store.

The federal government's response to the hijackings — creation of a massive, new security agency with 45,000 passenger screeners — created a more secure atmosphere at U.S. airports. But two years after its creation, the Transportation Security Administration (TSA) finds itself consistently criticized by politicians and the public. Occasional security gaffes — including a North Carolina college student's efforts last October to expose security glitches by hiding box cutters on two Southwest Airlines flights — have not helped the agency's image.

Moreover, lawmakers have complained the TSA is understaffed at some airports and overstaffed at others. For example, Rep. Harold Rogers, R-Ky., pointed out at a March hearing that the tiny Rutland, Vt., airport had seven screeners to handle just seven passengers a day. [1]

In addition, those lawmakers who in 2001 opposed the idea of taking airport security away from private contractors and making it a federal responsibility remain critical of the agency. Rep. John Mica, R-Fla., chairman of the Aviation Subcommittee of the House Transportation and Infrastructure Committee, believes more and more private companies should be given the opportunity to take screening back from the government in order to prove that businesses can do as good a job as the government in keeping terrorists off airplanes.

"Private screening companies are required to meet the same rigorous security standards as . . . federal screeners," Mica said. "As long as the highest-level security standards are met or exceeded, how that is accomplished should be determined by those most closely involved." [2]

But a recent investigation of five airports still using private security firms gave private screeners a mixed review. Clark Kent Ervin, inspector general of the Department of Homeland Security (DHS), said private contractors and the TSA performed "equally poorly." [3] But he blamed the problem largely on the slow hiring and screening process, which is still overseen by the TSA, even for the few airports still using private screeners.

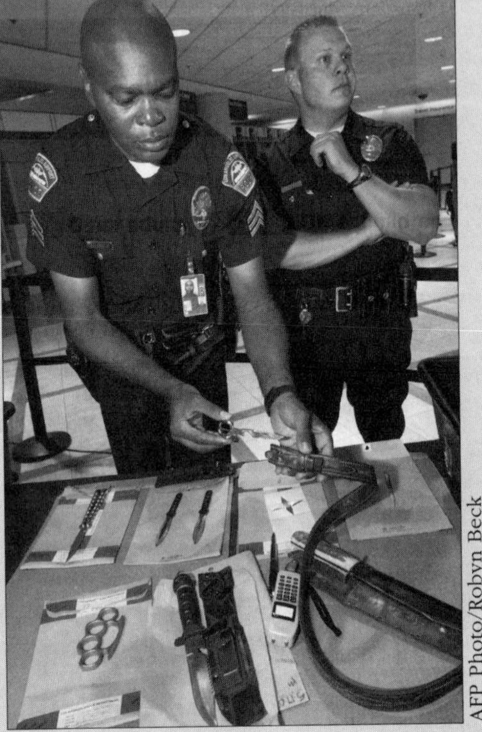

AFP Photo/Robyn Beck

Weapons confiscated from passengers at Los Angeles International Airport last year include a knife hidden inside a belt.

As the summer travel season unfolds and the commercial airline industry continues its financial recovery, the TSA is nearing a crossroads. [4] In November, airports will be able to "opt out" of the federalized screening programs and outsource the work to private contractors. Mica predicts up to 25 percent of the nation's airports will opt out, primarily out of frustration with the TSA's bureaucracy.

About the same time, controversial passenger database programs like the Computer Assisted Passenger Pre-screening System (CAPPS II) and the entry-exit immigration tracking system known as US VISIT will be in place at many airports, adding a new layer of scrutiny while raising questions about privacy.

TSA executives insist they have made the skies safer, noting that there have been no terrorist attacks on airlines since 9/11. In addition, the agency has confiscated 1.5 million knives and incendiary devices and 300 guns, just since last October, said TSA Deputy Administrator Stephen J. McHale. [5]

Despite the progress, several security gaps still exist in passenger aviation: There are no shields to protect commercial airliners from attacks with shoulder-fired missiles, and there is no mandatory screening of air cargo. Rep. Jim Turner, D-Texas, the top Democrat on the House Homeland Security Committee, has introduced a bill that would require cargo screening and hardened cockpit doors on foreign airliners flying in U.S. airspace.

"There are still some security gaps. We need to do more, faster on this troubled system. It's not foolproof," Turner says. "But the good news is that it is clearly more difficult for a terrorist to use an airplane as a weapon."

— Martin Kady II

[1] Martin Kady II, "TSA Shouldn't Expect an Easy Ride From This Appropriations Cardinal," *CQ Today*, March 12, 2004, p. 1.

[2] Quoted in *CQ Today*, April 23, 2004, p. 3.

[3] Testimony to House Transportation and Infrastructure Committee's Subcommittee on Aviation, April 22, 2004.

[4] Although some older airlines are still struggling, overall revenues for the industry have recovered somewhat since 9/11. See Eric Torbenson, "Airlines Get Lift from Rise in Revenue," *The Dallas Morning News*, May 21, 2004.

[5] Testimony to House Transportation and Infrastructure Committee Subcommittee on Aviation, May 13, 2004.

Continued from p. 499

the bombing of the *USS Cole* off Yemen in August 2000. But delays in linking the bombing to al Qaeda and reluctance to engage in a quick tit-for-tat response combined to quash any proposals to retaliate. Instead, Clinton and his national security team told incoming President Bush that he should put al Qaeda at the top of the list of national-security problems.

Did the Bush administration miss telltale clues that might have prevented the 9/11 attacks?

Intelligence agencies picked up a high volume of al Qaeda-related "threat reporting" in summer 2001. More than 30 possible overseas targets were identified in various intercepted communications. Officers at the CIA's Counterterrorism Center felt a sense of urgency, but some felt administration policymakers were too complacent. In fact, two veteran officers "were so worried about an impending disaster that . . . they considered resigning and going public with their concerns." [16]

Their frustration further buttresses the damning picture of the Bush administration's view of al Qaeda drawn by Clarke. He says in his book that his initial briefing on al Qaeda in January 2001 was greeted with sharp skepticism from Paul Wolfowitz, the deputy secretary of Defense. "I just don't understand why we are beginning by talking about this one man bin Laden," Clarke quotes Wolfowitz. Moreover, he describes Wolfowitz as linking the 1993 trade center bombing and other incidents to "Iraqi terrorism" — a theory Clarke says was "totally discredited." [17]

Experts representing a range of political views say Clarke's account rings true. "They took a long time to get off the mark studying this," the Manhattan Institute's Riebling says.

The American Federation of Scientist's Aftergood agrees: "In its first eight months, the Bush administration received warnings [about al Qaeda], but nevertheless moved at a leisurely pace until the crisis was upon us."

RAND's Treverton says the new administration apparently regarded state-sponsored terrorism as a greater threat than al Qaeda, and thus discounted Clinton officials' warnings. "It's pretty plain that terrorism — particularly, the brand represented by al Qaeda — was not quite on their radar scope," he says.

Some experts are less critical, acknowledging the difficulties that a new administration faced in taking office and setting policies on a range of foreign-policy and national-security issues. "Six months into a new administration, they were still getting their sea legs," says Pike of GlobalSecurity.org.

In both interviews and her sworn testimony before the 9/11 commission, national security adviser Rice insisted Bush understood the threat posed by al Qaeda. She told the commission on April 8 the administration was seeking to develop "a new and comprehensive strategy to eliminate" al Qaeda.

"I credit the administration with recognizing that at some point they were going to have to make really hard strategic choices," says James Jay Carafano, senior research fellow for defense and homeland security at the conservative Heritage Foundation. "That's a real testament to the administration."

Still, Carafano and others say the administration would have been hard-pressed to take stronger action against al Qaeda before 9/11. "Can you imagine if Bush had walked in the door and said let's invade Afghanistan?" Carafano asks. Pike says there were "missed opportunities, but they probably were not attainable, not realistic opportunities that you could have convinced people to implement."

The debate over the administration's response has come to focus on the now-famous PDB warning that bin Laden was "determined" to strike in the United States. The two-page document was first described in press accounts in May 2002, but the White House refused to provide it to the joint inquiry by House and Senate Intelligence committees investigating 9/11 and declassified it on April 10 only under pressure from the 9/11 commission. [18]

The brief describes bin Laden as wanting to retaliate "in Washington" for the 1998 missile strike in Afghanistan. It also quotes a source as saying in 1998 that a bin Laden cell in New York "was recruiting Muslim-American youths for attacks." Since that time, the brief continues, the FBI had noticed "patterns of suspicious activity" in the U.S. "consistent with preparations for hijackings or other types of attacks." Rice, in her testimony, described the brief as "historical," and Bush later insisted that it contained no "actionable intelligence."

Some experts agree. "That does not seem to me to be a case of something that was egregiously overlooked and that should have prompted a response that could have made a difference," says Columbia University's Betts. "I don't think that was politically realistic before the fact."

Aftergood is more critical. "The fact that Bush received the Aug. 6 PDB while on vacation in Texas tells us something," he says. "What it tells us is that more could have been done; greater vigor could have been exercised." As one example, Bush named Cheney on May 8, 2001, to head a task force to look into responding to a domestic attack with biological, chemical or radioactive weapons. The task force was just getting under way in September.

In line with existing procedure, the Aug. 6 PDB was not disseminated outside the White House. So, the Federal Aviation Administration (FAA) was given no special reason to step up airport security. Perhaps more significantly, the Justice Department never received the warning about possible domestic airline hijackings — which might have heightened attention to concerns raised by FBI agents in Phoenix and Minnesota in the months before Sept. 11.

Chronology I: The Clinton Years

1993-2000

Al Qaeda grows into worldwide terrorist organization under Osama bin Laden; U.S. attacked at home and abroad; Clinton administration tries but fails to stunt group's growth and kill or capture bin Laden.

Feb. 26, 1993
Truck bomb at World Trade Center kills six, injures more than 1,000; conspirators are later identified, indicted and some convicted.

June 1995
Presidential Decision Directive 39 labels terrorism a "potential threat to national security," vows to use "all appropriate means" to combat it; FBI designated lead agency.

January 1996
CIA's Counterterrorism Center creates special "Issue Station" devoted exclusively to bin Laden.

May 1996
Bin Laden leaves Sudan for Afghanistan.

June 25, 1996
Attack on Khobar Towers, U.S. Air Force residential complex, in Saudi Arabia kills 19 servicemembers.

April 1998
Taliban declines request to turn bin Laden over to United States.

May 1998
Presidential Decision Directive 62 lays out counterterrorism strategy; Richard A. Clarke named first national director for counterterrorism.

August 1998
U.S. embassies in Kenya and Tanzania bombed on Aug. 7; Clinton orders cruise missile strike ("Operation Infinite Reach") on al Qaeda base in Afghanistan; Aug. 20 strike hits camp, but after bin Laden had left. . . . Plan for follow-up strikes readied ("Operation Infinite Resolve") but not executed; Pentagon opposed.

December 1998
Plans prepared to use Special Operations forces to capture leaders of bin Laden network, but never executed; strikes readied after bin Laden possibly located, but intelligence deemed not sufficiently reliable, and strikes not ordered.

February, May 1999
Bin Laden located in February and again on several nights in May, but no strike ordered due to risk of killing visiting diplomats from United Arab Emirates (February), doubts about intelligence (May).

Summer 1999
High volume of threat reporting tied to Millennium celebrations.

July 1999
Clinton imposes sanctions on Taliban; U.N. sanctions added in October; through end of year, administration debates diplomatic vs. military approach but comes to no conclusion.

January 2000
Al Qaeda unsuccessfully tries to bomb *USS The Sullivans*; plot undisclosed until after attack on *USS Cole*. . . . Two future 9/11 hijackers tracked by CIA from al Qaeda meeting in Malaysia to United States; CIA and FBI trade accusations later over failure to place them on terrorism watch list.

Oct. 12, 2000
Attack on *Cole* kills 17 sailors; after the attack is linked to al Qaeda, strikes readied, but not ordered.

In Minnesota, FBI lawyer Coleen Rowley had raised suspicions about a French-Algerian man, Zacarias Moussaoui, who attended flight school without being able to identify who was paying his tuition. But FBI officials in Washington said Rowley did not have enough information to justify searching his computer. Moussaoui is now charged with conspiracy in the attacks. Meanwhile, an FBI counterterrorism agent in Phoenix had become suspicious of the number of Arab men taking flight lessons, but FBI headquarters also rejected his request for an investigation.

Are intelligence reforms needed to better guard against future terrorist attacks?

After weeks on the defensive following publication of Clarke's book and the 9/11 commission hearings, the Bush administration sought to regain control of the agenda by leaking word in mid-April of possible plans to back major changes in intelligence gathering. The White House was said to be considering a longstanding proposal from the intelligence community to create a new "director of national intelligence" with budgetary and operational control over all of the government's 15 intelligence agencies. In addition, the White House was said to be eyeing the creation of a new FBI domestic-intelligence unit. [19]

The proposed organizational changes draw mixed reactions. Some

Chronology II: The Bush Years

2001-Present

Bush administration developing anti-terrorism policies on eve of 9/11 attacks; president rallies nation, launches invasion of Afghanistan to eliminate haven for al Qaeda; later, investigations by congressional committees, independent commission focus on missed clues, possible reforms.

January 2001
President Bush takes office Jan. 20; administration officials briefed on *USS Cole* attack, but no strikes ordered; national security adviser Condoleezza Rice retains Richard A. Clarke in White House post but has him report to lower-level officials and asks him to draft new counterterrorism strategy.

March-July 2001
Various options for Afghanistan discussed at deputies level.

May 8, 2001
Bush names Vice President Dick Cheney to head counterterrorism task force; it was just getting organized in September.

Summer 2001
Increased threat reporting prompts concern by Clarke, CIA Director George J. Tenet.

June 2001
Draft presidential directive circulated by deputy national security adviser Stephen Hadley calls for new contingency military plans against al Qaeda and Taliban.

July 2001
Federal Aviation Administration issues several security directives; agency is aware that terrorist groups are active in United States and interested in targeting aviation, including hijacking. . . . Internal FBI memo urges closer scrutiny of civil aviation schools and use of schools by individuals who may be affiliated with terrorist organizations.

Aug. 6, 2001
Bush receives Presidential Daily Brief (PDB) warning, "Bin Ladin Determined to Strike in U.S."; two-page brief notes interest in hijacking; no immediate follow-up.

Late August 2001
Immigration and Naturalization Service arrests Zacarias Moussaoui in Minnesota after FBI lawyer raises suspicions about his enrollment in flight school; FBI headquarters rejects bid to search his computer.

Sept. 4, 2001
Top officials approve draft directive on terrorism for submission to Bush, calling for covert action, diplomacy, financial sanctions, military strikes.

Sept. 10, 2001
Three-phase strategy on Afghanistan agreed on at interdepartmental meeting of deputies.

Sept. 11, 2001
Hijackers fly airliners into World Trade Center and Pentagon as well as field in Pennsylvania; 3,000 persons killed; nation reacts with shock, anger.

October-December 2001
U.S.-led coalition ousts Taliban regime in Afghanistan.

2002
House, Senate Intelligence committees launch joint investigation of 9/11; under pressure, Bush administration also agrees to separate probe by independent commission.

2003
CIA, FBI, other intelligence agencies sharply criticized in report by joint congressional intelligence committees; panels call for intelligence overhaul, including new director of national intelligence.

2004
9/11 commission's interim staff reports fault CIA, FBI, other agencies for pre-9/11 lapses; Clarke book blasts Bush administration as slow and weak on terrorism; Bush, aides rebut criticisms; commission due to report in late July.

experts say the changes are long overdue, others that they would be ill-advised. Several say the greater need is for changes in procedures and attitudes better adapted to confronting the threat of terrorism in an age of instant global communication.

"I'm skeptical of large institutional changes," says Aftergood. Instead, he favors "steady, incremental reform and learning directly from experience, including, above all, learning from mistakes."

The proposal for a director of national intelligence, or DNI, at first seems simply a new title for the current director of central intelligence, or DCI. The 1947 National Security Act empowers the DCI to coordinate all the intelligence agencies with overseas operations.

In practice, however, the DCI has had no control over individual agency's budgets or other matters. "Almost every major study of the intelligence agencies has recommended bolstering the authority of the DCI," UCLA's Zegart says.

She would prefer to increase the DCI's power instead of creating a new position. "George Tenet needs more power over the entire community," she says. In particular, Zegart says the preponderant role of the military units — with around 80 percent of the estimated $40 billion intelligence budget — skews priorities in favor of identifying and locating military targets ("tactical intelligence") at the expense of broader research and analysis ("strategic intelligence").

Other experts, however, envision a DNI with a broad analytical role and no operational authority. "A director of national intelligence is probably a pretty good idea," RAND's Treverton says. "Someone looking across the spectrum and asking how we're spending the money, and what we're getting for it."

"You have to break up the two hats that Tenet wears," says Melvin Goodman, a former CIA officer who teaches at the National War College. "To be director of central intelligence and director of the CIA is an impossible task."

Tenet told the 9/11 commission, however, that he opposed separating the DCI's overall role from operational control of the CIA. The Defense Department has also resisted taking the military intelligence agencies' budgets out of the Pentagon. "Politically, it would be a very bloody fight to bring it about," says Columbia University's Betts, "and [very] expensive."

Proposals to reorganize the FBI reflect the view that the bureau's historic law enforcement role shortchanges intelligence collection and analysis. The methodical collection of evidence for use in courtroom prosecutions is "not quick enough" to prevent terrorist incidents, Zegart says. In addition, she says the FBI's "culture" is ill-suited to intelligence work.

Mueller says he is reorienting FBI policies and procedures to deal with the problems. "That kind of cultural change takes a long time," says a dubious Zegart. But Pike is more optimistic. "I found the argument compelling that the FBI has the matter in hand," he says.

In any event, Pike and other experts strongly oppose one widely discussed proposal: To create a freestanding domestic-intelligence unit comparable to Britain's MI-5. "We're citizens; we are not subjects," Pike remarks.

The Heritage Foundation's Carafano calls it "a really bad idea. We don't need another intelligence organization. We probably have too many now."

Zegart acknowledges the criticisms and suggests a "semiautonomous" domestic-intelligence unit within the FBI might be the answer. Other experts, however, say leadership is more important than organizational change. "If you've got a director who has a mission to reorient [the agency's priorities], it's not absolutely clear to me that a reformed FBI might not be able to do the job," Betts says.

Apart from organizational issues, several experts say 9/11 exposed above all the need for better information sharing. Much of the debate has focused on the "wall" — guidelines restricting the CIA's ability to provide intelligence to the FBI or other domestic agencies.

Several other experts, however, say cultural and organizational barriers may be more significant. "We have a CIA that is very much focused on secrets," Treverton says. The problem, he says, is "getting people to talk to people more."

Aftergood agrees. "The age of central intelligence is behind us," he says. "What we need to move toward is distributed intelligence" — making information more readily accessible for use in enhancing security and preventing terrorist incidents.

In any event, he says, organizational changes alone will not solve the problems. "Institutional arrangements are all less important than the ability of the people who are engaged," he says. ■

BACKGROUND

Dysfunctional Systems?

The 9/11 attacks disclosed huge gaps in the ability of U.S. intelligence, law enforcement and security systems to detect or prevent terrorist incidents at home. In hindsight, government agencies gave too little attention to domestic terrorist attacks, while airlines and the government agency that regulated them were lax in instituting and enforcing security measures. In addition, both the CIA and the FBI were constrained by reforms instituted after surveillance abuses by both agencies against domestic political groups in the 1960s and '70s.

Neither the CIA nor the FBI was created with counterterrorism in mind. [20] The FBI was established within the Justice Department by President Theodore Roosevelt. It first drew critical scrutiny during and after World War I for its aggressive investigations of sedition, espionage and anti-draft cases. A public and congressional backlash prompted Attorney General Harlan Fiske Stone in 1924 to appoint J. Edgar Hoover, then the bureau's assistant director, as director with a charge to professionalize the organization.

Hoover gained national celebrity by leading the FBI's anti-gangster efforts in the 1930s. With the Cold War, however, the bureau again turned its attention to suspected subversives. Hoover also directed FBI investigations of civil rights groups — notably, by eavesdropping on the Rev. Dr. Martin Luther King Jr. Investigations by journalists and congressional committees in the late '60s and early '70s uncovered a wide-ranging counterintelligence program — known as COINTELPRO — that used illegal or dubious practices to investigate or disrupt domestic political groups.

The Central Intelligence Agency traces its origins to the famed World War II Office of Strategic Services (OSS), which combined research and analysis functions with espionage, counterespionage, sabotage and propaganda. In late 1944, OSS chief Gen. William J. Donovan outlined to President Franklin D. Roosevelt a plan for a centralized peacetime civilian intelligence agency.

After Roosevelt's death, President Harry S Truman in 1946 created a weak coordinating body called the "Central Intelligence Group." A year later, the National Security Act created the CIA in its present form to coordinate and evaluate intelligence affecting national security.

The CIA became notorious for Cold War covert operations against communist or anti-American regimes in the 1950s and '60s. It toppled leftist governments in Iran and Guatemala, supported anti-Castro rebels in Cuba and encouraged U.S. entry into the war in Southeast Asia. The Watergate scandals under President Richard M. Nixon in the early 1970s led to evidence of illegal domestic political spying by the agency.

Despite its prominence, the CIA is actually dwarfed by Department of Defense intelligence agencies. The biggest is the National Security Agency (NSA), which grew from World War II codebreaking into intensely secretive, electronic surveillance worldwide. Another DoD unit, the National Reconnaissance Office, manages satellite-collection systems, and the National Geospatial Intelligence Agency processes images gleaned from the satellites. Each of the military services also has its own intelligence unit.

The Pentagon also has its own analytical office: the Defense Intelligence Agency, which — like the State Department's Bureau of Intelligence and Research — provides assessments and policy advice independent of, and often at variance with, CIA conclusions. Coast Guard Intelligence and the Department of Homeland Security's (DHS) Information Analysis and Infrastructure Protection Directorate have been added to the intelligence community since 9/11.

Aviation safety is the province of the Federal Aviation Administration (FAA). Hijacking and sabotage emerged gradually as a major FAA concern after hijackings of planes to and from Cuba became common in the early 1960s. After the first passenger death in a U.S. hijacking in 1971 and a rash of violent hijackings, the agency began scanning carry-on baggage and passengers for potential weapons in December 1972. [21] Additional security measures were adopted after other deadly incidents in the 1980s: air marshals in 1985 and X-raying of checked baggage following the bombing of Pan Am Flight 103 over Lockerbie, Scotland, in 1988.

During the '90s, there were no hijackings or aircraft bombings within the United States, possibly leading to increased security laxness. Two Department of Transportation reports in 1999 and 2000 faulted airport-security procedures — specifically for failing to control access to secure areas.

Meanwhile, several studies in 2000 and early 2001 found overall counterterrorism policies deficient. [22] The reports drew attention for short periods but then largely disappeared from the national agenda.

Frustrating Initiatives

Terrorism became a major domestic concern for the United States in the 1990s, but al Qaeda became a major focus of that concern only slowly. The deadly 1995 bombing of the federal office building in Oklahoma City turned out to be the work of domestic rather than international extremists. Meanwhile, bin Laden's buildup of his organization into a wide-ranging, paramilitary operation largely escaped attention — even from intelligence agencies — until the middle of the decade. Even after al Qaeda was linked to the 1998 bombings of two U.S. embassies in Africa, bin Laden remained little known to Americans.

Bin Laden began his path to international terrorism as a "freedom fighter" in Afghanistan in the 1980s, seeking to undo the Soviet invasion of the predominantly Islamic country. [23] He founded al Qaeda (Arabic for "the base") in 1987 to mount a global Islamic crusade. The son of a wealthy Saudi family, he turned against the Saudi government — and the United States — after the Saudis allowed U.S. troops on the Arabian peninsula during and after the Persian Gulf War (1991).

Bin Laden was known at the time only as a "terrorist financier" working from Sudan. [24] Clarke, who handled counterterrorism at the National Security Council (NSC) early in President Bill Clinton's first term, pressed the CIA for more information. In 1996, according to Clarke's account, the CIA got its first big break when a top aide to bin Laden defected. Jamal al-Fadl described bin Laden as the mastermind of a widespread terrorist network with affiliate groups or sleeper cells in 50 countries. By this time, bin Laden had moved his base of operations to Afghanistan.

The administration had tried without success while bin Laden was in Sudan to persuade Saudi Arabia to take him into custody for prosecution and trial. Once bin Laden was in Afghanistan, the Counterterrorism Security Group that Clarke headed drew up plans to abduct him — plans never executed because of logistical difficulties.

When al Qaeda was linked to the 1998 embassy bombings, however, Clinton authorized cruise missile strikes

Reorganizing Immigration Triggers Growing Pains

Rep. Harold Rogers, R-Ky., was so fed up with the Immigration and Naturalization Service's efforts to stop illegal immigrants from crossing the borders that he introduced a bill to abolish the agency. The 2000 measure went nowhere.

But the Sept. 11, 2001, terrorist attacks accomplished what Rogers could not: They ushered in the demise of the INS. The agency had spectacularly failed to track the comings and goings of the 19 hijackers, some of whom were in the United States on student visas — allowing them to operate without fear that the government would realize they had overstayed their visas.

AFP Photo/Robyn Beck

The Department of Homeland Security's US VISIT program uses digital cameras and computers to track immigrant entries and exits at airports.

The Homeland Security Act of 2002 broke up the old INS into separate pieces and assigned its duties to different divisions within the newly created Department of Homeland Security (DHS). Immigration investigations and administration were assigned to the new Bureau of Immigration and Customs Enforcement, while border enforcement became the responsibility of Customs and Border Protection.

However, reorganizing the INS has not come without bureaucratic growing pains. According to a May 11 General Accounting Office report, the department lacks adequate long-term estimates of the cost of its proposed US VISIT program, a multibillion-dollar computer system designed to track the entry and exit of every foreign visitor. [1] Meanwhile, the so-called "visa waiver" program, which allows citizens of 27 U.S.-friendly countries to travel in the United States without visas, is underfunded and poorly organized, according to an April report by the DHS's inspector general. That report also noted that DHS has not adequately tracked lost or stolen foreign passports to determine whether they were used to enter the country.

By October 2004, the passports of visitors without visas must include biometric data, such as fingerprint or facial recognition, to make them less susceptible to fraud. All 27 countries — which include England, France and Japan — will likely miss the deadline, according to DHS Secretary Tom Ridge and Secretary of State Colin L. Powell, who both asked Congress to extend the deadline.

"Rushing a solution to meet the current deadline virtually guarantees that we will have systems that are not operable," Powell said in April 21 testimony before the Senate Judiciary Committee's Subcommittee on Immigration. Sen. Saxby Chambliss, R-Ga., has introduced a bill to extend the deadline.

U.S. citizens will not be exempt from such biometric identities. This fall, the State Department will begin a pilot project to equip U.S. passports with biometric identifiers, with nationwide production of biometric passports beginning some time next year.

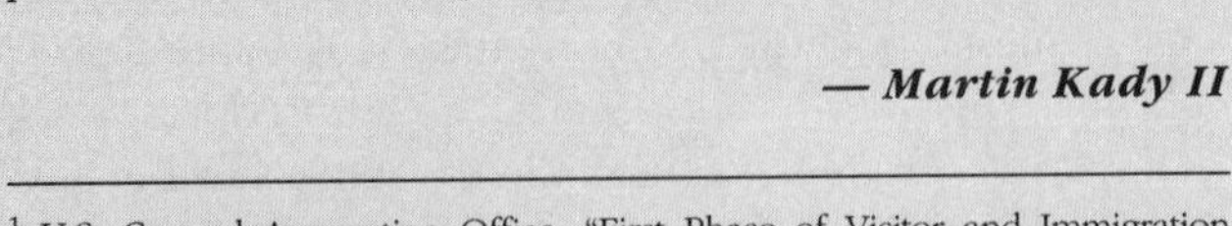

— *Martin Kady II*

[1] U.S. General Accounting Office, "First Phase of Visitor and Immigration Status Program Operating, but Improvements Needed," GAO-04-586 (May 11, 2004).

at an al Qaeda base in Afghanistan; they missed bin Laden by minutes. *

Tasked by Clinton, Clarke then designed a strategy to eliminate al Qaeda, including diplomatic efforts to eliminate its sanctuary in Afghanistan; covert action to disrupt terrorist cells; financial sanctions beginning with the freezing of funds of bin Laden-related businesses; and military action to attack targets as they developed.

In his book, Clarke voices great frustration with efforts to put the plan into effect — particularly the military's reluctance to get engaged. The 9/11 commission staff says the strategy "was not formally adopted" and that Cabinet-level officials have "little or no recollection of it."

Clarke writes that Clinton also approved assassinating bin Laden. Tenet told the 9/11 commission, however, that the agency considered the instructions unclear, at best. Clarke writes that he viewed the CIA's demurrals as an "excuse" for its inability to carry out the mission. Efforts to enlist the FBI's help in counterterrorism also proved difficult, according to the commission's staff report. Clinton's national security adviser, Samuel R. Berger, told the panel that despite regular meetings with Attorney General

* Clinton also approved a missile strike against a pharmaceutical plant near Khartoum, Sudan, suspected of manufacturing precursors of chemical weapons. The Sudanese government denied that the factory had any connection to chemical weapons — denials credited today by many U.S. intelligence experts.

Reno and FBI Director Freeh, the FBI "withheld" terrorism information, citing pending investigations.

In Clinton's final year in office, al Qaeda was viewed as an increasing threat in the United States and overseas. Al Qaeda had been linked to plans to disrupt celebrations of the new Millennium: A plot to plant bombs at Los Angeles International Airport was foiled when an Algerian man later linked to al Qaeda was stopped at the U.S.-Canadian border on Dec. 18, 1999, driving a car filled with bomb-making materials. Clarke reported afterward that al Qaeda "sleeper cells" might have taken root in the United States. [25]

In March, officials approved a four-part agenda that included disruption, law enforcement, immigration enforcement and U.S.-Canadian border controls. The White House also approved Predator aircraft attacks on al Qaeda bases — or on bin Laden himself. But CIA opposition to the flights derailed the plan. And Clinton left office in January 2001 with retaliation for al Qaeda's role in the October 2000 attack on the *Cole* still under consideration.

Postmortems

The Bush administration gave little visible attention to counterterrorism before 9/11. Bush drew wide public approval for rallying the nation immediately after the attacks and then leading a broad international coalition in ousting the pro-al Qaeda Taliban government in Afghanistan. But both the Clinton and Bush administrations have come under critical scrutiny since then — first from a joint inquiry by two congressional committees and now from the 9/11 commission.

Both administrations were blamed for not better coordinating the various agencies involved in counterterrorism. The Bush administration is also faulted for failing to appreciate the gravity of the threat that al Qaeda posed and for missing potential opportunities to disrupt or prevent the 9/11 attacks.

Clarke briefed Rice on al Qaeda during the transition period in January 2001. He writes that Rice seemed ill-informed about al Qaeda and voiced doubts about the need for a 12-person NSC unit devoted to counterterrorism. Rice told the 9/11 commission that Bush's national security team fully appreciated the threat from al Qaeda and wanted to make sure there was "no respite" in the fight against the organization. She says she took "the unusual step" of retaining Clarke and his staff despite the change in administrations. But Clarke says his position was downgraded so that he reported to deputies rather than to Cabinet-level "principals."

Rice directed Clarke to prepare a new counterterrorism strategy. Clarke says the work proceeded slowly, even with the spike in "threat reporting" in summer 2001. But Rice stressed in her testimony that the final document — approved by Cabinet-level officials on Sept. 4 — was the administration's first major national-security policy directive.

The multipart strategy parallels Clarke's unacted-on 1998 plan: diplomacy, financial sanctions, covert actions and military strikes. But Rice stressed to the 9/11 commission one difference: Whereas Clinton had called for bringing terrorists from Afghanistan to the United States for trial, the Bush plan directed the Pentagon to prepare for military action in Afghanistan itself.

When the war in Afghanistan ended, Congress in 2002 decided to examine the events leading up to 9/11. The House and Senate Intelligence committees completed their joint investigation in December 2002, but the 900-page report was not released until July 24, 2003 — while the Bush administration reviewed the document for classified material.

When finally released, the report painted a sharply critical portrait of both the CIA and the FBI. Prior to 9/11, intelligence agencies had received "a modest, but relatively steady, stream of intelligence reporting" indicating the possibility of terrorist attacks in the United States, but they "failed to capitalize on both the individual and collective significance" of the information, the panels reported. Intelligence agencies were "neither well organized, nor equipped, and did not adequately adapt" to meet the threats posed by global terrorism. [26]

The intelligence committees laid out ambitious recommendations, beginning with the proposal — periodically recommended by the intelligence community — to create a powerful director of national intelligence (DNI) over the entire intelligence apparatus. The Cabinet-level position would be separate from the CIA director. The panels also called for Congress and the executive branch to "consider promptly" whether the FBI should retain responsibility for domestic intelligence or whether "a new agency" should take over those functions.

The 16-page laundry list included a host of other recommended changes — less visible but equally or even more important, including developing "human sources" to penetrate terrorist organizations; upgrading technology to "better exploit terrorist communications"; maximizing "effective use" of covert actions; and developing programs to deal with financial support for international terrorism.

The panels also called for "joint tours" for intelligence and law enforcement personnel in order to "broaden their experience and help bridge existing organizational and cultural divides" between the different agencies.

In addition, the committees asked that the 9/11 commission study Congress' own record in monitoring the intelligence community, including whether to replace the separate House and Senate oversight panels with a single committee and whether to change committee membership rules. Currently, members are limited to eight-year terms, but many say the restriction prevents them from developing sufficient expertise on intelligence agencies before they are forced to leave the panel. [27] ■

CURRENT SITUATION

Ground Zero

Police, firefighters and other emergency personnel were universally celebrated for their rescue efforts on Sept. 11 once the World Trade Center towers had been turned into raging infernos. However, in emotional hearings on May 18 and 19 — punctuated by angry outbursts from several victims' family members in the audience — the 9/11 commission sharply criticized the Police and Fire departments' overall management of the disaster.

Inadequate planning, poor communications and interdepartmental rivalries significantly hampered rescue efforts, the commission staff suggested in two interim reports. [28] The critique — and barbed comments from some commissioners during the hearing — drew sharp retorts from current and former city officials. Former Mayor Rudolph W. Giuliani conceded "terrible mistakes" were made, but he denied any problems of coordination. [29]

But the staff reports said longstanding rivalry between the Police and Fire departments led each to consider itself "operationally autonomous" at emergency scenes. "The Mayor's Office of Emergency Management had not overcome this problem," the report said. Commissioner John Lehman called the command-and-control system "a scandal" and the city's disaster-response plans "not worthy of the Boy Scouts."

The staff reports also said 911 and Fire Department dispatchers had inadequate information and could not provide basic information to callers inside the buildings about the fires. "The 911 operators were clueless," said Commissioner Slade Gorton. The staff report also suggested that fire officials were slow to recognize the likelihood of the towers collapsing and therefore slow to order the buildings evacuated.

Thomas Von Essen, the fire commissioner at the time, called Lehman's remark "outrageous." For his part, Giuliani said firefighters were "standing their ground" in the building in order to get civilians out. Giuliani, who now runs his own security-consulting firm, called for Lehman to apologize. The former Navy secretary declined.

The staff reports also criticized the World Trade Center's owner, the Port Authority of New York and New Jersey. Despite biannual fire drills, civilians were not directed into stairwells or given information about evacuation routes, the report said. Civilians were "never instructed not to evacuate up" or informed that rooftop evacuations "were not part of the . . . evacuation plan." The report also noted that evacuation drills were not held and participation in fire drills "varied greatly from tenant to tenant."

The emergency response at the Pentagon, on the other hand, was "generally effective," the staff reports said, praising the "strong professional relationships and trust" established among emergency responders and "the pursuit of a regional approach to response" by departments from different jurisdictions.

New York's current mayor, Michael Bloomberg, told the commission on May 19 that the city was taking steps to "improve communications within and between the Police and Fire departments." Earlier, however, the commission's vice chairman, Lee H. Hamilton, had described the city's plan as a "prescription for confusion."

Bloomberg also criticized the allocation of post-9/11 federal emergency-preparedness assistance, saying that New York ranked 49th out of 50 states in per-capita funding received despite its prominence as a terrorist target. Homeland Security Secretary Tom Ridge told the commission the Bush administration had been trying to get Congress to change the allocation formulas, but he also said it was important to help each state.

In his appearance, Giuliani was asked about the significance of federal officials' failure to tell the city about the threat warnings described in Bush's Aug. 6 intelligence briefing. "I can't honestly tell you we would have done anything differently," Giuliani said. "We were doing, at the time, all that we could think of that was consistent with the city being able to move and to protect the city."

High Court Review

As President Bush was taking flak for his actions before Sept. 11, the administration was also awaiting Supreme Court rulings on the legality of aggressive detention policies adopted in the post-9/11 war on terrorism.

The justices will decide whether the government has crossed constitutional bounds by denying judicial review to some 600 foreign nationals detained at Guantánamo Bay Naval Base in Cuba since being captured in Afghanistan and Pakistan and to two U.S. citizens held as "enemy combatants" in the United States. One was captured in Afghanistan; the other was arrested at the Chicago airport in May 2002 and charged with conspiring to explode a radioactive bomb somewhere in the United States.

Continued on p. 510

At Issue:

Should Congress create the new position of director of national intelligence?

SEN. DIANNE FEINSTEIN, D-CALIF.
RANKING MINORITY MEMBER, SUBCOMMITTEE ON TERRORISM, TECHNOLOGY AND HOMELAND SECURITY

WRITTEN FOR *THE CQ RESEARCHER*, MAY 2004

yes

Intelligence failures on Iraq's weapons of mass destruction and in the months prior to Sept. 11, 2001, have made clear the need for reform within our nation's intelligence community. The place to start with this reform effort is at the top. We should begin by establishing a single director of national intelligence with the statutory and budgetary authority to truly oversee our nation's intelligence-gathering efforts.

The lack of coordination between intelligence agencies is well known. This disunity was described thoroughly in last summer's report by the Senate-House Inquiry into Sept. 11 and was echoed in the recent 9/11 commission hearings. Our intelligence-gathering efforts are plagued by territorial battles and reluctance among agencies to work together — reluctance that has caused the misreading of threats and endangered our nation.

This post-Cold War era of non-state, asymmetric threats demands cooperation among intelligence agencies. In an age when we must be prepared for the dangers of suitcase nukes, dirty bombs and bioterrorism, our entire government must share information to keep us safe.

The current intelligence structure is inadequate to address the threats posed by al Qaeda and other terrorist organizations. With 15 separate agencies, offices and departments charged with collecting or analyzing intelligence — including such little-known bodies as the National Reconnaissance Office and the National Geospatial-Intelligence Agency — our intelligence community is fragmented and inefficient.

The intelligence leadership structure exacerbates these divisions. The director of central intelligence (DCI) is charged with overseeing an agency while also acting as the leader of the entire intelligence community — two widely divergent functions that limit his effectiveness.

The DCI is further hampered by the fact that he oversees a mere one-fifth of the intelligence budget while the secretary of Defense controls most of the remaining 80 percent.

The best way to address this structural defect is to establish a single director of national intelligence with the statutory and budgetary authority to concentrate full time on coordinating intelligence resources, setting priorities and deciding strategies for the intelligence community and advising the president on intelligence matters.

Referring to the way we gather and analyze intelligence, 9/11 commission member and former Navy Secretary John Lehman recently said, "A revolution is coming."

Serious threats to our national security remain. We cannot afford to wait any longer to reform our intelligence community.

HAROLD BROWN
COUNSELOR/TRUSTEE, CENTER FOR STRATEGIC AND INTERNATIONAL STUDIES, SECRETARY OF DEFENSE (1977-1981)

WRITTEN FOR *THE CQ RESEARCHER*, MAY 2004

no

The present structure of the intelligence community is not working well. We need better connections between the various intelligence agencies. But there are reasons to be careful about inserting an additional position called director of national intelligence (DNI).

One suggestion is to have the DNI be a staff person in the White House. But that would merely add another layer to dealing with intelligence issues. If a referee among departments and agencies with intelligence functions is needed, the president's national security adviser or a deputy can do that.

Another suggestion is to have a DNI with line authority, budget authority and personnel authority over all of the intelligence agencies, including both CIA and those in the Department of Defense. But intelligence support is so important to military operations that any functions taken out of the Pentagon's control would likely be duplicated. And further centralizing of intelligence analysis would suppress alternative views and estimates, which recent history shows to be a mistake.

A DNI who is also director of the CIA cannot be an impartial overseer of the other agencies. But if there is a separate, subordinate, CIA head, the DNI will be too remote from the sensitive area of covert operations. Burying those further down the chain would provide more opportunity for uncontrolled activity.

Perhaps the biggest gap revealed by 9/11 is that between the FBI and the CIA. Discussion about the scope of DNI control usually omits the national security section of the FBI. If the Defense Department is recalcitrant about transferring large segments of its intelligence activities, that's nothing compared to the resistance from the Department of Justice and the FBI to taking away their national security functions.

Some suggestions for better organization can be found in the report of the Commission on the Roles and Capabilities of the U.S. Intelligence Community, which I headed in the mid-1990s. We suggested "double-hatting" heads of the separate intelligence agencies, so that they would report both to the secretary of Defense and the director of central intelligence. That's awkward, but it does correspond to the need for the DCI and the secretary of Defense to thrash out differences, which is necessary in any structure of intelligence. That report also proposed giving the DCI additional budgetary authority and training responsibility.

I would move in the direction of assuring better coordination of planning and operations, including across the sensitive boundary between domestic and foreign intelligence operations, but cautiously. Most of the proposals that have been suggested so far would likely make things worse, not better.

Continued from p. 508

Civil-liberties and human-rights organizations say the lack of access to courts is inconsistent with the U.S. Constitution and international law. But the government argues courts have very limited authority to review the president's authority as commander in chief to detain enemy combatants.

The justices seemed divided along their usual conservative-liberal fault line during arguments in the three cases in late April: Justices Sandra Day O'Connor and Anthony M. Kennedy, moderate-conservatives who often hold the balance of power on the court, gave mixed signals.

In the first case to be argued, a former federal appeals court judge told the justices on April 20 that the government had created "a lawless enclave" at Guantánamo by blocking the foreigners from going to court to challenge their detention. "What's at stake in this case is the authority of the federal courts to uphold the rule of law," said John Gibbons, a lawyer in Newark, N.J., and former chief judge of the federal appeals court in Philadelphia. [30]

Most of the 600 detainees being held at Guantánamo were captured during operations against al Qaeda or the Taliban in Afghanistan or Pakistan. The high court case stemmed from *habeas corpus* petitions filed by Kuwaiti, British and Australian nationals, all of whom claimed they had not been fighting the United States. Two lower federal courts dismissed the petitions, saying Guantánamo was outside U.S. jurisdiction.

In his argument, Solicitor General Theodore Olson noted that the United States was still fighting in Afghanistan and warned that judicial review of the detainees' cases would invite legal challenges to combat-zone treatment of captured enemy soldiers. "Judges would have to decide the circumstances of their detention, whether there had been adequate military process, what control existed over the territory in which they were kept," Olson said.

The administration urged a similarly broad view of executive authority in the cases of the two citizens, argued on April 28. [31] Deputy Solicitor General Paul Clement told the justices it was "well established and long established that the government has the authority to hold both unlawful enemy combatants and lawful prisoners of war captured on the battlefield to prevent them from returning to the battle."

Lawyers representing the two detainees, however, insisted the government's position amounted to authorizing "indefinite executive detention." Frank Dunham, a federal public defender, told the justices, "We could have people locked up all over the country tomorrow without any due process, without any opportunity to be heard."

Dunham was representing Yaser Hamdi, an American-born Saudi seized in Afghanistan. The second case involved José Padilla, a Chicagoan arrested at O'Hare Airport on May 8, 2002, after a flight originating in Pakistan. Both men were held at a Navy brig in Charleston, S.C., without charges and without access to lawyers. The federal appeals court in Richmond, Va., upheld Hamdi's detention, while the federal appeals court in New York ordered the government to charge Padilla or release him.

AFP Photo/Timothy A. Clary

The mother of a World Trade Center victim reacts angrily to former New York Mayor Rudolph W. Giuliani's testimony before the 9/11 commission in May 2004. While conceding "terrible mistakes" were made, Giuliani denied any problems of coordination between the Police and Fire departments. Commissioner John Lehman had called the city's disaster-response plans "not worthy of the Boy Scouts."

The cases raise legal questions that the high court has not considered since two pro-government rulings in World War II-era cases: One involved German saboteurs captured in the United States and later executed and the other German soldiers captured in China and later tried by military tribunals. [32]

The administration argued that both decisions supported its position in the current cases, while the detainees' attorneys maintained the rulings were factually and legally distinguishable. Decisions in the current cases are due before the justices' summer recess at the end of June. ■

OUTLOOK

Law of Averages?

Could 9/11 happen again? Federal officials warn that a new terrorist attack could come this summer or during the presidential campaign this fall. And they concede that despite tightened security measures, there is no assurance that an attack could be thwarted.

"Those charged with protecting us from attack have to succeed 100 percent of the time," national security adviser Rice told the 9/11 commission. "To inflict devastation on a massive scale, the terrorists only have to succeed once, and we know they are trying every day."

"I tend to be somewhat fatalistic about surprise attacks," says Columbia University's Betts. "We're dealing with a problem of batting averages. You're never going to bat 1,000."

The terrorist attacks have already brought about significant changes in the federal government and in Americans' daily routines. In Washington, the new Department of Homeland Security in 2002 consolidated existing border and transportation security functions and emergency preparedness and response under one department. And Americans in all walks of life have grown accustomed to tighter security, while aviation experts are warning of long security lines this summer. Meanwhile, many employers have increased their fire and evacuation drills.

Intelligence reorganization has emerged as the most significant issue in the two official investigations of 9/11. Leading Democratic members of the House and Senate Intelligence committees have proposed creating a new "director of national intelligence" with budget authority over all 15 intelligence agencies and who would no longer head the CIA itself.

A bill by Rep. Jane Harman, D-Calif., ranking member of the House panel, would give the proposed DNI substantial budgetary authority over the intelligence community but leave responsibility for "execution" with the Pentagon or other departments that house existing agencies. The DNI would serve at the pleasure of the president, while the bill would give the director of the CIA a 10-year term — the same as the FBI director. Senate Intelligence Committee member Dianne Feinstein, D-Calif., has sponsored similar legislation since 2002. Her current bill is somewhat less detailed than Harman's and does not give the CIA director a fixed term. [33]

Neither Feinstein nor Harman has any Republican cosponsors. Harman says there is "no reason" Republicans should not support the measure. "This is not a partisan bill," she says. GOP staffers on the Intelligence panels say Republican members are taking a wait-and-see approach. For its part, the administration has given no additional specifics since Bush said in mid-April that the intelligence agencies need to be overhauled.

"We will see no major reforms before another major catastrophic attack," says UCLA's Zegart. "Even then, I don't put the odds better than 50/50. The barriers to intelligence reform are exceptionally high."

The National War College's Goodman is more optimistic but sees the 9/11 commission report as the key to any significant changes. "The only hope is that this 9/11 report will be so strong and so shocking that people will suddenly say, 'Stop. Something's got to be done.' "

Commission Chairman Kean has repeatedly said he hopes the panel's final report will be unanimous. But some commission members are saying the panel may be divided on such major issues as intelligence reorganization. "Unanimity is a nice goal, but it isn't going to be a necessary goal," former Sen. Slade Gorton said. [34] A divided report is assumed likely to have less impact than a unanimous one.

Proposals to reorganize the FBI seem unlikely to advance, largely to allow time to evaluate the changes being put into effect by Director Mueller. Meanwhile, Rep. Christopher Cox, R-Calif., chairman of the House Select Homeland Security Committee, plans to give DHS' intelligence unit more authority over terrorism intelligence in the department's authorization bill. Cox says he is concerned that the unit — known as the Information Analysis and Infrastructure Protection Directorate — is not playing the role intended when the DHS was created.

As for local emergency preparedness, Homeland Security Secretary Ridge told the 9/11 commission his department has disbursed $8 billion to states, regions and cities to train and equip first responders. Noting the communications problems in New York City, Ridge also said the department was working to make communications and equipment "interoperable" between different departments and jurisdictions. Democrats have criticized the administration for not spending enough money to strengthen local emergency preparedness.

Republican and Democratic lawmakers are also squaring off already over re-

About the Author

Associate Editor **Kenneth Jost** graduated from Harvard College and Georgetown University Law Center, where he is an adjunct professor. He is the author of *The Supreme Court Yearbook* and editor of *The Supreme Court from A to Z* (both *CQ Press*). He was a member of *The CQ Researcher* team that won the 2002 American Bar Association Silver Gavel Award.

newing the USA Patriot Act, which Congress passed after 9/11 to strengthen law enforcement powers in anti-terrorism cases. Bush is urging Congress to extend the legislation this year, but Democrats are criticizing some of its provisions and questioning the need for action now. Some of the provisions expire in 2005.

Many observers fear that no matter how hard the government tries, the threat of terrorism cannot be eliminated. "There are going to be terrorist attacks, and there are going to be successful terrorist attacks," says the Heritage Foundation's Carafano. "We're never going to be immune from terrorism." ■

FOR MORE INFORMATION

Center for Strategic and International Studies, 1800 K St., N.W., Washington, DC 20006; (202) 887-0200; www.csis.org.

Families of September 11, 1560 Broadway, Suite 305, New York, NY 10036-1518; (212) 575-1878; www.familiesofseptember11.org.

Federation of American Scientists, 1717 K St., N.W., Suite 209, Washington, DC 20036; (202) 546-3300; www.fas.org.

National Commission on Terrorist Attacks Upon the United States, 301 7th St., S.W., Room 5125, Washington, DC 20407; (202) 331-4060; www.9-11commission.gov.

World Trade Center United Family Group, P.O. Box 2307, Wayne, NJ 07474-2307; (973) 216-2623; www.wtcufg.org.

Notes

[1] For background, see David Masci and Kenneth Jost, "War on Terrorism," *The CQ Researcher*, Oct. 12, 2001, pp. 817-848.

[2] Some eyewitness material taken from David Lightman, "A Frustrating Day for 9/11 Families," Knight Ridder/Tribune News Service, April 8, 2004.

[3] The Family Steering Committee's Web site can be found at www.911independentcommission.org. For other victims' organizations, see Families of Sept. 11 (www.familiesofseptember11.org) and World Trade Center United Family Group (www.wtcufg.org).

[4] The commission maintains a thorough and well-organized Web site: www.9-11commission.gov.

[5] For background, see Kenneth Jost, "Civil Liberties Debates," *The CQ Researcher*, Oct. 24, 2003, pp. 893-916, and David Masci and Patrick Marshall, "Civil Liberties in Wartime," *The CQ Researcher*, Dec. 14, 2001, pp. 1017-1040.

[6] For background, see Martin Kady II, "Homeland Security," *The CQ Researcher*, Sept. 12, 2003, pp. 749-772.

[7] Staff Statement No. 1 (immigration), Jan. 26, 2004. Staff Statement No. 3 (aviation security), Jan. 27, 2004.

[8] Staff Statement No. 11 (intelligence community), April 14, 2004. Staff Statement No. 9 (law enforcement), April 13, 2004.

[9] Richard A. Clarke, *Against All Enemies: Inside America's War on Terror* (2004), p. x. See also Masci, *op. cit.*

[10] For an overview, see the Intelligence Community's Web site: www.intelligence.gov.

[11] Zegart's book is tentatively titled *Stuck in the Moment: Why American National Securities Agencies Adapted Poorly to the Rise of Terrorism After the Cold War* (Princeton University Press, forthcoming 2005). Zegart notes as disclosure that Condoleezza Rice, President Bush's national security adviser, was her dissertation adviser at Stanford University.

[12] Staff Statement No. 7 (intelligence policy), March 24, 2004.

[13] For background, see Brian Hansen, "Intelligence Reforms," *The CQ Researcher*, Jan. 25, 2002, pp. 49-72.

[14] See Michael Isikoff and Daniel Klaidman, "The Hijackers We Let Escape," *Newsweek*, June 10, 2002; and David Johnston and James Risen, "Inquiry Into Attack on the Cole in 2000 Missed Clues to 9/11," *The New York Times*, April 11, 2004, Section 1, p. 1.

[15] Staff Statement No. 2 ("Three 9/11 Hijackers: Identification, Watchlisting, and Tracking") Jan. 26, 2004.

[16] Staff Statement No. 7, *op. cit.*

[17] Clarke, *op. cit.*, pp. 231-232.

[18] The document is appended to Staff Statement No. 10.

[19] See Douglas Jehl, "Administration Considers a Post for National Intelligence Director," *The New York Times*, April 16, 2004, p. A1.

[20] Background drawn from entries in George T. Kurian (ed.), *A Historical Guide to the U.S. Government* (1998).

[21] History drawn from undated "Aviation Security" entry on Web site of U.S. Centennial of Flight Commission: www.centennialofflight.gov/essay/Government_Role/security/POL18.htm.

[22] See Scott Kuzner, "U.S. Studied Terrorist Threat for Years," in David Masci and Kenneth Jost, *op. cit.*, p. 840.

[23] For a compact biography, see Charles S. Clark, "Bin Laden's War on America," in Masci and Jost, *op. cit.*, pp. 824-825.

[24] Remainder of section drawn from 9/11 commission Staff Statement No. 8; Clarke, *op. cit.*, pp. 134-154, 181-204.

[25] For background on computer-related Millennium problems, see Kathy Koch, "Y2K Dilemma," *The CQ Researcher*, Feb. 19, 1999, pp. 137-160.

[26] House Permanent Select Committee on Intelligence/Senate Select Committee on Intelligence, Report of the Joint Inquiry into Intelligence Community Activities before and after the Terrorist Attacks of Sept. 11, 2001, December 2002 (S. Rept. 107-351, H. Rept. 107-792; www.gpoaccess.gov/serialset/creports/911.html).

[27] See Dana Priest, "Congressional Oversight of Intelligence Criticized," *The Washington Post*, April 27, 2004, p. A1.

[28] Staff Statements Nos. 13 (emergency preparedness and response), May 18, 2004, and 14 (crisis management), May 19, 2004.

[29] Some quotes taken from coverage in *The New York Times*, May 19-20.

[30] The case is *Rasul v. Bush*, 03-334. For information, including a transcript of the oral argument, see the Supreme Court's Web site: www.supremecourtus.gov.

[31] The cases are *Hamdi v. Rumsfeld*, 03-6696, and *Rumsfeld v. Padilla*, 03-1027.

[32] The decisions are Ex parte Qirin, 323 U.S. 283 (1944) (saboteurs), and *Johnson v. Eisentrager*, 339 U.S. 763 (1950) (POWs).

[33] Harman's bill is HR 4104, Feinstein's S 190. Feinstein's legislation was also incorporated in a broad intelligence reorganization measure (S1520) introduced July 31, 2003, by Sen. Bob Graham, D-Fla.

[34] Quoted in Philip Shenon, "9/11 Panel May Not Reach Unanimity on Final Report," *The New York Times*, May 26, 2004, p. A19.

Bibliography

Selected Sources

Books

Bamford, James, *Body of Secrets: Anatomy of the Ultra-Secret National Security Agency from the Cold War Through the Dawn of a New Century*, Doubleday, 2001.
Published before 9/11, this informative general history of the NSA has two index entries for Osama bin Laden. Includes detailed notes.

Benjamin, Daniel, and Steven Simon, *The Age of Sacred Terror*, Random House, 2002.
Former National Security Council staffers in the Clinton administration provide a comprehensive account of the rise of al Qaeda. Benjamin is a senior fellow at the Center for Strategic and International Studies in Washington and Simon is an assistant director of the International Institute for Strategic Studies in London. Includes glossary, detailed notes.

Clarke, Richard A., *Against All Enemies: Inside America's War on Terror*, Free Press, 2004.
The former national coordinator for security, infrastructure and terrorism under both Clinton and Bush offers his controversial first-person account of the government's anti-terrorism efforts leading up to the 9/11 attacks.

Lowenthal, Mark M., *Intelligence: From Secrets to Policy* (2d ed.), CQ Press, 2003.
This updated overview of the structure, role and operations of the various agencies in the nation's intelligence community was written when Lowenthal worked with a security-consulting firm. He is now assistant director of central intelligence for analysis and production. Includes suggested readings, Web sites and other appendix material.

Riebling, Mark, *Wedge: From Pearl Harbor to 9/11. How the Secret War Between the FBI and CIA Has Endangered National Security*, Touchstone, 2002 (originally published, 1994).
The director of the Manhattan Institute for Policy Research provides a detailed history of policy differences and bureaucratic rivalry between the CIA (and its precursors) and the FBI. An epilogue and afterword in the paperback edition relate continuing tensions between the agencies through 9/11. A 14-page list of sources is included; sources for the epilogue and afterword are posted at secretpolicy.com/wedge/epilogue.

Treverton, Greg, *Reshaping National Intelligence for an Age of Information*, Cambridge University Press, 2001.
A RAND Corporation expert argues for a "sweeping" reshaping of national intelligence to make it more open and decentralized in the post-Cold War information age.

Articles

Dlouhy, Jennifer A., and Martin Kady II, "Lawmakers Eager to Weigh In on Overhaul of Intelligence," *CQ Weekly*, April 17, 2004, pp. 902-905.
Overview of lawmakers' views on various proposals to reorganize the U.S. intelligence community.

Gup, Ted, "The Failure of Intelligence," *The Village Voice*, April 13, 2004.
A veteran journalist and author provides a critical overview of terrorism-related intelligence collection and analysis before 9/11. Gup is now a journalism professor at Case Western Reserve University.

Johnston, David, and Eric Schmitt, "Uneven Response Seen to Terror Risk in Summer '01," *The New York Times*, April 4, 2004, Section 1, page 1.
The author reconstructs the Bush administration's limited follow-up to increased threat reporting during summer 2001; includes chart detailing some of the 33 intercepted messages with threat warnings.

Paltrow, Scot J., "Detailed Picture of U.S. Actions on Sept. 11 Remains Elusive," *The Wall Street Journal*, March 22, 2004, p. A1.
The reporter provides a meticulous reconstruction of the government's actions on Sept. 11, with some evidence contradicting previous official accounts.

Reports and Studies

House Permanent Select Committee on Intelligence/Senate Select Committee on Intelligence, *Report of the Joint Inquiry into Intelligence Community Activities before and after the Terrorist Attacks of September 11, 2001*, December 2002 (S. Rept. 107-351, H. Rept. 107-792; www.gpoaccess.gov/serialset/creports/911.html).
The 900-page report includes a summary of major findings and conclusions and a list of 17 recommendations. The report is dated December 2002 but was released in July 2003 following executive branch review for redaction of classified material.

National Commission on Terrorist Attacks upon the United States (www.9-11commission.gov).
The 9/11 commission's extensive Web site includes testimony and transcripts from all hearings and interim reports by the commission or staff. The commission's final report is scheduled to be released on July 26; the report will be published by W.W. Norton on the day of release and available for $10.

The Next Step:

Additional Articles from Current Periodicals

9/11 Commission

Jehl, Douglas, "'98 Terror Memo Disregarded, Report Says," *The New York Times*, April 15, 2004, p. A23.
CIA Director George J. Tenet declared war on terrorism in 1998, but his ardor failed to ignite major changes in the U.S. intelligence community.

Lichtblau, Eric, and David E. Sanger, "August '01 Brief Is Said to Warn of Attack Plans," *The New York Times*, April 10, 2004, p. A1.
A briefing warned the president a month before the attacks that al Qaeda wanted to hijack planes in the United States; the administration says the warning was not specific enough.

Meyer, Josh, "9/11 Panel Looks at Military," *Los Angeles Times*, April 16, 2004, p. A1.
The commission's final report in July will likely criticize the Pentagon for failures in confronting al Qaeda.

Miller, Greg, and Richard B. Schmitt, "9/11 Panel Finds CIA Slow to See Looming Threat From Al Qaeda," *Los Angeles Times*, April 15, 2004, p. A1.
Despite numerous warnings prior to the 9/11 attacks, the CIA never developed a comprehensive assessment of the threat posed by al Qaeda.

Bush and Terrorism

Eggen, Dan, and John Mintz, "9/11 Panel Critical of Clinton, Bush," *The Washington Post*, March 24, 2004, p. A1.
Officials from the Bush and Clinton administrations defend their counterterrorism actions against criticism from the Sept. 11 commission.

Elliott, Michael, "They Had a Plan," *Time*, Aug. 12, 2002, p. 28.
White House plans for dealing with bin Laden and his group were slow and indecisive until 9/11 blasted a hole in the national consciousness.

Johnston, David, and Jim Dwyer, "Pre-9/11 Files Show Warnings Were More Dire and Persistent," *The New York Times*, April 18, 2004, Section 1, p. 1.
The majority of the Sept. 11 commission agrees the attacks could have been prevented, but exactly when, how and by whom remain contentious questions.

Milbank, Dana, and Dan Eggen, "Bush, Clinton Varied Little on Terrorism," *The Washington Post*, March 27, 2004, p. A1.
The Clinton and pre-9/11 Bush terrorism strategies were not markedly different; a Clinton administration official says Richard A. Clarke was "despised."

Shenon, Philip, and Richard Stevenson, "Ex-Bush Aide Says Threat of Qaeda Was Not Priority," *The New York Times*, March 25, 2004, p. A1.
Former counterterrorism chief Richard A. Clarke's charges that President Bush did not take the al Qaeda threat seriously set off a partisan dispute.

Clinton Administration

Gellman, Barton, "U.S. Was Foiled Multiple Times in Efforts to Capture bin Laden or Have Him Killed," *The Washington Post*, Oct. 3, 2001, p. A1.
Officials hoped Saudi King Fahd would order a swift beheading, but a deal to get bin Laden ejected from Sudan and arrested in Saudi Arabia fell through.

Johnston, David, and Todd S. Purdum, "Missed Chances in a Long Hunt for bin Laden," *The New York Times*, March 25, 2004, p. A1.
Clinton's efforts to fight bin Laden were constrained by a finding that killing him would be illegal unless it were part of a capture operation.

Tyler, Patrick, "Feeling Secure, U.S. Failed to Grasp bin Laden Threat," *The New York Times*, Sept. 8, 2002, Section 1, p. 1.
Since the 1979 hostage-taking in Iran, America has been a prominent target for Islamist extremists, but outside of a few experts, the nation remained complacent.

Homeland Security

Alonso-Zaldivar, Ricardo, and Josh Meyer, "Box Cutters and Notes Found on Two Jets," *Los Angeles Times*, Oct. 18, 2003, p. A15.
Security officials are angered by someone who illustrated the imperfection of aviation security by sneaking box cutters aboard airplanes.

Gorman, Siobhan, "Second-Class Security," *National Journal*, May 1, 2004.
The Homeland Security Department remains very much a work in progress; its true authority is unclear and internally fractured into warring fiefdoms.

Hart, Gary, "Business as Usual for Chemical Plants," *The Washington Post*, Aug. 11, 2003, p. A17.
Plants producing large amounts of toxic chemicals have taken few or no steps to improve their security against terrorist attacks.

Rosen, Jeffrey, "Home Front," *The New Republic*, May 17, 2004, p. 14.
Preventive detention of alleged terrorists may be necessary, but it requires strong judicial oversight.

Intelligence Problems

"The Wrong People Doing the Right Job," *The Economist*, April 17, 2004.
Current and former leaders of the FBI and Justice Department advise against creating a domestic intelligence agency, but incremental changes to the FBI are insufficient.

Fessenden, Helen, "Director of National Intelligence: Hill Backs Idea, but Will It Sell?" *CQ Weekly*, Sept. 20, 2003, p. 2312.
Centralization of intelligence authority in the hands of one person faces stiff resistance from the Pentagon, which currently controls most of the intelligence budget.

Gladwell, Malcolm, "Connecting the Dots," *The New Yorker*, March 10, 2003, p. 83.
The difficulty of separating the countless thousands of worthless leads from the handful of real ones is often ignored when criticizing the intelligence agencies.

Hersh, Seymour M., "Missed Messages," *The New Yorker*, June 3, 2002, p. 40.
The FBI could not accurately respond to terrorist threats because of — among other things — outdated computers and a refusal to share information with other agencies.

Johnston, David, "Bush Sees a Need for Reorganizing U.S. Intelligence," *The New York Times*, April 13, 2004, p. A1.
President Bush indicates he may be willing to initiate many of the changes to America's intelligence services recommended since 9/11.

Miller, Greg, "9/11 Report Cites CIA, FBI Lapses," *Los Angeles Times*, July 25, 2003, p. A1.
A 900-page congressional report details the counterterrorism lapses that allowed al Qaeda to successfully mount their attack on the World Trade Center.

Pincus, Walter, "Intelligence Reform Will Not Be Quick," *The Washington Post*, May 4, 2004, p. A23.
It will be at least a year before any substantive intelligence reforms; the Pentagon's domination of the intelligence budget complicates the situation.

Priest, Dana, "Congressional Oversight of Intelligence Criticized," *The Washington Post*, April 27, 2004, p. A1.
Experts criticize Congress for paying scant attention to intelligence; only a handful of members reviewed the Iraq weapons of mass destruction material when given the chance.

Missed Chances

Isikoff, Michael, and Daniel Klaidman, "The Hijackers We Let Escape," *Newsweek*, June 10, 2002, p. 20.
The CIA tracked two 9/11 hijackers from a meeting in Malaysia until they entered the United States — then the agency did nothing.

Kaplan, David, *et al.*, "Pieces of the 9/11 Puzzle," *U.S. News & World Report*, March 15, 2004, p. 30.
Government eavesdroppers listened to 9/11 hijacker Khalid al-Mihdar when he called an al Qaeda safehouse in Yemen, but didn't bother to trace his call back to America.

Miller, Greg, and Josh Meyer, "Missed Opportunities Shadow 9/11 Attacks," *Los Angeles Times*, March 28, 2004, p. A1.
Thomas Kean, chairman of the 9/11 commission, says there were "16 or 17" opportunities that might have helped stop the attacks.

Smith, R. Jeffrey, "A History of Missed Connections," *The Washington Post*, July 25, 2003, p. A14.
In August 2001, an FBI agent predicted that "someone will die" when his request to investigate a 9/11 hijacker was rejected because of the "wall" between criminal and intelligence matters.

Citing *The CQ Researcher*

Sample formats for citing these reports in a bibliography include the ones listed below. Preferred styles and formats vary, so please check with your instructor or professor.

MLA Style

Jost, Kenneth. "Rethinking the Death Penalty." The CQ Researcher 16 Nov. 2001: 945-68.

APA Style

Jost, K. (2001, November 16). Rethinking the death penalty. *The CQ Researcher, 11*, 945-968.

Chicago Style

Jost, Kenneth. "Rethinking the Death Penalty." *CQ Researcher*, November 16, 2001, 945-968.

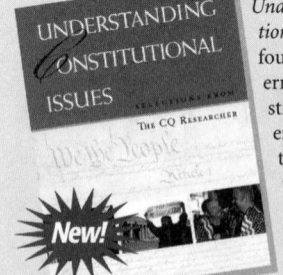

CQ Researcher

Published by CQ Press, a division of Congressional Quarterly Inc.

thecqresearcher.com

Nanotechnology

Does it pose environmental and health risks?

The future of nanotechnology — the science of creating molecule-size machines and materials — holds mind-boggling possibilities, according to proponents. Microscopic nanosensors someday will monitor criminals and detect chemical weapons. Nanobots, or tiny machines, will clean up toxic wastes, conduct surveillance, perform surgery and deliver drugs to targeted sites inside the body. Many products that use nanotechnology are already a reality, including dramatically faster computer chips and non-staining, wrinkle-free clothing. Some scientists warn, however, that the technology poses environmental and health risks, especially from easily ingested nanoparticles. Others worry that nanotechnology's potential is being over-hyped to investors. But advocates say the technology can be developed with proper safeguards and that it eventually could trigger the world's next Industrial Revolution, render oil obsolete and transform medical care.

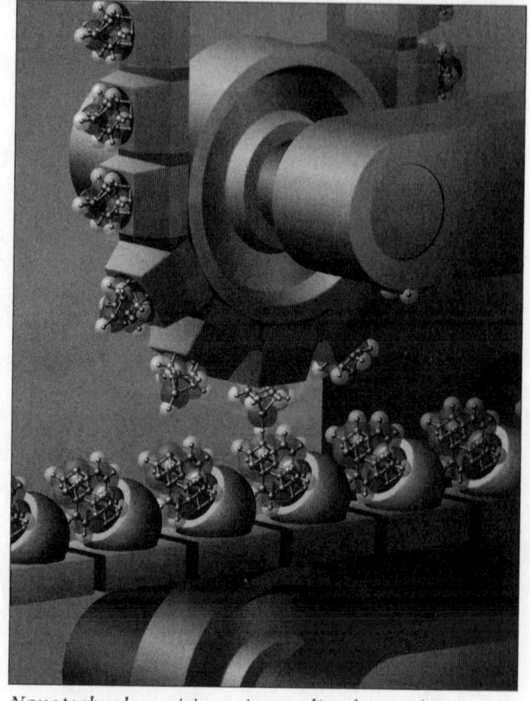

Nanotechnology visionaries predict that molecule-size machines like the one shown in this artist's rendering will be created in the future.

INSIDE THIS REPORT

The CQ Researcher • June 11, 2004 • www.thecqresearcher.com
Volume 14, Number 22 • Pages 517-540

RECIPIENT OF SOCIETY OF PROFESSIONAL JOURNALISTS AWARD FOR EXCELLENCE ◆ AMERICAN BAR ASSOCIATION SILVER GAVEL AWARD

THE ISSUES

BACKGROUND

CURRENT SITUATION

OUTLOOK

SIDEBARS AND GRAPHICS

FOR FURTHER RESEARCH

Cover: Some nanotechnology visionaries predict that molecule-size machines like this computer-generated example some day will be used as sensors injected into a patient's bloodstream to detect new disease or monitor a chronic condition. (Foresight Institute)

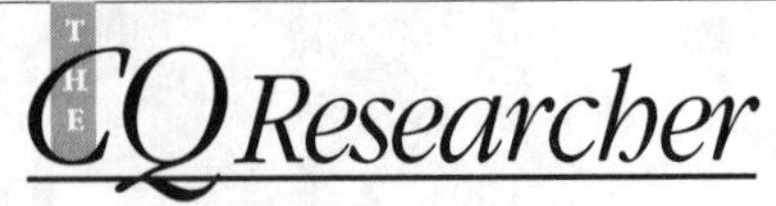

June 11, 2004
Volume 14, Number 22

MANAGING EDITOR: Thomas J. Colin

ASSISTANT MANAGING EDITOR: Kathy Koch

ASSOCIATE EDITOR: Kenneth Jost

STAFF WRITERS: Mary H. Cooper, David Masci, William Triplett

CONTRIBUTING WRITERS: Sarah Glazer, David Hatch, David Hosansky, Patrick Marshall, Tom Price, Jane Tanner

DESIGN/PRODUCTION EDITOR: Olu B. Davis

ASSISTANT EDITOR: Kenneth Lukas

A Division of
Congressional Quarterly Inc.

SENIOR VICE PRESIDENT/GENERAL MANAGER: John A. Jenkins

DIRECTOR, LIBRARY PUBLISHING: Kathryn C. Suárez

DIRECTOR, EDITORIAL OPERATIONS: Ann Davies

CONGRESSIONAL QUARTERLY INC.

CHAIRMAN: Paul C. Tash

VICE CHAIRMAN: Andrew P. Corty

PRESIDENT AND PUBLISHER: Robert W. Merry

The CQ Researcher (ISSN 1056-2036) is printed on acid-free paper. Published weekly, except Jan. 2, April 9, July 2, July 9, Aug. 6, Aug. 13, Nov. 26 and Dec. 31, by CQ Press, a division of Congressional Quarterly Inc. Annual subscription rates for institutions start at $625. For pricing, call 1-800-834-9020, ext. 1906. To purchase a *CQ Researcher* report in print or electronic format (PDF), visit www.cqpress.com or call 866-427-7737. A single report is $10. Bulk purchase discounts and electronic-rights licensing are also available. Periodicals postage paid at Washington, D.C., and additional mailing offices. POSTMASTER: Send address changes to *The CQ Researcher*, 1255 22nd St., N.W., Suite 400, Washington, D.C. 20037.

Nanotechnology

BY DAVID MASCI

THE ISSUES

If the predictions of nanotechnology visionaries come true, today's science-fiction writers may soon find that many of their best ideas actually exist.

Already, consumer products as diverse as wrinkle-free pants and ultrapowerful computer chips represent two of the latest advances created by the new science, which some experts say could trigger the world's next major Industrial Revolution.

In the future, some experts predict, nanotechnology may free the world from its dependence on oil and create products such as self-repairing highways and ingestible computerized particles that attack cancer cells.

IBM

Barely visible to the naked eye, the three tiny hard-drive components shown on the quarter were developed by IBM in 1997 and have been acclaimed as the first commercial nanotech products. Built with layers as narrow as a couple of atoms thick, they enable computers and other digital consumer products to store billions and billions of bits of data.

Nanotechnology — the science of the very small — involves the use of particles less than 100 nanometers long to create materials or simple machines at the atomic or molecular level.*

Although the ideas behind nanotechnology are decades old, scientists have put the science to wide-scale practical use only in the last few years. "We're really just at the earliest stages with this," says F. Mark Modzelewski, founder and executive director of the NanoBusiness Alliance, an industry trade group. "What we can do in terms of controlling atoms and molecules is still very limited."

Nonetheless, more than 1,200 firms now conduct nanotech research and development, ranging from recent startups, like Nano-Tex, an Emeryville, Calif., firm that develops anti-wrinkle chemicals for textiles, to large corporations like IBM, General Electric and Lucent. [1]

The technology already has been used to create a variety of industry-transforming products, such as computer hard drives that store 100 times more data than older models and special coatings that keep barnacles off ship hulls.

Several nanotech firms are developing cheaper, easier-to-use solar cells, which someday could help turn solar power into a major energy source. Others are using nanoparticles to improve screens for cell phones and large televisions or to create ever more powerful semiconductors for computers, cell phones and other electronic devices.

In medicine, researchers are exploring using nanoparticles to deliver anti-cancer drugs to targeted sites inside the body, making them much more effective while reducing side effects. Other expected advances include light, superstrong materials and dramatically more powerful computers.

Potential military uses of nanotechnology in the near-term include nanoarmor-lined turrets and doors for Humvees, nano foams and fibers to neutralize or protect against germ and chemical weapons and heat- and impact-resistant nanotech coatings for jet engines and ships. [2]

Nanotechnology inventions envisioned in the medium term include self-repairing concrete highways; materials 100 times stronger than steel with a fraction of the weight; energy-efficient lighting that could cut U.S. energy consumption by 10 percent, saving $100 billion annually; solutions for global warming and pollution-free manufacturing; and medical monitoring systems embedded in the body that sound an alert when a disease organism strikes or a cancer cell develops. [3]

Further into the future, some experts even foresee the creation of so-called nanobots, or molecular "machines," that will clean up toxic waste or conduct surveillance. That's not all. If molecular manufacturing based on self-replicating nanoassemblers becomes feasible, humans could make any item they desire — using only dirt and air. "Shovel in some dirt and out would pop a computer, a car, a pair of khakis, or a cabbage, depending on the recipe you specified," writes Ronald Bailey, *Reason* magazine's science correspondent. [4]

Not surprisingly, nanotech's great promise has drawn the federal government's interest. In December, President Bush signed legislation that will roughly retain the current level of funding — nearly $1 billion annually for research and development — for another four years.

"America's nanotechnology effort must be nothing less than the equivalent of President Kennedy's commitment to

---

A nanometer is one-billionth of a meter, or 80,000 times smaller than the width of a human hair.

How Small Is a Nanometer?

A nanometer (nm) is one-billionth of a meter long. A carbon molecule known as a "buckyball" is only 1 nm long, or the length of 10 hydrogen atoms lined up end to end. A human DNA molecule measures 2.5 nm. A single E. coli *bacterium is between 1,000 and 2,000 nm.*

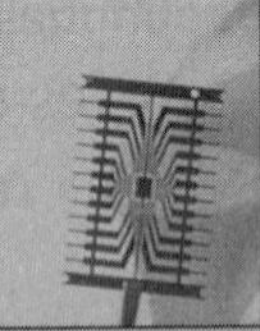

Buckyball (1 nm in diameter)

DNA (2.5 nm in diameter)

Transistor on computer chip (50 nm)

Blood cell (2,000-5,000 nm)

Human hair (60,000-120,000 nm)

Dust mite (200,000 nm)

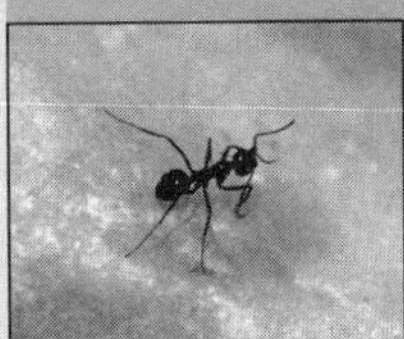

Head of a pin (1-2 million nm)

Ant (5 million nm)

Average-size man (1.8 billion nm)

Source: National Nanotechnology Initiative

landing a man on the moon," Sen. Ron Wyden, D-Ore., a co-sponsor of the legislation, told nanotech executives at an April 2 meeting in Washington, D.C. "In 2004, the idea of growing steel or highway pavement that can repair itself probably seems just as far-fetched to most Americans. But that's why America needs a nanotechnology 'moon shot' to make America see the possibilities of nanotechnology and realize its benefits."

"There is a vital role for the federal government to make sure there is adequate support for research and development," agrees Phillip Bond, undersecretary of Commerce for technology policy. "If this works out like we think it will, it will have a huge impact on our economy and society."

Indeed, the National Science Foundation (NSF) predicts that by 2015, nanotechnology products will be generating more than $1 trillion in revenue.

Investors are bullish about the industry's future. Most nanotech firms are less than a decade old, but some already are stock market favorites. And several stock indexes track the sector, including one created by Merrill Lynch. Some industry-watchers worry, however, that nanotech firms are being hyped in a way that recalls the Internet, or dot-com, boom and bust of a few years ago.

"The *Brave New World* of nanotechnology is actually a lot farther away than most people think, so investors need to be careful because there's a lot of unsubstantiated hype out there," says Michael Richardson, a senior analyst at the Freedonia Group, an industrial-research firm in Cleveland.

Industry growth also could be slowed by health and safety concerns, sparked by recent studies indicating that some nanoparticles could be harmful if ingested. Environmental groups like Canada's ETC and Greenpeace call for a global moratorium on new research until more is known about nanotech's impact.

But nanotech advocates counter that government and industry take very seriously their obligation to conduct safe research and to create safe products. "Of course, there are safety concerns, as in any industry, and we should address them," says Lynn E. Foster, a Los Angeles nanotechnology analyst. "But there is nothing here that warrants a moratorium."

A moratorium would be disastrous, supporters say, because the technology is already transforming many industries, and the progress is expected to accelerate.

"The impact of this is going to be as great, if not greater, than the steam engine or the computer," says Julie Chen, an NSF program director. "People are going to look back and see it as another Industrial Revolution."

Still, if nanotechnology does fulfill its great promise, it will also raise a host of new and possibly dangerous ethical concerns. Sun Microsystems co-founder Bill Joy worries that if scientists lose control of the technology it could actually threaten human existence. Mihail C. Roco, a senior adviser on nanotechnology for the NSF, worries that nanotech developments could widen the gap between rich and poor.

What Is Nanotechnology?

Broadly speaking, nanotechnology is the science of manipulating inorganic materials at the atomic or molecular level. Although scientists don't yet agree on a more precise definition of the new science, many say that something qualifies as nanotechnology when the work occurs at the scale of 100 nanometers* or less.

Matter behaves in different ways depending on size. Particles bigger than 100 nanometers generally adhere to the laws of physics laid out in the 17th century by Isaac Newton, such as gravity and the notion that for every action there is an equal and opposite reaction. But matter smaller than 100 nanometers is generally governed by quantum physics and behaves more erratically.

Some researchers believe that simply operating at less than 100 nanometers is not enough to qualify as nanotech. They hold that the matter must also be manipulated in ways that take into account quantum physics.

In this view, merely shrinking a transistor to 90 nanometers would not be nanotechnology because the technique still employs methods consistent with Newtonian laws. On the other hand, using holographic laser light to move nanotubes that are just a few nanometers wide would qualify, because the laser is aimed at overcoming the strange quantum properties that come into play at that tiny scale. [1]

Ironically, MIT engineer K. Eric Drexler had another definition in mind when he coined the term "nanotechnology" in the early 1980s. He simply wanted a "sexier" way to refer to "molecular manufacturing" — the science of assembling atoms and molecules into simple "machines."

Today, Drexler says his definition has been "hijacked" by scientists who wanted their work with small particles "to get more respect" than it did when it was just called material science or chemistry.

Drexler says he's willing to share the term, but he is angry because many scientists now say that molecular manufacturing should not be included in the definition of nanotechnology because they believe it is not scientifically possible.

"They want the original meaning to go away because they think [molecular manufacturing] is science fiction and, frankly, because they don't understand it," he says.

* A nanometer is one-billionth of a meter. The head of pin is 1-2 million nanometers wide. Red blood cells are 10,000 nanometers wide.

[1] Nicholas Varchaver, "Is Nanotech Ready for Its Close-up?" *Fortune*, May 17, 2004, p. 153.

As experts look at the field's future, here are some of the questions they are asking:

Does nanotechnology endanger the environment and human health?

In Michael Crichton's best-selling 2002 novel *Prey*, self-replicating and intelligent nanobots threaten to eliminate all life on Earth. Likewise, Joy's now famous piece for *Wired*, "The Future Doesn't Need Us," posits that nano-engineered plants or bacteria could destroy the biosphere, turning all life on the planet into "gray goo." [5]

The real nanotech revolution is not far enough along to wreak such havoc. But some scientists say industry and government thus far have ignored questions about nanotech's safety.

"No one really knows whether nanotechnology is [hazardous] or not," says Pat Mooney, executive director of ETC Group, in Winnipeg, Canada, which has spearheaded successful campaigns against genetically modified foods. "We have hundreds of products on the market right now, but few people have been looking into whether they pose any dangers."

Roger Kasperson, director of the Stockholm Environmental Institute, agrees that nanotechnology presents potentially dangerous unknowns. "Critics of nuclear power were called irrational," he says, "[But] we don't know what the risks of nano are, and we won't for some time." [6]

Early studies have raised warning flags, Mooney notes. "In the last year, not one of 12 major studies on nanotech has given the technology a clean bill of health," he says. "That doesn't inspire confidence."

Eva Oberdörster, an environmental toxicologist at Southern Methodist University in Dallas, found that a commonly used nanoparticle — a carbon molecule known as a "buckyball" — causes severe brain and liver damage when ingested by fish. [7]

Other studies suggest that similar nanoparticles might damage the lungs, creating the prospect of workplace injuries. [8] For instance, in 2002, when DuPont researchers "washed" nanotubes into rats' lungs, they began gasping for air, and 15 percent died almost immediately.

"It was the highest death rate we had ever seen," said lead researcher David B. Warheit. But the 85 percent that survived recovered within 24 hours, leading researchers to conclude that the rats suffocated because of nanotubes' tendency to clump rapidly — an area now being studied further. [9] The surviving rats eventually developed granulomas — abnormalities that disrupt oxygen absorption — but without the inflammatory response that normally accompanies such lesions.

"The response in the body was quite unique," said Vicki Colvin, director of the federally funded Center for Biological and Environmental Nanotechnology at Rice University. "They behaved differ-

Continued on p. 523

Where Is Nanotech Taking Us?

In a widely circulated essay four years ago, Sun Microsystems co-founder Bill Joy issued a dire warning about technology.

"The 21st-century technologies — genetics, nanotechnology and robotics — are so powerful that they can spawn whole new classes of accidents and abuses," Joy wrote in *Wired* magazine. [1]

Joy spun out a particularly terrifying scenario for nanotechnology, positing that intelligent, self-replicating nanomachines could cover the planet, wiping out all life.

The solution, Joy proposed, is to suspend research into nanobots until we've had a chance to think more deeply about the consequences of such new technology. "It would seem worthwhile to question whether we need to take such a high risk of total destruction to gain yet more knowledge and yet more things; common sense says that there is a limit to our material needs — and that certain knowledge is too dangerous and is best forgone." [2]

Vladimir Chaloupka, a professor of physics at the University of Washington in Seattle, says the warning was especially meaningful coming from one of Silicon Valley's leading figures. "It was good to have someone like him bring this up," he says, "because we are constantly bombarded by optimistic news about technology [implying that] science is good, by definition."

Joy and Chaloupka say the threat from nanotech is particularly insidious because nanotechnology — unlike earlier, potentially dangerous technologies, such as atomic weapons — does not require an enormous, government-funded Manhattan Project. "You won't need hundreds of millions of dollars and a huge facility that can be detected to do this," Chaloupka says. "You can do this with little more than a computer."

NASA Ames Research Center

Carbon nanotubes create millions of tiny electrical circuits on computer chips.

But many nanotech advocates dismiss such concerns as unnecessarily alarmist. "This is too wild, too soon," says F. Mark Modzelewski, founder and executive director of the NanoBusiness Alliance, an industry trade group. "This is the sort of stuff college professors talk about over their third glass of Merlot. It's not grounded in reality."

Mihail C. Roco, a senior adviser for nanotechnology at the National Science Foundation, agrees. "These opinions have not been embraced by people in the nanotech community, because what is predicted is so far from where we are in the field that it is not a realistic concern," he says. "This idea of nanobots multiplying into infinity is not realistic."

Even if doomsday scenarios don't occur, other ethical questions still need to be addressed before further technological development, Roco says. For instance, he worries that nanotechnology could "deepen the class divide" if it is not made available to everyone.

"There is already a big gap between the haves and the have-nots, and this could make it worse, particularly the advances coming in the medical field," he says. "So, along with our scientific work, we need to develop parallel social research to help us distribute research funds in ways that give us the best chance of this new technology benefiting the general public."

Nanotechnology also could significantly impact other important social paradigms. For instance, says Davis Baird, chairman of the Nanocenter at the University of South Carolina in Columbia, if nanotechnology significantly increases the human lifespan, as some predict, it would raise a number of important questions.

"There are the obvious issues: Like how will this affect insurance or pensions or employment? But there also are more subtle questions: What will this do to your relationship with your spouse and children? Will we be able to stay married to the same person for 120 years?"

Despite such challenges, and potential pitfalls, Phillip Bond, undersecretary of Commerce for technology policy, is confident about the future. "Every technological advance so far has brought with it an upside and a downside, and indeed, our history in this country is in many ways about managing the downside and harvesting the upside," Bond says "But I'm optimistic, because we're a democracy. Democracies are better equipped to handle both the good and bad because we're able to openly examine and debate these changes."

But Chaloupka is not so sanguine. "To have a chance to effectively deal with these issues, we have to be paying attention to them," he says. "And right now, we're not doing that."

---

[1] Quoted in Bill Joy, "Why the Future Doesn't Need Us," *Wired*, April 2000. www.wired.com/wired/archive/8.04/joy_pr.html

[2] Quoted in *ibid.*

Continued from p. 521

ently than other carbon-based ultrafine particles." [10]

Industry supporters have pointed out that dissolving nanoparticles in water before exposing them to lung tissue is unrealistic, since humans would most likely be exposed to nano materials through inhalation.

Researchers also have found that rodents' lung cells cannot detect and break down nanoparticles as easily as they do larger air-pollution particles. And nanoparticles have been found capable of crossing the blood-brain barrier, allowing particles to travel from the throat directly into the brain. If nanoparticles can enter the brain, some scientists ask, can they also cross the placenta and affect a developing fetus? Meanwhile, French researchers found that nanotubes can enter the cell nuclei, where the body's genetic code is located, and in some cases have caused the cells to die. [11]

"It would be unwise to claim that just because there are tiny amounts, it's harmless," said Jim Romine, director for materials science and engineering at DuPont's global research campus near Wilmington, Del. [12]

In preliminary studies, a study led by researchers at the National Aeronautics and Space Administration's (NASA) Johnson Space Center found that inhaling vast amounts of nanotubes is extremely dangerous. In another study, Vyvyan Howard, a pathology specialist at the University of Liverpool, found that nanoscale materials are toxic and can be easily ingested, inhaled or absorbed. [13]

Skeptics worry that safety concerns will only grow as technical advances proliferate, overwhelming society's ability to determine whether they are harmful or not. "Our understanding of the impact of nanotechnology is falling behind developments," says David Rejeski, director of the Foresight and Governance Project at the Woodrow Wilson International Center for Scholars. "This is only going to get worse."

Meanwhile, no one knows how much nanowaste is being produced each year from the hundreds of tons of nanomaterials being produced in U.S. laboratories and factories or the impact it is having on the environment, and no special regulations exist for its disposal. And no one knows the long-term effects of nanoparticles that accumulate in organic tissue. [14]

Mooney's group, Greenpeace and other environmental organizations have proposed a "moratorium" on nanotechnology research until laboratories have created tough safety standards and enforcement mechanisms. Mooney also has called for all nanotech products that touch human skin — like sunscreens and cosmetics — to be "pulled off the shelves" until they are shown to be safe by independent studies. "People are putting sunscreen [with nanoparticles] on their babies, and we don't know if it is safe or not," he adds.

But nanotechnology advocates say that while any potential risks should be studied, a moratorium on research or pulling products off the shelf is a gross overreaction, especially since no injuries or accidents have been associated with the technology.

"Safety is a perfectly legitimate issue and, by all means, it should be explored," says analyst Foster. "But I haven't seen any evidence that this is a dramatic problem that needs to be halted until we figure it out."

Nanotech advocates also point out that both industry and the federal government are exploring nanotech safety. According to E. Clayton Teague, director of the National Nanotechnology Coordination Office, $105.8 million — or 11 percent — of the $961 million the federal government is spending on nanotech research this fiscal year is earmarked for health and environmental studies. (*See graph, p. 528.*)

However, of that $105.8 million, only $8.5 million is being used to study the potential impact of nanotechnology on health and the environment. The rest is for basic research and environmental and health applications of the technology. [15] "We've been asking for a lot more federal environmental research," says Modzelewski, of the NanoBusiness Alliance.

"It's clear we are underinvesting in this area," said Tom Kalil, special assistant to the chancellor for science and technology at the University of California, Berkeley. [16]

AFP Photo/Stephen Jaffe

President Bush signs the 21st Century Nanotechnology Research and Development Act on Dec. 3, 2003, as industry and government officials watch, including Energy Secretary Spencer Abraham (second from left) and Sen. George Allen, R-Va. (third from right).

Nanotech Research Funding Is Rising

President Bill Clinton launched the National Nanotechnology Initiative in 2000 to coordinate the government's research and development (R&D) efforts. In November 2003, Congress expanded the initiative, authorizing $3.7 billion over four years beginning in 2005 — the biggest federal commitment to technology research in 40 years. The National Science Foundation and the Departments of Defense and Energy receive the largest share of the funding. The Environmental Protection Agency only received $5 million in 2004 and is slated to receive the same amount in 2005.

Federal Nanotech Research Funding

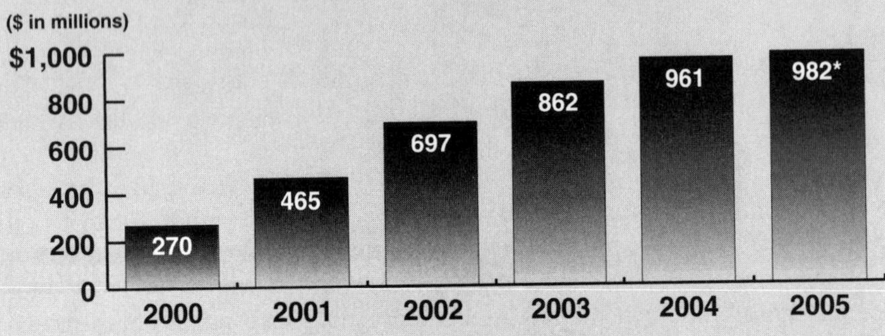

* *Enacted, not actual funds*

Source: National Science Foundation, April 1, 2004

But advocates counter that industry also is spending money on the environmental and health impacts of nanotechnology. "I get the sense that [nanotech proponents] are really trying to play it safe here and are pouring a lot of money into research," says Joshua Keller, a scientist at the Federation of American Scientists. "They want to avoid the debacle that occurred a few years ago with genetically modified [(GM)] food."

Moreover, a research moratorium would make it impossible to discover what is and isn't safe, nanotech advocates say. "You need to do research to determine if something is safe," says Davis Baird, chairman of the Nanocenter at the University of South Carolina, Columbia.

Furthermore, nanotech supporters say opponents are trying to set impossibly high standards for nanotechnology safety. "There is a feeling that unless you can prove that this is 100 percent safe, we shouldn't be doing it," says Christine Peterson, co-founder and president of the Foresight Institute, a nanotech think tank in Palo Alto, Calif.

"We produce many new chemicals every year, and about 85 percent of them are submitted to the EPA without human health data," she says. "This is very much the same thing."

In addition, most nanoproducts do not even release potentially dangerous particles into the air or water, she adds. "With most new things, like tennis rackets or clothes, the nanoparticles are embedded in the product," Peterson says. "So this idea that you have all these loose molecules all over the place is simply not true."

And even loose nanoparticles, so far, have not proven dangerous.

"People might not know this, but we're breathing in nanoparticles all the time," Baird says. "Diesel engines belch out nanoparticles and, so far, they haven't been identified as harmful to human health."

But some scientists and environmental advocates point out that nanoparticles behave differently — and sometimes unpredictably — due to the unique nature of nanophysics. For instance, gold is normally an inert metal, but gold nanoparticles become intensely chemically reactive, potentially disrupting biological processes. "The smaller the particles, the more toxic they become," said Howard of the University of Liverpool. [17]

Is the business community overestimating nanotechnology's potential?

A few years ago, the study of nanotechnology was largely confined to futurists and academic research laboratories. Today, it has gone commercial — and in a big way.

Many of the more than 1,200 firms in the field, like Nano-Tex, have attached the hot prefix "nano" to their names. Even older companies have embraced the trendy term. The Denver computer-engineering firm Sunlight Systems, for instance, is now Nano-Pierce Technologies. [18]

"It's like when companies added 'dot.com' during the Internet boom or 'tech' during the '80s PC boom," said Josh Wolfe, an analyst at a New York venture capital firm. "Being involved in nanotech opens up a whole new area of available resources." [19]

Meanwhile, stocks of several nano start-ups have jumped significantly in the last 18 months — sometimes by more than 100 percent. And on April 1, 2004, Merrill Lynch launched its "Nanotech Index," which tracks 25 bellwether nanotech firms.

"Nanotechnology could be the next growth innovation," said Steven Milunovich, Merrill Lynch's chief global-technology strategist. [20]

Still, the publicity surrounding nanotechnology sounds hyperbolic at times.

"We will make progress equivalent to that of the whole 20th century in the next 15 years," declared information-technology entrepreneur Ray Kurzweil, author of *The Age of Spiritual Machines*, at a 2002 nanotechnology conference. "Progress in the 21st century will be equivalent to 20,000 years of progress at today's rate." [21]

But some industry experts say the hype over nanotech's prospects recalls the way Internet stocks were promoted in the late 1990s, and later went bankrupt.

"You're buying the equivalent of an Internet stock a couple of years ago," says Thomas Theis, head of physical-science research at IBM. "If you think you're smart enough to get out before the bubble bursts, good luck."

Theis argues that nanotechnology should not be seen as a new miracle industry that will make every investor rich. Instead, he says, it is part of a broad historical trend toward miniaturization that began more than 100 years ago.

"This recent run-up in nanotech stocks — to two, three and five times their original value — is not warranted, at least not by anything I've seen in the last year or two," he says. "What we have here is a mini-bubble."

The Freedonia Group's Richardson points to other evidence of hype. "People keep talking about a $1 trillion industry in 10 years, but I have yet to see any good explanation of how they got to that figure and what it means," he says. He puts nanotech sales at a still impressive $35 billion by 2020.

Indeed, technological difficulties may slow industry growth, some experts say. Small particles behave strangely, making the manipulation of matter on the atomic or molecular level very difficult.

And manufacturing such tiny particles or machines poses a whole new set of challenges. While it may be possible to create an innovative and useful nanoparticle, it will be difficult to reliably and cheaply produce the millions or even billions needed to make an invention a viable product, experts say.

"I don't think people realize how hard it is to bring a lot of this great research from the laboratory to the marketplace," says the NSF's Chen, who awards research grants for studies aimed at overcoming nanotech's manufacturing hurdles. "We're just really starting to figure out how to do a lot of that."

But other industry-watchers say the investment climate surrounding nanotechnology is not being over-hyped.

"You just haven't seen the stupid money — people throwing their money into something without thinking simply because it's nanotech," analyst Foster says. "Compared to the dot-com trouble of a few years back, nanotech investors are being quite prudent."

"There's been a big backlash against overoptimism on Wall Street," Keller of the Federation of American Scientists says. "I see a lot of people approaching [nanotech] much more carefully."

Besides, experts on both sides of the argument agree that the level of investment in nanotech so far is relatively small. "You have to have a lot of money, a lot of investors in order to have a bubble," South Carolina's Baird says. "I don't see it happening. The level of venture capital just isn't there."

"Some of the larger venture capital firms that can afford to take chances have made some investments, but not a lot of smaller firms," Foster adds. "And you haven't seen this rush of companies going public" as they did during the dot-com bubble.

But enthusiasts say that even if there is some unwarranted hype, nanotech's prospects are enormous. "The potential for this field and, by association, for investors, is huge," says the Woodrow Wilson Center's Rejeski. "So there might be some hype that isn't justified, but if this field delivers in one or two areas — like medicine or information technology — then you're OK. All it takes is a few of your horses to cross the finish line, and most investors win."

Should the government provide substantial financial support to nanotechnology research?

On Dec. 3, 2003, President Bush signed the 21st Century Nanotechnology

The National Nanotech Initiative at a Glance

Research: *NNI supports about 2,500 active awards in about 300 academic organizations and 200 private organizations in all 50 states.*

Education: *7,000 students and teachers were trained in nanotechnology in 2003. Virtually all U.S. science and engineering colleges now have nanotech science and engineering courses.*

Significant infrastructure: *An estimated 40,000 people work in nanotech in the United States; 60 universities have nanotech user capabilities, and five research networks, including the National Nanofabrication Infrastructure Network and the Network for Computational Nanotechnology, have been established.*

Source: National Nanotechnology Coordination Office, April 2, 2004

Research and Development Act, which authorized $3.7 billion for nanotech research and development from 2005 to 2008. The government had already allotted $849 million for nanotech research in 2004, double the funding in 2001.

Supporters of the new law argue that government funding is necessary if the nascent field is to grow, particularly in the United States.

"Because of the complexity, cost and high risk associated with nanotechnology research, the private sector is often unable to assure itself of short-to-medium-term returns on R&D investments in this field," Richard M. Russell, associate director for technology for the Office of Science and Technology, told the House Committee on Science on March 19, 2003. "The [law] is a critical link between high-risk, novel research concepts and new technologies that can be developed by industry." [22]

Many nanotech proponents advocate even more government support. Citing already-intense competition from Japan, China and Europe, they say government money for basic research is vital to the United States keeping its lead in the field. Currently, Americans hold about 75 percent of the 7,000 patents on nanotechnology innovations. [23]

But Clyde Wayne Crews Jr., director of technical studies at the Competitive Enterprise Institute, a pro-free market think tank, argues that government funding smacks of central planning and that the market, not politicians, should decide whether the science has real commercial value.

"If there is so much promise in this exciting new technology, why do we need government money involved?" he asks "We ought to be treating this the same way we treated software, where we left the funding of research to the private sector — and look what happened."

James Gattuso, a research fellow in regulatory policy at the conservative Heritage Foundation, agrees. "Having the government involved in this kind of thing only makes sense if you believe that the government is better than venture capitalists, banks and the stock market at allocating research dollars," he says. "But the government has shown that, actually, it's not very good at it. The government could steer everything in one direction, but that might not be the most practical or useful direction. They're not the best at determining what is or isn't relevant."

Opponents cite several government science initiatives, including the never-completed super-conducting super-collider and the troubled, over-budget International Space Station, as examples of government scientific endeavors that they say wasted tens of billions of dollars and accomplished little. [24]

By contrast, adds Crews, the marketplace regulates risk: "You won't release something into the market unless it's relevant and reliable. That's the opposite of government-funded research, which doesn't do that because the funding doesn't depend on getting it right."

But supporters of government funding point out that the government is the only institution that can afford to do important basic research, which may not be profitable itself but which could provide the basis for a multitude of future ventures.

"At this stage, we need to be funding adventurous and speculative research, and private industry generally doesn't do that," IBM's Theis says. "There are many failures with this kind of research, but it's also the sort of research that is the foundation upon which successful industries are built."

Undersecretary Bond points to several areas where he says the government's role is vital, such as work by the National Institute of Standards and Technology to develop precise nanomeasurement standards so private equipment makers can make nanoscale measuring equipment. "That's the sort of basic research the government does," Bond says.

Supporters also dispute the notion that government funding will inevitably lead to the picking of winners and losers. "Nanotech is so broad," says Chen of the NSF, which distributes much of the government money set aside for scientific research. "We're not funding any one part of it, such as nanomedicine or nanoelectronics. We're funding basic R&D that industries will use as they see fit."

But Gattuso says that despite Chen's assurances, government money will be highly influential. "Whenever you talk about funding, you're ultimately talking about choices," he says. "What gets money and what doesn't will determine whether we go in one direction or another." ■

BACKGROUND

Seeing the Invisible

During the 5th century B.C., Greek philosophers began to wonder how many times matter could be divided. Leucippus reasoned that matter could not be divided infinitely, insisting that one would eventually find a particle that could not be broken into smaller components. [25] His student, the philosopher Democritus, called these smallest particles "atomos" (Greek for "unbreakable.") [26]

During the next 2,000 years, atomism was widely debated, but the theory of basic, indivisible particles remained unproven.

English scientist Robert Boyle, the "father" of chemistry, took the first step toward proving the existence of atoms. In the early 1660s, he showed that compressing air into a smaller and smaller space decreased its volume. Boyle reasoned that the volume had shrunk because air, like all other matter, had atoms and these atoms were

Continued on p. 528

Chronology

1940s-1970s

The rise of consumer culture, coupled with greater social mobility, increases the demand for smaller products, spurring miniaturization.

1947
Scientists at Bell Labs invent the transistor, which soon replaces vacuum tubes in electronic products and revolutionizes efforts at miniaturization.

1953
James Watson, an American, and Francis Crick, an Englishman, discover deoxyribonucleic acid or DNA, which carries the blueprints of life.

1959
American physicist Richard Feynman theorizes that the microscopic world will soon be harnessed for a variety of practical uses.

1965
Gordon Moore, a chemist at Intel, predicts that semiconductors will double in power every 18 months. His prediction, dubbed Moore's Law, has proven correct.

1971
Intel chips contain 2,000 transistors. The number will rise to 55 million by 2004.

1980s

Scientists begin thinking about the practical applications of nanotechnology.

1981
Two researchers at IBM's Zurich Research Lab invent the scanning tunneling microscope, which enables scientists to see atoms for the first time.

1984
Canadian environmentalists form the Action Group on Erosion, Technology and Concentration (ETC Group), dedicated to the socially responsible development of new technologies.

1985
Scientists Richard Smalley and Robert Curl at Rice University in Houston discover the nanocarbon particle known as the "buckyball."

1986
K. Eric Drexler publishes *Engines of Creation*, detailing his concept of molecular manufacturing and using the term "nanotechnology."

1989
Drexler and Christine L. Peterson establish the Foresight Institute to "help prepare society for anticipated advanced technologies."

1990-Present

Nanotechnology moves from the theoretical to the practical as many companies begin developing nanotech products.

1990
Scientists at IBM arrange 35 xenon atoms to form the company's logo.

1991
Japanese scientist Sumio Iijima invents carbon nanotubes.

1997
IBM uses nanotechnology to develop computer disk-drive heads that can store up to 100 times more memory than older heads.

2000
Wall Street's "dot-com bubble" bursts, causing hundreds of billions in losses for investors.

January 2000
Sixteen federal agencies establish the National Nanotechnology Initiative to coordinate nanotech activities.

April 2000
Sun Microsystems co-founder Bill Joy warns of the dangers of nanotech in "The Future Doesn't Need Us" in *Wired* magazine.

Sept. 28-29, 2000
National Science Foundation organizes the first conference to examine the ethical implications of nanotechnology.

May 2001
Nanotech start-up Nanosys is founded in Palo Alto, Calif.

October 2001
The first nanotechnology trade association, the NanoBusiness Alliance, is formed

2002
Best-selling author Michael Crichton publishes *Prey*, a novel about a swarm of self-replicating nanobots that tries to destroy humanity.

Dec. 3, 2003
President Bush signs the 21st Century Nanotechnology Research and Development Act, which authorizes $3.7 billion for research over four years.

March 28, 2004
Eva Oberdörster of Southern Methodist University in Dallas shows that fish that ingest "buckyballs" suffer from brain and liver damage.

April 1, 2004
Merrill Lynch launches the Nanotech Index to track nanotechnology stocks.

2015
Nanotechnology will be a $1 trillion industry by this date, the National Science Foundation predicts.

R&D Funding for Health and Environment

The National Nanotechnology Initiative allocated $106 million in 2004 for nanotech research and development related to health and environment, or 11 percent of the total $961 million nanotech research budget. But only 8 percent, or $8.5 million, of that was earmarked to study potential dangers of nanotechnology.

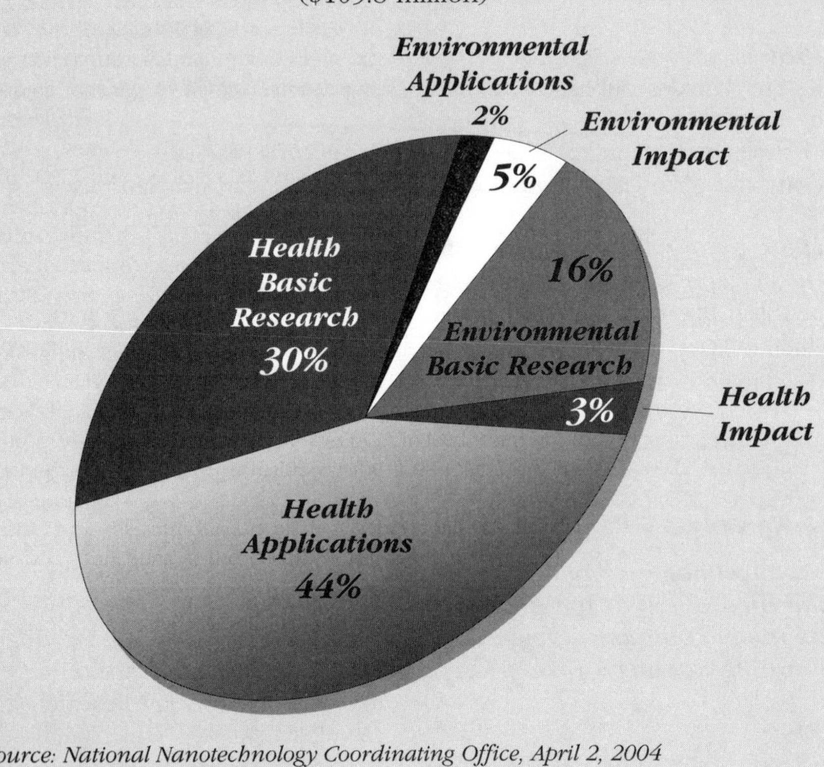

Source: National Nanotechnology Coordinating Office, April 2, 2004

Continued from p. 526

pushed closer together when the air was compressed. [27]

Boyle's laboratory assistant, Robert Hooke, went in a different direction. Although he did not invent the microscope, Hooke was among the first to use it for scientific discovery, examining such small wonders as the cellular structure of cork and the facets of a fly's eye. Along with the Dutch scientist Anton van Leeuwenhoek, who discovered the first microscopic organisms, Hooke sparked a scientific revolution that would witness a centuries-long search, as historian Daniel J. Boorstin observed, "to see the invisible" in nature's many realms. [28]

In the next three centuries, increasingly powerful microscopes helped discover smaller and smaller worlds. In 1953, James Watson, an American, and Englishman Francis Crick discovered the blueprints of life for every creature, the double helix of deoxyribonucleic acid (DNA) contained inside each cell. [29]

Meanwhile, other discoveries increased understanding of the broader physical universe. Over the course of the 19th and 20th centuries, scientists found that atoms cluster together in different combinations to form molecules, which in turn make up the basic elements of matter in the universe, like oxygen, hydrogen, lead and carbon. Led by England's Ernest Rutherford, researchers also determined the internal structure of atoms, with protons and neutrons surrounded by electrons. [30]

But the search for the small was not confined to the theoretical. By the 19th century, industrialization and the rise of a more mobile, consumer culture created a demand for lighter and more portable products. Perhaps the greatest advance in miniaturization came in 1947, when three scientists at Bell Laboratories invented the transistor. Made from several layers of super-conducting materials, transistors proved a cheap, reliable and low-power means to generate and control electrical signals. Most important, they were tiny.

Before transistors, electrical signals in radios, televisions and early computers were carried through bulky, expensive vacuum tubes, which made the products large and heavy. Once transistors began to be used commercially in the 1950s, products could be made smaller. Radios, for instance, were transformed from pieces of furniture into devices that could be held in the palm of one hand.

In addition to miniaturizing existing products, transistors helped create innumerable new ones, most notably the modern computer, through their use of the semiconductor — or the integrated chip.

In 1965, Gordon Moore, a chemist at chipmaker Intel, predicted that semiconductors would double in power every 18 months for the foreseeable future. That meant the number of transistors on each chip had to double, so they needed to continue to shrink.

So far, "Moore's Law" has proven accurate. In 1971, Intel chips contained 2,000 transistors. Today they contain a phenomenal 55 million; future chips will have more than a billion, some experts predict. [31]

Nanotech's Origins

Nobel Prize-winning physicist Richard Feynman is considered the theoretical father of nanotechnology. In 1959, he theorized that the microscopic world would soon be harnessed for a variety of practical uses. "The amount of space available to us for information storage (or other uses) is enormous," he said. "There is nothing besides our clumsy size that keeps us from using this space." [32]

Even though no tools to manipulate atoms or molecules then existed, Feynman predicted that manufacturing on the atomic level eventually would be a reality. Bottom-up production, as he called it, was the opposite of "top-down production," which created products by cutting, carving or molding parts and then piecing them together.

In the late 1970s, K. Eric Drexler, a young American scientist at Massachusetts Institute of Technology, began exploring the practical applications of Feynman's earlier musings.

"Even though my interests as a student were in engineering systems, I began to notice that the people in biochemistry were finding molecular 'machines' in living organisms," he says. "So I asked myself: Can we build machines like this?"

In 1986, Drexler set out his vision of "molecular manufacturing" in his far-sighted book *Engines of Creation.* He envisioned molecule-sized devices that acted like microscopic tools, putting atoms in specific places to form tiny machines.

Drexler pointed out that so-called "molecular assembly" differed from simple chemistry, in which substances are mixed together to create molecular reactions. Instead, he explained, he was describing actual manufacturing, but on the atomic level.

Meanwhile, as nanotechnology was beginning to coalesce conceptually, a number of important tools were created that could assist in practical research. In 1981, researchers at IBM's Zurich Research Lab invented the scanning tunneling microscope, which let scientists see atoms. Four years later, the same scientists developed the atomic force microscope, which further expanded this capability.

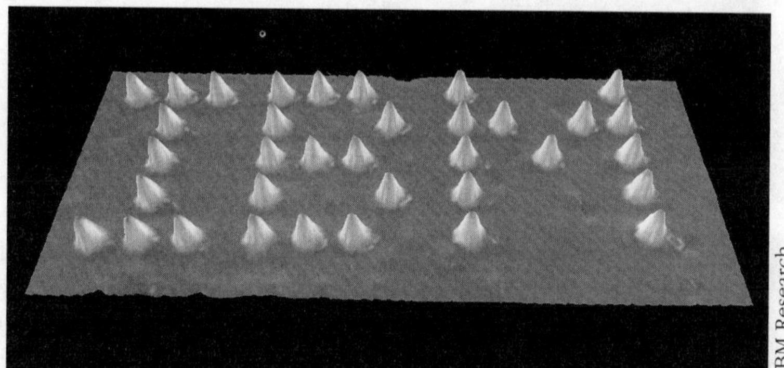

IBM Research

For the first time in history, IBM scientists in 1990 positioned atoms one at a time to spell the company's famous logo. The achievement created the potential for future applications, such as building custom-made molecules atom-by-atom.

"If you want to concentrate on nanotech, you have to be able to see things at that scale," says IBM spokesman William O'Leary. "So this work was a huge milestone."

The next milestone occurred at Rice University, when scientists in 1985 discovered a new carbon molecule containing 60 carbon atoms in the shape of a soccer ball. They called it a "buckyball" because it resembled the geodesic domes built by American architect Buckminster Fuller.

Buckyballs are smaller than a wavelength of light but so strong and stable they can withstand 3,000 atmospheres of pressure. Not surprisingly, they have become one of the key building blocks of nanotechnology products, such as fuel cells. [33]

In 1991, Sumio Iijima, a scientist working for the Japanese electronics firm NEC, transformed buckyballs into long tubes, called nanotubes. Like buckyballs, nanotubes have been used in a variety of nanotech products, including as reinforcing material for the latest lightweight tennis rackets and as a key component in liquid-crystal display screens.

The first efforts to work in nanotechnology were almost whimsical. In 1990, scientists at IBM arranged 35 xenon atoms to spell out the company's three-letter logo. A few years later, Cornell University researchers created a "nano-guitar," a microscopic instrument that could actually be played — using a laser beam to pluck the strings.

While these early demonstrations had little practical use, they spurred the scientific community to greatly expand nanotech research. By the mid-1990s, hundreds of university and corporate labs were working in the new science. ■

CURRENT SITUATION

Product Enhancements

Despite the fantastical predictions of nanotechnology visionaries, most early nanotech applications have been relatively ordinary.

Lucent Technologies Inc/Bell Labs (Both)

Droplets on Nanofields

Water forms a nearly perfect sphere (top) suspended on silicon nanoparticles. By electrically charging the surface, scientists at Bell Labs can drive the liquid through the nanoparticles, causing the droplet to spread (bottom). Potential applications for the new technique include thermal cooling circuits for powerful computers and components for optical communications.

"What we've seen so far has involved enhancing existing products rather than taking great leaps forward," says NSF's Chen.

Still, the "enhancements" already have touched products ranging from computers and digital cameras to clothing and cosmetics. And some of the developments have even been quite significant. For instance, in 1997 IBM developed a process to better control spinning electron particles on the magnetic heads in computer hard-drives. The resulting advance — known as giant megnetoresistive (GMR) disk drive heads — eventually allowed new computers to store up to 100 times more data than older models and accelerated the Internet revolution. [34]

Nanotech also has been used to enhance computer-display screens, specifically allowing electronics makers to produce organic, light-emitting diodes (OLEDs) — tiny particles that glow when electricity passes through them — to make lighter, better screens for notebook computers, cell phones and digital cameras. Although the diodes currently utilize glass backings, scientists say in a few years they will not need glass, making them so light and flexible consumers will be able to fold up computer screens and put them in their pockets. [35]

OLED technology already has led several high-tech firms, including Xerox and Phillips, to begin research on "e-paper," flexible screens with the look and weight of paper that will show black and white text. According to a market-research firm, the market for OLED screens will reach $2.7 billion by 2007. [36]

A different but nonetheless important nanotech enhancement involves the creation of stain- and wrinkle-free textiles. The NanoTex Co., for instance, has created nanoparticles that attach to cotton fibers and create a barrier that causes liquids and other substances to bead up rather than be absorbed by the cotton. The process is used by many clothing manufacturers, including GAP and Old Navy. Next year, the company plans to produce a coating that will help clothes absorb and neutralize body odors, giving clothes a fresh smell through repeat wearings.

Other products being improved with nanotechnology include:

- **Sunscreen:** The use of microscopic metal oxide particles produces a clear sun-blocking lotion without the "white smear" caused by older technologies. [37]
- **Cosmetics:** L'Oreal, Esteé Lauder and other companies are making skin creams and other products with nanoparticles that penetrate deep into the skin, allowing more effective and longer-lasting delivery of vitamins and other agents.
- **Paints and coatings:** Nanoparticles better protect surfaces from decay, scratches and corrosion, and window coatings reduce glare or provide greater insulation. In-

framat, a firm in Farmington, Conn., says its nanotech ceramic coating prevents barnacles from adhering to ship hulls. [38]

Nanotech's Future

Some of the most compelling and valuable advances in nanotechnology are likely to be in medicine. Scientists are particularily excited about targeted drug delivery.

"You put an 'intelligent' particle onto the delivery system so the drug only activates when it finds a tumor or whatever it is looking for," IBM's Theis says.

Nanotechnology also could enable delivery of drugs where traditional molecules are too big to go, such as across the very unporous barrier between the brain and the bloodstream. "They are working on ways to encapsulate medicine in particles small enough to get through," says the Wilson Center's Rejeski.

Using smaller particles also can improve overall drug absorption. In Ireland, the Elan Corp. has developed tiny "nanocrystals" that can carry drug doses. Breaking the dose up into tinier pieces increases the total surface area, allowing the patient to receive more of the medicine. [39]

Advances in diagnostic medical imaging also are in the offing. Researchers at Emory University in Atlanta, led by Shuming Nie, have created "quantum dots," or nanoparticles that light up in different colors when exposed to light. In early tests, they have proven excellent at finding cancerous tumors that might be missed by other methods, such as magnetic-resonance imaging (MRI).

Quantum dots are effective, in part, because they are small enough to pass through the leaky blood vessels found near cancerous cells and lodge near them. Nie has further boosted their detection skills by attaching cancer-finding antibodies to them. [40]

So far, research in mice with cancer has proven very promising. If successful in humans, quantum dots could be used to aid in drug delivery, guiding chemotherapy directly to a tumor. [41]

In the field of information technology, major advances are expected in nano-semiconductors. Since the 1960s, chip manufacturing has focused on shrinking transistors in order to place more of them onto a silicon wafer, increasing the chip's capabilities.

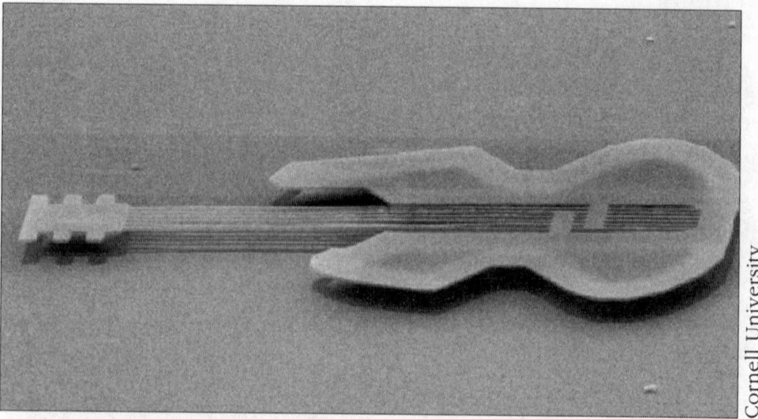
Cornell University

The world's smallest guitar is about the size of a single cell, with six strings each about 50 nanometers, or 100 atoms, wide. Cornell University scientists made it with silicon nanoparticles.

Today's chips have about 55 million transistors, each between 130 nanometers and 180 nanometers in length. But Intel recently announced a transistor just 90 nanometers long. If transistor miniaturization continues, chips will become immensely powerful, greatly increasing the computing power of all information-technology devices.

"Soon our PDAs [personal digital assistants] will have the kind of power that network computer servers do today," Undersecretary Bond says. "This will radically change how we do things."

Bond envisions what he calls "the era of the pervasive computer," whereby small devices (like cell phones and PDAs) will link people to computers that are literally everywhere around them. "We'll constantly be receiving data from the world around us, based on a set of pre-selected preferences we have established," he says. "So, for instance, you'll walk by a GAP store and your computer will automatically tell you that there is a sale on pants in your size."

Nanotech also is likely to dramatically alter the energy industry, with new solar cells that are finally cheap enough to compete with fossil fuels and other energy sources. One of the several nanotech firms working in this area, Nanosys, of Palo Alto, Calif., is developing liquid photovoltaic crystals that can literally be poured onto a surface to harden and create solar panels. That would allow solar cells to be incorporated into the roof of virtually every house and apartment building in America. Solar roofs could provide for an entire household's power needs, from running computers to air-conditioning systems. Extra energy would be stored in batteries for use at night. [42]

Moreover, nanotech is greatly enhancing the development of fuel cells — the hydrogen-powered devices that many believe eventually will power cars, laptops and even cities. Already, Japan's NEC Corp. has developed a new fuel cell for laptops and cell phones that uses specially shaped nanotubes that provide power three times longer than the standard lithium ion batteries now used in computers and wireless phones. [43]

Even the war on terrorism may benefit. For instance, researchers are making progress in producing nanoscale-size sensors to monitor people and detect bombs, chemical weapons and toxins. "We're already building various sensors on the micro scale," Rejeski says. "Nanoscale sensors are not far off."

"We are making great strides in making better, undetectable surveillance devices," agrees the University of South Carolina's Baird, citing "smart dust" reportedly being developed by the National Security Agency. "You could have a situation where you dump a box of this stuff from a helicopter over a house and it will measure the temperature of everything and everyone and use wireless technology to send back this data allowing you to track where everyone is."

Molecular Manufacturing?

Even more amazing, some scientists envision the rise of sophisticated machines built on the nanoscale by other nanomachines. Unlike most nanotech developments today — which involve creating particles with valuable properties — nanomachines would actually be sophisticated devices with moving parts, but on an incredibly small scale.

Even the most optimistic advocates for molecular manufacturing admit that it is at least 10 to 15 years away, if not more.

"We have a huge hump to get over, and that is building the molecular machines capable of building molecular machines," says the Foresight Institute's Drexler, who first proposed molecular manufacturing.

But some experts think Drexler is — at best — wildly optimistic. "I don't know of many real scientists in labs doing nanotechnology who think this is really credible," says Modzelewski of the NanoBusiness Alliance. "There are disruptions — quantum effects — when you work at that level, because every time you move one atom, other atoms in its orbit change position. So you can't simply transfer [building] techniques from the macro level to the nano level."

But if molecular manufacturing does become a reality, it will take nanotechnology to a new level, Drexler predicts. "The payoffs far exceed those we got sending a man to the moon," he says. "For starters, you'll be able to put a billion processors into the same space where you have one today, giving someone a billion times the computing power."

Other possible applications include nanomachines that clean toxins from the air or water or that can swim around a person's blood steam and perform surgical procedures or monitor certain conditions, like a recurrence of cancer.

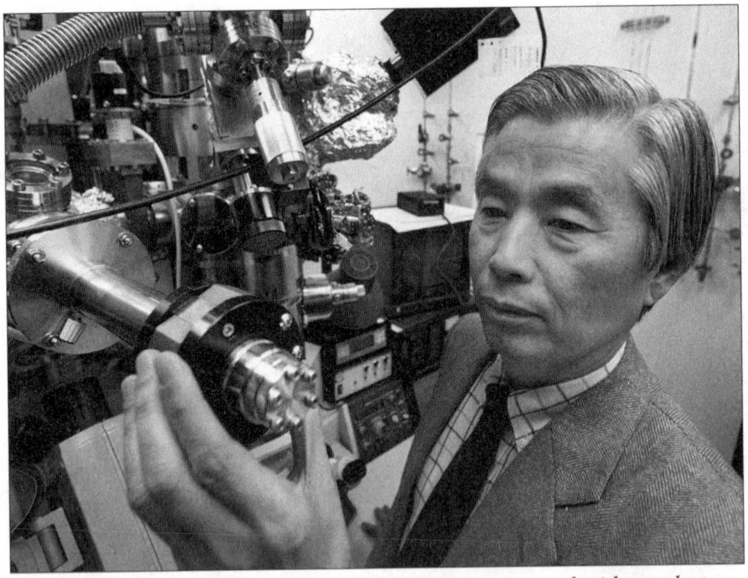

Molecular manufacturing also will have an impact on geopolitics, Drexler says. "If a country fails to do this, it'll be out of the great-power game, period," he says. "Those who get this will dominate almost every industry and by extension the world. Just think of the smart weapons you'd be able to make."

AFP Photo/Yoshikazu Tsuno

Japanese nanotechnology pioneer Sumio Iijima, pictured with an electron microscope, discovered carbon nanotubes in 1991. The narrowest carbon tubes known to science are used in tiny electrical circuits.

Congressional Action

Washington first embraced nanotechnology during the Clinton administration. "Most lawmakers are interested in jobs," said Modzelewski. "They see this as having a huge economic impact." [44]

Clinton had launched a National Nanotechnology Initiative in 2000 to coordinate the government's nanotech research and development efforts, but it was funded on a year-to-year basis. Federal nanotech research has since increased from $255 million in fiscal 1999 to $849 million in 2004. [45]

Then on Nov. 20, 2003, Congress greatly expanded the program, authorizing $3.7 billion over four years — the biggest federal commitment to technology research in 40 years. The 21st Century Nanotechnology Research and Development Act, sponsored by Sens. George Allen, R-Va., and Wyden, created a new National Nanotechnology Coordination Office and a National Nanotechnology Advisory Panel to coordinate federal research efforts. It also called for establishment of nanotech research centers at universities around the country, education and training programs and strategies for transferring nanotechnology — particularly nanomaterials manufacturing — to the marketplace.

"This legislation marshaled America's

Continued on p. 534

At Issue:

Should the government fund nanotechnology research?

F. MARK MODZELEWSKI
MANAGING DIRECTOR, LUX RESEARCH INC.
EXECUTIVE DIRECTOR, NANOBUSINESS ALLIANCE

WRITTEN FOR *THE CQ RESEARCHER*, JUNE 2004

yes

As a nation do we care about jobs? Do we care about our homeland defense? Do we care about the health of our families? Do we care about a cleaner environment? For all these reasons and more, a near-unanimous number of members of Congress — from the most conservative to the most liberal — made a strategic investment in our nation's future by passing the 21st Century Nanotechnology Research and Development Act.

Nanotechnology will affect almost every aspect of our lives, from our clothes to our computers to our medicines. Though nanotechnology discoveries are already entering the marketplace, it is just the beginning. Revenues are predicted to reach a trillion dollars in little over a decade. However, this level of economic impact and all the benefits that come with it doesn't happen by chance. It happens through planning, smarts, investment and hard work.

Americans believe in leaving the world a better place for our children, and our nation's nanotechnology efforts do just that. The act invests nearly $1 billion a year in basic research and support programs, almost all of which goes to universities. So we're not talking corporate welfare or industrial policy here. What companies, investors and entrepreneurs are doing is taking the discoveries the act finances at universities and government labs and turning them into products that will change our lives and economy. This is exactly what we saw from our government's commitment to the space race, the Internet and the Human Genome Project — all programs that even nanotechnology's biggest critics would admit pale in comparison to nanotech's potential impact.

Investment and planning in nanotechnology are particularly vital in the global economy. Unlike past technology-development waves, where the United States was a leader from the start, our nation doesn't have a clear lead in nanotechnology. Some would argue that we're falling behind in innovation and investment. Japan, China, the European Union and others have made major commitments to nanotechnology and are positioning themselves for international leadership.

We learned as kids the story of the grasshopper and the ant. Unlike the ant, the grasshopper fooled around, acted arrogantly and didn't plan for the future. Come winter, he starved while the ant and his family thrived. It's a simple lesson our political leaders have thankfully remembered in regards to nanotechnology.

CLYDE WAYNE CREWS JR.
DIRECTOR OF TECHNOLOGY STUDIES,
COMPETITIVE ENTERPRISE INSTITUTE

WRITTEN FOR *THE CQ RESEARCHER*, JUNE 2004

no

Nanotechnology advocates face a choice: They can work to assure that their industry remains as unregulated as possible. Or they can pursue government funding and promotion, which will assure heavy regulation and affect the evolution and market environment of the technology.

Apparently, an elated industry has chosen the latter, as evidenced by the recent signing of the 21st Century Nanotechnology Research and Development Act.

The industry already has its hands full fighting nanotech's opponents, who embrace a "precautionary principle" that could halt nanotechnology to avoid alleged risks. While nanotechnology poses risks, it also promises to reduce risks by making our environment cleaner.

Along with sound professional ethics, a prerequisite for managing risks associated with cutting-edge technologies is having healthy liability insurance markets backing up labs and products. Government dominance could take nanotech research out of the realm of insurability. This creates a problem for future innovation. For example, the Price Andersen Act limited nuclear power plant liability but resulted in total regulation. We'll never know if a more market-oriented development path might have made nuclear power more viable.

Nanotech is susceptible to government policy in other ways. Today's military and homeland security emphasis on nanotechnology can impact its evolution and the public policies affecting it. Homeland security legislation already indemnifies some companies from liability when their "security technologies" fail. Such interventions might pre-empt a private liability market for nano from ever emerging. Yet we need such risk-management instruments to incentivize the engineering of safety procedures and counterbalancing technologies to offset emerging risks.

Rather than funding particular lucky grantees, government should instead work to improve the business, tax and regulatory environment. Government funding would likely scatter nanotech research across multiple universities. But in a more rational world — and with reformed antitrust regulations — innovators could pool efforts or devise sophisticated sharing agreements, which might make more attractive targets for investment. Improved, private standard setting, joint research and other risk-sharing arrangements could overcome the problems that otherwise justify government funding.

We should abolish the federal National Nanotechnology Initiative, and instead improve the business climate. Nanotechnology needs a Bill Gates, not a Big Brother.

Continued from p. 532

nanotechnology research efforts into a single driving force," Wyden said. "It created a smart, accelerated and organized approach to our country's nanotechnology research, development and education." [46]

The bill's supporters argued that putting federal nanotech funding on a four-year rather than a year-to-year cycle would allow long-term planning. The money will be distributed to colleges, universities and research centers through the Energy Department, the EPA, NASA, the National Institute of Standards and Technology and the National Science Foundation. [47]

Among other things, the law mandates that the National Research Council (NRC) study whether self-replicating nanoscale devices can be created and whether standards, guidelines or strategies are needed to ensure the responsible development of such machines. The NRC will also oversee studies on how nanotechnology can improve encryption and defensive technologies, enhance human intelligence and develop artificial intelligence.

Additionally, the law calls for studies of the potential societal, ethical, environmental and work-force impacts of nanotechnology. Six months earlier, the House had rejected, 207-217, efforts by Democrats to require studies of the environmental and toxicological impacts of nanotechnology and its potential to help produce clean, inexpensive energy. The bill's sponsor, Science Committee Chairman Rep. Sherwood Boehlert, R-N.Y., argued the requirements were too restrictive. [48]

But Senate co-sponsor Allen warned nanotech executives and academics that they risk a public backlash similar to Europe's rejection of bioengineered foodstuffs if research on the environmental and health impacts of nanotech does not keep pace with development of practical uses of the technology.

"You only have to look at the field of genetically modified organisms to find a very promising field of science which lost public confidence, especially in Europe, and, therefore, dramatically lost support and funding," Allen told the National Nanotechnology Initiative Conference in Washington, on April 1, 2004. "If a large portion of the general public feels that science has overstepped its bounds — whether by misinformation or not — then general enthusiasm and support for further discovery of new technologies can whither away very quickly."

That's precisely why the law called for establishment of an American Nanotechnology Preparedness Center, charged with evaluating the societal, ethical, environmental, educational and workforce implications of nanotechnology, Wyden told the group.

Nano Backlash

Most scientists agree it will be years before enough studies are completed on nanotechnology's health and environmental impacts to provide a reliable body of evidence about its safety. "It's going to be 10 years before we can answer the 'so what should I do' question for people," said Oberdörster, of Southern Methodist University. [49]

But the recent studies on the negative health effects of nanoparticles and popular fiction portraying frightening nanotech scenarios have helped trigger public fears about nanotech's unknowns. [50] Activists have begun to organize a nascent anti-nano movement in both the United States and abroad, raising fears in the industry that it could face a public relations nightmare like Monsanto Corp. faced with its genetically engineered foods, which Europeans dubbed Frankenfoods. [51]

In 2002 Greenpeace raised questions about the technology's safety, and in 2003 Mooney's ETC Group published an 80-page manifesto about potential nanotech threats. [52] Britain's Prince Charles, who opposed genetically modified foods, also has raised alarms about nanotechnology, and residents of Berkeley, Calif., recently protested plans to build a local nanotech "molecular foundry." [53]

And ETC's Mooney has already approached the European Parliament about imposing a temporary moratorium on nanotech development and taking a more proactive role in regulating development of the new technology until more is known about its potential impacts. ETC wants international regulations for atom technology incorporated under a new International Convention for the Evaluation of New Technologies (ICENT). Already, committees of both the European Parliament and the United Nations Food and Agriculture Organization have called for the adoption of an ICENT. And in Britain, some members of Parliament have called for a moratorium on the sale of nanotech products that touch the skin, such as cosmetics. [54]

Meanwhile, some complain that industrial adoption of nanotechnology is outpacing the toxicological and environmental impact research. "The [nanotech] field is growing so rapidly in the discovery end that questions about their environmental consequences are still being generated," said Joseph B. Hughes, a professor at the Georgia Institute of Technology who oversees environmental engineering research at the Center for Biological and Environmental Nanotechnology, at Rice University in Houston. [55]

As nanotech research expenditures have increased worldwide, so have calls for regulation. "These two trends seem to be on a collision course toward a showdown of the type that we saw with GM [genetically modified] crops," bioethicists from the Joint Center for Bioethics at the University of Toronto wrote in the journal *Nanotechnology*. "As the science of [nanotechnology] leaps ahead, the ethics lags behind. . . . The ethical issues fall into the areas of equity, privacy, security, environment and metaphysical questions concerning human-machine interactions." [56]

Rita Colwell, director of the National Science Foundation, agrees that the fledgling industry could face public relations problems. "We can't risk making the same mistakes that were made with the introduction of biotechnology," she said. "We have to do this benignly and equitably." [57]

In addition to spending $105.8 million this year to study the environmental and health impacts of nanotechnology, an interagency working group — led by officials from the Food and Drug Administration and the National Institute for Occupational Safety and Health (NIOSH) — is studying whether current federal regulations can adequately deal with potential nanotechnology hazards.

In addition, NIOSH Director John Howard announced on May 7, 2004, that the institute plans to issue "best practices" guidelines for work with nanomaterials. "While we still don't know how harmful or benign these materials may be, it is important to provide basic information to manufacturers and users on how to minimize health risks based on what we do know now." [58]

Currently some nanotech factories require workers to wear sophisticated air-filtering equipment, while others only require inexpensive face masks. "It's like having a basketball net over your head to protect you from mosquitoes," ETC's Mooney said. [59] ■

OUTLOOK

A New Revolution?

Two major industrial revolutions shaped the modern age. The development of efficient steam power initiated the first — in the second half of the 18th century — leading to the creation of factories and the rise of urban society. The second — launched at the end of the 19th century — coincided with the development of electrical power and modern manufacturing techniques, most notably assembly-line production.

But the Industrial Revolution that could be triggered by nanotechnology "is going to be very big, much bigger than computers, because it will change everything around us," says the Foresight Institute's Peterson. "Computers only really altered one major aspect of our lives, but nanotechnology will change almost everything, from the consumer products we buy to the way we practice medicine."

Undersecretary Bond agrees that nanotech's impact could potentially rival past revolutions. "This is likely to affect every major industry at the basic level," he says. "When you add all this up, it sure looks like another Industrial Revolution to me."

But the changes produced by nanotech may be too "subtle and diffuse" to be called a revolution, nanotechnology analyst Foster says. "Nanotechnology is not one industry but is a more mixed animal affecting a lot of different industries, including computers and medicine. "So, yes, you'll have a lot of innovation, but it just won't be as visible as, say, what happened with computers, because it won't be a box on your desk; it will be spread out."

Bruce Lewenstein, associate professor of science communication at Cornell University, in Ithaca, N.Y., says predictions are premature. "People frequently speak about new technologies as world-changing events," he says. "They did that with many things that never fulfilled their promise, like atomic energy."

But the University of South Carolina's Baird argues that even one major innovation produced by nanotechnology could lead to epochal change. "Cars seemed to be a pretty straightforward improvement over the horse and buggy, and yet they completely changed our landscape, leading to the creation of suburbs," he says.

"Researchers talk about powering the entire United States by creating 100 square miles of [nanoenhanced solar cells] in the desert," he says. "Think about what that one change would do to our economy and our environment and to the geopolitical situation in the Middle East. And that's just one possibility."

Even nanotech skeptic Mooney realizes that if environmental and health risks can be overcome, nanotechnology has huge potential to solve many of the world's problems. "If nanotechnology is commercialized successfully, Armageddon may have to be put on the back burner," he wrote. [60] ■

Notes

[1] Figure cited in Rex Crum, "Nanotech Gambit Yields Small Players with Big Dreams," CBS Marketwatch, March 17, 2004.

[2] Doug Tsuruoka, "Military Key Customer For Nanotech Startups," *Investor's Business Daily*, May 27, 2004, p. A5.

About the Author

David Masci specializes in science, religion and foreign-policy issues. Before joining *The CQ Researcher* in 1996, he was a reporter at Congressional Quarterly's *Daily Monitor* and *CQ Weekly*. He holds a law degree from The George Washington University and a B.A. in medieval history from Syracuse University. His recent reports include "Rebuilding Iraq" and "Torture."

FOR MORE INFORMATION

Action Group on Erosion, Technology and Concentration, 478 River Ave., Suite 200, Winnipeg, MB, R3L 0C8, Canada; (204) 453-5259; www.etcgroup.org. The environmental and human rights activist group supports a global moratorium on nanotech research.

Foresight and Governance Project, Woodrow Wilson International Center for Scholars, One Woodrow Wilson Plaza, 1300 Pennsylvania Ave., N.W., Washington, DC 20004; (202) 691-4000; wwics.si.edu. Aims to facilitate long-term thinking on technology and the public sector.

Foresight Institute, P.O. Box 61058, Palo Alto CA 94306; (650) 917-1122; www.foresight.org. A nanotechnology think tank co-founded by nano pioneer K. Eric Drexler.

NanoBusiness Alliance, 244 Madison Ave., Suite 485, New York, NY 10016; (845) 247-8920; www.nanobusiness.org. A nanotechnology industry trade group.

National Science Foundation, 4201 Wilson Blvd., Arlington, VA 22230; (703) 292-5111; www.nsf.gov. Provides grants for nanotech R&D and other research.

[3] Ronald Bailey, "The smaller the better: the limitless promise of nanotechnology — and the growing peril of a moratorium," *Reason*, Dec. 1, 2003, p. 44.

[4] *Ibid.*

[5] Bill Joy, "Why the Future Doesn't Need Us," *Wired Magazine*, April 2000.

[6] See Rick Weiss, "Nanotech Poses Big Unknown to Science," *The Washington Post*, Feb. 1, 2004, p. A1.

[7] Rick Weiss, "Nanoparticles Toxic in Aquatic Habitat, Study Finds," *The Washington Post*, March 29, 2004, p. A2.

[8] *Ibid.*

[9] Quoted in Barnaby J. Feder, "As Uses Grow, Tiny Materials' Safety Is Hard to Pin Down," *The New York Times*, Nov. 3, 2003, Section C, p. 1.

[10] Weiss, Feb. 1, 2004, *op. cit.*

[11] *Ibid.*

[12] Feder, *op. cit.*

[13] From the Senate Report 108-147, Senate Commerce Committee Report accompanying S 189, Sept. 15, 2003.

[14] Weiss, Feb. 1, 2004, *op. cit.*

[15] See "Responsible Development of Nanotechnology," April 2, 2004, available at www.nano.gov/html/about/TeagueRegNNIConf04.html.

[16] Weiss, Feb. 1, 2004, *op. cit.*

[17] *Ibid.*

[18] James M. Pethokoukis, "Is Small the Next Big Thing?" *U.S. News & World Report*, Sept. 8, 2003, p. 29.

[19] Quoted in *Ibid.*

[20] Quoted in "Merrill Lynch Creates 'Nanotech Index' to Track Evolving Industry," *Business Wire*, April 1. 2004.

[21] Quoted in Bailey, *op. cit.*

[22] Quoted from www.house.gov/science/hearings/full03/mar19/russell.htm.

[23] Bailey, *op. cit.*

[24] For background, see David Masci, "NASA's Future," *The CQ Researcher*, May 23, 2003, pp. 473-496.

[25] Isaac Asimov, *The Atom: Journey Across the Subatomic Cosmos* (1991), p. 2.

[26] *Ibid.*, p. 3.

[27] *Ibid.*, p. 7.

[28] Daniel J. Boorstin, *The Discoverers* (1983), pp. 327-332.

[29] Mary H. Cooper, "Human Genome Research," *The CQ Researcher*, May 12, 2000, pp. 401-424.

[30] Asimov, *op. cit.*, p. 125.

[31] See National Nanotechnology Initiative Web site: www.nano.gov/html/facts/MooresLaw.htm.

[32] Quoted from Feynman's speech at www.zyvex.com/nanotech/feynman.html.

[33] Charles Choi, "Nanotubes, Buckyballs Surprise Investors," United Press International, May 19, 2004.

[34] Gary H. Anthes, "New Spin for Electronics," *Computerworld*, Aug. 18, 2003, p. 30.

[35] Rana Foroohar, "One Word: Plastics," *Newsweek*, Feb. 23, 2004, p. 54.

[36] *Ibid.*

[37] Harold Brubaker, "Mundane Products Benefit Now," *Akron Beacon Journal*, May 9, 2004, p. D1.

[38] "2003 Nanotech Product Guide," *Nanotech Report*, July 2003, p. 1.

[39] For a further explanation of nanocrystals see: www.elan.com/DrugDelivery/drug_delivery/nanocrystal_technology.asp.

[40] "Nanoprobes Are Destined for Major New Roles in Medicine," *Drug Week*, March 19, 2004, p. 173.

[41] Celia Henry, "Quantum Dot Advances," *Chemical and Engineering News*, June 9, 2003, p. 10.

[42] Mark Halper, "More Power to You," *Time*, Dec. 15, 2003, p. A10.

[43] Paul Kallender, "NEC Tries to Grab Fuel Cell Market by the Carbonnano Horns," *Small World*, March 25, 2003; www.smalltimes.com/document_display.cfm?document_id=5719.

[44] Quoted in Jon Van, "Nanotech wrapped in federal support; Law creates office, gives $3.7 billion over next 4 years," *Chicago Tribune*, Nov. 27, 2003, Zone C, p. 1.

[45] See "2003 Legislative Summary: Nanotechnology," *CQ Weekly*, Dec. 13, 2003, p. 3132, and S Rept. 108-147, *op. cit.*

[46] From remarks Wyden delivered to the National Nanotechnology Initiative Conference in Washington, D.C., on April 2, 2004.

[47] Van, *op. cit.*

[48] Quoted in Joseph C. Anselmo, "Senate Pushes For Quick Markup Of Bill Promoting Nanotechnology as the Next Big Thing," *CQ Weekly*, May 10, 2003, p. 1108.

[49] Feder, *op. cit.*

[50] In addition to Crichton's *Prey*, Dan Brown's new best-seller *Angels and Demons* has the Catholic Church denouncing nanotechnology as "evil."

[51] For background, see David Hosansky, "Biotech Foods," *The CQ Researcher*, March 30, 2001, pp. 249-272, and Kathy Koch, "Food Safety Battle: Organic vs. Biotech," *The CQ Researcher*, Sept. 4, 1998, pp. 761-784.

[52] Bailey, *op. cit.*

[53] Weiss, Feb. 1, 2004, *op. cit.*

[54] "Nanotech ingredients spark controversy," *Cosmetics International*, June 6, 2003, p. 7.

[55] Quoted in Feder, *op. cit.*

[56] Bailey, *op. cit.*

[57] Quoted in Weiss, *op. cit.*

[58] Quoted from the National Nanotechnology Initiative Web site, at www.nano.gov/html/facts/MooresLaw.htm.

[59] Weiss, Feb. 1, 2004, *op. cit.*

[60] Bailey, *op. cit.*

Bibliography

Selected Sources

Books

Drexler, K. Eric, *Engines of Creation: The Coming Age of Nanotechnology*, Anchor, 1987.
Drexler, who now directs the Foresight Institute, lays out his still-controversial vision for molecular manufacturing.

Ratner, Mark, and Daniel Ratner, *Nanotechnology: A Gentle Introduction to the Next Big Idea*, Prentice Hall, 2003.
Father and son scientists describe the new science and its current and future applications.

Regis, Ed, *Nano: The Emerging Science of Nanotechnology: Remaking the World Molecule by Molecule*, Little, Brown, 1995.
A science writer profiles nanotech's visionary thinkers.

Articles

"Nanotechnology's Unhappy Father," *The Economist*, March 13, 2004.
K. Eric Drexler coined the term nanotechnology and is fighting to continue to influence the science he helped define.

Bailey, Ronald, "The smaller the better: the limitless promise of nanotechnology — and the growing peril of a moratorium," *Reason*, Dec. 1, 2003, p. 44.
The magazine's science correspondent envisions an amazing nanofuture — and potentially devastating problems.

Brubaker, Harold, "Nanotechnology Is Hot: For Mundane Products," *Philadelphia Inquirer*, March 28, 2004, p. E01.
Nanotech's biggest impact so far is in improving common and often-stodgy products.

Feder, Barnaby J., "As Uses Grow, Tiny Materials' Safety Is Hard to Pin Down," *The New York Times*, Nov. 3, 2003, p. C1.
DuPont found that nanotubes inhaled by rats caused a 15 percent death rate.

Feder, Barnaby J., "It's a Tiny New World," *The New York Times*, Dec. 22, 2003, p. C1.
Nanotechnology's potential impact on the economy is examined.

Gillis, Justin, and Jonathan Krim, "If It's Nano, It's Big," *The Washington Post*, Feb. 22, 2004, p. F1.
Nanotechnology firms have become the new darlings of Wall Street and the venture-capital industry.

Joy, Bill, "The Future Doesn't Need Us," *Wired*, April 2000.
Joy's manifesto against what he sees as unbridled technological development has become both famous and infamous. The co-founder of Sun Microsystems envisions a possible future where developments in high-tech fields like nanotechnology lead to the extinction of all life.

"Much Ado About Almost Nothing," *The Economist*, March 20, 2004.
Industry and government want to shield nanotechnology from the kind of public-relations nightmare that greeted genetically modified foods.

Munro, Neil, "Big Plans from the Smallest Science," *National Journal*, March 6, 2004.
Munro reviews the public- and private-sector politics associated with nanotech.

New, William, "Nanotech Nation," *The National Journal*, June 14, 2003.
New clearly lays out the promise, politics and perils of nanotechnology.

Spotts, Peter N., "Big Questions for Tiny Particles," *The Christian Science Monitor*, Aug. 14, 2003, p. A11.
Health and safety issues have arisen from the use of nanoparticles in a host of new products.

Varchaver, Nicholas, "Is Nanotech Ready for Its Close-up?" *Fortune*, May 17, 2004, p. 153.
An examination of the nanotech industry that focuses on existing and future product development.

Weiss, Rick, "For Science, Nanotech Poses Big Unknowns," *The Washington Post*, Feb. 1, 2004, p. A1.
Weiss examines the potential risks that nanotechnology poses to human health and the environment.

Reports and Studies

"Nano's Troubled Waters," Action Group on Erosion, Technology and Concentration, April 1, 2004.
The Canadian environmental organization has compiled evidence from a number of studies questioning the safety of nanoparticles on people and the environment.

Roco, Mihail C., and William Sims Bainbridge, "Societal Implications of Nanoscience and Nanotechnology," National Science Foundation, March 2001.
An exhaustive look at the future social impact of nanotechnology.

The Next Step:

Additional Articles from Current Periodicals

Energy

"The Wizard of Small Things," *The Economist*, March 15, 2003.

Dr. Richard Smalley, renowned for helping to discover fullerenes, has turned his attention and talents to the world's energy needs and sees nanotechnology as part of the solution.

Feder, Barnaby J., "Small Thoughts for a Global Grid," *The New York Times*, Sept. 2, 2003, p. F3.

Carbon nanotubes, potentially far more efficient and lighter than copper, could help solve the world's energy needs by transporting wind and solar energy to where it is needed.

Maney, Kevin, "Tiny Technology That Could: Nanotech Could Solve Oil Issues," *USA Today*, Oct. 1, 2003, p. 3B.

Advances in improved photovoltaic cells could reduce America's dependence on imported oil, which accounts for one-third of the trade deficit.

Limitations

"Nanotechnology's Unhappy Father," *The Economist*, March 13, 2004.

Today's nanotechnology is more akin to traditional chemistry than the revolutionary manufacturing processes Eric Drexler imagined when he coined the term.

Chang, Kenneth, "Yes, They Can! No, They Can't: Charges Fly in Nanobot Debate," *The New York Times*, Dec. 9, 2003, p. F3.

The scientist who coined the term "nanotechnology" and a Nobel laureate hold a spirited debate on the possibility of producing nanobots.

Cowen, Robert C., "Tiny New Rulers for the 'Ultrasmall,' " *The Christian Science Monitor*, Feb. 26, 2004, p. 16.

Nanotechnology requires new measuring techniques that are precise enough to be useful at the scale of atoms.

Weiss, Rick, "Language of Science Lags Behind Nanotech," *The Washington Post*, May 17, 2004, p. A7.

As nanotechnology develops, a consistent nomenclature is needed so that scientists can quickly and easily convey important information about nanomaterials.

Little Tech, Big Business

Berger, Eric, "After Years of Promise, Nanotubes Can Deliver," *Houston Chronicle*, March 4, 2004, Business Section, p. 1.

A maker of carbon nanotubes will be able to manufacture 10,000 pounds daily by late 2005, compared to only a pound per year at first.

Feder, Barnaby J., "Bashful vs. Brash in the New Field of Nanotech," *The New York Times*, March 15, 2004, p. C1.

Nanosys is the poster child of the high-publicity start-up; nanofilm is an example of slow, steady progress.

Gillis, Justin, and Jonathan Krim, "If It's Nano, It's BIG," *The Washington Post*, Feb. 22, 2004, p. F1.

Some nanotechnology companies have become Wall Street darlings, but skeptics raise memories of the Internet's stock-market bubble.

Hearn, Kelly, "The Next Big Thing (Is Practically Invisible)," *The Christian Science Monitor*, March 24, 2003, p. 17.

The National Science Foundation says nanotechnology has the potential to create 2 million jobs and $1 trillion in revenue in the next decade.

Maney, Kevin, "Finally, a Purpose for Nanotech to Turn on Average Joe: Big-screen TVs," *USA Today*, July 9, 2003, p. 3B.

Motorola researchers develop a way to "grow" nanotubes that could greatly reduce the price of flat-screen televisions.

Pethokoukis, James M., "Is Small the Next Big Thing?" *U.S. News & World Report*, Sept. 8, 2003, p. 29.

Strapping the prefix "nano" onto a product seems to guarantee attention even for the most mundane manufacturer.

Roston, Eric, "Very Small Business," *Time*, Sept. 23, 2002, p. A12.

Businesses trying to create much more than nanoprofits are working on everything from AIDS treatments to tennis balls.

Military Applications

Brant, Martha, "Sci-Fi War Uniforms?" *Newsweek*, Feb. 24, 2003, p. 41.

MIT scientists are working to develop Army uniforms that are as light as silk and tough enough to stop bullets.

Feder, Barnaby J., "Frontier of Military Technology Is the Size of a Molecule," *The New York Times*, April 8, 2003, p. C2.

The Defense Department has been interested in nanotechnology for decades.

Ferdinand, Pamela, "Many Layers to Building a Super Soldier," *The Washington Post*, Jan. 20, 2003, p. A21.

Industrial partners DuPont and Raytheon team up with MIT to develop new technologies that include "intelligent" fabrics.

Questions About Nanotechnology

"Mega Questions About Nanotech," *Business Week*, May 31, 2004, p. IM4.

Prof. Kristen Kulinowski of Rice University discusses some questions surrounding the new frontiers of nanotechnology.

"Trouble in Nanoland," ***The Economist*, Dec. 7, 2002.**
Boosters have probably created unrealistic expectations that will eventually rebound, while nano-Luddites focus on the potential nano-horrors of the future.

Baum, Rudy, "Point-Counterpoint; Nanotechnology," ***Chemical & Engineering News*, Dec. 1, 2003, p. 37.**
Nobel laureate Dr. Richard Smalley debates the feasibility of molecular manufacturing with Dr. K. Eric Drexler.

Safety Concerns

"Much Ado About Almost Nothing," ***The Economist*, March 20, 2004.**
The outcry over genetically modified food may be repeated over nanotechnology.

Feder, Barnaby J., "From Nanotechnology's Sidelines, One More Warning," ***The New York Times*, Feb. 3, 2003, p. C1.**
A group that fought genetically modified foods warns about "green goo," or engineered microorganisms.

Graham, Sarah, "Nanotech: It's Not Easy Being Green," ***Scientific American*, August 2003.**
The Environmental Protection Agency is soliciting research proposals on the toxicity of manufactured nanomaterials.

Green, Heather, "Attack of the Killer Dust," ***Business Week*, Dec. 2, 2002, p. 103.**
Michael Crichton wrote about the horrors of nanotechnology in *Prey*; regarding new things, "there always is a downside," he says.

Rees, Martin, "The Dark Side of Science," ***Time Atlantic/British Isles*, May 12, 2003, p. 51.**
A British scientist warns that new technologies usually harbor the potential for danger.

Weiss, Rick, "Nanoparticles Toxic in Aquatic Habitat, Study Finds," ***The Washington Post*, March 29, 2004, p. A2.**
The changed physical properties that make nanoparticles so useful can also make them dangerous.

Witchalls, Clint, "The Next Asbestos?" ***Newsweek*, July 21, 2003, p. 49.**
There's little hard evidence about the safety of nanoparticles; but they are slathered on daily as sunscreen.

Soaring Interest, Soaring Funding

Epstein, Edward, "Silicon Valley Pins Hopes on Nanotechnology Boom," ***San Francisco Chronicle*, May 8, 2003, p. A1.**
California aims to establish itself as a nanotech powerhouse able to compete with other regions, like New York, that are investing heavily in the area.

Gavin, Robert, "Nanotech Being Seen as Next Big Thing," ***The Boston Globe*, March 8, 2004, p. C1.**
States are showering the nanotech industry with money in hopes of getting a piece of the action.

Hebel, Sara, "How SUNY-Albany Shocked the Research World and Reaped a Bonanza Worth $850 Million (and Counting)," ***The Chronicle of Higher Education*, Feb. 7, 2003, p. 16.**
The state university at Albany parlayed the interest of government leaders and corporate executives in nanoscience into a research windfall to make Stanford or Harvard envious.

McKinley, James, "Hope for the Upstate Economy in the Next Wave of Computer Chips," ***The New York Times*, Nov. 16, 2003, Section 1, p. 35.**
New York hopes nanotechnology can help replace lost manufacturing jobs.

CITING *THE CQ RESEARCHER*

Sample formats for citing these reports in a bibliography include the ones listed below. Preferred styles and formats vary, so please check with your instructor or professor.

MLA STYLE

Jost, Kenneth. "Rethinking the Death Penalty." The CQ Researcher 16 Nov. 2001: 945-68.

APA STYLE

Jost, K. (2001, November 16). Rethinking the death penalty. *The CQ Researcher, 11*, 945-968.

CHICAGO STYLE

Jost, Kenneth. "Rethinking the Death Penalty." *CQ Researcher*, November 16, 2001, 945-968.

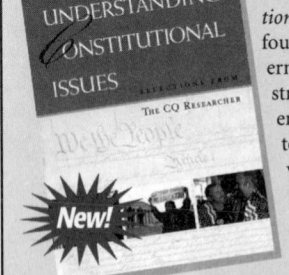

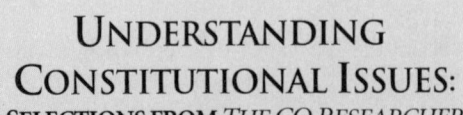

CQ Researcher

Published by CQ Press, a division of Congressional Quarterly Inc.

thecqresearcher.com

Ending Homelessness

Is the problem solvable?

More than 2 million Americans are homeless during the course of a year, and the number is rising. About 40 percent are families with children, 30 percent are substance abusers, 23 percent are severely mentally ill and 10 percent are veterans. Advocates blame the growing problem on the sluggish economy, Congress' refusal to raise the minimum wage, rising unemployment and stricter welfare-eligibility requirements. The Bush administration declared a commitment to ending chronic homelessness in 10 years and is pressing Congress to pass the Samaritan Initiative, which would provide $70 million for housing and attendant care specifically for the chronically homeless. Critics say the proposal does not go far enough because the chronically homeless represent only 10-20 percent of the problem. Meanwhile, although new research clearly shows that homelessness can indeed be solved, no consensus yet exists on a comprehensive approach to rooting out the causes of the problem.

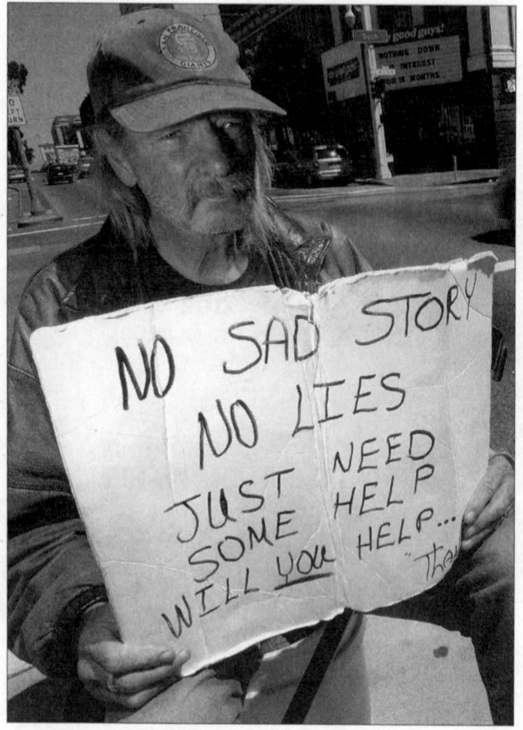

A homeless man in San Francisco holds a sign of the times.

INSIDE THIS REPORT

The CQ Researcher • June 18, 2004 • www.thecqresearcher.com
Volume 14, Number 23 • Pages 541-564

CQ PRESS

RECIPIENT OF SOCIETY OF PROFESSIONAL JOURNALISTS AWARD FOR EXCELLENCE ◆ AMERICAN BAR ASSOCIATION SILVER GAVEL AWARD

THE ISSUES

BACKGROUND

CURRENT SITUATION

OUTLOOK

SIDEBARS AND GRAPHICS

FOR FURTHER RESEARCH

Cover: A homeless man in San Francisco holds a sign of the times. The city's new Care Not Cash program lowered payments to the homeless but increased the number of available shelter rooms. (Getty Images/Justin Sullivan)

June 18, 2004
Volume 14, Number 23

MANAGING EDITOR: Thomas J. Colin

ASSISTANT MANAGING EDITOR: Kathy Koch

ASSOCIATE EDITOR: Kenneth Jost

STAFF WRITERS: Mary H. Cooper, David Masci, William Triplett

CONTRIBUTING WRITERS: Sarah Glazer, David Hatch, David Hosansky, Patrick Marshall, Tom Price, Jane Tanner

DESIGN/PRODUCTION EDITOR: Olu B. Davis

ASSISTANT EDITOR: Kenneth Lukas

A Division of
Congressional Quarterly Inc.

SENIOR VICE PRESIDENT/GENERAL MANAGER: John A. Jenkins

DIRECTOR, LIBRARY PUBLISHING: Kathryn C. Suárez

DIRECTOR, EDITORIAL OPERATIONS: Ann Davies

CONGRESSIONAL QUARTERLY INC.

CHAIRMAN: Paul C. Tash

VICE CHAIRMAN: Andrew P. Corty

PRESIDENT AND PUBLISHER: Robert W. Merry

The CQ Researcher (ISSN 1056-2036) is printed on acid-free paper. Published weekly, except Jan. 2, April 9, July 2, July 9, Aug. 6, Aug. 13, Nov. 26 and Dec. 31, by CQ Press, a division of Congressional Quarterly Inc. Annual subscription rates for institutions start at $625. For pricing, call 1-800-834-9020, ext. 1906. To purchase a *CQ Researcher* report in print or electronic format (PDF), visit www.cqpress.com or call 866-427-7737. A single report is $10. Bulk purchase discounts and electronic-rights licensing are also available. Periodicals postage paid at Washington, D.C., and additional mailing offices. POSTMASTER: Send address changes to *The CQ Researcher*, 1255 22nd St., N.W., Suite 400, Washington, D.C. 20037.

Ending Homelessness

BY WILLIAM TRIPLETT

THE ISSUES

City Commissioner Tomas Regalado advocates arresting anyone caught feeding the homeless in downtown Miami. [1]

In suburban Seattle, a homeless shelter has not brought the feared rise in crime, nor widespread opposition to its location. [2]

Outside Tucson, an elderly man and his 48-year-old son live in a filthy desert camp on the father's Social Security check and the son's panhandling, but neither has much interest in living in a shelter. [3]

In cities across the country, America's 2 to 3 million homeless people are increasingly visible — with all the complicated and sometimes contradictory realities associated with homelessness. In recent years, a shortage of affordable housing accompanied by a sluggish economy has put more Americans on the street, say advocates for the homeless. Meanwhile, requests for emergency shelter are up, but resources haven't kept pace, they say.

However, thanks to new research suggesting that homelessness could be solved if society addresses the many interrelated factors that cause it, advocates for the homeless are more optimistic now than perhaps ever before about the possibility of finally eliminating the perennial problem. But no consensus yet exists on a comprehensive approach to address all the causes.

Reflecting the new optimism, the Fannie Mae Foundation recently pledged $35 million in financing and challenge grants toward construction of new, subsidized housing. "In the late 1970s, we as a country were creating about 400,000 units of subsidized housing a year," says Paul Weech, director of market research and policy development at Fannie Mae (formerly the Federal National Mortgage Association). "For the last several years, it hasn't been above 60,000-70,000." Meanwhile, median housing prices rose 639 percent, contributing to a serious shortage of affordable housing nationwide. [4]

But according to Robert Rector, a senior research fellow at the conservative Heritage Foundation, homelessness is not just a housing problem. It is an "incidental symptom of other, more fundamental problems," like substance abuse or mental illness, he says. Homelessness exists "precisely because we have not succeeded in dealing with those other problems."

Fiscal conservatives maintain that with the federal government spending $3.2 billion a year on homelessness programs, anyone sleeping without a roof over his head should be held accountable for his behavior. But, they insist, anyone receiving a shelter berth should first earn it, even if that only means agreeing to take his anti-psychotic medication.

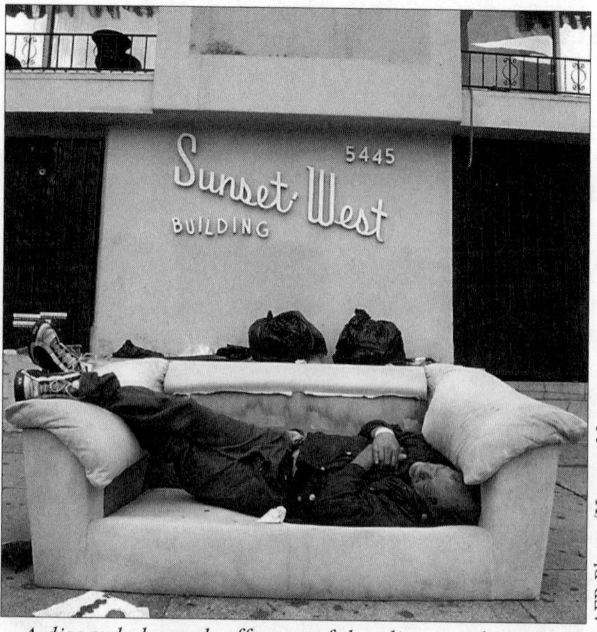

AFP Photo/Hector Mata

A discarded couch offers a soft landing to a homeless man on Sunset Boulevard in Hollywood, Calif. The U.S. Conference of Mayors estimates 840,000 people are homeless in America each day, with up to 3 million homeless over the course of a year.

But advocates for the homeless say that approach only works in some cases. "One size does not fit all," says Nan Roman, president of the National Alliance to End Homelessness, a nonprofit organization dedicated to mobilizing the nonprofit, public and private sectors to end homelessness within 10 years by addressing its root causes.

If one size does not fit all, it may be because the nation's homeless population is so diverse: 40 percent are families with children, 30 percent are substance abusers, 23 percent are severely mentally ill, 17 percent are employed and 10 percent are veterans. [5]

Despite the size and diversity of the problem, the federal government has never devoted enough resources to eliminate homelessness, and $3.2 billion really isn't enough, some advocates say.

Policy analysts and observers have only begun to understand the full complexity of homelessness in the last few years, many experts say. "People think that because they see people living on the streets, they understand homelessness," Roman says. "But so much of it is away from the public eye." To understand homelessness, she maintains, one needs to understand all the causes and effects of poverty.

Critics say the homeless — and their shelters — can drive down the value of real estate. And some homeless people refuse to go into shelters, often because of overcrowding or crime. But advocates question whether cities should be allowed to jail those

Who Are the Homeless?

America's homeless are primarily single men or families with children — a category that has grown from a third of the homeless population in 1988 to 40 percent today. Nearly equal percentages of blacks and whites are homeless, and significant percentages are mentally ill or substance abusers; a quarter were sexually abused as children.

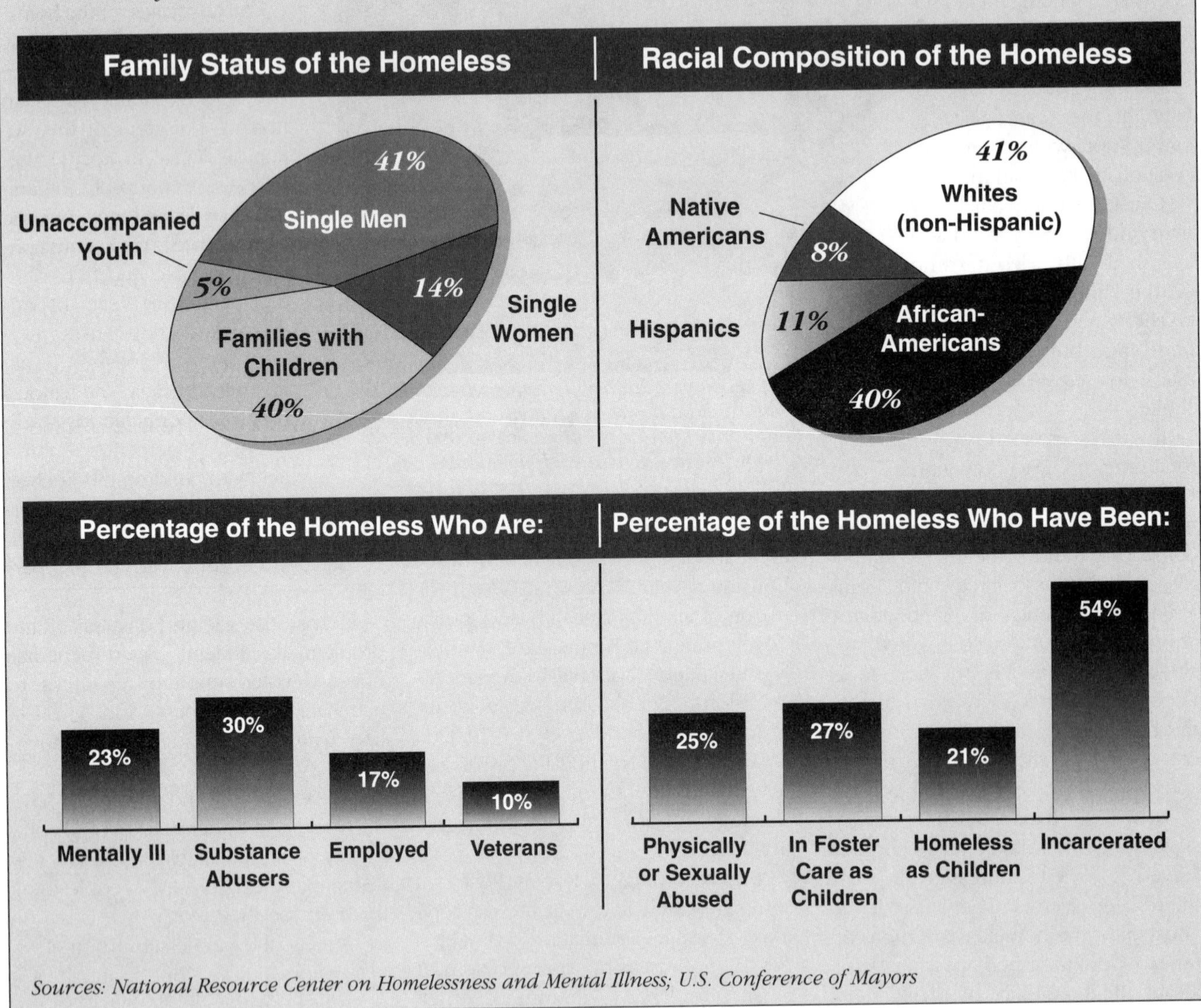

Sources: National Resource Center on Homelessness and Mental Illness; U.S. Conference of Mayors

who refuse to go to shelters, as some have chosen to do.

Experts also disagree about the size of the problem. The U.S. Conference of Mayors says 840,000 people are homeless on any given night, and that over the course of a year some 3 million people are homeless at one time or another. [6] Philip Mangano, executive director of the U.S. Interagency Council on Homelessness, estimates that 650,000 are homeless on any given night and 2 million to 2.5 million are without shelter at some point each year. Others say the U.S. Census Bureau's estimate of 470,000 people homeless on any given night is more realistic. [7]

Advocates say the numbers are increasing due to the recession, Congress' refusal to raise the minimum wage, rising unemployment and stricter welfare-eligibility requirements. They cite a recent Conference of Mayors survey showing that requests for shelter assistance in 2003 increased by 13 percent over the previous year. [8]

"Yes, [shelter requests] are up, but to some degree that reflects people moving from the streets to the shelters, and shelter availability fluctuates," notes Michael Tanner, director of health and welfare studies at the libertarian Cato Institute, who maintains that the nation's homeless population has not changed appreciably in the last 20 years.

Even the definition of homelessness remains disputed. Some observers say it means residing in a shelter (or outdoors) for more than six months; others say anyone without a home is homeless.

Most agree, however, that the homeless population consists of two types: the episodic, or transitionally homeless, who are experiencing a bad run of luck but will soon be back on their feet, and the chronically homeless — usually substance abusers, the handicapped or the mentally ill.

While the chronically homeless account for only 10 to 20 percent of the homeless, they pose the biggest challenges, most advocates for the homeless agree. They also agree that unless governments at all levels adopt new, coordinated strategies, homelessness will never be eliminated.

In 2002 the Bush administration declared a commitment to ending chronic homelessness in 10 years, and is pressing Congress to pass the Samaritan Initiative, a bill aimed at providing $70 million for housing and attendant care specifically for the chronically homeless. But critics say because the proposal only addresses the 10-20 percent who are chronically homeless, it does not go far enough or is rooted in failed approaches.

"We agree with ending chronic homelessness," Roman says. "But that doesn't mean we shouldn't address needs of other homeless people."

Mangano, the administration's point man on homelessness, maintains that ending homelessness will be a slow, incremental process, given its relatively low priority among lawmakers preoccupied with the war on terrorism and the occupation of Iraq. Addressing chronic homelessness is a sound first step, he says, because this subgroup consumes more than half the resources devoted to reducing homelessness.

Similarly, most agree that government — in particular, the federal government — should play the lead role in combating homelessness. But precisely what the government should do, and how much it should spend doing it, is still sharply contested. "In every respect, the private sector would probably do a better job than government," says Douglas Besharov, an expert on welfare at the American Enterprise Institute (AEI), a conservative think tank.

AFP Photo/Stephen Jaffe

President Bush greets volunteers during the December 2001 holidays at Martha's Table, a nonprofit in Washington, D.C., that feeds the homeless.

Meanwhile, public perceptions of homelessness have changed since the early 1980s, when the issue dominated media reports. General sympathy waned after years of federal programs and hundreds of local initiatives seemed to fail. In the mid-1990s, Congress limited welfare benefits, forcing some recipients off the program, and — according to homeless advocates, into the streets. [9] By decade's end, with the economy booming and unemployment low, many people assumed that if you were homeless, it was "your own damn fault." [10]

Cities began to rely more on law enforcement to deal with homelessness, such as anti-panhandling ordinances. Orlando, for instance, declared lying down on the sidewalk illegal. [11] In Manhattan, Mayor Rudolph W. Giuliani in 1999 ordered the arrest of any homeless person refusing to go into a city shelter. [12]

Some cities still criminalize homelessness, but because of the new research and the enthusiasm it has generated, alternatives are also developing.

As city officials and homeless advocates seek a solution to homelessness, here are some of the key questions under debate:

Is homelessness solvable?

"Absolutely," says Laurene Heybach, director of the Law Project at the Chicago Coalition for the Homeless. The key, she says, is to be clear about the ultimate goal. "Is it to solve every personal problem that every person who needs housing has? Not in my view, though I laud any program that assists people in overcoming their personal problems."

Heybach says history supports her viewpoint. "There was a time in our nation when many people with personal problems were housed." The rise of neoconservatism and its preference for private market forces over governmental programs has worsened the plight of the homeless, she argues. "There's been a tremendous loss of resources in [federally] funded programs since Ronald Reagan became president. We're in a neocon world now, which seeks to undo a number of programs that have worked very well over the years, though they've never been as big as they need to be."

For example, public housing projects have been extremely successful, she says, particularly for homeless children as well as the elderly and disabled. "Does that mean every public housing project is a success? Of course not. But neither is private housing. The private market can't solve the problem because it would be too expensive. In fact, the world is sliding backward because of a willingness to let market forces address homelessness."

But the AEI's Besharov thinks the homeless, like the poor, will always be with us. "It's a mistake to think we'll eradicate homelessness because there are always people who can't make it on their own" because of mental illness and alcoholism, he says.

"A certain level of homelessness is intractable," concurs Tanner of the Cato Institute. Since the first days of the Republic, he notes, "people lived on streets or in flophouses. Of course, you got a big explosion in the homeless population with deinstitutionalization [the widespread releasing of patients from state mental hospitals that began during the Kennedy administration] because those people used to be taken off the streets. You probably can help a few families of working poor who are temporarily having problems." But at least 400,000 people would still be homeless, he estimates.

The real obstacle to ending homelessness, he says, is often the homeless themselves. People experiencing temporary problems typically don't leave a shelter until they have a new permanent place to live. But substance abusers often will stay in a shelter for a few days, then leave to get drugs. "You can't tie people down and force them to stay," he says. "In winter, they'll stay longer because of the weather, but in summer, for some of these folks, life on the streets wasn't the worst thing in the world."

But homeless advocate Roman says the problem could be ended. "It's not that everyone's going to be living in a white house with a picket fence, but we don't have to have people living on the street or in shelters or transitional housing," she says. "And I don't think there are people who can't be helped. If people are rejecting what we're offering them" — such as refusing to enter shelters — "maybe we're not offering the right thing."

Homeless shelters, almost by definition, are only temporary accommodations, and many observers acknowledge a dire, nationwide shortage of affordable housing. According to Harvard University's Joint Center for Housing Studies, the total shortfall in low-cost rental housing was 4.7 million in 2002. [13]

Moreover, while the U.S. poverty rate declined slightly during the economic boom of the 1990s, it began to rise again in 2001, when the economy started to slow down rapidly. By 2003, almost 33 million Americans — 11.7 percent of the population — were living below the poverty line, according to census data. [14]

Thus, as the amount of affordable housing was decreasing, the number of poor people was increasing. With less money, poor families forced to choose between paying rent and buying groceries often opted for the food, ending up on the streets.

Until recently, one of the most effective antidotes to homelessness was single-room occupancy (SRO) housing, which offered simple but extended accommodations. "Even if you looked at Chicago 20 years ago," Heybach says, "we had lots of drunks on skid row, but they had a place to go at night because we had lots of SRO housing. But in the past 15 years, like in L.A. and San Francisco, SRO has disappeared."

Urban renewal and gentrification — replacing derelict buildings with expensive new offices or apartments — have eliminated much SRO housing and other traditional shelter space. And as advocacy groups have tried to establish new shelters in neighborhoods, residents often have raised the now-ubiquitous cry: "Not in My Back Yard!" (NIMBY).

"We had a struggle about two years ago," Heybach says. "A church proposed to convert a building into housing for recovering substance-abusing women who were homeless. There was lots of community opposition, and at the zoning hearing, people in this wealthy community were testifying that here would be people who we knew had used drugs. The very people articulating this were completely oblivious to the fact that on any given Friday night in this same community, many people with good jobs use drugs in their private residences."

"People are all for low-income housing as long as it is not in their suburb," Tanner observes.

Are we doing the right things to combat homelessness?

A few years ago, Amy Sherman, a senior fellow at the Hudson Institute and an urban policy adviser at Trinity Presbyterian Church in Charlottesville, Va., stopped her car to help a woman

Continued on p. 548

Crackdown in San Francisco

It used to pay to be homeless in San Francisco. For years, the city gave homeless people up to $410 a month. This past spring, about 2,500 of the city's estimated 9,500 homeless were receiving checks. [1]

"I was in Nebraska," a new arrival said in 2002, "and I met some guys on freight trains. They said, 'Hey, let's go to San Francisco. They give you a check.' I said, 'Why do they give you a check?' They said, 'Because you're homeless.' I said, 'I don't believe this.' " [2]

But it was true. A local television station even secretly videotaped some homeless people cashing their checks and then buying drugs or alcohol. [3]

Last month city officials began reducing the monthly homeless allowances to as little as $59 and instead will offer housing coupled with mental health and substance-abuse services. The new Care Not Cash program is similar to the Bush administration's proposed permanent supportive housing (PSH) program, a centerpiece of the administration's plan to ending chronic homelessness in 10 years.

Care Not Cash had a difficult birth. When an outline of the program was put on a ballot by then Supervisor Gavin Newsom two years ago as Proposition N, nearly 60 percent of residents voted for it. But the San Francisco Coalition on Homelessness, among others, denounced the measure as "another example of an aspiring politician using the homeless to advance his career." Another city official pointed out that the housing and services being promised by Care Not Cash did not yet exist. [4]

Proponents countered that the housing and services would be funded by the estimated $13.2 million in savings expected from reducing the monthly cash payments. However, the following year a homeless woman and an advocate for the poor challenged the validity of the Proposition N vote in court. A San Francisco judge ruled in their favor, saying that "only the city's elected Board of Supervisors, not voters, had the authority to reduce payments to the homeless." [5]

The program's proponents appealed, and in April an appeals court reversed the lower court's ruling. The vote was indeed valid, because it represented the will of the people, the court said.

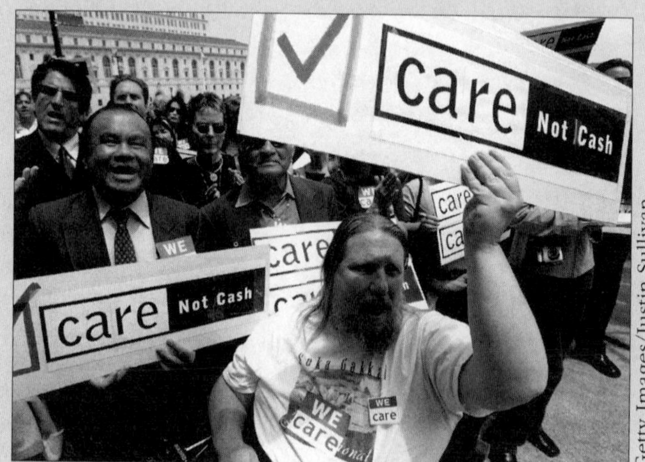

Getty Images/Justin Sullivan

Supporters of San Francisco's Care Not Cash program demonstrate during an address in May 2003 by then-mayoral candidate Gavin Newsom, who proposed the initiative.

Last month, San Francisco finally launched Care Not Cash by opening up two old residential hotels that the city had refurbished. Together, they have 154 rooms, one of which went to Cesar Ragsac, 53, who said he had been homeless since losing his electronics job nine years ago. "This is one of the best things that ever happened to me," he said. "My own home. My own." [6]

The city hopes to have 900 more rooms available by the end of the year, but that means nearly 1,500 people now receiving checks will still be homeless — and receiving only $59 a month. City officials claim that even more housing and services will be created as the savings begin to accrue from the reduced monthly payments. By next year, city funding for new residences will total $10 million, they say.

Critics say that may be too little, too late. Some 8,500 San Franciscans would still be competing for approximately 2,250 emergency shelter beds and 1,200 transitional housing slots, according to the National Law Center for Homelessness and Poverty. [7]

On the day the city opened the first of the two hotels to accept residents, about 100 activists and homeless people demonstrated against Care Not Cash. A homeless woman dressed as a monkey said, "Homeless people are being used like lab animals in experiments. Care Not Cash is the experiment. We are here because this is our Last Supper before being crucified by Care Not Cash." [8]

---

[1] Estimate of 9,500 from "Homelessness in the United States and the Human Right to Housing," National Law Center on Poverty and Homelessness, Jan. 14, 2004, p. 24. Some conservatives, however, estimate the city's homeless population is much closer to 6,000.

[2] Hank Plante, "5 Investigates: Can 'Care Not Cash' Help SF Homeless?", cbs5.com, Oct. 29, 2002; http://cbs5.com/news/local/2002/10/29/5_Investigates:_Can_'Care_Not_Cash'_Help_SF_Homeless%3F.html.

[3] *Ibid.*

[4] "San Francisco revamps homeless policy," CNN.com, Dec. 12, 2002; www.cnn.com/2002/US/West/12/12/homeless.evicted.ap.

[5] "Appeals Court Validates San Francisco's Homeless Initiative," The Associated Press, April 30, 2004.

[6] Kevin Fagan, "A home after years adrift — S.F. reduces payments to homeless people on welfare in exchange for providing housing," *The San Francisco Chronicle*, May 4, 2004, p. A1.

[7] National Law Center, *op. cit.*

[8] Fagan, *op. cit.*

Majority Opposes Criminalizing Panhandling

A majority of Americans oppose criminalizing panhandling by the homeless, and nearly half think homelessness is getting worse, according to a recent poll.

Do you favor or oppose laws that make it illegal for homeless people to panhandle?

Should it be legal or illegal for homeless people to sleep in public places, such as in parks or on sidewalks?

Is homelessness in the U.S. getting better, worse or has stayed about the same over the past few years?

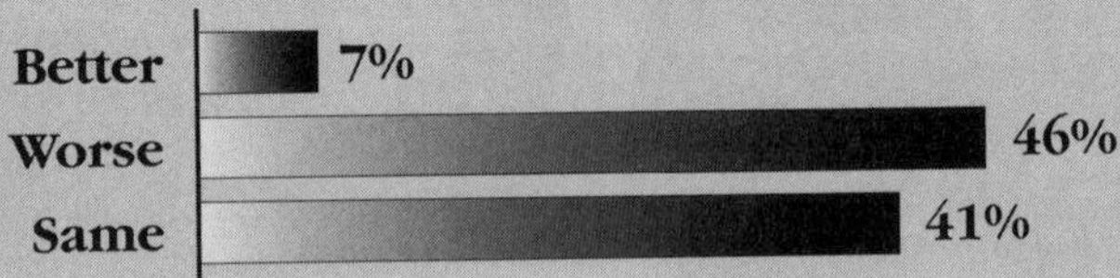

Source: Time/*CNN/Harris Interactive telephone poll of 1,006 adults, Nov.13-14, 2002. "Not sures" are not included.*

Continued from p. 546

holding a sign that read, "Homeless. Please Help." Sherman offered to take her to a clean, safe Salvation Army shelter, but the woman said she and her husband were fine sleeping under some nearby trees.

Sherman took the woman shopping, buying her food, clothing and some bug spray. Later, she visited the couple at their makeshift campsite, giving the husband job leads. Then one day they were gone. [15]

Some advocates would say that by offering tangible help, Sherman did exactly the right thing. But as she later wrote, "I'm convinced that handouts are basically wrongheaded." She shares author James L. Payne's view that handouts "demean recipients by implying [they] can't meet their own needs. [Handouts] can enable dysfunctional behavior and can be disincentives to work." [16]

By contrast, as Payne writes, " 'expectant giving' — a contribution that demands a constructive response from the supplicant — affirms people's God-given dignity and capacities. It's a 'hand-up,' not a handout." [17]

But the American social welfare system generally offers handouts, Sherman points out. The main reason for this, she says, is that "hand-up giving requires far more time, thought and personal investment than sympathetic [handout] giving. It's much easier to toss the homeless a few dollars than to build a relationship with them [that] can address the root causes of their condition." [18]

Critics of many programs targeting the homeless agree, saying the predominant strategy has only enabled the homeless by merely "warehousing" them and ignoring their personal problems. That's exactly what the nation's 50 federal programs, administered by eight different agencies, have done for the past 17 years, Housing Secretary Mel Martinez told the national convention of the National Alliance to End Homelessness shortly after he took office in 2001.

"Since 1987, the federal government has funneled more than $13 billion into easing the plight of the homeless . . . [b]ut we have not made much progress," he said. "It is time for the federal government to . . . invest in more permanent solutions [such as] moving the chronically homeless into permanent housing and permanent care." Martinez promised the administration would seek to remove Reagan-era "statutory barriers" that prevent the use of federal homeless dollars to develop housing.

But conservatives Rector and Besharov contend that homelessness is not, fundamentally, a housing problem. "Build a shelter, and it shall be filled, unless it is a rat hole," Besharov says. "If you build anything halfway decent and make it available for free, people are going to take it. It's just human nature. There'll always be shelters because they're too attractive, and they'll never kick people out."

"What we need in the shelters is a series of demands and requirements that begin to address the core reason why the individual is in the shelter," Rector says, such as requiring addicts to undergo a drug-withdrawal program and the mentally ill to take antipsychotic medication as prescribed. "Unfortunately a lot of homeless shelters seem to just operate as dumping grounds," with no requirements.

Maria Foscarinis, executive director of the National Law Center on Homelessness and Poverty (NLCHP), argues that many existing programs have been successful. "They have just not been at a large enough scale to solve the whole problem. Individual problems get solved, but not the whole problem." For example, she says, "We know that providing rent subsidies to people who just need help with housing costs can end homelessness — studies document this."

"Many of the shelter-plus-care programs have been very successful," adds Heybach. Indeed, permanent supportive housing (PSH) programs that also offer complementary supportive services, such as mental health care and detox programs designed to address the causes of homelessness, are becoming increasingly popular. In fact, 60,000 such units have been opened nationwide in recent years. [19]

PSH figures prominently in the Bush administration's strategy to end chronic homelessness in 10 years. "When you put housing together with services for vulnerable populations, then there's a high retention rate of tenancy," says the Interagency Council's Mangano, noting that a 10-year-old PSH program in New York has shown that "over 90 percent of people deemed intractably homeless retain tenancy with supportive housing."

Rep. Rick Renzi, R-Ariz., responded to the administration with the Samaritan Initiative Act of 2004, which he introduced in the House on March 30. The bill calls for the Departments of Health and Human Services, Housing and Urban Development and Veterans Affairs to create housing that provides health care, mental health and substance-abuse treatment and other services for the chronically homeless.

Reactions to the bill have been mixed. Many advocates and political insiders support the bill in spirit, but some have interpreted the White House's request for $70 million in funding as a cynical contradiction of that spirit. "Everybody knows $70 million won't buy you much," says Rep. Barney Frank, D-Mass. "If the Bush administration got its way on homelessness, the situation would be worse, not better."

Mangano hopes the $70 million is only the beginning of a regular stream of funding that will grow bigger as PSH begins to show positive effects. "We know more now about what works," he says, adding that political will to end homelessness is building, but only incrementally.

The focus on chronic homelessness is the first step in adopting a new, management-oriented strategy toward the problem. "We're not trying to service homeless people in place for years, as we have before," Mangano says. "We don't want to just fund more homeless programs because all you get are more homeless programs, and there are over 40,000 programs targeted to homeless people already."

As chronic homelessness shrinks, there will be more money to begin addressing the remaining homeless population, Mangano says. He notes that the chronically homeless account for no more than 10-20 percent of the total homeless population but absorb half the governmental resources devoted to the problem.

Heybach says the administration's focus on the chronically homeless leaves her unconvinced of its sincerity. "A cynic would say that represents an effort to get the most visible off the streets. We think there has to be a plan to house everyone."

Should government play a stronger leadership role in fighting homelessness?

Ending homelessness requires a partnership involving a wide range of government and private groups, but with government — in particular, the federal government — acting as the leading player, says Rep. Julia Carson, D-Ind.

"When you have people homeless in a community, it affects the whole community," she says. "It becomes like a disease — it starts out and then spreads. In suburban Indianapolis around shopping centers I see people pushing carts hoping to get cast-offs. The city has a blueprint to end homelessness, but it relies on federal support."

The support comes from the McKinney Act, which President Reagan signed into law in 1987. Among other provisions, it created the Interagency Council on Homelessness to coordinate the activities of 15 federal agencies (now 20) and designated $1 billion in federal funding the first two years for emergency food, shelter, care, education and job training for the homeless.

But Carson wants to broaden the federal government's role beyond the McKinney Act or the proposed Samaritan Initiative. In July 2003 she introduced the Bringing America Home Act, which would amend the McKinney Act to include donation of surplus federal property to assist the homeless and attempts to establish affordable housing as a basic human right. (*See "At Issue," p. 557.*) Lacking the administration's backing, however, the bill isn't moving through Congress as quickly as the Samaritan Initiative.

The NLCHP's Foscarinis also believes a full public-private partnership is necessary. "But the overwhelming responsibility is at the government level to make sure there's enough housing and other resources available to meet the basic needs of the poorest members of society," she says. But the policies needed to make those resources available aren't there yet, she says.

Indeed, says Heybach of the Chicago Coalition for the Homeless, the federal government should be doing the most to fight homelessness. "The federal government has put a lot of state and local entities into a fiscal crisis by grossly reducing taxes and raising the deficit and expenditures," she says. States simply can't afford to do enough. However, she cautions the federal government against any unilateral action. "Whatever they do must be in participation with those in the private sector and in advocacy groups who know about solutions." [20]

Mangano agrees the federal government could make a difference. But he also notes, "We've learned that no one level of government can get this job done alone."

The Interagency Council's leadership could best be used to build partnerships around the country, he says. An advocate on homelessness for more than two decades, Mangano is encouraging the nation's mayors to adopt 10-year plans to end chronic homelessness in conjunction with the administration's plan. To date, 117 mayors have adopted such plans, he says.

The Heritage Foundation's Rector stresses the government can do more, particularly in providing coordinated leadership involving shelters. "The general rule is that bad charity drives out good," he says. "If you have a few shelters in a community, and one of them tries to have rigorous behavioral requirements and the other shelters don't, guess who gets all the clients? It's very difficult for a private charity to run a constructive shelter program, one that's demanding, if down the street there's a bigger governmental facility that says, 'Hey, come on in and pass out!' "

Rector doesn't oppose the use of federal money as long as it's not wastefully spent. But historically, he says, federal spending on homelessness has achieved "nothing" at great expense.

Tanner of the Cato Institute says government at all levels needs to better recognize and address the ways in which government has contributed to homelessness through its zoning laws. "Are we zoning low-income housing out of existence?" he asks. He argues that local governments tend to bow to NIMBY pressure, which has helped restrict the amount of available affordable housing.

Advocates for the homeless also note that federal tax cuts have indirectly contributed to that loss of affordable housing by putting additional pressure on cash-strapped local governments, which often then turn to rezoning to enable gentrification of low-income areas, which increases local tax revenues.

"But I also think private charities and the private sector have enormous responsibility here, too," Tanner adds. "There are also issues of personal responsibility, and not just the individual's. It used to be that if your brother-in-law lost his job you put him on your couch. Now we send him to the shelter. We need to get back to taking care of each other."

For Besharov, government needs to play the leadership role because the private sector probably won't. "There are all sorts of reasons and challenges that make it difficult for the private sector to do it," including not having enough private money, he says. "But if there were enough of that, the private sector would do a better job than the government because in the end, judgments have to be made. Not about how much money to give, but about looking a homeless person in the eye and saying either, 'Get a job,' or, 'You need some counseling.' The private sector makes those judgments a lot better than the government."

Government certainly has a financial interest in ending homelessness. A recent study that followed 15 homeless people in San Diego for 18 months revealed that they were anything but inexpensive. Factoring in the number of ambulance rides and emergency-room services they needed, plus occasional law enforcement action, the cost to the city was $200,000 for each of the 15 people, according to Mangano.

"But at the end of 18 months, after $3 million was spent, these 15 people were in exactly the same situation they were at the beginning," Mangano says. ■

BACKGROUND

Perennial Problem

Homelessness has been a marginal feature of the American scene since the early days of the Republic. Over the years, though, perceptions of the jobless and homeless poor have changed.

In the past, according to a 1993 study, "the public was willing to admit that social isolation, alcoholism, drug abuse and mental illness were closely associated with homelessness, and from time to time reformers have designed programs intended to address these problems, some punitive, some generous." Today, in contrast, "fearful of blaming the victim, most people prefer to deny these conditions and view homelessness as a single problem: being without a home." [21]

Borrowing from the British experience, Americans of a century ago drew a sharp distinction between the "deserving" and "undeserving" poor. The little available assistance for the poor went to those whose impoverished condition was deemed beyond their control, such as incurably ill and physically handicapped persons, widows and orphans and men who suddenly lost their jobs. Paupers, generally able-bodied men who refused to work, received only contempt.

Meanwhile, social and economic upheavals left deep scars. Many wounded Civil War veterans, unable to regain their bearings, joined the ranks of the itinerant poor, along with widows and orphans of men killed in the conflict.

Continued on p. 552

Chronology

1930s *Stock market crash of 1929 wreaks economic havoc across the country.*

1933-1935
Federal Emergency Relief Administration (FERA) supplies shelter and other aid to the homeless.

1935
FERA is replaced by programs targeting individual needs. Works Progress Administration (WPA) creates jobs but requires applicants to meet strict residency tests.

1940s *World War II creates jobs nationwide, lessening the need for social programs.*

1949
Housing Act calls for "a decent home for every American."

1960s *Homelessness rises after years of seeming remission.*

1963
Community Health Centers Act deinstitutionalizes an estimated 430,000 mentally ill people.

1970s *Courts rule on homelessness for the first time.*

1972
Supreme Court decriminalizes vagrancy and declares laws making residency a condition for receiving public assistance unconstitutional.

Dec. 7, 1979
New York Supreme Court Justice Andrew R. Tyler declares in *Callahan v. Carey* that the state and the city must provide "clean bedding, wholesome food and adequate supervision and security" for the homeless.

1980s *Supplies of affordable housing begin to shrink as the nation awakens to the problems of homelessness.*

September 1982
Community for Creative Non-Violence estimates that 2.2 million Americans lack shelter.

October 1982
U.S. Conference of Mayors reports that cities are meeting only 43 percent of the demand for emergency services.

July 22, 1987
President Ronald Reagan signs into law the Stewart B. McKinney Homeless Assistance Act, which provides emergency shelters, job training and other programs.

1990s *Homelessness is increasingly perceived as a complex condition resistant to easy remedies.*

May 1992
Census Bureau says 459,000 persons are homeless; homeless advocates call the count far too low.

May 17, 1994
Interagency Council on the Homeless recommends "continuum of care" approach offering individuals and families a variety of services.

Dec. 6, 1995
President Clinton vetoes a balanced-budget bill that would have eliminated the preference for homeless-assistance groups in the disposal of surplus federal property.

Dec. 19, 1995
Conference of Mayors estimates that 24 percent of families' requests for emergency shelter were unmet in 1994.

1999
Fannie Mae Foundation finds that public housing has only "slight to modest" negative impact on property values.

2000s *New research leads to more effective strategies and approaches to fighting homelessness as private sector and government coordinate joint efforts.*

2002
Bush administration announces plan to end chronic homelessness in 10 years.

December 2003
Conference of Mayors' annual report on homelessness and poverty reveals that requests for emergency-shelter assistance increased an average of 13 percent in 25 cities.

January 2004
Bush administration's fiscal 2005 budget requests an increase of $113 million for affordable housing for low- and moderate-income individuals, and $70 million to fund the Samaritan Initiative; critics say the requests amount to a cutback and are too low to make a difference.

Continued from p. 550

The depressions that periodically shook post-Civil War economies plunged thousands of families into sudden indigence. Temple University historian Kenneth L. Kusmer noted that the "increasing number of homeless men during the very period when the United States was emerging as an industrial nation was no coincidence. The new vagrancy was an indigenous aspect of a country in rapid transition from an agricultural and small-town society to one centered in great cities." [22]

Before the 1930s, private charities and local governments furnished the bulk of services for poor, jobless and homeless people. But during the administration of Herbert Hoover, the Great Depression that followed the 1929 stock market crash overwhelmed the resources of traditional caregivers. As unemployment rose into double digits, breadlines and soup-kitchen queues grew steadily longer, while shantytowns derisively called "Hoovervilles" sprang up in large cities — including New York's Central Park.

Soon after Franklin D. Roosevelt took office as president in 1933, he initiated his New Deal program, in which the federal government began to assume a major role in combating poverty and homelessness. For instance, the Federal Emergency Relief Administration supplied shelter, food, medical care, clothing, jobs and cash to the homeless. And the Works Progress Administration also created jobs available to the homeless.

Most of the emergency-relief programs established in the early years of the New Deal were discontinued when World War II started. With war-production plants operating at peak capacity, unemployment vanished. Joblessness remained at low levels after peace returned, especially during the 1950s. By that time, homelessness seemed confined to the alcoholic and mentally disturbed single men who frequented impoverished neighborhoods like Lower Manhattan's Bowery.

Before long, though, homelessness resurfaced as a national concern. Social historians date the turnabout from February 1963, when President John F. Kennedy urged the creation of a nationwide network of community mental health centers to replace the state mental hospitals housing more than 500,000 mentally ill and mentally retarded people, where numerous abuses had come to light. [23]

Congress acceded to Kennedy's request, but from the outset many patients did not receive the aftercare they needed. States shuttered the state mental hospitals but did not provide enough support for the community mental health centers to replace inpatient treatment. Thousands of former patients ended up on the streets or in jails or prisons. [24]

In the mid-1960s, President Lyndon B. Johnson launched his Great Society program, a large part of which included his famous "War on Poverty." While Johnson's anti-poverty programs did not include any specific initiatives targeted at homelessness, many of its provisions benefited homeless people.

Library of Congress

At the end of the Great Depression in 1939, a homeless family walks along a highway near Brawley, Calif., on the way to San Diego, where the father hoped to get relief benefits. They were coming from Phoenix, Ariz., where they had picked cotton.

In the 1970s the courts confronted homelessness for the first time. In January 1972, the U.S. Supreme Court unanimously upheld lower court rulings barring one-year welfare residency laws in New York and Connecticut. The following month, the high court struck down as unconstitutionally vague a Jacksonville ordinance against loafing, "nightwalking" or avoiding work. The decision voided vagrancy laws in many other cities and states.

Callahan v. Carey, the nation's first right-to-shelter lawsuit, was filed in New York State Supreme Court in 1979 by homeless advocate Robert M. Hayes. In a ruling handed down on Dec. 7, Justice Andrew R. Tyler ordered New York City and New York state to create 750 new beds for the "helpless and homeless men of the Bowery."

In the early 1970s, veterans returning from the Vietnam War — particularly those suffering from post-traumatic stress disorder or who had become addicted to heroin in Vietnam — added to the homeless population. "Between the wounds of war and not being able to find a place to deal with it, many veterans turned to substance abuse, which then turned into homelessness," says Sharon Hodge, associate director of Vietnam Veterans of America. Approximately 10 percent of the current homeless population are veterans, almost half of whom are believed to be Vietnam vets. [25]

In 1980, President Jimmy Carter signed the Mental Health Systems Act, which would have helped the mental-health treatment problems of the homeless. But the law was repealed the following year under the new Reagan administration. The Omnibus Budget Reconciliation Act of 1981 essentially restructured the nation's mental health system by shifting direct federal funding to a more flexible program of community block grants that states could apply to mental health treatment if they so chose. Under the new system, funding for community mental health in 1982 dropped 30 percent. [26]

In the early 1980s, panhandlers and shabbily dressed people sleeping on outdoor steam grates began to attract the anxious notice of city residents and the news media. At first, the development was blamed on the 1981-82 recession and the federal budget cuts. It was assumed that once the economy improved, the number of homeless people would decline.

When that failed to happen, social commentators had to look for more deep-seated causes. The introduction of highly addictive crack cocaine in the mid-1980s obviously was a major factor. But changes in the work force and in housing availability may have been even more disruptive.

Disappearing Housing

The unskilled day-labor jobs transients had long relied on were rapidly disappearing, as was much of the nation's stock of low-rent housing. Many apartments in public housing complexes were being boarded up because of vandalism or lack of maintenance. And in some cities, entire high-rise public housing projects were being demolished as uninhabitable. The combination of fewer bottom-tier jobs and fewer affordable-housing units evidently tipped thousands of poor people out of their homes and into the streets. By this time, the crack epidemic had also begun turning many vulnerable inner-city residents into addicts who either lost their homes or were kicked out by their families. Many housing projects degenerated into crack havens or were so plagued by drug-related crime that many residents moved away.

Loss of privately owned, low-income shelter compounded the problem. Rooming houses, once a common residential option in big cities, became an endangered housing species. Many of the structures, especially those in gentrified neighborhoods, were returned to single-family use and sold at handsome profits.

The supply of single-room occupancy (SRO) hotels has fallen sharply for the same reason. Since the 1970s, numerous SRO buildings have been transformed into upscale rental apartments or condominiums or torn down as unsalvageable.

Christopher Jencks, a sociology professor at Northwestern University, has argued that construction of "cubicle hotels" modeled on the flophouses of yore could do much to alleviate homelessness. Cubicle housing would "provoke opposition in some neighborhoods," but it would also cost far less to build and maintain than regular SRO rooms, he says. [27]

But no one knows how much cubicle housing would be needed because of widely divergent estimates of homelessness. The debate dates at least from 1980, when Mitch Snyder, a homeless activist with the Community for Creative Non-Violence (CCNV) in Washington, D.C., began to draw frequent media coverage. In a 1982 report, "Homelessness in America: A Forced March to Nowhere," Snyder and a colleague, Mary Ellen Hombs, estimated that 2.2 million people lacked shelter nationwide and predicted that the number would reach 3 million or more in 1983.

"Lacking better figures, others repeated this guess, usually without attribution," Jencks noted. "In due course, it became so familiar that many people treated it as a well-established fact." [28]

Congress Responds

Snyder played a pivotal role in pressuring Congress to approve the sweeping 1987 Stewart B. McKinney Homeless Assistance Act. McKinney, a Connecticut Republican who suffered from AIDS, had fought for the homeless and the poor. He died weeks before the law passed, not long after he had joined a handful of other members of Congress to sleep on heating grates in downtown Washington to publicize the plight of the homeless. [29]

The measure was introduced on Jan. 8, 1987, ending a seven-week protest at the U.S. Capitol by homeless advocates. CCNV members had camped out near the Capitol's east entrance since Thanksgiving Day 1986 next to a homemade statue honoring the homeless. Snyder had defied police and court orders to remove the figure.

Congress' action was also triggered in part by two reports released the previous December showing that the nation's homeless population grew by 25 percent in 1986, and that families with children were the fastest-growing segment of that population. Advocates for the homeless blamed cuts of more than 70 percent in federal subsidized housing programs since Reagan became president. The administration, however, blamed continuing deinstitutionalization of mental patients, job losses and the disappearance of low-income housing due to local redevelopment projects. [30]

The law authorized $443 million in homeless aid for fiscal 1987 and an additional $616 million for fiscal 1988. The Interagency Council on the Homeless established by the act was directed to coordinate federal programs for the homeless and report to Congress and the president on the homeless problem. It also established nearly 20 programs to aid the homeless, including emergency food and shelter, medical and mental-health care, permanent housing, education and job training. The law also directed the secretary of the Department of Housing and Urban Development (HUD) to make underused federal buildings available for the homeless.

On Nov. 29, 1993, a homeless woman, Yetta M. Adams, 43, was found dead on a bench outside the offices of HUD Secretary Henry G. Cisneros. The low temperature that morning had been 34, two degrees above the threshold that sends city workers around in vans picking up the homeless and taking them to shelters. [31]

Cisneros promptly advanced several hundred thousand dollars to Washington to upgrade its homeless-outreach efforts. He also promised $25 million more to other cities. At the end of the month, the Clinton administration announced grants of $411 million to fund 187 homeless-assistance programs in 44 states. California ($75 million) and New York ($75 million) were the principal beneficiaries.

Then, in May 1994, the administration issued a blueprint for trimming the U.S. homeless population by one-third. The report, called "Priority: Home! The Federal Plan to End Homelessness," proposed $900 million in new HUD spending for homeless aid, bringing the total to a record $2.15 billion in fiscal 1995. Donald Whitehead, executive director of the National Coalition for the Homeless (NCH), says that while HUD Secretary Andrew Cuomo was "very responsive to the need for homelessness initiatives," and many new programs were begun, "many other initiatives were never implemented [and] HUD ended up with no real substantial increase in new funding."

Meanwhile, Democrats tried unsuccessfully during the Clinton administration to raise the nation's $5.15 minimum wage by $1 an hour. Some low-wage workers often must decide between paying rent and buying groceries, Sen. Edward M. Kennedy, D-Mass., said during the Senate's 2000 debate on raising the wage. At $5.15 per hour, an employee would have to work 80 hours a week to afford the fair-market rent established by the federal government for assisted housing. [32]

Republicans have said they would favor raising the minimum wage if it is phased in slowly and is accompanied by tax breaks for small business, but the measure has been stalled in Congress for nearly four years.

Cities Respond

City governments, however, were adopting harsher policies. New York's Giuliani announced in May 2000 that homeless persons would have to participate in job training, drug treatment and other self-help programs in order to qualify for shelter and other services. And the city began denying shelter to families who turned down more than three apartments offered by the city.

But the Giuliani approach soon appeared benign compared with those adopted by some other cities. A survey of 49 cities released in 1994 found that 42 "pursued efforts to criminalize activities associated with homelessness," mostly through anti-panhandling ordinances, restrictions on occupying public spaces and police sweeps. [33]

The National Law Center on Homelessness and Poverty conceded that some concerns about the use of public space were legitimate. "Ultimately, no city resident — homeless or housed — wants people living and begging in the streets. But criminalizing these activities is not the solution. Instead of attacking homeless people, cities should attack homelessness." [34]

Doe Fund

A formerly homeless man works cleaning streets in New York City after training by the Doe Fund's Ready, Willing and Able Program.

By the late 1990s and the start of the new millennium, consensus began to grow around causes of homelessness and workable solutions. For instance, homeless advocates once believed that substance abuse was a result of homelessness, but researchers eventually found instead that it was a principal cause of homelessness. Similarly, the notion that housing alone was the biggest problem gave way to the realization that — for the chronically homeless, in particular — supportive services had to accompany a roof and a bed.

The Bush administration also signaled a new attitude toward chronic homelessness when it claimed that the problem could indeed be eliminated. Throughout most of the 1990s, many politicians, researchers, analysts and even much of the general public had begun to view homelessness as intractable, causing many people to suffer so-called compassion fatigue.

But, as new research developed, the realization emerged that previous strategies were wrong or misdirected or, in the opinion of some, simply underfunded. ■

CURRENT SITUATION

Pending Bills

Rep. Renzi's pending Samaritan Initiative Act, cosponsored by 14 Republicans and two Democrats, is expected to clear Congress this year, given its strong White House support.

The $70 million requested by the White House for the program would be dispersed through three agencies: $50 million from HUD, $10 million from the Department of Health and Human Services and $10 million from the Department of Veterans Affairs.

Permanent supportive housing — the centerpiece of the initiative — was once derided as too costly by many members of Congress. But recent research has helped to change minds on both sides of the aisle. [35]

For example, a study of homeless facilities in New York showed that each chronically homeless person with severe mental illness cost the city on average almost $41,000 a year in shelter, corrections and health services. But residents in permanent supportive housing needed costly acute-care far less frequently, nearly offsetting the extra cost of PSH. [36]

By contrast, Rep. Carson's proposed Bringing America Home Act, cosponsored by 42 Democrats and an Independent, is far more ambitious than the Samaritan Initiative. It would establish a National Housing Trust Fund to underwrite construction and maintenance of 1.5 million affordable homes over the next 10 years. The bill would also provide job training and public transportation for the working homeless or those seeking work; child-care vouchers for working homeless parents; and emergency funding for families facing eviction. It also includes provisions on health, income and civil rights.

"We as a Congress need to look at everything that promotes homelessness and see what we can do to counteract it, if at all possible," Carson says. At the moment, the bill "is just hanging around," she says. "But we're getting more members interested in it once they understand the need for it, and that's a slow process."

Cutting Vouchers

Advocates for the homeless are disappointed in the Bush administration's fiscal 2005 budget for federal programs at agencies that deal with the homeless.

> **"For the third year in a row, the budget fails to demonstrate how the administration plans to implement its own goals of ending homelessness by 2012."**
>
> **— *National Alliance to End Homelessness***

"For the third year in a row, the budget fails to demonstrate, with either resources or a strategy, how the administration plans to implement its own goal of ending chronic homelessness by 2012," the National Alliance to End Homelessness said after the budget was released on Feb. 2. The group said the $70 million requested for the Samaritan Initiative was "wholly inadequate to the goal."

The administration's proposal would provide up to $2 billion less than is needed to maintain subsidized-rent vouchers — called Section 8 vouchers — at current levels, causing 250,000 households to lose federal housing aid, the group said.

But HUD spokesman Brian Sullivan says the administration is trying to hold the line on Section 8 spending, while

How You Can Help

America may have a shortage of shelter for the homeless, but it doesn't lack for programs to help. An estimated 40,000 public and private programs are dedicated to fighting homelessness.

For would-be volunteers, the key to success is to think specifically, according to the National Coalition for the Homeless (NCH). For instance, many shelters require filing, clerical or typing help. Many also need basic labor — sorting clothing, washing dishes, chopping vegetables. Volunteers should also consider whether they prefer working with individuals or groups, with men or women, with adults or children.

Start by contacting your local public housing authority or visit the NCH Web site (www.nationalhomeless.org/state/), which lists nearly 400 different advocacy groups across the country, to find out which goods or services are most needed in your area.

Ideally, you should say not only how you could best help but also when and for how long. Shelters and service providers are almost perpetually understaffed and underfunded, and providing as much information up front about what you can do saves them valuable time.

Here are some specific suggestions for volunteering from the NCH and National Alliance to End Homelessness:

- Volunteer for an evening or overnight shift at a shelter.
- Help build or renovate a house or shelter for the homeless.
- Assist with catering, plumbing, accounting, management, carpentry, public relations, fundraising, legal work, health care, dentistry, writing, child care, counseling, tutoring or mentoring.
- Offer to organize an event at a shelter, such as a board game or chess night, an open-mike poetry reading, a guest storytelling or musical performance or even a holiday party.
- Train homeless people for jobs.
- Register homeless people to vote.
- Donate food and used clothing.

Also consider becoming a part-time advocate by attending neighborhood and public meetings to speak in favor of low-income housing and shelters as well as homelessness-prevention programs. The implications of these measures are often complicated and not well understood by the general public; someone who knows their advantages and disadvantages can have a definite positive impact on any relevant vote or decision.

Call or write local officials and leaders to involve them on the issue. Are the area media covering homelessness sufficiently? If not, let them know. If yes, also let them know — the press often will continue reporting on stories they know are getting favorable attention.

Several advocacy groups also urge volunteers to contact their congressional representatives. For example, the National Student Campaign Against Hunger and Homelessness is currently asking visitors to its Web site to e-mail Washington with requests to support full federal funding for Section 8 housing.

For more specific advice on how to help, visit either www.nationalhomeless.org/help.html or www.naeh.org/do/index.htm.

providing a "record level" — about $1.3 billion — for homelessness.

That's not enough, maintains Foscarinis, of the National Law Center on Homelessness and Poverty. She cites last year's Conference of Mayors survey showing that more than 80 percent of cities surveyed had been forced to turn away homeless families in 2003, and expected unmet needs to increase in 2004. [37]

And holding the line on rent subsidies amounts to a cutback, say advocates for the homeless, because the ranks of the homeless are growing. "Losing that funding is going to do a lot of harm," says Roman of the National Alliance to End Homelessness. "The administration has committed to ending chronic homelessness in 10 years. It's going to be difficult to see how that's accomplished with their plans for Section 8."

But the Heritage Foundation's Rector strongly disagrees. "Section 8 is a bad program," he says. "In many respects it serves an able-bodied population similar to the [Temporary Assistance to Needy Families] program, but in TANF there are requirements to become self-sufficient. No requirements like that are in Section 8. This is essentially an old-style, War-on-Poverty, one-way handout program that facilitates dependence and certainly needs to be radically reformed."

Mangano of the Interagency Council agrees. "When I was an advocate in Massachusetts, for years I advocated for an increase in Section 8 funding. Very rarely did that happen. So one of the first things I did when I got to Washington was to look at Section 8, and I found that every year between $700 million and $1.2 billion of Section 8 resources were returned."

The money couldn't be used for a variety of reasons, Mangano says. For example, Section 8 vouchers cannot be applied to rents above a certain amount, and in some areas the rental markets had risen too high. Mangano immediately went to the White House Office of Management and Budget (OMB) to ask for some of the returned Section 8 funding to be made available for the Interagency Council on the Homeless for redistribution to other programs for the homeless.

Continued on p. 558

At Issue:

Is affordable housing a human right?

MARIA FOSCARINIS
EXECUTIVE DIRECTOR, NATIONAL LAW CENTER ON HOMELESSNESS AND POVERTY

WRITTEN FOR *THE CQ RESEARCHER*, JUNE 2004

yes

Over 50 years ago, the United States took the lead in drafting the Universal Declaration of Human Rights (UDHR). Adopted by the international community in 1948, it states: "Everyone has the right to a standard of living adequate for the health and well being of himself and his family, including . . . housing."

The right to housing is recognized in numerous subsequent treaties, including three that have been signed and ratified by the United States. As defined in human rights law, affordability is included as a component of the right.

Under the right to housing, each nation must maximize available resources to implement the right "progressively but fully." Implementing the right in the United States would not require government to provide free housing for everyone, but would require implementing a housing policy that ensures adequate housing for all — through subsidies, private-sector incentives, tax credits or a combination of means.

It would also require the United States to make implementation a priority and allocate resources accordingly. In effect, it would require our government to live up to the goal stated by Congress in the 1949 Housing Act: "The implementation as soon as feasible of a decent home and suitable living environment for every American family."

Yet today, due to inadequate funding, only about 25 percent of those low-income people eligible for federal housing assistance receive it. In contrast, the homeowners' tax deduction is available to all who qualify. Recognizing housing as a human right would mean extending housing benefits — of various kinds — to all, eliminating this inequity.

The universality of human rights can help counter the assumption that government involvement in housing benefits only the poor and broaden support for housing programs.

Economic and social rights are entwined with civil and political rights — and responsibilities. Nelson Mandela recently noted "the critical importance of social and economic rights in building true democracies," and observed, "this is nowhere more evident than in the right to housing. . . . Everyone needs a place which is a home."

Implementing the commitment to housing in the UDHR would make a positive difference in the lives of millions of Americans — and help re-establish the United States as a world leader in human rights.

MICHAEL TANNER
DIRECTOR, HEALTH AND WELFARE STUDIES CATO INSTITUTE

WRITTEN FOR *THE CQ RESEARCHER*, JUNE 2004

no

Affordable housing for every American is a desirable goal for public policy. But not every good policy can be translated into questions of human rights.

When properly defined, rights do not conflict. That is because rights are essentially negative in character. My exercise of my rights in no ways infringes on your exercise of your rights. Your only obligation is negative, to refrain from interfering with my exercise of rights. Thus, my right to speak freely requires no action on your part, takes nothing away from you. My right exists independent of you. Your only obligation is not to stop me from speaking.

But the same is not true of a right to affordable housing. It would impose a positive obligation. In order for me to exercise my right, something must be taken away from you. That may be your property, directly through taxes, or indirectly through limits on what you can charge for rent. But in theory, my claim on you could go still further. Suppose there simply was not enough housing being built. If housing is a right, I would have the authority to conscript you to become a carpenter.

This can be expanded even further. Rights are universal, not subject to national borders. Therefore, if housing is a right, people's property and liberty would be subject to appropriation not just to solve homelessness in this country, but until every person worldwide had housing.

And, of course, one shudders at the definitional question. What qualifies as housing sufficient to satisfy the right? A mud hut, a single room, a ranch-style bungalow?

Beyond the philosophical, there are practical questions involved. Simply declaring something a "right" does nothing to actually solve the problems leading to homelessness. Homelessness is not simply a question of lack of money or lack of inexpensive housing. The majority of homeless suffer from mental illness and/or drug and alcohol problems. If given a house or apartment today, many would be homeless again tomorrow.

The problems underlying homelessness are complex and the solutions subject to considerable debate. That is a debate worth having, but it is a debate that is not advanced by defining housing as a human right.

Continued from p. 556

"They told me that the reversion of Section 8 resources was so chronic that they already reprogrammed that money. Every year, they made the money available, but knowing about a billion was coming back, they allotted it elsewhere. So in that moment, it dawned on me, that in all those years I was begging for more Section 8 money, the policymakers' view of Section 8 was that it was a very dysfunctional program. And I then understood that something needed to be done to repair it."

In reducing the Section 8 subsidy, the Bush administration has only "made a corrective," Mangano says. "The hope is that the dire predictions of the sky falling will not be true. What will be true is what HUD and OMB are saying: That reform will allow the program to serve more people."

John Kerry, the presumptive Democratic nominee for president, has criticized the Bush administration for "working to dismantle many federal programs that help Americans find affordable housing." Citing statistics from the National Housing Conference, a nonprofit organization devoted to maintaining affordable housing, Kerry notes that more than 14 million working families were spending more than half of their income for housing in 2001. He further claims the administration's 2004 budget has worsened the problem by eliminating housing-assistance programs that help low-income families as well as the elderly and disabled. [38]

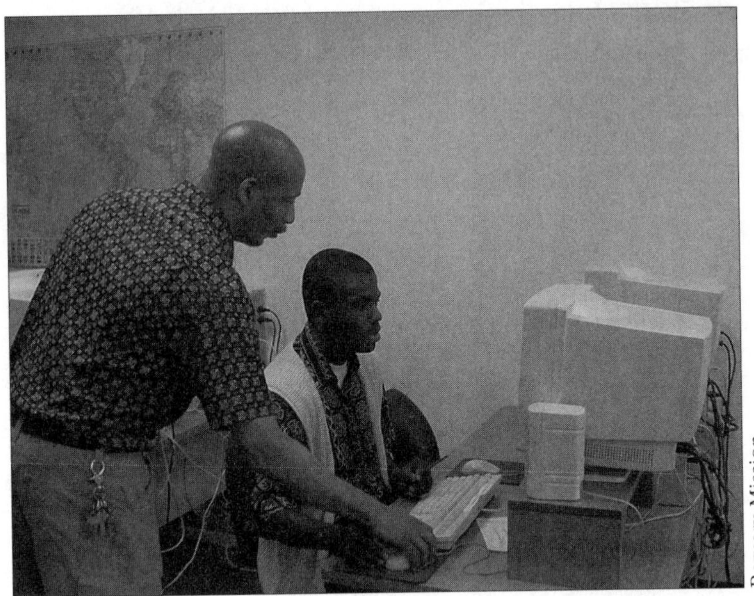

Bowery Mission

Homeless men receive computer training and employment counseling at New York City's Bowery Mission, in addition to meals, shelter and showers.

Local Alternatives

Some cities have begun developing alternative means of addressing homelessness. "Criminalizing [homelessness] continues and in some cases has gotten worse, but some cities are looking for a more constructive approach," The NLCHP's Foscarinis says. For instance, experts say Columbus, Ohio, has taken a model approach to homelessness, combining input from local officials and business leaders with up-to-date research and meticulous planning.

Advocates also hail "inclusionary zoning" initiatives adopted by some cities, which require high-rise developers to also erect low-cost housing elsewhere. "It's a great way to bring in the private sector to create more affordable housing without spending government dollars," Foscarinis says.

Other cities are focusing on preventive measures, such as targeting help to those already in the welfare system who are at risk of becoming homeless. In the absence of an increase in the minimum wage, Whitehead of the NCH says, several states, counties and cities around the country have passed living-wage ordinances as a way to prevent homelessness. [39]

While the federal government still holds the line on increasing the national minimum wage, he nonetheless believes that "as more of these ordinances are passed locally, we'll probably see an increase in the minimum wage. Not in the near future, but maybe the medium future."

Fannie Mae's Weech is optimistic. "There's a lot happening — a sense that this is the right thing to do — and that creates the sense of synergy and political will" to end homelessness, he says. "It will be very hard and resources required will be significant, but at the same time it feels like a very different environment from the one in which people said, 'This is an intractable problem!' " ■

OUTLOOK

Good News, Bad News

Optimism is indeed in the air, but so is pessimism.

"There's lots of opportunity," says Roman of the National Alliance to End Homelessness. For instance, if the Samaritan Initiative proves successful it could mean substantial federal funding for permanent supportive housing. And the Fannie Mae Foundation's recent pledge of $35 million for PSH programs could spur similar initiatives by other foundations.

"On the other hand, we kind of take three steps forward and two back, like with Section 8, so it's hard to know whether we'll end up ahead or behind," Roman says. "If we focus on end-game strategies, on prevention, on getting people out of the [temporary shelter] system faster, we're going to be better off than we would have been if we didn't do it. But if we can't make some key steps forward, like straightening out the Section 8 thing, then we're not going to end homelessness."

Foscarinis of the National Law Center on Homelessness and Poverty also sees a "good-news, bad-news" future. Federal appropriations for homelessness are low, she concedes, but the issue is getting increasing attention. "State and local governments are at least saying they want to end it, and even at the federal level there's a stated commitment to ending at least part of homelessness."

Rep. Carson, however, says, "I really don't see anything changing much. We're arguing the budget now, and it's a no-caring budget. As long as we keep misspending money, then we're not making an investment in human capital, as we should be."

The Cato Institute's Tanner also doubts the situation will change appreciably, but for different reasons. The recently improving economy will help families who had lost jobs "but [not] the chronic folks," he says.

But before the government starts "another round of spending on this," he insists, "there needs to be a rethinking of what it is we're trying to do. Do we want people off the streets temporarily so they don't freeze to death? Good idea. Or do we want to bring these people into the mainstream of society? If so, good luck. You're not going to see any large-scale changes over the next year or five years."

Politics and other vested interests are the two largest obstacles to improving the situation, says the Heritage Foundation's Rector. He chuckles on hearing that the Bush administration has proposed $70 million to address chronic homelessness, saying, "That's essentially the way these issues always get stuck. Welfare reform is a good paradigm for this. For almost 15 years, the liberals in Congress would say, 'Well, maybe having women on welfare work is a good idea, but you're going to have to fork up a lot of money for that.' And Republicans would say, 'We're not going to fork up any additional money for anything.'

"The reality is welfare reform was essentially self-funding," he continues. "The program was pretty expensive before reform, but when you put requirements on people, the numbers on the rolls dropped, and you were able to divert all those funds into things like day care. So, essentially it was a funding diversion. It would probably be similar with homelessness.

"The problem is that on a rhetorical level, everyone accepts the idea that we should no longer be giving . . . one-way handouts," he continues. "But as soon as you talk about [imposing] work or behavioral requirements, you immediately run into the same vested interests that opposed welfare reform."

Some advocates for the homeless and analysts — mostly liberals — still debate the success of welfare reform. [40] But even independent observers admit that, despite the promise of some new approaches and programs to end homelessness, success is hardly guaranteed.

Those approaches and programs "are extremely ambitious, requiring major changes to a variety of famously intractable social welfare and other public systems, not to mention significant allocation or reallocation of resources," writes Dennis P. Culhane, a welfare policy expert at the University of Pennsylvania.

"And the pitfalls are many — political and economic constraints can limit implementation, unintended consequences can undermine achievement of goals and external forces can overwhelm the best of intentions." [41]

But Housing Secretary Martinez is undaunted. "It will take optimism — and a healthy dose of strength, patience and persistence — to wrestle homelessness from our cities," Martinez says. "But these are qualities Americans have in abundance." ■

Notes

[1] "Feeding Homeless on the Street Opposed," *The Miami Herald*, May 24, 2004, p. B3.

[2] Keith Ervin and Justin Mayo, "Tent City Doesn't Seem to Affect Crime Rates," *The Seattle Times*, May 21, 2004, p. B1.

[3] Sheryl Kornman, "Homing in on Homeless," *Tucson Citizen*, April 29, 2004, p. 1A.

[4] National Association of Realtors.

[5] Conference of Mayors, *op. cit.*

[6] U.S. Conference of Mayors, Sodexho, "Homelessness and Hunger Survey," December 2003.

About the Author

William Triplett recently joined the *CQ Researcher* as a staff writer after covering science and the arts for such publications as *Smithsonian, Air & Space, Nature, Washingtonian* and *The Washington Post.* He also served as associate editor of *Capitol Style* magazine. He holds a B.A. in journalism from Ohio University and an M.A. in English literature from Georgetown University.

[7] Nina Bernstein, "Deep Poverty and Illness Found Among Homeless," *The New York Times*, Dec. 8, 1999, p. A16.
[8] Conference of Mayors, *op. cit.*
[9] For background, see "Welfare Reform," *The CQ Researcher*, Aug. 3, 2001, pp. 601-632.
[10] Jennifer A. Hurley, ed., *The Homeless: Opposing Viewpoints* (2002), p. 13.
[11] Mary E. Williams, ed., *Poverty and the Homeless* (2004), p. 14.
[12] Hurley, *op. cit.*, p. 13.
[13] "The State of the Nation's Housing 2003," Joint Center for Housing Studies, Harvard University, 2003, cited in *Homelessness in the United States and the Human Right to Housing*, National Law Center on Homelessness and Poverty, January 2004, p. i.
[14] Williams, *op. cit.*, p. 17.
[15] Amy L. Sherman, "Expectant Giving," *Christian Century*, vol. 116, Feb. 24, 1999, p. 206, reprinted in Williams, *op. cit.*, p. 166.
[16] *Ibid.*
[17] Quoted in *ibid*, p. 167.
[18] *Ibid.*
[19] Joel Stein, "The Real Face of Homelessness," *Time*, Jan. 20, 2003, p. 52.
[20] For background see William Triplett, "State Budget Crisis," *The CQ Researcher*, Oct. 3, 2003, pp. 821-844.
[21] Alice S. Baum and Donald W. Burnes, *A Nation in Denial: The Truth about Homelessness* (1993), p. 91.
[22] Quoted by Rick Beard in *On Being Homeless: Historical Perspectives* (1987), p. 23.
[23] For background, see Jane Tanner, "Mental Illness Medication Debate," *The CQ Researcher*, Feb. 6, 2004, pp. 101-124.
[24] See Bob Prentice, "Homelessness and Public Policy," in *Nursing and Health Care for the Homeless*, Juanita K. Hunter, ed. (1993), p. 21.
[25] See "Background and Statistics" page on Web site of National Coalition of Homeless Veterans; www.nchv.org/background.cfm.
[26] Tanner, *op. cit.*
[27] Christopher Jencks, "Housing the Homeless," *The New York Review of Books*, May 12, 1994, p. 43.
[28] Christopher Jencks, "The Homeless," *The New York Review of Books*, April 21, 1994, p. 20.
[29] For background, see *Congressional Quarterly Almanac* (1987), p. 53.
[30] *Ibid.*, pp. 508-509.
[31] Henry G. Cisneros, "The Lonely Death on my Doorstep," *The Washington Post*, Dec. 5, 1993, p. C1.

FOR MORE INFORMATION

American Bar Association Commission on Homelessness and Poverty, 740 15th St., N.W., Washington, DC 20005; (202) 662-1694; www.abanet.org/homeless/. Fosters pro bono legal programs for the homeless and educates the public about the legal problems of the very poor.

Beyond Shelter, 3255 Wilshire Blvd., Suite 815, Los Angeles, CA 90010; (213) 252-0772; www.beyondshelter.org. Combats chronic poverty, welfare dependency and homelessness among families with children.

Corporation for Supportive Housing, 50 Broadway, 17th Fl., New York, NY 10004; (212) 986-2966; www.csh.org. Supports the expansion of permanent housing opportunities linked to comprehensive services for people with chronic health challenges.

National Alliance to End Homelessness, 1518 K St., N.W., Washington, DC 20005; (202) 638-1526; www.naeh.org. Seeks to form a public-private partnership to reduce homelessness.

National Law Center on Homelessness and Poverty, 918 F St., N.W., Suite 412, Washington, DC 20004-1406; (202) 638-2535; www.nlchp.org. Monitors legislation affecting the homeless.

National Coalition for Homeless Veterans, 333-1/2 Pennsylvania Ave., S.E., Washington, DC 20003; (202) 546-1969; www.nchv.org. Works with government and community groups to build the capacity of service providers.

National Coalition for the Homeless, 1012 14th St., N.W., Suite 600, Washington, DC 20005; (202) 737-6444; www.nationalhomeless.org. Seeks to end homelessness through public education, grass-roots organizing and technical assistance.

U.S. Conference of Mayors Task Force on Hunger and Homelessness, 1620 Eye St., N.W., 4th floor, Washington, DC 20006; (202) 293-7330; http://usmayors.org. Studies trends in hunger, homelessness and community programs that address homelessness and hunger in U.S. cities.

U.S. Department of Housing and Urban Development, Special Needs Assistance Programs, HUD Building, Room 7262, Washington, DC 20410; (202) 708-4300; www.hud.gov/homeless/index.cfm. Promotes cooperation among federal agencies on homelessness issues.

[32] For background, see Kathy Koch, "Child Poverty," *The CQ Researcher*, April 7, 2000, pp. 281-304.
[33] National Law Center on Homelessness and Poverty, *No Homeless People Allowed*, December 1994, p. i.
[34] *Ibid.*, p. ii, vi.
[35] The Democratic cosponsors are Michael E. Capuano, Mass., and Jim Matheson, Utah.
[36] Dennis P. Culhane, "New Strategies and Collaborations Target Homelessness," *Housing Facts & Findings*, Fannie Mae Foundation, 2002; www.fanniemaefoundation.org/programs/hff/v4i5-strategies.shtml.
[37] "2004 Appropriations Fail to Keep Pace with Homelessness," press release, National Law Center on Homelessness and Poverty, Jan. 23, 2004.
[38] Statement is found at http://kerry.senate.gov/bandwidth/issues/housing.html.
[39] For background, see Jane Tanner, "Living-Wage Movement," *The CQ Researcher*, Sept. 27, 2002, pp. 769-792.
[40] For background, see Sarah Glazer, "Welfare Reform," *The CQ Researcher*, Aug. 3, 2001, pp. 601-632.
[41] Culhane, *op. cit.*

Bibliography

Selected Sources

Books

Anderson, Leon, and David A. Snow, *Down on Their Luck: A Study of Homeless Street People*, University of California Press, 1993.

Two sociology professors contend "any serious attempt to alleviate the problem of homelessness in the United States must move beyond a perspective based on individual pathology." Anderson is at Ohio State, Snow at the University of California, Irvine.

Burnes, Donald W., and Alice S. Baum, *A Nation in Denial: The Truth About Homelessness*, Westview Press, 1993.

Two homeless advocates dismiss claims that homelessness results from "lack of affordable housing, poverty, declining social benefits, and the nature of America's political and economic systems."

Hopper, Kim, *Reckoning with Homelessness*, Cornell University Press, 2003.

A research scientist at Columbia University analyzes the social and legal factors that cause or contribute to homelessness and the accomplishments and challenges of advocacy.

Hurley, Jennifer A., ed., *The Homeless: Opposing Viewpoints*, Greenhaven Press, 2002.

Essays, speeches, articles and book excerpts explore the big questions: Is homelessness a serious problem? What are its causes? How should society deal with it?

Williams, Mary E., ed., *Poverty and the Homeless*, Greenhaven Press, 2004.

A collection of articles explores whether unconditional charity is a positive or negative influence on reducing homelessness, and other questions.

Articles

Adams, Stacy Hawkins, "A New Light on the Homeless/ Study Attempts to Capture Information that could find ways to Prevent the Problem," *Richmond Times Dispatch*, April 9, 2004.

A focused research effort reveals that the demographics of the homeless in Richmond are not what officials have long believed them to be.

Bornemann, Thomas H., "Mental Health System Needs a Life," *The Washington Post*, May 29, 2004.

The director of the mental health program at the Carter Center argues that fragmentation of the mental health care system causes homelessness and other problems.

Hamill, Pete, "How to Save the Homeless — and Ourselves," *New York*, Sept. 20, 1993.

Hamill describes why many New Yorkers no longer sympathize with the homeless.

Jencks, Christopher, "The Homeless" and "Housing the Homeless," *The New York Review of Books*, April 21, 1994, and May 12, 1994.

A Northwestern University sociology professor examines the varying estimates of the U.S. homeless population.

Tunkieicz, Jennie, "Consolidation of emergency shelter services studied; Groups also want to address root causes of homelessness," *The Milwaukee Journal*, April 25, 2004.

Officials in Racine County, Wis., are joining together to evaluate and coordinate new integrated efforts to end homelessness in 10 years, beginning with a change in the way city shelters operate.

Von Bergen, Jane M., "The Job/Dancing with the Monster that Makes People Homeless; Navigating banking, bureaucracies to help the desperate," *The Philadelphia Inquirer*, May 31, 2004.

A city housing official disparages welfare policies that effectively "put people in situations where they [have] to turn to crime."

Reports and Studies

"Annual Report 2002," National Alliance to End Homelessness, July 2002.

A leading advocacy group says its blueprint for ending homelessness in 10 years is gaining increasing acceptance.

"Homelessness in the United States and the Human Right to Housing," National Law Center on Homelessness and Poverty, Jan. 14, 2004.

The advocacy group says "homelessness and the shortage of affordable housing that is its leading cause are growing crises in the United States."

"Hunger and Homelessness Survey 2003," U. S. Conference of Mayors, Sodexho, December 2003.

A survey of 25 cities concludes that homelessness rose last year.

Lee, Chang-Moo, Dennis P. Culhane and Susan M. Wachter, "The Differential Impacts of Federally Assisted Housing Programs on Nearby Property Values: A Philadelphia Case Study," *Housing Policy Debate*, Vol. 10, issue 1, Fannie Mae Foundation, 1999.

A study shows public housing has only a slight to moderate negative effect on surrounding real estate prices.

The Next Step:

Additional Articles from Current Periodicals

Families and Children

Dillon, Sam, "School Is Haven When Children Have No Home," *The New York Times*, Nov. 27, 2003, p. A1.
The number of homeless children nationwide is on the upswing, and many rely on school districts for immunizations, meals, transportation and even clothing.

Dwyer, Timothy, "Families as New Faces of Homeless," *The Washington Post*, Nov. 30, 2002, p. B1.
As housing costs rise, even families with a working parent are finding a place to live beyond their reach.

Fagan, Kevin, "Saving Foster Kids From the Streets," *San Francisco Chronicle*, April 11, 2004, p. A1.
In a nationwide trend, up to 50 percent of the 90,000 foster children in California will end up sleeping on the streets when they become adults.

Federal Efforts

Dardick, Hal, "Grants to Help Poorest of Poor," *Chicago Tribune*, Dec. 21, 2003, Metro Section, p. 1.
The Bush administration announced $1.3 billion in grants for homeless programs, but advocates called it a "trifle" in comparison to what is needed.

Fagan, Kevin, "Bush's Homeless Czar Is a Man on a Mission," *San Francisco Chronicle*, Jan. 14, 2004, p. A1.
Philip Mangano, the president's point man on homelessness, is convinced a 10-year plan to eliminate the problem can succeed.

Goldstein, Amy, "U.S. Plans Homeless Initiative," *The Washington Post*, July 19, 2002, p. A25.
The Department of Housing and Urban Development announced $350 million for rent subsidies and supportive services for the chronically homeless.

Rivera, Carla, "4 Big-City Mayors Ask Congress for $115 Million to Combat Homelessness," *Los Angeles Times*, April 30, 2004, p. B4.
The mayors of New York, Chicago, Los Angeles and San Francisco endorse the administration's Samaritan Initiative but ask for additional funding.

Stein, Joel, "The Real Face of Homelessness," *Time*, Jan. 20, 2003, p. 52.
President Bush appointed a homeless czar and announced a plan to end chronic homelessness in 10 years, but critics derided his efforts as underfunded.

Getting Tough

Brown, Lane Harvey, "Needed Shelters Face Opposition in Suburbs," *The Baltimore Sun*, Jan. 25, 2004, p. 1B.
Residents' fears of crime, sex offenders and decreased property values make it difficult to get permission to operate shelters.

Haynes, V. Dion, "Mean Streets Getting Meaner," *Chicago Tribune*, May 25, 2003, p. 1.
Business owners and developers oppose the presence of the chronically homeless, who scare off customers and lower property values.

Ritter, John, "Homeless Hurt on Several Fronts," *USA Today*, Dec. 27, 2002, p. 3A.
A growing number of cities are enacting ordinances outlawing begging and sleeping in public, while others disperse the homeless' tent camps.

Sanchez, Rene, "Exasperated Cities Move to Curb or Expel the Homeless," *The Washington Post*, Oct. 30, 2002, p. A1.
Whether banning sleeping in doorways, cutting stipends or discouraging handouts, cities are expressing their frustration with a festering problem.

Wood, Daniel, "As Homelessness Grows, Even Havens Toughen Up," *The Christian Science Monitor*, Nov. 21, 2002, p. 1.
Concerned their town was becoming a magnet for the homeless, Santa Monica, Calif., officials decided to discourage organizations that feed the homeless.

Helping the Homeless

Chan, Sewell, "Sweeping Streets Replaces Living on Them," *The Washington Post*, Sept. 3, 2003, p. B5.
A program that aims to accustom homeless men to working for pay is criticized as a "temporary, stopgap measure."

Gardner, Marilyn, "Small Towns Confront an Urban Problem," *The Christian Science Monitor*, March 7, 2003, p. 1.
Homelessness exists in less urban areas as well, but the resources to deal with it are far less than in places with an abundance of shelters and social services.

Higgins, Michael, "Mentally Ill Find Guidance After Jail," *Chicago Tribune*, Jan. 6, 2004, Metro Section, p. 1.
New programs that monitor and assist the mentally ill saved an estimated $1 million by keeping the homeless mentally ill off the streets and out of jails and hospitals.

Paulson, Amanda, "One City's Bold Approach to Chronic Homelessness," *The Christian Science Monitor*, Jan. 26, 2004, p. 1.
Columbus, Ohio, is taking the lead in providing supportive housing to the chronically homeless in an effort to permanently reduce the homeless population.

Housing

Cho, David, "For More Suburban Families, Affordable Housing Elusive," *The Washington Post*, April 15, 2003, p. B1.
One family with a moderate income found itself homeless and storing all its possessions in a pile of garbage bags in a dingy motel.

Harman, Danna, "The Struggle to Pay Rent Is About to Get Harder," *The Christian Science Monitor*, May 12, 2004, p. 14.
About 2 million low-income Americans use Section 8 housing vouchers to help pay the rent, but proposed budget cuts could cut the number of families benefiting from the program by a third.

MacDonald, G. Jeffrey, "Is Having a Home a Right?" *The Christian Science Monitor*, Feb. 4, 2004, p. 15.
Some advocates for the homeless would like to see the right to housing enshrined in law or in the Constitution, but the chances of that are slim.

Riley, Marianna, "Solutions, Not Shelters," *St. Louis Post-Dispatch*, March 9, 2004, p. B1.
A mentally ill homeless person uses $41,000 in publicly funded services; putting that person into supportive housing can decrease those costs by $16,000.

San Francisco

Fagan, Kevin, "A Rugged Refuge," *San Francisco Chronicle*, Dec. 2, 2003, p. A1.
At a tough homeless shelter, crack is $5 per rock; according to the staff, as long as no one gets hurt too badly, "it's all anybody can ask, really."

Fagan, Kevin, "A Way Out," *San Francisco Chronicle*, Dec. 4, 2003, p. A1.
San Francisco is urged to develop a master plan for ending chronic homelessness; creating enough supportive housing is estimated to cost $450 million.

Fagan, Kevin, "Care Not Cash Hits Streets Today," *San Francisco Chronicle*, May 3, 2004, p. A1.
Mayor Gavin Newsom's idea for reform in San Francisco is to drastically cut generous welfare payments to the homeless in return for housing.

Fagan, Kevin, "Signs of Hope in Helping S.F. Homeless Turn Lives Around," *San Francisco Chronicle*, May 9, 2004, p. A1.
Direct Access is a supportive housing program in San Francisco that houses 400 of the chronically homeless for $5.5 million per year in maintenance, a relative bargain.

Upsurge in Homelessness

Armour, Stephanie, "Homelessness Grows as More Live Check-to-Check," *USA Today*, Aug. 12, 2003, p. 1A.
With many Americans saving only a small portion of their income and accumulating high credit card debt, they have little cushion if the economy turns south.

Chan, Sewell, "Survey Indicates More Go Hungry, Homeless," *The Washington Post*, Dec. 19, 2003, p. A11.
A 25-city survey shows a 13 percent increase in requests for shelter while 30 percent of requests for shelter are unmet.

Partlow, Joshua, "Hidden Face of Homelessness," *The Washington Post*, Nov. 13, 2003, p. B1.
Wooded areas and out-of-the-way shelters make the problem less visible, but homelessness is increasing in suburban areas, as well.

Riley, Marianna, "Shelters Can't Keep Up," *St. Louis Post-Dispatch*, Nov. 6, 2003, p. C1.
As shelters close, requests for emergency shelter in St. Louis go up 46 percent in a single year.

CITING *THE CQ RESEARCHER*

Sample formats for citing these reports in a bibliography include the ones listed below. Preferred styles and formats vary, so please check with your instructor or professor.

MLA STYLE

Jost, Kenneth. "Rethinking the Death Penalty." The CQ Researcher 16 Nov. 2001: 945-68.

APA STYLE

Jost, K. (2001, November 16). Rethinking the death penalty. *The CQ Researcher, 11*, 945-968.

CHICAGO STYLE

Jost, Kenneth. "Rethinking the Death Penalty." *CQ Researcher*, November 16, 2001, 945-968.

CQ Researcher

Published by CQ Press, a division of Congressional Quarterly Inc.

thecqresearcher.com

Privatizing the Military

Does the Pentagon rely too much on private contractors?

Since the Cold War ended, a downsized U.S. military has increasingly turned to private contractors to fill positions once held by military personnel. In U.S.-occupied Iraq, most of the jobs involve logistical support, but several thousand contractors also work as armed security guards or help interrogate Iraqi prisoners. The privatization trend went largely unnoticed until April, when insurgents in Fallujah murdered four civilian security guards and burned and mutilated their bodies. Soon afterwards, at least two contract interrogators were implicated in prisoner abuses at Baghdad's Abu Ghraib prison. The incidents have renewed questions about the effectiveness and legal status of private contractors operating in war zones and the wisdom of the Pentagon's increasing reliance on private contractors. Supporters of privatization say the military's use of contractors saves taxpayers money and improves efficiency by freeing up soldiers for strictly combat operations.

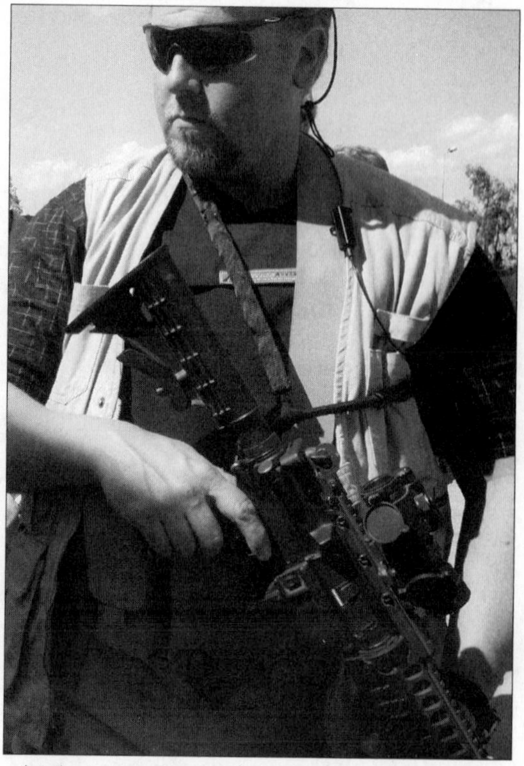

A private security guard protects U.S. administrator L. Paul Bremer III in Iraq.

INSIDE THIS REPORT

The CQ Researcher • June 25, 2004 • www.thecqresearcher.com
Volume 14, Number 24 • Pages 565-588

CQ PRESS

RECIPIENT OF SOCIETY OF PROFESSIONAL JOURNALISTS AWARD FOR EXCELLENCE ◆ AMERICAN BAR ASSOCIATION SILVER GAVEL AWARD

THE ISSUES

BACKGROUND

CURRENT SITUATION

OUTLOOK

SIDEBARS AND GRAPHICS

FOR FURTHER RESEARCH

Cover: A civilian bodyguard for L. Paul Bremer III, the U.S. administrator in Iraq, is among the 6,000 private security contractors in Iraq hired by the U.S. military. (AFP Photo/Ceerwan Aziz)

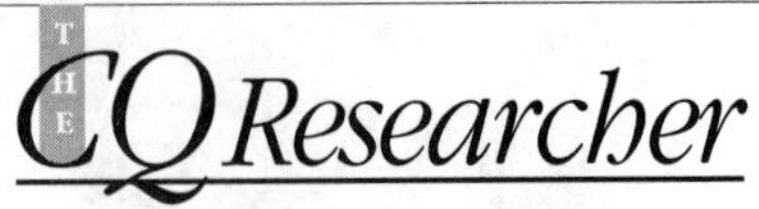

June 25, 2004
Volume 14, Number 24

MANAGING EDITOR: Thomas J. Colin

ASSISTANT MANAGING EDITOR: Kathy Koch

ASSOCIATE EDITOR: Kenneth Jost

STAFF WRITERS: Mary H. Cooper, David Masci, William Triplett

CONTRIBUTING WRITERS: Sarah Glazer, David Hatch, David Hosansky, Patrick Marshall, Tom Price, Jane Tanner

DESIGN/PRODUCTION EDITOR: Olu B. Davis

ASSISTANT EDITOR: Kenneth Lukas

CQ PRESS

A Division of Congressional Quarterly Inc.

SENIOR VICE PRESIDENT/GENERAL MANAGER: John A. Jenkins

DIRECTOR, LIBRARY PUBLISHING: Kathryn C. Suárez

DIRECTOR, EDITORIAL OPERATIONS: Ann Davies

CONGRESSIONAL QUARTERLY INC.

CHAIRMAN: Paul C. Tash

VICE CHAIRMAN: Andrew P. Corty

PRESIDENT AND PUBLISHER: Robert W. Merry

The CQ Researcher (ISSN 1056-2036) is printed on acid-free paper. Published weekly, except Jan. 2, April 9, July 2, July 9, Aug. 6, Aug. 13, Nov. 26 and Dec. 31, by CQ Press, a division of Congressional Quarterly Inc. Annual subscription rates for institutions start at $625. For pricing, call 1-800-834-9020, ext. 1906. To purchase a *CQ Researcher* report in print or electronic format (PDF), visit www.cqpress.com or call 866-427-7737. A single report is $10. Bulk purchase discounts and electronic-rights licensing are also available. Periodicals postage paid at Washington, D.C., and additional mailing offices. POSTMASTER: Send address changes to *The CQ Researcher*, 1255 22nd St., N.W., Suite 400, Washington, D.C. 20037.

Privatizing the Military

BY MARY H. COOPER

THE ISSUES

Iraqi insurgents in Fallujah recently gave Americans a horrific glimpse into a little-known and increasingly controversial aspect of U.S. military operations. After ambushing a truck convoy and killing four U.S. security guards on April 28, they burned and mutilated the bodies and hung them from a bridge.

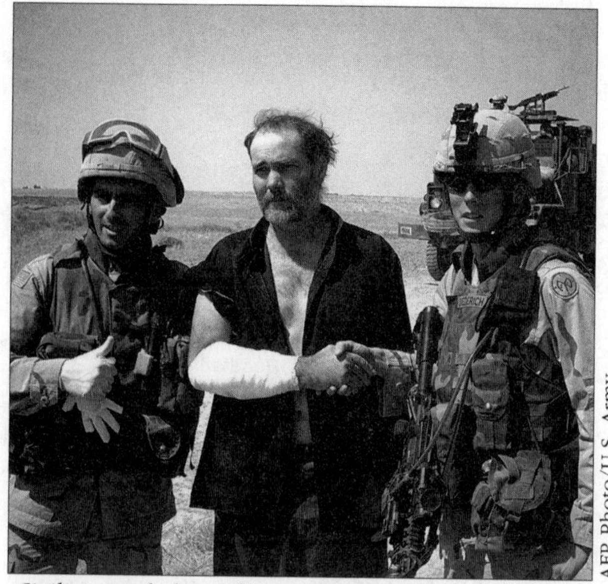

AFP Photo/U.S. Army

Civilian truck driver Thomas Hamill escaped from Iraqi kidnappers after 23 days in captivity. The Mississippi farmer came to Iraq to work for military contractor Kellogg, Brown and Root. Kidnapped contract workers have become pawns in the ongoing conflict in postwar Iraq. Private contractors serving as interrogators were also implicated in prisoner abuses at the U.S.-run Abu Ghraib prison in Baghdad.

The four deaths, however, were not included in the Pentagon's list of American casualties in Iraq that day. In fact, although the men worked for the military, they weren't GIs. They were civilians employed by the military.

"We know that somewhere around 50 private military people have been killed in Iraq," says Peter W. Singer, author of *Corporate Warriors: The Rise of the Privatized Military Industry* and director of the Project on U.S. Policy Towards the Islamic World at the Brookings Institution. "Another 300 or so have been wounded. But these are only estimates because private military casualties don't show up on the public record."

Private military contractors in Iraq made news again in May when widespread prisoner abuses were reported at the U.S.-run Abu Ghraib prison in Baghdad. Three civilian interrogators were among the six soldiers implicated in the shocking physical and sexual abuse of Iraqi detainees. [1] But unlike their military peers, the contractors were not subject to military law and have not been charged under civil law either.

However, on June 18 the Justice Department charged a contractor working for the CIA in Afghanistan with assault in the beating of an Afghan detainee who later died in a U.S. prison there. David A. Passaro, a former Army Ranger hired to conduct interrogations, is the first civilian to be charged in connection with alleged prisoner abuses in Afghanistan and Iraq. [2]

The slain guards in Fallujah and the civilian prison workers are part of a growing army of non-military personnel employed by scores of private contractors for the U.S. military in 50 countries around the world. Largely unnoticed by the American public, private contractors have assumed a growing role in the U.S. military for more than a decade.

Since the end of the Cold War in the early 1990s, policymakers have been reducing the size of the military and contracting out many non-combat jobs to private companies.

But after the U.S. victory in Iraq, violent resistance to the U.S.-led occupation forced the Pentagon to turn increasingly to private military contractors because the services were already stretched thin by downsizing and deployments in Afghanistan and other hot spots.

Private contractors now make up the second-largest contingent of forces in Iraq after the U.S. military itself — larger even than Britain's troop deployment. Most analysts say there are about 20,000 private military contractors (PMCs) in Iraq, including 6,000 who provide non-combat security, serving alongside 138,000 American GIs.

The armed personnel serve as guards, convoy escorts and bodyguards for U.S. officials in Iraq, including Ambassador L. Paul Bremer III, the American administrator of the Coalition Provisional Authority (CPA). [3]

"The role of private military contractors in Iraq is unprecedented, particularly given the numbers involved," says Marcus Corbin, senior analyst at the Center for Defense Information, an independent monitor of the military. "I can't think of any parallel in our military history."

Defense Secretary Donald H. Rumsfeld and other supporters of privatization say the military's use of contractors improves efficiency by freeing up soldiers for strictly combat operations. "There are a great many people [in Iraq] who are involved in various types of enterprises or activities that . . . need security," Rumsfeld said. "So a market [has been created] for security forces. And it's been a good thing that the security forces around this country and the world do a superb job." [4]

But some lawmakers and military experts worry that because contract workers are not bound by military law, privatization may erode accountability and blur the chain of command essential to military operations.

"How is it in our nation's interest to have civilian contractors, rather than military personnel, performing vital national-security functions such as prisoner interrogations in a war zone?" asked Michigan Sen. Carl Levin, senior Democrat on the Senate Armed Services Committee. "When soldiers break the law or fail to follow orders, commanders can hold them accountable for their misconduct. Military commanders don't have the same authority over civilian contractors." [5]

Privatization of military tasks has become a nearly $200-billion-a-year sector of the U.S. military-industrial complex. [6] In Iraq, previously obscure firms like North Carolina-based Blackwater Security Consulting, which employed the four guards killed in Fallujah, now operate beside well-known giants such as Halliburton Co., the oil and gas conglomerate formerly headed by Vice President Dick Cheney, and CACI, an information-technology firm based in Arlington, Va.

The value of civilian personnel services purchased by the Department of Defense increased from $100.5 billion in 1993 to $188 billion in 2004 — a rise of nearly 90 percent. [7] Many of those billions were earned through no-bid contracts. *(See sidebar, p. 570.)*

Rep. Janice D. Schakowsky, D-Ill., a longtime critic of the often-obscure process by which private companies receive government contracts, worries about the secrecy that surrounds Defense Department contracting. She has introduced legislation to expand congressional oversight and access to major contracts signed with private firms.

"I'm sure many important functions are done by these private contractors," she says. "But at the same time, the process masks just what the U.S. commitment is in places like Iraq and allows many of these activities to literally fly under the radar of the Congress and the consciousness of the American people."

Most Contractor Casualties Were in Iraq

More than 1,000 civilian contractors working for the U.S. government in Iraq and several other countries have died or been injured since September 2001, including more than 500 in Iraq.

	Deaths/Injuries
Iraq	529
Kuwait	317
Bosnia-Herzegovina	60
Colombia	52
Saudi Arabia	51
Germany	48
Afghanistan	44

Source: Department of Labor, based on insurance claims submitted to the U.S. government.

When the United States relinquishes sovereignty to the Iraqi interim government on June 30, the role of private contractors in Iraq will not end, but may even increase due to an expected escalation of violence and a continued need for security for Iraqi officials and the U.S.-led $18.4 billion reconstruction effort.

But the legal status of the military contractors has yet to be clarified. Iraq's new interim prime minister, Iyad Allawi, insists that civilian contractors come under Iraqi law on June 30, ending the immunity from prosecution in Iraq they now enjoy for any incident involving their work. The Bush administration wants to extend that immunity after the handover. [8]

As the role of private military contractors grows in Iraq and elsewhere, these are some of the questions being raised:

Can the military do its job without military contractors?

Private contractors have had a longstanding role in providing support services to the military, both at home and overseas, in peacetime and at war.

During the Vietnam War, one company alone had more than 30,000 employees providing logistical support to U.S. troops, according to Doug Brooks, president of the International Peace Operations Association, an organization of military service providers. During the 1968 Tet Offensive, contractors suffered more casualties than the regular troops, he adds.

"There's never been a war or a time in history when private contractors haven't been used for one thing or another," he says. "The U.S. military needs contractors, and it always has."

The military traditionally has turned to private companies to build weapons and vehicles, construct bases and camps and provide food and other services for troops. For the past 15 years, however, private companies have supplied a widening array of products and services. Highly sophisticated weapons and equipment like satellite phones, global-positioning systems and laser designators used to precisely locate targets require skilled technicians to maintain and repair, and the armed services often hire contractors trained by the equipment producers themselves.

"The modern military cannot function without private contractors for some key roles," says Michael P. Peters, executive vice president of the Council on Foreign Relations, a New York City think tank. "Take avionics for aircraft. You need people who've actually built this stuff to be with you and maintain it, because you simply can't train enough 18-to-22-year-olds to have the level of knowledge, background and experience to keep this very, very sophisticated equipment running. If they were to ban all civilian contractors, the military would have a difficult time functioning at all."

Going to war in countries like Iraq and Afghanistan poses additional language and cultural barriers that the downsized U.S. military is ill-equipped to surmount on its own, Peters says, citing the civilian translators and interrogators at Abu Ghraib.

"When you get into a circumstance that is as big as Iraq, you have almost no other option than to hire private contractors," Peters says. "The military just doesn't have enough people to perform those functions."

But critics say the widening prisoner-abuse scandal in Iraq and Afghanistan demonstrates a vital weakness in the military's growing reliance on civilian contractors to perform functions that traditionally have fallen to the military. "There is no room for U.S.-hired paramilitaries and mercenaries in an interrogation cell," said Rep. Schakowsky. "This is a dangerous and deadly mix that has contributed to the prisoner-abuse scandal in Iraq and could only lead to a more dangerous situation for U.S. military and civilian personnel at home and abroad, unless it is immediately stopped." [9]

Because many, if not most, security contractors are former soldiers, often with considerable combat experience, they are generally considered more effective at their jobs than new Army recruits. Young soldiers fresh out of training often suffer from the "22-year-old syndrome," panicking and firing their weapons in no particular direction when they come under fire, says an industry insider who requested he not be identified. "This tends to be damaging to local populations, buildings, that sort of thing."

On the other hand, Brooks says contractors, many of whom have as much as 20 years' experience in the field, tend to keep their cool under fire. "Combat is combat, of course, but security contractors tend to be far more professional," he says. "When you hire somebody with that kind of experience, you're getting quite a product."

But critics point out that, unlike GIs, private contractors are free to walk away from their posts when the going gets rough, endangering U.S. forces in hostile areas.

That hasn't happened, Brooks says, even during the recent escalation of hostilities in Iraq. "It's true that you can't order a contractor to stay, and there were predictions at the beginning of the war that as soon as the shooting started all of these private companies would pull out," he says. However, since the Fallujah incident, security firms not only have maintained their presence but also have received more job applications, Brooks says. "People keep saying that they're only there for the money, but it's not just about money," he says. "Sure, money's important. You have to have enough money to leave your home, your career and your family for six or 12 months, live in a tent, get shot at and bombed. But it's beyond money. Your money is useless if you get blown up."

But critics warn that privatization has been taken to such an extreme that it may undermine the effectiveness of U.S. military operations.

Defense Outsourcing Nearly Doubled

Spending on private contracts by the Department of Defense remained steady in the 1990s but nearly doubled in 2004.

Purchases of Private Services by Defense Department
(in $ billions)

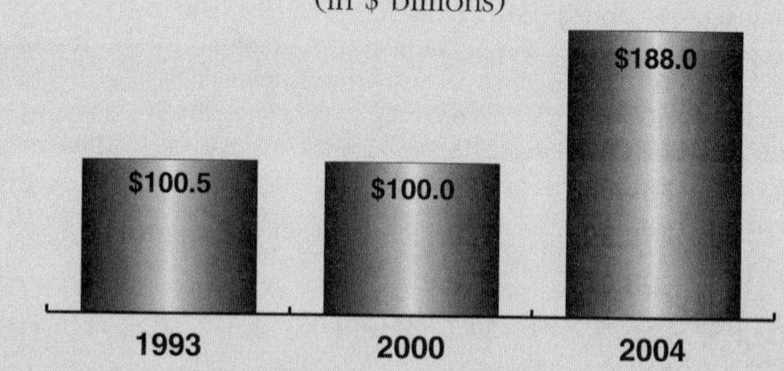

Increases in Outsourcing Outpace Spending

Purchases of private services by the Defense Department grew more than twice as fast as overall Defense spending in the last four years.

Increases in Defense Spending from 2000 to 2004*

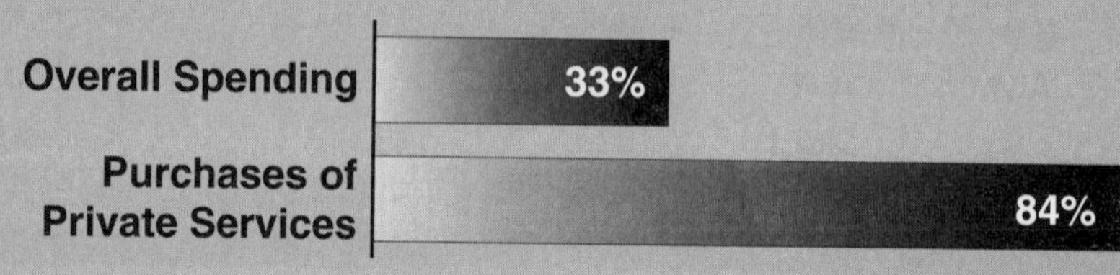

* *First quarter only*

Source: Charles L. Schultze, senior fellow emeritus, Brookings Institution, based on Commerce Department data (forthcoming report).

Controversy Surrounds Civilian Contractors

President Dwight D. Eisenhower's famous warning in 1961 about the rapidly growing "military-industrial complex" focused on the makers of tanks, ships and other military hardware.

His warning proved prescient. Hefty defense budgets and the emergence of the United States as the world's leading military power have turned the defense industry into a manufacturing behemoth. In fiscal 2003, procurement contracts to the top 100 Pentagon contractors totaled $209 billion. [1]

Since Eisenhower's prediction, a new category of defense contractors has emerged: Firms that provide workers to conduct security, interrogation and intelligence — work once performed exclusively by military personnel. After the Cold War ended more than a decade ago, the U.S. military turned increasingly to private military contractors to meet its security and intelligence needs around the world. About 60 such firms are operating in Iraq, and more than 20 in Afghanistan.

The multimillion-dollar global industry can be divided into three major sectors, according to Peter W. Singer, author of the 2003 book *Corporate Warriors: The Rise of the Privatized Military Industry*: [2]

- "Military provider firms" offer seasoned combatants — generally former members of U.S., British or South African special forces — to clients such as weak governments, insurgent forces or international oil or mining companies operating in hostile areas. Executive Outcomes provided forces in several African trouble spots in the 1990s, including Angola and Sierra Leone. London-based Sandline Co., which helped repel a 1998 coup attempt in Nigeria, embarrassed Britain by shipping arms to the region in violation of a U.N. arms embargo. Both firms have since disbanded.
- "Military consultant firms" train local police and military forces to fight in foreign conflicts. One of the leading such firms is Military Professional Resources Inc. (MPRI). Founded in 1987 and based in Alexandria, Va., it hires only American ex-soldiers and claims to work only on contracts approved by the U.S. government. MPRI's Defense Department contracts included training the Bosnian and Croatian armies in the 1990s.

Refraining from sending employees into battle has not protected military consultant firms from controversy, however. Employees of Falls Church, Va.-based DynCorp (purchased in 2003 by Computer Sciences Corp.), participated in a child-prostitution ring while working in Bosnia in the late 1990s, according to Human Rights Watch, Army investigators and two whistleblower lawsuits. [3] Although the employees were not immune from prosecution by local authorities for illegal acts committed outside their contractual mission, DynCorp fired them and returned them to the United States, where they did not face charges.

Lawmakers tried to close contractors' legal loopholes by passing the 2000 Military Extraterritorial Jurisdiction Act, which places Defense Department contractors overseas under U.S. legal jurisdiction. But because the alleged offenses in Bosnia preceded passage of the act, the DynCorp employees were not prosecuted. [4]

- "Military support firms" are farther removed from combat roles, at least in theory. The Halliburton Co. subsidiary Kellogg, Brown and Root (KBR) and other such firms provide logistics, intelligence, supply and other services to U.S. forces around the world. In Iraq, KBR truck convoys bring food and other supplies to a dozen or more Army camps. Ac-

"U.S. military doctrine says that we should not have private contractors in mission-critical roles, which are roles that affect the success or failure of operations," Singer says. "But there is a whole laundry list of roles that private contractors are playing in Iraq that violate that doctrine — everything from logistics, to training the Iraqi army, to protecting CPA installations and top government leaders, to escorting convoys, to conducting intelligence interrogations.

"If supplies break down," he continues, "if the local Iraqi army doesn't get trained properly, if CPA installations are overrun by rebels, if Paul Bremer gets killed, if our convoys are overrun by insurgent forces and if interrogators screw up at Abu Ghraib — all these things affect the success or failure of the operation."

Does privatization save taxpayers money?

In addition to freeing up military personnel for combat-related duties, privatization has been embraced by the Pentagon and other government agencies as a way to save money. The White House Office of Management and Budget recently projected that privatization would save more than $1 billion over the next three to five years, primarily because contractors bidding for government contacts are expected to find ways to reduce their costs. [10]

But that rationale has not always played out. During the 1980s, the Pentagon's payment of $640 for a toilet seat became the symbol of waste, fraud and abuse in military spending for goods and services and triggered efforts to increase oversight of the contracting process, including an effort to make contractors compete for government business. Later, Vice President Al Gore launched a campaign to "reinvent" a more efficient government, and reforms were introduced aimed at streamlining contracting procedures.

But charges of fraud and cronyism have continued to plague military contracting, as suggested by the current cording to several KBR drivers, the company bilked American taxpayers by charging the Pentagon for repeatedly moving convoys of empty trucks between U.S. encampments, exposing the truckers to attacks by Iraqi insurgents.

CACI International Inc., another support firm, provides interrogators to U.S. forces administering prisons overseas under a so-called "blanket purchase agreement" that was originally signed with the Interior Department but subsequently utilized by the Pentagon. Steven Stefanowicz, a CACI employee, was one of three private contractors implicated in the recent prisoner-abuse scandal in Iraq. A contract translator employed by another firm, Titan Corp., also was named in an extensive Army report on the abuses by Maj. Gen. Antonio M. Taguba.

Allegations of fraud and waste by private contractors in Iraq continue to mount. At least 14 major contracts in Iraq, including a $7 billion deal for Halliburton to restore the country's oil industry, were awarded with limited or no competition, according to a report issued on June 14, 2004, by the General Accounting Office. [5]

"Increasingly, the administration is turning over essential government functions to the private sector, and it has jettisoned basic safeguards like competition and supervision that are needed to protect the public interest," said Rep. Henry A. Waxman, D-Calif., a vocal critic of Bush administration contracting practices. "We need more competition, not less. And we need to place the interests of the taxpayer ahead of the interests of the contractors." [6]

Administration spokesmen reject the allegations of contracting misdeeds, including recent charges that the office of Vice President Cheney, formerly Halliburton's chief executive officer, was instrumental in granting the oil-services giant its no-bid contract in Iraq. "The vice president was not informed" that Halliburton would get the contract, said Kevin Kellems, Cheney's spokesman. [7]

Meanwhile, a report by the Center for Public Integrity, a nonprofit investigative organization in Washington, D.C., found that 14 of the top private contractors in Afghanistan and Iraq made campaign contributions in excess of $1 million from 1990 through fiscal 2002. "Combined, those companies gave nearly $23 million in political contributions since 1990," the report said.

In addition, in classic Washington revolving-door style, top officers of many of these firms are former Pentagon officials, while many civilian officials at the Pentagon are former employees of major defense contractors. "The center's investigation found that . . . 13 [of the 14 top contractors] employ former government officials or have close ties to various agencies and departments." [8]

[1] U.S. Defense Department, Directorate for Information Operations and Reports, www.dior.whs.mil.

[2] Unless otherwise noted, information in this section is based on Singer's book, pp. 73-184.

[3] See Kelly Patricia O'Meara, "DynCorp Disgrace," *Insight*, Jan. 14, 2002.

[4] See Gail Gibson, "Prosecuting Abuse of Prisoners," *The Baltimore Sun*, May 29, 2004, p. 4A.

[5] See General Accounting Office, "Rebuilding Iraq: Fiscal Year 2003 Contract Award Procedures and Management Challenges," June 14, 2004.

[6] From a statement issued May 27, 2004.

[7] Quoted by Larry Margasak, "Official: Cheney Not Briefed on Iraq Work," The Associated Press, June 16, 2004.

[8] Maud Beelman, "Winning Contractors: U.S. Contractors Reap the Windfalls of Post-war Reconstruction," Center for Public Integrity, Oct. 30, 2003.

controversy over Halliburton's $7 billion no-bid contract to rebuild Iraq's oil industry. [11]

Indeed, reform efforts actually opened the way for new loopholes that helped avoid congressional oversight of Pentagon contracting practices. For example, the new "blanket-purchase agreement" allows a government department to avoid bidding out contracts by piggybacking onto another department's existing contract with a firm for unrelated services. In this way, the Defense Department contracted with CACI to provide interrogators for Iraq using an existing agreement the firm had for unrelated services with the Interior Department.

"The theory behind the blanket-purchase agreement was that the Defense Department can save overhead costs by contracting through other agencies," says Danielle Brian, executive director of the Project on Government Oversight, a nonprofit government watchdog group. "But in practice, we've lost any kind of control over who is getting the contracts and what price we're paying for them because there is no competition anymore. We also have no control over how prime contractors subcontract out the work to other firms."

Thanks to blanket-purchase agreements, Brian says, "CACI has become one of several full-service government contractors, which basically say, 'We may not have the experience or expertise in what you're looking for, but we'll get it. Just tell us what you need, and we'll figure it out.' "

The General Accounting Office (GAO) found that all of the 14 new contracts it examined were awarded without open competition, but it didn't find anything illegal. The GAO said the law allows for limited or no competition in awarding contracts "when only one source is available or to meet urgent requirements." [12]

Using civilians to carry out functions traditionally delegated to soldiers and military police represents another exercise in false economy, critics

Top 10 Military Service Providers

Some of America's largest corporations supply the U.S. military with basic services such as health insurance and computer and food services. Many smaller companies provide security services but do not appear among the Top 10, such as Titan and CACI — whose employees have been implicated in the Abu Ghraib prisoner-abuse scandal in Baghdad. And some firms that provide interrogators and interpreters in Iraq do not appear on the Defense Department's list of contractors because they were hired through the Interior Department.*

Major Providers of Military Services
(in $ billions, for FY2003)

	Value of Contracts
Lockheed Martin Corp.	$4.4
Northrop Grumman Corp.	3.5
General Dynamics Corp.	2.4
Halliburton Co.	2.4
Humana Inc.	2.4
Computer Sciences Corp.	2.0
Science Applications International	1.9
Health Net Inc.	1.8
Raytheon Co.	1.7
Boeing Co.	1.3

** Lockheed Martin is in the process of acquiring Titan Corp.*

Source: "Procurement Statistics," Directorate for Information, Operations and Reports, Department of Defense

say. Many contractors are former Green Berets or Navy Seals — trained at government expense — who can make much more money doing the same work as private contractors rather than remaining in the military. Contract bodyguards in Iraq commonly earn twice as much or more than their military colleagues. [13]

"Military special forces are very expensive to train," Brian says. "By relying on contractors, the Defense Department is essentially spending a huge amount of money to train someone and then paying a company to make a profit off that taxpayers' investment."

Defenders of the "revolving door" between the military and the private sector say there's nothing wrong or novel about ex-soldiers using expertise gained at taxpayer expense to advance in the private sector. Airline pilots, for example, routinely get their training in the military. Indeed, Brooks, of the International Peace Operations Association, says the practice offers taxpayers a win-win opportunity.

"Basically, the taxpayer is getting double the service out of training a guy for one career," Brooks says. "When you train a military guy, you expect to use him while he's in the military. We're getting him when he's out of the military as well, so we're getting double the bang for the buck. I think it's brilliant."

Sometimes the savings to taxpayers is not obvious, say proponents of privatization, especially when contractors are often paid more than twice as much as a soldier for doing the same work. But proponents of military outsourcing point out that recruitment, training, equipment, housing and health care inflate the cost for every soldier far above the base salary paid by the government.

"Say you pay a soldier $40,000 to do a job you'd have to pay a contractor $100,000 to do," says Peters of the Council on Foreign Relations. "By the time you add all those other costs, the actual cost of putting that $40,000 soldier in place may well exceed $100,000."

Moreover, Peters says, the savings realized from outsourcing certain noncombat military services — such as translators and interrogators — are especially evident in places like Iraq. "Say we need 100 Arabic-speaking Army interrogators in Iraq," he says. "If you recruited 100 Arabic-speaking interrogators for Army service, you'd have to pay them to sit on the shelf to wait for a situation like Iraq. The overhead and investment [required] to keep that capacity in uniform is part of what you save when you're able to turn instead to the larger economy to find such people we can call upon when we need them for a discrete period of time — and without having to pay their retirement and other benefits."

Should there be more oversight of private military contractors?

The growing role of private contractors in the military has worried some lawmakers for years. Rep. Schakowsky has focused on the issue since visiting Colombia several years ago and learning that private contractors were playing a major role in U.S.-funded counternarcotics efforts. After the scandal erupted over the abuses of detainees in Iraq by both soldiers and contractors, Schakowsky wrote to

President Bush asking him to suspend the use of private contractors in all Iraqi prisons pending further investigations into their conduct. (*See "At Issue," p. 581.*)

AFP Photo

American personnel at the Abu Ghraib prison threaten an Iraqi prisoner with dogs. At least two private military contractors have been implicated in the prisoner abuses, leading critics to question how private contractors working for the military are held accountable for possible crimes.

But she says the White House has yet to respond to her request. "The administration continues to say that they use these private military contractors because they're trained to do the job," she says. "But I think that's a mistake, given the lack of clarity about whether they were involved in convincing or even ordering our military police to set the conditions for interrogations — in other words, to validate, if not direct, the abuses that occurred."

Corbin of the Center for Defense Information agrees, noting that their presence and participation in military operations, like the interrogations at Abu Ghraib, may make it unclear to soldiers who is actually in command.

"It's one thing if they're employed by and guarding private facilities," he says. "But having these semi-military, private contractors involved violates the fundamental military principle of having a chain of command."

Industry advocates dismiss this concern, noting that as civilians, private contractors are not under anybody's orders technically, nor allowed to give orders. "They're given a contract, which says what they can and cannot do, and that's essentially their chain of command," Brooks says.

While he concedes that combat conditions like those in Iraq may blur the separation of authority, he says it occurs in a way that decreases, not increases, contractors' autonomy. "Because this is a martial-law situation, the local military commander can order contractors to do just about anything," he says. "And the contractors have to jump."

That doesn't satisfy Corbin, who says the military needs to establish a body of rules and procedures governing private-contractor activities in war zones. "Just in terms of military operations, is the military supposed to go and rescue contractors when they come under fire?" he asks. "Or are contractors even supposed to go in to rescue the military? This is a new area, and both contractors and soldiers are woefully underserved in terms of operational procedures. They're just working it out on the fly."

Apart from confusion in the field, critics worry that contractors may answer more readily to their employers' and stockholders' interests than to those of the government's. "Who do they respond to?" Schakowsky asks. "Is it a CEO or a general?"

Singer of the Brookings Institution says a more worrisome ambiguity surrounding private contractors is their legal status. "We have folks within a military operation, carrying on military roles, who are not part of the military," he says. "While the soldier who commits crimes is held accountable under the code of military justice, for contractors the situation is a little bit more confused." Because private contractors can't be court-martialed, they fall under one of two other systems, local law or U.S. extraterritorial law.

Singer rules out local law because, "There is no local law in Iraq." In any case, he says, "CPA regulations stipulate that private military contractors are not subject to it."

Brooks says that concern is overstated because contractors are held to a higher legal standard when on overseas missions than civilians in the United States.

If a contractor commits an offense that is below the level of a felony, the individual generally gets fired, he says. "If you run a red light in the States, you're not going to get fired from your job, but that's what happens in Iraq because the companies don't want to cross the military at all. It's harsh, because there's no real avenue for a person to appeal getting fired. But we're in a war, right?"

Contractors who commit a felony, Brooks says, are subject to the 2000 Military Extraterritorial Jurisdiction Act (MEJA), which places contractors working overseas under U.S. legal jurisdiction. But Singer says MEJA contains two important loopholes. First, he says, "it applies only to Pentagon contractors, not to those working for other government agencies." The CACI employees implicated in the Abu Ghraib abuses were working under a contract let by the Interior Department. "Also, it's unclear whether the law applies to subcontractors or to third-party nationals." Many of the contractors are citizens of Iraq or other countries.

Equally important, Singer says, the Pentagon has never written the regulations needed to implement MEJA. As a result, he says, "Not one of the 20,000 private military contractors on the ground in Iraq has been tried under MEJA. And we're led to take the fantastic leap of the imagination to conclude that over the course of one year not one person of those 20,000 has committed a crime of any kind, let alone any on the scale of Abu Ghraib."

Passaro, the CIA contractor charged with assault in Afghanistan, is the first civilian to be charged in the widening prison-abuse scandal. Six soldiers implicated in the Abu Ghraib abuses are currently under prosecution in Iraq; a seventh has already pleaded guilty. [14] But the two private military contractors who also were implicated in the scandal have not faced formal charges. [15]

"Donald Rumsfeld continues to say that those who have committed crimes will be prosecuted under other U.S. laws," Schakowsky says. "But it's unclear what those sanctions will be or that anyone will be sanctioned at all. This is a very, very murky area with many problems that are now coming to light in Iraq."

That legal ambiguity can also enable the government to avoid taking responsibility for mistakes or even criminal behavior by private contractors. In 2001, for example, an American company on contract for the CIA in the U.S. war on drugs mistakenly identified a small aircraft flying over Peru as a possible drug transport. Acting on the tip, Peruvian pilots shot down the plane, killing a U.S. missionary and her infant daughter. U.S. lawmakers reportedly were unsuccessful in obtaining information about the incident from the State Department or the CIA.

The alleged implication of civilian contractors in torture could open the door to other avenues for prosecution. A 1994 law makes it a crime for Americans to commit torture outside the United States. But as long as administration officials refrain from calling the abuses at Abu Ghraib "torture," it's unlikely that the contractors will be prosecuted under that law. [16] ■

Background

Mercenary Armies

Throughout history, private armies have been the norm. Whether they were individual mercenaries signing on to bolster the ranks of organized armies or fully equipped professional armies, the ranks of the world's military forces more often than not have been driven by the profit motive. [17]

References to mercenaries date back more than 4,000 years to soldiers hired by King Shulgi of Ur (2094-2047 B.C.). The first record of a major conflict, the battle of Kadesh (1294 B.C.), speaks of hired Numidian soldiers in the army Egyptian Pharaoh Ramses II sent against the Hittites.

The first citizen armies mentioned in historical accounts were raised by Sparta and a few other ancient Greek city-states, but many other Greek forces relied on paid foreign soldiers who specialized in certain skills of war, such as cavalrymen from Thessaly and slingers from Crete.

Alexander the Great conquered the Persian Empire in 336 B.C. thanks in large part to mercenaries, including a 224-ship Phoenician armada. By the end of the First Punic War between the Romans and the Carthaginians in 241 B.C., the Carthaginians' reliance on mercenaries was so complete that failure to pay the victorious soldiers sparked a wholesale revolt known as the Mercenary War, which required yet more paid foreigners to quell. In 218 B.C., a largely mercenary force accompanied the Carthaginian general Hannibal in his march across the Alps in his campaign against Rome.

Like Greece, Rome relied initially on a citizen army but also on mercenaries with special skills, such as archery and cavalry. As the empire expanded and fewer Romans joined the far-flung forces, foreign mercenaries became key to Rome's military might; by the end of the third century A.D., the imperial army had more Germans than Romans in its ranks.

After the fall of the Roman Empire, European feudal rulers exacted military service from their serfs. But the feudal armies of Europe's Dark Ages continued to rely on mercenaries, especially for expertise in the latest war-making technologies of the time — the crossbow, early firearms and cannon. Nobles and kings often preferred mercenaries to conscripts, however, because arming serfs posed the risk of rebellion. The emergence of powerful cities, such as Venice and Florence, in 13th-century Italy gave rise to a new military organization. Units of contract soldiers and sailors participated in Europe's expanding local conflicts and in Crusades to the Middle East. By the end of the 14th century, mercenary troops had largely replaced feudal conscripts across Europe.

The growing power of mercenary armies posed a new threat to the European order. Rather than face unemployment at the end of hostilities, individual "free lances" began to form "companies" (from *con pane*, for the bread soldiers received for their services). These roving militias traveled the continent in search of war, offering their

Continued on p. 576

Chronology

1970s-1980s

U.S. military manpower peaks at more than 3 million personnel.

1973
The draft is dropped in favor of an all-volunteer military.

Dec. 4, 1989
The United Nations adopts the International Convention against the Recruitment, Use, Financing and Training of Mercenaries. To date, however, only 25 countries have signed and ratified or acceded to the treaty; the United States is not among them.

1990s

Military outsourcing picks up as the Pentagon downsizes U.S. forces at the end of the Cold War.

1993
A failed U.S. intervention to help the government of Somalia put down a rebellion galvanizes American public opinion against use of U.S. military forces in conflicts that pose no immediate threat to national security.

1994
The Federal Acquisition Streamlining Act expands agencies' authority to buy goods and services from private companies.

August 1995
After U.S. contractor Military Professional Resources Inc. (MPRI) helps Croatian forces defeat a Serbian attack, Croatia and Bosnia hire the Virginia-based firm to train their armed forces.

1996
The Clinger-Cohen Act allows the use of multi-agency contracts, enabling a single federal agency to handle contracts for other agencies.

2000s

Private military contractors serve in the "war on terrorism," prompting calls for greater oversight of these firms.

2000
The Military Extraterritorial Jurisdiction Act (MEJA) places Defense Department contractors working overseas under U.S. legal jurisdiction.

Sept. 11, 2001
Terrorists attack the World Trade Center in New York City and the Pentagon, prompting President Bush to declare war on terrorism.

Oct. 7, 2001
U.S.-led coalition forces invade Afghanistan and rout its Taliban rulers but fail to capture Osama bin Laden, leader of the al Qaeda terrorist organization responsible for the Sept. 11 attacks.

2002
U.S. active-duty troop levels stand at 1.4 million after falling by more than one-half in three decades.

January 2003
Rep. Charles B. Rangel, D-N.Y., and Sen. Ernest Hollings, D-S.C., introduce the Universal National Service Act, which would require all American men and women ages 18-26 to perform a period of military or civilian service.

April 15, 2003
The United States, with Britain and several smaller countries, invades Iraq, topples Saddam Hussein and occupies the country.

April 28, 2004
Insurgents kill four U.S. private military contractors in Fallujah, Iraq, and hang their burned and mutilated bodies from a bridge.

May 2004
Three civilian contractors are implicated in a prisoner-abuse scandal at U.S. prisons in Iraq and Afghanistan.

June 14, 2004
An amendment is proposed to the fiscal 2005 Pentagon reauthorization bill that would bar the government from outsourcing the oversight of Iraq reconstruction to private companies unless the government "is entirely unable" to do the job with federal employees. It also bars the letting of private contracts "if there is even an appearance of conflict of interest for the private company."

June 16, 2004
Senators reject Democrats' proposals to prohibit the use of private contractors in combat missions or to interrogate prisoners and to increase the penalties for war profiteering by making it a crime to overcharge the government for goods and services in military contracts.

June 30, 2004
The U.S.-led Coalition Provisional Authority in Iraq is due to hand over the reins of government to an interim Iraqi administration. Thousands of private security contractors are scheduled to remain in Iraq, along with U.S. military personnel.

Return of Draft Considered Unlikely

The unpopularity of the Vietnam War — and the widespread perception that it was fought mostly by men from poor families who couldn't get draft deferments — helped push lawmakers to replace the draft in 1973 with today's all-volunteer army.

Since then, the services have met their manpower needs by offering college scholarships, technical training and other perks intended to help recruits "be all you can be," as the Army promises.

In the post-Cold War 1990s, the military shed jobs. The number of active-duty military personnel now stands at about 1.5 million, half the total during the Vietnam War.

But conflicts in the Balkans, the Middle East, Somalia and other far-flung places posed new challenges to the U.S. military. The challenges have intensified since the Bush administration launched its war on terrorism following the attacks of Sept. 11, 2001. The invasions and occupations of Afghanistan and Iraq have further strained the downsized military's capabilities.

To meet its growing manpower needs, the Pentagon has repeatedly extended duty tours in Afghanistan and Iraq. In Iraq alone, tours have been extended for 20,000 soldiers. [1] In early June, the Army barred soldiers scheduled for deployment to either country from leaving the service, even if their enlistments were up. [2]

Critics say the administration is placing too great a burden on overstretched troops as well as on the National Guard and reserves. Sen. John F. Kerry, the presumptive Democratic presidential candidate, called the administration's policy "a backdoor draft" and promised that if elected, he would add 40,000 military personnel to the active-duty armed forces by shifting funds currently earmarked for a controversial missile-defense system. [3]

"Let's be honest," says Peter W. Singer, a national security expert at the Brookings Institution, "the military designed the system so that you would use the National Guard and reserves if you got into a major war. This was meant to be a checking mechanism so that you wouldn't get into wars lightly. If there are situations where you don't think it's worth sending in the National Guard or the reserves, then maybe it's not worth doing it at all."

Some administration critics say restoring the military draft would be a better — and fairer — way to bolster troop levels. In January 2003, Rep. Charles B. Rangel, D-N.Y., and Sen. Ernest Hollings, D-S.C., separately introduced the Universal National Service Act, which would require a period of military or civilian service for American men and women ages 18-26 "in furtherance of the national defense and homeland security."

Introduction of the bills and renewed talk of the draft have spawned a flurry of Internet rumors that the administration is secretly planning to reinstitute obligatory military service shortly after the fall presidential election. But most analysts dismiss such rumors. [4]

Although Rangel's House bill has gained 14 co-sponsors, neither chamber has acted on the measure. Indeed, support for the draft proposals seems to be more a vehicle for criticizing the Bush administration's invasion and occupation of Iraq and the social inequities in the U.S. military than determined calls for restoration of the draft.

"I do not think that members of this administration and Congress would have been so willing to launch a war if they had known that their own children might have to fight it," said Rangel.

Continued from p. 574

services to the highest bidder. During the Hundred Years War, companies were as feared as any official enemy, gaining a bloody reputation for extortion, killing unarmed civilians and destroying villages that refused to meet their demands for money and food.

As the free companies gained strength, kings mounted military campaigns away from home to keep them occupied. But the companies continued to grow more powerful, notably the 10,000-man Great Company in Italy and England's White Company. In Italy, nobles in Milan and other cities emulated their organization to mobilize local paid armies of *condottieri*, or contract soldiers, who eventually replaced their employers as the local ruling class. In 15th-century France, King Charles VII exploited the company model more successfully by taxing the country's growing middle class and permanently hiring several companies. In so doing, he kept them out of trouble and created Europe's first standing army since the Dark Ages.

Highly effective mercenary armies from Switzerland, southern Germany and Austria often determined the outcome of conflicts across Europe, and by the 17th century European armies were essentially collections of highly paid, specialized mercenary units. War became such a lucrative enterprise that brokers who recruited and armed units and then leased them to warring governments were among the wealthiest men on the continent.

Citizen Armies

The Thirty Years War (1618-1648) marked a major shift in notions of statehood and military organization. Like their predecessors during the Dark Ages, mercenary forces inspired public loathing by looting the countryside during the conflict. But the gradual dissolution of the Hapsburg Empire marked the rise of national sovereignty and citizenship, and mercenary armies were slowly replaced with domestic citizen armies.

"Fact is, we are currently a nation in which the poor fight our wars while the affluent stay at home." [5]

As American casualties in Iraq mounted this spring, some Republicans echoed Democrats' concerns about relying on an all-volunteer military to fight terrorism. "Should we continue to burden the middle class, who represents most all of our soldiers, and the lower middle class?" asked Sen. Chuck Hagel, R-Neb. [6]

AFP Photo/National Archives

U.S. Marines carry a wounded comrade to a helicopter while under heavy fire from North Vietnamese troops during Operation Hickory III in Vietnam in July 1967.

The Bush administration continues to support the all-volunteer army and reject suggestions that it is considering a return to the draft. "I don't know anyone in the executive branch of the government who believes it would be appropriate or necessary to reinstitute the draft," said Defense Secretary Donald H. Rumsfeld.

Although he acknowledged that the military is being stretched in Afghanistan and Iraq, Rumsfeld said the solution is better management of the professional military. "It simply requires changing the rules, changing the requirements, changing the regulations in ways that we can manage that force considerably better," he said. [7]

Military experts say the draft is unlikely to return anytime soon. "The political cost of cranking up something like the draft to meet a contingency that may not be there a couple of years from now would be tremendous," says Michael P. Peters, executive vice president of the Council on Foreign Relations, a New York City think tank.

"Frankly, most military people would not be in favor of reconstituting the draft because they've become very comfortable with the all-volunteer force. Despite what's been going on in Iraq, the military has been able to attract and bring into the active force a pretty steady flow of high-quality people to maintain the manpower levels they need."

[1] See Thomas E. Ricks, "Army Personnel Chief Aims to Keep Ranks Full," *The Washington Post*, May 28 2004, p. A21.

[2] See Bob Herbert, "Level With Americans," *The New York Times*, June 7, 2004, p. A27.

[3] See Dan Balz, "Kerry Says He Would Add 40,000 to Army," *The Washington Post*, June 4, 2004, p. A1. For background on missile defense, see Mary H. Cooper, "Missile Defense," *The CQ Researcher*, Sept. 8, 2000, pp. 689-712.

[4] See, for example, Jack Kelly, "Rumor Aside, Draft's Return Is Most Unlikely," *Pittsburgh Post-Gazette*, May 24, 2004.

[5] From a floor statement in the House of Representatives, May 5, 2004.

[6] Quoted in Robert Burns, "Defense Chief Sees No Need to Reintroduce the Military Draft," The Associated Press, April 22, 2004.

[7] Quoted in Guy Taylor, "Rumsfeld Rejects Idea of Returning to the Draft," *The Washington Times*, April 23, 2004, p. A1.

Advances in easy-to-use weaponry, notably the musket, contributed to the shift, since mercenaries had traditionally traded on their ability to offer specialized skills. In addition to requiring little training, muskets also gave a tactical advantage to the army with the largest number of soldiers to fire them, and rulers could more readily raise large numbers of troops through conscription than by hiring mercenaries. Meanwhile, Enlightenment notions of patriotism and citizenship made military service more appealing than during the era of serfdom.

"[P]eople were more willing to fight as citizens than as subjects," wrote Singer, of Brookings. "Those who fought for profit, rather than patriotism, were completely de-legitimated under these new conceptions." [18]

Paid military units continued to play an important role in conflicts, however. During the American Revolution, the British government hired some 30,000 mercenaries from the German state of Hesse-Kassel to help quell the colonists' uprising. Indeed, George Washington's 1776 defeat of the Hessian units was a key victory in the march to Independence.

Private military armies enjoyed a resurgence during the 200 years of European colonial expansion, when governments gave companies monopoly commercial rights to develop overseas holdings. The Dutch East India Co., English East India Co. and Hudson's Bay Co. fielded their own military units to defend their vast economic interests. Some of these private forces endured until the 20th century, when the companies' trade monopolies ended. But the legacy of the armed charter companies endured until the 1920s and '30s in parts of sub-Saharan Africa that lacked national governments and where private companies held sway — such as Rhodesia and Mozambique.

With the exception of elite units, such as the French Foreign Legion or the Nepalese Gurkhas who still serve in the British and Indian armies, citizen armies raised under the aegis of sovereign nation-states became the dominant form of military organization. Most private military actors were individual mercenaries who hired out to businesses or rebel organizations in parts of the world where governments were weak, especially Latin America and Africa.

"Once at the center of warfare, by the start of the 20th century the international trade in military services was marginalized and mostly pushed underground," Singer writes. [19]

With the ascendance of the nation-state, for-profit military forces fell increasingly out of favor, and many governments even prohibited them. Meanwhile, the Geneva Conventions denied mercenaries the legal protections they provide for soldiers in combat.

Mercenaries' notoriety increased in the 1950s and '60s, when they helped fill the security vacuum left as European colonial powers withdrew from most of their holdings in Africa. Led by such notorious figures as "Mad" Mike Hoare of Ireland and Frenchman Bob Denard, mercenaries known as *les Affreux* ("the Terrible Ones") fought in wars of succession in the former Belgian Congo and other areas throughout the decolonization period. Denard continued to participate in coups and attempted coups in Africa until 1995. Many mercenaries active in Africa received their training under the apartheid regime of South Africa, adding to their reputation for ruthless violence born of racism.

Downsizing the Military

The great wars of the 20th century were fought with conscripted or volunteer armies. After World War II, for almost the entire second half of the century, the United States and the Soviet Union, together with their respective allies in the North Atlantic Treaty Organization (NATO) and the Warsaw Pact, maintained huge standing armies, still composed almost entirely of citizen-soldiers.

AFP Photo/Ahmad Masood

Private security guards escort Afghan President Hamid Karzai (center) as he arrives in Afghanistan's Ghor province in July 2003. Many military contractors are retired Special Forces personnel.

But after the Soviet Union collapsed in 1991, ending the Cold War, the need for such large armies rapidly diminished. Buoyed by the promise of a "peace dividend" that could be invested in other public sectors or returned to taxpayers as tax cuts, the United States and other countries downsized their militaries.

Since 1988, the Pentagon has shuttered 97 major military installations and reduced personnel at 55 facilities, saving $17 billion immediately and $7 billion annually, according to Citizens Against Government Waste. [20]

As U.S. policymakers were downsizing the military, they were also encouraging privatization of non-combat jobs. Military outsourcing began in 1973, when the draft was discontinued, near the end of the Vietnam War. To lure recruits, the Pentagon began contracting mundane jobs like cleaning and cooking to private firms. Throughout the 1980s and '90s, the Pentagon privatized more service jobs, including heavy construction, fuel supply and, especially, technical support — paying defense contractors to maintain and service the military's increasingly complex weaponry. The parallel trends of downsizing and outsourcing more than halved the number of active-duty troops — from more than 3 million in 1970 to 1.4 million by 2002. [21] A third of the reduction occurred during the 1990s.

Another rationale for privatizing the military, which intensified during the Clinton-Gore efforts to "reinvent government," was that inviting private companies to bid for contracts to provide military goods and services would result in even more cost savings. [22]

"Competition enhances quality, economy and productivity," states the Office of Management Budget's "Circular A-76," the executive branch's document on outsourcing. To make it easier for the Pentagon and other agencies to purchase goods and services from the private sector, Congress passed the 1994 Federal Acquisition Streamlining Act. And in 1996 lawmakers approved the Clinger-Cohen

Act, enabling a single federal agency to handle contracts for other agencies. [23]

But the Cold War's end brought more than cost savings to the U.S. military. It also created a dangerous power vacuum that quickly sparked new and different threats to international security. As the superpowers withdrew from their previous areas of influence, long-simmering disputes erupted in countries — ranging from the former Yugoslavia to Rwanda and Sierra Leone — whose weak governments were unable to quell unrest on their own. These low-intensity conflicts were unlike those envisioned by Cold War planners, whose large armies and heavy equipment were ill suited to deal with the urban street-fighting and guerrilla tactics that characterized the new hostilities.

The United States learned this lesson the hard way in 1993 when it tried to help Somalia put down a rebellion. The effort ended with TV images of a dead GI being dragged through the streets of Mogadishu and galvanized U.S. public opinion against future interventions in conflicts that posed no immediate threat to national security.

Reflecting that reluctance, Congress restricted the role of U.S. troops in overseas conflicts. In trying to quell the supply of cocaine from Colombia, for example, the United States may deploy no more than 400 American soldiers. To get around the restriction, the U.S. is allowed to use up to 400 private military contractors to augment the official forces.

American private military contractors also played a major role in the Balkans. The August 1995 rout of Serbian forces in Croatia, for instance, was attributed to Virginia-based Military Professional Resources Inc. (MPRI), not Croatian forces. MPRI had first entered the region through a State Department contract to monitor sanctions against Serbia. After the battlefield victory, the governments of Croatia and Bosnia hired MPRI to help retrain and modernize their forces. [24]

Meanwhile, Western governments' fear of placing troops in harm's way and becoming mired in far-away conflicts has weakened the ability of multilateral forces to intervene in local and regional conflicts and subsequently keep the peace. Even as the number and intensity of global hostilities grew, the number of personnel in the United Nations' peacekeeping operations dropped from a peak of 76,000 in 1994 to about 15,000 just four years later. [25]

Yet the U.N. opposes the use of mercenary forces, having adopted on Dec. 4, 1989, the International Convention against the Recruitment, Use, Financing and Training of Mercenaries. So far, only 25 countries have signed and ratified or acceded to the treaty. The United States is not among them.

Despite continued societal ambivalence about private armies, mercenaries have flourished in the post-Cold War power vacuum, characterized by small wars and weak states. Military transformation and outsourcing have swollen the ranks of these modern freelancers, many of whom are former Warsaw Pact and NATO military personnel who found themselves out of work when their governments downsized them.

As demand for mercenaries' services has grown, new companies have emerged to provide a wide range of services, including logistical support; training local police forces; protecting officials and commercial sites; and armed combat. ■

Current Situation

Modern Mercenaries

The role of private contractors in U.S. military operations has expanded greatly since the Sept. 11 terrorist attacks and the Bush administration's subsequent declaration of a war on terrorism. [26] At least 85 U.S. companies have contracts in Afghanistan or Iraq; about 15 of the firms are playing key roles in both countries, often filling jobs that contractors have long performed for the military, such as maintenance and repair of vehicles and aircraft, supervising supply lines and running logistics, driving supply trucks carrying food

"The U.S. military is 35 percent smaller than it was at the end of the Cold War, but it has far more global commitments, and Iraq is the biggest military commitment in at least a generation. So there's a gap between the supply and demand of military personnel."

— Peter W. Singer
***Author,* Corporate Warriors: The Rise of the Privatized Military Industry**

and fuel, setting up warehouses, preparing meals, cleaning bases, washing clothes and building military housing. [27]

But as the Abu Ghraib scandal and numerous civilian casualties in Iraq's escalating violence have shown, private military contractors are now performing duties more closely related to combat functions. As interrogators, translators and transcribers, they are closely involved in intelligence operations. And armed private contractors also help train local Iraqi police and soldiers and guard officials, military installations and convoys and non-military installations, such as oil pipelines and electrical stations.

According to the Pentagon, private security companies in Iraq provide "only defensive services." [28] Brooks, of the contractors' association, says clear rules of engagement, established by the CPA, define what the approximately 6,000 security contractors may and may not do in Iraq. "They can defend themselves, they can defend what's in their contract — be it a person, a place or a convoy — and they can defend Iraqi citizens," he says.

The rules also define what types of weapons contractors may use on the job. "Essentially, they are limited to light weapons," Brooks says, "meaning weapons that one person can use alone, ranging from pistols to assault rifles," but not belted machine guns, grenade launchers or explosives. Companies may obtain special permits to carry larger weapons for convoy duty, he added.

Despite their conspicuous role, no one seems to know just how many private contractors are operating in Iraq. "The Defense Department doesn't care about the numbers; they hire a company to do something," Brooks says. "It's up to the companies that win contracts to determine how many people they're going to need to do the job. Some companies may use technology, and some may hire locals."

Likewise, the exact number of contractors who have been killed or wounded in Iraq is unknown because civilian casualties go largely unnoticed unless they are reported in the media. The Labor Department puts the death toll among civilian contractors in Iraq since April 2003 at 85, compared with 48 who have died in Afghanistan and other countries since 2001. But the totals do not reflect the mounting casualties resulting from the growing violence in Iraq over the past two months. [29] Meanwhile, as of June 15, 2004, 830 soldiers had died in Iraq, according to the Pentagon.

AFP Photo/Marwan Naamani

Armed guards aboard a helicopter operated by North Carolina-based Blackwater Security Co. patrol over Baghdad in May 2004. Four Blackwater guards were ambushed and killed in April.

Cheney and Halliburton

Despite efforts to reduce the incidence of fraud and waste in Pentagon contracting practices, critics continue to complain about the department's dealings with the private sector. Much of the criticism has centered on Halliburton, one of the Pentagon's main suppliers in Iraq; Vice President Cheney served as Halliburton CEO from 1995 until he became Bush's running mate in 2000. Cheney asserts that although he still receives deferred compensation from Halliburton he has no formal ties to the firm, which oversees the reconstruction of Iraq's oil industry, and provides other services through subsidiaries, such as Kellogg, Brown and Root. [30]

"I don't have anything to do with the contracting process," he said earlier this year, "and I wouldn't know how to manipulate the process if I wanted to." [31]

But new evidence appears to contradict Cheney's assertion. Rep. Henry A. Waxman, D-Calif., recently demanded information from Cheney's office about reports that he may have had a hand in Halliburton's winning its $7 billion, no-bid contract for the Iraqi oil-reconstruction project. [32] In addition, one of Halliburton's subsidiaries, Kellogg Brown and Root, is the military's single biggest contractor in Iraq, hired to transport food and other supplies to military installations around the country.

"Halliburton received $3.5 billion through its contract in Iraq last year alone," Rep. Schakowsky says. "So we're talking about a lot of money, but not a lot of oversight, accountability, clarity or sunlight on their activities." Schakowsky's proposed bill would require the Pentagon to show Congress any new contract worth more than $1 million for a private firm to do business

Continued on p. 582

At Issue:

Does the Pentagon rely too heavily on private contractors?

yes

REP. JANICE D. SCHAKOWSKY, D-ILL.
MEMBER, HOUSE ENERGY AND COMMERCE COMMITTEE, SUBCOMMITTEE ON OVERSIGHT AND INVESTIGATIONS

FROM A LETTER TO PRESIDENT BUSH, MAY 4, 2004

I am writing out of concern over recent news of abuse of prisoners being held by the United States at the Abu Ghraib prison in Iraq. In particular, I have questions about the role of civilian contractors in these abuses, the investigation into the abuses and rules of accountability for U.S. civilian contractors operating in Iraq. . . . This is yet another example of questionable adherence to international human rights laws by United States forces in Iraq.

It has been reported that, more than two months after a classified Army report found that contract workers were implicated in the illegal abuse of Iraqis, the companies that employ them (CACI International Inc. and Titan Corp.) say that they have heard nothing from the Pentagon and that they have not removed any employees from Iraq.

The sadistic abuses of Iraqis at a U.S. military prison raise serious questions about the accountability of U.S.-hired private military contractors who are involved in illegal activity. It has been widely reported that civilian contractors are not subject to the Uniform Code of Military Conduct and that the Department of Justice is reluctant to get involved in this issue. . . . I have long held that the use of civilian contractors to carry out military functions on behalf of the United States is a dangerous policy, in large part because of the lack of accountability and oversight that exists. In particular, I do not believe that private companies should be trusted with interrogation of Iraqi prisoners.

I believe that pending a thorough investigation and appropriate action, including but not limited to the dismissal and prosecution of those involved, all contracts with civilian firms for functions involving security, supervision and interrogation of prisoners, should be suspended. . . .

Furthermore, I would like to know the policy of your administration regarding the directives, rules and laws governing contractors that operate on behalf of the United States in Iraq. It is my hope that the individuals named in recent press reports were not ordered to conduct such atrocious activities by U.S. personnel. However, that is something your administration should unequivocally address. . . .

I maintain that the use of private military contractors by the United States military is a misguided policy [that costs] the American people untold amounts, in terms of dollars [and] U.S. lives and is damaging our reputation with the international community. It also impedes the ability of the Congress to conduct appropriate oversight and keeps the American public in the dark.

no

DOUG BROOKS
PRESIDENT, INTERNATIONAL PEACE OPERATIONS ASSOCIATION

WRITTEN FOR *THE CQ RESEARCHER*, JUNE, 2004

In times of war, the Department of Defense has always relied on the private sector for essential services. From Valley Forge to Vietnam, private companies have been flexible and able to endure remarkable risks while supporting our troops. Private companies are able to tap into a pool of highly specialized professionals and a large network of local and U.S. reconstruction capabilities. They regularly utilize experienced military veterans while supporting and enhancing U.S. policies, lessening the burden on our young soldiers serving on the front. Consequently, our military is more focused, professional and cost effective.

Attempts by partisan analysts to turn the practice of private sector support into a political football are worrying. We must ensure adequate standards, transparency and accountability. However, we should remember that redundant bureaucracy, regulations and restrictions dangerously limit the flexibility that makes the private sector so enormously cost effective. The U.S. military is immensely capable, but to demand that it radically curtail its utilization of contractors would place unnecessary stress on our soldiers struggling to bring stability to volatile regions of the world.

Contrary to public opinion, the overwhelming majority of private military contracts are restricted to logistical and support services. The fact that the Pentagon also chooses to contract with private companies to provide security services to protect our reconstruction efforts is neither surprising nor worrisome. In the United States we have three times as many private guards as we do police, and while the threat levels are substantially higher in Iraq and Afghanistan, contractors are limited to defensive roles.

The companies use former military personnel for this hazardous duty, and all employees are under strict rules of engagement and are limited to light weapons. They are clearly not the rogue private army that critics allege. Nor are critics honest about the numbers. Three-quarters of the 20,000-strong private security employees are, in fact, Iraqis — the very people who should be providing security for their own country.

Policymakers should decide where we draw the line between military and civilian operations, not contractors. Whether or not we support the policies that got us involved, it is in everyone's interest that Afghanistan and Iraq be stabilized, reconstructed and democratized. The more successful the Pentagon's stability operations are, the quicker American troops can be brought home. Partisan quarrels should not obscure the inherent usefulness of the private sector.

Continued from p. 580

in Iraq or Afghanistan. "Over the last four years, there have been more than $7 billion in contracts let for Iraq and Afghanistan," she says. "Let's remember, these are taxpayer dollars."

Allegations have also surfaced that Halliburton fraudulently charged the government — and exposed drivers to unnecessary danger — by repeatedly running convoys of empty trucks in some of the most violent areas of Iraq. According to 12 current and former employees, KBR drivers and escorts made more than 100 trips on trucks carrying nothing but "sailboat fuel." [33]

Under KBR's cost-plus contract, the firm can bill the government for every trip it makes, so frequent trips are in its interest. "No one knows exactly what they were charging," says Singer of the Brookings Institution. "The cost is estimated to be about $2,000 for each truck; there were 15 trucks in each convoy; and convoys run once or twice a day. So you can see how these services accrue over time."

KBR has said it never ran empty trucks unnecessarily. "KBR is not paid by the load or by the mission," said Patrice Mingo, the company's manager for public relations. "So we would not be running trucks if they did not need to be run." [34]

Despite Halliburton's large investment in Iraq, the mounting scrutiny into its operations could jeopardize its prospects there. "Everybody knows convoys are getting blown up by bombs as they travel down the highways," says Corbin of the Center for Defense Information. "This scandal may actually get Halliburton kicked out of Iraq because if it's true, it's just beyond belief."

Lawmakers and Pentagon officials are stepping up investigations into allegations of waste and cost overruns among private contractors in Iraq. On June 15, government auditors described poor oversight and overcharges by firms providing troop support and reconstruction projects.

Halliburton Co.

Private contractors help Iraqi and U.S. military experts assess damage to an Iraqi pipeline near Basra. The Pentagon contractors are employees of Kellogg, Brown and Root, a subsidiary of Halliburton, the oil and gas conglomerate formerly headed by Vice President Cheney.

"We have no evidence to say there was willful fraud, based on the work we've done so far," said David M. Walker, head of the General Accounting Office (GAO). "But there have been very serious problems." [35] The House Government Reform Committee is expected to hear testimony in July from former Halliburton employees about allegations of overcharging by the contractor.

Tightening Oversight

Even the most hardened critics were surprised by one of the Pentagon's latest contracts, which called for a foreign company headed by a controversial foreign mercenary to be in charge of overseeing contracts in Iraq and coordinating contractor activities in a U.S.-led military operation. In May, the Army awarded the three-year, $293 million contract to a British security firm to guard employees of the Program Management Office, responsible for U.S.-funded contracts in Iraq, and to run a new operations center for contractors to help coordinate convoy and staff movements. The firm, Aegis Defense Services, was founded just two years ago by Tom Spicer, a controversial former British special forces officer who worked for warring parties in Sierra Leone and Papua New Guinea in the 1990s. [36]

Contracts with Aegis and many other firms could run into trouble if a measure adopted by the Senate on June 14 becomes law. Included as an amendment to the fiscal 2005 Pentagon reauthorization bill, the measure introduced by Sens. Ron Wyden, D-Ore., and Byron Dorgan, D-N.D., prohibits the government from outsourcing the oversight of Iraq reconstruction to private companies unless the government "is entirely unable" to do the job with federal employees. It also bars the letting of private contracts "if there is even an appearance of conflict of interest for the private company."

"The outsourcing of oversight on Iraq reconstruction is a costly, unsound practice that never should have been permitted in the first place, and it's time to close the door on it now," Wyden said. "This amendment can save American taxpayers untold additional dollars by placing accountability for

Iraq reconstruction squarely with the Department of Defense." [37]

Senators have rejected two other Democratic amendments to the Pentagon bill aimed at enhancing congressional oversight of private military contractors. An amendment sponsored by Sen. Christopher Dodd, D-Conn., would have prohibited the use of private contractors in combat missions and to interrogate prisoners. Another, sponsored by Sen. Patrick Leahy, D-Vt., would have made it a crime to overcharge the government for goods and services in military contracts.

"It's unfortunate that Republican leaders have chosen to do the White House's bidding by killing stiff penalties for those who gouge the taxpayers," Leahy said after the June 16 vote defeating his measure. "We should be defending the public, not the war profiteers." [38]

Opponents said the proposals would jeopardize the effectiveness of U.S. forces at a time of growing violence in Iraq. "Congress should deliberate very carefully a criminal penalty of up to 20 years for these thousands upon thousands of companies that are currently engaged," said Senate Armed Services Committee Chairman John W. Warner, R-Va. [39] ■

OUTLOOK

After the Handover

The United States formally relinquishes its authority in Iraq on June 30, when it will turn over the reins of government to an interim administration, pending formal elections in January 2005. But the United States will maintain a robust military presence in the country long after the formal handover. It also will retain command over U.S. and Iraqi forces and control the $18.4 billion reconstruction effort. [40]

The Bush administration says it will maintain the current troop level of 138,000 in Iraq through 2005. But that may be hard to do. The Army has already extended soldiers' tours in Iraq, and while the service is currently meeting its recruiting goals, it may have trouble sustaining the planned troop levels over the long-term. [41]

"The U.S. military is 35 percent smaller than it was at the end of the Cold War, but it has far more global commitments, and Iraq is the biggest military commitment in at least a generation," says Singer. "So there's a gap between the supply and demand of military personnel."

All the options for increasing the number of troops on the ground in Iraq — expanding the military, calling up more National Guard reservists, reinstituting the draft and bringing in more allied forces — would be politically costly, he says. "Enlarging the military would force the administration to admit that they were wrong about how many troops would be needed to win the war in Iraq, restoring the draft would spark a huge outcry, and bringing in the allies would force the administration to make political compromises that it has shown it's not willing to make." Indeed, the leaders of NATO members France and Turkey rejected Bush's recent call to add NATO forces to the 138,000 U.S. contingent and 15,000 soldiers from Britain and 32 other coalition members after the handover. [42]

The manpower solution that imposes the least political cost to the administration, Singer says, is to rely even more heavily on private military contractors. "There are none of the costs associated with the other options, the public remains only limitedly aware of it, and when casualties happen there's not the same kind of outcry," he says. "In fact, they aren't even reported in the public record."

Indeed, most experts predict that private military contractors will continue to play an essential role in Iraq for the foreseeable future. "There aren't too many short-term solutions to the manpower problem in Iraq," says Peters of the Council on Foreign Relations. "Just about everybody in the active Army and Marine Corps is either in Iraq, on their way to Iraq or has just come back from Iraq. So there's not a lot of flexibility, and that's part of the challenge that the military faces." ■

Notes

[1] For background on Bush administration interpretations of prisoner protections, see David Masci, "Ethics of War," *The CQ Researcher*, Dec. 13, 2002, pp. 1013-1032.

[2] See Curt Anderson, "CIA Contractor Charged in Detainee Death," The Associated Press, June 18, 2004.

[3] The CPA, created by the United States in early 2003 to oversee reconstruction in post-conflict Iraq, will hand over authority to the interim Iraqi government on June 30. For background, see L. Elaine Halchin, "The Coalition Provisional Authority (CPA): Origins, Characteristics, and Institutional Authorities," CRS Report for Congress, Congressional Research Service, April 29, 2004.

About the Author

Mary H. Cooper specializes in defense, energy and environmental issues. Before joining *The CQ Researcher* as a staff writer in 1983, she was Washington correspondent for the Rome daily newspaper *l'Unitá*. She is the author of *The Business of Drugs* (CQ Press, 1990) and holds a B.A. in English from Hollins College in Virginia. Her recent reports include "Smart Growth," "Exporting Jobs," "Weapons of Mass Destruction" and "Bush and the Environment."

4 From a television interview with WAVY-TV in Hampton Roads, Va., April 6, 2004.
5 Levin spoke May 7, 2004, at a Senate Armed Services Committee hearing on Iraqi prison abuses.
6 See P.W. Singer, *Corporate Warriors* (2003), p. 78.
7 Charles L. Schultze, senior fellow emeritus, Brookings Institution, based on Commerce Department data (forthcoming report).
8 See Elisabeth Bumiller and Edward Wong, "Iraq Seeks Custody of Hussein; Bush Has Security Concerns," *The New York Times*, June 16, 2004, p. A1.
9 Schakowsky press release following the indictment of a CIA contractor for prisoner abuse in Afghanistan, June 17, 2004.
10 Office of Management and Budget, "Competitive Sourcing: Report on Competitive Sourcing Results, Fiscal Year 2003," May 2004.
11 Larry Margasak, "Committee to seek testimony from Halliburton executives," The Associated Press, June 15, 2004.
12 General Accounting Office, "Fiscal Year 2003 Contract Award Procedures and Management Challenges," June 2004.
13 See, for example, Andrew Buncombe, "You Don't Have to Be Poor to Work There, But It Helps," *The Independent* (London), June 15, 2004, p. 26.
14 See John Hendren and Mark Mezzetti, "U.S. Charges Contractor Over Beating of Afghan Detainee," *Los Angeles Times*, June 18, 2004 p. A6.
15 See Seymour M. Hersh, "Torture at Abu Ghraib," *The New Yorker*, June 15, 2004, p. 42.
16 See Adam Liptak, "Who Would Try Civilians of U.S.? No One in Iraq," *The New York Times*, May 26, 2004.
17 Unless otherwise noted, information in this section is based on Singer, *op. cit.*, pp. 19-39.
18 *Ibid.*, p. 31.
19 *Ibid.*, p. 37.
20 www.cagw.org.
21 See Council on Foreign Relations, "Iraq: Military Outsourcing," May 20, 2004, www.cfr.org.
22 For background on Clinton-era government downsizing efforts, see Susan Kellam, "Reinventing Government," *The CQ Researcher*, Feb. 17, 1995, pp. 145-168.
23 See Robert O'Harrow and Ellen McCarthy, "Private Sector Has Firm Role at the Pentagon," *The Washington Post*, June 9, 2004, p. E1.
24 See Eugene B. Smith, "The New Condottieri and U.S. Policy: The Privatization of Conflict and its Implications," *Parameters*, winter 2002-03, pp. 104-119. *Parameters* is a quarterly magazine published by the U.S. Army War College.
25 See David Shearer, "Outsourcing War," *Foreign Policy*, fall 1998, p. 70.
26 For background, see Kenneth Jost, "Re-examining 9/11," *The CQ Researcher*, June 4, 2004, pp. 493-516, and David Masci and Kenneth Jost, "War on Terrorism," *The CQ Researcher*, Oct. 12, 2001, pp. 817-848.
27 For more information, see Council on Foreign Relations, "Iraq: Military Outsourcing," www.cfr.org.
28 "Private Security Companies Operating in Iraq," an attachment to a letter from Defense Secretary Donald Rumsfeld to Rep. Ike Skelton, D-Mo., May 4, 2004.
29 James Cox, "Contractors Pay Rising Toll in Iraq," *USA Today*, June 16, 2004, p. 1A.
30 "Vice President Dick Cheney and Mrs. Cheney Release 2003 Income Tax Return," The White House, April 13, 2004, www.whitehouse.gov.
31 Quoted in "Cheney Faults 'Desperate' Attacks on Halliburton," CNN.com, Jan. 23, 2004. See also Robert O'Harrow Jr., "E-Mail Links Cheney's Office, Contract," *The Washington Post*, June 2, 2004, p. A6.
32 See Erik Eckholm, "Evidence Suggests Cheney Knew of Oil Contracts," *The International Herald Tribune*, June 15, 2004, p. 4.
33 See Seth Borenstein, "Trucks Made to Drive Without Cargo in Dangerous Areas of Iraq," Knight Ridder/Tribune News Service, May 23, 2004.
34 Quoted in Kathleen Schalch, "Halliburton Trucks Reportedly Traveling in Iraq Empty Instead of Hauling Supplies to Troops," National Public Radio, "Morning Edition," June 8, 2004.
35 Walker testified June 15, 2004, before the House Government Reform Committee. See Erik Eckholm, "Auditors Testify About Waste in Iraq Contracts," *The New York Times*, June 16, 2004, p. A13.
36 See Mary Pat Flaherty, "Iraq Work Awarded to Veteran of Civil Wars," *The Washington Post*, June 16, 2004, p. E1.
37 From a press release by Sen. Wyden's office, wyden.senate.gov.
38 From a press statement issued by Leahy's office on June 16, 2004.
39 Quoted in Carl Hulse, "Senate Rejects Harder Penalties on Companies, and Ban on Private Interrogators," *The New York Times*, June 17, 2004, p. A8.
40 See Jeffrey Gettelman, "Iraqis Start to Exercise Power Even Before Date for Turnover," *The New York Times*, June 13, 2004, p. A1.
41 See Monica Davey, "Recruiters Try New Tactics to Sell Wartime Army," *The New York Times*, June 14, 2004, p. A1.
42 See Glenn Kessler and Dana Milbank, "Leaders Dispute NATO Role in Iraq," *The Washington Post*, June 10, 2004, p. A6.

FOR MORE INFORMATION

Citizens Against Government Waste, 1301 Connecticut Ave., N.W., Suite 400, Washington, DC 20036; (202) 467-5300; www.cagw.org. Advocates the elimination of waste and inefficiency in government and publishes periodic exposés of pork-barrel spending.

Defense Procurement and Acquisition Policy, Defense Department, 3060 Defense, Pentagon, #3E1044, Arlington VA 20301; (703) 695-7145; www.acq.osd.mil/dpap. The Pentagon's office for assessing procurement policies serves as a liaison between the Defense Department and its civilian contractors.

General Accounting Office, 441 G St., N.W., Suite 1139, Washington, DC 20548; (202) 512-6071; www.gao.gov. The investigative arm of Congress has conducted many studies of contracting practices of federal agencies.

International Peace Operations Association, 1900 L St., N.W., Suite 320, Washington, DC 20036; (703) 516-7376; www.ipoaonline.org. Represents private military contractors.

Project on Government Oversight, 666 11th St., N.W., Suite 500, Washington, DC 20001; (202) 347-1122; www.pogo.org. A watchdog group dedicated to exposing government waste, fraud and corruption, especially in military contracting.

Bibliography

Selected Sources

Books

Pelton, Robert Young, *The Hunter, the Hammer, and Heaven: Journeys to Three Worlds Gone Mad*, The Lyons Press, 2002.

This journalistic account of wars in Sierra Leone, Chechnya and Bougainville (an island that recently seceded from New Guinea) includes a description of the role of private contractors in determining the outcome of modern conflicts.

Singer, P.W., *Corporate Warriors: The Rise of the Privatized Military Industry*, Cornell University Press, 2003.

Outsourcing military services enables the Defense Department to more efficiently manage U.S. military forces, but it also poses questions about congressional oversight of the military and the legal status of contractors overseas, the director of the Project on U.S. Policy Towards the Islamic World at the Brookings Institution writes.

Articles

Ante, Spencer E., "The Other U.S. Military," *Business Week*, May 31, 2004, p. 76.

Military contracting is a growing business, with billions of dollars in contracts in Iraq's reconstruction alone, but contractors appear to operate there with little oversight by Congress or executive agencies.

Avant, Deborah, "Mercenaries," *Foreign Policy*, July/August 2004, pp. 20-28.

A George Washington University political science professor answers several frequently asked questions about the use of private military contractors by the U.S. military.

Burger, Timothy J., and Adam Zagorin, "The Paper Trail," *Time*, May 30, 2004.

Vice President Dick Cheney's office rejects charges that Cheney, a former CEO of Halliburton, had a hand in the company's landing a lucrative, no-bid contract to restore Iraq's oil industry.

Cox, James, "Contractors Pay Rising Toll in Iraq, Insurgents Target Civilian Workers," *USA Today*, June 16, 2004, p. 1B.

Insurgents are attacking civilian contractors whose services are vital to Iraq's reconstruction.

Hersh, Seymour M., "Chain of Command," *The New Yorker*, May 17, 2004, pp. 38-43.

One in a series of articles by the author into the prisoner-abuse scandal at Abu Ghraib prison describes interrogation techniques used by U.S. soldiers and private contractors.

Schwartz, Nelson D., "The Pentagon's Private Army," *Fortune*, March 17, 2003, p. 100.

Even before the United States invaded Iraq last year, the U.S. military relied heavily on private contractors to provide essential services for troops.

Shearer, David, "Outsourcing War," *Foreign Policy*, fall 1998, pp. 68-81.

This review of the history of private military contractors raises the problem of their accountability to governments in an era of rapidly spreading regional conflicts.

Smith, Eugene B., "The New Condottieri and U.S. Policy: The Privatization of Conflict and Its Implications," *Parameters*, winter 2002-2003, pp. 104-119.

This article in the journal of the U.S. Army War College describes the rise of private military contractors in the wake of the Cold War's end and subsequent downsizing of the American military.

Reports and Studies

Beelman, Maud, "Winning Contractors: U.S. Contractors Reap the Windfalls of Post-War Reconstruction," Center for Public Integrity, Oct. 30, 2003.

The watchdog group examines allegations of fraud and cronyism between high-ranking government officials and companies that receive lucrative contracts with little congressional oversight.

General Accounting Office, "Military Operations: Contractors Provide Vital Services to Deployed Forces but Are Not Adequately Addressed in DOD Plans," June 2003.

The investigative arm of Congress finds that while the Pentagon considers private contractors to be part of U.S. forces in Iraq, it was unable to provide the cost of their contribution to the military mission.

House Committee on Government Reform, Minority Staff, Special Investigations Division, and Senate Democratic Policy Committee, "Contractors Overseeing Contractors: Conflicts of Interest Undermine Accountability in Iraq," May 18, 2004.

Democratic lawmakers criticize the Coalition Provisional Authority's hiring of private firms to oversee the work of private contractors in Iraq with which they have business ties.

The Next Step:

Additional Articles from Current Periodicals

Abu Ghraib

Brinkley, Joel, "9/11 Set Army Contractor on Path to Abu Ghraib," *The New York Times*, May 19, 2004, p. A13.

The exact actions of one of the contractors accused in the prison abuses are subject to dispute as friends call him "gentle as a lamb."

Epstein, Edward, and David Baker, "Abuse Raises Questions About Role of U.S. Contractors," *San Francisco Chronicle*, May 4, 2004, p. A11.

Interrogating prisoners is a highly sensitive task, but the use of private contractors in this area reflects how overwhelmed the United States is by the Iraqi occupation, experts say.

Miller, T. Christian, "U.S. Considers Barring Abu Ghraib Contractor," *Los Angeles Times*, May 28, 2004, p. A10.

The government launches an investigation into how a contract to provide computer equipment and training was used to hire private interrogators.

Sentementes, Gus G., and Tom Bowman, "Civilians' Role at Prison Studied," *The Baltimore Sun*, May 22, 2004, p. 4A.

According to some of the soldiers stationed at Abu Ghraib, some of the contractors said they did not have to answer to the officers at the prison.

Latin America

Forero, Juan, "Private U.S. Operatives on Risky Missions in Colombia," *The New York Times*, Feb. 14, 2004, p. A3.

Americans contractors captured or killed in Colombia generate little publicity — and some say that was the plan all along.

Marx, Gary, "U.S. Civilians Wage Drug War From Colombia's Skies," *Chicago Tribune*, Nov. 3, 2002, p. 4.

U.S. pilots help to fumigate Colombia's coca fields with helicopter gunship escorts; a Colombian newspaper calls them "gringo mercenaries."

Miller, T. Christian, "Foreign Pilots Hired to Boost U.S. Drug War," *Los Angeles Times*, April 18, 2001, p. A1.

The State Department evades the congressionally imposed limit on U.S. contractors in Colombia by hiring foreign citizens.

Legal Framework

Gibson, Gail, "Prosecuting Abuse of Prisoners," *The Baltimore Sun*, May 29, 2004, p. 4A.

The Military Extraterritorial Jurisdiction Act passed in 2000 may be the key to prosecuting any crimes by contractors, but it is relatively untested legally.

Liptak, Adam, "Who Would Try Civilians From U.S.? No One in Iraq," *The New York Times*, May 26, 2004, p. A11.

Granted immunity in Iraqi courts and not subject to courts-martial, contractors would have to be tried under U.S. laws.

Miller, T. Christian, "Contractors Fall Through Legal Cracks," *Los Angeles Times*, May 4, 2004, p. A8.

The credibility of the American legal system could be undermined if no action is taken against civilian contractors who abused prisoners at Abu Ghraib.

Shane, Scott, "Some U.S. Prison Contractors May Avoid Charges," *The Baltimore Sun*, May 24, 2004, p. 1A.

Since the civilian interrogators' contracts ran through the Interior Department, they may not be subject to a law allowing the prosecution of Defense Department contractors.

Military Outsourcing

"Dangerous Work," *The Economist*, April 10, 2004.

Deployments increased in the 1990s as the military's size was being reduced; private contractors, many former soldiers, filled the gap.

"Privatization and Peril in Iraq," *The Philadelphia Inquirer*, April 8, 2004, p. A19.

Peter Singer, an expert on military contracting, describes a "coalition of the billing" that has taken the place of support from traditional allies.

Bianco, Anthony, and Stephanie Anderson Forest, "Outsourcing War," *Business Week*, Sept. 15, 2003, p. 68.

Kellogg, Brown and Root, a subsidiary of Halliburton Co., is a ubiquitous presence wherever the U.S. military goes.

Bredemeier, Kenneth, "Thousands of Private Contractors Support U.S. Forces in Persian Gulf," *The Washington Post*, March 3, 2003, p. E1.

Despite the thousands of contractors working for it, the U.S. Central Command says it doesn't know how many contractors or companies are present.

Cha, Ariana Eunjung, and Renae Merle, "Line Increasingly Blurred Between Soldiers and Civilian Contractors," *The Washington Post*, May 13, 2004, p. A1.

The Army describes it as a mistake, but the awarding of battlefield commendations to private contractors illustrates their military role.

Dao, James, "Private Guards Take Big Risks, for Right Price," *The New York Times*, April 2, 2004, p. A1.

High pay is enticing so many Special Operations members into the private sector that a senior general described meeting contractors in Iraq as being "like a reunion."

Lee, Christopher, "Army Weighs Privatizing Close to 214,000 Jobs," *The Washington Post*, Nov. 3, 2002, p. A1.
Even as the Army considers privatizing more jobs, it is unaware how many contractors it employs.

McCarthy, Ellen, "CACI Contract: From Supplies to Interrogation," *The Washington Post*, May 17, 2004, p. E1.
Critics say that large, open-ended contracts given to private companies are intended to streamline procurement, but oversight and accountability are casualties.

Merle, Renae, "More Civilians Accompanying U.S. Military," *The Washington Post*, Jan. 22, 2003, p. A10.
The ratio of contractors to military personnel in the Persian Gulf War was one to 25 or even 50; now, the ratio is closer to one in 10.

Shane, Scott, "Uncle Sam Keeps SAIC on Call for Top Tasks," *The Baltimore Sun*, Oct. 26, 2003, p. 1A.
Science Applications International Corporation has grown into a giant that handles a variety of government tasks.

Private Armies

Borenstein, Seth, and Scott Dodd, "Civilian Security Jobs Abound in U.S. War Zones," *The Philadelphia Inquirer*, April 3, 2004, p. A8.
Industry leaders say standards are slipping in light of the high demand for security contractors; special-operations experience was the standard; now anyone who can handle a gun is in demand.

Collier, Robert, "Global Security Firms Fill in as Private Armies," *San Francisco Chronicle*, March 28, 2004, p. A1.
The 15,000 private fighters in Iraq are part of a global industry worth at least $100 billion per year and on which the fate of governments sometimes rides.

Fineman, Mark, "Privatized Army in Harm's Way," *Los Angeles Times*, Jan. 24, 2003, p. A1.
As contractors perform more and more essential duties on or near the front lines, experts say protecting them could be difficult and expensive.

Kady, Martin II, and Joseph Anselmo, " 'Private Army' Blurs the Lines," *CQ Weekly*, May 8, 2004, p. 1067.
The scale of contracting operations and the abuses at Abu Ghraib have Congress members shocked and demanding accountability in how Iraq funds are spent.

Wayne, Leslie, "America's For-Profit Secret Army," *The New York Times*, Oct. 13, 2002, Section 3, p. 1.
MPRI trained the Croatian army to execute an offensive that threw back the Serbs and then trained the Bosnian army as part of the Dayton peace accords.

Privatizing Conflict

Hukill, Tracy, "Should Peacekeepers Be Privatized?" *National Journal*, May 15, 2004.
United Nations officials staunchly oppose involving mercenaries in peacekeeping, but Secretary General Kofi Annan says he considered it during the Rwandan genocide.

Pape, Eric, and Michael Meyer, "Dogs of Peace," *Newsweek*, Aug. 25, 2003, p. 22.
Humanitarian crises in Africa led to offers by mercenary companies to step in and stabilize things when governments declined to intervene; some now say such offers might be worth accepting.

Tepperman, Jonathan, "Out of Service," *The New Republic*, Nov. 25, 2002, p. 10.
DynCorp contractors, like the ones hired to protect Hamid Karzai, can be responsible for key elements of foreign policy.

Citing *The CQ Researcher*

Sample formats for citing these reports in a bibliography include the ones listed below. Preferred styles and formats vary, so please check with your instructor or professor.

MLA Style

Jost, Kenneth. "Rethinking the Death Penalty." The CQ Researcher 16 Nov. 2001: 945-68.

APA Style

Jost, K. (2001, November 16). Rethinking the death penalty. *The CQ Researcher, 11*, 945-968.

Chicago Style

Jost, Kenneth. "Rethinking the Death Penalty." *CQ Researcher*, November 16, 2001, 945-968.

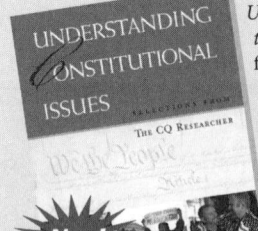

CQ Researcher

Published by CQ Press, a division of Congressional Quarterly Inc.

thecqresearcher.com

Medicaid Reform

Will efforts to cut costs hurt the poor?

Rising medical costs and declining tax revenues in recent years have forced many states to make deep cuts in services provided by Medicaid, the health care program for the poor. Both state and federal officials want to lower the program's spiraling costs — largely from prescription drugs and long-term care — but there is widespread disagreement about what changes are needed. Republicans say Medicaid — the nation's largest health insurance program — needs a radical overhaul. Instead of an unlimited entitlement program, they want to convert at least part of the program into a capped grant, which would give states more freedom from federal rules. Democrats say caps would be inequitable because they would lead to deeper cuts in tough economic times. Both liberals and conservatives agree, however, that the current growth of the program must be addressed.

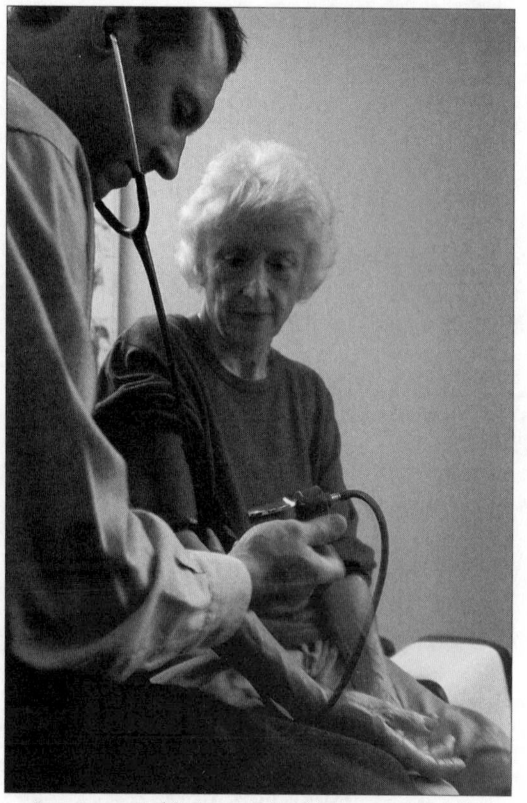

Low-income elderly and disabled Americans use 70 percent of Medicaid expenses.

INSIDE

THIS REPORT

The CQ Researcher • July 16, 2004 • www.thecqresearcher.com
Volume 14, Number 25 • Pages 589-612

CQ PRESS

RECIPIENT OF SOCIETY OF PROFESSIONAL JOURNALISTS AWARD FOR EXCELLENCE ◆ AMERICAN BAR ASSOCIATION SILVER GAVEL AWARD

Cover: The elderly and disabled account for 70 percent of Medicaid expenses, although most recipients are children and low-income parents. Facing swelling costs and dwindling revenues, some states are cutting Medicaid eligibility, benefits or payment rates. (PhotoDisc)

July 16, 2004
Volume 14, Number 25

MANAGING EDITOR: Thomas J. Colin

ASSISTANT MANAGING EDITOR: Kathy Koch

ASSOCIATE EDITOR: Kenneth Jost

STAFF WRITERS: Mary H. Cooper, David Masci, William Triplett

CONTRIBUTING WRITERS: Sarah Glazer, David Hatch, David Hosansky, Patrick Marshall, Tom Price, Jane Tanner

DESIGN/PRODUCTION EDITOR: Olu B. Davis

ASSISTANT EDITOR: Kenneth Lukas

A Division of Congressional Quarterly Inc.

SENIOR VICE PRESIDENT/GENERAL MANAGER: John A. Jenkins

DIRECTOR, LIBRARY PUBLISHING: Kathryn C. Suárez

DIRECTOR, EDITORIAL OPERATIONS: Ann Davies

CONGRESSIONAL QUARTERLY INC.

CHAIRMAN: Paul C. Tash

VICE CHAIRMAN: Andrew P. Corty

PRESIDENT AND PUBLISHER: Robert W. Merry

The CQ Researcher (ISSN 1056-2036) is printed on acid-free paper. Published weekly, except Jan. 2, April 9, July 2, July 9, Aug. 6, Aug. 13, Nov. 26 and Dec. 31, by CQ Press, a division of Congressional Quarterly Inc. Annual subscription rates for institutions start at $625. For pricing, call 1-800-834-9020, ext. 1906. To purchase a *CQ Researcher* report in print or electronic format (PDF), visit www.cqpress.com or call 866-427-7737. A single report is $10. Bulk purchase discounts and electronic-rights licensing are also available. Periodicals postage paid at Washington, D.C., and additional mailing offices. POSTMASTER: Send address changes to *The CQ Researcher*, 1255 22nd St., N.W., Suite 400, Washington, D.C. 20037.

Medicaid Reform

By Rebecca Adams

The Issues

Melvin Foote, a 47-year-old Marine veteran in Klamath Falls, Ore., relies on several drugs to treat his schizophrenia and bipolar disorder. He fears that if he stops taking them he will slip back into a cycle of deep depression, followed by frenzy.

But that possibility may soon become a reality as Oregon wrestles with skyrocketing health-care costs. Like cash-strapped state officials nationwide, Oregon lawmakers are struggling over the future of Medicaid, designed as a health-care safety net for low-income people — including children, pregnant women, the elderly and the blind and disabled.

"We can only serve half the population that we have," says Lynn Read, who oversees the state's Medicaid program. Eventually, state officials may have to shrink the number of people who qualify for Medicaid by lowering income eligibility, she says, adding, "These are all very vulnerable people."

The Medicaid program pays for one-third of all births nationwide, two-thirds of nursing-home stays and nearly half of the public funds spent on AIDS patients.

Foote, who speaks slowly and pauses to draw a breath before each answer, worries most about losing his coverage and facing an unforeseen emergency. "I'd have to get checked into a hospital without insurance, and I'd have to pay it off as well as I can," he says.

Oregon is one of many states that expanded their Medicaid programs during the 1990s, when states were flush with cash, to cover more of the nation's 43 million uninsured.

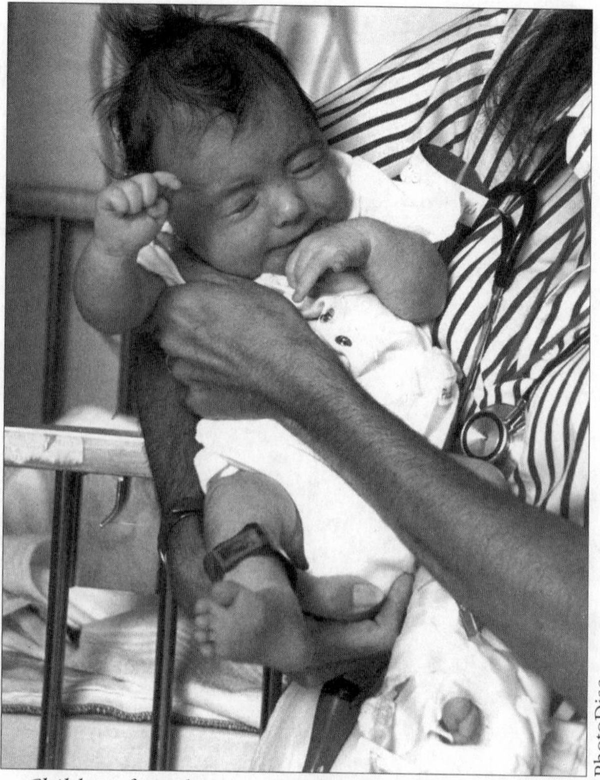

PhotoDisc

Children from low-income families make up nearly half of all Medicaid recipients, but they use less than 20 percent of total program expenditures. Rising Medicaid costs are largely due to the cost of caring for the disabled and the elderly, who account for 70 percent of Medicaid expenses.

Now facing plummeting revenues, many states are scaling back. Oregon already has had to cut some Medicaid benefits and services. [1] But with a reputation for adopting innovations to help the uninsured, state officials are considering ways to avoid deeper cuts, including taxing hospitals and other health care providers.

Pressure to overhaul Medicaid has increased in recent years as total federal and state expenses for the program jumped nearly $100 billion in five years: from $159.9 billion in 1997 to $258.2 billion in 2002. [2] In fact, the percentage of state resources consumed by Medicaid has doubled in the past 15 years — from 10 percent in 1989 to 20 percent today. [3]

Medicaid covers about 51 million people, according to the Congressional Budget Office. Children comprise 48.5 percent of the Medicaid population, while adults younger than 65, such as pregnant women, make up 24.5 percent. People with disabilities represent 17 percent and the elderly are almost 10 percent of Medicaid beneficiaries. Even though children and low-income parents make up the bulk of the population, their medical costs are far lower than the other groups. The elderly and disabled account for 70 percent of Medicaid expenses. [4]

Experts blame Medicaid's cost crunch on four trends:

- Skyrocketing health-care and drug expenses;
- Increased demands for long-term care for an aging population;
- State expansions of eligibility criteria during the booming 1990s; and
- Plunging state and federal tax revenues caused by tax cuts and a sagging economy.

Facing swelling costs and dwindling revenues, states have begun cutting Medicaid eligibility, benefits or provider-reimbursement rates. Many states have cut all three. For fiscal 2004, 49 states and the District of Columbia had implemented or planned to cut Medicaid, according to a report by the Kaiser Family Foundation. [5]

Anxiety about rising costs is fueling the debate over whether it is time to overhaul Medicaid. And with the adoption last year of a prescription drug benefit for seniors, Republicans who control Congress and the White House are turning their attention to health insurance and Medicaid issues. [6]

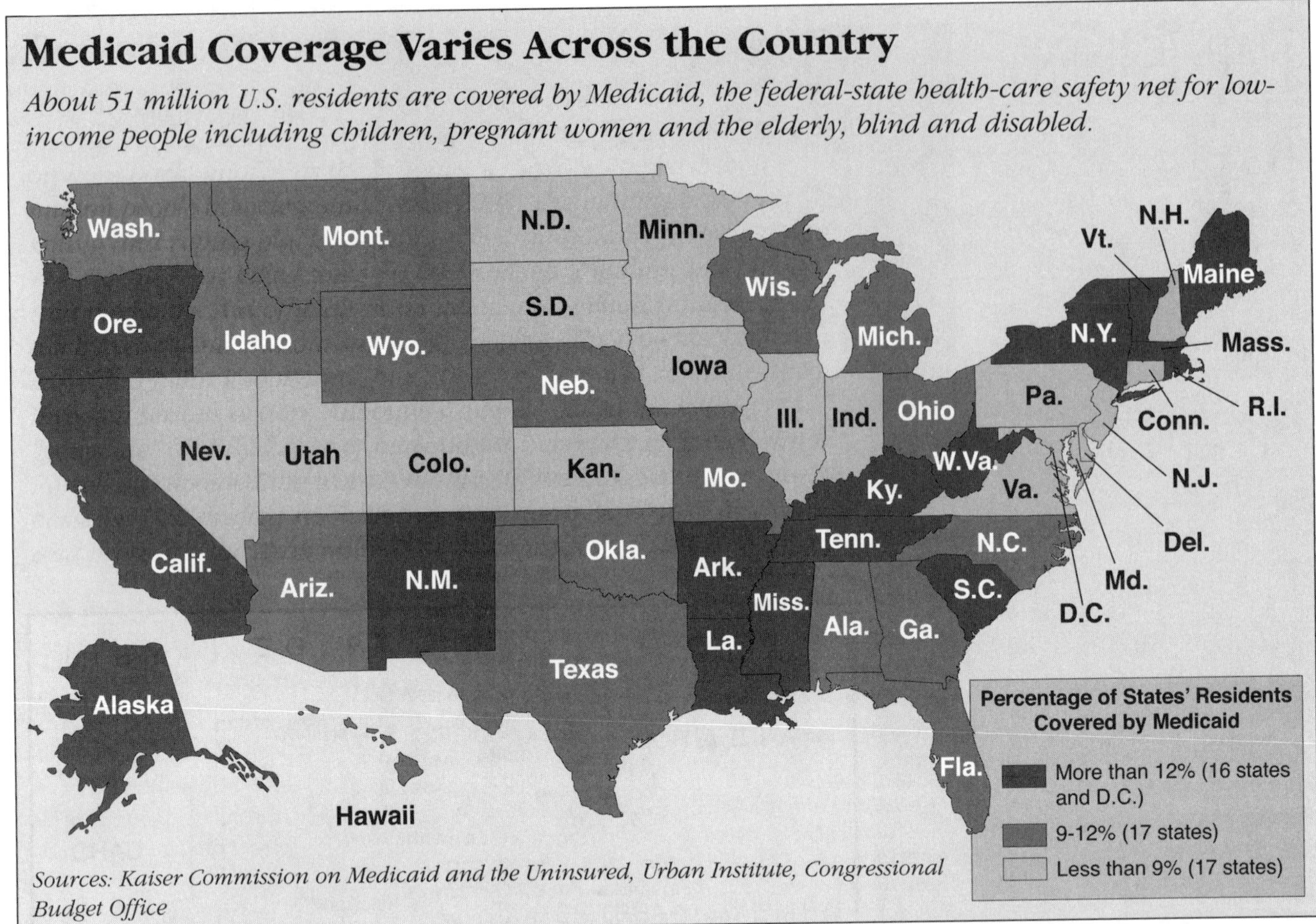

Medicaid Coverage Varies Across the Country

About 51 million U.S. residents are covered by Medicaid, the federal-state health-care safety net for low-income people including children, pregnant women and the elderly, blind and disabled.

Sources: Kaiser Commission on Medicaid and the Uninsured, Urban Institute, Congressional Budget Office

"Financing is at the core of all this," says Nina Owcharenko, senior health care analyst at the conservative Heritage Foundation. "In the end, it's all about the money."

Many Republicans in Washington, including President Bush, want to convert Medicaid from an unlimited federal entitlement program to one whose costs are capped. "You just can't have growth rates that high, and a program that is an open-ended check," Owcharenko warns.

But such a drastic move would prove enormously controversial, because it would transform the very nature of Medicaid, which receives less popular attention than Medicare — the health insurance program for the non-indigent elderly and disabled — even though Medicaid is larger. That's partly because average Americans do not view themselves as Medicaid beneficiaries.

"It's the ugly stepchild of health policy programs," Joy Johnson Wilson, a health care analyst at the National Conference of State Legislatures, says.

However, some say the program unfairly gets a bad rap. Democrats point out that Medicaid costs less per enrollee than private health insurance. [7]

Most governors adamantly oppose a cap, although at least five states have either accepted or are considering Bush administration offers of limits on federal funding in exchange for new flexibility in cutting benefits. "This way, they don't need legislation, and they achieve some of the same goals," Wilson says.

Critics say such individual deals allow policymakers to avoid accountability for important decisions that affect Medicaid beneficiaries. Instead, they argue, federal and state governments should develop more uniform policies. But state officials and some Republican leaders say each state is different and that experimentation allows legislatures to tailor programs to their individual populations.

In any case, most policymakers agree the current growth of the program should be addressed. Enacted in 1965, Medicaid has become the second-most-expensive domestic-entitlement program after Social Security. And costs will continue to climb as the population ages.

"This is the biggest issue we wrestle with," says Jim Frogue, health-policy director for the American Legislative Exchange Council, which represents state legislators.

Most governors — who, unlike Congress, must balance their budgets each year — say declining tax revenues force cuts in health care for the poor, which otherwise would crowd out demands for schools, roads and other services. After education, Medicaid is the largest drain on state budgets.

The federal government matches about 57 percent of state contributions to Medicaid. The arrangement gives state officials considerable latitude in determining eligibility standards, payment rates and covered services.

"We have to rethink the entire Medicaid program from the ground up," says former Rep. Newt Gingrich, R-Ga., who tried in 1995 as Speaker of the House to convert Medicaid from an open-ended entitlement program into fixed block grants. "There's far too much centralization . . . and we need to give states more flexibility to solve problems." The central question for conservatives like Gingrich is whether policymakers can provide better services to beneficiaries at lower costs. "It's not a question of hurting the poor but of getting better outcomes," Gingrich adds.

But advocates for the poor say that as states curb costs, the Medicaid safety net will deteriorate for low-income people, who have few other options for health coverage. They also say the nation cannot afford to allow more people to become uninsured or underinsured.

Losing insurance can have grave consequences. The Institute of Medicine reported recently that as many as 18,000 uninsured Americans die prematurely from treatable conditions, often because they delay checkups. And many of the uninsured do not have a primary physician, so they go to hospital emergency rooms — the most expensive form of care — further driving up costs. [8]

"Medicaid cannot be cut back to any significant degree without enormous harm," says Ron Pollack, executive director of Families USA, a liberal consumer-rights group. "The president is hell-bent on converting Medicaid to a block grant that would reduce federal and state spending and, in the process, push people into the ranks of the uninsured. That is going to be a huge battleground if the president is re-elected."

Given the polarization on the issue, enacting a legislative overhaul would be a challenge. The Bush administration is more likely to persuade individual states, one at a time, to accept federal caps in exchange for more freedom from federal regulations, according to many experts. "It makes sense for a lot of governors," says Thomas A. Scully, who recently resigned as administrator of the Centers for Medicare and Medicaid Services (CMS) and is now a health care consultant. "I'm sure you'll see a lot more of this."

Most policymakers agree on one thing: Controlling Medicaid costs while protecting the health care of the nation's needy is a daunting task. The program is more complex than Medicare, which cushions America's seniors from skyrocketing health costs. And the populations served by Medicaid are significantly more diverse than the seniors served by Medicare.

Moreover, each of the 56 state and territorial programs has been crafted from a series of local financial trade-offs, political compromises and individualized public demands. As a result, Medicaid benefits vary widely from state to state.

In addition, analysts agree that the current system should be more stable, instead of letting coverage decisions fluctuate wildly depending on budget conditions.

"We need to stabilize coverage so we're not giving it and jerking it back, because it really affects people's lives in the most basic ways," says Georgetown University researcher Cindy Mann, a former Medicaid official during the Clinton administration.

As Congress and the states consider revamping Medicaid, here are some of the questions being debated:

Medicaid Long-Term Care Costs Soar

Medicaid costs for long-term "institutional" care almost doubled from 1991 to 2001. As the baby boomers begin joining the ranks of the elderly, costs are expected to rise even more.

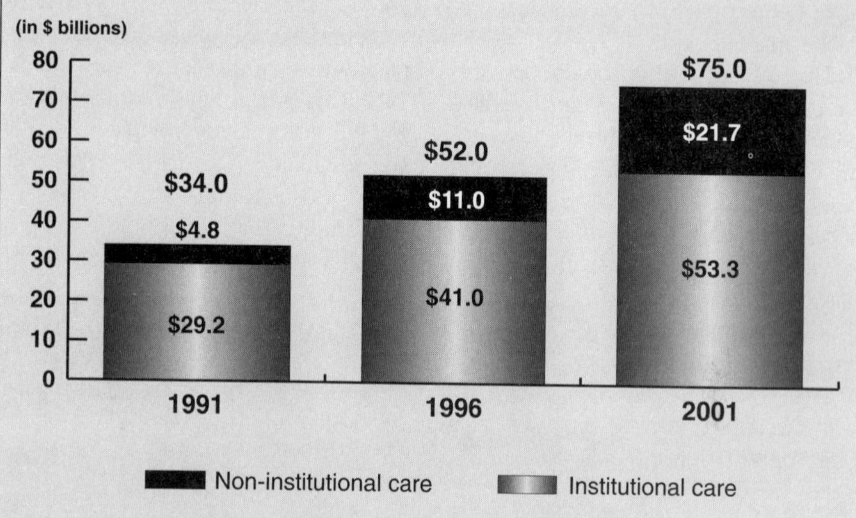

Source: Kaiser Commission on Medicaid and the Uninsured; Health Care Financing Administration

Should the federal government cap Medicaid spending?

Even before it was created, Medicaid generated debates about the most equitable way to offer medical care to low-income people — arguments that have been revived by recent state cutbacks in Medicaid.

Liberals argue that low-income citizens are entitled to standard medical benefits to protect their health. If spending were capped, they say, states would face difficulties when revenue fell or costs rose and would then have to consider cuts in services that people had come to expect.

The argument for capping Medicaid grants is consistent with the conservative philosophy of giving states freedom from federal rules and regulations as a way to reduce their dependence on Washington. According to this argument, states would be able to experiment to find the best solutions for their unique populations, the most effective innovations could serve as models for other states, and states would not have to follow rules that were not relevant for their citizens. Many governors say they could find more cost-effective ways of doing business if there were not so many federal rules.

For example, they may want to test a practice in a limited area before implementing it statewide. They also say that they could cover a wider range of people than is generally allowed.

Under the current system, Medicaid coverage depends on a complicated set of categories, based roughly on old welfare classifications, which have evolved into a confusing, arbitrary and, in some cases, even discriminatory patchwork system. Indeed, Medicaid's complex eligibility rules disqualify a significant number of people living below the federal poverty level.

Meanwhile, about one-third of current Medicaid beneficiaries fall into optional beneficiary groups created when state coffers were bulging in the 1990s. Policymakers now are scrutinizing these generally less needy people to see if their eligibility should be curtailed. [9]

The Bush administration wants to cap funding for the optional category in order to slow the growth of Medicaid spending. As an incentive, states would get more Medicaid funding during the first few years of a 10-year spending plan, but less in the final years.

But governors, even some Republicans, are reluctant to sign on to the plan because of the declining federal contributions. In the face of resistance from governors and lawmakers, the administration — preoccupied with efforts to add a prescription drug benefit to Medicare — has not pushed its plan aggressively.

AFP Photo/Paul J. Richards

More than 200 disabled citizens block traffic near the White House on May 13, 2002, to demand that President Bush expand Medicaid to cover in-home care for the disabled. With nursing-home care about three times as costly as in-home care, state Medicaid programs now increasingly cover in-home and community-based services, such as adult day-care centers.

Instead, the administration has been pursuing the approach via negotiations with individual states, such as California, Connecticut, Florida and New Hampshire.

In Connecticut, for instance, before he resigned on June 21, Republican Gov. John G. Rowland had been negotiating with federal officials over a waiver that would give more-generous coverage to the neediest low-income children, seniors and people with disabilities, but would reduce the services provided to poor single adults. But the legislature blocked Rowland's plan after advocates for Medicaid recipients said they feared the flexibility the state would have been given under the block grant would allow it to eliminate services for some beneficiaries, or coverage altogether.

But Rowland's support for capping spending is no surprise. In 2003, he and two other GOP governors — Colorado's Bill Owens and Florida's Jeb Bush — wrote to Congress supporting capped grants. "It is time to review and fundamentally rewrite the nation's Medicaid law," they said, suggesting that Medicaid "move away from [individual] entitlement without responsibility." The three also proposed that Medicaid programs operate more like private managed-care plans and that patients receive more "choices" in their coverage. [10]

Florida's recently passed fiscal 2005 state budget allows Gov. Bush to waive many federal rules if the CMS agrees. State health officials are discussing with federal policymakers a wide range of far-reaching changes.

For instance, Florida health officials have suggested they would probably

Administration Accused of Sidestepping Congress on Waivers

Members of Congress cannot stand seeing their legislative authority bypassed — especially if it leads to profound changes in a federal program. But many in Congress fear the Bush administration is using its executive powers to do just that.

Unable to get Congress to adopt controversial caps on some portions of federal Medicaid spending, the administration has been negotiating privately with individual states, granting them waivers from federal regulations if they agree to a limit on federal contributions to their state Medicaid programs. Some members of Congress say such agreements could undermine entitlements guaranteed to anyone eligible for Medicaid, fundamentally altering the program.

"If these waivers are put in place behind closed doors without the proper public input and congressional oversight, and if they are used to advance policies that would profoundly change the program, some of society's most helpless members will suffer," said Max Baucus, the senior Democrat on the Senate Finance Committee, after a June 16 meeting with Mark McClellan, administrator of the Centers for Medicare and Medicaid Services (CMS), which oversees the two programs.

Waivers were also used by the Clinton administration, but critics say the Bush administration is using them in a more far-reaching way than was ever intended. Opponents argue that because the Bush administration has been unable to convince Congress to agree to cap Medicaid spending, the administration is seeking to circumvent lawmakers and persuade individual states to accept caps.

Baucus and Senate Finance Committee Chairman Charles E. Grassley, R-Iowa, are considering holding a hearing on the waiver negotiations. "These proposals, and similar ones, if approved and implemented, could potentially make fundamental changes to the Medicaid program in ways that Congress did not anticipate or intend," Grassley and Baucus wrote to McClellan on June 16. "We strongly believe that, over time, these changes could have far-reaching implications, and debate over these changes should include the Congress."

The pair also has asked the General Accounting Office to study the issue of waivers, and Baucus has introduced a bill to limit the scope of waivers.

To be sure, some members of Congress are strongly supportive of the move to cap spending and see no problem with winning caps through waivers of federal law. Republican leaders in the House say they are happy to allow states to experiment with caps, as some states may be planning to do.

California, Connecticut, Florida and New Hampshire — among others — have been privately discussing changes to their Medicaid programs with CMS officials. Some of the states are facing scrutiny from CMS on other issues, such as questionable financing tactics known as "intergovernmental transfers." Some critics suggest that the federal government will be more lenient on states' use of intergovernmental transfers if the states will agree to caps on federal spending.

The waiver issue is expected to gain more attention in the coming months as the states move forward with their proposals.

In California, for instance, Republican Gov. Arnold Schwarzenegger is expected to unveil on Aug. 2 an outline of his waiver proposal, which he hopes to submit for CMS approval in September. The governor must get state legislative approval before it is implemented.

Discussion drafts of the proposal suggest that it will be a "comprehensive redesign" of the California Medicaid program. Options under consideration include adding $20 copays for each hospital admission for adults and, for adults who earn between $13,965 and $18,620, a $20 monthly premium. Another option would reduce benefits such as chiropractic care.

Members of Congress will be keeping a closer eye on the issue as the waivers become public. The Senate Finance Committee is asking McClellan to provide more information on the waiver process this summer.

accept five-year capped allotments if they could avoid federal requirements. Bush is considering proposing legislation that would cap Medicaid costs as a proportion of the state budget — with a ceiling of 20 percent, for example, down from the current 22.4 percent. Among other things, the state also wants to impose a lifetime cap on the number of years beneficiaries can receive the subsidized health coverage.

Proponents of capped grants point out that the popular State Children's Health Insurance Program, known as S-CHIP, is a joint state-federal block grant program rather than an entitlement program like Medicaid. Created in the 1997 Balanced Budget Act, it provides subsidized health insurance for low-income families with children who don't qualify for Medicaid because their incomes are too high.

But opponents of capped grants note that due to funding limits, several states — including Colorado and Florida — stopped enrolling children who would have been eligible if the money were available. In Florida, for instance, up to 110,000 children were put on a waiting list earlier this year until the legislature provided enough money to cover 90,000 of them. [11]

Some experts say the debate being played out in Florida — and the way that state is handling its S-CHIP program — may represent the future of Medicaid if it were to become a capped grant program. Under Florida's new law, for instance, fewer children will be eligible for S-CHIP. Children will not

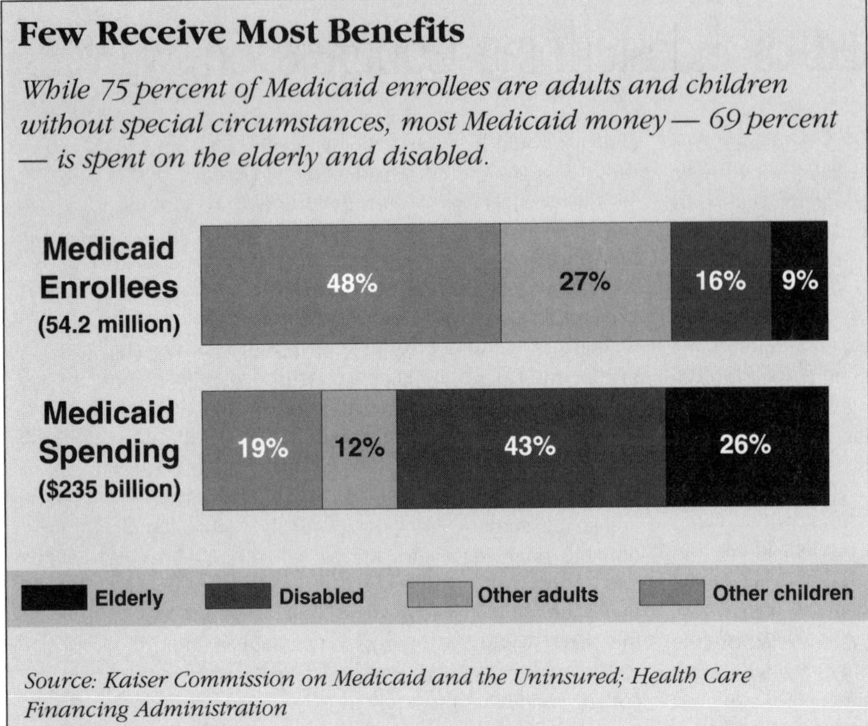

Few Receive Most Benefits

While 75 percent of Medicaid enrollees are adults and children without special circumstances, most Medicaid money — 69 percent — is spent on the elderly and disabled.

Source: Kaiser Commission on Medicaid and the Uninsured; Health Care Financing Administration

be covered, for example, if their families are eligible for any type of employer-sponsored insurance — even if it is inadequate for their needs. In addition, only two enrollment periods a year will be permitted, during which coverage will be available on a first-come, first-served basis, and the state will stop tracking how many children are turned away if there are not enough slots for all of them.

Republicans say slowing the growth of the children's program is responsible and necessary, and that allowing it to continue to grow could be a financial disaster. "The discipline the legislature has brought to this program protects the long-term viability" of the program, Gov. Bush said when it passed in March.

Echoing the debate in Congress, Florida Democrats challenged those assertions. "What could be more fiscally responsible than to provide health care for the children of the working poor in Florida?" asked state Rep. Suzanne Kosmas, of New Smyrna Beach. "It strikes me as fiscally responsible, and allows parents to be working and productive and allows these young people to go to school healthy, graduate . . . and [stay] out of the social services." [12]

"By shifting fiscal responsibility to states, the Medicaid block grant encourages states to limit their liability by capping enrollment, cutting benefits and increasing cost-sharing for millions of low-income people," Rep. Frank Pallone Jr., D-N.J., told a House Energy and Commerce Health Subcommittee hearing on March 18.

But federal officials counter that a capped grant system would put the future of each state's Medicaid program in the hands of local politicians and policymakers, making them accountable for any changes.

Should Medicare, rather than Medicaid, cover long-term care?

About 13 million people in the United States, or about 4 percent of the population, at some point in their lives need long-term care — such as home health services or care in a nursing home — to help with basic activities, such as eating and bathing. About 56 percent of those are over 65.

Although Medicare provides health insurance for the elderly and the disabled, it only pays for short-term stays in nursing facilities, such as after surgery. Medicaid pays for longer-term care for seniors.

Thus, Medicaid finances about 48 percent of all long-term care in the United States, making it the largest single purchaser of such services. For the 1.6 million Americans who use nursing homes, Medicaid pays for 70 percent of beds, according to former CMS administrator Scully.

But most governors, regardless of party, say the federal government should pay for long-term care for seniors. While Congress has not addressed the issue, some state officials are seeking a compromise in which the federal government would pay for the 7 million poor seniors who are old enough to qualify for Medicare, but who are also poor enough to receive additional benefits covered by Medicaid.

The issue will become more urgent as the population ages. In seven years, the 77 million baby boomers will begin to turn 65, and about six of every 10 Americans age 65 or older will use some type of long-term care services at some point. [13]

"Much of the increase in Medicaid spending over the past 10 years can be attributed to the ever-increasing costs of providing long-term care," said Scully in a 2003 congressional hearing.

Medicaid projects that it will spend approximately $90 billion in federal and state dollars on long-term services in fiscal 2004, with $49.1 billion going to nursing home care. And the costs are only expected to rise. [14]

"For state policymakers, long-term care for our seniors is at the center of a very difficult debate on exploding health care costs going on in virtually every statehouse in the nation," said Dirk Kempthorne, R-Idaho, chairman of the National Governors Association (NGA). Kempthorne has launched an initiative, called "A Lifetime of Health and Dignity," to publicize long-term care issues. [15]

Although many Americans think of Medicaid as the provider of health care for poor families, 70 percent of its budget pays for the more expensive services needed by the 26 percent of Medicaid beneficiaries who are elderly, blind or disabled. [16]

Governors insist they cannot continue contributing so much of their budgets to long-term care needs, noting that it is not just the poor who are relying on Medicaid to pay for these services. A middle-class person can become eligible for Medicaid-subsidized long-term care once he has spent down his family's resources for medical care until his bank accounts and stock holdings total no more than $2,000.

"It is . . . unacceptable for Medicaid to be the only long-term care program in this country," reads a plank in the Medicaid Reform Principles Policy of the NGA. The policy also states that the "federal government should assume full responsibility for the acute, primary, long-term and pharmaceutical care of the dual eligibles, individuals who are enrolled in the Medicare program but because of their low income, are also eligible for the Medicaid program."

But if Medicare does not begin to pick up more of the costs for long-term care, governors hope the public will better plan for their future long-term care needs. Kempthorne and other governors, along with the White House, are encouraging people to buy long-term care insurance. In some states, tax breaks are available for consumers who purchase the plans. The federal government is subsidizing long-term care insurance for its workers, and about five states allow people who buy state-approved long-term care insurance policies to qualify for Medicaid if necessary without "spending down" their life savings.

However, private insurance is still paying only about 13 percent of long-term care costs, according to CMS. "Private insurance hasn't done much on long-term care," Diane Rowland, executive director of the Kaiser Commission on Medicaid and the Uninsured, says. "So we should discuss what the role of Medicare should be in providing long-term care."

The alternative to shifting the costs of long-term care to Medicare is finding less expensive ways to meet long-term care needs. For example, the care for frail nursing home patients is more expensive than that for people who can remain in their homes. A year's stay in a nursing home costs roughly $57,000, and the average nursing home stay is about two-and-a-half years. Yet care at home costs only about $15,000 a year. [17]

Redesigning how people receive long-term care will take time, but the trend is toward more home or community-based care, such as home health services, assisted-living facilities or adult day-care centers, which can give family caregivers a break during the day.

In 1991, institutional facilities received 86 percent of Medicaid spending for long-term care, with 14 percent going to home or community care. Ten years later, institutional care represented only 71 percent of Medicaid's long-term care spending. [18] (*See graph, p. 593.*)

The trend was accelerated by a 1999 Supreme Court decision, *Olmstead v. L.C.*, which found that individuals who wanted to receive care at home or in less restrictive community settings should be able to do so. [19]

A year ago, the administration created a demonstration program that allows individuals in nursing homes or other institutions to take the money set aside for their care and use it in other settings. In a few states, Medicaid programs have experimented with "cash and counseling" projects that allow patients to cash out the funding that would be provided for their care and use it to hire people, including family members, to offer assistance.

Supporters of consumer-directed care say individuals, not the government, should make decisions about their own care. But critics fear beneficiaries might not be able to make the best judgments about their care, might abuse the system or could use the benefit to pay relatives for services they previously offered for free. Governors wonder whether Medicaid costs would rise.

Some officials believe at-home care will dominate future long-term care services. Government budget writers are hoping that home and community-based care can provide a solution to the problem of escalating long-term care costs.

"This issue is only going to grow in importance," Frogue of the American Legislative Exchange Council says. "This and other Medicaid issues are the ones that [legislators] understand least, and long-term care is growing on autopilot, so they will have to deal with it in very forceful ways."

Do Medicaid cuts affect private insurance?

Medicaid spending affects not only those who receive it but also consumers throughout the health care system.

Most significantly, Medicaid pays for many of the most expensive patients in society, such as people with disabilities and the elderly. If those patients were forced into private insurance, premiums for other members of those insured pools would probably increase, according to many health industry experts.

"By taking on that coverage, Medicaid has played an important role in holding down premiums for the rest of us," Rowland of the Kaiser Commission says.

Additionally, cuts in Medicaid could force hospitals, doctors and other providers to charge privately insured people more to make up the lost income. Although some economists say such cost-shifting should not happen, in theory, many practitioners and policymakers believe otherwise. "[If] reimbursement rates are cut, that cost shift has to be pushed onto private payers because there's nowhere else to go," Frogue says. "And that is a significant factor in rising health insurance premiums."

However, some economists vigorously debate whether such cost-shifting occurs, and, if it does, how it happens. Others question whether private insurers are forced to charge more to compensate for low government reimbursements in programs like Medicaid and Medicare.

"Our data provide no evidence that physicians respond to Medicare payment reductions by shifting costs to their privately insured patients," a 1996 study found. While other research had found that hospitals may shift costs, the study noted, "several forces combine to make this type of cost-shifting either difficult or unattractive" among physicians. For instance, it said, physicians already charge their private-insurance patients as much as possible; doctors facing competition wish to keep prices lower than their competitors; doctors may face resistance from insurers; and doctors may have other ways to increase revenues when public funding through Medicare or Medicaid declines. [20]

And some health-policy experts say Medicaid's impact should be considered by its impact on taxpayers, not patients. If Medicaid spending is high, then all taxpayers will have to contribute to its demands.

"The problem is that you create this program that grows exponentially without any curbing of growth of funding," Owcharenko of the Heritage Foundation says. "Medicaid is one of the biggest cost drivers for the government, and those are taxpayer dollars. What are you going to do with the unfunded liability of the program? You just can't have growth rates that high, and a program that is an open-ended check."

Others say it is only natural that when large programs such as Medicaid and Medicare pay less, the providers would have to charge others more. "Today, with the return of double-digit health care inflation . . . [h]ospital margins are being squeezed from all sides," the journal *Health Affairs* reported last fall. [21] "With increasing frequency and to a greater extent, the individual consumer is experiencing cost-shifting." The paper focused on Medicare payments, but its findings could be applied to Medicaid as well.

Even though it does not pay providers as generously as Medicare or private insurance, Medicaid financing is an important component in the mix of public and private funding received by medical providers. And health care providers say it is better than receiving nothing to care for the uninsured.

"Our resources are stretched piano-wire thin," says Art Kellerman, an emergency room physician at Grady Memorial Hospital in Atlanta and the co-chairman of a committee charged by the Institute of Medicine (IOM) to study the uninsured. "If Medicaid is cut more, we will be crushed like bugs."

Moreover, if providers are forced to limit or cut services overall because of lower Medicaid reimbursement rates, it could affect the quality of care for everyone else in a community. "The closure of a regional trauma center or a reduction in its scope of services puts the health of everyone in a community — whether insured or uninsured — at risk," the IOM noted recently. [22]

"All the financial bones are connected in this body, and if Medicaid is sore, that gets transmitted to other programs," said Joseph Antos, a former Medicare official who is now a policy expert at the conservative American Enterprise Institute. "We all are affected."

For instance, Kellerman pointed out, like many other regional trauma centers, Grady is the only hospital in Georgia equipped to address many life-threatening injuries. If a terrorist incident were to strike, Grady would be most likely to handle it. But with limited resources, the hospital could become overwhelmed in a crisis, and other hospitals would be even less prepared to help.

Even in less dramatic circumstances, Medicaid funding can affect the care — and the pocketbooks — of the privately insured, experts say. Cuts in Medicaid would lead uninsured people to seek care in more costly settings, such as hospital emergency rooms, which must stabilize patients without regard to their ability to pay. A high amount of uncompensated emergency-room care can lead to higher health-care costs for people with insurance.

Kellerman and other policy experts say that no matter what one's perspective about the solutions for Medicaid, it is clear that its problems affect all of society.

"This is not just an issue for poor folks," he said. "This affects the middle class. Everyone's health care is at risk unless we sort out this very messy, dysfunctional system." ■

BACKGROUND

Charity Care

In the early 20th century, charity care for the poor varied widely from state to state and even from city to city. The nation would debate for decades whether to establish a national medical-care program for all — a concept that was never wholly embraced.

An early movement by a group of economists known as the American Association for Labor Legislation lobbied

Continued on p. 601

Chronology

Early 1900s
Low-income and elderly residents live in almshouses, poor farms and homes for the aged.

1935
Social Security Act creates Old Age Assistance to bolster incomes of needy elderly.

1954
Amendments to the Hill-Burton Act allow federal grants to be used to build nursing homes.

1960s *Medical assistance for the poor evolves from largely charity-run care to limited government aid.*

1960
Kerr-Mills Act provides federal-state matching funds for medically indigent, including those in skilled nursing facilities.

1965
Social Security Act authorizes creation of Medicaid, to provide health-care services to low-income children deprived of parental support, their caretaker relatives, the elderly, the blind and those with disabilities.

1967
Congress establishes comprehensive health-services benefit for all Medicaid children under 21.

1970s *Federal and state support of health care for the poor expands.*

1972
Although some states choose to keep their more limited eligibility rules, Congress allows broader Medicaid eligibility standards for elderly, blind and disabled.

1980s *Conservatives attempt to rein in Medicaid, but Congress adds more benefits.*

1981
Federal government allows states to receive waivers that provide federal matching grants for home and community-based care. States are required to provide additional payments to hospitals that treat a disproportionate share of low-income patients.

1986
States are allowed to provide Medicaid coverage for pregnant women and infants with incomes equaling 100 percent of federal poverty level (FPL).

1988
Federal government mandates Medicaid coverage for pregnant women and infants with incomes up to 100 percent of FPL.

1989
Medicaid coverage expanded to include pregnant women and children under 6 in families with incomes up to 133 percent of FPL.

1990s *Congress severs the tie between welfare and Medicaid.*

1990
Congress increases Medicaid eligibility age from 6 to 18 and requires drug companies to allow state Medicaid programs to pay the same discount prices enjoyed by large purchasers like managed-care companies and the Department of Veterans Affairs.

1996
Congress replaces welfare entitlement program with Temporary Assistance for Needy Families block grants, severing link between welfare and Medicaid.

1997
Congress creates State Children's Health Insurance Program (S-CHIP). The federal government establishes new managed-care options and requirements for states.

1999
Ticket to Work and Work Incentives Improvement Act of 1999 expands availability of Medicare and Medicaid for certain disabled beneficiaries who return to work.

2000s *Economic downturn and tax cuts force states to grapple with difficult fiscal choices.*

2001
Governors begin cutting Medicaid.

2003
Medicare prescription drug law federalizes drug coverage for dual-eligible seniors but requires states to continue contributing to costs of drug benefits. . . . President Bush in May signs law providing $10 billion in temporary additional payments for state Medicaid programs.

June 2004
Temporary additional Medicaid payments expire.

States Wary of New Drug Bill

Congressional lawmakers predicted the Medicare prescription drug law passed last summer would ease the states' responsibility for "dual eligibles" — low-income seniors who qualify for both Medicare and Medicaid.

But state officials say the new law will provide little new money, force them to take on new tasks and pose difficult choices. [1]

"It sounds on the surface like a good thing, but there are concerns," says Christine Rackers, director of the Division of Medical Services in Missouri.

State officials are particularly disappointed that the law will offer scant new resources. "We expect no initial savings to the state," says Lynn Read, director of Oregon's Office of Medical Assistance Programs.

When discussions began over providing some drug coverage for seniors under the Medicare program, state officials had hoped the law would require the federal government to pay all the costs for low-income seniors receiving subsidized care under Medicaid. Indeed, many governors supported the Medicare bill because they believed it would reduce state costs dramatically, and both Democrats and Republicans said that was their goal.

But shifting all of those benefits from the states to the federal government was deemed too expensive, so Congress scaled back the federal funding to only cover prescription drugs. Now, Medicare will take over the state Medicaid drug programs for low-income seniors, covering a portion of the cost of the drugs, but the states will still be required to contribute almost as much as they did before. In fact, states will face the unusual prospect of sending funds back to the federal government in a sort of reverse block grant.

In 2006, the first year Medicare drug benefits will be available, states will pay 90 percent of what they were paying under their old state-run programs. That contribution will decline over time, but at the end of a 10-year phase-down period, the law will still require states to pay 75 percent of their previous costs.

But many state officials doubt they will see any savings at all, because the law also adds on several new duties, plus publicity for the new drug benefits may help more elderly people realize that they are eligible for Medicaid health-care coverage. In addition, some state officials criticize the way the formula for calculating their contribution is determined.

State officials also wonder what they will do if Medicare offers less-generous drug benefits than current state coverage under existing Medicaid programs. The list of drugs Medicare will cover has not been set, but many advocates for the poor worry that it will be more limited than the current state programs.

"We won't get any federal money for providing coverage" above the basic Medicare benefit, Rackers says. "What are we going to do? Just let it go?"

PhotoDisc

The federal government is taking over state Medicaid drug programs for low-income seniors, but the states still will be required to contribute almost as much as they did before.

State officials also fear that they cannot afford the additional administrative tasks required by the new law, such as determining eligibility for benefits. Furthermore, state Medicaid officials worry that the law could reduce their leverage in negotiating discounted drug prices for their other Medicaid populations because poor seniors will now get drug benefits through Medicare, shrinking the pool of recipients for Medicaid drug benefits and diminishing states' negotiating power.

State officials fear the law could raise costs in other ways as well. For instance, it would raise deductibles for doctors' visits. That also would increase costs for states, because state Medicaid programs fill in the gaps in Medicare to cover costs such as deductibles for low-income seniors who cannot afford them.

But federal policymakers say the states should count their blessings.

"The states wanted a huge dump truck full of money, and they ended up with a pickup truck," says Thomas A. Scully, former administrator of the Centers for Medicare and Medicaid Services. "This is a win for the states."

State officials remain unconvinced. "We'll be watching very carefully as this goes forward," says Joy Johnson Wilson, a health-care analyst at the National Conference of State Legislatures.

---

1 For background on prescription drug program, see Adriel Bettelheim, "Medicare Reform," *The CQ Researcher*, Aug. 22, 2003, pp. 673-696.

Continued from p. 598

state officials to pass health benefits and workman's compensation for employees, but standards for medical benefits were not adopted.

Ever since those early debates, American opinion has been split about how to protect the poor from catastrophic medical bills. Questions about the moral obligation of society to provide care for its most vulnerable citizens have been complicated by the desire to encourage individual responsibility and self-reliance.

Many of the issues under discussion decades ago are still debated today: Are subsidies for the needy fair to those who pay for them? Would the lack of a strong safety net end up indirectly costing society as a whole?

Library of Congress

President Lyndon B. Johnson's Great Society program championed the creation of Medicare in 1965, with Medicaid added to the legislation almost as an afterthought.

Such questions were debated during consideration of the Social Security Act of 1935. President Franklin D. Roosevelt considered proposing a national health care system but retreated in the face of political opposition. After the Social Security system was created, the debate intensified over two divergent visions for medical care — a universal or a piecemeal approach. Following Roosevelt's death in 1945, President Harry S Truman tried but failed to persuade a more conservative Congress to pass national health care. [23]

Subsequently, the federal government created two primary grant programs to provide states with aid for the poor. One benefited welfare recipients; the second helped those ineligible for public aid but still unable to cope with high medical bills.

In 1960, as seniors became a political force and medical costs continued to rise, Congress passed a law seeking to improve medical care for poor seniors. It was written by two Democrats, Rep. Wilbur Mills of Arkansas, chairman of the House Ways and Means Committee, and Sen. Robert Kerr of Oklahoma. By the end of 1962, 28 states had Kerr-Mills programs.

The 1960 law set precedents that were later reflected in Medicaid: It provided federal funds to states that covered needy seniors who earned too much to receive public aid but still could not afford their medical care; it let states administer benefits and control costs under broad federal guidelines; and it offered open-ended federal spending.

Kerr-Mills was "the most important predecessor" to Medicaid, says Andy Schneider, a health-care consultant who served as a Democratic health-care policy aide from 1979 to 1996. Kerr-Mills also boosted efforts to offer health care to all seniors, paving the way for Medicare.

Because the Kerr-Mills program was administered as a public aid rather than a health-care program, Medicaid has suffered, in the public's view, from its historical tie to welfare.

Medicaid Is Born

In 1965, seniors' rising demands for a more comprehensive health-insurance program led to the creation of Medicare, with Medicaid added almost as an afterthought to the legislation. [24]

Democrats — who in the 1964 elections retained the White House and picked up seats in Congress — used their majority status to expand government-financed health care. The Social Security Amendments of 1965 expanded the Kerr-Mills program.

How Medicaid Expenses Have Grown

Overall Medicaid spending rose about 13 percent from 2000-2002, but the cost of prescription drugs, home care and outpatient/clinic care jumped even more.

Average Annual Growth in Medicaid Expenditures, 2000-2002

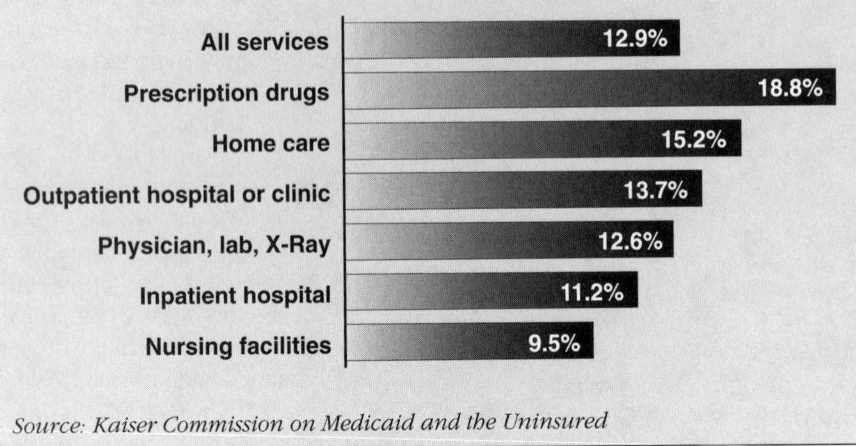

Source: Kaiser Commission on Medicaid and the Uninsured

In contrast to the more prescriptive benefits outlined by the federal legislation for Medicare beneficiaries, coverage for Medicaid beneficiaries was left partly to the states. The program was designed as a catchall system to assist a wide range of low-income people — although not everyone who was poor was eligible. As in the current system, Medicaid was available primarily to families with children, the elderly poor and the disabled. Most single men and women without children are not eligible unless their incomes are extremely low.

States could choose whether to join the new program, and, if so, how to implement it. They were required to cover a core group of recipients — such as anyone receiving welfare — but they could choose whether to cover others.

In addition, states joining the program had to offer at least five basic physician and hospitalization services, but they could choose to offer other services, such as dental care, prescription drugs, home health-care services, vision care or specialty care like podiatry and physical therapy. Within a year of enactment, 19 states had Medicaid programs.

Soon, policymakers were arguing about the intent of the law and who should be covered. Rising medical costs sparked a debate about the scope of the program after it quickly became apparent that Medicaid would be far more expensive than the $238 million annual cost projected in 1965.

Congress stepped in to change the program through the Social Security Amendments of 1967. On one hand, some new benefits were added, notably, the requirement that needy children receive "early and periodic screening, diagnosis and treatment." But the law also limited participation in the program by capping cash assistance for each state based on income-eligibility levels for the medically needy.

Additional limits were added through federal regulations written to implement the law. In 1969, for instance, federal rules admonished states to "safeguard against unnecessary utilization."

Even with the new limits, some states could not afford Medicaid. In 1965, health-care payments made up less than a third of welfare budgets, but four years later they had climbed above 40 percent.

Era of Expansion

In 1972, the federal government stepped in and took over state-administered public-assistance programs for the elderly and disabled. The new Supplemental Security Income (SSI) program became the primary way in which those persons became eligible for Medicaid.

Five years later, hoping to raise the profile of Medicaid in possible preparation for proposing national health insurance, President Jimmy Carter created the Health Care Financing Administration (HCFA) to consolidate oversight of Medicare and Medicaid. He also sought to broaden the Medicaid program in 1979, but his plan died in Congress. [25]

During the 1980s, President Ronald Reagan tried to shrink the program, but almost every year congressional Democrats expanded it. In 1981, Reagan proposed capping Medicaid growth at 5 percent a year, even though it was projected to grow 15 percent annually. Reagan also sought to consolidate 25 health-service grants into two main block grants for the states. Republicans said they wanted to give governors the ability to experiment with benefits and try to impose fiscal discipline. [26]

But the effort was stymied after protests from governors and health-care groups, who persuaded Congress to scale back the block grant proposals and reject the spending cap. Reagan did succeed in passing changes to welfare that effectively limited Medicaid.

He also won a cut in federal matching rates from fiscal years 1982 through 1984.

In 1984, Democrats joined with a few Republicans to ensure medical coverage for low-income women who were pregnant for the first time and poor pregnant women in two-parent unemployed households. The following year, Congress dropped the requirement that the families be unemployed. The law also required states to cover children up to age 5 if they met state welfare guidelines. [27]

In 1988, House Democrats helped pass several Medicaid expansions, including a requirement for states to cover pregnant women and babies under the federal poverty level and a measure that would protect the spouses of nursing home residents. In 1989, Congress required states to cover pregnant women and children under 6 who earned 133 percent or less of the federal poverty level. And in 1990, House Democrats used the budget bill to gradually raise the eligibility age from 6 to 18.

The 1990 budget reconciliation bill also created, over the objections of large drug companies, the Medicaid drug rebate program, which requires them to provide the same rebates to state Medicaid programs that they routinely give to large purchasers, such as big managed-care companies and the Department of Veterans Affairs. [28]

Back to Block Grants

When Republicans took control of Congress in 1995, they sought to stem the ballooning costs of Medicaid and control the burgeoning federal budget within seven years. House Republicans announced a sweeping proposal to end the Medicaid entitlement program, with its open-ended federal spending obligations, and replace it with capped grants.

The Republicans' MediGrant proposal would have replaced the federal eligibility and coverage entitlement with broad block grant guidelines. States would have gained free rein to design their own benefit and coverage plans. The plan also would have cut Medicaid by $163.4 billion from projected levels over seven years, and federal spending would have been limited to $791 billion over seven years — an average annual increase of 5.2 percent. The GOP proposal passed both houses of Congress, but President Bill Clinton vetoed it. Democrats, led by Clinton, balked at the cuts in spending and at the loss of the federal "entitlement," which guarantees coverage if a person meets specific criteria. [29]

The Republican Congress did make some significant changes to Medicaid in the 1996 welfare bill. It severed the traditional ties between welfare and Medicaid, so recipients in the new time-limited welfare system would no longer be automatically enrolled in Medicaid. The law also banned legal aliens who entered the United States after enactment of the law from obtaining any federal aid based on need, such as Medicaid, until they had been in the country for five years. However, some of those cuts were restored in the 1997 Balanced Budget Act. [30]

The 1997 act cut funds for Medicaid and allowed states to steer beneficiaries to managed-care plans without getting a waiver from federal rules. But it also expanded coverage for disabled persons and created a new block grant program, S-CHIP, for uninsured children in families with income slightly higher than Medicaid eligibility levels. It provides a higher federal matching rate than Medicaid. States can use the funds to expand their Medicaid programs or create new standalone programs.

Former House Speaker Gingrich today bemoans the fact that he and his fellow Republicans in the 1990s were not bolder. "We didn't put as much intellectual effort into Medicaid as we did in Medicare. We were significantly bolder and more reform-oriented in Medicare," Gingrich says. "In retrospect, I would've applied more of these ideas to Medicaid. The core principle is to get power back to states and increase experimentation." ■

CURRENT SITUATION

Reducing Costs

Now the Bush administration is trying to revive some of Gingrich's ideas, but with skeptical governors and a polarized Congress, few expect Medicaid to be overhauled in the next year. But if the Republicans maintain control of both houses of Congress and the White House after the fall elections, lawmakers are likely to show heightened interest in the issue.

"It's in crisis," said Georgetown University's Mann. "Changes are going to happen in the next few years, and some are needed."

To ease states' Medicaid burdens, lawmakers at both the state and federal levels are investigating new ways to reduce the program's costs. The economy is improving and state revenues are climbing, according to the National Conference of State Legislatures (NCSL) and the National Association of State Budget Officers (NASBO). However, total Medicaid spending is still expected to grow an average of 8.2 percent in fiscal 2004 — slower than the nearly 12 percent it grew in 2002, but still a significant increase.

That growth has fueled long-raging debates about the structure of the program, the proper balance between social responsibilities and funding concerns and the level of appropriate federal oversight for Medicaid.

"Medicaid is such a budget driver that some major changes have to occur," says Scott Pattison, executive director of NASBO.

The administration's 2003 proposal to transform part of Medicaid into a voluntary, capped grant program would have provided specified funding per person for chronic and acute care for the one-third of the Medicaid population that are optional beneficiaries — recipients that states choose to cover over and above those they are required to cover.

So far, Congress and the governors have strongly resisted the proposal, suggesting that such an overhaul would not come easily. Just as the Medicare debate of 2003 demonstrated, the current polarization in Congress has made major social policy legislation very difficult to enact, because the two parties come at the issue from very different perspectives.

"The White House and some Republicans would very much like it to be a more defined program and cap the amount spent," says Gail Wilensky, now a health care consultant at Project Hope, who formerly ran the Medicare and Medicaid programs in the first Bush administration. "But this is one of those areas in which there are substantial philosophical divisions. It would be very hard to resolve it without a clear majority in Congress."

Impact on States

Meanwhile, a handful of states already are poised to accept caps on federal spending in order to obtain more flexibility in how they cover the low-income program and what types of people would qualify.

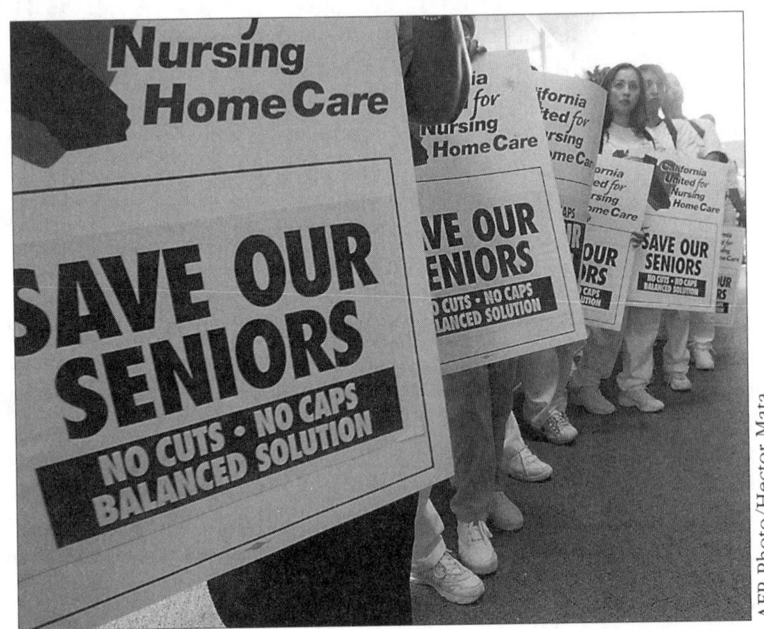

AFP Photo/Hector Mata

Members of a nursing-home caregivers' union in Los Angeles protest in July 2003 over proposed state budget cuts that they said would dramatically reduce health care for the poor.

Medicaid costs have outpaced its resources since 2001. Thus, with each new legislative session, more states have imposed a wider range of cost-control measures. For instance, some states cut benefits for "medical hardware" items — like eyeglasses, hearing aids, dentures and orthotics — or forced recipients to start making co-payments, despite their meager incomes. Some states began limiting the number of prescriptions patients could fill or provided coverage only for certain drugs — usually lower-priced versions — specified on state formulary lists. Other states cut reimbursement rates for providers, causing many doctors to stop seeing new Medicaid patients. Some patients lost coverage altogether.

Texas officials, for instance, reduced the number of pregnant women who could receive coverage. Massachusetts tightened eligibility standards for adults and capped enrollment for people with disabilities. In Washington, officials cut the number of people served and imposed premiums, a $150 deductible and 20 percent copays. [31]

Then in 2003, Congress stepped in to help. Federal lawmakers provided $10 billion in the tax cut legislation, to be divided among the states for Medicaid and $10 billion for other purposes. Many state lawmakers said the cuts in 2004 would have been much worse without the federal assistance.

But that aid ended in June. And not only did the fiscal relief expire, but the Bush administration and Republicans in Congress are calling for tighter control over the flow of federal dollars to the states — even though costs are still climbing.

"There are underlying factors that will continue to drive Medicaid spending to far exceed revenue growth, and this will keep pressure on the states," says Vern Smith, a consultant with Health Management Associates and former Michigan Medicaid director. "State resources are still extremely strained, and it will be some time before revenues are restored to previous levels. This will be an issue around the country for some time."

Continued on p. 606

At Issue:

Should the federal government crack down on Medicaid financing schemes used by the states to shore up their budgets?

REP. HEATHER WILSON, R-N.M.
MEMBER, HOUSE COMMERCE SUBCOMMITTEE ON HEALTH

FROM A STATEMENT BEFORE THE HOUSE ENERGY AND COMMERCE COMMITTEE, MARCH 18, 2004

yes

Medicaid is now the largest health care program in the country. It serves 48 million people and last year had a budget of $280 billion. It's about 7 percent of the federal budget, and it's close to between 15 and 20 percent of most state budgets.

In my view, Rube Goldberg would admire the financing scheme that underpins Medicaid. It's a scheme that's really set up to encourage states to maximize their federal expenditures with accounting tricks and kickback schemes and to have state Medicaid directors focused on what they can do to get the next percentage of a penny of federal match, rather than focusing on how to improve the health care of the people who depend upon Medicaid.

We know states are using upper payment limits and disproportionate share hospital payments for things other than health care [and that] in some cases, they transfer funds to public hospitals and then require those public hospitals to remit those funds [back to state governments] without using them for health care.

The federal match is based on per capita income. And when you have some states pursuing these schemes, that takes dollars from somebody else that needs those dollars to meet their own needs in health care. There are some circumstances where these intergovernmental transfers are completely legitimate ways of local governments contributing to the state and local match. . . . But there are other circumstances where there is an abuse of the Medicaid system. And I think we may need to take action to stop it.

I think also, though, that these tricks are only a symptom of a larger problem. Medicaid's whole financial structure is held together with baling wire and duct tape. And we need to look long term at how we change this structure.

We shouldn't be surprised that states play the game. We wrote the rules of the game. And the rules need to be changed so that the states win when the health of low-income Americans, children, pregnant women, disabled adults and seniors improves.

The system is not set up to improve anybody's health. It's set up to pay claims. And that's a fundamental problem with the financial structure of Medicaid. This system only continues to function because every state has multiple waivers to do something outside of the rules. . . . We need to change the rules. And the time is coming to fundamentally change the program.

REP. SHERROD BROWN, D-OHIO
RANKING MINORITY MEMBER, HOUSE COMMERCE SUBCOMMITTEE ON HEALTH

FROM A STATEMENT BEFORE THE HOUSE ENERGY AND COMMERCE COMMITTEE, MARCH 18, 2004

no

Medicaid coverage is at risk for tens of millions of Americans. What is our response? Rather than focusing on shoring up Medicaid, we focus on ways of cutting more dollars from it. The president's budget cuts $24 billion from Medicaid over the next 10 years. While the details are sketchy, CMS [Centers for Medicare and Medicaid Services] apparently intends to eliminate certain mechanisms states use to finance their share of the Medicaid program.

Previous administrations have worked with Congress and the states to address the misuse of intergovernmental transfers and other financing mechanisms. [As a result,] the opportunity to divert federal funds from Medicaid has been significantly curtailed.

Let's not fool ourselves. If we cut $24 billion from Medicaid . . . we'll be cutting people off from health care. Forty-nine states and the District of Columbia have plans to cut their Medicaid program this year. . . . Apparently to this administration, that just doesn't matter. The Bush administration is resurrecting old skeletons to justify the unjustifiable: Starving the Medicaid program instead of saving it. Medicaid isn't an extravagance. Medicaid isn't an afterthought. Medicaid anchors this nation's health care system.

Medicaid spending has increased dramatically over the past four years not because of fraud, not because of abuse, but because of enrollment increases associated with the economic downturn. . . . And the increase has been because prescription drug prices and hospital costs are pushing up spending for public and private insurance alike.

Medicaid is cost-efficient. Medicaid provides health care for fewer dollars per enrollee than the private health insurance system. Not only does Medicaid protect the individuals covered under the program, it plays a major role in financing the health and long-term care sectors of our economy. That means protecting the health professionals who serve all of us, and it means jobs.

The president won't replace the $24 billion he cuts from Medicaid, even though Medicaid is the only reason the uninsured rate in this country hasn't exploded under his watch. It's the only reason 1.3 million low-income seniors have access to nursing home care. It's the only reason children living in poverty receive care in a doctor's office rather than in an emergency room. . . .

Why are the most unfortunate among us the least important people in this country to our government? The government's role is to assist those in need, not to desert them.

Continued from p. 604

The issue has caused intense friction between states and the federal government, a tension analysts say they have not seen since the mid-1990s, when Republicans tried to convert the Medicaid entitlement into a block-grant program.

In his 2004 budget proposal, President Bush took a tough, new approach, which includes cutting $1.5 billion from Medicaid next year and $23.6 billion in the coming decade. During debate on the fiscal 2005 budget resolution on March 10, the Senate voted 53-43 to reject the cuts, but state officials say the proposed cuts will not be the last suggested by congressional Republicans and the administration.

The White House wants to require states to submit their Medicaid budget proposals to the federal government 150 days before they are implemented so federal officials can make sure state plans follow all federal rules correctly. Currently, federal officials do not review Medicaid budgets until after claims are paid.

State officials complain that the proposal would require them to produce new paperwork that would provide little significant, new information. Besides, the officials add, they often do not even have detailed budgets available that early.

When the administration published its proposal in January 2004, states were given only one day, rather than the typical 60-day comment period, to respond. After governors protested both the substance of the plan and the way it was released, the administration said it would work with state officials to revise it. But governors remain wary because federal officials say they still plan to implement some type of new requirements this year.

Already, federal officials are scrutinizing states' requests to update their programs with a more skeptical eye.

Financing Schemes

States are especially concerned that the federal government is more closely scrutinizing so-called "creative financing schemes" — bookkeeping maneuvers states use to increase the amounts they receive from the federal government. One such scheme involves the "intergovernmental transfers" (IGTs) used to transfer money from state to local governments and back. For example, a state may make a payment to a county nursing home, which the federal government must match, but then some of those funds go back to the states.

The CMS has estimated that as many as 35 states use some type of IGT mechanism to get federal funds in excess of their actual costs. In addition, 18 states use a particular type of scheme under which they obtain the "upper payment limit," or an amount intended to be a ceiling on federal matching rates for certain services. Critics say states are gaming the system to leverage federal matching dollars without paying their full share. These tactics are legal but seen by some as unfair. [32]

Moreover, critics say, because federal matching funds flow into the general state coffers and are not earmarked for health care, some states use the Medicaid funds they receive through intergovernmental transfers to improve or expand health care services for the poor.

"States can and do continue to claim excessive federal matching funds through [upper payment limit] arrangements, using them for non-Medicaid purposes or to inappropriately increase the federal share of Medicaid program expenditures," the General Accounting Office said. [33]

Three years ago, the federal government ordered the 18 states that use schemes to get the highest payments possible to phase out the practices on timetables of five to eight years. Now, federal officials are warning that they put a stop to them altogether. But some state officials charge that the federal government may be using these issues as ways to persuade states to accept caps on their federal dollars.

State officials say the tactics provide life-saving funds that states rely on. "Without the benefit of IGTs, large county-based states, such as New York, California, Wisconsin and North Carolina, would literally be unable to finance their Medicaid programs, destroying the safety net in many parts of the country and drastically increasing the numbers of the uninsured," Barbara Edwards, director of Ohio's Medicaid program, told the House Energy and Commerce Subcommittee on Health on April 1.

But federal officials say they have a duty to keep costs down. The federal government "has a strong interest in strengthening financial oversight and ensuring payment accuracy and fiscal integrity," says Dennis Smith, CMS' director of state operations. "Federal matching funds must be a match for real Medicaid expenditures." ■

OUTLOOK

Increasing Pressure

The tension between the states and the federal government will likely continue as long as funds for Medicaid are limited.

Meanwhile, funding for Medicaid and the S-CHIP program is expected to roughly double by 2013. And, as the population ages in the next decade, Medicaid costs for long-term care will climb precipitously, since seniors and people with disabilities consume nearly 70 percent of Medicaid resources.

"This is something we need to deal with now, but I have a feeling that Medicaid will be something we'll be hearing a lot about for the next 10 years," former CMS Director Scully says.

Advocates for the low-income say Medicaid should be a more reliable source of health care coverage. "Inevitably, these cuts do have an impact on real people," Ohio Medicaid Director Edwards says.

To be sure, some states now face more stable budget conditions than they did a year ago because they trimmed spending or collected more revenue. State tax collections rose 8.4 percent in the first three months of 2004, according to the Nelson Rockefeller Institute of Government in New York. [34]

"So far, fiscal 2004 looks to be a good year for state government revenues," said a Rockefeller Institute report released in May.

As a result, some states cut Medicaid less this year than they had initially proposed. For instance, in Missouri, the state legislature at first had considered cutting thousands from the Medicaid rolls, but ended up slicing coverage only for about 325 low-income parents. Other states actually restored some cuts previously made — such as in Connecticut, where the Democratic legislature found the money to eliminate new premiums and co-payments established last year.

But officials say they are not in the clear yet, because most states are not as strong financially as before the recent recession. And not only will rising Medicaid spending continue to be a factor, but the June 30 cutoff of additional federal payments will hit some states hard — especially those with many poor people.

"If states were a patient, the patient is certainly out of intensive care but still in the hospital," says Pattison of the state budget officers' group.

Some lawmakers, such as Sens. John D. Rockefeller IV, D-W.Va., and Gordon H. Smith, R-Ore., favor additional aid to states. But they face resistance, particularly from Republicans, who advocate cutting Medicaid below current levels.

Policymakers must decide, among other things, what level of coverage beneficiaries should receive. For instance, should Medicaid recipients receive benefits as generous as those provided by private insurance?

Advocates for the poor say paltry benefits not only hurt the poor but also taxpayers and private insurance consumers. If patients do not get the appropriate treatments, they end up sicker and require more costly care later, boosting overall public and private health care costs.

But others say cheaper substitutes are just as effective. "People with the most generous private insurance . . . get over-treated and mistreated at the same time," says Antos of the American Enterprise Institute. "Because it's free, so why not?"

Former Medicaid and Medicare chief Wilensky says the question deserves an honest and open discussion. "One of the most serious issues that we must address is how much we are willing to spend on the poor," she says. For other government benefits, such as housing or food stamps, people acknowledge that benefits may not equal those that individuals buy for themselves, she says, but "we have trouble saying the same thing when it comes to health care."

"How can we define a level of care that is adequate, even if it is not as convenient as the care for the privately insured?" she says. "It doesn't necessarily have to be what I want when I pay for it myself."

The outcome of this fall's elections will largely determine the outlook for the program. GOP leaders will continue their push for capped allotments that would reconfigure the shape of the program. Democrats say Medicaid needs more federal funding, not less, and that Medicaid can be credited with preventing more people from losing insurance.

Both sides agree that an evolution of the program is in store. "I do see it as a pivotal moment in Medicaid's history," former Medicaid official Mann says. "A solution is needed that would strengthen the program and allow it to do its job." ■

Notes

[1] For background see William Triplett, "State Budget Crisis," *The CQ Researcher*, Oct. 3, 2003, pp. 821-844.

[2] Centers for Medicare and Medicaid Services.

[3] National Association of State Budget Officers.

[4] See "The Long Term Budget Outlook," Congressional Budget Office, December 2003, Chapter 3, www.cbo.gov/showdoc.cfm?index=4916&sequence=4.

[5] See Vernon Smith, *et al.*, "States Respond to Fiscal Pressure: A 50 State Update of State Medicaid Spending Growth and Cost Containment Actions," Henry J. Kaiser Family Foundation, January 2004.

[6] For background on prescription drug program, see Adriel Bettelheim, "Medicare Reform," *The CQ Researcher*, Aug. 22, 2003, pp. 673-696.

About the Author

Rebecca Adams is a 2003-04 Kaiser Family Foundation health care media fellow. She has been a reporter for seven years at Congressional Quarterly. She previously reported for *The Macon Telegraph* and *The Chattanooga Times* and wrote for *The Arizona Republic* through the Pulliam fellowship program. She also writes for *The Washington Post* and other newspapers. She graduated from Emory University with a bachelor of arts in political science.

[7] Rep. Sherrod Brown, D-Ohio, from a statement at a hearing of the House Energy and Commerce Committee, March 18, 2004.

[8] See "Care Without Coverage: Too Little Too Late," Institute of Medicine, National Academy of Sciences, May 2002.

[9] See Robert Pear, "Medicaid Proposal Would Give States More Say on Costs," *The New York Times*, Feb. 1, 2003.

[10] Letter from Govs. Bill Owens and Jeb Bush.

[11] See David Royse, "Bush signs KidCare bill, removing 90,000 kids from waiting list," The Associated Press, March 11, 2004.

[12] Quoted in Mark Hollis, "Florida Legislature Makes Changes to KidCare Health Insurance Program," *Orlando Sentinel*, March 6, 2004, p. B5.

[13] See "Long-Term Care," *Alliance for Health Reform Sourcebook*, January 2003, www.allhealth.org/sourcebook2002/ch9_tc.html.

[14] *Ibid.*

[15] See National Governors Association, www.nga.org/chairman03/.

[16] See Congressional Budget Office, *op. cit.*

[17] Alliance for Health Reform sourcebook, *op. cit.*

[18] *Ibid.*

[19] See *Olmstead v. L. C.*, 527 U. S. 581, 1999. Supreme Court cases can be found on the court's Web site, www.supremecourtus.gov.

[20] Thomas Rice, *et al.*, "Do Physicians Cost Shift?" *Health Affairs*, fall 1996.

[21] Jason Lee, *et al.*, Medicare Payment Policy: Does Cost Shifting Matter?" *Health Affairs*, Web exclusive, Oct. 8, 2003.

[22] See "Insuring America's Health: Principles and Recommendations," Institute of Medicine, National Academy of Sciences, 2004.

[23] Unless otherwise noted, the following historical material is drawn from Robert Stevens and Rosemary Stevens, *Welfare Medicine in America* (2003).

[24] See Bettelheim, *op. cit.*

[25] *1979 CQ Almanac*, p. 499.

[26] *1981 CQ Almanac*, p. 477.

[27] Unless otherwise noted, the following historical material is drawn from Joseph Shatz, "Expanding Entitlements Bit by Bit: Waxman Shows How It's Done," *CQ Weekly*, Oct. 25, 2003, p. 2618.

[28] See Julie Rovner, *Health Care Policy and Politics A to Z* (2000), pp. 114-115.

FOR MORE INFORMATION

American Enterprise Institute, 1150 17th St., N.W., Washington, DC 20036; (202) 862-5800; www.aei.org. Conservative think tank that favors limited government.

Center on Budget and Policy Priorities, 820 1st St., N.E., #510, Washington, DC 20002; (202) 408-1080; www.cbpp.org. Liberal think tank focusing on fiscal policy and public programs that affect low- and moderate-income families and individuals.

Families USA, 1334 G St., N.W., Washington, DC 20005; (202) 628-3030; www.familiesusa.org. Liberal-leaning consumer-rights organization specializing in health-care issues.

Healthcare Leadership Council, 1001 Pennsylvania Ave., N.W., Suite 550 South, Washington, DC 20004; (202) 452-8700; www.hlc.org. Group of health care industry leaders that provides the private-sector perspective on issues.

Heritage Foundation, 214 Massachusetts Ave., N.E., Washington, DC 20002-4999; (202) 546-4400; www.heritage.org. Conservative think tank that favors limited government.

Kaiser Family Foundation, 1330 G St., N.W., Washington, DC 20005; (202) 347-5270; www.kff.org/about/kcmu.cfm. Nonprofit foundation focusing on health-policy issues.

National Association of State Budget Officers, Hall of the States Bldg., Suite 642, 444 North Capitol St., N.W., Washington, DC 20001-1511; (202) 624-5382; www.nasbo.org.

National Association of State Medicaid Directors, 810 First St., N.E., Washington, DC 20002; (202) 682-0100; www.nasmd.org.

National Conference of State Legislatures, 444 North Capitol St., N.W., Suite 515, Washington, DC 20001; (202) 624-5400; www.ncsl.org. Bipartisan organization serving the legislators and staffs of the states and territories.

National Governors Association, 444 North Capitol St., Washington, DC 20001-1512; (202) 624-5300; www.nga.org. Nonpartisan organization representing the nation's governors.

Urban Institute, 2100 M St., N.W., Washington, DC 20037; (202) 833-7200; www.urban.org. Liberal-leaning think tank that studies state and federal policies.

[29] See "Special Report: Social Policy," *CQ Weekly*, Jan. 6, 1996, p. 37.

[30] See Rovner, *op. cit.*, p. 113.

[31] See John Holahan, *et al.*, "State Responses to Budget Crisis in 2004: An Overview of Ten States," Kaiser Family Foundation, January 2004, p. 17.

[32] See "Medicaid: Improved Federal Oversight of State Financing Schemes Is Needed," General Accounting Office, Feb. 13, 2004.

[33] *Ibid.*

[34] See Nicholas W. Jenny, "State Tax Revenue Growth Add Momentum," *The Rockefeller Institute State Fiscal News*, Vol. 4, No. 3, May 2004.

Bibliography

Selected Sources

Books

Rovner, Julie, *Health Care Policy and Politics A to Z*, CQ Press, 2000.

This comprehensive handbook includes a detailed description of Medicaid. Former *CQ Weekly* reporter Rovner covers health care for National Public Radio.

Smith, David G., *Entitlement Politics: Medicare and Medicaid, 1995-2001*, Aldine de Gruyter, 2002.

A political science professor uses case studies and historical narrative to detail the political fights over attempts to cut the size of government by restructuring and privatizing aspects of the two federal health-care programs.

Stevens, Robert and Rosemary, *Welfare Medicine in America*, Transaction Publishers, 2003 Edition.

The latest edition of Rosemary Stevens' landmark 1974 work about Medicaid policy describes the creation of Medicaid and its early years.

Articles

Bettelheim, Adriel, "Medicare Reform," *The CQ Researcher*, Aug. 22, 2003, pp. 73-696.

The author provides a comprehensive review of efforts to add a prescription-drug program to Medicare, created along with Medicaid in the 1965 amendments to the Social Security Act.

Dubay, Lisa, and Genevieve Kenney, "Addressing Coverage Gaps for Low-Income Parents," *Health Affairs*, March/April 2004.

Low-income parents, especially those living in poverty, increasingly have no health insurance, but Medicaid and the State Children's Health Insurance Program could reduce uninsurance in this group and expand their access to medical services, the authors conclude.

Fong, Tony, "Safe zone; Medicaid will escape cuts for now, observers say," *Modern Healthcare*, May 24, 2004, p. 8.

Fong explains why additional Medicaid cuts failed to pass in Congress this year.

Pear, Robert, "Bush to Revisit Changes in Medicaid Rules," *The New York Times*, Feb. 23, 2004, p. 19.

Pear looks at recent concerns by governors about Medicaid and the administration's reaction.

Pear, Robert, "Medicaid Proposal Would Give States More Say on Costs," *The New York Times*, Feb. 1, 2003, p. A1.

President Bush's 2003 proposal to revise Medicaid is examined in depth.

Reports and Studies

Allen, Kathryn G., "Medicaid and SCHIP: States' Premium and Cost Sharing Requirements for Beneficiaries," General Accounting Office, March 31, 2004.

The director of Medicaid and private health insurance issues at the GAO describes how children are more likely to face cost-sharing requirements in the State Children's Health Insurance Program than in Medicaid.

Allen, Kathryn G., "Medicaid: Improved Federal Oversight of State Financing Schemes Is Needed," General Accounting Office, Feb. 13, 2004.

Allen describes how "upper payment limit" financing schemes in Medicaid are being phased out and regulated.

Allen, Kathryn G., "Medicaid: Intergovernmental Transfers Have Facilitated State Financing Schemes," General Accounting Office, March 18, 2004.

States have leveraged additional federal dollars through creative financing, Allen says.

Antos, Joseph, "Can Medicare and Medicaid Promote More Efficient Health Care?" Federal Trade Commission/Department of Justice, Sept. 30, 2003.

Medicaid has failed to promote innovation and efficiency in the health sector.

Mann, Cindy, and Samantha Artiga, "Impact of Recent Changes in Health Care Coverage for Low-Income People: A First Look at the Research Following Changes in Oregon's Medicaid Program," Kaiser Family Foundation, June 2004.

The authors summarize problems affecting Medicaid beneficiaries in Oregon in light of recent budget difficulties.

Davidoff, Ann, *et al.*, "Medicaid and State-Funded Coverage for Adults: Estimates of Eligibility and Enrollment," Kaiser Family Foundation, May 2004.

This overview of non-elderly adult eligibility for and enrollment in Medicaid and state-funded coverage shows that a lack of health insurance remains a difficult problem for low-income adults.

Williams, Claudia, *et al.*, "Challenges and Tradeoffs in Low-Income Family Budgets: Implications for Health Coverage," Kaiser Family Foundation, April 2004.

A study of families trying to make ends meet on limited budgets indicates that poor families spend 70 percent of their income on basic needs such as housing, transportation and food, and about 7 percent on health care.

The Next Step:

Additional Articles from Current Periodicals

Limiting Benefits

"Chopped Out," *The Economist*, Jan. 25, 2003.
Expanding Medicaid coverage during the prosperous 1990s was a noble goal, but one unaffordable in leaner times.

Kemper, Vicki, "Medicaid Feeling the Effects of the States' Fiscal Crisis," *Los Angeles Times*, Sept. 23, 2003, p. A13.
A steep drop in states' tax revenues led to the sharp Medicaid restrictions that are causing many people to lose coverage.

McMahon, Patrick, "States Reduce Services, Drop Many From Medicaid Rolls," *USA Today*, March 12, 2003, p. 3A.
Unlike the federal government, state governments aren't permitted to run budget deficits, and Medicaid cuts are the result.

Toner, Robin, and Robert Pear, "Cutbacks Imperil Health Coverage for States' Poor," *The New York Times*, April 28, 2003, p. A1.
State legislatures are acting to curb benefits and enrollment in Medicaid as costs jumped more than 50 percent since 1997.

Long-Term Care

Adler, Jane, "Don't Expect Government to Pay for Long-Term Care," *Chicago Tribune*, Jan. 11, 2004, Real Estate Section, p. 3A.
A poll reveals that many people who expect the government to pay for elder care may be in for an unpleasant surprise.

Perez-Pena, Richard, "Medicaid Plan Would Restrict Nursing Homes to Truly Poor," *The New York Times*, Dec. 23, 2003, p. B1.
New York plans to cut coverage for seniors' long-term care.

Salganik, M. William, "State Hopes More Elderly Can Be Cared For at Home," *The Baltimore Sun*, Jan. 15, 2004, p. 1A.
Maryland tries to persuade the elderly that living at home is a cost-effective alternative to expensive nursing homes.

Medicaid Abuse

Flaherty, Mary Pat, and Gilbert Gaul, "Medicaid Is Start of Drug Resale Trail," *The Washington Post*, Oct. 22, 2003, p. A17.
Some Medicaid recipients sell expensive drugs, preferably those costing $1,000 per dose or more, to criminal gangs.

Freudenheim, Milt, "Some Concerns Thrive on Medicaid Patients," *The New York Times*, Feb. 19, 2003, p. C1.
Companies that provide managed care for Medicaid recipients deny treatment too often and exploit the system to profit at public expense, critics say.

Halper, Evan, "Public Pays for Wealthy Seniors' Care," *Los Angeles Times*, May 2, 2004, p. A1.
Lawyers peddle strategies that hide assets so seniors whose incomes would otherwise be too high get Medicaid.

McIntire, Mike, "8 Are Arrested in a Medicaid Fraud That Used Agency Workers and Newspaper Ads," *The New York Times*, Nov. 22, 2003, p. B3.
Medicaid employees provided fraudulent Medicaid cards in return for kickbacks.

Roche, Walter F., "Health Funding Misuse Feared," *The Baltimore Sun*, May 2, 2004, p. 1B.
Maryland is losing $12 million per year to aliens who immigrate to inappropriately receive Medicaid-covered treatment.

Prescription Drugs

Austin, Marsha, "State Limits Prescriptions on Medicaid," *The Denver Post*, April 30, 2003, p. A1.
Colorado limits Medicaid recipients to eight prescriptions at a time unless their doctor gets a special exemption.

Harris, Gardiner, "States Try to Limit Drugs in Medicaid, but Makers Resist," *The New York Times*, Dec. 18, 2003, p. A1.
State efforts to require Medicaid recipients to use cheaper generic medications trigger opposition from patient advocates and drug companies.

Perez-Pena, Richard, "22 States Limiting Doctors' Latitude in Medicaid Drugs," *The New York Times*, June 16, 2003, p. A1.
Preferred drug lists have managed to slow the rise of Medicaid costs, but critics contend some patients lack access to necessary medication.

Stein, Charles, "Tough Medicine Is Paying Off for State," *The Boston Globe*, Feb. 17, 2004, p. C1.
Massachusetts manages to rein in the double-digit increases in prescription drug expenses by insisting on the use of more generics and limiting drug choices.

Proposals for Change

Caputo, Marc, "Medicaid Proposals Criticized," *The Miami Herald*, April 25, 2004, p. B1.
Proposals by Florida Republicans to cut down on Medicaid spending are controversial and convoluted.

Kemper, Vicki, "Bush Seeks Overhaul of Medicaid," *Los Angeles Times*, Feb. 1, 2003, p. A1.
Reactions are mixed to the Bush administration's plan to give states more authority in running their Medicaid programs in return for fewer federal dollars.

Kemper, Vicki, and James Gerstenzang, "Governors Wary of White House Medicaid Proposal," *Los Angeles Times*, Feb. 25, 2003, p. A13.
Governors seeking greater flexibility in running their Medicaid programs weren't willing to accept reduced federal funding as the trade-off.

Steinhauer, Jennifer, "New York, Which Made Medicaid Big, Looks to Cut It Back," *The New York Times*, March 3, 2003, p. B1.
A state known for its traditionally generous health spending confronts new fiscal realities.

Rising Health Care Costs

Appleby, Julie, "Finger Pointers Can't Settle on Who's to Blame for Health Costs," *USA Today*, Aug. 21, 2002, p. 1A.
Doctors, patients and drug manufacturers play a blame game, while medical costs register double-digit increases every year, far higher than inflation.

Francis, David R., "Healthcare Costs Are Up. Here Are the Culprits," *The Christian Science Monitor*, Dec. 15, 2003, p. 21.
Soaring health costs are devouring higher and higher percentages of the nation's gross domestic product.

White, Ronald D., "15% Rise Seen for Health Care Costs," *Chicago Tribune*, Dec. 10, 2002, Business Section, p. 8.
Higher prices for medical tests and treatments at hospitals bear a share of responsibility for the rapid growth of medical expenses.

State Troubles

Adams, Rebecca, "States Seek More Medicaid Help While GOP Eyes Program Overhaul," *CQ Weekly*, Feb. 1, 2003, p. 258.
Desperate state governments seek a federal bailout of their Medicaid programs, but Republicans focus on attempts to restructure the system.

Heath, Erin, "Medicaid: The Pendulum Swings," *National Journal*, Aug. 9, 2003.
State budgets are taking a pounding as Medicaid costs rise and fiscal overseers are taking a hard look at Medicaid.

Tough Times for the Needy

Austin, Marsha, "Legal Immigrants' Loss of Medicaid Benefits 'Like End of Life'," *The Denver Post*, March 9, 2003, p. A23.
Colorado removes Medicaid eligibility from elderly immigrants.

Austin, Marsha, "Poor Kids Feeling Poorly Have Fewer Choices in State," *The Denver Post*, April 29, 2004, p. A1.
Low Medicaid reimbursements mean that few pediatricians will accept patients covered only by Medicaid.

Paige, Connie, "Children Wait for Health Care," *The Boston Globe*, June 10, 2004, p. 1.
Children of the uninsured who earn too much to qualify for Medicaid create a burden on hospitals that must treat them for free if their parents can't afford to pay.

Sachdev, Ameet, "Health Care for Poor Kids on Trial," *Chicago Tribune*, May 1, 2004, p. 1.
Medicaid payments to doctors are so low that poor children have difficulties finding doctors willing to treat them; a class-action lawsuit is the result.

Salganik, William, "Medicaid Revolving Door Frustrates Many in Md.," *The Baltimore Sun*, Sept. 1, 2002, p. 1C.
People living just above the poverty level who are ineligible for Medicaid struggle with mounting medical debts.

CITING *THE CQ RESEARCHER*

Sample formats for citing these reports in a bibliography include the ones listed below. Preferred styles and formats vary, so please check with your instructor or professor.

MLA STYLE

Jost, Kenneth. "Rethinking the Death Penalty." The CQ Researcher 16 Nov. 2001: 945-68.

APA STYLE

Jost, K. (2001, November 16). Rethinking the death penalty. *The CQ Researcher, 11*, 945-968.

CHICAGO STYLE

Jost, Kenneth. "Rethinking the Death Penalty." *CQ Researcher*, November 16, 2001, 945-968.

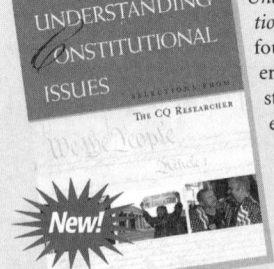

CQ Researcher

Published by CQ Press, a division of Congressional Quarterly Inc.

thecqresearcher.com

Sports and Drugs

Are stronger anti-doping policies needed?

With the Summer Olympic Games about to get under way, some of the best-known U.S. track and field stars are being investigated for allegedly using illegal performance-enhancing drugs. If the charges are proven, some could be banned from competition for life. The growing scandal over pharmaceutically pumped-up athletes also embraces other professional and collegiate athletes. Major League Baseball is under pressure to crack down on players who use steroids or other banned substances. Anti-doping advocates say the drugs hurt sports and risk players' health. A handful of dissidents disagree and call for lifting the anti-doping bans. A new international anti-doping code prescribes a two-year ban for a first offense, but drug testing is often circumvented, and some newly designed drugs cannot be detected. Meanwhile, the baseball players' association is resisting more rigorous testing, even though dozens of players tested positive in 2003.

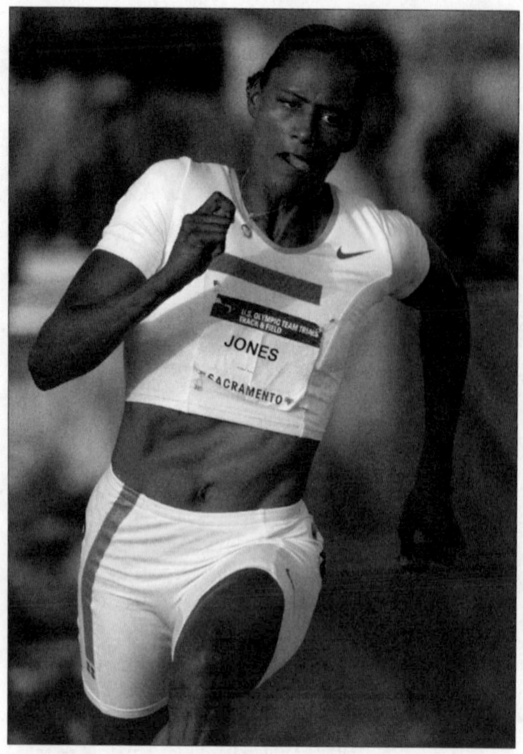

U.S. Olympic gold medallist Marion Jones denies that she used illegal steroids to run faster.

INSIDE THIS REPORT

The CQ Researcher • July 23, 2004 • www.thecqresearcher.com
Volume 14, Number 26 • Pages 613-636

RECIPIENT OF SOCIETY OF PROFESSIONAL JOURNALISTS AWARD FOR EXCELLENCE ◆ AMERICAN BAR ASSOCIATION SILVER GAVEL AWARD

July 23, 2004
Volume 14, Number 26

MANAGING EDITOR: Thomas J. Colin

ASSISTANT MANAGING EDITOR: Kathy Koch

ASSOCIATE EDITOR: Kenneth Jost

STAFF WRITERS: Mary H. Cooper, David Masci, William Triplett

CONTRIBUTING WRITERS: Sarah Glazer, David Hatch, David Hosansky, Patrick Marshall, Tom Price, Jane Tanner

DESIGN/PRODUCTION EDITOR: Olu B. Davis

ASSISTANT EDITOR: Kenneth Lukas

A Division of Congressional Quarterly Inc.

SENIOR VICE PRESIDENT/GENERAL MANAGER: John A. Jenkins

DIRECTOR, LIBRARY PUBLISHING: Kathryn C. Suárez

DIRECTOR, EDITORIAL OPERATIONS: Ann Davies

CONGRESSIONAL QUARTERLY INC.

CHAIRMAN: Paul C. Tash

VICE CHAIRMAN: Andrew P. Corty

PRESIDENT AND PUBLISHER: Robert W. Merry

The CQ Researcher (ISSN 1056-2036) is printed on acid-free paper. Published weekly, except Jan. 2, April 9, July 2, July 9, Aug. 6, Aug. 13, Nov. 26 and Dec. 31, by CQ Press, a division of Congressional Quarterly Inc. Annual subscription rates for institutions start at $625. For pricing, call 1-800-834-9020, ext. 1906. To purchase a *CQ Researcher* report in print or electronic format (PDF), visit www.cqpress.com or call 866-427-7737. A single report is $10. Bulk purchase discounts and electronic-rights licensing are also available. Periodicals postage paid at Washington, D.C., and additional mailing offices. POSTMASTER: Send address changes to *The CQ Researcher*, 1255 22nd St., N.W., Suite 400, Washington, D.C. 20037.

THE ISSUES

BACKGROUND

CURRENT SITUATION

OUTLOOK

SIDEBARS AND GRAPHICS

FOR FURTHER RESEARCH

Cover: Marion Jones runs in the Women's 200 Meters qualifying during the U.S. Olympic Track and Field Team Trials July 16, 2004, in Sacramento, Calif. (AFP Photo/Jeff Haynes)

Sports and Drugs

BY KENNETH JOST

THE ISSUES

Tim Montgomery's career has slowed considerably since the evening in Paris two years ago when he blazed to a record-setting 9.78 seconds in the 100-meter dash and earned the title of "world's fastest man." [1]

Today, however, Montgomery's future as an international track star is uncertain. On July 11 he failed to make the Olympic team. Moreover, the 29-year-old South Carolinian is one of several top U.S. track athletes who could be banned from competition for life for alleged use of illegal performance-enhancing drugs.

The charges enveloping Montgomery and the other track stars threaten not only their individual careers but also the United States' chances in the upcoming Olympic Games, set to open in Athens, Greece, on Aug. 13. The growing scandal over pharmaceutically pumped-up athletes — perhaps the largest in U.S. sports history — extends into professional baseball, possibly implicating, among others, Barry Bonds, the hulking San Francisco Giants outfielder who hit a record 73 homers in 2002.

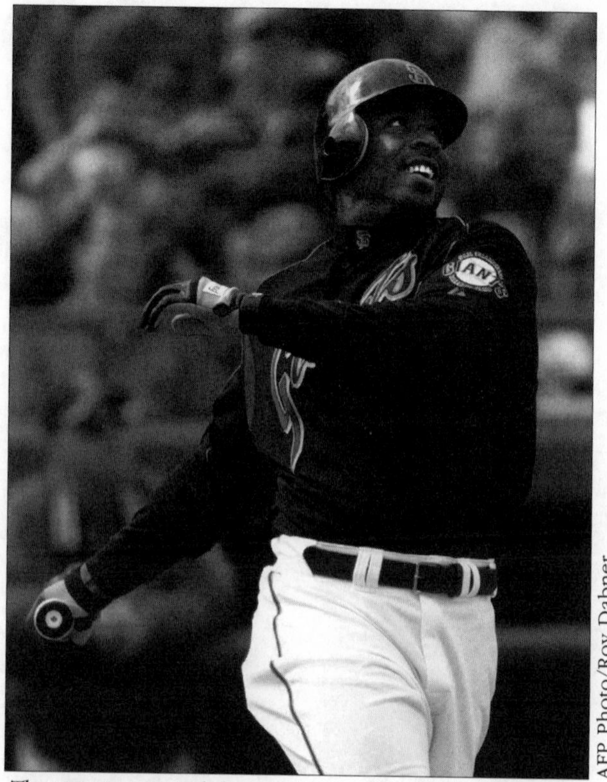

AFP Photo/Roy Dabner

The growing scandal over pharmaceutically pumped-up Olympic athletes extends into professional baseball, possibly implicating San Francisco Giants outfielder Barry Bonds, who hit a record 73 homers in 2002.

The athletes involved all publicly dispute the accusations, but the controversy underscores the undeniable fact that drugs have become a major part of elite athletic competition. A significant but unknown number of Olympic hopefuls in the United States and elsewhere, as well as many collegiate and other professional athletes, use chemical substances to increase strength and stamina beyond what they can achieve by nutrition and training alone. [2]

"It's human nature to obtain an edge, whether in combat, in business or in sports," says Charles Yesalis, a professor of health and human development at Pennsylvania State University and a leading expert on — and opponent of — performance-enhancing drugs.

Through the years, athletes have sought that edge from a variety of stimulants ranging from caffeine and brandy to heroin and cocaine. But the isolation of the male hormone testosterone in the 1930s paved the way for more sophisticated chemical agents known as anabolic ("tissue-building") steroids.

Steroids produce masculinizing effects comparable to those from naturally occurring testosterone. The resulting increase in muscle mass may be a boon for weightlifters, football players or athletes in track and field throwing events.

But steroids also produce undesirable side effects. Some, such as acne and increased body hair, are largely cosmetic. Others are more serious, including tumors and cancer in the liver, increased cholesterol levels and — in some men — shrunken testicles. Women who use steroids see many of the same effects, along with a deeper voice and — in some cases — an enlarged clitoris.

However, the medical effects of steroids are not fully researched, and some athletes and a handful of vocal critics of anti-drug enforcement efforts in sports dispute the health risks claimed by opponents or say they can be minimized. But their use in athletic competition has been widely viewed as unseemly at best ever since the practice first came to widespread attention in the 1960s.

Nonetheless, as the monetary and other rewards of elite competition have increased over the years, steroids have tempted many top-ranking athletes. "The pressure on people to try different things is very high," says William Roberts, an associate professor at the University of Minnesota's St. John's Hospital and president of the American College of Sports Medicine. "The difference between first and fifth place is the difference between fame and money and relative anonymity."

National and international sports federations and professional sports leagues were slow to respond to mounting evidence that steroid use has been increasing since the 1970s. In 1999, however, an international conference of governments and sports organizations led to the writing of a world "anti-doping" code that calls for a two-year suspension in most cases for athletes found to have used banned drugs. The conference also led

U.S. Attitudes Toward Athletes and Drugs

Most Americans disapprove of steroid use, but the young are more likely to view it as both more common and less of a concern.

How many professional athletes in the United States do you think use steroids or other performance-enhancing drugs?

Respondents' Age	Most	About half	About a quarter	Only a few	No answer
18-29	21%	34	29	13	3
30+	14%	26	24	21	15

How about American Olympic athletes?

Respondents' Age	Most	About half	About a quarter	Only a few	No answer
18-29	7%	17	17	59	
30+	5%	11	16	54	14

Does the use of performance-enhancing drugs by professional athletes bother you?

Respondents' Age	Yes, a lot	Yes, somewhat	No	No answer
18-29	15%	41	41	3
30+	31%	31	34	4

How about Olympic athletes?

Respondents' Age	Yes, a lot	Yes, somewhat	No	No answer
18-29	28%	41	30	1
30+	42%	35	20	3

Source: The New York Times, *interviews with 1,057 adults nationwide, Dec. 10-13, 2003*

to the creation of the independent World Anti-Doping Agency (WADA) to police the practice in international competitions, including the Olympics. *

* The term "doping" has been used to denote use of performance-enhancing drugs in sports at least since the 1930s. Some critics of anti-doping policies maintain the term is inherently pejorative and improperly skews the debate over the issue.

The charges against Montgomery and other U.S. track stars have been brought by WADA's counterpart in the United States: the U.S. Anti-Doping Agency (USADA). The agency sent letters on June 8 to Montgomery and three other Olympic hopefuls: sprinters Chryste Gaines, Michelle Collins and Alvin Harrison. The agency also has confirmed that it is investigating sprinter Marion Jones, a five-time Olympic gold medallist and Montgomery's live-in girlfriend.

The evidence against the athletes — not officially disclosed as of early July — appears to come from business records seized in a September 2003 raid by federal and state authorities on a San Francisco-area sports lab, the Bay Area Laboratory Cooperative (BALCO), run by sports nutritionist Victor Conte. [3] Federal authorities acted after USADA tipped them off to the existence of a new so-called designer drug — tetrahydrogestrinone or THG — similar to previously known steroids but altered slightly to avoid detection.

USADA itself had been tipped off by a then unidentified track coach, who sent the anti-doping agency a syringe in June containing the new steroid and named Conte as the source. [4] Conte's past clients include Bonds, who has tried unsuccessfully to dispel suspicions that his bulked-up physique and increased home run output in recent years are signs of steroid use.

The raids touched off a succession of high-profile events, including testimony before a federal grand jury by Bonds and many other well-known athletes and an eventual indictment of Conte and three others announced on Feb. 12 by Attorney General John Ashcroft. "This is not just a call to action," Ashcroft said. "It is a call to the values that make our nation and its people strong and free." *

Even before the BALCO investigation, Major League Baseball (MLB) was under pressure to more vigorously curb what several players publicly described as widespread use of steroids. President Bush added to the pressure in his

* The 42-count indictment charged Conte and three others with conspiracy to give athletes illegal steroids and prescription drugs. The other defendants are BALCO Vice President James Valente; Bonds' personal trainer Greg Anderson; and Remi Korchemny, a San Francisco Bay-area track coach.

State of the Union address on Jan. 20 by calling on "football, baseball and other sports" to "get rid of steroids now."

For years, the Major League Baseball Players Association had resisted drug testing, but the union agreed in 2002 to a year of anonymous random tests. If more than 5 percent of the samples tested positive, the agreement called for once-a-year testing of players by name. In fact, between 5 and 7 percent of the 2003 samples tested positive, so the league began testing all players by name this year. [5] *(See "At Issue," p. 629.)*

For Montgomery and the other track stars, USADA's allegations came at the worst of times — as they prepared for the U.S. Olympic trials in Sacramento, Calif., in mid-July. Montgomery and Jones both continued their training even as they and their lawyers publicly battled the accusations. "Tim's position is he's never done anything wrong, he's never failed any drug test, he'll be found not guilty," says his spokesman, Dan Goldberg.

Jones similarly insists on her innocence and is challenging USADA either to bring charges or drop the matter. "At this point, USADA ought to make clear that it doesn't have sufficient evidence, and that should be the end of the matter," says her attorney, Joseph Burton.

Despite the public denials, the *San Francisco Chronicle* reported in late June that Montgomery — in his federal grand jury testimony in November, given under a grant of immunity — acknowledged having used performance-enhancing drugs in the past. He also testified that Conte had admitted supplying steroids to Bonds, according to the *Chronicle*, which did not disclose its sources. Montgomery's lawyer declined to comment, and both Conte and Bonds angrily denied the accusations. [6]

For their part, USADA officials insist the procedures are fair. "Any suggestion that the USADA process compromises any athlete's rights or is unfair is a blatant distortion of the truth," says Legal Director Travis Tygart. As for speeding up action on Jones' case, Tygart says it would be "shortsighted" to rush the agency's review process "just to meet a competition deadline."

Whatever the outcome of the BALCO investigation, anti-doping officials acknowledge they face an uphill battle in trying to stay ahead of pharmacological advances. Some banned substances — such as human growth hormone (HGH) — cannot be detected under current technology, and new drugs such as THG are designed to escape detection. Moreover, looming on the horizon is the possibility of so-called gene doping — manipulation of an athlete's genes — to improve performance. *(See sidebar, p. 624.)*

As the debate over performance-enhancing drugs continues, here are some of the major questions being considered:

Does the use of performance-enhancing drugs hurt athletes and competitive sports?

Baseball fans were held spellbound in the late summer of 1998 as two of the game's leading sluggers — Mark McGwire and Sammy Sosa — chased one of the game's most daunting records: Roger Maris' mark of 61 home runs set nearly four decades earlier, in 1961. By the end of the season, the St. Louis Cardinals' first-baseman and Chicago Cubs' outfielder had both eclipsed the previous record, with Sosa at 66 and McGwire on top with a stunning 70 homers for the year.

As the home-run chase intensified, however, sports reporters noticed that the longtime power hitter had bottles of a dietary supplement called androstenedione — andro for short — in his locker. Questioned, McGwire openly acknowledged taking andro — a manufactured drug that the body converts into testosterone. Andro, which was legal for baseball players at the time, had already been banned in other sports — including football, collegiate athletics and the Olympics.

The disclosure stirred a debate over the legitimacy of McGwire's feat. Some critics suggested that the eventual record needed to be marked with a doubt-casting asterisk. [7] Most fans, however, appeared uninterested. And, tellingly, the sale of andro shot up thanks to the publicity.

Bowing to the controversy, MLB finally banned androstenedione on April 12, 2004.

The episode illuminates the opposing views about performance-enhancing drugs in sports. Many fans may share the discomfort of anti-doping advocates who say that drugs tarnish the mythic purity of sports. "The public likes to have a clean game," says Don Catlin, director of the Olympic drug-testing laboratory at the University of California at Los Angeles. "They like it to be fair and square."

But many fans also revel in the enhanced power, speed or endurance that steroids or other performance-enhancing drugs help make possible. "They love to see big, strong guys hit home runs," says Norman Fost, a professor of pediatrics at the University of Wisconsin Medical School and the most vocal academic opponent of anti-doping policies.

Fost has argued — all but alone in the United States — that anti-doping officials and advocates rely for their case on a fictitious image of pure athletic competition and exaggerated warnings of the health consequences of performance-enhancing drugs. He says they have been aided by compliant reporters who have conveyed those views to the public with little analysis and few doubts. "I can't think of a single subject that involves ethical and medical issues that's been so one-sided" in the media, Fost says. [8]

Anti-doping officials, however, insist that performance-enhancing drugs

More Younger Teens Use Steroids

Forty percent of high school seniors say steroids are easy to obtain. The other 60 percent may never have seriously considered the question, but if they tried a quick Google search, they'd probably agree. [1]

Typing in a few simple keywords produces a wealth of information about steroids, including forums where users trade tips on the most reliable and discreet sources. Many sellers purchase "sponsored links" on Google, or advertisements that appear when a steroid-related search term is entered. One such site even offers prescriptions for sale.

Perhaps because of their easy availability, steroids increasingly are being used by high-schoolers. The Centers for Disease Control and Prevention (CDC) says the number of boys who have used steroids at least once increased from 4.1 percent to 6.8 percent between 1991 and 2003. But girls' usage rocketed from 1.2 percent to 5.3 percent — more than a fourfold increase. That's a total of about 1 million high school steroid users. [2]

But the real numbers are probably even higher, warns Charles Yesalis, a professor of health and human development at Pennsylvania State University and a leading expert on performance-enhancing drugs.

At a recent Senate hearing on steroid use by teens and young adults, several witnesses said steroid use is widespread among adolescents and college students. A Division I college football player, testifying anonymously from beneath a hood, with his voice altered to protect his identity, told the panel: "My current friend and roommate lived with a player that supplied seven-to-eight other players on the team with these steroids." [3]

He said the NCAA's random-testing program was weak because testing comes at roughly the same time each year.

Moreover, steroid users are getting younger. The percentage of college steroid users who began using in junior high or before jumped from 4.2 percent in 1989 to 15.4 percent in 2001, according to an NCAA survey of substance abuse among student athletes. [4] In 1989, only 25 percent of NCAA steroid users had started taking the drugs before college; in 2001 the number had more than doubled to 57.2 percent. And steroid use among eighth-graders is higher now than it was among seniors in the mid-1990s. [5]

One reason for the increase may be that fewer teens view steroid use as dangerous. The percentage of teens who said steroid use is a "great risk" decreased from 70.7 percent in 1992 to 55 percent in 2003. [6]

Some observers blame growing teen complacency about steroid risks on slugger Mark McGwire's use of the steroid precursor androstenedione. They also point to steroids' increasing popularity among professional athletes — or at least the perception among the young that more pros are using steroids.

Not surprisingly, Internet sellers and steroid-user forums play down the risks of usage, capitalizing on uncertainty in the medical community on the exact risks associated with steroid use and the multiplicity of steroids available, some of which are reputed to be safer than others.

But the medical community unanimously opposes steroid use by adolescents. Steroids are definitively linked to permanent loss of height in adolescents due to the flood of artificial testosterone, which can cause bones to stop growing. Teenagers are also more likely to use extremely high doses or get steroids of questionable purity and production quality.

The motivations to use steroids by both girls and boys often

hurt not only the image of competitive sport but the athletes as well. And steroid use by professional and Olympic athletes encourages young people to try them as well, they argue. "It's clearly something that's infiltrated its way down to grade school and up," says Gary I. Wadler, a professor at New York University Medical School and a member of WADA.

Medical authorities generally say that — for otherwise healthy people — steroids have few if any clinical benefits and produce serious side effects, even if not completely documented. Steroids increase cholesterol levels and, by implication, the risk of heart disease, they say. Oral steroids — though not the more common injected versions — also appear to be associated with liver cancer, they say. Anecdotal evidence suggests that steroids can produce hyper-aggressiveness in some users — so-called 'roid rage. And, for young people, steroids cause bones to stop growing, effectively stunting growth.

However, anti-doping officials say some of the dangers are unproven and many exaggerated. "There's no study that steroids cause heart attacks," says Larry Bowers, USADA's senior managing director for technical and information resources.

Yesalis, who has chided the media for "sensationalizing" the dangers from steroids, adds, "That doesn't mean there aren't potentially serious consequences."

Fost, however, says the dangers are greatly exaggerated. "There is a nearly uniform claim as to steroids that they're very dangerous, they can cause death, cancer, heart attacks," he says. "None of that is supported by any medical evidence, or at least it's widely exaggerated." (*See "At Issue," p. 629.*)

But Fost agrees with anti-doping advocates on the risks steroids pose to young people. In fact, he favors continuing the ban for anyone under 18, pointing out that the most common use of steroids among young people is not by athletes but by bodybuilders. "It's middle- and high-school kids who want to look like Arnold Schwarzenegger," he says.

reflect a striking reversal of gender stereotypes. Participation rates of girls in high school athletics have increased substantially in recent years, including a 160 percent increase in female wrestlers. [7] The rising professionalism and profile of women's sports — like soccer and women's basketball — are probably also factors. [8]

As girls begin taking sports more seriously, boys are becoming — like their female friends — dissatisfied with their bodies. The percentage of men dissatisfied with their overall appearance jumped from 15 percent to 43 percent between 1972 and 1997. Thirty-eight percent of men want bigger pectoral muscles, while only 34 percent of women want bigger breasts. [9]

According to a 2001 survey, 20 percent of young people who take muscle-building supplements or steroids do so to look better. [10] The 2001 NCAA study supports that number.

Harrison Pope, a Harvard psychiatrist who has studied body-image disorders among men, found that most teenage boys have an unnaturally muscular "ideal physique," attainable only by using steroids.

"You feel a great sense of inadequacy, and steroids fill the gap," says "Joseph," an avid college weightlifter from New York who says he never used steroids but knew people who did.

Ironically, Pope's research has found that when female college students selected the most-desirable male bodies, they picked ones with 15 to 30 pounds less muscle than the bodies male college students rated as ideal. [11]

For those trying to quit steroids, losing an artificially enhanced physique can be hard to bear. "There's a serious bout of depression, because it comes to a point where normally you're looking like Superman and you're lifting a phenomenal amount, but once you stop, it's a precipitous decline.

"So it almost compels you to continue and continue and creates an addictive cycle," Joseph says.

Legislators acknowledge the lure of steroids for the young. "What this legislation does is protect our kids," said Rep. John Sweeney, R-N.Y., who sponsored the Anabolic Steroid Control Act of 2004, which would add androstenedione and other steroid precursors frequently sold over-the-counter to the list of drugs that require a doctor's prescription. [12]

— Kenneth Lukas

[1] The Monitoring the Future program at the University of Michigan (www.monitoringthefuture.org) tracks teenage drug use.

[2] The CDC's Youth Risk Behavior Surveillance System project (http://apps.nccd.cdc.gov/yrbss/) provides additional statistics on teen drug use. Figure for high school steroid users obtained by combining 2000 census data with CDC data.

[3] Hearing of the Senate Caucus on International Narcotics Control, July 13, 2004 (http://drugcaucus.senate.gov/steroids04doe.html).

[4] Available at www1.ncaa.org/membership/ed_outreach/research/index.html.

[5] See Monitoring the Future surveys, *op. cit.*

[6] *Ibid.*

[7] Erik Brady and MaryJo Sylwester, "More and More Girls Got Game," *USA Today*, July 1, 2003, p. 1C.

[8] For background, see Jane Tanner, "Women in Sports," *The CQ Researcher*, May 11, 2001, pp. 401-424.

[9] John Cloud, "Never Too Buff," *Time*, April 24, 2000, p. 64.

[10] Available at www.healthycompetition.org.

[11] William J. Cromie, "Drugs Muscle Their Way Into Men's Fitness," *The Harvard University Gazette*, June 15, 2000.

[12] Edward Epstein, "House Votes to Ban More Supplements," *San Francisco Chronicle*, June 4, 2004, p. A7.

For adults, however, Fost says steroids and other performance-enhancing drugs should be legal, and deciding whether to use them should be left up to the individual athlete. "There's not a single athlete in any competitive sport who's just running on his or her natural ability," he says. "Why pick steroids to be concerned about?"

Steroids, Fost says, are conceptually indistinguishable from other man-made aids, such as fiberglass pole-vaulting poles or super-efficient swimsuits. As for the health consequences, Fost says many sports — from gymnastics to football — involve the risk of injury. "It's morally incoherent to prohibit adult athletes from risking harming themselves," he says.

Anti-doping advocates vigorously rebut Fost's arguments. "Why don't you legalize all these drugs?" asks Marc Safran, director of sports medicine at the University of California at San Francisco. "The winner would be the person who comes closer to risking their life."

Yesalis adds that performance-enhancing drugs take away a real but intangible part of the enduring appeal of sport. "You do not need drugs to have a sense of fulfillment, to feel that you've left it all on the field," Yesalis says. "[Drugs have] taken something that God has given us — love of game and sport — and perverted us."

Is drug testing effective?

The controversy swirling around Montgomery, Jones and the other U.S. track stars stems not from failed drug tests but from a cloak-and-dagger story initiated by an anonymous tipster and a team of chemical sleuths. The newly discovered steroid THG was decoded by chemists at the Olympic drug-testing laboratory at UCLA from a sample delivered to USADA anonymously by someone who identified himself as a track and field coach.

Lab chief Catlin says it took three months of chemical testing to crack the code of the new steroid and develop a test to detect it — a chastening reminder of the difficulties of policing performance-enhancing drugs. "There are always new drugs moving in and the old ones moving out," he says. [9]

Cracking Down on Steroids

With the exception of the National Hockey League, major professional and college sports organizations test and penalize for steroid use.

National Football League

Testing: Random testing during the season; all players tested twice in the off-season and once in the preseason.

Penalties: 1st positive test — four-game suspension
2nd — six-game suspension
3rd — one-year suspension

Major League Baseball

Testing: Unannounced testing of all players once during the season, with a follow-up test five to seven days later.

Penalties: 1st positive test — mandatory drug-treatment program
2nd — 15-day suspension or up to a $10,000 fine
3rd — 25-day suspension or up to a $25,000 fine
4th — 50-day suspension or up to a $50,000 fine
5th — one-year suspension or up to a $100,000 fine

National Basketball Association

Testing: For first-year players, once during training camp and three times in regular season; for veterans, once during training camp.

Penalties: 1st positive test — five-game suspension
2nd — 10-game suspension
3rd — 25-game suspension

National Hockey League

Testing: None **Penalties:** None

National Collegiate Athletic Association

Testing: Random August-to-June testing for Division I and II football and Division I track and field; random testing for all competitors in Division I, II and III championships and Division I-A postseason bowl games

Penalties: loss of one year of eligibility

Drug testing — which involves chemical analysis of athletes' urine or blood samples — has been the principal tool for anti-doping enforcement since its introduction in the 1950s. [10] Drug testing snared its first Olympic medallist in 1972, when the teenage American swimmer Rick DeMont had to relinquish his gold medal after testing positive for the stimulant ephedrine, an ingredient in a prescription asthma medication he was taking. Then in 1984, Finnish runner Martti Vainio lost the silver medal he had won in the 10,000-meter race after testing positive for banned substances, and Canadian sprinter Ben Johnson was stripped of his gold medal in 1988 after testing positive for steroids.

The apparent simplicity and certainty of drug-test results, however, masks the complexity and uncertainty of the actual process. Testing is expensive — as much as $500 to $1,000 or more per test. Testing is susceptible to error, cover-up or even sabotage. And, testing can be circumvented.

Athletes can sometimes escape detection at scheduled tests by halting the use of any banned substances beforehand. They also use more ingenious subterfuges. For instance, NFL players have been known to "borrow" urine specimens from someone else, hide the urine vial inside their athletic supporters and then — shielded by a partition — provide the examiner with the clean samples. [11]

Such problems lead many anti-doping advocates to dismiss drug testing as a failure. "The drug testing system has loopholes big enough that I could navigate an Abrams tank through it," Yesalis says. "It's been a colossal flop. I don't know what other enterprise that has such a poor performance rating would still be in business."

Meanwhile, drug tests have yet to be developed for some banned substances — notably, the synthetic human-growth hormone (HGH) and erythropoietin (EPO), a hormone that stimulates production of oxygen-carrying red blood cells, which aid athletes in such endurance sports as cycling or marathons. And sports chemists are constantly developing new substances, such as THG, to evade detection.

"As long as there are people willing to cheat, there will be drugs that are undetectable," says Minnesota's Roberts. "This THG thing would never have come to light except that somebody blew the whistle."

Anti-doping critic Fost agrees. "The drugmakers and the athletes have kept ahead of the testers," he says. The inevitable futility of the effort is another reason to legalize performance-enhancing drugs, Fost suggests.

Moreover, legalizing the drugs would better protect athletes' health, he argues. "As long as they're banned, there will be people trying to avoid detection, and they'll have to do it underground," he says. "They'll be using drugs that won't be adequately tested or subject to [federal] oversight. The worst thing about the THG scandal is that anyone using it has no way of knowing what they're using."

Anti-doping officials acknowledge the difficulties but insist that testing is only one part of the overall effort to keep drugs out of sports. "What we're after is deterrence — not necessarily catching people and sanctioning them but deterring them from using drugs in the first place," USADA's Bowers says. "One of the tools we have for that is testing. We're better now than we were three years ago, and we're capable of seeing more things now than we were three years ago."

"You can't say that testing is going to stamp out drugs," says David Howman, WADA's director general. "You have to have effective education programs. We far prefer to be a preventive body than to be a detection body."

Are penalties for using performance-enhancing drugs stiff enough?

Anti-doping advocates achieved an important breakthrough in 1999 when an international conference of sports organizations and governments agreed to prescribe two-year suspensions for athletes' first doping violation and lifetime bans for a second offense. But U.S. Olympic sprinting champion Maurice Greene advocates even tougher penalties.

"There is no room in our sport for drug cheaters whatsoever," Greene said. "I don't think a year ban or a two-year ban is enough. I think it should be a life ban, if you get caught even once." [12]

USA Track & Field voted last Dec. 7, 2003, to impose a lifetime ban for first-time steroid offenses. It has not yet been implemented, pending a determination that it does not violate the Amateur Sports Act.

Greene's outburst may not have been solely about anti-doping policies. He and Montgomery have a history of bad relations: It was Greene's record of 9.79 seconds in the 100-meter dash that Montgomery clipped in 2002. Greene — who has three of the four fastest times in the event — likes to remind listeners that Montgomery set his mark with a tailwind right at the limit allowed for official records. [13]

Whatever Greene's motivation, some experts agree that a lifetime ban for a first doping violation is worth considering. "If you don't have very stiff penalties, you're not going to deter a lot of people," says the University of California's Safran. "A lifetime ban if you get caught would definitely get people to think twice about it."

But a lifetime ban might be too stringent to be enforceable, Bowers warns. "I'm not sure that we could get people to sanction athletes for life, particularly if that's their livelihood," he says. "If there's a repeat performance or lack of change in behavior after a first time, then I would support a lifetime ban."

In fact, the World Doping Code does allow reduced penalties for unintentional violations for banned substances found in generally available medicinal products. An athlete can also escape penalty by showing that he or she "bears no fault or negligence for the violation."

For his part, Catlin says improved detection is more important than stiffened penalties. "There's enough punishment. A two-year penalty, that's strong enough," he says.

The debate over penalties is most squarely joined today regarding Major League Baseball. The penalties established this season as a result of the 2003 testing include, for a first offense, mandatory referral to treatment and counseling. For a second offense, the player would be suspended for 15 days; only after a fifth offense would a player be suspended for as long as a year. Fines also escalate — to as much as $100,000 for a fifth offense. (*See box, p. 620.*)

AFP Photo/Paolo Cocco

U.S. cyclist Lance Armstrong, five-time Tour de France champion, has been accused of using performance-enhancing drugs but strongly denies the charge.

Wadler calls the MLB penalties "woefully inadequate," noting that on a first offense, the only response is " 'Go see a doctor.' "

For its part, the league is trying to reopen labor negotiations to provide for stiffer punishment. "The commissioner has been saying he'd like to see immediate discipline in the Major League policy," says Rob Manfred, MLB's executive vice president for labor relations.

But baseball association President Don Fehr insists mandatory treatment actually aids subsequent detection and prevention. " 'Go see a doctor' began with a premise: If you test positive . . . there are going to be a lot more tests for you," Fehr says. "The likelihood of the conduct recurring diminishes very greatly."

On the other hand, legalization advocates see no reason for any penalties for using performance-enhancing drugs. "Athletes ought to be able to use them . . . under the supervision of a sports expert after careful clinical trials showing the benefits and risks," Fost says.

But Minnesota's Roberts says that if performance-enhancing drugs were legal, all athletes would feel pressured to use them. "If you're caught, you should be penalized and penalized to the point that it's not worth getting caught," Roberts says. "And if you're caught twice, you should be penalized for life. I would like for athletes to be able to compete without having to use them. A zero-tolerance policy would make that less likely." ■

BACKGROUND

'The Chemical Athlete'

Athletes have always tried to improve their performance with various naturally occurring or chemically modified agents. Medical and pharmacological advances in the 19th and 20th centuries produced new performance-enhancing substances and more sophisticated understanding of their potential benefits — as well as their risks. By the 1960s, some sports organizations and medical associations were recognizing the widening use of performance-enhancing drugs in Olympic and professional sports and calling for steps to combat the practices. [14]

In ancient times, Greek athletes took mushrooms to improve their performance and trained on special diets that included dried figs. Egyptians believed that ingesting the ground rear hooves of the Abyssinian ass could boost performance. Roman gladiators took stimulants to overcome fatigue and injury. The 16th-century Spanish conquerors of Peru found widespread use among the native Incas of the coca leaf as a stimulant.

By the 19th century, athletes were experimenting with a variety of stimulants. Scientists in Europe first isolated cocaine around 1860; there were reports in 1869 of cyclists using heroin-cocaine mixtures to increase endurance. Through the late 19th and early 20th centuries, cyclists in various countries were reported to have used ether-soaked tablets (Belgium), caffeine tablets (France) or mixtures with some combinations of strychnine, heroin, brandy and cocaine (England). [15] In 1904, a U.S. marathoner, Tom Hicks, collapsed and died at the St. Louis Olympics after ingesting a strychnine-brandy cocktail.

The modern era of performance-enhancing drugs can be dated from various scientific developments in the 1930s, including the isolation of the male hormones androsterone (1931) and testosterone (1935) and the discovery of medical applications of the stimulant amphetamine (late-1930s). [16] The German military used testosterone in the 1930s and in World War II to increase the strength and aggressiveness of soldiers and similarly found that amphetamines helped overcome fatigue during combat. Scientific studies in the early 1940s showed improved strength and endurance from using anabolic steroids.

By the 1950s, steroids and amphetamines began spreading into competitive sports. The first recorded case of an "athlete" on steroids actually came earlier — in 1942 — when testosterone pellets were implanted in an 18-year-old trotting horse named Holloway. The results were dramatic. The testosterone, combined with months of training, reversed Holloway's decline and enabled the horse to set a record for trotters at the advanced age of 19. [17]

During the Cold War era, male and female Russian athletes reportedly used anabolic steroids to increase weight and power — prompting some in the United States to follow suit. John Ziegler, a U.S. team physician, returned from the 1956 World Games in Moscow convinced that the Soviet Union and other communist-bloc countries "were going to use every trick to win." He responded by developing and prescribing what he regarded as safe anabolic steroids — only to learn later that athletes were taking excessive dosages. [18]

Steroid use by Olympic participants and athletes in strength sports like football increased largely unchecked through the 1960s. An American Medical Association committee had warned that athletes were abusing amphetamines as early as 1957, and amphetamines were linked to the deaths of at least three world-class cyclists in the 1960s. [19] But steroids were legal, their use somewhat openly acknowledged, their benefits touted and their side effects either unknown or ignored.

The International Olympic Committee (IOC) finally established a medical commission to control drug use in 1967 and a year later instituted the first drug-testing program, during the Mexico City Olympics.

Continued on p. 624

Chronology

Before 1900

Athletes from ancient to modern times use primitive stimulants to try to improve performance.

1930s-1940s

Male hormone testosterone is isolated and synthetic variants are produced; German military uses steroids and amphetamines to increase strength, endurance.

1950s-1970s

Steroids come into widespread use among Olympic athletes; medical, sports authorities raise concerns about their use.

1957
American Medical Association panel warns athletes are abusing amphetamines.

1962
International Olympic Committee (IOC) passes anti-doping resolution.

Late 1960s
East German government systematically dopes Olympic athletes.

1967
Deaths of two elite cyclists linked to possible use of amphetamines.

1972
U.S. swimmer Rick DeMont loses his gold medal after testing positive for banned stimulant ephedrine, an ingredient in his asthma medication.

1980s ***Steroid use spreads in professional football, baseball.***

1987
National Football League (NFL) begins testing players for steroids after several players say steroids are widely used.

1988
Canadian sprinter Ben Johnson loses his Olympic gold medal after testing positive for steroids; Canada appoints special commission to study doping in sports.

1989
NFL begins suspending players who fail drug tests.

1990s ***Stronger anti-doping policies adopted by international and professional sports organizations.***

1990
NFL begins year-round, random-testing program, backed by immediate suspensions for any violations.

1993
NFL toughens drug-testing program.

1998
World's top cycling team is disqualified from Tour de France after coach admits supplying riders with banned drugs. . . . Mark McGwire tops single-season home run record after admitting using a then-legal steroid precursor.

1999
World Conference on Doping backs international code calling for two-year suspension for first-offense doping violation, lifetime ban for second; creates independent anti-doping agency to police Olympics, international events.

2000-Present

Use of performance-enhancing drugs becomes urgent issue for Olympics, baseball.

2002
Barry Bonds sets new single-season home-run record, heatedly denies steroid use. . . . Major League Baseball (MLB) Players Association agrees to random, anonymous testing for steroids during 2003 season.

2003
New steroid THG identified and test developed to detect it. . . . Federal, state authorities raid Bay Area Laboratory Cooperative (BALCO) in September; athletes on client list testify before federal grand jury in November. . . . Results from MLB drug tests trigger testing with penalties for 2004 season.

2004
President Bush urges professional sports leagues to "get rid of steroids now." . . . BALCO President Victor Conte, three others charged in February with conspiring to supply steroids to athletes. . . . Tough, new track and field penalties go into effect on March 1. . . . MLB bans steroid precursor androstenedione on April 12. . . . House votes to ban "andro" and 27 other steroid precursors; measure is pending in the Senate. . . . U.S. Anti-Doping Agency seeks lifetime ban in June against sprinter Tim Montgomery, three other track stars; confirms investigation of sprinter Marion Jones; all deny wrongdoing.

Experts Warn About Gene Doping

Steroid use has altered the face of competitive sports. But an even riskier — and potentially more effective — performance-enhancement method may be on the horizon. Gene doping, a form of gene therapy, could substantially increase a person's athletic ability for months or even years with a single injection — far surpassing the effects of the performance-enhancing steroids and drugs used today. And scientists say the effects could be almost undetectable through blood or urine testing currently used to catch most steroid or drug use. [1]

"The drug problem is the devil we know . . . and here we are at the beginning of a brave new world," World Anti-Doping Agency (WADA) President Richard Pound said last February. [2]

The world medical community has been exploring ways to alter DNA through gene therapy for decades in hopes of curing diseases and extending lives. But many doctors and scientists warn that such techniques might be misused by athletes looking for cutting-edge ways to bulk up and stand out in the increasingly competitive sports world.

These experts say it is highly unlikely that any athletes have undergone genetic alterations yet because the science is still too new. But it may be only a matter of a few years before gene doping is a serious problem, according to the scientists who advise the Montreal-based WADA. [3] Indeed, they say the science could easily be available by the 2008 Olympic Games in Beijing. [4]

Because the introduction of new genes could change how the body functions at the cellular level — strengthening muscles or increasing oxygen-carrying capacity, for example — scientists say gene doping would be particularly hard to detect. Changes in gene structure would be almost impossible to track, so doctors would have to do extensive muscle biopsies to reveal the precise spot where the injection was administered.

WADA has held several conferences, including one this past spring, to study the potential problems posed by gene doping. Theodore Friedmann, director of the gene-therapy program at the University of California, San Diego, and a member of WADA's health, medicine and research committee, says scientists who advise the agency are working on ways to detect genetic alteration.

"There is a much greater level of awareness, and that's the starting point," he says.

When genetic science becomes more readily available, experts assume many athletes will try to take advantage of it, based on 1995 survey in which more than half of about 200 aspiring U.S. Olympians said they would take a banned substance if it would enable them to win every competition for five years — even if it would eventually kill them. [5]

And gene doping could prove a risky enterprise. Friedmann says the main risks of gene doping are the low success factor and the potentially hazardous side effects. Some gene therapy experiments have resulted in death. Only one trial has succeeded — for a French boy born without an immune system, but he later developed leukemia.

Nevertheless, Friedmann believes some athletes probably have experimented with drugs that mimic the effects of ge-

Continued from p. 622

"We must obliterate the image of the chemical athlete," Col. F. Don Miller of the U.S. Olympic Committee declared. [20]

'Totally Juiced'

Far from being brought under control, the use of performance-enhancing drugs has increased exponentially since the 1970s — despite growing cries of alarm from public officials, journalists, sports organizations and even athletes themselves. Drug testing initiated by the IOC snared some Olympic athletes — most prominently, Canadian gold medallist Johnson in 1988. But athletes, observers and anti-doping opponents themselves acknowledged that steroid use was rampant among Olympic athletes, in such major U.S. professional sports as baseball and football and even in collegiate and high school athletics.

The Olympics' first anti-doping enforcement action came in 1972. In an action that remains a subject of controversy today, DeMont was stripped of his gold medal for the 400-meter freestyle at the Munich Games after testing positive for ephedrine. The swimmer, who was also barred from participating in other events at the games, had informed U.S. team physicians beforehand that he was taking an anti-asthma drug, but the information apparently did not reach IOC medical authorities. Three decades later, DeMont, now an assistant swimming coach at the University of Arizona, still believes the action unjustified. [21]

Meanwhile, the IOC essentially took no action against the seemingly blatant use of steroids by East German athletes through the 1970s and '80s. Beginning in the late 1960s, the communist government collaborated with the country's sports federations and team physicians in systematically administering steroids to elite athletes. In his book *Faust's Gold*, doping expert Steven Ungerleider says IOC officials, including Chairman Juan Samaranch, knew about the practices but felt constrained from acting because of possible damage to the image of the Olympics. In fact, Samaranch bestowed the Olympic Order on Manfred Ewald, the head of East German sports, in 1985 — only months benetic engineering, such as growth hormones or insulin-producing proteins that increase muscle size and strength. These drugs, used to treat dwarfism in children or counter the effects of old age, can be dangerous if not used correctly. Human growth hormone, for example, could cause muscles to outgrow the capacity of the blood supply. It could also dramatically enlarge the size of the head, hands or feet. [6]

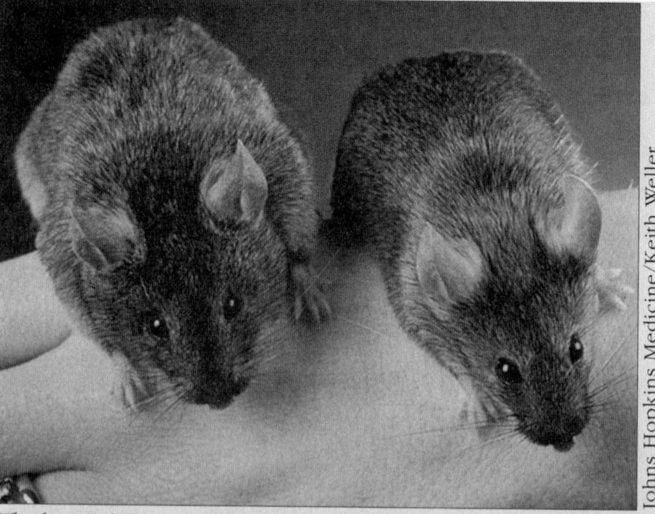

Johns Hopkins Medicine/Keith Weller

The leg and chest muscles of a genetically engineered mouse, left, are four times larger than those of a normal mouse, at right. Scientists fear that the infant medical technology will be used by athletes seeking non-detectable enhancements to their abilities.

Because of such problems, the medical community has been slow to advertise gene therapy as a potential cure-all. But some speculate that the black market for gene-therapy procedures is growing, creating fears that athletes could employ rogue scientists to make them stronger and faster. Russian officials say much of this market has developed in their country, where scientists for the former Soviet Union have lost funding and see gene doping as a potential windfall. [7]

Nikolai Durmanov, who heads Russia's anti-doping efforts, says gene doping is a real danger there, where scientists see few economic alternatives. "When it comes to doping, Russia will become to Europe what Colombia is to the United States" for drugs, he said. [8]

Friedmann says it is not likely that the problem will be limited to Russia and Europe. "I'm concerned that it could happen elsewhere, but I'm just as concerned that it could happen here," he said.

— Mary Clare Jalonick

[1] Toby Sterling, "Experts Believe Gene Doping Cases Are Around the Corner," The Associated Press, April 17, 2004.

[2] Bruce Lieberman, "Cheating in Sports Could Become Genetic," Copley News Service, Feb. 23, 2004.

[3] Sal Ruibal, "Gene Alteration Sets off Alarm in Doping Fight," *USA Today*, April 15, 2004, p. 3C.

[4] John Powers, "Despite Attempts to Track Down Athletes Using Banned Substances, USOC has Catching Up to Do," *The Boston Globe*, July 4, 2004, p. D1.

[5] Jere Longman, "Someday Soon, Athletic Edge May be From Altered Genes," *The New York Times*, May 11, 2001, p. A1.

[6] *Ibid.*

[7] Ruibal, *op. cit.*

[8] *Ibid.*

fore Ewald published a book acknowledging widespread doping. [22]

Johnson's disqualification after winning the 100-meter event at the Seoul Olympic Games in 1988 had a more galvanizing effect on anti-doping efforts. [23] Johnson — who had set a new world record for the event the year before — bested U.S. sprinter Carl Lewis in the race with another record-setting mark: 9.79 seconds. A few days later, however, Johnson's urine samples turned up steroids. He was disqualified and Lewis was awarded the medal. Later, after admitting he had used steroids before the 1987 race — his earlier world record was also wiped out. Tellingly, documents released in 2003 by former U.S. anti-doping official Wade Exum showed that Lewis had also taken the same types of banned stimulants in 1988 and had been caught at the U.S. Olympic trials.

The Canadian government responded to Johnson's disqualification by creating a special commission of inquiry headed by Ontario Chief Justice Charles Dubin. The commission's report, published in 1990, blamed widespread use of steroids — especially in weightlifting and track and field — for encouraging "hypocrisy and cynicism in athletes and young people." It recommended cutting off government financing for athletes who tested positive for drug use.

After the fall of the Iron Curtain, the reunification of Germany led to more damning evidence of the pervasive doping practices used by the former East German government and eventual criminal prosecutions of some participants. Evidence showed that many of the athletes — including teenagers — were administered steroids without their knowledge; some complained of lasting health effects. Leading sports officials were prosecuted and convicted, but most received only suspended sentences — including Ewald himself, in July 2000.

Anecdotal evidence about the use of steroids in U.S. professional football and baseball emerged during the 1980s and '90s. The growing bulk of football players on such vaunted teams as the Pittsburgh Steelers pointed unmistakably to the effects of steroids. In his 1991 book *False Glory*, former Steeler Steve Courson estimated at least half of the league's linemen used steroids. Other players made similar estimates. [24]

By the late 1980s and early '90s, suspicion was falling, too, on baseball, as players bulked up and home-run output increased. But Mark McGwire's use of the then-legal steroid precursor andro fell short of a scandal when acknowledged in 1998. Four years later, though, former San Diego Padre third-baseman Ken Caminiti admitted that he had heavily used steroids for years — including in 1996, when he won the National League's Most Valuable Player award. When it published Caminiti's admission — under the headline "Totally Juiced" — *Sports Illustrated* described the use of steroids and other performance-enhancing drugs as "rampant." [25]

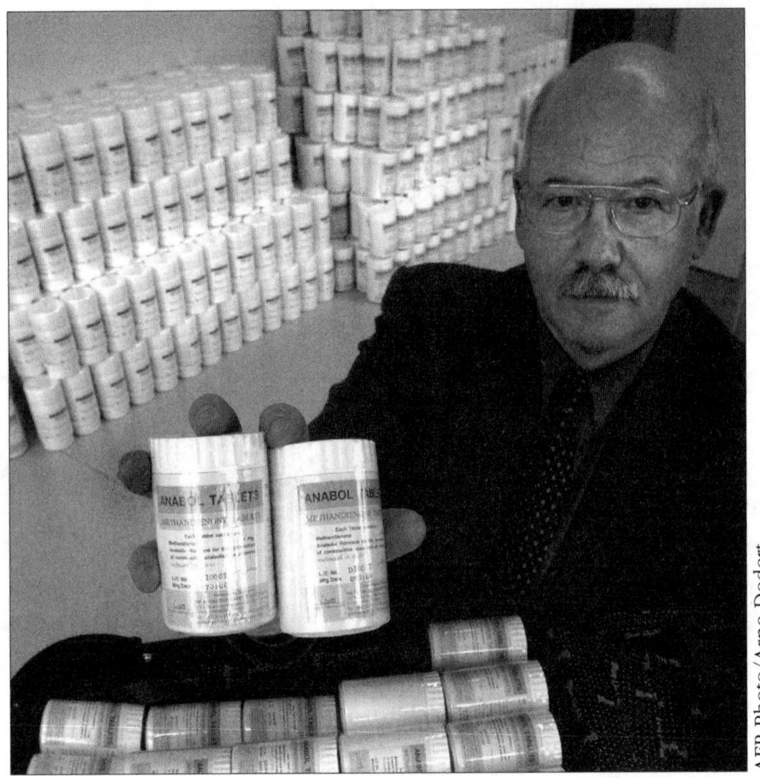

AFP Photo/Arne Dedert

Anabolic steroid tablets being smuggled from Thailand into Germany by a German drug-smuggling ring were seized at a Frankfurt airport in 2001 by customs officers.

Cracking Down

The continuing controversies about steroids in the 1990s led finally to stronger anti-doping policies. Most significantly, the IOC in 1999 adopted the World Anti-Doping Code and created WADA to combat performance-enhancing drug use in international sport. In the United States, the NFL claimed progress in reducing use of steroids after instituting random drug testing with significant penalties even for a first violation. Baseball proved more resistant to anti-doping policies, but the league and the players' association eventually agreed in 2002 to institute anonymous random testing and to move to "testing with consequences" if more than 5 percent of players tested positive.

The IOC convened an international conference in 1999 in Lausanne, Switzerland, against a backdrop of major sports controversies. In July 1998, all nine members of the world's leading cycling team were disqualified from the renowned Tour de France after the coach, Bruno Roussel, admitted supplying illegal steroids and the synthetic hormone EPO to the riders. [26]

Meanwhile, medical officials and some Olympic athletes themselves were saying that drug use was out of control at the quadrennial games. U.S. marathoner Mark Coogan said he was convinced the startling improvement in times for the event resulted from rampant use of EPO.

"It makes you want to quit running," he told *The New York Times.* [27] In a long article, the *Times* quoted a range of experts acknowledging that anti-doping enforcement was uneven at best.

"Only the dumb get caught," said Dick Schultz, executive director of the U.S. Olympic Committee.

When the anti-doping conference convened, the IOC was expected to emerge as the head of the new anti-doping agency. But the committee was under fire not only for ineffective anti-doping policies but also for a bribery scandal in connection with the impending 2002 Winter Games in Salt Lake City. Thus, the delegates — representatives of national governments as well as sports organizations — decided to create an independent agency.

The 18-member panel — to be established in time for the 2000 Summer Games in Sydney, Australia — was to be charged with overseeing out-of-competition testing, setting laboratory standards and improving detection methods. The conference also set in motion the writing of a new, world anti-doping code that was to prescribe a two-year suspension from all competition for any doping violations.

Through the 1980s and '90s, anti-doping advocates raised suspicions that steroids were implicated in the deaths of as many as two-dozen elite athletes. Doubts emerged when U.S. track star Florence Griffith Joyner — holder of the 100-meter and 200-meter Olympic records — died in her sleep in 1998, at age 38. Joyner had repeatedly denied using performance-enhancing drugs. The medical examiner said her death was unrelated to steroid use. [28]

Drug Testing

Among the nation's four major professional sports leagues, football has the strongest anti-doping program and hockey the weakest, with basketball and baseball in between.

The National Football League (NFL) began checking players for steroids in 1987; it started suspending violators in 1989. A year later, the NFL instituted year-round random testing, including off-season testing, with immediate suspensions for violations.

But Penn State's Yesalis and other critics call the NFL's approach a "façade." Because the testing is not conducted by an independent third party, the NFL can limit disclosure of positive tests or even decline to take action if it would mean outing a star player. [29]

Baseball did not institute its own much-maligned testing program until 2003, when it began anonymous testing. Critics complain that — in addition to having a weak regime with no off-season tests — baseball's penalties are too light. A first positive test allows a player to retain his anonymity and only requires him to enter a drug-treatment program. [30]

The National Basketball Association began testing for steroids in 1999. First-year players are tested once during training camp and up to three times during the regular season. Veteran players test only once, during training camp. Players are suspended for five games for a first violation, increasing to 25 games for the third and subsequent violations. [31]

The National Hockey League does not test its players for steroids, stimulants or any other performance-enhancing drugs. "We are fortunate not to have a problem with steroid use in our sport," said Ted Saskin, senior director of the NHL Players Association. [32] The league does, however, offer education and counseling for anyone who feels they need it.

But critics question how the league can be so sure it does not have a problem if it doesn't test. "The NHL absolutely, unequivocally needs a bona fide anti-doping program," says the WADA's Wadler. "To suggest the NHL is immune to problems of drug abuse borders on the absurd." [33]

In fact, he says, the league should look into whether stimulants or steroids are feeding the excessive aggressiveness associated with hockey. "Clearly, anabolic steroids make you more aggressive," Wadler says. [34]

For college athletes, testing regimens vary depending on the sport and level of play. The NCAA's August-to-June random testing applies only to football players in Division I and II programs, and track and field competitors at Division I schools; testing began in 1990 and 1992, respectively, for the two sports. All participants in any division championships and football players in Division I-A bowl games have been subject to testing since 1986. Players who test positive lose a year of eligibility.

Interestingly, it was a women's college track coach who mentioned her concern about steroid use by women to President Bush at a White House Christmas party, leading him to note the problem in his State of the Union address. [35] ■

CURRENT SITUATION

Agony of Defeat

After months of battling insinuations of steroid use, Marion Jones and Tim Montgomery saw their hopes of Olympic gold in their signature events dashed on the weekend of July 10-11. The finish-line pictures tell the story. Jones' face is etched with disappointment as she comes in fifth in the women's 100-meter final in the U.S. Olympic trials. Montgomery is all but out of the photo-finish picture in the men's 100-meter final the next day — ending up seventh in a race won by his longtime nemesis, Maurice Greene.

In defeat, Jones and Montgomery had bitter remarks about their treatment by the news media since their names were first linked to the BALCO drug scandal in September 2003. "When I talk, you guys have something negative to say," Jones told reporters. "When I don't talk . . . you guys have something negative to say. I'd much rather not talk and spend time with my son." [36]

Montgomery, Jones' live-in companion and father of their infant son, blamed the media for his loss. "I didn't win . . . because y'all were on my back," he said. "I have to deal with y'all every day." As he vanished from sight, however, he vowed: "This ain't my last race, man." [37]

The results were not completely unexpected. Montgomery and Jones had both run poorly in June in the Prefontaine Classic in Eugene, Ore. Regardless, the results eased the feared dilemma for the U.S. Olympics team of sending suspected users of performance-enhancing drugs to Athens in August to represent the United States.

During the 10 days of track and field Olympic qualifying trials in Sacramento, two other athletes facing doping charges failed to qualify for their events — Gaines (100 meters) and Alvin Harrison (400 meters) — while Collins withdrew from the 400 meters because of a hamstring injury. Regina Jacobs decided not to compete in the 1,500 meters and announced her retirement two days before the USADA banned her from competition for four years for having tested positive for THG. Calvin Harrison finished fifth in the 400-meter finals. Jones qualified in the women's long jump.

Among three athletes who had tested positive in the past for banned substances, Mickey Grimes failed to qualify in the 200-meter semifinals, and Larry Wade withdrew from the 110 hurdles after injuring an arm in practice.

Torri Edwards finished second in the 100 meters and third in the 200-meter race. But her eventual participation in the games was up in the air: On July19 she had to defend an earlier positive test for the banned stimulant nikethamide before an arbitration panel, where she faces up to a two-year suspension.

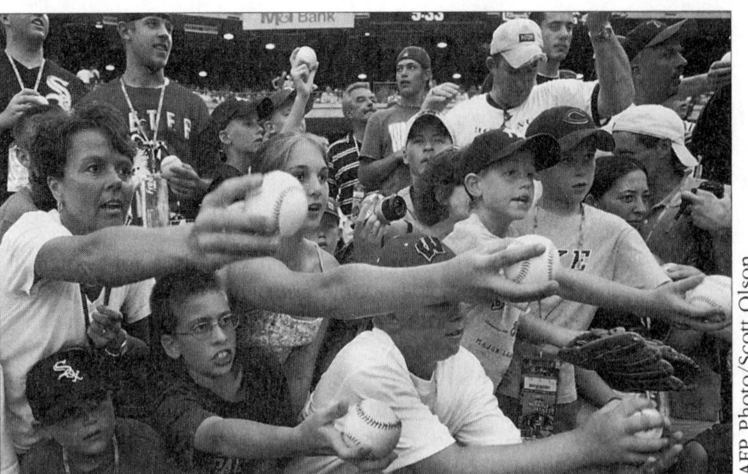
AFP Photo/Scott Olson

High attendance at baseball games suggests that Americans' love for sports has been little affected by the drug scandal and seems likely to endure even if a tougher crackdown fails to eliminate doping.

"These track performances take the edge off of USADA being up against the wall for the selection of the team," doping expert Ungerleider, said. "But when you look at the big picture, we still have to clean up the mess of cheating and drugs." [38]

Meanwhile, the International Association of Athletics Federations recommended on July 18 that the U.S. men's 1,600-meter relay team be stripped of its gold medal from the 2000 Olympics, because team member Jerome Young tested positive for steroids in 1999. The IOC is expected to endorse the recommendation.

The United States has been under special scrutiny because of its past reputation for doing little to try to stop doping. "There was no pressure in the United States to take anti-doping seriously," says Barrie Houlihan, a professor of sports policy at Loughborough University in Leicestershire, England. "People preferred to look away."

But Houlihan says USADA is helping the U.S. image abroad by "taking the issue more seriously."

In fact, four U.S. track and field athletes sat out this year's trials because they had been banned from competition for two years for doping violations, including Kelli White, the women's world 100-meter and 200-meter champion, who admitted using steroids and EPO. The three others — who all tested positive for THG — were shot put champion Toth, and hammer throw champions McEwen and Price.

Doping scandals are besetting many other countries as well. Dwain Chambers, Britain's top sprinter, was banned from competition for two years in February 2004 after testing positive for THG the previous August. Rio Ferdinand, a star defender for the Manchester United soccer team, was banned for eight months in 2003 for missing a scheduled drug test. The Italian Olympic Committee disclosed in June that Olympic hammer thrower Loris Paoluzzi failed a random drug test in April.

A major controversy is simmering in cycling, Europe's second-most-popular sport, after two leading riders described drug use in early 2004 as rampant among cyclists. The admissions came after the unexplained deaths of eight cyclists, ranging in age from 16 to 35, since January 2003. [39]

The U.S. cyclist Lance Armstrong, five-time Tour de France champion, is also being linked to use of performance-enhancing drugs in a new book, *L.A. Confidential: The Secrets of Lance Armstrong*. The book — by David Walsh and Pierre Ballester — relies in part on allegations by a former Armstrong assistant, Emma O'Reilly, who says she helped Armstrong dispose of used syringes and use make-up to disguise needle marks on his arms. Armstrong denies using drugs. [40]

WADA officials say European countries are among the most vigilant in anti-doping efforts. They cite limited progress in other regions, especially among poorer countries in Asia, Africa and Latin America. The most encouraging changes come from China, which has implemented an anti-doping policy four years after having withdrawn some 40 athletes from Sydney for doping issues. "They're doing everything we're asking of them," says Director General Howman. "Obviously," he adds, "the spur is the Beijing Olympics" — scheduled for 2008.

Points of Contention

The commissioner of baseball and the president of the players' association have many differences, but early this year they did agree on how best to handle suspected steroid use by players: The less said, the better.

Shortly after federal indictments were handed up in the BALCO scandal, Commissioner Bud Selig directed team officials and personnel to refrain from commenting on the case. Union President Fehr reportedly sent a similar advisory. "The best course of action for players is to do nothing about these matters," he reportedly said. [41]

Continued on p. 630

At Issue:

Should Major League Baseball adopt stricter policies on the use of steroids?

GARY I. WADLER, M.D.
ASSOCIATE PROFESSOR OF CLINICAL MEDICINE, NEW YORK UNIVERSITY SCHOOL OF MEDICINE MEMBER, WORLD ANTI-DOPING AGENCY

WRITTEN FOR *THE CQ RESEARCHER*, JULY 2004

yes

When it comes to eliminating doping, there can be no compromise, no middle ground, no rhetorical gymnastics.

Professional athletes awash with money and dazzled by fame feel pressure to win at any cost, even if it means using illicit drugs. Steroid abuse is the major problem regarding performance-enhancing drugs in baseball. Lest we forget, not long ago amphetamine use was the poster child of doping in baseball — giving rise to the Controlled Substances Act of 1970. Similarly, steroid abuse in the 1980s gave rise to the Controlled Substances (Anabolic Steroid) Act of 1990. Both laws recognized the threat to the public health from drug abuse.

Mark McGwire changed the steroid landscape in 1998, when it appeared that the dietary supplement androstenedione ("andro") may have contributed to his home-run record. The precursor of testosterone, androstenedione helped McGwire legally circumvent the Anabolic Steroid Act. McGwire did not break the laws of baseball or the laws of the land. Clearly, both laws needed to and have been strengthened.

Assertions that baseball is rife with steroids prompted baseball's new collective-bargaining agreement to ban Schedule III steroids and provide for testing in 2003 to assess the extent of the problem. The survey revealed 5 to 7 percent of the 1,438 tests were positive, and that there were between 72 and 101 failed tests — equivalent to two major league team rosters.

Fast forward. The Food and Drug Administration markedly limited androstenedione's availability. McGwire's name in the news has been replaced by Bonds, Giambi and others. The supplement/drug de jour is no longer "andro" but THG. And speculation continues to abound about who is using what, and which records are "drug free."

But steroid abuse is not only about records. It is also about a promising 16-year-old high school baseball player trying to put on 30 pounds who hanged himself in an anabolic steroid-induced depression. Despite those that would argue otherwise, the medical literature documenting the array of adverse effects of anabolic steroids is irrefutable.

Finally, the use of anabolic steroids other than for the treatment of a disease is against the law! In the final analysis, baseball must rid itself of steroids. A comprehensive drug-testing program, not what exists today, is essential to insure that baseball remains a contest of skill and character and not pharmacology.

NORMAN FOST, M.D.
PROFESSOR, PEDIATRICS AND BIOETHICS DIRECTOR, PROGRAM IN BIOETHICS UNIVERSITY OF WISCONSIN MEDICAL SCHOOL

WRITTEN FOR *THE CQ RESEARCHER*, JULY 2004

no

Let me be sure I understand this: Baseball Commissioner Bud Selig, speaking on behalf of the owners and allegedly the fans, wants stricter policies to prohibit anabolic steroid use. The effect of these policies might be to suspend, ban for life, or possibly even send to prison players like Barry Bonds.

Bonds is probably the biggest draw in the sport over the past decade. Why would the commissioner be so intent on taking him away from us? He says he's concerned about fair competition. This is hard to take seriously in a league where the Yankees have a payroll of $180 million, and my beloved Brewers have $30 million.

The commissioner says he also is concerned about the health and safety of the athletes. Then why doesn't he propose a lifetime ban for anyone using alcohol or tobacco? They account for 500,000 deaths each year in America, which is about 500,000 more than deaths due to anabolic steroids. If an umpire really thinks Roger Clemens is trying to hit someone in the head with a 95-mile-per-hour fastball, why eject him for just that game? Suspension for a year would convey a more sincere concern for players' safety.

The commissioner says the integrity of records is in jeopardy and that fans will lose interest if they think players are using performance-enhancing drugs. The last time I looked, the biggest draws in the past decade have been Mark McGwire, who admitted using steroids, and Bonds, who has been all but convicted by the press. Bad for baseball? Is Selig kidding?

With or without steroids, any claim that records are comparable is naive in the extreme. The fences are shorter, the pitching mound is lower, the seasons are longer and the ball is said to be livelier.

On the other hand, Bonds has to face set-up men and closers that hardly existed in Babe Ruth's time, when the Babe could hit against a tiring starter in the late innings. And the influx of African-American, Latino and Japanese players has expanded the pool of talented pitchers far beyond those available in Ruth's day.

The incoherent arguments that fuel steroid hysteria are, well — almost hysterical. As Myron Cohen, the great Jewish storyteller, used to say, "Somethin' fishy going on here!"

Continued from p. 628

Less than a week after the memos were disclosed, however, Selig and Fehr got a stern warning from a Senate committee investigating steroids. "The status quo is not acceptable," Commerce Chairman John McCain, R-Ariz., declared at a March 10 hearing. "We will have to act in some way unless the major league players' union acts in the affirmative and rapid fashion." [42]

Fehr insisted that the union does not "support or condone" the use of any illegal substance or the illegal use of any lawful substance. But he also said the union had gone far enough in its drug-testing program.

Fehr went on to criticize proposals for more extensive testing or penalties. "Each of us has an interest in preventing unwarranted invasions of privacy," Fehr said — adding, "even in the workplace of professional athletes."

For his part, Selig said drug testing had been "the most contentious issue" between the league and the union during the 2002 negotiations. Describing the agreement as "a compromise," Selig said the league would make it "a priority" in the next negotiations to try to win agreement for "more frequent and year-round testing of players."

As the season continues, baseball is enjoying record attendance and close races in most divisions. But the steroid issue continues to hang over some of the sport's top stars — most notably, Bonds.

The *San Francisco Chronicle* reported on June 24 that track star Montgomery had told the federal grand jury in fall 2003 that BALCO lab President Conte had provided the steroid Winstrol to Bonds. The newspaper also quoted a purported memo by an Internal Revenue Service investigator, Jeff Novitzky, as saying that Conte had acknowledged giving Bonds an undetectable steroid-like drug called "the clear" and a testosterone cream. [43]

Bonds lashed out at Montgomery the next day without specifically responding to the reported testimony. "I don't even know who he is," Bonds told reporters. "So how he's making accusations of me, I don't even know." [44]

Conte, on the other hand, issued a blanket denial. "I want to inform the world I have never given anabolic steroids or any other performance-enhancing drug to Barry Bonds," Conte said. [45]

Both Congress and baseball appear to be moving forward to silence one drug issue: the status of the steroid-precursor andro. The league banned the supplement in April, and the House voted on June 3 to ban it, as well as 26 other precursors; a comparable measure is pending in the Senate.

Selig is also becoming more vocal on the general issue of steroids. Speaking to a gathering of female journalists and sports information professionals in Milwaukee on June 4, he said he hopes to win the union's agreement "very soon" to what he called "a more comprehensive and far-reaching plan."

"This is about health. This is about fairness, this is about integrity, this is about social responsibility," Selig said. "This is about the long-term health of our players. This is about having a level playing field for our players to compete." [46]

Fehr, however, continues to do his best to deflect attention from the subject. In a 45-minute interview on June 29, the union chief contended that use of steroids by players is less widespread than believed. But he fended off questions whether steroids may be contributing to a reported increase in injuries among players or the recent surge in home runs.

Fehr declined to discuss negotiations with the league over additional testing. But he voiced confidence that use of steroids will be brought under control in the foreseeable future.

"We will have it very well under control either as a result of modifications that we make if they prove to be warranted or if they're a result of the things we've already put into place," he said. ■

OUTLOOK

The Values of Sports

Americans' love for sport has been little affected by the drug scandal. The multiple values that fans derive from sports — entertainment, excitement, solidarity — endure, as Michael Mandelbaum points out in his new book *The Meaning of Sports.* [47] And they seem likely to endure even if a tougher stand against performance-enhancing drugs fails — as seems likely — to eliminate their use.

Anti-doping advocates say they are making progress. Nearly half of the 34 international sports federations under the Olympic umbrella now have year-round "out of competition" drug testing. USADA officials are vigorously pushing cases stemming from the BALCO scandal, while also promising to increase research and education.

"We have taken some giant, giant steps around the globe and certainly in the country," says New York University's Wadler, a member of WADA.

For his part, Fost, the leading U.S. critic of anti-doping policies, acknowledges that what he calls "the mass hysteria" about performance-enhancing drugs is unlikely to change any time soon. "I don't think there are enough people who are looking at it carefully to turn the tide, at least in the foreseeable future," he says.

Still, anti-doping advocates concede that steroids continue to have a powerful appeal for many athletes, especially young people. "I sense that most athletes are young and don't feel their own mortality," says Roberts, the sports-medicine group's president. "To them, it's just another means of moving ahead."

Steroids also appear relatively easy to obtain despite their classification as controlled substances under federal law. A simple Internet search turns up several sites offering mail-ordered steroids; one site even sells prescriptions.

In addition, sports chemists appear likely to continue exploiting their knowledge of science to stay ahead of detection efforts. "There's always going to be the opportunity for small companies to produce slightly modified steroids," says Houlihan at Loughboro University.

At the UCLA testing lab, Catlin says he would be "quite surprised" if other designer drugs like the recently discovered THG did not already exist. "I believe they are out there," he said. "I hear about that every day." [48]

To get ahead of whatever other BALCOs may be out there, Catlin calls for concentrating drug-detection research efforts at a few well-funded institutes. "It doesn't work to have 30 or 40 research institutes around the world," Catlin says. "You only need two or three."

Penn State's Yesalis similarly wants to see more funding for drug detection. "The sports federations need to pool $100 million and distribute it to the top chemists around the world to develop new tests and close all those loopholes," he says. "I've never seen any credible funding that says they're being sincere about the problem."

In a world where sports are big business, however, some anti-doping advocates fear that performance-enhancing drugs actually offer financial incentives both for athletes and sports leagues. "One could make the argument that doping has been very good for the business of sports," Yesalis says. "Because it creates bigger-than-life individuals who perform bigger-than-life feats. And, after all, isn't that what people pay to see?"

But newly developing technologies — such as gene doping — may soon produce "bigger than life" genetically engineered super-athletes without using drugs, making the world's doping-detection apparatus obsolete.

"The world may be about to watch one of its last Olympic Games without genetically enhanced athletes," wrote H. Lee Sweeney, chairman of physiology at the University of Pennsylvania School of Medicine, in a recent cover story in *Scientific American*. [49]

In the meantime, both baseball and the Olympics appear to be holding fan support despite their entanglement with the BALCO scandal. Thomas Boswell, *The Washington Post*'s respected sports columnist, says the baseball public "has already digested the possibility" that one or more sluggers, including Bonds, may eventually be shown to be steroid users. The record-paced attendance during the season, he says, appears to represent the public's "broader verdict" on the game. [50]

As for the Olympics, most U.S. sports fans say that drug use is not a major problem. Among people who said they were interested in the Olympics, 43 percent said use of steroids and other performance-enhancing drugs was a major problem, but 49 percent described it as minor, and 6 percent called it no problem at all. [51]

With the Olympics about to get under way, Houlihan says he expects some progress in the anti-doping fight, but he says it will be slow — and also difficult to measure.

"The best indicator of progress would be that world records would stand still," he says. "We would probably see the average of the 10 best times in a particular event being steady or even declining. That might be in some ways the best indicator that it's becoming more difficult to compete in high-level athletic competitions and take drugs." ■

Notes

[1] See Tim Layden, "The New 100m World Record: 9.78 Seconds," *Sports Illustrated*, Sept. 23, 2002, p. 50.

[2] See Richard L. Worsnop, "Athletes and Drugs," *The CQ Researcher*, July 26, 1991, pp. 513-536.

[3] For background, see Mark Fainaru-Wada and Lance Williams, "How the Doping Scandal Unfolded," *The San Francisco Chronicle*, Dec. 21, 2003, p. B1. See also Jere Longman and Ford Fessenden, "Rivals Turn to Tattling in Steroids Case Involving Top Athletes," *The New York Times*, April 11, 2004, sec. 8, p. 1.

[4] *The San Jose Mercury News* identified Trevor Graham, who once coached both Jones and Montgomery, as the source. See Elliott Almond, *et al.*, "Feud lit fuse on Balco scandal; Track Coach Sent Smoking-Gun Syringe Filled With THG to Anti-Doping Agency," *San Jose Mercury News*, July 4, 2004, p. A1.

[5] Jack Curry and Jere Longman, "Results of Steroid Testing Spur Baseball to Set Tougher Rules," *The New York Times*, Nov. 14, 2003.

[6] See Mark Fainaru-Wada and Lance Wiliams, "Sprinter Admitted Use of BALCO 'Magic Potion'," *The San Francisco Chronicle*, June 24, 2004, p. A1; Lance Williams and Mark Fainaru-Wada, "Track Star's Testimony Linked Bonds to Steroid Use," *ibid.*, p. A16.

[7] For contrasting views, see Jack McCallum, "Swallow This Pill," *Sports Illustrated*, Aug. 31, 1998, p. 17; and Philip M. Boffey, "Post-Season Thoughts on McGwire's Pills," *The New York Times*, Sept. 30, 1998, p. A16.

[8] For a British academic who takes a similar view, see Ellis Cashmore, "Stop Testing and Legalise All Drugs," *The Observer*, Oct. 26, 2003, p. 9. Cashmore is a professor of culture, media and sport at Staffordshire University.

[9] For a detailed account, see Jere Longman and Joe Drape, "Decoding a Steroid: Hunches, Sweat, Vindication," *The New York Times*, Nov. 2, 2003, sec. 1, p. 1.

About the Author

Associate Editor **Kenneth Jost** graduated from Harvard College and Georgetown University Law Center, where he is an adjunct professor. He is the author of *The Supreme Court Yearbook* and editor of *The Supreme Court from A to Z* (both *CQ Press*). He was a member of *The CQ Researcher* team that won the 2002 American Bar Association Silver Gavel Award.

[10] Background drawn from Jim Ferstle, "Evolution and Politics of Drug Testing," in Charles E. Yesalis (ed.), *Anabolic Steroids in Sport and Exercise* (2d ed.), 2000, pp. 363-413.
[11] See Mike Freeman, "N.F.L. Is Told How Players Cheat on Drug Tests," *The New York Times*, Aug. 5, 1993, p. B2.
[12] Liz Robbins, "Greene Supports Lifetime Bans," *The New York Times*, May 18, 2004, p. D2.
[13] See Mike DeArmond, "Back Up to Speed: Greene Ran Into Some Injury Problems, but He's Ready to Go for More Gold," *The Kansas City Star*, May 18, 2004, p. C3.
[14] Background drawn from Barrie Houlihan, *Dying to Win: Doping in Sport and the Development of Anti-Doping Policy* (2d ed.), 2000, pp. 33-59; Gary I. Wadler and Brian Hainline, *Drugs and the Athlete* (1989), *passim*; Yesalis, (ed.), *op. cit.*, pp. 15-73.
[15] Robert Voy, *Drugs, Sport and Politics: The Inside Story about Drug Use in Sport and its Political Cover-up*, 1991, cited in Houlihan, *op. cit.*, p. 33.
[16] For background, see Erica R. Freeman, *et al.*, "A Brief History of Testosterone," *The Journal of Urology*, Vol. 165, pp. 371-373 (February 2001), at www.mastersmensclinic.com.
[17] B. Kearns, *et al.*, "Testosterone Implantation in the Gelding," *Journal of the American Veterinary Medicine Association* (1942), pp. 197-201, cited in Yesalis, *op. cit.*, pp. 52-53.
[18] John B. Ziegler, "Introduction," in Bob Goldman, *Death in the Locker Room: Steroids and Sports* (1984), pp. 1-3.
[19] See Goldman, *ibid.*, pp. 27-28.
[20] Quoted in Steven Ungerleider, *Faust's Gold: Inside the East German Doping Machine* (2001), p. 186.
[21] See Alan Abrahamson, "Thirty Years After Munich, IOC Battle Against Doping Is Far From Over," *Los Angeles Times*, Sept. 1, 2002, part 4, p. 3.
[22] Ungerleider, *op. cit.*, p. 23.
[23] See biographical entry in Wikipedia (http://en.wikipedia.org).
[24] Steve Courson and Lee R. Schreiber, *False Glory: Steelers and Steroids — The Steve Courson Story* (1991). For similar estimates, see Yesalis, *op. cit.*, pp. 60-61.
[25] Tom Verducci, "Totally Juiced," *Sports Illustrated*, June 3, 2002.
[26] Samuel Abt, "Top Team Expelled By Tour de France Over Drug Charges," *The New York Times*, July 18, 1998, p. A1.
[27] Jere Longman, "Widening Drug Use Compromises Faith in Sports," *The New York Times*, Dec. 26, 1998, p. A1.

FOR MORE INFORMATION

American College of Sports Medicine, 401 West Michigan St., Indianapolis, IN 46202-3233; (317) 637-9200; www.acsm.org.

Major League Baseball, 245 Park Ave., 31st floor, New York, NY 10167; (212) 931-7800; www.mlb.com.

Major League Baseball Players Association, 12 East 49th St., 24th floor, New York, NY 10017; (212) 826-0808; http://bigleaguers.yahoo.com.

USA Track & Field, One RCA Dome, Suite 140, Indianapolis, IN 46225; (317) 261-0500; www.usatf.org.

U.S. Anti-Doping Agency, 2550 Tenderfoot Hill St., Suite 200, Colorado Springs, CO 80906-7346; (719) 785-2000; www.usantidoping.org.

World Anti-Doping Agency, Stock Exchange Tower, 800 Place Victoria, Suite 1700, P.O. Box 120, Montreal (Quebec) H4Z 1B7, Canada; (514) 904-9232; www.wada-ama.org/en/t1.asp.

[28] Jere Longman, "Griffith Joyner Died After Seizure in Sleep," *The New York Times*, Oct. 23, 1998, p. D1.
[29] "PSU Prof Spots Big Drug Crisis," *Pittsburgh Post-Gazette*, May 27, 2004, p. D1.
[30] Baseball's current steroid policy is available, upon request only, as part of the 28-page Joint Drug Prevention and Treatment Program.
[31] See the NBA players' collective bargaining agreement at www.nbpa.com/cba/cba.html.
[32] Steve Wilstein, "NHL Needs Attitude Change in Support of Drug Testing," *Chattanooga Times Free Press*, March 21, 2004, p. C3.
[33] *Ibid.*
[34] *Ibid.*
[35] Steve Fainaru and Mike Allen, "MLB Players' Union Balks at Steroids Summit," *The New York Times*, Feb. 29, 2004, p. E1.
[36] For coverage, see Liz Robbins, "Jones Goes From Queen of 100 to Also-Ran," *The New York Times*, July 11, 2004, sec. 8, p. 1.
[37] See Liz Robbins, "Greene Leaves Montgomery Far Behind in 100," *The New York Times*, July 12, 2004, p. D1; Amy Shipley, "Jones Dashed in 100 Meters," *The Washington Post*, July 11, 2004, p. E1; "Not Easy Seeing Greene," July 12, 2004, p. D1; Mike Wise, "Greene Leaves No Doubt; Montgomery Simply Leaves," *The Washington Post*, July 12, 2004, p. D1.
[38] Quoted in Jere Longman, "Eligibility Is Decided on Track Instead of in Courtroom," *The New York Times*, July 12, 2004, p. D1.
[39] See Ron Kroichick, "Cycle of Tragedy: Baseball Has BALCO, but Europe Is Plagued With Its Own Sports Drug Scandal," *The San Francisco Chronicle*, May 9, 2004, p. C1.
[40] "French Judge Rejects Armstrong's Action," The Associated Press, June 21, 2004.
[41] Michael Hirsley, "Latest Steroid Policy: Zip It," *The Chicago Tribune*, March 4, 2004, p. C4.
[42] Quoted in Thomas Heath, "Senate Warns Baseball on Steroid Testing," *The Washington Post*, March 11, 2004, p. A1. See also Richard Sandomir, "Baseball Receives Steroid Warning," *The New York Times*, March 11, 2004, p. D1.
[43] Williams and Fainaru-Wada, *op. cit.*
[44] See Janie McCauley, "Furious Bonds: 'I Ain't Never Met Tim Montgomery'," The Associated Press, June 25, 2004.
[45] Carol Pogash, "Conte Disputes Report That He Gave Steroids to Bonds," *The New York Times*, June 26, 2004, p. D1.
[46] See Don Walker, "Selig Wants Tougher Testing," *The Milwaukee Journal-Sentinel*, June 5, 2004.
[47] Michael Mandelbaum, *The Meaning of Sports: Why Americans Watch Baseball, Football, and Basketball and What They See When They Do* (2004), pp. 280-284.
[48] Jere Longman and Liz Robbins, "Track World Fears Scandal May Widen," *The New York Times*, July 10, 2004, p. D5.
[49] H. Lee Sweeney, "Gene Doping," *Scientific American*, June 21, 2004, pp. 62-69.
[50] Thomas Boswell, "Baseball's Back on the Right Path," *The Washington Post*, July 13, 2004, p. D5.
[51] Rob Gloster, "Olympic Officials Want Federal Help in Banning Drug Cheaters," The Associated Press, April 27, 2004.

Bibliography

Selected Sources

Books

Goldman, Bob, with Patricia Bush and Ronald Klatz, *Death in the Locker Room: Steroids and Sports*, Icarus Press, 1984.

A competitive weightlifter who did not use steroids presents a strong critique of steroid use in sports combining research and personal accounts. Includes 135 pages of appendices, 44-page bibliography.

Houlihan, Barrie, *Dying to Win: Doping in Sport and the Development of Anti-Doping Policy* (2d ed.), Council of Europe Publishing, 2002.

A professor of sport policy at England's Loughboro University provides an overview of history and current policies toward use of performance-enhancing drugs. Includes up-to-date listing of prohibited substances, text of international anti-doping convention.

Ungerleider, Steven, *Faust's Gold: Inside the East German Doping Machine*, Thomas Dunne Books/St. Martin's Press, 2001.

A sports psychologist and adjunct professor at the University of Oregon presents a documented account of the officially sanctioned program for administering performance-enhancing drugs to East German athletes in the 1970s and '80s.

Wadler, Gary I., and Brian Hainline, *Drugs and the Athlete*, F.A. Davis Co., 1989.

Professors at New York University Medical School offer a comprehensive but now somewhat dated treatise on the history of performance-enhancing drugs in sport, their chemistry and physiology and methods of detection and prevention. Detailed references, appendices.

Yesalis, Charles E. (2d ed.), *Anabolic Steroids in Sport and Exercise*, Human Kinetics Publishers, 2000.

A professor of health and human development at Pennsylvania State University presents a comprehensive treatment by leading experts of the history of performance-enhancing drugs in sports, their medical efforts and policies aimed at detecting and preventing their use. References after each chapter.

Articles

Carey, Benedict, "A Bulked-Up Body of Knowledge," *Los Angeles Times*, June 10, 2002, p. S1.

A reporter provides a good overview of the health issues surrounding the use of steroids.

Dohrmann, George, "Who's Clean, Who's Not?", *Sports Illustrated*, May 31, 2004, p. 52.

Dohrmann provides an overview of investigations of suspected drug use by U.S. track and field athletes in the run-up to the Summer Olympics.

Fainaru-Wada, Mark, and Lance Williams, "How the Doping Scandal Unfolded: Fallout From BALCO Probe Could Taint Olympics, Pro Sports," *The San Francisco Chronicle*, Dec. 21, 2003, p. B1.

This thorough reconstruction of the BALCO investigation was published two months before indictments were returned.

Kolata, Gina, "With No Answers on Risks, Steroid Users Still Say 'Yes'," *The New York Times*, Dec. 2, 2002, p. A1.

The longtime science reporter provides a thorough overview of the health and policy issues surrounding the growing use of steroids among athletes, bodybuilders and others.

Paul, Noel C., "Whatever It Takes," *The Christian Science Monitor*, May 22, 2002, p. 11.

A reporter describes the growing use of dietary supplements and steroids by young men aiming for "the perfect body."

Sokolove, Michael, "In Pursuit of Doped Excellence: The Lab Animal," *The New York Times Magazine*, Jan. 18, 2004, pp. 28ff.

Sokolove takes a comprehensive look at the use of performance-enhancing drugs by elite Olympic and professional athletes.

Sweeney, H. Lee, "Gene Doping," *Scientific American*, June 21, 2004, pp. 62-69.

A professor at the University of Pennsylvania School of Medicine examines the potential clinical uses of gene therapy for restoring muscle lost to age or disease and the possibility that such techniques may be used for "high-tech cheating in athletics."

Verducci, Tom, "Totally Juiced," *Sports Illustrated*, June 3, 2002, p. 34.

Verducci comprehensively examines steroid use in Major League Baseball.

Wharton, David, "Voice of Dissent in Drug Wars," *Los Angeles Times*, May 9, 2004, p. D1.

A reporter interviews Norman Fost, the University of Wisconsin Medical School professor who says the risks of steroids have been exaggerated and calls for allowing athletes to use them.

The Next Step:

Additional Articles from Current Periodicals

Anti-Doping Efforts

Abrahamson, Alan, "IOC Chief Backs U.S. on Doping," *Los Angeles Times*, May 18, 2004, p. D1.
Jacques Rogge, head of the International Olympic Committee, voices his support for the U.S. Anti-Doping Agency's pursuit of steroid users.

Abrahamson, Alan, "Worldwide Perception Is a Harsh Reality for U.S.," *Los Angeles Times*, Aug. 27, 2003, p. D1.
International critics accuse American track and field officials of winking at doping by prominent U.S. athletes prior to the aggressive BALCO investigation.

Crumpacker, John, "Dick Pound; Hot on Trail of Cheaters," *San Francisco Chronicle*, Nov. 30, 2003, p. B1.
The head of the World Anti-Doping Agency, sometimes accused of anti-Americanism, is blunt with his criticism of lax drug-testing policies.

Kroichick, Ron, "Cycle of Tragedy," *San Francisco Chronicle*, May 9, 2004, p. A1.
A series of sudden heart-attack deaths among athletes punctuates a massive doping scandal that has rocked the world of competitive bicycling in Europe.

Litsky, Frank, "International Drug Code Is Adopted," *The New York Times*, March 6, 2003, p. D5.
For the first time, nations agree on a global anti-drug code that will regulate testing and penalties for Olympic athletes.

Meyer, John, "Doping War Broadens," *The Denver Post*, Oct. 26, 2003, p. C1.
Designer steroids provide the impetus for saving athletes' drug samples for retroactive testing if new drugs are later discovered.

Shipley, Amy, "USADA Eases Proof Standard," *The Washington Post*, June 13, 2004, p. E1.
By international agreement, the standard of evidence for guilt in doping cases is lowered, but accused athletes' attorneys vow to fight the new rules.

BALCO

Abrahamson, Alan, and Elliott Teaford, " 'Intentional Doping of the Worst Sort' Found Among U.S. Track Athletes," *Los Angeles Times*, Oct. 17, 2003, p. A1.
The story of BALCO and Victor Conte begins to break in 2003 and ultimately leads to a scandal that envelops American sports.

Fainaru-Wada, Mark, and Lance Williams, "Sprinter Admitted Use of BALCO 'Magic Potion'," *San Francisco Chronicle*, June 24, 2004, p. A1.
Sprinter Tim Montgomery admits using banned substances in leaked grand jury testimony filled with descriptions of back-stabbing coaches and athletes in sleazy deals.

Longman, Jere, "German Expert Warns Balco Investigators," *The New York Times*, June 26, 2004, p. D1.
A German doping expert says a strange pattern of urine testing by Marion Jones is similar to old East German methods of concealing steroid use.

Longman, Jere, and Joe Drape, "Decoding a Steroid: Hunches, Sweat, Vindication," *The New York Times*, Nov. 2, 2003, Section 1, p. 1.
After Donald Catlin received a syringe containing an allegedly undetectable steroid from a tipster, he reverse-engineered it and developed a test to detect it.

Gene Doping

Abrahamson, Alan, "Thirty Years After Munich, IOC Battle Against Doping Is Far From Over," *Los Angeles Times*, Sept. 1, 2002, Part 4, p. 3.
Athens in 2004 might be too early, but a leading biological researcher says genetic manipulation could be a factor in dramatic victories in Beijing in 2008.

Ruibal, Sal, "Gene Alteration Sets Off Alarm in Doping Fight," *USA Today*, April 15, 2004, p. 3C.
Ten million dollars and a graduate student's knowledge of molecular biology would be sufficient to start a lab for genetically altering athletes.

Stroh, Michael, "DNA 'Edge' Creates New Sports Worry," *The Baltimore Sun*, Feb. 3, 2002, p. 1A.
Genetically enhanced mice ripple with muscle whenever they move; scientists ask how long it will be until unethical athletes and doctors exploit the same techniques.

Major League Baseball

Fainaru, Steve, "Injecting Hope — And Risk," *The Washington Post*, June 23, 2003, p. A1.
Poverty-stricken Dominican teenagers hoping for a better life in the United States playing baseball turn to veterinary steroids with serious side effects.

Fainaru-Wada, Mark, "Steroid Issue Has Divided Baseball Like No Other," *San Francisco Chronicle*, March 28, 2004, p. C1.
With recent home-run records called into question, baseball's management and players struggle with their response to steroids.

Fainaru-Wada, Mark, and Lance Williams, "Steroid Scandal May Hit Olympics," *San Francisco Chronicle*, May 16, 2004, p. A1.

E-mails and other communications between Victor Conte and elite athletes form a trail, and anti-doping officials are on the hunt.

Longman, Jere, "Facing Marion Jones and a Lack of Options," *The New York Times*, June 10, 2004, p. D3.

USADA officials have a dilemma: To accuse an athlete without a positive drug test or face the possibility of revoked medals if new evidence surfaces after the Olympics.

Sandomir, Richard, "Baseball Receives Steroid Warning," *The New York Times*, March 11, 2004, p. D1.

Saying the sport is in danger of becoming a fraud, Sen. John McCain, R-Ariz., warns baseball officials to crack down on steroid use or the government might intervene.

Schmuck, Peter, "Baseball's Steroid Program Weighs In as Skimpy," *The Baltimore Sun*, Dec. 27, 2003, p. 1C.

Weak penalties in baseball's steroid program, such as undergoing treatment anonymously, may not deter many players when 10 extra home runs can be worth $1 million in salary.

Shaikin, Bill, "Steroid Standoff in Baseball May Force Someone's Hand," *Los Angeles Times*, May 3, 2004, p. D5.

Baseball Commissioner Bud Selig says he's unhappy with the steroid-testing status quo, but negotiations with the players' union appear stalled.

Williams, Lance, and Mark Fainaru-Wada, "Track Star's Testimony Linked Bonds to Steroid Use," *San Francisco Chronicle*, June 24, 2004, p. A16.

Home-run king Barry Bonds is alleged to have received steroids from Victor Conte, owner of BALCO.

Teens and Sports Drugs

Egan, Timothy, "Body-Conscious Boys Adopt Athletes' Taste for Steroids," *The New York Times*, Nov. 22, 2002, p. A1.

Police arrest students bringing steroids back from Tijuana, intending to sell them to fellow high school students, who apparently provide a lucrative market.

Kroichick, Ron, and Mitch Stephens, "More High School Athletes Risking Steroid Use," *San Francisco Chronicle*, Nov. 2, 2003, p. A1.

Steroid usage by teens is at all-time highs; recent athletic scandals may convince teens steroids are the path to big-time sports.

Longman, Jere, "An Athlete's Dangerous Experiment," *The New York Times*, Nov. 26, 2003, p. D1.

Erratic behavior that included stealing, violence and depression preceded the suicide of a teenage baseball player who had been using steroids.

Manning, Anita, "Kids, Steroids Don't Mix," *USA Today*, July 9, 2002, p. 1C.

In a culture that values winning above all, it's not unheard of for parents to push their kids toward steroids while coaches look the other way.

Wertheim, L. Jon, "Jolt of Reality," *Sports Illustrated*, April 7, 2003, p. 68.

Supplements are extremely popular among athletes of all ages; one young athlete died after taking a mixture of ephedra and caffeine known as a Yellow Jacket.

Citing *The CQ Researcher*

Sample formats for citing these reports in a bibliography include the ones listed below. Preferred styles and formats vary, so please check with your instructor or professor.

MLA Style

Jost, Kenneth. "Rethinking the Death Penalty." The CQ Researcher 16 Nov. 2001: 945-68.

APA Style

Jost, K. (2001, November 16). Rethinking the death penalty. *The CQ Researcher, 11*, 945-968.

Chicago Style

Jost, Kenneth. "Rethinking the Death Penalty." *CQ Researcher*, November 16, 2001, 945-968.

In-depth Reports on Issues in the News

Are you writing a paper?

Need backup for a debate?

Want to become an expert on an issue?

For 80 years, researchers have turned to *The CQ Researcher* for in-depth reporting and analysis of issues in the news. Reports on a full range of political and social issues are now available. Following is a selection of recent reports:

Civil Liberties
Civil Liberties Debates, 10/03
Gay Marriage, 9/03

Crime/Law
Serial Killers, 10/03
Corporate Crime, 10/02

Economy
Exporting Jobs, 2/04
Stock Market Troubles, 1/04

Education
Black Colleges, 12/03
Combating Plagiarism, 9/03

Energy/Transportation
SUV Debate, 5/03
Future of Amtrak, 10/02

Environment
Air Pollution Conflict, 11/03
Water Shortages, 8/03

Health/Safety
Homeopathy Debate, 12/04
Worker Safety, 5/04

International Affairs
Aiding Africa, 8/03
Rebuilding Iraq, 7/03

Politics/Public Policy
Redistricting Disputes, 3/04
Democracy in Arab World, 1/04

Social Trends
Future of Music Industry, 11/03
Latinos' Future, 10/03

Terrorism/Defense
North Korean Crisis, 4/03
Homeland Security, 9/03

Youth
Youth Suicide, 2/04
Hazing, 1/04

Upcoming Reports

Religion and Politics, 7/30/04
Science and Politics, 8/20/04
Social Security, 8/27/04
Big-Box Stores, 9/10/04
Gays on Campus, 10/1/04

ACCESS

The CQ Researcher is available in print and online. For access, visit your library or www.thecqresearcher.com.

STAY CURRENT

To receive notice of upcoming *CQ Researcher* reports, or learn more about *CQ Researcher* products, subscribe to the free e-mail newsletters, *CQ Researcher Alert!* and *CQ Researcher News*: www.cqpress.com/newsletters.

PURCHASE

To purchase a *CQ Researcher* report in print or electronic format (PDF), visit www.cqpress.com or call 866-427-7737. A single report is $10. Bulk purchase discounts and electronic rights licensing are also available.

SUBSCRIBE

A full-service *CQ Researcher* print subscription—including 44 reports a year, monthly index updates, and a bound volume—is $625 for academic and public libraries, $605 for high school libraries, and $750 for media libraries. Add $25 for domestic postage.

The CQ Researcher Online offers a backfile from 1991 and a number of tools to simplify research. Available in print and online, *The CQ Researcher en español* offers 36 reports a year on political and social issues of concern to Latinos in the U.S. For pricing and a free trial of either product, call 800-834-9020, ext. 1906, or e-mail librarysales@cqpress.com.

UNDERSTANDING CONSTITUTIONAL ISSUES:
SELECTIONS FROM *THE CQ RESEARCHER*

Understanding Constitutional Issues focuses on four key themes — governmental powers and structure, security, liberty, and equality — to help students develop a deeper understanding of the relation between current events and constitutional issues and principles. Integrating eighteen *CQ Researcher* reports, *Understanding Constitutional Issues* makes important connections clear, such as those between civil liberties and security; and privacy and liberty.

June 2004 • 8 1/2 x 11 • Approx. 432 pages • Paperback • ISBN 1-56802-885-7 • $39.95

To Order: Call Toll-Free: 866.4CQ.PRESS (427.7737)
Fax: 800.380.3810 • Web: www.cqpress.com
E-mail: customerservice@cqpress.com

CQ Press, 1255 22nd Street, NW, Suite 400 • Washington, DC 20037

CQ Researcher

Published by CQ Press, a division of Congressional Quarterly Inc.

thecqresearcher.com

Religion and Politics

Is President Bush too vocal about his faith?

Religion has always influenced American politics. But some analysts contend that President Bush's frequent use of religious language crosses the line separating church and state, alienating voters who don't share his beliefs. Critics also charge that Bush is using religion to appeal to conservative Christian congregations and has inappropriately asked them to campaign on his behalf. But others say references to God and the Bible are appropriate, especially in difficult times, and that the president has every right to approach churchgoers for votes. Meanwhile, recent polls show a "religion gap" between regular churchgoers, who overwhelmingly favor the GOP, and secular voters, who generally favor Democrats. Democratic strategists maintain they can still attract religious voters, but Republicans say the party is too liberal on social issues like abortion and gay marriage to appeal to many religious conservatives.

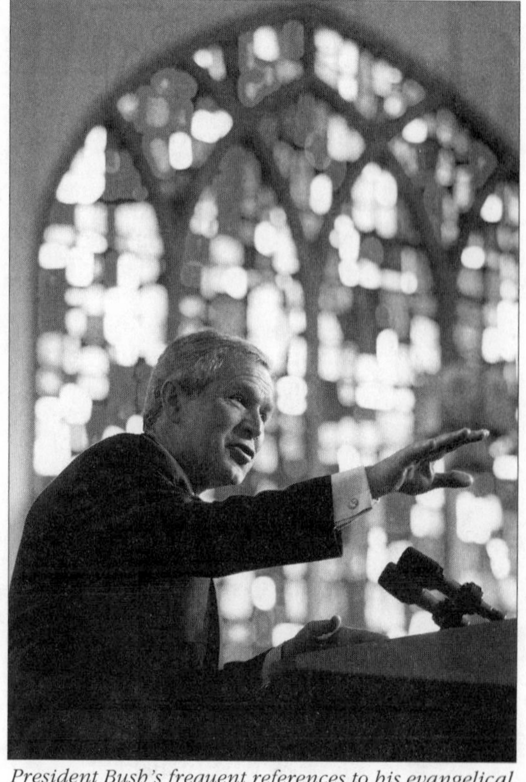

President Bush's frequent references to his evangelical Christian beliefs have rasied concerns among some critics.

INSIDE THIS REPORT

The CQ Researcher • July 30, 2004 • www.thecqresearcher.com
Volume 14, Number 27 • Pages 637-660

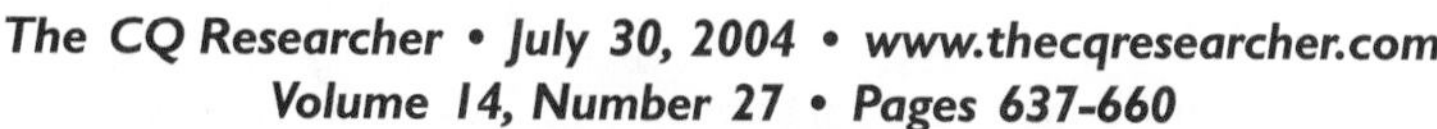

CQ Press

Recipient of Society of Professional Journalists Award for Excellence ◆ American Bar Association Silver Gavel Award

THE ISSUES

BACKGROUND

CURRENT SITUATION

OUTLOOK

SIDEBARS AND GRAPHICS

FOR FURTHER RESEARCH

Cover: President Bush's outspoken evangelicalism has raised concerns about whether the leader of a nation as religiously diverse as the United States should speak so forthrightly about his conservative Christian beliefs. (AFP Photo/Stephen Jaffe)

THE CQ Researcher

July 30, 2004
Volume 14, Number 27

MANAGING EDITOR: Thomas J. Colin

ASSISTANT MANAGING EDITOR: Kathy Koch

ASSOCIATE EDITOR: Kenneth Jost

STAFF WRITERS: Mary H. Cooper, David Masci, William Triplett

CONTRIBUTING WRITERS: Sarah Glazer, David Hatch, David Hosansky, Patrick Marshall, Tom Price, Jane Tanner

DESIGN/PRODUCTION EDITOR: Olu B. Davis

ASSISTANT EDITOR: Kenneth Lukas

A Division of Congressional Quarterly Inc.

SENIOR VICE PRESIDENT/GENERAL MANAGER: John A. Jenkins

DIRECTOR, LIBRARY PUBLISHING: Kathryn C. Suárez

DIRECTOR, EDITORIAL OPERATIONS: Ann Davies

CONGRESSIONAL QUARTERLY INC.

CHAIRMAN: Paul C. Tash

VICE CHAIRMAN: Andrew P. Corty

PRESIDENT AND PUBLISHER: Robert W. Merry

The CQ Researcher (ISSN 1056-2036) is printed on acid-free paper. Published weekly, except Jan. 2, April 9, July 2, July 9, Aug. 6, Aug. 13, Nov. 26 and Dec. 31, by CQ Press, a division of Congressional Quarterly Inc. Annual subscription rates for institutions start at $625. For pricing, call 1-800-834-9020, ext. 1906. To purchase a *CQ Researcher* report in print or electronic format (PDF), visit www.cqpress.com or call 866-427-7737. A single report is $10. Bulk purchase discounts and electronic-rights licensing are also available. Periodicals postage paid at Washington, D.C., and additional mailing offices. POSTMASTER: Send address changes to *The CQ Researcher*, 1255 22nd St., N.W., Suite 400, Washington, D.C. 20037.

Religion and Politics

By David Masci

The Issues

It has become known as the "Jesus moment" — the time when a reporter asked then-Gov. George W. Bush during the 2000 GOP presidential primary to name his favorite philosopher.

"Christ," the future president quickly responded, "because he changed my heart."

Bush's answer set off a heated debate about whether the potential leader of a country as diverse as the United States should be speaking so forthrightly about his Christian religion.

Some saw it as an honest declaration of deep faith. "Bush is very sincere in his religious expression, and I think that is what you were seeing that night," says John Green, a professor of political science at the University of Akron in Ohio. "Most ordinary Americans could see that, too, because they know people like George W. Bush."

Indeed, 62 percent of all Americans believe the president mentions his religious faith about the "right amount," compared with 14 percent who think he goes overboard. [1]

But Patrick Allitt, a professor of American History at Emory University in Atlanta, is among the cynics who see the president's frequent use of religious imagery — as well as the Jesus reference itself — as a bow to the evangelicals and other religious conservatives who are a key GOP constituency. "All of this religious language is about keeping his base happy," Allitt says. "That's what he was doing then, and that's what he's still doing."

Ron Reagan, the son of the late former president, appears to agree. Although he did not mention Bush by name, during a graveside eulogy in June, Reagan noted that his father had been devout but did not "wear his religion on his sleeve" for political gain, as some others do.

Others say the president's frequent use of religious imagery is actually harmful to the body politic, because it alienates and divides people. "By constantly referring to religion and faith in such a personal way, he's creating an impression that we're a spiritually monolithic country," says Melody Barnes, a senior fellow at the Center for American Progress, a liberal think tank. "He's excluding people of different faiths and beliefs, and that's wrong."

Regardless of Bush's motives, his so-called God talk has deep historical precedent. George Washington himself added the words, "so help me God," to the presidential oath, and Franklin D. Roosevelt prayed publicly in times of crisis. Thomas Jefferson also called Jesus his "favorite philosopher."

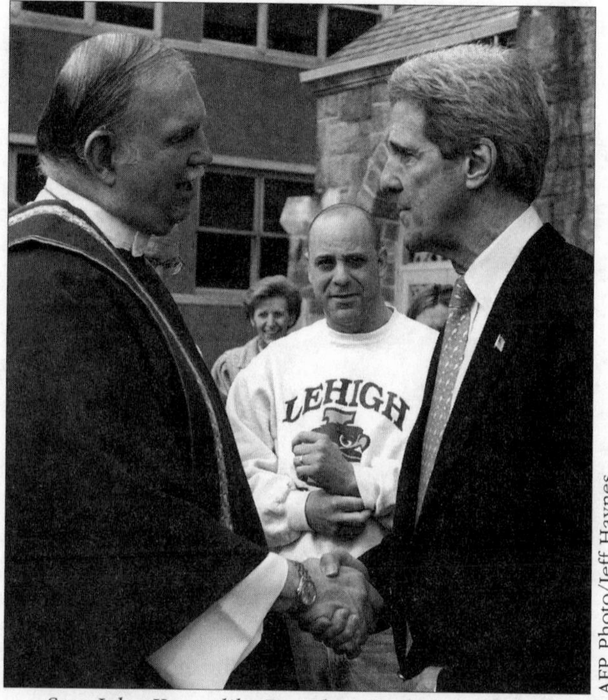

AFP Photo/Jeff Haynes

Sen. John Kerry, like President Bush, has sparked religious controversy during the presidential campaign. Several Roman Catholic bishops have vowed not to administer Holy Communion to pro-abortion rights supporters like Kerry, D-Mass. Here he greets the Rev. Michael J. Chaback (L) of the SS. Cyril & Methodius Parish in Bethlehem, Pa., after attending Sunday service on March 14, 2004.

The United States is one of the most religious countries in the world. Polls frequently show that more than 90 percent of Americans believe in God; roughly two-thirds say religion is important in their lives and almost 40 percent attend worship services regularly. [2]

Moreover, the evangelical movement and the number of Roman Catholics have grown enormously in the last few decades, due to immigration and the decline of other denominations. At the same time, evangelicals have made concerted efforts to gain political strength, led by charismatic ministers like the Rev. Pat Robertson. [3]

In this environment, Bush's efforts to portray himself as a deeply religious man have paid political dividends. During the 2000 election campaign, Bush won roughly two-thirds of those voters who attend worship regularly. Polls show that he is likely to repeat this showing in his upcoming presidential contest with Sen. John Kerry, the Democratic nominee.

Still, the Bush/Cheney campaign is taking no chances, contacting thousands of conservative religious supporters and urging them to organize other members of their churches on behalf of the president's re-election bid. Democrats and others responded angrily, charging that some of the things the administration is asking people and churches to do, such as sending the campaign a list of all the congregation's members, amount to illegal advocacy on behalf of a candidate. Under current federal law, churches, synagogues and

Religion 'Gap' Separates Kerry and Bush

Those who plan to vote for President Bush are more likely than Kerry's supporters to attend religious services on a regular basis and to believe that a candidate's faith is important to his leadership.

	All likely voters	Bush voters	Kerry voters
How important is it that the presidential candidate is a religious person?			
Percentage saying very important:	28%	42%	17%
Do you think the president should allow his personal religious faith to guide him in making decisions as president?			
Percentage saying yes:	48%	67%	29%
Does President Bush's religious faith make him a strong leader?			
Percentage saying yes:	48%	85%	15%
Does President Bush's religious faith make him too closed-minded?			
Percentage saying yes:	36%	5%	65%
Do you attend religious services once a week or more?			
Percentage saying yes:	47%	59%	35%

Source: Time, *from a telephone poll conducted June 2-4, 2004, among 1,280 adult Americans, of whom 880 were likely voters. The margin of error is 3.7%.*

other houses of worship that enjoy tax-exempt status (virtually all of them) are prohibited from endorsing or working on behalf of a candidate.

"Bush/Chaney is going out and asking churches to do things that could result in their losing their tax-exempt status," says the Rev. Barry W. Lynn, executive director of Americans United for the Separation of Church and State.

In response, some liberal-leaning religious groups like The Interfaith Alliance have sent brochures to church leaders outlining how to avoid stepping over a line that would threaten their tax-exempt status.

But the president's supporters say the way they are trying to reach conservative religious voters is completely legal. In addition, they predict Bush will make a good showing among religious conservatives in the fall not just due to skillful organizing but because the Democrats have essentially ceded the religious vote to the GOP. Decades of support for abortion and gay rights, they argue, have made the Democratic Party very secular in its outlook and hostile to religious conservatives and their views.

While the Democrats concede they need to do better at appealing to conservative religious voters, they say the party has the potential to attract many more people of faith than it has in recent elections. Core Democratic issues, including concern for the poor and the environment, make the party attractive to many religious people, they say.

And, indeed, Kerry and his running mate, North Carolina Sen. John Edwards, have been courting religious voters, speaking at churches and talking about "values." Recently, Kerry said that "values" will be at "the heart of our campaign." [4]

But Kerry's references to his faith also have drawn criticism, in this case from his own church. Several Roman Catholic bishops have said that they will not allow Kerry and other public officials who support abortion rights to receive Holy Communion in their dioceses. In Boston, Kerry's local bishop urged pro-choice politicians to voluntarily abstain from receiving communion.

Some conservative Catholics defend the action, arguing that opposition to abortion is a vital pillar of church doctrine and that candidates should not be regarded as good Catholics if they ignore the institution's teaching.

Critics of the bishops say, however, that the church should not single out abortion as a litmus test. And, indeed, the vast majority of bishops have not endorsed using communion as a sanction. Moreover, Kerry says he intends to continue receiving communion at Mass.

As the presidential election nears and the focus on religious voters intensifies, here are some of the questions being asked:

Have Democrats permanently lost the support of religious conservatives?

Several recent polls have identified a so-called religion gap in American politics. Voters who attend worship services regularly are much more likely to support GOP candidates than those who do not. Indeed, after party affiliation, religious practice is now the biggest predictor of how someone will vote.

According to a June poll commissioned by *Time,* 59 percent of those who consider themselves "very religious" support Bush, compared to 35 percent for Kerry. Those who classify themselves as "not religious," on the other hand, support Kerry, 69 percent to 22 percent, over Bush. [5]

"The gap between people who go to church regularly and those that don't is twice the gender gap," said Celinda Lake, a Democratic pollster. "It's huge." [6]

There hasn't always been a religion gap. During the 1930s, New Deal Democrats overwhelmingly won the support of Catholics as well as white and black Southern Protestants. And in the 1950s and '60s, religious leaders, like the Rev. Dr. Martin Luther King Jr., also helped to drive the civil rights movement.

But starting in the 1960s, the Democratic Party and its leadership began edging away from so-called traditional values. For instance, most Democrats applauded the 1962 Supreme Court decision outlawing prayer in public schools and the landmark 1973 *Roe v. Wade* decision protecting a woman's right to have an abortion. More recently, Democrats have championed gay rights.

Meanwhile, Republicans have become the political standard-bearers for the bellwether anti-abortion movement, probably the most important social issue for religious conservatives.

The GOP also has embraced other "traditional values" causes, including the fight against gay marriage. Recently, Republicans tried unsuccessfully to push a constitutional amendment banning gay marriage through the U.S. Senate, getting only 48 of the 60 votes needed to pass the measure. [7]

As a result, a solid majority of religious conservatives feel most at home in the Republican Party. "The Republicans have been able to get the overwhelming majority of these people because they are at least trying to address their concerns," says William Donohue, president of the Catholic League for Religious and Civil Rights. "The Democrats are simply too secular to speak to a lot of religious people."

Could the Democrats woo back people of faith? Even those who think the Democrats could increase their share

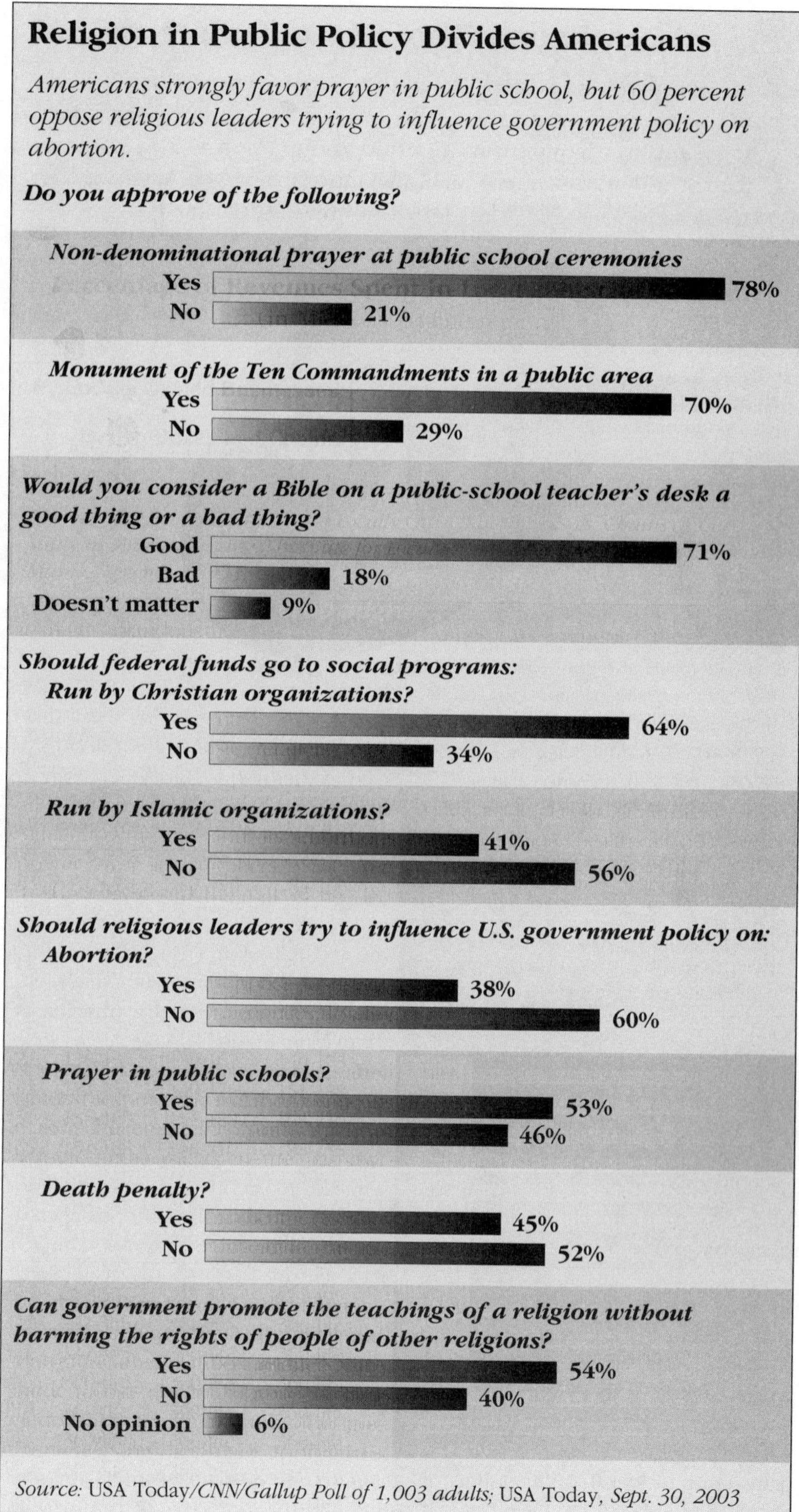

Religion in Public Policy Divides Americans
Americans strongly favor prayer in public school, but 60 percent oppose religious leaders trying to influence government policy on abortion.
Do you approve of the following?
Non-denominational prayer at public school ceremonies
Yes 78%
No 21%
Monument of the Ten Commandments in a public area
Yes 70%
No 29%
Would you consider a Bible on a public-school teacher's desk a good thing or a bad thing?
Good 71%
Bad 18%
Doesn't matter 9%
Should federal funds go to social programs:
Run by Christian organizations?
Yes 64%
No 34%
Run by Islamic organizations?
Yes 41%
No 56%
Should religious leaders try to influence U.S. government policy on:
Abortion?
Yes 38%
No 60%
Prayer in public schools?
Yes 53%
No 46%
Death penalty?
Yes 45%
No 52%
Can government promote the teachings of a religion without harming the rights of people of other religions?
Yes 54%
No 40%
No opinion 6%

Source: USA Today/*CNN/Gallup Poll of 1,003 adults;* USA Today, *Sept. 30, 2003*

Courting the Jewish Vote

American Jews traditionally are Democrats. In the last presidential election, 79 percent of Jewish voters supported Al Gore, compared with 19 percent for George W. Bush.

But some politics watchers believe Bush's consistently strong support for Israel might significantly boost his showing among Jews in November.

"The Jewish vote is more in play in this election than it was in the last," said Josh Block, a spokesman for the American Israel Public Affairs Committee (AIPAC), which lobbies for Israel in Washington. [1]

Time and again, President Bush has supported the Jewish state, most notably in 2002, when he distanced the United States from Yasser Arafat, arguing that the Palestinian leader's alleged involvement in terrorism disqualified him for a role in any future peace process. More recently, Bush endorsed Israeli Prime Minister Ariel Sharon's controversial plan to unilaterally withdraw from the Gaza Strip, a move that enraged many Muslims.

Moreover, Bush has repeatedly reminded Jewish groups of his support for Israel. At a recent AIPAC conference, the president told an enthusiastic crowd, "The United States is strongly committed, and I am strongly committed, to the security of Israel as a vibrant Jewish state."

All of this effort might seem odd, given that the Jewish community makes up less than 1.5 percent of the nation's population. (*See graph, p. 644.*) But a larger percentage of Jews — about 80 percent — go to the polls than most other ethnic groups, and they are big contributors to political causes and candidates.

In addition, several important states where neither candidate enjoys a clear advantage have sizable Jewish populations. "In some of these very close swing states — Florida, Pennsylvania, potentially Ohio, Nevada and Jersey — it could make a difference in a very close election," Block said. [2]

Traditionally, the Jewish piece of the electoral puzzle has been placed squarely in the Democratic camp. Even Ronald Reagan, a Republican who was unusually popular among Jews (due to his support for Israel and Jewish dissidents in the Soviet Union), received only 40 percent of the Jewish vote.

President Bush's chief campaign strategist, Matthew Dowd, concedes that his candidate is unlikely to match Reagan's share. Still, he expects the president to do much better among Jewish voters than he did in 2000. [3]

Besides his impressive pro-Israel credentials, the president won't be facing a Jewish candidate on the opposing ticket as he did in the first election, when Sen. Joseph I. Lieberman, D-Conn., was Gore's running mate.

Bush's standing in the Jewish community may also have been helped by Kerry, who criticized Israel last fall for building a security fence in the West Bank to separate the Israelis from the Palestinians. Soon after, Kerry upset Jewish groups again when he said he would consider sending former President Jimmy Carter to the Middle East as a special envoy. Many pro-Israel advocates consider Carter too sympathetic to the Palestinians. [4]

But many Democrats doubt that Bush could make more than marginal gains in the Jewish community, in part because he is out of step with most Jews on domestic issues, such as abortion.

"Bush enjoys an incredible perception as pro-Israel, but that's not the only issue Jews care about," says Steve Rabinowitz, a Democratic media strategist for several Jewish organizations. "Support for Israel is a litmus test, and a candidate must be very good on Israel even to be considered. Once they see that John Kerry is at least as good on Israel, and maybe has a longer and better record, then I think they pivot to domestic issues, and it's not even a close call."

Recently Kerry has tried to reassure Jewish voters that he is "good" on Israel, backing off his earlier controversial statements. And when the president came out in favor of Sharon's plan to withdraw from Gaza, the Democratic candidate immediately issued a statement supporting the move.

Finally, in a May 3 speech to the Anti-Defamation League, a Jewish civil rights organization, Kerry touted his pro-Israel voting record and echoed Bush's promise to protect Israel. "I will never force Israel to make concessions that cost or compromise any of Israel's security," he said. "The security of Israel is paramount." [5]

---

[1] Quoted in Joseph Curl, "Bush Campaign Courts Jewish Vote," *The Washington Times*, June 2, 2004, p. A8.

[2] Quoted in *ibid.*

[3] Richard W. Stevenson, "Bush Campaign Plays Up Pro-Israel Stance," *The New York Times*, May 15, 2004, p. A13.

[4] *Ibid.*

[5] For full text of the address, go to: www.adl.org/adl_in_action/conference_2004_kerry.asp.

of the religious vote acknowledge that the party has not tried hard enough to appeal to those voters. "There has been a tendency by the Democratic Party to write off religious believers, because the party came to feel that its position on abortion and gay rights and other cultural issues made it the enemy of religious people," says Alan Wolfe, director of the Boise Center for Religion and American Public Life at Boston College.

Jim Wallis, editor-in-chief of *Sojourners*, a Christian magazine on culture and public policy, agrees, adding, "Even when a Democrat speaks of religious faith they are always quick to add that it won't affect anything. That's a sign that the party is too secular."

But Wolfe and Wallis say the situation could change. Even many of the voters who don't agree with the Democrats on so-called cultural issues, like gay rights, might be swayed by other parts of the party's message. "The so-called cultural issues are not as salient as other issues," Wolfe says. "It's not that conservative Christians don't care about them . . . but more that they don't think they're as important as other issues, like the economy or Iraq."

These experts contend that Democrats can win over many more religious voters by talking core Democratic issues — such as tolerance, caring for the poor and stewardship of the environment — in religious terms.

"People forget that major Democratic issues, like civil rights, came out of a religious movement, in this case in the black churches," Wallis says. "If they could frame in religious terms those issues today that have a moral, they could compete for a lot of voters that have abandoned the party because they think it is hostile to religion."

But Jim Guth, a professor of political science at Furman University in Greenville, S.C. , says trying to repackage traditional Democratic issues won't carry much weight with those conservative voters who aren't already in the party's camp. "Religious voters who are sympathetic to the social justice appeal are usually already Democrats," he says. "So you're not really going to pick up a lot of new people by doing this."

Similarly, those who say the Democrats can't close the gap also dispute Wolfe's idea that the party's stand on cultural issues — such as gay and abortion rights — isn't that important to conservative voters.

"Take gay marriage, where you are talking about changing the basic foundation of our culture," says Bob Wenz, vice president of National Ministries at the National Association of Evangelicals. "You're talking about something that a lot of people care about very much, so of course it's going to influence who they support."

Democrats also are hindered by religious diversity within the party, Guth says. "They have traditionally been the party of religious minorities, like Jews and black Protestants and now Hindus, Buddhists and Muslims," he says.

AFP Photo/Stephen Jaffe

President Bush helps Talia Lefkowitz, 8, light a menorah at the White House on the second night of Hanukkah in 2001, as first lady Laura Bush watches. Many analysts believe that Bush could take a larger-than-usual portion of the Jewish vote because of his pro-Israel stance.

"And that makes it hard to find a common religious language. Republicans have it easier because they are more homogeneously Christian."

Finally, conservatives and others say, the Democratic Party's elite is simply too secular and too beholden to inherently secular causes to accept religious views.

"Within the Democratic Party, there is an increasingly aggressive secular left that has driven people of faith, especially conservative Catholics and evangelical Christians, into the Republican Party," said Grover Norquist, president of Americans for Tax Reform. "They recognize how damaging it is, but they can't fix it, given who pays the bills and who is in charge," he adds, referring to core constituencies of the party, such as women's and gay-rights advocates.

Moreover, the Catholic League's Donohue notes, the party's overwhelmingly secular nature makes it hard for Democratic candidates to connect with religious conservatives. "You have to talk the talk in a very meaningful way or else people will see through you," he says.

"So when you get someone like [former Vermont Gov. Howard] Dean, saying: 'I'll talk about Jesus and religion when I get down to the South and have to appeal to those more religious voters,' and then someone asks him what his favorite book of the New Testament is and he says 'the Book of Job,' people see through that."

But Barnes, of the Center for American Progress, rejects the notion that most Democrats or progressives are aggressively secular. "There are plenty of people who are pro-choice who are religious," she says, citing groups like Catholics for a Free Choice. "And many gays and lesbians are very religious, too. So this idea that you're only religious if you take specific positions on issues is ridiculous."

Should communion be denied to Catholic politicians who don't follow the church's teachings?

By his own description, Sen. Kerry is a "believing and practicing Catholic," regularly attending mass and taking Holy Communion. [8] But the Democra-

America's Changing Religious Makeup

The percentage of Americans who report having no religion has more than doubled in the past 30 years, while the percentage who identify with a non-mainstream group more than tripled. Meanwhile, the percentage of Protestants dropped from nearly two-thirds of Americans to slightly more than half, largely due to immigration of non-Protestants and fewer children being raised in that faith. At the same time, however, the number of evangelical Protestants increased dramatically.

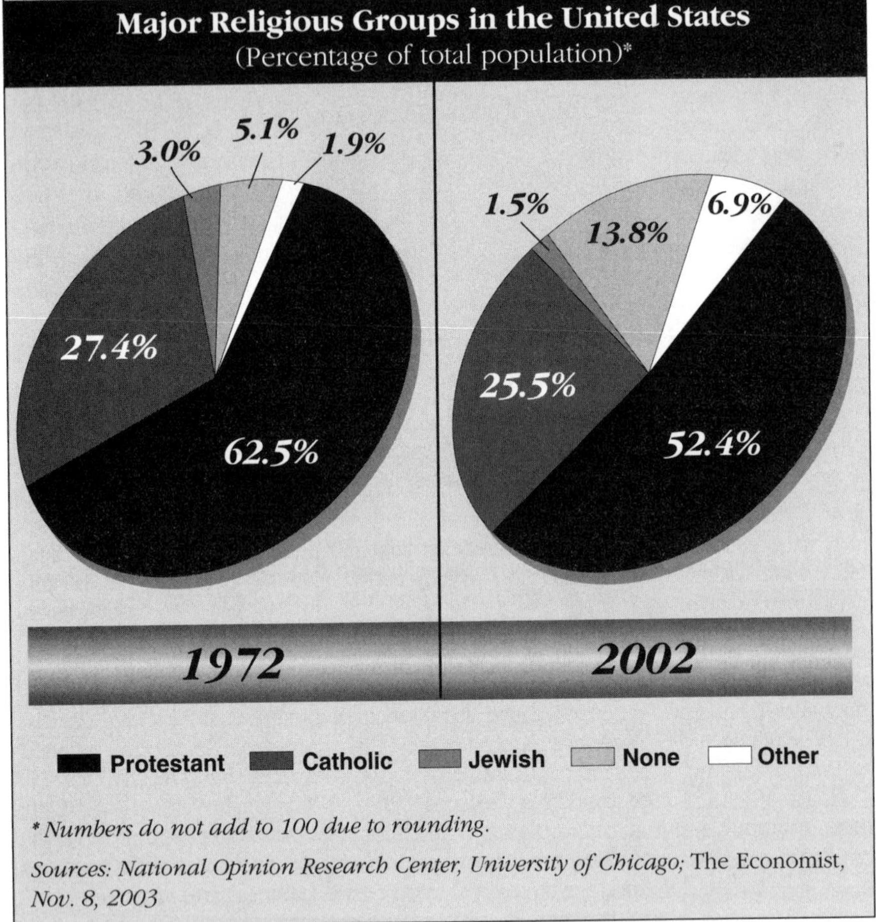

** Numbers do not add to 100 due to rounding.*

Sources: National Opinion Research Center, University of Chicago; The Economist, *Nov. 8, 2003*

tic nominee for president is also a strong supporter of abortion rights. Indeed, NARAL Pro-Choice America, the nation's largest abortion-rights advocacy group, gave the Massachusetts Democrat a 100 percent rating, based on his Senate voting record.

Kerry's strong support for abortion rights, however, puts him in direct conflict with one of the church's most important moral teachings — that a person is alive from the moment of conception and that terminating a pregnancy, at any stage, is murder.

Opposition to abortion has become the church's single most important political cause in the United States. Indeed, along with evangelical Christians, Catholics now form the cornerstone of the pro-life movement (*see p. 651*).

Some conservative Catholics say Kerry and other pro-choice politicians, by garnering support from abortion-rights advocates while presenting themselves as practicing Catholics, are trying to have it both ways and should not be regarded as good Catholics.

"Senators like Kerry and Kennedy want to call themselves Catholic when they go before the Knights of Columbus," Donohue says, referring to the nation's largest Roman Catholic fraternal men's organization. "But then they'll go out and vote against the partial-birth abortion ban. So it's natural that people ask: 'Why bother having rules unless we're going to enforce them?' "

Indeed, four American bishops say they will order the priests in their dioceses to deny Holy Communion to openly pro-choice public figures. One of the four, Bishop Michael J. Sheridan of Colorado Springs, also says members of his flock who vote for pro-choice candidates or support gay marriage or euthanasia should not receive communion unless they have confessed their sins and been absolved.

An additional 17 bishops — including Sean P. O'Malley, Kerry's hometown bishop in Boston — have taken a softer line, "suggesting" that politicians who support abortion rights voluntarily abstain from the sacrament.

So far, most of the nation's 276 bishops have either remained silent on the issue or declared that they will not use communion as a sanction. Cardinal Theodore McCarrick, who as head of the church in Washington, D.C., has taken a leadership role on the issue, opposes the denial of communion.

McCarrick and the other bishops released a statement on June 18 supporting the need to "teach" and "persuade" all Catholics, especially Catholic leaders, of the evils of abortion. However, they left the thorny question of denying communion up to each bishop.

The bishops' ambivalence echoes the position of Pope John Paul II, who two years ago directed Catholic politicians to "oppose any law that attacks human life." [9] But the pope himself has given Holy Communion to pro-choice Italian politicians, like Rome Mayor Francesco Rutelli, a former candidate for prime minister.

In the United States, meanwhile, the controversy has elicited a variety of responses from Catholic politicians. Kerry, for one, has said he has every intention of continuing to take communion. But New Jersey Gov. James McGreevey, also a pro-choice Democrat, has stopped receiving the sacrament after some bishops in his state urged him to do so. [10]

In early May, 48 Catholic Democratic members of Congress — all but three of them pro-choice — wrote to Cardinal McCarrick protesting what they saw as "deeply hurtful" threats by bishops. They argued that Catholic politicians should be judged on the totality of their records, such as support for the poor, and not purely on one issue.

But staunch Catholics counter that for the church, abortion is unlike most other public-policy issues. For instance, while the pope and many bishops in the United States and elsewhere oppose the death penalty, the church has not specifically called the practice immoral. Abortion, on the other hand, is considered "intrinsically evil" in church doctrine.

"There is a primacy in the fight to end abortion, and for a reason," says Joe Gigante, a spokesman for the American Life League, a Catholic pro-life group in Stafford, Va. "All other rights are irrelevant if you don't have the right to live. What do these other issues like poverty or health care mean to the 44 million children who have died [due to abortion] since [the Supreme Court's 1973 abortion decision in] *Roe v. Wade*."

However, opponents of denying communion say that even if abortion is the most important Catholic litmus test, refusal of the sacrament should not be used "to punish" those who do not fall in line behind church teaching.

"It is one thing for the church to preach what it believes — the sanctity of unborn human life," writes political commentator Andrew Sullivan, a Catholic. "It is another thing to use the sacraments of the church to enforce political uniformity on the matter." [11]

Library of Congress

In the 1960s, the Rev. Billy Graham and other evangelical leaders publicly worried that electing John F. Kennedy, a Catholic, would give the Roman Catholic Church too much influence over American governance.

Indeed, opponents say, using communion as a sanction turns an issue of conscience into a political concern. "All people go through a faith journey and struggle with various issues in their lives," says Barnes of the Center for American Progress. "So to take one of these issues and to make it some sort of a test, especially during the political season, seems very problematic to me."

For Father Thomas Reese, editor of *America*, one of the nation's largest Catholic magazines, using Holy Communion as a means to enforce orthodoxy on abortion is a "slippery slope" that could put the church in the difficult position of constantly having to split hairs.

"Where do we draw the line?" Reese asked at a June 23 discussion of the issue hosted by the Pew Forum on Religion and Public Life in Washington. "If a politician votes in favor of outlawing partial-birth abortion but does not support a constitutional amendment [outlawing abortion], does he get communion? Should Sen. [Rick] Santorum be denied communion for endorsing a pro-choice Republican for the U.S. Senate, even though Sen. Santorum has a pro-life voting record?" he asked, referring to the Pennsylvania Republican's recent backing of pro-choice Sen. Arlen Specter in the state's GOP primary over anti-abortion candidate Rep. Pat Toomey.

But Gigante disagrees, pointing out that the issue goes to the very heart of the church's most basic teachings. "This is not a slippery slope but the objective truth of the church, which says that abortion is intrinsically evil, period," he says. "It's that simple."

Finally, supporters say that by opposing pro-choice public officials, a few bishops have already raised awareness of the abortion issue, especially among Catholics. "Staying silent on this hasn't helped," Donohue says. "But taking this step has already galvanized the pro-life movement."

Nonetheless, opponents counter that denying communion will only end up hurting the pro-life movement. "This helps to brand abortion as a Catholic issue, rather than a human-rights issue," says Reese, who opposes abortion. "As long as this is a religious issue, the pro-life cause will fail."

Is President Bush too vocal about his faith?

Beginning with George Washington, every president has invoked God in political addresses. And many have peppered their speeches with references from the Bible and hymns.

"Just go read Lincoln's second inaugural, which sounds like a sermon, or Roosevelt's prayer when he announces the D-Day invasion in 1944," says Jim Land of the Southern Baptist Convention.

But observers say President Bush goes further than most of his predecessors, not only lacing his speeches and remarks with religious imagery but also invoking God's support on certain issues. They are particularly troubled by his remarks following the Sept. 11, 2001, terrorist attacks, in which the president casts the enemies of America as "evildoers" and puts God in the U.S. camp.

"When President Bush says that God blesses our policies or that God is on our side, we lose the self-reflection and accountability that comes with religion," says *Sojourners'* Wallis. "This is becoming a theology of righteous empire and turning aside Christian humility."

By contrast, Wallis says, past leaders frequently invoked God "to hold us accountable to His purpose," as in Lincoln's opposition to slavery and Dr. King's call for equal treatment of all Americans. "They pointed out to us what our religious values were and how we were falling short as a people — and they didn't use God to bless their policies."

Other critics say that many Americans are uncomfortable with the president's repeated references to the role religion plays in governing. "You've seen a lot of this sort of thing, especially with the Iraq war," says Boston College's Wolfe. "When he was asked whether he consulted with his father about the war, he said he had a 'higher father,' meaning God. I think that scares some people."

Bush's rhetoric also alienates Americans who don't share his particular religious beliefs. "It's become highly exclusionary, marginalizing those people who don't share his values," says Lynn of Americans United for the Separation of Church and State. "We've had highly religious presidents, like Jimmy Carter, who didn't speak so much of their religious beliefs because they didn't want to alienate people."

"We encourage public officials to speak about faith and values, but they need to keep that language inclusive," agrees Don Parker, a spokesman for the nonpartisan Interfaith Alliance.

But the University of Akron's Green finds the president's remarks — even his contention that God is on America's side — not unusual or inappropriate. "Most of his religious utterances are well within the bounds of American political discourse," Green says. "When you read the speeches of Washington, Lincoln or FDR, there is the notion that divine providence is with us and is supporting our cause."

Emory University's Allitt agrees. "I don't think you can say that he's out of the norm in the modern era of American politics," he says, "because even though he invokes God, he never says anything that is too religiously explicit. For instance, he doesn't say that 'America is a Christian republic,' which is something politicians used to say frequently in the 19th century."

Supporters also dismiss the argument that the president's remarks alienate people or other faiths or nonbelievers. Indeed, they say, Bush's remarks very much reflect the religious diversity of the country and strive not to exclude people of other faiths. "You'll notice that he will say 'church, synagogue and mosque,' which means he's trying to be evenhanded," Allitt says.

Allitt also sees nothing wrong with the president's use of biblical references in speeches. "This is still a Christian nation in that most people are still nominally Christian," he says. "So, it strikes me that referring back to the Bible is a legitimate reflection of the nation's beliefs and heritage." ■

BACKGROUND

Religious Tolerance

Unlike the Catholic Spanish missionaries who had been settling the Southwest for more than a century, the first Europeans to settle the Atlantic coast in the 1600s represented many Christian denominations and were often fleeing religious persecution.

Early Massachusetts was famously dominated by the Puritans, who worked to build their New Jerusalem amid the forests of New England. Other dissenting sects, such as the Quakers and Baptists, forged new societies in the Pennsylvania wilderness and elsewhere. Even Roman Catholics saw opportunities in English North America and established a colony in Maryland.

Only in the South, where most early settlers were Anglicans, was there something resembling the religious homogeneity found in much of Europe. But the first "Great Awakening — a religious revival that swept the

Continued on p. 648

Chronology

17th and 18th Centuries

American settlers stress religious tolerance and, eventually, a disengagement of church and state.

1620
Puritans land in America, hoping to build a "New Jerusalem" in a new land.

1776
Thomas Jefferson pens The Declaration of Independence, appealing to "Divine Providence" to help the new nation fight for freedom.

1787
The Constitutional Convention specifically leaves out any references to God and provides that there shall be no religious test for public office.

1789
The Bill of Rights is adopted, including the First Amendment, which provides for freedom of worship and government neutrality in religious matters.

19th Century

Religious groups champion social reform, including abolition of slavery and temperance.

1800
Jefferson, although accused of being an atheist, wins presidency.

1896
Populist Democrat William Jennings Bryan gives his famous "Cross of Gold" speech, but loses the presidential election to Republican William McKinley.

1900-1950

After repeal of Prohibition, conservative Protestants temporarily retreat from the public sphere. Roman Catholics become more politically active.

1919
The 18th Amendment, banning alcohol sales nationwide, is adopted.

1926
The Scopes "Monkey Trial" leads to ridicule of fundamentalist Christians.

1928
Democrat Al Smith, the first Catholic to run for president on a major party ticket, loses to Herbert Hoover.

1932
The 18th Amendment is repealed.

1950-Present

As black Protestants, Catholics and Jews gain new power, evangelicals reassert themselves politically.

1957
The Rev. Dr. Martin Luther King Jr. leads a church-based civil rights movement to end segregation.

1960
John F. Kennedy becomes the first Catholic elected president.

1964
The Civil Rights Act outlaws racial and ethnic discrimination.

1976
Evangelical Christian Jimmy Carter becomes president.

1979
The Rev. Jerry Falwell founds the conservative religious political group the Moral Majority. It claims credit for getting Republicans Ronald Reagan and George H. W. Bush elected president in 1982, '84 and '88.

1989
The Rev. Pat Robertson founds the Christian Coalition, which helps the GOP take over Congress in 1994.

1992
Democrat Bill Clinton is elected president, in part because Bush is unable to rally conservative Christians to his camp.

1994
Catholic and evangelical leaders issue *Catholics and Evangelicals Coming Together*, a call for both groups to work jointly on issues of common concern, notably abortion.

2000
Democratic Sen. Joseph I. Lieberman becomes the first Jew to run on a major national presidential ticket.

2001
George W. Bush, an evangelical Christian, becomes president.

2003
With support from religious conservatives, Congress in October bans a late-term abortion procedure known by opponents as a "partial-birth abortion."

2004
Several Roman Catholic bishops announce they will not administer communion to public officials who support abortion rights, like Sen. John Kerry. The Interfaith Alliance urges political candidates to refrain from using religion as a political strategy. Despite pressure from religious conservatives, Senate fails to pass a constitutional amendment banning gay marriage.

The Candidates' Spiritual Journeys

The Constitution specifically prohibits any religious test for public office. But voters often find candidates' religion of deep interest. Indeed, polls show that most Americans would not support a candidate for president who didn't believe in God.

George W. Bush and Sen. John Kerry both describe themselves as men of faith. And while they belong to different denominations, they both also came to their beliefs after periods of spiritual drift and doubt.

For Bush, his spiritual road was, by his own admission, long and bumpy. His famous father and mother were churchgoing Presbyterians, but the family was not especially religious.

After graduating from Yale in 1968, the future president spent his young, adult years drinking heavily, dating different women and jumping from job to job. Even after his 1977 marriage to Laura Welch, a demure public school librarian, Bush continued his wild ways, even after the birth of their daughters, Jenna and Barbara, in 1983. The following year, though, things began to change.

In 1984, Bush met Arthur Blessitt, a well-known minister who prayed with the then-vice president's son and urged him to make a serious commitment to Christ. [1] According to friends, Bush was "moved" by the experience.

The following year, he met evangelist Billy Graham who was visiting his father. During a private talk, Graham asked Bush: "Are you right with God?" The future president replied: "No, but I want to be." [2]

The talk with Graham set Bush on a new path. "Reverend Graham planted a mustard seed in my soul, a seed that grew over the next year," he later wrote, referring to Jesus' comparison of a mustard seed that grows into a great tree. "It was the beginning of a new walk where I would recommit my heart to Jesus Christ." [3]

Bush began to read the Bible regularly. Urged by his friend Don Evans (who would become his secretary of Commerce), he joined a men's Bible study group, in his hometown of Midland, Texas. According to Mark Leaverton, who ran the group, Bush made a dramatic transformation during the 18 months he attended. [4]

Today, the president regularly credits the "wonder-working power" of faith with helping him to stop drinking and to find meaning and direction in his life. He starts each morning by reading from the Bible and from a Christian devotional book, Oswald Chambers' *My Utmost for His Highest.*

Kerry and his three siblings were raised as Roman Catholics, and while the family attended mass regularly, they were not particularly devout.

At 10, Kerry was sent to boarding school in Switzerland, where his faith grew stronger. He became an altar boy and contemplated studying for the priesthood.

A few years later, he began to explore other religious traditions. Attendance at a prestigious Episcopal boarding school — St. Paul's in New Hampshire — led to a deep friendship with the institution's priest, the Rev. John Walker, who later became the bishop of Washington, D.C.

"He was always quite religious," says Daniel Barbiero, a St. Paul's classmate who said Kerry attended Mass every Sunday. [5]

But his faith was shaken by war. In 1966, the future senator enlisted in the Navy. Two years later, he was sent to Vietnam, where he commanded a Swift boat and patrolled dangerous inland waterways. He always carried a rosary during this time.

After his return to the United States in early 1970, Kerry suffered a crisis of faith. He only found his way back to his church after "a lot of reading and a lot of thinking," he said recently. [6]

Kerry has since come to view his Catholicism as a pillar in his life. "It's an important part of my getting through tough periods in my life and remains a bedrock of values — of sureness, I guess — about who I am, where we all fit, what our role is on this planet," he said. [7]

In 1970, Kerry married his first wife, Julia Thorne, an Episcopalian who agreed to be wed in a Catholic ceremony. The couple divorced in 1988, and Kerry later had the marriage annulled after marrying his current wife, Teresa Heinz, a devout Catholic.

Recently, the senator discovered that his paternal grandparents were Jewish immigrants who changed their name from Kohn to Kerry and converted to Catholicism. While Kerry has welcomed the news as "a revelation," he also has been quick to point out that it has done nothing to change his "Catholic heritage." [8]

---

1 Stephen Mansfield, *The Faith of George W. Bush,* (2003), p. 64.

2 Quoted in *ibid.* p. 68.

3 Quoted in *George W. Bush, A Charge to Keep,* (2000), p. 136.

4 Quoted from Frontline's Web site at: www.pbs.org/wgbh/pages/frontline/shows/jesus/president/cbs.html.

5 Quoted in Ann Rodgers, "John Kerry, Keeping the Catholic Faith," Scripps Howard News Service, May 10, 2004.

6 Quoted in Karen Tumulty, "Battling the Bishops," *Time,* June 21, 2004, p. 34.

7 Quoted in *ibid.*

8 Quoted in Rodgers, *op. cit.*

Continued from p. 646

East Coast in the 1730s and '40s — helped make the South more religiously diverse, too.

Indeed, by the outbreak of the American Revolution, the Colonies were more religiously pluralistic than anywhere on Earth. And efforts were under way to protect religious freedom and tolerance even before the Bill of Rights was ratified.

In 1779, for instance, the Virginia legislature passed a statute, drafted by Thomas Jefferson, protecting religious freedom. In the next decade, Jefferson would work with James Madison and others to disestablish the Anglican (Episcopal) Church in Virginia and beat back attempts by politicians to spend tax dollars on supporting churches in general. [12]

Religious tolerance took on a national dimension with ratification of the First Amendment to the Bill of Rights in 1789. In addition to guaranteeing free speech, press and assembly, it mandated that Congress "make no law respecting an establishment of religion, or prohibiting the free exercise thereof."

Many of the key drafters of the Constitution, including Madison, Benjamin Franklin, Alexander Hamilton, Gouverneur Morris and George Washington, were not deeply religious. The Constitution never asks for God's blessing or refers to the "divine." Indeed, they thought the states should maintain strict neutrality, working only to guarantee freedom of worship.

The founders believed that freeing religion from state interference would strengthen it. As Madison wrote in 1785, "faith depends on evidence, not on coercion." [13] Any church established by law, he warned, would itself become corrupt and, in turn, would corrupt the citizenry. [14]

Moreover, the founders did not seek to drive religion entirely from the public square. Jefferson referred to "the Creator" and appealed to "divine providence" in the Declaration of Independence. And federal and state legislatures routinely began sessions with a prayer, and still do.

Another Awakening

While some American clergy were troubled by the absence of God from the nation's founding law, the notion that churches would succeed without state interference proved prophetic. Many sects, new and old, thrived in an environment characterized by both tolerance and competition.

Indeed, the first decades of the 19th century witnessed a second "Great Awakening," an intense, evangelical movement that started in New England and spread south and west. It spawned new religions, notably the Seventh-Day Adventists and the Mormons, and greatly expanded others, such as the Baptists and Methodists. The movement also raised religious consciousness on political and social issues, particularly slavery.

Religion had already played a small political role in the early republic. For instance, charges that Jefferson was an atheist (a charge he denied) were raised during the hard-fought 1800 presidential election. The temperance movement also had taken hold in many churches. But slavery was the first cause that galvanized large numbers of religious people and pushed them into the political arena.

Protestants, especially evangelicals and Quakers, had opposed slavery as early as the mid-18th century. But the movement did not gain steam until the 1830s, when writer and editor William Lloyd Garrison urged all people of faith to abolish the practice.

Garrison's crusade spread throughout the North and West, where ministers frequently inveighed against slavery as being incompatible with Christianity. [15] The abolitionist movement also produced a political shift, as religious people outside the South came to see the Republican Party of Lincoln as the best hope for ending slavery. Abolitionists helped elect Lincoln president in 1860, sparking the secession of the Southern states and the Civil War.

As the war progressed, Lincoln's ambivalence about Christianity evolved into a view of the conflict as divinely ordained. During his famous second inaugural address, delivered a month before his assassination, Lincoln said, "American slavery is one of those offenses which, in the providence of God, must needs come, but which having continued through His appointed time, He now wills to remove, and that He gives to both North and South this terrible war as the woe due to those by whom the offense came. . . ." [16]

After the Civil War, religious Americans focused on other concerns. By the 1880s, liberal Protestants had embraced the "social gospel" movement, which inveighed against drunkenness, sexual immorality, economic inequality and other sins associated with the urbanization and industrialization sweeping the nation. It helped lead to the populist movement, which culminated in the 1896 presidential campaign of William Jennings Bryan. Populism was widespread throughout the rural South and West, where farmers and other low-income people embraced its anti-big business, pro-workingman message.

To attract religious voters to the Democratic Party, Bryan frequently used religious imagery to condemn big business. In his famous "Cross of Gold" speech, he likened the impact of the gold standard, which was believed to be depressing the wages of common laborers, to the crucifixion of Christ. "You shall not press down upon the brow of labor this crown of thorns, you shall not crucify mankind upon a cross of gold." [17]

Bryan lost, but populism and the social gospel movement survived. The energies of many liberal Protestants and evangelicals next were channeled into the temperance movement, which swept the country in the late 19th and early 20th centuries.

Banning alcohol had been a goal of religious reformers well before the movement reached fruition. Before the Civil War, 13 states had even experimented with prohibition, only to abandon the idea in all but two cases.

The modern temperance movement began in 1893 with the founding of the Anti-Saloon League in Oberlin, Ohio, where the league was active in politics and elected pro-temperance candidates.

By 1917, prohibition laws had been enacted in 26 states. In 1919, the movement scored a major victory with ratification of the 18th Amendment, banning the sale and consumption of alcohol nationwide. However, Prohibition proved very unpopular with most Americans and the amendment was repealed 13 years later.

The defeat of the temperance movement was actually the second major setback conservative Christians suffered during the early decades of the 20th century. The first occurred in 1925, when a high-school teacher from Dayton, Tenn., John Thomas Scopes, was arrested for violating the state's law prohibiting the teaching of Darwin's theory of evolution through natural selection rather than the biblical story of divine creation.

Scopes was convicted (and given a token fine) and the Tennessee law was upheld. But the infamous "monkey trial" was actually a defeat for conservative Christians, who were subjected to unprecedented ridicule in the national press.

New Players

As Protestants were flexing their political muscles through the populist and temperance movements, Roman Catholics were emerging onto the national scene. By 1900, immigration from Ireland and Southern and Central Europe had made Catholics the nation's largest, single Christian denomination, although they were still greatly outnumbered by Protestants.

Clustered in the industrial states of the Northeast and Midwest, Catholics became a key constituency of the pro-labor Democratic Party. In 1928, former Gov. Al Smith of New York became the first Roman Catholic to run for president on a national ticket against Republican Herbert Hoover. Still, Smith lost, in part because he was unable to overcome the fears of many Protestants, who said he would be beholden to the Vatican once in office.

Despite the loss, Catholics continued to play an important role in the Democratic Party. Along with African-Americans, Southern, white Protestants and smaller groups such as Jews — Catholics became a pillar of the winning New Deal Coalition that dominated politics throughout the 1930s and '40s.

In 1960, another Catholic, John F. Kennedy won the Democratic nomination for president and ran against Republican Richard M. Nixon, a Quaker from California. Kennedy worked hard to allay fears that had plagued Smith's candidacy, stating categorically that the Church would play no role in his administration. Kennedy's reassurances won him enough Protestant support to just squeak by Nixon and become the first, and so far only, Roman Catholic to win the White House.

As Catholics were emerging as major political players, African-Americans also were finding their political voice. In many parts of the country, especially the South, blacks had been shut out of the political process, leaving many to look to the pulpit for leadership and guidance.

Until the 1930s, most black ministers urged their flocks to vote for the GOP — the party of Lincoln. But the joblessness and economic misery created by the Great Depression that began in 1929 fell especially heavily on African-Americans. As a result, Roosevelt's New Deal, with its work programs and other government assistance, was able to attract a majority of black voters to the Democratic Party by the 1936 elections.

But Roosevelt did nothing to end the racial segregation that persited throughout the South and elsewhere. His successors, Democrat Harry S Truman and Republican Dwight D. Eisenhower, took some small steps toward racial equality — particularly in the military — but neither pushed for the significant changes African-Americans wanted.

By the mid-1950s, black clergymen were increasingly taking matters into their own hands. In 1957, King became head of the Southern Christian Leadership Conference and initiated a campaign to end segregation throughout the South.

Embracing Christian teachings on peace as well as those of India's founding father, Mohandas K. Gandhi, King urged his followers to use non-violent protest to call attention to unjust laws and racist practices. The strategy eventually culminated in passage of the 1964 Civil Rights Act and the end of institutional segregation.

New Alliances

Since the 1960s, the United States has witnessed a major political realignment of religious groups. Until about 40 years ago, a person's politics was often determined by religious affiliation. "We used to have antagonism between religious traditions, Catholics vs. Protestants vs. Jews," says the University of Akron's Green. "This was a politics of belonging."

Catholics — who were usually first- or second-generation urban immigrants with union jobs — tended to vote Democratic, because the party was more sympathetic to organized labor. White Protestants, on the other hand, were more likely to support the GOP.

This split was typified in 1960, when Kennedy, the Democratic Catholic nominee for president, received more than 80 percent of the Roman Catholic vote but only about 40 percent of the white Protestant vote.

Indeed, evangelical leaders like the Rev. Billy Graham publicly worried that electing Kennedy could result in the Catholic Church acquiring undue influence over American governance. In a 1960 article in *Christianity Today*, Graham warned that the Vatican would do "all in its power to control the governments of nations." [18]

Today, the landscape has changed dramatically. "Now we have a politics of believing and behaving," Green says. "Liberal Protestants linking up with liberal Catholics and liberal Jews against an alliance of conservative Protestants, conservative Catholics and conservative Jews."

That's not to say that religious affiliation no longer matters. Broadly speaking, Protestants are still more likely to vote Republican than Catholics, who in turn are more likely to support the GOP than Jews. But one's attitude toward religion is now a much more important indicator than religious affiliation.

By way of example, Green points out that the Catholic Democratic candidate Kerry is by no means assured of even a majority of the Catholic vote. Traditional, conservative Catholics overwhelmingly favor the very Protestant President Bush, and both candidates are fighting to win over moderates within both groups.

Much of the shift from "belonging" to "believing and behaving" can be traced to the transformation of conservative evangelical Christians into a political movement in the late 1970s and '80s. The move was sparked by the sexual revolution and other societal changes during the 1960s and '70s and the perception among many evangelicals that the country was heading in the wrong direction.

Groups like the Moral Majority, founded by the Rev. Jerry Falwell in 1979, galvanized evangelicals and other conservatives in the 1980 election, helping to put Republican Ronald Reagan in the White House in 1980 and 1984 and George H. W. Bush in 1988.

Many observers said the religious right was on the decline after the election of President Bill Clinton, but it came roaring back in the midterm elections of 1994, led in part by the Christian Coalition. Established in 1989 by the Rev. Pat Robertson, the coalition had grown steadily in the early 1990s, in part by converting lifelong Southern Democrats into Republicans by blaming "Clinton-style liberalism" for a decline in moral values in the United States. Robertson's group was a key factor in the Republicans' successful effort in 1994 to gain control of both houses of Congress.

Library of Congress

In 1779, the Virginia legislature passed a statute protecting religious freedom, drafted by Thomas Jefferson. He also worked to ensure churches do not receive state support.

As the ranks of evangelicals grew and they coalesced into a potent political force, they also increased their electoral punch by joining with conservative Catholics, even though the two groups have historically differed on many cultural and theological issues.

Cooperation between the two groups began in the 1980s, when they found themselves on the same side of a bitter fight over abortion. The partnership was formalized 10 years ago, when the Rev. John Neuhaus, a Catholic priest and intellectual, and Charles Colson, former Watergate felon who later became head of Prison Fellowship Ministries, convened a meeting between leaders of both traditions. The group, which also included Robertson and the late Cardinal John O'Connor of New York, issued a document entitled *Evangelicals and Catholics Together: The Christian Mission in the Third Millennium.*

The document enunciated the theological common ground between Catholics and evangelicals and pledged the two communities would work together on social and cultural issues like abortion. Today, the two groups also fight against gay marriage, euthanasia and stem cell research and battle for school vouchers. Although differences over religious style and substance remain, both sides view the other favorably.

"There is many an evangelical now who believes that they have more in common with the Catholics down the street than with mainline Protestants," says the Rev. Richard Cizik, director of government affairs for the National Association of Evangelicals.

Indeed, when actor, director and conservative Catholic Mel Gibson was about to release his controversial film, "The Passion of Christ," he appealed to and received enormous support from the evangelical community. Churches all over the country, like the 10,000-member McLean Bible Church in McLean, Va., bought blocks of thousands of tickets for congregants, helping the film gross over $350 million in the United States alone. [19]

In addition, a recent poll conducted for the PBS television program "Religion and Ethics Newsweekly" and *U.S. News & World Report*, showed that evangelicals had a more favorable view of Pope John Paul II (59 percent) than they did of either Robertson (54 percent) or Falwell (44 percent.) [20]

The increasing clout of religious conservatives has prompted the creation of more liberal and moderate religious organizations. For instance, The Interfaith Alliance, which includes Christians, Jews and people of other faiths, was created in 1994, partly in response to the growing political activity of conservative Christian groups. ■

Mel Gibson directs Jim Caviezel (Jesus) for his controversial film "The Passion of The Christ." Huge numbers of evangelical Protestants saw the film, reflecting the commonalities that exist today between conservative Catholics like Gibson and the evangelical movement.

CURRENT SITUATION

Crossing a Line?

Since late spring, the Bush-Cheney campaign has been working assiduously to mobilize religious voters. Recently, it sent a detailed plan to thousands of religious supporters directing them to distribute "issue guides" at church and to persuade their pastor or minister to hold a voter-registration drive. They also asked volunteers to provide the campaign with copies of church directories so other members could be contacted by campaign volunteers. [21]

The church voter-registration effort has particularly focused on key battleground or "swing" states, where neither candidate enjoys a big advantage. For instance, in June, the campaign sent an e-mail to religious supporters in Pennsylvania encouraging them to recruit volunteer networks at 1,600 "friendly congregations" in the state. [22]

Democrats immediately blasted the initiative, arguing that the Bush-Cheney campaign had "crossed a line" and was seeking to involve churches in unlawful political activity.

"It is sinful of them to encourage pastors and churches to engage in partisan political activity and run the risk of losing their tax-exempt status," Steve Rosenthal, chief executive officer of Americans Coming Together, a liberal group working to defeat President Bush in November, said. [23]

"This shows a reckless disregard for the welfare of churches," agrees Lynn of Americans United for the Separation of Church and State. "I really don't think they care if these churches lose their tax-exempt status."

Under Section 501(c)(3) of the federal code, religious organizations can be exempt from taxation if they refrain from participating, either directly or indirectly, in political campaigns.

The law does not mean that churches and other houses of worship must be completely uninvolved in politics. Churches frequently take positions on political issues and are allowed to conduct voter-registration drives. Candidates also frequently attend and speak at worship services, often turning them into political rallies.

But if a church or other house of worship specifically endorses or opposes a candidate or political party, it can lose its exemption. That is what happened to the Church at Pierce Creek, in upstate New York, which in 1992 took out a full-page ad in the local newspaper proclaiming that it was a "sin" to vote for then-Gov. Clinton in the upcoming presidential election. [24]

Critics are particularly troubled by the Bush-Cheney campaign's request for church directories. "To go into a church and use the directory, with its names and addresses and phone numbers, to enlist supporters clearly violates the law," says The Interfaith Alliance's Parker. "This sort of activity will hurt the sanctity of churches because it has the potential to drive a wedge between congregants based on political views. Soon people will be choosing a church not based on theology, but politics."

But Steve Schmidt, a spokesman for the Bush campaign says, "We are collecting all kinds of lists from many different sources, and it is completely appropriate to do so. People of faith have as much right to participate in the political process as anybody else."

Continued on p. 654

At Issue:

Should Congress relax the rules limiting political activities of tax-exempt churches?

REP. WALTER B. JONES, R-N.C.

WRITTEN FOR *THE CQ RESEARCHER*, JULY 2004

yes

Houses of worship play a critical role in shaping the moral character of the nation, and given their importance in American society, must retain their right to freedom of speech. That is the guarantee of the First Amendment. Yet the Internal Revenue Service (IRS) has reserved the right to determine that clerics' exercise of that First Amendment right to free speech may constitute "political activity."

Thus, while laws separating houses of worship from political campaigns should not be relaxed, laws limiting the content of a minister's sermon in a worship service should.

Prior to 1954 and the amendment that changed the tax code, there were no restrictions on the speech of religious leaders. But today the IRS is able to take away the tax-exempt status of a house of worship if someone brings a "political-speech violation" to the attention of the IRS.

The IRS attempts to prohibit not just the endorsement of candidates but also the use of what they have determined to be political code words, such as "pro-life" or "pro-choice." Such words can be central to a religious leader's faith, and thus to his or her role as a moral and religious teacher. The IRS' attempt to limit speech casts a pall over the First Amendment that no thinking person should tolerate.

Further, the current policy simply cannot be enforced uniformly. Current law says that third parties must present violations to the IRS in order for steps to be taken toward removing a church's tax-exempt status. Thus, by definition all churches are not equally scrutinized. In fact, this has become nothing more than another partisan issue. But its consequences are about much more: First Amendment rights to freedom of speech are in jeopardy.

The IRS should not be in the business of telling clerics what to say under any circumstances. Those who profess to champion a strict adherence to the principle of the separation of church and state should be similarly appalled. As current law stands, the IRS as a state actor is in direct violation of this principle by interfering with religious affairs.

It is time for Congress to restore the First Amendment rights of all ministers by passing legislation that gets the IRS out of the speech-police business.

THE REV. DR. C. WELTON GADDY
PRESIDENT, THE INTERFAITH ALLIANCE

WRITTEN FOR *THE CQ RESEARCHER*, JULY 2004

no

Houses of worship and their leaders can and should address politics — emphasizing the social nature of personal faith, examining social-political issues from the perspectives of sacred scriptures, challenging members of their congregations to participate in the political process and urging them to vote for the candidates of their respective choices. At the same time, houses of worship and their leaders have absolutely no business becoming involved in partisan politics — using spiritual authority to support partisan campaigns or bestowing a special blessing on one candidate alone.

No new rule or law is needed to allow houses of worship to do the political work that is rightfully theirs to do while maintaining their identity as houses of worship. To the contrary, every effort to weaken regulations that prevent houses of worship from engagements in partisan politics should be vigorously resisted — not only in the interest of good law but also in the interest of good religion. If a house of worship wants to take on the activity and identity of a partisan political entity, it can do so now; but political partisanship does not merit the special tax provisions given to a religious body.

Our Constitution provides brilliantly constructed guarantees of religious liberty that have allowed religion to thrive in this nation without religious bodies warring with each other. To encourage a wedding of religion with partisan politics is to risk the demise of the constitutional principle of religious liberty, to blunt the vitality of religion in the nation, to silence the religious community's voice of conscience calling the nation to its highest aspirations and to rob the nation of the one presence within it that can best enable diverse people to live together expressing goodwill for each other individually as well as for the nation as a whole.

The Interfaith Alliance, a nonpartisan, grassroots organization representing 150,000 members from more than 75 faith traditions, will continue to urge Congress to defeat all attempts to weaken laws that prohibit tax-exempt houses of worship from partisan political activities. Religion can best contribute to the nation by independent religious institutions speaking and acting with integrity on issues of morality and spirituality, not by turning houses of worship into halls for political meetings and further polarizing a public already too deeply divided by partisan politics.

Continued from p. 652

Republicans also point out that they are not alone in appealing to churches for support. For instance, when Kerry appeared at New Deliverance Evangelistic Church in Richmond, Va., a few days before that state's Feb. 10 primary, he was all but endorsed by the congregation's leader, Bishop Gerald Glenn. "We want to remember Election Day, Tuesday, the 10th of February," Glenn told his flock while Kerry sat behind him. "Sen. Kerry won in Michigan and in Washington state [and] I say to him this morning, 'Senator, I hope you can make it three for three.' I'd like to see him carry Virginia come November."

Congressional Republicans have been trying — so far unsuccessfully — to enact legislation to ease some of the political restrictions on churches. (*See At Issue, p. 653.*) The Houses of Worship Free Speech Restoration Act would allow clergy members to endorse and even raise funds for political candidates without their church losing its tax-exempt status. The bill has yet to be taken up in Congress.

Another proposal, the Safe Harbor for Churches Act, would allow a house of worship to make three "mistakes" before losing its tax-exempt status. Churches that unknowingly violated the law would still have to pay small tax penalties.

The language in the Safe Harbor bill was inserted into a jobs bill making its way through the House of Representatives. But the House Ways and Means Committee stripped out the language when it took up the overall bill on June 15.

Both provisions stand little chance of enactment any time soon, in part because they are opposed not only by civil liberties and liberal advocacy groups, such as People for the American Way, but also by some conservative religious organizations, including the Southern Baptist Convention and the Union of Orthodox Jewish Congregations. [25]

For his part, Land, of the Southern Baptists, believes that creating a system that allowed more wiggle room would require "an unacceptable intrusion of the IRS into the business of the church." [26] ■

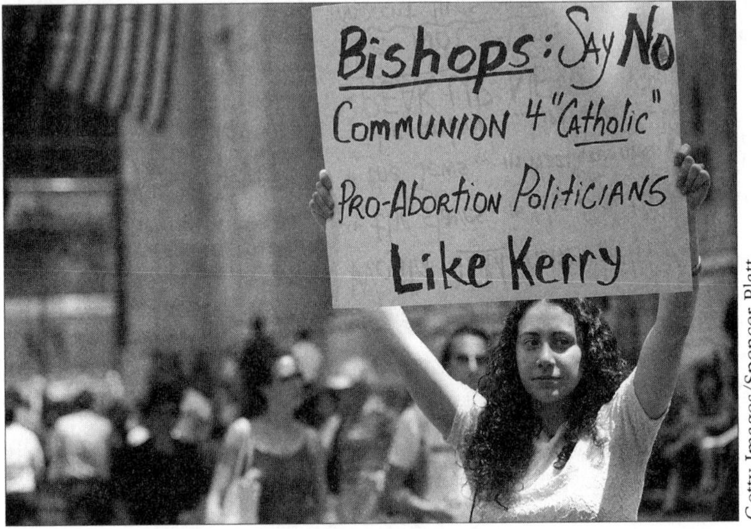

Getty Images/Spencer Platt

Protesters in New York City urge Catholic bishops to deny Democratic presidential nominee Sen. John Kerry the right to Holy Communion.

OUTLOOK

Impact on the Election

During the 1992 presidential election campaign, political strategist James Carville and other advisers working for then-Gov. Clinton made famous the phrase, "It's the economy, stupid," reflecting the belief by Clinton's strategists that one issue would dominate the campaign.

Twelve years later, the conventional wisdom seems to be that the 2004 presidential election will be decided by two issues: The war in Iraq and, once again, the state of the economy. But some political thinkers say moral or religious issues also may end up becoming important factors.

"It's possible that gay marriage may end up becoming very important in this campaign, because that's the issue that has the ability to stir the passions of a lot of voters," says the University of Akron's Green. "If it does become an issue, it will probably benefit Republicans because there are more fervent opponents [to same-sex unions] than fervent proponents."

Green predicts that the Bush campaign will move to bring the gay marriage issue up more prominently in the campaign. "They won't do it themselves, but will turn to proxies, like Christian leaders, to try to whip up the base on this," he says. "But they need to be careful: It helps to be on the side of traditional marriage, but if you go too far, you'll appear intolerant and lose the support of the voters in the center that you have to have to win."

Abortion may also come to the forefront, in part because of the controversy over Holy Communion. "The question over communion has certainly given the issue more visibility, and there is an effort by conservatives to use it as a wedge issue this year," Barnes says.

The passage last October of legislation banning "partial-birth abortions" and subsequent court challenges to the new law might also galvanize voters on both sides of the abortion debate.

But others predict that important moral or ethical issues will be marginalized this year.

"Gay marriage and abortion may have peaked too soon," Furman University's Guth says. "If gays [had] started marrying in September or October, or Congress had voted on the partial-birth abortion ban around that time, they might have become important issues in the campaign. But they've already lost a lot of traction, and I don't think they're going to get it back."

And that's just fine with candidates on both sides of the aisle, says Emory University's Allitt. "People on both sides are aware that these issues don't line up neatly along party lines," he says. "For instance, there are lots of Republicans on the libertarian wing of the party who would be OK with gay marriage and lots of more conservative Democrats who would be against it. So I don't think anyone is really going to push things like that."

Others agree that while moral issues won't be absent from the campaign, they probably will not make a huge difference in the overall election.

"They're going to be discussed and used by both sides to try to generate enthusiasm among supporters," says The Interfaith Alliance's Parker. "But I don't really see these moral issues having much of an impact on the election, because the people on both sides who will pay any attention to them have already made up their minds. They're already the true believers." ■

FOR MORE INFORMATION

Center for American Progress, 805 15th St., N.W., Suite 400, Washington, DC 20005; (202) 682-1611; www.americanprogress.org. Liberal think tank.

Christian Coalition of America, P.O. Box 37030, Washington, DC 20013; (202) 479-6900; www.cc.org. Conservative, religiously oriented political organization.

National Association of Evangelicals, P.O. Box 23269, Washington, DC 20026; (202) 789-1011; www.nae.net. Evangelical Christian advocacy group.

Pew Forum on Religion and Public Life, 1150 18th St., N.W., Suite 775, Washington, DC 20036; (202) 955-5075; http://pewforum.org. Nonpartisan research center that studies the intersection of religion and public affairs.

Southern Baptist Convention, 901 Commerce St., Nashville, TN 37203; (615) 244-2355; www.sbc.net. Association of the Southern Baptists.

The Interfaith Alliance, 1331 H St., N.W., Washington, DC 20005; (202) 639-6370; www.interfaithalliance.org. Founded by religious leaders of different faiths to oppose conservative groups, emphasizes inclusiveness and religious tolerance in public policy.

U.S. Conference of Catholic Bishops, 3211 Fourth St., N.E., Washington, DC 20017; (202) 541-3000; www.usccb.org. Organization of the nation's Roman Catholic bishops.

Notes

[1] Figures cited in "American Views on Religion, Politics, and Public Policy," The Pew Forum on Religion and Public Life and the Pew Research Center for People and the Press, July 2003, p. 4.

[2] Figures cited in Nancy Gibbs, "The Faith Factor," *Time*, June 21, 2004, p. 26.

[3] For background, see David Masci, "Evangelical Christians," *The CQ Researcher*, Sept. 14, 2001, pp. 713-736.

[4] Quoted in "The Politics of Virtue," *The Economist*, July 17, 2004, p. 34.

[5] Figures cited in Gibbs, *op. cit.*

[6] Quoted in Gail Russell, "Democrats Strike Back on Faith Issue," *The Christian Science Monitor*, June 9, 2004, p. A1. Women generally favor Democrats by 8-12 percentage points.

[7] Helen Dewar, "Ban on Gay Marriage Fails," *The Washington Post*, July 15, 2004, p. A1.

[8] Quoted in Katharine Q. Seelye, "Kerry Attends Easter Services and Receives Holy Communion," *The New York Times*, April 12, 2004, p. A15.

[9] Quoted in Terry Eastland, "John Kerry's Catholic Problem," *The Weekly Standard*, April 15, 2004.

[10] Andrew Sullivan, "Showdown at the Communion Rail," *Time*, May 24, 2004, p. 94.

[11] Quoted in *ibid.*

[12] Mark A. Noll, (ed), *Religion and Politics: From the Colonial Period to the 1800s* (1990), p. 29.

[13] Quoted in Gary Wills, *Under God: Religion and American Politics*, 1990, p. 375.

[14] Noll, *op. cit.*, p. 34.

[15] A. James Reichley, *Religion in American Public Life*, Brookings, 1985, p. 193.

[16] For the full text of President Lincoln's address see: www.bartleby.com/124/pres32.html.

[17] Quoted in Reichley, *op. cit.*, p. 210.

[18] Quoted in Laurie Goodstein, "How Evangelicals and Catholics Joined Forces," *The New York Times*, May 30, 2004, p. A4.

[19] Judith Person and John Ward, "Area Churches Will Use 'Passion' For Outreach," *The Washington Times*, Feb. 19, 2004, p. A1.

[20] Figures cited in Adelle M. Banks, "Along the Evangelical Divide," *The Kansas City Star*, April 17, 2004, p. F2.

[21] Alan Cooperman, "Churchgoers Get Direction from the Bush Campaign," *The Washington Post*, July 1, 2004, p. A6.

[22] David D. Kirkpatrick, "Bush Campaign Seeking Help from Congregations," *The New York Times*, June 3, 2004, p. A1.

[23] Cooperman, *op. cit.*

[24] David Ress, "Finding Votes in Churches," *Richmond Times Dispatch*, Feb. 17, 2004, p. A9.

[25] Alan Cooperman, "House Panel Drops 'Safe Harbor for Churches' Measure," *The Washington Post*, June 16, 2004, p. A25.

[26] Quoted in *ibid.*

About the Author

David Masci specializes in science, religion and foreign-policy issues. Before joining *The CQ Researcher* in 1996, he was a reporter at Congressional Quarterly's *Daily Monitor* and *CQ Weekly*. He holds a law degree from The George Washington University and a B.A. in medieval history from Syracuse University. His recent reports include "Rebuilding Iraq" and "Torture."

Bibliography

Selected Sources

Books

Dionne, E.J., Jean Bethke Elshtain and Kayla M. Drogosz (eds.), *One Electorate Under God?: A Dialogue on Religion and American Politics*, Brookings Institution Press, 2004.
The editors have collected essays from more than 40 journalists, thinkers and politicians on the role of faith in public life.

Greenberg, Stanley B., *The Two Americas: Our Current Political Deadlock and How to Break It*, St. Martin's Press, 2004.
The Democratic pollster explains how the United States has become a divided nation, with great differences on questions of values and faith.

Mansfield, Stephen, *The Faith of George W. Bush*, Penguin, 2003.
The author of several books on leadership explores President Bush's faith life, from his wild youth and aimless young adulthood to his conversion to evangelical Christianity soon after his 40th birthday.

Reichley, A. James, *Religion in American Public Life*, Brookings Institution Press, 1985.
A senior fellow at the Public Policy Institution at Georgetown University gives an overview of the interplay between religion and politics in U.S. history.

Articles

"The Politics of Virtue," *The Economist*, July 17, 2004, p. 34.
Democratic presidential candidate John Kerry is challenging President Bush on "values" issues like family, faith and patriotism.

Curl, Joseph, "Bush Campaign Courts Jewish Vote," *The Washington Times*, June 2, 2004, p. A8.
The article examines the Bush campaign's efforts to court the Jewish vote, an ethnic block that could make a crucial difference in several swing states, including Florida and Pennsylvania.

Goodstein, Laurie, "How Evangelicals and Catholics Joined Forces," *The New York Times*, May 30, 2004, p. D4.
Conservative Catholics and evangelical Christians, two groups that once viewed each other with distrust, have made common cause over issues like abortion and gay marriage.

Leo, John, "The Bishops and the Pols," *U.S. News & World Report*, May 17, 2004, p. 14.
The columnist examines the controversy over whether politicians who support abortion rights should take communion.

McDonald, G. Jeffrey, "When Prayer and Politics Intersect," *The Christian Science Monitor*, May 6, 2004, p. A1.
The clergy face challenges in addressing important public issues while not creating a hostile environment for those in the congregation who disagree.

Rogers, Ann, "John Kerry, Keeping the Catholic Faith," *Pittsburgh Post Gazette*, May 10, 2004.
Kerry's faith journey, from altar boy to agnostic to churchgoing Roman Catholic, is chronicled.

Sullivan, Andrew, "Showdown at the Communion Rail," *Time*, May 24, 2004, p. 94.
A well-known Catholic essayist argues that the bishops will politicize and ultimately hurt the church if they deny communion to pro-choice politicians.

Tumulty, Karen, "Is Kerry Catholic Enough? There's Evidence the Question is Backfiring on His Critics," *Time*, June 21, 2004, p. 34.
The reporter examines the conflict between Kerry and other pro-abortion rights politicians and some Catholic bishops who want to deny them Holy Communion.

Woodward, Kenneth, "A Political Sacrament," *The New York Times*, May 28, 2004, p. A21.
Newsweek's religion writer parses out the subtleties of the controversy over Holy Communion, arguing that many bishops may urge pro-choice politicians to voluntarily refrain from taking the sacrament rather than impose prohibitions on anyone.

Reports and Studies

Dessingue, Deirdre, "Politics and the Pulpit: A Guide to the Internal Revenue Code Restrictions on the Political Activity of Religious Organizations," The Pew Forum on Religion and Public Life, September 2002.
The associate general counsel for the United States Conference of Catholic Bishops provides a clear, readable guide to the complicated rules and regulations governing houses of worship and political activity.

The Interfaith Alliance, "Religion and Politics: Running for Office in a Multi-Faith Nation," www.interfaithalliance.org/elections.
The 14-page guide — distributed to hundreds of candidates from both parties this year by the nonpartisan, interdenominational organization — provides the group's views on proper and improper ways to incorporate religious language and references into political campaigns.

The Next Step:

Additional Articles from Current Periodicals

Bush and His Faith

Barnes, Fred, "God and Man in the Oval Office," *The Weekly Standard*, March 17, 2003.

The author defends Bush's frequent references to God and his faith as being well within the American mainstream and less than those of past presidents.

Cannon, Carl M., "Bush and God," *National Journal*, Jan. 3, 2004.

Bush's religious beliefs are sincere, but they could be a polarizing drawback in a conflict against religious fanaticism, some observers say.

Donnelly, John, "Some Voice Concern Over President's Religious Rhetoric," *The Boston Globe*, Feb. 16, 2003, p. A20.

Copious religious references in President Bush's speeches touch off a debate on whether such references help or hinder the fight against terrorism and al Qaeda.

Fineman, Howard, "Bush and God," *Newsweek*, March 10, 2003, p. 22.

The reporter chronicles George W. Bush's transition from hard-drinking partygoer to a man on a spiritual journey.

Schweizer, Peter, and Rochelle Schweizer, "Fundamentally, Bush Works on Faith," *Los Angeles Times*, April 11, 2004, p. M1.

According to an unnamed family member, George Bush sees the fight against al Qaeda as a religious war.

VandeHei, Jim, "Kerry Keeps His Faith in Reserve," *The Washington Post*, July 16, 2004, p. A1.

John Kerry's reticence regarding his personal religious faith is in stark contrast to President Bush's public declarations.

Catholic Voters

Feldmann, Linda, "Bush, Kerry, and a Battle for Catholics," *The Christian Science Monitor*, June 4, 2004, p. 1.

Once a reliably Democratic voting bloc, Catholics' views today tend to mirror those of the electorate as a whole.

La Ganga, Maria, "Changing Catholic Vote Appears Up for Grabs," *Los Angeles Times*, May 2, 2004, p. A24.

Catholics are seen as a desirable group of swing voters, but are so diverse that talk of a monolithic Catholic vote may be just an illusion.

Thomma, Steven, "Election Battle for Catholic Vote Heats Up," *The Philadelphia Inquirer*, June 5, 2004, p. A8.

Catholics are a large presence in swing states like Ohio and Pennsylvania, where neither candidate can afford to lose.

Toner, Robin, "The Catholic Vote; Testing the Church's Influence in Politics," *The New York Times*, Jan. 26, 2003, Section 4, p. 1.

The recent sex scandals have tainted the authority of the Catholic hierarchy in the U.S., lessening still further their ability to influence Catholics' voting behavior.

Communion Controversy

Cooperman, Alan, "Catholics Question Abortion Focus," *The Washington Post*, April 26, 2004, p. A2.

Some liberal Catholics see the church's focus on politicians who violate teachings on abortion as hypocritical, when, for example, pro-death penalty politicians are not also criticized.

Goodstein, Laurie, "Kerry, Candidate and Catholic, Creates Uneasiness for Church," *The New York Times*, April 2, 2004, p. A1.

Although diverging from Catholic orthodoxy on issues like abortion, he is closer to the bishops' positions on social-justice issues like poverty or immigration.

Gorski, Eric, "Bishops Blast Abortion, OK Local Decisions on Eucharist," *The Denver Post*, June 20, 2004, p. A21.

Catholic bishops fail to agree on a uniform national policy toward whether politicians violating church teachings should receive Holy Communion.

Lobdell, William, and Teresa Watanabe, "Church May Penalize Politicians," *Los Angeles Times*, Nov. 29, 2003, p. A14.

Frustration with "cafeteria Catholicism," where people choose which Vatican tenets to follow, leads to calls by some bishops to impose penalties on pro-abortion politicians.

O'Reilly, David, "Abortion Reemerging as a Litmus Test," *The Philadelphia Inquirer*, May 9, 2004, p. A9.

Calling it an "absolute wrong," bishops defend their criticism of Catholic politicians who support abortion rights.

Rainey, James, and Maria La Ganga, "Abortion Issue Pushes Kerry's Faith to Fore," *Los Angeles Times*, April 24, 2004, p. A20.

Talk among some Catholic clerics of denying Holy Communion to politicians who support abortion rights causes friction with John Kerry and other Catholic politicians.

Faith-Based Voting

"Belief and the Ballot Box," *The Economist*, June 5, 2004.

The primary political-religious conflict in America is shaping up between aggressive Republican evangelicals and aggressive Democratic secularists.

Gibbs, Nancy, "The Faith Factor," *Time*, June 21, 2004, p. 26.

The important role played by religion in politics makes candidates walk a fine line between attracting religious voters and alienating the more secular.

Lattin, Don, *et al.*, "Religious Groups on Common Ground," *San Francisco Chronicle*, March 14, 2004, p. A1.
Opposition to same-sex marriages unites a broad spectrum of people from many faiths, Christian and non-Christian.

Page, Susan, "Churchgoing Closely Tied to Voting Patterns," *USA Today*, June 3, 2004, p. 1A.
Beginning in the 1970s and ballooning in the 1990s, Americans' church attendance became a reliable indicator of their voting patterns.

Sheler, Jeffery, *et al.*, "Nearer My God to Thee," *U.S. News & World Report*, May 3, 2004, p. 59.
Many evangelical Christians could be key swing voters who would consider voting Democratic, but they are attracted to Bush's very public faith.

Steinfels, Peter, "Using How People Worship to Find Who Votes for Whom; Finding More Than One 'Religion Gap'," *The New York Times*, Jan. 31, 2004, p. B6.
The nuances of the religion gap are brushed over; it may be more accurate to speak of several religion gaps.

Wallsten, Peter, "Rumblings Are Felt at Base of Bush's Support," *Los Angeles Times*, July 17, 2004, p. A1.
Republicans are counting on a heavy turnout among evangelicals in November, but some express dissatisfaction with Bush's support for their causes.

Jews and Muslims

Blumenfeld, Laura, "Terrorism Jars Jewish, Arab Party Loyalties," *The Washington Post*, Dec. 7, 2003, p. A1.
While President Bush seems set to increase his share of the Jewish vote, Muslims are questioning his policies.

Lampman, Jane, "Mixing Prophecy and Politics," *The Christian Science Monitor*, July 7, 2004, p. 15.
Christian Zionists lobby for staunch U.S. backing for Israel based on their interpretation of biblical prophecies and are a political force.

Lattin, Don, "Muslim Voters Turn Away From Bush, Survey Finds," *San Francisco Chronicle*, June 30, 2004, p. A6.
Angry over the U.S. war in Iraq, U.S. policy toward Israel and the Palestinians, Muslims who strongly supported the GOP in 2000 are abandoning them.

Reynolds, Maura, and Peter Wallsten, "The Race to the White House," *Los Angeles Times*, May 19, 2004, p. A1.
President Bush is fighting hard to increase his share of the Jewish vote, but many Jews express reservations about his domestic policies.

Stone, Peter H., "Bush's Jewish Bloc," *National Journal*, Jan. 24, 2004.
The president's unstinting support for Israel during the last four years has been accompanied by aggressive fundraising efforts among the Jewish community.

Mixing Religion and Politics

Abdo, Geneive, "Religious Right Could Be Strong Pillar for Bush," *Chicago Tribune*, June 24, 2004, News Section, p. 13.
The "values" issues of the election, such as gay marriage, could mobilize religious voters who would otherwise not bother to vote.

Bumiller, Elisabeth, "Evangelicals Sway White House on Human Rights Issues Abroad," *The New York Times*, Oct. 26, 2003, Section 1, p. 1.
On issues like sex trafficking, AIDS and Sudan, evangelical groups have exercised significant sway on Bush's policies.

Dlouhy, Jennifer A., "Religion Takes Center Stage in Fight Over Judicial Nominees," *CQ Weekly*, Aug. 2, 2003, p. 1964.
A Senate fight over President Bush's judicial nominees engenders a debate among senators over the role of religion in the confirmation process.

Kirkpatrick, David, "Bush Campaign Seeking Help From Congregations," *The New York Times*, June 3, 2004, p. A1.
Efforts to enlist church congregations in political activities could cause churches to lose their tax-exempt status, leaving some church leaders uncomfortable.

Kirkpatrick, David, "Warily, a Religious Leader Lifts His Voice in Politics," *The New York Times*, May 13, 2004, p. A22.
James C. Dobson, perhaps the most influential evangelical leader, could risk his popular support wading into the political arena, experts say.

Kornblut, Anne, and Glen Johnson, "Report Says Bush Sought Vatican Help; Conservative Themes Addressed," *The Boston Globe*, June 14, 2004, p. A1.
John Kerry criticizes George Bush over an alleged appeal for Vatican help in getting Catholic bishops to support the president on social issues.

Roth, Bennett, "Politicians No Longer Avoid Separation of Church, Vote," *The Houston Chronicle*, June 23, 2004, p. A1.
In contrast to Kennedy, John Kerry is criticized for not adhering to church teachings; but he's hired an evangelical Christian to help reach out to religious voters.

Stammer, Larry B., "Faith-Based Stance on Environment," *Los Angeles Times*, July 4, 2004, p. A18.
Some evangelical leaders see themselves as doing God's work by trying to help the environment.

Stone, Peter H., "The Passion of the Religious Conservatives," *National Journal*, May 1, 2004.
Christian rockers and radio broadcasters are only a part of extensive voter mobilization efforts among religious voters that mostly benefit President Bush.

Religion and the Left

Chaddock, Gail Russell, "Democrats Strike Back on Faith Issue," *The Christian Science Monitor*, June 9, 2004, p. 1.
Some Democrats would like to do more to stress religious themes in their party to close the "church gap" among voters, but observers say the party's current culture makes that difficult.

Clemetson, Lynette, "Clergy Group to Counter Conservatives," *The New York Times*, Nov. 17, 2003, p. A17.
Clerics opposed to conservative religious groups establish their own partisan advocacy organization.

Pinsky, Mark, "Little Seems Left for Liberal Religious Activists," *The Philadelphia Inquirer*, Jan. 18, 2004, p. D4.
After riding popular social movements like civil rights in decades past, the religious left is splintered and unable to coalesce around an issue.

Sullivan, Amy, "Do the Democrats Have a Prayer?" *Washington Monthly*, June 2003, p. 30.
The Democrats need to get religion to win elections, the author says; they can and have fielded religious candidates, like Jimmy Carter, successfully.

Swarns, Rachel, and Diane Cardwell, "Democrats Try to Regain Ground on Moral Issues," *The New York Times*, Dec. 6, 2003, p. A11.
The Democratic presidential candidates struggled to attract religious conservatives without alienating secular supporters.

Religion in the Public Sphere

Copeland, Larry, "Church-and-State Standoffs Spread Over USA," *USA Today*, Sept. 30, 2003, p. 15A.
American attitudes toward religion in public life are complex, and so are judicial attitudes, as shown by several cases related to the displaying of the Ten Commandments.

Jacoby, Susan, "In Praise of Secularism," *The Nation*, April 19, 2004, p. 14.
The author criticizes President Bush for an assault on secularism and expounds on the necessity of separating church and state.

Milbank, Dana, "Bush Legislative Approach Failed in Faith Bill Battle," *The Washington Post*, April 23, 2003, p. A1.
Legislation encouraging faith-based initiatives, a favorite theme of the president, stumbled in Congress despite an initially promising outlook.

Padgett, Tim, "When God Is the Warden," *Time*, June 7, 2004, p. 50.
Two Florida prisons featuring religious teachings as a major component of rehabilitation attract the scrutiny of the American Civil Liberties Union.

Stevenson, Richard W., "In Order, President Eases Limits on U.S. Aid to Religious Groups," *The New York Times*, Dec. 13, 2002, p. A1.
President Bush signs an executive order making it easier for religious groups to receive federal funding for non-religious purposes, such as helping the needy.

Yen, Hope, "U.S. Judge Faults AmeriCorps Funding," *The Boston Globe*, July 7, 2004, p. A3.
A federal judge rules that AmeriCorps programs that place volunteers in Catholic schools violates the Constitution.

Citing *The CQ Researcher*

Sample formats for citing these reports in a bibliography include the ones listed below. Preferred styles and formats vary, so please check with your instructor or professor.

MLA Style

Jost, Kenneth. "Rethinking the Death Penalty." The CQ Researcher 16 Nov. 2001: 945-68.

APA Style

Jost, K. (2001, November 16). Rethinking the death penalty. *The CQ Researcher, 11*, 945-968.

Chicago Style

Jost, Kenneth. "Rethinking the Death Penalty." *CQ Researcher*, November 16, 2001, 945-968.

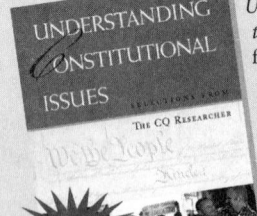

CQ Researcher

Published by CQ Press, a division of Congressional Quarterly Inc.

thecqresearcher.com

Science and Politics

Is political manipulation of science getting worse?

Political bickering over scientific research is intensifying. The Bush administration has attacked environmental laws like the Endangered Species Act and warnings about global warming, claiming they are not based on sound science. But a distinguished group of scientists contends the administration distorts scientific information in order to support policies favored by the religious right and business interests. Questions also have been raised about the influence of corporate money on the integrity of government and academic science. Recently, it was revealed that many scientists at the prestigious National Institutes of Health (NIH) were also working as paid consultants to drug companies whose fortunes could be affected by decisions the scientists made. And questions increasingly are being asked about the close ties developing between university researchers and corporations, which have become a growing source of funding for academic research.

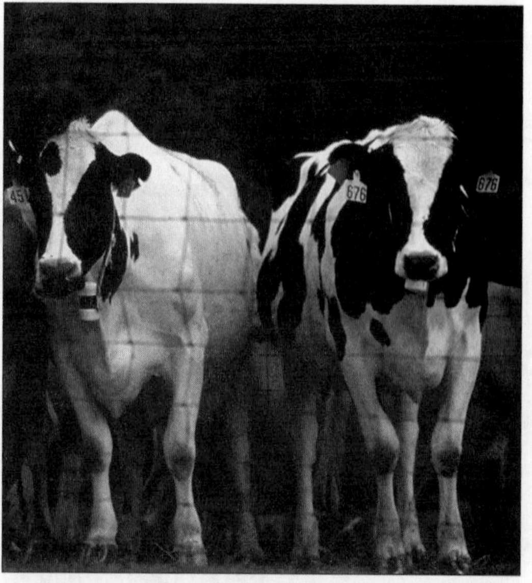

A university study on bovine growth hormone funded by Monsanto Co. raised early concerns about the influence of corporate money on research.

INSIDE THIS REPORT

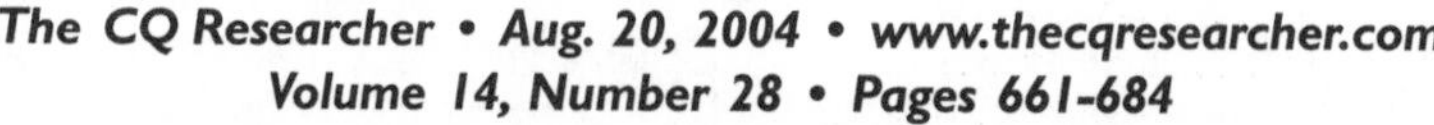

The CQ Researcher • Aug. 20, 2004 • www.thecqresearcher.com
Volume 14, Number 28 • Pages 661-684

CQ PRESS

RECIPIENT OF SOCIETY OF PROFESSIONAL JOURNALISTS AWARD FOR EXCELLENCE ◆ AMERICAN BAR ASSOCIATION SILVER GAVEL AWARD

THE ISSUES

BACKGROUND

CURRENT SITUATION

OUTLOOK

SIDEBARS AND GRAPHICS

FOR FURTHER RESEARCH

Cover: One of the first cases to draw attention to the alleged corrupting influence of corporate money on research involved a 1985 study Monsanto Co. asked Cornell University to conduct on bovine growth hormone. (USDA/Norman Watkins)

THE *CQ Researcher*

Aug. 20, 2004
Volume 14, Number 28

MANAGING EDITOR: Thomas J. Colin

ASSISTANT MANAGING EDITOR: Kathy Koch

ASSOCIATE EDITOR: Kenneth Jost

STAFF WRITERS: Mary H. Cooper, William Triplett

CONTRIBUTING WRITERS: Sarah Glazer, David Hatch, David Hosansky, Patrick Marshall, Tom Price, Jane Tanner

DESIGN/PRODUCTION EDITOR: Olu B. Davis

ASSISTANT EDITOR: Kenneth Lukas

CQ PRESS

A Division of Congressional Quarterly Inc.

SENIOR VICE PRESIDENT/GENERAL MANAGER: John A. Jenkins

DIRECTOR, LIBRARY PUBLISHING: Kathryn C. Suárez

DIRECTOR, EDITORIAL OPERATIONS: Ann Davies

CONGRESSIONAL QUARTERLY INC.

CHAIRMAN: Paul C. Tash

VICE CHAIRMAN: Andrew P. Corty

PRESIDENT AND PUBLISHER: Robert W. Merry

The CQ Researcher (ISSN 1056-2036) is printed on acid-free paper. Published weekly, except Jan. 2, April 9, July 2, July 9, Aug. 6, Aug. 13, Nov. 26 and Dec. 31, by CQ Press, a division of Congressional Quarterly Inc. Annual subscription rates for institutions start at $625. For pricing, call 1-800-834-9020, ext. 1906. To purchase a *CQ Researcher* report in print or electronic format (PDF), visit www.cqpress.com or call 866-427-7737. A single report is $10. Bulk purchase discounts and electronic-rights licensing are also available. Periodicals postage paid at Washington, D.C., and additional mailing offices. POSTMASTER: Send address changes to *The CQ Researcher*, 1255 22nd St., N.W., Suite 400, Washington, D.C. 20037.

Science and Politics

BY WILLIAM TRIPLETT

THE ISSUES

When Rep. Vernon Ehlers, the Michigan Republican who is one of only two research physicists in Congress, hears his colleagues call for the use of "sound science," he tells them they must be talking about acoustics. "Science is sound, period," he quips.

Not everyone, however, accepts that as a given. For instance, the chairman of the Senate Committee on Environment and Public Works, Sen. James Inhofe, R-Okla., frequently declares himself "an advocate of sound science," usually when discussing theories of global warming. He opposes federal regulation of the emission of greenhouse gases — created when fossil fuels are burned — claiming sound science does not support the theory that such gases are contributing to an increase in the Earth's climate temperature.

U.S. Fish and Wildlife Service

Threatened species like the coho salmon pit farmers in Oregon who use river water for their crops against environmentalists who try to limit irrigation, with both sides claiming their opponents use "junk science." Critics say the Bush administration frequently manipulates science for political gain, and the Endangered Species Act is a frequent target.

Inhofe and his supporters say President Bill Clinton's position that greenhouse gases cause global warming was based on a desire to retain the environmentalist vote, an increasingly important political bloc.

Conversely, Inhofe's critics say he ignores a plethora of sound science supporting the theory and instead elevates fringe scientists' opposing theories in order to protect the energy industry, which donates frequently to his campaigns. [1]

"This is definitely a bipartisan phenomenon," says Patrick Michaels, a climatology professor at the University of Virginia and a fellow at the libertarian Cato Institute.

And it's been going on for a long time. In 1990, for example, Sen. Steve Symms, R-Idaho, proclaimed that "if government standards and emission limitations must be set [on air pollutants], clean-air goals are best achieved when those standards are firmly founded in the soundest of science." [2]

But what exactly does the phrase mean? To Inhofe and those who agree with him, "sound science" means reliable, proven scientific data — the only kind the government should use in formulating public policy.

But to Ehlers and others, the term — at least as it's used in Washington — has devolved into little more than Orwellian code for bending scientific data to meet political ends. "It's what I believe in and you don't," says Michaels. "It's the science that gives me the policy I want."

Accusations of political misuse of science are not new, though many assert that they have reached new levels during the Bush administration. And science seems to have suffered more than its share of misuse — and in some cases, outright abuse — in recent times.

For example, in many ways the sound science debate is the political side of the "junk science" legal controversy, which has roiled civil courts for decades. Plaintiffs claiming their health has been damaged by exposure to a company's products, for example, often rely on scientific research to bolster their case. Typically the research suggests or asserts a health risk associated with exposure to the products. Corporate defendants have invariably attacked that research as "junk science," essentially speculative and not accepted or recognized by mainstream scientists.

In some cases, scientists themselves have contributed to the perception that some science may not be reliable. In the late 1980s and early '90s, several highly publicized cases of scientific misconduct involving fabricated evidence or results shook the nation's research community.

Questions also have been raised about the influence of corporate money on the integrity of government and academic science. Recently, many of the most highly paid scientists working for the prestigious National Institutes of Health (NIH) were revealed to be working as paid consultants to drug companies whose fortunes could be affected by decisions the scientists made. (*See sidebar, p. 672.*)

Similarly, critics complain about the close ties developing between univer-

Federal Research Funding Is Rising

Federal spending on research and development rose 37 percent from 2001 to 2004, to more than $107 billion.

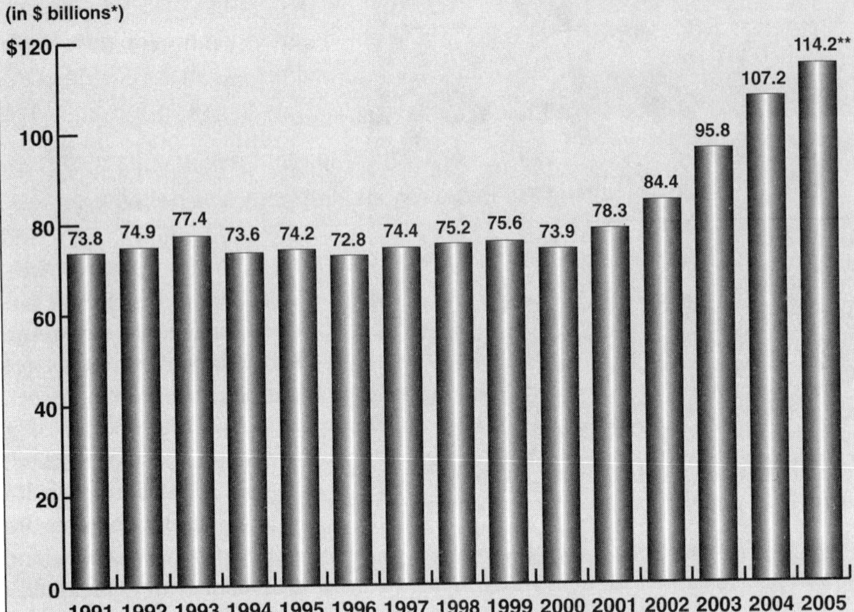

* *In constant 2000 dollars; funds for facilities not included.*
** *President's fiscal 2005 budget request*

Source: *White House Office of Science and Technology Policy*

sity researchers and corporations, which have become a growing source of funding for academic research as state and federal governments have cut back on their contributions to university research. Federal funding of academic research has dropped about 14 percent since the early 1960s, while industry funding has almost doubled. [3] Bemoaning the trend, *The New England Journal of Medicine* in 2000 ran an editorial under the headline, "Is Academic Medicine for Sale?" [4]

Last February, a distinguished scientific-advocacy group stoked the "sound science" controversy by charging that the Bush administration and its congressional allies were censoring or distorting scientific information on issues ranging from global warming and mercury emissions to reproductive health and the Endangered Species Act in order to support policies favored by the religious right and business interests — two of the GOP's most powerful constituencies. *

While acknowledging that charges of politicizing science are not unique, the report by the Union of Concerned Scientists (UCS) said: "The scope and scale of the manipulation, suppression and misrepresentation of science by the Bush administration are unprecedented." [5]

Among the examples cited in the report were a White House order to suppress part of a 2003 Environmental Protection Agency (EPA) report on the state of the environment that gave credence to the theory that human activity — particularly the burning of fossil fuels — contributes to global warming. Like Inhofe, the administration disputes the scientific validity of the theory, which could lead to costly restrictions on the energy industry if true. In fact, the White House ordered the EPA to replace the disputed section with text from a controversial report — funded largely by NASA and partly by the American Petroleum Institute — denying the human influence on global warming.

Environmentalists applauded the UCS report. "Across the board, there is an attempt to muzzle and silence scientists who disagree with either the administration's ideological agenda or the agenda of its corporate constituents," said Philip E. Clapp, president of the National Environmental Trust. [6]

But the Bush administration and others called the report politically motivated. Indeed, as longtime science journalist Gregg Easterbrook noted in the *Los Angeles Times*, the UCS "protests that Bush is being political with science, but the union is itself political with science. The group is best known for campaigning in the 1980s for the nuclear freeze — perhaps a just cause, but a quintessentially political cause." [7]

However, Chris Mooney, a science journalist working on a book about conservatives' alleged misuse of science, recently wrote, "Inhofe is a kind of scientific Attila the Hun. . . . That he now controls the Senate's environment committee suggests that today's GOP, run by dyed-in-the-wool

* Of the 60 scientists who signed the report, 20 were Nobel laureates, 11 had won the National Medal of Science, three had received the prestigious Crafoord Prize, many were heads of some of the country's leading universities and biomedical research institutes and two were former presidential science advisers.

conservatives instead of moderates like John McCain, [R-Ariz.], has developed a dangerous relationship with scientific knowledge itself." [8]

"Those who say the debate is more acrimonious now are absolutely correct," says Michaels, author of the forthcoming book, *Meltdown: The Predictable Distortion of Global Warming by Scientists, Politicians and the Media.*

Sen. John Kerry, the Democratic presidential nominee, recently sharply criticized President Bush as a "sound science" manipulator. [9] Indeed, assuming the mantle of protectors of scientific integrity, the Democrats have called for relaxing the Bush administration restrictions on stem-cell research. President Bush opposes making available more stem-cell lines — drawn from discarded embryos — claiming existing lines are enough. Most scientists disagree, and at the Democratic National Convention last month, Ron Reagan, son of the late president, criticized the administration for "playing politics" with stem-cell research, which some hope could help produce a cure for Alzheimer's disease, which Reagan's father suffered from for the last decade of his life.

Reagan's other son, Michael, who calls stem-cell research "junk science," will address the Republican National Convention next month.

Most R&D Funds Went to Defense

More than half the projected federal funding for research and development in 2004 was for the Defense Department.

Federal Research-and-Development Spending
(Budget authority, in $ millions)

Agency	2001 (Actual)	2004 (Projected)	% Change
Defense	$42,235	$65,484	55%
Health and Human Services	21,037	28,275	34.4
NASA	9,675	10,893	12.6
Energy	7,772	8,835	13.7
National Science Foundation	3,363	4,115	22.4
Agriculture	2,182	2,308	5.8
Homeland Security	N/A	1,053	N/A
Commerce	1,054	1,126	6.8
Veterans Affairs	748	824	10.2
Transportation	792	701	-11.5
Interior	622	675	8.5
EPA	598	575	-3.8
Education	264	N/A	N/A
Other	922	1,092	18.4
Total	$91,264	$125,956	38%

Source: White House Office of Science and Technology Policy

Environmentalists also say industry is using an obscure two-sentence provision — known as the Data Quality Act — quietly slipped into a 2000 appropriations bill to block implementation of environmental and health regulations by effectively shifting oversight for government science to the highly political White House Office of Management and Budget (OMB).

The act has "hamstrung EPA's ability to express anything that it couldn't back up with a mountain of data," said Jennifer Sass, a scientist with the Natural Resources Defense Council, essentially blocking EPA scientists "from expressing an expert opinion." [10]

Industry representatives defend the act — which requires regulators to attain an unprecedented level of scientific certainty before issuing federal rules — as being long overdue and a giant step toward basing federal regulations on "sound science."

Companies and industry trade groups have used the little-known law to challenge federal guidelines on sugar and salt intake and arsenic in wooden playground equipment; timber harvests on public lands; and use of the herbicide atrazine, banned by the European Union last year as being too dangerous to use. Some studies show it scrambles frogs' hormones until they become "chemically castrated," and may cause cancer in humans. [11]

As accusations fly that some scientists are letting themselves be used for political purposes, some observers say the "sound science" debate is just one more dark cloud among many casting shadows over the integrity of U.S. scientific research in general.

Here are some of the questions implicit in the ongoing debate:

Does the Bush administration play politics with science?

Two months after the UCS report called for congressional hearings into its allegations, White House science adviser John H. Marburger III — a Democrat — delivered a point-by-point rebuttal to lawmakers.

Addressing the charge that the White House had suppressed the climate-change section in the 2003 EPA report, Marburger explained that "following a standard interagency review," the EPA agreed that "the complexity of climate change science was not adequately addressed by the agency's short draft" on the subject. Accuracy, not suppression, was the motive for White House intervention, Marburger argued. [12]

Of the UCS report's 26 other allegations — including censoring information on mercury emissions, distorting science on reproductive-health issues and manipulating science regarding the Endangered Species Act — Marburger claimed that in each case the UCS relied primarily on quotes from people but never once provided "a single instance of an actual suppression of agency research." [13]

Marburger still bristles over some of the accusations. "The thesis that there's some kind of systematic undermining of science by the administration is simply wrong," he says. "That's the part of the report that I think is not responsible."

Yet some independent observers continue to criticize the Bush administration on many of the same points. Donald Kennedy, editor of the respected journal *Science*, characterizes some of the UCS charges as "overwrought," but he agrees the administration is politicizing science more than previous administrations. And Marburger's responses were "mixed," he says. "Some he really didn't do well on, including climate change."

"That, of course, is the mother of all political issues," says Utah Republican Chris Cannon, chairman of the House Science Committee and the newly formed House Science Caucus.

The Kyoto Protocol on global warming, which the Bush administration rejected just days after taking office, calls for reducing worldwide emissions of carbon dioxide and other greenhouse gases by 5.2 percent below 1990 levels by 2012. [14] But a study conducted in 1997 concluded that meeting those reductions could cost up to $300 billion, most of it to be borne by the U.S. energy industry — to which President Bush and Vice President Dick Cheney have extensive professional and personal ties. [15]

"Because of the very high cost of restricting energy production," Marburger argues, "you've got to look very carefully at exactly what the science says."

Most scientists and observers agree that during the last century, when manmade greenhouse gases began to rise dramatically, the Earth's temperature rose about 1 degree Fahrenheit.

"We know that rate of increase in average global temperature is out of skew with anything before, and that amount of warming has already produced significant changes on this planet," Kennedy says. "It has changed the times of flowering, the time of onset of breeding of birds, the times at which ice goes out of rivers in Alaska; it's thinning the west Antarctic ice sheet; it's thinning the edges of the Greenland glacier."

But disagreement arises over how much greenhouse gas emissions have contributed to the temperature rise and how much will they contribute to future increases. "To say that human activity is not a major environmental effect in climate change is ludicrous," says Rep. Rush Holt, D-N.J., Congress' other research physicist, along with Ehlers.

U.S. Fish and Wildlife Service

President Bush has called the "Clear Skies" initiative against air pollution his top environmental priority, but neither the Senate nor the House has taken significant action on the proposal. Meanwhile, a newly revised plan commissioned by Bush to research global warming has been endorsed by the National Academy of Sciences.

However, Earth's climate experienced changes long before humankind began filling the skies with greenhouse gases, others say. In fact, atmospheric temperature was warmer during medieval times than today — a fact global-warming advocates tend to ignore, Inhofe points out.

Many scientists regard the Intergovernmental Panel on Climate Change (IPCC), a U.N. body representing the work and opinions of some 2,000 scientists around the world, as the authority on global warming. Recent IPCC reports have forecast a rise of at least 3 degrees Fahrenheit and possibly as much as 12 degrees by 2100. Although the IPCC admits the precise influence caused by greenhouse gas emissions is unknown, many scientists and observers claim that enough is known to warrant reducing emissions now.

Others — like William O'Keefe, president of the George C. Marshall Institute, a think tank supported by business interests and conservative foundations — disagree. IPCC forecasts are based on assumptions put into computer models, but not all assumptions are accurate or justified, he and others claim.

"If you look at the pattern of warming in the past 100 years, it's not consistent with the theory" that human activity has been the major cause, O'Keefe says. "From 1900 to 1940, the temperature increased fairly dramatically, but emissions of greenhouse gases were lower. They really increased substantially after World War II, but from 1945 to 1975 there was a cooling of the Earth's temperature. Then, after 1975 the temperature began rising again."

O'Keefe admits he isn't a scientist, and, in fact, he is a registered lobbyist for ExxonMobil. But the Cato Institute's Michaels is, and he is even more skeptical of global warming. Careful analysis of IPCC data, he says, reveals that any rise in the Earth's temperature will be minimal. Both Michaels and O'Keefe say the Bush administration is right in not viewing global warming as a threat.

Both advocates and skeptics of the anthropogenic theory of global warming — that it is human-induced — claim growing numbers of scientists on their side; but neither side is free from controversial claims or studies. Most recently, when two scientists at the Harvard-Smithsonian Center for Astrophysics reviewed 240 papers on climate change and wrote in the journal *Climate Change* that the recent temperature rise is not out of skew with historical trends, several of the publication's editors resigned, claiming the conclusion could not be supported from the evidence cited by the authors.

Rep. Richard W. Pombo, a California Republican and administration supporter, bemoans the lack of consensus on global warming. "I've had well-respected scientists in my office who have argued both sides of it," he says. "When I listen to them and their arguments, they both make sense. But with no consensus, moving on something that would drastically impact the economy of the United States would be a huge mistake."

Some critics also say the administration plays politics with its appointments to governmental science-advisory panels. "Certainly, we hear more from scientists who are reporting from their own experience [about] the elimination of committees or saying the committee has been reappointed with other members more friendly to a particular administration position with respect to regulation," says *Science* Editor Kennedy.

But Marburger notes that the government has more than 600 scientific-advisory committees. "Every individual who serves on one of these committees undergoes extensive review, background checks and is recognized by peers for their contributions and expertise." [16]

Should scientific certainty be required before public policies are formulated?

Perhaps more than any other member of Congress, Inhofe has drawn fire from liberals, environmentalists and many scientists for asserting that global warming is "a hoax being perpetrated on the American people." But few might take exception when he says, "When you're trying to formulate public policy and you see one factor is going to destroy the economy, we would not want to do it unless we had some assurance on the accuracy of the science."

Most scientists say scientific certainty is a rarity, if not an impossibility. "We're pretty sure two plus two equals four, but once we get much beyond that, everything to some degree or another is an approximation," says Benn Tannenbaum, senior research analyst at the Federation of American Scientists, a nonprofit, anti-nuclear weapons group that traces its roots back to the Manhattan Project. "You measure something and you say, there is this much uncertainty in the measurement. That doesn't mean you don't know the answer you're seeking. It means that if you were to repeat the experiment, it's this much likely you'd get the same result."

White House Science Adviser Marburger concurs, saying that arriving at scientific consensus involves reducing the "error bars," or margins of error, in research as much as possible.

But Tannenbaum questions the Bush administration's repeatedly invoking uncertainty as a reason to delay regulatory action on a particular issue. "This is something that does seem to be new with this administration — either a misuse or misunderstanding of what scientific uncertainty is," he says.

"There's always going to be uncertainty," says science journalist Mooney, "but that's no reason to block action." He cites the administration's use of the uncertainty surrounding global warming as the "canonical example" of such a tactic.

However, the administration and its allies in Congress point to a newly revised plan commissioned by President Bush — and endorsed by the National Academy of Sciences (NAS) — for researching the remaining uncertainties about global warming.

The NAS — a private, nonprofit organization noted for its independence — advises Congress on science matters. It had faulted a previous version of the administration's global warming research plan, but recommended the revised version because advancing the science called for in the plan "will be of vital importance to the nation." Thus, the NAS seemed to side with the administration's view that the level of certainty on global warming may not yet be high enough to warrant regulation. [17]

However, the NAS also noted that "commitments to fund many of the newly proposed [research] activities are lacking," raising doubts about the sincerity of the administration's pledge to find answers.

Rep. Cannon acknowledges that "scientific certainty should almost never be the threshold [for formulating policy]. To my mind, it's a question of the quality of the research."

To address that issue, Oregon Republicans Rep. Greg Walden and Sen. Gordon H. Smith have introduced legislation that "gives greater weight to scientific or commercial data that [are] empirical or [have] been field-tested or peer-reviewed." [18]

But critics say such a standard is tantamount to requiring scientific certainty. "It essentially means forget using computer modeling," says Ana Unruh, legislative assistant to Rep. Edward J. Markey, D-Mass., a member of the House Resources Committee. "Modern wildlife biology requires both. You collect field data, but to interpret and understand it, you put it into models." Without modeling, to establish that a particular species might be endangered "you'd have to go out and find every single animal out there and show where they live."

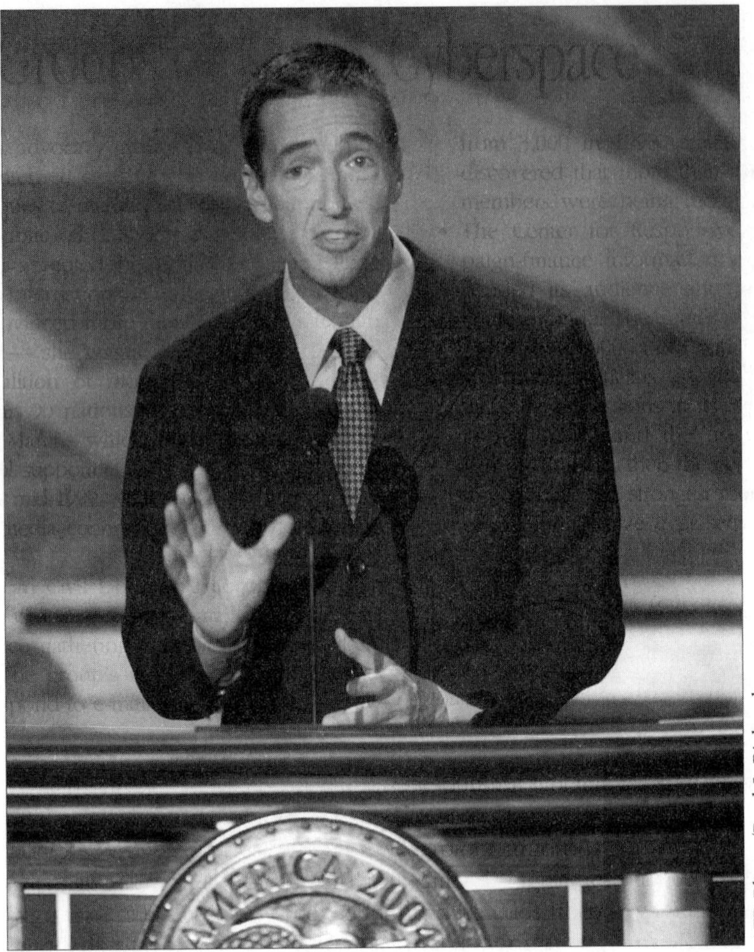

AFP Photo/Paul J. Richards

Ron Reagan urges support for stem-cell research at the recent Democratic National Convention, in Boston. Reagan is the son of the late president, who suffered from Alzheimer's disease. He shares the hope that stem-cell research could produce a cure for Parkinson's disease, diabetes and multiple schlerosis and has criticized Bush administration restrictions on stem-cell research as a purely political appeal to conservatives who oppose the research because it extracts cells from embryos.

Public health and the beef industry would also be put at risk under such a standard, says David Michaels, a professor of public health at The George Washington University. "Our entire federal program for mad cow [disease] prevention is based on a probabilistic model," he says. "If . . . this legislation were applied to the Department of Agriculture, they'd have to throw out the program. And with one case of mad cow, they might have to shut down the entire industry."

Having Congress instead of professional scientists decide what constitutes the best research is "reminiscent of Soviet science," he adds.

But Walden says his Oregon district's economy suffered up to $200 million in damages as a result of government actions based on insufficient scientific data. Because of federal regulations implementing the Endangered Species Act — which many in Congress and the administration say is not based on sound science — Oregon's heavily farmed Klamath Basin did not receive water for irrigation. More than 1,000 farms suffered losses, and nearly two-dozen went bankrupt. [19]

The National Research Council, an arm of the NAS, reviewed the incident and concluded that the federal orders to maintain upstream water levels for a listed species of salmon had been based on "doubtful" scientific evidence. Given the potential for such disastrous consequences, Walden said, the threshold must be raised for the accuracy of scientific data used to trigger federal action. [20]

Rep. Ehlers argues that too much uncertainty still shrouds several disputed issues, such as mercury emissions. "You read about all these 'terrible' mercury emissions out there," he says. "Yet most people are surprised when I tell them we get more mercury emissions out of volcanoes than out of power plants."

Mercury that settles in so-called "hot spots" around power plants is generally believed to have originated from the plants. "But by itself mercury isn't all that poisonous because the body doesn't absorb it quickly," Ehlers says. Mercury emissions enter the food chain, he explains, when they leach or wash into a body of water, where the mercury combines with other elements. "Then you get methylated mercury, which is readily absorbed," particularly by fish.

"But then you've got to ask, 'What level of mercury are you willing to live with in eating fish? How much fish do you eat?' " The list of still-unanswered questions, he says, "goes on and on."

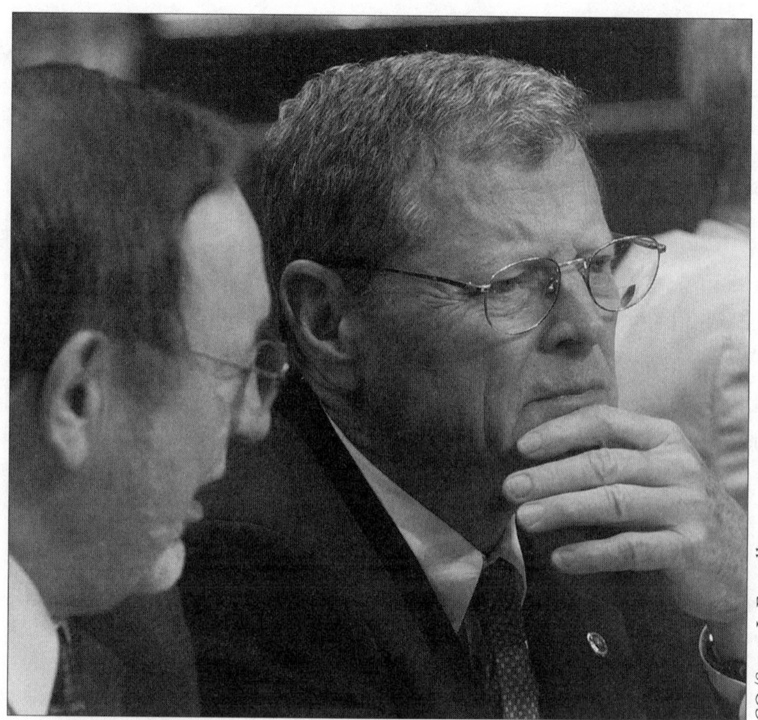

CQ/Scott J. Ferrell

Sen. James Inhofe, R-Okla., right, opposes federal regulation of greenhouse gases claiming burning fossil fuels doesn't contribute to global warming. Inhofe says President Bill Clinton's position against greenhouse gases was calculated to retain environmentalists' support. But Inhofe's critics say he supports opposing theories on global warming to protect the energy industry, which donates to his campaigns.

Science journalist Mooney and White House science adviser Marburger would appear to agree on one point: The threshold for initiating government action on a scientific issue will vary with each case. As Marburger explains, if the action called for is fairly inexpensive, and public concern is high, "then you can afford to do it" despite a possibly large margin of error.

"On the other hand, if the cost is great, then you want the [margin of error] to be smaller," he says. "And those kinds of judgments have to be made on a case-by-case basis. So you inevitably have a political weighing of the importance of responding to public concern, regardless of the science, and the costs. Governments are there to try to protect people even from their own misunderstanding."

However, as Mooney notes, "Uncertainty was also used by the tobacco industry," which, to avoid regulation, strategically exploited margins of error in research showing links between smoking and cancer.

In fact, environmentalists claim industry often intentionally sponsors conflicting studies, just to muddy the scientific waters and then use the Data Quality Act to claim that the science is too uncertain to proceed with federal restrictions. That is precisely what the Swiss manufacturer Syngenta did, they say, on the use of its pesticide atrazine. [21]

A scientist hired by Syngenta to study atrazine's effects on frog development found overwhelming evidence that when frogs are exposed to atrazine at one-thirtieth the level allowed in U.S. drinking water many develop both male and female sexual traits — conclusions since confirmed by four independent research teams in three countries. The company responded by sponsoring additional studies, which could not replicate the original findings.

Even though a special EPA science panel found major flaws in Syngenta's follow-up studies, the damage was done: The "weight of the evidence" against atrazine was fundamentally altered.

"I call this 'manufacturing uncertainty,' and there is a whole industry to do this," said Michaels, of George Washington University, who was the Energy Department's assistant secretary for environment, safety and health under Clinton. "They reanalyze the data to make [previously firm] conclusions disappear — poof. Then they say one study says yes and the other says no, so we're nowhere." [22]

Does corporate funding taint university research?

For decades, the federal government funded most academic scientific research in the United States, in areas ranging from plasma and fusion science to manure management at the National Swine Research Center.

But recent cutbacks in state and federal budgets have shifted more of the burden for funding academic research to the private sector. [23] In the early 1960s, the federal government funded slightly more than 70 percent of academic research; today it funds about 60 percent. Meanwhile, in the last 20 years the percentage of academic research funded by industry nearly doubled, from 4 percent to 7 percent. [24]

For instance, Harvard's Center for Risk Analysis, which frequently is asked to assess the cost of federal regulations, is funded by contributions from more than 100 industry and trade association donors. [25]

Most industry money goes for clinical drug trials conducted at the nation's universities, of which corporations now fund 70 percent. [26] Because industry funding often includes gifts to researchers, and researchers increasingly own stock in companies whose products they are evaluating, critics question the growing ties between business and academic scientists and whether the integrity of America's academic research is being compromised.

"Academic medical institutions are themselves growing increasingly beholden to industry," *The New England Journal of Medicine* editorialized. [27]

Both industry and scientists dispute allegations they have conflicts of interest. David Kay, a representative of the pharmaceutical company Amgen, Inc., has said, "[I]t would be foolish to try to bias researchers." [28]

One of the first cases to draw attention to the alleged corrupting influence of corporate money on research involved a 1985 study the Monsanto Co. asked Cornell University to conduct on bovine growth hormone, which the biotech company hoped to market. According to one account, before Monsanto would turn over the $557,000 to fund the study, Cornell "essentially had to agree to hand over control of its research." [29] Monsanto staff reviewed and interpreted the raw data Cornell scientists developed.

"I couldn't believe a university would agree to such restrictions," said Tess Hooks, a sociologist doing graduate work in ethics at Cornell at the time. [30] Although some Cornell researchers objected, in other similar cases university scientists did not.

Policymakers and observers disagree over the influence corporate funding may have on university research, which is often used to support or change public-policy decisions.

According to Tannenbaum of the FAS, scientific integrity depends on how the research is done. "My father worked for a large pharmaceutical company, and sometimes he'd farm out research to universities," he says. "Not because he wanted a specific answer, but to understand how a process works, and he didn't have time to do it himself. So research like that will be perfectly good."

"I sought corporate money for a dozen years as a university president," says *Science* Editor Kennedy, "and I had great confidence in the capacity of [Stanford] to make certain the money came without strings."

Indeed, says Marburger, "Industry labs with industry money developed much of the technology and science we rely on today. Industry research is good, in general. On the other hand, if government is going to use any research to inform its regulatory actions, then it's obligated to review it dispassionately."

O'Keefe of the Marshall Institute thinks the money source is irrelevant, and that corporate funding is unfairly singled out for suspicion or criticism. "People make a distinction between corporate funding and government funding. That's a false dichotomy," he says. "Because if someone knows that a government agency has a preferred policy, and they want government grants, they can write a grant application that'll be looked at more favorably because it'll be consistent with the policy preference. That's just as corrosive as a corporation giving money to a university and saying, 'I want you to produce this result.'

"But it's not who funds the work," O'Keefe continues. "It's how well the work stands up to complete scrutiny. You need to have a totally transparent process. If a work is the basis of a policy, all the models, data and hypotheses should be transparent to see if the conclusions can be replicated. If the results don't stand up under scrutiny, then the work is discredited, but not because of money."

O'Keefe, for instance, insists that his work for the Marshall Institute is "separate" from his work for ExxonMobil. [31]

Rep. Pombo agrees that government funding of academic research is not completely neutral, either. "Was a study clouded by possible federal grants going to the university?" he asks. "If you have a university that's been funded for years on climate change, chances are they're not going to say, 'No, the climate's not changing!' because the grants would end. Congress should take a really hard look at all the research — and how it's gathered and paid for."

Myron Ebell, director of global warming and international environmental policy at the pro-business, anti-regulatory Competitive Enterprise Institute (CEI), distrusts all funding, but, like O'Keefe, thinks it's ultimately irrelevant. But he also distrusts scientists in general.

"Politics puts a lot of pressure on scientists to come up with answers that politicians or bureaucrats or environmentalists or industrialists want," Ebell says. "But there's also lots of corruption of politics by scientists. We take what they say as if they're just giving us the unvarnished truth, when, in fact, they often have motives of ideology or self-interest.

"Everybody has motives," he continues, "and the only way you can decide whether a scientific paper is any good is [by asking], 'Does it withstand scrutiny?' You won't find that out by investigating the funding."

Cato Institute's Michaels argues that the solution is "to introduce competing biases into the funding stream. There's no way you can clean it up. So you broaden or diversify the biases funding the science."

For example, he continues, for global warming research, "Go to the Sierra Club, go to ExxonMobil, go to the federal government. Cover all the biases."

Continued on p. 672

Chronology

1860s-1920s

Regard for science grows as use of forensic evidence becomes popular.

1863
Republican President Abraham Lincoln creates the independent National Academy of Sciences.

1901
Republican President William McKinley asks Congress to establish the National Bureau of Standards.

1923
Appeals court rules in *Frye v. United States* that scientific evidence cannot be used in court unless it is "generally accepted" by scientists.

1930s

Lead industry becomes first industry to attack validity of scientific evidence.

1950s-1960s

Tobacco industry hires publicists and scientists to discredit the evidence linking smoking and cancer.

1957
Republican President Dwight D. Eisenhower creates position of White House science adviser.

1964
U.S. Surgeon General declares smoking dangerous to human health; manufacturers are required to put warning labels on cigarette packs.

1970s

Republican President Richard M. Nixon creates regulatory framework to protect environment and worker safety.

1970
Environmental Protection Agency is established.

1971
Occupational Safety and Health Administration is established.

1973
Nixon fires his White House science advisers, suspecting they are working against him.

1977
Democratic President Jimmy Carter creates Energy Department, which is to research energy-conservation technologies and non-fossil fuels.

1980s

Industries facing regulation begin questioning validity of what they call "junk science" supporting federal laws.

1988
Intergovernmental Panel on Climate Change (IPCC) is established to study global warming.

1990s

Concern arises over scientific misconduct and ties between the biomedical industry and university researchers. Political debates over "sound science" increase.

1995
An IPCC study suggests that a growing body of scientific opinion believes manmade greenhouse gases are causing global warming; the new GOP congressional majority leads move to abolish Congress' Office of Technology Assessment.

1997
Study says Kyoto Protocol would cost U.S. $300 billion to implement.

2000s

Liberals and conservatives exchange charges over politicizing science.

January 2001
Republican President Bush suspends Clinton administration's tighter limits on arsenic in water, claiming they were politically motivated; EPA later says the restrictions aren't necessary.

August 2001
President Bush bans research on new lines of stem cells.

2003
World Health Organization recommends restrictions on high-sugar foods; sugar-industry lobbyists call the scientific data "flawed." . . . In July Sen. James Inhofe, R-Okla., calls theories on global warming a "hoax" perpetrated by environmental "extremists." . . . *Los Angeles Times* discloses that up to "94 percent" of National Institutes of Health (NIH) senior scientists receive either payment or stock options from drug companies for consulting services.

2004
Union of Concerned Scientists (UCS) charges the Bush administration abuses science for conservative political purposes. Administration proponents say the UCS engages in leftist advocacy. . . . In July Congress forces the NIH to limit staff scientists' outside consulting.

Corporate Funding Questioned at NIH

The National Institutes of Health (NIH), just outside Washington, D.C., has long represented an international gold standard in medical research. Scientists and manufacturers of medical and pharmaceutical products worldwide pay close attention to the work of NIH researchers.

When President Richard M. Nixon declared war on cancer in 1971, he asked the NIH to lead the fight. The agency led the federal government's struggle against AIDS, and, most recently, assumed a lead role in developing countermeasures against potential bioterror attacks.

Margaret Heckler, secretary of Health and Human Services under President Ronald Reagan, once described the NIH as "an island of objective and pristine research, untainted by the influences of commercialization." [1]

Not anymore, according to recent media and congressional investigations. Last December a well-documented exposé in the *Los Angeles Times* disclosed that top NIH researchers had collected hundreds of stock options and consultant's fees from drug companies, with one scientist receiving more than $1 million. The dealings have raised serious questions about possible conflicts of interest. [2]

For example, early one morning in 1999 a patient in an NIH research clinic died following complications from an experimental treatment involving a drug made by a German company. Study participants were shocked to learn later that the doctor overseeing the study was a paid consultant of the drug company.

The doctor later said his consulting contract with the firm had not influenced any of his decisions in the study, and that top NIH officials were aware of the relationship. [3]

Indeed, as the *Times'* investigation revealed, the NIH leadership has routinely approved consulting agreements between staff and outside companies, some of which stood to benefit from NIH research. But a senior official involved in the approval process says the agreements posed no conflict with or compromise of NIH on behalf of the public.

But members of Congress are not convinced. Reps. W. J. "Billy" Tauzin, R-La., and James C. Greenwood, R-Pa., — both members of the Oversight and Investigations Subcommittee of the House Energy and Commerce Committee — called for hearings last spring on the propriety of NIH researchers receiving outside compensation from drug companies, and asked NIH Director Elias A. Zerhouni to provide a full account of all compensation that institute scientists have received from drug companies. Unlike most other federal agencies, the NIH allows employees to keep the amount of their consulting fees private.

"The receipt of outside payments, even though approved, raises concerns about whether the integrity of NIH clinical research has been affected and whether the honor system used by NIH to [monitor] NIH scientists and other conflict-of-interest rules has been violated," Tauzin and Greenwood wrote in a letter to Zerhouni. [4]

As a result of the hearings, the NIH prevented 66 of its most senior employees from taking consulting fees and stock options from drug companies. But the NIH did not comply with the Tauzin-Greenwood request for a full accounting of compensation. (Greenwood recently announced he will retire from Congress at the end of his term to become a lobbyist for the biotech industry, at a salary of $650,000 a year.)

Instead, the agency formed an internal review panel to determine whether rules or ethics had been violated. But its final report only provoked more congressional ire.

The report recommended no more industry compensation in any form for senior NIH scientists who review grant appli-

Continued from p. 670

Some observers say corporate campaign funding taints politicians' view of scientific research. For example, critics have questioned the sincerity of Inhofe's skepticism about global warming and other environmental issues, because in the last five years he has received nearly $500,000 in contributions from the energy industry, primarily oil and gas interests. [32]

"I have been strong on doing something about the energy crisis since the early 1980s," Inhofe responds, "so it's natural that I would get campaign contributions from people who share the belief that we have a crisis in America that's got to be addressed.

"The environmental extremists don't want any form of energy, no fossil fuels or nuclear energy, and now not even wind," he continues. "And yet we've got the largest machine in the world, called America, and we have to run it." ■

BACKGROUND

Elusive Certainty

The use of science to influence or effect a desired end is rooted in courtrooms of the early 1900s, when prosecutors began building cases based on new police investigative techniques, like fingerprinting and blood-typing. Defense lawyers initially challenged the scientific validity of the new techniques, but as forensic investigation became increasingly common, judges allowed prosecutors to introduce such evidence in trials.

Controversy arose, however, when police began using another new technique, the systolic blood pressure deception test, a precursor of the lie detector. In 1923, an appeals court in Washington, D.C., barred such evidence from being used in court, saying no scientific consensus existed on cations. It also limited the amount of outside income scientists can make and the amount of time they can devote to outside work.

But it did not address whether any violations had occurred, leading Rep. Peter Deutsch, D-Fla., to allege NIH was trying to "excuse the inexcusable." [5]

"This investigation has been slow-rolled and stonewalled," said Rep. John Dingell, D-Mich.

Rep. Joe Barton, R-Texas, declared, "We have found NIH to be less than cooperative, and that's going to change. They can cooperate cooperatively, or we will make them cooperate coercively." [6]

In a separate investigation, the Food and Drug Administration found that violations of federal rules had indeed occurred. For example, NIH scientists had entered into approximately 100 consulting arrangements without notifying agency managers, in violation of NIH rules. One scientist was receiving $100,000 a year. Another had allegedly lied under oath to a congressional committee, claiming he had terminated his consulting fees when he was still receiving thousands of dollars from a drug firm. [7]

As a result, the NIH plans to implement a new oversight system within six months that will prevent personnel with even indirect authority over NIH grants from consulting for drug or biotechnology companies, NIH Deputy Director Raynard S. Kington said on Aug. 3. [8]

Meanwhile, observers decry the apparently growing ties between the drug industry and academic as well as government researchers. "The threat is to the objectivity of scientific research," Sheldon Krimsky, a science policy expert at Tufts University, recently said. "It is reaching crisis proportions." [9]

National Institutes of Health

The National Institutes of Health recently came under fire because top NIH scientists were working as paid consultants to drug companies.

[1] See David Willman, "Stealth Merger; Drug Companies and Government Medical Research; Some of the National Institutes of Health's top scientists are also collecting paychecks and stock options from biomedical firms. Increasingly, such deals are kept secret," *Los Angeles Times*, Dec. 7, 2003, p. A1.

[2] *Ibid.*

[3] *Ibid.*

[4] See David Willman, "Records of Payments to NIH Staff Sought; Two congressmen ask health institutes' leader to detail researchers' links to drug companies," *Los Angeles Times*, Dec. 9, 2003, p. A12.

[5] See Rick Weiss, "House Panel Scolds NIH Chief, HHS; Members Threaten to Pursue New Ethics Legislation," *The Washington Post*, May 13, 2004, p. A27.

[6] *Ibid.*

[7] See Rick Weiss, "NIH Scientists Broke Rules, Panel Says; Deals With Companies Went Unreported, Probe of Potential Conflicts of Interest Finds," *The Washington Post*, June 23, 2004, p. A19.

[8] Rick Weiss, "NIH to Set Stiff Restrictions on Outside Consulting," *The Washington Post*, Aug. 4, 2004, p. A1.

[9] See Amy Barrett, "When Medicine and Money Don't Mix," *Business Week*, June 28, 2004, p. 68.

the validity of lie-detection technology. The court's ruling in the case (*Frye v. United States*) — that scientific evidence was only admissible if scientists "generally accepted" as scientifically valid the technology used to gather it — remains the nation's dominant ruling on using scientific evidence in court. [33]

But even the most seemingly indisputable forms of scientific data have their limits. When fingerprinting was introduced as evidence in U.S. courts, there was no definitive scientific proof that no two people have identical fingerprints, according to University of Iowa law Professor Michael Saks. And, although the theory has yet to be proven definitively, fingerprint experts long ago accepted consensus on the technology and routinely tell judges and juries in criminal cases that fingerprint matching is a conclusive method of identification. [34]

Debate over the validity of scientific evidence used in civil cases — typically in suits seeking compensation for alleged injury — began in the 1920s, when the lead industry disputed claims that its product was harming children. In an attempt to sway public opinion and juries, industry executives attacked the evidence as incomplete and inconclusive. [35]

Avoiding Regulation

The tobacco industry, however, was the first to use the elusiveness of scientific certainty in an orchestrated public relations campaign to avoid government regulation or payment of compensation. In the 1950s medical researchers began turning up evidence of a connection between smoking and lung cancer. But instead of trying to determine whether the evidence was sound, the industry commissioned scientists to produce research that would specifically undermine the connection.

The industry then began publishing a journal with the seemingly official and vaguely independent title, *Tobacco and Health Research*. However, according to a memo from a public relations firm hired by the industry for advice, the journal was to print only one kind of article — "that which casts doubt on the cause-and-effect theory of disease and smoking." [36] The industry also continued to deny the addictive quality of nicotine, although industry researchers had more or less confirmed it.

As the scientific evidence connecting smoking and cancer grew — declared officially by the Surgeon General in 1964 — tobacco companies were forced to print warning labels on cigarette packs. Still, they had avoided both regulation and paying compensation. [37]

The industry was not forced to acknowledge a causal link between smoking and lung cancer until the 1990s, when the industry was forced by a class-action lawsuit to enter a $246 billion compensation settlement with state governments. [38]

The tobacco industry was the "biggest and most effective" industry to combine a public relations approach with attacks on science "so they could continue to manufacture dangerous products without government interference," says Michaels of George Washington University.

For almost a century the Republican Party allied itself with science, beginning with establishment of the National Academy of Sciences under President Abraham Lincoln. In 1901 President William McKinley established the National Bureau of Standards, precursor of the National Institute of Science and Technology. McKinley had twice defeated Democratic nominee and creationist William Jennings Bryan, who would later assist the prosecution team in the Scopes "monkey" trial, passionately advance the theory of creationism. [39]

But science and Republicans began to split during Richard M. Nixon's presidency, when many U.S. scientists came out against the Vietnam War. Nixon contemptuously labeled them liberal Democrats and, fearing they had penetrated the White House, ordered his entire science advisory team disbanded in 1973. Nonetheless, he also oversaw the creation of the Environmental Protection Agency and the Occupational Safety and Health Administration, two agencies that would use scientific data to help regulate industries' impact on workers and the environment.

National Archives

During the Vietnam War, the United States extensively sprayed the foliage killer Agent Orange. Veterans groups later said that exposure to the herbicide caused cancer, and in the early 1990s scientists finally confirmed the link. In this 1966 photograph, helicopters airlift troops during a search and destroy mission northeast of Cu Chi, Vietnam.

During the presidency of Ronald Reagan, the wedge between Republicans and scientists grew. Reagan's refusal to endorse the theory of evolution lost him credibility among most scientists, but won him the support of Southern religious conservatives, who were lobbying local school boards to advance the teaching of creationism over evolution. In addition, Reagan championed development of an expensive, anti-missile shield (often derisively referred to as "Star Wars") that many scientists dismissed as unworkable. [40]

Since then, several industries — and even the U.S. government — have adopted the same public relations tactics perfected by the tobacco executives. For instance, in a 1981 news release alerting members to possible future federal regulation, the president of the National Agricultural Chemicals Association emphasized "the continuing need for the application of 'sound science' to risk-assessment decisions, including legislation which would create an 'independent panel of scientific experts' to assess and advise regulatory agencies on the risks of pesticides and other chemicals." [41]

Critics said the approach was designed to avoid or delay regulation or responsibility. For example, in the 1980s Vietnam veterans bitterly alleged that certain types of cancer, skin disorders and other health complaints of war returnees resulted from exposure to Agent Orange, a dioxin-containing herbicide the U.S. military sprayed extensively over Southeast Asia during the war.

Research on the possible causal links was often incomplete and sometimes contradictory. Agent Orange's manufacturers, Dow Chemical Co. and Monsanto, dismissed the research, while Republican Sen. Alan Simpson of Wyoming called the veterans whiners and complainers. Then in the early 1990s the Institute of Medicine (IOM) thoroughly reviewed all research literature on possible health risks associated with exposure to dioxin and concluded that a preponderance of reliable evidence showed a causal link between dioxin exposure and various forms of cancer — as well as a range of other diseases and disorders.

The Department of Veterans Affairs eventually began to grant service-connected benefits to exposed Vietnam veterans suffering from — among other diseases — prostate cancer, soft-tissue sarcomas, non-Hodgkins lymphoma, multiple myeloma and Type II diabetes. Subsequent IOM-sponsored research also confirmed a relationship between dioxin-exposed troops and spina bifida in their children.

Scientific Scandals

At about this same time, however, several high-profile cases of scientific misconduct cast a shadow over all research.

One case involved allegations of fabricated findings in an experiment conducted by a Massachusetts Institute of Technology scientist. Although the scientist, Thereza Imanishi-Kari, was eventually cleared of the charges, she was still criticized for having published an error-ridden account of her experiment in a prestigious journal. [42]

Meanwhile, Stephen J. Breuning, a prominent psychologist, was indicted in federal court for falsifying research projects for the National Institute of Mental Health. The implications were serious. His data — widely reported and used — represented at least one-third of all scientific articles on the topic and had been used to justify patient treatments. Although no harm occurred, the scandal cast a pall over scientific integrity and drew press and political attention to the issue. As one account noted, the Breuning case "demonstrated that science did not always self-correct." [43]

Another scientist fabricated as many as 113 of 117 data points in an experiment involving the transformation of carbon molecules into superconductors. [44]

So widespread were allegations of misconduct that the National Academy of Sciences' Committee on Science, Engineering and Public Policy issued a report in 1992 attempting to sort out exactly what constituted scientific misconduct and tried to establish guidelines for ensuring responsible scientific research.

The report helped reaffirm the need for absolute integrity in research but left a damaging impression that scientists, generally regarded as impartial, were not above corruption or distortion if it suited their purposes.

'Liberal Claptrap'

During his tenure (1957-89) as a Democratic senator from Wisconsin, William Proxmire created the annual "Golden Fleece" awards, which he handed out to federal programs he thought were wasting taxpayers' money. Often the winners involved some type of scientific research, such as the National Institute on Alcohol Abuse and Alcoholism's multimillion-dollar study in 1975 to find out if drunken fish are more aggressive than sober fish and whether young rats are more likely than adult rats to drink as a result of anxiety.

However, by the late 1980s and early '90s, congressional attacks on science were less about wastefulness and more about politics. Indeed, former Speaker of the House Rep. Newt Gingrich, R-Ga., saw scientists' purposes as distinctly partisan. In the mid-1990s the new GOP majority in Congress took aim at the ostensibly bipartisan Congressional Office of Technology Assessment (OTA), which had acquired a reputation among Republicans as being more responsive and helpful to Democrats, who for decades had been the majority party. Gingrich, who knew most scientists supported Democrats, felt the OTA represented partisan politics masquerading as scientific objectivity.

One of his first goals after becoming speaker in 1995 was to abolish the OTA, which informed lawmakers on technology and science issues affecting legislation. Gingrich claimed the office moved too slowly to help Congress make policy decisions.

Rep. Dana Rohrabacher, R-Calif., and later House Majority Whip Tom DeLay, R-Texas, shared Gingrich's view of scientists as partisans, calling them "liberal extremists" and dismissing their cautionary pronouncements on global warming as "liberal claptrap." [45]

Meanwhile, a Princeton University physicist claimed the Clinton administration's concern over global warming was more about retaining environmentalists' votes than pursuing sound science. William Happer — who had served as a Department of Energy science adviser under Republican President George H.W. Bush and for a period under Clinton — said the atmospheric content of carbon dioxide was not appreciably different now than a million years ago. The Clinton administration, Happer said, fired him for his views. [46]

Shortly before Republican George W. Bush took office in 2001, the outgoing Clinton administration issued rules lowering the amounts of arsenic allowed in drinking water. Environmentalists hailed a victory, but industry and some Republicans denounced the move as political. Clinton, they said, had issued them as a parting slap at the incoming Bush administration, which lost the environmentalist vote in the 2000 election to Democrat Vice President Al Gore. The new administration suspended the rules and ordered the EPA to review them, provoking charges the administration was trying to weaken the arsenic standard.

"That wasn't true," says Rep. Ehlers. "It wasn't clear the Clinton administration had done the science carefully to justify lower levels." The EPA eventually recommended the same levels that had existed before Clinton's guidelines were issued.

Science Adviser Gets Baptism by Fire

With advanced degrees and a solid experiment or two on their résumés, scientists usually don't have to continue proving anything except perhaps their newest theory.

But since becoming director of the White House Office of Science and Technology Policy (OSTP), John H. Marburger III has seen his status, relevance and even personal ethics questioned.

Amid charges and countercharges that the Bush administration is politicizing science to an unprecedented degree, Marburger — former director of the prestigious Brookhaven National Laboratory and co-founder of the University of Southern California's Center for Laser Studies — has been caught in the crossfire. Although critics have leveled their harshest accusations at those higher in the political pecking order, as the president's chief science adviser Marburger, a Democrat, has had to defend many of the administration's science-related actions.

Office of Science and Technology Policy

White House science adviser John H. Marburger III, a Democrat, has defended the Bush administration's use of scientific data.

For example, when the Union of Concerned Scientists (UCS) issued a report in March alleging "unprecedented" federal agency abuse of science to support administration policy, Marburger delivered to Congress the extensive, point-by-point response.

Observers like Donald Kennedy, editor in chief of the journal *Science*, thought Marburger answered some charges well, others not at all. One charge alleged the administration had appointed unqualified officials to government science advisory positions merely because they support administration policies. "He just said, 'We checked and they're qualified!' " says Kennedy of Marburger's comment to Congress. "You can't finesse the question that easily."

As a result, some suspect Marburger is growing more loyal to his boss than his scientific convictions. "I've known him for a while and have great respect for him," says Kennedy, "but he's been put now in a very defensive posture."

Another scientist said, "I have a great deal of sympathy for his position, because I don't believe he has the authority, the power, to go back into all the agencies and unearth all the facts about all these cases." [1]

Others, however, are more blunt. "I actually feel very sorry for Marburger, because I think he probably is enough of a scientist to realize that he basically has become a prostitute," said Howard Gardner, a Harvard cognitive psychologist. [2]

Arguing that President Bush is interested in science only as a political tool, critics have complained that the office of science adviser is no longer in the building next to the White House, supposedly indicating Marburger — and, by extension, science — have been excluded from the president's most intimate circle. They also note that the administration installed a former Republican congressional staffer, a non-scientist, as one of Marburger's associate directors.

Moreover, last January, *Science* reported that President Bush's plan for the U.S. space program to go back to the moon and later on to Mars was not drawn up or decided in Marburger's office, but by the National Security Council. [3]

"Nonsense!" replies Marburger. "My office was intimately involved in that decision. I think a lot of news stories that came out on that were based on selected leaks, which had somebody's spin on them." Several White House officials, including Chief of Staff Andrew H. Card Jr., have described Marburger as integral to not only daily senior staff meetings but also major budget decisions.

Marburger says any attempt to read a meaning into his office's location "is kind of laughable. What's that have to do with science? As far as I can tell, I'm taken very seriously, and I think science in general is taken more seriously by this administration than any previous one."

[1] See James Glanz, "At the Center of the Storm Over Bush and Science," *The New York Times*, March 30, 2004, p. F1.

[2] *Ibid.*

[3] Andrew Lawler, "How Much Space for Science?" *Science*, Jan. 30, 2004, pp. 610-612.

Still, Bush has challenged the science used to support a variety of policy decisions — sometimes dramatically more than his Republican predecessors. For instance, during Reagan's two-term presidency 253 species were added to the Endangered Species list; 234 were added during the first George Bush's term. But with one term almost complete, George W. Bush's administration has added only 31. [47] ■

Continued on p. 678

At Issue:

Should Congress reinstate the Office of Technology Assessment?

yes

REP. RUSH HOLT, D-N.J.
FORMER DIRECTOR, PRINCETON PLASMA PHYSICS LABORATORY; MEMBER, HOUSE PERMANENT SELECT COMMITTEE ON INTELLIGENCE; HOUSE COMMITTEE ON EDUCATION AND THE WORKFORCE

WRITTEN FOR *THE CQ RESEARCHER*, JULY 2004

Computer viruses. Forest fires. Medical research. Weapons of mass destruction. Crop production. High-speed rail. Internet regulation.

Every day, Congress legislates on a range of complex topics. These topics, though not "science issues" in the traditional sense, have significant scientific and technical components that are central to understanding and addressing them. And yet, Congress has no internal capacity to assess them thoroughly. As a result, critical aspects of these issues fall into Congress' collective blind spot.

That is not to say that Congress is lacking information. Quite the contrary. Congress is inundated with facts, figures, opinions and arguments from literally thousands of sources. But most of this information comes from interested parties who have motivation to disseminate information favorable to their side. And congressional staffs do not have the capacity to sift through, explore and objectively evaluate the information.

Congress needs timely, balanced analyses of key issues that are delivered by nonpartisan, objective experts who understand the needs and the language of legislators. Every year that passes without the capacity for in-house technical assessments represents lost opportunities for Congress to save lives, protect our towns and cities and commercialize new discoveries.

The Office of Technology Assessment (OTA) served Congress for two decades, ending in 1995. The OTA provided valuable, nonpartisan scientific advice on a host of issues, and many of its reports are still relevant today. Unfortunately, OTA's absence has left a void in congressional expertise.

Attempts to revive OTA have failed. So too, did my attempts to provide funding to the General Accounting Office [now the Government Accountability Office] (GAO) to do similar work. Rep. Amo Houghton and I have introduced legislation (H.R. 4670) to fill this void through the creation of the Center for Scientific and Technical Assessment (CSTA). The CSTA support staff would avoid the burden of too much hierarchy by building upon the current structure of the GAO. The GAO has shown its ability to perform independent and objective analysis for Congress, and creating the CSTA would enable it to respond to more member inquiries on technical matters.

For too long, Congress has been legislating without truly understanding scientific and technical components of our legislative issues. It's time to pass H.R. 4670 and help eliminate the blind spot.

no

PATRICK J. MICHAELS
SENIOR FELLOW IN ENVIRONMENTAL STUDIES, CATO INSTITUTE; PROFESSOR OF ENVIRONMENTAL SCIENCES, UNIVERSITY OF VIRGINIA

WRITTEN FOR *THE CQ RESEARCHER*, JULY 2004

In 1995, Congress killed its Office of Technology Assessment (OTA), a small operation costing about $40 million per year in today's dollars. OTA was Congress' own scientific think tank, specifically tasked with answering questions about science and technology.

Given the current ferment about "sound science" and accusations that the Republicans are spinning it for their own purposes, many people want OTA, or something like it, back.

Staffed mainly by some pretty high-quality Ph.D.s and networked with big-time academia, OTA produced reports in 1995 like "Telecommunications Technology and Native Americans: Opportunities and Challenges" and "Hospital Financing in Seven Countries."

All of these reports, and the 60 others OTA produced that year, were pretty good — as good as your average master's thesis from a top-tier university. Only, instead of being thought up by 23-year-olds, they were commissioned by members of Congress.

And that's my point. In a world dominated by increasingly sophisticated technology, there is a small army of young geniuses out there who will pay (as in graduate tuition) to do pretty much the same thing that OTA was paid by taxpayers to do. And, given that technology, their findings are as far away as "http."

What about the concern of "politicized" science? Try as it might, when an office is chartered to be at the beck and call of politicians, it is impossible to be free of politics. What are the chances that a report on Native Americans and technology would be commissioned by a libertarian Republican? Dozens of OTA reports from the Clinton administration required the signature of Jack Gibbons, his science adviser and a down-the-green-line Al Gore acolyte on global warming.

Publicly funded science can't avoid political strings. A new OTA won't stop that, nor can it stop any politician from highlighting aspects of science that serve the agenda, and disregarding those that don't. It happened, despite OTA's existence, when a Democratic Congress stacked hearings promoting the awful view of global warming, and it happened after Congress went Republican, only in the opposite direction. To the victor belongs the "delete" key.

Instead of replacing OTA, we should let our universities do its job while training the technological leaders of tomorrow.

Continued from p. 676

CURRENT SITUATION

Clear Skies Stymied

Bush's Climate Change Science Program (CCSP) — which calls for more research into global warming — and his "Clear Skies" initiative are his administration's two most significant environmental proposals.

The NAS lauded the administration for having consulted outside scientists for advice on devising the CCSP, but said the data gathered under the plan could benefit from outside peer review to avoid charges of politicization, especially since many officials involved with the plan are political appointees.

The CCSP has only recently begun soliciting comments for the first of 21 reports and assessments to be conducted under the plan, most by the National Oceanic and Atmospheric Administration. It is scheduled for completion in 2006.

President Bush announced his Clear Skies proposal in February 2002. According to the EPA, Clear Skies would set strict, mandatory emissions caps on three of the most harmful air pollutants from power plants — sulfur dioxide, nitrogen oxides and mercury, all of which would be reduced by 70 percent by 2018. [48]

During the 2000 presidential campaign, Bush had promised to reduce carbon dioxide (CO_2) emissions, the chief manmade greenhouse gas suspected in global warming. But Clear Skies measures introduced in both the House and Senate in 2002 contained no provision for reducing CO_2.

In June 2003, then EPA Administrator Christine Todd Whitman told the Senate's Clean Air Subcommittee, "There is no better time for Congress to be considering multi-pollutant legislation. President Bush has indicated that Clear Skies is his top environmental priority." [49] But neither the Senate nor the House has taken any significant action on the bills since then, largely because of disagreement among Republicans over the potential impact of the legislation.

"I really don't know what will happen to Clear Skies," says Rep. Ehlers.

Last August, the OMB proposed a controversial plan to establish a standard mandatory peer review of all scientific research or data supporting proposed federal regulations that might impact an "administration priority policy" or that would cost more than $100 million annually to implement. [50]

Many academic scientists charged that the plan was little more than a tactic to delay federal regulation. Perhaps even more worrying for the scientific community, however, was a provision that would bar from peer review panels any scientist who had received a federal grant from the agency considering the new regulation. Academic scientists felt the plan unfairly targeted them, because they usually rely more heavily on federal grants than industry scientists. The OMB later dropped the proposal.

Research Budgets

White House science adviser Marburger says if Congress approves Bush's proposed science budget for fiscal 2005, the president will have increased total research and development funding by 45 percent since taking office, from $91 billion in 2001 to $132 billion.

"There's a huge commitment to science here," he says.

However, Kei Koizumi, director of the research and development budget and policy program at the American Association for the Advancement of Science, has noted that most of the increase is earmarked for defense, homeland security and medicine rather than for basic science. [51] Yet, federal funding of basic scientific research has played a vital role in U.S. technological innovation in the past, leading to the development of magnetic resonance imaging, a global positioning system, human genome mapping and fiber optics, among other things. [52]

According to Marburger's Office of Science and Technology Policy (OSTP), the level of federal funding for basic science has increased about 26 percent since Bush became president, rising from $21.3 billion to a proposed $26.8 billion for fiscal year 2005. While Koizumi acknowledges that rise is "significant," he points out that most of the money has gone toward doubling the National Institutes of Health's budget, a process that began in 1998.

If Congress approves the administration's funding levels for 2005, OSTP figures show total federal R&D spending will be approximately 1.1 percent of gross domestic product, the first time it's been above 1 percent in 10 years. Koizumi welcomes the rise, but adds that in the mid-1980s total federal R&D spending was about 1.25 percent of GDP.

'Sound Science' Bills

In addition to Clear Skies, a sprinkling of "sound science" legislation is pending on Congress' plate, including the legislation introduced by Rep. Walden and Sen. Smith favoring empirical, field-tested and peer-reviewed scientific data over that derived from modeling in administering the Endangered Species Act.

A bipartisan bill to reinstate the OTA has been referred to four House subcommittees, but quick action does not appear urgent. For example, although House Science Committee Chairman Sherwood Boehlert. R-N.Y., is a cosponsor of the bill, the panel's staff director, David Goldston, says complaints that abolishing the OTA left Congress without scientific advice "have been way overblown." No companion bill yet exists in the Senate.

In July, the Senate Committee on Commerce, Science and Transportation passed a bill that would authorize $60 million for the administration's Climate Change Science Program. It is awaiting a date for a Senate debate, but no companion bill yet exists in the House.

Meanwhile, in March the House passed the so-called cheeseburger bill, which Republicans say will protect the food industry from frivolous lawsuits alleging their products make people fat. A Senate subcommittee held hearings on a companion bill last October, but it has not yet been scheduled for a vote.

The bill was a reaction to a March 2003 draft report by the World Health Organization and the U.N. Food and Agriculture Organization, recommending governmental limits on high-sugar foods, which some scientists have said are a major cause of obesity. Sugar industry scientists attacked the report, claiming its research was suggestive but not conclusive. ■

OUTLOOK

Election Friction

The partisan gridlock over science-related policies and issues is widely expected to intensify as the presidential election approaches and the increasingly contentious struggle for both the White House and control of Congress stifles most new legislation.

"I've watched Congress for a long time," says Utah Republican Cannon. "I love this institution, and I've seen it deteriorate to the lowest point of incivility and partisanship." [53]

"It has become way too political at this point to have a serious policy work its way through Congress," says California Republican Pombo. "I can pull out decisions made during the Clinton administration that I think were totally political, that had nothing to do with the science. And I'm sure those on the other side can make the same case about the Bush administration. Well, if that's so, then why don't we sit down and figure out a better way to do it? But between now and the election, it's not going to happen."

Science Editor Kennedy thinks if the Democrats win the White House the overall situation would change, "but maybe not permanently," he says, "because the scientific community will always maintain a sort of critical stance with respect to the way government handles science issues," regardless of who's in power.

But given how science issues are already figuring in the presidential campaign, charges of politicizing science will certainly continue if Kerry wins. For instance, Sen. Inhofe has denounced as hypocrisy Kerry's call for new technologies to enable less U.S. dependence on foreign oil because the Massachusetts senator opposes drilling in the Arctic National Wildlife Refuge, where Inhofe and others have long claimed oil exploration could be done without significant environmental impact.

Tannenbaum, of the Federation of American Scientists, fears widespread negative fallout if the sound science debate gets any more acrimonious. "The public's trust [and] ability to believe in science will be eroded, so when something does happen and it's real, and all scientists believe it but it's dismissed by politicians, the public will think it's nonsense," he says. "And that cannot be good."

If scientists end up discredited, they will only have themselves to blame, says Bush science adviser Marburger. "The worst damage to a scientist's reputation is the wholesale signing of letters and things like that by eminent scientists. I think that's a very bad practice," he says, alluding to the UCS report.

But after reflecting on those comments, Marburger then adds: "Let me soften that about signing letters. It's OK for scientists to act like normal people, as long as it's understood they're not expressing a scientific opinion when they do that.

"And I don't worry too much about this, because I think the public has a much deeper appreciation for what science is than most people think," he continues. "The public knows that science is about nature, and while you can manipulate opinions, you can't manipulate nature." ■

Notes

[1] For background, see Mary H. Cooper, "Global Warming Treaty," *The CQ Researcher*, Jan. 26, 2001, pp. 41-64.

[2] See Martin Kady II, Mary Clare Jalonick and Amol Sharma, "Science, Policy Mix Uneasily in Legislative Laboratory," *CQ Weekly*,

About the Author

William Triplett recently joined *The CQ Researcher* as a staff writer after covering science and the arts for such publications as *Smithsonian, Air & Space, Nature, Washingtonian* and *The Washington Post*. He also served as associate editor of *Capitol Style* magazine. He holds a B.A. in journalism from Ohio University and an M.A. in English literature from Georgetown University. His recent reports include "Search for Extraterrestrials" and "Broadcast Indecency."

March 20, 2004, p. 680.
[3] "Survey of Research and Development Expenditures at Universities and Colleges, Fiscal Year 2002," National Science Foundation/Division of Science Resources Statistics, 2002.
[4] "Is Academic Medicine for Sale?" *The New England Journal of Medicine*, May 18, 2000.
[5] Union of Concerned Scientists, "Scientific Integrity in Policymaking: An Investigation into the Bush Administration's Misuse of Science," March 2004, p. 2.
[6] Guy Gugliotta and Rick Weiss, "President's Science Policy Questioned; Scientists Worry That Any Politics Will Compromise Their Credibility," *The Washington Post*, Feb. 19, 2004, p. A2.
[7] Gregg Easterbrook, "Commentary: Politics and Science do Mix; Claims that Bush Misuses Science are Hypocritical," *Los Angeles Times*, April 6, 2004, p. B13.
[8] Chris Mooney, "Beware 'Sound Science.' It's Doublespeak for Trouble," *The Washington Post*, Feb. 29, 2004, p. B2.
[9] Nedra Pickler, "Kerry argues Bush relies on ideology, not facts, in science policies," The Associated Press, June 21, 2004.
[10] Rick Weiss, " 'Data Quality' Law Is Nemesis of Regulation," *The Washington Post*, Aug. 16, 2004, p. A1.
[11] *Ibid.*
[12] "The Union of Concerned Scientists Document: Administration Summary Response," Office of Science and Technology Policy, April 2, 2004, p. 1.
[13] *Ibid.*
[14] For background, see Cooper, *op. cit.*
[15] Kady, *et al*, *op. cit.*, p. 686, and Mary H. Cooper, "Air Pollution Conflict," *The CQ Researcher*, Nov. 14, 2003, pp. 965-988.
[16] "The Union of Concerned Scientists Document," *op. cit.*, p. 7.
[17] National Academy of Sciences press release, Feb. 18, 2004.
[18] "HR 1662, The Sound Science for Endangered Species Act Planning Act of 2003," http://walden.house.gov/issues/esa/108thcongress/index.html.
[19] Rep. Greg Walden, statement, Subcommittee on Energy and Minerals, House Committee on Resources, Feb. 4, 2003.
[20] *Ibid.*
[21] Weiss, *op. cit.*
[22] *Ibid.*
[23] For background, see William Triplett, "State Budget Crisis," *The CQ Researcher*, Oct. 3, 2003, pp. 821-844.
[24] National Science Foundation, *op. cit.*
[25] Weiss, *op. cit.*

FOR MORE INFORMATION

American Association for the Advancement of Science, 1200 New York Ave., N.W., Washington, DC 20005; (202) 326-6400; www.aaas.org. An international organization dedicated to advancing science; publishes the journal *Science*.

Intergovernmental Panel on Climate Change, c/o World Meteorological Organization, 7bis Avenue de la Paix, C.P. 2300, CH- 1211 Geneva 2, Switzerland; (41)-(22)-730-8208; www.ipcc.ch. Created in 1988 by the WMO and the United Nations to assess information on climate change.

National Academy of Sciences, 500 Fifth St., N.W., Washington, DC 2001; (202) 334-2000; www.nationalacademies.org. The NAS convenes experts who advise the government and general public on science and technology.

Petition Project, P.O. Box 1925, La Jolla, CA 92038-1925; www.oism.org/oism/s32p31.htm. Part of the Oregon Institute of Science and Medicine, the project is a leading organizer of skeptical opinion on human-induced climate change.

Union of Concerned Scientists, 2 Brattle Square, Cambridge, MA 02238-9105; (617) 547-5552; www.ucsusa.org. An independent, nonprofit alliance claiming more than 100,000 members dedicated to "rigorous scientific analysis with innovative thinking and committed citizen advocacy."

[26] Thomas Bodenheimer, "Uneasy Alliance — Clinical Investigators and the Pharmaceutical Industry," *The New England Journal of Medicine*, May 18, 2000, vol. 342, no. 20.
[27] "Is Academic Medicine for Sale?", *op. cit.*
[28] "Bias and conflicts of interest in medical research is funded by medical industry groups," National Public Radio, Oct. 21, 1999.
[29] Susan Benson, Mark Arax and Rachel Burstein, "Science for Sale: Conflicts of Interest Undermine Agricultural Biotechnology Research," *GeneWATCH*, April 1998, p. 12.
[30] *Ibid.*
[31] Mooney, *op. cit.*
[32] Center for Responsive Politics; www.opensecrets.org/politicians/indus.asp?CID=N00005582&cycle=2004.
[33] *Frye v. United States*, 293 F. 1013 (1923). For background see Kenneth Jost, "Science in the Courtroom," *The CQ Researcher*, Oct. 22, 1993, p. 920.
[34] *Ibid.*
[35] Interview, David Michaels, professor of public health, George Washington University.
[36] Kady, *et al.*, *op. cit.*
[37] Michaels interview, *op. cit.*
[38] For background, see Kenneth Jost, "Closing in on Tobacco," *The CQ Researcher*, Nov. 12, 1999, pp. 977-1000.
[39] For background, see David Masci, "Religion and Politics," *The CQ Researcher*, July 30, 2004, pp. 637-660.
[40] *Ibid.*
[41] Kady, *et al.*, *op. cit.*
[42] Marcel C. LaFollette, "The Evolution of the 'Scientific Misconduct' Issue: An Historical Overview," *Proceedings of the Society for Experimental Biology and Medicine*, 224:211-215 (2000); www.ebmonline.org/cgi/content/full/224/4/211.
[43] *Ibid.*
[44] Kenneth Chang, "On Scientific Fakery and the Systems to Catch It," *The New York Times*, Oct. 15, 2002, p. F1.
[45] See Nicholas Thompson, "Science Friction: the growing — and dangerous — divide between scientists and the GOP," *Washington Monthly*, July 1, 2003.
[46] Kady, *et al.*, *op. cit.*
[47] Juliet Eilperin, "Endangered Species Act's Protections Are Trimmed," *The Washington Post*, July 4, 2004, p. A1.
[48] Cooper, "Air Pollution Conflict," *op. cit.*
[49] www.epa.gov/air/clearskies/legis.html.
[50] Jeffrey Brainard, "How Sound is Bush's 'Sound Science'?" *The Chronicle of Higher Education*, March 5, 2004, p. 18.
[51] "Funding for Basic Science has Little Traction in Congress," *CQ Weekly*, July 3, 2004, p. 1610.
[52] *Ibid.*
[53] For background, see Alan Greenblatt, "The Partisan Divide," *The CQ Researcher*, April 30, 2004, pp. 373-396.

Bibliography

Selected Sources

Books

***Integrity in Scientific Research: Creating an Environment that Promotes Responsible Conduct*, National Academies Press, 2002.**

In response to an increase in scientific fraud and misconduct, the National Research Council attempts to identify practices that characterize and promote integrity in research and peer review.

Green, Kenneth P., *Global Warming: Understanding the Debate*, Enslow Publishers, 2002.

Writing for students, the chief scientist at the Fraser Institute explains the most prominent issues, theories and evidence in the global-warming debate.

Harrison, Neil E., and Gary C. Bryner, *Science and Politics in the International Environment*, Rowman & Littlefield, 2004.

Two scientists use case studies to explore how the interplay of science and politics influences international environmental policy.

Michaels, Patrick J., and Robert C. Balling, *The Satanic Gases: Clearing the Air about Global Warming*, Cato Institute, 2000.

Two climatologists rebut some of the key assertions made by advocates of global-warming theory.

Articles

Brainard, Jeffrey, "How Sound is Bush's 'Sound Science'?" *The Chronicle of Higher Education*, March 5, 2004.

Brainard evaluates the principal science-related issues and policies the Bush administration is said to have politicized.

Easterbrook, Gregg, "Politics and Science Do Mix; Claims That Bush Misuses Research are Hypocritical," *Los Angeles Times*, April 6, 2004, p. B13.

A science journalist critiques the Union of Concerned Scientists' recent allegations the Bush administration misused science.

Kady II, Martin, Mary Clare Jalonick and Amol Sharma, "Science, Policy Mix Uneasily in Legislative Laboratory," *CQ Weekly*, March 20, 2004, pp. 680-688.

Accusations of politicizing science on both sides of the aisle have intensified, causing deep partisan divides over science-related issues and legislation in Congress.

Mooney, Chris, "Beware 'Sound Science.' It's Doublespeak for Trouble," *The Washington Post*, Feb. 29, 2004, p. B2.

A science journalist presents alleged examples of how the Bush administration and its congressional allies try to make scientific data fit policy.

Thompson, Nicholas, "Science friction: the growing — and dangerous — divide between scientists and the GOP; Republican Party, George W. Bush and scientific policy," *Washington Monthly*, July 2003.

Thompson explores the genesis of the Bush administration's clash with much of the scientific community.

Weiss, Rick, " 'Data Quality' Law Is Nemesis of Regulation," *The Washington Post*, Aug. 16, 2004, p. A1.

Environmentalists charge that industry and the Bush administration use an obscure law to block or slow down environmental and health regulations under the guise of sound science.

Willman, David, "Stealth Merger: Drug Companies and Government Medical Research; Some of the National Institutes of Health's top scientists are also collecting paychecks and stock options from biomedical firms," *Los Angeles Times*, Dec. 7, 2003, p. A1.

Willman's exposé of consulting deals between NIH scientists and biomedical firms prompted congressional hearings.

Reports and Studies

"Climate Change 2001: IPCC Third Assessment Report," Intergovernmental Panel on Climate Change, 2001; www.grida.no/climate/ipcc_tar/.

This assessment concludes "there is new and stronger evidence that most of the warming observed over the last 50 years is attributable to human activities."

"Politics and Science in the Bush Administration," House Committee on Government Reform, Minority Staff, Special Investigations Division, August 2003.

Requested by Rep. Henry A. Waxman, D-Calif., this report alleges that the Bush administration "has repeatedly suppressed, distorted, or obstructed science to suit political and ideological goals."

"Scientific Integrity in Policymaking: An Investigation into the Bush Administration's Misuse of Science," Union of Concerned Scientists, March 2004.

The union arrived at essentially the same conclusions as the Waxman report. For White House science adviser John H. Marburger III's response, see www.ostp.gov/html/ucs/SummaryResponsetoCongressonUCSDocumentApril2004.pdf.

"The Science of Climate Change: Senate Floor Statement by U.S. Sen. James M. Inhofe, Chairman, Committee on Environment and Public Works," July 2003; http://inhofe.senate.gov/floorspeeches.htm.

Inhofe cites scientific opinion that doubts or disputes assertions of human-caused global warming.

The Next Step:

Additional Articles from Current Periodicals

Global Warming and Pollution

"Misleading Math About the Earth," ***Scientific American*****, January 2002.**
The publication leads an assault on the conclusions of the author of *The Skeptical Environmentalist,* who rejects current thinking on global warming (see below).

Lomborg, Bjorn, "The Skeptical Environmentalist Replies," ***Scientific American*****, May 2002.**
The author of the 2001 book *The Skeptical Environmentalist* criticizes conventional thinking about global warming.

Eilperin, Juliet, "Tougher Regulations Urged on Power Plant Emissions," ***The Washington Post*****, June 10, 2004, p. A3.**
A study finds that 23,600 premature deaths are caused by power plant emissions each year, but critics denounce it as bad science.

Shogren, Elizabeth, "EPA Plans 'Cap-and-Trade' Mercury Emission Reduction," ***Los Angeles Times*****, Dec. 16, 2003, p. A38.**
With the "Clear Skies" legislation stalled in Congress, the "cap-and-trade" approach allows power plants to buy and sell credits that permit some pollution.

Revkin, Andrew, and Katharine Seelye, "Report by E.P.A. Leaves Out Data on Climate Change," ***The New York Times*****, June 19, 2003, p. A1.**
Officials removed most of the information on global warming from a government report; environmentalists blame the White House.

Peer-Review Proposals

Kohn, David, "Foes Say Bush Plan Would Create 'Debating Society Over Science'," ***The Baltimore Sun*****, Dec. 18, 2003, p. 1A.**
Opponents of a proposal requiring more peer review for scientific studies say the requirements are designed to block new regulations.

Weiss, Rick, "OMB Modifies Peer-Review Proposal," ***The Washington Post*****, April 16, 2004, p. A19.**
Officials stepped back from their original research guidelines after strong criticism from the scientific community.

Weiss, Rick, "Peer Review Plan Draws Criticism," ***The Washington Post*****, Jan. 15, 2004, p. A19.**
Critics call proposed federal guidelines for regulation-related research studies "paralysis by analysis"; supporters call them a commitment to "sound science."

President Bush and Sound Science

"Cheating Nature?" ***The Economist*****, April 10, 2004.**
White House science adviser John Marburger III's response to charges of politicized science sometimes seems like spin rather than well-reasoned rebuttals.

Brainard, Jeffrey, "Bush's Science Adviser Rebuts Allegations That Research Findings Have Been Manipulated," ***The Chronicle of Higher Education*****, April 16, 2004, p. 27.**
Dr. John Marburger III answers the Union of Concerned Scientists.

Gugliotta, Guy, and Rick Weiss, "President's Science Policy Questioned," ***The Washington Post*****, Feb. 19, 2004, p. A2.**
Sixty scientists, including 12 Nobel laureates, claim the Bush administration is manipulating science to further political goals.

Kennedy Jr., Robert F., "The Junk Science of George W. Bush," ***The Nation*****, March 8, 2004, p. 11.**
An environmental lawyer slams the Bush administration's use of scientific data, comparing it to the Spanish Inquisition

Olinger, David, and Karen Crummy, "Kerry Makes a Splash," ***The Denver Post*****, June 22, 2004, p. A1.**
Endorsed by several Nobel laureates, the candidate pledges to support stem-cell research and to embrace better science.

Pianin, Eric, "Moving Target on Policy Battlefield," ***The Washington Post*****, May 2, 2002, p. A21.**
Much of the debate over President Bush's use of science turns on highly technical research.

Satel, Sally, "Science Fiction," ***The Weekly Standard*****, April 12-19, 2004.**
Satel says liberal litmus tests were applied to scientists during the Clinton administration, and that the left-wing tendencies of many scientists are well-documented.

Research Questions

Barrett, Amy, "When Medicine and Money Don't Mix," ***Business Week*****, June 28, 2004, p. 68.**
Concern has mounted that big drugmakers are selectively releasing the results of their medical studies.

Boser, Ulrich, "Who Foots Those Bills?" ***U.S. News & World Report*****, April 12, 2004, p. 50.**
Businesses are an essential source of research funds at many universities, but the funding attracts controversy because of fears the results are tainted.

Lawler, Andrew, "Last of the Big-Time Spenders?" ***Science*****, Jan. 17, 2003, p. 330.**

Mega-deals between universities and corporations raise eyebrows, but companies reconsider as the costs begin to outweigh the benefits.

Shankar, Vedantam, "Antidepressant Makers Withhold Data on Children," *The Washington Post*, Jan. 29, 2004, p. A1.
Questions about antidepressants' effects on children cause criticism of drug companies' practice of not publishing negative studies of their products.

Weiss, Rick, "NIH Scientists Broke Rules, Panel Says," *The Washington Post*, June 23, 2004, p. A19.
National Institutes of Health researchers didn't disclose connections to pharmaceutical and biotech companies, as required by ethics rules.

Willman, David, "NIH Staff Must Report Payments," *Los Angeles Times*, May 19, 2004, p. A15.
New NIH rules require scientists to disclose the consulting fees they have collected from businesses.

Restricting Sex Research

Kaiser, Jocelyn, "Studies of Gay Men, Prostitutes Come Under Scrutiny," *Science*, April 18, 2003, p. 403.
Health officials tell grant writers to remove certain terms from their applications to help avoid political scrutiny.

Navarro, Mireya, "Experts in Sex Field Say Conservatives Interfere With Health and Research," *The New York Times*, July 11, 2004, Section 1, p. 16.
Conservatives counter criticism of scientific interference by saying that most of the sex studies are frivolous.

Russell, Sabin, "AIDS, Sex Scientists on Federal List Fear Their Research Is in Jeopardy," *San Francisco Chronicle*, Oct. 28, 2003, p. A3.
An alleged "hit list" of sexual researchers is denounced as "scientific McCarthyism" by critics.

Science and Law

Faigman, David L., "Is Science Different for Lawyers?" *Science*, July 19, 2002, p. 339.
Recent legal decisions affecting the standards for scientific evidence used in court show that some judges misunderstand scientific principles.

Liptak, Adam, "Doctors' Testimony Under Scrutiny," *The New York Times*, July 6, 2003, Section 1, p. 10.
Under pressure from lawsuits, doctors' tribunals are beginning to review testimony from medical experts; expulsion from medical societies can be the result.

Zarembo, Alan, "Funding Studies to Suit Need," *Los Angeles Times*, Dec. 3, 2003, p. A1.
Controversy swirls around research paid for by Exxon that was used profitably in the courtroom.

Scientific Controversies

Graham, Judith, " 'Morning After' Pill Restricted by FDA," *Chicago Tribune*, May 7, 2004, News Section, p. 1.
Rejection of a contraceptive pill is allegedly a case of subordinating science to a conservative social agenda.

Martin, Andrew, "Flinging Mud in Nation's Food Fight," *Chicago Tribune*, Aug. 4, 2004, News Section, p. 1.
A lobbyist criticized for his own tactics says that "junk science" is being used in the debate about obesity and healthy eating.

Service, Robert F., " 'Combat Biology' on the Klamath: Biologists Charged With Protecting Endangered Species Are Caught in a Battle Over Water Rights," *Science*, April 4, 2003, p. 36.
Government environmental scientists are criticized by both farmers and a science review board over their recommendations for saving endangered fish.

Citing *The CQ Researcher*

Sample formats for citing these reports in a bibliography include the ones listed below. Preferred styles and formats vary, so please check with your instructor or professor.

MLA Style

Jost, Kenneth. "Rethinking the Death Penalty." The CQ Researcher 16 Nov. 2001: 945-68.

APA Style

Jost, K. (2001, November 16). Rethinking the death penalty. *The CQ Researcher, 11*, 945-968.

Chicago Style

Jost, Kenneth. "Rethinking the Death Penalty." *CQ Researcher*, November 16, 2001, 945-968.

In-depth Reports on Issues in the News

Are you writing a paper?

Need backup for a debate?

Want to become an expert on an issue?

For 80 years, researchers have turned to *The CQ Researcher* for in-depth reporting and analysis of issues in the news. Reports on a full range of political and social issues are now available. Following is a selection of recent reports:

Civil Liberties
Civil Liberties Debates, 10/03
Gay Marriage, 9/03

Crime/Law
Serial Killers, 10/03
Corporate Crime, 10/02

Economy
Exporting Jobs, 2/04
Stock Market Troubles, 1/04

Education
Black Colleges, 12/03
Combating Plagiarism, 9/03

Energy/Transportation
SUV Debate, 5/03
Future of Amtrak, 10/02

Environment
Air Pollution Conflict, 11/03
Water Shortages, 8/03

Health/Safety
Homeopathy Debate, 12/04
Worker Safety, 5/04

International Affairs
Aiding Africa, 8/03
Rebuilding Iraq, 7/03

Politics/Public Policy
Redistricting Disputes, 3/04
Democracy in Arab World, 1/04

Social Trends
Future of Music Industry, 11/03
Latinos' Future, 10/03

Terrorism/Defense
North Korean Crisis, 4/03
Homeland Security, 9/03

Youth
Youth Suicide, 2/04
Hazing, 1/04

Upcoming Reports

Ending Genocide, 8/27/04
Diet Supplements, 9/3/04
Big-Box Stores, 9/10/04
Cyber Politics, 9/17/04
Cloning, 9/24/04
Gays on Campus, 10/1/04

ACCESS

The CQ Researcher is available in print and online. For access, visit your library or www.thecqresearcher.com.

STAY CURRENT

To receive notice of upcoming *CQ Researcher* reports, or learn more about *CQ Researcher* products, subscribe to the free e-mail newsletters, *CQ Researcher Alert!* and *CQ Researcher News*: www.cqpress.com/newsletters.

PURCHASE

To purchase a *CQ Researcher* report in print or electronic format (PDF), visit www.cqpress.com or call 866-427-7737. A single report is $10. Bulk purchase discounts and electronic rights licensing are also available.

SUBSCRIBE

A full-service *CQ Researcher* print subscription—including 44 reports a year, monthly index updates, and a bound volume—is $625 for academic and public libraries, $605 for high school libraries, and $750 for media libraries. Add $25 for domestic postage.

The CQ Researcher Online offers a backfile from 1991 and a number of tools to simplify research. Available in print and online, *The CQ Researcher en español* offers 36 reports a year on political and social issues of concern to Latinos in the U.S. For pricing and a free trial of either product, call 800-834-9020, ext. 1906, or e-mail librarysales@cqpress.com.

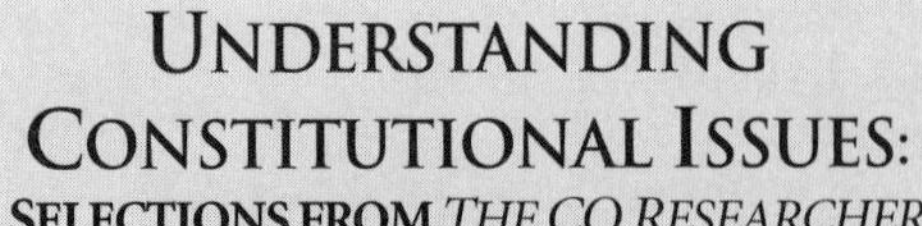

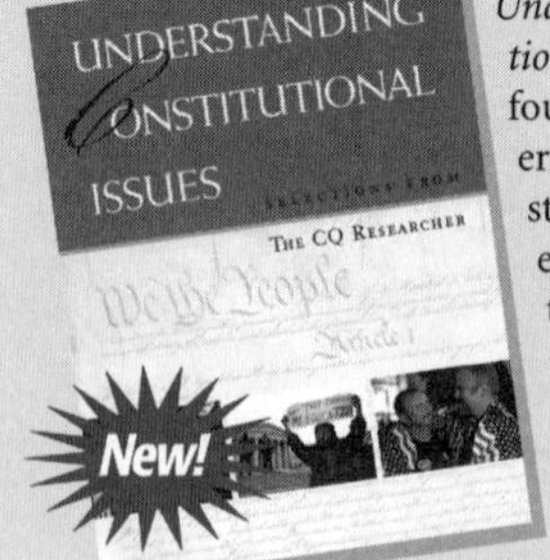

Understanding Constitutional Issues focuses on four key themes — governmental powers and structure, security, liberty, and equality — to help students develop a deeper understanding of the relation between current events and constitutional issues and principles. Integrating eighteen *CQ Researcher* reports, *Understanding Constitutional Issues* makes important connections clear, such as those between civil liberties and security; and privacy and liberty.

June 2004 • 8 1/2 x 11 • Approx. 432 pages • Paperback • ISBN 1-56802-885-7 • $39.95

To Order: Call Toll-Free: 866.4CQ.PRESS (427.7737)
Fax: 800.380.3810 • Web: www.cqpress.com
E-mail: customerservice@cqpress.com

CQ Press, 1255 22nd Street, NW, Suite 400 • Washington, DC 20037

CQ Researcher

Published by CQ Press, a division of Congressional Quarterly Inc.

thecqresearcher.com

Stopping Genocide

Should the U.S. and U.N. take action in Sudan?

Ten years ago, nearly a million ethnic-minority Rwandans died in a government-planned massacre. Political leaders in the United States and the United Nations later admitted they should have intervened and vowed "Never again" — just as they vowed after the Holocaust. But as ethnic killings occurring today in western Sudan make tragically clear, genocide still flourishes. The Bush administration supports sanctions against the Khartoum government, but human-rights activists say an international force is needed to protect civilians. With U.S. troops stretched thin in Iraq, however, the United States has been reluctant to act. Some question whether Americans, preoccupied with terrorism, have the appetite for humanitarian military actions. The U.N. has tried to improve its poor record of mobilizing troops by authorizing Western powers to lead forces in recent crises. But many believe the U.N. is politically paralyzed by the competing interests of the five major members of the Security Council, who can veto any military action.

A makeshift memorial in Cambodia exhibits the remains of victims of the Khmer Rouge regime in the late 1970s.

INSIDE

THIS REPORT

The CQ Researcher • Aug. 27, 2004 • www.thecqresearcher.com
Volume 14, Number 29 • Pages 685-708

CQ PRESS

RECIPIENT OF SOCIETY OF PROFESSIONAL JOURNALISTS AWARD FOR EXCELLENCE ◆ AMERICAN BAR ASSOCIATION SILVER GAVEL AWARD

STOPPING GENOCIDE

Cover: A youth examines the remains of victims of the Khmer Rouge in a makeshift memorial. Two million Cambodians died under the murderous regime in the late 1970s. (AFP Photo)

Aug. 27, 2004
Volume 14, Number 29

MANAGING EDITOR: Thomas J. Colin

ASSISTANT MANAGING EDITOR: Kathy Koch

ASSOCIATE EDITOR: Kenneth Jost

STAFF WRITERS: Mary H. Cooper, William Triplett

CONTRIBUTING WRITERS: Sarah Glazer, David Hatch, David Hosansky, Patrick Marshall, Tom Price, Jane Tanner

DESIGN/PRODUCTION EDITOR: Olu B. Davis

ASSISTANT EDITOR: Kenneth Lukas

A Division of Congressional Quarterly Inc.

SENIOR VICE PRESIDENT/GENERAL MANAGER: John A. Jenkins

DIRECTOR, LIBRARY PUBLISHING: Kathryn C. Suárez

DIRECTOR, EDITORIAL OPERATIONS: Ann Davies

CONGRESSIONAL QUARTERLY INC.

CHAIRMAN: Paul C. Tash

VICE CHAIRMAN: Andrew P. Corty

PRESIDENT AND PUBLISHER: Robert W. Merry

The CQ Researcher (ISSN 1056-2036) is printed on acid-free paper. Published weekly, except Jan. 2, April 9, July 2, July 9, Aug. 6, Aug. 13, Nov. 26 and Dec. 31, by CQ Press, a division of Congressional Quarterly Inc. Annual subscription rates for institutions start at $625. For pricing, call 1-800-834-9020, ext. 1906. To purchase a *CQ Researcher* report in print or electronic format (PDF), visit www.cqpress.com or call 866-427-7737. A single report is $10. Bulk purchase discounts and electronic-rights licensing are also available. Periodicals postage paid at Washington, D.C., and additional mailing offices. POSTMASTER: Send address changes to *The CQ Researcher*, 1255 22nd St., N.W., Suite 400, Washington, D.C. 20037.

Stopping Genocide

BY SARAH GLAZER

THE ISSUES

After Arab nomads raided the Sudanese village of Kornei and killed Hatum Atraman Bashir's husband, she fled with her seven children. But when Bashir and a few other mothers crept out one day to find food, the raiders raped them.

"They said, 'You are black women, and you are our slaves,' " she recalled, weeping softly. "One of the women cried, and they killed her. Then they told me, 'If you cry, we will kill you, too.' "

Bashir, already pregnant by one of the rapists when she told this story earlier this summer, was camping in the shade of a tree after stumbling across the border into Chad in search of help from one of the overburdened aid agencies serving Sudanese refugees. [1]

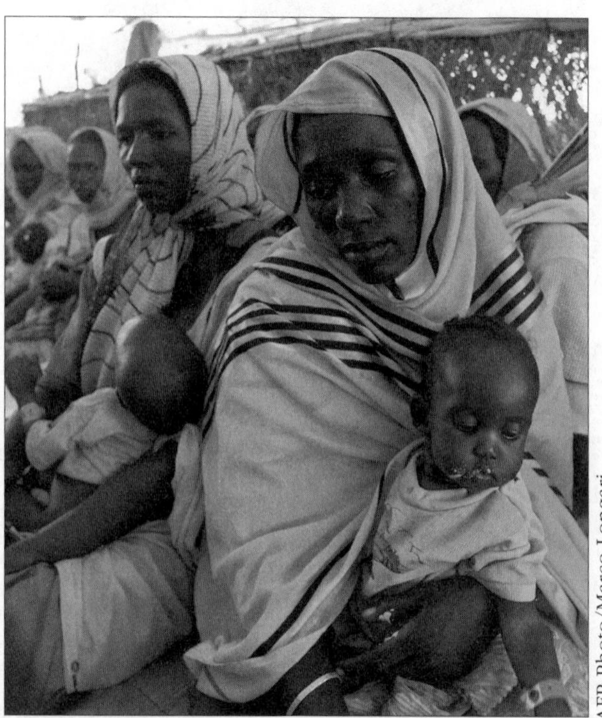
AFP Photo/Marco Longari

Survivors of ethnic violence rest in a refugee camp in western Sudan's embattled Darfur region, where 50,000 people have been killed and a million left homeless. On July 22, the U.S. Congress declared the violence "genocide."

Bashir is part of a wave of more than a million people from the western Darfur region of Sudan left homeless by rampaging nomadic militiamen on horseback, known as the Janjaweed. Since early 2003, the Arab militias have been killing and raping black Africans, who traditionally farm the land, and have burned many of their villages to the ground. The United Nations estimates that violence in Darfur has killed 50,000 and left 2 million short of food and medicine. [2] The Agency for International Development warns that between 300,000 and a million people could die by year's end, depending on how much aid reaches the refugees. [3]

Human-rights groups have accused the Sudanese government of arming the militias in an effort to root out and threaten rebels from Darfur's black African tribal groups. Some villages had been bombed by Sudan's air force and then attacked by Arab militias. [4]

Although the violence began in early 2003, it took until July of this year for the U.S. government and the international community to back up statements of concern with threats of serious action. On July 30, the United Nations Security Council passed a U.S.-drafted resolution giving the Sudanese government 30 days to disarm and prosecute the Arab militias or face unspecified sanctions. [5]

Congress declared the violence "genocide" on July 22 and urged President Bush to do the same. [6] But as of mid-August, Secretary of State Colin L. Powell studiously avoided using the word "genocide" on the advice of government lawyers, he explained. [7] Under the International Convention on the Prevention and Punishment of the Crime of Genocide, the United States and other participating countries are obliged "to prevent and punish" genocide, although experts say the 1948 treaty is not specific about what that entails. (*See box, p. 689.*)

Even some of the most committed activists have been reluctant to bandy about a word like genocide, concerned that it should be reserved for clear-cut cases. As of mid-August, groups like Amnesty International and Human Rights Watch said they did not have enough information to call the violence in Darfur genocide, even as they called for tougher action by the international community. The African Union also declined to label the situation genocide even as it was sending 150 troops to Darfur to protect its cease-fire monitors and was expressing interest in sending more troops with a broadened mandate to protect civilians. [8]

Complicating the question of whether the situation in Darfur could be called genocide is the fact that some of the victims of the militias are Arab, and not all Arab groups participated in the killings. [9]

Yet critics in Congress and human-rights groups called the response to Darfur too slow and — in some eyes — too weak. They said it bore a disturbing resemblance to the world's inaction 10 years ago, when close to a million Rwandans died in killings now widely described as genocide. [10] In 1994, the Clinton administration also had intentionally avoided describing the Rwanda crisis as genocide because Pentagon lawyers had advised that using the term could commit the United States "to actually do something" under the international genocide convention. [11]

Both former President Bill Clinton and U.N. Secretary-General Kofi Annan have since traveled to Rwanda to express regret over the world's failure to stop the genocide. "We did not act

Genocide in Sudan

Sudan is Africa's largest country — almost five times the size of France. In the western Darfur region, rampaging Arab militiamen on horseback, known as the Janjaweed, have left more than a million people homeless since early 2003. The militias have been killing and raping black Africans, who traditionally farm the land. The violence has killed some 50,000 and left 2 million short of food and medicine. Aid officials estimate up to a million refugees could die by year's end without sufficient supplies. The violence began in early 2003, but it took until July 2004 for the world community to threaten serious action. Although Congress called the killings "genocide" on July 22, as of mid-August, Secretary of State Colin L. Powell has avoided the word. On July 30, the U.N. Security Council passed a U.S.-drafted resolution giving Sudan 30 days to disarm and prosecute the Arab militias or face unspecified sanctions.

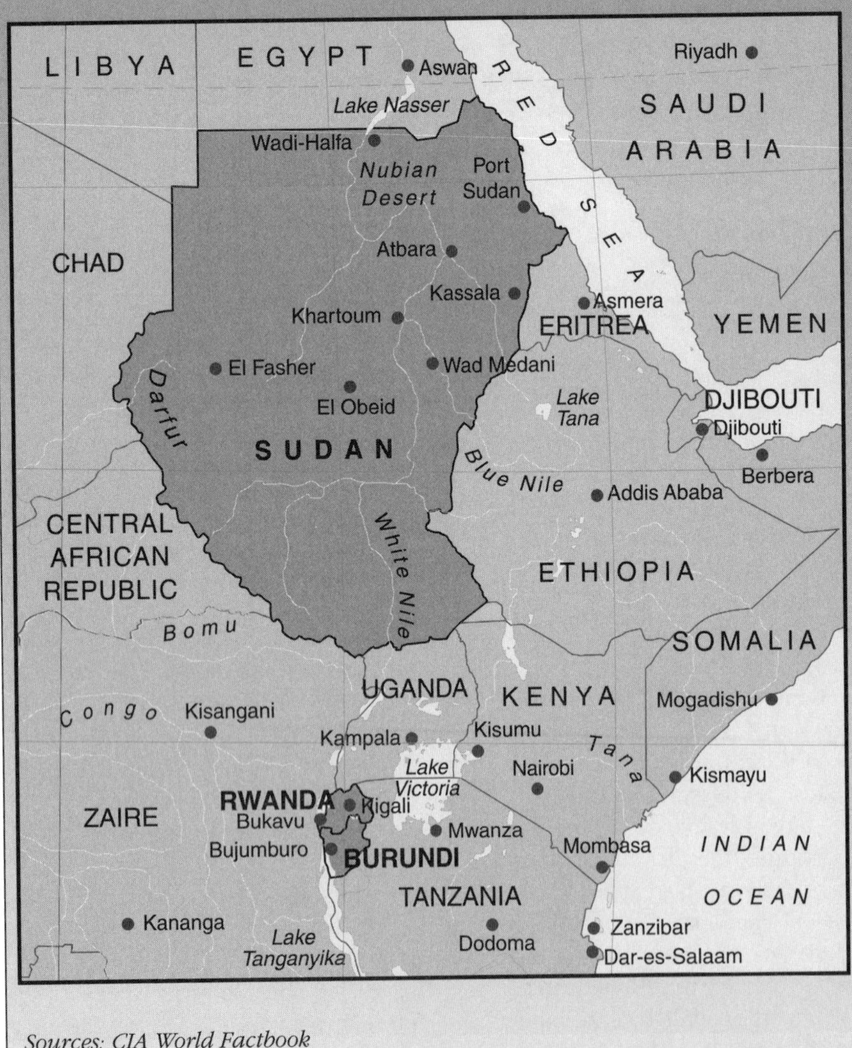

Sources: CIA World Factbook

quickly enough after the killing began," Clinton told hundreds of genocide survivors after hearing harrowing eyewitness accounts of the massacre. "We did not immediately call these crimes by their rightful name: genocide." [12]

Two months later, after touring a memorial containing the bones of 3,000 genocide victims, Annan somberly acknowledged, "The world failed Rwanda at that time of evil. The international community and the United Nations could not muster the political will to confront it." [13]

Instead, Clinton officials had urged the Rwandan government to negotiate with rebel militants from the Tutsi ethnic minority — the group the Hutu-led Rwandan government had targeted for killing. An estimated 800,000 minority Tutsi and moderate Hutu's were killed in three months — most hacked to death with machetes. The daily death rate exceeded even Hitler's killing machine. Many observers now agree Rwanda's leaders used their participation at the peace table as a cover for the killings they were planning and executing elsewhere in the country.

Similarly, Bush administration officials have stressed their role in encouraging north-south peace talks between the Sudan government and rebel groups, which want a share of Sudan's oil wealth. (The African rebel groups from Darfur charge they have been largely excluded from those agreements, which is one reason they are rebelling.)

"Once again, the world is turning its back on a defenseless people," said Rep. Tom Lantos, D-Calif., ranking minority member of the House International Relations Committee. He had warned State Department officials earlier this spring that Sudanese government leaders were "masters of manipulating" the international community, even as they engaged in the peace process. [14]

What does it take for a country like the United States to intervene in an ethnically driven massacre abroad — particularly if it puts American soldiers at

The Genocide Treaty

The United States and 135 other nations have signed the Convention on the Prevention and Punishment of the Crime of Genocide since the United Nations General Assembly approved it on Dec. 9, 1948. The treaty recognizes that genocide "is contrary to the spirit and aims of the United Nations and condemned by the civilized world" and that "in order to liberate mankind from such an odious scourge, international cooperation is required. . . ."

Key treaty provisions:

- The Contracting Parties confirm that genocide, whether committed in time of peace or in time of war, is a crime under international law which they undertake to prevent and to punish.
- In the present Convention, genocide means any of the following acts committed with intent to destroy, in whole or in part, a national, ethnical, racial or religious group, as such:
  - (a) Killing members of the group;
  - (b) Causing serious bodily or mental harm to members of the group;
  - (c) Deliberately inflicting on the group conditions of life calculated to bring about its physical destruction in whole or in part;
  - (d) Imposing measures intended to prevent births within the group;
  - (e) Forcibly transferring children of the group to another group.
- The Contracting Parties undertake to enact, in accordance with their respective Constitutions, the necessary legislation to give effect to the provisions of the present Convention, and, in particular, to provide effective penalties for persons guilty of genocide. . . .
- Persons charged with genocide [or attempted genocide or related crimes] . . . shall be tried by a competent tribunal of the State in the territory of which the act was committed, or by such international penal tribunal as may have jurisdiction with respect to those Contracting Parties which shall have accepted its jurisdiction.
- Any Contracting Party may call upon the competent organs of the United Nations to take such action under the Charter of the United Nations as they consider appropriate for the prevention and suppression of acts of genocide. . . .

risk? Increasingly, observers seem to concur with former journalist Samantha Power, a lecturer at Harvard's Kennedy School of Government. Her 2002 book, *A Problem from Hell*, argues that American presidents from Franklin D. Roosevelt to Clinton have been reluctant to intervene unless they perceive it to be in their political interest. And humanitarian intervention is widely viewed as unlikely to be popular with voters.

It's hard to argue for a compelling U.S. interest in far-off Sudan, even if it once harbored al-Qaeda terrorists. But proponents of humanitarian intervention say genocidal countries could indeed threaten the United States because they often become breeding grounds for terrorism and disease.

"Sudan's chaos is destabilizing surrounding countries, especially Chad, which is an increasing source of oil for us," *New York Times* columnist Nicholas D. Kristof recently argued, adding that recent outbreaks of ebola virus and polio in Sudan could also spread to neighboring countries. [15]

In a recent example of how ethnic persecution can spread to surrounding countries, a Hutu rebel faction in Burundi on Aug. 13 shot or hacked to death at least 189 Tutsi refugees from neighboring Congo, who had fled to a refugee camp in Burundi to escape a civil war at home. [16]

Rwandan President Paul Kagame later said the massacre "proves . . . that there have been incidents that are ignored by the international community and the U.N. where people are being killed in eastern Congo, being targeted for who they are." [17]

U.N. officials were investigating whether the killings were perpetrated by Hutu insurgents from neighboring Rwanda, who fled to Congo after participating in the 1994 genocide against Rwanda's minority Tutsi ethnic group.

Some of President Bush's harshest critics have given his administration credit for publicly condemning the killings in Sudan — if late in the game. In early July, Powell visited Sudan and received pledges from Sudanese officials to disarm the militias. The continuing killings in late July spurred the United States to push the Security Council to threaten punitive measures if a 30-day deadline was not met. [18]

According to Power, 10,000 peacekeeping troops would be needed to stop the killing. [19] But with its forces stretched thin in Iraq, the United States has so far been unwilling to commit troops to Darfur. In July, the United States was instead urging countries in the African Union and Europe to help, according to Pierre-Richard Prosper, U.S. ambassador-at-large for war crimes issues. [20] "What about the Europeans, Spain — all those people not helping us in Iraq?" he asks. "Why don't they help us? We're pretty locked down in Iraq right now."

American and U.N. reliance on Sudan's government to pacify the same Arab militias they have been charged with arming means "the wolf will guard the henhouse," in the opinion of John Prendergast, who handled African affairs during the Clinton administration. Only an international military force backed by the United States and Europe is likely to succeed, he has suggested. [21]

Complicating matters, the current scandal over American soldiers' abuse of Iraqi prisoners may have fatally undermined the United States' moral credibility if it calls for international military action in Sudan, argues Holly Burkhalter, U.S. policy director for Physicians for Human Rights.

"The U.S. has no authority in the world right now. We couldn't get consensus on a lemonade stand much less United Nations intervention," says Burkhalter, who favors sending troops to protect the delivery of food, medicine and shelter to Sudanese refugees, many of them in unprotected camps inside Sudan.

Some critics blame international inaction on the fact that the Security Council must approve the mobilization of U.N. peacekeepers. Any one of the five permanent members — including nations like Russia and China, which have themselves been accused of human-rights abuses — can veto a resolution. "In this case, it's not the U.S. that's the spoiler as we were with Rwanda," Burkhalter notes.

This time, however, the Security Council has an option that was not available in 1994: It could seek action by the International Criminal Court (ICC) in the Hague, Netherlands, established in 1998 to try crimes against humanity. [22] But such a move would be "difficult for us to even contemplate supporting," Prosper says. Expressing concern that American peacekeepers abroad could be hauled before the court on politically motivated war-crimes charges, the Bush administration has refused to join the court.

Human-rights activists say the administration's opposition to the court reflects its overall disdain for international law. Similarly, some see the administration's choice of an Iraqi-led tribunal to try Saddam Hussein on charges of genocide as just another chance to reject international justice.

"You've got an effort to deliberately hold at arms length international involvement and expertise in the name of an Iraqi-led effort while behind the scenes you have a U.S.-motored effort," says Richard Dicker, director of the International Justice Program at Human Rights Watch.

Bush administration officials counter that the Iraqi court could prove to be an improvement over the tribunals the U.N. set up after the genocides in Rwanda and Yugoslavia in the early 1990s. Those tribunals were criticized for being slow to bring cases to trial and for being held outside the countries where the crimes occurred.

As the United States struggles over its roles in Sudan and Iraq, here are some of the debates taking place in Congress and the international arena:

Is the United States doing enough to stop and prevent genocide?

Sudan may be the test case for determining whether the United States learned any lessons from Rwanda. Some human-rights activists have criticized the United States for doing too little too late, waiting more than a year after the attacks began on Sudanese civilians to consider stronger steps. But as of August, despite continued killing and raping, the administration still was not contemplating military action, despite the urging of some human-rights groups. [23]

Human rights in Darfur started to deteriorate after two rebel groups attacked Sudanese troops in February 2003 over the government's failure to protect civilians there or to include Darfur in ongoing peace negotiations. [24] Some activists say the Bush administration's slowness to act shows the United States has not learned the main lesson of Rwanda — act early, before crimes escalate to genocide.

"We wouldn't be facing hundreds of thousands of deaths in western Sudan today if we'd learned enough," Burkhalter says.

Yet other analysts say Rwanda has sensitized the administration to the need for earlier action. The United States has taken "the strongest public stance" of any nation against the situation in Darfur, Human Rights Watch declared in May, amid what it called a "shameful" void in international response. [25] In April, Bush called on Sudan to stop the militia attacks.

"I condemn these atrocities, which are displacing hundreds of thousands of civilians, and I have expressed my views directly to President [Omar Hassan Ahmed al] Bashir," Bush said.

Author Power saw Bush's statement as an improvement over Rwanda. "President Bush called Bashir, which is one more phone call than Clinton made to Rwanda in 1994," she said. "At least he's not saying, 'We're not going to send troops, so let's stay mute,' which is what happened before. That's a version of progress." [26]

It's too early to say how much more Bush might be willing to do in Sudan. But some experts say American presidents only risk military intervention if they see some political payoff.

"We don't intervene because the political risks of not acting are less than the political risks of acting," says Jerry Fowler, staff director of the Committee on Conscience, which guides the genocide-prevention activities of the United States Holocaust Memorial Museum. For the first time in its history, the committee declared a "genocide emergency" on July 26, saying that genocide in Sudan "was imminent or actually happening." [27]

Other observers suggest that Americans tend to be far less sympathetic to genocide in remote continents like Africa, where black people are victims, than to similar events in Europe. In 1999, an American-backed NATO bombing campaign to end ethnic killing in Kosovo, in the former Yugoslavia, came after enormous media attention and political pressure, in contrast to scant press attention to Rwanda. [28]

Noting the handful of reporters covering a May 6 hearing on Darfur before the International Relations Committee, Rep. Donald M. Payne, D-N.J., an African-American, said, "Perhaps if this was in Europe, we'd have TV cameras all over the place. But since it's just another government in Africa, we don't."

The country's attitude toward foreign disasters has also been influenced by the Sept. 11, 2001, terrorist attacks, *New York Times* columnist James Traub argued recently. "One of the consequences of 9/11 may be that vital interests have come to seem so pressing that humanitarianism has become an unaffordable luxury," he suggested. [29]

During his first presidential campaign, President Bush said the "best interests of the United States" would guide his international policies, not the well-being of foreign nations. He indicated he would not send troops if another Rwanda occurred on his watch. In justifying the invasions of Iraq and Afghanistan, however, Bush has recently borrowed the moral arguments used by liberal humanitarian interventionists during the 1990s to push for military action in Rwanda and Bosnia.

Over the summer, Secretary of State Powell came under fire for refusing to call the Sudan killings genocide. "Why would we call it a genocide when the genocide definition has to meet certain legal tests?" he told National Public Radio on June 30. "And based on what we have seen, there were some indicators but there was certainly no full accounting of all indicators that lead to a legal definition of genocide. And that's the advice of my lawyers." [30]

On July 1, the liberal grass-roots group MoveOn.org urged its members to lobby the administration to declare genocide in Darfur: "Formally recognizing the genocide would enable the U.N. Security Council to authorize other countries, like Germany, France, and Spain, which don't have troops in Iraq, to help stop the killing in Sudan."

AFP Photo/Alessandro Abbonizio

Former Rwandan Prime Minister Jean Kambanda receives a life sentence in September 1998 for his role in the deaths of 800,000 Rwandans in 1994. The special U.N. tribunal in Tanzania was the first international court to convict anyone for genocide and the first to hold a head of government responsible.

Contrary to MoveOn's perception, declaring a genocide is not needed to trigger military action by either the United States or the United Nations under the international genocide convention. The U.N. Charter empowers the Security Council to order military forces abroad to protect civilians, under its mission of protecting peace and security, notes Dicker of Human Rights Watch.

However, the international convention does commit participating countries to undertake to "prevent and punish genocide," an obligation weighty enough that administration lawyers have advised presidents against using the term. American presidents mistakenly — and repeatedly — assume their response to genocide must be either military action or nothing at all, Power observes. [31]

President Bush demonstrated that political clout could be exerted in other ways with his call to Sudan's President al Bashir on April 7 to denounce the killings in Darfur. Anxious to have economic sanctions lifted, Sudan announced an immediate cease-fire. When U.S. attention waned, however, the killings resumed.

Often forgotten in the debate over stopping genocide is another obligation of nations under the international convention — to make genocidal leaders accountable for their crimes. Many experts see the International Criminal Court as a crucial ingredient in preventing future genocides.

"By leaving perpetrators of genocide unpunished, we only make genocide more possible, not less," says Juan E. Mendez, the U.N.'s recently appointed special adviser on the prevention of genocide.

But the United States has refused to join the court and has sought exemptions from the court's jurisdiction for U.S. troops and officials, drawing fire from human-rights groups.

"The U.S should be leading the effort to have the Security Council refer the situation in Darfur to the International Criminal Court," Dicker argues.

Modern Genocides vs. the Holocaust

The horrendous death toll from the Nazi Holocaust — 6 million Jews and another 5 million Gypsies, homosexuals and communists — prompted U.S. political leaders to vow "Never again."

And yet genocides continue with little effort to stop them. One reason — or excuse — may be that ethnic killings since World War II look very different from the Nazi atrocities. Genocide today usually occurs in the context of wars or armed rebellions, with killing occurring on both sides. This fueled the argument against intervening during the Bosnian war, when Muslims and Serbs were killing each other. "It's been easy to analogize [the Bosnia situation] to the Holocaust," President Bill Clinton's secretary of State, Warren Christopher, told the House Foreign Affairs Committee on May 18, 1993, "but I never heard of any genocide by the Jews against the German people."

Historian Frank Chalk, co-director of the Montreal Institute for Genocide and Human Rights Studies at Concordia University, observes, "The public has in its mind cases like that of the Holocaust, where you could never sustain the argument that the Jewish people were lethal enemies of the Nazis or that the killing was part of military necessity."

But when both the government and the armed opposition are using famine as a weapon to starve civilians on the opposing side, he adds, "It's very hard to tell the public that both sides are doing that, and then mobilize the pressure for intervention."

Rwanda is a case in point. In 1994, the Rwandan government was battling an armed rebellion by the Tutsi Rwandan Patriotic Front at the same time that it was exhorting Hutu mothers and fathers to machete their Tutsi neighbors. But Joyce Leader, the U.S. deputy chief of mission to Rwanda in 1994, says her State Department superiors had enough information to distinguish military from civilian killings.

"That was a clear situation where the violence could have been stopped if there was a show of force by the international community; but the U.S. didn't want to get involved in a civil war — even when the killing of Tutsis was separate from the Tutsi rebel group fighting with government forces," Leader says. "We did inform the higher-ups that different kinds of killings were occurring, but they initially didn't hear it or didn't want to hear it."

"The court was created to go after those who are behind the Janjaweed and the Sudanese military authorities in their campaign of ethnic cleansing in Darfur."

The Bush administration's opposition to the court makes that unlikely. (*See "At Issue," p. 701.*) Instead, the administration supports setting up ad hoc courts to punish perpetrators as each new genocide arises — as in Rwanda, Yugoslavia and most recently Iraq. But the court's advocates say ad hoc tribunals take too long to establish and are too expensive.

Ambassador Prosper disagrees. "The world has learned over the years and is more efficient in creating those mechanisms," he maintains. He notes that a tribunal set up in about 45 days in Sierra Leone last year indicted those bearing the greatest responsibility for atrocities committed during a civil war that ended in 2002.

The administration also objects to the international court because it does not come under Security Council jurisdiction. If it did, State Department officials argue, the Security Council would prevent politicized prosecutions by the court. Moreover, as an independent entity, the international court doesn't have the political clout to force a state to give up a genocide suspect, Prosper argues.

On June 23, however, the Bush administration backed down from its attempt to get the U.N. to exempt U.S. military personnel serving as U.N. peacekeepers from international court jurisdiction. Secretary-General Annan had criticized the move in light of the accusations that American soldiers in Iraq were torturing prisoners.

"The U.S. is engaging in torture and pretending that it's not," Burkhalter says. "It puts us in a uniquely bad position to be rallying around a moral cause." [32]

Is the U.N. doing enough to stop and prevent genocide?

Annan has spoken out forcefully against the killings in Darfur and sent a special envoy there this summer. The U.N. also surprised some critics on July 30 when the Security Council threatened punitive measures if Sudan did not disarm the Arab militias. But human-rights activists say the U.N. has a weak record on genocide, citing what happened in Rwanda.

Some critics blame the weak record on the structure of the Security Council, the only U.N. organ empowered to authorize military force. Any one of the five permanent members — the United States, England, France, China or Russia — on the 15-member body can block council action. Human-rights groups have accused Russia of genocidal abuses in Chechnya, and China of violating human rights in Tibet.

The qualifications for Security Council membership need to be changed to eliminate members who practice genocide, says William Pace, who heads the Coalition for the International Criminal Court. Likening the council to a fire department, he says: "We shouldn't have pyromaniacs on the Security Council."

The Security Council's makeup has been blamed for the U.N.'s paralysis on several occasions. In June, the council failed to pass a U.S.-backed resolution criticizing Sudan because of opposition from Pakistan and Algeria, the two Muslim countries currently on the council, and China. [33]

When the Clinton administration wanted the Security Council to charge Iraq's Hussein with war crimes, the opposition of a few permanent members — China, Russia and France — blocked any action, according to David J. Scheffer, then-U.S. ambassador-at-large for war-crimes issues. They were more interested in protecting their oil interests in Iraq, he has charged. [34]

In Rwanda, the council responded to the 1994 ethnic killings by reducing its peacekeeping force to just 270 soldiers — one-tenth its original size. Many believe a larger contingent could have saved lives. Author Power has argued that Annan, who then headed U.N. peacekeeping operations, had so internalized the paralysis governing the veto-prone Security Council that he did not even bother to ask for a council vote in response to an urgent cable from the U.N. troop commander in Rwanda, Romeo Dallaire, warning of an impending massacre. In the cable, Dallaire said he planned to seize arms that he had been informed were being assembled by local Hutu militias to exterminate Tutsi's. Annan's cable rejected the proposed arm raids telling him, "the United States in particular would not support such an aggressive interpretation of his mandate," Power writes. [35]

"We've acknowledged our responsibilities in failing the people of Rwanda," says U.N. spokesman Farhan Haq.

However, Mendez, the special adviser, notes when it comes to genocide, "In the last 10 years there hasn't been a veto on action by any of the permanent five members. I don't see it as having been the main reason the international community failed to act."

Rather, the council's inaction may stem from individual members' desire to avoid a veto, Mendez suggests. In the case of Kosovo, for example, the NATO countries decided not even to seek Security Council authorization for military intervention because they feared a veto, Mendez notes. Instead, they acted on their own, sending in a NATO force in 1999. "It seems to me the U.N. is sometimes scapegoated for the lack of will of some member states: If you don't want to do something, you can argue, 'I can't do it because there will be a veto,' " Mendez says.

The U.N. General Assembly has discussed proposals to abolish the council's veto power, but U.N. spokesman Haq says, "Frankly, I don't think it will be resolved any time quickly."

In April, Annan announced that he wanted his main legacy to be a U.N. better equipped to prevent genocide. Saying regrets over Rwanda had "dominated" his thoughts ever since, Annan announced a plan built around giving early warning of wars and ethnic conflicts that have the potential to escalate into genocide.

"One of the reasons for our failure in Rwanda was that beforehand, we did not face the fact that genocide was a real possibility," he said in Geneva. "And once it started, for too long we could not bring ourselves to recognize it or call it by name." [36]

In that spirit, Annan created a new post this year — special adviser on the prevention of genocide. In July he appointed Mendez, an Argentinean lawyer who was tortured in Argentine prisons as a political prisoner. He will collect information on threats of genocide and recommend action to the Security Council. Human-rights activists have hailed this reform. In the case of Rwanda, for example, information often did not rise to the highest levels of international attention because genocide was not a career priority for either bureaucrats or appointed officials, some argue.

Annan also has called for the use of military force to prevent future genocides. In 1999, he argued for "humanitarian intervention" to protect people subjected to human-rights abuses by their governments. In September 2003 he cited the need for criteria for "coercive" action — an obligation to intervene with force if necessary. However, it usually takes months for the U.N. to gather forces from nations willing to contribute troops. Although the idea of a rapid-reaction force was in the original U.N. Charter, fears about creating a world army blocked its creation. U.N. peacekeepers are only authorized to maintain peace, not stop wars. Humanitarian intervention also sounds similar to the Bush administration's pre-emptive action in Iraq, making some countries nervous that a U.N. intervention could rationalize an act of aggression. [37]

Yet the current system has led to some disasters. The U.N. contingent protecting Srebrenica during the Bosnian war was so small that it was overrun by a Bosnian Serb invasion in 1995. Within days, Bosnian Serbs separated 7,000 Muslim men and boys from their families and executed them.

Following highly critical reports in 1999 highlighting the U.N.'s failures in Srebrenica and Rwanda, Annan appointed a panel of experts to advise the U.N. Led by former Algerian Prime Minister Lakhder Brahimi, it recommended in 2000 the U.N. not enter trouble spots until it could put adequate troops on the ground. [38]

Over the past five years, the Security Council, at Annan's request, has authorized individual nations instead of the U.N. to lead multinational peacekeeping forces in several cases.

For example, last year, in an incident disturbingly reminiscent of Srebrenica, U.N. peacekeepers in Congo's eastern Ituri region found themselves outnumbered, lightly armed and unable to prevent horrifying tribal killings. The Security Council approved a mandate for a French-led multilateral force to restore order with some success. And last year the council authorized a U.S.-led force in Liberia and a French-led force in Ivory Coast. Each time, U.N. troops followed. The council authorized an Australian-led force in East Timor in 1999.

Will the International Criminal Court prevent genocide?

Opponents of the court, including Bush administration officials, argue that any dictator bent on massacring his own people is unlikely to pause at the thought of ICC prosecution.

They note, for example, that in 1995, two years after a U.N. tribunal was created to prosecute genocide in the former Yugoslavia, Bosnian Serb leaders seized Srebrenica and carried out the largest massacre in Europe in 50 years. The commander of the Bosnian Serb army, Ratko Mladic, had the 7,000 Bosnian Muslims executed shortly after it became clear the tribunal was about to indict him.

It's little surprise that "weak tribunals" like the Yugoslavia tribunal "do little to deter potential offenders," writes Gary Bass, an assistant professor of politics and international affairs at Princeton University. But Bass argues that "even more credible efforts" like the Allied military action against Nazi Germany "met with little success when trying to dissuade genocide." [39]

Cornell Professor of Government Jeremy Rabkin says the ICC won't do any better because it has no power to make arrests. "If there are mass atrocities, is it likely the perpetrator is going to stop because people call him names?" he asks. "The ICC has no army, no police."

Supporters of the court answer that a nation's own police force or army is expected to do the physical arresting, much as they do now for the tribunals.

But some of the most likely candidates for genocide prosecution are heads of governments like Sudan that have never ratified the underlying treaty. That means they are not under the court's jurisdiction unless the Security Council unanimously votes to refer their case to the court. "If you are a butcher, you are not going to ratify it," Rabkin asserts.

If the United States ratified the treaty, it might be inhibited from using force to stop future genocides for fear of being accused of war crimes, Rabkin maintains. Under that scenario, he speculates, "We could have been indicted for attacking Saddam Hussein, but Saddam [who did not ratify the treaty] couldn't have been indicted for butchering his own people."

Brett Schaefer, a fellow at the conservative Heritage Foundation, a Washington think tank, argues that the new court could actually encourage genocidal despots to stay in power indefinitely: "What is the incentive for these folks to step aside if they know they'll be dragged before the ICC and possibly sentenced to life in prison?"

But supporters argue the court is already having a positive effect, such as the ICC prosecutor's announcement in June that he would begin investigating killings in eastern Congo.

"Warlords put down their AK-47s, put on business suits, picked up attaché cases and moved into the Grand Hotel in Kinshasha in hopes of getting jobs in the new transitional government," says Human Rights Watch's Dicker. "I don't want to attribute it all to the ICC, but it was crystal clear to everyone there that the threat of prosecution by this international court had a chilling effect on those associated with the most serious crimes."

History is not necessarily a good guide to whether the prospect of punishment could deter genocidists because it's hardly ever been tried, says historian Ben Kiernan, director of the Yale Genocide Studies Program. The United States didn't even ratify the 1948 international convention against genocide until 1988, he points out. Until the 1990s, he says, most genocidal leaders "didn't even know the genocide convention existed."

Perhaps surprisingly, genocide doesn't just flare up spontaneously during ethnic conflicts but is usually carefully planned and documented. The planning for the Khmer Rouge killings of 2 million people in Cambodia in the late 1970s was revealed in tens of thousands of documents, Kiernan discovered, which he has posted on the Web. [40]

An international court "will hamstring the killing and in a practical sense deter it if [the leaders] know the paperwork can be publicized and used in court against them," Kiernan maintains.

In the United States, however, the heart of the debate is whether the U.S. should bow to an international legal body. The Bush administration believes that ratifying the treaty could put American troops and officials overseas at risk of politicized prosecution. The underlying treaty creates an institution of "unchecked power," and "threatens the sovereignty of the United States" through the court's claim of authority over American citizens, said Undersecretary of State for Political Affairs Marc Grossman. [41]

United States government officials and British Prime Minister Tony Blair have already been accused of war crimes for invading Iraq in communications sent to the court, critics observe. Sally Eberhardt, media liaison at the Coalition for the International Criminal Court (CICC), responds that like any court, the ICC doesn't act on every charge — especially unfounded ones. For example, she notes, the court received 906 communications from individuals and organizations in 85 countries between its opening on July 1, 2002, and June 1, 2004. Of these, the court has publicly announced serious consideration or action in only two cases — Uganda and the Democratic Republic of the Congo.

The court had no jurisdiction over the United States concerning Iraq, according to Eberhardt. But because Britain has ratified the treaty, "Tony Blair could very well be brought up on charges," the Heritage Foundation's Schaefer asserts.

Defenders of the court argue there are enough built-in safeguards to make that unlikely. The ICC only has jurisdiction over a ratifying country if it is unwilling or unable to carry out

Continued on p. 696

Chronology

1900s-1940s

Ottoman Turkey enters World War I and declares intention to empty the country of Christians. In run-up to World War II, Adolf Hitler plans to kill Jews and other "undesirables."

1915-1916
Turks kill 1 million Armenians.

1939-1945
Nazis kill 11 million people.

1945
Allies establish Nuremburg war-crimes tribunal.

1948
U.N. passes a genocide treaty.

1970s ***U.S. supports radical regime in Cambodia.***

1975-1979
Communist Khmer Rouge regime kills 2 million Cambodians.

1980s ***U.S. views Iraq as ally against fundamentalist Muslim Iran; U.S. continues aid as Saddam Hussein kills thousands during Kurdish rebellion.***

1987-1988
Hussein uses chemical weapons and execution to kill 100,000 Kurds.

1988
U.S. signs U.N. genocide convention.

1990s ***U.S. intervenes in genocide in Bosnia but not Rwanda; genocide trials begin.***

1992-1995
An estimated 200,000 predominantly Muslim Bosnians are killed.

1993
Yugoslav genocide tribunal created.

1994
An estimated 800,000 Rwandans are killed by civilians and soldiers.

1995
Bosnian Serbs invade Srebrenica, executing 7,000 Muslims in a day.

1998
U.N. convention agrees to create international genocide court.

March 24, 1999
NATO starts bombing Serbs persecuting Albanians in Kosovo.

May 24, 1999
U.N. tribunal indicts Serbian President Slobodan Milosevic for genocide.

2000s ***International tribunals punish Rwandan leaders, stall over Cambodia and Yugoslavia; human-rights groups seek action in Sudan.***

May 23, 2002
President Bush withdraws U.S. support for International Criminal Court (ICC).

Aug. 3, 2002
Bush signs American Servicemembers' Protection Act, withholding military aid from countries that refuse to give Americans immunity from ICC.

December 2002
Milosevic trial begins.

2003
U.N. and Cambodian leaders agree to create tribunal to try Khmer Rouge leaders, but political deadlock in Cambodia stalls action. . . . Arab militias begin attacks on black civilians in Sudan.

May 2, 2003
President Bush declares end of U.S. war in Iraq.

April 7, 2004
Bush condemns Sudan killings, urges Sudanese president to act.

June 24, 2004
Bush administration drops attempt in U.N. to exempt U.S. soldiers from International Criminal Court.

June 30, 2004
U.S. hands over Hussein to provisional government of Iraq. . . . Secretary of State Colin L. Powell declines to call Sudan killings "genocide."

July 2004
Iraqi tribunal charges Hussein with war crimes; report finds U.N. has failed to assure Serbian rights in Kosovo; U.N. tribunal convicts 19th Rwandan leader for role in 1994 genocide; Human Rights Watch charges Sudanese government is behind ethnic cleansing in Darfur; Security Council gives Sudan 30 days to disarm and punish the militias operating in Darfur.

Aug. 5, 2004
Preliminary State Department report documents "a consistent and widespread pattern of atrocities" in Darfur, but stops short of terming it genocide.

Aug. 10, 2004
Senate Majority Leader Bill Frist, R-Tenn., calls Darfur killings "genocide."

Continued from p. 694

a prosecution or investigation. The CICC's Pace says the provision is aimed at a country whose court system is a sham. In the case of the United States, "The belief that would ever be a decision of the judges at the ICC is a fantasy," Pace says, because ICC judges are from democratic countries. "These are not [Muammar el] Quaddafi's and Saddam Hussein's judges," he says.

Pace's argument assumes that the United States will agree with the international court over the need to prosecute an American for a given war-related crime. But Johns Hopkins University Professor of International Law Ruth Wedgwood argues the United States could have "good faith differences of opinion in war-making doctrine" with the court, thereby subjecting it to the court's jurisdiction.

Disagreement would likely arise over the principle of "proportionality," which requires troops to distinguish between military and civilian targets, she predicts. "The U.S. is hardly likely to prosecute its own pilots for faithfully carrying out the air attacks assigned to them," Wedgwood has written. [42]

Still, the prosecution of an American or a Brit remains politically unlikely given the court's dependence on the major democracies for support, says Federico Borello, an international lawyer and senior associate at the International Center for Transitional Justice in New York City. "If the court decides to prosecute Bush, Blair and [France's Jacques] Chiraq, that court is finished," he says.

And finally there are moral arguments. "No criminal-justice system provides perfect deterrence — but it would be astonishing to conclude that we should therefore abandon criminal justice altogether," says Diane F. Orentlicher, a professor of international law at American University's Washington College of Law.

Even Princeton's Bass, a critic of international courts, concludes tribunals are better than the most likely alternative — revenge. ■

BACKGROUND

Genocide Convention

Historically, the United States has not acted on foreign genocides until domestic political pressure made inaction untenable. Indeed, some historians argue that the United States has never stopped a genocide in progress.

Author Power contends the United States usually had sufficient information that the genocide was occurring but felt intervention would have competed with other national interests. [43]

In 1915, for example, Henry Morgenthau Sr., the U.S. ambassador to Turkey, urged Washington to condemn Turkey's deportation and slaughter of its Armenian minority, but the U.S. refused to act because it wanted to maintain its position of neutrality with the European powers. Some 1 million Armenians were murdered or died of disease and starvation during the genocide.

Government officials dismissed the warnings of Raphael Lemkin, a Polish Jew and international lawyer, who told them about Hitler's extermination plans beginning in the early 1940s. Before and during the United States' entry into the war, the Allies resisted calls to denounce Hitler's atrocities, open their doors to Europe's Jewry or bomb the tracks to Nazi concentration camps. The Germans exterminated 6 million Jews and 5 million other "undesirables," including Jehovah's Witnesses, Poles, gypsies, homosexuals and political opponents during World War II.

Lemkin, haunted by the death of his family under Hitler, coined the word "genocide." Through unrelenting lobbying, he persuaded the fledgling United Nations in 1948 to pass the Convention on the Prevention and Punishment of the Crime of Genocide.

The convention commits participating countries to "prevent and punish" the crime of genocide and empowers them to call upon an organ of the United Nations to take action.

However, "That may mean nothing more than sending a letter to the U.N. Secretary-General," notes the Holocaust museum's Fowler. Just as important, however, may be the political or moral obligations incurred in the public's eyes once the government uses the "genocide" label. "If we call something genocide, we can't be seen not to do anything about it," he says.

The convention includes only two specific legal obligations for participating nations: pass legislation providing effective penalties for persons guilty of genocide and grant extradition of those indicted for genocide. However, because of Senate concerns about threats to U.S. sovereignty, so many conditions were inserted into the convention, Power has contended, "that it carried next to no force" after it was finally ratified by the United States in 1988. [44]

Warnings Ignored

In the 1970s, a few American diplomats and journalists in Cambodia warned of the widespread atrocities being committed in Cambodian villages by radical Maoist communists known as the Khmer Rouge. But America's political left ridiculed such warnings as falling for anti-communist propaganda. For its part, the U. S. government was leery of intervening in Southeast Asia so soon after the trauma of the Vietnam War.

The Khmer Rouge would eventually persecute ethnic Vietnamese, ethnic Chinese, educated citizens, academics and Buddhist monks — anyone seen as a potential political enemy. Between 1975 and 1979, the Khmer regime of leader Pol Pot killed 2 million people. But the Carter administration maintained diplomatic relations with the regime

Ethnic Cleansing in Bosnia

Within days after the citizens of Bosnia voted to secede from Yugoslavia in March 1992, Bosnian Serb soldiers and militiamen began rounding up non-Serbs — Muslims and Croats — savagely beating them and often killing them. They also shelled the city of Sarajevo, destroying most Muslim and Croat cultural and religious sites. The Serbs called their actions "ethnic cleansing," a term reminiscent of the Nazi euphemism — "cleansing" — for eliminating the Jews.

Over the next three years, a few State Department diplomats and members of Congress tried to convince the White House to bomb the Serb ethnic cleansers and lift the U.S. arms embargo against the outgunned Bosnian Muslims. Between 1992 and 1995, some 200,000 Bosnians were killed.

Clinton administration officials described the conflict as an ancient, intractable ethnic conflict they were powerless to end. Only when that stance became politically impossible did President Bill Clinton finally intervene, argues journalist Samantha Power, who covered the Bosnian conflict and authored the 2002 book *A Problem from Hell: America and the Age of Genocide.*

On July 11, 1995, Bosnian Serb military leaders seized an area of Srebrenica protected by a small force of U.N. troops, who were unable to resist the invasion. The Bosnians rounded up and slaughtered 7,000 Muslim men and boys.

Sen. Bob Dole of Kansas, then a Republican presidential challenger, pushed legislation through Congress ending the arms embargo. His crusade got editorial support and nightly news coverage, making Clinton's non-interventionist policy politically embarrassing. In a telling scene on the White House putting green, Clinton shouted at his top national security advisers over the mounting political costs: "I'm getting creamed!" [1]

Clinton reversed course, and with his blessings NATO undertook a three-week bombing campaign on Aug. 30, 1995. By then, however, "Bosnia's genocide had been largely completed, and a multiethnic state destroyed," Power writes. Nevertheless, backed by a credible threat of force, the United States convinced the Serbs to stop shelling civilians. That November, the Clinton administration brokered a peace accord between the parties in Dayton, Ohio.

Clinton responded more aggressively when Yugoslav President Slobodan Milosevic began brutalizing ethnic Albanians, mostly Muslims, in the southern Serbian province of Kosovo in the mid-1990s. In 1996, embittered Kosovo Albanians formed the Kosovo Liberation Army, gunning down several Serbian policemen in 1998. The following year, avenging Serbians killed 3,000 Muslims and drove another 300,000 from their homes.

Beginning on March 24, 1999, NATO jets commanded by U.S. General Wesley Clark began a two-and-a-half month bombing campaign. This was "the first time in history the United States or its allies had intervened to head off a potential genocide," Power writes. [2]

She attributes Clinton's decision to bomb to embarrassment over Srebrenica, guilt over Rwanda and fear the fighting could expand into a wider European war.

Two months into NATO's bombing campaign, a U.N. war-crimes tribunal indicted Milosevic for crimes against humanity and war crimes committed in Kosovo. It was the first time a head of state had been charged during a war with violating international law. On June 3, 1999, Milosevic surrendered. On June 9, he signed an agreement forcing Serbian troops to leave Kosovo and permitting 50,000 NATO peacekeepers to enter it.

After numerous delays, Milosovic's trial finally started in February 2002; it is still continuing.

[1] Samantha Power, *A Problem from Hell* (2002), pp. 436-437.
[2] *Ibid.*

even after its overthrow, in large part because the United States wanted to maintain good relations with China, Pol Pot's prime backer.

In 1988, Sen. Claiborne Pell, D-R.I., chairman of the Senate Foreign Relations Committee, tried to cut off agricultural and manufacturing credits to Iraq in retaliation for Hussein's attempt in the late 1980s to wipe out Iraq's rural Kurds. A coalition of the Reagan White House and the farm lobby defeated the sanctions package because they wanted to maintain friendly ties with Hussein's regime, then seen as a bulwark against the fundamentalist Muslim government in Iran, and sell wheat and rice to Iraq. As a result, Hussein was receiving more that $1 billion in American financial support as his regime was killing 100,000 Kurds.

Three months before the genocide began against Rwanda's minority Tutsis in April 1994, the Canadian commander of the U.N. peacekeeping troops there, Romeo Dallaire, sought permission to round up the Hutu militias' machetes, warning they had built up the capacity to kill "up to 1,000" Tutsi "every 20 minutes." [45]

Denied permission by U.N. headquarters, Dallaire watched the killings helplessly as the United States led the effort to remove most of the troops under his command. Clinton wanted to avoid repeating the country's humiliation in Somalia only eight months before, in October 1993, when 18 American soldiers on a peacekeeping mission had been killed.

The Clinton administration also refused requests from human-rights activists to jam a Hutu radio station that was exhorting Hutus to kill their Tutsi neighbors. A Defense Department memo in May 1994 argued that the jamming would be too expensive — $8,500 per hour — and ineffective compared to military action. [46]

But in the wake of Somalia, the Clinton administration had a firm policy of avoiding humanitarian situations that could lead to military entanglements, and neither the White House nor the Pentagon wanted a military solution in Rwanda. Just as important was the lack of ringing phones at the White House. "You must make more noise," Clinton foreign policy adviser Anthony Lake told human-rights activists in April 1994, when they asked how they could influence U.S. policy on Rwanda. [47] At the time, Human Rights Watch had not yet developed the grass-roots base to lobby the government, and the press was paying scant attention to Rwanda.

As government-supported radio propaganda warned of a fabricated Tutsi invasion, men and women became killers. An estimated 800,000 Rwandans were killed in 100 days. [48]

The failure of the United States to act in Rwanda has led some scholars to question whether the genocide convention's emphasis on proving genocidal "intent" is counter-productive. Genocide "is absolutely the hardest crime to prove," notes Frank Chalk, co-director of Concordia University's Montreal Institute for Genocide and Human Rights Studies, because the "intent" to destroy a particular group is hard to establish. In addition, he says, "We need to intervene earlier. We can't wait until we have an open-and-shut case."

Chalk is among a group of scholars calling for a broad category of "atrocity crimes" that would carry the international obligation to intervene without carrying such a heavy burden of proof. Former Ambassador Scheffer said that would more likely have produced action in Rwanda and the Balkans, as well as in Iraq. [49]

"Atrocity crimes" would include crimes against humanity and war crimes, which are easier to prove, cover many of the same actions and carry penalties just as great as genocide, Chalk says. Deportations, terror raids and killings, for example, are all considered war crimes and often signal the preliminary stages of a genocide. ■

AFP Photo/Paul Vreeker

Former Yugoslav President Slobodan Milosevic is being tried on charges he masterminded the slaughter of thousands of non-Serb civilians in the 1990s. The U.N. tribunal in The Hague, Netherlands, so far has indicted 101 people for war crimes and convicted 34.

CURRENT SITUATION

Punishing Genocide

In November 1994, seven months after the Rwandan genocide started, the Security Council authorized a special tribunal. It handed down its first indictments a few months later, eventually becoming the first international court to convict anyone for genocide and the first to hold a head of government — Prime Minister Jean Kambanda — responsible.

By mid-July, 68 individuals had been arrested for war crimes or genocide in Rwanda, according to the State Department's Office of War Crimes Issues. Of those, 19 had been convicted, including, former Finance Minister Emmanuel Ndindabahizi, who was sentenced to life imprisonment in July. [50]

"It's a good success record," says Alison DesForges, a senior adviser at Human Rights Watch and an expert witness at the Rwanda tribunal. "They've got the real leadership here."

Indeed, the Rwanda tribunal has a far better track record than its counterpart in The Hague, created by the Security Council in 1993 for Yugoslav war crimes. The trial of Slobodan Milosevic, the former Yugoslav president and Serbian leader accused of masterminding the slaughter of non-Serb civilians in the 1990s, did not get started until February 2002 and may not finish. On July 5, Milosevic's poor health prompted judges to postpone the beginning of his defense and to question whether the trial could continue. [51]

The Yugoslav tribunal has indicted 101 people and convicted 34, according to the war-crimes office. However, the government of Serbia-Montenegro has not turned over some of the most important suspects; 21 remain at large, and several reportedly even give media interviews.

NATO has been trying for almost nine years to apprehend the region's most wanted war-crimes suspect, former Bosnian Serb Leader Radovan Karadzic. NATO leaders also have been trying to find former Bosnian Serb army commander Mladic. Both men face accusations that they ordered the Srebrenica slaughter in 1995. [52]

Under congressional legislation conditioning foreign aid on cooperation with the Yugoslav tribunal, Secretary of State Powell told Congress in March that Serbia and Montenegro had not cooperated in apprehending accused war criminals. As a result, aid to the government was halted as of March 31, 2004. [53]

Hussein Tribunal

The world's attention was fixed on Saddam Hussein on July 1, when the former Iraqi leader was charged with war crimes and crimes against humanity in a makeshift courtroom at U.S. military headquarters near the Baghdad airport.

Four days before U.S. soldiers pulled Hussein out of what President Bush called his "spider hole" in December 2003, Iraq's Governing Council had announced that an Iraqi Special Tribunal composed of five-judge panels would hold trials for crimes against humanity, war crimes and genocide committed between July 17, 1968, when Hussein's Baath Party consolidated power, and May 1, 2003, when President Bush declared an end to the war in Iraq.

The starting date for Hussein's trial is uncertain. Ambassador Prosper says there's tension between Iraqis, "who want this done quickly," and the United States, which wants due process preserved. "We don't want to see Iraqis sacrificing quality for speed," he says.

What Iraqis want is "a quick process to judge Saddam guilty and just kill him," said Salem Chalabi, general director of the Special Tribunal. [54]

Human-rights activists fault Iraq for being insufficiently public in forming the tribunal and for not including international lawyers and judges, as in the U.N.'s Yugoslavia and Rwanda tribunals. Some have criticized the heavy involvement of the United States, which has spent years preparing the case against Hussein and is supplying the investigators. [55]

"We're working hard to reduce the active involvement we have," Prosper says. "We'll be there to assist and advise; it needs to be Iraqi, and it needs to be transparent."

As for making the tribunal international, he says, "No one wants a Milosevic trial, which was too long in coming and too long in going — that's a problem with full-blown international tribunals."

The Iraqi tribunal is similar to so-called mixed tribunals, which combine both international and national law. Many human-rights activists consider them a second-best to international tribunals, saying they are too dependent on the whim of a country's leadership. However, it's too early to say how well this relatively new type of tribunal will work.

Another mixed tribunal, which is supposed to try the aging leaders of the Khmer Rouge, has yet to get started. U.N. and Cambodian officials agreed in June 2003 to create the court, but the arrangement requires ratification by the National Assembly. The assembly is basically not functioning because the main political parties remain deadlocked over their roles in the government.

Some human-rights groups have questioned the objectivity of Cambodian judges — who will compose the majority of the tribunal's judges — to try the Khmer Rouge leaders. They note that Prime Minister Hun Sen and other government leaders were themselves once in the Khmer Rouge. Moreover, many of the Khmer Rouge leaders are now in their seventies and could die before the trials get under way. [56]

International Criminal Court

The difficulty of launching tribunals, sometimes years after genocide occurs, spurred support for the ICC. In 1998, 160 nations voted to establish the court. The United States was one of only seven nations voting against the Rome Statute, the treaty creating the court. The other dissenters were China, Iraq, Libya, Yemen, Qatar and Israel.

Although President Clinton signed the treaty, he called it "fundamentally flawed" and did not send it to the Senate for ratification. Currently, 140 countries have signed the treaty and 94 have ratified it.

The Bush administration actively opposes the treaty, arguing that American troops and government officials overseas could be subjected to politically motivated charges. On May 6, 2002, the administration withdrew from the treaty. The administration later negotiated a Security Council resolution providing a one-year exemption from ICC jurisdiction for American troops operating in U.N. peacekeeping operations.

However, the administration recently withdrew its proposal for another one-year exemption following opposition from Secretary-General Annan, who cited the scandal over American soldiers' abuse of Iraqi prisoners and possible violations of the Geneva Convention on torture. [57]

Despite this setback, the Bush administration is pursuing another strategy to avoid the ICC: It is negotiating bilateral agreements with individual allies requiring them not to surrender American citizens to the ICC. As of mid-July, 91 countries had agreed, Ambassador Prosper says.

The Bush administration also has received congressional assistance in enforcing the bilateral treaties. Under the American Servicemembers' Protection Act, signed by Bush on Aug. 3, 2002, the United States must refuse military aid to nations that sign the ICC treaty — unless the administration grants them a waiver. Washington has been using the threat of withdrawing military aid to pressure countries to sign the bilateral agreements, according to human-rights activists.

The legislation also prohibits U.S. participation in peacekeeping activities unless immunity from the ICC

Healing Rwanda After the Genocide

How does a country heal after ordinary citizens pick up machetes to kill their neighbors by the hundreds of thousands? If the response of Rwanda's increasingly repressive government is any sign, the news is not good.

An international tribunal set up by the United Nations has convicted the leadership of Rwanda's former government of genocide and other war crimes for leading a three-month killing frenzy in 1994. An estimated 800,000 men, women and children from the country's Tutsi minority died at the hands of citizens and soldiers from the majority Hutu ethnic group.

But even though some Tutsi rebel soldiers committed revenge atrocities against Hutu civilians at the time, not one has been arrested or indicted by the international tribunal, because the current Tutsi-backed government refuses to cooperate, according to Alison DesForges, senior adviser to the Africa division of Human Rights Watch.

Rwanda's government, born of the rebel army that stopped the genocide, has also come under criticism for human-rights violations in its efforts to bring other Rwandans to justice for their part in the genocide.

Over the past 10 years, the number of Rwandans held in overcrowded prisons grew to more than 100,000, of which the government has tried fewer than 10,000. Many were arrested in arbitrary sweeps of young Hutu men, according to human-rights activists. Some have remained behind bars the entire time without trial or evidence. "It's enough [simply] for someone to point a finger," says Sara Rakita, a consultant on Africa to the Ford Foundation.

To speed up the trials, the government recently decided to adopt *gacaca*, a traditional form of village justice that deals with minor squabbles, such as the theft of a neighbor's cattle; conventional courts still deal with serious crimes like murder and rape.

But the *gacaca* system has yet to hold a single trial, even though a quarter-million local judges were elected two years ago. Rwanda's rural communities have had trouble gathering the 100-person quorum demanded to attend long hearings held on the open ground in broiling sun or pouring rain.

In addition, the *gacaca* system is aimed solely at Hutu perpetrators. DesForges says many Hutus ask, "Why participate in a system that to them is unbalanced?"

Human-rights activists also question the fairness of the *gacaca* system. DesForges cites a Hutu teacher who was hiding seven Tutsi children in his house during the 1994 massacre. Afraid that his Hutu relatives and neighbors would discover the children, he helped man the roadblock set up to capture and kill Tutsis. Every day, he took a chair to the barrier and read a book. "He didn't hold a weapon. Is that person guilty of genocide?" DesForges asks. Some communities have so defined it; others not, she says.

Personal rivalries and old hatreds may also hold more sway in local courts. "I saw a proceeding where an old man's Hutu sons accused him [of genocidal crimes] because the sons wanted to get the old man's land," DesForges says, even though his Tutsi in-laws defended him.

The government often points to efforts like *gacaca* as an effort to achieve "reconciliation" between Hutu and Tutsis. But it's becoming increasing difficult for citizens of Rwanda to speak freely, according to human-rights groups.

In July, the Rwandan parliament asked the government to dissolve the country's four leading human-rights groups on the grounds that they were harboring "genocidal" ideas. [1] The groups had opposed the government's plans for consolidating land holdings and had asked for justice for victims of the Rwanda Patriotic Front (RPF), the rebel Tutsi group that took power after the genocide in 1994. Last year, the government dissolved the one party that could have successfully contested the RPF in elections. "It's simply an attempt to eliminate dissent," says DesForges.

Ironically, the main lesson Rwanda's ruling party seems to have learned from the U.N.'s failure to stop the 1994 genocide is that the only way to ensure survival of the Tutsis is "to stay in power indefinitely," *The Economist* magazine recently opined. Some of the government's efforts to protect its vulnerable Tutsi minority echo disturbingly of 1994. "It was justified in invading the Congo to disperse [Hutu] genocidaires who were using the place as a base for attacks on Rwanda," the magazine noted, "but it surely did not have to kill 200,000 people in the process." [2]

1 Human Rights Watch press release, "Rwanda: Parliament Seeks to Abolish Rights Group," July 2, 2004.

2 "Rwanda, remembered: Lessons of a genocide," *The Economist*, March 27, 2004.

is guaranteed for American personnel. It authorizes the president to use "all means necessary and appropriate," presumably including military force, to free Americans detained by the ICC. [58]

Human Rights Watch has charged that the Bush campaign against the ICC has diluted U.S. efforts against genocide, such as leading NATO in its efforts to arrest war criminals in the Balkans or bringing war-crimes charges against Hussein. [59]

Even more disturbing, according to Human Rights Watch Executive Director Kenneth Roth, "A court that exempts the world's superpower risks losing its legitimacy." [60]

For his part, Ambassador Prosper responds that his office has taken a lead role in supporting the tribunals for Yugoslavia, Rwanda, Sierra Leone and Iraq. "Everyone knows we share the same values," he says. "The only difference is the mechanism."

Continued on p. 702

At Issue:

Should the U.S. support the International Criminal Court?

WILLIAM PACE
CONVENOR, COALITION FOR THE INTERNATIONAL CRIMINAL COURT

WRITTEN FOR *THE CQ RESEARCHER*, AUGUST 2004

yes

The United States' needless opposition to the International Criminal Court (ICC) — which is supported by nearly 100 democracies — has seriously damaged America's international standing at a time when the U.S. needs to regain the trust of its global partners. The opposition began with the Bush administration's "unsigning" of the court's treaty in May 2002 and continues with the withholding of much-needed aid to economically vulnerable countries that refuse to grant ICC immunity to U.S. personnel.

In light of the many protections built into the ICC treaty, U.S. claims that Americans will be targeted by politically motivated ICC investigations are without merit. Indeed, rather than superceding national jurisdiction, the court's mandate allows it to act *only* where an individual state is unwilling or unable to try alleged criminals itself. As long as the U.S. military and civil judicial systems are functioning, U.S. personnel will *never* face the ICC. Additionally, the ICC has no jurisdiction over acts committed in the U.S. However, U.S. nationals are already prohibited from committing murders, much less war crimes, in other nations. Therefore, to insist that U.S. sovereignty is threatened unless Americans are granted blanket immunity is dangerous nonsense.

Rather than being criticised via unfounded allegations, the ICC should be judged by its track record. In July 2003, the ICC prosecutor announced he would not consider complaints submitted against the United States and United Kingdom's actions in Iraq. The ICC has no jurisdiction over the U.S., and in the case of the U.K,. which is an ICC party, the court would have to first allow for British national jurisdiction to be invoked. Instead, the court has initiated investigations requested by the Democratic Republic of the Congo and Uganda, which have suffered some of the most atrocious human-rights abuses.

By rejecting global consensus on international justice — embodied in effective structures such as the ICC, the U.N. and the Geneva Conventions — the United States has eroded its moral authority and squandered its outstanding legacy of leadership in support of international law. Even when treaty ratification is prolonged, most U.S. administrations sign or engage constructively while new international laws are being tested. Following the revelations of torture at Abu Ghraib prison, U.S. attempts to thwart international law now look all the more unjustifiable.

The ICC provides justice for the victims of the world's greatest atrocities and works to deter future atrocities. At this critical moment in U.S. diplomatic history, the United States should see that rather than the phantom menace it envisions, the ICC can contribute significantly to U.S. national-security interests.

MARC GROSSMAN
UNDERSECRETARY OF STATE FOR POLITICAL AFFAIRS

FROM REMARKS TO THE CENTER FOR STRATEGIC AND INTERNATIONAL STUDIES, MAY 6, 2002

no

We believe the ICC undermines the role of the United Nations Security Council in maintaining international peace and security.

We believe in checks and balances. The Rome Statute creates a prosecutorial system that is an unchecked power. We believe that in order to be bound by a treaty, a state must be party to that treaty. The ICC asserts jurisdiction over citizens of states that have not ratified the treaty. This threatens U.S. sovereignty.

We believe that the ICC is built on a flawed foundation. These flaws leave it open for exploitation and politically motivated prosecutions.

President Bush has come to the conclusion that the United States can no longer be a party to this process. . . .

Like many of the nations that gathered in Rome in 1998 for the negotiations to create a permanent International Criminal Court, the United States arrived with the firm belief that those who perpetrate genocide, crimes against humanity, and war crimes must be held accountable — and that horrendous deeds must not go unpunished. But the International Criminal Court that emerged from the Rome negotiations . . . will not effectively advance these worthy goals.

First, we believe the ICC is an institution of unchecked power.

Second, the treaty approved in Rome dilutes the authority of the U.N. Security Council and departs from the system that the framers of the U.N. Charter envisioned.

Third, the treaty threatens the sovereignty of the United States. The court, as constituted today, claims the authority to detain and try American citizens, even through our democratically elected representatives have not agreed to be bound by the treaty.

Fourth, the current structure of the International Criminal Court undermines the democratic rights of our people and could erode the fundamental elements of the United Nations Charter, specifically the right to self defense.

Fifth, we believe that by putting U.S. officials, and our men and women in uniform, at risk of politicized prosecutions, the ICC will complicate U.S. military cooperation with many friends and allies who will now have a treaty obligation to hand over U.S. nationals to the court — even over U.S. objections. . . .

We must ensure that our soldiers and government officials are not exposed to the prospect of politicized prosecutions and investigations. Our president is committed to a robust American engagement in the world to defend freedom and defeat terror; we cannot permit the ICC to disrupt that vital mission.

Continued from p. 700

Crisis in Darfur

This summer, aid workers returned to the United States with mounting evidence of genocide in Sudan. On July 17, former Clinton official Prendergast reported seeing mass graves of people who had been killed execution-style, shot in the back of the head. Refugees from Darfur told him their villages had first been bombed by the Sudanese air force and then attacked by Janjaweed militiamen shooting automatic weapons. "There's still mass raping going on," he reported. [61]

Peacekeepers prepare to leave for the troubled Darfur region, in western Sudan, on Aug. 14, 2004. The Rwandan troops are part of a 300-man force being sent by the African Union to restore order following attacks by Arab militiamen on black African villages.

AFP Photo/Gianluigi Guercia

On July 30, the Security Council passed a U.S.-drafted resolution threatening sanctions if the Sudanese government failed to disarm and prosecute the marauding Janjaweed militias within 30 days. But in mid-August, with little more than two weeks to go to the Aug. 31 deadline, the violence had deepened amid increasing raids on refugee camps and rapes carried out by Sudanese forces and Arab militamen. [62] Since the beginning of the conflict in 2003, the number of deaths has been estimated at a minimum of 50,000, according to the United Nations, and over a million have fled their homes in Darfur. In the overcrowded refugee camps, epidemics and widespread starvation threatened. Aid officials estimate that up to a million people could die by year's end. [63]

Activists have urged the United States to persuade the Security Council to back up demands for an end to the killing with the threat of U.N. troops, but no such proposal had been made. The Sudanese government was rejecting all proposals for peacekeeping troops to protect civilians and angrily accused the United States of being after its oil and gold. While the African Union was sending a few hundred troops to protect monitors of the cease-fire, it was unclear whether it had either the political power or the practical ability to send more troops to protect civilians. [64]

And some columnists doubted the American public wanted to engage in a humanitarian crusade so soon after the war in Iraq. As *New York Times* writer Traub suggested on July 18, "perhaps the Bush administration's effort to repackage the immensely unpopular war in Iraq as a Wilsonian crusade to free a subject people has discredited the very principle of humanitarian intervention." [65]

The chaos in Iraq vividly demonstrated the difficulty of rebuilding a country following a military intervention. Another sign of the difficulty came in a report in July that faulted the U.N. and local authorities that have run Kosovo for the past five years for not protecting the province's Serbian minority. [66]

The report appeared four months after thousands of ethnic Albanians — the group Milosevic persecuted in the 1990s — began attacking Serbian communities. The U.N. mission there had been established after Yugoslav and Serbian forces, which had been accused of widespread atrocities, were forced out of Kosovo by the NATO bombing campaign. ■

OUTLOOK

U.S. Role?

Following genocide, human-rights activists often stress, the international community needs to help rebuild a country's courts and democratic institutions to prevent the kind of revenge violence seen in Kosovo recently. But critics of humanitarian intervention suggest that the United States is not cut out for such ventures, as witnessed by its recent experience in Iraq.

"People may say abstractly, 'Let's do it,' " Cornell University's Rabkin says, "but when they face casualties it's not so pretty. We're not committed enough; we're not willing to shell out what it costs."

Yet humanitarian crises are only likely to proliferate as global struggles over dwindling resources like water and arable land become more desperate. "There are over 200 conflicts around the world. Any of those could be at risk of escalating to mass violence or to genocide," Ambassador Joyce Leader, who was deputy chief of mission in Rwanda during the 1994 genocide, says.

The United States is already involved in 100 peacekeeping operations around the world, according to the State Department, not to mention its major commitment in Iraq. That level of activity raises the question of how many other places the country can afford to send troops.

Other countries have similar problems. "We're all very thin," said Gunther Altenburg, an assistant secretary-general at NATO, which has peacekeeping troops in Afghanistan and Kosovo. Most NATO members are facing budget cuts, he noted. "When the call comes" asking for peacekeeping troops, "maybe they're already in the Balkans or in Afghanistan," he said, and are unwilling or unable to commit more troops. [67]

Practical problems aside, will nations have the political will to stop and punish the next genocide?

After the major genocides of the past century, leaders around the world have publicly pledged "Never again!" repeatedly. That increased consciousness gives some experts hope that this time, the shame over past massacres will mobilize democratic governments around the world. Genocide scholar Chalk notes that Secretary Powell's visit to Darfur this summer is a striking contrast to the U.S. response to Rwanda's massacres in 1994, when not a single prominent government official visited the killing grounds. "I think these guys are really going to do something this time," he says hopefully.

Yale Professor Kiernan sees two conflicting trends in the 1990s. On the one hand, increased world concern about bringing genocidal leaders to justice resulted in concrete solutions — the establishment of tribunals. On the other hand, longstanding ethnic conflicts were exacerbated as the Soviet bloc and Cold War alignments disintegrated — leading to genocide in places like Bosnia. On the negative side, Kiernan suspects that leaders of genocides in countries like Rwanda were encouraged by the slow international response to Bosnia. But on balance, "The story of the '90s is one of increasing awareness of the criminality of genocide and action to punish if not deter it," Kiernan says.

While governments and experts often show great conviction concerning genocides past and future, the Holocaust museum's Fowler notes that "it's very hard to get people to talk about the present" — actual cases in which military power, soldiers' lives and political prestige are at stake.

And it seems likely that there will continue to be despotic leaders who think they can act with impunity, counting on the indecisiveness of the rest of the world — as some experts believe is occurring in Sudan right now.

A reminder of that threat is contained in Adolf Hitler's famous expression of cynicism in August 1939 as he planned his military campaign. Assuring his generals that the Nazis would have the last word in the history books, Hitler said, "Who today still speaks of the massacre of the Armenians?" A week later, he invaded Poland. [68] ■

Notes

[1] Nicholas D. Kristof, "Magboula's Brush with Genocide," *The New York Times*, June 23, 2004.

[2] Reuters, "Factbox: What's Happening in Western Sudan," Aug. 11, 2004.

[3] Marc Lacey, "Despite Appeals, Chaos Still Stalks the Sudanese," *The New York Times*, July 18, 2004, p. A1.

[4] See Human Rights Watch and Amnesty International Web sites: www.hrw.org and www.amnesty.org.

[5] U.N. News Service, "Sudan Must Act on Darfur in 30 Days or Face Measures, Security Council Warns," July 30,2004.

[6] The Associated Press, "US Congress Declares Genocide in Sudan," July 23, 2004, at www.cnn.com.

[7] *Ibid.*

[8] See Reuters, "France Says Peacekeepers May be Needed in Darfur," Aug. 13, 2004, and Reuters, "Sudan Accuses West of Seeking its Oil and Gold," Aug. 12, 2004.

[9] Marc Lacey, "In Darfur, Appalling Atrocity, but is That Genocide?" *The New York Times*, July 23, 2004, p. A3.

[10] For background on Rwanda, see the following *CQ Researcher* reports by David Masci: "United Nations and Global Security," Feb. 27, 2004, pp. 173-196; "Ethics of War," Dec. 13, 2002, pp. 1013-1037; "Famine in Africa," Nov. 8, 2002, pp. 921-944.

[11] Testimony of author Samantha Power before House International Relations Subcommittee on Africa, April 22, 2004.

[12] The Associated Press, "Clinton in Africa; Clinton's Painful Words Of Sorrow and Chagrin," *The New York Times*, March 26, 1998, p. A12.

[13] James C. McKinley Jr., "Annan Given Cold Shoulder By Officials In Rwanda, *The New York Times*, May 8, 1998, p. A9.

[14] House International Relations Committee hearings on Darfur, May 6, 2004.

[15] Nicholas D. Kristof, "Dithering as Others Die," *The New York Times*, June 26, 2004.

[16] The Associated Press, "At Least 180 Killed in Attack on a Refugee Camp in Burundi," *The New York Times*, Aug. 15, 2004, p. A10.

[17] *Ibid.*

[18] Warren Hoge, "At UN, U.S. Threatens Penalties on Sudan," *The New York Times*, July 23, 2004.

About the Author

Sarah Glazer is a New York freelancer who specializes in health, education and social-policy issues. Her articles have appeared in *The New York Times*, *The Washington Post*, *The Public Interest* and *Gender and Work*, a book of essays. Her recent *CQ Researcher* reports include "Increase in Autism" and "Mothers' Movement." She graduated from the University of Chicago with a B.A. in American history.

FOR MORE INFORMATION

Amnesty International, 322 Eighth Ave., New York, NY 10001; (212) 807-8400; www.amnesty.org. Campaigns for human rights worldwide.

Coalition for the International Criminal Court, 777 U.N. Plaza, New York, NY 10017; (212) 687-2176; www.iccnow.org. A network of 2,000 non-governmental organizations.

Genocide Watch, P.O. Box 809, Washington, DC 20044, (703) 448-0222; www.genocidewatch.org. Coordinates an international campaign to end genocide.

Human Rights Watch, 350 Fifth Ave., 34th Floor, New York, NY 10118-3299; (212) 290-4700; www.humanrightswatch.org. Investigates and exposes human-rights violations around the world.

"Kristof Responds" Web site. *New York Times* columnist Nicholas D. Kristof posts his columns, answers reader e-mail and puts new developments on Darfur here. http://forums.nytimes.com/top/opinion/readersopinions/forums/editorialsoped/opedcolumnists/kristofresponds/index.html.

Office of War Crimes Issues, U.S. Department of State; 2201 C St., N.W., Washington, DC 20520; www.state.gov/s/wci. Formulates administration policy in response to atrocities committed around the world.

U.S. Holocaust Memorial Museum Committee on Conscience, 100 Raoul Wallenberg Place, S.W., Washington, DC 20024; www.ushmm.org/conscience. Publicizes present-day threats of genocide.

Yale University Genocide Studies Program, P.O. Box 208206, New Haven, CT 06520-8206; www.yale.edu/gsp. Posts genocide information on its Web site.

[19] Testimony before House International Relations Committee, April 22, 2004.
[20] For background, see Kenneth Jost, "War Crimes," *The CQ Researcher*, July 7, 1995, pp. 585-608.
[21] John Prendergast, "Sudan's Ravines of Death," *The New York Times*, July 15, 2004.
[22] For background on International Criminal Court, see Masci, "Ethics of War," *op. cit.*; David Masci, "Torture," *The CQ Researcher*, April 18, 2003, pp. 345-368, and Kenneth Jost, "War Crimes," *The CQ Researcher*, July 7, 1995, pp. 585-608.
[23] On July 18, Amnesty International blamed the Sudanese government for the Darfur attacks. See "Sudan: Darfur: Rape as a Weapon of War," www.amnestyusa.org.
[24] Reuters, "Factbox," *op. cit.*
[25] Human Rights Watch, "Too Little, Too Late: Sudanese and International Response 2004," May 2004; www.hrw.org.
[26] Maggie Farley, "Annan Calls on Humanity to be Ready to Fight Genocide," *Los Angeles Times*, April 2, 2004.
[27] "Holocaust Museum Declares Genocide Emergency," July 26, 2004 at www.ushm.org/conscience/Sudan/Darfur.
[28] For background, see Mary H. Cooper, "Future of NATO," *The CQ Researcher*, Feb. 23, 2003, pp. 177-200.
[29] James Traub, "Never Again, No Longer?" *The New York Times Magazine*, July 18, 2004, pp. 17-18.
[30] Available at www.npr.org.
[31] Power testimony, *op. cit.*
[32] For background, see Masci, "Torture," *op. cit.*
[33] Traub, *op. cit.*, p. 17.
[34] Peter Landesman, "Who v. Saddam?" *The New York Times Magazine*, July 11, 2004, p. 34.
[35] Samantha Power, A *Problem From Hell: America and the Age of Genocide* (2002), pp. 343-344.
[36] Farley, *op. cit.*
[37] *Ibid.*
[38] U.N. press release, "Report of the Panel on U.N. Peace Operations," Aug. 23, 2000.
[39] Gary Bass, *Stay the Hand of Vengeance* (2000), pp. 294-295.
[40] See www.yale.edu/gsp.
[41] Address to Center for Strategic and International Studies, May 6, 2002.
[42] Ruth Wedgwood, "An International Criminal Court is Still a Bad Idea," *The Wall Street Journal*, April 15, 2002.
[43] Power, *op. cit.*
[44] *Ibid.*, p. xix.
[45] Power testimony, *op. cit.*
[46] Power, *op. cit.*, pp. 377-378.
[47] *Ibid.*, p. 377.
[48] James Waller, *Becoming Evil* (2002), pp. 184-185.
[49] Doug Saunders, "Is the Brutality in Sudan Genocide?" *Globeandmail.com*, June 19, 2004, p. A1.
[50] "World Briefings: Africa: Rwanda: Ex-Minister Jailed for Life," *The New York Times*, July 16, 2004.
[51] Reuters, "Poor Health of Milosevic Delays Trial," *The New York Times*, July 6, 2004.
[52] Nicholas Wood, "NATO Tries Again, to Capture War Suspect," *The New York Times*, June 22, 2004.
[53] State Department press release, "Serbia and Montenegro Certification," March 31, 2004; also see State Department Daily Briefing, March 31, 2004.
[54] Landesman, *op. cit.*, p. 36.
[55] *Ibid.*
[56] Alan Sipress, "Khmer Rouge Trials Stalled by Political Deadlock," *The Washington Post*, May 5, 2004, p. A24.
[57] For coverage, see Warren Hoge, "Annan Rebukes U.S. for Move to Give its Troops Immunity," *The New York Times*, June 18, 2004, and Warren Hoge, "US Drops Plan to Exempt GI's from UN Court," *The New York Times*, June 24, 2004, p. A1. Note: "UN Court" is a misnomer; the ICC is an independent entity.
[58] See Human Rights Watch, "The United States and the International Criminal Court," www.hrw.org.
[59] *Ibid.*
[60] Remarks to the International Criminal Court Assembly of State Parties, Sept. 9, 2002; www.iccnow.org.
[61] "Is Sudan's Crisis a Case of Genocide?" "Weekend Edition," National Public Radio, July 17, 2004, at www.npr.org.
[62] Nima Elbagir, "New Violence Deepens Darfur Crisis," Reuters, Aug. 11, 2004.
[63] Lacey, *op. cit.*
[64] Somini Sengupta, "Crisis in Sudan," *The New York Times*, Aug. 16, 2004, p. A8.
[65] Traub, *op. cit.*, pp. 17-18.
[66] Nicholas Wood, "Kosovo Report Criticizes Rights Progress by UN and Local Leaders," *The New York Times*, July 14, 2004.
[67] The symposium, "The Responsibility to Protect, The Capacity to Prevent and the Capacity to Intervene," was held May 5, 2004, at the Woodrow Wilson International Center for Scholars, Washington, D.C.
[68] Quoted in Power, *op. cit.*, p. 23.

Bibliography

Selected Sources

Books

Bass, Gary Jonathan, *Stay the Hand of Vengeance: The Politics of War Crimes Tribunals*, Princeton University Press, 2000.

An assistant professor of politics and international affairs at Princeton University finds that war-crimes tribunals — from Napoleon to Milosevic — rarely deter genocide, but are better than the alternative — revenge.

Gourevitch, Philip, *We Wish to Inform You That Tomorrow We Will Be Killed with Our Families*, Picador, 1998.

Reporter Gourevitch visits Rwanda in the aftermath of the genocide and in a series of compelling interviews with Rwandans on both sides of the killings explores the themes of guilt, vengeance and responsibility.

Kuperman, Alan J., *The Limits of Humanitarian Intervention: Genocide in Rwanda*, Brookings Institution Press, 2001.

Countering the conventional wisdom, an assistant professor of political science at the Johns Hopkins School of Advanced International Studies argues that the Rwandan genocide happened too fast for the West to have prevented it.

Melvern, Linda, *A People Betrayed: The Role of the West in Rwanda's Genocide*, Zed Books, 2004.

An investigative journalist details the Rwandan genocide in 1994, the history leading up to it and the role of the Western powers.

Mills, Nicolaus, and Kira Brunner, eds., *The New Killing Fields: Massacre and the Politics of Intervention*, Basic Books, 2002.

War reporters and scholars examine why — and why not — the United States has intervened in state-sponsored massacres in Cambodia, Yugoslavia, Rwanda and East Timor.

Power, Samantha, *A Problem from Hell: America and the Age of Genocide*, Perennial, 2002.

A former journalist in Bosnia argues that American presidents rarely consider it in their political interest to stop genocides even when they know about them.

Waller, James, *Becoming Evil: How Ordinary People Commit Genocide and Mass Killing*, Oxford University Press, 2002.

A psychologist concludes that ordinary people get involved in genocide and do not have to be evil monsters to do so.

Articles

Sengupta, Somini, "Death and Sorrow Stalk Sudanese Across Border," *The New York Times*, Aug. 20, 2004, p. A1.

A month after Sudan pledged to crack down on marauding militias, the killings continue and an epidemic threatened to sweep overcrowded refugee camps.

Landesman, Peter, "Who v. Saddam?" *The New York Times Magazine*, July 11, 2004, pp. 34-39.

The special court that will try Saddam Hussein and other Iraqis for genocide has come under fire from human-rights activists, who want more international participation, and Iraqis, who want swift justice.

Traub, James, "Never Again, No Longer?" *The New York Times Magazine*, July 18, 2004.

The war in Iraq and the Sept. 11, 2001, terrorist attacks have muddied the waters about the legitimacy of intervention, making Americans' vulnerability to terror their prime concern and humanitarian intervention "yesterday's problem."

Reports, Studies and Transcripts

Amnesty International, "Sudan: Darfur: Rape as a Weapon of War," July 19, 2004; www.amnestyusa.org.

Rape, abduction and sexual slavery of young girls is being used on a mass scale by Janjaweed Arab militiamen to intimidate black Sudanese, but Amnesty stops short of calling it genocide.

Public Broadcasting Service, "Frontline," "Ghosts of Rwanda," April 9, 2004; www.pbs.org/wgbh/pages/frontline/shows/ghosts.

The transcript of this documentary about the 1994 Rwandan genocide describes the bureaucratic paralysis that seized Washington and the United Nations during the killings; the Web site has links to related interviews and reports.

Human Rights Watch, "Leave No One to Tell the Story: Ten Years Later," April 1, 2004; http://www.hrw.org/reports/1999/rwanda.

This update of the Rwandan story 10 years after the genocide describes how ethnic slaughters have spilled into neighboring Burundi and the Congo and how Rwanda's Tutsi-dominated government has become increasingly repressive.

Human Rights Watch, "Darfur Destroyed," May 2004; http://www.hrw.org/reports/2004/sudan0504.

The human-rights group concludes that Sudan has been working hand in glove with the Janjaweed militias attacking villages in Darfur and urges the U.N. to step in.

The Next Step:

Additional Articles from Current Periodicals

Darfur

Booker, Salih, and Ann-Louise Colgan, "Genocide in Darfur," *The Nation*, July 12, 2004, p. 27.
Diplomats worry that intervention by outside powers might jeopardize a recent peace agreement.

Dixon, Robyn, and Mary Curtius, "Help Will Come Too Late for Western Sudan," *Los Angeles Times*, June 28, 2004, p. A5.
The U.S. Agency for International Development estimates 320,000 people will die as a result of the carnage in Darfur.

Fowler, Jerry, "In Sudan, Staring Genocide in the Face," *The Washington Post*, June 6, 2004, p. B2.
More than 1 million Darfurians are fleeing the Janjaweed, nomadic raiders who are backed by the Sudanese government.

Marquis, Christopher, and Marc Lacey, "Powell and Annan See Hints of Disaster in Sudan," *The New York Times*, July 1, 2004, p. A1.
The secretary of State and U.N. secretary-general visit a refugee camp in Darfur, and government forces fire on students.

Farley, Maggie, "U.N. Council OKs Sudan Resolution," *Los Angeles Times*, July 31, 2004, p. A3.
The U.N. Security Council calls on the Sudanese government to clamp down on militias in Darfur.

Sengupta, Somini, "Crisis in Sudan: Thorny Issues Underlying Carnage in Darfur Complicate World's Response," *The New York Times*, Aug. 16, 2004, p. A8.
Hostility among Sudan and its neighbors toward any Western intervention illustrates the tension between national sovereignty and humanitarian impulses.

Wax, Emily, "In Sudan, a 'Big Sheik' Roams Free," *The Washington Post*, July 18, 2004, p. A1.
"No one can wipe out an ethnicity," says a Janjaweed leader with a criminal past as he denies allegations of genocide.

International Law

Anderson, Kenneth, "Who Owns the Rules of War?" *The New York Times Magazine*, April 13, 2003, p. 38.
The United States and international organizations are locked in a fight about who has the right to interpret and administer the laws of war.

Frankel, Glenn, "Belgian War Crimes Law Undone by Its Global Reach," *The Washington Post*, Sept. 30, 2003, p. A1.
A far-reaching Belgian law results in cases against George H.W. Bush, Colin Powell and the Belgian foreign minister before it is repealed.

Lacey, Marc, "In Darfur, Appalling Atrocity, But Is That Genocide?" *The New York Times*, July 23, 2004, p. A3.
The Genocide Convention requires governments to prevent and punish genocide, but deciding what constitutes genocide is something few agree on.

Lynch, Colum, "European Countries Cut Deal to Protect Afghan Peacekeepers," *The Washington Post*, June 20, 2002, p. A15.
Cries of hypocrisy are raised when nations that support the International Criminal Court get waivers for their troops from the Afghan government.

The U.N. and Genocide

"In Annan and Chirac's Words: 'Fork in the Road' and 'Call a Summit'," *The New York Times*, Sept. 24, 2003, p. A13.
U.N. Secretary-General Annan calls for "a discussion on the criteria for an early authorization of coercive measures" to be used in critical situations, such as cases of genocide.

Farley, Maggie, "Annan Calls on Humanity to Be Ready to Fight Genocide," *Los Angeles Times*, April 8, 2004, p. A3.
Annan, who headed U.N. peacekeeping operations in 1994, envisages a global warning system to help identify potential instances of genocide.

Holbrooke, Richard, "How Did 'Never Again' Become Just Words?" *The Washington Post*, April 4, 2004, p. B2.
The U.N. is only the sum of its parts, and its decision not to intervene in Rwanda was a joint decision by the nations of the Security Council.

The U.S. and the ICC

Cassel, Doug, "With or Without U.S., World Court Will Debut," *The Chicago Tribune*, May 12, 2002, Perspective Section, p. 1.
A legal expert says the ICC would be unlikely to abuse its power against Americans and argues that the world needs the ICC.

Chertoff, Michael, "Justice Denied," *The Weekly Standard*, April 12-19, 2004.
A federal judge criticizes the overly broad power of the ICC and its prosecutors, which could pose a danger to American businessmen.

Kissinger, Henry, "The Pitfalls of Universal Jurisdiction," *Foreign Affairs*, July-August 2001, p. 86.
The former secretary of State argues a just end does not permit the application of unjust means and that the ICC is flawed by prosecutorial discretion without accountability.

Matthews, Mark, "U.S. Drops Bid to Exempt GIs From War Crimes Prosecution," *The Baltimore Sun*, June 24, 2004, p. 1A.
Tainted by the events at Abu Ghraib, American attempts to win renewed immunity from the ICC while engaged in U.N. missions end in failure.

Orme, William, "Peace Missions Are Put in Doubt," *Los Angeles Times*, July 3, 2002, p. A1.
The Bush administration threatens to block peacekeeping missions unless Americans win immunity from prosecution by the ICC.

Roth, Kenneth, "The Case for Universal Jurisdiction," *Foreign Affairs*, Sept.-Oct. 2001, p. 150.
The director of Human Rights Watch rebuts Kissinger's fears (see above), saying the abuses of the legal system he fears are unlikely.

Trying the Accused

Bass, Gary J., "Milosevic in the Hague," *Foreign Affairs*, May-June 2003, p. 82.
The trial's most important aspect will not be legal, but political — whether it will shame bystanders, comfort the injured and deter future crimes.

Brooke, James, "25 Years Later, Cambodia Proposes Trials of Khmer Leaders," *The New York Times*, Jan. 8, 2004, p. A11.
Most people would resent a foreign invasion, but many Cambodians credit their survival to a lengthy Vietnamese invasion that toppled the Khmer Rouge.

Harman, Danna, "A Woman on Trial for Rwanda's Massacre," *The Christian Science Monitor*, March 7, 2003, p. 9.
The first woman to be accused of genocide also allegedly personally encouraged Hutu gangs to select the prettiest Tutsi women and rape them.

Kitfield, James, *et al.*, "A Tyrant's Trial," *National Journal*, Dec. 20, 2003.
Saddam's trial could stir even more resentment among Arabs enraged by "victor's justice" imposed on their defeated hero, or it could signal a new beginning for Iraq and the Arab world.

LaFraniere, Sharon, "3 Rwandan Media Execs Convicted of Genocide," *The Chicago Tribune*, Dec. 4, 2003, News Section, p. 1.
The three defendants used their radio station and newspaper to incite the murder of Tutsis, even reading out individual license plate numbers and names.

Sennott, Charles, "Doubt Aired on Genocide Case Against Milosevic," *The Boston Globe*, Feb. 26, 2004, p. A22.
As the prosecution rests its case, chief prosecutor Carla del Ponte expresses doubts over whether the genocide charge will stick.

Intervention

Boot, Max, "Shouldering the Load, and the Rifle," *Los Angeles Times*, Feb. 26, 2004, p. B13.
A senior fellow at the Council on Foreign Relations calls for a standing U.N. force to deal with failed states and their humanitarian catastrophes.

Evans, Gareth, and Mahomed Sahnoun, "The Responsibility to Protect," *Foreign Affairs*, November-December 2002, p. 89.
A former Australian foreign minister and high-ranking U.N. diplomat lay out principles the Security Council could use for authorizing humanitarian interventions.

Scheffer, David, "Shameful Inaction in Face of Genocide," *Los Angeles Times*, April 5, 2004, p. B11.
A former U.S. ambassador calls on America to recognize genocide for what it is and to have the courage to act.

Citing *The CQ Researcher*

Sample formats for citing these reports in a bibliography include the ones listed below. Preferred styles and formats vary, so please check with your instructor or professor.

MLA Style

Jost, Kenneth. "Rethinking the Death Penalty." The CQ Researcher 16 Nov. 2001: 945-68.

APA Style

Jost, K. (2001, November 16). Rethinking the death penalty. *The CQ Researcher, 11*, 945-968.

Chicago Style

Jost, Kenneth. "Rethinking the Death Penalty." *CQ Researcher*, November 16, 2001, 945-968.

CQ Researcher

Published by CQ Press, a division of Congressional Quarterly Inc.

thecqresearcher.com

Dietary Supplements

Is tougher regulation needed to protect consumers?

Americans spend at least $16 billion a year on nearly 30,000 kinds of dietary supplements, most of which seem safe. But critics contend that 10 years after Congress relaxed federal regulation of supplements manufacturing, little is really known about the long-term effects of many supplements, particularly herbals. Moreover, despite a federal ban against the once-popular weight-loss aid ephedra, critics say at least a dozen other supplements may also pose serious health risks. They want legislation to toughen safety rules and more money spent on enforcement. Questions also have emerged about the efficacy of supplements. Apart from vitamins and minerals, the health benefits of most supplements are minimal to non-existent, critics say. But supplement manufacturers counter that critics exaggerate the problems within the industry, ignore studies that suggest positive health effects of supplements and are hostile to alternative health care in general.

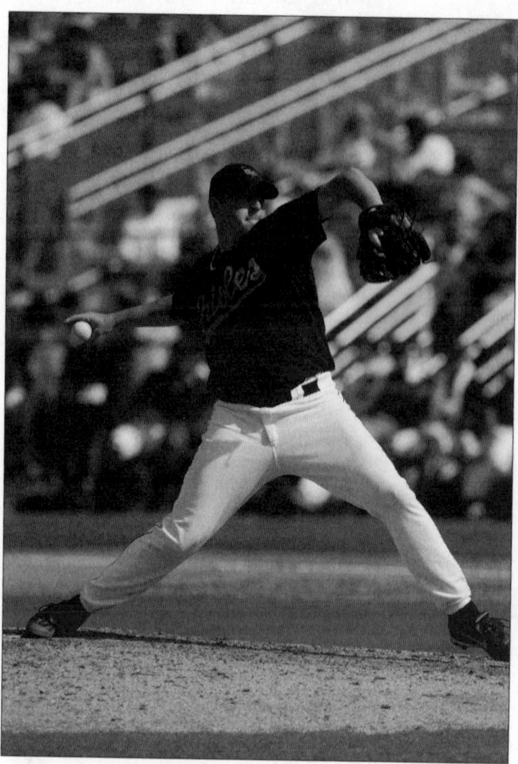

The sudden death of Baltimore Orioles pitcher Steve Bechler in 2003 was linked to his use of an ephedra-based stimulant.

INSIDE THIS REPORT

The CQ Researcher • Sept. 3, 2004 • www.thecqresearcher.com
Volume 14, Number 30 • Pages 709-732

CQ PRESS

RECIPIENT OF SOCIETY OF PROFESSIONAL JOURNALISTS AWARD FOR EXCELLENCE ◆ AMERICAN BAR ASSOCIATION SILVER GAVEL AWARD

THE ISSUES

BACKGROUND

CURRENT SITUATION

OUTLOOK

SIDEBARS AND GRAPHICS

FOR FURTHER RESEARCH

Cover: The sudden death of Baltimore Orioles pitcher Steve Bechler in 2003 was linked to his use of an ephedra-based stimulant he was taking for weight loss. (Getty Images/Eliot J. Schechter)

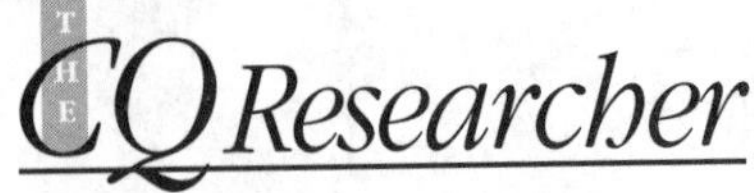

Sept. 3, 2004
Volume 14, Number 30

MANAGING EDITOR: Thomas J. Colin
ASSISTANT MANAGING EDITOR: Kathy Koch
ASSOCIATE EDITOR: Kenneth Jost
STAFF WRITERS: Mary H. Cooper, William Triplett
CONTRIBUTING WRITERS: Sarah Glazer, David Hatch, David Hosansky, Patrick Marshall, Tom Price, Jane Tanner
DESIGN/PRODUCTION EDITOR: Olu B. Davis
ASSISTANT EDITOR: Kenneth Lukas

CQ PRESS

A Division of Congressional Quarterly Inc.

SENIOR VICE PRESIDENT/GENERAL MANAGER: John A. Jenkins
DIRECTOR, LIBRARY PUBLISHING: Kathryn C. Suárez
DIRECTOR, EDITORIAL OPERATIONS: Ann Davies

CONGRESSIONAL QUARTERLY INC.

CHAIRMAN: Paul C. Tash
VICE CHAIRMAN: Andrew P. Corty
PRESIDENT AND PUBLISHER: Robert W. Merry

The CQ Researcher (ISSN 1056-2036) is printed on acid-free paper. Published weekly, except Jan. 2, April 9, July 2, July 9, Aug. 6, Aug. 13, Nov. 26 and Dec. 31, by CQ Press, a division of Congressional Quarterly Inc. Annual subscription rates for institutions start at $625. For pricing, call 1-800-834-9020, ext. 1906. To purchase a *CQ Researcher* report in print or electronic format (PDF), visit www.cqpress.com or call 866-427-7737. A single report is $10. Bulk purchase discounts and electronic-rights licensing are also available. Periodicals postage paid at Washington, D.C., and additional mailing offices. POSTMASTER: Send address changes to *The CQ Researcher*, 1255 22nd St., N.W., Suite 400, Washington, D.C. 20037.

Dietary Supplements

BY WILLIAM TRIPLETT

THE ISSUES

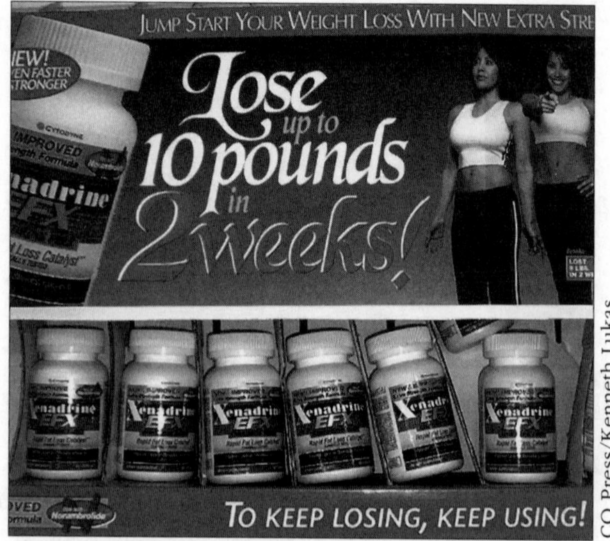

CQ Press/Kenneth Lukas

The manufacturer of the ephedra-containing stimulant linked to the death of baseball player Steve Bechler now makes ephedra-free products such as Xenadrine EFX. Health watchdogs worry about the safety of such dietary supplements, which are not required to undergo strict safety testing before being marketed.

About a year before Baltimore Orioles pitcher Steve Bechler's sudden death in 2003, U.S. airman Todd Lee, 21, was riding in the back seat of his mother's car in Oklahoma City. After a prolonged silence, his mother turned around to see if her son was alright. His hands were clenched and a tear seemed frozen on his face. He was dead. [1]

Lee's sudden death had one thing in common with Bechler's — both involved the dietary supplement ephedra, a popular weight-loss aid and energy booster. In the wake of more than 150 deaths linked to ephedra in the last 10 years, the supplement was finally banned last spring.

Yet some experts say diet supplements just as dangerous as ephedra are still on the market.

Some 30,000 different supplements are available in the United States today, and nearly 1,000 new ones enter the market each year. They range from run-of-the-mill vitamins and minerals to herbals, botanicals, homeopathic remedies, amino acids, enzymes and metabolites and come in a variety of forms — including tablets, capsules, softgels, gelcaps, liquids, powders, milkshakes and snackbars. [2] Some of the more popular supplements include echinacea, an herbal remedy for colds, and Zantrex-3, a pill for weight loss.

Millions of Americans take supplements and swear by their safety and benefits, like Rose Marie Pritts, a 63-year-old grandmother from Hawaii who takes a multivitamin and calcium. She recently completed her ninth 10K race in Hawaii. Each year she places closer to first, and is convinced she can win by the time she turns 80. "I feel like I'm 35," she said. [3]

Even ephedra continues to have enthusiastic fans among people who can "handle it," says Annette Dickinson, president of the Council for Responsible Nutrition (CRN), the principal lobbying group for the dietary supplements industry. "Millions of consumers used it and loved it and stockpiled it when they learned it was going away," she says.

Despite their popularity, little is known about the long-term health effects of most diet supplements. For example, ephedra had been on the market for years before reports began to surface of associated heart attacks, strokes, seizures and deaths. Industry critics blame the 10-year-old Dietary Supplement Health and Education Act, or DSHEA (often called "de-shay") for the problems.

"It is shocking . . . that dietary supplements are now subject to lower safety standards than are food additives and that consumers are provided with more information about the composition and nutritional value of a loaf of bread than about the ingredients and potential hazards of botanical medicines," Arthur Grollman, a professor of pharmacological sciences and medicine at the State University of New York, Stony Brook, told a congressional hearing last year on the law's effectiveness.

Designed to improve consumers' access to supplements, DSHEA loosened federal oversight of the supplements industry, largely exempting manufacturers from having to prove their products are safe. Instead, Congress classified dietary supplements the same as foods: Presumed safe unless the federal government proves otherwise. Most supplements appear to pose no significant risk, having been used safely in various forms for decades or even centuries.

Congressional efforts to leave the supplements industry largely unregulated coincided with Americans' growing interest in non-traditional ways to maintain good health. DSHEA also allowed supplement manufacturers to make certain health-benefit claims without submitting advance proof of effectiveness. Until then, only prescription-drug manufacturers had been allowed to make health-benefit claims about their products, but they were — and still are — required to first prove the drugs are effective.

As a result, a plethora of new products claim to do everything from "supporting" healthy cholesterol levels to improving memory. And sales are booming: 70 percent of Americans take supplements at least some of the time, and 40 to 50 percent take them regularly, according to the CRN. In the 10 years since the law was passed, the industry has grown from roughly

Fewer Deaths Linked to Ephedra

The banned supplement ephedra has been linked to 155 deaths in the last 10 years — far fewer than the number of deaths associated with food-borne illnesses or the use of prescription and common over-the-counter drugs in a single year.

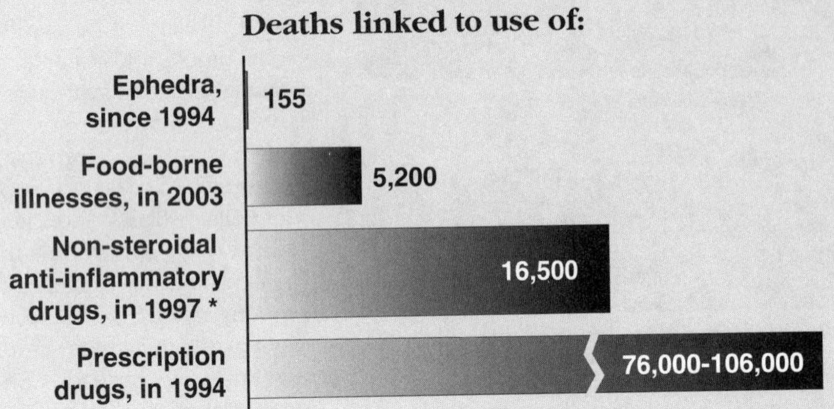

** Both over-the-counter and prescription types, such as aspirin, Motrin, Advil, Vioxx and Celebrex*

Sources: Food and Drug Administration; M. M. Wolfe, et al., *"Medical Progress: Gastrointestinal Toxicity of Nonsteroidal Antiinflammatory Drugs,"* The New England Journal of Medicine, *340:1888-1899 (1999); Jason Lazarou,* et al. *"Incidence of Adverse Drug Reactions in Hospitalized Patients: A Meta-analysis of Prospective Studies,"* Journal of the American Medical Association, *279:1200-1205 (1998); Centers for Disease Control and Prevention.*

$8 billion in annual sales to an estimated $16 billion to $19 billion. [4]

The industry is based largely in California and to some extent in Salt Lake City, Utah, hometown of powerful GOP Sen. Orrin G. Hatch, one of the industry's staunchest allies. Some companies adopt quasi-scientific sounding names, but have no laboratories or even offices, like Zoller Laboratories, maker of the popular diet-aid Zantrex-3. Critics say charlatans have penetrated the huge market, offering bogus claims about the beneficial properties of potentially unsafe products, mainly because of DSHEA. "The purpose of [DSHEA] was to remove the Food and Drug Administration [FDA] from having the ability to regulate the industry," says Marion Nestle, professor of nutrition and food studies at New York University (NYU) and author of *Food Politics: How the Food Industry Influences Nutrition and Health.* Supplement companies — led by the CRN, she says — were "extraordinarily successful" in getting DSHEA passed. "So now they're having to live with what they produced," she says. "And, of course, not all segments of the industry are as responsible as others."

But unscrupulous manufacturers and marketers exist in all industries, and they constitute only a tiny part of the supplements industry, say industry supporters. Most companies are reputable, they contend, claiming that critics and the media have blown the problems and risks of supplements completely out of proportion.

In addition to concerns about safety, questions have emerged about the efficacy of diet supplements. Apart from vitamins and minerals, the health benefits of almost all supplements are minimal to non-existent, say some critics. "This is an industry whose job it is to sell snake oil," Nestle says.

Industry representatives vehemently object, citing studies that have suggested positive effects of supplements such as saw palmetto on prostate health and St. John's wort on depression. Other studies found negligible to no positive effects for St. John's wort.

However, apart from vitamins and minerals, research into the effects of many nutrients and herbal products — and even foods — is a fairly recent phenomenon. "We used to not know that grapefruit juice interacts with drugs. Now we know it," says Michael McGuffin, president of the American Herbal Products Association (AHPA). "Who knows what other safety issues related to foods or drugs or dietary supplements or herbal ingredients we'll discover in the next 20 years?"

As for bogus claims, industry spokesmen point out that while manufacturers do not have to substantiate a claim before marketing a product, they must have evidence to back up any claim the FDA might question.

But the FDA has "never fully implemented or adequately enforced" the DSHEA requirements, David Seckman, executive director of the National Nutritional Foods Association (NNFA), told Congress last October. [5]

Critics say that's because Congress has never provided the FDA with enough enforcement funds. Since fiscal 2002, the first year the FDA received money specifically earmarked for DSHEA enforcement, Congress has appropriated a mere $500,000 annually for enforcement of the 1994 law.

Congress is considering tightening some DSHEA requirements and adding some new ones, as well as increasing funding for FDA enforcement. Another proposal would reclassify steroid precursors as controlled substances, making them available only through prescription. [6]

As the debate over dietary supplements continues, here are some of the major questions that have emerged:

Supplement Sales Rising Steadily

In the 10 years since Congress relaxed the federal regulations governing supplements, annual industry sales have more than doubled, to nearly $20 billion.

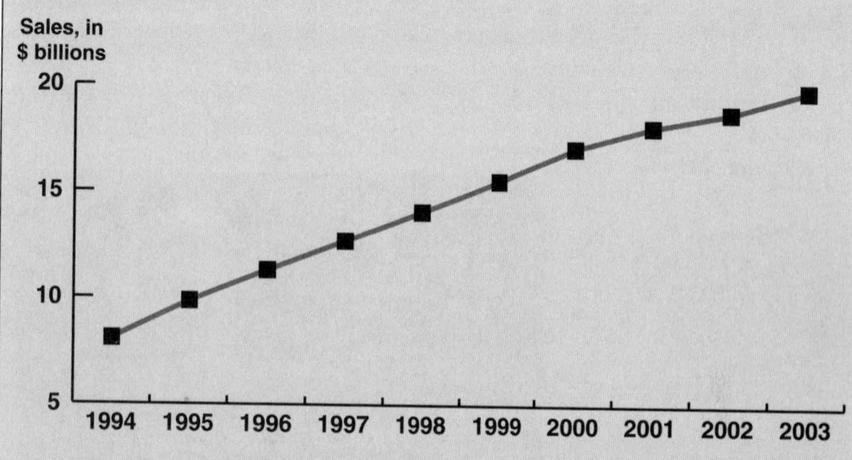

Source: Figures from 1994-2000 are from the FDA; figures for 2001-2003 are from the Nutrition Business Journal.

Are dietary supplements dangerous?

Some supplements — like Sigra, Stamina Rx, Y-Y, Spontane ES and Uroprin — are among the FDA's worst nightmares. Manufactured by NVE Pharmaceuticals Inc. in New Jersey and distributed by Hi-Tech Pharmaceuticals in Georgia, all were marketed as dietary supplements for sexual enhancement and obesity. Unbeknown to consumers, though, they also contained tadalafil, a controlled substance that is the active ingredient in Cialis, a prescription drug used to treat erectile dysfunction. Tadalafil can drastically lower blood pressure when combined with prescription drugs containing nitrates. [7]

Any product containing a controlled substance is considered a drug and thus subject to rigorous federal regulations regarding pre-market approval. But, despite FDA warnings in June 2003, Hi-Tech continued to label and sell the tadalafil-containing products as dietary supplements until a U.S. district court in September enjoined Hi-Tech from further distribution. Fortunately, no injuries or adverse reactions have been reported.

Beverly Hames of Beaverton, Ore., wasn't so lucky. In 1992, Hames was looking for a "safe, natural" treatment for chronic back pain. An acupuncturist gave her several herbal products. Four years later, facing kidney failure, Hames underwent a kidney transplant. [8] Analysis of the herbs later showed they contained aristolochic acid, a potent carcinogen associated with kidney failure and death.

The American Association of Poison Control Centers received 22,928 "adverse event" (bad reactions) reports involving herbal and homeopathic dietary supplements alone in 2002, according to Charles Bell, program director for Consumers Union, which publishes *Consumer Reports*. More than 8,800 of the events — nearly 40 percent — required treatment in health-care facilities. [9]

Representatives of the supplements industry say it is unfair to tar all supplement manufacturers and sellers with what they say are the actions of a few. "Those are the types of people who are on the fringes, but the main companies in the industry are not like that," says Seckman of the NNFA. "Whatever industry it is, there's always going to be that type of company doing things like that."

Compared to prescription medications or food-borne illnesses, Seckman says, "supplements are actually very safe." Every year more than 5,000 Americans are killed by some kind of food-borne illness, and common pain relievers like ibuprofen cause more than 17,000 deaths annually, he says. Moreover, prescription drugs kill 106,000 people a year — making them one of the five leading causes of death, he says.

However, critics of supplements note that because prescription and over-the-counter drugs are subject to stricter rules, they can be removed from the marketplace faster than dietary supplements. For example, the FDA removed the diet drug fen-phen within three months of learning that it was merely suspected in 33 cases of rare heart valvular disease. [10] Yet it took 155 deaths over 10 years before the FDA was able to get the supplement ephedra off the market. That's because the FDA, rather than the manufacturers, must prove safety risks for supplements — a laborious task — before it can remove supplements from the market.

Congress presumed that supplement ingredients already on the market at the time of DSHEA's enactment were safe. In Asia, ephedra has been used for centuries — for respiratory infections — in small doses and for relatively short periods. But ephedra proved Congress' presumption erroneous.

In America, ephedra became a popular weight-loss aid and energizer and was taken in larger doses and for longer periods than was customary in Asia — uses for which no research or even precedent existed. "These warranted oversight on the part of the industry, and I know we didn't do enough," Dickinson acknowledges. However, she and other industry representatives say the more important fact is that ephedra is now off the market.

Critics aren't impressed. First, they say, even one drug sold by a single company can cause a great deal of harm. "Take Metabolife, a manufacturer that had a big piece of the [ephedra] market before bad publicity hit," notes Ronald Davis, a physician and member of the American Medical Association's (AMA) Board of Trustees. According to the FDA, the San Diego company said it did not know of any adverse health effects or events associated with its products. In 2002, however, Metabolife admitted having received nearly 15,000 reports of adverse events over the previous five years. It was recently indicted for lying to the FDA. [11]

Moreover, a 2001 Department of Health and Human Services report estimated that less than 1 percent of adverse events are ever reported. [12]

Critics also say there are other dangers. For example, the May issue of *Consumer Reports* listed 12 dietary supplements it said warranted federal action. Among the so-called "dirty dozen" are aristolochia, the vine in which aristolochic acid naturally occurs; the steroid precursor androstenedione (andro), linked to increased cancer risk; and comfrey, chaparral, germander and kava, all of which are "known or likely causes of liver failure." [13]

"*Consumer Reports* is a biased adviser," counters McGuffin of AHPA. The FDA and the Federal Trade Commission already have issued warnings against many of the dozen listed, warnings the industry supports, he says. "The article didn't tell you everything."

"We stand by the list," responds Bell of Consumers Union. "The fact that the FDA has issued warnings doesn't mean that's sufficient means for dealing with them. They're still out there."

Others note that the ingredients of some supplements, particularly herbals, can vary in both quality and quantity — sometimes alarmingly. Manufacturers must ensure that their raw materials are untainted, but not all are successful. For instance, in 1998 health authorities found that 32 percent of Asian herbal medicines sold in California contained undeclared pharmaceuticals (such as ephedrine) or toxic levels of lead, mercury or arsenic.

"One hundred percent of those products were imported from China, Taiwan and Hong Kong," McGuffin says. "None were made in America, which is what's commonly sold in health foods stores." Stores in the Chinatown sections of U.S. cities are likely to have such herbals, "but not in the mass channels of retail trade. Those stores are selling American-made or finished goods," the vast majority of which, he says, are clean.

Supplements can also interact dangerously with prescription drugs or can even negate the effect of medicines, such as anti-cancer drugs. But supplement makers aren't required to warn of possible adverse interactions. For instance, St. John's wort induces enzymes that can seriously reduce the effectiveness of a crucial protease inhibitor commonly used to treat people infected with HIV.

The CRN's Dickinson points out, however, that while interactions are always a concern, "There are all kinds of interactions, including foods, some of which are contraindicated when you're taking certain medications."

CQ/Scott J. Ferrell

Dietary supplements are the third-largest industry in Utah, home of Republican Sen. Orrin G. Hatch, one of the industry's biggest supporters in Congress. Hatch co-authored the 1994 Dietary Supplement Health and Education Act, which consumer watchdog groups say weakened federal oversight over supplements. His son's lobbying firm has received substantial sums from the industry.

AHPA has recommended that member companies list known possible interactions on product labels. But as McGuffin notes, "There's no law saying dietary supplements must be absolutely free of any risk. If that were the law, we wouldn't sell anything — and your food supply would shrink markedly also."

Are dietary supplement manufacturers misleading the public?

"So potent it turns genetically average guys into supernatural studs no one messes with!"

"Medical evidence indicates it is an anti-inflammatory and antimicrobial agent and a possible treatment for asthma!"

"Take 3 capsules before bedtime. Watch the fat disappear!" [14]

Supplement manufacturers claim all sorts of benefits for their products; some of the claims adhere to federal restrictions better than others. But manufacturers cannot claim that dietary supplements "cure, prevent, treat or mitigate" a disease, according to Paul M. Coates, director of the Office of Dietary Supplements (ODS) at the National Institutes of Health (NIH). Only drugs, either prescription or over-the-counter, can make such claims.

However, if supplement manufacturers have supporting or suggestive evidence, they can say their products promote health or wellness. For example, a maker of garlic extract cannot say it reduces cholesterol, since no such proof exists. But "structure/function" statements — that something will improve some structure or function of the body, like "a diet that regularly includes garlic may help promote healthy heart function and regulate cholesterol levels" — are permissible.

Some experts say structure/function claims can evoke a false air of legitimacy or efficacy. As Coates points out, of the four verbs proscribed to the supplements industry — cure, prevent, treat and mitigate — "'prevent' is the challenge. The others are all clear. But what's disease prevention as opposed to health promotion?"

Often not knowing the difference, consumers are led to think that a supplement is more effective than it actually is, critics say. "People use dietary supplements most frequently because of the potential that they'll reduce their risk for chronic disease — cancer and heart disease, for example," Coates says. But only drugs, not dietary supplements, have been proven to do that.

With claims like gingko biloba "supports memory function," the supplements industry's most effective product is its artfully crafted marketing language, critics say. Nestle of New York University disparages "the cacophony of ridiculous health claims" made by the supplements industry because "as more research gets done, the less it shows" that diet supplements have any benefit, she says.

For example, the *Journal of the American Medical Association* (JAMA) recently reported that in a study of treating common colds among 400 children over a four-month period, a placebo worked just as well as echinacea. The U.S. military, always interested in keeping troops alert and energized, studied ginseng — long marketed as a natural energy booster — and found it useless. [15]

Making matters worse, critics say, are outright false and illegal claims that also proliferate. Until recently, for instance, Water Oz marketed dietary supplements it claimed were effective treatments for a variety of conditions, from AIDS to cancer. [16] Another supplements firm, Wildflower Pharmacal, was fined $2.4 million last December and convicted of three felonies for selling supplements that did not contain the amounts of numerous nutrients listed on the label. [17] And *JAMA* last year reported that more than half of 400 Internet sites were selling dietary supplements making illegal claims. [18]

"Consumers cannot be sure that what is written on the product label is what is actually in the bottle," Davis of the AMA told a congressional hearing on supplements last June. [19]

"Misleading claims are always a major problem for any industry," responds Dickinson of the CRN. "A misleading claim is an unfair trade practice. Companies trying to abide by the law aren't getting a fair shake if other companies are getting away with murder in terms of claiming to prevent or cure 400 diseases, as was the case with some of the coral calcium products a couple of years ago."

"But is it pervasive?" she asks. "Certainly on the edges, where companies . . . push the envelope. We may have more than our share of those companies in our industry, but we don't think that's typical of the mainstream."

According to the NNFA's Seckman, most dubious claims are made by Internet vendors, who, he says, account for only 1 percent of dietary supplement sales. In fact, the mainstream industry actively tries to marginalize or minimize the impact of charlatans, he says. When letters containing the deadly bacteria anthrax began arriving in Congress in 2001, NNFA members, suspecting attempts would be made online to cash in on public fear, drafted and released a joint statement saying no known natural or other kind of product exists that can cure anthrax.

"We knew people were going to get spammed about it," Seckman says, "and they certainly were."

Still, Internet sales remain extremely difficult to control. Teenagers, for example, have little trouble getting steroids or their precursors online. And buying supplements over the Internet can present dangerous health consequences if the products are adulterated. A recent Canadian study found that some herbal sex stimulants or aids were laced with the prescription drugs Viagra or Cialis, which can be toxic or fatal if taken with other drugs. [20]

Most Dangerous of 'The Dirty Dozen'

Among the dozen dietary supplements identified by Consumers Union (CU) as raising safety concerns, six have been linked to problems ranging from organ failure to being potential carcinogens. Supplement manufacturers say CU exaggerated the risks.

Regulatory Name (Common names)	Product Name	Dangers	Actions
Supplements Linked to Documented Cases of Organ Failure or Known to Have Carcinogenic Properties			
Aristolochic Acid (aristolochia, birthwort, birthwort, snakeroot, snakeweed, sangree root, sangrel, serpentary, serpentaria, asarum canadense, wild ginger)	Vaxa PMS-Ease, Shanghai Chinese Herbal Company Cardioflex (Guan Xin Su He Wan), Min Shan Brand Long Dan Xie Gan Wan	Potent human carcinogen; kidney failure, sometimes requiring transplant; deaths reported.	FDA warning to consumers and industry and import alert, in April 2001. Banned in seven European countries and Egypt, Japan and Venezuela.
Very Likely Hazardous (banned in some countries, FDA warning or adverse effects in studies)			
Comfrey (symphytum officinale, ass ear, black root, blackwort, bruisewort, consolidae radix, consound, gum plant, healing herb, knitback, knitbone, salsify, slippery root, symphytum radix, wallwort)	American Health & Herbs Ministry Asthma Formula 1040 Tincture	Abnormal liver function or damage, often irreversible; deaths reported.	FDA advised industry to remove from market, July 2001.

Sources: Consumer Reports, *May 2004, www.consumerreports.org/co/supplements*

Industry representatives and supporters also emphasize that when making structure/function claims, manufacturers must add the following disclaimer: "This statement has not been evaluated by the FDA. This product is not intended to diagnose, treat, cure, or prevent any disease." Consumers are immediately informed of the product's limitations.

But most people don't look at the "fine print," critics say. In fact, most people are misinformed on major issues involving dietary supplements. A nationwide 2002 Harris poll revealed that more than half the respondents believed — wrongly on all counts — that supplements couldn't be sold without government approval, that warnings of possible side effects had to appear on labels, and that claims of safety had to be backed by scientifically rigorous proof. [21]

"The federal government is awfully happy providing cautionary labels on drugs, on the assumption that people read those labels," says McGuffin of AHPA. "So it's hard for me to think that people's ability to read is somehow influenced by whether the information they're reading is associated with one class of consumer goods vs. another."

The industry is obligated to provide legible, understandable information that is relevant to the use of the goods, he says, adding, "We're not obliged to stand next to consumers and read it to them. Consumers have a responsibility, too."

Should the Dietary Supplement and Health Education Act of 1994 be strengthened?

The loopholes in DSHEA "are large enough to drive a tractor-trailer through," says Bell of Consumers Union. Other critics agree, noting that the law allows dietary supplements to be regulated essentially as foods, even though

Regulatory Name (Common names)	Product Name	Dangers	Actions
Androstenedione (4-androstene-3, 17-dione, andro, androstene)	AST Sports Science Andro100, SDI-Labs D-Bol Methadrostenol, Young Again Nutrients, Androstene Dione	Increased cancer risk, decrease in HDL cholesterol.	FDA warned 23 companies to stop manufacturing, marketing and distributing in March 2004. Banned by athletic associations.
Chaparral (larrea divaricata, creosote bush, greasewood, hediondilla, jarilla, larreastat)	Arizona Naturals Chaparral tablets, American Health & Herbs Ministry Bowel & Liver Cleanser Tincture, Larreacorp Ltd. Larreastat	Abnormal liver function or damage, often irreversible; deaths reported.	FDA warning to consumers in December 1992.
Germander (teucrium chamaedrys, wall germander, wild germander)	Nature's Wonderland Germander Herb Powder	Abnormal liver function or damage often irreversible; deaths reported.	Banned in France and Germany.
Kava (piper methysticum, ava, awa, gea, gi, intoxicating pepper, kao, kavain, kawa pfeffer, kew, long pepper, malohu, maluk, meruk, milik, rauschpfeffer, sakau, tonga, wurzelstock, yagona, yangona)	NutriBiotic Metarest, Ancient Herbs Relaxit, BlueBerry Matrix Herbal Stress Relief and Relaxation Enhancement Tablet	Abnormal liver function or damage, occasionally irreversible; deaths reported.	FDA warning to consumers in March 2002. Banned in Canada, Germany Singapore, South Africa and Switzerland.

supplement manufacturers increasingly claim their products provide health benefits similar to prescription drugs.

Moreover, among other things, the law does not require manufacturers to:

- Prove safety and benefit claims about their products; instead it forces the FDA to disprove manufacturers' claims.
- Register a complete business address and phone number with the FDA.
- List or disclose possible adverse interactions between supplements and medications.
- Notify the FDA of adverse-event reports (AERs) made by consumers.

"This single piece of legislation negated work conducted over decades to ensure that all medications were studied and evaluated for safety and efficacy before they reached the American public," SUNY's Grollman said. [22]

But the NNFA's Seckman strongly rejects the view that DSHEA weakened FDA authority over dietary supplements. If anything, "DSHEA provided the FDA . . . with increased enforcement powers," he said. [23]

Specifically, as spelled out in DSHEA, the FDA can:

- Seize dietary supplements that pose an "unreasonable or significant risk of illness or injury."
- Stop the sale of an entire class of supplements if they pose an imminent public health hazard.
- Refer for criminal action any company that sells a dietary supplement that is toxic or unsanitary.
- Obtain an injunction against the sale of a supplement that has false or unsubstantiated claims.

"Laws only work if their provisions are put into practice and the failure to abide by them is monitored and punished," Seckman said. [24] But in the

10 years since DSHEA was enacted, the FDA has yet to fully enforce the authority the law already confers on the agency, Seckman and other industry representatives argue.

Critics of DSHEA say the FDA is forced to meet an extraordinarily high burden of proof before it can take any of the actions cited by Seckman. "Because of the administrative process the agency has to go through, the FDA can only take on one fire at a time while the inferno is still raging," the AMA's Davis says.

The American Herbal Products Association maintains that when the FDA has exercised its authority, it has been extremely effective. For instance, under DSHEA the agency has premarket authority over any supplement containing an ingredient not available before 1994, when DSHEA was passed. Before selling anything with new ingredients, manufacturers must submit to the agency evidence supporting reasonable belief in the product's safety.

The FDA "is fulfilling its role as gatekeeper, ensuring that new dietary ingredients are safe prior to coming to market," says the AHPA, noting that the agency has rejected nearly half of the 145 notices of proposed new ingredients received since 1994. [25] "The idea that the FDA's hands are tied is false," AHPA's McGuffin says.

Both supporters and critics of the industry complain the FDA has not fulfilled another key DSHEA provision — developing a set of "good manufacturing practices" (GMPs) that would establish universal quality-control standards for the industry. Critics have often blamed the lack of GMPs for the fact that, for instance, eight of 21 brands of ginseng were found to contain unacceptable levels of pesticide residues. (Two brands contained more than 20 times the safe amount.) [26]

Bruce Silverglade, legal affairs director for the Center for Science in the Public Interest (CSPI), a consumer-advocacy organization, recently told a congressional hearing "some dietary supplements containing calcium made from bone meal and consumed by pregnant women have had high levels of lead that potentially could harm the fetus. Other supplements sold to improve brain function contain concentrated raw brain tissue from cows." [27] (Mad cow disease originates in bovine spinal and brain tissue.) Having GMPs, Silverglade said, could prevent these things. [28]

"It's not a trivial issue to develop GMPs, especially when you're starting from scratch," responds Barbara Schneeman, director of the FDA's Office of Nutritional Products, Labeling and Dietary Supplements. "We don't want to have to be changing the regulations frequently. I know it's frustrating about FDA, but it's also one of the strengths: we want to make sure that once something is published, it makes sense from our perspective and from the perspective of those who have to comply and from the public health perspective. That takes time."

Industry representatives say they welcome development of GMPs, but the industry opposed the FDA's first attempts at drafting guidelines in 1997, calling it too restrictive. The agency has since been revising its GMP proposal and hopes to publish it before the end of this year.

Meanwhile, the nongovernmental United States Pharmacopeia (USP) has set voluntary national quality standards, recognized by the FDA, for other-the-counter drugs and dietary supplements. It tests supplements for adherence to the standards; companies that comply can then use the USP seal of approval on their products. So far, less than 10 supplements manufacturers — representing 12 percent of the market — have joined the program.

Meanwhile, Congress is considering several bills that would boost the FDA's authority and enforcement capability. Currently, only $10 million of the FDA's $1.7 billion total budget is earmarked for all agency actions involving dietary supplements. Of that, only $500,000 is earmarked for enforcement, according to an agency spokesman.

A bill cosponsored by Sens. Hatch and Tom Harkin, D-Iowa, would increase FDA funding for enforcement of DSHEA by $20 million next year, rising to $65 million per year within five years. Another bill, introduced by Sen. Richard J. Durbin, D-Ill., would require manufacturers to report to the FDA any adverse reactions to supplements.

The major industry lobbying groups — AHPA, NNFA and CRN — say they would support an adverse-events reporting requirement and look forward to more aggressive policing by the FDA. But they oppose giving DSHEA more teeth.

"I don't think it's necessary," CRN's Dickinson says. "Many of the shortcomings people see in [the law] are because the FDA has only recently become truly active in implementing it."

Critics make a similar point about the industry's willingness to accept a slightly more regulated market. "Instead of condemning them for not offering it 10 years ago, I'll congratulate them for supporting it now," says the AMA's Davis. "But it's worth remembering that this might be a recent phenomenon that reflects the kind of regulatory pressure the industry is facing — congressional hearings and horrible publicity over ephedra. By looking responsible, they might be able to forestall some regulatory controls they don't like."

Furthermore, Davis testified in June, "Herbal remedies, anabolic steroids or their precursors and megadose vitamins are . . . substances that have biological activity in the human body, including side effects, and are really drugs. Thus the AMA believes these substances should be regulated as drugs by the FDA." [29]

However, Dickinson of the CRN maintains "reclassifying supplements as drugs would only serve to turn what is now an economically reasonable self-care choice into a less accessible, more expensive option." (*See "At Issue," p. 725.*) ■

Continued on p. 720

Chronology

19th Century

Amid industrialization, Americans begin recognizing links between nutrition and health; patent-medicine era reaches its zenith.

1866
Western Health Reform Institute, later renamed the Battle Creek Sanitarium, opens in Michigan.

Early-20th Century

Government recognizes need to regulate quality of foods and drugs.

1906
Congress passes Pure Food and Drug Act, requiring patent-medicine makers to disclose ingredients and rein in their more outrageous claims, slowly killing off the industry.

1920s-1930s

Wellness movement expands; manufacturers begin fortifying foods with vitamins and minerals; government tightens federal control over food and drugs.

1937
New liquid form of a drug commonly used to treat strep throat kills 137 children.

1938
Congress passes Food, Drug and Cosmetic Act, authorizing Food and Drug Administration (FDA) to regulate the manufacture and sale of all related products.

1940s

On the eve of World War II, the country boasts numerous fortified foods.

1941
Department of Agriculture issues first Recommended Daily Allowances for vitamins and minerals.

1950s

Postwar America indulges in prepackaged foods full of various additives; first fast-food chains emerge.

1958
Congress requires FDA to test some food additives for safety.

1960s

Environmental movement begins and counter-culture spurs resurgence of interest in natural and organic foods.

1962
Rachel Carson's *Silent Spring* draws attention to dangers of pesticides and other chemicals in food chain.

1970s

Studies increasingly link heart disease and diet, prompting the federal government to advise Americans to reduce fat and calories and eat more fruit, fiber and whole grains.

1980s

Grocery manufacturers try to capitalize on a growing desire for healthy diets.

1984
Circumventing federal regulations on health claims, Kellogg Co. advertises its All Bran cereal as part of a cancer-preventive diet. FDA tries unsuccessfully to stop the campaign; other manufacturers begin making similar claims.

1990s

Amid a growing demand for alternative medicine, dietary supplements become increasingly popular and receive favorable treatment from Congress.

1994
After intense industry lobbying, Congress passes Dietary Supplement Health and Education Act (DSHEA), which forces the FDA to no longer treat supplements like drugs.

2000s

Unscrupulous manufacturers proliferate in the largely unregulated dietary supplements market. Some supplement ingredients increasingly raise safety concerns.

April 2003
Autopsy concludes ephedra was a definite contributing factor in the sudden death of Major League Baseball pitcher Steve Bechler.

October 2003
Congress begins hearings on the effectiveness of DSHEA and whether the law needs to be strengthened.

April 2004
FDA bans ephedra due to links to 155 deaths.

The Martha Stewart of Snake Oil

We'll drink a, drink a, drink
To Lydia Pink a, Pink a, Pink
The savior of the human ra-hay-hayce
She invented a medicinal compound
Whose effects only God can replace. [1]

A lot of Americans sang that pub ditty in the late 19th century, if sales figures are any indication. Before she died in 1883, Massachusetts housewife Lydia E. Pinkham — the Martha Stewart and Ann Landers of her day — was grossing $300,000 a year from a homemade remedy she had been selling for less than a decade.

Pinkham, who became a fabulously wealthy icon of American businesswomen and feminism, offered help in a bottle to millions of women who swore by her "natural" cure-all, even though its many claimed benefits were never proven.

Although today's dietary supplements industry strongly denies it, some critics say the health benefits claimed by some supplement manufacturers often resemble those made by Pinkham and other early patent-medicine manufacturers. "This is an industry whose job it is to sell snake oil," says Marion Nestle, a professor of nutrition and food studies at New York University (NYU) and author of *Food Politics: How the Food Industry Influences Nutrition and Health.*

Pinkham began selling her homemade aches-and-pains remedy in 1875 to help tide the family over after several relatives died and her husband lost his real estate fortune. The remedy was based on an herbal-medication recipe her husband had once accepted as payment for a debt. Its primary ingredients were true unicorn root — from a yellow-flowered plant long used in alternative medicine — and pleurisy root, harvested from a type of milkweed.

Working from her kitchen, Pinkham began selling Lydia E. Pinkham's Vegetable Compound for $1 a bottle. An ardent abolitionist and an early supporter of women's rights, Pinkham targeted women as her primary customers, writing out handbills that read, "Only a woman can understand a woman's ills." Pinkham's product promised relief for cramps, gynecological complaints and even the "vapors" — a dizzy state caused by oxygen deprivation, usually produced by a too-tight corset.

Soon she was advertising in the Boston newspapers and demand was increasing, especially after her son Daniel advised her to include a picture of herself in the ad. Her pleasant, grandmotherly visage added a touch of the personal and homemade — qualities people feared were disappearing amid industrialization.

Sales soared. Soon production was moved into a facility where the Pinkhams brewed, bottled and shipped huge quantities. While the Vegetable Compound remained her staple, the Lydia Pinkham Medicine Co. branched out into all manner of women's issues. It published more than 100 booklets on such subjects as beauty tips, cooking, picnics and famous women, each plugging Pinkham's Vegetable Compound. Readers were encouraged to seek Pinkham's advice,

Continued from p. 718

BACKGROUND

'Snake Oil' Hucksters

American interest in consuming foods associated with good health largely began in the early 19th century, when the young nation slowly started to industrialize, creating a more urban and sedentary population. Cheap food, coupled with a less physical lifestyle, was already leaving many Americans obese, generating the first attempts to link diet to health.

The first major American nutrition pioneer was Sylvester Graham — originator of the Graham cracker. In the 1830s, he wrote and lectured against "gluttony," arguing that eating too much upset the body's natural digestive balance and could lead to a host of illnesses. [30] He also fought off Industrial Age efforts to process food. In particular, he warned against bread made with white flour, arguing that natural brown bread — containing bran — was much healthier.

Graham built a devoted following, and his ideas became part of a broader reform impulse sweeping the nation — from President Andrew Jackson's push for greater democracy to utopian, anti-industrialism schemes.

The 19th century also witnessed the rise of the patent-medicine phenomenon, in which legions of hucksters sold all manner of "natural" concoctions as cures or preventives for every ailment imaginable. Bonnore's Electro Magnetic Bathing Fluid, for example, claimed to cure cholera, neuralgia, epilepsy, scarlet fever, necrosis, mercurial eruptions, paralysis, hip diseases, chronic abscesses and "female complaints." [31]

Traveling "medicine shows" became notorious for selling so-called snake oils. They featured fast-talking salesmen in Conestoga wagons, flanked by bodybuilders claiming the elixir had given them great vigor and strength; shills in the crowd attested to the health benefits. The ingredients most often touted were natural herbs and potions. [32]

But patent medicines also often contained risky amounts of opium extracts, cocaine and grain alcohol — ingredients rarely touted or disclosed. Some even contained traces of uranium or radium. By the 20th century, death, severe injury or addiction from patent-medicine usage were common.

and so many letters poured in that the company created a Department of Advice. Soon, Pinkham was being called "the savior of her sex."

Claims for the compound grew bolder, appealing even to men as they touted more benefits for women: "A sure cure for PROLAPSUS UTERI, or falling of the womb, and all FEMALE WEAKNESSES including leucorrhoea, irregular and painful menstruation, inflammation and ulceration of the womb. . . . [F]or all weaknesses of the generative organs of either sex, it is second to no remedy that has ever been before the public, and for all diseases of the kidneys it is the GREATEST REMEDY IN THE WORLD." [2]

Eventually, the American Medical Association analyzed Pinkham's vegetable compound and found that up to 20 percent was alcohol — from a woman who espoused temperance — and the remainder was largely common vegetable extracts.

National Library of Medicine

A healthy child is featured in one of Lydia Pinkham's many ads for her popular alcohol-containing concoction.

Passage of the Pure Food and Drug Act in 1906, which forced patent-medicine makers to disclose more information about ingredients and reduce excessive claims, ended the company's staggering success.

Today's dietary supplement industry bristles at the suggestion it was spawned by patent medicines. "The origins of the dietary supplements industry is not with patent medicine but basically with health foods, natural foods, organic foods, the wellness movement," says Annette Dickinson, president of the Council for Responsible Nutrition, an industry trade group. "Patent medicines were more like over-the-counter drugs."

Still, she acknowledges that "there is crossover, then and now. At some end of the spectrum, natural drugs are not that different from dietary supplements derived from natural compounds."

[1] Song lyrics and background information are drawn from http://womenshistory.about.com.
[2] *Ibid.*

Opium-based preparations also were widely available in dozens of over-the-counter elixirs and products, ranging from cough medicines to hemorrhoid balms and nasal sprays. Some 250,000 Americans were addicted to either opiates or cocaine. [33]

Yet patent medicines were perfectly legal, and the single, largest source of newspaper ad revenue. After decades of largely ignoring the patent-medicine scam, however, muckraking journalists eventually began reporting on it, and did much to change the laws.

The most influential exposé was Samuel Hopkins Adams' "The Great American Fraud," published in 1905 in *Collier's Weekly*. Adams' article — as well as publication of Upton Sinclair's *The Jungle*, exposing conditions in the meat -packing industry — prompted the federal government to pass the Pure Food and Drug Act of 1906. It established the Bureau of Chemistry, the forerunner of the FDA, which forced manufacturers to disclose all ingredients and stop making fraudulent claims, effectively shutting down the entire patent-medicine industry.

However, Congress avoided strict regulation of the contents of medicines until 1937, when a new liquid version of sulfanilamide, used to treat streptococcal infections, killed 137 children. The deaths were so horrible that one mother was moved to describe her daughter's suffering in a letter to President Franklin D. Roosevelt: "Even the memory of her is mixed with sorrow, for we can see her little body tossing to and fro and hear that little voice screaming with pain, and it seems as though it would drive me insane." [34]

A year later, Congress passed the Food, Drug and Cosmetic Act, which finally allowed the FDA to fully regulate the contents and claims of foods and drugs. For the next three decades, the agency drew a distinct line between foods and drugs, defining the latter as any substance demonstrably effective in curing or treating a disease. Upon receiving such proof, the FDA would approve the drug for market. Manufacturers of foods — which included vitamins, minerals and herbs — could not claim curative or healing effects without facing severe regulatory action from the FDA.

Nutrition Worries

During the Gilded Age at the end of the 19th century, excess in just about everything — including eating — became a way of life for the affluent. But by the 1920s attitudes toward nutrition and health had become almost faddish reincarnations of Graham's ideas and values.

In Michigan, physician John Harvey Kellogg founded the Battle Creek Sanitarium, one of the nation's earliest and most renowned health spas. The Seventh-Day Adventists — for whom healthy eating is a religious tenet — originally launched the sanitarium, which novelist T. Coraghessan Boyle spoofed in his 1993 best-seller The Road to Wellville. The facility attracted such notables as Amelia Earhart, George Bernard Shaw, J. C. Penney, President William Howard Taft and Thomas A. Edison. [35]

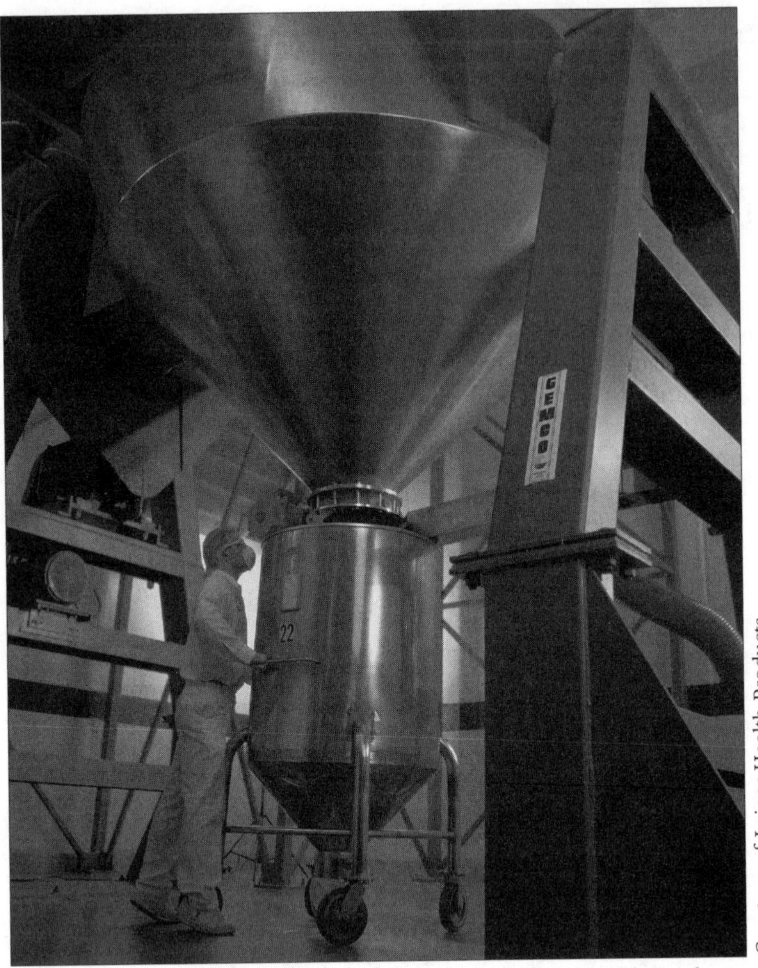

Courtesy of Leiner Health Products

An employee mixes dry powder in a blender at Leiner Health Products in Garden Grove, Calif. Leiner has voluntarily adopted so-called good manufacturing practices. The Food and Drug Administration is developing mandatory, industry-wide manufacturing standards after lax production practices at some other firms led to contaminated supplements.

Among other unconventional alternative therapies, Kellogg developed grain and nut products for the vegetarian diet of his sanitarium patients. His brother, W. K. Kellogg, later introduced Corn Flakes cereal to the meat-and-eggs-laden American breakfast table, and sanitarium patient C. W. Post would later make a fortune with his breakfast cereals.

The early 20th century also witnessed the discovery of vitamins. "For the first time, we started to realize that eating food meant more than filling our bellies," observed Manfred Kroger, emeritus professor of food science at Pennsylvania State University. "We began to understand the importance of nutrition." [36]

Food manufacturers quickly recognized the marketing value of vitamins and began "fortifying" their products — including milk, bread and cereals — with various vitamins and minerals. By the late 1930s, Americans could also buy vitamin supplements in pill form.

In 1941, on the eve of America's entry into World War II, the U.S. military discovered many of its young recruits were malnourished, and the U.S. Department of Agriculture began issuing its first Recommended Daily Allowances of key vitamins and minerals. But after the war, the country was in a mood to celebrate, not worry about nutrition. Thousands of new mass-produced foods flooded the market — including prepackaged, processed, usually sugary desserts and cookies — designed to taste and look good. Hundreds of new food additives, preservatives and dyes were developed to meet the need for brightly colored and tasty food.

It also was the era of malt shops and new fast-food chains. Americans had more disposable income than ever before, making eating out widely affordable. For many years after the war, the nutritional value of food was an afterthought — if a thought at all.

Then in 1958 Congress required the FDA to test food additives for safety. The publication of *Silent Spring* in 1962 brought the issue of food safety to the public's attention. Although Rachel Carson's landmark exposé dealt with the harmfulness of the insecticide DDT to the bird population, it also fostered greater awareness of the potential danger of synthetic chemicals to the nation's food supply.

Around the same time, reports linking cholesterol to heart disease began to appear, followed by similar warnings about saturated fat. For the first time in years, large numbers of Americans began worrying about what they were eating.

The 1960s also witnessed a popular return to equating food with identity. The decade's counterculture movement preferred natural foods to processed foods as part of an overall rejection of corporate goods and "the Establishment" in general. Often living on communal farms, hippies developed a philosophy of nutrition that emphasized organic farming, vegetarianism and natural foods.

Meanwhile, new information connecting diet to disease and disease-prevention began to be widely disseminated in best-sellers like Adelle Davis' *Let's Eat Right to Keep Fit* (originally published in 1954 but revised and issued in paperback 16 years later).

Nutritionist Davis explained what foods and, by extension, what vitamins and minerals readers needed to maintain good health. In particular, she showed how the typical American diet — high in sugar and fat — was nutritionally inadequate. Magazines devoted to diet and health were also founded in the 1970s and continue to flourish, such as *Natural Health* and *Nutrition Action Healthletter.*

Health Food Claims

In the late 1970s, spurred by several congressional health-and-nutrition reports, the National Academy of Sciences and other research groups, the federal government again advised Americans to reduce calories, fat and salt in their diets and add more fruits, vegetables and whole grains.

Sensing a new marketing opportunity, the food industry sought to link its products to healthy diets. However, the FDA still maintained its strict policy that only drugs, upon proving their efficacy and safety, could claim curative or treatment qualities.

The Kellogg Co. was the first to test the FDA limits on food claims with a 1984 marketing campaign for its All-Bran cereal. Citing a recent National Cancer Institute (NCI) recommendation that people eat high-fiber foods, cereal boxes proclaimed: "A growing body of evidence says high-fiber foods are important to good health. That's why a healthy diet includes high-fiber foods like bran cereals." [37]

Avoiding any claim to cure or treat a disease, the copy had artfully implied an association between eating All-Bran and cancer prevention. In the campaign's first six months, All-Bran increased market share by a staggering 47 percent, sending other food manufacturers into a mad scramble to come up with similar claims.

Kellogg had not submitted the copy to the FDA prior to putting the cereal on the market, as required. The agency tried to stop the campaign, but according to NYU's Nestle, the attempt failed largely because it was "inconsistent with the deregulatory ideology of the administration of President Ronald Reagan." [38]

Moreover, the NCI — like the FDA, part of the Department of Health and Human Services — didn't object to the campaign because it did not say that NCI endorsed the product. And the Federal Trade Commission, which monitors truth in advertising, heartily endorsed the campaign. Lacking any support, the FDA essentially agreed to allow the food industry to put similar, limited health claims on its products.

Not so, however, for dietary supplements, which the FDA asserted were more akin to drugs than foods.

The supplements industry — led chiefly by the influential Council for Responsible Nutrition — launched an aggressive movement to be allowed to make similar claims. A decade later Congress passed DSHEA, giving the industry most of what it wanted.

According to the council's Dickinson, DSHEA was needed to counter decades of FDA hostility toward supplements. For example, the agency had twice tried to limit the amount of vitamins Americans should be allowed to take — once in the 1960s and again in the '70s. Both times, courts prevented the agency from instituting such rules. In the early '90s, she says, the agency appeared likely to try instituting similar limits again. Thus, it seemed that only Congress could guarantee consumers access to products they had long been taking and were already spending roughly $8 billion on each year.

But Nestle maintains the industry simply wanted as regulatory-free an environment as possible in order to cash in as quickly as possible on Americans' growing desire to take a more active role in their own health care. And the industry was willing to exaggerate the truth, Nestle says. In her book, she documents the industry's massive pre-DSHEA publicity campaign scaring consumers into believing the FDA wanted to remove all dietary supplements from stores. In fact, the agency was only arguing that supplement makers should document safety and efficacy prior to selling products — arguments the industry campaign successfully quashed. [39]

DSHEA does grant FDA authority to remove products deemed unsafe, but since the law was enacted Congress has not provided the resources to police the market sufficiently. As problems with some supplements began to emerge following passage of DSHEA — most notably linked to ephedra — critics called for more restrictions on supplements. Congress responded last year by holding hearings on DSHEA's effectiveness and possible risks posed by some supplements. ■

CURRENT SITUATION

'The Dirty Dozen'

Dietary supplements that continue to raise safety concerns include *Consumer Reports'* so-called dirty dozen:

Functional Foods Growing in Popularity

Want a little St. John's wort with your soup? How about some echinacea with your tea, vitamins in your bottled water or maybe some plant sterols in your orange juice?

Even if you're not in the market for such tasty tidbits, be sure to check the labels on your groceries. Manufacturers increasingly are putting ingredients typically found in dietary supplements into so-called functional foods — products featuring added nutrients thought to promote health or help prevent disease. More and more companies are getting involved in functional foods, with a potential global market estimated at $26 billion. [1]

Manufacturers often make the same claims about the health benefits of functional foods that they make about dietary supplements, such as that eating soup with St. John's wort can help ease depression.

Although the term is relatively new, functional foods have been around since the early 20th century, when manufacturers began adding iodine to salt and vitamin D to milk. Foods fortified with vitamins and minerals now comprise a large part of what most Americans eat. But manufacturers now are also adding herbals.

A particularly popular segment of the functional foods market is "energy" drinks like Red Bull, which became a hit with its targeted market of 18-to-25-year-olds when it first appeared in 1997. The primary ingredients are water, sugar and caffeine, but competitors are now adding herbs and various so-called energy-enhancing extracts to their drinks, which bear provocative names like Piranha and Pimp Juice.

But not all extracts are as exotic as they may seem. For instance, Red Bull contains taurine, an energy-enhancing amino acid that was, according to urban legend, extracted from bulls' testicles. Taurine actually occurs naturally in human muscle and is found in scallops, fish, poultry and infant formula. [2]

Critics say any energy boost from drinking Red Bull or its competitors results from the 80 milligrams of caffeine they generally contain — about twice the amount in a typical can of cola. But the price can be up to six times higher than cola. "The margins are somewhere between excellent and obscene," John D. Sicher, editor and publisher of *Beverage Digest*, said recently. [3]

However, certain ingredients used in functional foods — such as plant sterols, are clearly beneficial. "Plant sterols have been researched for 40 years, and there's no doubt they interfere with cholesterol," says David Schardt, senior nutritionist at the Center for Science in the Public Interest, a consumer-advocacy group. For example, Benecol, a low-fat alternative to butter, contains plant sterols. "It's been tested, and it does help lower cholesterol. Benecol is an example of a good functional food."

Taken alone, plant sterols can reduce cholesterol levels by up to 15 percent, Schardt says. "If you take them in conjunction with [cholesterol drugs known as] statins, there's much more benefit."

But other herbs or botanicals may not be as beneficial, he says. Ginseng, for instance, is touted for its energy-boosting potential, and some energy drinks and power bars contain it instead of caffeine. "The U.S. and Canadian military have both tested it and found no energy benefit whatsoever," Schardt says. "But manufacturers continue to add it to drinks and [energy] bars as if it did."

Under federal law, functional foods containing ingredients commonly found in dietary supplements are regulated the same as foods. Dietary supplements are regulated similarly, but a food cannot be labeled as a dietary supplement, and vice versa, because of some differences in the regulations for each. Federal rules governing food are more stringent than those for dietary supplements, so experts have fewer safety concerns in general about functional foods than they do for dietary supplements.

"I can't say there are any harmful [functional foods], but maybe some useless ones," Schardt says. "Ginseng isn't hurting anyone unless you consider people wasting money is hurting them."

---

[1] See "Nutraceuticals: Company expands its product offerings within functional foods and beverages," *Health & Medicine Week*, Feb. 16, 2004, p. 602.

[2] See Sherri Day, "Energy Drinks Charm the Young and Caffeinated," *The New York Times*, April 4, 2004, sect. 3, p. 4.

[3] *Ibid.*

---

aristolochia, comfrey, andro, germander, chaparral, kava, bitter orange, lobelia, pennyroyal oil, skullcap, yohimbe and organ/glandular extracts. But industry representatives say most of the concerns have been addressed, either internally or by the government.

For instance, the FDA has banned aristolochia and certain extracts; advised industry to stop making, marketing or importing andro and comfrey; and issued warning letters to both industry and consumers against chaparral and kava. More to the point, however, consumers already know how to avoid some of the risks, McGuffin of AHPA says.

"It's well-known not to drink pennyroyal oil, and there's no problem with pennyroyal herb," he says. The warning on skullcap, he adds, is simply wrong. "That's based on an article from 20 years ago. Well, it's not skullcap, it's germander [that] shouldn't be sold." Consumers should also be warned against chaparral, he agrees, thus AHPA has advised for years that it be labeled as a "potential liver risk."

While Bell of Consumers Union continues to maintain that advice and warnings are not enough, other critics and experts warn of indirect risks

Continued on p. 726

At Issue:

Should dietary supplements be regulated like prescription drugs?

RONALD M. DAVIS, M.D.
TRUSTEE, AMERICAN MEDICAL ASSOCIATION

WRITTEN FOR *THE CQ RESEARCHER*, AUGUST 2004

yes

The truth is: Many dietary supplements are drugs. Like regulated prescription drugs, herbal remedies, megadose vitamins and anabolic steroids and their precursors cause biological activity in the human body — including potentially harmful side effects.

Currently, dietary supplements are inappropriately classified as "foods" under the Dietary Supplement Health and Education Act of 1994 (DSHEA). This must change. Many of these "natural" substances are harming American patients. For example, comfrey and kava are toxic to the liver, and aristolochic acid can cause kidney failure.

Patients with pre-existing medical conditions can be negatively affected by taking dietary supplements — as can those taking certain prescription drugs concurrently. Eight herbal remedies, including garlic, ginkgo and ginseng, are known to cause complications in patients undergoing surgery. The rising tide of adolescents abusing anabolic steroids and their precursors through dietary supplements raises serious safety concerns, particularly among the growing population of young female abusers.

The Food and Drug Administration's (FDA) current authority to regulate these supplements is insufficient to protect the health and welfare of the American public. Manufacturers of these substances are not required to provide premarket safety, efficacy or quality data to the FDA. They also do not have to include warnings or precautions on product labels or provide post-marketing data to the FDA about adverse events. If there is a problem with a dietary supplement, the burden falls upon the FDA to prove this is the case.

The effort and length of time it took for the FDA to remove ephedra from the market exemplifies the problems with the status quo. Because DSHEA makes it difficult for the FDA to prove that a dietary supplement is unsafe, dietary supplements containing ephedra were still available long after the risks of heart attack, stroke, seizure and death were documented.

It is particularly worrisome that most consumers believe dietary supplements are safe and approved by the government before sale, when, in fact, supplements are exempt from the same kind of expert scientific evaluation that helps ensure the safety and effectiveness of prescription drugs.

Regulating dietary supplements like prescription drugs would require manufacturers to submit efficacy and safety data on products for FDA approval prior to marketing, meet certain standards for product quality, provide post-marketing adverse event data to the FDA and be truthful in advertising. Only when this happens will consumers' safety perceptions meet reality.

ANNETTE DICKINSON
PRESIDENT, COUNCIL FOR RESPONSIBLE NUTRITION

WRITTEN FOR *THE CQ RESEARCHER*, AUGUST 2004

no

Foods and medicines are inextricably intertwined in science, philosophy and the public mind. Hence the old adage, "Let food be your medicine." Legally, however, foods and drugs are separate categories with different controlling statutes and regulations. On at least three different occasions, Congress has considered the legal status of dietary supplements and each time has opted to put supplements on the food side. That is where they should remain.

There are close parallels between some types of dietary supplements and some categories of conventional foods. Multivitamin supplements and fortified breakfast cereals both provide an array of nutrients that can help people ensure adequate intakes. Herbal supplements and herbal teas both provide access to specific botanical ingredients in a convenient form. Other supplements and so-called functional foods enable the public to increase consumption of beneficial substances such as glucosamine, lutein and omega-3 fatty acids. All of these products are and should be regulated as foods.

Many physicians, pharmacists, nurses and dietitians individually use and recommend dietary supplements to their patients or clients, and surveys show that seven out of 10 Americans use supplements. Institutionally, however, some organizations like the American Medical Association (AMA) are stuck in 1950s thought patterns, still arguing that regulating supplements like drugs would make them safer. But premarket approval, the basis of drug regulation, is no guarantee of safety. Numerous drug products have been approved by FDA, only to be recalled later for safety reasons.

Rather than truly addressing any safety issues, reclassifying supplements as drugs would only serve to turn what is now an economically reasonable self-care choice into a less accessible, more expensive option.

Consumers are passionate about dietary supplements. They don't want their senators, the FDA or the AMA dictating a rigid or conservative path that would unnecessarily limit their options. But the public also wants safe supplements, and the FDA has abundant authority under the law to oversee the safety of all foods, including supplements.

The agency has recently been flexing this considerable muscle, exercising some of its new clout provided by the Dietary Supplement Health and Education Act (DSHEA). Even if some additional oversight of supplements were warranted, nothing needs to be done that could not be accomplished under current food-safety laws. DSHEA provides the best framework for regulating supplements.

Continued from p. 724

that may be posed by supplements. For example, a review commissioned by the Agency for Healthcare Research and Quality concluded that garlic, touted for its ability to "promote healthy heart function and regulate cholesterol levels," does not appear to have any benefits enduring beyond six months on either heart function or cholesterol levels. [40]

Silverglade of the CSPI recently said the review's conclusion is "crucial because it is the prolonged elevation of blood cholesterol levels that raises the risk of cardiovascular disease." A supplement with only six months of benefit will be "virtually useless," he says, yet people will continue to take it thinking they're protecting themselves. [41]

Congress may intervene against one supplement — the steroid precursor known as andro. Precursors technically aren't steroids, which are controlled substances; however, when metabolized in the body, precursors have a steroidal effect. The Anabolic Steroid Control Act of 2004, introduced by Sen. Joseph R. Biden, Jr., D-Del., would classify andro and all precursors as drugs and thus place them under more stringent regulation.

Earlier this year, the Senate Judiciary Committee passed Biden's bill, and the House passed a companion bill with overwhelming bipartisan support (408-3).

Last spring, however, Sen. Durbin tried to attach his bill requiring supplement manufacturers to inform the FDA of all adverse-event reports as an amendment to the Defense reauthorization bill. That prompted Durbin's Democratic colleague, Sen. Harkin, and Republican Hatch to object. Since co-authoring DSHEA with Harkin in 1994, Hatch has received at least $137,000 in campaign contributions from the supplements industry, and lobbyists linked to his son have received nearly $2 million. Harkin, meanwhile, received $119,000 from supplement manufacturers between 1993 and 2002. [42]

Harkin and Hatch felt Durbin's bill was too narrow and discriminatory. According to congressional sources, Durbin withdrew the amendment as part of an agreement with Hatch, who wants to pass an unrelated measure from the Senate Health, Education, Labor and Pensions Committee. Harkin's bill to increase funding for FDA enforcement is awaiting a date for consideration by the committee.

Research and Enforcement

During its first five-year program, the NIH's Office of Dietary Supplements (ODS) reviewed existing data regarding some supplements, primarily the purported positive effects of omega-3 fatty acids on a variety of health conditions. The first and only review released so far looked at its impact on heart disease.

"The review said there's lots of evidence related to use of omega-3 fatty acids for cardiovascular disease prevention," says ODS Director Coates, "but [for] people who already have some pre-existing disease, omega-3-enriched foods and supplements will reduce the risk of further disease associated with whatever caused the disease in the first place. But in primary prevention, the data are rather weaker. So the question is, do we need more data? Yes."

ODS has recently begun assembling a research program to identify dietary supplements that could promote good health or help prevent disease. It will also develop analytic methods and reference materials for the most commonly used dietary supplements.

Meanwhile, the Federal Trade Commission (FTC) continues to monitor advertisements for dietary supplements. The commission oversees truth-in-advertising issues. According to Howard Beales, director of the FTC's Bureau of Consumer Protection, since DSHEA was passed in 1994 the commission has filed or settled more than 100 law-enforcement actions challenging allegedly false or misleading claims by supplements advertisers. Most recently, the FTC and FDA formed a joint task force to pursue similar claims. [43]

An FDA spokesman says the agency will be beefing up enforcement efforts in general when the new fiscal year begins in October. And Schneeman of the FDA says issuing good manufacturing practices (GMPs) remains a top agency priority.

Industry representatives continue to stress their ability to self-regulate. As the NNFA's Seckman says: "We started our own GMPs in January of 1999. We didn't want to wait for the FDA." However, getting GMPs from the FDA would help standardize the industry, he says.

"In 1996, we advised the industry to no longer use comfrey for internal use," adds McGuffin of AHPA. "We didn't do it because the FDA passed any law or because the FTC called us. We did it because we're experts in our field, and we came across information that [warranted it]," he says, acknowledging that some herbalists are still "seriously aggrieved that we took a position against it."

"Our objective is to deal with regulators and legislators and others who influence consumer decision-making," says the CRN's Dickinson. "We talk about it endlessly: What could be done that would change the views of some of these institutions?"

Because the group does not have a large budget, she says, it is focusing on promoting self-regulation to help weed out misleading claims and deal with product-safety issues.

"We are supporting the [adverse-event reports] requirement," she points out. "We're trying to show that the problems are being addressed." ■

OUTLOOK

Action in Congress

Both lawmakers on Capitol Hill and the dietary supplements industry predict passage soon of the various pending bills affecting supplements — increasing FDA enforcement resources, instituting AER requirements and reclassifying andro as a controlled substance. Aside from any additional political maneuverings that may occur in Congress, the determining factor likely will be the effect of the upcoming presidential election on legislative activity.

Dickinson of the CRN sees passage sooner rather than later and hopes the FDA's ephedra ban will survive a court challenge by companies that maintain the product is safe. "If all that happens," she says, "we'll start the next Congress addressing the issues that have been most controversial and damaging to us in this last Congress and get them off the table. If so, we'll have moved an enormous amount forward."

Meanwhile, Bell of Consumers Union would like to see more stringent labeling of herbal supplements. "There are serious problems with many of them," he says. "All the potential risks and interactions of those products are not routinely disclosed to consumers."

But he doubts that even the additional resources proposed in Sen. Harkin's bill would appreciably affect FDA enforcement. "The FDA might take action against a product for [false] claims, but it's just a drop in the bucket compared with all the products and all the claims being made."

NYU's Nestle also doubts DSHEA will be substantively strengthened. "It may be too late for that," she says. "One possibility was to make supplements a special case with special rules. But food manufacturers have said that if dietary supplements can make structure/function claims, they should be able to, too. That genie is now out of the bottle — food companies are now doing exactly what supplements have been doing — producing foods containing dietary supplements." (*See story, p. 724.*)

"Somebody really needs to take a look at this whole thing and try to rein in it in," she continues. "But I guarantee it's not going to happen under [the Bush] administration because this is a very industry-friendly administration."

According to Bell, the FDA is looking at three supplements in particular — kava, usnic acid and bitter orange — but they don't know when they'll have an announcement. Schneeman of the FDA says it would be inappropriate to discuss any dietary supplements the agency might be scrutinizing now or in the future.

However, the FDA, the Institute of Medicine (IOM) and the National Research Council (NRC) have outlined several procedures and policies that could be instituted to improve FDA's oversight of supplements.

For example, the study endorsed a mandatory adverse-event reporting system — similar to the one being considered by Congress — to help bring critical safety issues to the FDA's attention. But the study also suggested using data from animal research. While DSHEA does not require the FDA to have direct evidence of a safety threat, the agency must demonstrate "an unreasonable risk" — a difficult task that could be made easier with animal research. The FDA has embraced the recommendations and is continuing to evaluate how best to implement them.

Meanwhile, the industry plans to continue disseminating its message. "We need to educate Congress and the public and to work with FTC and FDA," says the National Nutritional Foods Association's Seckman.

"As in any industry, there will always be bad apples, but we think our safety record is fantastic," he says, "especially in comparison to some over-the-counter and prescription medicines and food-borne illnesses. Seven people out of 10 take a supplement every day. We have a really good story to get out there." ■

Notes

[1] See Julie E. Bisbee, "Mother says ephedra caused son's death," The Associated Press, July 8, 2004.

[2] See Jennifer LeClaire, "Happy, healthy and wise: Feel your best at any age," *Better Nutrition*, Aug. 1, 2004, p. 30.

[3] "Overview of Dietary Supplements," Center for Food Safety and Applied Nutrition, U.S. Food and Drug Administration, Jan. 3, 2001; www.cfsan.fda.gov/~dms/ds-oview.html.

[4] See testimony of Annette Dickinson, Senate Subcommittee on Oversight of Government Management, June 8, 2004. The $19 billion figure comes from Michael Specter, "Miracle in a Bottle; Dietary supplements are

About the Author

William Triplett recently joined *The CQ Researcher* as a staff writer after covering science and the arts for such publications as *Smithsonian, Air & Space, Nature, Washingtonian* and *The Washington Post.* He also served as associate editor of *Capitol Style* magazine. He holds a B.A. in journalism from Ohio University and an M.A. in English literature from Georgetown University. His recent reports include "Search for Extraterrestrials" and "Broadcast Indecency."

unregulated, some are unsafe — and Americans can't get enough of them," *The New Yorker*, Feb. 2, 2004, p. 64.

5 See testimony of David Seckman, Senate Commerce, Science and Transportation Committee, Oct. 28, 2003.

6 For background, see Kenneth Jost, "Sports and Drugs," *The CQ Researcher*, July 23, 2004, pp. 613-636.

7 See testimony of Robert Brackett, Senate Government Affairs Subcommittee on Oversight of Government Management, June 8, 2004.

8 "CR Investigates: Dangerous Supplements Still at Large," *Consumer Reports*, May 2004, p. 12.

9 See testimony, Senate Government Affairs Subcommittee on Oversight of Government Management, June 8, 2004.

10 "FDA Announces Withdrawal of Fenfluramine and Dexfenfluramine (Fen-Phen)," Press release (P97-32), Food and Drug Administration, Sept. 15, 1997.

11 See Julie Tamaki and Dan Morain, "Grand Jury Indicts Metabolife, Founder," *Los Angeles Times*, July 23, 2004, p. C1.

12 See testimony of Arthur Grollman, Senate Commerce, Science and Transportation Committee, Oct. 28, 2003.

13 *Consumer Reports* and Bell testimony, *op. cit.*

14 *Consumer Reports* and Brackett testimony, *op. cit.*

15 *Ibid.*

16 Brackett testimony, *op. cit.*

17 *Ibid.*

18 See testimony of Ronald Davis, Senate Government Affairs Subcommittee on Oversight of Government Management, June 8, 2004.

19 *Ibid.*

20 For background on teens and steroids, see Jost, *op. cit.*, pp. 618-619. Also, see Barbara Feder Ostrov, "Sex Pills' 'Secret' Additive; Prescription Chemicals Found in Herbal Options," *San Jose Mercury News*, May 11, 2004, p. A1.

21 *Consumer Reports*, *op. cit.*

22 Grollman testimony, *op. cit.*

23 Seckman testimony, *op. cit.*

24 *Ibid.*

25 "New Dietary Ingredient Safety Review Examined in Journal: FDA Shown to be a Strict Gatekeeper," American Herbal Products Association press release, July 23, 2004.

26 See testimony of Bruce Silverglade, Government Affairs Senate Subcommittee on Oversight of Government Management, June 8, 2004.

FOR MORE INFORMATION

American Herbal Products Association, 8484 Georgia Ave., Suite 370, Silver Spring, MD 20910; (301) 588-1171; www.ahpa.org.

American Medical Association, 515 N. State St., Chicago, IL 60610; (800) 621-8335; www.ama-assn.org.

Center for Science in the Public Interest, 1875 Connecticut Ave., N.W., Suite 300, Washington, DC 20009; (202) 332-9110; www.cspinet.org. Nonprofit consumer advocacy organization; publishes *Nutrition Action Healthletter*.

Consumers Union, 101 Truman Ave., Yonkers, NY 10703-1057; (914) 378-2000; www.consumersunion.org. Nonprofit organization that tests products for safety and efficacy; publishes *Consumer Reports*.

Council for Responsible Nutrition, 1828 L St., N.W., Suite 900, Washington, DC 20036-5114; (202) 776-7929; www.crnusa.org. Trade association representing major dietary supplement manufacturers.

Food and Drug Administration, 5600 Fishers Lane, Rockville, MD 20857-0001; 1-888-INFO-FDA; www.fda.gov/default.htm. Federal agency directly responsible for oversight of dietary supplements.

National Nutritional Foods Association, 1220 19th St., N.W., Suite 400, Washington, DC 20036; (202) 223-0101; www.nnfa.org. Represents more than 5,000 retailers, manufacturers, suppliers and distributors of health foods.

Office of Dietary Supplements, National Institutes of Health, 6100 Executive Blvd., Room 3B01, MSC 7517, Bethesda, MD 20892-7517; (301) 435-2920; http://dietary-supplements.info.nih.gov. Federal agency that identifies research needed to better understand effects of dietary supplements.

U.S. Pharmacopeia Verification Program, 12601 Twinbrook Parkway, Rockville, MD, 20852; (800) 822-8772; www.uspverified.org. A voluntary, nongovernmental organization that verifies national quality standards for over-the-counter drugs and for dietary supplement manufacturers.

27 *Ibid.*

28 For background, see Mary H. Cooper, "Mad Cow Disease," *The CQ Researcher*, March 2, 2001, pp. 161-184.

29 Davis testimony, *op. cit.*

30 For background see David Masci, "Diet and Health," *The CQ Researcher*, Feb. 23, 2001, pp. 129-160.

31 See http://encyclopedia.thefreedictionary.com/ patent%20medicine.

32 *Ibid.*

33 For background see Kathy Koch, "Medical Marijuana," *The CQ Researcher*, Aug. 20, 1999, pp. 705-728.

34 Specter, *op. cit.*

35 Masci, *op. cit.*

36 *Ibid.*

37 See Marion Nestle, *Food Politics: How the Food Industry Influences Nutrition and Health* (2002), p. 240.

38 *Ibid.*, p. 241.

39 *Ibid.*, pp. 247-271.

40 Silverglade testimony, *op. cit.*

41 *Ibid.*

42 See Chuck Neubauer, *et al.*, "Senator, His Son Get Boosts From Makers of Ephedra; Orrin Hatch has kept regulators at bay and benefited via campaign donations. Lobbyists linked to his son have received $2 million," *Los Angeles Times*, March 5, 2003, p. A1.

43 See testimony of Howard Beales, House Energy and Commerce Committee, Subcommittee on Oversight and Investigations, June 16, 2004.

Bibliography

Selected Sources

Books

Nestle, Marion, *Food Politics: How the Food Industry Influences Nutrition and Health*, University of California Press, 2002.

The chairman of New York University's Department of Nutrition and Food Studies chronicles the food industry's significant influence on federal regulation of the market, which includes dietary supplements; several chapters are devoted to the Dietary Supplement Health and Education Act (DSHEA) of 1994.

***Physicians' Desk Reference for Nonprescription Drugs and Dietary Supplements*, Thompson PDR, 2003.**

This guide to dietary supplements is intended to provide "all information necessary for informed use." For each product, the source is the manufacturer, which has "prepared, edited and approved" all information.

Articles

"Consumer Reports Investigates: Dangerous Supplements Still at Large," *Consumer Reports*, May 2004, p. 12.

The influential consumer magazine, published by the non-profit Consumers Union, asserts that at least 12 dietary supplements — some still available — threaten public health.

Dembner, Alice, "Herbal Industry Seen Fending Off FDA," *The Boston Globe*, March 26, 2004, p. A1.

Despite a federal ban against two supplements, ephedra and aristolochia, the herbal industry maintains considerable influence among Washington policymakers.

LeClaire, Jennifer, "Happy, healthy and wise: Feel your best at any age," *Better Nutrition*, Aug. 1, 2004, p. 30.

Some experts and natural-food nutritionists say regular use of dietary supplements can improve and maintain health.

McGuffin, Michael, and Anthony L. Young, "Premarket Notifications of New Dietary Ingredients — A Ten-Year Review," *Food and Drug Law Journal*, Vol. 59, No. 2, 2004, p. 229.

The president and general counsel, respectively, of the American Herbal Products Association write that the Food and Drug Administration's (FDA) regulation of dietary supplements with new ingredients has successfully kept undesirable ingredients out of the market.

Ottaway, Peter Berry, "A reflection on the impact of DSHEA on global supplement regs," *Nutraceuticals International*, March 2004.

A consultant in food sciences and European food law argues that DSHEA, with its comparatively relaxed standards and regulations, differs strongly from "almost all other regulatory" systems in other countries, which are generally far more stringent.

Roan, Shari, "Assessing black cohosh; Researchers attempt to determine how the popular herb works — and whether it's safe as a remedy for menopausal symptoms," *Los Angeles Times*, June 28, 2004, p. F1.

Some experts question whether enough is known about the prolonged use of an herb popular among menopausal women.

Specter, Michael, "Miracle in a Bottle; Dietary supplements are unregulated, some are unsafe — and Americans can't get enough of them," *The New Yorker*, Feb. 2, 2004, p. 64.

The author takes an in-depth look at the history and current practices and controversies surrounding the dietary supplements industry.

Vardi, Nathan, "Poison Pills: The dangerous world of diet supplements," *Forbes Global*, April 19, 2004, p. 56.

Some ephedra manufacturers vow to challenge the FDA's ban in court, but others are rushing to tout "replacements," such as the herb bitter orange.

Reports and Studies

"Dietary Supplements: A Framework for Evaluating Safety," Institute of Medicine and National Research Council, National Academies Press, April 2004.

At the request of the FDA, the IOM and NRC outlined a science-based process for assessing the ingredients in dietary supplements, particularly when data about a substance's safety in humans are scarce.

"Food Safety: Improvements Needed in Overseeing the Safety of Dietary Supplements and Functional Foods," U.S. General Accounting Office, July 2000.

The federal watchdog agency identifies principal areas of weakness in federal safety regulation of supplements.

Heller, Ilene Ringel, *et al.*, "Functional Foods: Public Health Boon or 21st Century Quackery?" Center for Science in the Public Interest, 1999.

A comparison of the effectiveness of governmental regulation of functional foods in Japan, Britain and the United States; recommendations made for each country.

The Next Step:

Additional Articles from Current Periodicals

Benefits of Supplements

Conis, Elena, "Antioxidants: Have They Been Hyped?" *Los Angeles Times*, Oct. 27, 2003, p. F1.

Mixed results in antioxidant studies cast doubts on the effectiveness of the much-touted substances; many doctors continue to support them.

Daley, Beth, "Fish Tale," *The Boston Globe*, April 20, 2004, p. E1.

Many recommend omega-3 fatty acids, available in fish oil supplements, for their health benefits.

Kotulak, Ronald, "Vitamin D Gains Favor as Health Key," *Chicago Tribune*, Feb. 29, 2004, News Section, p. 1.

Cases of rickets are increasing, and doctors say vitamin D is crucial not only for bone growth but also for a variety of crucial biological processes.

Packer-Tursman, Judy, "Pill 'Very Promising'," *The Washington Post*, Oct. 22, 2002, p. F1.

Coenzyme Q10 benefited Parkinson's disease sufferers, but definitive trials have not yet been performed.

Squires, Sally, "Some Fish Fats Protect the Heart. What If They Could Also Treat Your Brain?" *The Washington Post*, Aug. 19, 2003, p. F1.

Praised for improving cardiovascular health, researchers are now investigating whether omega-3 fatty acids also help treat depression.

Whiteman, Susan, "Joint Dilemma," *The Washington Post*, Jan. 27, 2004, p. F1.

A physician describes the research that persuaded her that taking glucosamine is worth trying to help with her osteoarthritis.

Business of Supplements

Carey, Benedict, "A Supplemental Pitch," *Los Angeles Times*, Aug. 26, 2002, p. S1.

Ethical concerns emerge when doctors who recommend — or even sell — dietary supplements to patients have a stake in the companies manufacturing the supplement.

Heller, Matthew, "Healthy, Wealthy, But Wise?" *Los Angeles Times Magazine*, Feb. 1, 2004, p. 10.

St. George, Utah, has experienced an economic and demographic boom thanks to supplement manufacturers locating their factories there, but now the town's future is tied to the industry's.

Ephedra

Duenwald, Mary, "Slim Pickings: Looking Beyond Ephedra," *The New York Times*, Jan. 6, 2004, p. F1.

Despite its side effects, ephedra helped people lose weight; other alternatives have disappointing results, too many side effects or both.

Manier, Jeremy, and Manya Brachear, "FDA Imposes Ephedra Ban," *Chicago Tribune*, Dec. 31, 2003, News Section, p. 1.

At its peak, 12 million people used ephedra, but it is "simply too risky to be used," according to Health and Human Services Secretary Tommy G. Thompson.

Russell, Sabin, "FDA Bans Diet Herb Blamed in 155 Deaths," *San Francisco Chronicle*, Dec. 31, 2003, p. A1.

After 16,000 adverse-reaction reports regarding ephedra, the government moves to halt its sale; California had already banned it.

Schmuck, Peter, "Report Lays Death Blame on Ephedrine," *The Baltimore Sun*, March 14, 2003, p. 1E.

Ephedrine played a significant role in the sudden death of Baltimore Orioles pitcher Steve Bechler.

Wolfe, Sidney M., "Ephedra — Scientific Evidence Versus Money/Politics," *Science*, April 18, 2003, p. 437.

A public health watchdog says campaign contributions were an impediment to enacting effective regulatory action for ephedra.

Regulating Supplements

Allen, Jane E., "A First Step Toward Standardizing Supplements," *Los Angeles Times*, March 17, 2003, p. F3.

Worried about consumer confidence, the supplements industry backs government plans to regulate quality control.

Dembner, Alice, "Herbal Industry Seen Fending Off FDA," *The Boston Globe*, March 26, 2004, p. A1.

Only 1 percent of the problems involving supplements come to the FDA's attention, making it difficult to investigate potentially dangerous products.

Grollman, Arthur, "Regulation of Dietary Drugs Is Long Overdue," *The New York Times*, Feb. 23, 2003, Section 8, p. 10.

A critic of the supplements industry argues strongly in favor of increased regulation for substances whose status as supplements rather than drugs is a "legal fiction."

Healy, Melissa, "Coral Calcium Scrutinized," *Los Angeles Times*, Sept. 29, 2003, p. F1.

The FDA moves against coral calcium sellers who are making unsubstantiated claims about its benefits.

Kaufman, Marc, "Oversight of Supplement Makers Advised," *The Washington Post*, April 2, 2004, p. A9.
An expert panel recommends that Congress give the FDA broader powers to regulate the approximately 29,000 dietary supplements now sold.

McNeil, Donald, and Sherri Day, "F.D.A. to Put New Rules on Dietary Supplements," *The New York Times*, March 8, 2003, p. A13.
Reports of supplements contaminated with glass, lead or pesticides trigger new regulatory action by the FDA to ensure consistent manufacturing quality.

Neubauer, Chuck, Judy Pasternak and Richard T. Cooper, "Senator, His Son Get Boosts From Makers of Ephedra," *Los Angeles Times*, March 5, 2003, p. A1.
Ties between supplement makers and lobbying shops that have employed the son of Sen. Orrin G. Hatch, R-Utah, raise conflict-of-interest questions.

Risks

Allen, Jane E., "Warning on Herb Widens," *Los Angeles Times*, Sept. 22, 2003, p. F1.
Supplements can interact with other medications to cause unintended side effects; St. John's wort, in particular, may cause problems with a long list of other medications.

Bell, Elizabeth, "Popular Herb May Severely Harm Liver," *San Francisco Chronicle*, March 26, 2002, p. A1.
Reports of severe liver damage attributed to kava use, while rare, elicit a warning letter from the FDA urging caution on consumers with liver problems.

Kolata, Gina, "Vitamins: More May Be Too Many," *The New York Times*, April 29, 2003, p. F1.
Some nutritionists are concerned that people may be ingesting too much of certain vitamins, particularly vitamin A, which can increase the risk of osteoporosis.

Tompkins, Joshua, "The Creatine Edge," *Los Angeles Times*, May 3, 2004, p. F1.
Creatine, a popular supplement among athletes young and old, is not linked to health problems but some doctors worry about the lack of long-term information.

Wharton, David, "Tainted Test Case," *Los Angeles Times*, March 28, 2004, p. D1.
Supplements are regularly contaminated with trace amounts of other substances; athletes must be careful, since a positive test, regardless of intent, is grounds for disqualification.

Scientific Evaluations

Agnvall, Elizabeth, "You Use That Stuff, Too?" *The Washington Post*, June 29, 2004, p. F1.
A rundown of the potential benefits and drawbacks of 10 popular alternative treatments, including echinacea, ginseng and garlic.

Carey, John, "Herbal Remedies: A $4 Billion Enigma," *Business Week*, April 28, 2003, p. 104.
Scientific tests show that most herbs, like ginseng or saw palmetto, are safe, but offer only mild benefits at best.

Fessenden, Ford, "Studies of Dietary Supplements Come Under Growing Scrutiny," *The New York Times*, June 23, 2003, p. A1.
A surge in litigation heralds concerns about the use and sometimes misuse of scientific data by supplement marketers trying to sell their wares.

Gold, Paul, Larry Cahill and Gary Wenk, "The Lowdown on Ginkgo Biloba," *Scientific American*, April 2003.
The available evidence on gingko's effectiveness is weak, but promising enough to encourage further study.

CITING *THE CQ RESEARCHER*

Sample formats for citing these reports in a bibliography include the ones listed below. Preferred styles and formats vary, so please check with your instructor or professor.

MLA STYLE

Jost, Kenneth. "Rethinking the Death Penalty." The CQ Researcher 16 Nov. 2001: 945-68.

APA STYLE

Jost, K. (2001, November 16). Rethinking the death penalty. *The CQ Researcher, 11*, 945-968.

CHICAGO STYLE

Jost, Kenneth. "Rethinking the Death Penalty." *CQ Researcher*, November 16, 2001, 945-968.

In-depth Reports on Issues in the News

Are you writing a paper?

Need backup for a debate?

Want to become an expert on an issue?

For 80 years, researchers have turned to *The CQ Researcher* for in-depth reporting and analysis of issues in the news. Reports on a full range of political and social issues are now available. Following is a selection of recent reports:

Civil Liberties
Civil Liberties Debates, 10/03
Gay Marriage, 9/03

Crime/Law
Serial Killers, 10/03
Corporate Crime, 10/02

Economy
Exporting Jobs, 2/04
Stock Market Troubles, 1/04

Education
Black Colleges, 12/03
Combating Plagiarism, 9/03

Energy/Transportation
SUV Debate, 5/03
Future of Amtrak, 10/02

Environment
Air Pollution Conflict, 11/03
Water Shortages, 8/03

Health/Safety
Homeopathy Debate, 12/04
Worker Safety, 5/04

International Affairs
Aiding Africa, 8/03
Rebuilding Iraq, 7/03

Politics/Public Policy
Redistricting Disputes, 3/04
Democracy in Arab World, 1/04

Social Trends
Future of Music Industry, 11/03
Latinos' Future, 10/03

Terrorism/Defense
North Korean Crisis, 4/03
Homeland Security, 9/03

Youth
Youth Suicide, 2/04
Hazing, 1/04

Upcoming Reports

Big-Box Stores, 9/10/04
Cyber Politics, 9/17/04
Social Security, 9/24/04
Gays on Campus, 10/1/04
Migrant Workers, 10/8/04
Media Bias, 10/15/04

ACCESS

The CQ Researcher is available in print and online. For access, visit your library or www.thecqresearcher.com.

STAY CURRENT

To receive notice of upcoming *CQ Researcher* reports, or learn more about *CQ Researcher* products, subscribe to the free e-mail newsletters, *CQ Researcher Alert!* and *CQ Researcher News*: www.cqpress.com/newsletters.

PURCHASE

To purchase a *CQ Researcher* report in print or electronic format (PDF), visit www.cqpress.com or call 866-427-7737. A single report is $10. Bulk purchase discounts and electronic rights licensing are also available.

SUBSCRIBE

A full-service *CQ Researcher* print subscription—including 44 reports a year, monthly index updates, and a bound volume—is $625 for academic and public libraries, $605 for high school libraries, and $750 for media libraries. Add $25 for domestic postage.

The CQ Researcher Online offers a backfile from 1991 and a number of tools to simplify research. Available in print and online, *The CQ Researcher en español* offers 36 reports a year on political and social issues of concern to Latinos in the U.S. For pricing and a free trial of either product, call 800-834-9020, ext. 1906, or e-mail librarysales@cqpress.com.

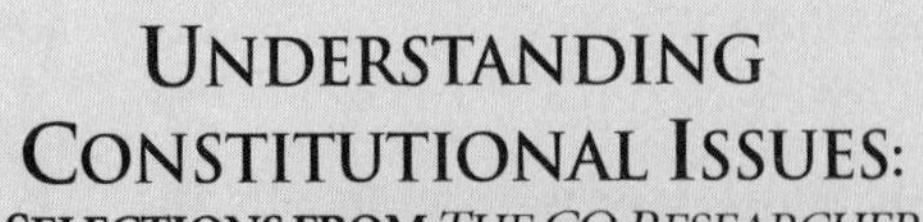

Understanding Constitutional Issues focuses on four key themes — governmental powers and structure, security, liberty, and equality — to help students develop a deeper understanding of the relation between current events and constitutional issues and principles. Integrating eighteen *CQ Researcher* reports, *Understanding Constitutional Issues* makes important connections clear, such as those between civil liberties and security; and privacy and liberty.

June 2004 • 8 1/2 x 11 • Approx. 432 pages • Paperback • ISBN 1-56802-885-7 • $39.95

To Order: Call Toll-Free: 866.4CQ.PRESS (427.7737)
Fax: 800.380.3810 • Web: www.cqpress.com
E-mail: customerservice@cqpress.com

CQ Press, 1255 22nd Street, NW, Suite 400 • Washington, DC 20037

CQ Researcher

Published by CQ Press, a division of Congressional Quarterly Inc.

thecqresearcher.com

Big-Box Stores

Are they good for America?

America is teeming with Wal-Marts, Home Depots and other "big-box" chain stores — some larger than five football fields. Millions of consumers like the low prices, free parking and one-stop shopping convenience offered by the megastores, while policymakers say the stores create jobs, enable customers to save money for other expenditures and pump much-needed tax dollars into community coffers. But critics say big-box stores actually harm local economies and flourish only because they receive public subsidies, pay low salaries and benefits and utilize unethical and possibly illegal practices to drive smaller, locally owned competitors out of business. Critics also say they cause added traffic congestion and suburban sprawl, force U.S. companies to ship high-paying manufacturing jobs overseas and cost more in local services than the taxes they generate. Communities increasingly are passing special ordinances to keep the big retailers out, but the chains are fighting back, saying they are simply giving consumers what they want.

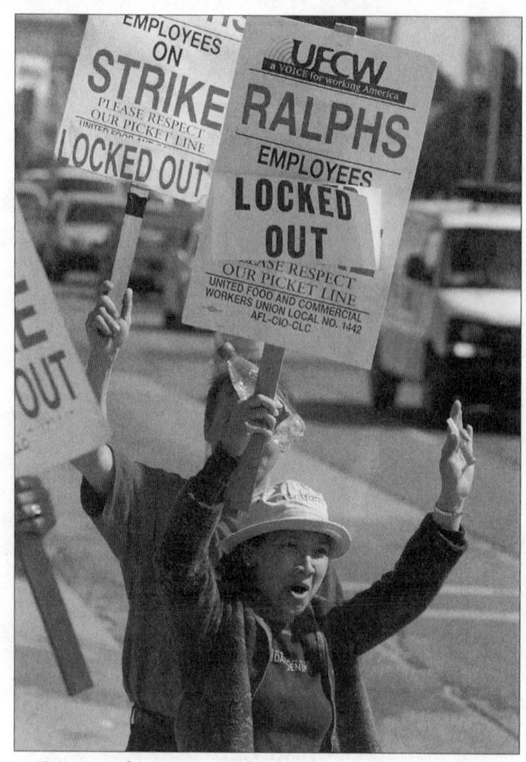

Unionized grocery workers in Los Angeles strike to retain benefits, as non-union Wal-Mart moves into the Southern California supermarket industry.

INSIDE THIS REPORT

The CQ Researcher • Sept. 10, 2004 • www.thecqresearcher.com
Volume 14, Number 31 • Pages 733-756

CQ PRESS

RECIPIENT OF SOCIETY OF PROFESSIONAL JOURNALISTS AWARD FOR EXCELLENCE ◆ AMERICAN BAR ASSOCIATION SILVER GAVEL AWARD

Cover: Worried about competition from non-union Wal-Mart, Los Angeles-area supermarket companies tried to cut union benefits last year. Workers struck for five months but were only partially successful. (AFP Photo/Robyn Beck)

Sept. 10, 2004
Volume 14, Number 31

A Division of Congressional Quarterly Inc.

The CQ Researcher (ISSN 1056-2036) is printed on acid-free paper. Published weekly, except Jan. 2, April 9, July 2, July 9, Aug. 6, Aug. 13, Nov. 26 and Dec. 31, by CQ Press, a division of Congressional Quarterly Inc. Annual subscription rates for institutions start at $625. For pricing, call 1-800-834-9020, ext. 1906. To purchase a *CQ Researcher* report in print or electronic format (PDF), visit www.cqpress.com or call 866-427-7737. A single report is $10. Bulk purchase discounts and electronic-rights licensing are also available. Periodicals postage paid at Washington, D.C., and additional mailing offices. POSTMASTER: Send address changes to *The CQ Researcher*, 1255 22nd St., N.W., Suite 400, Washington, D.C. 20037.

Big-Box Stores

By Brian Hansen

The Issues

It's hard to miss the Wal-Mart store in the Denver suburb of Commerce City. At 155,000 square feet, it is nearly as large as three football fields. The low-slung, largely windowless building sits just off the main drag, Dahlia Street, on a 15-acre tract. Its parking lot is frequently full, even late at night. That's because, like thousands of other Wal-Marts across the country, the store never closes.

CQ Press/Kenneth Lukas

Wal-Mart has grown into the world's largest company by offering "everyday low prices." But critics say big-box stores' ever-lower prices carry hidden costs for taxpayers, the community at large and the environment.

There are about 25 other Wal-Marts within 50 miles of Commerce City, as well as some 24 Home Depots, each store occupying at least 100,000 square feet. Other so-called big-box stores also abound, including Target, Kmart and Lowe's. In some Denver-area neighborhoods, mammoth, nationwide chain stores stand side by side like giant building blocks, with no local, independent businesses in sight.

Denver's experience is hardly unique. Big-box retailers in the United States are flourishing. More than 80 percent of American households purchased something last year from Wal-Mart, the nation's largest retailer — indeed, the world's biggest company of any kind. Home Depot is the nation's second-largest retailer and the fastest-growing retailer in U.S. history.

"People save time and money" by shopping at big-box retailers, says Jason Todd, government affairs manager at the International Mass Retail Association, which represents many big-box chains. "The stores also create quality jobs and generate tax revenues for the communities in which they're located."

But critics complain that the much-touted "everyday low prices" of big-box stores like Wal-Mart actually carry many hidden costs for taxpayers, the community at large and the environment, including: driving smaller stores out of business and turning downtown shopping areas into boarded-up ghost towns; exacerbating traffic congestion and suburban sprawl; undermining the nation's economy by creating a huge class of low-paid, non-union workers who can't afford basic needs such as health insurance or school lunches for their children; and forcing U.S. suppliers to manufacture products in low-wage countries overseas in order to meet demands for increasingly low prices. (*See sidebar, p. 744.*)

And because Wal-Mart is the world's largest wholesale buyer and employer, it has been able to crack the whip with both competitors and suppliers, forcing them to cope with its price-cutting policies in order to survive. And with some 1.5 million employees — more than the populations of 12 states — it is the world's largest private employer. As a result, the staunchly anti-union company — which is facing several class-action suits for allegedly violating fair-labor laws — is overhauling world employment practices, according to a report by the minority staff of the House Education and Workforce Committee.

"Wal-Mart's slogan should be 'Always low wages, always,' " Rep. George Miller, the committee's senior Democrat, said when he unveiled the report on Feb. 16, 2004. "Wal-Mart imposes a huge, often hidden, cost on its workers, our communities, and U.S. taxpayers. And Wal-Mart is in the driver's seat in the global race to the bottom, suppressing wage levels, workplace protections and labor laws."

But retail industry observers say Wal-Mart has wrung inefficiencies out of the supply chain and passed the savings along to consumers. "Wal-Mart is an outstanding operator, and suppliers learn how to supply goods faster, better, cheaper — in large part because of the challenges Wal-Mart puts toward them," says Dan Stanek, executive vice president of the retail consulting firm Retail Forward, Inc., of Columbus, Ohio. [1]

Nonetheless, many local policymakers have begun using zoning ordinances and other means to ban big-box retailers from their communities. The ordinances vary widely. Mequon, Wis., for example, prohibits retail stores larger than 20,000 square feet, while Santa Fe, N.M., sets the limit at 150,000 square feet.

Al Norman, an anti-big-box activist from Greenfield, Mass., estimates that the ordinances have derailed hundreds of proposed big-box stores in recent years. "More and more of these stores are being challenged, and it's slowing them down or stopping them in their tracks," Norman says.

The CBS television program "60 Minutes" dubbed Norman the "guru of the anti-Wal-Mart movement" after he kept Wal-Mart out of his hometown in the early 1990s. He now runs Sprawl-Busters, a group that opposes "mega-stores and other undesirable large-scale developments."

Study Cites Hidden Cost of Wal-Mart Jobs

The average Wal-Mart employee in California earns 31 percent less than the average employee at other large retail stores, according to the University of California at Berkeley Labor Institute. The study also found that fewer Wal-Mart workers are covered by company-based health insurance. As a result, Wal-Mart employees' families use more in taxpayer-subsidized public assistance — such as health care and food stamps — than the families of all large retail employees. Non-union Wal-Mart called the study biased because of the institute's strong ties to union labor.

Wal-Mart Wages vs. Other Large Retailers (in California in 2001)

	Average Wages
Wal-Mart	$9.70
All big retailers in California	$14.01

Percentage Covered by Employer-Based Health Insurance (in California in 2004)

Wal-Mart	48%
All large retailers	61%
Unionized grocers*	95%

Amount of Public Assistance Used Annually by Employees

Wal-Mart	$1,952
Large retailers	1,401

** In the San Francisco Bay area*

Source: "Hidden Cost of Wal-Mart Jobs," University of California-Berkeley Labor Center, Aug. 2, 2004

Big-box retailers denounce such efforts as illegal attempts to block competition. "There's nothing more going on here than an attempt by the unions and our competitors to try to stop our growth," says Robert S. McAdam, Wal-Mart's vice president of corporate affairs. "Instead of competing in the marketplace, they're trying to get government to preserve their profits."

But critics say big-box retailers themselves do not always operate on a level playing field with competitors, often demanding huge public subsidies from local and state governments before they will locate in an area. For instance, Wal-Mart — which last year made nearly $9 billion in profits — received at least $1 billion in state and local subsidies, according to a study released in May by the job-subsidy watchdog group Good Jobs First. [2] (*See sidebar, p. 740.*)

The anti-big-box movement has particularly targeted Arkansas-based Wal-Mart, which collected an astronomical $258 billion in revenues in 2003 — more than the combined revenues of General Motors, Microsoft and Coca-Cola. [3] And it is growing rapidly, having recently announced plans to move into perhaps its last marketing frontiers: big U.S. cities and overseas markets. On a single day last April, the giant chain opened 18 stores.

Big-box retailers come in two basic styles. Some, like Wal-Mart, Kmart and Target, sell everything from dog food to diamonds and operate "supercenters" that sell both groceries and general merchandise. Wal-Mart's supercenters are the biggest, sometimes covering 250,000 square feet, or nearly six acres, and carrying about 100,000 different products.

Other big-box retailers specialize in certain types of products, such as Barnes & Noble (books), Staples (office supplies) and Home Depot (home-improvement products). Atlanta-based Home Depot currently operates about 1,700 stores, each carrying about 40,000 different items. Stores average about 108,000 square feet, and have outdoor garden centers.

Americans love the convenience of big-box stores, especially the supercenters that feature one-hour photo centers, hair salons, banks, automotive centers and other services. Most also have acres of free parking — a huge attraction in today's car-cluttered culture. Brenda Hardy, of Montbello, Colo., patronizes Wal-Mart's Commerce City supercenter because, "Everything is under one roof, and you don't have to pay to park."

Wal-Mart's overarching business philosophy — to continuously cut prices — enables the Commerce City store to offer 50-foot garden hoses for just $4.96, large jars of Prego spaghetti sauce (with meat) for $1.72 and 20-inch flat-screen TVs for under $100.

McAdam says the low prices help bolster the nation's economy — and consumers' living standards — by allowing them to buy things they could not otherwise afford or to save for a rainy day. "If you're able to save 15 to 20 percent of your disposable income on what you have to buy for the necessities of life, you can spend that in other ways," McAdam says. "Maybe it's an extra night out on the town, or maybe you save up for a car or some other large purchase. Whatever it is, there's a benefit."

Wal-Mart's low prices also force competitors to lower their prices — a phenomenon known as the "Wal-Mart effect." Americans saved about $100 billion in 2002 thanks to Wal-Mart's low prices and the company's influence on its competitors, according to the New England Consulting Group, in Westport, Conn. [4]

Ira Kalish, global director of Deloitte Research in New York, says Wal-Mart has had a substantial positive impact on America's economy. "Wal-Mart has created a new economic model for retailing that focuses on low prices for consumers, and they've forced other retailers to do the same," he says. "This has effectively made consumers richer. It's like a tax cut, freeing up resources they can spend on other things."

Today, big-box retailers command large and growing market shares of many products. Nearly 40 percent of all book sales, for example, are captured by a handful of large chain stores, with just two companies — Barnes & Noble and Borders — accounting for more than a quarter of the total market. The office-supply market is similarly dominated by Office Max, Office Depot and Staples; and the hardware and building-supply markets by Home Depot and Lowe's.

No retailer, though, dominates more product markets than Wal-Mart. The company is the nation's top seller of many types of merchandise, including apparel, toys, cosmetics, diapers, CDs, DVDs and dog food. It currently commands the lion's share (about 30 percent) of sales of household staples such as toothpaste, shampoo and paper towels. Experts predict Wal-Mart will control half of this market by decade's end. [5]

But the intense competition from Wal-Mart and other discounters is taking a toll on other big retailers as well as mom-and-pop operations. For example, the once-dominant Toys "R" Us chain announced on Aug. 11 that it might abandon the toy business; it has about 17 percent of the $27 billion U.S. toy business, compared with Wal-Mart's 20 percent. [6]

Big-Box Stores Hurt Maine Economies

Three times as much money stays in the local economy when goods and services are bought from locally owned businesses instead of at national chains and big-box stores, according to an analysis of the revenue and expenditures of eight local businesses in Maine by an anti-big-box store organization.

Percentage of Revenues Spent in Local and State Economy
(in Midcoast Maine region)

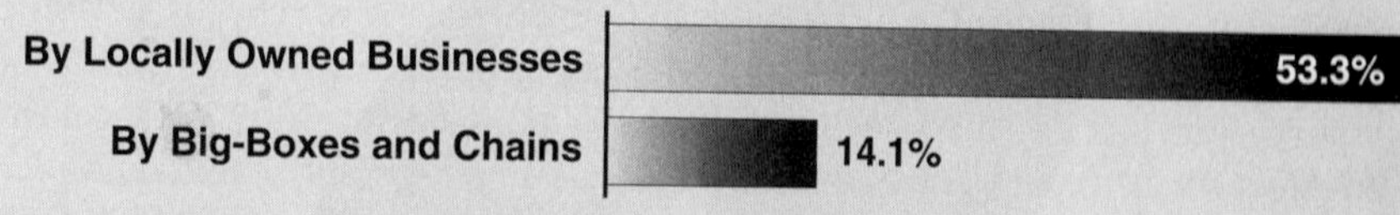

Source: "The Economic Impact of Locally Owned Businesses vs. Chains: A Case Study in Midcoast Maine," Institute for Local Self-Reliance and Friends of Midcoast Maine, September 2003.

"Bookstores, music retailers, electronics chains and supermarkets have all struggled to compete with Wal-Mart's low prices and its enormous power over its suppliers," *The New York Times* noted. [7]

Suppliers are equally squeezed by Wal-Mart's low-price policies. The company demands that suppliers constantly lower their wholesale prices, forcing some to close domestic manufacturing operations and ship jobs overseas. Levi Strauss & Co., America's iconic jeans maker, shuttered all its North American manufacturing plants in the past two years, eliminating some 5,600 jobs; foreign factories now handle the work. [8]

Stacy Mitchell, a researcher at the Washington, D.C.-based Institute for Local Self-Reliance, says the "savings" consumers derive by shopping at Wal-Mart and other big-box retailers carry hidden costs. In addition to millions of dollars in tax breaks and other government subsidies paid to big discounters, Mitchell notes, the companies often pay below-subsistence wages. According to the House report, the average Wal-Mart clerk made $8.23 an hour in 2001, or $13,861 a year — below the federal poverty line of $14,630 for a family of three.

Mitchell contends the company also offers inadequate health insurance plans, throwing more health-care responsibility onto taxpayers. "Wal-Mart encourages its employees to seek charitable and public assistance for meeting their health-care needs," the House study said.

Another study by researchers at the University of California, Berkeley, found that approximately 44,000 Wal-Mart employees in California cost taxpayers about $86 million annually due to their reliance on government services like public health care, subsidized housing, school lunches and food stamps. (*See table, p. 736.*) [9] Other studies have shown that local taxpayers often end up paying more for additional roads and public-safety services needed to support big-box stores than the extra tax revenues generated by the stores.

"There are lots of costs that don't show up on the price tags at stores like Wal-Mart," Mitchell says. "When you add it all up, these stores often don't even pay their own way, much less generate any net benefits for consumers and communities."

As Wal-Mart and other big-box retailers continue to expand, here are some of the issues being debated:

Do big-box retailers hurt locally owned businesses?

Independence, Iowa, population 6,000, once had a vibrant downtown. But after Wal-Mart opened a store nearby in 1984, local retailers began to disappear.

"Fourteen months later, the first local business went down: Anthony's, a department store that . . . had anchored Main Street for 30 years," *The New York Times Magazine* reported in 1989. Over the next four years, "about a dozen businesses closed . . . including a 100-year-old men's store, a furniture store and a sporting goods store. Most of the surviving shops are struggling to stay alive." [10]

A study by the National Trust for Historic Preservation found that 84 percent of all sales at new Wal-Mart stores came at the expense of existing businesses within the same county. Only 16 percent of sales came from outside the county — which critics say refutes the notion that Wal-Mart can act as a magnet drawing customers from a wide area and benefiting other businesses in town. [11]

While big-box stores usually get the blame for undercutting locally owned businesses, others say shoppers are at fault. "Wal-Mart offers consumers an additional shopping option," said Edward Fox, chairman of the J. C. Penney Center for Retail Excellence at Southern Methodist University. "If we choose to avail ourselves of that option, then we are the ones putting the downtown stores out of business." [12]

Wal-Mart's McAdam says the company is merely giving the customer what he wants. "It's not about whether you're small or large; it's about listening to your customers," he says. "Businesses that don't change and don't adapt to their customers' interests are the ones that may not succeed."

John Simley, a spokesman for Home Depot, says stores that struggle or close when his company comes to town are the ones that don't carry the right products, don't train their salespeople, or don't stay open in the evening. "The bottom line is, it's not us that's causing them problems — their customers are not choosing them anymore."

Small stores can co-exist with Home Depot if they adapt and find a niche, Simley says. He cites Curry Hardware in Quincy, Mass., which has a Home Depot practically next door and another a few miles away. Curry sells certain items, such as specialty paints, and provides services — like filling propane tanks and repairing windows and screens — that its big-box neighbors do not. "Business has been wonderful and we expect it to stay that way," said co-owner Sean Curry. "Home Depot hasn't been a problem for us." [13]

Bill Goldman, owner of Downtown Discount Fashions, a 6,000-square-foot independent clothing store and bridal shop in Rutland, Vt., tells a similar story: "They bring people into town [who then] filter around to the different specialty stores."

Locally owned businesses that can find a non-competitive niche do best, he says. "You don't try to compete with the big-box stores, because you can't. Wal-Mart is no competition to me. They don't carry what I carry [wedding gowns and bridal accessories]."

Brian Peltey, owner of Rutland Family Flooring, agrees. Although the Home Depot sells tile, carpeting and other flooring materials, it isn't hurting his much smaller, locally owned business. "I think they've driven some people to us," he says. "They fall down on the service end, so that's how we can compete.

But critics say more typically big-box retailers steamroll local competitors. Steinbaugh Hardware in Louisville, Colo., just east of Boulder, had served the quaint downtown corridor for 104 years when a Home Depot store opened outside of town in August 1996. Five months later, Eagle Hardware opened a big-box store in the same area. Tom Steinbaugh, the fourth-generation Steinbaugh to head the family business, reluctantly closed in June 1997.

"The big boxes — we could fight one, but not two," an angry Steinbaugh said. "It's a punch in the face." [14]

Steinbaugh says his big-box competitors undercut him significantly on price. Experts say the large retailers' dominance in the marketplace gives them the clout to demand extremely low wholesale prices from manufacturers and suppliers — prices mom-and-pop stores cannot get. The big stores can then undercut the small stores.

Some experts say big-box retailers routinely violate laws regulating volume-related discounts and other pricing practices that might be used to weaken competitors. For instance, Wal-Mart is accused of regularly violating the Robinson-Patman Act, enacted in 1936 to prevent large chain stores from conspiring with manufacturers to drive small retailers out of business.

A suit filed by James McCrory, an independent tire dealer in Pompano Beach, Fla., alleges Wal-Mart and the Goodyear tire company are running such a scheme. McCrory says Goodyear sells certain tires to Wal-Mart at or below cost and recoups its losses by charging him and other independent dealers more for the same tires. McCrory says the alleged scheme is significantly hurting his business.

"It doesn't take a rocket scientist to figure out what's going on," he says. "Wal-Mart is pulling this [expletive] all over the country."

Wal-Mart refutes the price-fixing allegation. "We are good bargainers; there's no question about that," McAdam says. "We just want a fair deal from our suppliers."

Wal-Mart and other big-box retailers also have been sued for violating state fair-pricing laws. Last year, for example, a judge in Oklahoma City ruled that three local Sam's Clubs, wholesale stores owned by Wal-Mart, had illegally sold gasoline at a loss to lure customers to buy other merchandise. He ordered the stores to raise their gas prices. The ruling helped "level the playing field" for independent gasoline marketers, said attorney Gary Chilton, who filed the lawsuit on behalf of several convenience stores. [15]

Critics say big-box retailers also violate state laws against "predatory pricing" — selling goods at a loss simply to eliminate competitors. However, such charges are difficult to prove. For example, three independent pharmacists in Conway, Ark., initially won their 1991 suit charging the local Wal-Mart with trying to drive them out of business by selling items below cost. But the Arkansas Supreme Court overturned the ruling two years later, dealing a major setback to small businesses that had hoped predatory-pricing laws would help them compete with big-box retailers.

Do big-box retailers make communities less livable?

Critics say the thousands of cars and trucks attracted by big discounters cause additional traffic, air pollution, noise, sprawl and other detriments to the quality of life.

The stores become prime drivers of suburban sprawl, critics maintain, because they usually locate on the outskirts of communities where land is cheap enough to provide abundant parking. This chews up green space, forces people to drive further to shop and raises taxpayers' costs for road maintenance, police protection and other public services, critics note. At the same time, the low prices wreak economic havoc on small, locally owned stores on traditional main streets.

"Most people wouldn't choose to spend their vacations in towns full of big-box stores and strip malls," says anti-big-box activist Steve Bercu, owner of Book People, an independent bookstore in Austin, Texas. "They'd go to places like Nantucket, where they don't have those things. And why would you want to live somewhere where there's no character?"

But John La Plante, an adjunct scholar at the Mackinac Center for Public Policy in Midland, Mich., scoffs at the "quality-of-life" crowd that opposes discount stores. He says it is comprised mainly of quixotic dreamers, who yearn for a return to a "Norman Rockwell" era, and affluent elitists, who simply don't want their chic communities sullied with stores that cater to lower-income people.

"There's a nostalgia for a sort of existence that's not realistic in this day and age," La Plante says, "and there's definitely a class element [to blocking big-box stores], because it hurts people of lower incomes."

"It's called NIMBYism [not in my backyard]," says Raymond Keating, chief economist at the Small Business Survival Committee, which advocates for small business. Those who complain that Wal-Mart will destroy their quality of life are usually "a very vocal minority who want to freeze [their community] in time. On the flip side are the countless people who shop at the Wal-Mart or Home Depot, and they're basically voting with their dollars. What about the families that want to save a little bit of money by having a local Wal-Mart? Doesn't that enhance their quality of life?"

Many zoning ordinances place no size restrictions on stores in commercial districts. In Fargo, N.D., for example, the main shopping district in the city of 91,000 features Wal-Mart, Sam's Club, Kmart, Target, Kohl's, Home Depot, Lowe's and Best Buy, among others.

"Our [zoning] is pretty friendly to big-box development," says Mark Williams, an assistant city planner. "We look at a Wal-Mart development in the same way we would a 2,000-square-foot bike shop."

"People really like the big-box stores," says Fargo Mayor Bruce Furness, because of the low prices, the wide selection of goods under one roof and the ample free parking. And the sales and property taxes generated by the big-box stores are "very important to our economy," he adds.

Yet Fargo's willingness to accommodate big-box retailers apparently hasn't hurt its quality of life: It consistently ranks among the nation's best small cities for livability and as a place to work and raise children. [16]

But other communities take a decidedly different approach to planning. Easton, Md., for example, a quaint town with about 12,000 residents on Maryland's Eastern Shore, decided to limit retail stores to 65,000 square feet, a threshold based on the size of the town's existing buildings.

Easton adopted its size-cap ordinance in 2000, largely to block three proposed stores of about 170,000 square feet each. The town's planning and zoning commission predicted that increased traffic and demands for public services would compromise Easton's "unique and attractive small-town character." [17]

Dozens of other communities have capped retail store sizes, including Boxborough, Mass. (25,000 sq. ft.); Ashland, Ore. (45,000); Flagstaff, Ariz. (70,000); Taos, N.M. (80,000); and Stoughton, Wis. (110,000).

Big-box retailers say such caps are designed not to legitimately regulate land use but to specifically keep them out. Some have sued cities over the caps, saying they violate retailers' constitutional rights to conduct interstate commerce and to enjoy equal protection under the law. Some also say the caps violate certain state laws by using zoning to regulate competition.

Legal issues aside, some experts say size caps are counterproductive and can foster the very quality-of-life problems — such as increased traffic — that supporters of caps say they are designed

Continued on p. 741

How Cities Subsidize Big-Box Stores

Lowe's is a $31 billion corporation. Yet the New Orleans City Council last year gave the giant home-improvement retailer $3.6 million in public funds to build a store near the French Quarter.

Target is a $48 billion corporation. But the Pennsylvania governor's office two years ago gave the company $5.8 million to build a distribution center in Chambersburg.

Even Wal-Mart — the world's largest company, with revenues of $258 billion in 2003 — caught a subsidy break. Birmingham, Ala., last year offered the giant retailer $10 million to build a store on the east side of town. And that's not all. According to a recent study, Wal-Mart — which last year made nearly $9 billion in profits — received at least $1 billion in various types of state and local government subsidies.

"The actual total is certainly far higher," said the study by the Washington, D.C.-based Good Jobs First, a subsidy watchdog group. "But the records are scattered in thousands of places, and many subsidies are undisclosed." [1]

To encourage new development, state and local governments often offer businesses various subsidies and tax exemptions on the premise that the jobs and future tax revenues they generate will outweigh the subsidy costs.

But critics say cities should not subsidize big-box stores, because studies show that the added financial burdens created by the huge stores — such as additional police services, employees' dependence on subsidized health care and other social benefits — far outweigh the jobs and tax revenues generated by the stores — even when they're not getting tax exemptions.

Moreover, says Jeff Milchen, executive director of the American Independent Business Alliance in Bozeman, Mont., when big-box stores receive subsidies, it unfairly disadvantages competitors who do not receive them. "Subsidies create a completely uneven, uncompetitive playing field," he says. "I have serious doubts as to whether Wal-Mart, Home Depot and other big-box retailers could succeed without the massive public subsidies they receive and use to support the operations of their stores."

The subsidies range from free or reduced-price land and infrastructure improvements to exemptions or rebates on sales, property and corporate income taxes; reduced utility rates, low-interest financing, subsidies to train and recruit workers, tax-exempt bond financing and outright grants.

For example, according to the Good Jobs First study, North Platte, Neb., gave Wal-Mart more than $15.2 million in subsidies to build a distribution center in 2003, including up to $9.45 million in tax abatements, $3.2 million for a racking system, $1 million in special financing for the city to purchase land that was then granted to Wal-Mart, $1 million in federal Community Development Block Grant funds, $170,000 in waived city fees, $400,000 in job training funds and infrastructure improvements worth an unknown amount.

Some subsidies are structured as tax abatements, which allow retailers to keep — usually for a limited time — some or all of the taxes they would normally pay. Birmingham's deal with Wal-Mart, for example, requires the city to refund 90 percent of the sales taxes the store collects — expected to top $2.2 million a year — until the $10 million mark is reached.

Some subsidies generate little opposition. Others spawn firestorms of protest, such as Denver's efforts to revitalize Alameda Square, a run-down strip mall housing an Asian grocery store, a nail parlor and a martial-arts center. The city declared the area "blighted" in 1991 and offered special subsidized financing to any company that would buy and redevelop the site. Wal-Mart proposed building a 209,000-square-foot supercenter on the site that would generate up to $12.2 million in tax revenues annually.

City officials were ecstatic, but many Denverites were outraged at plans to subsidize the world's richest company. Publicly, the city said it was giving Wal-Mart about $10 million in special funding to take on the project, but documents obtained by the Front Range Economic Strategy Center, a group opposed to the deal, indicated the subsidy could balloon to $25 million over several years.

"It was pretty horrific," says Chris Nevitt, the group's executive director. "A lot of people got worked up about it. It was not a popular deal, to say the least."

City officials defended the deal, arguing that Wal-Mart could revitalize the site in a way that a smaller company could not. But even a company of Wal-Mart's size would balk at paying for all the infrastructure improvements needed at a site as dilapidated as Alameda Square, said Tracy Huggins, executive director of the Denver Urban Renewal Authority.

"There's a belief that because [Wal-Mart is] a large company, they could pay for those costs," Huggins said. "And they're right; they could. But will they? If it doesn't make sense for them from a financial standpoint, they can't do it." [2]

Wal-Mart backed out of the deal in April, unable to come to terms with the property owners. While some Denverites were upset by the development, others cheered.

"There's no reason taxpayers should be subsidizing the world's largest corporation," says Al Norman, a well-known anti-big-box activist from Greenfield, Mass. "It's corporate welfare."

---

1 "Shopping for Subsidies: How Wal-Mart Uses Taxpayer Money to Finance Its Never-Ending Growth," Good Jobs First, May 2004.

2 Quoted in Erin Johansen, "DURA Relied on TIF to Bring in Projects," *The Denver Business Journal*, Feb. 6, 2004, p. A3.

Continued from p. 739

to curtail. "There are many, many occasions where our [non-capped] stores actually reduce traffic," says Wal-Mart's McAdam. "You don't have to make as many trips [to different stores] to get everything you need."

Home Depot sometimes agrees to scale back stores in response to community concerns — but only up to a point, Simley says. The company would not, for example, agree to build a 40,000 square-foot-store where there's a clear need for a 180,000-square-foot store, he says, because doing so would result in parking gridlock, more frequent truck deliveries and other unpleasant consequences.

"If we open a smaller store than what's recommended to us, it would still attract the same number of customers," he says. "We determine square footage based on demand; we don't just say, 'The bigger the better.' "

Wal-Mart, too, says it will make reasonable modifications to accommodate community quality-of-life concerns. When residents in Madison, Miss., voiced concerns about the design of a proposed Wal-Mart, the company agreed to build a store with a bricked exterior, a ceramic tile roof and white columns and arches. "The store is absolutely gorgeous; it should be a national model for Wal-Mart," said Mayor Mary Hawkins-Butler. [18]

But other communities haven't been swayed, such as the Denver suburb of Thornton, where Wal-Mart wanted to build a 24-hour supercenter near a golf course surrounded by large homes. Wal-Mart promised a "neighborhood-friendly" store with a unique, pleasing design and parking lot lights that didn't bleed into the neighborhood, plus a gift of eight acres for community open space.

But many Thornton residents feared the store would remain a hulking, ugly box despite efforts to dress it up while drawing as many as 10,000 cars per day to the quiet community, scaring off the bald eagles that sometimes roost in the area. More than 6,000 residents signed a petition opposing the store, and some threatened to mount a campaign to recall the six City Council members who initially supported the proposal.

Courtesy Madison Mayor's Office

When residents in Madison, Miss., complained about the design of a proposed Wal-Mart, the company built a store with a bricked exterior, a ceramic tile roof and white columns and arches to accommodate the community's quality-of-life concerns.

In June, the City Council reversed course and voted 7-2 against authorizing the rezoning proposal that Wal-Mart needed to build the store. "This was a real David vs. Goliath situation," said Thornton resident Joanne Flick, who spearheaded the grass-roots effort to block the store. "It wasn't appropriate to put a Wal-Mart or any other big box next to Thornton's only golf course." [19]

Do big-box retailers benefit local economies?

Supporters say the new jobs and additional sales- and property-tax revenues generated by big-box stores far outweigh any detrimental impacts. Plus, supporters say, by helping shoppers save money the stores foster job growth in other economic sectors through new consumer spending on everything from movies and health-club memberships to home improvements and new clothes.

Like hundreds of American communities, Hyannis, Mass., wrestled with the big-box question when BJ's Wholesale Club proposed a 69,000-square-foot grocery/general merchandise store in the picturesque town. The local policymaking body, the Cape Cod Commission, ultimately voted 7 to 6 (with two abstentions) to approve the store, which is slated for construction later this year.

"There were clear economic benefits for Hyannis and a substantial portion of the population," says Commissioner Lawrence Cole, who voted for the store. "If BJ's can provide people with what they want at lower prices, I can't see prohibiting them just because some people don't like big-box stores."

But Felicia Penn, executive director of the Cape Cod Smart Planning and Growth Coalition, which led the fight against BJ's, says it will hurt the town's few remaining local businesses. "It's not as if there's $35 million a year just sitting around unspent," says Penn, a local merchant herself, referring to BJ's projected first-year earnings. "All that money is going to have to come from other businesses, and that's going to suck the lifeblood out of our community."

Penn contends BJ's will produce a net loss of retail-sector jobs while drawing more traffic from neighboring communities. But the new tax revenues generated will not cover the additional road and infrastructure-maintenance costs required by the increased usage, she says.

A study commissioned by Barnstable, a community just north of Hyannis, supports Penn's hypothesis. The study by Tischler & Associates, a Bethesda, Md.-based consulting firm, found that locally owned "specialty retail" stores generate $326 in net tax revenues per 1,000 square feet per year. Conversely, the firm found, big-box stores cost Barnstable taxpayers more in services — such as road maintenance and police/fire protection — than the stores remit in taxes, creating net losses of $468 per 1,000 square feet annually. [20]

Other studies have reached similar conclusions. A 1993 study conducted for Greenfield, Mass., for example, concluded that a proposed Wal-Mart store would cost existing businesses $35 million in sales annually, leading to a net loss of 105,000 square feet of retail space (and the resulting lost property taxes). The study estimated that while the Wal-Mart would create 177 new jobs, it would cause local businesses to eliminate 148 jobs. [21] Greenfield residents rejected the proposed Wal-Mart in the wake of the study.

"What we find over and over again is that big-box retailers tend to destroy as many jobs as they create and end up costing taxpayers more than they contribute in revenues," says Mitchell of the Institute for Local Self-Reliance.

The National Trust study found that while local tax bases added about $2 million with each Wal-Mart, the decline in retail stores after the Wal-Mart opened depressed property values in downtowns and on shopping strips, offsetting the Wal-Mart tax gains. [22]

Some big-box advocates dismiss such studies outright, saying communities design them to produce the results they want to see. Others say they're inaccurate because they don't consider all of the relevant economic factors.

Home Depot's Simley says some studies ignore or gloss over the "multiplier" effect that Home Depot stores have on their host communities. The average Home Depot, Simley says, employs 150 to 175 people, creating a payroll of up to $5.5 million annually. About 80 percent of that stays in the local area, he says.

"That money goes to support other jobs in the community — jobs in grocery stores, clothing stores, restaurants and so forth," Simley says. "Depending on the locale, we've seen [job-creation] multipliers ranging from 1.8 to well over 3, so if we create 100 jobs, the net effect is between 180 to 300-plus new jobs."

Keating, of the Small Business Survival Committee, is skeptical about such studies, claiming, "If somebody is looking for a certain answer going in, they're going to get the answer coming out. When a Wal-Mart store opens, a lot of consumers go there and find wider selections and better prices, which are certainly good for those families and the economy in general."

Home Depot also benefits communities by providing residents with products to fix up their homes, which increases property values, Simley says. That creates more property tax revenues to spend on streets, parks, libraries and other amenities, he says.

"Where we go, assessments increase," Simley says. "There's no other retailer, except maybe Lowe's, that can say that."

Moreover, Simley notes, economic-impact studies often improperly misanalyze the impact of "leakage," or residents leaving their communities to shop. In Old Saybrook, Conn., for example, town officials rejected a proposed Home Depot store as "incompatible" with the community's small-town character, Simley says. As a result, many residents began patronizing Home Depots in adjacent communities. He estimates the leakage at $20 million annually.

"People are leaving Old Saybrook because they can't get what they need," Simley says. "The economic reality is that there's an overwhelming demand for what we sell, but the people there have to go elsewhere." ■

BACKGROUND

Early Retailers

Modern-day big-box retailers evolved from the department stores, chain stores and mail-order houses that began supplanting small general stores after the Civil War. Department stores began appearing in big cities in the 1860s and '70s, such as Macy's in New York, Wanamaker's in Philadelphia and Marshall Field's in Chicago. By the turn of the century, department stores were in smaller cities and towns. [23]

With their wide range of merchandise, early department stores resembled big-box retailers. But many were known for high-end merchandise and meticulous customer service, not bargain-basement goods that customers had to rummage through themselves. Moreover, unlike today's single-story big boxes, many early department stores boasted several floors and exquisitely designed facades and interiors.

The late-19th century also saw the first chain stores, or "junior department stores," viewed by some as the closest ancestors to big-box retailers. Instead of replicating the glamorous shopping environments of their bigger retail cousins, they emphasized simplicity and low prices.

The nation's first major chain, the Great Atlantic and Pacific Tea Co. (A&P), was founded in New York City in 1859. Eventually, it expanded from just dealing in tea into a full-blown grocery outlet; by 1929, A&P operated 15,000 stores nationwide — triple the 5,000 stores Wal-Mart has worldwide today.

General-merchandise companies soon jumped on the chain-store bandwagon. Among the most successful was the J. C. Penney Co. James Cash Penney

Continued on p. 744

Chronology

1850s-1890s

Department stores, chain stores and mail-order houses replace small general stores.

1858
R. H. Macy opens a small dry-goods store in New York City.

1859
The Great Atlantic and Pacific Tea Co. (A&P) is founded in New York City.

1872
Aaron Montgomery Ward distributes his first mail-order catalog.

1900-1930s

Small retailers say chain stores and mail-order houses are driving them out of business. State and federal efforts to level the playing field are unsuccessful.

1902
James Cash Penney opens his first store in Kemmerer, Wyo. The J. C. Penney chain expands to more than 1,400 stores by 1930.

1912
Small merchants unsuccessfully lobby Congress to abolish the parcel-post system, saying mail-order firms are driving them out of business.

1931
California enacts the first "fair trade" law, designed to help small merchants compete against chain stores. Dozens of states follow suit.

1936
Congress enacts Robinson-Patman Act to prevent chain stores from driving independent retailers out of business.

1960s-1980s

Discount stores give rise to big-box retailers.

1962
Kresge dime-store chain opens its first Kmart discount store in Garden City, Mich.; Dayton Corp. opens first Target store in Minneapolis; Sam Walton opens his first Wal-Mart in Rogers, Ark.

1970
Kmart is the nation's largest retailer with $2 billion in annual sales. Wal-Mart is far behind with $44.2 million.

1978
The first Home Depot opens in Decatur, Ga.

1979
Wal-Mart sales top $1 billion.

1988
The first Wal-Mart supercenter — a combination general merchandise/grocery store — opens in Washington, Mo.

1989
The first formal study of Wal-Mart's impact on rural America concludes that Wal-Mart raises overall retail sales in a community, but largely at the expense of small merchants.

1990s-Present

Local zoning laws try to limit the spread of big-box retailers.

1990
Wal-Mart becomes the nation's top retailer, with $32.6 billion in sales.

1991
Wal-Mart opens its first foreign store, in Mexico City.

1993
An Arkansas court rules that Wal-Mart engaged in predatory pricing to drive three independent pharmacies out of business. The state supreme court overturns the ruling.

August 2001
Kmart slashes prices to compete with Wal-Mart. Five months later, Kmart declares bankruptcy.

Oct. 11, 2003
Some 70,000 union grocery workers in California strike over grocery chains' efforts to cut wages and benefits to better compete with non-union Wal-Mart. The strike eventually ends, with the grocery chains getting most of what they wanted.

March 2, 2004
In a victory for Wal-Mart, voters in Contra Costa County, Calif., overturn a zoning ordinance banning supercenter-type stores.

April 6, 2004
Voters in Inglewood, Calif., reject a ballot initiative that would have allowed Wal-Mart to build a supercenter without adhering to city zoning codes.

June 22, 2004
A federal judge grants class-action status to a gender-discrimination suit filed against Wal-Mart, covering about 1.6 million current and former employees, making it the largest workplace-discrimination lawsuit in U.S. history.

Aug. 11, 2004
Under pressure from discounters, Toys "R" Us announces it may exit the toy business; the firm's share of the U.S. market has dropped to 17 percent, compared to Wal-Mart's 20 percent and Target's 18 percent.

Buy American? Not at Wal-Mart

Wal-Mart founder Sam Walton — the world's richest person when he died in 1992 — was a rags-to-riches billionaire. Raised in a backwater Arkansas town, he was famously frugal and down-to-earth: He shunned limousines, choosing instead to drive around in an old pickup truck.

"What am I supposed to haul my dogs around in, a Rolls-Royce?" Walton, an avid quail hunter, once quipped.

The first President George Bush extolled Walton as "an American original." Walton himself subtitled his autobiography, "Made in America."

Walton may have been made in America, but it's not easy to find American-made merchandise at Wal-Mart these days. The Levi Strauss jeans sold at Wal-Mart come from Mexico and Colombia. Fruit of the Loom boxer shorts are made in El Salvador, White Stag sweaters in the Philippines, Winnie-the-Pooh clocks in China — and the list goes on and on. Wal-Mart won't say what portion of its merchandise is imported, but the Columbus, Ohio, consulting firm Retail Forward estimates that it is about 60 percent.

However, in March 1985, Walton had announced that he was "firmly committed" to "buying everything possible from suppliers who manufacture their products in the United States." [1]

Walton touted the effort as a way to counteract the flood of cheap imports that was increasing the nation's trade deficit and prompting U.S. companies to eliminate manufacturing jobs. Wal-Mart pledged to buy U.S.-made items costing within 5 percent of equal-quality items from overseas. Some U.S. companies did lower their prices in order to sell to Wal-Mart. In 1988, Wal-Mart claimed it had converted some $1.2 billion in retail goods to U.S. manufacturers that otherwise would have been made overseas — creating or saving about 17,000 U.S. jobs.

Wal-Mart widely advertised its "Buy American" theme, and festooned its stores with red-white-and-blue banners that read, "Made in the USA," and "Keep America Working and Strong." It was a public relations windfall for Wal-Mart, especially among blue-collar Americans who had lost, or feared losing, their jobs due to foreign competition.

But eight months after Walton's death, NBC News correspondent Brian Ross interviewed then-Wal-Mart CEO David Glass on national television. Ross told Glass he'd recently visited numerous Wal-Mart stores and found clothing made in China and other countries on racks labeled "Made in the USA." Glass shrugged this off as a "mistake at the store level." [2]

Ross then played a videotape showing a Bangladesh factory where children as young as 9 were making shirts for Wal-Mart. Glass said Wal-Mart made a "concerted effort" not to buy merchandise made with child labor. But when Ross showed Glass photographs of the bodies of 25 children who had died in a fire at the same factory two years earlier, Glass replied, "Yeah. There are tragic things that happen all over the world." [3]

Other media investigations followed. After being forced to investigate its overseas suppliers, Wal-Mart announced it had adopted a set of standards to govern overseas suppliers. Other U.S. firms followed suit.

Wal-Mart's standards say the company "will not accept" products manufactured with any type of forced or prison labor. Workers must be at least 14 years old, even if local laws allow children to work at a lower age. Moreover, factory owners must "fairly compensate" workers and maintain

Continued from p. 742

opened his first store in Kemmerer, Wyo., in 1902. By the mid-1930s, he had more than 1,400 stores across the country.

Some early general-merchandise chains were known as variety stores, or "5 and dimes," because nothing cost more than 10 cents (at least initially). Pioneers in this category included W. T. Grant and F. W. Woolworth.

Two of the most successful chains started out as mail-order houses. Aaron Montgomery Ward distributed his first catalog — a single sheet of paper listing 163 items — in 1872. By 1904, Ward's catalog — known to millions of Americans as the "Wish Book" — exceeded 500 pages. Sears, Roebuck and Co. published its first mail-order catalog in 1896, and by the turn of the century its more than 1,000 pages listed tens of thousands of items. Mail-order firms were especially popular in rural areas, which often had only small general stores. Sears began opening retail outlets in 1925; Ward's followed suit the next year.

Backlash

The early chain stores and mail-order houses — and, to a lesser degree, department stores — provoked a backlash similar to today's criticism of big-box retailers. Independent retailers complained bitterly that their larger competitors engaged in unethical and illegal practices to drive them out of business, mainly using their buying power to obtain lower prices from suppliers.

Some independents responded by publicly burning mail-order catalogs, or by playing on the era's racism, spreading rumors that Richard Sears and Montgomery Ward were black. In 1912, a coalition of independent merchants unsuccessfully lobbied Congress to cancel the fledgling parcel-post service, the mail-order firms' lifeline.

But anti-chain fervor continued. In 1922, author Frank Farrington implored merchants, wholesalers and the general public in his book *Meeting Chain* "reasonable" work hours in accordance with prevailing labor laws. "Wal-Mart strives to do business only with factories run legally and ethically," the standards declare.

But critics say Wal-Mart and other U.S. retailers buy goods from countries like China precisely because they ignore their own labor laws. "U.S.-based corporations that invest in Chinese factories — a long list headed by Wal-Mart — owe some nice chunk of their profits to a work force toiling, to resurrect a line from Mao, under 'the barrel of a gun,' " Harold Meyerson, editor-at-large of the liberal *American Prospect* magazine, wrote recently. [4]

AFP Photo/Paul J. Richards

Wal-Mart remains popular with consumers even though most of its merchandise comes from overseas.

According to the House Education and Workforce Committee's recent minority staff report on Wal-Mart's labor abuses: "Workers in countries like China, Bangladesh and Honduras are suffering because of the stringent demands Wal-Mart makes of its suppliers. One factory worker reported working 19-hour days for 10- to 15-day stretches to meet Wal-Mart's price demands." [5]

Meanwhile, the Buy American program came under increasing attack. In 1998, the United Food and Commercial Workers International Union alleged that 80 percent of Wal-Mart's clothing was foreign-made and urged the Federal Trade Commission and all 50 state attorneys general to investigate Wal-Mart for "falsely" and "deceptively" concealing the practice.

"The time has come for American government officials to protect the integrity of our flag from crass, commercial abuse," said Doug Dority, then-president of the 1.4 million-member union. [6]

Wal-Mart abandoned its Buy American program in the late 1990s — not because of the union, it said, but rather because of the realities of economic globalization.

"There was a time when we really tried to buy product [domestically], but whether we like it or not, so much of everything is now sourced overseas," says Bob McAdam, Wal-Mart's vice president of corporate affairs. "And we are committed to providing people with the lowest possible price."

---

1 Wal-Mart press release, March 13, 1985.

2 Quoted in Bob Ortega, *In Sam We Trust* (1988), p. 223.

3 *Ibid*., p. 225.

4 Quoted in Harold Meyerson, "China's Workers — And Ours," *The Washington Post*, March 17, 2004, p. A25.

5 "Everyday Low Wages: The Hidden Price We All Pay for Wal-Mart," Democratic Staff of the House Committee on Education and the Workforce," Feb. 16, 2004.

6 Quoted in F.N. D'Alessio, "Major Union and AFL-CIO Join Attack on Wal-Mart's 'Buy American' Program," The Associated Press, July 30, 1998.

Store Competition to stop the proliferation of chains. And Shreveport, La., radio personality William K. Henderson urged listeners: "American people, wake up — we can whip these chain stores! We can drive them out in 30 days if you people will stay out of their stores."

But the chains' lower prices were just too seductive. Still, many state lawmakers were troubled by the chains' growing dominance and sought to level the retail playing field. Several states adopted "fair trade" laws that prohibited chains from selling a product for less than the manufacturer's suggested retail price. While the new restrictions had some effect, court decisions in the 1950s and '60s diluted or voided most of them.

Many states also taxed the chains according to the number of outlets they operated. By 1939, 27 states had chain-store tax laws. Ironically, the tax laws may have done the anti-chain movement more harm than good: They encouraged the chains to build larger stores (instead of more stores), giving the independents even tougher competition.

The growing tide of angry independents finally prompted Congress to act in 1936. The Robinson-Patman antitrust act, known as the "anti-chain store act," made it illegal for chains to pressure suppliers into giving them volume-related discounts not offered to smaller retailers. It also prohibited suppliers from giving volume-related discounts to retailers — no matter how much they bought — that did not reflect their actual savings in manufacturing and/or delivering the goods.

Robinson-Patman was expressly intended to kill off the most despised chain store of all: A&P. While the giant chain was found guilty of violating the act, the conviction did not sink the firm. But a few decades later modern supermarkets forced it to close most of its stores. As for the Robinson-Patman Act, the federal government essentially stopped enforcing it in the 1970s.

"There really hasn't been any enforcement since the Nixon administration," says Carl Person, a New York lawyer. "It's really been devastating for people who rely on the government to create a level playing field."

Rise of the Discounters

Retailing changed markedly again after World War II, when the development of "discounting" allowed merchants to profit while undercutting the competition. Strategies included bypassing "the middle man" and buying goods directly from manufacturers; eliminating home delivery and other services; and, especially, operating out of low-rent facilities, often on the outskirts of town.

Many chain and variety stores embraced discounting, and the technique ultimately evolved into big-box retailing. Among the movement's pioneers was the Kresge dime-store chain, which opened its first Kmart in Garden City, a Detroit suburb, in April 1962. By the end of 1963, there were 53 units.

Early Kmarts averaged about 100,000 square feet and typically were in shopping centers or strip malls, rather than crowded, downtown shopping districts. The outlying locations not only cut costs but also provided plenty of free parking — a convenience few downtown retailers could offer. By the late 1960s, Kmart was the largest discounter in America.

Woolworth launched a discount line, Woolco, in Columbus, Ohio, just three months after the first Kmart. Early Woolco stores were huge, up to 180,000 square feet. Like Kmarts, they usually were in shopping centers and strip malls with ample parking. Many also had restaurants, pharmacies and automobile service centers, presaging today's "one-stop shopping" trend.

Other early discounters included the Dayton Corp., which also opened its first Target store in 1962, J. C. Penney (Treasure Island stores) and Gamble-Skogmo (Tempo stores) in 1964.

Wal-Mart Emerges

The 1960s also saw the emergence of Wal-Mart. Founder Sam Walton began his career in 1940 at J. C. Penney's, earning $75 a month as a management trainee. After a stint in the Army, Walton opened several Ben Franklin variety stores in Arkansas, Missouri and Texas.

Walton thought full-scale discount stores would succeed in small- and medium-sized towns — which he believed were underserved by the big chains. After two retail firms declined to back him, Walton mortgaged everything he had to open his first discount store in Rogers, Ark., in 1962. He called it "Wal-Mart Discount City." A sign announced: "We Sell for Less."

Walton was fanatical about keeping his overhead — and thus his prices — down. He paid his clerks about 60 cents an hour, well below the federal minimum wage of $1.15.[24] He shunned expensive racks and display cases, instead stacking his merchandise on tables or hanging it from metal pipes. Walton had claimed he would sell only first-class goods, but much of his merchandise was of poor quality, because many manufacturers refused to sell their top goods to an unproven discounter.

Nevertheless, the first Wal-Mart was wildly successful. Walton rushed to open more outlets, and by 1970 he had 38 stores in five states. By 1979, he had 276 stores in 11 states, with sales topping the $1 billion mark for the first time.

In 1983, Walton launched "Sam's Club," a line of warehouse-like stores where a nominal membership fee permits shopping for deeply discounted merchandise, usually purchased in large quantities. His first Wal-Mart supercenter — a combination grocery/general merchandise store — opened in Washington, Mo., in 1988. Another milestone came in 1991, when Wal-Mart opened its first international store, in Mexico City.

At his death in 1992, Walton was the world's richest man, with a fortune of more than $20 billion. The company's growth continued, and during the 1990s it leapfrogged over legendary firms such as General Motors to become the largest company in the world, both in sales and employees.

As Wal-Mart expanded, many communities welcomed the giant retailer, but critics began to emerge.

Iowa State University economist Kenneth Stone conducted the first formal study of Wal-Marts' impact on retail sales in 1989, focusing on 10 Iowa towns where the company had stores, and 45 communities where it did not.

Stone's findings were mixed, however, prompting both Wal-Mart supporters and critics alike to tout them as proof of their arguments. To the delight of supporters, towns with Wal-Marts experienced overall sales increases. But the increases came largely at the expense of small, independent retailers — as Wal-Mart critics had contended.

"It's kind of a zero-sum game when Wal-Mart comes to town," Stone says today. "What they take in doesn't come out of thin air — it comes out of other merchants' cash registers." ■

CURRENT SITUATION

Union Busting?

One of the most contentious aspects of the big-box debate revolves around Wal-Mart's impact on the grocery industry, which it entered only 16 years ago. By contrast, Kroger, which operates Ralph's, King Soopers and other chains, has been selling groceries for 122 years.

Nevertheless, Wal-Mart is already America's largest grocery chain. Its grocery sales come mainly from its more than 1,500 supercenters, which can be as large as four football fields (230,000 square feet).

Wal-Mart's grocery success is due in large part to its low labor costs. The staunchly anti-union company typically pays its employees between $7.50 and $8.50 per hour, compared to $13 to $18 per hour paid by traditional supermarket chains, which are heavily unionized. [25] In any event, Wal-Mart's lower labor costs help customers save up to 30 percent on their grocery bills, studies have found.

But critics say the cheap groceries carry a tremendous societal cost: When traditional supermarket chains cannot compete with Wal-Mart, they either must close stores or eliminate well-paying union jobs — some of the last well-paying jobs available to single mothers, retirees and people without college degrees.

Albertson's, for example, shuttered some 450 stores in 2002, including all 95 in the Wal-Mart strongholds of Houston, Memphis, Nashville and San Antonio, at a cost of more than 3,000 union jobs. Wal-Mart denies frequent accusations that it engages in illegal "union busting," claiming a good labor-relations record. But at least 60 federal labor complaints have been filed against the company in the last 10 years. (*See sidebar, p. 748.*) [26]

Meanwhile, Wal-Mart faces other legal problems. It has denied knowingly using illegal immigrants to clean its stores and has reportedly been in talks to settle a Department of Justice probe into the matter. And a federal judge this year certified a class-action, workplace gender-bias suit against Wal-Mart, covering as many as 1.6 million current and former female employees.

Strike in California

California is the hottest spot in the grocery wars. For years Wal-Mart held off entering the state's heavily unionized grocery market, saying it needed time to build up its food-distribution system. But experts say the company really was mustering its resources to take on California's powerful unions.

In any event, in May 2002 Wal-Mart announced its intention to build 40 supercenters in California over the next four to six years. To prepare for the low-price competition, Kroger, Safeway and Albertson's scrambled to decrease the wages and benefits of thousands of workers at 852 California supermarkets.

Under the existing union contract, grocery clerks with just two years' experience could earn up to $17.90 per hour; $26.85 hourly on Sundays; and $53.70 per hour on holidays. Workers also received free, full health benefits. [27]

With the union contract set to expire last fall, the three companies jointly sought to charge workers for some of their health benefits, and lower the wages and benefits for new hires.

"We are seeking nothing more than a fair contract that will help us to remain competitive in the face of . . . increased competition from lower-cost operators," said John Burgon, president of the Ralph's chain. "The ability to manage costs is crucial to the long-term future of our businesses." [28]

But the United Food and Commercial Workers (UFCW) union rebuffed the companies' demands. Last Oct. 11, some 20,000 union workers in southern and central California went on strike at two Safeway subsidiaries, Vons and Pavilions. Kroger and Albertson's, in a show of support, locked out about 50,000 union workers the next day. In all, some 70,000 workers were walking picket lines.

As the strike dragged on, many observers said the outcome could have serious implications for middle-class wage earners everywhere. "If the union loses this and has to give back a significant portion of their benefits, you're really moving down the road to everybody [becoming like] a Wal-Mart worker, with low wages and low benefits," said Paul Clark, a labor-relations expert at Pennsylvania State University. [29]

In early March, nearly five months after the strike began, the two sides agreed to a three-year contract. While the UFCW declared victory, the companies got most of the salary and benefit cuts they had sought for new hires.

"You're not going to be able to make a career out of it anymore," said Kerry Renaud, a veteran produce worker at a supermarket in Hollywood. "We [got] squeezed." [30]

Zoning Lawsuits

Wal-Mart is vigorously contesting anti-big-box zoning ordinances across the country. In February, for example, the company challenged a Turlock, Calif., ordinance banning retail stores larger than 100,000 square feet that sell groceries on more than 5 percent of their floor space. Wal-Mart says the ordinance is illegal because it outlaws some big-box stores — namely, its supercenters — while allowing others, such as Home Depots.

"[The city] cannot discriminate against Wal-Mart as opposed to other businesses in the area," said Wal-Mart attorney Timothy Jones. "Our belief is that Wal-Mart was the subject of the ordinance." [31]

The first of Wal-Mart's two lawsuits against the city contends the ordinance violates the company's constitutional rights to conduct interstate commerce and to enjoy equal protection under the law. The second alleges the city violated state law by using a zoning ordinance to regulate competition.

Wal-Mart Accused of 'Union Busting'

When a pro-union flyer was found on the men's room floor at the Wal-Mart in Hillview, Ky., store manager Jon Lehman went into action. Following corporate policy, he immediately reported the incident to Wal-Mart headquarters in Bentonville, Ark., using the company's confidential "Union Hotline."

Within 24 hours, three company executives arrived in Hillview on a corporate jet. Lehman drove the officials to the store where he says they began "threatening, interrogating," making false promises to and "spying" on employees to determine who made the handbill. They scrutinized personnel files for clues and entered employees' biographical information and behavioral traits into a special matrix designed to identify likely union sympathizers. During the two-week investigation, they even monitored suspect employees' conversations.

The corporate sleuths didn't uncover the flyer's creator, but before departing they made employees watch two anti-union videos that portrayed union members as "crooks and thugs," Lehman says.

By spying on, intimidating and even firing employees thought to be union supporters, Wal-Mart routinely violates federal laws that protect workers' rights to unionize, according to officials at the United Food and Commercial Workers union (UFCW). "Union busting is a matter of policy at Wal-Mart," says Greg Denier, UFCW's director of communications. "Wal-Mart tells its managers that one of their primary duties is to identify and eliminate union activity. It's almost impossible to fulfill that mandate within the confines of the law."

Lehman resigned from Wal-Mart two years after the Hillview incident, feeling "outraged" over the incident and others like it and became a UFCW organizer. "I preached against the union for years," Lehman says now. "[Now] I'm trying to bring the truth back to Wal-Mart [employees] that the union can be a good thing."

So far, however, not one of Wal-Mart's 1.5 million employees — known as "associates" — is a union member. Wal-Mart says its stores are union-free because the employees are treated well — not because it is "anti-union," as critics charge. "We are not against unions; we just don't think they work for us and our associates," says Robert S. McAdam, Wal-Mart's vice president for state and local government relations.

Lehman says as a Wal-Mart manager he was given a 49-page policy manual, entitled "A Manager's Toolbox to Remaining Union-Free." It begins with the statement, "As a member of Wal-Mart's management team, you are our first line of defense against unionization," he says. The manual lists 25 early warning signs of union organizing, such as "associates spending an abnormal amount of time in the parking lot before and after work" and "frequent meetings at associates' homes."

The manual tells managers they need to "understand what is considered legal and illegal conduct" in responding to union activities. It lists 25 examples of illegal activities, such as, "You cannot threaten associates with loss of their job if they sign a union authorization card."

Lehman says the store managers he knew usually adhered to the manual's guidelines. But he adds: "If you had a legitimate union scare or union activity in your store, the people from Bentonville would come in, and they would throw the book out the window."

Wal-Mart's McAdam denies the charge. "We don't do anything that's illegal; that's just not true," he says.

However, the National Labor Relations Board (NLRB), an independent government agency that enforces federal labor law, has filed at least 60 complaints against Wal-Mart in the last 10 years alleging it violated workers' right to organize. [1] Few other companies have as many complaints filed against them. Some have been thrown out, and many are still pending. But others have been upheld. In 2002, for example, a judge ruled that managers at three Las Vegas Wal-Marts had broken the law dozens of times by interrogating workers, confiscating pro-union literature and denying a promotion because a worker supported a union. [2]

In another well-known case, meat-cutters in Jacksonville, Texas, voted to unionize — the first union election in a Wal-Mart store. Eleven days later, Wal-Mart announced plans to phase out its meat-cutting departments throughout the company and instead sell prepackaged meat. Wal-Mart said it had been considering the move for more than two years, and that the timing was just a coincidence. The company refused to enter into contract negotiations with the Jacksonville butchers.

Last June, an NLRB judge ruled that Wal-Mart had illegally refused to bargain with the meat-cutters; Wal-Mart is appealing the decision.

Meanwhile, the UFCW is still trying to organize Wal-Mart workers in Las Vegas, where other service-sector jobs are highly unionized. Lehman says he's making some progress but adds that it's tough to take on the largest corporation in the world.

"The most prevalent reaction I get [from Wal-Mart employees] is fear," he says. "They want to talk to me, but they don't want to be seen talking to the union because they're afraid they could lose their jobs."

[1] For more information, see Abigail Goldman and Nancy Cleeland, "The Wal-Mart Effect: An Empire Built on Bargains Remakes the Working World," *Los Angeles Times*, Nov. 23, 2003, p. A1; Steven Greenhouse, "Judge Rules Against Wal-Mart on Refusal to Talk to Workers," *The New York Times*, June 19, 2003, p. A16; and Bob Ortega, *In Sam We Trust: The Untold Story of Sam Walton and How Wal-Mart is Devouring America* (1998).

[2] See Steven Greenhouse, "Trying to Overcome Embarrassment, Labor Opens a Drive to Organize Wal-Mart," *The New York Times*, Nov. 8, 2002, p. A28.

Mayor Curt Andre says the city will "vigorously defend" its ordinance. "The overwhelming majority of people that have talked to me have been fervent in their desire to keep any kind of superstore out of Turlock," he said. [32]

But other communities are having second thoughts about taking on the

Continued on p. 750

At Issue:

Is Wal-Mart good for America?

ROBERT S. MCADAM
VICE PRESIDENT, STATE AND LOCAL GOVERNMENT RELATIONS, WAL-MART STORES, INC.

WRITTEN FOR THE *CQ RESEARCHER*, SEPTEMBER 2004

YES

Wal-Mart offers everyday, affordable prices for American families across the country while providing good jobs and serving communities through volunteerism and charitable contributions.

W. Michael Cox, chief economist at the Federal Reserve Bank of Dallas, noted in *The New York Times:* "Wal-Mart is the greatest thing that ever happened to low-income Americans. They can stretch their dollars and afford things they otherwise couldn't."

Communities also benefit from increased economic activity and the revitalization of economically depressed areas spurred by Wal-Mart. Often, new businesses are established and existing businesses relocate near a new Wal-Mart. In Columbia, Md., after Wal-Mart took over a space abandoned by another retailer, *The Washington Post* commented that "Wal-Mart has quickly turned into a magnet" for new businesses.

Increased economic activity and lower prices yield jobs and economic growth. A recent Los Angeles County Economic Development Corp. study found Wal-Mart supercenters would save residents in a seven-county region $589 per household per year and create 36,400 jobs. Two-thirds of Wal-Mart jobs are full time. All pay above the federal minimum. In fact, the average wage is $9.98 an hour — higher in larger cities.

Clearly, people find value in working here: Our turnover rate — 46 percent — is one-third below the retail average. Our benefits are ranked the best in the retail industry. Both full- and part-time associates are eligible for benefits.

We provide career growth, too. Nine thousand hourly associates moved into management last year, joining two-thirds of our store management who started as hourly employees.

Part of our company's culture is giving back to the communities we serve through charitable contributions to local organizations. Corporate giving totaled $158 million last year.

In our communities, we've generated more than $52 billion in sales taxes and $4 billion in property taxes in the past decade. Wal-Mart is proud to purchase goods from 10,000 U.S. suppliers and export $2 billion of U.S.-made goods to our stores in 10 foreign countries.

Wal-Mart's value can be calculated in jobs, economic growth and charitable partnerships in communities throughout the country. Those numbers don't compare, however, to the rising standard of living U.S. families experience because of Wal-Mart's commitment to lowering costs and prices on everyday needs.

AL NORMAN
FOUNDER, SPRAWL-BUSTERS.COM
***AUTHOR,* SLAM-DUNKING WAL-MART: HOW YOU CAN STOP SUPERSTORE SPRAWL IN YOUR HOMETOWN**

WRITTEN FOR THE *CQ RESEARCHER*, SEPTEMBER 2004

NO

The world's biggest retailer — some say the most admired retailer in America — is also the most reviled. Increasingly, Americans understand that Wal-Mart is more than just a chain store. It is a chain of exploitation that stretches from sweatshops in China to sales floors in California. Each link in the retail chain is forged in the heat of unfair advantage and abuse. Among other things, Wal-Mart:

- Watches 45 percent of its workers quit every year.
- Failed to make *Fortune* magazine's list of "100 Best Places to Work."
- Secretly collected life insurance benefits from its dead workers.
- Admits its wages are "not designed to fully support a family."
- Concealed violent crimes against shoppers at its stores.
- Asked taxpayers to subsidize the building of its empire.
- Spent 38 percent less on health care per worker than the average U.S. employer.
- Was sued in 32 states for forcing its employees to work "off the clock."
- Was sued by federal officials for discriminating on the basis of disability and sex.
- Has nearly 7,000 lawsuits pending against it at any point in time.
- Has more than 325 "dead" stores sitting empty in small-town America.
- Was busted for predatory pricing in the United States and Germany.
- Was caught using illegal workers to build and clean its stores.
- Imported more Chinese products ($12 billion) than any other retailer.
- Squeezes manufacturers on pricing so harshly that companies have been forced to transfer millions of factory jobs to Mexico or China.

Wal-Mart represents the end of competition, not the beginning. In 1989, its CEO, David Glass, predicted that half the nation's retailers would be out of business by the year 2000. The firm Retail Forward recently warned, "Wal-Mart will continue to steamroll the competitive landscape." Small-town America has been ravaged.

We are heading toward a "one-nation, one-store" marketplace. The battle will be won or lost in Wal-Mart's aisles. If Wal-Mart wins, America loses.

Continued from p. 748

world's largest corporation. On March 30, county officials in Oakland, Calif., voted to rescind an anti-big-box ordinance rather than contest a Wal-Mart lawsuit alleging that the measure imposed "unusual and unnecessary restrictions on lawful business enterprises."

The measure, which the county had enacted only three months earlier, was nearly identical to Turlock's. [33] Other communities that have rescinded ordinances after Wal-Mart took or threatened legal action include Clark County, Nev. (Las Vegas)

AFP Photo

Wal-Mart has been slashing prices in Beijing since July 11, 2003, when the world's biggest retailer made its first foray into a major Chinese city. Opera performers celebrate the launch of a Sam's Club warehouse store in the capital city.

In Los Angeles, meanwhile, the City Council voted, 14-1, on Aug. 11, 2004, to require developers seeking to build superstores — retail stores of 100,000 square feet or more that devote 10 percent or more of their floor space to food or other non-taxable items — to pay for an economic analysis before they can apply for, or get, a building permit.

The new law applies only to designated "economically vulnerable" areas of the city. City officials say the law is necessary because superstores like Wal-Mart supercenters and SuperTargets can have a devastating effect on local communities by lowering wages and driving out existing businesses.

Under the law, developers would have to analyze whether or not their proposed store would eliminate jobs, depress wages or harm surrounding businesses.

"This ordinance [ensures] that a superstore project would add to a neighborhood's economy and quality of life, not detract from them," said Mayor Jim Hahn.

Wal-Mart has spent millions of dollars lobbying city councils and residents in Los Angeles, Chicago and other large cities it hopes to move into, according to *The Washington Post.* [34]

Ballot Battles

Wal-Mart turned to voters instead of the courts to circumvent an anti-big box ordinance enacted in June 2003 in Contra Costa County, near Oakland. Using California's referendum process, Wal-Mart asked voters to reject the ordinance.

Wal-Mart spent some $1 million gathering signatures and distributing literature urging residents to overturn the measure — which they did on March 2, 2004, by a 54 percent to 46 percent vote.

"I hope this vote makes communities think twice about passing these ordinances," Wal-Mart spokeswoman Amy Hill said. [35]

Wal-Mart took an even more aggressive approach in Inglewood, a Los Angeles suburb that is 46 percent African-American and 46 percent Latino. The company first threatened a referendum and a lawsuit, which forced the City Council to repeal its 2002 anti-big-box ordinance. At that point, Wal-Mart could have built a store as long as it adhered to the rest of the city's zoning and environmental regulations.

Instead, Wal-Mart used the referendum process to ask voters to approve a supercenter on a 60-acre tract near The Forum, the former home of the Los Angeles Lakers. The 71-page ballot initiative described in minute detail Wal-Mart's plan for the site, from the design of the store's façade to the toilets in the restrooms.

It also declared the entire site would be exempt from Inglewood's planning, zoning and environmental regulations.

Wal-Mart spent more than $1 million promoting the initiative, inundating residents with phone calls, television commercials and mailers promising that the store would bring low-priced merchandise and good jobs to their community. "As far as I'm concerned, it's a no-brainer," Mayor Roosevelt Dorn said just before the vote, predicting the project would generate hundreds of jobs and millions of dollars in tax revenues. [36]

Supermarket workers and other UFCW union members mounted a campaign to defeat the plan, saying it would prompt other businesses to slash wages and benefits or eliminate good-paying jobs. Others were outraged over Wal-Mart's attempt to exempt itself from city regulations.

"They are driving a Mack truck through California land use, planning and environmental law and trying to create a Wal-Mart government on this 60-acre site," said Madeline Janis-Aparico, director of the Coalition for a Better Inglewood. "If they succeed in doing this, it will [become] their blueprint" for projects elsewhere. [37]

To the surprise of many pundits, Inglewood residents soundly rejected the proposal: 7,049 to 4,575.

"This shows . . . that Wal-Mart can't dupe people in this city to sign away their rights," said Inglewood resident Mike Shimpock. "If they spent $1 million here and lost by this margin, I doubt they'll try this elsewhere." [38]

But Wal-Mart officials said the defeat would not derail the company's expansion plans. "It's simply one store, one site in the list of hundreds we work on every year," McAdam said. "We're going to find ways to build stores and serve customers. We are not going to get pushed around by unions. We are here to state our case, and we are not going to go away quietly." [39] ■

OUTLOOK

More Expansion

Wal-Mart and Home Depot have especially aggressive growth agendas. Wal-Mart plans to open up to 495 new stores throughout the world this year, including 355 in the United States — an opening every 24 hours and 42 minutes. That would give Wal-Mart 3,368 stores in the United States and more than 5,000 stores worldwide. [40] Home Depot plans to open 175 new stores in 2004 — one every 50 hours. If the company stays on schedule, it will have more than 1,800 stores in North America by year's end. [41]

Many analysts speculate that Wal-Mart wants to get into other business sectors, such as automobile sales or banking. It has tried several times to buy a bank or a savings and loan but has been stymied by federal and state banking regulators. Nevertheless, the company recently partnered with a Memphis-based bank to establish Wal-Mart "Money Centers" in some stores. The banks carry Wal-Mart's imprimatur but are owned and operated by the Memphis firm.

Wal-Mart is tight-lipped about its banking aspirations, but many industry experts are worried. "Their goal is very clear: They want to have a Wal-Mart-owned bank branch in every store," said Kenneth Guenther, president of Independent Community Bankers of America. Wal-Mart banking would "inflict the black death" upon smaller competing banks, he warned. [42]

Meanwhile, most analysts say Wal-Mart will continue to consolidate its market share of product categories it now dominates, including groceries, sporting goods, household products, videogames, men's and women's apparel, toys and dog food. It is also rapidly expanding its overseas operations.

"The United States is 37 percent of the world's economy, which leaves 63 percent for international," said John Menzer, president of Wal-Mart's international division. "If we do our job, international operations should someday be twice as large as the United States." [43]

But critics like Sprawl-Busters' Norman say big-box retailers "will eventually take a hard fall. "If all you focus on is today, the siren-song of low prices will get you every time," he says. "It's important for people to understand that in the long run, their well- being and the well-being of their communities is bigger than the dimensions of their shopping carts." ■

Notes

[1] Quoted in Mary J. Thompson, "With low prices, Wal-Mart overwhelms competitors," *MSN Money*, Aug. 27, 2004.

[2] "Shopping for Subsidies: How Wal-Mart Uses Taxpayer Money to Finance Its Never-Ending Growth," Good Jobs First, May 2004.

[3] Revenues source: The companies' annual reports.

[4] For background, see *ibid*.

[5] See Anthony Bianco and Wendy Zellner, "Is Wal-Mart Too Powerful?" *Business Week*, Oct. 6, 2003, p. 100.

[6] Constance L. Hays, "Toys 'R' Us Says It May Leave the Toy Business," *The New York Times*, Aug. 12, 2004, p. A1

[7] *Ibid*.

[8] Quoted in "Levi Strauss Shuts All U.S. Plants," www.CBSNews.com, Sept. 25, 2003.

[9] See Arindrajit Dube and Ken Jacobs, "Hidden Costs of Wal-Mart Jobs: Use of Safety Net Programs by Wal-Mart Workers in California," University of California at Berkeley Labor Center, Aug. 2, 2004. Available online at http://laborcenter.berkeley.edu/lowwage/walmart.pdf.

[10] Quoted in Jon Bowermaster, "When Wal-Mart Comes To Town," *The New York Times Magazine*, April 2, 1989, p. 28.

[11] "What Happened When Wal-Mart Came to Town? A Report on Three Iowa Communities with a Statistical Analysis of Seven Iowa Counties," by Thomas Muller and Elizabeth Humstone, National Trust For Historic Preservation, 1996.

[12] Quoted in Rachel Sauer, " 'Wal-Mart Guilt' Doesn't Stop Shoppers," *The Milwaukee Journal Sentinel*, April 20, 2003, p. 5L.

[13] Quoted in Alexander Reid, "Local Stores Compete with 'Big-Box' Chains," *The Boston Globe*, Feb. 3, 2002, p. B1.

About the Author

Brian Hansen, a freelance writer in Boulder, Colo., specializes in educational and environmental issues. He previously was a staff writer for *The CQ Researcher* and a reporter for the *Colorado Daily* in Boulder and Environment News Service in Washington. His awards include the Scripps Howard Foundation award for public service reporting and the Education Writers Association award for investigative reporting. He holds a B.A. in political science and an M.A. in education from the University of Colorado.

FOR MORE INFORMATION

American Independent Business Alliance, 222 South Black Ave., Bozeman, MT 59715; (406) 582-1255; www.amiba.net. Helps communities start independent-business alliances to fight big-box chains.

Institute for Local Self-Reliance, 927 15th St., N.W., Washington, DC 20005; (202) 898-1610; www.ilsr.org. Promotes locally owned, independent retail businesses over the proliferation of chain stores.

National Trust for Historic Preservation, 1785 Massachusetts Ave., N.W., Washington, DC 20036; (202) 588-6219; www.nationaltrust.org. Generally anti-big-box, the Trust works to save historic commercial areas that "form our communities and enrich our lives."

Retail Industry Leaders Association, 1700 North Moore St., Suite 2250, Arlington, VA 22209; (703) 841-2300; www.imra.org. A trade group that promotes policies advantageous to big-box retailers. RILA members have more than $1 trillion in sales annually and operate more than 100,000 stores, manufacturing facilities and distribution centers nationwide.

Small Business Survival Committee, 1920 L St., N.W., Suite 200, Washington DC 20036; (202) 785-0238; www.sbsc.org. Supports policies that help small businesses and entrepreneurship but is generally supportive of policies that favor big-box retailers.

Sprawl-Busters, 21 Grinnell St., Greenfield, Mass. 01301; (413) 772-6289; www.sprawl-busters.com. Helps citizens' groups fight unwanted big-box retail stores and provides news on big-box battles across the country.

[14] Quoted in Gary Massaro, "Closing Store Leaves Big Gap," *The Rocky Mountain News* (Denver), April 6, 1997, p. A40.

[15] National Association of Convenience Stores press release, April 1, 2003.

[16] For example, *Expansion Management* magazine in May 2004 gave Fargo a "Five Star Community" rating, the highest level, in its annual Quality of Life Quotient. Components included affordable housing, available work force, standard of living, education levels, educational facilities, unemployment rates and peace of mind, described as the relative tranquility of a particular area. The same month, *Forbes* magazine named Fargo the second-best small city in the nation for businesses. For more information, see www.fmchamber.com/community/qualityoflife.html.

[17] The zoning ordinance and the commission's report are posted on the town's Web site: www.town-eastonmd.com.

[18] Quoted in Greg Harman, "Proposed Development Out of the Box," *The Biloxi* [Miss.] *Sun Herald*, Aug, 31, 2003, p. A1.

[19] Quoted in John Rebchook, "Thornton Decision 'Dismays' Wal-Mart," *The Rocky Mountain News* (Denver), June 17, 2004, p. B13.

[20] For more information, see the Smart Planning and Growth Coalition Web site at www.gotcommunity.org. The advocacy group is based in Barnstable, Mass.

[21] Land Use, Inc., and RGK Associates, "Greenfield, Massachusetts: Fiscal and Economic Impact Assessment of the Proposed Wal-Mart Development," April 2, 1993.

[22] Muller and Humstone, *op. cit.*

[23] Unless otherwise noted, information in this and following paragraphs is based on Bob Ortega, *In Sam We Trust* (1998), pp. 18-71; and Sandra S. Vance and Roy V. Scott, *Wal-Mart: The Story of Sam Walton's Retail Phenomenon* (1994), pp. 16-38.

[24] Ortega, *op. cit.*

[25] Wal-Mart does not release salary data, but the figures cited reflect estimates by several sources, including Retail Forward, a consulting firm in Columbus, Ohio; researchers at the University of California, Berkeley, Labor Center and legal depositions given by former Wal-Mart employees in civil lawsuits filed against the company. See Charles Williams, "Supermarket Sweepstakes: Traditional Grocery Chains Mull Responses to Wal-Mart's Dominance," *The Post and Courier* (Charleston, S.C.), Nov. 10, 2003, p. 16E.

[26] See Patricia Callahan and Ann Zimmerman, "Wal-Mart Tops Grocery List with its Supercenter Format," *The Wall Street Journal*, May 27, 2003.

[27] From a joint statement issued by Albertson's, Ralph's and Vons, Oct. 6, 2003.

[28] *Ibid.*

[29] Quoted in Steven Greenhouse, "Labor Raises Pressure on California Supermarkets," *The New York Times*, Feb. 10, 2004, p. A14.

[30] Quoted in Charlie LeDuff and Steven Greenhouse, "Grocery Workers Relieved, if Not Happy, at Strike's End," *The New York Times*, Feb. 28, 2004, p. A8.

[31] Quoted in John Holland, "Wal-Mart Sues Turlock Over Ban," *The Modesto Bee*, Feb. 12, 2004, p. A1.

[32] *Ibid.*

[33] For background, see Karen Holzmeister, "County Repeals Ban on Big-Box Stores," *The Oakland* [Calif.] *Tribune*, April 1, 2004.

[34] Michael Barbaro and Neil Irwin, "Wal-Mart in Talks to Build D.C. Store," *The Washington Post*, Aug. 11, 2004, p. E1.

[35] Quoted in Erin Hallissy, "Wal-Mart Win Sends Strong Message; Giant Retailer Warns Local Communities on Future Ordinances," *The San Francisco Chronicle*, March 4, 2004, p. A21.

[36] Quoted in John M. Broder, "Stymied by Politicians, Wal-Mart Turns to Voters," *The New York Times*, April 2, 2004, p. A1.

[37] *Ibid.*

[38] Quoted in Sara Lin and Monte Morin, "Voters in Inglewood Turn Away Wal-Mart," *Los Angeles Times*, April 7, 2004, p. A1.

[39] Quoted in Jessica Garrison, Abigail Goldman and David Pierson, "Wal-Mart to Push Southland Plan," *Los Angeles Times*, April 7, 2004 (on Web site only).

[40] Undated press release, "Wal-Mart Announces Expansion Plans for FY 2005."

[41] Press release, Jan. 16, 2004.

[42] Quoted in Alex Daniels, "Retailer Ties Name to Banking; Wal-Mart Venture Hints at Wider Ambitions, Observers Say," *The Arkansas Democrat-Gazette*, Jan. 21, 2004.

[43] Quoted in Andy Rowell, "Welcome to Wal-World: Wal-Mart's Inexhaustible March to Conquer the Globe," *The Multinational Monitor*, Oct. 1, 2003, p. 13.

Bibliography

Selected Sources

Books

Mitchell, Stacy, *The Home Town Advantage: How to Defend your Main Street Against Chain Stores — And Why it Matters*, Institute for Local Self-Reliance, 2000.
Mitchell argues that "megastores" are economically disastrous and documents how some communities are keeping them out with zoning ordinances.

Ortega, Bob, *In Sam We Trust: The Untold Story of Sam Walton and How Wal-Mart is Devouring America*, Times Business, 1998.
A former investigative reporter portrays Wal-Mart's founder as a ruthless businessman.

Slater, Robert, *The Wal-Mart Decade: How a New Generation of Leaders Turned Sam Walton's Legacy into the World's Number One Company*, Portfolio, 2003.
A former *Time* reporter documents how Wal-Mart grew exponentially after founder Sam Walton's death in 1992.

Walton, Sam, with John Huey, *Sam Walton: Made In America: My Story*, Doubleday, 1992.
Walton describes his business philosophy and responds to his critics in his autobiography.

Articles

Bianco, Anthony, and Wendy Zellner, "Is Wal-Mart Too Powerful?" *Business Week*, Oct. 6, 2003, p. 100.
The authors conclude Wal-Mart's "everyday low prices" come at a cost to consumers and the nation's economy.

Fishman, Charles, "The Wal-Mart You Don't Know," *Fast Company*, December 2003, p. 68.
The author examines the impact — both good and bad — of Wal-Mart's cost cutting on suppliers and the U.S. economy.

Goodman, Peter S., and Philip P. Pan, "Chinese Workers Pay for Wal-Mart's Low Prices," *The Washington Post*, Feb. 8, 2004, p. A1.
Two reporters examine conditions at Chinese factories that supply Wal-Mart.

Greenhouse, Steven, "Wal-Mart, a Nation Unto Itself," *The New York Times*, April 17, 2004, p. B1.
The author examines how Wal-Mart is affecting America's economy and culture.

Kline, Mitchell, "How Big is Too Big? Zoning Plan Says Build Up, Not Out," *The Tennessean*, July 8, 2004, p. 1W.
The town of Ranklin, Tenn., is using zoning ordinances to limit the size and impact of big-box stores.

Murphy, Edward D., "Small Maine Retailers Scurry for Niches; To Beat Back the Big Boxes, They Stress Their Unmatched Level of Service, Attention and Expertise," *Portland Press Herald*, June 27, 2004, p. A4.
Murphy focuses on how small mom-and-pop retailers in and around Portland, Maine, are competing with megastores.

Saporito, Bill, "Can Wal-Mart Get Any Bigger? Yes, a Lot Bigger — Here's How," *Time*, Jan. 13, 2003, p. 38.
The world's largest company could double or even triple in the next few years.

Useem, Jerry, "One Nation Under Wal-Mart: How Retailing's Superpower — And Our Biggest, Most Admired Company — is Changing the Rules for Corporate America," *Fortune*, March 3, 2003, p. 64.
The author examines how Wal-Mart's low prices affect U.S. manufacturers.

Weiss, Eric M., "'Big-Box' Stores Leave More Than a Void," *The Washington Post*, Jan. 20, 2004, p. B1.
Communities suffer when their local big-box store goes out of business or shuts down to move to an even bigger location.

Wysocki, Bernard, and Ann Zimmerman, "Wal-Mart Cost-Cutting Finds a Big Target in Health Benefits," *The Wall Street Journal*, Sept. 30, 2003, p. A1.
Wal-Mart allegedly skimps on health benefits.

Reports and Studies

Dube, Arindrajit, and Ken Jacobs, "Hidden Costs of Wal-Mart Jobs: Use of Safety Net Programs by Wal-Mart Workers in California," University of California at Berkeley Labor Center, Aug. 2, 2004.
A critical study concludes that Wal-Mart employees in California cost taxpayers about $86 million annually due to their heavy reliance on subsidized housing and other public benefits.

Freeman, Gregory, *Wal-Mart Supercenters: What's in Store for Southern California?* Los Angeles Economic Development Corporation, January 2004.
A pro-Wal-Mart study concludes that consumers in a seven-county region in Southern California would save $3.7 billion annually once the company attains a 20 percent share of the grocery market, and that communities that ban Wal-Mart will lose significant tax revenues due to "leakage."

The Next Step:

Additional Articles from Current Periodicals

Community Complaints

Alsever, Jennifer, "What Do You Do With the Empties? Abandoned Big-Box Stores Pose Problem," *The Denver Post*, July 4, 2004, p. K1.
Municipalities nationwide struggle with the question of what to do with vast, empty buildings left behind by big-box stores like Kmart and Wal-Mart.

Margolis, John, "Wal-Marts 'Endanger' Vermont, Group Says," *Chicago Tribune*, May 25, 2004, News Section, p. 1.
Vermont's quaint character makes it a convenient rallying point for those who dislike Wal-Mart as a symbol of the homogenization of American culture.

Sage, Alexandria, "Wal-Mart Can Attract Revenue — And Crime," *Los Angeles Times*, May 30, 2004, p. A16.
Small-town mayors appreciate the tax revenue, but large stores can also become magnets for petty crime and drunken driving.

Discrimination Suits

Armour, Stephanie, " 'Rife With Discrimination'," *USA Today*, June 24, 2004, p. 3B.
Wal-Mart's female employees were allegedly paid 15 to 20 percent less than male workers with comparable jobs, according to a discrimination lawsuit.

Greenhouse, Steven, and Constance Hays, "Wal-Mart Sex Bias Suit Given Class-Action Status," *The New York Times*, June 23, 2004, p. A1.
A judge granted class-action status to a sex-discrimination suit against Wal-Mart, making any prospective settlement a far more expensive proposition.

Masters, Brooke A., and Amy Joyce, "Costco Is the Latest Class-Action Target," *The Washington Post*, Aug. 18, 2004, p. A1.
Big-box stores, along with many other companies, are described as "green pastures" for lawyers seeking lucrative class-action suits.

Economics

Dang, Dan Thanh, "A Hard Bargain," *The Baltimore Sun*, July 7, 2004, p. 1E.
Despite all the ire, people continue to shop at Wal-Mart; the low prices are budget-savers for lower-income families.

Fernandez, Bob, "Great Deals Listed for, Not at, Wal-Mart," *The Philadelphia Inquirer*, June 1, 2004, p. C1.
Local governments have paid about $1 billion in subsidies to Wal-Mart; a store spokesman says the company has provided $56 billion in sales and property taxes.

Garrison, Jessica, "Battles Over Mega-Stores May Shift to New Studies," *Los Angeles Times*, Aug. 12, 2004, p. B1.
The Los Angeles City Council passed a law requiring large retailers to conduct economic-impact studies before building new stores.

Irwin, Neil, "The Urban Invasion of the 'Big Box'," *The Washington Post*, Sept. 16, 2002, p. E1.
Big-box stores in urban neighborhoods could potentially reverse the usual flow of dollars and jobs from the city to the suburbs.

Leeds, Jeff, "Universal Music Was Boxed In on CD Prices by Big Retail Chains," *Los Angeles Times*, Sept. 5, 2003, p. C1.
The music industry has been forced to cut prices by big retailers, which have been selling CDs at a loss to bring in business.

International Reach

Cummings, Jeanne, "Wal-Mart Opens for Business in a Tough Market: Washington," *The Wall Street Journal*, March 24, 2004, p. A1.
With free trade increasingly important to its global operations, Wal-Mart decided to become a Washington player in the late 1990s and in 2003 donated more money at the federal level than any other corporation.

Rowley, Ian, "Can Wal-Mart Woo Japan?" *Business Week*, May 10, 2004, p. 18.
Wal-Mart controls Japanese retailer Seiyu and is trying to conquer a big slice of Japan's $1.3 trillion retail market.

Upbin, Bruce, "Wall-to-Wall Wal-Mart," *Forbes*, April 12, 2004, p. 76.
Wal-Mart has succeeded wildly in Mexico, Canada and Britain, but ventures in Indonesia, Germany and South Korea have resulted in big losses so far.

Jobs and Wages

Cleeland, Nancy, and Abigail Goldman, "Grocery Unions Battle to Stop Invasions of the Giant Stores," *Los Angeles Times*, Nov. 25, 2003, p. A1.
Organized labor opposes Wal-Mart's California operations because union workers' relatively high wages — $19 per hour at traditional supermarkets — are threatened.

Daniels, Cora, "Up Against the Wal-Mart," *Fortune*, May 17, 2004, p. 112.
Union organizers face a challenge in Wal-Mart, which, according to critics, abolished its meat-cutting departments nationwide because one voted to unionize.

Featherstone, Liza, "Rollback Wages! Will Labor Take the

Wal-Mart Challenge?" *The Nation*, June 28, 2004, p. 11.**
Wal-Mart is staunchly opposed to union organizers: Its managers' manual tells employees that "the commitment to stay union-free must exist at all levels of management."

Greenhouse, Steven, "Illegally in the U.S., and Never a Day Off at Wal-Mart," *The New York Times*, Nov. 5, 2003, p. A1.
An investigation reveals widespread employment of poorly paid illegal immigrants by subcontractors responsible for Wal-Mart's cleaning crews.

Kinzer, Stephen, "Treading Carefully, Wal-Mart Enters Labor's Turf," *The New York Times*, July 6, 2004, p. A12.
Some speculate that as Wal-Mart moves into Chicago, a stronghold of organized labor, it will have to adapt to local conditions.

Opposition to Big-Box Stores

El Nasser, Haya, "Cities Put Shackles on Chain Stores," *USA Today*, July 20, 2004, p. 3A.
Towns, cities and neighborhoods act to ban not just big-box stores but all chain retailers, complaining that "sameness" cheapens their communities.

Hopkins, Jamie Smith, "Home Depot Drops Effort to Build in Rural Talbot," *The Baltimore Sun*, April 22, 2004, p. 1A.
After years of protests, Home Depot throws in the towel and drops plans to build a store in rural Maryland, echoing similar defeats for big retailers elsewhere in the state.

Nordlinger, Jay, "The New Colossus," *National Review*, April 19, 2004.
Wal-Mart epitomizes American economic values and growth, while Europeans sneer at the jobs it creates, despite their own stagnant economies.

Ritter, John, "California Tries to Slam Lid on Big-Boxed Wal-Mart," *USA Today*, March 2, 2004, p. 1B.
The Golden State represents untapped territory for Wal-Mart's supercenters, but it is a minefield of lawsuits and voter initiatives aimed at blocking the retail giant.

Schneider, Greg, "Wal-Mart's Damage Control," *The Washington Post*, Jan. 24, 2004, p. E1.
Facing a year of bad publicity and the latent public hostility toward corporate titans, Wal-Mart launches a public relations offensive against its critics.

Struggles of Traditional Retailers

Barbaro, Michael, "Wal-Mart Triggers Tumult in Toyland," *The Washington Post*, May 31, 2004, p. E1.
Controlling 22 percent of the toy market means paying lower wholesale prices and undercutting the competition; FAO Schwarz and KB Toys file for bankruptcy.

Byrne, Mary, "For Christian Retailers, It's David vs. Goliath," *The Washington Post*, July 3, 2004, p. B9.
Small, traditional religious stores are finding that secular leviathans' lower prices may be an irresistible temptation.

Douglass, Elizabeth, "Getting Pumped Up," *Los Angeles Times*, Sept. 21, 2003, p. C1.
Big stores have moved into the gasoline market, frightening some gas station owners, but analysts suspect the chains will claim only modest market share.

Fonda, Daren, "Plucky Little Competitors," *Time*, Oct. 21, 2002, p. 60.
Some independent retailers manage to thrive in the big-box environment by offering products and services more responsive to local tastes and needs.

Osegueda, Mike, "Are Music Stores Going Away?" *The Fresno Bee*, Nov. 30, 2003, p. J1.
Box stores and the Internet have combined to undercut traditional music stores like Tower Records.

CITING *THE CQ RESEARCHER*

Sample formats for citing these reports in a bibliography include the ones listed below. Preferred styles and formats vary, so please check with your instructor or professor.

MLA STYLE

Jost, Kenneth. "Rethinking the Death Penalty." The CQ Researcher 16 Nov. 2001: 945-68.

APA STYLE

Jost, K. (2001, November 16). Rethinking the death penalty. *The CQ Researcher, 11*, 945-968.

CHICAGO STYLE

Jost, Kenneth. "Rethinking the Death Penalty." *CQ Researcher*, November 16, 2001, 945-968.

CQ Researcher

Published by CQ Press, a division of Congressional Quarterly Inc.

thecqresearcher.com

Cyberpolitics

Do computers and the Internet enhance Democracy?

This is the year cyberpolitics came of age. Building his organization and fundraising efforts online, Howard Dean sped to an early lead in the race for the Democratic presidential nomination. Despite Dean's ultimate failure, other candidates emulated his online tactics, raising a record amount of campaign cash from small donors in the process. MoveOn.org — an Internet-based advocacy group started at home in 1998 by two California activists — became one of the most prominent players in the electoral and public-policy debate, cracking the $30-million mark in fundraising and claiming 3 million members. The Defense Department began, and then abandoned, an effort to enable military personnel overseas to vote over the Internet, while Michigan Democrats added online voting to their presidential caucuses. Exploiting other information technology, political organizations mined computer databases as never before, and election officials touched off heated controversies by switching to electronic voting machines.

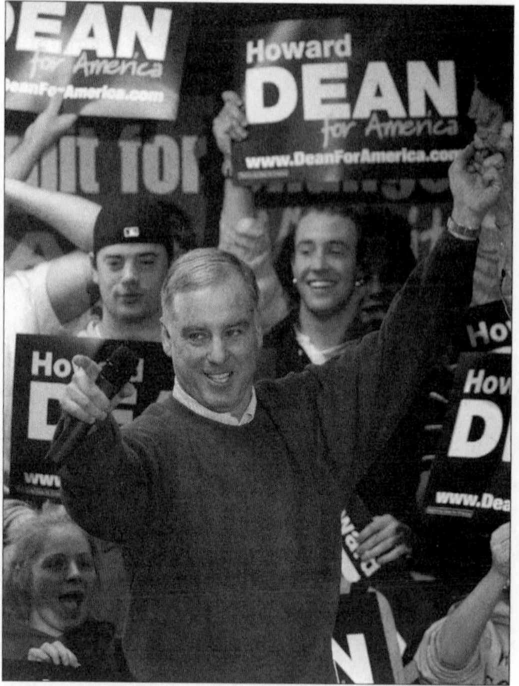

Howard Dean revolutionized the use of the Internet for organizing and fundraising during his unsuccessful bid for the Democratic presidential nomination.

INSIDE THIS REPORT

The CQ Researcher • Sept. 17, 2004 • www.thecqresearcher.com
Volume 14, Number 32 • Pages 757-780

CQ Press

Recipient of Society of Professional Journalists Award for Excellence ◆ American Bar Association Silver Gavel Award

THE ISSUES

BACKGROUND

CURRENT SITUATION

OUTLOOK

SIDEBARS AND GRAPHICS

FOR FURTHER RESEARCH

Cover: Howard Dean greets students at William Penn University, Oskaloosa, Iowa, on Jan. 16, 2004, just before the Iowa caucuses. He revolutionized the use of the Internet for organizing and fundraising during his unsuccessful bid for the Democratic presidential nomination. (AFP Photo/Timothy A. Clary)

Sept. 17, 2004
Volume 14, Number 32

MANAGING EDITOR: Thomas J. Colin

ASSISTANT MANAGING EDITOR: Kathy Koch

ASSOCIATE EDITOR: Kenneth Jost

STAFF WRITERS: Mary H. Cooper, William Triplett

CONTRIBUTING WRITERS: Sarah Glazer, David Hatch, David Hosansky, Patrick Marshall, Tom Price, Jane Tanner

DESIGN/PRODUCTION EDITOR: Olu B. Davis

ASSISTANT EDITOR: Kenneth Lukas

A Division of Congressional Quarterly Inc.

SENIOR VICE PRESIDENT/GENERAL MANAGER: John A. Jenkins

DIRECTOR, LIBRARY PUBLISHING: Kathryn C. Suárez

DIRECTOR, EDITORIAL OPERATIONS: Ann Davies

CONGRESSIONAL QUARTERLY INC.

CHAIRMAN: Paul C. Tash

VICE CHAIRMAN: Andrew P. Corty

PRESIDENT AND PUBLISHER: Robert W. Merry

The CQ Researcher (ISSN 1056-2036) is printed on acid-free paper. Published weekly, except Jan. 2, April 9, July 2, July 9, Aug. 6, Aug. 13, Nov. 26 and Dec. 31, by CQ Press, a division of Congressional Quarterly Inc. Annual subscription rates for institutions start at $625. For pricing, call 1-800-834-9020, ext. 1906. To purchase a *CQ Researcher* report in print or electronic format (PDF), visit www.cqpress.com or call 866-427-7737. A single report is $10. Bulk purchase discounts and electronic-rights licensing are also available. Periodicals postage paid at Washington, D.C., and additional mailing offices. POSTMASTER: Send address changes to *The CQ Researcher*, 1255 22nd St., N.W., Suite 400, Washington, D.C. 20037.

BY TOM PRICE

THE ISSUES

Even though he was the architect of the first Internet-based presidential campaign — former Vermont Gov. Howard Dean's run for the 2004 Democratic nomination — Joe Trippi found himself repeatedly astonished by the unpredictable power of cyberpolitics.

In early 2003, for instance, Trippi heard that supporters of presidential candidates were using the Meetup.com Internet site to schedule get-togethers. After putting a link to Meetup on the Dean Web site, Trippi watched as the number of pro-Dean Meetup participants soared from 400 to 2,700 to eventually 190,000. And Meetup was just one of many Internet tools Dean used to rise from obscure former governor of the second-smallest state in the Union to Democratic frontrunner.

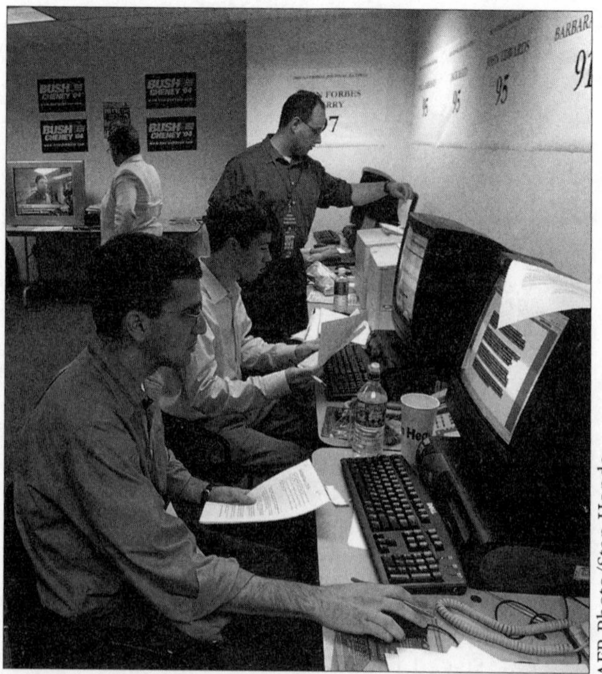

AFP Photo/Stan Honda

Republican "war room" staffers scan the Internet during the Democratic National Convention in Boston in July, ready to counter any claims by the John Kerry campaign. Following in the footsteps of advocacy groups and the Howard Dean campaign, both political parties widely use the Internet to raise funds and mobilize supporters. Meanwhile, the rising use of electronic voting machines is stirring controversy.

More than the other candidates, Dean used the Internet to organize supporters, publicize campaign events, raise funds and even seek advice. In November, he conducted an online referendum on whether he should forgo public campaign financing, and asked supporters to send contributions with their votes. They told him to give up the public funds and contributed more than $4 million a day at the beginning of the voting.

As a result, Dean became the most successful fundraiser in the history of the Democratic Party and was able to ignore the spending limits that accompany the federal funds. [1]

Although Dean crashed and burned in the Iowa caucuses in January, that did not obscure his phenomenal rise, or the Internet's coming of age as a formidable force in American politics.

"The Internet was his rocket ship, and nobody can deny how far and how fast the rocket ship took him up," says Phil Noble, an international political consultant and publisher of PoliticsOnline.com, a leading political Web site.

Republican President Bush and Massachusetts Sen. John Kerry — the eventual Democratic nominee and new Democratic fundraising champ — have copied at least some of Dean's online tactics. And advocacy groups of all stripes — long the most creative practitioners of Internet politics — continue to raise funds, organize and agitate online.

In addition, parties, candidates and advocacy groups mine computer databases to make their fundraising and organizing more efficient. The Defense Department worked on — then abandoned — a system to enable military personnel and other Americans overseas to vote online. The Michigan Democratic Party offered voters the option of voting on the Internet during its presidential caucuses.

Now election officials across the country are deploying computerized voting machines in an effort to avoid Florida's punch-card-counting fiasco of 2000. Rather than quell controversy, however, the machines have generated more, as advocates tout the machines' efficiency and critics warn of undetectable error and fraud.

"As computer scientists, unlike most people, we actually know what the vulnerabilities are in these systems," says David R. Jefferson, a consultant to California's secretary of state and a critic of the new voting machines.

In response, Harris Miller, president of the Information Technology Association of America, insists "there's not been one example of any fraud or misconduct."

But capturing the boldest headlines of the early 2003-4 election cycle, Dean and the MoveOn.org online advocacy group made a powerful case for cybervisionaries' dream that the Internet would level the political playing field — politically and financially. Both used the Internet to raise huge amounts of money and to organize their supporters for political activities.

By raising small contributions from large numbers of contributors online, Dean competed financially with candidates with better access to big donors, who traditionally dominate campaign fundraising. Dean's fundraising prowess fascinated the political press corps, heightening his visibility among the

Internet Users Seek Government Info Online

Two-thirds of Internet users surf government Web sites, while more than 40 percent research government documents online.

Percent of Internet Users Who Go Online to:

Obtain information from a government Web site	66%
Research government documents or statistics	41
Get recreational or tourist information	34
Get health or safety information from the government	28
Send e-mail to government officials	27
Get information about or apply for government benefits	23

Source: Pew Internet & American Life Project, July 2003

voters and turning him into the frontrunner in the polls.

Internet fundraising has helped to make the 2004 presidential campaign cycle the most expensive in history — and the one with the most small donors. From the beginning of 2003 until the end of July, the presidential campaign organizations, national political parties and independent political groups raised more than $1 billion, nearly double what they raised during the same period in 2000. Both parties reported attracting a million new donors since 2001.

During the entire two-year election cycle in 2000, Bush raised $104 million, compared to the $612 million he and national GOP organizations raised during the 18-month period ending June 30, 2004. By comparison, Gore raised $46 million during the 2000 campaign cycle, compared to the $409 million raised by Kerry and Democratic organizations in the recent 18-month cycle.

While the Bush campaign began fundraising in earnest in 2003, most of the Democratic fundraising has occurred this year: During the first six months of this year, Kerry and democratic party committees have out-raised their GOP counterparts by $20 million. [2]

Independent political organizations like MoveOn, known as 527 groups, helped make the flood of funding possible, largely because they are not covered by federal campaign regulations.

Started in 1998 by two Californians protesting the Clinton impeachment proceedings, MoveOn grew into a nationwide movement of liberal activists who have contributed some $30 million, most in small donations, to fund a variety of political ads and activities. Along with other liberal groups, MoveOn has helped Democrats cut into Republicans' traditional fundraising advantage in this presidential campaign.

The Internet's value as a fundraising tool was "just completely unexpected by everyone," says Steve Murphy, a veteran campaign manager who directed former House Democratic Leader Richard Gephardt's unsuccessful race for the presidential nomination.

While John McCain captured national attention by raising $2.7 million over the Internet in the three days after he upset Bush in the 2000 GOP primary in New Hampshire, Dean raised $4 million a day during a burst in 2003, and Kerry averaged $10 million a month over the first half of 2004.

Protesters — even, ironically, anarchists — have found the Internet to be an effective organizing tool, as well, whether they're putting together a peaceful demonstration or trying to disrupt a World Bank conference or a national political convention. And the Internet can be used for evil or good, Noble points out: "The single, most effective online organization in the world is arguably [the terrorist network] al Qaeda. They have used online communications to this day to develop and operate an enormous network of people."

Some advocates for the poor worry, however, that the Internet has not leveled the field for everyone. Internet access is directly related to income, education and race, with poorer, less-educated and black Americans less likely to go online than their wealthier, better educated and white fellow citizens.

As Election Day 2004 approaches, here are some of the questions being raised about the impact of computers on elections:

Does the Internet level the political playing field?

The Internet's capacity for instantaneous back-and-forth communication is enabling advocacy groups and individual citizens to become more politically knowledgeable and to speak with louder voices.

Moreover, Washington-based government employees, journalists and lobbyists no longer enjoy a monopoly on quick access to proposed legislation, government reports and other federal information. Anyone anywhere with Internet access can track federal legislation by visiting the Library of Congress' Web site: http://thomas.loc.gov. In addition, almost every federal agency provides online access to its reports, and congressional committees and individual lawmakers have their own Web sites. State and local governments make similar resources available, and the federal government maintains a portal to all of this at its FirstGov.gov Web site.

Advocacy groups mine this information and then use their own Web sites and e-mail to organize members for quick, targeted communications to key lawmakers or bureaucrats. The groups also use the Internet to attract new members and raise funds.

The Internet has "made it much easier to become a political entrepreneur," says Bruce Bimber, director of the Center for Information Technology and Society at the University of California, Santa Barbara. "It takes fewer resources and less political experience to identify and energize a group of like-minded people and to have a voice."

Because Internet activism is relatively inexpensive, liberal advocacy groups have been able to overcome some of the financial advantages traditionally enjoyed by business groups. By mastering — and often inventing — Internet tools, advocacy groups have become "more nimble, more flexible, more capable" than they were in the off-line age, Bimber says.

Indeed, advocacy groups took advantage of the Internet's political potential before businesses did, says Douglas Pinkham, president of the Public Affairs Council, the leading organization of U.S. public affairs professionals. And they've stayed ahead, partly because of the very nature of what they do: Advocacy groups exist to advocate, Pinkham notes, while businesses' primary purpose is selling products.

"When you're trying to motivate people, it helps if you can arouse passion," Pinkham explains. "It's a lot easier to arouse passion to save our children from lead paint than it is when you ask an employee to write your congressman to support us on the next trade deal."

The ability of the Internet to tap into passions has been especially helpful in leveling the fundraising playing field. Some political organizers think the emotional appeal of Dean's antiwar stance was the key to his Internet-based organizing and fundraising accomplishments. Similarly, they say Democrats' passionate dislike of President Bush fueled the contributions that cut deeply into Republicans' usual financial advantage.

'Digital Divide' Still Affects Poor, Less-Educated

Internet access has steadily increased among most segments of U.S. society, but blacks, the poor and the less educated have less access than other Americans. Alone among demographic groups studied, fewer blacks reported having Internet access in 2004 than in 2002.

Percentage of Groups Who Use the Internet

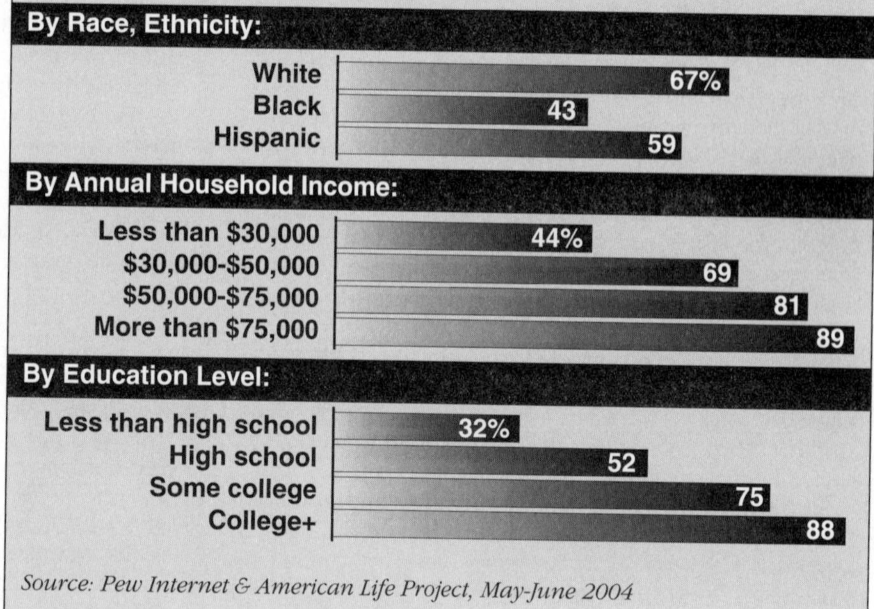

Source: Pew Internet & American Life Project, May-June 2004

Previously, the "dominant paradigm of American politics" had always been: "You line up fat, white guys to give you $1,000 checks and you use that to buy TV ads," PoliticsOnline publisher Noble says. "Dean showed you could build and run a campaign that says, 'I want people to make small contributions, and I want them to participate.' "

But major strides toward fundraising parity for Democrats this year also came from big contributions from wealthy liberals to so-called 527 groups: independent political committees not covered by federal campaign regulations and thus permitted to spend unlimited amounts on TV ads and mount get-out-the-vote campaigns. But the 527 phenomenon didn't emerge until substantial war chests were raised from small contributors online. [3]

MoveOn received $5 million from financier George Soros and insurance mogul Peter Lewis, Noble notes. "But they wouldn't have gotten [the money] if they didn't have millions of people" who had already contributed millions of dollars online in small donations, Noble says.

In fact, the Internet has clearly enabled more small donors to contribute to the campaign this year: Kerry received 35 percent of his funds in contributions of $200 or less, compared with 29 percent raised by Democratic presidential nominee Vice President Al Gore in 2000. Bush raised 28 percent in $200-or-less donations, compared with 20 percent four years ago. [4]

"Howard Dean has made a revolution in politics" by collecting 60 percent of his $51-million campaign treasury in contributions of less than $200, much of it online, said Elaine Kamarck, a lecturer in public policy at Harvard's Kennedy School of Government and

MoveOn.org Pioneers Online Activism

The liberal, online political activist organization MoveOn.org has recruited 3 million members, raised $30 million and become one of the most prominent players in American politics, fulfilling early cybervisionaries' predictions the Internet would facilitate political activity without the need for Industrial Age bureaucracies.

And it all started when Joan Blades and Wes Boyd got ticked off at Congress' obsession with the Clinton-Lewinsky affair in September 1998. The married couple e-mailed about 100 of their friends, asking them to sign an online petition demanding that Congress censure the president and "move on" to more important matters.

"Within a week," Blades recalls, "we knew we had a tiger by the tail." The first recipients forwarded the e-mail to their friends who passed it on to their friends, in a phenomenon known as "viral marketing." Within seven days, 100,000 people had signed the petition, Blades says, and "it's been an adventure ever since."

MoveOn had stepped into "a vacuum of voice," Blades explains, and gave those angered by the impeachment investigation an outlet for making themselves heard. "People aren't apathetic. They just, in many cases, have not known how to have a meaningful say in what's going on."

Blades and Boyd were astonished when the House impeached Clinton anyway, even though Republican congressional election losses that year were widely viewed as voter rejection of impeachment. [1]

"That's the point at which, as citizens, you say our next job is to elect people who better reflect our values," she says. So they launched a "We Will Remember" campaign, which sought pledges of contributions to candidates running against pro-impeachment legislators. Pledges totaled $5 million within a few days, [2] and $10 million in two weeks. [3]

It's impossible to know how many pledges were fulfilled, because MoveOn asked supporters to contribute directly to the candidates. Shortly thereafter, Blades and Boyd set up the MoveOn Political Action Committee, which can raise funds and contribute to candidates' campaigns.

Today the group has eight employees — beefed up to about 20 for the 2004 election year — who work from their homes scattered across the country. There are 2.5 million MoveOn members in the United States, another half-million around the world, who join simply by signing up to receive e-mail alerts, Blades says. The staff carries on a continual dialogue with members to determine what actions to take, she says.

"This is a huge advantage of the Internet," Blades explains. "We're getting thousands of e-mails every week. Our leadership [listens] as closely as it can and tries to identify opportunities where we think we can help our members participate in the political dialogue in an effective fashion."

That open approach left MoveOn open to attack when it sponsored a contest to create anti-Bush television ads. The 1,500 entries were posted online, so MoveOn members could vote which was best, and two likened Bush to Adolph Hitler. The Hitler ads drew few votes from MoveOn members, but they gave GOP Chairman Ed Gillespie the opportunity to accuse MoveOn of "the most vile form of political hate speech." [4]

While there is obvious risk in such wide-open discussions, political scientist Michael Cornfield notes that it makes Internet-based

former senior adviser to Al Gore's 2000 campaign. "I don't think in the future any candidate will pass up the Internet fundraising model." [5]

Dean may have led the fundraising revolution, but other Democrats quickly fell in line. By July, also having opted out of federal matching funds, Kerry was raising more than $10 million a month online and had far surpassed Bush in total online contributions — $65 million vs. $8.7 million. [6]

During the first six months of 2004, Kerry, the Democratic National Committee and the Democratic congressional campaign committees raised $292 million — $20 million more than Bush and the Republican committees. But because the Republicans had out-raised the Democrats in 2003, the GOP maintained the fundraising lead for the 2003-4 election cycle. But all of the Democratic presidential contenders combined raised more than Bush. And liberal 527 committees raised far more than their conservative counterparts.

With Kerry and Bush accepting federal funds for the general election campaign — while the parties and independent 527 committees could continue raising unlimited amounts — the Campaign Finance Institute at George Washington University declared the candidates to be "financially competitive" as they entered the home stretch. [7]

While all this may make the playing field less tilted, it doesn't level the field for everyone, particularly those without large amounts of cash, some observers argue. "The political playing field is never going to be level when [some groups] have large amounts of money," says MoveOn co-founder Joan Blades. "That gives you a louder voice."

Among advocacy groups, even on the Internet, "It helps to be big and to have an established brand," the Public Affairs Council's Pinkham says. "You have to be willing to do new and different things, [but] if you're big and you reinvent yourself well, you're going to be very, very successful."

Larry Noble, executive director of the Center for Responsive Politics, which monitors political funds, worries that "soft money" — large donations from wealthy individuals and organizations, which candidates and political parties no longer can accept

MoveOn different from traditional advocacy groups and heightens its effectiveness. "They don't need a [formal] membership," says Cornfield, research director of the Institute for Politics, Democracy and the Internet at George Washington University. "They have 2 million or more people because those 2 million people feel they're part of the decision-making."

MoveOn finances its activities with a pioneering fundraising strategy that Dean and other candidates have since copied, Cornfield adds. "You ask for the money in connection with a breaking news event and in connection with telethon-like goals and short-run objectives," he explains. "So the donor gets instant gratification."

Blades said MoveOn's leaders had "no idea" how much money they could raise that way until they asked for $35,000 to buy an anti-war ad in *The New York Times* in late 2002, and $400,000 poured in.

MoveOn's activity level soared this year when wealthy, liberal financier George Soros and insurance magnate Peter Lewis pledged to match up to $5 million of the group's usually small donations. Then the group's already-high profile spiked again when representatives of Bruce Springsteen and other music superstars asked for advice in organizing a concert tour in opposition to Bush's re-election.

The resulting "Vote for Change" tour in October is expected to swell MoveOn's membership and to raise millions of dollars for America Coming Together, another liberal group that is organizing get-out-the-vote drives in 17 battleground states.

Courtesy MoveOn.org

The online advocacy group MoveOn.org uses the Internet to raise money and mobilize protesters. These TV images were part of an anti-Iraq war campaign.

[1] Dan Balz and David S. Broder, "Shaken Republicans Count Losses, Debate Blame," *The Washington Post*, Nov. 5, 1998, p. A1. Laurie Goodstein, "Religious Conservatives, Stung by Vote Losses, Blame GOP for Focusing on Clinton," *The New York Times*, Nov. 5, 1998, p. B3. Ronald Brownstein, "Clinton's Pains Aided Democrats' Gains, Exit Poll Indicates," *Los Angeles Times*, Nov. 5, 1998, p. S1.

[2] Kim Zetter, "MoveOn Moves up in the World," *Wired News*, July 26, 2004. Available online at www.wired.com/news/politics/0,1283,64340,00.html.

[3] Jeri Clausing, "Anti-Impeachment Web Site Tallies Millions in Pledges," *The New York Times on the Web*, Jan. 8, 1999. Available online at www.nytimes.com/library/tech/99/01/cyber/articles/08move.html.

[4] John M. Glionna, "TV Ad Contest Targets President," *Los Angeles Times*, Jan. 11, 2004, p. A27. "Anti-Bush Ad Contest Includes Hitler Images," *The Washington Post*, Jan. 6, 2004, p. A4.

— is simply shifting to the new independent groups like the 527s.

However, Noble acknowledges, his organization exemplifies the leveling of the availability of information that computers and the Internet have accomplished. The center used to publish campaign finance information once every two years in a book that contained more than 1,300 pages, weighed nearly 10 pounds, cost nearly $200 per copy, sold only about 1,000 copies annually and came out 18 months after the election. Now, the center's OpenSecrets.org Web site contains substantially more information, is available free to anyone with Internet access and is updated almost as soon as candidates and organizations file reports with elections authorities.

Does a "digital divide" cut low-income citizens out of 21st-century politics?

Some experts say the greater Internet access enjoyed by affluent Americans compared to the poor and less educated prevents the Internet from truly leveling the political playing field. [8]

While no one argues there isn't a "digital divide," many political practitioners question its significance, noting that Internet access is steadily increasing and that new technologies always show up in wealthier homes first.

"There is a digital divide, and it is important, and it is diminishing every day," says Phil Noble, of PoliticsOnline, summing up both sides of the debate. Noting that the same concerns were raised about universal access to television when it first appeared, he says, the cost of Internet-access technology is diminishing so rapidly that it will eventually be available to all.

While Internet access has increased over the long term among all segments of U.S. society, according to the Pew Internet & American Life Project, the gap between the haves and have-nots has narrowed only slightly, and the digital divide between blacks and whites has actually grown. [9]

Nearly nine of 10 households with annual incomes above $75,000 have Internet access, compared to only 44 percent of those with incomes below $30,000. Nearly nine of 10 college graduates use the Internet from home compared with only a third of high school dropouts. And more than three-quarters

Advocacy Groups Flock to Cyberspace

Since the mid-1990s, advocacy groups have pioneered political use of the Internet, creating and deploying innovative online techniques to recruit and mobilize supporters, raise funds and lobby public officials. For example:

- When Jody Williams accepted the 1997 Nobel Peace Prize for organizing the International Campaign to Ban Land Mines — which convinced more than 100 nations to sign an anti-mine treaty — she was asked the secret to managing a global coalition of more than 1,400 advocacy groups in more than 90 nations. She replied: "E-mail." [1]
- The Million Mom March, which drew several hundred thousand gun-control supporters to Washington on Mother's Day 2000, began in mid-1999 with one angry mother with good political and media connections and a professionally designed Web site. [2]
- In 1998, the American Civil Liberties Union hired its first "cyber-organizer" to visit chat rooms, e-mail discussion lists and other cyberspace gathering spots in search of likely ACLU supporters. The group's roster of Internet activists — who agree to respond to e-mailed action alerts — grew from 3,000 in 1998 to 45,000 in 2000, when the ACLU discovered that more than a tenth of its new dues-paying members were being recruited online.
- The Center for Responsive Politics began putting campaign-finance information online in 1996 and vastly expanded its audience and the amount of information it could provide. The center — which each year in the early 1990s sold 1,000 books with information about candidates' and public officials' use of political money — recorded 95,000 user sessions at its Web site in April 1999, 270,000 in April 2000 and the use just kept growing. In 2000, Larry Makinson, then the center's executive director, called the Internet "the strongest tool for reinvigorating democracy of anything we've ever seen." [3]

[1] Thomas L. Friedman, *The Lexus and the Olive Tree: Understanding Globalization* (2000), p. 14.

[2] Tom Price, "Cyber Activism: Advocacy Groups and the Internet," Foundation for Public Affairs, 2000, p. 7.

[3] *Ibid.*, pp. 6, 11.

of 18-to-29-year-olds go online from home, compared with one-quarter of those 65 and older.

In each category, the gap narrowed by just 2 percentage points from 2000 to 2004. And availability among blacks, 43 percent of whom have in-home access, fell 8 percentage points further behind whites, two-thirds of whose homes are connected. Alone among the demographic groups studied, fewer blacks reported having Internet access in 2004 then in 2002, a fact that some analysts attributed to the weak economy. [10]

Overall, says Pew researcher Amanda Lenhart, "37 percent of Americans don't use the Internet, and that's a fairly significant group."

Wade Henderson, executive director of the Leadership Conference on Civil Rights, attributes the racial divide to America's highly segregated school system as well as to economics.

"Racially segregated schools generally correlate with schools that have poor quality instruction and the absence of technology," Henderson says. "If you don't have a school that emphasizes the use of technology or has the physical wherewithal to accommodate computers, then you're going to have a problem."

If black Americans aren't taught the value of the technology, he adds, they won't bother to go online.

Off-line Americans are disenfranchised in several ways, some analysts argue. "It's an issue in terms of delivery of government services," Lenhart says. As more of those services go online, and as more political campaigning moves online, "a subset of people is not participating in that dialogue."

When the Michigan Democratic Party added online voting to its presidential caucus system this year, Joel Ferguson, a black Democratic activist there, worried that minorities would be competing on "an uneven playing field." [11]

Although the Internet has boosted the effectiveness of the Center for Responsive Politics, Larry Noble observes, "When groups like ours look at using the Internet to reach people, we have to be aware there's still a whole segment of society that doesn't have daily access."

But Christine Iverson, press secretary at the Republican National Committee (RNC), plays down the significance of the divide. "If the Internet were the only form of political communication," she says, it would cut low-income citizens out of 21st-century politics. "But there are so many other ways to reach out to voters — phone, mail, television — the Internet is just one component of an overall plan. If you don't reach a voter through one method, you'll do anything you can to reach the voter through another."

Democratic Rep. Rick Boucher of Virginia, co-chair of the Congressional Internet Caucus, says the only digital divide he has observed is in access to high-speed Internet connections in rural areas.

"One cannot argue that computers are beyond the reach of people to afford," Boucher says. "Virtually everyone in America has a TV set, and computers can be purchased for the price of a moderately priced television. Internet connections today are the price of basic telephone service."

Campaign manager Murphy points out that an "audio divide" once existed — before everybody had telephones. "This is true with most [new] forms of technology," he says. "I'm optimistic that computers will become a more integral part of everybody's life in the coming years."

Lenhart acknowledges the cost of Internet access is dropping but adds that "it's still significant for a household that is at or just above the poverty line." Relying on public access sites, such as libraries, is not the same as having home access, she insists.

"In a perfect world," Henderson says, "the notion that the Internet can democratize public information and one's ability to participate in the debate is very real. It is potentially the ultimate democratizing medium. But, in practice, not yet."

Will electronic voting end vote-counting controversies?

"How many times can the state of Florida say 'oops'?" Bobbie Brinegar, president of the Miami-Dade County League of Women Voters, asked recently about the state's recurring Keystone Kops elections. [12]

Fortunately, Florida's Aug. 31 primary came off without its controversial, new electronic voting machines causing serious problems. [13] But the debate over those machines will rage for some time. And Florida isn't the only state to have suffered recent election snafus, or where voters are worried about potential disruptions in November's upcoming presidential voting.

Following Florida's 2000 vote-counting fiasco, which left the presidential contest undecided for five weeks, election officials across the country embraced e-voting machines. But the machines have been involved in numerous botched voting incidents. Computer scientists claim the machines are subject to invisible errors and undetectable fraud, and a movement is growing to require that the machines be able to produce paper copies of votes, so voters can verify their accuracy on the spot, and returns can be recounted.

The new machines were purchased in order to avoid the problems faced by Florida in 2000, when thousands of votes were thrown out because of poorly designed ballots or because machines either didn't punch ballots cleanly or punched them in the wrong spots. As a result, neither the ballot-counting machines nor the humans who tried to recount the ballots by hand could determine the voters' will.

Finally, on Dec. 12, the U.S. Supreme Court voted 5-4 to stop the recount, and Bush was declared the winner in Florida by 537 of nearly 6 million votes cast. [14] That gave him victory in the Electoral College, even though Gore won the nationwide popular vote by 543,895. [15]

A subsequent study by political and computer scientists at the California and Massachusetts institutes of technology determined that election problems weren't restricted to punch cards or to Florida. The CalTech/MIT Voting Technology Project estimated that between 4 and 6 million ballots nationwide were not counted in the 2000 election. The researchers attributed between 1.5 and 2 million ballot losses to faulty equipment or confusing ballot design, 1.5 to 3 million to registration mix-ups and up to 1 million to polling-place deficiencies, such as long lines or inconvenient locations. An unknown number went uncounted because of problems with absentee ballots.

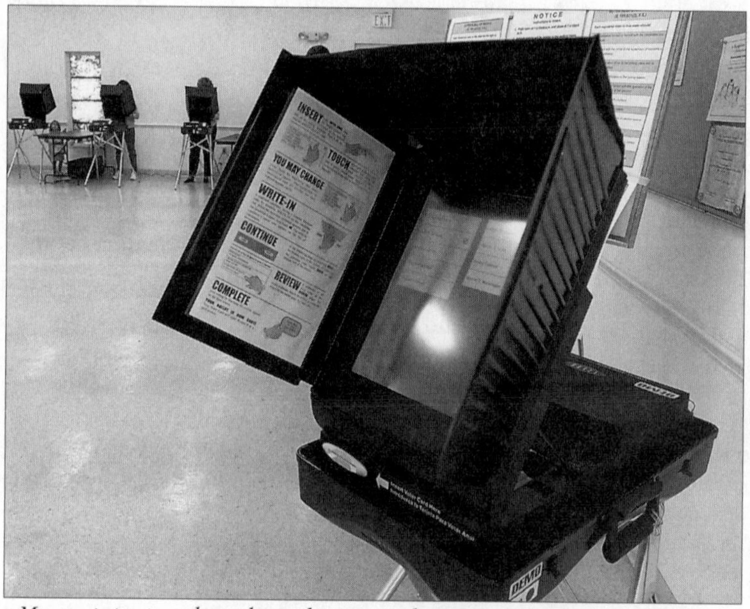

In the end, Illinois, South Carolina and Georgia all had higher rates of uncounted ballots than Florida in the 2000 presidential election. [16]

The researchers also found that in presidential, gubernatorial and U.S. Senate elections from 1988 through 2000, old-fashioned, pull-lever machines failed to count the largest percentage of votes, followed by electronic machines and punch-card systems, in that order. The fewest votes were lost using paper ballots — both hand-counted and machine-scanned. [17]

Congress responded to the Florida catastrophe by passing the Help America Vote Act (HAVA) in 2002, which authorized $3.9 billion to help states buy new voting equipment and make other election improvements.

The law also created the U.S. Election Assistance Commission, and charged it with developing voluntary standards for voting systems.

AFP Photo/Peter Muhly

Many states purchased touch-screen electronic voting machines after Congress authorized $3.9 billion in 2002 for new voting equipment and other election improvements following the 2000 Florida vote-counting debacle. This November, about a third of the voters are expected to use electronic machines.

The commission in June appointed a Technical Guidelines Development Committee to write proposed standards, but it will be some time before they take effect. The committee has nine months to produce proposals, which then will be reviewed by other panels before going before the full commission for adoption. [18]

Many states purchased electronic voting machines, particularly touch-screen models. The machines were touted as easy to use and meeting HAVA requirements by displaying ballots in multiple languages and offering audio voting for the blind. [19]

This November, about a third of the voters are expected to use electronic machines and another third machine-scanned paper ballots. About a quarter will use punch cards or lever machines and less than 1 percent hand-counted paper ballots. The rest of the votes will be cast in counties using a variety of systems. [20]

Critics complain the electronic machines are prone to errors that can't be caught without paper records, which few currently offer. Worse, critics charge, computer hackers could alter the results in undetectable ways without having a paper trail for verification.

The critics cite a lengthy list of e-voting foul-ups that have been discovered already:

- In Florida's Broward County (Fort Lauderdale), touch-screen machines used in January indicated that 134 voters, improbably, cast no votes in the only race on the ballot, which was decided by 12 votes. [21]
- In the 2000 general election in Espanola, N.M., 678 voters who cast early ballots on push-button e-voting machines were recorded as voting for no one because of a programming error. [22]
- Maryland this year discovered that a single key could open 16,000 electronic voting machines. [23]
- Officials in Dade County (Miami), Fla., reported in July that a computer crash erased almost all the electronic records from the September 2002 Democratic gubernatorial primary; three days later they announced the records had been found on a compact disc.

Florida's problems led Lida Rodriguez-Taseff, chairwoman of the Miami-Dade Election Reform Coalition, to describe touch-screen machines as "faith-based voting." [24] Such faith would be misplaced, says David R. Jefferson, a computer scientist at Lawrence Livermore National Laboratory.

"As computer scientists, unlike most people, we actually know what the vulnerabilities are in these systems," says Jefferson, a consultant to California Secretary of State Kevin Shelley, who has pushed for paper trails. "We know how exceedingly difficult it is to create software that cannot be broken, especially by insiders. We know what the threats are, so we're scared to death."

Fear of fraud was heightened by recent reports of political and financial ties between machine manufacturers, election officials and prominent politicians.

Walden O'Dell, a six-figure fundraiser for the Republican presidential ticket, is chairman and CEO of Diebold Inc., a leading manufacturer. He came under fire for a 2003 fundraising letter in which he pledged himself "to helping Ohio deliver its electoral votes to the president next year." [25]

Also raising eyebrows were the manufacturers' practices of hiring former election officials, bankrolling election officials' organizations, paying for events at the officials' meetings and even offering them gifts. [26]

Virginia Rep. Boucher — cosponsor of legislation requiring machines to print paper records — argues, "we have to be absolutely confident there is no possibility of fraud. You get a paper trail when you go to an ATM and make a financial transaction. We should demand no less when it comes to electronic voting."

But Miller, of the Information Technology Association of America, insists "there's not been one example of any fraud or misconduct" connected with electronic voting — an assertion Jefferson labels "nonsense" because "there's no way to know."

Miller retorts: "How do we know the results are accurate in any election?" Lever machines don't create paper trails, he notes, and they've been used for many decades. "Throughout history, whenever paper ballots are involved and it's a close race, someone always comes along and says someone else stuffed the ballot box or burned some ballots. There has never been a process that 100 percent guarantees every single vote is counted as the voter intended."

However, voting-machine manufacturers will add printers if that's what election officials want, Miller adds, and many jurisdictions seem likely to go that route. Nevada used printers in all polling places in its primary on Sept. 8, and they reportedly worked well. [27] California will require paper trails next year. [28] Lawmakers in at least 20 states have introduced legislation to require paper trails, and Democratic Rep. Rush Holt of New Jersey has introduced similar legislation in Congress. [29]

Miller argues that by demanding a paper trail, "all you're doing is adding to the complexity of the process."

MIT computer scientist Ted Selker, a member of the voting-technology project, argues that e-voting is getting an unfair rap. "When you have paper, you have people stuffing boxes, people changing things," he says. "And people can't count paper accurately."

He insists that electronic machines can be tested to assure that they're accurate and free of fraud. "The machines, I'm confident, will improve the results," Selker says. "We have to set up for all of the contingencies, but we don't just throw up our hands and freak out." ■

Continued on p. 768

Chronology

1960s-1980s
Origins of the Internet.

1967
Defense Department's Defense Advanced Research Projects Agency (DARPA) issues contract for studying "design and specification of a computer network."

1969
"DARPANET" links computers at Stanford Research Institute and universities of Utah, California at Los Angeles and California at Santa Barbara.

1971
E-mail invented.

1981
National Science Foundation creates Computer Science Network (CSNET).

1986
National Science Foundation creates higher-speed NSFNET.

1987
NSFNET assumes responsibility for DARPANET's civilian nodes.

1988-89
MCI Mail and CompuServe sell first commercial e-mail connections to Internet.

1990s
Internet comes of age as personal computers increase in popularity.

1990
DARPANET ceases to exist.

1991
Restrictions on commercial Internet activities rescinded; Tom Berners-Lee invents point-and-click hyperlink, names the World Wide Web.

1992
Clinton-Gore ticket posts campaign documents online.

1993
Scientists at University of Illinois unveil Mosaic, first graphical Internet browser. . . .White House Web site goes online.

1995
Library of Congress puts "Thomas" legislative-information service online.

1996
Major presidential nominees and national political organizations go online. . . . Center for Responsive Politics begins putting campaign-finance information online.

1997
Jody Williams accepts Nobel Peace Prize for International Campaign to Ban Land Mines, says secret weapon in campaign was e-mail.

1998
Internet campaigning plays key role in Jesse Ventura's surprise victory in Minnesota gubernatorial election. . . . American Civil Liberties Union hires "cyber-organizer" to recruit supporters online. . . . Cybergossip Matt Drudge reveals *Newsweek* investigation of Clinton-Lewinsky affair. . . . Online petition protesting Clinton impeachment investigation gets 100,000 names in a week, giving birth to MoveOn.org.

1999
Federal Election Commission OKs matching federal campaign funds for online credit-card donations. . . . Bill Bradley raises more than $600,000 online for his planned 2000 Democratic presidential campaign; John McCain raises $260,000 online for his GOP race. . . . Steve Forbes formally declares candidacy for Republican presidential nomination online. . . . Protesters use Internet to manage anti-globalization demonstrations at World Trade Organization meeting in Seattle.

2000-2004
Internet becomes key political tool.

2000
After upsetting George W. Bush in New Hampshire primary, McCain raises $2.7 million online in three days. . . . Million Mom March uses Internet to draw several hundred thousand gun-control supporters to Washington demonstration.

Oct. 29, 2002
President Bush signs Help America Vote Act.

2003
Howard Dean uses Internet to become front-runner for 2004 Democratic presidential nomination.

2004
Responding to criticism that Internet voting would not be secure, Defense Department scraps plan to let military personnel overseas vote online. . . . Michigan Democratic Party allows participants in presidential caucuses to vote over Internet; result is second-largest turnout in state party history. . . . Move to electronic voting machines in many states spurs controversy. . . . Online fundraising helps Democrats remain competitive with Republicans in campaign spending. . . . Protesters use Internet to organize demonstrations at Democratic and Republican national conventions. . . . Missouri Secretary of State Matt Blunt announces plan to let military personnel in combat areas vote by e-mail.

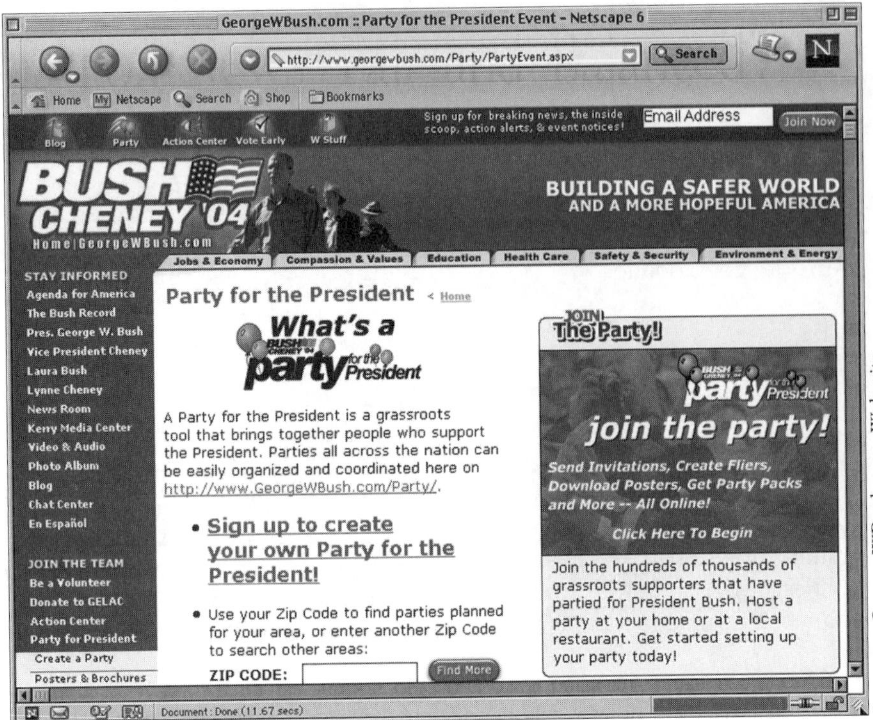

Courtesy GeorgeWBush.com Web site

Internet home pages for the Bush-Cheney campaign (above) and the Democratic National Committee reflect the increased use of the Internet by the major political parties for raising funds and mobilizing supporters. Thanks in large part to the Internet, Kerry and liberal advocacy groups have caught up with Bush in the fundraising department, virtually wiping out Republicans' traditional financial advantages.

Courtesy Democratic National Committee Web site

Continued from p. 766

BACKGROUND

Birth of the Internet

The history of politics on the Internet covers only about a decade, but the origins of the Internet itself can be traced back to the development of mechanical calculating machines and the telegraph in the mid-19th century. At least that's the argument in *History Of The Internet: A Chronology, 1843 To The Present.* [30]

Chris Casey, then-technology adviser to U.S. Senate Democrats, offered a similar analysis when he suggested at a 1999 conference that the telegraph is the earlier technology most similar to the Internet in its revolutionary impact on society. Before the telegraph permitted instant communication over long distances, "information traveled no faster than the fastest horse could run," Casey noted. The Internet transmits information no faster than television, telephone or radio. What is revolutionary is it enables instant back-and-forth communication among multiple parties and instant access to every piece of information offered by every computer linked to the Internet anyplace in the world. [31]

Whatever its debts to earlier technologies, the Internet traces its roots clearly to Dec. 16, 1967, when the Defense Department's Defense Advanced Research Projects Agency (DARPA) issued a $19,800 contract for studying the "design and specification of a computer network." DARPA wanted to link computers at remote locations to facilitate military research, and that wish was fulfilled late on Oct. 29, 1969, when DARPANET, the Internet precursor, "uttered its first words," according to Leonard Kleinrock, of the University of California, Los Angeles.

A UCLA computer, which Kleinrock oversaw, was to transmit the message "log," in order to log into another computer at the Stanford Research Institute. "We succeeded in transmitting the 'l' and the 'o,'" Kleinrock recalled, "and then the system crashed," demonstrating how some aspects of computing never change. [32] The message was sent successfully about an hour later.

DARPANET grew primarily as a device for sharing research files. As usage expanded beyond military needs, the National Science Foundation created the Computer Science Network (CSNET) in 1981. In 1986, NSF created a new, higher-speed network called NSFNET. The term Internet began to be used to mean a network of networks.

AFP Photo/Hector Mata

Then-California gubernatorial candidate Arnold Schwarzenegger throws T-shirts to supporters in Los Angeles in September 2003, just before Californians voted to recall Gov. Gray Davis and elected the popular movie actor. Petitions delivered online generated as many as one-third of the 1.4 million signatures used to launch the recall drive.

Also in the 1980s, companies began selling online services to home computer owners. But all they offered was slow, over-the-phone-line connections to private networks, not access to the Internet. MCI Mail and CompuServe sold the first commercial e-mail connections to the Internet in 1988 and 1989. The Software Tool and Die Co. of Brookline, Mass., offered the first full-service commercial access to the Internet in 1989, under the brand name "The World."

The Internet really begin its journey toward wide use in 1991, when rules restricting it to non-commercial activities were rescinded, and programmer Tom Berners-Lee invented the now-familiar process for clicking an on-screen link to jump from place to place throughout cyberspace. Berners-Lee referred to all the available linked information as the "World Wide Web."

Two years later, University of Illinois scientists unveiled Mosaic, the first graphical Internet browser. The stage was set for an explosion of Internet use by home computer users and political activists.

Cybercampaigning

Bill Clinton and Al Gore were the first politicians to actively use the Internet as a campaign tool. Primitive by today's standards, their campaign posted speech texts, position papers, biographies and copies of advertisements for those few voters with the wherewithal to find them.

Once in office, they quickly launched the first White House Web site, Whitehouse.gov. In 1995, the Library of Congress launched "Thomas," an online legislative information system named for Thomas Jefferson, who restocked the nation's library with his own books after the British burned its original collection during the War of 1812. House and Senate members gradually began setting up Web sites and using e-mail.

By 1996, all the major presidential nominees and national political organizations were on the Web. Now, Clinton and Republican presidential nominee Bob Dole included photos, links to like-minded sites, opportunities for e-mail feedback and animated graphics. Dole made Internet history by plugging his Web-site address during a televised debate and generating a spike of 500,000 extra hits over the next 24 hours.

Some strategists perceived the Internet's value even though few voters were trolling for political information online. Web-site visitors "are more politically active than a random sample of the electorate," House Republican Conference Communications Director John Czwartacki said. "And they're seeking you out — they're not a passive audience. So they're more likely to listen to what you have to say."

Most politicians were unconvinced, however. Ken Klein, former communications director for the Democratic Senatorial Campaign Committee, recalled debates about creating a Web site that "were probably the same as the discussions years ago about cars. People said: 'Why do we want to buy a car when we've already got a horse? Why do you want to take a chance on a mysterious purchase when you've already got a known product in hand?' "

Even as late as 1999, most campaign managers did not view the Internet as a tool that could win elections, consultant Murphy said at the time. They felt the need for a Web presence only to prove that "everything's up to date in Kansas City," he said. [33]

But Jesse Ventura's surprise victory in the 1998 Minnesota gubernatorial election forced politicians to sit up and take notice of the Internet's potential. Ventura overcame doubts stemming from his professional wrestling background by posting detailed position papers on his Web site. He built an e-mail list to motivate and manage supporters and raised $50,000 — nearly 10 percent of his campaign treasury — online.

"We didn't win the election because of the Internet," Ventura's Web master, Phil Madsen, said later. But Ventura "could not have won the election without the Internet." [34]

In 1999, Steve Forbes made Internet history by formally declaring his candidacy for the GOP presidential nomination online. But it was a bureaucratic decision that really set the stage for the brief flashes Sen. John McCain, R-Ariz., would make in the 2000 GOP contest and Dean would make in 2003 and early 2004: The Federal Election Commission agreed for the first time in 1999 that contributions charged to credit cards online would be eligible for matching federal funds.

Former U.S. Sen. Bill Bradley of New Jersey, Gore's unsuccessful challenger for the Democratic nomination, had asked for the ruling. He raised more than $600,000 online before the end of 1999; at the same time McCain raised $260,000 online.

After McCain upset Bush in the New Hampshire primary on Feb. 2, $2.7 million flooded his Web site over the next three days. The news media reported the phenomenon, which boosted his standing with voters and extended his financial windfall.

However, like Dean, neither McCain nor Bradley could parlay online achievements into sustained off-line victory. But they did make clear the Internet's exploding value. [35]

Meanwhile, Arizona became the first state to experiment with Internet voting on March 11, 2000, when the state's Democratic Party held the country's first-ever, binding online vote as part of its presidential primary. And Oregon officials predicted in 2000 that residents would be voting on the Internet within five years. [36] ■

AFP Photo/Shawn Thew

Demonstrators protest World Bank and International Monetary Fund policies in Washington, D.C., in September 2002. Advocacy groups pioneered the creative use of the Internet for organizing and agitating.

CURRENT SITUATION

Presidential e-Politicking

As the Nov. 2 general election approaches, the Internet is playing an integral part in nearly every serious effort to influence elections and government decisions.

At the most visible level, both the Bush and Kerry campaigns boast robust Web sites that encourage visitors to contribute funds, become volunteers, recruit friends and neighbors to the campaign, read good news about the favored candidate and view attacks on the opponent. [37] Both sites employ the latest, most sophisticated Internet technology, including video and audio files, searches and interactive features.

Kerry's Senate Web site and Bush's White House site supplement the online campaigns. The White House site is especially rich. In addition to numerous written documents that boost Bush's record, Cabinet members appear in audio and video files, visitors are invited to e-mail questions to the White House and government officials regularly engage in live chats.

The campaigns also have purchased advertisements on independent Web sites, exploiting the opportunity to target advertising to narrow audiences. The Bush campaign, for instance, produced an Internet-only video in which first lady Laura Bush discussed the

How Protesters Use the Internet

When the Justice Department launched a criminal investigation of an anti-GOP Web site in August, the American Civil Liberties Union (ACLU) charged the government with attempting to "chill free speech and intimidate protesters." [1]

Whatever the merits of the ACLU complaint, the government action spotlighted the importance of the Internet as a weapon in the arsenal of political protesters.

In this case, the Justice Department's target was the NYC Independent Media Center, which had posted online a list of Republican National Convention delegates, along with many of their addresses, phone numbers and New York hotels. [2] The group is among scores of so-called IndyMedia (independent media) organizations around the world that use the Internet and other computer technologies to facilitate activities by anarchists and other left-leaning activists.

The groups link with each other's Web sites and use online tools — such as digital video, instant messaging and e-mail — to organize protest marches and communicate with a global audience. Thousands of other activist groups use their own Web sites and e-mail lists for similar purposes. Typically, IndyMedia and others allow activists to post information without review by site editors. The NYC site's managers, for instance, said they didn't know who contributed the delegate list under the name "RNC Delegates Working Group."

The Justice Department said it was assisting a Secret Service investigation into possible violation of laws against voter intimidation by the groups protesting in New York. The ACLU called the claim "ironic," maintaining, "The only intimidation taking place here is [against] people who speak out against the government." [3]

But the protesters were admittedly intent on intimidating the Republicans — if not as voters then as unwanted interlopers into predominantly liberal and Democratic New York. For that purpose, numerous anti-GOP Web sites published schedules of convention events and urged protesters to attempt to disrupt them.

Protesters have been using Web sites and e-mail effectively since the late 1990s, first catching worldwide attention during the mass anti-globalization demonstrations that disrupted the World Trade Organization meeting in Seattle in 1999. [4]

At first, the Internet's primary value was to help protesters organize long-distance. Web sites contained calendars of events, information about food, housing and transportation and links that enabled participants to request and offer housing and to make transportation reservations. The Web sites used text, photos, drawings and audio and video files to bypass the establishment media and transmit the protesters' messages around the world.

The NYC IndyMedia group's Web site says it is one of more than 120 similar grass-roots organizations worldwide working online to bypass the "corporate media" to promote "social and economic justice" and empower people by providing "democratic access to available technologies and information."

And their arsenal expands as new technologies develop. This year's national political conventions saw the first use of TxtMob, for example, which enables subscribers to blast text messages in real time to hundreds of other subscribers' cell phones. Among its uses: warning roving bands of protesters about police movements or summoning protesters to a demonstration spot at a moment's notice. [5]

In addition, online radio stations — along with low-power broadcast stations, some of them violating Federal Communications Commission licensing rules — have formed networks to transmit alternative programming around the world. They broadcast live and recorded reports from demonstration sites. Some haul compact transmitting equipment to near protest sites and broadcast low-power signals that can be picked up by demonstrators with portable radios and others in the vicinity. [6]

The ease of using some new technology enables individuals to act alone or in very small groups. For instance, Gary Boston and Jeff Adler wanted New Yorkers to stage a general strike on Sept. 1 during the GOP convention. So Boston, who had no experience creating Internet sites, taught himself using Microsoft FrontPage Web software and the book *Front Page for Dummies*. The pair didn't shut the city down, but they did give the Internet a clever new Web page that features the Republican Party's stylized elephant lying on its back, an "x" where its eye should be in the universal cartoon symbol for sleep or death. [7]

---

[1] "ACLU Is Defending Web Host and Others Sought through Grand Jury Subpoena," ACLU statement available at www.aclu.org/FreeSpeech/FreeSpeech.cfm?ID=16341&c=86.

[2] www.nyc.indymedia.org.

[3] *Ibid*. Eric Lichtblau, "Subpoena Seeks Records About Delegate Lists on Web," *The New York Times*, Aug. 30, 2004, p. A10.

[4] Tom Price, "Cyber Activism: Advocacy Groups and the Internet," Foundation for Public Affairs, 2000, pp. 28-29. For background, see Brian Hansen, "Globalization Backlash," *The CQ Researcher*, Sept. 28, 2001, pp. 761-784.

[5] Daniel Terdiman, "Text Messages for Critical Masses," *Wired News*, Aug. 12, 2004. Available at www.wired.com/news/politics/0,1283,64536,00.html.

[6] Susan Carpenter, "Pirate Radio to Moor at Republican Convention," *Los Angeles Times*, Aug. 27, 2004, p. E1.

[7] shutitdownnyc.com. Ellen Simon, "Convention Protesters, Police Ready for Action," The Associated Press, in *The Washington Post*, Aug. 29, 2004, p. D1.

president's education positions. Posted on Web sites devoted to such topics as children, parenting and cooking — and to sites operated by such magazines as *Ladies' Home Journal* and *Family Circle* — the ad "provided the opportunity to show a longer-format video to people who would be interested in education but may not go to GeorgeWBush.com or to another political Web site," according to campaign press secretary Scott Stanzel.

But it's behind the public façade of the Web sites that the campaigns use the Internet and other information technology most effectively to communicate with voters, raise funds and manage campaign workers.

With the electorate highly polarized between the two parties and the undecided camp apparently at a record low, political strategists are coming to believe that this election will be decided by the kind of old-fashioned organizing that withered as high-cost television advertising came to dominate campaigns. [38] Ironically, the newest medium — the Internet — is proving the perfect tool for old-fashioned campaigning.

"Organizational politics has been in decline for 40 years or so, but the last few years they've been on the decided upswing," Democratic consultant Murphy says. "Because of the even, partisan split in the country — and the fact that a much higher proportion of voters today is aligning with one party or the other — simply turning out your party's supporters is probably the most critical factor.

"The Internet provides an effective means of communicating instantaneously with your supporters so they can be mobilized to do more," he continues. "You can't call them on the phone any more because nobody wants to talk on the phone because they've been inundated by telemarketers. You can't knock on the door anymore because nobody's ever home. But everybody's always home on the Internet."

Bush press secretary Stanzel notes that with 70 to 100 cable channels, hundreds of magazines and countless Internet sites, campaigns can no longer simply buy television ads and expect the results they achieved 20 years ago. "Our Internet effort empowers people to go to their neighbors and distribute information on their e-mail lists," he says. "So we are bringing the campaign back to a very grass-roots, neighbor-to-neighbor effort."

Both sides are crunching huge computer databases to make their old-fashioned, one-to-one tactics more effective. The idea is to identify individual voters, determine the issues they care most about, try to persuade them that Bush (or Kerry) deserves support on those issues and finally turn out those who are likely to vote for their candidate.

"You could ask me about any city block in America, and I could tell you how many on that block are likely to be health-care voters, or who's most concerned about education or job creation," Democratic National Committee Chairman Terence R. McAuliffe said. "We can then begin a conversation with these people that is much more sophisticated and personal than we ever could before." [39]

Similarly, GOP Chairman Ed Gillespie said the Republicans can tailor their message "to people who care about taxes, who care about health care, who care about jobs, who care about regulation." Then, "it's very, very important to us for people in the last 72 hours to e-mail their friends and knock on their doors and get Republicans to the polls." [40]

Bloggers captured attention from the mainstream media this year, and both parties invited some bloggers to attend the national conventions as credentialed members of the press. But, with some exceptions, blogs have few readers.

Blogs — Internet shorthand for Web logs, or personal cyberjournals — are another common component of both sides' efforts. Blogs are usually run by an individual, often contain the blogger's commentary as well as information and links to other Web sites, and allow others to join the conversation. Exceptions to traditional blogs, the Kerry and Bush blogs are run by the campaigns and appear on the candidates' Web sites.

Bloggers captured attention from the mainstream media this year, and both parties invited some bloggers to attend the national conventions as credentialed members of the press. But, with some exceptions, blogs have few readers. A Pew survey late last year found that between 2 and 7 percent of Internet users publish blogs, and about 11 percent read them. [41] That would give the average blogger between 1.5 and 5.5 readers, according to Pew researcher Lenhart.

In Dean's Internet-driven organization, however, blogs were "the nerve center of the campaign," Trippi said. [42]

And some bloggers can have major impact, says Phil Noble, of PoliticsOnline, pointing out that Matt Drudge, who first brought Monica Lewinsky to the world's attention, is a blogger. *The Drudge Report* now claims an average of more than 7 million visitors a day. [43]

Internet Voting

Among the many online innovations, however, Internet voting failed to catch fire this year. The Defense Department funded a project to

Continued on p. 774

At Issue:

Should electronic voting machines be required to produce paper records?

REP. RUSH HOLT, D-N.J.

WRITTEN FOR *THE CQ RESEARCHER*, SEPTEMBER 2004

Voting in a democracy was always intended to belong strictly to the voters who cast their ballots, and the election officials who count them. Such a system is "publicly" auditable, as it should be. But if a voter casts a vote on an electronic voting machine, how can the record of that vote be meaningfully audited? Neither the voter nor the election official can independently verify what is recorded only in cyberspace. That is why voter-verified and independently re-countable records of each vote must be required of all voting systems.

Harris Miller, president of the Information Technology Association of America, has argued that there has never been a demonstrated case of fraud on an electronic voting system. Yet how can one demonstrate that a fraud has occurred if there is no way to independently audit the results?

Published reports of irregularities on electronic voting equipment abound — 100,000 votes missing in Florida and "X"s jumping from one candidate to another in Virginia in 2002; a 144,000-vote irregularity in Indiana; machine failures resulting in the demand for a whole new election in Mississippi; and a hand count of paper optical-scan ballots proving the electronic count produced the wrong winners in Texas in 2003; Miami-Dade's 2002 touchscreen results reported missing altogether in 2004, then "found." Those are but a few examples.

Paper-ballot-based voting systems have a proven track record. A 2001 Caltech-MIT study reported "optically scanned paper and hand-counted paper ballots have consistently shown the best average performance. . . . Paper ballots have the highest degree of auditability."

A survey of the National Federation of Republican Women taken after it used voter-verified paper-trail voting systems in its own election reported that "over 97 percent of NFRW voters found the system easy to use" and 77 percent felt more confident that their vote would be recorded and counted accurately." Because paper ballots can be printed with bar codes, scanned and "read back" to sight-impaired voters, disabled voters can verify their votes as well.

Voter confidence in the electoral system is paramount, which is why I introduced The Voter Confidence and Increased Accessibility Act of 2003. My bipartisan bill has 150 cosponsors, and chapters of the Democratic, Conservative, Green and Libertarian parties have endorsed it. Moreover, the fight for verified voting is gaining steam. In July, pro-paper-trail rallies were held in 24 cities, and 350,000 petition signatures were delivered to secretaries of state in 20 states, urging them to use voter-verifiable, paper-based voting systems in November. When it comes to electronic voting, the public has spoken: Trust, but verify.

HARRIS N. MILLER
PRESIDENT, INFORMATION TECHNOLOGY ASSOCIATION OF AMERICA

WRITTEN FOR *THE CQ RESEARCHER*, SEPTEMBER 2004

This summer, former Vermont governor and presidential candidate Howard Dean, along with an ice-cream magnate and a college professor, launched The Computer Ate My Vote Day. The publicity stunt was ostensibly designed to bring public pressure on election officials to demand that voter-verified paper receipts be supplied with electronic voting machines. Whether Dean's endorsement of the widely covered event also served to undermine public confidence in electronic voting is another question.

But say that the issue is paper trails, not electronic votes. Supporters of paper receipts claim that because direct electronic recording (DRE) voting machines, or touch-screen machines, record a digital vote without paper-trail artifact, the results of such voting cannot be verified. Ignore the fact that DRE machines are built with multiple, redundant features for storing votes and can print out ballots cast, if necessary. Critics claim that, despite extensive testing, state certification and pre-election checking, machine programming can be tampered with.

There is nothing inherently bad — or good — about a voter-verified paper trail. History demonstrates that paper-based systems lose millions of votes in every presidential election. The issue becomes whether such technology introduces more problems than it solves. Elections officials have expressed concerns about the introduction of paper and printers into the electronic voting process:

- Printing voter-verifiable ballots will add several layers of cost and complexity to the voting process.
- Lines of voters will increase as voters take additional time to verify their votes.
- A lengthy set of ballot options would require a lengthy receipt for voters, and printers are likely to jam and run out of ink or paper.

Finally, the addition of printers to electronic voting systems would be a major defeat for the disabled and minority-language communities. Many visually impaired voters will cast their own ballots for the first time using DREs with audio capabilities. These visually impaired voters will be discriminated against by having a paper trail that they will not be able to read. Likewise, non-English language speakers will be discriminated against by having a paper trail only in English.

Electronic voting machine manufacturers respond to customer requirements and, if paper is what the customer wants, companies will add it (and most already are doing so). But vote-eating computers? Not likely. Electronic voting will cure the ills of the 2000 and previous elections. And introducing paper is no panacea.

Continued from p. 772

enable military personnel and other Americans living abroad to cast their votes online. But computer scientists warned that no Internet voting system could be made secure given the current state of Internet and personal computer technology, and the Pentagon scrapped the project.

"The idea is still attractive to the Pentagon, and for good reason," says computer scientist Jefferson, who opposed going forward this year. "It is much harder to vote when you're in Iraq than when you're at home. But Internet voting has problems so profound and so severe that I just do not believe there is any good solution now." [44]

MIT's Selker complains the critics overreacted, however. Unlike the controversial electronic voting machines that count votes and leave no paper trail, the Pentagon system would have transmitted encrypted, graphical copies of marked ballots that would have been printed and counted in the United States, he says.

"That would have been very hard to hack," Selker contends. And the original ballots could have been preserved for verification and recounting.

Cal Tech political scientist R. Michael Alvarez, who advocates scientific testing of Internet voting, also was disappointed by the Pentagon decision. "It was one of the few experiments on election reform we'd have been able to participate in in recent years," says Alvarez, who is co-director of the CalTech/MIT Project. "I fully understand there were concerns raised." But, he adds, every time a voting jurisdiction changes procedures, "they effectively run an experiment, and very rarely are they doing it under conditions that are controlled or being scientifically evaluated."

One of those unscientific experiments recently occurred in Michigan, when online voting was added to the Democratic caucuses. Democrats could vote from computers at home or elsewhere, such as libraries. They also could vote by mail or attend the regular caucuses.

Mark Brewer, executive chairman of the state's Democratic Party, says the caucuses were a great success. The turnout of 165,000 was the second-highest in history, and 28 percent voted online. It also was "a potent organizing tool for us," because online voters were asked to make contributions to the party and to fill out questionnaires to build the party's database.

Brewer admits the Michigan experience didn't prove that regular elections could be conducted successfully online, however.

"As a caucus," he explains, "we don't have a secret ballot. So we don't have all the problems of tracking who's already voted and preserving privacy that you'd have in regular election."

Lack of secrecy also spurred opposition to a last-minute plan to allow overseas military personnel to vote by e-mail in Missouri's general election. Secretary of State Matt Blunt, the Republican gubernatorial candidate, announced on Aug. 25 that personnel in combat areas could e-mail scanned copies of their ballots to the Pentagon, which would forward them to Missouri.

But workers at the Pentagon and in Missouri could see whom the soldiers voted for and even intentionally "lose" ballots for the wrong candidate, warned Bruce Schneier, of the National Committee for Voting Integrity. "There's been no discussion, no audits, no information about how will it prevent phony votes or hacking," Schneier charged. "Missouri is setting itself up to be the next Florida." [45]

And Elliot M. Mincberg, legal director for the People for the American Way Foundation, worried that personnel might even feel pressured by superiors to relinquish their right to a secret ballot. ■

OUTLOOK

Direct Democracy?

Political practitioners and scholars agree the Internet will get faster, more widely used and more important to public affairs. But it's impossible to know exactly how those developments will play out, they say, because the online world changes so fast.

"It's very difficult to predict how it's going to evolve, and what new applications will arise that truly are revolutionary in nature," says Rep. Boucher.

The RNC's Iverson agrees. "We're just beginning to discover the most effective ways to use the Internet. I think people are going to look back and marvel that there once was a day when campaigns didn't have Web pages or online advertising, the way people look back before television and marvel at how campaigns were run without TV."

The Public Affairs Council's Pinkham predicts that corporations, as well as government institutions, will be forced to become more open to public scrutiny as the Internet makes publication of information ever easier. "There will be a threefold increase in public expectations of transparency," he says, "and companies and politicians need to get ahead of that."

Conversely, Pinkham thinks that venerable communications institution — the Post Office — will have a longer and healthier life than many Internet visionaries predicted, because the flood of spam on home and office computers is diminishing the value of e-mail.

Advocacy groups also need to prepare for new demands from Internet activists, says Cornfield, at the Institute for Politics, Democracy and the Internet at George Washington University. "Once you start contacting people by the Internet and develop a network of supporters, those supporters want to do more than just give money and get a news report once in a while," he explains. "They want to be part of the decision-making."

Online advertising probably will come into its own over the next decade, Cornfield predicts, as practitioners educate themselves in the most effective ways to use it. "It's been slow to take off because the process of budgeting for online advertising, figuring out what kinds of ads you want to run and where you want to run them, is so complicated," he says. "You can contact a media buyer who knows how to buy television. The Internet is still a mystery. But I think gradually, over the next 10 years, that mystery will be solved."

Wider use of high-speed, broadband connections will boost online advertising by enabling Internet sites to sell the same kind of ads that now are effective only on television, PoliticsOnline publisher Noble says. "TV works because it's about emotion — visuals, motion, connecting in ways text can't do," he says. With its capacity for interaction and one-to-one communication, "broadband is going to push that in ways we haven't thought about yet."

In addition, he predicts, the Internet will spawn "a whole host of new players that exert enormous influence. There will be dozens of MoveOns. There will be lots of Howard Deans. And I think you're going to have new parties," if only on the local level.

Cornfield and Noble foresee the prospect — though not the certainty — that the Internet will produce a leader who, unlike Dean, will win. "I hold out the possibility that someone will figure out how to create a personal following through the Internet, and be charismatic through the Internet — who would be the FDR or JFK of the Internet," Cornfield says, "although I'm not sure it will happen."

Noble expects the Internet is more likely to produce a president who already is well-known off-line. "What if you had somebody who automatically had a national platform, and who said I'm running for president, and the way you can make that happen is to go to my Web site?" Noble asks. "If Oprah Winfrey decided she wanted to run for president as an independent, she might well be able to use the Internet to mobilize the people necessary to get on the ballot in 50 states."

No matter how profoundly the Internet changes the practice of politics, it's not going to convert America's representative democracy into direct democracy, as early online enthusiasts once predicted, according to political soothsayers.

"I believe in representative democracy, and I think there's a role for direct democracy, and part of the challenge for the next 50 years is the interplay between those two," Noble says. "Television did not replace radio. Radio did not replace newspapers. I don't think direct democracy will replace representative democracy, and I don't think it should.

"I've got no problem with 100 people going into a room, cutting deals, persuading, cajoling and convincing each other. I don't think it's a good thing for all Americans to get up every morning and punch a button to decide what our foreign policy should be." ■

Notes

[1] Joe Trippi, *The Revolution Will Not Be Televised: Democracy, the Internet and the Overthrow of Everything* (2004).

[2] Fundraising statistics from: *Ibid*; The Center for Responsive Politics, www.opensecrets.org; "CFI Analysis of the Presidential Candidates' Financial Reports Filed July 20, 2004," Campaign Finance Institute, George Washington University, July 20, 2004, available at www.cfinst.org/pr/072304.html; Jim VandeHei and Thomas B. Edsall, "Democrats Outraising the GOP This Year," *The Washington Post*, July 21, 2004, p. A1; Edsall, "Fundraising Doubles the Pace of 2000," *The Washington Post*, Aug. 21, 2004, p. A1; Lisa Getter, "Bush, Kerry Awash in Money," *Los Angeles Times*, May 4, 2004, p. A1. Edsall, James V. Grimaldi and Alice R. Crites, "Redefining Democratic Fundraising: Kerry Has Amassed Record Sums From Disparate Groups Opposed to Bush," *The Washington Post*, July 24, 2004, p. A1.

[3] For background, see Mary H. Cooper, "Campaign Finance Reform, *The CQ Researcher*, March 31, 2000, pp. 257-280, and Kenneth Jost, "Campaign Finance Showdown," *The CQ Researcher*, Nov. 22, 2002, pp. 969-992.

[4] "Contributions from All Donors," the Center for Responsive Politics, updated online when new reports filed, at www.opensecrets.org/presidential/donordems.asp.

[5] Kamarck quote from "NewsHour with Jim Lehrer," PBS, Nov. 10, 2003. Fundraising statistics from the Campaign Finance Institute.

[6] Edsall, *et al.*, *op. cit.*

About the Author

Tom Price, a Washington-based freelance journalist, has written about the Internet's impact on politics and government since the mid-1990s. He is author of three major studies on the topic published by the Foundation for Public Affairs: "Creating a Digital Democracy: The Impact of the Internet on Public Policy-Making" (1999); "Cyber Activism: Advocacy Groups and the Internet" (2000); and "Public Affairs Strategies in the Internet Age" (2002). His work has appeared in *The New York Times*, *Time*, *Rolling Stone* and other periodicals. He previously served as a correspondent in the Cox Newspapers Washington Bureau and chief politics writer for the *Dayton Daily News* and *The* [Dayton] *Journal Herald*. He earned a bachelor of science in journalism at Ohio University.

[7] Campaign Finance Institute, *op. cit.*, and VandeHei and Edsall, *op. cit.*

[8] For background, see Kathy Koch, "The Digital Divide," *The CQ Researcher*, Jan. 28, 2000, pp. 41-64.

[9] Pew Internet & American Life Project, available at www.PewInternet.org/trends/DemographicsofInternetUsers.htm. Figures for 2000 and 2002 are at www.PewInternet.org/pdfs/PIP_Shifting_Net_Pop_Report.pdf.

[10] *Ibid.*

[11] Charlie Cain, "Online Vote Triggers Worry," *The Detroit News*, Oct. 14, 2003, p. A1.

[12] Joe Mozingo and Erika Bolstad, "Touch-Screen Voting Fails to Ease Fear of More Blunders," *The Miami Herald*, Aug. 17, 2004. P. A1.

[13] Luisa Yanez, "Electronic Voting Machines Had Hitches, but No Glitches," *The Miami Herald*, Sept. 2, 2004, p. B5.

[14] Florida secretary of state. Available online at www.dos.state.fl.us.

[15] For background, see Kathy Koch, "Election Reform," *The CQ Researcher*, Nov. 2, 2001, pp. 897-920.

[16] "Voting: What Is, What Could Be," The Cal Tech/MIT Voting Technology Project, July 2001, p. 9. Available at www.vote.caltech.edu/Reports/2001report.html.

[17] *Ibid.*, p. 21.

[18] "U.S. EAC Forms Technical Committee to Create New Voting Standards," U.S. Election Assistance Commission, June 17, 2004, available on line at www.eac.gov/news_061704_2.asp.

[19] David Nather, "Provisions of the Federal Voting Standards and Procedures Law," *CQ Weekly*, Nov. 1, 2002.

[20] Caron Carlson, "Opposition Grows to Paperless Voting," *eWeek*, July 19, 2004, p. 20.

[21] Joe Mozingo and Erika Bolstad, "Touch-Screen Voting Fails to Ease Fear of More Blunders," *The Miami Herald*, Aug. 17, 2004, p. 1.

[22] Dan Keating, "Lost Votes in N.M. a Cautionary Tale," *The Washington Post*, Aug. 22, 2004, p. A5.

[23] "Insurance for Electronic Votes," editorial, *The New York Times*, July 23, 2004, p. A22.

[24] Mike Williams, "New Election Disputes Hit Florida," *The Austin American-Statesman*, Aug. 6, 2004, p. A29.

[25] Michael Shnayerson, "Hack the Vote," *Vanity Fair*, April 2004, p. 167.

[26] "On the Voting Machine Makers' Tab," *The New York Times*, Sept. 12, 2004, Section 4, p. 12.

[27] Adrienne Packer, "Machines to Print Voting Receipts," *Las Vegas Review-Journal*, July 13, 2004, p. 1B.

FOR MORE INFORMATION

CalTech/MIT Voting Technology Project, 1200 E. California Blvd., MC 228-77, Pasadena, CA 91125, or 77 Massachusetts Ave., E-15 315, Cambridge, MA 02139; www.vote.caltech.edu. Research group formed after 2000 election to recommend how voting systems can be improved. Members include scholars in political science, cognitive science, computer science, engineering and design from the California and Massachusetts institutes of technology.

Center for Information Technology and Society, 2215 North Hall, University of California, Santa Barbara, CA 93106; www.cits.ucsb.edu. Multidisciplinary research center that studies the social effects of information technology.

Center for Responsive Politics, 1101 14th St., N.W., Suite 1030, Washington, DC 20005-5635; www.opensecrets.org. Nonpartisan, nonprofit research organization that publishes an enormous amount of campaign-finance information online.

Institute for Politics, Democracy and the Internet, 805 21st St., N.W., Suite 401, Washington, DC 20052; www.ipdi.org. Research institute at The George Washington University that studies online politics.

Moving Ideas, www.movingideas.org. Portal to generally liberal public policy sites on the Internet.

Pew Internet & American Life Project, 1100 Connecticut Ave., N.W., Suite 710, Washington, DC 20036; www.PewInternet.org. Nonprofit research center that studies how the Internet affects Americans.

Town Hall, www.townhall.com. Portal to generally conservative public-policy sites on the Internet.

[28] Kristina Sauerwein, "Chadless Ballots, Puzzled Voters," *Los Angeles Times*, Feb. 29, 2004, p. B10.

[29] "Federal Panel Told E-Voting Is Unreliable," The Associated Press, May 6, 2004.

[30] Christos J. P. Moschovitis, Hilary Poole, Tami Schuyler and Theresa M. Senft, *History Of The Internet: A Chronology, 1843 To The Present* (1999), pp. 3-5.

[31] Tom Price, "Creating a Digital Democracy: The Impact of the Internet on Public Policy-Making," Foundation for Public Affairs, 1999, p. 6.

[32] Leonard Kleinrock, "The History of the Internet," available at www.lk.cs.ucla.edu/internet_history.html.

[33] Price, *op. cit.*

[34] *Ibid.*

[35] The preceding history of politics and government on the Internet was drawn from: Bruce Bimber and Richard Davis, *Campaigning Online: The Internet in U.S. Elections* (2003); Michael Cornfield, *Politics Moves Online: Campaigning and the Internet* (2004); Richard Davis, *The Web of Politics: The Internet's Impact on the American Political System* (1999); Price, *op. cit.* Price, "Political Combat in Cyberspace," FamilyPlanet.com, July 29, 1996.

[36] For background, see Mary H. Cooper, "Low Voter Turnout," *The CQ Researcher*, Oct. 20, 2000, pp. 833-856.

[37] www.georgewbush.com and www.johnkerry.com.

[38] For background, see Alan Greenblatt, "The Partisan Divide," *The CQ Researcher*, April 30, 2004, pp. 373-396.

[39] Paul Farhi, "Parties Square Off in a Database Duel," *The Washington Post*, July 20, 2004, p. A1.

[40] Jon Gertner, "The Very, Very Personal Is the Political," *The New York Times Magazine*, Feb. 15, 2004, p. 43.

[41] Pew Internet project, *op. cit.*

[42] Trippi, *op. cit.*, p. 141.

[43] www.DrudgeReport.com.

[44] See Cooper, "Low Voter Turnout," *op. cit.*

[45] Jo Becker, "Missouri Plan to Let Military Cast Votes by E-Mail Draws Criticism," *The Washington Post*, Aug. 27, 2004, p. A10.

Bibliography

Selected Sources

Books

Alvarez, R. Michael, and Thad E. Hall, *Point, Click and Vote: The Future of Internet Voting*, Brookings Institution Press, 2004.

Alvarez, a co-director of the CalTech/MIT Voting Technology Project, and Hall, program officer at The Century Foundation, argue for carefully crafted experiments in Internet voting, predicting that many Americans would benefit if they could vote online.

Bimber, Bruce, and Richard Davis, *Campaigning Online: The Internet in U.S. Elections*, Oxford University Press, 2003.

Two political scientists take a scholarly look at the role of the Internet in recent elections.

Cornfield, Michael, *Politics Moves Online: Campaigning and the Internet*, Century Foundation Press, 2004.

The research director of the Institute for Politics, Democracy and the Internet at George Washington University examines Internet politicking, particularly from 1999 through 2002.

Trippi, Joe, *The Revolution Will Not Be Televised: Democracy, the Internet and the Overthrow of Everything*, Regan Books, 2004.

The mastermind of the first Internet-based presidential campaign tells his insider's version of the amazing ascent and catastrophic crash of Howard Dean.

Articles

Gertner, Jon, "The Very, Very Personal Is the Political," *The New York Times Magazine*, Feb. 15, 2004, p. 43.

The author examines how politicians are mining computer databases to conduct person-to-person campaigning in the Information Age.

Jalonick, Mary Clare, "Consultant Q&A: Campaigning on the Internet," *Campaigns & Elections*, September 2002, p. 51.

Political consultants discuss the impact of the Internet on the 2002 campaigns.

Shapiro, Samantha M., "The Dean Machine Marches On," *Wired*, September 2004, p. 139.

Candidates in Senate and gubernatorial races are trying to apply the lessons learned in the Dean campaign about cyber-politicking.

Shnayerson, Michael, "Hack the Vote," *Vanity Fair*, April 2004, p. 158.

The author recounts some of the strongest attacks on electronic voting machines.

Reports and Studies

"Election Reform Briefing: Securing the Vote," electionline.org, April 2004. Available at http://electionline.org/site/docs/pdf/EB7.pdf.

This overview of the state of electronic voting includes a summary of the voting systems in use in each state.

"The Internet: Changing the Way We Communicate," National Science Foundation. Available at www.nsf.gov/od/lpa/news/publicat/nsf0050/internet/internet.htm.

An online history of the Internet provides a peak into the possible future.

***Voting: What Is, What Could Be*, The Cal Tech/MIT Voting Technology Project, July 2001, www.vote.caltech.edu/Reports/2001report.html.**

Political and computer scientists examine what went wrong in the 2000 vote — not only in Florida and with punch-card ballots but also around the country with all methods of voting.

Horrigan, John B., "How Americans Get in Touch With Government," Pew Internet & American Life Project, May 24, 2004. Available at www.pewinternet.org/pdfs/PIP_E-Gov_Report_0504.pdf.

A growing numbers of Americans use e-mail and government Web sites to contact government agencies, according to Pew, but the telephone remains an important tool for linking citizens and bureaucrats.

Jefferson, David, Aviel D. Rubin, Barbara Simons and David Wagner, "A Security Analysis of the Secure Electronic Registration and Voting Experiment," Jan. 20, 2004, available at http://servesecurityreport.org.

Computer experts hired to critique the Defense Department's plan to allow military personnel and other overseas Americans to vote via the Internet conclude the system would be highly vulnerable to cyber-attacks. The plan was abandoned based on the panel's findings.

Price, Tom, "Creating a Digital Democracy: The Impact of the Internet on Public Policy-Making," Foundation for Public Affairs, 1999; "Cyber Activism: Advocacy Groups and the Internet," Foundation for Public Affairs, 2000; "Public Affairs Strategies in the Internet Age," Foundation for Public Affairs, 2002.

Three reports by the author of this week's report look at the Internet's impact on government, public policy and activism.

The Next Step:

Additional Articles from Current Periodicals

Blogs

Grossman, Lev, and Anita Hamilton, "Meet Joe Blog," ***Time*****, June 21, 2004, p. 64.**

Major media outlets at first gave scant coverage to Trent Lott's controversial remarks about Strom Thurmond, but blogs aggressively resurrected the story, and Lott eventually resigned as Senate majority leader.

Kiely, Kathy, "Freewheeling 'Bloggers' Are Rewriting Rules of Journalism," ***USA Today*****, Dec. 30, 2003, p. 1A.**

The prominent reporters, producers and columnists who used to make and break candidates' reputations face some competition from the lowly bloggers.

Williams, Alex, "Blogged in Boston: Politics Gets an Unruly Spin," ***The New York Times*****, Aug. 1, 2004, Section 9, p. 1.**

Blog writers get accredited as journalists for the Democratic convention; though they provide more witty quips than hard facts, many readers find their irreverent style refreshing.

Digital Divide

Krim, Jonathan, "Program Aids Urban Poor in Accessing the Internet," ***The Washington Post*****, Aug. 9, 2004, p. A1.**

Only 38 percent of households with an income under $30,000 had Internet access in 2002, compared with 75 percent of households above $50,000.

Rose, Barbara, "Hispanic Market Targeted by AOL," ***Chicago Tribune*****, Aug. 12, 2004, Business Section, p. 1.**

AOL, facing declining subscriber numbers, targets Hispanic buyers with cut-rate computers requiring a subscription to AOL.

Toppo, Greg, "Schools Achieving a Dream: Near-Universal Net Access," ***USA Today*****, June 9, 2004, p. 6D.**

Helped by the federal E-rate program, the number of schools with Internet access rose from 65 percent to 99 percent between 1996 and 2002.

E-Voting

Davis, Julie Hirschfeld, "Michigan Voters Try an Online Ballot Box," ***The Baltimore Sun*****, Feb. 7, 2004, p. 1A.**

The state Democratic caucuses in Michigan provided one of the first times the Internet was used for voting in a presidential campaign.

Keating, Dan, "Lost Votes in N.M. a Cautionary Tale," ***The Washington Post*****, Aug. 22, 2004, p. A5.**

The 678 votes that were lost in New Mexico, a state won in 2000 by only 366 votes, serve as a stark warning, say critics of electronic voting machines.

McCormick, John, "Not All Voting for New Technology," ***Chicago Tribune*****, June 1, 2004, News Section, p. 1.**

Around 50 million voters, more than one-third of all those registered, are expected to use electronic voting machines in November.

Munro, Neil, "Are Chips the New Chads?" ***National Journal*****, Sept. 13, 2003.**

Congress gave the states $3.9 billion to replace their old punch-card voting machines, but buying new machines is proving more complex than anticipated.

Novak, Viveca, "The Vexations of Voting Machines," ***Time*****, May 3, 2004, p. 42.**

When a team led by a former government code breaker attempted to simulate efforts to manipulate voting machines, they easily wrought havoc.

Pfeifer, Stuart, "State Blocks Digital Voting," ***Los Angeles Times*****, May 1, 2004, p. A1.**

California's top election official withdraws his approval of electronic voting machines after repeated malfunctions.

Schulte, Brigid, "Jolted Over Electronic Voting; Report's Security Warning Shakes Some States' Trust," ***The Washington Post*****, Aug. 11, 2003, p. A1.**

Examinations reveal major flaws in electronic voting machines; "whoever certified that code as secure should be fired," said one security expert.

Sennott, Sarah, and Adam Piore, "The Age of E-Voting," ***Newsweek*****, April 5, 2004, p. 51.**

Europe is moving full speed ahead toward electronic voting machines and Internet voting; a variety of methods have been proposed to prevent vote tampering.

Fundraising

Baker, Stephen, "Click the Vote," ***Business Week*****, March 29, 2004, p. 102.**

Howard Dean's campaign brought in a dollar for every nickel spent on the Internet, according to a former staffer,

Jurkowitz, Mark, "Candidates Plug Into Net's Power as Never Before," ***The Boston Globe*****, June 12, 2004, p. A3.**

The Kerry campaign has targeted most of its Web ads to fundraising; an expert estimates the ads generate twice as much in donations as it costs to buy them.

Zeleny, Jeff, "Dean's Money Machine Tops Clinton's Best," ***Chicago Tribune*****, Oct. 1, 2003, News Section, p. 12.**

Dean's Internet-based fundraising operation raised more money in 2003 than former President Clinton's did in the same quarter of 1995.

Grass-roots Resurgence

Cochran, John, "Internet-Based Activist Group Puts Powerful Spin on Politics," *CQ Weekly*, Oct. 4, 2003, p. 2424.

The success of the MoveOn Web site's fundraising and organization has attracted the attention of Democratic politicians eager to harness its influence.

Gold, Matea, "Where Political Influence Is Only a Keyboard Away," *Los Angeles Times*, Dec. 21, 2003, p. A41.

Every month, 250,000 political supporters mobilize online to support their candidates and commune with their political fellow travelers.

Farhi, Paul, "Small Donors Grow Into Big Political Force," *The Washington Post*, May 3, 2004, p. A1.

Partially due to Internet fundraising, the number of small, first-time donors has increased dramatically.

Howard Dean's Rise and Fall

Getlin, Josh, "Web-Savvy Staff Helps Dean Weave His Way Up," *Los Angeles Times*, Sept. 24, 2003, p. A10.

Dean supporters dropped their lives in places like Moab, Utah, and moved to Vermont to create the online organization that made him a political phenomenon.

Kosterlitz, Julie, "The Internet Shows Its Muscles," *National Journal*, Oct. 4, 2003.

Politicos take notice when the Internet makes a serious candidate out of a "nobody from nowhere with no money in just six months."

Lizza, Ryan, "Dean.com," *The New Republic*, June 2, 2003, p. 10.

Joe Trippi, the architect of Dean's Internet outreach campaign, closely studied John McCain's online efforts four years ago and ultimately far surpassed them.

Rosenthal, Elisabeth, "Political Challenge 2.0: Make a Virtual Army a Reality," *The New York Times*, Dec. 21, 2003, Section 1, p. 42.

The Dean campaign eventually faced the challenge of turning a decentralized army of "netizens" into a centrally organized campaign.

Taylor, Chris, "How Dean Is Winning the Web," *Time*, July 14, 2003, p. 40.

Harnessing the power of the Internet as a tool for organizing and fundraising, Howard Dean tapped into a powerful well of disgruntled citizens willing to contribute time and money.

New Political Battleground

Birnbaum, Jeffrey, "Consultants Deliver Politics to Voters' Inboxes, at a Price," *The Washington Post*, Aug. 29, 2004, p. A1.

Companies supply politicians and organizations with voters' e-mail addresses for a price, outraging privacy advocates.

Drinkard, Jim, and Jill Lawrence, "Online, Off and Running: Web Gains Clout on Campaign Front," *USA Today*, July 15, 2003, p. 1A.

The decentralized, quasi-anarchic nature of online organizing is unsettling to modern campaigners whose playbook calls for a tightly focused, top-down message.

Faler, Brian, "Presidential Ad War Escalates Online," *The Washington Post*, May 30, 2004, p. A5.

The candidates can target specific demographics, such as when Kerry placed ads in the "Help wanted" section of an Iowa newspaper's Web site.

Miller, David, "Election Overview: Web Politics and Growing Pains," *CQ Weekly*, Feb. 21, 2004, p. 485.

Although Howard Dean's ultimate failure as a candidate popped the political Internet bubble, the parties continue to hone their Web-based tactics.

CITING *THE CQ RESEARCHER*

Sample formats for citing these reports in a bibliography include the ones listed below. Preferred styles and formats vary, so please check with your instructor or professor.

MLA STYLE

Jost, Kenneth. "Rethinking the Death Penalty." The CQ Researcher 16 Nov. 2001: 945-68.

APA STYLE

Jost, K. (2001, November 16). Rethinking the death penalty. *The CQ Researcher, 11*, 945-968.

CHICAGO STYLE

Jost, Kenneth. "Rethinking the Death Penalty." *CQ Researcher*, November 16, 2001, 945-968.

CQ Researcher

Published by CQ Press, a division of Congressional Quarterly Inc.

thecqresearcher.com

Social Security Reform

How should America's retirement system be saved?

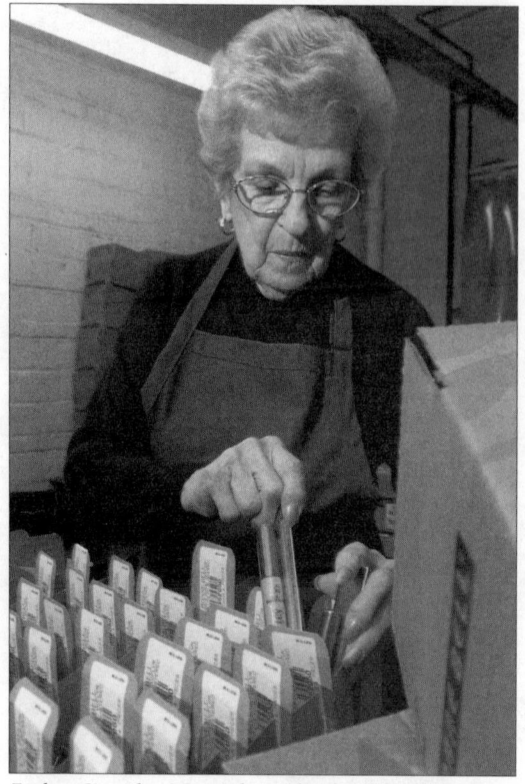

Evelyn Cicerchi, 90, works in the shipping department at Bonne Bell cosmetics in Lakewood, Ohio, to supplement her Social Security benefits.

Social Security has provided a guaranteed income for retirees, widows and disabled individuals for almost 70 years. But unless changes are made to the taxpayer-funded system, Social Security will begin paying more in benefits than it collects in payroll taxes in about 15 years. That's when the retirement of millions of baby-boom workers will overwhelm the system's pay-as-you-go funding mechanism. Moreover, by 2052, the program's trillion-dollar trust fund is expected to run dry. Experts continue to debate the seriousness of the program's problems and the best way to strengthen it. Three years ago, President Bush called for bolstering Social Security funding by allowing workers to invest part of their payroll contributions in personal investment accounts. Democratic presidential candidate Sen. John Kerry opposes privatization. Regardless of who wins this fall's presidential election, Social Security reform is likely to figure high on the legislative agenda next year.

INSIDE THIS REPORT

The CQ Researcher • Sept. 24, 2004 • www.thecqresearcher.com
Volume 14, Number 33 • Pages 781-804

CQ PRESS

RECIPIENT OF SOCIETY OF PROFESSIONAL JOURNALISTS AWARD FOR EXCELLENCE ◆ AMERICAN BAR ASSOCIATION SILVER GAVEL AWARD

Cover: Evelyn Cicerchi, 90, fills packages at Bonne Bell cosmetics in Lakewood, Ohio, to supplement her Social Security benefits. Low-income seniors received 82 percent of their retirement income from Social Security in 2001. (AFP Photo/David Maxwell)

Sept. 24, 2004
Volume 14, Number 33

MANAGING EDITOR: Thomas J. Colin
ASSISTANT MANAGING EDITOR: Kathy Koch
ASSOCIATE EDITOR: Kenneth Jost
STAFF WRITERS: Mary H. Cooper, William Triplett
CONTRIBUTING WRITERS: Sarah Glazer, David Hatch, David Hosansky, Patrick Marshall, Tom Price, Jane Tanner
DESIGN/PRODUCTION EDITOR: Olu B. Davis
ASSISTANT EDITOR: Kate Templin

CQ PRESS

A Division of Congressional Quarterly Inc.

SENIOR VICE PRESIDENT/GENERAL MANAGER: John A. Jenkins
DIRECTOR, LIBRARY PUBLISHING: Kathryn C. Suárez
DIRECTOR, EDITORIAL OPERATIONS: Ann Davies

CONGRESSIONAL QUARTERLY INC.

CHAIRMAN: Paul C. Tash
VICE CHAIRMAN: Andrew P. Corty
PRESIDENT AND PUBLISHER: Robert W. Merry

The CQ Researcher (ISSN 1056-2036) is printed on acid-free paper. Published weekly, except Jan. 2, April 9, July 2, July 9, Aug. 6, Aug. 13, Nov. 26 and Dec. 31, by CQ Press, a division of Congressional Quarterly Inc. Annual subscription rates for institutions start at $625. For pricing, call 1-800-834-9020, ext. 1906. To purchase a *CQ Researcher* report in print or electronic format (PDF), visit www.cqpress.com or call 866-427-7737. A single report is $10. Bulk purchase discounts and electronic-rights licensing are also available. Periodicals postage paid at Washington, D.C., and additional mailing offices. POSTMASTER: Send address changes to *The CQ Researcher*, 1255 22nd St., N.W., Suite 400, Washington, D.C. 20037.

Social Security Reform

BY MARY H. COOPER

THE ISSUES

Demographers often describe the huge generation of baby boomers as a pig in a python, a population bulge so big it dwarfs both their parents' generation and their children's.

By most measures, the 77 million Americans born during the prosperous postwar period from 1946 to 1964 have dominated culture and politics. New schools rose to accommodate them; their protests ended the Vietnam War; and their tastes drove entertainment and consumer trends.

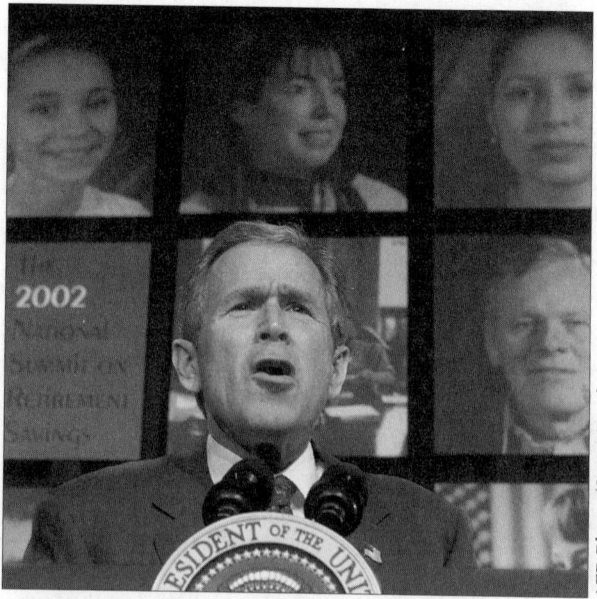

AFP Photo/Stan Honda

President Bush tells the National Summit on Retirement Savings he favors allowing workers to invest part of their Social Security payroll taxes in stocks. Democratic presidential nominee John Kerry opposes so-called privatization plans.

Now, as they near retirement, baby boomers may have yet another profound influence on American society: They could bankrupt the 70-year-old Social Security system.

"As the baby boomers start to retire, if the economy is slowing and the deficit is still bad, there's going to be some serious concern about whether or not they're even going to get all of their benefits," says Jeff Lemieux, executive director of the nonpartisan Centrist Policy Network, which analyzes Social Security reform proposals.

Only about 60 percent of the 47 million people who now receive Social Security benefits are retired, but the boomers' retirement will swell those ranks to the breaking point. Barring changes to current law, the Social Security trust fund will run out of money by 2053, according to the nonpartisan Congressional Budget Office (CBO). [1]

Demographers have warned for several decades that Social Security could not long survive the boomers' retirement without significant changes in the way the system collects and disburses revenue. [2] Spawned by the hardships of the Great Depression, Social Security was designed as a "pay-as-you-go" system, collecting payroll taxes from current workers and employers and using those funds to pay benefits to current retirees. Historically, the system stayed in the black because Social Security had a relatively large work force and small elderly population. In 1950, for example, 16 workers supported every retiree — more than enough to cover benefits. (*See graphs, p. 788.*)

Indeed, since 1983 payroll taxes have exceeded benefits paid, resulting in large surpluses in Social Security "trust funds" — the accounts used to pay benefits. [3] Money not needed to pay current benefits is invested in special-issue U.S. Treasury bonds. In early 2004, the Social Security system held $1.5 trillion in such bonds, which produced more than $80 billion a year in interest.

Over the years, the government has tapped into the trust funds to pay for unrelated programs, promising to pay the money back. But the boomers had fewer children than their parents, resulting in the "baby bust" of the 1970s and '80s. Thus, by 2040, when the last boomers will be well into retirement, only two workers will be supporting each Social Security recipient — too few to pay scheduled benefits at current tax rates.

Compounding the system's financial problems, medical advances have raised life expectancy, so future retirees will live longer and collect Social Security benefits longer than their predecessors. In fact, the combined impact of a larger retiree population and increased longevity suggests that Social Security's financial problems may outlive the boomers.

"This is not just a temporary problem that will go away when we get over the baby-boom bulge," says Michael Tanner, director of health and welfare studies at the libertarian Cato Institute. Rather than a "pig in a python," the boomers are "more like a python swallowing a telephone pole. The situation will never improve because life expectancies will continue to increase, while birth rates will likely continue to decline."

Policymakers have been reluctant to take on the politically thankless task of reforming Social Security. Indeed, the program is so popular it's known as the electrified "third rail" of U.S. politics — touching it can be political suicide. But with the approach of 2008, when the first boomers become eligible for Social Security benefits, politicians are acknowledging the system must be changed if it is to survive. *

* Retiring workers may begin to receive reduced benefits at age 62. They receive full benefits by deferring retirement until their normal retirement age of 66.

Low-Income Retirees Depend on Social Security

Low-income seniors received 82 percent of their retirement income from Social Security in 2001, while wealthy seniors depended on Social Security for only 19 percent of their income.

Sources of Income for Seniors, 2001

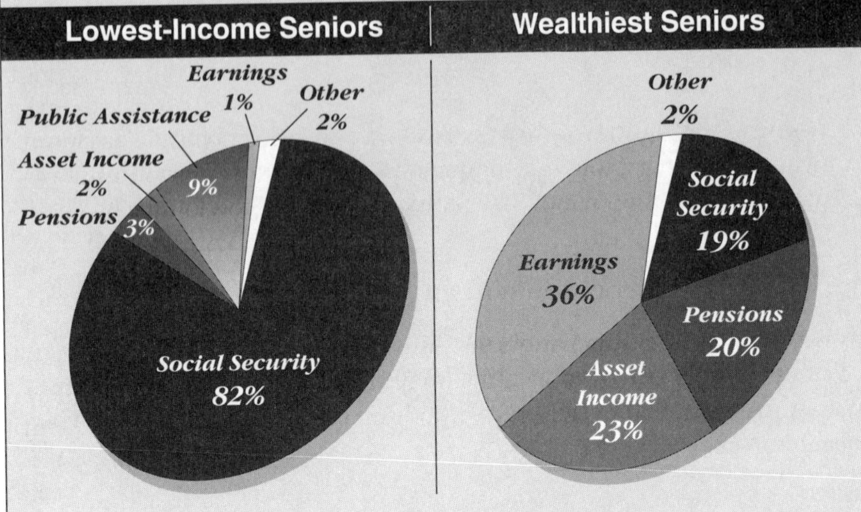

Note: Percentages for low-income seniors do not add to 100 due to rounding.

Source: "Income of the Aged Chartbook, 2001," Social Security Administration, 2003

The question is how. Early in his administration, President Bush set up a commission that recommended ways to "privatize" part of Social Security by allowing workers to invest a small portion of their payroll contributions in stocks held in personal investment accounts. The theory was that stocks would return higher dividends than the government's conservative bond investments.

Support for personal investment accounts runs high among conservatives eager to reduce the size and role of government in general — a sentiment famously characterized by Grover Norquist, president of Americans for Tax Reform: "I don't want to abolish government; I simply want to reduce it to the size where I can drag it into the bathroom and drown it in the bathtub." [4]

Some proposals to privatize Social Security reflect the view that the private-enterprise system is a superior source of financial security for retirees than a government-funded entitlement program. Peter J. Ferrara, an associate law professor at the George Mason University School of Law, in Arlington, Va., and a former senior policy adviser on Social Security for Norquist's organization, has authored a plan that relies heavily on private investments. "Even though the stock market has a lot of ups and downs, over a lifetime of investment workers are certainly going to end up with a lot more through a system like this than they would under the pay-as-you-go Social Security system," Ferrara says.

Critics, including many Democrats, say personal accounts amount to a backdoor assault on one of the country's most successful entitlement programs. "What the folks who want to drown government in the bathtub are really trying to do with privatization is bankrupt the federal government," says Joan Entmacher, vice president for economic security at the National Women's Law Center, a Washington advocacy group. "It's terrifying."

The "dirty little secret" about personal investment accounts, she continues, is that rather than improving Social Security's long-term financial shortfall, "they would make it worse." A full 85 percent of payroll taxes paid by all of today's workers "go to pay benefits for our fathers, our grandmothers and the kid down the street whose parents were killed. If — instead of going into the Social Security trust fund — that money goes into private accounts [unavailable to Social Security], how are we going to pay those benefits?"

The stock market's recent plunge and recent corporate and stock market scandals that resulted in thousands of Americans losing their retirement nest-eggs raise more red flags for critics of privatization plans. [5] Further, corporate America is abandoning traditional, defined-benefit pension plans in favor of defined-contribution schemes like 401(k)s that shift pension investment risks to workers, making Social Security the only secure source of retirement income that retirees can count on, they say. [6]

"In today's 401(k) world, 40 percent of workers work for employers who don't even offer a 401(k) plan, and fewer than 50 percent of private-sector workers take advantage of those plans," says Christian Weller, senior economist at the Center for American Progress, a liberal think tank in Washington. "Even those who favor privatization are aware of Social Security's value as an insurance system."

To date, the contenders in this fall's presidential election have taken a cautious approach to Social Security reform. Even Bush, who earlier spearheaded the call for privatization, has downplayed the issue. Sen. John Kerry, D-Mass., the Democratic nominee, rejects Bush's privatization scheme for Social Security but has yet to offer a detailed plan to resolve the system's impending funding shortfall. And neither candidate is thought likely to offer a detailed solution to the shortfall before the election.

"The candidates have been quiet on Social Security all year, and that's largely because it's an election year," says Jeffrey R. Brown, a Social Security expert and professor of finance at the University of Illinois, Urbana-Champaign. "This, more than any other issue, is a topic that is difficult to express nuanced views about in a way that is easily digested by the electorate."

But even if both candidates continue to dodge the issue through the November elections, the next administration will face fundamental choices about the best way to ensure the system's long-term survival. Meanwhile, these are some of the questions policymakers are asking:

Outlays to Surpass Revenues in 15 Years

Social Security benefit payments will exceed revenues coming into the system beginning in 2019, according to Congressional Budget Office predictions. The revenue shortfall will force the program to pay benefits by drawing down its trust funds, which are expected to run dry by 2053.

Social Security Outlays and Revenues, 2003 to 2100

(As a percentage of gross domestic product)

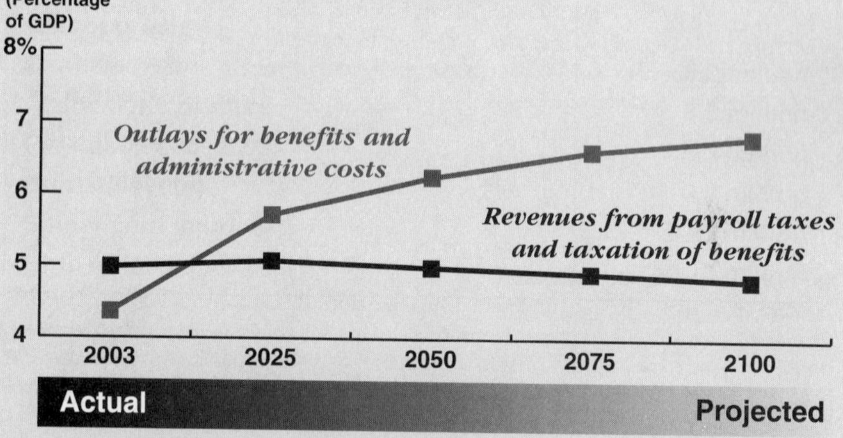

Source: Congressional Budget Office, "The Outlook for Social Security," June 2004

Does Social Security face an immediate funding crisis?

Government analysts predict that Social Security will begin taking in less revenue than it pays out in benefits in about 15 years. After that, the system will be able to continue paying scheduled benefits for another three decades by drawing down the surplus in the Social Security trust funds. Around the middle of the century, however, that cushion will run out.

"We have a huge fiscal gap, a huge generational imbalance, which has been built up over years through this pay-as-you-go program," says Laurence J. Kotlikoff, an economics professor at Boston University. "It's now time for us to recognize that fact and collectively deal with it." In his recently published *The Coming Generational Storm*, Kotlikoff says it's not the boomers, but their children and grandchildren, who stand to suffer if Social Security reform is put off any longer. [7] "We do need social insurance; we just need to pay for it," he says. "And we can't let one generation's social insurance be paid for by bankrupting another generation."

Social Security's funding shortfall is even more worrisome, some analysts say, in the context of a rapidly worsening federal budget deficit and even graver financial shortfalls facing Medicare and Medicaid, the federal programs that provide health insurance program for seniors and the poor, respectively. [8]

"People often say that no action is taken until a crisis is upon us," says Maya MacGuineas, executive director of the Committee for a Responsible Federal Budget, a bipartisan, nonprofit group in Washington. "Today that crisis is really upon us. We have structural budget deficits, a huge deficit in Social Security and even larger deficits in our health-care programs. Then we have tax cuts that they're talking about making permanent with no plan for how to pay for them. Hopefully, this will push Congress to come up with a real kind of budget agreement, which is what we need to get back on the path towards fiscal soundness."

But other experts say predictions of Social Security's impending demise are overblown. "It's very important to consider the financial problems that Social Security is supposed to encounter from a long-term perspective," says Weller of the Center for American Progress. He points out that in their most recent annual report on the program's financial sustainability, the Social Security trustees predicted that the costs associated with the baby boomers' retirement would level off by about 2038. "Once the baby boomers have all died off, the program's cost stabilizes," he says. "Other than this demographic bulge, there's nothing really that makes the system unsustainable."

Major Proposals to Reform Social Security

Proposals to reform Social Security are designed to eliminate the funding gap that the program likely would face over the next several decades as baby boomers start retiring in droves.

Plans to "privatize" Social Security would supplement the current system, which pays defined, or guaranteed, benefits, with a voluntary system enabling workers to shift part of their payroll-tax contribution into government-managed personal investment accounts. [1] Returns on those investments would replace part of the defined benefits provided to retirees who choose to participate. Most of the plans offer several investment options in index funds, like the existing federal Thrift Savings Plan (TSP) that covers government employees. The plans differ in the amount of transition costs they entail, which result from the diversion of payroll-tax revenue from the Social Security trust funds to personal accounts.* Most plans include benefit cuts with or without payroll-tax increases. Among the plans being debated are proposals from:

Rep. Paul Ryan, R-Wis., and Sen. John Sununu, R-N.H. — Based on a proposal by Peter J. Ferrara of George Mason University, the plan allows workers to divert an average of 6.4 percent of earnings into personal investment account, more than any other major proposal. It would not cut Social Security benefits or raise payroll taxes. Workers who choose to stay with the current Social Security system would receive the benefits promised under current law; those who open investment accounts would be guaranteed to receive at least as much as they would receive in benefits under current law. The plan incurs much higher transition costs than other major proposals, according to Centrists.org, a nonpartisan group that analyzes public policy. [2]

Michael Tanner, Cato Institute — Workers could divert half of their payroll taxes — 6.2 percent — to private accounts. (The other half would pay disability and survivor benefits and part of the transition costs.) Workers who choose the private accounts would forgo the accrual of future traditional Social Security benefits. Workers who remain in the traditional Social Security system would receive benefits payable with the current level of revenue. The government would guarantee that workers' retirement incomes would be at least 120 percent of the poverty level. The plan requires Congress to figure out how to pay for remaining transition costs, suggesting cutting corporate subsidies and redirecting the savings to Social Security. [3]

President's Commission to Strengthen Social Security — The most closely watched of the commission's three proposals, Model 2, would allow workers to place up to 4 percent or $1,000 per year of payroll taxes into personal investment accounts, with the remainder going to the Social Security trust funds to pay current beneficiaries. Once retired, account holders would receive reduced benefits, based on the total amount diverted into their personal accounts. The plan would offer several investment options for Social Security retirement accounts, and those who fail to stipulate their investment allocations would have their holdings split among stocks and bonds. The plan would reduce retirees' initial benefits but continue to allow later benefits to rise with inflation.

Sen. Lindsey Graham, R-S.C. — Workers under age 55 either could "pay to stay" in the current system or join a hybrid system with personal accounts similar to the TSP. (Workers over 55 would remain in the current system.) Eligible workers could stay in the current system by paying an additional payroll tax of 2 percent. The hybrid system would pay lower benefits but increased minimum benefits for low-income workers. The government would match voluntary contributions up to $500 for workers making less than $30,000 a year and guarantee a min-

In fact, supporters of Social Security's current funding mechanism say calls for diverting payroll tax revenues to private investment accounts are little more than fear-mongering on the part of those, like Norquist, who want to reduce the size of the government. "This is precisely a backdoor way of achieving that goal," says Entmacher of the National Women's Law Center. "While we might want to make some adjustments to the payroll tax, Social Security really is in a strong financial position."

Entmacher cites annual reports by the Social Security trustees and the recent CBO report as evidence that the system's projected shortfalls hardly amount to a crisis. The trustees' most recent annual report, published in March, predicted that the system's trust funds won't run out until 2042, 13 years later than the 2029 date the trustees forecasted in 1997, thanks in part to rising real wages since 1997. [9] And the CBO was even more optimistic, predicting the program wouldn't run out of trust fund money until 2052. "The privatizers aren't able to sell fear because the CBO confirms that Social Security can pay 100 percent of benefits until 2052," Entmacher says. "That's 50 more years."

But long before the trust funds actually run out of money, the surplus will begin to shrink. It's uncertain exactly when the system will begin paying more in benefits than it collects in payroll taxes — the trustees predict that will occur in 2018; the CBO says it won't happen until 2019. Such differences among the official forecasts are unimportant, some experts say. "The evidence is overwhelming that we are going to begin to run large deficits in the Social Security system sometime in the next two decades," says Brown of the University of Illinois. "Whether it's in 2018 or 2019, once we pass over imum benefit. Centrists.org calls the proposal moderately sized and somewhat more progressive — lower-income workers get relatively higher benefits, and higher-income workers get relatively lower benefits — than under current law, but with significant transition costs.

Reps. Jim Kolbe, R-Ariz., and Charles Stenholm, D-Texas — Beginning in 2006, workers under 55 could redirect 3 percent of their first $10,000 in earnings and 2 percent of their remaining taxable earnings to personal accounts. (For someone earning $30,000, the amount that could be invested would be about $733.) The government would match 50 percent of the contributions for workers earning less than $30,000 a year. Low-wage workers would receive a new minimum benefit. It would speed up the increase in Social Security's normal retirement age to 67 by 2011, with a small reduction in benefits for workers who retire early and a small increase in benefits for those who work beyond the normal retirement age. Centrists.org describes this personal-account plan as moderately sized, probably more progressive than current law and better than Graham's plan at limiting and paying for transition costs.

Laurence J. Kotlikoff, economist, Boston University, and Scott Burns, finance columnist — A new "personal security system" (PSS) would replace the retirement portion of Social Security (survivor and disability insurance would remain unchanged). The retirement portion of Social Security would cease to collect revenue, and a new federal retail sales tax would be used to pay off the transition costs. Current retirees would continue to receive their promised benefits, and current workers, once they retire, would receive all the benefits owed them as of the plan's implementation date. Workers continue to pay payroll taxes to cover Social Security's survivor and disability benefits; the portion of payroll taxes no longer collected for Social Security's retirement system would go instead to PSS accounts. The government guarantees the principal amount that workers contribute to their PSS accounts. [4]

Robert M. Ball, former Social Security commissioner — Retains the system's current structure with minor benefit cuts and tax increases and offers private investment accounts. Part of the Social Security trust funds, now held only in Treasury bonds, would be invested in a broad index of stocks, overseen by a Federal Reserve-type board. Workers could choose to invest up to an additional 2 percent of their earnings in supplemental retirement savings accounts administered by Social Security.

Peter Orszag and Peter Diamond, economists, Brookings Institution — Plan offers no personal accounts and relies on tax increases to solve Social Security's funding shortfall, with a gradual increase in the $87,900 cap on taxable income and a new tax of 3 percent on earnings above the cap. It cuts benefits for higher-income workers and raises benefits for low-income workers, widows and widowers and workers qualifying for disability benefits. With no personal accounts, there are no transition costs. Centrists.org says the plan's downside is its permanent increase in the payroll tax, and that overall the plan is probably more progressive than current law.

* Transition costs are the payroll tax revenues diverted to private accounts and thus unavailable to pay benefits under the existing system.

[1] Social Security payroll taxes currently total 12.4 percent of earnings up to $87,900, half of which are paid by employers and half by employees.

[2] Centrists.org. The Web site provides assessments of most major Social Security reform proposals.

[3] See Michael Tanner, "Cato's Plan for Reforming Social Security," *Cato Policy Report*, May/June 2004, p. 3.

[4] See Laurence J. Kotlikoff and Scott Burns, *The Coming Generational Storm* (2004), pp. 155-162.

into that period, absent some sort of a change in the way the system is structured, those deficits are going to grow larger every year."

Indeed, while experts differ widely over the gravity of Social Security's funding shortfall and the best way to solve it, everyone agrees that some adjustments are needed to ensure the system's long-term survival. They also agree that the sooner lawmakers make those changes, the easier it will be to pay for them. "There's no miracle here," says Alicia Munnell, director of the Center for Retirement Research at Boston College. "We just have to bite the bullet and acknowledge that it's going to require money. Then we can talk about what's the best way to do it."

Inaction — the path taken thus far — is no longer a viable option, most experts agree. "We could do nothing for a couple of decades, but then we would have very few options on the table apart from big tax increases or big benefit cuts," Brown says. "To do nothing is completely irresponsible and unrealistic."

Would privatization be good for future retirees?

Most proposals to privatize Social Security are voluntary and would allow workers to invest part of the money they now contribute as payroll taxes in stocks, bonds or a mix of the two, in privately held, government-administered accounts. In return, they would receive smaller monthly benefits when they retire than they would under the current system. Current beneficiaries and workers nearing retirement would retain promised benefits under most proposals.

Beyond those general terms, however, privatization schemes vary widely. The most sweeping proposal — by George Mason's Ferrara — would require the federal government to guar-

Fewer Workers Support Each Beneficiary

The number of workers paying into Social Security per beneficiary has dropped from 16 in 1950 to 3.3 today. In 2033, only two workers will be supporting each beneficiary, severely straining Social Security's financial soundness.

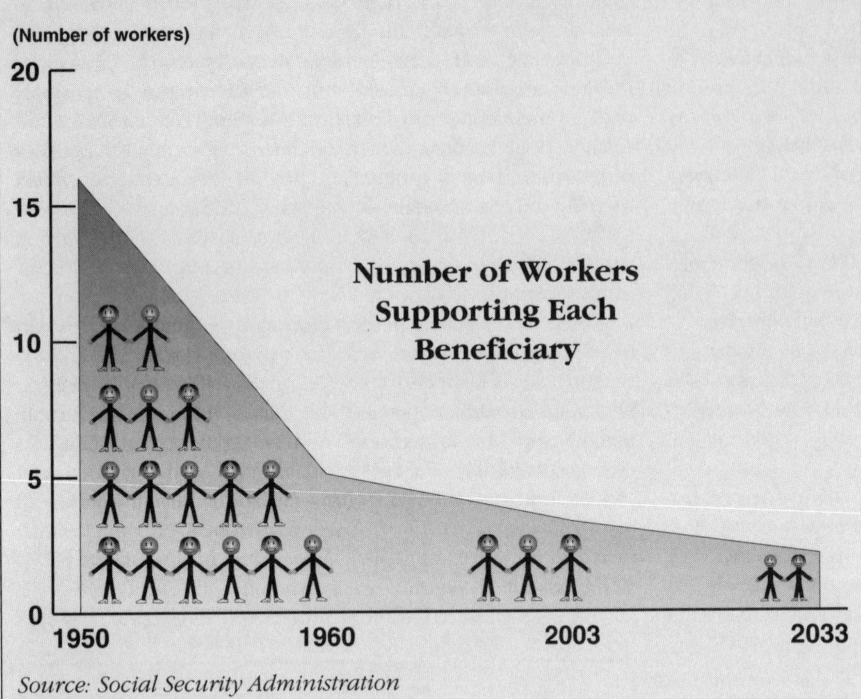

Source: Social Security Administration

antee that beneficiaries' personal accounts return no less than the benefits they would have received through Social Security under current law.

"Even if Social Security could pay all its promised benefits, the real rate of return for most workers would be no more than 1.5 percent," says Ferrara. "The long-term return on stocks after inflation is 7 to 7.5 percent. So even if stocks during certain periods go up or down, the large gulf between private capital returns and the pay-as-you-go return means that we can take the risk off the worker so that he's guaranteed current-law benefits in any event."

Those higher investment returns, supporters of this approach maintain, will translate into greater consumer spending, boosting the overall U.S. economy. But critics say Ferrara's plan could bankrupt the system because it relies too heavily on the consistently robust growth of the stock market, an assumption they say is invalidated by the recent volatility of stock prices. "Peter Ferrara's proposal is a prime example of the notion that somehow privatization will accelerate economic growth and that over the long run it will ultimately pay for itself," says Weller of the Center for American Progress. "That's just silly economics."

Under some privatization proposals, administrative costs — mainly fees charged by brokers to manage workers' personal accounts — could reduce participants' account balances at retirement by as much as 30 percent, according to CBO estimates. [10] Boston University's Kotlikoff would reduce that burden by offering a single, internationally diversified portfolio. "This plan offers private investment in a collective, global mutual fund of stocks and bonds," he says. "Instead of having everybody investing on their own and paying whatever fees their brokers want to charge, everybody in our plan would be invested in exactly the same portfolio, and the whole thing would be administered by the Social Security Administration."

But critics say privatization would divert revenue from the Social Security trust funds to private accounts, reducing the amount of money available to pay benefits to current beneficiaries. Over time, when workers holding personal investment accounts retire and use the returns on those investments as part of their retirement income, privatization could save the system money. But until then, the payroll taxes diverted to those accounts would be a drain on Social Security, commonly described as the "transition costs" of privatization.

"Giving workers accounts costs money in the short run, because at the same time you're funding those accounts you're also paying Social Security benefits," says Lemieux of the Centrist Policy Network. "It's only in the long run, when people holding personal accounts get smaller regular Social Security benefits, that the savings to the system begin to take effect."

Many experts assess the viability of privatization plans according to the magnitude of the transition costs they would incur. Ferrara's plan has attracted the broadest criticism from supporters of Social Security because it would allow workers to divert a larger portion of their payroll to private accounts. "Some of the more conservative Republicans are entertaining a pie-in-the-sky or free-lunch proposal," says Lemieux. "This plan is just nuts. The transition costs would be so enormous they would greatly upset capital markets and possibly the economy. Over the next 75 years, Ferrara's plan would cost more than current law, and it would raise Social Security spending much higher than it would get even after all the baby boomers retire."

Other critics say privatization is the wrong approach to solving Social Security's funding problem because it undermines the federally guaranteed program at a time when other sources of retiree income are becoming less certain. U.S. employers are abandoning traditional, defined-benefit pension plans, which promise a monthly payment for life, in favor of defined-contribution plans, which shift the investment risk to the employee and future retiree. [11] Moreover, because employees generally are not required to participate in the defined-contribution plans — known as 401(k) plans — it's usually the lower-paid or less-educated workers who fare the worst, because they either feel they can't afford to set aside money for retirement or are unaware of the need to do so.

"We need a part of our retirement income that's secure and that we can count on," says Entmacher of the National Women's Law Center. "So much risk is already being shifted to workers, while employers are bearing less and less of that risk in private pensions. For that reason, we need Social Security to really be secure."

But many analysts who dismiss sweeping reforms such as Ferrara's still favor partial privatization as the only way to ensure Social Security's long-range survival. In addition, some proposals — such as one introduced by Reps. Jim Kolbe, R-Ariz., and Charles W. Stenholm, D-Texas — seek to enhance the system's progressivity by tailoring it in favor of low-income workers. * "The good reform proposals don't cut benefits so much for people who earned small amounts during their working careers, and they specifically boost personal accounts for those people," Lemieux says. "So I feel pretty confident that they would be even more progressive than current law."

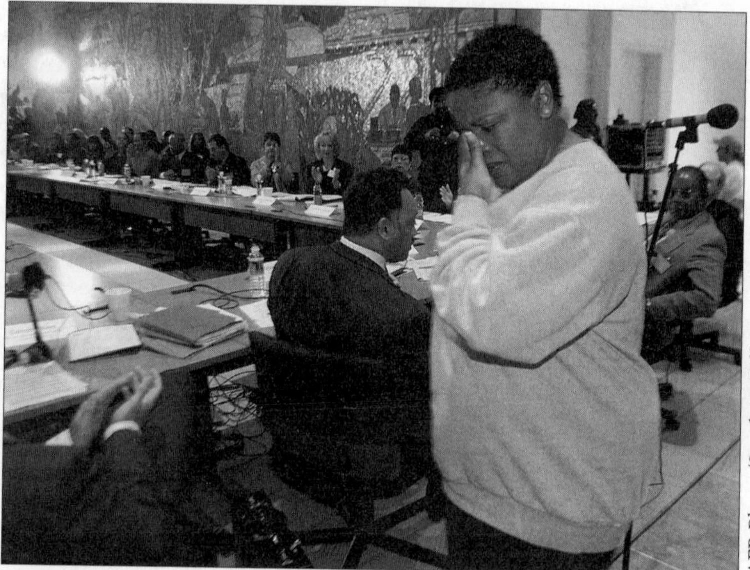

AFP Photo/Stephen Jaffe

Former Enron employee Gwen Gray cries after telling union officials in Washington about her job layoff and her husband's death. The failure of many corporate pension funds has complicated the debate over Social Security reform.

Are benefit cuts or payroll-tax increases better alternatives to privatization?

Reducing benefits or increasing payroll taxes are the only alternatives to partial privatization to resolve Social Security's funding shortfall.

Lawmakers cut benefits in 1983 by gradually raising the age at which retirees become eligible to receive full benefits. Under current law, only workers born before 1938 may begin receiving benefits at the traditional eligibility age of 65. Anticipating Americans' increasing longevity, Congress phased in a gradual increase in the eligibility age, which eventually will reach 67 for those born after 1959. Workers of all ages may continue to take early retirement at 62 with reduced benefits, based on the expectation that they will receive them for a longer time than if they began receiving them at their normal retirement age.

Federal Reserve Board Chairman Alan Greenspan has suggested that the retirement age continue to increase to reflect longer life expectancies. But many analysts say further benefit cuts would deal an unacceptable blow to the entitlement program's promise to keep retirees and the disabled out of poverty.

"Social Security is already a bare-bones system," says Weller, of the Center for American Progress, who calculates that each one-year increase in the normal retirement age amounts to an 8 percent benefit cut. "About a third of households enter retirement woefully inadequately prepared, often with just Social Security to live on, which was never the intention. Cutting back Social Security benefits from their already low level is a dangerous proposition."

Some reform proposals would cut benefits less directly by changing the way they are calculated. Currently, Social Security adjusts benefits based on two formulas: Initial benefits are adjusted to reflect average wage increases in the economy, based on a wage-indexation formula, and subsequent benefits are adjusted for infla-

* Progressivity means that poor workers get proportionally more benefits than wealthy ones.

tion using the cost-of-living index. But some reform plans would eliminate wage indexation and adjust benefits according to consumer price increases alone. "That would shrink the replacement ratio [the portion of pre-retirement earnings beneficiaries receive each month] of Social Security over time, from about 40 percent [of workers' earnings] right now to 20 percent or less within the next two or three decades," says Weller. "That's basically death by a thousand cuts, because every year relative benefits would be cut a little bit more. That's just a recipe for disaster."

Some analysts say changing the ways benefits are indexed is not only necessary but also fair. "You can call it a benefit cut, or you can call it a reduction in the growth of benefits," says Brown of the University of Illinois. "If you have future benefits grow with inflation rather than with real wage growth, future generations will continue to pay the current 12.4 percent payroll tax, but their benefits will grow with inflation and nothing more. Over 60 years, that would rebalance the system and do it in a very gradual way. People who are near retirement wouldn't be greatly affected, while people in their 20s and 30s today would have plenty of time to adjust. That would be a lot more feasible politically than cutting everybody's benefits today."

Others say increasing the payroll tax would make Social Security solvent over time. Today workers and employers split the cost of Social Security, with each paying 6.2 percent of workers' earnings, up to a maximum of $87,900 a year. Earnings above that cap are not subject to the payroll tax. Some analysts say raising the wage cap would be the fairest solution to the system's funding problems.

"Why should a secretary pay the Social Security tax on 100 percent of her income while her boss, who is more likely to be male, only pays tax on a portion of his?" asks Entmacher of the National Women's Law Center.

Some proposals, including the Kolbe-Stenholm bill, would increase tax payments by raising the earnings cap. "Most of the reform community is actually in favor of that to some extent," says Lemieux, including some privatizers who see an increase in the wage cap as a necessary means to cover the transition costs resulting from any shift to private accounts. "These transition costs amount to over a trillion dollars over the next 10 years, and we'd have to pay for that somehow."

Munnell, of the Center for Retirement Research, points out that benefits are already going to diminish, even without any additional changes to the system, thanks to the rising retirement age, an increase in Medicare premiums and the taxation of Social Security benefits. [12] Medicare Part B premiums, which are automatically deducted from Social Security benefits, are expected to rise from 6 percent of benefits for someone retiring today to 9 percent for those retiring in 2030. Because Social Security benefits are taxed at a fixed rate, and future benefits will rise with inflation, the number of beneficiaries whose benefits will be taxed will grow over time.

"It's quite reasonable to fix the current system and keep its existing structure, but you need more money or benefit cuts to do that," Munnell says. "My preference is more money, because I'm not sure we want wage-replacement rates to go down further than they're already scheduled to go."

She supports an increase in the taxable-wage base, which former Social Security Commissioner Robert M. Ball and a few other reformers have proposed. "This can easily be done without going to personal accounts." ■

BACKGROUND

Roots in Industrialization

Social Security began during the Depression, but the concept of a publicly funded safety net to protect citizens from poverty is rooted in long-standing theory and practice. In his pamphlet, "Agrarian Justice," written shortly after the Revolutionary War, American patriot Thomas Paine described a social program to ensure the economic well being of the young and the elderly. Paine proposed creating a fund, financed through an inheritance tax, to provide a single payment of 15 pounds sterling to citizens reaching age 21, to help them get started in life, and annual benefits of 10 pounds sterling to everyone 50 and older to prevent poverty in old age.

Paine's idea never made its way into public policy. Before the Industrial Revolution drew workers off the farms and into urban factories, in fact, people who could no longer work as a result of injury or old age relied on family for support and care. But the move to cities eroded that safety net, as extended families broke up into smaller, "nuclear" households composed of only parents and their children. Charities and a patchwork of state welfare programs were a poor substitute for family-based support. [13]

Only one segment of American society — war veterans — enjoyed government-provided income protection. The first solders' pension program started in 1776, before the signing of the Declaration of Independence. The Civil War Pension program, created in 1862, initially provided benefits to combat-disabled Union veterans and to widows and orphans of Union soldiers killed in action. Confederate veterans

Continued on p. 792

Chronology

1930s *Social Security is created to combat widespread poverty during the Great Depression.*

Aug. 14, 1935
President Franklin D. Roosevelt signs the Social Security Act, the nation's first major anti-poverty insurance program providing benefits to older Americans.

1939
Ida May Fuller of Ludlow, Vt., becomes the first retiree to receive a monthly Social Security check. Social Security is expanded to provide benefits to workers' survivors and the disabled.

1940s-1960s
A postwar population boom sets the stage for Social Security's future funding shortfall.

1946
The first year of the baby boom starts a demographic bulge that will last for the next 18 years.

1950
Cost-of-living adjustments are applied to Social Security to protect benefits from inflation. . . . There are 16 workers for every retiree in the United States, more than enough to cover Social Security benefits.

1954
Congress expands Social Security to include benefits for disabled older workers and disabled adult dependents.

1960
Disability insurance is extended to cover disabled workers of all ages and their dependents.

1961
All workers are permitted to receive reduced, early-retirement benefits at age 62.

July 30, 1965
Medicare, the most far-reaching change to the Social Security system, becomes law, providing health insurance to Americans ages 65 and older.

1970s-1980s
Concern mounts over Social Security's solvency, as demographers warn of the coming baby-boom bulge.

1972
Social Security's new Supplemental Security Income (SSI) program provides additional benefits to poor seniors and begins covering the blind and the disabled — groups previously served by the states and localities.

1977
As Social Security benefit expenditures rapidly mount due to expanded coverage, Congress raises payroll taxes and increases the wage base — the maximum earnings subject to Social Security taxes — to restore the trust funds' financial soundness.

1983
Congress authorizes taxation of Social Security benefits, brings federal employees into the system and calls for an increase in the normal retirement age from 65 to 67, beginning in the 21st century.

2000s *Privatization proposals gather momentum.*

2001
President Bush's Commission to Strengthen Social Security recommends ways to reform the program that would introduce personal investment accounts.

2008
The first baby boomers reach age 62, making them eligible to receive reduced, early-retirement Social Security benefits.

2019
Social Security begins paying more in benefits than it receives in payroll tax revenues, forcing it to draw down its trust funds in order to pay benefits, according to Congressional Budget Office (CBO) predictions.

2009
The normal retirement age — the age at which retirees may receive full Social Security benefits — rises to 66.

2012
The first baby boomers turn 66, enabling them to receive full Social Security benefits.

2027
The normal retirement age rises to 67.

2040
With most boomers well into retirement, there are just two workers for each Social Security recipient, too few to pay scheduled benefits at current tax rates.

2052
The Social Security trust funds will run out of money, the CBO predicts.

Benefits Crucial to Older Women

Almost two-thirds of U.S. retirees now rely on Social Security for most of their income, largely due to the decline of traditional pensions in recent decades.

Social Security is especially vital for elderly women, but it does less to meet women's retirement needs than it does for men. Because of their longevity and work patterns, "women rely much more heavily on Social Security than men do for their economic security in old age," says Joan Entmacher, vice president for economic security at the National Women's Law Center.

The average American woman who reaches age 65 will live for another 20 years, four years longer than her male counterpart. But after her spouse dies, a widow receives only half her husbands' benefits, leaving her with reduced income to cover the higher medical costs that typically come with old age. Single women often fare even worse, having only their own benefits to live on in retirement.

Women also have fewer alternative sources of income during retirement than men, so they're more dependent on Social Security. They tend to accumulate less in savings and pension credits than men during their working years, mainly because they are more likely to work part time or take time off to raise children. [1]

Indeed, women typically work for 32 years, compared with 44 years for men. Part-time employment generally pays less than full-time work, and rarely provides pension coverage. Full-time female workers still make 75 cents for every dollar earned by men, a wage gap that makes it harder for women to save money for retirement. Because traditional pension benefits usually are calculated on the basis of years worked and earnings, even women with full pension coverage tend to receive lower benefits during retirement than their male counterparts.

Advocates of Social Security privatization say allowing women to save part of their payroll taxes in managed retirement investment accounts would help them prepare for a more comfortable old age.

But many women's-rights activists say privatization would further erode women's retirement security. For one thing, the current system favors lower-income recipients, a group that includes a disproportionate share of women. "Social Security has a progressive benefit formula, so that lower earners get a higher percentage of their pre-retirement earnings as benefits," says Alicia Munnell, director of the Center for Retirement Research at Boston College. "So to the extent that we move away from that benefit formula and into individual accounts, women would be hurt."

Another advantage of Social Security as it's currently designed is the automatic cost-of-living increase, which protects benefits from inflation. Virtually no private investment scheme or annuity offers such protection. "Because women live much longer than men, Social Security's inflation-indexed annuities are particularly valuable for women," Munnell says. "Again, to the extent that you move away from that, women will be hurt."

[1] See Alicia H. Munnell, "Why Are So Many Older Women Poor? Just the Facts on Retirement Issues," Center for Retirement Research at Boston College, April 2004.

Continued from p. 790

and their dependents received no benefits. The program was expanded in 1906 to include all surviving Union veterans and their widows. The last Civil War Pension recipient, a woman who married an elderly veteran while in her teens, died earlier this year. [14]

Working Americans became eligible for old-age benefits with the advent of company pensions, first introduced in 1882 by the Alfred Dolge Co., a piano and organ manufacturer. But private pensions were slow to gain acceptance. In 1900, only five companies in the United States offered pensions to workers.

Meanwhile, the steady move to cities, the breakdown of the extended family, increasing reliance on wage income for survival, together with an increase in life expectancy, were undermining the living standards of older Americans. By 1920, more people were living in cities than on farms. The vast majority of aging workers were simply fired when they were no longer able to perform up to standard. With no one to care for them and no income, millions of former workers faced the prospect of dying in poverty. Because of improvements in sanitation and health care, life expectancy increased by 10 years between 1900 and 1930, the fastest increase in recorded history. By 1935, the number of elderly Americans had reached nearly 8 million at a time when the traditional sources of care for this population were fast disappearing.

The plight of America's growing elderly population deteriorated even more rapidly after Oct. 24, 1929, when the stock market crashed, setting off the Great Depression. More than a quarter of working Americans lost their jobs, about 10,000 banks failed, and the gross national product — the value of economic output — plummeted from $150 billion before the crash to just $55 billion in 1932.

With few federal resources available to fight poverty, President Herbert Hoover (1929-33) called on Americans to volunteer their services and charitable contributions to alleviate the plight of the unemployed and the elderly. But with so much of the population facing financial hardship, Hoover's call went largely unanswered, leaving it up to the states to support the poor and elderly. By the 1930s, most states had established limited workers' compensation programs and state old-age "pensions" for older Americans who met financial-need standards. But these programs were of little value; none offered more than $1 a day to qualified beneficiaries.

As Congress began considering proposals for a new nationwide old-age safety net, conservative lawmakers favored adopting the state model, arguing that its need-based structure would limit the scope of the program and make it easy to end it once the economy recovered. But as the Depression persisted, calls for a different approach to social welfare — one that would reflect the permanent societal changes wrought by industrialization — began to take hold.

Average Low-Wage Worker Receives $701 Monthly

A typical low-wage worker who retired at age 65 in 2003 received $701 a month from Social Security, compared to $1,721 received by the average high-wage earner. Workers can maximize their monthly income by working until age 70 before claiming benefits.

Typical Social Security Benefits, 2003

Earnings	Age 62	Age 65	Age 70
Low	$572	$701	$833
Average	943	1,158	1,387
High	1,236	1,513	1,786
Maximum	1,404	1,721	2,045

Source: "Fast Facts & Figures About Social Security, 2003," Social Security Administration

Social Security Act

President Franklin D. Roosevelt (1933-45) took office promising to shift the model for federal economic security policy from the state-based welfare assistance programs to new federal programs similar to "social insurance" plans then prevalent in Europe. First adopted in 1889 in Chancellor Otto von Bismarck's Germany, social insurance plans worked like commercial insurance plans, collecting premiums, or taxes, from a large pool of individuals (in this case working-age citizens) to pay benefits to those who meet eligibility conditions, such as disability and old age.

On June 8, 1934, Roosevelt announced his support for a similar approach in the United States. "Security was attained in the earlier days through the interdependence of members of families upon each other and of the families within a small community upon each other," he said in an address to Congress. "The complexities of great communities and of organized industry make less real these simple means of security. Therefore, we are compelled to employ the active interest of the nation as a whole through government in order to encourage a greater security for each individual who composes it."

Roosevelt sought to placate critics of such an expanded role for the federal government by adding: "This seeking for a greater measure of welfare and happiness does not indicate a change in values. It is rather a return to values lost in the course of our economic development and expansion."

On Aug. 14, 1935, Roosevelt signed into law the Social Security Act, which codified various recommendations of the presidential Committee on Economic Security. The new law created a social insurance program to pay retired workers age 65 or older a steady income for the rest of their lives.

"We can never insure 100 percent of the population against 100 percent of the hazards and vicissitudes of life," Roosevelt said. "But we have tried to frame a law which will give some measure of protection to the average citizen and to his family against the loss of a job and against poverty-ridden old age."

Though the law fell short of some supporters' goals, it provided the basic structure for today's Social Security program. Initially it paid benefits only to covered workers when they retired at 65. And, unlike the state old-age pension plans, it was funded through a contributory system, in which future beneficiaries contribute to their own retirement through payroll deductions made during their working lives. The law established a Social Security Board, made up of three presidential appointees, to administer the new program, but the Social Security Administration (SSA) replaced it in 1946, later incorporated into the Department of Health and Human Services.

Within two years all employers were registered, workers were assigned Social Security numbers and field offices were built. On Jan. 1, 1937, workers began acquiring credits toward their old-age benefits, and they and their employers began paying payroll taxes, known as FICA taxes (after the Federal Insurance Contributions Act, which authorized their collection). FICA taxes were placed in dedicated Social Security trust funds, to be used for paying benefits.

For the first three years Social Security paid each beneficiary a small, single, lump-sum payment because

America's Changing Population

Most Americans were under age 50 at the end of the 19th century. But by 2080, because of the coming retirement of the baby boomers, longer life expectancies and the popularity of smaller families, there will be relatively fewer young people and more Americans over 50 — creating a demographic bulge resembling a "python swallowing a telephone pole," according to some demographers.

Makeup of U.S. Population, by Age and Gender

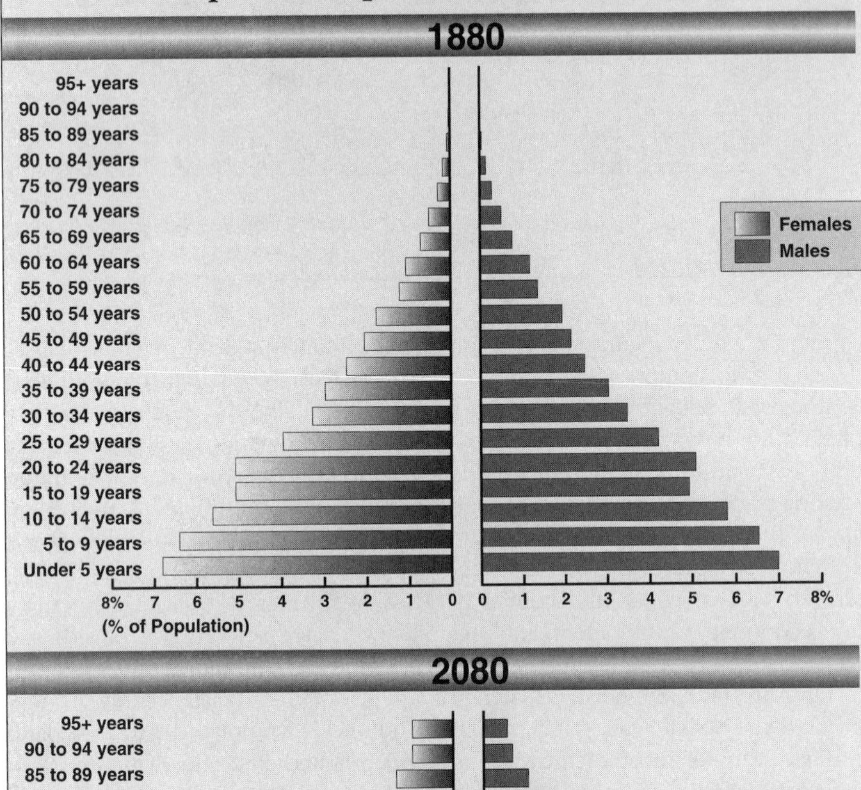

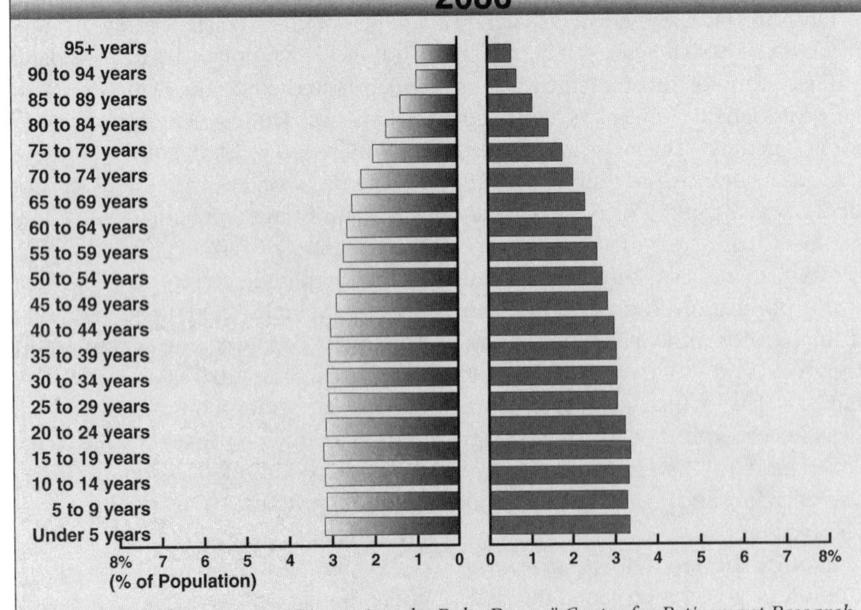

Source: "Population Aging: It's not just the Baby Boom," Center for Retirement Research

early recipients had not paid enough into the system to be vested for monthly benefits. By 1940, the trust funds had collected enough revenues to begin paying monthly payments.

In 1939 Congress expanded Social Security to cover workers' spouses, children under 18 and aged parents and provided survivors' benefits in the event of a worker's premature death. Lawmakers thus transformed the program from a retirement system for workers into a broader family income-security system.

The first retiree to receive a monthly Social Security check was Ida May Fuller of Ludlow, Vt., who retired in 1939 at age 65. Because of Social Security's pay-as-you-go financing arrangement, the retired legal secretary got a great return on her contribution. After contributing just $24.75 into the system over three years, she collected $22,888.92 in Social Security benefits before she died in 1975 at 100.

Later Amendments

By 1950, inflation had eaten away at the value of Social Security benefits, so Congress incorporated cost-of-living allowances (COLAs) that provided retroactive adjustments for beneficiaries in 1950 and 1952. A 1972 amendment made the COLA provision permanent.

Then, in 1954 Congress expanded the program to include disability insurance, initially limited to disabled older workers and disabled adult dependents. In September 1960, President Dwight D. Eisenhower (1953-61) signed into law an amendment extending coverage to all disabled workers and their dependents.

In 1956, Congress reduced from 65 to 62 the age at which women could choose to begin receiving their old-age benefits. Women who took the earlier benefits would receive smaller monthly checks, based on the actuarial notion that they would receive benefits for a longer period of time than if they waited until age 65. The same early-retirement option was extended to men in 1961.

In the 1960s, building on Roosevelt's vision of a strong governmental role in protecting Americans from poverty, President Lyndon B. Johnson launched a series of federal programs — known as the Great Society — including measures that strengthened the safety net provided by Social Security.

Johnson's primary proposal was Medicare — the federal program that provides health insurance to nearly all Americans age 65 and older. Signed into law on July 30, 1965, Medicare would become the most far-reaching change to the Social Security system. Within the next three years, nearly 20 million Americans enrolled in Medicare.

By the end of the 1960s there were calls to bring the old state and local welfare programs into the federal Social Security system to reduce waste and redundancy. In 1969, President Richard M. Nixon (1969-74) called on Congress to "bring reason, order and purpose into a tangle of overlapping programs."

The 1972 Social Security Amendments brought three "adult categories" — needy aged, blind and disabled — previously served by the states and localities with partial federal funding — under a single new Social Security program called Supplemental Security Income (SSI). More than 3 million people were shifted from the state welfare rolls to SSI.

The 1972 amendments also increased Social Security benefits for elderly widows and widowers, extended Medicare to individuals receiving disability benefits and those with chronic renal disease and increased Social Security benefits for workers who delay retirement past age 65.

Concerns about Social Security's soundness began to surface in the late 1970s. An economy beset by "stagflation" — inflation and minimal economic growth — and the demographic time bomb posed by the baby boom fueled predictions that the trust funds would soon be exhausted. To address the coming shortfall, Congress passed the 1977 Social Security Amendments, which increased the payroll tax, increased the maximum earnings subject to Social Security taxes and adjusted the way COLAs and the wage base are calculated. These changes restored the trust funds' long-term financial soundness for the next 50 years.

But within only a few years Social Security faced a serious short-term funding crisis due to the rapid growth in benefit expenditures. The crisis prompted President Ronald Reagan (1981-89) to appoint a panel headed by Greenspan (who began his tenure as Federal Reserve chairman in 1987) to recommend changes to the system. The 1983 amendments, based on those recommendations, authorized taxation of Social Security benefits, brought federal employees into the system and called for the gradual increase in the normal retirement age from 65 to 66 in 2009 and 67 in 2027.

Courtesy Social Security Administration

President Franklin D. Roosevelt signs the Social Security Act on Aug. 14, 1935. "We have tried to . . . give some measure of protection to the average citizen and to his family against the loss of a job and against poverty-ridden old age," he said.

Reagan oversaw the beginnings of a shift in philosophy toward the social safety net that had protected Americans from poverty since the Great Depression. He repeatedly called for tightening eligibility standards for welfare programs, decrying "welfare queens" he said were working the system to gain a free ride at the expense of honest, hardworking Americans. In 1995 Republicans took control of Congress, and began passing laws reflecting this philosophical shift.

The 1996 Contract with America Advancement Act, signed by Democratic President Bill Clinton on March 29, for the first time disqualified applicants for disability benefits under Social Security or SSI if drug or alcohol addiction contributed to their disabilities. The Personal Responsibility and Work Opportunity Act, signed five months later, ended the unlimited welfare entitlements provided under the Aid to Families with Dependent Children program that had been established by the 1935 Social Security Act.

The 1996 law limited the amount of time beneficiaries could receive welfare benefits and required recipients to work; it also ended SSI eligibility for most legal non-citizen aliens and tightened up eligibility standards for disabled children. After public outcry, Congress later relaxed some of the new restrictions on non-citizens and children.

Clinton signed two other bills aimed at encouraging Social Security beneficiaries to work. The 1999 Ticket to Work and Work Incentives Improvement Act established a new program providing vocational rehabilitation and employment services to help disability beneficiaries find productive work. The 2000 Senior Citizens' Freedom to Work Act allowed workers to receive benefits even if they continued to work past the normal retirement age. ■

AFP Photo/Stan Honda

Privatization supporters say stocks typically return higher dividends than the government's conservative bond investments. But critics say the stock market's recent plunge and numerous corporate and stock market scandals make personal investment accounts too risky for average workers.

CURRENT SITUATION

Privatization

When he made his acceptance speech at the Republican National Convention on Sept. 2, President Bush said, "We'll always keep the promise of Social Security for our older workers. With the huge baby-boom generation approaching retirement, many of our children and grandchildren understandably worry whether Social Security will be there when they need it. We must strengthen Social Security by allowing younger workers to save some of their taxes in a personal account, a nest egg you can call your own and government can never take away."

President Bush's support for shifting part of the Social Security tax revenues into personal accounts marks another philosophical departure from the social-insurance concept championed by Roosevelt. Like many of his supporters, Bush has often called for reducing the size of the federal government. As the main entitlement programs in the federal budget, Social Security and Medicare are prime targets for this effort.

Bush announced during his January 2001 inaugural address that he intended to reform Social Security and Medicare. That May he appointed the President's Commission to Strengthen Social Security and directed it to recommend ways to reform the program that would ensure three major goals: preserve the benefits of current retirees and those nearing retirement; return Social Security to sound financial footing; and enable younger workers to invest part of their payroll taxes in individual savings accounts outside of the Social Security system.

Supporters of the current system immediately denounced the commission as a rubber stamp for privatization. "The president, his staff and his allies are already committed to privatization," declared the liberal Campaign for America's Future after the commission was created. "Calling their process of arranging the details a 'commission' is an attempt to mislead the public about its process and purpose. In reality, it will amount to no more than a collection of individuals who support privatization." [15]

Treasury Secretary Paul H. O'Neill responded by defining Social Security as "a revolutionary idea for its time" that was fast running out of money. "This is all about happy times and doing the right thing while our generation is able to act," he said. [16]

The commission's final report, issued in December 2001, recommended several measures to meet Bush's goals. It offered three different models to ensure that Social Security would remain afloat over the long term. Model 2 of the report, widely viewed as the likely basis for the Bush administration's reform proposal, if it wins a second term, would eliminate wage indexation and rely entirely on consumer prices to adjust future benefits. Apart from changing the benefits formula, Model 2 would retain the current system for all who prefer it while allowing workers who wish to set up a private investment account with part of their payroll-tax contribution to do so.

Several reform plans have been introduced in recent months — including the Kolbe-Stenholm bill and one authored by Sen. Lindsey Graham, R-S.C. — both of which would provide for moderately sized, progressive per-

Continued on p. 798

At Issue:

Is privatization the best way to save Social Security?

yes

PETER J. FERRARA
SENIOR FELLOW, INSTITUTE FOR POLICY INNOVATION

FROM TESTIMONY BEFORE THE SENATE SPECIAL COMMITTEE ON AGING, JUNE 15, 2004

I'm here to discuss . . . providing a progressive option for personal retirement accounts as a choice as compared to Social Security. The option . . . is designed to be progressive, which means lower-income workers can contribute a higher percentage of their taxes to the account than higher-income workers.

The option provides [for] . . . an average of 6.4 percent of the 12.4 percent [payroll-tax contribution] to go into personal accounts, a much larger account than has been proposed before. . . . The proposal makes no change in disability and survivors' benefits, and there is no change in Social Security benefits otherwise for anybody at any point — now or in the future. Because the advantages of a large personal account are so great, no other changes are necessary. . . . It preserves within the personal account the progressivity of Social Security so workers across the board would gain roughly the same percentage. . . .

There are five ways this proposal enhances progressivity for low- and moderate-income workers. First of all, it sharply increases future retirement benefits. . . . Large accounts do that much more than any other alternative because they're able to take more advantage of the better return in the private sector, so they provide very sharp increases. . . . [Workers who] invest over a lifetime, half-and-half in stocks and bonds at standard, market-investment returns, I calculate would gain a benefit increase of two-thirds compared to currently promised Social Security benefits. . . .

For most workers today, the real rate of return promised by Social Security — let alone what it could pay — is 1 to 1.5 percent. The long-term, real rate of return on corporate bonds is 3 to 3.5 percent. On stocks, I think the record will bear out 7 to 7.5 percent, so [there will be] much higher returns. And you see what we've done here is a vast improvement both on the basis of adequacy and of equity, because the returns are much higher, the future benefits are higher.

Also, under the reform plan low- and moderate-income workers would gain much greater accumulations of personal wealth than under Social Security. The chief actuary of Social Security has already officially scored this plan. He estimates that by 15 years after the reform plan is adopted working people would have gained $7 trillion in today's dollars in their own personal accounts. [T]his is the greatest advantage and breakthrough for working people that we could possibly adopt today.

no

CHRISTIAN WELLER
SENIOR ECONOMIST, CENTER FOR AMERICAN PROGRESS

FROM TESTIMONY BEFORE THE SENATE SPECIAL COMMITTEE ON AGING, JUNE 15, 2004

Privatization as an alternative to fixing Social Security within the parameters of the system is too risky and too costly, especially for low-income families. Usually 80 percent of pre-retirement income is considered adequate for a decent standard of living. A substantial minority of households, typically one-third, falls short of this standard. The shortfalls are especially large for minorities, single women, workers with less education and low-wage workers. To make ends meet in retirement, these households will have to curtail their consumption, often severely, and rely on public assistance in retirement.

Retirement income adequacy also has worsened for the typical household over the past few years. Underlying this trend are three factors. First, pension coverage has remained low and declined in recent years. Second, retirement wealth has become increasingly unequally distributed. And, third, with the proliferation of defined-contribution plans, such as 401(k) plans, risks have shifted onto workers.

Against this backdrop, Social Security gains in relative importance. Its coverage is almost universal, [and] its benefits favor lifetime earners and [have] guaranteed, lifetime, inflation-adjusted benefits. Part of Social Security's importance results . . . from its other benefits, in particular disability and survivorship benefits. These benefits are often also at stake when Social Security benefits are reduced to pay for privatization. But we've got to keep in mind that Social Security benefits are bare bones. The average replacement ratio [the percentage of one's pre-retirement earnings provided by Social Security] in the United States is about half of that in Germany or Italy, and the average monthly benefit [for Social Security] was about $850 in 2002.

Social Security benefits were 80 percent of retirement income for households in the bottom 40 percent of the income distribution in 2000, meaning that the private sector is still not doing its job to help low-income workers. Yet Social Security trustees predict a financial shortfall in the long run. It is anticipated that by 2042 Social Security will have exhausted its trust funds and that tax revenue will cover only two-thirds of promised benefits. An immediate and permanent increase of the payroll tax by 1.9 percent would allow Social Security to cover all of that shortfall. . . .

With privatization, insurance is replaced with savings accounts. That is, the risks are privatized. These risks include the risk of misjudging the market and investing in losing assets. Another risk is the possibility of financial markets staying low for long periods of time. Moreover, workers face the risk that they will exhaust their savings during their retirement.

Continued from p. 796

sonal accounts. In July, Rep. Paul Ryan, R-Wis., introduced a bill that incorporates Ferrara's more-radical privatization plan. "We're going to try to translate that into a very broad co-sponsorship on the Hill," George Mason University's Ferrara says, "ultimately with the goal of presenting it to the administration and making the case to them that this is, in fact, what they should adopt."

But with much of Congress facing re-election and concerns about the wars against Iraq and terrorism, proposals to overhaul Social Security have yet to receive extensive congressional consideration. Other than being introduced, says Lemieux of the Centrist Policy Network, "there hasn't been a lot of legislative activity on Social Security."

Eroding Pensions

Recent trends in private pension coverage add additional uncertainties to the debate over Social Security reform. Many traditional pension funds have been failing, threatening a major source of retirement income for American workers. Most recently, in a move that may be emulated by other troubled companies, United Airlines is considering scrapping its defined-benefit pension plan, which covers 120,000 workers, as part of a bankruptcy proceeding. The federal Pension Benefit Guaranty Corp. (PBGC), which protects pension benefits from corporate bankruptcies, would assume the airline's $8.3 billion pension obligations, but the move likely would mean reduced benefits for United workers. If other companies follow United's lead, the PBGC could be unable to cover benefits, requiring a taxpayer bailout reminiscent of the savings and loan crisis of the 1980s. [17]

That prospect — or the possibility that many retirees may stop receiving their pension checks altogether — gained further credence with a new study that concludes the agency will go broke by 2023 if pension funds continue to fail at the pace of recent years. [18]

Meanwhile, a study by Munnell, of the Center for Retirement Research, documents the inability of 401(k)s and other defined-contribution plans to fill the gap created as private companies scale back or abandon their traditional pension programs. Despite the popularity of 401(k)s, she found that less than half of American workers are covered by an employer-provided pension plan, a figure that hasn't changed since 1979. And only one in four workers whose employers do offer 401(k)s chooses to participate in the plan, and fewer than one in 10 contribute the maximum allowable portion of their income. In addition, many employers offering 401(k)s have responded to hard economic times by cutting their matching contributions to the plans. [19]

These findings constitute a strong case against relying on private markets to solve Social Security's funding problems, Munnell says.

"We were stunned to find out what a poor mechanism 401(k) plans are, as currently structured, to provide retirement income," she says. Like 401(k)s, private investment accounts within Social Security require workers to be involved in the management of their retirement incomes, she notes. "These financial decisions are hard for people to make. They're not trained to do it, they don't have the time to do it, and to shift an even greater burden to the individual doesn't make any sense."

Ferrara says his plan addresses those concerns. "We designed the investment structure of the fund to make it easy for unsophisticated investors," he says. "There would be a list of private, managed investment funds approved and regulated by the government expressly for this purpose, and the investor only needs to pick one of those funds. Then the managers of those funds make all the sophisticated investment decisions for the investor."

Budget Concerns

When President Bush announced the formation of his Commission to Strengthen Social Security in May 2001, he said federal budget surpluses were enough to cover any costs incurred by the transition to a partially privatized system. "Our government will run large budget surpluses over the next 10 years," Bush said. "These surpluses provide an opportunity to move to a stronger Social Security system." [20]

That was before the terrorist attacks of Sept. 11, 2001. Since then, administration-supported tax cuts coupled with spending for counterterrorism initiatives and the war against Iraq have obliterated the budget surplus. This year, the deficit is expected to reach a record high of $445 billion, up from $375 billion in fiscal 2003.

Bush's initiative to add a drug benefit to Medicare, signed into law Dec. 8, 2003, will place an additional drain on the federal budget. The Medicare Prescription Drug, Improvement and Modernization Act, which would expand the federal health insurance program for some 41 million elderly and disabled Americans by offering partial coverage of prescription drug costs, is now expected to cost $534 billion over the next 10 years, $134 billion more than the administration had originally claimed. [21]

"Congress is still in shock and denial about the deteriorating budget," says Lemieux of the Centrist Policy Network. "They're still doing things the way they did a couple of years ago, when they thought they had a budget surplus and could pass tax cuts without paying for them and keep spending growing fast."

In light of the budget deficit, some analysts say moderate privatization plans offer a promising solution to Social Security's funding shortfall. "We have Medicare and Medicaid growing much faster than the gross domestic product, and we're looking at a very uncertain future in terms of how much money we're going to be spending on homeland security, defense and other programs," says University of Illinois Social Security expert Brown. He supports the commission's Model 2 plan for partial privatization of Social Security. "We have to put some serious constraints on how quickly Social Security can grow."

An essential and fair cost-saving element of the plan, Brown says, is its elimination of wage indexation in calculating initial benefits. "I don't see why the program has to grow faster than inflation," he says. "Why should my children get Social Security benefits that, after adjusting for inflation, are 30 percent higher than mine, even if we're [making the same amount of money today?]"

But other experts say the case for privatization evaporated with the federal budget surplus. "When some of the privatization proposals were developed we had a surplus, and they said we could take some of the surplus and use it to create private accounts," says Entmacher, of the National Women's Law Center. "Well, hello, not only is there no surplus anymore, but we're running gigantic deficits as far as the eye can see, and privatization actually makes it worse." ■

OUTLOOK

Campaign Debate

As the November presidential election nears, both major candidates are declaring their support for Social Security but skirting the details of plans to ensure the program survives the baby boomers' retirement.

Bush continues to push for partial privatization through private investment accounts, and he has not ruled out raising the retirement age. "It's very important in the Social Security system to say to boomers like me, nothing's going to change," Bush said at a campaign rally in Wheeling, W.Va. "We're in good shape. But if you're a younger worker, you better listen very carefully to the presidential debates on Social Security. The fiscal solvency of Social Security is in doubt for the young workers coming up. Therefore, I think young workers ought to be able to own a personal retirement account, a personal savings account, in order for Social Security to work."

Candidate Kerry opposes privatization, raising the retirement age or cutting payments. "As president, I will not privatize Social Security," Kerry said in accepting his party's nomination in July. "I will not cut benefits. And together, we will make sure that senior citizens never have to cut their pills in half because they can't afford life-saving medicine."

The Democratic Party platform pledges to support "reform" but to fight privatization of either Social Security or Medicare. But it has provided no details about how to strengthen either program beyond fiscal discipline for Social Security and expanded prescription-drug coverage for Medicare. [22]

"I don't see anything that either the Republicans or the Democrats are advocating right now that would really responsibly deal with the long-term problems either with Social Security or Medicare," says Kotlikoff of Boston University. "The privatization proposal that the president is likely to propose if he's re-elected could well make things worse because it could cut taxes by more than it cuts benefits."

Meanwhile, Federal Reserve Chairman Greenspan is trying to heat up the debate by warning policymakers that reforms are urgently needed. "We owe it to our retirees to promise only the benefits that can be delivered," he said, suggesting that even the boomers — not just their children — may be in for an ugly surprise if changes are postponed much longer. "If we have promised more than our economy has the ability to deliver . . . as I fear we may have, we must recalibrate our public programs so that pending retirees have time to adjust through other channels. . . . If we delay, the adjustments could be abrupt and painful." [23]

Most analysts hope that the candidates will heed that warning and inform voters of their plans to resolve Social Security's fiscal problems as the campaign progresses. "Even if they don't provide highly detailed proposals, both candidates need to flesh out how they would reform the program," says MacGuineas of the Committee for a Responsible Budget. "If someone wants to lead this country, we need to know how they would fix the federal government's largest program. That's something the voters should have insight on." ■

About the Author

Mary H. Cooper specializes in defense, energy and environmental issues. Before joining *The CQ Researcher* as a staff writer in 1983, she was Washington correspondent for the Rome daily newspaper *l'Unitá*. She is the author of *The Business of Drugs* (CQ Press, 1990) and holds a B.A. in English from Hollins College in Virginia. Her recent reports include "Smart Growth," "Exporting Jobs," "Weapons of Mass Destruction" and "Bush and the Environment."

Notes

[1] Congressional Budget Office, "The Outlook for Social Security," June 2004.
[2] For background, see Adriel Bettelheim, "Saving Social Security," *The CQ Researcher*, Oct. 2, 1998, pp. 857-880.
[3] See David Cay Johnston, "The Social Security Promise Not Yet Kept," *The New York Times*, Feb. 29, 2004.
[4] From an interview with Mara Liasson, "Morning Edition," National Public Radio, May 25, 2001.
[5] For background, see Kenneth Jost, "Corporate Crime," *The CQ Researcher*, Oct. 11, 2002, pp. 817-840, and David Masci, "Stock Market Troubles," *The CQ Researcher*, Jan. 16, 2004, pp. 25-48.
[6] For background, see Mary H. Cooper, "Retirement Security," *The CQ Researcher*, May 31, 2002, pp. 481-504.
[7] Laurence J. Kotlikoff and Scott Burns, *The Coming Generational Storm* (2004).
[8] For background, see Adriel Bettelheim, "Medicare Reform," *The CQ Researcher*, Aug. 22, 2003, pp. 673-696; and Rebecca Adams, "Medicaid Reform," *The CQ Researcher*, July 16, 2004, pp. 589-612.
[9] For more information on these estimates, see Thomas J. Healey, "Social Security's Surprising Turn," *The Washington Post*, June 25, 2004.
[10] Congressional Budget Office, "Administrative Costs of Private Accounts in Social Security," March 2004.
[11] See Cooper, *op. cit.*
[12] See Alicia H. Munnell, "Just the Facts: The Declining Role of Social Security," Center for Retirement Research, February 2003.
[13] Unless otherwise noted, information in this section is drawn from Social Security Online, "Brief History," March 2003.
[14] Melissa Nelson, "Woman Recognized as Confederate Widow," The Associated Press, June 15, 2004.
[15] Campaign for America's Future, press advisory, May 2, 2001.
[16] Quoted in Glenn Kessler, "O'Neill Faults 'No Assets' Social Security," *The Washington Post*, June 19, 2001, p. E1.

FOR MORE INFORMATION

Cato Institute, 1000 Massachusetts Ave., N.W., Washington, DC 20001; (202) 842-0200; www.cato.org. This libertarian think tank supports the introduction of private investment accounts to Social Security.

Center for American Progress, 805 15th St., N.W., Washington, DC 20005; (202) 682-1611; www.americanprogress.org. A liberal think tank that supports the current structure of Social Security and opposes efforts to privatize them.

Center for Retirement Research, Boston College, Fulton Hall 550, 140 Commonwealth Ave., Chestnut Hill, MA 02467; (617) 552-1762; www.bc.edu/centers.crr. Directed by Alicia Munnell, a former research director at the Federal Reserve Bank of Boston, the center studies issues related to Social Security and other sources of retirement income.

Centrist Policy Network Inc., 236 Massachusetts Ave., N.E., Suite 205, Washington, DC 20002; (202) 546-4090; www.centrists.org. A nonpartisan group that analyzes most of the major proposals to reform Social Security.

Committee for a Responsible Federal Budget, 163 Connecticut Ave., N.W., 7th floor, Washington, DC 20009; (202) 986-6599; www.crfb.org. This nonprofit group analyzes all aspects of the federal budget and supports policies, including Social Security reform proposals, that strive to avoid deficit spending.

Institute for Policy Innovation, 1660 S. Stemmons Freeway, Suite 475, Lewisville, TX 75067; (972) 874-5139; www.ipi.org. A conservative group that supports Social Security privatization and other initiatives to reduce the size of the federal government.

National Women's Law Center, 11 Dupont Circle, N.W., Suite 80, Washington, DC 20036; (202) 588-5180; www.nwlc.org. A nonprofit group that analyzes the impact of public policy, including Social Security, on women and criticizes privatization efforts that would erode benefits to elderly women.

Social Security Administration, 6401 Security Blvd., Baltimore, MD 21235; (410) 965-3120; www.ssa.gov. The federal agency that administers Social Security and Medicare.

[17] See Mary Williams Walsh, "Bailout Feared if Airlines Shed Their Pensions," *The New York Times*, Aug. 1, 2004, p. A1.
[18] Douglas J. Elliott, "PBGC: When Will the Cash Run Out?" Center on Federal Financial Institutions, Sept. 13, 2004.
[19] Alicia H. Munnell and Anika Sundén, *Coming Up Short: The Challenge of 401(k) Plans* (2004).
[20] From remarks in the Rose Garden, May 2, 2001.
[21] See Walter Shapiro, "Politicians Fool Only Themselves with Medicare Bribe," *USA Today*, Aug. 13, 2004. For background, see Bettelheim, "Medicare Reform," *op. cit.*
[22] See Dan Balz, "Democratic Platform Assails Administration," *The Washington Post*, July 4, 2004, p. A4.
[23] Quoted in Martin Crutsinger, "Social Security Crisis Warned," The Associated Press, Aug. 28, 2004.

Bibliography

Selected Sources

Books

Katz, Michael B., *In the Shadow of the Poorhouse: A Social History of Welfare in America*, Basic Books, 1996.
A professor of history from the University of Pennsylvania traces the development of social policy in the United States, including Social Security.

Kotlikoff, Laurence J., and Scott Burns, *The Coming Generational Storm: What You Need to Know about America's Economic Future*, MIT Press, 2004.
A Boston University economist (Kotlikoff) and a finance columnist (Burns) suggest how Social Security and Medicare can survive the onslaught of 77 million retiring baby boomers and how individuals can protect their private savings.

Articles

Kirchoff, Sue, "Greenspan Urges Cuts to Benefits for Retirees," *USA Today*, Aug. 30, 2004.
Federal Reserve Chairman Alan Greenspan renews his controversial call to reduce Social Security benefits, even for baby boomers nearing retirement, to save the system from collapse.

Krugman, Paul, "Maestro of Chutzpah," *The New York Times*, March 2, 2004.
The liberal columnist argues that in the face of deepening federal budget deficits, Federal Reserve Chairman Greenspan should drop his call to cut Social Security benefits and instead push for a repeal or roll-back of the Bush-supported tax cuts that he says primarily benefit wealthy Americans.

McNeil, Donald G., Jr., "Demographic 'Bomb' May Only Go 'Pop!' " *The New York Times*, Aug. 29, 2004, "Week in Review," p. 1.
Falling birth rates are lessening the threat of global overpopulation and fueling concern over the negative impact of aging populations, especially in industrialized countries.

Porter, Eduardo, "Coming Soon: The Vanishing Work Force," *The New York Times*, Aug. 29, 2004, Section 3, p. 1.
The coming retirement of millions of baby boomers will create shortages of skilled workers in many fields and may force many boomers to postpone retirement.

Tanner, Michael, "Cato's Plan for Reforming Social Security," *Cato Policy Report*, May/June 2004, p. 3.
The libertarian think tank's solution for Social Security's shortfall is a combination of personal investment accounts and reduced benefits.

Reports and Studies

Congressional Budget Office, "The Outlook for Social Security," June 2004.
The CBO predicts Social Security's financial shortfall is not as imminent as earlier estimates indicated: Payments will start exceeding revenues in 2019, but the trust funds will not run out of money to pay benefits until 2052.

__, "Social Security: A Primer," September 2001.
This exhaustive analysis provides historical background, a description of Social Security's organization and programs and options for its future.

Favreault, Melissa M., and Frank J. Sammartino, "The Impact of Social Security Reform on Low-Income and Older Women," Urban Institute, July 2002.
Social Security benefits affect women of different ages, marital status and income levels in different ways. The authors point out the impact of several reform options on older women.

Ferrara, Peter, "A Progressive Proposal for Social Security Private Accounts," *IPI Reports*, Institute for Policy Innovation, June 13, 2003.
The most far-reaching and controversial of the major privatization plans would allow workers to divert a large portion of their payroll-tax contributions to private accounts.

Munnell, Alicia H., "Population and Aging: It's Not Just the Baby Boom," *Issue Brief*, Center for Retirement Research, April 2004.
The director of the Boston College-based center warns that the baby boomers' retirements will radically change U.S. society. Low birth rates since the mid-1960s and steady increases in longevity ensure that the United States will remain an aging society for the foreseeable future.

President's Commission to Strengthen Social Security, "Strengthening Social Security and Creating Personal Wealth for All Americans," December 2001.
The panel appointed by President Bush to devise ways to incorporate personal investment accounts into Social Security offers three main alternatives, one of which is expected to provide the model for a legislative proposal in 2005 if Bush wins re-election.

Social Security Administration, "The Future of Social Security," January 2004.
The report outlines current funding problems facing the program and proposals to allow workers to use part of their payroll-tax contributions to fund personal investment accounts.

The Next Step:

Additional Articles from Current Periodicals

Budget Problems

"Enough to Live On," *The Economist*, March 27, 2004.
Compared to some European countries, Americans' budget problems seem relatively easy to solve.

Bernasek, Anna, "The $44 Trillion Abyss," *Fortune*, Nov. 24, 2003, p. 113.
Economists working for former Treasury Secretary Paul O'Neill calculated that $44 trillion of government debt will accumulate in the future if no policy changes are made.

Bettelheim, Adriel, "A Wide Open 'Lockbox'," *CQ Weekly*, Jan. 17, 2004, p. 157.
A Social Security "lockbox" of secured reserves to pay retirees was widely discussed by politicians but never actually implemented.

Taylor Jr., Stuart, "The Threat That Bush, Kerry — and the Voters — Ignore," *National Journal*, Aug. 21, 2004.
Experts calculate that the budget deficit will increase from 3.8 percent to 20 percent of GDP in 2040 due in part to soaring Social Security costs.

Updegrave, Walter, "Your Greatest Retirement Fear," *Money*, fall 2002, p. 112.
According to forecasts, payroll and income taxes will only be able to provide 75 percent of scheduled Social Security benefits.

Lack of Resources

Atkinson, Bill, "Many Forced Into Hard Work in Retirement," *The Baltimore Sun*, Sept. 28, 2003, p. 1A.
A hundred years ago, most people worked until they died, a fate increasingly shared by today's elderly, who often spend their time driving buses and stocking shelves.

Chaddock, Gail Russell, "Baby Boomers Face Retirement Squeeze," *The Christian Science Monitor*, Feb. 27, 2004, p. 1.
Only 22 percent of working-age Americans contribute to a 401(k) plan, and barely 1 in 3 has saved more than $100,000 for retirement.

Dugas, Christine, "Retirement Crisis Looms as Many Come Up Short," *USA Today*, July 19, 2002, p. 1A.
Retirees need about 75 percent of their pre-retirement income, says one study, yet 40 percent of middle-age households won't even be able to replace half.

Quinn, Jane Bryant, "The Retirement Race," *Newsweek*, March 15, 2004, p. 65.
Many boomers haven't saved much for their retirement, and others have been hit hard by stock market losses.

Pension Troubles

Byrnes, Nanette, "The Benefits Trap," *Business Week*, July 19, 2004, p. 64.
Many corporations are dumping pensions and health benefits for retirees, potentially creating massive, new government liabilities in providing pension and health-care relief.

Hulse, Carl, and Micheline Maynard, "Pension Relief Legislation Is Approved by the Senate," *The New York Times*, April 9, 2004, p. C5.
Newer corporations without pension plans or many retired employees opposed legislation making it easier for established companies to pay their pension obligations.

Maynard, Micheline, and Mary Williams Walsh, "United Warns It May Jettison Pension Plans to Stay Afloat," *The New York Times*, Aug. 20, 2004, p. C1.
United Airlines prepares to renege on its pension liabilities in order to leave bankruptcy, potentially setting off a chain reaction in the airline industry.

Perry, Tony, "Fall From Frugality Puts San Diego on Fiscal Brink," *Los Angeles Times*, Sept. 1, 2004, p. A1.
San Diego is being forced to cut city services to help cover a pension shortfall of more than $1 billion.

Privatization Plans

Kinsley, Michael, "A Guided Tour of the 'Ownership Society'," *Los Angeles Times*, Sept. 5, 2004, p. M5.
A prominent commentator on the left attacks the reasoning behind privatization plans.

Krueger, Alan, "Some Lessons From Sweden on the Pros and Cons of Privatizing Social Security," *The New York Times*, Feb. 5, 2004, p. C2.
Sweden has adopted a system somewhat similar to Social Security privatization plans, and its experience holds lessons for the United States.

Ota, Alan K., "Bush Renews Effort to Create Tax-Free Savings Accounts," *CQ Weekly*, Jan. 31, 2004, p. 280.
Proposed retirement savings accounts (RSAs) could replace IRA plans and 401(k) retirement accounts.

Walczak, Lee, *et al.*, "Selling the Ownership Society," *Business Week*, Sept. 6, 2004, p. 34.
Transition costs for any privatization plan could top $1 trillion, making such a plan a hard sell in Congress while budget deficits mount.

Weisman, Jonathan, "GOP Disavows Social Security

'Privatization'," *The Washington Post*, Sept. 13, 2002, p. A10.**
Fearing voter backlash, Republicans distance themselves from privatization-reform plans prior to the November 2002 congressional elections.

Pozen, Robert C., "Retiring on a Budget," *The New York Times*, Feb. 7, 2004, p. A15.
Shifting from wage indexing to price indexing when determining Social Security's benefits would generate substantial savings, an expert says.

Reform Measures

Atkinson, Bill, and Eileen Ambrose, "Social Security Cuts Will Be Necessary, Greenspan Warns," *The Baltimore Sun*, Feb. 26, 2004, p. 1A.
The Federal Reserve chairman predicts that Social Security benefits will require cuts and recommends increasing the eligibility age for benefits.

Ball, Robert M., "Just a Little Maintenance," *The Washington Post*, July 18, 2004, p. B4.
An official involved in the 1983 Social Security reform outlines his plans for reforming Social Security.

Bernasek, Anna, "The Next Greenspan?" *Fortune*, June 14, 2004, p. 124.
Economist Martin Feldstein is close to the Bush administration and has been influential in forming privatization plans.

Kosterlitz, Julie, and Lisa Caruso, "Social Security's Ticking Bomb," *National Journal*, May 22, 2004.
Ideas to reform Social Security while providing continued benefits and saving the budget cover a wide spectrum of views, but all agree that action is needed.

Kristof, Kathy, "Coalition Offers Fix for Social Security," *Los Angeles Times*, March 21, 2004, p. C3.
A coalition of groups favoring optional personal investment accounts says its plans can fix Social Security while guaranteeing today's level of benefits.

Social Security Politics

Andrews, Edmund, "Tough Issues, Awaiting Their Turn," *The New York Times*, April 13, 2004, p. G1.
Whether Americans should prepare for old age collectively or individually is a basic philosophical dispute between the parties.

Calmes, Jackie, "Ambitions to Fix Social Security Present Big Hurdles for Bush," *The Wall Street Journal*, Sept. 2, 2004, p. A1.
Needing a big idea to help his campaign, President Bush looks to Social Security reform; other Republicans are "scared as hell" of touching this political nerve.

Page, Susan, "Social Security Debate May Be Ready to Reignite," *USA Today*, Dec. 3, 2002, p. 11A.
Polls show that the younger the voters, the more likely they are to favor personal-investment accounts.

Wallsten, Peter, "Bush Opening Social Security Debate Without Saying Much," *Los Angeles Times*, Aug. 20, 2004, p. A1.
President Bush remains unlikely to get specific on his plans for Social Security prior to the election due to fears of disturbing seniors.

Weisman, Jonathan, "Bush Faces Pressure on Social Security," *The Washington Post*, Dec. 28, 2003, p. A4.
Congressional Republicans say President Bush must take a leading role in reform proposals rather than leaving details to Congress.

CITING *THE CQ RESEARCHER*

Sample formats for citing these reports in a bibliography include the ones listed below. Preferred styles and formats vary, so please check with your instructor or professor.

MLA STYLE

Jost, Kenneth. "Rethinking the Death Penalty." The CQ Researcher 16 Nov. 2001: 945-68.

APA STYLE

Jost, K. (2001, November 16). Rethinking the death penalty. *The CQ Researcher, 11*, 945-968.

CHICAGO STYLE

Jost, Kenneth. "Rethinking the Death Penalty." *CQ Researcher*, November 16, 2001, 945-968.

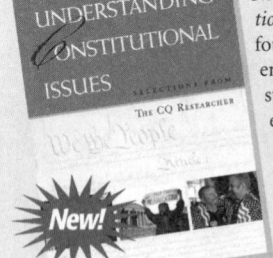

CQ Researcher

Published by CQ Press, a division of Congressional Quarterly Inc.

thecqresearcher.com

Gays on Campus

Should colleges offer gay and lesbian studies?

Gay and lesbian students are increasingly visible and vocal on U.S. college campuses. They are also finding a more welcoming climate at many, though not all, schools. Still, some gay students suffer harassment or threats because of their sexual orientation, and many, particularly athletes, stay "in the closet" for fear of unfavorable treatment. At least 100 universities have established resource centers to help gay, lesbian, bisexual and transgender (GLBT) students cope with the distinctive issues they face in college life. More than 150 colleges now offer courses in lesbian and gay studies — with some schools even offering academic majors or minors in the specialty. But anti-gay organizations and some academics contend that lesbian and gay studies is not a legitimate discipline and that the courses are inherently ideological, immoral or both. And some religiously affiliated schools maintain policies that bar recognition of gay student groups, limit public advocacy of gay causes and prohibit homosexual behavior.

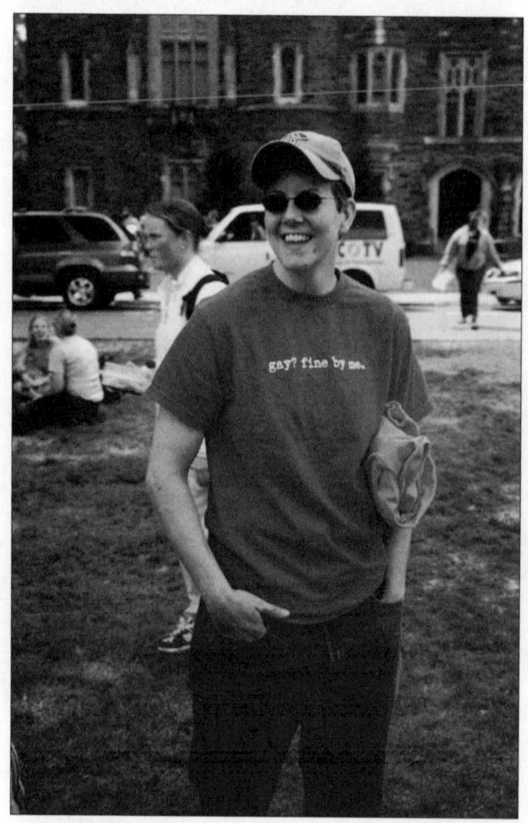

Duke University senior Tyler Pulis wears a T-shirt urging students to be gay-friendly.

INSIDE THIS REPORT

The CQ Researcher • Oct. 1, 2004 • www.thecqresearcher.com
Volume 14, Number 34 • Pages 805-828

CQ PRESS

RECIPIENT OF SOCIETY OF PROFESSIONAL JOURNALISTS AWARD FOR EXCELLENCE ◆ AMERICAN BAR ASSOCIATION SILVER GAVEL AWARD

THE ISSUES

BACKGROUND

CURRENT SITUATION

OUTLOOK

SIDEBARS AND GRAPHICS

FOR FURTHER RESEARCH

Cover: Duke University students began wearing "gay? fine by me" T-shirts in 2003 after the *Princeton Review* ranked Duke the nation's most homophobic school. Tyler Pulis, pictured here as a senior, graduated and is now teaching in Durham, N.C. (Leila Nesson/Fine By Me)

Oct. 1, 2004
Volume 14, Number 34

MANAGING EDITOR: Thomas J. Colin

ASSISTANT MANAGING EDITOR: Kathy Koch

ASSOCIATE EDITOR: Kenneth Jost

STAFF WRITERS: Mary H. Cooper, William Triplett

CONTRIBUTING WRITERS: Sarah Glazer, David Hatch, David Hosansky, Patrick Marshall, Tom Price, Jane Tanner

DESIGN/PRODUCTION EDITOR: Olu B. Davis

ASSISTANT EDITOR: Kate Templin

A Division of
Congressional Quarterly Inc.

SENIOR VICE PRESIDENT/GENERAL MANAGER: John A. Jenkins

DIRECTOR, LIBRARY PUBLISHING: Kathryn C. Suárez

DIRECTOR, EDITORIAL OPERATIONS: Ann Davies

CONGRESSIONAL QUARTERLY INC.

CHAIRMAN: Paul C. Tash

VICE CHAIRMAN: Andrew P. Corty

PRESIDENT AND PUBLISHER: Robert W. Merry

The CQ Researcher (ISSN 1056-2036) is printed on acid-free paper. Published weekly, except Jan. 2, April 9, July 2, July 9, Aug. 6, Aug. 13, Nov. 26 and Dec. 31, by CQ Press, a division of Congressional Quarterly Inc. Annual subscription rates for institutions start at $625. For pricing, call 1-800-834-9020, ext. 1906. To purchase a *CQ Researcher* report in print or electronic format (PDF), visit www.cqpress.com or call 866-427-7737. A single report is $10. Bulk purchase discounts and electronic-rights licensing are also available. Periodicals postage paid at Washington, D.C., and additional mailing offices. POSTMASTER: Send address changes to *The CQ Researcher*, 1255 22nd St., N.W., Suite 400, Washington, D.C. 20037.

Gays on Campus

BY KENNETH JOST

THE ISSUES

Early in the academic year, Yale undergraduates are busy shopping courses, signing up for student groups and settling into college life. School spirit runs high on the campus of the prestigious, 300-year-old university.

Many Yale students, however, are taking pride these days not in traditional measures of the school's pre-eminence, like the number of Nobel Prize laureates on the faculty or the competition between two alumni to be the next president of the United States. Instead, Yale's gay and lesbian students are basking in the school's reputation as "the gay Ivy."

More than 100 universities around the country provide support services for gay and lesbian students. At the University of Vermont, program coordinator Dorothea "Dot" Brauer, rear left, hangs out with students at the Lesbian, Gay, Bisexual, Transgender, Questioning and Ally (LGBTQA) Student Services office.

Getty Images/Jordan Silverman

"One in four and maybe more," says freshman Noah Mamis, of Watchung, N.J., quoting a totally unscientific, two-decade-old description of Yale's approximately 5,300 undergraduates.

The campus climate is "very gay-friendly," says Ruth, a Louisiana senior and co-president of Prism, an organization for gay students of color, who asks that her last name not be used. "I don't feel like there's any rift" between the gay and straight students. "We're a minority, but not a silent minority."

"Being gay isn't much different from being straight," says Gabriel Arana, a junior from Nogales, Ariz. There is "a general consensus" among students, faculty and administrators that discrimination against gay people is unacceptable, he says.

Yale's queer students — the all-embracing term increasingly preferred on college campuses despite its epithetic history — have a smorgasbord of academic and extracurricular offerings to choose from. The Lesbian, Gay, Bisexual and Transgender (LGBT) Co-operative, an umbrella organization, hosts an introductory meeting in early September with presentations by leaders of the various groups for gay men, lesbians, bisexuals, transgender people, students of color and "not-straight frosh." Then in October, the group hosts its Co-op Dance, typically attended by more than 700 students — gay, straight or in between.

The 100 or so students gathered in Yale's Gothic-style chapel also hear from Jonathan D. Katz, who coordinates what he calls the "largest and best-funded lesbian and gay studies program in the country — and the only one in an Ivy institution." The program was established with a $1 million donation in honor of the gay playwright-activist Larry Kramer, a Yale alumnus. Yale accepted the money in 2001 only after having turned down the contribution four years earlier, in part because of questions about the legitimacy of the field.

(Actually, Brown University, an Ivy League school in Providence, R.I., has offered since 1994 a concentration in "Sexuality and Society." The curriculum is coordinated by the University Committee for Lesbian, Gay and Bisexual Concerns.)

Katz, who gained the nation's first tenured position in gay and lesbian studies at City College of San Francisco in 1989, invites students to enroll in any of the 25 courses listed in a two-page brochure called "The Pink Book" — a self-mocking allusion to Yale's official course catalog, known as "The Blue Book." Courses range from "The History of Sexuality in the United States" to "Sex and Race as Performance," which covers such erotic performers as Michael Jackson, Madonna and the black drag queen RuPaul. *(See box, p. 809.)*

Yale's embrace of lesbian and gay students may be distinctively warm, but it is by no means unusual among the nation's 2,551 four-year colleges and universities. Gay students today will find accepting or even welcoming attitudes among students, faculty and administrators at many, perhaps even most, campuses. Rainbow flags hang from dorm windows, and same-sex couples walk arm in arm on campuses across the country, while student newspapers endorse gay marriage — even at such conservative schools as Baptist-affiliated Baylor University, in Waco, Texas.

"We've evolved from a period when students could be and were thrown out of college simply for being gay to

Ten Most, Least Gay-Friendly Campuses

Eugene Lang College, part of New York's New School University, is the nation's most gay-friendly campus, according to the 2005 Princeton Review *compilation of the nation's best 357 colleges and universities. The University of Notre Dame was rated as the least accepting of gay and lesbian students, one of seven church-affiliated or explicitly religious schools among the 10 campuses in that category.* The Review's *rankings — based on student surveys at the respective schools — are widely circulated, but viewed as flawed by many university administrators and faculty.*

Gay Community Accepted

1. Eugene Lang College, New York, N.Y.
2. New York University, New York, N.Y.
3. Sarah Lawrence College, Bronxville, N.Y.
4. New College of Florida, Sarasota, Fla.
5. Brandeis University, Waltham, Mass.
6. Mount Holyoke College, South Hadley, Mass.
7. Reed College, Portland, Ore.
8. Hendrix College, Conway, Ark.
9. Smith College, Northampton, Mass.
10. Bryn Mawr College, Bryn Mawr, Pa.

Alternative Lifestyle Not an Alternative

1. University of Notre Dame, South Bend, Ind. (Catholic)
2. Baylor University, Waco, Tex. (Baptist)
3. Grove City College, Grove City, Pa. (Christian)
4. Wheaton College, Wheaton, Ill. (Christian)
5. Boston College, Boston, Mass. (Catholic)
6. Birmingham-Southern College, Birmingham, Ala. (Methodist)
7. Brigham Young University, Salt Lake City, Utah (Mormon)
8. Texas A&M University, College Station, Texas
9. Hampden-Sydney College, Hampden-Sydney, Va.
10. Washington and Lee University, Lexington, Va.

Source: The Princeton Review *(www.princetonreview.com)*

a period where colleges offer courses on gay/lesbian issues," says gay author Eric Marcus.

Institutionally, at least 100 universities have centers to provide support services for LGBT students, says Chicora Martin, co-director of the National Consortium of Directors of Lesbian Gay Bisexual and Transgender Resources in Higher Education. * More than 150 schools offer some courses in lesbian and gay studies, including more than 20 that recognize a minor or major in the field, according to John G. Younger, a professor at the University of Kansas in Lawrence, who maintains a Web site listing the programs. (*See chart, p. 820.*)

A spring 2004 survey of college registrars and admissions officials found that more than half — 54 percent — described the climate on their campuses as "somewhat" or "very" accepting of GLBT persons, while 31 percent called the climate unaccepting. About 83 percent of the 355 respondents said there was no significant hostility toward GLBT students on campus. [1]

In a survey of students published a year earlier, 43 percent of GLBT respondents described the overall climate on their campuses as homophobic, and more than one-third said they had experienced harassment during the previous year. Sponsored by an arm of the National Gay and Lesbian Task Force (known simply as the Task Force), the report was based on a student survey conducted between October 2000 and December 2001 at 14 universities with gay/lesbian resource centers. [2]

"You can say the climate is improving," says Martin, who directs the LGBT center at the University of Oregon in Eugene. "But that doesn't mean that improvement for one campus is the same as for another."

"There are a number of campuses, particularly Catholic universities, where it's not even welcome to discuss GLBT issues, let alone make a space for students to meet each other," says Jason Cianciotto, research director for the Task Force Policy Institute.

Anti-gay organizations view the establishment of GLBT resource centers and gay and lesbian studies with disdain, if not disgust. "We believe that homosexual behavior is harmful to society and harmful to people who engage in it," says Peter Sprigg, senior director of policy studies for the Fam-

* The acronyms GLBT and LGBT are both used in titles, written materials and interviews to refer to gay men, lesbians, bisexuals and transgender persons and are used interchangeably in this report.

Inside Yale's 'Pink Book'

Yale University offers a major in lesbian and gay studies within its Women, Gender and Sexuality program. Here are some of the current courses, with condensed descriptions from the 2004-05 catalog, known as the "Pink Book" (www.yale.edu/lesbiangay):

AIDS and Society: The natural history, biology and epidemiology of AIDS; social, ethical, public policy and political aspects of AIDS and of the ways societies address a medical crisis.

American Queer Studies: Theorizing Race, Gender, Sexuality: Study of interdisciplinary methodologies shaping the field of lesbian/gay studies and its attendant queer theory.

History of Feminist Thought: Key works from the history of feminist thought in Britain, France and the United States from the Enlightenment to the present, with related writings on gender.

History of Sexuality in the United States: Selected topics in the history of sexuality in the 19th and 20th centuries.

Psychology of Gender: Exploration of the relationship between gender and psychological processes at individual, interpersonal, institutional and cross-cultural levels.

Regulating Love, Sex and Marriage: Seminar: Examination and exploration — against the backdrop of the same-sex marriage controversy — of the justifications that have been advanced for a state role in regulating the entry by adults into intimate, consensual relationships.

Sex and Gender in 17th-Century Theater: Examination of the remarkably rich site of gender ambiguity and sexual confusion in 17th-century French theater.

Sex and Race as Performance: Examination of how erotic performers inform contemporary film, club music, dance, performance art and photography.

Sexual Meanings: Human sexuality in historical and cross-cultural perspective.

ily Research Council, a Washington-based Christian advocacy group. "The vast majority of these programs tend to deny that fundamental reality."

Gay and lesbian studies "isn't true academic work but rather an utterly polemic exercise in justifying homosexuality," says Robert Knight, director of the Culture & Family Institute at Concerned Women for America, which promotes biblical values in public policy.

Despite such views, anti-gay groups are giving scant attention to campus issues while waging the fight against gay marriage in Washington and in the states. [3] But battles do occasionally flare up.

In 2000, when David Halperin began offering a course at the University of Michigan, Ann Arbor, entitled "How to Be Gay," the head of the Michigan chapter of the conservative American Family Association mounted a public-relations campaign attacking it. The course continues. [4] But some other schools, public and private, have shied away from gay studies for fear of stirring up political controversy.

Others are slow on the uptake: Harvard began concrete moves to create a program only in spring 2004. "We're playing catch-up," says Brad Epps, a professor of romance languages and literatures who is working to establish the program.

Scholars in the field defend its importance and dismiss the criticisms. "This is a group of people who have a history, and people have an attitude toward them," says Younger. "It's interesting to study that history and the history of these attitudes."

For his part, Cianciotto mocks the accusation from critics that gay and lesbian studies may seduce students into homosexuality. "There's no roving band of gay and lesbian students who kidnap unexpecting freshmen from their dorms and perform some sort of ceremony to make them gay or lesbian," he says.

Law schools are the focus of another gay-rights debate — this one over on-campus recruitment by the military. Law schools require employers using campus facilities and services for recruiting to adopt anti-discrimination policies. When some schools moved to limit assistance to military recruiters because of the military's "don't ask, don't tell" policy barring service by "out" gays or lesbians, Congress and the Pentagon retaliated by passing a law — and later regulations — to cut off federal funds for any university adopting such restrictions.

A coalition of some 20 law schools is challenging those regulations as a violation of academic freedom. The case is awaiting decision by the federal appeals court in Philadelphia. Similar cases filed by groups of professors at Yale Law School and the University of Pennsylvania Law School also are pending.

As gay and lesbian students continue to come out on college and university campuses, here are some of the questions being debated:

Should colleges adopt policies to create a favorable campus climate for GLBT students?

As a Roman Catholic school, the University of Notre Dame views homosexual behavior as sinful and refuses to recognize gay student groups. For several years, Notre Dame has also been rated among the nation's least gay-friendly colleges, according to the widely quoted rankings by the private *Princeton Review*. (*See chart, p. 808.*)

Still, Notre Dame also has a standing committee on gay and lesbian students' needs. And in March 2004, Notre Dame students borrowed a consciousness-raising device from Duke University — previously ranked as the least gay-friendly school — and distributed 1,600 T-shirts on campus with the slogan, "gay? fine by me." [5]

Notre Dame's ambivalence combines two of the strains of thought toward homosexuality found on campuses today. More and more, gay and lesbian students find a welcoming attitude among other students as well as faculty and administrators. Yale's first-year students, for example, are welcomed with a 48-page brochure, "Queer Life at Yale," that includes a message from Yale's president, Richard Levin. "We stand committed to the belief that, by reaching out to support Yale's lesbian and gay students, staff, faculty, and administrators, we aid the university in achieving its mission, and we benefit the nation as well," Levin writes.

But gay and lesbian students at Baptist-affiliated Baylor receive a different message. The online handbook for students includes a statement that "affirms" what it calls "the biblical understanding of human sexuality" as prohibiting either heterosexual sex outside of marriage or homosexual behavior.

"It is thus expected," the statement continues, "that Baylor students will not participate in advocacy groups which promote understandings of sexuality that are contrary to biblical teaching." Students "struggling with these issues" are then encouraged "to avail themselves of opportunities for serious, confidential discussion and support through the University Ministries Office."

Within the range defined by those polar opposites, gay and lesbian students will find that the climate "differs dramatically from school to school," according to Sheldon Steinbach, general counsel of the American Council on Education, a coordinating body for higher-education groups.

In an online survey by the gay network PlanetOut, gay and lesbian students rated positively big state universities and small liberal arts colleges in all parts of the country — in so-called red and blue states alike. The *Princeton Review* lists religiously affiliated institutions, along with a current and a formerly all-male school, as the least gay-friendly.

Martin says LGBT centers like the one at the University of Oregon help ensure that students get needed support, providing "a safe space for individuals to come out in a healthy way and to identify in whatever way they feel comfortable."

Anti-gay organizations, however, say these centers give students inaccurate information about homosexuality. "They don't offer true information about the dangers of homosexual behavior, for example, the health risks," Sprigg says. "They don't offer accurate information about the possibility of changing your

AP Photo/*Waco Tribune-Herald*, Duane A. Laverty

Students at Baylor University, in Waco, Texas, discard school hats and T-shirts to protest the Baptist school's anti-gay policies. The rally on March 27, 2004, was held in downtown Waco, because gay-rights activities are prohibited on campus.

sexual behavior and even your sexual orientation. They are geared toward celebrating homosexual behavior, and we feel that's harmful."

The 14-campus survey by the Task Force found that a majority of gay and lesbian students responding had concealed their sexual orientation within the previous year to "avoid intimidation." Slightly over one-third said they had avoided disclosing their orientation to a teacher or administrator for fear of negative consequences.

More than one-third of the GLBT undergraduates and 29 percent of all respondents said they had been harassed because of their sexual orientation. Derogatory remarks or verbal harassment were most common, but the survey found 10 reported instances of physical assaults against GLBT students on campus and 11 other threats of physical violence.

Martin says religious opposition to homosexuality can encourage harassment against gay and lesbian students. "By calling it a sin, you can now devalue these people as human beings," she says. "That creates hateful rhetoric and gives people an excuse to commit acts of violence and hate crimes."

Sprigg calls the accusation "a slander without empirical support." If anything, he notes, "Playing the 'hate-crimes' card gives people an excuse to snuff out religious liberty, which cannot exist if believers are not free to label as 'sins' acts they sincerely believe to be sinful."

Susan R. Rankin, a senior planning analyst at Pennsylvania State University and author of the Task Force report, says colleges need to do more to improve the campus climate for gay and lesbian students. "It's still difficult to be out if you're a student, faculty, administrator or staff on college campuses," she says. "We've actually improved, but we need to continue to improve."

Anti-gay organizations, however, say that schools are already going too far. "Colleges can encourage all students to be treated fairly and decently without promoting homosexuality," says Knight of the Culture & Family Institute.

Should colleges and universities offer academic programs in gay and lesbian studies?

When professors at the College of Charleston in South Carolina began planning to offer a minor in gay and lesbian studies in September 2003, opposition quickly emerged.[6] "What about a course in the history of stable, monogamous, heterosexual marriages in the state?" Robert Baker, the bishop of the Catholic diocese of Charleston, asked. State Rep. John Graham Altman warned that the plan could jeopardize the school's public funding.

Within days, the university president, Lee Higdon, and Provost Elise Jorgens acted to squelch the idea, stressing in a letter to the Charleston newspaper that there was "no such minor in any stage of formal review process." When the faculty Senate later passed a resolution criticizing the political pressure, Higdon and Jorgens responded that the stillborn proposal was not "in the best interest of the college."

Since the first courses were offered in 1970, lesbian and gay studies programs have spread to many U.S. college campuses. But they are still encountering resistance — more from politicians and advocacy groups, however, than from academia.

"If students form a gay students organization as an expression of their freedom of association and speech, that's within their freedom to do that," Sprigg says. "But when you begin establishing these kinds of programs as part of the curriculum and hiring faculty specifically to teach gay and lesbian studies, it becomes problematic."

Scholars in the field insist that the discipline has proved its worth with important new insights into human sexuality. Jonathan Ned Katz, an author and independent scholar (no relation to Yale's Katz), says gay/lesbian studies "deepen everyone's appreciation of the diversity of human beings and human societies and the different ways that sexuality and affection have been organized socially. That's a new kind of insight."

Anti-gay groups, however, view any scholarship in the field as inherently flawed. Gay and lesbian studies "is an attempt to put an academic gloss on a movement that preys on vulnerable people," Knight says.

"I can't imagine a gay studies program that takes seriously the traditional Christian moral position on sexuality, which is still the belief of the vast majority of Americans," says John Zmirak, editor of *Choosing the Right College*, a guide published by the conservative Intercollegiate Studies Institute.

"It's like having a department of Marxism or a department of neoconservatism," says Zmirak, who graduated from Yale in 1986 with a degree in Christianity and literature. "It's taking a prefabricated position and pretending it's an academic discipline."

Some gay and lesbian scholars give critics ammunition by explicitly adopting a political stance. Halperin, the University of Michigan professor, has called gay studies "the academic wing of the lesbian, bisexual, gay and transgender movement." Seth Clark Silberman — one of the two lecturers currently holding two-year appointments at Yale's program — says he sees lesbian and gay studies "as part of a broader social and political movement."

But Yale's Katz disagrees. "Lesbian and gay studies isn't tied disciplinarily to a social and political movement," he says. "What we study may have been engendered by a progressive social movement but is not tied to it."

Katz acknowledges some skepticism about the field even within the gay community or among gay-rights supporters. For instance, some argue that gay and lesbian studies courses are "preaching to the choir" — teaching students who are either gay or lesbian

Gay Athletes Often Encounter Bias

Mike Crosby was a standout water polo player in high school in California and then at Harvard, where he was elected co-captain in his senior year and helped lead the team to a national ranking at the end of the 2001-2002 season.

Crosby is also gay. He began to come out to his teammates in his sophomore year and found fellow players and coaches totally supportive.

"I don't even think about Mike's sexuality," coach Jim Floerchinger told the gay magazine *Genre*. "It's something that never crosses my mind." [1]

Crosby showed it is possible to be a college athlete and openly gay. But his story is hardly typical. More common among the relatively few openly gay college athletes are experiences like those of former Stanford lineman Dwight Slater and University of Florida catcher Andrea Zimbardi, who both left their teams after coming out because of reactions from their coaches or teammates.

More common still are the countless untold stories of gay college athletes who keep their sexual orientation hidden. When the *St. Petersburg Times* did a story in summer 2004 about gay athletes, five college athletes who initially agreed to talk to the reporter eventually backed out. [2] A gay soccer player at an unidentified New England college similarly declined to let his name be used for an earlier story in *The Chronicle of Higher Education*. [3]

"There are isolated instances where athletes, most likely women, are able to come out and have the support of their teammates," says Susan Cahn, an associate professor of history at the State University of New York, Buffalo, and author of a history of women's sports. "But, on the whole, at best, people are gay and it's not talked about. It's sort of a 'don't ask, don't tell' situation. At worst, it's something about which people are really terrified of being discovered."

Gay and lesbian athletes often feel "ostracized, isolated, made fun of," according to Rosie Stallman, director of education outreach for the National Collegiate Athletic Association (NCAA). There are instances of physical violence against gay athletes in men's programs, she says. In women's programs, gay athletes are more likely to be excluded from team activities.

Slater came out in his first year on Stanford's highly ranked football team. [4] Initially, his classmates were supportive. But when he told his coach, the coach pressured Slater to tell his parents and then told other coaches. "I was forced out of football," Slater said later. When he decided to leave, Slater added, his coach "seemed relieved."

Zimbardi was co-captain of the University of Florida's women's softball team in 2002, a star catcher and a popular teammate. [5] She had come out to some of her teammates earlier. "It never really affected their thinking," she says today. But the team's new coach in June 2000 brought her strong Christian views into the locker room, including evident disapproval of homosexuality. A new assistant coach with similar views made the situation more uncomfortable. Zimbardi also felt she was being frozen out of some of the team activities.

Zimbardi complained about her treatment to the university's administration. A meeting in February 2003 with an administrator and the coaches seemed to be conciliatory, but two days later Zimbardi was told she was suspended for a week — supposedly for having lied about the assistant coach. She believes she was kicked off for taking a stand against homophobic treatment.

The National Center for Lesbian Rights (NCLR) helped Zimbardi file a complaint with the university. Without admitting discrimination, the university settled the complaint in January 2004 by agreeing to provide training to combat homophobia. The school also petitioned the NCAA on Zimbardi's behalf to reinstate her eligibility for a final year. The petition is pending even though Zimbardi has now graduated. "It matters a great deal to Andrea even if she decides not to use that final year of eligibility," says NCLR attorney Karen Doering.

The NCAA itself is taking some steps to combat homophobia in college sports. It included a panel on the issue at its national convention in January 2002, added sexual orientation to its non-discrimination policy and continues to put on regional workshops on the subject. "It's an issue, and we're dealing with it," Stallman says.

Zimbardi has spoken on her experiences in a number of forums and says she has met several other athletes with similar stories. "It makes you sad, but it also makes you happy in a way that we're talking about it," Zimbardi says. "People have to start accepting the fact that gays and lesbians are everywhere, even in the athletic arena."

---

[1] Cyd Zeigler Jr., "Harvard Water Polo Player Makes a Splash," *Genre* (available at www.outsports.com/gaygames/profiles/03crosby.htm).

[2] Antonya English, "Out Isn't In," *The St. Petersburg Times*, July 18, 2004, p. 1C.

[3] Jennifer Jacobson, "Facing Derision in a Macho Culture, Many Gay Athletes In," *The Chronicle of Higher Education*, Nov. 1, 2002, p. 36.

[4] Background drawn from Chris Bull, "The College Sports Closet," *The Advocate*, March 5, 2002. For a first-person account, see Cyd Zeigler, "In Their Own Words: Dwight Slater, Stanford Football," www.outsports.com.

[5] For coverage, see Jim Buzinski, "Was Andrea Zimbardi outed, then ousted?", www.outsports.com; Patrick Letellier, "A home run against homophobia," *The Advocate*, April 13, 2004.

themselves or already sympathetic to gay and lesbian causes.

"To some extent, that's fair," Katz says. "In a cultural and social context that sees sexuality as so fraught, how do you get students who are fearful, whose parents refuse to allow them to take the courses [or] who have religious or moral objections to take the courses? I don't think ultimately there's much we can do about that. Once the larger culture shifts, this will shift, too."

Despite the criticisms, Katz believes serious academic opposition to gay and lesbian studies has ended. "That debate is over," he says. His assessment appears to be correct as far as Yale is concerned. Editors at the *Yale Daily News* say there have been no recent controversies on campus.

Public universities, however, are likely to see continuing fights. "If people speak out and taxpayers speak out regarding the way their money is being spent, they can have an impact on this," Sprigg says.

Younger at the University of Kansas concedes that pressure from state legislatures is "a fact of life," but calls for university administrators and governing boards to resist it. "They need to stand up and say that sex is a proper subject and should be taught, and we don't need oversight from supervisors who are not experts."

Should law schools be forced to help military recruiters despite the Pentagon's "don't ask, don't tell" policy on gays?

For the past 10 years, Congress and the Pentagon have been in a slow-motion showdown with law schools over the schools' objections to the military's "don't ask, don't tell" policy barring service by out gay men or lesbians. [7] Most law schools prohibit any recruiting help to employers that discriminate on the basis of, among other things, sexual orientation. Congress and the Pentagon responded with laws and regulations to cut off most federal funds for any university that did not give military recruiters the same access to students provided to other employers.

So far, only one school has been ruled ineligible for federal funding: William Mitchell College of Law, an independent school in St. Paul, Minn., which, in fact, receives no federal assistance. For law schools affiliated with big universities, however, the Pentagon's threat could mean the loss of millions of dollars in research grants or other assistance from federal departments covered by the law: Defense, Education, Labor and Health and Human Services.

Courtesy of Desiree Herrera

Gays and straights mix easily at events on many campuses, such as Oberlin College's popular "Drag Ball." Fencing team members Desiree Herrera (right) and Benjamin Brown attended the ball on April 10, 2004.

Yale, for example, reportedly could lose $300 million if the so-called Solomon amendment — named after Rep. Gerald B. H. Solomon, the New York Republican who authored the law in 1994 — is enforced under the Pentagon's interpretation. The issue simmered uneventfully during the Clinton administration. But under President Bush, the Pentagon has stepped up the conflict, issuing official warnings to university presidents that their institutions face financial sanctions because of the law schools' refusal to aid military recruiters.

In the face of the threats, many law schools have changed their policies, but Yale law professors decided to fight. "We should be free to decide whether we should assist the military in the implementation of a hiring policy that is degrading and insulting to gays and lesbians who are our students," says Robert Burt, the lead plaintiff in a federal court suit by more than 40 Yale law professors challenging the law. [8]

The Pentagon, however, says the law takes precedence over the law schools' policies. "Public law supersedes a [private association's] policy when the two are in conflict," says Lt. Col. Ellen Krenke, a Pentagon spokeswoman.

The dispute is as much symbolic as real. Law schools' career-service offices regularly assist law firms and other legal employers by helping them schedule recruiting interviews — on campus at some schools, off campus at others. Even without that assistance, however, military recruiters typically can obtain names and contact information of law students interested in talking with them, according to Joshua Rosenkranz, lead attorney for the coalition of law schools that brought the main court challenge to the law. In addition, students or student groups can invite military recruiters onto campus, Rosenkranz points out.

However, under policies adopted by the Association of American Law Schools and the American Bar Association, law schools must obtain pledges of non-discrimination from any employers using their facilities or services for recruitment.

When originally passed in 1994, the Solomon amendment said the federal government could cut off funds for any school that denied military recruiters access to campus. Yale, like other schools, maintained that it was only refusing to assist military recruiters, not denying them access. The Pentagon disagreed but did not impose financial penalties.

The dispute escalated after the terrorist attacks of Sept. 11, 2001. The Pentagon began interpreting the law as requiring schools to actively assist military recruiters. The Defense Department also had adopted regulations in 2000 that called for penalizing an entire university if any of its separate schools violated the law.

By fall 2003, law schools decided to go to court over the issue. A coalition of 21 law schools, called the Forum for Academic and Individual Rights (FAIR), filed the first suit on Sept. 19, 2003, in federal court in New Jersey. Suits were filed in October by University of Pennsylvania law professors in Pennsylvania and separately by Yale law professors and students in Connecticut.

The suits generally contend that the Defense Department's interpretation of the law is wrong or, if correct, that it violates the schools' First Amendment rights. "We are being forced to affiliate ourselves with a policy that we oppose," Burt says.

The Pentagon counters that the Solomon amendment "is directed not at what law schools or other educational institutions wish to say, but instead at what they wish to do — namely, to deny military recruiters entry to campus and access to students."

U.S. District Court Judge John Lifland rejected the First Amendment arguments in a ruling on Nov. 5, 2003, although he criticized the Pentagon's interpretation of the law. The law schools appealed, and arguments were held before the Third U.S. Circuit Court of Appeals in Philadelphia on June 30, 2004.

Meanwhile, both houses of Congress have approved a provision codifying the Pentagon's interpretation of the law by requiring schools to give military recruiters access "equal in quality and scope" to that provided other employers. "Our nation's military should be treated just like any other employer recruiting on campus and given fair and equal access to our nation's most highly educated students," says Rep. Mike Rogers, R-Ala., who sponsored the provision as part of the Defense Department authorization bill. The measure is awaiting final action.

But attorney Rosenkranz insists the military is seeking special treatment. "We do not discriminate, and we do not assist others who discriminate — no exceptions," he says. "The military is demanding an exception." ■

BACKGROUND

Sexual Awakenings

The college years often are a time of sexual awakening for coming-of-age men and women. For most of U.S. history, however, college students who found themselves physically attracted to persons of the same sex either repressed their inclinations or expressed them only furtively. Only since the 1960s has it become comfortable for gay men or lesbians — students, faculty members or administrators — to be open in their sexuality on many, but still not all, college and university campuses.

The diaries of Ralph Waldo Emerson show that the future author was greatly smitten with a younger schoolmate, Martin Gay, while attending Harvard College in the early 19th century. [9] In an entry dated Aug. 8, 1820, Emerson — about to enter his senior year — wrote of "the singular sensations" produced by the freshman's presence. Two months later, he wrote that the two men had exchanged "two or three long profound stares." Later entries, along with a love poem addressed to "Malcolm," bespeak the frustrations of unrequited romance. Emerson and Gay remained friends, but no more.

Decades later, Yale student John William Sterling lived a different life, according to evidence assembled by historian Katz. "Last night I slept with Jim Mitchell," the future lawyer wrote in a diary entry in fall 1863. In 1870, six years after his graduation, Sterling met his future life companion, James Orville Bloss. Sterling went on to help found the still prominent New York-based law firm, Shearman & Sterling. His will provided that Bloss could remain in the house they had shared and that the two would be buried together in a stately mausoleum in New York. The will also provided for a $15 million bequest to Yale, a gift memorialized in the naming of the university's main library at the center of the New Haven, Conn., campus. [10]

Administrators and faculty also had to be discreet — or risk consequences. The turn-of-the-century president of Bryn Mawr College, Helen Carey Thomas, appears to have had an intimate but unacknowledged relationship with another woman, according to a diary entry by the English mathematician Bertrand Russell after a visit in 1896.

At Amherst College, a prominent professor, Stark Young, provoked resentment from his faculty colleague, the poet Robert Frost, because of Young's apparent flirtation with a young male student who enrolled in 1915. Frost sought to have Young fired, according to historian Katz, but the university's president "thought Young too

Continued on p. 816

Chronology

1940s-1950s
Gay men and lesbians begin to emerge from closet; first stirrings of U.S. gay-rights movement.

1948
Kinsey Report finds evidence of same-sex behavior by many men, women for some part of their lives.

1950s
Mattachine Society founded as first gay-rights advocacy group in 1951; Daughters of Bilitis, counterpart group for lesbians, established in 1955.

1960s-1970s
College campuses become centers for visible, aggressive gay-rights movement.

1966
Columbia undergraduates establish Student Homophile League, nation's first campus-based gay-rights organization; recognized by university in April 1967. . . . Stanford students follow suit in 1968.

1969
Riot breaks out after police raid the Stonewall Inn, a New York City gay bar; event marks beginning of modern gay-rights movement in the U.S.

1972
City College of San Francisco becomes first school to offer formal course in gay/lesbian studies.

1973
Gay Academic Union formed at meeting in New York City attended by more than 300 academics. . . . Homosexuality removed from list of mental disorders by American Psychiatric Association.

1980s
Gay and lesbian students gain visibility, acceptance on many college campuses; lesbian and gay studies programs advance.

1986
Historian Martin Duberman begins pushing for gay-studies center; Yale University, other schools say no; Center for Lesbian and Gay Studies established at City University of New York in 1991.

1987
Yale hosts first national conference on lesbian and gay studies; attendance grows from 200 at first conference to 2,000 five years later.

1989
City College of San Francisco establishes department of gay and lesbian studies, hires Jonathan D. Katz as nation's first tenured faculty member in field.

1990s
Gay and lesbian studies draw criticism from anti-gay organizations, politicians as they grow in number and visibility.

1994
Brown University begins offering concentration in "Sexuality and Society," with curriculum coordinated by committee on lesbian, gay and bisexual concerns. . . . Congress passes Solomon amendment to penalize schools that limit military recruiters over "don't ask, don't tell" policy.

1997
Yale declines $1 million gift from playwright Larry Kramer to fund gay-studies program. . . . "Revolting Behavior," women's studies conference held in November at State University of New York, New Paltz, draws fire for graphic sexual information.

2000-Present
Lesbian and gay studies — often called "queer studies" by proponents — continue to advance despite continuing opposition.

2001
Yale reaches agreement with Kramer for donation of papers, $1 million contribution to establish Larry Kramer Initiative for Lesbian and Gay Studies at the university. . . . National Center for Lesbian Rights establishes Homophobia in Sport Project to advocate for rights of gay and lesbian student athletes.

2002
National Collegiate Athletic Association adds sexual orientation to non-discrimination policy for college athletic programs.

2003
Duke University students launch "Gay? Fine by me" T-shirt campaign to counter school's ranking as least gay-friendly of major U.S. colleges. . . . Law schools challenge Solomon amendment on First Amendment grounds; main case argued before federal appeals court in June 2004.

2004
University of Notre Dame hosts "Queer Film Festival," a first for a Catholic university . . . Larry Kramer Initiative mounts exhibit, "The Pink and the Blue," documenting lesbian and gay life at Yale and in Connecticut, 1642-2004.

Baylor Says No to Gay Student's Activism

Darrin Adams knew he was gay when he enrolled at Baylor University in 2000, but he did not know his sexual orientation would jeopardize his graduation four years later.

Raised in a Baptist family in Pawnee, Okla., Adams chose the Baptist-affiliated school in Waco, Texas, because of its relative proximity and small classes. He had started to disclose his sexual orientation as a high school senior but did not think about the issue in selecting a college.

"Baylor doesn't advertise that it's a homophobic school," Adams says. "It's a Baptist school, but it doesn't say in the brochure that gay people shouldn't apply."

In fact, Baylor's student handbook formally disapproved of homosexuality and admonished students not to participate in advocacy groups that "promote understandings of sexuality that are contrary to biblical teaching." The school is affiliated with the Baptist General Convention of Texas.

For a while, Adams thought he was the only gay person on the 14,000-student campus. He heard enough snide comments about homosexuality to decide to keep his sexual orientation to himself. With few friends, he was lonely and thought about transferring.

One day in his sophomore year, however, Adams saw a sidewalk chalking that read, "Want to come out and not get kicked out?" He replied to the Web site address provided and, with another organizer, helped assemble an e-mail circle of gay and lesbian students. He also helped found a student group, Baylor Freedom, to advocate for gay rights.

That summer, Adams wore a Baylor Freedom T-shirt while marching in a gay-rights parade in Houston, about 200 miles from campus. His picture appeared in a newspaper, and an irate alumnus complained to the school. Adams was called in and warned against using the school's name.

But Adams kept up his activism. He persuaded the university to amend its policy statement to disapprove of "homosexual behavior," not homosexuality. At another student's invitation, he planned to speak about homosexuality to a social-work class until a dean barred the appearance.

Then, in March 2004, just before graduation, Adams helped organize a gay-rights rally in downtown Waco to protest the school seminary's decision to deny a friend of his a scholarship because the friend was gay. News reports estimated the crowd at around 200.

Adams was summoned again to see the associate dean for judicial affairs. The school was already embroiled in controversy over an editorial in the student-edited newspaper in February endorsing gay marriage. This time, Adams was told that he had violated university policy and that he needed to sign an admission or face formal hearings — proceedings that could jeopardize his scheduled graduation. [1]

"I didn't want to sign it because I didn't think what I did was wrong," Adams says. After conferring with a lawyer, however, he signed.

Baylor officials defend their stance. "If a student went out and held a rally and wore a Baylor T-shirt and advocated a stance on homosexuality that's at odds with [the university's handbook statement], they're probably going to be disciplined," says Larry Brumley, associate vice president for external affairs.

Adams, who is now interning for a public relations firm in Washington, says he no longer considers himself a Baptist. "My experience with the Baptist religion is that it focuses on that one part of the biblical teaching and excludes everything else," he says.

On the other hand, Adams says he does not regret going to Baylor — and would do it again. "My experiences at Baylor made me who I am now," he says. "Because of my trials at Baylor, I had time to grow and develop skills and really help out. Of course, I would do it again."

[1] For other coverage, see Angela K. Brown, "Baylor student disciplined for gay rights rally," The Associated Press, May 15, 2004; "Ex-student organizes rally over gay rights at Baylor," *ibid.*, March 27, 2004.

Continued from p. 814

fine a teacher to fire simply because of his homoerotic proclivities." [11]

By the 1930s, gay men and lesbians were starting to come out of campus closets but still with as little attention as possible from heterosexual classmates and colleagues, according to a history of 20th-century gay life by the author John Loughery. [12] Covert homosexual societies could be found in such heartland campuses as the University of Nebraska and Iowa State University, Loughery reports. At Texas Christian University, gay students met under the cover of an Oscar Wilde study group. A prominent music professor at the University of Colorado in the late 1930s opened his home as an "unofficial social center" for gay students and faculty. The professor's activities were known and tolerated, Loughery says, though he was fired in the anti-homosexual purges that followed World War II.

Researchers helped open the closet door in the years after World War II by documenting the previously unacknowledged extent of homosexual activity among men and women. Most importantly, the entomologist-turned-sex researcher Alfred Kinsey showed in his landmark work *Sexual Behavior in the American Male* in 1948 that a significant number of American men engaged in sexual activity with other men for some portion of their lives. [13] The precise numbers are subject to methodological criticism, but Kinsey found that one-third of the 30-something single men in his study had had some same-sex experience and that 10 percent of all male respondents had been exclusively homosexual for at least three years. His later study, *Sexual Behavior in the Human Female*, found a lower incidence of homosexual behavior among women despite lesser "social concern" about such activities by women than by men. [14]

Intriguingly, Kinsey found homosexual behavior was more frequent among high-school educated men than among college graduates. But Benjamin Glover, a doctor at the University of Wisconsin, wrote ominously in a medical journal in 1951 of "a noticeable increase in cases of homosexuality as well as other socially offending cases." [15]

Glover's alarm reflected the conventional wisdom of the times. A homosexual scandal at the University of Texas during World War II resulted in the dismissal of several teachers and a story in *Time*, according to Loughery. A decade later, an investigation by a Florida legislative committee uncovered evidence of homosexuality at the state university in Gainesville. Several professors were allowed to resign quietly. When the story hit the news, the local newspaper editorially complained that the teachers had gotten off too lightly. [16]

Liberation Movements

The overt repression of the 1950s had the paradoxical result of fostering the creation of the first organizations in the United States to actively defend the rights of homosexuals. College campuses began in the mid-1960s to emerge as the centers of a publicly visible gay-liberation movement. By the 1990s, gay-rights advocates could count more than 400 campuses with gay student organizations, but only a handful of schools had formal policies to protect gay and lesbian students and faculty members from discriminatory treatment. [17]

The first gay-rights organization, the Mattachine Society, can be traced to a 1948 "beer bust" bull session involving Harry Hay, an avowedly Marxist labor organizer in his mid-30s, and several gay undergraduates at the University of Southern California in Los Angeles. [18] Years later, Hay recalled that the group formulated plans that night for a gay political-advocacy organization, but the next morning no one remembered the idea except Hay. Two years later, though, Hay and six other gay men established a consciousness-raising and political-advocacy group that took its name from masked Venetian court jesters of medieval times. In 1955, Del Martin and Phyllis Lyon, two San Francisco women then in their third year as a couple, formed a comparable organization for lesbians: the Daughters of Bilitis. [19]

In 1966, students at Columbia University sought to form a chapter of the Mattachine Society, but the society's leaders rebuffed them in order to avoid any insinuations of pedophilia. So the dozen undergraduates instead formed the Student Homophile League, the country's first campus gay-rights organization. The university was "none too keen" on the idea, according to one historian's account, and the leader used a pseudonym — Stephen Donaldson — instead of his real name, Robert Martin. *The New York Times* took note when the group won university recognition in spring 1967. [20]

Stanford counts itself the second university to have a student gay-rights organization: the Student Homophile League of Stanford University, founded in 1968. [21] In announcing the new group, an unnamed spokesman said it would be a "civil libertarian organization" and not "a social organization for introductions." The group was short-lived, but a successor organization — the Gay People's Union — was founded in 1971 and survives today under the name Stanford Pride.

Two off-campus events gave birth and then an added a measure of objective legitimacy to the modern gay-liberation movement. A police raid on June 28, 1969, at the Stonewall Inn, a gay bar in New York's Greenwich Village, touched off a riot by patrons and others that became the template for a new assertiveness by gay men and lesbians. Four years later the American Psychiatric Association removed homosexuality from its list of mental disorders — an action that helped gay men and lesbians over time displace the public's view of homosexuality as a disease to be treated.

The developments combined to encourage uncounted numbers of gay men and lesbians to come out, on college campuses and elsewhere. One of those was Randy Shilts, later a prominent journalist and author, who announced his homosexuality to a sophomore anthropology class at a community college in Portland, Ore., in 1972. He later founded the Gay People's Alliance at the University of Oregon in Eugene. The group brought speakers to campus and sponsored gay-pride parades as well as the school's first gay-straight sock hop. [22]

By the 1980s, gay and lesbian students had achieved acceptance on many campuses. Gay events at the University of Wisconsin were "as commonplace as the homecoming football game," *Newsweek* reported in a long overview in 1982. [23] Many colleges had gay and lesbian awareness days, residential advisers were instructed on counseling gay and lesbian students, and openly gay men or lesbians won student-government elections at some schools. Georgetown University, a Jesuit school, was forced to recognize a gay-student group under the District of Columbia's law prohibiting discrimination on the basis of sexual orientation.

By 1987, a Yale alumna could write in *The Wall Street Journal* of the increased visibility of gay and lesbian students on her former campus. The article by freelance writer Julie Iovine appears to be the first in-print reference to the "one-in-four" statistic, which she attributed to "a notice" that one student said she received before registering as a freshman. [24] (Stephen Lee, a later Yale graduate and now part-time Internet journalist, says no evidence of such a notice has ever been found.) [25]

On many other campuses, however, gay and lesbian students were still mostly in the closet. A woman who graduated from Pennsylvania State University in 1987 recalled years later a "Coming Out Day" on campus that attracted just three people: her, her lesbian partner and a gay male student. At Penn State, she said, "everybody goes to football games, everybody gets involved in the university." But "being a Penn Stater was elusive for us." [26]

A decade later, the brutal slaying of a gay University of Wyoming student, Matthew Shepard, brought new attention to the problem of homophobia on and off college campuses. Shepard died on Oct. 12, 1998, from injuries received six days earlier after two men he met in a Laramie bar drove him outside of town, where they tied him to a fence, beat him senseless and left him hanging there. A fellow student, a girlfriend of one of the perpetrators, was charged as an accessory.

Shepard's death produced an outpouring of anti-violence protests and rallies at colleges and universities around the country, including on the Laramie campus. News coverage at the time also noted that many studies found significant percentages of gay students in high schools and colleges continued to experience verbal threats or harassment. [27]

Academic Pursuits

From scattered beginnings in the 1970s, lesbian and gay studies has now become a staple of course catalogs at a growing minority of colleges and universities throughout the United States. Some course titles broadly encompass "sexuality," but syllabuses make plain a major focus on homosexuality. Other courses may be provocatively labeled as "queer studies" — a field premised in part on sexual ambiguity and fluidity. Whatever the title, the courses have remained somewhat controversial outside academia but proved to be popular on campuses — increasingly among straight as well as gay and lesbian students. [28]

Homosexuality is an inevitable aspect of courses in many fields, most evidently literature and art. Oscar Wilde's plays and Walt Whitman's poems, for example — not to mention Plato's *Symposium* — cannot be fully taught without discussing their homoeroticism. But college courses with specific references to homosexuality in their titles appear to date only from the 1970s.

City College of San Francisco — a community college serving a city with a large gay population — is usually given credit for offering the first such course, "Survey of Gay and Lesbian Literature," in 1972. [29] Seventeen years later, the college inaugurated a lesbian and gay studies department and hired Jonathan D. Katz as the first tenured faculty member in the field. "When I arrived, the founding of the department was greeted with a kind of relief and a recognition that, if anything, this was overdue," Katz recalls.

The gradual spread of gay-themed courses stemmed in part from post-Stonewall comings-out by gay and lesbian faculty members. More than 300 met in New York in November 1973 for the first meeting of the Gay Academic Union. Some returned to their home campuses emboldened to disclose their sexuality to their students, colleagues and administrators. John Graves, a philosophy instructor at the Massachusetts Institute of Technology in Cambridge, recalled that his students were "absolutely rapt." He went on to teach MIT's first course in gay studies. [30]

The poet Louie Crew, then at Georgia State University and now at Rutgers University, said that coming out enhanced his students' understanding of gay literature because he stopped referring to gay writers as they, them and their "when I really mean we, us and our." [31]

By the mid-1980s, the field was "quickening," according to the University of Kansas' Younger, and gaining acceptance. In 1986, gay historian Martin Duberman at the City University of New York (CUNY) began efforts that eventually resulted in the establishment of the Center for Lesbian and Gay Studies (CLAGS) at CUNY's Graduate School. Yale University — which offered its first gay course in 1973 — was among several schools that spurned Duberman's proposal. But in 1987 it hosted the first U.S. academic conference on gay and lesbian studies, with 200 participants. The conference grew quickly. Five years later, the event was held at Rutgers, with more than 2,000 in attendance and 200 papers presented. [32]

As gay and lesbian studies programs grew in number and size, they drew criticisms from alumni, politicians and religious and conservative organizations. Younger, who helped found Duke University's program, said the school received many calls from alumni threatening to withhold contributions. "Most of the reaction has been from outside universities," Younger says. "And many times the universities have responded very vigorously and said that universities are areas where we need controversies."

News media reported on some of the controversies, generating more controversy. A conference at the State University of New York in New Paltz in November 1997 entitled "Revolting Behavior: The Challenges of Women's Sexual Freedom" included among 21 workshops a session on sadomasochism with graphic instruction on sexual techniques. Candace de Russy, a university trustee who attended the event, said the program amounted to "recruitment" for sadomasochism and "proselytization for lesbian, anal and public sex." [33] (A review by an outside committee found no evidence of recruitment.)

Halperin, who dresses in leather for his "How to Be Gay" course at the University of Michigan, faces similar accusations of recruitment. "The course is about how gay people acquire a group identity and the role that dissident cultural practices play in that process," he told the *Advocate*, a gay newsmagazine, in September 2003. "It has nothing to do with turning heterosexuals into homosexuals. If there is a recipe for that, I don't have it." [34]

Even before these controversies, Yale had shied away from accepting playwright Kramer's offer to fund two full professorships in gay and lesbian studies. [35] The explanation at the time was multifaceted: Yale had frozen faculty hiring; Kramer proposed specific conditions; the field was unproven. "It's also fair to say that Yale was weak-kneed, nervous, scared about lesbian and gay studies," Katz says today.

Kramer and university officials kept talking, however, and four years later reached agreement for the playwright to donate his literary and political papers to Yale's Beinecke Library while his brother Arthur, a money manager and also a Yale alumnus, would give $1 million to fund the Larry Kramer Initiative for Lesbian and Gay Studies. [36] Kramer, who is HIV-positive, said he was still considering leaving his estate — valued at several million dollars — to the university.

"This is Yale, so it puts the imprimatur of a major institution on lesbian and gay studies," William B. Rubenstein, a friend of Kramer's and a law professor at UCLA, told *The New York Times*. "It is recognition that the field is acknowledged to be important by people who are not gay." [37] ■

CURRENT SITUATION

Seeking Understanding

When Colby College President William Adams appointed a nine-member task force on gay, lesbian, bisexual and transgender issues in 2002, the group decided to rename itself the "Queer Task Force" and then issued a 71-page report that called for, among other things, a minor in queer studies. Adams warmly praised the report after receiving it in December 2002, but the new program and the new faculty position to go along with it are still on the academic drawing board. [38]

"That request was heard," explains Stephen Collins, director of communications at the Waterville, Maine, liberal arts college. "All requests for new programs and [positions] to staff new programs have to go into the request pool, and they would compete with all the other requests that are in."

"We never make it to the top," says Margaret McFadden, an associate professor in American studies and one of three faculty members who served on the task force. "Something else is always more important."

To critics, however, moves to create gay and lesbian studies programs are proceeding at an alarming rate. "I see no way to stop this without profound changes taking place outside universities," says Paul Gottfried, a professor of humanities at Elizabethtown College in Pennsylvania. Supporters, however, say the programs face daunting obstacles, including the often-glacial pace of academic decision-making. "There are a lot of burned out and disheartened faculty who are pushing this large boulder and not getting so terribly far," McFadden says.

City College of San Francisco remains the only school to have a full-fledged gay and lesbian studies department and to offer a bachelor's degree in the field, according to Professor Younger's online compilation. A few schools offer a minor in the field, while another two dozen or so give students other options to focus on lesbian and gay studies. Some offer "certificate" programs in LGBT or sexuality studies. Others recognize "concentrations" in lesbian and gay studies within a major — most commonly, women's and gender studies. Gay and lesbian material is also taught in courses without those terms in the title.

"It's pervasive," says Elizabeth Fox-Genovese, a traditionalist professor of history at Emory University in Atlanta.

Colby itself offers a concentration in queer studies within its women's, gender and sexuality studies major. Students have to take three courses from a list of 19 with what the college catalog calls "significant relevant content." McFadden says that a queer studies minor would give students more courses and a different perspective. "There's a distinction between a queer studies course and a sexuality course," she says.

At Yale, most of the courses in "The Pink Book" are taught by tenured or tenure-track professors from various departments outside the women's, gender and sexuality studies program. Silberman, one of the two lecturers hired specifically for the lesbian and gay studies program, offers a course in American Queer Studies as well as Sex, Race and Performance. The other lecturer, Megan Sinnott, is teaching Cross-Cultural Sexualities and Women's Sexuality.

Katz says professors in other departments are glad to have their courses cross-listed under lesbian and gay studies. He aims "to look at the panoply of courses" and try to make sure that the school is offering "a wide range" of lesbian and gay studies.

Yale students who have taken the courses acknowledge some of the problems cited by critics and skeptics. "My

Gay and Lesbian Studies Programs Nationwide

More than 150 colleges and universities offer courses in lesbian and gay studies. At least 28 recognize a minor or major in the field or offer a concentration, including City College of San Francisco, which boasts a Department of Gay, Lesbian and Bisexual Studies:

Allegheny College (Meadville, Pa.) — Minor in Lesbian and Gay Studies.

Barnard College, Columbia University (New York, N.Y.) — Concentration in Gender and Sexualities through Department of Women's Studies.

Bowdoin College (Brunswick, Maine) — Minor in Gay and Lesbian Studies.

Brown University (Providence, R.I.) — Concentration in Sexuality and Society.

City College of San Francisco — Concentration in Queer Studies through Department of Gay, Lesbian and Bisexual Studies.

Cornell University (Ithaca, N.Y.) — Undergraduate concentration and graduate minor in Lesbian, Bisexual and Gay Studies through College of Arts and Sciences.

Denison University (Granville, Ohio) — Concentration in Queer Studies.

Duke University (Durham, N.C.) — Undergraduate certificate program in the Study of Sexualities.

Hobart and William Smith Colleges (Geneva, N.Y.) — Major and Minor in Lesbian, Gay, and Bisexual Studies.

Macalester College (St. Paul, Minn.) — Major and minor in Women's and Gender Studies

Purchase College, State University of New York (Purchase) — Minor in Lesbian and Gay Studies through Lesbian and Gay Studies Program in School of Humanities.

Rice University (Houston) — Major in Study of Women and Gender.

San Francisco State University — Minor in Gay, Lesbian, and Bisexual Studies through College of Behavioral and Social Sciences.

Smith College (Northampton, Mass.) — Concentration in Queer Studies through Department of Women's Studies.

Temple University (Philadelphia) — Minor in Lesbian, Gay, Bisexual and Transgender Studies through Department of Women's Studies in College of Liberal Arts.

City University of New York — Home to Center for Lesbian and Gay Studies, a research center.

University of California (Berkeley) — Minor in Lesbian, Gay, Bisexual and Transgender Studies through Division of Undergraduate and Interdisciplinary Studies.

University of California (Los Angeles) — Minor in Lesbian, Gay, Bisexual and Transgender Studies.

University of California (Riverside) — Minor in Lesbian, Gay, Bisexual, Intersexual and Transgender Studies through Department of English.

University of Chicago — The Lesbian and Gay Studies Project coordinates graduate and undergraduate courses and organizes conferences and ongoing workshops.

University of Colorado (Boulder) — Certificate in Lesbian, Gay, Bisexual, Transgender Studies through College of Arts and Sciences.

University of Illinois (Chicago) — Undergraduate minor and graduate concentration in Women's and Gender Studies (including gay, lesbian, and transgender studies and queer theory) through College of Liberal Arts and Sciences.

University of Iowa (Iowa City) — Certificate in Sexuality Studies through Division of Interdisciplinary Programs.

University of Maryland (College Park) — Undergraduate certificate in Lesbian, Gay, Bisexual and Transgender Studies.

University of Southern California (Los Angeles) — Minor in Gender Studies through College of Letters, Arts and Sciences.

University of Wisconsin (Milwaukee) — Certificate Program in Gay and Lesbian Studies.

Western Washington University (Bellingham) — Minor in Lesbian, Gay, Bisexual Studies through Department of American Cultural Studies.

Yale University (New Haven, Conn.) — Undergraduate major and graduate concentration for qualification in Gay & Lesbian Studies within the Women's, Gender and Sexuality Studies program.

Source: Individual university Web sites.

fear is that it is preaching to the choir," says Nathan Kitada, a senior from the San Francisco area and one of the straight students in Silberman's current course. "A lot of the people who would benefit from taking the class aren't there."

Candice, a junior from Pomona, Calif., and one of the co-presidents of the people-of-color group Prism, agrees with critics that the program is not ideally suited to a future career. "I definitely don't think it's a business-making major," she says. She asks that her last name not be used.

Despite any reservations, students gathered for the LGBT Co-op's initial meeting are uniformly proud of Yale's program and certain of its value. "Understanding sexuality is pretty key since so much of our lives center around sex and sexuality," says Chad Sell, a senior from Wisconsin. "Understanding queer sexuality is part of understanding sexuality in general."

Looking for Comfort

When the online gay news service PlanetOut asked users to rank the most gay-friendly U.S. colleges and universities, many of the schools on the list came as no surprise.[39] Yale was there, along with its formerly all-women sister school Vassar. So were the all-women's schools of Smith and

Continued on p. 822

At Issue:

Should colleges offer lesbian and gay studies programs?

PROF. JOHN G. YOUNGER
ACTING CHAIRMAN, DEPARTMENT OF CLASSICS, PROFESSOR OF CLASSICS, HUMANITIES AND WESTERN CIVILIZATION, UNIVERSITY OF KANSAS

WRITTEN FOR *THE CQ RESEARCHER*, SEPTEMBER 2004

yes

Many universities offer Lesbian, Gay, Bisexual, Transgender and Questioning (LGBTQ) Studies: There are major programs at some 10 universities, minors at about 15 and "concentrations" at another 10. Scores of other institutions offer LGBTQ courses, support services, benefits and event programming.

What is LGBTQ Studies? Since most LGBTQ people come to their sexual orientation after childhood, their culture is constantly being reinvented. Most of us, therefore, do not learn our culture the way, say, African-Americans do; we come to it out of a diaspora. Likewise, LGBTQ history usually does not concern us but rather society's attitudes about us. Many of these attitudes take the form of religious, legal and economic sanctions and are at the forefront of hot-button political issues, such as "family values" and "sanctity of marriage." Such attitudes have histories that deserve scrutiny.

The biggest obstacle to establishing LGBTQ programs is the continuing prejudice against LGBTQ people — a prejudice the federal government does little to discourage. Although universities and colleges have been actively establishing minority programs, like women's studies or African-American studies, since the early 1970s, LGBTQ programs are only now gaining visibility.

Despite the government's silence about LGBTQ people, most universities include "sexual orientation" in their anti-discrimination clause for the convenience of the campus (after all, should discrimination against an Asian-American lesbian be tolerated if it's only against her lesbianism?).

Most recent LGBTQ programs involve a "concentration" (usually six courses thematically linked); these allow students to study issues of sexual orientation in disparate departments like English, sociology, anthropology, religion, psychology — even classics.

Once universities offering such programs were considered on the "cutting edge," large places like Duke, Yale, Cornell, Chicago, Berkeley and most recently Minnesota. But smaller schools are now jumping on the bandwagon (e.g., Humboldt State, Allegheny and Hobart and William Smith).

Universities should establish such programs — if there is student and faculty interest. At Kansas University, for example, there seems to be little such interest, but next door, at the University of Nebraska, Lincoln, students and faculty have just begun planning an LGBTQ program.

As to the academic legitimacy of such programs, however, there is no doubt: Studying sexuality is a powerful tool for understanding society in all its forms.

JOHN ZMIRAK
EDITOR,* CHOOSING THE RIGHT COLLEGE, *ISI BOOKS, WILMINGTON, DEL.

WRITTEN FOR *THE CQ RESEARCHER*, SEPTEMBER 2004

no

Let's think outside of the box for a moment. Instead of asking about lesbian and gay studies, imagine the question is whether universities should establish programs in Creation Science.

It seems to me an improper use of university resources to support such a department or interdisciplinary program. This not merely for the reasons usually cited, for instance, against black- or women's-studies programs: that creating such a department would prove needlessly divisive, or produce graduates with degrees in what is not currently an established discipline, and who are therefore handicapped in the job market.

However valid such objections might be from a pragmatic perspective, the real reason to oppose the creation of such a major is philosophical: As thinking people, we are compelled to question, if not dismiss outright, the very basis of the discipline, as founded not upon knowledge and the quest for truth, but on opinion.

By its very definition, such a discipline seems locked into a set of doctrinally regulated responses. This may be acceptable in the narrow context of a specifically religious school, which is at least candid about its catechetical mission. It seems totally inappropriate for a non-sectarian university.

The above argument about Creation Science is in every particular applicable to the so-called discipline of "Gay Studies." Like creationism, Gay Studies is predicated upon a long list of unexamined, unquestioned premises, which dictate in advance the outcome of debates that ought rather to be open, subject both to input from the heritage of the past and the democratic politics of the present.

While creationism is rejected by the overwhelming verdict of contemporary science, the unexamined assumption of Gay Studies — that homosexual activity is morally equivalent to heterosexual — conflicts with the orthodox teachings of the three major world religions: Judaism, Christianity and Islam, and the beliefs of most Americans. Secular elites may disagree with these beliefs; but they do not have a scientific basis for disproving them.

Evolution is empirically demonstrable as the most probable hypothesis for explaining the origins of life. Acceptance of homosexuality is not similarly provable. It may be held with equal fervor, but it is not an empirically arguable proposition; rather, it's a plank in a liberal social platform, and one that should remain open to dispute.

Continued from p. 820

Mt. Holyoke in Massachusetts, both long known as lesbian-friendly. There were two schools from the gay mecca of San Francisco and six others from elsewhere in California.

Some of the top-ranked schools, however, may seem less likely to be hospitable to gay and lesbian students, including big state schools in states like Arizona, Indiana, Iowa and Kentucky. But perhaps no school on the list seems more improbable than tiny Hendrix College in Conway, Ark., about 30 miles north of Little Rock.

"This college is amazingly liberal for being such a small private school with a religious affiliation (Methodist) in the Bible Belt region," writes Jeremy, apparently a current student. "Gay people are not only 'tolerated' here, but they are viewed as an integral part of the Hendrix community."

Jay Barth, an alumnus and now an openly gay associate professor of politics, attributes the school's favorable climate for gays to a long tradition of openness along with the absence of a Greek fraternity and sorority system. "Gay and straight students live together, they hang out together," he says. "There's not that demarcation that is arguably as troubling in some ways as the closetedness of the past."

Students at several of the other schools also attest on PlanetOut's posting to the easy mixing of gays and straights on their campuses. Bard College in Annandale-on-Hudson, N.Y. has an annual "Drag Race" described as one of the top campus parties in the country. "Everyone cross-dresses, and the whole school attends," K.C. writes. An anonymous writer — seemingly an alumnus — brags that Oberlin University's "Drag Ball" is "the most fabulicious event at a college EVER."

Gay solidarity finds expression on many of the campuses in celebrations for Pride Week or National Coming Out Day. Many dorms or offices display rainbow flags or pink triangle "Safe Zone" stickers. Several of the online posts point to GLBT resource centers as helpful.

However, anti-gay organizations say the centers are hurting, not helping, students. "If they truly cared about their gay and lesbian students, they'd point them toward counseling that would help them overcome the sexual detour they've taken," says Knight of Concerned Women for America. "It's all geared toward seduction of college kids into homosexuality," he adds. "Nobody's fated to be homosexual."

Martin at the University of Oregon dismisses the accusation of recruitment. "I am 100 percent sure that even if we did not have GLBT centers, we would have queer students on campus," says Martin. "We would have gay students, and they would suffer greatly if they did not have that support."

Homophobic incidents were reported at a few of the schools posted on PlanetOut. Derek, the president of Pride Student Union at the University of Florida in Gainesville, reported that a fraternity member "was tied to a tree and the word 'fag' written across his exposed chest" — ostensibly as a joke. The school then instituted a mandatory sensitivity program for fraternities and sororities. Tom, a student at Grinnell College in Iowa, said there had been two homophobic incidents at the school. "In both cases, the entire campus community has rallied around those targeted," he wrote.

Yale students also tell a visitor of a few anti-gay incidents. Justin Ross, a sophomore from Victoria, British Columbia, and one of the co-chairs of the GLBT Co-op, recalls an instance of minor harassment at a fraternity party during his first year. On another occasion, fellow students defaced a sidewalk chalking that was announcing a GLBT event.

Most gay and lesbian students, however, appear to have few complaints. "You're able to do what you want, within your own sphere," says Danny Gusman, a senior from Lancaster, Calif. A straight editor at the *Yale Daily News* agrees. "It's very tolerant," says City Editor Adam Click. "For people of that persuasion, it's about as good as it can be. There's a very high comfort level." ■

OUTLOOK

Vanishing Identities?

The word "homosexual" is defined in the brochure "Queer Life at Yale" as "a term dating from the steam engine. Came to be used to pathologize and segregate queer people. Sometimes reclaimed ironically."

For the heterosexual majority, the thought may seem strange, but scholars in gay and lesbian studies say that the current dichotomy between gay and straight is a recent invention or — in their phraseology — social construction. The word "homosexual" itself dates only from the late 19th century. And they say attitudes toward same-sex relationships have been more varied and fluid through history than was commonly believed before the advent of their field.

"The tendency in the academy is to see lesbian and gay identity as historically specific and in no way essential," says Yale's Katz. On that basis, he says, there is "a powerful paradox" between the academic and political movements.

"Lesbian and gay studies is pleading the imminent demise of the lesbian and gay category as an identity, which is the opposite of the political movement," he says. His own gay identity, Katz says, "is of recent vintage and a fairly short half-life." In time, he says, the importance of gay or lesbian identity will diminish — just as the importance of Jewish identity decreased in U.S. social and political life through the 20th century.

Anti-gay organizations also hope for the demise of gay and lesbian identity, but through a different route. They argue strongly that people can overcome same-sex inclinations and that gay-studies programs and GLBT resource centers serve only to mislead students whom Knight of Concerned Women for America describes as "seriously confused."

"Colleges ought to be honest and acknowledge that there's no scientific evidence that you're born gay and that they should stop aiding and abetting the effort to entice people into homosexual behavior and keep them there," Knight says.

For his part, Sprigg at the Family Research Council says — like Katz — that offering gay and lesbian studies "in some ways contradicts the political agenda" of the gay-rights movement, which views homosexuality as innate. "In these studies programs, we have courses on how to be gay, which suggest all along that homosexuality is a social construct. The actual content of these programs undermines the arguments that are made in the public square."

For the moment, however, gay and lesbian self-identification is growing among students on U.S. college campuses. Even universities that teach religious doctrines opposed to homosexuality are finding that they must deal with the real-life problems and real-life interests. At Notre Dame, for example, a standing committee on gay and lesbian students' needs sponsors speakers on gay subjects and helps observe national coming out day. DiversityND, an unrecognized student group, sponsored a queer film festival on campus in February 2004.

"We're in a situation of what I would call tension," says Sister M. L. Gude, the committee's head. The university upholds Catholic teaching against "homogenital acts," she says. "On the other hand, gay and lesbian Catholics are people, and the law of love supersedes all. Whatever you think of people's activities, that doesn't mean you shun people."

At Baptist-affiliated Baylor, students with same-sex inclinations are urged to seek ministerial counseling. "No one ever went to the ministries," says Darrin Adams, a recent graduate and gay activist on campus. "A lot of the people were very distrustful of the school. They felt that if they went to counseling and didn't change, they would get kicked out."

The advancing trend at the vast majority of secular colleges and universities is toward greater acceptance of and support for gay and lesbian students. But GLBT support centers have "a lot more to do," says Martin at the University of Oregon.

In her report, Pennsylvania State University's Rankin concludes with a laundry list of recommended actions for colleges and universities to improve the climate for gay and lesbian students. For students, colleges should include sexual orientation and gender-identity issues in orientation, address GLBT issues within residence life and address homophobia within fraternities, sororities and intercollegiate athletic teams. For administrators, faculty and staff, universities are urged to include sexual orientation in non-discrimination policies and to extend employee spousal benefits to domestic partners.

"Cultural change takes longer than two or three years," Rankin says. "I see us having a great discourse, and my hope is that in five to 10 years you won't need people doing the kind of work that I do." ■

Notes

[1] American Association of Collegiate Registrars and Admissions Officials, "Gay, Lesbian, Bisexual and Transgender Survey," April 2004 (www.aacrao.org).

[2] Susan R. Rankin, "Campus Climate for Gay, Lesbian, Bisexual, and Transgender People: A National Perspective," The Policy Institute of the National Gay and Lesbian Task Force, April 2003.

[3] For background, see Kenneth Jost, "Gay Marriage," *The CQ Researcher*, Sept. 5, 2003, pp. 721-748.

[4] See George Archibald, " 'How to Be Gay' Course Draws Fire at Michigan," *The Washington Times*, Aug. 18, 2003, p. A1.

[5] See Claire Heininger, "Despite Rocky Beginnings, Groups Continue to Support Homosexual Students at Notre Dame," *The Observer*, March 18, 2004. *The Observer* is Notre Dame's independent, student-edited newspaper. For more coverage, see the various articles published under the title " 'The Love That Dare Not Speak Its Name,' " in *Notre Dame Magazine*, summer 2004.

[6] For coverage, see these stories by Seanna Adcox in *The* (Charleston, S.C.) *Post and Courier*: "C of C Weighs Minor in Gay, Lesbian Studies," Sept. 4, 2003, p. 1B; "Talk of C of C Gay, Lesbian Minor Squelched," Sept. 12, 2003; "College of Charleston Faculty Senate Resolution Takes Aim at Intolerance," Oct. 8, 2003, p. 1B.

[7] For an overview of the dispute, see Alice Gomstyn, "Military Recruiting Goes to Court," *The Chronicle of Higher Education*, Dec. 12, 2003, p. 17. For background on gays in the military, see Kenneth Jost, "Gay Rights Update," *The CQ Researcher*, April 14, 2000, pp. 305-328.

[8] The case is *Burt v. Rumsfeld*, filed Oct. 16, 2003, in U.S. District Court for Connecticut. The furthest advanced case is *Forum for Academic and Individual Rights (FAIR) v. Rumsfeld*, filed on Sept. 19, 2003, in U.S. District Court for New Jersey and argued on June

About the Author

Associate Editor **Kenneth Jost** graduated from Harvard College and Georgetown University Law Center, where he is an adjunct professor. He is the author of *The Supreme Court Yearbook* and editor of *The Supreme Court from A to Z* (both *CQ Press*). He was a member of *The CQ Researcher* team that won the 2002 American Bar Association Silver Gavel Award.

30, 2004, before the Third U.S. Circuit Court of Appeals. A separate case, *Burbank v. Rumsfeld*, was filed in U.S. District Court for the Eastern District of Pennsylvania, on Oct. 1, 2003, by University of Pennsylvania Law School professors.

9 See Jonathan Ned Katz (ed.), *Gay American History: Lesbians & Gay Men in the U.S.A.* (rev. ed.), 1992, pp. 456-460.

10 Jonathan Ned Katz, "Our Struggle for a History of Sexualities," lecture, Yale University, April 2, 2003, summarized in Yale news release, March 31, 2003 (www.yale.edu/opa/newsr/03-03-31-05.all.html). Bloss is actually buried in Syracuse; Katz says no one knows why.

11 Katz, *Gay American History*, *op. cit.*, pp. 58-60 (Russell diary), 74-76 (Young-Frost episode).

12 John Loughery, *The Other Side of Silence: Men's Lives and Gay Identities: A Twentieth-Century History* (1998), pp. 76-78, 171-173.

13 Alfred C. Kinsey, Wardell B. Pomeroy, and Clyde E. Martin, *Sexual Behavior in the American Male* (1948), pp. 610-667. Summary taken from Loughery, *op. cit.*, pp. 191-196.

14 Alfred C. Kinsey, Wardell B. Pomeroy, Clyde E. Martin, and Paul H. Gerhard, *Sexual Behavior in the Human Female* (1953), pp. 446-489.

15 Benjamin Glover, "Observations on Homosexuality Among University Students," in *Journal of Nervous and Medical Diseases* (1951), cited in Loughery, *op. cit.*, p. 172.

16 *Ibid.*, pp. 173 (Texas), pp. 244-248 (Florida).

17 See John D'Emilio, "The Campus Environment for Gay and Lesbian Life," *Academe*, Vol. 76, no. 1 (January-February 1990), pp. 16-19.

18 Katz, *Gay American History*, *op. cit.*, pp. 406-414.

19 Hay died in 2002; Martin and Lyon are still living in San Francisco and were granted the city's first same-sex marriage license on Feb. 12, 2004 — later nullified by the California Supreme Court.

20 See Wayne R. Dynes, "Stephen Donaldson (Robert A. Martin), 1946-1996," in Vern L. Bullough (ed.), *Before Stonewall: Activists for Gay and Lesbian Rights in Historical Context* (2002), pp. 268-269. The *Times'* story, "Columbia Charters Homosexual Group," by Murray Schumach, appeared on May 3, 1967. A plaque in Donaldson's memory now hangs in Columbia's "Queer Lounge."

21 See Stanford Pride, "Pridestones," www.stanfordalumni.org/stanfordclub/pride/pridestones.htm (visited September 2004). As noted, an earlier group, the Stanford Sexual Rights Forum, founded in 1965, addressed issues concerning heterosexual and homosexual behavior. It lasted only six months.

22 Marcus, *op. cit.*, pp. 165-167. Shilts went on to become a reporter at *The San Francisco Chronicle* and wrote books on AIDS and gays in the military. He died of AIDS in 1994.

23 Gerald C. Lubenow with others, "Gays and Lesbians on Campus," *Newsweek*, April 5, 1982, p. 75. Some other material drawn from the article.

24 Julie V. Iovine, "'Lipsticks and Lords': Yale's New Look," *The Wall Street Journal*, Aug. 4, 1987, Leisure & Arts section, p. 1.

25 Stephen Lee, "Yale: "One in Four, Maybe More," *Newsaic* (www.newsaic.com), last updated Aug. 25, 2001, visited September 2004.

26 Quoted in Kim Strosnider, "Gay and Lesbian Alumni Groups Seek Bigger Roles at Their Alma Maters," *The Chronicle of Higher Education*, Sept. 5, 1997, p. A59.

27 James Brooke, "Homophobia Often Found in Schools, Data Show," *The New York Times*, Oct. 14, 1998, p. A19.

28 Some background drawn from John G. Younger, "Academic Developments, Opportunities, and Resources for Queer Studies," in Neil Schlager, ed., *St. James Press: Gay & Lesbian Almanac* (1998), pp. 205-230. For a recent journalistic overview, see Dan Kening, "Gay Studies Flourish in Academia as Topic Gains Urgency," *The Chicago Tribune*, March 7, 2004, "Education Today," p. 1.

29 See M. C. Cage, "A Course on Homosexuality," *The Chronicle of Higher Education*, Dec. 14, 1994, pp. A19-20, cited in Younger, *op. cit.*

30 See Loughery, *op. cit.*, pp. 344-345.

31 Louie Crew, "The Gay Academic Unmasks," *The Chronicle of Higher Education*, Feb. 20, 1974, p. 20. Crew, a poet, is also known as Quean Lutibelle.

32 See Ethan Bronner, "Study of Sex Experiencing 2d Revolution," *The New York Times*, Dec. 8, 1997, sec. 1, p. 1.

33 See Candace de Russy, " 'Revolting Behavior': The Irresponsible Exercise of Academic Freedom," *The Chronicle of Higher Education*, March 6, 1998, p. B9. For a reply, see letters to the editor in the same publication by two professors at the school: Susan Lehrer and William Rhoads (March 27, 1998, p. B10).

34 Jay Blotcher, "Recipe for Recruiting?" *The Advocate*, Sept. 30, 2003.

35 For contemporaneous coverage, see Karen W. Arenson, "Playwright Is Denied a Final Act," *The New York Times*, July 9, 1997, p. B1.

36 Karen W. Arenson, "Gay Writer and Yale Finally Agree on Donation," *The New York Times*, April 2, 2001, p. B6.

37 *Ibid.*

38 For coverage, see Stephen Collins, "Harassment, Invisibility Concerns for Queer Task Force," *colbymagazine*, spring 2003 (www.colby.edu/colby.mag/issues/spr03/stu/4qtf.shtml); "Q&A" (interview with Margaret McFadden), *colbymagazine*, spring 2004 (www.colby.edu/colby.mag/issues/current/articles.php?issueid=16&articleid=140&dept=fromthehill).

39 "The Queer Fifty," PlanetOut (www.planetout.com/people/features/2001/01/collegges) (visited September 2004).

FOR MORE INFORMATION

Concerned Women for America, 1015 15th St., N.W., Suite 1100, Washington, DC 20005; (202) 488-7000; www.cwfa.org. Conservative religious group opposed to homosexuality.

Family Research Council, 801 G St., N.W., Washington, DC 20001; (202) 393-2100; www.frc.org. Conservative group opposed to homosexuality.

Larry Kramer Initiative for Lesbian and Gay Studies at Yale University, 100 Wall St., 311 William L. Harkness Hall, P.O. Box 208334, New Haven, Ct. 06520-8334; (203) 432-7737; www.yale.edu/lesbiangay/homepage.html. Sponsors lectures, conferences and symposia, special events and community-building activities.

National Consortium of Directors of Lesbian Gay Bisexual and Transgender Resources in Higher Education; www.lgbtcampus.org. Organization of campus LGBT services directors.

The Task Force (formerly, National Gay and Lesbian Task Force), 1325 Massachusetts Ave., N.W., Suite 600, Washington, DC 20005; (202) 393-5177; www.thetaskforce.org. National civil rights and advocacy organization for GLBT persons.

Bibliography

Selected Sources

Books

Cahn, Susan K., *Coming On Strong: Gender and Sexuality in Twentieth-Century Women's Sport*, Free Press, 1994.
An overview by an associate professor of history at the State University of New York, Buffalo, describes women's sports as a haven for lesbians as long as they obscure their sexual orientation: "Play it, don't say it."

Katz, Jonathan Ned (ed.), *Gay American History: Lesbians and Gay Men in the U.S.A.* (rev. ed.), Meridian, 1992.
A documentary history by an independent scholar illuminates the history of gay men and lesbians in the United States from Colonial times to the present day.

Loughery, John, *The Other Side of Silence: Men's Lives and Gay Identities: A Twentieth-Century History*, Henry Holt, 1998.
A broad, historical account by a nonfiction author describes the campus climate for gays and lesbians through the 20th century and the role of college organizations in the gay-liberation movement.

Marcus, Eric, *Making Gay History: The Half-Century Fight for Lesbian and Gay Equal Rights*, Perennial, 2002.
Marcus' interviews with more than 60 people involved in gay and lesbian advocacy since 1950 include several accounts of experiences in college. His other books include *Breaking the Surface*, a biography of the gay Olympic diver Greg Louganis.

Articles

Branch, Mark Alden, "Back in the Fold," *Yale Alumni Magazine*, April 2003.
The article details how talks between Yale University and gay playwright and Yale alumnus Larry Kramer led to his $1 million donation for a gay-studies program.

Bull, Chris, "The College Sports Closet," *The Advocate*, March 5, 2002.
The writer provides an overview of homophobia's "stranglehold" on college athletics and the NCAA's initial steps to deal with the issue.

Cohen, Ed, "Resolving Family Differences," *Notre Dame Magazine*, summer 2004.
Notre Dame's refusal to add sexual orientation to its nondiscrimination policy or to recognize gay/lesbian student organizations is examined at length. Other articles in the issue included first-person accounts by a gay student and the father of a gay student, examination of Roman Catholic doctrine on homosexuality, and an interview with the chair of the university's Standing Committee for Gay and Lesbian Student Needs.

English, Antonya, "Out Isn't In," *The St. Petersburg Times*, July 18, 2004, p. 1C.
The article depicts the climate for gay and lesbian athletes, collegiate or professional, as "mostly hostile."

Gomstyn, Alice, "Military Recruiting Goes to Court," *The Chronicle of Higher Education*, Dec. 12, 2003, p. 17.
The author provides a thorough overview of the dispute between law schools and the Pentagon over a federal law penalizing schools that restrict use of school facilities and services by military recruiters because of objections to the military's "don't ask, don't tell" policy against gays and lesbians.

Kening, Dan, "Gay Studies Flourish in Academia as Topic Gains Urgency," *The Chicago Tribune*, March 7, 2004, "Education Today," p. 1.
The writer examines the current status of lesbian and gay studies at U.S. colleges and universities.

McLemee, Scott, "A Queer Notion of History," *The Chronicle of Higher Education*, Sept. 12, 2003, p. 14.
The growth of gay history scholarship is detailed.

Reports and Studies

Rankin, Susan R., "Campus Climate for Gay, Lesbian, Bisexual, and Transgender People: A National Perspective," National Gay and Lesbian Task Force, fall 2003.
Sexual-minority students on college campuses continue to encounter distinctive challenges because of their sexual orientation or gender identity, according to this 64-page report written by a senior planning analyst at Pennsylvania State University for the National Gay and Lesbian Task Force.

Younger, John G., "Education and Scholarship: Academic Developments, Opportunities, and Resources for Queer Studies," in Neil Schlager, ed., *St. James Press: Gay & Lesbian Almanac*, St. James Press, 1998, pp. 205-30.
A professor of classics at the University of Kansas and a leading advocate of the field takes a comprehensive overview of the status of lesbian and gay studies programs. Includes short first-person accounts by seven prominent scholars in the field.

The Next Step:

Additional Articles from Current Periodicals

Campus Climate

Buchanan, Joy, "Pepperdine Rejects Club for Campus Gays," *Los Angeles Times*, Feb. 20, 2004, p. B4.
Pepperdine University denied recognition for a proposed club called "Students Against Homophobia," saying it would conflict with the California school's Christian mission.

Cavanagh, Sean, "Colleges Increasingly Look to Attract Gay, Lesbian Applicants," *Education Week*, June 19, 2002, p. 12.
Admissions officials seek out homosexual students for reasons similar to those driving the recruitment of racial and ethnic minorities: to increase campus diversity.

DeQuine, Jeanne, "Out of the Closet and On to Fraternity Row," *Time*, March 17, 2003, p. 8.
Approximately 25 gay fraternities now exist around the country — with half emerging in the conservative Greek system during the past five years.

Gold, Scott, "Student Stand on Gay Unions Roils Baylor," *Los Angeles Times*, March 3, 2004, p. A26.
The president of Baptist-oriented Baylor University condemned an editorial in the student newspaper supporting gay marriage and said he would exert more control over the paper's content.

Grossman, Ron, "At Notre Dame, Gay Film Fest a First," *Chicago Tribune*, Feb. 11, 2004, p. 1.
Only a year after the *Princeton Review* ranked Notre Dame the university most unfriendly to homosexuals comes the debut of a school-sponsored "Queer Film Festival."

Marklein, Mary Beth, "Colleges Grow Gay-Friendlier," *USA Today*, June 22, 2004, p. 1D.
A small, but increasingly visible, group of universities is targeting potential gay and lesbian students through college fairs, online recruitment and mentor programs.

May, Meredith, "National Gay Support Group Offers College Scholarships," *San Francisco Chronicle*, Jan. 23, 2004, p. E2.
Parents, Families and Friends of Lesbians and Gays is offering scholarships of up to $2,500 for high-school seniors who have been active in the gay community.

Schevit, Tanya, " 'Out' is in on Campus," *The San Francisco Chronicle*, Nov. 23, 2002, p. A15.
Universities have begun to tailor their recruiting materials to target a gay population that is coming out younger and looking for supportive college environments.

Seymour, Craig, "Gays Feel Left Out of Morehouse Brotherhood," *Atlanta Journal-Constitution*, Dec. 29, 2002, p. 1A.
The 3,000 black men attending Morehouse College are united by honor and achievement but are often divided by background and, as shown by a brutal attack, sexual orientation.

Toy, Vivian S., "Hofstra Breaks New Ground With Gay Law Fellowship," *The New York Times*, Sept. 28, 2003, Section 14LI, p. 1.
Each year Hofstra University's law school awards three three-year fellowships that pay 70 percent of tuition in return for a commitment to study legal issues important to gays and lesbians.

Gay America

Cloud, John, "The New Face of Gay Power," *Time*, Oct. 13, 2003, p. 52.
Five years after gay student Matthew Shepard's murder, the state of Wyoming has learned a harsh lesson and is now living with a slowly growing homosexual culture.

Ricci, James, and Patricia Ward Biederman, "Acceptance of Gays on Rise, Polls Show," *Los Angeles Times*, March 30, 2004, p. B1.
While the American public might not be ready for same-sex marriages, a study shows increasing support for other gay issues.

Gay Athletes

Jacobson, Jennifer, "Facing Derision in a Macho Culture, Many Gay Athletes In," *The Chronicle of Higher Education*, Nov. 1, 2002, p. 36.
At many colleges, the athletics department is the most homophobic place on campus, but gay athletes make it through their sports programs, albeit uncomfortably.

Lopez, Kathryn, "Leagues of Their Own: The Delicate Question of Lesbians and Softball," *National Review*, Oct. 14, 2002.
The lesbian softball-player stereotype often rings true at colleges, but few coaches or university officials will discuss how the sport is about more than friendly competition.

Orth, Maureen, "Out of the Locker Room, and the Closet," *The New York Times*, Nov. 30, 2003, Section 9, p. 1.
Former Washington Redskins football player Roy Simmons reveals he is HIV-positive and discusses the psychological effects of being a homosexual and a professional athlete.

Sandoval, Greg, "Going Behind the Back," *The Washington Post*, Jan. 24, 2003, p. D1.
As the popularity of female sports has risen, so have recruiters' attempts to dissuade athletes from attending rival schools — by implying the female coach at the other school is a lesbian.

Gay Studies

Kening, Dan, "Gay Studies Flourish in Academia as Topic Gains Urgency," *Chicago Tribune*, March 7, 2004, p. 1.
Gay and lesbian studies, including history, sexuality and contributions to literature and art, flourish at many major universities.

McLemee, Scott, "A Queer Notion of History," *The Chronicle of Higher Education*, Sept. 12, 2003, p. 14.
The recently opened Tulsa Center for Gay and Lesbian History is home to a field of study growing at a remarkable rate but not always taken seriously by academia.

Wilson, Robin, " 'Dr. Sex'," *The Chronicle of Higher Education*, June 20, 2003, p. 8.
Human-sexuality expert and psychology Professor J. Michael Bailey created controversy with his book and academic studies, which some say stereotype gay men and transsexuals.

Gay Teenagers

Gewertz, Catherine, "Expansion of N.Y.C. School Ignites Debate Over Gay Students' Needs," *Education Week*, Sept. 3, 2003, p. 7.
Controversy surrounds a new gay city high school, which some criticize as advancing a homosexual agenda and others see as setting a precedent for segregation.

Reid, Karla, "School Pride," *Education Week*, Oct. 15, 2003, p. 31.
Insults about homosexuality have long been fixtures at high schools, but in recent years, more students are striving to redefine the culture by forming "gay-straight alliances."

Richard, Alan, "Alternative Proms Gain in Popularity," *Education Week*, May 19, 2004, p. 1.
Alternative proms for students based on race, religion and sexual orientation are causing observers to consider the tension between integration and separation.

Scelfo, Julie, "Out at the Prom," *Newsweek*, June 9, 2003.
As kids are coming out at younger ages — an average of age 16 for males and 17 for females, according to one study — the prom has become a rite of passage for both gay and straight teens.

Tuller, David, "A New Dimension in Snapshot of Gay Teenager," *The New York Times*, Dec. 24, 2002, p. F7.
Conflicting images of gay teens have researchers and academics in disagreement about the psychological health of the typical homosexual teenager and the kind of outreach programs that still are needed.

Military Issues

Schodolski, Vincent, "Military Loses Able Recruits With Gay Rule," *Chicago Tribune*, Jan. 23, 2003, p. 8.
Despite an increased need for soldiers with foreign language knowledge, many gay men studying at the armed forces' language school have been discharged for violating the military's homosexuality policy.

Stern, Seth, "Law Schools Revolt Over Pentagon Recruitment on Campus," *The Christian Science Monitor*, Nov. 6, 2003, p. 2.
Suits filed by law schools, professors and students charge the Pentagon with forcing them to violate anti-discrimination rules by demanding access to campuses.

Trounson, Rebecca, "Law Schools Bow to Pentagon on Recruiters," *Los Angeles Times*, Oct. 12, 2002, p. B1.
Law schools at several universities are being forced to give military recruiters greater access to students or risk the loss of federal funds.

Citing *The CQ Researcher*

Sample formats for citing these reports in a bibliography include the ones listed below. Preferred styles and formats vary, so please check with your instructor or professor.

MLA Style

Jost, Kenneth. "Rethinking the Death Penalty." The CQ Researcher 16 Nov. 2001: 945-68.

APA Style

Jost, K. (2001, November 16). Rethinking the death penalty. *The CQ Researcher, 11*, 945-968.

Chicago Style

Jost, Kenneth. "Rethinking the Death Penalty." *CQ Researcher*, November 16, 2001, 945-968.

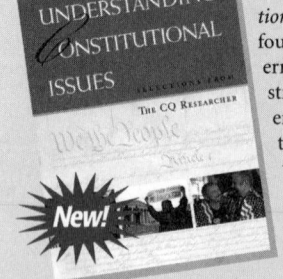

CQ Researcher

Published by CQ Press, a division of Congressional Quarterly Inc.

thecqresearcher.com

Migrant Farmworkers

Is government doing enough to protect them?

Much as they did 100 years ago, farmworkers today still face "back-breaking jobs with impossibly long hours for skinflint wages in filthy conditions," as a newspaper editorial described it. Wages have not kept pace with inflation, and in some labor camps, living conditions range from the deplorable to the unconscionable. Some farm bosses even have been convicted in recent years of enslaving workers, most of whom are illegal aliens afraid to speak out for fear of deportation. Human-rights advocates say the only way to improve conditions is to give undocumented workers legal residency. But opponents say that would reward illegals for breaking U.S. immigration laws and ultimately spark more illegal immigration. Meanwhile, many state and federal laws protecting workers go unenforced, and growers say Americans increasingly do not want to do farm work.

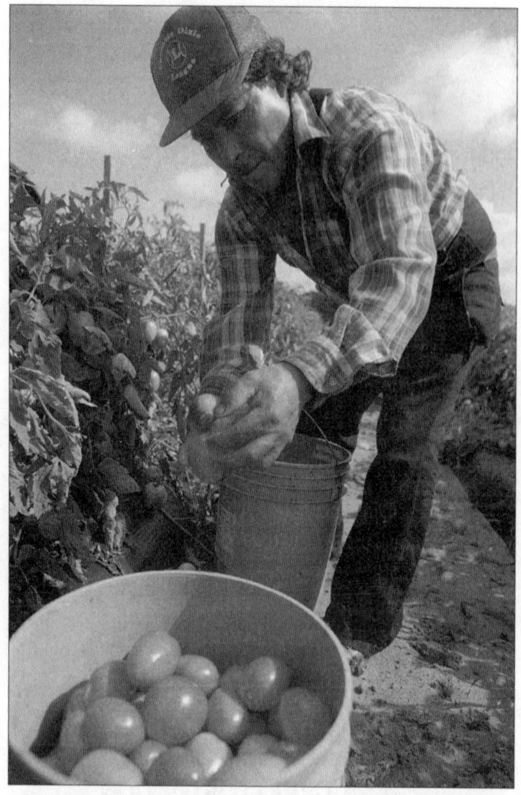

Gumaro Cortes, an undocumented farmworker from Mexico, picks tomatoes in Mississippi.

INSIDE THIS REPORT

The CQ Researcher • Oct. 8, 2004 • www.thecqresearcher.com
Volume 14, Number 35 • Pages 829-852

CQ PRESS

RECIPIENT OF SOCIETY OF PROFESSIONAL JOURNALISTS AWARD FOR EXCELLENCE ◆ AMERICAN BAR ASSOCIATION SILVER GAVEL AWARD

THE ISSUES

BACKGROUND

CURRENT SITUATION

OUTLOOK

SIDEBARS AND GRAPHICS

FOR FURTHER RESEARCH

Cover: Gumaro Cortes, an undocumented farmworker from Mexico, picks tomatoes in Mississippi. Most U.S. farmworkers are Mexican. (AP Photo/The Mississippi Press, James Edward Bates)

THE CQ Researcher

Oct. 8, 2004
Volume 14, Number 35

MANAGING EDITOR: Thomas J. Colin
ASSISTANT MANAGING EDITOR: Kathy Koch
ASSOCIATE EDITOR: Kenneth Jost
STAFF WRITERS: Mary H. Cooper, William Triplett
CONTRIBUTING WRITERS: Sarah Glazer, David Hatch, David Hosansky, Patrick Marshall, Tom Price, Jane Tanner
DESIGN/PRODUCTION EDITOR: Olu B. Davis
ASSISTANT EDITOR: Kate Templin

CQ PRESS

A Division of Congressional Quarterly Inc.

SENIOR VICE PRESIDENT/GENERAL MANAGER: John A. Jenkins
DIRECTOR, LIBRARY PUBLISHING: Kathryn C. Suárez
DIRECTOR, EDITORIAL OPERATIONS: Ann Davies

CONGRESSIONAL QUARTERLY INC.
CHAIRMAN: Paul C. Tash
VICE CHAIRMAN: Andrew P. Corty
PRESIDENT AND PUBLISHER: Robert W. Merry

The CQ Researcher (ISSN 1056-2036) is printed on acid-free paper. Published weekly, except Jan. 2, April 9, July 2, July 9, Aug. 6, Aug. 13, Nov. 26 and Dec. 31, by CQ Press, a division of Congressional Quarterly Inc. Annual subscription rates for institutions start at $625. For pricing, call 1-800-834-9020, ext. 1906. To purchase a *CQ Researcher* report in print or electronic format (PDF), visit www.cqpress.com or call 866-427-7737. A single report is $10. Bulk purchase discounts and electronic-rights licensing are also available. Periodicals postage paid at Washington, D.C., and additional mailing offices. POSTMASTER: Send address changes to *The CQ Researcher*, 1255 22nd St., N.W., Suite 400, Washington, D.C. 20037.

Migrant Farmworkers

By William Triplett

The Issues

In July 2003, after picking grapes for 10 hours in 100-degree heat in California's San Joaquin Valley, Asuncion Valdivia collapsed. Coworkers poured water on the 53-year-old farmworker, and he regained consciousness.

But the crew boss didn't summon an ambulance, even though Valdivia couldn't walk without help. Instead, the boss told Valdivia's son to take his father home. Minutes after being put in a car, however, Valdivia started foaming at the mouth and died. [1]

Migrant farmworkers harvest lettuce in Belle Glade, Fla. Most U.S. farmworkers are undocumented Mexicans, who often endure substandard living conditions, low pay, abusive crew bosses and over-exposure to dangerous pesticides. Human-rights advocates say granting amnesty to illegal workers would improve working conditions. Critics say it would just encourage more illegal border crossings.

The Palm Beach Post/Gary Coronado

Heatstroke deaths are not uncommon among the nation's estimated 1.7 million farmworkers. [2] Nor are wretched living conditions or abusive crew bosses.

Crew bosses — independent contractors who hire migrants for temporary work on farms — have been notorious for years in some parts of Florida and other states for treating workers, especially those who are undocumented, like slaves. They cheat them out of their meager wages and routinely intimidate and sometimes even assault them.

In Florida more than 200 bosses and their assistants have been barred from the industry — about 40 percent of the total bosses barred nationwide. Twelve Florida contractors, smugglers and their enforcers have been imprisoned in recent years for criminal abuse of farmworkers, including smuggling them across the Mexican border in often deadly conditions and enslaving them until they pay off exorbitant "transportation costs." The Justice Department has prosecuted five such cases since 1996, the most recent in 2003. But no grower has ever been prosecuted. [3]

"I thought I was going to die there," Antonio Martinez, a farm laborer, said of the Florida fields where he once worked essentially as a slave. "And I knew if I escaped, [the contractor] would beat me. But when I escaped, I felt liberated." [4]

Besides coping with abusive crew bosses, farmworkers must endure substandard living conditions. For example, migrants working in the citrus groves near Lake Placid, Fla., northwest of Lake Okeechobee in South-Central Florida, were discovered last year living in crowded shacks with no running water or bathroom facilities. In one of the ramshackle buildings, snakes were plainly visible through holes in the floor. [5]

Some farmworkers are treated fairly by growers and labor contractors and have gained some protections and improvements in their living conditions, particularly those whose employers do not use labor contractors. To a large extent, the improvements were brought about by the United Farm Workers (UFW) union, founded in the 1960s with the help of California labor leader Cesar Chavez.

Since then, however, the migrant labor force has been increasingly made up of illegal immigrants from poor Central American and Caribbean countries, which has weakened the union's power to demand better wages and conditions. Eager to work, the newcomers readily accept lower-than-union wages and are too terrified of being deported to demand decent wages, benefits or better working conditions, or even to talk to union officials.

Thus, wages and conditions for many migrant workers have not proportionally improved since novelist John Steinbeck's searing 1930 classic, *The Grapes of Wrath*, portrayed the horrific working and living conditions endured by migrants in California's Central Valley, experts say. In fact, because today's migrant workers are predominantly illegal aliens, conditions are worsening, most advocates and observers agree.

Since the late 1990s, the percentage of migrant workers who are illegal immigrants — primarily from Mexico, Central America and the Caribbean — has grown from 52 percent to around 85 percent. [6]

Passage of the North American Free Trade Agreement (NAFTA) has contributed to the increased influx of illegal farmworkers, particularly from Mexico. By eliminating trade barriers between Mexico, Canada and the United States, NAFTA displaced many farmworkers in Mexico, because it became cheaper for Mexicans to buy imported corn, for instance, from mechanized farms in Iowa, than to produce it on their own family farms. As Mexico struggles to transform itself from a predominantly agrarian economy into a manufacturing society, many out-of-work Mexican farmworkers who cannot find factory work are

The Hazards Farmworkers Face

Nearly 40 percent of California farmworkers reported blurry vision, which experts blame on proximity to pesticides and drinking contaminated water. A third reported musculoskeletal conditions, such as backache and swollen joints. Farmworkers also have higher risks of leukemia and stomach cancer compared to other Latinos.

Health Problems Reported by California Agricultural Workers

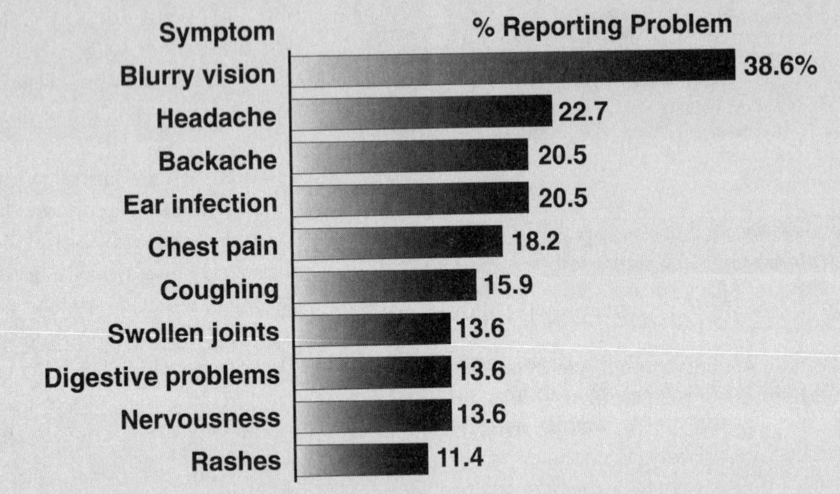

Source: U.S. Department of Labor, "Findings from the National Agricultural Workers Survey, 1997-98," March 2000

willing to risk the hazardous trip to the United States to find field work.

"The biggest impediment to farmworkers standing up for themselves is the abject fear they feel over their immigration status, and it makes them especially vulnerable to abuses," says Marc Grossman, chief spokesman for the UFW. Even legal immigrants are sometimes hesitant to report abuses, advocates say, for fear of retaliation.

Legally here or not, migrant workers face a difficult life. Migrant farmworkers' median annual income was $7,500, and 61 percent had incomes below the poverty level, according to a Labor Department survey in the late 1990s. Over the previous decade, farmworkers had lost 11 percent of their purchasing power — more than the losses suffered by non-agricultural workers. Since 1989, their average real hourly wages (in 1998 dollars) had dropped from $6.89 to $6.18, the Labor Department survey found. [7]

Besides the salary disparity, farmworkers face increased health risks and a shorter life expectancy than the average American, due largely to excessive pesticide exposure. The U.S. Bureau of Labor Statistics says farmworkers suffer the highest rate of chemically related illness of any occupational group — 300,000 acute pesticide-related illnesses every year, according to the Environmental Protection Agency (EPA). [8]

"The risk of death for a farmworker is more than 31 times that of a clerical employee," said Rosemary Sokas, associate director for science at the National Institute for Occupational Safety and Health (NIOSH). [9]

Indeed, just standing in a field can be lethal. In California, growers use driverless tractors to slowly pull flatbeds through the fields so pickers can drop harvested produce into crates or boxes on the flatbed. But the tractors sometimes "derail" from the deep furrows they were designed to follow, injuring or even killing workers, UFW President Arturo Rodriguez told Congress in 2002. [10]

Farmworker advocates largely blame the terrible conditions on growers, who they say prefer to use immigrants — particularly illegals, who are cheaper and less demanding of safer conditions. Growers, in turn, complain that they must contend with forged work documents and the fact that U.S. citizens increasingly do not want farm jobs.

"Nobody comes to our farms but the Mexican and Central American workers," American Nursery and Landscape Association President Peter Orum recently told the UFW. [11]

Sen. Larry E. Craig, R-Idaho, says many of the abuses could be reduced if the government provided temporary work permits for undocumented farmworkers — a solution he has outlined in his proposed AgJOBS bill. Notably, the measure is supported by both migrants' advocates and large growers.

"This landmark, bipartisan legislation hopes to provide long-term solutions for the serious problems facing farmers and farmworkers alike," Craig's Web site explains. "This bill is a practical and achievable approach to resolve the seriously flawed farm-labor program our country currently operates under. It will head off a growing crisis that threatens American agriculture, workers, and consumers." [12]

Critics of U.S. immigration policy argue that Americans would happily take farm jobs if growers paid higher wages but that legalizing undocumented workers would take the pressure off growers to pay higher wages. Instead, they argue, the government should better control the country's borders and enforce existing laws designed to protect farmworkers.

Several bills addressing the plight of farmworkers through immigration reform are pending in Congress, including Sen. Craig's proposal. Craig says the bill is stalled because of opposition by the Bush administration, which appears unwilling to alienate its more conservative, anti-immigration base in an election year. Earlier this year, Bush proposed an alternative to the AgJOBS bill, essentially a grant of temporary residency to some undocumented workers. [13]

Rosemary Jenks, government relations director at Numbers USA, a non-profit organization that advocates reduced immigration, opposes both the AgJOBs bill and Bush's guest-worker proposal. "If there is really a shortage of workers, then we have a legal, temporary visa program to give employers the [seasonal] workers they need," she said. "But we should allow market forces to work in the agriculture industry, just like everywhere else, and let market pressures drive up the wages."

As the debate over conditions for migrant farmworkers continues, here are some of the questions being discussed:

Most Farmworkers Are Migrants

The majority of U.S. farmworkers in the late 1990s were migrants — defined as workers who travel at least 75 miles to find jobs.

Migration and U.S. Farmworkers

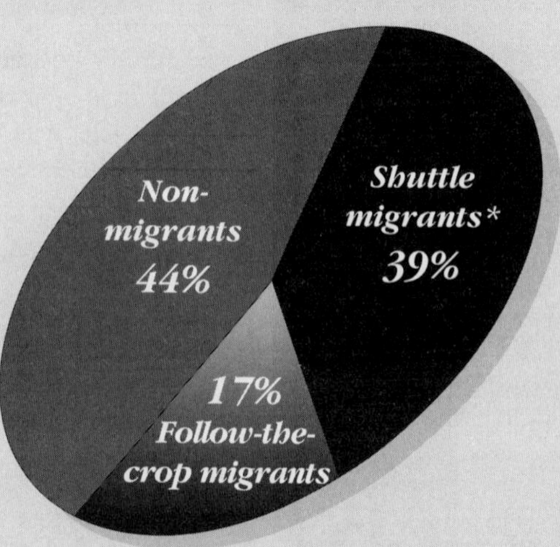

** Shuttle migrants move between jobs clustered at a location far from their home base.*

Source: U.S. Department of Labor, "Findings from the National Agricultural Workers Survey, 1997-98," March 2000

Should Congress pass the AgJOBS bill?

Craig's bill, which has 62 bipartisan sponsors, would grant temporary work permits to workers who can prove they have worked at least 100 days in the previous 18 months and who agree to fingerprinting and background checks. They can attain permanent residency status if they work at least 360 more days within the next three to six years.

Both farmworker advocates and growers — traditional antagonists — have joined forces to support AgJOBS. Indeed, ANLA President Orum told the UFW's biennial convention in July 2004, "I am here today because we are fighting together for the future of American agriculture." [14] It was the first time a grower has ever addressed the UFW.

Supporters say the bill is needed for several reasons, including the inadequacy of the Department of Labor's temporary H-2A visa program, which allows foreign agricultural guest workers to work for limited periods of time in the United States, after which they must leave the country.

"The current H-2A process is so expensive and hard to use," Craig said, explaining that growers find it extremely bureaucratic and cumbersome. In addition, only about 40,000-50,000 workers a year — 2 to 3 percent of the total agricultural work force — enter the country under the program. A 1997 General Accounting Office study found that the Labor Department had missed statutory deadlines for processing employer applications to participate in H-2A more than a third of the time. [15]

Bruce Goldstein, executive director of the Farmworker Justice Fund (FJF), says AgJOBS "would help stabilize the agricultural labor force by helping employers find workers when they need them. It also will empower workers to demand improvements in their wages and working conditions, because they'll have a legal status."

"AgJOBS has been a work in progress for a lot of years," says Craig J. Regelbrugge, co-chairman of the Agriculture Coalition for Immigration Reform, a group of growers supporting the bill. "There have been compromises all around, and it's not perfect by anybody's standards. But it reflects a realization that the medium- and long-term interests of workers and employers are totally intertwined."

However, anti-illegal-immigration groups maintain that those intertwined interests conflict with the country's best interests. "AgJOBS is an amnesty bill, and we have learned through experience that any amnesty program acts as an incentive for more illegal immigration," says Jenks of Numbers USA.

In 1986, facing a somewhat smaller version of today's migrant-laborer problem, Congress passed the Immigration Reform and Control Act (IRCA), which eventually enabled 3 million undocumented workers to apply for and receive legal status.

But once illegal laborers received their green cards, they quit farm work to find better jobs, critics complain. When word reached Mexico that thousands of farm jobs were subsequently available, they say, the inevitable happened. "The 1986 amnesty just set off another tidal wave of illegal immigration," says Dan Stein, executive director of the Federation for American Immigration Reform (FAIR), an immigration-reduction group.

"If we pass AgJOBS, we're going to be in the same position again in a couple years," Jenks adds.

But supporters of the AgJOBS bill counter that unlike IRCA, Craig's bill would not grant unlimited amnesty but would require undocumented workers to prove they have been working and that they will continue to work at least another three years before receiving a green card. AgJOBS represents "earned legalization," the UFW's Grossman says.

"You can redefine words to suit your needs, but the legal definition of amnesty is basically a pardon by government of a certain violation for a group of people," Jenks responds. "The AgJOBS bill states you have to be here illegally, so you have to have broken the law, but we're going to waive the penalties for that right up front. That's an amnesty.

"Then you hand them a reward — the temporary permission to stay and a work permit," she continues. "Then you go further and give them a green card, which is a pass to citizenship. You cannot legitimately define this bill as anything but an amnesty. It looks silly when proponents call it 'earned legalization.' It's become this word game that's reaching a point of absurdity."

As for Americans refusing to do farm work, Jenks says, "There's not a single job in this country — digging ditches, cleaning sewers or picking fruits and vegetables — that Americans will not do if the wages compensate for it. But growers don't want to increase wages."

Sharon Hughes, executive vice president of the National Council of Agriculture Employers, acknowledges that farm labor is extremely punishing. But she says the primary reason Americans avoid farm work is "because it's seasonal, only maybe three months out of the year." She adds that legal farmworkers generally get, on average, $8.55 an hour. Illegal farmworkers often got considerably less. Federal minimum wage is $5.15 an hour.

Stein says better control of the country's borders and tougher sanctions against employers who hire undocumented workers would help legal farm laborers gain strength.

"When you flood the market with substitutable labor" — as AgJOBS will, he says — it will "erode the bargaining leverage of people here." While that might help some employers, it also has "profound socio-economic consequences . . . [such as] rising poverty rates, the growing percentage of workers without health insurance and the loss of benefits in general."

The Palm Beach Post/Paul J. Milette

Lauro Almanza, left, grieves at the grave of her husband and her two brothers, in their hometown in Mexico. The three men were found dead in June 2003 along with 16 other undocumented workers in a locked tractor-trailer in Victoria, Texas, abandoned by the "coyote" who had smuggled them into the U.S.

Should growers be held responsible for abuses committed by farm-labor contractors?

Many growers hire their workers through labor contractors, who recruit and pay the workers at rates the contractors set. When working for ethical contractors, many laborers make more than minimum wage.

However, that is not always the case. Florida labor contractors Ramiro "the Devil" Ramos and his brother Juan recruited workers in Mexico and illegally transported them into the United States for $1,000 each. The brothers told the workers they could pay off the fee gradually from the wages they'd make working for growers in Lake Placid. The brothers also promised to provide housing. [16]

But the housing turned out to be a "filthy and overcrowded camp," as authorities later described it, for 700 workers. The Ramos brothers constantly deducted bogus charges from the Mexicans' pay, from assessing outrageous interest on the $1,000 smuggling loan to "fees" for almost anything, including food, soap and transportation to the fields. The charges essentially shackled the workers to indentured servitude. The brothers maintained order through intimidation and violence.

When the brothers were tried on slavery charges in 2003, growers denied knowing about any abuses. But U.S. District Judge K. Michael Moore, who sentenced the Ramoses to a minimum of 10 years in jail, was skeptical.

"It seems that there are others at another level in this system of fruit picking, at a higher level, that to some extent are complicit in one way or another in how these activities occur," he said. "They rely on migrant workers, and they create a legal fiction or corporation [i.e., a labor contractor] between them and the workers themselves so that they can be relieved of any liability for the hiring of illegal immigrants. And yet they stand to benefit the most."

Indeed, one of the brothers' attorneys, Joaquin Perez, said during the trial, "Do you not think for one moment . . . that the growers don't know what's going on?"

Goldstein of the Farmworker Justice Fund says unethical contractors constitute "probably the primary mechanism by which labor-law violations occur. A few years ago, between a third and half of California farmworkers were hired through labor contractors, and it's increased. It's a massive problem."

For instance, up to 70 percent of workers at the California vineyards operated by Gallo — the world's largest winery — are hired through labor contractors, the UFW's Grossman says.

Due to the growing problem, many advocates argue that growers should be held equally accountable for violations committed by contractors they employ. The UFW has tried three times to get California to pass such a law, but each time the growers convinced the legislature not to act. "Three times we got our heads handed to us," Grossman says.

Farmworkers' Homeownership Declined

One-third of all U.S. farmworkers owned or were buying a home in the mid-1990s, but by the end of the decade less than half as many were homeowners. The decline reflects the increasing number of farmworkers who are recent illegal, economically disadvantaged immigrants.

Own or Are Buying a Home

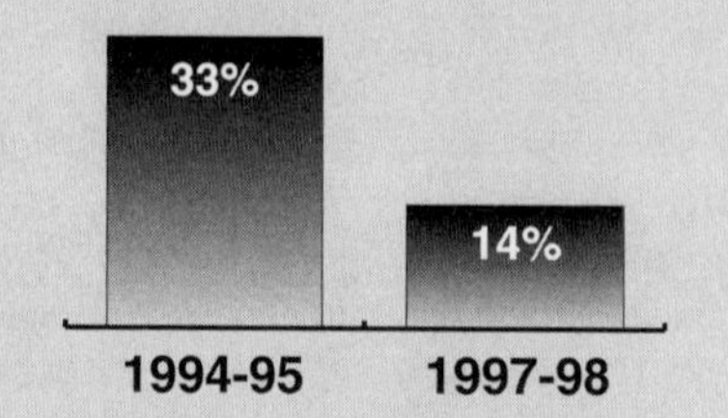

Source: U.S. Department of Labor, "Findings from the National Agricultural Workers Survey, 1997-98," March 2000

Growers counter that unscrupulous contractors cheat or otherwise abuse workers away from the growers' fields, usually at the labor camps they operate. "How can you hold anybody accountable outside of the work environment, where you have no control?" asked Walter Kates, director of labor relations for the Florida Fruit and Vegetable Association, a growers' trade group. [17]

Besides, says Susan Howard, president of the Agriculture Institute of Florida (AIF), which represents a wide range of agricultural businesses, "There are myriad [state] laws that protect farmworkers," and, in fact, the legislature last spring passed new legislation to toughen enforcement of labor laws.

But Max Perez, a staff member of the Coalition of Immokalee Workers, says, "The laws aren't really enforced. Not long ago, contractors used to beat up people in the fields. The only way that stopped was when we organized the coalition and marched in front of the houses of the contractors. The state authorities were no help."

Hughes, of the agriculture employers group, points out that federal law already holds growers jointly accountable with labor contractors. During the Clinton administration the Department of Labor amended the Fair Labor Standards Act to eliminate the separation of responsibility between growers and independent contractors. "The way the regulations are now written, it's nearly impossible for a grower not to be found as a joint employer," Hughes says.

But in actuality, that rarely happens, Perez says. "In the last big case of slavery we had here" — the Ramos brothers case — "not a single grower was touched. Sometimes growers don't know what's happening, but in cases that big, they should make sure things are in place to prevent it from happening, or be held responsible."

Using unscrupulous contractors helps growers keep their overhead down, so they can charge less for their produce than competitors who use legitimate contractors. Eventually many competitors feel pressured to make a choice: Go out of business, or also start using unscrupulous contractors.

Thus, taking California's approach, and only focusing enforcement on contractors, is not a solution either, said Rob Williams, director of the Migrant Farmworker Justice Project of Florida Legal Services in Tallahassee. "You take away their license and their brother gets a license or their wife gets a license or their kid gets a license. Or they operate without a license. The bad contractors move the good contractors out. The grower gives the job to the lowest bidder, and

Most Migrant Children Get Little Schooling

Most migrant children, like their parents, never graduate from high school. In fact, rather than attending school, many migrant children follow their parents into the fields, ensuring that the only thing they will learn is how to be a migrant worker.

The average migrant worker has only a sixth-grade education, and his child has only a 40 percent chance of entering the ninth grade. [1] One out of five migrant children completes less than three years of school, according to the Labor Department. [2]

But because "no definitive study" has been done on the subject, no one knows how many migrant children graduate from high school, says Reid Maki, communications director for the Association of Farmworker Opportunity Programs. "We estimate the dropout rate to be about 65 percent. Anecdotally, we've heard reports from some areas that it's as high as 80 percent."

Poverty and the transient nature of migrant work make it extremely difficult for migrant children to finish high school. Because migrant wages are so low, both parents usually have to work, and many families need their children to work in the fields as well.

"Since farmworkers are paid by how many buckets they fill, it's advantageous for the parents to have the kids helping," says Sylvia Partida, director of operations at the National Center for Farmworker Health (NCFH).

Federal labor law allows children as young as 10 to work in the fields, but Partida says children even younger than that work alongside their parents on a regular basis. Indeed, the Department of Labor has photographed children as young as 6 doing farm work. [3] In 1998, the General Accounting Office (GAO) estimated that 300,000 migrant children were working in the fields. The United Farm Workers union (UFW) estimates that the number may be closer to 800,000.

At least a third of all migrant children work in the fields either to contribute to the family income or because no child-care is available at their labor camps, Manda Lopez Klein, executive director of the Migrant and Seasonal Head Start Association (MSHSA), told the House Education Reform Subcommittee in 2003. The lack of migrant child-care services "contributes to child labor in this country," she added.

Even when migrant children do manage to enroll, many find it hard to stay in school because most migrant families move at least once every two years — sometimes more often — searching for work. Children who change schools more than four times in their lifetime are at higher risk of dropping out, according to the NCFH.

Experts say moving often takes a greater emotional toll on migrants' children than on their parents, making it harder to constantly be newcomers or outsiders in a new school. Moreover, curricula in America vary from school district to school district, making it harder for children of migrant workers to keep up academically and increasing their sense of social displacement or alienation.

A special Head Start program for migrant children runs Head Start centers where some 34,000 migrants' infants, toddlers and preschoolers spend the day while their parents are working.

The Department of Education's Migrant Education Program (MEP) helps older children finish high school or obtain GEDs. Since entire migrant communities sometimes move together in search of work, the MEP occasionally employs teachers who travel with the communities. Other MEP programs help migrant children remain in their school when their parents have to move; participating area universities usually provide room and board for the students.

But, as Klein notes, the Migrant and Seasonal Head Start Program only serves a fraction of the eligible children, because until recently no one knew how many migrant children were in the United States.

"We've never had a really solid count of migrant farmworkers in this country, let alone migrant farmworker children," Klein says. "So no one really knew" the extent of the problem.

But in 2001 a Department of Health and Human Services (HHS) study showed that more than 161,000 migrant children are eligible for the Migrant and Seasonal Head Start Program. Thus, the program currently serves only 19 percent of needy migrant children, says Klein. By comparison, Head Start programs targeting non-migrant children reach 60 percent of eligible children.

"Our position now is, 'OK, you've done a study, so now do something about it,' " Klein says. But with record-high budget deficits, Congress has no money to expand the program, she says.

Windy Hill, associate commissioner for the Head Start Bureau in Washington, says she's "unfamiliar with the HHS study," but confirms that to increase funding of the migrant program, "we would have to have money made available" by Congress.

1 "Findings from the National Agricultural Workers Survey, 1997-98," Research Report No. 8, U.S. Department of Labor, March 2000. By comparison, the average non-migrant child is 96 percent likely to enter the ninth grade.

2 Paul E. Green, "The Undocumented: Educating the Children of Migrant Workers in America," *Bilingual Research Journal*, 27:1, spring 2003, p. 64.

3 "Pesticides: Improvements Needed to Protect Farmworkers and Their Children," U.S. General Accounting Office, March 2000, p. 18.

when something goes wrong, they point to the contractors." [18]

Is government doing enough to protect farmworkers?

"Whenever you hear horror stories about farmworker abuses in California," says the UFW's Grossman, "the first thing you hear growers say is, 'Well, California has the toughest laws in the nation protecting farmworkers!' "

California does have a wide variety of laws to protect farmworkers, including a state minimum wage — $6.75 an hour — $1.60 above the federal minimum wage.

But enforcement is weak in California, as in most other states, Grossman says. Massive state budget deficits have led to widespread cuts in enforcement resources and personnel in almost every state program. And, while most states are back in the black again, California is still struggling with a large deficit.

Nevertheless, in summer 2004 the state began cracking down on labor-law violations, and officials uncovered the kinds of abuses farmworkers' advocates have been complaining about for years. [19]

Near a Fresno vineyard, for example, officials stopped a 1989 Ford van lacking insurance, seatbelts and a licensed driver. In the back were seven Mixtec Indians, all illegal workers from southern Mexico, who spoke no English and little Spanish. They had been hired at $40 a day, which at only eight hours a day (pickers often toil longer), would earn them less than either the state and federal minimum wages. [20]

In another case, authorities conducting an unannounced inspection at a vineyard found a young Mixtec Indian who wasn't even sure how much he was being paid. All he knew was that he hadn't been paid in more than two weeks, although state law requires payment every week. The law also requires drinking water to be available nearby; none was. [21]

UFW President Rodriguez also points out that state workers'-compensation laws often deny farmworkers the same coverage and benefits for work-related injuries and illnesses granted to other occupations. "The lack of coverage often precludes farmworkers from affording medical care," he said. "Such workers either do not get health care or, if they do go to the hospital for treatment, the taxpayers are forced to absorb the medical costs that workers'-compensation insurance could cover." [22]

AP Photo/Pat Sullivan

Eleven-year-old Chris Nino carries chili pepper bags on a Plainview, Texas, farm. Federal law allows children as young as 10 to work in the fields.

Rodriguez said the lack of coverage resulted in a dangerous, self-perpetuating paradox: When employers do not have to pay workers'-compensation premiums, they have little incentive to create a safer work environment, increasing workers' need for compensation insurance.

In Florida, two recent bills to improve farmworker conditions — one that would have granted farmworkers the right to sue growers if cheated on pay, the other the right to data on pesticides — died without even a vote. [23]

Advocates say the quick death was hardly a surprise: Florida agricultural interests contributed at least $35 million to state and federal political campaigns between 1996 and 2003 — and half the members of the Florida House Committee on Agriculture, including the chairwoman, were growers. [24]

The federal government hasn't been much help, either, advocates say, even though it is responsible for enforcing the Migrant and Seasonal Agricultural Worker Protection Act of 1983, which regulates how farmworkers are to be paid, housed and transported.

"The amount of money allocated to labor-law enforcement in agriculture is utterly inadequate," says Goldstein of the Farmworkers Justice Fund. "And the penalties are very minor. As a result, employers feel like there's very little risk of getting caught."

Indeed, the number of Labor Department investigators charged with enforcing the worker protection act, has decreased since President Bush took office. The Wage and Hour Division (WHD) had 945 investigators in 2001; it currently has 810, according to Dolline Hatchett, a Labor Department spokeswoman.

Moreover, the WHD's enforcement budget has increased more slowly under Bush. In fiscal 2001, the last Clinton administration budget, the WHD enforcement budget grew by more than $10 million from the previous year — from $141.7 million to $152.4 million. But under Bush, the budget has only grown by less than $8 million over three years, to $160.1 million in fiscal 2004, which ended on Sept. 30.

Enforcement actions dipped significantly shortly after the Bush administration took office. During the last year of the Clinton administration, the WHD completed 8,800 enforcement cases. In fiscal 2002, it completed 6,300. "But we climbed back up to about 8,000 in 2003," WHD Acting Administrator Al Robinson says. However, according to Labor Department figures, while 30 percent more agricultural workers received back wages in 2003 than in 2002, they only collected 21 percent more in wages than were collected the previous year. [25]

"We have been active, are active, and will continue to be active," Robinson responds. "Hopefully, resources permitting, we'll be able to supplement our investigator level in the coming year."

Federal law sometimes even undermines state law, advocates say. In California, for example, following several horrific road accidents — including one that killed 13 farmworkers — the legislature required employers to transport workers in vehicles with seatbelts certified as safe by the California Highway Patrol. But when farmworkers are transported across the state line for work in Nevada or Arizona, federal law — which doesn't require seatbelts or even seats — applies. [26]

California labor officials say that under Democratic Gov. Gray Davis, farm-labor violations were not a priority, but they are for Republican Gov. Arnold Schwarzenegger.

"This is the beginning of what we hope is a long process," said Vicky Bradshaw, head of the California Labor and Workforce Development Agency. "We want to make long-term positive change in an industry with a large number of vulnerable workers." [27]

But Cindy Hahamovitch, a labor-history professor at the College of William and Mary, in Williamsburg, Va., says, "We have all these laws on the books, [but] how do we get them enforced? You're never going to get enough officials to be able to inspect every labor camp, to make sure wage and hour rules are observed. The only way rules are enforced is when workers are empowered enough to enforce them themselves." ■

BACKGROUND

Rise of Migrants

Migratory farm labor in the United States began emerging in the mid- to late-19th century, after slavery ended in the South and keeping year-round, live-in field help eventually gave way to tenant farms and the hiring of seasonal workers. In addition, family-owned farms were being transformed and consolidated into large mechanized business enterprises that needed fewer year-round workers and even seasonal harvesters.

By the 1940s, there were only 1 million migrant farmworkers in the United States, down from 2 million in the 1920s, according to Philip L. Martin, chairman of the University of California Comparative Immigration and Integration Program and editor of *Migration News* and *Rural Migration News*. The numbers dropped to about 800,000 in the 1970s.

Due to the transient nature and difficulty of the work, picker jobs were increasingly filled with the poor, minorities and, eventually, almost entirely by recent immigrants. [28]

Migrant workers follow three general streams. In the East, they travel from South Florida up to Ohio, New York and Maine — following the crops from citrus to tobacco to blueberries. From southern Texas they stream north throughout the Midwest, and from Southern California they follow the coast up to Washington or head inland to North Dakota.

Those migrant populations have fluctuated during the 20th century, as the federal government opened or closed its borders — officially or unofficially — to foreign farmworkers depending on growers' labor needs. Some economists argue that the waxing and waning of strict immigration enforcement is the result of the government's longstanding goal of providing Americans with the cheapest food in the world. [29]

But Martin says laborers' wages are only a minor component of food prices. "Most of the value-added costs come after the product leaves the farm," Martin says, added by middlemen like food processors, truckers and grocers.

Rather than being motivated by a cheap food policy, Martin says, "Congress doesn't like to see crops rotting in the fields. It doesn't look good."

Apart from the slaves in the South, the first significant population of foreign farmworkers came to the United States from China in the 19th century. In the 1860s nearly 200,000 Chinese men and women worked under contract as field hands in California.

The second wave of immigrant farmworkers came from Mexico to work on cattle ranches in the Southwest and fruit orchards in California. About 55,000 Mexican laborers came to the United States between 1850 and 1880. U.S. involvement in World War I opened more doors for Mexican workers because of the void in the labor force created by Americans fighting in Europe.

By the time the U.S. stock market crashed in 1929, American agriculture had been suffering its own depression for most of the decade. Demand for U.S. farm goods had shot up during World War I, causing a massive increase in agricultural output across the country. After the war, though, European farms began to produce again, and American farmers found themselves drowning in a sea of overproduction.

With the onset of the Great Depression, thousands of struggling farmers saw already-weak crop prices nearly collapse. But with millions of Americans unemployed, anti-immigrant hostility turned toward the Mexican migrant-worker population. In the early 1930s, the U.S. expelled about 500,000 Mexican laborers to create jobs for Americans. [30]

No Rights for Migrants

Ongoing battles between American laborers and management, combined with huge numbers of workers trying to find a livable wage, led President Franklin D. Roosevelt to sign into law the landmark National Labor

Continued on p. 840

Chronology

Early 20th Century

War and the Great Depression stoke anti-immigrant sentiment.

1917-18
U.S. involvement in World War I creates labor shortage; more Mexican workers are allowed into the U.S.

1920s
American agriculture suffers from surplus of goods, caused by overly increased wartime production.

1929
The stock market crashes, triggering the Great Depression.

1930s
With millions of Americans out of work, the U.S. expels 500,000 Mexican laborers. Severe drought turns the Great Plains into a Dust Bowl, forcing thousands of farmers to head West as migrant workers.

1935
Field workers and domestics are excluded from protection under the landmark National Labor Relations Act giving workers the right to collective bargaining.

1940s
With millions of Americans serving in World War II, growers complain of a labor shortage. The government initiates the Bracero Program, importing workers from Mexico.

Postwar America
The agriculture industry takes over control of the Bracero Program.

1960s

Bracero Program continues as some unscrupulous growers and farmers take advantage of workers . . . . Efforts to unionize farmworkers begin.

1962
Former migrant worker Cesar Chavez and activist Dolores Huerta found the National Farm Workers of America (NFWA).

1964
U.S. ends Bracero Program.

1965
NFWA collaborates with the Agricultural Workers Organizing Committee (AWOC) to pressure grape growers for better wages. The effort increases the power of farmworkers.

1970s

NFWA and AWOC become the United Farm Workers (UFW). Membership grows to 50,000.

1975
UFW activism prompts California to pass the Agricultural Labor Relations Act, granting farmworkers new rights.

1980s

A flood of illegal, low-wage agricultural workers enters the U.S.

1983
Congress passes Migrant and Seasonal Agricultural Worker Protection Act.

1986
Congress passes Immigration Reform and Control Act (IRCA), which penalizes employers who hire illegal workers. The new law also grants amnesty to an estimated 1-3 million illegal aliens.

1990s

Illegal aliens who win amnesty under IRCA leave farm work for better jobs, creating a farmworker shortage that sparks another wave of illegal border crossings from Mexico.

1997-98
Department of Labor survey finds farmworkers are increasingly disadvantaged, and that at least 52 percent are undocumented.

2000s

The number of illegal aliens in the U.S. soars to an estimated 10 million. The Sept. 11, 2001, terrorist attacks prompt a crackdown on illegal entry into the country.

October 2001
Congress passes the USA Patriot Act, which is intended to stop terrorists from entering the country.

2003
Idaho Republican Sen. Larry E. Craig introduces the AgJOBS bill, which would legalize undocumented workers, enabling them to advocate for themselves without fear of deportation.

January 2004
President Bush proposes temporary legal residency for current undocumented workers; conservative and immigration-reform groups strongly oppose the plan.

July 2004
Sen. Craig's AgJOBS bill is blocked by Majority Leader Bill Frist, R-Tenn., reportedly on behalf of the White House.

Developers Trap Naive Buyers

Green Valley Farms sounds like a nice place to live, but it is far from idyllic. The low-income community along the Texas-Mexico border was built on a dry lakebed, making it vulnerable to intensive flooding. But the developers never told the purchasers. So residents like Rosie De Leija live in constant fear of rain.

"I knew nothing about it flooding or anything," she said. "It was a big surprise. We have septic tanks that get overflowed, and this is very hazardous to the children's health, to our health." Bloated animal carcasses float for days among the houses until the water recedes enough for the health department to come and remove them, she explains. [1]

Green Valley Farms is known as a "colonia." The Spanish word means neighborhood, but for the 500,000 residents in the nation's 1,600 colonias, in reality it is often just a fancy name for a slum. Most of the residents are Latino, and many are migrants. Colonias dot the barren, unincorporated areas along the U.S.-Mexico border, from Texas to California. [2] Most are in Texas — almost 1,500 with 400,000 inhabitants.

The number of colonias is up markedly from the 1,200 that existed in 1992, due largely to passage of the North American Free Trade Agreement (NAFTA). The agreement prompted many U.S. and Canadian companies to build factories just south of the border, and many of the workers bought land in the colonias. [3]

Although numerous improvements in housing and infrastructure have been made since the colonias were first established 50 years ago, many still have ramshackle dwellings, dusty unpaved roads, open sewage and lack of indoor plumbing, clean water or proper drainage.

"In colonias, people are living in Third World conditions," says Richard Lopez, a colonias program specialist in San Antonio for the U.S. Department of Housing and Urban Development (HUD). "The communities are very poor and very desolate."

Colonias were largely created by developers who prey on people whose limited knowledge of either English or real estate law makes them vulnerable. "It's unscrupulous land dealing," says Craig Griffith, assistant dean for finance and administration at Texas A&M University's college of architecture, which supervises the university's Colonias Program. It sets up partnerships between colonias residents and county, state and federal agencies and nonprofit groups, and has helped establish 14 community-resource centers for colonias residents. At the centers, outreach workers provide education, health services, job training and programs for youth and the elderly.

The colonias began sprouting in the 1950s, when unethical developers bought up agriculturally worthless land along the border, subdivided it and then sold pieces — unimproved — to poor people who wanted to own property. Nearly 65 percent of the buyers were born in the United States. The developers offered questionable financing in the form of "contracts for deed," which stipulated low down payments but withheld transfer of title until the buyer made the final payment. [4]

County clerks did not record contracts for deed, unlike the traditional deeds of trust provided in normal financing. Thus, if the resident fell behind on payments, developers could easily repossess their property — along with any improvements the resident may have made — without going through the normal foreclosure process.

Moreover, since the developers held the deed, they paid the property taxes, so they could legally demand that the buyers reimburse them for those taxes. Usually the buyer couldn't afford to, and the developer could then take back the property.

Yvette Sanchez, director of colonias initiatives for the state of Texas, says officials were not aware of such predatory practices until the early 1990s, when the colonias population began

Continued from p. 838

Relations Act (NLRA) in 1935. Among several protections it conferred on workers, arguably the most important was the right to collective bargaining: American labor for the first time had some leverage with employers.

However, two classes of laborers — field workers and domestic help — were deliberately excluded from protection. "This had an enormous impact, but the striking thing is there was so little discussion of it at the time, which is kind of horrifying," historian Hahamovitch says. "It's still an open question" as to why FDR allowed it, she says, "but the general reading is that Southern Democrats did not want the rights of labor organizing to extend to African-Americans."

At the time, about 65 percent of U.S. blacks were field workers or domestics. FDR needed the support of all Democrats to enact the legislation, which would profoundly affect future migrant workers.

On the heels of the Depression came the Dust Bowl, an ecological disaster that wiped out thousands of farms across the Great Plains due to crop erosion. For years farmers in the region had used planting methods that failed to protect vital topsoil; when severe drought and heavy winds struck in the early 1930s, erosion turned much of the Great Plains into desert-like landscapes.

Oklahoma was one of the hardest-hit states. Hundreds of thousands of Oklahomans and other Midwest farmers packed up their meager belongings and headed to California, where they had heard — through growers' advertisements — that plentiful farming jobs awaited them. But when they arrived they discovered the pitiful pay and conditions that migrant farmworkers had known for decades, wrenchingly memorialized in Steinbeck's *Grapes of Wrath.*

to grow rapidly. "People were not really speaking up about it before then," largely because colonias residents thought the real estate practices were normal.

In 1995, Texas passed the Colonias Fair Land Sales Act to redress some of the inequities. Developers must now record contracts for deed with the county clerk and advise prospective buyers of what services and amenities are — or are not — available with a piece of property.

The contract for deed, however, is still the principal means of sale in colonias, and low-income families and migrant workers still have few housing options in the region. Unemployment among colonias dwellers hovers around 40 percent. Average per capita income in Texas is roughly $16,700; within colonias, it is only about $7,300. [5]

For residents, a colonia offers what appears to be not just a haven but also a piece of the American dream. As little as $40 down and a monthly mortgage payment of $60 buys a piece of property in a colonia. But as Donald Lee, executive director of the Texas Conference of Urban Counties, recently said, buyers don't realize "they're buying into a nightmare." [6]

Because many colonias are located in floodplains, heavy rains strike fear in residents. After flooding in Tierra Grande, a colonia near Corpus Christi, in summer 2004: "Septic tanks overflowed, and human waste saturated the floodwaters inside and outside the ramshackle houses. Snakes slithered into homes, and huge water beetles that look like leeches crawled out of the flooded vegetation and into residents' damp mattresses," *The Washington Post* reported. [7]

Since owners do not have title to their property, they have no collateral to offer lenders who might finance construction of a house. So owners typically build their own homes at a slow pace, or just live in tents or lean-to's. Some put dilapidated trailers or buses on their lots and add to them. Some eventually construct permanent houses, but they usually lack electricity, plumbing or other amenities.

Few houses meet code. Potable water must be bought and stored. Because of insufficient or non-existent wastewater disposal systems, sewage often collects in pools, posing serious human health hazards. "Texas Department of Health data show that hepatitis A, salmonellosis, dysentery, cholera and other diseases occur at much higher rates in colonias than in Texas as a whole," state officials said. "Tuberculosis is also a common health threat, occurring almost twice as frequently along the border than in Texas as a whole." [8]

Today, the Texas Department of Housing and Community Affairs and the state attorney general's office say they are trying to ensure that colonias residents are not cheated in their housing transactions.

Most enforcement actions, however, are handled at the county level. But Frank Davis, director of the office of departmental operations and coordination at HUD, points out that colonias are located outside county limits, and that county governments must "take care of people within county limits first."

---

1 "The Forgotten Americans," documentary aired on PBS, Dec. 14, 2000.

2 National Colonia Clearing House, University of Texas; http://coserve1.panam.edu/copc/colonias.html.

3 Office of the Texas Secretary of State; http://www.sos.state.tx.us/border/colonias/faqs.shtml.

4 Ariel Cisneros, "Texas Colonias: Housing and Infrastructure Issues," Federal Reserve Bank of Dallas, June 2001, www.dallasfed.org/research/border/tbe_cisneros.html.

5 Texas Secretary of State, *op. cit.*

6 *Ibid.*

7 See Sylvia Moreno, "Shantytowns Migrate Far North of the Border in Texas; Weak County Laws Tied to the Spread of Squalid Developments," *The Washington Post*, Aug. 2, 2004, p. A3.

8 Texas Secretary of State, *op. cit.*

Bracero Program

The U.S. economy recovered after the outbreak of World War II, which mobilized the country for wartime production. Migrants working on California farms took better-paying jobs in shipyards and other industrial sectors. And with millions of other Americans in uniform, Southern borders were again opened for migrant "guest workers."

However, Hahamovitch says, debate still rages over whether a war-driven labor shortage actually existed at the time. "Some federal officials argued that it wasn't so much a dearth of labor but that growers were accustomed to the kind of [low] wages they'd been paying during a 20-year agricultural depression," she says. "There was enough of a reduction of workers because of the war that farmworkers could say, 'No, I won't work for your wage.' That drove growers absolutely ballistic. So, they got organized and put pressure on [Congress] and, lo and behold, they got a guest-worker program."

It was called the Bracero Program, for *brazo*, the Mexican word for arm, although workers came from the Caribbean as well as Mexico. For instance, Florida growers sought West Indian laborers, primarily Bahamians, who had been working intermittently in the state since the 19th century. Florida's sugarcane industry, which didn't really take root until the 1930s, also relied heavily on Mexicans and black Americans. In California and the Southwest, Mexican workers predominated.

The federal government ran the Bracero Program from 1942 to 1947, brokering deals between American growers and the countries that agreed to supply workers. Salary was to be set at market value, but no less than 30 cents an hour, and workers had to be guaranteed a minimum amount of pay even in periods of no work due to weather or other uncontrollable circumstances.

But abuses were common. For example, the government originally sent Jamaican laborers to farms north of the Mason-Dixon Line for fear they would be mistreated in the South. However, when winter came and there was no work in the North, the government had to transfer them to the South. "They went to Florida, and pretty much all hell broke loose," Hahamovitch says. "They were not treated as British workers who happened to be black, but like [former slaves]. They were greeted by labor camp supervisors carrying bullwhips and pistols."

Each ethnic group was housed in separate camps — one for the Jamaicans, one for the Bahamians and one for the African-Americans — so growers could play them off against one another in driving down wages, she says. The growers would go into one camp, claiming that the other camps would work for a lower wage. If no workers would agree to accept the lower wage, the growers would drive to the next camp and do the same thing until finally one camp agreed, she says.

In 1947, the federal government turned control of the Bracero Program over to the growers, who could now set all terms of a contract, including wages. Wages dropped so low that Americans would no longer work in the fields. By decade's end, only West Indians were cutting sugarcane in Florida.

For the majority of the ultimately 4 million Mexicans who worked as braceros over the next 17 years, the jobs were a decidedly mixed blessing. Before, most had been dirt poor in their home villages, so even a low American wage was good. But the conditions were inhuman.

"They treated us like animals," a former bracero said. "The [bosses] insulted us. If you did something wrong, they'd yell, 'What are you? An idiot? A fool?' There was a lot of discrimination. They kept the American workers and the Mexican braceros in separate crews. The Americans said terrible things about us. We weren't allowed to enter restaurants. Some employers even beat their workers. But, as a bracero, you knew you couldn't complain." [31]

The federal government finally halted the program in 1964, after labor unions, religious groups and community organizations vigorously protested the abuses. Florida's sugarcane growers, however, were allowed to continue importing West Indian cutters.

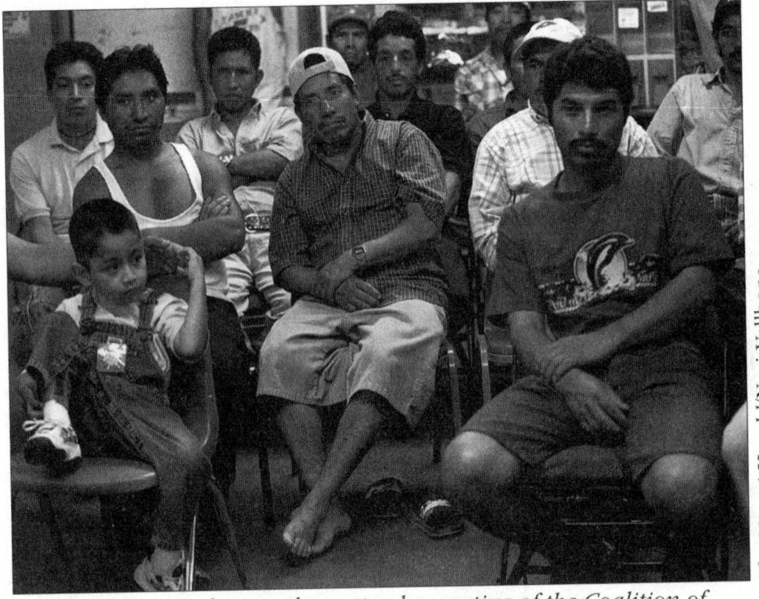

The Miami Herald/Nuri Vallbona

South Florida farmworkers attend a meeting of the Coalition of Immokalee Workers, where they learn about their rights and coalition efforts to better conditions for migrants.

'Harvest of Shame' Redux

At Thanksgiving in 1960, CBS-TV brought the plight of migrants into America's living rooms, with its broadcast of Edward R. Murrow's famous "Harvest of Shame" documentary. The nation was shocked by the report's graphic portrayal of the squalid living conditions, miserable wages and abuses suffered by the migrant farmworkers who help put food on America's tables.

As one Southern farmer told Murrow, "We used to own our slaves; now we just rent them." [32]

The report focused on migrant conditions in Belle Glade, Fla., on the outer reaches of wealthy Palm Beach County.

The resulting public outcry spurred passage two years later of the Migrant Health Act, which, among other things, provided grants for public and nonprofit private agencies to provide health services to migrants.

But 30 years later, in April 1990, the PBS-TV show "Frontline" revisited Florida's migrants. Its documentary, "New Harvest, Old Shame," concluded that little had changed since Murrow's report. Despite immigration-law reform and union organizing, the black Americans who did the picking when Murrow did his investigation had been replaced by a steady stream of undocumented Mexicans and Salvadorans and more recently Guatemalans and Haitians, depressing the wages of those already here, Frontline found. Thus, there were three farmworkers for each available job, and wages were not keeping up with inflation, reporter David Marash found. Moreover, most were getting no health insurance, sick days, vacations or pensions, and the transient life of their children made them unlikely to finish school — and thus more likely to end up as migrants themselves.

"This ain't no life," Pedro Silva, a 40-year-old migrant worker who had been working in the fields since the Murrow documentary aired, told the 1990 documentary makers. [33]

Meanwhile, Marash found, big growers lobbied for loopholes in labor and immigration laws and then discouraged strict enforcement. As one rural organizer observed, "Farm workers are not anyone's constituency in Congress." [34]

More than a decade later, investigative journalists found once again that not much had changed, and, indeed, the situation may have even worsened for a new wave of immigrants. In a 2003 series entitled "Modern Day Slavery," reporters at *The Palm Beach Post* spent nine months investigating the deplorable living and working conditions among Florida's migrants, many of whom had been smuggled into the country from Mexico under life-threatening conditions and were being held in indentured servitude by labor bosses. [35] The same year, *The Miami Herald* ran a similar series, uncovering the same types of abuses.

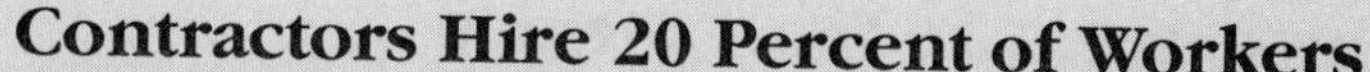

Contractors Hire 20 Percent of Workers

More than 40 percent of all farmworkers worked in vegetables and field crops, and one-third in fruit and nut crops in 1997-98. One-fifth of the workers were hired by independent farm labor contractors, mostly frequently for work in horticulture and field crops.

Crops Farmed by Farmworkers
(By percentage of workers)

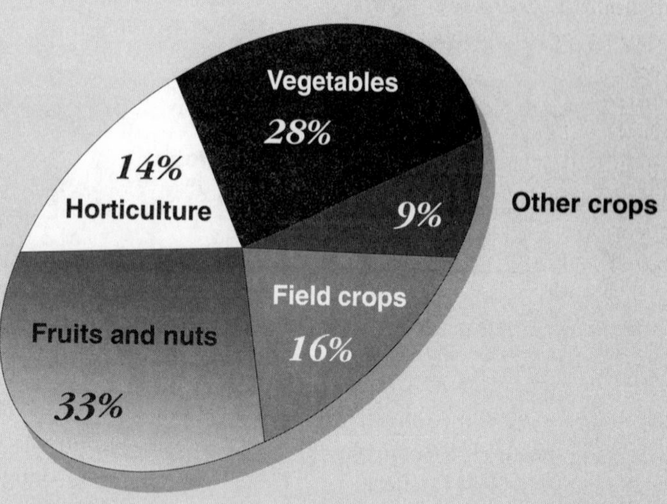

Source: U.S. Department of Labor, "Findings from the National Agricultural Workers Survey, 1997-98," March 2000

Birth of a Union

Attempts during the 1950s to organize farmworkers into a union had failed, largely because braceros — who made up a sizable portion of migrant workers — were afraid to join unions since their immigration status was only temporary and they feared deportation.

So when the federal Bracero Program ended in the early 1960s, labor organizers saw new possibilities for unions — and none too soon.

Grape pickers in 1965 were making an average of $.90/hour, plus 10 cents per "lug" (basket) picked. State laws regarding working standards were simply ignored by growers. At one farm, the boss made the workers all drink from the same cup, a beer can, in the field; at another ranch workers were forced to pay a quarter per cup. No ranches had portable field toilets. Workers' temporary housing was strictly segregated by race, and they paid two dollars or more per day for unheated metal shacks — often infested with mosquitoes — with no indoor plumbing or cooking facilities. Farm-labor contractors played favorites with workers, selecting friends first, sometimes accepting bribes. Child labor was rampant, and many workers were injured or died in easily preventable accidents. The average life expectancy of a farmworker was 49 years. [36]

In 1962, Cesar Chavez, a former migrant worker, and Dolores Huerta, an activist who had been raised in an agricultural community, founded the National Farmworkers of America (NFWA). Their early efforts focused on recruiting members, registering farmworkers to vote and generally trying to improve working conditions. But the NFWA gained substantial power in 1965 by working with another farmworkers group, the Agricultural Workers Organizing Committee (AWOC), to pressure grape growers for better wages.

Though farmworkers were still not covered by the National Labor Relations Act, which, among other things, offered job protections for striking union members, they benefited from Chavez's public-relations genius. In 1966, he led 70 striking California grape pickers on a 340-mile, 25-day march from Delano to Sacramento, the state capital. Along the way, thousands of supporters and well-wishers cheered them on,

Most Farmworkers Are From Mexico

People from Mexico made up more than three-quarters of all U.S. farmworkers in 1997-98. Overall, 81 percent of the farmworkers were foreign-born.

Farmworker Ethnicity and Place of Birth

Mexican-born	77%
Asian-born	1
Other foreign-born	1
U.S.-born white	7
U.S.-born Hispanic	9
U.S.-born African-American	1
Other U.S.-born	2
Latin American-born	2

Source: U.S. Department of Labor, "Findings from the National Agricultural Workers Survey, 1997-98," March 2000

and many joined the march. By the time they reached Sacramento, there were nearly 10,000 marchers.

Chavez turned the farmworkers' exclusion from the NLRA into an advantage. Under the NLRA, unions could boycott their employer but could not simultaneously boycott any outlet (such as a retail store) or affiliated company (like a shipper). Because they were not restricted by the law, farmworkers could mount as many simultaneous boycotts as they wanted. Chavez focused on grape growers and grocery stores that sold the grapes, drawing widespread public sympathy in the 1960s.

Eventually the NFWA and AWOC merged to become the United Farm Workers. By 1970, membership had reached 50,000, and many growers were negotiating contracts with the new union. UFW activism even played a role in passing the California Agricultural Labor Relations Act (CALRA) in 1975; essentially the law conferred on California farmworkers all the rights and protections guaranteed other workers under the NLRA.

For a brief period in the 1970s, the International Brotherhood of Teamsters competed with the UFW to represent farmworkers. But the UFW accused the Teamsters of favoring the growers. By the end of the decade, the UFW represented most farmworkers nationwide.

But in the 1980s California began to relax CALRA enforcement, emboldening growers not to sign union contracts. About the same time, California and Florida experienced waves of illegal immigration, and many of the aliens went to work in the fields. Chavez continued to lead boycotts, but UFW membership dropped to 15,000 by the middle of the decade.

In 1986, Congress passed the Immigration Reform and Control Act, aimed at preventing employers from hiring the illegal aliens. But while the act specified penalties for such employers, it also granted amnesty to the majority of illegal aliens in the country since 1982. As a result, the now-legal farmworkers sought other better-paying jobs. A new wave of illegal immigration followed — particularly in California and Florida — as impoverished people from Mexico and the Caribbean learned that U.S. farm jobs once again were available.

In 1996, Congress passed another major immigration-reform bill designed to limit the number of immigrants and make it easier to deport illegal aliens. But enforcement again declined during the economic boom of the late 1990s, incensing groups opposed to illegal immigration.

In 2001, Congress passed the most recent legislation affecting immigration — the USA Patriot Act, which focuses on preventing terrorists from entering the country. ■

CURRENT SITUATION

Blocking AgJOBS

Until last July, Sen. Craig's AgJOBS bill seemed likely to pass. With more than 60 bipartisan co-sponsors, the measure is filibuster-proof. Craig planned to attach the bill as an amendment to a class-action litigation bill that the Senate Republican majority and some Democrats wanted to enact over the summer. But Craig's spokesman, Dan Whiting, says shortly before the Senate met to consider the class-action bill the White House asked the Idaho Republican not to offer his bill as an amendment. [37]

Given conservatives' hostile reaction to a proposal by President Bush last January to extend temporary legal residency to undocumented workers, the administration was determined to avoid any such reform during an election year, insiders said.

Ignoring the White House request, Craig tried to attach AgJOBS to the class-action litigation bill, only to find himself blocked by Senate Majority Leader Bill Frist, R-Tenn., who, according to both Republican and Democratic sources, was doing the White House's

Continued on p. 846

At Issue:

Should Congress pass the AgJOBS bill?

yes

SEN. LARRY E. CRAIG, R-IDAHO

FROM A STATEMENT BEFORE THE SENATE FOREIGN RELATIONS COMMITTEE, MARCH 23, 2004

With an estimated 8 to 12 million undocumented persons in the country, we need to identify them, treat them humanely and reasonably, and bring them out of the underground economy.

We need to face facts and realize that entire sectors of our economy are dependent on the labor of these workers — the vast majority of whom want nothing more than to work under decent conditions at jobs that, quite frankly, American citizens often do not want.

We also need to realize that putting more locks on the border works both ways. As our borders have been tightened, many undocumented workers now are trapped here, because getting smuggled home has become as dangerous as coming here in the first place.

We also need to consider the humanitarian side of this issue. Every year, more than 300 human beings die in the desert, in boxcars, in trunks, or otherwise being smuggled into this country. That is intolerable.

Increased enforcement is part of the solution — but only part. Those who say, "Just round 'em up, just enforce the law," are only proposing an excuse, not a solution.

A key part of any solution will be the fair, humane treatment of those undocumented workers already here, already contributing to our economy and paying taxes.

The AgJOBS bill is a mature, thoroughly developed product. [It] represents more than seven years of work on these issues, and four years of tough, bipartisan negotiations.

With AgJOBS, we could begin immediately to improve our homeland security — and especially ensure the safety and security of our food supply — by knowing who is planting and harvesting our crops, where those workers came from and where they are working.

This is not amnesty. Conditioning the right to stay here on a worker's commitment to three to six more years of physically challenging agricultural work is not a reward — it is an opportunity for the worker to rehabilitate his or her status under the law and earn the right to stay.

The AgJOBS bill has something no other proposal has: A historic, nationwide, broad bipartisan coalition of grass-roots support. Four hundred organizations — national, state, and local organizations — [support] AgJOBS.

no

DAN STEIN

EXECUTIVE DIRECTOR, FEDERATION FOR AMERICAN IMMIGRATION REFORM

WRITTEN FOR *THE CQ RESEARCHER*, OCTOBER 2004

Amnesty for the estimated 10-12 million illegal aliens in the United States is a radioactive issue with the U.S. electorate. Yet that remains a cherished goal for the Bush administration and many in Congress.

With a sweeping amnesty politically unfeasible, the objective has become to enact it in small pieces. The AgJOBS bill — which would legalize untold numbers who have violated our immigration laws and establish an open-ended pipeline of guest workers, who, in time, would qualify for legal residency themselves — is merely the first step toward this objective.

Aside from helping to pry open the doors of amnesty for millions of illegal immigrants, the AgJOBS bill would likely touch off an even greater wave of illegal immigration. Millions around the world will interpret it as a signal that coming to the U.S. illegally will be rewarded; but it would do nothing to end the shameful exploitation of farm labor that has existed for decades.

A similar agricultural amnesty in 1986 legalized some 1.3 million illegal aliens — the majority of whom received amnesty fraudulently. It did nothing to stop new illegal aliens from coming to the United States or employers from hiring workers who are easily exploited. Why should anyone believe that if we grant yet another amnesty this time the government will get serious about preventing another influx of illegal aliens and crack down on the agribusinesses that employ them?

Amnesty also has profound homeland security implications. More than two-thirds of the agricultural amnesty beneficiaries in 1986 received amnesty fraudulently. The government simply lacks the time and resources to conduct even minimal background checks on the millions who are likely to apply for amnesty, or even verify that they had indeed worked in agriculture.

The results can be fatal. Two brothers who were beneficiaries of the 1986 agricultural amnesty — Egyptian taxi drivers in New York City — later were convicted in the 1993 bombing of the World Trade Center. The proposed AgJOBS amnesty contains even fewer measures to prevent that kind of dangerous fraud from happening again.

Rather than rewarding illegal immigrants with amnesty and appeasing a powerful economic interest group with more low-wage labor, the United States must, once and for all, control its borders and punish employers who hire illegal aliens.

Continued from p. 844

bidding. Frist prevented a vote on the AgJOBS bill, saying, "To take issues that are even bigger than class action and try to address those as amendments is absurd. It can't be done." [38]

However, Craig still insists he is committed to getting a vote on the measure before the 108th Congress adjourns, either as stand-alone legislation or as an amendment to another bill. "I believe we will have a vote, and I'll continue to work with leadership to find the best means to accomplish that goal," Craig says.

Utah Republican Rep. Chris Cannon introduced a companion AgJOBS bill in the House, which has 146 bipartisan sponsors. It has been referred to both the Judiciary and the Education committees, but no action is expected on it before the presidential election.

Health and Safety

NIOSH is examining the environmental health risks faced by migrant farmworkers. The agency is particularly concerned that immigrant farmworkers — due to their poor English-language skills — rarely understand their rights and thus allow themselves to be exposed to working conditions they should — and legally could — avoid. Their different cultural beliefs also can influence their understanding of health risks, disease causation and treatment options.

For instance, farmworkers have a 59 percent higher risk of leukemia and a 69 percent higher risk for stomach cancer compared to other Latinos, according to the *American Journal of Industrial Medicine.* But because they usually put off reporting medical problems promptly, farmworkers' diagnoses and treatment for serious illnesses are delayed, making the diseases harder and more costly to treat. [39]

Since the mid-1990s, NIOSH advisory teams, made up of farmworkers and people knowledgeable about workers' customs and concerns, have helped the agency raise farmworker awareness of occupational health and safety issues. They have also documented the prevalence of musculoskeletal disorders, skin and eye irritation, field sanitation and potential pesticide exposure among farmworkers.

NIOSH is now using education programs to develop more cooperation and trust between researchers, workers and advocates. One program, for example, uses English-as-a-second-language classes to inform younger farmworkers about workplace safety issues and their relevant rights. Another program uses theater to convey information, minimizing the impact of literacy limitations.

The agency is also trying to determine how many farmworkers have limited English proficiency so it can better communicate information on injury risk and prevention. For instance, farmworkers most frequently suffer pain in the back, shoulders, arms and hands. NIOSH recently published a visual guide showing how to make or modify tools that reduce the risk of such pain.

Meanwhile, following *The Miami Herald's* three-part exposé last year, both the FBI and the U.S. Justice Department's Civil Rights Division (CRD) have opened investigations into systemic abuses by field bosses against Florida's migrants. The CRD's involvement stems from the Justice Department's ongoing pursuit of human trafficking, which Attorney General John Ashcroft has made a priority. [40] Since early 2001, the CRD has charged 132 traffickers — including the Ramos brothers — nearly three times more than were charged in the three preceding years. Over the same period, the CRD opened 250 new investigations into trafficking allegations. [41]

Union Dispute

In addition to lobbying for the AgJOBS bill, the United Farm Workers is embroiled in a heated contract dispute with Gallo Wineries of Sonoma. A major flashpoint in the negotiations has involved farmworkers supplied by labor contractors, who provide 60 percent of the huge vineyard's pickers. Under the previous contract, which expired last November, the workers received only modest raises and no sick days, vacation pay or medical benefits. The UFW says Gallo is offering even less for a new contract.

The UFW has been accused of coercing workers and bargaining in bad faith, all of which it denies. Last December, a judge ruled that Gallo officials had illegally interfered with a union election; Gallo is appealing. Both sides say they want a settlement. [42]

Because budgets have been cut for government-funded legal aid programs in recent years, the privately funded Farmworker Justice Fund has been trying to assist farmworkers in their grievances against employers. In addition, the federal Legal Services Corporation, a private, nonprofit corporation established and funded by Congress, underwrites some legal aid programs, but recipients are prohibited from representing undocumented workers, who make up the majority of farmworkers today.

The House Rules Committee was meeting at press time to set ground rules for the floor debate of that chamber's GOP-crafted intelligence overhaul bill, called the 9/11 bill, which, unlike the Senate's version, contains several provisions that crack down on illegal immigration. However, the White House opposes the provisions and is pressing House Republicans to remove them from the bill. But the Rules Committee is expected to continue considering the provisions, which, among other things, would make it harder for immigrants to get drivers' licenses. ■

OUTLOOK

Continuing Support?

There is wide agreement that the nation's increasing reliance on undocumented migrant farmworkers to harvest its food supply needs to change — but equally wide disagreement on how to do it.

Most farmworker advocates favor enacting the AgJOBS bill. Give workers a legal status, their theory goes, and they will no longer fear reprisal for standing up for themselves. In short, they will be the primary engine driving the movement toward reform.

Some supporters say that despite its uncertain future, AgJOBS will probably be passed at some point, perhaps even sooner than later.

"There's a steady drumbeat coming from the agriculture community that's saying, 'Hey, we've done the hard work on this, so let's move on it, let's get it done!' " says Regelbrugge of the Agriculture Coalition for Immigration Reform. "[Sen.] Craig has also showed every sign of being committed, and so there's a chance it'll still happen, maybe before the election, though that would be against the odds."

Change will come from looking beyond symptoms to focus on causes, labor historian Hahamovitch says, but she's not optimistic that will happen soon.

"Fixating on farm-labor contractor abuses gives the impression that federal policy has nothing to do with farm-labor conditions and that growers have nothing to do with them," she says. "The fact is, it's the banal, everyday stuff that we have to take a look at — such as, how could it be that farm-labor conditions could be pretty much the same now as they were in the 1930s?"

Not all farmworkers are poor or destitute, she acknowledges, "but there are some policies that are keeping things the way they are."

President Bush's temporary-guest-worker counterproposal to AgJOBS, she points out, followed the federal tradition of allowing employers to contract for workers. "As long as employers can say who gets in and who doesn't, then a guest-worker program is going to be exploited. Our system right now is employer-controlled, which is what South Africa's system was for a long time. Not a very good model."

Opponents of the AgJOBS bill, like Stein of the Federation for American Immigration Reform and Jenks of Numbers USA, say it would allow lawmakers to avoid reckoning with the seismic labor-policy shift that's already begun in the United States — in effect, the globalization of the work force.

"Somewhere in the 1980s, there became a new ethic in this country," says Stein, in which "if you couldn't get workers to work at wages you wanted to pay, then you had the right to bring in new people who would" or ship the jobs overseas to lower-wage countries. [43]

Union support for legislation that has effectively allowed this to continue, Stein says, is an anomaly. "In the 1910s and '20s, the American labor movement was always very much committed to controlling the labor supply, because that's the surest practical way of increasing bargaining leverage."

The AgJOBS bill would only facilitate the status quo, he says. "What we need is a broader debate about immigration and why we need so much of it, and who are the winners and losers and what's the agenda, because immigration is really about redistribution of wealth.

"It's not about growing the economy," he continues. "It's about redistributing wealth in a way that benefits elites. It's about big money and cheap labor. There's a big change going on, and it seems to be happening without any real debate."

But given the strong bipartisan support for AgJOBS and similar bills waiving penalties for illegal entry into the U.S., Stein expects no real change to result from the upcoming presidential election, regardless of who wins. Both Republicans and Democrats will continue their "Hispandering," as he puts it.

"If we allow growers to keep bringing in cheap foreign workers or illegal aliens, then we ensure that farm work will always remain a poverty-level occupation in this country," Jenks says.

"As a society, that's a choice we need to make, and it looks like we're making it in favor of poverty," she continues. "So we have to ask: Do we really want to have an industry where the workers are condemned to poverty for their lives, and their children too? Because it's a self-perpetuating cycle." ■

Notes

[1] See Mark Arax, "Bitter Taste in the Grape Fields; Farmworker says his father, 53, didn't have to die of heatstroke," *Los Angeles Times*, Aug. 30, 2004, p. B1.

About the Author

William Triplett recently joined *The CQ Researcher* as a staff writer after covering science and the arts for such publications as *Smithsonian, Air & Space, Nature, Washingtonian* and *The Washington Post*. He also served as associate editor of *Capitol Style* magazine. He holds a B.A. in journalism from Ohio University and an M.A. in English literature from Georgetown University. His recent reports include "Search for Extraterrestrials" and "Broadcast Indecency."

FOR MORE INFORMATION

Association of Farmworker Opportunity Programs, 4350 North Fairfax Dr., Suite 410, Arlington VA 22203; (703) 528-4141; www.afop.org. Promotes better training and education for farmworkers.

Center for Housing and Urban Development, Texas A&M University, College of Architecture, College Station, TX 77843; (979) 845-3211; www.chud.tamu.edu. Works to improve the lives of Texas residents, including those in colonias.

Coalition of Immokalee Workers, P. O. Box 603, Immokalee, FL 34143; (239) 657-8311; www.ciw-online.org. A community-based union consisting of largely Latino, Haitian and Mayan Indian immigrants working in low-wage jobs throughout Florida.

Farmworker Justice Fund, Inc., 1010 Vermont Ave., N.W., Suite 915, Washington, DC 20005; (202) 783-2628; www.fwjustice.org. Litigates and lobbies for better wages and working conditions for farmworkers.

Federation for American Immigration Reform, 1666 Connecticut Ave., N.W., Suite 400, Washington, DC 20009; (202) 328-7004; www.fairus.org. Nonprofit group that opposes unlimited immigration.

National Center for Farmworker Health, 1770 FM 967, Buda, TX 78610; (512) 312-2700; www.ncfh.org. Provides information and services to 500 health centers and other organizations serving farmworkers.

National Council of Agriculture Employers, 1112 16th St., N.W., Suite 920, Washington, DC 20036; (202) 728-0300; www.ncaeonline.org. A nonprofit organization focusing on farm-labor issues from the growers' viewpoint.

United Farm Workers of America, P.O. Box 62, Keene, CA 93531; www.ufw.org. The largest farmworker union represents about 27,000 members.

[2] Testimony of United Farm Workers President Arturo S. Rodriguez before the Senate Health, Education, Labor and Pensions Committee, Feb. 27, 2002. Other experts, such as University of California, Davis, professor of agricultural economics Philip L. Martin, says only about 250,000 workers actually "follow the crops." Hunderds of thousands of others are classified as "migrants" if they moved to the United States to work in agriculture.

[3] See Ronnie Greene, "Fields of Despair: Brutal farm labor bosses punished, but not growers who hire them," *The Miami Herald*, Sept. 1, 2003.

[4] *Ibid.*

[5] *Ibid.*

[6] The 52 percent figure is from "Findings from the National Agricultural Workers Survey, 1997-98; A Demographic and Employment Profile of United States Farmworkers," U.S. Department of Labor, March 2000. The 85 percent figure is from Sen. Larry E. Craig, at http://craig.senate.gov.

[7] "Findings from the National Agricultural Workers Survey, 1997-98," *ibid.*

[8] "Farmworker Exposure to Pesticide," testimony of Daniel G. Ford before the Washington State Board of Health, June 13, 2001.

[9] Testimony of Rosemary Sokas before the Senate Health, Education, Labor and Pensions Committee, Feb. 27, 2002.

[10] Rodriguez testimony, Feb. 27, 2002, *op. cit.*

[11] "Remarks of Peter Orum, President, American Nursery and Landscape Association, to United Farmworkers, AFL-CIO, Fresno, CA," speech, Aug. 29, 2004.

[12] See http://craig.senate.gov/.

[13] For background, see David Masci, "U.S.-Mexico Relations," *The CQ Researcher*, Nov. 9, 2001, pp. 921-944.

[14] "Remarks of Peter Orum," *op. cit.*

[15] See "H-2A Agricultural Guestworker Program: Changes Could Improve Services to Employers and Better Protect Workers," General Accounting Office, Dec. 24, 1997, www.gao.gov/archive/1998/he98020.pdf.

[16] Unless otherwise noted, the information in this section comes from Greene, *op. cit.*

[17] *Ibid.*

[18] *Ibid.*

[19] See Sam Quinones, "Roadblocks Signal Crackdown on Labor Issues; State inspectors return to California's fields after years of lax enforcement," *Los Angeles Times*, Sept. 1, 2004, p. B1.

[20] *Ibid.*

[21] *Ibid.*

[22] Rodriguez testimony, *op. cit.*

[23] See Ronnie Greene, "Fields of Despair; Politicians' farming interests led to drought of laws for workers," *The Miami Herald*, Sept. 2, 2003.

[24] *Ibid.*

[25] "New Data Show Record-Breaking Results from Strong Enforcement, Compliance Assistance," press release, U.S. Department of Labor, Nov. 18, 2003; http://www.dol.gov/opa/media/press/opa/OPA2003750.htm.

[26] Rodriguez testimony, *op. cit.*

[27] Quinones, *op. cit.*

[28] See "Now With Bill Moyers," Web site: http://www.pbs.org/now/politics/migrants.html.

[29] Americans spend about 12 percent of their disposable income on food, less than consumers in nearly every other industrialized nation. For background, see Kathy Koch, "Food Safety Battle: Organic vs. Biotech," *The CQ Researcher*, Sept. 4, 1998, pp. 761-784.

[30] Cindy Hahamovitch, *The Fruits of Their Labor: Atlantic Coast Farmworkers and the Making of Migrant Poverty* (1997).

[31] Daniel Rothenberg, *With These Hands: The Hidden World of Migrant Farmworkers Today* (1998), p. 38.

[32] See Moyers, *op. cit.*

[33] See Walter Goodman, " 'New Harvest, Old Shame,' About Farm Workers," *The New York Times*, April 17, 1990.

[34] *Ibid.*

[35] The *Post* series can be found at www.palmbeachpost.com/moderndayslavery/content/moderndayslavery/index.html.

[36] United Farm Workers Web site.

[37] See Elizabeth Shogren, "Bush Is Taken to Task on Immigration," *Los Angeles Times*, July 17, 2004, p. A13.

[38] See Emily Pierce, "Frist Blocks Craig's Immigration Measure," *Roll Call*, July 12, 2004.

[39] See Paul K. Mills and Sandy Kwong, "Cancer Incidence in the United Farmworkers of America, 1987-1997," *American Journal of Industrial Medicine*, 40:596-603 (2001).

[40] For background, see David Masci, "Human Trafficking and Slavery," *The CQ Researcher*, March 26, 2004, pp. 273-296.

[41] See www.usdoj.gov/trafficking.htm.

[42] See Lee Romney, "Union Takes Attack on Gallo to Net; United Farm Workers threatens a boycott if demands aren't met as contract talks resume," *Los Angeles Times*, Aug. 3, 2004, p. B9.

[43] For background, see Mary H. Cooper, "Exporting Jobs," *The CQ Researcher*, Feb. 20, 2004, pp. 149-172.

Bibliography

Selected Sources

Books

Daniel, Cletus E., *Bitter Harvest: A History of California Farmworkers, 1870-1941*, Cornell University Press, 1981.

A former farm laborer chronicles the rise of farm labor in California.

Hahamovitch, Cindy, *The Fruits of Their Labor: Atlantic Coast Farmworkers and the Making of Migrant Poverty, 1870-1945*, University of North Carolina Press, 1997.

A professor of labor history at The College of William and Mary examines the industrial forces behind the hardships of East Coast farmworkers.

Rothenberg, Daniel, *With These Hands: The Hidden World of Migrant Farmworkers Today*, Harcourt Brace, 1998.

A professor in the University of California's Law and Society Program interviewed 250 farmworkers.

Wilkinson, Alec, *Big Sugar: Seasons in the Cane Fields of Florida*, Alfred A. Knopf, 1989.

An exposé of the exploitation of West Indian workers.

Articles

"Migrants' misery; Many of the immigrant farmworkers who help grow and harvest North Carolina crops are caught in a cycle of exploitation," *The* [Raleigh, N.C.] *News & Observer*, Sept. 15, 2004, p. A20.

An editorial laments that "a porous U.S.-Mexican border and weak state laws on migrant labor continue to funnel farm workers into back-breaking jobs with impossibly long hours for skinflint wages in filthy conditions."

Bormann, Dawn, "La Raza calls for changes in immigration law," *The Kansas City Star*, Sept. 22, 2004, p. B8.

The country's largest Latino civil rights organization is demanding that Congress enact immigration reform, particularly by passing the AgJOBS bill.

Evans, Christine, *et al.*, "Modern Day Slavery," *The Palm Beach Post*, Dec. 7-9, 2003.

This three-part, award-winning exposé found undocumented workers in Florida being held against their will.

Greene, Ronnie, "Fields of Despair," *The Miami Herald*, Aug. 31-Sept. 2, 2003.

A three-part series found widespread violations of farmworkers' rights, ranging from underpayment of wages to assault.

Greene, Ronnie, "New Farmhand Abuse Claims Probed; Federal investigators and prosecutors are probing new allegations that farmworkers have been criminally abused in Florida," *The Miami Herald*, Dec. 4, 2003.

FBI agents investigate possible human trafficking.

Quinones, Sam, "Roadblocks Signal Crackdown on Labor Issues; State inspectors return to California's fields after years of lax enforcement of laws," *Los Angeles Times*, Sept. 1, 2004, p. B1.

California authorities make surprise inspections and discover rampant violations.

Romney, Lee, "Union Takes Attack on Gallo to Net," *Los Angeles Times*, Aug. 3, 2004, p. B9.

The relationship between the United Farm Workers and the world's largest winery sinks to a record low.

Shogren, Elizabeth, "Bush Is Taken to Task on Immigration," *Los Angeles Times*, July 17, 2004, p. A13.

The White House blocked a Senate vote on a key bill aimed at helping undocumented farmworkers.

Reports and Studies

"Findings from the National Agricultural Workers Survey (NAWS), 1997-98; A Demographic and Employment Profile of United States Farmworkers," Research Report No. 8, U.S. Department of Labor, March 2000.

The first detailed federal research into U.S. farm labor reveals that farmworkers face a variety of inequities.

"Fingers to the Bone: United States Failure to Protect Child Farmworkers," Human Rights Watch, June 2000.

The international advocacy group charges the federal government with failing to protect farmworkers and their children.

"Pesticides: Improvements Needed to Protect Farmworkers and Their Children," General Accounting Office, March 2000.

The GAO found that workers, and particularly their children, are at high risk of pesticide poisoning.

"Undocumented Immigrants: Facts and Figures," The Urban Institute, January 12, 2004.

Using data from the Department of Homeland Security, the nonpartisan research group draws a statistical picture of illegal aliens.

Mills, Paul K., and Sally Kwong, "Cancer Incidence in the United Farmworkers of America (UFW), 1987-97," *American Journal of Industrial Medicine*, Vol. 40, 2001, pp. 596-603.

UFW members, most of whom are Hispanic, have an elevated risk of leukemia, stomach, uterine cervix, and endometrial cancer in comparison to all Hispanics in California.

The Next Step:

Additional Articles from Current Periodicals

Foreign Migrant Workers

Magnier, Mark, "China's Migrant Workers Ask for Little and Receive Nothing," *Los Angeles Times*, Jan. 21, 2004, p. A4.

Even the Chinese government's notoriously unreliable statistics peg unpaid wages for the country's almost 100 million migrant workers at only $12.1 billion.

Perlez, Jane, "For Some Indonesians, Echoes of 'Coolie' Nation," *The New York Times*, Aug. 18, 2002, p. A10.

Thousands of Indonesian migrant workers are returning home, fleeing new laws in Malaysia that call for the imprisonment and caning of illegal workers.

Samuelson, Robert, "China: The New America?" *The Washington Post*, March 31, 2004, p. A25.

The AFL-CIO says exploitive labor practices — including the bondage of millions of migrant workers — have depressed China's factory wages and lowered export prices.

Yardley, Jim, "The New Uprooted," *The New York Times*, Sept. 12, 2004, Section 4, p. 6.

China has approximately 114 million migrant workers, not including the millions of family members who moved with them, and the government predicts the number will rise to 300 million by 2020.

Hardships and Abuses

Avila, Oscar, "Cut Off From Their World," *Chicago Tribune*, Sept. 8, 2004, p. C1.

The latest wave of migrant workers, speaking neither Spanish nor English, is vulnerable to mistreatment from employers and even faces racism from fellow workers.

Easterbrook, Michael, "Law Takes Beating in Migrant Camps," *The* [Raleigh, N.C.] *News & Observer*, Sept. 12, 2004, p. A1.

North Carolina's migrant workers, who make up half of the state's agricultural laborers, are paid paltry wages and live in substandard conditions.

Lee, Jennifer, "Lost Fruit in Central Florida Means Lost Jobs for Migrants," *The New York Times*, Sept. 10, 2004, p. A22.

Hurricanes Frances and Charley destroyed 90 percent of Polk County's grapefruit harvest, 50 percent of the orange crop and thousands of migrant workers' livelihoods.

Song, Jason, "Limbo of the Migrant Worker," *The Baltimore Sun*, May 14, 2003, p. 2A.

The nomadic fruit pickers in Carlsbad, Calif., who usually go home to Mexico in the winter have been wary of returning because of increased border security since Sept. 11, 2001.

Song, Jason, "Migrants' Job Hopes Clouded by Heavy Rains," *The Baltimore Sun*, July 28, 2003, p. 1A.

Thousands of migrant workers on the East Coast are jobless after almost four inches more rain than normal stunted crop growth and pushed back the work season.

Helping Migrant Workers

Belluck, Pam, "Maine Looks to Improve Conditions for Forestry Workers," *The New York Times*, Jan. 7, 2003, p. A12.

Two state legislators want to improve working conditions for migrant loggers by increasing pay and requiring companies to make the work environment safer.

Broadway, Bill, "Churches Back Boycotts Over Migrant Workers," *The Washington Post*, Nov. 22, 2003, p. B9.

The National Council of Churches endorsed consumer boycotts of Taco Bell and the Mt. Olive Pickle Co. in an effort to improve conditions for migrant workers in Florida and North Carolina.

Furhman, Janice, "Napa Vintners Work to Increase Farm-Worker Housing," *The San Francisco Chronicle*, March 23, 2001, p. 14.

Housing advocates, vintners and county offices worked to organize better housing for migrant workers and to raise the issue of homeless workers in affluent Napa.

Gorman, Tom, "Groups Try to Protect Low-wage Workers," *Los Angeles Times*, Jan. 21, 2001, p. A28.

Government, labor unions and church officials have joined together to create an outreach program to protect exploited migrant workers in Los Angeles.

Lofholm, Nancy, "Photographer Brings Farmworkers' Lives into Focus," *The Denver Post*, Jan. 25, 2004, p. A27.

Photographer Celia Roberts creates a calendar each year showing migrant workers in fields and camps across America and donates the proceeds and her time to improve workers' lives.

Lydersen, Kari, "Immigrant Advocates Win Award," *The Washington Post*, Nov. 20, 2003, p. A3.

Members of an advocacy group working to improve the lives of South Florida's migrant workers exposed five slavery rings where workers were beaten and held hostage.

Romney, Lee, "Workers' Medical Records Can Now Follow the Harvest," *Los Angeles Times*, Oct. 9, 2003, p. B6.

A new pilot program enables doctors to use the Internet to obtain the health histories of migrant patients, who suffer disproportionately from chronic health problems and rarely have medical records.

Immigration Laws

Boudreaux, Richard, and Maura Reynolds, "Fox Backs Bush's Reforms," *Los Angeles Times*, Jan. 13, 2004, p. A1.
Mexican President Vicente Fox supports President Bush's proposed plan to offer temporary work permits to millions of illegal Mexican immigrants working in the United States.

Madrick, Jeff, "The Bush Proposal on Illegal Immigrants is a Tentative but Important First Step," *The New York Times*, Jan. 22, 2004, p. C2.
By providing migrant workers legal status, including eligibility for domestic social programs, businesses could not as easily pay low wages or ignore payroll taxes.

Reza, H. G., "Bush Plan No Migrant Lure," *Los Angeles Times*, Feb. 15, 2004, p. B1.
The president's plan to allow guest workers in the United States is not finding a huge demand among Mexicans who would not have otherwise crossed the border.

Rucker, Patrick, "Immigrants Face Taxing Times," *Chicago Tribune*, April 14, 2004, p. C1.
Filing income-tax returns does nothing to benefit the immigration status of illegal workers, but an increasing number believe their tax returns will prove they could be good citizens.

Living Conditions

Akhtar, Faiza, "The Changing Face of the Suffolk Harvest," *The New York Times*, Oct. 6, 2002, Section 14, p. 1.
Southern agricultural workers used to migrate to Long Island in the 1940s and '50s by the thousands, but illegal Latinos are now the core group of the area's migrant workers.

Angel, Amanda, "Working in Foreign Fields," *The Baltimore Sun*, Oct. 19, 2003, p. 1B.
About 50,000 foreign migrant workers come into the United States each year to provide seasonal agricultural work on H-2A visas, an increasingly popular program.

Blanding, Michael, "The Invisible Harvest," *Boston Magazine*, October 2002.
The harvest of tobacco leaves in Massachusetts requires backbreaking, repetitive labor in poor conditions.

Ellingwood, Ken, "Town's Migrant Workers Living and Leaving in Fear," *Los Angeles Times*, Aug. 18, 2003, p. 13.
Immigrants in Canton, Miss., are scattering after the fatal shooting of a coworker, a series of firings at a local plant and a roundup threat by the county sheriff.

Sebastian, Simone, "Faith in the Field," *Chicago Tribune*, July 24, 2003, p. N1.
Each summer, an Indiana farm is transformed from a place of labor to a place of worship in an effort to bring church services to the workplace of Spanish-speaking migrant workers.

Migrant Money

Dwyer, Timothy, "Under the Trees, the Gift of Community," *The Washington Post*, Dec. 7, 2002, p. A1.
As the Christmas tree business in southwestern Virginia has grown, so has farmers' utter dependence on migrant workers.

"Monetary lifeline," *The Economist*, July 31, 2004, Finance & Economics Section.
Remittances sent back home by migrant workers in rich countries — and totaling some $93 billion last year — are increasingly important to developing economies.

Rawe, Julie, "The Fastest Way to Make Money," *Time*, June 23, 2003, p. A6.
As the pace of global migration quickens, so does the business of Western Union, a makeshift bank for millions of migrant workers who send money back home.

CITING *THE CQ RESEARCHER*

Sample formats for citing these reports in a bibliography include the ones listed below. Preferred styles and formats vary, so please check with your instructor or professor.

MLA STYLE

Jost, Kenneth. "Rethinking the Death Penalty." The CQ Researcher 16 Nov. 2001: 945-68.

APA STYLE

Jost, K. (2001, November 16). Rethinking the death penalty. *The CQ Researcher, 11*, 945-968.

CHICAGO STYLE

Jost, Kenneth. "Rethinking the Death Penalty." *CQ Researcher*, November 16, 2001, 945-968.

CQ Researcher

Published by CQ Press, a division of Congressional Quarterly Inc.

thecqresearcher.com

Media Bias

Are the major sources of news trustworthy?

Charges of media bias have never been louder than they are today. Both liberals and conservatives complain about slanted coverage of central events such as the war in Iraq and the presidential campaign. CBS was universally condemned in September for basing a report about President Bush on fake documents, but every major media outlet has come in for its share of criticism. The Fox News Channel and popular commentator Bill O'Reilly have been called little more than spokesmen for the Republican Party. And Fox, *The Wall Street Journal* and MSNBC have all come under fire recently for the perceived right-wing slant of their reporters and political commentators. With distrust so rampant, experts are asking whether the American public as a whole can ever agree about what constitutes the truth. In an era of polarized politics, if citizens can't even agree about what the facts are because they don't trust major sources of information, it is that much more unlikely that the populace will be able reach consensus on the major issues of the day.

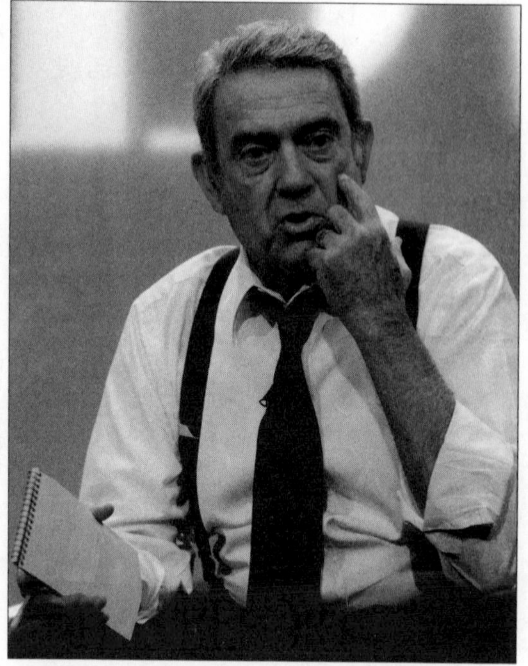

CBS News anchor Dan Rather lost credibility when memos he aired on Sept. 4, 2004, about President Bush's stint in the Texas Air National Guard turned out to be fake.

INSIDE THIS REPORT

The CQ Researcher • Oct. 15, 2004 • www.thecqresearcher.com
Volume 14, Number 36 • Pages 853-876

CQ Press

Recipient of Society of Professional Journalists Award for Excellence ◆ American Bar Association Silver Gavel Award

THE ISSUES

BACKGROUND

CURRENT SITUATION

OUTLOOK

SIDEBARS AND GRAPHICS

FOR FURTHER RESEARCH

Cover: After conservative bloggers questioned the memos aired on Sept. 4 by CBS News anchor Dan Rather about President Bush's Air National Guard service, CBS admitted the documents were fake and that it had been tricked by a partisan source. (AFP Photo/Stan Honda)

Oct. 15, 2004
Volume 14, Number 36

MANAGING EDITOR: Thomas J. Colin
ASSISTANT MANAGING EDITOR: Kathy Koch
ASSOCIATE EDITOR: Kenneth Jost
STAFF WRITERS: Mary H. Cooper, William Triplett
CONTRIBUTING WRITERS: Sarah Glazer, David Hatch, David Hosansky, Patrick Marshall, Tom Price, Jane Tanner
DESIGN/PRODUCTION EDITOR: Olu B. Davis
ASSISTANT EDITOR: Kate Templin

A Division of
Congressional Quarterly Inc.

SENIOR VICE PRESIDENT/GENERAL MANAGER: John A. Jenkins
DIRECTOR, LIBRARY PUBLISHING: Kathryn C. Suárez
DIRECTOR, EDITORIAL OPERATIONS: Ann Davies

CONGRESSIONAL QUARTERLY INC.
CHAIRMAN: Paul C. Tash
VICE CHAIRMAN: Andrew P. Corty
PRESIDENT AND PUBLISHER: Robert W. Merry

The CQ Researcher (ISSN 1056-2036) is printed on acid-free paper. Published weekly, except Jan. 2, April 9, July 2, July 9, Aug. 6, Aug. 13, Nov. 26 and Dec. 31, by CQ Press, a division of Congressional Quarterly Inc. Annual subscription rates for institutions start at $625. For pricing, call 1-800-834-9020, ext. 1906. To purchase a *CQ Researcher* report in print or electronic format (PDF), visit www.cqpress.com or call 866-427-7737. A single report is $10. Bulk purchase discounts and electronic-rights licensing are also available. Periodicals postage paid at Washington, D.C., and additional mailing offices. POSTMASTER: Send address changes to *The CQ Researcher*, 1255 22nd St., N.W., Suite 400, Washington, D.C. 20037.

BY ALAN GREENBLATT

THE ISSUES

Washington Post media critic Howard Kurtz thought minority journalists behaved appallingly when President Bush and Sen. John Kerry addressed their convention in Washington in August. [1]

Kerry's speech was interrupted by applause about 50 times. Bush, by contrast, received polite clapping. Some in attendance, in fact, laughed derisively at Bush's answers to questions about terrorism and tribal sovereignty.

"As a journalist, I don't applaud — or boo — politicians," said Kurtz. "Three-quarters of the Unity convention gave Kerry a standing ovation, but was much more tepid toward President Bush. I think that's way out of line and opens the minority organizations involved to accusations of political bias. Especially during a campaign, it's important for journalists not to appear to take sides." [2]

Nevertheless, the event illustrated something that many conservatives have long believed — that much of the media have a liberal bias. "As a registered Republican, I tend to feel that a lot of journalists lean to the left wing and just don't take President Bush seriously," said Val Canez, a photographer for the *Tucson Citizen* who attended the Unity conference. "How people reacted today proved that for me." [3]

Most mainstream journalists are more discreet about their political leanings, but surveys continually show that reporters tend to be more liberal than Americans as a whole, particularly on social issues such as abortion, gun control and gay rights. A recent poll by the Pew Research Center for the People & the Press confirmed that there is the perception among conservatives that CBS, NPR, *The New York Times* and other mainstream outlets have a liberal bias. [4] Journalists insist that they keep their own opinions out of their newspapers or television stories, and that editors monitor their work for fairness.

AFP Photo

Conservative Fox News commentator Bill O'Reilly, right, interviews filmmaker Michael Moore during the Democratic National Convention in July 2004. Moore's movie "Fahrenheit 9/11" has made him a leading critic of President Bush. Both liberals and conservatives are complaining about perceived bias in news coverage of critical events such as the war in Iraq.

Moreover, right-leaning bloggers were the first to call into question the authenticity of memos used by CBS News anchor Dan Rather on Sept. 8, when he reported that Bush had received special treatment during his National Guard career. Within two weeks, Rather had admitted that the documents were fake and that CBS had been gulled by a partisan source. Even though a secretary later confirmed on the air that the allegations in the fake memos were indeed accurate, the damage to CBS' credibility had already been done.

Yet critics on the other side of the political spectrum complain that the mainstream media have become little more than stenographic services for government and corporate powerbrokers or — in the case of Fox News — for the Republican Party. (*See sidebar, p. 864.*) Fox, *The Wall Street Journal* and MSNBC have all come under fire within recent weeks for the perceived right-wing slant of their reporters and political commentators. [5]

Many media critics trace the problems to the recent takeover of America's major media outlets by corporate conglomerates and what they see as the press' fear of offending official sources that control access to the White House and other government news. An overdependence on official sources, critics say, was especially evident during coverage of the recent Iraq war. Indeed, this past summer after no weapons of mass destruction had been found in Iraq, *The New York Times* and *The Washington Post* questioned the accuracy of their own coverage leading up to the war, and *The New Republic* ran several articles under the cover headline, "Were We Wrong?" All three publications concluded they had given too much weight to administration claims, and a recent liberal documentary, "Uncovered: The Whole Truth About the Iraq War," implied that the U.S. press did not treat the administration's justification for going to war with enough skepticism. [6]

In the 19th century, American journalists were openly biased, with papers actively promoting the fortunes of one political party over another. In contemporary practice, however, journalists are taught to strive for fairness. But some critics complain that the press lost that appearance of fairness when it adopted a propensity to offer analysis.

"If you don't have any analysis in a story, you haven't done your job," says Martin Johnson, a political scientist at the University of California, Riverside, who has studied the media. "But

Democrats Have Most Faith in the Media

With the sole exception of the Fox News Channel, Republicans believe far less in the credibility of major news organizations than Democrats.

Partisanship and Credibility

	Believe all or most of what the news organization says	
	Republicans	Democrats
Broadcast and cable outlets:		
CNN	26	45
CBS News	15	34
NPR	15	33
NewsHour	12	29
60 Minutes	25	42
ABC News	17	34
MSNBC	14	29
C-SPAN	22	36
NBC News	16	30
Local TV News	21	29
Fox News Channel	29	24
Print Outlets:		
The Associated Press	12	29
New York Times	14	31
Time	15	30
Newsweek	12	26
USA Today	14	25
Daily newspaper	16	23
Wall Street Journal	23	29

Source: "News Audiences Increasingly Politicized," The Pew Research Center for the People & the Press, June 8, 2004

then you're open to the criticism of injecting bias. We want reporters to be thoughtful and analytical, but at the same time we want them to be objective and not tell us what they really think about things, and those are two entirely contradictory propositions."

As a result, many Americans today — convinced that news outlets are biased — are seeking out networks and publications that gibe with their own political views. The recent explosion in the availability of news outlets — with the advent of round-the-clock cable television news and the Internet — enables them to do that easily. Americans who once had to get their news from one or two local newspapers or a 30-minute broadcast by one of three networks can pick their own "politically appropriate" media — from right-leaning talk radio, Internet sites and Fox News to left-leaning independent media sources or newspapers from around the world via the Internet.

And thanks to new technology, news junkies can keep up with the news 24 hours a day, using Palm Pilots and cell phones or reading headlines on their Internet service providers' home pages. And Internet users who haven't found a Web blog — as Internet journals are called — that shares their political viewpoint just haven't been looking.

"The old line in broadcasting that there is one message that is going to make sense to everybody is just not the model that we're working under any more," says Barbie Zelizer, a professor at the Annenberg School of Communications at the University of Pennsylvania.

Some fear that this "Balkanization" of the nation's news media will exacerbate the partisan divide that already afflicts the political landscape.[7] "After Sept. 11, American mainstream culture has become much more politicized than it was before and probably more than it's been in a generation. The media are contributing to that," says Matthew Felling, media director of the Center for Media and Public Affairs.

The splintering of the nation's news media and the profusion of technology have also radically changed the way news is covered, amply demonstrated in the coverage of the presidential campaign this year by fully accredited bloggers.

In addition, critics say the political press has expended too much time and energy on charges and countercharges, rather than investigating the candidates' plans for Medicare, Social Security or national defense. "Bush, Kerry and their operatives drown reporters with an around-the-clock deluge of spin — via e-mail, fax, cell phone and Web blogs — leaving them little time to report and reflect on what is true and what isn't," the *Columbia Journalism Review* complained this summer.[8]

Some critics say Kerry has been slow to adapt to the realities of the new media. For instance, in August he did not immediately respond to commercials by the Swift Boat Veterans for

Confidence in Media Dropped

Americans' confidence in the media dropped "a significant" 10 percentage points in the past year, according to a recent Gallup Poll. The September 2004 poll was taken after questions were raised about the credibility of a report by CBS News anchorman Dan Rather about President George W. Bush's Vietnam-era National Guard service. Gallup called the poll results "particularly striking" because public confidence previously had been very stable — fluctuating only between 51% and 55% from 1997-2003.

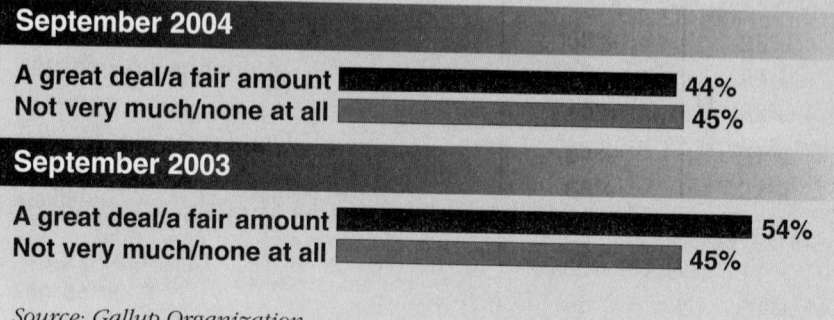

Do you have confidence in the media's ability to report news stories accurately and fairly?

Source: Gallup Organization

Truth attacking his Vietnam War record. In a classic example of the modern media "echo chamber" — which can magnify the impact of the smallest news item — the initial ads, despite running in just seven media markets in three states, were heavily covered by the television and cable networks.

Indeed, a Kerry friend said the candidate focuses too much on traditional outlets and does not understand the modern media market. "You would think he would have recognized this five years ago," the friend said. [9]

The Rather affair revealed the new media reality: The traditional media — the three biggest broadcast networks and the large national daily newspapers — no longer control the agenda for the political debate. With the networks ratcheting down their election coverage, outlets that didn't even exist five years ago now dominate the field.

"A big difference is that Democrats continue to try to play within the traditional media, such as the TV networks, *The New York Times*, the *Post* and the major papers," says Elizabeth Wilner, political director for NBC News, "while the Republicans have done a far better job of using alternative news sources and new news sources, such as the Internet and the Fox cable network and talk radio." [10]

"This is potentially a big cultural moment," editorialized *The Wall Street Journal* in September. "For decades, liberal media elites were able to define current debates by all kicking in the same direction, like the Rockettes." [11]

Of course, liberals have long lambasted *The Wall Street Journal* editorial page, Fox News and conservative talk radio hosts like Rush Limbaugh as kicking in a distinctly right-wing direction. With so many charges of bias flying in all directions and the growing intensity of media criticism (and self-criticism) many Americans now believe the media simply can't be trusted to tell the truth. The media's credibility also has taken major body blows in recent years after reporters at some of the nation's most venerable news outlets were found to have fabricated news stories. [12]

"The common ground for public understanding and public information may be destroyed in all this," warns Frank Sesno, a communications professor at George Mason University in Virginia and former TV broadcaster and CNN executive. "The simple question of 'what happened today?' becomes something we're in danger of arguing over." [13]

"The danger is conveying to people that there's no trustworthy source of news," says the University of California's Johnson. "If that's the message that people ultimately get, that makes it really difficult for them to evaluate the actions of people in government."

As observers consider current changes in the media, here are some of the questions they are asking:

Is the news audience fracturing along partisan lines?

Patty Cron travels regularly for business and puts up with a lot from hotels, but if there's one thing she can't stand it's a place that offers CNN as the only cable news choice on the room televisions. She prefers Fox News Channel. "When that happens, I check out and switch hotels," she told *The Dallas Morning News*." [14]

Most people probably wouldn't go to that much effort. But in the increasingly fragmented media world, millions of Americans are seeking a "journalism of affirmation" — news presentations that explain or contextualize events in a way that accords with their political outlook.

"Political polarization is increasingly reflected in the public's news habits," concluded the Pew Research Center for the People & the Press. "In an era of deep-seated political divisions, conservatives and liberals are increasingly choosing sides in their TV news preferences."[15]

A Pew poll of 3,000 adults found that 41 percent of Republicans regularly watched Fox, and 25 percent watched CNN. By contrast, only 20 percent of Democrats watched Fox, while 44 percent watched CNN. In general, Pew found that Republicans were more skeptical about the credibility of major media outlets than Democrats.[16]

"The audience is fracturing on partisan lines, and a big contributor to that are 24-hour cable-news networks," says Richard Campbell, director of the journalism program at Miami University in Ohio. Not only do ratings-sensitive cable networks exacerbate partisanship, he says, but they raise the decibel level of the political debate. "If you look at those shows over a long period of time, the goal is conflict, the goal is to create drama by getting people to yell at each other."

When the media, blogs, talk radio and "shouting heads" cable programming accentuate division, it leaves less of a market for straight, seemingly unbiased accounts, such as those appearing on low-key discussion programs like "The NewsHour With Jim Lehrer," "The Charlie Rose Show" and radio's "The Diane Rehm Show."

"It's a very lonely business to present the facts, because what sells is opinion-mongering," agrees Felling, at the Center for Media and Public Affairs. He argues that because Americans are so deluged with information, "People are hungry for someone to contextualize the news. They go to opinion-makers because it saves time."

Some media observers see this as a positive development. They believe that all news outlets have their hidden biases and should be upfront about them, like the press in Europe. "For the first time in decades, it's become transparently clear that America has an ideological media, that our TV networks, newspapers, magazines and radio talk shows all represent particular points of view," writes *LA Weekly* media columnist John Powers.[17]

Others think the trend is worrisome. If people look for outlets that confirm their preconceived ideas and views and don't trust others, says Charlotte Grimes, who holds Syracuse University's Knight Chair in Political Reporting, it becomes harder for society to reach a general consensus about the meaning of events and the right policy course for responding to them. "When I was growing up, there were far fewer media options, giving Americans a far larger body of shared cultural experience," Powers writes.[18]

While the number of Americans seeking partisan affirmation is growing, it has not reached a critical mass. The majority of the U.S. news audience is not shopping for news outlets with a political bias, say media experts. "The bulk of the population is not necessarily going to be seeking out partisan journalism," says Robert McChesney, a professor of communication at the University of Illinois.

Indeed, the Pew Research Center's survey found that 58 percent of Americans do not care whether a news source shares their views, while only 36 percent do. "It's not yet a majority perspective," says Scott Keeter, associate director of the center. "It isn't that a majority of the public really wants to see news with a view, but some do. For some conservatives and Republicans, they may feel they have found that in Fox."

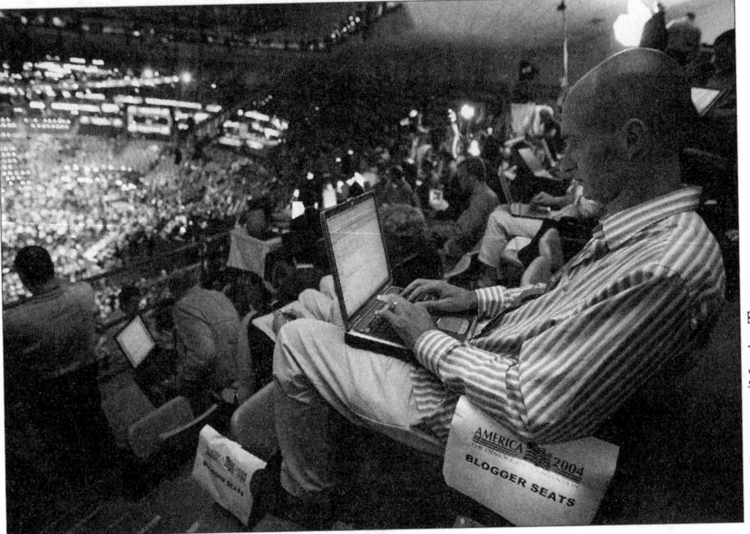

Getty Images/Mario Tama

Internet bloggers served as credentialed members of the press during the Democratic National Convention in July 2004, helping to change the way news is covered.

Fox News is now the leading source for news on cable; CNN, for example, gets about two-thirds of the Fox News Channel's viewers. But Fox's audience is only a fraction of the broadcast networks' audience share; each network news show gets about three times as many viewers as Fox's top news show.

"At this point, what's called the mainstream news — at the networks and the cable networks aside from Fox — has significant influence about what people think about, if not what they think," McChesney says.

Does having more news outlets mean the public is better informed?

The function of the news media in a democracy is to produce an informed electorate. Thirty years ago, the electorate had limited choices for news: three newsweeklies, three television networks and the nation's daily newspapers. Today, Americans can choose between a seemingly infinite number of broadcast, cable, newspaper and magazine outlets, both in print and online, domestic and international.

Jack Shafer, a media columnist with the online magazine *Slate*, says the proliferation of news sources makes Americans better informed. "There is undoubtedly a greater flow of information," he says. "If people have a taste for media and want to spend time with a variety of channels and Web sites, absolutely" they will be better informed than under the "old media" regime.

In addition to having more news outlets, he adds, consumers have easier access to everything from raw government data to live coverage of major events, including White House news briefings and daily sessions of Congress. It's not clear, however, how well people are taking advantage of all the information that's available.

"In the same way that you are what you eat, you become what you consume in the news business," says former *Boston Globe* Associate Editor David Nyhan, who worries that shrill sources of information are starving their listeners except for "a cadre of people with an appetite for serious news." He adds: "You can't force people to eat their broccoli."

Tom Rosenstiel, director of the Project for Excellence in Journalism, makes a similar comparison: Even though today more fruits and vegetables and other healthy foods are more readily available year-round, people seem to be eating more junk food than ever.

"There's a similar risk here in our information diet," he says. "Some people are better informed, while some have become expert in the trivial, and some have just engrossed themselves in propaganda. We're faced with a Scandinavian smorgasbord every day, and you don't always eat healthy food at a smorgasbord."

Still, cable and the Internet have been a boon to Nyhan's broccoli eaters — those who seek out hard news. Steve Rendall, a senior analyst at Fairness and Accuracy in Reporting (FAIR), a left-leaning media-watchdog group, notes that the British Broadcasting Corporation's (BBC) Web site received a million more hits a day during the run-up to the Iraq war and during the war in Afghanistan.

"They thought the vast majority of the hits were from the United States," he says, adding that Americans were surfing British Web sites because they felt they weren't getting adequate information from the U.S. press.

Critics of the U.S. media complain that it is obsessed with gore and gossip. "If it bleeds, it leads," critics say about local TV news. Similarly, cable networks often dedicate the majority of their 24 hours a day of news to murder trials and celebrity gossip. Seemingly incessant updates about the legal troubles of Kobe Bryant, Martha Stewart or Scott Peterson sometimes crowd out reporting on the environment, foreign affairs and other serious topics, critics say.

"We have a lot more voices, but I don't know how much journalism we've got going on, at least journalism as it's taught at universities like mine — digging out stories," says the University of Illinois' McChesney. "Most of what they do is regurgitate what someone else has uncovered or what someone in power is talking about."

Felling, at the Center for Media and Public Affairs, agrees. "The paradox of the new media landscape is that there are more outlets and less information." Picking up on the food metaphor, he says, "Print news is the protein of the news diet; all the rest is junk food. The 24-hour news outlets are all sizzle and no steak."

Lee Rainie of the Pew Internet and American Life Project, says the Internet has become a great tool for those who want to know more about serious issues. "It's so much easier now," he says. "The Internet absolutely helps you know more."

But Rainie notes that people can just as easily turn away from general news — accessing information in cyberspace about their church or favorite football team, while their neighbors are turning to Web sites dedicated to knitting or cats. "They're better informed about the things that they care about."

That's not necessarily going to be the great issues of the day. "There are just a lot of people out there who are really inattentive to politics," says the University of California's Johnson. "A lot of people think what's really going on is Spider Man."

Other observers worry that the fracturing of the news audience — combined with media and business changes that are leading to overconcentration on a few big, dramatic stories at the expense of duller government reporting — could cause some real problems for democracy.

There have been numerous instances in recent years of public opinion forcing changes in policy. During the 1980s, Congress repealed major changes in Medicare it had passed the year before after seniors protested. During the 1990s, the lack of public support for a universal health plan proposed by President Bill Clinton led to the death of that proposal — and was a prime contributor to Republicans taking control of Congress in 1995 after years in the minority. Outrage over photographs taken in the Abu Ghraib prison in Iraq forced the Bush administration to clarify its anti-torture policies.

For every case in which public opinion was roused, there are hundreds of examples of government decisions that didn't receive press coverage sufficient to awaken constituent ire. There's a cliché in politics — "sunshine is the best disinfectant" — meaning the more people know about government decisions, the more likely they're going to be made in the public interest. When the press fails to perform its watchdog role, last-minute changes can be made to legislation designed to benefit special interests, or government contracts rewarded to campaign contributors or friends of public officials.

"I can't be in Washington or in my statehouse all the time paying attention to politics," says the University of California's Johnson. "I entrust that job to people in the press who can be there, paying attention for me."

Is There an al Qaeda-Iraq Link?

A far higher percentage of people who get their news primarily from Fox than from PBS-NPR incorrectly thought that the U.S. had found clear evidence in Iraq that Saddam Hussein was working closely with the al Qaeda terrorist network.

Americans Who Thought There Was a Link

(By percentage of those who depend primarily on each source for news)

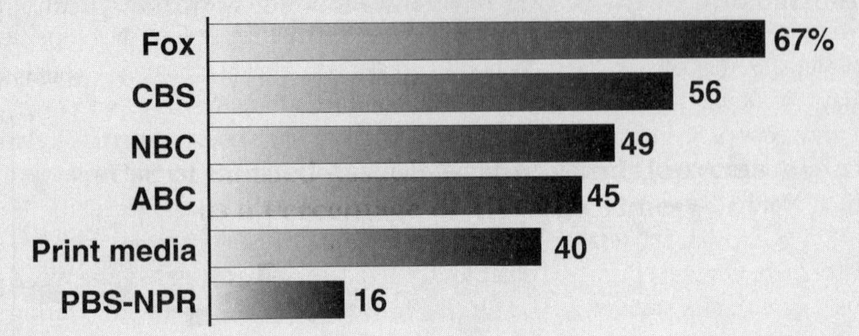

Source: "Misperceptions, the Media and the Iraq War," The PIPA/Knowledge Networks Poll, Oct. 2, 2003

But Bruce Bartlett, a senior fellow at the National Center for Policy Analysis, celebrates the proliferation of sources for political information as a vast improvement over the "old paradigm," when information was controlled by a few chosen media outlets.

"Today, cable news, C-SPAN, talk radio and the Internet raise questions and disseminate raw material to millions of people who are no longer bound by the quasi-monopoly of three television networks and one-newspaper towns," Bartlett writes. "They can now get news that otherwise would be suppressed or ignored, check original sources for themselves and draw their own conclusions." [19]

Has the press been sufficiently skeptical in its coverage of Iraq?

No event in recent years has caused such intense media self-examination as the war in Iraq. And perhaps no other event demonstrates the difficulty the press has in balancing its mandate to report the news — including repeating official statements — while at the same time questioning official sources. Many journalists now wonder whether the media were rigorous enough in challenging Bush administration rationales for war that have proved, in retrospect, mostly wrong.

The conclusions last summer by *The New York Times*, *The Washington Post* and *The New Republic* that they had given too much weight to administration claims may have been unprecedented.

"Before the war, U.S. journalists were far too reliant on sources sympathetic to the administration," wrote Michael Massing, a *Columbia Journalism Review* contributing editor. "Despite abundant evidence of the administration's brazen misuse of intelligence in this matter, the press repeatedly let officials get away with it." [20]

But Dana Priest, a national security reporter at the *Post*, says she "never felt any pressure to be on board [with the war], or less skeptical. All these people who criticize the press now — it's not like we had the information that there were no WMD [weapons of mass destruction] and we didn't put it out. We didn't have the information."

In fact, the *Post* and other publications did question the validity of the claim that Iraq had WMD, but the volume and frequency of administration claims — and the front-page treatment they received — tended to drown out the doubt. According to a study by FAIR, the media-watchdog group, 76 percent of the sources in network stories about Iraq during the war were current or former government officials. [21]

"War is far too important to be left to the ex-generals, and that's basically what we were left with," FAIR's Rendall says.

Many reporters point out that part of their job is to report official statements by administration officials and that the skepticism should have started with the opposition party or members of the broader intelligence community. But the Democratic leadership in Congress supported the decision to go to war and, as John Diamond, who covers intelligence issues for *USA Today*, puts it, "Regrettably, there was no country in the world with an intelligence community robust enough to question U.S. and British intelligence."

Diamond says the fact that the Bush administration had ramped up its rhetoric so strongly from earlier Clinton administration claims that Iraq was reconstituting its WMD programs suggested that it must have had some compelling evidence. And when the press demanded proof, the administration's response that America couldn't afford to wait for proof of a smoking gun to emerge in the form of a mushroom cloud was a tacit admission that proof was lacking, he says.

"They were essentially saying we're willing to act without proof," he says. "There was nothing for reporters to hang their hats on other than Iraqi denials, and they had a long history of lying."

Rosenstiel, of the Project for Excellence in Journalism, says covering the run-up to the war in Iraq was different

Continued on p. 862

Documentaries Giving Partisans New Voice

Like many conservatives and critics, Peter Rollins, editor-in-chief of the journal *Film & History*, takes issue with Michael Moore's portrayal of the Bush administration in his controversial film "Fahrenheit 9/11." Rollins calls Moore "wacky but thrilling" and says he has a "sophomoric, simplistic view."

But unlike other Moore critics, Rollins has no doubts that "Fahrenheit" belongs in the category of documentary film. "They say it's not objective," Rollins says, "but no documentary has ever tried to be objective. Moore's film is very much in the tradition of the persuasive film."

If "Fahrenheit 9/11" has plenty of antecedents, from the late Leni Riefenstal's movies about Nazi Germany to the 1974 anti-Vietnam War documentary "Hearts and Minds," Moore also has plenty of company these days. Every week seems to bring the release of yet another anti-Bush movie, such as "The Oil Factor Behind the War on Terror"; "Hijacking Catastrophe: 9/11, Fear & the Selling of the American Empire" and two recent films by Robert Greenwald that are achieving underground celebrity: "Uncovered: The Whole Truth About the Iraq War," and "Outfoxed: Rupert Murdoch's War on Journalism." Several, including "Bush's Brain," illustrate and elaborate arguments that had already been put forward in books.

"To a certain extent, I believe liberals have found their message vehicle in popular documentaries, just as Republicans did in talk radio," says Matthew Felling, media director at the Washington-based Center for Media and Public Affairs.

Liberals may not hold onto such a monopoly much longer. On Oct. 5, the day Moore's film was released on DVD, conservative groups released the DVD of "George W. Bush: Faith in the White House," a documentary about Bush's Christian faith — which is being sent to thousands of churches as the conservative response to "Fahrenheit 9/11." Then, conservative Sinclair Broadcasting announced it would broadcast a 90-minute anti-Kerry documentary on its 62 television stations. And two festivals devoted to conservative documentaries have recently been held in Dallas and Los Angeles. "There hasn't been an appetite for it, but I have a feeling that's about to change," says Roger Aronoff, a conservative media critic who has just completed "Confronting Iraq," a documentary about the war.

Liberals and conservatives — and non-political storytellers — are crafting documentaries in unprecedented number for two reasons: technology and money. Digital video cameras and editing have made the creation and manipulation of images neater and easier.

"It's so quick and inexpensive," says William McDonald, head of the cinematography program at the UCLA School of Theater, Film and Television. "In the past, people might have had an idea for a documentary but wouldn't have known how to pay for it, and production would have been cumbersome. Now you just pick up a camcorder and make a film."

Homemade documentaries are sometimes passed around among partisans on DVD and videotape, similar to the way *samizdat* — underground literature — was circulated in the old Soviet Union. But other, more carefully crafted films are making serious money. Documentary filmmakers used to consider themselves lucky to get a one-time screening at a festival, but now they can set their sights on a long run at the multiplex.

"Supersize Me," which documented the effects of eating a month's worth of meals at McDonald's, spent several weeks among the Top 10 box office leaders last spring. "The Fog of War," an Oscar winner about the career of former Defense Secretary Robert S. McNamara, grossed about $10 million. "Fahrenheit 9/11," which made $120 million in theaters and will probably earn even more as a DVD, shattered Moore's previous record, for 2002's "Bowling for Columbine," as the top-grossing non-Imax documentary of all time.

That kind of financial return will only encourage more people to invest in documentaries, says David Thomson, a film historian in San Francisco. Much of the audience, he suggests, is made up of adults who are tired of the preponderance of Hollywood films targeted at children and teenagers. "There are a lot of people — it's a minority, but still enough to make an audience — who are pretty well sick of the fiction films that are being made in America today," Thomson says.

Rick McKay, director of the recent documentary "Broadway: The Golden Age," agrees. "Feature films these days tend to be for the lowest common denominator, and people are demanding something that makes them think and inspires them," he said in an online chat. "There is a huge void to be filled that documentary filmmakers are filling without the support of a studio. Documentaries are the last vestige of free speech and passion in the film industry that literally one person can make alone." [1]

Thomson says that the documentary tradition in this country, particularly on television, is not as rich as in his native England, but he's not surprised that the medium has become hot in a time of polarization. "Whenever people are politically aroused, and we definitely live in a time when the country is fiercely divided, I think people want to know more about what's going on," he says.

But Thomson warns that, with documentaries, seeing is not necessarily believing. Images can be manipulated and moments captured on film can take on new meanings when put in a different context.

"Documentary is not naturally, inherently factual," Thomson says. "It's very open to trickery of one kind or another."

---

[1] "Film: 'Broadway: The Golden Age,'" Aug. 6, 2004, http://www.washingtonpost.com/wp-dyn/articles/A43460-2004Aug5.html.

Continued from p. 860

from covering a big domestic story, such as Medicare, which would allow reporters to check for themselves whether the program is working as advertised. Because Iraq was a closed society, it was even different than covering the 1999 war in Kosovo, where reporters could witness for themselves evidence of ethnic cleansing.

"Virtually no one was in Iraq, and if they were, there weren't a lot of people they could ask about WMD," Rosenstiel says. "It's easy to say that they should have known, but the fact is, it may well be that the secretary of State was misled, and he's got a lot more clearance than the national security correspondent of *The Washington Post*."

Reporters and media critics have lamented the fact that major news outlets such as *The New York Times* relied so heavily on self-promoting sources, particularly from Ahmed Chalabi and his defector group, the Iraqi National Congress (INC), while giving little credence to minority voices arguing that there were no WMD. "The INC's agenda was to get us into a war," wrote *New York Daily News* reporter Helen Kennedy. "The really damaging stories all came from those guys, not the CIA." [22]

After the war started, the press focused more on how the war was being fought — highlighting sophisticated new weapons and communications systems, for example — than on why the United States was at war. Once the occupation began to sour, however, press questioning of administration plans and tactics became more aggressive. Indeed, administration officials and some members of Congress have criticized the press for focusing too much on negative stories about Iraq and not highlighting successes there.

Even after all this time, "they still don't cover Iraq adequately," says Laurie Mylroie, a scholar at the American Enterprise Institute and the author of several books and articles about Iraq. "A year and a half later, when the war is still going on, the coverage becomes thin and ill-informed and politicized."

Indeed, views of war coverage have become politicized. The press has been criticized from the left for being too slow to break the story of prisoner abuses at the Abu Ghraib prison and from the right for concentrating too much on such stories. Although liberal opponents of the war were chagrined at the U.S. flag emblems regularly displayed as graphics decorating news broadcasts, supporters cheered the literal flag-waving.

Administration defenders note that the belief Saddam Hussein possessed WMD was held not only by the Bush administration but also by foreign leaders. They argued there was an ongoing connection between Hussein and Osama bin Laden's al Qaeda terrorist network, for months after the 9/11 Commission report to the contrary. [23]

"I would be willing to bet lunch or dinner at a good restaurant," says Michael Schudson, a professor of media studies at the University of California, San Diego, that the question of whether coverage of the Iraq war and its aftermath has been fair "would break down entirely by party affiliation."

The fact that the debate about Iraq retains its partisan charge has not kept many reporters from wishing they had questioned the Bush administration more critically about its justifications for the war. But, for the most part, they believe they did the best they could, given the unfavorable circumstances.

"It's very difficult in the run-up to a war because a president has access to information that the press does not, but there's probably no more important job for the press than to question the reasons for going to war," Rosenstiel says. "Throughout American history, if a president misleads the public, or is misled by the intelligence community, the press is not going to catch that. They should, but it's never happened." ■

BACKGROUND

Revolutionary Change

At times it seems that the news has not changed at all over the last several hundred years. The type of news once delivered at fairs and markets by balladeers — stories of wars in foreign lands, murder and other crimes — would sound familiar to any contemporary cable viewer.

However, changes in the technology have periodically revolutionized the news business over the course of American history, leading to profound shifts in both the stories being told and the nature of the audience.

During Colonial times, printers, who acted, in effect, as editors and publishers, sometimes allowed governors to approve their copy before going to press. "Printers avoided offending the powerful by keeping divisive issues out of their newspapers, stifling debate rather than promoting it," writes Princeton University sociologist Paul Starr in his new book, *The Creation of the Media*. [24]

Such practices changed drastically during the Revolutionary War. The Founding Fathers were great pamphleteers, and newspaper circulation, already higher in America than in England, rose dramatically. Papers took a leading role in disseminating news not only of the conflict but also the texts of essential documents, such as the Declaration of Independence. The central idea of the American Revolution — that ordinary people could govern themselves — made it imperative that information be shared as widely as possible. As Starr notes, democracy gave politicians and parties the incentive to promote a medium that could influence public opinion.

Accordingly, in 1792, the new government — which had created an unusually extensive postal network — set

Continued on p. 864

Chronology

1960s-1970s

Television comes to dominate the news landscape.

1960
KFAX, in San Francisco, is launched as the nation's first 24-hour news radio station but goes out of business after just four months

1963
Television surpasses newspapers as the leading source of daily news.

1969
PBS is created . . . . Moon landing is watched by 94 percent of American households with TV.

1971
U.S. Supreme Court rules the government cannot prevent *The Washington Post* and *The New York Times* from printing the Pentagon Papers.

1972
CBS News anchor Walter Cronkite is named "most trusted man in America."

1973
The Washington Post wins the Pulitzer Prize for public service for its coverage of the Watergate scandal.

1980s

Cable grows exponentially while newspapers continue to decline

1980
Ted Turner creates CNN (Cable News Network), ushering in an era of 24-hour news

1981
Federal Communications Commission (FCC) determines there are enough radio stations to guarantee sufficient competition and exempts the medium from devoting minimum daily time to news and public affairs programming; the ruling is extended to TV in 1984

1982
USA Today, a national newspaper with colorful graphics, short stories and less government reporting, is founded and soon widely imitated

1988
Cable Communications Act releases cable networks from state and local regulations and many of the competitive constraints sought by broadcasters, leading to explosive growth in the new industry

1990s

Major media companies continue to consolidate, leaving fewer big players.

1991
CNN is the only TV news organization with correspondents and a direct satellite hookup in Baghdad during the first Persian Gulf War.

1992
NBC's "Dateline" rigs explosives under a GM truck to make a fuel tank explosion look more dramatic . . . Ross Perot announces his candidacy for president on CNN's "Larry King Live."

1995
Former football star O. J. Simpson's trial for murder receives unprecedented coverage from all media.

1996
Disney acquires Capital Cities-ABC, combining a movie studio with a TV network . . . Telecommunications Act loosens broadcast ownership restrictions . . . Fox News Channel founded.

1997
U.S. Supreme Court finds the Communications Decency Act unconstitutional, extending First Amendment rights to the Internet.

1998
Plagiarism and fabrication scandals at *The New Republic* and *The Boston Globe* add to journalism's credibility woes.

2000s

New players threaten traditional media's audience and credibility.

2001
Fox becomes most-watched network in cable news.

2003
New York Times reporter Jayson Blair is fired after fabricating stories.

Feb. 9, 2004
FCC recommends a $550,000 fine for CBS stations and calls for tighter decency regulation following a televised glimpse of Janet Jackson's right breast during the Super Bowl.

Sept. 2, 2004
Fox reaps higher ratings during the Republican National Convention than any other network.

Sept. 20, 2004
CBS anchor Dan Rather admits his "60 Minutes" report about President Bush's National Guard service was based on phony documents.

Oct. 12, 2004
Federal Communications Commission proposes record-setting $1.2 million fine against 169 Fox television stations for an April 2003 broadcast of "Married by America" that featured whipped-cream-covered strippers.

Is Fox News 'Fair and Balanced'?

As the Republican National Convention was winding down on Sept. 2, dozens of GOP delegates gathered near the CNN booth and began chanting loudly, "Watch Fox News! Watch Fox News!" [1]

The apparently spontaneous demonstration came just days after protesters of a more liberal persuasion gathered outside Fox's New York headquarters, holding signs that said, "Faux News" and "Shut Up!" (the retort popular Fox commentator Bill O'Reilly sometimes shouts at guests who annoy him).

It may seem surprising that a news outlet could engender such passionate demonstrations from partisans at either end of the ideological spectrum. But, to the extent that the general public concerns itself with questions about media bias, Fox has become the most heated flashpoint — and just a few years after its 1996 founding.

Liberals have decried Fox as the "the most biased name in news," claiming it does little more than spread Republican propaganda. The cable network's owner, Rupert Murdoch, is a media mogul with newspapers, cable and satellite networks and TV stations worldwide, reaching three-quarters of the world's population; he is known for his support of conservative politicians in this country and others. Fox President Roger Ailes was an adviser to Republican presidents from Richard M. Nixon to the first President George Bush.

In fact, some critics charge, Murdoch is using the Fox News Channel (FNC) to import party-affiliated news coverage to the United States. Former Fox producers and reporters claim that they got marching orders each day from management that echoed the Republican Party's line. Rep. Bernie Sanders, I-Vt., contends that Fox pounds away at the GOP's "message of the day," which usually focuses on divisive "wedge" issues like gay rights and abortion instead of issues of concern to the broader population, like the economy, the environment and health care. [2]

Moreover, Sanders and other critics say, Fox reporters and commentators use the same language, word for word, used that day by the GOP on the House or Senate floor and on conservative talk radio, producing an "echo chamber that resonates throughout America."

"I don't think any serious observer at this point does not think Fox leans to the right," says Steve Rendall, senior analyst at Fairness and Accuracy in Reporting (FAIR), a liberal, media-watchdog group.

Jeff Chester, executive director of the Center for Digital Democracy, is blunter: "Fox News is nothing more than a 24/7 political ad for the GOP," he says in the documentary "Outfoxed: Rupert Murdoch's War on Journalism."

Rendall has done studies suggesting that on Fox's flagship news program, "Special Report," Republican guests make up 83 percent of the one-on-one guests vs. 17 percent for Democrats, and that the few Democrats who do appear on the show are centrist or conservative.

"My problem with Fox is not that they are conservative," says Jeff Cohen, a former news contributor to both MSNBC and Fox News. "It's the consumer fraud of them claiming to be 'fair and balanced.' It's nothing of the sort." [3]

But Bill Shine, vice president for production at Fox, counters that "fair and balanced" is more than just the network's slogan. He says that Fox goes so far as to take a stopwatch into the studio to ensure that speakers representing different viewpoints get equal time. [4]

Political scientists Tim Groseclose and Jeff Milyo determined in a study that Fox's "Special Report" was more centrist than other sources for news including ABC News' "World News Tonight," *USA Today* and the *Los Angeles Times.* Their study was based on the number of times the outlets quoted various think tanks, comparing these to citations of the same think tanks in speeches by members of Congress. "All of the news outlets, except for Fox News' 'Special Report,' received a score to the left of the average member of Congress," they say. [5]

Groseclose and Milyo, however, acknowledge that their study did not include editorials and commentary. There seems to be little debate that Fox's commentary programs are dominated by conservative voices. Much of the growth of Fox's audience — it has surpassed both CNN and MSNBC to become the top-rated 24-hour news channel — has come from self-identified conservative viewers. [6]

Continued from p. 862

low postal rates for newspapers. By 1832, newspapers accounted for 95 percent of postal weight but contributed only 15 percent of postal revenues. [25] Such postal subsidies helped papers reach a wider area and increase circulation.

When U.S. politics grew more competitive during the 1820s, openly partisan newspapers played a leading role in helping to promote Whigs and other parties.

In the 1830s, the press became more of a popular medium through the rise of "penny papers." Where earlier papers were written mainly for an elite audience and concerned themselves mainly with commercial news, the low, one-cent price of the "penny press" enabled it to reach a broader audience with content focused on political controversies of the day.

But the press' growing reliance on money from advertisers, who didn't want newspapers to offend readers, along with the rise of the telegraph, led to increasing efforts at journalistic objectivity. The Associated Press wire service came to dominate foreign news and contributed a great deal of copy to local newspapers, particularly in the Midwest. Knowing that their client papers held a variety of partisan leanings, AP tried to send out stories that would offend neither advertisers nor readers of any political persuasion.

The falling cost of newsprint, faster presses and improvements in ink and typecasting fostered further growth in the

"There is a group of conservatives dissatisfied by an impression that the mainstream press isn't conservative enough," says Martin Johnson, a political scientist at the University of California, Riverside. "If I'm a conservative and know that Fox is going to present the news from a conservative standpoint, then it makes sense for me to watch it."

Indeed, many viewers applaud Fox's openly patriotic productions, with American flags much in evidence. During the Iraq war, concluded the conservative Media Research Center, "FNC aided viewers by rejecting the standard liberal idea that objective war news requires an indifference to whether America succeeds or fails." [7]

"I have always felt that the major media networks have been liberal in their bias," said Bonnie Dunbar, a delegate to the Republican National Convention from Findlay, Ohio. "Then along comes Fox that presents both sides and gives conservatives their due without putting a negative slant on everything conservatives have to offer." [8]

Even some critics of the news content on Fox acknowledge its skill at transforming television, including the networks' much-imitated moving-graphics style. It presents the news with more emotion than its rivals and understands that conflict makes for good viewing. "Part of Fox News Channel's recipe for success is some of its political agenda, but also its masterful showmanship," says Matthew Felling, director of the Center for Media and Public Affairs. "It presents the news in an entertaining fashion, in a smash-mouth style that's the key to talk radio as well."

Showmanship has its downsides, say Fox critics, who also complain that the network's predominant format of focusing on anchors diminishes news by generating less of it. "Fox is kind of leading the way in cheapening the news in a financial sense," says Robert Greenwald, director of "Outfoxed." "It takes a lot less resources to put two people into a studio screaming at each other than to send reporters all over the world and have them spend months digging."

Regardless of the complaints, Fox News Channel's ratings are a rare area of rapid growth for the beleaguered news industry. The GOP delegates need not have bothered with their catcalling at CNN's convention booth. Fox's ratings for President Bush's acceptance speech that night peaked at more than 7 million viewers — not only higher than any broadcast network but also more than double CNN's 2.7 million viewers. [9]

Seeing the financial success of Fox, other networks are now mimicking its methods, giving more air time to conservative viewpoints, say critics of Fox. "It's called the 'Fox Effect,' " said Cohen, describing how when he was a senior producer for MSNBC's "Phil Donahue Show" he was directed to "out-fox Fox" by putting more conservative guests on the show than liberals. "They mandated that if we had two left-wing guests, we had to have three right-wing guests."

If the "Fox Effect" takes hold of other news outlets, the critics say, objectivity and, eventually, democracy will be the victims.

"Murdoch doesn't believe in objectivity," said David Brock, president and CEO of Media Matters for America. "He has contempt for journalism. He wants all news to be a matter of opinion, because opinion can't be proven false. That's very dangerous, because if people don't have a set of facts they can believe in, it's difficult to reach consensus on public policy." [10]

---

1 Alan Murray, "As In Olden Days, U.S. Media Reflect the Partisan Divide," *The Wall Street Journal*, Sept. 14, 2004, p. A4.

2 Quoted in "Outfoxed: Rupert Murdoch's War on Journalism."

3 *Ibid.*

4 See Colleen McCain Nelson, "America's Split Screen: It's Fox News vs. CNN," *The Dallas Morning News*, July 18, 2004, p. 1A.

5 Tim Groseclose and John Milyo, "A Measure of Media Bias," Stanford University Working Paper, September 2003, p. 2.

6 "News Audiences Increasingly Politicized," Pew Research Center for the People & the Press, June 8, 2004, p. 1.

7 Brent Baker and Rich Noyes, "Grading TV's War News," Media Research Center, April 23, 2003, *Executive Summary*, p. 1.

8 Leon Lazaroff and John Cook, "Fox News scores with GOP, spurs protesters," *Chicago Tribune*, Sept. 3, 2004, p. 14.

9 Lisa de Moraes, "Fox Tops GOP Parley Stats," *The Washington Post*, Sept. 9, 2004, p. C7.

10 Quoted in "Outfoxed," *op. cit.*

---

news business. By 1909, about 2,600 daily papers existed in the United States — up from 574 in the 1870s. [26] Editors sought the attention of readers — including new immigrants — with bolder headlines, a greater emphasis on storytelling and occasional crusades and stunts.

Newspaper barons such as Joseph Pulitzer and William Randolph Hearst engaged in circulation wars, running sensational headlines and poaching each other's star reporters.

But newspapers soon faced a major threat from yet another new technology — radio.

Electronic Media

Americans embraced the radio. Even as the Depression forced many families to drop phone service, the proportion of homes with radios grew from under 25 percent in 1927 to 65 percent in 1934. The Communications Act of 1934 created the Federal Communications Commission (FCC), which regulated radio more tightly than the freewheeling press.

Anyone could, in theory, print a newspaper, but there was a limited amount of broadcasting spectrum. Much of the radio dial was soon dominated by national networks such as NBC, which tightly controlled affiliated stations and diminished localism by appealing to a broad audience. As with the telegraph, radio helped shape the modern news style, with clear, concise reports. Even then, listeners complained broadcasters were dumbing things down to reach the broadest possible audience.

Technology made political coverage more candidate-centered. With parties unable to influence radio as they had the newspaper business, radio focused more on personalities, especially the incumbent president, which helped President Franklin D. Roosevelt — a natural performer. A study of the 1940 presidential campaign found that the two major parties dominated different media: "In exposure, in congeniality of ideas, in trust and in influence . . . the Republicans inclined in favor of the newspaper and the Democrats in favor of the radio." [27]

During World War II, radio's live broadcasts gave the medium an advantage over newspapers, which were being hurt by a shortage of newsprint. Radio owned the story of Pearl Harbor for about 17 hours, because networks could break into coverage of football games, but no afternoon papers were published on Sundays. By 1943, radio ad revenues surpassed those of newspapers. [28]

As television began to emerge after World War II as the dominant news medium of the second half of the 20th century, broadcasters were subject to regulation aimed at opening the airwaves to all points of view. The so-called "Fairness Doctrine" — formalized by the FCC in 1949 — required radio and television stations to devote a reasonable percentage of time to the coverage of public issues and to provide an opportunity for the presentation of contrasting points of view. The Supreme Court upheld the policy as constitutional in 1969, based largely on the limited number of radio and TV stations. Two decades later, in 1987, the FCC dropped enforcement of the doctrine, citing the growth of broadcast and cable outlets and legal and policy doubts about the rule.

A statutory provision still on the books — Section 315 of the Communications Act — requires any broadcaster that allows a candidate to "use" its facilities to grant "equal opportunities" to all legally qualified candidates for the office. Congress in 1959 amended the "equal time" rule to exempt "bona fide" newscasts and documentaries. But the rule is usually interpreted to apply to entertainment programs so that, for example, the popular NBC comedy show "Saturday Night Live" could not feature one candidate for president without providing equal time to all others. [29]

As early as 1953, about half of U.S. households had a TV. The networks that dominated radio took over television. Radio stations survived through narrowcasting — appealing to limited audiences that advertisers wanted to reach, such as teenagers, African-Americans and farmers, without having to buy ads on the TV networks.

The watershed year for television news may have been 1963, when TV surpassed newspapers as Americans' leading source of daily news. That year, CBS and NBC extended their daily news programs from 15 to 30 minutes. (ABC followed suit four years later.) [30] It was also the year that a stunned nation watched four days of broadcasts surrounding the John F. Kennedy assassination and funeral. A few years later, gruesome war images broadcast into people's homes would help turn public opinion against U.S. involvement in Vietnam.

Relations between the press and the government, strained by Vietnam, worsened with the 1972 Watergate presidential scandal, which led to a more adversarial press culture. *The Washington Post's* initially lonely pursuit of the story, portrayed as heroic in the 1976 film "All the President's Men," led to a spike in enrollment in college journalism programs, helping to foster the more educated, professional culture of the modern press corps.

Tabloid Culture

Consistently beaten on breaking stories by the electronic media, newspapers adapted by changing the nature of their content, according to press historian Mitchell Stephens. "[Newspapers] are moving away from pure news reporting toward some hybrid of news, opinion, history and pop sociology," Stephens wrote in 1988. [31] The same changes would later take place in broadcast television, signaling what many see as a decline in the broadcast networks' quality and quantity of news, as well as their commitment to providing news as a public service.

During one 18-month period between 1985 and 1986, non-journalistic corporations purchased each of the three major U.S. broadcast networks. Cost-cutting and staff layoffs in news divisions soon followed.

"When the new generation of owners at ABC, CBS and NBC began to analyze their acquisitions for ways to improve profitability, the news divisions — with their sprawling, highly paid staffs, lavish operating budgets and perishable product and ratings that would prevent ad sales from ever reliably covering costs — presented them with an obvious target," wrote author Susan Bridge, describing a dynamic that was soon dramatized in the satiric 1987 film "Broadcast News." [32]

The networks also cut back dramatically on their foreign coverage, documentaries and investigations and devoted more time to sensationalistic and celebrity news. They devoted extensive coverage in 1986 to the nation's crack epidemic, but when the Drug Enforcement Agency in September released a report calling the attention "excessive," NBC was the only network even to briefly mention it. [33]

The explosive growth of cable television further heightened the single-minded devotion to sensational stories.

The Freewheeling World of Blogs

Terry Teachout regularly writes about the arts for *The Wall Street Journal* and *The Washington Post*, but he gets a lot more feedback when he writes about the arts for a much smaller audience — the people who read his blog, "About Last Night."

The ease of e-mailing a response just by clicking on the writer's name is one big reason. But part of the fun of blogs — short for Web logs — is their immediacy. Bloggers generally post their thoughts about their particular area of interest daily, or even several times a day, while providing links to postings, documents and images elsewhere.

Bloggers are sometimes criticized for being too insular — linking, for instance, to postings on other blogs about themselves. Like the entertainment media promoting a new movie, the blogosphere can become temporarily obsessed with one hot topic. But blogs do open up an unending dialogue about any and every subject.

No blog has an audience that comes close to the circulation of either of the daily papers that Teachout writes for. Out of the 2 million or so active blogs, only a handful has regular readerships that are even in the five figures. (Teachout is not one of them, although he's received about a half-million hits in just over a year of posting.)

According to a survey conducted in spring 2004 by the Pew Internet and American Life Project, about 5 percent of the 128 million American adults on the Web have their own blog, while 17 percent of Internet users have read blog postings. Those numbers, says Lee Rainie, director of the project, suggest that blogging is still a smaller Web phenomenon than weather reports, online dating or stock trading.

But blog audiences, if small, tend to be deeply engaged in a topic, whether it's the arts, the Boston Celtics or the behavior of pet dachshunds. "A blog is a way of identifying a specific interest and playing to it," says Barbie Zelizer, an associate professor of communication at the University of Pennsylvania. "How is that any different from MTV or BET or *The Nation?*"

For one thing, blogs are different because they aren't under any pressure from advertisers to deliver an audience. That reality allows blogs to become freewheeling areas of discussion, known for their individual voices and sharp commentary. Bloggers become characters that their readers can follow, noting their likes and peeves and getting the latest word about their head colds.

Technology has allowed amateurs and professionals alike to compete on fairly even terms for attention. That's why, Teachout says, professional writers tend not to like blogs — although it's become pretty common for authors promoting books to start their own sites.

"It's the most meritocratic marketplace of ideas out there right now," says Matthew Felling, media director at the Center for Media and Public Affairs. "On TV, you can just shout louder or refuse to talk to a guest. On a blog, you rely strictly on the strength of your ideas."

Blogging is thus an attractive medium to a critic such as Teachout. Indeed, rather than containing news, blogs are more likely to contain criticism or commentary on events or other media. "By its nature, just like conversation itself, a lot of it is reactive," Rainie says. "If there's an organizing principle to what bloggers do, it is to react to something that is in the mainstream media already."

Blogs also signal journalists about controversies raging within certain specialized communities that might resonate within the broader public. Certainly, other outlets have often repeated stories (and rumors) first posted on the *Drudge Report*. In 2002, bloggers such as Glenn Harlan Reynolds (aka InstaPundit) and Joshua Micah Marshall (talkingpointsmemo.com) made a stink about a racially insensitive remark from then-Senate Majority Leader Trent Lott, R-Miss. The bloggers kept beating the drum for days until the mainstream media made it a major story, forcing Lott to step down from his leadership post.

Their biggest coup, however, came in September, when the validity of documents used by CBS News in its report critical of President Bush's National Guard record was first picked apart by bloggers. CBS anchor Dan Rather eventually apologized on air for using bogus evidence.

The accusations that Sen. John Kerry, D-Mass., may have lied about his war record were also aired widely on the Web before coming to dominate network television coverage for a time in August. (Kerry and other politicians, notably former Vermont Gov. Howard Dean, have successfully used blogs to link to their own fundraising pages.)

"Blogs bring attention to things the press is not paying attention to," says Jack Shafer, an editor and media columnist for the online magazine *Slate*. "They're sort of an aggregated reader mind."

But because blogs produce more criticism than original information, they're likely to remain a secondary source. "Blogging is perfectly suited to short reviews," Teachout says. "Reportage is a different matter; there I suspect blogs will always be epiphenomena of old-media publications with large staffs."

The Cable Communications Policy Act of 1988 released cable operators from competitive constraints (sought by broadcasters) and from state and local government regulation. Cable penetration of U.S. households leapt from 20 percent in 1980 to 60 percent a decade later. [34]

A wave of mergers, prompted by the 1996 Telecommunications Act, led to further media cost-cutting. Over the next several years, Clear Channel Communications purchased more than 1,200 radio stations, and newspapers declined in both number and circulation. By 1997, only

37 cities had competing dailies (and in 17 of those cities competing papers had joint printing arrangements). [35]

As media consolidation continued, huge fortunes were made, but investment in newsgathering did not keep pace. "The object of these mergers is never to improve the service," said noted journalist and author David Halberstam. "I don't think there's anybody at the head of one of these large corporations that cares very much about journalism." [36]

Cable and satellite technology made possible the proliferation of hundreds of channels, giving birth to tabloid journalism. Faced with 24 hours to fill, all-news channels such as CNN and MSNBC have given wall-to-wall coverage to crime and celebrity stories that cost comparatively little to cover, such as the 1995 murder trial of O. J. Simpson. The line between gossip and reporting became forever blurred, as correspondents rushed to put new information on the air.

"We are a one-story business — there's only room for one big story, because the news managers have decided to cut costs and give less space to difficult, complex and hard-to-understand stories," says former *Boston Globe* Associate Editor Nyhan.

In the late 1990s, the ultimate tabloid story involved President Bill Clinton's affair with White House intern Monica Lewinsky. For the first time, the mainstream press followed up on reports in tabloids like the *National Enquirer*. "We didn't become more like the media — the media became more like us," said *Enquirer* Editor-in-Chief Iain Calder. "I see our DNA in magazines, newspapers and television all over America." [37]

The Lewinsky story took off when *Newsweek* was scooped on its own story through use of the latest technology to alter the news business — the Internet. On Jan. 17, 1998, *Newsweek* editors had decided not to run with the Lewinsky story. Two days later, Matt Drudge posted news of the decision and the content of the story on his online blog, the *Drudge Report*. Two days later, *The Washington Post* and ABC News presented their initial stories about the affair, followed by *Newsweek*, which finally posted its story online. [38]

Reflecting the priority now given to such stories, the networks brought home their anchors, who had been in Cuba to cover a papal visit. Over the course of the year, the networks would air on their nightly news programs more than 1,500 stories about the Lewinsky affair. [39]

On March 4, 1999, when ABC broadcast Barbara Walters' interview with Lewinsky, 49 million people tuned in — the largest audience ever for a network news broadcast. [40] ■

CURRENT SITUATION

Merger Mania

On Sept. 8, 2004, CBS anchor Dan Rather reported on "60 Minutes" that CBS had obtained documents showing that President Bush had received favorable treatment during his stint in the Texas Air National Guard. The documents were quickly derided by bloggers and other news organizations as forgeries that could not have been made on the typewriters of the time. After defending its story for nearly two weeks, CBS admitted on Sept. 20 that it had been misled by its source — who turned out to be a former Guardsman who has urged Democrats to wage "war" against Republican "dirty tricks."

The blog chatter that helped sink Rather's account illustrated a curious fact about the modern media: The number of news outlets has grown exponentially, despite the rapid consolidation of media ownership.

Since passage of the 1996 Telecommunications Act, there has been a seemingly unending wave of media mergers, affecting all aspects of the news business. [41] In television, the 10 biggest companies own 30 percent of all stations, reaching 85 percent of U.S. households. The networks make up less than 30 percent of the total business of their new corporate owners. In radio, the top 20 companies control more than a fifth of all stations nationwide. Clear Channel, with its 1,200 stations, is a presence in 191 of the top 300 markets. Twenty-two companies now control 70 percent of daily newspaper circulation. [42]

More than half the journalists surveyed by the Pew Research Center in spring 2004 thought their profession was being "seriously hurt" by financial pressures brought about by mergers. [43] (Journalists at the Unity conference applauded Kerry vigorously when he stated his opposition to continuing mergers.)

Corporate profits are rising, but newsroom staffs are being cut. More money is being invested in new technologies for disseminating the news than in collecting it. But even as the number of major news companies dwindles, other voices have proliferated. Cable and satellite technology provide hundreds of new channels, offering a much larger choice of programming. And the Internet allows the emergence of new voices in the form of blogs, as well as instant access to newspapers and other sources of information — both reliable and spurious — around the world.

In a decision that displayed both the influence of a single company in the age of media consolidation and the decline of enforcement in equal time and fairness rules, the family-owned Sinclair Broadcasting Corp. in October ordered the 62 TV stations it owns — many of them in states contested in the 2004 presidential race — to air a documentary highly critical of Kerry. [44] The Kerry campaign called charges made in the documentary about his

Continued on p. 870

At Issue:

Do mainstream media outlets have a partisan bias?

yes

CLIFF KINCAID
***EDITOR*, ACCURACY IN MEDIA REPORT**

FROM A WEB COMMENTARY, JUNE 14, 2004

It's finally starting to dawn on some in the media that diversity should mean something other than hiring minorities and homosexuals. In an article in *The Weekly Standard*, Fred Barnes quoted Tom Rosenstiel of the Project for Excellence in Journalism as saying it's necessary not to think just of diversity that makes newsrooms "look like America," but to create a press corps that "thinks like America."

"In truth," said Barnes, "the effort to hire more minorities and women has had the effect of making the media more liberal. Both these groups tend to have liberal politics, and this is accentuated by the fact that many of the women recruited into journalism are young and single, precisely those with the most liberal views." Rosenstiel says, "By diversifying the profession in one way, they were making it more homogenous in another."

This discussion comes in the wake of a survey by the Pew Research Center and Project on Excellence in Journalism, finding that "news people, especially national journalists, are more liberal, and far less conservative, than the general public." Picking up on the "diversity" problem, Howard Kurtz of *The Washington Post* quoted Rosenstiel as saying that "the growing proportion of self-identified liberals in the national media — and the fact that 'conservatives are not very well represented' — is having an impact." Rosenstiel said, "This is something journalists should worry about."

The survey found a relatively small number of conservatives at national and local news organizations: "Just 7 percent of national news people and 12 percent of local journalists describe themselves as conservatives, compared with a third of all Americans." The liberal bias is most apparent in coverage of social issues. It found, for instance, that "journalists are much more accepting of homosexuality than is the general public."

Thomas Bray of the *Detroit News* suggests that the Pew survey may substantially understate the degree of the bias. Bray suggests that liberal media bias has affected the public's view of Bush and the economy. He notes a Gallup Poll of 1,000 Americans showed that 51 percent of Americans say the economy is getting worse, "even as gross domestic product, employment and other indicators continue to forge ahead."

Bray says Bush may be able to overcome this bias, but that he "shouldn't rely too heavily on the notion that voters will be able to sort things out based on what they read, see and hear in the press."

no

CHARLOTTE GRIMES
KNIGHT CHAIR IN POLITICAL REPORTING
S. I. NEWHOUSE SCHOOL OF PUBLIC COMMUNICATIONS, SYRACUSE UNIVERSITY

WRITTEN FOR *THE CQ RESEARCHER*, OCTOBER 2004

"Bias" is a four-letter expletive that partisans of all stripes throw at the press. To dispute the accusation is like spitting into a hurricane. The blowback is fierce and ugly. In short, this is an argument that cannot be won. It usually can't even be conducted civilly.

But, to spit into the hurricane: The press does have biases toward conflict and controversy. Reporters and editors are drawn to a verbal brawl like rubberneckers to a highway accident. In our competitive mode, we too often sacrifice accuracy, precision and clarity for speed. In the modern media echo chamber of talk shows, blogs and 24-hour cycle of relentless repetition, the press also plays a part in magnifying and distorting the trivial into the monumental.

Does any or all of that make us partisan? No. So why this widespread — and intensifying — perception of bias?

Partly it's all the above flaws, which partisans and ordinary folks looking for the simplest answers can easily misinterpret as "Aha, bias." Partly it's the bitter fruit of the general decline in public respect for all institutions. Partly it's the age-old "kill the messenger" syndrome. Partly it's the eye of the beholder, with Democrats and Republicans alike making the bias charge ("Why did the press wait so long to publish the Abu Ghraib photographs?" vs. "Why is the press making such a big deal out of the Abu Ghraib photos?") Partly it's the polarization — remember those red and blue states? — of the nation. And partly it's the failures of the press to explain its ethics, professional skills and job — and to make the case that journalists do try to police themselves.

Much is made by partisans, for example, of surveys of journalists showing a majority of respondents have voted for Democrats. Little is said about the independent studies of journalists' work that show, indeed, partisan bias in coverage is generally rare and usually slight. Few, especially among the partisans, notice or credit that often the journalists themselves are those most outraged by the lapses.

Sure, there are some reporters and editors who can't or won't exercise the essential professional skills for impartiality, like asking "What or who's left out?" or "Are any words or phrases loaded?" or "Is this true and accurate?" Those journalists usually end up as columnists or out of the newsroom. True, the press has its sins, weaknesses and flaws. But, if anything, we're bipolar — not partisan.

Continued from p. 868

Vietnam-era activities scurrilous, but it had no recourse for demanding equal time. Equal-time requirements do not apply to news reports, which this documentary is being billed as. But even if Kerry can convince the FCC the program doesn't constitute news, he probably can't win the argument, because it's Kerry who is being showcased, after all, even if in an unflattering light. (Under the equal-time rules, candidates only get to complain if their opponent is being shown and they are not.)

Blurring the Lines

With the advent of Web blogs, anybody can be a journalist (or consider himself one), as the bloggers who were credentialed at the party conventions proved this year. Journalism has become a wide-open market, making it harder for the working press to set itself apart.

Coincidentally, the emergence of bloggers as journalists raises sticky questions about whether journalists can shield their sources. "Do bloggers also have confidentiality of sources?" asks Syracuse University's Grimes, referring to an ongoing investigation into who leaked to reporters the identify of CIA operative Valerie Plame.

"How do we reclaim our distinctive identity in the press," Grimes continues. "People confuse the reporters with the commentators. We've cooperated a lot with that confusion — to our detriment." Grimes, a veteran journalist, says she became an academic after meeting a woman in a shopping mall who said she loved the news. When Grimes asked what news programs she watched, the woman mentioned Montel Williams and Oprah Winfrey, two talk show hosts.

Talk show programs like that are "virtual journalism," Grimes says, "a combination of innuendo and rumor and factoid, and we're presenting it as the real thing."

Two recent incidents involving a non-journalist demonstrate just how fuzzy the line between news, gossip and entertainment has become.

James Carville has been a Democratic political consultant for many years. In 2003, he played a fictionalized version of himself as an ongoing character in an HBO series, "K Street," which mixed its narrative with appearances from real Washington insiders. On the show, Carville told former Vermont Gov. Howard Dean, then still a presidential hopeful, a joke about Sen. Trent Lott, R-Miss., that he thought Dean should use in the campaign. Dean went ahead and told the joke at a real-world presidential debate. Carville then watched the actual political debate on a TV monitor in a subsequent "K Street" episode. [45] For many people, it was a demonstration of how the media have helped muddy the distinction between reality and fiction.

More recently, Carville served as an illustration of the interchangeability of political commentators and political operators. He recently joined the ranks of other political aides-turned-journalists — such as NBC's Tim Russert and George Stephanopoulos and *New York Times* columnist William Safire — appearing as a co-host on CNN's "Crossfire," which features both liberal and conservative commentators. But unlike Russert and the others, Carville did not surrender his role as a cog in the political machinery after he joined the media.

It became clear this fall that Carville and his "Crossfire" colleague Paul Begala were acting as advisers to the Kerry campaign, even as they kept their jobs on the show. "No matter how [brief] the overlap between Mr. Carville and Mr. Begala's TV and campaign roles ["Crossfire"] and CNN are now inextricably bound to the Democrats," wrote liberal columnist Frank Rich in *The New York Times*.

"[CNN's] casual abandonment of even a fig leaf of impartiality ratifies a larger shift in the news landscape." [46]

Some see today's media environment as topsy-turvy. Major media companies are investing more money in new ways to disseminate information than to gather it. Print reporters appear as commentators on TV and people read their stories as links from other Web sites. It's becoming nearly impossible for the average person to know where they first heard or read a particular story, which makes it more difficult, of course, for them to build up a sense of trust toward a particular outlet. In fact, quality standards now often vary within a single organization, with NBC, for instance, remaining more rigorous than MSNBC.

The diminishing credibility of news institutions, some say, will ultimately prove more damaging than a recent series of scandals involving individual reporters who plagiarized or fictionalized stories, most notably Jayson Blair of *The New York Times* and Jack Kelley of *USA Today*. [47] Although those were isolated cases, the amount of criticism of the media in general will prove more damaging in the long run, says Felling of the Center for Media and Public Affairs. "Media credibility is spiraling downward because media is eating itself," he says.

Media criticism has become more than a cottage industry. Entire organizations are devoted to critiquing the media. Numerous books such as Bernard Goldberg's *Bias*, Al Franken's *Lies and the Lying Liars Who Tell Them* and Ann Coulter's *Treason and Slander* have been bestsellers. The fact that Goldberg and Coulter impute bias from the left while Franken lampoons pundits on the right hardly matters.

"There are shelves at the bookstore devoted to the idea that the media is horrible because it's liberal," Felling says. "Or because it's conservative. All that tells the average person is that that the media is horrible, period."

"At a time when America's mass media becomes ever more centralized . . . the public's relationship to the media is more decentered than ever before," writes

L.A. Weekly columnist Powers. "Just as the proliferation of blurbs in movie ads has made all critics appear to be idiots or flacks, so the rabbitlike proliferation of news sources — many of them slipshod, understaffed or insanely partisan — has inevitably devalued the authority of any individual source." [48] ■

OUTLOOK

Abandon Objectivity?

Rumors are flying that one of the major broadcast networks may get out of the news business altogether. Except for Fox News Channel, the audience for television news has been in decline and corporate pressures in TV often fall hardest on the labor-intensive newsgathering operations. And with the audience for news fracturing, the only areas of growth lie outside the traditional mainstream media — in Hispanic broadcasting and publications, the Internet and Fox.

While it once made sense to aspire to objectivity so as to offend no one, in today's splintered media market it may make more sense to adopt the European model — appealing ardently to partisans of one stripe or another in hopes of securing their allegiance. The popularity of conservative talk radio and Fox News' financial success have prompted other networks — in a trend nicknamed the "Fox Effect" — to change formats and hosts: Both MSNBC and PBS have recently hired more conservative hosts. Meanwhile, in an effort to appeal to liberals, the Air America radio network began broadcasting in March, and former Vice President Al Gore is exploring a cable television venture.

In many cases, Americans are changing their news-intake habits to reflect the changing media. As news coverage on local radio stations has shrunk — due to consolidation — National Public Radio has seen Its audience more than doubled over the last decade. Niches still exist for serious news, and, even if one of the major networks does shut down its news division, the remaining networks will benefit. The most-viewed Web news pages still belong to well-established media brands.

And in a new trend this election year, both liberals and conservatives who feel the mainstream media is not properly covering the presidential election have turned to books and documentaries for information about their candidates. Book store shelves are bulging with titles about both candidates, and the documentary market is flourishing, ranging from Michael Moore's anti-Bush "Fahrenheit 9/11" to "George W. Bush: Faith in the White House," a documentary about Bush's Christian faith.

Meanwhile, the audience for news is shrinking. According to the Pew survey, Americans spend about 66 minutes each day watching, reading or listening to the news — a 10 percent decline since 1994. [49] The future doesn't necessarily look any brighter: Younger Americans are even less likely to pay attention to the news than their elders. Only 29 percent of young people read a newspaper regularly and are much more likely to turn for information to entertainment shows such as "The Daily Show" or "The Tonight Show," substituting jokes about the news for the real thing.

All of today's media still rely on mainstream news organizations as primary sources of information, even if they occasionally question the credibility of that information. However, as old-line news organizations invest less and less in newsgathering, and the new media have no budget or inclination to engage in original reporting, the business will diminish, says Rosenstiel, of the Project for Excellence in Journalism.

The new news business likes its information raw, whether it's a Web site linking to documents or TV stations concentrating on events that can be filmed from a helicopter. There is plenty of opinion espoused in the media today, but less analysis that interprets what the staged events of the day really mean. And independent analyses of official statements are increasingly dismissed as partisan.

"As citizens in a democracy, we need access to independent, accurate facts in order to make responsible decisions," says Rendall, the FAIR senior analyst. Rendall says news outlets should own up to their opinions and pursue a more European model in which they announce their biases openly, while presenting solid reporting to back it up.

As "Daily Show" host Jon Stewart commented to ABC newsman Ted Koppel during the convention, the mainstream press is not doing its job when it merely acts as a referee in partisan debates without providing a "reality check" on the misstatements and exaggerations made by the two parties. [50]

"The major networks and major newspapers are losing ground as agenda-setters and as referees," says Nyhan, the former *Boston Globe* editor. "When the media drop the ball, the politicians go crazy. No one is watching these very complex decisions and mistakes get made."

Jeff Cohen, a television producer and former MSNBC and Fox news

About the Author

Alan Greenblatt is a staff writer at *Governing* magazine and contributor to *The New York Times*. He previously covered elections, agriculture and military spending for *CQ Weekly*, where he won the National Press Club's Sandy Hume Award for political journalism. He graduated from San Francisco State University and received a master's degree in English literature from the University of Virginia.

contributor, sees a more serious outcome of the media changes. "The media is the nervous system of a democracy," he said. "If it's not functioning well, democracy can't function." [51] ■

FOR MORE INFORMATION

Accuracy in Media, 4455 Connecticut Ave., N.W., Suite 330, Washington, DC 20008; (202) 364-4401; www.aim.org. A conservative media-watchdog organization.

Center for Media and Public Affairs, 2100 L St., N.W., Suite 300, Washington, DC 20037; (202) 223-2942; www.cmpa.com. A nonpartisan research organization.

Center for Excellence in Journalism, 1850 K St., N.W., Suite 850, Washington, DC 20006; (202) 293-7394; www.journalism.org. Represents the Committee of Concerned Journalists and the Project for Excellence in Journalism.

Fairness and Accuracy in Reporting, 112 W. 27th St. New York, NY 10001; (212) 633-6700; www.fair.org. A progressive national media-watchdog organization.

Media Research Center, 325 S. Patrick St., Alexandria, VA 22314; (703) 683-9733; www.mediaresearch.org/welcome.asp. A conservative media-watchdog group.

Pew Research Center for the People & the Press, 1150 18th St., N.W., Suite 975, Washington, DC 20036; (202) 293-3126; www.people-press.org. An independent media-research organization funded by the Pew Charitable Trusts.

Notes

[1] Unity is a joint convention held every five years by the four principal minority journalist groups: the National Association of Black Journalists (NABJ), National Association of Hispanic Journalists (NAHJ), Asian American Journalists Association (AAJA), and the Native American Journalists Association (NAJA).

[2] Howard Kurtz, "Media Backtalk," washingtonpost.com, Aug. 16, 2004, http://www.washingtonpost.com/wp-dyn/articles/A46374-2004Aug6.html.

[3] Kimberly A. C. Wilson, "Applause Raises Specter of Bias," *The Baltimore Sun*, Aug. 7, 2004, p. 4A.

[4] "News Audience Increasingly Politicized," The Pew Research Center for the People & the Press, June 8, 2004, p. 1.

[5] David Folkenflik, "More grist for those seeking 'bias' in the news media," *The Baltimore Sun*, Oct. 6, 2004, p. 1E.

[6] See "A Pause for Hindsight," *The New York Times*, July 16, 2004, p. 20; Howard Kurtz, "The Post on WMDs: An Inside Story," *The Washington Post*, Aug. 12, 2004, p. A1; and "Were We Wrong?" *The New Republic*, June 28, 2004, p. 8.

[7] For background, see Alan Greenblatt, "The Partisan Divide," *The CQ Researcher*, April 30, 2004, pp. 373-396.

[8] "Summer of Lies," *Columbia Journalism Review*, July/August 2004, p. 3.

[9] Jim VandeHei, "Kerry Sharpens Contrast With Bush," *The Washington Post*, Sept. 2, 2004, p. A1.

[10] Elizabeth Wilner, "Outlook: Just Wired Differently," washingtonpost.com, Sept. 21, 2004, http://www.washingtonpost.com/wp-dyn/articles/A29834-2004Sep17.html.

[11] "A Media Watershed," *The Wall Street Journal*, Sept. 16, 2004, p. A16.

[12] For background, see Brian Hansen, "Combating Plagiarism," *The CQ Researcher*, Sept. 19, 2003, pp. 773-796.

[13] Colleen McCain Nelson, "America's Split Screen: It's Fox News vs. CNN," *The Dallas Morning News*, July 18, 2004, p. 1A.

[14] *Ibid.*

[15] Pew Research Center, *op. cit.*

[16] *Ibid.*, p. 13.

[17] John Powers, *Sore Winners (and the Rest of Us) in George Bush's America* (2004), p. 199.

[18] *Ibid.*, p. 247.

[19] Bruce Bartlett, "The Fall of the News Oligopoly," *National Review Online*, Sept. 20, 2004, http://www.nationalreview.com/nrof_bartlett/bartlett200409200822.asp.

[20] Michael Massing, "Now They Tell Us," *The New York Review of Books*, Feb. 26, 2004, p. 43.

[21] Steve Rendall and Zara Broughel, "Amplifying Officials, Squelching Debate," *FAIR*, May/June 2003.

[22] Quoted in Douglas McCollam, "How Chalabi Played the Press," *Columbia Journalism Review*, July/August 2004, p. 31.

[23] Walter Pincus and Dana Millbank, "Al Qaeda-Hussein Link Is Dismissed," *The Washington Post*, June 17, 2004, p. A1.

[24] Paul Starr, *The Creation of the Media* (2004), p. 61.

[25] *Ibid.*, p. 90.

[26] Jerry W. Knudson, *In the News* (2000), p. 89.

[27] Paul F. Lazarsfeld, Bernard Berelson and Hazel Gaudet, *The People's Choice* (1944), p. 129.

[28] Susan Bridge, *Monitoring the News* (1998), p. 7.

[29] Harvey Zuckman, et al., *Modern Communications Law* (1999), p. 1234.

[30] Edward Bliss Jr., *Now the News: The Story of Broadcast Journalism* (1991), p. 311.

[31] Mitchell Stephens, *A History of News* (1988), p. 287.

[32] Bridge, *op. cit.*, p. 19.

[33] Edwin Diamond, *The Media Show* (1991), p. 100.

[34] Bliss, *op. cit.*, p. 435.

[35] Knudson, *op. cit.*, p. 89.

[36] Quoted in Herbert N. Foerstel, *From Watergate to Monicagate* (2001), p. 19.

[37] Quoted in Tom Maurstad, "Enquiring Media: Tabloids Make Vivid Impression on Pop Culture," *The Dallas Morning News*, Aug. 29, 2004, p. 10E.

[38] Knudson, *op. cit.*, p. 256.

[39] Foerstel, *op. cit.*, p. 122.

[40] Leonard Downie Jr. and Robert G. Kaiser, *The News About the News* (2002), p. 28.

[41] For background, see David Hatch, "Media Consolidation," *The CQ Researcher*, Oct. 10, 2003, pp. 845-868.

[42] "The State of the News Media 2004," Project for Excellence in Journalism, March 15, 2004, http://www.stateofthenewsmedia.org/narrative_overview_ownership.asp?media=1.

[43] "Bottom-Line Pressures Now Hurting Coverage, Say Journalists," Pew Research Center for the People & the Press, May 23, 2004, p. 1. For background, see Kathy Koch, "Journalism Under Fire," *The CQ Researcher*, Dec. 25, 1998, pp. 1121-1144.

[44] Howard Kurtz and Frank Ahrens, "Family's TV Clout In Bush's Corner," *The Washington Post*, Oct. 12, 2004, p. 1A.

[45] Powers, *op. cit.*, p. 260.

[46] Frank Rich, "This Time Bill O'Reilly Got It Right," *The New York Times*, Sept. 19, 2004, Section 2, p. 1.

[47] Hansen, *op. cit.*

[48] Powers, *op. cit.*, p. 194.

[49] Pew Research Center, *op. cit.*

[50] "Nightline" ABC News, July 28, 2004.

[51] Quoted in "Outfoxed: Rupert Murdoch's War on Journalism."

Bibliography

Selected Sources

Books

Alterman, Eric, *What Liberal Media?: The Truth about Bias and the News*, Basic Books, 2003.

The Nation columnist argues that accusations of a liberal bias in the mainstream media are not only overstated but miss a tendency toward conservatism.

Bozell III, L. Brent, *Weapons of Mass Distortion: The Coming Meltdown of the Liberal Media*, Crown Forum, 2004.

The president of the Media Research Center offers evidence that major media outlets are liberal and argues that they are going to continue to lose market share as a result.

Downie Jr., Leonard, and Robert G. Kaiser, *The News About the News: American Journalism in Peril*, Knopf, 2002.

Two top *Washington Post* editors worry that good journalism — providing crucial information about government and issues of interest — is too often crowded out by sloppy journalism.

Powers, John, *Sore Winners (and the Rest of Us) in George Bush's America*, Doubleday, 2004.

The *LA Weekly* editor and columnist explains how Bush's presidency both exemplifies and takes advantage of changes in contemporary media culture.

Starr, Paul, *The Creation of the Media: Political Origins of Modern Communications*, Basic Books, 2004.

A Princeton University sociologist shows how the U.S. government helped make the media vital and competitive through regulatory decisions and investments in technology.

Articles

"A Media Watershed," *The Wall Street Journal*, Sept. 16, 2004, p. A16.

An editorial argues that CBS' embarrassment in using fake documents in a report critical of Bush signals the moment when the liberal media lost its power to control the public agenda.

Kurtz, Howard, "The Post on WMDs: An Inside Story," *The Washington Post*, Aug. 12, 2004, p. A1.

The Post's media critic takes the paper to task for not being sufficiently rigorous of its coverage of the war in Iraq.

Massing, Michael, "Now They Tell Us," *The New York Review of Books*, Feb. 26, 2004, p. 43.

Massing argues that reporters relied too heavily on outside sources arguing the case for war against Iraq and too little on critics.

Menand, Louis, "Nanook and Me," *The New Yorker*, Aug. 9, 2004, p. 90.

Examining "Fahrenheit 9/11" within the documentary tradition, the author concludes that the art of making documentaries tends to be practiced by liberals.

Navarette Jr., Ruben, "Once Journalists Show Their Politics Can They Still Claim Impartiality?" *Chicago Tribune*, Aug.13, 2004.

The columnist worries that the minority journalists who applauded John Kerry and booed President Bush embarrassed their profession by revealing partisan colors.

Samuelson, Robert J., "Picking Sides for the News," *Newsweek*, June 28, 2004, p. 37.

The economics columnist notes that surveys show the public increasingly finds media outlets politically biased.

Reports and Studies

"News Audiences Increasingly Politicized," The Pew Research Center for the People & the Press, June 8, 2004.

The group found that political polarization is increasingly reflected in American viewing and reading habits.

"The State of the News Media 2004," Center for Excellence in Journalism, March 15, 2004.

The center finds the long-term outlook for many traditional news outlets is "problematic."

Groseclose, Tim and Jeff Milyo, "A Measure of Media Bias," *Stanford University Working Paper*, September 2003.

Two political scientists devise a way to measure bias in the media.

Kull, Steven, *et al.*, "Misperceptions, the Media and the Iraq War," Program on International Policy Attitudes/Knowledge Networks, Oct. 2, 2003.

Seven polls conducted during 2003 concerning the public's knowledge of the war in Iraq indicate that the audiences for different news outlets have very different grasps of the facts.

Lott Jr., John R. and Kevin A. Hassett, "Is News Coverage of Economic Events Politically Biased?" American Enterprise Institute, Sept. 1, 2004.

The AEI scholars conclude that economic data is about 20 percent more likely to receive positive coverage under Democratic administrations than Republican ones.

The Next Step:

Additional Articles from Current Periodicals

Blog Bias

Billmon, "Blogging Sells, and Sells Out," *Los Angeles Times*, Sept. 26, 2004, p. M6.
Famous for their anti-establishment views, bloggers are already being domesticated and are now on the verge of being absorbed by the media complex they claim to despise.

Grossman, Lev, and Anita Hamilton, "Meet Joe Blog," *Time*, June 21, 2004, p. 64.
More and more people get their news from amateur Web sites called blogs, now a genuine alternative to mainstream news, because they're fast, funny and totally biased.

Kurtz, Howard, "Who Cares What You Think? Blog, and Find Out," *The Washington Post*, April 22, 2002, p. C1.
Blogs have been dismissed as a "medium where no thought goes unpublished," but the arena has produced fresh, clever musings by people whose voices would not be heard otherwise.

Witt, Howard, "True or False: Blogs Always Tell It Straight," *Chicago Tribune*, Sept. 19, 2004, p. C1.
Editors and TV directors are disdainful of bloggers, who assume the façade of the free press but operate outside of the journalistic rules of fairness and rigorous fact-checking.

Covering a World at War

Goodman, Tim, "Media Get a Bit Combative," *The San Francisco Chronicle*, March 26, 2003, p. W2.
An emboldened press may come too late for critics in the United States and abroad who believe the media are too soft on the administration and are not providing a real look at the war.

Kinsley, Michael, "The Rush To Pressure The Press," *The Washington Post*, Nov. 9, 2001, p. A37.
In the aftermath of Sept. 11, 2001, journalists, often criticized for being too opinionated, were critiqued for remaining "neutral" and not expressing bias against terrorism.

Stanley, Alessandra, "A Nation at War: The TV Watch," *The New York Times*, March 30, 2003, p. B15.
As the conflict in Iraq deepens, so has the debate about television coverage, with complaints coming from politicians, anti-war groups and conservatives.

Fox News

Cook, John, "Glimpse at the Future Looks Neither Fair nor Balanced," *Chicago Tribune*, Sept. 19, 2004, p. C1.
Many television news executives fear that Fox News' dominant coverage of the Republican National Convention marks a turning point toward a more partisan news culture.

Folkenflik, David, "Fair Game," *The Baltimore Sun*, Aug. 13, 2003, p. 1E.
As Fox News forges ahead with its successful pursuit of conservative viewers, CEO Roger Ailes says those alleging bias are the ones playing politics.

Getlin, Josh, "Fox News' Patriotic Fervor Sets It Apart in Ratings Race," *Los Angeles Times*, April 11, 2003, Part 1, p. 16.
After the fall of Baghdad, Fox News racked up the largest audiences in its six-year history with its, some say, biased approach, solidifying its lead over CNN and MSNBC.

Rich, Frank, "This Time Bill O'Reilly Got It Right," *The New York Times*, Sept. 19, 2004, Sect. 2, p. 1.
Fox News' O'Reilly correctly criticized CNN for keeping James Carville and Paul Begala as hosts after they joined the Kerry campaign.

Rutten, Tim, "Miles from 'Fair and Balanced,' " *Los Angeles Times*, Nov. 1, 2003, p. E1.
A producer alleged that Fox News executives issue a daily memo asking the staff to bend the network's reporting to conform with management's political views.

Mainstream Bias

Cunningham, Brent, "Re-thinking Objectivity," *Columbia Journalism Review*, July/August 2003, p. 24.
This 7,000-word commentary by the *Review's* managing editor says editors should admit that being totally objective is almost humanly impossible and that journalists should become experts in their specialties so they can "adjudicate factual disputes" in political debates.

Chiat, Jonathan, "Bad Press," *The New Republic*, Nov. 10, 2003, p. 20.
Bad habits, biases and a new breed of politicians adept at exploiting those weaknesses have political reporters producing misleading coverage.

Gabler, Neal, "The Media Bias Myth," *Los Angeles Times*, Dec. 22, 2002, p. M1.
The media war isn't between liberals and conservatives but between two entirely different journalistic mind-sets: those who believe in advocacy and those who believe in objectivity.

Kurtz, Stanley, "Media Blackout," *National Review*, Sept. 8, 2003, National Review Online.
The Washington Post, *New York Times* and *Boston Globe* failed to cover the proposed Federal Marriage Amendment, leading to an argument of bias by omission.

Nunberg, Geoffrey, "Who Knew? It's Not Just the Media.

These Days, Everybody's Biased," ***The New York Times*, Nov. 9, 2003, Sect. 4, p. 4.**

The meaning of "media bias" has changed in the last 50 years from an implication of deliberately distorting events to a more covert, subconscious manipulation.

Shaw, David, "The More Pernicious Bias is Less Substance, More Fluff," *Los Angeles Times*, Jan. 19, 2003, Part 5, p. 37.

The real bias in media is not liberal but one aimed at sensationalism, scandal, celebrities and violence as opposed to serious, insightful coverage of important issues.

Smolkin, Rachel, "Are the News Media Soft on Bush?" *American Journalism Review*, October, 2003/November, 2003, p. 16.

The so-called liberal press was much tougher on President Clinton than it has been on President Bush, the author argues, because the media are more interested in personal peccadilloes like Clintons that on Bush's controversies, which involve complicated policy debates.

Partisan Journalism

Anderson, Brian, "Culture Clash; Right Wing's Mass-Media Insurgency Heralds a Real Change," *Los Angeles Times*, Nov. 23, 2003, p. M1.

Cable TV, the Internet and book publishing have injected conservative ideas into the country's political and cultural debates.

Campbell, Kim, "A Call to the Right," *The Christian Science Monitor*, July 25, 2002, p. 11.

Conservative groups are growing their own journalistic ranks as an alternative to complaining about liberal media bias.

Gibbs, Nancy, "Blue Truth, Red Truth," *Time*, Sept. 27, 2004, p. 24.

Americans in the Blue (Democratic) or Red (Republican) worlds have two separate realities.

Harden, Blaine, "In Virginia, Young Conservatives Learn How to Develop and Use Their Political Voices," *The New York Times*, June 11, 2001, p. A10.

The Leadership Institute, financed by about $8 million a year in contributions from wealthy conservatives, trains "a new generation of conservative journalists."

Perlstein, Rick, "Eyes Right; Conservatives Are Winning the Media War. How Do They Do It?" *Columbia Journalism Review*, March, 2003/April, 2003, p. 52.

In reviewing Eric Alterman's *What Liberal Media?*, author Perlstein describes "conservative bunkerism" vs. "liberal openness." While conservative media fight politics as a "life-and-death struggle," he argues, liberals are busy trying to promote fairness, openness and diversity. The result, he says: Conservatives "fight the media war ruthlessly, and they are winning."

Research Supporting Bias Claims

Goldberg, Jonah, "Occam's Spoon," *National Review*, May 7, 2001, National Review Online.

Seventy percent of self-defined liberals think the media has a liberal bias, but journalists, who value objectivity over all, refuse to acknowledge it.

Porter, Eduardo, "Do Newspapers Make Good News Look Bad?" *The New York Times*, Sept. 12, 2004, Sec. 3, p. 6.

Economists at a conservative research organization say economic reporters slant the news to favor the Democrats.

Samuelson, Robert, "Bull Market for Media Bias," *The Washington Post*, June 23, 2004, p. A21.

A Pew survey confirms that people are increasingly picking their media on the basis of partisanship.

Tolson, Jay, "The Media on Trial," *U.S. News & World Report*, Sept. 6, 2004, p. 78.

The Pew Research Center says 53 percent of Americans don't trust news reports — up from 30 percent in 1976.

CITING *THE CQ RESEARCHER*

Sample formats for citing these reports in a bibliography include the ones listed below. Preferred styles and formats vary, so please check with your instructor or professor.

MLA STYLE

Jost, Kenneth. "Rethinking the Death Penalty." The CQ Researcher 16 Nov. 2001: 945-68.

APA STYLE

Jost, K. (2001, November 16). Rethinking the death penalty. *The CQ Researcher, 11*, 945-968.

CHICAGO STYLE

Jost, Kenneth. "Rethinking the Death Penalty." *CQ Researcher*, November 16, 2001, 945-968.

In-depth Reports on Issues in the News

Are you writing a paper?
Need backup for a debate?
Want to become an expert on an issue?

For 80 years, researchers have turned to *The CQ Researcher* for in-depth reporting on issues in the news. Reports on a full range of political and social issues are now available. Following is a selection of recent reports:

Civil Liberties
Civil Liberties Debates, 10/03
Gay Marriage, 9/03

Crime/Law
Stopping Genocide, 8/04
Serial Killers, 10/03

Economy
Big-Box Stores, 9/04
Exporting Jobs, 2/04
Stock Market Troubles, 1/04

Education
School Desegregation, 4/04
Black Colleges, 12/03
Combating Plagiarism, 9/03

Energy/Transportation
SUV Debate, 5/03
Future of Amtrak, 10/03

Environment
Smart Growth, 5/04
Air Pollution Conflict, 11/03

Health/Safety
Dietary Supplements, 9/04
Homeopathy Debate, 12/03
Worker Safety, 5/04

International Affairs
Stopping Genocide, 8/04
Aiding Africa, 8/03

Politics/Public Policy
Redistricting Disputes, 3/04
Democracy in Arab World, 1/04

Social Trends
Future of Music Industry, 11/03
Latinos' Future, 10/03

Terrorism/Defense
North Korean Crisis, 4/03
Homeland Security, 9/03

Youth
Athletes and Drugs, 7/04
Youth Suicide, 2/04
Hazing, 1/04

Upcoming Reports

Cloning, 10/22/04
Voting Rights, 10/29/04
Gun Control, 11/5/04
Sentencing Debates, 11/12/04
Treatment of Veterans, 11/19/04
Tobacco Industry, 12/3/04

ACCESS

The CQ Researcher is available in print and online. For access, visit your library or www.thecqresearcher.com.

STAY CURRENT

To receive notice of upcoming *CQ Researcher* reports, or learn more about *CQ Researcher* products, subscribe to the free e-mail newsletters, *CQ Researcher Alert!* and *CQ Researcher News*: www.cqpress.com/newsletters.

PURCHASE

To purchase a *CQ Researcher* report in print or electronic format (PDF), visit www.cqpress.com or call 866-427-7737. A single report is $10. Bulk purchase discounts and electronic rights licensing are also available.

SUBSCRIBE

A full-service *CQ Researcher* print subscription—including 44 reports a year, monthly index updates, and a bound volume—is $625 for academic and public libraries, $605 for high school libraries, and $750 for media libraries. Add $25 for domestic postage.

The CQ Researcher Online offers a backfile from 1991 and a number of tools to simplify research. Available in print and online, *The CQ Researcher en español* offers 36 reports a year on political and social issues of concern to Latinos in the U.S. For pricing and a free trial of either product, call 800-834-9020, ext. 1906, or e-mail librarysales@cqpress.com.

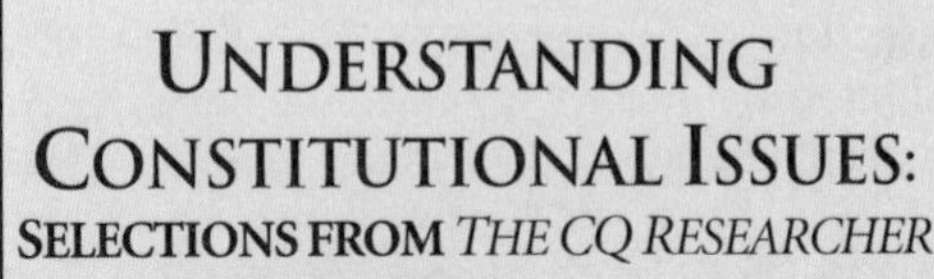

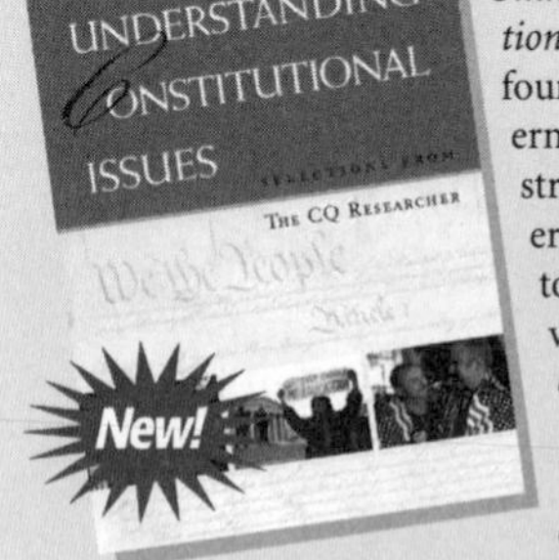

Understanding Constitutional Issues focuses on four key themes — governmental powers and structure, security, liberty, and equality — to help students develop a deeper understanding of the relation between current events and constitutional issues and principles. Integrating eighteen *CQ Researcher* reports, *Understanding Constitutional Issues* makes important connections clear, such as those between civil liberties and security; and privacy and liberty.

June 2004 • 8 1/2 x 11 • Approx. 432 pages • Paperback • ISBN 1-56802-885-7 • $39.95

To Order: Call Toll-Free: 866.4CQ.PRESS (427.7737)
Fax: 800.380.3810 • Web: www.cqpress.com
E-mail: customerservice@cqpress.com

CQ Press, 1255 22nd Street, NW, Suite 400 • Washington, DC 20037

CQ Researcher

Published by CQ Press, a division of Congressional Quarterly Inc.

thecqresearcher.com

Cloning Debate

Should all forms of human cloning be banned?

Cloning became a hot issue in this year's presidential race after scientists in South Korea announced that they had created human embryos by cloning, and former first lady Nancy Reagan urged President Bush to reconsider his policies on so-called therapeutic cloning and embryonic stem-cell research. Some scientists think embryonic stem-cell research could someday produce cures for Parkinson's disease, diabetes and other maladies that afflict millions of people, including Alzheimer's disease, which killed President Ronald Reagan. Others say the procedure offers more hype than hope. Still others, including President Bush, say the research is grossly unethical because it destroys human embryos. They also fear that therapeutic cloning could lead to human cloning and even the creation of human clones as organ sources. Presidential candidate Sen. John Kerry opposes human cloning but has vowed to quadruple federal funding for embryonic stem-cell research.

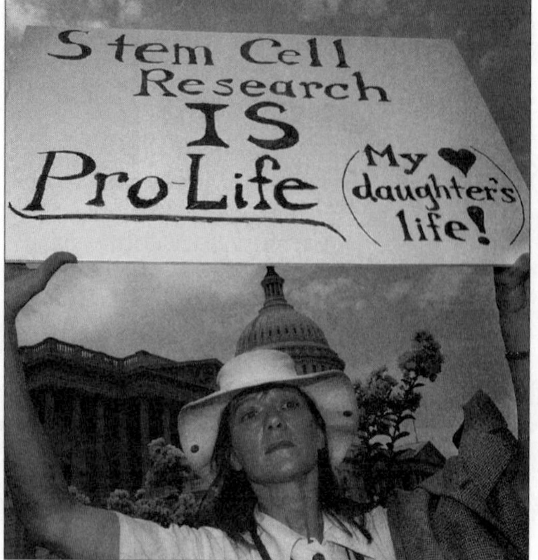

The mother of a child with juvenile diabetes demonstrates at the Capitol in support of stem-cell research.

INSIDE THIS REPORT

The CQ Researcher • Oct. 22, 2004 • www.thecqresearcher.com
Volume 14, Number 37 • Pages 877-900

CQ PRESS

RECIPIENT OF SOCIETY OF PROFESSIONAL JOURNALISTS AWARD FOR EXCELLENCE ◆ AMERICAN BAR ASSOCIATION SILVER GAVEL AWARD

THE ISSUES

BACKGROUND

CURRENT SITUATION

OUTLOOK

SIDEBARS AND GRAPHICS

FOR FURTHER RESEARCH

Cover: The mother of a child with juvenile diabetes demonstrates at the Capitol in support of embryonic stem-cell research. (Getty Images/Shawn Thew)

The CQ Researcher

Oct. 22, 2004
Volume 14, Number 37

MANAGING EDITOR: Thomas J. Colin

ASSISTANT MANAGING EDITOR: Kathy Koch

ASSOCIATE EDITOR: Kenneth Jost

STAFF WRITERS: Mary H. Cooper, William Triplett

CONTRIBUTING WRITERS: Sarah Glazer, David Hatch, David Hosansky, Patrick Marshall, Tom Price, Jane Tanner

DESIGN/PRODUCTION EDITOR: Olu B. Davis

ASSISTANT EDITOR: Kate Templin

CQ PRESS

A Division of Congressional Quarterly Inc.

SENIOR VICE PRESIDENT/GENERAL MANAGER: John A. Jenkins

DIRECTOR, LIBRARY PUBLISHING: Kathryn C. Suárez

DIRECTOR, EDITORIAL OPERATIONS: Ann Davies

CONGRESSIONAL QUARTERLY INC.

CHAIRMAN: Paul C. Tash

VICE CHAIRMAN: Andrew P. Corty

PRESIDENT AND PUBLISHER: Robert W. Merry

The CQ Researcher (ISSN 1056-2036) is printed on acid-free paper. Published weekly, except Jan. 2, April 9, July 2, July 9, Aug. 6, Aug. 13, Nov. 26 and Dec. 31, by CQ Press, a division of Congressional Quarterly Inc. Annual subscription rates for institutions start at $625. For pricing, call 1-800-834-9020, ext. 1906. To purchase a *CQ Researcher* report in print or electronic format (PDF), visit www.cqpress.com or call 866-427-7737. A single report is $10. Bulk purchase discounts and electronic-rights licensing are also available. Periodicals postage paid at Washington, D.C., and additional mailing offices. POSTMASTER: Send address changes to *The CQ Researcher*, 1255 22nd St., N.W., Suite 400, Washington, D.C. 20037.

Cloning Debate

BY BRIAN HANSEN

THE ISSUES

Brigitte Boisselier holds two Ph.D.s in chemistry and has worked in both industry and academia.

Yet it's easy to dismiss Boisselier as, well . . . a crackpot. After all, she belongs to the fringe Raelian religious sect, which believes that humans are descendants of clones created 25,000 years ago by space aliens.

Boisselier made headlines two years ago when she announced that the Raelians had facilitated the birth of the world's first human clone. Most people scoffed, but Boisselier not only stands by her story but also claims that Clonaid — the Raelians' biotechnology company — has produced 13 other human clones.

"We are doing around 10 implantations a month," says Boisselier, a native of France and a part-time resident of Las Vegas. "And we're getting thousands and thousands of requests from people who are interested in cloning."

Cloning is a form of asexual reproduction in which an embryo is created, not by the "natural" method of a sperm (male) cell fertilizing an egg (female) cell, but by using technology to replicate the genetic makeup of a single individual. (*See diagram, p. 880.*)

Boisselier contends that cloning is the first step to immortality, a tenet of the Raelian religion. But she also views it as a legitimate way of helping infertile couples and homosexuals bear genetically related children. Two other scientists — Panayiotis Zavos, a fertility clinic operator in Lexington, Ky., and Severino Antinori, an Italian gynecologist — are publicly offering cloning services to help infertile couples and homosexuals.

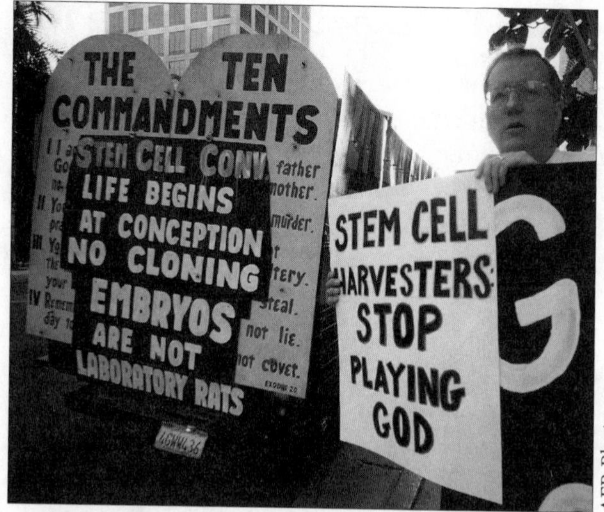

Signs held by a protester in San Diego, Calif., and on a passing truck oppose all embryonic stem-cell research, which two-thirds of Americans support. President Bush has imposed strict funding limits on stem-cell research; Democratic presidential challenger Sen. John Kerry supports more funding. Many scientists say Bush's policy is causing private investors — as well as young scientists just starting their careers — to avoid embryonic research.

Antinori claimed in May that at least three human clones have been born with his assistance. "I confirm the facts," he told a Rome news conference. "It happened, and I am repeating it." [1]

Many experts also scoff at Antinori's claims, which have not been independently verified. Nonetheless, the idea of cloning humans deeply troubles many experts and ethicists.

They argue that so-called reproductive cloning would undermine the fundamental concept of humanness. Moreover, they note, only about 5 percent of all mammalian cloning attempts result in live births, which often exhibit severe genetic abnormalities.

"It would be grossly unethical to try and make a human baby by cloning, given what we know about failure rates in other mammals," says Thomas Murray, president of the Hastings Center, a bioethics research center in Garrison, N.Y.

While scientists and policymakers overwhelmingly oppose reproductive cloning, many support "therapeutic" cloning — creating human embryos through cloning, not to produce babies, but to harvest their stem cells for medical research. Embryonic stem cells are undifferentiated "master" cells capable of developing into any type of tissue in the body. Many scientists think they could someday be used to repair or "regenerate" mature organs and tissues damaged by Parkinson's disease, diabetes and other afflictions.

In a stunning cloning breakthrough, South Korean scientists announced in February 2004 that they had created human embryos by cloning and had successfully harvested stem cells from them.

"Our goal is not to clone humans, but to understand the causes of diseases," said project director Hwang Woo-suk, of Seoul National University.

Meanwhile, Harvard University's ethical review board revealed early this month it is considering proposals from two teams of university scientists to conduct similar experiments. "This is cutting-edge research," says Professor Douglas Melton, the senior researcher on one of the teams. We want new ways to study and hopefully cure diseases."

But the scientists pursuing therapeutic cloning are quick to point out that they oppose reproductive cloning. "We'd like to ask every country or nation to have a law to prohibit reproductive cloning," Korean obstetrician Moon Shin-yong said. [2]

The United States has not banned reproductive cloning, however, and neither have most other countries.

Most embryonic stem cells held in research facilities were harvested from "natural" (uncloned) embryos that people donated to science, mostly unused embryos from fertility clinics. So far, scientists have

Continued on p. 881

How Reproductive and Therapeutic Cloning Differ

*Therapeutic cloning creates human embryos through cloning in order to harvest their stem cells for medical research; reproductive cloning creates the embryos for human reproduction. But the two procedures are initially identical. The first step in the process — known as somatic cell nuclear transfer, or SCNT — is to remove the nucleus from a female egg cell, stripping out most of its genetic material (**1**). This produces a denucleated egg. Next, the nucleus is removed from a body (somatic) cell — a skin cell, for example, and inserted (**2**) into the denucleated egg. Then the egg is stimulated with a tiny jolt of electricity or a few drops of chemicals (**3**) to "trick" it into dividing, a process normally triggered by a sperm cell.*

Embryos created in this manner are almost — though not quite — exact genetic replicas of the body (somatic) cell donors. About 2 percent of a donor's genetic material is not passed along because it resides in a cell's mitochondria, not its nucleus. Cloned embryos receive this 2 percent from the mitochondria of their denucleated egg cells.

*Once an embryo starts to divide, the cloning process is technically complete (**4**).*

*In the case of reproductive cloning, the cloned embryo is implanted into a woman's womb in the hope that she will give birth (**5**). In therapeutic cloning, the cloned embryo is allowed to develop in a laboratory petri dish long enough for embryonic stem cells to be harvested, which destroys the embryo (**6**).*

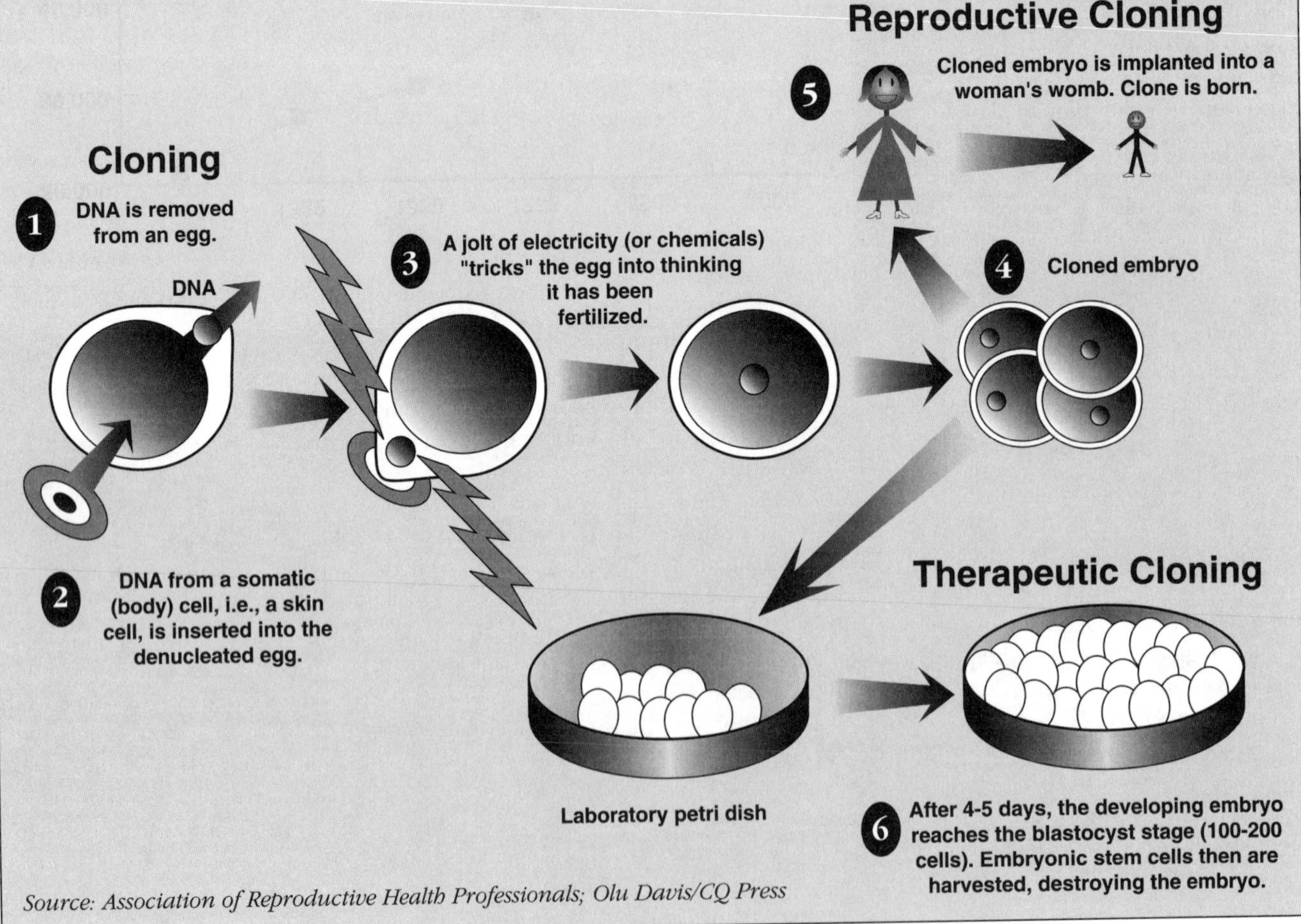
Reproductive Cloning
5 Cloned embryo is implanted into a woman's womb. Clone is born.
Cloning
1 DNA is removed from an egg.
DNA
3 A jolt of electricity (or chemicals) "tricks" the egg into thinking it has been fertilized.
4 Cloned embryo
2 DNA from a somatic (body) cell, i.e., a skin cell, is inserted into the denucleated egg.
Therapeutic Cloning
Laboratory petri dish
6 After 4-5 days, the developing embryo reaches the blastocyst stage (100-200 cells). Embryonic stem cells then are harvested, destroying the embryo.

Source: Association of Reproductive Health Professionals; Olu Davis/CQ Press

Continued from p. 879

tested these cells only on animals, no embryonic stem-cell therapies have been used on humans in the United States.

But many scientists predict embryonic stem cells someday will be used to treat human diseases, thanks especially to Hwang and Moon. "The South Korean work is staggeringly important," says Gerald Schatten, a cloning expert at the University of Pittsburgh School of Medicine. "It ushers in a new era of medical promise."

"It's a major medical milestone," agrees Robert Lanza, vice president of medical and scientific development at Advanced Cell Technology, in Worcester, Mass. "It offers hope to millions of patients suffering from a long list of diseases." [3]

Experts say creating embryonic stem cells through cloning rather than the normal method of combining egg and sperm cells could provide a huge medical advantage: People being treated for Parkinson's disease, for instance, could be injected with cells bearing their exact genetic makeup, eliminating the risk of immunological rejection.

The late Christopher Reeve, who was tragically paralyzed in a 1995 equestrian accident, was an outspoken supporter of therapeutic cloning and embryonic stem-cell research. Reeve, who was best known for starring in the "Superman" films of the 1970s and '80s, died of heart failure this fall. Testifying before Congress two years ago, Reeve said the two technologies could help "100 million Americans [who] suffer from serious or currently incurable diseases." [4]

But some scientists say the promises of embryonic stem-cell research — and, by extension, therapeutic cloning — are being oversold. "They have yet to treat one human patient, and their success in animal models has been very limited," says David Prentice, a senior fellow in life sciences at the Family Research Council, a pro-life organization in Washington, D.C.

Stem-Cell Therapies Could Aid Millions

Many scientists say more than 100 million Americans could potentially be aided by therapies developed through stem-cell research. Critics deride the figure as vastly inflated.

Condition	Number of patients
Cardiovascular disease	58 million
Autoimmune diseases	30 million
Diabetes	16 million
Osteoporosis	10 million
Cancers	8.2 million
Alzheimer's disease	5.5 million
Parkinson's disease	5.5 million
Burns (severe)	0.3 million
Spinal-cord injuries	0.25 million
Birth defects (per year)	0.15 million

Source: National Academies of Science, Committee on the Biological and Biomedical Applications of Stem Cell Research, 2002

Moreover, critics like Prentice say embryonic stem-cell research and therapeutic cloning are unethical and should be banned because they destroy human embryos destined to become human beings. Some critics — especially Catholics, Christians and conservative Republicans — equate the practice with murder.

But to be sure, there are exceptions to this rule. Nancy Reagan, for example, the widow of former President Ronald Reagan, a Republican Party icon, supports both therapeutic cloning and embryonic stem-cell research. The Reagans' son, Ron, even spoke at the Democratic National Convention in Boston this summer in support of the technologies. On the other hand, Sen. Mary Landrieu, D-La., who is "pro-choice" on the issue of abortion, favors banning expanded therapeutic (as well as reproductive) cloning. Landrieu supports federally funded embryonic stem-cell research, but only if it is conducted with embryos that had already been destroyed before Aug. 9, 2001. [5]

President Bush has a similar policy. Bush imposed strict limits on federal funding for embryonic stem-cell research in August 2001, saying it raised "profound ethical questions" because it "destroys" an embryo's "potential for life." Bush limited federal spending on such research to the approximately 60 cell lines that he claimed were then available, arguing that "the life and death decision has already been made" for the embryos from which they were harvested. [6]

To date, there are no federal restrictions on privately funded embryo research, but many scientists say Bush's policy is causing private investors — as well as young scientists just starting their careers — to avoid embryonic research.

"People are not committing to it because they don't want to waste money or years of effort," says Elizabeth Blackburn, a biology professor at the University of California, San Francisco.

While U.S. policymakers widely view reproductive cloning as unethical,

Support Rose for Stem-Cell Research

The number of Americans who approve of embryonic stem-cell research has increased four percentage points from three years ago, while the number who disapprove has fallen by almost half.

Do you agree or disagree:

If most scientists believe that stem-cell research will greatly increase our ability to prevent or treat serious diseases, we should trust them and let them do it:

	Tend to Agree	Tend to Disagree	Not sure/ refused
2001	63%	29%	7%
2004	67	16	18

Source: Harris Poll, conducted online among 2,242 Americans age 18 and over, July 18-24, 2004

Congress has not moved to ban the practice, because some lawmakers are holding out for a ban on reproductive but not therapeutic cloning; others want to criminalize both types.

Meanwhile, some experts worry that the Koreans' widely publicized findings could serve as a roadmap for rogue doctors or mad scientists bent on cloning humans.

"I'm afraid some nitwit is going to try," said Larry Goldstein, a cellular and molecular biologist at the University of California, San Diego. [7]

"It is going to happen," said Lee M. Silver, a professor of molecular biology at Princeton University. "I'm not saying it's good, but I think it's going to happen." [8]

As scientists and policymakers grapple with the South Korean cloning achievement, here are some of the questions being asked:

Is reproductive cloning unsafe?

Many experts say reproductive cloning is grossly unethical because it jeopardizes the health of would-be child clones. They note that efforts to clone sheep, pigs, goats and other animals yield few live births, and that many live-born mammal clones die within weeks or months because of organ abnormalities.

"There is no such thing as a normal, healthy clone," says renowned animal-cloning expert Rudolf Jaenisch, of the Massachusetts Institute of Technology (MIT). "It would be totally irresponsible to attempt human cloning at this point, given what we know about animal cloning."

Reproductive cloning also would likely endanger the birth mothers, critics say. With animals, pregnancies involving cloned fetuses regularly result in life-threatening complications for the mother. In one prominent study, nearly a third of the pregnant cows died from complications late in pregnancy. [9]

Meanwhile, 88 percent of Americans polled in May 2004 said cloning humans would be "morally wrong" for a variety of reasons, even if it could be done safely. (*See graph, p. 883.*) Other polls show similar results. [10]

Reproductive cloning is fundamentally wrong, critics say, because it would undermine the basic concept of human identity. As a result, they say, clones would be seen by society — and themselves — not as unique individuals, but as carbon copies of their "original" genetic twins.

Cloning also would allow adults to "customize" their children's genes in the hope that they would look or act a certain way, critics say. That would lead, they argue, to the diminution of individual uniqueness: Children would become mere consumer goods. [11]

"Human cloning turns procreation into a manufacturing process, treating human life as a commodity made to preset specifications," said Cardinal William Keeler, chairman of the Committee for Pro-Life Activities of the United States Conference of Catholic Bishops. "This is a sign of moral regress." [12]

Leon Kass, chairman of the President's Council on Bioethics, agrees. "It is the first step toward a . . . world in which children become objects of manipulation and products of will," Kass told a Senate panel last year. [13]

Advocates of reproductive cloning acknowledge the procedure could be abused, but they insist that with government oversight it can be carried out safely and morally.

"Human cloning will be done whether we like it or not," said Zavos, who runs the fertility clinic in Kentucky, as well as other clinics overseas. "We should accept it, make it legal, regulate it and make sure it is done in a responsible, scientifically correct way." [14]

As for the notion that clones would suffer from identity crises, Boisselier, of the Raelians, says they would be "loved and cherished even more" because their parents cannot have children any other way. "We are talking about babies, not monsters," she says. "They have their own identities and are seen as individuals."

Mark Eibert, a San Mateo, Calif., attorney who advocates for infertile couples, argues that there are no such identity problems with identical twins, which he calls "naturally occurring clones."

"They don't seem to have any identity crisis," says Eibert, the father of 4-year-old twin boys. "There is no evidence — as opposed to speculation — to suggest that cloned children would feel bad about the way they were conceived, or that they would wish they had never been born. They are not going to be freaks leading secondhand lives; they are going to be ordinary people and unique individuals with as much of an open future as anybody has."

Eibert also rejects the "designer children" argument: that people would use reproductive cloning to create kids who look like movie stars or have great musical talent or athletic ability. Ninety-nine percent of the demand for cloning is going to come from infertile people," Eibert says, "and they're just interested in having normal, healthy children who are biologically related to them."

Eibert says cloning is needed because infertility treatments, such as *in vitro* fertilization (IVF), can't help people who cannot produce viable eggs or sperm. "IVF doesn't work for everyone," he says, calling cloning "revolutionary" because it is the only infertility treatment that does not require the patients to produce viable eggs or viable sperm. If they can spare a few cells scraped from the inside of their cheek, they too can have biologically related children and families, just like healthy people do."

Zavos maintains that reproductive cloning is not only morally justifiable but also medically safe. Testifying before Congress in 2002, Zavos said the "poor success rates noted by the animal cloners" were because of "experiments that were poorly designed, poorly executed, poorly approached and poorly understood and interpreted." In fact, Zavos says, "it may be technically easier and safer" to clone humans than animals. [15]

Zavos, Boisselier and Antinori say they have developed sophisticated testing procedures to "prescreen" cloned embryos for genetic defects before they are implanted in women. But none has disclosed details of the procedures, which sparks further suspicion and outrage among many of the world's top scientists.

"Zavos and the others are really renegades to science," says MIT's Jaenisch. "They're totally ignoring all the scientific evidence, and that's completely unethical. There is no way to use cloning to create a normal baby."

Most Americans Oppose Human Cloning

Nearly 90 percent of Americans polled in 2004 said cloning humans is morally wrong. The percentage has stayed about the same since 2001.

Do you personally believe that cloning humans is morally acceptable or morally wrong?

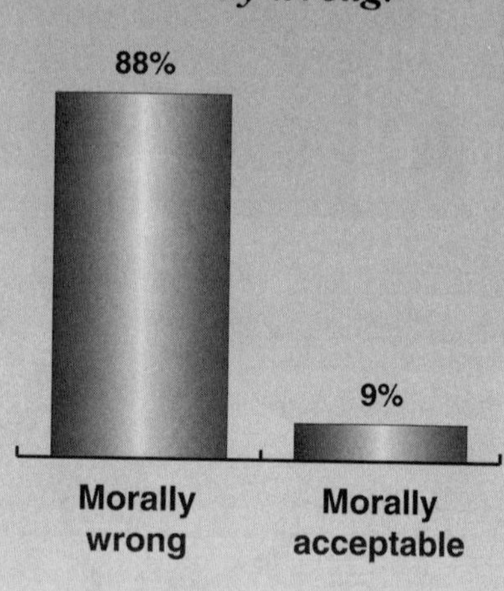

Source: Gallup Poll, of 1,000 Americans age 18 and over, May 2-4, 2004

Will therapeutic cloning and embryonic stem-cell therapies revolutionize medicine?

Therapeutic cloning produces embryonic stem cells that are used to research potential treatments for conditions ranging from Parkinson's and Alzheimer's diseases to diabetes, spinal-cord injuries and cancer. Eventually, scientists hope, the cells can be used to treat the actual diseases, using stem-cell therapy.

So far, embryonic stem-cell therapies have only been tested on mice and other animals. Most of the cells used in stem-cell research have been harvested from "natural" embryos discarded by clients of fertility clinics. The South Korean work announced in February marked the only time that researchers have extracted stem cells from cloned embryos.

Nevertheless, many experts believe that therapeutic cloning and embryonic stem-cell research could revolutionize medical science. The Coalition for the Advancement of Medical Research (CAMR), representing scientific societies and patient organizations, estimates stem-cell research could save the lives or ease the suffering of 100 million Americans and untold millions worldwide.

"This is an incredibly promising area," says Sean Tipton, CAMR's vice president. "It looks very promising for a whole host of human conditions where a new way to generate tissue is needed."

Researchers hope doctors eventually will be able to repair or "regenerate" damaged tissue by injecting or transplanting embryonic stem cells into patients. Because the cells are so biologically flexible, scientists believe they can be "coaxed" into becoming whatever type of tissue patients need, such as healthy brain cells for Parkinson's patients and insulin-producing pancreatic cells for diabetics.

Supporters of so-called regenerative medicine cite animal studies and laboratory experiments with human embryonic stem cells as evidence the approach will work. Researchers have coaxed mouse embryonic stem cells into becoming a wide variety of tissues, including blood, brain, bone and muscle cells. In an experiment at the National Institutes of Health (NIH) in Bethesda,

Are There Clones Among Us?

So far, no one has presented any hard scientific evidence, such as a DNA test, to prove that a human clone has been born. But some claim that — like something out of a science fiction movie — clones already walk among us.

Brigitte Boisselier, a member of the Raelian religious sect (who believe humans are descendants of clones created 25,000 years ago by space aliens) and Italian gynecologist Severino Antinori both say they have facilitated the births of more than a dozen human clones. And Kentucky-based fertility specialist Panayiotis Zavos says he has implanted a cloned embryo in a woman, but that she failed to become pregnant. He plans to implant other women soon, he says.

Boisselier, Zavos and Antinori say they have good reasons for not providing proof of their purported cloning accomplishments: Doing so would violate their clients' privacy and could even subject them to violence by anti-cloning zealots.

The three say they also fear arrest. Reproductive cloning is illegal in France and Italy, Boisselier's and Antinori's native countries, respectively. Even if Boisselier offered proof while in a country where reproductive cloning is still legal (such as the United States), Boisselier could be extradited back to her native France to stand trial.

"Why should I give the world the proof that will put me in jail?" asks Boisselier, who says she's currently negotiating with several foreign governments to allow her to take up residence without fear of extradition. "I will not give the proof unless there is a place I can stay, and I am very confident that no extradition can happen." If those conditions were met, she continues, "Then, of course, I will give every detail."

Here are the three scientists' claims:

- Boisselier runs Clonaid, the Raelians' human cloning project. On Dec. 27, 2002, She announced that Clonaid had facilitated the birth of the world's first human clone. She said the baby, nicknamed Eve, was born the previous day to a 31-year-old American woman at an undisclosed overseas location. Boisselier promised to provide proof of the claim but never did, claiming that Eve's parents refused to allow any genetic testing. Boisselier says Eve is currently living in Israel, and that Clonaid has since facilitated the births of more than a dozen other clones.
- Antinori became known in the 1990s for his controversial work in helping post-menopausal women have children. In 2001, he announced his intention to facilitate the birth of a human clone. In 2002 and 2003 he made several inconsistent claims that clonal pregnancies were under way. In May 2004, he said at least three babies had been born, but that he had played only an "advisory" role in their births. Although Antinori's medical and research credentials make his claims at least somewhat plausible, there is no evidence to support his announcements.
- Zavos runs fertility clinics in Lexington, Ky., London and Limassol, Cyprus. In May 2002, Zavos said he had assembled a team of scientists and had approved 12 couples for participation in cloning experiments. In April 2003, he published a picture said to be of a four-day-old cloned embryo, but the peer-reviewed analysis he promised did not follow. In January 2004, he announced that he had implanted a cloned embryo in one of his clients, but two weeks later said the woman had failed to become pregnant.

Md., mice given diabetes regained some insulin-producing ability after receiving injections of mouse embryonic stem cells. In another, mouse stem cells became brain cells that produce dopamine, a chemical lacking in Parkinson's sufferers. When the dopamine-producing cells were then transplanted into laboratory rats inflicted with Parkinson's, the rats were partially cured.

"We're absolutely confident that we have the right type of cell, and we can clearly show it affects the behavior of the animal," said project director Ron McKay, an NIH biologist. While the research is far from proof of a cure, McKay added, "It's absolutely definitive evidence that these cells can work in the brain." [16]

Scientists also have successfully induced human embryonic stem cells into becoming brain, liver and other types of cells (in laboratory petri dishes). Although no therapies have been developed using them, many experts believe that if that day ever arrives, patients could be treated with cells of their own genetic makeup, by having themselves, in effect, "therapeutically cloned." In theory, this would eliminate the risk that a person's immune system would reject the injected cells as foreign bodies; thus patients wouldn't have to take expensive immune-suppressing drugs that sometimes cause painful side effects, or don't work at all.

"That's the hypothesis, but we still need to prove it," said Jose Cibelli, a Michigan State University biotechnology professor who collaborated on the South Korean experiment. "If we can circumvent the rejection issue, life will be happy thereafter." [17]

Ron Reagan Jr., the son of the late former president, Ronald Reagan, touted that argument in a speech at the Democratic National Convention in Boston last summer.

"How'd you like to have your own, personal biological repair kit standing by at the hospital?" asked Reagan. "Sound like magic? Welcome to the future of medicine."

But critics say the potential for therapeutic cloning and embryonic stem-cell therapy is being oversold. This summer, for example, more than 2,400 doctors, scientists and other professionals affiliated with the Christian Medical & Dental Association (CMDA) wrote to Congress arguing that embryonic stem-cell research has yielded "only very limited and/or questionable success in animal models" and "no therapeutic application whatsoever in human beings." The letter accused some researchers of "hyping" the science "far beyond scientific integrity" in order to secure federal research funding. [18]

To be sure, groups like the CMDA have strong moral objections to embryonic stem-cell research. But they also say the approach has serious scientific shortcomings that should be troubling to everyone — including those who do not share their religious or moral views. For example, the prospect of treating diabetes with embryonic stem cells is far less promising than supporters claim, according to the critics. They argue that the much-touted 2001 experiment in which researchers claimed to have produced insulin-generating pancreatic islet cells was, in fact, a failure because all of the lab rats that received the supposedly therapeutic cells died of diabetes.

Moreover, they point out that in 2003 another team of researchers concluded that the first team had not created insulin-producing pancreatic cells but that the cells had only absorbed insulin from the culture medium and released it again. Critics also note that researchers at the University of Calgary, in Canada, found that while pancreatic cells derived from embryonic stem cells produced some insulin, they did not do so in response to changing glucose levels, as needed. Furthermore, when the Calgary researchers transplanted the cells into mice, they formed tumors. [19]

Critics are even more skeptical that embryonic stem-cell research will produce a cure for Alzheimer's disease, a brain disorder that affects as many as 5 million Americans. Because the disease kills huge numbers of many different varieties of cells, the therapy probably will not work on it, they say.

AFP photo/Tim Sloan

Controversial human-cloning researchers, from left, Severino Antinori, Panayiotis Zavos and Brigitte Boisselier attend a conference at the National Academy of Sciences.

"The complex architecture of the brain, the fact that it's a diffuse disease with neuronal loss in numerous places and with synaptic loss, all this is a problem" for any approach involving cell replacement, said Huntington Potter, a brain researcher at the University of South Florida in Tampa and chief executive of the Johnnie B. Byrd Institute for Alzheimer's Research. [20]

Critics are also skeptical of the claim that therapeutic cloning will yield cells that will not be rejected by recipients' immune systems. Unless the eggs used in the procedure are donated by the transplant recipients themselves, the resulting embryos will contain divergent DNA that could trigger an immune-system rejection, they point out.

Even MIT's Jaenisch concedes that tissue rejection could be a problem. In 2002, he created cloned mouse embryos and transplanted their stem cells back into the same animals. Although the cells were genetically identical to the recipients' other cells, they were rejected.

"Our results raise the provocative possibility that even genetically matched cells derived by therapeutic cloning may still face barriers to effective transplantation for some disorders," Jaenisch wrote. [21]

Critics have seized on Jaenisch's pronouncement as evidence that the rejection problem will forever hamper therapeutic cloning. But Jaenisch — and many other scientists — say it is simply too early for such sweeping conclusions. "The science is inefficient at this point, and much has to be learned," he says. "Technically, there are some issues that need to be resolved, and they can be resolved."

Meanwhile, many opponents of cloning and embryo research support regenerative medicine using adult, rather than embryonic, stem cells. So-called adult stem cells have been found in many kinds of mature tissues, including bone marrow, some organs and blood. Adult stem-cell therapies have already been used on people, with some success. And the approach is not controversial like embryonic stem-cell research and therapeutic cloning, because no embryos are destroyed in the process. [22]

Scientists generally agree that adult stem cells have medical promise. But most believe that embryonic cells have much greater potential.

"We are all for research into adult stem cells," says Tipton, of CAMR, "but the overwhelming scientific opinion is they are not going to be nearly as good."

Is therapeutic cloning immoral?

Some people argue that therapeutic cloning is immoral because it creates and then destroys human embryos, which they say are destined to become human beings.

"All human cloning produces another human life," said Sen. Sam Brownback, R-Kan., who advocates criminalizing all forms of the practice. "The deliberate creation and destruction of young humans through the process of [therapeutic] human cloning is morally wrong." [23]

John Kilner, president of the Center for Bioethics and Human Dignity, a Christian-oriented think tank in Bannockburn, Ill., agrees. "So-called therapeutic cloning destroys embryonic human beings," says Kilner, a Harvard-trained religious ethicist. "It produces human embryos for the explicit purpose of fatally mining them to obtain bodily materials for experimental purposes."

Some critics also argue that therapeutic cloning would not necessarily stop at the embryonic level. Clones could be kept alive in laboratories for months or even years until their organs could be harvested for "therapeutic" purposes, they speculate.

Princeton's Silver, who believes that therapeutic and reproductive cloning would be moral if they could be performed safely, touched off a firestorm a few years ago when he said, "it would almost certainly be possible to produce human bodies without a forebrain." Lee added that "these human bodies without any semblance of consciousness would not be considered persons, and thus it would be perfectly legal to keep them 'alive' as a future source of organs." [24]

Critics say Silver's "organ farm" scenario is not so far-fetched: Imagine a grief-stricken couple whose child desperately needs a heart transplant. Faced with such a scenario, critics say, the couple might agree to have doctors clone their sick child and genetically modify the embryo so that it would develop without a forebrain. The couple could then pay a surrogate mother to carry the embryo to term, or at least to a point where the fetus' heart is fully developed. Doctors could then remove the heart from the cloned, brainless fetus — which would have died anyway — and transplant it into the couple's sick child.

Charles Krauthammer, excoriates this scenario as morally reprehensible. "There is no grosser corruption of biotechnology than creating a human mutant and disemboweling it at our pleasure for spare parts," wrote Krauthammer, a conservative columnist and a medical doctor, in *Time*. "If we flinch in the face of this high-tech barbarity, we'll deserve to live in the hell it heralds." [25]

Other critics argue that even if reproductive cloning were criminalized and therapeutic cloning did not result in organ-farm practices, it would facilitate the cloning of people. The "slippery slope" argument they make goes this way: If the federal government or the states embraced therapeutic cloning, they would have to fund — or at least permit — research in order for the practice to be performed safely and efficiently. Because therapeutic and reproductive cloning are procedurally identical at the laboratory stage, the perfected technique for therapeutic cloning would inevitably be used for reproductive purposes, they argue.

Simply banning reproductive cloning could not prevent this from occurring, critics say, because rogue doctors could fly their patients to countries where the practice is legal. "Today, cloned [embryos] for research, tomorrow cloned [embryos] for babymaking," White House bioethics adviser Kass said in response to South Korea's therapeutic-cloning triumph. "In my opinion . . . the only way to prevent this from happening here is for Congress to enact a comprehensive ban or moratorium on all human cloning." [26]

Others argue that therapeutic cloning would endanger and exploit women who donate eggs for the procedure, because of the dangers inherent in the hormone treatments and surgery endured by egg donors. And if donors are offered financial compensation to donate their eggs, critics say, it would result in poor women selling their body parts for financial recompense.

"[Therapeutic cloning would] usher in an era where women will be exploited by experimental research cloning by corporations in order to get their eggs. Millions of women's eggs will be purchased for use in cloning experiments," said Rep. Dave Weldon, R-Fla., a physician. "Eventually, these companies will . . . exploit poor women in Third World countries to get their eggs."

But proponents of therapeutic cloning say it would be morally wrong not to allow the procedure (as well as embryonic stem-cell research), given the untold suffering that could be ameliorated.

"It is a weighing of morals," says Blackburn, of the University of California. "[Nobody] is hurt by therapeutic cloning or embryonic stem-cell research, but . . . a great many people could be harmed by banning them."

She and others reject the argument that therapeutic cloning and embryonic stem-cell research destroy actual or nascent human beingsbecause many "naturally" fertilized eggs never develop into full-fledged fetuses. The American Society for Reproductive Medicine estimates that 40 to 50 percent of all fertilized eggs expire on their own accord.

"It is true that every human life begins with an embryo, but it is not at all true that every embryo begins a human life," says Arthur Caplan, director of the Center for Bioethics at the University of Pennsylvania in Philadelphia. "Scientifically, it is not correct to say that every embryo has the potential to become a person, because many embryos are simply miswired and do not develop into anything at

Continued on p. 888

Chronology

1850s-1950s

Scientists make first attempts at cloning.

1938
German scientist Hans Spemann articulates the principles of modern cloning.

1952
American embryologists Robert Briggs and Thomas J. King transfer genetic material from frog cells to denucleated frog eggs. Many of the eggs develop into juvenile frogs.

1960s-1980s

Scientists begin cloning mammals.

1962
In the first successful cloning experiment using adult cells, Oxford University zoologist John Gurdon transfers genetic material from tadpole intestinal cells into denucleated frog eggs. The result: tadpole clones.

1970
Theologian Paul Ramsey argues against cloning humans in his book *The Fabricated Man.*

1984
Danish embryologist Steen Willadsen clones a sheep using embryonic cells. Other researchers subsequently clone cattle, pigs and other farm animals.

1990s

The first animal is born cloned from adult cells. Scientists also isolate human embryonic stem cells, raising hopes of revolutionary new medical treatments.

January 1996
English scientist Ian Wilmut and his colleagues clone first mammal ever created using adult stem cells. Six months later, on Feb. 22, 1997, Wilmut announces birth of "Dolly" the sheep.

December 1997
A furor ensues when Princeton biologist Lee Silver says that cloning might someday be used to create brainless human clones as sources of organs.

November 1998
Scientists at the University of Wisconsin and Johns Hopkins University announce that they isolated human embryonic stem cells for the first time.

2000-Present

A few scientists announce their intentions to clone humans. Other experts say cloning could be used for "therapeutic" purposes. Lawmakers clash over how to regulate cloning.

Nov. 26, 2001
Advanced Cell Technology of Worcester, Mass., clones human embryos for stem-cell research, but none develop past the six-cell stage.

Jan. 26, 2001
American fertility expert Panayiotis Zavos announces his intentions to clone human beings. Italian gynecologist Severino Antinori and Raelian religious cult member Brigitte Boisselier soon follow suit.

July 31, 2001
The House of Representatives passes legislation banning all forms of human cloning, but the measure stalls in the Senate because some members want to allow therapeutic cloning.

Aug. 9, 2001
President Bush says scientists may use federal funds to study human embryonic stem-cell lines created before this date, but that the government will not fund the "destruction" of more embryos.

Dec. 26, 2002
Boisselier claims that the world's first human clone, a girl nicknamed Eve, has been born.

Feb. 27, 2003
The House once again votes to ban all forms of human cloning, and the Senate once again refuses to do so.

Feb. 12, 2004
South Korean scientists create human embryos by cloning and harvest stem cells from them to use in therapeutic research.

May 2004
Antinori announces the birth of three human clones. He provides no proof, and most scientists doubt the claim.

June 5, 2004
Former President Ronald Reagan dies of Alzheimer's disease. His widow rebukes Bush's policy by calling for more federal support for embryonic stem-cell research. Democratic presidential candidate Sen. John Kerry does the same.

October 2004
Harvard University's ethical review board reveals it is considering proposals from two teams of university scientists to conduct embryonic stem-cell research. . . . Gov. Arnold Schwarzenegger, R-Calif., breaks with the state Republican Party and the Bush administration and supports a $3 billion bond measure that would fund embryonic stem-cell research.

Animal Cloning Spurs Controversy, Too

Scientists have cloned or are trying to clone livestock, pets, endangered species and even genetically engineered animals that could be harvested for organs or specific substances they produce. But the research has produced a plethora of ethical controversies.

Livestock producers say cloning would allow the unlimited replication of animals with desired characteristics, such as abundant muscle mass (meat), less fat or disease-resistance. "Cloning produces healthier animals [that] yield more nutritious food products," says Barbara Glenn, director of animal biotechnology at the Biotechnology Industry Organization (BIO), in Washington, D.C.

Only a fraction of U.S. livestock has been produced through cloning so far, and the U.S. Food and Drug Administration (FDA) has asked livestock producers to voluntarily withhold such products from the marketplace while the agency studies the matter. But many observers expect the agency to approve the sale of food products from cloned animals by the end of the year. The agency telegraphed its intentions last fall, when it published a draft report concluding that food products derived from animal clones and their offspring "are likely to be as safe to eat as food from their non-clone counterparts." [1]

While critics generally do not argue that food from cloned animals is unsafe to eat, they do argue that cloning reduces the biological diversity of a species, leaving it vulnerable to unanticipated disorders and diseases. Indeed, they say, this is already happening with conventional "selective" breeding practices and the creation of genetically engineered, or "transgenic," animals. Such animals carry genes from other animals, bacterium or plants inserted into their genetic codes to create entirely new species with desired traits.

"Already animals are suffering from maladies at a rate unheard of before we applied biotechnology to the barnyard," says Michael Appleby, vice president for farm animals and sustainable agriculture at the Humane Society of the United States. "A single pathogen could wipe out countless numbers of genetically identical animals, putting . . . the world's food supply at risk."

Appleby and other critics also argue that livestock cloning harms the animals themselves, because a large percentage of animal clones die before or shortly after birth, and those that survive often suffer from serious health problems.

Cloning transgenic animals with the desired medicinal traits is also controversial. Researchers have developed transgenic goats, for example, that produce substances in their milk that can dissolve blood clots in heart attack and stroke victims. Scientists have also created transgenic pigs that could someday be used as organ donors for humans — a procedure known as xenotransplantation. The pigs are genetically modified at the embryonic stage so that their organs will not be rejected by the human immune system.

Once researchers develop the first version of an animal with the desired genetic prototype — an extremely difficult process — they can replicate it indefinitely through cloning. "Cloning could theoretically provide a limitless supply of cells and organs for xenotransplantation," says Michael Lanza, medical director at Advanced Cell Technology, a biotechnology company in Worcester, Mass.

But critics decry such practices on both scientific and ethical grounds. Some argue that xenotransplantation could transmit animal viruses to transplant recipients, who could in turn infect others. They note that in 1918 a viral strain of influenza (flu) was transferred from pigs to people and swept the globe, killing an estimated 20-to-40 million people. Human immunodeficiency virus (HIV), the virus responsible for the AIDS pandemic, most likely originated in chimpanzees.

Others question the ethics of treating animals as organ factories. "We don't have the right to use pigs or any other animals as spare parts for people," says Peter Wood, a research associate at People for the Ethical Treatment of Animals (PETA) in Washington, D.C. "Animals are independent entities with their own interests, not a means to an end for humans. We have no right to create and then dismember animals at will."

Cloning may not bring back extinct species, like the dinosaurs in Michael Crichton's novel *Jurassic Park*, but it is keeping some endangered species from disappearing altogether. Earlier this year, Chinese scientists cloned a rare Siberian ibex, and they have long

Continued from p. 886

all. And philosophically, it's a terrible mistake to mix up potential people with real people. That's like saying acorns are the same as oak trees."

Some right-to-life advocates, though, even lament the fact that many fertilized eggs die off naturally before producing viable pregnancies. "There's lots of suffering and death in the world, but that's one of the great evidences of how out-of-kilter things are," says Kilner, who also believes that it's unethical for people to discard "extra" embryos created for *in vitro* fertilization purposes. Those people should instead arrange for "embryo adoptions," Kilner says.

Caplan, meanwhile, also rejects the "slippery slope" argument — that therapeutic cloning would inevitably lead to reproductive cloning.

"That's like arguing you have to ban all uses of matches because there are arsonists," he says. "You can certainly draw a line and say you can't use cloning to make people, and anybody who makes an embryo into a human being is going to be penalized." ■

BACKGROUND

Scientific Milestones

German embryologist Hans Spemann articulated the principles of modern cloning science in 1938. He wondered if animals could be replicated by transferring the genetic material of differentiated (somatic) body cells —

been trying to clone the endangered giant panda. In Australia, efforts are under way to clone the endangered northern hairy nosed wombat.

Three years ago, U.S. scientists cloned an oxlike gaur, a rare Asian species of wild cattle. And last April, Lanza's company cloned two bantegs, wild cowlike creatures native to Southeast Asia. The clones were derived from the cells of a male banteng that died at the San Diego Zoo in 1980 without producing offspring. Tissue samples taken from the animal were kept frozen for 23 years.

In Great Britain, a much more ambitious project — known as the "Frozen Ark" initiative — aims to freeze tissue samples of thousands of endangered animals to ensure their long-term survival. This summer, the first tissue samples — from an Arabian oryx, a spotted sea horse and a British field cricket — were frozen. In the future, scientists could thaw out the samples and attempt to clone new animals. [2]

Critics complain that cloning does not address the real reason animals become endangered: the destruction of their habitats. "Cloning endangered species gives a false sense that we're saving species, when it would be better to . . . preserve species in the wild," said Susan Lieberman, director of the species-preservation program at the World Wildlife Fund. [3]

AFP photo/Phil Shofield

In a scientific breakthrough, the first cloned mule, Idaho Gem, is born in May 2003.

Meanwhile, grief-stricken pet owners can now clone their departed animals. Three U.S. companies now clone pets: PerPETuate, Lazaron and Genetic Savings & Clone (GSC). The companies may have lighthearted names, but they practice serious science. Their prices are serious, too: GSC charges $50,000 to clone a cat. Next year the company plans to start cloning dogs. And the company offers a "gene banking" service — costing from $295-$1,395 — that allows people to keep their pets' genetic material frozen.

"It's a multibillion-dollar business waiting to happen," Lou Hawthorne, the company's founder and CEO, said. [4]

"I'm very worried that people are putting a piece of Fluffy in the fridge with the hope that cloning will restore it," says Arthur Caplan, director of the Center for Bioethics at the University of Pennsylvania. "Cloning is an echo; it is not a copy. These companies border on deceiving people."

[1] The letter is available on the FDA's Web site at www.fda.gov/bbs/topics/NEWS/2003/NEW00968.html

[2] More information about the Frozen Ark initiative is available on the British Natural History Museum's Web site at www.nhm.ac.uk/services/press/items/frozenark.htm

[3] Quoted in Tim Johnson, "China Announces Cloning of Endangered Siberian Ibex," *The San Jose Mercury News*, Jan. 30, 2004.

[4] Television interview, "CBS Evening News," Sept. 8, 2004.

skin cells, for example — to egg cells whose own nuclei had been removed. The procedure Spemann envisioned was essentially identical to somatic cell nuclear transfer (SCNT), the process used today in both therapeutic and — purportedly — reproductive cloning. Spemann didn't know how to perform the procedure, but he speculated it would be "somewhat fantastical" in nature. [27]

In 1952, American embryologists Robert Briggs and Thomas J. King made progress towards Spemann's "fantastical" vision by transferring genetic material taken from embryonic cells of leopard frogs to denucleated leopard frog eggs. Many of the eggs developed into tadpoles, and some grew into juvenile frogs. Other scientists repeated the experiment with other species of frogs.

But these experiments were not the type that Spemann envisioned, because they involved transferring genetic material from embryonic cells, not somatic cells, which are mature or adult cells. Cloning with embryonic cells is relatively easy, because the genes in the transplanted nuclei are all functioning and thus can be used as genetic blueprints to create new, duplicate animals. With adult cells, by contrast, many genes are genetically "turned off," making the blueprint incomplete.

Nevertheless, scientists employed the embryonic cell-transfer technique to replicate animals. In 1984, Steen Willadsen of Denmark cloned a sheep using embryonic cells. Other researchers subsequently cloned cattle, pigs, goats and rats using the same approach. An early exception to the embryonic-only procedure occurred in 1962, when Oxford University zoologist John Gurdon transferred genetic material from adult tadpole intestinal cells into denucleated frog eggs. The result was embryos that developed into cloned tadpoles.

Fear and Loathing

These experiments sparked debate over whether scientists could — and should — clone humans. Some experts believed cloning could improve the human race. This belief, known as eugenics, originated in ancient Greece, where the philosopher Plato spoke of selectively breeding "superior" people and eliminating the "feeble" in order to improve the quality of the republic's population. [28]

The eugenics movement took root in the United States in the early 20th century. Many white Americans embraced the concept as a way to keep their race from being genetically "degraded" by non-Northern European immigrants who were flooding into the country at the time.

Eugenics was used to justify the 1924 Immigration and Restriction Act, which set strict immigration quotas based on race and ethnicity. Then-President Calvin Coolidge emphasized the eugenic underpinnings of the new law: "America must be kept American. Biological laws show that Nordics deteriorate when mixed with other races."

About that time, several states launched forced-sterilization programs to prevent "defective people" from breeding. By the early 1930s, 27 states had sterilization laws, and tens of thousands of Americans had been sterilized. The U.S. Supreme Court upheld the laws on the basis of eugenics. In a famous 1927 case, Justice Oliver Wendell Holmes applauded the forced sterilization of a mentally retarded plaintiff, writing: "Three generations of imbeciles is enough."

But such ideas horrified society in the aftermath of World War II and the Nazis' attempt to create an Aryan master race by sterilizing and ultimately murdering some 12 million Jews, Slavs, Gypsies and other "undesirable" members of society. By the 1950s, most state forced-sterilization programs had been dismantled.

But the eugenics rationale for cloning didn't disappear entirely. In a controversial 1996 article, Nobel Prize-winning biologist Joshua Lederberg outlined how cloning might be used to improve the human race. "If a superior individual is identified, why not copy it directly, rather than suffer all the risks of recombinational disruption, including those of sex?" Lederberg asked. "The same solace is accorded the carrier of genetic disease: Why not be sure of an exact copy of yourself rather than risk a homozygous segregant" — a baby born with two copies of the same mutant gene. Such babies would likely suffer from a genetic disease. [29]

Ethicist Joseph Fletcher had made similar points in his 1974 book *The Ethics of Genetic Control: Ending Reproductive Roulette.* He argued that human cloning would provide a way around genetic diseases and infertility, and would allow people to bear children that resembled them or members of their families.

But theologian and ethicist Paul Ramsey excoriated the prospect of human cloning in his 1970 book *Fabricated Man: The Ethics of Genetic Control.* He argued that human cloning would violate the ethical responsibilities of both science and parenthood because it would involve experiments on nascent children, it would transform parenthood into a manufacturing process, and it would deny children their individuality. Human cloning, Ramsey wrote, would result in a "vast technological alienation of man" and the "abolition of man's embodied personhood."

British author Aldous Huxley had painted a similarly chilling picture in his 1931 novel *Brave New World,* where babies are produced in identical batches through a government-run cloning program, the family is obsolete and human beings are merely well-satisfied animals. To this day, cloning opponents invoke Huxley's horrors when discussing the procedure.

Hello Dolly!

In the meantime, scientists continued trying to clone animals using adult cells. The goal, they said, was to replicate animals with desired traits such as cows with more meat, less fat and a greater resistance to disease. Cloning, in theory, would allow ranchers to breed unlimited numbers of "archetype" cows, pigs or other animals.

In 1994, a team of U.S. researchers found a way to "turn off" and then "turn on" again the genes of embryonic cells by putting them into a chemically induced state of quiescence, or hibernation. In January 1996, scientists at the Roslin Institute in Scotland adapted the technique in a bid to clone a sheep from an adult sheep cell.

Led by Englishman Ian Wilmut, the team transplanted adult sheep nuclei into 277 denucleated eggs. After subjecting them to chemicals and weak electric shocks, 29 embryos were "tricked" into thinking they had been fertilized and were then implanted into surrogate mother sheep.

On July 5, 1996, one of the ewes gave birth, marking the first mammal ever cloned from an adult cell. The cloned sheep was named Dolly, after the popular country-western singer, Dolly Parton. [30]

When Wilmut announced Dolly's birth six months later, on Feb. 22, 1997, speculation ran wild that the technology that produced Dolly could lead to human cloning. In the United States, Congress held hearings on the subject, and in early 1998 the Senate considered legislation, proposed by a trio of Republican lawmakers, to permanently ban all human cloning.

Nearly all senators denounced human cloning, but many argued that the proposed ban would undermine potentially valuable scientific research. Democratic Sens. Edward M. Kennedy of Massachusetts and Tom Harkin of Iowa led the effort to kill the bill, which was also opposed by patient-advocacy groups, scientific and medical organizations and the biotechnology industry.

"Congress can and should act to ban cloning of human beings during this session," Kennedy said in February 1998. "But it should not act in haste, and it should not pass legislation that goes far beyond what the American people want or what the scientific and medical community understands is necessary or appropriate." [31]

Although Harkin and Kennedy introduced their own version of the bill, banning reproductive cloning but allowing therapeutic cloning, the measure died, and Congress remains stalemated on the issue.

The stakes of the cloning debate changed again just nine months later, in November 1998, when researchers at the University of Wisconsin and Johns Hopkins University announced that they had isolated human embryonic stem cells, the undifferentiated "master" cells that can become any type of tissue in the body. The discovery sparked enduring scientific and ethical questions. ■

CURRENT SITUATION

Competing Legislation

In Washington, policymakers are taking two general approaches to cloning. Some want to outlaw the practice entirely, while others want to ban reproductive cloning but allow therapeutic cloning. The House has twice passed legislation that would ban all cloning, most recently in February 2003. The legislation, sponsored by Reps. Dave Weldon, R-Fla., and Bart Stupak, D-Mich., would make cloning punishable by up to 10 years in prison and a $1 million fine.

The Senate version of the bill is sponsored by Sens. Brownback, the Kansas Republican, and Landrieu, a Democrat from Louisiana. "All cloning is reproductive," Brownback maintains. "So-called 'therapeutic' cloning is the process by which an embryo is created for the purpose of subsequently killing it for its parts . . . and [that] is certainly not 'therapeutic' for the clone who has been created and then disemboweled for the purported benefit of its adult twin." [32]

President Bush says he will sign the Brownback-Landrieu legislation into law if it reaches his desk. He cites three main reasons for his support. Like Brownback and others in the anti-cloning camp, Bush views the promised medical benefits of therapeutic cloning — Bush calls it "research" cloning — as "highly speculative." He also argues that anything other than a total ban would be "virtually impossible to enforce." Cloned human embryos created for research, he says, would inevitably find their way into the hands of rogue scientists who would use them for reproductive purposes.

But the president's main concern is that all cloning is unethical. "Research cloning would contradict the most fundamental principle of medical ethics: that no human life should be exploited or extinguished for the benefit of another," Bush said. "Yet a law permitting research cloning, while forbidding the birth of a cloned child, would require the destruction of nascent human life."

But Bush probably won't get a chance to sign the Brownback-Landrieu bill. Several influential senators — including some Republicans — back a competing bill that would prohibit only reproductive cloning. Much to the chagrin of the ban-all-cloning camp, Sen. Orrin G. Hatch — the staunchly conservative, anti-abortion Utah Republican — is sponsoring the bill that would permit therapeutic cloning to continue.

"In our attempt to ban human reproductive cloning, we should not close the door on a form of scientific research (therapeutic cloning) that has the potential of curing millions of debilitating and life-threatening diseases," Hatch said in introducing the bill in 2003. "As a right-to-life senator, I believe that a critical part of a pro-life, pro-family philosophy is helping the living."

Global Ban?

Stymied by the Senate, Bush has been pushing the United Nations to enact an international treaty banning all forms of human cloning worldwide.

Last fall, the United States was the driving force behind a draft U.N. treaty, introduced by Costa Rica, to ban the creation of cloned human embryos "for any purpose whatsoever" — including therapeutic uses. The proposal described human cloning as "morally repugnant, unethical and . . . a grave violation of fundamental human rights." [33] It was tabled last November without an up-or-down vote, and was scheduled to be reconsidered on Oct. 21. The United States will once again vigorously lobby for it. But a host of countries, led by the United Kingdom, oppose the U.S. approach for the same reason Bush's critics do at home: They do not want to ban therapeutic cloning.

The United Kingdom, Singapore, South Korea, Japan and China have all banned reproductive cloning but allow therapeutic cloning. The five countries — along with other countries with thriving biotechnology industries — support a Belgium-authored U.N. proposal that would ban reproductive cloning but permit therapeutic cloning.

"It would be indefensible to stop this research and deny millions of people — and their families — the opportunity to save their lives," Adam Thomson, a British representative to the U.N., told the General Assembly in December. [34]

Genetics Policy Institute, a think tank in Coral Gables, Fla., that supports therapeutic cloning, lobbied for the Belgium proposal last year. Bernard Siegel, the institute's executive director, says the U.S. delegation worked vigorously behind the scenes to dissuade other countries from backing it. "It was hardball politics," he says.

But Siegel and others familiar with the issue say politics is behind the Bush administration's actions. Even if the U.N. adopts a comprehensive cloning treaty, they note, it would not be binding on the United States without Senate ratification — a highly unlikely prospect. The same goes for other countries: Thompson stated flatly last year that the U.K. would "not apply" such a ban to its national law.

Nevertheless, a U.N. treaty "would be a tremendous propaganda victory for the foes of therapeutic cloning," Siegel says. "Bush could then say that the world's greatest international body had condemned it as morally indefensible, and that they [the Senate] had to follow suit."

Getty Images/Vince Bucci

Actor Michael J. Fox presents an award to former first lady Nancy Reagan at a May 2004 fund-raising event in Beverly Hills, Calif., for stem-cell and juvenile diabetes research. Fox has Parkinson's disease; the late President Ronald Reagan had advanced Alzheimer's disease, which some scientists say might be cured with the help of stem-cell research.

Stem-Cell Showdown

Bush is also facing pressure to lift the restrictions that he placed on federal spending for embryonic stem-cell research in August 2001. Bush said at the time that there were "more than 60" embryonic stem-cell lines existing in laboratories around the world. Reasoning that the embryos that had given rise to them had already been destroyed, Bush made federal funds available to researchers who wanted to study them. But he prohibited federal spending on research using other, newer lines.

Critics have long maintained that Bush greatly overestimated the number of useable lines that existed at the time of his announcement. Indeed, the National Institutes of Health, a division of the U.S. Department of Health and Human Services, estimated in March that only 19 lines were available for federal funding, far fewer than Bush originally indicated. Consequently, the federal government doled out only $24.8 million for embryonic stem-cell research in 2003.

In June, more than 140 scientific societies, patient organizations and other groups sent a letter to Bush urging him to expand his policy and allow federal funds to be spent on additional embryonic stem-cell lines (more than 100 have been created with private funds and in other countries since Bush announced his policy).

"[F]or the full potential of embryonic stem-cell research to be reached, the number of stem-cell lines readily available to scientists must increase," the letter stated. "For those of us with a personal stake in the possibilities of embryonic stem-cell research, this really is a race against time. In the past three years, more than 4 million Americans have died from diseases that embryonic stem cells have the potential to treat." [35]

Continued on p. 894

At Issue:

Should Congress ban all forms of human cloning?

DAVID PRENTICE
SENIOR FELLOW FOR LIFE SCIENCES, FAMILY RESEARCH COUNCIL

WRITTEN FOR *THE CQ RESEARCHER*, OCTOBER 2004

yes

human cloning starts with construction of an embryo. In a technique called somatic cell nuclear transfer (SCNT), the chromosomes of an egg cell are replaced with the nucleus of a somatic (body) cell. If the resulting embryo is then inserted into a womb in hopes of a live birth, it is called "reproductive cloning." If the embryo is destroyed to harvest its stem cells for experiments, it is called "therapeutic cloning." But these are not two separate types of cloning: The same embryo — produced by the same technique — is the starting point for both uses.

While most are opposed to reproductive cloning, some favor therapeutic cloning. The premise is that embryonic stem cells from a cloned embryo will produce matched transplant tissue for the patient whose cells were cloned. Yet, even proponents of therapeutic cloning have disputed this supposed transplant match, and when tested in mice, the cells were indeed rejected. Embryonic stem-cell researchers have noted that therapeutic cloning is unlikely to be of clinical significance. On the other hand, research using adult stem cells — which does not destroy any embryos — continues to show success at treating human patients.

However, any use of human cloning poses a health risk to women. A tremendous number of eggs are required for creation of just one cloned embryo, with minimal estimates of 50-100 (the South Koreans required 242 eggs to produce one embryonic stem-cell line.) A simple calculation shows that to treat just one disease group in the U.S. — the 17 million diabetes patients — would require a minimum of 850 million-1.7 billion human eggs, requiring the "harvest" of eggs from women on a global basis.

Allowing therapeutic cloning will likely lead to reproductive cloning. The same embryo is used for both procedures, and practice with the technique to produce embryos for research would refine the technique for producing embryos for implantation in a womb, as noted by the American Society for Reproductive Medicine Ethics Committee in November 2000. The lead author of the Korean study admitted at a news conference that the technique developed in his lab "cannot be separated from reproductive cloning."

Creating human embryos for research raises grave ethical concerns. It instrumentalizes human life and creates a caste of humans only to serve the needs of others. There is no evidence that cloning is necessary or useful for medical science, it poses a risk to women's health and crosses an ethical line in creation of human beings.

DANIEL PERRY
PRESIDENT, COALITION FOR THE ADVANCEMENT OF MEDICAL RESEARCH

WRITTEN FOR *THE CQ RESEARCHER*, OCTOBER 2004

no

banning all forms of cloning would slam the door on hope for up to 100 million Americans by outlawing vital research on some of the most debilitating diseases known to humankind.

There are very different kinds of "cloning," which simply means making copies of a single molecule, cell, virus or bacterium. Reproductive cloning — creating babies that are genetically identical to a parent — is unsafe and morally repugnant. I agree with the vast majority of Americans and virtually all responsible scientists that it should be banned.

Therapeutic cloning, or somatic cell nuclear transfer technology (SCNT), as scientists call it) is fundamentally different. SCNT involves removing the nucleus of an egg cell, replacing it with the material from the nucleus of a skin, heart, nerve or any other non-germ cell, then stimulating this cell to begin dividing. It is important to remember that this tiny batch of cells — smaller than the period at the end of this sentence — never leaves the lab, nor is it transplanted into a womb. No sperm is used. Instead, researchers store the unfertilized egg cells in a lab, where they are used to produce stem cells.

Leading medical researchers say these cells may be able to treat or even cure several debilitating diseases. They also say the clear differences between reproductive and therapeutic cloning would make it easy to devise a ban that prevents the former while allowing the latter.

Therapeutic cloning could produce patient-specific embryonic stem cells that could be used to cure certain conditions without being rejected by the patient's immune system. It might also provide scientists with cells or tissues carrying certain diseases, which researchers could analyze for insights into what causes certain diseases and why they develop in certain ways. This type of cloning could also bring new hope to people suffering from cancer, diabetes, Alzheimer's, spinal cord injury and many other now-incurable conditions.

This is why pro-life Republican Sen. Orrin Hatch, former Presidents Jimmy Carter and Gerald Ford and Nancy Reagan support therapeutic cloning. Two years ago, 40 U.S. Nobel laureates, including pioneers in research on cancer and other life-threatening diseases, released a joint statement strongly supporting therapeutic cloning. They warned that legislation then before Congress to ban this vital research, "would have a chilling effect on all scientific research in the United States."

Those words are even more true today.

Continued from p. 892

Lawmakers, too, are hounding Bush to expand the policy. And the pressure is coming not just from Democrats, but conservative, right-to-life Republicans as well. Earlier this year, 206 House members and 58 senators signed letters calling on Bush to expand federal funding for embryonic stem-cell research. Three-dozen Republicans signed the House letter, and 14 Republicans signed the Senate letter.

Bush is even getting heat from Mrs. Reagan, a GOP luminary. Reagan died this summer after a long struggle with Alzheimer's disease, a condition that some scientists say could be addressed with embryonic stem cell and therapeutic cloning therapies.

In May, a month before her husband died, Mrs. Reagan described how the devastating brain-wasting disease had "taken him to a distant place where I can no longer reach him." She expressed hope that stem-cell research and therapeutic cloning might provide new treatments for many diseases.

"I just don't see how we can turn our backs on this," she said at a fund-raiser for the Juvenile Diabetes Research Foundation. "We have lost so much time already, and I just really can't bear to lose any more."

Sen. John Kerry of Massachusetts, the Democratic Party's presidential candidate, says he'd quadruple federal funding for embryonic stem-cell research to at least $100 million annually if elected in November. Kerry says Bush's position on the issue amounts to "sacrificing science for ideology."

"We're going to listen to our scientists and stand up for science," Kerry said at a campaign event this summer. "We're going to say 'yes' to knowledge, 'yes' to discovery and 'yes' to a new era of hope for all Americans."

A solid majority of Americans support embryonic stem-cell research. [36]

Action in the States

Nine states ban reproductive cloning: Arkansas, California, Iowa, Michigan, New Jersey, North Dakota, Rhode Island, South Dakota and Virginia. Five of these — Arkansas, Iowa, Michigan and the Dakotas — criminalize therapeutic cloning as well.

State laws on embryonic stem-cell research vary widely. A few states — Louisiana, Illinois, Michigan, Arkansas, Iowa and the Dakotas — specifically prohibit research on embryos created in certain ways, such as therapeutic cloning. Louisiana is the only state that specifically prohibits the research on the largest source of embryos — those discarded by clients of *in vitro* fertilization clinics.

The majority of the states place no restrictions on embryonic stem-cell research. But some states are going much further, in a clear rebuke of the restrictions imposed by the Bush White House, by committing public monies for the research.

In May, Gov. James E. McGreevey, D-N.J., signed legislation establishing the nation's first state-funded stem-cell research institute, which is to be built in downtown New Brunswick and run jointly by Rutgers University and the University of Medicine and Dentistry of New Jersey. The bill allocates $6.5 million in state funds for equipment and to help recruit top researchers to the facility. McGreevey expects that the seed money will attract more than $20 million in public and private investments in the first five years. He says the facility could find cures for people suffering from conditions such as heart disease, Alzheimer's disease, diabetes, cancer and spinal cord injuries.

"People are suffering today, and what we offer them is hope," McGreevey said in dedicating the facility last spring. "We have the opportunity to change lives throughout the world. We have no higher calling."

But no state is doing more to promote stem-cell research — and therapeutic cloning — than California. In November, Californians will vote on a ballot proposal that would authorize the state to spend $3 billion on the two research areas over the next decade. That averages out to $300 million per year — 12 times what the federal government spent on embryonic stem-cell research in 2003. The funds would be spent for research conducted at the state's medical schools and other nonprofit scientific institutions.

"We have more than 50 percent of the biotech capacity in the United States and more than most other countries," said Robert Klein, a real estate developer in Palo Alto, Calif., who is a leading backer of the proposal. "We can run a substitute national program." [37]

Joseph Lacob, an investment banker in Menlo Park, Calif., who voted for Bush in 2000, agrees. Lacob says he's angry with Bush for limiting federal funding on the research, which he considers to be medically promising.

"This country is falling behind because of an administration directive that I think is totally in error," Lacob said. "I felt something had to be done to send a message to the Bush administration and the world that the United States and particularly California is going to take a leadership role." [38] ■

OUTLOOK

Human Cloning?

The future of U.S. cloning and embryonic stem-cell research hinges in part on who wins the presidential election in November. Bush, despite the criticism he's receiving over embryonic stem-cell research, has not indicated he would change positions on the issue if he wins; Kerry has promised to quadruple federal funding for the research if elected. Bush supporters say Kerry's policy would cause untold numbers of nascent human beings to be slaughtered; Kerry supporters say Bush is letting his personal religious beliefs block research that could help millions of those already living.

Bush and Kerry also differ on cloning policy. Bush wants to criminalize all forms of cloning. Kerry wants to ban only reproductive cloning. But, realistically, neither is likely to prevail unless there's a major reshuffling of Congress. Thus, Washington's cloning stalemate will undoubtedly continue for the foreseeable future — leaving both types of cloning legal except where prohibited by state law.

Meanwhile, will human cloning become a verifiable reality? Opinions vary.

"Never," says the University of Pennsylvania's Caplan. "If you look at the animal data, the outcomes are so poor that I'm suspicious that cloning may not work in people."

Kilner, of the Center for Bioethics and Human Dignity, isn't so sure. "I wouldn't be surprised if it were announced tomorrow that a clone had been born," he says. "It's conceivable to me that whatever obstacles there are can be bypassed or overcome."

Some experts — even those opposed to reproductive cloning — say the therapeutic-cloning experiment carried out by South Korean researchers earlier this year went a long way in overcoming those obstacles.

"It would be naive to say we aren't a step closer to irresponsible people attempting reproductive cloning," says Schatten, of the University of Pittsburgh School of Medicine.

Only a "worldwide, enforceable ban" on any attempts at human reproductive cloning will prevent someone from cloning humans, he says.

Zavos, the controversial fertility specialist, says it's too late for that. He vows to push ahead with his effort to clone a human being. "Ban it?" he asks wryly, "That time has passed a long time ago. The genie is out of the bottle." [39] ■

Notes

[1] Quoted in Joanne Laucius, "'It Happened,' Doctor Says of Three Cloned Babies," *The Ottawa Citizen* [Canada], May 6, 2004, p. A9.

[2] Quoted in John von Radowitz, "Cloned Embryo Pioneers Say Duplicating of Humans Must be Outlawed," The Press Association Limited, Feb. 12, 2004.

[3] Quoted in Steve Mitchell, "Human Embryonic Stem Cells Cloned," United Press International, Feb. 12, 2004.

[4] Reeve testified before the Senate Health, Education, Labor and Pensions Committee on March 5, 2002.

[5] For more information on Landrieu's positions on stem cell and embryo research, see Bruce Alpert, "Senators Urge More Stem Cell Research," *The Times-Picayune* (New Orleans), June 9, 2004, p. A6.

[6] A transcript of Bush's remarks is available on the White House Web site at www.whitehouse.gov/news/releases/2001/08/20010809-2.html.

[7] Quoted in Michael D. Lemonick, "Cloning Gets Closer," *Time*, Feb. 23, 2004, p. 48.

[8] Laurie Goodstein and Denise Grady, "Split on Clones of Embryos: Research vs. Reproduction," *The New York Times*, Feb. 13, 2004, p. A1.

[9] See J. R. Hill, *et al.*, "Clinical and Pathologic Features of Cloned Transgenic Calves and Fetuses," *Theriogenology*, Vol. 8, pp. 1451-1465, 1999.

[10] See, for example, CNN/*USA Today*/Gallup Poll, Jan. 3-5, 2003, of 1,000 adults nationwide.

[11] For background, see David Masci, "Designer Humans," *The CQ Researcher*, May 18, 2001, pp. 425-448.

[12] www.usccb.org/comm/archives/2004/04-025.htm.

[13] Kass testified before the Senate Judiciary Committee on March 19, 2003.

[14] Quoted in Panos Zavos, "Should Human Beings be Cloned?" *The New York Times Upfront*, April 30, 2001, p. 26.

[15] Zavos testified before the House Government Reform Subcommittee on Criminal Justice, Drug Policy and Human Resources on May 15, 2002.

[16] Quoted in Michele Grygotis, "New Studies Bolster Promise of Both Adult and Embryonic Stem Cells," *Transplant News*, June 30, 2002.

[17] Quoted in Jonathan Bor, "Stem cells: A Long Road Ahead," *The Baltimore Sun*, March 8, 2004, p. A12.

[18] The letter was sent to every member of the House and Senate on July 30, 2004.

[19] See "Fact Sheet: Juvenile Diabetes Patients Need Real Hope, Not Hype, Embryonic Stem Cells, Cloning, Are Not Path To Cures," March 2, 2004, www.stemcellresearch.org/facts/fact-sheet-04-03-02.htm#_ftn2.

[20] Quoted in Rick Weiss, "Stem Cells An Unlikely Therapy for Alzheimer's," *The Washington Post*, June 10, 2004, p. A3.

[21] William M. Rideout III and Rudolf Jaenisch, *et al.*, "Correction of a Genetic Defect by Nuclear Transplantation and Combined Cell and Gene Therapy," *Cell*, Vol. 109, No. 1, p. 17.

[22] For more information on adult stem cells, see the National Institutes of Health, online at http://stemcells.nih.gov/info/basics/basics4.asp. See also "Do No Harm," The Coalition of Americans for Research Ethics, online at www.stemcellresearch.org. (The coalition is an advocacy group that opposes embryo research for ethical reasons.)

[23] Testimony before the U.S. Senate Subcommittee on Science, Technology and Space, Jan. 29, 2003.

About the Author

Brian Hansen, a freelance writer in Boulder, Colo., specializes in educational and environmental issues. He previously was a staff writer for *The CQ Researcher* and a reporter for the *Colorado Daily* in Boulder and Environment News Service in Washington. His awards include the Scripps Howard Foundation award for public service reporting and the Education Writers Association award for investigative reporting. He holds a B.A. in political science and an M.A. in education from the University of Colorado.

[24] Quoted in Steve Connor, "Cloners Hatch Headless Embryos of Mice — and Men?" *The Australian*, Dec. 22, 1997, p. 7.

[25] Charles Krauthammer, "Of Headless Mice . . . And Men; The Ultimate Cloning Horror: Human Organ Farms," *Time*, Feb. 19, 1998, p. 76.

[26] Quoted in Gina Kolata, "Cloning Creates Human Embryos," *The New York Times*, Feb. 12, 2004, p. A1.

[27] See Hans Spemann, *Embryonic Development and Induction* (1938). As quoted in G. Kolata, *Clone: The Road to Dolly and the Path Ahead* (1998), p. 61.

[28] Unless otherwise noted, this material comes from Masci, *op. cit.*

[29] Quoted in Joshua Lederberg, "Experimental Genetics and Human Evolution," *The American Naturalist*, September-October 1966, p. 527.

[30] See Michael Specter and Gina Kolata, "A New Creation: The Path to Cloning — A Special Report.; After Decades of Missteps, How Cloning Succeeded," *The New York Times*, March 3, 1997, p. A1.

[31] *Congressional Record*, Feb. 9, 1998, pp. S513-514.

[32] Brownback originally made this comment on Jan. 29, 2003, during a Senate subcommittee hearing. He has subsequently repeated it in a number of different venues.

[33] Quoted in Asif Ismail, "Dim Chance for Global Cloning Ban," The Center for Public Integrity, June 4, 2004. Online at www.publicintegrity.org/genetics/report.aspx?aid=276&sid=200.

[34] Remarks before the U.N. General Assembly, Dec. 9, 2003.

[35] The letter is available on the Coalition for the Advancement of Medical Research's Web site at www.camradvocacy.org/fastaction/Change6-17-20042.pdf.

[36] Quoted in "Scientists, Patients Fight U.N. Stem-Cell Study Ban," CNN.com, Oct. 14, 2004.

[37] Quoted in John M. Broder and Andrew Pollack, "Californians to Vote on Spending $3 Billion on Stem Cell Research," *The New York Times*, Sept. 20, 2004, p. A1.

[38] *Ibid.*

[39] Quoted in Nell Boyce, "The Clone is Out of the Bottle," *U.S. News & World Report*, Feb. 23, 2004, p. 40.

FOR MORE INFORMATION

Center for Bioethics and Human Dignity, 2065 Half Day Road, Bannockburn, IL 60015; (847) 317-8180; www.cbhd.org. Christian-oriented think tank that approaches cloning, embryonic stem-cell research and other bioethics issues from the perspective of "biblical values."

The Reprogen Organization, 17 Gr. Xenopoulou St., Suite 2A, P.O. Box 53117, 3300 Limassol, Cyprus; 357-5-866300; www.reprogen.org. Company run by American embryologist Panayiotis Zavos that calls itself the "international center for the study of reproductive DNA cloning technology."

Christian Medical and Dental Association, P.O. Box 7500, Bristol, TN 37621; (423) 844-1000; www.cmdahome.org. Membership organization representing more than 17,000 Christian medical professionals that opposes all forms of cloning and embryonic stem-cell research.

Clonaid, www.clonaid.com. Company affiliated with the Raelian religious sect that calls itself the "world's first human cloning company."

Coalition for the Advancement of Medical Research, 2021 K St., N.W., Suite 305, Washington, DC 20006; (202) 833-0355; www.camradvocacy.org. An association of scientific societies, patient organizations and other institutions that works to promote therapeutic cloning and embryonic stem-cell research.

Do No Harm, The Coalition of Americans for Research Ethics, 1101 Pennsylvania Ave., N.W., Suite 600, Washington, DC 20004; (202) 756-4947; www.stemcellresearch.org. An association of doctors, ethicists and theologians opposed to cloning and embryonic stem-cell research.

Family Research Council, 801 G Street, N.W., Washington, DC 20001; (202) 393-2100; www.frc.org. Think tank that "promotes the Judeo-Christian worldview as the basis for a just, free and stable society." Maintains that the "right to life is the most fundamental of political rights." Opposes all forms of cloning and embryonic stem-cell research.

Genetics Policy Institute, 4000 Ponce De Leon Blvd., Coral Gables, FL 33146; (305) 777-0268; www.genpol.org. International nonprofit organization dedicated to establishing a legal framework to advance therapeutic cloning and embryonic stem-cell research.

The Hastings Center, 21 Malcolm Gordon Rd., Garrison NY 10524; (845) 424-4040; www.thehastingscenter.org. Nonpartisan research institute devoted to ethical issues in health and medicine, the life sciences and the environment. Its president supports therapeutic cloning and embryonic stem-cell research.

National Institutes of Health, 1 Center Dr., Building 1, Suite 126, Bethesda, MD 20892; (301) 496-2433; www.nih.gov. The federal government's leading biomedical research organization; funds research on human embryonic stem cells in keeping with the restrictions imposed by President Bush in August 2001.

President's Council on Bioethics, 1801 Pennsylvania Ave., N.W., Suite 700, Washington, DC 20006; (202) 296-4669; www.bioethics.gov. Advises the president on cloning, embryonic stem-cell research and other bioethics issues; most members oppose both reproductive and therapeutic cloning.

Bibliography

Selected Sources

Books

Bonnicksen, Andrea L., *Crafting a Cloning Policy: From Dolly to Stem Cells*, Georgetown University Press, 2002.
A Northern Illinois University political science professor examines the political responses to advances in cloning and embryonic stem-cell research as well as proposed federal and state laws, research funding and other countries' cloning policies.

Kolata, Gina, *Clone: The Road to Dolly and the Path Ahead*, Morrow and Company, 1998.
An acclaimed science journalist documents the story behind Dolly, the first mammal to be cloned from an adult cell; she chronicles the history of cloning and how the Dolly breakthrough could relate to the cloning of humans.

Kunich, John Charles, *The Naked Clone: How Cloning Bans Threaten Our Personal Rights*, Praeger Publishers, 2003.
A law professor at Roger Williams University in Bristol, R.I., argues that banning therapeutic and reproductive cloning would violate Americans' rights to personal autonomy, privacy, reproduction and freedom of expression.

Maienschein, Jane, *Whose View of Life? Embryos, Cloning, and Stem Cells*, Harvard University Press, 2003.
The director of the Center for Biology and Society at Arizona State University examines developments in stem-cell research, cloning and embryology from both scientific and philosophical viewpoints.

Silver, Lee, *Remaking Eden: How Genetic Engineering and Cloning Will Transform the American Family*, Avon, 1998.
A biology professor at Princeton University looks at how cloning and other forms of genetic engineering could be used to reshape the human race.

Articles

Broder, John M., and Andrew Pollack, "Californians to Vote on Spending $3 Billion on Stem Cell Research," *The New York Times*, Sept. 20, 2004, p. A1.
Some Californians, frustrated by President Bush's policy on embryonic stem-cell research, are backing a ballot initiative that would pump billions of dollars of state funds into the research.

Goodstein, Laurie, and Denise Grady, "Split on Clones of Embryos: Research vs. Reproduction," *The New York Times*, Feb. 13, 2004, p. 22.
This overview chronicles recent scientific developments in cloning and stem-cell research and outlines the main arguments for and against the technologies.

Ismail, Asif M., "Dim Chance for Global Cloning Ban," The Center for Public Integrity, June 4, 2004 (online at www.publicintegrity.org/genetics).
A journalist describes why there is only a slim chance the international community will ban all forms of cloning.

Kolata, Gina, "Cloning Creates Human Embryos," *The New York Times*, Feb. 12, 2004, p. A1.
A science writer describes how a team of researchers from South Korea created human embryos by cloning and harvested embryonic stem cells from them.

Lemonick, Michael D., "Cloning Gets Closer," *Time*, Feb. 23, 2004, p. 48.
This easy-to-read feature story explores how the South Korean therapeutic cloning achievement could revolutionize medical science and/or lead to the cloning of human beings.

Weiss, Rick, "Stem Cells An Unlikely Therapy for Alzheimer's," *The Washington Post*, June 10, 2004, p. A3.
A veteran journalist, citing some of the top Alzheimer's researchers in the nation, casts doubt on the claim that embryonic stem-cell research could lead to a cure for the devastating condition.

Reports

"Human Cloning and Human Dignity: An Ethical Inquiry," The President's Council on Bioethics, July 2002.
This comprehensive report on both reproductive and therapeutic cloning concludes that reproductive cloning should be banned outright, and calls for a four-year moratorium on therapeutic cloning.

"Scientific and Medical Aspects of Human Reproductive Cloning," National Academy of Sciences, Committee on Science, Engineering and Public Policy, National Academies Press, 2002.
Human reproductive cloning should "not now" be practiced because "it is dangerous and likely to fail," but the scientific and medical aspects should be reviewed again in five years, the national science panel recommends.

"Stem Cells and the Future of Regenerative Medicine," National Academy of Sciences, Committee on the Biological and Biomedical Applications of Stem Cell Research, National Academies Press, 2002.
A federal scientific advisory panel describes the promise of embryonic and adult stem-cell research, as well as the barriers to accomplishing it.

The Next Step:

Additional Articles from Current Periodicals

Animal Cloning

Monaghan, Peter, "Meet Idaho Gem and His Siblings, Triplet Stars of Science," ***The Chronicle of Higher Education*****, Aug. 6, 2004, p. 32.**
Students at the University of Idaho and Utah State University have become experts in the science of cloning, working with three identical, cloned horses — the first of their kind.

Pollack, Andrew, "F.D.A. Finds Cloned Animals Safe for Food," ***The New York Times*****, Oct. 31, 2003, p. A20.**
According to the Food and Drug Administration, milk and meat from cloned animals are safe to consume, a finding that could eventually clear the way for such products to reach supermarkets and for cloning to be used to breed livestock.

Said, Carolyn, "$10 Million Bengal Kittens Pave Way for Pet Cloning," ***The San Francisco Chronicle*****, Aug. 6, 2004, p. A1.**
A Sausalito, Calif., firm that wants to clone pets says it has created two cloned cats and is now ready to start filling customers' orders.

Politics and Science

Cohen, Eric, "The Party of Cloning: The Democrats Embrace the Gospel of Stem Cells," ***The Weekly Standard*****, Aug. 30, 2004.**
Democrats are poised to cross an ethical and political boundary — federal funding for the creation, study and destruction of cloned human embryos.

Cohen, Eric, "Sen. Kerry's Stem-Cell Fairy Tales," ***Los Angeles Times*****, Aug. 22, 2004, p. M3.**
Democrats make the powerful, but false claims that Bush has banned stem-cell research and that cures for everything from AIDS to Alzheimer's are just around the corner.

Graham, Judith, "Key Issue: Stem Cell Research," ***Chicago Tribune*****, July 27, 2004, p. C16.**
Stem-cell research is a major issue in the November 2004 presidential race between George W. Bush and Sen. John Kerry, even causing some voters to change parties.

Lawrence, Jill, "Kerry's Scientific Approach," ***USA Today*****, Oct. 5, 2004, p. 20A.**
Science is a hot issue in the presidential election, with Sen. John Kerry arguing that President Bush favors special interests over science and made the wrong choices on stem-cell research.

Niedowski, Erika, and David Kohn, "Stem Cell Dispute Pulls Science Into Political Arena," ***The Baltimore Sun*****, Aug. 15, 2004, p. 1A.**
Scientists say President Bush's stem-cell research policy has hindered their work, and Sen. John Kerry says he will lift the restrictions if he wins in November.

Semple, Kirk, "U.N. to Consider Whether to Ban Some, or All, Forms of Cloning of Human Embryos," ***The New York Times*****, Nov. 3, 2003, p. A1.**
The United Nations will consider two competing resolutions that propose bans on human cloning and seek to establish international legal boundaries in the field of life sciences.

President's Council on Bioethics

Blackburn, Elizabeth, "A 'Full Range' of Bioethical Views Just Got Narrower," ***The Washington Post*****, March 7, 2004, p. B2.**
An ex-member of the bioethics council explains how her removal from the council represents a narrowing of views on the embryonic stem-cell research debate.

Brainard, Jeffrey, "A New Kind of Bioethics," ***The Chronicle of Higher Education*****, May 21, 2004, p. 22.**
Some academics say the bioethics council is driven by conservative ideology, rushing to alarmist conclusions and ignoring relevant topics like access to medical care.

Hall, Stephen, "U.S. Panel About to Weigh In On Rules for Assisted Fertility," ***The New York Times*****, March 30, 2004, p. F1.**
The Council on Bioethics plans to release a report that recommends regulations that affect the research and practice of *in vitro* fertilization and embryo research.

Lamb, Gregory, "In Cloning Debate, a Compromise," ***The Christian Science Monitor*****, April 8, 2004, p. 14.**
The council offered liberals and conservatives a way out in their debate over human cloning by recommending a ban on reproductive cloning but not cloning research.

Rothstein, Edward, "The Meaning of 'Human' In Embryonic Research," ***The New York Times*****, March 13, 2004, p. B9.**
An unusual 628-page publication of the bioethics council tries to address "the human and moral significance of developments in biomedical and behavioral science and technology."

Stem-Cell Research

"Baby Steps," ***The Economist*****, Jan. 3, 2004.**
Researchers at the U.S. biotechnology firm Advanced Cell Technology reportedly have created human embryos healthy enough to make it through at least the earliest stages of development.

Hall, Stephen, "Specter of Cloning May Prove A Mirage," ***The New York Times*****, Feb. 17, 2004, p. F1.**
The future of human therapeutic cloning — the laws governing it, the knowledge gained from it and the ethical costs of doing it — may hinge on the biological and moral subtleties of a tiny dot of tissue.

Kolata, Gina, "Stem Cell Science Gets Limelight; Now It Needs a Cure," *The New York Times*, Aug. 24, 2004, p. F1.
The challenge for scientists studying stem cells in the midst of a fierce political debate, many say, is to be realistic about how hard it is to develop treatments.

Munro, Neil, and Mark Kukis, "A Brave New World?" *The National Journal*, May 22, 2004.
Critics argue that while they share the goal of developing new therapies, bioengineering will change and fragment people's understanding of nature and humanity.

Pollack, Andrew, "Cloning and Stem Cells: The Research," *The New York Times*, Feb. 13, 2004, p. A22.
In cloning human embryos and extracting stem cells, scientists have taken a big step, but significant scientific and ethical barriers still lie between this feat and actual therapy.

South Korean Breakthrough

Faiola, Anthony, "Dr. Clone: Creating Life or Trying to Save It?" *The Washington Post*, Feb. 29, 2004, p. A1.
Woo Suk Hwang, leader of a South Korean team of scientists who created the world's first cloned human embryos, views cloning as essential for the chronically ill.

Kolata, Gina, "Cloning Creates Human Embryos," *The New York Times*, Feb. 12, 2004, p. A1.
South Korean scientists report they have created human embryos through cloning embryonic stem cells, reigniting the debate over the ethics of human cloning.

Lee, B. J., "Cloning College," *Newsweek*, March 1, 2004, p. 48.
While well-endowed labs in the United States, Britain and France are constrained by a political backlash against cloning research, South Korea has quietly filled the void.

Lemonick, Michael, "Cloning Gets Closer," *Time*, Feb. 23, 2004.
Two South Korean scientists announced they created more than 200 embryos by cloning human cells in an effort to fight disease with the slow-moving technology.

State Cloning Laws

Broder, John, and Andrew Pollack, "Californians to Vote on Spending $3 Billion on Stem Cell Research," *The New York Times*, Sept. 20, 2004, p. A1.
Proposition 71, an initiative on the Nov. 2 ballot, would authorize the state to issue $3 billion in bonds to pay for a range of stem-cell research now severely limited by the Bush administration's policy.

Davidson, Keay, "Stem Cell Initiative Leads by Small Margin," *The San Francisco Chronicle*, Aug. 15, 2004, p. B1.
A close race in the campaign to pass a California initiative for stem-cell research appears to have become a microcosm of the equally polarized presidential race.

Roosevelt, Margot, "Stem-Cell Rebels," *Time*, May 17, 2004, p. 49.
Given the nature of the stem-cell debate, the Bush administration is unlikely to make any moves before the election, but several states are filling the vacuum.

Smith, Wesley, "California's Other Senator; Jon Corzine Wants to Help California Lure Biotech Cloning Companies Away from New Jersey," *The Daily Standard*, Aug. 26, 2004.
Jon Corzine, a senator from New Jersey, donated $100,000 to help pass Proposition 71, which would force Californians to borrow billions for embryonic stem-cell research.

Vregano, Dan, "States Dive into Stem Cell Debates," *USA Today*, April 21, 2004, p. 1D.
An annual Senate debate has hit the road, moving to 33 state legislatures considering 100 bills that alternately condemn, condone or fund embryonic stem-cell research.

CITING *THE CQ RESEARCHER*

Sample formats for citing these reports in a bibliography include the ones listed below. Preferred styles and formats vary, so please check with your instructor or professor.

MLA STYLE

Jost, Kenneth. "Rethinking the Death Penalty." The CQ Researcher 16 Nov. 2001: 945-68.

APA STYLE

Jost, K. (2001, November 16). Rethinking the death penalty. *The CQ Researcher, 11*, 945-968.

CHICAGO STYLE

Jost, Kenneth. "Rethinking the Death Penalty." *CQ Researcher*, November 16, 2001, 945-968.

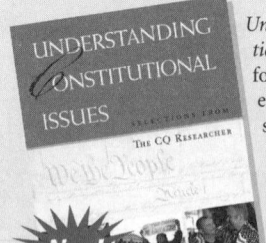

CQ Researcher

Published by CQ Press, a division of Congressional Quarterly Inc.

thecqresearcher.com

Voting Rights

Will the votes of all Americans be counted on Nov. 2?

As the heated presidential campaign enters its final days, unprecedented concern surrounds the fairness of the voting process. Indeed, four years after a vote-counting scandal in Florida had to be resolved by the U.S. Supreme Court — and four decades after passage of the landmark Voting Rights Act — civil-rights advocates say the votes of many Americans are still at risk. Republicans charge that Democrats are padding registration lists; Democrats say Republicans are trying to intimidate African-Americans and suppress the votes of Hispanics, former felons and other likely Democratic voters to keep them away from the polls. Voting experts worry that new electronic voting machines purchased by funds from the 2002 Help America Vote Act are susceptible to tampering and do not allow for an accurate recount if the election — once again — is contested. Meanwhile, both parties are dispatching thousands of poll watchers and lawyers to pounce on any voting irregularities, especially in the too-close-to-call "battleground" states.

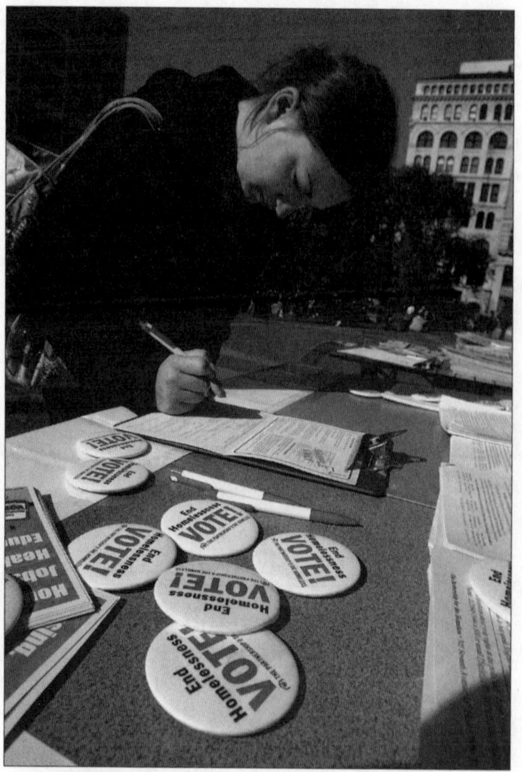

A young New Yorker registers to vote, joining thousands of others who responded to an aggressive registration campaign by voting advocates.

The CQ Researcher • Oct. 29, 2004 • www.thecqresearcher.com
Volume 14, Number 38 • Pages 901-924

RECIPIENT OF SOCIETY OF PROFESSIONAL JOURNALISTS AWARD FOR EXCELLENCE ◆ AMERICAN BAR ASSOCIATION SILVER GAVEL AWARD

INSIDE THIS REPORT

THE ISSUES

BACKGROUND

CURRENT SITUATION

OUTLOOK

SIDEBARS AND GRAPHICS

FOR FURTHER RESEARCH

Cover: One day before the Oct. 8 deadline, a young New Yorker registers to vote, joining thousands of others who responded to an aggressive registration campaign by voting advocates. (Getty Images/Spencer Platt)

THE CQ Researcher

Oct. 29, 2004
Volume 14, Number 38

CQ PRESS

A Division of Congressional Quarterly Inc.

The CQ Researcher (ISSN 1056-2036) is printed on acid-free paper. Published weekly, except Jan. 2, April 9, July 2, July 9, Aug. 6, Aug. 13, Nov. 26 and Dec. 31, by CQ Press, a division of Congressional Quarterly Inc. Annual subscription rates for institutions start at $625. For pricing, call 1-800-834-9020, ext. 1906. To purchase a *CQ Researcher* report in print or electronic format (PDF), visit www.cqpress.com or call 866-427-7737. A single report is $10. Bulk purchase discounts and electronic-rights licensing are also available. Periodicals postage paid at Washington, D.C., and additional mailing offices. POSTMASTER: Send address changes to *The CQ Researcher*, 1255 22nd St., N.W., Suite 400, Washington, D.C. 20037.

Voting Rights

BY MARY H. COOPER

THE ISSUES

As the heated election between President Bush and Sen. John Kerry approaches, unprecedented concern surrounds the fairness of the voting process.

Republicans charge that Democrats are padding registration lists; Democrats say Republicans are trying to disenfranchise African-Americans, Hispanics, former felons and others thought likely to vote Democratic. Voting experts worry that new electronic voting machines are susceptible to tampering and do not allow for an accurate recount if the election is contested.

Indeed, four years after a vote-counting scandal in Florida had to be resolved by the U.S. Supreme Court — and four decades after passage of the landmark Voting Rights Act — civil rights advocates say the voting rights of many Americans are still at risk.

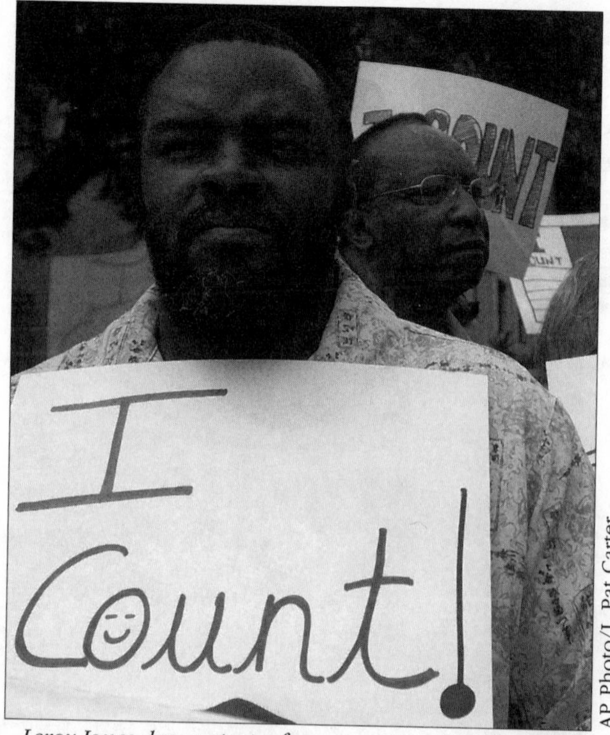

AP Photo/J. Pat Carter

Leroy Jones demonstrates for restoration of voting rights for himself and his fellow ex-felons outside a federal court in Miami in April 2003. In 2000, Florida purged thousands of names from voter registration rolls, erroneously identifying them as felons. This year, Democrats have accused Republicans of intimidating minority voters, and Republicans have charged Democrats with padding the lists of newly registered voters.

Public confidence also has been undermined by persistent allegations of voter suppression, including attempts to intimidate minority voters to keep them from going to the nation's 193,000 polling places.

In the run-up to the election, both parties are dispatching thousands of poll watchers and lawyers to pounce on any possible voting irregularities, especially in the too-close-to-call "battleground" states. Meanwhile, the charges and countercharges are coming non-stop:

- In Colorado, the Republican secretary of state accused the Democratic attorney general of failing to investigate charges that his party is fraudulently registering ineligible voters. [1]
- In Pennsylvania, Republicans are suspicious of the Democratic governor's plan to dispatch government workers to monitor the polls. [2]
- In Michigan, a GOP state legislator, John Pappageorge, was quoted in July as saying, "If we do not suppress the Detroit vote, we're going to have a tough time in this election." More that 80 percent of Detroit's electorate are African-Americans. [3]
- In Nevada and Oregon, GOP-sponsored groups registering voters were alleged to have systematically destroyed hundreds of registration forms filled out by Democrats. [4]
- Republicans claimed on Oct. 25 that Democratic partisans have engaged in more than 40 instances of protests, violence, vandalism and burglaries at Bush headquarters across the country since July, all aimed at intimidating GOP voters. [5]
- And Florida's Republican secretary of state was forced to withdraw a "purge list" of convicted felons, ineligible to vote under state law, after it was discovered that the list contained the names of many eligible — and likely Democratic — voters. [6]

These and similar reports have been appearing almost daily in the final weeks of Campaign 2004. "Both parties are very assiduously courting and trying to register new voters, and all sorts of lines are being crossed," says Paul Herrnson, director of the Center for American Politics and Citizenship at the University of Maryland. "We have a polarized electorate, and the stakes are very high in this extremely competitive election, so people are resorting to things that they otherwise would not do."

Congress responded to the 2000 Florida voting debacle by enacting the Help America Vote Act (HAVA). Signed by Bush on Oct. 29, 2002, the law authorized $3.89 billion to help states update their voting equipment in an effort to avoid the problems that plagued Florida in the 2000 election. [7] Poorly punched cards used in punch-card machines produced the infamous "hanging" and "pregnant" chads that made it difficult to count thousands of paper ballots. Many states used HAVA funds to replace outdated punch-card and lever-activated voting machines. Largely as a result, almost a third of the nation's voters will cast ballots electronically this year. (*See sidebar, p. 908.*)

Many Counties Still Use Old Voting Equipment

The nation's 3,142 counties use five basic balloting methods. Almost half the counties — with more than a third of all registered voters — use optical devices that read ballots marked by the voters. Almost a third of all voters use computers that flash the ballot onscreen. The rest of the voters use old-style lever machines, punch cards or hand-counted paper ballots.

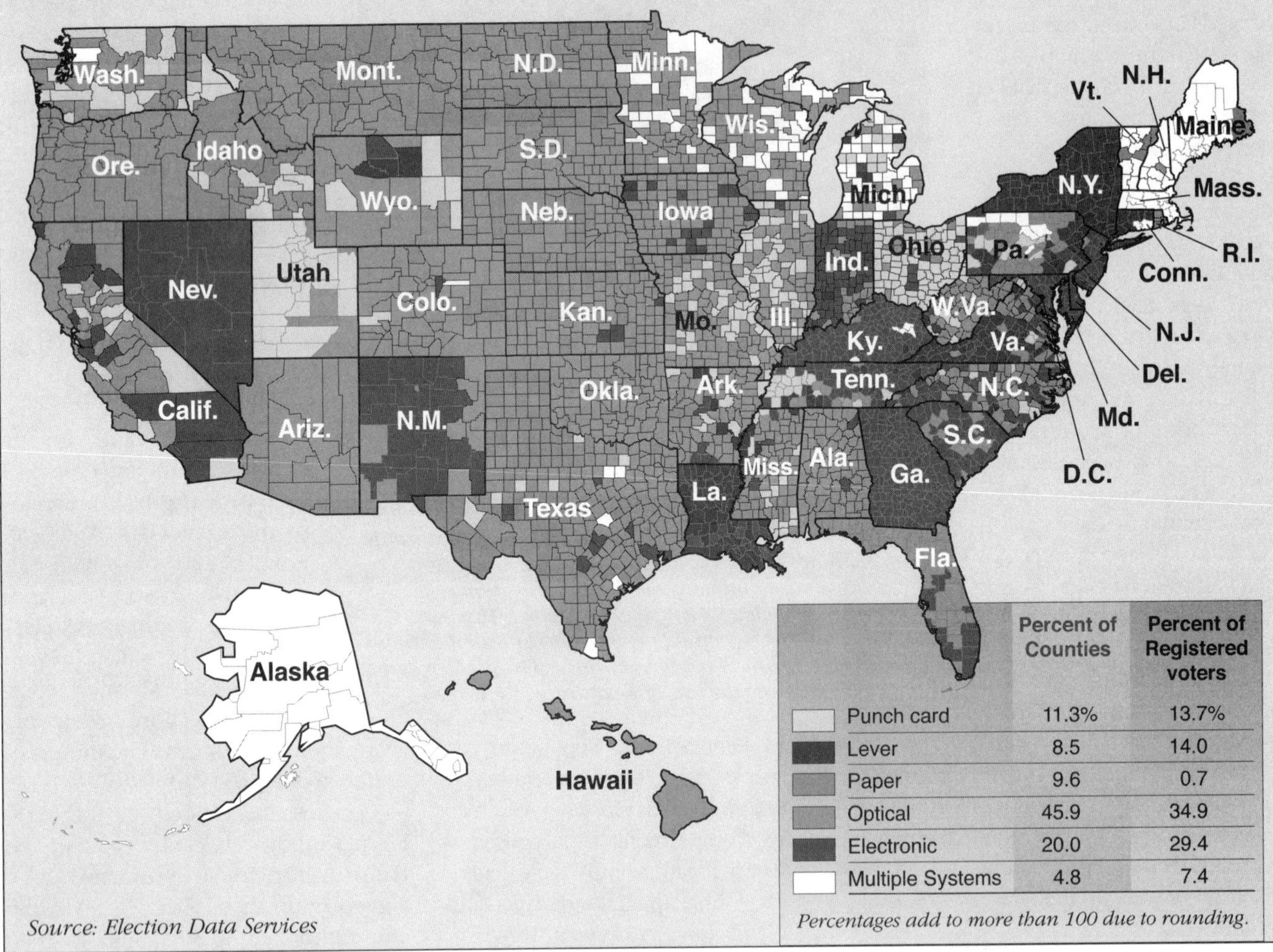

	Percent of Counties	Percent of Registered voters
Punch card	11.3%	13.7%
Lever	8.5	14.0
Paper	9.6	0.7
Optical	45.9	34.9
Electronic	20.0	29.4
Multiple Systems	4.8	7.4

Percentages add to more than 100 due to rounding.

Source: Election Data Services

But the new machines are not foolproof, and critics say their failings may become apparent on Election Day. "HAVA was overly ambitious about upgrading the voting technology," says Aviel D. Rubin, a professor of computer science at Johns Hopkins University who has studied some of the new systems and found them susceptible to technical failure and tampering. "States purchased these machines, but nobody really looked at security. Now, most people realize that they moved too quickly."

HAVA also required states to adopt procedures to ensure fair and accurate voting and set up the federal Election Assistance Commission (EAC) to help states make the improvements and establish federal standards for election-equipment accuracy.

But even HAVA's strongest supporters concede that the law's impact may be overshadowed by the cloud of uncertainty about the integrity of the election process generated by the 2000 election debacle.

"The problems of 2000 got so much publicity that any progress made since then has often not been noticed," says EAC Chairman DeForest B. Soaries Jr. And, although the law took effect two years ago, he adds, "More people know about hanging chads than know about HAVA."

As it turned out, the problems exposed in 2000 went far beyond the Sunshine State. According to "What Is, What Could Be," a post-election study by the California and Massachusetts Institutes of

Technology, up to 6 million of the 100 million Americans who went to the polls on Nov. 7, 2000, might just as well have stayed home: Their ballots were never counted. The problems ranged from inadequate registration data and faulty voting equipment to inaccurate vote counts.

"Minority voters are more sensitive to the possibility of what happened in Florida and elsewhere in 2000," says Julian Bond, chairman of the National Association for the Advancement of Colored People (NAACP). "It wasn't just Florida; it happened in many states across the country, and minority voters who were the victims are, of course, more sensitive to it."

In this year's election not only will there be thousands of new voting machines but also many thousands of new voters trying to figure out how to use them. The closeness of the race has spurred organizers from both parties to mount aggressive voter-registration drives, especially in the battleground states, where polls suggest the addition of several thousand new voters could tip the balance in either direction. According to an Associated Press analysis, Democrats have registered more new voters than Republicans in all states except Florida, where the two parties are tied for new registrations. [8] The NAACP's National Voter Fund alone says it has registered 225,000 new voters this year. [9]

Equipment Changes Since 2000

More than 30 percent of voters — 44 million Americans — used punch-card ballots in the 2000 election, including those in the disputed Florida election. On Nov. 2, 2004, fewer than half as many will get punch cards, none of them in Florida.

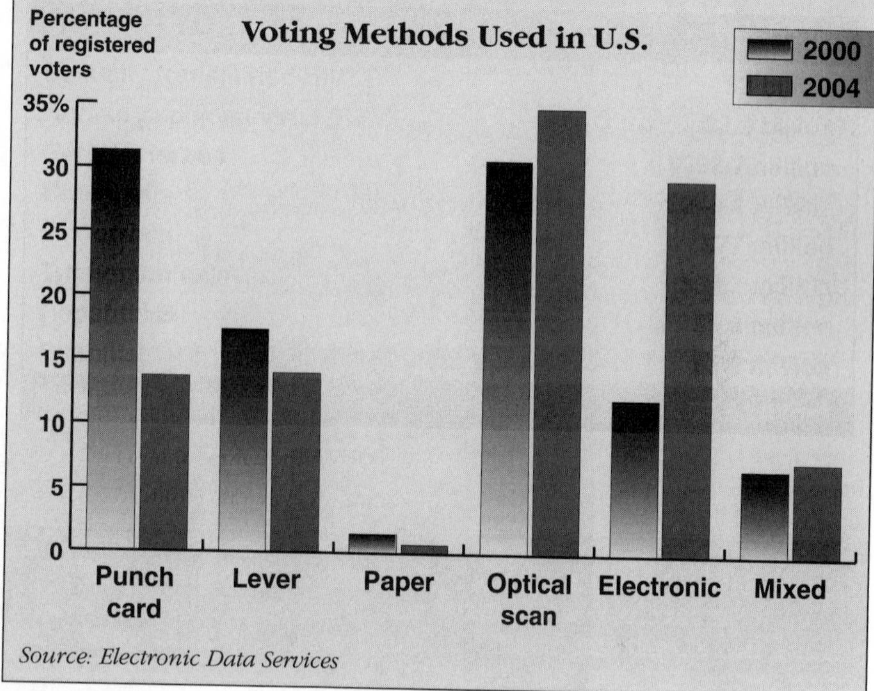

Source: Electronic Data Services

As new and long-time voters struggle to adjust to all the changes, the eyes of the world will be focused on both Florida and the nation. New grass-roots organizations, such as Election Protection — a civic group formed by the Lawyers' Committee for Civil Rights Under Law, People for the American Way Foundation and the National Coalition on Black Civic Participation — are enlisting thousands of volunteers to watch the polls and offer help to voters who encounter problems casting their votes.

Likewise, Republican groups plan to look for evidence of voter fraud. "We will have poll watchers in precincts all across the country who are trained to look out for any problems and report them immediately to the local officials," said Robert Traynham, senior adviser to the Republican National Committee. [10]

International monitors also will scrutinize the U.S. vote. The Organization for Security and Cooperation in Europe, a 55-nation security watchdog based in Vienna, Austria, plans to send 100 observers to follow the election.

If all the newly registered voters actually turn out on Nov. 2, there may be long lines at the polls, especially where voters face unfamiliar voting machines. [11] To avoid such logjams — and to ensure that there is a "paper trail" in case of recounts — the liberal, pro-Kerry group, MoveOn.org, and other voting-rights advocacy groups for weeks have been urging voters to send in absentee ballots.

As concern about the upcoming election mounts, here are some of the questions being asked by voters'-rights advocates, election officials and policymakers.

Are voting irregularities by party operatives undermining the election system?

The 1965 Voting Rights Act took action against the most egregious forms of voter intimidation and suppression, notably the poll taxes, literacy tests and other obstacles many Southern states had erected after the Civil War to keep former slaves away from the voting booth. But activists quickly found ways to circumvent the law and prevent African- and Native Americans — as well as recent immigrants and other minority groups — from voting.

Such practices are still common, and not just in the South. The People for the American Way Foundation and the NAACP recently released a compendium of alleged voter intimidation and suppression over the past decade that have occurred around the country. In California and other states with large immigrant populations, anti-immigrant activists have deployed uniformed security guards in heavily Hispanic precincts warning would-be voters that election officials "will be watching." In New York, Philadelphia and other cities, streets signs have appeared before Election Day threatening illegal voters with prosecution and deportation. Fliers encouraging citizens to come to the polls — a day or two *after* Election Day — have cropped up in minority neighborhoods. [12]

"There is some fairly specific evidence of those kinds of things happening, especially in the last couple of years," says Elliot Mincberg, legal director of People for the American Way. As recently as last year, during the Philadelphia mayoral election, he says, people dressed in official-looking uniforms and carrying clipboards asked voters for identification outside several polling stations in minority precincts. "Nine percent of African-Americans in Philadelphia's central city area reported that they had encountered somebody like that," Mincberg says. "That sort of intimidation continues to happen."

Not all efforts to prevent voters from exercising their rights are illegal. "Both federal law and most state laws bar voter suppression and intimidation," Mincberg says. "But when does something cross the line to become prohibited activity? It's certainly not illegal for people to challenge other people at the polls, but there comes a point where that goes too far. Wholesale challenges at the poll and intimidating activities, as in Philadelphia, are illegal under the federal Voting Rights Act and most states' laws."

Unlike the era before the civil rights movement, most allegations of voter intimidation today are aimed at Republicans, who stand to lose if African-Americans, Hispanics and other minority groups show up in droves on Election Day. "What used to be a Democratic practice until the late 1960s of frightening, scaring, intimidating and terrorizing minority voters has now become an exclusive Republican practice," says the NAACP's Bond, who also played a key role in the civil rights movement that led to passage of the Voting Rights Act. "There is abundant evidence to back that up."

AFP/Getty Images/Scott Gries

The Black Eyed Peas perform at a fundraiser to increase minority voter registration, at New York City's Apollo Theater in May 2004. Twenty million more Americans are expected to vote in this year's presidential election than in 2000.

Democratic supporters are not the only ones making that claim. Curtis Gans, director of the Committee for the Study of the American Electorate, a nonpartisan, nonprofit research institution that focuses on issues surrounding citizen engagement in politics, agrees. "There's plenty of historical evidence that the Republican Party has resorted to tactics that come close to intimidation," he says.

The usual victims of alleged voter suppression — blacks and Native Americans — tend to vote overwhelmingly Democratic. [13] And 64 percent of Hispanics favor Democrats — except in South Florida, where the large Cuban-American community favors Republicans — according to the Zogby International polling firm. [14]

GOP spokesmen deny that their party is involved in voter suppression and intimidation. "We certainly don't condone any alleged voter intimidation," says Traynham. "That is not something that the Republican Party wants to be associated with, and it's obviously something that we do not condone."

Indeed, Republicans charge that Democrats fraudulently register ineligible voters to boost the ranks of potential supporters of Democratic candidates. "We are concerned about our friends on the other side doing just that," Traynham says.

But Gans says the number of instances of fraudulent registration by supporters of Democratic candidates is far outweighed by reports of voter intimidation by Republicans. "Voter fraud is not non-existent," Gans says, "but it's not a huge problem."

Some political observers say voter intimidation and fraud are not sufficiently widespread to seriously undermine credibility in the country's election system. "I've heard reports from all over the country that leaflets are put in minority communities announcing that Election Day will be one or two days after it really is," says Larry J. Sabato, a politics professor and director of the Center for Politics at the University of Virginia. "Leaflets in Hispanic areas tell voters to be sure to bring their immigration papers to the polls. There's also no question that Democratic operatives visit nursing homes and find an incredible number of Democratic votes there in some places. But let's keep things in perspective. We're talking about a relatively small effort affecting a relatively tiny portion of the electorate."

But to some election officials, intimidation and fraud — however widespread they may be — damage the U.S. election system's credibility. "The negative impact of suspicion and the acrimony caused by these activities cannot be underestimated," says Election Assistance Commission Chairman Soaries. Although he served as the New Jersey secretary of state in the Republican administration of former Gov. Christine Todd Whitman, he and fellow commissioners have agreed to refrain from all political activity as long as they serve on the commission.

"The onus is on us, who are responsible for the rights of voters, to demonstrate to the American people that we assume that responsibility without regard to political or partisan interests," he says.

Should felons who have completed their sentences continue to be denied the right to vote?

Voting rights have been expanded over the years through constitutional amendments and laws, culminating in the 1965 Voting Rights Act. But the Constitution leaves the administration of elections up to the individual states, and in seven states convicted felons are still not allowed to vote — even after they have finished serving their sentences. (*See sidebar, p. 912.*)

Felon-disenfranchisement laws are relics of Jim Crow laws that emerged in the post-Civil War South. They gained legal strength from the U.S. Supreme Court in a 1974 opinion penned by Associate Justice (now Chief Justice) William H. Rehnquist in *Richardson v. Ramirez.* The court found that Section 2 of the 14th Amendment, which granted citizenship to former slaves after the Civil War, authorized states to deny voting rights to anyone convicted of a crime.

To prevent former slave states from denying these new citizens the right to vote, Section 2 stipulates that whenever a state denies voting rights to otherwise qualified inhabitants, it will lose representation in Congress in direct proportion to the number of citizens denied the right to vote — except when that right is denied because of "participation in rebellion or other crime." Rehnquist's opinion interpreted that provision as an exception to the amendment's Equal Protection Clause and determined that it allowed states to disenfranchise felons.

Today, including the seven states that bar convicted felons from voting after they have served their time, a total of 48 states restrict felons' voting rights in some way or another, such as requiring ex-felons to apply to the governor for special dispensation.

Challenged by civil rights activists, felon disenfranchisement continues to be hotly debated. The Supreme Court returned to the issue in 1985, ruling in *Hunter v. Underwood* that while states can deny felons the right to vote, they cannot do so if it can be shown that the disenfranchisement was racist in intent. Since that ruling, challenges to felon disenfranchisement laws have mounted.

"The core argument in most of these cases is that the disenfranchisement laws were both racist in intent as well as racist in practice," says Ryan S. King, research associate at the Sentencing Project, a nonprofit, criminal-justice advocacy group. Most felon disenfranchisement challenges are based on the Voting Rights Act, which bars the denial of those rights on the basis of race.

Civil rights advocates are focusing on a Washington state case pending before the 9th U.S. Circuit Court of Appeals, which ruled that the Voting Rights Act does, in fact, recognize a state law's practical impact on individuals' ability to vote. (The case was remanded to the lower court for a determination of whether the facts in the case show that felon disenfranchisement in Washington is having a discernible impact on voting rights.)

"There are still challenges out there," King says. "But the Constitution does still permit felon disenfranchisement."

Whatever the outcome of the legal challenges, state laws barring felons from voting unquestionably reduce the turnout of black and Hispanic Americans at the polls. The Sentencing Project estimates that about 5 million Americans cannot vote due to felony disenfranchisement laws, and African-Americans are disproportionately denied their voting rights under the laws. Black men, who comprise about 8 percent of the U.S. population, account for 40 percent of the prison population. [15]

Southern states have some of the most sweeping laws disenfranchising African-Americans. In Atlanta alone, the Sentencing Project reports, 14 percent of the city's black male inhabitants are unable to vote because they are in prison, on probation or on parole.

"We know that these laws . . . were imposed as Reconstruction was closing down, and that their purpose was then to limit the votes of the newly freed slaves," says Bond of the NAACP. "We also know that they've remained in place because they serve the present-day purpose of disproportionately discriminating against racial minorities."

The denial of voting rights to convicted felons does not stop at the Mason-Dixon Line, however. According to the Rhode Island Family Life Center, 20 percent of that state's African-American men and more than 10 percent of its Hispanic men cannot vote because they have been convicted of a felony. The vast majority — 86 percent — are no longer in prison. [16] In Ohio, after prisoner-rights groups sued the state, it notified 34,000 felons on parole and probation that they are, in fact, allowed to vote next month. The lawsuit had charged that the felons had been wrongly told they were ineligible to vote. Ohio law disenfranchises felons only while they are in prison. [17]

Continued on p. 909

Voting Machines Still Problematical

Thanks to funds from the 2002 Help America Vote Act (HAVA), almost a third of the nation's registered voters will find electronic equipment at their polling places on Nov. 2, up significantly from the presidential contest in 2000. But many experts say the devices are flawed.

Some 35 percent of U.S. voters will still use decades-old optical-scanning devices, the most widely used technology. After marking their choices in boxes or circles on a voting card next to the names of candidates or ballot measures, voters either place the ballot into a sealed box or feed it directly into a tabulating device, which scans the card and registers the votes.

More than a quarter of registered voters this year will use either punch-card machines or lever machines, considered the two most antiquated voting devices. In use for more than a century, lever machines accounted for more than half the nation's voting devices by the 1960s. The voter flips down a horizontal lever next to the candidate's name or issue of choice, and after the polls close a mechanical counter records the number of times each lever was depressed. Many jurisdictions — predominantly in Connecticut, Louisiana, New York and Virginia — still use them.

AFP/Getty Images/Roberto Schmidt

Touch-screen voting booths replaced punch-card machines in Florida and other states following the vote-count debacle in 2000. Some voting experts worry the machines are hard to operate, susceptible to tampering and do not allow for an accurate recount if the election is contested.

Punch-card systems, first introduced in 1964 in Georgia, require voters to use a stylus to punch holes in their ballots next to their choices. As the controversial 2000 Florida vote made clear, such systems are prone to error. After the election, poll workers spent more than a month poring over incompletely punched ballots, whose "hanging" and "pregnant" chads made it hard to interpret the results. Only 13.7 percent of voters will use punch-card machines this year, compared with 31 percent in 2000. [1]

The most recent innovation in voting technology is the direct-recording electronic (DRE) device. Like lever machines, they do not use paper ballots. Voters either touch a screen, as with a bank ATM, or use a keyboard to record their choices. The machine's software tabulates the votes. The percentage of voters using e-voting systems has grown from 12.2 percent in 2000 to almost a third this fall. [2]

"Our reliable systems accurately and securely capture each vote," claims Diebold Election Systems, which has provided more than 75,000 electronic voting stations across the country.

But the new devices are far from foolproof, critics say. The wrong ballots appeared on touch screens in some California precincts last March, for example, while machines in other precincts failed altogether. [3] In Maryland, studies have warned that Diebold's AccuVote-TS System is "at high risk of compromise" [4] and "contains considerable security risks that can cause moderate to severe disruption in an election." [5]

According to Aviel D. Rubin, a professor of computer science at Johns Hopkins University and co-author of another study of Maryland's new equipment, the AccuVote-TS also is vulnerable to vote tampering. The Diebold machines are really awful," he says. "They should not be used without a paper trail, but they will be."

Indeed, Rubin and other experts recommend that all electronic systems be able to print a paper ballot that voters could read and verify. "That way it really wouldn't matter how secure the machines are because we could go back and count the paper ballots again if we had to," Rubin says.

But some election experts have their doubts. "The paper trail is still new technology and is not supported by sufficient research," says DeForest B. Soaries Jr., chairman of the U.S. Election Assistance Commission, created by HAVA to distribute the funds to upgrade voting equipment and to help states improve the election process. "More specifically, I don't think the federal government should mandate a particular type of voting equipment on the states."

---

[1] See David Nether, "Problems Old and New Lurk in the Voting Booth," *CQ Weekly*, Oct. 9, 2004, p. 2359.

[2] *Ibid.*

[3] See Stuart Pfeifer, "State's E-Vote Trust Builds Slowly," *Los Angeles Times*, Sept. 27, 2004, p. B1.

[4] Science Applications International Corp., "Risk Assessment Report: Diebold AccuVote-TX Voting System and Processes," Sept. 2, 2003, p. v.

[5] RABA Technologies, "Trusted Agent Report: Diebold AccuVote-TS Voting System," Jan. 20, 2004, p. 3.

Continued from p. 907

Civil rights activists say felon disenfranchisement should end, as it does in Ohio, when a convicted felon has served the sentence meted out by his peers in a court of law — and that they should not have to apply for special dispensation to vote. "Rules saying felons cannot vote unless they apply for special permission are vestiges of segregation and discrimination being used to try to make it more difficult for minorities to vote," says Mincberg of the ACLU. "Someone who has been convicted of a crime and has served his time, is becoming a citizen and is paying taxes, ought to have his right to vote restored."

But supporters of felon disenfranchisement say it is a just form of punishment for serious crime. "Just because a criminal serves his time in prison — 'pays his or her debt to society' — does not mean that society has to ignore the fact that the individual has seriously breached the social contract," wrote Roger Clegg, general counsel at the conservative Center for Equal Opportunity in Sterling, Va. "People who are not willing to follow the law should not be allowed to make the law for others, which is what voting is. The right to vote can be earned back by those who committed a less serious felony — though all felonies are serious, by definition — and thereafter keep a clean record, but that determination should be made case by case." [18]

Other supporters of felon-disenfranchisement laws argue that felons do not deserve to have the same say on matters regarding law-enforcement policies as law-abiding citizens. "It is simply false to say that a felon has served his entire debt to society upon the completion of his prison sentence," said Todd F. Gaziano, director of the Center for Legal & Judicial Studies at the Heritage Foundation, a conservative think tank. "The fact that so many states have these felon-disenfranchisement laws is strong evidence that many citizens do not want their ability to influence crime-control decisions to be diluted by convicted felons on parole or otherwise." [19]

Some governors intent on gaining minority support for their parties' candidates in this fall's election are emphasizing their records in restoring voting rights to felons. Virginia Gov. Mark Warner, a Democrat, for instance, recently announced that he had restored the voting rights of 1,892 convicted felons.

But civil rights advocates are not impressed. "The governor of Virginia has just congratulated himself for allowing [1,892] felons to vote," Bond says. "But when thousands of other ex-felon Virginians are still kept from voting, his self-congratulation is just a little much."

Do electronic voting machines help Americans exercise their right to vote?

States, counties and localities decide what kind of voting machines will be used in their precincts. But after hanging chads and inscrutable "butterfly ballots" disrupted the vote count in Florida in 2000, election officials across the country have tried to modernize their voting equipment. HAVA authorized $3.89 billion in 2001 to help states improve their election systems, but so far only about $2 billion has been disbursed to the states, much of it to buy the latest in electronic voting machines. [20]

So-called direct-recording electronic (DRE) systems offer several advantages over earlier technology. With systems like those used in Florida in 2000, the voter uses a stylus to punch a hole in a card next to the chosen candidate. Most new electronic machines, on the other hand, work like a bank ATM: The voter simply touches a box on the screen next to the candidate's name. If the machine senses the touch, the vote is tabulated; if not, the voter tries again until the machine registers his choice.

Almost 30 percent of American voters will cast their votes this November on new electronic equipment, according to Election Data Services, a political consulting firm.

Electronic machines are hardly foolproof, however. Most of them produce no "paper trail" because they eliminate paper from the voting process. In January, paperless, touch-screen voting machines used in Florida's Broward County (Fort Lauderdale), failed to record 134 ballots cast in a special election where the margin of victory was just 12 votes. With no paper trail, a recount was impossible. [21] In May, a computer chip coding error caused one candidate to receive all the votes cast in a local election in Arkansas. [22]

Critics say many states moved too quickly to replace older voting devices with electronic machines. "One of the big dangers is that there will be some kind of glitch or unintentional bug in the machines, and they just won't get the right answer," says Rubin, at Johns Hopkins University, who was one of the first experts to expose the flaws in electronic voting systems. "In that case we'll have no recourse, because there won't be a paper trail or any way to audit them to determine the real results. What will we do on Nov. 3 if the results we get from a lot of precincts just don't make any sense?"

Moreover, says Mincberg, elderly or marginally literate voters may find the new technology confusing or hard to use. "The machines may be intimidating to some voters, partly because of all the concern about the machines' reliability, and partly because they are just more complex," he says.

But Soaries of the EAC contends that voters with impaired vision or arthritis in their hands might have had more trouble using the punch-card system, with its stylus and small print. "The touch-screen machine is not as challenging as some might imagine, even among the elderly," he says.

To ensure that the machines will improve voters' ability to exercise their rights, the EAC is pressing election officials to let voters practice in as many settings as possible before they go to the polls. "In Florida, Nevada and other states that have gone to all electronic equipment, they're taking the machines to churches, shopping malls and other places to ensure that people practice using the equipment before Election Day," Soaries says.

And the efforts are paying off, he says. "Elderly people I saw using touch-screen machines for the first time in Nevada's primary a few weeks ago were thrilled," he says. "Election officials there were not surprised by that reaction because there had been so much voter education taking place in the state."

But non-government analysts say that few voters have had a chance to acquaint themselves with the new machines. "Any time you move from one technology to another, there is an adjustment that takes place, and very few polling places are offering voters the opportunity to practice," says Herrnson, of the Center for American Politics and Citizenship at the University of Maryland.

Herrnson is leading a study comparing voting machines and ballot styles, but the results will not be released until after this year's election. "For some voters, particularly those who are not used to computers, the learning curve may be steep."

Some critics say the lack of a paper trail is a major, if fixable, flaw in electronic voting machines that will arise if a close election prompts recounts. "The only way that you can maintain a checkable election is with a paper trail," says election expert Gans.

Verified Voting, a grass-roots movement, is calling for the use of voter-verified paper ballots for all elections. "Our primary concern is the threat that unverifiable electronic voting poses to elections in the United States," the group states. "What if the miscounts we know of are only the tip of an undetected iceberg of electronic miscounts? They might be. We have no way of knowing." [23]

Nevada is the only jurisdiction to have adopted in time for this fall's election a statewide system of electronic machines that produce paper records of each vote. California recently passed a law mandating a paper trail on all its electronic voting machines by 2006. On Oct. 25, a federal judge in Florida threw out a lawsuit that would have required voter-verified paper ballots on touch-screen machines. However, several states are considering mandating paper trails on any e-voting system they may purchase. [24] Meanwhile, a bill by Rep. Rush Holt, D-N.J., to require paper records in all U.S. voting precincts has not garnered enough support for passage.

A nationwide mandate that all voting devices provide a paper trail would infringe on the states' authority to administer elections, say critics of the bill. "It is an appropriate role for the federal government to help the states secure the kind of technology that they need because that's an extension of voting rights," Soaries says. "However, when we get into things that should best be defined locally, like voting equipment, that's when the federal government should not overstep its bounds because the country's so diverse. In Nevada they adopted a paper trail because Nevadans decided that if they could secure their gambling machines, they could secure their voting machines. But Nevada has a different culture than New Hampshire or Georgia."

For his part, Gans is unconvinced that even the Nevada machines can ensure an accurate vote count. "From my point of view, the only two valid systems are optical scans * and paper ballots," Gans says.

In any event, some election experts say the technology used at the polls is less important than the individual voter's responsibility to use it correctly. "One of the lessons the electorate learned in 2000 is that they themselves had made most of the mistakes," says Sabato of the University of Virginia's Center for Politics. He observed the Florida recount, which involved optical scanners as well as punch-card ballots. "Some of the machines malfunctioned, but most of the discounted votes were filled out — or not filled out — by real people."

The key to overcoming technical barriers to accurate and fair elections, Sabato says, is voter education. His center runs a voter-education program in all 50 states with 1.5 million student participants. "We should have been doing this decades ago," he says. "It's a long, hard process taking students to the local registrar and letting them use the voting machines. But it will have an impact in 10 or 15 years." ■

* Optical-scanning machines count ballots marked by voters.

BACKGROUND

Fighting for Rights

Democracy, including the right to vote on which it rests, was the guiding beacon that Colonial Americans followed in rejecting the English monarchy. Thomas Jefferson clearly enshrined the concept in the Declaration of Independence: "Governments are instituted among Men, deriving their just Powers from the Consent of the Governed." [25]

Beyond that lofty statement of principle, however, it quickly became apparent that the right to vote would apply to only a small segment of "the Governed." Women were automatically excluded — the Declaration clearly states that "all men are created equal" — while slaves and Native Americans had no legal rights. Indeed, the Founding Fathers worried about allowing men without property to vote, lest, in James Madison's words, "the rights of property [owners] . . . may be overruled by a majority without property."

In the end, the Founding Fathers threw up their hands over what Madison termed "a task of peculiar delicacy" and made the fateful decision to leave the whole issue of voting

Continued on p. 912

Chronology

1870s-1960s

Voting rights are gradually expanded to include women, African-Americans and other citizens.

1870
Two years after the 14th Amendment granted citizenship to former slaves, Congress approves the 15th Amendment to halt the continuing disenfranchisement of former slaves.

1876
Republican Rutherford B. Hayes defeats Democrat Samuel J. Tilden for the presidency after a special commission created by Congress settles a dispute over vote tallies in Florida, South Carolina, and Louisiana.

1919
Congress passes the 19th Amendment extending vote to women.

1924
The Snyder Act grants full citizenship to Native Americans.

1962
New Mexico becomes the last state to strike down state laws preventing Indians from voting.

1964
Congress bans poll taxes, used to keep African-Americans and other poor citizens from voting. Punch-card voting debuts in Georgia.

1965
Voting Rights Act adds literacy tests to the list of barred activities used to disenfranchise African-Americans.

1970s-1990s

Congress makes it easier for most Americans to register and vote, but not ex-felons.

1971
The 26th Amendment extends voting rights to Americans ages 18-21.

1974
U.S. Supreme Court, in *Richardson v. Ramirez*, upholds the states' right to deny the vote to anyone convicted of a felony.

1984
The Polling Place Accessibility for the Elderly and Handicapped Act eases access to polling places.

1985
U.S. Supreme Court rules in *Hunter v. Underwood* that denying voting rights to felons is not permissible if it can be shown that the disenfranchisement is racist in intent.

1993
National Voter Registration Act — the "Motor Voter Act" — allows citizens to register at the same time they get their driver's licenses. The law also bars states from purging voters from rolls for not voting in previous elections.

2000s

The close presidential race reveals flaws in the election process.

Nov. 7, 2000
Poor voting technology and legal challenges delay the final result of the presidential election in Florida until a 5-4 ruling by the U.S. Supreme Court on Dec. 12 bars further recounts in Florida. Gov. George W. Bush, R-Texas, is declared the winner over Vice President Al Gore.

August 2001
Bipartisan National Commission on Federal Election Reform recommends changes in state election laws, including the restoration of felons' voting rights.

Oct. 29, 2002
President Bush signs the Help America Vote Act (HAVA), which authorizes almost $4 billion to help states upgrade their voting equipment and requires them to permit voters whose names do not appear on voter lists to cast provisional ballots.

May 2003
Rep. Rush Holt, D-N.J., introduces a bill that would require states using electronic voting machines to equip the devices with a "paper trail" to allow for vote recounts in close elections.

January 2004
Election Assistance Commission, created by HAVA, begins to help states strengthen their election systems.

Oct. 12, 2004
A federal judge in Missouri rules that provisional ballots cast at the wrong polling place can be thrown out. The ruling comes in the first of several lawsuits involving the HAVA mandate requiring states to allow voters to cast provisional ballots if their names do not appear on voting lists.

Nov. 2, 2004
About a third of voters will use electronic voting machines.

2005
HAVA must establish federal standards for electronic voting machines.

2006
Congress expected to consider reauthorization of the Voting Rights Act, due to expire in 2007.

Felon Disenfranchisement Varies by State

After thousands of Floridians were barred from voting in 2000 because they were erroneously identified as felons — and President Bush was subsequently elected by a 537-vote margin in that state — national attention has focused on the practice of preventing felons from voting.

Felon-disenfranchisement laws — with roots in English law, Colonial law and early state laws — have evolved over the last 40 years. Many states have narrowed the list of relevant crimes or eliminated lifetime disenfranchisement by allowing ex-felons to petition the state for restoration of voting rights after a certain number of years of good behavior. [1]

Proponents of disenfranchisement say lawbreakers should not have a say in the voting process. But opponents say felon-disenfranchisement laws are vestiges of a time when states sought to block blacks from voting and amount to de facto disenfranchisement of African-American males. Black males make up nearly a third of all disenfranchised ex-felons — a rate that is seven times the national average for all races, according to the Sentencing Project, a nonprofit advocacy group that promotes alternatives to imprisonment. [2]

State laws vary in how they treat felons' voting rights. Most states require felons to finish both their prison time and their parole or probation before being allowed to vote; only Maine and Vermont allow felons to vote while still in prison. Seven states — Alabama, Florida, Iowa, Kentucky, Mississippi, Nebraska and Virginia — disenfranchise felons for life unless specifically pardoned by the governor.

After holding public hearings and studying the matter for more than six months, the bipartisan National Commission on Federal Election Reform, headed by former Presidents Jimmy Carter and Gerald R. Ford, recommended in 2001 that ex-felons' voting rights be restored once they are no longer on parole or probation. [3]

In response, several state legislatures either tightened their laws or liberalized them. Massachusetts — which had allowed prison inmates to vote — disenfranchised them, while Kansas added probationers to the list of felons not allowed to vote. Connecticut extended voting rights to felons on probation, adding 36,000 people to the state's eligible voters; New Mexico repealed its lifetime ban on voting by ex-felons; and Maryland passed a law to automatically restore voting rights to additional categories of non-violent ex-felons.

Three of the seven states that disenfranchise ex-felons for life — Alabama, Kentucky and Virginia — have recently made it easier for ex-felons to petition for restoration of voting rights. In Virginia, a 2000 law allowed certain non-violent ex-felons to apply to the circuit court to have their voting rights restored five years after completing their sentences, subject to the governor's approval.

In 2003, the Virginia General Assembly approved a resolution calling for a constitutional amendment to be put before the voters allowing non-violent felons to be granted the right to vote. [4] But the legislature killed the measure last spring.

Meanwhile, Virginia's Democratic Gov. Mark R. Warner has streamlined the procedure for seeking restoration of voting rights for non-violent ex-felons and has restored voting rights to 1,892 ex-felons — more than any of his predecessors since World War II. But more than 200,000 ex-felons remain disenfranchised in Virginia.

State Rep. Bradley P. Marrs, a GOP delegate from Chesterfield, said Warner was restoring felons' voting rights much more quickly than his Republican predecessor Gov. James Gilmore, who restored rights to 238 felons during his tenure. [5]

Warner explained that he is only restoring rights to non-violent felons and that each must have a clean record for at least five years, complete a 13-page application, write full explanations of their crimes and obtain three letters of recommendation.

---

[1] See "To Assure Pride and Confidence in the Electoral Process," National Commission on Federal Election Reform, August 2001, p. 45.

[2] Sentencing Project, "Felony Disenfranchisement Laws in the United States," September 2004. While about 4.7 million ex-felons have lost their voting rights, 1.4 million black men are disenfranchised felons.

[3] National Commission on Federal Election Reform, *op. cit.*

[4] Tyler Whitley, "Assembly Clears Felon Rights Plans; Statewide Vote on Issue Sought," *Richmond Times-Dispatch*, Feb. 15, 2003, p. A8.

[5] Tyler Whitley, "Voting Rights Issue Draws Ire, Warner Challenged on High Rate of Felons Getting Rights Back," *Richmond Times-Dispatch*, Oct. 21, 2004, p. B4.

Continued from p. 910

rights and election administration to the states. Article I, Section 4 of the Constitution states: "The times, places and manner of holding elections for Senators and Representatives, shall be prescribed in each state by the legislature thereof; but the Congress may at any time by law make or alter such regulations."

Thanks to efforts by President Andrew Jackson (1829-37), most white men without property were enfranchised by 1860. But women, African-Americans, Native Americans and young people ages 18-21 would have to struggle for their voting rights over the next century.

Women began their struggle for suffrage in 1848, when anti-slavery and women's-rights leaders Lucretia Mott and Elizabeth Cady Stanton hosted the first women's-rights convention in the United States, at Seneca Falls, N.Y. But 20 years later, when Congress approved the 14th Amendment to the Constitution, it defined voters as "male citizens twenty-one years of age."

Stanton and fellow suffragist Susan B. Anthony launched a campaign to amend the Constitution to allow for universal suffrage. Meanwhile, another suffragist movement, led by Lucy Stone, her husband Henry Blackwell and reformer Julia Ward Howe (author of "The Battle Hymn of the Republic"), focused on persuading Western states to extend voting rights to women.

By 1910, the two movements had joined forces, and women had won the right to vote in Colorado, Idaho, Utah, Washington and Wyoming. The National American Woman Suffrage Association quickly gained strength, despite the controversial arrest of 10 suffragists who had picketed outside the White House in 1917. Then, in 1919 Congress passed the 19th Amendment, which extended voting rights to about half the U.S. population with these words: "The right of citizens of the United States to vote shall not be denied or abridged by the United States or by any state on account of sex."

African-Americans have fought a harder and longer struggle to win suffrage. The 14th Amendment, approved in 1868 after the Civil War, granted citizenship to former slaves. But many states, especially former Confederate states, found ways to prevent African-Americans from voting. Two years later, in 1870, Congress approved the 15th Amendment with sweeping language to halt the widespread disenfranchisement of former slaves: "The right of citizens of the United States to vote shall not be denied or abridged by the United States or by any State on account of race, color, or previous condition of servitude."

Compromise of 1876

Barely 10 years after the Civil War, disputed election results in the contest between Republican presidential candidate Rutherford B. Hayes and Democrat Samuel J. Tilden created a constitutional crisis and raised fears of another civil war.

Hayes, the three-time governor of Ohio, lost the popular vote and had a questionable hold on the Electoral College vote, but he eventually won the presidency after a special commission created by Congress settled the election. (Hayes won 4.0 million votes to Tilden's 4.3 million.)

The problem arose when the vote tallies in Florida, South Carolina, and Louisiana were called into question. There was good reason to be suspicious of any vote count in these and other Southern states. Republicans controlled the balloting places and mounted vigorous drives to get newly enfranchised blacks to the polls, but Democrats used physical intimidation and bribery to keep blacks away.

When state election board recounts and investigations did not settle the issue, Congress appointed a commission to do so composed of five senators, five representatives and five Supreme Court justices; eight commission members were Republican, seven Democratic. Weeks of bargaining finally gave Republicans the presidency in exchange for a pledge to pull federal troops out of the states of the Confederacy and to commit federal money to making internal improvements in the South. [26]

But some states, particularly in the South, continued to circumvent the intent of Congress. "Grandfather clauses" stipulating that a citizen could vote only if his grandfather had done so — which excluded former slaves — were used until the Supreme Court barred them in 1915. For the next half-century, most black Americans were prevented from exercising their right to vote through a variety of tactics, including poll taxes, literacy tests, ballot-box tampering, intimidation and even violence by Ku Klux Klansmen.

Meanwhile, the 15th Amendment had not granted Native Americans the right to vote, because they were not considered citizens. Not until passage of the Snyder Act in 1924 did Native Americans born in the United States gain full citizenship and, thus, under the 15th Amendment, the right to vote. Nevertheless, just as Southern states tried to prevent blacks from voting, many states used fraud, intimidation, poll taxes and literacy tests to disenfranchise Indians until civil and voting-rights laws in the 1960s banned such practices.

Those voting-rights laws were hard-fought. During the 1960s, under the leadership of the Rev. Martin Luther King Jr., the civil rights movement used marches, boycotts and other non-violent techniques to demand voting rights for blacks. Hundreds were arrested and jailed, including King. Protesters frequently encountered violence at the hands of racist police and citizens: Police turned water hoses on child marchers, homes and churches were firebombed and some protesters — white as well as black — were murdered.

The violent response to the peaceful protests — broadcast around the nation by television news — shocked the nation and focused public opinion on black disenfranchisement. In 1964, the 24th Amendment outlawing poll taxes was ratified.

The next year, eight days after horrified television viewers watched policemen clubbing and tear-gassing peaceful protesters marching from Selma to Montgomery, Ala., President Lyndon B. Johnson vowed to send Congress a tough, new voting-rights bill. Adopting the slogan of the civil rights movement, Johnson told a televised joint session of Congress: "We shall overcome." [27]

Five months later, Congress passed the landmark 1965 Voting Rights Act, which Johnson signed into law on Aug. 6. It outlawed literacy tests and other disenfranchisement tactics and provided for federal enforcement of its provisions. It also authorized federal supervision of voter registration in any state, city or county that had used voter-qualification tests before the November 1964 elections and where fewer than 50 percent of voting-age residents had voted. Further, it barred any state or political subdivision from adopting any election procedures that would deny or hamper the right to vote.

On Aug. 25, Johnson announced that in the first 19 days under the new law, federal election examiners had registered 27,385 blacks in three Southern states. In Selma, on Aug. 14 alone, 381 African-Americans were put on the rolls — more than had been registered in the previous 60 years.

By the end of the 1960s, the civil rights movement had achieved many of its goals, and registration among voting-age African-Americans nationwide had risen from 23 percent to 61 percent.

Subsequent revisions to the Voting Rights Act in 1970, 1975 and 1982 extended and strengthened voting rights for short-term residents, non-English-speaking citizens and victims of racial discrimination, respectively. In 1984, Congress passed the Polling Place Accessibility for the Elderly and Handicapped Act, which made it easier for voters to gain access to polling places and receive help, where needed, to cast their ballots.

Young citizens, ages 18-21, are the most recent group of Americans to win their voting rights. At the height of the Vietnam War, lawmakers decided to end the double standard inherent in drafting 18-year-old soldiers to fight and die for their country when they weren't allowed to vote. With ratification of the 26th Amendment in 1971, young men and women over 18 won their voting rights.

In 1993, President Bill Clinton signed the National Voter Registration Act, also known as the Motor Voter Act, which enabled prospective voters to register at the same time they apply for or renew their driver's licenses. The law also barred states from purging the names of voters from rolls for not voting in previous elections.

After Florida, HAVA

Then-Gov. George W. Bush led Democratic Vice President Al Gore in Florida by 1,784 votes the day after the 2000 election. Under state law, the narrow margin required a recount. Completed by week's end, that recount narrowed Bush's lead to 327 votes.

Gore, meanwhile had requested a manual recount of the votes in four of the state's 67 counties — Volusia, Palm Beach, Broward and Miami-Dade.

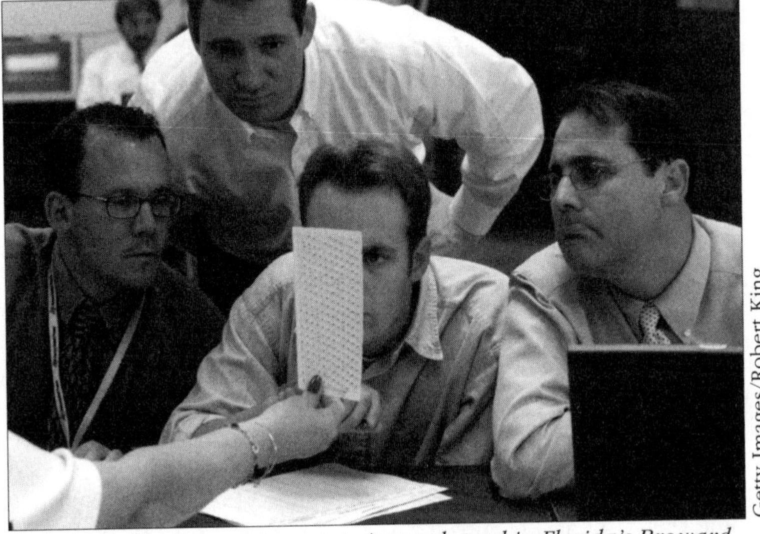

Getty Images/Robert King

Election officials examine a voter's punch card in Florida's Broward County (Fort Lauderdale) during the recount of the disputed 2000 presidential election.

Those recounts began even though Bush had asked a federal court to block them. [28]

The recount took an unprecedented 36 days and was delayed repeatedly by confusion over how to count ballots that were not completely punched out, leaving so-called "hanging" and "pregnant" chads. Moreover, suspicions of high-level maneuvering arose when it emerged that Florida Secretary of State Katherine Harris — the official in charge of elections — was also co-chair of the state Republican campaign committee; Florida Gov. Jeb Bush was the GOP contender's brother.

Ultimately, the U.S. Supreme Court decided the matter, handing Florida — and the White House — to Bush. The margin was 537 votes. But the court's decision did little to lift the cloud of bitterness that followed the election fiasco.

During the next two years, several high-level panels and academic groups examined what went wrong in the election, not just in Florida but elsewhere in the country. In addition to the Caltech-MIT study, the U.S. Commission on Civil Rights examined voter irregularities and administrative problems in polling places nationwide. It found, for example, that up to 3 million votes were lost due to clerical and administrative errors on voter-registration lists. [29]

The April 2004 study also found that while 30 states required no voter identification at the polls, the rest required some form of identification and tended to single out minority and immigrant voters when enforcing that requirement — a tactic civil rights advocates said was intimidating. Poor training of poll workers also contributed to disenfranchisement on Election Day, the commission concluded. The commission recommended several measures to improve election systems and enhance voting rights, some of which found their way into the Help America Vote Act.

The greatest number of recommendations came from a bipartisan, blue-ribbon panel co-chaired by former Presidents Jimmy Carter and Gerald R. Ford. After six months of hearings around the country, it issued an exhaustive study and a long list of recommendations.

The House passed its version of HAVA in December 2001, just after the Sept. 11 terrorist attacks. The Senate followed suit with its bill the following April. Bush signed the compromise version on Oct. 29, 2002 — nearly two years after the Florida election debacle.

"The vitality of America's democracy depends on the fairness and accuracy of America's election," Bush said upon signing HAVA into law. "Every registered voter deserves to have confidence that the system is fair and elections are honest, that every vote is recorded and that the rules are consistently applied."

Besides authorizing the $3.89 billion to help local jurisdictions upgrade their voting systems and creating the Election Assistance Commission, HAVA also requires:

- States to create computerized voter-registration lists;
- First-time voters who did not submit identification with their mail-in registration forms to present an I.D. (such as a driver's license, utility bill or bank statement) at the polls;
- That voters whose names don't appear on registration lists at the polls be allowed to cast provisional ballots that must be counted in the final tally if the voters later proved to be eligible.

CURRENT SITUATION

Charges and Countercharges

With Bush and Kerry running neck and neck just before the election, supporters of both candidates are pouring resources and volunteers into voter-registration campaigns across the country. Kerry supporters are focused on increasing voter turnout in minority communities, which traditionally vote Democratic. Registration drives in Ohio, for example, pulled in about a million new voters, a majority of whom are expected to vote Democratic. [30] The NAACP reports that its registration drive has signed up nearly a half-million new voters since 2000. [31]

Republican critics of these targeted registration efforts charge that overzealous Kerry supporters are fraudulently padding registration lists with the names of ineligible voters, including deceased individuals and even pets.

In the close, pivotal race in Ohio, the Republican Party says it will place 3,600 election challengers at polling places on Nov. 2. The Republicans say they are only trying to guard against fraud. But in an Oct. 26 editorial entitled "Election Day Misdeeds," *The New York Times* warned: It is likely that some voters will be challenged [in Ohio] next week not because they appear to be ineligible, but because partisan challengers think they will vote for the other side. There is a long history of challengers targeting minority precincts and minority voters. It is troubling in Ohio this year the Republicans appear to be focusing much of their effort on Cleveland, Dayton and other cities with large African-American and Latino populations."

In New Mexico, Republicans unsuccessfully sued the state's Democratic secretary of state to require that all new voters present identification at the polls. Colorado's Republican secretary of state also accused the state's Democratic attorney general of failing to investigate allegations of registration fraud. [32]

Democratic spokesmen flatly deny the charges. "Our stance is that there shouldn't be any voter fraud, period," says Tony Welch, press secretary for the Democratic National Committee. "The Republicans seem to believe voter fraud only exists in areas that are likely to vote against George W. Bush. If it's fraud they're interested in, they might want to investigate a few areas that are friendly to Bush. That way they'd at least have the appearance of wanting to do something more than suppress the African-American vote."

Indeed, civil rights advocates and Kerry supporters charge that Republican operatives are using dirty tricks to intimidate minority voters and suppress the minority vote. They cite a "purge list" distributed earlier this year by Florida's Republican secretary of state, Glenda E. Hood, which listed 47,000 names of individuals alleged to be felons and thus ineligible to vote. After a press report revealed that about 2,000 of the individuals were not felons, that most of them were African-Americans and that hardly any were Hispanic — in a state where Cuban-Americans tend to vote Republican — Hood withdrew the list. [33] But according to press reports, few of the wrongly purged names have reappeared on voting lists. [34]

"This might not technically fall into the category of fraud, but if you're interested in voting fairness, you'd think that [GOP officials] would let Jeb [Bush] know they were very concerned about such an incident," Welch says. "But to my knowledge, no such letter went out to Gov. Bush."

Again in Florida, Hood issued a directive instructing election officials to reject registration applications in which applicants failed to check a box affirming their U.S. citizenship, even though by signing the application itself the applicants pledged that they were indeed U.S. citizens. Although many counties reportedly are ignoring the directive, election officials in Duval County have followed it. According to one report, three times as many of the rejected applications there were from Democrats than from Republicans. [35]

Just weeks before his state's registration deadline, Ohio's Republican secretary of state, J. Kenneth Blackwell, announced that mail-in voter registration applications would be rejected unless they were submitted on official, 80-pound bond forms. After a groundswell of negative publicity, he reversed the decision. In Milwaukee, the GOP county executive, who also co-chairs Wisconsin's Bush-Cheney campaign, decided to print 300,000 fewer ballots than the City of Milwaukee had requested, citing his concern about fraud in the Democratic stronghold (He too later reversed the decision.) [36]

In Nevada and Oregon, employees of groups hired by the GOP to register voters told reporters they were told to discourage Democrats from registering and that leaders of the groups destroyed thousands of registration forms filled out by Democrats. [37]

"There is a central difference between the Democratic Party and the Republican Party," Democratic spokesman Welch says. "Our goal is to work toward allowing and ensuring that as many people who are eligible to vote can successfully cast that ballot."

The Republican Party rejects allegations of voter intimidation across the board. "With 15 days left until the election, Democrats have admitted they have nothing to offer the American people but fear and bold-faced untruths," said Republican National Committee Chairman Ed Gillespie. "Fear is not an agenda, and Democrats will learn this lesson on Election Day." [38]

HAVA's Impact

The 2002 Help America Vote Act will bring a number of changes to polling places this fall, primarily in the form of new voting machines. States have used most of the money authorized under the law to buy electronic machines to replace paper ballots and lever machines.

But according to the U.S. Civil Rights Commission, the speed with which states have implemented HAVA varies greatly. "Although nearly every state has a plan, reform efforts vary widely from state to state," the commission found earlier this year. "Some have made measurable changes; others are progressing more slowly, either because of the lengthy legislative process, lack of funding, or an absence of political leadership." [39]

Some observers are disappointed at the EAC's pace of distributing HAVA funds in time to make a bigger difference in time for this fall's elections. "The money just hasn't been there to implement the law in the way that it needed to be," says Mincberg of People for the American Way.

But EAC Chairman Soaries defends the commission's record in distributing funds to the states, especially in view of the short time it has had to get under way and the overwhelming priority given to defense and homeland security needs in the wake of the Sept. 11 attacks. "I think it's a miracle we have any money," Soaries says. "Of the $3 billion that has been appropriated, $2 billion has been distributed. We're rolling."

HAVA's mandate that states allow voters whose names do not appear on voter lists to cast provisional ballots has already run into problems in several jurisdictions. A number of states where the outcome is expected to be especially close — including Colorado, Florida, Michigan, Missouri and Ohio — have announced that they will not count the provisional ballots cast by eligible voters at the wrong polling place. Several court rulings on legal challenges to these exceptions to HAVA's provisional-ballot mandate — including federal appeals court rulings on Oct. 19 and 23 — have affirmed local officials' right to enforce such a requirement. "Provisional ballots could be the hanging chads of 2004," said Tony Sirvello, a Texas elections official. "If there's a state as close as Florida was in 2000, this could have a major effect." [40]

Gans of the Committee for the Study of the American Electorate is hopeful that HAVA will make a bigger difference in future elections. "HAVA has been slow to be funded and slow to be implemented," he says, "but it is a step in the right direction." Meanwhile, Gans says some of the registration problems that HAVA has not resolved could be easily overcome by setting up a computer match with the U.S. Postal Service's change of address system and by making sure the names match. "Some states are doing a better job than others of checking the bona fides of newly registered voters," he says. "Alaska, for example, regularly has registration rates that are over 100 percent of its eligible population, which means they haven't cleaned their list."

Another mandate under HAVA — that first-time voters who did not submit identification with their registration applications present I.D.'s at the polls — also appears likely to cause confusion at the polls. Some states, such as Georgia, already require all voters to present identification at the polls, while others have had to rewrite state laws to comply with HAVA.

Some critics say the law doesn't go far enough to eliminate fraud by newly registered voters. Sen. Pete V. Domenici, R-N.M., recently introduced a measure to amend HAVA and require all new voters who did not register in person at their local election offices to present identification at the polls. After the New Mexico Supreme Court rejected the Republican challenge to a new state law that requires only new voters who registered by mail to produce an I.D. in November, Domenici predicted massive voter fraud in November: "As it stands now, there will be few if any checks at the polls this fall to ensure that a voter is who they say they are."

Democratic secretary of state Rebecca Vigil-Giron dismissed the challenge as a "frivolous attempt to disrupt the election process." [41]

Continued on p. 918

At Issue:

Are Americans' voting rights in peril?

PEOPLE FOR THE AMERICAN WAY FOUNDATION AND NATIONAL ASSOCIATION FOR THE ADVANCEMENT OF COLORED PEOPLE (NAACP)

FROM "THE LONG SHADOW OF JIM CROW: VOTER INTIMIDATION AND SUPPRESSION IN AMERICA TODAY," 2004

yes

In a nation where children [learn] that every citizen has the right to vote, it would be comforting to think that the last vestiges of voter intimidation, oppression and suppression were swept away by the passage and subsequent enforcement of the historic Voting Rights Act of 1965. It would be good to know that voters are no longer turned away from the polls based on their race, never knowingly misdirected, misinformed, deceived or threatened.

Unfortunately, it would be a grave mistake to believe it.

In every national American election since Reconstruction, voters — particularly African-American voters and other minorities — have faced calculated and determined efforts at intimidation and suppression. [The] poll taxes, literacy tests and physical violence of the Jim Crow era have disappeared. Today, more subtle, cynical and creative tactics have taken their place. . . .

Voter intimidation and suppression is not a problem limited to the Southern United States. It takes place from California to New York, Texas to Illinois. It is not the province of a single political party, although patterns of intimidation have changed as the party allegiances of minority communities have changed over the years. . . .

The election problems in Florida and elsewhere that led to the disenfranchisement of some 4 million American voters in the 2000 elections cast a harsh spotlight on flaws in our voting system [resulting from] both illegal actions and incompetence by public officials, as well as outdated machines and inadequate voter education. As election officials nationwide struggle to put new voting technology into place, redesign confusing ballots and educate voters, the opportunities for voter intimidation and suppression have proliferated along with opportunities for disenfranchisement caused by voter confusion and technical problems.

With widespread predictions of a close national election, and an unprecedented wave of new voter registration, unscrupulous political operatives will look for any advantage, including suppression and intimidation efforts. As in the past, minority voters and low-income populations will be the most likely targets of dirty tricks at the polls.

Robbing voters of their right to vote and to have their vote counted undermines the very foundations of our democratic society. Politicians, political strategists and party officials who may consider voter intimidation and suppression efforts as part of their tactical arsenal should prepare to be exposed and prosecuted.

R. ALEXANDER ACOSTA
ASSISTANT ATTORNEY GENERAL FOR CIVIL RIGHTS, U.S. DEPARTMENT OF JUSTICE

FROM TESTIMONY BEFORE THE HOUSE JUDICIARY SUBCOMMITTEE ON THE CONSTITUTION, MARCH 2, 2004

no

The right to vote is among the most fundamental in our democracy. Protecting access to and integrity of the franchise is a top priority.

Providing access to polling places is part of this effort. We have dispatched record numbers of federal monitors and observers to polling places around the country. . . . In 2002, we deployed a total of 829 federal employees: 608 observers and 221 department personnel to monitor elections in 17 states. By contrast, in 1992, the department dispatched 571 observers and monitors. During this year's general election, we anticipate similarly proactive prevention efforts . . . .

Our Disability Rights Section has actively enforced federal requirements that polling places be accessible to individuals with disabilities. . . . In addition, we recently issued guidance for local election officials instructing them in how to make polling places fully accessible. . . .

We have similarly taken significant steps toward protecting the voting rights of language minorities under Section 203 of the Voting Rights Act [which requires translated signs and ballots in jurisdictions with many non-English-speaking voters]. In July 2002, the Census Bureau determined [that] 296 such jurisdictions [exist] across 30 states. We conducted an extensive outreach campaign to ensure compliance by these . . . jurisdictions, sending letters to all affected officials and offering substantial technical assistance. We also initiated a comprehensive review of the compliance efforts of all covered jurisdictions.

We have now monitored elections in a number of covered jurisdictions across the country. Where we identified problems, we are investigating. Where appropriate, we are prepared to sue and to negotiate settlement agreements and consent decrees to ensure that deficiencies are fixed and that language minorities receive . . . the assistance required by law.

We likewise have begun a vigorous process of implementing the Help America Vote Act of 2002 (HAVA). Some provisions . . . took effect on Jan. 1, 2004. Jurisdictions are now required to provide for provisional voting, provide voter information at polling places, comply with federal rules for mail-in registration and properly manage statewide voter registration lists.

In preparation for HAVA, we have been monitoring states' implementation efforts and have offered substantial technical assistance for over a year. Now that those provisions have taken effect, we stand ready to enforce HAVA's requirements as needed. We intend to work with the Election Assistance Commission to help states ensure that voters know their rights under this new law.

Continued from p. 916

Democrats, meanwhile, are concerned that the large number of voters, especially minority voters, expected to turn out at this year's closely contested election will face widespread intimidation. Although overt efforts to intimidate would-be voters have been less visible so far this year, Mincberg says, most such incidents are not reported until Election Day. "Unfortunately, there's no question that voter intimidation has continued and probably will happen in some places this November," he says. "Exactly where is very hard to say."

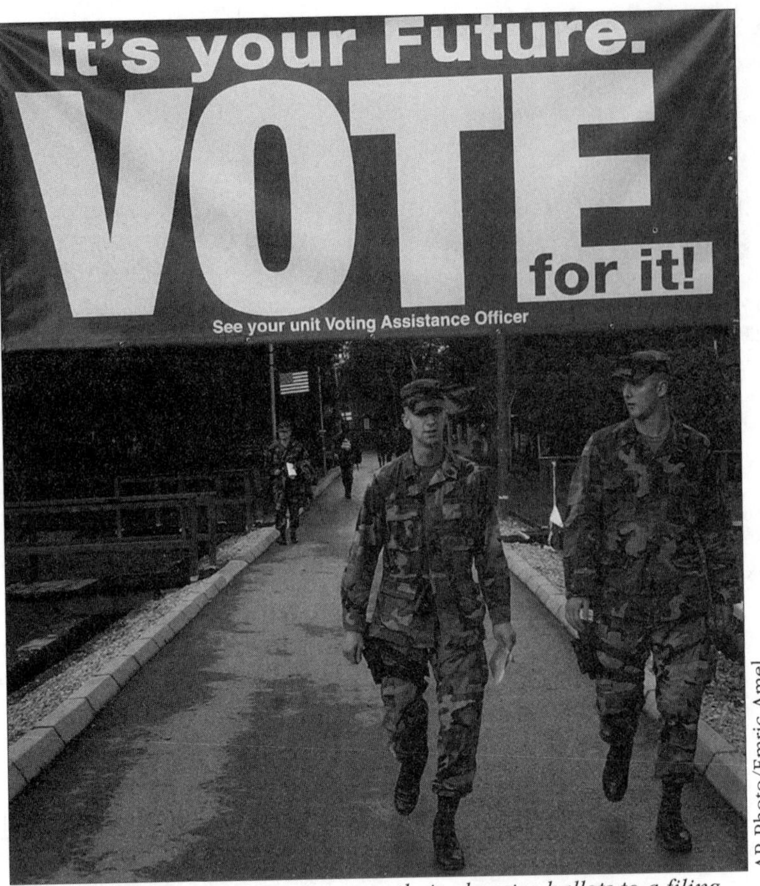

It's your Future.
VOTE
for it!
See your unit Voting Assistance Officer

AP Photo/Emric Amel

U.S. peacekeepers in Bosnia, carry their absentee ballots to a filing center on Oct. 20, 2004. Thousands of overseas U.S. military personnel were unable to vote in 2000, prompting the Pentagon to launch a special voter program this year.

Terror Threat

Concern that terrorists might try to disrupt the Nov. 2 presidential election intensified after terrorists bombed commuter trains outside Madrid on March 11, 2004, killing 191 people. Days later, Spanish voters ousted the conservative government of Prime Minister Jose Maria Aznar, who had sent troops to Iraq in support of the U.S.-led war to topple Saddam Hussein. Aznar's successor, socialist Jose Luis Zapatero, promptly withdrew the Spanish forces.

Since Madrid, FBI and Homeland Security Department officials have warned repeatedly that terrorists might have similar designs on the United States, and on Sept. 24, Attorney General John Ashcroft ordered federal law-enforcement agencies to help state and local election officials beef up security at the nation's 193,000 polling places.

President Bush recently restated that concern. "Ever since the Madrid bombings," he said in an Oct. 18 interview with The Associated Press, "we have been concerned, as have other nations, about the terrorists trying to disrupt our election. . . . We have no specific threat information. Otherwise, we would have let everyone know." [42]

Some observers say the administration's warnings may intimidate voters. "Like all Americans, we want the government to take the proper steps to safeguard the nation from terrorists, but without specific intelligence about possible attacks during the presidential election in November, we think that sending hundreds of armed police officers to polling places could be seen as an effort to depress the vote, given the experience of the Florida election in 2000," NAACP President Kweisi Mfume said on Oct. 8. "The NAACP's concern is that security forces will be placed disproportionately in African-American and Hispanic voting districts."

Overseas Military

In 2000, more than a quarter of the 2.7 million U.S. military personnel posted overseas were unable to vote because they didn't get absentee ballots or received them too late. [43] So this year the Pentagon launched an Internet-voting program. But after technical experts said the system was insecure, the Defense Department decided to enable service members to vote by fax or e-mail instead. The Pentagon then hired a private company to process the military ballots and forward them to local jurisdictions.

But the open handling of ballots by the firm violates the rights of military personnel to a secret ballot, critics say. "Military disenfranchisement was one of the first things that was recognized to go wrong in Florida in 2000, but very little has been done to correct it," says Sabato of the Center for Politics. "These people are fighting [in Iraq and Afghanistan] to preserve democracy, and they deserve the right to vote. It really is disappointing." [44]

Herrnson of the Center for American Politics and Citizenship adds that the Pentagon's solution leaves low-ranking soldiers especially vulnerable to violations of their rights. "If you can't vote privately, and people can see your votes, then you're open to all sorts of pressure," Herrnson says. "In a hierarchical situation like the military, that would be a disaster. It shows the extremes that America has gone to in terms of privatizing government, and in such a way that it denies people their basic rights."

The Pentagon defends the method it has chosen to enable overseas military personnel to vote. "We're confident that we're providing all the information and the capability that our servicememebers, as well as U.S. citizens living overseas, need to obtain and return absentee ballots in a timely manner," said Lt. Col. Ellen Kranke, a Pentagon spokeswoman. [45] ■

OUTLOOK

Scenario for 2006

While HAVA has helped put electronic voting machines in many polling places this Election Day, computer experts warn that the new devices may fall short of expectations in many jurisdictions.

"When you buy a microwave oven, you assume that the manufacturer is subject to government standards to protect you from any negative effects from microwaves," says Election Assistance Commission Chairman Soaries. "We don't yet have that kind of scrutiny over our voting machines."

But in the years ahead, if HAVA is implemented on its planned schedule, new technical standards for voting machines should improve their reliability in time for the next broad election cycle, the midterm contests of 2006.

The last provision of HAVA to go into effect, scheduled for the summer of 2005, is the establishment of voting-machine standards. "The most important job that we now have is the creation of minimum standards against which states can test their machines," Soaries says. "We'll start feeling the benefits of these standards in 2006."

Another HAVA requirement, calling for all the states to have computerized voter-registration lists in place by 2006, should eliminate additional flaws in the current system. "These centralized databases will give states the prerogative to become much more flexible and allow people to vote anywhere in the state," Soaries says.

The databases also should help address Republican concerns about voter-registration fraud as well as Democratic concerns about voter suppression and intimidation. Poll workers will be able to verify new voters' names on statewide lists, reducing the need for provisional ballots. Also, Soaries says, "it's less likely that your name will get lost, or that if you show up at the wrong polling place five minutes before the polls close, you'll lose your right to vote."

Critics of the nation's voting system say more could have been done, and sooner, to eliminate obstacles to fair and accurate elections. High on the list is equipping electronic voting machines to produce paper receipts for every vote, like the credit-card receipts printed by gas pumps. Electronic machines in most jurisdictions do not provide paper "trails."

Wall Street Journal columnist John Fund, author of *Stealing Elections*, says requiring paper trails, reducing absentee voting and requiring voters to present identification at the polls would significantly reduce voter fraud.

"It is strange that we have to show a photo I.D. to travel, we have to show a photo I.D. to get a video from Blockbuster, but we don't have to show a photo I.D. for the sacred act of voting," he said.

"Whatever it costs, it's cheaper than going through another Florida nightmare." [46] ■

Notes

[1] Valerie Richardson, "Colorado to Tackle Voter-Fraud Fears," *The Washington Times*, Oct. 14, 2004.

[2] "Rendell to Put State Bureaucrats at Election Offices; Republicans Suspicious of Move," freerepublic.com, Oct. 14, 2004.

[3] The Associated Press, "Democrats Blast GOP Lawmaker's 'suppress the Detroit vote' remark," *The Detroit Free Press*, July 21, 2004.

[4] Adam Goldman, "Executive Denies Voter-Registration Forms Destroyed in Nevada," *San Francisco Chronicle*, Oct. 13, 2004.

[5] David D. Kirkpatrick, "Republicans Claim Democrats Are Behind Office Attacks," *The New York Times*, Oct. 26, 2004, p. A 19.

[6] Garrett Therolf, "Voter-Purge List of Felons Made Public," *The Tampa Tribune*, July 3, 2004.

[7] For background on the 2000 election, see Kathy Koch, "Election Reform," *The CQ Researcher*, Nov. 2, 2001, pp. 897-920.

[8] See Robert Tanner, "Democrats Signing Up More New Voters," The Associated Press, Oct. 18, 2004.

[9] NAACP National Voter Fund press release, Oct. 6, 2004.

[10] "Worldwide Scrutiny Is Coming to the U.S. National Election," *The New York Times*, Oct. 10, 2004.

[11] For background, see Tom Price, "Cyberpolitics," *The CQ Researcher*, Sept. 17, 2004, pp. 757-780.

About the Author

Mary H. Cooper specializes in defense, energy and environmental issues. Before joining *The CQ Researcher* as a staff writer in 1983, she was Washington correspondent for the Rome daily newspaper *l'Unità*. She is the author of *The Business of Drugs* (CQ Press, 1990) and holds a B.A. in English from Hollins College in Virginia. Her recent reports include "Smart Growth," "Exporting Jobs," "Weapons of Mass Destruction" and "Bush and the Environment."

12 People for the American Way and NAACP, "Special Report: The Long Shadow of Jim Crow: Voter Intimidation and Suppression in America Today," Aug. 25, 2004.

13 See Patrick Reddy, "Analysis: Black Vote Key to Kerry's Charge," *Insight on the News*, March 2, 1004.

14 John Zogby, "Hispanic Vote," *Zogby International*, www.zogby.com.

15 See Darryl Fears, "In Atlanta, 14% of Black Men Can't Vote," *The Washington Post*, Sept. 23, 2004.

16 Marshall Clement and Nina Keough, "Political Punishment: The Consequences of Felon Disenfranchisement for Rhode Island Communities," Rhode Island Family Life Center, Sept. 23, 2004.

17 See Scott Hiaasen, "Ohio Will Notify Parolees by Letter That They Can Vote," *The* [Cleveland] *Plain Dealer*, Sept. 14, 2004, p. B1.

18 From a letter to the editor, *The Washington Post*, June 24, 2004, p. A24.

19 Todd F. Gaziano, "Election Reform," March 14, 2001, posted at www.heritage.org.

20 See Price, *op. cit.*

21 See Erika Bolstad, "New System No Easy Touch for 134 Voters in Broward," *The Miami Herald*, Jan. 8 2004.

22 See LeAnn Askins, "Commission OKs Results of Elections," *Jonesboro* [Arkansas] *Sun*, May 28, 2004.

23 See www.verifiedvoting.org.

24 See Susan Llewelyn Leach, "E-voting Machines' Confidence Gap," *The Christian Science Monitor*, Oct. 4, 2004, p. 11.

25 Unless otherwise noted, material in this section is based on "Voters," Library of Congress, at www.memory.loc.gov.

26 CQ Electronic Library, *CQ Encyclopedia of American Government.*

27 Unless otherwise noted, this background comes from Nadine Cohodas, "Electing Minorities," *The CQ Researcher*, Aug. 12, 1994, pp. 697-720.

28 Kenneth Jost, *The Supreme Court Yearbook: 2000-2001* (2002), pp. 37-38.

29 U.S. Commission on Civil Rights, "Is America Ready to Vote? Election Readiness Briefing Paper," April 2004.

30 See Darrel Rowland, "Punch Cards May Hurt Blacks," *The Columbus* [Ohio] *Dispatch*, Oct. 17, 2004, p. A1.

31 NAACP National Voter Fund, *op. cit.*

32 See James Dao, "As Election Nears, Parties Begin Another Round of Legal Battles," *The New York Times*, Oct. 18, 2004, p. A1.

33 See Marc Caputo, "Felons Get New Boost on Vote," *The Miami Herald*, July 15, 2004, p. 1.

FOR MORE INFORMATION

Center for Equal Opportunity, 14 Pidgeon Hill Dr., Sterling, VA 20165; (703) 421-5443; www.ceousa.org. A conservative think that opposes the use of racial preferences in employment, education and voting.

Democratic National Committee, 430 S. Capitol St., S.E., Washington, DC 20003; (202) 863-8000; www.democrats.org. The Democratic Party charges that Republicans are systematically intimidating minority voters, considered likely to vote Democratic.

Heritage Foundation, Center for Legal and Judicial Studies, 214 Massachusetts Ave., N.E., Washington, DC 20002-4999; (202) 546-4400. www.heritage.org. Oppose what it considers an unconstitutional trend toward judges and regulators exercising more power.

National Association for the Advancement of Colored People — NAACP, 4805 Mt. Hope Dr., Baltimore, MD 21215; (877) 622-2798; www.naacp.org. The country's leading civil rights organization supports voting rights for all minorities through its National Voter Fund.

People for the American Way Foundation, 2000 M St., N.W., Suite 400, Washington, DC 20036; (202) 467-4999; www.pfaw.org. The liberal organization is promoting voting rights by sending volunteers to watch the polls under its Election Protection program.

Republican National Committee, 310 First St., S.E., Washington, DC 20003; (202) 863-8614; www.rnc.org. The Republican Party accuses Democrats of committing voter fraud by registering ineligible voters.

Sentencing Project, 514 10th St., N.W., Suite 1000, Washington DC 20004; (202) 628-0871; www.sentencingproject.org. Develops and promotes sentencing programs that reduce reliance on incarceration.

U.S. Election Assistance Commission, 1225 New York Ave., N.W., Suite 1100, Washington, DC 20005; (202) 566-3100; www.eac.org. Created by the 2002 Help America Vote Act, the four-member commission serves as a clearinghouse of election administration information and funnels federal assistance to the states to upgrade their voting equipment and improve the election process.

34 See Paul Krugman, "Block the Vote," *The New York Times*, Oct. 15, 2004, p. A23.

35 See Jo Becker, "Pushing to Be Counted in Fla.," *The Washington Post*, Oct. 13, 2004, p. A1; see also Jo Becker and Thomas B. Edsall, "Registering Voters: Add One, Take Away Two," *The Washington Post*, Oct. 14, 2004, p. A8.

36 "Milwaukee Ballot Dispute Resolved; More Ballots Available," The Associated Press, Oct. 15, 2004.

37 See David Sarasohn, "In Oregon, Florida Seems to Inch Closer," *The Sunday Oregonian*, Oct. 17, 2004, p. D4.

38 Statement of Oct. 18, 2004, posted at www.gop.com.

39 U.S. Commission on Civil Rights, *op. cit.*, p. 23.

40 Quoted by Jim Drinkard, "Standby Ballots Already Disputed," *USA Today*, Oct. 11, 2004, p. 1A.

41 Quoted by Deborah Baker, "Court Sides with Secretary of State in New Mexico Voter ID Dispute," The Associated Press, Sept. 29, 2004.

42 Quoted by Walter Shapiro, "With Scare Tactics Aplenty, Election Rivals Halloween," *USA Today*, Oct. 20, 2004, p. 4A.

43 See Jo Becker and Steve Fainaru, "Military Voter Education Underway," *The Washington Post*, Oct. 1, 2004, p. A5.

44 *Ibid.*

45 *Ibid.*

46 Fund was interviewed on "Marketplace," National Public Radio, Oct. 15, 2004.

Bibliography

Selected Sources

Books

Bugliosi, Vincent, Molly Ivins and Gerry Spence, *The Betrayal of America: How the Supreme Court Undermined the Constitution and Chose Our President*, Thunder's Mouth Press, 2001.

The Supreme Court decision to end the recount of presidential votes in Florida in 2000 amounted to a "judicial coup d'etat" that stole the election from U.S. voters.

Fund, John H., *Stealing Elections: How Voter Fraud Threatens Our Democracy*, Encounter Books, 2004.

A member of *The Wall Street Journal* editorial board warns that technical problems with new electronic voting machines and fraudulent manipulation of registration applications and ballots may skew the presidential election.

Hewitt, Hugh, *If It's Not Close, They Can't Cheat: Crushing the Democrats in Every Election and Why Your Life Depends on It*, 2004.

A talk-radio host argues that Democrats are fraudulently manipulating registration rolls.

Sammon, Bill, *At Any Cost: How Al Gore Tried to Steal the Election*, Regnery Publishing, 2001.

A *Washington Times* reporter accuses the former Democratic vice president of undermining the U.S. Supreme Court ruling that decided the 2000 presidential election.

Articles

Cusac, Anne-Marie, "Bullies at the Voting Booth," *The Progressive*, October 2004.

Republican dirty tricks aimed at keeping minority groups who tend to vote Democratic from casting their votes this fall may determine the outcome of the presidential race.

Gibbs, Nancy, "The Morning After," *Time*, Nov. 1, 2004, p. 28.

A close outcome in the 2004 presidential election could lead to a repeat of the 2000 Florida voting-counting debacle.

Kosova, Weston, "A Clean Count?" *Newsweek*, Oct. 18, 2004, pp. 30-40.

Unfamiliar voting machines, millions of new voters and challenges to close results could disrupt Election Day.

Toobin, Jeffrey, "Poll Position: Is the Justice Department Poised to Stop Voter Fraud — or to Keep Voters from Voting," *The New Yorker*, Sept. 20, 2004, p. 56.

Under Attorney General John Ashcroft, the Justice Department's focus in enforcing the 1965 Voting Rights Act has shifted from voter intimidation based on racial discrimination to voter "integrity" campaigns aimed at preventing voter fraud.

Zeller, Tom, Jr., "Why We Fear the Digital Ballot," *The New York Times*, Sept. 26, 2004.

Reports that manufacturers of electronic voting machines may be conspiring to sway the election have undermined voter confidence in the voting process, but computer experts say it would be hard to coordinate massive manipulation of the voting results.

Reports & Studies

Caltech-MIT Voting Technology Project, "Voting: What Is, What Could Be," California Institute of Technology and Massachusetts Institute of Technology, July 2001.

Two leading technical-learning centers say "unsound technology" undermined the accuracy of both casting and recounting ballots in Florida in 2000.

Clement, Marshall, and Nina Keough, "Political Punishment: The Consequences of Felon Disenfranchisement for Rhode Island Communities," Rhode Island Family Life Center, September 2004.

While many Southern states suspend the voting rights of convicted felons, Rhode Island is the only state in New England to do so for the duration of the prisoner's sentence.

Election Reform Information Project, "The Business of Elections," Election Reform Briefing, August 2004.

A nonpartisan group says electronic voting machines may be vulnerable to technical failure and intentional ballot manipulation.

National Commission on Federal Election Reform, "To Assure Pride and Confidence in the Electoral Process," August 2001.

A bipartisan commission headed by former Presidents Jimmy Carter and Gerald R. Ford examined the flaws in the 2000 election process and issued recommendations for change, some of which were incorporated in the Help America Vote Act.

People for the American Way Foundation and National Association for the Advancement of Colored People (NAACP), "The Long Shadow of Jim Crow: Voter Intimidation and Suppression in America Today," 2004.

Deliberate efforts to keep members of minority communities from the polls continue. While neither major political party can claim innocence, most recent instances of intimidation have been linked to the Republican Party.

U.S. Commission on Civil Rights, "Is America Ready to Vote?" April 2004.

The commission cites numerous reports of voter intimidation during the current presidential campaign.

The Next Step:

Additional Articles from Current Periodicals

Electronic Voting

Dugger, Ronnie, "How They Could Steal the Election This Time," *The Nation*, Aug. 16, 2004, p. 11.

Some fear that millions of voters will be sending their votes into computers that programmers, working for private corporations and election officials, could use to invisibly falsify the outcomes.

Keating, Dan, "Electronic Voting Raises New Issues," *The Washington Post*, Oct. 25, 2004, p. A6.

Electronic voting systems were advertised as the solution to the "hanging chads" of the 2000 election in Florida, but they have become a new source of controversy as experts debate software reliability, recount possibilities and the competence of local election officials.

Palast, Greg, "Vanishing Votes," *The Nation*, May 17, 2004, p. 20.

The Help America Vote Act (HAVA) stresses reform through complex computerization and does not address — in fact, worsens — the racial bias of the uncounted vote.

Zeller, Tom, "Ready or Not (and Maybe Not), Electronic Voting Goes National," *The New York Times*, Sept. 19, 2004, Sect. 1, p. 1.

Weeks before the first election in which touch-screen voting will play a major role, specialists agree that questions remain about the technology's readiness, but it is too late to make changes.

Florida Fallout

Goodnough, Abby, "In Palm Beach, Results of 2000 Still Stir a Fight," *The New York Times*, Aug. 28, 2004, p. A1.

Four years after the infamous "butterfly ballot," election officials in Palm Beach County are determined things will run smoothly in 2004.

Goodnough, Abby, "Reassurance for the Florida Voters Made Wary by the Electoral Chaos of 2000," *The New York Times*, May 24, 2004, p. A1.

Florida's 27 electoral votes could be crucial to the presidential victor once again, prompting a movement in poor, black communities to register, educate and reassure.

Rosen, Jeffrey, "Rematch," *The New Republic*, Oct. 4, 2004, p. 17.

Bush v. Gore has emboldened political candidates to challenge election procedures and create Democratic and GOP legal swat teams.

Wildermuth, John, "Parties Anticipate Chaotic Election," *The San Francisco Chronicle*, Sept. 18, 2004, p. A1.

Lingering bitterness from Florida's 2000 vote could explode into Election Day chaos, triggering preparation by both parties to fight the battle again, anywhere in the country.

Help America Vote Act (HAVA)

Cannon, Angie, "Election Chaos?" *U.S. News & World Report*, Sept. 27, 2004, p. 30.

HAVA offered nearly $4 billion for states to replace equipment, improve poll-worker training and create registration databases, but reforms have been slow and have created confusion.

Fessenden, Ford, "A Rule to Avert Balloting Woes Adds to Them," *The New York Times*, Aug. 6, 2004, p. A1.

Provisional voting, the centerpiece of the 2002 Help America Vote Act, goes into effect this year to ensure more votes are counted.

Pear, Robert, "Congress Passes Bill to Clean Up Election System," *The New York Times*, Oct. 17, 2002, p. A1.

Congress passes the HAVA bill, calling for a major expansion of the federal role in regulating voter registration and conducting elections, but states keep the primary responsibility.

Minority Groups

"Black Voters in Florida Deserve Some Real Answers," *USA Today*, Jan. 11, 2001, p. 14A.

Probes into how the black vote was handled in Florida's 2000 election should carry one goal: Never again should minorities believe they were denied the right to vote.

Bardach, Ann Louise, "How Florida Republicans Keep Blacks From Voting," *Los Angeles Times*, Sept. 26, 2004, p. M3.

Since 92 percent of blacks voted for Al Gore in 2000, the state is abuzz with suspicions about how Gov. Jeb Bush will limit the effect of black voters this November.

Dwyer, Jim, "Among Black Voters, a Fervor To Make Their Ballots Count," *The New York Times*, Oct. 11, 2004, p. A1.

African-Americans are speaking about the act of voting with renewed passion, still angry about disqualified ballots and the contentious outcome of the 2000 election.

Glanton, Dahleen, "Florida's Ex-Convicts Seek Right to Vote," *Chicago Tribune*, July 20, 2004, Zone CN, p. 10.

Florida requires most former inmates to appear before the governor to regain their right to vote, a fact critics say is a Republican effort to sway the presidential election.

Hayes, Stephen, "The Democrats' Race Conspiracy Theory," *The Daily Standard*, Nov. 6, 2002.
Terry McAuliffe, head of the Democratic National Committee, has suggested Republicans try to intimidate minority voters, but scant evidence exists to support the claim.

Judis, John, "Soft Sell," *The New Republic*, Nov. 11, 2002, p. 12.
Republicans try to convince blacks not to vote by spreading cynicism about white Democrats and subtly intimidating black voters with dubious charges of election fraud.

O'Connor, Anne-Marie, "Getting Every Vote Counted," *Los Angeles Times*, July 27, 2004, p. E1.
The Mississippi Freedom delegation fought for voting rights for black Americans 40 years ago, but many people still see more to do before all voters are treated equally.

Vedantam, Shankar, "Dementia and the Voter; Research Raises Ethical, Constitutional Questions," *The Washington Post*, Sept. 14, 2004, p. A1.
As swing states with large elderly populations get ready for another presidential election, two studies show that many people with advanced dementia are still voting.

Vote Fraud

Dionne Jr., E. J., "An Election Day Nightmare," *The Washington Post*, Nov. 5, 2002, p. A25.
Republicans claim Democratic efforts to register supporters are tainted by illegality, and Democrats retort that Republicans engage in intimidation and suppression to hold down minority turnout.

La Ganga, Maria, "Election Day Becomes 'Just the Last Day to Vote,' " *Los Angeles Times*, Sept. 26, 2004, p. A33.
More than 70 percent of voters can cast their ballots early this year, leading some to believe that the process could increase fraud or voter intimidation.

Moss, Michael, "Absentee Votes Worry Officials As Nov. 2 Nears," *The New York Times*, Sept. 13, 2004, p. A1.
As both major political parties promote absentee balloting, election officials say they are struggling to cope with coercive tactics and fraudulent vote-gathering involving absentee ballots.

Vote Fraud Prevention

Becker, Jo, and Dan Eggen, "Voter Probes Raise Partisan Suspicions," *The Washington Post*, Sept. 20, 2004, p. A5.
Attorney General John Ashcroft launched several inquiries into alleged voter fraud in key presidential battlegrounds, putting the Justice Department in the middle of a debate over when aggressive fraud enforcement becomes intimidation.

Britt, Donna, "Ensuring That Voting's Sanctity Wins Out," *The Washington Post*, Oct. 1, 2004, p. B1.
Thousands have volunteered to be poll watchers through the nonpartisan Election Protection Coalition.

Getter, Lisa, "Major Parties Already Honing Recount Strategy," *Los Angeles Times*, Oct. 3, 2004, p. A23.
Both major presidential campaigns are lining up thousands of lawyers in case the election is too close to call again, and Democratic lawyers are filing lawsuits over election policies they believe will disenfranchise voters.

Halbfinger, David, "Kerry Building Legal Network For Vote Fights," *The New York Times*, July 19, 2004, p. A1.
John Kerry's campaign has set up a nationwide legal network under its own umbrella, rather than relying on lawyers associated with state Democratic parties.

Moss, Michael, "Big G.O.P. Bid to Challenge Voters at Polls in Key State," *The New York Times*, Oct. 23, 2004, p. A1.
GOP officials in the hotly contested swing state of Ohio have hired 3,600 volunteers to monitor the election at polling places on Nov. 2 to help weed out ineligible voters.

Citing *The CQ Researcher*

Sample formats for citing these reports in a bibliography include the ones listed below. Preferred styles and formats vary, so please check with your instructor or professor.

MLA Style

Jost, Kenneth. "Rethinking the Death Penalty." The CQ Researcher 16 Nov. 2001: 945-68.

APA Style

Jost, K. (2001, November 16). Rethinking the death penalty. *The CQ Researcher, 11*, 945-968.

Chicago Style

Jost, Kenneth. "Rethinking the Death Penalty." *CQ Researcher*, November 16, 2001, 945-968.

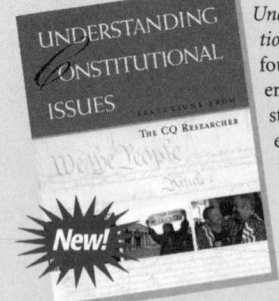

CQ Researcher

Published by CQ Press, a division of Congressional Quarterly Inc.

thecqresearcher.com

Sentencing Debates

Are the federal guidelines unconstitutional?

The Supreme Court has cast doubt on the constitutionality of the federal sentencing guidelines used for nearly two decades. Congress created the complex system to eliminate disparities and increase certainty in sentencing federal defendants. The system requires judges to apply detailed numerical guidelines to calculate individual sentences, often based on new information never presented to the jury. Federal judges and defense lawyers have long complained that the procedures are too rigid and the sentences too harsh. But several recent Supreme Court decisions in state cases have required that juries, not judges, decide factual issues needed to raise or lower a defendant's sentence. The justices are now considering whether the same rule applies to the federal guidelines. A decision to throw out the guidelines could prompt Congress to step in with even tougher sentencing policies. The justices are also considering the constitutionality of imposing the death penalty on 16- and 17-year-olds — a practice some argue is "cruel and unusual punishment" prohibited by the Eighth Amendment.

The U.S. Supreme Court overturned Ralph Blakely's kidnapping sentence in Washington state in June 2004, ruling that the state's sentencing system was unconstitutional.

INSIDE THIS REPORT

The CQ Researcher • Nov. 5, 2004 • www.thecqresearcher.com
Volume 14, Number 39 • Pages 925-948

CQ PRESS

RECIPIENT OF SOCIETY OF PROFESSIONAL JOURNALISTS AWARD FOR EXCELLENCE ◆ AMERICAN BAR ASSOCIATION SILVER GAVEL AWARD

SENTENCING DEBATES

Cover: The U.S. Supreme Court overturned Ralph Blakely's kidnapping sentence in Washington state in June 2004, ruling that the state's sentencing system was unconstitutional. The court held that a state judge had improperly bypassed the jury in increasing Blakely's sentence because he had committed the offense with "deliberate cruelty."

THE *CQ Researcher*

Nov. 5, 2004
Volume 14, Number 39

MANAGING EDITOR: Thomas J. Colin

ASSISTANT MANAGING EDITOR: Kathy Koch

ASSOCIATE EDITOR: Kenneth Jost

STAFF WRITERS: Mary H. Cooper, William Triplett

CONTRIBUTING WRITERS: Sarah Glazer, David Hatch, David Hosansky, Patrick Marshall, Tom Price, Jane Tanner

DESIGN/PRODUCTION EDITOR: Olu B. Davis

ASSISTANT EDITOR: Kate Templin

CQ PRESS

A Division of Congressional Quarterly Inc.

SENIOR VICE PRESIDENT/GENERAL MANAGER: John A. Jenkins

DIRECTOR, LIBRARY PUBLISHING: Kathryn C. Suárez

DIRECTOR, EDITORIAL OPERATIONS: Ann Davies

CONGRESSIONAL QUARTERLY INC.

CHAIRMAN: Paul C. Tash

VICE CHAIRMAN: Andrew P. Corty

PRESIDENT AND PUBLISHER: Robert W. Merry

The CQ Researcher (ISSN 1056-2036) is printed on acid-free paper. Published weekly, except Jan. 2, April 9, July 2, July 9, Aug. 6, Aug. 13, Nov. 26 and Dec. 31, by CQ Press, a division of Congressional Quarterly Inc. Annual subscription rates for institutions start at $625. For pricing, call 1-800-834-9020, ext. 1906. To purchase a *CQ Researcher* report in print or electronic format (PDF), visit www.cqpress.com or call 866-427-7737. A single report is $10. Bulk purchase discounts and electronic-rights licensing are also available. Periodicals postage paid at Washington, D.C., and additional mailing offices. POSTMASTER: Send address changes to *The CQ Researcher*, 1255 22nd St., N.W., Suite 400, Washington, D.C. 20037.

Sentencing Debates

BY KENNETH JOST

THE ISSUES

Freddie Booker was caught almost red-handed after a $90 drug deal in Beloit, Wis., and sentenced to 30 years in prison after a two-day trial that drew little attention locally and no notice elsewhere. But now the U.S. Supreme Court may use Booker's case to dismantle the complex and controversial system of federal sentencing guidelines created two decades ago.

A big part of Booker's prison sentence — more than eight years — was based on findings made by the federal judge who heard his case, not by the jury. Christopher Kelly, Booker's court-appointed lawyer, says judicial fact-finding, which is mandated by the guidelines, violates defendants' constitutional rights to a jury trial under the Sixth Amendment.

AP Photo/Missouri Department of Corrections

Christopher Simmons was sentenced to death for a gruesome murder he committed when he was 17. Now the Supreme Court is considering Simmons' case to decide whether executing 16- and 17-year-olds is "cruel and unusual punishment" prohibited by the Constitution. Simmons is one of 72 death row inmates facing execution for crimes committed at age 16 or 17. The court is also weighing the constitutionality of the controversial federal sentencing guidelines, which federal judges and defense lawyers say produce overly harsh sentences.

"It undermines the right to a jury trial," Kelly says. "It allows a judge to decide what facts determine a punishment when it's historically been a jury's job to do that."

Government lawyers, however, defend the guidelines system as an effort to regularize criminal sentencing while relying on what they say is a tradition of broad judicial discretion in setting prison terms.

"Legally and historically, judges have done post-verdict fact-finding forever," says Deborah Rhode, counselor to the head of the Justice Department's criminal division. "The concept is not new."

Nevertheless, the Supreme Court threw the constitutionality of the federal sentencing scheme into doubt in June 2004, when it struck down a somewhat comparable system in Washington state. In that decision (*Blakely v. Washington*), a 5-4 majority held that a state judge had improperly increased the sentence of defendant Ralph Blakely in a kidnapping case by finding — after Blakely's guilty plea — that he had committed the offense with "deliberate cruelty." [1]

Washington's law, like systems adopted in many other states since the 1980s, gave state judges power to increase or "enhance" a defendant's sentence based on specific factors. However, writing for the majority in Blakely's case, Justice Antonin Scalia said the procedure was constitutionally defective. "When a judge inflicts punishment that the jury's verdict alone does not allow," Scalia wrote, "the judge exceeds his proper authority."

The federal guidelines, in use since 1987, give federal judges detailed instructions for calculating a defendant's sentence after a jury verdict or guilty plea. [2] Booker's trial and sentencing in September and December 2003 provide a typical example of the guidelines in operation.

Police in Beloit arrested Booker on Feb. 26, 2003, after responding to a reported trespass at a vacant house. The officers found a friend of Booker's leaving the house, with a mouthful of crack cocaine. Moments later, Booker came around the corner.

Booker's friend told police he had bought the cocaine from Booker. Booker — who had been out of prison for only a few months after serving four years for a state drug conviction — claimed he had come to collect money on a loan. But inside the house, police found a satchel belonging to Booker containing 92.5 grams (about three ounces) of cocaine.

Booker admitted to police that he had sold his friend "an eight-ball" for $90 — and that he had also sold about 20 ounces of cocaine in the previous month. But during the trial Booker insisted he had been joking with the officers when he confessed. A federal court jury convicted Booker of possession with intent to distribute at least 50 grams of cocaine. Because of his previous conviction, the offense was punishable by a prison term of 20 to 22 years.

U.S. District Judge John Shabaz then applied the federal guidelines to raise the sentence to 30 years after finding that Booker had sold the additional cocaine not charged in the indictment and that he had lied on the witness stand. The guidelines generally require judges to consider all "relevant conduct" — even if the evidence was not considered by the jury.

U.S. Attorney J. B. van Hollen, whose office prosecuted the case, says Booker's sentence is fair. "He's proven, based on his activity and his prior criminal history, that the only way that society can be protected from him at this juncture is for him to be incarcerated for that period," van Hollen says.

The federal prosecutor also believes the guidelines are constitutional, but adds, "I will not be surprised if the Supreme Court decides otherwise."

For their part, defense lawyers criticize the guidelines for taking factual issues out of the jury's hands and simultaneously dictating to judges how to calculate a defendant's sentence. "We're taking away virtually all of their discretion," says David Porter, a federal defender in Sacramento, Calif., and coauthor of a friend-of-the-court brief in Booker's case submitted by the National Association of Criminal Defense Lawyers. "That's a terrible, terrible mistake."

Many academic experts agree. "It is a system that has a lot of injustices built into it," says Douglas Berman, a law professor at Ohio State University in Columbus.

Kate Stith, a Yale University law professor, calls the guidelines "too complicated, too severe and too arbitrary."

Justice Department lawyers, on the other hand, support the system. Rhode says the guidelines result in "individualized sentencing — individually tailored defendant by defendant, case by case." The government vigorously defended the constitutionality of the guidelines before the Supreme Court in Booker's case and in a second drug case from Maine. In that case, a federal district court judge — citing *Blakely* — sentenced Ducan Fanfan to 78 months' imprisonment for conspiracy to distribute cocaine instead of a guideline-calculated sentence of 188-235 months — more than twice as long.

Outside the Justice Department, the guidelines appear to have few unconditional supporters. "The guidelines badly

How the Sentencing Guidelines Work

Judges calculate defendants' sentences in federal court using a complex, 258-square grid (at right) and a series of possible sentence adjustments. On the vertical axis, crimes are assigned to an Offense Level from 1 to 43 based on the severity of the offense; on the horizontal axis, a defendant is placed in one of six Criminal History Categories mainly based on prior convictions. Zones indicate the confinement alternatives judges have for the offenses in that zone, such as weekend detention. Zone A has the most flexibility; Zone D requires prison.

Here's how the guidelines might be used to calculate the sentence for a defendant who pleaded guilty in a telemarketing scam in which 40 people lost a total of $80,000. He had two prior criminal offenses and assisted law enforcement in prosecuting others.

Factors to consider	Calculation of sentence
Step 1: Determine Offense Level (from 1 to 43)	Offense Level 7: 0-6 mos.
Step 2: Determine presence of aggravating or mitigating circumstances ("specific offense characteristics").	• Loss of > $70,000: Increases Offense Level by 8, to Level 15. 10 or more victims: Increases Offense Level by 2, to Level 17.
Step 3: Apply adjustments for factors such as victim's status, offender's role or acceptance of responsibility.	Accepted responsibility: Reduces Offense Level by 2, back to Level 15.
Step 4: Determine "Criminal History Category" (from 1 to 6).	Two prior offenses: Category III.
Step 5: Locate presumed sentencing range on grid (intersection of final offense number with Criminal History Category).	Offense Level 15, Criminal History Category 3: 24-30 mos. (Shaded in table)
Step 6: Decide whether any options concerning probation, incarceration, supervision, fines or restitution apply.	Ineligible for probation (Zone D); restitution ordered; fine permitted, $3,000-$30,000.
Step 7: Determine whether a "departure" is warranted for offender's assistance to law enforcement or for aggravating or mitigating factors "not adequately taken into consideration by Sentencing Commission."	Judge makes "downward departure" of 9 months for "substantial assistance" to law enforcement, reducing the sentence range to 15-21 months.

Sources: Arthur W. Campbell, The Law of Sentencing *(2d ed.), 1991; Thomas W. Hutchison* et al., Federal Sentencing Law and Practice, *2004.*

Sentencing Table
(in months of imprisonment)

Zone	Offense Level	Criminal History Category I (0 or 1)	II (2 or 3)	III (4, 5, 6)	IV (7, 8, 9)	V (10, 11, 12)	VI (13 or more)
A	1	0-6	0-6	0-6	0-6	0-6	0-6
A	2	0-6	0-6	0-6	0-6	0-6	1-7
A	3	0-6	0-6	0-6	0-6	2-8	3-9
A	4	0-6	0-6	0-6	2-8	4-10	6-12
A	5	0-6	0-6	1-7	4-10	6-12	9-15
A	6	0-6	1-7	2-8	6-12	9-15	12-18
A	7	0-6	2-8	4-10	8-14	12-18	15-21
A	8	0-6	4-10	6-12	10-16	15-21	18-24
B	9	4-10	6-12	8-14	12-18	18-24	21-27
B	10	6-12	8-14	10-16	15-21	21-27	24-30
C	11	8-14	10-16	12-18	18-24	24-30	27-33
C	12	10-16	12-18	15-21	21-27	27-33	30-37
D	13	12-18	15-21	18-24	24-30	30-37	33-41
D	14	15-21	18-24	21-27	27-33	33-41	37-46
D	15	18-24	21-27	**24-30**	30-37	37-46	41-51
D	16	21-27	24-30	27-33	33-41	41-51	46-57
D	17	24-30	27-33	30-37	37-46	46-57	51-63
D	18	27-33	30-37	33-41	41-51	51-63	57-71
D	19	30-37	33-41	37-46	46-57	57-71	63-78
D	20	33-41	37-46	41-51	51-63	63-78	70-87
D	21	37-46	41-51	46-57	57-71	70-87	77-96
D	22	41-51	46-57	51-63	63-78	77-96	84-105
D	23	46-57	51-63	57-71	70-87	84-105	92-115
D	24	51-63	57-71	63-78	77-96	92-115	100-125
D	25	57-71	63-78	70-87	84-105	100-125	110-137
D	26	63-78	70-87	78-97	92-115	110-137	120-150
D	27	70-87	78-97	87-108	100-125	120-150	130-162
D	28	78-97	87-108	97-121	110-137	130-162	140-175
D	29	87-108	97-121	108-135	121-151	140-175	151-188
D	30	97-121	108-135	121-151	135-168	151-188	168-210
D	31	108-135	121-151	135-168	151-188	168-210	188-235
D	32	121-151	135-168	151-188	168-210	188-235	210-262
D	33	135-168	151-188	168-210	188-235	210-262	235-293
D	34	151-188	168-210	188-235	210-262	235-293	262-327
D	35	168-210	188-235	210-262	235-293	262-327	292-365
D	36	188-235	210-262	235-293	262-327	292-365	324-405
D	37	210-262	235-293	262-327	292-365	324-405	360-life
D	38	235-293	262-327	292-365	324-405	360-life	360-life
D	39	262-327	292-365	324-405	360-life	360-life	360-life
D	40	292-365	324-405	360-life	360-life	360-life	360-life
D	41	324-405	360-life	360-life	360-life	360-life	360-life
D	42	360-life	360-life	360-life	360-life	360-life	360-life
D	43	life	life	life	life	life	life

need shaking up," says Frank Bowman, a professor at Indiana University School of Law and a former federal prosecutor who describes himself as a "longtime supporter."

While disputing some of the criticisms of the guidelines' length and complexity, Bowman agrees with critics that they have given prosecutors growing control over sentencing. He also says Congress has shown "a persistent and growing tendency to micro-manage" the work of the seven-member U.S. Sentencing Commission, established in 1984 to write the guidelines. [3]

Both supporters and critics, however, worry that a Supreme Court ruling against the guidelines may make federal sentencing worse, not better. "I fear the court may tear down a structure that is the only hope for rational sentencing," says Ronald Weich, a Washington, D.C., lawyer and former state prosecutor and Sentencing Commission counsel.

In particular, he and many others fear that if the guidelines are struck down, Congress will call for even more severe sentencing: longer mandatory minimums and higher maximums for many offenses. At the least, these observers say, requiring jury trials on all of the guideline factors — so-called "*Blakely*-ization" — will make federal criminal cases longer, more complex and more expensive.

Criminal defense lawyers minimize the potential burdens on federal courts. "A sentencing jury can and should be entrusted with those sentence-enhancing facts," Porter says. "There is a similar procedure for sentencing juries in death-penalty cases that's been going on for years."

As for the danger of a congressional backlash, Porter says: "I don't think we can plan our litigation strategies on what Congress will or might do," he says. "There are too many imponderables. Sixth Amendment principles are what they are."

The court's ruling also may affect sentencing schemes in a dozen or more states besides Washington. But none of the states relies on as many sentence-enhancing factors for their judicial fact-finding as the federal scheme does. "Most states don't share the magnitude of the problem that the feds have," says Daniel Wilhelm, director of the state sentencing and corrections program at the New York City-based Vera Institute of Justice.

Meanwhile, the high court has taken under advisement a second contested sentencing issue: the constitutionality of imposing the death penalty for crimes committed by 16- or 17-year-olds. [4] The issue reached the justices in a Missouri case, in which the state supreme court ruled that the execution of juvenile offenders is "cruel and unusual punishment" prohibited by the Eighth Amendment.

The U.S. Supreme Court, in successive decisions in 1988 and 1989, barred executions of anyone for offenses committed before the age of 16 but allowed the death penalty for older teens. In its ruling, the Missouri high court said there was now a "national consensus" against executing juveniles — citing a parallel to the U.S. Supreme Court's 2002 decision barring execution of mentally retarded offenders.

As judges, prosecutors and defense lawyers await the court's rulings, here are the major questions being debated:

Should federal sentencing guidelines be ruled unconstitutional?

When Congress created the U.S. Sentencing Commission in 1984, supporters worried that the new body charged with writing sentencing guidelines might be ruled unconstitutional as an improper legislative intrusion into judicial decision-making. So Congress designated the commission as a part of the judicial branch, and the Supreme Court accepted that view in upholding the law in 1989.

The constitutional issue that now threatens the federal sentencing guidelines — the right to a jury trial — was barely mentioned during the congressional debate or in subsequent debates. The issue emerged only after 1999, when a series of Supreme Court decisions began to gradually strengthen the role of juries *vis-à-vis* judges in fact-finding used to set defendants' sentences.

The Justice Department and other defenders of the guidelines say the jury-trial issue surfaced belatedly because the critics' premise — that the guidelines give judges additional powers — is simply wrong. "The guidelines do not allow judges to find facts that they could not find before," says Rhode.

In briefs before the Supreme Court, both the Justice Department and the Sentencing Commission try to differentiate between the federal scheme and the Washington state system — with guidelines imposed by statute — that was struck down in the *Blakely* decision. They rely in part on the structural argument the Supreme Court accepted in the earlier ruling. "Congress placed the commission within the judicial branch so that the judiciary would retain its traditional sentencing function," the Sentencing Commission says in its brief.

In addition, both government agencies argue the guidelines allow judges to set penalties within the maximum sentences prescribed by Congress, while the Washington system established "standard range" sentences that judges could raise based on additional fact-finding. "The guidelines do not alter the statutorily prescribed range of penalties to which a criminal defendant is exposed," the commission contends.

But lawyers for Booker and Fanfan and the criminal defense and other groups supporting them say that neither of those distinctions makes the federal guidelines constitutional. In its brief, the defense bar group says judge fact-finding to increase a defendant's sentence violates due process and jury-trial rights "whether the sentencing rules . . . were promulgated by a legislature, by courts, by an executive agency or by an independent commission."

The defense lawyers also insist that the *Blakely* principle prevents a federal judge from raising a defendant's sentence above the "base level" specified in the guidelines based on facts not presented to the jury. "If the fact is necessary to a sentence," attorney Kelly writes in his brief for Booker, "a defendant has the right to have the government prove the fact to a jury."

Yale's Stith notes that *Blakely* also requires that defendants be given notice before trial of charges that will be brought against them. Under the federal guidelines, sentencing factors are routinely introduced for the first time by prosecutors or probation officers after a jury verdict or guilty plea.

"One of the things that has always shocked me about the guidelines is that a person can plead guilty to an offense, and at his hearing no one has to say anything about other conduct," Stith says. "Then in one or two days the government can charge you with other conduct and, if the judge finds you did it, he's going to have to sentence you [to a longer term]."

Defenders of the guidelines maintain that they have partly achieved the goal of promoting greater uniformity in federal sentencing by giving judges rules for exercising discretion. "What the judge used to do in his or her mind now becomes part of a book, part of a worksheet," says Roscoe Howard, a former U.S. attorney for the District of Columbia. He says the guidelines are "clearly tolerated by the Sixth Amendment" if they are only guidelines for judges, not mandatory rules.

However, most federal judges and outside observers agree with defense lawyers that the guidelines have increasingly been applied in a mechanistic fashion. "They're a straitjacket," federal defender Porter says. One group of former federal judges has urged in a friend-of-the-court brief that the Supreme Court uphold the guidelines by stressing that they allow judges to "depart" from a prescribed sentence — either upward or downward — "in appropriate cases."

Despite disagreements about the constitutionality of the guidelines, court watchers were nearly unanimous prior to the Supreme Court arguments in predicting that the guidelines would be ruled invalid — and the justices' questions during the Oct. 4 argument appear to confirm that prediction.

Would invalidating the federal sentencing guidelines improve sentencing policies?

Three years before the *Blakely* decision, the Kansas Supreme Court ruled to the same effect that juries, not judges, must make any factual findings needed to raise a defendant's sentence above the statutory level. Defense lawyers and their supporters cite Kansas' experience since then as evidence that applying *Blakely* to the federal sentencing guidelines would not require far-reaching changes in federal court procedures.

Defenders of the guidelines, however, say that federal jury trials on all of the sentencing factors would be complicated for jurors and time-consuming and expensive for courts. They also warn that Congress is likely to respond to a Supreme Court decision invalidating the guidelines by making sentencing more severe and more rigid — fears freely acknowledged by defense lawyers as well.

In Kansas, the legislature responded to the state supreme court's ruling in May 2001 by adopting a law the next year requiring prosecutors to prove any facts needed to impose a longer sentence either in the main trial or at a separate jury proceeding. "It has not turned out to be an overly burdensome process, and in fact it's rarely used," says Wilhelm of the state sentencing and corrections program at the reformist Vera Institute of Justice. [5]

Lawyers for Booker and Fanfan in the U.S. Supreme Court cases contend nothing more is needed to "fix" the federal system if the justices rule in their favor. "Jury fact-finding is a familiar, workable system," Boston attorney Rosemary Scapicchio writes in her brief for Fanfan. "Both current and historical practice confirm the constitutional, democratic understanding that juries are fully equipped to handle complicated fact-finding."

In its arguments, however, the government says jury trials on all of the guideline factors would be "unfeasibly complex" — especially in big securities fraud and other white-collar crime cases. The "inevitable result," the government brief reads, "would be, in some cases, jury confusion and a decrease in the accuracy of jury fact-finding." Instead, the government urges the high court to rule that the guidelines are merely advisory.

The argument over what is called "*Blakely*-izing" the guidelines turns in part on a question of congressional intent: What would Congress have done if it had known that judicial fact-finding would be ruled unconstitutional? The government says that judicial sentencing using the guidelines as advisory better serves Congress' goals of uniformity and proportionality than jury fact-finding would.

Lawyers for Booker and Fanfan disagree. "Congress did not intend judges to impose wholly discretionary sentences," Kelly writes.

The dispute over past congressional intent may become moot, however, if Congress responds to a Supreme Court decision as expected by revising the sentencing system itself. "Whatever happens to the guidelines, whatever happens to the commission, it's clear that Congress is going to remain in control of sentencing," says the Justice Department's Rhode.

Congressional intervention is especially likely if, as defense lawyers hope, a Supreme Court-mandated shift to jury fact-finding under the guidelines results — or is seen as likely to result — in lower sentences. "There will be fewer enhancements under that system," Porter says. "But that is perfectly consonant with how our criminal-justice system is supposed to work."

Observers generally think Congress would respond by raising federal sentences further. In the past decade Congress has passed some 70 provisions aimed at increasing federal sentences — most recently, in a 2003 amendment requiring the Justice Department to report to Congress when a judge hands down a sentence that is lower than recommended in the guidelines. [6]

"It's quite possible that this will backfire on [defense lawyers]," says Kent Scheidegger, legal director for the California-based Criminal Justice Legal Foundation, which frequently files pro-law enforcement briefs before the Supreme Court.

Bowman, in a law journal article completed not long after the *Blakely* ruling, forecast three possible responses by Congress to a similar ruling on the federal system. [7] One option he calls "topless guidelines" — eliminating the tops of the current ranges on the sentencing table and substituting the statutory maximum for the offense. A second possibility — "guidelines turned upside down" — would apply the maximum statutory sentence to any offense unless the defendant could prove mitigating factors. A final "fallback" position, Bowman says, would be for Congress to enact more mandatory minimum sentences for federal offenses.

"I don't think Congress has proven itself either responsible or wise in terms of the things it has done in the sentencing arena," says Nora V. Demleitner, a professor at Hofstra University School of Law, Hempstead, N.Y.

John Martin, a New York lawyer who served as a federal judge from 1990 to 1993 agrees. "Nothing Congress has done in the last 10 years suggests that they're going to make anything better."

Juvenile Killers Face Execution in 19 States

The Supreme Court is considering whether juveniles ages 16 or 17 should face the death penalty. Nineteen states now permit executions of older teens. The issue reached the justices in a Missouri case, in which the state supreme court ruled that the execution of older juvenile offenders is "cruel and unusual punishment" prohibited by the Eighth Amendment. The Missouri court said there was now a "national consensus" against executing juveniles. U.S. Supreme Court rulings currently bar executions for offenses committed before age 16 but allow the death penalty for teens 16 and 17.

Minimum Death Penalty Ages in the States

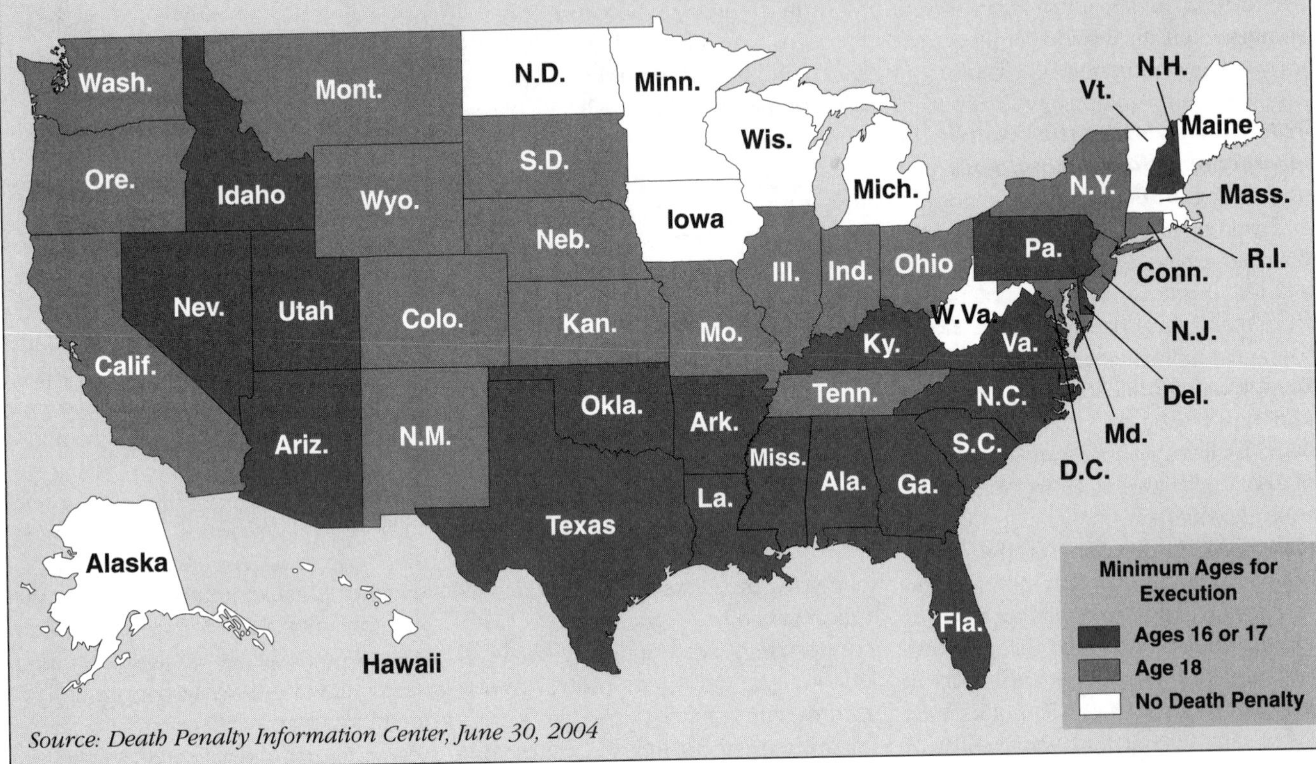

Source: Death Penalty Information Center, June 30, 2004

But Berman of Ohio State University says the fear of congressional reaction should not deter the Supreme Court from striking down the guidelines system in its present form. "That's a reason for trying to do something about the reaction to it, not that the principle ought not to be vindicated itself," he says.

Should the death penalty for juvenile offenders be abolished?

Christopher Simmons was sentenced to death by a St. Louis court for a gruesome murder that he helped commit in 1993, when he was 17. Now, the U.S. Supreme Court is using Simmons' case to decide whether — as four of the nine justices have already said — executing juvenile offenders is "cruel and unusual punishment" and thus prohibited by the Eighth Amendment of the Constitution.

Lawyers for Simmons and an array of medical, civil liberties and human rights groups are urging the court to rule that executing juvenile offenders is wrong because they are too immature and impulsive to be held fully responsible for capital crimes. In addition, they say that a national and international consensus has emerged against the practice, as reflected in the small number of executions of juvenile offenders in the United States and the even smaller number of other countries that permit the practice. (*See chart, p. 933.*)

But lawyers for the state of Missouri say that making the death penalty available for juveniles who commit the most heinous capital crimes serves society's interests in retribution and deterrence. They also say that any decision to outlaw the practice should be made by state legislatures, not the Supreme Court.

The high court now has the case under advisement after having heard arguments on Oct. 13. Observers say the hour-long session provides few clues about whether the four liberal justices who have already signed opinions condemning capital punishment for juvenile offenders are going to pick up the needed fifth vote from either or both of the court's swing-vote conservatives: Sandra Day O'Connor and Anthony M. Kennedy.

Simmons is one of 72 inmates in the United States facing the death penalty for crimes committed at age 16 or 17. In a pair of decisions in 1988 and 1989, the high court effectively barred the death penalty for offenses committed by anyone under the age of 16 but then upheld capital punishment for older adolescents. O'Connor, who cast the pivotal votes in the narrowly divided decisions, said in the second case that there was no "national consensus" against the death penalty for juvenile offenders but left the door open to re-examine the issue later. [8]

The St. Louis jury recommended death for Simmons after convicting him of capital murder in the abduction-drowning of an elderly woman after a home burglary. Simmons and a 16-year-old accomplice bound the woman's hands and feet and threw her from a bridge into a river in a state park. The trial included testimony — disputed by Simmons' lawyer — that Simmons had previously talked to friends about committing such a crime and assured them that as juveniles they could "get away with it."

Whether true or not, opponents of the death penalty for juveniles say Simmons' purported statement exemplifies the undeveloped reasoning and judgment common among adolescents. "They don't appreciate the consequences of their conduct," says Marsha Levick, legal director of the Juvenile Law Center in Philadelphia, which filed a brief in support of Simmons' plea. The brief cites new studies showing that adolescents' brains function differently from those of adults, particularly in the areas affecting reasoning, impulse control and decision-making. [9]

In a brief on the opposite side, a victims' advocacy group says juries and judges should be free to weigh such factors in individual cases. "The [Supreme Court] shouldn't group all juveniles together as a class but should recognize that they are all different with respect to their development and to their moral culpability," says Dan Cutrer, a Houston attorney who authored the brief for the group Justice for All. "The trial court should have the option to look very closely at whether the perpetrator is of sufficient age, maturity and judgment that they could no longer be considered as a child."

Opponents, however, say juries are hampered in making such judgments because the offender is always older by the time his case comes to trial. In addition, they say, prosecutors often point to a defendant's youth as an aggravating factor: evidence of extreme violence or dangerousness warranting the death penalty.

The opposing sides in the case also disagree about what may be the pivotal issue: whether there is a national consensus against executing juvenile offenders. In 2002, the court reversed a 1989 decision and barred execution of mentally retarded offenders after finding a national consensus against the practice. The ruling in *Atkins v. Virginia* emphasized that most states did

Death Rows Hold 72 Juvenile Offenders

Texas leads the nation in both the number of juvenile offenders on death row and the number who have been executed since 1976.

Juvenile Offenders on Death Row or Executed * (1976-2004)

State	On Death Row	Executed
Texas	29	13
Alabama	14	0
Mississippi	5	0
Arizona	4	0
Louisiana	4	0
North Carolina	4	1
Florida	3	0
South Carolina	3	1
Georgia	2	1
Pennsylvania	2	0
Virginia	1	3
Nevada	1	0
Oklahoma	0	2
Missouri	0	1
Total	72	22

** Execution data through April 1, 2004; Death Row data through Sept. 30, 2004*

Source: Death Penalty Information Center, Oct. 20, 2004

not permit execution of mentally retarded offenders: 12 states had no death penalty and 18 others exempted the mentally retarded. [10]

Lawyers for Simmons perform a similar count today. They say that 31 states — including 12 with no death penalty — do not allow capital punishment for juvenile offenders. Moreover, they say that death sentences for juvenile offenders are rare and actual executions even rarer. In the past 10 years, only three states — Texas, Virginia and Oklahoma — have executed inmates for crimes committed under age 18. Representing Simmons, former U.S. Solicitor General Seth Waxman told the justices the evidence showed "a substantial consensus" against executing juvenile offenders.

In its arguments, however, Missouri emphasizes that only a few states have raised the age limit for the death penalty since 1989 and that several have specifically reaffirmed making 16- and 17-year-olds subject to capital punishment. Most broadly, the state's lawyers insist the question is "a political question" for legislatures, not the courts. "Legislatures and juries are capable of evaluating these things and deciding for themselves," Missouri State Solicitor James R. Layton told the court. ■

BACKGROUND

Judges' Discretion

Judicial discretion in sentencing has been a fundamental part of the federal criminal-justice system and most state systems for most of U.S. history. The broad leeway given to judges — and, later, to parole boards — reflected the optimistic goal of tailoring punishment to individual offenders, in part to promote their rehabilitation into society after imprisonment. The system — or non-system, as one influential critic called it — came under sharp attack by the 1970s for what liberals viewed as its wide disparities and what conservatives regarded as its excessive leniency. The dual lines of criticism resulted in passage of guideline systems aimed at producing greater uniformity and certainty in criminal sentencing. [11]

The earliest criminal statutes passed by Congress established the pattern for the federal system that prevailed into the late 20th century. Judges had responsibility for sentencing and could impose fines and/or prison terms up to the statutory maximum. For most federal offenses, no minimum term was specified. And until the 20th century, federal appeals courts had virtually no power to reverse a sentencing decision.

In the states, juries often played a role in sentencing, but judicial sentencing gradually became the norm. And state judges typically had broad leeway in sentencing.

A new system of executive branch discretion — parole — was laid over the state and federal criminal-justice systems in the late 19th and early 20th centuries. Beginning with New York in 1881, states enacted so-called indeterminate sentencing laws that called for judges to commit defendants to the custody of correctional authorities and gave prison officials or parole boards power to determine the time an inmate actually served, within the statutory maximum. Congress introduced parole into the federal system in 1910 while preserving most judicial discretion. The legislation specified that inmates could not be released before serving one-third of their nominal sentences unless the judge specified immediate parole eligibility.

State laws also gave judges the power to suspend a defendant's sentence — or to reimpose the suspended sentence later if conditions of probation were not met. The Supreme Court in 1916 ruled that federal judges had no power to suspend a minimum sentence, but Congress in 1925 passed the National Probation Act to restore that authority.

Indeterminate sentencing prevailed in state and federal systems until two separate lines of attack combined in the 1970s to weaken both its theoretical rationale and its political support. One critique — found in academic articles as early as the 1920s — focused on sentencing disparities. Judges and parole boards were said to have no semblance of uniformity in trying to make the punishment fit the crime. In their account, Yale's Stith and federal appeals court Judge José Cabranes explain that some experts attributed the discrepancies to the backgrounds and personalities of individual judges, while others saw systemic biases on the basis of race, income, education or other factors. Both groups, however, "shared the view that illegitimate considerations were influencing the exercise of judicial discretion." [12]

This critique gained prominence and influence with the 1973 book *Criminal Sentences: Law Without Order*, by a highly respected federal judge, Marvin Frankel. Frankel argued that federal judges varied greatly in skills and temperament and that their broad sentencing discretion resulted in "arbitrary cruelties perpetrated daily." He proposed an alternative approach: an administrative sentencing commission that would develop "a detailed chart or calculus" to be used in determining an individual sentence — relying "wherever possible, on some form of numerical or other objective grading." [13]

Meanwhile, an anti-crime backlash — fostered by rising crime rates and controversial Supreme Court criminal-law rulings of the 1960s — focused on the perceived leniency of judicial sentencing and parole board decision-making. Retribution had, in fact, long taken second place to rehabilitation as the dominant goal of sentencing among penologists and criminologists. From the 1950s through the advent of the federal sen-

Continued on p. 936

Chronology

Before 1960

Judges in federal and state systems generally have broad discretion in sentencing criminal defendants.

1960s-1970s

Calls for sentencing reform: Liberals seek to reduce disparities; conservatives want to provide certainty, check "leniency" by judges, parole boards.

1973

Federal Judge Marvin Frankel, in *Criminal Sentences: Law Without Order*, criticizes "almost wholly unchecked" power given to judges in sentencing decisions; calls for creation of sentencing commission to devise numerical guidelines.

1975

Sen. Edward M. Kennedy, D-Mass., introduces first in a series of bills to create federal sentencing guidelines; enlists support from key conservative senators.

1980s

Congress creates sentencing guidelines system for federal courts; sentencing reform advances in states, with similar plans adopted in many.

1984

President Ronald Reagan signs Sentencing Reform Act, which calls for creation of seven-member commission to write sentencing guidelines for federal judges. . . . Reagan's appointees to commission have conservative cast.

1987

U.S. Sentencing Commission issues federal sentencing guidelines, effective Nov. 1, which draw from existing sentencing patterns but raise penalties for drug, white-collar offenses; rules also suggest judges consider all "relevant conduct" by defendants in calculating sentences.

1988

Supreme Court effectively bars execution for crimes committed by juveniles 15 or under.

1989

Supreme Court upholds structure of Sentencing Commission (*Mistretta v. United States*) . . . Justices later uphold executions of 16- and 17-year-olds and mentally retarded offenders.

1990s

Federal sentencing guidelines draw criticism; Congress raises penalties outlined in the guidelines by imposing mandatory minimums for drug, other offenses; Supreme Court spurns challenges to guideline procedures.

1995

Congress vetoes Sentencing Commission proposal to reduce penalties for use of crack cocaine — used more among minority populations than powdered cocaine; critics said lesser penalties for powdered cocaine resulted in harsher treatment for black defendants.

1999

Supreme Court, in little-noticed decision affecting federal carjacking law, limits judges' power to raise sentences.

2000-Present

Supreme Court decisions strengthening power of juries vis-à-vis judges cast doubt on state, federal sentencing guideline systems.

2000

Supreme Court ruling on a New Jersey hate-crime law requires that a jury find, beyond a reasonable doubt, any fact needed to raise defendant's sentence above statutory maximum (*Apprendi v. New Jersey*); potential impact of decision not immediately recognized.

2002

Supreme Court extends *Apprendi* decision to require jury role for any fact necessary to impose death penalty (*Ring v. Arizona*). Separately, justices bar execution of mentally retarded offenders.

2003

Congress passes and President Bush signs bill limiting federal judges' ability to impose lighter sentences than those dictated by guidelines for crimes against children.

2004

Supreme Court, in 5-4 decision, extends jury trial right to sentencing factors in Washington state's guideline system (*Blakely v. Washington*); June 24 ruling immediately casts doubt on federal scheme. . . . Justices on Aug. 2 agree to review two federal cases to resolve issue (*United States v. Booker*, *United States v. Fanfan*); hear arguments on first day of new term, Oct. 4. . . . Constitutionality of death penalty for juvenile offenders argued before justices in Missouri case on Oct. 13 (*Roper v. Simmons*). . . . California voters retain tough "three-strikes" law.

Mandatory Minimums Hit Non-violent First-timers

Tammi Bloom, a nurse and mother of two from Miami, says she had no idea her husband of 15 years, Ronald, was having an affair. Or that he and his mistress were distributing cocaine.

After Ronald and his mistress were arrested on federal charges in Ocala, Fla. — about 250 miles away — police searched the Blooms' Miami home and found cocaine, three firearms and a drug ledger hidden in the backyard. A confidential informant countered Tammi Bloom's claims of innocence, saying he had witnessed her participation in a drug deal.

Tammi was held accountable for the drugs found at her home and sold by Ronald in Miami, and in 1999, because of mandatory minimum sentencing, she was sent to prison for almost 20 years — two more than her husband and 13 more than his mistress. While Bloom's level of involvement in the drug scheme remains disputed, her status as a first-time, non-violent offender is not. But mandatory-sentencing policies prevented her judge from giving her a lesser and — many would argue — more just sentence.

Federal mandatory minimum sentencing laws have been beefed up and expanded since the late 1980s, when lawmakers faced what many described as a nationwide, crack cocaine-related crime wave. The laws were designed to target the most violent drug offenders and to catch people high on the drug-distribution food chain. Although meted out at both the state and federal levels, mandatory minimum sentences have been most contentious at the federal level because of successive congressional actions increasing mandatory penalties for federal crimes, especially for drug offenses.

"Drug trafficking is an evil, and criminal law enforcement — including the imposition of significant prison sentences in appropriate cases — plays a vital role in combating that evil," Indiana University law Professor Frank Bowman told the House Judiciary Subcommittee on Crime, Terrorism and Homeland Security in July. [1]

In practice, however, the laws have clogged the country's prisons with addicts and low-level and first-time offenders like Bloom, but few drug kingpins, says Monica Pratt, director of communications for Families Against Mandatory Minimums. State and federal prisons now hold 2 million inmates — twice as many as 15 years ago, according to the Department of Justice. [2] Fifty-four percent of the federal inmates are serving time for drug-related crimes, according to the Bureau of Prisons, and 58 percent are non-violent, first-time offenders. [3]

"Mandatory minimums are perhaps a good example of the law of unintended consequences," said Chief Justice William H. Rehnquist. "There is a respectable body of opinion [that] believes mandatory minimums impose unduly harsh punishment for first-time offenders — particularly for 'mules' who played only a minor role in a drug-distribution scheme." [4]

Others besides Rehnquist question the wisdom and effectiveness of mandatory minimum policies, especially given rising prison populations and the costs of building and maintaining them. Bloom's incarceration, for example, costs taxpayers about $25,000 a year — almost what it costs to pay a Florida policeman's salary for a year.

Moreover, according to the Drug Enforcement Administration, the minimums have not affected the availability or price of drugs on the street. [5] "We have half a million non-violent drug offenders in jail, yet drugs are readily available in our community — the prices of both cocaine and heroine are at record lows, and purity is at a record high — so mandatory minimums have failed," says Bill Piper, the director of national affairs at the Drug Policy Alliance, a nonprofit organization.

Julie Stewart, president and founder of Families Against Mandatory Minimums, says that while many elected officials agree the sentencing system is flawed, most will not abandon tough-on-crime stances to push for change. "Members of Congress don't give a damn about who goes to prison," she says. "It is a win-win to be tough on crime and tough on drugs. It requires a brave and thoughtful and rational member of Congress to say, 'The system is broken, and we need to fix it to make it more fair.' There just aren't that many members of Congress who are that brave."

Indeed, some congressmen advocate increasing federal mandatory minimums. Rep. James Sensenbrenner, R-Wis., introduced a bill in June calling for tougher penalties for use of a firearm while committing a drug crime and imposing a mandatory life

Continued from p. 934

tencing guidelines in the late 1980s, nearly half of defendants sentenced in federal court received no prison time. [14]

In the states, judges and parole boards were routinely blamed for giving criminals inadequate sentences and sending prisoners back to the streets too soon. The criticism gained public support from recurrent news media accounts of violent crimes committed by paroled inmates.

Frankel's work gained the attention of Senate Judiciary Committee Chairman Edward M. Kennedy, D-Mass., who hosted a dinner for the judge and other criminal-justice experts in 1975 and later that year introduced the first in a succession of federal sentencing guidelines bills. Kennedy's bill had what Stith and Cabranes describe as "a liberal, reformist aura." Over the next decade, anti-crime lawmakers refashioned the proposal into a more conservative instrument, with less discretion for judges and more political influence on sentencing policies.

Sentencing Guidelines

The movement to establish federal sentencing guidelines began with support from both conservative and liberal forces but became more conservative at every stage: as the legislation moved through Congress, as the new U.S. Sentencing Commission wrote the initial guidelines and as Congress passed new sentencing laws after the guidelines went into effect in 1987. [15]

sentence for three-time drug offenders. The congressman said he wanted to prevent judges from trivializing serious crimes and from imposing vastly different sentences for similar crimes.

Congress tried to standardize sentencing practices nationwide in 1984, when it created the seven-member U.S. Sentencing Commission and asked it to draft federal sentencing guidelines outlining specific factors judges could consider when handing down sentences. In force since 1987, the guidelines offer judges a range of sentences — based on the nature and severity of the crime.

Families Against Mandatory Minimums

First-time offender Tammi Bloom, with her children Antuan and Taronda, is serving almost 20 years in prison.

Since then, however, some tough-on-crime lawmakers — unhappy with the way judges interpreted the guidelines — have pushed for stricter sentences by passing mandatory minimum sentences for a variety of crimes. "Opponents of mandatory minimums would have a far stronger argument if they could assure Congress that federal judges were faithfully adhering to the federal sentencing guidelines," Rep. Howard Coble, R-N.C., told the House panel during the July hearing. "Sadly, that is not always the case." [6]

No action was taken on Sensenbrenner's bill before Congress recessed this year.

Mandatory minimums also could be affected by the Supreme Court's decisions in *United States v. Booker* and *United States v. Fanfan*, which challenge the constitutionality of federal sentencing guidelines. Stewart worries that if federal sentencing guidelines are struck down, the door will be opened for Congress to impose additional and harsher mandatory minimums. "If the guidelines have the floor pulled out from under them, members of Congress could make a mandatory minimum for every federal crime du jour," she says. The Supreme Court is expected to issue an opinion about the consolidated cases as early as year's end.

With the future of mandatory minimums unclear, the more than 20,000 people whose drug-related cases will go to trial in the next 12 months will have to wait to see how their sentences will by determined.

Supreme Court Justice Anthony Kennedy, in testimony to the House Appropriations Committee in 2003, explained what he sees as the downside to mandatory minimums. "You'll have a young man, and he shouldn't be doing this, but he's raising marijuana in the woods. That makes him a distributor. And he's got his dad's hunting rifle in the car. He forgot about it, and he wants to do target practice. That makes him armed. He's looking at 15 years. An 18-year-old doesn't know how long 15 years is.

"It's not so much the sentencing guidelines," he continues. "It's the mandatory minimums. That's the problem." [7]

— Kate Templin

---

[1] Testimony in support of the Safe Access to Drug Treatment and Child Protection Act of 2004, July 6, 2004.

[2] "Key Facts at a Glance," Bureau of Justice Statistics, U.S. Department of Justice, http://www.ojp.usdoj.gov/bjs/glance/tables/corr2tab.htm.

[3] "Quick Facts," Federal Bureau of Prisons, www.bop.gov.

[4] Quoted in David Kopel, "Prison Blues: How America's Foolish Sentencing Policies Endanger Public Safety," Cato Institute, *Policy Analysis*, May 1994, p. 19.

[5] "Illegal Drug Price and Purity Report," Department of Justice, Drug Enforcement Administration, http://www.usdoj.gov/dea/pubs/intel/02058/02058.html.

[6] Testimony in support of the Safe Access to Drug Treatment and Child Protection Act of 2004, July 6, 2004.

[7] Brad Wright, "Justice Kennedy criticizes mandatory minimum sentences," CNN.com, April 9, 2003, www.cnn.com/2003/LAW/04/09/kennedy.congress.

From the start, Kennedy, a leading liberal, forged an alliance in support of sentencing reform with two prominent conservative senators: John L. McClellan, D-Ark., and Strom Thurmond, R-S.C. Kennedy's successive bills included the same basic features: creation of a commission to develop detailed sentencing guidelines; instruction to the commission to "consider" the relevance of offense and personal offender characteristics in setting guidelines; provision for appellate review of sentencing and elimination of parole.

The final Sentencing Reform Act — enacted as part of the Comprehensive Crime Control Act of 1984 — included those basic provisions but differed in several significant respects from Kennedy's original. For one thing, it gave the power to appoint commission members to the president, not to the U.S. Judicial Conference as in Kennedy's proposal. It also stipulated that federal judges were presumed to follow the guidelines; Kennedy had made the guidelines only advisory. The final bill also broadened appellate courts' power to review lower court sentencing decisions.

President Ronald Reagan's appointments to the commission gave it a generally conservative cast. [16] Several pivotal commission decisions made the guidelines more rigid and severe than required, according to Stith and Cabranes. The commission claimed to derive base sentences for most offenses by looking to past practice in federal courts, but it increased sentences for the vast majority of federal cases: those including drugs, fraud and violence. The guidelines also discouraged the then-prevalent use of probation instead of incarceration.

Most significantly, the commission required judges to consider all "relevant conduct" by an offender — not merely the charged crimes. By also requiring judges to consider an offender's criminal record while discouraging consideration of mitigating personal characteristics, the guidelines often resulted in longer prison terms.

The commission released the guidelines in April 1987. Under the law, the 300 pages of directives were to go into effect in six months unless disapproved by Congress. Many judges, academics and criminal defense lawyers opposed the guidelines altogether, while some judges and the American Bar Association urged a delay. But the Justice Department and conservative lawmakers opposed any delay. Congress ended up taking no action, allowing the guidelines to take effect as scheduled on Nov. 1.

AFP/Getty Images/Joyce Naltchayan

The U.S. Supreme Court is weighing the constitutionality of federal sentencing guidelines after Justices Stevens, Scalia, Souter, Thomas and Ginsburg invalidated a somewhat similar state system on Oct. 4, 2000. From left: Antonin Scalia, Ruth Bader Ginsburg, John Paul Stevens, David H. Souter, Chief Justice William H. Rehnquist, Clarence Thomas, Sandra Day O'Connor, Stephen G. Breyer and Anthony M. Kennedy.

Once in effect, the guidelines provoked widespread judicial resistance. At least 200 district courts went on record saying they were unconstitutional on separation-of-powers grounds, according to Ohio State's Berman. But the Supreme Court upheld the guidelines in an 8-1 decision in 1989, *Mistretta v. United States*. The majority said Congress had not delegated excessive power to the commission or upset the balance of powers by placing the commission within the judicial branch. Scalia was the lone dissenter. [17]

Over the next decade, the court's decisions generally supported Sentencing Commission policies. "The court at that time and thereafter was composed of guidelines hawks," says attorney Weich. In 1993 and 1995, the court ruled it constitutional to use the guidelines to raise sentences on the basis of perjury committed at trial or a prior conviction. Two years later the court rejected a challenge to the use of acquitted conduct to enhance a sentence. Justice John Paul Stevens was the lone dissenter. [18]

Only once did the court seem to disturb the trend toward longer sentences under the guidelines. In 1996, the justices said appellate courts should generally defer to district court judges when they made "downward departures" from the guidelines. [19]

Meanwhile, Congress had begun ratcheting up sentences by adopting new mandatory minimum prison terms, in particular for drug crimes. The practice began in 1986 — even while the guidelines were being written — and continued every two years through 1996 — "timed with the election year cycle," Berman notes.

In a different vein, Congress intruded on the commission's responsibilities in 1995 by vetoing its proposed new guideline aimed at eliminating the substantial disparity in punishment for powdered cocaine and "crack" cocaine. The commission had acted in response to widespread criticism of the sharply higher sentences imposed disproportionately on African-American defendants for crack cocaine than on predominantly white defendants in powdered-cocaine cases. [20]

Congressional micromanagement of Sentencing Commission policies culminated with the Feeney amendment in 2003. Added to a child-safety law by Rep. Thomas Feeney, R-Fla., it limits the ability of judges to reduce sentences for crimes against children below guideline levels. It also permits the commission to review the use of so-called downward departures by all judges — not just those in sex and child-crime cases — and to amend the guidelines to reduce the number of lighter sentences. In addition, the amendment cap at three the number of judges who can serve on the seven-member commission, which opponents said would limit the voice of judges in deciding such issues. [21]

Jury Trials

During the 1990s — as Congress was making the sentencing guidelines tougher — judges, criminal-defense lawyers and civil liberties groups grew ever more discontented with the rules. The discontent failed, however, to produce significant changes. But a series of Supreme Court decisions beginning in 1999 cast constitutional doubts on guideline sentencing procedures as an infringement of defendants' rights to jury trials. Over increasingly sharp dissents, the justices in the majority eventually struck down Washington state's guideline system in June 2004. Legal experts immediately saw the ruling as possibly dooming the federal scheme.

The high court began grappling with how to allocate responsibility between judge and jury in the new sentencing regime in a 1998 decision that upheld, by a 5-4 vote, a judge's use of a prior conviction to substantially increase a defendant's prison sentence. The majority said a judge could consider a prior conviction in fixing a prison term — even if the information had not been presented to a jury.

A year later, however, the court effectively required a jury trial for federal defendants under a recently enacted carjacking law that called for enhanced sentences if the offense resulted in serious bodily injury or death. By a 5-4 vote, the court held that to avoid constitutional problems "serious bodily injury" had to be considered not as a sentencing factor for the judge but a separate element of the offense to be found by a jury beyond a reasonable doubt. The majority in the new case included the four dissenters from the previous ruling — Stevens, Scalia, David H. Souter and Ruth Bader Ginsburg — plus Justice Clarence Thomas, who did not explain his change in position. [22]

In 2000, the same five-justice majority stuck down on due-process grounds a provision of New Jersey's hate-crimes law that allowed a judge to increase a defendant's sentence if the offense was motivated by racial or other bias. For the majority, Stevens phrased the holding in *Apprendi v. New Jersey* in unexpectedly broad terms. "Other than the fact of a prior conviction, any fact that increases the penalty for a crime beyond the prescribed statutory maximum must be submitted to a jury, and proved beyond a reasonable doubt," he wrote. In a sharp dissent, O'Connor said the ruling would have the effect of invalidating "three decades' worth of nationwide reform." [23]

Apprendi drew somewhat more attention than the earlier decision, but O'Connor's warning produced no widespread reaction from opponents of federal sentencing guidelines. Two years later, the court extended the *Apprendi* ruling to state capital punishment laws by holding in an Arizona case that any "aggravating factor" needed to make a defendant eligible for the death penalty must be found by the jury, not the judge alone. [24]

The court's decision in October 2003 to hear the *Blakely* case again drew little public attention, but criminal-law specialists took notice. Blakely had abducted his estranged wife and held her at gunpoint for a day trying to get her to drop her divorce suit and control of a family trust. He pleaded guilty to second-degree kidnapping, which under Washington state law carried a "standard range" sentence of 49-53 months. The judge, however, imposed a 90-month sentence after finding that Blakely acted with "deliberate cruelty" — an aggravating factor under Washington's sentencing guidelines law. Blakely argued on appeal that the judge's action violated *Apprendi*, but the Washington Court of Appeal said the final sentence was within the maximum permitted under the statute.

Criminal-defense lawyers and the American Civil Liberties Union backed Blakely's appeal to the Supreme Court. The Justice Department and several states warned that a ruling for Blakely would imperil state and federal sentencing-guideline systems alike. In its June 24 ruling, the court expanded its *Apprendi* ruling by holding that the right to a jury trial applied to any fact necessary to raise a sentence above the normal range — not only above the statutory maximum.

Within weeks, a few federal courts ruled the guidelines invalid because of *Blakely*. The Justice Department advised prosecutors to begin refashioning indictments to include all facts intended to be used in sentencing. Within weeks the solicitor general's office also filed urgent appeals in the *Booker* and *Fanfan* cases, asking the justices to consider them on an expedited basis to resolve what the government lawyers called "the deep uncertainty and disarray about the constitutional validity of the federal sentencing-guidelines system." The justices agreed to hear the cases on Aug. 2 and set argument for the first day of the new term, Oct. 4. ■

CURRENT SITUATION

Mixed Reactions

State and federal courts are grappling with confusion and uncertainty in the wake of the Supreme Court's decision nullifying part of Washington's sentencing-guideline system, even as the justices consider extending the ruling to the federal scheme. [25]

Within weeks of the court's decision, two federal appeals courts and half a dozen federal district courts concluded that *Blakely* also applied to the federal sentencing guidelines and required juries, not judges, to find facts necessary to raise defendants' sentences. A third appeals court issued an unusual request that the Supreme Court act quickly to answer the question.

By contrast, many state courts apparently are minimizing the impact of *Blakely* on their sentencing systems,

California's Tough Three-Strikes Law Survives

With days to go before the election, Californians appeared ready to narrow the state's harsh "three-strikes" law that has resulted in life prison terms for tens of thousands of repeat offenders. But a late campaign by the state's popular Republican governor, Arnold Schwarzenegger, helped defeat the ballot initiative by a 7 percent margin.

The measure — Proposition 66 on the Nov. 2, 2004, ballot — would have required life prison terms only if a defendant's third offense was for a violent or serious felony and also would have reduced the number of felonies classified as violent or serious. Supporters promoted the initiative as a way to reduce the state's spiraling costs of housing a growing prison inmate population.

Polls in the final week before the election suggested the measure would pass by a comfortable margin. But Schwarzenegger stepped in to warn that passage would result in the release of as many as 26,000 offenders from California prisons. "Proposition 66 is nothing but a loophole for violent criminals, and it will lead to more crime and more victims in California," Schwarzenegger said in a joint news conference with three of the state's former chief executives: Republican Pete Wilson and Democrats Jerry Brown and Gray Davis. [1]

AFP Photo

California Gov. Arnold Schwarzenegger

Supporters disputed Schwarzenegger's description of the potential effects of the measure, noting that it would have allowed inmates to be released only after a hearing. But the governor's intervention apparently helped turned the tide. Nearly final returns from the California Secretary of State's office showed the measure losing by a margin of 53.4 percent to 46.6 percent. The initiative won in coastal counties from Los Angeles to San Francisco and the Oregon border, but lost in inland regions and in Republican areas south of Los Angeles.

The California law was the most severe of anti-recidivist measures enacted by some 25 states in the 1990s. Efforts to soften the law failed in the state legislature, and the U.S. Supreme Court in 2003 rejected constitutional challenges contending the penalties amounted to cruel and unusual punishment under the Eighth Amendment. [2]

The defendants in the two cases were given long prison sentences under the three-strikes law after new convictions for stealing $150 worth of children's video tapes in one case and golf clubs worth $1,200 in the other.

An expert on state sentencing policies says the initiative underscores the problems California and other states face from the increasing costs and rates of incarceration. "States will continue to face the same kinds of budgetary and prison pressures that they faced the day before the election," says Daniel Wilhelm, director of the state sentencing and corrections program of the Vera Institute of Justice, a New York-based court-reform organization.

Many states have taken steps to stem their growing prison populations, Wilhelm notes. Texas, for example, is one of several states to have recently moved to channel first- or second-time non-violent drug offenders into treatment rather than prison. Some states — most notably, Michigan in 2002 — also have reduced or repealed some mandatory sentence provisions.

Three-strikes laws, however, appear to remain popular, Wilhelm says: "Other states have not rolled back three-strikes laws."

[1] Quoted in Eric Slater and Peter Nicholas, "Battle Over 3-Strikes Measure Heats Up," *Los Angeles Times*, Oct. 29, 2004, p. A1.

[2] The cases are *Ewing v. California*, 538 U.S. 11 (2003) and *Lockyer v. Andrade*, 538 U.S. 63 (2003).

although at least three state supreme courts — California, Colorado and Indiana — are considering *Blakely* challenges. Similar appeals are popping up in other states.

The July 9 ruling by the 7th U.S. Circuit Court of Appeals in Chicago in the *Booker* case was the first at that level to extend *Blakely* to the federal scheme. Interestingly, the majority 2-1 opinion was written by a leading conservative judge, Richard Posner, while another prominent conservative, Frank Easterbrook, dissented.

On July 21 the 9th U.S. Circuit Court of Appeals issued a similar decision in a drug case against a Montana man, Alfred Ameline. The San Francisco-based court covers California and eight other Western states. Coincidentally, O'Connor the next day told a regularly scheduled meeting of 9th Circuit judges and prosecutors that *Blakely* "looks like a number 10 earthquake to me."

Even before the *Booker* and *Ameline* rulings, the Justice Department on July 2 had advised prosecutors to take precautions that would "safeguard against

Continued on p. 942

At Issue:

Is the death penalty constitutional for 16- and 17-year-olds?

YES

***FROM BRIEF FOR PETITIONER DONALD P. ROPER, SUPERINTENDENT, PETOSI CORRECTIONAL CENTER, IN* ROPER V. SIMMONS**

IN THE SUPREME COURT OF THE UNITED STATES

The people in many states have chosen, through their legislatures, to make capital punishment available to prosecutors and juries when they find persons guilty of committing heinous crimes at age 17. This Court affirmed that choice in *Stanford v. Kentucky* (1989).

The Supreme Court of Missouri assumed authority to effectively overrule this Court's interpretation of the Constitution in *Stanford* in favor of its own. That is wrong. It is for this Court, and not lower courts, to declare whether a particular punishment has become "cruel and unusual" and is thus newly barred by the Eighth Amendment.

Moreover, the Court should not abandon *Stanford.* States, prosecutors and juries have relied on that precedent for the last 15 years. The Missouri court concluded that societal standards have evolved to the point that *Stanford* is no longer good law. That conclusion is incorrect.

This Court has consistently and appropriately refused to declare a particular punishment "cruel and unusual" unless and until there is a national consensus to that effect. To determine whether there is a consensus, the Court looks at the objective record in two areas: legislative action and jury verdicts.

Since *Stanford*, a few state legislatures have raised the minimum age from 16 to 18. But most have retained the age limit affirmed in *Stanford*; the picture has not appreciably changed. The consensus the Court looked for in *Stanford* still does not exist.

Jury verdicts confirm that result. Capital sentences and executions of those who commit crimes before age 18 are more common today than they were when the Court decided *Stanford.*

Capital punishment serves societal interests today just as it did in 1989. Polling data leads to the ambiguous conclusion that many oppose capital punishment for juveniles in the abstract, but they support it when faced with specific cases. Some self-appointed expert groups opine that the practice should be barred, but they do not speak with the authority of a legislature, and their opinions do not establish a national consensus. And though foreign countries that have capital punishment may have chosen a higher minimum age, the question here is whether there is an American consensus that a particular age is mandated by the United States Constitution.

If there is an American consensus today, it is a consensus that the States should be allowed to preserve capital punishment for use in the extraordinary case where a 17-year-old commits a particularly heinous crime.

NO

***FROM BRIEF FOR RESPONDENT CHRISTOPHER SIMMONS, IN* ROPER V. SIMMONS**

IN THE SUPREME COURT OF THE UNITED STATES

Punishment is "cruel and unusual" within the meaning of the Eighth Amendment either if there is a general societal consensus against its imposition or it is disproportionate to the moral culpability of the offender.

This Court first considered the constitutionality of the death penalty for 16- and 17-year-old offenders in 1989. In the 15 years since *Stanford v. Kentucky*, advances in the scientific understanding of adolescent development, and the consistent movement by legislatures and juries away from imposition of death on juvenile offenders, have demonstrated that capital punishment of those under 18 is inconsistent with our society's evolving standards of decency. The execution of juvenile offenders is both disproportionate to their personal moral culpability and contrary to national and worldwide consensus.

First, research in developmental psychology and neurology over the last 15 years has confirmed that 16- and 17-year-olds differ from adults in ways that both diminish their culpability and impair the reliability of the sentencing process. Adolescents of that age are less able than adults to weigh risks and benefits, less able to envision the future and apprehend the consequences of their actions and less able to control their impulses.

The maturity of 16- and 17-year-olds, of course, varies. But because of their developmental deficits and their inherent changeability, the case-by-case consideration that suffices for adults cannot provide the reliable assessment of character and culpability that the Eighth Amendment demands. The rapid pace of change during adolescence means that a jury evaluating an adolescent defendant at sentencing cannot assess with any certainty that defendant's maturity and moral responsibility at the time of the crime.

Second, over the last 15 years, our nation has witnessed a general legislative rejection of the death penalty for juvenile offenders. Since *Stanford*, seven additional states and the federal government have expressly set the minimum age for the death penalty at 18, and not one state has lowered the minimum age for the death penalty. Thirty-one jurisdictions and the federal government now expressly prohibit the death penalty for juvenile offenders. Even among states that theoretically permit the execution of juvenile offenders, just three have actually conducted such executions in the last 10 years.

Both executions and death sentences imposed on juvenile offenders are now exceedingly rare. And the handful of United States jurisdictions that continue to impose the death penalty on juveniles offenders now stand alone in a world that has almost universally set its face against that punishment.

Continued from p. 940

the possibility of a changed legal landscape." A memo signed by Deputy Attorney General James Comey told federal prosecutors to include "readily provable" aggravating factors in indictments and to seek waivers of *Blakely* rights from defendants in plea agreements. [26]

Some defense lawyers are balking at such agreements. "If the guidelines are unconstitutional, they are unconstitutional, and our clients cannot and should not be sentenced under them," Maria Stratton, chief federal public defender in Los Angeles, wrote in a letter to the U.S. attorney's office there. [27]

Bowman says applying *Blakely* could, in many cases, reduce judges' ability to mitigate the guidelines' harsh effects. "There's always a certain amount of discretion in judicial fact-finding," he says. "Judge are going to lose power over sentencing outcomes" if *Blakely* applies.

Ohio State's Berman, however, says applying *Blakely* would probably reduce some defendants' sentences, at least in the short-term. Regardless, he adds, "*Blakely* articulates a very important principle that is fundamental to our criminal-justice system, and I certainly don't see why that principle shouldn't be applied to the federal system."

Oral Arguments

The Supreme Court now holds the fate of the federal sentencing guidelines in its hands. In an unusual two-hour argument on Oct. 4, the Bush administration's top courtroom advocate vigorously defended the constitutionality of the guidelines. But court watchers say Acting Solicitor General Paul Clement appeared to make little headway with any of the five justices who previously voted to strike down a similar state scheme in the *Blakely* case.

Clement began by reminding the justices that the court had upheld the guidelines in several previous decisions. He then warned that "a majority" of the 1,200 federal criminal sentencings each week would become "constitutionally dubious" if the guidelines were struck down. Later, he urged as a back-up position that if the court does rule the scheme unconstitutional, it should leave the guidelines on the books as "advisory" for judges.

Four of the five justices in the *Blakely* majority — all but the customarily silent Thomas — challenged Clement sharply and repeatedly during his allotted hour. Scalia opened by refuting Clement's suggestion that the court had dealt with jury-trial rights in any of the prior cases.

Scalia and Ginsburg also insisted the guidelines could not be analogized to the traditional idea of broad discretion for judges. "There is a huge difference between a judge taking account of many, many factors [and] giving them a specific quantity as the guidelines require," Ginsburg said.

Stevens suggested that Clement was exaggerating the possible impact of invalidating the guidelines. The government lawyer said about 65 percent of cases examined raised "potential" *Blakely* issues. But Stevens said the effect would be much smaller because most federal criminal cases — 97 percent in the most recent year — were resolved by guilty pleas, not trials.

Neither did the justices seem to buy Clement's argument that the guidelines could be made advisory. "It seems contrary to what Congress intended," said O'Connor, one of the *Blakely* dissenters. But Clement closed by warning that ruling against the guidelines would wreak "carnage and wreckage" in the federal system.

Lawyers representing Booker and Fanfan drew challenging questions from Rehnquist, Kennedy and Breyer — three of the four *Blakely* dissenters — but none of the interplays appeared to raise doubts among the *Blakely* majority. By the end, Fanfan's lawyer, Scapicchio, appeared confident enough that she left the lectern with 10 minutes of her time remaining.

For Booker, attorney Kelly opened by noting that eight years of Booker's 30-year term were "based on crimes never proved to a jury beyond a reasonable doubt." Breyer suggested that an appellate court or parole board could constitutionally adjust a defendant's sentence after a jury verdict, and that the guideline scheme simply combined such judicial and executive decision-making into one body. Kelly noted that Breyer's hypotheticals did not entail raising a defendant's sentence above the maximum authorized by the jury.

Later, Rehnquist asked Scapicchio if applying *Blakely* to the federal system would favor defendants by allowing judges to lower but not to raise sentences. Scapicchio said Congress would be free to revise the guidelines if it saw fit.

"You don't have to throw out 20 years of sentencing reform," the attorney continued. "The bulk of the guidelines remain. We're just changing the fact-finder."

Although the justices gave no indication when they would rule, observers speculated that they would try to speed the decision to eliminate uncertainty among federal prosecutors and judges.

When the court heard arguments nine days later in the juvenile death-penalty case, attention focused on the two justices with pivotal votes on the issue: O'Connor and Kennedy. But O'Connor gave only the slightest clue about her inclination, and Kennedy sent mixed signals about his.

O'Connor asked one question during the hour-long debate: Had "about the same" number of states barred executions of juvenile offenders as had barred executions of mentally retarded offenders before the court's 2002 ruling on that issue?

Kennedy appeared sympathetic to the argument by attorney Waxman, representing Simmons, that the prevailing world practice against executing juvenile offenders indicated that the death penalty would be "unusual" punishment for Eighth Amendment purposes.

Later, however, Kennedy indicated concerns that youth gangs might pressure 16- and 17-year-olds to carry out assigned killings if they were ineligible for capital punishment. ■

OUTLOOK

'Transition Period'

When the Senate Judiciary Committee held a hearing on the future of the federal sentencing guidelines just 19 days after the Supreme Court's *Blakely* decision, senators from both parties foresaw serious — even dire — results.

"We're in somewhat of a mess," Chairman Orrin G. Hatch, R-Utah, said as he opened the July 13 hearing.

Alabama's Sen. Jeff Sessions, a fellow Republican and former federal prosecutor, bluntly said the high court ruling was "going to create havoc."

Even liberal Vermont Democrat Sen. Patrick J. Leahy voiced concerns. By making it harder to increase defendants' sentences than to lower them, applying *Blakely* to the federal system might create what he called "a prosecutor's nightmare and a defense counsel's dream."

But Paul Cassell, a recently appointed federal judge from Utah and former conservative law professor, was more phlegmatic. "We are certainly in a transition period, and there are going to be some problems," Cassell told the panel. "But once the Supreme Court gives us some guidance in this area . . . things will sort themselves out considerably."

The committee's hearing ended with no legislative "fixes" on the table, and none are expected to emerge until after the court rules in the *Booker* and *Fanfan* cases. But between them, Sens. Hatch and Kennedy defined the range of possible congressional actions. Hatch foresaw Congress adopting more mandatory minimums for federal offenses, while Kennedy voiced hopes for reducing sentences, simplifying the guidelines and increasing judges' ability to go below the prescribed prison terms.

Most court watchers expect the court to divide along the same lines it did in *Blakely*, with a 5-4 majority holding that any fact used to raise a defendant's sentence must be found by a jury, not a judge. "Why would the court, having taken half a step, not take the next?" Yale Professor Stith asks rhetorically.

The ruling, however, is likely to leave a host of unanswered questions, such as whether to apply *Blakely* or the new decision retroactively to cases that have already gone through the appellate process. Judging from other recent decisions on retroactivity issues, the court seems unlikely to allow closed cases to be reopened. On the same day that *Blakely* was decided, for example, the court refused to give retroactive effect to its decision limiting judges' role in death penalty cases. [28]

In addition, state courts are already grappling with secondary questions raised by *Blakely*, such as whether judges still have a free hand to require separate sentences to be served consecutively — one after another — instead of concurrently. Some state laws require that sentences be concurrent except in specified circumstances. Will *Blakely* require that a jury make those findings?

Similarly, some state laws prohibit defendants convicted of certain lesser felonies from being sentenced to prison except in special circumstances. A Tennessee appellate judge suggested a jury, not a judge, must make those decisions.

Nonetheless, Congress and state legislatures have perhaps the major role in overhauling sentencing systems after the Supreme Court speaks. Kansas, for example, made changes with minimal controversy. Legal experts and Capitol Hill observers alike say they expect any congressional debates to be more protracted and more contentious.

However, even critics of the federal guidelines do not want to return to the unstructured sentencing that prevailed before the guidelines were adopted. "I would not want to go back to a totally guidelineless world," Hofstra's Demleitner says.

Speaking from a pro-law enforcement perspective, Scheidegger of the Criminal Justice Legal Foundation agrees. "The guidelines are better than the system that preceded them," he says. "They're certainly subject to a lot of criticism, and they may be replaced by something less rigid. But I certainly hope it won't go back to what it was before." ■

About the Author

Associate Editor **Kenneth Jost** graduated from Harvard College and Georgetown University Law Center. He is the author of *The Supreme Court Yearbook* and editor of *The Supreme Court from A to Z* (both *CQ Press*). He was a member of *The CQ Researcher* team that won the 2002 American Bar Association Silver Gavel Award. His recent reports include "Gays on Campus" and "Sports and Drugs."

Notes

[1] See Kenneth Jost, *Blakely v. Washington*, CQ Electronic Library, *CQ Supreme Court Collection*, (2004), at http://library.cqpress.com/scc/scyb03-223-9935-641100.
[2] The text of the guidelines and other material can be found on the U.S. Sentencing Commission's Web site: www.ussc.gov.
[3] Frank O. Bowman III, "Train Wreck? Or Can the Federal Sentencing System Be Saved? A Plea for Rapid Reversal of *Blakely v. Washington*," *American Criminal Law Review*, Vol. 41, No. 2 (spring 2004), pp. 220-263.
[4] For background, see Brian Hansen, "Kids in Prison," *The CQ Researcher*, April 27, 2001, pp. 345-376, and Kenneth Jost, "Rethinking the Death Penalty," *The CQ Researcher*, Nov. 16, 2001, pp. 945-968.
[5] The Kansas Supreme Court decision is *State v. Gould* (www.kscourts.org/kscases/supct/2001/20010525/82641.htm). For coverage, see Adam Liptak, "Justices' Sentencing Ruling May Have Model in Kansas," *The New York Times*, July 13, 2004, p. A12.
[6] The list appears as an appendix to NACDL's brief in the *Booker* and *Fanfan* cases.
[7] Bowman, *op. cit.*, pp. 257-263.
[8] The cases are *Thompson v. Oklahoma*, 487 U.S. 815 (1988), and *Stanford v. Kentucky*, 492 U.S. 361 (1989).
[9] For background, see Mary Beckman, "Crime, Culpability and the Adolescent Brain," *Science*, July 30, 2004.
[10] The citation is 536 U.S. 304 (2002). The earlier decision was *Penry v. Lynaugh*, 492 U.S. 302 (1989).
[11] Background drawn from Arthur W. Campbell, *Law of Sentencing* (2d ed.), 1991, pp. 1-15; Kate Stith and José A. Cabranes, *Fear of Judging: Sentencing Guidelines in the Federal Courts* (1998), pp. 1-37.
[12] Stith and Cabranes, *op. cit.*, p. 31. Stith and Cabranes are married to each other.
[13] Marvin E. Frankel, *Criminal Sentences: Law without Order* (1973), pp. 103, 113-114, cited in *ibid.*, pp. 35-36. For a longer excerpt, see Nora V. Demleitner, *et al.*, *Sentencing Law and Policy: Cases, Statutes, and Guidelines* (2004), pp. 118-123.
[14] Bureau of Justice Statistics, *1994 Sourcebook of Criminal Justice Statistics*, table 5.27, cited in Stith and Cabranes, *op. cit.*, p. 20.
[15] Background drawn from Stith and Cabranes, *op. cit.*, pp. 38-77.
[16] The three judges on the panel included two conservatives: one a protégé of Thurmond's, the other a close friend of Chief Justice Warren E. Burger. The third was the more liberal future Supreme Court justice, Stephen Breyer, a one-time Kennedy aide then serving on the federal appeals court in Boston. Among three academics, two reflected conservative schools of thought. The seventh member, then serving on the U.S. Parole Commission, was seen as having little influence. *Ibid.*, pp. 49-50.
[17] The citation is 488 U.S. 361 (1989).
[18] The cases are *United States v. Dunnigan*, 507 U.S. 87 (1993) (perjury); *Witte v. United States*, 515 U.S. 389 (1995) (prior conviction); *United States v. Watts*, 519 U.S. 148 (1997) (acquitted conduct).
[19] The case is *Koon v. United States*, 518 U.S. 81 (1996).
[20] For background, see Mary H. Cooper, "Drug-Policy Debate," *The CQ Researcher*, July 28, 2000, pp. 593-624.
[21] Jennifer A. Dlouhy, "Kennedy Still Seeing Red Over Sentencing Restrictions Enacted as Part of AMBER Alert Law," *CQ Today*, May 20, 2003.
[22] The contrasting cases are *Almendarez-Torres v. United States*, 523 U.S. 244 (1998), and *Jones v. United States*, 526 U.S. 227 (1999).
[23] The citation is 530 U.S. 466 (2000).
[24] The case is *Ring v. Arizona*, 536 U.S. 584 (2002).
[25] For detailed post-*Blakely* developments, see Professor Douglas Berman's blog: Sentencing Law and Policy (http://sentencing.typepad.com), from which much of this section is drawn.
[26] See Dan Eggen and Jerry Markon, "High Court Decision Sows Confusion on Sentencing Rules," *The Washington Post*, July 13, 2004, p. A1.
[27] Cited in David Rosenzweig, "Rulings Throw U.S. Sentencing Guides Into Limbo," *Los Angeles Times*, Oct. 22, 2004, p. B2.
[28] The case is *Schriro v. Summerlin* (June 24, 2004).

FOR MORE INFORMATION

The Constitution Project, 1120 19th St., N.W., 8th floor, Washington, DC 20036; (202) 721-5624; www.constitutionproject.org. Sponsors bipartisan Sentencing Initiative to examine issues raised by pending Supreme Court decision on federal sentencing guidelines.

Death Penalty Information Center, 1320 18th Ave., N.W., Washington, DC 20036; (202) 293-6970; www.deathpenaltyinfo.org. Opposes capital punishment generally and specifically for juvenile offenders.

Justice For All, P.O. Box 55159, Houston, TX 77089; (713) 935-9300; www.jfa.net. Supports capital punishment, including for juvenile offenders.

National Association of Criminal Defense Lawyers, 1150 18th St., N.W., Suite 950, Washington, DC 20036; (202) 872-8600; www.nacdl.org. Challenges constitutionality of federal sentencing guidelines.

U.S. Department of Justice, 950 Pennsylvania Ave., N.W., Washington, DC 20530; (202) 514-2001; www.usdoj.gov. Defends constitutionality of federal sentencing guidelines.

U.S. Sentencing Commission, One Columbus Circle, N.E., Washington, DC 20002-8002; (202) 502-4500; www.ussc.gov. Seven-member commission created by Congress to promulgate federal sentencing guidelines.

Vera Institute of Justice, 233 Broadway, 12th floor, New York, NY 10279; (212) 334-1300; www.vera.org. Law enforcement- and court-reform group studies state sentencing and corrections issues.

Bibliography

Selected Sources

Books

Campbell, Arthur W., *Law of Sentencing* (2d ed.), Clark Boardman Callaghan, 1991.
The treatise introduces the history and philosophy of sentencing; summarizes different sentencing systems, including the federal sentencing guidelines; analyzes constitutional considerations; and covers individual topics, including the death penalty. Supplemented periodically, most recently in 2003. Campbell is a professor at California Western School of Law.

Demleitner, Nora V., Douglas Berman, Ronald F. Wright and Marc L. Miller, *Sentencing Law and Policy: Cases, Statutes, and Guidelines*, Aspen, 2004.
The legal textbook covers the range of criminal sentencing issues with a variety of materials, including case excerpts, selected statutes and federal sentencing guidelines, prosecutors' and defense lawyers' manuals and commentary. The authors are law professors at, respectively, Hofstra, Ohio State, Wake Forest and Emory universities.

Frankel, Marvin E., *Criminal Sentences: Law without Order*, Hill & Wang, 1973.
The strongly argued book by a highly regarded federal judge laid the basis for the federal sentencing guidelines by criticizing standardless judicial discretion and suggesting instead a system of quantifiable rules for calculating sentences.

Hutchison, Thomas W., Peter B. Hoffman, Deborah Young and Sigmund G. Popko, *Federal Sentencing Law and Practice*, Thomson-West, 2004.
The massive volume includes the complete text of the federal sentencing guidelines, with case annotations and authors' comments. Hutchison and Hoffman are attorneys in Washington, D.C., and Silver Spring, Md., respectively; Young and Popko are professors at Cumberland School of Law and Arizona State University College of Law, respectively.

Stith, Kate, and José A. Carbanes, *Fear of Judging: Sentencing Guidelines in the Federal Courts*, University of Chicago Press, 1998.
The book provides a succinct history of sentencing reform in the United States since the 19th century, followed by a somewhat critical account and analysis of the "invention" and operation of the federal sentencing guidelines. Stith is a professor at Yale Law School; Carbanes, her husband, is a judge on the 2nd U.S. Circuit Court of Appeals.

Articles

Cohen, Laurie P., and Gary Fields, "How Unproven Allegations Can Lengthen Time in Prison," *The Wall Street Journal*, Sept. 20, 2004, p. A1.
The article examines five cases in which defendants received longer prison terms under the federal sentencing guidelines because of allegations not proven according to the ordinary standards of criminal trials. An accompanying article examined the potential impact on the federal probation system of limiting judicial fact-finding in calculating sentences. (Gary Fields, "Federal Sentencing Changes Could Strain Probation System," *The Wall Street Journal*, Sept. 20, 2004, p. B1).

Fields, Gary, and Laurie P. Cohen, "Mandatory Sentences Loom as Issue," *The Wall Street Journal*, Sept. 30, 2004, p. A4.
The article examines the growing number and severity of mandatory minimum sentence provisions adopted by Congress for federal offenses.

Streib, Victor L., "The Juvenile Death Penalty Today: Death Sentences and Executions for Juvenile Crimes, Jan. 1, 1973-Sept. 30, 2004," www.law.onu.edu/faculty/streib/documents/JuvDeathSept302004.pdf.
The compilation, updated quarterly, provides comprehensive statistics and individual case summaries on death sentences and executions of juvenile offenders. Streib is a professor at Ohio Northern University College of Law.

Reports and Studies

U.S. Senate, Judiciary Committee, *Blakely v. Washington and the Future of the Federal Sentencing Guidelines*, July 13, 2004, (http://judiciary.senate.gov).
The committee heard testimony from nine witnesses, including representatives of the Justice Department, U.S. Sentencing Commission and federal judiciary as well as academic experts.

Wool, Jon, and Don Stemen, "Aggravated Sentencing: *Blakely v. Washington*. Practical Implications for State Sentencing Systems," Vera Institute of Justice, State Sentencing and Corrections (August 2004).
The report by the New York court-reform group estimates that sentencing systems in 12 other states are likely jeopardized and another six to eight possibly endangered by the Supreme Court's ruling striking down the guidelines system in Washington state. A later report examined legal issues for states considering how to respond to the ruling. (Jon Wool, "Aggravated Sentencing: *Blakely v. Washington*. Legal Considerations for State Sentencing System," Vera Institute of Justice, State Sentencing and Corrections; September 2004.)

The Next Step:

Additional Articles from Current Periodicals

Blakely v. Washington

Hardaway, Robert, "Protecting the Right to a Jury Trial," *The Denver Post*, Aug. 1, 2004, p. E1.

A landmark U.S. Supreme Court case, *Blakely v. Washington,* has revisited the scope of the Sixth Amendment and might call into question the practice of depriving an accused of the right to a jury during sentencing.

Lane, Charles, "Jury Role In Raising Sentences Affirmed," *The Washington Post*, June 25, 2004, p. A1.

A bitterly divided Supreme Court ruled that only juries, not judges, may increase criminal sentences beyond the maximums suggested by statutory guidelines.

Stith, Kate, and William Stuntz, "Sense and Sentencing," *The New York Times*, June 29, 2004, p. A27.

The Supreme Court threw a very large wrench into the machinery of the criminal-justice system in *Blakely v. Washington,* striking down the sentencing guidelines used in Washington state — and, most likely, federal sentencing guidelines.

Weinstein, Henry, "Ruling Causes Uncertainty in Sentencing," *Los Angeles Times*, July 22, 2004, p. A14.

Asserting that Blakely created instability in the federal sentencing system, the Justice Department asked the Supreme Court to review two federal cases that question sentencing guidelines.

Criticism of Sentencing Guidelines

Abramsky, Sasha, "The Drug War Goes Up in Smoke: A Budget Crisis and a Prison Boom Make the States a Vanguard for Drug Reform," *The Nation*, Aug. 18, 2003, p. 25.

The war on drugs has led to more than a million people serving lengthy minimum sentences in prisons, but the realization that tough drug laws have failed to make progress toward a drug-free America has many states reforming their policies.

Bowman, Frank, "When Sentences Don't Make Sense," *The Washington Post*, Aug. 15, 2003, p. A27.

The fact that judges impose sentences that are "downward departures" from sentencing guidelines almost 40 percent of the time does not mean they are soft on crime.

Hill, Michael, "Rules Shackle Judges' Hands," *The Baltimore Sun*, Jan. 11, 2004, p. 1C.

Many call federal mandatory sentencing guidelines a failed experiment, and 27 federal judges from around the country signed a statement calling for a repeal of the guidelines.

Urbina, Ian, "New York's Federal Judges Protest Sentencing Procedures," *The New York Times*, Dec. 8, 2003, p. B1.

Federal judges in New York, who tend to avoid politics and public debate, have been vocal in their criticism of a new sentencing law that they say bullies them into handing down harsher sentences.

Willing, Richard, "Judges Go Soft on Sentences More Often," *USA Today*, Aug. 28, 2003, p. 1A.

Federal judges are expressing disapproval of strict sentencing guidelines by giving convicted offenders less time than the law requires almost 20 percent of the time.

Future of Sentencing Guidelines

Butterfield, Fox, "With Cash Tight, States Reassess Long Jail Terms," *The New York Times*, Nov. 10, 2003, p. A1.

In the past year, about 25 states have eliminated some mandatory minimum sentences, and politicians say they are discovering a new motto: Instead of being tough on crime, it is more effective to be smart on crime.

Crawford, Jan, "Justices Seem Skeptical Over Sentencing," *Chicago Tribune*, Oct. 5, 2004, p. C11.

A majority of the Supreme Court appears to see constitutional problems with federal sentencing guidelines and grapples with whether to change the way criminal defendants are sentenced in federal cases.

Greenhouse, Linda, "Justices Show Inclination To Scrap Sentencing Rules," *The New York Times*, Oct. 5, 2004, p. A14.

Criminal sentencing will inevitably change, but what form the change might take, how drastic it might be and whether defendants or prosecutors would benefit the most remains open to question.

Witt, Howard, "U.S. Courts Await Clarity on Sentencing Guidelines," *Chicago Tribune*, Aug. 29, 2004, p. C13.

The Supreme Court did not rule on whether a Washington state decision on sentencing should apply to the federal system, which has led to a series of conflicting rulings regarding the constitutionality of the federal guidelines.

Juvenile Death Sentence

Farrell, Michael, "Is It Wrong to Put a Juvenile on Death Row?" *The Christian Science Monitor*, Oct. 13, 2004, p. 15.

The *Simmons* case will most heavily impact the 72 inmates now on death row for crimes committed as juveniles and the families of victims and offenders.

Greenburg, Jan, "Court to Weigh Death for Juvenile Murderers," *Chicago Tribune*, Oct. 11, 2004, p. CN1.

The Supreme Court, including several justices who have publicly questioned whether the death penalty is being fairly administered, will take up the question of whether the government can execute those who were 16 or 17 when they killed.

Greenhouse, Linda, "Justices Consider Executions of Young Killers," *The New York Times*, Oct. 14, 2004, p. A1.
The Supreme Court appears deeply divided about whether giving the death penalty for acts committed while a juvenile should be seen as "cruel and unusual punishment" in violation of the Eighth Amendment.

Liptak, Adam, "Penalty for Young Sniper Could Spur Change in Law," *The New York Times*, Dec. 25, 2003, p. A12.
The decision by a jury to spare Lee Malvo's life after finding him guilty in last year's Washington-area sniper rampage may hasten a movement to abolish the death penalty for juvenile killers.

Raeburn, Paul, "Too Immature for the Death Penalty?" *The New York Times*, Oct. 17, 2004, Sect. 6, p. 26.
The death-penalty case of Christopher Simmons, who was 17 years old when he murdered a woman, has drawn intense interest from the American Medical Association and the nation's psychiatrists and psychologists.

Rimer, Sara, and Raymond Bonner, "Young and Condemned, A Special Report: Whether to Kill Those Who Killed as Youths," *The New York Times*, Aug. 22, 2000, p. A1.
The practice of executing teenagers reflects the country's complex attitudes about capital punishment; 23 of the 38 states that have the death penalty permit the execution of juvenile offenders, but only a handful have actually carried out such executions.

Mandatory Minimums

Jenkins, Chris, "State Is Paying Higher Price for Crime Crackdown," *The Washington Post*, March 4, 2004, p. B4.
Since 1991, mandatory minimum sentences have contributed to the more than $400 million increase in the annual cost of operating Virginia's prisons, which now stands at $900 million.

Liptak, Adam, "Long Term in Drug Case Fuels Debate on Sentencing," *The New York Times*, Sept. 12, 2004, p. A20.
A drug offender faces 55 years in prison — 30 years more than if he had hijacked an airplane and 41 years more than if he had committed a second-degree murder.

Liptak, Adam, "Sentencing Decision's Reach is Far and Wide," *The New York Times*, Sept. 12, 2004, p. A16.
The Supreme Court has almost certainly doomed the federal guidelines that generated a man's 24-year sentence for financial fraud; without guidelines, it would likely be zero to six months.

Romero, Simon, "Stiff Sentence Is Possibility For a Name Not So Known," *The New York Times*, March 24, 2004, p. C1.
While skeptics predict the executives responsible for a wave of corporate misdeeds might get off easy, a federal judge may prove them wrong if he hands down the recommended sentence for a former executive convicted of fraud.

Schmitt, Richard, "U.S. Attorneys Required to Seek Maximum Sentence," *Los Angeles Times*, Sept. 23, 2003, p. A13.
The Justice Department adopted guidelines that require federal prosecutors to seek the toughest punishment, reversing a Clinton administration policy that allowed more discretion.

Volokh, Eugene, "Congress Has Every Right to Judge the Judges," *Los Angeles Times*, Feb. 8, 2004, p. M3.
Congress seeks information on how federal judges are applying sentencing guidelines, and judges respond that the action "is a power grab by one branch of government over another branch."

CITING *THE CQ RESEARCHER*

Sample formats for citing these reports in a bibliography include the ones listed below. Preferred styles and formats vary, so please check with your instructor or professor.

MLA STYLE

Jost, Kenneth. "Rethinking the Death Penalty." The CQ Researcher 16 Nov. 2001: 945-68.

APA STYLE

Jost, K. (2001, November 16). Rethinking the death penalty. *The CQ Researcher, 11*, 945-968.

CHICAGO STYLE

Jost, Kenneth. "Rethinking the Death Penalty." *CQ Researcher*, November 16, 2001, 945-968.

CQ Researcher

Published by CQ Press, a division of Congressional Quarterly Inc.

thecqresearcher.com

Gun Control Debate

Do gun bans violate Americans' Second Amendment rights?

On Sept. 13, 2004, Congress allowed a 10-year ban on assault weapons to expire, once again legalizing rapid-fire, semiautomatic weapons like the AK-47, the TEC-9 and the Uzi. Two weeks later, despite 10 years of declining murder rates, the House of Representatives voted to abolish the District of Columbia's strict gun laws. Gun control supporters and major police organizations said the laws had protected civilians and police officers. But the powerful National Rifle Association (NRA) argued that the laws were ineffective and trampled constitutional rights. Meanwhile, victims of gun violence have won $4.4 million in damages from gun dealers and a manufacturer. As the industry lobbies Congress and the states to immunize it against such suits, gun control advocates vow to renew the assault-weapons ban and strengthen the 1993 Brady law. However, given the results of the Nov. 2 presidential and congressional elections, it is considered highly unlikely that the new Congress will pass additional gun control measures.

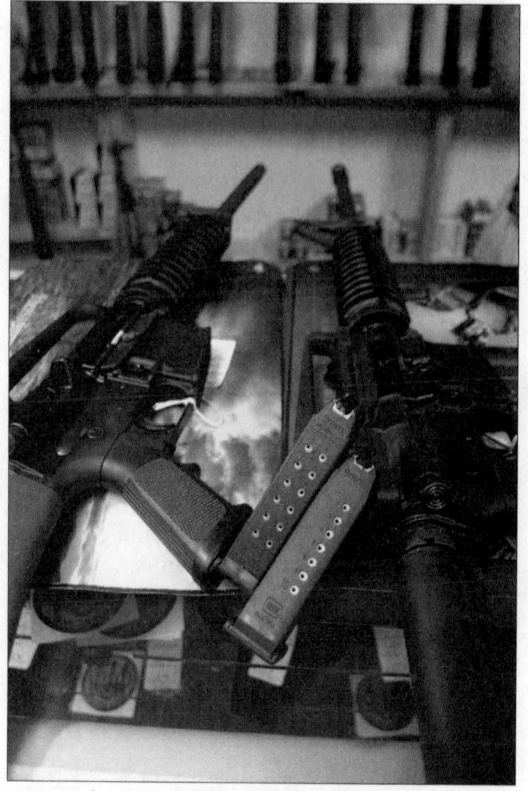

Assault weapons became legal in September after Congress allowed the 10-year ban on the rapid-fire weapons to expire.

INSIDE THIS REPORT

The CQ Researcher • Nov. 12, 2004 • www.thecqresearcher.com
Volume 14, Number 40 • Pages 949-972

CQ PRESS

RECIPIENT OF SOCIETY OF PROFESSIONAL JOURNALISTS AWARD FOR EXCELLENCE ◆ AMERICAN BAR ASSOCIATION SILVER GAVEL AWARD

THE ISSUES

BACKGROUND

CURRENT SITUATION

OUTLOOK

SIDEBARS AND GRAPHICS

FOR FURTHER RESEARCH

Cover: Congress allowed the 10-year ban on assault weapons to expire in September despite overwhelming public support for the law and a 50 percent drop in illegal use of the rapid-fire guns. (Getty Images/Thomas Cooper)

Nov. 12, 2004
Volume 14, Number 40

MANAGING EDITOR: Thomas J. Colin

ASSISTANT MANAGING EDITOR: Kathy Koch

ASSOCIATE EDITOR: Kenneth Jost

STAFF WRITERS: Mary H. Cooper, William Triplett

CONTRIBUTING WRITERS: Sarah Glazer, David Hatch, David Hosansky, Patrick Marshall, Tom Price, Jane Tanner

DESIGN/PRODUCTION EDITOR: Olu B. Davis

ASSISTANT EDITOR: Kate Templin

A Division of Congressional Quarterly Inc.

SENIOR VICE PRESIDENT/GENERAL MANAGER: John A. Jenkins

DIRECTOR, LIBRARY PUBLISHING: Kathryn C. Suárez

DIRECTOR, EDITORIAL OPERATIONS: Ann Davies

CONGRESSIONAL QUARTERLY INC.

CHAIRMAN: Paul C. Tash

VICE CHAIRMAN: Andrew P. Corty

PRESIDENT AND PUBLISHER: Robert W. Merry

The CQ Researcher (ISSN 1056-2036) is printed on acid-free paper. Published weekly, except Jan. 2, April 9, July 2, July 9, Aug. 6, Aug. 13, Nov. 26 and Dec. 31, by CQ Press, a division of Congressional Quarterly Inc. Annual subscription rates for institutions start at $625. For pricing, call 1-800-834-9020, ext. 1906. To purchase a *CQ Researcher* report in print or electronic format (PDF), visit www.cqpress.com or call 866-427-7737. A single report is $10. Bulk purchase discounts and electronic-rights licensing are also available. Periodicals postage paid at Washington, D.C., and additional mailing offices. POSTMASTER: Send address changes to *The CQ Researcher*, 1255 22nd St., N.W., Suite 400, Washington, D.C. 20037.

Gun Control Debate

BY BOB ADAMS

THE ISSUES

Lying dazed and bleeding after being ambushed in a dark alley one night in January 2001, Orange, N.J., police officer Kenny McGuire wasn't thinking about making legal history. He was thinking about survival.

"I thought he was going to get on top of me and kill me," McGuire, now 29, recalls. "I thought he was never going to stop shooting."

However, fellow officers stopped the shooter, and in June 2004, McGuire and his partner that night, David Lemongello, were awarded $1 million in damages from the West Virginia dealer who sold the gun used to shoot both men. It was the first time a dealer had ever been forced to pay for the damage caused by guns he had sold.

"It's a breakthrough," says Dennis A. Henigan, legal director for the Brady Campaign to Prevent Gun Violence, who was co-counsel on the case. "It will encourage other victims to seek legal remedies if they or their families have been shot."

But three months later, the National Rifle Association (NRA) trumped the victory. On Sept. 13, Congress and President Bush bowed to the NRA and allowed a 10-year-old ban on so-called assault weapons to expire, once again legalizing semiautomatic weapons like the AK-47, the TEC-9 and the Uzi.

In the NRA's view, the ban not only didn't prevent crime but also violated the Second Amendment to the Constitution, which grants citizens the right to bear arms. "It's proven to be a failed experiment," says Chris W. Cox, chief lobbyist for the NRA. "It's bad policy, and bad politics."

But police and gun control groups say failing to extend the ban puts lives at risk. "Let the carnage begin on Monday," Los Angeles Police Chief William Bratton said sarcastically in a furious last-minute campaign to save the ban.

The assault-weapons battle was the latest in the continuing war over gun control, largely led by the NRA and the Brady Campaign. * And the contest goes on: As the gun industry lobbies Congress to pass a law immunizing it against damage suits, the Brady Campaign and its allies have vowed to renew the assault-weapons ban.

During the recent presidential campaign, Democratic nominee Sen. John F. Kerry was quick to attack Bush over the ban's expiration. "Today George Bush chose to make the job of terrorists easier and make the job of police officers harder, and that's just plain wrong," he declared. Kerry noted that the commission that investigated the Sept. 11 terrorist attacks found that terrorist leaders encouraged their followers to buy assault weapons in the United States because they were relatively easy to buy here — even during the ban. [1]

For his part, the president had said in 2000 that he favored the ban, but he did little or nothing to keep it from expiring this year — a fact some attribute to his successful bid for the endorsement of the NRA, one of Washington's most powerful lobbies. House Majority Leader Tom DeLay, R-Texas, had refused to bring bills extending the ban to the House floor without the president's blessing. Bush, in turn, pointed the finger back at Congress.

Although Kerry has touted his support for hunting and gun ownership — TV ads in late October showed him goose hunting in full camouflage gear — the NRA has given his Senate performance an "F" rating on gun-rights legislation.

AFP/Getty Images/Staci McKee

Yvette Mouton-Tucker-Griffin, a mother from Hampton, Va., wipes away a tear as she remembers her son during an anti-gun Mother's Day rally in Washington, D.C., on May 9, 2004. He was murdered in 2003 by a robber who held him up for $6. The "Halt the Assault" rally kicked off an unsuccessful nationwide lobbying campaign to retain the assault-weapons ban, which Congress allowed to expire in September after heavy lobbying by the National Rifle Association.

* The campaign is named after President Ronald Reagan's press secretary, James Brady, who was shot and partly paralyzed in John Hinckley's attempt on Reagan's life in 1981.

State Anti-Gun Laws Get Mixed Grades

More than half the states received a grade of "D" or "F" from the Brady Campaign for the quality of their laws designed to protect children from firearms. Only 10 states received "A's" or "B's." The report card measures such factors as whether state laws ban gun possession by juveniles, require safety locks on guns and prohibit the carrying of concealed weapons. States received demerits if they recently prohibited local governments from suing gun manufacturers. Last year, some 2,900 Americans age 19 and under were killed with firearms.

Grading the States on Gun Laws That Protect Children

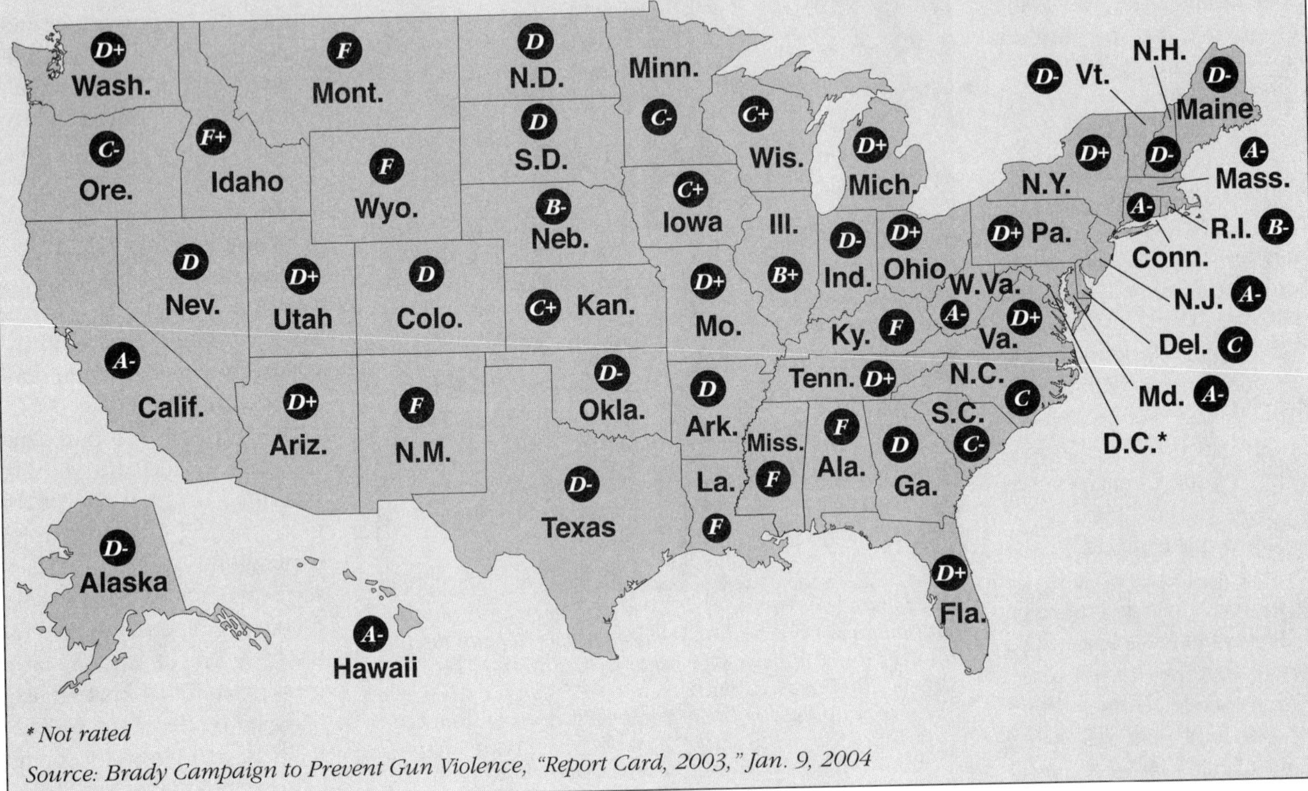

* Not rated

Source: Brady Campaign to Prevent Gun Violence, "Report Card, 2003," Jan. 9, 2004

"He's pretending to be a defender of the Second Amendment, after voting against it for 20 years," Cox says. "It's not surprising that he and others are trying to run from their anti-gun past. We're going to do everything we can to make sure people know that Kerry isn't a hunter — he just plays one on TV."

The NRA estimates it spent $20 million rewarding friends and punishing enemies during the 2004 elections. Former President Bill Clinton, among others, has said that during the GOP takeover of the House in 1994, gun-rights groups helped defeat as many as 20 Democrats. And many say former Vice President Al Gore's support for gun control cost him his home state of Tennessee in 2000 — and the White House along with it.

The 192 million firearms owned by roughly 44 million Americans have a considerable impact on the nation. [2] Firearms killed more than 29,700 Americans in 2002 — more than the number of U.S. soldiers killed during the bloodiest year of the Vietnam War. Guns are the second-leading cause of death (after motor vehicle accidents) among Americans under age 20 and the leading cause of death among African-American men ages 15 to 24. [3]

Physicians for Social Responsibility estimates that gun violence costs the United States $100 billion a year. David Hemenway, a professor of health policy at Harvard University, calls gun violence "a major public health problem." [4]

But the NRA's Cox says more gun control won't help. "The answer to criminals with guns is to put the full force of the law on them," he says.

One thing is certain: For good or evil, guns are a fundamental part of American culture — from Michigan's Upper Peninsula, where there are two deer per person and hunting is deeply embedded in the local culture, to Detroit, Los Angeles, Washington and other cities where drug-turf shoot-outs take the lives of innocent bystanders and gang members alike.

Clinton summed up the paradox on Nov. 30, 1993, when he signed the Brady Handgun Violence Protection Act, which requires a background check for gun purchases from retail dealers (but not for sales at gun shows):

"I come from a state where half the folks have hunting and fishing licenses. . . . I can still remember the first time I pulled a trigger on a .410 shotgun. . . . This is part of the culture of a big part of America. . . . We still close schools and plants on the first day of deer season. [But] we have taken this important part of the life of millions of Americans and turned it into an instrument of maintaining madness. It is crazy." [5]

The Consumer Federation of America predicts gun manufacturers will take full advantage of the demise of the assault-weapons ban, especially since the Brady Campaign has vowed to seek another ban. In fact, a gun-industry source told the federation, " 'We may move to shorter barrels on long guns, and might even produce the 1928 version of the Tommy Gun. We will reintroduce the 50-round drum for our Thompson semiautomatic. I believe there is pent-up demand for pre-ban items.' " [6]

"We're going to see the market flooded again," declared Joseph Vince, former chief of gun-crime analysis for the Bureau of Alcohol, Tobacco, Firearms and Explosives (ATF). "It will negate everything that's been done all these years. We're reverting back to the 1980s." [7]

Indeed, before the ban expired, the Web site of Illinois gunmaker ArmaLite Inc., offered special "Pre-

Americans Supported Assault-Weapons Ban

Americans of all races, ages, economic backgrounds and political orientations, including gun owners, supported the assault-weapons ban, which Congress allowed to expire in September 2004. Members of the National Rifle Association strongly opposed it.

Do you favor or oppose extending the federal law banning assault weapons?

Percentage	Favor	Oppose
Total	68%	28%
Men	65%	32%
Women	71%	24%
Whites	68%	28%
African-Americans	67%	29%
Latinos	75%	23%
High school or less	64%	31%
Some college	68%	27%
College degree or more	75%	22%
18-29 years old	63%	34%
30-44	68%	28%
45-64	70%	26%
65 and over	69%	23%
Household income below $35,000	68%	27%
$35,000 to less than $75,000	67%	29%
$75,000 and over	71%	26%
Northeast	73%	23%
Midwest	66%	29%
South	67%	28%
West	67%	29%
Urban	69%	26%
Suburban	71%	26%
Rural	61%	33%
Republican	61%	34%
Democrat	73%	23%
Independent	69%	27%
Conservative	62%	33%
Moderate	70%	26%
Liberal	75%	22%
Gun owner in household	57%	38%
NRA member	32%	63%

Source: 2004 National Annenberg Election Survey; 4,959 adults were interviewed by telephone from Aug. 10-Sept. 4, 2004.

'Mamma, I Shot a Little Girl'

"Mamma, I shot a little girl. I didn't mean to. I'm sorry." Thus did a 6-year-old first-grader at Buell Elementary School outside Flint, Mich., explain how he killed Kayla Rolland, also a first-grader, on Feb. 29, 2000. [1]

His mother, Tamarla Owens, and her three children had been evicted from their home a week earlier for failure to pay the rent. Owens, who worked two jobs, had sent her two sons to live with her brother. She didn't know, she said, that the place was a haven for drugs and guns.

One night, her 6-year-old found a .32 caliber semiautomatic pistol in a shoebox in his uncle's bedroom. He took it to school the next day. A few hours later, his classmate was dead.

Last year, some 2,900 Americans age 19 and under were killed by firearms, according to the Centers for Disease Control and Prevention (CDC). That's about one every three hours. Countless more were injured.

The figures are especially striking when compared with those in other countries. In 1997, the CDC studied firearms deaths in the United States and 25 other industrialized countries, including England, France and Japan. The U.S. rate of firearms death among children ages 15 and under was nearly 12 times the average number of deaths in the other countries.

Morna Murray, who studies juvenile-justice issues for the Children's Defense Fund, says the killings are, among other things, a powerful argument for requiring trigger locks on handguns. So far, Congress hasn't passed such a law.

She also notes that it is ultimately adults, not children, who are responsible for shootings. Guns and ammunition shouldn't be stored in the same place, she says, let alone in a shoebox where a child could find it.

"It's tragic in every aspect," Murray says. "It's tragic for the 6-year-old who was killed, and for her family. And it's tragic for the boy, who will be stigmatized and will have to live with this for the rest of his life. It's just so unnecessary — and so heartbreaking."

She also notes that guns are popular among many older children in low-income urban areas. "There's a culture of violence," she says, noting the larger problems of racism and poverty that contribute. "Guns are something of a trading tool. They're basically a commodity on the street. The media glamorize guns. They're part of being 'cool' — of being the ultimate guy in today's world."

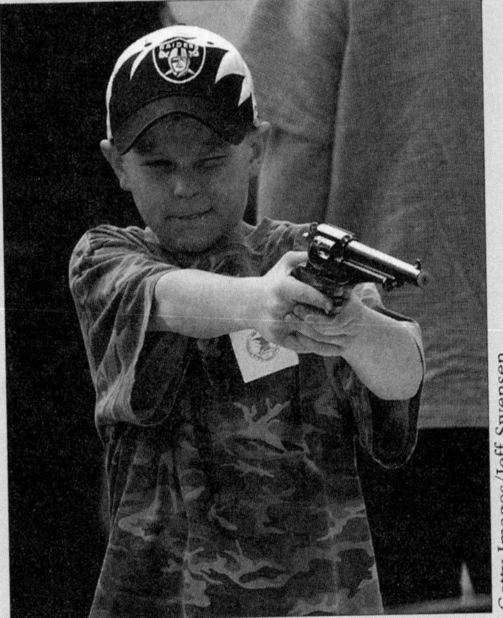

Getty Images/Jeff Swensen

A boy tries a laser pistol at the 133rd National Rifle Association convention, in Pittsburgh, on April 18, 2004. More American children are killed with firearms than in any other industrialized nation.

In some areas, she said, kids see all the guns around them and, fearfully, decide to get one of their own. Andrew Arulanandam, a spokesman for the National Rifle Association (NRA), also called the shooting a tragedy. He noted that the NRA has an educational program called "Eddie the Eagle" targeted toward children. "If they find a gun, they should stop, don't touch, leave the area and tell an adult," he said. "We also need to make sure they have proper parenting and proper mentoring. It's incumbent on every head of household to figure out the most effective means to keep children away from guns."

The day after the death of Kayla Rolland, Sen. Carl Levin, D-Mich., urged his colleagues to "wake up and pass legislation" that would require firearms to be sold with storage or safety devices. The Senate passed such a bill earlier this year. The House, so far, has not.

The 6-year-old boy was placed in a foster home after a court found his mother unable to deal with his behavioral problems.

Michigan's state legislature took action of its own.

In December 2000, less than a year after Kayla was killed, lawmakers made it legal to carry a concealed weapon — a recipe, say gun control advocates, to put still more guns on the streets.

---

[1] Shawn Windsor, "Shooter's Mom Takes Blame," *The Detroit Free Press*, Feb. 28, 2001, p. A1.

paid-PreBan" deals, with weapons to be shipped once the ban expired, including a "pin-on flash suppressor." (Flash suppressors turned rifles into illegal assault weapons under the ban.)

But company President Mark A. Westrom said that as of early September, there had not been much demand for his special deals. Thanks to its ingenuity, the gun industry had already "designed around" many of the forbidden items, so customers were already getting replicas of the banned rifles anyway. [8]

As the gun control debate continues, here are some of the key questions being asked:

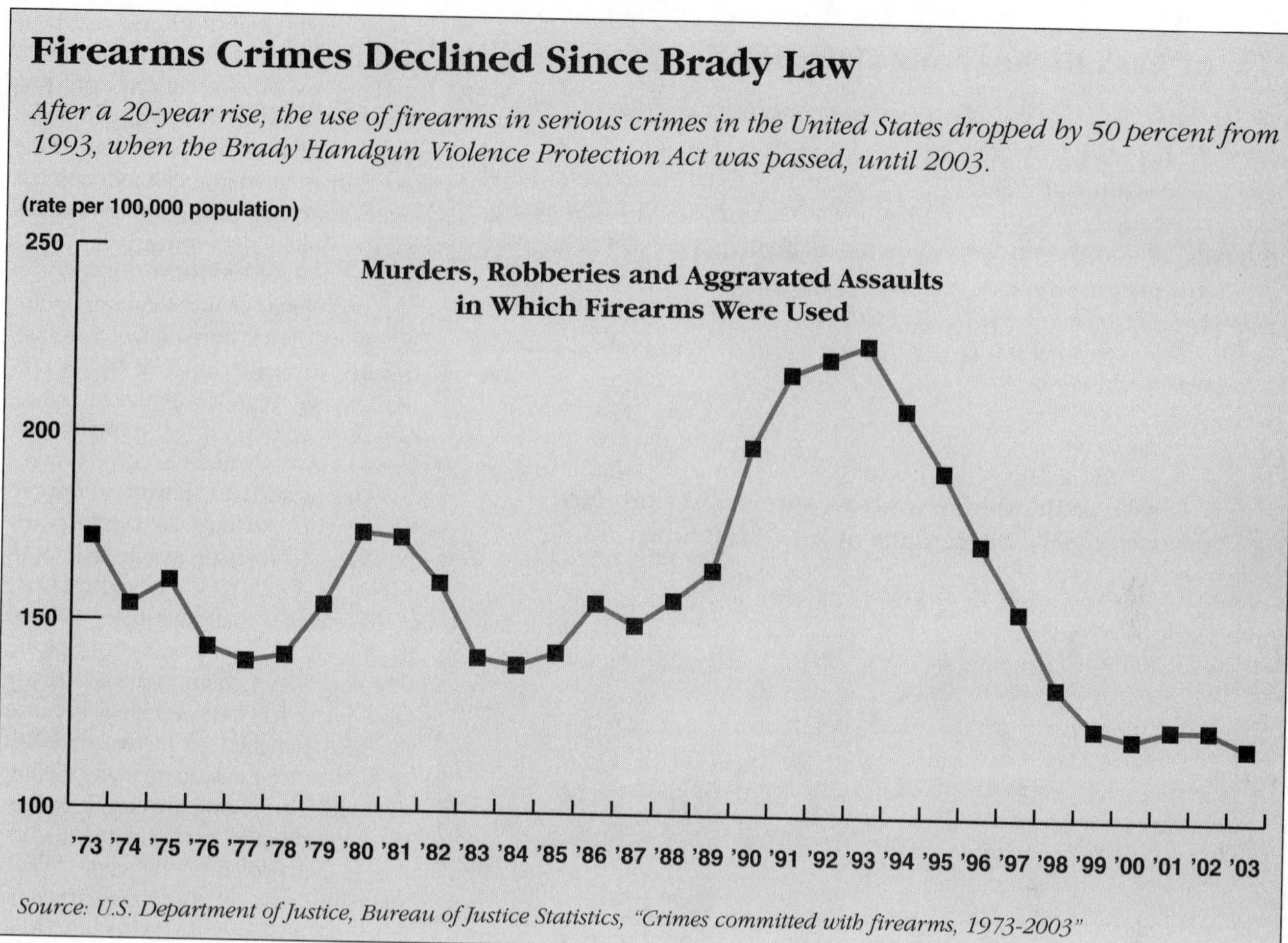

Source: U.S. Department of Justice, Bureau of Justice Statistics, "Crimes committed with firearms, 1973-2003"

Did the assault-weapons ban and the Brady law reduce crime?

Public support for gun control grew in the late 1980s, after a series of shocking mass murders. In January 1989, a man with a Chinese-made AK-47 assault rifle killed five children and wounded 29 others in a Stockton, Calif., schoolyard. Two years later, in the worst mass shooting in American history, a man used a Glock 9-millimeter semiautomatic pistol to kill 22 people and wound 23 more in a Killeen, Texas, cafeteria before killing himself. (*See sidebar, p. 963.*) [9]

The assault-weapons ban — passed in 1994 with a "sunset" provision that ended the ban after 10 years — outlawed 19 specific models and two-dozen copycat versions, while exempting more than 600 types of hunting rifles. It also listed characteristics, such as a large magazine and a pistol grip, which defined a rifle as a banned weapon. (*See sidebar, p. 963.*)

A year earlier, the Brady law had imposed a five-day waiting period and background check for anyone purchasing a handgun from a retail dealer. Criminals and anyone judged by a court to be mentally incompetent were not allowed to buy handguns. (The list was later expanded to include anyone under restraining orders for domestic violence.) It also required that multiple handgun sales be reported to the police; provided $200 million a year for states to computerize their handgun-purchase records, and increased federal firearm licensing fees from $30 to $200.

Raw statistics suggest the new laws have been a success. Deaths from firearms in the United States dropped sharply, from almost 40,000 in 1993 to 29,700 in 2002. [10] And the number of licensed gun dealers dropped from 285,000 to 104,000 in three years. [11]

In September 2004, the Department of Justice reported that homicides were at their lowest rate since the 1960s. Moreover, the rate of violent crime was at its lowest since the department began keeping those statistics in 1973, and the percentage of violent crimes involving firearms decreased from 11 percent in 1993 to 7 percent in 2003. [12]

Virtually every major police organization supported the assault-weapons ban, along with a majority of gun owners, according to numerous polls. (*See poll, p. 953.*)

Use of Assault Weapons Declined

The use of illegal assault weapons in gun crimes dropped by half after the Federal Assault Weapons Act banned the sale of 19 specific assault weapons and two-dozen "copycat" models in 1994. Under pressure from the National Rifle Association, congressional lawmakers allowed the ban to expire in September 2004. The NRA contends the ban did not prevent crime and violated the Second Amendment to the Constitution. But police and gun-control groups say failing to extend the ban endangers police officers and citizens.

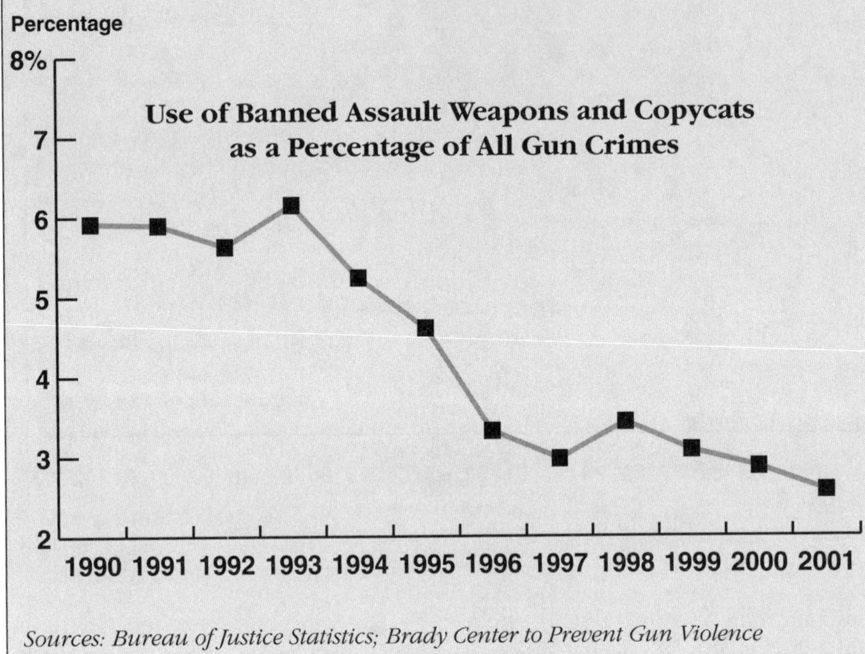

Sources: Bureau of Justice Statistics; Brady Center to Prevent Gun Violence

"We're sick and tired of picking up these young bodies off the streets," says Atlanta Police Chief Richard Pennington. Sen. Charles Schumer, D-N.Y., told a press conference shortly before the ban expired: "We're in this Alice-in-Wonderland position of repealing a law that everyone agrees has been overwhelmingly successful."

Others disagree, however, on whether the lower crime statistics can be attributed to either the assault-weapons ban or the Brady law. Criminologists note that population shifts play a part in violent-crime cycles. Today there are fewer men in their late teens and early 20s — the age when people are most likely to commit crimes using guns. Also, many large cities put more police on the street as part of former President Clinton's anti-crime push. And many judges are imposing longer mandatory sentences. [13]

"Probably no single factor" explains the drop in crime, says Lawrence A. Greenfeld, director of the Bureau of Justice Statistics. "It probably has to do with demographics, and with having a lot of very high-rate offenders behind bars."

Indeed, some foes of gun control believe that firearms are part of the solution, not part of the problem. "If a fellow is a criminal, he's not going to sign a paper and wait for a background check," declared John Snyder, chief lobbyist for the Citizens' Committee for the Right to Keep and Bear Arms. "It disarms the innocent."

He believes the recent spate of NRA-backed state laws allowing people to carry concealed weapons has done more than anything else to combat crime. Since 1987, the number of states with so-called right-to-carry laws has jumped from 10 to 38.

Florida State University criminologist Gary Kleck says Americans use firearms to resist crime up to 2.4 million times a year. "Bad-guy gun owners drive crime up," he maintains. "Good-guy owners drive crime down."

Other academics, however, dispute Kleck's data. Robert J. Spitzer, a political science professor at the State University of New York College at Cortland, estimates that guns deter 100,000 to 200,000 crimes a year. But Spitzer, who favors gun control, says the Brady law's effect has been minimal because the NRA punched so many loopholes in it. "I don't think there's any definitive study that shows a causal link" between the Brady law and the reduction in gun violence," he said.

Philip Cook, a Duke University professor of public policy who has studied the gun issue for 30 years, compared 32 states where the Brady law took effect with 18 others that already had similar restrictions. In the 32 states, the number of suicides by firearm declined among those age 55 and over — perhaps as a result of the five-day "cooling off" period, Cook found. (The waiting period has since been superseded by so-called instant checks.) But he found "no evidence" that the Brady act had reduced homicide rates. [14]

Tony Orza, the Brady Campaign's legislative counsel, acknowledges the impact of the population changes and the increase in police. But since the law took effect, he notes, some 1 million gun sales have been prevented. "If you limit the access of criminals to guns, common sense dictates that there will be fewer gun deaths," Orza says. "The Brady law is playing a role."

The law would play an even bigger role, gun control advocates say, if NRA-backed loopholes were plugged. Most important, they say, is closing the gun-show loophole. Background checks aren't required at gun shows, where an estimated 40 percent of all gun sales take place. The Brady Campaign also wants to deny sales to people convicted of violent misdemeanors, use "ballistic fingerprinting" to help trace guns used in crimes and promote the manufacture of so-called "smart guns" — weapons that, because of advanced technology, can be used only by their owners.

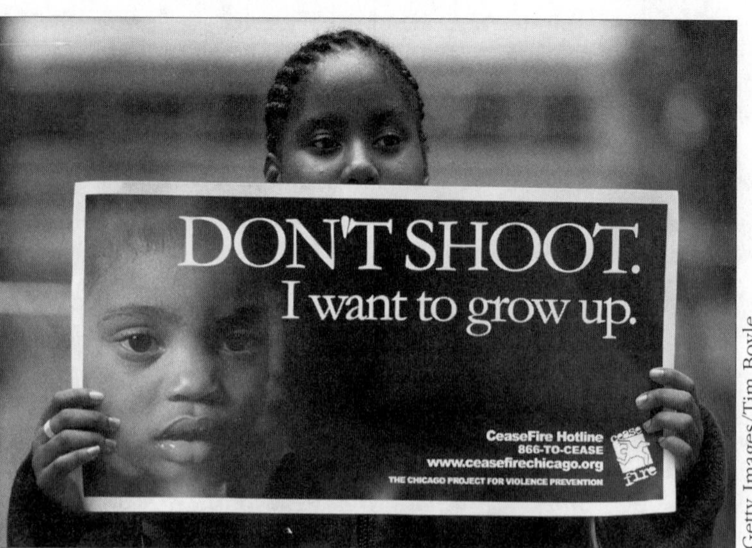

Getty Images/Tim Boyle

Seventh-grader DeAnna Belt demonstrates against handgun violence in Chicago on Oct. 20, 2004, during a rally sponsored by the Illinois Council Against Handgun Violence.

Do gun control laws threaten constitutional rights?

Gun control opponents invariably cite the Second Amendment, which states, "the right of the people to keep and bear arms shall not be infringed."

But supporters say the opponents deliberately overlook the preamble to that section — "A well regulated Militia, being necessary to the security of a free State" — as well as the amendment's history. Virtually all the discussion of arms had to do with serving in a militia; there was no mention of an individual right to hunt or shoot.

Some gun advocates say there exists not only a constitutional right to own a gun but also a natural right. "You have a right to live, and therefore a right to defend that life," Snyder says.

The NRA's Cox adds: "The Second Amendment has nothing to do with hunting. It has to do with our God-given right to defend ourselves."

SUNY's Spitzer traces the history of the Second Amendment in detail — from the Constitutional Convention of 1787 to the *Federalist Papers* defending it, to various state convention debates over ratification and the first Congress that drafted the Bill of Rights. The Second Amendment, he concludes, was always mentioned in the context of a militia. The debate was about the role of armed state militias as opposed to a national, standing army.

"Absent from this extended history is any connection between the Second Amendment and any personal use of weapons, for purposes including hunting, sporting, recreation, or even personal protection," Spitzer writes. [15] Colonial militias, he notes, declined in the 19th century. Today's descendent of the old state militias is the National Guard — controlled by state governors but subject to a federal call to duty, as in the current war in Iraq.

Interpretations of the Second Amendment have thus been split between "collectivists" — those who believe it applies only to militias and thus is a dead letter today — and "individualists," who believe it confers a right on each person.

Even the late Chief Justice Warren E. Burger, a conservative, said the amendment should be interpreted as if it began with the word "Because." The right to carry a gun, he said, was inextricably linked to state militias. Historians and legal scholars generally agree.

In recent years, however, some "collectivists" have re-evaluated their opinions — most notably, Harvard's liberal and respected constitutional lawyer Laurence H. Tribe. In an op-ed article in *The New York Times* in 1999, Tribe accused both sides of tunnel vision, of looking only at its favorite half of the amendment, instead of the whole thing.

He acknowledged the link to militias. "But the Second Amendment's reference to the people's 'right' to be armed cannot be trumped by the amendment's preamble," Tribe wrote. An individual right was there after all, he argued.

On the other hand, he derided pro-gun forces for thinking the Second Amendment gave "every citizen a nearly absolute right to own guns . . . it has been a terrible mistake for both sides in the gun controversy to insist that the Second Amendment bans virtually everything or virtually nothing." Gun control laws, he said, can still be a valid public safety regulation even if the Constitution confers an individual right to own firearms. [16]

Then, along came Timothy Joe Emerson, a San Angelo, Texas, physician who owned a handgun and whose wife, Sacha, was filing for divorce. A local court placed a restraining order on Emerson. He was later indicted by a grand jury for violating the Brady law, which said that people under restraining orders in domestic disputes couldn't own guns.

To the surprise of both sides, U.S. District Judge Sam Cummings threw out the indictment on the grounds that it violated Emerson's "individual right to bear arms." Emerson's lawyer had tossed in the Second Amendment almost as an afterthought. For the first time in U.S. history, a federal judge had proclaimed an "individual right" to own a gun. [17]

The ruling drew national attention. The NRA, the Brady Campaign and others got involved. The prosecution immediately appealed the case, and on Oct. 16, 2001, the 5th U.S. Circuit Court of Appeals, in New Orleans, issued its 2-1 decision. It was a classic good news-bad news ruling — for both sides.

On the one hand, it reinstated the indictment. The right to bear arms, the judges said, was subject to reasonable limits. But two of the three judges agreed with Cummings, ruling that the Second Amendment conferred an individual right to carry a gun.

"The plain meaning of the right of the people to keep arms," they wrote, "is that it is an individual, rather than a collective, right and is not limited to keeping arms while engaged in active military service or as a member of a select militia such as the National Guard." [18]

Both sides claimed victory. The Brady Campaign noted that, even with the "individual right" interpretation of the Second Amendment, the court had upheld the federal gun control law. The NRA and its allies were buoyant that a U.S. Court of Appeals had endorsed the "individual right" view.

Legal scholars who had previously written of "the embarrassing Second Amendment," "this orphan of the Constitution" or "the infamous dependent clause" started taking another look.

The U.S. Supreme Court has historically shied away from Second Amendment cases. Its last decision came in 1939, in the case of Jack Miller and Frank Layton, who had been convicted for transporting a sawed-off shotgun across state lines. The court ruled unanimously against their challenge of their conviction on Second Amendment grounds, among others.

In the absence of evidence that the shotgun "has some reasonable relationship to the preservation or efficiency of a well regulated militia," the court wrote, "we cannot say that the Second Amendment guarantees the right to keep and bear such an instrument." [19]

If the Miller-Layton case, or a similar one, were to reach today's current Supreme Court, the outcome would be uncertain. But gun advocates hope it will happen and that the court will produce a landmark decision favoring individual rights.

Should gun manufacturers and dealers be held accountable for gun crimes?

The $1 million settlement for New Jersey policemen McGuire and Lemongello was the first requiring a dealer to pay damages for the criminal use of a gun he had sold. But it wasn't the last. The Brady Campaign quickly followed it with two similar cases — one involving the manufacturer as well as the dealer. Altogether, three dealers and one gunmaker have paid $4.4 million in damages since last June. Similar suits are pending.

"We were ecstatic — primarily for the officers, who had their careers ended by this tragedy," says the Brady Campaign's Henigan. "It sends a message to the gun dealers that there's a very high price to be paid for irresponsible gun practices."

Cox, of the NRA, accuses the Brady Campaign of filing "bogus and reckless lawsuits." These aren't typical cases involving damages for a faulty product, he notes. "This is about suing gun manufacturers for criminals that illegally own firearms.

"These suits are not designed to win," Cox continues. "They're designed to bleed the industry. And it will only take one to bankrupt this industry. This is a very serious threat."

Gun control advocates, for their part, compare the suits to those successfully brought by smokers against the cigarette industry, and by motorists injured when the gas tanks of Ford Pintos exploded several years ago. If Congress won't pass laws to protect people, they say, the only remedy is in civil court.

At the urging of the NRA, several states already have passed laws prohibiting such suits, and the House of Representatives passed a similar bill earlier this year. But the Senate rejected the bill after stiffer gun controls were added. [20]

In the McGuire-Lemongello case, a buyer with a clean record who easily passed a background check purchased the guns for the criminal at a pawnshop in South Charleston, W.Va., in July 2000. Such third-party "straw" purchases are illegal.

According to court papers, the scene was almost surreal. James Gray, a convicted felon, paid drugs and money to Tammi Lea Songer, a local taxi driver with no criminal record, to buy 12 semiautomatic handguns. Songer, high on drugs, made the $4,000 purchase. Gray told her which guns he wanted, and she filled out the paperwork. The clerk phoned the owner to ask if it was legal to sell 12 guns at once. Yes, he was told, and the sale was made. The next day the store manager notified the authorities. [21]

But one of the 12 guns was already on its way to Shuntez Everett, who was wanted for attempted murder in Orange, N.J. On Jan. 12, 2001, Everett shot McGuire and Lemongello as they staked out a gas station that had been robbed six times in a month. Everett was shot dead, McGuire and Lemongello seriously wounded.

"I lost about 17 units of blood," McGuire recalled. A large portion of his colon was removed. His right femur was shattered; a metal rod had to be inserted from his knee to his hip. He spent 21 days in intensive care. "It's better than taking a dirt nap," McGuire says now, using a slang term for dying. "Hopefully, this will put some sense of responsibility into the gun dealers and manufacturers."

Continued on p. 960

Chronology

1900-1960s

Outbreaks of crime and the assassinations of prominent Americans spur enactment of gun laws.

1911
New York state passes Sullivan law, the first modern-day gun control measure, which bans the sale, possession or carrying of deadly weapons.

1934
Concern about organized crime spurs Congress to pass National Firearms Act, banning private ownership of sawed-off shotguns and machine guns.

1939
Supreme Court takes "collectivist" view of Second Amendment; upholds National Firearms Act as long as it doesn't interfere with state militias.

1968
Following the assassinations of President John F. Kennedy, Sen. Robert F. Kennedy, D-N.Y., and the Rev. Martin Luther King Jr., Congress passes the Gun Control Act of 1968 banning the interstate sale of rifles and handguns and barring the importation of cheap handguns called "Saturday night specials."

1970s

Gun control laws continue to pass while National Rifle Association (NRA) takes increasingly harder line against them.

1976
District of Columbia passes one of the nation's toughest gun control laws, requiring residents to keep firearms disassembled or trigger-locked.

1977
Hard-liners opposed to any form of gun control take control of NRA.

1980s

Pro-gun lobbyists take battle to state and local governments; federal law weakened.

1981
Morton Grove, Ill., becomes first town to ban possession or sale of handguns. Law is upheld following court challenge but not enforced.

1982
Kennesaw, Ga., passes law requiring all heads of households to have guns; later amended to let citizens decide for themselves.

1986
Congress passes McClure-Volkmer bill, weakening 1968 Gun Control Act and legalizing, again, interstate sale of rifles and shotguns.

1990s

Gun control advocates achieve major victories, but at steep political cost.

Nov. 30, 1993
President Bill Clinton signs Brady law, mandating five-day waiting period and background check before guns can be purchased from gun stores.

Sept. 13, 1994
Clinton signs law banning military-style assault weapons; partly as a result, GOP wins control of House and Senate.

Nov. 6, 1997
In a striking turnabout in public opinion, Washington state voters reject gun-safety initiative, 71 to 29 percent.

2000s

For the first time, gun dealers are forced to pay damages caused by their products. Assault-weapons ban is allowed to expire.

June 23, 2004
Backed by the Brady Campaign to Prevent Gun Violence, two Orange, N.J., police officers injured by guns receive $1 million in damages from a gun dealer.

September 2004
On Sept. 13 the nation's 1994 ban on assault weapons expires after President Bush and congressional leaders make little effort to extend it. Presidential challenger Sen. John F. Kerry responds: "Today George Bush chose to make the job of terrorists easier and make the job of police officers harder." He based his charge on the Sept. 11 Commission, which reported that terrorists are encouraged to purchase assault weapons in the United States. . . . The House on Sept. 29 passes legislation to end the strict ban on handguns in the District of Columbia and remove a prohibition against semiautomatic weapons in the city.

Continued from p. 958

The National Shooting Sports Foundation, a gun industry trade association, refused to criticize the settlement or defend the gun store operators. "If there was an illegal straw purchase, they should be prosecuted and sent to prison and the same for the dealer, if he was complicit," said Lawrence Keane, senior vice president and general counsel. "Nobody is in favor of straw purchases."

A similar settlement soon followed in Philadelphia. A court there approved payment of $850,000 from a gun dealer in Williamsport, Pa., to the mother of a child accidentally shot by a playmate who found a gun on a Philadelphia street. It was one of 10 guns the dealer had sold to the same person.

In September 2004, Bull's Eye Shooter Supply in Washington state — which "lost" the rifle used in the 2002 Washington-area sniper shootings — paid $2 million to six families and two victims of the snipers in still another lawsuit. Bushmaster Firearms of Wyndham, Maine, paid $550,000 in the same suit — the first time a manufacturer had paid damages in such a case.

In denying motions by Bull's Eye and Bushmaster to dismiss the case, Superior Court Judge Frank Cuthbertson said the dealer had created "a high degree of risk" in his gun-selling practices. Although the semiautomatic Bushmaster rifle used to murder 10 Washington-area residents during the weeks-long shooting spree was exempt from the assault-weapons ban, the judge concluded that the manufacturer "knew or should have known that Bull's Eye Shooter Supply was operating in a reckless or incompetent manner."

The ATF says 57 percent of all guns recovered in crimes can be traced to 1 percent of the nation's gun dealers. Thus, hitting the few irresponsible dealers with big fines could significantly reduce gun trafficking, gun control advocates believe. [22]

Some cities are using the same technique, suing gunmakers for the damage their products cause on the streets. None has won any money so far, but courts in several states have ruled that the cities have the right to sue on those grounds. Pressed by the NRA, however, legislators in some 33 states have passed laws granting the gun industry immunity from such suits.

Some legal experts are uncomfortable with using lawsuits to bring about gun control, fearing the courts are taking on a role that the Framers intended for Congress and the executive branch.

But the Brady Campaign's Henigan defends the right of citizens to turn to the courts when lawmakers fail them. He calls it "a quiet revolution." As for the NRA and its allies, he says, "They can read the number of zeros in $1,000,000, and they can read the legal decisions that say gun dealers and manufacturers have liability." ■

BACKGROUND

Gun Culture?

The gun has been romanticized into an icon of U.S. history. As schoolchildren often learn, swashbuckling early settlers carried rifles to hunt game and fend off hostile natives, while Westerners wielded Colts and Winchesters to tame the wild, 19th-century Western frontier.

But some historians say the role of firearms in the nation's early history has been greatly exaggerated. Michael Bellesiles claims to have studied probate records for the 18th and 19th centuries and found that until around 1850, no more than 10 percent of Americans owned guns. [23] And Richard Shenkman writes that rifles and six-shooters played a relatively small role in the settling of the West.

"The truth is many more people have died in Hollywood westerns than ever died on the real frontier," Shenkman says. "In the worst year in Tombstone [Ariz.], home of the shootout at the OK Corral, only five people were killed." [24]

Moreover, Americans showed an early ambivalence about guns. In 1692, the Massachusetts colony passed the first gun control law, which forbade the carrying of "offensive" weapons. In the early 19th century, four states banned concealed weapons, starting with Kentucky in 1813, Indiana in 1819, Georgia and Arkansas in 1837. [25]

Rise of NRA

Two Civil War veterans founded the NRA in 1871, mainly to improve marksmanship. By the early 20th century, the NRA was affiliated with 2,000 local sporting clubs. By the 1930s it was the largest citizens' group of firearms owners in the country and began using its clout to influence federal gun laws. Returning veterans from World War II added to its numbers.

Today the NRA has about 4 million members, according to its own and independent figures, and an annual budget of around $190 million. It also boasts 500 employees, including more than 70 in the group's political arm, the Institute for Legislative Action. Its principal opponent, the Brady Campaign, has only a fraction of the NRA's resources.

For years, the NRA opposed any regulations on firearms, fearing they would be a "slippery slope" to an outright ban on guns. Today the group supports the limited background checks for retail gun buyers embodied in the Brady law but opposes gun registration and checks on purchases at gun shows.

The group's ability to intimidate state and national legislators has made it one of the country's strongest lobbying groups. Known simply as the "gun lobby," the NRA has watered down or killed even relatively mild restrictions on gun ownership. [26]

A striking example of NRA power was the attempt in 1996 to pass a ballot initiative in Washington state requiring trigger-locking devices on handguns and handgun safety licenses.

Just a month before the election, polls showed 62 percent support for the measure. Yet on Election Day it was overwhelmingly rejected, 71 to 29 percent. Foes of the initiative say they simply outworked their competition. But advocates say the real blow was a $2 million ad blitz by the NRA.

Andrew Arulanandam, an NRA spokesman, prefers to talk about the group's role in training police officers and citizens in gun use and safety: "We have more than 43,000 NRA-certified instructors. We train more than 800,000 people a year."

As for gun control advocates, he says, "Why even negotiate with someone whose end game is to drive you into the sea? They're just trying to put us out of business."

Robert Ricker, a former NRA lawyer who now works for the Coalition to Stop Gun Violence, says the 1999 massacre at Columbine High School in Littleton, Colo., opened his eyes to the potentially catastrophic danger of unregulated gun use. [27] That was also the period when the NRA was pushing "right to carry" laws in the states.

In March 2000, Ricker helped Smith & Wesson, the nation's oldest gun manufacturer, negotiate a voluntary agreement with the Clinton administration. The firm agreed to put trigger locks on its guns and to select its dealers more carefully. The company hoped, in return, that various cities would drop their lawsuits against it.

But the NRA launched a costly boycott of Smith & Wesson, and three months later the company was sold. In 2001, the new owners and the Bush administration canceled the pact.

"I think the NRA is irresponsible when it comes to gun safety," Ricker says. "There are proactive things the gun industry could do, like policing its own dealers and manufacturers. But the industry chose to circle the wagons and follow the NRA."

Getty Images/Jeff Swensen

Vice President Dick Cheney inspects a flintlock rifle given to him at the National Rifle Association's annual convention in Pittsburgh, on April 17, 2004, where Cheney spoke in support of Second Amendment rights. From left: NRA Vice President Sandra Froman, CEO Wayne LaPierre, Cheney and President Kayne Robinson.

20th-Century Crime

Crime waves have spurred repeated gun control campaigns in America. The first came in 1910-11, when New York Mayor William J. Gaynor was shot and wounded by a former city employee. Five months later, popular novelist David Graham Phillips was shot to death on a New York sidewalk.

In response to the public outcry, New York state Sen. Timothy D. Sullivan proposed banning the sale, possession or carrying of deadly weapons. To get a license to carry a handgun, a citizen had to show "proper cause" for needing it — and carrying a gun without a license could bring a prison term. One of the toughest gun laws ever passed, the Sullivan law of 1911 is still on the books.

In the 1930s, concern about organized crime led Congress to pass the first major federal gun control law. The 1934 statute curtailed ownership of sawed-off shotguns and machine guns. Those who wanted the so-called gangster weapons had to register and pay a hefty tax of $200 per weapon. Before the decade was over, gun dealers had to have a federal license.

In the 1960s, a wave of assassinations shocked the country: President John F. Kennedy in 1963 and Sen. Robert F. Kennedy and the Rev. Dr. Martin Luther King Jr. in 1968. In response, Congress passed the Gun Control Act of 1968, which prohibited minors, felons and the mentally ill from buying firearms. It also banned the interstate sale of rifles and handguns (such a sale enabled Lee Harvey Oswald to purchase the rifle he allegedly used to kill President Kennedy); barred the importing of "Saturday night special" pistols, a cheap, favorite tool of street criminals; and required gun dealers to keep records of their sales.

But gun control opponents weakened the law in 1986. A bill sponsored by Sen. James A. McClure, R-Idaho, and Rep. Harold L. Volkmer, D-Mo., once again legalized interstate sales of rifles and shotguns. The NRA-backed McClure-Volkmer bill also made it easier to get a dealer's license.

After a decade of lobbying by gun control advocates, Congress passed the Brady law in 1993, followed by the as-

Brady Center to Prevent Gun Violence (All)

Lethal and Legal

The 19 specific models of assault weapons banned by Congress in September 1993, including those above, are now legal again, along with two-dozen copycat models; lawmakers let the ban expire in September 2004. Assault rifles tend to be smaller than traditional hunting rifles, allowing them to be easily hidden. They also can have larger magazines; pistol grips, which allow firing from the hip; and attachments that let the shooter grip the gun's hot barrel and spray bullets across a wide swath.

sault-weapons ban in 1994. The period was a high-water mark for gun control. Clinton also worked out a deal with gun manufacturers in 1997 that required safety locks on about 80 percent of the handguns made in the U.S.

In another high-water mark for gun control advocates, in May 2000 tens of thousands of women and families marched in Washington and in rallies in about 70 other cities — dubbed the Million Mom March — demanding stricter gun controls.

But the Clinton-era legal gains and the growing public display of anti-gun sentiments triggered the wrath of the NRA, which mounted a full-court press to help defeat Gore in the 2000 presidential race. "They hurt us bad," Clinton later told, the online magazine *Salon* in June 2004, positing that his own anti-gun battles may have cost Gore Arkansas, Missouri, Tennessee and New Hampshire.

Perhaps realizing the power of the NRA over electoral politics, gun control was not a major campaign issue in 2004, and only 3,000 people showed up for a May 2004 Million Mom March to demand extension of the assault-weapons ban. ■

CURRENT SITUATION

Weapons Bans

Gun control advocates wasted no time in condemning President Bush and congressional Republicans for letting the ban expire. Presidential candidate Kerry declared that Bush had failed a "test of character." But partly because Democrats feared the power of the NRA, gun control didn't become a major issue in the fall 2004 presidential campaign. Indeed, Kerry noted that he, himself, owns a hunting rifle and even donned camouflage and hunted geese on a campaign stop.

With military-style weapons once again legal on American streets, "People are going to die," declares Steve Lenkart, chief lobbyist for the International Brotherhood of Police Officers. "Cops are going to die; civilians are going to die. I don't think it will be Armageddon, but I think there will be a flood of weapons."

Meanwhile, guns remain one of the few consumer products exempt from regulation by the Consumer Product Safety Commission, even though, unlike other potentially lethal objects, guns have only one purpose — to kill or wound. Gun control advocates want firearms put under the commission's control, arguing that faulty parts alone cause accidental shootings every year. But the gun lobby has avoided such regulation since the commission was created in 1972.

Roughly a million handgun purchases have been denied by the FBI or by local police since the Brady law took effect. Every year for the past five years, the FBI alone has turned down more than 60,000 would-be buyers.

But the NRA and other gun advocates say the law has been a failure because it has merely inconvenienced criminals, who eventually get guns anyway.

But gun control supporters say the sheer number of turndowns — about 2 percent of the would-be purchasers — shows that many guns are being kept out of the wrong hands. Moreover, they say, the law would be more effective if the three- to five-day waiting period for gun purchases were restored, gun show sales were covered by the law and private gun sales were conducted only through federally licensed dealers, complete with a background check.

Continued on p. 964

Designed to Kill Humans

What, exactly, are assault weapons? They are not machine-guns. Those are automatic rifles that fire several bullets a second with just one pull of the trigger. They've been outlawed in the civilian population since 1934.

Assault weapons are semiautomatic, requiring a separate squeeze of the trigger for each shot, just like hunting rifles. Assault weapons "function exactly the same way your grandfather's deer rifle did," declares Chris W. Cox, chief lobbyist for the National Rifle Association (NRA).

But traditional hunting rifles — 661 varieties of them — were excluded from the 10-year ban on assault weapons passed by Congress in 1994. However, the Federal Assault Weapons Act, which was allowed to expire on Sept. 13, 2004, outlawed 19 specific models of assault rifles, along with some two-dozen copycat versions.

Several distinct characteristics made the banned assault weapons more lethal than sporting rifles:

- *Size:* They tend to be smaller, with shorter barrels and sometimes folding stocks so they can be easily hidden, for example, under a coat.
- *Capacity:* They also have magazines that can hold 100 rounds of ammunition, which means the shooter doesn't have to reload as often. (The ban limited rifle magazines to 10 rounds.)
- *Pistol grips:* allow them to be fired, literally, from the hip. Hunting rifles are fired from the shoulder.
- *Barrel shrouds:* Many assault rifles allow an attachment that lets the shooter grip the hot barrel of the gun — making it easy to spray bullets across a wide swath.

"They're designed to do one thing: kill a lot of people very quickly."

— Gene Voegtlin, Legislative Counsel, International Association of Chiefs of Police

Opponents say assault weapons are, in essence, military weapons. Some even have bayonet mounts. "They're designed to do one thing: kill a lot of people very quickly," says Gene Voegtlin, legislative counsel for the International Association of Chiefs of Police. "And they have no place on our streets."

Robert Ricker, a former NRA lawyer now with the Coalition to Stop Gun Violence, explains, "The lethality comes especially from the magazine. It allows you to fire, fire, fire, fire."

"Anyone who says assault weapons can kill a lot of people quickly is intentionally misleading people," says NRA spokesman Andrew Arulanandam. "With semiautomatic firearms, you have to depress the trigger every time you want a bullet to fire. The picture that comes to mind when most people think of an assault weapon is a machine gun. This does not accurately describe the guns covered by the 1994 act, which are guns that are widely used by sportsmen, hunters and even athletes in Olympic sports."

Assault weapons also have been used in some of the nation's worst mass murders, most of which occurred before the ban. All of the following incidents — except for the Columbine school shootings — involved weapons later banned by the act:

- **McDonald's Shooting:** Armed with an Uzi assault pistol and a shotgun, James Huberty killed 21 people and wounded 19 others when he opened fire on patrons at a San Ysidro, Calif., McDonald's on July 18, 1984.
- **Stockton Schoolyard Massacre:** Patrick Purdy killed five children and wounded 29 others and a teacher on Jan. 17, 1989, when he shot 106 rounds in less than two minutes into a playground in Stockton, Calif., using an AK-47 assault rifle with a 75-round "drum" magazine.
- **Louisville Printing Plant Massacre:** Joseph Wesbecker killed eight people and wounded 13 others at the plant where he used to work in Louisville, Ky., on Sept. 14, 1989, before committing suicide. He used an AK-47 rifle and two MAC-11 assault pistols.
- **CIA Headquarters:** Pakistani national Mir Aimal Kasi used an AK-47 with a 30-round magazine to kill two CIA employees and wound three others outside the agency's Langley, Va., headquarters on Jan. 25, 1993.
- **Branch-Davidian Standoff:** Four ATF agents were killed and 16 others were wounded on Feb. 28, 1993, during a shootout at the religious cult's Waco, Texas, compound. The group had an arsenal of assault weapons, including: 123 AR-15s, 44 AK-47s, two Barrett .50 calibers, two "Street Sweepers," an unknown number of MAC-10 and MAC-11s.
- **San Francisco Pettit & Martin shootings:** Gian Luigi Ferri used two TEC-DC9 assault pistols with 50-round magazines to kill eight people and wound six others at the San Francisco law offices of Pettit & Martin and other offices on July 1, 1993.
- **Columbine High School, Littleton, Colo.:** On April 20, 1999, students Eric Harris and Dylan Klebold killed 13 people and wounded 23 others before killing themselves at their high school. Among their weapons were a Hi-Point Carbine and a TEC-DC9. The boys were too young to legally buy such weapons, but the guns were either not covered by the ban or were "grandfathered in" because they were manufactured before the ban was enacted.

Continued from p. 962

Juvenile records should also be searched as part of background checks, they argue, and those with violent misdemeanors on their records should be denied gun purchases. Reformed criminals could petition to remove their names from the no-sale list. Finally, gun control advocates call for the use of "ballistic fingerprinting." Before any gun is sold, it would be fired, and the unique marks made on the bullet as it travels through the barrel would be recorded in a national data bank so bullets later shot from the weapon would be easier to trace.

"What if we'd been able to do that during the D.C. sniper shootings?" asks Henigan of the Brady Campaign. As it was, the rifle used to murder and terrorize Washington, D.C.-area residents in the fall of 2002 wasn't traced to its seller until the suspects were caught.

"The best we can do now is to determine that two bullets came from the same gun," Henigan observes. "But we can't identify the gun. Don't you think it would discourage criminals from using guns if they could be traced that easily?"

The NRA opposes waiting periods at gun shows. "They're proposing 72-hour waiting periods, and gun shows only last 48 hours," Arulanandam says.

He also questions the technique of ballistic fingerprinting. "Talking about 'ballistic DNA' is highly misleading," he says. "All a person would have to do is run a file through the barrel of the gun. Also, over the months and years of usage, the markings of the barrel change."

Weapons experts, however, defend the technique. "It's more difficult than just running a file through," Ricker says. "You would have to file the entire inner surface of the barrel. And you run the risk of damaging the gun in the process."

"They're proposing 72-hour waiting periods, and gun shows only last 48 hours."

— NRA spokesman Andrew Arulanandam, explaining the NRA's opposition to waiting periods for purchases at gun shows.

The Beleaguered ATF

The NRA derides the ATF as intrusive and inept, creating "phony gun laws" to harass innocent citizens and an already overregulated industry. After all, the group says, there are 20,000 local and state laws governing gun ownership.

But advocates of stronger gun laws call the ATF the "lap dog" of the gun industry. Clinton aides lambasted the agency in 1997 for speeding up the approval of import permits for 150,000 modified assault weapons at the same time the White House was trying to reduce the presence of assault weapons. Clinton himself eventually stepped in and suspended the permits. [28]

In a blistering July 2004 report, the Justice Department's inspector general complained the ATF often granted licenses to dealers after merely a phone call rather than a personal visit by an inspector. Moreover, the report said, the ATF inspects only about 4.5 percent of the 104,000 gun dealers every year. [29]

"At that rate, it would take the ATF more than 22 years to inspect" all dealers, the report said. The goal was a "compliance inspection" every three years.

The report noted that one gun dealer had been cited "for selling guns to a minor and for numerous record-keeping violations" but was never reinspected. Inspectors found another dealer had "missing sales records and sales to out-of-state residents — all strong indicators of (illegal) gun trafficking," but they never reported the dealer to ATF's special agents for investigation.

Carl J. Truscott, who became director of the ATF last May, agreed with most of the criticisms and promised to do better. Both he and the report cited lack of resources as a reason for the agency's failures.

The agency, which enforces all federal gun laws, has only 420 inspectors to monitor the nation's gun dealers.

Courts and State Initiatives

With three legal victories under its belt, the Brady Campaign, plans to pursue more lawsuits against gun dealers and manufacturers.

For its part, the NRA plans to keep trying to get laws banning such suits. "This exploitation of tragedy is not only intellectually dishonest, it's shameful," declares Cox.

The Brady Campaign counters that lawsuits are the only way to bring justice to victims of irresponsible gun traffickers — and that maybe they will cause dealers and gun-makers to change their ways.

Continued on p. 966

At Issue:

Have the assault-weapons ban and the Brady law helped to prevent crime?

DENNIS A. HENIGAN
LEGAL DIRECTOR, BRADY CENTER TO PREVENT GUN VIOLENCE

WRITTEN FOR *THE CQ RESEARCHER*, OCTOBER 2004

yes

A decade ago, our nation took two giant steps toward a sensible, national gun policy. In 1993, President Bill Clinton signed the Brady Handgun Violence Protection Act, requiring licensed gun dealers to conduct background checks on gun buyers. A year later, he signed legislation banning production of military-style assault weapons and high-capacity ammunition magazines.

Since these landmark laws were enacted, violent crime has dropped dramatically. Yet President Bush and the Congress recently allowed the ban on assault weapons to expire. In the 1990s we had begun to win the fight against violent crime. Why are we now turning back the clock?

Brady act background checks have stopped more than 1 million felons, fugitives and other high-risk individuals from buying guns over-the-counter. During the period 1993-2001, as violent crime dropped 54 percent, violent crime committed with guns dropped 63 percent. Gun homicides, which had increased 43 percent from 1987 to a peak of over 17,000 in 1993, plunged 37 percent between 1994 and 2000.

This dramatic success story is no doubt due to many factors. Is it plausible to believe that the Brady act is not one of them?

The assault-weapons ban was enacted to reduce the lethal firepower available to criminals. It banned not only semiautomatic assault weapons like the Uzi and the TEC-9, but also the high-capacity magazines that turn ordinary pistols into killing machines. According to a recent report from the National Institute of Justice (NIJ), attacks with these high-capacity guns "result in more shots fired, more persons hit and more wounds per victim than do attacks with other firearms."

The Brady Center to Prevent Gun Violence recently reported that the frequency of banned assault weapons used in crime has declined 66 percent since the law went into effect. The NIJ report concluded that the ban had prevented thousands of crimes with assault weapons annually.

Every major, national law-enforcement organization has called for the ban to be extended. President Bush's leadership, however, has been missing-in-action. With a wink to the gun lobby, he refused even to meet with the police on this issue.

The lesson of the 1990s is that sensible gun laws save lives. Yet every two weeks, we still lose more Americans to gunfire than we have lost in the entire Iraq war. Our success in curbing criminal violence should be a mandate to strengthen, not weaken, the nation's gun laws.

CHRIS W. COX
CHIEF LOBBYIST, NATIONAL RIFLE ASSOCIATION

WRITTEN FOR *THE CQ RESEARCHER*, OCTOBER 2004

no

Despite the distressed rhetoric of the gun control lobby, the so-called "assault-weapons" ban expired on Sept. 13. That's because a clear majority of Congress recognized that this 10-year ban on semiautomatic firearms was bad policy and bad politics. Like the Brady law, it was just another failed experiment for nationwide gun control.

Dozens of reports by criminologists, journalists and federal, state and local law-enforcement agencies have found that these firearms were involved in only 1 percent of crimes — before, during and after this ban was adopted. In fact, there isn't one statistic showing the ban had any effect on reducing crime. Even President Bill Clinton's own Justice Department study proved this law was ineffective.

In the elections following enactment of the ban, gun owners voiced their opposition at ballot boxes across the country, removing many politicians — including the sitting Speaker of the House, Tom Foley — who voted for the ill-conceived measure. Former President Clinton acknowledged to the *Cleveland Plain Dealer* in January 1995: "The fight for the assault-weapons ban cost 20 members their seats in Congress."

Still, some in Washington were determined to play politics with the Second Amendment. That's because the debate is not about so-called "assault weapons." Very simply, it's about banning guns.

A day after this gun ban was signed into law in 1994, a *Washington Post* editorial admitted, "Assault weapons play a part in only a small percentage of crime. The provision is mainly symbolic; its virtue will be if it turns out to be, as hoped, a stepping stone to broader gun control."

Bill sponsor Sen. Dianne Feinstein, D-Calif., confirmed her true agenda to CBS' "60 Minutes." "If I could have gotten 51 votes in the Senate of the United States for an outright ban, picking up every one of them — Mr. and Mrs. America, turn them all in — I would have done it."

Those are the only words gun owners should ever need to remember. Never has the anti-gun agenda been stated more succinctly or honestly.

Undoubtedly, the gun control lobby will wait for the next tragedy to try to push their agenda. They will continue to say that gun control measures like the Brady law are the panacea for a safe society. Those with an ounce of logic will reject this nonsense and opt for stricter laws that target criminals — not law-abiding Americans.

Continued from p. 964

The NRA is also continuing to press for state "shall carry" laws that allow citizens to carry concealed weapons. Thirty-eight states now have such laws, and separate laws banning lawsuits have prevented several cities from pursuing legal action against the gun industry.

The Supreme Court continues to avoid ruling on the substance of the Second Amendment. But Justice Clarence Thomas has issued what some see as an open invitation to bring the "individual right" interpretation to the court. In 1997, Thomas — in a decision involving the Brady law — wrote that if the Second Amendment "is read to confer a personal right to 'keep and bear arms,' a colorable argument exists that the Federal Government's regulatory scheme, at least as it pertains to the purely intrastate sale or possession of firearms, runs afoul of that Amendment's protections.

"Perhaps at some future date," he continued, "this Court will have the opportunity to determine whether Justice [Joseph] Story was correct when he wrote that the right to bear arms 'has justly been considered, as the palladium of the liberties of a republic.' " [30]

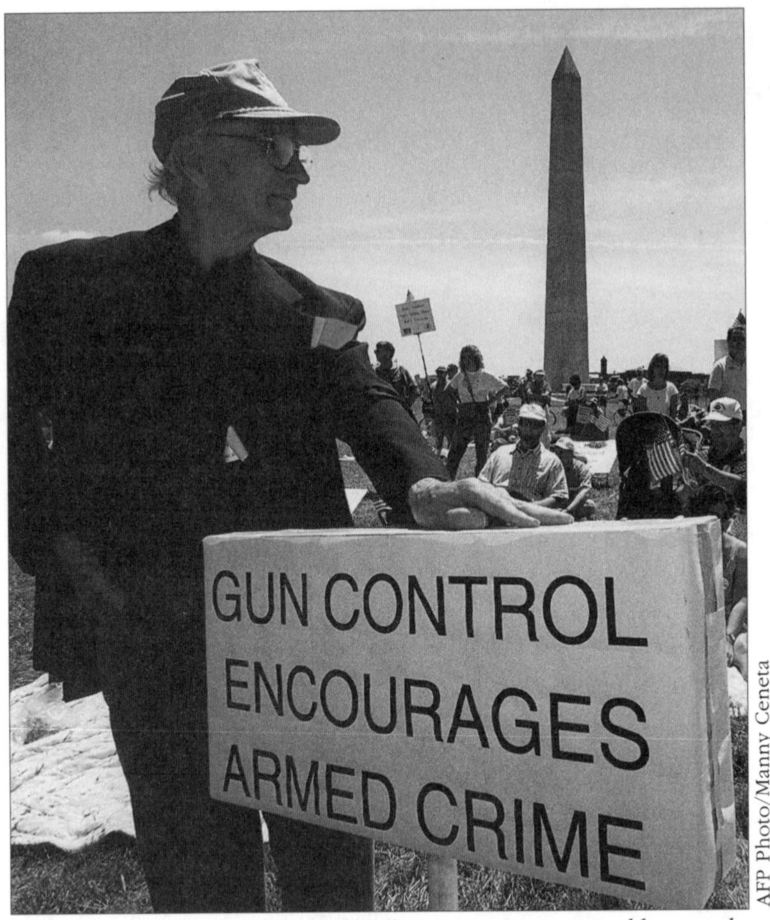

AFP Photo/Manny Ceneta

Retired Navy Capt. Charles Rozek rallies against gun control laws at the Washington Monument on May 14, 2000. The rally was held to counter the Million Mom March, which supported stricter gun laws.

District of Columbia

Washington, D.C., has some of the nation's toughest gun laws. It has its own assault-weapons ban, independent of the expired federal law, and requires residents to keep their firearms disassembled or trigger-locked. Police believe the restrictions have helped cut the number of murders in the District from 454 in 1993 to 248 in 2003.

Yet in September 2004, Rep. Mark Souder, R-Ind., announced that he had 228 cosponsors on a bill to abolish the city's gun control laws. Moreover, the bill would forbid the city's mayor and council from passing any "laws or regulations that discourage or eliminate the private ownership or use of firearms." Sen. Larry Craig, R-Idaho, is sponsoring a similar bill in the Senate. Despite "home rule," Congress is still the ultimate authority in the District of Columbia.

"The folly of gun control is shown time and again in cities that have strict gun control laws," Souder said. "Washington, D.C., has the most restrictive gun control laws in the country, yet it is known foremost for its violent criminal activity." His bill, he said, "would allow law-abiding people to use guns to protect their homes and families."

Infuriated local officials vowed to fight. Mayor Anthony Williams called the bill "outrageous" and "an attack on the limited democracy we have here for D.C. residents." And District of Columbia House Delegate Eleanor Holmes Norton declared: "The intrusion into our local home rule is not simply about the pride of self-government. It has meaning for how we live, up to and including whether we live." [31]

Hannah Hawkins, who heads a youth center in crime-ridden Anacostia, saw a touch of hypocrisy in House members, safe in their tightly guarded offices, taking the District's gun protections away. "If the U.S. Capitol can be handgun-free, why can't we?" she asked. [32]

Others noted that of the 1,385 guns recovered from crimes in the District between Jan. 1 and Sept. 8 of this year, 97 percent were purchased elsewhere. [33]

On Sept. 29, the bill passed the House, 250 to 171. The "yes" votes included 52 Democrats. Political observers decried the bill as a partisan ploy. A *New York Times* editorial called the effort "sickening," "shameful" and "a brazen insult" to District residents. It said the bill "would make D.C. stand for Dodge City" and "may answer the question of how low congressional politicians will go in bowing to the gun lobby." [34]

Having served its political purpose — forcing lawmakers to take a position on gun control six weeks before the election — the bill then went to the Senate, where it was expected to die quietly. As of early November, the Senate had taken no action. ■

OUTLOOK

The Fight Continues

The Nov. 2 election results were seen as a major setback for the NRA's adversaries. President Bush, with NRA backing, won re-election with 51 percent of the popular vote. Republicans, who are less inclined toward gun control than Democrats, picked up four seats in the Senate, giving them a majority of 55 to 44, with one Independent. The GOP also strengthened its hold on the House, winning at least 231 seats out of 435.

The NRA claimed victory in 14 of the 18 Senate races and 241 of the 251 House races where it had made endorsements. "This was a good election for us," spokesman Arulanandam says. "It's a testament to the will of the people. The NRA position on gun rights is the mainstream position. I think it's important that Democratic leaders stop taking their party over a cliff on gun control."

In fact, a recent poll showed that Americans of all races, ages, economic backgrounds and political orientation — including a majority of gun owners — strongly supported the 10-year assault-weapons ban, which the NRA opposed. (*See poll, p. 953.*)

Brady Campaign leader Sarah Brady acknowledges that the new congressional ratios are not in her favor, but she vows to fight on. "I'm sure [the NRA] will move full speed ahead," she says. "And we'll be doing the same on our side."

An early priority for the Brady camp will be the renewal of the assault-weapons ban. Gun control advocates point to Bush's restatement of his support for the ban in his third debate with Kerry. Bush's failure to ask Congress to renew the ban, however, was instrumental in its demise on Sept. 13.

Brady noted the strong public and police support for the ban. "Was it perfect? No," she said. "But we'll start with what we had and work from there. We don't want to take guns away from people, but we do want to strengthen the law."

Gun control advocates also will try to close loopholes in the Brady law, particularly to cover gun shows, where some 40 percent of firearms sales take place.

Of course, the NRA will strongly resist such changes, and with the new configuration of the House and Senate, Bush's support for gun rights and a wariness among Democrats to confront the gun lobby, new gun laws will likely be defeated.

Gun control advocates' best hope may be the courts. Henigan says the next legal showdown could come in New York City, where the government is suing a Who's Who of prominent gun manufacturers for allegedly careless practices that help create a "public nuisance." The city accuses the manufacturers of selling to reckless dealers, thus aiding the illegal traffic in guns. The trial is scheduled for April 2005.

The NRA plans to vigorously challenge the city's suits. And with its renewed clout on Capitol Hill, the NRA sees the coming 109th Congress as fertile ground for banning similar suits. Although such a measure passed the House this session, the Senate could be a problem. Republicans picked up four seats and ousted Senate Democratic leader Thomas A. Daschle of South Dakota, but the GOP still lacks the 60 votes necessary to cut off a filibuster. Thus Democrats might be able to frustrate legislation that would protect the gun industry against damage suits at the national level.

At the state level, the NRA will continue to press for legislation blocking suits in the 17 states that do not ban lawsuits against gun dealers and manufacturers.

Both sides are gearing up for the confrontations ahead.

"There will be another ban on assault weapons," Brady predicts.

"We've been around for 133 years," Arulanandam says. "You can bet we'll be around to fight these battles for a while." ■

Notes

[1] Spencer S. Hsu, "House GOP Proposes to Repeal D.C. Gun Bans," *The Washington Post*, Sept. 14, 2004, p. A1.

[2] Robert J. Spitzer, *The Politics of Gun Control*, CQ Press (2004), p. 6. Cox, of the NRA, uses

About the Author

Bob Adams is a veteran Washington journalist who specializes in foreign policy and national politics. He covered the civil wars in El Salvador and Nicaragua in the 1980s, the Persian Gulf War in 1991 and four presidential campaigns and served for 10 years as Washington bureau chief of the *St. Louis Post-Dispatch*. He has received two awards from the Overseas Press Club (for reporting on the Soviet Union and Central America); the Raymond Clapper Award from the White House Correspondents' Association (for best reporting by a Washington correspondent on any topic) and the National Headliner Award for exposing defense fraud and has been a judge for the Pulitzer Prizes. His previous *CQ Researcher* reports include the "Glass Ceiling" and "Primary Health Care." He has a B.S. in journalism from the University of Illinois.

a figure of 80 million gun owners and more than 200 million guns.

[3] Centers for Disease Control and Prevention, September 2004.

[4] David Hemenway, *Private Guns, Public Health* (2004), p. 19.

[5] Spitzer, *op. cit.*

[6] Quoted in "Back in Busine$$," Consumer Federation of America, Sept. 7, 2004.

[7] *Ibid.*, p. 14.

[8] Fox Butterfield, "As Expiration Looms, Gun Ban's Effect Is Debated," *The New York Times*, Sept. 10, 2004, p. A14.

[9] Reuters, Oct. 16, 1991.

[10] Figures obtained from the Centers for Disease Control and Prevention, September 2004.

[11] Spitzer, *op. cit.*, p. 130.

[12] Bureau of Justice Statistics, U.S. Department of Justice, September 2004.

[13] For background, see Kenneth Jost, "Sentencing Debates," *The CQ Researcher*, Nov. 5, 2004, pp. 925-948.

[14] Phillip Cook and Jens Ludwig, "Homicide and Suicide Rates Associated with Implementation of the Brady Handgun Violence Prevention Act," *Journal of the American Medical Association*, Aug. 2, 2000, pp. 585-591.

[15] Spitzer, *op. cit.*, pp. 16-40.

[16] Laurence H. Tribe and Akhil Reed Amar "Well-Regulated Militias, and More," *The New York Times*, Oct. 28, 1999, p. A31.

[17] Richard Willing, "Texas Case Could Shape the Future of Gun Control," *USA Today*, Oct. 27, 1999, p. A1.

[18] *U.S. v. Emerson*, 5th U.S. Circuit Court of Appeals, Oct. 16, 2001.

[19] Spitzer, *op. cit.*, p. 30.

[20] Helen Dewar, "Congress Leaves Some Priority Bills Unfinished," *The Washington Post*, Oct. 14, p. A29.

[21] Fox Butterfield, "Gun Dealer Settles Case Over Sale to Straw Buyer," *The New York Times*, June 23, 2004, p. A14.

[22] *Ibid.*

[23] Michael A. Bellesiles, "The Origins of Gun Culture in the United States, 1760-1865," *Journal of American History*, September 1996, pp. 426-428. Bellesiles' work has been widely criticized. Some experts even contend that he never actually studied probate records.

[24] Richard Shenkman, *Legends, Lies, and Cherished Myths of American History* (1988), p. 112.

[25] See Richard Worsnop, "Gun Control," *The CQ Researcher*, June 10, 1994, pp. 505-528.

[26] For a history of the NRA and an analysis of its power, see Spitzer, *op. cit.*, Chapter 4.

FOR MORE INFORMATION

Brady Campaign to Prevent Gun Violence, 1225 I St., N.W., Suite 1100, Washington, DC 20005; (202) 898-0792; www.bradycampaign.org. The leading voice for gun control; headed by Sarah Brady.

Bureau of Alcohol, Tobacco, Firearms and Explosives, 650 Massachusetts Ave., N.W., Washington, DC 20226; (202) 927-8500; www.atf.gov. Enforces federal gun regulations.

Children's Defense Fund, 25 E St., N.W., Washington, DC 20001; (202) 628-8787; www.childrensdefense.org. Advocates on a broad range of children's issues.

Citizens Committee for the Right to Keep and Bear Arms, Liberty Park, 12500 N.E., 10th Place, Bellevue, WA 98005; 1-800-426-4302; www.ccrkba.org. Calls itself "the common sense gun lobby."

Coalition to Stop Gun Violence, 1023 15th St., N.W., Suite 600, Washington, DC 20005; (202) 408-0061; www.csgv.org. Successor to the National Coalition to Ban Handguns; concentrates on achieving gun restrictions.

Consumer Federation of America, 1424 16th St., N.W., Suite 604, Washington, DC 20036; (202) 387-6121; www.consumerfed.org. Issued report on gun manufacturers' intentions prior to the expiration of the ban on assault weapons.

International Association of Chiefs of Police, 515 N. Washington St., Alexandria, VA 22314; (703) 836-6767; www.theiapc.org. Oldest and largest nonprofit membership organization of police executives.

International Brotherhood of Police Officers, 159 Burgin Parkway, Quincy, MA 02169; (617) 376-0220; www.ibpo.org. Lobbies on behalf of police and public safety.

National Rifle Association, 11250 Waples Mill Road, Fairfax, VA 22030; (703) 267-1000; www.nra.org. A powerful and vocal opponent of gun control.

National Shooting Sports Foundation, 11 Mile Hill Road, Newton, CT 06470; (203) 426-1320; www.nssf.org. The trade association for the firearms industry.

Police Foundation, 1201 Connecticut Ave., N.W., Washington, DC 20036; (202) 833-1460; www.policefoundation.org. Founded by the Ford Foundation, the nonprofit group studies ways to increase police effectiveness; supports assault-weapons ban.

Violence Policy Center, 1140 19th St., N.W., Suite 600, Washington, DC 20036; (202) 822-8200; www.vpc.org. A research and advocacy group for gun control.

[27] See Kathy Koch, "School Violence," *The CQ Researcher*, Oct. 9, 1998, pp. 881-904.

[28] For background, see Kenneth Jost, "Gun Control Standoff," *The CQ Researcher*, Dec. 19, 1997, pp. 1105-1128.

[29] "Inspection of Firearms Dealers by the Bureau of Alcohol, Tobacco, Firearms and Explosives," U.S. Department of Justice, Office of the Inspector General, July 2004.

[30] *Printz v. United States*, 521 U.S. (1997). The reference to Justice Story was from Story's book *Commentaries*, published in 1833.

[31] Maureen Fan, "Gun Vote Brings Out the Fight in Norton," *The Washington Post*, Sept. 30, 2004, p. B1.

[32] Spencer S. Hsu, "D.C. Gun Ban Repeal Is Set Aside," *The Washington Post*, Sept. 21, 2004, p. B1.

[33] Spencer S. Hsu, "Bush Challenged on D.C. Gun Ban," *The Washington Post*, Sept. 28, 2004, p. A4.

[34] Editorial, "Bang Bang, You're Elected," *The New York Times*, Sept. 19, 2004, "News of the Week in Review," p. 10.

Bibliography

Selected Sources

Books

Bijlefeld, Marjolijn, *The Gun Control Debate: A Documentary History*, Greenwood Publishing Group, 1997.

For those who seek primary sources in the gun control debate, a freelance writer and editor provides more than 200 basic documents on the subject from the past 200 years.

Hemenway, David, *Private Guns, Public Health*, University of Michigan Press, 2004.

A Harvard professor of health policy argues that the high cost of gun deaths and injuries caused by firearms should not be tolerated.

Kleck, Gary, *Targeting Guns: Firearms and Their Control*, Aldine de Gruyter, 1997.

Taking a minority view among criminologists, a professor of criminology at Florida State University maintains that as many as 2.5 million crimes a year are prevented by the use or presence of a firearm. The figure has been challenged by other experts.

Lott, John R., Jr., *More Guns, Less Crime*, University of Chicago Press, 2000.

A University of Chicago criminology professor disputes the methods and conclusions of other academics who study gun control. Like Kleck, he believes gun control laws are inherently flawed and supports the carrying of concealed weapons.

Spitzer, Robert J., *The Politics of Gun Control*, CQ Press, 2004.

A professor of political science at the State University of New York at Cortland describes the National Rifle Association's drift to the right and its lobbying power and argues that the logic of international arms control also applies to the gun control debate in America.

Articles

Butterfield, Fox, "As Expiration Looms, Gun Ban's Effect Is Debated," *The New York Times*, Sept. 10, 2004, p. A14.

Defects in the assault-weapons ban limited its effectiveness.

Hsu, Spencer, "D.C. Gun Bill May Be Linked to Budget," *The Washington Post*, Sept. 17, 2004, p. B3.

A move to repeal virtually all of D.C.'s gun restrictions received a boost in the Senate, where gun rights supporters are seeking to pass the measure as an amendment to the city's 2005 budget.

Jost, Kenneth, "Gun Control Standoff," *The CQ Researcher*, Dec. 19, 1997, pp. 1105-1128.

The author's comprehensive analysis of current research on gun control includes a discussion of the NRA's role in defeating the 1997 gun-safety initiative in Washington state.

Stolberg, Sheryl Gay, "Effort to Renew Weapons Ban Falters on Hill," *The New York Times*, Sept. 9, 2004, p. A1.

The reporter discusses the fear of the gun control issue among Democrats and describes the political gamesmanship being played between House Republicans and President Bush in declining to renew the 10-year-old ban on assault weapons.

Tribe, Laurence H., and Akhil Reed Amar, "Well-Regulated Militias, and More," *The New York Times*, Oct. 28, 1999, p. A31.

Two constitutional scholars re-evaluate the traditional analyses of the Second Amendment, arguing that its "reference to the people's 'right' to be armed cannot be trumped by the Amendment's preamble."

Tucker, Neely, "Handguns With A Safety Catch," *The Washington Post*, Sept. 29, 2004, p. C1.

The House is scheduled to vote on the D.C. Personal Protection Act, which would end the District's ban on handguns and allow residents to carry handguns.

Reports and Studies

Cook, Philip J., and Jens Ludwig, *Guns in America: Results of a Comprehensive National Survey on Firearms Ownership and Use*, Police Foundation, May 1997.

The survey indicates widespread use of guns by Americans to defend themselves, and then proceeds to debunk the survey.

Levinson, Sanford, "The Embarrassing Second Amendment," *Yale Law Journal*, December 1989.

The author's argument that the Second Amendment, in spite of its "militia" clause, confers an individual right to carry guns touched off a re-examination of the Second Amendment by other scholars.

Peschin, Susan, *et. al.*, *Back in Busine$$: Gun Industry Plans for the Expiration of the Federal Assault Weapons Ban*, Consumer Federation of America, Sept. 7, 2004.

Based on interviews with gun-industry executives, the report says the ban's demise will put more lethal and less expensive weapons on the street, even though domestic gun manufacturers had already been able to evade import restrictions on assault weapons.

The Next Step:

Additional Articles from Current Periodicals

Assault-Weapons Ban

Hirschfeld Davis, Julie, "Kerry Assails Bush Over Lapse of Gun Ban," *The Baltimore Sun*, Sept. 14, 2004, p. 1A.
As the 10-year-old federal ban on assault weapons expired, John Kerry accused President Bush of making life easier for terrorists and harder for police officers by letting the law lapse.

Simon, Richard, "Assault Weapons Ban Ends Quietly," *Los Angeles Times*, Sept. 10 2004, p. A1.
With a decade-long ban on assault weapons set to expire, Congress will allow once demonized semiautomatic weapons to again be sold to the public, and manufacturers are competing to reap the most out of their return.

Stockwell, Jamie, and Karin Brulliard, "No Cheers Over Gun Ban's End," *The Washington Post*, Sept. 14, 2004, p. B1.
Gun dealers said lifting the federal ban on assault weapons would have little effect on business because stores wouldn't have a fresh stock for weeks, and customers aren't that eager to buy them.

Weinstein, Henry, "Court Upholds State Assault Weapons Ban," *Los Angeles Times*, Dec. 6, 2002, p. 1.
A federal appeals court upheld California's assault-weapons control act, ruling that there is no constitutional right for individuals to keep and bear arms, a decision at odds with the Bush administration.

Children and Guns

Brody, Jane, "Keeping Guns Out of Children's Hands," *The New York Times*, Aug. 17, 2004, p. F7.
The rate of fatal and non-fatal injuries inflicted by guns on children 14 and younger declined by more than 50 percent in the 1990s, but firearm injuries to children remain a serious public health concern.

Haynes, Karima, "Mothers Push Fight Against Gun Violence," *Los Angeles Times*, Aug. 5, 2002, Part 2, p. A3.
Almost 750,000 people gathered in Washington on Mother's Day 2000 to support sensible gun laws, and they have continued to mobilize people in their hometowns in the war against gun violence.

Rich, Eric, and Theola Labbe, "Moms Unleash Their Anguish, Anger; Thousands March to End Gun Violence, Renew Assault Weapons Ban," *The Washington Post*, May 10, 2004, p. B1.
Moms joined with the Brady Campaign for the largest gun control demonstration in four years, hoping President Bush will support renewal of the ban on assault weapons.

Gun-Related Lawsuits

Anton, Mike, "Gun Foes Might Buy Arms Firm," *Los Angeles Times*, June 17, 2004, p. B1.
The legal team representing a teenager who was left a quadriplegic after being accidentally shot with a Bryco pistol might make a bid to buy the company, which went bankrupt after being ordered by pay the boy $24 million.

Dolan, Maura, "Gun Makers Not Liable in Crimes, State Justices Say," *Los Angeles Times*, Aug. 7, 2001, p. A1.
The California Supreme Court ruled that gunmakers could not be held responsible when their products are used to commit crimes.

Leonnig, Carol, "Suit Takes Aim at Gun Maker's Role; Case Survives Bid in Congress to Halt Litigation Against Arms Manufacturers," *The Washington Post*, March 11, 2004, p. T10.
The family of one of the D.C. snipers' victims sues the gun's manufacturer with the help of a Washington law firm and the nation's leading gun control experts.

Stolberg, Sheryl Gay, "Senate Leaders Scuttle Gun Bill Over Changes," *The New York Times*, March 3, 2004, p. A1.
The Senate rejected a bill that would shield gun manufacturers and dealers from lawsuits because of attached amendments that renewed the assault-weapons ban and required background checks on customers at gun shows.

VandeHei, Jim, "Gun Firms On Verge Of Winning New Shield," *The Washington Post*, May 5, 2003, p. A1.
President Bush and many lawmakers support legislation that would prevent victims of gun crimes from making civil claims against companies that manufactured, imported or sold the weapons.

National Rifle Association

Collier, Lorna, "Weapons of Mass Possession," *Chicago Tribune*, May 5, 2004, p. C1.
An estimated 17 million women in America own guns — a number that could be on the rise — and the NRA is targeting them with specialized classes and a magazine.

Dao, James, "N.R.A. Opens an All-Out Drive for Bush and Its Views," *The New York Times*, April 16, 2004, p. A1.
The National Rifle Association not only celebrates the Second Amendment at its annual meeting but also kicks off a campaign to drum up support for President Bush's re-election.

Lichtblau, Eric, "Irking N.R.A., Bush Supports The Ban on Assault Weapons," *The New York Times*, May 8, 2003, p. A1.
President Bush and the NRA, long regarded as allies, find

themselves at odds over the extension of the ban on assault weapons, which will soon be introduced by Congress.

Mangu-Ward, Katherine, "Trigger Happy; The NRA Outguns Its Opponents," *The Weekly Standard*, Sept. 27, 2004.
Gun sellers say the assault-weapons ban didn't make a difference, but it's been a thorn in the NRA's side for a decade.

Powers, Thom, "Don't Tread on the NRA," *Los Angeles Times*, May 18, 2003, p. R6.
"Outgunned: Up Against the NRA" tells the story of how gun control activists and lawyers terrified the gun industry and how the NRA battled back with its profound political influence.

Slater, Eric, "Gun Groups May Not Be Bush Campaign Weapon," *Los Angeles Times*, April 13, 2004, p. A1.
Some gun owners and NRA members have grown so disenchanted with President Bush that they may cast protest votes against Bush.

Strom, Stephanie, "A Deficit of $100 Million Is Confronting the N.R.A.," *The New York Times*, Dec. 21, 2003, p. A1.
Legal, legislative and political battles in the last decade have left the NRA with a $100 million deficit, reopening a bitter debate within the group about how it manages its money.

Politics and Guns

Baer, Susan, "Attitudes Toward Guns Predict Places in a Divided Electorate," *The Baltimore Sun*, Oct. 4, 2004, p. 1A.
In this election year, politicians faced with the reality that nearly 50 percent of voting households own guns are revisiting the gun debate with political pragmatism.

Bendavid, Naftali, "Law-Enforcement Groups Divided on Presidential Candidates," *Chicago Tribune*, Sept. 28, 2004, p. C15.
Controversies over the assault-weapons ban and Bush's budget cuts have split the law-enforcement community.

Crowley, Michael, "Muzzled," *The New Republic*, Sept. 27, 2004, p. 11.
Capitol Hill Democrats fail to challenge the expiration of the 10-year-old assault-weapons ban, struggling to appeal to pro-gun-control voters but avoid the wrath of the NRA.

Epstein, Edward, "NRA Huff—Weapon Ban Falls; Politicians Loath to Tangle with the Power of the Gun Lobby," *The San Francisco Chronicle*, Sept. 13, 2004, p. A1.
The assault-weapons ban — which enjoys support from two-thirds of Americans — expired due to the enduring power of the National Rifle Association over politicians.

Heinzmann, David, and Rudolph Bush, "Report Takes Aim at Area Gun Sellers," *Chicago Tribune*, Jan. 13, 2004, p. C1.
Gun-law reform advocates say the federal government has been lax in prosecuting a minority of dealers who sell guns that are responsible for the majority of gun crimes.

James, Frank, "Assault Gun Ban is Political Ammo for Democrats," *Chicago Tribune*, Aug. 1, 2004, p. C15.
With the majority of the public in favor of keeping the assault-weapons ban, some Democrats hope to use the issue against President Bush and members of Congress in their campaigns.

Parker, Laura, "Gun-Control Debate Gets Muzzled," *USA Today*, Aug. 8, 2003, p. 3A.
The national debate over gun control has been mostly silent, with Democrats less willing to take on the gun lobby, and the gun industry racking up legislative wins.

Tumulty, Karen, and Viveca Novak, "Dodging the Bullet," *Time*, Nov. 4, 2002, p. 45.
Considering the regularity with which Democratic candidates now tout the Second Amendment, gun control advocates don't expect the Washington-area sniper attacks to produce any new gun laws.

Citing *The CQ Researcher*

Sample formats for citing these reports in a bibliography include the ones listed below. Preferred styles and formats vary, so please check with your instructor or professor.

MLA Style

Jost, Kenneth. "Rethinking the Death Penalty." The CQ Researcher 16 Nov. 2001: 945-68.

APA Style

Jost, K. (2001, November 16). Rethinking the death penalty. *The CQ Researcher, 11*, 945-968.

Chicago Style

Jost, Kenneth. "Rethinking the Death Penalty." *CQ Researcher*, November 16, 2001, 945-968.

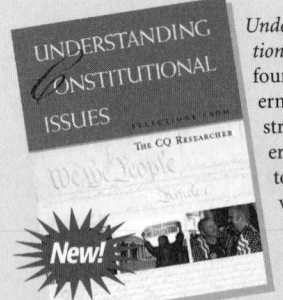

CQ Researcher

Published by CQ Press, a division of Congressional Quarterly Inc.

thecqresearcher.com

Treatment of Veterans

Is the nation keeping its promises to veterans?

America has always promised good care and benefits to veterans for their service to the nation. But an estimated 1.7 million uninsured veterans — including U.S. troops who served in Iraq and Afghanistan, as well as veterans from the Vietnam and Persian Gulf wars — were unable to get the promised support last year. While the military and Department of Veterans Affairs (VA) provide state-of-the-art medical treatment, ex-warriors must often fight dispiriting bureaucratic battles to get their care and benefits. The Bush administration points to record VA budgets and new procedures to make VA services more accessible to veterans. But veterans say they are increasingly losing benefits because the VA is underfunded; they want veterans' health services to become a mandatory part of the federal budget. Meanwhile, today's GI Bill offers fewer benefits than the landmark 1944 legislation that helped millions of veterans go to college and establish comfortable civilian lives after World War II.

Former Army Spec. Robert Jackson of Des Moines lost his legs in an explosion while serving in Iraq with the Iowa National Guard.

INSIDE THIS REPORT

The CQ Researcher • Nov. 19, 2004 • www.thecqresearcher.com
Volume 14, Number 41 • Pages 973-996

CQ PRESS

RECIPIENT OF SOCIETY OF PROFESSIONAL JOURNALISTS AWARD FOR EXCELLENCE ◆ AMERICAN BAR ASSOCIATION SILVER GAVEL AWARD

THE ISSUES

BACKGROUND

CURRENT SITUATION

OUTLOOK

SIDEBARS AND GRAPHICS

FOR FURTHER RESEARCH

Cover: Former Army Spec. Robert Jackson lost his legs in an explosion while serving in Iraq with the Iowa National Guard. About 6,000 U.S. soldiers have been wounded in Afghanistan and Iraq, and almost 900 have suffered serious injuries, such as lost limbs or eyesight. The Department of Veterans Affairs has become a specialist in prosthetics. (AP Photo/Charlie Niebergall)

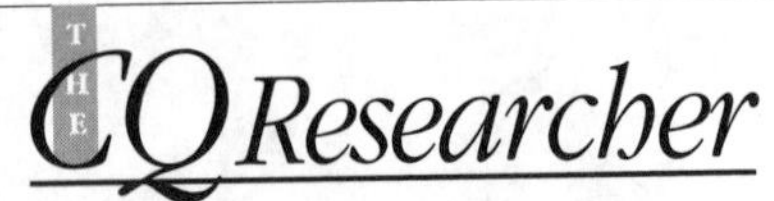

Nov. 19, 2004
Volume 14, Number 41

MANAGING EDITOR: Thomas J. Colin
ASSISTANT MANAGING EDITOR: Kathy Koch
ASSOCIATE EDITOR: Kenneth Jost
STAFF WRITERS: Mary H. Cooper, William Triplett
CONTRIBUTING WRITERS: Sarah Glazer, David Hatch, David Hosansky, Patrick Marshall, Tom Price, Jane Tanner
DESIGN/PRODUCTION EDITOR: Olu B. Davis
ASSISTANT EDITOR: Kate Templin

CQ PRESS

A Division of
Congressional Quarterly Inc.

SENIOR VICE PRESIDENT/GENERAL MANAGER: John A. Jenkins
DIRECTOR, LIBRARY PUBLISHING: Kathryn C. Suárez
DIRECTOR, EDITORIAL OPERATIONS: Ann Davies

CONGRESSIONAL QUARTERLY INC.

CHAIRMAN: Paul C. Tash
VICE CHAIRMAN: Andrew P. Corty
PRESIDENT AND PUBLISHER: Robert W. Merry

The CQ Researcher (ISSN 1056-2036) is printed on acid-free paper. Published weekly, except Jan. 2, April 9, July 2, July 9, Aug. 6, Aug. 13, Nov. 26 and Dec. 31, by CQ Press, a division of Congressional Quarterly Inc. Annual subscription rates for institutions start at $625. For pricing, call 1-800-834-9020, ext. 1906. To purchase a *CQ Researcher* report in print or electronic format (PDF), visit www.cqpress.com or call 866-427-7737. A single report is $10. Bulk purchase discounts and electronic-rights licensing are also available. Periodicals postage paid at Washington, D.C., and additional mailing offices. POSTMASTER: Send address changes to *The CQ Researcher*, 1255 22nd St., N.W., Suite 400, Washington, D.C. 20037.

Treatment of Veterans

BY WILLIAM TRIPLETT

THE ISSUES

While serving as a company commander with the 101st Airborne Division in Vietnam, Gordon H. Mansfield suffered a paralyzing spinal cord injury. Two years ago, Mansfield went on an undercover mission for his boss, Veterans Affairs (VA) Secretary Anthony J. Principi. His mission: Try to get doctors' appointments at VA medical centers around the country.

Helping veterans with "service-connected" disabilities like Mansfield's is the VA's top priority. But as the highly decorated veteran told Principi, also a decorated Vietnam veteran, getting the help isn't always easy. Of the eight centers contacted by Mansfield, the VA's deputy director, six were overbooked and could not see him. [1]

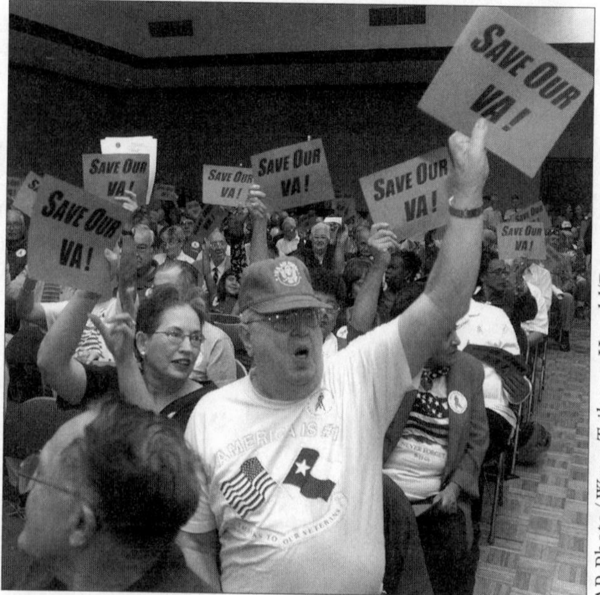

AP Photo/*Waco Tribune-Herald*/Duane A. Laverty

Veterans and their families protest on Oct. 3, 2003, after plans were announced to close the veterans hospital in Waco, Texas. Department of Veterans Affairs (VA) Secretary Anthony J. Principi later put the decision on hold. While veterans praise the VA and Department of Defense for their medical care, they criticize long waits for appointments with doctors, delays in processing claims, suspensions of many veterans' benefits and increased costs for veterans' prescription drugs.

The delay was no surprise to fellow Vietnam vet Rick Burk, of Columbia, Md. In 2002, Burk filed a claim for disability compensation with the VA for hearing loss.

But he had not been in a combat unit, he says, "So I had to prove I was involved in combat actions" that would have caused a hearing loss. He hit a dead-end, however, because he was told his unit records were probably stored at a facility in the Marshall Islands, in the South Pacific.

Then a researcher sent him to the main National Archives repository outside Washington, D.C., where he found a Special Forces logbook that chronicled several rocket attacks on his unit.

After one night attack, he recalls, "My ears rang for days." Worse, reading details of that night brought back memories of other barrages and people being blown up, triggering panic attacks, night sweats, nightmares and massive depression. So Burk also sought treatment for his psychological wounds as well.

In October 2004, two years and two months after he started the claims process, the VA finally gave him a 70 percent disability rating for his PTSD and hearing loss.

Though the wait was long, Burk finally started receiving his monthly disability check. World War II Navy veteran John Savage of Quincy, Mass., didn't fare so well. Last summer, at age 77, his area VA hospital told him he was not eligible for care. [2]

Savage, it turned out, was one of an estimated 200,000 "low-priority" veterans — those not disabled from military service and not indigent — whose benefits were suspended by Principi due to budget shortages in January 2003. [3]

Meanwhile, a new study reveals that 1.7 million uninsured veterans could not receive VA health care in 2003 because they either made too much money, were on VA waiting lists, could not afford VA co-payments for specialty care or had no VA facilities in their communities.

"Millions of American veterans and their family members . . . face grave difficulties in [obtaining] even the most basic medical care," the report by the Harvard/Cambridge Hospital Group said. "It seems particularly abhorrent that services are denied to those who have served." More than two-thirds of the uninsured veterans were employed, and 86 percent had worked in the past year. [4]

Veterans' benefits are eroding in other ways as well. In the VA's proposed 2005 budget, the administration seeks to more than double — from $7 to $15 — the co-payment veterans must make for prescription drugs. It also wants certain classes of low-priority veterans to pay an enrollment fee of $250 to participate in VA benefits.

In addition, veterans who want education benefits under today's GI Bill must contribute $100 per month for a year, and the fee is not refundable if the soldier decides not to use the benefit. Under previous GI Bills, veterans received education benefits for free. (*See sidebar, p. 977.*)

"Veterans know they're getting screwed, and they want us to do something about it," says Rep. Lane Evans, D-Ill., a Vietnam combat veteran.

Advocates say that with a staggering federal deficit approaching $500 billion, the government is trying to save money any way it can, even if it means breaking promises to its veterans.

Funding for Veterans Has Tripled

Funding for veterans' services has increased more than threefold in the last quarter-century, from $22 billion in 1980 to more than $65 billion under President Bush's proposed 2005 budget request.

Net Funding for Department of Veterans Affairs

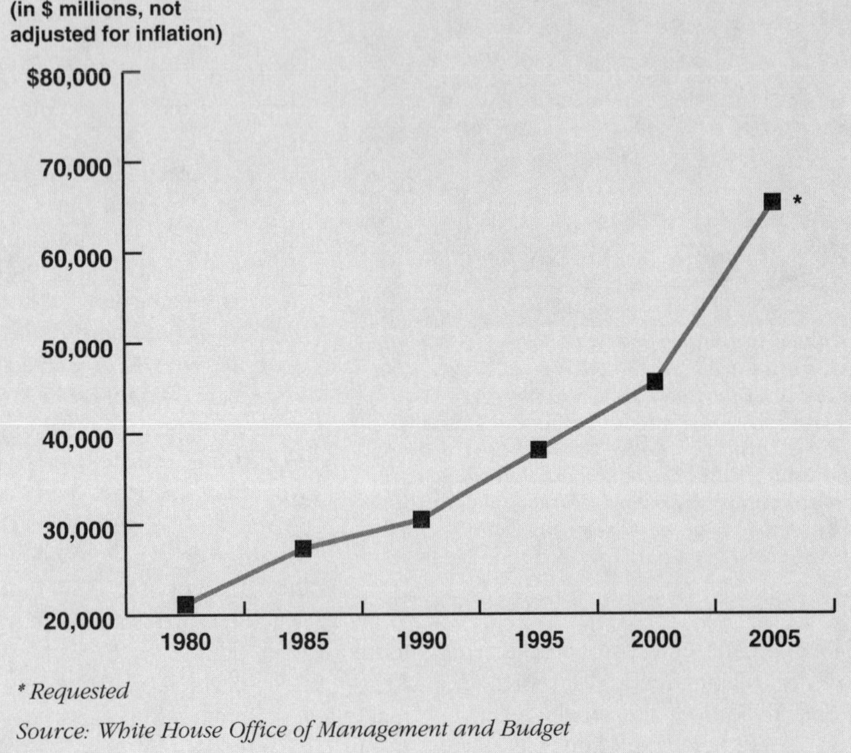

* *Requested*

Source: White House Office of Management and Budget

"The policies of the administration are very suspect to me," says Steve Robinson, executive director of the National Gulf War Resources Center (NGWRC), a veterans' advocacy group. "I know that when you spend billions in Iraq and have billions in deficit, there's got to be belt tightening. But I'm not sure it fulfills the commitment from a grateful nation to make those cost savings on the backs of people you have sent to war."

Even when they do receive their benefits, many veterans feel they have to struggle — like Burk — to get them. Getting a first appointment to see a VA physician can take up to a year; waiting for the VA to process a claim can take more than twice as long. In Southern California, for example, almost 10,000 veterans — 2,500 more than last year — are waiting for decisions on their disability claims from the VA regional office in Los Angeles. [5] The VA says processing the average claim takes about five months; veterans' organizations say it's more like six months to a year.

Janice Jacobs, acting deputy director of the VA's compensation and pension service, says the entire system has 334,000 unprocessed claims in its backlog. Yet the administration has proposed reducing the VA's staff of claims processors by 500, or slightly less than 10 percent. The VA currently has 5,293 processors. [6]

"If you ask veterans, 'Have you gained or lost benefits in the last 10 years?' nine out of 10 would say lost," says Steve Robertson, legislative director for the American Legion.

However, the VA, congressional Republicans and the administration contend that benefits and services for veterans have significantly improved during President Bush's time in office.

For instance, since fiscal 2001, the last budget year prepared by the administration of President Bill Clinton, overall funding for the VA has risen nearly 50 percent, from $48 billion to almost $71 billion. Funding for veterans' medical care — the benefit most in demand — has risen about 40 percent since 2001, from $20.2 billion to $27.8 billion. [7]

"We've increased health care alone by over 40 percent, and the overall budget has increased by a third — the largest dollar increase in the history of my department, which goes back about 75 years," Principi said on Veterans' Day. [8]

Moreover, says VA Deputy Undersecretary for Health Laura Miller, as of Oct. 1, only about 6,000 new veterans were waiting for their first medical appointment, down from 136,000 since January 2003. "So we've made huge progress," she says. "But we want to get that number down more."

In fiscal 2003, VA health-care facilities treated a record-breaking 4.8 million patients and exceeded that number this year, with nearly 5 million veterans passing through the system. [9] In 1996, by comparison, 2.9 million vets were treated.

To meet the growing demand for health-care services from aging World War II vets and wounded soldiers from the Iraq and Afghanistan wars, the VA has built new outpatient clinics, which are extremely popular with veterans in rural areas. In addition to its 158 mostly urban-area hospitals, 132 nursing homes, 42 residential rehabilitation treatment programs and 88 comprehensive home-care programs, the VA now operates 854 ambulatory care and community-based outpatient clinics across the country. [10]

However, the VA says it must close, move or consolidate some facilities because they are too old to maintain economically, or no longer in demand. Some, like the facility in Waco, Texas, are listed in the National Register of Historic Places and under federal law must be maintained, often at prohibitive expense. Or, explains Elizabeth Crossan, a VA media officer in Texas, long-term demographic projections show a local facility, like the one in Waco, will lose patients in the future while Austin will gain them. "So we need to shift things around," she says.

Indeed, congressional Republicans maintain that despite the swelling federal deficit, the government continues to stand firmly by its veterans. A briefing paper recently issued by the House Veterans' Affairs Committee flatly states: "NO CUTS in veterans' benefits have occurred during the past four years." [11]

Bill Bradshaw, director of national veterans' services for the Veterans of Foreign Wars (VFW), acknowledges that no cuts have been made, but he notes, "They have not kept pace with the need." If the agency were keeping up with the growing demand, he adds, there would be no eligibility suspensions or delays in obtaining benefits or appointments.

Already, the VA has received applications for claims from nearly 27,000 veterans of the wars in Iraq and Afghanistan, who are given top priority by the VA. Yet more than a third of their claims have not yet been processed. [12]

"The system just isn't working," says Dave Gorman, executive director of Disabled American Veterans (DAV). "Going along the way it is now, the VA is going to come to a cliff and fall over."

Here are some of the key questions from the current debate over veterans' benefits:

Earlier GI Bills Offered More Benefits

Veterans returning from World War II received more benefits than veterans of modern wars. The current bill offers only education and training benefits.

Serviceman's Readjustment Act of 1944 (Original World War II-era GI Bill of Rights)

- *Education and training* — Paid tuition, books, fees and other training costs and provided a monthly living allowance
- *Loan guarantees* — For a home, farm or business
- *Unemployment pay* — $20 a week for up to 52 weeks
- *Job-search assistance*

Total educated: 7.8 million
Total cost: $14.5 billion
Expired: July 25, 1956

Veterans Readjustment Assistance Act of 1952 (Korean War GI Bill)

- *Education and training* — Up to $110 per month
- *Loan guarantees* — For a home, farm or business

Total educated: 2.4 million
Total cost: $4.5 billion
Expired: Jan. 31, 1965

Veterans Readjustment Benefits Act of 1966 (Vietnam-era GI Bill)

- *Education and training* — One month of coverage provided for each month of service, for a maximum of 36 months, later extended to 45 months; payment increased from $100 a month in 1966 to $376 per month in 1984
- *Loan guarantees* — For a home or farm
- *Job counseling;* employment placement service

Total educated: 8.2 million
Total cost: $42 billion
Expired: Dec. 31, 1989

Montgomery GI Bill (current program, passed in 1986)

- *Education and training* — Active-duty service member pays $100 per month for 12 months ($1,200 total, non-refundable); can receive payments of $1,004 per month starting Oct. 1, 2004, for up to 36 months after three years of service; must use benefit within 10 years of discharge

Total educated: 400,000 in 2003 (More than 75 percent of enlistees have enrolled in the program.)

Source: "GI Bill History," GI Bill Web site, Department of Veterans Affairs, http://www.gibill.va.gov/education/GI_Bill.htm.

Is the VA adequately serving all veterans?

After World War II, and for many years afterwards, the VA's medical care and its facilities were widely seen as inadequate. Indeed, veterans' advocates railed against the shortage of medical personnel and the "warehousing" of patients in depressing, poorly equipped hospitals.

"Fifteen years ago, the No. 1 complaint against the VA was the quality of its health care," says the American Legion's Robertson. "That's changed. Now it's, 'I can't get into the facility!' That's because the quality of health care in the VA is outstanding now, so many veterans want access to it."

Indeed, almost 5 million veterans are seeking care today, largely due to the growing needs of the estimated 5 million World War II veterans and aging Korean War and Vietnam War veterans. "They need specialized, long-term care," says the DAV's Gorman.

And today, the VA can deliver it, Robertson says. Until recently, the agency's health-care system was largely inpatient-focused, he explains. "But just as the rest of the health-care industry was changing in the 1990s, the VA transformed itself during the Clinton years," he says, adding outpatient clinics with first-rate equipment and personnel. "This is not your grandfather's VA any more," Robertson says.

But, actually, it is. With millions of veterans in their 70s and 80s, the VA has become a national leader in geriatric care. Moreover, improved medical technologies and quick battlefield evacuations in Vietnam saved the lives of many soldiers who would have otherwise died from booby-traps that blew off arms and legs. Thus, the agency has also become a specialist in prosthetics.

Mansfield's field report prompted Principi, with Congress' help, to organize veterans into eight priority groups, focusing first on veterans with service-connected disabilities, low-incomes or catastrophic disabilities.

Veterans' advocates welcomed the refocusing, but objected when Principi added means testing in January 2003. Under the new rules, a veteran with a relatively mild service-connected disability (recurring pain from shrapnel wounds, for example) seeking care for a condition unrelated to that disability would have to disclose his income level; if it exceeded the threshold (from $25,000-$34,000 a year, depending on the location), he would be classified among the 200,000 veterans in Priority Group 8 — the lowest-priority group. Principi suspended their eligibility for health care, effective Jan. 1, 2004, because the VA could not keep pace with the demand.

"A guy could've landed at Normandy, fought the Battle of the Bulge — the whole nine yards — and he's on a fixed income now, on Medicare, but he wants to go to the VA because he knows they have a super geriatrics program," Robertson says. "Even though he has medals out the ying-yang, unless he's got a service-connected disability or is indigent, they're going to say to him, 'Sorry, there's no room at the inn.' "

The Priority Group 8 suspension, Undersecretary Miller says, "was a very difficult decision," but one that had to be made given "our available resources." She also notes that during fiscal 2004, which ended Sept. 30, "we added about 600 new physicians to both hospitals and outpatient clinics."

The VA's overall goal is to see 93 percent of patients within 30 days of the desired date for an appointment. "Last September, for all our clinics, we were hitting that number, though there are still some patients who are waiting longer than we'd like," Miller says. "But we're working on it, tracking it, clinic by clinic."

On another positive note, veterans generally praise the VA's support and treatment services for post-traumatic stress disorder (PTSD). Studies show that nearly one-third of Vietnam veterans alone have suffered from the debilitating psychological condition. [13] The VA says it is currently paying disability compensation on 211,250 PTSD claims. (*See sidebar, p. 987.*)

But veterans criticize the VA's handling of Vietnam veterans exposed to the herbicide Agent Orange, many of whom developed prostate cancer and other serious health problems. Rick Weidman, director of government relations for the Vietnam Veterans of America (VVA), says the VA could do more to help those veterans who are eligible for health care and compensation for conditions the VA now acknowledges were caused by Agent Orange.

"We estimate that maybe 75 percent of Vietnam veterans with prostate cancer have no clue it's connected to their service in Vietnam, because the VA doesn't do squat for outreach," Weidman says. "A lot of these guys die bankrupt from medical bills, and they're dying as surely as a result of their Vietnam service as if they'd caught an AK-47 round. It's outrageous."

The VA has increased its outreach efforts, but only for the newest generation of veterans. In May, it mailed benefits information to more than 150,000 veterans of the wars in Afghanistan and Iraq. It expects to continue mailing about 10,000 such letters each month, as the conflicts continue in those countries. [14]

Dealing with the 334,000 unprocessed claims won't be as easy, Jacobs says. "The time for a claim to move through the system varies depending on the complexity of the claim," she says. "Generally, if it's just one issue, it can be done very quickly. But these days, most claims have anywhere from three to 21 issues, and we need evidence on each issue."

Moreover, Jacobs says, learning to be a good claims adjudicator "takes a good two years of on-the-job training. We've got a lot of new people with less than two years." (VA spokesman Jose Llamas says 21 percent of the adjudicators have less than two years' experience.) And many of the experienced adjudicators are nearing retirement age, she adds. Still, "We handle claims a lot better than most people realize," she says.

Aside from the processing delay, some veterans say the VA is insensitive to how difficult it is to file a claim. "Especially for people with PTSD, the benefits-application process is extremely stressful," says Vietnam veteran Burk. "You have to relive [the traumatic event], write it down and then deal with the bureaucracy. Most guys can't withstand that."

Last year, the VA paid disability compensation or pensions to 2.8 million veterans and 568,146 spouses, children and parents of deceased veterans. Among them are 147,291 survivors of Vietnam-era veterans and 272,883 survivors of World War II veterans. [15]

The VA's other major failure, according to some critics, involves dealing with homeless veterans. Estimates of the number of homeless veterans vary from roughly 10 percent of the homeless population to nearly 25 percent. "Nine percent of the U.S. population are veterans, yet they account for 23 percent of the homeless population," says Linda Boone, executive director of the National Coalition for Homeless Veterans. About 275,000 veterans are homeless on any given night, she says, and about twice as many experience homelessness at some point in any given year. [16]

"The VA has increased its attention and resources to this problem, and that's good," Boone says "They didn't always do it willingly, but they did it. But is it enough? No."

Jacobs responds: "We have a homeless coordinator in each of the 57 VA regional offices. Teams go on the streets and look for veterans. Of all the subpopulations of veterans we serve, the homeless subpopulation is one about which I've never heard any complaints. We've only had praise about our outreach to homeless veterans."

AP Photo/Pat Crowe II

Korean War veteran William A. Richardson joins other veterans in Dover, Del., on April 28, 2004, in a rally supporting construction of the state's first home for aging and disabled veterans, which the legislature approved unanimously. States vary widely in the kinds of services and benefits they offer veterans.

Should Congress make VA funding mandatory?

Veterans' advocates say money is behind the VA's problems in serving veterans and that the money problems are caused by the method in which the agency's appropriations are determined every year.

Like all Cabinet-level agencies, the VA submits a budget request every year to the White House Office of Management and Budget (OMB), which determines whether to ask Congress for that amount (or more or less) based on the administration's overall priorities and needs.

After OMB submits the president's budget proposal to Congress, lawmakers then essentially go through the same process: Based on what they believe the country — and their constituents — need most, they decide how much money to appropriate for every request in the proposal. This is called discretionary funding.

And that's the problem, says the DAV's Gorman. "The VA isn't funded correctly," he says. "We couldn't praise VA employees more. They do their best. But they can only do so much with the limited budget they have. It's all up to the whim of Congress every year. As a result, the VA can't really plan for anything. They don't know how much money they're going to get, when they'll get it, or even if they'll get it."

Conversely, in so-called mandatory funding, Congress must appropriate whatever money is needed to cover all expenses. Social Security, Medicaid and Medicare — known as entitlement programs — have mandatory funding.

Actually, about half the VA's budget — its non-medical-care funding — is already under mandatory funding. Nine veterans' service organizations want Congress to put the entire VA budget under mandatory funding as well.

Under mandatory funding, advocates maintain, the VA would be assured of getting the money and resources it needs to offer health care to all eight priority groups. The

Number of Veterans Expected to Drop

Today's population of 25 million veterans, according to OMB estimates, is expected to drop by one-third, to 17 million, in the next 20 years as World War II, Korean War and Vietnam-era veterans die.

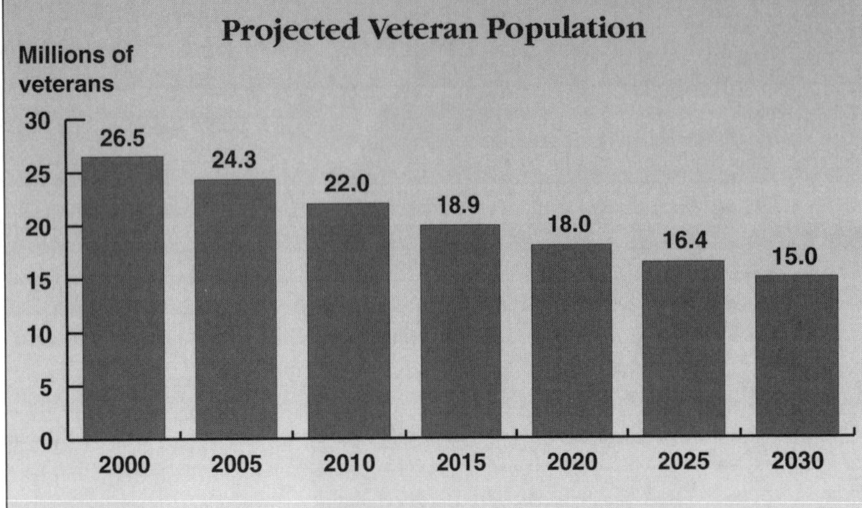

Source: White House Office of Management and Budget (OMB)

claims process, they say, would also be expedited because the agency would be able to offer experienced adjudicators reason to stay.

"After they get experience, a lot of VA claims adjudicators move to the Social Security Administration or somewhere else," the American Legion's Robertson says. "You've got to have salaries that make people want to stay working for the VA."

According to VA spokesman Llamas, however, the department boasted a 93 percent retention rate last year for its adjudication staff. Meanwhile, the VA says it is doing the best it can with its current funding. "We're doing a very good job," Jacobs says. "We could always use more resources — any federal agency could — but we're doing so much more with less."

In the 1990s, all federal agencies were forced to trim costs and waste as part of a general trend toward downsizing the government. "Some would argue that the Veterans Health Administration has cut down to the bone," Gorman says. "What the VA needs is an infusion of cash and resources."

Indeed, in unusually candid testimony before the House Veterans' Affairs Committee in February, Principi said the VA budget request that OMB had submitted to Congress was $1.2 billion less than the amount he had requested. [17]

"Even Principi knows there's a need that's unmet, and he voiced it in a way that most administrators would not," says Robinson of the National Gulf War Resources Center (NGWRC). "That alone should make people stand up and pay attention."

Others say mandatory funding isn't the answer. "It would make VA funding inflexible," says Christopher Hellman, a budget analyst at the Center for Arms Control and Nonproliferation. "Congress would have to fund the VA even if there's a [fiscal] crisis elsewhere."

Chris Edwards, director of tax policy at the libertarian Cato Institute, says the VA budget has received steady increases under the Bush administration, enabling the VA to plan ahead. "There hasn't been any problem with a gyrating budget," he says, adding that he sees no reason to think that's going to change.

Brian Riedl, senior budget analyst at the conservative Heritage Foundation, concurs. "If it turns out that veterans' health-care funding needs to be determined more than a year in advance, Congress can solve that by using advance appropriations," Riedl says.

Indeed, he says, mandatory funding would be a mistake because, "Mandatory programs grow faster than discretionary programs. They put more pressure on the budget, and other budgets would have to be cut. It basically takes control of the program out of the hands of Congress, and that's not good for government."

But according to a 2003 White House task force report, the lack of available and adequate resources "could threaten the quality of VA health care." The report recommended that the VA budget be placed under "a mandatory funding mechanism, or some other . . . process that achieves the desired goal." [18]

After the report was released, Rep. Evans, the ranking Democrat on the Veterans' Affairs Committee, introduced legislation calling for a mandatory funding formula to calculate the VA's annual budget needs. However, committee Republicans responded, "This approach relies upon a static formula, so if the baseline is set too high or too low, VA health care could be permanently underfunded or overfunded." [19] Evans disputes the criticism.

For his part, committee Chairman Christopher Smith, R-N.J., introduced legislation to create an independent board of experts to determine the VA's annual health-care funding needs, but retaining the discretionary nature of the agency's funding.

Though neither bill has been debated yet, veterans' groups support

Evans' bill. "Mandatory funding isn't a panacea, and there's no guarantee we'd get it right the first time," says Dennis Cullinan, director of the VFW's national legislative service. "But right away, the VA would know how much money it's going to get, and the money would arrive on time."

While he doubts the wisdom of mandatory funding, Hellman acknowledges that something will have to change, inasmuch as the VA hasn't been able to cover the needs of existing veterans, much less those of future veterans. "If the war in Iraq continues over the next three to five years, and casualties continue at the same rate," he says, "you're going to see a crisis in VA health care."

Is the Department of Defense meeting its responsibilities to veterans and the VA?

About 6,000 U.S. soldiers have been wounded in Afghanistan and Iraq; almost 900 have suffered a 30 percent or greater disability, such as loss of limbs or eyesight. [20]

Yet, when those disabled service members are discharged from the military, it can take months — sometimes even years — for the Defense Department to provide the VA with service records verifying that service personnel are eligible for continuing health care and other VA services.

To help those severely injured transition out of the military, the Department of Defense (DOD) last spring initiated the Disabled Soldier Support System (DS3) to help with the discharge process and provide information on VA benefits.

DS3 is part of a joint effort by DOD and the VA to help those disabled in Operation Enduring Freedom in Afghanistan and Operation Iraqi Freedom make a "seamless transition" from active duty to veteran status. Among other things, the agencies are trying to share critical medical information electronically so personnel can easily file claims.

Dr. Michael Kilpatrick, DOD's deputy director of deployment health support, says that current and future veterans will find claims for VA health benefits easier to file thanks to a new practice being followed by military doctors.

"We ask about lots of different experiences they may have had and any medical treatment they had and any concerns they might've had in theater.

"The point," he continues, "is that veterans' records will have more information in them about their health status during service and their experiences. Also, this information will be electronically stored as well as on paper, and the VA will have access to it. So VA benefits people can look at that instead of waiting for DOD to provide paper."

Before service personnel are transferred to the VA's care, they receive medical care at one of the country's 163 military hospitals, like Walter Reed Army Medical Center, in Washington, D.C. Veterans' advocates say that DOD — in particular, the Army, which has suffered the most casualties — has provided good care to troops wounded in Iraq and Afghanistan, helping them to readjust. "These guys are getting top-notch, state-of-the-art care," says Gorman of the DAV. "They are being taken care of."

The NGWRC's Robinson, who visited five Army hospitals around the country, agrees — but only to a point. "The commands seem to do well treating the acutely wounded, who return with bullet, bomb and blast injury," he says. "However, they fail miserably in treating the psychological and other wounds of war."

Lt. J. Philip Goodrum, an Army reserve veteran from Tennessee being treated at Walter Reed, agrees. He developed severe carpal tunnel syndrome while serving in Iraq, but before he could be sent back to the United States for surgery, combat triggered PTSD flashbacks from his earlier service in the Persian Gulf War. Indeed, his greatest fear came to pass: A soldier under his command was killed — literally cut in half in a convoy accident when the truck he was driving slammed into the truck in front, and his vehicle was hit from behind.

In his room at Walter Reed, more than a dozen pill bottles cover a table. Some are for the pain in his hands; most are for PTSD and associated depression. The psychiatric treatment he receives, Goodrum says, is not very good, primarily because the Army doctors are young and not experienced in treating PTSD. Many of those with psychological wounds are reluctant to seek care for fear of "being treated like dirt . . . mostly by people who didn't deploy to this war or experience the dangers of it."

A recent study of PTSD among veterans of Iraq and Afghanistan, published in *The New England Journal of Medicine*, noted that up to 17 percent of Iraq veterans were exhibiting signs of "major depression, generalized anxiety or PTSD" but that only 23 to 40 percent sought mental health care because of fear of being stigmatized. [21]

Robinson says many recent veterans with PTSD end up languishing in Army medical facilities, waiting for their case to be reviewed by a medical evaluation board (MEB) — "a bureaucratic, paper-driven monster that can take anywhere from three months to a year for the soldier to get some form of resolution."

The MEB determines the extent of a soldier's disability and is a key factor in any disability claim filed with the VA. Robinson says that out of severe frustration with the time it takes to receive an MEB, a growing number of soldiers are checking themselves out of medical facilities before the MEB adjudicates their disability claims, jeopardizing their chances for VA benefits later on.

Those feeling most frustrated — and discriminated against — are members of Reserve or National Guard units, or "reserve component," according to Capt. Kent E. LaGasse, an Army Reserve officer who oversees the processing of reserve component soldiers at Walter Reed. "The first question these guys are asked here isn't about their condition or wounds," he says. "It's, 'Are you regular Army or reserve component?' When they say 'reserve,' they get segregated, treated differently and get less attention."

Jaime Cavazos, a civilian media relations officer for the Army Medical Command, responds that hospitals have to ask which branch soldiers are in simply for accountability, "to see who they've got on their patient list. But everybody gets treated as an individual, not based on his affiliation or ethnicity. You hear rumblings about this, but I don't put much credence in it."

Delays on MEBs, Cavazos says, are often the result of prolonged treatment. "Health needs must be addressed before an MEB can be convened, and that's for every soldier, irrespective of branch."

Indeed, according to DOD's Kilpatrick, "When someone has a medical condition that requires hospitalization, the goal of treatment is to see if they can recuperate enough to stay on active duty. That treatment, in general, can [take] up to a year. I don't think the troops really understand this, and the most who have problems with this are Reserve and Guard, who don't have a lot of experience with military medicine and processes."

As for the quality of health care, either physical or psychological, Cavazos says, "Everybody's got opinions about their health care, and sometimes soldiers don't feel like they've been given the best. But ultimately, our health-care professionals are among the best and have the soldiers' best interests at heart."

Kilpatrick also points out that DOD has initiated another collaborative program with the VA to expedite the benefits claim that a disabled soldier will eventually file. Until recently, personnel mustering out of the service had to undergo both an exit physical exam from the military, and then later another physical exam by the VA to substantiate a claim.

"We've now got a uniform exit physical exam that makes the VA exam no longer necessary," Kilpatrick says. "And we're supplying the medical information from the exit exam to the VA even before the GI is discharged." ■

BACKGROUND

Early Complaints

Americans first began looking after their ex-soldiers in the 17th century, when the Plymouth Colony Pilgrims wiped out the Pequot Indians and passed a law in 1636 requiring the colony to support soldiers disabled in the conflict. [22]

The idea expanded as the scale and scope of succeeding wars grew, increasing the country's need for soldiers. For instance, to entice young men to fight the British "Red Coats," the Continental Congress of 1776 promised that any soldier disabled in the Revolutionary War would receive a government pension. After the war, the newly born states provided direct medical and hospital care to veterans.

The first American veteran to publicly complain about unfair treatment from the government he had fought for may have been Daniel Shays. He returned to his farm in western Massachusetts after the war, but the economic depression that descended over the new nation caused him and many other Massachusetts farmers to default on their taxes. Showing no mercy for men who had driven the British from the colonies, the state began to foreclose on debtors' farms.

When their pleas for more time were ignored, Shays and other veterans and farmers rose up, sparking Shays' Rebellion. A mercenary militia put down the uprising, and Shays passed into history largely as an outlaw rebel. But to many, Shays is still remembered as an exemplar of "standing up when things aren't right."

During the early 19th century, the federal government authorized the first combined shelter and medical facility for veterans, the Naval Home in Philadelphia. The government also extended benefits and pensions to the widows and dependents of veterans.

About this time, however, the federal government began having the first of its ongoing reservations about its benefits for veterans. In 1818, at President James Monroe's behest, Congress authorized funding to expand federal benefits to veterans. Monroe had felt that, regardless of whether they had been injured, all poor and infirm veterans of the Revolutionary War — and now the War of 1812 — deserved the government's support.

Some in Congress warned of bogus claims and other abuses, and their fears seemed justified when so many claims arrived that $3 million — six times the amount Congress had authorized — would be needed to pay them. Taxpayers ended up covering all the claims, but in the aftermath, the federal government reduced its assistance to veterans.

To Richard Severo and Lewis Milford, respected authors of *The Wages of War: When America's Soldiers Came Home — From Valley Forge to Vietnam*, both Shays' Rebellion and the reduced veterans' assistance epitomized what would become the country's frequent ambivalence toward its veterans:

"From the very beginning, we thought of ourselves as a generous and compassionate people but invariably fell to judging harshly the objects of our compassion and generosity. We urged our best young men to fight hard for us, even if we did not always believe in what the fight was all about. We venerated patriotism, but

Continued on p. 984

Chronology

Colonial Era

Continental Congress promises in 1776 that any soldier disabled in the Revolutionary War will receive a government pension.

19th Century

In the early 1800s, the government expands veterans' benefits to their widows and dependents. After the Civil War, many states establish veterans' homes; Congress establishes the National Home for Disabled Volunteer Soldiers.

Early 20th Century

Congress increases veterans' benefits and programs, such as insurance policies and vocational rehabilitation for the disabled.

1930
Veterans Administration (VA) replaces the Veterans Bureau.

1940-1960

More than 16 million American men and women serve in uniform during World War II, the largest mobilized force in U.S. history; the nation unites to support soldiers and veterans alike.

1944
President Franklin D. Roosevelt signs the Servicemen's Readjustment Act of 1944 — the GI Bill of Rights — offering home loan and education benefits to veterans.

1960s-1980s

Americans are bitterly divided over the Vietnam War and its veterans, who fight with the government over the herbicide Agent Orange, which they say caused cancer and other diseases in exposed troops.

1984
Agent Orange's manufacturers agree to a $180 million out-of-court settlement with Vietnam veterans who sued them.

1990s

Fighting in the Middle East produces another generation of U.S. veterans suffering from ill health.

1991
United States leads a coalition to oust Iraq after it occupies neighboring Kuwait. Of nearly 700,000 American troops deployed, 100,000 eventually report a variety of mysterious ailments. The Pentagon says no troops were exposed to chemical weapons; military and VA doctors initially ascribe the illnesses to stress.

1994
Institute of Medicine confirms that sufficient scientific evidence links at least two cancers and several other diseases and conditions to exposure to Agent Orange.

1997
Pentagon admits that as many as 100,000 U.S. soldiers may have been exposed to nerve gas in Persian Gulf War. VA begins paying veterans disability compensation.

2000s

Two more wars create a new generation of veterans, straining VA's ability to provide health care.

2001
After terrorists attack the World Trade Center and the Pentagon on Sept. 11, President Bush sends the U.S. military into Afghanistan to root out Al Qaeda and its Taliban supporters.

2003
In January, the VA suspends the health-care benefits of 200,000 veterans. . . . In March President Bush launches Operation Iraqi Freedom to find and destroy Iraq's alleged weapons of mass destruction.

2004
In February veterans' organizations sharply criticize the proposed VA budget as inadequate and object to a plan to charge veterans an annual enrollment fee for health care. . . . VA sends letters in May to more than 150,000 veterans of the Iraq and Afghanistan wars, outlining their eligibility for VA benefits; 27,000 veterans file for benefits, but as of October at least one-third of the claims are not yet processed; VA has a backlog of 334,000 claims. In October the Senate approves a bill that increases veterans' education, employment and housing benefits, including a 10 percent hike in monthly stipends while pursuing on-the-job training and more time to pay the $1,200 enrollment fee for participating in the Montgomery GI Bill. The House followed suit on Nov. 17, clearing the bill for the president's signature.

Today's GI Bill Confronts Economic Reality

When President Franklin D. Roosevelt signed the Serviceman's Readjustment Act of 1944, few foresaw the profound impact it would have on American society. In less a decade, the measure — better known as the GI Bill of Rights — provided education and job-training vouchers to 8 million veterans. More than 2 million former GIs flooded college campuses. The law's home-loan benefit doubled the ratio of homeowners from one in three before the war to two in three afterwards — essentially creating modern suburbia.

Many economists attribute the post-World War II emergence of the middle class — with its higher wages and resultant additional tax revenues — to the GI Bill. In fact, for every dollar invested in Roosevelt's GI Bill, the government and economy received at least $6.90 in return, according to government estimates. [1]

But government budget restraints and the rapidly rising cost of tuition have reduced GI Bill benefits over the years. While a World War II veteran could have attended Harvard University entirely on the government's dime under the original GI Bill, today's veterans struggle to pay even community college costs with the benefits provided under the Montgomery GI Bill.

VA officials say the differences in the two bills reflect the differences in post-World War II America. And, while the VA's critics say a grateful nation should provide additional benefits to returning soldiers, they are realistic about the current budgetary limitations.

"My biggest hope would be that the GI Bill would be returned to 1944 levels. I hope the nation will take a serious look at the transitional assistance that veterans need when coming back from serving honorably," says Steve Robertson, legislative director at the American Legion. "But I don't think the chances are very good with the deficit the way it is."

Under previous GI Bills, veterans received benefits for free, but service members who want to sign up for VA educational benefits today must contribute $100 per month for a year; it is not refundable if the soldier decides not to use it. Veterans with three years of service can receive $1,004 per month for up to 36 months of schooling (approximately $9,036 per year for a four-year education). [2]

Out of those payments, veterans must pay for tuition, books, room and board and other personal expenses. According to the College Board, the average yearly cost of tuition for the 2004-2005 school year — not including books, supplies, room and board, is $5,312 for public colleges and $20,082 for private colleges. [3]

The financial strain is compounded by the large percentage of veterans who are married and have children (most World War II veterans were single). Today education often takes a back seat to providing for a family and finding a job that offers health insurance, Robertson says. Moreover, today's benefits expire 10 years after the soldier is discharged. (Previous bills died when the programs ended — 15 years after the WW II and Korean War GI bills, and 25 years after the Vietnam War bill were enacted.)

Critics say those obstacles affect how many eligible service members take advantage of the GI Bill. According to VA estimates, almost 95 percent of new recruits opt to pay into the program, but only 57 percent use the education benefits. [4]

Those percentages lead to a host of underutilized talent, Robertson says. "This is a volunteer service of the youngest and the brightest. These kids learn so much about management in basic training and their early years in the military, and once they leave the military, they have all kinds of potential. The only handicap is whether they can afford to go to school," he says.

Congress has tried to improve the benefits and the number who take advantage of them with varying degrees of success. About 20 measures designed to increase Montgomery GI Bill benefits are pending in Congress, says Dennis Douglass, deputy director of education service for the Veterans Benefits Administration. At least one bill — sponsored by Sen. Arlen Specter, R-Pa., and containing multiple benefits, including some for ed-

Continued from p. 982

found something pesky in the expense vouchers of our patriots."

After the Civil War, many states established veterans' homes, which provided medical and hospital treatment for all injuries and diseases — service-connected or not. The facilities welcomed indigent and disabled veterans of the Civil War, Indian Wars, Spanish-American War and Mexican War, as well as discharged regular members of the armed forces.

But because only veterans of the regular Army and Navy were eligible for care in these facilities, Congress also established, in 1865, the National Home for Disabled Volunteer Soldiers. One of the last acts signed by President Abraham Lincoln before his assassination, the legislation marked the entrance of the United States into the direct provision of care for the temporary vs. career military man.

Yet, despite Lincoln's famous concern "to care for him who should have borne the battle, and for his widow and orphan," the prevailing attitude throughout the victorious North was that veterans should be encouraged toward self-reliance and self-sufficiency, not dependence.

For example, the carnage of the war and deprivations of prison camps had left thousands of shattered and maimed men. Even those not requiring acute medical care needed extended periods of government-provided ucation — cleared Congress on Nov. 17 and was sent to President Bush for his signature. But the other measures will likely have to be reintroduced in the 109th Congress.

One of the pending bills, sponsored by House Veterans' Affairs Committee Chairman Christopher H. Smith, R-N.J., would eliminate the $1,200 pay-in and increase the monthly payout to $1,200. Smith also sponsored a bill, which President Bush signed into law in 2001, increasing the dollar benefit of Montgomery GI Bill education from $24,192 to $35,460. [5]

"The cost of a college education has come to greatly exceed the monthly tuition benefit," Smith said in December 2001, after the bill was signed into law. "Helping our vets attain the American dream of a college education is the least we can do to reward them for their work ensuring our freedom."

A commission created by Congress to analyze veterans' benefits in 1999 suggested increasing the benefits even more. It argued that, in order to promote leadership and spark recruitment, the $1,200 pay-in should be eliminated and eligible veterans should be paid full tuition, fees and books at any public or private institution, as well as a $400-per-month stipend — much like the benefits received under the post-World War II GI Bill.

"Today, the Services face increasing difficulties in meeting their recruiting goals," the commission report says. "The . . . GI Bill benefit is the principal enticement for recruiting new service personnel. However, recruiting shortfalls indicate that the benefit should be enhanced if it is to successfully assist the services in recruiting the young men and women that they will need in the next century." [6]

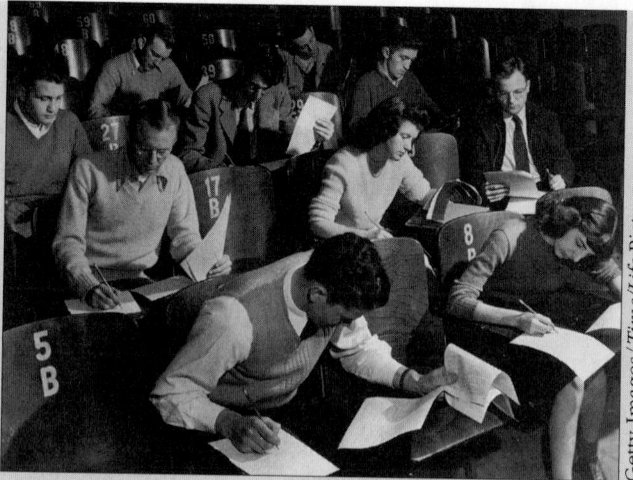

Getty Images/*Time/Life* Pictures

World War II veterans attend class at the University of Iowa in 1947, funded by the 1944 GI Bill. The landmark program enabled more than 2 million vets to attend college in 10 years. Famed photographer Margaret Bourke-White took the photo.

Douglass acknowledges that restoring Montgomery GI Bill benefits to 1944 levels would be a powerful recruitment tool but says it is improbable in such a drastically changed society: There is no longer a draft, college enrollments are bulging and more tuition funds are available through other avenues. Still, he says, the military is one of the best ways to pay for college for those who could not afford it on their own.

"The GI Bill can't be today what it was in 1945," Douglass says. "But that doesn't mean it is less important."

— Kate Templin

[1] Calculated in 1952 dollars, factoring out inflation, from "A Cost-Benefit Analysis of Government Investment in Post-Secondary Education Under the World War II GI Bill," Subcommittee on Education and Health of the Joint Economic Committee, Dec. 14, 1988.

[2] Information from the GI Bill Web Site, www.gibill.va.gov.

[3] Figures from the College Board, "Break Down the Bill; What's It Going To Cost?" www.collegeboard.com.

[4] "Final report from the Congressional Commission on Servicemembers and Veterans Transition Assistance," Jan. 14, 1999, www.vetbiz.gov/library/Transition%20Commission%20Report.pdf.

[5] Press release on Veterans' Education and Benefits Expansion Act, from Web site of Rep. Christopher Smith, R-N.J., www.house.gov/chrissmith/news/press2001/prgibillincrease.htm.

[6] "Final Report," *op. cit.*

shelter during their readjustment to civilian life. Some got it, but not all.

After Lincoln's death, the federal government offered payments to Union soldiers who had lost limbs in the war and couldn't get into a shelter. A veteran who lost a leg was entitled to $75; a lost arm merited $50. If the payment were declined, the government would provide the veteran with an artificial limb, to be replaced every three years. Most opted for the cash.

U.S. entry into World War I in 1917 prompted Congress to initiate new veterans' programs that included insurance policies and vocational rehabilitation for the disabled. But according to authors Severo and Milford, World War I veterans received few benefits immediately after the war's end in 1918. Vocational training had been promised to approximately 110,000 eligible veterans, for example, but by the advent of the 1920s, only 217 men had been retrained.

Veterans Bureau Created

In 1921, the federal government created the Veterans' Bureau, which, along with the Bureau of Pensions and the National Home for Disabled Volunteer Soldiers, administered all federal benefits and programs for veterans. President Warren G. Harding appointed Charles R. Forbes as the bureau's first director. It proved a huge mistake.

Forbes essentially used bureau funds as his own private bank account. For example, although the bureau had $33 million for new hospitals and medical facilities, Forbes managed to add only 200 beds to an existing veterans' hospital in Tennessee during his two-year tenure. Yet the money was gone. Senate investigators concluded he had secreted away most of it. Forbes was eventually tried and convicted of defrauding the U.S. government.

Meanwhile, more than 200,000 letters from veterans seeking information about their claims accumulated unanswered within the bureau. And in every case, the burden was on veterans to prove the validity of their claims. A disgusted columnist eventually wrote, "Congress little realizes that its creature, the Veterans' Bureau, has probably made wrecks of more men since the war than the war itself took in dead and maimed."

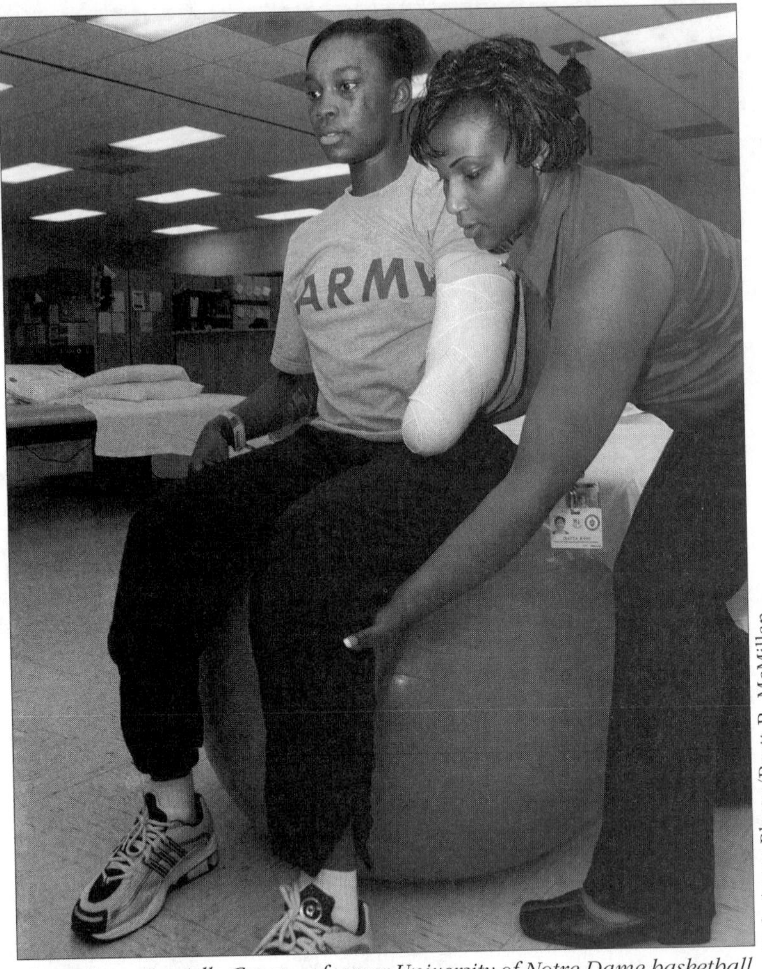

U.S. Army Photo/Brett B. McMillan

Army Spec. Danielle Green, a former University of Notre Dame basketball star, receives physical therapy at Walter Reed Army Medical Center after being wounded in Iraq in May 2004. Veterans' organizations praise the quality of services provided at the nation's military hospitals but say veterans often must wait months to obtain services at VA facilities after leaving the military.

The Veterans Administration, created by Congress in 1930, consolidated all programs and initiatives of the Veterans Bureau, the Bureau of Pensions and the National Home for Disabled Volunteer Soldiers under one roof.

The Japanese attack on Pearl Harbor in 1941 and Hitler's expanding assault on Europe, where many Americans claimed ancestry, unified the United States behind its soldiers during World War II, regardless of religion, race, ethnicity or class. The eventual defeat of the Axis powers and the ensuing economic boom in the United States generated admiration and honor for the more than 16 million American men and women who had served in the war. Never before had the citizenry and the government displayed such unalloyed gratitude toward veterans' service and sacrifice.

GI Bill Enacted

The most concrete expression of that gratitude was the G.I. Bill of Rights. Enacted by Congress in 1944, it profoundly affected the nature of the country and the economy.

Perhaps most important was its education funding: Millions of men who otherwise couldn't have afforded to go college were given the opportunity, turning higher education into a staple of middle-class life. In addition, the GI Bill's discount rates for home loans enabled veterans to buy houses in the suburbs, contributing heavily to the postwar flight from the inner cities.

In the early 1950s, as World War II veterans were enjoying the nation's postwar prosperity, the nation went to war in Korea. But when the Korean War veterans returned in 1953, many encountered national ambivalence toward their service as well as virulent anti-communist sentiment that even put some soldiers under suspicion.

During the war, North Korea had captured about 4,500 American soldiers and held them in brutal conditions. Repatriated after a truce was signed, many of them faced accusations of collaborating or sympathizing with their captors. Even though nearly all the charges were groundless, a 1943 law allowed the VA to revoke benefits to anyone guilty of treason, sabotage or mutiny. Thus the VA formed its own version of the notorious, communist-hunting House Un-American Activities Committee to investigate subversives. It found none.

Meanwhile, other Korean War veterans received benefits and care they were due, but they also encountered the indifference of a nation that perceived the war as a loss.

The Challenge of Post-Traumatic Stress

As a gunner's mate on the *USS Missouri* during the Persian Gulf War in 1991, J. Philip Goodrum, thought his number was up when an incoming Iraqi missile was spotted coming straight at his position. Although a nearby warship downed the missile 30 yards in front of the *Missouri*, the explosion and its heat-blast are seared in Goodrum's memory.

More recently, as a platoon leader during Operation Iraqi Freedom, Goodrum, 34, constantly feared for the safety of the soldiers in his transportation company. "We were always being sent on unsafe convoys," he says. "We had no maps, no armor, no escort. We had lousy vehicle maintenance and were always low on fuel. There's no worse feeling than having little fuel out in the field and you're being fired on, and you're responsible for the lives of 18 kids."

Goodrum is now being treated at Walter Reed Army Medical Center in Washington, D.C., for post-traumatic stress disorder (PTSD), but he's not pleased with the help. [1] "I'd rather be an amputee than a psychological patient," he says. The physically disabled earn sympathy and respect from the military, he says, while the psychologically wounded draw mostly suspicions of malingering or weakness.

"The doctors here are only three or four years out of school," he adds. "They don't seem to know much about PTSD, and I don't think they even really believe in it."

CQ Press/Olu Davis

Lt. J. Philip Goodrum, right, is seeking service-connected benefits with help from Steve Robinson, executive director of the National Gulf War Resources Center.

Goodrum's sense that Army doctors don't have much patience for PTSD sufferers is shared by Steve Robinson, executive director of the National Gulf War Resources Center. "The military is in the job of projecting power and fighting wars and procuring weapons and developing weapons systems," says Robinson, an Army veteran of the Persian Gulf War. "They're not in the business of taking care of people who can't do any of those things."

Goodrum supplements his treatments at Walter Reed by going to a Department of Veterans Affairs "Vet Center." Among other things, the nation's 183 Vet Centers offer job and education advice, as well as PTSD counseling.

Many of the VA's PTSD programs are staffed by Vietnam veterans who often have first-hand experience with PTSD. "They've seen a lot worse," Goodrum says. "They know the problem."

Indeed, of the approximately 3 million men and women who served in Vietnam, up to 1 million have suffered from PTSD. [2] In previous wars, PTSD was often referred to as "shell shock." But Vietnam produced an extraordinarily high number of PTSD cases, due to the unusually high stresses produced by a war with no clear front lines, an enemy that melded into the civilian population and frequent, sudden violence and death.

Combat conditions in Iraq mimic those in Vietnam, creating a new wave of PTSD sufferers. In fact, *The New England Journal of Medicine* recently reported that as many as 17 percent of Operation Iraqi Freedom veterans exhibit PTSD symptoms. [3]

In addition to its Vet Centers, the VA offers more than 100 hospital-based PTSD programs, ranging from education about the disorder and how to evaluate it to inpatient treatment. In 1989, in response to a congressional mandate to address the needs of veterans with service-related PTSD, the VA established the National Center for Post-Traumatic Stress Disorder.

The disorder often eludes diagnosis by general physicians, despite volumes published about it in the last 20 years. But experts widely credit the VA with developing expertise in both diagnosis and treatment.

"A lot of us are really looking forward to getting more help from the VA," Goodrum says. "But we worry that they won't be able to handle all the demand."

---

[1] For background, see Sarah Glazer, "Treating Anxiety," *The CQ Researcher*, Feb. 8, 2002, pp. 97-120.

[2] "Epidemiological Facts about PTSD," National Center for PTSD, National Vietnam Veterans Readjustment Survey, www.ncptsd.org/facts/general/fs_epidemiological.html.

[3] See Charles W. Hoge, M.D., *et al.*, "Combat Duty in Iraq and Afghanistan, Mental Health Problems, and Barriers to Care," *The New England Journal of Medicine*, Vol. 351, No. 1, July 1, 2004.

Agent Orange

Likewise, veterans of the Vietnam War (1959-75) often encountered outright hostility from the American people. As with the Korean War, U.S. involvement in Vietnam was rooted in Cold War fears that communism was spreading throughout the world. But as the war dragged on with no clear end in sight, the American public became deeply divided over the conflict. [23] As a result, returning veterans encountered a public that largely didn't want to see or think about them.

Worse, thousands of veterans returned with serious physical or psychological illnesses, including the then-obscure PTSD. The physical ailments involved, among others, odd skin rashes and unusual cancers that seemed to have no cause. Then in the late 1970s a suspect emerged — Agent Orange.

Between 1961 and 1970, U.S. forces had sprayed 11.2 million gallons of the defoliant over the Vietnamese countryside in an attempt to destroy the thick jungle canopy that hid enemy forces. But a 1969 scientific report showed that an ingredient in Agent Orange could cause birth defects in laboratory animals, and use of the herbicide in Vietnam ceased the following year. [24]

As many as 3 million U.S. service personnel were exposed to potentially harmful levels of Agent Orange in Vietnam, but the Defense Department refused to acknowledge any connection between exposure to the herbicide and the veterans' illnesses. During the late 1970s and early '80s, thousands of Vietnam veterans joined a class-action lawsuit against Agent Orange's seven manufacturers — Dow Chemical, Monsanto, Uniroyal, Hercules, Diamond Shamrock, Thompson Chemical and T. H. Agriculture and Nutrition.

The VA had been offering medical care to veterans whose health problems might have resulted from exposure to Agent Orange. However, when veterans applied for disability compensation, the VA resisted. Such payments are required under federal law for any disability incurred or aggravated by military service. The veterans accused the agency of trying to avoid costly payouts; the VA and others insisted that not enough scientific evidence existed to support the veterans' claims.

Then in 1984, the manufacturers of Agent Orange agreed to a $180 million out-of-court settlement, while admitting no wrongdoing. But as scientists conducted more studies throughout the decade, evidence mounted suggesting a link between many of the health problems veterans were reporting and exposure to Agent Orange. In 1991, Congress passed a bill providing compensation to Vietnam veterans suffering from two illnesses that seemed most likely to be connected to exposure — soft tissue sarcomas and non-Hodgkin's lymphoma.

To settle the controversy, the federal government a year later asked the Institute of Medicine (IOM) to review the enormous body of research on Agent Orange. In 1994, the IOM found that in addition to soft tissue sarcomas and non-Hodgkin's lymphoma, evidence also supported links between Agent Orange exposure and Hodgkin's disease, a skin and nerve disorder. Since then, more evidence has emerged to support links with numerous other forms of cancer, type-2 diabetes and at least one birth defect.

Vietnam veterans welcomed the VA's acceptance of their claims about Agent Orange, but many remain resentful that without sustained outside pressure, the VA might have never done so.

Gulf War Syndrome

While most troops in the first Persian Gulf War returned home unharmed to parades and warm welcomes — and many veterans have received proper care and attention from the VA — some observers saw a replay of the Agent Orange debacle when approximately 100,000 of the 697,000 U.S. troops deployed to the Gulf began complaining of mysterious ailments.

The multiple symptoms included joint pain, aches and fevers, chronic fatigue and neurological problems. Military and VA physicians initially said they were caused by stress. But the veterans suspected exposure to chemical weapons. Military officials at first dismissed the suspicion, saying maybe only 5,000 troops had been in the vicinity of chemical weapons. Later the Pentagon acknowledged that certain combat actions and disposal of chemical weapons had released some toxic chemicals into heavy winds that might have affected as many as 100,000 troops, causing so-called Gulf War Syndrome. [25]

In the mid- and late-1990s, two reports — one from a committee appointed by President Clinton, the other from the IOM — said chemical exposure probably did not cause the veterans' illnesses. However, a new report commissioned by the VA has concluded that direct exposure to toxic chemicals is indeed the likely cause. [26]

The report recommended that, based on the new findings, the VA conduct further research on treatments, which VA Secretary Principi has agreed to do. Meanwhile, the VA is treating and compensating veterans with the syndrome. For instance, the agency already provides disability benefits to Gulf veterans who have developed amyotrophic lateral sclerosis (ALS), or Lou Gehrig's disease. Studies show that Gulf veterans face almost twice the risk of developing the disease as veterans who did not serve in the Gulf. [27] ■

CURRENT SITUATION

Renovation Program

The VA is planning its largest renovation program in history: the modernization of its 4,900 medical buildings, which are an average of 50 years old. "VA's medical infra-

Continued on p. 990

At Issue:

Should Congress make VA funding mandatory?

yes

JOHN FURGESS
COMMANDER-IN-CHIEF, VETERANS OF FOREIGN WARS OF THE U.S.

WRITTEN FOR *THE CQ RESEARCHER*, NOVEMBER 2004

From the smallest store to the largest international corporation, managers must know how much operating capital they have to work with — and when it will be available — in order to make sound fiscal decisions. This basic business principle should certainly apply to our nation's largest integrated health-care system, the Veterans Health Administration (VHA). But unfortunately it doesn't.

As part of the Department of Veterans Affairs (VA), VHA provides health care to more than 5 million disabled military veterans every year at more than 160 hospitals, 850 clinics and 130 nursing homes. But VHA must bear the annual uncertainty of not knowing precisely what its budget will be or when it will become available.

This unfortunate situation exists because Congress funds VA health care on a discretionary basis. It is here, due to political strife and a variety of other reasons, that budget uncertainty is created, and it has resulted in a late budget for the past six years in a row — once by almost five months. This uncertainty impacts everything from the hiring of sorely needed health-care professionals to equipment acquisitions and construction projects. As a result, waiting times and veterans' access to health care are negatively affected.

For these reasons, veterans' service organizations support funding VA health care on a mandatory basis. We understand that money isn't the only answer — we also want accountability so that when dollars are spent, it's on the right equipment, services and people — but clearly, discretionary funding isn't working. It's time for a change.

Mandatory funding will not establish an individual entitlement, such as Social Security, but it would fund VHA on a formula that factors in known costs from previous years. It would not, as suggested by some, alter the eligibility criteria for VA health care. Nor would it eliminate the secretary's authority to annually assess which veteran-priority categories would continue to have access to VA health care.

Mandatory funding will allow managers to know in advance the budget they have to work with in a given fiscal year, and that it will be provided on time. This is essential to effective business planning and helps ensure the most efficient use of taxpayer dollars. Only when this is done will the greatest possible number of veterans be afforded top-quality health care on a timely basis.

The mandatory funding of VA health care is simply the right thing to do.

no

PETER VAN DOREN, EDITOR, AND
THOMAS A. FIREY, MANAGING EDITOR
***REGULATION* (PUBLISHED BY THE CATO INSTITUTE)**

WRITTEN FOR *THE CQ RESEARCHER*, NOVEMBER 2004

The Veterans Affairs problem is well known: The nation enters into a contract with the young men and women of its armed forces whereby they give up considerable personal freedom and take on significant risk. In return, they receive a bundle of benefits that includes money for college, home-financing help and such services as health care and counseling for injuries and illnesses incurred through military service.

But when veterans begin drawing on those benefits, they too often find that they're receiving socialized medicine and other services on the cheap: long waits for adjudication of medical claims; delayed or rationed resources; department strategy that is set by political calculations instead of veterans' needs; and the stifling, unreformed bureaucracies of the VA, against which too many veterans feel overwhelmed, lost or powerless.

Those shortcomings are not the result of malevolent, negligent or incompetent VA employees; the caregivers, administrators and other VA professionals we know are well trained and dedicated to helping American veterans. But they must work within an entrenched bureaucracy that treats veterans as simple input and output in a machine. The VA manages services that are intensely important and personal to each veteran, but — as with any bureaucracy — the quality of those services comes second to the department's rationing and political goals. The VA is largely unaccountable to those whom it's supposed to serve — the veterans.

The best — and only — way to improve this situation and give veterans the benefits they deserve is to empower them to manage their own care. The VA has, for some time, considered using vouchers — giving money to capable clients so that they can go out in the marketplace (or to the VA) and procure the treatment and other services they find most useful. Nothing would improve veterans' care more than giving them control over those very personal transactions. And nothing would more positively affect the VA than to make it compete with private care providers.

Proponents of moving the VA off the discretionary budget believe that doing so will somehow improve matters. But changing the department's budget stream will likely further entrench its bureaucratic machinations by pushing it further away from congressional oversight and public view.

Instead of worrying about how the money is allocated, veterans' advocates should focus more on who decides how that money is spent — the VA bureaucracy or the veterans.

Continued from p. 988

structure has become old and outdated," Principi has said." [28]

Congress had been reluctant to appropriate funds toward such a massive project until the VA in the late 1990s detailed which facilities would be shut and what new construction and equipment it needed and for what purpose. In 1998, the agency initiated a process it called CARES — for Capital Asset Realignment for Enhanced Services — to produce the blueprint for change. Early this year, the VA's CARES Commission released its report.

The plan anticipates steady growth in the percentage of veterans who will want VA health care in the future. Currently, about 7 million of the nation's 29 million veterans, or 24 percent, are enrolled in the VA health-care system. CARES predicts that by 2022, one-third of all veterans will be enrolled.

Veterans' advocates are eager to see CARES put into effect, and Principi enthusiastically endorses the plan. But some are skeptical, especially budget analysts at the OMB. The VA secretary announced that $1 billion would be included in the agency's fiscal 2005 budget for CARES, with another $1 billion per year for the next five years. [29] But in the budget request sent to Capitol Hill, the $1 billion for CARES had been deleted.

As of mid-November 2004, more than a month into the new fiscal year, Congress is still debating the budget for the year. "It's possible they'll add that billion into the budget," says Robertson of the American Legion, "but we don't know for sure."

The agency's collaboration with the Pentagon on "seamless" transition from military to VA health care remains another VA priority, and the Pentagon continues to strongly support the VA-originated idea. "It wasn't easy to infiltrate the military-treatment facilities at first," says Jacobs of the VA's compensation and pension service. "But now that we're there, they don't want us to leave. We're now part of their system."

In mid-November, five VA staff members were working full time and one part time with patients at both Walter Reed and the Bethesda Naval Medical Center in Maryland, helping service members move from military to VA care. Similar teams assist at three other DOD medical centers serving as evacuation and treatment points for seriously injured troops: Eisenhower Army Medical Center, Ft. Gordon, Ga.; Brooke Army Medical Center, Ft. Sam Houston, Texas; and Madigan Army Medical Center at Western Regional Medical Command, Tacoma, Wash.

But Robinson of the NGWRC says more personnel are needed. "There's not enough to help all the soldiers," he says.

Meanwhile, the Army is trying to address concerns raised by injured Reserve and National Guard soldiers, unaccustomed to long separation from family and home. The Army's Community-Based Health Care Initiative (CBHCI) allows reserve component soldiers to receive treatment and recuperate in Army or VA facilities near their homes. It is staffed primarily by Reservists and Guardsmen.

And veterans' advocates are watching to see if the VA will lift its suspension of Priority Group 8 veterans' eligibility to enroll in VA health care. Principi has given no indication he will any time soon.

Top Priority

Veterans' advocates, however, are focused primarily on securing mandatory funding for the VA budget. But chances of success aren't promising in light of the fact that Rep. Smith's bill calling for mandatory funding, introduced at the end of the 107th Congress, never budged.

In February 2003, when he tried to spark congressional debate over the issue as a prelude to reintroducing the legislation, he attracted the wrath of the House leadership. Congressional Republicans were angry because Smith had given Democrats a tool to use in attacking the Bush administration's budget cuts and because mandatory funding could swell an already ballooning deficit, a sensitive issue for both Congress and the White House. Moreover, Republican appropriators felt Smith had encroached on their authority. House Speaker J. Dennis Hastert, R-Ill., reportedly warned Smith he could lose his chairmanship if he continued to press the issue. [30]

In response, Smith introduced a compromise bill in June 2003 calling for an independent panel of experts to determine the VA's annual budget needs. Their determination would become the administration's budget proposal for VA health care, bypassing the OMB, but Congress would retain discretionary authority to raise or lower the funding. The bill, which has 46 co-sponsors, is still in the Veterans' Affairs Committee but no action has been scheduled on it.

Democrat Evans' proposal calling for mandatory funding, meanwhile, has 184 sponsors, including 14 Republicans. The House leadership continues to oppose it as well, and it is still awaiting action by the Veterans' Affairs Committee.

Although Evans and Smith have had cordial working relations, Evans' attempt to run with a ball that Smith was clearly told by the House leadership to drop could put the two lawmakers at odds. But Evans remains upbeat.

"I'm very optimistic that starting next year we'll probably be able to get something done," he says. "We can have a real impact."

Benefits in the States

According to Charles Sheehan-Miles, executive director of the Veterans for Common Sense advocacy group, some states offer veterans benefits, but "typically they're very limited." For example, South Carolina provides emergency relief for deployed soldiers' families that are strapped for cash and, say, possibly losing a home. Virginia pays the college tuition of children of service personnel killed in war. Texas offers multiple benefits: free college tuition, special, low-interest rates for buying land and retirement housing for veterans.

Six states have home-loan programs for veterans, and nearly every state maintains a veterans' cemetery, usually financed by the VA, says Robertson, of the American Legion. Some states have county shelters for homeless veterans, while other states simply help veterans apply for VA benefits.

Both Sheehan-Miles and Robertson point out, however, that the state programs vary widely, leaving the VA as veterans' sole source for major, substantive benefits. ■

OUTLOOK

More Cuts?

The wars in Iraq and Afghanistan make the newest generation of veterans the VA's priority for the immediate future. "We've seen everyone [wounded] who has needed to be seen," says the VA's Miller. "We aren't turning anybody away, and we're prepared to assist in every way feasible. There may be here or there a gap or snafu, but overall I think it's working well."

While veterans' advocates applaud the help new veterans are getting, they say the VA is serving them at the expense of older veterans. And Weidman, of the Vietnam Veterans of America, predicts things will get worse. "We expect Congress and the VA will try to redefine 'service-connected disability' in such a way as to reduce the rolls."

Neither Congress nor the VA, however, has indicated it plans any redefinition, and some observers, like Hellman, of the Center for Arms Control and Nonproliferation, question the wisdom of such a move.

"Change someone from 30 percent disabled to 20 percent?" he asks. "Scaling back benefits for people already receiving them is always bad politically. Nothing worse than taking away a promise."

Gorman of Disabled American Veterans says that could happen to disabled veterans from the Iraq and Afghanistan conflicts, even though the DOD currently takes care of them with state-of-the-art equipment. "But that's the short term," says Gorman, "and I can tell you, I lost both legs in Vietnam, and over the course of a year or so, the wounds start to play on you, and you need more attention. Other things start to break down later. And that's what's going to happen with these kids. At 18, 20 years old, a lot of them look at disabilities as challenges, not obstacles. But you've got maybe another 60 years in front of you, and where are you going to get your care then?

"Nobody seems to realize that there's this aftermath, a continuing cost of war, and that's the VA system," Gorman continues. Funding needs to keep pace with the demand, he says, but he doesn't expect it to happen anytime soon.

Robertson of the American Legion is also doubtful. "We in the veterans world get confused when we go and ask the government for more money to help take care of veterans per the benefits they've earned, and we're told there's no money.

"Then out of the clear blue, somebody comes up with a $17 billion appropriation to fight AIDS in Africa. And we scratch our heads and say, 'OK, if we go to Africa and develop AIDS, we'll get access to full health care.' I wish I could tell you that regardless of who's elected they'll do the right thing, but every year we have to fight from day one for every increase we get."

For his part, Secretary Principi is putting his faith in updating the VA's health-care infrastructure. "With the acceptance of the CARES Commission Report," he said, "I am confident that the Department of Veterans Affairs stands more ready than ever to continue to meet President Lincoln's solemn promise today and into the future." [31] ■

Notes

[1] See Alicia Caldwell, "VA System Flooded," *St. Petersburg Times*, Sept. 29, 2002, p. 1A.

[2] See Mark Strassmann, "Veterans' Benefits," CBS News, Aug. 12, 2004, www.cbsnews.com/stories/2004/08/12/eveningnews/main635591.shtml.

[3] See Thomas Oliphant, "Broken promises to veterans," *The Boston Globe*, June 27, 2004.

[4] "America's Neglected Veterans: 1.7 Million Who Served Have No Health Coverage," Harvard/Cambridge Hospital Study Group on Veterans' Health Insurance, Oct. 19, 2004.

[5] "Southern California Veterans Must Wait Months for Benefits," press release, House Committee on Government Reform, Minority, Oct. 12, 2004.

[6] See Josh White, "Influx of Wounded Strains VA; Claims Backlog Besets Returning U.S. Troops," *The Washington Post*, Oct. 3, 2004, p. A1.

About the Author

William Triplett covered science and the arts for such publications as *Smithsonian, Air & Space, Nature, Washingtonian* and *The Washington Post* before joining the *CQ Researcher* staff. He also served as associate editor of *Capitol Style* magazine. He holds a B.A. in journalism from Ohio University and an M.A. in English literature from Georgetown University. His recent reports include "Search for Extraterrestrials" and "Broadcast Indecency."

FOR MORE INFORMATION

American Legion, 700 N. Pennsylvania St., Indianapolis, IN 46204; (317) 630-1200; www.legion.org. Chartered by Congress in 1919 as a mutual-help, wartime veterans' organization, the world's largest veterans' organization has nearly 3 million members worldwide.

AMVETS, 4647 Forbes Blvd., Lanham, MD 20706; (301) 459-9600; www.amvets.org. Founded by soldiers returning from World War II, tracks veterans-related legislative issues and advocates for improved veterans' benefits.

Department of Veterans Affairs, 810 Vermont Ave., N.W., Washington, DC 20420; (202) 273-5400; www.va.gov. The Cabinet agency responsible for veterans' benefits and health care.

Disabled American Veterans, 3725 Alexandria Pike, Cold Spring, KY, 41076; (859) 441-7300; www.dav.org. Represents more than 1 million veterans disabled in war or armed conflict.

National Coalition for Homeless Veterans, 3331/2 Pennsylvania Ave., S.E., Washington, DC 20003; (202) 546-1969; www.nchv.org. Founded in 1990 by a group of community-based providers of services for homeless veterans, seeks to eliminate homelessness in the veteran community.

National Gulf War Resources Center, 8605 Cameron St., Suite 400, Silver Spring, MD 20910; (800) VVA-1316; www.ngwrc.org. Founded in 1995 to represent Gulf War veterans seeking compensation for illnesses they alleged were connected to their exposure in Iraq to oil-well fires, depleted uranium, chemical and biological warfare agents and pesticides, as well as negative effects of mandatory anthrax vaccines.

Veterans for Common Sense, c/o EPIC, 1101 Pennsylvania Ave., S.E., Washington, DC 20003; (202) 543-6176; www.veteransforcommonsense.org. Focuses on foreign policy issues in addition to advocating for veterans.

Veterans of Foreign Wars, 406 West 34th St., Kansas City, MO 64111; (816) 756-3390; www.vfw.org. Founded in 1899 by veterans of the Spanish-American War and the Philippine Insurrection to secure rights and benefits for veterans; has 2.7 million members (including its Ladies Auxiliary).

Vietnam Veterans of America, 8605 Cameron St., Suite 400, Silver Spring, MD 20910; (800) VVA-1316; www.vva.org. Founded in 1978, the only national organization congressionally chartered and exclusively dedicated to Vietnam-era veterans and their families.

[7] "Veterans Issue Briefs," House Committee on Veterans Affairs, p. 2.

[8] Interview on CNN's "Lou Dobbs Tonight," Nov. 11, 2004.

[9] "Highlights of Congressional Accomplishments for Veterans," House Committee on Veterans Affairs, p. 2.

[10] Fact Sheet, Department of Veterans Affairs, May 2004.

[11] "Veterans Issue Briefs," *op. cit.*

[12] See White, *op. cit.*

[13] "Epidemiological Facts about PTSD," National Center for PTSD, National Vietnam Veterans Readjustment Survey, www.ncptsd.org/facts/general/fs_epidemiological.html. For background, see Sarah Glazer, "Treating Anxiety," *The CQ Researcher*, Feb. 8, 2002, pp. 97-120.

[14] "VA Services for Veterans of Operation Iraqi Freedom and Operation Enduring Freedom," Fact Sheet, Department of Veterans Affairs, January 2004.

[15] "Facts About the Department of Veterans Affairs," Fact Sheet, Department of Veterans Affairs, May 2004.

[16] For background, see William Triplett, "Helping the Homeless," *The CQ Researcher*, June 18, 2004, pp. 541-564.

[17] See Niels. C. Sorrells, "VA Secretary Tells Lawmakers White House Rebuffed Pleas for More Money," *CQ Today*, Feb. 4, 2004. See also Suzanne Gamboa, "Principi wanted $1.2 billion more for Veterans Affairs' budget," The Associated Press, Feb. 4, 2004.

[18] Quoted in "Chairman simmons praises presidential task force recommendations for stronger commitment to VA health funding," press release, Rep. Rob Simmons, May 29, 2003.

[19] "Veterans Issue Brief," *op. cit.*

[20] See Donna Miles, "Disabled Soldier Support System Helping Wounded Troops," American Forces Information Service, Oct. 20, 2004, www.defenselink.mil/news/oct2004/n10202004_200410202007.html.

[21] See Charles W. Hoge, M.D., *et al.*, "Combat Duty in Iraq and Afghanistan, Mental Health Problems, and Barriers to Care," *The New England Journal of Medicine*, Vol. 351, No. 1, July 1, 2004.

[22] Except where noted, principal sources for this section are "A Brief History," Department of Veterans Affairs, www.va.gov/vafhis.htm, and Richard Severo and Lewis Milford, *The Wages of War: When America's Soldiers Came Home — From Valley Forge to Vietnam*, Simon & Schuster (1989).

[23] For background, see Harry Summers, *On Strategy: A Critical Analysis of the Vietnam War* (1982).

[24] See "Agent Orange: Information for Veterans Who Served in Vietnam," Environmental Agents Service, Department of Veterans Affairs, July 2003, and "Veterans and Agent Orange: Health Effects of Herbicides Used in Vietnam," Committee to Review the Health Effects in Vietnam Veterans of Exposure to Herbicides, Institute of Medicine, 1994.

[25] See Patrick G. Eddington, *Gassed in the Gulf: The Inside Story of the Pentagon-CIA Cover-up of Gulf War Syndrome* (1997).

[26] See Scott Shane, "Chemicals Sickened '91 Gulf War Veterans, Latest Study Finds," *The New York Times*, Oct. 15, 2004, p. A1.

[27] *Ibid.*

[28] Anthony J. Principi, "Secretary's Opening Statement and Acceptance of CARES Commission Report," The CARES Commission Report, Department of Veterans Affairs, 2004.

[29] *Ibid.*

[30] See Niels C. Sorrells, "Smith Plan for Veterans' Health Heats Already Turbulent Issue," *CQ Today*, May 5, 2003.

[31] Principi, *op. cit.*

Bibliography

Selected Sources

Books

Eddington, Patrick G., *Gassed in the Gulf: The Inside Story of the Pentagon-CIA Cover-up of Gulf War Syndrome*, Insignia Publishing, 1997.

A former award-winning CIA analyst uses declassified and unclassified information to argue that the spy agency — along with U.S. military leaders — sought to deceive the public about illnesses Persian Gulf War veterans were suffering.

Schuck, Peter H., *Agent Orange on Trial: Mass Toxic Disasters in the Courts*, Harvard University Press, 1986.

A Yale University law professor chronicles the legal and human consequences of the largest personal-injury, class-action lawsuit in the country's history.

Severo, Richard, and Lewis Milford, *The Wages of War: When America's Soldiers Came Home — From Valley Forge to Vietnam*, Simon & Schuster, 1989.

A former prize-winning *New York Times* reporter (Severo) and a former lawyer for the National Veterans Law Center document how the hostility that greeted soldiers returning from Vietnam was the rule, and the celebrations for World War II veterans were the exception in how America's veterans are treated.

Articles

"Senators: Open VA to all vets," The Associated Press, July 26, 2004.

Thirty-four Democratic senators asked VA Secretary Anthony J. Principi to lift the 2003 moratorium on Priority Group 8 veterans, barring them from receiving health care. Some senators estimate that as many as 500,000 veterans could be affected by the exclusion.

Caldwell, Alicia, "VA Medical System Flooded," *The St. Petersburg Times*, Sept. 29, 2002, p. 1A.

A surge in demand for VA health care causes lengthy delays for appointments and even prevents veterans with service-connected disabilities from being seen.

Higgins, Richard, "Bush budget takes a beating from veterans," *The Sebastian* [Florida] *Sun*, Feb. 13, 2004, p. A5.

At a House Veterans' Affairs Committee hearing, veterans' advocates criticize the proposed White House VA budget as "too little and too late."

Oliphant, Thomas, "Broken Promises to Veterans," *The Boston Globe*, June 27, 2004.

A columnist argues that President Bush and congressional allies are breaking promises to veterans by denying them health care and "gouging them with escalating out-of-pocket charges."

Shane, Scott, "Chemicals Sickened '91 Gulf War Veterans, Latest Study Finds," *The New York Times*, Oct. 15, 2004, p. A1.

A new VA study, contradicting previous reports, finds substantial evidence to confirm chemical exposure did cause Gulf War Syndrome.

Sorrells, Niels C., "Smith Plan for Veterans' Health Heats Already Turbulent Issue," *CQ Today*, May 5, 2003.

Plans by House Veterans' Affairs Committee Chairman Christopher Smith to change VA funding from discretionary to mandatory could become politically explosive.

Sorrells, Niels C., "VA Secretary Tells Lawmakers White House Rebuffed Pleas for More Money," *CQ Today*, Feb. 4, 2004.

In a rare disclosure, a Cabinet secretary acknowledged to Congress that the White House's proposed fiscal 2005 VA budget is $1.2 billion less than he requested.

White, Josh, "Influx of Wounded Strains VA; Claims Backlog Besets Returning U.S. Troops," *The Washington Post*, Oct. 3, 2004, p. A1.

U.S. troops returning from Iraq and Afghanistan with physical injuries and mental health problems are encountering an overburdened health-care system, and experts worry the situation will worsen.

Reports and Studies

"Agent Orange: Information for Veterans Who Served in Vietnam," Environmental Agents Service, Department of Veterans Affairs, July 2003.

The report covers the use and known health effects of Agent Orange and the VA's related responsibilities, plus how veterans can get treatment and compensation.

"Veterans and Agent Orange: Health Effects of Herbicides Used in Vietnam," Committee to Review the Health Effects in Vietnam Veterans of Exposure to Herbicides, Institute of Medicine, 1994.

The National Academy of Sciences agency found substantial evidence linking Agent Orange to several diseases and conditions.

Hoge, Charles W., M.D., *et al.*, "Combat Duty in Iraq and Afghanistan, Mental Health Problems, and Barriers to Care," *The New England Journal of Medicine*, July 1, 2004, p. 13.

Approximately 17 percent of soldiers returning from Operations Enduring Freedom and Iraqi Freedom exhibit symptoms of post-traumatic stress disorder (PTSD).

The Next Step:

Additional Articles from Current Periodicals

Bush Administration

Loeb, Vernon, "Bush Threatens Veto of Defense Bill," *The Washington Post*, Oct. 7, 2002, p. A2.

President Bush has threatened to veto the defense authorization bill if it includes new pension benefits for disabled military retirees that would allow them to collect retirement and disability benefits at the same time.

Pear, Robert, "U.S. to Review Research at Hospitals for Veterans," *The New York Times*, April 13, 2003, p. A5.

The Bush administration has ordered a review of medical research at all veterans' hospitals and has halted some studies after investigators found violations of federal rules that may have contributed to the deaths of patients.

Rosenblatt, Bob, "Dollars and Sense; Healing Veterans Injured During Service," *Los Angeles Times*, Sept. 10, 2001, p. S1.

President Bush is promising a better deal for 600,000 veterans seeking benefit payments to compensate for physical or mental problems and receive treatment through hospitals and clinics.

Walsh, Edward, "Veterans' Groups Critical of Bush's VA Budget," *The Washington Post*, March 3, 2004, p. A25.

Leaders of veterans' organizations say Bush's budget would worsen the backlog of VA disability claims, reduce the number of nursing home beds and force some veterans to pay a fee to gain access to VA health care.

GI Bill

Davenport, Christian, "The Middle Class Rose, As Did Expectations," *The Washington Post*, May 27, 2004, p. B1.

By providing guaranteed loans to veterans to help with college tuition, the GI Bill became a vehicle for upward mobility.

Greenberg, Milton, "How the GI Bill Changed Higher Education," *The Chronicle of Higher Education*, June 18, 2004, p. 9.

When the GI Bill was passed in June 1944, few anticipated how it would instantly change the nation's social landscape.

Madhani, Aamer, "For Ex-GIs, Fitting In on Campus a Struggle," *Chicago Tribune*, Oct. 27, 2004, p. C1.

Campuses have been flooded with veterans looking to collect their education benefits under the Montgomery GI Bill, but universities have no one to help the GIs transition from battlefield to classroom.

Marklein, Mary Beth, "Going Online to Be All They Can Be," *USA Today*, June 12, 2001, p. 9D.

The Army debuts an online education program designed to complement the GI Bill, in which soldiers can take college courses on the Web with the Army paying for the laptops, Internet service, books and tuition.

Sturrock, Carrie, "Student Finds GI Bill Doesn't Cover All Costs," *The San Francisco Chronicle*, Aug. 8, 2004, p. B1.

Military recruiters use the promise of money for college to entice recruits, who often don't know they have to pay into the program to access benefits and that receiving military supplements can hinder their ability to obtain standard financial aid.

Homeless Veterans

Barry, Dan, "War Veteran's Homecoming Is Spent in Homeless Shelters," *The New York Times*, April 24, 2004, p. B1.

A 23-year-old single mother honorably discharged from the Army after serving in Iraq finds herself living on the streets with her 1-year-old daughter.

Stewart, Jocelyn, "From the Ranks to the Street," *Los Angeles Times*, May 29, 2004, p. A1.

Veterans make up 9 percent of the U.S. population but 23 percent of the homeless population, according to the federal government.

Walsh, Edward, "Changes at VA Vex Advocates For Homeless," *The Washington Post*, March 20, 2003, p. A27.

Many veterans' organizations and shelters are being denied federal funding due to the vastly increased competition for the limited amount of money that the VA made available for homeless veterans' programs.

Overburdened System

Freedberg, Sydney, "Filling the Veterans' Medical Care Gap," *National Journal*, June 14, 2003.

The 2003 budget for veterans' health care tops $23 billion, but the Veterans Affairs Department still struggles to serve its 4.5 million regular patients — a fifth of those eligible.

Rosenblatt, Susannah, "VA Health System Failing," *Los Angeles Times*, July 15, 2003, Part 1, p. 18.

Veterans are waiting six months or more for medical care as a severely overburdened Veterans Affairs health system fails to keep pace with growing demand, according to a report to Congress.

Schrader, Esther, "Military's Retirees Due Healthy Bonus," *Los Angeles Times*, Aug. 5, 2001, p. A18.

Ten months after Congress voted to guarantee free medical coverage to 1.5 million aging military retirees, the Pentagon is struggling to implement the costly program.

Walsh, Edward, "VA Eyes Hospital Closings in Health-Care Overhaul," *The Washington Post*, Oct. 9, 2003, p. A35.

With little notice outside the veterans' community, the Department of Veterans Affairs has embarked on a major overhaul of its health-care system to streamline its operation and relieve budget pressure.

Vogel, Steve, "Battling Bankruptcy in D.C.," *The Washington Post*, Jan. 25, 2004, p. C1.
The Armed Forces Retirement Home in Washington, D.C., facing the threat of bankruptcy for years, is reducing the size of its operation, selling surplus land and closing its 24-hour medical treatment center and funeral home.

Veterans' Health Care

Hobbs, Erika, "Family Fights for Veteran's Medical Care," *The Baltimore Sun*, Oct. 10, 2004, p. 1B.
A family battles for continued health-care coverage for a decorated Vietnam veteran who suffered a stroke last year and is now paralyzed on his left side, but the VA says its underfunded program cannot afford his care.

Schrader, Esther, "Back Home, Disabled Vets Fight Injuries, Red Tape," *Los Angeles Times*, Aug. 8, 2004, p. 1A.
Thousands of service personnel wounded in the Iraq war will face a future filled with frustration and pain as they leave efficient Army hospitals and find themselves on their own in an unfamiliar and difficult-to-navigate maze of VA benefits and services.

Welch, William M., "VA Offers Medicines at Bargain Prices," *USA Today*, June 18, 2003, p. 1A.
The federal government runs a health-care system for military veterans that provides affordable care, has hospitals and clinics around the country and charges patients just $7 a month for each prescription.

Welch, William M., "VA to Reorganize Hospital System," *USA Today*, May 7, 2004, p. 4A.
The biggest-ever reorganization of the veterans' health system comes five years after the General Accounting Office found the VA wastes as much as $1 million a day maintaining vacant, underused and obsolete properties.

Wars' Impact on Veteran Health

Carey, Benedict, "On the Lookout for Gulf War Illness," *Los Angeles Times*, April 7, 2003, Part 6, p. 1.
As U.S. forces prepare for battle in the same hostile desert of the Gulf War, veterans of the 1991 conflict wonder whether a new generation will face the same mysterious health problems.

Chau, Doan Bao, "Agent Orange, the Next Generation," *The New York Times*, Aug. 8, 2004, Sect. 1, p. 25.
Twenty years after American chemical companies paid $180 million to settle Agent Orange lawsuits, American veterans and Vietnamese citizens filed new suits over the lasting and nightmarish problems caused by the defoliant.

Cohen, Sharon, "Vet Believes His Military Service May Have Led to Lou Gehrig's Disease," *Los Angeles Times*, Feb. 17, 2002, p. A1.
The VA announced Gulf War veterans were twice as likely as other military personnel to develop Lou Gehrig's disease (ALS) — and a group of ALS veterans has received their first benefits.

Farley, Maggie, "Effect of Munitions Debated," *Los Angeles Times*, June 15, 2003, Part 1, p. 21.
Scientists differ on the danger posed by exposure to depleted-uranium weapons, but they agree that troops returning from Iraq should be tested for exposure, and the army should clean up the hazardous mess left behind.

Goode, Erica, "Learning From the Last Time; Treatment and Training Help Reduce Stress of War," *The New York Times*, March 25, 2003, p. F1.
The American armed forces, schooled by Vietnam and the first Gulf War, have grown far more sophisticated in their approach to the psychological pressures of battle.

Citing *The CQ Researcher*

Sample formats for citing these reports in a bibliography include the ones listed below. Preferred styles and formats vary, so please check with your instructor or professor.

MLA Style

Jost, Kenneth. "Rethinking the Death Penalty." The CQ Researcher 16 Nov. 2001: 945-68.

APA Style

Jost, K. (2001, November 16). Rethinking the death penalty. *The CQ Researcher, 11*, 945-968.

Chicago Style

Jost, Kenneth. "Rethinking the Death Penalty." *CQ Researcher*, November 16, 2001, 945-968.

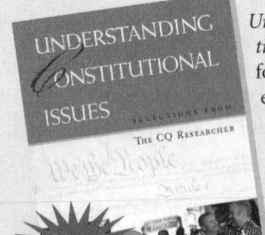

CQ Researcher

Published by CQ Press, a division of Congressional Quarterly Inc.

thecqresearcher.com

Sexually Transmitted Diseases

Is abstinence the best approach to prevention?

The United States has the highest rate of sexually transmitted diseases (STDs) of any industrialized nation. Yet some experts contend the U.S. has no concerted, national campaign to prevent and cure infection. While new AIDS cases have fallen dramatically in the U.S., adolescents, minorities and women suffer disproportionately high rates of all sexual infections. The Bush administration says abstinence is the only 100 percent effective approach to avoiding STDs and bars any organization receiving federal funding for abstinence-only education from discussing contraceptives, except to point out their failure rates. But public health officials see condoms as an essential protective device against STDs and say the abstinence-only message deprives teenagers of crucial, life-saving information and makes little sense in developing countries, where married women are the fastest-growing group infected with AIDS.

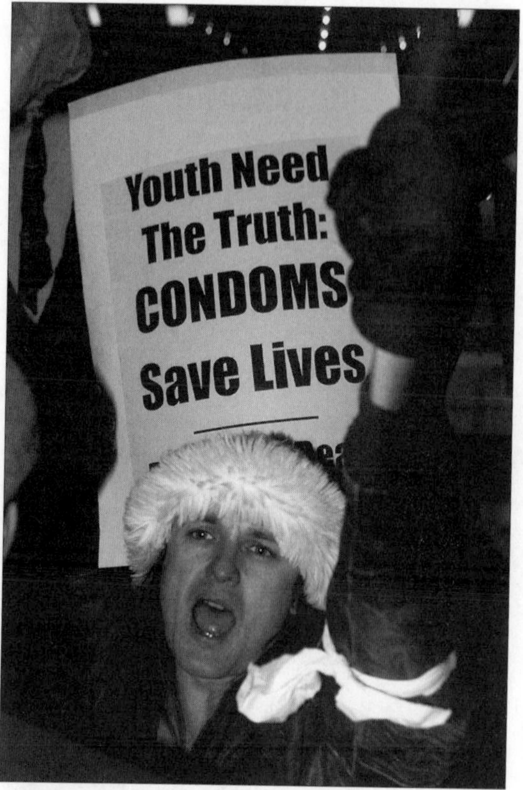

A protester at the STD prevention conference held by the Centers for Disease Control and Prevention in Philadelphia in March 2004 criticizes President Bush's plan to expand abstinence-only education.

INSIDE THIS REPORT

The CQ Researcher • Dec. 3, 2004 • www.thecqresearcher.com
Volume 14, Number 42 • Pages 997-1024

CQ PRESS

RECIPIENT OF SOCIETY OF PROFESSIONAL JOURNALISTS AWARD FOR EXCELLENCE ◆ AMERICAN BAR ASSOCIATION SILVER GAVEL AWARD

THE ISSUES

BACKGROUND

CURRENT SITUATION

OUTLOOK

SIDEBARS AND GRAPHICS

FOR FURTHER RESEARCH

Cover: A protester at the STD prevention conference held by the Centers for Disease Control and Prevention in Philadelphia in March 2004 criticizes President Bush's plan to expand abstinence-only education. (Getty Images/Jeff Fusco)

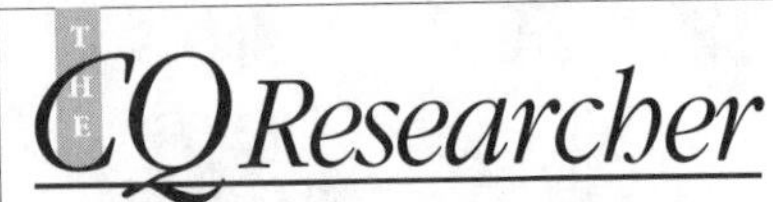

Dec. 3, 2004
Volume 14, Number 42

MANAGING EDITOR: Thomas J. Colin

ASSISTANT MANAGING EDITOR: Kathy Koch

ASSOCIATE EDITOR: Kenneth Jost

STAFF WRITERS: Mary H. Cooper, William Triplett

CONTRIBUTING WRITERS: Sarah Glazer, David Hatch, David Hosansky, Patrick Marshall, Tom Price, Jane Tanner

DESIGN/PRODUCTION EDITOR: Olu B. Davis

ASSISTANT EDITOR: Kate Templin

A Division of
Congressional Quarterly Inc.

SENIOR VICE PRESIDENT/GENERAL MANAGER: John A. Jenkins

DIRECTOR, LIBRARY PUBLISHING: Kathryn C. Suárez

DIRECTOR, EDITORIAL OPERATIONS: Ann Davies

CONGRESSIONAL QUARTERLY INC.

CHAIRMAN: Paul C. Tash

VICE CHAIRMAN: Andrew P. Corty

PRESIDENT AND PUBLISHER: Robert W. Merry

The CQ Researcher (ISSN 1056-2036) is printed on acid-free paper. Published weekly, except Jan. 2, April 9, July 2, July 9, Aug. 6, Aug. 13, Nov. 26 and Dec. 31, by CQ Press, a division of Congressional Quarterly Inc. Annual subscription rates for institutions start at $625. For pricing, call 1-800-834-9020, ext. 1906. To purchase a *CQ Researcher* report in print or electronic format (PDF), visit www.cqpress.com or call 866-427-7737. A single report is $10. Bulk purchase discounts and electronic-rights licensing are also available. Periodicals postage paid at Washington, D.C., and additional mailing offices. POSTMASTER: Send address changes to *The CQ Researcher*, 1255 22nd St., N.W., Suite 400, Washington, D.C. 20037.

Sexually Transmitted Diseases

BY SARAH GLAZER

THE ISSUES

The United States has the highest rates of sexually transmitted diseases (STDs) of any industrialized nation, and sexually active youth account for about half the new cases of infection occurring annually. Indeed, more than half of all Americans will get an STD at some point in their lifetime. [1] Yet the nation has no concerted, national campaign to prevent, treat and cure these infections, according to the American Social Health Association, a public health advocacy and information group in Research Triangle Park, N.C. [2]

Children's Aid Society/Felipe Ayala

High school students in the Children's Aid Society's sexuality-education program in New York City visit Binghamton University last summer. The "abstinence-plus" program has been called the nation's most successful approach to reducing teen sex and pregnancy. It urges youths to wait until they are older to have sex and then to use contraceptives conscientiously. The Bush administration says abstinence is the only 100 percent effective approach to avoiding STDs and is providing funding to spread the message in U.S. schools and overseas.

What the public needs is more information — not less, many public health advocates argue. Not much has changed since 1997, when "The Hidden Epidemic," a report by the Institute of Medicine (IOM), singled out secrecy as a major societal obstacle to curbing a problem that costs the United States up to $15.5 billion annually in direct medical expenses." [3] (*See chart, p. 1001.*)

The shame Americans feel about sex-related infection continues to inhibit people from talking about it to their sexual partners, a crucial factor in preventing it from spreading. It also prevents doctors from asking their patients about their sexual history and doing the kind of testing that could catch many of these infections in the early stages when they are easily curable, says Edward Hook, a professor of medicine at the University of Alabama, who served on the IOM committee.

"There is this really curious American ambivalence about sex being everywhere — from the sidelines of the football game to merchandising — but we can't advertise doing it safely or the untoward consequences of doing it unsafely," Hook says. "If I had one thing I could change it would be the stigma." In other developed countries, people are more likely to tell their partners if they're infected and talk to their doctors about it, he maintains, because there is less shame.

Most young girls won't even know they have chlamydia, one of the most common and curable STDs, unless their doctor tests them for it. In approximately three-quarters of infected men and women, this bacterial infection has no early symptoms, but it can be easily cured with antibiotics if caught early. If not, in 10 percent of girls it can lead to serious consequences like infertility or a tubal pregnancy years later.

Similarly, many of the other most common STD infections — including genital herpes and human papillomavirus (HPV) — have few if any recognizable symptoms, another serious obstacle to rousing public awareness. (*See chart, p. 1004.*)

STDs have been around for centuries but were once fewer and curable. Syphilis and gonorrhea, two of the oldest, are deadly bacterial diseases that were almost eliminated after the discovery of antibiotics. But both have recently made a comeback, most notably in the gay community. With the rise of drug-resistant strains of gonorrhea, the number of effective antibiotics against that infection is dwindling, posing a potential public health crisis. Moreover, in recent decades, the variety of viral STDs — like herpes and HPV, which are treatable but not curable — has multiplied.

If left untreated, STDs can produce tragic results, especially for women — including infertility, tubal pregnancy and cervical cancer. In some cases, pregnant women can transmit the infection to their babies, which can be life threatening.

And most Americans underestimate their risk of contracting an STD. According to recent survey data, only 14 percent of men and 8 percent of women think they are at risk of being infected. [4]

Meanwhile, despite dire predictions in the 1980s of a growing AIDS epidemic, the number of new HIV infections diagnosed in the United States each year appears to have stabilized during the 1990s to about 40,000 new infections. [5] While still unacceptably high, it is a remarkable decrease from more than 150,000 cases a year in the mid-1980s. [6]

STD Rates in U.S. Are Higher

The reported rates of curable STDs in the United States are several times higher than in other developed countries, according to the most recent available data.

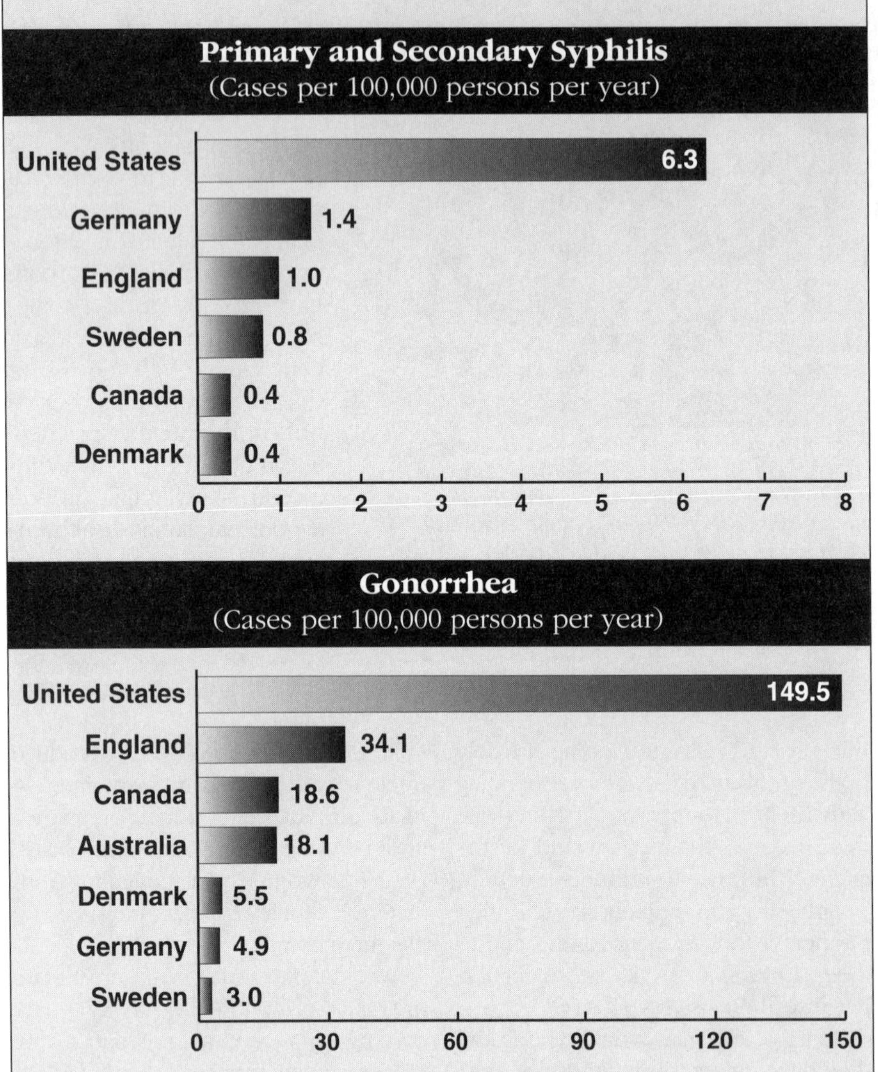

Source: "The Hidden Epidemic," Institute of Medicine, 1997

That success story has included dramatic decreases in HIV among gay men, injection drug users and newborn infants. Recent reports of rising syphilis and HIV rates in the male, gay community have some experts worried, however, about the possibility of a new resurgence of HIV, which is more easily transmitted among people with STDs.

AIDS also remains among the top three causes of death for African-American women between ages 35 and 44 and African-American men 25 to 54. During the televised vice presidential debate, a question from moderator Gwen Ifill, senior correspondent of PBS' "The NewsHour with Jim Lehrer," drew national attention to the fact that African-American women are diagnosed with AIDS at a rate 23 times higher than white women and die from AIDS at a much higher rate than their white counterparts.

African-Americans also have the poorest survival rate of all racial and ethnic groups, according to the Centers for Disease Control and Prevention (CDC). [7] One possible reason for the lower survival rate: Blacks have a much higher rate than whites of other STDs — 20 times more gonorrhea and five times more syphilis.

Women and adolescents are also disproportionately affected by STDs. Worldwide, approximately half the new HIV infections are occurring among women, and the rate of HIV infection is growing faster in women than in men. [8]

Because of the inconsistent reporting system for STDs in this country, it's unclear whether STD rates are on the rise among young Americans. Some experts worry that rising chlamydia rates among young people indicate a growing number may be turning to hormonal birth control, which doesn't protect against STDs, instead of condoms, which do. But those rates may be merely a result of increased testing, according to government officials.

On the whole, teens are engaging in less risky sexual behavior than in previous years, possibly in response to widespread public education campaigns about HIV. A recent study found that more than half of sexually active teenage girls now use condoms. [9] Indeed, among 15-to-24-year-olds, HIV is far less common than chlamydia, genital herpes, HPV or gonorrhea.

The stunning 33 percent decline in teen pregnancy rates between 1991 and 2000 appears to have been driven as much by teens' concerns about STDs as their fear of becoming pregnant, a recent CDC study suggests. According to the analysis, delaying the age of first intercourse and improved contraceptive use both contributed equally to the drop in teen pregnancy. The proportion of teenagers who ever had sexual intercourse by the time they finished high school dropped from 51 percent in 1991 to 43 percent in 2001. [10]

Abstinence advocates credit this trend at least in part to "virginity pledges," a church-led movement in which teens pledge publicly to abstain from sex until marriage. But a recent study found that teens who took the pledge had the same rate of STDs and pregnancy as those who didn't, probably because they were less likely to use contraception the first time they had sex and less likely to seek medical treatment. (*See sidebar, p. 1015.*) [11]

Sarah Brown, director of the National Campaign to Prevent Teen Pregnancy, suggests that abstinence has become increasingly cool because of the way it's portrayed in the media. On TV, "You see hot characters saying 'No.' So I'm not surprised to see a few more young people delaying sexual activity."

Sex education advocates forecast doom as programs preaching abstinence-until-marriage proliferate with the prod of greatly expanded federal funding under the Bush administration. Such programs are not permitted to instruct students about condoms or contraception except to discuss their failure rates.

"There's a real danger that many people are not getting the information they need to protect themselves against sexually transmitted diseases," says Cynthia Dailard, senior public policy associate at the Alan Guttmacher Institute, a private research organization in New York, who has surveyed sex education in the schools.

Abstinence advocates argue that condoms are not 100 percent effective against all STDs, as abstinence is, and that teaching kids about the benefits of condoms gives them a mixed moral message about premarital sex.

STDs Cost U.S. $15.5 Billion Annually

The direct cost of eight major STDs among Americans ages 15-24 was $6.5 billion in 2000. Overall, STDs cost the U.S. $15.5 billion. The CDC estimates that 19 million STD infections occur annually, almost half among youth ages 15-24.

STD	Total Cost
Sexually transmitted HIV	$3 billion
Human papillomavirus (HPV)	$2.9 billion
Genital Herpes	$292.7 million
Chlamydia	$248.4 million
Gonorrhea	$77 million
Trichomoniasis	$34.2 million
Hepatitis B	$5.8 million
Syphilis	$3.6 million
Total	$6.5 billion*

** Does not add up exactly due to rounding.*

Source: The Alan Guttmacher Institute

It's like an anti-drug program that says, "Here are the drugs just in case you decide to do it," argues Leslee Unruh, executive director of the Abstinence Clearinghouse, a private group in Sioux Falls, S.D., that promotes abstinence education. "We've been doing sex education in our schools for almost 30 years, and what's happened?" she asks, noting that the variety of sexually transmitted diseases has proliferated over that period.

The evaluations Brown's organization has sponsored have so far found no abstinence program to be effective in reducing risky behavior. But she is skeptical that teenage ignorance is a real danger in an age when teens spend more time in front of the computer and TV than in school. "A lot of us underestimate the number of sources young people draw on for information," she says.

As President Bush begins his second term with a strengthened mandate, here are some of the issues being debated in Congress, the schools and the media:

Should abstinence be the sole focus of sex education?

There's little dispute that avoiding sex is the only 100 percent certain way to avoid getting a sexually transmitted disease. But the question is whether educational programs designed to convey this message almost exclusively are successful in reducing both intercourse and risky sexual behavior that exposes teens to infection.

The most rigorous evaluations have not found a single abstinence-only program that is effective in reducing the kind of behavior that leads to STDs. In May 2001, a National Campaign to Prevent Teen Pregnancy report concluded that programs that emphasized abstinence as the best and safest approach but that also stressed using protection against pregnancy and STDs were the most effective in reducing teen pregnancy or reducing risky sexual behavior. The widely publicized report was backed up by a research task force that included outspoken advocates of abstinence-only education, such

Black Women Have Highest AIDS Rate

Experts are still trying to puzzle out why African-American straight women are contracting AIDS faster than any other demographic group. Black women are 23 times more likely to have AIDS than white women.

The Centers for Disease Control and Prevention (CDC) suggests that the higher rate of poverty among blacks might contribute to the higher infection rates, because poverty limits access to the quality health care that could help prevent progression of the disease.

In addition, black men in heterosexual relationships may be more likely to secretly engage in risky anal sex — known as sex "on the down low" — with other men than white men. A higher percentage of black males have used intravenous drugs and spent time in prison, where they are likely to be exposed to anal sex, increasing their risk of contracting HIV. [1]

Finally, black men and women have the highest sexually transmitted disease (STD) rates of any ethnic group in the nation. Compared to whites, blacks are 20 times more likely to have gonorrhea and five times more likely to have syphilis. [2] Open sores caused by STDs like herpes can serve as an entry point for HIV, and the presence of certain STDs can increase the chances of contracting HIV by three- to fivefold, according to recent studies. Similarly a person infected with both HIV and another STD has a greater chance of spreading HIV to other sexual partners.

---

[1] See, Jon Cohen, "A Silent Epidemic," www.slate.com, Oct. 27, 2004.

[2] CDC, "STD Surveillance 2003," www.cdc.gov.

---

as Texas ob-gyn Joe S. McIlhaney, Jr., president of the Austin-based pro-abstinence Medical Institute for Sexual Health and a member of the Presidential Advisory Council on HIV/AIDS, as well as representatives from groups that favor contraceptive education, such as the Guttmacher Institute — the former research arm of Planned Parenthood. [12]

According to report author Douglas Kirby, senior research scientist at ETR Associates in Scotts Valley, Calif., so-called "abstinence-plus" programs were effective in producing four types of changes in behavior known to lower the risk of STDs:

- delaying first intercourse;
- reducing the number of sex partners;
- reducing the frequency of sex, or
- increasing condom use.

The most impressive results came from an after-school program that provides tutoring, counseling and medical services in addition to sexuality education. The program, run by the Children's Aid Society in New York City, delayed the date of first intercourse and reduced pregnancy rates among girls by 50 percent. Participants in the program were also more likely than a comparison group to be vaccinated for hepatitis B, which can be sexually transmitted. (*See sidebar, p. 1010.*)

But none of the abstinence-only programs Kirby studied produced those kinds of results. "I'm in the process of doing an international search and have not found any abstinence-only programs that delay the initiation of sex," Kirby says of studies of sex-education curricula. "That is not to say they do not work; it's mostly due to the fact that there are very few studies that meet reasonable criteria. So the jury is still out."

Advocates of abstinence education reject the conclusion that abstinence-only programs are ineffective. But they do acknowledge that so far there have been only a handful of studies that meet the most rigorous research standard: assigning students randomly to a group that receives the program and a control group that does not.

According to Robert Rector, senior research fellow at the conservative Heritage Foundation in Washington, D.C., a number of programs show results that are not statistically significant "but close." Rector, who has conducted his own survey of sex-education studies, says, "Certainly by the time we get as many studies as we have on the other side, abstinence is going to look pretty good."

Abstinence advocates also argue that abstinence-plus curricula contain very little emphasis on abstinence, "other than a random sentence or two which says, 'The safest thing you can do is abstain; now let's talk about where to get your condoms,' " according to Rector. A Heritage Foundation analysis of nine programs described by Kirby as abstinence-plus concluded that only 4.7 percent of the curricula's content discusses abstinence compared to 71 percent in an "authentic" abstinence program. [13]

"There's no moral message that says, 'We really want you to abstain' even through high school — or even until marriage," Rector maintains. "They have a lot of content that's nearly pornographic; it's just completely outrageous and unacceptable to most parents."

If traditional sex education is so successful, asks Unruh of the Abstinence Clearinghouse, why is there such a high rate of STDs among teens?

"We continue to promote sex and sex education in the schools and make the kids feel like there's something wrong with them if they're not having sex; that's why," she says, answering her own question.

"There's no such thing as responsible sex outside of marriage," she stresses, echoing the prime warning

Blacks Have Highest Gonorrhea Rate

Gonorrhea rates among African-Americans are 20 times higher than rates among whites and 9 times higher than rates for Hispanics. The higher rates are most likely due to differences in access to prevention and treatment services. A bacterial infection curable with antibiotics, gonorrhea most easily infects adolescent girls because of changes in the cervix due to puberty. Public health officials warn of growing problems with drug-resistant gonorrhea.

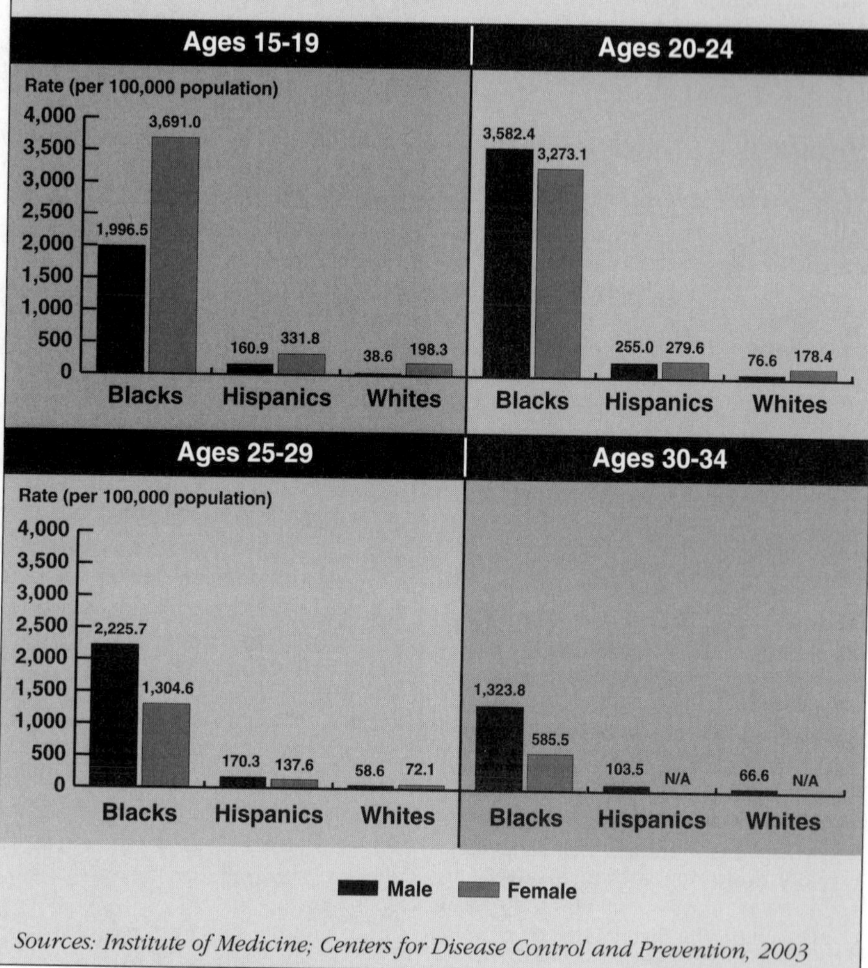

Sources: Institute of Medicine; Centers for Disease Control and Prevention, 2003

of abstinence educators. "If you are a person having sex outside marriage, a condom may break or may come off; you may be allergic to latex. HPV [human papillomavirus] is caused by skin-to-skin contact; a condom will not protect against that."

Unruh's statement that condoms won't protect against HPV is only partially correct. According to the American Social Health Association (ASHA), "Using condoms consistently and correctly can reduce the risk of getting HPV-related diseases such as genital warts and cervical cell abnormalities. However condoms do not protect against all genital areas and therefore, cannot completely prevent the spread of HPV." [14]

Statements like Unruh's about HPV are actually dangerous, because they leave out or distort important information teens need to protect themselves, public health experts say. In a recent review of abstinence-until-marriage programs around the country, the Sexual Information and Education Council of the United States (SIECUS), a private group in New York that advocates contraceptive instruction in the schools, charged that the programs are "based on religious beliefs, rely on fear and shame, omit important information, include inaccurate information and present stereotypes and biases as fact." [15]

As an example, SIECUS cites this statement from the abstinence-only FACTS * curricula, which is taught in Arizona, Nebraska, Oregon and Utah: "You know people talk about you behind your back because you have had sex with so many people. . . . Finally you get sick of it and commit suicide." [16]

Concerns have heightened with the expansion of federally funded programs that bar any mention of contraception except to discuss failure rates. "Our tradition of commitment to truth-telling makes those programs immoral," says the Rev. Debra Haffner, a Unitarian-Universalist minister and director of the Religious Institute, which represents 2,300 religious leaders from more than 40 denominations in the United States that support sexuality education. [17]

Some experts are disturbed by the psychological effects such programs could have on teens. "What does it mean to sit in a classroom and be told to be abstinent after you've already had sex? How does that help you?" asks Deborah L. Tolman, professor of Human Sexuality Studies at San Francisco State University and author of the 2002 book *Dilemmas of Desire: Teenage Girls Talk about Sexuality.*

"I have concerns about a lot of the abstinence programs, because the ultimate result is going to be a generation that's terrified of sexuality, unable

* Family Accountability Communicationg Teen Sexuality.

Common STDs and Their Outcomes

STD	Symptoms	Curable	Long-Term Outcomes
Chlamydia	Women usually have no symptoms; men may have a penile discharge.	Yes.	In women, may cause pelvic inflammatory disease (PID), which can lead to infertility, tubal pregnancy and chronic pain. In men, may cause scrotal infection. In infants, may cause eye and lung infections.
Genital herpes	May cause no symptoms, or itching, irritation or painful blisters. The disease is chronic, so symptoms can recur with subsequent outbreaks.	No. Medicines can help manage outbreaks.	Most cases are mild. If a woman acquires herpes during pregnancy, the virus can be life-threatening for the infant.
Gonorrhea	Women usually have no symptoms; men may have a penile discharge.	Yes. But new strains are becoming antibiotic-resistant	In women, may cause PID, which can lead to infertility, tubal pregnancy and chronic pain. In men, may cause scrotal infection.
Hepatitis B	May cause no symptoms, or "yellow jaundice" or abdominal problems.	No. Can be prevented with a vaccine.	May lead to liver cancer and sometimes death.
HIV/AIDS	HIV may cause no symptoms but may progress to AIDS. In AIDS, the body's immune system is compromised, so it cannot fight off many infections and cancers.	No. Medicines may extend life.	Opportunistic infections and cancers may lead to death. Pregnant women may transmit HIV to the fetus or infant.
Human papillomavirus (HPV)	Untreated, some HPV types may lead to cervical abnormalities or genital warts.	No, but the immune system may suppress or eliminate the virus.	Untreated, some HPV types may lead to cervical cancer or genital warts. Pap testing can usually detect cervical disease in time to prevent cancer. Genital warts can be treated.
Syphilis	Painless sores and rashes that go away without treatment.	Yes.	Untreated, may cause serious neurological, cardiac and other diseases, or death. Increases risk of contracting or transmitting HIV. In pregnancy, can lead to severe abnormalities or death of infant.
Trichomoniasis	In women, may cause heavy discharge and genital irritation. Men may have no symptoms.	Yes.	Could have no long-term consequences; may cause adverse pregnancy outcomes.

Source: J. R. Cates, et al., *"Our Voices, Our Lives, Our Futures: Youth and Sexually Transmitted Diseases," School of Journalism and Mass Communication, University of North Carolina at Chapel Hill, 2004*

to embrace their sexuality. At what point does it become a good thing, and how do you make yourself and your body go from bad to good?" asks Tolman, observing that many people don't get married until their mid- to late-20s, and 90 percent will have had intercourse by age 20.

Abstinence advocates counter that their message does not prevent teenagers from getting information about contraception and protection about STDs in other ways. "Most kids get several hits of sex education" in health and science classes, maintains Rector, including information about contraception. But he says "on the three days that they're taught about abstinence, do you also want them to be taught about contraception? An abstinence provider would say that's the worst thing you could do — to send a very strong mixed message at that point."

Counters Tolman: "If you take abstinence-only money, you can't talk about contraception anywhere in the school." Of Rector's assertion that kids will get sex education in other classes, she says, "It's an acknowledgement of the profound need for the information and the sense of responsibility ultimately for public education to provide the information."

But the Campaign to Prevent Teen Pregnancy's Brown cautions against dismissing abstinence-only sex education. "The Bush administration has tapped into a widely shared value: Most people would prefer teenagers not to have sex in middle school or high school." She adds, "The idea that nobody can get teens to delay first intercourse with a strong abstinence-only program doesn't strike me as reasonable."

An answer should be forthcoming in the next three to four years, after ongoing evaluations of abstinence-only programs funded by the federal government are completed.

Is the United States doing enough to prevent STDs?

The values war over abstinence also has invaded the nation's public health campaign to prevent STDs. For years, a central message of government health campaigns has been that condoms are a crucial weapon in the war against HIV and other STDs. But in the last two years, social conservatives have claimed that condoms are not very effective against sexually transmitted diseases and have pressed federal agencies to adopt this viewpoint, sometimes successfully.

For example, until recently a CDC Web page said that education about condom use did not lead young people to earlier or increased sexual activity, a statement that conflicted with the views of abstinence-only advocates. In October 2002, however, the CDC dropped that information, which was based on several studies, from a revised version of its online fact sheet about condoms. It also dropped instructions on condom use and specific information on the effectiveness of different types of condoms. [18]

The revised fact sheet posted on the Web site emphasizes condom failure rates and the effectiveness of abstinence, beginning in boldface: "The surest way to avoid transmission of sexually transmitted diseases is to abstain from sexual intercourse or to be in a long-term mutually monogamous relationship with a partner who has been tested and you know is uninfected. . . . [C]ondom use cannot guarantee absolute protection against any STD." [19]

The Democratic staff of the House Government Reform Committee has charged these revisions were made under pressure from conservative Republicans. "Under the Bush administration, scientific evidence on the effectiveness of condoms has been suppressed or distorted" in support of the claim that condoms are not very effective in preventing sexually transmitted diseases, charges the staff Web site sponsored by Rep. Henry A. Waxman, ranking California Democrat on the committee. [20]

Conservatives like Rep. Mark Souder, R-Ind., have focused their criticism on HPV, a common STD that can lead to cervical cancer in a small percentage of women. Because HPV is transmitted by skin-to-skin contact and because condoms do not cover all the areas of skin where HPV manifests itself — in genital warts, for example — they may not provide the same protection as they do against STDs transmitted by bodily fluids, according to the CDC. [21]

A law authored by former Rep. Tom Coburn, R-Okla., and signed by President Bill Clinton days before leaving office in 2001 requires the CDC and the Food and Drug Administration (FDA) to inform the public about the "effectiveness of condoms to protect against HPV" and "to determine if condom labels are medically accurate."

"Nearly 5,000 women die every year in the U.S. as a result of HPV-related cancers, and millions more are treated for other health conditions related to HPV infection," Souder says. "This is a serious health issue, and Congress passed and President Clinton signed the HPV prevention law four years ago specifically because FDA and CDC had failed to properly address it. These agencies continue to thumb their nose at Congress and undermine their own scientific integrity and — most importantly — the health of the public with their continued cover-up of the HPV epidemic."

In March, Souder called hearings to confront the CDC and FDA with his contention that the agencies had not complied with the law. A fact sheet from his office claims that government Web sites "continue to omit" medically accurate information, including "the lack of effectiveness of condoms in preventing infection." He also charges that the FDA has yet to rewrite condom labels to ensure that they "reflect the effectiveness or lack of effectiveness in preventing HPV and other STDs." [22]

But as news reports noted at the time of the hearings, this debate is as much about ideology — premarital abstinence vs. condom use — as it is about preventing disease. [23]

"People like Rep. Souder are taking this small piece of the puzzle and running with it, saying condoms don't work . . . instead of saying condoms are really good at preventing HIV and other diseases," said Julie Davids, executive director of CHAMP, a New York-based HIV/AIDS organization that cosponsored a March rally protesting the Souder hearings. [24]

As evidence of condoms' alleged ineffectiveness, for example, the Abstinence Clearinghouse in its promotional materials prominently cites a 2001 study by the National Institutes of Health, which concluded, "There is no scientific evidence that condoms prevent the transmission of most sexually transmitted disease, including chlamydia, syphilis, chancroid, trichomoniasis, genital herpes and HPV." [25]

Syphilis Poses New Threat

A recent rise in syphilis cases among gay men is raising concern that the trend may signal a return to promiscuous, unprotected sex and possibly to a new surge in sexually transmitted diseases (STDs) reaching beyond the gay community.

Although the number of new syphilis cases remains relatively low — about 7,000 new cases a year — recent studies suggest that syphilis is on the rise for the third consecutive year. And more than 60 percent of syphilis cases in 2003 occurred among men who have sex with men, researchers at the Centers for Disease Control and Prevention (CDC) estimate. [1]

"There's a lot of concern this may be a warning signal that risky behavior in subsets of gay men may be increasing, potentially leading to increasing rates of HIV transmission," says John Douglas, director of the CDC's Division of STD Prevention.

Untreated syphilis can cause serious neurological, cardiac and other diseases. It also increases the risk of getting or transmitting HIV. In pregnancy, syphilis can lead to severe infant abnormalities or even death.

Use of the illegal recreational drug crystal methamphetamine and the prescription impotence drug Viagra appears to be fueling increases not only in syphilis but also in HIV and other STDs among gay men, according to CDC researchers. When crystal meth users get high from the drug, they are twice as likely as non-users to engage in anal intercourse without a condom. Condoms are protective against both HIV and syphilis. [2]

Now that anti-retroviral therapy has made living with HIV possible, some experts speculate that complacency about HIV may be behind the increases in unsafe sex.

"People without HIV are saying, 'I see these people [treated with anti-retroviral therapy] walking around, climbing mountains and looking great; maybe I don't need to be so worried anymore," Douglas suggests.

The annual number of new HIV infections in the United States appears to have stabilized during the 1990s to about 40,000 new infections each year, a significant decrease from more than 150,000 cases a year in the mid-1980s. Still, King K. Holmes, director of the Center for AIDS and STD at the University of Washington, Seattle, notes that "40,000 cases a year of a fatal disease is disastrous."

---

[1] CDC press release from 2004 National STD Prevention Conference, "New U.S. Data Show Fewer Americans Have Herpes but Rates of Other Sexually Transmitted Diseases High," March 8, 2004.

[2] "Viagra, Methamphetamine, Internet Use Linked to Increase in Number of Syphilis, HIV Cases Among MSM, Studies Say," *Kaiser Daily HIV/AIDS Report*, March 11, 2004. at www.kff.org.

What it doesn't say is that the study found strong evidence for condoms' effectiveness against HIV and gonorrhea. And a January 2004 CDC report notes that there is evidence that condom use may actually reduce the risk of cervical cancer, public health advocates note. [26]

"If we want to beat cervical cancer, we must focus on making sure all women have access to cervical cancer screening and follow-up care instead of turning cervical cancer into an excuse to disparage condoms," said James R. Allen, president and CEO of ASHA.

"Scaring sexually active individuals away from using condoms will not reduce the prevalence of HPV," says Theresa Raphael, executive director of the National Coalition of STD Directors. "Instead, it will put millions of Americans at risk of contracting a range of preventable STDs."

As for the other diseases, the study was inconclusive. "Scientifically, this is an enormously difficult thing to study; people aren't guinea pigs; you can't put people in cages and expose them to STDs with and without condom use," explains John Douglas, director of the CDC's Division of STD Prevention. He notes that more recent studies have found condoms reduce the risk of herpes and chlamydia. While "condoms are not perfect, "he says," it's quite clear that the absence of their use is worse than using them imperfectly."

When asked about the CDC's new abstinence emphasis and removal of condom information from in its Web site, Douglas sounds like a government official caught between a rock and a hard place. "I feel the fact sheet we have up there is an accurate fact sheet; it does take more pains to point out the imperfections of condoms than previous fact sheets." As for the impact of the controversy over condoms' effectiveness, he says, "I don't have any data that condom use has diminished because of that, but we have lots of concerns that it could be."

Ideally, the best way to prevent sexually transmitted diseases would be to develop vaccines. The only STD for which a vaccine is currently available is hepatitis B. The recent flu vaccine crisis has demonstrated that the nation can no longer rely on pharmaceutical companies to develop vaccines, some researchers argue, because the profit margins just aren't big enough. Vaccines against HPV and herpes are currently in the final phase of clinical trials.

"Pharmaceutical companies don't want to invest in something that would be high-risk for liability and low-risk for profitability," says Willard "Ward" Cates Jr., president and CEO of the Institute for Family Health, Family Health International in Research Triangle Park, N.C., which has conducted research to bring new contraceptive products to market. He says his organization has not been able to find a pharmaceutical company to underwrite similar research efforts in the area of HIV and genital herpes vaccines.

Given the industry's lack of interest, the federal government should step up to the plate and fund special research institutes around the country to develop vaccines against STDs, argues Lawrence Corey, professor of medicine at the University of Washington in Seattle and principal investigator in HIV vaccine trials funded by the National Institutes of Health (NIH).

Getty Images/Ian Waldie

A member of the U.S. teen-celibacy group Silver Ring Thing waits for customers at its merchandise table at a church in Claygate, England, during the group's tour of the United Kingdom. Abstinence advocates credit stunning declines in teen pregnancy rates in recent years in part to "virginity pledges" until marriage.

"There's no culture that has controlled an STD without a vaccine," contends Corey. In the case of genital herpes, for example, 22 percent of the population has it, according to one recent study Corey cites, but 95 percent of those who have it don't know it. Consequently, "You can't screen and test everybody," Corey says. But work on developing a herpes vaccine has been extremely slow. The third pharmaceutical company to work with Corey's group on a herpes vaccine recently dropped out, he says, "because the risk is high and the amount of capital they can put into it is low."

The NIH is currently sponsoring a large clinical trial of a herpes vaccine that appears to work in women, but not men. So even if this trial proves successful after three or four years, it's not the ultimate solution, Corey observes.

Of course, the kind of commitment that Corey is talking about would take a lot more federal funding. In the world of medical researchers, "You get a grant for $350,000 it's a big grant; $1 million is a huge grant," says Corey. By contrast, he notes, "If a company is doing vaccine development, it's 5, 8, 10 million dollars a year." Today's limited government funding means that vaccine development will be slower than if the government made a big commitment, he argues. Worldwide, barely 20 researchers are working on a herpes vaccine, Corey estimates. "What kind of a commitment is that?" he asks.

HIV vaccine research has more generous government funding and more interest from pharmaceutical companies than other STDs partly because HIV is fatal, while most other STDs are not. Corey's group is starting a trial this month in cooperation with drug maker Merck, which will be the first to test the efficacy of a vaccine for HIV based on T-cell responses, currently seen as a highly promising approach. But the HIV vaccine search has run into failure before and remains a difficult scientific problem. As a result most medical researchers, who survive by applying for grants based on past successes, are reluctant to devote themselves to it full time, he says.

"If you put people full time in a risky venture, you've got to give them some job security. You can't continue to have negative data; no one will keep on funding you," Corey says. "So you've got to be like a broker; you diversify your portfolio so you can have a success. But that's not the best way to make a vaccine. So we have a lot of people spending 25 percent of their time on it; it would move a lot quicker if we had people spending 100 percent of their time on it."

Researchers like Cates say STDs have been the poor stepchild of HIV ever since HIV was recognized as the most serious global disease. "You have HIV getting billions of dollars and STDs tens of millions of dollars," he estimates, even though herpes causes premature death in infants, and untreated HPV can lead to cervical cancer in women. Moreover, having an STD can increase the risk of HIV transmission. "Is it fatal? No. Is it serious? Absolutely," he says.

When it comes to prevention, years of inadequate flat funding at both federal and state levels (*see p. 1014*) have forced numerous cutbacks in the public health system's ability to prevent STDs at clinics throughout the country, says Gail Bolan chair of the national Coalition of STD Directors and chief of the STD Control Branch at the California Department of Health Services.

In California, the number of publicly funded clinics that specialize in STDs has dwindled, and the health department has difficulty getting the word out to doctors about growing problems with drug-resistant gonorrhea, according to Bolan. With bioterrorism at the top of the agenda, public health staff is increasingly diverted from routine public health problems like STDs, federal and state officials say.

Regarding inadequately funded STD prevention, the CDC's Douglas says, "We have a lot of social and health issues in this country and lots of choices to make, and those choices are getting tougher all the time. It's rare for any program to get to all the funding it needs to address the problem. STDs are not an exception. We're using the resources we have to reach those people at the greatest risk."

But he adds, "In this country we put greater priorities on the things we see than the things we don't see. The public sees curative medicine in all of its glorious forms in a much clearer light than they do the background work of public health; clean water is not as sexy as organ transplants."

Some experts say the government should urge mass screening for STDs, especially when a patient has no symptoms. In the case of chlamydia, the CDC and other prominent medical organizations are now recommending that sexually active women up to age 25 be screened for chlamydia. But less than half of the nation's medical providers follow those guidelines. Experts say doctors feel uncomfortable suggesting a patient is sexually active or even promiscuous.

"I've had providers say, 'I don't have those kinds of patients in my practice,' " recalls Bolan.

Similarly, controversy continues about whether all adults should be tested routinely for herpes. "People concerned about the spread of herpes have been saying we have to do a better job of identifying people affected," says Charles Ebel, senior director of program development at ASHA.

"We have some blood tests that work well to identify HSV-2 [the most common type of genital herpes] with people who have ambiguous symptoms or are in situations suggestive of being at risk — because they have a past or present partner with herpes — but don't have symptoms," Ebel notes. "But a lot of people in clinical care don't want to have to identify someone and tell them they have an STD when the person ostensibly doesn't have any problem, because there's a social stigma associated with STDs and a certain psychological and social distress burden experienced by those diagnosed."

Proponents of mass screening point out that herpes affects one in five American adults, and open herpes sores can increase the risk of getting HIV. "It's not the most severe disease, but in the long term it could be important in controlling HIV rates and in minimizing neonatal infection because sometimes it is transmitted from mother to baby," Ebel says.

Similar issues have been raised when it comes to routinely running a DNA test that is now available to test for HPV, a mostly benign infection that in a small percentage of women can lead to cervical cancer later on. Running the test requires doctors to explain that HPV is sexually transmitted.

"If they have to go there with patients, they have to get into the whole sexual-history piece, which is complicated, time-consuming, sometimes embarrassing and relates back to the social stigma," Ebel says. "There's controversy about how much these DNA tests should be used and how much clinicians should be expected to bite off counseling about this."

"It's a total waste of money to get tested for strains of HPV," Cates argues, because HPV is so widespread. In the majority of cases, HPV goes away on its own without the patient even being aware she had it. "In this country, using the Pap smear as the main cancer control approach is the most cost-efficient, time-efficient way for clients to proceed."

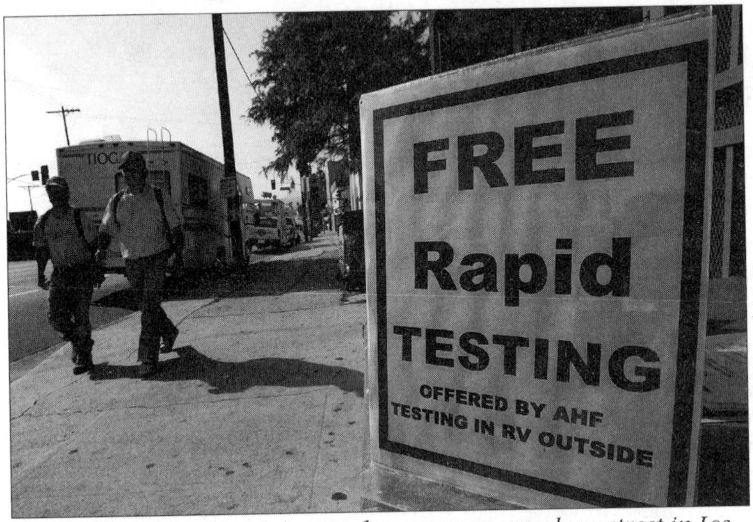

Getty Images/David McNew

A mobile AIDS testing lab waits for customers on a busy street in Los Angeles last spring. The number of new HIV infections in the United States appears to have stabilized during the 1990s to about 40,000 new infections each year, down from more than 150,000 cases a year in the mid-1980s.

Will President Bush's abstinence-only policy hurt the global effort to prevent AIDS?

President Bush's five-year, $15 billion plan to tackle AIDS overseas requires that one-third of the prevention funds be spent on encouraging abstinence. The Global AIDS bill, the legal mandate for the strategy, would provide a minimum of $133 million annually to abstinence-until-marriage programs in 15 countries. The administration points to Uganda's stunning success in reducing HIV as the justification, saying it wishes to replicate its approach.

Continued on p. 1010

Chronology

1940s-1950s

Penicillin contributes to aggressive public health treatment of venereal disease.

1941
Penicillin becomes the first modern antibiotic found effective against bacterial infections.

1946
Early-stage syphilis peaks in U.S. at 94,957 cases

1956
Drop to 6,392 cases of syphilis spurs reduction in funding for public health treatment.

1960s-1970s

Complacency about venereal disease leads to resurgence; birth control pill, sexual revolution and gay liberation movement increase promiscuous sexual behavior.

1961
Early-stage syphilis cases nearly triple from low point in mid-1950s.

1962
Food and Drug Administration (FDA) approves birth control pill.

1969
Riot at gay Stonewall Bar in New York City's Greenwich Village marks beginning of gay rights movement.

1980s

AIDS (Acquired Immune Deficiency Syndrome) discovered in gay men; spreads to intravenous (IV) drug users; chlamydia rises; gonorrhea rates decline; U.S. government begins campaign against AIDS; syphilis rates climb in minorities, fueled by crack cocaine epidemic.

1981
Centers for Disease Control (CDC) reports rare form of pneumonia in five gay men, later determined to be AIDS; program to promote teen chastity begun under Adolescent and Family Life Act.

1982
AIDS officially recognized by CDC.

1983
CDC adds female sex partners of men with AIDS as risk group.

1984
HIV (Human Immune Deficiency Virus) isolated as cause of AIDS.

1987
AZT, the first anti-retroviral drug against AIDS, comes on the market.

1990s

AIDS deaths peak, then fall with new therapy; sexual behavior in U.S. becomes less risky following public health campaigns; federal government expands sexual-abstinence programs.

1992
AIDS becomes No.1 cause of death in U.S. for men ages 25-44.

1995
FDA approves first protease inhibitor, ushering in new era of highly effective anti-retroviral AIDS therapy.

1996
Welfare reform act signed into law, funding states for new abstinence-until-marriage initiative; number of new AIDS cases declines for first time, but AIDS remains leading cause of death for African-Americans ages 25-44.

1997
AIDS deaths decline by more than 40 percent over previous year due to anti-retroviral therapy.

1998
First large-scale human trials for HIV vaccine begin.

2000s

AIDS begins infecting large numbers of women; President Bush expands funding for abstinence, worldwide AIDS program; scientists make breakthroughs in developing HPV (human papillomavirus) vaccine.

October 2001
Bush administration creates third grant program for abstinence education.

2002
U.N. reports women comprise half of all adults with HIV/AIDS.

Jan. 28, 2003
Bush announces $15 billion plan for AIDS relief overseas during his State of the Union address.

2004
Bush global AIDS program begins first round of funding. . . . In October GlaxoSmithKline announces it will bring HPV vaccine to market in 2006 . . . . On Nov. 20, Congress passes omnibus spending bill increasing abstinence funding for fourth consecutive year. . . . On Nov. 23, U.N. reports a record 39.4 million people are living with AIDS worldwide and that the number of women with HIV/AIDS is increasing throughout world.

This Sex-Education Program Works

Joel, a high school senior with a mop of curly black hair, wears hip-hop-style jeans favored by many teenagers in Washington Heights, a low-income New York City neighborhood heavily populated with Dominican immigrants.

But unlike many of his peers, he plans to apply for college. He also has a different attitude about sex than most of his buddies. "I'd like to try it, but if I get a girl pregnant, I don't know what I would do. I'm putting it on pause," Joel says, adding that he plans to wait to have sex until he is 18 or 19 — "when I'm more mature." (Joel is a pseudonym.)

Since the sixth grade, Joel has participated every day after school in a sexuality-education program run by the Children's Aid Society, a curriculum used at several schools around the country. It is the nation's most successful program for reducing teen sex and pregnancy, according to a three-year study of 600 children — half in the program and half randomly assigned to a control group. Girls in the program had one-third of the pregnancies and half as many births as the comparison group. Teens in the program, who are mainly minority and low-income, also waited until they were older to have sex for the first time and used contraceptives more conscientiously when they did have sex. [1]

"Paradoxically, we are the only proven program that has abstinence-only results but we can get no money from the federal government," observes the program's founder, Michael A. Carrera, director of the National Adolescent Sexuality Training Center at Children's Aid. The program is ineligible for federal funding because it instructs teens in the importance of condoms and birth control and also provides contraceptives as part of its comprehensive package of medical and dental services.

The program has not had a single case of HIV in its 20 years, according to Carrera. The rate of other STDs has not been evaluated, but teens in the program were more likely to have received a hepatitis B vaccine. Boys also were more likely to make regular medical visits and discuss sexual health with a doctor, according to Jackie Williams Kaye, who co-directed the evaluation for Philliber Research Associates in New York.

Carrera said he developed his comprehensive approach because, after decades as a traditional sex-education teacher, he felt that his message wasn't really sticking with kids. "What I learned," Carrera says, "was that I was separating it from all the other things that make a kid whole" — most significantly, their hopes for the future.

Joel, for example, is getting preparation for the future that includes one-on-one tutoring to prepare him for the mandatory state graduation test; visits to colleges; and meetings with a college adviser — all services supplied by the program.

"When young people feel there's hope in the future and possibilities, then they themselves will take many of the steps to avoid the risks," Carrera maintains. One indication may be that 61 percent of the program's high school graduates enrolled in college, compared to 39 percent of their peers from similar backgrounds.

But not everyone is convinced the program is a success. "Carrera believes kids will be sexually active and that it's pointless to spend much effort trying to teach them to delay," says Robert Rector, senior research fellow at the conservative Heritage Foundation, who favors preaching abstinence.

Continued from p. 1008

In the most dramatic decline seen in any country, Uganda's HIV prevalence decreased from a peak of 15 percent of the population in 1991 to 5 percent in 2001. Most experts attribute that drop to the high-visibility campaign waged personally by President Yoweri K. Museveni known as ABC — in which A stands for abstinence, B stands for Be faithful and C stands for condoms. [27]

William Shepherd Smith, president of the Institute for Youth Development, a pro-abstinence group in Sterling, Va., says he has traveled to African countries like Mozambique, where HIV rates have been as high as 40 percent among young people. "The message we saw was condoms, condoms and more condoms," an approach he says was failing. By contrast, he says, the answer in Uganda was to get young people to wait till marriage to have sex. "It wasn't ABC take your pick; it was A to young people, B to couples and C 'If you don't have self control, yes use a condom,' " with condoms particularly targeted to promiscuous groups like prostitutes and truck drivers.

Indeed, a video about Uganda made by Sterling's group emphasizes the role of abstinence and plays down the role of condoms, quoting Harvard medical anthropologist Edward Green saying, "Rates were coming down in 1993, and very few people were using condoms." Smith says in the video, "Much of the message to young people is about character development, about making the right choices in life." [28]

The abstinence emphasis of Bush's program, which also plans to rely heavily on faith-based groups, smacks of religion to some critics, who say the administration is neglecting the important role of condoms. Deborah Arrindell, senior director of health policy at ASHA, calls the policy "exporting ideology."

William Smith, director of public policy at SIECUS, charges, "These funds are going to missionary groups that haven't done public health in these countries; so again, the Bush administration is building up an entire new industry to promote an ideology of marriage promotion just like they've done here."

The Children's Aid Society's Millennium after-school sexuality program in New York City teaches about postponing sex and also using contraceptives.

Carrera also prefers that kids delay sex, but adds, "Look, if our own children decided, against whatever we said, that they were going to do something their own way, we would make sure they wouldn't get hurt or hurt somebody else," by providing contraceptives.

However, the dramatic drops in unintended pregnancies were not replicated among the boys, leading Kaye to speculate that perhaps the boys were having sex with girls outside the program who were not getting its message.

Rector suggests the program's success with girls is "because they shoot the girls up with Depo-Provera," a contraceptive hormone. Kaye says fewer than a quarter of the girls in the program use the hormone, a rate that is admittedly higher than the Depo-Provera usage rate among their peers who are not in the program. Eighty-five percent of the teens in both groups used condoms.

Moreover, older teens who already have had sex are harder to engage, and boys who had already had sex were the least conscientious attendees and showed the least success, according to the evaluation. In response to that finding, the program has shifted its focus to including sixth- and seventh-graders, who are on the verge of puberty.

Can Carrera's success be replicated elsewhere? A similar program in Florida failed to achieve the same success, according to evaluator Douglas Kirby, senior research scientist at ETR Associates in Scotts Valley, Calif. But Carrera did not personally provide the training, Kirby says, adding, "Michael Carrera is very charismatic, and he certainly enters into the equation."

Carrera agrees, to some extent. The Florida program was not an exact replica of his approach, he says. He says that only 21 of the 50 programs in 20 states that claim to use his curriculum are exact replications. The others have not been able to raise enough money — $4,000 per child annually — to include all the services. But at $17 a day, Kaye says, it's a bargain for a program proven to work, compared to other highly regarded after-school programs.

[1] Children's Aid Society, "2001 Data," fact sheet on findings from evaluation by Philliber Research Associates. See Douglas Kirby, "Emerging Answers," May 2001, National Campaign to Prevent Teen Pregnancy, at www.teen-pregnancy.org.

Several groups that work with AIDS in the developing world say the concept of preaching abstinence to unmarried, sexually active teens is a supremely American idea. "It's not valid for millions of adolescents in the developing world, because they're married. In the developing world, teen pregnancy is a concept that occurs within marriage," says Geeta Rao Gupta, president of the International Center for Research on Women (ICRW) in Washington, D.C., a private research organization. [29] Married women are the fastest-growing group of people being infected with HIV in India, which will soon outpace South Africa as the country with the world's highest infection rate. [30] In fact, marriage does not appear to be a protective factor in these countries as abstinence advocates often assume.

"Young married girls are more likely to be HIV-positive than their unmarried peers because they have sex more often, use condoms less often, are unable to refuse sex and have partners who are more likely to be HIV-positive," according to a report by ICRW citing research in Kenya and Zambia. [31] Young women are expected to prove their fertility quickly once married and rarely have the social status to insist that their husbands abstain or put on a condom, Gupta points out.

Experts at the Alan Guttmacher Institute argue that all three components of ABC were important in reducing Uganda's HIV rates. The abstinence message appears to have had a strong impact on young people. The median age at which young women began having sex rose from 15.9 in 1988 to 16.3 in 1995.

But experts now think a reduction in partners may be the most important behavior change. The "Be Faithful" message produced increasing levels of monogamy among sexually active men and women of all ages; the unmarried particularly were less likely to have more than one sexual partner in 1995 than in 1989. Condom use rose steeply among unmarried sexually active men — from 2 percent in 1989 to 22 percent in 1995. [32]

In Zambia, where HIV rates also appear to be declining among urban youth,

The Guttmacher Institute gives much of the credit to a program that promotes both abstinence and condom use, noting that young people exposed to a U.S. Agency for International Development-funded media campaign are 67 percent more likely to have used a condom than those not exposed.

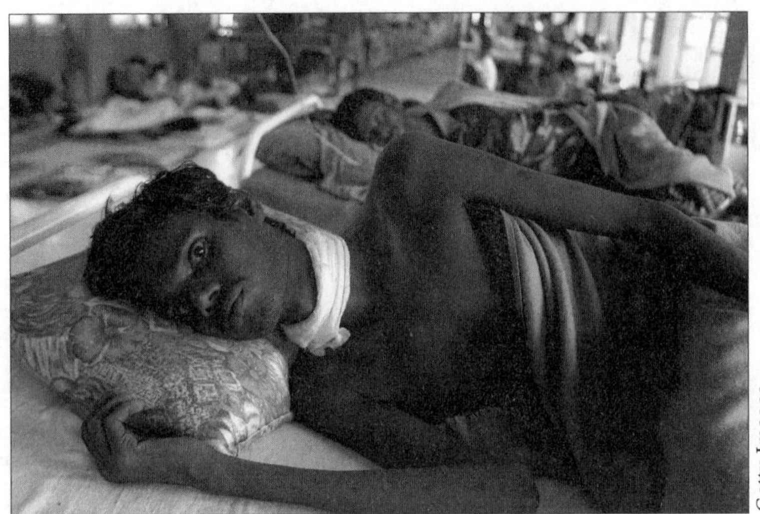

Men and women with HIV or AIDS crowd a hospital ward in India's Tamil Nadu state. President Bush's $15 billion plan to tackle AIDS overseas requires that one-third of the prevention funds be spent on encouraging abstinence. But several groups that battle AIDS overseas say that preaching abstinence to unmarried, sexually active teens in the developing world is pointless since adolescents often marry and have children.

A field study published earlier this year charges that the administration's Global AIDS program puts excessive emphasis on abstinence and discriminates against any group that provides information on safe abortion. The United States "is prohibiting organizations from providing condoms or condom information," said Jodi Jacobson, executive director of the Center for Health and Gender Equity, an international reproductive health and rights organization based in Takoma Park, Md., which authored the study. [33]

The organization contends that the Bush strategy limits condom use to narrowly defined "high risk" groups, including prostitutes and substance abusers. By so stigmatizing condoms, the group argues, it contributes to the perception that risk is something that only occurs outside of marriage. For example, in a recent survey of 300 HIV-positive married women in Zimbabwe, the majority of the women knew about HIV but did not insist on condom use with their husbands or partners because they thought that condom use was only for those who visited prostitutes. [34] Faith-based groups that receive U.S. funds may exclude information about contraceptive methods, including condoms, if such information is inconsistent with their religious beliefs, the group said.

Government officials have stated that abstinence will be only one part of a broad-based strategy and have denied the claims that the program is discriminating against groups that provide abortion. Since only 20 percent of the entire program is slated for prevention, the one-third devoted to abstinence represents a very small fraction of the entire effort, they say.

"To say that condoms alone are going to solve this problem is crazy," Mark Dybul, the plan's deputy chief medical officer, said in response to the recent study from the Center for Health and Gender Equity. "You need the full ABC message, which was really initiated by President Museveni of Uganda." [35]

In an interview earlier this year, the Bush administration's point man, Ambassador Randall L. Tobias, U.S. Global AIDS Coordinator, answered criticisms that some groups couldn't get access to funding because they wanted to emphasize condoms as a prevention approach. "The U.S. doesn't discourage that; we're buying as many condoms now as has ever been the case," he said. "But . . . the evidence really shows that condoms have never been effective anywhere in the world in curtailing broad-based general epidemics in the broad population." [36]

He added, "Changing behavior is what is really making the difference in Uganda and other places, and that means getting people to do two things: To delay the age at which they become sexually active, and then reducing the number of partners they have when they are sexually active."

Smith, of the Institute for Youth Development, argues that it's highly unlikely that public health officials will be able to persuade a man to wear a condom if he's irresponsible enough to be promiscuous. "Irresponsible men like them less," he says. "The better message to these same men is if you want to live and have a lot of sex, 'Reduce partners.' " He adds that handing out condoms is "an absurd approach but the approach we've bought into because we don't want to give a moralistic message. We should have recognized that it was the right public health message — not a religious message — to reduce partners." ■

BACKGROUND

Early Anti-STD Efforts

Some sexually transmitted diseases, such as syphilis and gonorrhea, have been known for centuries while others, such as HIV, have only been identified in the past few decades. STDs are caused by more than 25 infectious organisms, and as more organisms are identified, the number of STDs continues to expand.

In the early part of the 20th century, syphilis was responsible for populating the mental hospitals with victims who suffered dementia and for the deaths of adults or babies (who caught it in utero).

The social hygiene movement of the early 1900s, which sought to unite moral cleanliness with health, tried to combat these deadly diseases by arguing that prostitution spread venereal disease, and by preaching the values of sexual abstinence and self-discipline. [37] In the 1930s many hospitals refused to admit patients with venereal disease because they considered the sufferers immoral, a lack of treatment that contributed to a growing epidemic. [38]

With the advent of penicillin in the 1940s, the control of the disease shifted from moralistic preaching to medical treatment. Syphilis can be cured by antibiotics in its early stages. If left untreated, late-stage syphilis can cause paralysis, blindness, dementia and death.

Beginning in the late 1940s and continuing through the early 1950s, aggressive national programs against syphilis succeeded in nearly eliminating early-stage syphilis in the United States. By the mid-1950s, the apparent success of the program led to sharp funding reductions for combating it. But within a few years of the funding reductions, the number of primary and secondary syphilis cases in the United States nearly tripled. [39]

"Historically, anytime we start to pat ourselves on the back and think control efforts have helped, the diseases come back," notes the university of Alabama's Hook. "In the U.S., we thought we eliminated syphilis three times, in 1997 most recently." But recent statistics indicate syphilis is on the rise again.

The sexual revolution that began in the 1960s with the birth control pill, gay liberation and the cocaine epidemic were all factors that contributed to an epidemic of STDs and the spread of HIV during the 1970s and '80s. In the United States and Britain, symptomatic genital herpes and genital warts increased up to 15-fold during the '70s and '80s. During the '70s, chlamydial infections became the most prevalent bacterial STD in the developed world. [40]

AIDS Leads to Restraint

AIDS first came to the attention of the health community in 1981, when CDC scientists reported a strange immune-system disorder in five homosexual men from Los Angeles. The following year, when new cases of the disease appeared in heterosexual women, drug users and Haitian immigrants, the CDC officially recognized it as a new disease and named it Acquired Immune Deficiency Syndrome (AIDS).

From the mid-1980s to the '90s, public health campaigns against HIV urged the use of condoms and the reduction of sexual partners. Sexual behavior over that period, especially among young people, became more moderate, with greater use of condoms and later initiation of sex. [41] The waning of the cocaine epidemic, which many believe helped fuel unprotected sex by loosening inhibitions, and improvements in diagnosing STDs also contributed to the decline of STDS and AIDS through this period.

For example, cases of gonorrhea, a bacterial infection curable with antibiotics, fell 59 percent between 1978 and 1994 through a combination of public health programs, safer sexual practices stemming from concerns about HIV and changes in contraceptive methods, according to the Institute of Medicine. [42] However, gonorrhea remained high among minorities and adolescents. [43]

In 1987, the first anti-AIDS drug, AZT, came on the market. The next big advance in AIDS treatment came in 1995 when drug companies released a new class of medicines known as protease inhibitors, ushering in the new era of highly effective anti-retroviral therapy. Researchers found that protease inhibitors were most effective when patients were given a cocktail of three or four types at a time. Since then, the FDA has approved other drugs to be given in combination. Although not a cure, anti-retroviral therapy has permitted many people with AIDS to live longer, high-quality lives.

In 1997, an expert committee organized by the Institute of Medicine issued a report warning that STDs were "hidden epidemics" that represented "a growing threat to the nation's health." The committee estimated the annual direct and indirect cost of STDs, including HIV, was $17 billion. The committee singled out the social stigma attached to STDs and the resulting secrecy surrounding the subject as one of the primary obstacles to curbing the epidemic — both historically and today. [44] It noted that this view was particularly evident early in the AIDS epidemic, when some considered the disease a symbol of deviant sexual behavior. [45]

King K. Holmes, director of the Center for AIDS and STDs at the University of Washington and a member of the IOM Committee, worries that the abstinence-only movement is a return to the moralistic approach of old. "What we need is less of these simplistic approaches — abstinence only or condom only," he says. "We need multi-component interventions like ABC together with biomedical interventions and services for kids with STDs."

Young People at Risk

The number of people infected with STDs in the United States is difficult to determine, and trends over time are even more difficult to discern. Only some STDS — chlamydia, gonorrhea, HIV and AIDS, hepatitis B and syphilis — are nationally "reportable," which means that state health authorities report the number of cases to the CDC. However, the reports are generally believed to be an undercount of the actual number of cases. [46] As a result of expanded screening programs and improved detection tests, there has been some improvement in tracking these diseases since 1996.

Bacterial STDs such as gonorrhea and chlamydia can be cured. Viral STDs — such as herpes, hepatitis B and HIV — can be effectively treated but at present there is no cure for them.

Sexually active youth have the highest STD rates of any age group in the country. By age 25, at least half of sexually active youth will have acquired an STD. Almost half of the approximately 18.9 million new cases of STDs occurring annually are among 15-to-24-year-olds. Three types of infection (HPV, chlamydia and trichomoniasis) account for 88 percent of all new cases in this age group. [47]

Females are particularly prone to STD infection because of the anatomy of the female reproductive tract. STDs are more easily passed from men to women, which results in higher female rates of infection. Moreover, the consequences of untreated STDS are often more serious for women ranging from infertility, tubal pregnancy and chronic pain to other complications.

Some STDs are especially common among young people for biological reasons. The bacterial infections chlamydia and gonorrhea most easily infect adolescent girls because of changes in the cervix during puberty. Young people are also more likely to be unmarried, to have more than one partner over time or have a partner who has an STD. ■

CURRENT SITUATION

Focus on Vaccines

The budget for prevention of STDs, directed by the CDC, remained flat over the past two years at $168 million. Congress just passed a $2.4 million dollar increase for FY 2005, but it still falls far short of what is needed to promote awareness and screening, according to public health advocates. [48]

ASHA was pushing for another $115 million, which it says is needed to help prevent STDs in women, adolescents and people of color, groups that are disproportionately impacted by STDs. "If these were common ear infections that could lead to pain and hearing loss, screening would be part of every physical," says the ASHA's Arrindell, who argues that because of squeamishness about sexual matters they're not.

For example, even though the CDC has made a big push to get sexually active young women tested for chlamydia, it is estimated that less than half of them do. Public health experts blame the expense of the tests, lack of awareness among young people and the reluctance of doctors to imply that an unmarried patient is sexually active.

"Every time a teenage girl gets chlamydia, she has a 10 percent chance of being infertile or having an ectopic pregnancy," complications that won't become apparent for years or decades, Hook notes. Yet only about 40 percent of primary-care providers are following the CDC's recommendation to test sexually active young women annually, Hook says, a reluctance he attributes at least partly to embarrassment.

Given how difficult it is to nudge both patients and doctors toward regular testing for these often-silent diseases, many experts agree the ultimate preventive solution is vaccines. Currently the only STD for which a vaccine exists is hepatitis B, a virus that can result in cirrhosis of the liver, liver cancer and even death.

Although the vaccine has been available for years, few adults availed themselves of it when it was advertised as effective against an STD. "Now in the 1990s, when it's been made into a baby shot and people are not told [hepatitis B is] an STD, rates are declining, and we're making a huge difference," Hook says.

Recently, breakthroughs were announced in the development of a vaccine for women against HPV strains linked to cervical cancer. The pharmaceutical company GlaxoSmithKline announced in October that it had moved up its government filing date to 2006, two years ahead of schedule, for a vaccine that could prevent 70 percent of all cervical cancers worldwide. Merck and Co. is developing a similar vaccine that industry analysts expect to be filed late in 2005. [49]

Progress remains frustratingly slow, however, in the search for a vaccine against HIV and herpes.

Research Funding

The federal government is currently spending $18.5 billion on HIV/AIDS, with the largest wedge of the pie going into health care for people living with HIV/AIDS in the United States. About 15 percent of the total, or $3 billion, is allocated to research. President Bush proposed a 7 percent increase for fiscal 2005 for the entire AIDS budget, mostly for mandatory funding for domestic care and for his global AIDS program. [50]

Congress allocated a total of $2.3 billion for the global fight against HIV and AIDS, tuberculosis and malaria in fiscal 2005. This is $99 million more than the president requested and $690 million more than last year. [51]

By contrast, research funding for other STDs at the National Institute of Allergies and Infectious Diseases was $51.5 million in fiscal 2004 with only a $1 million increase requested by the administration for 2005.

The so-called values debate has also threatened research into risky sexual behavior. Last year, the Traditional Values Coalition, an organization of 43,000 churches, publicly objected to some $100 million worth of government-

Continued on p. 1016

Do Virginity Pledges Reduce STD Risks?

Lifeway Christian Resources, the world's largest provider of religious products, initiated a movement in 1993 called "True Love Waits," which encourages adolescents to pledge to abstain from sex until marriage. The goal: follow "God's plan for purity." [1] Within two years, an estimated 2.2 million teens — 12 percent of all American adolescents — had taken the pledge, often in church-sponsored gatherings.

In 2000, the first study of the sexual behavior of virginity pledgers found that they waited 18 months longer than non-pledgers to have their first sexual intercourse, had fewer sexual partners and married earlier. [2] Advocates of the faith-based approach to reducing teen pregnancy seized on the results as proof that the program works to both reduce pregnancy and sexually transmitted diseases (STDs).

But Columbia University sociology Professor Peter Bearman, who conducted the survey, found just the opposite when he did a follow-up study with more than 11,000 pledgers between the ages of 18 and 24. [3]

Urine samples revealed that pledgers were just as likely to have sexually transmitted diseases as non-pledgers. Communities in which at least 20 percent of teens had been pledgers had higher rates of STDs than other communities, according to the study. The study also found that pledgers were less likely to use condoms the first time they had intercourse, and were less likely to have ever been tested for an STD or to have seen a doctor over worry about an STD.

Bearman speculates that if teens are breaking their public virginity pledges, they will hide the fact. In addition, there will probably be less discussion of sex and STDs among pledgers in schools with large numbers of pledgers.

"If they have burning urination, and there's no discussion in the peer community about what it means as an STD symptom, there's generalized ignorance," he suggests. Pledgers who remained virgins were also more likely to have oral and anal sex, which can increase teens' risk of acquiring STDs, the study found.

Public health officials are most concerned about untreated human papillomavirus (HPV), which affects 20-25 percent of girls in the age group studied. Untreated HPV cases can "facilitate cancer in early adulthood," Bearman notes.

Virginity-pledge advocates say Bearman's study doesn't represent their personal experience. "I've met these kids," says Leslee Unruh, director of the Abstinence Clearinghouse in Sioux Falls, S.D. "We had pictures of their weddings; we saw their purity rings."

She cites a study by Robert Rector, a senior research fellow at the conservative Heritage Foundation, which found that virginity pledgers are less likely to engage in unprotected sex or experience teen pregnancy. [4] Bearman calls that study "a nonsense analysis of our data" and says he found no difference in the pregnancy rate.

True Love Waits

Olympic champion Carl Lewis addresses a True Love Waits rally held during the 2004 summer Olympics in Athens, Greece.

Rector counters that while it's true that pledgers aren't particularly good about using contraception the first time they have intercourse, over time they use protection at the same rates as non-pledgers. He says he has been unable to replicate Bearman's finding that teens who take the pledge have as high a rate of STDs as teens who don't.

Both sides agree, however, that delaying sex is beneficial from a developmental perspective. One out of five adolescents has sex before age 15, a trend that disturbs experts on both sides of the virginity divide. [5]

"A lot of kids have sex way before they're able to handle relationships and intimacy," Bearman agrees. But he stresses that the two big public health concerns — STDs and teen pregnancy — are not affected by virginity pledges and may even be exacerbated by them. "The pledge doesn't really help kids," he says.

---

[1] See www.lifeway.com.

[2] Peter S. Bearman and Hannah Bruckner, "Promising the Future: Virginity Pledges as They Affect Transition to First Intercourse," July 15, 2000.

[3] Peter Bearman and Hannah Bruckner, "After the Promise: The STD Consequences of Adolescent Virginity Pledges," Sept. 2, 2004. Forthcoming in the *Journal of Adolescent Health*.

[4] Robert Rector, *et al.*, "Teens Who Make Virginity Pledges Have Substantially Improved Life Outcomes," Heritage Foundation, Sept. 21, 2004.

[5] National Campaign to Prevent Teen Pregnancy, "14 and Younger: The Sexual Behavior of Young Adolescents," 2003, at www.teenpregnancy.org.

Continued from p. 1014

backed research, much of it on sexual behavior. It compiled a "hit list" of 150 researchers who had done sex studies that looked, for example, at behavior that puts people at risk for STDs.

In July 2003, Rep. Patrick J. Toomey, R-Pa., introduced an amendment to withdraw financing from a list of more than 200 studies on the hit list. The proposal fell short on the House floor by two votes. [52]

The University of Washington's Holmes called this the latest example of moralistic blocking of basic scientific research — and "frightening." [53]

Teachers' Reaction

Much of the controversy over the Bush administration's expansion of abstinence programs stems from a definition in the 1996 welfare reform act (Temporary Assistance to Needy Families Act), to which all federally funded abstinence programs must adhere. The definition requires that programs have as their "exclusive purpose" to teach the benefits of abstaining from sexual activity. Among other things, the definition requires programs to teach "sexual activity outside of marriage is likely to have harmful psychological and physical effects."

Teaching about contraceptives is not permitted except in the context of their failure rates, according to federal officials, a guideline that has raised the hackles of some states and educators. California was for many years the only state that did not apply for funds under this act, because state laws authorized comprehensive sexuality-education programs that teach about contraception. California had experimented with its own abstinence-only initiative in the early 1990s. The program was terminated in February 1996, when evaluation results found the program to be ineffective. [54] Governors in Arizona and Pennsylvania also rejected those funds last year.

The restrictions have had a "chilling effect" on teachers of sexuality education, according to David Hoover, a senior project coordinator and clinical social worker with the National Education Association (NEA), which represents teachers. "Teachers are often forbidden to answer questions" from students about condoms and birth control, Hoover says. "It's about the only topic we approach where we say people shouldn't know anything."

Unruh of the Abstinence Clearinghouse claims the chilling effect works in the opposite direction, too. According to Unruh, school administrators in liberal "blue" states like New York are barring abstinence programs from their doors. "We don't want to give out names of teachers that are having us come in [to discuss abstinence] because we know they'll give them a hard time."

Abstinence Funding

Despite the lack of definitive studies showing that they work, President Bush has proposed a major boost for two of the three programs that fund abstinence programs. Although the welfare reform act has expired, Congress has authorized the welfare system and the abstinence funding within it to continue unchanged. The initiative has channeled $50 million per year for five years into the states. States that choose to accept the funds are required to match every four federal dollars with three state-raised dollars and then disperse the funds to schools and community organizations.

Bush proposed doubling funding this year for the largest abstinence program, Special Projects of Regional and National Significance (SPRANS), to $186 million from last year's level of $76 million. The program already has grown exponentially during the Bush's administration from a mere $20 million in 2001, its first year. Congress provided $105 million for the program for fiscal 2005 in an omnibus-spending bill passed last month. [55]

Bush also proposed doubling funding to $26 million for programs under the Adolescent and Family Life Act, the first of the three federal program designed to prevent teen pregnancy by promoting chastity. However, Congress appropriated $13 million, the same as last year.

It is unclear exactly how many schools receive federally funded abstinence-only programs since private groups that are the direct grant recipients often provide instructors and curriculum to the schools. According to Unruh, 700 groups receive funding under welfare reform, 119 under SPRANS and 58 under the Adolescent and Family Life Act.

According to the most recent data, compiled by the Alan Guttmacher Institute in 1999, 35 percent of school districts with a sex-education policy taught an abstinence-only curriculum. According to the CDC, 96 percent of the nation's high schools taught abstinence as the best way to prevent HIV.

Even before the Bush administration expanded funding, schools were already moving toward an abstinence philosophy during the 1990s, according to the Guttmacher Institute. "It was a time when social conservatives were getting organized from the school-board level on up," says study author Dailard. "Schools were reacting to the vocal minority. It's why we see teachers not being able to teach contraception in the classroom — either because of school district policy that prevented them or because they feared possible community reprisal."

According to Dailard, 22 states have a sex-education mandate. But that policy, she cautions, may not tell the whole story about what schools are teaching because the real decision-making occurs at the local level. According to a survey by the institute, four in 10 sex-education teachers either do not teach about contraceptives

Continued on p. 1018

At Issue:

Is "abstinence-only" the best sex-education policy for schools to implement?

yes

ELIZABETH BRADLEY
MATH TEACHER, LEWISTON HIGH SCHOOL, LEWISTON, MAINE; 2000 PRESIDENTIAL AWARD RECIPIENT

FROM NATIONAL EDUCATION ASSOCIATION WEB SITE, WWW.NEA.ORG/NEATODAY/0302/DEBATE.HTML

Consider this: "Good morning, class. Today we're going to talk about how to drive a car safely, even if you've been drinking. Now, it's really better not to drink and drive, because you might end up dead, but there are some ways to do it so that you cut your risk of becoming injured or dying."

The fact is that the true message sent by adults, the media, and the schools is the exact opposite: "Don't drink and drive." And we don't offer training in how to do it safely.

Now, let's change the scene just a little.

"Good morning, class. Today we're going to learn how to have safe sex (now referred to as 'safer sex' because safe sex doesn't really exist).

"We'll show you how to put a condom on a banana, and some other things you can do to minimize your risk of contracting an incurable disease, which may make you sterile (chlamydia), be a precursor to cervical cancer (HPV) or cause death (HIV).

"Oh, and you might end up pregnant. Then your choices are abortion ('one dead, one wounded,' to quote a recent bumper sticker), adoption (a lifelong hole in your heart), or parenthood (a 24/7 commitment that will make school, college, work, independence and emotional stability very difficult)."

Why can't we take the drinking-and-driving approach of "Just don't do it"? Statistics show that kids do care about what the adults in their lives have to say.

To me, teen promiscuity is in the same category as Russian roulette, and promoting safe sex is just handing them the gun.

If you knew that within the next 12 months your child would have a child, an incurable disease or be HIV positive, how far would you be willing to go today to prevent that? [Four] million teens a year [must] deal with these consequences.

Let's raise the standard and tell kids, unequivocally, what is in their best interest.

Why is it that we want so much to protect their sexual activity, but not their very lives?

no

EILEEN TOLEDO
ENGLISH TEACHER, PABLO AVILA JUNIOR HIGH SCHOOL, CAMUY, PUERTO RICO; ADMINISTERS THE "BABY, THINK IT OVER" PROGRAM

FROM NATIONAL EDUCATION ASSOCIATION WEB SITE, WWW.NEA.ORG/NEATODAY/0302/DEBATE.HTML

More students are becoming sexually active at earlier ages. As an educator, I had to get involved. I have been using "Baby, Think It Over" at my junior high school for five years. Pregnancy dropped from 15 the first year, to three last semester, and zero this year!

This program has a "baby" simulator. Students, male and female, are given "baby" to take home for five days. They experience the endless cries, waking at night, feeding, changing diapers.

Meanwhile, at school, we talk about child abuse, how to place babies to sleep correctly, and more. Students budget the weekly costs of caring for a baby. They inquire about jobs available to them at their age (13-16). Students realize how hard raising a baby can be for them.

One girl who loved baby-sitting became so frustrated after two days that "baby" was thrown in a clothes hamper and covered to drown out the cries. Her parents explained the consequences had this been a real baby. The student learned that this is not the time for her to become a parent.

We also discuss STDs, and we talk about how making love is different from sex, which is what teens are having. Making love is a beautiful experience in a true relationship between adults ready and able to take on responsibilities. . . .

We do role-plays: You're with your boyfriend, lose control, go all the way and don't even think about birth control, and a while later the girl is pregnant and all dreams are now put on hold. Or, things get hot but you stop and say, "Wait a second, I'm not ready for this."

Yet, I cannot be so naive [as] not to see that most teens become sexually active at an early age. So I must also talk about birth control. But schools that accept federal "abstinence-only" funds are not allowed to teach any factual information about the effectiveness of any form of birth control.

Students who have complete information about disease transmission and contraceptive use are the most likely to remain abstinent and will protect themselves if they choose to be sexually active.

We have worked with more than 400 students, and only three became pregnant in high school.

Continued from p. 1016

at all or teach they are ineffective in preventing pregnancy and STDs. [56] That number has risen from one in 50 at the beginning of the decade, according to Dailard. ■

OUTLOOK

New Focus on Women

Worldwide, the focus is shifting to women as the fastest-growing group contracting HIV. The number of women with HIV has risen in every region in the world, according to a United Nations report released last month; women account for nearly 60 percent of infected people in Africa, the most heavily affected continent. [57]

Microbicides — gels and creams under development that women could use on themselves to prevent STDs instead of depending on men to use condoms — could eliminate the disease in the future, advocates claim.

"When 50 percent of the new infections worldwide are happening among women, and the rate of new infection among women is increasing more rapidly than among men, that tells us there's a big gap in our prevention strategy," says Anna Forbes, a program coordinator for the Global Campaign for Microbicides, headquartered in Washington, D.C. "A condom can only go so far. When the man refuses to wear a condom and it's left in the drawer, it's not protective."

Microbicides could be invaluable for married women in the developing world who want protection against HIV but want to bear more children, Forbes adds.

Although microbicides are being developed primarily to prevent HIV, several under development would also protect against other STDs. Some advocates say a commercial product could be as close as five years away; other experts are more skeptical. Since 1990, five clinical trials have found the now commercially available microbicide Nonoxynol 9 was not effective against HIV and in some cases increased the risk, according to the University of Washington's Holmes, who participated in the first such study. Other microbicides have proven effective against HIV in the laboratory and in animals but have yet to be proven in clinical trials with people.

Other solutions — vaccines — will depend on funding and biological breakthroughs. Most experts think it will be at least a decade before a safe, affordable HIV vaccine can be developed, according to the American Foundation for AIDS Research. [58]

In the meantime, experts are concerned about growing rates of STDs in the gay community and high rates among poor people and minorities. Considering the growing numbers of the medically uninsured, Hook says, there's a question about how they will obtain either preventive care or treatment if they become infected. And the homeless and indigent are likely to have the most trouble sticking to the complex treatment regimen required for treating HIV.

While increases in syphilis and HIV are currently confined to the gay community, some experts worry the trend could spread to the general population.

"We're not yet seeing major increases in adolescents," says Holmes, "but it would not be surprising if we saw this phenomenon become more generalized if we don't strengthen our interventions." Moreover, over the past five years, heterosexuals have accounted for the greatest proportionate increase of reported AIDS cases in the United States. [59]

The increasingly female face of HIV means that more advocates from all sides and international groups like the U.N. are recognizing prevention efforts will have to change to take women's situation into account. Paradoxically, some abstinence advocates are singing the same song as women's advocates about the dangers women face in trying to influence men's sexual behavior, especially in societies where violence against wives is accepted.

"The woman who demands that the partner wear a condom will subject herself to great abuse," says abstinence proponent Smith of the Institute for Youth Development. But Smith vehemently rejects a biomedical breakthrough like microbicides as the solution. In fact, he says, "It worries me. We have to change the fundamental behaviors of men and women to be abstinent until they meet that partner in a faithful, lifetime way. If we don't, and we develop microbicides, another disease will come along that we won't have a microbicide for."

In many ways the same debate is being played out domestically in the debate over whether STDs should be prevented through a moral strategy — abstinent behavior — or modern science — through vaccines.

"We also believe it's important to delay sexual activity," SIECUS' Smith says of high school teens. But he contends the abstinence movement's approach is "to censor; to not give people information. Ours is to respect that young people are sexual beings and need information to protect themselves for lifelong sexual health."

As the recent presidential election showed, the country is deeply divided over moral values. And one might assume that division extends to sex education — except if one looks at the polls. Over 90 percent of adults and teens say it is important for teens to be given a strong message from society that they should not have sex until they are at least out of high school. A hefty majority also wishes that teens were getting more information not just about abstinence but also about contraception and protection against sexually transmitted diseases. And most adults don't think it's a "mixed message" to stress abstinence while also providing information about using birth control and protection against infection. [60]

As a parent, the University of Alabama's Hook sees the importance of both. "I have 12-year-old and 9-year-old girls. I think abstinence is great. I'm all for it; that's what I'm promoting in my kids," he says. "At the same time, if my kids make a wrong decision, I don't want to penalize them and have them not talk to me about it."

Moreover, Hook notes, "We're now seeing the resurgence of diseases like gonorrhea and syphilis in gay men, and that is happening because of the perception that modern treatment has transformed a previously fatal disease to a disease that can be managed as chronic illness." ■

Notes

1 American Social Health Association, "Overview Fact Sheet on Sexually Transmitted Diseases," at www.ashastd.org.
2 *Ibid.*
3 Thomas R. Eng and William T. Butler, eds., *The Hidden Epidemic*, Institute of Medicine (1997); See also www.cdc.gov.
4 American Social Health Association, *op. cit.*
5 For background, see Adriel Bettelheim, "AIDS Update," *The CQ Researcher*, Dec. 4, 1998, pp. 1049-1072.
6 Centers for Disease Control and Prevention (CDC), "HIV/AIDS Among African Americans," at www.cdc.gov/hiv/pubs/Facts/afam.htm.
7 *Ibid.*
8 For background, see David Masci, "Global AIDS Crisis," *The CQ Researcher*, Oct. 13, 2000, pp. 809-832.
9 John S. Santelli *et al.*, "Can Changes in Sexual Behaviors among High School Students Explain the Decline in Teen Pregnancy Rates in the 1990s?" *Journal of Adolescent Health*, August 2004, pp. 80-90, see p. 89.
10 *Ibid.*
11 Peter Bearman, "After the Promise: The STD Consequences of Adolescent Virginity Pledges," forthcoming in *Journal of Adolescent Health*. For background, see Kathy Koch, "Encouraging Teen Abstinence," *The CQ Researcher*, July 10, 1998, pp. 577-600.
12 Douglas Kirby, "Emerging Answers," May 2001, National Campaign to Prevent Teen Pregnancy, at www.teenpregnancy.org.
13 Shannan Martin, *et al.*, "Comprehensive Sex Education vs. Authentic Abstinence: A Study of Competing Curricula," Heritage Foundation, 2004.
14 ASHA, "Fact Sheet on HPV," www.ashastd.org.
15 SIECUS press release, "SIECUS Releases Review of Fear-Based, Abstinence-Only-Until-Marriage Curricula Used in Federally-Funded Programs," Sept. 29, 2004. Full report at www.siecus.org/reviews.html.
16 *Ibid.*
17 See www.religiousinstitute.org.
18 See "Condom Effectiveness," Politics and Science Web site, and Adam Clymer, "U.S. Revises Sex Information and a Fight Goes on," *The New York Times*, Dec. 27, 2002.
19 CDC, "Male Latex Condoms and Sexually Transmitted Diseases," at www.cdc.gov/nchstp/od/latex.htm.
20 "Condom Effectiveness," at http://democrats.reform.house.gov/features/politics_and_science/example_condoms.htm.
21 Abby Christopher, "Hearing Addresses condoms for HPV Prevention," *Journal of the National Cancer Institute*, July 7, 2004, p. 985.
22 "Status of HPV-related Provisions of Public Law 106-554," fact sheet from office of Rep. Mark Souder, e-mailed Nov. 2004.
23 Abby Christopher, "Hearing Addresses condoms for HPV Prevention," *Journal of the National Cancer Institute*, July 7, 2004, p. 985.
24 "200 Public Health Advocates Rally Against Bush's Abstinence-Only Sex Education Policy at Close of STD Conference," March 11, 2004, *Kaiser Daily HIV/AIDS Report* at www.kff.org.
25 National Institutes of Health, "Scientific Evidence on Condom Effectiveness for STD Prevention," 2001.
26 ASHA, "Major Health Organizations Call for Science — Not Politics — to Drive Sexual Health Policy," press release, March 11, 2004.
27 U.S. Agency for International Development, "What Happened in Uganda?" *Project Lessons Learned Case Study*, September 2002.
28 Institute for Youth Development, "What Happened in Uganda?" (Video), March 2004.
29 See www.icrw.org.
30 Dara Mayers, "Our Bodies, Our Lives," *Ford Foundation Report*, summer 2004, pp. 8-13.
31 See Susan A. Cohen, "Delayed Marriage and Abstinence-until-Marriage: On a Collision Course?" June 2004, *The Guttmacher Report on Public Policy*, June 2004.
32 *Ibid.*
33 Robert Walgate, "Bush's AIDS plan criticized for emphasizing abstinence and forbidding Condoms," *British Medical Journal*, July 24, 2004. at www.bmj.com.
34 "Debunking the Myths in the U.S. Global AIDS Strategy: An Evidence Based Analysis," Center for Health and Gender Equity, March 2004.
35 Walgate, *op. cit.*
36 Interview on "The NewsHour with Jim Lehrer," May 18, 2004.
37 Elizabeth Feder, "Social Hygiene," Reader's Companion to U.S. Women's History (on-line).
38 Eng and Butler, *op. cit.*, p. 88.
39 *Ibid*, p. 208.

About the Author

Sarah Glazer, a New York freelancer, is a regular contributor to *The CQ Researcher*. Her articles on health, education and social-policy issues have appeared in *The New York Times, The Washington Post, The Public Interest* and *Gender and Work*, a book of essays. Her recent *CQ Researcher* reports include "Increase in Autism" and "Mothers' Movement." She graduated from the University of Chicago with a B.A. in American history.

[40] Willard Cates, Jr., "Treating STDs to Help Control HIV Infection," *Contemporary OB/GYN*, Oct. 1, 2001.

[41] See Nina Bernstein, "Behind Fall in Pregnancy, a New Teenage Culture of Restraint," *The New York Times*, March 7, 2004.

[42] Eng and Butler, *op. cit.*, p. 208.

[43] Cates, *op. cit.*

[44] Eng and Butler, *op. cit*, pp. 1, 88.

[45] *Ibid.*, pp. 88-89.

[46] Cates, J. R. *et al*, "Our Voices, Our Lives, Our Futures: Youth and Sexually Transmitted Diseases, School of Journalism and Mass Communication, University of North Carolina at Chapel Hill, February 2004.

[47] These figures are for 2000. Hillard Weinstock, *et al.*, "Sexually Transmitted Diseases Among American Youth: Incidence and Prevalence Estimates, 2000," *Perspectives on Sexual and Reproductive Health*, January/February 2004, pp. 6-10.

[48] Some funding for HIV/AIDS is also included in CDC's HIV/AIDS, STD and TB prevention program, which has also been level-funded at $1.1 billion for the last two years. Congress passed an increase of about 4 percent over last year's budget for CDC overall for FY 2005, more than the president requested.

[49] Reuters, "Glaxo Vaccine Stops Virus Linked to Cancer-Study," Nov. 12, 2004.

[50] Kaiser Family Foundation, "HIV/AIDS Policy Fact Sheet: Federal Funding for HIV/AIDS: The FY 2005 Budget Request," February 2004 at www.kff.org.

[51] Katharine Q. Seelye and David E. Rosenbaum, "Big Spending Bill Makes a Winner of Mars Program but Many Losers Elsewhere," *The New York Times*, Nov. 23, 2004.

[52] Benedict Carey, "Long After Kinsey, Only the Brave Study Sex," *The New York Times*, Nov. 9, 2004, p. F1.

[53] For background, see William Triplett, "Science and Politics," *The CQ Reseacher*, Aug. 20, 2004, pp. 661-684.

[54] Debra Hauser, "Five Years of Abstinence-only-Until-Marriage Education: Assessing the Impact," Advocates for Youth, 2004, at www.advocatesforyouth.org.

[55] Seelye and Rosenbaum, *op. cit.*

[56] Alan Guttmacher Institute, "Sex Education: Needs, Programs and Policies," April 2004, p. 21, at www.agi-usa.org.

[57] Lawrence K. Altman, "AIDS Infections Reach Record High, U.N. Says," *The New York Times*, Nov. 23, 2004.

[58] www.amfar.org.

FOR MORE INFORMATION

Abstinence Clearinghouse, 801 East 41st St., Sioux Falls, SD 57105; (605) 335-3643; www.abstinence.net. A nonprofit educational organization that promotes sexual abstinence.

Advocates for Youth, 2000 M St., N.W., Suite 750, Washington, DC 20036; (202) 419-3420; www.advocatesforyouth.org. Established in 1980 to help young people make informed decisions about their sexual health through comprehensive sex education, including all birth-control options.

Alan Guttmacher Institute, 120 Wall St., New York, NY 10005; (212) 248-1111; www.guttmacher.org. A private research organization (formerly the research arm of Planned Parenthood) that publishes special reports on topics pertaining to sexual and reproductive health and rights with the mission to protect all reproductive choices.

American Foundation for AIDS Research, 120 Wall St., 13th Floor, New York, NY 10005-3908; (212) 806-1600; www.amfar.org. One of the world's leading organizations dedicated to supporting AIDS research, prevention and funding.

American Social Health Association, P.O. Box 13287, Research Triangle Park, NC 27709; (919) 361-8400; www.ashastd.org. A non-governmental group that seeks to improve public health, focusing specifically on sexually transmitted diseases and prevention.

Centers for Disease Control and Prevention, 1600 Clifton Rd., Atlanta, GA 30333; (404) 639-3311; www.cdc.gov/std. The federal agency charged with improving Americans' health and quality of life by preventing and controlling disease and injury.

Heritage Foundation, 214 Massachusetts Avenue, N.E., Washington, DC 20002; (202) 546-4400; www.heritage.org. A research institute that formulates and promotes conservative public policies, including abstinence-only sex education.

Institute for Youth Development, P.O. Box 16560, Washington, DC 20041; (703) 471-8750; www.youthdevelopment.org. Advocates a comprehensive message to youth to completely avoid five risk behaviors — alcohol, drugs, sex, tobacco and violence.

International Center for Research on Women, 1717 Massachusetts Ave., N.W., Suite 302, Washington, DC; (202) 797-0007; www.icrw.org. A nonprofit organization that seeks to improve the lives of women in poverty, focusing on issues affecting their economic, health and social status.

National Campaign to Prevent Teen Pregnancy, 1776 Massachusetts Ave., N.W., Suite 200, Washington, DC 20036; (202) 478-8500; www.teenpregnancy.org. Seeks to reduce teen pregnancy by one-third by 2005; works to try to find common ground between the advocates of abstinence-only and comprehensive sex education.

Sexuality Information and Education Council of the U.S. (SIECUS), 130 West 42nd St., Suite 350, New York, NY 10036-7802; (212) 819-9770; www.siecus.org. Since 1964, SIECUS has worked to promote sexuality education, protect sexual rights and expand access to sexual health.

[59] Willard Cates, *op. cit.*

[60] The National Campaign to Prevent Teen Pregnancy, "Teens Continue to Express Cautious Attitudes Toward Sex," press release, Dec. 16, 2003. Available at www.teenpregnancy.org.

Bibliography

Selected Sources

Books

Eng, Thomas R., and William T. Butler, eds., *The Hidden Epidemic: Confronting Sexually Transmitted Diseases*, National Academy Press, 1997.

An Institute of Medicine panel called secrecy one of the biggest obstacles to curbing a hidden epidemic of STDs.

Richardson, Justin, and Mark A. Schuster, *Everything You Never Wanted Your Kids to Know About Sex (but Were Afraid They'd Ask): The Secrets to Surviving Your Child's Sexual Development from Birth to the Teens*, Crown, 2003.

Two Harvard-trained doctors provide a humorous, compassionate and informative guide for parents.

Articles

Bernstein, Nina, "Behind Fall in Pregnancy, a New Teenage Culture of Restraint," *The New York Times*, March 7, 2004.

In tracing the romance of two 16-year-old sweethearts in the Bronx, Bernstein cites a new interest in virginity as one of the reasons teen pregnancy rates are falling

Cohen, Jon, "A Silent Epidemic," Oct. 27, 2004, www.slate.com.

Cohen reviews possible explanations for the high percentage of HIV and AIDS among black women.

Epstein, Helen, "The Fidelity Fix," *The New York Times Magazine*, June 13, 2004, p. 54.

Reducing the number of sexual partners, especially through fidelity in marriage, has helped reduce HIV in Uganda.

Lane, Earl, "White House Policy: Aiding Abstinence," *Newsday*, Oct. 22, 2004.

The Bush administration has exhibited an unusual interest in ideological purity for its appointees, critics charge.

Santelli, John, "Can Changes in Sexual Behaviors Among High School Students Explain the Decline in Teen Pregnancy Rates in the 1990s?" *Journal of Adolescent Health*, May 11, 2004, at www.teenpregnancy.org.

Santelli concludes that 53 percent of the recent decline in teen pregnancy can be attributed to abstinence and 47 percent to increased contraceptive use.

Weinstock, Hillar, *et. al*, "Sexually Transmitted Diseases Among American Youth: Incidence and Prevalence Estimates, 2000," *Perspectives on Sexual and Reproductive Health*, January/February 2004, pp. 6-10. at www.agi-usa.org.

CDC researchers conclude that Americans between 15 and 24 account for nearly half the new cases of STDs.

Reports and Studies

Alan Guttmacher Institute, "Sex Education: Needs, Programs and Policies," April 2004.

The latest information about sex education as it relates to STDs. At www.agi-usa.org.

Bearman, Peter S., and Hannah Bruckner, "Promising the Future: Virginity Pledges as They Affect Transition to First Intercourse," July 15, 2000. at http://www.sociology.columbia.edu/people/faculty/bearman/papers/virginity.pdf

Teens who took virginity pledges delayed their first sexual intercourse by many months, a study found.

Cates, J.R., *et al*, "Our Voices, Our Lives, Our Futures: Youth and Sexually Transmitted Diseases," School of Journalism and Mass Communication, University of North Carolina at Chapel Hill, February 2004.

This report includes a primer on the most common STDs.

Committee on Government Reform, U.S. House of Representatives, Minority Staff, "The Content of Federally Funded Abstinence-only Education Programs," December 2004, at www.democrats.reform.house.gov.

This report concludes that 80 percent of the most popular abstinence-education curricula contain "false, misleading or distorted" information.

Kirby, Douglas, "Emerging Answers," May 2001, The National Campaign to Prevent Teen Pregnancy, at www.teenpregnancy.org.

This widely cited report concludes that advising teens to delay sex but also providing information about contraceptives constitutes the most effective approach to sex education.

Rector, Robert, and Kirk A. Johnson, "Teens Who Make Virginity Pledges Have Substantially Improved Life Outcomes," Heritage Foundation, Sept. 21, 2004.

Researchers for the conservative think tank conclude that teens who take virginity pledges have better life outcomes.

Web Sites

Justice Talking; http://www.justicetalking.org/viewprogram.asp?progID=426#laws.

The Dec. 9, 2003, "Justice Talking," a radio program distributed by National Public Radio was a debate on the topic, "Abstinence-Only" between a Bush administration official and an advocate for sexuality education.

Kaiser Family Foundation: www.kff.org.

This Web site contains daily news reports on HIV/AIDS and STDs.

The Next Step:

Additional Articles from Current Periodicals

Abstinence-Only Sex Education

Brody, Jane, "Abstinence-Only: Does It Work?" *The New York Times*, June 1, 2004, p. F7.

Proponents of comprehensive sex education and abstinence-only advocates both take credit for declining teen pregnancy rates, but the jury is still out on which sex-education approach works better at preventing unwanted pregnancies.

Connolly, Ceci, "Texas Teaches Abstinence," *The Washington Post*, Jan. 21, 2003, p. A1.

In 1995, George W. Bush, who was then governor of Texas, signed a law requiring schools to teach abstinence-only sex education, and now President Bush is promoting abstinence-until-marriage programs nationwide.

Kohn, David, "Only Abstinence as the Answer," *The Baltimore Sun*, Feb. 29, 2004, p. 1A.

Since 1998, federal and state governments have given out almost $1 billion to abstinence-only education programs, and President Bush has promised to double annual funding for such programs to $270 million.

Sternberg, Steve, "Sex Education Stirs Controversy," *USA Today*, July 11, 2002, p. 8D.

Congress will decide whether to approve a $500 million, five-year effort to narrow the focus of sex education in public schools from teaching broadly about sexuality and contraception to teaching the benefits of abstaining from sex before marriage.

Witt, Howard, " 'Just Say No' to Sex? Educators Not Sure," *Chicago Tribune*, April 18, 2004, News Section, p. 1.

Proponents of abstinence education argue that young people are inundated with messages proclaiming that sex has no costs, and to counteract that influence, youths need a clear message that sex has many risks that are reduced by waiting until marriage.

AIDS and AIDS Funding

Bernstein, Sharon, "Rising Rate of HIV Infection Renews Bathhouse Debate," *Los Angeles Times*, March 23, 2004, p. B1.

L.A. County officials are considering tougher enforcement of existing laws that require bathhouse patrons to use condoms and whether to require that clubs offer information on safe sex and on-site testing for HIV and other STDs.

Daruvalla, Abi, and Jeff Israely, *et al.*, "Risky Business," *Time International*, June 3, 2002, p. 68.

New cases of STDs are soaring in Europe — British officials predict a 50 percent increase in HIV infection from 2000 to 2005 — as young people forget the lessons of the AIDS era.

Lauerman, Connie, "Lack of Education, Risky Behavior Put Teens in Danger," *Chicago Tribune*, Sept. 1, 2004, Woman News section, p. 1.

A recent federal study showed that from 1999 to 2002, 64 percent of new HIV infections occurred in women — and girls age 13 to 19 account for the majority of new heterosexually acquired HIV cases.

McKeough, Kevin, "With STDs, Many Still Wind Up Sorry Instead of Safe," *Chicago Tribune*, July 31, 2002, Woman News Section, p. 1.

U.S. health officials estimate that 40,000 Americans — including 12,000 women — are infected with HIV each year, with heterosexual sex accounting for one-third of all new cases.

Russell, Sabin, "Rich Countries Urged to Boost AIDS Funding," *The San Francisco Chronicle*, July 13, 2004, p. A1.

The ability to deliver cheap but effective drugs to millions of AIDS patients in poor countries is close, but experts warn that wealthier nations might not be able to come up with the billions to pay for such programs.

Stein, Jeannine, "It Hasn't Gone Away," *Los Angeles Times*, Aug. 13, 2003, Part 6, p. 1.

Rising HIV infection rates are raising concerns that AIDS may be making a resurgence after years of progress, and that there is a growing sense of public complacency about the disease

Contraception

Bernstein, Nina, "Behind Fall in Pregnancy, a New Teenage Culture of Restraint," *The New York Times*, March 7, 2004, p. A1.

A decline in the teen birth rate is linked to an increase in high school students abstaining from sex and a drastic increase in condom use among those who are sexually active — 65 percent of all teens and 73 percent of black male teens say they use condoms.

Brody, Jane, "Fact of Life: Condoms Can Keep Disease at Bay," *The New York Times*, Jan. 21, 2003, p. F7.

A large percentage of sexually active young adults often delay condom use or use them ineffectively, even though the proper and consistent use of condoms protects against STDs and unwanted pregnancies.

Carberry, Maegan, "Unsound Barrier; Condoms Far From Perfect in Stopping Certain Diseases," *Chicago Tribune*, March 9, 2004, RedEye Edition, p. 12.

HPV, or the human papilloma virus that causes genital warts and cervical cancer, can be transmitted even with condom use, and as many as 20 million Americans have the sexually transmitted disease.

Internet Effect

Ornstein, Charles, "Online Access to Risky Sex," *Los Angeles Times*, July 26, 2002, Part 1, p. 1.

Gay and bisexual men looking for quick-turnaround sex are turning increasingly to the Internet, and public health experts say the result is an uptick in the spread of HIV and other sexually transmitted diseases.

Purdom, Candace, "Hooking Up On the Internet," *Chicago Tribune*, Sept. 28, 2003, Sect. Q, p. 9.

As more people seek sex online, STD fighters are finding a new way to reach people exposed to a sexually transmitted disease and to promote safe sex and STD testing.

Tuller, David, "Health Officials Put Safer-Sex Message Online," *The New York Times*, Oct. 26, 2004, p. F8.

Health officials discovered that several gay men with syphilis all met sexual partners on the same Web site, highlighting what many health experts feared: Trysts arranged on the Internet often fuel the spread of STDs among gay men.

Sex Education

Clymer, Adam, "U.S. Revises Sex Information, and a Fight Goes On," *The New York Times*, Dec. 27, 2002, p. A17.

Critics say changes in sex information on government Web sites illustrate how the Bush administration can satisfy conservative constituents with relatively little exposure to the kind of attack that a legislative proposal or a White House statement would invite.

Coeyman, Marjorie, "Schools Stumble Over Sex Education," *The Christian Science Monitor*, July 22, 2003, p. 13.

There are few topics in public education that ignite more emotion or present more divergent viewpoints than sex education. In an age when Americans talk about sex more openly than ever, they still struggle with what to tell their children.

Kelleher, Kathleen, "Birds & Bees; Starting Kids on Right Path Pays Off in Long Run," *Los Angeles Times*, May 20, 2002, Part 5, p. 2.

A new study says the best deterrent against high-risk sexual activity among teens may be programs aimed at keeping kids off drugs, away from violence and in school.

Lauerman, Connie, "Two Schools of Thought," *Chicago Tribune*, Oct. 20, 2004, Woman News Section, p. 1.

Nearly half of U.S. teens have sexual intercourse by the time they finish high school, but there's controversy around the two ways of dealing with the birds and the bees — abstinence-until-marriage sex education vs. comprehensive sex education.

Teens and Sex

Lally, Kathy, "Sexual Experience Before 15," *The Baltimore Sun*, May 21, 2003, p. 2A.

Even though teen-age pregnancy rates have dropped during the past 10 years, the National Campaign to Prevent Teen Pregnancy found that about 20 percent of teenagers report having sex before the age of 15.

Morse, Jodie, "An Rx For Teen Sex," *Time*, Oct. 7, 2002, p. 64.

Historically, major medical organizations have backed comprehensive sex education curriculums, contending it is irresponsible to deny kids information about condoms, but a small but vocal group of doctors has begun promoting abstinence.

Villarosa, Linda, "More Teenagers Say No to Sex, and Experts Aren't Sure Why," *The New York Times*, Dec. 23, 2003, p. F6.

Declines in the teenage birthrate over the last decade combined with a decrease in abortions among teenagers point to a promising trend: fewer teenagers are becoming pregnant.

Citing *The CQ Researcher*

Sample formats for citing these reports in a bibliography include the ones listed below. Preferred styles and formats vary, so please check with your instructor or professor.

MLA Style

Jost, Kenneth. "Rethinking the Death Penalty." The CQ Researcher 16 Nov. 2001: 945-68.

APA Style

Jost, K. (2001, November 16). Rethinking the death penalty. *The CQ Researcher, 11*, 945-968.

Chicago Style

Jost, Kenneth. "Rethinking the Death Penalty." *CQ Researcher*, November 16, 2001, 945-968.

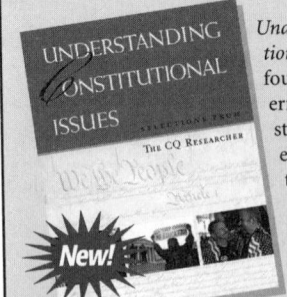

CQ Researcher

Published by CQ Press, a division of Congressional Quarterly Inc.

thecqresearcher.com

Tobacco Industry

Do ads and new products still target teen smokers?

Six years after major U.S. tobacco companies agreed to restrict cigarette advertising as part of a $246 billion settlement, "Big Tobacco" is fighting for survival. U.S. sales have plummeted in the past three years, tobacco taxes have risen, and smoking has been banned in airplanes, buses and restaurants. Nonetheless, a quarter of American teens are smokers by the time they leave high school, tobacco exports to Asia are booming, and lawmakers recently defeated a bill authorizing the Food and Drug Administration to regulate tobacco products. But tobacco use is still the leading preventable cause of death in the United States, and industry critics complain that cigarette ads and controversial, new products — including flavored cigarettes — target minors. The industry's prospects may well rest on the outcome of two suits by smokers and a $280 billion Justice Department action charging cigarette makers conspired to defraud the public about the risks of smoking.

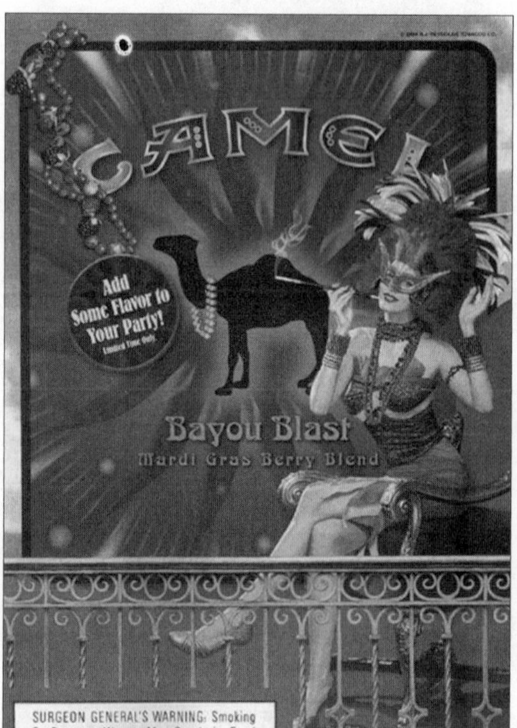

After ads aimed at children were banned, R.J. Reynolds Tobacco Co. introduced flavored cigarettes and other specialty products, which it claims target adults. But critics say minors are still the industry's focus.

INSIDE THIS REPORT

The CQ Researcher • Dec. 10, 2004 • www.thecqresearcher.com
Volume 14, Number 43 • Pages 1025-1048

CQ Press

Recipient of Society of Professional Journalists Award for Excellence ◆ American Bar Association Silver Gavel Award

THE ISSUES

BACKGROUND

CURRENT SITUATION

OUTLOOK

SIDEBARS AND GRAPHICS

FOR FURTHER RESEARCH

Cover: R.J. Reynolds introduced flavored cigarettes after ads aimed at children were banned. But critics say cigarette makers still target young smokers. Nonetheless, smoking by high-school students is dropping. (R.J. Reynolds)

THE CQ Researcher

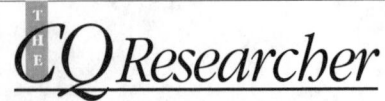

Dec. 10, 2004
Volume 14, Number 43

MANAGING EDITOR: Thomas J. Colin
ASSISTANT MANAGING EDITOR: Kathy Koch
ASSOCIATE EDITOR: Kenneth Jost
STAFF WRITERS: Mary H. Cooper, William Triplett
CONTRIBUTING WRITERS: Sarah Glazer, David Hatch, David Hosansky, Patrick Marshall, Tom Price, Jane Tanner
DESIGN/PRODUCTION EDITOR: Olu B. Davis
ASSISTANT EDITOR: Kate Templin

CQ PRESS

A Division of
Congressional Quarterly Inc.

SENIOR VICE PRESIDENT/GENERAL MANAGER: John A. Jenkins
DIRECTOR, LIBRARY PUBLISHING: Kathryn C. Suárez
DIRECTOR, EDITORIAL OPERATIONS: Ann Davies

CONGRESSIONAL QUARTERLY INC.

CHAIRMAN: Paul C. Tash
VICE CHAIRMAN: Andrew P. Corty
PRESIDENT AND PUBLISHER: Robert W. Merry

The CQ Researcher (ISSN 1056-2036) is printed on acid-free paper. Published weekly, except Jan. 2, April 9, July 2, July 9, Aug. 6, Aug. 13, Nov. 26, Dec. 24 and Dec. 31, by CQ Press, a division of Congressional Quarterly Inc. Annual subscription rates for institutions start at $625. For pricing, call 1-800-834-9020, ext. 1906. To purchase a *CQ Researcher* report in print or electronic format (PDF), visit www.cqpress.com or call 866-427-7737. A single report is $10. Bulk purchase discounts and electronic-rights licensing are also available. Periodicals postage paid at Washington, D.C., and additional mailing offices. POSTMASTER: Send address changes to *The CQ Researcher*, 1255 22nd St., N.W., Suite 400, Washington, D.C. 20037.

Tobacco Industry

BY MARY H. COOPER

THE ISSUES

It's the crack of dawn, and Mary, a 20-something professional woman, is out on the balcony of her apartment, lighting up what she hopes will be one of the last cigarettes she ever smokes.

"If I don't have this one," she admits, "I won't make it through the rest of the day."

Mary started smoking during her second year in college, but now, seven years later, she's determined to quit.

Three weeks later, Mary is working out at a downtown gym in Washington, D.C., and feeling better than she has in years. "I am that chick that I wanted to be, and she keeps getting better. It's like a whole new life beginning," Mary says.

Mary is one of an estimated 45 million American smokers — about 23 percent of the adult population. [1] If she does manage to kick her habit for good, she will join an estimated 46 million Americans who have weaned themselves from nicotine — an ingredient in cigarettes and smokeless tobacco that is one of the most addictive substances known to man.

For help, Mary turned to the antismoking American Legacy Foundation (ALF), which is posting her story online (www.maryquits.com). ALF President Cheryl G. Healton, a professor of clinical public health at Columbia University, says the best way to quit smoking is to combine counseling with nicotine-withdrawal medication and nicotine-replacement therapy, if necessary. "But 70 percent of our effort is aimed at reaching teenagers with a message that will stop them from starting at all," she adds.

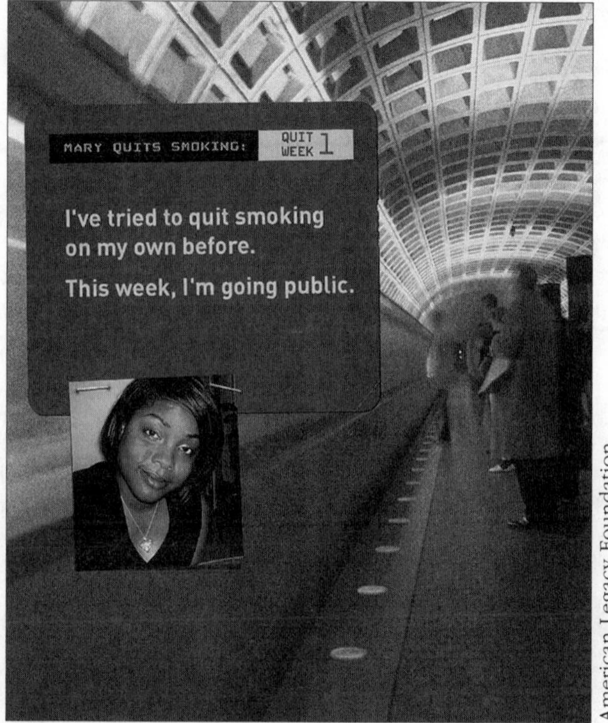

MARY QUITS SMOKING:
QUIT WEEK 1
I've tried to quit smoking on my own before.
This week, I'm going public.

American Legacy Foundation

A no-smoking campaign featuring a young woman from Washington, D.C., is being watched by millions of Americans. The campaign is produced by the American Legacy Foundation, founded as part of the $246 billion settlement between cigarette makers and the states. The settlement, along with declining consumption and competition from overseas, spells an uncertain future for the tobacco industry.

The foundation was founded as a result of the 1998 Master Settlement Agreement (MSA) that ended lawsuits against the U.S. tobacco industry brought by 46 state attorneys general. [2] The landmark settlement obligated major U.S. cigarette manufacturers to pay the states $206 billion over 25 years to compensate state Medicaid programs for the costs of treating cancer and other diseases resulting from tobacco use. Manufacturers also agreed to limit advertising and promotions targeted at minors. [3]

Separate settlements with the remaining four states brought the industry's total liability to $246 billion. States spend about $7.3 billion a year treating smoking-related diseases. The federal government spends another $20.5 billion a year to subsidize treatment of seniors for smoking-related diseases through Medicare. [4]

Tobacco smoke contains more than 4,000 chemicals — including benzene, arsenic, butane, DDT, toluene and vinyl chloride — 69 of which are known or suspected carcinogens. [5] (*See box, p. 1036.*) Smoking increases the risk of stroke and is responsible for 90 percent of all lung cancers, 75 percent of chronic bronchitis and emphysema and 25 percent of ischemic heart disease. [6] (*See sidebar, p. 1033.*)

In the six years since the MSA took effect, the U.S. tobacco industry has changed dramatically. Manufacturers have passed along to their customers the cost of the MSA payouts, causing retail cigarette prices to jump from an average of $2.03 per pack in 1998 to $3.59 in 2003. [7] And despite tobacco's highly addictive nature, American smokers have proved sensitive to the price increases: Per capita cigarette consumption has fallen by half since peaking in the early 1960s, to about 10 cartons a year. [8]

Actually, cigarette smoking has been declining in the United States since the surgeon general first linked lung cancer to smoking in the mid-1960s. "Ninety percent of young people start smoking before age 19," Healton says. "Our media campaigns reach out to children from 12 to 17, with an emphasis on older teens."

As smoking has declined, a growing non-smoking public has pushed for protection from the dangers of secondhand smoke, which can cause lung cancer and heart disease in non-smokers. [9] States and local governments have increased tobacco taxes and banned smoking in airplanes, buses, restaurants, bars

Fewer High-School Students Smoke

The percentage of high-school smokers decreased by 8 percentage points from 1997 to 2001, the lowest level in a decade. About 39 percent of white students smoke, compared to 33 percent of Hispanics and 20 percent of blacks. The government's "Healthy People" initiative seeks to reduce high-school smoking to 16 percent by 2010 through anti-smoking campaigns and increased cigarette taxes.

Percentage of U.S. High School Students Who Smoke*

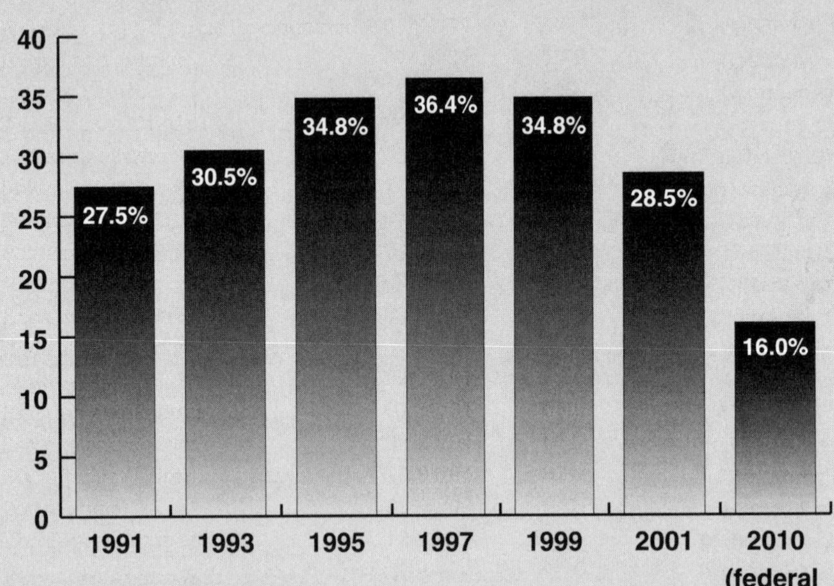

* *Based on students who said they had smoked at least one cigarette within the previous 30 days.*

Source: Centers for Disease Control and Prevention, "Targeting Tobacco Use: The Nation's Leading Cause of Death," 2004

and other public places. Aggressive anti-smoking campaigns by organizations like American Legacy and the Campaign for Tobacco-Free Kids have stigmatized smoking.

"There's been a change in attitudes toward the acceptability of smoking," says David A. Logan, dean of Roger Williams University School of Law in Bristol, R.I., and a tobacco industry expert. "Twenty years ago, a lot of people smoked in the workplace. But during the 1990s, the Protestant, Calvinistic notion that drinking is bad spread over into smoking. Now the few people who do smoke are huddled outside [their offices] looking like they've got typhoid. Students even complain about having to walk by them."

Nonetheless, tobacco use contributes to the deaths each year of nearly 440,000 Americans from tobacco-related diseases. "Tobacco remains the No. 1 preventable cause of premature death and disease," says Matthew L. Myers, president of the Campaign for Tobacco-Free Kids. "We know that by increasing tobacco taxes, expanding clean indoor-air protection, funding tobacco prevention and regulating the industry, we could dramatically reduce the costs of tobacco use on our society."

The MSA, competition from overseas growers and falling U.S. consumption have forced the tobacco industry to undergo sweeping changes. Eager to hold down prices, manufacturers have shifted production to countries with lower labor costs like Brazil, Zimbabwe and Malawi, which now grow tobacco that appeals to American smokers. Imports comprised about 35 percent of tobacco used in the United States in 2002, compared with less than 2 percent in 1972. [10]

The tobacco imports and outsourcing of production have undermined the longtime cohesive alliance between U.S. tobacco farmers and cigarette manufacturers, weakening the powerful lobby that had helped retain a Depression-era tobacco quota and price-support system. But the subsidies have not been able to protect domestic growers from plummeting world tobacco prices. In October, Congress finally agreed to end the subsidies as part of a $10.1 billion buyout of growers' tobacco quotas, enabling them to sell as much tobacco as they want in a free market or abandon tobacco farming altogether. (*See sidebar, p. 1039.*)

Public-health and taxpayers' groups had fought for decades to abolish the subsidies as well as another provision that was initially part of the Senate version of the buyout measure: authorization for the Food and Drug Administration (FDA) to regulate tobacco. Health groups had sought the provision since the U.S. Supreme Court ruled in 2000 that the FDA did not have authority to regulate tobacco. But the provision became a victim of election-year politics after House GOP leaders stripped it from the final bill — a tactic seen to aid GOP candidates running in key tobacco states in November's congressional elections.

"The majority of the farmers are pleased with the buyout," says Daniel Green, a lobbyist for the Burley Tobacco Growers Cooperative Association in Lexington, Ky., noting that even with the federal subsidies, many small farmers could not afford to continue growing tobacco because of the falling world prices. "There was just a very grim outlook for the federal program we were operating under. Most farmers are pleased to see it over with so they can move forward."

For their part, the cigarette manufacturers present a radically different image from the negative one created in 1994, when seven industry executives swore before a House subcommittee that tobacco was not addictive. [11] Relentless legal and financial setbacks since then have triggered an industry shakeout that has left the domestic tobacco market in the hands of three major players — Philip Morris USA, R.J. Reynolds Tobacco Co. (RJR) and Lorillard Tobacco Co. Big Tobacco, as they are known, now must compete with a growing number of small cigarette producers selling discount brands to a dwindling population of smokers.

But the tobacco industry has been nimble in the face of adversity. Philip Morris, which claims just over half of the U.S. market with its top-selling Marlboro brand, stunned its competitors by breaking ranks and declaring its support for FDA regulation of the industry — a move that many believe could improve prospects for future FDA regulation.

Meanwhile, Philip Morris' main competitors are seeking to expand their market share with new, controversial products, including flavored cigarettes, which critics say are targeted at minors in clear violation of the MSA. All three major producers are also pursuing supposedly "safer" tobacco products, such as cigarettes that produce less smoke.

Ultimately, the industry's prospects may rest on the outcome of a new spate of tobacco litigation, including two class-action smokers' suits — in Florida and Illinois — and a massive, $280 billion Justice Department racketeering suit charging that cigarette makers conspired to defraud the public about the health risks of smoking.

As the courts consider the latest tobacco litigation, these are some of the questions being asked about Big Tobacco:

Are cigarette manufacturers still targeting minors?

If young people make it to age 20 without lighting up, the odds are overwhelming they will never take up smoking, which is why anti-smoking campaigns focus on teenagers and the MSA-banned advertising aimed at youngsters. In particular, RJR was required to stop featuring its Joe Camel cartoon figure in its ads.

The restrictions are paying off. The percentage of high-school students who smoke dropped from 36.4 percent in 1997 to 28.5 percent in 2001, according to the Centers for Disease Control and Prevention (CDC). [12]

But the American Legacy Foundation (ALF) sees a worrisome trend. Two ALF surveys found that a quarter of young women, ages 16-24, smoke and that while 83 percent of them believe they can quit, only 3 percent succeeded in quitting for a year or more. [13] Girls are more likely than boys to try to quit but are less successful. [14]

Anti-smoking advocates cite such findings when they criticize the industry's rising advertising expenditures, including coupons and "buy two packs, get one free" promotions, which critics say target vulnerable young people.

"Since the MSA settlement, the industry has been circumventing the intent of advertising restrictions by increasing expenditures on those areas not covered by the settlement," says Myers of the Campaign for Tobacco-Free Kids, citing a record $12.5 billion spent on cigarette marketing in 2002. [15] "The largest increases have

Cigarettes Kill 440,000 Americans Annually

Tobacco use is the leading cause of preventable disease and death in the United States, contributing to the deaths of more than 440,000 Americans each year. Lung cancer causes almost 30 percent of all tobacco-related deaths.

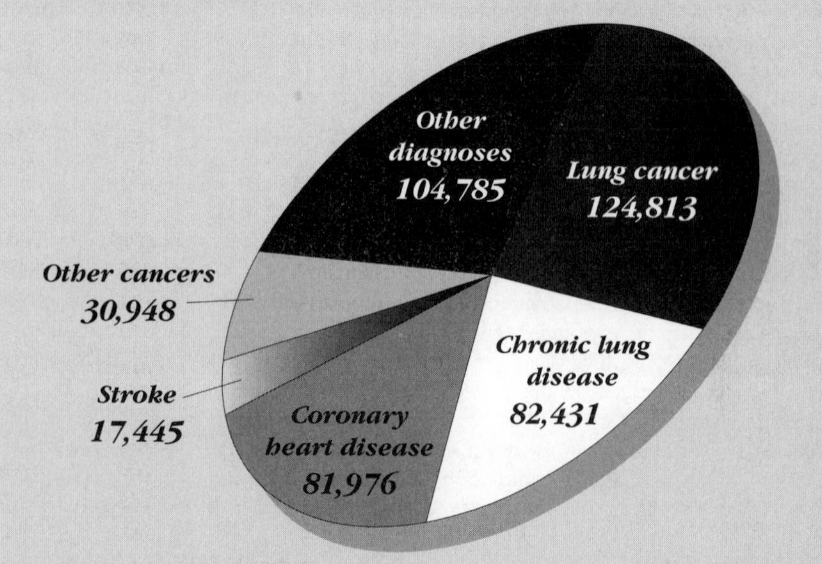

Source: Centers for Disease Control and Prevention, "Targeting Tobacco Use: The Nation's Leading Cause of Death," 2004

Reeling Tobacco Firms Seek Markets Overseas

Faced with lawsuits, advertising restrictions and falling cigarette consumption in the United States, Big Tobacco, like other major manufacturers, has gone overseas in its search for more promising labor conditions and consumer markets.

Affluent countries in Europe are experiencing the same gradual decline in smoking levels seen in the United States. Some European countries are imposing even stronger restrictions against smoking. Ireland banned smoking in pubs, restaurants and offices in March 2004, and Scotland is poised to take similar action.

"We believe that the bans in Ireland and Scotland are symptomatic of a larger trend in Western Europe and the United States," says Robert Campagnino, tobacco analyst for Prudential Securities in New York City.

That leaves less-developed countries as the most promising markets for cigarette exporters. "There are a whole lot more people in China who might start smoking American cigarettes than there are teenagers in the United States who might start smoking cigarettes," says David A. Logan, dean of Roger Williams University School of Law in Bristol, R.I.

But the World Health Organization (WHO) hopes to slow sales down. After four years of debate, the WHO's 192 member states overcame opposition by the global tobacco industry and the United States and adopted the first international treaty to regulate tobacco products on May 10, 2003. [1] The Framework Convention on Tobacco Control (FCTC), which the United States signed on May 10, 2004, calls on countries to establish smoking-cessation programs, restrict tobacco advertising and publicize tobacco's health risks but imposes no penalties for failing to implement the treaty. Peru became the 40th nation to ratify the FCTC on Nov. 30, 2004, which means the treaty will become part of international law on March 1, 2005. The Bush administration has yet to indicate whether it will send the treaty to the Senate for ratification.

"Now the real work must start, said WHO Assistant Director-General Catherine le Gales-Camus. "The convention sets forth the ideal goals and a roadmap for the work that needs to be implemented in countries. WHO will continue to support all countries in the vital work of building capacity and implementing the treaty." [2]

Meanwhile, the tobacco companies' marketing efforts are aided by the lag time between tobacco addiction and the appearance of tobacco-related diseases.

This pattern has repeated itself so predictably around the world that researchers have identified four universal, distinct stages of tobacco addiction and disease. During the first stage, essentially limited now to sub-Saharan Africa, smoking increases quickly among males.

In the second stage, male smoking rates skyrocket, female smoking grows more gradually, and tobacco-related diseases begin to kill a significant number of men, as in China, Japan, Southeast Asia, North Africa and some Latin American countries.

Eastern Europe, Southern Europe and part of Latin America are in the third stage, when male, smoking-related deaths rise rapidly, male smoking rates start falling, but female smoking rates continue to grow.

During the fourth and final stage, now being experienced by the United States, Canada, Western Europe and Australia, smoking levels among men continue to fall as death rates among male

been in areas like price promotions and product giveaways, both of which have a significant impact on youth smoking."

Indeed, testifying in the Justice Department's racketeering lawsuit, Lorillard's chief executive, Martin L. Orlowsky, admitted that his company had sent millions of direct-mail ads and coupons to consumers without ensuring they were over 21. [16]

Anti-smoking advocates are especially critical of new, flavored cigarettes they say are targeted specifically at teenagers. R.J. Reynolds, for example has launched citrus-flavored Camels called "Twista Lime" and coconut-flavored "Kauai Kolada," while Brown & Williamson Tobacco Co. — which merged with Reynolds on July 30 to form a new corporation, Reynolds American — features hip-hop artists on its Kool Mix packages. The flavored brands are being primarily marketed as limited-edition, seasonal products. For instance, the Nov. 22 issue of *Newsweek* includes a full-page ad featuring a sexy, young ice-skater enjoying the "Winter MochaMint" version of Camel.

Reynolds insists such products target adults. "All of the blends in these specialty products are developed for and tested with adult smokers," says David Howard, a Reynolds spokesman. He likens flavored cigarettes to the increasingly popular flavored coffees, alcoholic beverages and other consumer items. "Flavored cigarettes are a response to adult consumers who have said that there definitely is an interest in differentiated products like these," he says. "They are specialty products that are more in line with a special occasion, like that unique night out, when you want something different."

But Myers argues, "The same people who told us that Joe Camel wasn't aimed at children are now telling us that Twista Lime isn't aimed at children, and the claim deserves the same credibility. Confirmed smokers don't pick up Twista Lime Camels. The only people who would smoke candy-flavored cigarettes are people who are not yet committed smokers, and that means young people."

Reynolds' main competitors, Philip Morris and Lorillard, do not manufacture flavored cigarettes. "We don't think smokers peak and begin to decline, while women, who never reach smoking levels of men (except in New Zealand, Norway and Sweden), also begin to abandon the habit. [3]

If these patterns continue to hold true, the tobacco industry's days are numbered. But despite the likely continued decline in smoking levels, demographic trends promise a prosperous future for at least the next few decades. Because there will be 2 billion more people in the world by 2030, the WHO estimates, the total number of smokers will continue to rise, even in the face of declining smoking rates.

Asia and Australia are the largest consumers of cigarettes. According to the WHO, Asia is by far the main current and future market for tobacco sales. Even at the relatively early second stage of tobacco addiction, there are more male smokers in China — more than 300 million — than the entire population of the United States. [4]

To meet the escalating demand, China has rapidly emerged as the world's leading cigarette-manufacturing country, with production controlled by a state monopoly. Altria Group, formerly Philip Morris Companies, which accounts for about half the U.S. market, is the world's leading corporate cigarette manufacturer, with $47 billion in sales, led by Marlboro, the world's best-selling cigarette, followed by Hongtashan, made by the Chinese monopoly. The United Kingdom's British-American Tobacco Co. is the second-biggest maker, with $31 billion in sales. Japan Tobacco International, Reemsta of Germany and Altadis, a Spanish-French consortium, make up the rest of the global Big Five cigarette manufacturers.

Philip Morris Is Top Transnational Company

U.S. manufacturer Philip Morris is the world's largest transnational tobacco company, with more than 16 percent of the global market and $47 billion in revenue. State monopolies, mainly in China and the Middle East, control 40 percent of the global market.

Leading Transnational Tobacco Companies

	Percentage of World Market
Philip Morris (Altria Group)	16.4%
British-American Tobacco	15.4
Japan Tobacco International	7.2
Reemsta (Germany)	2.6
Altadis (Spain, France)	1.9

Source: World Health Organization

[1] See Kirsten B. Mitchell, "Tobacco Flip-Flop a Safe Bet; Reversal by Bush Poses Little Risk," *Richmond Times Dispatch*, May 22, 2003, p. A-8; and Ben Coates, "Cigarette Company Documents outline Strategy to Derail Global Tobacco Treaty," Center for Public Integrity, May 16, 2003, publicintegrity.org.

[2] World Health Organization, "WHO Tobacco Treaty Set to Become Law, Making Global Public Health History," Dec. 1, 2004; www.who.int.

[3] See A.D. Lopez, *et al.*, "A Descriptive Model of the Cigarette Epidemic in Developed Countries," Tobacco Control, No. 3, 1994, pp. 242-247, illustrated in Omar Shafey, *et al.*, eds., *Tobacco Control Country Profiles* (2003).

[4] World Health Organization, *The Tobacco Atlas* (2002).

it's the right thing to do for our business," says Peggy Roberts, senior director of communications for Philip Morris USA, stopping short of agreeing that flavored cigarettes are aimed at enticing youngsters to smoke.

Lorillard's leading brand, Newport, is a longstanding leader among mentholated cigarettes. But menthol is not a flavor, says Lorillard spokesman Steve Watson. "We don't have a specific flavor characteristic in our brand," he says. But unlike Roberts, he emphatically rejects the notion that marketing flavored cigarettes violates the MSA.

"If we were marketing to kids, the Federal Trade Commission would be obligated under the law to prosecute criminally the tobacco manufacturers," he says. "Furthermore, if any attorneys general in the country who signed that agreement felt that we were in violation of the MSA, they would take action. No one has, to this point, felt that we have done anything but be 100 percent compliant with the MSA, and that's what we intend to do."

Are higher cigarette taxes an effective way to reduce tobacco consumption?

Numerous studies have confirmed that even though tobacco is highly addictive, smokers are sensitive to price increases: Every 10 percent jump in cigarette prices produces a 3-5 percent drop in demand. [17] Governments can raise cigarette prices by imposing or increasing tobacco taxes.

"Substantial tax increases have been shown time and time again in both studies and real-life situations to be the quickest way to dramatically reduce tobacco use, particularly among children, because they are the most price-sensitive consumers," says Myers of the Campaign for Tobacco-Free Kids. "Since the MSA, there has been a 40 percent decline in tobacco use among children in this country," he says, "while state tobacco taxes have more than doubled." Moreover, the most significant decreases in cigarette consumption by minors have occurred in states with the highest tobacco-tax increases.

Indeed, in the past two years alone 38 states have raised tobacco taxes. In fall 2004 voters in Colorado, Montana and Oklahoma voted overwhelmingly

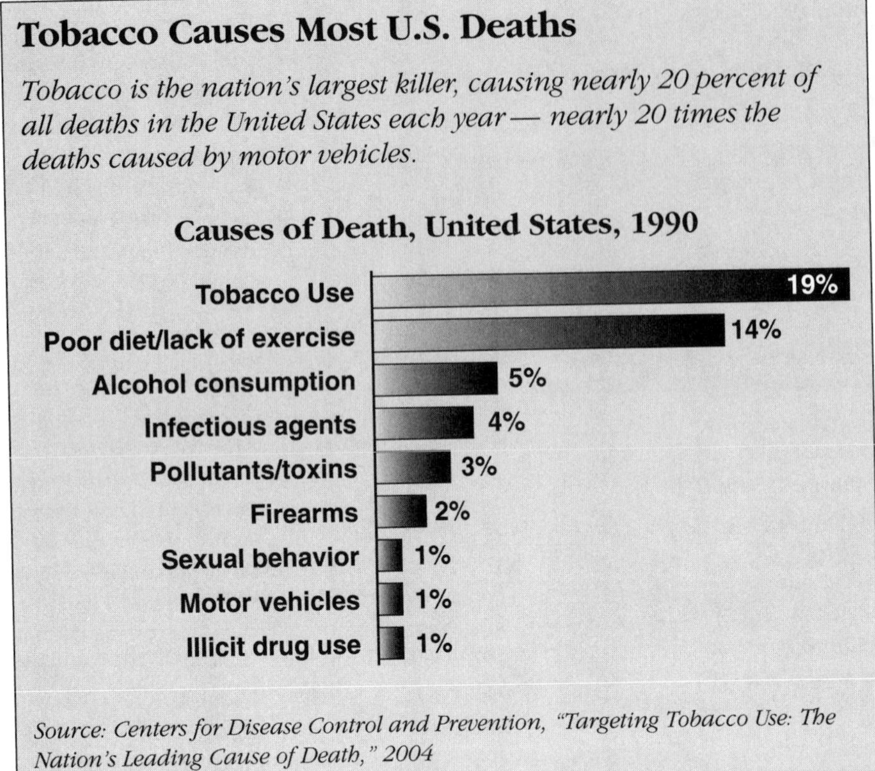

to raise tobacco taxes, despite wins in all three states by the GOP, which frowns on increases.

The tobacco industry lobbied hard to defeat the increases, spending $1.5 million on anti-tax advertising in Oklahoma alone. [18] Industry spokesmen openly acknowledge that tobacco taxes eat into corporate profits. "Taxes do increase the cost of cigarettes, and whenever they raise taxes, a certain number of smokers will trade down to less expensive products that either we or our competitors make," says Seth Moskowitz, spokesman for Reynolds. "Then, a certain number of smokers will decide they don't need to be spending that kind of money on cigarettes anymore and quit. So taxes, obviously, have an impact on our business."

To avoid higher prices, some smokers buy cigarettes smuggled from low-tax to high-tax states. "Tobacco taxes do have unintended consequences, and the black market in cigarettes is one," Roberts says. As a result, Philip Morris opposes "excessive" tobacco taxes, which Roberts defines somewhat ambiguously as "taxes that would promote black-market cigarettes." Sales of tax-free cigarettes on the Internet and by Indian tribes are also increasing. [19]

Cigarette smuggling is particularly high in jurisdictions with high taxes adjacent to low-tax states, such as the District of Columbia, where a $1-a-pack tobacco tax has fueled a thriving black market in cigarettes from Virginia, where the tax is only 20 cents a pack. State tobacco taxes average 84 cents a pack, ranging from a low of three cents in tobacco-producing Kentucky to $2.46 in Rhode Island. Some cities add a municipal tax as well. New York City, for example, imposes $1.50 on each pack of cigarettes, in addition to the state's $1.50 tax, boosting the average price to more than $7 a pack. [20]

Patrick Fleenor, chief economist at the Tax Foundation, a nonprofit advocacy organization that supports lower taxes, says any beneficial impact tobacco taxes may have on consumption is outweighed by their negative impacts. "Cigarettes are an ideal product to bootleg and smuggle across international and national borders because they're small and light. It's become a very profitable business," he says. "The tobacco tax is so easily avoided that I estimate that in places like New York City only about a quarter of the total demand for cigarettes is filled by the legal market."

Between 1993 and 2002 the federal tax on a pack of cigarettes rose from 24 cents to 39 cents, where it stands today. A federal committee created by Health and Human Services Secretary Tommy G. Thompson recommended that the federal cigarette tax be increased to $2.39, in an effort to discourage smoking, but the Bush administration ignored the recommendation. [21]

In March, Democratic Sens. Tom Harkin (Iowa) and Dianne Feinstein (California) proposed raising the federal cigarette tax to $1 and using the revenue to fund the CDC's tobacco-prevention programs. The measure failed, but Myers hopes public support for state cigarette-tax increases ultimately will spill over to the federal level.

"We would hope that as Congress figures out how to deal with the massive budget deficit and the need to fund tobacco prevention and other health-related programs, it would give serious consideration to a substantial tobacco-tax increase," he says.

Is there a safe way to use tobacco?

Long before it acknowledged links between smoking and disease, the tobacco industry began developing ways to reduce smokers' contact with harmful ingredients in tobacco smoke. Early efforts focused on reducing the amount of tar and nicotine reaching

Smokers Face Lethal Odds

The statistics are stark: Cigarettes kill half of all lifetime smokers. Half of those will die between ages 39 and 69. According to the World Health Organization (WHO), tobacco is the world's most lethal consumer product, killing more people than AIDS, legal and illegal drugs, auto accidents, murder and suicide combined. [1]

Since the 1960s, U.S. public health officials have linked tobacco with a number of serious and often deadly diseases. Smokers are at much greater risk than non-smokers of developing cancer of the lungs, mouth, throat, liver, kidneys, bladder, esophagus, stomach, pancreas and colon — as well as the cervix in women. Tobacco chewers are more likely than non-users to develop disfiguring and often fatal cancers of the lip, tongue and mouth.

Smokers are at far greater risk than non-smokers of heart disease, stroke and emphysema, as well. In addition, an estimated 3,000 non-smokers, or passive smokers, die each year of lung cancer contracted from exposure to second-hand smoke in the United States alone. Developing fetuses of pregnant smokers are at risk of low birth weight and diseases of early infancy, including sudden infant death syndrome (SIDS).

Because men began smoking in the United States many years before women took up the habit, cancer and other smoking-related diseases afflicted many more men than women until recent decades. But as women's smoking rates crept up, so too has the incidence of tobacco-caused illness in women.

In fact, while women's public health advocacy campaigns still devote the lion's share of publicity and fund-raising efforts to preventing and treating breast cancer, lung cancer has actually claimed more female lives than breast cancer each year since 1987. [2]

Thanks to anti-smoking advertising campaigns and programs to help smokers quit, the incidence of tobacco-related diseases is expected to peak and then begin declining in the United States and other developed countries in coming years. But global mortality due to smoking will continue to escalate as smoking rates continue to rise in developing countries.

In 2030, some 3 million people in industrialized countries are projected to die of smoking-related diseases, up from 2.1 million in 2000. But tobacco deaths in developing countries are projected to skyrocket, from 2.1 million in 2000 to 7 million by 2030.

---

[1] Unless otherwise noted, all data are from World Health Organization, "The Tobacco Atlas" (2002).

[2] Centers for Disease Control and Prevention (CDC), "Women and Tobacco," May 2004.

smokers' lungs by altering tobacco blends and putting filter tips on cigarettes. In the 1970s and '80s, as the evidence linking smoking and disease mounted, cigarette makers marketed "light" and "ultra-light" cigarettes that incorporated stronger filters and perforated paper that mixed more air with the smoke drawn from the cigarette, reducing the amount of smoke inhaled.

But light cigarettes proved no less harmful than regular cigarettes. To compensate for the lower levels of nicotine they were getting from light cigarettes, some smokers smoked more cigarettes. Others "put their fingers over the air holes, inhale deeper to get more tobacco and nicotine, and some even tear off the filter," says Mark Smith, an RJR spokesman.

A class-action lawsuit pending before the Illinois Supreme Court alleges that manufacturers marketed light cigarettes as safer products even though they knew the cigarettes offered no meaningful protection from the harmful ingredients in smoke. In response, the tobacco industry now emphatically declares that, in the words of a Philip Morris ad: "There's no such thing as a safe cigarette."

However, manufacturers are aggressively researching ways to reduce the harm associated with cigarette consumption. "We are working diligently, and have been for some time, on technologies that may eventually result in somewhat reduced exposure to the harmful constituents in tobacco smoke," Roberts of Philip Morris says, "but we're not there yet."

For now, RJR has taken the lead in pursuing safer cigarettes and marketing new brands. In 1988, the company introduced Premier cigarettes, which produced smoke by heating, rather than burning, tobacco. But consumers rejected that alternative, so in 1996 the company introduced Eclipse, which burns tobacco, but less intensely than conventional cigarettes. "Eclipse may present smokers with less risk of some, but not all, smoking-related diseases, compared to other cigarettes," the company's Eclipse ads said. [22] In 2001, Brown & Williamson developed another light cigarette, called Advance.

But consumers were still disinterested. Eclipse accounts for less than 1 percent of cigarettes sold in the United States, Smith says. "We're constantly trying to improve the taste so more people will smoke it," he says, acknowledging the dilemma posed by trying to develop safer cigarettes. "People smoke for the pleasure and the nicotine it brings," Smith says.

"There needs to be a balance, to come up with a product that is good enough that consumers will want to smoke it. Otherwise, what's the use of even offering it?"

Other tobacco products deliver nicotine in ways that do not involve exposure to tobacco smoke, such as chewing tobacco and snuff. But they have been associated with oral and esophageal cancers, indicating that exposure to the tobacco leaf, and not just its smoke, is harmful. A Swedish brand of snuff, called Snuss, has become popular in Sweden following reports that it has not been linked to serious health problems. Healton is skeptical of such reports, however. "As Snuss became the most popular form of nicotine and tobacco use in the country, lung cancer rates plummeted," she says. "But that doesn't say anything about nicotine-related heart disease."

Other products deliver extracted nicotine through patches, gums, oral inhalers and nasal sprays, which often are used by smokers trying to wean themselves slowly from nicotine. But they have not gained widespread use as long-term alternatives to smoking.

Three years ago, after studying whether these products offer a safer alternative to conventional cigarettes, a panel of experts appointed by the Institute of Medicine (IOM) found that while some products reduce exposure to tobacco toxins, reduced exposure "does not necessarily assure reduced risk to the individual user or reduced harm to the larger population."

Indeed, the panel concluded that the mere availability of such products could cancel out any of their health benefits if they reduced consumers' concerns about the danger of tobacco use. Thus, the panel concluded, despite the potential harm reduction the alternatives might offer, "use of tobacco in any form poses greater risk than having no exposure to tobacco at all." [23] ■

BACKGROUND

Tobacco Economy

Tobacco use was widespread throughout the Western Hemisphere for centuries before Christopher Columbus "discovered" it for Spain in 1492. [24] Central America's Mayan Indians are believed to have discovered the pleasures of chewing and smoking the leaves of *Nicotania tabacum*, a distinctively American plant species, and introduced the habit to other cultures. Tobacco use spread rapidly among Native American societies, many of which venerated tobacco and incorporated the plant into creation legends and religious ceremonies.

European explorers were initially aghast at the spectacle of Native Americans smoking. Rodrigo de Jerez, a member of Columbus' crew, reportedly was the first to observe the practice in present-day Cuba, where he said that natives wrapped dried tobacco leaves in palm leaves or corn husks "in the manner of a musket formed of paper," lit one end and proceeded to "drink" the smoke through the other.

When Jerez became the first European to light up back in Spain, startled officials, believing he was possessed by the devil, threw him in jail for seven years.

By the time Jerez was released, smoking had taken hold in Spain and spread to other parts of Europe and Asia, as sailors introduced the practice in ports around the world during the 16th century's Age of Exploration. The wealthy often inhaled tobacco in the form of snuff (ground-up leaves), but most users smoked it, either in cigars or pipes.

Even before the cultivation of tobacco in Europe began around 1600, scientists and physicians began studying its effect on humans. French diplomat Jean Nicot de Villemain, who first wrote favorably of the plant's medicinal value in 1561, lent his name to the plant's main mind-altering chemical — nicotine. Tobacco was widely welcomed as a cure for a number of ailments, including worms, halitosis, toothache and — ironically — cancer.

Some of the first cautions about potentially negative health effects of tobacco use emerged in Germany, where a 1586 tract called the plant a "violent herb." It was the first of what would become many subsequent warnings linking smoking and disease.

During the 17th century, as tobacco emerged as the economic anchor of Europe's colonies in the New World, it became the focus of deepening controversy, triggering a religious and social backlash against its use. Several countries in Europe and Asia banned tobacco imports in the early years of the century.

England's King James I decreed in a 1604 treatise, "Counterblaste to Tobacco," that smoking was "loathsome to the eye, hatefull to the Nose, harmfull to the brain, [and] dangerous to the lungs." In Rome, several popes recommended excommunicating smokers, and in China, Turkey, Persia and Russia smokers were executed, flogged or had their nostrils slit. But, eventually, it became apparent that such draconian measures were powerless to halt tobacco addiction.

In addition, the revenues levied on tobacco imports from Virginia's expanding tobacco plantations eventually outweighed the king's distaste for smoking, and England and Spain were soon competing for domination of a fast-growing global trade in tobacco. Reflecting the burgeoning industry's strength, by 1619 tobacco leaves were being used for currency in Virginia. Ominously, that same year the first African slaves were imported and sold to Virginia planters to plant and harvest their vast tobacco crops, beginning a practice that would spread throughout much of the South, launch

Continued on p. 1036

Chronology

1930s-1960s

U.S. tobacco industry prospers despite early health warnings about smoking.

1933
Agricultural Adjustment Act imposes acreage restrictions on tobacco cultivation, introduces tobacco price supports and provides for government loans to tobacco farmers.

1950
Morton Levin of the Roswell Park Memorial Institute in Buffalo, a state cancer research and treatment center, publishes first major U.S. study definitively linking smoking to lung cancer.

1964
First "Surgeon General's Report on Smoking and Health" establishes a direct link between smoking and lung cancer.

1965
Federal Cigarette Labeling and Advertising Act requires all cigarette packages to bear the surgeon general's warning.

1970s-1990s

Efforts to regulate tobacco intensify amid new evidence linking smoking with disease.

1971
Congress bans all broadcast cigarette ads.

1990
Smoking is banned on interstate buses and domestic airline flights less than six hours in duration. The ban will later apply to all flights.

April 14, 1994
Seven tobacco-company executives swear before the House Commerce Subcommittee on Health and the Environment that they do not believe that nicotine is addictive.

1997
Cigarette advertisements featuring the Joe Camel cartoon character are banned on evidence that they encourage children to smoke.

April 1998
Senate Commerce Committee approves a bill sponsored by Sen. John McCain, R-Ariz., to impose tight restrictions on cigarette advertising, grant the FDA authority to regulate tobacco products and raise the federal tobacco tax. The bill never comes to a vote in the full Senate.

November 1998
Under the Master Settlement Agreement, 46 state attorneys general agree to drop their suits against the tobacco companies to recover their states' Medicaid expenses for treating tobacco-related diseases, in return for the industry's payment to the states of $246 billion over 25 years.

2000s

Tobacco companies face steadily declining U.S. sales.

March 21, 2000
U.S. Supreme Court rules Food and Drug Administration does not have legal authority under existing law to regulate tobacco as a drug.

2001
Federal Centers for Disease Control and Prevention (CDC) reports that the percentage of high school students who smoke has dropped to 28.5 percent, down from 36.4 percent in 1997.

2002
Cigarette makers spend a record $12.5 billion on advertising and marketing, but U.S. sales fall by 5.5 percent to 376 billion "sticks."

July 2000
Florida jury awards $145 billion in punitive damages to as many as 700,000 state smokers in a personal-injury class action, *Howard A. Engle v. Liggett Group.* After an appeals court throws out the award, the Florida Supreme Court agrees to review the case.

March 2003
Illinois judge orders Philip Morris to pay $10.1 billion to 1.14 million smokers in a class action, *Sharon Price v. Philip Morris,* alleging consumer fraud by marketing light cigarettes as safer alternatives to conventional cigarettes. The tobacco company appeals, and the case later goes to the Illinois Supreme Court.

Sept. 22, 2004
Justice Department sues the tobacco industry under RICO anti-racketeering statute, alleging that cigarette makers fraudulently misled the public over their products' safety; suit seeks $280 billion in damages, which would be the highest damage award ever for a U.S. civil suit.

Oct. 22, 2004
President Bush signs Job Creation Act, which includes a provision eliminating the tobacco subsidy and quota program, but not a Senate-approved proposal to bring tobacco under FDA regulation.

Spring 2005
Decisions expected in class-action and Justice Department suits.

Deadly Chemicals Pollute Tobacco Smoke

Tobacco smoke contains more than 4,000 chemicals, at least 60 of which are known or suspected carcinogens. Most are byproducts of combustion itself, or the chemical reactions of chemicals produced by the smoke; several are additives used for flavoring, to facilitate inhalation, to increase nicotine absorption and to mask the smell and invisibility of sidestream smoke.

Ingredients of Tobacco Smoke	As found in:
Acetone	Paint stripper
Ammonia	Floor cleaner
Arsenic	Ant poison
Butane	Lighter fluid
Cadmium	Car batteries
Carbon monoxide	Car exhaust
DDT	Insecticide
Hydrogen cyanide	Gas chambers
Methanol	Rocket fuel
Napthalene	Moth balls
Toluene	Industrial solvent
Vinyl chloride	Plastics

Source: World Health Organization "The Tobacco Atlas," 2002

Continued from p. 1034

the Civil War and cause untold misery for generations to come.

By the 18th century, many countries and cities had experimented with tobacco bans — mostly to little avail — as tobacco use continued to spread, including among the ruling elites, who preferred snuff. Napoleon was reputed to use seven pounds of snuff a month; King George III's wife was known as "snuffy Charlotte."

To meet the growing demand, the first American tobacco factories — small snuff manufacturers — appeared in Virginia around 1730. British taxes on tobacco exports helped fuel Colonial discontent leading up to the American Revolution, but the Colonies' tobacco wealth also helped Benjamin Franklin obtain French loans to pay for the war. Meanwhile, the first clinical reports of lung cancer — previously an extremely rare disease — appeared. Reports of other cancers to smoking soon followed.

Tobacco fashions came and went, but demand continued to grow during the 19th century. In England, snuff was largely abandoned in favor of cigars, the specialty product of Cuba and other former Spanish colonies in Latin America and the Caribbean. By 1830, England's cigar imports reached 250,000 pounds, up from just 26 pounds four years earlier.

The modern cigarette made its first appearance in the 1830s, thanks to an inventive Egyptian artilleryman who, in a "Eureka!" moment, stuffed tobacco into a paper tube designed to hold gunpowder and lit up. The technique spread quickly, especially after British soldiers in the Crimean War brought cigarettes back to England in the 1850s.

Big Tobacco's Rise

For many years, tobacco users in the United States — virtually all men — preferred chewing tobacco. As late as 1860 Virginia and North Carolina, the leading tobacco producers, had 348 chewing-tobacco factories and only six plants that also made smoking tobacco out of scraps left over from plug production. The use of chewing tobacco spread after the Civil War, when returning Union soldiers introduced their new habit to the North as well as the fast-expanding frontier territories and states. Several leading tobacco companies, including RJR and Liggett & Myers Co. got their start in the 1870s producing plug tobacco.

By 1890, sales of chewing tobacco had peaked and been rapidly overtaken by cigarettes and cigars. In 1881, James Buchanan "Buck" Duke opened a cigarette factory in Durham, N.C. From that base, Duke cornered the American tobacco market until the U.S. Supreme Court in 1911 ordered his $240 million-a-year American Tobacco Co. dismantled for violating the Sherman Antitrust Act.

During the same period, temperance advocates opposed smoking because they felt it encouraged alcohol use; health reformers linked smoking to cancer, tooth decay, baldness and licentiousness; and middle-class reformers linked smoking with the decadent wealthy, foreign immigrants and the corruption of youth.

The anti-smoking backlash gained steam after mass production made tobacco products widely available. An anti-cigarette league, headed by Chicagoan Lucy Page Gaston, claimed a membership of 300,000 in the United States and Canada and lobbied for states to ban tobacco. (In 1901, the Supreme Court ruled that cigarettes were a legitimate article of commerce, but that states had the right to prohibit their sale.)

But efforts to curtail tobacco use and regulate the industry failed. Congress had begun taxing tobacco sales in 1862, primarily to generate revenue to help pay for the war. In 1892 federal lawmakers rejected a proposal to bar cigarettes, leaving tobacco regulation to the states. By that time most states and territories had barred the sale of cigarettes to minors (although the definition of "minor" varied widely). By 1909, 15 states had imposed total, albeit short-lived, bans on cigarette sales.

Tobacco slipped through the regulatory fingers of the new Food and Drug Administration (FDA), established in 1906 to oversee the sale of adulterated foods and drugs and the accurate listing of product ingredients on labels. In exchange for their support for the establishment of the FDA, tobacco-state lawmakers insisted that nicotine be dropped from the official list of drugs to be regulated — effectively barring federal regulatory oversight of tobacco products.

By 1910, the inexpensive cigarette had eclipsed the cigar as the most popular form of tobacco consumption. After American Tobacco's break-up a year later, a handful of large firms focused on cigarette production, setting the pattern for the growing U.S. tobacco industry for the rest of the century. Besides a pared-down American Tobacco Co., the industry leaders that emerged from the demise of Duke's "tobacco trust" were RJR, Liggett & Myers Co., P. Lorillard and British-American Tobacco Co.

Reynolds took the early lead in the burgeoning market by introducing Camel, the first pre-blended, packaged cigarette, in 1913, followed by Liggett & Myers' Chesterfield and RJR's Lucky Strike. World War I further solidified demand for cigarettes, which were included as essential rations for soldiers in the field. Asked what he needed to ensure the Allied victory, Gen. John J. Pershing famously replied, "Tobacco is as indispensable as the daily ration; we must have thousands of tons without delay."

As an entire generation of young men returned from Europe addicted to nicotine, calls to treat tobacco like alcohol (prohibited by the 18th Amendment in 1919) fell on deaf ears. [25] In 1927, Kansas became the last state to drop its ban on cigarette sales. Cigarettes were iconic accessories of the Roaring Twenties, as women joined men in the pleasures of smoking. In 1924, Philip Morris introduced Marlboro, advertised as "mild as May," specifically for the fast-growing female market. Brown & Williamson, established in 1894, also marketed its innovative menthol cigarette, Kool, to women. By the end of the 1920s, more than 70 billion cigarettes were being sold in the United States.

Americans' desire to light up even in the face of economic hardship saved the tobacco industry from economic ruin during the Great Depression of the 1930s. Congress provided help with the 1933 Agricultural Adjustment Act, which imposed price supports and acreage restrictions on tobacco cultivation to prevent overproduction and thus a drop in crop prices, and also provided for government loans to tobacco farmers.

By 1949, after a new generation of GIs had become addicted to the free cigarettes included in their World War II field rations, more than half of U.S. men and a third of the women were smokers.

'Tar Wars'

Although sporadic health warnings had appeared since tobacco was introduced to Europe, scientists began reporting a strong correlation between smoking and lung cancer only in the early 20th century. Deaths from lung cancer began to grow perceptibly with the rise of tobacco smoking: from 0.6 per 100,000 population in the United States in 1914 to more than six times that many — 3.8 per 100,000 — by 1930.

But the U.S. medical community was slow to react. *The Journal of the American Medical Association*, while repudiating tobacco-company claims that tobacco actually helped cure lung ailments and other diseases, continued to publish advertisements that made such claims until the 1950s. Indeed, many of the warnings about smoking and cancer emanated from Nazi Germany, where researchers wrote of the dangers of secondhand smoke and the potential damage to developing fetuses posed by pregnant women smoking. Such issues would not be taken seriously in the United States for decades.

Still, the U.S. tobacco industry began responding to health concerns by introducing new products. As early as 1936, for example, Brown & Williamson unveiled the first nationwide brand of filtered cigarettes, Viceroys, claiming the cellulose filter removed half the particles found in smoke.

But consumers ignored the health warnings. By 1949, after a new generation of GIs had become addicted to the free cigarettes included in their World War II field rations, more than half of U.S. men and a third of the women were smokers. Lung cancer had become the second-most-common form of the disease, after stomach cancer.

The tide began to turn against the industry's health claims in 1950, when Dr. Morton Levin of the Roswell Park Memorial Institute in Buffalo, a state cancer research and treatment center, published the first major U.S. study definitively linking smoking to lung cancer. [26] Cigarette manufacturers responded by engaging in "tar wars" — advertising campaigns aimed at convincing consumers that their filter cigarettes offered better protection from tar and nicotine than the competition.

Then, in 1954, to counter the sickly image emanating from the nation's cancer-treatment centers, Philip Morris launched its "Marlboro Man" ads, featuring an American cowboy smoking Marlboros and equating the cigarette with manly strength and freedom. The industry also joined together to create the Tobacco Industry Research Committee, which enlisted scientists to dispute Levin's findings. But their claims flew in the face of the evidence. No longer a rare disease, lung cancer claimed 31 lives per 100,000 population in 1956, a tenfold increase over the previous 15 years.

The 1960s marked the turning point for public awareness of the dangers of tobacco use. In 1964, a year when 70 million Americans smoked and tobacco was an $8 billion industry, the first "Surgeon General's Report on Smoking and Health" was published. [27] The landmark report found a direct link between smoking and lung cancer. It launched what became a series of annual reports detailing an ever-growing list of the dangers posed by tobacco.

Getty Images/Mario Tama

Some cities add a municipal tax to state cigarette taxes, driving prices up and consumption down. New York City, for example, imposes $1.50 on each pack of cigarettes, in addition to the state's $1.50 tax, boosting the average price to more than $7 a pack.

The report triggered a new era of tightening industry regulation, beginning with the 1965 Federal Cigarette Labeling and Advertising Act, which required cigarette packages to warn about the dangers of smoking. In 1971, Congress banned all broadcast cigarette ads; in 1990, smoking was banned on interstate buses and domestic airline flights less than six hours in duration; in 1997, advertisements featuring Joe Camel were banned on evidence that they encouraged children to smoke; and in 1995 President Bill Clinton announced plans to place tobacco under FDA regulation.

Tobacco on Trial

Smokers with cancer, respiratory disease and other illnesses related to their habit have been suing the tobacco industry for 50 years. [28] For decades, the tobacco industry has beat back consumer lawsuits, initially by rejecting charges that tobacco posed health risks and later by arguing that smokers were responsible for any risks involved in using their products.

Their most serious legal challenge before the 1990s came in 1983, when the husband of Rose Cipollone, who had smoked a pack and a half a day since she was 17, sued Liggett & Myers Co., charging that the company had failed to warn her that smoking their L&M cigarettes threatened her health. He won a $400,000 judgment against the company, which was later overturned. After Cipollone died of lung cancer, the case was argued twice before the U.S. Supreme Court, but her family, unable to pay the costs of further litigation, eventually dropped the suit.

In 1994, bolstered by internal company documents revealing that Brown & Williamson executives had discussed the negative health effects of smoking for years while publicly rejecting such evidence, FDA Commissioner David A. Kessler asserted that his agency had the authority to regulate tobacco. [29] The same year, Mississippi Attorney General Michael Moore and Minnesota Attorney General Hubert Humphrey III sued the major cigarette manufacturers to recover the costs of treating tobacco-related

The $10 Billion Buyout

Tobacco growers got their Christmas present early this year. In October, Congress finally agreed to spend $10.1 billion to end the nation's tobacco quota and subsidy program, freeing growers to sell as much as they want in a free market or abandon tobacco farming altogether.

Since the Depression era, the subsidy system has provided tobacco-price supports to ensure tobacco growers a minimum price for their crops in exchange for accepting quota limits on the amount of land they can farm. Growers depended on the subsidy program to protect them from volatile price swings, but in recent years the system had lost growers' support as prices fell. [1]

"Due largely to the federal support program that sets a market price for tobacco that is much higher than the price of tobacco produced in places such as Brazil and Malawi, domestic U.S. and foreign purchasers of leaf tobacco have turned increasingly to non-U.S. suppliers," says Robert Campagnino, tobacco analyst for Prudential Securities in New York City. "Consequently, we have seen a sharp decline in recent years of sales of U.S.-grown leaf tobacco."

The decline in sales has shattered the historic coalition between tobacco farmers and cigarette makers. [2] "As recently as the early 1990s, whenever there was a debate about tobacco issues on Capital Hill, the industry would routinely trot out farmers to say how tobacco regulation would drive them out of business," says David A. Logan, a tobacco industry expert and dean of Roger Williams University School of Law.

Today, Logan says, far more acres of productive land are owned by corporations than by individuals. "But to the extent that there are any Farmer Joneses left in the tobacco-growing business," he says, "Farmer Jones is not happy with the tobacco industry because he sees depressed prices as a result of the availability of overseas tobacco."

Tobacco growers stand to gain by the buyout, which will pay out the $10.1 billion over the next 10 years. After the 2005 season, growers will be free to sell their tobacco on the open market, and grow as much tobacco as they wish. But some are likely to quit.

"The farmer who is near retirement will probably go ahead and retire, but a 40-year-old farmer who's already invested in the [mechanized] planter, harvester and curing barns that you can't use for anything but tobacco will probably keep on growing," says Lioneil Edwards, general manager of the Flue-Cured Tobacco Cooperative Stabilization Corp. in Raleigh, N.C.

The only other crop that mechanical tobacco planters can be used for is sweet potatoes, Edwards says, making it hard for many growers to plant major alternative crops like corn or soybeans. "Farmers are very ingenious people, and they've been growing alternative crops along with tobacco for some time," he says. But with soybean prices at half their level of just six months ago, it's no simple matter to shift to alternative crops. "One of the big problems with U.S. farmers is if you turn them loose they will overproduce, and when you get oversupply of any commodity, you know what happens to demand."

Shifting to alternative crops is even more problematic for growers of burley tobacco, concentrated in the hills of Kentucky, Tennessee and West Virginia. "Our farmers don't have the resources to switch to row crops like corn and soybeans," says Daniel Green, a lobbyist for the Burley Tobacco Growers Cooperative Association in Lexington, Ky. "Unfortunately, the best alternative for many of these growers is to find off-farm income."

Green says most growers welcomed the buyout as the best they could hope for in a depressed market. "This buyout allows the larger growers to expand their production and make a better living with tobacco," he says. "It also provides the income needed for smaller growers to diversify or get out of the tobacco business altogether."

[1] For background, see Thomas C. Capehart Jr., "U.S. Tobacco Industry Responding to New Competitors, New Challenges," *Amber Waves* (published by the U.S. Agriculture Department), September 2003.

[2] See Eric N. Lindblom, "False Friends: The U.S. Cigarette Companies' Betrayal of American Tobacco Growers," American Heart Assocation, American Cancer Society and Campaign for Tobacco-Free Kids, December 1999.

disease incurred by their state Medicaid programs. Every state in the country quickly followed their lead. In 1996, as meetings began on a settlement between the tobacco companies and 46 of the states, four states (Florida, Mississippi, Minnesota and Texas) settled with the tobacco companies on their own.

In June 1997, the proposed agreement between the 46 states and Big Tobacco was announced. It required Congress to grant the cigarette makers limited immunity from new lawsuits for past actions and called for FDA regulation of tobacco. In April 1998, the Senate Commerce Committee approved, 19-1, a bill sponsored by Sen. John McCain, R-Ariz., to implement the agreement. (Then-Sen. John Ashcroft, R-Mo., who later became President Bush's first attorney general, cast the sole "No" vote). The agreement would have cost the industry more than $500 billion, tightly restricted cigarette advertising, allowed the FDA to regulate tobacco products and raised the federal tobacco tax.

But both Kessler and former Surgeon General C. Everett Koop argued the legislation did not go far enough to punish the tobacco companies.

The industry then withdrew its support for the bill and launched a $50 million campaign condemning it. McCain could not overcome a filibuster, and the measure never came to a vote by the full Senate.

Six months later, in November 1998, the 46 state attorneys general reached the Master Settlement Agreement (MSA) with the four major cigarette makers to recover state Medicaid expenses and to penalize the companies for deceptive practices. In exchange for the states dropping their suits against the tobacco companies, the companies agreed to pay the states $206 billion over 25 years. The states were free to use the funds as they saw fit, though many vowed to use it to help pay for treating smoking-related disease through Medicaid. Only $1.7 billion was specifically earmarked — to establish the American Legacy Foundation and support its anti-teen-smoking and smoking-cessation programs. The MSA also ordered the dissolution of the Tobacco Institute, barred cigarette ads targeting minors — including those featuring Joe Camel and other cartoon characters — and banned billboard tobacco ads.

In the end, the MSA was less stringent than the 1997 agreement that had formed the basis of the ill-fated McCain bill. The settlement made no mention of FDA regulation, placing implementation of the measure beyond Congress' control. It also dropped earlier requirements of stronger warnings on cigarette packages and stiffer regulations to reduce indoor air pollution. Nor did the agreement grant limited immunity from future lawsuits, as the 1997 proposal had.

Because the states were not required to use the tobacco-company payouts for health-related programs, many financially strapped states used the money for unrelated programs. In fact, more than half the money paid in 2004 was slated to offset budget shortfalls, and just 17 percent for health programs. [30] Some, such as Florida, also cut spending for highly effective, existing anti-smoking programs. ■

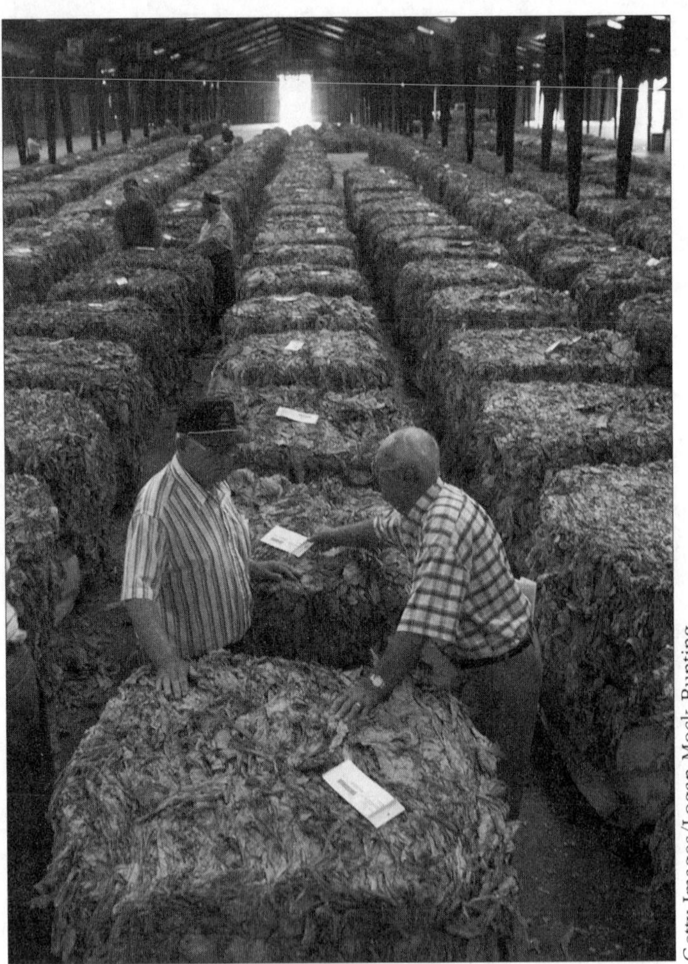

Getty Images/Logan Mock-Bunting

Tobacco buyers await the start of the big tobacco auction in Wilson, N.C., in August 2004. In October 2004, Congress voted to pay growers $10.1 billion over 10 years to end the nation's system of tobacco quotas and subsidies.

CURRENT SITUATION

Tobacco After the MSA

The Master Settlement Agreement has dramatically altered the playing field on which the tobacco industry operates. By agreeing to pay the states $246 billion over the next 25 years and forgoing key advertising venues, manufacturers also had agreed to forgo significant future earnings.

"There's been a lot of shuffling, related to the enormous pressures created by both the actual financial aspects of the master settlement and also some of the changes to business practices that were required by the settlement of those suits," says Logan of Roger Williams University School of Law. "So they're facing a very different business climate."

In addition, mergers have eliminated some industry stalwarts. Philip Morris USA has solidified its hold over the industry, claiming half the U.S. market in cigarettes. Second-ranked Reynolds American only sells to the U.S. market after Japan Tobacco bought its overseas business, as does third-ranked Lorillard, now a division of Loews Corp.

Today, what is left of Big Tobacco controls about 87 percent of domestic cigarette sales — down from 98 percent in 1997. [31] The MSA has enabled

Continued on p. 1042

At Issue:

Are the states doing their part to fight tobacco use?

yes

RAYMOND C. SCHEPPACH
EXECUTIVE DIRECTOR, NATIONAL GOVERNORS ASSOCIATION

FROM TESTIMONY BEFORE THE SENATE COMMERCE, SCIENCE AND TRANSPORTATION COMMITTEE, NOV. 12, 2003.

The tobacco Master Settlement Agreement (MSA) was reached on behalf of the attorneys general of 46 states, five commonwealths and territories and the District of Columbia on Nov. 23, 1998. That agreement, worth $206 billion over a 25-year period, is actually worth $246 billion when combined with previous settlements on behalf of Florida, Minnesota, Mississippi and Texas. . . .

On May 21, 1999, President Clinton signed into law a measure recognizing that decisions about how to spend the tobacco settlement dollars were most appropriately made at the state level, where governors and legislators could be the most responsive to the unique needs and circumstances of their citizens. . . .

Over the 2000-2003 period, states have received $37.5 billion from the Master Settlement Agreement. . . . About 36 percent went to health services and long-term care. About 4 percent went to tobacco-use prevention. Another 12 percent went to research, education and services for children. Also, states allocated 3 percent to tobacco farmers for crop-diversification efforts to reduce their states' dependence on tobacco production. The remainder went to endowments, budget reserves and other programs.

The one area that witnessed a major change over the three-year period was the percent allocated to endowments and budget reserves, which went from 29 percent in 2000 to . . . 2 percent in 2004. This was caused by the worst state fiscal crisis since World War II. [Nonetheless], 37 states continued to spend funds on health services, and about 33 maintained their commitment to tobacco-use prevention. . . .

The current state crises are likely to endure well into 2005. These fiscal conditions are driven by two major factors: sagging revenues and exploding Medicaid costs. . . .

The nation's governors feel strongly that the states are entitled to all of the funds awarded to them . . . without federal restrictions. . . .

Given the long history of state expenditures for smoking-related illnesses and the fiscal pressures facing states, the financial flexibility provided to states in the MSA is not only appropriate but vitally necessary.

The state fiscal crisis will continue, and without flexible use of MSA funds to target emerging priorities, states will be forced to cut education spending and make painful cuts in Medicaid expenditures for prescription drugs and long-tem care, as well as other public health and health-promotion activities.

no

MICHAEL MOORE*
ATTORNEY GENERAL, MISSISSIPPI

FROM TESTIMONY BEFORE THE SENATE COMMERCE, SCIENCE AND TRANSPORTATION COMMITTEE, NOV. 12, 2003.

Mississippi filed the first case against the tobacco industry in May 1994. We claimed the tobacco companies were killing 430,000 people a year, attracting 3,000 new teenage smokers every day by their marketing and advertising and costing our state millions of dollars a year in medical treatment for those indigent citizens in our health-care programs. . . .

Since the tobacco settlements, I have been in 44 states, giving a speech called "Spend the money on what the fight was about." I have discovered that some governors and state legislators must believe that the tobacco settlement dollars fell out of heaven, that the dollars have no connection to the public-health lawsuit that we brought. The money is being spent on one-time budget deficits, college scholarships, tobacco warehouses, roads — anything but prevention, cessation and improving the public health of this country.

If tobacco really kills 430,000 people a year in America, if tobacco-related disease really is the No. 1 cause of preventable death in America, then why is it we get $246 billion to do something about the problem and only a few states are using the money at a substantial level to make a difference? Comprehensive tobacco-prevention programs work. They have worked everywhere they have been implemented. The only place they don't work is where they have not been tried. . . .

I have heard all the arguments by those states that have chosen not to live up to the purposes of the tobacco fight:

- That the settlement documents don't say we have to spend the money on tobacco prevention and cessation. To them I say the preamble of the settlement provides ample language that public-health improvement, protection of our children and the reduction of death and disease from tobacco form the basis of the agreement. . . .
- I also hear, "We have a budget problem, a huge deficit, so we need this money to fill the hole." This short-term thinking makes little sense when compared with the dollars saved by a long-term investment in reducing deaths and disease from tobacco use and preventing our children from starting [to smoke]. . . .

I congratulate all those states like Maine, who just announced dramatic reductions in youth smoking this month. Florida, Massachusetts and California all had great results but have now been cut back. I know we can do better. The attorneys general of this country fought long and hard to achieve this important public-health victory.

** Moore was succeeded as attorney general by Jim Hood in November 2003.*

Continued from p. 1040

numerous, small makers of deeply discounted cigarettes — who are not part of the MSA — to enjoy a competitive advantage over the big companies, which are passing on the cost of their MSA payouts to customers. According to Robert Campagnino, tobacco analyst for Prudential Securities in New York City, the average price for a pack of Marlboros in mid-2004 was $3.53 per pack, compared to $2.53 for discount brands. "The large companies used to be able to [raise prices] anywhere from 6 to 10 percent a year, which is not normal for a consumer product," he says. "That's gone, and there hasn't been a cigarette price increase since March 2002."

Meanwhile, the customer base for all cigarette manufacturers is declining, as the number of U.S. smokers continues its slow, steady decline. The Federal Trade Commission recently reported that despite Big Tobacco's record $12.5 billion spending on advertising and promotions in 2002, U.S. cigarette sales fell by 5.5 percent that year to 376 billion "sticks." [32]

Philip Morris' decision to support FDA regulation of tobacco is another "pretty amazing development," Logan says. "I can't think of any other examples of companies urging legislation to be regulated more closely."

After the defeat of McCain's proposal for FDA jurisdiction over tobacco, the Supreme Court ruled on March 21, 2000, that the FDA did not have legal authority under existing law to regulate tobacco as a drug. Since then, congressional supporters of tobacco regulation — with Philip Morris' support — have redoubled efforts to extend the FDA's authority over tobacco products. A bipartisan measure sponsored by Sens. Mike DeWine, R-Ohio, and Edward M. Kennedy, D-Mass., won overwhelming Senate approval this year as part of the massive corporate tax-cut proposal — the same measure that ended the tobacco-subsidy system.

Getty Images/Scott Olson

Illinois Attorney General Lisa Madigan holds packs of Kool cigarettes during a July 2004 press conference in Chicago. She has sued Brown & Williamson Tobacco Co., charging its "Kool Mixx 2004" promotion targets African-American children and teenagers.

The provision was struck from the final House version of the tax bill, however, after heavy lobbying from tobacco-state legislators and competitors of Philip Morris, who argued that the company stood to solidify its competitive advantage under the proposed regulatory framework. The FDA undoubtedly would rigidly restrict cigarette advertising, which would benefit Philip Morris, with its best-selling Marlboro brand.

"If you walk into a 7-11, and there's no form of advertising whatsoever as to what brands are available, the biggest brand will only get bigger," Lorillard spokesman Watson says. "You'd be locking in the share of the big guy, and the other companies would have no way to compete."

Watson says his company in principle supports FDA regulation that would require safety testing of tobacco products, but not the bill that Congress rejected this year. "The way this legislation was written, the chairman of the FDA would decide on his own, based on what he believes is in the best interest of public health," Watson says. "It eliminated the rulemaking process, which involves scientific fact-finding, technological-feasibility studies and cost-benefit analyses, that all other consumer products have to adhere to."

Philip Morris denies charges that it is seeking FDA regulation to advance its competitive advantage in the domestic market. "We've always believed that it would provide a level playing field for everybody involved," spokeswoman Roberts says. While she downplays Philip Morris' record in developing a safer cigarette, critics say the company's determination to beat out the competition in this area as well as conventional brands explains why it came out so strongly in favor of extending FDA regulation over tobacco.

"Philip Morris is planning to bring out the biggest blockbuster [alternative] product," says Healton of the American Legacy Foundation. "But all of these products will collectively behave the same way that 'light' cigarettes did. The biggest risk is that they will dissuade smokers who are contemplating quitting . . . as lights and ultra lights did in the past." ■

OUTLOOK

Crucial Lawsuits

While the sweeping 1998 MSA protected Big Tobacco firms from additional state lawsuits, it did not grant them immunity from future lawsuits by others. Today, as a result, the industry is battling three major cases — two state-level class actions and a federal conspiracy suit. Legal experts widely agree the industry's future hinges on the outcome of the cases, which are likely to be decided by spring 2005.

The Florida Supreme Court is considering a personal-injury class action, *Howard A. Engle v. Liggett Group*, which could cost cigarette manufacturers $145 billion in punitive damages. A Florida jury awarded that sum in July 2000 on behalf of up to 700,000 smokers seeking compensation for smoking-related diseases. After an appeals court threw out the award in 2003, the state Supreme Court agreed to review the case.

Another class-action suit — alleging consumer fraud rather than personal injury — is before the Illinois Supreme Court. The plaintiffs in *Sharon Price v. Philip Morris* charged that the biggest U.S. cigarette maker fraudulently marketed Marlboro Lights and Cambridge Lights as safer alternatives to conventional cigarettes. In March 2003, an Illinois judge ordered Philip Morris to pay $10.1 billion to the 1.14 million smokers represented in the suit. The company appealed the ruling.

The most sweeping, and perhaps most surprising, of the current tobacco cases is the Justice Department's conspiracy case against Big Tobacco. *U.S. v. Philip Morris* is a so-called RICO case, based on the Racketeer Influenced Corrupt Organization Act, which was initially devised to go after organized crime. The case, the largest civil racketeering action ever brought by the Justice Department, seeks to force the industry to "disgorge" $280 billion of what the government claims are ill-gotten gains from defrauding and misleading the American public for 50 years about the health risks of smoking cigarettes. [33] The suit was originally filed during the Clinton administration, and most observers were surprised when Bush administration Attorney General Ashcroft decided to pursue it.

"We were pleased that after several initial efforts either to settle or undermine this case, the Bush administration has allowed the Justice Department to pursue it aggressively," says Myers of the Campaign for Tobacco-Free Kids. "We hope that after the election, the political people in the White House and the Justice Department don't try to undermine the case as a political payback for the tobacco industry's support in the presidential election." Myers' group estimates that tobacco companies contributed $2.8 million to candidates, mostly Republicans, running for office in November 2004. [34]

Industry spokesmen say they would not survive if they lose the non-jury federal case, which opened on Sept. 21 before U.S. District Judge Gladys Kessler, who alone will rule on the non-jury suit. "This is the largest amount of money ever sought in any civil lawsuit," say Moskowitz of Reynolds American. "If a judgment were upheld for that amount, it would bankrupt the entire tobacco industry."

Most observers give the government little chance of winning, however. "While we think it's possible that the Justice Department may be able to convince the relatively liberal Judge Kessler that the tobacco industry has done wrong in the past, we do not believe that it will be able to convince her that there is a reasonable likelihood that the industry will do wrong in the future," says Campagnino of Prudential Securities. "We continue to believe that the Justice Department's $208 billion claim is vastly overblown and that the tobacco industry will ultimately prevail." ■

Notes

[1] Centers for Disease Control and Prevention, "Cigarette Smoking Among Adults — United States, 2002," *Morbidity and Mortality Weekly Report*, May 28, 2004, pp. 427-431.

[2] For background on events leading to the Master Settlement Agreement, see Kenneth Jost, "Closing In on Tobacco," *The CQ Researcher*, Nov. 12, 1999, pp. 977-1000.

[3] For background, see Patrick Marshall, "Advertising Overload," *The CQ Researcher*, Jan. 23, 2004, pp. 49-72.

[4] National Governors Association, "Tobacco Prevention and Control," 2004, www.nga.org. A federal government claim against the tobacco industry for Medicare reimbursement of tobacco-related expenses was thrown out by a federal judge in 2000. In May 2004, the U.S. Supreme Court rejected an appeal on behalf of smokers' Medicare costs. That private suit sought to recover $100 billion from tobacco companies. See Mark H. Anderson,

About the Author

Mary H. Cooper specializes in defense, energy and environmental issues. Before joining *The CQ Researcher* as a staff writer in 1983, she was Washington correspondent for the Rome daily newspaper *l'Unitá*. She is the author of *The Business of Drugs* (CQ Press, 1990) and holds a B.A. in English from Hollins College in Virginia. Her recent reports include "Smart Growth," "Exporting Jobs," "Weapons of Mass Destruction" and "Bush and the Environment."

"Tobacco Cos. Dodge Medicare Lawsuit at Supreme Court," *The Wall Street Journal*, May 17, 2004.

5 "Risks Associated with Smoking Cigarettes with Low Machine-Measured Yields of Tar and Nicotine," *Smoking and Tobacco Control Monograph No. 13*, National Cancer Institute, October 2001.

6 See World Health Organization "The Tobacco Atlas," October 2002.

7 IRI/Capstone, cited on R.J. Reynolds Tobacco Co.'s Web site, rjrt.com.

8 World Health Organization, *op. cit.*

9 *Ibid.*

10 Tom Capehart, "U.S. Tobacco Import Update," Economic Research Service, U.S. Agriculture Department, February 2004.

11 For background, see Mary H. Cooper, "Regulating Tobacco," *The CQ Researcher*, Sept. 30, 1994, pp. 841-864.

12 CDC, "Targeting Tobacco Use: The Nation's Leading Cause of Death," 2004.

13 For background, see David Masci, "Women's Health," *The CQ Researcher*, Nov. 7, 2003, pp. 941-964.

14 American Legacy Foundation, "Legacy Media Tracking Survey" and "National Youth Tobacco Survey," 2004.

15 "Federal Trade Commission Cigarette Report for 2002," Oct. 22, 2004.

16 Bloomberg News, "Tobacco Trial Focuses on Mailings," Oct. 14, 2003.

17 Department of Health and Human Services, "Reducing Tobacco Use: A Report of the Surgeon General," 2000.

18 Campaign for Tobacco-Free Kids, "If Philip Morris and RJR Don't Want Kids to Smoke, Why Are They Spending $1.5 Million in Oklahoma to Defeat Cigarette Tax Increase?" Oct. 27, 2004.

19 See Eduardo Porter, "Indian Web Sales of Taxless Tobacco Face New Pressure," *The New York Times*, Sept. 26, 2004, p. A1.

20 See Steven A. Schroeder, "Tobacco Control in the Wake of the 1998 Master Settlement Agreement," *The New England Journal of Medicine*, Jan. 15, 2004, pp. 293-301.

21 See Ceci Connolly, "$2 a Pack Increase in Tax on Cigarettes is Rejected," *The Washington Post*, Feb. 27, 2003, p. A25.

22 "Eclipse and Premier," rjrt.com.

23 Institute of Medicine, "Clearing the Smoke: Assessing the Science Base for Tobacco Harm Reduction," Feb. 22, 2001.

24 Unless otherwise indicated, material in this section is based on Gene Borio, "Tobacco BBS," www.tobacco.org, a Web site that collects tobacco news and information.

25 The 18th Amendment was repealed by the 21st Amendment in 1933.

26 Morton L. Levin, Hyman Goldstein and Paul R. Gerhardt, "Cancer and Tobacco Smoking," *Journal of the American Medical Association (JAMA)*, May 27, 1950, pp. 336-338.

27 The report was issued on Jan. 11, 1964, by Surgeon General Luther L. Terry. All the surgeon general's reports can be found at www.surgeongeneral.gov.

28 For more information on tobacco litigation, see Jost, *op. cit.* See also Kenneth Jost, "High-Impact Litigation," *The CQ Researcher*, Feb. 11, 2000, pp. 89-112.

29 Information in this section is based on Schroeder, *op. cit.*

30 Government Accountability Office, "Tobacco Settlement: States' Allocation of Fiscal Year 2003 and Expected Fiscal Year 2004 Payments," March 2004.

31 "A Smoke Ring? That'll Cost You $280 Billion," *The Economist*, Sept. 16, 2004.

32 Federal Trade Commission, *op. cit.*

33 See Mark Kaufman, "U.S. Racketeering Trial Against Tobacco Industry Is Set to Start," *The Washington Post*, Sept. 19, 2004, p. A14.

34 "Buying Influence, Selling Death: Campaign Contributions by Tobacco Interests," Tobacco-Free Kids Action Fund and Common Cause, October 2004.

FOR MORE INFORMATION

American Legacy Foundation, 2030 M St., N.W., 6th Floor, Washington, DC 20036; 202-454-5555; www.americanlegacy.org. Created as part of the 1998 Master Settlement Agreement between the tobacco industry and the states, the foundation sponsors anti-smoking programs around the country.

Burley Tobacco Growers Cooperative Association, 620 S. Broadway, Lexington, KY 40508; 859-252-3561; www.burleytobacco.com. Represents growers in Kentucky, Ohio, Indiana, Missouri and West Virginia.

Campaign for Tobacco-Free Kids, 1400 I St., N.W., Suite 1200, Washington DC 20005; 202-296-5469; www.tobaccofreekids.org. One of the nation's largest non-governmental initiatives to protect children from tobacco addiction and exposure to secondhand smoke.

Flue-Cured Tobacco Cooperative Stabilization Corp., P.O. Box 12300, Raleigh, NC 27605; 919-821-4560; www.ustobaccofarmer.com. Serves tobacco farmers from the "bright leaf" area of Florida, Alabama, Georgia, South Carolina, North Carolina and Virginia.

Lorillard Tobacco Co., Customer Relations, P.O. Box 21688, Greensboro, NC 27420; 877-703-0386; www.lorillard.com. The third-largest U.S. tobacco company makes Newport and other brands.

Philip Morris USA, Consumer Response Center, P.O. Box 26603, Richmond, VA 23261; 800-343-0975; www.philipmorrisusa.com. The maker of Marlboro, the world's best-selling cigarette, also is the industry leader in the United States.

R.J. Reynolds Tobacco Co., Consumer Relations Department, P. O. Box 2959, Winston-Salem, NC 27102; 800-372-9300; www.rjrt.com. The second-largest cigarette manufacturer makes Camel and other brands and recently merged with Brown & Williamson Tobacco Co.

Tax Foundation, 1900 M St., N.W., Suite 550, Washington DC, 20036; 202-464-6200; www.taxfoundation.org. This nonprofit organization analyzes tax policy, including tobacco taxes, and generally advocates reduced tax burdens.

Bibliography

Selected Sources

Books

Gately, Iain, *Tobacco: A Cultural History of How an Exotic Plant Seduced Civilization*, Grove Press, 2003.
This sweeping history of the world's most prevalent addiction by a British journalist and author examines virtually every aspect of tobacco use, beginning in pre-Columbian America and continuing through the smoking litigation of the 1990s and beyond.

Glantz, Stanton A., *et al.*, *The Cigarette Papers*, University of California Press, 1998.
Glantz, a professor of medicine at the University of California, San Francisco, and director of its Center for Tobacco Control Research and Education, analyzes thousands of pages of internal documents he received from a whistleblower revealing that Brown & Williamson executives knew the risks of cigarette smoking.

Kluger, Richard, *Ashes to Ashes: America's Hundred-Year Cigarette War, the Public Health, and the Unabashed Triumph of Philip Morris*, Vintage, 1997.
The author, a former journalist and executive editor of publisher Simon & Schuster, presents a detailed history of the tobacco industry, focusing on industry leader Philip Morris.

Articles

Capehart, Thomas C. Jr., "U.S. Tobacco Industry Responding to New Competitors, New Challenges," *Amber Waves* (U.S. Agriculture Department), September 2003.
Falling cigarette consumption and foreign competition are driving U.S. tobacco growers out of business and prompting calls to end the Depression-era price-support and quota system controlling the tobacco-leaf market.

Fleenor, Patrick, "Cigarette Taxes, Black Markets, and Crime: Lessons from New York's 50-Year Losing Battle," *Policy Analysis* (Cato Institute), Feb. 6, 2003.
An economist at the conservative think tank attributes the development of cigarette smuggling across international and state lines in large part to high tobacco taxes in some jurisdictions.

Parloff, Roger, "Tobacco's Month of Living Dangerously," *Fortune*, Nov. 29, 2004, p. 137.
U.S. cigarette makers face three potentially devastating lawsuits — class actions in Florida and Illinois as well as a conspiracy case brought by the Justice Department — but analysts predict the companies will escape bankruptcy from this latest round of anti-smoking litigation.

Rosenthal, Elisabeth, "Across Europe, Women Are Lighting Up," *International Herald Tribune*, Nov. 22, 2004, p. 1.
Smoking rates among men are falling in Europe, but women are slow to follow suit. In Germany, half of young women under 30 are smokers.

Tiplady, Rachel, "Europe: Where the Smoke Is Clearing," *Business Week*, Nov. 22, 2004, p. 62.
Anti-smoking campaigns are beginning to take effect in many European countries, thanks to smoking bans and rising tobacco taxes.

Reports and Studies

American Heart Association, American Cancer Society and Campaign for Tobacco-Free Kids, "False Friends: Cigarette Companies' Betrayal of American Tobacco Growers," December 1999.
Three public-health advocacy organizations describe the U.S. tobacco industry's outsourcing of tobacco leaf to lower-cost countries, leaving American growers with declining demand and little support to grow alternative crops.

Federal Trade Commission, "Cigarette Report for 2002," 2004.
The FTC reports that even as domestic cigarette sales continued to decline, U.S. tobacco companies spent a record $12 billion on advertising and promotions from 2001 to 2002.

General Accounting Office, "Tobacco: Issues Surrounding a National Tobacco Settlement," April 1998.
This report examines the background behind the Master Settlement Agreement (MSA), the massive settlement between the largest U.S. tobacco companies and state attorneys general, which is expected to have a profound impact on youth smoking, cigarette excise taxes and smuggling.

—, "Tobacco Settlement: States' Allocations of Fiscal Year 2003 and Expected Fiscal Year 2004 Payments," March 2004.
Most of the $12.8 billion paid by tobacco companies in 2003 to 46 states under the 1998 MSA was used for budget shortfalls and health-related programs instead of for smoking-cessation programs, as many states had promised.

World Health Organization, "The Tobacco Atlas," 2001.
The United Nations agency presents dozens of tables and graphs about the tobacco industry, including the incidence of smoking, tobacco-related diseases and international trade in tobacco products; online at www.who.int.

The Next Step:

Additional Articles from Current Periodicals

Cigarette Advertising and Promotion

Cushman, John, "Big Tobacco Pays This Foundation to Bash Tobacco," *The New York Times*, Nov. 17, 2003, p. F10.

Commercials and Internet campaigns aimed at persuading young people not to smoke are produced by the American Legacy Foundation, which is financed by Big Tobacco companies.

Ives, Nat, "Flavored Kool Cigarettes Are Attracting Criticism," *The New York Times*, March 9, 2004, p. C11.

New versions of Kool cigarettes draw attention for their flavors — Caribbean Chill, Midnight Berry, Mocha Taboo and Mintrigue — which critics say are designed to appeal to adolescent non-smokers.

Kasindorf, Martin, "Tobacco Execs Launch Attack on Anti-Smoking Ads," *USA Today*, June 9, 2003, p. 4A.

Tobacco executives have filed a lawsuit in California asking the courts to ban anti-smoking ads that portray them as callous killers who try to get kids addicted to nicotine.

Ligos, Melinda, "Enthusiastic Promoter of a Reviled Product," *The New York Times*, July 1, 2004, p. C6.

The creators of a boutique alternative to mass-produced cigarettes respond to the constraints on their product with entrepreneurial flair, elbowing their way into niche outlets and pulling off publicity stunts.

McLure, Jason, "Changing Habits," *Newsweek*, Aug. 14, 2003, Newsweek Web Exclusive.

As public-smoking bans get tougher, snuff companies that make products like Skoal and Copenhagen are devising new strategies to lure tobacco users to their products.

Farmer Buyouts

Gately, Gary, "Tobacco Barns Becoming Endangered in Maryland," *The New York Time*, Sept. 12, 2004, p. A20.

Government buyouts designed to discourage tobacco growing have led to the crop's fast fading after 40 years as southern Maryland's main cash crop.

Jonsson, Patrik, "Along Tobacco Row, A Changed Culture," *The Christian Science Monitor*, Oct. 21, 2004, p. 1.

Congress passed legislation that requires cigarette makers to fund $10 billion in payouts to growers in return for the end of price supports.

Kaufman, Marc, "Tobacco States Fume Over Bush Remarks," *The Washington Post*, May 16, 2004, p. A4.

In a campaign comment, President Bush opposed a buyout for hard-pressed tobacco growers and set off a firestorm in the generally Republican states where relief for the farmers is a potent political issue.

Romero, Simon, "Growers Keep Their Fingers Crossed for a Windfall," *The New York Times*, July 26, 2004, p. A10.

Tobacco growers are challenged by anti-smoking campaigns, international competition and lack of rain, but help is on the way — a Senate-approved tobacco buyout plan.

Federal Tobacco Regulation

Hulse, Carl, "In Hard Times, Tobacco Growers Consider the Unthinkable: Giving Up Price Supports," *The New York Times*, Aug. 20, 2003, p. A13.

With foreign competition increasing and income falling steadily, tobacco farmers and senators from tobacco states say they are prepared to give up the government crop limits and price supports.

Hulse, Carl, "Senate Approves Tobacco Buyout and New Curbs," *The New York Times*, July 16, 2004, p. A1.

After years of resistance by the cigarette industry, the Senate overwhelmingly approved new federal regulation of tobacco products and advertising as part of a deal to end Depression-era tobacco price supports.

Kaufman, Marc, "Unusual Alliance Seeks Deal on Tobacco Curbs," *The Washington Post*, Oct. 3, 2003, p. A3.

Tobacco growers and public-health advocates are unlikely allies, but are both pushing for a compromise in which financially strained tobacco growers would get federal relief in exchange for the FDA gaining regulatory control over tobacco products.

Lazarus, David, "Strange Tobacco Reaction," *The San Francisco Chronicle*, Oct. 17, 2004, p. J1.

A historic provision that would allow the FDA to regulate tobacco was dropped from a corporate tax bill, disappointing anti-smoking crusaders and, more surprisingly, Philip Morris executives.

Morgan, Dan, and Helen Dewar, "House Blocks FDA Oversight of Tobacco," *The Washington Post*, Oct. 12, 2004, p. A4.

Tobacco interests prevail over pro-regulatory forces as House Republicans outmaneuver Senate negotiators and push through a tax bill that omits Senate-approved FDA regulation of cigarettes.

Health Effects and Quitting

Gerstenzang, James, "Health Risks From Smoking More Widespread," *Los Angeles Times*, May 28, 2004, p. A1.

The federal government reports that cigarette smoking harms nearly every human organ and is increasingly a habit of the poorest Americans; also, cigarettes offering lower tar and nicotine than conventional cigarettes provide no clear health benefits.

Malcolm, Ginger, "Young Smokers Often Kicked By Habit," *Chicago Tribune*, Sept. 3, 2003, Woman News Section, p. 1.
One-quarter of women ages 16 to 24 in the United States smoke. Of the 60 percent of female smokers who tried to quit in the past year, only 3 percent succeeded.

Reitman, Valerie, "Is Smokeless Safer?" *Los Angeles Times*, June 14, 2004, p. F1.
Anti-smoking researchers and public health advocates suggest that smokers who can't kick the habit would be better off switching to new clean, smokeless tobacco products.

Smoking Bans and Restrictions

Craig, Tim, "Studies Cloud Smoking Ban Issue," *The Washington Post*, Dec. 28, 2003, p. C1.
Studies indicating that restaurants and bars are hurt financially by smoking bans are largely funded by the tobacco industry and often use flawed data, according to an analysis of 97 studies from 30 states and eight countries.

Holmes, William, "Colleges Snuff Out Tobacco Sales," *The Washington Post*, May 23, 2004, p. A17.
Ironically, schools built using tobacco fortunes, such as Duke University, Wake Forest and the University of North Carolina, are restricting smoking and on-campus cigarette sales.

Perez-Pena, Richard, "A City of Quitters? In Strict New York, 11% Fewer Smokers," *The New York Times*, May 12, 2004, p. A1.
In the wake of tobacco tax increases and a ban on smoking in bars, the number of adult smokers in New York City fell 11 percent from 2002 to 2003.

Tizon, Tomas Alex, "Without Smokes, There May Be Fire," *Los Angeles Times*, June 23, 2004, p. A10.
Guards and prisoners worry that a prison smoking ban that would force inmates to quit smoking cold turkey could create mass tension and lead to an increase in violence.

Tobacco Lawsuits

Glaberson, William, "A Revenge Not So Sweet," *The New York Times*, Jan. 6, 2004, p. B1.
A jury ordered the Brown & Williamson Tobacco Corp. to pay a widow whose husband died of lung cancer $175,000 in actual damages, the first defeat in New York for a tobacco company in a suit over an individual smoker's death.

Glaberson, William, "U.S. Court Considers a Once-and-for-All Tobacco Lawsuit," *The New York Times*, Sept. 14, 2004, p. B1.
The federal appeals court in New York is considering a case that could radically reshape the national legal battle over the health effects of cigarettes and could set the stage for the largest verdict ever against the tobacco industry.

Janofsky, Michael, "Tobacco Firms Face U.S. in High-Stakes Trial," *The New York Times*, Sept. 20, 2004, p. A16.
In a trial that has the potential to put tobacco companies out of business, the government is seeking to strip tobacco companies of $280 billion that Justice Department lawyers say was earned through fraud.

Leonnig, Carol, "U.S. Trial Against Tobacco Industry Opens," *The Washington Post*, Sept. 22, 2004, p. A3.
The U.S. government accused the nation's largest tobacco companies of conspiring over the past 50 years to deceive the public about the proven dangers of smoking to protect billions of dollars in cigarette profits.

Levin, Myron, "Tobacco Giant, In a Shift, Pays Victim," *Los Angeles Times*, Oct. 2, 2003, p. A1.
Philip Morris paid $2 million to settle the case of a child injured in a fire allegedly caused by a smoldering cigarette; it is the first time the cigarette maker has agreed to pay damages in a personal-injury case.

Citing *The CQ Researcher*

Sample formats for citing these reports in a bibliography include the ones listed below. Preferred styles and formats vary, so please check with your instructor or professor.

MLA Style

Jost, Kenneth. "Rethinking the Death Penalty." The CQ Researcher 16 Nov. 2001: 945-68.

APA Style

Jost, K. (2001, November 16). Rethinking the death penalty. *The CQ Researcher, 11*, 945-968.

Chicago Style

Jost, Kenneth. "Rethinking the Death Penalty." *CQ Researcher*, November 16, 2001, 945-968.

CQ Researcher

Published by CQ Press, a division of Congressional Quarterly Inc.

thecqresearcher.com

International Law

Should U.S. policy give it more weight?

The Bush administration has been widely condemned for skirting international law in its harsh handling of enemy combatants after the war in Afghanistan and bypassing the United Nations in the invasion of Iraq. Critics at home and abroad say the policies weakened international support for U.S. actions and could endanger any U.S. service members captured in future conflicts. Liberal advocacy groups are also urging the U.S. Supreme Court to consider foreign and international law in making decisions and lower courts to be open to suits against foreign officials or multinational corporations for human rights violations abroad. Conservatives counter that foreign law has no role in U.S. constitutional issues and join with business groups in urging U.S. courts to restrict litigation for overseas offenses. Meanwhile, there is growing concern that international trade laws grant dispute-settlement tribunals powers so broad they can challenge U.S. court decisions and domestic laws that protect health, safety, the environment and workers' rights.

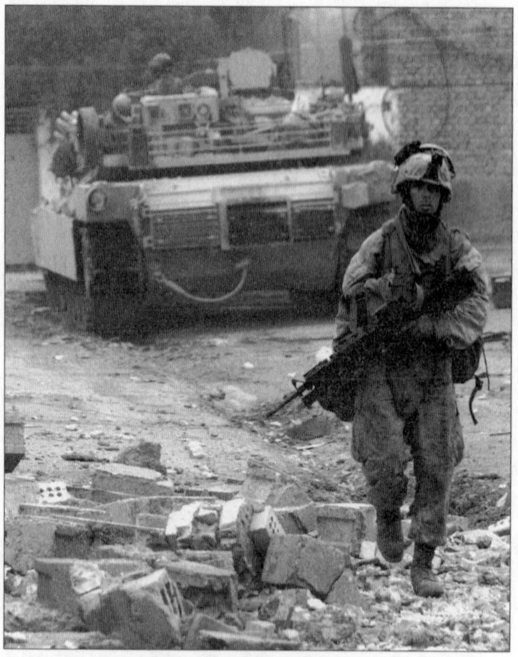

U.S. Marines patrol the battered Iraqi city of Fallujah in November 2004 after a week of combat between U.S. forces and rebels.

INSIDE THIS REPORT

The CQ Researcher • Dec. 17, 2004 • www.thecqresearcher.com
Volume 14, Number 44 • Pages 1049-1072

Cover: U.S. Marines patrol the battered Iraqi city of Fallujah in November 2004 after a week of combat between U.S. forces and rebels. (AFP/Getty Images/Patrick Baz)

THE CQ Researcher

Dec. 17, 2004
Volume 14, Number 44

MANAGING EDITOR: Thomas J. Colin
ASSISTANT MANAGING EDITOR: Kathy Koch
ASSOCIATE EDITOR: Kenneth Jost
STAFF WRITERS: Mary H. Cooper, William Triplett
CONTRIBUTING WRITERS: Sarah Glazer, David Hatch, David Hosansky, Patrick Marshall, Tom Price, Jane Tanner
DESIGN/PRODUCTION EDITOR: Olu B. Davis
ASSISTANT EDITOR: Kate Templin

CQ PRESS

A Division of Congressional Quarterly Inc.

SENIOR VICE PRESIDENT/GENERAL MANAGER: John A. Jenkins
DIRECTOR, LIBRARY PUBLISHING: Kathryn C. Suárez
DIRECTOR, EDITORIAL OPERATIONS: Ann Davies

CONGRESSIONAL QUARTERLY INC.
CHAIRMAN: Paul C. Tash
VICE CHAIRMAN: Andrew P. Corty
PRESIDENT AND PUBLISHER: Robert W. Merry

The CQ Researcher (ISSN 1056-2036) is printed on acid-free paper. Published weekly, except Jan. 2, April 9, July 2, July 9, Aug. 6, Aug. 13, Nov. 26, Dec. 24 and Dec. 31, by CQ Press, a division of Congressional Quarterly Inc. Annual subscription rates for institutions start at $625. For pricing, call 1-800-834-9020, ext. 1906. To purchase a *CQ Researcher* report in print or electronic format (PDF), visit www.cqpress.com or call 866-427-7737. A single report is $10. Bulk purchase discounts and electronic-rights licensing are also available. Periodicals postage paid at Washington, D.C., and additional mailing offices. POSTMASTER: Send address changes to *The CQ Researcher*, 1255 22nd St., N.W., Suite 400, Washington, D.C. 20037.

International Law

By Kenneth Jost

The Issues

At first glance, the U.S. government's terrorism case against Salim Ahmed Hamdan seems rock solid. For nearly five years, the Yemeni native served as driver and sometimes bodyguard for Osama bin Laden, the infamous head of the al Qaeda terrorist network.

Hamdan also delivered weapons, munitions and other supplies to al Qaeda training camps inside Afghanistan, the government says, and learned of al Qaeda's role in the 1998 bombings of U.S. embassies in Kenya and Tanzania, the 2000 bombing of the *USS Cole* and the Sept. 11, 2001, attacks on the World Trade Center and the Pentagon.

But Hamdan — now in his third year of detention at the U.S. Naval Base at Guantanamo Bay, Cuba — insists he is not a terrorist. He says he took the job as bin Laden's driver in 1996 simply to earn a living.

Hamdan says Afghan bounty hunters turned him over to U.S. forces in Afghanistan in October 2001 and that he cooperated with the Americans in every way. For his troubles, he says he was physically abused in Afghanistan and then held in solitary confinement at Guantanamo Bay since June 2002.

Such factual disputes are regularly resolved in trials based on direct testimony and circumstantial evidence offered by prosecution and defense. For more than two years, however, the government has insisted that Hamdan be tried before a special military commission with limited procedural rights and no review in the regular judicial system.

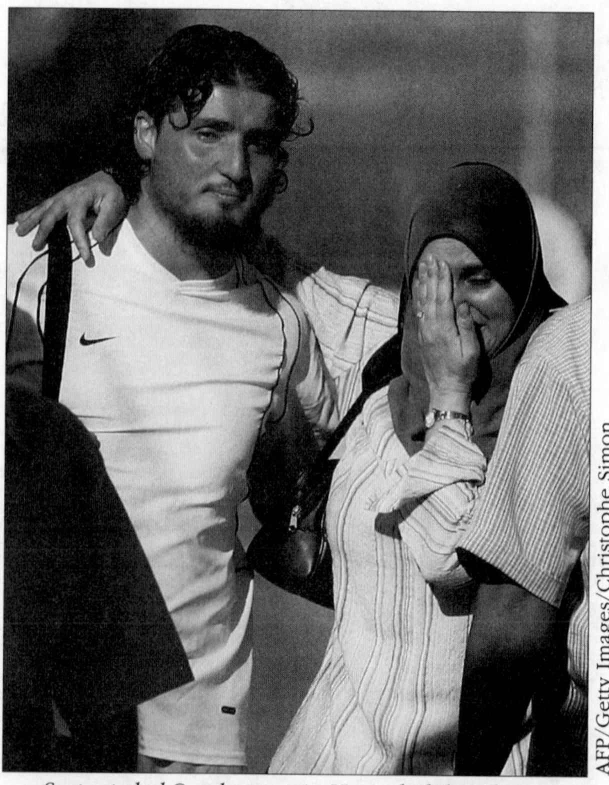

AFP/Getty Images/Christophe Simon

Suspected al Qaeda terrorist Hamed Abderrahman Ahmed, a Spanish Muslim, was released after two years in custody at the U.S. Naval Base in Guantanamo Bay, Cuba. He will be tried in Spain and faces life in prison. Critics contend the Bush administration's harsh treatment of the Guantanamo detainees defies international law.

The government suffered a major setback in the case on Nov. 28, 2004, when a federal judge in Washington, D.C., ruled the proceedings unlawful. U.S. District Judge James Robertson said the military commissions not only violated the Uniform Code of Military Justice (UCMJ) but also international law — specifically, the Geneva Conventions — by denying Hamdan prisoner-of-war status without a prior hearing to decide the question.

"The government must convene a competent tribunal . . . and seek a specific determination as to Hamdan's status under the Geneva Conventions," Robertson wrote in the 45-page ruling. "Until or unless such a tribunal decides otherwise, Hamdan has, and must be accorded, the full protections of a prisoner of war." [1]

Robertson's ruling represents the latest and perhaps the highest-profile example of the growing role of international law in legal disputes within the United States — and the growing controversy over that role. An increasing number of civil plaintiffs or criminal defendants are basing claims or defenses on international law, including — but not limited to — provisions of treaties ratified by the United States.

In recent cases, for example, the Supreme Court has been asked to look to decisions by international and foreign courts to determine the constitutionality of capital punishment of juvenile offenders or state anti-sodomy laws. The justices are also being asked to order a new hearing for a Mexican national facing execution in Texas on the ground that he was not allowed to see a Mexican consul before trial as required by an international treaty signed — and actively pushed — by the United States.

Meanwhile, lower federal courts have been asked to award damages to foreign plaintiffs for human rights violations committed overseas by foreign government officials or, in some cases, big multinational corporations. A Supreme Court ruling in June 2004 limited but did not completely bar such suits brought under a 1789 law, the Alien Tort Statute.

International law is a hard-to-grasp concept that inspires idealistic hopes for world peace among supporters and fears of loss of national sovereignty among skeptics. Its origins lie in what is called "customary international law" — practices such as diplomatic immunity or freedom of the seas that came to be accepted as binding by nation-states despite the lack of any international court or enforcement bodies.

U.S. Businesses Sued for Rights Abuses Overseas

Foreign plaintiffs are using the federal Alien Tort Statute to try to win damages from U.S. and other multinational corporations for their roles in alleged human rights abuses in countries around the world. None of the plaintiffs has won a judgment since the first case was filed against Unocal Corp. in 1995. But business groups say the suits represent a major financial threat to companies operating overseas. Here are summaries of a few of the major cases:

Name of Case Issues. *Status*	(Citation/Case Number)
Aguinda v. Texaco, Inc. Ecuadorians sued Texaco for environmental damage attributed to an oil pipeline leak. *Dismissed on ground suit should be tried in Ecuador.*	303 F.3d 470 (2d Cir. 2002)
In re South African Apartheid Litigation Consolidated cases by South African citizens against more than 100, mostly U.S.-based, corporations seeking more than $200 billion in damages for alleged collaboration in murder, torture, forced relocation and other abuses under former apartheid policies. *Dismissed on ground complaints did not sufficiently allege violations of international law.*	MDL 1499 (S.D.N.Y. 2004)
Bano v. Union Carbide Corp. Victims of 1984 toxic gas disaster at Bhopal, India, chemical plant sued in U.S. court in 1999, for damages beyond a settlement approved in Indian court in 1991. *Alien Tort Statute claims dismissed; environmental claims reinstated.*	273 F.3d 120 (2d Cir. 2001)
Doe v. Exxon Mobil Corp. Eleven Indonesian villagers in northern region of Aceh, Sumatra, claim Exxon Mobil responsible for human rights abuses by military unit assigned to guard facilities. *Pending on defendants' motion to dismiss, supported by U.S. government.*	01-CV-1357 (D.D.C.)
Doe v. Unocal Corp. Plaintiffs filed parallel federal, state court suits claiming Unocal is liable for human rights abuses by Myanmar military in conjunction with construction of gas pipeline. *Unocal agreed to settle the case in December 2004 for a still-to-be negotiated amount.*	BC 237-980 (Los Angeles County Superior Court)
Sarei v. Rio Tinto PLC Plaintiffs charged a British-based company with destruction of a Papua New Guinea (PNG) rain forest as a result of copper-mining operations and with PNG government collaboration to suppress a civilian uprising against reopening of the mine. *Dismissed under "political question doctrine."*	221 F. Supp. 2d 1116 (C.D. Cal. 2002)
Sinaltrainal v. Coca-Cola Co. A Colombian trade union claims Coca-Cola hired paramilitary units to terrorize and murder trade union organizers at bottling plants in Colombia. *Pending trial.*	01-CV-03208 (S.D. Fla.)
Wiwa v. Royal Dutch Petroleum Co. Current or former Nigerians claim Royal Dutch Shell conspired with military government to unlawfully suppress Nigerian opposition movement. *Pending after appeal court reversed lower court's decision that case should be tried in Nigeria.*	226 F.3d 88 (2d Circ. 2000)

Sources: Center for Constitutional Rights; Institute for International Economics; International Labor Rights Fund

Historically, the United States has favored and promoted an expanded scope of international law — through bilateral and multilateral treaties and creation of international forums, including the United Nations.

"International law has been an important vehicle for the United States to advance its interests and values and to mobilize international support for actions it wants to pursue," says Jane Stromseth, who teaches international law at Georgetown University Law Center in Washington.

Conservatives in the United States have often resisted these efforts — for example, by blocking U.S. participation in the League of Nations after World

War I and periodically complaining about loss of U.S. sovereignty because of various international treaties or actions of the United Nations. More recently, consumer, environmental and labor groups have charged that the World Trade Organization (WTO) infringes U.S. sovereignty by establishing free-trade rules that limit the ability to support domestic producers or set strict environmental or consumer protection standards. (*See sidebar, p. 1056.*)

The Bush administration has drawn waves of criticism for policies that critics say amount to defiance of or contempt for international law, including the decision to deny POW status to detainees at Guantanamo Bay. In explaining the decision to go to war against Iraq, Bush at times has advocated a policy of "preventive" or "pre-emptive" war that critics say violates the U.N. Charter's provisions on the use of military force. (*See "At Issue," p. 1065.*)

The administration also has strongly opposed U.S. participation in the International Criminal Court (ICC), the permanent U.N. war crimes tribunal established in 2002 under terms of a 1998 treaty signed by 120 countries. Bush in 2002 revoked the U.S. signature to the treaty, fearing that American service members would be subject to prosecution before the tribunal. The administration insists that countries receiving American military aid agree to shield U.S. service members from prosecution before the tribunal.

"This administration has pursued more of a line that says if the rules don't suit us, we'll ignore them," says Anne-Marie Slaughter, dean of the Woodrow Wilson School of Public and International Affairs at Princeton University in New Jersey. "The view has been that we can afford to do that."

For now, Hamdan's lawyers are asking the Supreme Court to review his case quickly in hopes of an early resolution of the rules for military commissions at Guantanamo. The government says the case should follow normal procedure and go first to the U.S. Court of Appeals for the District of Columbia. The justices are expected to decide how to handle the case in January 2005.

AFP/Getty Images/Stan Honda

U.N. Secretary-General Kofi Annan challenged President Bush's doctrine of "pre-emptive, unilateral, military force" in attacking Iraq. "From our point of view and from the [U.N.] Charter point of view, it was illegal," he said.

As the administration continues to fend off criticisms of its policies, and U.S. courts continue to deal with a variety of international-law issues, here are some of the major questions being debated:

Should the United States give more weight to international law in foreign policy?

Barely two weeks after the 9/11 terrorist attacks, the Bush administration asked the United Nations Security Council to stiffen the international community's stand against terrorism. Unanimously and with unusual speed, the council approved a resolution requiring nations to seek to suppress terrorists and terrorist organizations by, among other things, freezing their assets, denying them safe haven and preventing movement across borders. "We are very encouraged by the Security Council's strong support and rapid, unanimous action," U.S. Delegate John Negroponte declared. [2]

Two years later, however, the administration bypassed the Security Council when it launched the U.S.-led invasion of Iraq. In his message to Congress on March 19, 2003, President Bush sought to justify the war as a means "to bring Iraq into compliance with its obligations" under Security Council resolutions. But the administration started the war without council approval because it could not muster the necessary nine votes in the 15-member council nor would it have been able to avert a possible veto from France and Russia — two of the five permanent members with veto power over resolutions. [3]

Administration officials and their supporters defend the invasion in terms of international law in part by claiming a right of self-defense under the United Nations Charter for either an actual attack or an "imminent threat" of attack. "The right to use force pre-emptively is not a novel concept in international law or in the history of the United States," says William Howard Taft IV, the State Department's legal adviser.

Critics disagree with the administration's so-called pre-emptive war doctrine, both as theory and in practice. And U.N. Secretary-General Kofi Annan told the BBC unequivocally that he considers the war in Iraq was not in conformity with the U.N. Charter. Asked pointedly about its legality, he said, "From our point of view and from the charter point of view it was illegal." [4]

"It is controversial that a country can act to prevent states from acquiring certain weapons in the future," says Stromseth, referring to the administration's claimed rationale to find and destroy Iraq's alleged weapons of mass destruction. The disputes over the legality of the invasion, she adds, left many countries reluctant to commit troops to the war or help support the post-conflict reconstruction.

Critics also say the administration weakened international support for its policies by skirting international law with its treatment of detainees after the Afghanistan war and prisoners captured in the Iraq war. "We have always been the strongest proponent of the Geneva Conventions," says Slaughter. "Effectively, we just said none of those rules applies here," leaving the impression "that this administration is inventing its own rules."

The administration, however, insists that the Geneva Conventions are out of date — written to govern the treatment of uniformed soldiers of nation-states, not clandestine members of terrorist networks. "This is a new circumstance that we've never seen before," says John Yoo, a law professor at the University of California, Berkeley, who helped devise the legal rationale for the administration's policies while serving as deputy director of the Justice Department's Office of Legal Counsel. "The last thing you would do is to say we ought to stay with the same categories and rules that we had on Sept. 10 — because those failed."

Even sympathetic international-law experts acknowledge misgivings with the administration's stances. "The U.S. legal case didn't quite make it, but I am strongly in favor of the invasion," says John Murphy, a law professor at Villanova University in Pennsylvania. "It pains me to say that, as an international lawyer."

The United States was forced to take action to oust Iraqi President Saddam Hussein because of obstructionism by France and Russia at the Security Council, Murphy says. "When you have . . . an ally actively undermining the efforts of the Security Council to require Saddam Hussein to comply with all the obligations, . . . and you have a person who's as evil as he was, it was necessary to remove him," Murphy says.

But Slaughter says the United States risks longer-term costs to foreign policy interests by acting unilaterally instead of following international law. "It's a way of reassuring other nations that we are not going to be a rogue elephant, that we're not simply going to crash around the international system and do what we want," she says. "It's important that other nations be reassured because otherwise they have every reason to start balancing against us."

Yoo counters that critics misunderstand international law, which he says depends as much on what nations do as what treaties they sign. "Some people . . . think nations cannot use force unless they're under threat of imminent attack or the U.N. Security Council authorizes it," he says. "Anyone who looks at the practice of states since 1945 can see that that's not the practice states have followed."

Slaughter and Stromseth see some need to change international law in the post-9/11 era. "There is scope for a new understanding of the right of self-defense against non-state actors," Stromseth says. Slaughter says some of the provisions of the Geneva Conventions do not apply in conflicts with a non-state enemy.

But they and others say the United States would be better served by seeking international agreement on any changes instead of acting on its own. "When we end up doing something unilaterally, we pay the price somewhere else," says Harold Hongju Koh, dean of Yale Law School and the State Department's human rights chief under President Bill Clinton. "We strain our alliance and we end up having trouble in other areas of our foreign policy."

Should the Supreme Court consider international and foreign law in making decisions?

Lawyers seeking to bar the execution of juvenile offenders in the United States often cite the prohibition against the practice by international treaty and by national law or practice in all but four other countries. * But when a lawyer for the state of Missouri was asked during recent Supreme Court arguments whether the justices should take international or foreign law into account in deciding the issue, he bluntly said no.

"That's not for this court to decide," Missouri state solicitor James Layton said during the Oct. 13 argument in a case brought by death row inmate Christopher Simmons. "Congress should consider that. The legislatures should consider that. It's an important consideration, but it is not a consideration under the Eighth Amendment." [5]

* The countries are: Iran, Saudi Arabia, Nigeria and Congo, according to Amnesty International.

The arguments provided the latest airing of an issue that has become a flash point between conservatives and liberals and some moderates both on and off the court. Liberal advocacy groups want the court to look to international and foreign law for possible guidance on some constitutional issues. "We can and, I believe, should look to international law as a way of informing our own judgments about our laws and our policies," says Virginia Sloan, executive director of the Constitution Project, a bipartisan group in Washington that filed a brief in support of Simmons' plea to the Supreme Court.

Conservatives strongly object, saying that international law has no place in interpretation of the U.S. laws and constitutional provisions. "The [Supreme Court's] limited role is to interpret the Constitution," Yoo says. "It's not to ask other countries what our Constitution means or what their constitution means."

AFP/Getty Images/Joyce Nalchayan

Defense Secretary Donald Rumsfeld and Chairman of the Joint Chiefs Gen. Richard Myers have maintained that holding the Guantanamo Bay detainees without trial does not violate the Geneva Conventions.

The court itself has cited international law in two recent, high-profile decisions. When the court in 2002 prohibited execution of mentally retarded offenders, Justice John Paul Stevens noted in a footnote that "within the world community" the practice was "overwhelmingly disapproved." A year later, Justice Anthony M. Kennedy pointed to the invalidation of anti-sodomy laws by the European Court of Human Rights as a factor in the decision to declare laws banning gay sex unconstitutional in the United States as well. [6]

At least three other justices have commented favorably in public speeches about the use of international law: Sandra Day O'Connor, like Kennedy a moderate conservative, and liberals Ruth Bader Ginsburg and Stephen G. Breyer. On the other hand, Antonin Scalia, the high court's most outspoken conservative, has strongly criticized the practice.

Scalia complained about the citation of international law in his dissents in the earlier capital punishment and gay sex cases. He also sharply questioned Simmons' lawyer on the practice in the pending death penalty case. "It is my view that modern, foreign legal material can never be relevant to any interpretation of, that is to say, to the meaning of the U.S. Constitution," Scalia declared in a speech to the American Society of International Law in April 2004. [7]

Despite the sharp debate, some observers on both sides say the practical effect of the practice is minimal. "You get the sense that it's almost ornamental," Yoo says.

Likewise, Louis Michael Seidman, a liberal constitutional law expert at Georgetown University Law Center, doesn't think the citations "amount to much."

Still, conservative academics and advocacy groups are mounting a full-bore attack on the practice. "The idea that it makes one whit of a difference that many other countries do not execute people who are 16 or 17 makes no sense to me," says Richard Samp, chief counsel of the conservative Washington Legal Foundation. "World opinion is not what gives the authority to federal judges. It is the Constitution."

Speaking to a meeting of the conservative Federalist Society in Washington in November 2004, Pepperdine Law School Professor Roger Alford called the practice "inherently undemocratic" and "prone to judicial hegemony."

Michael Ramsey, a professor at the University of San Diego School of Law, agreed. "No one has adopted a principled theory for deciding when to look at foreign practices other than picking the ones they like," he said. "The use of international practices expressly adopts the view of courts as policy makers."

Liberal academics insist that the practice is far from new, but dates actually from the earliest days of the United States. "The earliest justices were all former diplomats," Koh says. "There was no federal law, only state law and international law."

International-law advocates also liken the practice to judicial decision-making within the United States. "Knowing how a very distinguished judge [in another country] has thought about the issue is no more troubling than a New Jersey judge considering how a California judge has ruled on the issue," Slaughter says.

"The fear among conservatives is that we'll somehow fall prey to some strange, exotic cultural practice from somewhere else," adds Richard Wilson, who directs an international human rights clinic at American University's law school in Washington. "There's very little likelihood that that will happen, and there's a possibility that we may learn something."

Do Trade Treaties Challenge U.S. Authority?

The tiny Caribbean nation of Antigua and Barbuda recently taught the United States a potentially costly lesson in the power of international law. It won a ruling from the World Trade Organization (WTO) in November 2004 that two U.S. laws prohibiting Internet gambling — along with four similar state laws — violate a global agreement liberalizing trade in services. Antiqua and Barbuda had complained before the WTO that its offshore gambling industry declined more than 50 percent after the United States cracked down on Internet gambling.

The Bush administration is appealing the ruling, arguing that states and the federal government can regulate gambling under their longstanding authority to protect public morals and public order. But legal scholars say the Antigua decision could encourage other countries to challenge any law restricting gambling, including gambling monopolies run by state lotteries and Indian tribes and limits on the number of slot machines or casinos allowed in a state.

"If Antiqua can challenge federal and state laws related to Internet gambling, then other countries can challenge state laws related to bricks-and-mortar gambling," says Georgetown University law Professor Robert K. Stumberg. Moreover, he adds, "lots and lots of state laws" could conceivably be seen as restraints of trade and are now vulnerable to challenges from overseas corporations.

Antigua's WTO triumph underscores growing concern that international trade laws grant dispute-settlement tribunals broad, new powers that enable them to challenge the legality of a variety of federal, state and local laws both here and abroad, and, in at least two cases, have even challenged U.S. court decisions.

"There are grave implications here," California Supreme Court Chief Justice Ronald M. George said. "It's rather shocking that the highest courts of the state and federal governments could have their judgments circumvented by these tribunals." [1]

The controversial tribunals have been established by the WTO, created in 1995 to regulate global trade, and the North American Free Trade Agreement (NAFTA), adopted in 1994 to open up trade between Canada, Mexico and the United States. But because the trade arbitration panels give top priority to the free flow of goods and services above all other considerations, critics say they can force local, state and federal governments to either eliminate or weaken domestic laws that protect health, safety, the environment and worker rights.

WTO rulings that have raised concerns include cases in which countries have challenged U.S. laws designed to protect dolphins and sea turtles; Clean Air Act rules requiring clean-burning gasoline; and regulations to prevent the importation of invasive species into the United States. For its part, the United States has challenged or threatened to challenge, among other things, Japan's automobile efficiency and emission policies designed to meet an international anti-global warming treaty and a European Union ban on the sale of furs from animals caught with steel jaw leg traps.

Global trade advocates point out that a WTO tribunal cannot actually overturn or nullify a domestic law. The government whose law is declared a barrier to trade can either change the offending law or keep it on the books. But by retaining the law, the government must pay damages, which can range in the hundreds of millions of dollars. Most governments choose to change their laws rather than pay the damages. Often, say critics of the current global trade regime, the mere threat of a WTO challenge discourages lawmakers from even proposing certain environmental, safety or workers'-rights laws.

Moreover, under a little-known provision of NAFTA, called Chapter 11, broad, new powers are granted to corporations that some legal scholars and critics say redefine property rights in a way that goes far beyond the rights recognized by U.S. courts or enjoyed by U.S. companies. In fact, the U.S. Congress has repeatedly rejected the broader definition of property rights allowed under the new NAFTA provision. [2]

Under Chapter 11, any foreign corporation that might potentially lose money due to a government action, such as a local zoning law or a state court decision, may sue the national government for damages. The provision ostensibly was included to protect international investors from having their property expropriated by foreign governments, as Mexico did in 1938 when it nationalized its oil industry.

However, under the NAFTA provision corporations are claiming damages even though no actual property has been seized, but when the company perceives that a government action could *potentially* cut into a portion of its future profits. Already, more than 20 Chapter 11 cases have been filed, demanding almost $14 billion from U.S., Canadian and Mexican taxpayers as compensation for corporate "losses" that allegedly occurred due to local land-use decisions, environmental and public health policies, and even adverse court rulings. (American companies are not allowed to file such cases in U.S. courts.) [3]

For instance, in 1999 the Canadian methanol manufacturer Methanex Corp. sued the United States, demanding $970 million in damages from U.S. taxpayers to compensate the company's anticipated loss of profits due to California's ban on the use of the gasoline additive methyl tertiary butyl ether (MTBE),

Should U.S. courts hear suits for human rights violations abroad?

The accounts in two federal court suits depict widespread abuses of Burmese workers by the Myanmar military during the construction of a natural gas pipeline in the Southeast Asian country — abuses ranging from forced labor and torture to rape and even killings. The suits' principal target is not Myanmar's military junta, however, but the Unocal Corp., the giant California-based, multinational oil and gas company.

The suits, filed under an obscure 18th-century U.S. law alternately called the a potentially carcinogenic chemical that was leaking into groundwater. Despite the environmental damage, Methanex claimed California's ban was an unfair restraint of trade under NAFTA. The case is still pending. [4]

In two unprecedented Chapter 11 cases foreign corporations that lost cases in U.S. domestic courts have taken those cases to be "reheard" under NAFTA's Chapter 11 provision. One case challenged the concept of sovereign immunity involving a contract dispute with the City of Boston, and the other challenged the rules of civil procedure, the jury system and a damage award in a Mississippi state court contract dispute. [5]

Having an international tribunal reviewing U.S. court judgments amounts to "the biggest threat to United States judicial independence that no one has heard of, and even fewer people understand," said Georgetown University law Professor John D. Echeverria. [6]

Recently, the Conference of Chief Justices, the National Association of State Attorneys General, the National League of Cities and the National Conference of State Legislatures have criticized the Chapter 11 provisions for impinging on state and court authorities.

University of Chicago law Professor Alan O. Sykes says concerns about NAFTA's two Chapter 11 challenges of U.S. court decisions are largely a tempest in a teapot — at least so far. "It could turn out to be a bigger deal down the road, but so far no great damage has been done by these cases." Technically, he points out, trade tribunals cannot overturn a U.S. court decision; they can only hold a state liable for damages if the tribunal finds the court's decision discriminated against a foreign corporation.

With regard to Chapter 11 decisions redefining corporate property rights, Sykes says, the NAFTA governments have issued a clarification that the provision was not meant to do that. "My feeling is that the arbiters have gotten the message that their decisions have gone too far. They've figured out which end is up, and are trying not to create all sorts of mess."

Critics of the global trading system particularly chafe at the secretiveness and lack of accountability of the often-anonymous three-judge panels that make WTO and NAFTA decisions. "Hidden beneath the 'free trade' cover was an entire, anti-democratic governance system under which policies affecting our daily lives in innumerable ways are decided out of our sight or control," says a Public Citizen assessment of NAFTA. [7]

Indeed, the Methanex case was heard by a three-judge panel in closed-door proceedings, and no one from the California state government or the environmental and consumer-protection groups that had fought for the MTBE ban were notified of the hearings, nor were they allowed to file briefs supporting the measure.

But Sykes dismisses charges that the international trade regime threatens democracy. "Democratically elected leaders signed these treaties because they felt it was in their national interest," he says. "Any time you agree to something under international law, you restrict a country's freedom of action." In exchange, the United States "gets a lot out of these treaties. We get less-expensive imported goods, lower inflation, access to foreign markets and protection for intellectual property abroad."

However, Georgetown's Stumberg says the secrecy is part of a pattern in which a growing number of "hot-button issues" that conservatives have long sought unsuccessfully in Congress and the U.S. courts — such as tort reform, "regulatory takings" reform, sovereign immunity, curtailment of states' regulatory powers and local permitting authority — are now being debated in inaccessible international venues.

"All the kinds of things that investors and governments fight about in U.S. courts are migrating over to these international forums," says Stumberg, adding that he did not think the migration was "by accident."

Indeed, NAFTA's architects knew exactly what they were doing when they wrote Chapter 11, contends Daniel Price, a Washington lawyer who helped to write the provisions. "The parties did not stumble into this. This was a carefully crafted definition. NAFTA checks the excesses of unilateral sovereignty." [8]

---

[1] Quoted in Adam Liptak, "Review of U.S. Rulings by Nafta Tribunals Stirs Worries," *The New York Times*, April 18, 2004, Sec. 1, p. 20.

[2] Under U.S. law, a company can claim damages from a "regulatory taking" only if its actual property has been rendered almost 100 percent useless because of a government action. But the international trade panels are interpreting Chapter 11 to mean that a company's property has been "taken" if a small percentage of its estimated future profits has been impacted. The U.S. government is including Chapter 11 powers in other bilateral and regional trade agreements currently being negotiated, and would eventually like to expand the powers to cover the entire Western Hemisphere under the proposed Free Trade Agreement of the Americas.

[3] "The Ten Year Track Record of the North American Free Trade Agreement: Undermining Sovereignty and Democracy," Public Citizen, 2004.

[4] See William Greider, "The Right and US Trade Law: Invalidating the 20th Century," *The Nation*, Oct. 15, 2001.

[5] The cases are *Loewen v. United States* (Mississippi) and *Mondev International Ltd. v. United States* (Massachusetts).

[6] Greider, *op. cit.*

[7] Public Citizen, *op. cit.*

[8] Greider, *op. cit.*

Alien Tort Claims Act or Alien Tort Statute, seek millions of dollars in damages from Unocal on the theory that the company knowingly aided the enslavement and mistreatment of Burmese workers by the Myanmar military. Unocal denied wrongdoing, but after seeking to have the suits dismissed on legal grounds agreed with the plaintiffs' lawyers in December 2004 to settle the case by paying a still-to-be-negotiated amount for compensation and programs to improve living conditions in the region. [8]

The Unocal cases are the furthest advanced pending suits among dozens filed against current or former foreign government officials or multinational corporations since 1980, when a federal appeals court first opened the door to such suits. The so-called *Filártiga* decision by the New York-based 2nd U.S. Circuit Court of Appeals allowed a Paraguayan physician to sue a former Paraguayan police official for the torture death of his son. [9]

Human rights groups say the suits serve a valuable purpose by enlisting U.S. courts in the cause of promoting compliance with international law. "If we believe in a system of international law, it has to apply here," says Jennifer Green, a senior staff attorney with the New York-based Center of Constitutional Rights, which represents plaintiffs in the Unocal case. "It's necessary if we are committed to human rights law and the rule of universal standards."

But conservative groups and business lobbies say such suits threaten U.S. business and foreign policy interests and typically are out of place in U.S. courts. "The idea that somehow we owe it to the international human rights community to open up our courts to any and all violations of human rights that have occurred around the world is absurd," says the Washington Legal Foundation's Samp.

The dispute turns in part on the meaning of the elliptically phrased statute, contained in the original Judiciary Act of 1789. The law states that federal courts "shall have original jurisdiction of any civil action by an alien for a tort only, committed in violation of the law of nations or a treaty of the United States." Human rights groups say the statute broadly recognizes suits for violations of international law, while conservative and business groups say Congress must specifically authorize any such legal actions.

The Supreme Court split the difference between those views in June 2004 in its first ruling on the law since *Filártiga.* Six justices joined a majority opinion in *Sosa v. Alvarez-Machain* that limited use of the act to international-law violations recognized in the 18th century, such as piracy, or to other violations of norms "accepted by the civilized world and defined with . . . specificity." In a separate opinion for three members of the court, Justice Scalia said he would have limited the acts to suits specifically authorized by Congress. [10]

Human rights groups claimed the decision as a victory. The ruling "endorsed the standard used in the *Filártiga* case," Green says. Business groups took some comfort from restrictive language in the decision, but voiced disappointment that the majority left lower courts with some discretion to recognize new suits. "It leaves wiggle room," Samp says.

Business groups and business-oriented experts complain that suits open multinational corporations to the danger of huge damage awards or costly settlements. "Whenever there exists a deep-pocket defendant, there necessarily exist incentives to bring claims 'on spec' that involve both bold conjectures about facts and ambitious claims about unwritten law," says Paul Stephan, an international business expert at the University of Virginia School of Law in Charlottesville. One recent study found that more than 50 multinational corporations are defendants in alien tort suits with claims exceeding $200 billion. [11]

"I would hope that businesses in general don't subscribe to the theory that these gross human rights violations are a normal part of doing business," counters Green. "We're talking about things that are well defined in international law: torture, genocide. If they engage in those practices, they can expect to be hauled into court."

Critics also say the law can put U.S. courts at odds with the government's diplomatic stance toward other countries. "This kind of litigation has got to be limited because otherwise federal courts are going to be interfering with foreign policy of the executive branches," says former Justice Department official Yoo.

Koh, the State Department's human rights chief for three years, calls that argument "a red herring," arguing that the government "is always free to file a brief, and the court should take that into account." In the Unocal suit, Koh notes that the United States has had "a policy of wholesale condemnation" of the Myanmar government for three administrations. ■

BACKGROUND

'The Law of Nations'

The United States has professed allegiance to international law since its founding, championed international law throughout its history and played the major role in building the superstructure of international law institutions established since the end of World War II. Even when the United States flexed its diplomatic, economic or military muscle, it has only rarely challenged the idea that it was bound, like all countries, to follow the "law of nations." [12]

The authors of the Declaration of Independence in 1776 felt obliged by "a decent respect to the opinions of mankind" to set forth the causes for breaking away from Britain. They proceeded to lay out a detailed indictment of British rule to be judged by "a candid world." Two decades later, with a new nation and a new Constitution, the Supreme Court in 1793 explicitly recognized the applicability of international law. "The United States, by taking a place among the nations of the earth, [became] amenable to the law of nations," Chief Justice John Jay wrote. [13]

Later, as secretary of State, Jay made the first important U.S. contribution to international law by negotiating a treaty with Britain that called for the use of

Continued on p. 1060

Chronology

1945-1970s

United Nations founded under U.S. leadership, but peacekeeping machinery paralyzed by Cold War rivalry with Soviet Union.

1945
U.N. Charter formally approved by 51 countries; creates Security Council as peacekeeping body, with U.S., Soviet Union among five nations with veto power; also establishes International Court of Justice (World Court).

1947
General Agreement on Tariffs and Trade (GATT) binds U.S., other signatories to free-trade rules; superseded by World Trade Organization in 1995.

1949
Geneva Conventions codify rules on treatment of prisoners of war, civilians.

1977
Geneva Conventions expanded to cover civil war, liberation conflicts.

1980s-1990s

Terrorist attacks on U.S. citizens, facilities here and abroad.

1980
Federal appeals court in *Filártiga* case allows suit under Alien Tort Statute by Paraguayan dissident against Paraguayan police inspector for torture-murder of son; ruling revives use of previously obscure 1789 provision.

1983
U.S. invades Grenada, saying action necessary to protect U.S. citizens; invasion condemned by U.N. General Assembly.

1984-1986
World Court in 1984 backs jurisdiction over suit by Nicaragua claiming U.S. support for contras violates international law; Reagan administration next year terminates U.S. agreement to compulsory jurisdiction; court rules against U.S. in 1986.

1989
U.S. invades Panama, claiming right of self-defense; invasion later condemned by U.N. General Assembly, Organization of American States.

1993
Bombing of World Trade Center, later linked to al Qaeda; Clinton administration initiates criminal prosecutions of perpetrators.

1995
U.S. backs special international war crime tribunals for former Yugoslavia, Rwanda.

1996
Burmese citizens are first to use Alien Tort Statute to sue corporate defendant for rights abuses abroad.

1997
Kyoto Protocol calls on developed nations to reduce "greenhouse gas" emissions to reduce global warming.

1998
U.S. signs treaty to create permanent International Criminal Court to try war crimes cases, but President Bill Clinton does not submit it for ratification. . . . Bombing of U.S. embassies in Kenya, Tanzania, later linked to al Qaeda.

2000-Present

Bush administration often differs with other countries, world opinion on international-law issues.

2001
President Bush rejects Kyoto Protocol . . . Terrorist attacks on World Trade Center and Pentagon by al Qaeda operatives on Sept. 11 leave nearly 3,000 people dead; U.N. Security Council passes U.S.-backed anti-terrorism resolution on Sept. 28. . . . U.S. leads international coalition to oust Taliban regime in Afghanistan for harboring al Qaeda; hundreds of detainees later transported to Guantanamo Bay Naval Base in Cuba.

2002
Bush revokes U.S. signature on International Criminal Court treaty . . . Supreme Court cites international practice in barring execution of mentally retarded offenders. . . .

2003
President Bush, bypassing U.N. Security Council, launches U.S-led invasion of Iraq in March. . . . Supreme Court in June cites ruling by European Court of Human Rights in striking down state anti-sodomy laws. . . .

2004
Supreme Court on June 28 rejects Bush administration's effort to bar court challenges by Guantanamo detainees; in separate decision next day, justices narrow scope of cases under Alien Tort Statute. . . . Justices in October consider plea to bar execution of juvenile offenders; decision due by June 2005. . . . Federal judge in November says military violating Geneva Conventions by failure to give Guantanamo detainees hearing on POW status. . . . High-level U.N. panel in November rejects doctrine of "preventive" use of force except when authorized by Security Council; U.S. disagrees.

Continued from p. 1058

arbitration to resolve remaining Revolutionary War disputes. The Jay Treaty settled most issues between the two countries but provided that three disputes would be resolved by "commissions" composed of one or two members appointed by each party and a third or fifth member chosen by agreement or lot. The two countries also resorted to arbitration after the end of the War of 1812 and again after the Civil War, when the United States in the so-called *Alabama Claims* arbitration successfully sought damages from Britain for building warships for the Confederacy while professing neutrality. [14]

The United States claimed international law on its side in each of its three major international wars of the 19th century. The United States launched the War of 1812 by claiming that Britain — then at war with Napoleonic France — was violating its rights of neutral shipping by seizing U.S. ships and impressing American sailors along with any captured British subjects. President James K. Polk launched the U.S.-Mexican War in 1845 by depicting Mexico's land claims as a violation of the treaty ending the war of Texan independence. And the United States claimed to be backing Cuba's independence from its colonial ruler when it declared war against Spain in 1898. Territorial expansion may have been the main motive in 1845 and economic imperialism in 1898, but the cloak of international law was thrown over both conflicts.

In the aftermath of the Spanish-American War, the Supreme Court once again declared the country's commitment to international law, this time in a dispute arising from the seizure of two Spanish fishing boats off the Cuban coast. The owners of the boats sued to recover damages after the ships and their cargo had been sold as prizes of war. They claimed that international law exempted fishing vessels from capture during war. "International law is part of our law," the Supreme Court declared in its ruling in the boat owners' favor. The court noted that in imposing the blockade of Cuba, President William McKinley had instructed the Navy to follow "the law of nations applicable in such cases." [15]

AFP/Getty Images/ Michael Porro

The International Court of Justice, or World Court, cannot require participation or enforce its decisions. Judges arrive at the beginning of hearings to discuss Israel's controversial wall in the Occupied Territories.

The United States was primed to enter World War I by Germany's alleged violations of neutral shipping rights with its submarine warfare against U.S. passenger and freight-carrying vessels. In his message asking Congress to declare war against Germany in 1917, President Woodrow Wilson enlarged U.S. goals into "a crusade to make the world safe for democracy." With the war won, Wilson sought to create a new international body that would protect nations against foreign aggression and ensure worldwide peace. The League of Nations failed in both goals, in part because the United States declined to join and in part because its charter included no enforcement powers.

As the world's sole superpower after World War II, the United States set out to establish a new and more effective international body — the United Nations. In one crucial change from the League of Nations, the U.N. Charter created an enforcement tribunal: the Security Council.

The council — which now has 15 members — was given authority to determine the existence of a threat to the peace or an act of aggression and to authorize economic sanctions or military action in response. Security Council resolutions are theoretically binding on all member states. But in a bow to geopolitical realities, the five major World War II victors — the United States, Britain, France, the Soviet Union and China — were each given veto power over any council action. "We set about establishing a set of rules that would take power realities into account but would nevertheless establish rules that everyone would comply with," says Princeton University's Slaughter. [16]

The Rule of Law

The Cold War rivalry between the United States and the Soviet Union largely paralyzed the United Nations' peacekeeping machinery whenever the two nations clashed because both had veto power in the Security Council. Meanwhile, the body of international law was growing through the operations of U.N. agencies and U.N.-supported treaty-making conferences.

The United States sometimes supported and sometimes resisted the growing web of international laws.

Only once during the Cold War did the U.N. Security Council authorize military action against the wishes of one of the two rival superpowers. That came in 1950 when communist North Korea invaded the pro-Western South Korea, and the Soviet Union boycotted the Security Council meeting called to consider the crisis. Without a Soviet veto, the council authorized the United States to lead a multinational force to repel the invasion.

Over the next 40 years, the Security Council frequently voted to dispatch "peacekeeping" forces to trouble spots: the Suez Canal in 1956, Congo in1960, the Kashmir region along the India-Pakistan border in 1965. But the council authorized military intervention only in 1990 — after the end of the Cold War — when it approved a resolution for a U.S.-led force to repel Iraq's invasion of Kuwait.

In the meantime, the laws of war had been consolidated and expanded in two major diplomatic conferences, both times with strong backing from the United States. The four Geneva Conventions — signed on Aug. 12, 1949 — codified rules for treatment of combatants and prisoners of war and extended protections to civilians. To distinguish combatants from civilians, troops are required to wear uniforms and carry arms openly. Combatants who follow the guidelines enjoy various protections, including requirements for humane treatment and limits on interrogation if held as POWs. The fourth convention bars attacks on civilians or the use of civilians as hostages. Two additional protocols signed in 1977 extended the rules to wars of self-determination and other internal conflicts.

The U.N. Charter also established the International Court of Justice (the ICJ or, colloquially, the World Court) as a successor to a comparable tribunal under the League of Nations. The 15-member court, which sits in The Hague, Netherlands, "has not lived up to hopes of many of its early supporters," according to the authors of a leading textbook. [17]

The court has jurisdiction only over countries, not individuals, and cannot require participation or enforce its decisions. In 1980, for example, Iran refused to comply with the court's judgment to release U.S. hostages.

The United States similarly refused to abide by the court's 1986 decision that its support for the Nicaraguan contras violated international law. [18] While the case was pending, the Reagan administration in 1985 decided to terminate U.S. agreement to compulsory ICJ jurisdiction over treaty or other international-law disputes — reversing a policy dating from the Truman administration.

The United States also drew criticism from the U.N. General Assembly for two military actions during the 1980s — the invasions of Grenada in 1983 and Panama in 1989 — though it was designated to lead the Security Council-approved intervention to expel Iraq from Kuwait in 1990.

In the 1990s, however, the Clinton administration strongly supported creation of limited-jurisdiction international tribunals to hear war crimes cases involving genocide and mass murder in the former Yugoslavia and Rwanda. [19] President Clinton also approved use of U.S. troops as part of a U.N. peacekeeping force in Somalia (1993) and backed NATO's intervention — without U.N. approval — twice in the former Yugoslavia: Bosnia (1996) and Kosovo (1999). Clinton also signed the international treaty establishing the International Criminal Court. Upon taking office, President Bush withdrew U.S. approval of the treaty.

International treaties covered an ever-growing list of activities during the second half of the 20th century. One of the first post-war treaties, the General Agreement on Tariffs and Trade (GATT), sought to liberalize trade rules by generally requiring member states to grant other nations equal access to markets and limiting preferential treatment of domestic producers. Signed in 1947, the GATT established a voluntary dispute-settlement system, which was superseded in 1995 by the WTO's mandatory dispute-settlement system.

Among other major treaties, the United States strongly supported pacts in 1970 and 1971 aimed at preventing airline hijackings and the 1987 Montreal Protocol restricting the use of ozone-depleting chlorofluorocarbons. On the other hand, the United States refused to sign the 1982 Law of the Sea Convention because of restrictions on deep-seabed mining. And currently the Bush administration opposes participation in the 1997 Kyoto Protocol, which calls on developed nations to reduce emission of so-called greenhouse gases implicated in causing global warming. [20]

Within the United States, meanwhile, the 2nd U.S. Circuit Court of Appeals in New York created a major new venue for international law disputes with its 1980 decision allowing two Paraguayan citizens to use the Alien Tort Statute to sue a former Paraguayan police official for the torture death of a family member. After the appeals court refused to throw the case out, a lower federal court awarded Joel Filártiga and his daughter $10 million in punitive damages, but they are believed never to have been able to collect any significant amount of the judgment. The 2nd Circuit later allowed Croats and Muslims from Bosnia-Herzegovina to bring a suit for torture and genocide against Radovan Karadzic, the former Serb paramilitary leader now believed to be hiding in Bosnia. A jury in 2000 awarded $4.5 billion in damages, but prospects of any recovery are nil.

Legal conservatives criticized the *Filártiga* case on the grounds that the federal courts' role in international disputes was unwarranted and unhelpful. Criticism grew as foreign plaintiffs sued multinational corporations for a variety of alleged international law violations overseas. Besides the suit by Burmese plaintiffs against Unocal, other noteworthy cases included suits against Royal Dutch Shell for allegedly conspiring with the Nigerian government to crush opposition to oil drilling in the country's Ogoni region; against Texaco for alleged environmental degradation in the Ecuadorian rain forest; and against an array of companies for alleged complicity with South Africa's former apartheid policies. As of summer 2004, plaintiffs had won judgments in none of the two-dozen such cases. [21]

The Post-9/11 World

The Sept. 11, 2001, terrorist attacks became a watershed in official U.S. attitudes toward international law. The United States won worldwide support for its initial response to the attacks. But a month later President Bush drew domestic and international criticism for his decision to circumvent Geneva Conventions provisions in the treatment of prisoners captured in Afghanistan.

Eighteen months later, in March 2003, Bush bypassed the U.N. Security Council in launching the invasion of Iraq. The administration then drew a new round of criticism with disclosures of alleged abuses of detainees at Guantanamo Bay and in Iraq. With criticism mounting, the Supreme Court in June 2004 issued two rulings rejecting the administration's legal basis for its policies toward the detainees.

Through the 1990s, the Clinton administration had sought criminal prosecutions for terrorist attacks on the World Trade Center (1993) and U.S. embassies in Kenya and Tanzania (1998). However, Clinton rejected an all-out military response other than a failed cruise missile attack on an al Qaeda base in Afghanistan and an alleged chemical weapons factory in Sudan after the embassy bombings. [22]

In September 2001, however, President Bush immediately promised military retaliation for the attacks on the World Trade Center and the Pentagon against al Qaeda and Afghanistan's Taliban government for harboring the terrorist network. Missile strikes on Oct. 7 marked the beginning of a military campaign that toppled the Taliban within two months and left thousands of Afghans and other, mostly Muslim foreigners in U.S. captivity.

In a speech to the U.N. General Assembly on Nov. 10, Bush vowed that the United States would defend itself "against terror and lawless violence." Three days later, Bush signed an order authorizing special military tribunals to try foreigners charged with terrorism, including acts unrelated to the Sept. 11 attacks. The order promised detainees would be treated "humanely," but administration officials said the Geneva Conventions did not apply.

The order prescribed loosened rules of evidence before the tribunals barred detainees from seeking legal review in any U.S., foreign or international court. "The conventional way of bringing people to justice doesn't apply to these times," White House Communications Director Dan Bartlett told reporters. An American Civil Liberties Union official called the order "deeply disturbing." [23]

By early 2002, some 600 foreigners had been transported from Afghanistan to the U.S. naval base at Guantanamo Bay, Cuba. Despite the order, lawyers representing some of the detainees filed *habeas corpus* petitions in federal courts challenging the conditions and procedures as violations of both U.S. and international law. The administration vigorously defended its position in and out of court. Through February 2004, Defense Secretary Donald H. Rumsfeld and other Pentagon officials were suggesting that the detainees could be held without trial for the duration of the war on terrorism.

Behind the scenes, however, Secretary of State Colin L. Powell and others reportedly were calling as early as October 2002 for releasing or transferring some of the less important detainees. [24] The State Department was responding in part to diplomatic pressure from such staunch U.S. allies as Australia and Britain about the detentions; a small number of Australians and Britons were among the captives, and four of them brought one of the *habeas corpus* petitions. Eventually, the administration began releasing some of the detainees, including one of the Britons. But the administration won a significant victory in March 2003 when the federal appeals court in Washington ruled that the Guantanamo detainees had no right to contest their confinement.

Meanwhile, Bush provoked new waves of criticism for advocating what came to be called a right of "preemptive self-defense" against potential attacks from enemy countries or terrorist organizations. In a May 2002 speech at the U.S. Military Academy at West Point, Bush said the United States would "impose pre-emptive, unilateral, military force when and where it chooses." Bush and other administration officials elaborated on the doctrine through the run-up to the war against Iraq even while seeking Security Council support for the planned invasion on other grounds — chiefly, enforcement of previous U.N. resolutions requiring Iraq to disarm.

Within the United States, the doctrine was widely criticized, though criticism receded as leading Democrats became reluctant to oppose Bush's evident intention to go to war. But U.N. Secretary-General Annan publicly challenged the Bush doctrine, as did France and Germany among other countries in opposing Security Council sanction for the invasion. Once major combat had ended in Iraq, criticism increased as doubts grew about Bush's allegations that Iraq had developed weapons of mass destruction

— the administration's main justification for the war.

By late 2003 and early 2004, the Supreme Court had also stepped into the debate by agreeing to hear legal challenges to the Guantanamo policies along with separate cases brought by U.S. citizens held as enemy combatants in the United States. In June 2004, the court delivered an unmistakable rebuke to the administration by ruling, 6-3, that federal courts had jurisdiction under U.S. law to hear the detainees' challenges. Neither the majority opinion nor the dissent dealt with the detainees' international-law claims.[25]

In one of the U.S. citizen cases, however, six of the justices said the administration violated either international law or U.S. military regulations by refusing to give the detainee a chance to challenge his confinement before some impartial tribunal.[26] ■

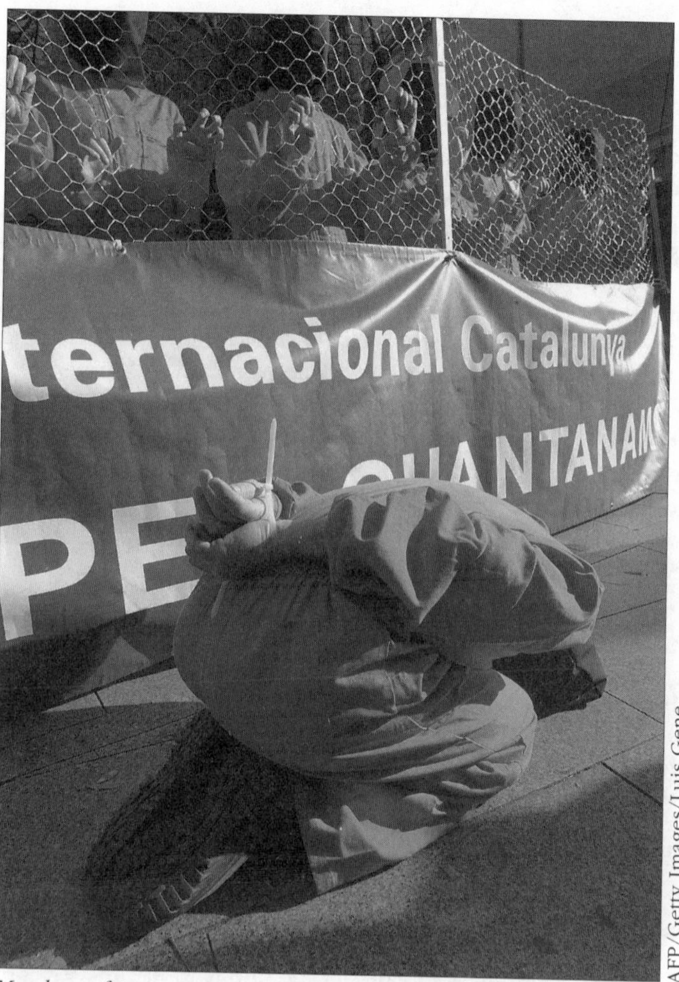

AFP/Getty Images/Luis Gene

Members of Amnesty International in Barcelona, Spain, call for the liberation of hundreds of detainees being harshly treated and held without trial at the U.S. Naval Base in Guantanamo Bay, Cuba.

CURRENT SITUATION

Policies Challenged

The Bush administration continues to face criticism at home and abroad for its policies in the war on terror and in Iraq. In perhaps the most stinging criticism, the International Committee of the Red Cross (ICRC) has charged that the military has subjected detainees at Guantanamo Bay to coercive interrogation and treatment "tantamount to torture."

Reports of the ICRC's claim surfaced in late November as federal courts in Washington were dealing with legal challenges to plans for military commissions to try some of the detainees on terrorism-related charges.

Barely a week later, the American Civil Liberties Union (ACLU) released a trove of government records documenting concerns lodged by Defense Department and FBI personnel about treatment of U.S. captives in Iraq, Afghanistan and Guantanamo.

Meanwhile, the New York-based Center for Constitutional Rights (CCR) is asking a German court to initiate a war-crimes investigation of U.S. officials and military personnel for alleged U.S. mistreatment of Iraqi captives at the Abu Ghraib prison in Baghdad.

"We vehemently deny any allegations of torture at Guantanamo, and reject categorically allegations that the treatment of detainees at Guantanamo is improper," the Pentagon said on Nov. 30, the day *The New York Times* detailed the ICRC's findings.[27]

The Geneva-based ICRC, which is not affiliated with the American Red Cross, declined to release the report. But the organization said it "remains concerned that significant problems regarding conditions and treatment at Guantanamo Bay have not yet been adequately addressed."

The Geneva Conventions specifically mention the ICRC as an organization to monitor treatment of POWs. It regularly sends inspection teams to POW detention centers while promising that any findings will be submitted in confidence to the host government. ICRC teams began visiting the Guantanamo facility in January 2002. In a report publicized in October 2003, the ICRC charged that holding detainees indefinitely without initiating legal proceedings was adversely affecting their mental health.

The Times story disclosed that an unreleased report in January 2003 raised the question of whether "psychological torture" was taking place. The July 2004 report went further, the *Times* said, by depicting the treatment as amounting to physical and psychological coercion aimed at breaking the prisoners' will.

Techniques used, according to the *Times*, included subjecting detainees to "humiliating acts, solitary confinement, temperature extremes and use of forced positions." The report continued: "The construction of such a system, whose stated purpose is the production of intelligence, cannot be considered other than an intentional system of cruel, unusual and degrading treatment and a form of torture."

The ICRC also charged that some medical personnel at the base were participating in planning for interrogation in what it described as "a flagrant violation of medical ethics." The Pentagon replied that detainees were receiving first-rate medical care and denied that medical files were "used to harm detainees." [28]

The documents released by the ACLU included reports by Defense Intelligence Agency (DIA) "debriefers" on allegedly abusive interrogation at Abu Ghraib in violation of the Geneva Conventions as late as May 2004. The DIA personnel said the military interrogation teams obstructed their work by ordering them out of rooms during questioning and confiscating evidence of the alleged abuses. The records were obtained in Freedom of Information Act lawsuits brought by the ACLU in conjunction with CCR, Physicians for Human Rights, Veterans for Common Sense and Veterans for Peace. [29]

In Washington, meanwhile, a ranking government attorney acknowledged in court that evidence obtained by torture could be used in the military commissions planned for some of the Guantanamo detainees. Brian Boyle, principal deputy associate attorney general, made the statement in a hearing Dec. 2 in one of the challenges brought by detainees.

U.S. District Judge Richard Leon asked whether evidence obtained by torture would be admissible before the military's so-called combatant status review tribunals. Boyle answered that if the tribunals "determine that evidence of questionable provenance were reliable, nothing in the Due Process Clause [of the Constitution] prohibits them from relying on it." Boyle later specified that he did not believe torture had taken place at Guantanamo. [30]

Leon, hearing challenges filed by five detainees, expressed some doubts about interfering with the government's plans for the tribunals. The previous day, Senior Judge Joyce Hens Green, who was presiding over consolidated cases brought by 54 detainees, seemed more sympathetic to their objections. Both judges said they would try to issue rulings promptly. [31]

In the other development, CCR invoked a German law claiming universal jurisdiction over alleged war crimes in filing a 102-page complaint stemming from the reported abuses at Abu Ghraib. Those named include Defense Secretary Rumsfeld, former CIA Director George Tenet and various U.S. military personnel.

'We vehemently deny any allegations of torture at Guantanamo, and reject categorically allegations that the treatment of detainees at Guantanamo is improper.'

— Department of Defense, Nov. 30, 2004

Death Case Reviewed

The International Court of Justice (ICJ) wants U.S. courts to reconsider death sentences imposed on any foreign nationals denied treaty-granted rights to assistance from consular officials from their home countries before their trials. But the effect of the ICJ's ruling is uncertain as the U.S. Supreme Court considers a Mexican national's effort to use the decision to block his execution for participating in a 1993 gang-related murder in Texas. [32]

The international tribunal's 14-1 ruling on March 31, 2004, came in a case brought by Mexico on behalf of 51 Mexican nationals facing the death penalty for capital murder convictions in the United States. [33] Mexico charged the United States with violating the 1963 Vienna Convention on Consular Relations, which allows people arrested in a foreign nation to meet with diplomatic representatives from their own country and requires officials to advise detainees of that right.

An 18-member U.S. legal team, headed by State Department legal adviser Taft, argued before the tribunal in December 2003 that the Mexicans' rights had not been violated or, alternatively, that any failure to advise them of their rights had not affected their trials. But the court ruled that it was "clear" that the United States had committed "internationally wrongful acts" by "the failure of its competent authorities to inform the Mexican nationals concerned, to notify Mexican consular posts and to enable Mexico to provide consular assistance."

The court rejected Mexico's argument, however, that the violations required nullification of all the convictions. Instead, it said the United States should "permit review and reconsideration" of each case in order to determine whether

Continued on p. 1066

At Issue:

Should there be a right of pre-emptive self-defense?

JOHN YOO
PROFESSOR OF LAW, UNIVERSITY OF CALIFORNIA AT BERKELEY SCHOOL OF LAW

WRITTEN FOR *THE CQ RESEARCHER*, DECEMBER 2004

yes

In the last five years, the United States has launched three wars against other sovereign nations — in Kosovo, Afghanistan and Iraq. It has also engaged in a global conflict against the al Qaeda terrorist organization. While other countries and legal scholars claim that these interventions violate international law, in reality they recognize an emerging standard for the use of force to prevent threats to international peace and security.

A narrow reading of the U.N. Charter requires that nations use force only in two circumstances: in self-defense against a cross-border attack or when authorized by the U.N. Security Council. By historical practice, nations have also recognized that force may be used to pre-empt attacks that have not yet occurred but are "imminent." Obviously, neither the United States nor other nations have obeyed this standard. During the Cold War, for example, the United States resorted to armed force many times in places like Vietnam, Grenada and Panama, yet the U.N. authorized the use of force only twice (in Korea and the first Iraq war).

A more flexible approach to the use of force is demanded by the significant changes in the international and technological environment. A strict U.N. standard might have made sense at the end of World War II, when the problem was vast wars between nation-states, and the U.S. wanted to reduce the level of international violence to zero.

Today, however, we are faced with the threat of terrorism, rogue nations and the proliferation of weapons of mass destruction (WMD). As we learned on Sept. 11, 2001, we may have little or no warning that a terrorist attack is "imminent." Nations may only have narrow windows of opportunity to strike at threats before they become difficult or impossible to stop. Rather than ask whether an attack is about to occur, we should ask whether the use of force is reasonable in light of the magnitude of potential harm that a terrorist or rogue nation could inflict.

The wars in Kosovo, Afghanistan and Iraq also make clear that the use of force cannot be limited to self-defense alone. A failed state, which can allow terrorists to flourish, or the reckless ambitions of a despotic tyrant present threats to international peace and security.

Requiring approval from the Security Council — filled with nations only too happy to use their vetoes to protect their parochial interests — to stop threats of terrorism, rogue nations and WMD only discourages efforts to supply the world with the most valuable international public good of all: stability and security.

MARY ELLEN O'CONNELL
WILLIAM B. SAXBE DESIGNATED PROFESSOR OF LAW AND FELLOW, MERSHON CENTER FOR INTERNATIONAL SECURITY, THE OHIO STATE UNIVERSITY

WRITTEN FOR *THE CQ RESEARCHER*, DECEMBER 2004

no

Today's law on self-defense is found in the United Nations Charter. It was written largely by the United States, and it allows unilateral force in self-defense only when an armed attack occurs. Any other situation in which a state wants to use significant armed force requires authorization through the collective decision-making process of the U.N. Security Council.

Thus, the law prohibits the use of armed force to pre-empt a future attack unless prior authorization is received from the Security Council. (The charter's rules on self-defense parallel very closely the self-defense rules in U.S. criminal law: You can't fight back until attacked and, anticipating an attack, you go to the authorities to prevent the attack.)

The United States wrote these rules with the Nazi example very much in mind — the Germans had claimed to be exercising lawful pre-emptive self-defense when they invaded their neighbors prior to and during World War II. Hard experience taught that states must be held to a standard where the necessity for using force is objectively demonstrated. The system of international law, perhaps more than other legal systems, needs such objective, bright-line rules. In the absence of an international police force and regular courts, it needs rules that are self-implementing.

The Iraq case reveals the genius of this system. Iraq never attacked the United States, therefore the United States had no right to "counterattack" in self-defense. The United States could not persuade the Security Council of the need to use force against Iraq. Nevertheless, the United States invaded, only to find that indeed there was no actual threat. Our country would have been far better off had it heeded the council's collective wisdom.

It is not surprising, and is perhaps hopeful, that the United States has turned back to the council for help regarding Iran and North Korea.

Until Iraq, the United States stood steadfastly by the charter rules as written, knowing that a breach of the rules sets a dangerous precedent. States are equal under international law; the rules work largely on the basis of reciprocity.

There is no special set of rules for superpowers. If the United States wants a rule prohibiting force — and it always has for the most basic moral considerations — it needs to respect that rule itself.

Continued from p. 1064

the violation "caused actual prejudice" to the defendant. The court also said the United States had been making "considerable efforts" to ensure that law enforcement authorities comply with the treaty.

The enforceability of the tribunal's judgment in U.S. courts is uncertain. Six weeks after the ruling, the Oklahoma Court of Criminal Appeals on May 13 halted the execution of one of the Mexicans in the case, Osbaldo Torres; and Gov. Brad Henry commuted Torres' sentence later the same day. But the 5th U.S. Circuit Court of Appeals refused to bow to the ruling six days later in a case involving a Texas death row inmate, Jose Ernesto Medellin. The appeals court said Medellin's claim was "procedurally defaulted" because he had failed to raise the issue until after his trial and appeals in Texas courts.

In its ruling — and in an earlier decision in a case brought by Germany — the ICJ said use of procedural default rules to block review of a foreign national's plea violated the Vienna convention. But the 5th Circuit court said the U.S. Supreme Court had ruled the opposite way in a brief, unsigned decision in 1998 involving a Paraguayan facing execution in Virginia. [34]

Now, Medellin is asking the Supreme Court to determine whether U.S. courts must follow the ICJ's decision "as a matter of international comity and in the interest of uniform treaty interpretation." Medellin's petition is being supported by Mexico and 13 other Latin American countries, the European Union and Amnesty International.

In addition, former U.S. diplomat L. Bruce Laingen, who was charge d'affaires in the U.S. Embassy in Tehran during the 1979 hostage crisis, is also backing Medellin's plea. Laingen argues that unless U.S. courts respect the consular treaty, other countries will retaliate, and U.S. citizens' rights abroad will be endangered.

Texas officials are urging the high court to stick with its 1998 decision, which it described as holding that Vienna Convention claims, "like constitutional claims, can be procedurally defaulted, even in a death penalty case." The Bush administration has not filed a brief with the Supreme Court, nor has any other state or private organization joined on Texas' side at this stage.

The justices had Medellin's case on their schedule for three consecutive weekly conferences in late November and early December 2004 before finally granting review on Dec. 10. Argument will be held in the spring with a decision due by the end of June.

Meanwhile, lower federal courts are beginning to apply the Supreme Court's decision narrowing the scope of suits brought under the federal Alien Tort Statute. In the first decision to apply the high court's ruling, a federal court judge in New York City has dismissed a sprawling suit by South Africans against U.S. and other multinational corporations for collaboration with the country's former apartheid policy of racial discrimination.

U.S. District Judge John Sprizzo sharply criticized the apartheid policy's other abuses to the more than 100 companies named as defendants. But he said that holding multinational companies liable for "doing business in countries with less than stellar human rights records" could have "significant, if not disastrous, effects on international commerce." [35] ■

OUTLOOK

Preventive Action

Nearly two years after the launch of the Iraq war, the United States remains at odds with the United Nations over the use of force in the post-9/11 world. The dispute is one of several international-law issues where the Bush administration is taking stands in conflict with U.S. allies and much of world opinion.

In a report released on Nov. 30, 2004, a high-level panel created a year earlier by U.N. Secretary-General Annan acknowledged the need for "a broader-based approach" to fighting terrorism and singled out al Qaeda as a "universal threat." But the report rejected arguments that an individual country could exercise a right of "anticipatory self-defense" and instead said only the Security Council could authorize preventive action in cases where no attack had occurred or was imminent.

"The risk to the global order and the norm of non-intervention on which it continues to be based is simply too great for the legality of unilateral preventive action, as distinct from collectively endorsed action, to be accepted," the report states. "Allowing one to so act is to allow all." [36]

A week later, Kim Hughes, assistant U.S. secretary of State for international organizations, commended the report for urging the Security Council to be "more proactive" in dealing with terrorism and nuclear proliferation. But Hughes said the United States has "serious concerns" about the panel's limited view of self-defense and would not feel obliged to seek Security Council approval to use force preventively.

"Even in a case where terrorists have a nuclear weapon, the report says a state should go to the Security Council first for authorization to take preventative military action," Hughes said in a Dec. 6 speech to the Baltimore Council on Foreign Relations. "Whether the council could decide soon enough for effective military action is another matter. Such constraints will never be acceptable to the United States."

The administration also continues to oppose two major international treaties negotiated in recent years: the

Kyoto Protocol to limit emission of gases thought to cause climate change and the pact to establish the permanent International Criminal Court (ICC). The Kyoto treaty is set to take effect in February 2005. Bush rejected the treaty in 2001, calling for voluntary measures instead.

The administration has used diplomatic pressure, including the threat to cut off military aid, to persuade 97 of the 139 countries that have now signed the ICC treaty to protect U.S. service members from prosecution before the tribunal. [37]

Some observers say the administration's skeptical stance toward international law reduces international support for U.S. policies. "Increasingly, the United States has found itself at odds with several key players," says Villanova law Professor Murphy.

Berkeley's Professor Yoo minimizes the problem. "The cost to our reputation is probably not that much," he says.

The disputes over these and other treaties underscore the widening scope and complexity of multilateral agreements and what one professor calls the "receding importance" of so-called customary international law. J. Patrick Kelly, a professor at Widener University School of Law in Wilmington, Del., welcomes the trend, saying treaties provide more specific formulations of international law and also give a greater voice to developing nations — but at the expense of reducing the influence of the United States and other developed countries. [38]

Under the Constitution, treaties ratified by the Senate are part of "the supreme law of the land" (Article VI). Still, members of Congress and others periodically complain about the loss of U.S. sovereignty under international law even when treaties have been approved by the Senate. Specialists in the field generally discount the problem.

"It does interfere with our national sovereignty to some extent, but that's not a bad thing," says Michael Ramsey, a professor at the University of San Diego School of Law and self-described "mild skeptic" of international law.

"We decided it would be better for our national security and our national interests if we agreed to these things," Ramsey says, referring to the U.N. Charter and other treaties. "Sometimes you can promote your long-term interests best by giving up things. That's the nature of a contract."

"The world is too big for us to deal with by ourselves," says Yale's Koh. "We need to have mechanisms for dealing with problems globally, and international law is the means to do that. We need to have a strategy for using international law to achieve our own ends." ■

Notes

[1] The case is *Hamdan v. Rumsfeld*, Civ. No. 04-1519 (Nov. 8, 2004). Factual background drawn from documents filed with Hamdan's petition for *certiorari* before U.S. Supreme Court (docket number 04-702, filed Nov. 22), available at SCOTUSblog (http://www.goldsteinhowe.com/blog/).

[2] For the text of Resolution 1373, see http://ods-dds-ny.un.org/doc/UNDOC/GEN/N01/557/43/PDF/N0155743.pdf?OpenElement. For coverage, see Serge Schmemann, "U.N. Requires Members to Act Against Terror," *The New York Times*, Sept. 29, 2001, p. A1.

[3] See David E. Sanger with John F. Burns, "Bush Orders Start of War on Iraq; Missiles Apparently Miss Hussein," *The New York Times*, March 20, 2003, p. A1.

[4] Quoted in Patrick E. Tyler, "U.N. Chief Ignites Firestorm By Calling Iraq War 'Illegal,' " *The New York Times*, Sept. 17, 2004, p. A1.

[5] The case is *Roper v. Simmons*, 03-633. For background, see Kenneth Jost, "Sentencing Debates," *The CQ Researcher*, Nov. 12, 2004, pp. 932-934.

[6] The cases are *Atkins v. Virginia*, 536 U.S. 304 (2002), and *Lawrence v. Texas*, 539 U.S. 558 (2003).

[7] See Anne Gearan, "Supreme Court Justice Skeptical of Value of International Law to U.S. Courts," The Associated Press, April 2, 2004.

[8] See Lisa Girion, "Unocal to Settle Rights Claim," *Los Angeles Times*, Dec. 14, 2004, p. A1.

[9] The case is *Filártiga v. Pena-Irala*, 630 F.2d 876 (2d Cir. 1980).

[10] The citation is 540 U.S. — (June 29, 2004). The decision barred a suit by a Mexican physician, Humberto Alvarez-Machain, against a former Mexican police inspector for abducting him and bringing him to the United States for trial.

[11] Gary Clyde Hufbauer and Nicholas K. Mitrokostas, "Awakening Monster: The Alien Tort Statute of 1789," Institute for International Economics, July 2003, p. 7. The study was financed in part by a business lobby, the National Foreign Trade Council.

[12] Background drawn in part from John F. Murphy, *The United States and the Rule of Law in International Affairs* (2004). See also Barry E. Carter, Phillip R. Trimble and Curtis A. Bradley, *International Law* (4th ed.), 2003.

[13] *Chisholm v. Georgia*, 2 Dall. 419 (1793), cited in Louis Henkin, *Foreign Affairs and the Constitution* (1972), p. 127.

[14] See Carter, *et al., op. cit.*, p. 342.

[15] The case is *Paquete Habana*, 175 U.S. 677 (1900).

[16] For background on the Security Council, see David Masci, "The United Nations and Global Security," *The CQ Researcher*, Feb. 27, 2004, pp. 173-196.

[17] Carter, *et al., op. cit.*, p. 287.

[18] The case is titled *Case Concerning Military and Paramilitary Activities In and Against Nicaragua* (*Nicaragua v. United States of America*), [1986] I.C.J. Rep. 14 (Judgment).

[19] For background, see Kenneth Jost, "War Crimes," *The CQ Researcher*, July 7, 1995, pp. 585-608.

About the Author

Associate Editor **Kenneth Jost** graduated from Harvard College and Georgetown University Law Center. He is the author of *The Supreme Court Yearbook* and editor of *The Supreme Court from A to Z* (both *CQ Press*). He was a member of *The CQ Researcher* team that won the 2002 American Bar Association Silver Gavel Award. His recent reports include "Gays on Campus" and "Sports and Drugs."

[20] For background, see Mary H. Cooper, "Global Warming Treaty," *The CQ Researcher*, Jan. 26, 2001, pp. 41-64, and Mary H. Cooper, "Bush and the Environment," *The CQ Researcher*, Oct. 25, 2002, pp. 865-896.
[21] See Hufbauer and Mitrokostas, *op. cit.*, pp. 63-72.
[22] See Kenneth Jost, "Re-examining 9/11," *The CQ Researcher*, June 4, 2004, pp. 493-516.
[23] "Military Order of November 13, 2001: Detention, Treatment and Trial of Certain Non-Citizens in the War Against Terrorism," 66 Fed. Reg. 57,833 (Nov. 16, 2001), excerpted in Sean D. Murphy, *United States Practice in International Law, Volume 1: 1999-2001* (2003), pp. 438-441. For coverage, see Elisabeth Bumiller and David Johnston, "Bush Sets Option of Military Trials in Terrorism Cases," *The New York Times*, Nov. 14, 2001, p. A1.
[24] See Tim Golden, "Administration Officials Split Over Military Tribunals," *The New York Times*, Oct. 25, 2004, p. A1.
[25] The case is *Rasul v. Bush*, 540 U.S. — (June 28, 2004).
[26] The case is *Hamdi v. Rumsfeld*, 540 U.S. — (June 28, 2004). Four of the justices, in a plurality opinion by Justice Sandra Day O'Connor, said the procedure violated military regulations; two justices, in a partial concurrence by Justice David H. Souter, said the procedure violated the Third Geneva Convention. The court dismissed on procedural grounds the second U.S. citizen case, *Rumsfeld v. Padilla*, 540 U.S. — (June 28, 2004).
[27] Neil A. Lewis, "Red Cross Finds Detainee Abuse in Guantanamo," *The New York Times*, Nov. 30, 2004, p. A1. *The Times* said it had obtained a memorandum describing and quoting from the ICRC report but not the report itself.
[28] *The Washington Post* had previously reported on the ICRC criticism of allowing military interrogators access to detainees' medical files. See Peter Slevin and Joe Stephens, "Detainees' Medical Files Shared; Guantanamo Interrogators' Access Criticized," *The Washington Post*, June 10, 2004, p. A1.
[29] See Barton Gellman and R. Jeffrey Smith, "Report to Defense Alleged Abuse by Prison Interrogation Teams," *The Washington Post*, Dec. 8, 2004, p. A1.
[30] The ACLU posted the documents at www.aclu.org/torturefoia. For coverage, see Michael J. Sniffen, "Evidence gained by torture can be used to detain enemy combatants at Guantanamo," The Associated Press, Dec. 3, 2004.
[31] See Neil A. Lewis, "Fate of Guantanamo Detainees Is Debated in Federal Court," *The New York Times*, Dec. 2, 2004, p. A29, and Carol D. Leonnig, "Judge Questions Sweep of Bush's War on Terrorism," *The New York Times*, Dec. 2, 2004, p. A4.
[32] Background drawn in part from Tony Mauro, "High Court on Collision Course With Int'l Law," *Legal Times*, Nov. 22, 2004, p. 1.
[33] The case is *Avena and Other Mexican Nationals (Mexico v. United States of America)*, 2004 ICJ 128 (Judgment of March 31), www.icj-cji.org. For coverage, see Marlisle Simmons and Tim Weiner, "World Court Rules U.S. Should Review 51 Death Sentences," *The New York Times*, April 1, 2004, p. A1.
[34] The earlier ICJ decision is the *LaGrand* case (*Germany v. United States of America*), 2001 ICJ 104 (judgment of June 27). The Supreme Court decision is *Breard v. Greene*, 523 U.S. 371 (1998).
[35] The case is *In re South African Apartheid Litigation*, MDL No. 1499 (S.D.N.Y. Nov. 29, 2004) For coverage, see Larry Neumeister, "Judge tosses out lawsuits seeking billions from U.S. companies," The Associated Press, Nov. 29, 2004.
[36] United Nations, "A More Secure World: Our Shared Responsibility: Report of the Secretary-General's High-Level Panel on Threats, Challenges, and Change," Nov. 30, 2004 (http://www.un.org/secureworld/report2.pdf). For coverage, see Warren Hoge, "Report Urges Big Changes for U.N.," *The New York Times*, Dec. 1, 2004, p. A1.
[37] See Joe Lauria and Farah Stockman, "Aid Cuts Threatened by U.S. Over Tribunal," *The Boston Globe*, Dec. 5, 2004, p. A1.
[38] See J. Patrick Kelly, "The Twilight of Customary International Law," *Virginia Journal of International Law*, Vol. 49 (winter 2000), pp. 449-538.

FOR MORE INFORMATION

American Constitution Society for Law and Policy, 50 F St., N.W., Suite 5200, Washington, DC 20001; (202) 393-6181; www.acslaw.org. A progressive legal organization "working to ensure that the fundamental principles of human dignity, individual rights and liberties, genuine equality, and access to justice are in their rightful, central place in American law."

The American Society for International Law, 2223 Massachusetts Ave., N.W., Washington, DC 20008; (202) 939-6000; www.asil.org. Fosters the study of international law and promotes the establishment and maintenance of international relations "on the basis of law and justice."

Center for Constitutional Rights, 666 Broadway, 7th Floor, New York, NY 10012; (212) 614-6464; www.ccr-ny.org. "Dedicated to protecting and advancing the rights guaranteed by the U.S. Constitution and the Universal Declaration of Human Rights."

Federalist Society, 1015 18th St., N.W., Suite 425, Washington DC 20036; (202) 822-8138; www.fed-soc.org. A "group of conservatives and libertarians . . . founded on the principles that the state exists to preserve freedom, that the separation of governmental powers is central to our Constitution, and that it is emphatically the province and duty of the judiciary to say what the law is, not what it should be."

Institute for International Economics, 1750 Massachusetts Ave., N.W., Washington, DC 20036; (202) 328-9000 Fax: (202) 695-3225; www.iie.com. A nonpartisan research institution devoted to the study of international economic policy.

International Law Association, Charles Clore House, 17 Russell Square, London, WC1B 5 DR, England; (44) 20-7323-2978; www.ila-hq.org. American branch: c/o Carlos Pelayo, Davis Polk and Wardwell; 450 Lexington Ave., Room 1938; New York, NY 10017. Devoted to the study, clarification and development of both public and private international law, with about 50 branches worldwide.

Washington Legal Foundation, 2009 Massachusetts Ave., N.W., Washington, DC 20036; (202) 588-0302; www.wlf.org. Works "to maintain balance" in the courts and help the U.S. government "strengthen America's free-enterprise system" through litigation, publishing and educational efforts.

Bibliography

Selected Sources

Books

Carter, Barry E., Phillip R. Trimble and Curtis A. Bradley, *International Law* (4th ed.), Aspen Law & Business, 2003.
The law school casebook provides comprehensive coverage of court decisions, executive branch action and other materials on international law issues. Carter is a law professor at Georgetown University; Trimble at the University of California, Los Angeles; and Bradley at the University of Virginia.

Damrosch, Lori F., Louis Henkin, Richard Crawford Pugh, Oscar Schachter, and Hans Smith, *International Law: Cases and Materials* (4th ed.), West, 2001.
The law school casebook thoroughly covers international law topics, including a succinct introduction to the history of international law. Includes a four-page guide to official and private Internet sources on international law. Damrosch and Smith are professors and Henkin and Schachter professors emeriti at Columbia University School of Law; Pugh is a professor at the University of San Diego School of Law.

Murphy, John F., *The United States and the Rule of Law in International Affairs*, Cambridge University Press, 2004.
The book analyzes and assesses the role of international law in U.S. foreign policy. Includes chapter notes. Murphy is a professor at Villanova Law School.

Murphy, Sean D., *United States Practice in International Law: Volume 1, 1999-2001*, Cambridge University Press, 2002.
The reference book combines original source material with explanatory narratives to cover U.S. practice in international law, topic by topic, from 1999-2001. The next volume covers 2002-2004 [forthcoming, 2005]. Murphy, a professor at George Washington University School of Law, is also coauthor with Thomas Buergenthal of *Public International Law in a Nutshell* (3d ed.), West, 2002.

Rose, David, *Guantanamo: The War on Human Rights*, New Press, 2004.
The British journalist presents a highly critical account of detention and interrogation policies at the Guantanamo Bay Naval Base as inconsistent with international law standards.

White, Richard Alan, *Breaking Silence: The Case That Changed the Face of Human Rights*, Georgetown University Press, 2004.
The book vividly recounts the torture-murder of Joelito Filártiga, teenaged son of a prominent Paraguayan opposition leader; the Filártiga family's use of the Alien Tort Claims Act to sue the responsible police inspector in U.S. courts and the impact of the court decisions in favor of the suit. White is a senior fellow at the Council of Hemispheric Affairs in Washington.

Articles

Alford, Roger P., "Misusing International Sources to Interpret the Constitution," *American Journal of International Law*, January 2004.
An associate professor at Pepperdine University School of Law argues against the Supreme Court's use of foreign and international law in constitutional interpretation.

Greene, Jenna, "Gathering Storm: Suits That Claim Overseas Abuse Are Putting U.S. Executives on Alert and Their Lawyers on Call," *Legal Times*, July 21, 2003.
The story gives an overview of issues surrounding suits against corporate defendants under the Alien Tort Statute.

Kelly, J. Patrick, "The Twilight of Customary International Law," *Virginia Journal of International Law*, Vol. 40, winter 2000, pp. 445-539.
A professor at Widener University School of Law argues that treaties are replacing customs and practices as the major sources of international law.

Neuman, Gerald L., "The Uses of International Law in Constitutional Interpretation," *American Journal of International Law*, January 2004.
A professor at Columbia University School of Law argues in favor of the Supreme Court's use of foreign and international law in constitutional interpretation.

Reports and Studies

Hufbauer, Gary Clyde, and Nicholas K. Mitrokostas, "Awakening Monster: The Alien Tort Statute of 1789," Institute for International Economics, July 2003.
The tract traces the history of the Alien Tort Statute and strongly criticizes its recent use in broad-based human rights suits in U.S. courts against foreign officials and, in particular, multinational corporations. Includes summaries of 23 suits brought under the act since the seminal case, *Filártiga v. Pena-Irala* (1980). The study was partially funded by the National Council on Foreign Trade, a business group that opposes expansive use of the act.

United Nations, "A More Secure World: Our Shared Responsibility: Report of the Secretary-General's High-level Panel on Threats, Challenges and Change," Nov. 30, 2004 (www.un.org/secureworld/report2.pdf).
The report is aimed at forging a "new security consensus" to deal with threats to peace and order posed by terrorism, failed states and nuclear proliferation. The United States, however, rejected one of the major premises — that only the Security Council can authorize the use of force as preventive action against a threat to stability.

The Next Step:

Additional Articles from Current Periodicals

Global Law

Cassel, Doug, "With or Without U.S., World Court Will Debut," ***Chicago Tribune*****, May 12, 2002, Perspective Section, p. 1.**

The United States withdraws its signature from the treaty to establish an International Criminal Court to prosecute genocide, serious war crimes and crimes against humanity.

Chertoff, Michael, "Justice Denied: The International Criminal Court Is Even Worse Than Its Critics Have Said," ***The Weekly Standard*****, April 12, 2004.**

Americans are accused of showing contempt for international law by challenging the International Criminal Court, but even the critics may have underestimated the risks posed by the new tribunal.

Ford, Peter, "Belgium Makes Justice Less Global," ***The Christian Science Monitor*****, June 24, 2003, p. 6.**

Swamped by a host of lawsuits against U.S. and other world leaders, Belgium will limit a war-crimes law that angered Washington and prompted warnings of a NATO boycott.

International Outlook

Morgan, Dan, "Even Bush Submits To These Global Tests," ***The Washington Post*****, Oct. 17, 2004, p. B3.**

Though President Bush ridiculed John Kerry's concept of the "global test," on the economic front the nation has obediently participated in a host of global institutions, and U.S. companies are routinely subject to the actions of foreign entities.

Schell, Jonathan, "Healing the Law," ***The Nation*****, Aug. 2, 2004, No. 4, Vol. 279, p. 12.**

The imperial policies of the Bush administration show contempt for international law, and their global adoption would introduce additional preventative wars and regime change, bringing international chaos.

Sellers, Frances, "A World Wishing To Cast a Vote," ***The Washington Post*****, Nov. 21, 2004, p. B1.**

Non-Americans wish to have a greater voice in U.S. elections and their legislative outcomes, saying they affect the entire world and suggesting that changes be made to reflect that stake in the form of a global democratic forum.

Taylor, Stuart, "It's Time for Bush to Take Our Treaty Obligations Seriously," ***National Journal*****, April 10, 2004, Vol. 36, No. 15.**

Conservatives discount the idea that the United States should heed international law and honor rulings by international tribunals, a self-defeating attitude at a time when much of the world sees America as an international scofflaw.

Multinational Corporations

Brown, David, "U.S. Urged to Monitor Global Labor Policies," ***The Washington Post*****, Jan. 12, 2004, p. A15.**

Even globalization's biggest advocates oppose child labor or inhumane working conditions, but without global manufacturing regulations or restrictive trade policies, the goal of abolishing such practices remains elusive.

Engardio, Pete, "Global Compact, Little Impact," ***Business Week*****, July 12, 2004, p. 86.**

The U.N.'s corporate-responsibility plan, which has brought together multinationals and activist groups to help ensure that company activities conform to basic human rights and environmental standards, is falling short of expectations.

Greider, William, "The Right and US Trade Law: Invalidating the 20th Century," ***The Nation*****, Oct. 15, 2001, p. 21.**

NAFTA's investor protections are a manifestation of a broad, backdoor effort to restore the primacy of property against society's broader claims, expanding the definition of property rights far beyond the established terms in U.S. jurisprudence.

Liptak, Adam, "Review of U.S. Rulings by NAFTA Tribunals Stirs Worries," ***The New York Times*****, April 18, 2004, p. 20.**

Multi-national cases ruled upon in U.S. state and federal courts could be challenged by NAFTA tribunals, potentially leaving American and international governments liable for hundreds of millions of dollars.

Post-9/11 Justice

Carter, Phillip, "The Road to Abu Ghraib: The Biggest Scandal of the Bush Administration Began at the Top," ***Washington Monthly*****, Nov. 1, 2004, No. 11, Vol. 35, p. 20.**

The Abu Ghraib scandal was a direct result of a post-9/11 Bush administration policy, in which the need for intelligence via interrogations was pressing, but the limits placed by international law on interrogation techniques were constricting.

Glaberson, William, "Critics' Attack On Tribunals Turns to Law Among Nations," ***The New York Times*****, Dec. 26, 2001, p. B1.**

Beyond claims that the military tribunals authorized by President Bush would violate civil liberties guaranteed by American law, some experts argue that they would also breach international law guaranteeing fair treatment of prisoners of war.

Golden, Tim, "After Terror, a Secret Rewriting of Military Law," ***The New York Times*****, Oct. 24, 2004, p. A1.**

White House officials worked in great secrecy post-9/11 to devise a system of justice for the war on terrorism that bypassed federal courts and their constitutional guarantees and gave the military the authority to detain foreign suspects indefinitely.

Hendren, John, "Trials of Terror Suspects Halted," *Los Angeles Times*, Nov. 13, 2004, p. A1.
The Bush administration suspended its system for putting accused terrorists on trial in Guantanamo Bay after a court ruling declared the practice below U.S. standards of justice and in violation of the Geneva Conventions.

Isikoff, Michael, "Double Standards?" *Newsweek*, May 21, 2004, Newsweek Web Exclusive.
In a memo written four months after Sept. 11, Justice Department lawyers advised that President Bush and the U.S. military did not have to comply with any international laws in the handling of detainees in the war on terrorism.

Schmitt, Eric, and Douglas Jehl, "Army Says CIA Hid More Iraqis Than It Claimed," *The New York Times*, Sept. 10, 2004, p. A1.
Army investigators find that as many as 100 Iraqi detainees at Abu Ghraib prison were hidden from the International Red Cross at the request of the CIA and not registered as required by Army regulations and international law.

Shanker, Thom, and Katharine Seelye, "Who Is a Prisoner of War? You Could Look It Up. Maybe," *The New York Times*, March 10, 2002, Sect. 4, p. 9.
Although the Bush administration conceded that the detainees at Guantanamo Bay deserve to be covered by the Geneva Conventions, it refused to allow them prisoner-of-war status, leaving unclear how they would be protected.

Supreme Court

Greenhouse, Linda, "Human Rights Abuses Worldwide Are Held to Fall Under U.S. Courts," *The New York Times*, June 30, 2004, p. A21.
Federal courts will remain open to lawsuits by foreigners claiming to be victims of serious human rights violations anywhere in the world, according to a Supreme Court decision.

Richey, Warren, "Global Legal Trends Make Waves at High Court," *The Christian Science Monitor*, Oct. 21, 2004, p. 2.
In arguments about the juvenile death penalty, the Supreme Court reveals an emerging trend in which a majority of justices are increasingly willing to cite international law.

Scelfo, Julie, "The Longer Arm of the Law," *Newsweek*, June 30, 2004, Newsweek Web Exclusive.
A Supreme Court decision permitting foreigners to use U.S. courts to seek redress for human rights violations may have implications for organizations doing business overseas.

United Nations

"Fighting For Survival — United Nations," *The Economist*, U.S. Edition, Nov. 20, 2004.
The United Nations is in crisis after last year's Iraq war, which left many wondering whether a body increasingly seen as ineffective should survive.

Kraul, Chris, "Mexicans on U.S. Death Row Denied Rights, Court Says," *Los Angles Times*, April 1, 2004, p. A1.
In a rebuke of the U.S. legal system, the judicial body of the United Nations ruled that 51 Mexicans on death row in U.S. states were illegally deprived of consular assistance.

Priest, Dana, and Charles Babington, "Plan Would Let U.S. Deport Suspects To Nations That Might Torture Them," *The Washington Post*, Sept. 30, 2004, p. A1.
The Bush administration is supporting the deportation of certain foreigners to countries where they are likely to be tortured, an action prohibited by the U.N.'s international laws against torture that the United States signed 20 years ago.

Tharoor, Shashi, "Why America Still Needs the United Nations," *Foreign Affairs*, September 2003, p. 67.
Working with the United Nations gives the United States the ability to attract and persuade others to adopt the American agenda without using military force.

CITING *THE CQ RESEARCHER*

Sample formats for citing these reports in a bibliography include the ones listed below. Preferred styles and formats vary, so please check with your instructor or professor.

MLA STYLE

Jost, Kenneth. "Rethinking the Death Penalty." The CQ Researcher 16 Nov. 2001: 945-68.

APA STYLE

Jost, K. (2001, November 16). Rethinking the death penalty. *The CQ Researcher, 11*, 945-968.

CHICAGO STYLE

Jost, Kenneth. "Rethinking the Death Penalty." *CQ Researcher*, November 16, 2001, 945-968.

Published by CQ Press, a division of Congressional Quarterly Inc.

thecqresearcher.com

Index

January 1991–December 2004

❖ *CQ Researcher* reports are indexed by title under boldface topic headings.

- Titles are followed by the date the report appeared and the first page number of its print version.
- Page numbers followed by an asterisk refer to a sidebar or the "At Issue" (Pro/Con) feature.

❖ This index is updated monthly and available at: www.thecqresearcher.com/researcher_index.pdf

❖ The *CQ Researcher* can be accessed online at: www.thecqresearcher.com

Published by CQ Press, a division of Congressional Quarterly Inc.

 *Indicates sidebar or "At Issue" report section.

 *Indicates sidebar or "At Issue" report section.

 *Indicates sidebar or "At Issue" report section.

 *Indicates sidebar or "At Issue" report section.

Business and industry — Environmental issues

Cable television

California

 *Indicates sidebar or "At Issue" report section.

 *Indicates sidebar or "At Issue" report section.

 *Indicates sidebar or "At Issue" report section.

 *Indicates sidebar or "At Issue" report section.

 *Indicates sidebar or "At Issue" report section.

 *Indicates sidebar or "At Issue" report section.

 *Indicates sidebar or "At Issue" report section.

 *Indicates sidebar or "At Issue" report section.

 *Indicates sidebar or "At Issue" report section.

 *Indicates sidebar or "At Issue" report section.

 *Indicates sidebar or "At Issue" report section.

 *Indicates sidebar or "At Issue" report section.

 *Indicates sidebar or "At Issue" report section.

 *Indicates sidebar or "At Issue" report section.

 *Indicates sidebar or "At Issue" report section.

 *Indicates sidebar or "At Issue" report section.

 *Indicates sidebar or "At Issue" report section.

 *Indicates sidebar or "At Issue" report section.

 *Indicates sidebar or "At Issue" report section.

 *Indicates sidebar or "At Issue" report section.

 *Indicates sidebar or "At Issue" report section.

 *Indicates sidebar or "At Issue" report section.

 *Indicates sidebar or "At Issue" report section.

 *Indicates sidebar or "At Issue" report section.

 *Indicates sidebar or "At Issue" report section.

 *Indicates sidebar or "At Issue" report section.

 *Indicates sidebar or "At Issue" report section.

 *Indicates sidebar or "At Issue" report section.

 *Indicates sidebar or "At Issue" report section.

 *Indicates sidebar or "At Issue" report section.